CARSWELL

THE 2017 ANNOTATED

IMMIGRATION AND REFUGEE PROTECTION ACT OF CANADA

Edited & annotated by

Henry M. Goslett

and

Barbara Jo Caruso

Formerly Frank N. Marrocco & Henry M. Goslett

STATUTES OF CANADA ANNOTATED

THOMSON REUTERS

A cataloguing record for this publication is available from Library and Archives Canada.

ISSN 1709-2051
ISBN 978-0-7798-7104-9 (2017 edition: bound)   ISBN 978-0-7798-7103-2 (2017 edition: pbk.)

Printed in the United States by Thomson Reuters

TELL US HOW WE'RE DOING
Scan the QR code to the right with your smartphone to send your comments regarding our products and services. Free QR Code Readers are available from your mobile device app store. You can also email us at carswell.feedback@thomsonreuters.com

THOMSON REUTERS

THOMSON REUTERS CANADA, A DIVISION OF THOMSON REUTERS CANADA LIMITED

One Corporate Plaza
2075 Kennedy Road
Toronto, Ontario
M1T 3V4

Customer Relations
Toronto 1-416-609-3800
Elsewhere in Canada/U.S. 1-800-387-5164
Fax 1-416-298-5082
www.carswell.com
Contact www.carswell.com/email

To

Frank and Debbie

And to

Douglas, Allison, Jessica, Alexandra and Jacqueline

PREFACE

The starting point for anyone interested in immigration law is the position of the alien at common law. In this regard, Lord Denning M.R.'s concise summary of the common law in the case of *R. v. The Governor of the Pentonville Prison, ex parte Azam*, [1973] 2 All E.R. 741 at 747 is most helpful:

> At common law no alien has any right to enter this country except by leave of the Crown; and the Crown can refuse leave without giving any reason: see *Schmidt v. Secretary of State for Home Affairs*, [1969] 2 Ch. 49 at 168. If he comes by leave, the Crown can impose such conditions as it thinks fit, as to his length of stay, or otherwise. He has no right whatever to remain here. He is liable to be sent home to his own country at any time if, in the opinion of the Crown, his presence here is not conducive to the public good; and for this purpose, the executive may arrest him and put him on board a ship or aircraft bound for his own country: see *R. v. Brixton Prison (Governor), ex parte Soblen*, [1963] 2 Q.B. 243 at 300, 301. The position of aliens at common law has since been covered by the various regulations; but the principles remain the same.

This annotation is directed at the question of the extent to which the common law has been affected by the *Charter of Rights and Freedoms*, the *Immigration and Refugee Protection Act of Canada* and the Regulations passed pursuant to that Act.

A number of Supreme Court of Canada decisions have confirmed that although ". . .the most fundamental principle of immigration law is that non-citizens do not have an unqualified right to enter or remain in Canada" this does not mean that the proceedings related to deportation in the immigration context are immune from scrutiny under section 7 of the *Charter*.

Considerable judicial resources have been applied to marking the boundary between national security obligations and individual rights. We have included, at the beginning of Part 1, Division 9, annotations of decisions taken under Section 40.1 of the former Immigration Act and under former Division 9 of IRPA. Division 9 was replaced on March 5, 2008 as a result of the Supreme Court of Canada's decision in *Charkaoui, Re* (2007), 59 Imm. L.R. (3d) 1, that concluded there were two defects in the legislation that were inconsistent with the *Charter*. While the security provisions of the former Act and the sections under former Division 9 are differently worded, it is thought that these annotations may contribute to the development of the law in this very difficult area.

We have preserved summaries of decisions annotated under the former *Immigration Act* which dealt with the definition of a Convention Refugee. These case summaries are included under sections 96 and 108 of IRPA. Cases concerning the Schedule, Sections E and F of Article 1 of the United Nations Convention Relating to the Status of Refugees, decided under the former Act, follow the Schedule to the IRPA. In addition, procedural decisions regarding refugee hearings under the former Act are collected under the Refugee Protection Division Rules, section 67.

Cases under the former legislation dealing with the requirements to obtain a stay of a removal order are collected under section 18.2 of the *Federal Courts Act*. It is recognized that in some cases the application for a stay is made because an H&C application is pending. Such orders are perhaps inherently different than those described in section 18.2. We decided that it was better to collect all of the decisions involving judicial stays under the former Act in one place and chose section 18.2 of the *Federal Courts Act* for that purpose.

We have included the IRB Guidelines issued by the Chairperson pursuant to section 65(3) of the former Act and section 159(1)(h) of IRPA.

Bill C-11, entitled the *Balanced Refugee Reform Act*, passed but only after significant evolution prior to Royal Assent. Please note, although the provisions in Bill C-11 came into force immediately, the appeal provisions (section 31) in the existing legislation came into force on December 15, 2012. This annotation now includes summaries of cases challenging both the jurisdiction and correctness of decisions of the Refugee Appeal Division.

Changes to the Regulations dealing with Temporary Foreign Workers and changes to the Regulations dealing with the sponsorship of parents and grandparents came into force in 2014, along with changes to the definition of a dependent child which came into force on August 1, 2014. As anticipated, these changes had a profound impact on foreign workers in Canada and prospective immigrants to Canada and their families. Consequently, it is not surprising that the Federal Government elected in the fall of 2015 has made it a priority to address these issues. Regulations to change the definition of the age of a dependent child back to under 21 years old were published October 29, 2016. Announcements from the Minister, Immigration Refugee Citizenship Canada ("the Minister"), to address some of the issues surrounding work permits are expected in late 2016. Meanwhile the Minister has already increased the number of applications to sponsor parents and grandparents that will be received each year.

There have been many procedural changes that have taken place in the last few years, including closures of visa offices abroad and Citizenship and Immigration Offices in Canada, resulting in the redistribution of numerous applications and on January 1, 2015, the introduction of Express Entry, a new case management system to process permanent resident cases. Initially we saw some positive impact on the delivery of immigration services to those wishing to come to Canada and those wanting to stay in Canada, but we have observed that the rights of many applicants and prospective applicants have been negatively impacted by these changes. Consequently these matters are also ending up before the courts. Unfortunately in many instances the result has been a denial of processing within a reasonable period of time and often no ability to administratively resolve issues since calls and emails to Government of Canada representatives are often unanswered. Furthermore, Express Entry has been an obstacle to many foreign workers and students in Canada who meet the criteria for permanent residence and are unable to secure an invitation to apply. The Minister has indicated that there will be announcements in the near future to alleviate some of the issues for these temporary residents.

The procedural changes and the numerous changes in policy to the Temporary Foreign Worker Program have had a negative impact on economic activity in Canada. Companies routinely find it difficult to obtain approvals for key positions including for senior executives responsible for growing Canadian businesses. Employers and businesses are treated as if they have previously failed to comply with immigration requirements and the onus is put on the employer to satisfy Federal Government officials that they have complied with requirements, which are not clearly defined. The result is employers may inadvertently fail to comply by merely giving a foreign worker an annual wage increase. Regulations that came into force December 1, 2015, to provide for administrative monetary penalties to be imposed against employers found to be non-compliant with terms of labour market impact assessments or work permits issued under the Temporary Foreign Worker Program or the International Mobility Program.

Preface

The rules and policies of the former Government of Canada lacked clarity and openness and discouraged the facilitation of foreign workers, business visitors and tourists. They were counterintuitive and changed the Canadian Immigration landscape. One year after the new Government was sworn in, there have been a number of announcements and promises of change, but it is too early to know if there will be meaningful change

Once again, we have observed counsel advocating and litigating various issues under the *Immigration and Refugee Protection Act* and we have been impressed with the extent to which they have pursued litigation, not only in the interest of their clients but in the interest of the evolution of the interpretation and application of this legislation. Both the Immigration Bar and the Minister's representatives have made a significant contribution in this regard. Often, it is more cost efficient to reapply or at least, to avoid the risk of having a negative decision for the client in a judicial forum; however, countless times over this past year, cases have been judicially reviewed for the benefit of all future applicants applying under the provisions of IRPA. These litigants, their counsel and the Minister's representatives should all be commended for their advocacy skills.

Again this year we want to recognize the significant contribution the judiciary makes to the development of immigration law. Federal Court Judges face many challenges, including an increasing case load due to significant legislative changes; difficult and complex factual and legal cases due to international events that impact many refugee claimants; and criticism by the current government that challenges their role as independent decision makers. We expect the judiciary will continue to play an important role in immigration law.

We are indebted once again to those members of the legal profession, Citizenship and Immigration Canada, the Canada Border Service Agency, Employment and Social Development Canada and the Immigration and Refugee Board who have provided constructive criticism to us throughout the year. All of these comments were most gratefully received and many of them have been incorporated into this year's edition.

We wish to thank our publisher for its assistance in providing us with decisions, the citations which appear in our text, the table of cases and the index. We wish to express our thanks to Brenda Wong, Donna Pyza, Natalie Lofeudo, Sjarif Jonathan Ismail, Natallia Valynchuk, Jacqueline Bonisteel, and Douglas Tsoi for their assistance in the preparation of the 2017 edition. We also wish to recognize the contribution of Frank Marrocco and Pamela Hudson to previous editions of our text. Without the care and attention of these persons, this edition would not have been possible. This edition contains all relevant cases which have come to our attention as of June 30, 2016.

October 31, 2016
Toronto, Ontario

Henry M. Goslett
Barbara Jo Caruso

SUMMARY TABLE OF CONTENTS

TABLE OF CONTENTS

IMMIGRATION AND REFUGEE PROTECTION ACT

Table of Contents

Table of Contents

Table of Contents

Table of Contents

Table of Contents

Table of Contents

Table of Contents

Table of Contents

s

Coming Into Force

SOR 2002-227 — IMMIGRATION AND REFUGEE PROTECTION REGULATIONS

PART 1 — INTERPRETATION AND APPLICATION

DIVISION 1 — INTERPRETATION

DIVISION 2 — FAMILY RELATIONSHIPS

PART 2 — GENERAL REQUIREMENTS

DIVISION 1 — DOCUMENTS REQUIRED BEFORE ENTRY

DIVISION 2 — APPLICATIONS

Table of Contents

Table of Contents

Table of Contents

Table of Contents

Transitional Federal Skilled Workers
Transitional Federal Skilled Worker Class

Requirements

Quebec Skilled Worker Class

Provincial Nominee Class

Canadian Experience Class

Federal Skilled Trades Class

DIVISION 2 — BUSINESS IMMIGRANTS
Interpretation

Investors
Investors Class

Fund

Investor Selected by a Province

Entrepreneurs
Entrepreneur Class

Conditions

Entrepreneur Selected by a Province

Self-employed Persons
Self-employed Persons Class

Self-employed Person Selected by a Province

Table of Contents

Selection Criteria
General

Experience

Adaptability

Requirements

Selection

Transitional Federal Investors, Entrepreneurs and Self-employed Persons
Transitional Federal Business Classes

Requirements

DIVISION 3 — LIVE-IN CAREGIVERS

PART 7 — FAMILY CLASSES
DIVISION 1 — FAMILY CLASS

DIVISION 2 — SPOUSE OR COMMON-LAW PARTNER IN CANADA CLASS

Table of Contents

Table of Contents

Table of Contents

Table of Contents

Table of Contents

Table of Contents

Table of Contents

Table of Contents

Table of Contents

Table of Contents

SOR 2011-142 — REGULATIONS DESIGNATING A BODY FOR THE PURPOSES OF PARAGRAPH 91(2)(C) OF THE IMMIGRATION AND REFUGEE PROTECTION ACT

Table of Contents

COMING INTO FORCE

SOR 2012-256 — REFUGEE PROTECTION DIVISION RULES

Table of Contents

Table of Contents

SCHEDULE 1 — CLAIMANT'S INFORMATION AND BASIS OF CLAIM

SCHEDULE 2 — INFORMATION TO BE PROVIDED ABOUT THE CLAIMANT BY AN OFFICER

SCHEDULE 3 — INFORMATION AND DECLARATIONS — COUNSEL NOT REPRESENTING OR ADVISING FOR CONSIDERATION

SOR 2012-257 — REFUGEE APPEAL DIVISION RULES

INTERPRETATION

PART 1 — RULES APPLICABLE TO APPEALS MADE BY A PERSON WHO IS THE SUBJECT OF AN APPEAL

Filing and Perfecting an Appeal

Intervention by the Minister

Reply

Extension of Time

Disposition of an Appeal

PART 2 — RULES APPLICABLE TO APPEALS MADE BY THE MINISTER

Filing and Perfecting an Appeal

Response to an Appeal

Reply

Extension of Time

Disposition of an Appeal

PART 3 — RULES APPLICABLE TO ALL APPEALS

Communicating with the Division

Counsel

Table of Contents

Table of Contents

Table of Contents

Table of Contents

Table of Contents

SOR 2002-230 — IMMIGRATION APPEAL DIVISION RULES

Table of Contents

Table of Contents

SOR 2012-255 — OATH OR SOLEMN AFFIRMATION OF OFFICE RULES (IMMIGRATION AND REFUGEE BOARD)

FEDERAL COURTS ACT

Table of Contents

PART 4 — ACTIONS
Summary Judgment and Summary Trial
Motion and Service

Striking Out Pleadings

PART 5 — APPLICATIONS
General

PART 7 — MOTIONS

PART 9 — CASE MANAGEMENT AND DISPUTE RESOLUTION SERVICES
Case Management
Specially Managed Proceedings

PART 10 — ORDERS

PART 11 — COSTS
Awarding of Costs Between Parties

SOR 93-22 — FEDERAL COURTS CITIZENSHIP, IMMIGRATION AND REFUGEE PROTECTION RULES

INTERPRETATION

APPLICATION

FORM OF APPLICATION FOR LEAVE

EXTENSION OF TIME TO FILE AND SERVE APPLICATION FOR LEAVE

FILING AND SERVICE OF APPLICATION FOR LEAVE

NOTICE OF APPEARANCE

OBTAINING TRIBUNAL'S DECISION AND REASONS

CANADA EVIDENCE ACT

PART I

Specified Public Interest

Table of Contents

PRIVACY ACT
ACCESS TO PERSONAL INFORMATION
Right of Access

APPENDIX I
GUIDELINES ISSUED BY THE CHAIRPERSON

APPENDIX II

AN ACT RESPECTING IMMIGRATION TO QUÉBEC
DIVISION I — DEFINITION

DIVISION II — SELECTION OF FOREIGN NATIONALS

DIVISION III — INTEGRATION OF FOREIGN NATIONALS

APPENDIX III

QUÉBEC IMMIGRATION ACT [PROPOSED]

Table of Contents

Chapter III — Temporary and Permanent Immigration

DIVISION I — IMMIGRATION CLASSES AND PROGRAMS

DIVISION II — TEMPORARY IMMIGRATION

DIVISION III — TRANSITION TO PERMANENT IMMIGRATION

DIVISION IV — PERMANENT IMMIGRATION

§1. — General provisions

1. — Selection for Permanent Immigration

2. — Sponsorship Undertaking

§2. — Economic class

§3. — Family class

§4. — Humanitarian class

Chapter IV — Override Power

Table of Contents

Table of Contents

Chapter IX — Required Fees

Chapter X — Delegation and Agreements

Chapter XI — Inspection and Investigation
DIVISION I — INSPECTION

DIVISION II — INVESTIGATION

DIVISION III — MISCELLANEOUS PROVISIONS

Chapter XII — Penal Provisions

Chapter XIII — Regulations

APPENDIX X

CONSTITUTION ACT, 1982

PART I — CANADIAN CHARTER OF RIGHTS AND FREEDOMS

Table of Contents

Equality Rights

Official Languages of Canada

Minority Language Educational Rights

Enforcement

Application of Charter

Citation

TABLE OF CASES

Table of Cases

Table of Cases

Table of Cases

Table of Cases

Table of Cases

Table of Cases

Table of Cases

Table of Cases

Table of Cases

Table of Cases

Table of Cases

Table of Cases

Table of Cases

Table of Cases

Table of Cases

Table of Cases

Table of Cases

Table of Cases

Table of Cases

Table of Cases

Table of Cases

Table of Cases

Table of Cases

Table of Cases

Table of Cases

Table of Cases

Table of Cases

Table of Cases

Table of Cases

Table of Cases

Table of Cases

Table of Cases

Table of Cases

Table of Cases

Table of Cases

Table of Cases

Table of Cases

IMMIGRATION AND REFUGEE PROTECTION ACT

An Act respecting immigration to Canada and the granting of refugee protection to persons who are displaced, persecuted or in danger

S.C. 2001, c. 27 [s. 245 not in force at date of publication. Repealed 2004, c. 15, s. 110.], as am. S.C. 2001, c. 27, s. 273.1(3); 2001, c. 32, s. 81(3); 2001, c. 41, s. 123; 2002, c. 8, s. 194; 2003, c. 22, ss. 172, 173, 225(z.3); 2004, c. 15, ss. 70–72, 110; 2005, c. 10, s. 34(1)(o), (2); 2005, c. 20, s. 81; 2005, c. 38, ss. 118, 119; 2008, c. 3, ss. 1–5; 2008, c. 28, ss. 116–119; 2010, c. 8, ss. 2, 3, 4(1), (2) (Fr.), 5–9, 10 (Fr.), 11–27.1, 28(1), (2) (Fr.), 29–31 [ss. 8, 15(1), (2), (5), 16, 24, 25, 27(1), 27.1 not in force at date of publication.] [s. 8 repealed 2011, c. 8, s. 6(2).] [ss. 11, 11.1, 12, 14.1, 15, 20, 23 amended 2012, c. 17, ss. 56–61, 63.] [ss. 21, 24 repealed 2012, c. 17, ss. 62, 64.]; 2011, c. 8, ss. 1–4; 2012, c. 1, ss. 149, 150, 205–208; 2012, c. 17, ss. 2–12, 13(1), (2) (Fr.), (3), (4) (Fr.), 14–40, 41(1), (2) (Fr.), (3) (Fr.), (4), 42(1), (2) (Fr.), (3), 43, 44(1) (Fr.), (2), 45 (Fr.), 46, 47(1) (Fr.), (2), 48, 49, 50(1), (2) (Fr.), (3), 51–55, 84 [ss. 11(1), 31, 40, 54 not in force at date of publication.] [s. 30 amended 2012, c. 31, s. 313(4).]; 2012, c. 19, ss. 311, 700–705, 706(1), (2)–(4) (Fr.), (5), 707, 708, 710; 2012, c. 31, ss. 308–312, 313(2), 314; 2013, c. 16, ss. 2–27, 36(2), (3), (10), (11), 37(2)(b) [ss. 19, 22, 23, 25–27 not in force at date of publication; s. 36(10), (11) conditions not yet satisfied.] [s. 12 repealed 2013, c. 16, s. 37(2)(a); ss. 22, 23 amended 2013, c. 16, ss. 36(4), (7)(a).]; 2013, c. 33, ss. 161–166; 2013, c. 40, ss. 235, 237(1)(i), 238(1)(h), 290–292 [s. 290 amended 2014, c. 20, s. 306.]; 2014, c. 20, ss. 299–305; 2014, c. 22, ss. 42, 43; 2014, c. 39, ss. 306–313 [ss. 306, 308, 309(1), 311, 313(2) not in force at date of publication.]; 2015, c. 3, ss. 108–111, 112 (Fr.), 113 (Fr.), 114, 115–117; 2015, c. 20, ss. 52–60; 2015, c. 29, s. 2 [Not in force at date of publication.]; 2015, c. 36, ss. 168–175 [Not in force at date of publication.].

[Editor's Note: The Immigration Act, *R.S.C. 1985, c. I-2 has been repealed by 2001, c. 27, s. 274(a) and replaced by the* Immigration and Refugee Protection Act, *S.C. 2001, c. 27, effective June 28, 2002.]*

Despite the repeal of the Immigration Act, *R.S.C. 1985, c. I-2, the "former Act", there are substantial transitional provisions that may apply to the particular proceeding or transaction. Reference should be made to the transitional provisions which speak to the continuing application of the former Act in certain situations in S.C. 2001, c. 27, ss. 187–201, either by express reference therein or as prescribed by the new* Immigration and Refugee Protection Regulations, *SOR/2002-227.*

The Immigration Regulations, *1978, SOR/78-172, the* Refugee Claimants Designated Class Regulations, *SOR/90-40, the* Immigration Act Fees Regulations, *SOR/97-22, and the* Humanitarian Designated Classes Regulations, *SOR/97-183, the "former Regulations", have been repealed and replaced by ss. 364(a), (b), (c), (d), respectively, of the*

Immigration and Refugee Protection Regulations, *SOR/2002-227, effective June 28, 2002. Despite the repeal of the former Regulations, there are substantial transitional provisions that may apply to the particular proceeding or transaction. Reference should be made to the transitional provisions which speak to the continuing application of the former Act in certain situations and as previously prescribed by the former Regulations in SOR/2002-227, ss. 316–363.]*

Her Majesty, by and with the advice and consent of the Senate and House of Commons of Canada, enacts as follows:

SHORT TITLE

1. Short title — This Act may be cited as the *Immigration and Refugee Protection Act.*

INTERPRETATION

2. (1) Definitions — The definitions in this subsection apply in this Act.

"Board" means the Immigration and Refugee Board, which consists of the Refugee Protection Division, Refugee Appeal Division, Immigration Division and Immigration Appeal Division. *("Commission")*

"Convention Against Torture" means the Convention Against Torture and Other Cruel, Inhuman or Degrading Treatment or Punishment, signed at New York on December 10, 1984. Article 1 of the Convention Against Torture is set out in the schedule. *("Convention contre la torture")*

"designated foreign national" has the meaning assigned by subsection 20.1(2). *("étranger désigné")*

"foreign national" means a person who is not a Canadian citizen or a permanent resident, and includes a stateless person. *("étranger")*

"permanent resident" means a person who has acquired permanent resident status and has not subsequently lost that status under section 46. *("résident permanent")*

[Editor's Note: SOR/2002-227, s. 328(1) provides that a person who was a permanent resident immediately before June 28, 2002 is a permanent resident under the new Immigration and Refugee Protection Act, S.C. 2001, c. 27.]

"Refugee Convention" means the United Nations Convention Relating to the Status of Refugees, signed at Geneva on July 28, 1951, and the Protocol to that Convention, signed at New York on January 31, 1967. Sections E and F of Article 1 of the Refugee Convention are set out in the schedule. *("Convention sur les réfugiés")*

(2) Act includes regulations and instructions — Unless otherwise indicated, references in this Act to "this Act" include regulations made under it and instructions given under subsection 14.1(1).

2012, c. 17, s. 2; 2012, c. 19, s. 700

OBJECTIVES AND APPLICATION

3. (1) **Objectives — immigration** — The objectives of this Act with respect to immigration are

(a) to permit Canada to pursue the maximum social, cultural and economic benefits of immigration;

(b) to enrich and strengthen the social and cultural fabric of Canadian society, while respecting the federal, bilingual and multi-cultural character of Canada;

(b.1) to support and assist the development of minority official languages communities in Canada;

(c) to support the development of a strong and prosperous Canadian economy, in which the benefits of immigration are shared across all regions of Canada;

(d) to see that families are reunited in Canada;

(e) to promote the successful integration of permanent residents into Canada, while recognizing that integration involves mutual obligations for new immigrants and Canadian society;

(f) to support, by means of consistent standards and prompt processing, the attainment of immigration goals established by the Government of Canada in consultation with the provinces;

(g) to facilitate the entry of visitors, students and temporary workers for purposes such as trade, commerce, tourism, international understanding and cultural, educational and scientific activities;

(h) to protect public health and safety and to maintain the security of Canadian society;

(i) to promote international justice and security by fostering respect for human rights and by denying access to Canadian territory to persons who are criminals or security risks; and

(j) to work in cooperation with the provinces to secure better recognition of the foreign credentials of permanent residents and their more rapid integration into society.

(2) **Objectives — refugees** — The objectives of this Act with respect to refugees are

(a) to recognize that the refugee program is in the first instance about saving lives and offering protection to the displaced and persecuted;

(b) to fulfil Canada's international legal obligations with respect to refugees and affirm Canada's commitment to international efforts to provide assistance to those in need of resettlement;

(c) to grant, as a fundamental expression of Canada's humanitarian ideals, fair consideration to those who come to Canada claiming persecution;

(d) to offer safe haven to persons with a well-founded fear of persecution based on race, religion, nationality, political opinion or membership in a particular social group, as well as those at risk of torture or cruel and unusual treatment or punishment;

IRP Act

(e) to establish fair and efficient procedures that will maintain the integrity of the Canadian refugee protection system, while upholding Canada's respect for the human rights and fundamental freedoms of all human beings;

(f) to support the self-sufficiency and the social and economic well-being of refugees by facilitating reunification with their family members in Canada;

(g) to protect the health and safety of Canadians and to maintain the security of Canadian society; and

(h) to promote international justice and security by denying access to Canadian territory to persons, including refugee claimants, who are security risks or serious criminals.

[Editor's Note: SOR/2002-227, s. 320(1) provides that a person is inadmissible under the new Immigration and Refugee Protection Act, *S.C. 2001, c. 27 on security grounds if, on June 28, 2002, the person had been determined to be a member of an inadmissible class described in paragraph 19(1)(e), (f), (g) or (k) of the former* Immigration Act, *R.S.C. 1985, c. I-2.]*

(3) **Application** — This Act is to be construed and applied in a manner that

(a) furthers the domestic and international interests of Canada;

(b) promotes accountability and transparency by enhancing public awareness of immigration and refugee programs;

(c) facilitates cooperation between the Government of Canada, provincial governments, foreign states, international organizations and non-governmental organizations;

(d) ensures that decisions taken under this Act are consistent with the *Canadian Charter of Rights and Freedoms*, including its principles of equality and freedom from discrimination and of the equality of English and French as the official languages of Canada;

(e) supports the commitment of the Government of Canada to enhance the vitality of the English and French linguistic minority communities in Canada; and

(f) complies with international human rights instruments to which Canada is signatory.

2012, c. 1, s. 205

Case Law

Section 3(1)

Agraira v. Canada (Minister of Public Safety & Emergency Preparedness) (2013), 16 Imm. L.R. (4th) 173, 52 Admin. L.R. (5th) 183, 360 D.L.R. (4th) 411, 2013 SCC 36, 2013 CarswellNat 1983, 2013 CarswellNat 1984 — The appellant, a citizen of Libya, had been residing in Canada continuously since 1997, despite having been found to be inadmissible on security grounds in 2002. The finding of inadmissibility was based on his membership in a Libyan National Salvation Front ("LNSF"), a terrorist organization according to CIC. The appellant applied in 2002 under s. 34(2) of the *Immigration and Refugee Protection Act* for ministerial relief from the determination of inadmissibility, but his application was denied in 2009. The Minister of Public Safety and Emergency

Preparedness ("Minister") concluded that it was not in the national interest to admit individuals who have had substantial contact with known terrorist and/or terrorist-connected organizations. The appellant's application for permanent residence was denied. The Federal Court granted the application for judicial review. The Federal Court of Appeal, however, allowed the appeal and dismissed the application for judicial review concluding that the Minister's decision was reasonable. The Supreme Court of Canada concluded that the Minister's decision under s. 34(2) of the IRPA should be allowed to stand and dismissed the appeal. The standard of review applicable in the case at bar is reasonableness.

The meaning of the term "national interest" in s. 34(2) of the IRPA was central to the Minister's exercise of discretion in this case. As is plain from the statute, the Minister exercises this discretion by determining whether he or she is satisfied by the applicant and the applicant's presence in Canada would not be detrimental to the national interest. The meaning of "national interest" in the context of this section is accordingly key, as it defines the standard the Minister must apply to assess the effect of the applicant's presence in Canada in order to exercise his or her discretion. The Minister, in making his decision with respect to the appellant, did not expressly define the term "national interest." The Minister's interpretation of the term "national interest," namely that it focussed on matters related to national security and public safety, but also encompasses the other important considerations outlined in the Guidelines and any analogous considerations, is reasonable. The Guidelines did not constitute a fixed and rigid code. Rather, they contained a set of factors, which appeared to be relevant and reasonable, for the evaluation of applications for ministerial relief. The Minister did not have to apply them formulaically, but they guided the exercise of his discretion and assisted in framing a fair administrative process for such applications.

The Minister's implied interpretation of the term "national interest" encompasses all the factors referred to in the Guidelines. The appellant acknowledged, these factors included humanitarian and compassionate factors. The Minister "reviewed and considered the material in evidence submitted in its entirety." Therefore, if the appellant had a legitimate expectation that the Minister would consider certain factors, including humanitarian and compassionate factors, in determining his application for relief, this expectation was fulfilled.

[Editor's note: Although s. 34(2) of IRPA was repealed June 19, 2013, it may still have relevance as it relates to the objective and application of the Act.]

Yazdani v. Canada (Minister of Citizenship & Immigration) (2010), 92 Imm. L.R. (3d) 97, 324 D.L.R. (4th) 552, 14 Admin. L.R. (5th) 74, 374 F.T.R. 149 (Eng.), 2010 FC 885, 2010 CarswellNat 3204, 2010 CarswellNat 3631 — The court considered who bears the risk when email notices are sent by a reviewing visa officer but are not received by the applicant's agent who has exercised due diligence. In the case at hand, there had been no prior successful email transmission between the Warsaw visa office and the consultant's office. Nor did the [CIC] Protocol or Email Communications contemplate and provide safeguard measures for email transmission failures (such as alternate follow-up by mailing the letter). Finally, the visa application system does not provide for reconsideration in such circumstances. The respondent chose to send an important and crucial notice to the applicant via email without safeguards in place. The respondent therefore bears the risk of an email transmission failure when it sent the crucial request to the applicant. The application for judicial review was allowed.

Alavi v. Canada (Minister of Citizenship & Immigration) (2010), 92 Imm. L.R. (3d) 170, 2010 FC 969, 2010 CarswellNat 3633 — The court quashed the refusal of the applicant's application which was based on a failure to supply information requested in a communication which the applicant's representative, in affidavit evidence, said was never received and because the respondent Minister did not put proper evidence before the court that the communication was sent. The so called "risk" involved in a failure of communication is to be borne by the Minister if it cannot be proved that the communication in question was sent by the Minister's officials. However, once the Minister proves that the communication was sent, the applicant bears the risk involved in a failure to receive the communication.

Shahid v. Canada (Minister of Citizenship & Immigration) (2010), 89 Imm. L.R. (3d) 19, 2010 FC 405, 2010 CarswellNat 2897, 2010 CarswellNat 931 — This was an application for judicial review of the Minister's failure to take a decision on their application for landing and a remedy in the nature of *mandamus*. The applicant was granted refugee status in May 2001 and applied for permanent residence in 2002. He was notified on September 5, 2001, that he met the eligibility requirements and that a decision would be made within 18 months. No decision had been made yet.

There is no dispute that the Minister has a duty to process the applicants' application. There is also no dispute that the applicants have satisfied all conditions precedent to the performance of the Minister's duty by providing all the necessary information. Nor is there any dispute as to the fact that they have repeatedly demanded that the Minister perform the duty. The sole issue in this case is whether enough time has passed since the applicant made this demand, and whether the Minister can be inferred to have refused to act. An inference may be drawn from "unreasonable" delay in making a decision. Eight years is, *prima facie*, a much longer delay than routine background checks require. CIC's lack of diligence in the applicant's file is shocking and in direct contradiction with IRPA's objective set out in para. 3(1)(f): "to support, by means of consistent standards and prompt processing, the attainment of immigration goals established by the government of Canada." An order in the nature of *mandamus* requiring the respondent to process the applicant's application for permanent residence in accordance with the law was issued. A decision was to be provided to the applicant within three months of the order.

Singh v. Canada (Minister of Citizenship & Immigration) (2010), 89 Imm. L.R. (3d) 36, 2010 FC 378, 2010 CarswellNat 3016, 2010 CarswellNat 817, [2010] F.C.J. No. 426 — The applicant was recently found to be inadmissible for misrepresenting or withholding a material fact when he immigrated to Canada in 1993. At that time, he did not disclose that he had fathered a child who remained in India. His defence is that he did not know he had fathered a child. Paternity has now been scientifically established by DNA tests. As a result, the Immigration Division of the Immigration and Refugee Board of Canada issued an exclusion order and he was ordered removed from Canada. His appeal to the Immigration Appeal Division was dismissed. He sought judicial review of that decision.

The applicant's submission is that he could not have misrepresented or withheld facts within the meaning of s. 40 of IRPA or its predecessor, since subjectively he had no knowledge at the time that he was the girl Shilpa's biological father. The Minister's position is that it does not matter what the applicant knew or did not know, it is a scientifically proven fact that he is Shilpa's biological father, and that is the end of the matter.

Given that the wording "knowingly" does not appear in s. 40, it follows, that knowledge is not a prerequisite to a finding of misrepresentation or withholding material facts. Undoubtedly, the existence of a child is a material fact. In this case, the alleged misrepresentation was a misstatement of fact. Such misrepresentations may be fraudulent, negligent or innocent. The panel found that the applicant was not credible. Even if he did not know that he was Shilpa's father, the circumstances, *i.e.* his long sexual relationship with Shilpa's mother while her husband was out of India, should, at the very least, have put him on inquiry. He had a duty of candour which required him to disclose upon his arrival in Canada in 1993 the strong possibility that he had fathered a child. The panel's assessment of facts was not unreasonable and so it follows that the applicant, a permanent resident, is inadmissible for misrepresentation.

One of the objectives of IRPA, as set out in s. 3, is "to see that families are reunited in Canada," not to remove someone against his will so that he may be reunited with his wife and daughter in India. The panel noted that the applicant had been here for many years, and had been gainfully employed, however, it made no assessment of the job prospects of a 50-year-old man in India, taking into account his obligation to support his wife and child. How the couple manages their affairs is their business. It would appear that they would prefer that the applicant work in Canada. There is nothing preventing him from visiting his wife and daughter in India on a regular basis. Perhaps after he has saved more money, he will return to and retire in India. It was not for the panel to say that they would be better off if reunited in India now. This smacked of "big brotherhood." This aspect of the decision was unreasonable. The matter was referred back to a differently constituted panel for reconsideration.

Koromila v. Canada (Minister of Citizenship & Immigration), 2009 CarswellNat 1167, 2009 FC 393 — The applicant sought judicial review of a decision to refuse an application on H&C grounds pursuant to s. 25 of the IRPA. The applicant's mother died when she was aged 3 and her father never remarried. The applicant and her sister were raised in Greece by their father and their aunt. Their father died of a heart attack when they were teenagers and their aunt continued to care for them. The applicant's sister met a Canadian citizen and immigrated to Canada. The applicant remained in Greece to live and help support her aunt. It was their intention to join her sister and her husband in Canada. Subsequently, the aunt had a very bad stroke and was paralyzed. The applicant remained in Greece to look after her aunt. The aunt died in December 2002. The applicant is alone in Greece and is currently an elderly woman. The applicant says that, as they age, it will become more difficult for her and her sister to visit each other. The applicant applied for permanent residence in Canada in June of 2007 and was refused by the officer.

The officer's stated understanding of the scope of s. 3(1)(d) of the Act is that "the objective of the law was to reunite parents with their children or children with parents or spouses." The officer either misunderstood the scope of s. 3(1)(d) and so fettered his discretion or he made a mistake of law. There was no evidence before the court that the officer was cognizant of the principle enunciated in para. 3(1)(d) of the Act or of the considerations to be taken into account as enunciated in the elements of the OP 4 in considering whether a *de facto* family member should qualify for relief on humanitarian and compassionate considerations. This error was compounded by the officer's assessment that the applicant's coming to Canada permanently was simply a matter of convenience and that the applicant was not a *de facto* family member who had been left behind. The visa officer ignored the evidence of emotional dependency. There is a significant factual difference between living together and sharing day-to-day life and an occasional visit. Such matters seem to have been left entirely out of account by the officer to an unreasonable extent. The officer did not consider the application of subs. 3(1)(d) of the Act to this case. The application for judicial review was allowed.

Khalil v. R. (2007), 65 Imm. L.R. (3d) 8, 317 F.T.R. 32, 160 C.R.R. (2d) 234, 2007 FC 923, 2007 CarswellNat 2910, 2007 CarswellNat 5360, [2007] F.C.J. No. 1221; affirmed (2009), 78 Imm. L.R. (3d) 1, 64 C.C.L.T. (3d) 199, 2009 CarswellNat 550, 2009 CarswellNat 1303, 2009 FCA 66 — The plaintiffs alleged that the defendant's delay in processing their application for permanent residence caused some harm for which they claimed damages. They asserted that their entitlement to damages arises from the defendant's negligence and the infringement of their s. 7 and 15 rights under the *Canadian Charter of Rights and Freedoms*. For this infringement, they claim a remedy under subs. 24(1) of the *Charter*. Although the plaintiffs established that there was unreasonable and inordinate delay in the processing of their applications for permanent residence, delay is not a free-standing cause of action. There was insufficient proximity between the plaintiffs and the defendant to find a private law duty of care. Additionally, there are compelling policy reasons that militate against the imposition of such a duty. Even if it were otherwise, causation was not established. Consequently, the plaintiffs could not succeed in negligence. The plaintiffs did not establish that their liberty interests under s. 7 of the *Charter* were engaged on the facts of this matter. The s. 7 security of the person interests are not engaged because the alleged harm is not state imposed.

To impose a private law duty of care on the relationship between the plaintiffs' and the defendant's officials "creates a general potential for serious and significant conflict" with the statutory duty to protect the public interest, including the health and safety of Canadians and the maintenance of the security of Canadian society. In this case, the delay in processing the plaintiffs' application for permanent residence arose in large part as a result of potential inadmissibility under para. 34(1)(f) of the IRPA. The purpose of the legislated inadmissibility provisions is protection of the public.

David v. Canada (Minister of Citizenship & Immigration), 2007 CarswellNat 1385, 2007 FC 546 — This was an application for judicial review of a decision of the First Secretary, Immigration, of the Canadian Embassy in the Philippines denying an application for permanent residence based on humanitarian and compassionate grounds. The applicant filed a sponsorship application for his wife and three sons requesting that the application for his wife and eldest son be considered under humanitarian and compassionate grounds and that they be exempted from the application of para. 117(9)(d) of the Regulations.

The exclusion mentioned at para. 117(9)(d) of the Regulations is a very harsh one, but does not prevent a sponsor from invoking H&C grounds considerations. Indeed, the very reason why the Court of Appeal in *De Guzman* (2005), 51 Imm. L.R. (3d) 17, found that this provision is compliant with the international instruments to which Canada is a signatory is that s. 25 of the Act enables the Act to be administered in a compliant manner.

The First Secretary, Immigration, at the Canadian Embassy did not make any findings of fact with respect to the evidence tendered by the applicants, such as the relationship between the sponsor and his wife and son, the fact that the sponsor had been supporting the family financially, the frequency of their contact, as well as the letters tendered by various members of the family and others in support of their application. It is clear in this case that the First Secretary did not make a separate assessment for the oldest son's application and as such, did not address his best interest as the child of the sponsor. Instead, he simply stated that the application of the two youngest son's would proceed "but it is sponsor's choice if he wants to split his family further and take his two youngest children from their mother in the Philippines." The officer's notes do not provide a clear rationale of why any of the public policy considerations mentioned by the First Secretary (such as the past misrepresentations) should prevail here over the objective at para. 3(1)(d) of the Act "to see that families are reunited in Canada." Nor do they reveal whether the First Secretary considered that the *de facto* family members excluded from the family class because of para. 117(9)(d) of the Regulations may suffer hardship indefinitely.

Nalbandian v. Canada (Minister of Citizenship & Immigration) (2006), 56 Imm. L.R. (3d) 67, 2006 CarswellNat 2899, 2006 FC 1128 — The applicant sought judicial review of the decision that humanitarian and compassionate considerations did not justify granting the applicant permanent residence in Canada. The applicant was a citizen of Iraq in her late 60s or early 70s. She was a Christian and fled to Jordan with her daughter in 1990 due to horrific circumstances in Iraq. She did not have permanent status in Jordan. The applicant's daughter and her son subsequently fled to the Netherlands and claimed refugee status. Neither was in a position to support immigration of the applicant to the Netherlands. The applicant's three brothers and sisters all fled directly to Canada and were all citizens of Canada. They were well established in Canada and providing economic support to the applicant. They provided a detailed plan to support the applicant's settlement in Canada. The applicant also has 13 nephews and nieces who are all Canadian citizens. While the decision arrived at by the officer might well be open to her, against a standard of review of reasonableness *simpliciter*, and against the terms of para. 3(1)(d) of the Act and the guidance provided in OP4 to persons such as the officer, the officer erred in a reviewable manner in not documenting her decision against the prescribed criteria. The judicial review was allowed and the applicant's application for permanent residence in Canada referred back for reconsideration.

Six years elapsed between the filing of the application and a decision which represented "special circumstances" justifying an award of costs.

R. v. Premakumaran (2006), 53 Imm. L.R. (3d) 161, [2007] 2 F.C.R. 191, 2006 CarswellNat 1590, 2006 FCA 213 — The appellants were immigrants to Canada from the United Kingdom who were living comfortably when they began to investigate the idea of coming to Canada. They had relatives in Canada and they believed there was work opportunity for accountants, a field in which Mr. Premakumaran was involved. They were accepted as immigrants in the skilled immigrant category but had difficulty finding suitable work. For eight years they had to do menial work to keep them and their four children alive, causing them severe economic, physical and psychological damage. The appellants instituted a lawsuit alleging fraudulent and negligent misrepresentation causing them financial, physical and psychological harm. They also claim that the false information was disseminated about certain job categories that were supposed to be in high demand and about the use of the processing fees which were charged to applicants for immigration. As remedies, damages were sought for expenses and pain and suffering, as well as a *mandamus* ordering the Federal Court to do certain things to fix the immigration system and to apologize publicly. The defendant brought a motion for summary judgment and the motions judge dismissed the action including the claims of fraudulent and negligent misrepresentation. The Federal Court concluded the motions judge correctly exercised his discretion in dismissing the case in its entirety. There was no evidence of fraud, the complaint about the alleged misuse of the processing fees was unfounded and the unusual remedies sought were not among those available to the court to grant. No duty of care existed as there was no special relationship of proximity and reliance in this case. There were no personal, specific representations of fact made to these particular appellants upon which they could reasonably have relied. The printed documentation and information given to them was merely general material for them to use in making an application for immigrant status. It is not correct to say that someone "who picks up a brochure or reads a poster at the High Commission is a 'neighbour'" and is owed a duty as a result. More is required. The information given to the appellants contained no guarantees of work, no guarantee of success in the licensing procedure or that any particular assistance would be forthcoming. The appeal was dismissed.

Paszkowski v. Canada (Attorney General) (2006), 51 Imm. L.R. (3d) 299, 2006 CarswellNat 359, 2006 FC 198 — The plaintiff claimed that Citizenship and Immigration officials committed torts of public misfeasance and malfeasance by delaying the processing of her June 5, 1990, permanent residence application and that her rights under the *Canadian Charter of Rights and Freedoms* were violated. As a result, the plaintiff claimed that she was deprived of opportunities to become a Canadian citizen, to travel abroad, to continue her education, to earn a living and to have more children.

The plaintiff did not establish, *prima facie*, that she was owed a duty of care by the immigration officials who dealt with her application for permanent residence. The necessary proximity required by the jurisprudence was not established. Specifically, the relationship between the plaintiff and the immigration officers arose from the implementation of the immigration policy imposed by the statute and not as a result of any misfeasance committed by the immigration officers. At the time the decision was made to deny the plaintiff's application, the legislation precluded the admissibility of the plaintiff by reason of her husband's criminal conviction. Neither the legislation nor common law imposed any duty on the immigration officers to inform the plaintiff when the law was changed such as to allow her first application to be processed or to file a fresh application.

Medovarski v. Canada (Minister of Citizenship & Immigration), [2005] 2 S.C.R. 539, 50 Imm. L.R. (3d) 1, 135 C.R.R. (2d) 1, 258 D.L.R. (4th) 193, [2005] S.C.J. No. 31, 339 N.R. 1, EYB 2005-95306, 2005 CarswellNat 2943, 2005 CarswellNat 2944, 2005 SCC 51 — The appellant was a permanent resident and had been ordered deported for serious criminality. Her removal order was automatically stayed when she appealed the deportation order to the Immigration Appeal Division. The appeal was discontinued as a result of s. 196 of the IRPA (a transitional provision), which took away the right to appeal an order for removal unless a party had, under the former Act, been "granted a stay." The trial judge set aside the decision to discontinue. However, the Federal Court of Appeal allowed the Minister of Citizenship and Immigration's appeal, holding that the purpose of the IRPA transitional provision was to deny the right of appeal in the case of an automatic stay. Section 196 of the IRPA, properly interpreted, applies only to actively granted stays. The objectives of the IRPA, as expressed in s. 3, indicate an intent to prioritize security. In keeping with these objectives, the IRPA creates a new scheme whereby a person sentenced to more than six months in prison is inadmissible pursuant to s. 36; if they have been sentenced to a prison term of more than two years, they are denied a right to appeal their removal order under s. 64 of the IRPA. The purpose in enacting the IRPA, and in particular s. 64, was to efficiently remove from the country persons who have engaged in serious criminality. Since s. 196 refers explicitly to s. 64, the transitional provision should be interpreted in light of these legislative objectives.

The deportation of a non-citizen cannot in itself implicate the liberty and security interests protected by s. 7 of the *Canadian Charter of Rights and Freedoms*. Even if the liberty and security of the person were engaged, any unfairness resulting from s. 196 would be inadequate to constitute a breach of principles of fundamental justice.

Charkaoui, Re, 2005 CarswellNat 410, 2005 CarswellNat 5111, 2005 FC 258 — This judgment has to do with the fourth review of the detention of Mr. Charkaoui that is provided for in s. 83(2). The court decided that the phrase "danger to national security" had the same meaning as the phrase "danger to the security of Canada," the meaning of which was discussed in *Suresh v. Canada (Minister of Citizenship & Immigration)*, [2002] 1 S.C.R. 3, at para. 90. The other phrase in subs. 83(3) "danger . . . to the safety of any person" includes awareness of danger before the terrorist act occurs. It applies to more than persons who have been convicted of a serious offence. Danger to national security or the safety of any person have in common the fact that Parliament has asked the designated judge when considering the release of the person concerned to analyse the evidence and consider whether either of these two dangers still exist. The wording of the section suggests that a danger to national security or the safety of any person may exist at one moment and not at another. There is a possibility the danger may be imminent but subsequently neutralized. The other phrase used in s. 83 is the phrase "unlikely to appear at a proceeding or for removal." This phrase indicates that Parliament intended a degree of probability to be taken into account by the designated judge when weighing the evidence.

In considering a conditional release, the designated judge must be satisfied, on reasonable grounds, that the person concerned is not a danger to national security or the safety of any person. If there is a danger, the judge cannot consider release, even with exceptional conditions.

When the Ministers signed the warrant for the arrest and detention of Mr. Charkaoui, they did so not in order to lay charges or eventually secure a conviction, but to make an arrest and detention that would prevent events that might occur. This tool, given to the Ministers by Parliament pursuant to subs. 82(1), is intended to "maintain the security of Canadian society" — one of the objectives of immigration as set out in para. 3(1)(h).

Detention reviews involve questions of fact peculiar to each situation. In the case at bar, the imprisonment, the passage of time, the media attention to the proceedings, the presence of the family, the community support, and the testimony of the person concerned are examples of situations to be taken into account in assessing whether a danger still exists or whether the person concerned will likely appear at a proceeding or for removal.

The court set terms for Mr. Charkaoui's release.

Chen v. Canada (Minister of Citizenship & Immigration) (2003), 232 F.T.R. 118, 2003 FCT 447, 2003 CarswellNat 2908, 2003 CarswellNat 1052 — The applicant sought to review a negative decision on an H&C application. In 1959 the applicant and his wife put their daughter in the care of her aunt and uncle when only a baby. In 1961, the aunt and uncle moved from Tianjin to Hong Kong. In order to bring the little girl with them to Hong Kong the aunt and uncle needed to show a document indicating that the child had been adopted. Therefore, the applicant and his wife signed an agreement to that effect. In 1975, the aunt and uncle immigrated to Canada and brought their adopted daughter with them. The daughter was landed as a dependent daughter and not as an adopted daughter. In 1993, the applicant and his wife were reunited with their daughter. Since their reunification the applicant has been living with his daughter who was providing him with all the necessary care. The officer found that the daughter was not an eligible sponsor as she was not satisfied that a parent/child relationship existed between the applicant and daughter. Under subs. 3(c) of the *Immigration Act*, the immigration objective established is "to facilitate the reunion in Canada of Canadian citizens and permanent residents with their close relatives from abroad." In the new *Immigration and Refugee Protection Act*, 2001, at subs. 3(1)(d), the related objective is "to see that families are reunited in Canada." In IRPA, s. 2, the word "relatives" means a person who is related by blood or adoption. There is room for interpretation of the law with respect to the immigration objectives and the new definition of "relative" so as not to preclude a person from sponsoring a biological parent if he or she already has an adoptive parent. There is enough evidence to show that there is a sufficient parent/child relationship to conclude that the immigration officer made a capricious finding of fact, which fettered her discretion.

Section 3(2)

Canadian Doctors for Refugee Care v. Canada (Attorney General) (2014), 28 Imm. L.R. (4th) 1, [2015] 2 F.C.R. 267, 2014 FC 651, 2014 CarswellNat 2430, 2014 CarswellNat 2431 — The Government of Canada has funded comprehensive health insurance coverage for refugee claimants and others who have come to Canada seeking its protection through the interim federal health program for more than 50 years. In 2012, the Governor in Council passed two Orders in Council which significantly reduced the level of health care coverage available to many such individuals, and all but eliminated it for others pursuing risk-based claims. The effect of these changes is to deny funding for life-saving medications such as insulin and cardiac drugs to impoverished refugee claimants from war-torn countries such as Afghanistan and Iraq. The effect of these changes is also to deny funding for basic pre-natal, obstetrical and paediatric care to women and children seeking the protection of Canada from "Designated Countries of Origin." The effect of these changes is to deny funding for any medical care whatsoever to individuals seeking refuge in Canada who are only entitled to a pre-removal risk assessment, even if they suffer from a health condition that poses a risk to the public health and safety of Canadians.

The Orders in Council are not *ultra vires* the prerogative powers of the Governor in Council, nor has there been a denial of procedural fairness in this case. The s. 7 *Charter* claim was dismissed on the basis that it would impose a positive obligation on the Government of Canada to fund health care for individuals seeking the protection of Canada. While it is open to the government to assign priorities and set limits of social benefit plans such as the interim federal health program, the intentional targeting of an admittedly poor, vulnerable and disadvantaged group for adverse treatment takes this situation beyond the realm of traditional *Charter* challenges to social benefit programs. The executive branch of the Canadian government has intentionally set out to make the lives of these disadvantaged individuals even more difficult than they already are in an effort to force those who have sought the protection of this country to leave Canada more quickly, and to deter others from coming here. The affected individuals are being subjected to "treatment" as contemplated by s. 12 of the *Charter*, and that this treatment is indeed "cruel and unusual." This is particularly, but not exclusively so as it affects children who have been brought to this country by their parents. The 2012 modifications to the interim federal health program potentially jeopardize the health, the safety and indeed the very lives, of these innocent and vulnerable children in a manner that shocks the conscience and outrages our standards of decency. These changes also violate s. 15 of the *Charter* inasmuch as the program now provides a lesser level of health insurance coverage to refugee claimants from Designated Countries of Origin in comparison to that provided to refugee claimants from Non-Designated Countries of Origin. This distinction is based upon the national origin of the refugee claimants, and does not form part of an ameliorative program. This distinction serves to perpetuate the historical disadvantage suffered by members of an admittedly vulnerable, poor and disadvantaged group.

The court declared that the Orders in Council were inconsistent with ss. 12 and 15 of the *Charter* and are of no force or affect. The effect of the declaratory order was suspended for a period of four months. The government was to provide the applicant with health insurance coverage that is equivalent to that to which he was entitled under the provisions of the pre-2012 interim federal health program.

3(3)

Adolph v. Canada (Minister of Public Safety & Emergency Preparedness) (2009), 357 F.T.R. 216 (Eng.), 2009 FC 1271, 2009 CarswellNat 4277 — This "sad and disturbing" case involved a minor child who remains alone in Canada after having been sent to Toronto by his mother and aunt on a one-way ticket from St. Lucia, purportedly to offer him an opportunity for a better life. To compound this unacceptable situation, two government agencies are working at cross purposes from each other in this case, each claiming to be taking into account the true best interest of the child. A motion to stay the removal procedure was brought pursuant to s. 18.2 of the *Federal Courts Act*. The applicant argued that the enforcement officer ignored compelling factors demonstrating that the best interests of the applicant were such that his removal should be deferred and that the officer failed to take into account Canada's obligations under the *Convention on the Rights of the Child* to provide protection and assistance to the applicant and act in his best interest. The Minister argued that contrary to the allegations of the Children's Aid Society of Toronto the best interests of the applicant do not include an entitlement to remain in Canada to obtain a better life than he would otherwise have in St. Lucia. The Minister also adds that non-citizen parents from foreign countries should not be encouraged to send and abandon their children in Canada in the hopes of better opportunities for them.

ENABLING AUTHORITY

4. (1) Minister of Citizenship and Immigration — Except as otherwise provided in this section, the Minister of Citizenship and Immigration is responsible for the administration of this Act.

(1.1) Designated Minister — The Governor in Council may, by order, designate a minister of the Crown as the Minister responsible for all matters under this Act relating to special advocates. If none is designated, the Minister of Justice is responsible for those matters.

(2) Minister of Public Safety and Emergency Preparedness — The Minister of Public Safety and Emergency Preparedness is responsible for the administration of this Act as it relates to

    (a) examinations at ports of entry;

    (b) the enforcement of this Act, including arrest, detention and removal;

    (c) the establishment of policies respecting the enforcement of this Act and inadmissibility on grounds of security, organized criminality or violating human or international rights; or

    (d) declarations referred to in section 42.1.

IRP Act

(2.1) Minister of Employment and Social Development — In making regulations under paragraphs 32(d.1) to (d.4), the Governor in Council may confer powers and duties on the Minister of Employment and Social Development.

Proposed Amendment — 4(2.1)

(2.1) Minister of Employment and Social Development — In making regulations under paragraphs 32(b.1) and (d.1) to (d.4), the Governor in Council may confer powers and duties on the Minister of Employment and Social Development.
2014, c. 39, s. 306 [Not in force at date of publication.]

(3) Specification — Subject to subsections (1) to (2), the Governor in Council may, by order,

(a) specify which Minister referred to in any of subsections (1) to (2) is the Minister for the purposes of any provision of this Act; and

(b) specify that more than one Minister may be the Minister for the purposes of any provision of this Act and specify the circumstances under which each Minister is the Minister.

(4) Publication — Any order made under subsection (3) must be published in Part II of the *Canada Gazette*.
2005, c. 38, s. 118; 2008, c. 3, s. 1; 2012, c. 19, s. 701; 2013, c. 16, s. 2; 2013, c. 40, s. 238(1)(h)(i); 2014, c. 20, s. 299

Case Law

Paszkowski v. Canada (Attorney General) (2006), 51 Imm. L.R. (3d) 299, 2006 CarswellNat 359, 2006 FC 198 — The plaintiff claimed that Citizenship and Immigration officials committed torts of public misfeasance and malfeasance by delaying the processing of her June 5, 1990, permanent residence application and that her rights under the *Canadian Charter of Rights and Freedoms* were violated. As a result, the plaintiff claimed that she was deprived of opportunities to become a Canadian citizen, to travel abroad, to continue her education, to earn a living and to have more children.

The plaintiff did not establish, *prima facie*, that she was owed a duty of care by the immigration officials who dealt with her application for permanent residence. The necessary proximity required by the jurisprudence was not established. Specifically, the relationship between the plaintiff and the immigration officers arose from the implementation of the immigration policy imposed by the statute and not as a result of any misfeasance committed by the immigration officers. At the time the decision was made to deny the plaintiff's application, the legislation precluded the admissibility of the plaintiff by reason of her husband's criminal conviction. Neither the legislation nor common law imposed any duty on the immigration officers to inform the plaintiff when the law was changed such as to allow her first application to be processed or to file a fresh application.

5. (1) Regulations — Except as otherwise provided, the Governor in Council may make any regulation that is referred to in this Act or that prescribes any matter whose prescription is referred to in this Act.

(1.1) Application — Regulations made under this Act that apply in respect of sponsorship applications or applications for permanent or temporary resident visas, permanent or temporary resident status or work or study permits may, if they so provide, apply in respect of any such applications that are pending on the day on which the regulations are made, other than

(a) applications to become a permanent resident made in Canada by protected persons; and

(b) applications for permanent resident visas made by persons referred to in subsection 99(2) and sponsorship applications made in respect of those applications.

(2) **Tabling and referral of proposed regulations** — The Minister shall cause a copy of each proposed regulation made under sections 17, 32, 53, 61, 87.2, 102, 116, 150 and 150.1 to be laid before each House of Parliament, and each House shall refer the proposed regulation to the appropriate Committee of that House.

(3) **Alteration of proposed regulation** — A proposed regulation that has been laid before each House of Parliament under subsection (2) does not need to be so laid again, whether or not it has been altered.

(4) **Making of regulations** — The Governor in Council may make the regulation at any time after the proposed regulation has been laid before each House of Parliament under subsection (2).

2004, c. 15, s. 70; 2008, c. 3, s. 2; 2012, c. 19, s. 702

Case Law

Vaziri v. Canada (Minister of Citizenship & Immigration) (2006), 55 Imm. L.R. (3d) 247, 52 Admin. L.R. (4th) 118, 2006 CarswellNat 3014, 2006 FC 1159 — A father and son jointly applied to the court for an order of *mandamus* requiring the Minister of Citizenship and Immigration to render a decision on the father's sponsored application for permanent residence.

The applicants assert that consideration of their applications was severely and negatively impacted beginning in 2001 or 2002 when the Minister, acting administratively, established target levels for immigration to Canada that incorporated a 60:40 ratio between the economic and non-economic classes. The Minister placed further restrictions on the processing of applications for parents and grandparents by giving priority to spouses and dependent children within the family class. The effect was the sponsorship applications for parents and grandparents have been processed at much slower rates. The applicants submit that the Minister had no legal authority to establish the targets or to put into place a process that seriously detracts from the rights of parents and grandparents to become sponsored permanent residents, unless authorized by regulation made under s. 14(2) of the IRPA. There are no such regulations.

There is no dispute that the Minister and CIC, as public bodies, can only act within the constraints of their legislated jurisdiction, since their authority derives from statute. The court concluded that there is nothing in the IRPA or the Regulations that appears to detract from the Minister's power to manage the immigration flow on the basis of social and economic policy considerations. In the absence of regulations made under s. 14(2) of the IRPA, the Minister acted lawfully in establishing the 60:40 ratio, in establishing targets for visa approvals by class and in setting procedures for prioritizing sponsored applications within the family class. While the Governor in Council may make regulations to address all of these matters, there is no obligation on the Governor in Council to do so. The existence of a non-mandatory Governor in Council regulation-making power does not preclude the Minister responsible for the administration of the IRPA from taking these policies in administrative decisions. The applicants did not satisfy the court that the discretionary remedy of *mandamus* should be granted.

Although several questions were certified, the Federal Court of Appeal did not hear the appeal, since the Minister issued the applicant a visa, rendering the appeal moot.

6. (1) Designation of officers — The Minister may designate any persons or class of persons as officers to carry out any purpose of any provision of this Act, and shall specify the powers and duties of the officers so designated.

(2) Delegation of powers — Anything that may be done by the Minister under this Act may be done by a person that the Minister authorizes in writing, without proof of the authenticity of the authorization.

(3) Exception — Despite subsection (2), the Minister may not delegate the power conferred by subsection 20.1(1), section 22.1 or subsection 42.1(1) or (2) or 77(1).

2012, c. 17, s. 3; 2013, c. 16, ss. 3, 36(2)

Case Law

Khalil v. R. (2007), 65 Imm. L.R. (3d) 8, 317 F.T.R. 32, 160 C.R.R. (2d) 234, 2007 FC 923, 2007 CarswellNat 2910, 2007 CarswellNat 5360, [2007] F.C.J. No. 1221; affirmed (2009), 78 Imm. L.R. (3d) 1, 64 C.C.L.T. (3d) 199, 2009 CarswellNat 550, 2009 CarswellNat 1303, 2009 FCA 66 — The plaintiffs alleged that the defendant's delay in processing their application for permanent residence caused some harm for which they claimed damages. They asserted that their entitlement to damages arises from the defendant's negligence and the infringement of their s. 7 and 15 rights under the *Canadian Charter of Rights and Freedoms*. For this infringement, they claim a remedy under subs. 24(1) of the *Charter*. Although the plaintiffs established that there was unreasonable and inordinate delay in the processing of their applications for permanent residence, delay is not a free-standing cause of action. There was insufficient proximity between the plaintiffs and the defendant to find a private law duty of care. Additionally, there are compelling policy reasons that militate against the imposition of such a duty. Even if it were otherwise, causation was not established. Consequently, the plaintiffs could not succeed in negligence. The plaintiffs did not establish that their liberty interests under s. 7 of the *Charter* were engaged on the facts of this matter. The s. 7 security of the person interests are not engaged because the alleged harm is not state imposed.

To impose a private law duty of care on the relationship between the plaintiffs' and the defendant's officials "creates a general potential for serious and significant conflict" with the statutory duty to protect the public interest, including the health and safety of Canadians and the maintenance of the security of Canadian society. In this case, the delay in processing the plaintiffs' application for permanent residence arose in large part as a result of potential inadmissibility under para. 34(1)(f) of the IRPA. The purpose of the legislated inadmissibility provisions is protection of the public.

Szebenyi v. R., 2007 CarswellNat 660, 2007 FCA 118 — This was an appeal from the Federal Court wherein the action by the appellant against the respondent seeking $6,000,000 in damages for alleged negligence in the handling of his mother's sponsorship application was dismissed. The trial judge concluded that the facts did not give rise to an action in tort against the respondent. Although the appellant had suffered depression, the trial judge was not prepared to conclude that this condition or any emotional stress suffered by the appellant was caused by the servants or agents of the respondent. The trial judge concluded that the respondent owed no duty of care to the appellant in the circumstances. The trial judge found that the appellant had no right to issuance of a visa to his mother, but only to make the sponsorship application and to appeal a negative decision in respect of the application to the Immigration Appeal Division. In these circumstances, there was an insufficiently close relationship between the respondent and the appellant to give rise to a *prima facie* duty of care. There was no basis to depart from the conclusion of the trial judge.

Samimifar v. Canada (Minister of Citizenship & Immigration) (2006), 58 Imm. L.R. (3d) 24, 2006 CarswellNat 5309, 2006 FC 1301, [2006] F.C.J. No. 1626 — The applicant was granted approval-in-principle to accept and process an application for permanent residence from within Canada. He submitted his application in 1994 and until January 2003, his application appears to have been subject to inattention, inaction and delay for reasons which he alleges amount to negligence and breach of his s. 7 *Charter* rights. In January 2003, he was informed that his PR application was refused on the basis of inadmissibility to Canada under s. 34(1)(f) of the IRPA because there were reasonable grounds to believe he was a member of a terrorist organization.

In addition to pursuing his administrative efforts to become a permanent resident, the applicant commenced an action against the Minister of Citizenship and Immigration by filing a Statement of Claim. The respondent brought a motion seeking summary judgment to dismiss all or part of the claim. The court concluded that the policy considerations did not preclude the imposition of the duty of care where an immigration officer completely ignores a file. At trial, it may be possible for the defendant to be able to provide a satisfactory explanation as to why this matter languished for at least seven years. However, given the unusual nature of the claim involving allegations against a particular immigration officer in the context of the harm allegedly suffered by the applicant, the action should not be summarily dismissed on broad policy grounds.

Paszkowski v. Canada (Attorney General) (2006), 51 Imm. L.R. (3d) 299, 2006 CarswellNat 359, 2006 FC 198 — The plaintiff claimed that Citizenship and Immigration officials committed torts of public misfeasance and malfeasance by delaying the processing of her June 5, 1990, permanent residence application and that her rights under the *Canadian Charter of Rights and Freedoms* were violated. As a result, the plaintiff claimed that she was deprived of opportunities to become a Canadian citizen, to travel abroad, to continue her education, to earn a living and to have more children.

The plaintiff did not establish, *prima facie*, that she was owed a duty of care by the immigration officials who dealt with her application for permanent residence. The necessary proximity required by the jurisprudence was not established. Specifically, the relationship between the plaintiff and the immigration officers arose from the implementation of the immigration policy imposed by the statute and not as a result of any misfeasance committed by the immigration officers. At the time the decision was made to deny the plaintiff's application, the legislation precluded the admissibility of the plaintiff by reason of her husband's criminal conviction. Neither the legislation nor common law imposed any duty on the immigration officers to inform the plaintiff when the law was changed such as to allow her first application to be processed or to file a fresh application.

AGREEMENTS

7. International agreements — The Minister, with the approval of the Governor in Council, may enter into an agreement with the government of a foreign state or with an international organization for the purposes of this Act.

8. (1) Federal-provincial agreements — The Minister, with the approval of the Governor in Council, may enter into an agreement with the government of any province for the purposes of this Act. The Minister must publish, once a year, a list of the federal-provincial agreements that are in force.

(2) Consistency with agreement — Subject to subsection (3) but despite the other provisions of this Act, the following must be consistent with the federal-provincial agreements:

(a) the selection and sponsorship of, and the acquisition of status by, foreign nationals under this Act; and

(b) regulations governing those matters, including regulations respecting the examination in Canada of applications to become a permanent resident, or respecting the foreign nationals who may be selected on the basis of an investment in Canada.

(3) Inadmissibility not limited — Subsection (2) is not to be interpreted as limiting the application of any provision of this Act concerning inadmissibility to Canada.

9. (1) Sole provincial responsibility — permanent residents — Where a province has, under a federal-provincial agreement, sole responsibility for the selection of a foreign national who intends to reside in that province as a permanent resident, the following provisions apply to that foreign national, unless the agreement provides otherwise:

(a) the foreign national, unless inadmissible under this Act, shall be granted permanent resident status if the foreign national meets the province's selection criteria;

(b) the foreign national shall not be granted permanent resident status if the foreign national does not meet the province's selection criteria;

(c) the foreign national shall not be granted permanent resident status contrary to the provisions of the law of the province governing the number of foreign nationals who may settle in the province as permanent residents, whether that number is an estimate or a maximum, or governing the distribution of that number among classes of foreign nationals; and

(d) conditions imposed in accordance with the law of the province have the same force and effect as if they were made under this Act, if they are imposed on a foreign national on or before the grant of permanent resident status.

[Editor's Note: SOR/2002-227, s. 328(1) provides that a person who was a permanent resident immediately before June 28, 2002 is a permanent resident under the new Immigration and Refugee Protection Act, *S.C. 2001, c. 27.]*

(2) Sole provincial responsibility — appeals — If a federal-provincial agreement gives a province sole responsibility to establish and apply financial criteria with respect to undertakings that sponsors living in that province may make in respect of a foreign national who applies to become a permanent resident, then, unless the agreement provides otherwise, the existence of a right of appeal under the law of that province respecting rejections by provincial officials of applications for sponsorship, for reasons of failing to meet financial criteria or failing to comply with a prior undertaking, prevents the sponsor, except on humanitarian and compassionate grounds, from appealing under this Act against a refusal, based on those reasons, of a visa or permanent resident status.

Case Law

Ransanz v. Canada (Minister of Public Safety and Emergency Preparedness), 2015 FC 1109, 2015 CarswellNat 7829, 2015 CarswellNat 7830, [2015] F.C.J. No. 1136 — The applicant sought judicial review of a decision by a visa officer to deny the application for permanent residence as an investor in the economic immigration class destined for the province of Quebec on the basis that the officer was not satisfied that the applicant intended to reside in Quebec. The court found that the officer did not lack the jurisdiction to refuse the applicant's application, in light of the fact that he had already been selected as an investor in the economic immigration class destined to the province of Quebec and had not been found inadmissible. The court also concluded that the officer did not have a duty to consult the province of Quebec or to obtain a concurring decision from a different officer prior to refusing the applicant's permanent residency application. However, the officer breached procedural fairness or ignored relevant evidence, or otherwise failed to provide the applicant with a meaningful opportunity during his in-person interview to respond to the credibility concerns he may have had with respect to the evidence related to the travel to Montreal prior to the interview and the documentary evidence in this regard. The application for judicial review was allowed.

10. (1) Consultations with the provinces — The Minister may consult with the governments of the provinces on immigration and refugee protection policies and programs, in order to facilitate cooperation and to take into consideration the effects that the implementation of this Act may have on the provinces.

(2) Required consultations — The Minister must consult with the governments of the provinces respecting the number of foreign nationals in each class who will become permanent residents each year, their distribution in Canada taking into account regional economic and demographic requirements, and the measures to be undertaken to facilitate their integration into Canadian society.

PART 1 — IMMIGRATION TO CANADA

Proposed Addition — 10.01, 10.02

DIVISION 0.01 — BIOMETRIC INFORMATION
[Heading added 2015, c. 36, s. 168. Not in force at date of publication.]

10.01 Biometric information — A person who makes a claim, application or request under this Act must follow the procedures set out in the regulations for the collection and verification of biometric information, including procedures for the collection of further biometric information for verification purposes after a person's claim, application or request is allowed or accepted.

2015, c. 36, s. 168 [Not in force at date of publication.]

10.02 Regulations — The regulations may provide for any matter relating to the application of section 10.01 and may include provisions respecting

(a) restrictions on the persons to whom that section applies and on the claims, applications or requests to which it applies;

(b) the procedures for the collection and verification of biometric information;

(c) the biometric information that is to be collected;

(d) the circumstances in which a person is not required to provide certain biometric information;

(e) the processing of the collected biometric information, including the creation of biometric templates or the conversion of the information into digital biometric formats; and

(f) the circumstances in which a person is exempt from the application of that section.

2015, c. 36, s. 168 [Not in force at date of publication.]

DIVISION 0.1 — INVITATION TO MAKE AN APPLICATION
[Heading added 2013, c. 40, s. 290.]

10.1 (1) Application for permanent residence — invitation to apply — A foreign national who seeks to enter or remain in Canada as a member of a class that is referred to in an instruction given under paragraph 10.3(1)(a) may make an application for permanent residence only if the Minister has issued them an invitation to do so, the invitation has not been cancelled under subsection 10.2(5) and the applicable period specified in an instruction given under paragraph 10.3(1)(k) has not expired.

(2) Limitation — An instruction may be given under paragraph 10.3(1)(a) only in respect of a class that is part of the economic class referred to in subsection 12(2).

(2.1) Provincial nominees — In the case of the prescribed class of provincial nominees, an instruction may be given under paragraph 10.3(1)(a) in respect of the foreign nationals who are nominated by the government of a particular province in accordance with an agreement referred to in section 8, or in respect of a portion of those foreign nationals.

(3) Expression of interest — A foreign national who wishes to be invited to make an application must submit an expression of interest to the Minister by means of an electronic system in accordance with instructions given under section 10.3 unless the instructions provide that they may do so by other means.

(4) Inadmissible foreign national — A foreign national may not submit an expression of interest if they have been determined to be — and continue to be — inadmissible for misrepresentation.

(5) New expression of interest — A foreign national who has submitted an expression of interest may not submit another one before the expiry of the period referred to in an instruction given under paragraph 10.3(1)(f).

(6) Failure to make application — A foreign national who is invited to make an application and does not do so within the period specified in an instruction given under paragraph 10.3(1)(k) is not eligible to be invited to make an application in relation to the expression of interest on the basis of which the invitation was issued.

2013, c. 40, s. 290 [Amended 2014, c. 20, s. 306(1), (2).]

10.2 (1) Expression of interest — processing — In processing an expression of interest, the Minister

(a) is to determine whether the foreign national is eligible to be invited to make an application by applying the criteria set out in instructions given under paragraph 10.3(1)(e) and is to advise the foreign national of the determination in accordance with instructions given under paragraph 10.3(1)(l); and

(b) subject to subsection (2), is to determine whether, in accordance with instructions given under paragraph 10.3(1)(i), the foreign national occupies the rank required to be invited to make an application and, if so, is to issue the invitation in accordance with instructions given under paragraph 10.3 (1)(l).

(2) Limitation — A determination under paragraph (1)(b) may be made only if the number of invitations that have been issued is less than the number provided for in an instruction given under paragraph 10.3(1)(j).

(3) Electronic system — The Minister is to use an electronic system to carry out any applicable instruction given under subsection 10.3(1) and to make a determination under paragraph (1)(a) or (b).

(4) Compliance with instructions — An expression of interest must be processed in compliance with any applicable instruction.

(5) Cancellation of invitation — The Minister may cancel an invitation to make an application if the invitation was issued in error.

2013, c. 40, s. 290 [Amended 2014, c. 20, s. 306(3).]

10.3 (1) Instructions — The Minister may give instructions governing any matter relating to the application of this Division, including instructions respecting

(a) the classes in respect of which subsection 10.1(1) applies;

(b) the electronic system referred to in subsections 10.1(3) and 10.2(3);

(c) the submission and processing of an expression of interest, including by means of the electronic system;

(d) the circumstances in which an expression of interest may be submitted by means other than the electronic system and respecting those other means;

(e) the criteria that a foreign national must meet to be eligible to be invited to make an application;

(f) the period during which a foreign national remains eligible to be invited to make an application;

(g) the personal information that the Minister may disclose under section 10.4 and the entities to which that information may be disclosed;

(h) the basis on which an eligible foreign national may be ranked relative to other eligible foreign nationals;

(i) the rank an eligible foreign national must occupy to be invited to make an application;

(j) the number of invitations that may be issued within a specified period, including in respect of a class referred to in an instruction given under paragraph (a);

(k) the period within which an application must be made once an invitation has been issued;

(l) the means by which a foreign national is to be advised of any matter relating to their expression of interest, including an invitation to make an application; and

(m) any matter for which a recommendation to the Minister or a decision may or must be made by a designated person, institution or organization with respect to a foreign national.

(2) Clarification — For greater certainty, an instruction given under paragraph (1)(j) may provide that the number of invitations that may be issued in any specified period in respect of a class be zero.

(3) Application of instructions — An instruction given under any of paragraphs (1)(a), (b) and (f) to (l) applies in respect of an expression of interest that is submitted before the day on which the instruction takes effect, unless the instruction provides otherwise.

(4) Publication — Instructions given under subsection (1) must be published on the Department of Citizenship and Immigration's Internet site. Instructions given under any of paragraphs (1)(a), (d) to (g), (k) and (l) must also be published in the *Canada Gazette*.

(5) Criteria provided for under other Divisions — For greater certainty, an instruction given under subsection (1) may provide for criteria that are more stringent than the criteria or requirements provided for in or under any other Division of this Act regarding applications for permanent residence.

2013, c. 40, s. 290 [Amended 2014, c. 20, s. 306(4)–(6).]

10.4 Disclosure of information — For the purpose of facilitating the selection of a foreign national as a member of the economic class or as a temporary resident, the Minister may disclose personal information provided to him or her by the foreign national under section 10.1 and referred to in an instruction given under paragraph 10.3(1)(g) to an entity that is referred to in an instruction given under that paragraph.

2013, c. 40, s. 290

DIVISION 1 — REQUIREMENTS AND SELECTION
[Heading amended 2012, c. 17, s. 4.]

Requirements
[Heading amended 2012, c. 17, s. 4.]

11. (1) Application before entering Canada — A foreign national must, before entering Canada, apply to an officer for a visa or for any other document required by the regulations. The visa or document may be issued if, following an examination, the officer is satisfied that the foreign national is not inadmissible and meets the requirements of this Act.

(1.01) Electronic travel authorization — Despite subsection (1), a foreign national must, before entering Canada, apply for an electronic travel authorization required by the regulations by means of an electronic system, unless the regulations provide that the application may be made by other means. The application may be examined by the system or by an officer and, if the system or officer determines that the foreign national is not inadmissible and meets the requirements of this Act, the authorization may be issued by the system or officer.

Proposed Amendment — 11(1.01)

(1.01) Electronic travel authorization — Despite subsection (1), a foreign national must, before entering Canada, apply for an electronic travel authorization required by the regulations by means of an electronic system, unless the regulations provide that the application may be made by other means. The application may be examined by an officer and, if the officer determines that the foreign national is not inadmissible and meets the requirements of this Act, the authorization may be issued by the officer.

2015, c. 36, s. 169(1) [Not in force at date of publication.]

Proposed Addition — 11(1.02)

(1.02) Applications from within Canada — Subject to the regulations, a foreign national who has temporary resident status may apply for a visa or other document during their stay in Canada.

2015, c. 36, s. 169(2) [Not in force at date of publication.]

(1.1) Restriction — A designated foreign national may not make an application for permanent residence under subsection (1)

(a) if they have made a claim for refugee protection but have not made an application for protection, until five years after the day on which a final determination in respect of the claim is made;

(b) if they have made an application for protection, until five years after the day on which a final determination in respect of the application is made; or

(c) in any other case, until five years after the day on which they become a designated foreign national.

(1.2) Suspension of application — The processing of an application for permanent residence under subsection (1) of a foreign national who, after the application is made, becomes a designated foreign national is suspended

(a) if the foreign national has made a claim for refugee protection but has not made an application for protection, until five years after the day on which a final determination in respect of the claim is made;

(b) if the foreign national has made an application for protection, until five years after the day on which a final determination in respect of the application is made; or

(c) in any other case, until five years after the day on which the foreign national becomes a designated foreign national.

(1.3) Refusal to consider application — The officer may refuse to consider an application for permanent residence made under subsection (1) if

(a) the designated foreign national fails, without reasonable excuse, to comply with any condition imposed on them under subsection 58(4) or section 58.1 or any requirement imposed on them under section 98.1; and

(b) less than 12 months have passed since the end of the applicable period referred to in subsection (1.1) or (1.2).

(2) If sponsor does not meet requirements — The officer may not issue a visa or other document to a foreign national whose sponsor does not meet the sponsorship requirements of this Act.

2008, c. 28, s. 116; 2012, c. 17, s. 5; 2012, c. 31, s. 308

Case Law

Section 11(1)

Abbasi v. Canada (Minister of Citizenship & Immigration) (2010), 88 Imm. L.R. (3d) 174, 2010 FC 288, 2010 CarswellNat 1675, 2010 CarswellNat 560 — The applicant challenged a refusal of a visa officer to grant him a permanent resident visa as a member of the family class. The applicant was a Pakistan national being sponsored for landing in Canada by his wife. The refusal of the sponsorship application was based on the finding that the marriage was not genuine. Two grounds were advanced for setting aside the visa officer's decision: the finding that the marriage is not genuine is unreasonable; and that the process applied to reaching the decision offends the *Official Languages Act*, R.S.C.

1985, c. 31 (4th Supp.), because the visa officer's interview of the applicant was conducted in Urdu.

The circumstances of the marriage were unusual which, not surprisingly, raised suspicion. But the unusual circumstances should give cause for very careful consideration. A marriage is a union between two individuals, and where suspicion exists as to the genuineness of the union because an expected standard of conduct is not met, to fairly and properly deal with the suspicion, the evidence of each individual must be carefully considered. There is no evidence on the record that the visa officer provided the applicant's spouse with an opportunity to give her evidence with respect to the quality of the marriage before the decision under review was made. In a case such as this, the visa officer was required to interview both the applicant and his spouse by the best means available whether by teleconference, video conference, or personal interview. The decision under review was unreasonable.

In this case there was no breach of the *Official Languages Act*. The interview was conducted in Urdu at the applicant's request. This choice was confirmed by the visa officer at the opening of the interview. No interpreter was required as the visa officer was fluent in this language. The applicant argued that as a matter of law the visa officer was required to conduct the interview in either English or French through an interpreter who could interpret the visa officer's questions to the applicant in Urdu and his answers back in English or French to the visa officer.

Section 20(1) of the *Charter* provides a right to any member of the public in Canada to communicate with and receive available services from federal institutions in English and French. This right imposes an obligation and practical requirement on federal institutions to comply with the right. This rights based concept does not inhibit federal institutions to offer services in languages other than English or French if the members of the public involved do not wish to exercise their right under s. 20(1) of the *Charter*, and, indeed wish to conduct business in any other language to which the institution's officials are capable of reliably communicating without an interpreter. This point was made by Justice Pinard in *Toma v. Canada (Minister of Citizenships & Immigration)* (2006), 295 F.T.R. 158 (Eng.) at para. 33 where a visa officer conducted an interview in Arabic without an interpreter:

> If the officer speaks the applicant's language — as was the case here — it would be strange indeed for the officer to use an interpreter. There would be no need to do so. The preferable options, as the Manual suggests [Overseas Processing Manual (OP) 5], is to conduct the interview in the applicant's language.

The application for judicial review was allowed on the first ground.

Lopez v. Canada (Minister of Citizenship & Immigration), 2008 CarswellNat 1325, 2008 CarswellNat 1326, 2008 FC 582 — This was the judicial review of a PRRA officer's dismissal of an application for permanent residence made from within Canada. The officer failed to take into account that s. 25 of the IRPA is driven either on humanitarian and compassionate considerations or public policy considerations. Put another way, is it Canada's public policy that a person who is not inadmissible in terms of the United Nations Convention Relating to the Status of Refugees and whose record of criminality in Canada cannot be considered because of the pardon granted to him (s. 36(3) IRPA) should nevertheless have to busk in the Montreal Metro for the rest of his life without legal status? The decision of the PRRA officer was an important one which affected the applicant's life in a fundamental way. In this case, the officer failed to assure himself that there was a public policy consideration present. The question was not whether there would be an unusual, underserved or disproportionate hardship if the applicant had to leave Canada. The truth was that he cannot leave Canada since Cuba won't take him back and the authorities know it. The applicant had not applied for permanent residence from abroad because he could not. The application for judicial review was granted and the matter referred back to another officer for redetermination.

Tantash v. Canada (Minister of Citizenship & Immigration), 2008 CarswellNat 1366, 2008 FC 565 — The applicant sought judicial review of a decision to refuse his application for permanent residence in Canada under the economic skilled workers class, on the ground that he had not submitted the requested documents, and he was therefore inadmissible. Although the applicant made a request for an extension of time to submit an FBI clearance, at no time did the applicant attempt to provide the officer with reasons for the lengthy wait in providing the FBI clearances, nor did he provide her with any timeframe in which he anticipated receiving the documents.

The refusal resulted from the applicant's failure to provide the officer with the evidence and documents that were reasonably required. Reasonable timeframes must be respected in order to allow that applications be processed in an expeditious manner. Therefore, the officer's decision to refuse the application and refuse any further extension of time was free of any breach of procedural fairness or natural justice.

Tran v. Canada (Minister of Citizenship & Immigration) (2006), 59 Imm. L.R. (3d) 217, 2006 CarswellNat 3833, 2006 FC 1377 — The applicant sought to overturn the decision of an immigration officer who denied his application for a study permit. The visa officer was not satisfied that he was either a *bona fide* student or a *bona fide* temporary resident, sufficiently well established in Vietnam, that he would leave Canada after his authorized stay in Canada. Procedural protection that arises in the context of a student visa application is "relaxed." In other words, there is no clear requirement that an applicant be permitted to respond to an officer's concerns as they arise. Immigration manuals are primary guidelines for the assistance of the visa officers in the assessment of applications for either permanent residence or temporary visas. As such, manuals cannot be relied upon by applicants to argue lack of fairness simply because the officer did not strictly adhere to the guidelines found in the manual in question. It is trite law that the onus is on the applicant to provide a visa officer with all relevant information and documentation to satisfy the visa officer that the applicant meets the statutory requirements of the IRPA and the Regulations. In this case, the visa officer conducted a fulsome and diligent assessment of the applicant's application for a study permit. The visa officer considered a variety of factors in her assessment, including the low income of the applicant's parents in Vietnam and no proof of their employment, income or any assets. The fact that the same type of education is available locally and at a fraction of the cost is a relevant factor in determining the credibility and intentions of a potential foreign student. It was not patently unreasonable for the visa officer to consider the availability of similar courses in Vietnam and South Asia at a much less cost. The applicant's very weak English and his inability to carry even a basic conversation in English, as was revealed during his telephone conversation with the case analyst and reflected in the CAIPS notes, was a relevant factor for the visa officer to consider, given that his acceptance into Algonquin College was conditional upon him meeting the English language requirement. There were no reviewable errors in the visa officer's refusal to issue a study permit. The application for judicial review was dismissed.

Dhoot v. Canada (Minister of Citizenship & Immigration), 57 Imm. L.R. (3d) 153, 2006 CarswellNat 3480, 2006 FC 1295, [2006] F.C.J. No. 1625 — This is an application for judicial review of a visa officer's decision of the applicant's application for a permanent resident visa which was denied on the basis that the applicant failed to attend an interview scheduled on October 26, 2005. The applicant states that he was never informed of the interview. The visa officer insisted that the notice of the interview was provided to the applicant by letter dated August 19, 2005.

The visa officer, for whatever reason, did not send the notice by mail as would be expected given the significantly prejudicial impact non-delivery would have on the applicant's interest in obtaining a permanent resident visa. It is reasonable to expect that there will be mistakes by the respondent when dealing with thousands of immigration files. When the evidence shows that there has been such a mistake the court expects that the respondent cure the mistake, *i.e.*, invite the applicant to attend another interview. It was wrong for the respondent, in a case such as this, to oppose the applicant's court case. The application for judicial review was allowed and the applicant was awarded legal costs.

Wong v. Canada (Minister of Citizenship & Immigration), 2006 CarswellNat 3951, 2006 FC 1410 — In deciding whether to grant the applicant an exemption from the processing requirements under subs. 11(1) of the IRPA, the decision maker erred in placing undue emphasis on the applicant's suspected medical inadmissibility and potential for establishment in Canada. The decision maker's assessment of these factors ought to have been deferred until the second stage of the H&C application. The decision to deny the applicant's application on humanitarian and compassionate grounds for an exemption from their requirement to obtain an immigration visa before coming to Canada was quashed.

Adegbayi v. Canada (Minister of Citizenship & Immigration), 2004 CarswellNat 5097, 2004 CarswellNat 3436, 2004 FC 1348 — This was an application to review a negative H&C decision. The officer who made the decision had concerns about whether the applicant and her spouse were in fact cohabiting. Procedural fairness dictated that the officer should have given the applicant an opportunity to address this concern.

Khan v. Canada (Minister of Citizenship & Immigration), 2003 CarswellNat 113, 2003 CarswellNat 664, 2003 FCT 58 (T.D.) — The applicants sought to review a negative decision by a visa officer refusing their immigration application in the investor category. At the interview, the applicants were unable to provide proof of ownership for a business that they claimed to own, nor were they able to provide balance sheets, accountants' reports or income tax returns.

There is a statutory obligation on an applicant to establish that she and her dependents are qualified for admission to Canada in accord with the Act and Regulations relating to investors. All of the instructions sent with the call-in notice did not warrant a conclusion that the visa officer failed to meet her obligation to fairly consider the application by the principal applicant. The officer had no obligation to provide an opportunity for the applicants to bolster their application by the submission of documents that in a normal course were required to be submitted before or at the interview.

11.1 Biometric information — **A prescribed foreign national who makes an application for a temporary resident visa, study permit or work permit must follow the prescribed procedures for the collection of prescribed biometric information.**

Proposed Repeal — 11.1

11.1 [Repealed 2015, c. 36, s. 170. Not in force at date of publication.]

2012, c. 17, s. 6

11.2 Visa or other document not to be issued — An officer may not issue a visa or other document in respect of an application for permanent residence to a foreign national who was issued an invitation under Division 0.1 to make that application if — at the time the invitation was issued or at the time the officer received their application — the foreign national did not meet the criteria set out in an instruction given under paragraph 10.3(1)(e) or did not have the qualifications on the basis of which they were ranked under an instruction given under paragraph 10.3(1)(h) and were issued the invitation.

2014, c. 20, s. 300

Selection of Permanent Residents

12. (1) Family reunification — A foreign national may be selected as a member of the family class on the basis of their relationship as the spouse, common-law partner, child, parent or other prescribed family member of a Canadian citizen or permanent resident.

(2) Economic immigration — A foreign national may be selected as a member of the economic class on the basis of their ability to become economically established in Canada.

(3) Refugees — A foreign national, inside or outside Canada, may be selected as a person who under this Act is a Convention refugee or as a person in similar circumstances, taking into account Canada's humanitarian tradition with respect to the displaced and the persecuted.

Sponsorship of Foreign Nationals

13. (1) Sponsorship of foreign nationals — A Canadian citizen or permanent resident, or a group of Canadian citizens or permanent residents, a corporation incorporated under a law of Canada or of a province or an unincorporated organization or association under federal or provincial law — or any combination of them — may sponsor a foreign national, subject to the regulations.

(2) [Repealed 2012, c. 17, s. 7.]

(3) [Repealed 2012, c. 17, s. 7.]

(4) Instructions of Minister — An officer shall apply the regulations on sponsorship referred to in paragraph 14(2)(e) in accordance with any instructions that the Minister may make.

2012, c. 17, s. 7

Undertakings

[Heading added 2012, c. 17, s. 8.]

13.1 Undertaking binding — An undertaking given under this Act in respect of a foreign national — including a sponsorship undertaking — is binding on the person who gives it.

2012, c. 17, s. 8

Case Law

Manitoba v. Barkman (2007), 213 Man. R. (2d) 273, 2007 CarswellMan 86, 2007 MBQB 54 — The plaintiff sued the defendant to recover the amount of income assistance payments which the plaintiff paid to immigrants sponsored by the defendant pursuant to an "undertaking of assistance," whereby the defendant undertook to provide and guaranteed their maintenance or support. The defendant maintains that the immigrants did not need to apply for social assistance; that any application for such was made at the instance of agents of the plaintiff. The defendant had sponsored his wife and four children. His wife and the children abruptly left. The defendant submitted that his wife and the children did not need to go on income assistance because he was always prepared to support them. The plaintiff's officials were quite right in concluding that the defendant's wife was genuinely in need of income assistance. The plaintiff did not follow their policy with respect to notifying the sponsor by registered mail (or at all) that legal action may be taken to recover the assistance as a result of the sponsor's breach of the undertaking. The plaintiff obtained judgment against the defendant.

13.2 (1) Undertaking required — If required to do so by the regulations, a foreign national who makes an application for a visa or for permanent or temporary resident status must obtain the undertaking specified in the regulations.

(2) Minister's instructions — An officer must apply the regulations made under paragraph 14(2)(e.1) in accordance with any instructions that the Minister may give.

2012, c. 17, s. 8

Regulations

14. (1) Regulations — The regulations may provide for any matter relating to the application of this Division, and may define, for the purposes of this Act, the terms used in this Division.

(2) Regulations — The regulations may prescribe, and govern any matter relating to, classes of permanent residents or foreign nationals, including the classes referred to in section 12, and may include provisions respecting

(a) selection criteria, the weight, if any, to be given to all or some of those criteria, the procedures to be followed in evaluating all or some of those criteria and the circumstances in which an officer may substitute for those criteria their evaluation of the likelihood of a foreign national's ability to become economically established in Canada;

(b) applications for visas and other documents and their issuance or refusal, with respect to foreign nationals and their family members;

(c) the number of applications that may be processed or approved in a year, the number of visas and other documents that may be issued in a year, and the measures to be taken when that number is exceeded;

(d) conditions that may or must be imposed, varied or cancelled, individually or by class, on permanent residents and foreign nationals;

(e) sponsorships;

(e.1) undertakings, and penalties for failure to comply with undertakings;

(f) deposits or guarantees of the performance of obligations under this Act that are to be given by any person to the Minister;

(f.1) the power to inspect, including the power to require documents to be provided for inspection, for the purpose of verifying compliance with undertakings; and

(g) any matter for which a recommendation to the Minister or a decision may or must be made by a designated person, institution or organization with respect to a foreign national or sponsor.

(3) **Electronic travel authorization** — For the purposes of subsection 11(1.01), the regulations may include provisions respecting the circumstances in which an application may be made by other means and respecting those other means.

Proposed Repeal — 14(3)

(3) [Repealed 2015, c. 36, s. 171(1). Not in force at date of publication.]

(4) **Biometric information** — The regulations may provide for any matter relating to the application of section 11.1, including

(a) the circumstances in which a foreign national is exempt from the requirement to follow the procedures prescribed under that section;

(b) the circumstances in which a foreign national is not required to provide certain biometric information; and

(c) the processing of the collected biometric information, including creating biometric templates or converting the information into digital biometric formats.

Proposed Repeal — 14(4)

(4) [Repealed 2015, c. 36, s. 171(2). Not in force at date of publication.]

(5) **Applications to be made electronically** — The regulations may require foreign nationals who make an application for a visa or other document under subsection 11(1) and foreign nationals who were issued an invitation under Division 0.1 to apply for permanent residence to make those applications by means of an electronic system and may include provisions respecting that system, respecting the circumstances in which those applications may be made by other means and respecting those other means.

Proposed Repeal — 14(5)

(5) [Repealed 2015, c. 36, s. 171(3). Not in force at date of publication.]

2012, c. 17, s. 9; 2012, c. 31, ss. 309, 313(2); 2013, c. 16, s. 4; 2014, c. 20, s. 301

Case Law

Vaziri v. Canada (Minister of Citizenship & Immigration) (2006), 55 Imm. L.R. (3d) 247, 52 Admin. L.R. (4th) 118, 2006 CarswellNat 3014, 2006 FC 1159 — A father and son jointly applied to the court for an order of *mandamus* requiring the Minister of Citizenship and Immigration to render a decision on the father's sponsored application for permanent residence.

The applicants assert that consideration of their applications was severely and negatively impacted beginning in 2001 or 2002 when the Minister, acting administratively, established target levels for immigration to Canada that incorporated a 60:40 ratio between the economic and non-economic classes. The Minister placed further restrictions on the processing of applications for parents and grandparents by giving priority to spouses and dependent children within the family class. The effect was the sponsorship applications for parents and grandparents have been processed at much slower rates. The applicants submit that the Minister had no legal authority to establish the targets or to put into place a process that seriously detracts from the rights of parents and grandparents to become sponsored permanent residents, unless authorized by regulation made under s. 14(2) of the IRPA. There are no such regulations.

There is no dispute that the Minister and CIC, as public bodies, can only act within the constraints of their legislated jurisdiction, since their authority derives from statute. The court concluded that there is nothing in the IRPA or the Regulations that appears to detract from the Minister's power to manage the immigration flow on the basis of social and economic policy considerations. In the absence of regulations made under s. 14(2) of the IRPA, the Minister acted lawfully in establishing the 60:40 ratio, in establishing targets for visa approvals by class and in setting procedures for prioritizing sponsored applications within the family class. While the Governor in Council may make regulations to address all of these matters, there is no obligation on the Governor in Council to do so. The existence of a non-mandatory Governor in Council regulation-making power does not preclude the Minister responsible for the administration of the IRPA from taking these policies in administrative decisions. The applicants did not satisfy the court that the discretionary remedy of *mandamus* should be granted.

Although several questions were certified, the Federal Court of Appeal did not hear the appeal, since the Minister issued the applicant a visa, rendering the appeal moot.

Minister's Instructions

[Heading added 2012, c. 19, s. 703.]

14.1 (1) Economic immigration — **For the purpose of supporting the attainment of economic goals established by the Government of Canada, the Minister may give instructions establishing a class of permanent residents as part of the economic class referred to in subsection 12(2) and, in respect of the class that is established, governing any matter referred to in paragraphs 14(2)(a) to (g), 26(a), (b), (d) and (e) and 32(d) and the fees for processing applications for permanent resident visas or**

for permanent resident status and providing for cases in which those fees may be waived.

(2) Limitation — Despite any instruction given by the Minister under paragraph 87.3(3)(c), no more than 2,750 applications in a class established under subsection (1) may be processed in any year.

(3) Application of regulations — Subject to subsection (4), regulations that apply to all classes prescribed under subsection 14(2) that are part of the economic class referred to in subsection 12(2) apply to a class established under subsection (1).

(4) Exception — The Minister may specify in an instruction that regulations made under subsection 14(2), paragraph 26(a), (b), (d) or (e) or 32(d) or subsection 89(1) do not apply to a class established under subsection (1).

(5) Non-application of regulations — For greater certainty, regulations that apply to only one class prescribed under subsection 14(2) that is part of the economic class referred to in subsection 12(2) — or to only certain classes that are part of that economic class — do not apply to a class established under subsection (1). However, an instruction given under that subsection may specify otherwise.

(6) Non-application of instructions — The instructions do not apply in respect of a class prescribed by the regulations.

(7) Compliance with instructions — An officer must comply with the instructions before processing an application and when processing one.

(8) Amendments to instructions — An instruction that amends another instruction may, if it so provides, apply in respect of applications in a class established by the original instruction that are pending on the day on which the amending instruction takes effect.

(9) Effective period — limitation — An instruction given under subsection (1) has effect for the period specified in the instruction, which is not to exceed five years starting on the day on which the instruction first takes effect. No amendment to or renewal of an instruction may extend the five-year period.

(10) Pending applications — Despite subsection (9), the Minister may direct officers to process, after the end of the effective period of an instruction, applications in a class established by the instruction that were made during the period in which the instruction had effect.

(11) User Fees Act — The *User Fees Act* does not apply in respect of the fees referred to in subsection (1).

(12) Publication — Instructions must be published in the *Canada Gazette*.

2012, c. 19, ss. 703, 710(3)

DIVISION 2 — EXAMINATION

15. (1) Examination by officer — An officer is authorized to proceed with an examination if a person makes an application to the officer in accordance with this Act or if an application is made under subsection 11(1.01).

(2) Provincial criteria — In the case of a foreign national referred to in subsection 9(1), an examination of whether the foreign national complies with the applicable selection criteria shall be conducted solely on the basis of documents delivered by the province indicating that the competent authority of the province is of the opinion that the foreign national complies with the province's selection criteria.

(3) Inspection — An officer may board and inspect any means of transportation bringing persons to Canada, examine any person carried by that means of transportation and any record or document respecting that person, seize and remove the record or document to obtain copies or extracts and hold the means of transportation until the inspection and the examination are completed.

[Editor's Note: SOR/2002-227, s. 332 provides that a thing seized under the former Immigration Act, R.S.C. 1985, c. I-2 *continues to be seized on June 28, 2002, and the seizure is governed by the provisions of the new* Immigration and Refugee Protection Act, S.C. 2001, c. 27.]

(4) Instructions — The officer shall conduct the examination in accordance with any instructions that the Minister may give.

2012, c. 31, s. 310

Case Law

Section 15(1)

J. (G.) v. Canada (Minister of Public Safety & Emergency Preparedness), 2012 FC 1489, 2012 CarswellNat 4993, 2012 CarswellNat 5404 — This was an application for review of the CBSA's decision to convoke the applicant to an interview on December 7, 2011, with a representative of CSIS under the authority of s. 15(1) of the IRPA. There was no evidence that CBSA explained to the applicant that when it convoked her to the CSIS interview, she was compelled to appear but was not compelled to submit to the interview. The exercise of an authority granted by statute carries with it the responsibility to ensure that the discretion is employed fairly. Here, the applicant would not have known that she was not required to participate in the interview with the CSIS officer had she been unrepresented. The CBSA abused its authority. CBSA indeed had the power to compel attendance. However, it exceeded the scope of its mandate when it used this power for a purpose not granted to the agency by its home statute, however desirable this purpose may have seemed. Appropriate discretion to coordinate activity with security agencies does not extend to compel attendance at interviews in which a person is not obligated to participate, with the strong implication that it would be better for them if they did participate. The application was granted in part and it was declared that CBSA does have the authority to convoke refugee claimants to interviews with CSIS under the authority of s. 15(1) of the IRPA.

IRP Act

The following question was certified:

> Is it an abuse of power for a CBSA officer to compel a person to attend an interview with CSIS where CBSA has no authority to compel the person to participate in that interview?

R. v Ellis (2009), 82 Imm. L.R. (3d) 142, 194 C.R.R. (2d) 94, 2009 ONCJ 319, 2009 CarswellOnt 4002 — The accused was charged with two counts of entering Canada without the required visa, and misrepresentation or withholding facts of his loss of status as a U.S. Resident Alien contrary to ss. 124(1)(a) and 127(a) of IRPA. This is a ruling on the admissibility of a disputed item of evidence sought to be tendered by the Crown. The Crown submitted that the conversation between a senior immigration officer and the accused heard in *voir dire* ought to be admitted. Defence counsel submitted that the conversation was inadmissible as it was a compelled statement taken in violation of s. 7 and s. 10(b) of the *Canadian Charter of Rights and Freedoms* before the accused could implement his right to counsel.

The *Immigration and Refugee Protection Act* requires that persons answer the questions of the immigration officials at the point of entry to Canada, and such statements are the product of statutory compulsion. It was conceded that during the initial routine questioning of the accused at the border, he was not detained for the purposes of s. 10 of the *Charter* nor was he detained when he was directed to the secondary area where he was further questioned by an officer. The referral to secondary examination is "a continuation or completion of the initial examination which takes place in the primary inspection line."

At the time that the senior immigration officer interviewed the accused he had been arrested and detained by the secondary officer. He had also indicated that he wished to exercise his right to counsel, and had not yet been afforded that call. While it was clear that the senior immigration officer had a duty to present his removal report to the accused to read, and to ask him if he wanted to add anything to it, before making a removal order; it is not so clear that he ought to ask him other questions going to the heart of the allegations here without implementing his right to counsel. The court found that questions of the senior immigration officer were interrogatory and not merely clarification. The attempt to use those answers in the subsequent criminal proceeding runs afoul of the principle of self incrimination protected by s. 7 of the *Charter*; and in this case also infringes s. 10(b) of the *Charter*, since the accused had not yet had the opportunity to speak to counsel, although he had expressly requested to do so. There was no urgency or necessity to ask additional questions to the removal report. That could have been dealt with after the accused was permitted to speak to duty counsel. The admission of the statement was found to tend to render the trial unfair and the applicant satisfied the burden of establishing that it ought to be excluded. Therefore the statements made to the senior officer were not admissible at trial.

Zhong v. Canada (Minister of Citizenship & Immigration) (2009), 350 F.T.R. 43 (Eng.), 2009 FC 632, 2009 CarswellNat 1867 — This application exposes a fundamental fault in the refugee claim process applied at the time the applicant made his initial statements claiming refugee protection. The initial interview was conducted through a Cantonese interpreter. The applicant gave his statements in Cantonese which were in turn given in English by the interpreter and written in English by the interviewing officer. No independent means, such as a recording, was used to verify what was said by either the applicant or the interpreter, or whether the interviewing officer's writing accurately recorded what the Cantonese interpreter said. This "Record of Examination" is the centre of a fundamental controversy in the present application. Following the preparation of the personal information form by the applicant with the help of legal counsel, the Record of Examination was made available to the applicant and his counsel. The applicant immediately asserted to his counsel that the Record of Examination did not correctly record what he said in the interview, and, as a result, counsel for the applicant made this known to the Refugee Protection Division well in advance of the hearing. Nevertheless, the RPD member who conducted the hearing chose to use the Record of Examination as accurate and relied on the statements made in it to find contradictions between it and the PIF and oral evidence produced at the hearing. This process resulted in a negative credibility finding made against the applicant. This process constituted a breach of due process.

In the absence of a verifiable record of what was said by the applicant at his interview, I find it is a breach of due process for the RPD to have accepted the Record of Examination as accurate in the face of the applicant's sworn statement that it was not accurate. The Record of Examination is the result of a fundamentally flawed record keeping process and should not be used with respect to the applicant's claim for refugee protection. The application for judicial review was allowed. Counsel for the respondents requested a question for certification, however, the applicant objected and the court agreed that the finding of breach of due process in the present case was based on the facts.

Toronto Coalition to Stop the War v. Canada (Minister of Public Safety & Emergency Preparedness) (2009), 80 Imm. L.R. (3d) 72, 2009 CarswellNat 775, 2009 FC 326 — The applicants brought a motion to seek an order of the Federal Court to permit a Mr. Galloway to enter Canada. Mr. Galloway was a British citizen and member of Parliament of the UK. He was to speak at a public forum entitled "Resisting War from Gaza to Kandahar," hosted by the Toronto Coalition to Stop the War.

Every person seeking to enter Canada must appear for an examination to determine whether the person has a right to enter Canada or is or may become authorized to enter and remain in Canada under subs. 18(1) of the IRPA. Mr. Galloway's personal views and open sympathies for the Palestinians and their cause became a matter of public record. An official of the High Commission of Canada, Immigration Section, by letter dated March 20, 2009, advised the applicant Galloway, apparently as a matter of "courtesy," that according to the "preliminary assessment" of the CBSA, he is inadmissible to Canada on security grounds pursuant to subs. 34 of the IRPA. Mr. Galloway was invited by the letter to make submissions and that a CBSA officer will make a final determination of admissibility based on this preliminary assessment and any submissions he may make should he present himself at a port of entry.

The court denied the applicant's request for an interim order or interlocutory injunction to enjoin the respondents and their officials from denying Mr. Galloway entry to Canada.

At one time, the court was reluctant to grant mandatory interlocutory injunctions but, over time, has been somewhat more willing to do so. Still, some greater level of caution arises when, particularly at an interlocutory stage, the court is asked to order somebody to take a positive action that will change the *status quo*. It is only in clear cases that mandatory injunction relief against the enforcement of a law will likely be granted by the court before a full hearing of the application for judicial review. In such instances, public interests and the relative strength of the parties' arguments are relevant factors to consider in the assessment of balance of convenience.

A fundamental principle of immigration law is that non-citizens do not have an unqualified right to enter Canada. The admission of a foreign national to this country is a privilege determined by statute, regulation or otherwise, and not a matter of right. In this respect, Parliament has expressly given the CBSA officers legal authority to exclusively determine whether a foreign national who seeks to enter this country is admissible (s. 15 and 18 of the Act). Yet there had been no final determination made by an officer with respect to the admission in Canada of Mr. Galloway.

The court was not prepared to exempt Mr. Galloway from the application of the provisions in the Act and Regulations respecting entry and examination, or to order the respondents' officials to allow him to come to Canada, without any final decision made on his admissibility.

Dhoot v. Canada (Minister of Citizenship & Immigration), 57 Imm. L.R. (3d) 153, 2006 CarswellNat 3480, 2006 FC 1295, [2006] F.C.J. No. 1625 — This is an application for judicial review of a visa officer's decision of the applicant's application for a permanent resident visa which was denied on the basis that the applicant failed to attend an interview scheduled on October 26, 2005. The applicant states that he was never informed of the interview. The visa officer insisted that the notice of the interview was provided to the applicant by letter dated August 19, 2005.

The visa officer, for whatever reason, did not send the notice by mail as would be expected given the significantly prejudicial impact non-delivery would have on the applicant's interest in obtaining a permanent resident visa. It is reasonable to expect that there will be mistakes by the respondent when dealing with thousands of immigration files. When the evidence shows that there has been such a mistake the court expects that the respondent cure the mistake, *i.e.*, invite the applicant to attend another interview. It was wrong for the respondent, in a case such as this, to oppose the applicant's court case. The application for judicial review was allowed and the applicant was awarded legal costs.

Dehghani v. Canada (Minister of Employment & Immigration), [1993] 1 S.C.R. 1053, 18 Imm. L.R. (2d) 245, 10 Admin. L.R. (2d) 1, 20 C.R. (4th) 34, 101 D.L.R. (4th) 654, 150 N.R. 241, 14 C.R.R. (2d) 1, 1993 CarswellNat 57, 1993 CarswellNat 1380, EYB 1993-67290, [1993] S.C.J. No. 38 — The appellant, a citizen of Iran, arrived in Canada without valid travel or identity documents and claimed Convention refugee status. He was interviewed at the secondary examination and extensive written notes were made by an immigration officer, which notes were later entered in evidence at the credible-basis hearing. At the conclusion of that hearing the first level tribunal decided that there was no credible basis to the appellant's claim.

When the appellant was taken to a secondary examination at Canadian Immigration at Pearson International Airport, he was not detained in the sense contemplated by s. 10(b) of the *Charter*. Further, the principles of s. 10(b) do not require that the appellant be provided with counsel at the pre-inquiry or pre-hearing stage of the refugee claim determination process. The secondary examination of the appellant at the port-of-entry is not analogous to a hearing. The purpose of the port-of entry interview was to aid in the processing of the appellant's application for entry and to determine the appropriate procedures which should be invoked in order to deal with the appellant's application for Convention refugee status. The principles of fundamental justice do not include a right to counsel in these circumstances of routine information gathering.

[Editor's note: Although Dehghani *was decided under the former Act, it may still be relevant.]*

IRP Act

16. (1) Obligation — answer truthfully — A person who makes an application must answer truthfully all questions put to them for the purpose of the examination and must produce a visa and all relevant evidence and documents that the officer reasonably requires.

(1.1) Obligation — appear for examination — A person who makes an application must, on request of an officer, appear for an examination.

(2) Obligation — relevant evidence — In the case of a foreign national,

(a) the relevant evidence referred to in subsection (1) includes photographic and fingerprint evidence; and

(b) subject to the regulations, the foreign national must submit to a medical examination.

(2.1) Obligation — interview — A foreign national who makes an application must, on request of an officer, appear for an interview for the purpose of an investigation conducted by the Canadian Security Intelligence Service under section 15 of the *Canadian Security Intelligence Service Act* for the purpose of providing advice or information to the Minister under section 14 of that Act and must answer truthfully all questions put to them during the interview.

(3) Evidence relating to identity — An officer may require or obtain from a permanent resident or a foreign national who is arrested, detained, subject to an examination or subject to a removal order, any evidence — photographic, fingerprint or otherwise — that may be used to establish their identity or compliance with this Act.

2010, c. 8, s. 2; 2013, c. 16, s. 5; 2015, c. 3, s. 108

Case Law

Garcia Porfirio v. Canada (Minister of Citizenship & Immigration) (2011), 99 Imm. L.R. (3d) 320, 2011 FC 794, 2011 CarswellNat 2704 — The applicant sought judicial review of his application for permanent residence as a skilled worker. The officer was not satisfied that the applicant had a genuine arranged employment offer as required by the ministerial instructions. HRSDC and CIC have different goals and benchmarks to meet, and it is equally clear that they each have a different realm of expertise. In this regard, CIC has chosen to use the specialized knowledge of HRSDC to help to streamline the processing of skilled workers. However, the immigration or visa officer is still the final check and balance in the system. Although an officer might be directed to take the HRSDC arranged employment opinion (AEO) at face value, they are instructed and required to consider whether the applicant is able and likely to carry out the offer of employment by s. 82 of the Regulations. Even if an immigration officer is precluded from considering the genuineness of the job offer she is certainly not precluded from assessing the genuineness of the applicant's intentions as needed to ensure that the requirements of IRPA are fulfilled.

Generally it would be unusual for the officer to question the window-washing needs of southern Ontario and dismiss out of hand the positive AEO obtained by the window cleaners. However that is not what occurred, and the officer did not act beyond her jurisdiction in rendering her decision. The officer was entitled to refuse the application since she found the applicant to be untruthful.

Subsection 16(1) of IRPA states that a person who makes an application must answer truthfully all questions put to them for the purpose of the examination and must produce a visa and all relevant evidence and documents that the officer reasonably requires. Though the officer might be precluded from evaluating the genuineness of the offer in Canada, she is not barred from assessing the legitimacy of the applicant's overall application. In this case, that is what she attempted to do. The applicant effectively shot himself in the foot when he lied in the interview. Clearly, there was a reasonable basis for the officer's decision. The application for judicial review was dismissed.

Yazdani v. Canada (Minister of Citizenship & Immigration) (2010), 92 Imm. L.R. (3d) 97, 324 D.L.R. (4th) 552, 14 Admin. L.R. (5th) 74, 374 F.T.R. 149 (Eng.), 2010 FC 885, 2010 CarswellNat 3204, 2010 CarswellNat 3631 — The court considered who bears the risk when email notices are sent by a reviewing visa officer but are not received by the applicant's agent who has exercised due diligence. In the case at hand, there had been no prior successful email transmission between the Warsaw visa office and the consultant's office. Nor did the [CIC] Protocol or Email Communications contemplate and provide safeguard measures for email transmission failures (such as alternate follow-up by mailing the letter). Finally, the visa application system does not provide for reconsideration in such circumstances. The respondent chose to send an important and crucial notice to the applicant via email without safeguards in place. The respondent therefore bears the risk of an email transmission failure when it sent the crucial request to the applicant. The application for judicial review was allowed.

Alavi v. Canada (Minister of Citizenship & Immigration) (2010), 92 Imm. L.R. (3d) 170, 2010 FC 969, 2010 CarswellNat 3633 — The court quashed the refusal of the applicant's application which was based on a failure to supply information requested in a communication which the applicant's representative, in affidavit evidence, said was never received and because the respondent Minister did not put proper evidence before the court that the communication was sent. The so called "risk" involved in a failure of communication is to be borne by the Minister if it cannot be proved that the communication in question was sent by the Minister's officials. However, once the Minister proves that the communication was sent, the applicant bears the risk involved in a failure to receive the communication.

Ghasemzadeh v. Canada (Minister of Citizenship & Immigration) (2010), 372 F.T.R. 247 (Eng.), 2010 FC 716, 2010 CarswellNat 2941, 2010 CarswellNat 1997 — The applicant, a citizen of Iran, refused to answer questions asked of him during interviews with Canadian Security Intelligence Service agents and a Canadian visa officer regarding projects he worked on as an employee with the Iranian Defense Industries Organization ("DIO") as part of his compulsory military obligations as a citizen of Iran. It was determined that he was inadmissible to Canada on the basis of misrepresentation, pursuant to subs. 40(1)(a) of IRPA. The applicant sought to quash the decision.

The onus is on the applicant to show that he meets the requirements of IRPA. Section 16(1) of IRPA imposes a duty on the applicant to answer truthfully all questions asked during an examination. A visa may be issued if, following an examination, an officer is satisfied that a foreign national is not inadmissible and meets the requirements of IRPA. To facilitate the visa officer's decision, the applicant is required to answer truthfully all questions put to him for the purposes of the examination. Should the Minister deny the visa on the basis of inadmissibility, the onus is on the Minister to show the grounds for a finding of inadmissibility.

It was not disputed that the refusal to answer questions constituted a withholding of information for the purposes of s. 40(1)(a) of IRPA. Although the visa officer did not cite the specific ground of inadmissibility, this omission did not constitute an error because the totality of facts led to only one reasonable conclusion: he knew he was a security concern and remained so. The materiality of the questions regarding the applicant's activities at the DIO is without doubt. The effect of refusal to answer questions, specifically the failure to disclose his employment activities, was to foreclose or avert further inquiries. Ultimately, the purpose of the officer's inquiry regarding inadmissibility was frustrated. The withholding could have induced an error in the determination of the applicant's inadmissibility under IRPA. The application for judicial review was dismissed.

Lu v. Canada (Minister of Citizenship & Immigration), 2007 CarswellNat 415, 2007 FC 159 — This is an application for judicial review of a decision to refuse an application for permanent residence on the basis that the applicant was inadmissible to Canada due to a misrepresentation. The Consulate General made inquiries to confirm the authenticity of a capital validation report. The visa officer concluded that the applicant was inadmissible to Canada. In her letter to the applicant, the visa officer wrote ". . . because you, a person described under subs. 16(1) of IRPA and ss. 34 to 42 of the *Immigration and Refugee Protection Act . . .* you are therefore criminally inadmissible to Canada." Although the officer did overstep her role in the evaluation of the applicant's permanent resident application, her actions did not constitute an error of law. The fact that the officer wrote in her letter to the applicant that "you are therefore criminally inadmissible to Canada" was an error which can be associated to a typographical error and it was not of a conclusive nature. There was no indication in the officer's letter that she misunderstood the evidence before her and as such believed the applicant was inadmissible under s. 36 of the IRPA due to criminality, or that the officer believed that providing untruthful information made the applicant inadmissible due to criminality. The application for judicial review was dismissed.

Li v. Canada (Minister of Citizenship & Immigration), 2006 CarswellNat 1300, 2006 CarswellNat 2280, 2006 FC 599 — The applicant applied for permanent resident status under the Canada-Quebec Investor Program. His application was denied on the basis that he failed to adequately account for the origins of his net worth. The applicant argued that the officer's decision was patently unreasonable as the decision was based on irrelevant considerations. He also argued that the information the officer requested imposed too heavy a burden on the applicant as the documents were from many years prior to the interview, and were not relevant to the current assets that had been primarily accumulated in recent years. The court held that given the money in question was the seed money that allowed the applicant to establish his own business, it was very relevant to the application and the officer was merely doing her duty under s. 16 of IRPA when enquiring into the source of the funds.

Shi v. Canada (Minister of Citizenship & Immigration) (2005), 50 Imm. L.R. (3d) 277, 2005 CarswellNat 2715, 2005 CarswellNat 5376, 2005 FC 1224 — The applicant applied for permanent residence status to Canada as an investor in the business category. His application was refused on the basis that the visa officer was not satisfied by how the applicant accumulated his personal net worth. In applying a high degree of deference to the decision of the visa officer, it is not sufficient to show that the evidence before the visa officer could have led to a different conclusion. Rather, to show an error, the applicant would have to demonstrate that there was no evidence before the officer that could have led to the conclusion in question. The visa officer was not satisfied that the applicant

IRP Act

had answered truthfully to all the questions put to him. Specifically, the visa officer had discovered that the tax document filed by the applicant was fraudulent. The court upheld the visa officer's decision and concluded that s. 16(1) of the IRPA applied to the applicant even though he did not already hold a visa. Section 16(1) applies whenever an applicant under the IRPA is the subject of an examination and not just when he already holds a visa.

Lan v. Canada (Ministre de la Citoyenneté & de l'Immigration) (2004), 42 Imm. L.R. (3d) 280, 2004 CarswellNat 3167, 2004 CarswellNat 1576, 2004 FC 770 — This was an application to review a decision of a visa officer dismissing an application for permanent residence made by the applicant in the immigrant investor class.

In order to allow a visa application, the officer must be convinced that the prospective immigrant is a person admissible to Canada. The officer is bound to refuse a visa to an applicant who has not fulfilled the obligations provided in subs. 16(1).

In order for the failure to provide documents to justify the refusal of a visa, these documents must be relevant, in light of the circumstances of the file under review. Thus, the officer's request for documents must be reasonable.

The evidence in the record showed that at the hearing the applicant submitted her financial statements dating back to 1996, as well as bank certificates, in order to establish the value of her current assets. The value of the applicant's shares in her company, which made up the majority of the assets declared on her application, was established by financial statements going back to 1996.

The officer did not dispute the authenticity of these documents or their probative value. Accordingly, it was possible to determine based on these documents that the applicant's current assets, primarily accumulated in recent years, were obtained legally and therefore it was not necessary to require documentary evidence for the period between 1984 and 1989. Accordingly, the application for judicial review was allowed.

17. Regulations — **The regulations may provide for any matter relating to the application of this Division, and may include provisions respecting the conduct of examinations.**

DIVISION 3 — ENTERING AND REMAINING IN CANADA

Entering and Remaining

18. (1) Examination by officer — **Every person seeking to enter Canada must appear for an examination to determine whether that person has a right to enter Canada or is or may become authorized to enter and remain in Canada.**

(2) Transit — **Subsection (1) also applies to persons who, without leaving Canada, seek to leave an area at an airport that is reserved for passengers who are in transit or who are waiting to depart Canada.**

Case Law

Toronto Coalition to Stop the War v. Canada (Minister of Public Safety & Emergency Preparedness) (2009), 80 Imm. L.R. (3d) 72, 2009 CarswellNat 775, 2009 FC 326 —

The applicants brought a motion to seek an order of the Federal Court to permit a Mr. Galloway to enter Canada. Mr. Galloway was a British citizen and member of Parliament of the UK. He was to speak at a public forum entitled "Resisting War from Gaza to Kandahar," hosted by the Toronto Coalition to Stop the War.

Every person seeking to enter Canada must appear for an examination to determine whether the person has a right to enter Canada or is or may become authorized to enter and remain in Canada under subs. 18(1) of the IRPA. Mr. Galloway's personal views and open sympathies for the Palestinians and their cause became a matter of public record. An official of the High Commission of Canada, Immigration Section, by letter dated March 20, 2009, advised the applicant Galloway, apparently as a matter of "courtesy," that according to the "preliminary assessment" of the CBSA, he is inadmissible to Canada on security grounds pursuant to subs. 34 of the IRPA. Mr. Galloway was invited by the letter to make submissions and that a CBSA officer will make a final determination of admissibility based on this preliminary assessment and any submissions he may make should he present himself at a port of entry.

The court denied the applicant's request for an interim order or interlocutory injunction to enjoin the respondents and their officials from denying Mr. Galloway entry to Canada.

At one time, the court was reluctant to grant mandatory interlocutory injunctions but, over time, has been somewhat more willing to do so. Still, some greater level of caution arises when, particularly at an interlocutory stage, the court is asked to order somebody to take a positive action that will change the *status quo*. It is only in clear cases that mandatory injunction relief against the enforcement of a law will likely be granted by the court before a full hearing of the application for judicial review. In such instances, public interests and the relative strength of the parties' arguments are relevant factors to consider in the assessment of balance of convenience.

A fundamental principle of immigration law is that non-citizens do not have an unqualified right to enter Canada. The admission of a foreign national to this country is a privilege determined by statute, regulation or otherwise, and not a matter of right. In this respect, Parliament has expressly given the CBSA officers legal authority to exclusively determine whether a foreign national who seeks to enter this country is admissible (ss. 15 and 18 of the Act). Yet there had been no final determination made by an officer with respect to the admission in Canada of Mr. Galloway.

The court was not prepared to exempt Mr. Galloway from the application of the provisions in the Act and Regulations respecting entry and examination, or to order the respondents' officials to allow him to come to Canada, without any final decision made on his admissibility.

Dehghani v. Canada (Minister of Employment & Immigration), [1993] 1 S.C.R. 1053, 18 Imm. L.R. (2d) 245, 10 Admin. L.R. (2d) 1, 20 C.R. (4th) 34, 101 D.L.R. (4th) 654, 150 N.R. 241, 14 C.R.R. (2d) 1, 1993 CarswellNat 57, 1993 CarswellNat 1380, EYB 1993-67290, [1993] S.C.J. No. 38 — The appellant, a citizen of Iran, arrived in Canada without valid travel or identity documents and claimed Convention refugee status. He was interviewed at the secondary examination and extensive written notes were made by an immigration officer, which notes were later entered in evidence at the credible-basis hearing. At the conclusion of that hearing the first level tribunal decided that there was no credible basis to the appellant's claim.

When the appellant was taken to a secondary examination at Canadian Immigration at Pearson International Airport, he was not detained in the sense contemplated by s. 10(b) of the *Charter*. Further, the principles of s. 10(b) do not require that the appellant be provided with counsel at the pre-inquiry or pre-hearing stage of the refugee claim determination process. The secondary examination of the appellant at the port-of-entry is not analogous to a hearing. The purpose of the port-of entry interview was to aid in the processing of the appellant's application for entry and to determine the appropriate procedures which should be invoked in order to deal with the appellant's application for Convention refugee status. The principles of fundamental justice do not include a right to counsel in these circumstances of routine information gathering.

[Editor's note: Although Dehghani *was decided under the former Act, it may still be relevant.]*

19. (1) Right of entry of citizens and Indians — Every Canadian citizen within the meaning of the *Citizenship Act* and every person registered as an Indian under the *Indian Act* has the right to enter and remain in Canada in accordance with this Act, and an officer shall allow the person to enter Canada if satisfied following an examination on their entry that the person is a citizen or registered Indian.

(2) Right of entry of permanent residents — An officer shall allow a permanent resident to enter Canada if satisfied following an examination on their entry that they have that status.

20. (1) Obligation on entry — Every foreign national, other than a foreign national referred to in section 19, who seeks to enter or remain in Canada must establish,

> **(a)** to become a permanent resident, that they hold the visa or other document required under the regulations and have come to Canada in order to establish permanent residence; and

> **(b)** to become a temporary resident, that they hold the visa or other document required under the regulations and will leave Canada by the end of the period authorized for their stay.

(1.1) Declaration — A foreign national who is the subject of a declaration made under subsection 22.1(1) must not seek to enter or remain in Canada as a temporary resident.

(2) Provincial criteria — A foreign national referred to in subsection 9(1) must also establish, to become a permanent resident, that they hold a document issued by the province indicating that the competent authority of the province is of the opinion that the foreign national complies with the province's selection criteria.

2013, c. 16, s. 6

Case Law

Section 20(1)

Momi v. Canada (Minister of Citizenship & Immigration) (2013), 427 F.T.R. 273 (Eng.), 2013 FC 162, 2013 CarswellNat 275, 2013 CarswellNat 864 — The applicant sought judicial review of the decision of a visa officer to refuse a temporary work permit. The officer concluded that the foreign national would not leave Canada by the end of the period authorized for his stay. The considerations relied on by the officer were irrelevant or neutral, or even worse, draw an inference that is not reasonable given the state of the record. The fact that the applicant sought to obtain the appropriate visa from Canada because his immigration situation in Australia would become precarious militates in favour of considering the applicant as law abiding. Past, previous immigration encounters are good indicators of an applicant's likelihood of future compliance. The fact the applicant had stayed in Australia since 2009 was not sufficient to conclude that if he were awarded a temporary work permit to Canada, he would not return to India at its expiration. At best, not wishing to return to India following a stint in Australia by seeking to obtain a temporary work visa in Canada should be considered as neutral as to whether or not the applicant will leave Canada by the end of the period authorized for their stay. Similarly, having a "permanent job" in Canada does not allow for an inference that the applicant will break the law and remain in Canada past the expiry of the work permit. There was no evidence on the record that the applicant would have ties in Canada such that he would be tempted to stay for that reason alone. Conversely, his ties with India remain as his family is there. The officer's reasons appear to be speculations, without adequate consideration given to the countervailing factors. As such, they appear to be arbitrary and do not meet the standard of reasonableness. The application for judicial review was allowed.

Calaunan v. Canada (Minister of Citizenship & Immigration), 2011 FC 1494, 2011 CarswellNat 5388, 2011 CarswellNat 5978 — The applicant's application for a work permit under the pilot project for hiring foreign workers in occupations that require lower levels of formal training was refused on the basis that the officer was not satisfied that the applicant had sufficient ties to his home country to ensure incentive to leave Canada by the end of the authorized stay.

Previous immigration encounters are the best indicators of an applicant's likelihood of future compliance. In the case at hand, there was no evidence to suggest that the applicant had previous immigration encounters, which was reaffirmed by the statements in the applicant's affidavit.

The court further noted that according to the applicable legislation, the officer must be satisfied that an applicant will not remain illegally in Canada after his authorized period of stay. It was the duty of the applicant to prove that he would leave Canada by the end of his authorized period of stay and to provide relevant documentation to that effect. However, in light of the lack of evidence supporting his strong ties to the Philippines, the existence of his ties to Canada, the apparent economic advantage of relocating to Canada — which is a necessary component of the decision — the court concluded that it was not unreasonable for the officer to reject his application. The applicant's parents, his two brothers, his cousin and his two uncles lived in Canada. Also, the applicant listed no spouse, children or any other family members in the Philippines. Although the applicant mentioned a family farm in his application, no evidence was provided in this regard. Officers are entitled to rely on their common sense and rationality in their analysis of an applicant's incentive to leave Canada at the end of their stay. As these are findings of fact, the court may not re-evaluate or reconsider the objective evidence and must defer to the decision of the officer. The application for judicial review was dismissed.

See *Loveridge* summary at s. 22(2) of IRPA. And see *Alvarez* under s. 24(1).

And see *Abdulateef v. Canada (Minister of Citizenship & Immigration)* summary at Reg. 216.

Tran v. Canada (Minister of Citizenship & Immigration) (2006), 59 Imm. L.R. (3d) 217, 2006 CarswellNat 3833, 2006 FC 1377 — The applicant sought to overturn the decision of an immigration officer who denied his application for a study permit. The visa officer was not satisfied that he was either a *bona fide* student or a *bona fide* temporary resident, sufficiently well established in Vietnam, that he would leave Canada after his authorized stay in Canada. Procedural protection that arises in the context of a student visa application is "relaxed." In other words, there is no clear requirement that an applicant be permitted to respond to an officer's concerns as they arise. Immigration manuals are primary guidelines for the assistance of the visa officers in the assessment of applications for either permanent residence or temporary visas. As such, manuals cannot be relied upon by applicants to argue lack of fairness simply because the officer did not strictly adhere to the guidelines found in the manual in question. It is trite law that the onus is on the applicant to provide a visa officer with all relevant information and documentation to satisfy the visa officer that the applicant meets the statutory requirements of the IRPA and the Regulations. In this case, the visa officer conducted a fulsome and diligent assessment of the applicant's application for a study permit. The visa officer considered a variety of factors in her assessment, including the low income of the applicant's parents in Vietnam and no proof of their employment, income or any assets. The fact that the same type of education is available locally and at a fraction of the cost is a relevant factor in determining the credibility and intentions of a potential foreign student. It was not patently unreasonable for the visa officer to consider the availability of similar courses in Vietnam and South Asia at a much less cost. The applicant's very weak English and his inability to carry even a basic conversation in English, as was revealed during his telephone conversation with the case analyst and reflected in the CAIPS notes, was a relevant factor for the visa officer to consider, given that his acceptance into Algonquin College was conditional upon him meeting the English language requirement. There were no reviewable errors in the visa officer's refusal to issue a study permit. The application for judicial review was dismissed.

Murai v. Canada (Minister of Citizenship & Immigration) (2006), 53 Imm. L.R. (3d) 218, 2006 CarswellNat 367, 2006 FC 186 — The applicant came to Canada without a visa as it was not required. Her application for an extension of time to remain in Canada was refused. Her subsequent application for refugee status was denied and her leave application for judicial review was refused. Her application to defer the removal order was denied. Her pre-removal risk assessment was denied and leave for judicial review was denied. Her humanitarian and compassionate leave application was denied and leave for judicial review was also denied. She left Canada. She then made an application for a work permit as a live-in caregiver. This application was denied as the visa officer was not satisfied that the applicant would leave Canada at the end of the authorized stay period per s. 183(1)(a) of the Regulations. The officer came to this conclusion on the basis of the applicant's previous immigration history.

The officer was entitled to satisfy himself that the applicant for the Live-In Caregiver Program had an intention of leaving Canada should the application for permanent residence be refused. In this case, however, the court concluded that the officer's decision was unreasonable since the record revealed that the applicant was a law-abiding citizen, who after exhausting her remedies returned to her home country and subsequently applied under the Live-In Caregiver Program. In fact, the evidence of her previous immigration encounters supported the applicant's contention that she was law abiding and would continue to comply with the rules in the future.

The visa officer should have asked himself "will this person stay illegally in Canada if not successful under the program?" Based on the applicant's past performance, any reasonable person would say "no, she would not stay in Canada illegally."

Toor v. Canada (Minister of Citizenship & Immigration), 2006 CarswellNat 1342, 2006 FC 573 — The applicant applied for judicial review of a decision of an immigration officer at the New Delhi High Commission, wherein the officer refused the applicant's application for a temporary resident visa. The officer was not satisfied as to the *bona fides* of the application. The applicant had been invited to an interview by a provincial government. However, the officer noted that the letter from the province of Manitoba referred to funds claimed by the applicant which could not be verified on documents and accordingly concluded there were large inconsistencies. The officer also noted the applicant had no previous travel and only previous refusals from the United States and New Zealand.

The applicant argued that it would have been proper for the visa officer to give him an opportunity to reply to his concerns.

The court concluded that the obligation to confront an applicant with adverse conclusions applies when the conclusions arise from material not known to the applicant. Where the issue arises out of material provided by the applicant, there is no obligation to provide an opportunity for explanation since the provider of the material is taken to know of the contents of the material. There was no breach of procedural fairness.

Boni c. Canada (Ministre de la Citoyenneté & de l'Immigration) (2005), 57 Imm. L.R. (3d) 4, 2005 FC 31, 2005 CarswellNat 176, 2005 CarswellNat 4646, [2005] F.C.J. No. 43; affirmed (2006), 57 Imm. L.R. (3d) 4, 2006 CarswellNat 414, 2006 FCA 68, [2006] F.C.J. No. 275 — The applicant applied for judicial review of a visa officer's decision to deny the applicant's application for a study permit. The risk that study permit applicants will not leave Canada once the period of their stay ends is a very important factor to be considered. An officer may examine the applicant's long-term objective. That objective is a relevant point which carries some weight, in view of the evidence as a whole on whether a study permit would be granted. A visa officer's conclusions will not be disturbed unless they are so unreasonable as to require the court's intervention.

Malhi v. Canada (Minister of Citizenship & Immigration) (2005), 53 Imm. L.R. (3d) 71, 2005 CarswellNat 2444, 2005 CarswellNat 5062, 2005 FC 1120 — This was an application for judicial review of an officer's decision to refuse an application for temporary resident status with a work permit. The applicant was a citizen of India and received a job offer, which was certified by Human Resources and Development Canada, to work in Ontario as a teacher. He then applied for a work permit but was refused, as the officer was not satisfied that he would leave Canada at the end of the 12-month term. The officer based his decision on the fact that the applicant had applied for a visitor visa to Canada in 2002 but had been denied, and the applicant did not have sufficient ties to India. The court found the officer erred in concluding that the applicant did not have sufficient ties to India, given all of the presented information, mainly, that his whole family including his wife and two children would remain in India; his wife owns a trucking business in India; he completed 70 per cent of his PhD studies and that he will not be able to complete these studies if he did not return to India; that his employment in Canada was for a duration of 12 months, after which he would become unemployed; and finally, that the assets belonging to the applicant and his wife totalled approximately $60,000, and that if the assets of his mother and father were included, that amount jumped to approximately

$350,000. The officer seemed to rely mainly on the fact that the salary the applicant would receive in Canada was more than seven times that which he receives in India.

The court found that it was patently unreasonable for the officer to determine that the applicant did not have sufficient ties to India, given all of the presented information. The application for judicial review was granted and the officer's decision quashed.

Moghaddam v. Canada (Minister of Citizenship & Immigration) (2004), 39 Imm. L.R. (3d) 239, 2004 CarswellNat 2502, 2004 CarswellNat 1346, 2004 FC 680 — The applicant sought to review a decision by a visa officer refusing the applicant's request for a study permit. The visa officer refused the application on the basis that the applicant had weak ties with her family in Iran.

Evidence of the intention to leave Canada upon the expiry of the period authorized for a temporary stay is a requirement under the Act. Section 22(2) addresses the situation where a person seeking temporary entry also holds the intention of establishing permanent residence. The applicant's family had an outstanding application for permanent residence in which she was named as a dependent. The officer's reference to the family application for permanent residence was improper. That application was not before him for a decision and was irrelevant to the matter before him. The issue of dual intent arose only in relation to that application which did not form part of the record before the visa officer. The family's application for permanent residence was irrelevant to the assessment of the applicant's application for a study permit. By referring to that application the visa officer relied on an extraneous consideration. The decision of the visa officer was set aside.

Thompson v. Canada (Minister of Citizenship & Immigration) (2003), 35 Imm. L.R. (3d) 308, 2003 CarswellNat 4562 (Imm. & Ref. Bd. (App. Div.) — The appellant appealed from a departure order made against her. She was found described in para. 20(1)(a).

The law of residency obligations has changed under IRPA in two ways. A permanent resident complies with the residency obligation with respect to a five-year period if, for at least 730 days of that five-year period, the permanent resident is physically present in Canada. IRPA also provides recourse to humanitarian and compassionate relief. The Appeal Division considered the following factors with respect to the appellant's case: 1) the reason for the departure order; 2) the number of years the appellant lived in Canada as a landed resident and her degree of establishment here; 3) her reasons for leaving Canada and remaining outside of Canada; 4) the time of her return to Canada; 5) her ability to re-establish in Canada; 6) her ties to Canada; 7) the best interest of the appellant's daughter; 8) hardship to the appellant in having to leave Canada; 9) hardship to others if the appellant was required to leave Canada; and 10) hardship to the appellant in returning to Trinidad and Tobago.

The appellant's failure to establish residence here is not the result of malfeasance and this makes her departure order appeal different from a removal order appeal of someone whose removal is the result of criminality or misrepresentation. The appellant did not misrepresent herself to immigration in order to obtain her status and she did not commit criminal offences while she lived here.

There are three types of removal orders. For the most serious matters deportation orders are issued which require the person to obtain written permission to ever return to Canada. Exclusion orders prohibit a person returning to Canada for a two- or three-year period, but written permission is not required. A departure order is the least onerous sanction. It allows the person to leave on his or her own within 30 days of the order being made. There are no bars to applying to return to Canada.

In the circumstances of this case the court granted humanitarian and compassionate relief.

20.1 (1) Designation — human smuggling or other irregular arrival — The Minister may, by order, having regard to the public interest, designate as an irregular arrival the arrival in Canada of a group of persons if he or she

(a) is of the opinion that examinations of the persons in the group, particularly for the purpose of establishing identity or determining inadmissibility — and any investigations concerning persons in the group — cannot be conducted in a timely manner; or

(b) has reasonable grounds to suspect that, in relation to the arrival in Canada of the group, there has been, or will be, a contravention of subsection 117(1) for profit, or for the benefit of, at the direction of or in association with a criminal organization or terrorist group.

(2) Effect of designation — When a designation is made under subsection (1), a foreign national — other than a foreign national referred to in section 19 — who is part of the group whose arrival is the subject of the designation becomes a designated foreign national unless, on arrival, they hold the visa or other document required under the regulations and, on examination, the officer is satisfied that they are not inadmissible.

(3) Statutory Instruments Act — An order made under subsection (1) is not a statutory instrument for the purposes of the *Statutory Instruments Act*. However, it must be published in the *Canada Gazette*.

2012, c. 17, s. 10

20.2 (1) Application for permanent residence — restriction — A designated foreign national may not apply to become a permanent resident

(a) if they have made a claim for refugee protection but have not made an application for protection, until five years after the day on which a final determination in respect of the claim is made;

(b) if they have made an application for protection, until five years after the day on which a final determination in respect of the application is made; or

(c) in any other case, until five years after the day on which they become a designated foreign national.

(2) Suspension of application for permanent residence — The processing of an application for permanent residence of a foreign national who, after the application is made, becomes a designated foreign national is suspended

(a) if the foreign national has made a claim for refugee protection but has not made an application for protection, until five years after the day on which a final determination in respect of the claim is made;

(b) if the foreign national has made an application for protection, until five years after the day on which a final determination in respect of the application is made; or

(c) in any other case, until five years after the day on which the foreign national becomes a designated foreign national.

(3) Refusal to consider application — The officer may refuse to consider an application for permanent residence if

(a) the designated foreign national fails, without reasonable excuse, to comply with any condition imposed on them under subsection 58(4) or section 58.1 or any requirement imposed on them under section 98.1; and

(b) less than 12 months have passed since the end of the applicable period referred to in subsection (1) or (2).

2012, c. 17, s. 10

Status and Authorization to Enter

21. (1) Permanent resident — A foreign national becomes a permanent resident if an officer is satisfied that the foreign national has applied for that status, has met the obligations set out in paragraph 20(1)(a) and subsection 20(2) and is not inadmissible.

[Editor's Note: SOR/2002-227, s. 328(1) provides that a person who was a permanent resident immediately before June 28, 2002 is a permanent resident under the new Immigration and Refugee Protection Act, S.C. 2001, c. 27.]

(2) Protected person — Except in the case of a person described in subsection 112(3) or a person who is a member of a prescribed class of persons, a person whose application for protection has been finally determined by the Board to be a Convention refugee or to be a person in need of protection, or a person whose application for protection has been allowed by the Minister, becomes, subject to any federal-provincial agreement referred to in subsection 9(1), a permanent resident if the officer is satisfied that they have made their application in accordance with the regulations and that they are not inadmissible on any ground referred to in section 34 or 35, subsection 36(1) or section 37 or 38.

Proposed Amendment — 21(2)

(2) Protected person — Except in the case of a person who is a member of a prescribed class of persons, a person who has made a claim for refugee protection or an application for protection and who has been finally determined by the Board to be a Convention refugee or to be a person in need of protection, becomes, subject to any federal-provincial agreement referred to in subsection 9(1), a permanent resident if the officer is satisfied that they have made their application in accordance with the regulations and that they are not inadmissible on any ground referred to in section 34 or 35, subsection 36(1) or section 37 or 38.

2012, c. 17, s. 11(1) [Not in force at date of publication.]

[Editor's Note: SOR/2002-227, s. 347(1) provides that if landing was not granted before June 28, 2002, an application for landing submitted under s. 46.04 of the former Immigration and Refugee Protection Act, R.S.C. 1985, c. I-2 *is an application to remain in Canada as a permanent resident under s. 21(2) of the* Immigration and Refugee Protection Act, S.C. 2001, c. 27 *(the "new Act").*]

SOR/2002-227, s. 347(2) provides that if landing was not granted before June 28, 2002, an application for landing as a member of the undocumented Convention refugee in Canada class is an application to remain in Canada as a permanent resident under s. 21(2) of the new Act and is not subject to the requirement in s. 175(1) of the new Immigration and Refugee Protection Regulations, SOR/2002-227, that the application be received within 180 days after a determination is made by the Immigration and Refugee Board).

SOR/2002-227, s. 347(3) provides that if landing was not granted before June 28, 2002, an application for landing submitted by a person pursuant to a determination that the person is a member of the post-determination refugee claimants in Canada class is an application to remain in Canada as a permanent resident under s. 21(2) of the new Act.]

(3) Pending application — subsection 108(2) — A person in respect of whom the Minister has made an application under subsection 108(2) may not become a permanent resident under subsection (2) while the application is pending.

2012, c. 17, s. 11(2)

Case Law

Section 21(1)

Hamalipoor v. Canada (Minister of Citizenship & Immigration) (2005), 47 Imm. L.R. (3d) 245, 2005 CarswellNat 1629, 2005 CarswellNat 3611, 2005 FC 803 — The applicant obtained refugee status in September 2000 and in November 2000 applied for permanent residence status. In February 2001, the case processing centre acknowledged receipt of his application for permanent residence. In March 2001, the applicant's CSIS check was completed and was valid for 18 months. In November 2001, the applicant was told he had to submit a certified translation of his identity card. Apparently, the translation submitted was not certified as required and it took $9\frac{1}{2}$ months for the Minister to advise the applicant of this deficiency. The required certified translation was filed within weeks. At the year end of 2001, all documents had been filed and a valid CSIS clearance was in place. However, it was not until March 2004, and only after repeated requests by his counsel, that the applicant was informed that the Minister was awaiting an updated CSIS clearance, the previous one having lapsed through the passage of time. The applicant was interviewed by CSIS in February 2005.

The applicant brought an application for *mandamus* to compel the Minister to complete the processing of his application for permanent residence. The Minister claimed it had a satisfactory justification for the delay, in that it was awaiting the CSIS update. The court pointed out that a review of the file showed a considerable amount of balancing of the file or parts of it between various parts of the respondent's organization, as well as between it and other government agencies and that this internal scurrying about with no actual progress was not a satisfactory justification for delay. Furthermore, the court held that it was not adequate to pass the buck and avoid responsibility by blaming delays on another government organization. An applicant's right to a decision is an obligation on the Government of Canada acting through the responsible minister. It is the Minister of Citizenship and Immigration's obligation to cause the necessary steps within the government so that the rights under the statute are fulfilled. The court concluded that there had been excessive delay beyond that which the nature of the process required, which was not attributable to the applicant, and for which there was no adequate justification; accordingly, the applicant was entitled to an order of *mandamus*.

Rukmangathan v. Canada (Minister of Citizenship & Immigration), 2004 CarswellNat 1673, 2004 CarswellNat 488, 247 F.T.R. 147, 2004 FC 284, [2004] F.C.J. No. 317 — This was an application for judicial review of the decision of a visa officer denying an application for permanent residence.

Procedural fairness requires that an applicant be given an opportunity to respond to extrinsic evidence relied upon by the visa officer and to be apprised of the officer's concerns arising from such evidence. The duty of fairness may require immigration officials to inform applicants of their concerns with applications even where such concerns arise from evidence tendered by the applicant. A visa officer should apprise an applicant at an interview of her negative impressions of evidence tendered by the applicant. However, procedural fairness does not stretch to the point of requiring a visa officer to provide an applicant with a running score of the weaknesses in their application.

Visa officers deal with many applications. The court was not prepared to adopt the approach that visa officers have no interest in the application and therefore their version is to be believed when it conflicts with that of an applicant. The court observed that once a visa officer's decision is challenged, that person has an interest in justifying his or her decision. At that point the officer is not a disinterested person.

Section 21(2)

Starovic v. Canada (Minister of Citizenship & Immigration), 2004 CarswellNat 5561, 2004 CarswellNat 4398, 2004 FC 1681 — The applicant met the eligibility requirements to apply for permanent residence as a Convention refugee. After the applicant had been determined to be a refugee, she left the country to be with her husband.

There is no provision of the law that requires an applicant who has been found to be a Convention refugee and who has applied for permanent residence in Canada to attend an interview in Canada as a condition precedent to determination of his or her application. Undoubtedly, in circumstances where the applicant has been found to be a Convention refugee, he or she would, in most instances, remain in Canada while applying for permanent residence. This is one of those rare instances where the applicant had to leave Canada after having been found to be a refugee. Interviews of persons seeking to come to Canada as permanent residents are routinely conducted at Canada's diplomatic premises abroad. Accordingly, the decision to declare the application for permanent residence to have been abandoned by reason of the fact that the applicant could not attend in Canada for an interview was set aside.

22. (1) Temporary resident — **A foreign national becomes a temporary resident if an officer is satisfied that the foreign national has applied for that status, has met the obligations set out in paragraph 20(1)(b), is not inadmissible and is not the subject of a declaration made under subsection 22.1(1).**

(2) Dual intent — **An intention by a foreign national to become a permanent resident does not preclude them from becoming a temporary resident if the officer is satisfied that they will leave Canada by the end of the period authorized for their stay.**

2013, c. 16, s. 7

Case Law

Section 22(1)

Boni c. Canada (Ministre de la Citoyenneté & de l'Immigration) (2005), 57 Imm. L.R. (3d) 4, 2005 FC 31, 2005 CarswellNat 176, 2005 CarswellNat 4646, [2005] F.C.J. No. 43; affirmed (2006), 57 Imm. L.R. (3d) 4, 2006 CarswellNat 414, 2006 FCA 68, [2006] F.C.J. No. 275 — The applicant applied for judicial review of a visa officer's decision to deny the applicant's application for a study permit. The risk that study permit applicants will not leave Canada once the period of their stay ends is a very important factor to be considered. An officer may examine the applicant's long-term objective. That objective is a relevant point which carries some weight, in view of the evidence as a whole on whether a study permit would be granted. A visa officer's conclusions will not be disturbed unless they are so unreasonable as to require the court's intervention.

Section 22(2)

Loveridge v. Canada (Minister of Citizenship & Immigration) (2011), 390 F.T.R. 316 (Eng.), 2011 FC 694, 2011 CarswellNat 2120 — The applicant was a citizen of the U.K. and had attended a college there where she studied animal care and animal management. In 2010, she was accepted into a Pre-Health Sciences program at a college in Ontario. She was also conditionally accepted into the school's Veterinary Technician program for the subsequent year. She applied for a study permit. She indicated in her application that her husband would be accompanying her to Canada. A visa officer found that the applicant had not met the requirements set out in IRPA to warrant granting a study permit. Specifically, the officer found that the applicant had not demonstrated sufficient ties to the U.K. to satisfy the officer that she had dual intent and would leave Canada at the end of the period authorized to stay. The applicant had included a motivation letter that indicated both an intention to stay in Canada as well as an intention to leave Canada and return to the U.K. This is different from indicating a "dual intent" within the meaning of subs. 22(2) of IRPA, because that type of a "dual intent" is actually an intention to remain permanently in Canada, coupled with an intention to abide by immigration laws as required — i.e. a willingness to leave Canada if required to do so. The two intentions involved under subs. 22(2) are complementary, not contradictory.

Given that the intentions appear to be contradictory, it cannot be said that the officer acted unreasonably in finding that the letter provided little support for the proposition that the applicant would leave Canada by the end of the period authorized for her stay. The burden was with the applicant to demonstrate that she would leave at the end of her study period. The officer noted that both the applicant and her husband were unemployed in the UK and had experienced difficulty becoming established there. She also noted that there was no proof of property ownership in the U.K. Even if the officer erred in considering the bank statements, given the contradictory nature of the applicant's motivation letter, combined with the dearth of other evidence indicating that the applicant would leave Canada at the end of the period authorized for her stay, it cannot be said that the officer erred in finding that the applicant had not demonstrated dual intent. It is not the court's role to reassess the evidence. The officer's determination fell within the range of possible, acceptable outcomes defensible in respect of the facts and law and was reasonable. The application for judicial review was dismissed.

Odewole v. Canada (Minister of Citizenship & Immigration), 2008 CarswellNat 1667, 2008 CarswellNat 2786, 2008 FC 697 — The applicant sought judicial review of a visa officer's decision to refuse an application for a study permit. The application was refused because the applicant failed to demonstrate that her obligations or ties to her home country are such that they would compel her to leave Canada following the completion of her studies and because the officer was not satisfied that the applicant had dual intent pursuant to s. 22(2) of the Act. The applicant's sister had applied to sponsor the applicant's mother and the applicant was included as a dependent child in her mother's application for permanent residence.

Pursuant to subs. 22(2) of the Act, a person seeking a temporary entry into Canada may also hold the intention of establishing permanent residence. The officer was therefore required to weigh the evidence in connection with the application for a study permit and assess the applicant's intention to leave Canada at the end of her studies under para. 20(1)(b) of the Act and subs. 216(1) of the Regulations. The officer was not dealing with the family application for permanent residence, and the issue of dual intent arose only in relation to that application. The application for permanent residence was an irrelevant consideration for the purposes of the applicant's application for a study permit. Although in her affidavit the officer acknowledged that she lacked jurisdiction to assess the applicant's eligibility for permanent residence under the family class sponsorship, she nevertheless took this factor into account. Thus, the officer committed a reviewable error. The decision was set aside.

Bonilla v. Canada (Minister of Citizenship & Immigration), 2007 CarswellNat 26, 2007 FC 20 — The applicant applied for a study permit. The application was refused. The visa officer found that living in Canada during her formative high school years would have a negative impact upon the applicant's ability to function in Colombia. The applicant was therefore unable to establish that she would return to her home country following the expiration of her study permit, should she be given one. The officer concluded that the applicant's separation from her family, community, language and Colombia's education system, for such a long period of time, would result in the severance of her ties to Colombia.

The visa officer relied upon a generalization when he refused the applicant's application. The generalization in question is that all applicants who apply for a study permit which cover four years of high school should be denied, since they would automatically be unlikely to return to their home country due to long-term separation from their families and cultures. Clearly, any individual who applies to study in Canada for four years of high school would be away from the aspects of their home country noted by the visa officer. However, it is not necessarily the case that all young people in these circumstances would become unable to function in their home countries following the four-year period, and as a result, would be unlikely to leave Canada. The officer subjectively formed an opinion and should have allowed the applicant an opportunity to respond to his concerns. The applicant had no way of knowing that the visa officer would act upon his view that those in their "formative years" may not study in Canada for a four-year period, since they would be unlikely to leave the country. The visa officer's failure to give the applicant an opportunity to respond to his concerns, on the facts of this case, amounted to a breach of the rules of natural justice. The application for judicial review was allowed.

Dang v. Canada (Minister of Citizenship & Immigration), 2007 CarswellNat 25, 2007 FC 15 — The immigration officer's decision not to grant a study permit was based on a factual finding that the applicant had not established that she would leave Canada at the end of her authorized stay. To obtain a renewal of a study permit, the Regulations require that applicants maintain good standing at their educational institution, have sufficient and available financial resources to support their studies, and establish that they will leave Canada after the expiry of their authorized stay. The evidence before the immigration officer, which included progress reports issued to the applicant by the Canadian Conversation College, indicated that the applicant maintained satisfactory standing in her classes. The immigration officer's finding of fact that the applicant was progressing slowly was patently unreasonable. Moreover, the immigration officer erroneously found that the applicant has been studying for 4 1/2 years, when in fact it was three years. The fact that the applicant had pursued an application to permanently reside in Canada with her husband does not establish that she would not leave Canada at the end of the period authorized for her study permit as required under para. 216(1)(b) of the Regulations. The visa officer failed to recognize that the IRPA expressly allows the applicant to simultaneously seek permanent resident status and temporary resident status as a student. Without an evidentiary basis on which to support the immigration officer's findings, the conclusion that the applicant would not leave Canada at the end of the period authorized for her stay was patently unreasonable. By determining that the applicant had taken an unreasonable amount of time to learn the English language, the immigration officer based her conclusion on irrelevant factors. The Regulations in this respect only require that an applicant maintain "good standing" at her educational institution, which she had done. The application for judicial review was allowed.

Ogunfowora v. Canada (Minister of Citizenship & Immigration), 2007 CarswellNat 1022, 2007 FC 471 — This was an application for judicial review of a decision of a visa officer denying the applicants a temporary resident visa. The officer stated that he was not convinced the applicants would return to Nigeria at the end of the period authorized by their stay, as mandated by para. 20(1)(b) of the IRPA.

Legally, an officer is obligated to consider each application on its own merits. The officer was not entitled to use the fact that the applicants had an outstanding application for permanent residence to deny them their temporary resident visas and this is evident from the plain language of the legislation. Subsection 22(2) of the IRPA explicitly precludes denying an application for temporary status on the basis that there is an outstanding permanent resident application if the decision maker believes the person will return. Thus, the legislation appears to demand that a decision maker determine on the basis of objective evidence whether the person will return, irrespective of any outstanding permanent resident applications. Most of the objective evidence in this case was disregarded for no valid reason. In order to satisfy himself, the officer must look objectively at the request and all the supporting information; he should not, as he obviously did here, decide subjectively, and ignore what favoured the applicants. The officer's decision on the evidence available appears to be patently unreasonable. The application for judicial review was allowed and the matter referred back to the respondent for re-determination by a different visa officer.

Farhat v. Canada (Minister of Citizenship & Immigration), 2006 CarswellNat 3418, 2006 FC 1275 — The Minister's delegate of the Consulate General of Canada in New York was of the opinion that the applicant's circumstances did not warrant the issuance of a temporary resident permit (TRP). The applicant sought judicial review of the decision. The applicant was married to a Canadian citizen who applied to sponsor him from within Canada. This application was refused as the applicant did not have temporary resident status at the time the application was filed. The applicant was then convicted of theft under $5,000 and a s. 44 report was prepared because the Minister was of the opinion that the applicant was inadmissible on grounds of criminality. The applicant was excluded from Canada for one year. The applicant's counsel was made aware that the applicant needed to apply for an authorization to return to Canada. The applicant then made an application for a TRP to the Canadian Consulate. The Minister concluded that the circumstances did not warrant the issuance of a TRP. The Minister was not satisfied that the applicant would leave Canada at its expiry. The Minister indicated that the applicant could apply for a pardon. The Minister also found that the applicant had to obtain an authorization to return to Canada.

The applicant has the onus of establishing the compelling reasons and did not satisfy the Minister that the particular circumstances of his case warranted the granting of a TRP. A person seeking a TRP must have the intention of staying in Canada for temporary purpose and an officer must be satisfied that such a person will leave upon the expiry of status. Albeit, it is true that an intention by a foreign national to become a permanent resident does not preclude an individual from becoming a temporary resident; nevertheless, the officer has to be satisfied that the foreign national will leave Canada by the end of the period authorized by his or her stay. Considering the applicant's history of noncompliance with the Canadian immigration laws and regulations, and his overstay in Canada, it was not patently unreasonable for the applicant to be obliged to leave at the end of the period authorized for his stay. The applicant did not present, in regard to the existence of his spouse and child, any "compelling reasons" which would allow him to be granted a TRP. It was not patently unreasonable for the Minister to consider the interest of the child, in this case, did not amount to "compelling reasons" in light of the evidence presented.

The decision of the Minister concerning the TRP application was not irrational or perverse or so gratuitous and oppressive that no reasonable person could think it justified. Consequently, this application for judicial review was dismissed.

Murai v. Canada (Minister of Citizenship & Immigration) (2006), 53 Imm. L.R. (3d) 218, 2006 CarswellNat 367, 2006 FC 186 — The applicant came to Canada without a visa as it was not required. Her application for an extension of time to remain in Canada was refused. Her subsequent application for refugee status was denied and her leave application for judicial review was refused. Her application to defer the removal order was denied. Her pre-removal risk assessment was denied and leave for judicial review was denied. Her humanitarian and compassionate leave application was denied and leave for judicial review was also denied. She left Canada. She then made an application for a work permit as a live-in caregiver. This application was denied as the visa officer was not satisfied that the applicant would leave Canada at the end of the authorized stay period per s. 183(1)(a) of the Regulations. The officer came to this conclusion on the basis of the applicant's previous immigration history.

The officer was entitled to satisfy himself that the applicant for the Live-In Caregiver Program had an intention of leaving Canada should the application for permanent residence be refused. In this case, however, the court concluded that the officer's decision was unreasonable since the record revealed that the applicant was a law-abiding citizen, who after exhausting her remedies returned to her home country and subsequently applied under the Live-In Caregiver Program. In fact, the evidence of her previous immigration encounters supported the applicant's contention that she was law abiding and would continue to comply with the rules in the future.

The visa officer should have asked himself "will this person stay illegally in Canada if not successful under the program?" Based on the applicant's past performance, any reasonable person would say "no, she would not stay in Canada illegally."

Patel v. Canada (Minister of Citizenship & Immigration) (2006), 54 Imm. L.R. (3d) 180, 2006 CarswellNat 454, 2006 CarswellNat 2375, 2006 FC 224 — The applicant was aged 79 and a citizen of India. She had five children and 11 grandchildren living in Canada, all of whom were Canadian citizens. Her husband was deceased and she had no more family living in India. She first came to Canada to attend the wedding of her granddaughter. Subsequently, her Canadian children decided they would sponsor her to stay in Canada as she would be alone in her mother country. She obtained three extensions of her status as a temporary resident. Her request for a fourth extension was denied after consideration of dual intent and determination that she was not a *bona fide* temporary resident. An application for restoration was denied.

The standard of review applicable to a decision refusing restoration of status is that of reasonableness *simpliciter*.

A permanent residence application does not necessarily preclude a temporary purpose for being in Canada. The current statutory and regulatory scheme does not say that a person's initial temporary purpose must remain constant and unchanged. The only requirement is the existence of a temporary purpose. The application for restoration of temporary status was not refused on the basis that the applicant would not be in Canada for a temporary purpose. On the contrary, it was denied because the applicant's stay in Canada would be for a "longer" temporary purpose, that is, while awaiting a decision on the application for permanent residence. The conclusion reached by the officer contained a reviewable error. The application was granted and the matter referred back to a different officer for redetermination.

Rebmann v. Canada (Solicitor General), 2005 CarswellNat 628, 2005 CarswellNat 1413, 2005 FC 310 — A person may have the dual intent of immigrating and of abiding by the immigration law respecting temporary entry. At the time the exclusion order was issued the applicant had a valid status of temporary resident despite the fact that the applicant was married to a Canadian citizen, was the father to a son born in Canada, owned a house and started a corporation in Toronto. It also appears that the applicant was travelling extensively inside and outside of Canada. As long as there was an intention to leave Canada when his temporary status expired, even if the applicant had been contemplating obtaining permanent residence, it was not a violation of the Act to enter Canada with dual intent. Given that the Act contemplates that persons who are married to spouses in Canada can apply for a permanent residence from within Canada it is incongruous to suggest that a person who is married to a Canadian spouse and who wishes to seek admission into Canada as a temporary resident can be inadmissible as a permanent resident without a visa. This is inconsistent with the provisions of the Act.

Moghaddam v. Canada (Minister of Citizenship & Immigration) (2004), 39 Imm. L.R. (3d) 239, 2004 CarswellNat 2502, 2004 CarswellNat 1346, 2004 FC 680 — The applicant sought to review a decision by a visa officer refusing the applicant's request for a study permit. The visa officer refused the application on the basis that the applicant had weak ties with her family in Iran.

Evidence of the intention to leave Canada upon the expiry of the period authorized for a temporary stay is a requirement under the Act. Section 22(2) addresses the situation where a person seeking temporary entry also holds the intention of establishing permanent residence. The applicant's family had an outstanding application for permanent residence in which she was named as a dependent. The officer's reference to the family application for permanent residence was improper. That application was not before him for a decision and was irrelevant to the matter before him. The issue of dual intent arose only in relation to that application which did not form part of the record before the visa officer. The family's application for permanent residence was irrelevant to the assessment of the applicant's application for a study permit. By referring to that application the visa officer relied on an extraneous consideration. The decision of the visa officer was set aside.

22.1 (1) Declaration — The Minister may, on the Minister's own initiative, declare that a foreign national, other than a foreign national referred to in section 19, may not become a temporary resident if the Minister is of the opinion that it is justified by public policy considerations.

(2) Effective period — A declaration has effect for the period specified by the Minister, which is not to exceed 36 months.

(3) Revocation — The Minister may, at any time, revoke a declaration or shorten its effective period.

(4) Report to Parliament — The report required under section 94 must include the number of declarations made under subsection (1) and set out the public policy considerations that led to the making of the declarations.

2013, c. 16, s. 8

23. Entry to complete examination or hearing — An officer may authorize a person to enter Canada for the purpose of further examination or an admissibility hearing under this Part.

[Editor's Note: SOR/2002-227, s. 330 provides that any of the following persons who were in Canada immediately before June 28, 2002 are deemed to have been authorized under s. 23 of the new Immigration and Refugee Protection Act, *S.C. 2001, c. 27 to enter Canada:*

(a) a person in respect of whom an examination remains incomplete and whose examination was adjourned and referred to another immigration officer for completion under s. 12(3) of the Immigration Act, *R.S.C. 1985, c. I-2 (the "former Act");*

(b) a person in respect of whom an examination remains incomplete and whose examination was deferred under paragraph 13(1)(a) of the former Act;

(c) a person in respect of whom an examination remains incomplete and who was authorized to come into Canada for further examination under paragraph 14(2)(b) of the former Act;

(d) a person in respect of whom an examination remains incomplete and who was authorized to come into Canada for further examination under paragraph 23(1)(b) of the former Act; and

(e) a person who has made a claim to be a Convention refugee in respect of which a determination of eligibility was not made before June 28, 2002.]

24. (1) Temporary resident permit — A foreign national who, in the opinion of an officer, is inadmissible or does not meet the requirements of this Act becomes a temporary resident If an officer is of the opinion that it is justified in the circumstances and issues a temporary resident permit, which may be cancelled at any time.

(2) Exception — A foreign national referred to in subsection (1) to whom an officer issues a temporary resident permit outside Canada does not become a temporary resident until they have been examined upon arrival in Canada.

(3) Instructions of Minister — In applying subsection (1), the officer shall act in accordance with any instructions that the Minister may make.

(4) Restriction — A foreign national whose claim for refugee protection has been rejected or determined to be withdrawn or abandoned by the Refugee Protection Division or the Refugee Appeal Division may not request a temporary resident permit if less than 12 months have passed since their claim was last rejected or determined to be withdrawn or abandoned.

(5) Restriction — designated foreign national — A designated foreign national may not request a temporary resident permit

(a) if they have made a claim for refugee protection but have not made an application for protection, until five years after the day on which a final determination in respect of the claim is made;

(b) if they have made an application for protection, until five years after the day on which a final determination in respect of the application is made; or

(c) in any other case, until five years after the day on which the foreign national becomes a designated foreign national.

(6) Suspension of request — The processing of a request for a temporary resident permit of a foreign national who, after the request is made, becomes a designated foreign national is suspended

(a) if the foreign national has made a claim for refugee protection but has not made an application for protection, until five years after the day on which a final determination in respect of the claim is made;

(b) if the foreign national has made an application for protection, until five years after the day on which a final determination in respect of the application is made; or

(c) in any other case, until five years after the day on which the foreign national becomes a designated foreign national.

(7) Refusal to consider request — The officer may refuse to consider a request for a temporary resident permit if

(a) the designated foreign national fails, without reasonable excuse, to comply with any condition imposed on them under subsection 58(4) or section 58.1 or any requirement imposed on them under section 98.1; and

(b) less than 12 months have passed since the end of the applicable period referred to in subsection (5) or (6).

[Editor's Note: SOR/2002-227, s. 329(2) provides that a permit issued by the Minister under s. 37 of the former Immigration Act, *R.S.C. 1985, c. I-2 is deemed to be a temporary resident permit referred to in s. 24 of the new* Immigration and Refugee Protection Act, *S.C. 2001, c. 27.]*

2010, c. 8, s. 3; 2012, c. 17, s. 12

Case Law

Section 24

Dhaliwal v. Canada (Minister of Citizenship and Immigration), 2015 FC 762, 2015 CarswellNat 2303, 2015 CarswellNat 3885 — The applicant challenges a decision of Citizenship and Immigration Canada to reject his application for a temporary resident permit. The authority to grant a TRP pursuant to subs. 24(1) of the IRPA is highly discretionary and exceptional in nature. In exercising this discretion in respect of either an application to extend a TRP, or an application for a subsequent TRP after one or more TRPs have already been granted, CIC is not prevented from refusing the application where there is no change in circumstances, relative to those that existed when the prior TRPs were granted. If that were so, a person who receives a TRP would be able to stay in Canada indefinitely, so long as there was no change in circumstances, as the applicant claims he should be permitted to do. This would be entirely inconsistent with the "temporary" nature of the discretionary and exceptional authority provided under subs. 24(1). It would also seriously undermine the government's ability to manage the TRP program from year to year. The application for judicial review was dismissed.

Vaguedano Alvarez v. Canada (Minister of Citizenship & Immigration), 2011 CarswellNat 2091, 2011 FC 667 — An officer determined there were insufficient grounds to merit the issuance of a TRP to the applicant. The applicant was an ordained pastor and had been issued a temporary resident entry visa to work at a Hispanic church in Ontario. The applicant was convicted of operation of a motor vehicle while impaired, contrary to s. 253(1)(a) of the *Criminal Code.*

The applicant's request for an extension of his visitor's record was refused. The refusal letter advised the applicant that he must leave Canada on or before the expiry of his current document, as the failure to do so could result in an enforcement action against him. He subsequently made an application for a TRP under s. 24 of IRPA. While the TRP decision was pending, the applicant was informed that a report had been prepared under s. 44 of IRPA based on reasonable grounds to believe that he was inadmissible to Canada. The applicant's request for a TRP was rejected. The applicant and his family were subsequently ordered deported.

The level of procedural fairness required in this context is rather low. The officer listed the appropriate factors as set out in the guidelines — the infraction, that the applicant was enrolled in the back-on-track program, that he provided ministry to the Hispanic community — and found nonetheless that there were not sufficient grounds to merit the issuance of a permit. Clearly the officer did not consider the need of the applicant to remain in Canada to be so compelling as to outweigh any risk he presented. A detailed written analysis is not required. Although the officer's reasons were brief, there was a chain of reasoning, and it is implicit that she put more weight on the applicant's failure to leave Canada than the contribution he makes to the community as the reference letters attest. That he failed to leave Canada because he misunderstood the provisions of the IRPR was unfortunate, but did not raise a breach of procedural fairness in the context of sufficiency of the reasons. The application for judicial review was dismissed.

See the *Ferraro* summary under s. 25(1) of IRPA.

Shah v. Canada (Minister of Citizenship & Immigration) (2011), 3 Imm. L.R. (4th) 269, 2011 FC 1269, 2011 CarswellNat 4567, 2011 CarswellNat 5677, [2011] F.C.J. No. 1553 — The applicant's application for permanent residence from within Canada based on humanitarian and compassionate considerations under s. 25 of IRPA were refused. As well, she requested a temporary resident permit (TRP) in hopes of becoming eligible for a pardon for her shoplifting offences. The officer did not consider the TRP request.

Where an applicant makes a TRP request, it must be considered and a failure to do so is a reviewable error. Even if there is no basis for the issuance of a TRP, the officer should indicate the request was considered. The application for judicial review was granted.

Dhandal v. Canada (Minister of Citizenship & Immigration) (2009), 82 Imm. L.R. (3d) 214, 2009 FC 865, 2009 CarswellNat 5809, 2009 CarswellNat 2582 — This is an application for judicial review of the decision of a visa officer in refusing to consider the issuance of a temporary resident permit (TRP). The applicants were citizens of India. They applied for permanent residence on January 9, 2007. On July 25, 2008 an immigration counsellor determined that the applicants were inadmissible pursuant to para. 40(1)(a) of IRPA for misrepresenting the age of Simrajit Kaur Dhandal. In accordance with para. 40(1)(b) of the Act, the applicants continued to be inadmissible for two years following the date of that decision. On September 4, 2008, the applicants requested that the visa officer consider issuing a TRP pursuant to s. 24 of the Act. Additional submissions supporting the request for the TRP were sent by the applicants in September 2008. The visa officer informed them that their file had been closed following the refusal in July 2008 and no further reconsideration would be given.

The applicants submit that the failure of the visa officer to even consider the TRP request was an error of law. The respondent submitted that the request for a TRP was not properly constituted as it was filed one month after the file was closed and no separate application or fee was provided.

A request for temporary residence is implicit in an application for permanent residence. A new application is not necessary if the applicant is found to be inadmissible for permanent residence. A simple letter is sufficient to trigger the request for temporary residence, based upon the existing application (for permanent residence) if the applicant has been found to be inadmissible for permanent residence. In the present instance, the permanent resident application was denied, a letter was subsequently sent to the visa officer requesting temporary residence. In refusing to consider the request, the visa officer committed an error of law. The application for judicial review was granted.

Ali v. Canada (Minister of Citizenship & Immigration) (2008), 73 Imm. L.R. (3d) 258, 2008 FC 784, 2008 CarswellNat 2902, 2008 CarswellNat 2061, [2008] F.C.J. No. 985 — Section 24 requires an officer to decide whether a TRP is justified "in the circumstances." That phrase must mean the relevant circumstances. Both the CIC Policy Manual and the immigration officer's own analysis (as well as the applicant's submission) made family ties and the existence and interest of children a relevant circumstance. The evidence of the minor child's interest was material to this case. Therefore, the failure to address the minor child was a legal error in failing to consider the "circumstances" of this particular applicant. The application for judicial review was granted.

Rodgers v. Canada (Minister of Citizenship & Immigration) (2006), 56 Imm. L.R. (3d) 63, 2006 CarswellNat 2849, 2006 FC 1093 — The granting of TRPs under s. 24 is clearly discretionary. Depending on the circumstances, issuing a TRP may be justified or not. The mere fact that there is a provision for issuing TRPs does not mean that there cannot be circumstances where the issuing of TRPs would undermine the entire procedure for dealing with applicants under the IRPA.

The considerations under s. 24 only have to be justified under the circumstances. It is not a full-scale H&C consideration as mandated by s. 25. In this case, the applicant's immigration history was such that the immigration officer's decision was not unreasonable. The applicant came illegally to Canada and by using every available means including a false diabetes claim and an unjustified refugee claim managed to stay 15 years. Under these circumstances, the denial of the TRP was hardly unreasonable. Given that this was not a full-scale H&C assessment under s. 25, there is no requirement to consider and deal with each submission of the applicant. The application for judicial review of a decision not to grant a TRP was set aside.

Malicia v. Canada (Minister of Citizenship & Immigration), 2006 CarswellNat 3208, 2006 FC 755 — This is an application for judicial review of the decision of an immigration officer to refuse to seek authority to issue a temporary resident permit (TRP) for the applicant. The applicant argued that a positive "stage one" H&C decision provides the foundation for considering whether to issue a TRP. The applicant claims that there is no form or formal, legislated process for applying for a TRP; in practice, an applicant is only invited to apply for a TRP after a positive "Stage One" and a negative "Stage Two" H&C decision has been made. The parties have agreed that this matter should be returned for reconsideration for lack of reasons. The applicant claims that when the decision goes back, the court should direct that the exemption from stage one or the PR application should continue to apply.

The court concluded that when the matter is returned for reconsideration, the officer responsible is required to re-examine all aspects of the decision, and the court should not interfere with this process by isolating one aspect and placing it outside the scope of reconsideration. The court should not issue a direction that has the effect of making a decision that is for the decision maker to make and, while the court may guide the decision-making process, it cannot make the actual decision.

Lee v. Canada (Minister of Citizenship & Immigration) (2006), 60 Imm. L.R. (3d) 62, 2006 FC 1461, 2006 CarswellNat 4260 — The applicant was found to be inadmissible pursuant to s. 38(1) of the IRPA. On the basis of medical evidence, the officer found that the applicant's health conditions, which included polycystic kidney disease, hypertension, moderate mitral regurgitation and chronic renal failure, would reasonably be expected to cause "excessive demands" on Canada's health services. The applicant argued that, as he is an entrepreneur with considerable net worth, the officer erred in law by failing to consider his ability to provide for his own health care if admitted to Canada, and further, the officer breached procedural fairness by not considering his request for a temporary resident permit. Specifically, the applicant relied on the Supreme Court of Canada's decision in *Hilewitz v. Canada (Minister of Citizenship and Immigration)*. Hilewitz dealt specifically with an applicant's ability to pay for *social services* and not *health services*; therefore the applicant's argument that the reasoning in *Hilewitz* applied equally to health services was dismissed. The officer did not err in law by not considering the applicant's financial ability to pay for his own health care.

In a letter to the Canadian Consulate, the applicant requested the officer consider granting him a TRP. The officer was required to respond to this request without the necessity of a separate submission. The failure of the officer to deal with this request constituted an error in due process. A different immigration officer was ordered to assess the applicant's temporary resident permit application on the basis of the existing evidentiary record.

Farhat v. Canada (Minister of Citizenship & Immigration), 2006 CarswellNat 3418, 2006 FC 1275 — The Minister's delegate of the Consulate General of Canada in New York was of the opinion that the applicant's circumstances did not warrant the issuance of a temporary resident permit (TRP). The applicant sought judicial review of the decision. The applicant was married to a Canadian citizen who applied to sponsor him from within Canada. This application was refused as the applicant did not have temporary resident status at the time the application was filed. The applicant was then convicted of theft under $5,000 and a s. 44 report was prepared because the Minister was of the opinion that the applicant was inadmissible on grounds of criminality. The applicant was excluded from Canada for one year. The applicant's counsel was made aware that the applicant needed to apply for an authorization to return to Canada. The applicant then made an application for a TRP to the Canadian Consulate. The Minister concluded that the circumstances did not warrant the issuance of a TRP. The Minister was not satisfied that the applicant would leave Canada at its expiry. The Minister indicated that the applicant could apply for a pardon. The Minister also found that the applicant had to obtain an authorization to return to Canada.

The applicant has the onus of establishing the compelling reasons and did not satisfy the Minister that the particular circumstances of his case warranted the granting of a TRP. A person seeking a TRP must have the intention of staying in Canada for temporary purpose and an officer must be satisfied that such a person will leave upon the expiry of status. Albeit, it is true that an intention by a foreign national to become a permanent resident does not preclude an individual from becoming a temporary resident; nevertheless, the officer has to be satisfied that the foreign national will leave Canada by the end of the period authorized by his or her stay. Considering the applicant's history of non-compliance with the Canadian immigration laws and regulations, and his overstay in Canada, it was not patently unreasonable for the applicant to be obliged to leave at the end of the period authorized for his stay. The applicant did not present, in regard to the existence of his spouse and child, any "compelling reasons" which would allow him to be granted a TRP. It was not patently unreasonable for the Minister to consider the interest of the child, in this case, did not amount to "compelling reasons" in light of the evidence presented.

The decision of the Minister concerning the TRP application was not irrational or perverse or so gratuitous and oppressive that no reasonable person could think it justified. Consequently, this application for judicial review was dismissed.

Figueroa v. Canada (Minister of Citizenship & Immigration), 2003 CarswellNat 3657, 2003 CarswellNat 4507, 2003 FC 1339 — The applicant sought to review a decision of an immigration officer refusing the applicant's request for an extension of her temporary resident status.

The applicant is a citizen of Cuba. She met her husband, Mr. Cecil Stein, a Canadian citizen, when he was vacationing there. Mr. Stein continued to visit the applicant in Cuba after his holiday and eventually proposed to her. The applicant sought a Canadian visitor visa but was refused. Mr. Stein contacted his member of Parliament and eventually a

Minister's permit was obtained for the applicant in the summer of 2002. This permit allowed the applicant temporary residence in Canada until September 30, 2002. On August 21, 2002, the applicant married Mr. Stein and on August 26, 2002, more than 30 days before the expiration of her temporary resident permit, the applicant sought an extension pending a final determination of her permanent resident application. The permanent resident application was filed in September 2002, the applicant applied as a member of the Spouse In-Canada class. Her application was supported by Mr. Stein's sponsorship application. In December 2002, the applicant's request for an extension of her temporary resident status was refused.

The covering letter from the immigration officer indicated that she was attaching copies of the decision giving written reasons for the decision. However, it is clear that the decision did not include any written reasons.

The respondent took the position that the immigration officer acted in accordance with the instructions from the Minister. The record, however, was silent as to the content of those instructions. In the absence of any evidence as to those instructions, and without reasons, a question arose as to how the immigration officer followed the instructions. In those circumstances, the lack of reasons raised an appearance of arbitrariness on the part of the officer. Accordingly the officer's decision was set aside.

25. (1) Humanitarian and compassionate considerations — request of foreign national — Subject to subsection (1.2), the Minister must, on request of a foreign national in Canada who applies for permanent resident status and who is inadmissible — other than under section 34, 35 or 37 — or who does not meet the requirements of this Act, and may, on request of a foreign national outside Canada — other than a foreign national who is inadmissible under section 34, 35 or 37 — who applies for a permanent resident visa, examine the circumstances concerning the foreign national and may grant the foreign national permanent resident status or an exemption from any applicable criteria or obligations of this Act if the Minister is of the opinion that it is justified by humanitarian and compassionate considerations relating to the foreign national, taking into account the best interests of a child directly affected.

(1.01) Restriction — designated foreign national — A designated foreign national may not make a request under subsection (1)

(a) if they have made a claim for refugee protection but have not made an application for protection, until five years after the day on which a final determination in respect of the claim is made;

(b) if they have made an application for protection, until five years after the day on which a final determination in respect of the application is made; or

(c) in any other case, until five years after the day on which they become a designated foreign national.

(1.02) Suspension of request — The processing of a request under subsection (1) of a foreign national who, after the request is made, becomes a designated foreign national is suspended

(a) if the foreign national has made a claim for refugee protection but has not made an application for protection, until five years after the day on which a final determination in respect of the claim is made;

(b) if the foreign national has made an application for protection, until five years after the day on which a final determination in respect of the application is made; or

(c) in any other case, until five years after the day on which they become a designated foreign national.

(1.03) Refusal to consider request — The Minister may refuse to consider a request under subsection (1) if

(a) the designated foreign national fails, without reasonable excuse, to comply with any condition imposed on them under subsection 58(4) or section 58.1 or any requirement imposed on them under section 98.1; and

(b) less than 12 months have passed since the end of the applicable period referred to in subsection (1.01) or (1.02).

(1.1) Payment of fees — The Minister is seized of a request referred to in subsection (1) only if the applicable fees in respect of that request have been paid.

(1.2) Exceptions — The Minister may not examine the request if

(a) the foreign national has already made such a request and the request is pending;

(a.1) the request is for an exemption from any of the criteria or obligations of Division 0.1;

(b) the foreign national has made a claim for refugee protection that is pending before the Refugee Protection Division or the Refugee Appeal Division; or

(c) subject to subsection (1.21), less than 12 months have passed since the foreign national's claim for refugee protection was last rejected, determined to be withdrawn after substantive evidence was heard or determined to be abandoned by the Refugee Protection Division or the Refugee Appeal Division.

(1.21) Exception to paragraph (1.2)(c) — Paragraph (1.2)(c) does not apply in respect of a foreign national

(a) who, in the case of removal, would be subjected to a risk to their life, caused by the inability of each of their countries of nationality or, if they do not have a country of nationality, their country of former habitual residence, to provide adequate health or medical care; or

(b) whose removal would have an adverse effect on the best interests of a child directly affected.

(1.3) Non-application of certain factors — In examining the request of a foreign national in Canada, the Minister may not consider the factors that are taken into account in the determination of whether a person is a Convention refugee under section 96 or a person in need of protection under subsection 97(1) but must consider elements related to the hardships that affect the foreign national.

(2) Provincial criteria — The Minister may not grant permanent resident status to a foreign national referred to in subsection 9(1) if the foreign national does not meet the province's selection criteria applicable to that foreign national.

2008, c. 28, s. 117; 2010, c. 8, s. 4(1); 2012, c. 17, s. 13(1), (3); 2013, c. 16, ss. 9, 36(3); 2013, c. 40, s. 291

Case Law

Section 25(1)

Gan v. Canada (Minister of Citizenship and Immigration), 2014 FC 824, 2014 CarswellNat 3366, 2014 CarswellNat 3533 — The applicant sought judicial review of an immigration officer's decision to refuse her application for permanent residence under the family class due to her exclusion under para. 117(9)(d) of the *Immigration and Refugee Protection Regulations*, finding that H&C considerations under subs. 25(1) of the Act did not overcome the applicant's exclusion under the Regulations due to non-disclosure by her mother. The officer referred to the mother's misconduct on more than 30 occasions. While some such references are undoubtedly fair comments in relation to the issue of the mother's credibility as the applicant's sponsor, many, if not the majority, are made in contexts other than assessing the credibility of the mother, or their reunification plans. This excessive concern with the mother's actions, as serious as her misconduct was, creates the appearance that the rejection of the H&C, which was brought to overcome her ineligibility, was instead decided because of the very facts underlying that ineligibility, namely the mother's failure to disclose the applicant. The officer's assessment is tainted by the repeated references to the mother's misrepresentations. The application for judicial review was allowed.

Akyol v. Canada (Minister of Citizenship and Immigration) (2014), 32 Imm. L.R. (4th) 132, 2014 FC 1252, 2014 CarswellNat 6618, 2014 CarswellNat 5560 — The applicant sought to set aside the decision of a senior immigration officer refusing their permanent resident application from within Canada based on H&C grounds. The principal applicant and his wife are citizens of Turkey. Their oldest child was born in Turkey but moved to the United States when he was 2. Their second child was born in the United States and third child in Canada. Their refugee status claim in Canada was dismissed in 2012. They then made a request for permanent residence based on H&C grounds pursuant to subs. 25(1) of IRPA. Their request cited consideration of the risk of discrimination and harassment in Turkey as Kurds; their relatives' opposition to the couple's mixed marriage; the best interests of the children; and level of establishment in Canada. Their second child had significant learning disabilities. The evidence before the officer demonstrated that the child's learning challenges were significant. This was not a case where the evidence of learning disabilities consisted of a statement of a family physician or school teacher. Here his abilities were tested across the range of functions and skills by professionals using recognized methods and assessed against established norms. Given their conclusion as to the nature and extent of the disability the officer's reasoning did not meet the *Baker* standard. The interests of the child, in the unique circumstances of this case, could not be disposed of by a mere reference in a single country condition report to an obligation on the receiving country to accommodate disabled students. This is not to negate the empirical value of country condition reports. They are very often the best and most reliable source of information available. Here, however, the *Baker* standard was not satisfied. The officer erred in requiring evidence of the severe harm or hardship to a child. The question is not: "is the child suffering enough that his 'best interests' are not being met?" Rather, the question is "what is in the child's best interests?" It is the child that must, first and foremost, be considered when conducting a best interest of child analysis, rather than whether the child could adapt to another country, or accompany parents. The application for judicial review was granted.

Weng (Litigation guardian of) v. Canada (Minister of Citizenship and Immigration) (2014), 29 Imm. L.R. (4th) 152, 2014 CarswellNat 3016, 2014 CarswellNat 3673 — The applicant sought judicial review of a decision of a visa officer that determined pursuant to s. 25(1) of IRPA that there were insufficient H&C grounds to grant permanent residence or an exemption from a family class exclusion arising from s. 117(9)(d) of the Regulations. The applicant was a 12-year-old minor child and a citizen of China. In February 2001, her mother submitted an application for permanent residence. The first daughter, Angela, had been born on July 14, 1999. The applicant's mother became pregnant again in the fall of 2001 which was contrary to China's one-child policy. Her parents took steps to hide the pregnancy and the applicant was born on July 20, 2002. Her parents arranged for her to be cared for by a family in a remote village where she stayed until she was 18 months old. Her mother then took her to live with her maternal grandparents. When she was aged 3, her paternal grandparents took over her care. Her parents registered her birth but did not change their *hukou* (household registration). The parents immigrated to Canada with the older sister in July of 2006. The parents claim that their immigration consultant advised them not to update and declare the applicant's birth in their permanent resident application as they could sponsor her once they were in Canada. They were afraid that her birth would be discovered by the Chinese government if they made this declaration. Soon after they landed, they applied to sponsor the applicant. After five years, on September 5, 2011, her application was denied. Meanwhile, the parents had a third child, a son born in Canada on January 10, 2008. In December 2011, the second application to sponsor based on H&C grounds was made.

The visa officer failed to address the best interest of the applicant's siblings. The visa officer must consider the scenario of the family being reunited in Canada when considering the best interests of the child. Further, where more than one child is directly affected, the officer must consider their separate interests and needs. Here, the applicant's siblings are both Canadian children and were directly affected by their sister's presence in China. As Canadian citizens being forced to move back to China with their parents, their situation was very different from that of their sister. The visa officer should have used the applicant's potential life in Canada as a point of comparison in considering her best interests. Instead, the visa officer considered only the status quo of the applicant's life in China, and whether there was any impediment to her remaining there. When an applicant has been excluded pursuant to s. 117(9)(d) of the Regulations, it is an error for an officer to give undue weight to the misrepresentation. The visa officer's fixation on the reason for the non-disclosure prevented him from genuinely assessing the H&C considerations that the applicant had raised. The application for judicial review was allowed.

Tiangha v. Canada (Minister of Citizenship & Immigration) (2013), 15 Imm. L.R. (4th) 271, 2013 CarswellNat 1049, 2013 CarswellNat 483, 2013 FC 211 — This was an application for judicial review of a decision by an immigration officer to refuse the applicant's request for permanent residence under the Live-In Caregiver class. While the applicant met the eligibility requirements, he had also undertaken additional work without authorization and did not satisfy the officer that an exemption on humanitarian and compassionate grounds should be granted. The officer made no attempt to appreciate the difficulties the applicant was faced with and drew unreasonable inferences about the options that were open to him. The record shows that after completing all the requirements of the caregiver program and submitting his application for permanent residence, he continually sought more jobs as a nurse-caregiver and only turned to manual labour to pay the unexpected and substantial expenses incurred by his father's illness and funeral when he was unsuccessful in this search. It was not reasonable of the officer to have speculated that the applicant could draw on unlimited funding and free accommodation from presumed friends and relatives in Canada instead of working, or to fail to understand that the debts resulting from his father's final illness did not cease to exist upon his father's death. The officer's conclusions did not represent a possible or acceptable outcome. The application for judicial review was allowed.

Pokhan v. Canada (Minister of Citizenship & Immigration), 2012 FC 1453, 2012 CarswellNat 4895, 2012 CarswellNat 5374 — The applicant sought judicial review of her request for humanitarian and compassionate relief and for a pre-removal risk assessment. The officer considered the best interests of the Canadian child and in doing so considered the circumstances that would face a child in Guyana. The officer noted that education and health care resources in Guyana are poor; however, the child would not be personally affected by those problems because they are not experienced by the entire population. Further, the child would not be denied basic amenities.

It is clearly an error for an officer to indicate that the best interests of a child will only be relevant where basic amenities will be denied. The question is not whether the child will face undue, undeserved or disproportionate hardship. The officer must consider the benefit to the child if the parent is allowed to remain in Canada and the hardship the parent's removal would cause. In this case, the officer never considered the possibility of the applicant remaining in Canada and the implications for the child in such circumstances. The application for judicial review was allowed.

Kobita v. Canada (Minister of Citizenship & Immigration) (2012), 15 Imm. L.R. (4th) 205, 2012 FC 1479, 2012 CarswellNat 4952, 2012 CarswellNat 5403 — The applicant and her two sons were denied a permanent residence visa following the sponsorship by her husband. The immigration officer concluded that the applicant and her children were not members of the family class pursuant to paragraph 117(9)(d) of the Regulations because her husband had failed to declare them as dependants upon his arrival in Canada in 2005 and in his application for permanent residence, which was made in 1999. The officer also found there was insufficient evidence of H&C grounds under s. 25(1) of the Act to overcome the exclusion.

The court considered the decision of *Williams v. Canada (Minister of Citizenship & Immigration)*, 2012 FC 166, at para 64, that there is no "hardship threshold" that must be met, but rather that the best interests of the child is truly the starting point of the analysis. The court also considered the three-step approach set out in the *Williams* decision, which held that the decision maker, when assessing the best interest of the child, must first establish what is in the child's best interest, second the degree to which the child's interest are compromised by one potential decision over another, and then finally, in light of the foregoing assessment determine the weight that this factor should play in the ultimate balancing of positive and negative factors assessed in the application. The court also pointed out that the *Williams* decision did not have the mandatory effect that a decision of the Supreme Court of Canada or Federal Court of Appeal would have.

In the present case, the officer concluded that the best interests of the children would be to continue to reside with their mother in Bangladesh as they did not appear to be suffering undue hardship as a result of their exclusion. The court found that the officer's assessment of the best interests of the child was unreasonable. The officer took the status quo as her starting point and determined the status quo was sufficient without considering other options, including life in Canada with both parents. The officer focused on the fact that the children were not suffering "undue hardship" due to their exclusion. There was no need to find that the children were suffering undue hardship before considering if their best interests could be met by moving them to Canada. The application for judicial review was allowed.

Jacob v. Canada (Minister of Citizenship & Immigration) (2012), 14 Imm. L.R. (4th) 324, 2012 FC 1382, 2012 CarswellNat 4680, 2012 CarswellNat 5040 — The applicant sought judicial review of a decision to refuse his application for permanent residence in Canada on humanitarian and compassionate grounds. The applicant came to Canada as a student and following the school's closure looked into options for employment as a caregiver to an elderly, bed-ridden man whose wife had advertised for the job after obtaining a Labour Market Opinion. The applicant had two years' experience as a live-in caregiver in India. He applied for a work permit from within Canada on the basis of being in Canada on a study permit and on the basis of the positive LMO. The work permit was not issued under the live-in caregiver program ("LCP"). The applicant eventually made an in-Canada application for permanent resident status under the LCP. He was advised initially that he met the requirements to apply under the live-in caregiver class, and subsequently was told in order to be considered under that class he must have been assessed under the LCP from abroad. Since his work permits were not issued under the LCP, he was never in the LCP. The applicant responded and provided an explanation as to how he had become a caregiver in Canada and his oversight in not being under the LCP and referred to the initial positive letter he had received from CIC. He asked for forgiveness and requested the continuing of the processing of the application. The application was refused. He sought judicial review arguing that he had requested that his application be assessed in the live-in caregiver class and requested he be exempted from the requirement that he enters as a live-in caregiver, and in particular from paragraph 113(d) of the Regulations.

The officer did not consider that the purpose of the regulatory scheme underlying an LCP was to encourage people to come into Canada to fill a void that exists in the Canadian labour market, and in consideration for their commitment to work in the domestic field participants are virtually guaranteed permanent residence. The officer's failure led him to ignore a relevant consideration. The officer also erred in processing the application as if it was a simple exemption request from having to apply for permanent residency to Canada from abroad; in fact, the applicant was applying for permanent residency in Canada because that is what he was entitled to as a live-in caregiver, which he was, but had entered in Canada legally as a student. Finally the officer ignored the letter of evidence of the applicant's interdependency with the Thomas family and ignored Mrs. Thomas's letter as well as the doctor's letter. The application for judicial review was granted.

Sebbe v. Canada (Minister of Citizenship & Immigration) (2012), 10 Imm. L.R. (4th) 321, 414 F.T.R. 268 Eng., 2012 FC 813, 2012 CarswellNat 2169, 2012 CarswellNat 2911 — The applicant sought judicial review of the senior immigration office's decision to refuse an application for permanent residence on humanitarian and compassionate grounds. The officer had found that the refugee application had taken some time and the applicants had established themselves to some degree during that time; however, the officer was required to analyze and assess the degree of establishment of the applicants and how it weighs in favour of granting an exemption. The officer cannot merely discount what the applicants had done by crediting the Canadian immigration and refugee system for having given them the time to do these things without giving credit for the initiatives they undertook. The officer must examine whether the disruption of that establishment weighs in favour of granting the exemption.

The officer also concluded that the applicant had knowingly purchased various items including a house, with the full knowledge that he was a failed refugee claimant and there was a possibility that he may have to return to Brazil. The court concluded that the officer took a perverse view of the evidence of establishment. The court stated: "Is every investment, purchase, business established, residence purchased, etc. to be discounted on the basis that it was done knowing that it might have to be given up or left behind? Is the officer suggesting that it is the preference of Canadians that failed claimants do nothing to succeed and support themselves while in Canada? Is he suggesting that any steps taken to succeed will be worthless, because they knew that they were subject to removal? In my view, the answers to these questions show that it is entirely irrelevant whether the person knew he or she was subject to removal when they took steps to establish themselves and their families in Canada. While some may suggest that in establishing themselves applicants are using a backdoor to gain entry into Canada, that view can only be valid if the applicants have no real hope to remain in the country. In virtually all these cases applicants retain hope that they will ultimately be successful in remaining here. Given the time frame most of these applicants spend in Canada, it is unrealistic to presume that they would put their lives on hold awaiting the final decision."

The proper question was not what knowledge the applicants had when they took these steps, but what were the steps they took, were they done legally, and what will the impact be if they must leave them behind. The application for judicial review was allowed.

Medina Moya v. Canada (Minister of Citizenship & Immigration) (2012), 11 Imm. L.R. (4th) 276, 2012 FC 971, 2012 CarswellNat 3435, 2012 CarswellNat 2934 — This was an application for judicial review of a decision of a senior immigration officer wherein the applicants' application for permanent residence in Canada on humanitarian and compassionate grounds was not granted. The officer did not consider the best interest of the two eldest children, aged 18 and 20. The court concluded that the officer was correct in not considering these children under the provisions of s. 25 of IRPA: "best interests of a child." The court did not agree that dependency and vulnerability are the defining characteristics of "childhood" for the purposes of s. 25. The court found that dependent adults should not be included in the analysis of the best interests of the child.

The court went on to conclude that it was unreasonable and incorrect for an officer to consider the "best interests of a child" against a standard of unusual or disproportionate hardship and therefore allowed the application for judicial review on the grounds that the officer applied the wrong test in considering the best interests of the minor children. The court did certify the following question: "Is the 'child' spoken of in s. 25 of IRPA restricted to a person under the age of 18 years?"

Kaur v. Canada (Minister of Citizenship & Immigration), 2012 CarswellNat 2797, 2012 CarswellNat 3429, 2012 FC 964 — The applicant sought judicial review of a decision denying her application for an exemption on humanitarian and compassionate grounds from the requirement of applying for permanent residence from outside Canada. She left

India as a young dependent child and had no knowledge of the Indian economy or its cultural milieu. She grew up in the United States which has a culture similar to Canada and not India. She had no family in India. Her immediate family was in Canada. Her lack of status was strangely at odds with the acceptance of her father, mother and brother as permanent residents. The applicant had not been part of that application because she was too old to qualify as a dependant possibly due to her previous counsel's carelessness or error. The officer failed to conduct a realistic assessment of the hardships that the applicant would face on return to India to apply for permanent residence from outside the country. There was no assessment of how long that process may take. Nor was there any assessment of the applicant's opportunities to adapt given the fact she did not speak the language or have experience with the economy, culture and mores of India. The officer also failed to assess the restrictive attitudes in India towards single women as they would relate to this applicant given she would be in India without family support in that country. The application for judicial review was allowed.

Kwon v. Canada (Minister of Citizenship & Immigration), 2012 FC 50, 2012 CarswellNat 67, 2012 CarswellNat 332 — The applicant sought judicial review of a decision of an immigration officer to refuse the request for permanent residence from within Canada on humanitarian and compassionate grounds. The applicants were a husband and wife from South Korea with three adult children in Korea. Their fourth child is a Canadian citizen and the mother of her own two daughters aged 9 and 11 (the granddaughters). The daughter's married life in Canada was a nightmare. Her young family lived with her husband's parents who were abusive. There was physical violence. As well, the daughter's husband was an alcoholic who accumulated serious debts. The daughter eventually ended the marriage but was left alone as a student with no money and two young children. Her parents moved to Canada, purchased a home for their daughter and granddaughters, learned basic English and provided a loving, stable and safe environment for them. Their granddaughters are doing well at school and their daughter has completed her studies and secured employment as a registered nurse. However, her shift work means that she is often not home in the evening and on weekends. After the marriage ended, the daughter's husband suffered a brain injury in a motorcycle accident and is permanently mentally disabled. He is not able to play any role in the upbringing of the children. The applicants are effectively parenting their granddaughters.

Given that the officer recognized that the granddaughters needed emotional and psychological support on an ongoing basis, his failure to squarely address the impact of the applicants' departure on their granddaughters was unreasonable. There was a suggestion in the decision that there should have been psychologists' reports on the granddaughters showing evidence of ongoing or permanent trauma to justify the H&C application. However, expert opinions were not required. On these facts, it is obvious that the departure of the applicants would deprive the granddaughters of the emotional and psychological support which the officer concluded they required. The judicial review was allowed and the H&C application was sent back for reconsideration by another officer.

Zazai v. Canada (Minister of Citizenship & Immigration), 2012 FC 162, 2012 CarswellNat 428, 2012 CarswellNat 1046 — The applicant sought judicial review of an officer's decision that there were insufficient H&C grounds to warrant an exception allowing the applicant's permanent residence application to be made from within Canada. In assessing PRRA applications, officers must consider new, credible, relevant and material evidence of facts that might have affected the outcome of the applicant's refugee claim hearing if this evidence had been presented and thereby assess the risk against the country of removal. Conversely, when assessing H&C applications, officers must "have regard to public policy considerations and humanitarian grounds, including family-related interests." Compared to PRRA assessments, H&C assessments are a lower threshold and are not limited to specific parameters of persecution.

Due to these differences between the two processes, the officer's reliance in this case on a future PRRA assessment, and a "restricted" one at that, did not show how the best interests of the children would be considered prior to removal. Further, although the officer clearly stated that the best interests of the children were the most compelling H&C considerations in this case, her limited discussion on these interests did not meet the standard of examining them in great detail. The existence of a TRP that can be cancelled at any time did not remove the requirement to consider these interests thoroughly and carefully.

Although it was up to the officer to determine what weight to grant the best interests of the children, she did not conduct an adequate analysis of these interests before proceeding with the balancing exercise. The officer's reliance on a future restricted PRRA did not guarantee that these interests would be addressed prior to a future removal that remained a possibility due to the impermanent nature of TRPs. The application for judicial review was allowed.

Ferraro v. Canada (Minister of Citizenship & Immigration), 2011 CarswellNat 2533, 2011 FC 801 — The applicant sought judicial review of a decision denying his request for a temporary resident permit and for H&C consideration to overcome inadmissibility for serious criminality. There was no error with respect to the rejection of the applicant's request for a temporary resident permit without a distinct analysis. In effect, given that the applicant's request was clearly based on the same grounds as those of his H&C application, it was proper for the decision maker to simply refer to her same analysis. The application for judicial review was dismissed.

Divakaran v. Canada (Minister of Citizenship & Immigration), 2011 CarswellNat 2079, 2011 FC 633 — The applicant sought judicial review of two decisions by a pre-removal risk assessment officer wherein the officer refused the applicant's application under subs. 25(1) of the Act to have his application for permanent residence processed from within Canada on H&C grounds, and the officer determined that the applicant would not be subject to risk of persecution, torture, risk to life or risk of cruel and unusual treatment or punishment, if he returned to Sri Lanka.

The Federal Court of Appeal and the Federal Court have both held that a series of discriminatory events that individually do not give rise to persecution may amount to persecution when considered cumulatively. The officer failed to consider cumulative persecution. For example, in the H&C decision, the officer accepted that the applicant may have to register with police and be questioned by state security agencies if he wishes to reside in Colombo, or, if he resides in Jaffna, the applicant might be required to proceed through security checkpoints and register with the police. These findings of facts were absent from the PRRA decision. As both decisions were made on the same day by the same officer, these findings should have formed part of the PRRA decision and the officer should have assessed whether the applicant would face more than a mere possibility of persecution on the basis of these discriminatory actions. The application for judicial review for both the PRRA and H&C applications was allowed. If the PRRA is faulty, then the same would follow for the H&C.

Sinniah v. Canada (Minister of Citizenship & Immigration) (2011), 5 Imm. L.R. (4th) 313, 2011 FC 1285, 2011 CarswellNat 4688, 2011 CarswellNat 5749, [2011] F.C.J. No.

1568 — The officer in this case did precisely what the Federal Court of Appeal and the Federal Court have said should not be done when assessing the best interests of affected children. On page 6 of the decision the officer says that "there is little before me to suggest that removing the applicant from the current role he plays in the children's lives would cause them an unusual and undeserved or disproportionate hardship." Again, at the conclusion of the best interests portion of the officer's analysis, she says "I do not find sufficient evidence to establish that either child or the applicant would likely face an unusual and undeserved or disproportionate hardship if he were required to leave Canada to Sri Lanka to apply for permanent residence from abroad." By requiring the applicant to establish unusual and undeserved or disproportionate hardship in relation to the affected children, the officer has misconceived the nature of the weighing process that was required of her in this case and has placed too high a burden on the applicant. It is an error to incorporate such threshold standards into the exercise of that aspect of the H&C discretion which requires the interests of the children be weighted. The end result is that the officer either applied the wrong legal test by imposing the burden of showing "disproportionate hardship" rather than the "best interests" test, or unreasonably fettered her discretion by requiring that unusual and undeserved or disproportionate hardship related to the child must be established before the best interests of the affected children can be weighed against the other factors at play in this case. Either way, a reviewable error occurred. The application for judicial review was allowed.

Walcott v. Canada (Minister of Citizenship & Immigration), 2011 FC 415, 2011 CarswellNat 1122, 2011 CarswellNat 2777 — While state protection may be a relevant consideration in an assessment of an H&C application, the officer erred when her analysis stopped with the consideration of state protection. In contrast to a PRRA application or a refugee claim, state protection is not a determinative factor. Deciding that state protection may exist in a country of removal does not relieve the officer from the task of assessing whether, regardless of any available protection, the applicant's circumstances warrant receiving an exemption from the requirements of IRPA based on humanitarian and compassionate considerations.

It is no doubt true that conscientious objection based on political, moral, or religious grounds does not provide a sufficient basis on which to establish a claim for refugee protection. There is clearly a trend towards accepting that punishing people who refuse military service on conscientious grounds amounts to persecution: *Hinzman, Re* (2006), 55 Imm. L.R. (3d) 54 at ¶232-33 (F.C.); *Lebedev v. Canada (Minister of Citizenship & Immigration)* (2007), 62 Imm. L.R. (3d) 161 at ¶47–50 (F.C.). Notwithstanding the fact that punishment for refusing to serve in the military as a result of sincerely held objection to a particular war does not constitute persecution under Canadian law, the officer was nevertheless required to determine whether the judicial and non-judicial punishments faced by the applicant if returned to the U.S. because of his sincerely held beliefs, as well as the hazing and the imprisonment while suffering from PTSD, amounted to unusual and undeserved or disproportionate hardship.

By failing to recognize that filing a conscientious objector status application would not in any way alleviate any of the hardships asserted by the applicant, by failing to recognize that the applicant does not qualify as a conscientious objector under the applicable Army regulation, and by ignoring evidence that filing such an application may in fact increase the hardship suffered by the applicant, the officer's decision is unreasonable in that it did not meet the standard of justification, transparency, and intelligibility. The application for judicial review was granted.

Da Silva v. Canada (Minister of Citizenship & Immigration), 2011 FC 347, 2011 CarswellNat 895, 2011 CarswellNat 1735 — The applicant was a citizen of Brazil who came to Canada in April 2001 on a temporary resident permit and remained in Canada without status. She applied for H&C in October 2005. At a young age the nieces lost three primary caregivers in a span of three years: their mother, father, and then grandmother. The applicant claims that she is like a mother to the nieces and a grandmother to one of the niece's sons. The applicant never married and has no children of her own. The court agreed with Justice Martineau in *Frank v. Canada (Minister of Citizenship & Immigration)*, 2010 FC 270, where he stated at para. 30 of the decision:

> I do not believe *John* [2010 FC 85] created an obligation for all immigration officers to explicitly consider the issue of *de facto* family members in every case. It is clear in the present application that the officer considered the applicant's relationship with his family in Canada, and, without evidence the officer failed to consider any other relevant criteria in determining the H&C application, the Court should not intervene.

In the present case, the officer considered the applicant's relationship with her family in Canada. The officer's failure to consider whether the applicant was a *de facto* family member is reasonable because it was clear from the evidence in the record that the applicant was not a *de facto* family member. Although the applicant certainly had a close emotional bond with her nieces, *de facto* family member is a defined concept in the immigration context and the applicant simply did not meet the definition. The applicant claimed to be financially self-sufficient, and she did not demonstrate emotional dependence on the nieces that would render her a *de facto* family member. The applicant is an independent and functional adult, as was the applicant in *Frank*, above, and so is not a *de facto* family member. The application for judicial review was dismissed.

Toussaint v. Canada (Minister of Citizenship & Immigration), 2011 FCA 146, 2011 CarswellNat 1943, 2011 CarswellNat 1446; application/notice of appeal to S.C.C. filed 2011 CarswellNat 2875 (S.C.C.) — On a proper interpretation of subs. 25(1) of IRPA, the Minister is obligated to consider a request for an exemption from the requirement in para. 10(1)(d) of the Regulations to pay a fee for processing an application under subs. 25(1). The Governor in Council's failure to enact regulations permitting the waiver of fees for foreign nationals living in poverty who wish to make an in-Canada application for permanent residence status pursuant to subs. 25(1) of IRPA does not infringe an applicant's ss. 7 or 15 of the *Charter of Rights* nor does it infringe the rule of law or the common law constitutional right of access to the courts.

Hinzman v. Canada (Minister of Citizenship & Immigration) (2010), 10 Admin. L.R. (5th) 89, 405 N.R. 275, 321 D.L.R. (4th) 111, 2010 FCA 177, 2010 CarswellNat 2094, 2010 CarswellNat 3626 — The appellants asked the court to find that the H&C officer failed to have regard to Mr. Hinzman's personal circumstances, including his sincerely held moral, political and religious objections to service with the United States army in Iraq.

The H&C officer had the duty to look at all of the appellants' personal circumstances, including Mr. Hinzman's beliefs and motivations, before determining if there was sufficient reasons to make a positive H&C decision. She did not. The H&C decision was significantly flawed and therefore unreasonable. The appeal was allowed.

John v. Canada (Minister of Citizenship & Immigration), 2010 FC 85, 2010 CarswellNat 1134, 2010 CarswellNat 126 — This is a judicial review of the immigration officer's refusal to grant an application for permanent residence from within Canada on humanitarian and compassionate grounds. The applicant was aged 18 when she came to Canada in order to care for her ailing mother. She never left despite her visa expiring in 1991 and her mother passing away in 1994. She remained with her uncle's family which included her grandmother, of whom she takes care.

Paragraph 13.8 of the guidelines IP-5 suggests that an important consideration is to what extent the applicant would have difficulty in meeting financial or emotional needs without the support and assistance of the family unit in Canada. "Separation of persons in such a genuine dependent relationship may be grounds for a positive decision." The guidelines list a number of factors the officer should consider which include whether the dependency is *bona fide*, the level thereof, the stability and the length of the relationship, the ability and willingness of the family in Canada to provide support, alternatives such as siblings outside of Canada "able and willing to provide support" and whether there has been a significant degree of establishment in Canada. The facts were clearly set out in the application, and not only were staring the officer in the face, but indeed were noted by the officer and therefore it was not necessary that s. 13.8 of the guidelines dealing with *de facto* family relationships be specifically brought to the officer's attention. The officer's decision was unreasonable. The application for judicial review was allowed.

Kisson v. Canada (Minister of Citizenship and Immigration) (2010), 88 Imm. L.R. (3d) 66, 2010 FC 99, 2010 CarswellNat 803, 2010 CarswellNat 161 — This was an application for judicial review of a visa officer's decision rejecting the applicant's application for permanent residence under the federal skilled worker category. The applicant requested a substitute evaluation and exemption from the requirements of IRPA pursuant to humanitarian and compassionate considerations. The visa officer did not demonstrate that he looked beyond the selection criteria listed at subs. 76(1) of the Regulations (*i.e.* education, language, experience, age, arranged employment, adaptability). There was no evidence that the visa officer's substituted evaluation broadly assessed the likelihood of the ability of the applicant to become economically established in Canada according to his set of circumstances. The clear intent of subs. 76(3) is to allow the visa officer to substitute their evaluation taking into account a number of factors, and not just the factors listed in s. 76(1). In this case, the applicant had an existing employment offer and previous establishment in Canada which were indicative of the possibility that the applicant will once again be able to establish himself successfully in Canada. It was unreasonable that these factors do not appear to have been considered by the officer when he assessed the humanitarian and compassionate considerations under s. 25 of IRPA. Application for judicial review was allowed.

Kisana v. Canada (Minister of Citizenship & Immigration) (2010), 392 N.R. 163, [2010] 1 F.C.R. 360, 2009 FCA 189, 2009 CarswellNat 1626, 2009 CarswellNat 4008, [2009] F.C.J. No. 713 — The minor appellants were the twins of Sushil and Seema Kisana, born in India on August 20, 1991, before their parents were married. Sushil immigrated to Canada on February 16, 1993, and was landed as an unmarried dependant of his parents. He married Seema upon his return to India in 1994 and subsequently sponsored her for permanent residence in Canada. Seema was landed on April 25, 1999. Both are now Canadian citizens. Neither listed their daughters as dependants on their permanent residence applications. Seema further denied having any children during her two call-in interviews while her application was being processed. Their explanation for failing to make the disclosure is that they were ashamed of having had children out of wedlock and that they had not disclosed the fact that they had children to their parents. The girls' aunt had been caring for them in India since Seema left for Canada. An application to sponsor the girls in 2005 was made with a request that the application be considered on H&C grounds. Specifically, the appellants requested that the visa officer consider the emotional impact of continued separation and indicated that the aunt was no longer in a position to adequately care for their daughters. The Federal Court judge concluded that the officer had not erred in determining that the girls had not suffered undue hardship because of the separation from their parents and their having to live in India. The Federal Court judge also held that the parents' misrepresentation with respect to their daughters was a proper consideration for the officer in determining the H&C application. The Federal Court of Appeal reviewed whether the officer's decision was reasonable and whether adequate consideration was given to the children's best interest. The appeal was dismissed.

An officer who is "alert, alive and sensitive" to the best interest of the child will take these vulnerabilities into account. Generally officers should endeavour to ask age-appropriate questions, satisfy themselves that the questions are understood and ask open-ended questions or follow-up questions where appropriate. Particularly in cases involving very young children, it may be appropriate for an adult to accompany the child in the interview room. In short, while an officer is under no obligation to attempt to illicit all evidence that may help a child's case, being "alert, alive and sensitive" to the child's best interest requires that an interview be conducted in a manner that will allow the child to express him or herself effectively. An officer must keep in mind the linguistic, cognitive and emotional difference between children and adults when conducting an interview. A child confronted with pointed, close-ended questions will likely give simply "yes" or "no" responses and not make efforts to volunteer any additional information. He or she may be reluctant to ask for clarification if a question is not understood. Younger children may not be capable of comprehending the nature of the interview at all.

In obiter, Justice Trudel commented that it is wholly inappropriate to import the "best interest of the child" framework that is used in custody and access cases into immigration applications. The best interests of the child are the determinative factor in a family law case — not so in an immigration context, where it is but one factor to be weighed along with others.

Kandhai v. Canada (Minister of Citizenship & Immigration) (2009), 81 Imm. L.R. (3d) 144, 2009 FC 656, 2009 CarswellNat 1919, 2009 CarswellNat 5681 — The applicant sought judicial review of a decision refusing his application for humanitarian and compassionate exemption. The court determined it was appropriate to consider the application, notwithstanding the applicant's history of repeatedly lying to Canadian immigration authorities. The reasons given for refusing the H&C application were also insufficient. The officer's "reasons" essentially consisted of a review of facts coupled with a statement of conclusion, without any analysis to back it up. Consequently the application for judicial review was allowed. The decision under review was the applicant's third H&C application. He admitted that he was not truthful on his most recent H&C application, as he indicated on the form that he was divorced when in fact he was living in a common-law relationship with his ex-wife. The applicant argued that while the misrepresentation as to his marital situation was undoubtedly an error in judgment, it was not made with the intent of securing an advantage in relation to his H&C application, and thus had no negative effect on the integrity of the Canadian immigration process. In fact, the presence of a common-law partner in Canada may have strengthened his H&C application. In two prior H&C applications, the applicant indicated that he had never been charged with, or convicted of, a criminal offence in another country, when that was not, in fact, the case.

These misrepresentations were made in order to gain an advantage in relation to those applications, and thus had the potential to undermine the integrity of the immigration process. In this case, since the misrepresentations did not appear to be made to gain an advantage, and the applicant appeared to have come forward voluntarily with his admission of misrepresentation, the court concluded that for the purposes of this "clean hands" analysis it was a very strong case.

The court relied on the Federal Court of Appeal decision in *Thanabalasingham v. Canada (Minister of Citizenship & Immigration)* (2006), 51 Imm. L.R. (3d) 1, where the court held that the task for the reviewing court is to strike a balance between "maintaining the integrity of, and preventing the abuse of, judicial and administrative processes," and "the public interest in ensuring the lawful conduct of government in the protection of fundamental human rights."

Rakheja v. Canada (Minister of Citizenship & Immigration) (2009), 81 Imm. L.R. (3d) 219, 345 F.T.R. 159 (Eng.), 2009 FC 633, 2009 CarswellNat 5615, 2009 CarswellNat 1875 — An immigration officer found that the applicant did not meet the requirements of the spouse or common-law partner in Canada class as outlined in section 5.14 of the Operational Manual for Inland Processing 8 (IP8). Specifically the officer found that the applicant did not meet the requirement of possessing a valid non-expired passport, and did not qualify for the discretionary exemption available where a passport has expired during the processing of an application. During his interview, the applicant stated that he would not be able to obtain a new passport because there was an outstanding arrest warrant against him in India. The applicant argued that the immigration officer erred in concluding that he was ineligible for a passport waiver and that, under the guidelines, he should have been given an opportunity to obtain a passport before his application was refused.

Section 72(1)(e)(ii) and s. 50(1)(a) of the Regulations require that an individual must provide a passport or travel document. One reason for the passport requirement is to prove the identity of the applicant. Under the policy, individuals whose passports expire during processing may submit their expired passports if there is no question as to their identity. The guidelines in the Operational Manual IP8 do not provide that an immigration officer may accept an expired passport where the expired date pre-dates the application for permanent residence. However, the intent of the public policy is to facilitate family reunification of spouses under s. 25 of IRPA, even where the applicant is not in status as required by the Act.

An application for permanent residence under the spouse or common-law partner in Canada class is a discretionary exemption by the respondent under s. 25 of IRPA. The respondent has set out a policy for situations granting that exemption which include that the applicant have a valid passport at the time the application is made. According to the respondent the applicant can now make another application under s. 25 for an exemption from the requirement that he have a valid passport, and then the applicant can make another application for permanent residence under the spouse or common-law partner in Canada class. While this two-step process seems illogical, the court acknowledges that it was reasonably open to the respondent to require that the applicant have a valid passport before bringing his current application. Accordingly, the immigration officer's decision in this matter was reasonably open to her and the application for judicial review was dismissed.

Ferrer v. Canada (Minister of Citizenship & Immigration), 2009 CarswellNat 899, 2009 CarswellNat 2095, 2009 FC 356 — The applicant sought judicial review of a decision of the IAD which dismissed his plea for humanitarian and compassionate relief pursuant to s. 67(1)(c) of the IRPA. An exclusion order had been issued against the applicant based on a finding of inadmissibility for a misrepresentation made in September 1998 with respect to his permanent resident application. In his permanent resident application, the applicant testified that he was single with no children. It was not disputed that at the time he was the father of two dependent children living with their mother in the Philippines. The applicant married his spouse who was the mother of his two children on a trip back to the Philippines after he was granted permanent residence status in Canada. The applicant's spouse is not excluded from the family class pursuant to s. 117(9)(d) of the Regulations. Accordingly, the applicant's two children would be eligible to be included on the applicant's spouse's application for permanent residence as her dependent children, provided the applicant's appeal before the IAD was allowed as he would be in a position to sponsor his wife and both of his children as members of the family class.

The IAD considered only two possibilities with respect to the best interests of the children. The first possibility was that the children could remain in the Philippines and that their father would continue to have a geographically distant relationship with them while at the same time supporting them financially at a higher level than possible if he were returned to the Philippines. The second alternative was that the applicant could be returned to the Philippines where he would be able to better meet their emotional needs by having close contact with them, though he would not be able to provide the higher level of financial support in the event that he was removed from Canada. It was argued that the analysis was erroneous and that it did not take into consideration the most probable outcome should the applicant's appeal be allowed. The tribunal's failure to consider the likely chain of events should the appeal be allowed led to its conclusion that the best interests of the children were a neutral factor; in fact the best interests of the applicant's children were a positive factor which weighed in favour of allowing the appeal. In other words, the tribunal failed to appreciate that the applicant's children could have the best of both worlds by being reunited with him in Canada. Had the tribunal not committed this error, it would certainly have considered the best interests of the applicant's children to be a factor in favour of allowing his appeal and not a neutral factor — thereby negating its value. It appears that the IAD's reasoning was dominated by a consideration of the "integrity of the Canadian immigration system." This might be an important factor to consider, but only after the best interest of the children are properly addressed; only in this way can a fair and balanced approach be taken to this important statutory requirement. The application for judicial review was allowed and the matter sent back for redetermination.

Okoye v. Canada (Minister of Citizenship & Immigration), 2008 CarswellNat 4570, 2008 CarswellNat 3690, 2008 FC 1133 — Subsection 25 of the IRPA imposes a statutory duty on the officer to consider the best interests of a child. At the same time, the best interests of a child are not determinative of the parent's status. In the present case, Ms. Okoye expressly raised her daughter Bianca's best interests in her humanitarian and compassionate application, and provided medical evidence from Bianca's pediatrician that she requires treatment for acute asthma attacks. This distinguishes the decision of *Ahmad*, 2008 FC 646, where it was not clear that the parents raised as an issue their children's best interests. The officer's reference in her reasons to Bianca was almost passing in nature. While the officer referred to the doctor's letter, Bianca's medical needs were not mentioned in the analysis portion of the officer's reasons. The officer does not address how Bianca's interests will be affected by her mother's departure from Canada, does not address what hardship Bianca would face in Nigeria, and does not address Bianca's best interests. This analysis was particularly required when country condition documentation otherwise relied upon by the officer reported that in Nigeria public schools are substandard, and many children do not have access to education. Application for judicial review was allowed.

Okoloubu v. Canada (Minister of Citizenship & Immigration) (2008), 75 Imm. L.R. (3d) 1, 301 D.L.R. (4th) 591, 382 N.R. 35, 2008 CarswellNat 3852, 2008 CarswellNat 5576, 2008 FCA 326 — The applicant sought an exemption to apply for permanent residence from within Canada. Were it not for a criminal conviction, he would have been entitled to remain in Canada while his application for a permanent resident visa was being considered. However, his conviction disqualified him from being a member of the spouse or common-law partner in Canada class. He argued that protection of the family and the rights of his wife and the child had to be properly considered. The pre-removal risk assessment officer said she did not have jurisdiction to deal with international law and constitutional issues, and that a request for exemption from permanent resident visa requirements was not the proper venue for resolving such complex legal issues. The officer concluded that the applicant's family situation, links within Canadian society, and the risk factors upon his return to his country did not justify an exemption. The applicant successfully had the decision set aside by the Federal Court. The Federal Court agreed and concluded that the officer's refusal to consider the applicant's rights and those of his wife and Canadian child under the *Charter* and the International Convention on Civil and Political Rights resulted in an unfair hearing. The Minister appealed this decision to the Federal Court of Appeal.

The Federal Court of Appeal held that para. 3(3)(f) of the IRPA does not require that an officer exercising discretion under s. 25 specifically refer to and analyze the international human rights instruments to which Canada is signatory. It is sufficient if the officer addresses the substance of the issues raised. While the officer stated that she did "not have jurisdiction to deal with international law" it was clear that she addressed in substance the different and important interests at stake, giving careful weight to the interest of the child and the importance of the family unit. Therefore, the Federal Court of Appeal's intervention was not warranted and it became unnecessary to address the Federal Court judge's finding that the respondent was deprived a fair hearing. The Federal Court of Appeal found that the certified question "Does an immigration officer in charge of assessing an application under s. 25 of the *Immigration Refugee and Protection Act* (for an exemption from the obligation to present an application for an immigrant visa from outside Canada) have jurisdiction to consider whether an applicant's removal would breach the *International Covenant on Civil and Political Rights*, more specifically Article 17, 23 and 24?" was irrelevant and not dispositive of the appeal and therefore it need not be answered. The appeal was allowed, the judgment of the Federal Court set aside and the applicant's application for judicial review dismissed.

Alie v. Canada (Minister of Citizenship & Immigration), 2008 CarswellNat 2627, 2008 CarswellNat 3911, 2008 FC 925 — The applicants were denied permanent residency in Canada on humanitarian and compassionate grounds. When considering the best interests of the Canadian born child of the adult applicants, the officer failed to properly focus her analysis on the needs of that child; her analysis was focused on the benefit or harm to the family if they were moved from Canada. Proper focus of those considerations must be on the child herself. In this case, the officer failed to focus on the child and the hardship the removal of her family, with or without her, would have on her. Instead, the officer focused her analysis on the hardship to the family if they were removed from Canada, with or without the child. The application for judicial review was allowed.

Odicho v. Canada (Minister of Citizenship & Immigration) (2008), 75 Imm. L.R. (3d) 45, 2008 CarswellNat 4011, 2008 CarswellNat 3442, 2008 FC 1039 — Mr. and Mrs. Odicho sought judicial review of a visa officer's decision to refuse to issue a permanent resident visa to Mrs. Odicho. The applicants argued that the visa officer erred by failing to consider H&C grounds, pursuant to subs. 25 of the IRPA. They submit that they specifically requested that the wife's application for permanent residence in Canada be considered on the basis of s. 25. Mr. Odicho had been landed in Canada in January 2005 and his initial application to sponsor his wife in May 2005 was refused on the basis that he had not disclosed his marriage when he was landed. The application on behalf of a dependent child was refused for the same reason but was subsequently reversed. The visa officer, however, maintained the rejection of the application on behalf of the wife on the basis of para. 117(9)(d) of the Regulations.

There was no dispute that the husband failed to declare his wife as a non-accompanying dependant when he landed in Canada in January 2005. There is no evidence to challenge the *bona fides* of the marriage of the applicants. There is no evidence to challenge the status of the infant as their child. The failure of the husband to declare the change in marital status when he landed in Canada gave rise to the exclusion of his wife pursuant to the terms of para. 117(9)(d) of the Regulations. The court held that the visa officer apparently ignored the material that was submitted concerning the "circumstances" of the husband's failure to declare the change in his marital status at the time he landed in Canada. The applicants carry the burden of establishing the evidence to justify an exercise of discretion, but the discharge of this burden does not require superfluity. The visa officer's decision does not demonstrate an understanding of the purpose of subs. 25(1), which is to overcome the consequences of being in breach of statutory requirements. The initial decision which excluded the child, as well as the wife, illustrates an excess of zeal on the part of that decision maker, if not a misunderstanding of s. 117 of the Regulations. The application for judicial review was allowed. The matter was remitted for reconsideration by a different member of the Canadian Embassy.

Lopez v. Canada (Minister of Citizenship & Immigration), 2008 CarswellNat 1325, 2008 CarswellNat 1326, 2008 FC 582 — This was the judicial review of a PRRA officer's dismissal of an application for permanent residence made from within Canada. The officer failed to take into account that s. 25 of the IRPA is driven either on humanitarian and compassionate considerations or public policy considerations. Put another way, is it Canada's public policy that a person who is not inadmissible in terms of the United Nations Convention Relating to the Status of Refugees and whose record of criminality in Canada cannot be considered because of the pardon granted to him (s. 36(3) IRPA) should nevertheless have to busk in the Montreal Metro for the rest of his life without legal status? The decision of the PRRA officer was an important one which affected the applicant's life in a fundamental way. In this case, the officer failed to assure himself that there was a public policy consideration present. The question was not whether there would be an unusual, underserved or disproportionate hardship if the applicant had to leave Canada. The truth was that he cannot leave Canada since Cuba won't take him back and the authorities know it. The applicant had not applied for permanent residence from abroad because he could not. The application for judicial review was granted and the matter referred back to another officer for redetermination.

Yoon v. Canada (Minister of Citizenship & Immigration), 2008 CarswellNat 844, 2008 CarswellNat 1862, 2008 FC 439 — The applicants, an elderly couple from Korea, applied for permanent residence from within Canada based on humanitarian and compassionate considerations. The officer refused the case stating that the applicants' daughters were "established enough to meet the LICO standards for sponsorship of their parents after eight years in Canada." A scrutiny of the record discloses that there was no evidence to support this statement. There was absolutely no evidence on the record to substantiate the notion that the applicants would only be temporarily separated from their children should they be required to return to Korea. The decision under review was unreasonable and was set aside.

Thandal v. Canada (Minister of Citizenship & Immigration), 2008 CarswellNat 1085, 2008 CarswellNat 1958, 2008 FC 489 — The applicant sought judicial review of a decision to refuse her application for permanent residence as a skilled worker and her H&C application from outside Canada. With the Supreme Court of Canada's decision in *New Brunswick (Board of Management) v. Dunsmuir,* 2008 SCC 9, it is settled that procedural fairness is to be reviewed on a correctness standard while the H&C decision is to be reviewed on a reasonableness standard. The reasonableness standard admits a range of reasonable outcomes. The court was aware that an H&C decision is discretionary, an exception to the normal rules. The officer, by virtue of familiarity and having interviewed the applicant, was in an excellent position to assess the merits of the applicant's story.

It is well established that an applicant has the burden of establishing her case. Generally, an applicant is to do that once, rather than on the basis of some sort of rolling story of reply, sur-reply and so forth. The applicant had an interview at which all the relevant issues were canvassed. There is nothing unfair in the officer deciding the case on the evidence as provided by the applicant at that time. The judicial review was dismissed.

Thalang v. Canada (Minister of Citizenship & Immigration) (2008), 71 Imm. L.R. (3d) 60, 2008 CarswellNat 1270, 2008 FC 340, 2008 CarswellNat 668 — The applicant made both a PRRA application and an H&C application both of which were considered by the same officer at the same time. The officer based the H&C assessment on the wrong test. The officer's assessment was based on risk, which was a PRRA criteria, not an H&C criteria. The proper H&C criteria are unusual and undeserved or disproportionate hardship. This was an error of law in respect of which the standard of review is that of correctness.

Johnson v. Canada (Minister of Citizenship & Immigration), 2008 FC 2, 2008 CarswellNat 1327, 2008 CarswellNat 11, [2008] F.C.J. No. 10 — The applicant's inland application for permanent residence was refused because he was found to be inadmissible on grounds of serious criminality. The criminal convictions that led to the finding of inadmissibility were later set aside. The applicant argued that the officer erred in reaching the decision to refuse his permanent residence application by ignoring relevant evidence, specifically that the applicant's conviction was under appeal and that the officer breached the duty of fairness he owed to the applicant by failing to provide the applicant with an opportunity to respond to his criminal convictions.

A deportation order has a clear and imminent effect upon a person's right to remain in Canada. If, in that context, there is no obligation to await the result of an appeal of a criminal conviction, it is the court's view that there can be no obligation to defer consideration of a humanitarian and compassionate application because of an outstanding appeal. This is so because one may file a new inland application for permanent residence if circumstances later change as a result of a successful appeal. In the absence of compelling circumstances, it would be contrary to the scheme of the Act to require decisions about inadmissibility, made in the context of humanitarian and compassionate application, to be delayed until all criminal proceedings, including all rights of appeal are exhausted. The failure of the applicant to advise immigration of his convictions did not shift the onus to the officer to communicate with the applicant about his convictions. It was always open to the applicant to advise the officer of both his convictions and his appeal, and to request a deferral of the officer's decision until the appeal had been decided. The applicant requested no postponement of the officer's decision. The application for judicial review was dismissed.

Montivero v. Canada (Minister of Citizenship & Immigration), 2008 CarswellNat 1705, 2008 CarswellNat 2802, 2008 FC 720 — The applicants sought to quash the decision of an immigration officer denying their application for an exemption on humanitarian and compassionate (H&C) grounds. The selection of the appropriate test in the context of an H&C application should be assessed by the court on a correctness standard. There is an importance of holding officers to the tests prescribed by Parliament. The correctness standard should be applied here. The applicants submitted that the test for personalized risk under ss. 96 and 97 of the IRPA is different from that of undue hardship under s. 25 H&C applications. They claim that the assessment of the availability of state protection to the applicants is unnecessary under a s. 25 undue hardship analysis. They assert that the officer's assessment of this factor shows that the officer erroneously imposed the higher ss. 96 and 97 threshold to the applicants' s. 25 application. The court concluded that the applicants did not show that the officer applied an incorrect test or threshold to their application. The court pointed out that the applicants raised the question of state protection in their submissions on the H&C application and therefore could not now argue that such an issue was irrelevant to that assessment. In this case, the officer's analysis that the question of alleged risk on an H&C assessment revealed that it was considered in the context of hardship. Accordingly, the decision was not based on the wrong legal test and the decision was not set aside.

Thiara v. Canada (Minister of Citizenship & Immigration) (2008), 70 Imm. L.R. (3d) 80, 2008 FCA 151, 2008 CarswellNat 1220 — Paragraph 3(3)(f) of the IRPA does not require that an officer exercising discretion under s. 25 of the IRPA specifically refer to and analyze the international human rights instruments to which Canada is a signatory. It is sufficient if the officer addresses the substance of the issues raised.

Phillip v. Canada (Minister of Citizenship & Immigration) (2008), 67 Imm. L.R. (3d) 132, 2008 CarswellNat 989, 2008 CarswellNat 16, 2008 FC 19 — This was the case of a 64-year-old grandmother who had resided in Canada for 19 years and was the *de facto* mother of her daughter's children (if not the only caregiver). In the respondent's decision, the officer noted the applicant's accomplishments but did not regard her establishment as "exceptional." The respondent relied upon the content of the father's successful H&C application in which he included another daughter as evidence of the father's commitment to his two other children, the applicant's grandchildren. On the issue of the best interests of the children, the officer assumed that the grandchildren would be taken care of by extended family and that their father would be involved. There was no analysis of the father's ability to care for the children despite the father's admission that he had not been able to care for them. The officer's reliance on the father's H&C application and the inclusion of another daughter therein, was not only procedurally unsound but lead to a *non sequitur* of reasoning. Not only was the use of the father's H&C application a breach of fairness, it led to, or compounded, a substantive error in the consideration of the best interests of the children.

Aguilar Espino v. Canada (Minister of Citizenship & Immigration), 2007 FC 74, 2007 CarswellNat 143, [2007] F.C.J. No. 102 — The applicant, his wife and their two children applied for permanent residence from within Canada on humanitarian and compassionate grounds. Their application was rejected by an officer. The guidelines in the Inland Processing Manual (IP 5) direct that an application to remain in Canada on humanitarian and compassionate grounds be assessed in two steps. The two-step process is explained in ss. 5.6, 5.7 and 5.9. The first step requires the applicants satisfy the decision maker that the H&C factors present in their individual circumstances are sufficient to warrant an exemption. The second step requires that the applicant must meet the requirements for permanent residence in Regulation 68, including that the applicant and their family members, whether accompanying or not, are not inadmissible and otherwise meet the requirements of the Act and Regulations. The two-step assessment process for considering humanitarian and compassionate applications set out in the guidelines applicable to subs. 25(1) of the Act is not contrary to the Act. The two-step assessment process is not contrary to the intent of the legislation but it is supportable within the terms of the Act. The application for judicial review was dismissed.

The following questions were certified:

1. Is the Minister legally entitled to fragment an application under s. 25 of the *Immigration and Refugee Protection Act* into a two-step assessment, the first step being an assessment whether individual humanitarian and compassionate circumstances are sufficient to warrant an exemption from subs. 11(1) and 20(1) of the IRPA and the second step being a determination whether the person is inadmissible?

2. Is the Minister obliged, when considering an application under s. 25 of the IRPA, to weigh or balance the degree of compelling humanitarian and compassionate circumstances on which the individual relies against the nature and extent of the legal obstacle to admissibility?

Wong v. Canada (Minister of Citizenship & Immigration), 2006 CarswellNat 3951, 2006 FC 1410 — In deciding whether to grant the applicant an exemption from the processing requirements under subs. 11(1) of the IRPA, the decision maker erred in placing undue emphasis on the applicant's suspected medical inadmissibility and potential for establishment in Canada. The decision maker's assessment of these factors ought to have been deferred until the second stage of the H&C application. The decision to deny the applicant's application on humanitarian and compassionate grounds for an exemption from their requirement to obtain an immigration visa before coming to Canada was quashed.

Oshurova c. Canada (Ministre de la Citoyenneté & de l'Immigration), 2006 CarswellNat 5301, 2006 FCA 301 — The Federal Court of Appeal was asked to answer whether there was an appearance of bias, *in this case*, because the same officer decided the application for a visa exemption on humanitarian and compassionate grounds as well as the pre-removal risk assessment.

There is no apprehension of institutional bias of all officers who have been, or are involved with these two types of applications. The appeal was dismissed.

Williams v. Canada (Minister of Citizenship & Immigration), 2006 CarswellNat 4593, 2006 FC 1474 — An applicant bears the onus of establishing that he or she has met the standard required to succeed in an H&C application. A successful H&C application usually requires an applicant to demonstrate that an "unusual, underserved or disproportionate hardship" would arise should he or she be required to apply for permanent resident status from outside Canada. An applicant in an H&C application is entitled to present any facts he or she believes to be relevant. The law is clear that some hardship accruing to a separation from family will not necessarily satisfy the requirements of an H&C application. The fact that one leaves behind friends or family, employment or residence, as well as the cost of, or inconvenience of, having to return home to apply in the normal manner would not generally be enough to constitute hardship and thus warrant a positive H&C determination. An applicant has a high threshold to meet when requesting an exemption from the IRPA.

Yue v. Canada (Minister of Citizenship & Immigration), 2006 FC 717, 2006 CarswellNat 1600, [2006] F.C.J. No. 914 — This is an application for judicial review of a decision of a visa officer denying the applicant's request to be granted permanent residence status and exemption from a requirement of the IRPA. The applicant's mother, who is a resident and citizen of Canada, sought to sponsor her for permanent residence some years after the mother had gained permanent residence in Canada. She had not, in her application for permanent residence, included the name of the applicant as a member of the family class and is now unable to sponsor the applicant unless the applicant obtains an exemption on humanitarian and compassionate grounds under subs. 25(1) of the Act.

The applicant was born to her mother and her mother's first husband in China in 1988. In 1989, her father committed suicide. Her mother remarried in October of 1992 and had a daughter by that marriage as well. The applicant did not live with her mother after 1992 but lived with her maternal grandparents. The mother's second husband went to the United States in 1995 to study and in 1997 the mother joined him there. They immigrated to Canada in 1999. The mother, when applying for permanent residence, did not list the applicant as a family member. The mother returned to China in 2000 and 2004 to see her daughter. She talked to her daughter frequently on the telephone and sent her money regularly. The applicant lived with her maternal grandparents until she entered a boarding school where she was still a student. She visits her grandparents on weekends. The applicant is now 18 years old and her mother stated that she has not visited her daughter more often in China because while she was in the United States, she was a student who could not leave and return on a student visa, and later when in Canada she could not afford to do so.

The court concluded that the visa officer adequately addressed herself to issues of hardship. While taking into account that it is the wish of the applicant to live with her mother she observed such facts as: that the applicant had not lived with her mother since 1992; that she was then 17 (now 18); that she lives at a boarding school and sees her grandparents on weekends; that her mother's contacts with her, at least since the mother left for the United States in 1997, have been limited to phone calls three or four times a week and two visits by her mother to China in 2000 and 2004; and that her mother sends her money periodically. The officer had no indication before her that the applicant was a needy person because of her presence in China nor was there any specific evidence as to how her life would be materially better in Canada. It is not for the Federal Court to review that balancing of factors where it is apparent that the visa officer had them in mind when she made her decision.

Terigho v. Canada (Minister of Citizenship & Immigration), 2006 FC 835, 2006 CarswellNat 1901, [2006] F.C.J. No. 1061 — This is an application for judicial review of the

decision of an immigration officer not to recommend an exemption from visa requirements due to humanitarian and compassionate considerations pursuant to subs. 25(1) of
the IRPA. In her decision, the officer indicated that she had considered the applicant's
case under both H&C considerations and the spousal support policy, but did not believe
the marriage was genuine. The main issue in the application was whether the officer erred
in her assessment that the marriage of the applicant and his Canadian wife was not genuine, and had ignored relevant evidence before her. The officer made no mention of the
documentary evidence filed in support of the application. Although there is generally a
presumption that a tribunal, such as an officer conducting a H&C assessment, will have
considered all of the evidence that was before it, where there is relevant evidence that
contradicts the tribunal's finding on a central issue, there is an obligation on the tribunal
to analyze that evidence and to explain in its decision why it does not accept it or prefers
other evidence on the point in question. The greater the relevance of the evidence, the
greater the need for the tribunal to explain its reasons for not attributing weight to it.

In this case, there was no question that the documentary evidence was highly relevant to
the issue of the genuineness of the marriage. When cross-examined on her affidavit as to
why she made no mention of the documents in her decision, the officer's response was, in
essence, that they were only one piece of the evidence and that she preferred to rely upon
the face to face interviews and her assessment of the spouses' consistency in answer to
her questions. Thus it appears that the officer totally discounted the documents and based
her decision entirely upon the opinion she formed from the interviews. The court concluded that while the interviews can be an effective tool in uncovering fraud in the H&C
process, the results achieved do not relieve the officer of the responsibility to properly
analyze the other evidence. The officer's failure to do so was a reviewable error and
consequently the application for judicial review was allowed.

Somasundram v. Canada (Minister of Citizenship & Immigration) (2006), 56 Imm. L.R.
(3d) 105, 2006 CarswellNat 2180, 2006 FC 925 — The applicant, a single, Tamil, female
citizen of Sri Lanka fled Colombo where she was seized and detained by the police. The
police abused her and demanded information as to the warring factions in her local area.
Upon her release by the police she fled to Canada claiming refugee protection. Once in
Canada, she took up residence with relatives in the Toronto area. She has been steadily
employed as a cashier in a local business and settled into the community without incident. Her refugee claim was rejected in July of 2001 and in November 2001 she made a
claim for exemption from visa requirements on humanitarian and compassionate grounds.
This application was dismissed in October 2005 and she sought judicial review of that
decision.

The application for judicial review was allowed on the basis that the reasons for the decision did not stand up to a reasonably probative examination as required. The court found
that the last of the quotations from the reasons were nothing more than a recital of the
general categories of materials reviewed, following which was a recital of the criteria set
out by the guidelines and of the decision made. The reasons failed to address any consideration given to the major points at issue. No issues were stated, no points of evidence
were discussed, and no explanation of the thought process engaged by the officers is
given.

Espino v. Canada (Minister of Citizenship & Immigration), 2006 FC 1255, 2006 CarswellNat 3331, [2006] F.C.J. No. 1578 — The Ministry showed little compassion in its
decision to deny the applicant the opportunity of applying for permanent residence status
from within Canada. The applicant came to Canada under a valid employment authoriza-

tion as a live-in caregiver. When she completed the first phase of that program, she was entitled to and did submit an inland application for permanent residence. That application took nine years to process before it was refused. In the interim, she was given unrestricted work permits. She bettered herself and built a career with a prominent Canadian bank. A good part of her earnings go back to the Philippines to help her handicapped child. The officer was of the view that there would be only minimal adjustments to allow her to resettle, to find a job and to be self-supporting in the Philippines. The officer made no analysis as to why it took the Minister nine years to come to a final decision with respect to her initial application for permanent residence filed pursuant to the live-in caregiver program. The officer also made no analysis to contradict the applicant's assertion that a 51-year-old single woman who had not lived in the Philippines for 15 years would have difficulty finding a suitable job. The decision was unreasonable and the application for judicial review was allowed.

Yu v. Canada (Minister of Citizenship & Immigration) (2006), 55 Imm. L.R. (3d) 159, 2006 CarswellNat 2405, 2006 FC 956 — The applicant sought judicial review of a decision of the Immigration Program Manager at the Canadian Embassy in the Philippines, wherein the applicant's application for humanitarian and compassionate (H&C) consideration pursuant to subs. 25(1) of the IRPA was refused. The applicant was a 61-year-old citizen of the Philippines and was single without children. She and her twin sister were the youngest of nine siblings, only four of whom were still alive: her and her twin sister and two other sisters. The applicant's father was killed when she was less than one year old and she was only age 12 when her mother died. She and her twin sister moved in with their oldest brother who raised them and financed their education. When they graduated from high school, they moved into a dormitory together for their college education in Manila. After graduating, they moved back to San Pablo City to work at their oldest brother's auto supply business. After about a year, they both moved to Naga City to work at another auto supply business until 1969. They then moved to Manila and lived together for over two years. In 1974, the applicant's twin sister married and they lived separately for one year but they could not stand being away from each other and the applicant was invited to live with her twin sister and her husband. The applicant lived with them until they immigrated to Canada in 1993. The applicant applied for permanent residence to Canada as a bookkeeper shortly after her sister moved to Canada. Her application was refused in 1996. She applied again in July 2000. The applicant was advised that she would need to attend an interview at the Canadian Embassy in Manila and that the waiting period was up to 36 months. In April 2002, the applicant's sister was diagnosed with cancer and following surgery was released from hospital and the applicant was by her side following her release.

In February 2005, the applicant was interviewed by a visa officer. She subsequently received a letter from the Canadian Embassy in Manila stating that she did not meet the minimum number of points required for a permanent resident visa and therefore did not satisfy the officer that she would be able to become established in Canada.

The court considered whether the Immigration Program Manager erred in finding no sufficient humanitarian and compassionate grounds to grant the applicant's request, specifically that she is not a *de facto* family member. The court concluded that the decision maker did not consider the relevant H&C factors in finding that the applicant was not a *de facto* family member. This application for judicial review was allowed.

In *obiter*, the judge stated that it was not the court's role to substitute itself for the H&C decision maker. Exceptional cases require exceptional consideration. Humanitarian and compassionate grounds are those grounds that do not fit conveniently into set parameters but rather look further to extenuating circumstances in order to address the fragility of the human condition while it can still be addressed. The anatomy of humanitarian and compassionate grounds is based on exceptional criteria in a differently constituted framework. That framework is established to examine extenuating circumstances.

It is Canada's unique response to the fragility of the human condition.

Liang v. Canada (Minister of Citizenship & Immigration), 2006 CarswellNat 2412, 2006 FC 967 — The applicant was a citizen of China who applied for permanent residence in Canada and requested that his case be assessed on humanitarian and compassionate grounds because he is the last remaining member of his family in China. The visa officer refused the request for special relief. The application for judicial review was dismissed. The court concluded the officer examined the evidence put before him, including that relating to the level of dependency, the impact of separation, the financial and emotional needs of the applicant in relation to the family unit, and the ability and willingness of the family in Canada to provide support. Since the officer gave tenable reasons for that conclusion, the court was precluded from intervening on judicial review.

The applicant argued that under prior policies (specifically the Last Remaining Family Member policy) the Minister recognized that humanitarian and compassionate grounds existed in circumstances when a last remaining single son or daughter was left alone, abroad. The court dismissed this argument stating "to argue that what amounted to sufficient humanitarian and compassionate considerations under prior guidelines must of necessity meet the current guidelines, is to say that in every case where an officer finds a last remaining single son or daughter to be alone abroad when their parents are in Canada as permanent residents, an officer must find sufficient humanitarian and compassionate considerations to exist. The court concluded this view does violence to Parliament's intent as evidenced in s. 25 of the Act. It is inconsistent with the granting of a broad discretion to the Minister in that section to say that there are circumstances which in every case must lead to a positive exercise of that discretion."

Nalbandian v. Canada (Minister of Citizenship & Immigration) (2006), 56 Imm. L.R. (3d) 67, 2006 CarswellNat 2899, 2006 FC 1128 — The applicant sought judicial review of the decision that humanitarian and compassionate considerations did not justify granting the applicant permanent residence in Canada. The applicant was a citizen of Iraq in her late 60s or early 70s. She was a Christian and fled to Jordan with her daughter in 1990 due to horrific circumstances in Iraq. She did not have permanent status in Jordan. The applicant's daughter and her son subsequently fled to the Netherlands and claimed refugee status. Neither was in a position to support immigration of the applicant to the Netherlands. The applicant's three brothers and sisters all fled directly to Canada and were all citizens of Canada. They were well established in Canada and providing economic support to the applicant. They provided a detailed plan to support the applicant's settlement in Canada. The applicant also has 13 nephews and nieces who are all Canadian citizens. While the decision arrived at by the officer might well be open to her, against a standard of review of reasonableness *simpliciter*, and against the terms of para. 3(1)(d) of the Act and the guidance provided in OP4 to persons such as the officer, the officer erred in a reviewable manner in not documenting her decision against the prescribed criteria. The judicial review was allowed and the applicant's application for permanent residence in Canada referred back for reconsideration.

Six years elapsed between the filing of the application and a decision which represented "special circumstances" justifying an award of costs.

John v. Canada (Minister of Citizenship & Immigration) (2006), 59 Imm. L.R. (3d) 314, 2006 CarswellNat 3889, 2006 FC 1422 — The applicant came to Canada in 1986 but was deported in 1998 after her application for humanitarian and compassionate consideration was denied. In 2002, she was allowed to return to Canada after her application was re-opened. On her return, the applicant was permitted to work while she waited for her application to be assessed. She was employed in 2002 and 2003, but then was injured in a fall. As a result, she had been on social assistance ever since. According to s. 39 of the IRPA, persons who are dependent on social assistance are inadmissible to Canada. An immigration officer denied her request for permanent residence on the ground that she was receiving social assistance.

The applicant sought judicial review and argued that the officer failed to follow guidelines applicable to applications based on humanitarian and compassionate grounds (IP5 — *Immigration Applications in Canada made on Humanitarian or Compassionate Grounds*). The only guideline that was relevant to the decision under review states that applications should not be automatically rejected on the ground that the applicant is receiving social assistance (Guideline 16.14 — see Annex). Applicants may be dependent on social assistance temporarily and may be self-sufficient by the time the application is processed. However, the guideline states that officers must reject applications where the applicant is still on social assistance after the other steps in the process had been completed. The officer in this case concluded that the applicant was inadmissible to Canada, given that she had been on social assistance since 2003 and the situation was unlikely to change. In 2005, her physician advised her not to seek employment. The officer's decision was not unreasonable.

Bansal v. Canada (Minister of Citizenship & Immigration) (2006), 52 Imm. L.R. (3d) 11, 2006 CarswellNat 480, 2006 CarswellNat 1356, 2006 FC 226 — A "prolonged inability to leave Canada" is a relevant factor in determining establishment of an applicant with respect to a H&C application. In this case, the immigration officer found that the applicant's stay in Canada had not been due to a situation beyond his control. However, the court concluded that the only evidence was contrary to this finding in that the applicant could not get a passport although he had cooperated with removals officials attempting to arrange his departure from Canada. This evidence was relevant to the establishment of the applicant in Canada.

Delcid v. Canada (Minister of Citizenship & Immigration), 2006 CarswellNat 601, 2006 FC 326 — The applicant applied for judicial review of a decision of an immigration officer refusing an H&C application to permit inland processing of the applicant's permanent residence application.

A humanitarian and compassionate officer must make further inquiries when a Canadian-born child is involved in order to show that he or she has been attentive and sensitive to the importance of the rights of the child, the child's best interests and the hardship that may be caused to the child by a negative decision. In this case, the immigration officer's assessment did not address how the best interests of the five- and three-year-old children would be jeopardized if their mother were removed from Canada, other than the children would have the love, support and care of the custodial parent. Specifically, the immigration officer did not consider who would care for the children when the father was at work. The immigration officer also did not address the situation of the two children should the applicant take them with her outside of Canada and specifically that English was not the first language in the foreign country, and the fact that English was the children's first language. It is essential for an H&C decision to be made in a reasonable manner. The application for judicial review was allowed and the matter remitted for re-determination by a different officer.

Keymanesh v. Canada (Minister of Citizenship & Immigration), 2006 CarswellNat 1392, 2006 FC 641 — The applicant challenged a decision made by the officer denying his application for permanent resident status because of a failure to obtain a pardon from a conviction for impaired driving in 1998. In the absence of a pardon, the applicant was ineligible for landing and, in the result, subject to removal. The court considered whether the department owed a duty to give notice to the applicant that it was intending to determine his application for permanent residence in the absence of proof of a pardon, and if so, did it fulfill that duty. The department wrote the applicant giving him a notice to respond to its request for the pardon which was returned "undeliverable." Not hearing from the applicant they sent him a "final notice" which was also returned as "undeliverable." The department refused the application for permanent residence. The applicant claimed not to have received the three notification letters and deposed that he had advised the department of his change of address. The applicant had a clear indication that the department required proof of a pardon before his application for landing would be finalized. However, when the department began to contemplate the possibility of revoking his interim status, it did have a duty to inform him of that risk. Indeed, the department's lengthy acquiescence may well have created some expectation in the mind of the applicant that time was not of the essence and that he would be informed of any change in the department's position.

It is difficult to contemplate any decision by the department which would have greater significance to the applicant than the one taken here. The finalization of his application for permanent residence without the required pardon had only one possible outcome: deportation. The obligation to give effective notice of a potentially adverse administrative decision is different than a situation involving the obligation to produce evidence or to meet a burden of proof. From the department's record, it was not clear that the officer who decided to refuse the application for landing was even aware that its notification correspondence had been returned as undelivered. Although the department need not exhaust every tracing possibility, some effort to that end is essential in cases like this, at least to the extent recognized by the Department's own guidelines.

IP5-Immigration Application in Canada Made on Humanitarian and Compassionate Grounds, s. 17.3, suggests that where contact has been lost some effort should be made to locate the subject. The recommendations imply that where the department is aware that its notification letters have not been received there is some responsibility to make some enquiries with respect to whereabouts.

The department did not meet the duty of fairness owed to the applicant with respect to giving effective notice. The failure was entirely inadvertent but does require that the decision to refuse the applicant's application for permanent residence be set aside.

Kim v. Canada (Minister of Citizenship & Immigration) (2005), 51 Imm. L.R. (3d) 262, 2005 CarswellNat 3129, 2005 CarswellNat 4949, 2005 FC 1357 — The applicant applied for permanent residency under the skilled worker category, but was refused as he was inadmissible due to his son's medical disability. The applicant then made an H&C application, which required him to attend an oral hearing with an immigration officer. The applicant provided little in support of his application; on her own initiative, the immigration officer sought third party information concerning services available to the applicant's disabled child. The officer did not disclose this information to the applicant. After receiving that information, the officer recommended to her manager that the case be dismissed. The manager claimed that he did not consider the third party information, but that on the evidence before him, there were insufficient H&C factors present to grant the application.

The applicant's procedural fairness had been breached. The immigration officer made formal efforts to obtain third party information which was not disclosed to the applicant and she relied on this information to make her recommendation to her manager. Although the immigration officer was not the final decision maker, she had relied on that information, and the manager was found to have implicitly accepted the findings of the third party.

Tikaprasad v. Canada (Minister of Citizenship & Immigration) (2005), 48 Imm. L.R. (3d) 130, 2005 CarswellNat 1689, 2005 CarswellNat 5406, 2005 FC 843 — The duty of fairness requires an officer who consults a third party and obtains information from that source to disclose it so that the applicant is aware of it and can respond.

Miranda v. Canada (Minister of Citizenship & Immigration) (2005), 52 Imm. L.R. (3d) 113, 2005 CarswellNat 3691, 2005 CarswellNat 5032, 2005 FC 1533 — Although the Federal Court is reluctant to interfere with an H&C determination, in this case, the officer's conclusion was unreasonable. Specifically the officer concluded that the applicant's grown children would support the applicant's wife following his removal from Canada. It was not reasonable for the officer to proceed from the presumption that the children were able and willing to support the applicant's wife. The children could be living elsewhere; they might be indigent, incapacitated, or incarcerated.

Bui v. Canada (Minister of Citizenship & Immigration), 2005 CarswellNat 1636, 2005 CarswellNat 5429, 2005 FC 816 — The applicant was a citizen of Vietnam and Norway and he came to Canada on a visitor's visa and subsequently overstayed. He then married a Canadian citizen and he applied under the former *Immigration Act* for an exemption from the landing requirements as a sponsored spouse. Upon the coming into force of the IRPA, the application was converted to a humanitarian and compassionate application as the applicant was in Canada without status. This application was refused on the basis that the marriage was not genuine and that the applicant had not established himself in Canada. The applicant argued that his rights to procedural fairness were violated because he was not granted an oral interview. It was his responsibility to ensure the information was accurate and he bore the onus of satisfying the decision maker. An officer cannot be faulted for not convening an interview to determine what was false and what was accurate in the material.

Singh (B.) v. Canada (Minister of Citizenship & Immigration), 2005 CarswellNat 1419, 2005 FC 718 — The applicant carries the burden of adducing evidence in support of an H&C application. When considering the best interests of the child, however, it can generally be presumed that the presence of the parent will be consistent with those interests. The applicant provided affidavit and oral evidence to the effect that he was the primary source of financial support for his child and the child's mother, the applicant's wife. Ignoring, for all practical purposes, the financial implications of the parent's removal for the child is not akin to being alert, alive and sensitive to the child's best interests.

Adu v. Canada (Minister of Citizenship & Immigration), 2005 CarswellNat 1047, 2005 FC 565, [2005] F.C.J. No. 693 — This was an application to review a negative decision respecting an H&C application. A review of the facts and the statement by conclusion, without analysis to back it up, are not reasons at all. The officer simply reviewed the positive factors militating in favour of granting the application and concluded, without any explanation, that these factors were not sufficient to justify granting the exemption. This was not sufficient, as it leaves the applicants in the unenviable position of not knowing why their application was rejected.

Lee v. Canada (Minister of Citizenship & Immigration) (2005), 45 Imm. L.R. (3d) 129, 2005 CarswellNat 2020, 2005 CarswellNat 783, 2005 FC 413, [2005] F.C.J. No. 507 — The decision of the ministerial delegate with respect to an H & C application is a discretionary one. The standard of review is reasonableness *simpliciter*. The onus on an application for an H&C exemption is on the applicant. The ministerial guidelines are not law and the Minister and her agents are not bound by them but they are accessible to the public and of great assistance to the court. An H&C decision must be supported by reasons. It is inappropriate to require administrative officers to give as detailed reasons for their decisions as may be expected of an administrative tribunal that renders its decisions after an adjudicative hearing.

Pinter v. Canada (Minister of Citizenship & Immigration) (2005), 44 Imm. L.R. (3d) 118, 2005 CarswellNat 530, 2005 FC 296 — The applicants are failed refugee claimants. They applied for relief under s. 25. It was an error in law for the immigration officer to conclude that she was not required to deal with risk factors in her assessment of the humanitarian and compassionate application. She should not have closed her mind to risk factors even though a valid negative pre-removal risk assessment may have been made. There may well be risk considerations which are relevant to an application for permanent residence from within Canada.

Raposo v. Canada (Minister of Citizenship & Immigration) (2005), 45 Imm. L.R. (3d) 291, 2005 FC 118, 2005 CarswellNat 248 — The applicants sought to review a negative decision respecting their H&C application. The officer's analysis of the best interests of the Canadian-born child should deal firstly with the fact that the child is a Canadian citizen and then determine what effect his parents' removal would have on him. How would the removal affect his best interests? In the present case, the analysis dealt with the fact that the child would adapt to life in the Azores. This is not an adequate assessment of a child's best interests.

Momcilovic v. Canada (Minister of Citizenship & Immigration) (2005), 42 Imm. L.R. (3d) 61, 2005 CarswellNat 92, 2005 FC 79 — A plain reading of subs. 25(1) indicates that it is broader than the best interests of a parent's own child. The section does not use wording such as "child of the marriage" or "the applicant's child." It refers to the best interests of a "child directly affected." In this case the applicant had cared for the child for six years and was her primary caregiver. The applicant was the only mother that the child knew. The applicant looked after the child before she went to school and was there when the child returned home. The applicant did the child's laundry and took the child on outings. There was no one else caring for the child. Accordingly, the court was of the view that the child in this case was a "child directly affected" and, therefore, her best interests must be assessed. The officer's decision was set aside.

Cordeiro v. Canada (Minister of Citizenship & Immigration), 2004 CarswellNat 3116, 2004 CarswellNat 3963, 2004 FC 1231 — The applicants were seeking to overturn a negative decision concerning their H&C application. The applicants were citizens of Brazil.

They had a nine-year-old Canadian-born child and a married daughter. The married daughter was a permanent resident of Canada having married a Canadian citizen in 2001. The family originally came to Canada in 1989. Their son was born in this country and then the family returned to Brazil in February of 1994. They remained there until 1998 when they came back to Canada and made an unsuccessful refugee claim based upon allegations of persecution due to crime and violence in Brazil. The male applicant is a carpenter and had been employed in Canada in that trade. At the time of the application he had his own carpentry business. His wife worked as a cleaner and had completed caregiver training programs while she was in Canada. Both were active in their church and in their community. In their time in Canada, the applicants had been steadily employed, had amassed significant savings and had paid their taxes every year.

The interests of the Canadian-born child were not sufficiently well identified or defined by the officer. It was apparent that the Canadian-born child enjoyed an exceptionally close relationship with his older sister and her husband who lived next door. While the officer addressed the impact that removing the family would have on the female applicant, virtually no attention was paid to the consequences for the Canadian-born child if he were separated from his older sister. The H&C decision was set aside.

Osadolor v. Canada (Minister of Citizenship & Immigration) (2004), 36 Imm. L.R. (3d) 127, 252 F.T.R. 314, 2004 CarswellNat 1499, 2004 FC 737, 2004 CarswellNat 5947, [2004] F.C.J. No. 895 — IRPA changed the law and policy for immigrants married to Canadians. After June 26, 2002, a new class of persons who may apply for permanent residence within Canada was created. This class is called the spouse or common-law partner in Canada class." To qualify as a member of this class, an applicant is required to meet the requirements of s. 124 of the Regulations.

Legal immigrants do not need to make an H&C application, if they are married to, or a common-law spouse of, a Canadian citizen.

Pramauntanyath v. Canada (Minister of Citizenship & Immigration) (2004), 39 Imm. L.R. (3d) 243, 2004 CarswellNat 230, 2004 CarswellNat 2892, [2004] F.C.J. No. 184, 2004 FC 174 — The applicant sought to review a negative H&C decision. The applicant made an application for a humanitarian and compassionate exemption in November 2000. By letter dated January 2, 2003, Immigration Canada advised the applicant that his application was now being reviewed and he was asked to provide updated information within 30 days. The applicant's former counsel mailed updated information to the commission within the 30 day period. The H&C application was refused and a review of the officer's reasons makes it clear that the officer did not have this updated information when the H&C application was refused.

The information in question revealed that the applicant had opened a very successful restaurant in Toronto, a restaurant which employed 10 people and had received positive reviews in the Toronto media. The updated information indicated that the applicant had worked hard, lived frugally, had become fluent in English and was active in his community.

The negative decision was set aside. The applicant was directed to send supplementary information to immigration and he took advantage of this opportunity. There was no obligation on the applicant to follow-up and make sure that the information was in fact received by the immigration officer assigned to the file.

Étienne v. Canada (Ministre de la Citoyenneté & de l'Immigration), 2003 CarswellNat 3527, 2003 CarswellNat 4455, 2003 FC 1314 — The applicants sought to review a decision refusing their request for humanitarian and compassionate exemption.

An interview is not a general requirement for decisions made on applications based on humanitarian grounds.

The doctrine of "legitimate expectation" is based on the principle that the circumstances effecting procedural fairness take into account the promises or regular practices of administrative decision makers. Generally, it will be unfair for decision makers to act in contravention of representations as to procedure, or to back track on substantive promises without according significant procedural rights.

Nothing in the record suggested that the officer had affirmed, implicitly or explicitly, that the applicants would have an interview. Nothing in the evidence established the existence of a systematic practice of granting an interview. There was no legitimate expectation of an interview established in this case.

Jasim v. Canada (Minister of Citizenship & Immigration), 32 Imm. L.R. (3d) 118, 2003 CarswellNat 4413, 2003 CarswellNat 2658, 2003 FC 1017 — This is an application to review a negative humanitarian and compassionate decision. The existence of a humanitarian or compassionate review offers an individual special and additional consideration from an exemption from Canadian immigration laws that are otherwise universally applied. The process is highly discretionary and, as such, the onus is on the applicant to satisfy the officer that sufficient grounds exist to warrant a favourable decision. The decision of an officer not to grant a exemption takes no right away from an applicant who may still apply for landing from outside of Canada which is the usual requirement under Canadian immigration legislation.

The reasons for decision in this case consisted of a list of the factors which the officer considered. A list of factors considered does not constitute sufficient analysis. The officer thus failed to provide reasons for the decision which was a reviewable error.

Section 25(1.3)

Kanthasamy v. Canada (Minister of Citizenship and Immigration), [2015] 3 S.C.R. 909, 93 Admin. L.R. (5th) 1, 391 D.L.R. (4th) 644, 36 Imm. L.R. (4th) 1, 347 C.R.R. (2d) 163, 479 N.R. 103, 2015 SCC 61, 2015 CarswellNat 6500, 2015 CarswellNat 6501, [2015] S.C.J. No. 61 — The applicant was a Tamil aged 16 from northern Sri Lanka. Fearing for his safety after being detained and questioned by the Sri Lankan army and police, his family arranged for him to travel to Canada to live with an uncle. When he arrived in Canada, he made a claim for refugee protection which was refused. His application for a pre-removal risk assessment was also rejected. He additionally filed an application for humanitarian and compassionate relief under s. 25 and the officer reviewing that application concluded that relief was not justified as she was not satisfied that a return to Sri Lanka would result in hardship that was unusual and undeserved or disproportionate. The Federal Court of Appeal agreed. The Supreme Court of Canada allowed the appeal concluding that the officer's decision was unreasonable and should be set aside and the matter remitted for reconsideration. Ministerial guidelines intended to assist immigration officers in determining whether humanitarian and compassionate considerations warrant relief under s. 25(1) state that applicants must demonstrate either "unusual and undeserved" *or* "disproportionate" hardship for relief under s. 25(1) to be granted. "Unusual and undeserved hardship" is defined in the guidelines as hardship that is "not anticipated or addressed" by the Act or its Regulations, and is "beyond the person's control." "Disproportionate hardship" is defined as "an unreasonable impact on the applicant due to their personal circumstances."

While the guidelines are useful, they are not legally binding and are not intended to be either exhaustive or restrictive. Officers should not fetter their discretion by treating them as if they were mandatory requirements that limit the equitable H&C discretion anticipated by s. 25(1). The words "unusual and undeserved or disproportionate hardship" should instead be treated as descriptive, not as creating three new thresholds for relief separate and apart from the humanitarian purpose of s. 25(1). As a result, officers should not look at s. 25(1) through the lens of the three adjectives as discrete and high thresholds. This has the result of using the language of "unusual and undeserved or disproportionate hardship" in a way that limits the officer's ability to consider and give weight to *all* relevant H&C considerations in a particular case. The three adjectives should be seen as instructive but not determinative.

Section 25[(1)] refers to the need to take into account the best interest of a child directly affected. The "best interest" principle is highly contextual because of the multitude of factors that may impinge on the child's best interests. A decision under s. 25(1) will therefore be found to be unreasonable if the interests of children affected by the decision are not sufficiently considered. The status of the applicant as a child triggered not only the requirement that the "best interests" be treated as a significant factor in the analysis, it should have also influenced the manner in which the child's circumstances were evaluated. Children will rarely, if ever, be deserving of *any* hardship, therefore the concept of unusual or undeserved hardship is presumptively inapplicable to the assessment of the hardship invoked by a child to support his or her application for humanitarian and compassionate relief. Because children may experience greater hardship than adults faced with a comparable situation, circumstances which may not warrant humanitarian and compassionate relief when applied to an adult, may nonetheless entitle a child to relief.

In this case, the officer failed to give sufficiently serious consideration to K's youth, his mental health, and the evidence that he would suffer discrimination if he were returned to Sri Lanka. The officer took a segmented approach, assessing each factor to see whether it represented hardship that was "unusual and undeserved or disproportionate." This literal obedience to those words, that do not appear anywhere in s. 25(1), led her to see each of them as a distinctive legal test, rather than as words designed to help reify the equitable purpose of the provision and look at the applicant's circumstances as a whole. This rendered her decision unreasonable.

Section 25(2)

Koroghli v. Canada (Minister of Citizenship & Immigration), 2010 FC 1067, 2010 CarswellNat 4910, 2010 CarswellNat 4911 — This was an application for judicial review of a visa officer's decision to reject the application for a permanent resident visa for a child under tutorship, on the ground that he was not a member of the family class category. The officer also refused to exercise his humanitarian discretion to grant permanent residence to this child because subs. 25(2) of IRPA prohibited him from doing so. All that the OP-5 Manual states is that the applicants must be informed that they can move to another province where the adoption could theoretically be possible, in which case the local office in the new province of residence will be responsible for the application. Even if the manual could apply or if this scenario took place, the applicant would still have to satisfy the s. 25 requirements and the exception in subs. 25(2). Even when the sponsors were taking steps to obtain tutorship of the child, it was their responsibility to find out whether this child could immigrate to Quebec. If they had done so in a timely manner, they would have known that the adoption was not possible. They could have taken steps to reside in another province. The officer did not err in law. The application for judicial review was dismissed.

25.1 (1) Humanitarian and compassionate considerations — Minister's own initiative — The Minister may, on the Minister's own initiative, examine the circumstances concerning a foreign national who is inadmissible — other than under section 34, 35 or 37 — or who does not meet the requirements of this Act and may grant the foreign national permanent resident status or an exemption from any applicable criteria or obligations of this Act if the Minister is of the opinion that it is justified by humanitarian and compassionate considerations relating to the foreign national, taking into account the best interests of a child directly affected.

(2) Exemption — The Minister may exempt the foreign national from the payment of any applicable fees in respect of the examination of their circumstances under subsection (1).

(3) Provincial criteria — The Minister may not grant permanent resident status to a foreign national referred to in subsection 9(1) if the foreign national does not meet the province's selection criteria applicable to that foreign national.

2010, c. 8, s. 5; 2013, c. 16, s. 10

25.2 (1) Public policy considerations — The Minister may, in examining the circumstances concerning a foreign national who is inadmissible or who does not meet the requirements of this Act, grant that person permanent resident status or an exemption from any applicable criteria or obligations of this Act if the foreign national complies with any conditions imposed by the Minister and the Minister is of the opinion that it is justified by public policy considerations.

(2) Exemption — The Minister may exempt the foreign national from the payment of any applicable fees in respect of the examination of their circumstances under subsection (1).

(3) Provincial criteria — The Minister may not grant permanent resident status to a foreign national referred to in subsection 9(1) if the foreign national does not meet the province's selection criteria applicable to that foreign national.

(4) Conditions — The conditions referred to in subsection (1) may include a requirement for the foreign national to obtain an undertaking or to obtain a determination of their eligibility from a third party that meets any criteria specified by the Minister.

2010, c. 8, s. 5; 2012, c. 17, s. 14

Case Law

Enabulele v. Canada (Ministry of Public Safety & Emergency Preparedness) (2009), 81 Imm. L.R. (3d) 78, 347 F.T.R. 309 (Eng.), 2009 FC 641, 2009 CarswellNat 1876, 2009 CarswellNat 5904 — The applicant, a citizen of Nigeria married to a Canadian citizen, applied for permanent residence under the spouse or common-law partner in Canada class, pursuant to the ministerial policy, released in February 2005, and contained in Appendix H of the Citizenship and Immigration of Canada's Operational Manual for Inland Processing IP8. This policy is designed to allow spouses or common-law partners in Canada to apply for permanent residence from within Canada in accordance with the same criteria as members of the spouse or common-law partner in Canada class regardless of their immigration status. The applicant was advised, by reason of having been charged with two counts of sexual assault, that he was not entitled to a 60-day administrative deferral of removal under the policy. The applicant sought to challenge the policy on the basis that it violated his s. 7 and s. 11(d) Charter rights. The court accepted the respondent's submission that the administrative deferral under the policy sought by the applicant would have expired even if the officer had found that the applicant was eligible for it. Notwithstanding this, the court considered the Charter issues raised in the application.

The applicant argued that the policy compromised his security in that it did not allow him to defend his innocence of the charges laid against him. He says the policy stigmatizes those charged but not convicted of criminal charges. The court found the applicant's argument without merit and concluded his s. 7 Charter rights were not engaged in the circumstances. The impugned policy renders the applicant ineligible for an administrative deferral by reason of his criminal charges. It does not follow, however that the applicant will be removed without a proper risk assessment. The PRRA process, to which the applicant is entitled, is designed to assist foreign nationals who may be required to leave Canada. It is the means by which the applicant can have his risk assessed prior to his departure. It is the very process which provides for consideration of the applicant's life, liberty and security interest in a pre-removal context. The applicant's access to that process was in no way affected by the policy. The application for judicial review was dismissed. The following question was certified:

> Does the Minister's policy on administrative deferral of removal found under IP8 offend the applicant's sections 7 and 11(d) rights of the *Canadian Charter of Rights and Freedoms*?

26. Regulations — The regulations may provide for any matter relating to the application of sections 18 to 25.2, and may include provisions respecting

(a) entering, remaining in and re-entering Canada;

(b) permanent resident status or temporary resident status, including acquisition of that status;

(b.1) declarations referred to in subsection 22.1(1);

(c) the circumstances in which all or part of the considerations referred to in section 24 may be taken into account;

(d) conditions that may or must be imposed, varied or cancelled, individually or by class, on permanent residents and foreign nationals;

(d.1) undertakings that may or must be given in respect of requests made under subsection 25(1) or undertakings referred to in subsection 25.2(4), and penalties for failure to comply with undertakings;

(d.2) the determination of eligibility referred to in subsection 25.2(4); and

(e) deposits or guarantees of the performance of obligations under this Act that are to be given to the Minister.

2010, c. 8, s. 6; 2012, c. 17, s. 15; 2013, c. 16, s. 11

Rights and Obligations of Permanent and Temporary Residents

27. (1) Right of permanent residents — **A permanent resident of Canada has the right to enter and remain in Canada, subject to the provisions of this Act.**

(2) Conditions — **A permanent resident must comply with any conditions imposed under the regulations or under instructions given under subsection 14.1(1).**

[Editor's Note: SOR/2002-227, s. 328(1) provides that a person who was a permanent resident immediately before June 28, 2002 is a permanent resident under the new Immigration and Refugee Protection Act, *S.C. 2001, c. 27.]*

2012, c. 19, s. 704

Case Law

Section 27(2)

Chang v. Canada (Minister of Citizenship & Immigration), 2006 FC 157, 2006 CarswellNat 329, 2006 CarswellNat 2194, [2006] F.C.J. No. 217 — The legislatively established conditions of the entrepreneur category, if flaunted knowingly, without serious consequence, would make a mockery of the purpose for which they were established. The act of creating or participating in a front operation or a sham investment, if left unchecked, strikes a blow at the very integrity of the immigration system. In this case, the applicants were found to be in non-compliance with subs. 27(2) and s. 28. The applicants' children were also found to be in non-compliance with subs. 27(2) as they were dependants of an entrepreneur and bound by the same terms and conditions of landing as provided in para. 23.1(1)(a) to (d) of the previous Regulations. Both the applicants as well as their children sought special relief on appeal in light of the circumstances of their case, specifically, that there were sufficient humanitarian and compassionate considerations that warranted the setting aside of departure orders. The IAD was of the view that the parents did not merit discretionary relief as they took part in a sham arrangement to try to fulfill the conditions of the entrepreneur category. Even though the IAD felt that the children would be excellent candidates for permanent residence, it refused to grant discretionary relief to the children, because once the children became permanent residents they would be entitled to sponsor their parents which would render the removal of the parents moot.

The granting of special relief is a weighing process. Even though there were some positive elements in favour of discretionary relief being allowed to the three children, these elements did not outweigh the importance given to the integrity of maintaining the conditions in the entrepreneur category. It was open to the IAD to find that special relief should not be granted to the children because this would benefit the parents who had not respected the conditions under which they entered Canada.

28. (1) Residency obligation — **A permanent resident must comply with a residency obligation with respect to every five-year period.**

(2) Application — The following provisions govern the residency obligation under subsection (1):

(a) a permanent resident complies with the residency obligation with respect to a five-year period if, on each of a total of at least 730 days in that five-year period, they are

(i) physically present in Canada,

(ii) outside Canada accompanying a Canadian citizen who is their spouse or common-law partner or, in the case of a child, their parent,

(iii) outside Canada employed on a full-time basis by a Canadian business or in the federal public administration or the public service of a province,

(iv) outside Canada accompanying a permanent resident who is their spouse or common-law partner or, in the case of a child, their parent and who is employed on a full-time basis by a Canadian business or in the federal public administration or the public service of a province, or

(v) referred to in regulations providing for other means of compliance;

(b) it is sufficient for a permanent resident to demonstrate at examination

(i) if they have been a permanent resident for less than five years, that they will be able to meet the residency obligation in respect of the five-year period immediately after they became a permanent resident;

(ii) if they have been a permanent resident for five years or more, that they have met the residency obligation in respect of the five-year period immediately before the examination; and

(c) a determination by an officer that humanitarian and compassionate considerations relating to a permanent resident, taking into account the best interests of a child directly affected by the determination, justify the retention of permanent resident status overcomes any breach of the residency obligation prior to the determination.

[Editor's Note: SOR/2002-227, s. 328(1) provides that a person who was a permanent resident immediately before June 28, 2002 is a permanent resident under the new Immigration and Refugee Protection Act, S.C. 2001, c. 27 (the "new Act").

SOR/2002-227, s. 328(2) provides that any period spent outside Canada within five years preceding June 28, 2002 by a permanent resident holding a returning resident permit is considered to be a period spent in Canada for the purpose of satisfying the residency obligation under s. 28 of the new Act if that period is included in the five-year period referred to in s. 28 of the new Act.

SOR/2002-227, s. 328(3) provides that any period spent outside Canada within the two years immediately following June 28, 2002 by a permanent resident holding a returning resident permit is considered to be a period spent in Canada for the purpose of satisfying the residency obligation under s. 28 of the new Act if that period is included in the five year period referred to in s. 28 of the new Act.]

2003, c. 22, s. 172

Case Law

Osba v Canada (Minister of Citizenship and Immigration), 2015 FC 1294, 2015 CarswellNat 3907, 2015 CarswellNat 10087 — The IAD accepted that SUBCOE was a Canadian company. However, since the applicant's employment contract with SUBCOE referred only to part-time employment for 16 hours a week, they concluded he did not work full-time for a Canadian business. Further, while the applicant may have worked full time for GOS, it was not a Canadian business. Therefore, the IAD concluded that the applicant did not meet the residency requirement in IRPA. The IAD then went on to consider humanitarian and compassionate factors. It found that the applicant's ties to Canada, the best interests of his children, and the hardship the removal order would have imposed on him favoured a positive decision on his behalf. On the other hand, the IAD found the negative factors outweighed the positive ones — the degree of the applicant's non-compliance with the residency requirement, his lack of establishment in Canada, and the absence of convincing reasons to remain outside Canada. The IAD dismissed the applicant's appeal.

The Federal Court found the IAD's analysis of the legality of the removal order was deficient because it did not take into account the exception set out in the IRPA, and did not address the evidence that was relevant to the issue. The evidence before the IAD clearly showed that the applicant worked full time, on assignment, for a client of SUB-COE, GOS, from June 2006 to October 2009. According to IRPA, working full time on assignment for a Canadian business or a client of that business qualifies as time spent working for the Canadian business itself. This possibility was not considered by the officer who issued the removal order, or by the IAD. Council for the Minister before the Board argued that working for a non-Canadian client of a Canadian business does not count as employment for a Canadian business. The court concluded that if the applicant had been credited for the time spent working for GOS, he would have met his residency requirement. The Board's decision was unreasonable and was set aside.

Canada (Minister of Citizenship and Immigration) v. Wright (2015), 32 Imm. L.R. (4th) 179, 2015 FC 3, 2015 CarswellNat 120, 2015 CarswellNat 3480 — The Minister of Citizenship and Immigration brought the application for judicial review of a decision of the Immigration Appeal Division ("IAD") which found that there were sufficient humanitarian and compassionate grounds to grant relief pursuant to s. 67(1)(c) of the IRPA, to overcome the respondents' inadmissibility to Canada for failure to comply with their residency requirements as permanent residents. The court has considered many applications for judicial review arising from H&C determinations in the context that other provisions of the Act, including ss. 25, 28 and 67 and, although the wording of the provisions varies slightly, the provisions do not refer specifically to "hardship" but to "humanitarian and compassionate considerations" or "sufficient humanitarian and compassionate considerations." However, the jurisprudence has consistently confirmed that the hardship to be considered along with other factors to determine whether sufficient H&C considerations exist must be more than the hardship that would normally result from removal. The respondents' argument that the considerations relevant to an H&C decision pursuant to s. 67 differ from those under s. 25, and that unusual or disproportionate hardship is not required, fails to appreciate the overall guidance of the analogous jurisprudence. There is no reason for *some* hardship to be sufficient in the context of considering H&C grounds to overcome a breach of permanent resident status when in other contexts, such as refugee protection, the criteria established by the IRB and IAD and confirmed by the courts calls for *unusual, undue or disproportionate* hardship; more than the normal and expected consequences of removal from Canada.

In this case, the IAD did find the consequences of the respondents' removal would be serious hardship, which appears to acknowledge its understanding that more than the expected or normal hardship of removal is required for such a finding. The evidence before the IAD was of inconvenience, disappointment and emotional upheaval, along with the economic impact of maintaining two residences. The IAD failed to consider that the respondents would not be destitute nor would they be homeless in the United States and that their age was no more an impediment to relocation than it was in 2012 when they divested themselves of their home in the United States and returned to Canada. The IAD did not consider relevant evidence that would have had a bearing on its findings with respect to several of the factors, in particular the serious hardship they would suffer if removed. This evidence would have a bearing on the weight to be attached to those factors and on the overall assessment of whether there were *sufficient* — not just *some* — humanitarian and compassionate grounds to justify the exceptional relief of overcoming the breach of their obligation to be physically present in Canada 730 days in each five-year period. The application for judicial review was allowed.

Samad c. Canada (Ministre de la Sécurité publique et de la Protection civile), 2015 FC 30, 2015 CarswellNat 2827, 2015 CarswellNat 55, [2015] F.C.J. No. 2; application for judicial review refused 2013 CarswellNat 5224, 2013 CarswellNat 5225 (Imm. & Ref. Bd. (App. Div.)) — The Federal Court upheld a decision of the Immigration Appeal Division which upheld the decision of the Canada Border Services Agency that the applicants had breached their residency obligation in Canada under s. 28 of IRPA. The applicants had a significant shortfall of physical presence in Canada within the relevant five-year period; they validated their permanent residency knowing they would not be able to settle in Canada; their efforts to settle in Canada were belated and all post-dated the issuance of the removal order; despite their combined contribution potential, they had not contributed to any significant degree to the Canadian economy over a seven-year period of permanent residency; and they could easily return to live in Egypt where their immediate family members still resided, in a family home that they still owned. The IAD's findings were owed a high degree of deference and there was no basis to interfere with them. The application for judicial review was dismissed.

Durve v. Canada (Minister of Citizenship and Immigration) (2014), 27 Imm. L.R. (4th) 251, 2014 FC 874, 2014 CarswellNat 3544, 2014 CarswellNat 4618 — The applicant sought judicial review of the decision of the Appeal Division which found that he had failed to comply with the residency requirements and upheld the decision to not renew his permanent resident status. The applicant, a citizen of India, landed in Canada in 2002 and was later granted permanent resident status. He incorporated a business best described as a "one-man operation" in Ontario in 2004. He frequently travelled to India and other countries for significant periods of time. In May 2009, Citizenship and Immigration Canada did not renew his permanent resident card because he failed to meet the residency requirement of 730 days in Canada in a five-year period. The Board conducted a *de novo* hearing and again dismissed the appeal. The Board found that his business was not an "ongoing operation in Canada."

The Board identified several indicia or considerations and did not rule out that one-man operations could fit within s. 28. It is not possible to anticipate all the potential fact scenarios and set out a list of some criteria which if met will weigh more heavily than others depending on the nature of the business, the time spent within and outside of Canada and, importantly, the nexus or connection between the work outside Canada and the business in Canada. Where the business is a one-man operation with no employees in Canada, more focus will be put on the nature of the business in Canada and how the work conducted by the one-man operation or self-employed person relates to the Canadian business. The basic principles remain that: the onus is on the permanent resident to provide clear and cogent evidence that his business is a Canadian business (an ongoing operation in Canada) and that work done outside Canada is full-time work for the Canadian business; the inquiry is a question of fact to be determined by the nature and the degree of the applicant's business activities in each individual case; and the focus is on the nature of an applicant's business activities while outside of Canada in relation to the business of his Canadian company. An ongoing business is a business with continuing activities in Canada. This determination takes into account what the business actually does within Canada, and how this is demonstrated or documented. Where the business is a self-employed person or a very small business, the goods or services, which would include advice, must be identifiable. The decision-maker should consider whether there are employees, associates or contractors in Canada; the corporation's physical office is a consideration; and it is not essential that all work and every business activity or service be carried out in Canada but that a sufficient connection or nexus exist between work done abroad and the ongoing operation of the business in Canada. The nature of business activities outside Canada and how they advance the overall goal of the business in Canada, and their connection or nexus to the Canadian business is a significant consideration. The permanent resident's pattern of travel, residence in Canada and residence outside of Canada are also relevant considerations. Records of time spent for specific services provided and clients' businesses will be informative, including time spent for work that is not remunerated and the reason for this. The revenue of the business should be considered, including whether the financial statements of the business reflect the described business activities and can be reconciled with invoices. If the permanent resident's personal income exceeds the income from the claimed business activities, it will be more difficult to establish that it is full time work for the Canadian business. The application for judicial review was dismissed.

Xi v. Canada (Minister of Citizenship & Immigration), 2013 FC 796, 2013 CarswellNat 2565, 2013 CarswellNat 4270 — The applicant sought judicial review of a decision of the Immigration Appeal Division ("IAD") wherein it was determined that he, his wife, and their daughter failed to satisfy their residency obligation under s. 28 and that their personal circumstances did not raise H&C considerations sufficient to overcome any breach of their residency obligation. The IAD concluded that the principal applicant's employment with 2727056 Canada Inc. did not satisfy s. 61 because, while he had established employment on a full-time basis by a Canadian business outside Canada, he did not show that his was a temporary assignment. Instead, the principal applicant's position, which was essentially that of an overseas manager, was created locally for an indeterminate period in China to exploit his expertise in the Chinese garment business. The IAD stressed that, before the principal applicant was hired by 2727056, he had only been in Canada for one week and had spent the previous 19 months in China. The IAD also reasoned that the contract of employment did not indicate that the principal applicant's employment in China would be temporary, nor was there any indication that he would be promoted by 2727056 to a permanent position in Canada after working in China. The court concluded that it was reasonable to conclude that, while the principal applicant maintained some connection to a business in Canada, (1) he was essentially the agent of 2727056 and its customers in China; (2) his employment in China was not temporary, and (3) he may not, in the future, become its employee in Canada. The H&C analysis is in the range of possible, acceptable outcomes. The IAD applied the appropriate factors and the court may not intervene because the applicants are "not happy with the manner in which the IAD weighed" these factors. The application for judicial review was dismissed.

Zhang v. Canada (Minister of Citizenship & Immigration), 2014 CarswellNat 1075, 2014 CarswellNat 1693, 2014 FC 362 — An immigration officer was of the opinion that the applicant had failed to maintain his residency obligation set out in s. 28 of IRPA. The officer prepared a report to the Minister pursuant to s. 44. The Minister's delegate issued a removal order in accordance with s. 44(2). The applicant appealed to the Immigration Appeal Division. The IAD found that he was approximately eight months short on his residency requirement and that there were insufficient humanitarian and compassionate considerations to warrant relief. The applicant sought judicial review of that decision. There was a discrepancy in the number of days that the officer concluded the applicant was short physical residence and the number of days he claimed. The amount of the shortfall may have been a relevant factor in the H&C considerations. It was clear that an error had been made by the officer and that he failed to take into account a passport stamp indicating an arrival of the applicant in July 2011. A clear error as to the shortfall in the number of required days was a point which has considerable bearing on humanitarian and compassionate considerations. The application for judicial review was allowed.

Sarfaraz v. Canada (Minister of Public Safety & Emergency Preparedness), 2012 FC 735, 2012 CarswellNat 3373, 2012 CarswellNat 2273 — The applicant sought judicial review of a decision of the Immigration Appeal Division to refuse an appeal of his removal order. A departure order had been issued against the applicant for failure to comply with his residency requirement under s. 28 of the Act.

On June 20, 2008, an immigration officer allowed the applicant to re-enter Canada as a permanent resident. However, this re-entry did not bar an examination of the applicant's compliance with the residency requirements once he applied for a permanent resident card. Upon application for a permanent resident card, an immigration officer has to examine whether the applicant complies with the residency requirements under s. 28 of the Act. A decision under subs.19(2) to allow a permanent resident to re-enter Canada is not a decision barring an examination of the residency requirements under the Act, when the applicant is applying for a permanent resident card, even if such an application is made only ten days after having been readmitted, especially when the first officer noted that "[c]lient should be examined closely for residency obligations." The applicant's re-entry to Canada on June 20, 2008, as a permanent resident did not have an effect of *res judicata*.

Khan v. Canada (Minister of Citizenship & Immigration) (2012), 15 Imm. L.R. (4th) 101, 2012 FC 1471, 2012 CarswellNat 4944, 2012 CarswellNat 5401 — The applicant was a permanent resident of Canada who had been issued a permanent resident card as proof of his status. PR cards are time limited and this application arises out of the applicant's failed attempt to renew his expired card. The PR card does not create or maintain one's status as a permanent resident: it merely serves as proof of that status. The applicant's application to obtain a replacement card was processed by CIC at its Case Processing Centre — Sydney (CPCS). He received a letter informing him that he could pick up his new PR card at CIC GTA Central. The letter also advised that all permanent residents of Canada are subject to a residency assessment at the time of distribution of their new PR card, and that an immigration officer would review his documents and may require additional information to determine his eligibility. The applicant went to CIC GTA Central on

June 28, 2011, to pick up his new card where the CIC officer examined his former and current passport and asked why he had taken so long to pick up his new card. He told her that he had been in Pakistan for the birth of his daughter. He was then asked to list his absences in the five years preceding the appointment at CIC GTA and was advised that it appeared he did not meet the residency requirement and that she could not issue him the card. He protested saying that he thought the five-year period was from the date of his application, not the date when he picked up the card. The officer sent his file for investigation.

The court considered whether the CIC GTA Central representative acted lawfully in refusing to provide the applicant with his validly issued permanent resident card because the respondent was *functus officio* after granting the card. The court further considered whether the CIC GTA Central representative otherwise acted unlawfully since nothing in the Act mandated the review of the residency requirement when providing the card.

The court concluded that the Act requires that every permanent resident meet the residency obligation in every rolling five-year period. Therefore, although not required, it was open to the officer at CIC GTA Central to question whether the applicant met the residency obligation as at that date or as at any other earlier date. What was not open to her was to refuse to issue him the PR card once he had met the conditions set out in subs. 59(1) of the Regulations. There was a refusal to acknowledge that the applicant was entitled to be issued his new card notwithstanding questions as to whether he had completed the residency obligation. Those questions could and should have been addressed later and, if it was determined that he had failed to meet the residency obligation, appropriate steps taken which would provide the applicant with appeal rights to the IAD from any adverse decision. The applicant was entitled to be placed back in the position he ought to have been on June 28, 2011, provided he produced the relevant original documents.

Although an application for a PR card must be made in Canada, there is no requirement in the Act that it must be issued to an applicant in Canada.

The court allowed the application for judicial review and directed the respondent to issue a new card to the applicant. The issuance of the card and the residency obligation are two distinct matters. The respondent is entitled to pursue an investigation as to whether the applicant has met the residency obligation if it continues to have any concerns in that regard. The court did not therefore order that the applicant was free from responding to inquiries made by the respondent in this respect.

The applicant was ordered to advise the respondent in writing within 30 days of the date of the order as to whether he is in Pakistan or Canada and to provide his current address.

The following question was certified:

> Who has the jurisdiction to make the final determination on the merits of an application for a permanent resident card application — CPCS who may authorize the production of the PR Card or the CIC local office whose mandate is to issue the PR Card pursuant to s. 59 of the Regulations?

Wei v. Canada (Minister of Citizenship & Immigration) (2012), 12 Imm. L.R. (4th) 256, 2012 FC 1084, 2012 CarswellNat 3506, 2012 CarswellNat 5054, [2012] F.C.J. No. 1173 — This was an application for judicial review of a decision of the Immigration Appeal Division under subs. 63(4) of the Act. The Appeal Division held that a visa officer's determination that the applicant had failed to comply with the residency obligations was valid in law and there were insufficient H&C grounds to warrant special relief. The applicant became a permanent resident in May 1999 and was employed by a sea product company and a chicken farm in Vancouver. In 2004, he was hired by a B.C. pharmaceutical company to represent that company in China to find a business partner for it there. The applicant's salary was paid every three months and employment and Canadian taxes were deducted. The applicant applied for a travel document in 2009 which was refused by the Canadian Embassy for failure to meet the residency obligations. The Board found that the applicant was hired for a local position in China and therefore there was no assignment within the meaning of the Regulation, s. 61(3). Accordingly, the time that he was employed in China did not count toward the fulfilment of his residence obligation. The Board found the visa officer's decision reasonable but noted it retained the discretion to allow the applicant's appeal on H&C grounds taking into account the best interest of a child directly affected by the decision. The Board noted that the applicant was not hired to work in Canada and there was no position for him in Canada should the position in China cease. The Board therefore concluded that the applicant was hired for a local job in China and thus there was no assignment as per the Regulations. The applicant argued that the Board erred in finding that his employment was full time; as his position was subject to annual renewal, it was temporary rather than full time. Further, there were several connecting factors between the applicant and his Canadian employer including his work duties, his payment of taxes and other employment deductions in accordance with Canadian law and the fact that the Canadian company controlled his assignment from its head office in Canada. The court found that the Board came to a reasonable decision in finding that there was no assignment ultimately due to the lack of a job available for the applicant to return to in Canada. There were also insufficient H&C grounds and the application for judicial review was dismissed.

Bi v. Canada (Minister of Citizenship & Immigration), 2012 CarswellNat 870, 2012 FC 293 — The IAD rejected the applicant's appeal of a determination that he had failed to comply with the residency obligation of s. 28 of IRPA. The applicant was a Chinese citizen who became a permanent resident on September 3, 2005, along with his parents and sister. He returned to China approximately one month later. Upon his return to China, the applicant remained unemployed from October 2005 to February 21, 2007, when he entered into an agreement with a Canadian business to work as an assistant general manager in China until January 20, 2010. In an application for a travel document dated April 3, 2010, the applicant indicated that he had spent 130 days in Canada over the previous 4½ years. The visa officer refused his application for a travel document based on a lack of supporting evidence and, moreover, determined he had also failed to satisfy his residency obligation. The Federal Court in *Canada (Minister of Citizenship & Immigration) v. Jiang*, 2011 FC 349, was clearly opposed to an employee accumulating days toward meeting their residency requirement simply by being hired on a full-time basis outside of Canada by a Canadian business. Instead, it was the court's view that the permanent resident must be assigned temporarily, maintain a connection with his or her employer, and to continue working for his or her employer in Canada following the assignment. *Jiang* does not mandate that the permanent resident first worked in Canada. The emphasis is instead on the temporary nature of the assignment that requires the employee to maintain a connection with the Canadian business and then remain employed for that business in Canada.

In this case, even if a translation error occurred during the hearing which caused a misunderstanding as to the applicant's continued connection with his employer, there was no doubt that the applicant was not assigned to temporarily work abroad. Instead, his work abroad began from the moment he was hired and continued to the expiry of his contract nearly three years later. Furthermore, there was simply no evidence that his employer had agreed to keep the applicant on in Canada after this period. The applicant only indicated at the hearing that he now wanted to talk to the employer to tell him or her that he wanted to work in Canada and inquire as to whether another employee could be sent abroad in his place. As a result, the IAD's conclusion that the applicant did not meet the burden of establishing that he had satisfied the requirements under subs. 61(3) of the IRPR was reasonable. The application for judicial review was dismissed.

Wong v. Canada (Minister of Citizenship & Immigration) (2011), 1 Imm. L.R. (4th) 287, 2011 FC 971, 2011 CarswellNat 3013, [2011] F.C.J. No. 1193 — The applicants were found not to satisfy the residency obligations pursuant to subs. 28(2) of IRPA and were issued departure orders. The applicants appealed the decision to the IAD. The IAD found the applicants were not truthful when they attempted to enter Canada as visitors in November, 2008, that the removal orders were validly made, and that there were insufficient humanitarian and compassionate considerations to warrant quashing the removal orders.

The court found that the reasonings of the tribunal were flawed for a number of reasons. Its conclusion that the removal orders were valid in law was simply contrary to law, and furthermore, did not constitute a defensible and acceptable outcome in light of the law and the relevant facts of the case. Here, the applicants had discharged their onus of proving that the removal orders were not valid by adducing documentary evidence establishing that the review was conducted after the removal orders. The tribunal did not question this evidence. The tribunal should have allowed the appeal, according to subs. 67(2) of the Act; its only power in this regard would have been to refer the matter back to the appropriate decision maker for reconsideration.

The two-step process mentioned in s. 44 of the Act had to start again, this time before a different officer and a different Minister's delegate. The decision makers, if they choose to start the examination again, will have to render their decision based on new calculations, taking into account that some two years and eight months have elapsed since November 2008. The whole process may take months before the issue of whether either or both of the two applicants comply with the residency obligation set out in subs. 28(2) of the Act is finally decided again. Since it was impossible to predict the result at this point, the court saw no useful purpose in referring the matter back to the IAD and made a declaration that the removal orders were null and void.

Canada (Minister of Citizenship & Immigration) v. Sidhu (2011), 4 Imm. L.R. (4th) 196, 397 F.T.R. 29 (Eng.), 2011 FC 1056, 2011 CarswellNat 3541, 2011 CarswellNat 4225 — The respondent's permanent resident card expired on February 16, 2009, while he was in India. On December 31, 2009, he applied to a visa office in India for a travel document indicating his permanent resident status to allow him to return to Canada. In order to issue the travel document, s. 31 of the Act required a visa officer to be satisfied that, among other things, the applicant had complied with the residency obligation under s. 28. The visa officer concluded that the applicant did not meet the residency obligations. The visa officer considered whether humanitarian or compassionate considerations should alter the decision. The respondent filed an appeal. The Board found that all of the respondent's immediate family — his wife, four children, and five or six grandchildren — all lived in Alberta. The Board found this to be highly significant. The Board emphasized that the fact that the respondent could probably be sponsored by his family to come to Canada was not a factor in allowing the appeal. The Department of Citizenship & Immigration sought judicial review of the Board's decision.

The Board had a duty to consider all of the evidence. In this case, the evidence was that the respondent was present in Canada for only 26 days in the five years between 2004 and 2009. Although there was some testimony that his wife and a son lived with him in India at some point during the past 15 years and that his family members have come to visit him in India, there was no specific evidence of the dates or length of these visits. Thus, the evidence suggested that the family has been thriving in the respondent's absence and that they are able to visit him in India. Moreover, the respondent had been living separate and apart from his wife and family in Canada since 1995 — i.e. for 15 years. In preferring the respondent's evidence that he would suffer extreme hardship, the Board had a duty to confront this contrary evidence. The Board's decision was not reasonably open to it based on the evidence and lacked the degree of transparency, justification, and intelligibility required. The application for judicial review was allowed and the matter remitted to a new panel of the Board for redetermination.

Canada (Minister of Public Safety & Emergency Preparedness) v. Baig, 2011 FC 1191, 2011 CarswellNat 4392, 2011 CarswellNat 4630 — In its decision, the IAD allowed the respondent's appeal under subs. 63(3) of the Act against the removal order issued against her for her failure to comply with the permanent residency requirements on the basis of humanitarian and compassionate grounds. The IAD attached the greatest weight to the best interest of the respondent's son; significant weight to the respondent's family ties with Canada, having a maternal aunt and cousin in Toronto; to the fact that she no longer has any contact with her family in Pakistan; to her lengthy stay abroad due to her mother's illness and her inability to return to Canada due to the confiscation of her passport; and to the special circumstances of the present case, specifically her fear of returning to Pakistan due to the risk she and her child would face. The court held that the Minister failed to show that the IAD did not provide adequate reasons for its decision or that the IAD's conclusions were unreasonable; accordingly the application for judicial review was dismissed.

Durve v. Canada (Minister of Citizenship & Immigration) (2011), 99 Imm. L.R. (3d) 334, 2011 FC 995, 2011 CarswellNat 3202 — A visa officer refused to renew the applicant's permanent resident status because he had failed to comply with the residency obligations. The IAD upheld the decision and the applicant sought judicial review of the IAD's decision.

The determination of whether a Canadian corporation has an "ongoing operation" is essentially a question of fact to be determined by the nature and the degree of the activity of the companies in each individual case and no particular *indicia* is determinative. In this case, all the consulting fees were paid to the Canadian corporation; there was no evidence of any salary being paid by any other company to the applicant; and the incorporation of the Canadian company did not coincide with the applicant's entry in Canada.

It is important to examine the nature of the applicant's activities while outside of Canada in relation to the business of his or her Canadian company. It is also clear that the application of subs. 61(1) and (2) of the Regulations involves two distinct concepts. A company that does not have an ongoing operation is not necessarily a company incorporated primarily for the purpose of allowing an applicant to meet its residency obligations.

The court found that the presumption that the decision maker had considered all the evidence had been rebutted and that the decision did not meet the requirements of justification and transparency applicable under the standard of reasonableness. Although the decision was set aside, it did not imply accepting that the applicant's company fell within the parameters of subs. 61(1) of the Regulations. Instead, the court simply found that the matter had not been properly assessed on all the facts and the evidence before the decision maker, and that the decision maker had not sufficiently explained its reasonings to enable the court to properly assess the validity of its conclusion. In that respect, the court indicated it would be helpful if the IAD could be more precise as to the *indicia* it will look at when considering the application of the above-mentioned provisions to businesses started by new permanent residents on a very small scale and which involved developing clientele abroad. For example, if a one-man operation is not acceptable, it should be clearly spelled out. The application for judicial review was granted.

Rodriguez v. Canada (Minister of Citizenship & Immigration) (2011), 1 Imm. L.R. (4th) 304, (sub nom. *Martinez Rodriguez v. Canada (Minister of Citizenship & Immigration)*) 395 F.T.R. 21 (Eng.), 2011 FC 946, 2011 CarswellNat 2890 — The applicant accompanied her parents to Canada when they obtained permanent resident status in 1991. At the time, she was six years old. Two months later, her parents returned to El Salvador and she accompanied them. She visited Canada in 1998 and in 2000, both times on a visitor's visa. In 2010, she applied for another temporary visitor's visa in order to visit her aunt who lives in Canada. The visa officer realized that she had obtained permanent resident status in 1991. However, it was clear that she had not maintained her residency requirement, as she had not been in Canada a single day in the past 10 years. Under s. 31(3) the visa officer was prohibited from issuing the applicant a travel document, and as a permanent resident she could not be given a temporary resident visa. She was asked to sign, in English, a Consent to Decision on Residency Obligation and Waiver of Appeal Rights Resulting in Loss of Status under s. 46(1)(b). While the visa officer may well have thought she was doing the applicant a favour, since she was not entitled to a travel document as a permanent resident, if the only alternative was to renounce that status, she should not have been given that opportunity. She should have been sent back to El Salvador, and given a full opportunity to consider her options and to take advice. Renunciation of permanent resident status is a very important step in a person's life. It should not be decided on the spur of the moment. Although she clearly had not maintained the residence requirement, it was up to the IAD, not the Federal Court, to determine if there were humanitarian and compassionate considerations which override that defect. The IAD's decision that it had no jurisdiction to hear her appeal because she had lost her status as a permanent resident was set aside and sent back to a newly constituted panel of the IAD for redetermination.

Tai v. Canada (Minister of Citizenship & Immigration), 2011 FC 248, 2011 CarswellNat 1933, 2011 CarswellNat 471 — The applicants became permanent residents of Canada in 2001 but did not move to, or reside in, Canada. In April 2008, when the Tai family members sought to enter Canada, they were issued removal orders for failing to comply with their residency obligation. Ms. Chang and their daughters remained in Canada. Mr. Tai returned to his job in Taiwan and did not move to Canada until one year later at the end of April 2009. At the IAD, the family members admitted they had failed to meet their residency obligation and asked that their appeals be allowed based on discretionary jurisdiction. The IAD concluded there were insufficient H&C considerations to warrant special relief.

The IAD reasons were adequate when reviewed as a whole. The IAD considered all the circumstances of the case, and not just the failure to meet the residency obligation. The IAD is required to consider all of the circumstances in the case and not just the Tai family's recent efforts to establish itself (para. 67(1)(c) and s. 68(1) of IRPA). The Tai family argued that the IAD should have placed greater weight on the *Ribic* factor of "rehabilitation," in that it had apologized for the breach and now worked hard to establish itself in Canada. "Rehabilitation" is a factor that is considered by the IAD in exercising its discretionary jurisdiction with respect to criminal inadmissibility. The Tai family's positive contribution to Canada is only one factor that is considered under the *Ribic* test that is applied by the IAD. These factors are adapted in cases that do not involve criminal inadmissibility to consider "the circumstances surrounding the failure to meet the conditions of admission which led to the deportation order," instead of rehabilitation. The IAD reached a reasonable conclusion. The application for judicial review was dismissed.

Canada (Minister of Citizenship & Immigration) v. Jiang, 2011 FC 349, 2011 CarswellNat 1527 — This was an application for judicial review by the Minister of Citizenship and Immigration of a decision by the Immigration Appeal Division (the "panel"). The panel allowed the appellant's appeal and determined that she had met the residency obligation imposed on permanent residents under s. 28 of IRPA. The panel found that the appellant, through her employment with Investissement Québec in China, was "assigned full-time as a term of one's employment to a position outside of Canada" within the meaning of subs. 61(3) of the *Immigration and Refugee Protection Regulations*. The panel determined that being hired locally outside Canada, i.e. in China, met the requirements of the Act and the Regulations. The Minister sought judicial review of the panel's decision.

In this case, it is difficult to argue that the appellant met the "assignment" criterion set out in the Regulations. The word "assignment" in the context of permanent resident status interpreted in light of the Act and Regulations necessarily implies a connecting factor to the employer located in Canada. The word "assigned" in s. 61 of the Regulations means that an individual who is assigned to a position outside Canada on a temporary basis and who maintains a connection to a Canadian business or to the public service of Canada or of a province, may therefore return to Canada. The memorandum's definitions of advisors and local recruited professional employees (attachés) are convincing in this regard. The appellant was hired as a local employee, where the concept of assignment is absent from the definition. The ENF 23 also refers to "assignment" and to "duration of the assignment." The clarification added by Parliament to subs. 61(3) of the Regulations creates an equilibrium between the obligation imposed on the permanent resident to accumulate the required number of days under the Act while recognizing there may be opportunities for permanent residents to work abroad. Consequently, the court was of the opinion that, in light of the evidence in the record, the panel's finding that permanent residents holding full-time positions outside Canada with an eligible Canadian company can accumulate days that would enable them to comply with the residency obligations set out in s. 25 of the Act, is unreasonable.

In *obiter*, the court sympathized with the appellant's situation and noted she was a highly qualified person and her contribution was without a doubt an asset to Canadian society in general and to Quebec society in particular. However, it was not within the purview of the court to grant special relief under the current Act in order to proceed with an assessment of the genuine connections between the appellant and Canada and the fact that she enriches and strengthens the social and cultural fabric of Canadian society in addition to being a benefit to the Canadian economy, which in and of itself reflects the purpose of the Act (s. 3(2)). The appellant's particular circumstances lend themselves to an application for humanitarian and compassionate relief. The application for judicial review was allowed.

Ambat v. Canada (Minister of Citizenship & Immigration), 2011 FC 292, 2011 CarswellNat 1632, 2011 CarswellNat 623 — The IAD dismissed the applicant's appeal of a visa officer's determination that he was inadmissible for failing to meet the residency obligation for permanent residence, as set out in s. 28 of IRPA. The IAD was not satisfied that Conares Canada was a Canadian business for the purposes of IRPA and the Regulations. Since Conares Canada had no employees in Canada and no financial information was provided by the company after 2006, the IAD was unable to find that it had ongoing operations in Canada. Moreover, the IAD found that the timing of Conares Canada's creation and incorporation, which coincided with the applicant's landing in Canada, strongly indicated that it was a business of convenience, serving primarily to allow the applicant to meet his residency obligation while living outside of Canada.

The applicant's permanent resident card ("PRC") was set to expire in July 2008 so he applied to have it renewed while he was in Canada in April 2008, providing the necessary supporting documentation. He received notice that his application for renewal of his PRC had been accepted and approved and that the card was ready to be picked up. He was working in Dubai at the time and visited the UAE visa office to apply for a travel document for travel to Canada to pick up his PRC. A visa officer refused his request for a travel document, indicating that he had failed to meet the residency requirement under s. 28. The visa officer did not accept that the applicant was outside Canada employed by a Canadian business. The applicant was subsequently able to obtain a travel document based on his intention to appeal the negative residency determination pursuant to para. 31(3)(c) of IRPA. Once in Canada, he collected his renewed PRC card and submitted a notice of appeal to the IAD.

Section 31 of IRPA provides that a rebuttable presumption is raised if a person is in possession of a PRC. This provision makes it clear that a permanent resident must comply with the residency requirements at the time of examination. The applicant in this case was not in possession of his PRC when he applied for a travel document, and there was therefore no presumption that he was a permanent resident. There is no basis in IRPA for finding that the overseas visa officer was precluded from assessing whether or not the applicant met the residency obligation simply because he had a letter from the CIC inland office showing that his renewed PRC was ready for pickup. The application for judicial review was dismissed.

Shaath v. Canada (Minister of Citizenship & Immigration) (2009), 349 F.T.R. 81 (Eng.), 2009 FC 731, 2009 CarswellNat 2251, 2009 CarswellNat 4145 — The applicant sought judicial review of a decision dismissing his appeal from a departure order issued against him, by reason of his failure to comply with s. 28 of IRPA, which provides that a permanent resident meets his residency obligations in each five-year period if he/she was physically present in Canada at least 730 days during that period.

The tribunal reached its conclusion despite the fact counsel for the Minister appearing before the tribunal agreed the appeal should be allowed on humanitarian grounds mainly because of the family's establishment in Canada who, except for the applicant, are Canadian citizens. Counsel for the Minister also recognized his important financial investment in Canada and "he had been credible in his efforts to obtain his certification in Canada in order to get a job in his own specialty in the near future." Counsel's main reason for recommending the applicant's appeal be allowed was that she thought it was "nonsense to ask for a denial of the appeal since Mr. Shaath could apply tomorrow as a member of the family class, sponsored by his wife and it would be really easy to obtain his permanent residency and start the whole thing again." She considered that in all of the circumstances, "the punishment of losing his permanent residency would be disproportionate in all of the circumstances." The tribunal disagreed with counsel for the Minister's recommendation.

The Supreme Court of Canada's decision in *Canada (Citizenship & Immigration) v. Khosa* (2009), 77 Imm. L.R. (3d) 1, has a considerable impact upon this case because it dealt with the exercise by the IAD of its discretion under para. 67(1)(c) of IRPA. *Khosa* makes it clear where reasonableness standard applies, it requires deference and reviewing courts are not allowed to substitute their own appreciation of the appropriate solution but rather must determine if the outcome falls "within a range of possible, acceptable outcomes which are defensible in respect of the facts and the law." Paragraph 67(1)(c) provides a power to grant "exceptionable relief" and calls for a fact-dependent and policy-driven assessment. An applicant has the burden of adducing proof of any claim upon which a humanitarian and compassionate application relies. The application for judicial review was dismissed.

Dudhnath v. Canada (Minister of Citizenship & Immigration), 2009 CarswellNat 941, 2009 FC 386 — This was an application for judicial review of a decision of the IAD which dismissed the applicant's appeal of a visa officer's decision that he had failed to comply with his residency obligations as a permanent resident under s. 28 of the IRPA. The applicant placed too much reliance on "intent," both as an applicable principle and as to its application in this case. Intent may be a relevant factor under H&C considerations in s. 67 of the IRPA but it does not dominate the analysis of factors. The IAD did a thorough analysis of the relevant factors. The critical factor was the 1997 decision to deny the request for a returning resident permit. That decision, based on allegations that the applicant had sold his Record of Landing, concluded that the applicant had abandoned Canada. In the absence of any challenge to the 1997 decision, the High Commission and the IAD had to accept that finding. Given that finding, the sporadic and ineffective efforts to return to Canada are not sufficient evidence of intent to remain or to acquire residency. The IAD's consideration of the H&C factors was sufficient and comprehensive. Although the analysis of the best interests of the children may have raised issues, it is not for the court to reweigh the evidence. The applicant's efforts to rebut any finding of abandonment or to establish H&C grounds to permit a return to Canada were "too little and too late." The applicant was left with the option of applying to enter Canada in the same way most others must. The application for judicial review was dismissed.

Ikhuiwu v. Canada (Minister of Citizenship & Immigration), 2008 FC 35, 2008 CarswellNat 42, [2008] F.C.J. No. 35 — This was an application for judicial review of an IAD decision, confirming the decision of an overseas visa officer. The visa officer concluded that the applicant was inadmissible pursuant to ss. 28 and 41(b) of the IRPA as he did not reside in Canada for the required 730 days within a five-year period.

The legislative scheme under the IRPA makes it clear that the mere possession of a permanent resident card is not conclusive proof of a person's status in Canada. Pursuant to s. 31(2) of the IRPA, the presumption that the holder of a permanent resident card is a permanent resident is clearly a rebuttable one. In this case, it is clear that the permanent resident card, which was issued in error after it was determined by the visa officer in Nigeria that the applicant had lost his permanent residence status, could not possibly confer legal status on him as a permanent resident, nor could it have the effect of restoring his permanent resident status which he had previously lost because he didn't meet the residency requirements under s. 28 of the IRPA. There is no provision in the IRPA or the Regulations which suggests that the mere possession of a permanent resident card, which was improperly issued, could have the effect of restoring or reinstating a person's prior permanent resident status.

Section 59(1)(a) of the Regulations also makes it clear that an officer can only validly issue a new permanent resident card where an applicant has not lost his or her status under s. 46(1) of the IRPA. In this case, the applicant lost his permanent resident status after failing to meet the residency requirements under s. 28 of the IRPA and failed to appeal the decision within the 60 days as prescribed by Regulation 63(4). This regulatory scheme confirms that it was not possible for the issuing officer of the permanent resident card to have validly and properly issued it in light of the fact that the applicant had previously lost his permanent resident card. The application for judicial review was dismissed.

Chen v. Canada (Minister of Public Safety & Emergency Preparedness), 2007 CarswellNat 2175 (Imm. & Ref. Bd. (App. Div.)) — The appellant was found to be a person described in subs. 41(b) of the IRPA as inadmissible for failing to comply with the residency obligation of s. 28 of the Act. The appellant had made no reasonable attempts to return to Canada to reside at the earliest opportunity. There were no satisfactory explanations as to why the appellant chose to spend most of his time in the last nine years in Taiwan separated from his children. His actions were consistent with the intentions of continuing to live in Taiwan, to manage his properties in Taiwan and to pursue his education in Taiwan, settling his children in Canada for a better future and attempting to maintain a potential future option to return to Canada. Even after the removal order was issued, the appellant did not remain in Canada. He had limited assets in Canada. There was no evidence of social attachments to Canada and no letters of support from friends in Canada or community or business organizations. Although he had other family members in Canada who were likely supportive of him, there was limited evidence of close relationships with other family members in Canada. The appellant's two daughters were currently aged 22 and 23 and were Canadian citizens. They are not considered to be "dependent" children under the Act and as such the panel need not consider the best interests of children directly affected by this decision. There was limited evidence of any undue hardship that the appellant would face from losing his status in Canada. There was no credible evidence of country conditions that would create hardship to the appellant. He has close family in Taiwan as well. He had significant assets in Taiwan. While the appellant's medical condition may create some concerns or delays in future applications, there are avenues the appellant can pursue to overcome them and therefore this factor does not, in the circumstances, create undue hardship to the appellant. The removal order was valid in law. The appeal was dismissed.

Chu v. Canada (Minister of Citizenship & Immigration), 2007 CarswellNat 1469, 2007 FCA 205 — The five-year period in s. 28 of the IRPA applies to periods prior to June 28, 2002. Applying s. 28 retroactively does not breach s. 7 of the *Canadian Charter of Rights and Freedoms*.

Lai v. Canada (Minister of Citizenship & Immigration) (2006), 60 Imm. L.R. (3d) 17, 2006 CarswellNat 3669, 2006 FC 1359 — The applicant was landed in Canada in 1996 at the age of nine. She came to Canada as a dependant but she and her family returned to Taiwan within 12 days of their arrival. The family returned to Canada on occasion but did not take up residency here. The family purchased an apartment but never occupied that property and eventually it was sold. In August 2002, the applicant returned to Canada to take up high school studies. Apart from some vacations to Taiwan, the applicant has lived continuously in British Columbia since August 2002 attending full-time high school studies. In 2004, the applicant applied for a travel document in Taiwan to permit her to return to Canada as a permanent resident. That request was denied by a visa officer because it was determined that she had not fulfilled the residency requirement of the IRPA. These provisions required that she actually reside in Canada for a minimum of 730 days in the preceding five-year period. At that point the applicant had been physically present in Canada for only 443 days during the relevant five-year period.

In the case of a dependent child of relatively tender years there is little, if any, opportunity to independently fulfil the residency obligation required to preserve landed status or to create the genuine ties to Canada that are typically necessary for H&C relief. In most cases, the child can only accomplish that which the parents are prepared to allow and support. The applicant's status in Canada may have been jeopardized by the decision of her parents, but her claim to relief should not be enhanced by those parental decisions. The application for judicial review was dismissed.

The court adopted the decision of the Federal Court in *Chu v. Canada (Minister of Citizenship & Immigration)* (2006), [2007] 2 F.C.R. 578, 54 Imm. L.R. (3d) 216, 2006 FC 893, [2006] F.C.J. No. 119. In *Chu*, the court concluded that the current legislative scheme represented by the IRPA is retrospective in effect, relative to compliance with the residency requirements. In this case the applicant did not have a vested legal right to the application of the previous residency rules. The status she enjoyed under the former Act was contingent upon her ability to fulfil and to establish compliance with those rules on an ongoing basis. When those rules were changed by the IRPA, she had no right to their continued application to her situation.

Chu certified a question: "five-year period in s. 28 of the IRPA apply to periods prior to June 28, 2002?" The court in this case certified the same question.

El Idrissi c. Canada (Ministre de la Citoyenneté & de l'Immigration), 2005 CarswellNat 2421, 2005 CarswellNat 5248, 2005 FC 1105 — The applicant was given permanent residence status in 1991. In 1999, the applicant left Canada to visit his sick father and manage a family business in his home country. He did not return until June 15, 2003. He fell under the purview of s. 41 of the IRPA and a departure order was made against him by the Minister. He filed an appeal to the Immigration Appeal Division but conceded that the removal order against him was legally valid and the only issue he argued was that there were humanitarian and compassionate grounds to explain his failure to meet the residency obligation.

Simply having a wife in Canada was not sufficient for this situation to be considered a humanitarian and compassionate ground. The Appeal Division was entitled to consider that the applicant's plans for the future were vague. The applicant had the burden of establishing the existence of humanitarian and compassionate grounds.

Yu v. Canada (Minister of Citizenship & Immigration), 2005 CarswellNat 2998, 2005 CarswellNat 4835, 2005 FC 1323 — The applicant, having been granted permanent residence status in the independent category, was denied re-admission as a resident by a visa officer in November, 2003. The visa officer's decision was appealed to the IAD who determined that the applicant failed to comply with the residency obligation under s. 28 of the IRPA. The Immigration Appeal Board determined that pursuant to s. 41 of the IRPA there was non-compliance and upheld the visa officer's determination. The Board also determined that there were insufficient humanitarian and compassionate considerations justifying the retention of permanent residence status; therefore the applicant was unable to overcome the breach of her residency obligations.

The applicant planned to work in her native land until able to retire with full pension benefits, in 2006. In 2005, the law concerning her pension benefits was changed and the applicant was able to retire earlier. This important new evidence was forwarded by way of affidavit to the Board on December 10, 2004.

The issue of "intention" should have been discussed or at least canvassed, as well as the change of circumstances regarding the applicant's retirement. The Board's decision was set aside and the matter was sent back to be reheard.

29. (1) Right of temporary residents — **A temporary resident is, subject to the other provisions of this Act, authorized to enter and remain in Canada on a temporary basis as a visitor or as a holder of a temporary resident permit.**

(2) Obligation — temporary resident — **A temporary resident must comply with any conditions imposed under the regulations and with any requirements under this Act, must leave Canada by the end of the period authorized for their stay and may re-enter Canada only if their authorization provides for re-entry.**

[Editor's Note: SOR/2002-227, s. 329(1) provides that any of the following persons who were in Canada immediately before June 28, 2002 are temporary residents under the new Immigration and Refugee Protection Act, *S.C. 2001, c. 27 and are subject to its provisions:*

> *(a) a visitor under the* Immigration Act, *R.S.C. 1985, c. I-2 (the "former Act"); and*

> *(b) a person issued a permit under s. 37 of the former Act.]*

Case Law

Section 29(2)

Sui v. Canada (Minister of Public Safety & Emergency Preparedness) (2006), 58 Imm. L.R. (3d) 135, [2007] 3 F.C.R. 218, 2006 CarswellNat 3554, 2006 FC 1314 — The applicant was in Canada for several years as a temporary resident on a study permit. Before his study permit expired he applied for a post-graduation work permit. He received a letter from CIC informing him that he did not meet the requirements for a work permit and that he should leave Canada immediately, failing which enforcement action would be taken against him. Within 90 days of the expiration of his study permit and within 90 days of losing his temporary resident status he applied to have his status restored pursuant to Regulation 182. While awaiting a decision on his application for restoration, two immigration officers attended his home and questioned him. Two inadmissibility reports were issued, the first based on para. 40(1)(a) of the IRPA and the fact that "there were reasonable grounds to believe that this foreign national was inadmissible for directly or indirectly misrepresenting or withholding material facts relating to a relevant matter that induces or could induce an error in administration of this Act." The second report was based on para. 41(a) and subs. 29(2) of the IRPA and the fact that the applicant was inadmissible for failing to comply with his obligation as a temporary resident to leave Canada by the end of the period authorized for his stay. A Minister's delegate decided to issue an exclusion order based on para. 41(a) and subs. 29(2) of the IRPA. In light of s. 225 of the Regulations, this meant that the applicant could not come back to Canada without written consent of the Minister for a period of one year following his departure. The applicant left Canada. No decision with respect to the application for restoration was ever made. In this case, the Minister's delegate had the discretion and even the duty to consider the fact that the applicant had applied for restoration well before a s. 44(1) report was issued against him in respect of his failure to leave Canada at the end of his authorized stay. It was an error of law to consider that the applicant was not entitled to make such an application for restoration simply because after the filing of his application in accordance with the Regulations, a s. 44(1) report had been issued on the sole basis of subs. 29(2) of the IRPA. The decision was set aside.

The following questions were certified:

1. Is an application for restoration pursuant to s. 182 of the Regulations a relevant consideration when the Minister's delegate considers whether or not to make an exclusion order based on a failure to comply with s. 29(2) of the IRPA?

2. foreign national who has a applied for restoration within the delay set out in s. 182 of the Regulations, automatically lose the benefit of his or her application when an enforcement officer considers issuing a report under s. 44(1) on the basis of a failure to comply with s. 29(2) of the IRPA.

Brar v. Canada (Minister of Citizenship & Immigration) (2006), 59 Imm. L.R. (3d) 293, 2006 CarswellNat 4324, 2006 FC 1502 — The applicants sought judicial review in respect of a decision by a member of the Immigration and Refugee Board of Canada given collectively, but pertaining to them. It determined that each of the applicants had contravened the terms of the work permit issued to each of them and therefore each was to be excluded from Canada. The applicants were all adult male citizens of India. They applied for and received temporary work permits. The work permit stated:

Employer: Bombay Paradise

    Conditions:

- not authorized to work in any occupation other than stated;
- not authorized to work for any employer other than stated; and
- not authorized for work in any location other than stated.

When the applicants arrived in Calgary they found that the Bombay Paradise Restaurant was under construction and far from being completed. The owner of that business was a numbered company run by a person known as Vic. He placed them in another establishment known as Bombay Sweet House & Restaurant. Apparently, the ownership was not the same as Bombay Paradise, although pay cheques issued to the applicants were from the numbered company which was the owner of the Bombay Paradise business.

It came to the Minister's attention that the applicants were working for an employer whom the Minister believed to be other than that named in the work permit. As a result, an exclusion order was issued. Following that order, an admissibility hearing was held on March 1, 2006. The issue of the hearing was whether each of the applicants was inadmissible under s. 41(a) of the IRPA, as having contravened s. 29(2) of that Act.

The court concluded that Bombay Paradise paid the applicants and the applicants worked in Calgary, and therefore, no term as set out in the work permit had been breached. A work permit should be understandable to all interested persons, not just the worker or the government, on the face of it. The Minister has the resources to ensure that the permit is complete and understandable. If it is not, the Minister cannot be seen to rely on self-created ambiguities to derive a beneficial interpretation. It is the same concept as *contra proferentum* in the interpretation of a contract. If the contract was prepared by a party, any ambiguity must be interpreted against the interests of that party.

The applicants did not breach the terms of their work permits. Their employer, the person who pays them, was Bombay Paradise. They worked in Calgary. As a result, the exclusion order was set aside and the matter was returned to be determined by a different person.

30. (1) Work and study in Canada — A foreign national may not work or study in Canada unless authorized to do so under this Act.

(1.1) Authorization — An officer may, on application, authorize a foreign national to work or study in Canada if the foreign national meets the conditions set out in the regulations.

(1.2) Instructions — Despite subsection (1.1), the officer shall refuse to authorize the foreign national to work in Canada if, in the officer's opinion, public policy considerations that are specified in the instructions given by the Minister justify such a refusal.

(1.3) Concurrence of second officer — In applying subsection (1.2), any refusal to give authorization to work in Canada requires the concurrence of a second officer.

(1.4) Purpose — The instructions referred to in subsection (1.2) shall prescribe public policy considerations that aim to protect foreign nationals who are at risk of being subjected to humiliating or degrading treatment, including sexual exploitation.

(1.41) Revocation of work permit — An officer may revoke a work permit if, in the officer's opinion, public policy considerations that are specified in instructions given by the Minister justify the revocation.

(1.42) For greater certainty — For greater certainty, subsection (1.41) does not affect any other lawful authority to revoke a work permit.

(1.43) Revocation or suspension of opinion — If, in the view of the Department of Employment and Social Development, public policy considerations that are specified in instructions given by the Minister of Employment and Social Development justify it, that Department may

(a) revoke an assessment provided by that Department with respect to an application for a work permit;

(b) suspend the effects of the assessment; or

(c) refuse to process a request for such an assessment.

(1.44) For greater certainty — For greater certainty, subsection (1.43) does not affect any other lawful authority to revoke an assessment referred to in that subsection.

(1.5) Publication — Instructions given under this section shall be published in the *Canada Gazette*.

(1.6) Application — The instructions take effect on the day on which they are published, or on any later day specified in the instructions, and apply in respect of all applications for authorization to work in Canada and requests to provide an assessment with respect to an application for a work permit, including those applications and requests that were made before that day and for which a final decision has not been made.

(1.7) Revocation — The instructions cease to have effect on the day on which a notice of revocation is published in the *Canada Gazette*.

(2) Minor children — Every minor child in Canada, other than a child of a temporary resident not authorized to work or study, is authorized to study at the preschool, primary or secondary level.

2012, c. 1, s. 206; 2013, c. 33, s. 161; 2013, c. 40, s. 235; 2014, c. 39, s. 307

Case Law

Section 30(1)

Juneja v. Canada (Minister of Citizenship & Immigration), 2007 CarswellNat 636, 2007 FC 301 — While in Canada on a valid study permit, the applicant was observed to be working at a local car dealership in Edmonton. He was arrested for working without authorization contrary to s. 30(1) of the Act. An admissibility hearing was then convoked under s. 44(2) of the Act. The applicant was declared inadmissible and was issued an exclusion order requiring him to leave Canada. The Board was satisfied that his activity did constitute "work" under the Act and Regulations. The applicant was performing work-like tasks for the dealership but was not being paid. The employer was banking or keeping track of his hours, presumably for the purposes of paying wages if and when the applicant received an authorization to work from the department. The agreed wage was $8 per hour. The employer's agreement to bank the applicant's hours and to pay a wage of $8.00 per hour — albeit conditionally — was either an activity for which wages are paid or was, otherwise, in direct competition with the employment activities of Canadians or permanent residents. The Board's finding was upheld and the application for judicial review was dismissed.

Proposed Addition — 30.1

30.1 Publication of employer names and addresses — (1) The Minister or the Minister of Employment and Social Development may, in accordance with the regulations, publish on a list the name and address of an employer who has been found guilty of an offence arising out of the contravention of a provision of this Act that is designated in the regulations or an offence under any other federal or provincial law that regulates employment or the recruiting of employees and who

(a) has provided information in accordance with regulations made under paragraph 32(d.5) or employs or has employed a foreign national for whom a work permit is required; or

(b) has requested an assessment from the Department of Employment and Social Development with respect to an application for a work permit.

(2) Removal of names and addresses — The Minister or the Minister of Employment and Social Development may also, in accordance with the regulations, remove such a name and address from the list.

2014, c. 39, s. 308 [Not in force at date of publication.]

Status Document

31. (1) Status document — A permanent resident and a protected person shall be provided with a document indicating their status.

[Editor's Note: S.C. 2001, c. 27, s. 200 provides that s. 31(1) of the Immigration and Refugee Protection Act, *S.C. 2001, c. 27 (the "new Act") does not apply with respect to persons who were permanent residents, within the meaning of the* Immigration Act, *R.S.C. 1985, c. I-2, on June 28, 2002.*

SOR/2002-227, s. 328(1) provides that a person who was a permanent resident immediately before June 28, 2002 is a permanent resident under the new Act.]

(2) Effect — For the purposes of this Act, unless an officer determines otherwise

(a) a person in possession of a status document referred to in subsection (1) is presumed to have the status indicated; and

(b) a person who is outside Canada and who does not present a status document indicating permanent resident status is presumed not to have permanent resident status.

(3) Travel document — A permanent resident outside Canada who is not in possession of a status document indicating permanent resident status shall, following an examination, be issued a travel document if an officer is satisfied that

(a) they comply with the residency obligation under section 28;

(b) an officer has made the determination referred to in paragraph 28(2)(c); or

(c) they were physically present in Canada at least once within the 365 days before the examination and they have made an appeal under subsection 63(4) that has not been finally determined or the period for making such an appeal has not yet expired.

Case Law

Ambat v. Canada (Minister of Citizenship & Immigration), 2011 FC 292, 2011 CarswellNat 1632, 2011 CarswellNat 623 — The IAD dismissed the applicant's appeal of a visa officer's determination that he was inadmissible for failing to meet the residency obligation for permanent residence, as set out in s. 28 of IRPA. The IAD was not satisfied that Conares Canada was a Canadian business for the purposes of IRPA and the Regulations. Since Conares Canada had no employees in Canada and no financial information was provided by the company after 2006, the IAD was unable to find that it had ongoing operations in Canada. Moreover, the IAD found that the timing of Conares Canada's creation and incorporation, which coincided with the applicant's landing in Canada, strongly indicated that it was a business of convenience, serving primarily to allow the applicant to meet his residency obligation while living outside of Canada.

The applicant's permanent resident card ("PRC") was set to expire in July 2008 so he applied to have it renewed while he was in Canada in April 2008, providing the necessary supporting documentation. He received notice that his application for renewal of his PRC had been accepted and approved and that the card was ready to be picked up. He was working in Dubai at the time and visited the UAE visa office to apply for a travel document for travel to Canada to pick up his PRC. A visa officer refused his request for a travel document, indicating that he had failed to meet the residency requirement under s. 28. The visa officer did not accept that the applicant was outside Canada employed by a Canadian business. The applicant was subsequently able to obtain a travel document based on his intention to appeal the negative residency determination pursuant to para. 31(3)(c) of IRPA. Once in Canada, he collected his renewed PRC card and submitted a notice of appeal to the IAD.

Section 31 of IRPA provides that a rebuttable presumption is raised if a person is in possession of a PRC. This provision makes it clear that a permanent resident must comply with the residency requirements at the time of examination. The applicant in this case was not in possession of his PRC when he applied for a travel document, and there was therefore no presumption that he was a permanent resident. There is no basis in IRPA for finding that the overseas visa officer was precluded from assessing whether or not the applicant met the residency obligation simply because he had a letter from the CIC inland office showing that his renewed PRC was ready for pickup. The application for judicial review was dismissed.

Refugee Travel Document
[Heading added 2012, c. 17, s. 16.]

31.1 Designated foreign national — For the purposes of Article 28 of the Refugee Convention, a designated foreign national whose claim for refugee protection or application for protection is accepted is lawfully staying in Canada only if they become a permanent resident or are issued a temporary resident permit under section 24.

2012, c. 17, s. 16

Regulations

32. Regulations — The regulations may provide for any matter relating to the application of sections 27 to 31, may define, for the purposes of this Act, the terms used in those sections, and may include provisions respecting

(a) classes of temporary residents, such as students and workers;

(b) selection criteria for each class of foreign national and for their family members, and the procedures for evaluating all or some of those criteria;

Proposed Addition — 32(b.1)

(b.1) the publication and removal of the names and addresses of employers, the circumstances under which the names and addresses must not be published and the designation of provisions of this Act, for the purposes of section 30.1;
2014, c. 39, s. 309(1) [Not in force at date of publication.]

(c) anything referred to in paragraph (b) for which a decision or recommendation may or must be made by a designated person, institution or organization;

(d) the conditions that must or may be imposed, varied or cancelled, individually or by class, on permanent residents and foreign nationals, including conditions respecting work or study;

(d.1) the conditions that must or may be imposed, individually or by class, on individuals and entities — including employers and educational institutions — in respect of permanent residents and foreign nationals, or that must or may be varied or cancelled;

(d.2) the power to inspect — including the power to require documents to be provided by individuals and entities, including employers and educational institutions, for inspection — for the purpose of verifying compliance with the conditions imposed under paragraphs **(d)** and **(d.1)**;

(d.3) the consequences of a failure to comply with the conditions referred to in paragraphs **(d)** and **(d.1)**;

(d.4) a system of administrative monetary penalties applicable to the contravention by an employer of any conditions referred to in paragraph **(d.1)** and the amounts of those penalties;

(d.5) the requirement for an employer to provide a prescribed person with prescribed information in relation to a foreign national's authorization to work in Canada for the employer, the electronic system by which that information must be provided, the circumstances in which that information may be provided by other means and those other means;

Proposed Amendment — 32(d.5)

(d.5) the requirement for an employer to provide a prescribed person with prescribed information in relation to a foreign national's authorization to work in Canada for the employer;

2015, c. 36, s. 172 [Not in force at date of publication.]

(e) the residency obligation under section 28, including rules for calculating applicable days and periods; and

(f) the circumstances in which a document indicating status or a travel document may or must be issued, renewed or revoked.

2012, c. 19, s. 705; 2013, c. 16, s. 37(2)(b); 2014, c. 20, s. 302; 2014, c. 39, s. 309(2), (3)

DIVISION 4 — INADMISSIBILITY

33. Rules of interpretation — The facts that constitute inadmissibility under sections 34 to 37 include facts arising from omissions and, unless otherwise provided, include facts for which there are reasonable grounds to believe that they have occurred, are occurring or may occur.

Case Law

Tang v. Canada (Minister of Citizenship & Immigration), 2009 CarswellNat 1497, 2009 CarswellNat 2096, 2009 FC 292 — A potential permanent resident was held to be inadmissible on the grounds of organized criminality, a determination first made in 1996 and communicated to the principal applicant in 2007 after many twists and turns between federal government offices. The applicant's conviction for claiming to be a member of a triad was advanced as reasonable grounds for believing that he was in fact a member of a triad. In other cases, that might well be sufficient, but not in this case. First, there was no consideration of the circumstances surrounding the conviction which called into question whether the claim was true. The conviction arose from a guilty plea and resulted in a minimal penalty. Secondly, if the Minister of Citizenship and Immigration had a *"bona fide* belief" that the applicant was or had been a member of a triad, it had had that belief since 1997 and yet continued to permit the applicant to enter Canada on a regular basis. The Minister's actions and acquiescence belied its stated belief. Thirdly, there was a certain element of disingenuousness in the manner in which officials relied on the conviction as if the 1995 admissions by the applicant, where he denied actual membership in a triad and claimed that he had not gone through a traditional initiation ceremony but elaborated on his allegedly limited role and other aspects of his "non-membership," were never made. The Minister made no reference to the admissions and used a more convenient pretext of a conviction to ground the admissibility decision. In light of the inconsistency between what the Minister has said, done and relied upon for its decision, the decision was not reasonable. The judicial review was granted and the decision quashed, and the matter remitted back to the Minister for a proper determination.

Thanaratnam v. Canada (Minister of Citizenship & Immigration), [2004] 3 F.C.R. 301, 37 Imm. L.R. (3d) 96, 2004 CarswellNat 2193, 2004 CarswellNat 569, 2004 FC 349, [2004] F.C.J. No. 395; reversed (2005), 45 Imm. L.R. (3d) 1, 2005 FCA 122, 2005 CarswellNat 887 — The words "reasonable grounds to believe" create a relatively low evidentiary threshold. "Reasonable grounds to believe" is more than mere suspicion. It connotes a degree of probability based on credible evidence. The standard of "reasonable grounds to believe" can be met by way of hearsay evidence and other forms of proof that would not normally be admissible at a trial, including evidence about a person's reputation or criminal record.

Unresolved criminal charges are, until proven otherwise, nothing more than mere allegations against the accused. They are not indicative of guilt and obviously therefore, are not indicative of a propensity to re-offend either, until they are proven beyond a reasonable doubt by the Crown in a court of law. The reasonable grounds standard operates as a protection against arbitrary, capricious or ill-founded state action.

34. (1) Security — **A permanent resident or a foreign national is inadmissible on security grounds for**

(a) engaging in an act of espionage that is against Canada or that is contrary to Canada's interests;

(b) engaging in or instigating the subversion by force of any government;

(b.1) engaging in an act of subversion against a democratic government, institution or process as they are understood in Canada;

(c) engaging in terrorism;

(d) being a danger to the security of Canada;

(e) engaging in acts of violence that would or might endanger the lives or safety of persons in Canada; or

(f) being a member of an organization that there are reasonable grounds to believe engages, has engaged or will engage in acts referred to in paragraph (a), (b), (b.1) or (c).

(2) [Repealed 2013, c. 16, s. 13(3).]

[Editor's Note: SOR/2002-227, s. 320(1) provides that a person is inadmissible under the new *Immigration and Refugee Protection Act, S.C. 2001, c. 27 on security grounds if, on June 28, 2002, the person had been determined to be a member of an inadmissible class described in paragraph 19(1)(e), (f), (g) or (k) of the former* Immigration Act, R.S.C. *1985, c. I-2.]*

2013, c. 16, s. 13

Case Law

Kanagendren v Canada (Minister of Citizenship and Immigration) (2015), 382 D.L.R. (4th) 562, 2015 FCA 86, 2015 CarswellNat 815, [2015] F.C.J. No. 382 — The Immigration Division found the appellant inadmissible under s. 34(1)(f) of IRPA as a member of an organization that there are reasonable grounds to believe engages or will engage in terrorism.

The Supreme Court decision in *Ezokola v Canada (Minister of Citizenship and Immigration)* (2013), 18 Imm. L.R. (4th) 175, does not require modification of the legal test for membership in a terrorist organization under para. 34(1)(f) of the IRPA. Article 1F(a) of the United Nations Convention Relating to the Status of Refugees excludes individuals from the definition of "refugee" if there are "serious reasons for considering that they have committed a crime against peace, a war crime, or a crime against humanity." Article 1F(a) is incorporated into Canadian law by s. 98 of IRPA. As a matter of law, criminal liability is not confined to the direct perpetrators of a crime. The court in *Ezokola* found that complicity arises by contribution. Article 1F(a) requires serious reasons for considering that an individual has voluntarily made a significant and knowing contribution to a group's crime or criminal purpose.

Read together, clear differences exist between subss. 34(1) and 35(1). Under s. 34(1) an inadmissibility finding flows from engaging in terrorism or membership in an organization that engages in terrorism; under s. 35(1) an inadmissibility finding flows from the commission of an offence. Since criminal liability attaches to both the direct perpetrators and their accomplices, complicity is relevant to the s. 35(1) analysis.

There is no provision under s. 35(1)(a) that gives the Minister discretion to grant relief against inadmissibility. A relieving provision is not required where inadmissibility flows from the commission of an offence whether as perpetrator or accomplice.

The underlying purpose of s. 34(1) is security concerns, which is served by a wide definition of membership. In contrast s. 35(1)(a) guards against abuse of the Refugee Convention by those who create refugees: those who create refugees are not refugees themselves.

The decision was reasonable. The appeal was dismissed.

Najafi v. Canada (Minister of Public Safety and Emergency Preparedness) (2014), 31 Imm. L.R. (4th) 1, 86 Admin. L.R. (5th) 235, 379 D.L.R. (4th) 542, 466 N.R. 82, 2014 FCA 262, 2014 CarswellNat 5396; leave to appeal to S.C.C. refused 2015 CarswellNat 1116, 2015 CarswellNat 1117 (S.C.C.) — The appellant was a citizen of Iran of Kurdish ethnicity. His refugee claim was accepted. However, he did not obtain permanent resident status because the Minister sought a declaration of his inadmissibility under s. 34 of IRPA, seeking to have the applicant declared inadmissible due to his involvement with the Kurdish Democratic Party of Iran (the "KDPI"). The Minister claimed that there were reasonable grounds to believe that the appellant was a member of the KDPI and that the KDPI had engaged in the "subversion by force" of the Iranian government. The Immigration Division agreed and issued a deportation order. The appellant admitted to collecting medicines and money for the KDPI. He admitted he was active in the KDPI verbally promoting the party's goals and ideology and distributing their monthly publication and that he solicited funds and medications for the party. These facts, coupled with the requirement to interpret the notion of membership broadly, afforded the Immigration Division a reasonable basis for concluding that he was a member of the KDPI. Therefore, the Immigration Division's membership finding was reasonable.

The Legislature chose to render individuals inadmissible in the first instance if, among other things, they or their organizations engaged in the use of force to subvert any government. This includes despotic or oppressive regimes and even regimes that engaged in widespread human rights abuses, like the former government in South Africa. The Division did not err in declining to consult international law to interpret para. 34(1)(b) of the IRPA. It appropriately premised its decision regarding the meaning to be given to "subversion by force" on settled jurisprudence, which lead to the conclusion that the KDPI was an organization that attempted to subvert the government in Iran by force.

In answer to the Federal Court's certified question the Federal Court of Appeal stated that Canada's international law obligations do not require the Immigration Division, in interpreting para. 34(1)(b) of the *Immigration and Refugee Protection Act*, to exclude from inadmissibility those who participate in an organization that uses force in an attempt to subvert a government in furtherance of an oppressed people's claimed right to self-determination.

Perez Villegas v. Canada (Minister of Citizenship & Immigration) (2011), 95 Imm. L.R. (3d) 261, 2011 FC 105, 2011 CarswellNat 1008, 2011 CarswellNat 232 — The applicant requested an order quashing the decision of an officer who found the applicant inadmissible pursuant to para. 34(1)(f). There is no definition of "terrorism" in the Act. A decision maker must show the evidentiary foundation to support a finding that an organization was engaged in acts of terrorism. The decision maker must make specific findings of fact about what the organization engaged in that are contained in paragraphs 34(1)(a), (b) or (c). Then, the decision maker must provide analysis of the acts the organization has committed and explain how they meet the definition of terrorism. This requires showing a link between the acts and the definition of terrorism provided (see *Naeem v. Canada (Minister of Citizenship & Immigration)* (2008), 78 Imm. L.R. (3d) 23, 2008 FC 1735. Significantly, the decision maker must explain how the acts were intended to harm civilians — as the definition of terrorism focuses on the protection of civilians.

In this case, the analysis did not meet the requirements set down by the jurisprudence. The application for judicial review was allowed and the matter was referred to a different officer for redetermination.

Toronto Coalition to Stop the War v. Canada (Minister of Public Safety & Emergency Preparedness) (2010), 91 Imm. L.R. (3d) 123, 219 C.R.R. (2d) 226, 17 Admin. L.R. (5th) 1, 374 F.T.R. 177 (Eng.), 2010 FC 957, 2010 CarswellNat 3438, 2010 CarswellNat 3439 — The applicant was found to be inadmissible to Canada. The decision was communicated by way of a letter from the Canadian High Commission in London. The applicants are groups and individuals who are involved in bringing the applicant to Canada for a speaking tour. His topics related to the wars in Iraq and in Afghanistan and to the situation in the Palestinian territories. As a matter of law, this application had to be dismissed. The applicant made the decision not to attempt to enter Canada because he might be detained. Consequently the respondents' intention and actions did not result in a reviewable decision to exclude him. There is therefore no decision which the court can review. These findings should not be taken as agreement with the respondents' position that there are reasonable grounds to believe that the applicant may be inadmissible pursuant to s. 34 of the Act.

In *obiter* the court indicated that it was under no illusions about the character of the organization in question, Hamas. But the evidence considered by the respondents fell far short of providing reasonable grounds to believe that the applicant was a member of that organization. It was clear that the efforts to keep the applicant out of the country had more to do with antipathy to his political views than with any real concern that he had engaged in terrorism or was a member of a terrorist organization. No consideration appeared to have been given to the interest of those Canadians who wished to hear the applicant speak or the values of freedom of expression and association enshrined in the *Canadian Charter of Rights and Freedoms*. The application for judicial review was dismissed. The following questions were certified:

1. With respect to a visa-exempt, foreign national who indicates a future intention to visit Canada, is a "preliminary assessment" of inadmissibility a decision, order, act or proceeding properly subject to judicial review in the Federal Court pursuant to s. 18.1 of the *Federal Courts Act*?

2. Does the voluntary contribution of cash and goods to an organization listed as a "terrorist entity" pursuant to the *Criminal Code*, without other acts or indicia of membership, constitute reasonable grounds to believe that the donor has engaged in a terrorist act or is a member of a terrorist organization so as to make the donor inadmissible on security grounds under section 34(1)(c) or (f) of IRPA?

Peer v. Canada (Minister of Citizenship & Immigration) (2010), 91 Imm. L.R. (3d) 17, 372 F.T.R. 28 (Eng.), 2010 FC 752, 2010 CarswellNat 3628, 2010 CarswellNat 2396; affirmed (2011), 96 Imm. L.R. (3d) 18, 2011 FCA 91, 2011 CarswellNat 1917, 2011 CarswellNat 575 — The record before the court, even without the evidence that the respondent had failed to properly enter into evidence, strongly supported a conclusion that the applicant was engaged in espionage against a democratic government, institution or process, specifically India, as well as Canada. The visa officer did not err in finding the applicant inadmissible for security reasons and rejecting his application for permanent resident visa.

The court certified the following question:

Is a person inadmissible to Canada for "engaging in an active espionage . . . against a democratic government, institution or process" within the meaning of subs. 34(1)(a) of the *Immigration Refugee Protection Act*, if the person's activities consist of intelligence gathering activities that are legal in the country where they take place, do not violate international law and where there is no evidence of hostile intent against the persons who are being observed?

Saleh v. Canada (Minister of Citizenship & Immigration), 2010 FC 303, 2010 CarswellNat 2930, 2010 CarswellNat 645 — The applicant sought judicial review of a decision of an immigration officer wherein the officer determined the applicant to be inadmissible pursuant to paragraphs 36(2)(a) and 34(1)(f) of IRPA by reason, in the case of the first citation, of the applicant's conviction in Canada on March 9, 2007, for theft under $5,000 and, in the case of the second citation, for being a member of the General Union of Palestinian Students (GUPS), and the Fatah faction of the Palestinian Liberation Organization (PLO) and the Popular Committee of the PLO, organizations in which, in the view of the decision-maker, there are reasonable grounds to believe engaged, have engaged, or will engage in acts of terrorism referred to in para. 34(1)(c) of IRPA. The officer concluded that the applicant had been a member of GUPS, the Fatah faction of the PLO and a Popular Committee of the PLO and this finding was not disputed. The officer concluded on the issue of "engaging in terrorism" that the applicant's limited activities in the GUPS, the Fatah faction of the PLO and the Popular Committee of the PLO, as a member of such organizations, constituted his membership in organizations that there are reasonable grounds to believe have engaged in terrorism.

The burden of jurisprudence of this court and the Federal Court of Appeal appears to be contrary to the applicant's position that mere formal membership should not inevitably constitute "membership" for the purposes of para. 34(1)(f) of IRPA. The Federal Court concluded "in short, if one is a 'member' then he or she is a 'member' for the purposes of para. 34(1)(f) with all the implications that membership carries with it and with relief, if warranted, lying in the discretion of a Minister of the Crown under subs. 34(2) of IRPA and not in the discretion of immigration officers or this court." Therefore, the decision of the officer was reasonably open to the officer in the sense that it demonstrates the existence of justification, transparency and intelligibility within the decision-making process and fell within a range of possible, acceptable outcomes which are defensible in respect of the facts underlying the matter and the applicable provisions of law. The application for judicial review was dismissed.

The following question was certified:

> Is formal membership in an organization that has engaged in acts of terrorism determinative of whether a person is to be considered inadmissible to Canada pursuant to paragraph 34(1)(f) of the *Immigration and Refugee Protection Act*?

Gebreab v. Canada (Minister of Public Safety & Emergency Preparedness) (2009), 85 Imm. L.R. (3d) 265, 359 F.T.R. 296 (Eng.), 2009 FC 1213, 2009 CarswellNat 5482, 2009 CarswellNat 3919 — This was an application for judicial review of the Immigration Division's decision pursuant to s. 44 of IRPA that the applicant was inadmissible to Canada pursuant to para. 34(1)(f) of IRPA for being a member of an organization in which there are reasonable grounds to believe engages, has engaged or will engage in the Acts referred to in paragraphs 34(1)(b) and (c), namely subversion by force of a government and terrorism. The applicant argued that the Board applied the wrong test for determining whether the Ethiopian Peoples' Revolutionary Party (EPRP), at the time the applicant was a member, was an organization that met the criteria of s. 34(1)(b) and (c). The court concluded that the decision in *Sittambalam* (2006), 56 Imm. L.R. (3d) 161 (Fed. C.A.), does not establish any "test" for the definition of an "organization." Instead the factors are considered to be helpful, but no one of them is essential. In any event, the factors also do not address the question of changes within an organization. The court in *Sittampalam* also favoured a broad interpretation of membership and organization — one that is not limited by temporal qualifications or changes in the organization. By finding that the EPRP is not an "organization" because at the time of the applicant's membership, it did not engage in acts of terrorism or subversion, the Board would, in effect, eliminate the words "they have occurred" from s. 33 and the words "has engaged" from s. 34(1)(f).

Having concluded that there were no required factors, the issue is whether the Board, in determining s. 37(1) issues, asked itself the right questions. In this case there was no question as to the applicant's membership in the EPRP and it was undisputed that the acts of the EPRP in the 1970s would meet the test for a terrorist or subversive organization as those terms are used in s. 34(1)(b) and (c) of IRPA. Therefore, the only issue before the Board dealt with the "organization" that called itself the EPRP in the 1970s and the "organization" that called itself the EPRP in the 1980s. The Board considered whether the organization the applicant belonged to in the 1980s was that of the 1970s, or whether there were two separate and different organizations that shared the same name. The Board correctly identified the question before it and correctly applied the test for determining whether the EPRP was an organization as contemplated by s. 34(1) of IRPA. The Board's finding of inadmissibility under s. 34(1)(f) was not unreasonable. Accordingly the application for judicial review was dismissed.

The Federal Court of Appeal in *Gebreab v. Canada (Minister of Public Safety & Emergency Preparedness)*, 2010 CarswellNat 4040 (Fed. C.A.), upheld Justice Sneider's decision and concluded that it was not a requirement for inadmissibility under s. 34(1)(f) of IRPA that the dates of an individual's membership in the organization correspond with the dates on which that organization committed acts of terrorism or subversion by force.

Toronto Coalition to Stop the War v. Canada (Minister of Public Safety & Emergency Preparedness) (2009), 80 Imm. L.R. (3d) 72, 2009 CarswellNat 775, 2009 FC 326 — The applicants brought a motion to seek an order of the Federal Court to permit a Mr. Galloway to enter Canada. Mr. Galloway was a British citizen and member of Parliament of the UK. He was to speak at a public forum entitled "Resisting War from Gaza to Kandahar," hosted by the Toronto Coalition to Stop the War.

Every person seeking to enter Canada must appear for an examination to determine whether the person has a right to enter Canada or is or may become authorized to enter and remain in Canada under subs. 18(1) of the IRPA. Mr. Galloway's personal views and open sympathies for the Palestinians and their cause became a matter of public record. An official of the High Commission of Canada, Immigration Section, by letter dated March 20, 2009, advised the applicant Galloway, apparently as a matter of "courtesy," that according to the "preliminary assessment" of the CBSA, he is inadmissible to Canada on security grounds pursuant to subs. 34 of the IRPA. Mr. Galloway was invited by the letter to make submissions and that a CBSA officer will make a final determination of admissibility based on this preliminary assessment and any submissions he may make should he present himself at a port of entry.

The court denied the applicant's request for an interim order or interlocutory injunction to enjoin the respondents and their officials from denying Mr. Galloway entry to Canada.

At one time, the court was reluctant to grant mandatory interlocutory injunctions but, over time, has been somewhat more willing to do so. Still, some greater level of caution arises when, particularly at an interlocutory stage, the court is asked to order somebody to take a positive action that will change the *status quo*. It is only in clear cases that mandatory injunction relief against the enforcement of a law will likely be granted by the court before a full hearing of the application for judicial review. In such instances, public interests and the relative strength of the parties' arguments are relevant factors to consider in the assessment of balance of convenience.

A fundamental principle of immigration law is that non-citizens do not have an unqualified right to enter Canada. The admission of a foreign national to this country is a privilege determined by statute, regulation or otherwise, and not a matter of right. In this respect, Parliament has expressly given the CBSA officers legal authority to exclusively determine whether a foreign national who seeks to enter this country is admissible (s. 15

and 18 of the Act). Yet there had been no final determination made by an officer with respect to the admission in Canada of Mr. Galloway.

The court was not prepared to exempt Mr. Galloway from the application of the provisions in the Act and Regulations respecting entry and examination, or to order the respondents' officials to allow him to come to Canada, without any final decision made on his admissibility.

Daud v. Canada (Minister of Citizenship & Immigration), 2008 CarswellNat 1800, 2008 FC 701 — This was an application for leave for judicial review of a decision by an immigration officer in which the applicant was found to be inadmissible for permanent residence by reason of being a member of a terrorist organization pursuant to s. 34(1)(f) of the Act. The crux of the present case involves determining whether the officer committed a reviewable error when he concluded that the applicant was inadmissible on security grounds for being a member of a terrorist organization. Since the applicant was granted refugee status and thus was found to face persecution should he be returned to Pakistan, any subsequent finding of inadmissibility should be carried out with prudence, and established with the outmost clarity. Given the applicant admitted to being a member of the MQM-A organization, the court was to review the officer's determination that the MQM-A is "an organization that there are reasonable grounds to believe engages, has engaged or will engage in acts referred to in para. (a), (b), or (c)" (s. 34(1)(f) of the Act). The assessment of whether there are reasonable grounds to believe that an organization has engaged in acts of terrorism is a two-step analysis. The first step involves a factual determination of whether there are reasonable grounds to believe that the organization in question committed the acts of violence attributed to it. At the second step of the analysis, a determination is made as to whether those constitute acts of terrorism. The officer must provide the definition of terrorism relied upon and explain how the listed acts meet that definition.

Given the evidence before the officer, the court was unable to conclude that the officer's determination that MQM-A committed violent acts, including murder and torture, was unreasonable.

The existence of general violence does not preclude a determination that an organization engages in terrorism. The existence of generalized violence is part of the context within which the officer conducts his analysis, but it is not dispositive of the end determination. Indeed, terrorist acts are committed during an array of country conditions ranging from periods of relative peace to those of widespread strife and conflict. In this case the officer made reference to s. 83.01 of the *Criminal Code*, as well as the annexed list of treaties to the United Nations Convention for the Suppression of the Financing of Terrorism as fundamental guidelines in his analysis. Furthermore, he reproduced the definition of terrorism provided by the Supreme Court of Canada in *Suresh v. Canada (Minister of Citizenship & Immigration)*, [2002] 1 S.C.R. 3. The court was unable to conclude that the officer's analysis with respect to the second step was unreasonable. To the contrary, the "decision fell within a range of possible, acceptable outcomes which are defensible in respect of the facts in law." The application for judicial review was dismissed.

Mekonen v. Canada (Minister of Citizenship & Immigration) (2008), 66 Imm. L.R. (3d) 222, 2007 CarswellNat 3655, 2007 FC 1133 — The applicant brought an application for judicial review of a decision of a visa officer that, as a member of the Eritrean Liberation Front ("ELF"), the applicant was captured by para. 34(1)(f) of the IRPA, and therefore was inadmissible to Canada. The court found that the officer should have provided the applicant with a CBSA memorandum and an open source document, to allow him to make submissions that were responsive to that material. The court adopted the Federal Court of Appeal decision in *B. (S.) v. Canada (Minister of Citizenship & Immigration)*, 2001 CarswellNat 2008, that the question is not whether the report is or contains extrinsic evidence of facts unknown to the person affected by the decision, but whether the disclosure of the report is required to provide the person with a reasonable opportunity to participate in a meaningful manner in the decision-making process. In this case, meaningful participation included the right to highlight weaknesses in the material before the officer. Because the officer breached the duty of procedural fairness, the application for judicial review was allowed.

Jalil v. Canada (Minister of Citizenship & Immigration), 2007 CarswellNat 1440, 2007 FC 568 — While there is no legal requirement that there be evidence that an organization sanctioned or approved the terrorist acts, in making an assessment under paragraphs 34(1)(f) of the Act, an immigration officer must determine whether there is enough evidence to establish that the organization sanctions the acts.

Golestaneh v. Canada (Minister of Public Safety & Emergency Preparedness), 2007 CarswellNat 1233, 2007 FC 509 — Pursuant to subs. 44(1) of IRPA an enforcement officer at the Canadian Border Services Agency prepared a report alleging that the applicant was inadmissible, as per paragraphs 34(1)(f) and 35(1)(a) of the Act, by reason of his involvement with a listed terrorist entity in Canada. The report prepared by the enforcement officer was referred by the Minister of Public Safety and Emergency Preparedness to the Immigration Division of the Immigration Refugee Board for an admissibility hearing. The applicant sought judicial review of the decisions made under subs. 44(1) and 44(2) of the Act.

The enforcement officer did not have access to the documentation supporting the security intelligence report prepared by the Canadian Security Intelligence Services (CSIS). The enforcement officer's decision was limited to reading the report itself. This alone was a serious error of law that justified setting aside the decision of the enforcement officer. Although the CSIS document may set out precisely the grounds on inadmissibility of the applicant, the officer who must decide whether to issue a subs. 44(1) report has a duty, when examining the file for the first time, to consult all of the reference documents, including the appendices to the CSIS report and the information on the sources underlying this report, before making a decision. This is necessary in order to ensure that the procedure followed will sufficiently guarantee the independence of the decision maker and thus protect the rights of the individual concerned.

The decision of the enforcement officer to prepare a report for the Minister, and the subsequent decision by the Minister to refer the report to the Immigration Division for an admissibility hearing, was set aside and the file was referred back to a different enforcement officer for re-determination.

Oremade v. Canada (Minister of Citizenship & Immigration) (2005), [2006] 1 F.C.R. 393, 2005 CarswellNat 2211, 2005 CarswellNat 2942, 2005 FC 1077 — For purposes of para. 34(1)(b) of the IRPA, the permanent resident or foreign national has to have the intention of actually using force in subverting a government. Given the context in which the words "by force" appear, the intention to subvert by force, rather than by some other means, is critical to the applicability of para. 34(1)(b). However, this intent to subvert by force is not to be measured solely from the subjective perspective of the applicant. It may well be that there was a hope or expectation that the coup would be bloodless but it is also reasonable for persons on the street to assume, upon seeing armed soldiers occupying lands and buildings, that force could or would be used if thought necessary. The use of force in the subversion must be more than an accident: it must be the intended means by which to affect the overthrow of the government. It is the Board's function to weigh all the subjective and objective evidence related to the impugned act. Subjective intent is but one element, albeit, in assessing all of the evidence of intent, it is appropriate to presume that a person knows or ought to have known and to have intended the natural consequences of their action.

Poshteh v. Canada (Minister of Citizenship & Immigration) (2005), 331 N.R. 129, 252 D.L.R. (4th) 316, 2005 CarswellNat 564, 2005 CarswellNat 2047, 2005 FCA 85, [2005] F.C.J. No. 381; reconsideration refused 2005 CarswellNat 949, 332 N.R. 374, 252 D.L.R. (4th) 335, 2005 FCA 121 — Under subs. 34(2) of IRPA, membership in a terrorist organization does not constitute inadmissibility if the individual in question satisfies the Minister that their presence in Canada would not be detrimental to the national interest. The court was satisfied that the term "member," under the Act, should continue to be interpreted broadly due to the fact that the Minister has the discretion to exclude an individual from the operation of s. 34. There is no blanket exemption for minors from the provisions of s. 34. An individual status as a minor is still relevant under para. 34(1)(f). It would be highly unusual for there to be a finding of membership in the case of a young child, say under the age of 12. Although it would depend on the evidence in each case, it would seem self evident that in the case of such children, the presumption would be that they do not possess the requisite knowledge or mental capacity to understand the nature and effect of their actions. In the case of young children, the age of the child itself would be *prima facie* evidence of an absence of the requisite knowledge or mental capacity. At common law there was an irrebuttable presumption that a child under the age of seven was incapable of possessing a criminal intent. Once a child reached the age of fourteen, the common law presumption of criminal incapacity disappeared and was replaced by a rebuttable presumption of capacity for criminal intent. For the purpose of determining membership in a terrorist organization by a minor, the requisite knowledge or mental capacity should be viewed on a continuum. Just as there would be a presumption against the requisite knowledge or mental capacity in the case of young children, there would be a presumption that the closer the minor is to eighteen years, the greater will be the likelihood that the minor possesses the requisite knowledge or mental capacity. It is open to the minor to raise issues of duress or coercion although those particular issues did not arise on the facts of this case. It would be very difficult for a minor to argue that he should not be found to be a member of a terrorist organization if he had been directly involved in violent activities or had held a leadership role in the terrorist organization. Matters such as knowledge or mental capacity are the types of considerations to be taken into account in deciding whether a determination of membership in a terrorist organization in the case of a minor is to be different than in the case of an adult.

[Editor's note: Although s. 34(2) was repealed on June 19, 2013, this case may still be of some relevance here.]

Abdolkhaleghi v. Canada (Minister of Citizenship & Immigration) (2005), 46 Imm. L.R. (3d) 19, 2005 CarswellNat 1601, 2005 FC 729 — The applicants sought an order of *mandamus*. Their applications for permanent residence were not being processed because the respondent was waiting for the results of security checks being conducted by CSIS. The fact of an ongoing investigation by CSIS is not an absolute bar to ordering *mandamus*. If there is a long delay without adequate explanation, then *mandamus* can follow. To simply state, in response to the applicants' requests for information respecting the length of time it was taking to process their applications, that a security investigation by CSIS is ongoing, is not an adequate explanation. A blanket statement to the effect that a security check investigation is pending, prevents an analysis of the adequacy of the explanation. For security reasons, immigration authorities may not think it appropriate to disclose or provide more detailed information about why the security checks are taking so long. This concern can be addressed in the *mandamus* order itself, by providing the respondent with an opportunity to return to court for an extension of time within which to process the application.

Ali v. Canada (Minister of Citizenship & Immigration) (2004), 42 Imm. L.R. (3d) 237, 2004 CarswellNat 4035, 2004 CarswellNat 2940, 2004 FC 1174 — Judicial review does lie from a decision of an immigration officer made pursuant to subs. 34(1). It is appropriate for the court to entertain an application for judicial review notwithstanding that an application for Ministerial relief under subs. 34(2) is pending.

35. (1) Human or international rights violations — A permanent resident or a foreign national is inadmissible on grounds of violating human or international rights for

(a) committing an act outside Canada that constitutes an offence referred to in sections 4 to 7 of the *Crimes Against Humanity and War Crimes Act*;

(b) being a prescribed senior official in the service of a government that, in the opinion of the Minister, engages or has engaged in terrorism, systematic or gross human rights violations, or genocide, a war crime or a crime against humanity within the meaning of subsections 6(3) to (5) of the *Crimes Against Humanity and War Crimes Act*; or

(c) being a person, other than a permanent resident, whose entry into or stay in Canada is restricted pursuant to a decision, resolution or measure of an international organization of states or association of states, of which Canada is a member, that imposes sanctions on a country against which Canada has imposed or has agreed to impose sanctions in concert with that organization or association.

(2) [Repealed 2013, c. 16, s. 14.]

[Editor's Note: SOR/2002-227, s. 320(2) provides that a person is inadmissible under the new Immigration and Refugee Protection Act, *S.C. 2001, c. 27 on grounds of violating human or international rights if, on June 28, 2002, the person had been determined to be a member of an inadmissible class described in paragraph 19(1)(j) or (l) of the former* Immigration Act, *R.S.C. 1985, c. I-2.]*

2013, c. 16, s. 14

Case Law

Concepcion v. Canada (Minister of Citizenship and Immigration), 2016 FC 544, 2016 CarswellNat 1603, 2016 CarswellNat 3053 — The applicant wished to sponsor her husband for permanent residence in Canada. He currently resides in the Philippines. A visa officer found him to be inadmissible to Canada for having committed crimes against humanity when he served as a radio operator in the Philippine Army. The test for inadmissibility under s. 35(1)(a) requires serious reasons for considering that a person has voluntarily made a significant and knowing contribution to an offence contrary to the *Crimes Against Humanity and War Crimes Act*, or to a group's criminal purpose. The Minister maintained that the officer made no error in applying the test in *Ramirez v. Canada (Minister of Employment & Immigration)*, [1992] 2 F.C. 306, as it amounts, in substance, to the same standard articulated and applied by the Supreme Court of Canada in *Ezokola v. Canada (Minister of Citizenship and Immigration)*, [2013] 2 S.C.R. 678. While there were many common elements in *Ramirez* and *Ezokola*, there are also, significant differences. Specifically, in *Ezokola*, the Supreme Court explicitly departed from the concept of complicity by association (a notion that derives not from *Ramirez* itself, but from its progeny; See, *e.g*, *Sivakumar v. Canada (Minister of Employment & Immigration)*, [1994] 1 F.C. 433 at para 9). The test now requires proof of a significant contribution to an international crime. The Minister maintained that the test was met in this case by evidence showing that the applicant's husband made a "voluntary, significant and knowing contribution to the Philippines Military for many years when it was committing atrocities." This is not the proper test. The evidence must show, at least, that the person made a significant contribution to a crime or the organization's criminal purpose, not just a contribution to the organization. In this case, the officer found that an association with an international crime group would amount to complicity if the person knew about and acquiesced in the group's activities. That standard can no longer be applied after *Ezokola*, which requires evidence that a person made a significant contribution to a crime or a group's criminal purpose. The officer should have applied the principles of liability set out in *Ezokola*. Failure to do so amounted to an error of law. The judicial review was allowed.

Segasayo v. Canada (Minister of Citizenship & Immigration) (2010), 89 Imm. L.R. (3d) 7, 2010 FC 173, 2010 CarswellNat 323, 2010 CarswellNat 324 — The applicant was Rwanda's ambassador to Canada from 1991 to 1995. After the new government in Rwanda recalled him, he and his family applied for and were given refugee status by the Immigration and Refugee Board in 1996. He submitted that as a member of the Hutu intelligentsia and as ambassador to Canada appointed by the former government he feared persecution and reprisal by the new Tutsi government. He is now subject to a deportation order because he was found inadmissible to Canada for violating human or international rights. He sought judicial review of that decision. The Board determined that the applicant was a person described in s. 35(1)(a) of IRPA. The member was of the view that the deeming provision in s. 16 of the Regulations created an irrebuttable presumption that an ambassador in the service of a government on the Minister's list was inadmissible on the grounds of violating human or international rights. In other words, once it was shown that the applicant was the ambassador of the government designated by the Minister (facts that the applicant had never disputed), then he was inadmissible and had no defence based on lack of complicity in crimes against humanity or human rights violations. The member also dismissed the argument that the provisions in question were unconstitutional as violating s. 7 of the *Canadian Charter of Rights and Freedoms*. The court upheld the Board's decision that the applicant was inadmissible, dismissed his *Charter* argument and dismissed the application for judicial review

The following question was certified:

> Are ss. 35(1) of the *Immigration and Refugee Protection Act* and 16 of the *Immigration and Refugee Protection Regulations* in accordance with the principles stated by the Supreme Court in *Singh v. Canada (Minister of Citizenship & Immigration)*, [1985] 1 S.C.R. 177 and *Charkaoui v. Canada (Citizenship & Immi-*

gration) (2007), 59 Imm. L.R. (3d) 1, and with s. 7 of the *Canadian Charter of Rights and Freedoms* when a person targeted by those provisions had already obtained the refugee or protective person status and does not have the right to defend him/herself against the allegations made against him/her under those provisions?

Varela v. Canada (Minister of Citizenship & Immigration) (2009), 80 Imm. L.R. (3d) 1, 2009 CarswellNat 1228, 2009 FCA 145; affirming (2008), 72 Imm. L.R. (3d) 236, [2009] 1 F.C.R. 605, 2008 FC 436, 2008 CarswellNat 928, 2008 CarswellNat 2790, [2008] F.C.J. No. 568 — This was a judicial review of a decision of the Immigration and Refugee Board which held that the applicant had violated human or international rights for having committed an act outside Canada that constituted an offence referred to in ss. 4 to 7 of the *Crimes Against Humanity and War Crimes Act*, S.C. 2000, c. 24. Section 36 of the IRPA specifically provides that inadmissibility on the grounds of serious criminality may not be based on a conviction in respect of which a pardon has been granted, or if there has been a final acquittal. Furthermore, rehabilitation is taken into account. Although s. 35, which deals with war crimes and crimes against humanity, is silent on these matters, given the international context of the case, the United Nations Guidelines cannot simply be ignored. The applicant's participation in a death squad and in the treatment of prisoners was so grave and heinous that as a matter of law the full application of s. 35 of the IRPA cannot be mitigated.

The Federal Court of Appeal determined it was not necessary to send this matter back for a new determination, as there was only one legal conclusion open to the Board. It would be a waste of resources to start the whole matter over on what is an included offence, as murder is certainly a serious crime, even if other requirements of a crime against humanity, or a war crime, were not met.

Although several questions were certified, the Federal Court of Appeal concluded there were no serious questions of general importance and dismissed the appeal.

Golestaneh v. Canada (Minister of Public Safety & Emergency Preparedness), 2007 CarswellNat 1233, 2007 FC 509 — Pursuant to subs. 44(1) of IRPA an enforcement officer at the Canadian Border Services Agency prepared a report alleging that the applicant was inadmissible, as per paragraphs 34(1)(f) and 35(1)(a) of the Act, by reason of his involvement with a listed terrorist entity in Canada. The report prepared by the enforcement officer was referred by the Minister of Public Safety and Emergency Preparedness to the Immigration Division of the Immigration Refugee Board for an admissibility hearing. The applicant sought judicial review of the decisions made under subs. 44(1) and 44(2) of the Act.

The enforcement officer did not have access to the documentation supporting the security intelligence report prepared by the Canadian Security Intelligence Services (CSIS). The enforcement officer's decision was limited to reading the report itself. This alone was a serious error of law that justified setting aside the decision of the enforcement officer. Although the CSIS document may set out precisely the grounds on inadmissibility of the applicant, the officer who must decide whether to issue a subs. 44(1) report has a duty, when examining the file for the first time, to consult all of the reference documents, including the appendices to the CSIS report and the information on the sources underlying this report, before making a decision. This is necessary in order to ensure that the procedure followed will sufficiently guarantee the independence of the decision maker and thus protect the rights of the individual concerned.

The decision of the enforcement officer to prepare a report for the Minister, and the subsequent decision by the Minister to refer the report to the Immigration Division for an admissibility hearing, was set aside and the file was referred back to a different enforcement officer for re-determination.

Beltran Velasquez v. Canada (Minister of Citizenship & Immigration), 2006 CarswellNat 2616, 2006 FC 1024 — A decision to deny the applicant a visa to enter Canada as a permanent resident was set aside, since the officer did not give notice of concerns respecting the nature and scope of the applicant's activities nor was the applicant given a reasonable opportunity to respond. Specifically, the visa officer concluded that the applicant was involved or complicit in crimes against humanity following disclosure by the applicant during a telephone interview that he was with Mobile Brigade #2 in a particular location in Colombia in October 1992. The applicant was never confronted with the opinion formed, and was never asked questions as to what he was doing or what others known to him were doing at the relevant time or place. The visa officer concluded he was inadmissible under subs. 35(1)(a) of the IRPA.

Perez v. Canada (Minister of Citizenship & Immigration) (2006), 55 Imm. L.R. (3d) 227, 2006 CarswellNat 2610, 2006 FC 1000 — The applicant's wife applied to sponsor the applicant, but the sponsorship was refused by a visa officer on the basis that there were reasonable grounds to believe that the applicant was inadmissible pursuant to s. 35(1)(a) of the IRPA for having violated human or international rights "by committing an act outside Canada that constitutes an offence referred to in ss. 4 to 7 of the *Crimes Against Humanity and War Crimes Act*." Although the Minister conceded that the visa officer had failed to observe principles of natural justice in rendering the decision and that consequently the matter should be sent back for re-determination, the applicant argued that the visa officer was precluded from re-examining the issue of inadmissibility pursuant to s. 35(1)(a) of the IRPA by virtue of the doctrine of *res judicata*, as an earlier binding, final decision on the issue had already been rendered in 1997. In 1997 the applicant, in the context of a refugee claim, stated that he had been a member of a Guatemalan death squad and an adjudicator held that the applicant was not inadmissible under s. 19(1)(j) of the then applicable , as there were no reasonable grounds to believe that the applicant committed an offence referred to in any of ss. 4 to 7 of the *Crimes Against Humanity and War Crimes Act*. The applicant argued that there was no new relevant evidence before the visa officer and therefore, the visa officer erred both by re-examining the issue of inadmissibility, and by reaching the unsustainable conclusion that the applicant is inadmissible.

Section 34 of the former *Immigration Act* clearly excludes res judicata in the specific context of s. 27 of the Act. Accordingly, s. 34 of the former *Immigration Act* makes it abundantly clear that the adjudicator's decision was not a final decision regarding inadmissibility. The applicant argued in the alternative that if inadmissibility could be examined, then the visa officer made his inadmissibility finding without proper regard to relevant evidence by failing to consider the adjudicator's finding that the applicant was not inadmissible for war crimes or crimes against humanity. The court agreed with this argument and quashed the visa officer's decision, sending the matter back for a new hearing before a new visa officer and directing that the new visa officer, in rendering his or her decision, must consider all the facts and evidence of this case, including the adjudicator's decision of May 29, 1997.

Mugesera c. Canada (Ministre de la Citoyenneté & de l'Immigration), [2005] 2 S.C.R. 91, 47 Imm. L.R. (3d) 1, EYB 2005-91970, [2005] S.C.J. No. 40, 197 C.C.C. (3d) 225,

254 D.L.R. (4th) 193, 30 C.R. (6th) 107, 335 N.R. 220, 15 C.P.C. (6th) 51, 2005 Car-swellNat 1738, 2005 CarswellNat 1739, 2005 SCC 39 — At the secondary level of appellate review, the Federal Court of Appeal should proceed with the review of the Minister's allegations on the basis of the facts as found by the Immigration Appeal Division. On questions of law, however, the standard of review is correctness and the Immigration Appeal Division is not entitled to deference when it comes to defining the elements of a crime or whether the Minister's burden of proof has been discharged. Where the Minister relies on a crime committed abroad, a conclusion that the elements of the crime in Canadian criminal law had been made out will be deemed to be determinative in respect of the commission of crimes under the foreign criminal law. With respect to the specific allegations made pursuant to s. 27(1) of the former *Immigration Act*, the evidence adduced by the Minister must meet the civil standard of the balance of probabilities. The appellant, an active member of a hard-line Hutu political party opposed to a negotiation process then under way to end the war, spoke to about 1,000 people at a meeting of the party in Rwanda. The content of the speech eventually led the Rwandan authorities to issue the equivalent of an arrest warrant against the appellant. He fled the country and successfully applied for permanent residence in Canada. After the immigrant landed in Canada, the Minister became aware of allegations against him and commenced proceeding to deport him, on the basis that he committed criminal acts or offences. Specifically, the issue was whether a speech delivered by the appellant in Rwanda triggered a series of events that led to murder, hatred and genocide. In this case, the Minister had to prove that, on the facts of the case as found on a balance of probabilities, the speech constituted an incitement to murder, genocide or hatred. The Supreme Court of Canada upheld the validity of the deportation order on the basis that each element of the offence under the *Criminal Code* had been made out and that there were reasonable grounds to believe that the immigrant committed a crime against humanity and was therefore inadmissible under the former *Immigration Act*. The "reasonable grounds to believe" standard requires more than mere suspicion, but less than the normal civil litigation standard of proof on the balance of probabilities.

Zazai v. Canada (Minister of Citizenship & Immigration) (2005), 50 Imm. L.R. (3d) 107, 259 D.L.R. (4th) 281, 339 N.R. 201, [2005] F.C.J. No. 1567, 2005 CarswellNat 2933, 2005 CarswellNat 4771, 2005 FCA 303 — The appellant came to Canada as a stowaway and made a refugee claim. The Refugee Board determined that he was excluded from the definition of Convention refugee under subs. 2(1) of the *Immigration Act*, R.S.C. 1985, because of section F(a) of Article 1 of the United Nations Convention relating to the status of refugees. The Board found that there were serious reasons for considering that he had committed crimes against humanity. His application for leave with respect to the Refugee Board's decision was denied. He subsequently submitted an application for landing as a post-determination refugee claimant in Canada. A report under s. 27(2) of the former Act was prepared and a s. 27(3) direction for inquiry was issued. The inquiry was held before an adjudicator who concluded that the appellant was a person described in para. 27(2)(a) coupled with para. 19(1)(j) of the former Act. As a result, the adjudicator determined that he was subject to a deportation order. The appellant successfully sought leave to apply for judicial review of the adjudicator's decision. The Federal Court Trial Division allowed the application and the Minister appealed. The appeal to the Federal Court of Appeal was allowed and the order of the applications judge was set aside and remitted back to the Federal Court for re-determination.

The Federal Court of Appeal concluded that the definition of "crime against humanity" found at subs. 6(3) of the *Crimes Against Humanity and War Crimes Act* includes complicity.

As a matter of fact, as found by the adjudicator and agreed by the reviewing judge, there was sufficient cogent evidence that the appellant was, knowingly and voluntarily, a participating and active member for five years in a secret service organization within the Ministry of State Security known as KHAD that tortured and eliminated people who were against the government. The evidence revealed that the appellant entered as a lieutenant and rose to the level of captain. Not only did he share and espouse the views of the brutal organization, he attended training sessions and provided the names of those who did not cooperate.

According to the evidence, the appellant was willingly and to his benefit a member of an organization that only existed for a limited brutal purpose. Under both Canadian and international jurisprudence, the behaviour of the appellant amounted to complicity in the commission of crimes against humanity. Consequently, the Federal Court judge properly confirmed the decision of the adjudicator that the appellant was inadmissible pursuant to para. 19(1)(j) of the former Act or para. 35(1)(a) of the new Act.

The Supreme Court's decision in *Mugesera v. Canada (Minister of Citizenship & Immigration)*, [2005] S.C.J. No. 39, was distinguished on the basis that the Supreme Court in that case was not confronted with an issue of complicity in the commission of a crime by someone else. In that case Mr. Mugesera was the actual perpetrator. Complicity is not a crime at common law and under Canadian criminal law, it was, and still is, a mode of commission of a crime. It refers to the act or omission of a person who helps, or is done for the purpose of helping, the furtherance of a crime. An accomplice is then charged with, and tried for, the crime that was actually committed and that he assisted or furthered. In other words whether one looks at it from the perspective of our domestic law or of international law, complicity contemplates a contribution to the commission of a crime. Complicity must not be confused with the inchoate crimes of conspiracy, attempt and incitement to commit a crime. Unlike complicity, they are not modes or means of committing a crime.

Matti v. Canada (Minister of Citizenship & Immigration), 2005 CarswellNat 3799, 2005 CarswellNat 4785, 2005 FC 1561 — The visa officer refused the applicant's application for permanent residence on the basis that there were reasonable grounds to believe that the applicant, by his denial and silence with respect to certain facts based on evidence, was complicit in crimes against humanity. Although denial and silence are valid reasons for questioning credibility, they do not amount to evidence of complicity in crimes against humanity. Whether one is complicit will depend on the facts of the case, particularly the extent of knowledge of an organization's crimes and the degree of participation in or support of those crimes.

36. (1) Serious criminality — A permanent resident or a foreign national is inadmissible on grounds of serious criminality for

> **(a) having been convicted in Canada of an offence under an Act of Parliament punishable by a maximum term of imprisonment of at least 10 years, or of an offence under an Act of Parliament for which a term of imprisonment of more than six months has been imposed;**

(b) having been convicted of an offence outside Canada that, if committed in Canada, would constitute an offence under an Act of Parliament punishable by a maximum term of imprisonment of at least 10 years; or

(c) committing an act outside Canada that is an offence in the place where it was committed and that, if committed in Canada, would constitute an offence under an Act of Parliament punishable by a maximum term of imprisonment of at least 10 years.

[Editor's Note: SOR/2002-227, s. 320(3) provides that a person is inadmissible under the Immigration and Refugee Protection Act, *S.C. 2001, c. 27 (the "new Act") on grounds of serious criminality if, on June 28, 2002, the person had been determined to be a member of an inadmissible class described in paragraph 19(1)(c) or (c.1) of the* Immigration Act, *R.S.C. 1985, c. I-2 (the "former Act") or had been determined to be inadmissible on the basis of paragraph 27(1)(a.1) of the former Act.*

SOR/2002-227, s. 320(5)(a) provides that a person who on June 28, 2002 had been determined to be inadmissible on the basis of paragraph 27(1)(d) of the former Act is inadmissible under the new Act on grounds of serious criminality if the person was convicted of an offence and a term of imprisonment of more than six months has been imposed or a term of imprisonment of 10 years or more could have been imposed.]

(2) Criminality — **A foreign national is inadmissible on grounds of criminality for**

(a) having been convicted in Canada of an offence under an Act of Parliament punishable by way of indictment, or of two offences under any Act of Parliament not arising out of a single occurrence;

(b) having been convicted outside Canada of an offence that, if committed in Canada, would constitute an indictable offence under an Act of Parliament, or of two offences not arising out of a single occurrence that, if committed in Canada, would constitute offences under an Act of Parliament;

(c) committing an act outside Canada that is an offence in the place where it was committed and that, if committed in Canada, would constitute an indictable offence under an Act of Parliament; or

(d) committing, on entering Canada, an offence under an Act of Parliament prescribed by regulations.

[Editor's Note: SOR/2002-227, s. 320(4) provides that a person is inadmissible under the Immigration and Refugee Protection Act, *S.C. 2001, c. 27 (the "new Act") on grounds of criminality if, on June 28, 2002, the person had been determined to be a member of an inadmissible class described in paragraph 19(2)(a), (a.1) or (b) of the* Immigration Act, *R.S.C. 1985, c. I-2 (the "former Act"), or had been determined to be inadmissible on the basis of paragraph 27(1)(a.2) or (a.3) or (2)(d) of the former Act.*

SOR/2002-227, s. 320(5)(b) further provides that a person who on June 28, 2002 had been determined to be inadmissible under the new Act on the basis of paragraph 27(1)(d) of the former Act is inadmissible under the new Act on grounds of criminality if the offence was punishable by a maximum term of imprisonment of five years or more but less than 10 years.]

(3) Application — The following provisions govern subsections (1) and (2):

(a) an offence that may be prosecuted either summarily or by way of indictment is deemed to be an indictable offence, even if it has been prosecuted summarily;

(b) inadmissibility under subsections (1) and (2) may not be based on a conviction in respect of which a record suspension has been ordered and has not been revoked or ceased to have effect under the *Criminal Records Act*, or in respect of which there has been a final determination of an acquittal;

(c) the matters referred to in paragraphs (1)(b) and (c) and (2)(b) and (c) do not constitute inadmissibility in respect of a permanent resident or foreign national who, after the prescribed period, satisfies the Minister that they have been rehabilitated or who is a member of a prescribed class that is deemed to have been rehabilitated;

(d) a determination of whether a permanent resident has committed an act described in paragraph (1)(c) must be based on a balance of probabilities; and

(e) inadmissibility under subsections (1) and (2) may not be based on an offence

(i) designated as a contravention under the *Contraventions Act*,

(ii) for which the permanent resident or foreign national is found guilty under the *Young Offenders Act*, chapter Y-1 of the Revised Statutes of Canada, 1985, or

(iii) for which the permanent resident or foreign national received a youth sentence under the *Youth Criminal Justice Act*.

2008, c. 3, s. 3; 2010, c. 8, s. 7; 2012, c. 1, s. 149

Case Law

Section 36(1)

Tran v. Canada (Minister of Public Safety and Emergency Preparedness) (2014), 31 Imm. L.R. (4th) 160, 2014 FC 1040, 2014 CarswellNat 4405, 2014 CarswellNat 4866; additional reasons 2014 CarswellNat 8412, 2015 FC 899; reversed (2015), 38 Imm. L.R. (4th) 175, [2016] 2 F.C.R. 459, 392 D.L.R. (4th) 351, 478 N.R. 165, 2015 FCA 237, 2015 CarswellNat 5677, 2015 CarswellNat 9252; leave to appeal to S.C.C. allowed 2016 CarswellNat 1065 (S.C.C.) — The applicant became a permanent resident in 1989. In 2013, he was convicted of a charge of producing marijuana and the court imposed a sentence of 12 months to be served in the community (i.e. a conditional sentence). A Canadian Border Services Agency officer referred the applicant's file to the Immigration Division to decide whether he should be found to be inadmissible for having been convicted of an offence for which a term of imprisonment greater than six months had been imposed, or an offence punishable by a maximum term of imprisonment of at least 10 years under s. 36(1)(a) of IRPA. The Federal Court agreed that the applicant's conditional sentence of 12 months did not represent a term of imprisonment greater than six months; that his offence was punishable by a maximum of seven years' incarceration (not 10 or more); and that the officer should not have considered allegations that did not result in convictions. The application for judicial review was allowed.

The Federal Court of Appeal considered whether a conditional sentence of imprisonment imposed pursuant to the regime set out in ss. 742 to 742.7 of the *Criminal Code* was "a term of imprisonment" under s. 36(1)(a) of the IRPA and whether the phrase "punishable by a maximum term of imprisonment of at least ten years" in s. 36(1)(a) of the IRPA refers to the maximum term of imprisonment available at the time the person was sentenced or to the maximum term of imprisonment under the law in force at the time admissibility is determined. The Federal Court of Appeal also considered whether the decision of the officer was unreasonable because he relied in part on unproven allegations — arrests, charges and police reports. The Federal Court of Appeal concluded that the phrase "punishable by a maximum term of imprisonment of at least ten years" in para. 36(1)(a) of the IRPA can reasonably be interpreted as the maximum term of imprisonment under the law in force at the time admissibility is determined. The Court of Appeal also concluded that a conditional sentence of imprisonment imposed pursuant to the regime set out in ss. 742 to 742.7 of the *Criminal Code* may reasonably be construed as a term of imprisonment under para. 36(1)(a) of the IRPA. The interpretation adopted by the Minister's delegate was not unreasonable. Obviously the deference granted to administrative decision makers is in part meant to give them flexibility to adjust to new arguments and circumstances. It is thus obviously open to the ID and the IAD to adopt another interpretation should they believe that it is warranted by the inconsistent consequences, such as potential unfairness of precluding appeals for those on whom a conditional sentence of imprisonment of more than six months had been imposed, whereas those on whom jail terms of lesser lengths were imposed were not so precluded, even though these punitive measures are considered equivalent or harsher.

Finally, the court concluded that the officer was well aware of the distinction between arrests, stayed charges and criminal convictions and felt that he could consider this information, as well as the information contained in the police reports, for his broader assessment of the appellant's behaviour and rehabilitation prospects. The court agreed with the officer that he was entitled to consider the information to assess whether certain statements made by the appellant, such as that his behaviour was pristine for a long period before his two convictions and whether he was taking full responsibility for his past behaviour.

The decision to refer the appellant to the ID was within the range of outcomes defensible on the law and the facts. The appeal was allowed.

Wang v. Canada (Minister of Citizenship & Immigration), 2011 FC 1510, 2011 CarswellNat 5444, 2011 CarswellNat 6043, [2011] F.C.J. No. 1832 — The Canadian wife's application to sponsor the applicant was put on hold pending the determination of whether there were reasonable grounds to believe that he was inadmissible to Canada under para. 36(1)(b) of IRPA. The Immigration Appeal Division found that the applicant was inadmissible as he had been convicted of an offence outside Canada that, if committed in Canada, would constitute an offence punishable by a maximum term of imprisonment of at least 10 years. He sought judicial review of this decision, asserting that the Board erred in its equivalency analysis.

The law does not require that offences be identical in every aspect. What is required is "essentially the similarity of definitions of offences." In this case, the definition of the degree of injury required in the two offences was sufficiently similar as to render the offences equivalent for the purposes of a s. 36 analysis. If anything, the "serious physical injury" element of the New York Penal Code offence is more onerous than the "bodily harm" of the Canadian offence. That is, harm that qualifies as the "serious physical injury" for the purposes of the *NYPC* offence would necessarily qualify as "bodily harm" for the purposes of s. 267 of the Criminal Code. The Board did not err as alleged. The application for judicial review was dismissed.

See *Farenas* (2011), 391 F.T.R. 60, 2011 FC 660, 2011 CarswellNat 2104, [2011] F.C.J. No. 833, under s. 40(1) of IRPA.

Bankole v. Canada (Minister of Citizenship & Immigration), 2011 FC 373, 2011 CarswellNat 985, 2011 CarswellNat 1796 — An officer denied the applicant's application for permanent residence on the basis that he was inadmissible pursuant to para. 36(1)(c) of the Act. The applicant was stopped at Pearson International Airport in Toronto returning from the Bahamas, allegedly escorting an undocumented person, Mr. Prince Sarumi. The applicant alleged that he had only just met Mr. Sarumi, but an address book attributed to the applicant was found containing Mr. Sarumi's contact information in several locations. The applicant alleged that this address book did not belong to him. Charges were laid against the applicant for counseling/abetting a person to misrepresent a matter to induce error in the administration of the Act, contrary to s. 126. Reports were made pursuant to s. 44 of the Act. The charges were ultimately dropped and the applicant submitted a Provincial Court document to Canadian Border Services Agency indicating as much. As a result of this, the applicant's application for permanent residence was referred to a local CIC office for further investigation.

The officer found reasonable grounds to believe that the applicant had committed abetting personation contrary to s. 135 of the Ghana Criminal Code. The officer found that the Canadian offence of abetting personation with intent contrary to para. 403(a) of the Criminal Code of Canada is an equivalent offence punishable by a maximum term of imprisonment of at least 10 years. While the RCMP report indicated that there was insufficient evidence to charge the applicant, it was clear that this was because the imposter was being detained in Ghana and the witnesses and evidence were in Ghana. Otherwise, the report reiterated the information that the officer relied on in her finding. An officer is not required to refer to all the evidence before her. The officer need only convince the court that she considered the totality of the evidence. A reading of the police report suggests that it neither supports nor detracts from the officer's finding. As such, the officer did not err in not referring to the police report in her decision. The officer did not commit an error in finding the applicant was inadmissible. The application for judicial review was dismissed.

Wajaras v. Canada (Minister of Citizenship & Immigration), 2009 FC 200, 2009 CarswellNat 530, 2009 CarswellNat 1116 — The applicant sought to set aside a decision of the Immigration Division that found him to be inadmissible to Canada on the ground of serious criminality in accordance with s. 36(1)(a) of IRPA. The applicant entered Canada in 1997 as a Convention refugee and was granted permanent resident status at that time. He subsequently committed a serious assault and was criminally charged and sentenced to three years imprisonment in 2005.

The CBSA made an inadmissibility report which lead to an inadmissibility hearing before the Board under s. 44(2) of the IRPA. The applicant was advised of the CBSA's intention to have him declared a danger to the public. Notwithstanding his refugee status, such a finding would have permitted his return to Sudan in the event that he was also found to be inadmissible. The Minister determined that the applicant did not represent a danger to the public. In the result he could not be returned to Sudan even though he had been determined to be inadmissible and was the subject of a corresponding removal order. The applicant argued before the Board that it was an abuse of process for the Minister to seek a removal order against him with the resulting loss of permanent resident status in circumstances where his removal could not be lawfully effected.

The Federal Court concluded that notwithstanding that the Board erred in law by stating that the doctrine of abuse of process required evidence of malice or animus, a question remained as to whether an abuse of process argument could be sustained on this particular record. The Federal Court concluded it could not and the Board's mistake, therefore, was of no consequence. The application for judicial review was set aside. The applicant was solely responsible for the position he found himself in. He is not without potential future recourse. If administrative decisions are made which unlawfully interfere with his interests, including the opportunity to work, he would have the right to seek judicial review. If he stays out of legal trouble, enhances his Canadian establishment and continues to make positive social and economic contributions, he would be in a position at some point to pursue humanitarian and compassionate relief under s. 25 of the IRPA.

An abuse of process argument cannot be built around selective references to the purposes of the IRPA. The legislation serves many purposes, not the least of which is protecting Canadians by imposing consequences for the criminal behaviour of a few of those who have emigrated here.

The Federal Court judge certified a question and the Federal Court of Appeal in *Wajaras v. Canada (Minister of Citizenship & Immigration)* (2010), 399 N.R. 31, 2010 FCA 41, 2010 CarswellNat 266, 2010 CarswellNat 623 concluded that the Minister of Citizenship and Immigration does not engage in abuse of process in continuing to seek a removal order where the effected individual has been determined not to be a danger to the public. The Federal Court of Appeal concluded that it was not improper for the Minister to seek a deportation order for the purpose of depriving a permanent resident of this status as a result of serious criminality, even where there are impediments to removal. The appeal was dismissed.

Capra v. Canada (Attorney General) (2008), 76 Imm. L.R. (3d) 21, 335 F.T.R. 299 (Eng.), 2008 CarswellNat 3875, 2008 CarswellNat 5267, 2008 FC 1212 — This was an application for a declaration that subs. 128(4) of the *Corrections and Conditional Release Act*, S.C. 1992, c. 20 ("CCRA") is invalid on the ground that it breaches ss. 7, 9 and 15 of the *Canadian Charter of Rights and Freedoms*, Part 1 of the *Constitution Act, 1982*. The applicant had been granted Convention refugee status and became a permanent resident on December 2, 1992. The applicant was subsequently convicted of 80 counts of fraud in connection with credit cards and automatic bank teller machines in 2001. A deportation order was issued on the grounds of serious criminality. Both the appeal of the deportation order and his application were dismissed and the applicant lost his permanent residence status. However, because of his refugee status, he could not be removed to Romania unless the Minister of Citizenship and Immigration issued an opinion that the applicant constitutes a danger to the public. The CBSA sought the opinion of the Minister that he was a danger to the public in Canada. In the meantime, the applicant served his sentence in a medium security federal correctional facility and underwent a rehabilitation program. He became eligible for an unescorted temporary absence ("UTA") and day parole on July 2008. The CBSA informed the sentence management office of the deportation order previously issued against the applicant. As a result, by operation of subs. 128(4) of the CCRA, the applicant was ineligible for release on a UTA or day parole until his full parole eligibility date. The applicant believed that he was being treated differently in relation to day parole eligibility because he was not a Canadian citizen. He claimed that he was the subject of discrimination and regardless of whether he was allowed to stay in Canada or not, he perceived that he was being denied an opportunity to work towards his own rehabilitation simply because of his identity.

The court held that s. 128(4) of the CCRA was directed at inmates subject to removal. The operation of the subsection is triggered by the issuance of a removal order. A stay of that removal order suspends the section's effect. The application of the section is rationally tied to its purpose and cannot be called arbitrary in relation to the objectives sought to be attained. Accordingly this was not arbitrary detention within the meaning of s. 9. Furthermore, the Supreme Court of Canada had made it clear that a "change in the form in which a sentence is served, whether it be favourable or unfavourable to the prisoner, is not, in itself, contrary to any principle of fundamental justice."

Parliament has decided that offenders subject to removal should serve their sentences in different ways from other offenders, including Canadian citizens. This is to ensure that their status as offenders does not enhance their access to Canadian society over that of non-offenders who face deportation; it is also intended to ensure that their removal status does not result in their serving shorter sentences than either Canadian citizens or non-citizens who are not subject to removal. Parliament has chosen to deal with these issues by suspending day parole and UTA for offenders who are subject to removal. It is possible to disagree with this approach and with whether it achieves the objectives it is intended to achieve, but that was not the issue before the court. What is relevant is that the variation in the form of the sentence that comes about as a result of subs. 128(4) of CCRA is triggered by the existence of a removal order and whether this fact makes it part of a deportation scheme.

The court was not convinced that, if the purpose of parole is to protect society, that the loss of the possibility of that protection because of the loss of eligibility for day parole under subs. 128(4) was a disadvantage to the applicant, whether or not he was removed from Canada. Furthermore if parole was a benefit to offenders, the court was not convinced that the applicant had been disadvantaged by the loss of any such benefit in a situation where the evidence showed his deportation was being actively pursued and he did not fall into one of the exceptions specifically provided for under subs. 128(6). The applicant failed to demonstrate differential treatment between citizens and non-citizens. The application was dismissed.

Younis v. Canada (Minister of Citizenship & Immigration) (2008), 74 Imm. L.R. (3d) 115, 332 F.T.R. 99 (Eng.), 2008 CarswellNat 2744, 2008 FC 944 — The applicant had a number of criminal convictions. The Immigration Division issued a deportation order against the applicant on the basis that he was inadmissible for serious criminality under s. 36(1)(a) of the Act because of his conviction for drug trafficking. The applicant appealed the deportation order and sought special relief on humanitarian and compassionate grounds under the Act. He did not challenge the legal validity of the deportation order. The IAD denied the applicant's appeal. He then sought judicial review of that decision. The issues raised in the application were whether the IAD erred in admitting the applicant's juvenile criminal record into evidence and whether the IAD erred in taking into consideration the report to Crown counsel. The Youth Criminal Justice Act ("YCJA") contains prohibitions against the release of records of convictions of young persons as well as some exceptions to the prohibition against the release of records of convictions of young persons. The question of whether or not the applicant's juvenile record fell within the period of access and is accessible turned on whether the sexual assault conviction was for a summary or indictable offence. There was no indication in the evidence before the

IAD whether the applicant, as a youth, was convicted of a summary or indictable offence. Without such evidence, the IAD had no way of determining whether the applicant's juvenile conviction was releasable under the YCJA. The IAD is responsible for determining the admissibility, reliability and weight to be given to evidence presented before it. Although the IAD is not bound by the same legal or technical rules of evidence as a court of law, this does not confer upon the IAD the authority to admit a youth criminal record where the second conviction falls outside the period of access. The release of such a report would not only constitute a breach of s. 118 of the YCJA, it would also amount to a breach of the procedural fairness guarantees in hearings before the IAD. The IAD was found to have a duty to determine the admissibility of the applicant's youth criminal record before considering whether the record was credible and trustworthy and before determining the weight to be given to the record.

The IAD relied on the report to Crown counsel which contained a list of proposed criminal charges against the applicant. The IAD failed to make the necessary distinction between the fact that the proposed charges were mere allegations and that the applicant had not been convicted of the offences. Although it was open to the IAD to consider the evidence underlying the charges in question, it was not open to the IAD to conclude that this evidence was sufficient to find that the applicant was guilty of the offences proposed in the report. The IAD's decision was also void of any discussion regarding the reliability and credibility of the report. The absence of any analysis in this regard suggested that the IAD failed to turn its mind to whether the report was reliable and credible. This omission constituted an error of law. The application for judicial review was allowed.

Johnson v. Canada (Minister of Citizenship & Immigration), 2008 FC 2, 2008 CarswellNat 1327, 2008 CarswellNat 11, [2008] F.C.J. No. 10 — The applicant's inland application for permanent residence was refused because he was found to be inadmissible on grounds of serious criminality. The criminal convictions that led to the finding of inadmissibility were later set aside. The applicant argued that the officer erred in reaching the decision to refuse his permanent residence application by ignoring relevant evidence, specifically that the applicant's conviction was under appeal and that the officer breached the duty of fairness he owed to the applicant by failing to provide the applicant with an opportunity to respond to his criminal convictions.

A deportation order has a clear and imminent effect upon a person's right to remain in Canada. If, in that context, there is no obligation to await the result of an appeal of a criminal conviction, it is the court's view that there can be no obligation to defer consideration of a humanitarian and compassionate application because of an outstanding appeal. This is so because one may file a new inland application for permanent residence if circumstances later change as a result of a successful appeal. In the absence of compelling circumstances, it would be contrary to the scheme of the Act to require decisions about inadmissibility, made in the context of humanitarian and compassionate application, to be delayed until all criminal proceedings, including all rights of appeal are exhausted. The failure of the applicant to advise immigration of his convictions did not shift the onus to the officer to communicate with Mr. Johnson about his convictions. It was always open to the applicant to advise the officer of both his convictions and his appeal, and to request a deferral of the officer's decision until the appeal had been decided. Mr. Johnson requested no postponement of the officer's decision. The application for judicial review was dismissed.

Canada (Minister of Citizenship & Immigration) v. Malarski, 2006 CarswellNat 2612, 2006 FC 1007 — Where a permanent resident who is subject of a deportation order which has been stayed is subsequently convicted of an offence that constitutes serious criminality under subs. 36(1), the stay is cancelled by operation of law pursuant to subs. 68(4) of the IRPA and an appeal to the IAD is terminated. Once this happens, the IAD loses jurisdiction over the matter.

Cheddesingh v. Canada (Minister of Citizenship & Immigration) (2006), 52 Imm. L.R. (3d) 247, 2006 CarswellNat 259, 2006 FC 124 — Subsection 64(2) of the IRPA is not concerned with the length of the sentence imposed on the offender, but with the punishment. It is clear from the jurisprudence that once a person is convicted of a crime, time served by that individual in pre-trial detention will be deemed to be part of the offender's punishment.

In this case, the applicant argued that the proper interpretation was to compute the time a person is sentenced to spend in custody as of the date of the sentence, and the time spent in pre-sentence custody should not be taken into account. According to this interpretation, the applicant's term of imprisonment would only amount to a year instead of 30 months. The applicant's proposed interpretation was contrary to the intent of Parliament in drafting subs. 64(2) of the Act. Accordingly, the Board did not commit a reviewable error in determining that the period the applicant spent in pre-sentence custody formed part of her "term of imprisonment."

Medovarski v. Canada (Minister of Citizenship & Immigration), [2005] 2 S.C.R. 539, 50 Imm. L.R. (3d) 1, 135 C.R.R. (2d) 1, 258 D.L.R. (4th) 193, [2005] S.C.J. No. 31, 339 N.R. 1, EYB 2005-95306, 2005 CarswellNat 2943, 2005 CarswellNat 2944, 2005 SCC 51 — The appellant was a permanent resident and had been ordered deported for serious criminality. Her removal order was automatically stayed when she appealed the deportation order to the Immigration Appeal Division. The appeal was discontinued as a result of s. 196 of the IRPA (a transitional provision), which took away the right to appeal an order for removal unless a party had, under the former Act, been "granted a stay." The trial judge set aside the decision to discontinue. However, the Federal Court of Appeal allowed the Minister of Citizenship and Immigration's appeal, holding that the purpose of the IRPA transitional provision was to deny the right of appeal in the case of an automatic stay. Section 196 of the IRPA, properly interpreted, applies only to actively granted stays. The objectives of the IRPA, as expressed in s. 3, indicate an intent to prioritize security. In keeping with these objectives, the IRPA creates a new scheme whereby a person sentenced to more than six months in prison is inadmissible pursuant to s. 36; if they have been sentenced to a prison term of more than two years, they are denied a right to appeal their removal order under s. 64 of the IRPA. The purpose in enacting the IRPA, and in particular s. 64, was to efficiently remove from the country persons who have engaged in serious criminality. Since s. 196 refers explicitly to s. 64, the transitional provision should be interpreted in light of these legislative objectives.

The deportation of a non-citizen cannot in itself implicate the liberty and security interests protected by s. 7 of the Charter. Even if the liberty and security of the person were engaged, any unfairness resulting from s. 196 would be inadequate to constitute a breach of principles of fundamental justice.

Shepherd v. Canada (Minister of Citizenship & Immigration) (2005), 48 Imm. L.R. (3d) 118, 2005 CarswellNat 2115, 2005 CarswellNat 3490, 2005 FC 1033 — The IAD concluded that the pre-sentencing custodial terms that had been expressly taken into account and credited to the applicant's sentence formed part of the term of imprisonment for the purposes of subs. 64(2) of the Act. Accordingly, the IAD ruled that the applicant had lost his right to appeal in light of subs. 64(2). Subsection 719(3) of the Criminal Code specifically provides that pre-sentence detention can be taken into account when a court is imposing a sentence and in this case it was clear that the sentencing judge considered the pre-sentencing detention to be part of the punishment imposed on the applicant. The record showed that the applicant was punished by a term of imprisonment of at least two years and that falls within the definition of "serious criminality" pursuant to subs. 64(2). In these circumstances, the applicant had no right of appeal to the IAD.

Magtibay v. Canada (Minister of Citizenship & Immigration), 2005 CarswellNat 2019, 2005 CarswellNat 757, 2005 FC 397 — The applicant applied for permanent residence under the live-in caregiver class. The applicant's spouse had been acquitted of a criminal offence; however, the court in giving judgment in the Philippines had found that the offence had in fact been committed but since the victim had pardoned her aggressor, no conviction would result.

It should be made clear that para. 36(1)(c) of the Act does not require a conviction for the crime but simply its commission. This is in contrast to para. 36(1)(b) which requires a conviction and not simply that the crime was committed. It is clear that Parliament intended to allow for the inadmissibility of a permanent resident or foreign national not only on conviction but also on the commission of certain acts. The immigration officer did not err in concluding that the offence had been committed. Accordingly the judicial review application was dismissed.

Marshall v. Canada (Minister of Citizenship & Immigration), 2004 CarswellNat 127, 2004 CarswellNat 877, 2004 FC 34 — The member conducting the hearing under s. 36(1)(a) has to make the determination that an applicant is or is not a Canadian citizen. It is the member's decision and not the decision of Citizenship and Immigration.

Meerza v. Canada (Minister of Citizenship & Immigration) (2003), 34 Imm. L.R. (3d) 309, 2003 CarswellNat 4531 (Imm. & Ref. Bd. (App. Div.)) — A conditional sentence qualifies as a term of imprisonment within the meaning of that term in s. 36(1)(a).

[Editor's note: Although decided under the former Act, the following two decisions may still be relevant.]

Barnett v. Canada (Minister of Citizenship & Immigration) (1996), 33 Imm. L.R. (2d) 1, 109 F.T.R. 154, 1996 CarswellNat 319, [1996] F.C.J. No. 363 — This was an application to set aside the decision of an adjudicator which held that the applicant was the member of an inadmissible class pursuant to para. 19(1)(c.1)(i). The applicant, a UK citizen, entered Canada in September 1993. In May 1994 he was reported for working without an employment authorization. An inquiry opened in May 1994 and was adjourned. The applicant was subsequently served with a report alleging that he had been convicted in the United Kingdom for impaired driving. Later, a further s. 27 report was served alleging that the applicant, in 1977, had been convicted of burglary. The applicant's position was that pursuant to the UK Rehabilitation of Offenders Act, 1974, his conviction for burglary was spent on October 7, 1982, and he was no longer deemed to be convicted of the offence. The adjudicator decided that although the conviction for burglary was spent under United Kingdom law, it was not spent for purposes of the Canadian Immigration Act.

Where another country, whose legal system is based on similar foundations and values as our own, has enacted legislation which reflects goals and objectives analogous to those encompassed within our own system, then that law should be accorded respect and recognized for purposes of Canadian immigration law. The question is not whether Canada has identical legislation in place but whether the underlying rationale of the foreign legislation is consistent with some fundamental principle of justice esteemed within our society.

The applicant has been treated in the United Kingdom as not having been convicted of the offence of burglary and there is no solid rationale for refusing to recognize the Rehabilitation of Offenders Act, 1974 of the UK. Accordingly, the applicant had not been convicted as that term is used in para. 19(1)(c.1)(i) of the *Immigration Act*, and was not excluded on that basis.

Canada (Minister of Employment & Immigration) v. Burgon (1991), 13 Imm. L.R. (2d) 102, 78 D.L.R (4th) 103, [1991] 3 F.C. 44, (sub nom. *Burgon v. Canada (Minister of Employment & Immigration))* 122 N.R. 228, [1991] F.C.J. No. 149, 1991 CarswellNat 33, 1991 CarswellNat 777 (C.A.) — This was an appeal from a decision of the Appeal Division allowing the respondent to remain in Canada. The respondent was arrested on drug charges in the United Kingdom in 1987. While awaiting trial in prison she learned her elder son had also become involved in drug trafficking. This caused her to give a statement to the police which led to the imprisonment of her son, her father and a well-known drug dealer. The respondent had pleaded guilty in England to conspiracy to supply a controlled drug and was given a suspended sentence. In March 1987 the respondent, who had married a Canadian citizen, was the subject of a sponsorship application by her husband. On December 7, 1987, with the help of her probation officer, she received an English discharge order which had the effect of clearing her completely.

The respondent's application for permanent residence was rejected. It was refused on two bases: initially, because of her "conviction" it was the opinion of Immigration that she was caught by s. 19(1)(c) of the Immigration Act; and secondly, because of her previous addiction she was thought to be inadmissible by virtue of s. 19(1)(a).

The more complex question was whether the respondent was excluded pursuant to s. 19(1)(c). It is clear that the word "convicted" does not have a universal immutable meaning. This word, like so many other words, may have different meanings depending on the context in which it is used.

What must be decided is whether the policy of the *Immigration Act* predominates in arriving at the meaning of the word "convicted," whether the policy of the criminal law should be controlling, or whether the court should seek to harmonize the legislation in these two areas. Also, in this case, there was a foreign element which required the court to consider what recognition, if any, should be given to the laws of the foreign country in this interpretation exercise.

The policy of the criminal law in Canada in relation to criminal records has been changed in recent years to reflect altering social attitudes towards those who violated the criminal law. The first legislative response was the *Criminal Records Act*, S.C. 1969-70, c. 40, which permitted a pardon by the Governor in Council, after the lapse of a certain period of time, upon the recommendation of the National Parole Board. The effect of such a pardon was that the conviction was vacated. Not long after, the *Criminal Code* was amended to allow judges to impose absolute and conditional discharges in appropriate cases. This amendment had the effect of the accused being deemed not to have been convicted of the offence in question.

Similar provisions aimed at helping those convicted of crimes to make a new beginning were enacted in the United Kingdom as well as other countries. The British went further than Canada: in addition to allowing absolute and conditional discharges Britain enacted the *Powers of Criminal Courts Act*, 1973, to the effect that when an offender was placed on probation his conviction would be deemed not to be a conviction. It was this provision which enabled the respondent to have her conviction expunged in the UK.

When Parliament reenacted the *Immigration Act* in 1976 it must be taken to have known about its own earlier penal legislation which allowed for the elimination of criminal convictions from records of deserving individuals. In using the word "convicted" in s. 19(1)(c) Parliament meant a conviction that had not been expunged. If a conviction had been erased by the provisions of another law of Parliament, it was not meant to be treated in the same way as a conviction that had not been removed. In this way the policy of the criminal law is incorporated within the *Immigration Act*. The further question to consider was whether the UK legislation, which was similar in purpose, but not identical to the Canadian law, should be treated in the same way. In both countries certain offenders are granted the advantage of avoiding the stigma of a criminal record to facilitate their rehabilitation. There is no good reason for immigration law to thwart the goal of this British legislation which is consistent with the Canadian law. The two legal systems are based on similar foundations and share similar values. Unless there is a valid basis for deciding otherwise, the legislation of countries similar to our own, especially when their aims are identical, ought to be accorded respect. While a court is not required to go so far as to "attorn" to the law of all foreign jurisdictions, it is appropriate to do so in this case because the laws and the legal systems of the other country are similar to ours.

Accordingly, the court ruled that there being no conviction in the United Kingdom, and there being no reason to refuse to grant recognition to the law of the United Kingdom, the respondent was not "convicted" for the purpose of s. 19(1)(c).

Section 36(2)

R. v. Roy, [2012] 2 S.C.R. 60, 281 C.C.C. (3d) 433, 93 C.R. (6th) 1, 345 D.L.R. (4th) 193, 28 M.V.R. (6th) 1, 321 B.C.A.C. 112, 259 C.R.R. (2d) 361, 430 N.R. 201, 547 W.A.C. 112, 2012 SCC 26, 2012 CarswellBC 1573, 2012 CarswellBC 1574, [2012] S.C.J. No. 26 — The accused was convicted of dangerous driving causing death and his appeal to the Court of Appeal was dismissed. The trial judge had concluded that his conduct was objectively dangerous. He then immediately concluded that the accused's driving had constituted a marked departure from the standard of care a reasonable person would observe in the circumstances. The Court of Appeal concluded that the trial judge had made a legal error but was of the view that the error was harmless as it occasioned no substantial wrong or miscarriage of justice. On appeal to the Supreme Court of Canada, the conviction was set aside and an acquittal entered. The Court of Appeal erred in finding that the trial court's error was not a substantial wrong or a miscarriage of justice. There was no evidence to support the finding that the accused was aware of the risk he was creating and deliberately chose to run that risk, and fault could not be inferred from the fact that the driving was, objectively viewed, dangerous. The record disclosed a single and momentary error in judgment with tragic consequences. Since the record did not provide evidence on which a properly instructed trier of fact, acting reasonably, could have concluded that the accused's standard of care was a marked departure from that expected of a reasonable person in the circumstances, an acquittal was appropriate.

It is important, in the case of a charge of dangerous driving, to ensure that the fault requirement is established. Failing to do so unduly extends the reach of the criminal law and wrongly brands as criminals those who are not morally blameworthy. The distinction between a *mere* departure, which may support civil liability, and the marked departure required for criminal fault is a matter of degree. The trier of fact must identify how and in what way the departure from the standard goes *markedly* beyond mere carelessness.

The Supreme Court of Canada in *R. v. Beatty*, [2008] 1 S.C.R. 49 clarified the importance of insisting on a significant fault element in order to distinguish between negligence for the purpose of imposing civil liability and that necessary for the imposition of criminal punishment. In considering whether the *actus reus* has been established, the question is whether the driving, viewed objectively, was dangerous to the public in all circumstances. Focus of the inquiry must be on the risk created by the accused's manner of driving, not the consequences, such as an accident in which he or she was involved.

Casimiro Santos v. Canada (Minister of Citizenship & Immigration), 2013 CarswellNat 5764, 2013 FC 425, 2013 CarswellNat 5763 — The applicant alleged that the IAD erred in finding that there is equivalency between the foreign law under which he was convicted and s. 252 of the *Criminal Code of Canada*. There is nothing in para. 36(2)(b) that in any way limits or modifies the nature of the offences outside Canada for which a foreign national may have been convicted. It is difficult to conceive a conduct that is prohibited as an indictable offence in Canada and that may simply be treated as an administrative offence or misdemeanor in certain parts of the world. Foreign nationals may not escape the purview of para. 36(2)(b) just because the foreign offence for which they were convicted cannot be characterised as being criminal in nature in that jurisdiction. Permitting them scope to do so would undermine the important objectives of protecting the Canadian public. The fact that the Florida statute in this case may also be equivalent to s. 68 of the *Motor Vehicle Act* (B.C.) is not particularly relevant. The IAD's decision to find the applicant inadmissible was reasonable and the application for judicial review was dismissed.

R. v. Lu, 2013 ONCA 324, 2013 CarswellOnt 5866, [2013] O.J. No. 2222; notice of appeal filed 2013 CarswellOnt 12395 (S.C.C.) — The appellant, a citizen of Taiwan, had been convicted in Canada of a serious offence but wished to be admissible to Canada where her Canadian husband lives. She pleaded guilty to obstruction of a peace officer in the execution of his duties, contrary to s. 129(a) of the *Criminal Code*. At the sentencing hearing, the appellant requested a conditional discharge. The Crown sought a suspended sentence with a period of probation and community service. In light of new evidence regarding the consequences of the conviction on the appellant's immigration status, the summary appeal court judge (SCAJ) conducted a *de novo* sentencing hearing. While the SCAJ was sympathetic to the appellant's immigration plight, she dismissed her sentence appeal. The appellant then sought leave to appeal to the Ontario Court of Appeal.

While a sentencing judge may exercise his or her discretion to take collateral immigration consequences into account, the sentence ultimately imposed must be proportionate to the gravity of the offence and the degree of responsibility of the offender. The collateral immigration consequences must not be allowed to dominate the sentencing exercise or skew the process. The SCAJ made a case specific determination that a discharge would be contrary to the public interest. It was open to her to reach this conclusion and there was no basis for interfering with it. Leave to appeal was granted but the sentence appeal was dismissed.

See *Farenas* (2011), 391 F.T.R. 60, 2011 FC 660, 2011 CarswellNat 2104, [2011] F.C.J. No. 833, under s. 40(1) of IRPA.

R. v. Daskalov, 2011 BCCA 169, 2011 CarswellBC 793, [2011] B.C.J. No. 623 — The respondent was convicted under s. 122(1)(a) of IRPA and pled guilty in Provincial Court.

The respondent was sentenced to a conditional discharge and six months' probation. The Crown appealed the sentence arguing that the trial judge gave improper consideration to the immigration consequences of the sentence, and allowed that factor to override the purpose and principles of sentencing. The Crown further argued that a conditional discharge fell outside the range of sentences for an offence of this nature, which typically include a period of imprisonment, and that the discharge was granted in order to avoid recording a conviction for the offence against the respondent and thus avoid the effect of s. 36(2)(a) of IRPA.

The B.C. Court of Appeal concluded that the sentencing judge erred in principle by taking into account an irrelevant fact, that being the effect of s. 36(2)(a) of IRPA on the respondent's future inadmissibility into Canada, which resulted in his granting the respondent a conditional discharge with a period of six months' probation. Given the absence of an exceptional or unique circumstances, the sentence was unfit, the appeal was allowed and the sentence was varied to a period of imprisonment of one day resulting in an effective sentence of four months.

Qi v. Canada (Minister of Citizenship & Immigration) (2009), 79 Imm. L.R. (3d) 229, 2009 CarswellNat 505, 2009 CarswellNat 1115, 2009 FC 195 — The applicant, a citizen of the People's Republic of China, sought leave for judicial review of a visa officer's decision refusing his application for a permanent resident visa. The visa officer found that the applicant's son was inadmissible for criminality because he committed an act in Hong Kong that is an offence in Hong Kong and that, if committed in Canada, would be an indictable offence under an Act of Parliament. The visa officer concluded that the applicant's son committed an offence under s. 42(2)(i) of the Immigration Ordinance of Hong Kong as a result of possessing and using an altered passport. He concluded that if committed in Canada, this would constitute an offence under s. 122(1)(b) of the IRPA, punishable by way of indictment.

The court concluded that the visa officer could not reasonably conclude that the main applicant's son had committed acts or an offence in Hong Kong, and therefore find him criminally inadmissible in Canada, in light of the expert opinion to the contrary provided by a Mr. Blanchflower and in the absence of any contrary expert opinion. Mr. Blanchflower was of the opinion that the passport with the missing pages did not constitute an "altered travel document" within s. 42(2)(c)(i) of the Ordinance for two reasons: first, there was no evidence that the alteration was done "unlawfully," and second, the missing pages did not constitute an alteration under that provision. He relied for those propositions on the legislative history of the provision, on arguments of legislative construction, and on the case law.

This is not to say that the visa officer himself should have sought an independent legal opinion; in the normal course of events, the respondent should bear the burden of providing expert opinion supporting his position. These reasons should not be interpreted as requiring expert opinion in all circumstances where immigration officials make decisions predicated on foreign law. However, when an applicant's position is buttressed by credible and well-articulated opinions authored by an expert whose credentials are not in dispute, it will most likely be unreasonable to come to an opposite conclusion without the benefit of any expert evidence to the contrary. The application for judicial review was allowed.

Zeon v. Canada (Minister of Citizenship & Immigration) (2005), 49 Imm. L.R. (3d) 146, 2005 CarswellNat 3061, 2005 CarswellNat 4879, 2005 FC 1338 — The applicant's application for permanent residence was refused on the basis that he was inadmissible to Canada for criminality pursuant to s. 36(2)(c) of the IRPA. To render a reasonable decision under s. 36(2)(c), it is incumbent on a visa officer to provide critical analysis of how a visa applicant can be said, on reasonable grounds to believe, to have had committed an act which constitutes an offence in a foreign jurisdiction, and then to also provide critical analysis of how it can be said, on reasonable grounds to believe, that the same act would constitute an offence in Canada.

In this case, there was no evidence that this critical analysis required between the foreign law and Canadian law had been undertaken and concluded before the decision was announced during the interview.

The court set aside the officer's decision and referred the matter back to a different visa officer for re-determination based on a fresh record of evidence and to be conducted in the presence of counsel for the applicant if the applicant so wished.

Barnett v. Canada (Minister of Citizenship & Immigration) (1996), 33 Imm. L.R. (2d) 1, 109 F.T.R. 154, 1996 CarswellNat 319, [1996] F.C.J. No. 363 — See the *Barnett* case summary above, in s. 36(1).

Canada (Minister of Employment & Immigration) v. Burgon (1991), 13 Imm. L.R. (2d) 102, 78 D.L.R (4th) 103, [1991] 3 F.C. 44, (sub nom. *Burgon v. Canada (Minister of Employment & Immigration))* 122 N.R. 228, 1991 CarswellNat 777, 1991 CarswellNat 33, [1991] F.C.J. No. 149 (C.A.) — See the *Burgon* case summary above, in s. 36(1).

Section 36(3)

Hadad v. Canada (Minister of Citizenship, Immigration & Multiculturalism), 2011 CarswellNat 5390, 2011 FC 1503, 2011 CarswellNat 5885 — The applicant's application for criminal rehabilitation was denied. This conclusion was based on the officer's finding that she was not satisfied that the applicant had been rehabilitated under para. 36(3)(c) of IRPA. The purpose of para. 36(3)(c) of the Act is "to allow the Minister to take into consideration the unique facts of each particular case and to consider whether the overall situation warrants a finding that the individual has been rehabilitated." Information significant to this determination would include: the nature of the offence; the circumstances under which it was committed; the length of time that has elapsed; and whether there have been previous or subsequent offences. Implicit in the concept of rehabilitation is the acknowledgment that the person has already participated in some type of conduct from which he or she needs to be rehabilitated. In the present case, for the applicant, that conduct was the criminal convictions and the breach of immigration laws. Rehabilitation is forward looking, that is, is he/she likely to continue in this or similar conduct?

In this case, the officer attributed too much importance to the fact that the applicant had past criminal activity as opposed to the likelihood that he would be involved in future criminal or unlawful activity. For this reason, the decision was unreasonable and was set aside. The application for judicial review was allowed.

Sun v. Canada (Minister of Citizenship & Immigration), 2011 FC 708, 2011 CarswellNat 3443, 2011 CarswellNat 2305 — The applicant's application for permanent residence as a skilled worker was refused on the basis of criminal inadmissibility pursuant to para. 36(1)(b) of IRPA. The applicant had been convicted of a criminal offence pursuant to article 268 of the *Korean Criminal Act*, namely, "death and injury by occupational gross negligence." The applicant had been driving with a blood-alcohol level of 0.12 percent when he crossed the centre line and collided with a truck, seriously injuring its passengers. As a result of the conviction, he paid a fine. The applicant had a clean criminal record otherwise. The applicant argued that he was deemed to be rehabilitated. It was agreed that more than 10 years had lapsed since his conviction and the payment of the fine when the officer reviewed his application and that he met all the conditions set out in para. 18(2)(a) of the Regulations except for subparagraph 18(2)(a)(i), namely that the offence is punishable in Canada by a maximum term of imprisonment of *less than 10 years*, which is at the centre of the dispute. The only issue in this application is whether the term "not exceeding 10 years" in the Criminal Code falls within the maximum term of "less than 10 years" in s. 18 of the Regulations. The following was held to apply:

a) Serious criminality is defined at subs. 36(1) as including offences committed outside of Canada that could have been punishable by a maximum term of at least 10 years, meaning 10 years or more.

b) Subs. 249(3) of the Criminal Code provides for a term not exceeding 10 years, meaning 10 years or less.

c) Pursuant to paragraph 36(3)(c) of IRPA and s. 18 of the Regulations, the benefit of deemed rehabilitation only applies to offences punishable by a maximum of less than 10 years, meaning up to nine years, 364 days.

The application was dismissed.

Aksenova v. Canada (Minister of Public Safety & Emergency Preparedness), 2006 FC 557, 2006 CarswellNat 1204, [2006] F.C.J. No. 699 — The immigration officer issued a report against the applicant under subs. 44(1) of the IRPA because she was deemed inadmissible to Canada pursuant to para. 36(2)(a), having been convicted in Canada of an offence punishable by indictment. On the basis of that report, a deportation order was then issued by the Minister's delegate under subs. 44(2). The court considered whether in exercising its discretion to issue a report and make a deportation order, the officer and the Minister's delegate considered that the applicant was granted admission to Canada twice after she was convicted of an offence in Canada. The court concluded that the fact that the applicant was admitted to Canada twice after being convicted of an offence in Canada is not included in the exceptions set out under subs. 36(3) of IRPA dealing with inadmissibility to Canada. Therefore, the officer and delegate made no error by not considering them before they acted as they did. The particular circumstances of a person are irrelevant considerations and at most, the delegate could have stayed or deferred the making of the order if the applicant had already been subjected to an effective removal order, if plans had been made to leave Canada or if the applicant had been a witness called to testify in proceedings held in Canada. None of these considerations were applicable in this case. "Particular circumstances of the person" were said to be irrelevant. Although both subs. 44(1) and (2) use the term "may" in enabling the officer to prepare a report and the delegate to make a removal order, the statutory scheme enacted by the IRPA limits the discretion vested in the officer and the delegate. The term "may" in subs. 44(1) and (2) must be read in conjunction with subs. 36(3), which sets out the exceptions to inadmissibility.

Kok v. Canada (Minister of Citizenship & Immigration), 2005 CarswellNat 135, 2005 FC 77 — This was an application to review a negative decision on an application for rehabilitation. The Minister's delegate acknowledged some of the mitigating factors in a very general way in the decision but there was significant evidence in the form of supporting documentation. As well there was evidence that the applicant had not been convicted of an offence since 1985 and between 2001 and 2004 had found a religious commitment.

The failure to address important issues suggests that they were not really taken into account. The delegate should have addressed the strong documentary evidence in favour of rehabilitation.

Tessma v. Canada (Minister of Citizenship & Immigration), 2003 CarswellNat 4883, 2003 CarswellNat 3064, 240 F.T.R. 43, 2003 FC 1126 — This was an application to review the decision of the Immigration Division that the applicant was inadmissible to Canada on grounds of serious criminality. The applicant came to Canada when he was 12 years old in 1992, and at the age of 16 years was charged with several criminal offences under the Young Offenders Act, which was the law in effect at that time. The case was transferred to the ordinary courts and the applicant was tried and convicted as an adult of offences under the Criminal Code relating to pimping and assault.

The proper interpretation of the Young Offenders Act is that when an order is made transferring charges from youth court to ordinary court the applicant is not being tried for offences under the Young Offenders Act. The convictions against the applicant, in this case, were therefore convictions for indictable offences under the Criminal Code. Therefore, the exception contained in s. 36(3) of IRPA was not applicable and the applicant was properly found to be criminally inadmissible and the application for judicial review was dismissed.

37. (1) Organized criminality — **A permanent resident or a foreign national is inadmissible on grounds of organized criminality for**

    (a) being a member of an organization that is believed on reasonable grounds to be or to have been engaged in activity that is part of a pattern of criminal activity planned and organized by a number of persons acting in concert in furtherance of the commission of an offence punishable under an Act of Parliament by way of indictment, or in furtherance of the commission of an offence outside Canada that, if committed in Canada, would constitute such an offence, or engaging in activity that is part of such a pattern; or

    (b) engaging, in the context of transnational crime, in activities such as people smuggling, trafficking in persons or laundering of money or other proceeds of crime.

(2) Application — **Paragraph (1)(a) does not lead to a determination of inadmissibility by reason only of the fact that the permanent resident or foreign national entered Canada with the assistance of a person who is involved in organized criminal activity.**

[Editor's Note: SOR/2002-227, s. 320(6) provides that a person is inadmissible under the new Immigration and Refugee Protection Act, S.C. 2001 c. 27 on grounds of organized criminality if, on June 28, 2002, the person had been determined to be a member of an inadmissible class described in paragraph 19(1)(c.2) or subparagraph 19(1)(d)(ii) of the former Immigration Act, R.S.C. 1985, c. I-2.]

2013, c. 16, s. 15; 2015, c. 3, s. 109

Case Law

Saif v. Canada (Minister of Citizenship and Immigration), 2016 FC 437, 2016 CarswellNat 1267, 2016 CarswellNat 2727 — The applicant challenged the Immigration and Refugee Board's finding that he had been in engaged in activity that is part of a pattern of criminal activity planned and organized by a number of persons acting in concert in furtherance of the commission of an indictable offence. The applicant had plead guilty to an offence under para. 465(1)(d) of the *Criminal Code* involving a conspiracy to commit a summary offence and received a conditional sentence of five months. The conspiracy in question involved a scheme orchestrated by another whereby more than 300 Canadian permanent residents were afforded addresses of convenience and other documentation to fraudulently establish their Canadian residency. The applicant's involvement was secondary to that of another. The applicant allowed his address to be used as a mail drop and his name to be used on falsified lease documents. He also carried out errands to facilitate the scheme for which he received payment.

Although an unrestricted and broad interpretation for this to be given to the word "organization" as it is used in subs. 37(1), the provision still requires the existence of common organizational characteristics such as "identity, leadership, a loose hierarchy and a basic organizational structure." Third parties who individually transact with a criminal organization cannot reasonably be seen to be "members" nor can they be considered to be "engaged in activity that is part of a pattern of criminal activity planned and organized by a number of persons acting in concert in furtherance of the commission of an indictable offence." By way of analogy, no one would consider a purchaser of narcotics, without further involvement, to be either a member of, or acting in concert with, a criminal organization established to sell the narcotics, even though both are engaged in common in a criminal transaction. The Board apparently concluded in this case that the long-standing criminal conspiracy between the applicant and one other also involved "numerous people" and therefore fell within that part of para. 37(1)(a) concerned with a "pattern of activity." The court concluded that "organized criminality" was not established. The requirement of "organized criminality" was not established where the pattern of criminal conduct was carried out by only two persons. This requirement is not overcome by the peripheral involvement of third parties whose participation falls outside of the underlying criminal conspiracy. Under any reasonable interpretation of para. 37(1)(a), those persons cannot be said to have been engaged in activity that is part of a pattern of criminal activity planned and organized in concert with the applicant and another in furtherance of the commission of an indictable offence. The decision under review was set aside.

Lai v. Canada (Minister of Public Safety and Emergency Preparedness) (2015), 29 Imm. L.R. (4th) 211, 467 N.R. 198, 2015 FCA 21, 2015 CarswellNat 194, [2015] F.C.J. No. 125 — This was an appeal of a decision of a judicial review before the Federal Court of the decision of a member of the Immigration Division wherein it was determined that the applicant was inadmissible. The Federal Court judge took a broad view of the provisions of IRPA respecting removal for criminal activity. There was abundant evidence on the record including a book and an article directly implicating the applicant as a prominent Triad member. The Federal Court concluded there was no basis for setting the decision aside on this issue. The Federal Court of Appeal agreed that the judge's conclusion was consistent with the prior jurisprudence of the Federal Court. However, the Federal Court judge certified the question related to the interpretation in subs. 37(1)(a) of the IRPA. Specifically, whether the phrase "in furtherance of the commission of an offence outside Canada that, if committed in Canada, would constitute such an offence" required evidence of the elements of a specific foreign offence and an equivalency analysis and finding of dual criminality between the foreign offence and an offence punishable under an Act of Parliament by way of indictment. The Federal Court of Appeal concluded that the question certified by the Federal Court judge was not dispositive of the appeal. An issue that need not be decided, in this case a discrete comparative analysis of the specific elements of foreign and domestic offences, can never be an issue that grounds a properly certified question. In this case, the alleged offences were such that regardless of the jurisdiction, most civilized countries would have laws condemning such offences and it would be ludicrous to expect that expert evidence would have to be led in such circumstances. The appeal was dismissed.

B010 v. Canada (Minister of Citizenship and Immigration), [2015] 3 S.C.R. 704, 92 Admin. L.R. (5th) 1, 390 D.L.R. (4th) 385, 36 Imm. L.R. (4th) 64, 478 N.R. 57, 2015 CarswellNat 6186, 2015 SCC 58, 2015 CarswellNat 6186, 2015 CarswellNat 6187, [2015] S.C.J. No. 58 — The appellants were among nearly 500 Tamils from Sri Lanka who boarded the cargo ship *Sun Sea* in Thailand. The organizers of the voyage promised to transport them to Canada for sums ranging from $20,000 to $30,000 per person. Shortly after departure, the Thai crew abandoned the ship, leaving the asylum seekers on board to their own devices. Twelve of the migrants took over various duties during the three-month voyage across the Pacific Ocean to Canada. The Immigration and Refugee Board found the migrants inadmissible to Canada, on the basis that s. 37(1)(b) of the IRPA covers all acts of assistance to illegal migrants and does not require a profit motive. On judicial review to the Federal Court, B010's application was rejected while the applications of J.P., G.J., B306 and H were allowed. The Federal Court of Appeal rejected B010's appeal and in the remaining cases, the court allowed the appeals and reinstated the Board's decisions of inadmissibility. The Supreme Court allowed the appeals and the cases were remitted to the Board for reconsideration.

> Acts committed by people who are not themselves members of criminal organizations, who do not act in knowing furtherance of a criminal aim of such organizations, or who do not organize, abet or counsel serious crimes involving such organizations, do not fall within s. 37(1)(b). The tools of statutory interpretation — plain and grammatical meaning of the words, statutory and international contexts, and legislative intent — all point inexorably to the conclusion that s. 37(1)(b) applies only to people who act to further illegal entry of asylum seekers in order to obtain, directly or indirectly, a financial or other material benefit in the context of transnational organized crime.

> A migrant who aids in his own illegal entry or the illegal entry of other refugees or asylum seekers in their collective flight to safety is not inadmissible under s. 37(1)(b). Acts of humanitarian and mutual aid (including aid between family members) do not constitute people smuggling under the IRPA. To justify a finding of inadmissibility on the grounds of people smuggling under s. 37(1)(b), the respondent Ministers must establish before the Board that the migrants are people smugglers in this sense. The migrants can escape inadmissibility under s. 37(1)(b) if they merely aided in the illegal entry of the other refugees or asylum seekers in the course of their collective flight to safety. The Board's interpretation of s. 37(1)(b) was not within the range of reasonable interpretations. The migrants were found inadmissible on an erroneous interpretation of s. 37(1)(b) and are therefore entitled to have their admissibility reconsidered.

Also see *R. v. Appulonappa*, [2015] 3 S.C.R. 754, 332 C.C.C. (3d) 1, 24 C.R. (7th) 385, 390 D.L.R. (4th) 425, 35 Imm. L.R. (4th) 171, 379 B.C.A.C. 3, 345 C.R.R. (2d) 74, 478 N.R. 3, 654 W.A.C. 3, 2015 SCC 59, 2015 CarswellBC 3427, 2015 CarswellBC 3428, [2015] S.C.J. No. 59, at s. 117(1) of the Act.

Canada (Minister of Citizenship & Immigration) v. Dhillon, 2012 CarswellNat 1904, 2012 FC 726 — This application raised one issue: can the IAD's conclusion that the applicant is not inadmissible under s. 37(1)(b) of IRPA for having been convicted of conspiracy to import marijuana into the United States withstand scrutiny on the applicable standard of review? There was no dispute that the applicant fell under the provision of s. 36(1)(b) which provides that a person is inadmissible on grounds of serious criminality for "having been convicted of an offence outside Canada that, if committed in Canada, would constitute an offence under an Act of Parliament punishable by a maximum term of imprisonment of at least 10 years." If the applicant was inadmissible for serious criminality under s. 36(1)(b), he would have a right of appeal to the IAD that he could argue that sufficient H&C considerations warrant "special relief." However, if the applicant is inadmissible on grounds of organized criminality under s. 37(1)(b), he loses his right of appeal to the IAD.

The court concluded that the use of the words "such as" did not limit the application of s. 37(1)(b) to the crimes of people smuggling, trafficking in persons and money laundering; the loss of the applicant's right to an appeal to the IAD on H&C grounds is consistent with the objective of Parliament to prioritize security for Canadians; and a textual, contextual and purposive analysis to find a meaning that is harmonious with IRPA as a whole results in a conclusion that the transnational crime of drug smuggling is included in s. 37(1)(b). Accordingly, the application for judicial review was allowed. The court certified the following question of general importance: "Is the importation of narcotics into another state an activity 'such as people smuggling, trafficking in persons or money laundering' within the meaning of s. 37(1)(b) of *IRPA*?"

Baybazarov v. Canada (Minister of Citizenship & Immigration), 2010 FC 665, 2010 CarswellNat 2427, 2010 CarswellNat 2428 — The applicant applied in the investor category after a positive selection as a Prince Edward Island Provincial Nominee. The visa officer determined the applicant inadmissible under s. 37(1)(b) of IRPA on grounds of engaging, in the context of transnational crime, in activity such as money laundering. The officer relied on a document classified as "secret," from the Canadian Border Services Agency's Organized Crime Section, and a report from the Financial Transactions and Reports Analysis Centre of Canada citing suspicious financial activity relating to the applicant, his business partner in Canada and their corporation.

The CBSA report is an instrument of advocacy. The CBSA report discloses a number of serious allegations in considerable detail. The allegations appear to tie the applicant or his publishing company to known organized crime figures. Because of the officer's admitted reliance on the CBSA report, and the officer's suspicions of the applicant's employment income, the CBSA report ought to have been disclosed in the fairness letter. Without this disclosure, the applicant had no way of meaningfully responding to concerns that his source of income was illegitimate. The officer breached procedural fairness. The application for judicial review was allowed.

Castelly c. Canada (Ministre de la Citoyenneté & de l'Immigration) (2008), 74 Imm. L.R. (3d) 209, (sub nom. *Castelly v. Canada (Minister of Citizenship & Immigration)*) 329 F.T.R. 311 (Eng.), [2009] 2 F.C.R. 327, 2008 CarswellNat 2009, 2008 CarswellNat 3508, 2008 FC 788 — This was an application to consider the lawfulness of a decision dated October 24, 2007, of a member of the Immigration Division of the Immigration and Refugee Board to make a removal order against the applicant because she was inadmissible to Canada under para. 37(1)(a) of the IRPA. A report was issued on July 28, 2005, under subs. 44(1) of the IRPA. The departmental official was of the opinion that the applicant should be inadmissible on grounds of "organized criminality" under para. 37(1)(a). The Minister referred the matter to the panel for investigation. The applicant was invited to make additional written submissions in answer to the question "are there reasonable grounds to believe that Ms. Castelly was a member of the Wolf Pack organization?" The applicant had testified before the panel that she was "simply a mother who at the time was not working outside the home, was overtaken by events, and had no knowledge about the activity of her son and his friends."

The Act does not define the term "member" and the courts have not established a precise definition of the term or a test for "belonging to" an organization described in para. 37(1)(a) of the Act. In the last few years at least, case law of the Federal Court and Federal Court of Appeal has not been consistent on the issue of a test relevant to determining whether someone is a member of a criminal organization. While the evidence on the tribunal record does not demonstrate that the applicant *personally* took part in serious crimes, the panel was able to support its findings because of the fact that the applicant had direct knowledge of the criminal activity of other members of the Wolf Pack who acted on behalf of the gang. The Federal Court held that it was not unreasonable for the panel to find that the applicant was a member of the Wolf Pack, an "organization" that engaged in the types of crime described in s. 37. Moreover, it was not necessary to prove that someone belongs to a criminal organization described in s. 37; it is sufficient to have reasonable grounds to believe that he or she is or was a member of such an organization. In that regard, the panel did not have to apply the test developed by the Canadian courts concerning belonging to a criminal organization for the purposes of subs. 467.1(1) of the Criminal Code. The panel's decision was not unreasonable because it did not make reference to tests used by the police to determine whether someone is a member of a street gang or because it did not mention in the impugned decision the existence of an "institutional link" between the Wolf Pack and the applicant. The application for judicial review was dismissed. The following question of general importance was certified:

> For the purposes of paragraph 37(1)(a) of the *Immigration and Refugee Protection Act*, what is the general definition of "member," and what test must one apply to determine whether a person is or was a "member" of an "organization" described in that paragraph?

Sittambalam v. Canada (Minister of Citizenship & Immigration) (2006), 56 Imm. L.R. (3d) 161, (sub nom. *Sittampalam v. Canada (Minister of Citizenship & Immigration)*) 272 D.L.R. (4th) 1, [2007] 3 F.C.R. 198, (sub nom. *Sittampalam v. Canada (Minister of Citizenship & Immigration)*) 354 N.R. 34, 2006 CarswellNat 3236, 2006 FCA 326, [2006] F.C.J. No. 1512 — The issue in this appeal is whether the appellant is a member of a criminal organization so as to deny him the right of appeal to the Immigration Appeal Division on the question of whether he is inadmissible pursuant to para. 37(1)(a) of the IRPA. The appeal was dismissed. The phrase "being a member of an organization" in para. 37(1)(a) includes a person who was not a member at the time of the reporting, but was a member before that time. The word "organization," as it is used in para. 37(1)(a), is to be given a broad unrestricted interpretation. While no precise definition can be established here, the factors listed by O'Reilly J. in *Thanaratnam v. Canada (Minister of Citizenship & Immigration)*, [2004] 3 F.C.R. 301 (T.D.) by the Board member, and possibly others, are helpful in making a determination, but no one of them is an essential element. The structure of criminal organizations is varied, and the Board must be given flexibility to evaluate all of the evidence in light of the legislative purpose of the IRPA to prioritize security in deciding whether a group is an organization for the purpose of para. 37(1)(a) of the IRPA.

38. (1) Health grounds — A foreign national is inadmissible on health grounds if their health condition

(a) is likely to be a danger to public health;

(b) is likely to be a danger to public safety; or

(c) might reasonably be expected to cause excessive demand on health or social services.

(2) Exception — Paragraph (1)(c) does not apply in the case of a foreign national who

(a) has been determined to be a member of the family class and to be the spouse, common-law partner or child of a sponsor within the meaning of the regulations;

(b) has applied for a permanent resident visa as a Convention refugee or a person in similar circumstances;

(c) is a protected person; or

(d) is, where prescribed by the regulations, the spouse, common-law partner, child or other family member of a foreign national referred to in any of paragraphs (a) to (c).

[Editor's Note: SOR/2002-227, s. 320(7) provides that a person — other than an applicant described in s. 7 of the Immigration Regulations, 1978, *SOR/78-172, or s. 4 of the* Humanitarian Designated Classes Regulations, *SOR/97-183, who made an application for admission under the* Immigration Act, R.S.C. 1985, c. I-2 *(the "former Act") — is inadmissible under the new* Immigration and Refugee Protection Act, S.C. 2001 c. 27 *on health grounds if, on June 28, 2002, the person had been determined to be a member of the inadmissible class described in paragraph 19(1)(a) of the former Act.]*

Case Law

Section 38(1)

Muzeka-Harasim v. Canada (Minister of Citizenship and Immigration) (2016), 41 Imm. L.R. (4th) 87, 2016 FC 438, 2016 CarswellNat 1307, 2016 CarswellNat 2280 — The applicant sought judicial review of a decision of the IAD to deny permanent resident visas to her parents. The officer had denied the visas after finding that the applicant's father was medically inadmissible to Canada. The applicant claimed that the IAD erred when it held that it was not allowed to depart from the medical officer's diagnosis. Thus the applicant stated that "the IAD can review expert evidence from medical experts at the *de novo* hearing stage that demonstrates that CIC's medical findings were erroneous." The Federal Court did not agree and referred to the Federal Court of Appeal's decision in *Jiwanpuri v. Canada (Minister of Employment & Immigration)* (1990), 10 Imm. L.R. (2d) 241 (Fed. C.A.), whereby the Federal Court of Appeal indicated that members of the IAD do not have the expertise required to question the correctness of the medical diagnosis reached by the officers. Although it was not up to the IAD to revisit the medical officer's diagnosis, it could consider whether the health condition specified in that medical diagnosis might reasonably be expected to cause excessive demand on health or social services, in light of the new medical evidence. In this case, the IAD did, in fact, consider this issue and concluded that the new evidence failed to "sufficiently speak to the issue of excessive demand of medical and social services." Furthermore, even if the new medical evidence had adequately addressed the issue of "excessive demand," the findings on this point would have been tainted by the fact that they were based on an alternative diagnosis of the father's health condition, which had not been accepted by the IAD. The application was dismissed.

Smiraglia v. Canada (Minister of Citizenship and Immigration) (2014), 456 F.T.R. 295, 2014 FC 576, 2014 CarswellNat 3155, 2014 CarswellNat 2512 — The applicant's application for permanent residence was refused on the basis of his dependant spouse being medically inadmissible because he had HIV virus and required expensive antiviral medications which, it is accepted, would cost in excess of the current threshold for demand on Canada's health system. His spouse was employed as a Music Technical Services Librarian at the University of Pennsylvania. He was covered by a lifetime employment-based insurance policy which covered all of his prescription medications less co-payments of $2,000 per year. The coverage was conditional on him maintaining a permanent and valid street address in the United States of America and remaining eligible for Medicare. The officer asked for proof that the insurance would cover him if he became a permanent resident of Canada and moved to Canada on a permanent basis. The court concluded it was reasonable for the officer to require proof of continued coverage from the insurer. The fact that the policy required the insured to permanently maintain a valid street address in the U.S. did not raise the question of whether the insured's physical presence in the U.S. was required for continued coverage. The failure to establish that continued coverage was possible was sufficient to support the reasonableness of the decision. The application for judicial review was dismissed.

Lawrence v. Canada (Minister of Citizenship & Immigration) (2013), 454 N.R. 199, 2013 FCA 257, 2013 CarswellNat 4142 — The applicant was denied permanent residence in Canada due to his son's medical condition. The visa officer concluded that the applicant's plan to mitigate the cost of excessive demands on Canadian social systems was inadequate, in part because there was no indication of the nature of the schools in question nor whether either or both had agreed to accept the child. Medical officers are intended to be the experts on how social services operate in the provinces. The medical officer in this case would have known that the named schools were fully private and that the child would have to be assessed by the schools in Canada before he could be admitted. The responsibility for providing an opinion on such matters is assigned by OB 63 to the medical officer. The visa officer acknowledged this in her affidavit but asserted that she did not think it was necessary in this case to consult the medical officer based on the wording of OB 63B. She believed that anything non-medical related to social services need not go to the medical officer. This was an error of law that could not be cured by the subsequent review and declaration by the medical officer that he stood by his earlier opinion. The application for judicial review was granted.

On appeal by the Minister to the Federal Court of Appeal, the appeal was dismissed and the Federal Court of Appeal held that when a principal applicant in response to a fairness letter submits a proposal to mitigate the costs of publicly funded social services and the proposal raises matters that fall within the mandate of the medical officer, that proposal must be submitted to the medical officer for consideration even if the applicant does not dispute any of the medical officer's initial conclusions.

Zhang v. Canada (Minister of Citizenship & Immigration) (2012), 13 Imm. L.R. (4th) 95, 2012 FC 1093, 2012 CarswellNat 3526, 2012 CarswellNat 4190, [2012] F.C.J. No. 1179; affirmed (2013), 446 N.R. 382, 2013 FCA 168, 2013 CarswellNat 2197, [2013] F.C.J. No. 764 — Despite the fact that the applicant's son, who was diagnosed with "moderate mental retardation," was a non-accompanying family member, the applicant and the other accompanying family members were deemed to be inadmissible in conformity with para. 38(1)(c) and s. 42 of IRPA on the grounds that the son suffers from a health condition that might reasonably be expected to cause excessive demand on health or social services. There was no clear undertaking by the applicant that he would not sponsor the son, while it was even questionable whether an applicant seeking the issuance of a visa to gain permanent resident status, can legally renounce to the right to sponsor a non-accompanying family member. It was up to the applicant to discharge the onus by providing a credible plan for mitigating the excessive demand on social services in Canada. The fact that the son would apparently be taken care of in China by an aunt did not really respond to the visa officer's concern that nothing prevented the applicant, in the future, from sponsoring his son once he himself gained permanent resident status. Accordingly, it was reasonable to require the applicant to submit an individualized plan addressing the problem of excessive demand on social services in Canada, considering that the son could be sponsored in the future without regard to his inadmissibility. The application for judicial review was dismissed and the following question was certified:

> In the aftermath of *Hilewitz v. Canada (Minister of Citizenship & Immigration*, 2005 SCC 57, when an applicant is required to submit an individualized plan to ensure that his family member's admission will not cause an excessive demand on social services, is it acceptable for this applicant to state that the inadmissible family member will not be accompanying him to Canada, considering that he could be sponsored in the future without regard to his inadmissibility pursuant to paragraph 38(2) of the *Immigration and Refugee Protection Act*?

The Federal Court of Appeal dismissed the applicant's appeal because the certified question did not meet the test for certification and could not be determinative of the appeal. The Court of Appeal affirmed that pursuant to subpara. 23(b)(iii) of the regulations, in circumstances where a child is in the legal custody of someone other than an applicant or an accompanying family member of an applicant, a visa officer might conclude that the child's inadmissibility does not render the applicant inadmissible.

Cuarte v. Canada (Minister of Citizenship & Immigration), 2012 CarswellNat 647, 2012 FC 261 — The application for permanent residence was refused. The refusal was based on the medical officer's opinion that the applicant's son, having been diagnosed with global development delay, "might reasonably be expected to cause excessive demand on health or social services" as per s. 38(1)(c) of IRPA. The Saskatchewan *Education Act* does not establish a mechanism allowing reimbursement of publically funded educational services in the circumstances of the applicant. However, it is possible to voluntarily enter into an agreement with the school board to contribute to the applicant's son's expenses. The visa officer concluded that since there was no reimbursement mechanism, the applicant had not proven his ability to pay for the costs of the special education services. The court held that the immigration officer failed to adequately consider the applicant's declaration of intent and ability to pay by relying solely on the absence of a mechanism for reimbursement. Since the immigration officer failed to conduct an individualized assessment and acted unreasonably in requiring that there be evidence of a reimbursement mechanism, the application for judicial review was allowed.

Cramer v. Canada (Minister of Citizenship & Immigration) (2011), 1 Imm. L.R. (4th) 282, 294 F.T.R. 86 (Eng.), 2011 FC 854, 2011 CarswellNat 2802, 2011 CarswellNat 3665 — The applicant sought permanent residence in Canada as a skilled worker. Her application was denied because her daughter Grace suffered from a health condition that might reasonably be expected to cause an excess demand on health and social services in Canada. Specifically, Grace suffered from developmental delay issues. At birth she was slow to breathe and suffered mild cerebral palsy. In response to a fairness letter, the applicants provided a plan for Grace that included keeping her in a normal classroom environment at a private school and continued home therapy from her parents, who had been trained by specialists to conduct such sessions. Parental support would be augmented by assistance from Grace's grandparents with whom the family intended to reside. The officer concluded that the plan was inadequate as it did not include an estimated cost of social services to be used. The officer further highlighted that it was not clear what the backup plan would be if Grace's grandparents were to become infirm or die as they were both approximately aged 70. The medical officer reviewed the file and was of the opinion that the submitted plan did not alter the initial determination of medical inadmissibility.

In assessing the reasonable probability of excessive demand, the medical officer's opinion on which the visa officer relies must be sufficient to explain the decision to the parties, provide public accountability and permit effective review. Here, there were effectively no reasons in support of the medical officer's opinion on record other than the passing reference in the CAIPS notes. The CAIPS notes did not provide any information as to why the medical officer considered Grace inadmissible. When considering the reasons supporting a medical officer's opinion, the concern is whether any inadequacy prevented the visa officer from assessing the reasonableness of the opinion. Statements by the medical officer that are found to be insufficient and constitute a breach of procedural fairness cannot be saved by the greater detail provided by a visa officer's CAIPS notes. The failure of the visa officer to identify what additional costs were considered to constitute excessive demand in the fairness letter and the inadequacy of the medical officer's reasons amounted to a denial of natural justice. Accordingly, the application for judicial review was allowed.

Firouz-Abadi v. Canada (Minister of Citizenship & Immigration) (2011), 99 Imm. L.R. (3d) 346, 2011 FC 835, 2011 CarswellNat 2661, 2011 CarswellNat 3587, [2011] F.C.J. No. 1036 — The applicant applied to the Manitoba Provincial Business Nominee Program and was approved by the provincial authorities. As required, he then applied for permanent residence which included his wife and two sons. In order to obtain visas, all of the family members were required to disclose their medical histories. In the case of the children, medical disclosures confirmed a common diagnosis of mucopolysaccharidosis, a genetic metabolic disorder commonly manifesting in skeletal and neurological impairments of varying degrees of severity.

The approach taken in this case came close to the line drawn by the court in *Hilewitz*. The only information that the medical officer had to support his social services findings was the diagnosis of mucopolysaccharidosis manifesting in mental impairment, and a largely undefined level of dependency. The treating physician had indicated that both boys were able to manage most of their daily needs but were dependent upon the continuing support and supervision of their parents. Notwithstanding the paucity of information about where these children fell on the medical and personal care continuum, the medical officer concluded that they would require vocational training and respite care. No one denied that the children were dependent, but the level of their dependency was described only in very general terms. This is precisely the type of situation where detailed specialists' evaluations were necessary and, indeed, clearly indicated by immigration's Handbook for Designated Medical Practitioners. Under the statutory scheme, a visa officer is not entitled to ignore the stated intentions and assurances of the parents, particularly in a case like this where the identified social services are optional and where the parents have already provided the necessary support to their disabled children well into their adult years. Visa officers are told that fairness letters must explain to applicants that they are obligated to demonstrate a detailed plan indicating how they will obtain anticipated social services or provide for alternative arrangements. Where the response received from an applicant is deemed insufficient, the visa officer is told that a follow-up request may be sent. The fairness letter used here merely sought additional information relating to the medical condition or diagnosis and tepidly invited "any information addressing the issue of excessive demand if it applies to your case." The officer also failed to send a Declaration of Ability and Intent to the applicants to be signed and returned. Had it been sent it would have drawn the applicants' attention to the need to present a detailed plan for the avoidance of excess of demand on Canadian social services. The content of the fairness letter fell well short of the standard required. Although immigration Operational Guidelines are not rules of law, they are ignored by administrative decision makers at some peril because they can create expectations and they may also be seen to express the immigration department's view of what is necessary to achieve a fair outcome. The visa officer's assessment of the principal applicants' financial means was deficient. Some consideration of their expected financial prospects in Manitoba was essential to an understanding of their ability to meet the future financial demands of caring for their two children.

Chaudhry v. Canada (Minister of Citizenship & Immigration) (2011), 95 Imm. L.R. (3d) 93, 2011 FC 22, 2011 CarswellNat 60 — The applicant received a renal transplant in 2004 and required daily immunosuppressive medication. Nonetheless, he had excellent health and expected to remain so for many years, a claim which was supported by letters from two medical doctors in the U.S. His application for permanent residence was refused on the basis that his medical condition might require services, the costs of which would likely exceed the average Canadian per capita cost over five years. The court reviewed the fairness letter and concluded that the documents made it clear that the applicant knew perfectly well what the decisive issue was: drug cost and excessive demands upon the public health system in Canada. He understood this because, in his response, he said that the problems can be overcome and he can make arrangements for a private or group plan that will mean he does not make excessive demands on the public purse. Although the applicant did indicate his willingness to enrol in a private health insurance plan in Canada just as he had done in the United States, his plans were inchoate. Personal undertakings not to access government programs are not enforceable. The application for judicial review was dismissed.

Sharpe v. Canada (Minister of Citizenship & Immigration), 2011 FC 21, 2011 CarswellNat 62 — This was a second judicial review of the respondent's refusal to grant a visa because of the family's developmentally challenged child. The case turned on whether a child's learning disability was moderate or severe. The applicant's son was found to have a sensory-neuro and conductive hearing, severe speech and language delay, fine and gross motor difficulties and significant learning delays. The applicant challenged the description of Conor's disability as "severe" and contended that his disabilities were mild/moderate. Documentary evidence which showed Conor's school was designated as a school for pupils with moderate learning disabilities and did not admit pupils with severe, profound or multiple learning disabilities was provided as well as a conditional acceptance to a private school in Alberta, a psychological report which assessed Conor against the Alberta Department of Education criteria and concluded that he was placed within the mild cognitive disability range for Alberta's education. The second medical officer then concluded that the demand on Canadian health and social services was likely to be reduced to a degree such that it was no longer excessive. However, the visa officer had difficulty drawing the same conclusion. The final result was that the second medical officer changed his assessment and concluded that Conor was severely disabled as regards to his cognitive skills.

When a government body such as immigration requests information of an individual, it is duty-bound to consider that information when received. This is especially so in the case where the information requested is in the form of expert opinion, which is time consuming as well as costly to acquire. If a decision is rendered that runs contrary to the information requested, the decision maker must at least make reference to the contrary information, and account for its rejection. To put it bluntly, if immigration requests certain medical reports and receives two positive medical reports and one negative report, and a medical assessment is rendered apparently solely on the negative medical report, reasons must be given as to why the positive reports are absent from the analysis. Even if the decision makers had considered the requested information, and had placed it in the context of the circumstances of the case, there is nothing on the face of this record communicated to the applicant to indicate that consideration of the favourable material was seriously made. There is no appearance of justice. The decision makers thus failed the applicant in three basic duties of procedural fairness and natural justice in this case. The application for judicial review was allowed.

Sapru v. Canada (Minister of Citizenship & Immigration) (2011), 93 Imm. L.R. (3d) 167, 413 N.R. 70, 330 D.L.R. (4th) 670, 2011 FCA 35, 2011 CarswellNat 1930, 2011 CarswellNat 229 — A medical officer is not obligated to seek out information about the applicants' ability and intent to mitigate excessive demands on social services from the outset of the inquiry. It is sufficient for the medical officer to provide a fairness letter that clearly sets out all the relevant concerns and provides a true opportunity to meaningfully respond to all of the concerns of the medical officer.

When assessing whether a foreign national's health condition might reasonably be expected to cause excessive demand, a medical officer is under a duty to provide sufficient information to an immigration officer to allow the immigration officer to be satisfied that the medical officer's opinion is reasonable.

The judge found the reasons of the medical officer to be inadequate. The judge went on to hold, however, that the inadequacy of the medical officer's reasons was "saved" by the detailed reasons of the immigration officer. The Federal Court of Appeal disagreed with the judge's conclusion that the inadequacies of the medical officer's reasons were overcome by the reasons of the immigration officer. The immigration officer was under an obligation to assess the reasonableness of the medical officer's opinion. No meaningful assessment could be performed on the basis of the inadequate reasons of the medical officer. The judge relied upon an Operational Bulletin 063 which states that "immigration and medical officers should work closely together during the process [of assessing excessive demand on social services] and document this collaboration." However, there is no documentation of such collaborative process in the certified tribunal record in the present case. The sole reference to any communication between the officers is an entry in the CAIPS notes that records a conversation between the two officers prior to receipt of the

Fairness Response. Finally, the judge's conclusion may well have been influenced by his prior finding that the medical officer "considered the non-medical evidence in this case as she was required to do so." Yet the judge recognized that the medical officer's statement and her reasons to the effect that she had read the Fairness Response was insufficient to render her reasons adequate. Little weight could be given to such a generic statement that is silent about what the medical officer did, and whether the principles articulated in *Hilewitz* were applied. The appeal was allowed and the decision of the Federal Court set aside. The matter was remitted to another immigration officer to be redetermined on the basis of a valid medical opinion prepared by a different medical officer.

Aleksic v. Canada (Minister of Citizenship & Immigration), 2010 FC 1285, 2010 CarswellNat 4916, 2010 CarswellNat 5669 — The IAD denied the applicant's appeal of the refusal of the visa officer to grant residence under a family class sponsorship for the applicant's elderly parents because of the inadmissibility of the applicant's father due to poor health. The medical evidence showed that the applicant's father would require more than medication and oxygen, and was expected to likely require ongoing care and management by specialists in various fields of medicine, and health services provided by government. The IAD did not misapprehend the scope of health care services that the applicant's father would have required in the future. The IAD did not err in rejecting the *Hilewitz* arrangement of having the applicant privately pay for the father's medical costs, since *Hilewitz* dealt specifically with an applicant's ability to pay for social services and not health services. The application for judicial review was dismissed.

Aguinaldo v. Canada (Minister of Citizenship & Immigration), 2010 FC 682, 2010 CarswellNat 1975, 2010 CarswellNat 3623 — The applicant, a citizen of the Philippines, had worked for several years as a nurse in a remote hospital north of Saskatoon. She applied for permanent residence status so that her husband and son could immigrate to Canada. The son Jon has autism spectrum disorder. A visa officer denied her application as s. 38(1) of the *Immigration Refugee Protection Act* provides that a foreign national is inadmissible on health grounds if his or her conditions might reasonably be expected to cause excessive demand on health or social services. By virtue of s. 42, this inadmissibility extended to the whole family. The applicant put forth a series of possibilities including one where her son and husband would reside in Saskatoon and her son would attend a private school. Another where her husband who had been taking special courses would soon be in a position to home school Jon. The visa officer made assumptions that the family could not bear the expense should she continue to work in the remote community while her husband and son lived in Saskatoon. No inquiry whatsoever was made as to her current cost of living, and what the cost of living would be in Saskatoon. The record indicated that she earned around $150,000 per year. There was nothing in the record to suggest that that would not be sufficient income to maintain a household for her husband and son in Saskatoon and a separate residence for herself, and pay for Jon's social services. The decision was made without an evidentiary basis, and was procedurally unfair. A judicial review was granted.

In *obiter*, Justice Harrington stated, "I refuse to accept that Canadian immigration law is so rigid as to deny the inhabitants of a northern community the services of a desperately-needed nurse because her son's condition may pose a demand on social services that the applicable payor government would, if necessary, be happy to absorb. Our immigration law creates at least three possible paths to a favourable outcome. First, she may have the ability and intent to offset these costs per *Hilewitz*. Second, s. 24 of IRPA allows an officer to issue a temporary resident permit which can lead to permanent residence. Finally, s. 25 of IRPA allows the Minister to grant a foreign national permanent residence status or an exemption from any applicable criteria, if of the opinion that such is justified by humanitarian and compassionate considerations, taking into account the best interest of the child directly affected. Is it in Jon's best interest that he only be able to see his mother a few weeks a year? Is it in the best interest of the community of La Loche, which desperately needs Mrs. Aguinaldo's services, that she pack up her bags in frustration and go home to her family?"

Bichari v. Canada (Minister of Citizenship & Immigration), 2010 FC 127, 2010 CarswellNat 1166, 2010 CarswellNat 258 — The applicants were an elderly couple from Algeria with 11 children, two of whom reside in Canada. They arrived as visitors in November 1999 and applied for refugee status, which was subsequently refused. They then made an application for permanent residence on H&C grounds. Mrs. Bichari received a kidney transplant and is dependent on anti-rejection medicines for survival. On April 27, 2006, their H&C application was approved in principle. On January 22, 2007, Mrs. Bachari was informed that she was medically inadmissible due to her renal insufficiency post-transplantation. Since the prescription medicines were guaranteed by provincial health insurance, the medical officer concluded that Mrs. Bichari's medical condition might reasonably be expected to cause excessive demand on Canadian health services.

According to Operational Bulletin 021 — June 26, 2006, immigration officers are not allowed to grant exemptions from the application of s. 38 of the Act. If they are of the opinion that an exemption on humanitarian and compassionate grounds may be warranted, or if one is sought, the file must be forwarded to the Director of Case Review at national headquarters. The director refused the applicants' application for permanent residence status finding there were insufficient H&C considerations to issue a temporary resident permit or to exempt Mrs. Bichari's medical inadmissibility. The director relied on articles disclosed to the Bicharis' counsel that renal transplantation does take place in Algeria and that 40 had been done by 1994. The director concluded that there was adequate post-renal transplant care available in Algeria. The court held that if the applicants wanted to question the conclusions of the inferences that could be drawn from these articles, they had ample opportunity to submit, and should have submitted their own evidence, which they failed to do. The applicants also disagreed with the director's reliance on the medical officer's comments concerning the availability of health services in Algeria. Again, if the applicants did not agree with her conclusion it was up to them to submit documentation to the contrary. The standard on H&C applications cannot be whether the applicants will get better or more affordable treatment in Canada; if this were the case, virtually all medically and inadmissible persons would be entitled to stay. Without evidence to the contrary that the medical services were not available in Algeria, it was reasonable for the director to decide how she did. The applicant cannot simply rest his or her case on the fact that the evidence relied upon by the decision maker is speculative when he or she has simply failed to discharge the burden of proof in establishing that proper medical care is not available in their country. The application for judicial review was dismissed.

Mazhari v. Canada (Minister of Citizenship & Immigration), 2010 CarswellNat 1261, 2010 FC 467 — The applicant, a citizen of Iran, applied to come to Canada as a permanent resident. During his medical assessment it was discovered that he had lung cancer. The discovery of the applicant's cancer led to a request from Citizenship & Immigration for further medical examinations. The court concluded that the medical officer's report was not generic but instead met the requirement of being individualized as stipulated by

Hilewitz v. Canada (Minister of Citizenship & Immigration); De Jong v. Canada (Minister of Citizenship & Immigration) (2005), 50 Imm. L.R. (3d) 40 (S.C.C.). In this case, the medical assessment of the applicant was made within a few months of his original diagnosis and surgery. This made the task of evaluating the potential for recurrence more difficult; he had minimal personal history of surviving with the disease post-surgery. Accordingly, the use of statistical information as contained in the medical literature became the only reasonable way of assessing the likelihood that he will require treatment in the future. The fact that the medical officer relied on such statistical data did not necessarily make the evaluation non-personalized. The application for judicial review was dismissed.

Rashid v. Canada (Minister of Citizenship & Immigration) (2010), 88 Imm. L.R. (3d) 165, 2010 FC 157, 2010 CarswellNat 318, [2010] F.C.J. No. 183 — The visa officer found the applicant to be medically inadmissible to Canada and refused the application for permanent residence under the federal skilled worker program. The applicant was HIV positive and asymptomatic, meaning the virus was present but did not manifest any visible symptoms. He contracted HIV in 1996 from contaminated blood in Tanzania. A medical officer determined that the cost of the treatment required for the applicant's condition would likely exceed the amount spent on the average Canadian and would delay or deny provision of those services to those in Canada who might need them. Acknowledging that some HIV-infected applicants will not cross the threshold of excessive demand and thereby qualify for admittance into Canada, the medical officer found that the applicant was on a regimen of medication costing about US$10,000 per year. There is no dispute between the parties that this amount is well in excess of the health cost threshold.

The applicant relied on the Supreme Court of Canada's decision in *Hilewitz v. Canada (Minister of Citizenship & Immigration); De Jong v. Canada (Minister of Citizenship & Immigration)* (2005), 50 Imm. L.R. (3d) 40 (S.C.C.), to argue that, as in the case of social services, a person in the applicant's position can pay for his own medical health services: in this case, the cost of out-patient prescription anti-viral drugs.

The applicant would be eligible for coverage under the provincial Trillium Drug Program if he was to become resident in Ontario, as intended, once a valid Ontario health card was issued to him and upon demonstrating high prescription drug cost in relation to his net household income. The plan to pay for the prescription drugs put forward by the applicant was based upon personal commitments to pay for the required health services. Given the non-enforceability of those commitments and the expected eligibility of the applicant under Ontario's Trillium Drug Program, the visa officer's determination that the applicant did not meet the requirements for immigration to Canada pursuant to para. 38(1)(c) of IRPA, was reasonable and within the range of possible and acceptable outcomes.

The facts of this case were distinguishable from those in *Companioni v. Canada (Minister of Citizenship & Immigration)* (2009), 87 Imm. L.R. (3d) 271 (F.C.), where one of the two applicants had a personal insurance policy that covered prescription drug costs and the second was covered by an employer-based group policy, either or both of which might have continued to apply if the applicants relocated to Canada. In the present matter, the applicant was relying on the personal commitments of his sister and two others.

The following question was certified:

> When a medical officer has determined that an applicant will be in need of prescription drugs, the cost of which would place the applicant over the threshold of "excessive demand" as set out in the *Immigration and Refugee Protection Regulations*, must the visa officer assess the applicant's ability to pay for the prescrip-

IRP Act

tion drugs privately when those same drugs are covered by a government program for which the applicant would be eligible in the province/territory of intended residence?

Jafarian v. Canada (Minister of Citizenship & Immigration) (2010), 87 Imm. L.R. (3d) 262, 360 F.T.R. 150 (Eng.), 2010 FC 40, 2010 CarswellNat 1171, 2010 CarswellNat 241 — The applicant, an Iranian, was selected by Quebec as an investor. His daughter was afflicted with multiple sclerosis. The visa officer came to the conclusion that the family was inadmissible because the daughter's condition might reasonably be expected to cause excess demand on health services. Although the disease is degenerative, it has been controlled by the drug Rebif. In Canada the daughter's prescription would cost some $15,000 a year. The concerns of the visa officer were certainly justified. Pursuant to the Regulations, health services include the cost of both medical personnel and prescription drugs. An "excessive demand" is one which exceeds the average annual Canadian per capita cost, which at the time was just over $5,000. However, and this is crucial to this case, a health service is one for which the majority of the funds is contributed by the governments. The officer referred to the medical diagnosis and quoted from the Health Canada doctor that Rebif ". . . is a very expensive drug which would be provided by provincial medical care plans." In the "fairness letter" the visa officer declared that the daughter's Rebif would be government funded. However, this is not necessarily the case.

The principles enunciated by the Supreme Court in *Hilewitz* and *DeJong* (2005), 50 Imm. L.R. (3d) 40, although expressly limited to social services, are equally applicable to prescription drugs and other health services as long as the majority of the funds for the prescription drug in question are not contributed by governments. The court held that assessments must be individualized and take into account not merely eligibility for services, but also likely demand as well as the applicant's ability and intention to pay. These circumstances are quite unlike *Hilewitz*, where, as a matter of Ontario law, the cost of most if not all the social services in questions were recoverable, irrespective of Mr. Hilewitz's representations. If the majority of the cost of Rebif is not covered by the Quebec government, this issue is moot. If the majority is so covered, then his intentions and good faith are simply not relevant. The law does not permit him to opt out. If this latter scenario is the case, the refusal to grant permanent resident visas to the applicant and his family was correct in law.

The application for judicial review was granted on the basis of a procedural fairness argument. The decision as to whether the care would constitute "excessive demand" was not the Health Canada doctor's decision but rather the decision of the visa officer and he abrogated his responsibility.

Ma v. Canada (Minister of Public Safety & Emergency Preparedness) (2009), 84 Imm. L.R. (3d) 280, 2009 FC 1042, 2009 CarswellNat 4937, 2009 CarswellNat 3234 — This was an application for judicial review of a visa officer's decision to refuse the applicant's application for permanent residence under the British Columbia Provincial Nominee Program (PNP) on the basis that the visa officer was not satisfied that the applicant had both the ability and intent to offset the excessive demand on social services that would be required of his son, Jun Ma.

Jun had a moderate intellectual disability that would necessitate special education. The officer believed that Jun's health condition might cause excessive demand on health or social services in Canada. Such a finding would render the family inadmissible to Canada by virtue of ss. 38 and 42 of IRPA. The officer found that the fact that Jun had been enrolled in a public school in Canada significantly undermined the assertion that, in future, his educational and social services expenses would be paid for privately. Only recently was Jun enrolled in a private school, a fact that raised the question of whether this was done primarily for the purpose of securing immigrant visas rather than as part of a genuine plan to assume responsibility for the cost of Jun's special education services. The court agreed with the applicant that the officer seemed to have unduly been concerned about the fact that Jun had been initially enrolled in public school. The family was under no legal obligation to proceed differently until the issue of inadmissibility was raised, and it was only then that their actions could be fairly scrutinized. The officer's pejorative characterization of the motive for enrolling Jun in private school was troubling since there is nothing inherently objectionable about taking a step with the view to improving an application for landing provided that the process is carried out openly. The officer also failed to inform the applicant that the officer was not satisfied that their future intentions were honourable. It is clear that the officer did not accept these declarations at face value and, without saying so directly, found them to be untrue and sworn only for the purpose of obtaining visas. This was an inference that was based on a negative credibility determination which itself rested upon a tenuous factual underpinning. It was also made without an interview and in the absence of an explicit warning that the credibility of the applicant and his wife and his brother were an issue. The Department has created a form of declaration for visa applicants and, in doing so, it leaves an impression that this will suffice. The fact that these declarations apparently cannot be enforced, and that there are presently no other methods to legally bind someone in the situation of the applicant, is an issue for the Department to solve. Until it does, it needs to show more patience and greater guidance to applicants than was afforded to the applicant in this case. The application for judicial review was allowed.

Companioni v. Canada (Minister of Citizenship & Immigration) (2009), 87 Imm. L.R. (3d) 271, 360 F.T.R. 157 (Eng.), 2009 FC 1315, 2009 CarswellNat 4596, 2009 CarswellNat 4965, [2009] F.C.J. No. 1688 — The officer refused to issue permanent resident visas on the grounds that the applicants were inadmissible as their condition, within the meaning of s. 38 of IRPA, might reasonably be expected to cause excessive demand on health services. Specifically, the cost of out-patient prescription drugs to control their HIV totaling some $33,500 per year made them inadmissible. The general rule in the province of Ontario is that the cost of out-patient drugs is not government funded. It follows that the cost of such drugs is not a demand on health services. There are, however, exceptions to that exception and this is where the difficulty in this case lies.

The principles annunciated in *Hilewitz* (2005), 50 Imm. L.R. (3d) 40 (S.C.C.) are equally applicable in any consideration as to whether the cost of out-patient drugs would constitute an excessive demand on health services. The fundamental distinction, however, is that when it comes to social services, at least in Ontario, as a matter of law the province is entitled to recover most, if not all, of those costs from those who can afford it. But when it comes to the supply of out-patient drugs in Ontario, by virtue of the provincial Trillium Drug Program, most of the cost of the drugs in question would be paid by the province. Promises not to access this program are simply not enforceable.

The visa officer took into account Operational Bulletin 063 which was originally designed to assess the applications of business investors who had medical or social service issues. However, since the Federal Court of Appeal held in *Colaco v. Canada (Minister of Citizenship & Immigration)* (2007), 64 Imm. L.R. (3d) 161, that individual assessments would also be required for skilled workers, hers was a perfectly sensible approach.

She asked herself if the applicants had advanced a credible plan. She also asked herself if the applicants had the financial ability to cover the projected expenses over the full period. However, she was ambivalent as to whether the period was five or 10 years. It appeared to the court that the only possible answer was 10 years, and that the visa officer attempted to give the applicants the benefit of the doubt. Absent a viable insurance plan, most of the cost of the drugs in question would be borne by the province of Ontario, would constitute an excessive demand and would render the applicants inadmissible. Although the evidence on file was far from perfect, there was specific mention of employer-based insurance. However, there was nothing in the record to substantiate the visa officer's belief that employer-based prescription drug coverage would be uninsurable due to their pre-existing condition. Accordingly, the application for judicial review was granted and the matter returned to a different officer for a fresh determination limited to medical inadmissibility. The following question was certified:

> Is the ability and willingness of applicants to defray the cost of their out-patient prescription drug medication (in keeping with the provincial/territorial regulations regulating the government payment of prescription drugs) a relevant consideration in accessing whether the demands presented by an applicant's health condition constitute an excessive demand?

Vazirizadeh v. Canada (Minister of Citizenship & Immigration), 2009 CarswellNat 4932, 2009 FC 807, 2009 CarswellNat 2387, [2009] F.C.J. No. 919 — This was a judicial review of a decision of the IAD to dismiss the appeal of a sponsorship of a parent who was found to be medically inadmissible pursuant to para. 38(1)(c) of the Act because her health condition "might reasonably be expected to cause excessive demand on health or social services" in Canada. Six months after the visa officer's decision, she underwent right knee replacement surgery in Iran. The applicant argued that the IAD hearing, which was a *de novo* hearing, did not consider the appellant's changed medical status. The court, however, concluded that the IAD analyzed the medical condition both at the time of the visa officer's decision in 2007 and the IAD hearing in 2008, including the evidence of right knee replacement surgery, physiotherapy and the opinion of the appellant's orthopedic specialist. However, the IAD reiterated or quoted the original medical opinion which, besides the likelihood of specialized knee replacement surgery, stated that the appellant's mother suffers from other medical problems, *i.e.* hypertension, obesity, osteoporosis and osteoarthritis, degenerative changes of the spine and hands and also degenerative osteoporosis of the thoracic vertebrae.

The Federal Court referred to *Mohamed v. Canada (Minister of Employment & Immigration)*, [1986] 3 F.C. 90, a Federal Court of Appeal decision which held that the medical condition at the time the visa officer refused the visa was the only relevant one and subsequent improvement in the medical condition was only relevant as to whether special relief should be granted on appeal.

The Federal Court concluded that the IAD's decision was well founded in fact and in law and amply satisfied the test of falling within an acceptable range of reasonable decisions and therefore the application for judicial review was dismissed. The Federal Court also refused to certify a question.

Vashishat v. Canada (Minister of Citizenship & Immigration) (2008), 77 Imm. L.R. (3d) 220, 337 F.T.R. 283 (Eng.), 2008 CarswellNat 5282, 2008 CarswellNat 4632, 2008 FC 1346 — The applicant applied to sponsor her father and younger brother as members of the family class. The visa officer found the brother inadmissible pursuant to para.

38(1)(c) of the IRPA on the ground that his state of mental development might reasonably be expected to cause excessive demands on health or social services. The applicant appealed to the IAD which dismissed her appeal and she sought judicial review of that decision. *Colaco v. Canada (Minister of Citizenship & Immigration), infra*, does not stand for the proposition that there has to be evidence of an ability to pay for the services if there is some alternative means to provide them. If a skilled worker applicant can establish that his or her admissibility in Canada cannot reasonably be expected to cause excessive demands on social services, there is no reason to exclude that applicant on that basis.

As was articulated in *Hilewitz v. Canada (Minister of Citizenship & Immigration), infra*, any anticipated burden on the public purse must be tethered to the realities of the applicants' circumstances, including the extent of the family's willingness and ability to contribute time and resources. Here, the family stated that it was prepared to make alternative arrangements to provide employment for him on a farm which would attenuate any anticipated burden or excessive demand on social services. The IAD focused on the family's ability to pay without taking into consideration the alternative arrangements they had made for the younger brother. The IAD did not properly consider the applicants' actual circumstances in determining what "demands" would be made on Canada's services.

The wording of the provision of s. 38 indicates that medical officers must assess likely *demands* on social services, not mere *eligibility* for them. In its reasons, the IAD maintained that "the Appellant might not, at this time, have the intention of using any of the social services for which her brother would be eligible; however, the applicant will have a right to these publicly funded services." This rationale does not meet the threshold required for establishing that the brother's medical condition would or might reasonably be expected to result in an excessive demand on social services. The application was allowed and the matter sent back to another panel.

Colaco v. Canada (Minister of Citizenship & Immigration) (2007), 64 Imm. L.R. (3d) 161, 2007 CarswellNat 2909, 2007 FCA 282 — The applicants and their two children applied under the skilled worker category for permanent resident status. Their application was refused pursuant to subs. 38(1) of the IRPA on the basis that a family member whose health condition — mild mental retardation — might reasonably be expected to cause excessive demand on health or social services.

The rationale enunciated by the Supreme Court of Canada in *Hilewitz v. Canada* [2005] 2 S.C.R. 706 applied and an individualized assessment of the applicant's needs for social services support, as well as their capacity to assume the cost of them is required to determine whether the needs might reasonably be expected to cause excessive demand on these social services.

Kirec v. Canada (Minister of Citizenship & Immigration), 2006 FC 800, 2006 CarswellNat 1770, [2006] F.C.J. No. 1017 — This was an application for judicial review of the decision of a visa officer which refused the applicant's application for permanent residence. The refusal was based on the conclusion that the applicant was inadmissible to Canada pursuant to subs. 38(1) of the IRPA because his daughter might reasonably be expected to cause excessive demand on health or social services as a result of her diagnosis of cerebral palsy. She utilizes the services of occupational and speech therapy, physiotherapy, and assistive technology equipment for communication. In school she is in a modified special education learning environment with a support worker.

Canadian social philosophy has a commitment to equality, full participation and integration of all individuals, and thus an extensive social support system is available. Currently her disability would make her eligible for intensive Special Education and support for required medical and assisted technology devices.

The applicant argued that a fairness letter was issued but did not provide detailed information relied upon by the medical officer. The court disagreed and concluded that the letter outlined the grounds for which the applicant's daughter was found to be inadmissible due to her medical condition. The applicant also argued that the medical notification was flawed because it did not provide evidence as to the actual cost to be incurred by reason of the applicant's daughter's medical condition. The court concluded that despite not providing an exact dollar amount of all the services the applicant's daughter would probably use, it was reasonable for the medical officer to conclude that the total cost would be in excess of the average Canadian per capita cost over a period of five years. It was perfectly reasonable for the visa officer to trust the findings of the medical officer's report in this regard.

The applicant also argued that the medical officer's conclusions were flawed because he had failed to take into consideration the applicant's daughter's personal circumstances, particularly the degree of support that would be provided by the family so as not to place excessive demand on social services. The respondent argued that the family support should not be assessed in the present matter seeing as the applicant was applying for permanent residency based on the skilled worker category and not as a business class category. The court concluded the applicant's daughter had a long history of using social services while living in Canada. Furthermore, the applicant never made any submissions to the fact that his daughter would not place an excessive demand on such services if the family were to move back to Canada from the United States. The visa officer, therefore, clearly took into consideration the personal circumstances of the applicant's daughter. As such, the visa officer did not err in rejecting the applicant's application for permanent residence based on the medical inadmissibility of his daughter.

Cohen v. Canada (Minister of Citizenship & Immigration) (2006), 55 Imm. L.R. (3d) 21, 2006 CarswellNat 1745, 2006 FC 804 — This was an application for judicial review of the decision of a visa officer which refused the applicant's application for permanent residence. The refusal was based on the conclusion that the applicant was inadmissible to Canada pursuant to subs. 38(1) of IRPA because his wife might reasonably be expected to cause excessive demand on health and social services as a result of her diagnosis of rheumatoid arthritis.

The applicant argued that the visa officer's and medical officer's analysis of excessive demand was flawed because both failed in their obligation to calculate the health services costs and social services costs over a period of five years for the average Canadian and the applicant's spouse. The applicant argued that the officer's decision to deny permanent residency was based on the perception that the applicant's spouse needs the expensive drug Entanercept to control her medical condition. However, the applicant argued if the officer had considered the applicant's submissions in response to the fairness letter, she would have concluded that the applicant's spouse does not need this drug to control her condition.

The court concluded that both the visa officer and the medical officer were not precise enough in their conclusions and, accordingly, the conclusions were based on imprecise assessments by both the visa and medical officers. The application for judicial review was granted.

Newton-Juliard c. Canada (Ministre de la Citoyenneté & de l'Immigration) (2006), 57 Imm. L.R. (3d) 15, 2006 CarswellNat 2925, 2006 FC 177 — This was an application for judicial review of a decision by a visa officer to deny the applicant permanent residence based on the health condition (autism) of her daughter, as admitting her to Canada might reasonably be expected to cause excessive demand on health or social services pursuant to subs. 38(1) of the IRPA. One of the grounds raised by the applicant was that the visa officer erred in failing to consider, with regard to the question of excessive demand, the financial situation of the family, which would probably be able to defray the costs of the services required by the applicant's daughter. In other words, the family would itself contribute to reduce the additional costs which would otherwise be assumed by the community in education and care for her autistic daughter through the volunteer work, for example, that the applicant would give to the school, assistance that could certainly be given a monetary value and/or through the purchase of a private insurance policy. The court dismissed the applicant's argument on the basis that the school was a public school financed by the municipality as well as income tax. Further, the court concluded it was purely speculative to take the applicant's volunteer work at the school into account, since nothing in the evidence would have allowed the medical doctor to quantify the time. The court also concluded that since the case did not involve a question of health care for the daughter, but mostly of social services that she needed, the proposal to take out private insurance for health care would have nothing to do with the specialized education in the school. The application for judicial review was dismissed.

Lee v. Canada (Minister of Citizenship & Immigration) (2006), 60 Imm. L.R. (3d) 62, 2006 FC 1461, 2006 CarswellNat 4260 — The applicant was found to be inadmissible pursuant to s. 38(1) of the IRPA. On the basis of medical evidence, the officer found that the applicant's health conditions, which included polycystic kidney disease, hypertension, moderate mitral regurgitation and chronic renal failure, would reasonably be expected to cause "excessive demands" on Canada's health services. The applicant argued that, as he is an entrepreneur with considerable net worth, the officer erred in law by failing to consider his ability to provide for his own health care if admitted to Canada, and further, the officer breached procedural fairness by not considering his request for a temporary resident permit. Specifically, the applicant relied on the Supreme Court of Canada's decision in *Hilewitz v. Canada (Minister of Citizenship and Immigration)*. *Hilewitz* dealt specifically with an applicant's ability to pay for *social services* and not *health services*; therefore the applicant's argument that the reasoning in Hilewitz applied equally to health services was dismissed. The officer did not err in law by not considering the applicant's financial ability to pay for his own health care.

In a letter to the Canadian Consulate, the applicant requested the officer consider granting him a TRP. The officer was required to respond to this request without the necessity of a separate submission. The failure of the officer to deal with this request constituted an error in due process. A different immigration officer was ordered to assess the applicant's temporary resident permit application on the basis of the existing evidentiary record.

Hilewitz v. Canada (Minister of Citizenship & Immigration), [2005] 2 S.C.R. 706, 50 Imm. L.R. (3d) 40, 33 Admin. L.R. (4th) 1, 340 N.R. 102, 259 D.L.R. (4th) 244, [2005] S.C.J. No. 58, 2005 CarswellNat 3234, 2005 CarswellNat 3235, 2005 SCC 57 — The appellant and another both applied for permanent residence, respectively, under the "investor" and "self-employed" classes set out in the *Immigration Act*. These categories require that applicants have substantial financial resources to qualify. Both qualified, but were denied admission because the intellectual disability of a dependent child "would cause or might reasonably be expected to cause excessive demands on . . . social services" in Canada, which made them inadmissible pursuant to s. 19(1)(a)(ii) of the former *Immigration Act.*

The visa officers' decisions were set aside by the Supreme Court of Canada. The Supreme Court of Canada concluded that the personal circumstances of the families of disabled dependants are relevant factors in an assessment of their anticipated impact on social services. Since the "investor" and "self-employed" categories under which the appellants were qualified for admission to Canada were, to a large extent, concerned with an individual's assets, it would be incongruous to interpret the legislation in such a way that the very assets that qualify these individuals for admission to Canada can simultaneously be ignored in determining the admissibility of their disabled children.

The applicants' ability and willingness to attenuate the burden on the public purse that would otherwise be created by their intellectually disabled children was a relevant factor in determining whether those children could reasonably be expected to cause excessive demands on Canada's social services. The fears were articulated in the rejections of the applications, such as possible bankruptcy, mobility, school closure or parental death, represent contingencies that could be raised in relation to any applicant. Using such contingencies to negate a family's genuine ability and willingness to absorb some of the burdens created by a child's disabilities anchors an applicant's admissibility to conjecture, not reality. The visa officers erred by confirming the medical officers' refusal to account for the potential impact of the families' willingness to assist. Moreover, the visa officers' failure to read the families' responses to the fairness letters sent to them meant that their decisions were not based on all the relevant available information.

[Note: Although decided under former legislation (the Immigration Act, *R.S.C. 1985, c. I-2) this decision may still be useful.]*

39. Financial reasons — **A foreign national is inadmissible for financial reasons if they are or will be unable or unwilling to support themself or any other person who is dependent on them, and have not satisfied an officer that adequate arrangements for care and support, other than those that involve social assistance, have been made.**

[Editor's Note: SOR/2002-227, s. 320(8) provides that a person is inadmissible under the new Immigration and Refugee Protection Act, *S.C. 2001 c. 27 for financial reasons if, on June 28, 2002, the person had been determined to be a member of the inadmissible class described in paragraph 19(1)(b) of the* Immigration Act, *R.S.C. 1985, c. I-2 (the "former Act") or had been determined to be inadmissible on the basis of paragraph 27(1)(f) or (2)(l) of the former Act.]*

Case Law

Delisa v. Canada (Minister of Citizenship & Immigration) (2010), 87 Imm. L.R. (3d) 125, 2010 FC 88, 2010 CarswellNat 946, 2010 CarswellNat 165 — The immigration officer refused the applicant's application for permanent resident status under the spouse or common-law partner in Canada based on the applicant's receipt of Income Support from the Ontario Disabilities Support Program (ODSP). The phrase "social assistance" is undefined in the legislation or regulations, but the Federal Court of Appeal has held that it connotes "welfare." It is evident that social assistance is a flexible term that can include among other things "public assistance, in the form of government subsidized housing." There can be no doubt that benefits under the ODSP are a form of social assistance, notwithstanding the fact that the applicant is in receipt of those benefits by virtue of being a dependant of the sponsor who receives those benefits by reason of disability. While a sponsor may be approved as a sponsor despite relying on social assistance by reason of a disability, the applicant must nevertheless satisfy the immigration officer that she is not inadmissible for any of the myriad grounds of inadmissibility pursuant to s. 11 of IRPA. One of those grounds is in s. 39 of IRPA which bars the applicant for financial reasons. Pursuant to s. 39, if applicants cannot show that they are willing and able to support themselves, they must show that adequate arrangement for their care and support have been made, other than those that involve social assistance. The officer's decision on this ground was reasonable. However, the officer breached the duty of procedural fairness by failing to alert the applicant that her receipt of ODSP benefits could render her inadmissible to Canada pursuant to s. 39 of IRPA and to give her an opportunity to address those concerns. The application for judicial review was allowed.

40. (1) Misrepresentation — **A permanent resident or a foreign national is inadmissible for misrepresentation**

(a) for directly or indirectly misrepresenting or witholding material facts relating to a relevant matter that induces or could induce an error in the administration of this Act;

(b) for being or having been sponsored by a person who is determined to be inadmissible for misrepresentation;

(c) on a final determination to vacate a decision to allow their claim for refugee protection or application for protection; or

(d) on ceasing to be a citizen under

(i) paragraph 10(1)(a) of the *Citizenship Act*, as it read immediately before the coming into force of section 8 of the *Strengthening Canadian Citizenship Act*, in the circumstances set out in subsection 10(2) of the *Citizenship Act*, as it read immediately before that coming into force,

(ii) subsection 10(1) of the *Citizenship Act*, in the circumstances set out in section 10.2 of that Act, or

(iii) Paragraph 10.1(3)(a) of the *Citizenship Act*, in the circumstances set out in section 10.2 of that Act.

(2) Application — **The following provisions govern subsection (1):**

(a) the permanent resident or the foreign national continues to be inadmissible for misrepresentation for a period of five years following, in the case of a determination outside Canada, a final determination of inadmissibility under subsection (1) or, in the case of a determination in Canada, the date the removal order is enforced; and

(b) paragraph (1)(b) does not apply unless the Minister is satisfied that the facts of the case justify the inadmissibility.

(3) Inadmissible — **A foreign national who is inadmissible under this section may not apply for permanent resident status during the period referred to in paragraph (2)(a).**

[Editor's Note: SOR/2002-227, s. 320(9) provides that a person is inadmissible under the new Immigration and Refugee Protection Act, *S.C. 2001 c. 27 for misrepresentation if, on June 28, 2002, the person had been determined to be inadmissible on the basis of paragraph 27(1)(e) or (2)(g) or (i) of the former* Immigration Act, *R.S.C. 1985, c. I-2.]*
2012, c. 17, s. 17; 2013, c. 16, s. 16; 2014, c. 22, s. 42

Case Law

Canada (Minister of Citizenship and Immigration) v. Liu, 2016 FC 460, 2016 CarswellNat 1379, 2016 CarswellNat 2883 — The Minister sought judicial review of a decision by the IAD allowing the applicant's appeal of a decision of the Immigration Division. The applicant had obtained permanent residence by way of a marriage of convenience and she was therefore held to be inadmissible for misrepresentation. On appeal, she admitted that the marriage had been a fraud and she thus accepted the ID's finding of inadmissibility; however, she asked that the appeal be allowed on H&C grounds. The IAD accepted this submission. ·

The court agreed with the Minister's submission that the decision was unreasonable because the IAD in considering the issue of establishment did not feel the applicant's misrepresentation was a relevant factor. The misrepresentation is a relevant factor when considering a person's degree of establishment. To do otherwise is to place the immigration cheat on an equal footing with the person who has complied with the law. Whether the impact of the fraud is to reduce the establishment to zero or to something more is a question for the discretion of the decision maker based on the particular facts before him or her. But it must be considered. The application for judicial review was allowed.

Chughtai v. Canada (Minister of Citizenship and Immigration) (2016), 40 Imm. L.R. (4th) 157, 2016 FC 416, 2016 CarswellNat 1384, 2016 CarswellNat 3240 — The applicant sought judicial review of an officer's decision to refuse his application for permanent residence as a skilled worker due to a finding that he was inadmissible to Canada on the basis of misrepresentation, pursuant to para. 40(1)(a) of IRPA. In particular, the officer reviewing the applicant's file found that the applicant had submitted an AEO for a position that was not genuine, and that this submission was relevant to whether or not he met the selection criteria as a skilled worker under the ministerial instructions. This misrepresentation was material to the disposition of the application, and could have led to an error in the administration of IRPA.

The determination of misrepresentation under para. 40(1)(a) is factual in nature and calls for a differential standard of review. The court should not intervene if the decision falls within a range of possible acceptable outcomes which are defensible in respect of the facts and law.

A visa officer has the discretion to refuse an application for permanent residence as a skilled worker, even in cases where HRSDC has issued an AEO. Pursuant to s. 203(1)(a) of the Regulations, an officer must determine on the basis of an assessment provided by the Department of Employment and Social Development if the job offer is genuine. The visa officer must be satisfied that the criteria specified in s. 82 of the Regulations are met. Furthermore, HRSDC's opinion is not determinative of whether a visa should be issued. The immigration officer is the ultimate decision maker. While the officer was permitted to determine the genuineness of the job offer, taking into account the assessment provided by HRSDC, the respondent missed the crux of the issue by a mischaracterization of the impugned decision. It is true that in this case, the officer's finding that the AEO was not genuine led the officer to award the applicant zero points for that category, presumably resulting in the applicant's failure to reach the necessary 67-point threshold. The officer's primary reason for rejecting the application was the finding that the applicant was inadmissible for misrepresentation.

The officer alleged that the employer changed the education requirements of the AEO; however, the court held that rather than altering any of the employment requirements the employer simply stated in his first letter that he was aware of the applicant's educational credentials at the time the AEO was made, that he was familiar with the educational institution from which the applicant received his degree, and that he was satisfied that these credentials were sufficient, particularly in conjunction with the applicant's overall training, background and work experience. This did not rise to the level of clear and convincing evidence of a misrepresentation. Nor did the court conclude that the record suggested that the applicant or the employer misrepresented their familial relationship. While misrepresentation can occur by omission, there does not appear to be any indication that the applicant or the employer believed they were withholding material information with respect to their relationship. The information was volunteered during the interview and was not solicited prior to that time. Although, a relationship between applicant and the employer may be a factor that the officer can take into account in assessing the *bona fide* character of the contract, there is nothing in the Act or the Regulations to prevent family ties between future employer and employee. Overall, it appears that the only evidence the officer used to support the misrepresentation finding was the determination that the employer may not have had an actual business need for the position of office manager. The reasons did not support the officer's finding of misrepresentation on the basis of clear and convincing evidence. The determination of inadmissibility did not fall within the range of possible, acceptable outcomes which are defensible in respect of the facts and law. The application for judicial review was allowed.

Murugan v. Canada (Minister of Citizenship and Immigration), 2015 FC 547, 2015 CarswellNat 1323, 2015 CarswellNat 2283 — The visa officer refused an application for permanent residence on the basis that the applicants were inadmissible to Canada for misrepresentation. The applicant and his daughter were being sponsored by his son who resided in Toronto. Both applicants incorrectly answered "no" on Schedule A with respect to there ever having been refused a visitor visa. The officer refused the application on the basis that the applicants had misrepresented this information on their application for permanent residence. In this case, the issue is whether the misrepresentation — the answer "no" — could have induced an error in the administration of the IRPA. When considered at a "macro" level, or put another way, at a level that does not factor in the reasons for the refusal, there is no doubt that if an applicant fails to disclose a refusal, the reasons for their refusal may not be investigated and a wrong decision on an application for permanent residence could be made. However, in this case, the fact that the applicant's visitor's visa was refused because he might have stayed in Canada could not have had any impact on the decision reached on his application for permanent residence. In other words, it could not have caused the officer to reach an erroneous decision, and therefore could not have induced an error in the administration of the Act. Consideration of the circumstances includes consideration of whether, on the facts of each case, the misrepresentation could have induced an error in the administration of the Act. The application for judicial review was allowed.

Xu v. Canada (Minister of Citizenship and Immigration) (2011), 392 F.T.R. 339 (Eng.), 2011 FC 784, 2011 CarswellNat 7220, 2011 CarswellNat 7221 — The visa officer found that the applicant had misrepresented an offer of arranged Canadian employment and, in the result, she was determined to be inadmissible under s. 40(1) of IRPA. In order to verify the genuineness of the employer's offer of employment, a visa officer asked the applicant to provide corroborating income tax information for it and photographs of its business premises. The employer provided the available documentation and pointed out that two of the requested Canada Revenue Agency forms were not applicable. The visa officer then requested corporate tax return and payroll lists and its 2008 Business Notice of Assessment. The employer refused to provide the additional requested documentation. The visa officer was not satisfied with the response and sent a fairness letter to the applicant. It indicated that the officer had concerns and believed that the applicant had been engaged in a misrepresentation in submitting her application for permanent residence. The employer responded and attempted to explain the significance of some of the information he had previously provided but again refused to submit corporate tax information on the basis that he was "not obliged to do so." The officer concluded that the applicant had misrepresented the fact that there was a genuine offer of employment by providing an arranged employment opinion from a company that, based on financial documents provided, does not have the ability to pay the wage offered in the arranged employment opinion.

The employer may have been correct in its assertion that it had no legal obligation to provide the supporting payroll and income tax evidence required by the visa officer. However, this information was clearly relevant and reasonably considered to be necessary to address the visa officer's concern about the genuineness of the employment offer. While withholding material information may be a basis of finding misrepresentation, here the refusal to do so was that of the employer and not the applicant. There is nothing in the record to show that the applicant was complicit in the employer's decision — a decision that was apparently made for business reasons. The visa officer's decision makes a completely unsupported leap from the reasonable finding of insufficiency of evidence to one of misrepresentation. A misrepresentation is not proved where the evidence is found only insufficient to establish the necessary criteria for admissibility. As a result, the misrepresentation finding was made without regard to the evidence and must be set aside. The application for judicial review was allowed in part.

Kaur v. Canada (Minister of Citizenship & Immigration), 2013 FC 1023, 2013 CarswellNat 3634, 2013 CarswellNat 3916 — The applicant sought judicial review of the finding of inadmissibility by reason of misrepresentation. The officer concluded that documents concerning the applicant's son were fraudulent. As a result, he concluded that the applicant was inadmissible. Procedural fairness was not afforded. Hence, the matter was returned for redetermination by a different officer. The record showed that there were other documents which supported the contention that the applicant's son was a student in university. The officer proceeded to send the letter advising the applicant of the finding of inadmissibility despite two requests for an extension of time. Efficient decision-making cannot alleviate the need to allow for representations to be made.

Dhatt v. Canada (Minister of Citizenship & Immigration), 2013 FC 556, 2013 CarswellNat 2130, 2013 CarswellNat 1631 — The applicant sought judicial review of a decision of a visa officer to refuse his application for permanent residence on the basis he was inadmissible for misrepresentation pursuant to s. 40 of IRPA. Specifically, the applicant was being sponsored by his son and included in his application was his adopted daughter, Kirandeep. The applicant admitted during the interview that Kirandeep's birth certificate had been obtained by providing false information to the Indian authorities.

Having regard to the broad interpretation that must be given to s. 40 of the Act, the court found the officer's decision unreasonable. Simply stated, the material fact that Kirandeep was adopted was never concealed or otherwise misrepresented to the Canadian authorities. Indeed, the deed of adoption indicating that Kirandeep had been adopted was provided to CIC at the very beginning of the application process. The information was thus available to the officer throughout the entire course of the application; there was no attempt to conceal the fact that Kirandeep was adopted. Nor was there an initial misrepresentation that the applicant later attempted to rectify. Also, the birth certificate, though it was obtained fraudulently from the Indian authorities, does not specify that the applicant and his wife are Kirandeep's biological parents. Rather, it merely lists their names under "Name of Father" and "Name of Mother." Finally, nothing suggested that the birth certificate was provided to the Canadian authorities for the purposes of misrepresenting his relationship with Kirandeep, or that the applicant knew or believed he was misrepresenting material information. The officer's notes indicated that during the interview the applicant had clearly stated that Kirandeep was adopted. It cannot be said that the applicant attempted to pass Kirandeep off as his biological daughter. It was unreasonable for the officer to conclude that the applicant misrepresented his relationship with Kirandeep since there was no attempt to conceal the fact that she was adopted. The officer's finding to the contrary fell outside the range of possible, acceptable outcomes and therefore was quashed.

Borazjani v. Canada (Minister of Citizenship & Immigration), 2013 CarswellNat 527, 2013 FC 225 — The applicant sought judicial review of a decision to refuse his application for permanent residence as a skilled worker . The visa officer denied the application and concluded he was inadmissible to Canada for having filed a fraudulent document with this application. Included with the application was a test result form ("TRF") showing his competence in the English language as measured by the International English Language Testing System ("IELTS"). On his original application, he provided a 2001 photocopy of the TRF but subsequently provided an updated, original version of his 2010 TRF. The visa officer informed him that the 2001 TRF could not be verified and warned him that he could be found inadmissible to Canada for misrepresentation. He responded by explaining the TRF was genuine but he no longer had an original copy so that any problems with the document could be explained by the poor photocopy. Further, he explained that since it was more than two years old, IELTS could not verify its contents. At an interview, the authenticity of the TRF was discussed but the officer's current concerns were not alleviated.

The authenticity of the 2010 TRF was not questioned. The applicant had not been required to provide the 2001 TRF with his application but had done so voluntarily. The reasons did not disclose how the officer came to the conclusion that parts of the document were scanned while other parts were photocopied. Further, the officer was concerned that the "test report form number" was improperly formatted; however, the 2001 TRF does not bear a "test report form number." Further, the appearance of a strange watermark on the photocopy of the TRF does not, in itself, suggest that the document was fraudulent; it may have been a feature of the paper on which the copy was made.

A finding of misrepresentation can only be made where there is "clear and convincing evidence" to support it. The evidence before the officer here did not meet that threshold. There was no reasonable basis to conclude the applicant had misrepresented his language skills by way of a fake TRF. The application for judicial review was allowed.

Kaur v. Canada (Minister of Citizenship & Immigration), 2012 CarswellNat 659, 2012 FC 273 — The applicant first applied for a permanent resident visa under the skilled worker class but subsequently withdrew her application. She then married and reapplied for permanent residence on January 4, 2010, including her husband as an accompanying spouse. A visa officer assigned the applicant a score of 69 points but determined that an interview was required due to concerns that the applicant's husband was seven years older than her, which was not common in local culture; that the spouse held a master's degree but had been unemployed since he graduated in April 2007; that the applicant and spouse had been married only one month before she applied for permanent residence; that her new passport issued February 2010 did not indicate she was married; and the applicant's PCC from India issued in May 2010 did not indicate she was married. The visa officer concluded that the applicant had misrepresented her marital status in order to bring her husband to Canada and to pass selection with enough points gained from the spouse's education. After review the manager determined on a balance of probabilities it was more probable that the applicant had misrepresented the facts and deemed the applicant inadmissible for misrepresentation under s. 40 of IRPA.

The court concluded that the manager's decision was taken under s. 40 and that no determination was made under s. 4 of the Regulations. As a result, the manager was not guided by the proper legal considerations and committed a reviewable error. The officer and manager made their findings based strictly on concerns about the *bona fides* of the marriage. Such a determination should have been made under s. 4 of the Regulations. It would then have been open to them to also conclude there was a misrepresentation based on s. 40. Without first determining under s. 4 that the marriage was entered into in bad faith, however, the officer and manager could not simply conclude misrepresentation had occurred based on an unconfirmed doubt as to the *bona fides* of the marriage. The application for judicial review was allowed.

Goudarzi v. Canada (Minister of Citizenship & Immigration), 2012 CarswellNat 1120, 2012 FC 425 — The applicants were found inadmissible pursuant to s. 40(1)(a) of the Act, due to misrepresentation of a material fact in their application for permanent residence. The applicants hired an immigration consultant who was not an authorized immigration consultant or lawyer. The principal applicant states that, unbeknownst to her, the consultant included an International English Language Testing System (IELTS) test result that turned out to be fraudulent.

In keeping with the duty of candour, there is a duty for an applicant to make sure that when making an application, the documents are complete and accurate. It is too easy to later claim innocence and blame a third party when, as in the present case, the application form *clearly* stated that the language results were to be attached, and the form was signed by the applicants. It is only in exceptional cases where an applicant can demonstrate that they honestly and *reasonably* believed that they were not withholding material information, where "the knowledge of which was beyond their control," that an applicant may be able to take advantage of an exception to the application of s. 40(1)(a). This was not such a case. The court acknowledged that the problem of fraudulent immigration consultants was a serious one. However, this problem does not amount to a *defence* against the operation of s. 40(1)(a). Furthermore, subject to the narrow exception, that the negligence of counsel should not cause an applicant who has acted with care to suffer, the court has consistently found that an applicant can be inadmissible under s. 40(1)(a) for misrepresentations made by another without the applicant's knowledge. There can thus clearly be no subjective intent or knowledge requirement to s. 40; this would be contrary to the broad interpretation that the wording and purpose of the provision requires. The application was dismissed.

Farenas v. Canada (Minister of Citizenship & Immigration) (2011), 391 F.T.R. 60, 2011 FC 660, 2011 CarswellNat 2104, [2011] F.C.J. No. 833 — The applicant came to Canada as a caregiver and applied for permanent residence from within Canada. She included both her husband and her son on the application. The visa office in Manila determined that the birth certificate the applicant provided for her son contained fraudulent information. The visa office discovered that there was a registration of the child's birth in 1993 that listed a different father than the birth certificate submitted by the applicant, which was issued in 2003. The officer believed that this act constituted an offence in the Philippines that if committed in Canada would constitute an offence under para. 337(1)(b) of the Criminal Code — causing false information to be inserted into a birth registration. Furthermore, the officer had information that the applicant was still married to the father listed on the 1993 birth registration, when she married her current husband. In the officer's opinion, this constituted the crime of bigamy which is punishable in Canada pursuant to s. 290 of the Code. The officer also opined that the applicant might be inadmissible under para. 36(1)(c) of IRPA for serious criminality. Moreover, she might also be inadmissible due to material misrepresentation under s. 40(1) of IRPA.

The applicant argued that she lacked the required *mens rea* to have committed bigamy and perjury, and the officer conducted no analysis at all regarding the offence of defacing a birth registry. In the absence of a conviction, the officer must look at the facts and Filipino law to determine whether or not there are reasonable grounds to believe that the applicant can be said to have committed the alleged crime in the Philippines, and then he must explain how that same act would constitute a crime in Canada. To be reasonable, it is incumbent on the officer to provide a critical analysis. In the present matter, there is no evidence to suggest that the officer conducted an adequate, critical, equivalency analysis. Consequently, he failed to provide sufficient reasons to support his finding. While the misrepresentations allegedly made by the applicant regarding her first marriage and the father of her child were troubling and breached the duty of candour required by IRPA, they were not sufficient in and of themselves to overcome the deficiencies found in the equivalency analysis and defeat this application for judicial review. The application for judicial review was allowed and remitted to a different decision maker.

Osisanwo v. Canada (Minister of Citizenship & Immigration) (2011), 3 Imm. L.R. (4th) 52, 2011 FC 1126, 2011 CarswellNat 4812, 2011 CarswellNat 3886, [2011] F.C.J. No. 1386 — The applicants filed an application for permanent residence under the family class category. Among the documents they filed included a document bearing a stamp and signature of the local registrar of births. For some unstated reason, officials at Citizenship and Immigration Canada were not satisfied with this document and required DNA testing. That testing led to the conclusion that one of the applicants was the mother of one of the dependent children but the other applicant was not the father. Without requesting an explanation, it appears that the officer determined that the registration of birth document was fraudulent and a material misrepresentation had been made. Therefore, the application was refused. The applicant stated in her affidavit that she did not know that her husband was not the biological father of her son. In the present case, the applicant was clearly the mother of the child. A birth certificate attests to the father being the other applicant. The uncontradicted evidence was that the father had accepted the child and raised the child as his own. He had no reason to believe otherwise. History is replete with children born to and raised by a married couple, believing it to be their own. Must an applicant seeking entry into Canada disclose every extra-marital relationship where there is any possibility that a child might have been fathered by someone other than the husband? Surely our society has not found itself at that point. Here, the husband and wife believed the child to be theirs; a birth certificate attests to that fact. There was no reasonable basis for concluding that there was any *mens rea* to mislead. The application for judicial review was allowed. The following question was certified:

> Is a foreign national inadmissible for misrepresenting a material fact if at the time of filing his/her application for permanent residence or at the time of granting permanent residence he/she has no knowledge of the material fact that constituted such misrepresentation?

Jiang v. Canada (Minister of Citizenship & Immigration), 2011 CarswellNat 3786, 2011 FC 942 — The applicant's Canadian husband filed an application to sponsor her to Canada as a member of the family class. The applicant's daughter was listed on the application as an accompanying dependant. The applicant claimed that, in February 2002, she was raped. The applicant did not inform the sponsor or Citizenship & Immigration Canada of the incident; she revealed it later during an admissibility hearing in 2007. In March or April of 2002, the applicant discovered that she was pregnant. The sponsorship application was successful and the applicant and her daughter were landed in April 2003. As the applicant had claimed that her son was also the biological son of the sponsor, a Canadian citizen, the child was able to immigrate to Canada as a Canadian citizen with his mother and half-sister. In May 2003, the sponsor took samples himself and arranged for a paternity test. The results of that test determined that he was not the biological father of the applicant's son. The marriage disintegrated, and the couple divorced in 2004. In June 2006, the applicant was interviewed by CIC. CIC requested DNA results confirming the parentage of the child. Removal orders were issued against the appellant and her daughter in 2008. The removal orders were based on the finding that the applicant had intentionally misrepresented that the sponsor was the father of her son and on the finding that the daughter had indirectly made the same misrepresentation. The applicant and her daughter appealed these orders. The appeal was allowed for the daughter and dismissed for the applicant. The applicant sought judicial review of the decision dismissing her appeal.

Under subs. 40(1) of the Act, a misrepresentation includes a fact that induces or could induce an error in the administration of IRPA. The court has repeatedly found that a visa applicant seeking to enter Canada has a duty of candour. This duty is codified in subs. 16(1) of the Act. The court has repeatedly held that the purpose of para. (a) of s. 40(1) is to ensure that applicants provide complete, honest and truthful information in every manner when applying for entry into Canada. Since it was assumed that the applicant's son was a Canadian citizen, the normal admissibility checks that would take place when a foreign national seeks entry to Canada did not take place. As a result, the applicant's misrepresentation led to an error in the administration of the Act. The applicant also argued that the misrepresentation was not material because it did not induce an error under the Act. She claimed that the son came to Canada by way of the *Citizenship Act* and not IRPA. Realistically speaking, the misrepresentation induced an error under both statutes. It resulted in the son receiving a benefit under the *Citizenship Act* to which he was not entitled, and it also allowed him to avoid the processes and checks that would have occurred under IRPA if the misrepresentation had not been made. The application for judicial review was dismissed.

Kumar v. Canada (Minister of Citizenship & Immigration), 2011 FC 781, 2011 CarswellNat 2431, 2011 CarswellNat 3513 — Ms. Kumar was a permanent resident of Canada who applied in 2006 to sponsor her family under s. 117 of IRPA. Her father, her mother and their dependent son, Sumit Kumar (her brother) were included in the application. The visa officer twice requested a statutory declaration from Sumit verifying his marital status. Ms. Kumar sent an email to the consulate advising that her brother declares that he is engaged to his girlfriend and they have a daughter together. The brother also sent a note to the consulate indicating that he was engaged. The officer sent out a fairness letter stating that because the applicants had failed to declare the existence of a child at the time of applying for permanent residence, the officer had come to the conclusion that Sumit misrepresented himself and that all of the applicants could possibly be inadmissible for permanent residence. The officer gave the applicants an opportunity to respond. Ms. Kumar wrote stating that Sumit had not been in touch with his ex-girlfriend for four years and only became aware of the child in November 2009, after the application had been filed. The court held that it was reasonable for the officer to conclude that Sumit's withholding of a fact that he had a daughter on the original application for permanent residence amounted to misrepresentation under para. 40(1)(a) because it could have induced an error in the administration of the Act. There was no satisfactory explanation given for withholding the information.

Mai v. Canada (Minister of Public Safety & Emergency Preparedness), 2011 FC 101, 2011 CarswellNat 211 — The applicant challenged the legality of a decision made by the Immigration Appeal Division to uphold the removal order issued for misrepresentation. The applicant was born in Vietnam and applied for permanent residence under the family class as an unmarried dependant of his father who lived in Canada and acted as sponsor. He obtained his visa and arrived in Canada in March 2005. However, in the interim, the applicant married his pregnant girlfriend in a Catholic ceremony on August 17, 2004. The marriage was not registered at the time with the Vietnamese government. Their child was born on September 18, 2004. The birth was not registered at the time with the Vietnamese government either. The applicant did not report either his marriage or the birth of his child to immigration officials. In 2006, the applicant decided to sponsor his wife and child and disclosed that they were married in August 2004 and their son was born in September 2004. The applicant's wife indicated that they had lived together from 2000 to 2004. The applicant argued that he honestly believed his religious marriage was not required to be reported, and as such he should not be punished by having made an inadvertent error.

While the general argument could be made that common-law marriages can often be difficult to define or prove, this is patently not the case. Even if the applicant had believed that his religious marriage was not a real marriage in the eyes of the Vietnamese and Canadian governments, he repeatedly stated that he viewed the marriage as valid, as per his Catholic faith. Indeed, the applicant and his wife supposedly underwent the religious ceremony in 2004 in order to save their families from the shame of an illegitimate child. Furthermore, since the applicant's wife indicated on her application that they had lived together since 2000, the applicant's relationship with his wife clearly qualified as, at the very least, a common-law marriage. Thus the applicant was obliged to report that his spouse or conjugal status had changed, which he did not do. The application for judicial review was dismissed.

Mahmood v. Canada (Minister of Citizenship & Immigration), 2011 FC 433, 2011 Car-swellNat 1103, 2011 CarswellNat 1935 — The applicant, a Canadian citizen, applied to sponsor his mother for permanent residence. The applicant included the applicant's sister who at the time was aged 22 and was a dependant of the mother. When the application was reviewed, concerns were raised regarding the authenticity of the sister's educational documents. The visa post sent a fairness letter alleging that the educational certificates were counterfeit. The mother responded explaining that her daughter was an established doctor in Pakistan and was shocked to learn that her educational documents were coun-terfeit. The mother indicated that the daughter was no longer interested in immigrating to Canada. The officer concluded that the mother's misrepresentation was material in that it could induce an error in the administration of the Act. She was found inadmissible.

In some instances it might be difficult to parse credibility concerns from the mere fact or substance of an alleged misrepresentation. However, in the present case the mother was given a reasonable opportunity to present evidence to refute the officer's concerns. She failed to do so. The duty of fairness does not relieve an applicant from having to dis-charge the onus to satisfy the officer that she has met all the requirements of IRPA and is entitled to a visa. The application for judicial review was dismissed.

Haque v. Canada (Minister of Citizenship & Immigration), 2011 FC 315, 2011 Car-swellNat 1638, 2011 CarswellNat 626 — The principal applicant, Mr. Haque, was found inadmissible to Canada under para. 40(1)(a) for having omitted and misrepresented cer-tain information in his application for permanent residence pertaining to his prior studies, residency and work history. His application failed to disclose that he had formerly lived and studied in the United States for over one year. He also omitted or misrepresented details with respect to his places of residence, his education and his employment history. A foreign national seeking to enter Canada has a "duty of candour" which requires dis-closure of material facts. Mr. Haque did not disclose the information that, had it not been discovered, could have resulted in a visa issued without the required police and conduct certificates from the United States. This information was material to the application and without it, an investigation would have been foregone that could have had the effect of inducing an error in the administration of the Act. If the information was deliberately omitted to avoid a delay in conducting such inquiries, it was a costly mistake. The court did not accept Mr. Haque's argument that he had corrected his misrepresentation. Al-though para. 40(1)(a) is written broadly, it should not be read to mean that it applies in all situations where a misrepresentation is clarified prior to a decision being rendered. The application for judicial review was dismissed.

Tabungar v. Canada (Minister of Citizenship & Immigration), 2010 FC 735, 2010 Car-swellNat 3036, 2010 CarswellNat 2089 — The applicant's application for permanent res-idence was refused. The applicant claimed she had work experience for more than four years in certain listed occupations. She provided a letter from Tower Languages Tutorial Centre and a letter from Johnson Controls giving details as to her employment with those organizations. A clerk at the Canadian Embassy phoned Tower and what she believed was the correct branch of Johnson Controls and spoke to some otherwise unidentified persons there. The clerk's notation in the CAIPS notes as to the conversation with Tower is to the effect that she was told the applicant's employment there was part-time. The clerk's notation in the CAIPS notes as to the conversation with Johnson Controls is to the effect that she was told no such person by the applicant's name worked there. The file was then forwarded to an officer who made a notation on the cover of the file: "Appears fraud employ cert." The application was ultimately refused. The evidence in the record showed that the clerk phoned the wrong office. The clerical error appears to have resulted in an endorsement on the corner of the file of "fraud" and raised concerns as to "credibility" by the officer who made the decision. Where the notation "fraud" is made on the file by a visa officer a red flag has been raised requiring serious investigation by the decision-making officer and, in the case of any doubt, even if the matter is not directly relevant, the applicant should be given a reasonable opportunity to respond. The application for judicial review was allowed.

Ghasemzadeh v. Canada (Minister of Citizenship & Immigration) (2010), 372 F.T.R. 247 (Eng.), 2010 FC 716, 2010 CarswellNat 2941, 2010 CarswellNat 1997 — The applicant is a citizen of Iran who applied to immigrate to Canada. He refused to answer questions asked of him during interviews with Canadian Security Intelligence Service agents and a Canadian visa officer regarding projects he worked on as an employee with the Iranian Defense Industries Organization ("DIO") as part of his compulsory military obligations as a citizen of Iran. It was determined that he was inadmissible to Canada on the basis of misrepresentation, pursuant to subs. 40(1)(a) of IRPA. The applicant sought to quash the decision.

The onus is on the applicant to show that he meets the requirements of IRPA. Section 16(1) of IRPA imposes a duty on the applicant to answer truthfully all questions asked during an examination. A visa may be issued if, following an examination, an officer is satisfied that a foreign national is not inadmissible and meets the requirements of IRPA. To facilitate the visa officer's decision, the applicant is required to answer truthfully all questions put to him for the purposes of the examination. Should the Minister deny the visa on the basis of inadmissibility, the onus is on the Minister to show the grounds for a finding of inadmissibility.

It was not disputed that the refusal to answer questions constituted a withholding of information for the purposes of s. 40(1)(a) of IRPA. Although the visa officer did not cite the specific ground of inadmissibility, this omission did not constitute an error because the totality of facts led to only one reasonable conclusion: he knew he was a security concern and remains so. The materiality of the questions regarding the applicant's activities at the DIO is without doubt. The effect of refusal to answer questions, specifically the failure to disclose his employment activities, was to foreclose or avert further inquiries. Ultimately, the purpose of the officer's inquiry regarding inadmissibility was frustrated. The withholding could have induced an error in the determination of the applicant's inadmissibility under IRPA. The application for judicial review was dismissed.

Singh v. Canada (Minister of Citizenship & Immigration) (2010), 89 Imm. L.R. (3d) 36, 2010 FC 378, 2010 CarswellNat 3016, 2010 CarswellNat 817, [2010] F.C.J. No. 426 — The applicant was recently found to be inadmissible for misrepresenting or withholding a material fact when he immigrated to Canada in 1993. At that time, he did not disclose that he had fathered a child, Shilpa, who remained in India. His defence is that he did not know he had fathered a child. Paternity had been scientifically established by DNA tests. As a result, the Immigration Division of the Immigration and Refugee Board of Canada issued an exclusion order and he was ordered removed from Canada. His appeal to the Immigration Appeal Division was dismissed. He sought judicial review of that decision.

The applicant's submission is that he could not have misrepresented or withheld facts within the meaning of s. 40 of IRPA or its predecessor, since subjectively he had no knowledge at the time that he was Shilpa's biological father. The Minister's position is that it does not matter what the applicant knew or did not know, it is a scientifically proven fact that he is Shilpa's biological father, and that is the end of the matter.

Given that the wording "knowingly" does not appear in s. 40, it follows that knowledge is not a prerequisite to a finding of misrepresentation or withholding material facts. Undoubtedly, the existence of a child is a material fact. In this case, the alleged misrepresentation was a misstatement of fact. Such misrepresentations may be fraudulent, negligent or innocent. The panel found that the applicant was not credible. Even if he did not know that he was Shilpa's father, the circumstances, *i.e.* his long sexual relationship with Shilpa's mother while her husband was out of India, should, at the very least, have put him on inquiry. He had a duty of candour which required him to disclose upon his arrival in Canada in 1993 the strong possibility that he had fathered a child. The panel's assessment of facts was not unreasonable and so it follows that the applicant, a permanent resident, is inadmissible for misrepresentation.

One of the objectives of IRPA, as set out in s. 3, is "to see that families are reunited in Canada," not to remove someone against his will so that he may be reunited with his wife and daughter in India. The panel noted that the applicant had been here for many years, and had been gainfully employed, however, it made no assessment of the job prospects of a 50-year-old man in India, taking into account his obligation to support his wife and child. How the couple manages their affairs is their business. It would appear that they would prefer that the applicant work in Canada. There is nothing preventing him from visiting his wife and daughter in India on a regular basis. Perhaps after he has saved more money, he will return to and retire in India. It was not for the panel to say that they would be better off if reunited in India now. This smacked of "big brotherhood." This aspect of the decision was unreasonable. The matter was referred back to a differently constituted panel for reconsideration.

Chen v. Canada (Minister of Public Safety & Emergency Preparedness), 2010 FC 584, 2010 CarswellNat 2957, 2010 CarswellNat 1506 — The applicant, a Chinese citizen, married Ms. Zou, a Canadian resident. She then sponsored him for permanent residence. When he arrived in Canada about a year later, he found her pregnant with another man's child. After a month or two, the marriage fell apart. After their divorce, he married an old flame in China and as a Canadian permanent resident endeavoured to sponsor her. At this stage, the immigration authorities became suspicious. Not only was the sponsorship of his second wife disallowed, he was also declared inadmissible for misrepresentation by directly withholding information and representing that his first marriage was genuine. The applicant appealed that decision to the Immigration Appeal Division of the Immigration and Refugee Board. His appeal was dismissed. This was the judicial review of that decision.

The basis for holding that the marriage was not genuine was that it only lasted for a short time, and that he did not immediately return to China when the marriage broke up but returned a short time later to pursue a former flame. These facts cannot establish an evidentiary basis that the marriage was not genuine in the first place. He could not know at the time of the marriage that his wife would become pregnant with another man's child a year later. As to not immediately returning to China when the marriage broke down, he said that as a cuckold he would be the laughing stock of his village. There was no evidence to contradict that statement. When he returned thereafter, it was in a different context altogether. As to not sharing the rumours regarding his wife's affair at the time of the interview, he withheld no material fact. The only fact was that he had heard rumours. Even if they were true, it did not mean that the marriage was necessarily at an end. The

Divorce Act specifically contemplates a possible reconciliation and the divorce papers jointly signed by the parties, which are to be found in the tribunal record, contain their joint statement that reconciliation was not possible. The duty of candour did not oblige the applicant to share his worries with an immigration officer. There was no misrepresentation and no fact was withheld. The application for judicial review was granted.

Uppal v. Canada (Minister of Citizenship & Immigration), 2009 CarswellNat 1209, 2009 FC 445 — The applicant family sought judicial review of a decision refusing their applications for permanent residence through a family sponsorship. While acknowledging that they had initially misrepresented the nature of their familial relationships, the applicants submit that the misrepresentation was withdrawn prior to a decision being made in relation to their application. Accordingly, they argued there was no material misrepresentation that induced or could induce an error in the administration of the IRPA. The applicants argued that the officer erred in failing to give any weight to the documents provided by them to demonstrate the validity of the marriage between two of them, Mr. Uppal and Ms. Kaur. It was clear that the applicants concealed the fact of Mr. Uppal's first marriage, and misrepresented the true nature of the relationship between Ms. Kaur and his two older children. The family history and the nature of the familial relationships between the various parties to the application for permanent residence were clearly both relevant and material in a family sponsorship application. Although counsel endeavoured to portray the "clarification" letter sent as a voluntary correction of the record by the applicants, the reality is that they only acknowledged the true nature of the relationships between the various individuals once it was clear that their misrepresentation was about to be revealed through DNA testing.

The misrepresentations in this case were made in the context of the applications for permanent residence that were under consideration by the officer. In such circumstances, the fact that the misrepresentations were disclosed by the applicants prior to a final decision having actually been taken in relation to their application does not assist them. The court has previously held in *Khan v. Canada (Minister of Citizenship & Immigration)*, 2008 FC 512 at paragraphs 27–29, that such an interpretation would lead to situations where individuals could knowingly misrepresent their circumstances, but nevertheless escape an inadmissibility finding as long as they disclose a misrepresentation right before a decision was made. Not only would such an interpretation encourage the abuse of the Act, it also ignores the requirement to provide truthful information in applications under it. The application for judicial review was dismissed.

Nazim v. Canada (Minister of Citizenship & Immigration), 2009 CarswellNat 1216, 2009 FC 471 — The applicant sought judicial review of a decision rejecting his application for permanent residence as a member of the spouse in Canada class. The immigration officer found that the applicant had misrepresented a material fact in relation to his application. The applicant initially came to Canada in 1997 and made a refugee claim based on his alleged fear of persecution in Pakistan as a result of his membership in the Mohajir (or Muttahida) Quami Movement (or "MQM"). He was called in for an interview with the Canadian Security Intelligence Service. During questioning by these officials, the applicant changed his story, and claimed that he had never in fact been a member of the MQM. He claimed that an immigration consultant had counseled him to provide the fabricated story of the MQM membership and persecution by Pakistani forces. When the applicant was later interviewed by representatives of Citizenship and Immigration Canada, he repeated his new story and provided CIC with a revised application form that made no mention of either membership in, or association with, the MQM. An immigration officer subsequently found him to be inadmissible to Canada pursuant to s. 40(1)(a) of the IRPA for having misrepresented or withheld material facts in connection with his application for permanent residency.

This case was somewhat unusual in that rather than enhancing his application for permanent residency, the misrepresentation made by the applicant could actually have led to him having been found to be inadmissible to Canada on security grounds. As such, it was clearly material to his application. It appears, however, that the applicant only came to understand the potential implications of his misrepresentation in the course of his CSIS interview. It was at this point that he changed his story and denied ever having been a member of the MQM. The court was satisfied that the officer's conclusion was reasonably available and the application for judicial review was dismissed.

Mukamutara v. Canada (Minister of Citizenship & Immigration), 2008 CarswellNat 923, 2008 FC 451 — The decision challenged was a refusal by a visa officer to grant an application for permanent residence to the applicant's adopted daughters. The basis for the decision was that the officer found the two girls to be untruthful about the date of their father's death, although only one had been interviewed. The effect of the decision was to keep the daughters away from their adoptive mother. This case turns on the confusion surrounding the date of death of the girls' father. On the application it was listed as July 12, 1990. An undated death certificate was provided with the July 12, 1990 date of death filled in. One of the daughters was interviewed and she clarified that her father died on August 2, 1992. A corrected and dated death certificate was provided to the officer. The applicant claimed that when filling in the application, she had relied on the July 12, 1990 date of death from the erroneous certificate. The officer did not believe that the girls' father had died or at least not on the dates in issue, that they had lied on their application and concluded that neither of them fit within the class of persons who could be sponsored.

The issue of misrepresentation comes down to the materiality of the representation or withholding. The date of death in this case may have been material, particularly if it had any relevance to the validity of the adoption. However, there was insufficient clarity in the record to consider that the officer was questioning the validity of the adoption on the basis that the father was not dead at the time of adoption. Rather, the issue that troubled the officer was more related to the *timing* of death than the *fact* of death. Therefore, it was not possible to determine if there was some materiality to the misrepresentation other than that the officer may have felt that persons who misrepresent in any circumstance should not be admitted to Canada. As such, the officer erred in law in concluding that she had a discretion to refuse the application because of a misrepresentation, the materiality of which was never addressed. The officer never directly challenged the validity of the adoption — a most material fact.

Koo v. Canada (Minister of Citizenship & Immigration) (2008), 74 Imm. L.R. (3d) 99, 2008 CarswellNat 2630, 2008 CarswellNat 5631, 2008 FC 931 — This was an application for judicial review of an immigration officer's decision which refused the applicant's permanent residence visa under the skilled worker category. The scope of this application was limited to the officer's finding that the applicant was inadmissible to Canada on the basis that he had misrepresented or withheld material facts within the meaning of s. 40(1)(a) of the IRPA. The officer refused the applicant's application for permanent residence because she determined that he did not meet the necessary points required to be granted permanent residence in Canada and because she had found that the applicant has misrepresented or withheld material facts which could have induced errors in the administration of the Act. Specifically, she concluded that he did not admit to having previously applied for and been refused permanent residence in Canada and that he did not admit to having previously used another name. She also found that he stated on his application that the highest level of education was a trade/apprenticeship credential when in fact his highest level of education was a secondary diploma.

The applicant swore an affidavit that he believed that both his previous and current names had been provided on the forms included with his application for permanent residence submitted by his former representative. He argued that despite both names not being disclosed on the forms that the officer should have found his previous legal name as it appeared throughout the supporting documentation submitted with the application. The court concluded that this was clear evidence that the applicant did not mislead Citizenship and Immigration authorities. At his interview, the applicant advised the officer that he had not thoroughly read the completed application forms before signing them. In light of this explanation and the fact that the applicant had clearly not attempted to conceal his previous name because he had provided numerous supporting documents in his previous name and had also disclosed his previous name at the interview, it was unreasonable for the officer to conclude that the failure to include his previous name on the application forms was not simply a human error in transcription, as his former representative recognized, and did rise to the level of misrepresentation under s. 40(1)(a) of the Act.

The applicant checked off the "yes" box to the question whether he had "previously sought refugee status in Canada or applied for a Canadian immigrant or permanent resident visa or visitor or temporary resident visa," but checked off the "no" box to the question as to whether he had been refused such status. The applicant stated that this was an oversight on both the part of himself and his former representative and it was in no way intentional. Further, when the applicant was asked at the interview about whether he had previously submitted any immigration application, the CAIPS notes reflected that he advised the officer that he had previously submitted an application for permanent residence in Canada, which was refused in 1995. The applicant's previous disclosure was found to support his claim that he misread the question on the application form and inadvertently ticked off the wrong box. Moreover, no assessment of the materiality of the inadvertent failure to disclose that the applicant had previously applied for permanent residence was conducted. Such an assessment is necessary in order to properly evaluate whether a misrepresentation was material in accordance with s. 40(1)(a) of the Act. The officer's failure to conduct such an assessment constituted a reviewable error.

Finally, the officer's finding that a misrepresentation was made with respect to the applicant's educational credentials also constituted a reviewable error. The applicant's former representative interpreted the applicant's experience and training to have constituted an apprenticeship level of education. While this may have been an inaccurate interpretation, it is not an entirely unreasonable conclusion given the fact that the applicant had undergone a significant amount of practical training and had been accredited by the government of Taiwan in the field of Chinese cuisine as the result of successfully completing a government-administered examination. The awarding of points was a matter to be evaluated by the officer and the officer did just that. She questioned the applicant about his education and he answered her honestly and openly. It is as a result of her review of his educational documentation, the information provided by the applicant himself at interview and her subsequent analysis that she came to the conclusion that the applicant should not be awarded the points requested by his former representative. This is the role of a visa officer and it is the work they conduct on a daily basis.

The inadvertent errors made by the applicant and his consultant did not in any way meet the threshold of s. 40 of the Act. Not only were they not misrepresentations, but neither were they material. The officer failed to conduct the proper analysis as to the materiality of the alleged misrepresentations, which was also a reviewable error. The officer had a duty to consider the totality of the information that was in the applicant's file with immigration for almost two years, which she did not do. The application for judicial review was granted.

Bodine v. Canada (Minister of Citizenship & Immigration), 2008 CarswellNat 2300, 2008 FC 848 — The applicant, a citizen of the United States of America, attempted to enter Canada at the Peace Arch border crossing. The applicant stated that she was seeking entry as a visitor to stay with a friend in Canada for two or three months. The applicant was refused entry by a CBSA officer. The officer concluded that the applicant would not leave Canada at the end of her stay because she was unemployed and did not have proof of funds to support herself during her stay in Canada. Also, she did not have documents proving her ties to the United States or proof of an address in the United States to which she would return. Further, the number and nature of the items in her vehicle suggested that the applicant was coming to Canada to live. These items included personal documents (pay stubs, journals, and old mail), sheets of return address stickers with a Vancouver address, a wooden chest, bicycle and a bicycle rack, and several bags of personal goods. The applicant voluntarily withdrew her application for entry to Canada. Later, the same morning, the applicant's boyfriend, a Canadian citizen, met the applicant and transferred a number of articles from her car to his vehicle. The applicant also obtained an ATM receipt as proof of the funds in her bank account and a bank statement showing her home address in Colorado. The applicant then proceeded to the Peace Arch border crossing and was admitted into Canada without being referred to secondary examination. The officer who admitted the applicant into Canada was not aware that the applicant had voluntarily withdrawn her application earlier that morning or of the reasons for that withdrawal. Shortly thereafter, the applicant's boyfriend attempted to re-enter Canada and was referred to secondary examination. A number of articles were found in his car, including: a bicycle and bicycle rack; a wooden chest containing anti-war and cannabis literature; personal file folders filled with personal information and art work; photo albums; old letters; old bills; unopened letters; several notebooks; old books; women's clothing and shoes; a certificate of achievement for a course that was completed; and the applicant's expired passport and expired driver's license. Upon discovering that the applicant had entered Canada, the items were seized and a warrant was issued for the applicant's arrest on the grounds that she was inadmissible for a misrepresentation pursuant to s. 40(1)(a) of the Act. The applicant was arrested and at an inadmissibility hearing, the Board found that the applicant had indirectly withheld information or made a direct misrepresentation, noting that when she entered Canada she "was not asked . . . . about the quantity of belongings she was bringing into Canada . . . because she was displaying only a minimal of personal effects." The Board held that the purpose of transferring most of her belongings to her boyfriend's car was unquestionably to mislead the examining officer into believing she was bringing into Canada less than she actually was. The Board found that this misrepresentation was material because, by removing the bulk of the belongings, the applicant foreclosed or averted further inquiries, or in other words, she cut off an avenue of investigation for the officer. The Board concluded that the misrepresentation induced, or could have induced, an error in the administration of the Act. The applicant sought judicial review of the Board's decision.

It is clear that a duty of candor exists and that the surrounding circumstances are important for deciding what that duty entails in any particular instance. This case presents the question of the extent to which an applicant must disclose information when not expressly asked for that information by an examining officer. Section 40 of the Act does not require that a person must spontaneously disclose *any* fact that could *possibly* be relevant. Instead, to determine whether the withholding of information constitutes a misrepresentation under the Act, it is necessary to consider the surrounding circumstances in each instance. Here, the applicant knew or ought to have known that the amount and the kind of goods she was bringing into Canada was a relevant fact that the examining border services officer would need to know in order to assess whether she was admissible under the Act.

On the specific facts of this case, there was an obligation on the part of the applicant to fully disclose the number of articles she was bringing into Canada, since only a few hours earlier the applicant, to her knowledge, was refused entry because of, *inter alia*, the quantity and nature of the articles in her possession. The application for judicial review was dismissed.

Ali v. Canada (Minister of Citizenship & Immigration), 2008 CarswellNat 905, 2008 CarswellNat 279, 2008 FC 166 — A visa officer held a dependent of a convention refugee from Bangladesh to be inadmissible for landing in Canada due to misrepresentation under s. 40(1) of the IRPA. The visa officer's CAIPS notes disclose that, prior to the misrepresentation being detected, there was no outstanding issue with respect to the applicant's age or his family relationships. The misrepresentation issue arising thereafter was due to the fact that the applicant submitted a fraudulent school record. The applicant subsequently filed a further school record and stated that the misrepresentation was made without his knowledge.

In order for an applicant to be inadmissible due to misrepresentation, s. 40(1) of the IRPA requires that the misrepresented facts be material to the application. Therefore, by Citizenship & Immigration Canada's policy guidelines with respect to evaluating whether a misrepresentation will render an applicant inadmissible, the materiality of the misrepresentation must first be determined. The CAIPS notes do not reflect any analysis by the visa officer on the issue of the materiality of the misrepresentation under consideration. In the evaluation of the applicant's admissibility, his age, identity, and family relationships were not in doubt prior to the detection of the misrepresentation. As a result, the reasons given in the rejection letter do not constitute an analysis of materiality warranting the applicant's rejection. On this basis, the visa officer's decision was not in accordance with s. 40(1) of the IRPA, and further, is factually erroneous. The visa officer's decision was set aside and referred back for redetermination by a different visa officer.

Walia v. Canada (Minister of Citizenship & Immigration), 2008 CarswellNat 1079, 2008 CarswellNat 2640, 2008 FC 486 — The applicants sought judicial review of a decision that they were inadmissible to Canada for directly or indirectly misrepresenting or withholding material facts contrary to para. 40(1)(a) of the IRPA. The principal applicant had indicated that she was divorced and did not cohabitate with one Mr. Ashok Raikhywalia. An officer from the High Commission visited the applicant's village and house and discovered that she was still in cohabitation with Mr. Ashok Raikhywalia. The applicant was given an opportunity to address the officer's concerns about the misrepresentation.

The officer's finding as to the making of a material misrepresentation within the scope of para. 40(2)(a) of the Act was grounded in the finding that Mrs. Raikhywalia continued to cohabitate with her former husband. The question of "cohabitation," means more than simple shared residence, if that is indeed the situation here. The word "cohabitate" has been interpreted as meaning a "marriage-like" relationship characterized by the features of financial interdependence, a sexual relationship, a common principal residence, mutual obligations to share the responsibility of running the home and the "expectation each day that there be continued mutual dependency." The evidence in the record fell short of establishing these facts. The decision of the visa officer did not meet the standard of reasonableness. The application for judicial review was allowed.

Baro v. Canada (Minister of Citizenship & Immigration), 2007 CarswellNat 4369, 2007 CarswellNat 5117, 2007 FC 1299 — The applicant was found to be inadmissible to Canada on the basis that he had misrepresented or withheld material facts from immigration authorities when his spouse, a Canadian resident, sponsored his application for permanent residence. The applicant admits that he had a previous marriage. He says that he became estranged from his spouse and then having lost touch with her entirely obtained a declaration from a court in the Philippines presuming her to be dead. He did not mention these facts to Canadian immigration officials. His second wife notified authorities after she learned, on a visit to the Philippines, that the applicant's first wife had reappeared. The Board concluded that the applicant was inadmissible to Canada. It found that the Canadian official had requested a "marriage check" in the form of a certificate from the National Statistics Office. In providing a certificate indicating that no marriage was registered in his name, the applicant had misrepresented the facts. Further, by omitting to mention the existence of an order recognizing that his first wife was presumed dead, he had failed to disclose a material fact. The court considered whether the applicant had a duty to disclose his marital history in the circumstances even in the absence of a specific request from Canadian authorities.

In general terms, an applicant for permanent residence has a "duty of candour" which requires disclosure of marital facts. This duty extends to variations in his or her personal circumstances, including a change of marital status. Even an innocent failure to provide material information can result in a finding of inadmissibility. An exception arises where applicants can show that they honestly and reasonably believed that they were not withholding material information. An applicant's marital history is clearly relevant to an application for permanent residence based on a spousal sponsorship. Canadian officials will want to ensure that the union is genuine and the applicant's marital background is a valid factor for them to take into account. In this case, Mr. Baro was obligated to disclose his marital history. While he complied with the request for an official certificate of marriage registration, his compliance with that request did not absolve him of the obligation to divulge his previous marriage and the steps he took to have his first wife presumed dead. The Board's decision that the applicant had failed to comply with s. 40(1)(a) was upheld.

Maruquin v. Canada (Minister of Citizenship & Immigration) (2007), 68 Imm. L.R. (3d) 273, 2007 CarswellNat 4562, 2007 CarswellNat 5785, 2007 FC 1349 — The applicants were sponsored as permanent residents to Canada and completed their forms in April 2003. In early March 2006, the applicants' application was approved and their visas were printed. On March 21, 2006, the sponsor faxed the immigration officer advising that one of the applicants, Cheryl Maruquin, gave birth to a baby during the processing of her immigration paper. The child was born in July 2004. Cheryl was a single mother and at the time, the family had decided to leave the baby in the Philippines and petition him in the near future. When the birth of Cheryl's son was disclosed to the immigration officials, the applicants' visas had been approved but had not been delivered to the applicants. On

July 14, 2006, the application for permanent residence was refused "... for directly or indirectly misrepresenting or withholding material facts relating to a relevant matter that induces or could induce an error in the administration of this Act," pursuant to para. 40(1)(a) of the IRPA. The basis of the misrepresentation was the failure of the principal applicant and his daughter, Cheryl, to disclose the birth of her son in a timely fashion. The applicants' principal position was that the birth of the child was disclosed on their own initiative after the printing but prior to the delivery of the visas and, in any event, prior to any of them being landed in Canada. Accordingly, in their view, the disclosure of the child's birth on March 21, 2006, some 21 months after the fact but prior to the delivery of the visas, rendered impossible any misrepresentation or withholding of a material fact that induced or could have induced an error in the administration of the Act.

The court held, that the special circumstances of this case, the non-disclosure of the information concerning the birth of Cheryl's son until March 21, 2006 cannot be said to be the withholding of a material fact relating to a relevant matter that induced or could have induced an error in the administration of the Act. The forms made available in this proceeding could not be the basis of a requirement, in any practical sense, that Cheryl report the change of information immediately. In the end, the birth of the son was disclosed prior to any legal requirement to do so in the regulations. There was no evidence in the tribunal record that the information was "deliberately" withheld. There was no information in the CAIPS notes to suggest that the applicants had any incentive not to disclose the birth of the child, let alone the non-disclosure was deliberate.

Lu v. Canada (Minister of Citizenship & Immigration), 2007 CarswellNat 415, 2007 FC 159 — This is an application for judicial review of a decision to refuse an application for permanent residence on the basis that the applicant was inadmissible to Canada due to a misrepresentation. The Consulate General made inquiries to confirm the authenticity of a capital validation report. The visa officer concluded that the applicant was inadmissible to Canada. In her letter to the applicant, the visa officer wrote ". . . because you, a person described under subs. 16(1) of IRPA and ss. 34 to 42 of the *Immigration and Refugee Protection Act* . . . you are therefore criminally inadmissible to Canada." Although the officer did overstep her role in the evaluation of the applicant's permanent resident application, her actions did not constitute an error of law. The fact that the officer wrote in her letter to the applicant that "you are therefore criminally inadmissible to Canada" was an error which can be associated to a typographical error and it was not of a conclusive nature. There was no indication in the officer's letter that she misunderstood the evidence before her and as such believed the applicant was inadmissible under s. 36 of the IRPA due to criminality, or that the officer believed that providing untruthful information made the applicant inadmissible due to criminality. The application for judicial review was dismissed.

Calixto v. Canada (Minister of Citizenship & Immigration) (2005), 49 Imm. L.R. (3d) 36, 2005 CarswellNat 2165, 2005 CarswellNat 4919, 2005 FC 1037 — The applicant arrived in Canada and was granted refugee status, and then applied for landed immigrant status. At a CSIS interview the applicant was confronted with information that he had lied about his past activities, including a criminal record in the United States that arose during the time he claimed he was being persecuted in Mexico. The applicant admitted this misrepresentation and as a result of the admission, the applicant's refugee status was vacated pursuant to s. 109(1) of the IRPA. A report was prepared pursuant to s. 44(1) setting out that the applicant was inadmissible pursuant to s. 40(1)(c). An immigration officer found the report well founded and consequently made a deportation order against the applicant pursuant to s. 44(2). The applicant argued that s. 40(1)(c) would render him inadmissible only if he made a misrepresentation in the course of the vacation proceeding before the Refugee Protection Division. The court held that whether the applicant made any misrepresentations during the vacation hearing was not a relevant consideration. Instead, the use of the term "misrepresentation" in s. 40(1)(c) should be read as denoting statements of fact which operate to make a person inadmissible, that is, if either of the events mentioned in this section are proved to have occurred, a person is considered, or "deemed," inadmissible for "misrepresentation."

Menon v. Canada (Minister of Citizenship & Immigration) (2005), 53 Imm. L.R. (3d) 85, 2005 FC 1273, 2005 CarswellNat 2826, 2005 CarswellNat 5329, [2005] F.C.J. No. 1548 — The principal applicant misrepresented material facts in that he presented what purported to be an original certificate from the University of Bombay and an original marks transcript from the same university which were determined, following verification, to be false. During the interview, the visa officer gave the applicant notice of his concerns regarding the false educational documents. The applicant returned to Mumbai and obtained genuine evidence that he had graduated from the University of Bombay. He couriered this evidence to the High Commission in London. The Computer Assisted Immigration Processing System (CAIPS) did not reflect that the High Commission in London or the visa office in Abu Dhabi had received any further documents from the applicant after the interview. The court concluded that the duty of fairness had not been met, since the supplementary material filed by the applicant was not entered into CAIPS by the visa officer. A very high standard of fairness is to be applied in the application of s. 40(1) where a permanent resident or a foreign national is determined to be inadmissible for misrepresentation.

40.1 (1) Cessation of refugee protection — foreign national — A foreign national is inadmissible on a final determination under subsection 108(2) that their refugee protection has ceased.

(2) Cessation of refugee protection — permanent resident — A permanent resident is inadmissible on a final determination that their refugee protection has ceased for any of the reasons described in paragraphs 108(1)(a) to (d).

2012, c. 17, s. 18

41. Non-compliance with Act — A person is inadmissible for failing to comply with this Act

    (a) in the case of a foreign national, through an act or omission which contravenes, directly or indirectly, a provision of this Act; and

    (b) in the case of a permanent resident, through failing to comply with subsection 27(2) or section 28.

[Editor's Note: SOR/2002-227, s. 320(10) provides that a person is inadmissible under the Immigration and Refugee Protection Act, S.C. 2001 c. 27 (the "new Act") for failing to comply with the new Act if, on June 28, 2002, the person had been determined to be a member of an inadmissible class described in paragraph 19(1)(h) or (i) or (2)(c) or (d) of the Immigration Act, R.S.C. 1985, c. I-2 (the "former Act") or had been determined to be inadmissible on the basis of paragraph 27(1)(b) or (2)(b), (e), (f), (h), (i) or (k) of the former Act.]

Case Law

Ikhuiwu v. Canada (Minister of Citizenship & Immigration), 2008 FC 35, 2008 CarswellNat 42, [2008] F.C.J. No. 35 — This was an application for judicial review of an IAD decision, confirming the decision of an overseas visa officer. The visa officer concluded that the applicant was inadmissible pursuant to ss. 28 and 41(b) of the IRPA as he did not reside in Canada for the required 730 days within a five-year period.

The legislative scheme under the IRPA makes it clear that the mere possession of a permanent resident card is not conclusive proof of a person's status in Canada. Pursuant to s. 31(2) of the IRPA, the presumption that the holder of a permanent resident card is a permanent resident is clearly a rebuttable one. In this case, it is clear that the permanent resident card, which was issued in error after it was determined by the visa officer in Nigeria that the applicant had lost his permanent residence status, could not possibly confer legal status on him as a permanent resident, nor could it have the effect of restoring his permanent resident status which he had previously lost because he didn't meet the residency requirements under s. 28 of the IRPA. There is no provision in the IRPA or the Regulations which suggests that the mere possession of a permanent resident card, which was improperly issued, could have the effect of restoring or reinstating a person's prior permanent resident status.

Section 59(1)(a) of the Regulations also makes it clear that an officer can only validly issue a new permanent resident card where an applicant has not lost his or her status under s. 46(1) of the IRPA. In this case, the applicant lost his permanent resident status after failing to meet the residency requirements under s. 28 of the IRPA and failed to appeal the decision within the 60 days as prescribed by Regulation 63(4). This regulatory scheme confirms that it was not possible for the issuing officer of the permanent resident card to have validly and properly issued it in light of the fact that the applicant had previously lost his permanent resident card. The application for judicial review was dismissed.

Ivanov v. Canada (Minister of Citizenship & Immigration) (2006), 56 Imm. L.R. (3d) 56, 2006 CarswellNat 2335 (Imm. & Ref. Bd. (App. Div.)) — The appellant made an application for permanent residence as an independent in May 2001. At the time he disclosed that he had never been married and had no dependants. The application was successful and he was issued a permanent resident visa in June 2003. The appellant married his girlfriend on October 3, 2003. The appellant arrived in Canada on October 7, 2003. He disclosed his recent marriage to Canadian immigration officials upon his arrival in Toronto. At the time of his examination at Pearson Airport, he could not establish that his wife met the requirements of IRPA and the Regulations. His counsel wrote to the Canadian Embassy in Vienna in November 2003 advising that the immigration official at the port of entry had no objection regarding the release of the landed documents to the appellant subject to the appellant's wife meeting the medical and security requirements. The Embassy replied that there was no legal basis on which they were required to assess the wife against the admissibility criteria of IRPA. The appellant was issued an exclusion order on the basis that he was unable to establish, at the time of his examination, that his wife met the requirement of the Act and the Regulations. The appellant appealed the exclusion order.

The Appeal Board concluded that the exclusion order was valid in law. The appeal, however, was allowed under s. 67(1)(c) and the matter referred back to an immigration officer at the port of entry for reconsideration. The Board found that the appellant made an honest mistake in not informing the visa officer of his marriage prior to appearing for landing, but had disclosed the marriage immediately upon landing. As a result of the appellant's error, the Board concluded that he had suffered financial hardship upon his arrival in Canada, exhausting his savings because he could not legally work here. The Board found that the appellant had established humanitarian and compassionate considerations to warrant the granting of special relief in light of all the circumstances of the case. The Board directed that the department take all steps required to facilitate the examination of the appellant's wife and to provide the appellant with the necessary immigration documents to allow the appellant to attend before an immigration officer at a port of entry for reconsideration.

Brar v. Canada (Minister of Citizenship & Immigration) (2006), 59 Imm. L.R. (3d) 293, 2006 CarswellNat 4324, 2006 FC 1502 — The applicants sought judicial review in respect of a decision by a member of the Immigration and Refugee Board of Canada given collectively, but pertaining to each of them, that determined that each of the applicants had contravened the terms of the work permit issued to each of them and therefore each was to be excluded from Canada. The applicants were all adult male citizens of India. They applied for and received temporary work permits. The work permit stated:

> Employer: Bombay Paradise
>
> > Conditions:
> >
> > * not authorized to work in any occupation other than stated;
> > * not authorized to work for any employer other than stated; and
> > * not authorized for work in any location other than stated.

When the applicants arrived in Calgary, they found that the Bombay Paradise Restaurant was under construction and far from being completed. The owner of that business was a numbered company run by a person known as Vic. He placed them in another establishment known as Bombay Sweet House & Restaurant. Apparently, the ownership was not the same as Bombay Paradise, although pay cheques issued to the applicants were from the numbered company which was the owner of the Bombay Paradise business.

It came to the Minister's attention that the applicants were working for an employer whom the Minister believed to be other than that named in the work permit. As a result, an exclusion order was issued. Following that order, an admissibility hearing was held on March 1, 2006. The issue of the hearing was whether each of the applicants was inadmissible under s. 41(a) of the IRPA, as having contravened s. 29(2) of that Act.

The court concluded that Bombay Paradise paid the applicants and the applicants worked in Calgary, and therefore, no term as set out in the work permit had been breached. A work permit should be understandable to all interested persons, not just the worker or the government, on the face of it. The Minister has the resources to ensure that the permit is complete and understandable. If it is not, the Minister cannot be seen to rely on self-created ambiguities to derive a beneficial interpretation. It is the same concept as *contra proferentum* in the interpretation of a contract. If the contract was prepared by a party, any ambiguity must be interpreted against the interests of that party.

The applicants did not breach the terms of their work permits. Their employer, the person who pays them, was Bombay Paradise. They worked in Calgary. As a result, the exclusion order was set aside and the matter was returned to be determined by a different person.

Chang v. Canada (Minister of Citizenship & Immigration), 2006 FC 157, 2006 CarswellNat 329, 2006 CarswellNat 2194, [2006] F.C.J. No. 217 — The legislatively established conditions of the entrepreneur category, if flaunted knowingly, without serious consequence, would make a mockery of the purpose for which they were established. The act of creating or participating in a front operation or a sham investment, if left unchecked, strikes a blow at the very integrity of the immigration system. In this case, the applicants were found to be in non-compliance with subs. 27(2) and s. 28. The applicants' children were also found to be in non-compliance with subs. 27(2) as they were dependants of an entrepreneur and bound by the same terms and conditions of landing as provided in para. 23.1 of the previous Regulations. Both the applicants, as well as their children, sought special relief on appeal in light of the circumstances of their case, specifically, that there were sufficient humanitarian and compassionate considerations that warranted the setting aside of departure orders. The IAD was of the view that the parents did not merit discretionary relief as they took part in a sham arrangement to try to fulfill the conditions of the entrepreneur category. Even though the IAD felt that the children would be excellent candidates for permanent residence, it refused to grant discretionary relief to the children because, once the children became permanent residents, they would be entitled to sponsor their parents which would render the removal of the parents moot.

The granting of special relief is a weighing process. Even though there were some positive elements in favour of discretionary relief being allowed to the three children, these elements did not outweigh the importance given to the integrity of maintaining the conditions in the entrepreneur category. It was open to the IAD to find that special relief should not be granted to the children because this would benefit the parents who had not respected the conditions under which they entered Canada.

Yu v. Canada (Minister of Citizenship & Immigration), 2005 CarswellNat 2998, 2005 CarswellNat 4835, 2005 FC 1323 — The applicant, having been granted permanent residence status in the independent category, was denied re-admission as a resident by a visa officer in November, 2003. The visa officer's decision was appealed to the IAD who determined that the applicant failed to comply with the residency obligation under s. 28 of the IRPA. The Immigration Appeal Board determined that pursuant to s. 41 of the IRPA there was non-compliance and upheld the visa officer's determination. The Board also determined that there were insufficient humanitarian and compassionate considerations justifying the retention of permanent residence status; therefore, the applicant was unable to overcome the breach of her residency obligations.

The applicant planned to work in her native land until able to retire with full pension benefits, in 2006. In 2005, the law concerning her pension benefits was changed and the applicant was able to retire earlier. This important new evidence was forwarded by way of affidavit to the Board on December 10, 2004.

The issue of "intention" should have been discussed or at least canvassed, as well as the change of circumstances regarding the applicant's retirement. The Board's decision was set aside and the matter was sent back to be reheard.

Mand v. Canada (Minister of Citizenship & Immigration) (2005), 51 Imm. L.R. (3d) 272, 2005 FC 1637, 2005 CarswellNat 3970, [2005] F.C.J. No. 2016 — The principal applicant came to Canada under the entrepreneurial category. He was accompanied to Canada by his spouse and three children. They did not meet their obligations under the terms and conditions of their landing and, as a result, deportation orders were issued against them. They filed appeals against the deportation orders and were granted a two-year stay subject to following certain terms and conditions. The appeals were subsequently rejected when the applicants did not respect the conditions. The IAD also concluded that the applicants failed to demonstrate that having regard to all the circumstances of the case, they should not be removed from Canada for humanitarian and compassionate considerations. Although the Federal Court concluded that the IAD erred in concluding that the principal applicant's daughter did have strong ties to Canada, the Federal Court concluded the IAD's decision to cancel the stay of the deportation orders was not patently unreasonable, as it would be unjust and against the principles of the Canadian immigration process to decide otherwise. The principal applicant was given a second chance and failed to respect the rules; he should not be rewarded for being able to abuse the system to the point of allowing his family to remain in Canada long enough to build strong ties and qualify for a further stay of deportation orders based on humanitarian and compassionate grounds.

El Idrissi c. Canada (Ministre de la Citoyenneté & de l'Immigration), 2005 CarswellNat 2421, 2005 CarswellNat 5248, 2005 FC 1105 — The applicant was given permanent residence status in 1991. In 1999, the applicant left Canada to visit his sick father and manage a family business in his home country. He did not return until June 15, 2003. He fell under the purview of s. 41 of the IRPA and a departure order was made against him by the Minister. He filed an appeal to the Immigration Appeal Division but conceded that the removal order against him was legally valid and the only issue he argued was that there were humanitarian and compassionate grounds to explain his failure to meet the residency obligation.

Simply having a wife in Canada was not sufficient for this situation to be considered a humanitarian and compassionate ground. The Appeal Division was entitled to consider that the applicant's plans for the future were vague. The applicant had the burden of establishing the existence of humanitarian and compassionate grounds.

Proposed Addition — 41.1

41.1 (1) Polygamy — A permanent resident or a foreign national is inadmissible on grounds of practising polygamy if they are or will be practising polygamy with a person who is or will be physically present in Canada at the same time as the permanent resident or foreign national.

(2) Interpretation — For the purposes of subsection (1), polygamy shall be interpreted in a manner consistent with paragraph 293(1)(a) of the *Criminal Code*.

2015, c. 29, s. 2 [Not in force at date of publication.]

42. (1) Inadmissible family member — A foreign national, other than a protected person, is inadmissible on grounds of an inadmissible family member if

   (a) their accompanying family member or, in prescribed circumstances, their non-accompanying family member is inadmissible; or

   (b) they are an accompanying family member of an inadmissible person.

(2) Exception — In the case of a foreign national referred to in subsection (1) who is a temporary resident or who has made an application for temporary resident status or an application to remain in Canada as a temporary resident,

   (a) the matters referred to in paragraph (1)(a) constitute inadmissibility only if the family member is inadmissible under section 34, 35 or 37; and

(b) the matters referred to in paragraph (1)(b) constitute inadmissibility only if the foreign national is an accompanying family member of a person who is inadmissible under section 34, 35 or 37.

[Editor's Note: SOR/2002-227, s. 352 provides that a person is not required to include in an application a non-accompanying common-law partner or a non-accompanying child who is not a dependant son or a dependant daughter within the meaning of s. 2(1) of the Immigration Regulations, 1978, *SOR/98-172 and is a dependant child as defined in s. 2 of the* Immigration and Refugee Protection Regulations, *SOR/2002-227 (the "new Regulations") if the application was made under the* Immigration Act, R.S.C. 1985, c. I-2 (the *"former Act") before June 28, 2002.*

SOR/2002-227, s. 353 provides that if a person has made an application under the former Act before June 28, 2002, the following provisions of the new Regulations do not apply to the person in respect of any of their non-accompanying dependent children, referred to in s. 352 of the new Regulations, or their non-accompanying common-law partner:

(a) paragraph 70(1)(e);

(b) subparagraph 72(1)(e)(i); and

(c) paragraph 108(1)(a).

SOR/2002-227, s. 354 further provides that if a person makes an application before June 28, 2002, their non-accompanying dependent children, referred to in s. 352 of the new Regulations, and their non-accompanying common-law partner shall not, for the purposes of that application, be considered inadmissible non-accompanying family members referred to in paragraph 42(a) of the Immigration and Refugee Protection Act, *S.C. 2001, c. 27 (the "new Act"), and are not subject to the requirements of paragraph 30(1)(a) or 51(b) of the new Regulations.*

SOR/2002-227, s. 355 still further provides that if a person who made an application under the former Act before June 28, 2002 sponsors a non-accompanying dependent child referred to in s. 352 of the new Regulations, who makes an application as a member of the family class or the spouse or common-law partner in Canada class, or sponsors a non-accompanying common-law partner who makes such an application, paragraph 117(9)(d) of the new Regulations does not apply in respect of that dependent child or common-law partner.]

2013, c. 16, s. 17

42.1 (1) Exception — application to Minister — The Minister may, on application by a foreign national, declare that the matters referred to in section 34, paragraphs 35(1)(b) and (c) and subsection 37(1) do not constitute inadmissibility in respect of the foreign national if they satisfy the Minister that it is not contrary to the national interest.

(2) Exception — Minister's own initiative — The Minister may, on the Minister's own initiative, declare that the matters referred to in section 34, paragraphs 35(1)(b) and (c) and subsection 37(1) do not constitute inadmissibility in respect of a foreign national if the Minister is satisfied that it is not contrary to the national interest.

(3) Considerations — In determining whether to make a declaration, the Minister may only take into account national security and public safety considerations, but, in his or her analysis, is not limited to considering the danger that the foreign national presents to the public or the security of Canada.

2013, c. 16, s. 18

43. Regulations — The regulations may provide for any matter relating to the application of this Division, may define, for the purposes of this Act, any of the terms used in this Division, and may include provisions respecting the circumstances in which a class of permanent residents or foreign nationals is exempted from any of the provisions of this Division.

DIVISION 5 — LOSS OF STATUS AND REMOVAL

Report on Inadmissibility

44. (1) Preparation of report — An officer who is of the opinion that a permanent resident or a foreign national who is in Canada is inadmissible may prepare a report setting out the relevant facts, which report shall be transmitted to the Minister.

(2) Referral or removal order — If the Minister is of the opinion that the report is well-founded, the Minister may refer the report to the Immigration Division for an admissibility hearing, except in the case of a permanent resident who is inadmissible solely on the grounds that they have failed to comply with the residency obligation under section 28 and except, in the circumstances prescribed by the regulations, in the case of a foreign national. In those cases, the Minister may make a removal order.

(3) Conditions — An officer or the Immigration Division may impose any conditions, including the payment of a deposit or the posting of a guarantee for compliance with the conditions, that the officer or the Division considers necessary on a permanent resident or a foreign national who is the subject of a report, an admissibility hearing or, being in Canada, a removal order.

Proposed Addition — 44(4), (5)

(4) Conditions — inadmissibility on grounds of security — If a report on inadmissibility on grounds of security is referred to the Immigration Division and the permanent resident or the foreign national who is the subject of the report is not detained, an officer shall also impose the prescribed conditions on the person.

(5) Duration of conditions — The prescribed conditions imposed under subsection (4) cease to apply only when

    (a) the person is detained;

    (b) the report on inadmissibility on grounds of security is withdrawn;

    (c) a final determination is made not to make a removal order against the person for inadmissibility on grounds of security;

    (d) the Minister makes a declaration under subsection 42.1(1) or (2) in relation to the person; or

(e) a removal order is enforced against the person in accordance with the regulations.

2013, c. 16, s. 19 [Not in force at date of publication.]

[Editor's Note: SOR/2002-227, s. 331 provides that a performance bond posted or security deposited under the former Immigration Act, R.S.C. 1985, c. I-2 that remains posted or deposited immediately before June 28, 2002 continues as a deposit or a guarantee under the new Immigration and Refugee Protection Act, S.C. 2001, c. 27 and is governed by its provisions.]

[Editor's Note: SOR/2002-227, s. 321(1) provides that a report made under s. 20 or s. 27 of the Immigration Act, R.S.C. 1985, c. I-2 (the "former Act") is a report under s. 44(1) of the Immigration and Refugee Protection Act, S.C. 2001 c. 27 (the "new Act").

SOR/2002-227, s. 321(3) provides that a report that was forwarded to a senior immigration officer under the former Act and in respect of which a decision has not been made on June 28, 2002 is a report transmitted to the Minister.

SOR/2002-227, s. 321(4) further provides that the causing by a senior immigration officer of an inquiry to be held under former Act is the referring by the Minister of a report to the Immigration Division under s. 44(2) of the new Act unless s. 44(2) of the new Act allows the Minister to make a removal order.

SOR/2002-227, s. 321(5) still further provides that if no substantive evidence was adduced before the Adjudication Division, the causing by a senior immigration officer of an inquiry to be held under the former Act is, if s. 44(2) of the new Act allows the Minister to make a removal order, a report on the basis of which the Minister may make a removal order.]

Case Law

Section 44(1)

Fabbiano v. Canada (Minister of Citizenship and Immigration) (2014), 32 Imm. L.R. (4th) 84, 2014 FC 1219, 2014 CarswellNat 8341, 2014 CarswellNat 5231 — The applicant was born in Italy in 1957 but has lived in Canada since 1963. During the 1990s, he "became" involved with the Hells Angels. He was convicted of drug trafficking in 1999 and served a one-year sentence in the community. In 2006, a representative of the Canadian Border Services Agency wrote to the applicant informing him that, as a member of a criminal organization, he might be inadmissible to Canada.

In 2008, after he had made submissions to CBSA on the subject of his admissibility, an enforcement officer recommended he be referred to an admissibility hearing. A senior CBSA analyst concurred with the recommendation. In 2009, a delegate of the Minister of Public Safety and Emergency Preparedness referred the applicant for an admissibility hearing. He did not learn of any of these decisions until 2013. The applicant challenges the Minister's delegate's decision arguing that the delay in notifying him of the delegate's decision constitutes an abuse of process.

Since the applicant heard nothing until 2013 about his potential inadmissibility after having made submissions in 2007, he reasonably believed that officials were no longer pursuing the issue, and was obviously surprised when he received the 2013 decision. There was nothing that would have suggested to him that he ought to file supplementary submissions. This was not an application on his part, in respect of which he might have had an obligation to inform the decision-maker of any additional information. He was being pursued by the respondents. At the time the decision was communicated to him, the information underlying it was nearly seven years old. Undoubtedly, the circumstances of his children and other family members would have evolved during that time, as would his own situation, including his employment, health and, perhaps, his relationship, if any, with the Hells Angels. Issuing a decision in 2013 related to his admissibility based on information gathered in 2007 clearly prejudiced him. The delay in dealing with his inadmissibility resulted in his inability to present evidence to counter his removal from Canada. If his case goes to an admissibility hearing, the issuance of a removal order will be inevitable, and he will have no further remedies available to him. Clearly, the delay has prejudiced him. The circumstances amounted to an abuse of process based both on unfairness and a breach of the integrity of the justice system. The application was allowed and an order that the inadmissibility proceedings relating to the applicant be permanently stayed.

Mudalige Don v. Canada (Minister of Citizenship & Immigration) (2014), 20 Imm. L.R. (4th) 249, 369 D.L.R. (4th) 356, 455 N.R. 132, 2014 FCA 4, 2014 CarswellNat 14; leave to appeal to S.C.C. refused 2014 CarswellNat 1959, 2014 CarswellNat 1960 (S.C.C.) — The delegate of the Minister of Citizenship and Immigration issued an exclusion order against the applicant for his failure to respect the requirement under subs. 184(1) of the *IRPA Regulations* to leave Canada within 72 hours after ceasing to be a member of the crew. The Federal Court judge allowed the judicial review and certified a question. The Federal Court of Appeal concluded that a Minister's issuance of an exclusion order pursuant to subpara. 228(1)(c)(v) of the Regulations before the member of a crew subject to an exclusion order has any contact with the immigration authorities does not constitute a breach of procedural fairness by depriving the foreign national of the opportunity to make a refugee claim. The Federal Court of Appeal concluded that the lower court judge's reasoning disregarded both the wording of the relevant legislation and its intent. In allowing for the timely issuance of a removal order, the Legislature must be taken to have acted coherently, in full knowledge of the impact that such order has on the right to claim refugee protection (subs. 99(3) of the Act). The result is that persons who desert a ship in Canada in order to claim refugee protection should report to the immigration authorities and make their claim promptly. The 72-hour limitation makes it clear that they cannot expect to claim this status at a time of their choice. The appeal was allowed and the decision of the Federal Court judge set aside, and the application for judicial review by the applicant was dismissed.

Beltran v. Canada (Minister of Citizenship & Immigration) (2011), 1 Imm. L.R. (4th) 317, 2011 FC 606, 2011 CarswellNat 2897 — The goal of a judicial review of a s. 44 report is to right a wrong quite different from that targeted by a permanent stay of proceedings. A judicial review targets the reasonableness (or in some cases, the correctness) of a decision. A permanent stay has nothing to do with the reasonableness of that decision. Rather, its purpose is to halt an abuse of process. Furthermore, a stay is based on a different record. In this case, the Minister proposed a two-stage process. If leave was not granted or if leave was granted and then the judicial review was dismissed, the applicant would still have been able to move for a permanent stay on the grounds of an abuse of process. Adding such a step would unnecessarily complicate the process and create additional expense for both parties. The court must be attuned to fundamental access to justice through procedures that minimize unnecessary costs and complexity.

The court declared that the admissibility proceeding against the applicant based on the s. 44(1) report constituted an abuse of process and prohibited the Minister from issuing any further s. 44 reports against the applicant regarding an allegation of inadmissibility under s. 34(1)(f) due to his membership in the 28th of February Popular Leagues (LP-28), unless the Minister obtained new, credible and trustworthy evidence about his membership that the Minister would not otherwise have obtained prior to the date of the order through due diligence efforts. Similarly, the Immigration Division was prohibited from continuing the admissibility hearing against the applicant on similar conditions as those imposed against the Minister.

Canada (Minister of Citizenship & Immigration) v. Peirovdinnadi (2010), 92 Imm. L.R. (3d) 1, 409 N.R. 161, 2010 FCA 267, 2010 CarswellNat 3780 — The IAD was obliged to determine the genuineness of the marriage in this case because it was the misrepresentation alleged in the immigration officer's report under IRPA, subs. 44(1), and was closely related to the misrepresentation found by the ID and in issue in the IAD. That is, if the marriage was not genuine, the respondent was not living with his wife as his spouse and, as his counsel conceded, his statement on the form that he was living with his spouse constituted a misrepresentation. The appeal was allowed, the decision of the Federal Court was set aside, the Minister's application for judicial review was granted, the decision of the IAD set aside and the matter remitted for redetermination by the IAD, differently constituted.

Kainth v. Canada (Minister of Citizenship & Immigration), 2009 FC 100, 2009 CarswellNat 278, [2009] F.C.J. No. 134 — The applicant sought judicial review of a decision of the IAD confirming an order for his removal to India, pursuant to a breach of his residency obligation set out at s. 28 of the IRPA. The applicant was a citizen of India who immigrated to Canada in June 2000. He subsequently left Canada in August 2001 to elope with an Indian woman whom he had met over the internet and who lived in the United States. He made a refugee claim in the United States based on a false name and was granted asylum there in 2002. During a police investigation of assault charges in the United States, his true name and Canadian identity documentation came to light. His U.S. refugee claim was cancelled and he was given the option of appealing the decision or being expulsed to India or Canada. He chose to return to Canada and U.S. authorities escorted him in January 2006 to the Vancouver International Airport. The officer told him that he was in breach of his residency obligation which might result in his removal to India. She explained to him that she was not convinced that he had raised sufficient humanitarian considerations to warrant the exercise of her discretion not to report him. He was asked if he had anything else to add to her consideration, in answer to which he only referred to his desire to stay in Canada. The officer gave evidence that before reporting to the Minister's delegate, she spoke with the applicant's lawyer to advise him that she would be issuing a report under subs. 44(1) of the IRPA recommending the issuance of a removal order as she had found the applicant to be inadmissible. Said counsel simply asked the officer to fax him a copy of her report after its issuance. The officer spoke to counsel regarding the terms of a bond and shortly thereafter the applicant was released on a bond.

The application for leave and judicial review of the removal order alleged a breach of the applicant's rights under subs. 10(b) of the *Charter* and of the duty of procedural fairness of a POE officer for having: (1) failed to advise him that unless he made a refugee claim before the removal order was issues, he would lose his right to do so; and (2) failed to respect his right to counsel during his interview in respect of his residency obligation.

The court found that: (1) there are minimal participatory rights included in the duty of fairness of the POE officer in this case; (2) those rights were respected on the facts of this case; and, (3) the court is simply not willing to say that here, the duty of fairness incumbent on the officer included expressly confirming with counsel that he had no submissions to make and felt no need for an adjournment or to speak with his client prior to the issuance of the report. Keeping in mind the undisputed findings of the IAD that the applicant properly understood the reasons for the interview, the possibility of removal to India and his answers to the POE officer's questions in respect of his refugee claim in the United States, the court agreed that the IAD and the POE officer could, in this matter, reasonably infer that the applicant was not facing nor fearing any particular danger in India. She simply had no duty to expressly ask him if he intended to make a refugee claim in Canada. The application for judicial review was dismissed.

Clark v. Canada (Minister of Public Safety & Emergency Preparedness) (2009), 79 Imm. L.R. (3d) 54, 2009 CarswellNat 753, 2009 FC 311 — At the time of his birth, the applicant's parents ran a farm in Southern Manitoba, near the Canada-U.S. border. The applicant was born on June 5, 1947, in West Hope, North Dakota, the site of the nearest hospital. He has lived in Canada his whole life believing he was a Canadian citizen. Persons in the applicant's circumstances are sometimes referred to as "lost Canadians." Mr. Clark was convicted of various drug-related and smuggling offences in April 2006. After his conviction it came to the CBSA's attention that he had been convicted of serious criminality under the IRPA and a delegate confirmed the CBSA's finding that he was inadmissible and issued a deportation order against the applicant while he was in prison. The applicant requested that the deportation order be stayed pending the final disposition of an application for judicial review of the Minister's delegate's decision.

The applicant raised at least a serious question regarding his citizenship. The Federal Court need not resolve the dispute between the parties on the issue of the applicant's claim to Canadian citizenship. The decision maker should adjourn the proceeding to allow the person to have the citizenship issue resolved. Here, given that the delegate could only issue a deportation against a non-citizen, he should have waited until a determination of the applicant's citizenship had been made before finding him to be inadmissible. The Minister's delegate treated the applicant unfairly by failing to provide reasons for finding him inadmissible to Canada and by doing so in advance of the decision on the applicant's citizenship. Accordingly, the decision was overturned.

Richter v. Canada (Minister of Citizenship & Immigration) (2008), 73 Imm. L.R. (3d) 131, [2009] 1 F.C.R. 675, 2008 FC 806, 2008 CarswellNat 3180, 2008 CarswellNat 2182, [2008] F.C.J. No. 1033; affirmed (2009), 79 Imm. L.R. (3d) 2, 2009 CarswellNat 593, 2009 FCA 73 — The applicant immigrated to Canada with her husband in 1970. In 2003 the applicant was arrested in Toronto and charged with trafficking in firearms and related offences. The applicant was convicted and sentenced to 37 months imprisonment. The applicant was imprisoned at Grand Valley Institute for Women where she was interviewed by at least two officers with respect to her immigration status. At some point, she was informed of her right to contact counsel and says she tried without success to contact her counsel from the criminal trial. When she was eventually informed she was being arrested on an immigration hold, she took steps to retain a lawyer specializing in immigration matters. A report on the factual grounds for proceeding with an admissibility hearing was written on May 29, 2007. The immigration officer reviewing the case interviewed the applicant and recommended that she seek legal advice on June 4th. She provided her telephone number should the applicant wish to contact her. The applicant made no contact with the officer over the next two weeks. The manager acting as a Ministerial delegate on June 18 referred the case for an admissibility hearing on the basis of the officer's report. These steps were taken pursuant to s. 44 of the IRPA. On July 4, 2007, the applicant's counsel wrote to the manager requesting the opportunity to provide further information before the s. 44 report was written. On July 11, the enforcement officer replied noting that the applicant had already been referred for an admissibility hearing and had been arrested and detained for that purpose. The officer also noted that she had been contacted by the applicant's criminal law firm and that she had offered to forward any submissions they wished to make to the enforcement office which would be scheduling the admissibility hearing. The applicant challenged the decision of the enforcement officer to prepare the report and the decision of the manager to refer the report for an admissibility hearing. The applicant alleged a heightened duty on immigration officials when dealing with the person in custody, given the restrictions on their liberty, and suggested that the officer should have contacted the criminal lawyer herself or gone back to the applicant after the two weeks to inquire whether the applicant had done anything about her situation.

While it is true that persons in the custody of the state are subject to limits on their freedom, they are not barred from seeking and obtaining legal services. Immigration officers cannot be required to act as the bridge between incarcerated persons who are the subject of s. 44 report and whatever counsel they have or may wish to have. In this case, the application was dismissed.

The Court of Appeal did not answer the general question certified by the applications judge stating it was too vague, and that the scope and content of the duty of fairness will vary depending on the circumstances of each case. The Court of Appeal dismissed the appeal.

Hernandez v. Canada (Minister of Public Safety & Emergency Preparedness) (2007), 62 Imm. L.R. (3d) 236, [2008] 2 F.C.R. 450, 2007 CarswellNat 1902, 2007 CarswellNat 4085, 2007 FC 725 — The applicant was a permanent resident of Canada and was convicted of an indictable offence and was sentenced to 30 months imprisonment. An enforcement officer of Canada Border Services Agency made a report under s. 44(1) of the IRPA stating that the applicant was inadmissible to Canada pursuant to s. 36(1)(a). Neither IRPA nor its regulations define what a "report" under s. 44(1) is to comprise. The court considered whether the failure to provide the "Recommendation and appendixes" constituted a breach of fairness that could provide a basis for setting aside the s. 44(1) or 44(2) decisions.

In the circumstances of the present case the officer prepared and delivered to the Minister not only the "report" but also a detailed "recommendation" with many appendixes. These latter documents were undoubtedly intended to provide to the Minister detail as to what was contained in the report and substantiation as to its conclusions. Having been prepared, having been sent to the Minister, being pertinent to the "report" and substantiating what is in the "report," they must be considered to be part of the "report." The issue is *not* whether there was any requirement to create the "recommendation" and appendixes. Rather, the issue was *having created* them, *having delivered them* to the Minister, and *given their pertinence* to the "report," they should have been delivered to the applicant. In particular, when a clear and specific request for delivery of such material was made by the applicant's lawyer before the admissibility hearing, there was no proper basis for withholding that material.

Where a relevant document was created and put before the Minister, yet withheld from the applicant, this is sufficient to require that the s. 44(1) determination be set aside and done again.

Golestaneh v. Canada (Minister of Public Safety & Emergency Preparedness), 2007 CarswellNat 1233, 2007 FC 509 — Pursuant to subs. 44(1) of IRPA an enforcement officer at the Canadian Border Services Agency prepared a report alleging that the applicant was inadmissible, as per paragraphs 34(1)(f) and 35(1)(a) of the Act, by reason of his involvement with a listed terrorist entity in Canada. The report prepared by the enforcement officer was referred by the Minister of Public Safety and Emergency Preparedness to the Immigration Division of the Immigration Refugee Board for an admissibility hearing. The applicant sought judicial review of the decisions made under subs. 44(1) and 44(2) of the Act.

The enforcement officer did not have access to the documentation supporting the security intelligence report prepared by the Canadian Security Intelligence Services (CSIS). The enforcement officer's decision was limited to reading the report itself. This alone was a serious error of law that justified setting aside the decision of the enforcement officer. Although the CSIS document may set out precisely the grounds on inadmissibility of the applicant, the officer who must decide whether to issue a subs. 44(1) report has a duty, when examining the file for the first time, to consult all of the reference documents, including the appendices to the CSIS report and the information on the sources underlying this report, before making a decision. This is necessary in order to ensure that the procedure followed will sufficiently guarantee the independence of the decision maker and thus, protect the rights of the individual concerned.

The decision of the enforcement officer to prepare a report for the Minister, and the subsequent decision by the Minister to refer the report to the Immigration Division for an admissibility hearing, was set aside and the file was referred back to a different enforcement officer for re-determination.

Sui v. Canada (Minister of Public Safety & Emergency Preparedness) (2006), 58 Imm. L.R. (3d) 135, [2007] 3 F.C.R. 218, 2006 CarswellNat 3554, 2006 FC 1314 — The applicant was in Canada for several years as a temporary resident on a study permit. Before his study permit expired, he applied for a post-graduation work permit. He received a letter from CIC informing him that he did not meet the requirements for a work permit and that he should leave Canada immediately, failing which enforcement action would be taken against him. Within 90 days of the expiration of his study permit and within 90 days of losing his temporary resident status, he applied to have his status restored pursuant to Regulation 182. While awaiting a decision on his application for restoration, two immigration officers attended his home and questioned him. Two inadmissibility reports were issued, the first based on para. 40(1)(a) of the IRPA and the fact that "there were reasonable grounds to believe that this foreign national was inadmissible for directly or indirectly misrepresenting or withholding material facts relating to a relevant matter that induces or could induce an error in administration of this Act." The second report was based on para. 41(a) and subs. 29(2) of the IRPA and the fact that the applicant was inadmissible for failing to comply with his obligation as a temporary resident to leave Canada by the end of the period authorized for his stay. A Minister's delegate decided to issue an exclusion order based on para. 41(a) and subs. 29(2) of the IRPA. In light of s. 225 of the Regulations, this meant that the applicant could not come back to Canada without written consent of the Minister for a period of one year following his departure. The applicant left Canada. No decision with respect to the application for restoration was ever made. In this case, the Minister's delegate had the discretion and even the duty to consider the fact that the applicant had applied for restoration well before a s. 44(1) report was issued against him in respect of his failure to leave Canada at the end of his authorized stay. It was an error of law to consider that the applicant was not entitled to make such an application for restoration simply because after the filing of his application in accordance with the Regulations, a s. 44(1) report had been issued on the sole basis of subs. 29(2) of the IRPA. The decision was set aside.

The following questions were certified:

1. Is an application for restoration pursuant to s. 182 of the Regulations a relevant consideration when the Minister's delegate considers whether or not to make an exclusion order based on a failure to comply with s. 29(2) of the IRPA?

2. Does a foreign national who has applied for restoration within the delay set out in s. 182 of the Regulations, automatically lose the benefit of his or her application when an enforcement officer considers issuing a report under s. 44(1) on the basis of a failure to comply with s. 29(2) of the IRPA?

Uppal v. Canada (Minister of Citizenship & Immigration) (2006), 53 Imm. L.R. (3d) 284, 289 F.T.R. 196, 2006 CarswellNat 697, 2006 FC 338 — When the applicant came from the United Kingdom claiming to be a visitor, he produced a British passport which the Canadian authorities had been notified had been obtained fraudulently. A report was written under subs. 44(1) of the IRPA alleging that the applicant was inadmissible under para. 36(1)(c) in that there were reasonable grounds to believe the applicant was inadmissible on grounds of serious criminality because of his commission of an act outside of Canada, that if committed in Canada would be an offence under an Act of Parliament punishable by a maximum term of at least 10 years.

The report set out the factual information upon which the report was based. It also referred to the Canadian equivalent offence of the Criminal Code and recited the wording of that provision. The matter was referred to an admissibility hearing. Prior to the hearing, the report was amended to substitute another section of the Criminal Code as the Canadian equivalent offence.

The substitution of an equivalent Canadian offence that better conforms to the offence alleged to have been committed does not affect the substance of the subs. 44(1) report. It follows that the substitution of one particular provision of the Code that better depicts or corresponds to the impugned act than another, does not necessitate a withdrawal of the report such that the subs. 44(2) decision is returned to its preliminary stage.

The applicant received formal notice of the substitution of the equivalent offence along with a supplemental disclosure package. Furthermore, no objection was taken to the amendment of the subs. 44(1) report prior to or during the hearing. The failure to make a timely objection constitutes, if not an unequivocal waiver, an implied waiver.

Aksenova v. Canada (Minister of Public Safety & Emergency Preparedness), 2006 FC 557, 2006 CarswellNat 1204, [2006] F.C.J. No. 699 — The immigration officer issued a report against the applicant under subs. 44(1) of the IRPA because she was deemed inadmissible to Canada pursuant to para. 36(2)(a), having been convicted in Canada of an offence punishable by indictment. On the basis of that report, a deportation order was then issued by the Minister's delegate under subs. 44(2). The court considered whether in exercising its discretion to issue a report and make a deportation order, the officer and the Minister's delegate considered that the applicant was granted admission to Canada twice after she was convicted of an offence in Canada. The court concluded that the fact that the applicant was admitted to Canada twice after being convicted of an offence in Canada is not included in the exceptions set out under subs. 36(3) of IRPA dealing with inadmissibility to Canada. Therefore, the officer and delegate made no error by not considering them before they acted as they did. The particular circumstances of a person are irrelevant considerations and at most, the delegate could have stayed or deferred the making of the order if the applicant had already been subjected to an effective removal order, if plans had been made to leave Canada or if the applicant had been a witness called to testify in proceedings held in Canada. None of these considerations were applicable in this case. "Particular circumstances of the person" were said to be irrelevant. Although both subs. 44(1) and (2) use the term "may" in enabling the officer to prepare a report and the delegate to make a removal order, the statutory scheme enacted by the IRPA limits the discretion vested in the officer and the delegate. The term "may" in subs. 44(1) and (2) must be read in conjunction with subs. 36(3), which sets out the exceptions to inadmissibility.

Awed v. Canada (Minister of Citizenship & Immigration), 2006 CarswellNat 1077, 2006 FC 469 — The purpose of the interview under s. 44(1) is simply to confirm the facts that may support the formation of an opinion by the officer that a permanent resident or foreign national present in Canada is inadmissible. The use of the word "may" in s. 44(1) does not connote discretion but merely that the officer is authorized to perform an administrative function.

While it may be more efficient to allow the officer to exercise discretion at this stage of the process, such as to decide whether a criminal conviction should be discounted because of mental illness, the officer is not empowered by the enactment to make such a determination. The formation of the officer's opinion merely initiates a process which may or may not result in removal. In every case, it remains open to the applicant to seek an exception on humanitarian and compassionate grounds or a pre-removal risk assessment.

Where an immigration officer calls a permanent resident or foreign national for an interview in order to confirm the facts that would support a s. 44(1) opinion and report, the content of the duty of fairness is minimal. However, even a minimal degree of fairness would require that the officer advise the person of the purpose of the interview if only to put the person on notice of the possible consequences and to consider his options.

The officer, in this case, breached the duty of fairness by not informing the applicant that the status of his presence in Canada was in question because of his criminal convictions. Since there was nothing in the material to indicate that the officer's opinion was incorrect, the outcome would have been the same had another officer been directed to make the same inquiry. Accordingly, the decision was not set aside.

Mugesera c. Canada (Ministre de la Citoyenneté & de l'Immigration), [2005] 2 S.C.R. 91, 47 Imm. L.R. (3d) 1, EYB 2005-91970, [2005] S.C.J. No. 40, 197 C.C.C. (3d) 225, 254 D.L.R. (4th) 193, 30 C.R. (6th) 107, 335 N.R. 220, 15 C.P.C. (6th) 51, 2005 CarswellNat 1738, 2005 CarswellNat 1739, 2005 SCC 39 — At the secondary level of appellate review, the Federal Court of Appeal should proceed with the review of the Minister's allegations on the basis of the facts as found by the Immigration Appeal Division. On questions of law, however, the standard of review is correctness and the Immigration Appeal Division is not entitled to deference when it comes to defining the elements of a crime or whether the Minister's burden of proof has been discharged. Where the Minister relies on a crime committed abroad, a conclusion that the elements of the crime in Canadian criminal law had been made out will be deemed to be determinative in respect of the commission of crimes under the foreign criminal law. With respect to the specific allegations made pursuant to s. 27(1) of the former *Immigration Act*, the evidence adduced by the Minister must meet the civil standard of the balance of probabilities. The appellant, an active member of a hard-line Hutu political party opposed to a negotiation process then under way to end the war, spoke to about 1,000 people at a meeting of the party in Rwanda. The content of the speech eventually led the Rwandan authorities to issue the equivalent of an arrest warrant against the appellant. He fled the country and successfully applied for permanent residence in Canada. After the immigrant landed in Canada, the Minister became aware of allegations against him and commenced proceeding to deport him, on the basis that he committed criminal acts or offences. Specifically, the issue was whether a speech delivered by the appellant in Rwanda triggered a series of events that led to murder, hatred and genocide. In this case, the Minister had to prove that, on the facts of the case as found on a balance of probabilities, the speech constituted an incitement to murder, genocide or hatred. The Supreme Court of Canada upheld the validity of the deportation order on the basis that each element of the offence under the Criminal Code had been made out and that there were reasonable grounds to believe that the immigrant committed a crime against humanity and was therefore inadmissible under the former *Immigration Act*. The "reasonable grounds to believe" standard requires more than mere suspicion, but less than the normal civil litigation standard of proof on the balance of probabilities.

Lasin v. Canada (Minister of Citizenship & Immigration), 2005 FC 1356, 2005 CarswellNat 3130, 2005 CarswellNat 4337, [2005] F.C.J. No. 1655 — The failure of the immigration officer to provide a reasonable opportunity for the applicant to present evidence on mitigating factors over the course of the subs. 44(2) proceeding, such as his two-year marriage to a Canadian citizen and his outstanding H&C application, does not constitute a breach of procedural fairness. Decisions under s. 44(1) and (2) are routine administrative decisions. Issues relating to humanitarian and compassionate considerations or the safety of the applicant are obviously vital to the applicant, however, they have no place in these routine administrative proceedings. Rather, the Act provides specific procedures for dealing with them in ss. 25 and 112, respectively.

Hernandez v. Canada (Minister of Citizenship & Immigration) (2005), 45 Imm. L.R. (3d) 249, 2005 CarswellNat 825, 2005 FC 429 — The applicant, a permanent resident of Canada, was sentenced to 30 months for possession of cocaine for the purposes of trafficking.

An immigration officer interviewed the applicant. The purpose of this interview was to decide whether to write a report under s. 44(1). The officer decided to write a report and sent it to the director of case management. The officer recommended that an admissibility hearing be held. The Minister's delegate concurred in the officer's recommendation and an admissibility hearing was held. The applicant was ordered deported.

In this application, the applicant sought to review three decisions: the officer's report; the decision to refer the matter for an admissibility hearing; and the decision to issue the deportation order. This proceeding involved a combination of three different Federal Court files. Sections 44(1) and 44(2) are broad enough to allow the Minister's delegate to consider the factors outlined in the relevant sections of the CIC procedure manual.

The duty of fairness required in a s. 44 decision is more relaxed. The affected person should have the right to make submissions, either orally or in writing, and to obtain a copy of the report. Implicit in the duty of fairness is a requirement that the person being interviewed is informed of the purpose of the interview. The interviewing officer should put to the person concerned any information which the person would not reasonably be expected to have. The person concerned should be offered the opportunity to have counsel present at the interview or to assist in the preparation of written submissions. An oral interview may not always be required as long as the affected person is given an opportunity to make submissions and to know the case against him or her. The duty of fairness does not require that the applicant be given a further opportunity to respond prior to the s. 44(2) referral.

Aguillar v. Canada (Minister of Citizenship & Immigration) (2005), 45 Imm. L.R. (3d) 16, 2005 CarswellNat 313, 2005 FC 152 — The applicant sought to overturn a decision that determined that he was inadmissible and ordered his deportation. Under subs. 86(1) the Minister may make an application for non-disclosure of information. The determination is made in accordance with s. 78. The application will be allowed if the information is injurious to national security or the safety of any person.

The immunity from disclosure which is accorded in relation to information furnished to the police in the course of their performance of their duties is general in its scope. This has become recognized as a rule of law with only one recognized exception, namely, where upon the trial of the defendant for a criminal offence, disclosure of the identity of the informer could help show that the defendant was innocent. The value of informers to police investigations has long been recognized. As long as crimes have been committed, informers have played an important role in their investigation. Some informers act for compensation or for self-serving purposes. Whatever their motives, the position of informers is always precarious and their role is fraught with danger.

Leong v. Canada (Solicitor General), 41 Imm. L.R. (3d) 48, 256 F.T.R. 298, 2004 CarswellNat 4848, 2004 CarswellNat 2842, 2004 FC 1126, [2004] F.C.J. No. 1369 — A relatively low level of procedural fairness is owed when the initial s. 44(1) report is being prepared. Consequently, the officer did not err by failing to inform the applicant that a report was being considered, nor was the applicant entitled to make written submissions before the decision was made.

Correia v. Canada (Minister of Citizenship & Immigration), 36 Imm. L.R. (3d) 139, 253 F.T.R. 153, 2004 CarswellNat 2982, 2004 CarswellNat 1561, 2004 FC 782, [2004] F.C.J. No. 964 — The applicant was a 56-year-old citizen of Guyana who had been a permanent resident of Canada since 1968 and had a history of criminal activity. Immigration officials began the process of removing the applicant and on April 7, 2003, an officer made a report pursuant to s. 44(1) of the Act that the applicant was inadmissible by reason of serious criminality. On the next day a delegate of the Minister referred the report to the Immigration Division for an admissibility hearing. A removal order was issued by the Immigration Division and the applicant brought this application for judicial review as a result.

Section 44(1) involves two different acts by the officer: first there is the formation of an opinion concerning inadmissibility, and second, there is the decision to make a report. The discretion not to report is extremely limited and rare, otherwise, it would give officials a level of discretion not even enjoyed by the responsible Minister.

For the purposes of s. 44(1) the report is restricted to "relevant facts." In the case of serious criminality, those facts relate to the fact of the conviction. The nature of the inquiry does not involve issues of humanitarian and compassionate matters, rehabilitation or other such factors. The facts essentially involve the fact of the conviction and the length of the sentence. The officer has no jurisdiction to consider humanitarian and compassionate issues in issuing his or her report. The inquiry regarding serious criminality can be contrasted with that involving organized criminality, health grounds or misrepresentation, and on these other grounds of inadmissibility, officials are required to make judgements both as to fact and law. Therefore, the nature of those inquiries is quite different from the very straight forward inquiry as to serious criminality.

It is difficult to see what purpose an interview would serve in this type of inquiry. The fact that the interview, in this case, was held after the decision to refer was made was a breach of procedural fairness, but there was no reason to quash the decision because the applicant was unable to suggest what relevant facts could have been put to the delegate which would in any way have altered the decision to refer the matter.

Section 44(2)

See *Wong* summary under s. 28 of IRPA.

Rosenberry v. Canada (Minister of Citizenship & Immigration) (2010), 221 C.R.R. (2d) 128, 374 F.T.R. 116 (Eng.), 2010 FC 882, 2010 CarswellNat 3998, 2010 CarswellNat 3201 — The Minister's delegate issued a removal order against each of the applicants pursuant to s. 44 of IRPA due to the applicants' violations of subs. 41(a) and 29(2) of the Act. The applicants raised the question of whether the procedure laid out in s. 44 of the Act violated the constitutional principle of the separation of powers.

The applicants were citizens of the United States whose daughter was a permanent resident of Canada and had sponsored the applicants to Canada as members of the family class. Before the applicants had obtained a decision, they chose to come to Canada. To that end, the applicants sold their house in California and sent their belongings to their daughter's residence. They were turned back at the Idaho-Canada border because they failed to satisfy the officer that they were entering Canada for a temporary purpose. In June 2008, the applicants entered Canada at a different border crossing and without proper authorization. They flew to Edmonton where they had purchased a home prior to entering. They applied for an extension of their visitor's status. The applicants were to attend an interview regarding the extension and following that interview they were directed to leave Canada forthwith. The allegation of inadmissibility was relatively straightforward: the applicants were foreign nationals who were inadmissible pursuant to subs. 41(a) and 29(2) of the Act and they had failed to leave Canada at the end of the period authorized for their stay. While the Minister's delegate dealt with the request swiftly and with a negative result for the applicants, there is no indication that she prevented them from making any important submission in favour of the adjournment. The process was administrative in nature, with no requirement for the hallmarks of the quasi-judicial procedure. It was entirely appropriate for the Minister's delegate to consider the entire submission and especially the last submission, to be more adequately and appropriately handled in a request under s. 48 of the Act. The applicants were afforded a fair procedure. The application for judicial review was dismissed.

Lee v. Canada (Minister of Citizenship & Immigration), 2006 FC 158, 2006 CarswellNat 381, [2006] F.C.J. No. 260 — Subsection 44(2) of the IRPA confers the power to refer a report to the Immigration Division in subjective terms. The test is not whether the report is well founded, but whether the Minister is "of the opinion" that the report is well founded. There is ample authority that unless the overall scheme of the Act indicated otherwise, such subjective decisions cannot be judicially reviewed except on grounds that the decision maker acted in bad faith, erred in law, or acted on the basis of irrelevant considerations. When confronted with the record which was before the decision maker and there is no evidence to the contrary, the court must assume that the decision maker acted in good faith having regard to the material.

The fact is, under the IRPA, a permanent resident will not have his case reviewed in the same manner and with as much formality as he would have under the previous legislation. That is the clear effect of the legislation. It is consistent with the purposes of the legislation. It is more difficult under the IRPA for serious criminals to prevent their removal.

Cha v. Canada (Minister of Citizenship & Immigration) (2006), 53 Imm. L.R. (3d) 1, 267 D.L.R. (4th) 324, 349 N.R. 233, 2006 CarswellNat 751, 2006 FCA 126, [2006] F.C.J. No. 491 — The intent of Parliament is clear. The Minister's delegate is only empowered under subs. 44(2) of the Act to make the removal orders in prescribed cases which are clear and non-controversial and where the facts simply dictate the remedy. The Minister's delegate could not look at the gravity of the offence, and the particular circumstances of the applicant and his conviction, in determining not to issue the removal order. It is simply not open to the Minister's delegate to indirectly or collaterally go beyond the actual conviction. To do so would ignore Parliament's clearly expressed intent that the breaking of the condition of non-criminality be determinative. Although the manual indicates that the personal circumstances of the offender will be considered at the front-end of the process before any decision is taken to remove an individual from Canada, these views and statements have been expressed in respect to permanent residents convicted of serious offences in Canada. No such assurances were given by specific reference to foreign nationals. A foreign national may wish to invoke humanitarian and compassionate considerations and is at liberty to make a request to the Minister pursuant to s. 25 of the Act or to stay a removal order pursuant to s. 233 of the Regulations, or avail himself of the pre-removal risk assessment proceeding pursuant to s. 112 of the Act.

Absent a *Charter* right to be notified of a right to counsel on arrest or detention, there is no authority for the proposition that a person is entitled as of right to be notified before a hearing that he or she has either a statutory right or a duty-of-fairness right to counsel. Once a person is sufficiently informed of the object and possible effects of a forthcoming hearing — absent sufficient notice, the decision rendered will in all likelihood be set aside — the decision maker is under no duty to go further.

It may be sound practice, in certain cases, to give notice in advance that counsel may be retained, but there is no duty to do so unless the statute requires it. The responsibility lies with the person to seek leave from the decision maker to be accompanied by counsel or to come to the hearing accompanied by counsel.

In the recent IRPA, the right to be informed of one's right to counsel in admissibility matters has disappeared and the right to counsel has been preserved only with respect to hearings before the Immigration Division. There is no provision concerning the right to counsel and proceedings before the immigration officer or the Minister's delegate under subs. 44(1) and (2) of the IRPA. In this case, the respondent did not seek leave to have counsel present during the interview or to attend accompanied by counsel.

If leave is denied or if counsel is not allowed to be present, that could become an issue in a judicial review of the decision ultimately rendered.

Also see *Aksenova v. Canada (Minister of Public Safety & Emergency Preparedness)*, 2006 FC 557, 2006 CarswellNat 1204, [2006] F.C.J. No. 699 and *Lasin v. Canada*

(Minister of Citizenship & Immigration), 2005 FC 1356, 2005 CarswellNat 3130, 2005 CarswellNat 4337, [2005] F.C.J. No. 1655, both at s. 44(1).

Hernandez v. Canada (Minister of Citizenship & Immigration) (2005), 45 Imm. L.R. (3d) 249, 2005 CarswellNat 825, 2005 FC 429 — The applicant, a permanent resident of Canada, was sentenced to thirty months for possession of cocaine for the purposes of trafficking.

An immigration officer interviewed the applicant. The purpose of this interview was to decide whether to write a report under s. 44(1). The officer decided to write a report and sent it to the director of case management. The officer recommended that an admissibility hearing be held. The Minister's delegate concurred in the officer's recommendation and an admissibility hearing was held. The applicant was ordered deported.

In this application the applicant sought to review three decisions: the officer's report; the decision to refer the matter for an admissibility hearing; and the decision to issue the deportation order. This proceeding involved a combination of three different Federal Court files. Sections 44(1) and 44(2) are broad enough to allow the Minister's delegate to consider the factors outlined in the relevant sections of the CIC procedure manual.

The duty of fairness required in a s. 44 decision is more relaxed. The affected person should have the right to make submissions, either orally or in writing, and to obtain a copy of the report. Implicit in the duty of fairness is a requirement that the person being interviewed is informed of the purpose of the interview. The interviewing officer should put to the person concerned any information which the person would not reasonably be expected to have. The person concerned should be offered the opportunity to have counsel present at the interview or to assist in the preparation of written submissions. An oral interview may not always be required as long as the affected person is given an opportunity to make submissions and to know the case against him or her. The duty of fairness does not require that the applicant be given a further opportunity to respond prior to the s. 44(2) referral.

Admissibility Hearing by the Immigration Division

45. Decision — **The Immigration Division, at the conclusion of an admissibility hearing, shall make one of the following decisions:**

(a) recognize the right to enter Canada of a Canadian citizen within the meaning of the *Citizenship Act*, a person registered as an Indian under the *Indian Act* or a permanent resident;

(b) grant permanent resident status or temporary resident status to a foreign national if it is satisfied that the foreign national meets the requirements of this Act;

(c) authorize a permanent resident or a foreign national, with or without conditions, to enter Canada for further examination; or

(d) make the applicable removal order against a foreign national who has not been authorized to enter Canada, if it is not satisfied that the foreign national is not inadmissible, or against a foreign national who has been authorized to enter Canada or a permanent resident, if it is satisfied that the foreign national or the permanent resident is inadmissible.

IRP Act

Case Law

Wajaras v. Canada (Minister of Citizenship & Immigration), 2009 FC 200, 2009 CarswellNat 530, 2009 CarswellNat 1116 — The applicant sought to set aside a decision of the Immigration Division that found him to be inadmissible to Canada on the ground of serious criminality in accordance with s. 36(1)(a) of IRPA. The applicant entered Canada in 1997 as a Convention refugee and was granted permanent resident status at that time. He subsequently committed a serious assault and was criminally charged and sentenced to three years imprisonment in 2005.

The CBSA made an inadmissibility report which lead to an inadmissibility hearing before the Board under s. 44(2) of the IRPA. The applicant was advised of the CBSA's intention to have him declared a danger to the public. Notwithstanding his refugee status, such a finding would have permitted his return to Sudan in the event that he was also found to be inadmissible. The Minister determined that the applicant did not represent a danger to the public. In the result he could not be returned to Sudan even though he had been determined to be inadmissible and was the subject of a corresponding removal order. The applicant argued before the Board that it was an abuse of process for the Minister to seek a removal order against him with the resulting loss of permanent resident status in circumstances where his removal could not be lawfully effected.

The Federal Court concluded that notwithstanding that the Board erred in law by stating that the doctrine of abuse of process required evidence of malice or animus, a question remained as to whether an abuse of process argument could be sustained on this particular record. The Federal Court concluded it could not and the Board's mistake, therefore, was of no consequence. The application for judicial review was set aside. The applicant was solely responsible for the position he found himself in. He is not without potential future recourse. If administrative decisions are made which unlawfully interfere with his interests, including the opportunity to work, he would have the right to seek judicial review. If he stays out of legal trouble, enhances his Canadian establishment and continues to make positive social and economic contributions, he would be in a position at some point to pursue humanitarian and compassionate relief under s. 25 of the IRPA.

An abuse of process argument cannot be built around selective references to the purposes of the IRPA. The legislation serves many purposes, not the least of which is protecting Canadians by imposing consequences for the criminal behaviour of a few of those who have emigrated here.

The Federal Court judge certified a question and the Federal Court of Appeal in *Wajaras v. Canada (Minister of Citizenship & Immigration)* (2010), 399 N.R. 31, 2010 FCA 41, 2010 CarswellNat 266, 2010 CarswellNat 623 concluded that the Minister of Citizenship and Immigration does not engage in abuse of process in continuing to seek a removal order where the effected individual has been determined not to be a danger to the public. The Federal Court of Appeal concluded that it was not improper for the Minister to seek a deportation order for the purpose of depriving a permanent resident of this status as a result of serious criminality, even where there are impediments to removal. The appeal was dismissed.

Powell v. Canada (Minister of Citizenship & Immigration) (2005), 45 Imm. L.R. (3d) 210, 2005 CarswellNat 1489, 2005 FCA 202 — Assuming, without deciding, that the appellant's liberty interest is engaged, the scheme of the IRPA which may result in the removal of the appellant, a foreign national, pursuant to subs. 45(d), does not violate the principles of fundamental justice.

Loss of Status

46. (1) Permanent resident — A person loses permanent resident status

(a) when they become a Canadian citizen;

(b) on a final determination of a decision made outside of Canada that they have failed to comply with the residency obligation under section 28;

(c) when a removal order made against them comes into force;

(c.1) on a final determination under subsection 108(2) that their refugee protection has ceased for any of the reasons described in paragraphs 108(1)(a) to (d);

(d) on a final determination under section 109 to vacate a decision to allow their claim for refugee protection or a final determination to vacate a decision to allow their application for protection; or

(e) on approval by an officer of their application to renounce their permanent resident status.

(1.1) Effect of renunciation — A person who loses their permanent resident status under paragraph (1)(e) becomes a temporary resident for a period of six months unless they make their application to renounce their permanent resident status at a port of entry or are not physically present in Canada on the day on which their application is approved.

(2) Effect of ceasing to be citizen — A person becomes a permanent resident if he or she ceases to be a citizen under

(a) paragraph 10(1)(a) of the *Citizenship Act*, as it read immediately before the coming into force of section 8 of the *Strengthening Canadian Citizenship Act*, other than in the circumstances set out in subsection 10(2) of the *Citizenship Act*, as it read immediately before that coming into force;

(b) subsection 10(1) of the *Citizenship Act*, other than in the circumstances set out in section 10.2 of that Act; or

(c) paragraph 10.1(3)(a) of the *Citizenship Act*, other than in the circumstances set out in section 10.2 of that Act.

[Editor's Note: SOR/2002-227, s. 328(1) provides that a person who was a permanent resident immediately before June 28, 2002 is a permanent resident under the new Immigration and Refugee Protection Act, S.C. 2001, c. 27.]

2012, c. 17, s. 19; 2013, c. 16, s. 20; 2014, c. 22, s. 43

Case Law

Rodriguez v. Canada (Minister of Citizenship & Immigration) (2011), 1 Imm. L.R. (4th) 304, (sub nom. *Martinez Rodriguez v. Canada (Minister of Citizenship & Immigration)*) 395 F.T.R. 21 (Eng.), 2011 FC 946, 2011 CarswellNat 2890 — The applicant accompanied her parents to Canada when they obtained permanent resident status in 1991. At the time, she was six years old. Two months later, her parents returned to El Salvador and she accompanied them. She visited Canada in 1998 and in 2000, both times on a visitor's visa. In 2010, she applied for another temporary visitor's visa in order to visit her aunt who lives in Canada. The visa officer realized that she had obtained permanent resident status in 1991. However, it was clear that she had not maintained her residency requirement, as she had not been in Canada a single day in the past 10 years. Under s. 31(3) the visa officer was prohibited from issuing the applicant a travel document, and as a permanent resident she could not be given a temporary resident visa. She was asked to sign, in English, a Consent to Decision on Residency Obligation and Waiver of Appeal Rights Resulting in Loss of Status under s. 46(1)(b). While the visa officer may well have thought she was doing the applicant a favour, since she was not entitled to a travel document as a permanent resident, if the only alternative was to renounce that status, she should not have been given that opportunity. She should have been sent back to El Salvador, and given a full opportunity to consider her options and to take advice. Renunciation of permanent resident status is a very important step in a person's life. It should not be decided on the spur of the moment. Although she clearly had not maintained the residence requirement, it was up to the IAD, not the Federal Court, to determine if there were humanitarian and compassionate considerations which override that defect. The IAD's decision that it had no jurisdiction to hear her appeal because she had lost her status as a permanent resident was set aside and sent back to a newly constituted panel of the IAD for redetermination.

47. Temporary resident — A foreign national loses temporary resident status

    (a) at the end of the period for which they are authorized to remain in Canada;

    (b) on a determination by an officer or the Immigration Division that they have failed to comply with any other requirement of this Act; or

    (c) on cancellation of their temporary resident permit.

[Editor's Note: SOR/2002-227, s. 329(1) provides that any of the following persons who were in Canada immediately before June 28, 2002 are temporary residents under the new Immigration and Refugee Protection Act, *S.C. 2001, c. 27 and are subject to its provisions:*

    (a) a visitor under the Immigration Act, *R.S.C. 1985, c. I-2 (the "former Act"); and*

    (b) a person issued a permit under s. 37 of the former Act.]

Case Law

Zhang v. Canada (Minister of Citizenship & Immigration) (2006), 59 Imm. L.R. (3d) 165, 2006 CarswellNat 3831, 2006 FC 1381 — The applicant moved to British Columbia in 2002 on a temporary student permit that was valid until August 2004. He applied for and was granted an extension to August 30, 2005. Since he wanted to continue his studies, he applied for a further extension in August 2005. The officer concluded he was not a *bona fide* student and did not intend to leave Canada at the end of his stay. The applicant did not leave Canada, nor did he seek leave of the court to challenge the decision to refuse his extension application. Instead, the applicant submitted a restoration application seeking to re-acquire the temporary status he had lost. The applicant's restoration application was refused. The officer's letter essentially quoted para. 47(a) of the IRPA and s. 182 of its accompanying Regulations, and simply stated that the applicant was refused as he was not satisfied the applicant met those criteria. It was perfectly legitimate for the applicant to apply for restoration instead of judicial review of the initial decision to extend his study permit. While the immigration officer could take the extension decision into consideration, he also had to assess the applicant's new evidence in support of his claim that the initial decision was mistaken or did not reflect his true intentions. It is true that there is nothing in the IRPA requiring an immigration officer to provide reasons to an applicant. But it is well established that the duty of procedural fairness sometimes requires that explanations be given for a particular decision. In the present case, the mere recital of the relevant sections of the IRPA and the Regulations was clearly not sufficient. The applicant submitted further evidence that he was a *bona fide* student. He is certainly entitled to some explanation as to why these further documents were inadequate to show that he was a *bona fide* student. As a result of the negative restoration decision, the applicant was found to be inadmissible to Canada and the decision that he challenged before the Federal Court would have profound implications for him. The more important a decision is to the lives of those affected and the greater its impact on that person or those persons, the more stringent the procedural protections that will be mandated. Although a relatively low degree of procedural fairness is warranted in an immigration officer's decision to grant or deny an application to restore temporary resident status, a low level of procedural fairness still imposes some obligations on officers to provide reasons for negative decisions. The application for judicial review was granted.

Enforcement of Removal Orders

48. (1) Enforceable removal order — A removal order is enforceable if it has come into force and is not stayed.

(2) Effect — If a removal order is enforceable, the foreign national against whom it was made must leave Canada immediately and the order must be enforced as soon as possible.

2012, c. 17, s. 20

Case Law

Section 48(1)

Begum v. Canada (Minister of Citizenship & Immigration), 2013 FC 550, 2013 CarswellNat 1753, 2013 CarswellNat 1754 — The applicant and her son sought a stay of a removal order. They had a long and convoluted history in Canada. They arrived in 1999 when the son was less than 2 years old. They were denied refugee status and their application for leave to judicially review that decision was dismissed. A PRRA was also negative. They had been removal ready since 2004. The underlying decision in this case was a refusal in 2012 to permit them to apply for permanent residence from within Canada. The applicant had been considered a flight risk and was in detention for the past year. Leave was granted. The applicants requested the deferral of their removal. An enforcement officer concluded that a deferral of the execution of the removal order was not appropriate in the circumstances.

This motion deals with the administration of justice, and disrespect of this court. It is not quite contempt, but not far off. The *sub judice* rule is almost on point. Not only were proceedings ongoing, but a hearing on the merits of the judicial review had taken place. The Minister conceded there was a serious question. The court held there would be irreparable harm if the applicants were removed without the wherewithal to return should they ultimately be successful. The balance of convenience was found to favour the applicants. The motion to stay the removal order was granted.

Strungmann v. Canada (Minister of Citizenship & Immigration), 2011 FC 1229, 2011 CarswellNat 4487, 2011 CarswellNat 4840 — The applicant sought judicial review to have the deportation order against him quashed on the grounds of absolute nullity. While in Canada as a visitor, the applicant pled guilty to a count of mischief for having sprayed graffiti on a wall and was convicted of that charge in Montreal. The same day, he was found inadmissible under para. 36(2)(a) of IRPA and was issued a deportation order by the Minister's delegate. The removal order was enforced. Following his departure from Canada, he appealed his conviction and his appeal was allowed and a new trial was ordered. Eventually the case was dismissed. As a result, the applicant argued that the removal order was void *ab initio* and should no longer stand, since the applicant had been acquitted of the charge upon which the inadmissibility decision, and consequently, the deportation order, was based. He argued the deportation order was illegal retroactive to the date it was made.

A decision taken from a fundamental change in evidence is not a nullity or void *ab initio*. However, on a going-forward basis, any such decision could not be enforced or otherwise acted or relied on. The application was dismissed.

Dhurmu v. Canada (Minister of Public Safety & Emergency Preparedness), 2011 FC 511, 2011 CarswellNat 1434, 2011 CarswellNat 2498 — While the Federal Court of Appeal in *Perez v. Canada (Minister of Citizenship & Immigration)* (2009), 82 Imm. L.R. (3d) 167, 393 N.R. 332, 2009 FCA 171, 2009 CarswellNat 1522, 2009 CarswellNat 5164, [2009] F.C.J. No. 691, stated that a judicial review application of a negative PRRA decision would be rendered moot if the applicant were to be removed from Canada before the application was heard, it did not say that the applicant's removal should be stayed in every case where there is an outstanding PRRA judicial review. Thus, while it is an issue that the enforcement officer will have to take into consideration, the exercise of an application for judicial review of a negative PRRA decision cannot be said to be determinative as to the issue of removal. In the case at bar, however, the officer skirted the issue entirely, declaring that there may in fact be time for the judicial review application to be heard, when the reality was that given the timeline this would make such a reality impossible.

In determining whether to defer a removal, it is not for the officer to decide the likelihood of success for the applicant in her judicial review proceedings but merely to decide whether the existence of a judicial review application is a compelling enough reason. It was unreasonable and perhaps also outside of the very narrow jurisdiction of the officer to delve into her opinions as to the merits of the applicant's application for judicial review. The judicial review was allowed.

Baron v. Canada (Minister of Public Safety & Emergency Preparedness) (2009), 79 Imm. L.R. (3d) 157, 387 N.R. 278, 2009 CarswellNat 596, 2009 FCA 81, [2009] F.C.J. No. 314 — The court considered whether an application for judicial review of an enforcement officer's decision not to defer an applicant's scheduled removal from Canada becomes moot where the court has stayed the removal and the applicant has remained in Canada.

The jurisprudence is conclusive that the enforcement officer's discretion is limited. However, ultimately an enforcement officer is intended to do nothing more than enforce a removal order. While enforcement officers are granted the discretion to fix new removal dates, they are not intended to defer removal to an indeterminate date. On the facts before the court, the date of the decision on the H&C application was unknown and unlikely to be imminent, and thus, the enforcement officer was being asked to delay removal indeterminately. An indeterminate deferral was simply not within the enforcement officer's powers.

Over the years, the duties of enforcement officers have not changed, and yet, the basis upon which applicants rely to obtain deferrals have dramatically increased. The scope of the enforcement officer's discretion cannot be changed by virtue of the request made. An enforcement officer's role is not to assess the best interest of the children or the probability of success of any application. The enforcement officer's role should remain limited and deferral should be contemplated in very limited circumstances. The legislation has not provided a new step to claimants who desire yet another assessment of their circumstances. Claimants already have the refugee application process, the pre-removal risk assessment process and the H&C application in addition to judicial reviews of these processes and the stay before removal. In this case, it appears that the claimants want to open yet another avenue of review by asking the enforcement officer to reassess information that has already been examined by administrative tribunals and that was a subject of judicial review. For the enforcement officer to comply with this request for reassessment would be akin to the enforcement officer making a quasi-judicial order without the benefit of hearing from opposing counsel. It is time to stop this abusive cycle.

The appeal was dismissed. The removal date having passed, the determination of the reasonableness of the enforcement officer's refusal to defer the removal date in January 2007 was without consequence; the matter was rendered moot.

Palka v. Canada (Minister of Public Safety & Emergency Preparedness), 2008 CarswellNat 1309, 2008 FCA 165 — The Palkas appealed from a decision of the Federal Court dismissing their application for judicial review of a refusal by an enforcement officer to defer their removal from Canada, until their application for permanent residence on humanitarian and compassionate grounds ("H&C") had been decided. The lower court judge held that the application for judicial review was moot, and did not consider its merits. She based her finding of mootness on the fact that another judge of the Federal Court had stayed the Palkas' removal scheduled for June 13, 2007, pending the disposition of their application for judicial review of the officer's refusal to defer their removal. The lower court judge rejected the position taken by both the Palkas and the respondent Minister of Public Safety & Emergency Preparedness, that the passing of the scheduled removal date did not render the application for judicial review moot because an application for permanent residence on H&C grounds was outstanding. The lower court judge certified a question for appeal on the mootness issue. The Palkas then brought a motion for a stay of removal to their country of nationality, pending the disposition of the appeal.

They argue that, if they are denied a stay, their appeal on the mootness decision will be nugatory. They claim that this would constitute irreparable harm. The court did not agree. Even if their appeal was moot, the court may decide to hear it in its discretion, on the ground that the question certified may arise repeatedly and be evasive of review. Even if a refusal of a stay does not render the appeal nugatory, this does not necessarily constitute irreparable harm. It all depends on the facts of the individual case.

Despite numerous attempts, through administrative and legal channels, the Palkas have been denied status in Canada. There has to be some finality. To grant yet another deferral of their removal is contrary to the public interest as expressed in the Act. Motion to defer removal was dismissed.

Level (Litigation Guardian of) v. Canada (Minister of Public Safety & Emergency Preparedness) (2008), 71 Imm. L.R. (3d) 52, 2008 CarswellNat 423, 2008 FC 227 — This was an application for judicial review of an enforcement officer's decision to deny the applicant's request for a deferral of removal pending a decision on his application for permanent residence based on an H&C application.

An enforcement officer is statutorily bound to remove an applicant as soon as reasonably practical. However, if the officer relies on extrinsic evidence not brought forward by the applicant, the applicant must be given an opportunity to respond to that evidence. This is a minimal duty of procedural fairness. In the application at bar, the enforcement officer relied on detailed evidence about medical conditions in Jamaica that the applicant contested in an affidavit filed in support of the applicant's successful motion for a stay of removal. With respect to tight time frames, the applicant has been in Canada for 20 years, and the duty of fairness should not be sacrificed because of an artificial deadline established by the respondent for the applicant's removal. There was no harm in allowing the applicant another week or two in order to respond to extrinsic evidence upon which the enforcement officer intends to rely. If that extrinsic evidence is incorrect, the applicant will suffer great harm. The application for judicial review was allowed.

Maruthalingam v. Canada (Minister of Public Safety & Emergency Preparedness) (2007), 63 Imm. L.R. (3d) 242, 2007 FC 823, 2007 CarswellNat 3088, 2007 CarswellNat 2278, [2007] F.C.J. No. 1079 — The applicants were ordered to report for deportation and an enforcement officer refused the applicants' request that the removal from Canada be deferred. The applicants filed a notice of application for leave and judicial review of the enforcement officer's decision and brought a motion for a stay of their removal until the court had disposed of the application for judicial review. The motion for the stay was granted. The applicants were not removed. By the time this judicial review application was heard by the court, the serious issues identified in the stay motion were, in practical terms, academic. This application for judicial review was dismissed. The applicants raised the issue of whether the court should still rule that the issue was moot where it was asked to stay the removal until the outcome of another process. The court refused to opine as to whether the court could grant a remedy to the applicants on a free-standing basis. The applicants had not sought an order to stay the removal until the final determination of their outstanding application on humanitarian and compassionate grounds. Instead, their sole request was that the matter be referred to another enforcement officer for reconsideration.

See also *Vu v. Canada (Minister of Citizenship & Immigration)*, 2007 CarswellNat 3591 (F.C.)

Higgins v. Canada (Minister of Public Safety & Emergency Preparedness) (2007), 64 Imm. L.R. (3d) 98, 2007 FC 377, 2007 CarswellNat 1841, 2007 CarswellNat 832, [2007] F.C.J. No. 516 — By order dated June 29, 2006, the court stayed the removal of the applicant from Canada pending final determination of this application for judicial review. The granting of the stay gave the applicant his remedy before the merits of the application for judicial review were addressed.

If the respondent remains determined to remove the applicant before his humanitarian and compassionate grounds application is determined, it would be open to the applicant to request a new deferral of removal, based on all of the current circumstances and evidence. If that request is denied, a further application for leave and for judicial review would be open to him together with a further motion before the court seeking a stay of removal pending the final determination of that new application for leave and for judicial review.

The application for judicial review must. The court refused to exercise discretion to hear the matter.

Kovacs v. Canada (Minister of Public Safety & Emergency Preparedness) (2007), 68 Imm. L.R. (3d) 218, 2007 FC 1247, 2007 CarswellNat 4247, 2007 CarswellNat 5009, [2007] F.C.J. No. 1625 — There will no doubt be cases where the court can provide an important precedent; in such a situation the court may decide to exercise its discretion. This is not such a case. The issue in this judicial review is simply whether the enforcement officer had regard to the evidence before him. A ruling on this issue would not have any practical side effects on the rights of the parties.

The judicial review was dismissed.

See also *Islami v. Canada (Minister of Citizenship & Immigration)*, 2008 FC 364, 2008 CarswellNat 702, 2008 CarswellNat 2952.

Tesoro v. Canada (Minister of Citizenship & Immigration), 2005 CarswellNat 2049, 2005 CarswellNat 1083, 2005 FCA 148, [2005] F.C.J. No. 698 — The appellant brought a motion to stay his removal pending the disposition of an appeal to the Federal Court of Appeal from a decision of a motions judge. In that decision, the motions judge dismissed his application for judicial review of the refusal of the Immigration Appeal Division to re-open its rejection of his appeal.

The IAD does not lose jurisdiction over an application for the re-opening of an appeal because the applicant, who was in Canada when the application was filed, left under a removal order before the IAD considered it.

On a motion to stay a removal pending the disposition of an application for judicial review or an appeal, the focus is limited to the effect of the deportee's temporary absence from Canada pending the disposition of the legal proceedings.

Decisions on the grant of stays tend to be fact specific. Motions can come on at very short notice and decisions are often rendered under severe time constraints. Hence, it is not surprising to find some inconsistency in the case law. Irreparable harm, in this context, may include family separation and is not limited to threats to a deportee's life and limb. The more difficult issue is to delineate the circumstances in which family separation and the disruption of personal and other important relationships constitute irreparable harm. The question is the impact of removal on the appellant and his family as a result of the separation and whether that will be more than the usual consequences of deportation. It is relevant, when considering the separation of the appellant from his parents, that his parents are getting on in years and that his mother has health problems and may not be able to travel to Italy to visit him.

If the court had determined the appellant's removal would cause irreparable harm on the ground that the effects of family separation were more than mere inconveniences, the court would have to balance that harm against the public interest in the prompt removal from Canada of those persons found to be inadmissible for serious criminality. If the administration of immigration law is to be credible, the prompt removal of those ordered deported must be the rule and the grant of a stay pending the disposition of legal proceedings the exception.

Griffiths v. Canada (Minister of Citizenship & Immigration), 2005 CarswellNat 638, 2005 FC 329 — This was an application for a stay. The applicant came to Canada from

Jamaica when he was six years old and has not been back since he arrived here. His mother and three siblings are all Canadian citizens. The applicant was ordered deported in 1994. He appealed and in 1995 was granted a four-year stay on conditions. One condition was that he remain crime-free. However, the applicant was convicted in 1996. In 1998, the stay of the deportation order was lifted; however, the applicant was not deported because he was facing two criminal charges. In January 2001, the applicant was acquitted of one criminal charge and pleaded guilty to the other. From that point on he could have been deported but the authorities were content to leave him alone until late 2003.

The applicant was given one working day's notice of the respondent's intention to remove him from Canada. The respondents argued that the motion for a stay should not be considered because the applicant's counsel had not submitted a full written memorandum of fact and law. Having required the applicant to seek an abridgement of the normal delays because of the extremely short notice given him, the respondents cannot be heard to complain that they were prejudiced because applicant's counsel did not have the time to generate a full set of written submissions. The expulsion officer refused to defer removal without considering the interests of the applicant's children. Although an expulsion officer is not required to carry out a full H&C analysis, he must take some account of the children.

Finally, the fact that the Minister waited three years before attempting to remove the applicant was taken into consideration in deciding to make the Minister wait for the outcome of the matters before the Federal Court before affecting removal.

El Ouardi v. Canada (Solicitor General), 2005 CarswellNat 254, 2005 CarswellNat 1822, 332 N.R. 76, 2005 FCA 42, [2005] F.C.J. No. 189 — On the question of irreparable harm, the fact that an appeal will be rendered nugatory if a stay is not granted, will not always succeed in demonstrating irreparable harm. The difficulty with the argument is that it would apply to virtually all removal cases in which a stay is sought and would essentially deprive the court of the discretion to decide questions of irreparable harm on the facts of each case.

Canada (Solicitor General) v. Subhaschandran, 249 D.L.R. (4th) 269, 331 N.R. 182, 2005 CarswellNat 1129, 2005 CarswellNat 184, 2005 FCA 27, [2005] F.C.J. No. 107 — The respondents brought a motion for a stay of the order for their deportation. At the conclusion of the argument the motions judge adjourned the motion. The Minister launched a motion for reconsideration which was dismissed. The motions judge issued a clarification and ordered that the applicants not be removed from Canada pending a determination of their motion for a stay.

It is true that, generally, interlocutory orders including adjournments cannot be appealed. An exception to this rule, however, occurs where a judge refuses to exercise his jurisdiction and deal with the case. In the present case, the motions judge, by adjourning the motion, has deprived the parties of ever having a decision on the stay motion. This amounts to a refusal to exercise his jurisdiction and a remedy must be available.

Accordingly, the Court of Appeal took jurisdiction despite the fact that there was no serious question certified by the motions judge, allowed the appeal, set aside the order of the motions judge and remitted the matter back to the motions judge to make a decision on the application for a stay.

Mahjoub v. Canada (Minister of Citizenship & Immigration), 2004 CarswellNat 3440, 2004 FC 1315 — The applicant sought an order granting a stay of a removal order which provided for his imminent removal to Egypt, his country of nationality.

As to what constitutes at law a serious issue, the jurisprudence simply requires that an applicant show that the application is not frivolous or vexatious. This is a low threshold. The second requirement is irreparable harm. Irreparable harm must be harm which will occur in the interim between now and the time the application for leave and judicial review is adjudicated upon. Irreparable harm is harm which cannot be cured. An applicant for a stay must establish on a balance of probabilities that he or she faces a serious likelihood of harm. The existence of irreparable harm is fact-specific. The evidence must be credible and the harm non-speculative.

With respect to the balance of convenience test, the court found that so long as the applicant remained in detention, the third branch of the test should be determined in his favour.

In this case, a stay was granted.

Section 48(2)

Molnar v. Canada (Minister of Citizenship and Immigration), 2015 FC 345, 2015 CarswellNat 637, 2015 CarswellNat 3846 — The applicants brought an application for judicial review to challenge the decision of the Refugee Protection Division in which the Board determined that the applicants are neither Convention refugees nor persons in need of protection. The Minister brought a motion to dismiss the application on the ground that it was rendered moot as a result of the applicants' return to their country of nationality. The Minister's motion to dismiss the application was denied and the application was set down for a hearing on its merits. The court was not persuaded that Parliament intended to preclude the court and the Board from hearing a claim for refugee protection after a person has been removed from Canada pursuant to s. 48(2) of the IRPA. In the absence of express statutory language, the court was not prepared to read the rights conferred on the applicants by the IRPA in such a manner that they are rendered nugatory by the performance of the Minister's duty to execute a removal order as soon as reasonably practicable. In any event, it was an appropriate case in which the court should exercise its discretion to deal with the matter on its merits.

The following question was certified:

> Is an application for judicial review of a decision of the Refugee Protection Division moot where the individual who is the subject of the decision has involuntarily returned to his or her country of nationality, and, if yes, should the court normally refuse to exercise its discretion to hear it?

See *Strungmann* summary, 2011 FC 1229, 2011 CarswellNat 4487, 2011 CarswellNat 4840, under s. 48(1).

Villanueva v. Canada (Minister of Public Safety & Emergency Preparedness), 2010 FC 543, 2010 CarswellNat 1422, 2010 CarswellNat 2441 — This was an application for judicial review of a decision of an enforcement officer with the Canadian Border Services Agency, refusing the applicant's application for a deferral of the execution of the removal order against him. The officer was asked to consider the significant backlogs in the system in the case of a timely H&C application that had been outstanding for a considerable time, 15 months. The officer ignored this request and refused to defer on the basis of, *inter alia*, "imminence," *i.e.* whether a decision of the H&C grounds was about to be

IRP Act

made, irrespective of the amount of time it had been in the system and the reasons for the delay. There was no evidence that the backlog factor was given consideration. The officer did recognize that the H&C application was timely, but in focusing upon "imminence" he neglected to consider whether significant backlogs in the system and a long-outstanding H&C application should impact his decision. This was a reviewable error and the application for judicial review was allowed.

Vieira v. Canada (Minister of Public Safety & Emergency Preparedness) (2007), 64 Imm. L.R. (3d) 32, 2007 CarswellNat 1637, 2007 FC 626 — The inconvenience, which the applicants may suffer as a result of their removal from Canada, does not outweigh the public interest in executing removal orders as soon as reasonably practicable in accordance with subs. 48(2) of the IRPA. The Minister's obligation under subs. 48(2) of the IRPA is not simply a question of administrative convenience, but implicates the integrity and fairness of, and public confidence in, Canada's system of immigration control. The motion for the stay of removal was dismissed.

Cortes v. Canada (Minister of Citizenship & Immigration), 2007 CarswellNat 190, 2007 FC 78 — The applicants challenged a decision of a removals officer to deny of deferral of removal to Costa Rica. The court concluded a deferral decision was not a question of fact, but is a question of mixed law and fact. The question of mixed law and fact involves the application of general principles of the statutory provision concerned to specific circumstances. The onus is on the applicants to establish that the officer's refusal to defer is untenable. A deferral decision is intricate. The legal requirement is clear: the removal is to be immediate, but enforcement is based on practicalities; that is, a removal is to occur as soon as it is "able to [be] put into practice." But there is an important additional qualifier: what is practical must be reasonable, that is, "sensible." With respect to what is practical, the line of analysis on this element of a deferral decision revolves around what is possible at the time. A decision on this factor only amounts to a conclusion being drawn on features such as: is the whereabouts of the failed refugee claimant known; is the claimant accessible; is there an available method whereby the claimant may be transported out of the country; and are there persons who can escort the claimant to the airport or drive the claimant to the border? These are not complex operational considerations. However, the factor of reasonability adds complexity to the decision-making process being conducted. It is on this factor that there is wide judicial agreement that a removals officer has discretion. There is disagreement on the scope of this discretion. Some review decisions say that only "exceptional circumstances" are reasonable, while others take in a more flexible view, and find that humanitarian considerations can be applied. In these instances, the fact that a humanitarian and compassionate application is before the Minister of Citizenship and Immigration pursuant to s. 25(1) of the IRPA can be found to make it reasonable that a claimant not be removed until the application is decided.

The applicants' main appeal to the officer on the reasonableness factor was that their removal should be deferred until their H&C application is decided. The officer analyzed the health issues which were the basis of the request. This consideration could only properly occur within the form designed for the purpose: the H&C application process which the applicants have invoked. The officer's decision was set aside and the matter referred back for re-determination before another removals officer, but with a direction that the redetermination not occur until after the applicants' outstanding H&C application is finally determined. The court certified the following question:

> What is the correct standard of review of an officer's decision, made pursuant to the discretion set out in s. 48 of the IRPA to defer removal of persons from Canada?

Bastien v. Canada (Minister of Citizenship & Immigration), 2006 CarswellNat 1598, 2006 FC 711 — This is an application for judicial review of the decision of an expulsion officer to refuse to stay the removal of the applicant from Canada to Dominica. The applicant came to Canada in 1996 as a visitor and her permit was extended a number of times. She was sponsored under the care-giver program, but ended up living illegally. Her claim for refugee status was denied and a PRRA application that followed was negative. She submitted an application for humanitarian and compassionate consideration under s. 25 of the IRPA, arguing that she supports her ailing mother, her sister and her sister's three children, all of whom reside in Dominica. She also argued that the three children of her employer in Canada were dependent on her as a surrogate parent. She was advised that she would be deported from Canada and an application for a motion for stay pending the current judicial review was allowed. The applicant sought judicial review of the decision of the expulsion officer to deport her. Essentially, the removals officer did not exercise her discretion to defer the applicant's request for a deferral of removal. The officer noted that she had an obligation under s. 48 of the IRPA to carry out removal orders as soon as reasonably practicable.

The application for humanitarian and compassionate consideration was processed and a negative decision was returned. Consequently the issue to be considered was now moot. Nevertheless, the court wished to comment on the submissions regarding the exercise of discretion by a removals officer. The first issue was whether the expulsion officer had a duty to acknowledge that he or she has some discretion to defer removal. In this case, the court concluded that the officer did acknowledge such discretion. The second issue was whether the expulsion officer was required to give reasons and elaborate a subjective analysis of the issue. The court concluded that an expulsion officer has very limited discretion, and should not be required to give extensive reasons for a very limited decision-making process. The application for judicial review was dismissed.

M. (R.A.) v. M (Y.Y.), [2005] B.C.J. No. 1507, 48 Imm. L.R. (3d) 301, 2005 CarswellBC 1604, 2005 BCPC 259 — The B.C. Provincial Court does not have jurisdiction to decide issues under the *Family Relations Act* with respect to a child who is not born in Canada, is not a Canadian citizen, and who is subject to a valid and outstanding deportation order under the *Immigration and Refugee Protection Act*. The Provincial Court's jurisdiction under the *Family Relations Act* should not be used to override the comprehensive immigration scheme created by federal legislation in order to enjoin federal authorities and the Federal Courts from enforcing valid removal orders. Even where there is concurrent jurisdiction between the Provincial Court and the Federal Court, the Provincial Court should decline to assume or exercise the jurisdiction in immigration matters, and leave them to the Federal Court.

Hailu v. Canada (Solicitor General) (2005), 27 Admin. L.R. (4th) 222, 2005 CarswellNat 362, 2005 FC 229 — The standard of review applied to the decisions of removal officers is a patently unreasonable standard. The decisions of a removal officer, given the very limited nature and extent of the powers of such officers, do not require a formal decision with reasons. The keeping of notes is useful and to be encouraged but is not an absolute requirement. The onus rests on the applicant to make out the case to the removals officer that would compel him or her to defer removal.

Bharat v. Canada (Solicitor General), 2004 FC 1720, 2004 CarswellNat 4671, [2004] F.C.J. No. 2094 — The patently unreasonable standard should be applied to the decisions of removals officers, given the nature of the statutory scheme and, in particular, the limited and fact-driven discretion they exercise.

Labiyi v. Canada (Solicitor General), 2004 CarswellNat 5911, 2004 CarswellNat 3808, 2004 FC 1493 — The applicant made a request that his removal be deferred and this request was denied in November 2003. Eight weeks later, on January 23, 2004, a further request for deferral was made. The officer declined to consider their request on the basis that her director had made a decision not to defer removal some eight weeks earlier.

The decision of the officer was set aside. In the eight weeks that passed, events could have occurred which might have justified deferring removal. It is not merely because a decision has been previously made that an enforcement officer loses his or her power to reassess a situation. The officer had an obligation and a duty to assess the situation and to make a decision whether to exercise his or her discretion. This had not been done and the decision of the officer was set aside.

Boniowski v. Canada (Minister of Citizenship & Immigration) (2004), 44 Imm. L.R. (3d) 31, 2004 FC 1161, 2004 CarswellNat 5616, 2004 CarswellNat 2741, [2004] F.C.J. No. 1397 — The purpose of s. 48(2) is to allow for some limited discretion in the timing of a person's removal. The requirement for reasons was fulfilled in the decision letter where the officer indicated that she had received and reviewed the applicants' submissions in her decision not to defer removal. The nature of this decision is one where an officer has a very limited discretion and no actual formal decision is mandated in the legislation or regulations. The jurisprudence instructs that an officer must acknowledge that she has some discretion to defer removal, if it would not be "reasonably practicable" to enforce a removal order at a particular point in time. For example, the existence of a pending H&C application that was filed in timely manner, medical factors, and the arrangement of travel documents are some of the factors that may be considered by the officer.

The notes of the officer were filed as part of the judicial review proceeding but need not, as a regular procedure, be provided to applicants given the nature of this decision. The recording of written notes that set out the reasons for an administrative decision fosters better decision-making and provides a basis of explanation, if such a decision is challenged on judicial review. Therefore, while not obligatory, note keeping should be encouraged as a regular practice.

On the facts of this particular case, the decision of the officer not to defer removal was upheld.

49. (1) In force — A removal order comes into force on the latest of the following dates:

    (a) the day the removal order is made, if there is no right to appeal;

    (b) the day the appeal period expires, if there is a right to appeal and no appeal is made; and

    (c) the day of the final determination of the appeal, if an appeal is made.

(2) In force — claimants — Despite subsection (1), a removal order made with respect to a refugee protection claimant is conditional and comes into force on the latest of the following dates.

(a) the day the claim is determined to be ineligible only under paragraph 101(1)(e);

(b) in a case other than that set out in paragraph (a), seven days after the claim is determined to be ineligible;

(c) if the claim is rejected by the Refugee Protection Division, on the expiry of the time limit referred to in subsection 110(2.1) or, if an appeal is made, 15 days after notification by the Refugee Appeal Division that the claim is rejected;

(d) 15 days after notification that the claim is declared withdrawn or abandoned; and

(e) 15 days after proceedings are terminated as a result of notice under paragraph 104(1)(c) or (d).

[Editor's Note: SOR/2002-227, s. 319(1), provides that subject to SOR/2002-227, s. 319(2), a removal order made under the Immigration Act, *R.S.C. 1985, c. I-2 (the "former Act") that was unexecuted on June 28, 2002 continues in force and is subject to the provisions of the* Immigration and Refugee Protection Act, *S.C. 2001, c. 27 (the "new Act").*

SOR/2002-227, s. 319(2) provides that the execution of a removal order that had been stayed on June 28, 2002 under paragraphs 49(1)(c) to (f) of the former Act continues to be stayed until the earliest of the events described in paragraphs 231(1)(a) to (e) of the new Immigration and Refugee Protection Regulations, *SOR/2002-227.*

However, SOR/2002-227, s. 319(3) provides that SOR/2002-227, s. 319(2) does not apply if

(a) the subject of the removal order was determined by the Convention Refugee Determination Division not to have a credible basis for his or her claim; or

(b) the subject of the removal order

(i) is subject to a removal order because he or she is inadmissible on grounds of serious criminality, or

(ii) resides or sojourns in the United States or St. Pierre and Miquelon and is the subject of a report prepared under s. 44(1) of the new Act on his or her entry into Canada.

SOR/2002-227, s. 319(4) provides that a conditional removal order made under the former Act continues in force and is subject to s. 49(2) of the new Act.]

2012, c. 17, s. 21

50. Stay — A removal order is stayed

(a) if a decision that was made in a judicial proceeding — at which the Minister shall be given the opportunity to make submissions — would be directly contravened by the enforcement of the removal order;

(b) in the case of a foreign national sentenced to a term of imprisonment in Canada, until the sentence is completed;

(c) **for the duration of a stay imposed by the Immigration Appeal Division or any other court of competent jurisdiction;**

(d) **for the duration of a stay under paragraph 114(1)(b); and**

(e) **for the duration of a stay imposed by the Minister.**

Case Law

Editor's note: For cases dealing with judicial stays of removal orders see the cases collected under section 18.2 of the Federal Courts Act.

Moretto v. Canada (Minister of Citizenship & Immigration) (2011), 96 Imm. L.R. (3d) 320, 2011 FC 132, 2011 CarswellNat 260 — The applicant, a citizen of Italy where he was born in 1969, became a permanent resident in Canada before his first birthday. He lived in Canada his whole life and only had a vague recollection, if any at all, of a one-month family vacation in Italy when he was aged approximately 8. In 2009, a removal order was issued against the applicant on the basis of his serious criminality. The member refused the applicant's request for a stay of the removal order. The stay had been sought based on humanitarian and compassionate considerations, including the best interest of his daughter, who was born in 2001.

The member's assessment of hardship did not take into account that the applicant was facing removal to Italy, a place he does not know. The reference to the applicant's ability to "reintegrate" himself in that country suggests he will be returning to a place he was familiar with. The member failed to consider how separation from his family support would affect his ability to manage his mental health and addiction issues. The member inferred that the assistance the applicant received from his family in Canada could be replaced by his relatives in Italy; however, he does not know these people. Third, the member ignored the impact removal would have on an individual with serious mental health and addiction issues. Finally, and significantly, the member ignored the uncontradicted evidence that the applicant had a positive and loving relationship with his daughter. The applicant is a virtual Canadian. The member's decision would have the applicant returned to a place where he has never lived and does not know. The member misapprehended the evidence in this exceptional case. Her findings were made without regard to the material before her. This resulted in an outcome which was unreasonable. The application for judicial review was granted.

Idahosa v. Canada (Minister of Public Safety and Emergency Preparedness) (2008), 77 Imm. L.R. (3d) 130, 385 N.R. 134, 2008 CarswellNat 4895, 2008 FCA 418 — The mother sought to stay a deportation to Nigeria indefinitely on the basis that since arriving in Canada, and while her status in Canada was uncertain, she gave birth to two children in Canada. Those children are the subject of an order of the Ontario court precluding their removal from Ontario. That order, however, can be varied. Further, the endorsement on the record of the judge making the order makes it clear that the Ontario court is not dealing with the immigration issues. On the basis of the decision of the Federal Court in *Alexander v. Canada (Solicitor General)* (2005), 49 Imm. L.R. (3d) 5, the court found that the order of the Ontario court would not be "directly contravened" within the meaning of s. 50(a) were the removal to be carried out. The application was dismissed. The applicant appealed to the Federal Court of Appeal who dismissed the appeal and found that para. 50(a) does not apply to a provincial court's order awarding custody to a parent of Canadian-born children for the purpose of delaying or preventing the enforcement of a removal order against the parent, when there is no *lis* respecting custody that is unrelated to the removal. On the facts of this case it did not make a difference that the order could be varied and that the Minister had an opportunity to speak to the order.

Blake v. Canada (Minister of Public Safety & Emergency Preparedness), 2008 CarswellNat 2816, 2008 CarswellNat 1324, 2008 FC 572 — The applicant sought judicial review of the decision made by an enforcement officer. In that decision, the officer determined that an order of the Ontario court of Justice granting the applicant sole custody of her children and prohibiting their removal from Ontario did not constitute a statutory stay pursuant to subs. 50(a) of the IRPA. The applicant then sought an order quashing the decision to remove her to Jamaica, a declaration that a statutory stay arises by virtue of the order of the Ontario Court of Justice for the purposes of subs. 50(a) of the Act, and an order prohibiting her removal from Canada pending the determination of her application for landing in Canada on the basis of humanitarian and compassionate grounds.

The scheme of the Act is to regulate the entry of non-citizens into Canada. At the same time the Act identifies, as one of its objectives, the reunification of families, that is in para. 3(1)(d). The Act also refers to the respect for international conventions in para. 3(3)(f). However, the courts have repeatedly ruled that the best interest of the children are not paramount in the scheme of immigration law. The Act does not contemplate that the making of a custody order *per se* will give rise to a statutory stay pursuant to subs. 50(a). The Custody and Non-Removal Order in question was made pursuant to a provincial statute. The intent, purpose and scope of that legislation did not trump the legislative scheme set out in the IRPA. Insofar as the order in question arises under a statutory scheme enacted by the province of Ontario for the purposes and objectives that are unrelated to the purposes of the IRPA, the court was not required to apply provincial law.

In the scheme of the IRPA, only Canadian citizens and permanent residents have an unqualified right to remain in Canada. Permanent residents may be removed, under certain circumstances. The applicant, as a result of criminal activities and convictions, became vulnerable to removal. Once the removal order against her became effective, the respondent was obligated to discharge his statutory duty pursuant to s. 48 to effect that removal as soon as practicable, unless that removal was stayed by an order of the court or by operation of law. This statutory obligation cannot be displaced by the making of a custody order pursuant to another statutory scheme. The Custody and Non-Removal Order made by the Provincial Court judge pursuant to the provincial legislation is not an "order" that gives rise to a stay pursuant to s. 50 of the IRPA. The application for judicial review was dismissed. The following questions were certified:

1. In the circumstances of this case where:

> 1. A parent is a foreign national who is subject to a valid removal order;

> 2. A family court issues an order, granting custody to the parent of his or her Canadian born child and prohibiting the removal of the child from the province; and

> 3. The Minister is given the opportunity to make submissions before the family court before the order is pronounced.

Would the family court order be directly contravened, within the contemplation of subs. 50(a) of the Act, if the parent, but not the child, is removed from Canada?

2. If it does not create a statutory stay pursuant to s. 50(a) of the IRPA, then does removal of the mother/parent constitute a violation of s. 7 of the *Charter*?

H. (J.) v. A. (D.) (2008), 290 D.L.R. (4th) 732, 51 R.F.L. (6th) 181, 89 O.R. (3d) 514, 2008 CarswellOnt 1053 (S.C.J.); affirmed (2009), 77 Imm. L.R. (3d) 123, 306 D.L.R. (4th) 496, 2009 CarswellOnt 85, 2009 ONCA 17 — The Minister of Citizenship & Immigration and the Minister of Public Safety & Emergency Preparedness appealed the order of the Ontario Court of Justice prohibiting the removal of a mother and one daughter, subject to a deportation order, from the province of Ontario pending a further order of the Ontario court. The Minister sought to have the motion's judge's order vacated to the extent that its effect was to stay the deportation order.

The court pointed out that rather than seek a stay of the deportation order from the Federal Court, which was open to the mother to do, the mother brought a motion for custody before the Ontario Court of Justice. The Ontario Court of Justice has jurisdiction to determine issues of custody and access as between the parents. The issue was whether the court did in fact determine an issue of custody as between the parents or whether it ordered a stay of the deportation order and wrongly assumed jurisdiction. The court concluded that the motions judge did not have jurisdiction to make the order that temporarily stayed the removal order pending the consideration of the mother's H&C claim. The motions judge committed material errors in wrongly assuming jurisdiction of an immigration proceeding; in circumventing a legitimate application of law using private custody litigation; in filling a "legislative gap" in the IRPA; and in exceeding his jurisdiction by effectively precluding the mother's removal from Canada by ordering that the child not be removed from Ontario. The order of the motions judge to the extent that it stayed the removal was vacated. There are other avenues that the mother may consider in order to properly address the question of the best interests of her children. It was open to the mother to bring a motion in Federal Court for a stay of the removal order that was issued against her.

On further appeal to the Ontario Court of Appeal, there was a finding that the appeal court judge did not err in vacating the non-removal order. The IRPA provides opportunities for consideration of the best interests of the children of those subject to deportation. The reasoning in *Idahosa* is consistent with the Ontario cases which indicate that non-removal orders under the CLRA should not be granted for the purpose of frustrating removal orders in immigration proceedings.

Laranjo v. Canada (Minister of Citizenship & Immigration), 2007 CarswellNat 5161, 2007 FC 726 — The applicant immigrated to Canada in 1961. He never acquired Canadian citizenship. In 1981, he was convicted of first degree murder for the sexual assault and killing of a female hitchhiker. He was sentenced to a term of life imprisonment without eligibility of parole for 25 years. He filed a humanitarian and compassionate application pursuant to s. 25 of the IRPA. This application was denied. He argued that his deportation violated his s. 7 *Charter* rights because he would be deprived of the National Parole Board programs for the duration of his sentence to life imprisonment. Paragraph 50(b) of the IRPA provides that a removal order is stayed until a foreign national's sentence to a term of imprisonment is completed. However, for the purposes of para. 50(b) of the IRPA, the sentence of an offender on parole is deemed to be completed according to subs. 128(3) of the *Corrections and Conditional Release Act*, S.C. 1992, c. 20. Parliament's enactment of subs. 128(3) is a complete answer to the absurd consequences that would result if the applicant, because of his life sentence, could be said to have greater constitutional rights than a person in similar circumstances who had fully served a sentence of 20 years. The Supreme Court of Canada has affirmed that deportation is not a punishment. The applicant did not show that his deprivation of rehabilitation services is a punishment, let alone one that comes within the scope of s. 12 of the *Charter*. The issue of returning to their country of citizenship, persons who have lived virtually all of their lives in Canada, is a matter of policy enacted by Parliament. The constitutionality of the relevant provisions of the IRPA which enact this policy was not challenged in this proceeding. The application for judicial review was dismissed.

Garcia c. Canada (Ministre de la Citoyenneté & de l'Immigration), 2007 CarswellNat 3016, 2007 CarswellNat 576, 2007 FCA 75 — A judgment by a Provincial Court refusing to order the return of a child in accordance with the Convention on the Civil Aspects of International Abduction, [1989] R.T. Can. No. 35, and s. 20 of An Act respecting the Civil aspects of international and inter-provincial child abduction, R.S.Q., c. A-23.01, cannot have the effect of directly and indefinitely preventing the enforcement of a removal order which is effective under the IRPA.

Clark v. Canada (Minister of Public Safety & Emergency Preparedness) (2006), 59 Imm. L.R. (3d) 299, 2006 CarswellNat 4518, 2006 FC 1512 — The applicant brought a motion for an order staying a deportation order against him. The applicant has lived in Canada for all of his 59 years, and was the son of Canadian-born parents. The applicant did not register the fact of his birth within two years of its occurrence as required under s. 5(1)(b) of the former *Citizenship Act*. The applicant was currently incarcerated; he was convicted of several offences. The Minister's delegate wrote a report under s. 44(1) of the IRPA stating that the applicant was a foreign national or permanent resident for whom there were reasonable grounds to believe was inadmissible. The Minister's delegate issued a deportation order stating the applicant was inadmissible on grounds of serious criminality. The applicant claimed that he is a citizen of Canada and that the issuance of the deportation order triggered a serious consequence, specifically, the automatic ineligibility for day parole for which the applicant would otherwise be eligible. The applicant raised a serious issue as to whether he was a Canadian citizen. There was a minimal prejudice to the respondents in staying the deportation order since the applicant had lived in Canada for 59 years. Therefore the balance of convenience favoured the applicant and the deportation order was stayed.

Alexander v. Canada (Solicitor General) (2005), 49 Imm. L.R. (3d) 5, [2006] 2 F.C.R. 681, 279 F.T.R. 45, 2005 CarswellNat 2396, 2005 FC 1147, [2005] F.C.J. No. 1416; affirmed (2006), 57 Imm. L.R. (3d) 1, 360 N.R. 167, 2006 CarswellNat 4243, 2006 FCA 386 — An order of the Ontario Court of Justice granting sole custody of two Canadian-born children to an individual who is subject to a deportation order under the IRPA, and further ordering that the children not be removed from Ontario does not create a statutory stay pursuant to subs. 50(a) of the IRPA.

The applicant sought to have determined whether the family court order would be directly contravened, within the contemplation of subs. 50(a) of the Act, if the parent, but not the child, was removed from Canada. The application for judicial review was dismissed. The applicant obtained a stay on humanitarian and compassionate grounds, rendering the appeal moot. The conditions required for the Federal Court of Appeal to decide moot questions in special circumstances were not met. The appeal was dismissed.

Wozniak v. Brunton (2004), 1 R.F.L. (6th) 429, 2004 CarswellOnt 943 (Ont. S.C.J.) — The mother brought an application for temporary custody of her child with specified access to the father and a non-removal order for the child. The father brought an application for temporary joint custody, specified access and non-removal order. He argued that if the mother were removed, the child would be deprived of the social and economic benefits of Canada. There was no evidence Trinidad presented an environment harmful to the child. The court held that separation of a child from a parent may be an unfortunate but inevitable consequence incidental to, for example, the incarceration of a parent, the deportation of a parent, or the divorce of two parents. Considerations as to whether the best interests of the child should warrant a stay of a deportation, pending an application of humanitarian and compassionate grounds, can be canvassed by the Federal Court. An order for temporary custody was awarded to the mother.

Varvara v. Costantino, [2003] O.J. No. 5980, 36 Imm. L.R. (3d) 256, 2003 CarswellOnt 5903 (Ont. C.J.) — The mother sought an order pursuant to para. 2 amending an order of the court to include a provision preventing any persons from removing her three children from the jurisdiction. The court ordered the non-removal of the children be an incident of custody, in spite of the pending deportation of the mother. The non-removal order was in the children's best interest because there was evidence that the children would be at risk of harm from the father if returned to Italy.

51. Void — permanent residence — A removal order that has not been enforced becomes void if the foreign national becomes a permanent resident.

52. (1) No return without prescribed authorization — If a removal order has been enforced, the foreign national shall not return to Canada, unless authorized by an officer or in other prescribed circumstances.

(2) Return to Canada — If a removal order for which there is no right of appeal has been enforced and is subsequently set aside in a judicial review, the foreign national is entitled to return to Canada at the expense of the Minister.

Case Law

Section 52(1)

Manoo v. Canada (Minister of Citizenship and Immigration), 2015 FC 396, 2015 CarswellNat 671, 2015 CarswellNat 2274 — The applicant sought judicial review of a decision denying the applicant's application for Authorization to Return to Canada ("ARC"). The applicant is a 65-year-old citizen and resident of Trinidad and Tobago. His wife passed away in 1985. His 102-year-old mother is a Canadian citizen. He has seven brothers and sisters, all of whom currently live in and around Toronto. He first came to Canada in September 2002, at which time he made a refugee claim, in which he alleged persecution at the hands of criminals in Trinidad and Tobago. A conditional removal order was issued upon his arrival. His refugee claim was denied. He then applied for a pre-removal risk assessment which was later denied. He submitted an application for permanent residence for humanitarian and compassionate reasons that was also refused. He then applied for a temporary resident visa to visit family. This application was refused. Several years later, he made an application for a multiple entry visa and an application for an ARC. The visa officer refused the ARC. The decision was unreasonable. The officer's conclusion that the applicant had remained without authorization was inaccurate. In fact, he remained as a refugee claimant and a PRRA applicant. The officer's statement that the applicant had egregiously manipulated the immigration system was also inaccurate. The applicant had availed himself of applications that he was entitled to make under Canadian law. The decision was also unreasonable because the statement "purpose of travel is to visit family" minimized the importance of the applicant's trip. In fact, he wished to visit a sick mother, a sister who had had a stroke, a niece who was in a wheelchair, and a brother who had been in a car accident. The application was allowed.

Parra Andujo v. Canada (Minister of Citizenship & Immigration) (2011), 391 F.T.R. 292, (sub nom. *Andujo v. Canada (Minister of Citizenship & Immigration)*) 2011 FC 730, 2011 CarswellNat 2341, 2011 CarswellNat 3358 — The applicant was refused an Authorization to Return to Canada (ARC). A visa officer subsequently denied the applicant's application for permanent residence. The visa officer had no discretion to entertain the applicant's permanent resident application. The deportation order affecting the applicant had been enforced and she was unsuccessful in obtaining an ARC pursuant to s. 52 of IRPA. A visa may be issued only if an applicant is not inadmissible and meets the requirements of IRPA. A person, who required an ARC, does not meet the requirements of IRPA unless this person obtains such an authorization. The application for judicial review was denied.

Gutierrez v. Canada (Minister of Citizenship & Immigration), 2010 FC 32, 2010 CarswellNat 944, 2010 CarswellNat 90 — This was an application for judicial review of a decision to refuse the applicant's application for Authorization to Return to Canada.

Parliament did not want anyone who had ever committed an offence against the Act to be permanently banned from Canada. On the contrary, the possibility of returning would be kept open, contingent on the authorization of an officer. The mere fact that an applicant did not comply with the Act is not a reason for rejecting the applicant's claim. The officer must take into consideration the seriousness of the offence, as noted in the "OP-1 Procedures" document.

In this case, the applicant did not leave Canada when the removal order became enforceable, before filing her PRRA application which, under a new regime, automatically imposed a stay on her departure order. Up until the date of the PRRA application, the applicant never received instructions from CIC, and was therefore never given a departure date. It was only after she withdrew her PRRA application that the 30-day deadline was reinstated. She left four days later. She failed to notify Canadian authorities of her departure and did not obtain the required certificate. Ignorance of the Act does not excuse a violation. Under the circumstances, however, it appeared to be carelessness or negligence on the applicant's part. She did not act in bad faith. It is true that this negligence allowed the applicant to return to Canada in 2003 without authorization and to work. However, the applicant was always honest with Canadian authorities and when she was given the order to leave Canada in December 2003, she complied. The technical failings of the applicant did not justify banning her from returning to Canada when in fact there was a "compelling reason" as spelled out in the CIC document for allowing her to return. The application for judicial review was allowed and the matter referred back to a different immigration officer for redetermination.

Bravo v. Canada (Minister of Citizenship & Immigration) (2010), 89 Imm. L.R. (3d) 123, 2010 FC 411, 2010 CarswellNat 958 — The applicant sought judicial review of a decision rejecting his application for a work permit. He first came to Canada in 2002 as a visitor. He overstayed his visit and subsequently made a refugee claim which gave him the ability to work in Canada. His refugee claim was rejected and he sought judicial review in the Federal Court but leave was denied. In November 2004 he left Canada. Even though his departure was voluntary under s. 240 of the *Immigration and Refugee*

Protection Regulations, the removal order against him was deemed to have been enforced. This meant that s. 52(1) of IRPA required an Authorization to Return to Canada. It is well established that one's past history with Canadian immigration officials is one of the best indicators of their likelihood of future compliance. In the applicant's case, his history is at best ambiguous, if not troubling: in 2002-2003, he first misrepresented his intentions in order to obtain a visitor's visa, then made a refugee claim only to acquire a work permit. It may or may not be that he has since learned from his mistakes, but this is what he had to show. The court could not conclude that the decision fell outside the "range of possible, acceptable outcomes which are defensible with respect to the facts and law." The application for judicial review was dismissed.

R. v. Beltran (2010), 89 Imm. L.R. (3d) 1, 2010 ABPC 113, 2010 CarswellAlta 602 — The accused entered a guilty plea to an offence of returning to Canada without the prescribed authorization, contrary to IRPA. The Crown sought a sentence of five months' incarceration. The accused sought a conditional discharge. A discharge was not a fit disposition in this case. The offence is a problematic one in that it is difficult to detect and quantify the cost to taxpayers. The accused entered Canada unauthorized for his own personal gain and to avoid the proper and lawful mechanisms in place for application. The offence was planned, deliberate and ongoing. There were no facts presented to show that the accused intended at any time to address his unlawful act or remove himself from the country to properly apply for admission. He is currently willing to leave Canada but it appears only because he was prosecuted.

Any hardship on the accused's family was inflicted by his act. There are no exceptional circumstances in this case that would compel the court to put the accused in a position he would have been in but for his third illegal entry. The accused was sentenced to four months and 13 days in custody. Without credit for pre-sentence custody, the jail term imposed would have been five months. The time spent in custody prior to this sentencing hearing was nine days. The amount of time credited was 18 days.

Khakh v. Canada (Minister of Citizenship & Immigration), 2008 CarswellNat 1682, 2008 CarswellNat 2788, 2008 FC 710 — The applicant and his wife arrived in Canada illegally in December 2003 after three failed attempts to obtain Canadian visitor visas. In January 2004, the applicants filed a claim for refugee protection. That claim was dismissed. In November 2004 an application for leave and judicial review of that decision was dismissed. In July 2005, the applicants applied for a pre-removal risk assessment. The applicants withdrew their PRRA application in November 2005 and left Canada in compliance with a removal order in March 2006. Prior to leaving Canada, the applicants applied as provincial nominees under the Provincial Nominee Program of Prince Edward Island. Having been accepted as provincial nominees, the applicants applied for permanent residence in Canada. Their applications were received at the Canadian High Commission in New Delhi in September 2005. Due to the fact that they had previously been subject to an enforced removal order, the applicants' permanent residence application could not be processed unless they first obtained authorization to return to Canada pursuant to subs. 52(1) of the Act. The visa officer recommended that the Immigration Program Manager refuse the applicants' request for authorization to return to Canada. The Program Manager concluded that the applicants should not be granted an authorization to return to Canada. The visa officer refused the applicants' application for permanent residence in Canada.

The Program Manager's reliance on the applicants' illegal entry into Canada in 2003, which along with their late departure in March 2006 combined to form the "multiple violations" referred to in the decision, was unreasonable in that no consideration was given to the applicants' purpose for illegally entering Canada in 2003, namely, filing a claim for refugee protection, which they were entitled to do under the law. While respecting immigration laws is a legitimate policy consideration in the Program Manager's exercise of discretion, the evidence before the court established that the applicants' only true violation was their failure to leave Canada within the timeframe mandated. Moreover, the Program Manager's decision was not made with regard to all the circumstances of the case and the underlying objectives of Canadian immigration law. First, while the Program Manager attempted to balance the economic benefit to Canada of granting the applicants' request for authorization, at no point did he consider the applicants' reasons for not leaving Canada until March 2006. The applicants stated that their late departure was largely due to trouble renewing their Indian passports. They explained that despite paying extra fees to have their renewal applications expedited, they could not secure renewed passports until March 2006, the very same month in which they left Canada. Further, at no time in the Program Manager's decision or the visa officer's recommendation, is any consideration given to the fact that deportation orders are often applied to those individuals who have been found inadmissible to Canada on various grounds including serious criminality, national security, or violations of human and international rights. Unlike in those situations, the applicants in the case at bar were not security risks, nor did they possess criminal records. While they entered Canada illegally, they made a valid, albeit unsuccessful claim for refugee protection. It was unreasonable that the applicants would be denied authorization to return under such circumstances, especially considering that no consideration was given to their reasons for not departing Canada before March 2006. The application for judicial review was allowed.

Akbari v. Canada (Minister of Citizenship & Immigration) (2006), 59 Imm. L.R. (3d) 207, 2006 CarswellNat 3882, 2006 FC 1421 — The applicant had a reasonably lengthy immigration history. She is an Iranian citizen and a failed refugee claimant. She had been married to a Canadian citizen since July 2002. The *bona fides* of the marriage were not in issue. An application under the spousal sponsorship provisions of the IRPA had been submitted. A previous application was refused. A spousal sponsorship application was pending.

The applicant had earlier applied for a green card in the United States although it was unclear from the record precisely when that application was made. When her green card was approved in August of 2004, she traveled to the United States. In so doing, she was deemed deported (as a failed refugee claimant) and therefore required authorization under subs. 52(1) of the IRPA and subs. 226(1) of the *Immigration and Refugee Protection Regulations*, to return to Canada.

The applicant claimed not to have been aware, at the time of her departure, that by leaving voluntarily she was effecting her deportation and would thus require authorization to return. When she returned to Canada she was intercepted at the airport. She completed a pre-removal risk assessment application, which was ultimately determined to be negative. Her passport was seized and subsequently lost by the Canada Border Services Agency officials. She was removed from Canada. She made another attempt to return in April 2005, but the applicant's application for an authorization to return to Canada was refused. She sought judicial review of the refusal alleging that the officer failed to consider the totality of the evidence upon which the application was based. The court did not agree with the applicant's suggestion that an interview was required. Nor is there a requirement that formal reasons be provided. The notes of the immigration officer may be taken as the reasons for the decision. An authorization to return to Canada should not be construed as a mini-humanitarian and compassionate application. However, regard must be had to the various factors. This requirement necessitates that consideration be given to the totality of the factual circumstances that are presented to the immigration officer. Here, the notes of the immigration officer revealed a focus on the applicant's immigration history. The officer also indicated apprehension with respect to the applicant remaining beyond her authorization. There was no indication that consideration was given to any of the factual circumstances presented by, and of concern to the applicant — more specifically, that she had left Canada voluntarily, that she and her husband could not reunite in North America or elsewhere, and that she was not inadmissible for reasons of criminality. The immigration officer's notes did not reflect consideration of the specific submissions. Absent some indication in the notes that the officer at least turned his mind to the applicant's circumstances, it was assumed that he did not. The failure of the officer to consider the totality of the evidence resulted in a denial of procedural fairness to the applicant. The application for judicial review was allowed.

Regulations

53. Regulations — The regulations may provide for any matter relating to the application of this Division, and may include provisions respecting

(a) conditions that may or must be imposed, varied, or cancelled, individually or by class, on permanent residents and foreign nationals;

(a.1) the form and manner in which an application to renounce permanent resident status must be made and the conditions that must be met before such an application may be approved;

(b) the circumstances in which a removal order shall be made or confirmed against a permanent resident or a foreign national;

(c) the circumstances in which status may be restored;

(d) the circumstances in which a removal order may be stayed, including a stay imposed by the Minister and a stay that is not expressly provided for by this Act;

(e) the effect and enforcement of removal orders, including the consideration of factors in the determination of when enforcement is possible;

(f) the effect of a record suspension under the *Criminal Records Act* on the status of permanent residents and foreign nationals and removal orders made against them; and

(g) the financial obligations that may be imposed with respect to a removal order.

2012, c. 1, s. 150; 2012, c. 17, s. 22; 2013, c. 16, s. 21

Division 6 — Detention and Release

54. Immigration Division — The Immigration Division is the competent Division of the Board with respect to the review of reasons for detention under this Division.

55. (1) Arrest and detention with warrant — An officer may issue a warrant for the arrest and detention of a permanent resident or a foreign national who the officer has reasonable grounds to believe is inadmissible and is a danger to the public or is unlikely to appear for examination, for an admissibility hearing, for removal from Canada or at a proceeding that could lead to the making of a removal order by the Minister under subsection 44(2).

[Editor's Note: SOR/2002-227, s. 325(1) provides that a warrant for arrest and detention made under the Immigration Act, R.S.C. 1985, c. I-2 *(the "former Act") is a warrant for arrest and detention made under the* Immigration and Refugee Protection Act, S.C. 2001, c. 27 *(the "new Act").*

SOR/2002-227, s. 325(2) provides that an order for the detention of a person made under the former Act is an order to detain made under the new Act.]

(2) Arrest and detention without warrant — An officer may, without a warrant, arrest and detain a foreign national, other than a protected person,

(a) who the officer has reasonable grounds to believe is inadmissible and is a danger to the public or is unlikely to appear for examination, an admissibility hearing, removal from Canada, or at a proceeding that could lead to the making of a removal order by the Minister under subsection 44(2); or

(b) if the officer is not satisfied of the identity of the foreign national in the course of any procedure under this Act.

(3) Detention on entry — A permanent resident or a foreign national may, on entry into Canada, be detained if an officer

(a) considers it necessary to do so in order for the examination to be completed; or

(b) has reasonable grounds to suspect that the permanent resident or the foreign national is inadmissible on grounds of security, violating human or international rights, serious criminality, criminality or organized criminality.

(3.1) Mandatory arrest and detention — designated foreign national — If a designation is made under subsection 20.1(1), an officer must

(a) detain, on their entry into Canada, a foreign national who, as a result of the designation, is a designated foreign national and who is 16 years of age or older on the day of the arrival that is the subject of the designation; or

(b) arrest and detain without a warrant — or issue a warrant for the arrest and detention of — a foreign national who, after their entry into Canada, becomes a designated foreign national as a result of the designation and who was 16 years of age or older on the day of the arrival that is the subject of the designation.

231

(4) Notice — If a permanent resident or a foreign national is taken into detention, an officer shall without delay give notice to the Immigration Division.

2012, c. 17, s. 23

56. (1) Release — officer — An officer may order the release from detention of a permanent resident or a foreign national before the first detention review by the Immigration Division if the officer is of the opinion that the reasons for the detention no longer exist. The officer may impose any conditions, including the payment of a deposit or the posting of a guarantee for compliance with the conditions, that the officer considers necessary.

(2) Period of detention — designated foreign national — Despite subsection (1), a designated foreign national who is detained under this Division and who was 16 years of age or older on the day of the arrival that is the subject of the designation in question must be detained until

(a) a final determination is made to allow their claim for refugee protection or application for protection;

(b) they are released as a result of the Immigration Division ordering their release under section 58; or

(c) they are released as a result of the Minister ordering their release under section 58.1.

Proposed Addition — 56(3), (4)

(3) Conditions — inadmissibility on grounds of security — If an officer orders the release of a permanent resident or foreign national who is the subject of either a report on inadmissibility on grounds of security that is referred to the Immigration Division or a removal order for inadmissibility on grounds of security, the officer must also impose the prescribed conditions on the person.

(4) Duration of conditions — The prescribed conditions imposed under subsection (3) cease to apply only when one of the events described in paragraphs 44(5)(a) to (e) occurs.

2013, c. 16, s. 22 [Not in force at date of publication. Amended 2013, c. 16, s. 36(4).]

[Editor's Note: SOR/2002-227, s. 331 provides that a performance bond posted or security deposited under the former Immigration Act, R.S.C. 1985, c. I-2 *that remains posted or deposited immediately before June 28, 2002 continues as a deposit or a guarantee under the new* Immigration and Refugee Protection Act, S.C. 2001, c. 27 *and is governed by its provisions.]*

2012, c. 17, s. 24

57. (1) Review of detention — Within 48 hours after a permanent resident or a foreign national is taken into detention, or without delay afterward, the Immigration Division must review the reasons for the continued detention.

(2) Further review — At least once during the seven days following the review under subsection (1), and at least once during each 30-day period following each previous review, the Immigration Division must review the reasons for the continued detention.

(3) Presence — **In a review under subsection (1) or (2), an officer shall bring the permanent resident or the foreign national before the Immigration Division or to a place specified by it**

Case Law

Canada (Minister of Citizenship & Immigration) v. Li, 2009 CarswellNat 598, 2009 FCA 85 — This appeal demonstrates the delicate balancing act required when issues of criminality, long-term detention and human rights collide under the IRPA and the *Charter of Rights and Freedoms*. The Federal Court dismissed an application by the appellant for judicial review of the Immigration Division's decision that ordered the release of the respondents from detention. In the order that it issued on December 29, 2008, the Federal Court certified a question. The certified question did not lend itself to a simple "yes" or "no" answer. What was in issue in the certified question is the appropriateness of making estimates of anticipated future length of detention on a mere anticipation of available processes under the IRPA and the Regulations, including Federal Court proceedings.

The Division proceeded on a basis that was both unreasonable and erroneous in law when it determined the anticipated future length of detention of the appellants. It speculated on potential proceedings that the parties could bring rather than making its estimation on actual pending proceedings. In addition, the speculation was too far reaching, unwarranted, unreasonable and unnecessary since there was a review at least once every 30 days. It was also an error to assume that the Federal Court and the Federal Court of Appeal would entertain the speculative remedies. Finally, the Division failed to take into account and assess relevant factors as well as the impact of another appropriate available and less drastic recourse to prevent a breach of the *Charter*, i.e., expediting the proceedings. The Federal Court should have intervened to remedy these errors of law.

The Federal Court of Appeal concluded that the basis of the estimation of anticipated future length of detention should be the proceedings as they exist at the time of each monthly review and not on an anticipation of available processes not yet underway. This conclusion with others disposed of the appeal and accordingly the appeal was allowed and the decision of the Federal Court was set aside. The matter was referred back to the Immigration Division for a redetermination.

Canada (Minister of Citizenship & Immigration) v. Sittampalam (2004), 43 Imm. L.R. (3d) 1, 2004 CarswellNat 4867, 2004 CarswellNat 5765, 2004 FC 1756 — The respondent was a subject of two release orders both of which were being reviewed by the Minister in this proceeding.

Simply because the Minister established a *prima facie* case at one time does not mean it stands indefinitely. There will be a time, dependent on the facts, where a danger will be perceived to have dissipated at some point in the future. If at that point the Minister wishes the continued detention of the respondent, it is entirely reasonable that evidence of a current danger must be presented. The presiding member must decide afresh at each hearing whether continued detention is warranted. A detention review is not precisely a trial *de novo* because the member is expected to take into account the evidence and reasons pertaining to previous detention orders. The member is not entitled to rely on speculation instead of evidence. In this case, the decisions were quashed and the matter returned to be heard by a differently constituted panel.

Canada (Minister of Citizenship & Immigration) v. Thanabalasingham, [2004] 3 F.C.R. 572, 38 Imm. L.R. (3d) 1, 247 F.T.R. 159 (note), 236 D.L.R. (4th) 329, 10 Admin. L.R.

(4th) 285, 315 N.R. 91, [2004] F.C.J. No. 15, 2004 CarswellNat 22, 2004 CarswellNat 782, 2004 FCA 4 — This was an appeal on a certified question from a decision of the motions judge. The certified question asked whether detention reviews were hearings *de novo* and whether the detained person bears the burden of establishing that he or she was not a danger to the public or a flight risk. The respondent was arrested in October 2001 on an immigration warrant and detained on grounds that he was a danger to the public because he was the leader of a Tamil gang. His detention was reviewed under that Act and, after it came into force, under ss. 57 and 58 of IRPA. At his first five reviews, the continued detention of the respondent was ordered. At his sixth review, the respondent was ordered released. The Minister applied for judicial review and obtained a stay of that order until the next detention review was completed. The next detention review was completed in March 2003 and the respondent was once again ordered released. The Minister once again obtained a stay of that order and sought judicial review and it was this judicial review that was the subject of the matter in this case.

Detention reviews are the kind of essentially fact-based decisions to which deference is usually shown. While prior decisions are not binding on a member, if a member chooses to depart from prior decisions to detain, clear and compelling reasons for doing so must be set out. The best way for the member to provide clear and compelling reasons would be to expressly explain what has given rise to the changed opinion. It would be unacceptable for a member to give a cursory decision which does not advert to the prior reasons for detention in a meaningful way.

Sections 57 and 58 allow persons to be detained for potentially lengthy if not indefinite periods of time without having been charged let alone having been convicted of any crime. As a result, detention decisions must be made with s. 7 of the *Charter* in mind.

It is the Minister who must establish, on a balance of probabilities, that the respondent is a danger to the public if he wants the detention to continue. The onus is always on the Minister to demonstrate that there are reasons which warrant detention or continue detention. Once the Minister has made out a *prima facie* case for the continued detention, the individual must lead some evidence or risk continued detention. The Minister may establish a *prima facie* case in a variety of ways including reliance on reasons for prior detention.

Canada (Minister of Citizenship & Immigration) v. Gill (2003), 33 Imm. L.R. (3d) 204, 2003 CarswellNat 3918, 2003 CarswellNat 4422, 2003 FC 1398, 242 F.T.R. 126 — The Minister sought to review the decision of a member of the Immigration Division who after conducting a 48-hour first detention review ordered the respondent released. The decision of the member was set aside. The member failed to take into consideration, when exercising her discretion, the two factors, one referred to in s. 247(1)(c) of the Regulations and the other in 247(1)(e) of the Regulations. Further, the member made an erroneous finding of fact to the effect that the immigration authorities were satisfied with the respondent's identity because they decided to issue a departure order in the name reflected in the documents of doubtful authenticity. Such a finding was contrary to the opinion given by the Minister under s. 58 of the Act.

57.1 (1) Initial review — designated foreign national — Despite subsections 57(1) and (2), in the case of a designated foreign national who was 16 years of age or older on the day of the arrival that is the subject of the designation in question, the Immigration Division must review the reasons for their continued detention within

14 days after the day on which that person is taken into detention, or without delay afterward.

(2) Further review — designated foreign national — Despite subsection 57(2), in the case of the designated foreign national referred to in subsection (1), the Immigration Division must review again the reasons for their continued detention on the expiry of six months following the conclusion of the previous review and may not do so before the expiry of that period.

(3) Presence — In a review under subsection (1) or (2), the officer must bring the designated foreign national before the Immigration Division or to a place specified by it.

2012, c. 17, s. 25

58. (1) Release — Immigration Division — The Immigration Division shall order the release of a permanent resident or a foreign national unless it is satisfied, taking into account prescribed factors, that

(a) they are a danger to the public;

(b) they are unlikely to appear for examination, an admissibility hearing, removal from Canada, or at a proceeding that could lead to the making of a removal order by the Minister under subsection 44(2);

(c) the Minister is taking necessary steps to inquire into a reasonable suspicion that they are inadmissible on grounds of security, violating human or international rights, serious criminality, criminality or organized criminality;

(d) the Minister is of the opinion that the identity of the foreign national — other than a designated foreign national who was 16 years of age or older on the day of the arrival that is the subject of the designation in question — has not been, but may be, established and they have not reasonably cooperated with the Minister by providing relevant information for the purpose of establishing their identity or the Minister is making reasonable efforts to establish their identity; or

(e) the Minister is of the opinion that the identity of the foreign national who is a designated foreign national and who was 16 years of age or older on the day of the arrival that is the subject of the designation in question has not been established.

[Editor's Note: SOR/2002-227, s. 324 provides that a release from detention under the former Immigration Act, R.S.C. 1985, c. I-2 is the ordering of release from detention under the new Immigration and Refugee Protection Act, S.C. 2001, c. 27 and any terms and conditions imposed under the former Act become conditions imposed under the new Act.]

(1.1) Continued detention — designated foreign national — Despite subsection (1), on the conclusion of a review under subsection 57.1(1), the Immigration Division shall order the continued detention of the designated foreign national if it is satisfied that any of the grounds described in paragraphs (1)(a) to (c) and (e) exist, and it may not consider any other factors.

(2) Detention — Immigration Division — The Immigration Division may order the detention of a permanent resident or a foreign national if it is satisfied that the permanent resident or the foreign national is the subject of an examination or an admissibility hearing or is subject to a removal order and that the permanent resident or the foreign national is a danger to the public or is unlikely to appear for examination, an admissibility hearing or removal from Canada.

(3) Conditions — If the Immigration Division orders the release of a permanent resident or a foreign national, it may impose any conditions that it considers necessary, including the payment of a deposit or the posting of a guarantee for compliance with the conditions.

[Editor's Note: SOR/2002-227, s. 331 provides that a performance bond posted or security deposited under the former Immigration Act, *R.S.C. 1985, c. I-2 that remains posted or deposited immediately before June 28, 2002 continues as a deposit or a guarantee under the new* Immigration and Refugee Protection Act, *S.C. 2001, c. 27 and is governed by its provisions.]*

(4) Conditions — designated foreign national — If the Immigration Division orders the release of a designated foreign national who was 16 years of age or older on the day of the arrival that is the subject of the designation in question, it shall also impose any condition that is prescribed.

Proposed Addition — 58(5), (6)

(5) Conditions — inadmissibility on grounds of security — If the Immigration Division orders the release of a permanent resident or foreign national who is the subject of either a report on inadmissibility on grounds of security that is referred to the Immigration Division or a removal order for inadmissibility on grounds of security, it shall also impose the prescribed conditions on the person.

(6) Duration of conditions — The prescribed conditions imposed under subsection (5) cease to apply only when one of the events described in paragraphs 44(5)(a) to (e) occurs.

> 2013, c. 16, s. 23 [Not in force at date of publication. Amended 2013, c. 16, s. 36(7)(a).]

2012, c. 17, s. 26

Case Law

Section 58(1)

Wang v. Canada (Minister of Public Safety and Emergency Preparedness), 2015 FC 720, 2015 CarswellNat 1943, 2015 CarswellNat 4226 — The applicants sought judicial review of the Immigration and Refugee Board decision to continue detention on the ground that they are unlikely to appear for removal pursuant to subs. 58(1) of IRPA and s. 245 of the Regulations. The application for judicial review was allowed on the basis that the member did not consider the applicants' refugee hearing as an important consideration in analyzing whether there were alternatives to detention that could attenuate their flight risk.

Canada (Minister of Public Safety & Emergency Preparedness) v. Ismail (2014), 25 Imm. L.R. (4th) 151, 373 D.L.R. (4th) 748, 2014 FC 390, 2014 CarswellNat 1240, 2014 CarswellNat 1871 — At issue in this application for judicial review is the relationship between the grounds for arresting and detaining an individual under *IRPA*, and the grounds that permit the continued detention of that individual by the Immigration Division of the Immigration and Refugee Board. The specific question is whether an individual who has initially been detained on the basis that there are reasonable grounds to believe that he is inadmissible to Canada and is unlikely to appear for an admissibility hearing can subsequently have his detention continued on the basis that the Minister is taking necessary steps to inquire into a reasonable suspicion that the individual is inadmissible on security grounds. The Immigration Division concluded that detention could only be continued on the basis that the Minister is taking necessary steps to inquire into a reasonable suspicion that the individual is inadmissible on security grounds in cases where the original detention was made on the same ground. Notwithstanding the deference owed to the Immigration Division's interpretation of its home statute, its interpretation of the legislation at issue was unreasonable. To interpret para. 58(1)(c) of *IRPA* so as to permit the detention of an individual in order to allow the Minister to take necessary steps to inquire into a reasonable suspicion that the individual is inadmissible on grounds of security, when that suspicion only arises after the person has entered Canada, accords with the priority that the legislation ascribes to security. The Minister's application for judicial review should be granted.

The following question was certified:

> Is paragraph 58(1)(c) of the *Immigration Refugee Protection Act* only available as a ground for continued detention where it follows a detention under subsec. 55(3) of the *IRPA*?

An appeal was discontinued by the appellant on August 14, 2014.

Canada (Minister of Citizenship & Immigration) v. B072, 2012 CarswellNat 1493, 2012 FC 563 — The applications for judicial review were brought by the Minister of Citizenship and Immigration concerning the release of the respondent from immigration detention by decisions rendered by the Immigration Division.

Immigration detention is not a form of punishment. It can only be imposed if the statutory conditions for detention have been satisfied. In this case, the relevant issue was whether the respondent's detention should continue because he is unlikely to appear for a hearing or for removal. The respondent's apparent involvement in a sophisticated human smuggling operation and his lack of credibility were relevant factors but so were the presence of his family in Canada, their ongoing attempts to obtain Canadian protection, the strength of the surety and the amount of the bond, the Minister's inability to accurately estimate the time required to complete the respondent's PRRA, the time needed to resolve his judicial challenge to the inadmissibility ruling and the fact that he had been in detention for 19 months. The member weighted those factors appropriately and concluded that the conditions for continuing the respondent's detention were no longer compelling.

The Immigration Division's responsibility over detention reviews is onerous. At its heart lies the difficult task of predicting future behaviour on the basis of past events and conduct. The Immigration Division must also balance the competing interests of a detainee not to be unduly deprived of freedom with the public interest in upholding the law including the effective execution of immigration removals. Every person facing removal from Canada to a place that is less desirable represents, at some level, a flight risk. The member understood that fact, weighed the available evidence and concluded that the risk was manageable with onerous conditions of release. It is not the role of the court on judicial review to substitute its judgment for that of the responsible decision maker and, even if the court had authority, this is not a decision that this court would have been inclined to set aside. The decision was amply supported by the evidence and reasonable in the sense that it fell within a range of possible, acceptable outcomes which are defensible in respect of the facts and law.

Canada (Minister of Citizenship & Immigration) v. X (2010), 93 Imm. L.R. (3d) 209, 375 F.T.R. 204 (Eng.), 2010 FC 1095, 2010 CarswellNat 4201 — The Minister of Citizenship and Immigration challenged a decision of the member of the Immigration and Refugee Board in which he ordered the release of the respondent from detention upon terms. The member erred in not recognizing that the obligation to establish one's identity rests first and always with the claimant. The Minister's obligation is to make reasonable efforts. Neither has the complete onus of proof; neither can sit back and do nothing. The determination of "reasonable efforts" is conditioned to some extent by the efforts of a claimant. This is over and above the obligation to not obstruct and to cooperate. It requires the member to make a qualitative evaluation of the efforts on the part of both parties. The term "reasonable steps" in s. 58(1)(d) connotes a broader range of actions than "necessary steps" but the analytical framework is essentially the same. Under s. 58 both parties have obligations and the fulfilment of one party's obligations, in this case the Minister's, is influenced by the other party's conduct. The member failed to consider this reciprocal and reciprocating legal obligation. In assessing the reasonableness of a decision, it is appropriate to consider whether the decision is balanced in view of all the facts and whether the terms and conditions were a disproportionate response to the frailties of the respondent's position and the risks inherent in releasing an unidentified individual. The member erred in not considering these competing factors and therefore reached an unreasonable conclusion. The application for judicial review was granted.

Canada (Minister of Public Safety & Emergency Preparedness) v. Welch, 2006 CarswellNat 2416, 2006 FC 924 — The Minister sought judicial review of the decision of a member of the Immigration Division of the Immigration and Refugee Board, allowing the conditional release from detention of the respondents. This was the fifth review of the detention of the respondents. The Minister argued that the member did not provide clear and compelling reasons as to why he should depart from the four previous decisions and release the respondents on terms and conditions. The Minister's view was that these terms and conditions were less stringent than those considered at the previous reviews.

The respondents are citizens of the United States and are wanted in the State of Colorado on a number of charges. They fled to Canada following release on bail pending their trial in the United States. Shortly after their arrival in Canada, they were arrested by the RCMP and a decision was made to detain them, and a removal order pursuant to s. 44 of the IRPA was issued against them. The respondents claimed refugee status and this claim had yet to be determined. At the first detention hearing, it was determined that they were a flight risk but the duration of the detention contemplated was very short. It was mentioned that they had two children. At a second detention hearing, the member came to the same conclusion and continued the detention. The two respondents' children were in the audience during the second hearing. It became clear that they had been with their parents when the latter were apprehended. The children were by then in the care of their grandmother in Canada, having been in the custody of the Ministry of Children and Families. It was argued that it was not in the best interest of the children to be separated from their parents. However, the presence of the children was not found to supersede the other factors listed in s. 245 of the Regulations. A proposal for release including a curfew and a

$4,000 bond was rejected. At the third detention hearing, the member considered physical restriction to an area, $25,000 cash bond for each of the respondents, a prohibition to carry weapons, daily reporting and, alternatively, the release of only one of the respondents to enable the children, who were back in the United States with their grandmother, to visit and spend some time with her. At this hearing, the Minister argued for the first time that the respondents posed a danger to the public. This argument was rejected. The member concluded that even a release subject to cash bond and very stringent reporting conditions would not be effective considering that the respondents failed to appear for their trial in the United States, in spite of significant bail bonds in existence there (US$25,000 and US$100,000).

At the fourth hearing, the member concluded the detention was necessary to ensure the respondents would appear for their removal. At that time, in addition to the three conditions of release discussed earlier, the respondents proposed a release be made subject to a review once a decision was made on the refugee claim. They also alluded to the possibility of electronic tracking as an alternative to detention, but had been advised by the Minister that this was not a viable alternative as no such system was currently available. Despite the fact that the respondents were likely to remain in detention for several months pending the determination of their refugee claim, the member concluded that their continued detention was necessary and found he had no authority to give any direction to the Minister with respect to the quality of the detention and the electronic monitoring. At the fifth detention hearing, the respondents called a representative of the company Trace Canada as a witness to explain how Trace Canada would equip them with electronic tracking devices that would keep a record of their movements at all times. The company could then report this information to immigration officials who would know immediately if the respondents had breached their conditions of release. Their submission was that the flight risk would be considerably reduced if such a mechanism were in use. The member took the matter under advisement. When the hearing resumed, the member specified that he was not "reopening" the detention review, but simply wished to obtain some clarification with regard to the services offered by Trace Canada. He questioned the representative about the functioning of the electronic tracking system. The member concluded that he considered electronic monitoring to be more responsive than a self-monitored curfew and no-go zone. He also stated it was more responsive than periodic physical reporting where, according to him, the respondents could be long gone by the time they failed to show up to report. It was thus a more immediate form of reporting. He also noted that, in the end, if the person's intention is to abscond, they will do so whatever the type of monitoring and explained that:

> Alternatives to detention are not meant to provide absolute certainty of appearance for removal. They need only have the effect of reducing the risk to an acceptable degree. The fact that the persons concerned have proposed electronic monitoring and have made the effort to bring a proposal for consideration is an indication of their sincerity in seeking to address the Minister's concerns of flight.

The question the court considered was not whether or not the member was justified in ordering the release on the conditions he did, but whether he had provided clear, compelling reasons for departing from the previous decisions reached at the detention reviews. Had the superiority of electronic monitoring been the sole basis of the decision, the court would have concluded that the reasons given by the member met the low threshold set out by the Court of Appeal in *Thanabalasingham*. However, the member clearly distinguishes the situation before him from those reviewed by his colleagues on the basis of the "new evidence" with respect to the respondents' children. Since the member believed the information relating to the existence of the respondents' children was new, he could not properly turn his mind to the decisions of his colleagues on this point and consider why he should depart from the course of action they took. Since the member clearly failed to consider the contrary view expressed by the previous member on this particular point, the decision was set aside.

Canada (Minister of Citizenship & Immigration) v. Singh (R.) (2004), 263 F.T.R. 106, 2004 CarswellNat 5904, 2004 CarswellNat 4215, 2004 FC 1634 — This was an application by the Minister for judicial review of a decision of the Refugee Protection Division which ordered the applicant released. The Board member required the Minister to be satisfied with respect to the respondent's identity by a fixed date failing which the respondent would be released. Such a condition was beyond the Board member's jurisdiction.

Section 58(2)

Canada (Minister of Public Safety & Emergency Preparedness) v. Samuels (2009), 85 Imm. L.R. (3d) 226, 2009 FC 1152, 2009 CarswellNat 5632, 2009 CarswellNat 3739 — This is an application by the Minister for judicial review of an order of a member of the Immigration Division to release the respondent from detention. The respondent was born in Panama but lived for 39 years in Jamaica. He is a citizen of both countries and came to Canada in 1991 and became a permanent resident. By September 1992, he was diagnosed as having schizophrenia. In total, the respondent has 27 or 30 criminal convictions, as well as over 10 provincial convictions. Following his last criminal conviction on March 14, 2005, he was immediately placed in immigration hold. He was released from immigration hold on October 12, 2006, under the Toronto Bail Program, for which he was supervised by Steven Sharp. Contrary to the terms of his release, the respondent repeatedly left his residence unescorted. Mr. Sharp was of the opinion that public safety would be a concern if the respondent remained in the community. The respondent was re-arrested and returned to immigration hold, remaining in detention ever since. A risk assessment officer reached a positive decision in June 2009 and the Minister then sought a danger opinion against the respondent, which would lead to his removal from Canada. Following the success of the PRRA application, the respondent sought to be released from detention. The member of the Immigration Division determined that while a danger opinion was being sought, it was likely to take a considerable time — and might yet turn out to be negative, so that it "wouldn't be fair" to keep the respondent in detention. Although the member noted that the respondent had "a pretty impressive criminal file," the member concluded that "if there's no removal in sight, the Immigration Division is not responsible to protect Canadian society anymore."

The court held that the Immigration Division had jurisdiction to order the respondent's continued detention if it was satisfied that he was a danger to the public. The court also found that the Immigration Division member failed to exercise its statutory duty, and quashed the decision to release the respondent. A removal order that is stayed is not void. Although it cannot be executed pending a ruling on a protected person's application for permanent residence or the passing of the deadline to file such an application, it still exists and is valid and, in the opinion of the court, the person against whom it was issued is still "subject to it." Accordingly, the Immigration Division had jurisdiction to order the continued detention of the respondent, if it was satisfied that he was a danger to the public.

Section 58(3)

Canada (Minister of Public Safety & Emergency Preparedness) v. Sittampalam (2009), 83 Imm. L.R. (3d) 147, 350 F.T.R. 101 (Eng.), 2009 FC 863, 2009 CarswellNat 5808, 2009 CarswellNat 2593 — This is an application for judicial review of a decision of the Immigration Refugee Board whereby the tribunal ordered changes in the terms and conditions of the respondent's release from custody. The applicant, the Minister of Public Safety and Emergency Preparedness, submits that the member's order compromises the ability of the Canadian Border Services Agency to properly monitor the respondent.

In August 2008, the respondent requested a variance to the conditions of his release to the Immigration Division. An agreement was made between counsel for the parties. The respondent requested an oral hearing to amend the conditions of release. An oral hearing was held before the member on October 8, 2008. At that hearing, the parties made submissions on the amendments requested in the respondent's motion. On November 13, 2008, the member released her order. She granted the respondent's motion and made additional amendments to the respondent's terms and conditions. The applicant sought judicial review of the decision to make additional amendments to the respondent's terms and conditions.

The member made significant changes to conditions which were not argued and which were not raised as being an issue in the hearing. In failing to provide the parties with an opportunity to make submissions and in altering and deleting conditions that were not requested by the respondent, the member breached the principles of procedural fairness, specifically the right to be heard and to know the case to be met. This error warranted the court's intervention. The application for judicial review was allowed.

The following question was certified:

> Do the principles set forth by the Supreme Court of Canada in *Charkaoui v. M.C.I.* (2007), 59 Imm. L.R. (3d) 1, respecting a review of the conditions of release from detention, where the detention is based on a "Security Certificate," apply as well to detention reviews under subs. 58(3) of IRPA?

Kang v. Canada (Minister of Public Safety & Emergency Preparedness), 2006 CarswellNat 1441, 2006 FC 652 — The applicant paid a cash deposit of $5,000 to secure her elderly mother's release from immigration detention. One of the release conditions was that the mother reside at her daughter's address "at all times." The mother was absent one day when Canada Border Services Agency officers visited to enquire about other family members. Several months later, after the mother had returned to Korea, the operations manager of the greater Toronto Enforcement Centre declared the $5,000 deposit forfeited. The applicant sought judicial review of that decision. The decision to forfeit a cash bond should withstand scrutiny on the reasonableness standard.

The applicant contended that the notes contained the interviewing officer's conclusions rather than statements fairly attributable to her or her mother. A close reading of the notes suggests that what may appear to be admissions against interest by the applicant and her mother are no more than a repetition of the conclusion reached by the immigration officer based on what the applicant's son may have mistakenly told the officer during the visit to the applicant's house. The case, therefore, was complicated by the involvement of other members of the family subject to arrest and removal and the language barrier. There was no fault on the part of the immigration officers, but the possibility of confusion and error should have been considered by the operations manager when there was contradictory affidavit evidence before her. The manager's factual finding that the release condition had been breached was patently unreasonable in light of that evidence. Furthermore, no rational explanation was provided as to why the evidence did not provide a justification for not forfeiting the deposit. Accordingly the decision was found to be unreasonable and was overturned.

The current Act is silent on the question of ministerial discretion for the forfeiture of security deposits or performance bonds but provides, in s. 61, for the making of regulations for the application of Division 6 with respect to detention and release. It was clear from the evidence that the operations manager did not consider whether a lesser amount, including no amount, would be sufficient to satisfy the purpose of imposing the cash deposit, particularly where, as here, the subject of the release condition had returned to her country of origin. Further, it was impossible to ascertain from the brief reasons endorsed on the applicant's submissions or from the terse letter communicating the decision what factors the manager took into consideration in deciding that the bond should be forfeited. The court had no way to determine whether the manager relied upon considerations that were irrelevant or extraneous to the legislative purpose for which she exercised discretion. Accordingly, the manager's error in this regard amounted to another ground for concluding that the application must be granted and remitted for reconsideration by another officer.

Khalife v. Canada (Minister of Citizenship & Immigration) (2006), 52 Imm. L.R. (3d) 267, 2006 CarswellNat 456, 2006 CarswellNat 1135, 2006 FC 221, [2006] F.C.J. No. 293 — The statute and the Regulations say little about the decisions to impose and to forfeit a cash deposit. The authority to require a cash deposit is found in the IRPA at subs. 58(3). The manager's decision to forfeit the deposit appears to have been made in accordance with the principles in the Immigration Canada Enforcement Manual. The manager exercised his statutory discretion in good faith, in accordance with the principles of natural justice and did not rely upon considerations irrelevant or extraneous to the statutory purpose. Instead, the manager verified that the applicant was fully aware of the conditions of his release and determined that the applicant had in fact breached these terms. The manager received and considered the applicant's representations and then followed the direction provided by s. 49(4) of the Regulations and the Manual and determined on the merits that it was appropriate to forfeit only part of the applicant's deposit.

Tsang v. Canada (Minister of Public Safety & Emergency Preparedness), 2006 FC 474, 2006 CarswellNat 941, 2006 CarswellNat 2380, [2006] F.C.J. No. 576 — A regional director of the Canadian Border Services Agency decided that a performance bond granted by the applicant in the amount of $80,000 was forfeited. The bond had been provided for the release of the applicant's husband. He had violated a term of the release order and as a result was arrested. In consequence of this violation, the performance bond was forfeited. The decision to forfeit the $80,000 bond was set aside since the officer failed to appreciate that he had the discretion to make a decision that resulted in less than $80,000 being forfeited.

58.1 (1) Release — on request — The Minister may, on request of a designated foreign national who was 16 years of age or older on the day of the arrival that is the subject of the designation in question, order their release from detention if, in the Minister's opinion, exceptional circumstances exist that warrant the release.

(2) Release — Minister's own initiative — The Minister may, on the Minister's own initiative, order the release of a designated foreign national who was 16 years of age or older on the day of the arrival that is the subject of the designation in question if, in the Minister's opinion, the reasons for the detention no longer exist.

(3) Conditions — If the Minister orders the release of a designated foreign national, the Minister may impose any conditions, including the payment of a deposit or the posting of a guarantee for compliance with the conditions, that he or she considers necessary.

Proposed Addition — Conditional Amendment — 58.1(4), (5)

On the coming into force of both S.C. 2012, c. 17, s. 27 [In force June 28, 2012.] and S.C. 2013, c. 16, s. 23 [Not in force at date of publication.], s. 58.1 is amended by adding the following:

> **(4) Conditions — inadmissibility on grounds of security** — If the Minister orders the release of a designated foreign national who is the subject of either a report on inadmissibility on grounds of security that is referred to the Immigration Division or a removal order for inadmissibility on grounds of security, the Minister must also impose the prescribed conditions on the person.
>
> **(5) Duration of conditions** — The prescribed conditions imposed under subsection (4) cease to apply only when one of the events described in paragraphs 44(5)(a) to (e) occurs.
>
> 2013, c. 16, s. 36(10) [Conditions not yet satisfied.]

2012, c. 17, s. 27

59. Incarcerated foreign nationals — If a warrant for arrest and detention under this Act is issued with respect to a permanent resident or a foreign national who is detained under another Act of Parliament in an institution, the person in charge of the institution shall deliver the inmate to an officer at the end of the inmate's period of detention in the institution.

60. Minor children — For the purposes of this Division, it is affirmed as a principle that a minor child shall be detained only as a measure of last resort, taking into account the other applicable grounds and criteria including the best interests of the child.

61. Regulations — The regulations may provide for the application of this Division, and may include provisions respecting

(a) grounds for and criteria with respect to the release of persons from detention;

(a.1) the type of conditions that an officer, the Immigration Division or the Minister may impose with respect to the release of a person from detention;

(a.2) the type of conditions that the Immigration Division must impose with respect to the release of a designated foreign national who was 16 years of age or older on the day of the arrival that is the subject of the designation in question;

Proposed Addition — Conditional Amendment — 61(a.3)

On the coming into force of both S.C. 2012, c. 17, s. 28 [In force June 28, 2012.] and S.C. 2013, c. 16, s. 23 [Not in force at date of publication.], s. 61 is amended by adding the following:

(a.3) the conditions that an officer, the Immigration Division or the Minister must impose with respect to the release of a permanent resident or foreign national who is the subject of either a report on inadmissibility on grounds of security or a removal order for inadmissibility on grounds of security;

2013, c. 16, s. 36(11) [Conditions not yet satisfied.]

(b) factors to be considered by an officer or the Immigration Division; and

(c) special considerations that may apply in relation to the detention of minor children.

2012, c. 17, s. 28

DIVISION 7 — RIGHT OF APPEAL

62. Competent jurisdiction — The Immigration Appeal Division is the competent Division of the Board with respect to appeals under this Division.

63. (1) Right to appeal — visa refusal of family class — A person who has filed in the prescribed manner an application to sponsor a foreign national as a member of the family class may appeal to the Immigration Appeal Division against a decision not to issue the foreign national a permanent resident visa.

(2) Right to appeal — visa and removal order — A foreign national who holds a permanent resident visa may appeal to the Immigration Appeal Division against a decision to make a removal order against them made under subsection 44(2) or made at an admissibility hearing.

(3) Right to appeal removal order — A permanent resident or a protected person may appeal to the Immigration Appeal Division against a decision to make a removal order against them made under subsection 44(2) or made at an admissibility hearing.

(4) Right of appeal — residency obligation — A permanent resident may appeal to the Immigration Appeal Division against a decision made outside of Canada on the residency obligation under section 28.

[Editor's Note: SOR/2002-227, s. 328(1) provides that a person who was a permanent resident immediately before June 28, 2002 is a permanent resident under the new Immigration and Refugee Protection Act, S.C. 2001, c. 27.]

(5) Right of appeal — Minister — The Minister may appeal to the Immigration Appeal Division against a decision of the Immigration Division in an admissibility hearing.

2015, c. 3, s. 110

Case Law

Section 63(1)

Fang v. Canada (Minister of Citizenship and Immigration), 2014 FC 733, 2014 CarswellNat 2739, 2014 CarswellNat 3279 — The applicant appealed the decision of a visa officer finding that her daughter was excluded from the family class for sponsorship for permanent residence, pursuant to 117(9)(d) of the Regulations. The Board also found that it did not have jurisdiction to review the officer's conclusion with respect to H&C considerations pursuant to s. 25 of IRPA. The applicant had disclosed her daughter as a non-accompanying family member in her application for permanent resident status, but her daughter was not medically examined at that time.

Section 65 of the Act limits the jurisdiction of the Board with respect to H&C factors where an individual is found not to be a member of the family class. In this case, the applicant's daughter was not examined at the time the applicant immigrated to Canada. Pursuant to para. 117(9)(d) of the Regulations, she is not a member of the family class. Consequently, according to s. 65 of the Act, the Board had no jurisdiction to consider H&C factors in its consideration of the appeal.

The court certified the following question:

> In an appeal under subsection 63(1) of the *Immigration and Refugee Protection Act*, S.C. 2001, s. 27 ("IRPA"), and considering the statutory bar under section 65 of IRPA, does the Immigration Appeal Division have jurisdiction to determine whether a visa officer made an error pursuant to paragraph 67(1)(a) of IRPA when assessing a family class permanent resident visa application, as regards the visa officer's determination of the foreign national's request under section 25(1) of the IRPA for an exemption based on Humanitarian and Compassionate considerations from a given requirement of the IRPA and associated Regulations?

Nguyen v. Canada (Minister of Citizenship & Immigration), 2012 FC 331, 2012 CarswellNat 866 (F.C.) — The applicant tried to sponsor his daughter to become a permanent resident of Canada. A visa officer dismissed the application on the basis he had not disclosed his daughter's existence when he previously sponsored his three sons. In fact, he was unaware of his daughter's existence at that point. The applicant asked the officer to consider H&C grounds supporting his application, but the officer appeared not to have considered them. The applicant appealed the officer's decision to the IAD. The IAD confirmed that the applicant's daughter could not be sponsored because she had not been identified in his earlier application. It also stated it had no jurisdiction to consider H&C factors in the circumstances and only the Minister of Citizenship and Immigration could do so. The applicant argued that the IAD erred by failing to appreciate that he was not asking the IAD to consider the H&C factors; rather, he had argued that the officer had committed an error of law by failing to consider the H&C factors. The IAD has jurisdiction to overturn an officer's decision if it is based on an error of law. The IAD misapprehended the grounds of the applicant's appeal. The question was whether the officer had erred in law, a matter over which the IAD clearly had jurisdiction. The application for judicial review was allowed and the IAD was ordered to reconsider the appeal. The sole issue was whether the IAD erred in law by failing to consider the basis of the applicant's appeal.

Somodi v. Canada (Minister of Citizenship & Immigration) (2009), 82 Imm. L.R. (3d) 159, 311 D.L.R. (4th) 335, 395 N.R. 270, 2009 FCA 288, 2009 CarswellNat 3062, 2009 CarswellNat 5060 — The appellant sought, in the Federal Court, judicial review of a decision of a visa officer which refused his spousal sponsorship application for permanent residence status as a member of the family class. At the same time as the appellant made his judicial review application, his sponsor appealed the decision of the visa officer. The appellant's application was dismissed by a judge of the Federal Court on the ground that para. 72(2)(a) of IRPA required the appellant's sponsor to exhaust her right of appeal to the Immigration Appeal Division (IAD) before an application for judicial review could be made. While the appellant's appeal was pending before the Federal Court of Appeal the IAD granted his sponsor's appeal and set aside the decision of the visa officer. In effect, the IAD, by setting aside the visa officer's decision, rendered the appellant's appeal moot since the decision which is the subject of the application for judicial review no longer exists. However, the Federal Court judge certified a question on an issue which has not been considered by the Federal Court of Appeal. Specifically the question reads:

> Does section 72 of the IRPA bar an application for judicial review by the applicant of a spousal application, while the sponsor exercises the rights of appeal pursuant to section 63 of the IRPA?

Both parties at the hearing submitted that it would be in the interest of justice that the Federal Court of Appeal answer the certified question.

It should be remembered that, on a family sponsorship application, the interest of the parties are congruent. Both the sponsor and the foreign national seek a reunification of the family. It would be illogical and detrimental to the objectives of the scheme to allow multiplicity of proceedings on the same issue, in different forms, to parties pursuing the same interest. It would also be detrimental to the administration of justice as it would open the door to conflict in decisions and fuel more litigation. This is precisely what Parliament intended to avoid. In addition, the appellant is not deprived of all remedies. He has other avenues such as an application to the Minister based on H&C considerations pursuant to s. 25 of IRPA. The appeal was dismissed for mootness and the court answered the certified question in the affirmative.

Sandhu v. Canada (Minister of Citizenship & Immigration) (2005), 48 Imm. L.R. (3d) 104, 34 Admin. L.R. (4th) 307, 2005 CarswellNat 2101, 2005 CarswellNat 5263, 2005 FC 1046 — The Immigration Appeal Division dismissed the applicant's appeal of a visa officer's decision to refuse the applicant's application to sponsor his son as a member of the family class. The IAD concluded that the applicant had not shown that the visa officer's refusal was wrong in law. Accordingly, the IAD concluded that the person who was sponsored by the applicant was not a member of the family class and therefore under s. 65 of the IRPA, the IAD had no discretionary jurisdiction to consider humanitarian and compassionate considerations. The application for judicial review was allowed as the IAD provided no explanation or analysis whatsoever to conclude that the visa officer's refusal of the applicant's sponsorship application was wrong in law. Accordingly, the reasons provided by the IAD were entirely insufficient to allow the applicant and his family members to understand why they had been denied the opportunity to unite their family in Canada. The reasons were equally insufficient to allow the Federal Court to determine whether or not the tribunal was justified in deciding as it did.

Singh v. Canada (Minister of Citizenship & Immigration), 2005 FC 1673, 2005 CarswellNat 4126, 2005 CarswellNat 4892, 2006 FC 474, [2005] F.C.J. No. 2071 — An appeal heard under s. 63(1) of the IRPA results in a hearing *de novo*. In such a hearing, the IAD does not need to comment on every piece of new evidence that is proffered, but it must deal with evidence that directly contradicts, or at least addresses, the concerns of the original decision maker.

de Guzman v. Canada (Minister of Citizenship & Immigration) (2005), 51 Imm. L.R. (3d) 17, 262 D.L.R. (4th) 13, 137 C.R.R. (2d) 20, 345 N.R. 73, 2005 CarswellNat 4381, 2005 FCA 436, [2005] F.C.J. No. 2119; leave to appeal to S.C.C. refused 2006 CarswellNat 1695, [2006] S.C.C.A. No. 70, 356 N.R. 399 — In 1993, the appellant came to live in Canada. When she was landed in Canada, she told the immigration officials that she was single and had no dependants, other than her daughter who was accompanying her. This was not true: she also had two sons whom she left in the Philippines with their father. Eight years later, after establishing herself in Canada and becoming a citizen, the appellant applied to sponsor her sons as members of the family class. They were refused visas under para. 117(9)(d) of the Regulations on the ground that they were not members of the family class because they had not been examined for immigration purposes when the appellant applied to come to Canada.

The appellant's misrepresentation was highly material to the success of her application for a visa in the family class as an unmarried daughter. Her daughter's birth certificate stated that the appellant was unmarried, unlike her sons' birth certificates.

The Immigration Appeal Division was correct in law to dismiss the appellant's appeal pursuant to para. 74(d) of the IRPA. Specifically, the Board concluded that since the sons were not members of the family class, the Board, under s. 65 of the IRPA, had no discretionary jurisdiction to consider humanitarian and compassionate circumstances.

The Federal Court of Appeal concluded that para. 117(9)(d) of the Regulations was not invalid or inoperative. It was not unconstitutional nor did it deprive the applicant of her right to liberty and/or her right to security of person, in a manner not in accordance with the principles of fundamental justice contrary to s. 7 of the *Charter*.

Section 63(2)

Canada (Minister of Citizenship and Immigration) v. Liu, 2016 FC 460, 2016 CarswellNat 1379, 2016 CarswellNat 2883 — The Minister sought judicial review of a decision by the IAD allowing the applicant's appeal of a decision of the Immigration Division. The applicant had obtained permanent residence by way of a marriage of convenience and she was therefore held to be inadmissible for misrepresentation. On appeal, she admitted that the marriage had been a fraud and she thus accepted the ID's finding of inadmissibility; however, she asked that the appeal be allowed on H&C grounds. The IAD accepted this submission.

The court agreed with the Minister's submission that the decision was unreasonable because the IAD in considering the issue of establishment did not feel the applicant's misrepresentation was a relevant factor. The misrepresentation is a relevant factor when considering a person's degree of establishment. To do otherwise is to place the immigration cheat on an equal footing with the person who has complied with the law. Whether the impact of the fraud is to reduce the establishment to zero or to something more is a question for the discretion of the decision maker based on the particular facts before him or her. But it must be considered. The application for judicial review was allowed.

Ismail v. Canada (Minister of Citizenship and Immigration), 2015 FC 338, 2015 CarswellNat 571, 2015 CarswellNat 2180 — The applicants arrived at Pearson airport and presented their permanent resident visas and were examined by an immigration officer. When the applicant was unable to answer simple questions in English, the officer checked the computer database and noticed that a visa officer in Cairo had determined that the language testing results submitted were fraudulent. The visas were nonetheless issued. The applicants were not landed but were permitted to enter Canada under s. 23 of IRPA for the purpose of attending an examination at a later date. Prior to the examination, a visa officer revoked the applicants' permanent resident visas. The applicants then attended an examination and exclusion orders were issued against all three, given that they did not have valid visas. The applicants sought to appeal the exclusion orders to the IAD, pursuant to subs. 63(2) of the IRPA. The determinative issue in the appeal was whether the IAD had jurisdiction to hear the appeal, given that the applicants' visas were cancelled on November 23, 2011, before the examination, resulting in exclusion orders issued on December 2, 2011. The IAD concluded that, once there had been a finding in a report under s. 44 of the IRPA that the permanent resident visas were invalid, the foreign national did not have a right of appeal to the IAD and the proper recourse for the applicants would have been an application for judicial review.

There is no doubt that a visa can be revoked at any time after having been issued. This is indeed one of the exceptions to the presumption that a visa once issued is presumed to be valid. There was no dispute between the parties that, had the permanent resident visa been revoked prior to the applicants' arrival in Canada, the IAD would clearly not have had jurisdiction to hear their appeal. The only issue was whether it made any difference that at the time the applicants presented themselves to the port-of-entry, they were in possession of valid visas. The court concluded that the examination at the port-of-entry would not constitute a cut-off point after which the validity of the permanent visas could not be assessed to ascertain whether one of the four exceptions set out in *Canada (MCI) v Hundal* (1995), 30 Imm. L.R. (2d) 52 (Fed. T.D.), would apply. The examination process is not completed until a determination is made that a person has a right or is entitled to enter Canada as a temporary or permanent resident, and the visa can be revoked until that determination is made. The fact that a person has entered Canada and triggered the examination process has no bearing on the power to revoke the visa.

It is clear from a textual, contextual and purposive analysis of both s. 63(2) and the IRPA as a whole that a right of appeal is granted only to a person who "holds" a valid permanent resident visa at the time the exclusion report is issued. A finding that the appeal right in subs. 63(2) of the IRPA would apply to an invalid or revoked visa would lead to the absurd consequence of granting persons with no right to be in Canada the right to appeal a removal order denying their ability to be in Canada. In the absence of clear words to the contrary, Parliament cannot be taken to have had that intention. Foreign nationals who are found to be inadmissible at the port-of-entry or at a deferred examination will have a right of appeal to that tribunal only when their inadmissibility does not relate to the absence of a permanent resident visa. Such will be the case where there has been a change in circumstances since the visa was issued, for example, as a result of a criminal conviction or of a new medical condition. In those circumstances, an exclusion order will be appealable before the IAD, and H&C factors may then be taken into consideration. When the inadmissibility relates to the absence of a permanent resident visa, the only recourse will be an application for judicial review to the Federal Court. The application for judicial review was dismissed.

The following question was certified:

> For the purposes of determining its jurisdiction to hear an appeal pursuant to subsection 63(2) of the IRPA, shall the validity of the permanent resident visa be assessed by the IAD at the time of arrival in Canada or at the time the exclusion order is made?

Canada (Minister of Citizenship & Immigration) v. Peirovdinnadi (2010), 92 Imm. L.R. (3d) 1, 409 N.R. 161, 2010 FCA 267, 2010 CarswellNat 3780 — The IAD was obliged to determine the genuineness of the marriage in this case because it was the misrepresentation alleged in the immigration officer's report under IRPA, subs. 44(1), and was closely related to the misrepresentation found by the ID and in issue in the IAD. That is, if the marriage was not genuine, the respondent was not living with his wife as his spouse and, as his counsel conceded, his statement on the form that he was living with his spouse constituted a misrepresentation. The appeal was allowed, the decision of the Federal Court was set aside, the Minister's application for judicial review was granted, the decision of the IAD set aside and the matter remitted for redetermination by the IAD, differently constituted.

Zhang v. Canada (Minister of Citizenship & Immigration), 2007 CarswellNat 1498, 2007 FC 593 — In January 2004, the applicant received a visa in the mail from Canadian immigration authorities. Roughly one month after it was issued, her visa was revoked. She was asked to return it. Instead, she flew to Canada with the invalid document and tried to use it to enter the country. When the applicant arrived in Canada, immigration authorities realized her visa had been revoked and referred her to an admissibility hearing. An immigration officer found the applicant inadmissible to Canada under ss. 20(1)(a) and 41(a) of the *Immigration and Refugee Protection Act*. The applicant tried to appeal the officer's decision to the Immigration and Refugee Board's Immigration Appeal Division. The Board has jurisdiction to hear appeals against removal orders from admissibility hearings. However, its jurisdiction is set out specifically at s. 63(2) of the IRPA. This section limits the Board's appeal jurisdiction to foreign nationals who hold permanent resident visas.

To find that s. 63(2) of the IRPA applies to the applicants with invalid permanent resident visas would give persons, with no right to be in Canada, the right to appeal a removal order denying their ability to be in Canada. The fact the applicant still held the physical copy of her visa did not change the legal consequence of its revocation. Rather than pursuing an appeal of the immigration officer's removal order before the Board, she should have sought judicial review of the officer's decision in the Federal Court.

Section 63(3)

See *Baig*, 2011 FC 1191, 2011 CarswellNat 4392, 2011 CarswellNat 4630, under s. 28 of IRPA.

Khan v. Canada (Minister of Citizenship & Immigration), 2009 FC 762, 2009 CarswellNat 2396, 2009 CarswellNat 5352 — This was an application for judicial review of an appeal brought under subs. 63(3) of the Act with respect to a deportation order against the applicant who was a permanent resident of Canada. The applicant had been convicted of sexual assault and had been found inadmissible and ordered deported. The Board is entitled to consider the list of factors set out in *Ribic* and may also consider other factors and the Board's findings regarding humanitarian and compassionate considerations merit curial deference. It is also well recognized that the weight given to the evidence is within the Board's competence, and it is not the role of the Federal Court to second guess the decisions of the Board with respect to the weight assigned to the factors considered by it.

While it is true that the court should not reweigh the evidence, it must intervene when reviewable errors are demonstrated. This attracts a reasonableness standard which was applied in this case.

The Federal Court allowed the application for judicial review on the basis that the Board ignored the details of the hardship the applicant had provided and misconstrued an experts psychological report as inconclusive, when in fact the report stated that the applicant was unlikely to be danger to Canadian society in the sense that it was improbable that he would again infringe the law or commit a criminal act. Accordingly, the application for judicial review was allowed.

Canada (Minister of Citizenship & Immigration) v. Rumpler (2008), 76 Imm. L.R. (3d) 237, 336 F.T.R. 285 (Eng.), 2008 CarswellNat 4258, 2008 CarswellNat 5085, 2008 FC 1264, 2008 CarswellNat 4258 — This was an application for judicial review of the decision of the IAD wherein the Division concluded it had jurisdiction to hear an appeal of the respondent's removal order. Returning to Canada from Israel, an immigration officer determined that the respondent did not satisfy the residency requirements of s. 28 of the Act, and undertook measures to have him removed. The period to appeal the removal order expired and the respondent voluntarily left Canada for the United States. The respondent then requested of the IAD an extension of the period to allow him to lodge an appeal of the removal order. The IAD decided that, according to subs. 63(3) of the Act, it did not have the competence to extend the period of appeal after its expiration, because the respondent had lost his status as permanent resident by failing to appeal. Justice Blanchard of the Federal Court granted the respondent's application for judicial review, and held that the IAD did have competence under the said provision to grant the extension. Accordingly, an extension was granted by a different member of the IAD and at a new hearing before the IAD, the Minister asked the tribunal to reject the appeal of the removal order on the ground of mootness, because the respondent had voluntarily left the country and thus executed the order. The Minister's motion was rejected and the Minister brought an application for judicial review of the IAD's decision.

The IAD erred in law in finding that it had continuing jurisdiction in spite of the fact that the respondent had left Canada and had executed the removal order before he filed a notice of appeal. It is trite law that the IAD does not have jurisdiction to reopen an appeal where the motion to reopen has been filed after an appellant is removed from Canada. Since the IAD did not have the jurisdiction to cancel the removal order once it had already been executed, it necessarily had no jurisdiction to grant a request (filed after such an execution) for an extension of time to lodge an appeal of the removal order. Consequently, the application for judicial review was allowed.

Elias c. Canada (Ministre de la Citoyenneté & de l'Immigration), 2005 CarswellNat 5708, 2005 FC 1329 — The applicant sought judicial review of the IAD's decision dismissing their appeal from a removal order. The principal applicant was born in Lebanon and emigrated to Brazil, where he lived for 20 years and became a citizen of that country. The applicant was granted landing in Canada as an entrepreneur and accepted the conditions provided under para. 23.1 of the Immigration Regulations. The Immigration Division decided that the applicants were persons contemplated by s. 41 of the IRPA since the principal applicant had not respected the conditions imposed for entrepreneurs when he was granted landing. The IAD dismissed the applicant's appeal concluding that an order to stay the removal order would have the effect of not only calling into question the integrity of the program conceived to attract entrepreneurs, but also the integrity of the Canadian immigration system as a whole. The principal applicant argued that he had provided plausible explanations and reasons why he was unable to respect the conditions within the two-year time period. In this case, the court concluded that the IAD weighed the best interests of the children directly affected as well as the other factors alleged by the applicants in support of their appeal but, considering the other circumstances of the matter, determined that special relief was not justified. The applicants' eldest son was born in Brazil while the younger son was born in Canada. The applicants did not submit any evidence regarding the effects that the removal to Brazil could have on the eldest child, or the effects of a possible migration on the younger child. The applicants' argument regarding the children amounted to saying that the presence of children in Canada automatically implies humanitarian considerations justifying special measures. The court concluded that Parliament has not decided that the presence of children in Canada constitutes in itself an impediment to any *refoulement* of a parent illegally residing in Canada. The application for judicial review was dismissed.

64. (1) No appeal for inadmissibility — **No appeal may be made to the Immigration Appeal Division by a foreign national or their sponsor or by a permanent resident if the foreign national or permanent resident has been found to be inadmissible on grounds of security, violating human or international rights, serious criminality or organized criminality.**

(2) Serious criminality — **For the purpose of subsection (1), serious criminality must be with respect to a crime that was punished in Canada by a term of imprisonment of at least six months or that is described in paragraph 36(1)(b) or (c).**

(3) Misrepresentation — **No appeal may be made under subsection 63(1) in respect of a decision that was based on a finding of inadmissibility on the ground of misrepresentation, unless the foreign national in question is the sponsor's spouse, common-law partner or child.**

[Editor's Note: S.C. 2001, c. 27, s. 190 provides that every application, proceeding or matter under the Immigration Act, R.S.C. 1985, c. I-2 (the "former Act") that is pending or in progress immediately before June 28, 2002 shall be governed by the Immigration and Refugee Protection Act, S.C. 2001, c. 27 (the "new Act"), effective June 28, 2002.

S.C. 2001, c. 27, s. 192 provides that if a notice of appeal has been filed with the Immigration Appeal Division immediately before June 28, 2002, the appeal shall be continued under the Immigration Act, R.S.C. 1985, c. I-2 (the "former Act") by the Immigration Appeal Division of the Immigration and Refugee Board.

S.C. 2001, c. 27, s. 196 provides that despite S.C. 2001, c. 27, s. 192, an appeal made to the Immigration Appeal Division before June 28, 2002 shall be discontinued if the appellant has not been granted a stay under the former Act and the appeal could not have been made because of s. 64 of the Immigration and Refugee Protection Act, S.C. 2001, c. 27 (the "new Act")

S.C. 2001, c. 27, s. 197 further provides that despite S.C. 2001, c. 27, s. 192, if an appellant who has been granted a stay under the former Act breaches a condition of the stay, the appellant shall be subject to the provisions of s. 64 and s. 68(4) of the new Act.

SOR/2002-227, s. 326(2) provides that a person in respect of whom s. 70(5) or paragraph 77(3.01)(b) of the former Act applied on June 28, 2002 is a person in respect of whom s. 64(1) of the new Act applies.]

2013, c. 16, s. 24

Case Law

Section 64(1)

R. v. Pham (2013), 76 Alta. L.R. (5th) 206, 293 C.C.C. (3d) 530, 99 C.R. (6th) 219, 357 D.L.R. (4th) 1, *(sub nom. R. v. Ly (T.Q.))* 441 N.R. 375, 2013 SCC 15, 2013 Carswell-Alta 296, 2013 CarswellAlta 297, EYB 2013-219399, [2013] S.C.J. No. 100 — The appellant was a Vietnamese citizen who came to Canada under the sponsorship of his father. He was convicted of producing and possessing marijuana for the purposes of trafficking. Pursuant to a joint submission on sentence, he was sentenced to two years' imprisonment. Despite the joint submission, the applicant appealed, arguing that the consequences of the sentence with respect to the IRPA ought to have triggered a reduced sentence. The Crown consented to the reduction. The majority of the Court of Appeal dismissed the appeal. In its view, the particular circumstances of the case, and in particular, the applicant's prior convictions, did not warrant varying the sentence or undermining the provisions of the IRPA. The appellant appealed the Court of Appeal's decision to refuse to vary his sentence. The Supreme Court of Canada allowed the appeal and reduced the sentence of imprisonment to two years less a day.

The sentencing judge was not aware of the sentence's collateral immigration consequences, and the appellate court accordingly had the authority to intervene. The Crown conceded both in the Court of Appeal and at the hearing in this court that a reduced sentence of two years less a day remains within the range of otherwise fit sentences and that the imposed sentence of two years' imprisonment should be reduced by one day. The Crown also agreed that the reduced sentence is what the sentencing judge would have imposed had he been aware of the collateral immigration consequences. It was wrong for the Court of Appeal to refuse the one-day reduction solely on the basis that the appellant had a prior criminal record or that it felt that he had "abused the hospitality that [had] been afforded to him by Canada." It was therefore appropriate to grant the variation of the sentence.

Where the issue of immigration consequences is brought to the trial judge's attention and the trial judge applies the proper sentencing principles but nonetheless decides on a two-year sentence, then, absent fresh evidence, deference is owed to that decision. Where this issue has not been raised before the trial judge and the Crown does not give its consent, an affidavit or some other type of evidence should then be adduced for consideration by the Court of Appeal.

An appellate court has the authority to intervene if the sentencing judge was not aware of the collateral immigration consequences of the sentence for the offender, or if counsel had failed to advise the judge on this issue. In such circumstances, the court's intervention is justified because the sentencing judge decided on the fitness of the sentence without considering a relevant factor. Although there will be cases in which it is appropriate to reduce the sentence to ensure that it does not have an adverse consequence for the offender's immigration status, there will be other cases in which it is not appropriate to do so.

R. v. Hennessey (2007), 63 Imm. L.R. (3d) 8, 228 O.A.C. 29, 2007 CarswellOnt 5272, 2007 ONCA 581 — The appellant plead guilty to five counts of robbery. In addition to seven months credit for pre-sentence custody, he was sentenced to 35 months imprisonment, concurrent, on each charge. The appellant asked the court to vary his sentence to seven months imprisonment, consecutive, on each charge. The reason for this request was that an order was made deporting the appellant and, under s. 64(1) of the IRPA, the appellant had no right to appeal the deportation order if he received a sentence of two years imprisonment or more for any single offence. This circumstance was unknown to the appellant when he was sentenced. He had been in Canada since age five, his family is here and he wished to remain. On these particular facts, given the Crown's concession that a 35-month sentence imposed in addition to pre-sentence custody was appropriate in terms of totality, it would not circumvent the provisions and policies of the IRPA to impose sentences of 23 months on individual counts but a global sentence equivalent to that imposed by the trial judge.

Holway v. Canada (Minister of Citizenship & Immigration) (2005), 49 Imm. L.R. (3d) 281, 2005 CarswellNat 2927, 2005 FC 1261 — The applicant, a Canadian citizen, sought to sponsor his parents to come to Canada as permanent residents. A visa officer denied the sponsorship application on the basis that the applicant's father was a person described in s. 35(1)(b) of the IRPA. The applicant sought leave for judicial review and concurrently filed an appeal of the same decision with the Immigration Appeal Division (IAD). The Minister argued against leave being granted on the basis that the application was premature and that the applicant had not exhausted all rights of appeal under the IRPA, namely an appeal to the IAD. Without reasons, the Federal Court denied the application for leave. The IAD, in turn, ruled that it did not have jurisdiction to hear the applicant's appeal based on s. 64(1) of the IRPA. The plain wording of s. 64, read in the context of the IRPA as a whole, and in conjunction with the issue paper published before the IRPA, together with the clause by clause analysis prepared by the Department of Citizenship and Immigration, and provided to both the Standing Committee on Citizenship and Immigration and the Standing Senate Committee on Social Affairs, Science and Technology, confirm that Parliament's intent in enacting s. 64 of the IRPA was to foreclose any right of appeal to the IAD that may have been available to the applicant on the facts of this case.

The Minister conceded that a mistake was made by counsel in opposing the leave application that sought to challenge the visa officer's decision, specifically that the judicial review of the visa officer's decision was premature because the applicant had not exhausted his rights of appeal to the IAD. The Minister acknowledged the mistake and agreed to consent to a motion to the Federal Court to reconsider the order denying leave to review the visa officer's decision.

Thevasagayampillai v. Canada (Minister of Citizenship & Immigration), 2005 CarswellNat 1094, 2005 FC 596 — The clear wording of s. 64(1) of IRPA together with the object of the IRPA and its scheme preclude the Appeal Division from reconsidering the finding of inadmissibility made by an authorized decision maker. If Parliament had intended to grant the right of appeal *de novo* with respect to the existence of one of the enumerated grounds mentioned in subs. 64(1), clearer language would have been used.

R. v. Hamilton, 22 C.R. (6th) 1, 72 O.R. (3d) 1, 186 C.C.C. (3d) 129, 241 D.L.R. (4th) 490, 189 O.A.C. 90, 2004 CarswellOnt 3214, [2004] O.J. No. 3252 (C.A.) — The risk of deportation can be a factor to be taken into consideration among the appropriate sentencing responses in tailoring the sentence to best fit the crime and the offender. However, the sentencing process cannot be used to circumvent the provisions and policies of the IRPA.

Kroon v. Canada (Minister of Citizenship & Immigration (2004), 36 Imm. L.R. (3d) 244, 252 F.T.R. 257, 15 Admin. L.R. (4th) 315, 2004 CarswellNat 2884, 2004 CarswellNat 1404, 2004 FC 697, [2004] F.C.J. No. 857 — The IAD lacks jurisdiction to determine the constitutionality of s. 64 of IRPA. There is nothing in the legislation which either expressly or explicitly grants this jurisdiction. The challenge provisions expressly limit the jurisdiction of the IAD insofar as they remove any right of appeal to the tribunal by a permanent resident who has been found to be inadmissible on grounds of serious criminality. Parliament could not have been more clear in its intention to limit the IAD's jurisdiction with respect to individuals who fall within para. 36(1)(a) of the Act. Although the IAD has exclusive jurisdiction to consider questions of law and determine its own jurisdiction, its general powers do not extend to finding that a statutory section, which contain an express limitation on its jurisdiction, is unconstitutional.

Section 64(2)

Editor's note: On February 22, 2010, important amendments to the Criminal Code came into force regarding sentencing. These were enacted under S.C. 2009, c. 29, the Truth in Sentencing Act. Under the new Criminal Code rules, the sentencing judge will have to state in the record whether any time of pre-sentence custody has been taken into consideration and, if so, whether the credit is granted on a 1:1 or (exceptionally) on a 1.5:1 basis. The new 1.5 credit rate will be the maximum permitted compared with the previous practice of crediting two or even three days per day detained.

The Federal Court continues to accept CBSA's position that pre-sentence custody forms part of the period of punishment under s. 64(2) of IRPA, despite the Supreme Court of Canada's decision in R. v. Mathieu, *[2008] 1 S.C.R. 723, which held that, as a general rule, pre-sentence custody was not part of the sentence.*

R. v. Freckleton (2016), 39 Imm. L.R. (4th) 158, 2016 ONCA 130, 2016 CarswellOnt 2175, [2016] O.J. No. 777 — The appellant sought to reduce his sentence to avoid the prospect of deportation resulting from the retrospective application of the *Faster Removal of Foreign Criminals Act*, S.C. 2013, c. 16. Section 24 of that Act amended s. 64(2) of IRPA to allow a person found inadmissible for serious criminality to appeal to the Immigration Appeal Division only if he or she had been punished by a term of imprisonment of less than six months. Prior to the amendment, anyone receiving a sentence of less than two years had a right of appeal to the Immigration Appeal Division. Both appellants were sentenced before the amendment and would have had a right to appeal but for the subsequent retrospective amendment.

Parliament's clear intent in enacting s. 24 of the *Faster Removal of Foreign Criminals Act* is that persons subjected to a fit sentence of at least six months of imprisonment may not appeal a finding that they are inadmissible to Canada because of "serious criminality" to the Immigration Appeal Division. The substantial reduction the appellant sought in his effective sentence would circumvent this clear parliamentary intent. His sentence appeal was dismissed.

R. v. Nassri, 2015 ONCA 316, 2015 CarswellOnt 6562, [2015] O.J. No. 2311 — The appellant was sentenced to nine months imprisonment following his convictions for robbery and possession of a weapon for a dangerous purpose. It was not known at the time of his sentencing that as a result of a recent change in the law, the appellant, a permanent resident, faced more or less automatic deportation to war-torn Syria if sentenced to a term of six months or more. Applying the principles stated in *R. v. Pham*, [2013] 1 S.C.R. 739, a fit sentence in this case was one that "better contributes to the offender's rehabilitation." It is self-evident that depriving the appellant of the right to appeal deportation to one of the most dangerous places on earth would be grossly disproportionate to this offence and this offender and would contravene the sentencing principle of individualization. The court granted leave to appeal the sentence and allow the appeal, reducing the custodial portion of the sentence to one of six months less 15 days.

R. v. Duhra, [2011] A T No. 608, 2011 ABCA 165, 2011 CarswellAlta 914 — The appellant was a permanent resident of Canada and pled guilty to a count of robbery and was sentenced to a term of imprisonment that (with double credit for pre-trial custody) was regarded by the sentencing judge as an effective sentence of imprisonment for two years plus 18 months' probation. Although double credit for pre-sentence custody figures in the analysis, it has been stated that the effective prison term will be treated in law as two years if that is what the sentencing judge stated. At the time the sentence was imposed, no one raised with the sentencing judge the implications under those circumstances of IRPA. Counsel did not put their minds to the possibility that a practical sentence of two months, additional to 22 months' credit for 11 months in pre-sentence custody, was something that would trigger the loss of a right of appeal by operation of s. 64 of IRPA. The Court of Appeal recognized the illogic of reducing a sentence for an offender either to a disproportionately low sentence or a lower sentence than a citizen might reasonably receive for the same crime in order to assist an offender guilty of serious criminality towards a lighter burden under s. 64. However, the Court of Appeal was not persuaded that citizenship should be a disadvantage for sentencing purposes. The justice of this case, as well as the proportionality principle and relevant considerations and recommendations, led to the conclusion to allow the appeal and cut the prison sentence to an effective term of two years less one day.

Nguyen v. Canada (Minister of Citizenship & Immigration), 2010 FC 30, 2010 CarswellNat 78, 2010 CarswellNat 725 — The determinative issue for the IAD was whether the applicant's appeal of his deportation order was barred pursuant to subs. 64(2) of IRPA. The IAD concluded that a sentence of less than two years (in this case 18 months) does, for the purpose of subs. 64(2), become a sentence of more than two years simply because the trial judge, in imposing the sentence of less than two years, took into account the time already spent in custody as a result of the offence. Thus the sentence was 29 months (11 months of pre-sentence custody and an 18-month term of imprisonment after conviction) for the purposes of subs. 64(2). Because the IAD determined the applicant met the definition of "serious criminality," s. 64 was engaged and the IAD had no jurisdiction upon which it could consider an appeal of inadmissibility. See also *Ariri v. Canada (Minister of Public Safety & Emergency Preparedness)* (2009), 83 Imm. L.R. (3d) 162 (F.C.), where Justice Tannenbaum found that considering the pre-trial custody as part of the term of imprisonment for the purposes of determining that the applicant has serious criminality is an acceptable exemption to the ruling in *Mathieu*.

R. v. Amon (2009), 82 Imm. L.R. (3d) 41, 241 Man. R. (2d) 192, 2009 MBQB 163, 2009 CarswellMan 297 (Q.B.) — The accused had entered a plea of guilty to a charge of aggravated assault. The defence argued that a sentence of two years or more will affect the accused's immigration status and should be an important factor in assessing a fit and just sentence. The practice of the court was to indicate at the time of sentence what time had been attributed to pre-sentence custody, and to record that time on the disposition sheet; it is only the measurements imposed at the time of the sentence that actually form part of the sentence. Therefore, no further time in custody was warranted in this case. Unfortunately, this did not apply to the accused because a series of Federal Court decisions have held that the time that an individual spends in pre-trial custody does form part of the "term of imprisonment" for the purposes of s. 64(2) of IRPA. Since it appears that the Immigration Appeal Division does not itself take on the task of calculating the pre-trial custody in order to determine appeal eligibility, but instead relies on how much pre-trial custody has been attributed to the sentence by the sentencing judge, the court designated some portion of the pre-trial custody to the accused's sentence. But for the immigration issue, the court might not have engaged in that calculation at all. However, the Crown would also want the court to refer to a specific amount of pre-trial custody in imposing a sentence in order to provide a record of the extent of the sentence for future reference. In the event that an accused re-offends, the length of the period of incarceration attributed to an offence will be relevant in sentencing for a subsequent offence. Therefore, engaging in this calculation was not simply for the purpose of determining the accused's eligibility to appeal his removal order. The court ordered that the disposition show pre-trial custody of two years less a day.

Capra v. Canada (Attorney General) (2008), 76 Imm. L.R. (3d) 21, 335 F.T.R. 299 (Eng.), 2008 CarswellNat 3875, 2008 CarswellNat 5267, 2008 FC 1212 — This was an application for a declaration that subs. 128(4) of the *Corrections and Conditional Release Act*, S.C. 1992, c. 20 ("CCRA") is invalid on the ground that it breaches ss. 7, 9 and 15 of the *Charter of Rights and Freedoms*. The applicant had been granted Convention refugee status and became a permanent resident on December 2, 1992. The applicant was subsequently convicted of 80 counts of fraud in connection with credit cards and automatic bank teller machines in 2001. A deportation order was issued on the grounds of serious criminality. Both the appeal of the deportation order and his application were dismissed and the applicant lost his permanent residence status. However, because of his refugee status, he could not be removed to Romania unless the Minister of Citizenship and Immigration issued an opinion that the applicant constitutes a danger to the public. The CBSA sought the opinion of the Minister that he was a danger to the public in Canada. In the meantime, the applicant served his sentence in a medium security federal correctional facility and underwent a rehabilitation program. He became eligible for an unescorted temporary absence ("UTA") and day parole in July 2008. The CBSA informed the sentence management office of the deportation order previously issued against the applicant. As a result, by operation of subs. 128(4) of the CCRA, the applicant was ineligible for release on a UTA or day parole until his full parole eligibility date. The applicant believed that he was being treated differently in relation to day parole eligibility because he was not a Canadian citizen. He claimed that he was the subject of discrimination and regardless of whether he was allowed to stay in Canada or not, he perceived that he was being denied an opportunity to work towards his own rehabilitation simply because of his identity.

The court held that s. 128(4) of the CCRA was directed at inmates subject to removal. The operation of the subsection is triggered by the issuance of a removal order. A stay of that removal order suspends the section's effect. The application of the section is rationally tied to its purpose and cannot be called arbitrary in relation to the objectives sought to be attained. Accordingly this was not arbitrary detention within the meaning of s. 9. Furthermore, the Supreme Court of Canada had made it clear that a "change in the form in which a sentence is served, whether it be favourable or unfavourable to the prisoner, is not, in itself, contrary to any principle of fundamental justice."

Parliament has decided that offenders subject to removal should serve their sentences in different ways from other offenders, including Canadian citizens. This is to ensure that their status as offenders does not enhance their access to Canadian society over that of non-offenders who face deportation; it is also intended to ensure that their removal status does not result in their serving shorter sentences than either Canadian citizens or non-citizens who are not subject to removal. Parliament has chosen to deal with these issues by suspending day parole and UTA for offenders who are subject to removal. It is possible to disagree with this approach and with whether it achieves the objectives it is intended to achieve, but that was not the issue before the court. What is relevant is that the variation in the form of the sentence that comes about as a result of subs. 128(4) of CCRA is triggered by the existence of a removal order and whether this fact makes it part of a deportation scheme.

The court was not convinced that, if the purpose of parole is to protect society, the loss of the possibility of that protection because of the loss of eligibility for day parole under subs. 128(4) was a disadvantage to the applicant, whether or not he was removed from Canada. Furthermore if parole was a benefit to offenders, the court was not convinced that the applicant had been disadvantaged by the loss of any such benefit in a situation where the evidence showed his deportation was being actively pursued and he did not fall into one of the exceptions specifically provided for under subs. 128(6). The applicant failed to demonstrate differential treatment between citizens and non-citizens. The application was dismissed.

R. v. Mathieu, [2008] S.C.J. No. 21, 292 D.L.R. (4th) 385, 373 N.R. 370, 56 C.R. (6th) 1, 231 C.C.C. (3d) 1, 2008 SCC 21, 2008 CarswellQue 3114, 2008 CarswellQue 3115 — "Pre-sentence custody is not part of the sentence, but is only one factor taken into account by the judge in determining the sentence." This means that a sentence of less than two years does not, for the purposes of s. 731(1)(b), become a sentence of more than two years simply because the trial judge, in imposing the sentence of less than two years, took into account the time already spent in custody as a result of the offence. It is not solely because of the law and s. 719 of the Code that pre-sentence custody is taken into account as a factor in sentencing. This result can also be inferred from a conceptual interpretation of pre-sentence custody. Pre-sentence custody generally refers to custody before the verdict is rendered, at a time when the accused is presumed innocent. In the context of these appeals, this custody is, in principle, preventive rather than punitive. Pre-sentence custody cannot really be characterized as a "sentence": if the accused is convicted, the judge does take it into account as a relevant factor in sentencing, but what if the accused is *acquitted*? Whether the pre-sentence custody was part of a sentence for the purposes of the Code would thus fall to be determined retroactively in light of the verdict — a subsequent and separate event.

Manifestly, the words "imprisonment for a term not exceeding two years" used by Parliament in s. 731(1)(b) refer to the custodial term imposed at the time of sentence — the actual term of imprisonment imposed by the court after taking into account any time spent in pre-sentence custody. This interpretation of the word "sentence" is also justified by the purpose of a probation order, namely to facilitate the offender's rehabilitation. To conclude that a probation order is not available in cases where the total of the time spent in pre-sentence custody and the sentence of imprisonment imposed by the judge is more than two years, could have a harmful consequence, as the judge might decide to impose a longer period of incarceration. This interpretation must be rejected, since it would have the unfortunate effect of unjustifiably increasing the length of time to be served in prison. In addition, the probation order's effect of facilitating an offender's reintegration into society would be unavailable to offenders who might benefit from it.

R. v. Leila (2008), 67 Imm. L.R. (3d) 82, 250 B.C.A.C. 117, 416 W.A.C. 117, 2008 BCCA 8 — Leave to appeal sentence is advanced on the ground that there is a serious and unintended collateral consequence to the sentence imposed by the trial judge in that a custodial sentence of two years or more results in the automatic termination of the appellant's right to appeal a deportation order to the IAD. The loss of the appellant's immigration appeal rights is a disproportionately severe collateral sanction, which was unforeseen by the appellant and his counsel at the sentencing hearing and apparently unintended by the sentencing judge. In the circumstances of this case, reducing the appellant's sentence to one which will allow him to preserve his immigration appeal rights is inconsequential to the sentencing principles relied upon by the sentencing judge. The appellant spent 57 days in pre-trial custody. The judge imposed a sentence of two years "plus time spent in custody." There was no indication that the judge gave credit beyond the 57 days spent in pre-trial custody and, therefore, the effective sentence appears to be one of two years and 57 days. Leave was granted and the appeal allowed to the extent of reducing the effective sentence so that it is one day under two years.

Cheddesingh v. Canada (Minister of Citizenship & Immigration) (2006), 52 Imm. L.R. (3d) 247, 2006 CarswellNat 259, 2006 FC 124 — Subsection 64(2) of the IRPA is not concerned with the length of the sentence imposed on the offender, but with the punishment. It is clear from the jurisprudence that once a person is convicted of a crime, time served by that individual in pre-trial detention will be deemed to be part of the offender's punishment.

In this case, the applicant argued that the proper interpretation was to compute the time a person is sentenced to spend in custody as of the date of the sentence, and the time spent in pre-sentence custody should not be taken into account. According to this interpretation, the applicant's term of imprisonment would only amount to a year instead of 30 months. The applicant's proposed interpretation was contrary to the intent of Parliament in drafting subs. 64(2) of the Act. Accordingly, the Board did not commit a reviewable error in determining that the period the applicant spent in pre-sentence custody formed part of her "term of imprisonment."

Medovarski v. Canada (Minister of Citizenship & Immigration), [2005] 2 S.C.R. 539, 50 Imm. L.R. (3d) 1, 135 C.R.R. (2d) 1, 258 D.L.R. (4th) 193, [2005] S.C.J. No. 31, 339 N.R. 1, EYB 2005-95306, 2005 CarswellNat 2943, 2005 CarswellNat 2944, 2005 SCC 51 — The appellant was a permanent resident and had been ordered deported for serious criminality. Her removal order was automatically stayed when she appealed the deportation order to the Immigration Appeal Division. The appeal was discontinued as a result of s. 196 of the IRPA (a transitional provision), which took away the right to appeal an order for removal unless a party had, under the former Act, been "granted a stay." The trial judge set aside the decision to discontinue. However, the Federal Court of Appeal allowed the Minister of Citizenship and Immigration's appeal, holding that the purpose of the IRPA transitional provision was to deny the right of appeal in the case of an automatic stay. Section 196 of the IRPA, properly interpreted, applies only to actively granted stays. The objectives of the IRPA, as expressed in s. 3, indicate an intent to prioritize security. In keeping with these objectives, the IRPA creates a new scheme whereby a person sentenced to more than six months in prison is inadmissible pursuant to s. 36; if they have been sentenced to a prison term of more than two years, they are denied a right to appeal their removal order under s. 64 of the IRPA. The purpose in enacting the IRPA, and in particular s. 64, was to efficiently remove from the country persons who have engaged in serious criminality. Since s. 196 refers explicitly to s. 64, the transitional provision should be interpreted in light of these legislative objectives.

The deportation of a non-citizen cannot in itself implicate the liberty and security interests protected by s. 7 of the *Canadian Charter of Rights and Freedoms*. Even if the liberty and security of the person were engaged, any unfairness resulting from s. 196 would be inadequate to constitute a breach of principles of fundamental justice.

Shepherd v. Canada (Minister of Citizenship & Immigration) (2005), 48 Imm. L.R. (3d) 118, 2005 CarswellNat 2115, 2005 CarswellNat 3490, 2005 FC 1033 — The IAD concluded that the pre-sentencing custodial terms that had been expressly taken into account and credited to the applicant's sentence formed part of the term of imprisonment for the purposes of subs. 64(2) of the Act. Accordingly, the IAD ruled that the applicant had lost his right to appeal in light of subs. 64(2). Subsection 719(3) of the Criminal Code specifically provides that pre-sentence detention can be taken into account when a court is imposing a sentence and in this case it was clear that the sentencing judge considered the pre-sentencing detention to be part of the punishment imposed on the applicant. The record showed that the applicant was punished by a term of imprisonment of at least two years and that falls within the definition of "serious criminality" pursuant to subs. 64(2). In these circumstances, the applicant had no right of appeal to the IAD.

Bouttavong v. Canada (Minister of Citizenship & Immigration) (2005), 344 N.R. 134, 2005 CarswellNat 3527, 2005 CarswellNat 5559, 2005 FCA 341 — Former public danger opinions are irrelevant to the determination of danger to the public under subs. 113(d)(i). This does not mean that the underlying criminal convictions may not be taken into account, only that the danger opinions are irrelevant.

Sherzad v. Canada (Minister of Citizenship & Immigration), 2005 CarswellNat 1493, 2005 FC 757 — In determining whether a crime was one that was punished in Canada by a term of imprisonment of at least two years, regard may be had to the time spent in pre-trial custody which resulted in a reduction of the sentence that was ultimately imposed.

Martin v. Canada (Minister of Citizenship & Immigration) (2005), 42 Imm. L.R. (3d) 104, 2005 CarswellNat 86, 2005 CarswellNat 1819, 2005 FC 60, [2005] F.C.J. No. 83 — Section 64(2) must be interpreted as referring to the term of imprisonment for which an offender was sentenced. That is, the punishment imposed rather than the actual amount of time served prior to being granted parole.

Canada (Minister of Citizenship & Immigration) v. Smith (2004), 42 Imm. L.R. (3d) 254, 2004 CarswellNat 4933, 2004 CarswellNat 5740, 2004 FC 63, [2004] F.C.J. No. 2159 — Pre-sentence custody is included in the phrase "term of imprisonment" under s. 64(2) of the IRPA.

Canada (Minister of Citizenship & Immigration) v. Atwal, 2004 CarswellNat 23, 2004 CarswellNat 1623, 2004 FC 7, [2004] F.C.J. No. 63, 245 F.T.R. 170 — This was an application to review a decision of the Appeal Division refusing to discontinue the respondent's appeal. The respondent had received a sentence of 6 months which sentence took into account 20 months of pre-sentence custody.

The time spent in pre-sentence custody is to be taken into consideration under s. 64.

Cartwright v. Canada (Minister of Citizenship & Immigration) (2003), 32 Imm. L.R. (3d) 79, 2003 CarswellNat 3179, 2003 CarswellNat 1899, 236 F.T.R. 98, 2003 FCT 792, [2003] F.C.J. No. 1024 — The applicant sought to review a decision of the Adjudicator declining to hear the applicant's appeal against the deportation. The applicant was born in the Bahamas and came to Canada when he was 4 years old. He never applied for Canadian citizenship. The applicant had a history of criminal offences, and was sentenced on January 25, 2001 to a four year term in a Federal Penitentiary. Section 64(2) must be interpreted as referring to the term of imprisonment for which an offender is sentenced, rather than the actual amount of time served prior to being granted parole.

65. Humanitarian and compassionate considerations — In an appeal under subsection **63(1) or (2) respecting an application based on membership in the family class, the Immigration Appeal Division may not consider humanitarian and compassionate considerations unless it has decided that the foreign national is a member of the family class and that their sponsor is a sponsor within the meaning of the regulations.**

Case Law

O'Brien v. Canada (Minister of Citizenship and Immigration) (2015), [2016] 2 F.C.R. 56, 2015 FC 1047, 2015 CarswellNat 4247, 2015 CarswellNat 5925; affirmed (2016), 40 Imm. L.R. (4th) 213, 2016 CarswellNat 1854, [2016] F.C.J. No. 567 (C.A.) — The applicant appealed a removal order to the IAD under s. 63(2) of the IRPA on the basis of humanitarian and compassionate considerations. The IAD hearing took place on July 22, 2014, and, in his direct testimony, the applicant indicated that he and his sponsor had separated. This raised questions surrounding the jurisdiction of the IAD to consider the appeal. The IAD adjourned the hearing to seek written submissions on the jurisdictional issue and, following receipt of such submissions, concluded that it was without jurisdiction to consider the appeal.

The court was mindful of the policy arguments advanced by the applicant, to the effect that the IAD's interpretation of s. 65 could drive certain undesirable behaviours, as appellants remain in relationships, or rekindle them, in an effort to preserve their right to seek H&C consideration on appeal. However, the court noted the government's position on the policy considerations, that it would be less desirable that a foreign national be afforded a guaranteed status notwithstanding a change in circumstances impacting eligibility for that status prior to an IAD appeal hearing. The court was not persuaded by the policy arguments to depart from the conclusion that the legislative intent in this particular case can be found in the plain reading of the language of s. 65. Accordingly, the IAD's decision was both reasonable and correctly interpreted s. 65 of IRPA by finding that it must consider the applicant's membership in the family class as of the time of the IAD hearing. The application for judicial review was dismissed.

The following question was certified:

> In an appeal pursuant to s. 63(2) of the *Immigration and Refugee Protection Act*, in relation to what period in time should an assessment of membership in the family class under s. 65 be conducted by the Immigration Appeal Division?

Habtenkiel v. Canada (Minister of Citizenship and Immigration) (2014), 29 Imm. L.R. (4th) 1, 461 N.R. 240, 2014 FCA 180, 2014 CarswellNat 2800, 2014 CarswellNat 6288 — The applicant was a young woman who sought to join her father in Canada. Her father had not identified her as a non-accompanying family member when he immigrated to Canada, so that she was not examined at that time by a visa officer. As a result, she was excluded from the family class and may only come to Canada if the Minister exercises his discretion under s. 25 of IRPA, to exempt her from the requirements of the Act on humanitarian and compassionate grounds. Her application for H&C consideration was refused. She sought to have that decision judicially reviewed but her application was dismissed on the ground that she must wait until her sponsor (her father) exercises his right of appeal to the Immigration Appeal Division, thereby exhausting other remedies before bringing an application for judicial review. The Federal Court of Appeal found that the application judge erred in the analysis of the applicant's right to bring an application for judicial review; however, as there was no basis for interfering with the visa officer's decision, the appeal was dismissed.

The Federal Court of Appeal concluded that where an applicant has made a family class sponsorship application and requested H&C considerations within the application, the applicant is not precluded from seeking judicial review by the Federal Court before exhausting their right of appeal to the Immigration Appeal Division where the right of appeal is limited pursuant to para. 117(9)(d) of the *Immigration Refugee Protection Regulations*.

See *Nguyen* summary, 2012 FC 331, 2012 CarswellNat 866, under s. 63(1) of IRPA.

de Guzman v. Canada (Minister of Citizenship & Immigration) (2005), 51 Imm. L.R. (3d) 17, 262 D.L.R. (4th) 13, 137 C.R.R. (2d) 20, 345 N.R. 73, 2005 CarswellNat 4381, 2005 FCA 436, [2005] F.C.J. No. 2119; leave to appeal to S.C.C. refused 2006 CarswellNat 1695, [2006] S.C.C.A. No. 70, 356 N.R. 399 — In 1993, the appellant came to live in Canada. When she was landed in Canada, she told the immigration officials that she was single and had no dependants, other than her daughter who was accompanying her. This was not true: she also had two sons whom she left in the Philippines with their father. Eight years later, after establishing herself in Canada and becoming a citizen, the appellant applied to sponsor her sons as members of the family class. They were refused visas under para. 117(9)(d) of the Regulations on the ground that they were not members of the family class because they had not been examined for immigration purposes when the appellant applied to come to Canada.

The appellant's misrepresentation was highly material to the success of her application for a visa in the family class as an unmarried daughter. Her daughter's birth certificate stated that the appellant was unmarried, unlike her sons' birth certificates.

The Immigration Appeal Division was correct in law to dismiss the appellant's appeal pursuant to para. 74(d) of the IRPA. Specifically, the Board concluded that since the sons were not members of the family class, the Board, under s. 65 of the IRPA, had no discretionary jurisdiction to consider humanitarian and compassionate circumstances.

The Federal Court of Appeal concluded that para. 117(9)(d) of the Regulations was not invalid or inoperative. It was not unconstitutional nor did it deprive the applicant of her right to liberty and/or her right to security of person, in a manner not in accordance with the principles of fundamental justice contrary to s. 7 of the *Charter*.

66. Disposition — After considering the appeal of a decision, the Immigration Appeal Division shall

    (a) allow the appeal in accordance with section 67;

    (b) stay the removal order in accordance with section 68; or

    (c) dismiss the appeal in accordance with section 69.

Case Law

Younis v. Canada (Minister of Citizenship & Immigration) (2008), 74 Imm. L.R. (3d) 115, 332 F.T.R. 99 (Eng.), 2008 CarswellNat 2744, 2008 FC 944 — The applicant had a number of criminal convictions. The Immigration Division issued a deportation order against the applicant on the basis that he was inadmissible for serious criminality under s. 36(1)(a) of the Act because of his conviction for drug trafficking. The applicant appealed the deportation order and sought special relief on humanitarian and compassionate grounds under the Act. He did not challenge the legal validity of the deportation order. The IAD denied the applicant's appeal. The applicant then sought judicial review of that decision. The issues raised in the application were whether the IAD erred in admitting the applicant's juvenile criminal record into evidence, and whether the IAD erred in taking into consideration the report to Crown counsel. The *Youth Criminal Justice Act* ("YCJA") contains prohibitions against the release of records of convictions of young persons as well as some exceptions to the prohibition against the release of records of convictions of young persons. The question of whether or not the applicant's juvenile record fell within the period of access and is accessible turned on whether the sexual assault conviction was for a summary or indictable offence. There was no indication in the evidence before the IAD whether the applicant, as a youth, was convicted of a summary or indictable offence. Without such evidence, the IAD had no way of determining whether the applicant's juvenile conviction was releasable under the YCJA. The IAD is responsible for determining the admissibility, reliability and weight to be given to evidence presented before it. Although the IAD is not bound by the same legal or technical rules of evidence as a court of law, this does not confer upon the IAD the authority to admit a youth criminal record where the second conviction falls outside the period of access. The release of such a report would not only constitute a breach of s. 118 of the YCJA, it would also amount to a breach of the procedural fairness guarantees in hearings before the IAD. The IAD was found to have a duty to determine the admissibility of the applicant's youth criminal record before considering whether the record was credible and trustworthy and before determining the weight to be given to the record.

The IAD relied on the report to Crown counsel which contained a list of proposed criminal charges against the applicant. The IAD failed to make the necessary distinction between the fact that the proposed charges were mere allegations and that the applicant had not been convicted of the offences. Although it was open to the IAD to consider the evidence underlying the charges in question, it was not open to the IAD to conclude that this evidence was sufficient to find that the applicant was guilty of the offences proposed in the report. The IAD's decision was also void of any discussion regarding the reliability and credibility of the report. The absence of any analysis in this regard suggested that the IAD failed to turn its mind to whether the report was reliable and credible. This omission constituted an error of law. The application for judicial review was allowed.

67. (1) Appeal allowed — To allow an appeal, the Immigration Appeal Division must be satisfied that, at the time that the appeal is disposed of,

    (a) the decision appealed is wrong in law or fact or mixed law and fact;

    (b) a principle of natural justice has not been observed; or

    (c) other than in the case of an appeal by the Minister, taking into account the best interests of a child directly affected by the decision, sufficient humanitarian and compassionate considerations warrant special relief in light of all the circumstances of the case.

(2) Effect — If the Immigration Appeal Division allows the appeal, it shall set aside the original decision and substitute a determination that, in its opinion, should have been made, including the making of a removal order, or refer the matter to the appropriate decision-maker for reconsideration.

Case Law

Chung v. Canada (Minister of Citizenship and Immigration), 2015 FC 1329, 2015 CarswellNat 6287, 2015 CarswellNat 10289 — The applicant was previously ordered deported on grounds of a criminal conviction and successfully appealed the order in November, 2006, after having been granted a stay in November, 1999. He was subsequently convicted of a criminal offence and was ordered removed a second time on August 26, 2013. The applicant appealed that removal order on humanitarian and compassionate grounds, and challenges the IAD's dismissal of the appeal in this judicial review. The applicant argued that when an accused pleads not guilty, it is an error of law to consider lack of remorse as an aggravating factor for the purpose of sentencing. Relying upon this principle culled from criminal sentencing the applicant says, in the present immigration context, that while it is legitimate to consider remorse to be mitigating, it is not legitimate to consider a lack of remorse to be aggravating where an accused pleads not guilty even if he is subsequently convicted. The court was not prepared to accept the applicant's bald statement that criminal sentencing principle should be imported into the present context. To do so would require the IAD and also the Federal Court to ignore the fact that he was convicted of this offence beyond a reasonable doubt and now refuses to assume responsibility for the crime. The applicant may be entitled to maintain his innocence but the IAD cannot leave out of account what a competent court has found when the IAD is considering rehabilitation. In the court's view, the conviction was a reasonable basis for the IAD to conclude that the applicant committed a recent offence for which he refused to accept responsibility and which, when looked at in conjunction with his past criminal conduct and his past experience with deportation proceedings, meant that there was little possibility of rehabilitation in the future. The application for judicial review was dismissed.

The following question was certified:

> Does the Immigration Appeal Division of the Immigration and Refugee Board, in the exercise of its humanitarian jurisdiction, err in law in considering adverse to an applicant lack of remorse for an offence for which the applicant has pled not guilty but was convicted?

Canada (Minister of Citizenship and Immigration) v. Wright (2015), 32 Imm. L.R. (4th) 179, 2015 FC 3, 2015 CarswellNat 120, 2015 CarswellNat 3480 — The Minister of Citizenship and Immigration brought the application for judicial review of a decision of the Immigration Appeal Division ("IAD") which found that there were sufficient humanitarian and compassionate grounds to grant relief pursuant to s. 67(1)(c) of the IRPA, to overcome the respondents' inadmissibility to Canada for failure to comply with their residency requirements as permanent residents. The court has considered many applications for judicial review arising from H&C determinations in the context that other provisions of the Act, including ss. 25, 28 and 67 and, although the wording of the provisions varies slightly, the provisions do not refer specifically to "hardship" but to "humanitarian and compassionate considerations" or "sufficient humanitarian and compassionate considerations." However, the jurisprudence has consistently confirmed that the hardship to be considered along with other factors to determine whether sufficient H&C considerations exist must be more than the hardship that would normally result from removal. The respondents' argument that the considerations relevant to an H&C decision pursuant to s. 67 differ from those under s. 25, and that unusual or disproportionate hardship is not required, fails to appreciate the overall guidance of the analogous jurisprudence. There is no reason for *some* hardship to be sufficient in the context of considering H&C grounds to overcome a breach of permanent resident status when in other contexts, such as refugee protection, the criteria established by the IRB and IAD and confirmed by the courts calls for *unusual, undue or disproportionate* hardship; more than the normal and expected consequences of removal from Canada.

In this case, the IAD did find the consequences of the respondents' removal would be serious hardship, which appears to acknowledge its understanding that more than the expected or normal hardship of removal is required for such a finding. The evidence before the IAD was of inconvenience, disappointment and emotional upheaval, along with the economic impact of maintaining two residences. The IAD failed to consider that the respondents would not be destitute nor would they be homeless in the United States and that their age was no more an impediment to relocation than it was in 2012 when they divested themselves of their home in the United States and returned to Canada. The IAD did not consider relevant evidence that would have had a bearing on its findings with respect to several of the factors, in particular the serious hardship they would suffer if removed. This evidence would have a bearing on the weight to be attached to those factors and on the overall assessment of whether there were *sufficient* — not just *some* — humanitarian and compassionate grounds to justify the exceptional relief of overcoming the breach of their obligation to be physically present in Canada 730 days in each five-year period. The application for judicial review was allowed.

See *Wong*, (2011), 1 Imm. L.R. (4th) 287, 2011 FC 971, 2011 CarswellNat 3013, [2011] F.C.J. No. 1193, under s. 28 of IRPA.

Tai v. Canada (Minister of Citizenship & Immigration), 2011 FC 248, 2011 CarswellNat 1933, 2011 CarswellNat 471 — The applicants became permanent residents of Canada in 2001 but did not move to, or reside in, Canada. In April 2008, when the Tai family members sought to enter Canada, they were issued removal orders for failing to comply with their residency obligation. Ms. Chang and their daughters remained in Canada. Mr. Tai returned to his job in Taiwan and did not move to Canada until one year later at the end of April 2009. At the IAD, the family members admitted they had failed to meet their residency obligation and asked that their appeals be allowed based on discretionary jurisdiction. The IAD concluded there were insufficient H&C considerations to warrant special relief.

The IAD reasons were adequate when reviewed as a whole. The IAD considered all the circumstances of the case, and not just the failure to meet the residency obligation. The IAD is required to consider all of the circumstances in the case and not just the Tai family's recent efforts to establish itself (para. 67(1)(c) and s. 68(1) of IRPA). The Tai family argued that the IAD should have placed greater weight on the *Ribic* factor of "rehabilitation," in that it had apologized for the breach and now worked hard to establish itself in Canada. "Rehabilitation" is a factor that is considered by the IAD in exercising it's discretionary jurisdiction with respect to criminal inadmissibility. The Tai family's positive contribution to Canada is only one factor that is considered under the *Ribic* test that is applied by the IAD. These factors are adapted in cases that do not involve criminal inadmissibility to consider "the circumstances surrounding the failure to meet the conditions of admission which led to the deportation order," instead of rehabilitation. The IAD reached a reasonable conclusion. The application for judicial review was dismissed.

Singh v. Canada (Minister of Citizenship & Immigration) (2010), 89 Imm. L.R. (3d) 36, 2010 FC 378, 2010 CarswellNat 3016, 2010 CarswellNat 817, [2010] F.C.J. No. 426 — The applicant was recently found to be inadmissible for misrepresenting or withholding a material fact when he immigrated to Canada in 1993. At that time, he did not disclose that he had fathered a child who remained in India. His defence is that he did not know he had fathered a child. Paternity has now been scientifically established by DNA tests. As a result, the Immigration Division of the Immigration and Refugee Board of Canada issued an exclusion order and he was ordered removed from Canada. His appeal to the Immigration Appeal Division was dismissed. He sought judicial review of that decision.

The applicant's submission is that he could not have misrepresented or withheld facts within the meaning of s. 40 of IRPA or its predecessor, since subjectively he had no knowledge at the time that he was the girl Shilpa's biological father. The Minister's position is that it does not matter what the applicant knew or did not know, it is a scientifically proven fact that he is Shilpa's biological father, and that is the end of the matter.

Given that the wording "knowingly" does not appear in s. 40, it follows, that knowledge is not a prerequisite to a finding of misrepresentation or withholding material facts. Undoubtedly, the existence of a child is a material fact. In this case, the alleged misrepresentation was a misstatement of fact. Such misrepresentations may be fraudulent, negligent or innocent. The panel found that the applicant was not credible. Even if he did not know that he was Shilpa's father, the circumstances, *i.e.* his long sexual relationship with Shilpa's mother while her husband was out of India, should, at the very least, have put him on inquiry. He had a duty of candour which required him to disclose upon his arrival in Canada in 1993 the strong possibility that he had fathered a child. The panel's assessment of facts was not unreasonable and so it follows that the applicant, a permanent resident, is inadmissible for misrepresentation.

One of the objectives of IRPA, as set out in s. 3, is "to see that families are reunited in Canada," not to remove someone against his will so that he may be reunited with his wife and daughter in India. The panel noted that the applicant had been here for many years, and had been gainfully employed, however, it made no assessment of the job prospects of a 50-year-old man in India, taking into account his obligation to support his wife and child. How the couple manages their affairs is their business. It would appear that they would prefer that the applicant work in Canada. There is nothing preventing him from visiting his wife and daughter in India on a regular basis. Perhaps after he has saved more money, he will return to and retire in India. It was not for the panel to say that they would be better off if reunited in India now. This smacked of "big brotherhood." This aspect of the decision was unreasonable. The matter was referred back to a differently constituted panel for reconsideration.

Malfeo v. Canada (Minister of Citizenship & Immigration), 2010 CarswellNat 372, 2010 CarswellNat 2169, 2010 FC 193 — The main question raised by this judicial review application was whether a member of the Immigration Appeal Division (IAD) breached the principles of natural justice and/or the requirements of the law when she dismissed the applicant's request to stay his deportation to Italy. This application had been made pursuant to s. 67(1)(c) of IRPA, which enables the tribunal to grant relief if sufficient humanitarian and compassionate considerations are demonstrated in light of the circumstances.

The use of joint submissions is a concept well known in criminal law where the Crown and the defence make joint submissions, for example, in sentencing. It is not unknown in administrative law cases and has been applied by this court in the context of immigration law (see *Nguyen v. Canada (Minister of Citizenship & Immigration)* (2000), 10 Imm. L.R. (3d) 252, 196 F.T.R. 236), a case which bears similarity with the case at hand since it involved an application by Mr. Nguyen to the then Appeal Division for the exercise of its humanitarian and compassionate jurisdiction under a provision of the now repealed *Immigration Act* similar to para. 67(1)(c) of IRPA. That case involved the failure of the tribunal to explain why the joint submissions of counsel proposing a five-year stay was not endorsed. The purpose of staying the deportation is, in that case as it is in this one, to give the applicant an opportunity to demonstrate, on the ground so to speak, becoming a decent law-abiding resident of the country.

Having received the joint submission albeit unexpectedly, the tribunal breached procedural fairness by rejecting it outright without asking for further input. The applicant in these circumstances was not given a fair hearing. The tribunal provided no analysis and did not even refer to the proposed terms and conditions. It was also clear that the tribunal did not give serious consideration to the joint submissions. Again, it provided no analysis of its terms and dismissed the joint submission in a perfunctory manner. The reasons put forward for rejecting the joint submission also lacked analysis. The application for judicial review was granted.

Shaath v. Canada (Minister of Citizenship & Immigration) (2009), 349 F.T.R. 81 (Eng.), 2009 FC 731, 2009 CarswellNat 2251, 2009 CarswellNat 4145 — The applicant sought judicial review of a decision dismissing his appeal from a departure order issued against him, by reason of his failure to comply with s. 28 of IRPA, which provides that a permanent resident meets his residency obligations in each five-year period if he/she was physically present in Canada at least 730 days during that period.

The tribunal reached its conclusion despite the fact counsel for the Minister appearing before the tribunal agreed the appeal should be allowed on humanitarian grounds mainly because of the family's establishment in Canada who, except for the applicant, are Canadian citizens. Counsel for the Minister also recognized his important financial investment in Canada and "he had been credible in his efforts to obtain his certification in Canada in order to get a job in his own specialty in the near future." Counsel's main reason for recommending the applicant's appeal be allowed was that she thought it was "nonsense to ask for a denial of the appeal since Mr. Shaath could apply tomorrow as a member of the family class, sponsored by his wife and it would be really easy to obtain his permanent residency and start the whole thing again." She considered that in all of the circumstances, "the punishment of losing his permanent residency would be disproportionate in all of the circumstances." The tribunal disagreed with counsel for the Minister's recommendation.

The Supreme Court of Canada's decision in *Canada (Citizenship & Immigration) v. Khosa* (2009), 77 Imm. L.R. (3d) 1, has a considerable impact upon this case because it dealt with the exercise by the IAD of its discretion under para. 67(1)(c) of IRPA. *Khosa* makes it clear where reasonableness standard applies, it requires deference and reviewing courts are not allowed to substitute their own appreciation of the appropriate solution but rather must determine if the outcome falls "within a range of possible, acceptable outcomes which are defensible in respect of the facts and the law." Paragraph 67(1)(c) provides a power to grant "exceptional relief" and calls for a fact-dependent and policy-driven assessment. An applicant has the burden of adducing proof of any claim upon which a humanitarian and compassionate application relies. The application for judicial review was dismissed.

Vazirizadeh v. Canada (Minister of Citizenship & Immigration), 2009 CarswellNat 4932, 2009 FC 807, 2009 CarswellNat 2387, [2009] F.C.J. No. 919 — This was a judicial review of a decision of the IAD to dismiss the appeal of a sponsorship of a parent who was found to be medically inadmissible pursuant to para. 38(1)(c) of the Act because her health condition "might reasonably be expected to cause excessive demand on health or social services" in Canada. Six months after the visa officer's decision, she underwent right knee replacement surgery in Iran. The applicant argued that the IAD hearing, which was a *de novo* hearing, did not consider the appellant's changed medical status. The court, however, concluded that the IAD analyzed the medical condition both at the time of the visa officer's decision in 2007 and the IAD hearing in 2008, including the evidence of right knee replacement surgery, physiotherapy and the opinion of the appellant's orthopedic specialist. However, the IAD reiterated or quoted the original medical opinion which, besides the likelihood of specialized knee replacement surgery, stated that the appellant's mother suffers from other medical problems, *i.e.* hypertension, obesity, osteoporosis and osteoarthritis, degenerative changes of the spine and hands and also degenerative osteoporosis of the thoracic vertebrae.

The Federal Court referred to *Mohamed v. Canada (Minister of Employment & Immigration)*, [1986] 3 F.C. 90, a Federal Court of Appeal decision which held that the medical condition at the time the visa officer refused the visa was the only relevant one and subsequent improvement in the medical condition was only relevant as to whether special relief should be granted on appeal.

The Federal Court concluded that the IAD's decision was well founded in fact and in law and amply satisfied the test of falling within an acceptable range of reasonable decisions and therefore the application for judicial review was dismissed. The Federal Court also refused to certify a question.

Canlas v. Canada (Minister of Public Safety & Emergency Preparedness), 2009 CarswellNat 1492, 2009 FC 303 — This is an application for judicial review of the decision of a member of the IAD which dismissed the applicants' appeal of a removal order made against them pursuant to subs. 40(2) of the IRPA. The principal applicant obtained permanent residence status for herself and her daughters under false representations about their civil status and their identities as well as her own identity. The applicant obtained false birth certificates for her two daughters in order for them to leave the Philippines without the knowledge of their biological father, and misrepresented their paternity by indicating falsely that she was married to another man and that he was their biological father. The Canadian authorities discovered the applicants' false representations in September 2004, when the other man applied for a temporary resident visa in which he declared names of his wife and his children. The applicants requested that the exclusion orders issued against them be quashed on the basis of sufficient H&C warranting special relief supported by the best interests of her Canadian-born son.

The IAD ignored the medical report stating that since an early age, the applicant's Canadian-born son was followed and treated in a Canadian pediatric clinic with specialized multi-disciplinary care, and that two of the medications needed for his treatment were not readily available in developing countries such as the Philippines. In addition, the IAD found that there was no reason why the Canadian-born child could not remain with his father in Canada. The father, however, was not called as a witness and no material or information was filed on his behalf to confirm his willingness and/or ability to care for his son. Obligation to inquire as to whether a child will be adequately looked after if a parent is removed from Canada stems from dicta in *Adams v. Canada (Minister of Citizenship & Immigration)* (March 28, 2008), Doc. IMM-1470-08 (F.C.).

The IAD acknowledged that in *Adams*, the facts were "strikingly similar to those in the instant case," inasmuch as a Canadian-born child is concerned. In order to be able to distinguish the present case from *Adams*, the IAD erred in assuming the father was available to care for the minor child in Canada in replacement of the mother and her two daughters, and this without any evidence to support such finding. The application for judicial review was allowed.

Ferrer v. Canada (Minister of Citizenship & Immigration), 2009 CarswellNat 899, 2009 CarswellNat 2095, 2009 FC 356 — The applicant sought judicial review of a decision of the IAD which dismissed his plea for humanitarian and compassionate relief pursuant to s. 67(1)(c) of the IRPA. An exclusion order had been issued against the applicant based on a finding of inadmissibility for a misrepresentation made in September, 1998 with respect to his permanent resident application. In his application, the applicant testified that he was single with no children. It was not disputed that at the time he was the father of two dependent children living with their mother in the Philippines. The applicant married his spouse who was the mother of his two children on a trip back to the Philippines after he was granted permanent residence status in Canada. The spouse is not excluded from the family class pursuant to s. 117(9)(d) of the Regulations. Accordingly, the applicant's two children would be eligible to be included on the spouse's application for permanent residence as her dependent children, provided the applicant's appeal before the IAD was allowed as he would be in a position to sponsor his wife and both of his children as members of the family class.

The IAD considered only two possibilities with respect to the best interests of the children. The first possibility was that the children could remain in the Philippines and that their father would continue to have a geographically distant relationship with them while at the same time supporting them financially at a higher level than possible if he were returned to the Philippines. The second alternative was that the applicant could be returned to the Philippines where he would be able to better meet their emotional needs by having close contact with them, though he would not be able to provide the higher level of financial support in the event that he was removed from Canada. It was argued that the analysis was erroneous and that it did not take into consideration the most probable outcome should the applicant's appeal be allowed. The tribunal's failure to consider this probable outcome led to its conclusion that the best interests of the children were a neutral factor when in fact the best interests of the children were a positive factor which weighed in favour of allowing the appeal. In other words, the tribunal failed to appreciate that the applicant's children could have the best of both worlds by being reunited with him in Canada. Had the tribunal not committed this error, it would certainly have considered the best interests of the applicant's children to be a factor in favour of allowing his appeal and not a neutral factor — thereby negating its value. It appears that the IAD's reasoning was dominated by a consideration of the "integrity of the Canadian immigration system." This might be an important factor to consider, but only after the best interest of the children are properly addressed; only in this way can a fair and balanced approach be taken to this important statutory requirement. The application for judicial review was allowed and the matter sent back for redetermination.

Khosa v. Canada (Minister of Citizenship & Immigration), [2009] S.C.J. No. 12, 77 Imm. L.R. (3d) 1, 82 Admin. L.R. (4th) 1, 2009 SCC 12, 304 D.L.R. (4th) 1, 385 N.R. 206, 2009 CarswellNat 434, 2009 CarswellNat 435 — The applicant, a permanent resident of Canada, was convicted of criminal negligence causing death as a result of his participation in an automobile race. It ended with the death of an innocent pedestrian who was struck by the applicant's vehicle. The applicant received a conditional sentence of two years less a day with various conditions. He was declared inadmissible for serious criminality pursuant to s. 36(1)(a) of the Act and was ordered removed from Canada. He appealed. He did not challenge the validity of his removal order but rather sought special relief on the basis of humanitarian and compassionate considerations. The majority of the IAD dismissed his appeal. The application for judicial review was dismissed. The Court of Appeal concluded that the applicable standard of review should be reasonableness, essentially because the decision was not protected by a full privative clause, was not a polycentric one, related to human interest and did not, so far as the possibility of rehabilitation factors was concerned, engage the Board's expertise. The Federal Court of Appeal reviewed the Board's decision on the correct standard of review, reasonableness. Accordingly, the Board's decision was found to be unreasonable as it appeared that the Board was trying to second guess decisions of the criminal court and disagreed with the criminal sentence imposed on the applicant and saw in the H&C decision an opportunity to readdress the situation.

On appeal to the Supreme Court of Canada, the appeal restored the decision of the IAD. The majority of the court concluded that in *New Brunswick (Board of Management) v. Dunsmuir*, [2008] 1 S.C.R. 190, (sub nom. *Dunsmuir v. New Brunswick*) [2008] S.C.J. No. 9, 372 N.R. 1, 69 Admin. L.R. (4th) 1, 2008 C.L.L.C. 220-020, D.T.E. 2008T-223, 329 N.B.R. (2d) 1, 170 L.A.C. (4th) 1, 291 D.L.R. (4th) 577, 64 C.C.E.L. (3d) 1, 2008 CarswellNB 124, 2008 CarswellNB 125, 2008 SCC 9, did away with the distinction between "patent unreasonableness" and "reasonableness *simpliciter*" and substituted a more context-driven view of "reasonableness" that nevertheless "does not pave the way for a more intrusive review by courts." *Dunsmuir* teaches that judicial review should be less concerned with the formation of different standards of review and more focused on substance, particularly on the nature of the issue that was before the administrative tribunal under review. Here, the decision of the IAD required the application of broad policy considerations to the facts as found to be relevant, and weighed for importance, by the IAD itself. The question whether the applicant had shown "sufficient humanitarian and compassionate considerations" to warrant relief from his removal, which all parties acknowledged to be valid, was a decision which Parliament confided to the IAD, not to the courts. On general principles of administrative law, including the Supreme Court of Canada's recent decision in *Dunsmuir*, the applications judge was right to give a high degree of deference to the IAD decision. The majority of the IAD was within a range of reasonable outcomes and the majority of the Federal Court of Appeal erred in intervening in this case to quash it. The appeal was therefore allowed and the decision of the IAD was restored.

Tamber v. Canada (Minister of Citizenship & Immigration), 2008 CarswellNat 2867, 2008 CarswellNat 3913, 2008 FC 951 — Both the visa officer and the Board concluded that the marriage between the applicant and a Mr. Singh was not genuine. The applicant sought judicial review of the Board's decision. She had given birth to a baby boy on March 11, 2005, and DNA testing confirmed Mr. Singh as the alleged father with a 99.98 per cent probability of paternity. The Board rejected the DNA evidence even though the supporting test documentation was on its face reliable and the respondent acknowledged that the analysis had been carried out by a reputable Canadian laboratory. That, however, was not the primary problem with the Board's approach to this highly determinative evidence. If the Board had reservations about the reliability of this testing or about the continuity of the blood samples, it had a clear duty to advise the applicant's counsel of its concerns. This was a proceeding that spanned two hearings separated by almost three months and there was no justification for ambushing the applicant by essentially ignoring the issue during the testimonial phase. It was open to the Minister to supervise the DNA testing and to control the continuity of the evidence obtained; it was not appropriate for the Minister to sit silently until all the evidence was in and then criticize the process as deficient. For the same reason it was unfair for the Board to reject this evidence as unreliable. It is a well-accepted principle of natural justice that the Board's concerns about the reliability of important documentary evidence must be put to the claimant either for an explanation or to allow for additional corroboration. The application was allowed.

Ivanov v. Canada (Minister of Citizenship & Immigration) (2006), 56 Imm. L.R. (3d) 56, 2006 CarswellNat 2335 (Imm. & Ref. Bd. (App. Div.)) — The appellant made an application for permanent residence as an independent in May 2001. At the time he disclosed that he had never been married and had no dependants. The application was successful and he was issued a permanent resident visa in June 2003. The appellant married his girlfriend on October 3, 2003. The appellant arrived in Canada on October 7, 2003. He disclosed his recent marriage to Canadian immigration officials upon his arrival in Toronto. At the time of his examination at Pearson Airport, he could not establish that his wife met the requirements of IRPA and the Regulations. His counsel wrote to the Canadian Embassy in Vienna in November 2003 advising that the immigration official at the port of entry had no objection regarding the release of the landed documents to the appellant subject to the appellant's wife meeting the medical and security requirements. The Embassy replied that there was no legal basis on which they were required to assess the wife against the admissibility criteria of IRPA. The appellant was issued an exclusion order on the basis that he was unable to establish at the time of his examination that his wife met the requirement of the Act and the Regulations. The appellant appealed the exclusion order.

The Appeal Board concluded that the exclusion order was valid in law. The appeal, however, was allowed under s. 67(1)(c) and the matter referred back to an immigration officer at the port of entry for reconsideration. The Board found that the appellant made an honest mistake in not informing the visa officer of his marriage prior to appearing for landing, but had disclosed the marriage immediately upon landing. As a result of the appellant's error, the Board concluded that he had suffered financial hardship upon his arrival in Canada, exhausting his savings because he could not legally work here. The Board found that the appellant had established humanitarian and compassionate considerations to warrant the granting of special relief in light of all the circumstances of the case. The Board directed that the department take all steps required to facilitate the examination of the appellant's wife and to provide the appellant with the necessary immigration documents to allow the appellant to attend before an immigration officer at a port of entry for reconsideration.

Vong v. Canada (Minister of Citizenship & Immigration) (2006), 60 Imm. L.R. (3d) 98, 2006 CarswellNat 4315, 2006 FC 1480 — The Immigration Appeal Division concluded the applicant failed to comply with the residency obligations of s. 28 of the Act during the five-year period immediately preceding August 2, 2004. The applicant appealed this decision and in the *de novo* proceedings before the Board, he produced new evidence in support of his insistence that he met the two-year residency requirement. The Board did not find the evidence credible and refused his appeal. The applicant argued the Board committed an error of law in not considering humanitarian and compassionate factors. During the Board hearing, the applicant waived his right to invoke a grant for special relief pursuant to para. 67(1)(c) of the Act (H&C). The applicant sought instead to provide evidence that would prove he met the residency requirements.

There is very little jurisprudence on this matter regarding the onus of the Board to consider H&C factors in spite of the stated position of the applicant not to pursue such factors. Even if the Board is required to consider H&C factors against the express wishes of the applicant, the onus will not shift from the applicant to establish exceptional reasons why he should be allowed to remain in Canada. The Board has no obligation to assume such a burden. The applicant failed to establish that the Board committed an error that would warrant intervention with respect to the H&C factors. The court did conclude that the Board's decision regarding the credibility of the applicant and his documentary evidence should be set aside and the matter was sent back for the re-determination before a different Board member.

Chang v. Canada (Minister of Citizenship & Immigration), 2006 FC 157, 2006 CarswellNat 329, 2006 CarswellNat 2194, [2006] F.C.J. No. 217 — The legislatively established conditions of the entrepreneur category, if flaunted knowingly, without serious consequence, would make a mockery of the purpose for which they were established. The act of creating or participating in a front operation or a sham investment, if left unchecked, strikes a blow at the very integrity of the immigration system. In this case, the applicants were found to be in non-compliance with subs. 27(2) and s. 28. The applicants' children were also found to be in non-compliance with subs. 27(2) as they were dependants of an entrepreneur and bound by the same terms and conditions of landing as provided in para. 23.1 of the previous regulations. Both the applicants as well as their children sought special relief on appeal in light of the circumstances of their case, specifically, that there were sufficient humanitarian and compassionate considerations that warranted the setting aside of departure orders. The IAD was of the view that the parents did not merit discretionary relief as they took part in a sham arrangement to try to fulfill the conditions of the entrepreneur category. Even though the IAD felt that the children would be excellent candidates for permanent residence, it refused to grant discretionary relief to the children because once the children became permanent residents they would be entitled to sponsor their parents which would render the removal of the parents moot.

The granting of special relief is a weighing process. Even though there were some positive elements in favour of discretionary relief being allowed to the three children, these elements did not outweigh the importance given to the integrity of maintaining the conditions in the entrepreneur category. It was open to the IAD to find that special relief should not be granted to the children because this would benefit the parents who had not respected the conditions under which they entered Canada.

Elias c. Canada (Ministre de la Citoyenneté & de l'Immigration), 2005 CarswellNat 5708, 2005 FC 1329 — The applicant sought judicial review of the IAD's decision dismissing their appeal from a removal order. The principal applicant was born in Lebanon and emigrated to Brazil, where he lived for 20 years and became a citizen of that country. The applicant was granted landing in Canada as an entrepreneur and accepted the conditions provided under para. 23.1 of the Immigration Regulations. The Immigration Division decided that the applicants were persons contemplated by s. 41 of the IRPA since the principal applicant had not respected the conditions imposed for entrepreneurs when he was granted landing. The IAD dismissed the applicant's appeal concluding that an order to stay the removal order would have the effect of not only calling into question the integrity of the program conceived to attract entrepreneurs, but also the integrity of the Canadian immigration system as a whole. The principal applicant argued that he had provided plausible explanations and reasons why he was unable to respect the conditions within the two-year time period. In this case, the court concluded that the IAD weighed the best interests of the children directly affected as well as the other factors alleged by the applicants in support of their appeal but, considering the other circumstances of the matter, determined that special relief was not justified. The applicants' eldest son was born in Brazil while the younger son was born in Canada. The applicants did not submit any evidence regarding the effects that the removal to Brazil could have on the eldest child, or the effects of a possible migration on the younger child. The applicants' argument regarding the children amounted to saying that the presence of children in Canada automatically implies humanitarian considerations justifying special measures. The court concluded that Parliament has not decided that the presence of children in Canada constitutes in itself an impediment to any *refoulement* of a parent illegally residing in Canada. The application for judicial review was dismissed.

Mand v. Canada (Minister of Citizenship & Immigration) (2005), 51 Imm. L.R. (3d) 272, 2005 FC 1637, 2005 CarswellNat 3970, [2005] F.C.J. No. 2016 — The principal applicant came to Canada under the entrepreneurial category. He was accompanied to Canada by his spouse and three children. They did not meet their obligations under the terms and conditions of their landing and, as a result, deportation orders were issued against them. They filed appeals against the deportation orders and were granted a two-year stay subject to following certain terms and conditions. The appeals were subsequently rejected when the applicants did not respect the conditions. The IAD also concluded that the applicants failed to demonstrate that having regard to all the circumstances of the case, they should not be removed from Canada for humanitarian and compassionate considerations. Although the Federal Court concluded that the IAD erred in concluding that the principal applicant's daughter did have strong ties to Canada, the Federal Court concluded the IAD's decision to cancel the stay of the deportation orders was not patently unreasonable, as it would be unjust and against the principles of the Canadian immigration process to decide otherwise. The principal applicant was given a second chance and failed to respect the rules; he should not be rewarded for being able to abuse the system to the point of allowing his family to remain in Canada long enough to build strong ties and qualify for a further stay of deportation orders based on humanitarian and compassionate grounds.

El Idrissi c. Canada (Ministre de la Citoyenneté & de l'Immigration), 2005 CarswellNat 2421, 2005 CarswellNat 5248, 2005 FC 1105 — The applicant was given permanent residence status in 1991. In 1999, the applicant left Canada to visit his sick father and manage a family business in his home country. He did not return until June 15, 2003. He fell under the purview of s. 41 of the IRPA and a departure order was made against him by the Minister. He filed an appeal to the Immigration Appeal Division but conceded that the removal order against him was legally valid and the only issue he argued was that there were humanitarian and compassionate grounds to explain his failure to meet the residency obligation.

Simply having a wife in Canada was not sufficient for this situation to be considered a humanitarian and compassionate ground. The Appeal Division was entitled to consider that the applicant's plans for the future were vague. The applicant had the burden of establishing the existence of humanitarian and compassionate grounds.

68. (1) Removal order stayed — To stay a removal order, the Immigration Appeal Division must be satisfied, taking into account the best interests of a child directly affected by the decision, that sufficient humanitarian and compassionate considerations warrant special relief in light of all the circumstances of the case.

(2) Effoot — Where the Immigration Appeal Division stays the removal order

(a) it shall impose any condition that is prescribed and may impose any condition that it considers necessary;

(b) all conditions imposed by the Immigration Division are cancelled;

(c) it may vary or cancel any non-prescribed condition imposed under paragraph (a); and

(d) it may cancel the stay, on application or on its own initiative.

(3) Reconsideration — If the Immigration Appeal Division has stayed a removal order, it may at any time, on application or on its own initiative, reconsider the appeal under this Division.

(4) Termination and cancellation — If the Immigration Appeal Division has stayed a removal order against a permanent resident or a foreign national who was found inadmissible on grounds of serious criminality or criminality, and they are convicted of another offence referred to in subsection 36(1), the stay is cancelled by operation of law and the appeal is terminated.

[Editor's Note: S.C. 2001, c. 27, s. 190 provides that every application, proceeding or matter under the Immigration Act, R.S.C. 1985, c. I-2 (the "former Act") that is pending or in progress immediately before June 28, 2002 shall be governed by the Immigration and Refugee Protection Act, S.C. 2001, c. 27 (the "new Act"), effective June 28, 2002.

S.C. 2001, c. 27, s. 192 provides that if a notice of appeal has been filed with the Immigration Appeal Division immediately before June 28, 2002, the appeal shall be continued under the Immigration Act, R.S.C. 1985, c. I-2 (the "former Act") by the Immigration Appeal Division of the Immigration and Refugee Board.

S.C. 2001, c. 27, s. 196 provides that despite S.C. 2001, c. 27, s. 192, an appeal made to the Immigration Appeal Division before June 28, 2002 shall be discontinued if the appellant has not been granted a stay under the former Act and the appeal could not have been made because of s. 64 of the Immigration and Refugee Protection Act, S.C. 2001, c. 27 (the "new Act")

S.C. 2001, c. 27, s. 197 further provides that despite S.C. 2001, c. 27, s. 192, if an appellant who has been granted a stay under the former Act breaches a condition of the stay, the appellant shall be subject to the provisions of s. 64 and s. 68(4) of the new Act.

SOR/2002-227, s. 326(2) provides that a person in respect of whom s. 70(5) or paragraph 77(3.01)(b) of the former Act applied on June 28, 2002 is a person in respect of whom s. 64(1) of the new Act applies.]

Case Law

Section 68(1)

Tai v. Canada (Minister of Citizenship & Immigration), 2011 FC 248, 2011 CarswellNat 1933, 2011 CarswellNat 471 — The applicants became permanent residents of Canada in 2001 but did not move to, or reside in, Canada. In April 2008, when the Tai family members sought to enter Canada, they were issued removal orders for failing to comply with their residency obligation. Ms. Chang and their daughters remained in Canada. Mr. Tai returned to his job in Taiwan and did not move to Canada until one year later at the end of April 2009. At the IAD, the family members admitted they had failed to meet their residency obligation and asked that their appeals be allowed based on discretionary jurisdiction. The IAD concluded there were insufficient H&C considerations to warrant special relief.

The IAD reasons were adequate when reviewed as a whole. The IAD considered all the circumstances of the case, and not just the failure to meet the residency obligation. The IAD is required to consider all of the circumstances in the case and not just the Tai family's recent efforts to establish itself (para. 67(1)(c) and s. 68(1) of IRPA). The Tai family argued that the IAD should have placed greater weight on the *Ribic* factor of "rehabilitation," in that it had apologized for the breach and now worked hard to establish itself in Canada. "Rehabilitation" is a factor that is considered by the IAD in exercising it's discretionary jurisdiction with respect to criminal inadmissibility. The Tai family's positive contribution to Canada is only one factor that is considered under the *Ribic* test that is applied by the IAD. These factors are adapted in cases that do not involve criminal inadmissibility to consider "the circumstances surrounding the failure to meet the conditions of admission which led to the deportation order," instead of rehabilitation. The IAD reached a reasonable conclusion. The application for judicial review was dismissed.

Ivanov v. Canada (Minister of Citizenship & Immigration) (2007), 64 Imm. L.R. (3d) 3, 368 N.R. 380, [2008] 2 F.C.R. 502, 2007 FCA 315, 2007 CarswellNat 3194, 2007 CarswellNat 4159, [2007] F.C.J. No. 1295 — The Immigration and Refugee Board, Immigration Appeal Division is obligated to consider all the relevant factors raised by the applicant's evidence even if the applicant has neither referred to, nor relied on, these factors in his submissions as a basis for staying a deportation order. Once there is evidence that relates to a *Ribic* factor, the IAD must consider that *Ribic* factor in its reasons. This is not tantamount to an obligation to elicit evidence. The evidentiary burden to demonstrate why a stay ought not to be cancelled remains on the permanent resident facing deportation.

[Editor's note: This case was decided under s. 74(3)(b)(i) of the former Act.]

Zlobinski v. Canada (Minister of Citizenship & Immigration), 2006 CarswellNat 1747, 2006 FC 810 — The applicant came to Canada with his mother in 1992 when he was 14 years old. He is now a person who is inadmissible to Canada on grounds of serious criminality and he is the subject of a valid deportation order. As a result, the applicant moved before the IAD for an order staying the deportation order. The IAD was not satisfied that "sufficient humanitarian and compassionate considerations warranted special relief in light of all the circumstances of the case." The applicant sought judicial review.

The applicant had been convicted of nine offences. The IAD found that he was not a good candidate for rehabilitation, given his past failed attempts to do so. The IAD noted that the applicant had used heroin for 10 years and that his criminal record reflected his need to finance his drug habit. The IAD concluded that he had little establishment in Canada and a spotty work history, little money in the bank and no ownership or interest in any property. Although the IAD noted that he had no family in Ukraine, they concluded that he had not sought out the support of his family in dealing with his issues in Canada.

Although the IAD did not specifically refer in its reasons to the evidence of the applicant's father, the IAD did consider the hardship to the applicant and his family if he were

IRP Act

to be deported to Ukraine. The Federal Court was not persuaded that this evidence was of such a nature that the failure of the IAD to mention it specifically gave rise to an inference that material evidence was ignored. Further, a misstatement as to the date in which the applicant came into Canada in 1995 was found not to be a material error. The application for judicial review was dismissed.

Chieu v. Canada (Minister of Citizenship & Immigration), [2002] 1 S.C.R. 84, [2002] S.C.J. No. 1, REJB 2002-27421, 37 Admin. L.R. (3d) 252, 18 Imm. L.R. (3d) 93, 208 D.L.R. (4th) 107, 280 N.R. 268, 2002 CarswellNat 5, 2002 CarswellNat 6, 2002 SCC 3 — The court considered whether the words "having regard to all the circumstances of the case" in s. 70(1)(b) of the *Immigration Act* allow the IAD to consider potential foreign hardship when reviewing a removal made against a permanent resident. The IAD has considered the potential foreign hardship an individual would face upon removal for well over a decade, following *Ribic v. Canada (Minister of Employment & Immigration)*, 1986 CarswellNat 135 (Imm. App. Bd.). There is no evidence that this consideration prolonged hearings before the IAD by any significant extent. The IAD is entitled to consider potential foreign hardships when exercising its discretionary jurisdiction under s. 70(1)(b) of the Act, provided that the likely country of removal has been established by the individual being removed on a balance of probabilities. The Minister should facilitate the determination of the likely country of removal before the IAD whenever possible, as this improves the efficient functioning of the Act. The factors set out in *Ribic, supra*, remain the proper ones for the IAD to consider during the appeal under s. 70(1)(b). On such an appeal, the onus is on the individual facing removal to establish exceptional reasons as to why they should be allowed to remain in Canada.

[Editor's note: This case was decided under the former Immigration Act; *however, we think it continues to have relevance as the jurisprudence under the IRPA has developed.]*

Ribic v. Canada (Minister of Employment & Immigration), 1986 CarswellNat 1357, [1985] I.A.B.D. No. 4 (Imm. App. Bd.) — Whenever the Board exercises its equitable jurisdiction pursuant to para. 72(1)(b) (the former *Immigration Act*) it does so only after having found that the deportation order is valid in law. In each case the Board looks to the same general areas to determine if having regard to all the circumstances of the case, the person should not be removed from Canada. These circumstances include the seriousness of the offence or offences leading to the deportation and the possibility of rehabilitation or in the alternative, the circumstances surrounding the failure to meet the conditions of admission which led to the deportation order. The Board looks to the length of time spent in Canada and the degree to which the appellant has established; family in Canada and the dislocation to that family that deportation of the appellant would cause; the support available for the appellant not only within the family but also within the community; and the degree of hardship that would be caused to the appellant by his return to his country of nationality.

[Editor's note: This case was decided under the former Immigration Act; *however, we think it continues to have relevance as the jurisprudence under the IRPA has developed.]*

Section 68(2)

Canada (Minister of Citizenship & Immigration) v. Stephenson (2008), 68 Imm. L.R. (3d) 297, 2008 CarswellNat 959, 2008 FC 82, 2008 CarswellNat 141 — Mr. Stephenson was a permanent resident of Canada and was ordered to be removed because he had been convicted of trafficking in a narcotic. He appealed the issuance of the removal order and the IAD stayed the removal order for a period of three years on a number of conditions.

One condition was that he keep the peace and be of good behaviour. The IAD notified the parties that, pursuant to subs. 68(3) of the IRPA it would reconsider Mr. Stephenson's appeal. The IAD requested each party to provide a written statement about whether Mr. Stephenson had complied with the conditions of his stay of removal. The IAD was not convinced that three convictions in respect of the Ontario *Highway Traffic Act* offences constituted a breach of the condition to keep the peace and be of good behaviour. In order to "be of good behaviour," a person must abide by federal, provincial, and municipal statutes and regulations. In this case, given the evidence that convictions had been entered under the Ontario *Highway Traffic Act* against Mr. Stephenson, it was not, as a matter of law, open to the IAD to find that the convictions did not constitute a breach of the condition to "be of good behaviour." It was, however, open to the IAD to consider all the circumstances of Mr. Stephenson's case, including the nature and severity of his breach of conditions of the stay, and to determine how it should exercise its discretion. The application for judicial review was allowed.

Cooper v. Canada (Minister of Citizenship & Immigration) (2005), 49 Imm. L.R. (3d) 263, 2005 CarswellNat 2843, 2005 CarswellNat 4265, 2005 FC 1253 — The applicant had lived in Canada since the age of 12 and was ordered deported as a consequence of his having been convicted of four counts of armed robbery and two counts of using an imitation firearm. The IAD stayed the deportation for two years, provided that the applicant comply with a number of conditions, including the condition that he "keep the peace and be of good behaviour and not commit further criminal offences." Upon review by the IAD, evidence was provided that the applicant had been convicted of several speeding and parking offences, as well as one count of breaching the Ontario *Highway Traffic Act* and one offence contrary to the provision of the *Compulsory Automobile Insurance Act* of Ontario. The court held the requirement that the applicant "not commit any criminal offences" was implicit in the requirement that he be of good behaviour. The court also stated that a conditional order made in the immigration context requiring that the individual be "of good behaviour" includes, abiding by federal, provincial and municipal statutes and regulatory provisions.

Section 68(3)

Canada (Minister of Public Safety & Emergency Preparedness) v. Ali, 2008 CarswellNat 1829, 2008 CarswellNat 855, 2008 FC 431 — The Minister challenged the decision rendered by the IAD pursuant to the transitional provision of s. 197 of the IRPA. On the facts presented to the IAD, the question was whether contraventions of the *Ontario Highway Traffic Act* (HTA) constituted a breach of a condition of the stay granted to the applicant "to keep the peace and be of good behaviour." Mr. Ali had five convictions under the HTA since his stay was imposed. The IAD panel agreed that a failure to be of "good behaviour" may result from a failure to abide by a federal, provincial or municipal statute or regulatory provision, but that a failure to abide by a federal, provincial or municipal statute or regulatory provision does not necessarily mean there has been a failure to be of "good behaviour." A relatively minor or trivial conviction under a federal, provincial or municipal statute or regulatory provision does not mean that a breach of the condition "to keep the peace and be of good behaviour" has necessarily occurred and that the appellant should be given no opportunity to argue this. While not condoning Mr. Ali's HTA offences, the incidences for which he had been convicted under the HTA were relatively minor in nature. The panel did not find they were sufficiently serious to be considered failures to "keep the peace and be of good behaviour."

In order to engage in an analysis of whether a person has breached "good behaviour," it is first necessary to establish that the person has contravened a federal, provincial or municipal statute or regulatory measure and, upon so finding, the opportunity is triggered to evaluate whether the contravention results in a further finding that a breach of "good behaviour" has occurred. Therefore, in this analysis, a person's general conduct is an important factor which must be taken into consideration. The court found that this case was distinguishable from *Canada (Minister of Citizenship & Immigration) v. Stevenson*, 2008 FC 82, which supported the Minister's argument on the law, since it was not decided under the transition provision of the IRPA. The court concluded that there was no reviewable error of the IAD's decision. The court certified the following question:

> Is the condition "keep the peace and be of good behaviour" as imposed in stay of deportation orders by the IAD of the IRB breached each and every time the person concerned is convicted of an offence under and/or found to have violated any federal, provincial and/or municipal statute and regulation throughout Canada?

Canada (Minister of Citizenship & Immigration) v. Newman (2007), 65 Imm. L.R. (3d) 302, 2007 CarswellNat 3869, 2007 CarswellNat 5264, 2007 FC 1150 — Mr. Newman, a permanent resident, was ordered deported from Canada after having been convicted of welfare fraud, attempting to obstruct justice and failing to appear. The IAD granted Mr. Newman a stay of his deportation for three years on certain conditions. Three years later, the IAD decided that the original deportation order should be quashed. The Minister argued that the IAD's decision was not supported by the evidence before it. The IAD was aware that Mr. Newman had committed numerous driving offences, had failed to pay his fines, and had been sentenced to a term of imprisonment for driving while suspended. The IAD emphasized the fact that Mr. Newman had not committed any criminal offences in the preceding five years. The court found that the IAD failed to explain how the evidence relating to Mr. Newman's conduct over recent years supported a finding of rehabilitation. The court allowed the application for judicial review and ordered a new hearing before a different panel of the IAD.

Section 68(4)

Caraan v. Canada (Minister of Public Safety & Emergency Preparedness), 2013 FC 360, 2013 CarswellNat 924, 2013 CarswellNat 138 — On July 13, 2012, the IAD cancelled the stay of the deportation order against the applicant and the applicant's appeal was terminated by operation of the law under subs. 68(4) of IRPA. In its reasons, the IAD noted that the conditions for the automatic application of subs. 68(4) were met, namely: (1) the applicant was convicted of a crime referred to in subs. 36(1) of IRPA, and; (2) the conviction was entered during the period of the stay of the deportation order. IAD noted that subs. 68(4) applied to cancel a stay and terminate an appeal even where the acts giving rise to the convictions occurred prior to the stay being issued. The IAD noted there was no condition included in the IAD's stay excluding the application of subs. 68(4) for charges based on acts occurring before it.

The court found that subs. 68(4) was enacted to remove the discretionary power normally held by the IAD to grant a stay of a removal order when a person who has already benefited from a positive decision of the IAD commits another serious offence, as defined in subs. 36(1) of IRPA, thereby demonstrating that he is not rehabilitated. It automatically cancels their stay and their appeal is terminated.

The words of the statute are clear and must be assigned their ordinary meaning. The word "convicted" as used in subs. 68(4) means a finding of guilt or a conviction. Parliament was well aware of the presumption of innocence — hence the use of the words "and they are convicted of another offence." The applicant also still had the option of making a s. 25 claim for humanitarian and compassionate considerations. The application for judicial review was dismissed. The following question was certified:

> During a stay of removal order, does subsec. 68(4) of the IRPA only apply to convictions for subsec. 36(1) offences committed after the beginning of the stay?

Canada (Minister of Citizenship & Immigration) v. Hyde (2007), 57 Imm. L.R. (3d) 165, 359 N.R. 165, 2006 FCA 379, 2006 CarswellNat 4146, [2006] F.C.J. No. 1747 — The effect of s. 197 of IRPA is to terminate the IAD's jurisdiction with respect to a person who falls within the sections ambit. Section 197 precludes the IAD from staying a removal order in the exercise of its jurisdiction under s. 68 of IRPA. A permanent resident whose removal the IAD stayed before IRPA came into effect, and who breaches a condition of the stay, cannot continue an appeal to the IAD if either the basis of the deportation order was a criminal conviction with a sentence of two years or more, or if the offence committed after the IAD had stayed the removal was punishable by a maximum of 10 years or a sentence of more than six months was imposed.

The appellant had been ordered deported on the basis of a s. 64 offence (that is, one for which he received a sentence of two years or more). Therefore, his appeal was automatically terminated by IRPA when he breached the conditions imposed on his stay. It is irrelevant that the breaches did not involve the commission of offences referred to in subs. 68(4). The appeal was allowed.

Canada (Minister of Citizenship & Immigration) v. Malarski, 2006 CarswellNat 2612, 2006 FC 1007 — Where a permanent resident who is subject of a deportation order which has been stayed is subsequently convicted of an offence that constitutes serious criminality under subs. 36(1), the stay is cancelled by operation of law pursuant to subs. 68(4) of the IRPA and an appeal to the IAD is terminated. Once this happens, the IAD loses jurisdiction over the matter.

Singh v. Canada (Minister of Citizenship & Immigration), [2006] 3 F.C.R. 70, 344 N.R. 244, 51 Imm. L.R. (3d) 49, 2005 CarswellNat 4113, 2005 CarswellNat 5141, 2005 FCA 417 — The appellant was a permanent resident of Canada. After being convicted of robbery he was found inadmissible on the grounds of serious criminality and ordered deported. He appealed his deportation and was granted a stay of removal that contained, among others, the condition "keep the peace and be of good behaviour." Subsequently, the appellant committed another serious offence and was convicted of that crime. It is the offence itself that constitutes the breach of the condition to keep the peace and to be of good behaviour. In this regard, a breach may be established without a conviction where there is other clear evidence of the offensive behaviour.

Between the time of the assault and the conviction, on June 28, 2002, the *Immigration Act*, R.S.C. 1985, c. I-2, was replaced by the IRPA. A provision of the IRPA addressed individuals such as the appellant, who were found inadmissible on grounds of serious criminality, had obtained a stay of their removal order, and were then convicted of another serious offence. Specifically, the IRPA mandates the cancellation of the stay and the termination of the appeal.

The appellant argued that the transitional provision of the IRPA, s. 197(1) should not apply to a breach of condition that occurred before s. 197 was enacted. The Federal Court concluded that Parliament clearly intended that the provision of the IRPA that cancels the stay and terminates the appeal apply to individuals such as the appellant, regardless of whether the condition of the stay was breached before or after the IRPA came into force.

Leite v. Canada (Minister of Citizenship & Immigration), 2005 CarswellNat 2006, 2005 CarswellNat 5148, 2005 FC 984 — In this case, the applicant was subject to a stay order. The IAD had issued a stay of a deportation and had attached specific terms and conditions to the stay, including detailed reporting requirements and an oral review of the case. The actual stay order did not refer to a four-year term. The applicant was convicted of trafficking a controlled substance and the conviction triggered the application of s. 197 of the IRPA which required the stay to be cancelled by operation of law pursuant to subs. 68(4) of the IRPA. The applicant argued that the stay had expired at the time the conviction occurred and that the applicant should have a hearing where he could lead new evidence and the Board could determine what to do with his case on the merits. The court concluded the stay ordered by the Board was in effect and the applicant was convicted of an offence during that time and, consequently, s. 68(4) applied.

Ferri v. Canada (Minister of Citizenship & Immigration) (2005), 51 Imm. L.R. (3d) 177, [2006] 3 F.C.R. 53, 2005 FC 1580, 2005 CarswellNat 3878, 2005 CarswellNat 5009, [2005] F.C.J. No. 1941 — Subsection 68(4) of the IRPA limits the jurisdiction of the IAD to determining whether the factual requirements of this subsection are met. The IAD can only consider whether it has previously stayed a removal order; whether the individual in question is a permanent resident or a foreign national who was found inadmissible on grounds of serious criminality or criminality; and whether the individual has been convicted of another offence coming within subs. 36(1) of the IRPA. Once the IAD determines that the factual requirements of this subsection have been met, it then loses jurisdiction over the individual, by operation of law. The IAD does not have jurisdiction to consider the constitutionality of subs. 68(4).

69. (1) Dismissal — The Immigration Appeal Division shall dismiss an appeal if it does not allow the appeal or stay the removal order, if any.

(2) Minister's Appeal — In the case of an appeal by the Minister respecting a permanent resident or a protected person, other than a person referred to in subsection 64(1), if the Immigration Appeal Division is satisfied that, taking into account the best interests of a child directly affected by the decision, sufficient humanitarian and compassionate considerations warrant special relief in light of all the circumstances of the case, it may make and may stay the applicable removal order, or dismiss the appeal, despite being satisfied of a matter set out in paragraph 67(1)(a) or (b).

(3) Removal order — If the Immigration Appeal Division dismisses an appeal made under subsection 63(4) and the permanent resident is in Canada, it shall make a removal order.

70. (1) Decision binding — An officer, in examining a permanent resident or a foreign national, is bound by the decision of the Immigration Appeal Division to allow an appeal in respect of the permanent resident or foreign national.

(2) Examination suspended — If the Minister makes an application for leave to commence an application for judicial review of a decision of the Immigration Appeal Division with respect to a permanent resident or a foreign national, an ex-

amination of the permanent resident or the foreign national under this Act is suspended until the final determination of the application.

2015, c. 3, s. 111

71. Reopening appeal — The Immigration Appeal Division, on application by a foreign national who has not left Canada under a removal order, may reopen an appeal if it is satisfied that it failed to observe a principle of natural justice.

Case Law

Nazifpour v. Canada (Minister of Citizenship & Immigration) (2007), 60 Imm. L.R. (3d) 159, 360 N.R. 199, 278 D.L.R. (4th) 268, 2007 CarswellNat 324, 2007 FCA 35 — The issue in this appeal was whether the statutory context and purpose supply Parliament's omission, so that s. 71 should be interpreted as *implicitly* removing the unusual and long-established jurisdiction of the IAD to reopen a decision to consider new evidence before an appellant is deported. The appellant, a citizen of Iran, appealed from a decision of the Federal Court dismissing his application for judicial review to set aside a decision of the IAD. The applications judge held that the IAD was correct to conclude that s. 71 had removed its jurisdiction to entertain the appellant's motion to reopen its dismissal of his appeal against a deportation order on the basis of new evidence.

The Federal Court of Appeal concluded that s. 71 of the IRPA extinguishes the common law continuing "equitable jurisdiction" of the IAD to reopen an appeal except where the IAD had failed to observe a principle of natural justice. It is true that the drafter could easily have avoided all ambiguity by including the word "only" in the test of s. 71. However, the reading which best effectuates the general objects of the IRPA, and attributes a plausible function to s. 71 itself, is that the section *implicitly* removes the IAD's jurisdiction to reopen appeals on the ground of new evidence, a jurisdiction which would otherwise be judicially inferred from the nature of the statutory discretion to relieve against deportation.

Griffiths v. Canada (Minister of Citizenship & Immigration) (2005), 49 Imm. L.R. (3d) 268, 2005 FC 971, 2005 CarswellNat 2427, 2005 CarswellNat 4659, [2005] F.C.J. No. 1194 — Under the old *Immigration Act*, the IAD had a continuing equitable jurisdiction until the moment of deportation to decide if a person should be allowed to remain in Canada upon the presentation of new evidence, as well as subsequent case law. Under s. 71 of the IRPA (no equivalent section existed in the old *Immigration Act*), the IAD's jurisdiction to reopen appeals is limited and implicitly excludes the common law jurisdiction to reopen appeals to permit the appellant to present additional or new evidence. Section 71 limits or restricts the jurisdiction of the IAD to reopen appeals with respect to breaches of the rules of natural justice.

Ye v. Canada (Minister of Citizenship & Immigration) (2004), 40 Imm. L.R. (3d) 42, 2004 CarswellNat 2163, 18 Admin. L.R. (4th) 166, 254 F.T.R. 238, 2004 FC 964 — Section 71 limits the jurisdiction of the IAD to reopen appeals and implicitly excludes the common law jurisdiction to reopen appeals to permit the appellant to present additional or new evidence.

Lawal v. Canada (Minister of Citizenship & Immigration) (2002), 26 Imm. L.R. (3d) 226, 2002 CarswellNat 4340 (Imm. & Ref. Bd. (App. Div.)) — The applicant moved to reopen an appeal. The applicant was ordered deported on the basis that she had misrepresented a material fact by not declaring her dependent son when applying for permanent residence. Her appeal was dismissed and the applicant filed a motion to reopen on May 30, 2002.

The panel does not have continuing equitable jurisdiction in the matter given the changes in the immigration law. The specific language in IRPA clearly forecloses a reopening on the principle of continuing equitable jurisdiction. Section 71 explicitly defines the only grounds upon which a motion to reopen a removal order appeal by a foreign national can be made. The panel was of the view that there was no failure to observe a principle of natural justice in the appeal, and therefore, dismissed the motion to reopen.

DIVISION 8 — JUDICIAL REVIEW

72. (1) Application for judicial review — Judicial review by the Federal Court with respect to any matter — a decision, determination or order made, a measure taken or a question raised — under this Act is, subject to section 86.1, commenced by making an application for leave to the Court.

[Editor's Note: SOR/2002-227, s. 348(1) provides that, on June 28, 2002, any applica tion for leave to commence an application for judicial review and any application for judicial review or appeal from an application that was brought under the Immigration Act, *R.S.C. 1985, c. I-2 (the "former Act") that is pending before the Federal Court or the Supreme Court of Canada is deemed to have been commenced under Division 8 of Part 1 of the* Immigration and Refugee Protection Act, *S.C. 2001, c. 27 (the "new Act") and is governed by the provisions of that Division and s. 87 of the new Act.*

SOR/2002-227, s. 348(3) provides that, despite SOR/2002-227, s. 348(1), an application for judicial review that was not subject to the requirement of an application for leave under the former Act and was pending on June 28, 2002 does not require such an appli- cation under the new Act.

SOR/2002-227, s. 348(4) provides that any judicial review proceeding brought in respect of any decision or order made or any matter arising under the former Act after June 28, 2002 is governed by Division 8 of Part 1 and s. 87 of the new Act.

SOR/2002-227, s. 348(5) provides that a person in respect of whom the 30-day period provided by s. 18.1 of the Federal Courts Act, *R.S.C. 1985, c. F-7 for making an applica- tion for judicial review from a decision or matter referred to in s. 82.1(2) of the former Act has not elapsed on June 28, 2002 and who has not made such an application has 60 days from June 28, 2002 to file an application for leave under s. 72 of the new Act.*

SOR/2002-227, s. 348(6) provides that the validity or lawfulness of a decision or act made under the former Act that is the subject of a judicial review procedure or appeal referred to in SOR/2002-227, s. 348(1) is determined in accordance with the provisions of the former Act.

SOR/2002-227, s. 349 provides that, on June 28, 2002, an appeal made under s. 102.17 of the former Act or an application for an order made under s. 102.2 of the former Act that is pending remains governed by the provisions of the former Act.]

(2) Application — The following provisions govern an application under subsec- tion (1):

> **(a) the application may not be made until any right of appeal that may be pro- vided by this Act is exhausted;**

(b) subject to paragraph 169(f), notice of the application shall be served on the other party and the application shall be filed in the Registry of the Federal Court ("the Court") within 15 days, in the case of a matter arising in Canada, or within 60 days, in the case of a matter arising outside Canada, after the day on which the applicant is notified of or otherwise becomes aware of the matter;

(c) a judge of the Court may, for special reasons, allow an extended time for filing and serving the application or notice;

(d) a judge of the Court shall dispose of the application without delay and in a summary way and, unless a judge of the Court directs otherwise, without personal appearance; and

(e) no appeal lies from the decision of the Court with respect to the application or with respect to an interlocutory judgment.

[Editor's Note: SOR/2002-227, s. 350(1) provides that, subject to SOR/2002-227, ss. 350(2) and 350(3), if a decision or an act of the Minister or an immigration officer under the Immigration Act, *R.S.C. 1985, c. I-2 (the "former Act") is referred back by the Federal Court or Supreme Court of Canada for determination and the determination is not made before June 28, 2002, the determination shall be made in accordance with the* Immigration and Refugee Protection Act, *S.C. 2001, c. 27 (the "new Act").*

SOR/2002-227, s. 350(2) provides that if the decision or act was made under paragraph 46.01(1)(e), s. 70(5) or paragraph 77(3.01)(b) of the former Act and the new Act makes no provision for the decision or act, no determination shall be made.

SOR/2002-227, s. 350(3) provides that if a decision or an act of the Minister or an immigration officer under the former Act in respect of a person described in subparagraph 9(1)(b)(i) or paragraph 10(1)(b) of the Immigration Regulations, 1978, *SOR/98-172 (the "former Regulations") is referred back by the Federal Court or Supreme Court of Canada for determination and the determination is not made before June 28, 2002, the determination shall be made in accordance with ss. 361(3) and (5) of the* Immigration and Refugee Protection Regulations, *SOR/2002-227 (the "new Regulations").*

SOR/2002-227, s. 350(4) provides that if a decision or an act of the Minister or an immigration officer under the former Act in respect of a person described in subparagraphs 9(1)(b)(ii) or (iii) of the former Regulations is referred back by the Federal Court or Supreme Court of Canada for determination and the determination is not made before June 28, 2002, the determination shall be made in accordance with s. 361(3) of the new Regulations.

SOR/2002-227, s. 350(5) provides that if a decision of the Immigration Appeal Division made under the former Act is referred back by the Federal Court or Supreme Court of Canada for determination and the determination is not made before June 28, 2002, the Immigration Appeal Division shall dispose of the matter in accordance with the former Act.

SOR/2002-227, s. 350(6) provides that if a decision of the Adjudication Division made under the former Act is referred back by the Federal Court or Supreme Court of Canada for determination and the determination is not made before June 28, 2002, the Immigration Division shall dispose of the matter in accordance with the new Act.]

2002, c. 8, s. 194(a)(i); 2015, c. 20, s. 52

Case Law

Section 72(1)

Chaudhary v. Canada (Minister of Public Safety & Emergency Preparedness) (2015), 38 Imm. L.R. (4th) 210, 127 O.R. (3d) 401, 92 Admin. L.R. (5th) 147, 390 D.L.R. (4th) 598, 343 C.R.R. (2d) 146, 340 O.A.C. 211, 2015 ONCA 700, 2015 CarswellOnt 15828, [2015] O.J. No. 5438 — The applications judge concluded that the court should decline to exercise its *habeas corpus* jurisdiction, in light of the fact that IRPA put into place a comprehensive statutory review mechanism as broad and advantageous as *habeas corpus*. The Ontario Court of Appeal disagreed and allowed the appeals.

The prerogative writ of *habeas corpus* is "a cornerstone of liberty" and "a means of judicial control over the arbitrary behaviour of the executive government." It is "one of the most important safeguards of the liberty of the subject": M. Groves, "*habeas corpus*, Justiciability and Foreign Affairs" (2013) 11:3 N.Z. J. Pub. & Int'l L. 587, at p. 588. It is also "the most significant means of protecting individual liberty": R.S. Sharpe, J. Farbey & S. Atrill, *The Law of Habeas Corpus*, 3rd ed. (New York: Oxford University Press, 2011), at p. 1. Most significantly in Canada, it is guaranteed by s. 10(c) of the Charter which reads as follows: "Everyone has the right on arrest or detention . . . to have the validity of the detention determined by way of *habeas corpus* and to be released if the detention is not lawful."

The question a *habeas corpus* application would answer is whether the detentions, because of their length and their uncertain duration, have become illegal and in violation of the appellants' ss. 7 and 9 Charter rights. As such, the immigration status of the applicants will not be affected. They will still be subject to removal. All that will be decided is whether there continues to be a constitutionally valid basis for their detentions pending those immigration decisions and dispositions. This court has previously held that, although immigration matters will generally be best dealt with under the comprehensive scheme established under the immigration legislation, "there will be situations in which the Federal Court is not an effective and appropriate forum in which to seek the relief claimed. In those rare cases, the Superior Court can properly exercise its jurisdiction": *Francis (Litigation Guardian of) v. Canada (Minister of Citizenship and Immigration)* (1999), 49 O.R. (3rd) 136 (C.A.); leave to appeal granted (2000), 138 O.A.C. 199 (note) (S.C.C.), at para. 12. The exception set out in *Peiroo v. Minister of Employment and Immigration* (1989), 69 O.R. (2d) 253 (C.A.); leave to appeal refused (1989), 37 O.A.C. 160 (note) (S.C.C.), is not a blanket exclusion of *habeas corpus* in all matters related to immigration law. Therefore, because the issue raised by the appellants is not a core immigration issue as was *Peiroo* and seeks only the determination of the legality of the appellants' continued detentions, these are cases that warrant a "careful evaluation" as prescribed in *May v. Ferndale Institution*, [2005] 3 S.C.R. 809. There are three critical differences between the IRPA process and *habeas corpus* that, taken together, make *habeas corpus* broader and more advantageous to the appellants when the issue is whether continued detentions have become illegal due to their length and the uncertainty of their continued duration. Those three differences are:

   (i) the question the court is to answer;

   (ii) the onus; and

   (iii) the review process.

In addition, the Supreme Court in *May v. Ferndale Institution* identified the weaknesses in the statutory process for the review of prisoner transfer decisions, went on to assess the differences between the statutory scheme and *habeas corpus* purposively.

This involved consideration of five factors that the court found mitigated in favour of concurrent jurisdiction and provided additional support for allowing federal prisoners access to *habeas corpus*. The following five factors were also considered in this case:

    (i) the choice of remedies and forum;

    (ii) the expertise of provincial superior courts;

    (iii) the timeliness of the remedy;

    (iv) local access to the remedy; and

    (v) the nature of the remedy and the burden of proof.

In conclusion, the applicants, who have been in immigration detentions for lengthy periods and whose detentions are to continue for uncertain duration, should not be deprived of their Charter right to *habeas corpus*. They have the right to choose whether to have their detention-related issues heard in the Federal Court through judicial review of the ID decisions, or in the Superior Court through *habeas corpus* applications. The appeals were allowed.

Somodi v. Canada (Minister of Citizenship & Immigration) (2009), 82 Imm. L.R. (3d) 159, 311 D.L.R. (4th) 335, 395 N.R. 270, 2009 FCA 288, 2009 CarswellNat 3062, 2009 CarswellNat 5060 — The appellant sought, in the Federal Court, judicial review of a decision of a visa officer which refused his spousal sponsorship application for permanent residence status as a member of the family class. At the same time as the appellant made his judicial review application, his sponsor appealed the decision of the visa officer. The appellant's application was dismissed by a judge of the Federal Court on the ground that para. 72(2)(a) of IRPA required the appellant's sponsor to exhaust her right of appeal to the Immigration Appeal Division (IAD) before an application for judicial review could be made. While the appellant's appeal was pending before the Federal Court of Appeal, the IAD granted his sponsor's appeal and set aside the decision of the visa officer. In effect, the IAD, by setting aside the visa officer's decision, rendered the appellant's appeal moot since the decision which is the subject of the application for judicial review no longer exists. However, the Federal Court judge certified a question on an issue which has not been considered by the Federal Court of Appeal. Specifically the question reads:

> Does section 72 of the IRPA bar an application for judicial review by the applicant of a spousal application, while the sponsor exercises the rights of appeal pursuant to section 63 of the IRPA?

Both parties at the hearing submitted that it would be in the interest of justice that the Federal Court of Appeal answer the certified question.

It should be remembered that, on a family sponsorship application, the interest of the parties are congruent. Both the sponsor and the foreign national seek a reunification of the family. It would be illogical and detrimental to the objectives of the scheme to allow multiplicity of proceedings on the same issue, in different forms, to parties pursuing the same interest. It would also be detrimental to the administration of justice as it would open the door to conflict in decisions and fuel more litigation. This is precisely what Parliament intended to avoid. In addition, the appellant is not deprived of all remedies. He has other avenues such as an application to the Minister based on H&C considerations pursuant to s. 25 of IRPA. The appeal was dismissed for mootness and the court answered the certified question in the affirmative.

New Brunswick (Board of Management) v. Dunsmuir, [2008] 1 S.C.R. 190, *(sub nom. Dunsmuir v. New Brunswick)* [2008] S.C.J. No. 9, 372 N.R. 1, 69 Admin. L.R. (4th) 1, 2008 C.L.L.C. 220-020, D.T.E. 2008T-223, 329 N.B.R. (2d) 1, 170 L.A.C. (4th) 1, 291 D.L.R. (4th) 577, 64 C.C.E.L. (3d) 1, 2008 CarswellNB 124, 2008 CarswellNB 125, 2008 SCC 9 — The operation of three standards of review has not been without practical and theoretical difficulties; neither has it been free of criticism. One major problem lies in distinguishing between the patent unreasonableness standard and the reasonableness simpliciter standard. The difficulty in distinguishing between those standards contributes to the problem of choosing the right standard of review. An even greater problem lies in the application of the patent unreasonableness standard, which at times seems to require parties to accept an unreasonable decision.

Even if one could conceive of a situation in which a clearly or highly irrational decision were distinguishable from a merely irrational decision, it would be unpalatable to require parties to accept an irrational decision simply because, on a deferential standard, the irrationality of the decision is not clear enough. It is also inconsistent with the rule of law to retain an irrational decision. A simpler test is needed.

In judicial review, reasonableness is concerned mostly with the existence of justification, transparency and intelligibility within the decision-making process. But it is also concerned with whether the decision falls within a range of possible, acceptable outcomes which are defensible in respect of the facts and law. The move towards a single reasonableness standard does not pave the way for a more intrusive review by courts and does not represent a return to pre-*Southam* formalism. In this respect, the concept of deference, so central to judicial review in administrative law, has perhaps been insufficiently explored in the case law.

Deference is both an attitude of the court and a requirement of the law of judicial review. It does not mean that courts are subservient to the determinations of decision makers, or that courts must show blind reverence to their interpretations, or that they may be content to pay lip service to the concept of reasonableness review while in fact imposing their own view. Rather, deference imports respect for the decision-making process of adjudicative bodies with regard to both the facts and the law. The notion of deference "is rooted in part in a respect for governmental decisions to create administrative bodies with delegated powers." There are now only two standards, reasonableness and correctness. The process of judicial review involves two steps. First, courts ascertain whether the jurisprudence has already determined in a satisfactory manner the degree of deference to be accorded with regard to a particular category of question. Secondly, where the first inquiry proves unfruitful, courts must proceed to an analysis of the factors making it possible to identify the proper standard of review.

The existing approach to determining the appropriate standard of review has in the past commonly been referred to as "pragmatic and functional." In the future, it should simply be referred to as the "standard of review analysis." The analysis must be contextual. It is dependent on the application of a number of relevant factors, including: (1) the presence or absence of a privative clause; (2) the purpose of the tribunal as determined by interpretation of enabling legislation; (3) the nature of the question at issue; and (4) the expertise of the tribunal.

The existence of a privative or preclusive clause gives rise to a strong indication of review pursuant to the reasonableness standard. Where the question is one of fact, discretion or policy, as well as questions where the legal issues cannot be easily separated from the factual issues, a standard of reasonableness is appropriate. Where an administrative tribunal has developed particular expertise, a reasonableness test is applied. A question of law that is of "central importance to the legal system. . .and outside the. . .specialized area of expertise" of the administrative decision maker will always attract a correctness standard, while a question of law that does not rise to this level may be compatible with a reasonableness standard.

Padda v. Canada (Minister of Citizenship & Immigration), 2006 CarswellNat 2516, 2006 FC 995 — The applicants brought a motion for an extension of time within which to perfect their record in support of their application for leave and for judicial review. Rather than bringing their motion in writing pursuant to Rule 369 of the *Federal Court Rules*, as is the norm in immigration leave applications, the applicants elected to proceed orally, making their motion returnable at the general sittings. Such practice should be discouraged. To allow an applicant to obtain an oral hearing for an interlocutory motion in a leave application that is intended to be conducted entirely in writing appears antithetical to the statutory and regulatory objectives of efficiency and expediency. It could easily be abused by an unscrupulous applicant who could obtain an extended stay of removal pending determination of the application for leave by making his or her motion for extension of time returnable in the distant future. The registry should, as a rule, seek directions from the court with respect to any motion in an immigration leave application that is not brought in writing pursuant to Rule 369 of the *Federal Courts Rules*.

Logeswaren v. Canada (Minister of Citizenship & Immigration) (2004), 43 Imm. L.R. (3d) 225, 2004 FC 1374, 2004 CarswellNat 5644, 2004 CarswellNat 3571, [2004] F.C.J. No. 1659 — The court granted the Respondent Minister's motion for a reconsideration.

The Minister commenced proceedings to vacate the grant of refugee status. The Applicant filed a motion to dismiss the vacation application on the basis of *res judicata* — a previous motion to vacate having been dismissed.

The *res judicata* motion was dismissed by the Board. Leave to review that interlocutory motion was granted and the judicial review was heard on March 15, 2004.

The court rendered its decision on June 22, 2004 and concurred with the Board's conclusion as to the inapplicability of *res judicata*; however, the court referred the matter back to the Board for a redetermination to be made on the basis of Rule 56 of the IRB Rules.

Prior to the hearing by the court on March 15, 2004, the Board had held its hearing on the merits of the application to vacate. This event was not brought to the attention of the court despite the fact that counsel for the respondent had direct, personal knowledge that the hearing on the merits of the application to vacate had been held. On the same day as the judicial review hearing in this Court, but after the hearing had concluded, the applicant and his counsel received the Board's decision which granted the Minister's motion to vacate. This fact was also not brought to the court's attention until the Minister's motion to re-open. The requirement that the Board reconsider the matter under Rule 56 is irrelevant. Accordingly, the application for judicial review was dismissed.

The adversarial system cannot properly function unless counsel conduct themselves in a professional manner and unless courts are satisfied that counsel are doing so. Lawyers must be able to confidently assume that their colleagues will not act in a fashion designed to improperly take advantage of a situation. judges must be able to assume that the merits on which they are being asked to adjudicate are, indeed, the merits. If these principles are not adhered to, the whole administration of justice is called into question. The most important and primary consideration must be to avoid subjecting the integrity of the judicial process to abuse.

Lee v. Canada (Minister of Citizenship & Immigration) (2004), 34 Imm. L.R. (3d) 182, 2004 CarswellNat 1380, 2004 CarswellNat 924, 320 N.R. 184, 2004 FCA 143 — Where a visa officer refuses an application for permanent residence on re-determination after a previous decision was set aside by the Court, the visa officer is not obliged to specifically state or set out the differences between the two decisions.

Sarmis v. Canada (Minister of Citizenship & Immigration) (2004), 40 Imm. L.R. (3d) 111, 245 F.T.R. 312, 2004 CarswellNat 167, 2004 CarswellNat 2524, 2004 FC 110 — The applicants failed to file their own affidavits based on personal knowledge in support of their application for leave. They filed the affidavit of a paralegal who lacked personal knowledge of the matter.

The failure of an application to be supported by affidavits based on personal knowledge is not automatically fatal to an application for judicial review. The affidavit before the court was sufficient to establish the fact of the application and its rejection.

Ranganathan v. Canada (Minister of Citizenship & Immigration) (2003), 34 Imm. L.R. (3d) 302, 2003 CarswellNat 3722, 2003 CarswellNat 4418, 2003 FC 1367, [2003] F.C.J. No. 1741 — This was an application to challenge a decision of a panel of the Refugee Protection Division refusing to recuse a panel member.

The hearing before the Board occurred over 2 days. On the second day of the hearing the applicants agreed to proceed with a one member panel after being advised that the other panel member would be unable to attend that day. At this hearing, the member conducting the panel stated that he considered photographs tendered by the applicants not to be probative and engaged in extensive questioning of the witnesses called by the applicants. One month later, counsel for the applicants submitted a written motion in which he requested the member to remove himself due to an alleged reasonable apprehension of bias.

The applicants' counsel only brought the formal motion after having checked the case law and having sought the view of other counsel. While this may have been prudent it did not amount to raising the issue at the earliest opportunity. Counsel's failure to raise the issue of a reasonable apprehension of bias formally at the first opportunity was held to be an implied waiver of his right to raise the issue of an apprehension of bias.

Waraich v. Canada (Minister of Citizenship & Immigration), 33 Imm. L.R. (3d) 78, 2003 CarswellNat 4268, 2003 CarswellNat 2951, 2003 FC 1099 — This was a motion by an immigration consultant seeking leave to intervene in the judicial review application. The applicant applied for recognition as a Convention refugee and was rejected. The applicant applied for leave to judicially review the negative decision. The proposed intervener in his capacity as an immigration consultant and a citizen of Canada suggests that he has a juridical interest which clearly requires him to intervene in the present debate. Applicants for intervener status must have an interest of more than a jurisprudential nature. This application was rejected. Whatever decision the Court was going to give on the application, it could have no direct impact on the rights of the proposed intervener. The immigration consultant was also denied a status as *"amicus curiae"* because he failed to satisfy the court as to the nature of his expertise and how this expertise would be of assistance to the court. The application was dismissed.

Kalachnikov v. Canada (Minister of Citizenship & Immigration) (2003), 236 F.T.R. 142, 2003 CarswellNat 1950, 2003 FCT 777, 2003 CarswellNat 3436, [2003] F.C.J. No. 1016 — This is an application for an order of *mandamus* directing the respondent to process the application of the applicant and issue a final decision within 60 days.

Mandamus is a discretionary equitable remedy subject to the following conditions precedent:

1. There is a public duty to act.

2. This duty must be owed to the applicant.

3. There is a clear right to performance of that duty, in particular:

> (a) The applicant must have satisfied all conditions precedent giving rise to the duty;

> (b) There must have been a prior demand for performance of the duty, a reasonable time to comply with the demand and a subsequent refusal which can either be expressed or implied.

4. There must be no other adequate remedy.

5. The balance of convenience must favour the applicant.

If the applicant tends to rely on the fact that there has been an implied refusal to perform the duty due to an unreasonable delay, then the following conditions must be met:

1. The delay must have been longer than the nature of the process required.

2. The applicant and his counsel must not be responsible for the delay; and

3. The authority responsible for the delay must not have provided a satisfactory justification.

Prior jurisprudence is not particularly helpful except for the purposes of outlining the parameters in which the court has issued an order in the nature of *mandamus* where it has found an unusual delay. Based on the facts of this case *mandamus* issued.

The court declined to order costs, finding that special reasons as contemplated by Rule 22 of the *Federal Court Immigration and Refugee Protection Rules* have not been demonstrated.

Marshall v. R., 2002 CarswellNat 2901, 2002 CarswellNat 3965, 2002 FCT 1099 (T.D.) — The applicant applied to the court for an order restraining an adjudicator from continuing a hearing against the applicant until the action commenced by the applicant was heard and determined. The court concluded that it did not have jurisdiction to issue the order requested because no application for judicial review had been filed with the court. Section 18(1) of the *Federal Court Act* grants the Federal Court the jurisdiction to grant certain remedies, but subs. 18(3) requires that the application for judicial review be commenced. In the present motion, the motion for an interim injunction is made incidental to an action, not an application for judicial review. The court has jurisdiction to grant a stay pursuant to s. 18.2 of the *Federal Court Act*, but only if a judicial review application has been filed. Subsection 50(1) of the *Federal Court Act* gives the court jurisdiction to grant a stay, but only provides for stays in proceedings being conducted before the Federal Court. Accordingly, the motion for an injunction was dismissed.

Section 72(2)

Somodi v. Canada (Minister of Citizenship & Immigration) (2009), 82 Imm. L.R. (3d) 159, 311 D.L.R. (4th) 335, 395 N.R. 270, 2009 FCA 288, 2009 CarswellNat 3062, 2009 CarswellNat 5060 — See the *Somodi* summary under s. 72(1).

Canada (Minister of Citizenship & Immigration) v. Edwards, 2005 CarswellNat 1238, 2005 FCA 176 — The Minister appealed the decision of a motions judge granting the respondent a stay of a departure order. The motions judge had the requisite jurisdiction to entertain the stay motion and make an order disposing of that motion. Paragraph 72(2)(e) precludes the Court of Appeal from entertaining an appeal from that judgement without a certified question.

Mabrouki c. Canada (Ministre de la Citoyenneté & de l'Immigration), 2003 CarswellNat 3854, 2003 CarswellNat 2948, 2003 FC 1104, 242 F.T.R. 171 — A motions judge does not have jurisdiction to hear an appeal from a decision of a prothonotary which dismissed an application for an extension of time.

Dydyuk v. Canada (Minister of Citizenship & Immigration) (2003), 245 F.T.R. 161, 2003 CarswellNat 2807, 2003 FCT 717, 2003 CarswellNat 1687 — The applicant was seeking to review a negative determination of her refugee claim. Six days before the application for judicial review was to be heard in the Federal Court, a letter was sent by a person purporting to be counsel for the applicant requesting a short adjournment because counsel was unable to attend due to a family emergency. Counsel was overseas and would be returning on June 10, 2003, one day after the date scheduled for the judicial review application.

The request for an adjournment was refused. On February 17, 1993, the Trial Division issued a practice direction advising parties that scheduled trials and hearings would only be adjourned in exceptional cases. The practice direction advises that the Federal Court does not overbook its trial sittings. Adjournments, therefore, cause serious inconvenience and expense. It is therefore expected that all counsel will be able to proceed on the date fixed. Requests to adjourn must be made to the Associate Chief Justice and, unless made promptly after the fixing of a hearing date, will be considered only in the most exceptional circumstances.

Accordingly, the request for an adjournment was refused and the judicial application proceeded.

Yogalingam v. Canada (Minister of Citizenship & Immigration) (2003), 27 Imm. L.R. (3d) 198, 233 F.T.R. 74, 2003 CarswellNat 1175, 2003 FCT 540, 2003 CarswellNat 2696, [2003] F.C.J. No. 697 — The applicant sought an extension of time to file an application record. This motion was dismissed by the prothonotary and the applicant appealed. Section 72(2)(e) of the IRPA removes jurisdiction to hear an appeal of the prothonotary's decision.

Canada (Attorney General) v. Hennelly (1999), 244 N.R. 399, 167 F.T.R. 158 (note), [1999] F.C.J. No. 846, 1999 CarswellNat 967 (C.A.) — The proper test for granting an extension of time is whether the applicant has demonstrated:

  1. a continuing intention to pursue his or her application;

  2. that the application has some merit;

  3. that no prejudice to the respondent arises from the delay; and

  4. that a reasonable explanation for delay exists

Any determination of whether or not the applicant's explanation justifies the granting of the necessary extension of time will turn on the fact of each particular case.

73. Right of Minister — The Minister may make an application for leave to commence an application for judicial review with respect to any decision of the Refugee Appeal Division, whether or not the Minister took part in the proceedings before the Refugee Protection Division or Refugee Appeal Division.

74. Judicial review — Judicial review is subject to the following provisions:

(a) the judge who grants leave shall fix the day and place for the hearing of the application;

(b) the hearing shall be no sooner than 30 days and no later than 90 days after leave was granted, unless the parties agree to an earlier day;

(c) the judge shall dispose of the application without delay and in a summary way; and

(d) subject to section 87.01, an appeal to the Federal Court of Appeal may be made only if, in rendering judgment, the judge certifies that a serious question of general importance is involved and states the question.

2015, c. 20, s. 53

Case Law

Felipa v. Canada (Minister of Citizenship & Immigration) (2011), 2 Imm. L.R. (4th) 177, 340 D.L.R. (4th) 227, 422 N.R. 288, 32 Admin. L.R. (5th) 1, 2011 FCA 272, 2011 CarswellNat 3921, 2011 CarswellNat 6334, [2012] 1 F.C.R. 3 — The Chief Justice does not have the authority under subs. 10(1.1) of the *Federal Courts Act* to request that a retired judge of a superior court act as a deputy judge of the Federal Court after attaining the age of 75.

Ismail v. Canada (Minister of Citizenship & Immigration) (2006), 58 Imm. L.R. (3d) 179, 358 N.R. 160, 2006 CarswellNat 4247, 2006 FCA 396 — The statutory prohibition on appeals in immigration matters, unless a question is certified pursuant to para. 74(d) of the IRPA, would be meaningless if it could be circumvented simply by filing a motion under Rule 397 or 399 (Federal Court Rules).

Lazareva v. Canada (Minister of Citizenship & Immigration) (2005), 335 N.R. 21, 2005 CarswellNat 1240, 2005 FCA 181 — This was the second attempt in two days by the Minister to appeal a decision of the Federal Court in the absence of a certified question. It is not open to the court to disregard the provisions of the *Immigration and Refugee Protection Act* that preclude an appeal or an appeal without a certified question. Accordingly, the appeal was quashed and costs were awarded to the respondent.

Canada (Solicitor General) v. Subhaschandran, 2005 FCA 27, 2005 CarswellNat 1129, [2005] F.C.J. No. 107, (sub nom. *Subhaschandran v. Canada (Solicitor General)*) 249 D.L.R. (4th) 269, 331 N.R. 182, 2005 CarswellNat 184 — The respondents brought a motion for a stay of the order for their deportation. At the conclusion of the argument, the motions judge adjourned the motion. The Minister launched a motion for reconsideration which was dismissed. The motions judge issued a clarification and ordered that the applicants not be removed from Canada pending a determination of their motion for a stay.

It is true that, generally, interlocutory orders including adjournments cannot be appealed. An exception to this rule, however, occurs where a judge refuses to exercise his jurisdiction and deal with the case. In the present case, the motions Judge, by adjourning the motion, has deprived the parties of ever having a decision on the stay motion. This amounts to a refusal to exercise his jurisdiction and a remedy must be available.

Accordingly, the Court of Appeal took jurisdiction despite the fact that there was no serious question certified by the motions judge, allowed the appeal, set aside the order of the motions judge and remitted the matter back to the motions judge to make a decision on the application for a stay.

Li v. Canada (Minister of Citizenship & Immigration) (2004), 40 Imm. L.R. (3d) 161, 2004 CarswellNat 2338, 2004 CarswellNat 3952, 2004 FCA 267, 327 N.R. 253, [2004] F.C.J. No. 1264; leave to appeal refused (2004), 2004 CarswellNat 4253, 2004 CarswellNat 4254 (S.C.C.) — The IRB applied to intervene in an appeal before the Federal Court of Appeal. The Board intended to address a substantive issue raised in the appeal, namely the standard of proof under s. 97 of IRPA and to add fresh evidence with respect to this issue. Where the parent or authorizing statute is silent as to the role or status of the tribunal in appeal or review proceedings, the tribunal is confined to the issue of its jurisdiction to make the order in question. Even where the right to appear is given by statute, the Supreme Court of Canada has held that the administrative tribunal's role in such a situation is limited to an explanatory role with reference to the record and to making representations relating to jurisdiction. In this case, therefore, the Board was denied permission to intervene.

Khalil v. R. (2004), 252 F.T.R. 292, 2004 CarswellNat 3067, 2004 CarswellNat 1451, 2004 FC 732 — The standard of review applicable to appeals from a prothonotary requires that unless the decision is clearly wrong, insofar as it was based upon a wrong legal principle or a misapprehension of the facts, involved the misuse of judicial discretion, or raised issues vital to the final disposition of the action, the decision should remain undisturbed on appeal. The Court decided that a *de novo* standard should apply when the decision could terminate the plaintiff's action. It was that standard which was applied in this case.

The plaintiffs have a right to frame their action. It is not open to the defendant to impute a different manner of proceeding, that is, an application for judicial review, when the plaintiffs themselves did not choose that forum.

Joseph v. Canada (Minister of Citizenship & Immigration), 2004 FC 682, 2004 CarswellNat 3074, 2004 CarswellNat 1347, [2004] F.C.J. No. 838 — Any lack of fairness in the hearing process generally voids a hearing and requires that a new hearing be held unless the demerits of the claim are such that the remission of the claim would be hopeless.

Amado-Cordeiro v. Canada (Minister of Citizenship & Immigration) (2004), 36 Imm. L.R. (3d) 35, 2004 CarswellNat 1515, 2004 CarswellNat 742, 2004 FCA 120, 320 N.R. 319 — The Court of Appeal will not overrule its own prior decisions in the absence of manifest error.

Zazai v. Canada (Minister of Citizenship & Immigration) (2004), 36 Imm. L.R. (3d) 167, 2004 CarswellNat 544, 318 N.R. 365, 2004 FCA 89, 2004 CarswellNat 4792, (sub nom. *Canada (Minister of Citizenship & Immigration) v. Zazai)* 247 F.T.R. 320 (note) — The certification of a question of general importance allows for an appeal from the judgement of the Trial Division which would otherwise not be permitted. Such an appeal does not confine the court to answering the stated question or issues directly related to it. All issues raised by the appeal may be considered.

The threshold for certifying a question is this: is there a serious question of general importance which would be dispositive of an appeal? The corollary of the fact that a question must be dispositive of the appeal is that it must be a question which has been raised and dealt with in the decision below. In this case, the certified question was not dealt with by the applications judge, so the court remitted the matter for a decision by a Federal Court judge.

75. (1) Rules — **Subject to the approval of the Governor in Council, the rules committee established under section 45.1 of the *Federal Courts Act* may make rules governing the practice and procedure in relation to applications for leave to commence an application for judicial review, for judicial review and for appeals. The rules are binding despite any rule or practice that would otherwise apply.**

(2) Inconsistencies — **In the event of an inconsistency between this Division and any provision of the *Federal Courts Act*, this Division prevails to the extent of the inconsistency.**

2002, c. 8, s. 194(b)(i), (c)

DIVISION 9 — CERTIFICATES AND PROTECTION OF INFORMATION
[Heading amended 2008, c. 3, s. 4.]

Interpretation
[Heading amended 2005, c. 10, s. 34(1)(o)(i); 2008, c. 3, s. 4.]

Editor's Note

[Included below are the annotations of decisions taken under section 40.1 of the former Immigration Act. While the security provisions of the former Act are differently worded than the security provisions of IRPA, it is thought that these annotations may still be of assistance.]

Case Law

Section 40.1(1) of the Former Act

Canada (Minister of Citizenship & Immigration) v. Singh (I.) (1998), 44 Imm. L.R. (2d) 309, 151 F.T.R. 101 — This was a decision on the merits under para. 40.1(4)(d) dealing with whether a certificate filed by the applicants in relation to the respondent was reasonable. In s. 40.1 proceedings, where there are reasonable grounds to believe that a person is a member of an organization, there must also be reasonable grounds to believe that the organization is engaged in subversion or terrorism. Standard of proof is on a balance of probabilities.

In his testimony, a supervisor with the counter-terrorist branch of CSIS expressed the opinion that terrorism included politically motivated violence often with an indiscriminate target. A politically motivated organization, which sets off bombs killing innocent people or which engages in assassinations, is an organization engaged in terrorism.

The court concluded that the term "member" incorporated into s. 40.1 by reference to s. 19 was to be interpreted broadly. The context of this provision in immigration legislation is public safety and national security, the most serious concerns of government. Terrorist organizations do not issue membership cards, there is no formal test for membership and members are therefore not easily identifiable. In this context, it is obvious that Parliament intended that the term "member" be given an unrestricted and broad interpretation.

Ahani v. R. (1996), 37 C.R.R. (2d) 181, 201 N.R. 233, 119 F.T.R. 80 (note) (C.A.); leave to appeal to S.C.C. refused [1997] 2 S.C.R. v, 44 C.R.R. (2d) 376 (note), 223 N.R. 72 (note) — The court adopted the reasons of the trial judge in this matter and affirmed her decision.

Between a determination by the designated judge that the s. 40.1 certificate is reasonable and a possible removal of the person concerned to the country where he or she fears persecution, there must be a second opinion formed by the Minister of Immigration, based on a determination that the person constitutes "a danger to the public in Canada," or "a danger to the security of Canada." Such a determination will have to be made in accordance with the principles of fundamental justice and will be subject to judicial review.

Section 40.1 is in no way akin to a criminal proceeding. In a s. 40.1 proceeding there exists an alien who may lose the qualified right to stay in Canada that he or she gained by being given refugee status, but whose liberty will not then be otherwise impeded. While it is true that the filing of the certificate has the immediate unfortunate effect of leading to the arrest and detention of the person concerned, it must not be forgotten that this detention is not imposed as a punishment, but rather as a means of providing preventative protection to the Canadian public. This detention is not arbitrary or excessive. The test for the issuance of the certificate is the reasoned opinion of two Ministers based on security information. The scheme provides for the obligatory judicial scrutiny of the reasonableness of those opinions within an acceptably short period of time; further, at any time, the person can agree to leave the country and thereby end his or her detention. Finally, this procedure deals with a type or class of individual who is believed to be associated with terrorism.

Baroud, Re (1995), 98 F.T.R. 99 — The purpose of subparagraphs 19(1)(f)(ii) and (iii) of the *Immigration Act*, in very general terms, is to prevent the arrival of persons considered to be a danger to Canadian society. The term terrorism must therefore receive an unrestrictive interpretation and will unavoidably include the political connotations which it entails. In the light of the evidence submitted to the court, there existed reasonable grounds to believe that the applicant was described in s. 19(1)(f)(iii).

Section 40.1(4) of the Former Act

Suresh, Re (1997), 40 Imm. L.R. (2d) 247, 140 F.T.R. 88 — These were the reasons of the court determining that reasonable grounds existed for the Solicitor General and the Minister of Employment and Immigration to have issued a certificate pursuant to s. 40.1 of the *Immigration Act*. It was not necessary to define the content of the term "terrorist" or "terrorist act" as it is referred to in s. 19. The Act "must be seen through the eyes of a Canadian for the purposes of a s. 40.1 application." The term "terrorism or terrorist act" must receive a wide and unrestricted interpretation for the purposes of a s. 40.1 application.

Membership in an organization cannot and should not be narrowly interpreted when it involves the issue of Canada's national security. Membership does not only refer to persons who have engaged in or who might engage in terrorist activities. The court looked at the nature of the applicant's activities in support of the organization that he was supposed to be a member of and his own admission of his close association with that organization.

Farahi-Mahdavieh, Re (1993), 19 Imm. L.R. (2d) 222, 63 F.T.R. 120 — The applicant illegally entered Canada from the United States at the border near Vancouver. While preparing to fly to Toronto, she was stopped and detained by immigration officials acting under a certificate issued under s. 40.1(1) and (2) of the *Immigration Act*. The certificate stated that the applicant was a member of an inadmissible class described in s. 19(1)(g).

The court must determine whether on the basis of the evidence and information available, the certificate is reasonable when it identifies the applicant as a person who, there is reasonable grounds to believe, will engage in acts of violence that would or might endanger the lives or safety of persons in Canada, or is a member of, or likely to participate in the unlawful activities of, an organization that is likely to engage in such acts of violence (s. 19(1)(g)).

As the person named in such a certificate is subject to mandatory detention, a higher standard of reasonableness should be applied in reviewing this type of administrative action. Actual membership in an organization described in s. 19(1)(g) is not required. It is sufficient to meet the statutory requirement that the evidence show that there are reasonable grounds to believe that the person is a member of such an organization. The test is the one understood in *Canada (Attorney General) v. Jolly*, [1975] F.C. 216 (C.A.). In this case the court found the certificate to be reasonable.

[Editor's note: Although the sections in question have been amended, the principles in this case may still be applicable.]

Section 40.1(9) of the Former Act

Baroud v. Canada (Minister of Citizenship & Immigration) (1995), 121 D.L.R. (4th) 308, 22 O.R. (3d) 255, 77 O.A.C. 26, 26 C.R.R. (2d) 318 (C.A.) — The appellant, a stateless refugee claimant who had been detained pursuant to a certificate issued under s. 40.1, applied for release from detention by means of a writ of *habeas corpus* with *certiorari* in aid. The appellant was a Palestinian who entered Canada and claimed refugee status in 1991. About 3 years later the Minister of Employment and Immigration and the Solicitor General of Canada certified their belief that the appellant was not admissible to Canada under s. 19(1)(f) of the *Immigration Act*. The appellant was detained in June, 1994 and remained in detention when this application was heard.

The Federal Court trial division has no jurisdiction to grant *habeas corpus*. The hearing, available under s. 40.1, would take place approximately the same time as the argument on the return of *habeas corpus* and, accordingly, the Federal Court trial procedure was an adequate and effective alternative remedy which provided relief to the appellant in a forum where proceedings relating to the appellant's detention were in progress. The mandatory language of s. 10 of the *Charter* was subject to s. 1 of the *Charter*. Once there is a finding that an alternative remedy is equally effective, it is axiomatic that the denial of the right to the issuance of a writ of *habeas corpus* is a justifiable limit. Accordingly, the *habeas corpus* application was dismissed.

Author's Note

[Included below are the annotations of decisions taken under the former Division 9 of Part I of the IRPA which was replaced on March 5, 2008, as a result of the Supreme Court of Canada's decision in Charkaoui, Re, *[2007] S.C.J. No. 9, that concluded there were two defects in the legislation that were inconsistent with the Charter.]*

Case Law

Former Section 78

Charkaoui, Re, [2007] 1 S.C.R. 350, 59 Imm. L.R. (3d) 1, 54 Admin. L.R. (4th) 1, 44 C.R. (6th) 1, 358 N.R. 1, 276 D.L.R. (4th) 594, 2007 CarswellNat 325, 2007 SCC 9, [2007] S.C.J. No. 9 — Mr. Charkaoui is a permanent resident, while Messrs. Harkat and Almrei are foreign nationals who had been recognized as Convention refugees. All were living in Canada when they were arrested and detained. At the time of the decisions on appeal, all had been detained for some time — since 2003, 2002 and 2001 respectively. In 2001, a judge of the Federal Court determined Mr. Almrei's certificate to be reasonable; another determined Mr. Harkat's certificate to be reasonable in 2005. The reasonableness of Mr. Charkaoui's certificate had not yet been determined. Messrs. Charkaoui and Harkat were released on conditions in 2005 and 2006 respectively, but Mr. Harkat has been advised that he will be deported to Algeria, which he is contesting in other proceedings. Mr. Almrei remains in detention. In all three cases, the detentions were based on allegations that the individuals constituted a threat to the security of Canada by reason of involvement in terrorist activities. In the course of their detentions, all three appellants challenged, unsuccessfully, the constitutionality of the IRPA's certificate scheme and detention review processes.

The IRPA's procedure for determining whether a certificate is reasonable does not conform to the principles of fundamental justice as embodied in s. 7 of the *Charter*. The same conclusion necessarily applies to the detention review procedures under ss. 83 and 84 of the IRPA. The secrecy required by the scheme denies the named person the opportunity to know the case put against him or her, and hence to challenge the government's case. This, in turn, undermines the judge's ability to come to a decision based on all the relevant facts and law. Despite the best efforts of judges of the Federal Court to breathe judicial life into the IRPA procedure, it fails to assure the fair hearing that s. 7 of the *Charter* requires before the state deprives a person of life, liberty or security of the person.

While the deportation of a non-citizen in the immigration context may not in *itself* engage s. 7 of the *Charter*, some features associated with deportation, such as detention in the course of the certificate process or the prospect of deportation to torture, may do so.

The IRPA's procedures for determining whether a certificate is reasonable and for detention cannot be justified as minimal impairments of the individual's right to a judicial determination on the facts and the law and right to know and meet the case. Mechanisms developed in Canada and abroad illustrate that the government can do more to protect the individual while keeping critical information confidential than it has done in the IRPA. Precisely what more should be done is a matter for Parliament to decide.

Permanent residents, who pose a danger to national security, are also meant to be removed expeditiously. If this objective can be pursued while providing permanent residents with a mandatory detention review within 48 hours, then how can a denial of review for foreign nationals for 120 days after the certificate is confirmed be considered a minimal impairment? The lack of timely review of the detention of foreign nationals violates s. 9 and s. 10(c) and cannot be saved by s. 1.

Extended periods of detention under the certificate provisions of the IRPA do not violate ss. 7 and 12 of the *Charter* if accompanied by a process that provides regular opportunities for review of detention, taking into account all relevant factors, including the following: reasons for detention; length of detention; reasons for the delay in deportation; anticipated future length of detentions; availability of alternatives to detention.

The IRPA, interpreted in conformity with the *Charter*, permits robust ongoing judicial review of the continued need for, and justice of, the detainee's detention pending deportation. On this basis, extended periods of detention pending deportation under the certificate provisions of the IRPA do not violate s. 7 or s. 12 of the *Charter*, provided that reviewing courts adhere to the guidelines set out above. Thus, the IRPA procedure itself is not unconstitutional on this ground. However, this does not preclude the possibility of a judge concluding at a certain point that a particular detention constitutes cruel and unusual treatment or is inconsistent with the principles of fundamental justice, and therefore, infringes the *Charter* in a manner that is remediable under s. 24(1) of the *Charter*.

Mr. Charkaoui argued that the IRPA certificate scheme discriminated against non-citizens, contrary to s. 15(1) of the *Charter*. However, s. 6 of the *Charter* specifically allows for different treatment of citizens and non-citizens in deportation matters: only citizens are accorded the right to enter, remain or leave Canada (s. 6(1)). A deportation scheme that applies to non-citizens, but not to citizens, does not, for that reason alone, violate s. 15 of the *Charter*.

The scheme set up under Division 9 of Pt.1 of the IRPA suffers from two defects that are inconsistent with the *Charter*. The first is that s. 78(g) allows for the use of evidence that is never disclosed to the named person without providing adequate measures to compensate for this non-disclosure and the constitutional problems it causes. It is clear from approaches adopted in other democracies, and in Canada itself in other security situations, that solutions can be devised that protect confidential security information and at the same time are less intrusive on the person's rights. It follows that the IRPA's procedure for judicial confirmation of certificates and review of detention violates s. 7 of the *Charter* and has not been shown to be justified under s. 1 of the *Charter*.

In order to give Parliament time to amend the law, the Supreme Court of Canada suspended its declaration for one year from the date of its judgment. After one year, the certificates of any individuals whose certificates have been deemed reasonable will lose the "reasonable" status that has been conferred on them, and it will be open to them to apply to have the certificates quashed. If the government intends to employ a certificate after the one-year delay, it will need to seek a fresh determination of reasonableness under the new process devised by Parliament. Any detention review occurring after the delay will be subject to the new process.

The second defect is found in s. 84(2) of the IRPA, which denies a prompt hearing to foreign nationals by imposing a 120-day embargo, after confirmation of the certificate, on applications for release. Section 84(2) was struck and "foreign nationals" was read into s. 83 and the words "until a determination is made under subs. 80(1)" were struck from s. 83(2).

Harkat, Re (2004), 48 Imm. L.R. (3d) 211, 2004 CarswellNat 5369, 2004 CarswellNat 4688, 259 F.T.R. 98 (Eng.), 2004 FC 1717, [2004] F.C.J. No. 2101 — The Federal Court is not a court of general or inherent jurisdiction. It is a statutory court, constituted pursuant to Parliament's authority under s. 101 of the *Constitution Act*, 1867. Section 3 of the *Federal Courts Act* provides that the court is a court of law, equity, and admiralty and a superior court of record having civil and criminal jurisdiction. The designation of the Federal Court, as a superior court, has been held to confer no jurisdiction by itself. The Federal Court can only exercise those powers that are given to it by Parliament.

A power may be conferred by implication to the extent that the existence and exercise of such power is necessary for the court to properly and fully exercise the jurisdiction expressly conferred upon it. The evidence does not establish that the appointment of an *amicus curiae* is necessary in order for the court to exercise its responsibility under ss. 78 and 80.

In security proceedings, the court is obliged to isolate the facts relied upon to support the security certificate and then review such evidence with intense scrutiny and weigh the evidence with an eye to the quality and number of sources of information. Such an exercise will require the court to consider the potential for error caused by a number of factors including misidentification, mistake, misdirection, incompetence and malevolence.

The court denied the applicant's request for an *amicus curiae* to assist the court.

Harkat, Re (2003), 27 Imm. L.R. (3d) 47, 231 F.T.R. 19, 2003 CarswellNat 556, 2003 FCT 285, 2003 CarswellNat 3392, [2003] F.C.J. No. 400 — This proceeding was instituted by the Solicitor General of Canada and the Minister of Citizenship and Immigration for a determination as to whether the certificate signed by them, stating that Mohamed Harkat is inadmissible to Canada under s. 34 of the IRPA, was reasonable. Mr. Harkat made a motion for an order directing the disclosure of relevant information in order to make full answer in defence. In the absence of a judicial determination, a disclosure of information put before the judge would be injurious to national security or the safety of any person. The information or evidence put before the judge should be disclosed to the subject of the certificate. The right of the subject of the certificate to be reasonably informed of the circumstances, giving rise to the certificate, is subject to the restriction that the disclosure would be injurious to national security or the safety of any person. Criminal law principles as articulated in Stinchcombe are not applicable. The Court approved of the statement of Lord Denning in *R. v. Secretary of State for the Home Department*, [1977] 3 All. E.R. 452 (Eng. C.A.); affirmed [1977] 1 W.L.R. 789 (Eng. H.L.): "The information supplied to the Home Secretary by the Security Service is, and must be, highly confidential. The public interest in the security of the realm is so great that the sources of information must not be disclosed, nor should the nature of the information itself be disclosed, if there is any risk that it would lead to the sources being discovered. The reason is because, in this very secretive field, our enemies might try to eliminate the source of information."

In security matters, there is a requirement to not only protect the identity of human sources of information but to recognize that the following types of information might require to be protected, with due regard, of course, to the administration of justice and more particularly to the openness of proceedings: (1) information pertaining to the identity of targets of surveillance whether they be individuals or groups; (2) the technical means and sources of surveillance; (3) the methods of operation of the service; (4) the identity of certain members of the service; (5) the telecommunications and cypher systems; (6) the fact that a surveillance is being, or is not being, carried out. Evidence which of itself might not be of any particular use in actually identifying the threat might nevertheless require to be protected if the divulging of the fact that CSIS is in possession of such information would alert the targeted organization to the fact that it is subject to electronic surveillance or to a wiretap or to a leak from some human source within the organization. An informed reader of information, that is a person who is both knowledgeable regarding security matters and a member of, or associated with a group which constitutes a threat or potential threat to the security of Canada, will be quite familiar with the minute details of its organization and of the ramifications of its operations. As a result, such an informed reader may, by fitting a piece of apparently innocuous information into the general picture, be in a position to arrive at some damaging deductions regarding the investigation being conducted by CSIS. The target or targeted group might for instance be in a position to determine: (1) the duration, scope, intensity and degree of success or lack of success of an investigation; (2) the investigative techniques of the service; (3) the typographic and teleprinter systems employed by this service; (4) internal security procedures; (5) the nature and content of other classified documents; (6) the identities of service personnel or other persons involved in an investigation.

Former Section 80(1)

Harkat, Re (2005), 45 Imm. L.R. (3d) 65, 2005 FC 393, 2005 CarswellNat 737, [2005] F.C.J. No. 481 — The court decided that the security certificate in this case was reasonable. Courts both here and abroad have recognized the need for security intelligence information to be kept secret in order to protect national security. The need to preserve the secrecy of security information flows from the fact that security intelligence investigations are directed towards future events. They attempt to predict future events by discovering from past and present events patterns of occurrences and relationships. This requires piecing together bits of information that may, at first, not appear to be related.

A group or organization with hostile intentions has an ongoing existence with a continuity of operations. A security intelligence investigation does not end with the detention or apprehension of one member, rather investigations are long range and ongoing. This is one of the principal factors that distinguishes intelligence investigations from criminal investigations. Furthermore, there is no completed offence to provide a framework for the investigation. Criminal law principles and policies do not apply to security certificate proceedings.

When security information is disclosed it must be assumed that the information will reach persons who have knowledge about the suspect of an investigation and his activities. In the hands of an informed reader, unrelated pieces of information can provide an insight into the scope or progress of an ongoing intelligence operation. Equally, disclosure of the fact that certain information is not known by the authorities may allow an informed reader to learn about subjects of investigation, methods of investigation, sources of information or that certain activities are not under investigation.

The designated judge is responsible to ensure the confidentiality of the information upon which the security certificate is based and of any other evidence provided to the judge which disclosure would be injurious to national security or the safety of any person. This obligation and its companion obligation to provide a summary to the person concerned, reflect the tension between the democratic requirement of open court proceedings and the equally compelling necessity of keeping security information secret.

If confidential information is provided by a human source, some relevant inquiries and areas for examination by the court include matters such as the origin and length of the relationship between the service and the human source, whether the source was paid for the information, what is known about the source's motive for providing information, whether the source has provided information about other persons and if so, particulars of that, the extent to which information provided by the source has been corroborated, the citizenship/immigration status of the source and whether that status has changed throughout the source's relationship with the service, whether the source has been subject to any form of pressure to provide information, if so, why and by whom, whether the source was or is under investigation by the service or any other intelligence agency or police force, whether the source has a criminal record or any outstanding criminal charges, the nature of any relationship between the source and the subject of the investigation, whether there is any known or inferred motive for the source to provide false information.

If any confidential information is provided from another agency, some relevant inquiries are: the manner in which the service assesses the reliability of information, the extent to which the information is corroborated, is there any suggestion the agency may have a motive for colouring the information provided, what is the human rights record of the agency and the agency's home country, how does the foreign agency itself assess the reliability of the information it has provided, and is the agency a conduit for information originating from a less reliable agent.

If confidential information is provided through technical sources, relevant inquiries may include: the accuracy of any document that records intercepted information, the accuracy of any translation, the objectivity or bias of any summary made of the intercepted information, and how the parties to any conversation are identified.

Reasons delivered in security intelligence cases cannot fully justify and explain a result publicly when the evidence the court relies upon cannot be disclosed.

Former Section 82(1)

Charkaoui, Re, 2005 CarswellNat 410, 2005 CarswellNat 5111, 2005 FC 258 — This judgment has to do with the fourth review of the detention of Mr. Charkaoui that is provided for in s. 83(2). The court decided that the phrase "danger to national security" had the same meaning as the phrase "danger to the security of Canada," the meaning of which was discussed in *Suresh v. Canada (Minister of Citizenship & Immigration)*, [2002] 1 S.C.R. 3 at para. 90. The other phrase in subs. 83(3) "danger. . .to the safety of any person" includes awareness of danger before the terrorist act occurs. It applies to more than persons who have been convicted of a serious offence. Danger to national security or the safety of any person have in common the fact that Parliament has asked the designated judge, when considering the release of the person concerned, to analyse the evidence and consider whether either of these two dangers still exist. The wording of the section suggests that a danger to national security or the safety of any person may exist at one moment and not at another. There is a possibility the danger may be imminent but subsequently neutralized. The other phrase used in s. 83 is the phrase "unlikely to appear at a proceeding or for removal." This phrase indicates that Parliament intended a degree of probability to be taken into account by the designated judge when weighing the evidence.

In considering a conditional release, the designated judge must be satisfied, on reasonable grounds, that the person concerned is not a danger to national security or the safety of any person. If there is a danger, the judge cannot consider release, even with exceptional conditions.

When the Ministers signed the warrant for the arrest and detention of Mr. Charkaoui, they did so not in order to lay charges or eventually secure a conviction, but to make an arrest and detention that would prevent events that might occur. This tool, given to the Ministers by Parliament pursuant to subs. 82(1), is intended to "maintain the security of Canadian society" — one of the objectives of immigration as set out in para. 3(1)(h).

Detention reviews involve questions of fact peculiar to each situation. In the case at bar, the imprisonment, the passage of time, the media attention to the proceedings, the presence of the family, the community support, and the testimony of the person concerned are examples of situations to be taken into account in assessing whether a danger still exists or whether the person concerned will likely appear at a proceeding or for removal.

The court set terms for Mr. Charkaoui's release.

Former Section 83

Jaballah v. Canada (Attorney General), [2005] O.J. No. 3681, 258 D.L.R. (4th) 161, 49 Imm. L.R. (3d) 305, 2005 CarswellOnt 3869 (S.C.J.) — The applicant sought declaratory and other just and appropriate relief because, in his submission, his continued detention pursuant to ss. 82 to 85 of the IRPA, which provide for the automatic and mandatory detention of a foreign national subject to a security certificate issued under s. 77 and which prohibit any possibility of review of the need to detain the foreign national until the security certificate is upheld and the person is not removed within the next 120 days, was unconstitutional. The Ontario Superior Court of Justice refused to deal with the *habeas corpus* application as it could lead to a decision on the constitutional validity of any impugned provisions of the IRPA that is inconsistent with any decisions of the Federal Court dealing with the same, or similar, issues. The Federal Court has the expertise and experience that is necessary to develop a coherent body of law on these constitutional issues. The Ontario Superior Court should defer to that expertise and experience where the constitutionality of the IRPA is at issue, since the danger of inconsistent decisions between the Ontario Superior Court and the Federal Court must be avoided as any such inconsistencies are not in the public interest and may undermine the public confidence in the administration of justice.

Zündel, Re (2004), 39 Imm. L.R. (3d) 271, 2004 CarswellNat 66, 2004 CarswellNat 439, 2004 FC 86, 245 F.T.R. 61 — The Minister of Citizenship and the Solicitor General signed a certificate stating that the respondent was inadmissible on grounds of security. A warrant for the respondent's arrest was issued and, in this case, the judge sitting as a designated judge pursuant to s. 76 and subs. 83(1) was reviewing the continued detention of the respondent.

The grounds to continue detention are much narrower than the grounds of inadmissibility. Inadmissibility covers more than security and includes such grounds as human rights violations or criminality. The test for continued detention requires the designated judge to consider whether the person is a danger to national security or the safety of any person and whether the person is unlikely to appear at a proceeding for removal. The onus is on the Ministers to prove that the permanent resident presents a danger. The standard of proof is "a *bona fide* belief in a serious possibility based on credible evidence."

A person constitutes a danger to the security of Canada if he or she poses a serious threat the security of Canada, whether direct or indirect, and one must bear in mind the fact that the security of one country is often dependent on the security of other nations. The threat must be serious in the sense that it must be grounded on objectively reasonable suspicion based on evidence and in the sense that the threat and harm must be substantial rather than negligible.

The court found that the threat to national security in this case was sufficient to justify the respondent's detention.

Former Section 84(2)

Harkat v. Canada (Minister of Citizenship & Immigration), 2006 CarswellNat 1310, 2006 CarswellNat 2434, 2006 FC 628 — The applicant applied to the court for release from incarceration following a determination that a security certificate signed by the Minister of Citizenship and Immigration and the Solicitor General of Canada was reasonable. The certificate stated that the applicant, a foreign national, was inadmissible to Canada on grounds of security because there were reasonable grounds to believe that he has engaged in terrorism by supporting terrorist activities.

The applicant established a material or substantial change of circumstances since his previous application. The applicant also met the onus placed upon him by subs. 84(2) of the Act, to satisfy the court that he would not be removed from Canada within a reasonable time and that his release would not pose a danger to national security or to the safety of any person.

The court concluded that if the delay in appointing a delegate and the resultant delay in considering whether the applicant may be removed from Canada were known in December of 2005, the previous decision of the Federal Court made by Mr. Justice Lemieux may well have been different. Mr. Justice Lemieux set out seven factors that led him to conclude that the applicant had not discharged the onus upon him to satisfy the court that he would not be removed in a reasonable time. The unexpected delay in the appointment of the Minister's delegate, and the consequent failure of the delegate to begin to consider his decision, are facts that are inconsistent with Justice Lemieux's conclusions that the authorities were "proceeding expeditiously in this matter" and that the Minister's delegate's decision is pending.

The court also concluded that no cogent evidence of imminent removal had been put before it. Instead, the court pointed out that the advice from the Canadian Border Services Agency to the applicant's counsel was that the delegate's decision would not be made within the time originally contemplated.

Finally, the court concluded it would be erroneous to reject the applicant's application for release if there were conditions that, on a balance of probabilities, would neutralize or contain the danger posed by his release. In that circumstance, his continued incarceration could not be justified because of Canada's respect for human and civil rights, and the values protected by our *Charter*.

In considering whether there were terms and conditions that would neutralize and contain the danger posed by the applicant's release, the court considered the need for terms and conditions to be specific and tailored to the applicant's precise circumstances. These terms and conditions had to be designed to prevent his involvement in any activity that commits, encourages, facilitates, assists or instigates an act of terrorism or any similar activity. The terms and conditions had to be proportionate to the risk posed by the applicant.

The applicant, having satisfied the court that there had been a material or substantive change of circumstance since his previous application, that he would not be removed from Canada within a reasonable time and that his release would not pose a danger to national security or the safety of any person, was ordered released.

Canada (Minister of Citizenship & Immigration) v. Mahjoub (2005), 270 F.T.R. 101, 2005 CarswellNat 3933, 2005 FC 1596 — The applicant sought to be released from detention. The presence of sureties and the imposition of conditions would not be sufficient to neutralize the danger posed by the release of the applicant. The applicant did not satisfy the court he could be trusted to abide by those conditions. Furthermore, the medical evidence did not support that the applicant would comply with the conditions and the sureties did not know the applicant sufficiently well to have the ability to control his actions.

Almrei v. Canada (Attorney General) (2005), 50 Imm. L.R. (3d) 310, 2005 CarswellOnt 6822 ((S.C.J.)) — There is a long line of authority in Ontario's Superior Court and in the Ontario Court of Appeal that holds that the Ontario courts should decline to assume jurisdiction in matters relating to immigration, except in the rarest of cases, because of the expertise and experience that the Federal Court possesses in immigration matters. The court issued a stay of the applicant's application for a writ of *habeas corpus* and *certiorari* and other declaratory relief pertaining to his conditions of detention.

Almrei v. Canada (Minister of Citizenship & Immigration) (2005), 50 Imm. L.R. (3d) 160, 270 F.T.R. 1, [2005] F.C.J. No. 1994, 2005 CarswellNat 4022, 2005 CarswellNat 5881, 2005 FC 1645 — On an application for relief brought under subs. 84(2) of the IRPA, the onus of proof is on the applicant to establish, on a balance of probabilities, that he will not be removed within a reasonable time and that he is not a danger to national security or to the safety of any person. The statutory criteria in the provision are conjunctive. In this case, the applicant premised his application wholly on the grounds that he will not be removed within a reasonable time and that he is not such a danger. The applicant only met one criteria but not the other. Accordingly, the statute mandates that the application be dismissed.

Almrei v. Canada (Minister of Citizenship & Immigration) (2005), 45 Imm. L.R. (3d) 163, 2005 CarswellNat 319, 2005 CarswellNat 869, 2005 FCA 54, 330 N.R. 73, 251 D.L.R. (4th) 13, [2005] F.C.J. No. 213 — This was an appeal against a decision dismissing an application for a judicial release from detention. Subsection 27(1) of the *Federal Courts Act* gives the appellant a right of appeal against a decision on a subs. 84(2) application for judicial release. The onus of proof rests with the person who brings the application for judicial release and it has to be discharged on a balance of probabilities. The decision on the reasonableness of the security certificate is not determinative of the merit, opportunity and legality of the detention of the person concerned.

Where the removal of a foreign national is delayed so as to bring into play the reasonable time requirement, the judge hearing the judicial release application must consider the delay and look at the causes of such delay. Judicial remedies have to be pursued diligently and in a timely fashion. The same goes for the Government's responses and the judicial hearing of these remedies. Courts, as they must do, have given priority to the hearing of challenges to the legality of detention. Thus, in determining whether there will be execution or enforcement of the removal order within a reasonable period of time, a judge must look at the delay generated by the parties as well as the institutional delay which is inherent in the exercise of a remedy. Where an applicant, rightly or wrongly, tries to prevent his removal from Canada and delay ensues as a result of his action, he cannot be heard to complain that his removal has not occurred within a reasonable period of time, unless the delay is unreasonable or inordinate and not attributable to him.

Section 78, which deals with the protection of information relating to national security, applies to an application for judicial release under subs. 84(2) of IRPA.

The test for granting or refusing a subs. 84(2) application is future-oriented. Evidence has to be provided that the applicant will not be removed within a reasonable period of time. If the government produces, at the hearing, credible and compelling evidence of an imminent removal, the time already served and the conditions of detention lose much of their significance. The length and conditions of past detention are relevant in assessing the credibility of the evidence submitted that the removal of the person concerned is imminent. The history of events may cast doubt on the reliability of the assertion and evidence submitted that the moment of removal is close. Conditions of detention, especially when coupled with a lengthy detention, may cause the phrase "within a reasonable time" to take on some urgency. The removal would then have to be effected more expeditiously in order to be in compliance with the requirements of subs. 84(2).

The possibility that the removal of a detainee may be to a country where the detainee may face torture and serious violations of human rights requires that more substantial procedural protections and safeguards be given in the preparation of the danger opinion. The person facing deportation to torture must be informed of the case to be met and must be given an opportunity to respond to the case presented by the Minister. He or she is entitled to disclosure, subject to privilege and other lawful exceptions. He or she has a right to present evidence both on the issue of lack of danger to the security of Canada and on the risk of torture. Consultations with other government departments and with the countries to which the person could be removed may be necessary to obtain and implement safeguards for the life and integrity of the individual.

Canada (Minister of Citizenship & Immigration) v. Mahjoub (2004), 260 F.T.R. 226 (Eng.), 2004 CarswellNat 2644, 2004 CarswellNat 5396, 2004 FC 1028, [2004] F.C.J. No. 1335 — The respondent was seeking an order releasing him from detention and was requesting an order, during the course of that proceeding, to give part of his evidence *in camera*. It is a fundamental principle that the proceedings of Canadian courts are open and accessible to the public. The court is obliged to determine where such a restriction is necessary to prevent a real and substantial risk to the fairness of the hearing, because reasonably available alternative measures will not prevent the risk, and secondly whether the salutary effects of the restriction outweigh the deleterious effects of the free expression of those affected by the ban. The respondent's request that he be permitted to testify *in camera* was dismissed.

Jaballah v. Canada (Minister of Citizenship & Immigration) (2004), 38 Imm. L.R. (3d) 179, 2004 FC 299, 2004 CarswellNat 645, (sub nom. *Jaballah, Re)* 247 F.T.R. 68, [2004] F.C.J. No. 420 — This was an application for release made more than 120 days after the determination by the court that a certificate signed by the two respondent Ministers was reasonable in stating that Mr. Jaballah was inadmissible to Canada on the grounds of national security.

The applicant applied for release under s. 84(2) of IRPA. This provision carries forward a process established under s. 40.1(8) and (9) of the former *Immigration Act*. Jurisprudence under the former Act remains relevant to applications under subs. 84(2). The standard of proof is the ordinary civil standard. The certificate is conclusive proof that the person is inadmissible to Canada. Release under subs. 84(2) is not automatic. A person cannot be detained indefinitely, at least without good reason. The 120-day detention, which must occur before an application for release can be initiated, is measured from the date the Minister's certificate is found to be reasonable so that time spent in detention before that is not ordinarily a factor. Similarly, the 120 days after the certificate is upheld is also not a factor in assessing whether release in the future will not be in a reasonable time.

The burden to establish the requirements under subs. 84(2) is that of the applicant. Release under subs. 84(2) is not automatic nor is it easily achieved. One would expect the applicant to show change in circumstances or new evidence not previously available to obtain release.

While the applicant was entitled to pursue his legal rights in Canada, he is not entitled to rely on any uncertainty in predicting when those matters may be determined as a basis to claim uncertainty about when his removal would be effective.

This type of application is not similar to a bail application in a criminal proceeding. Such a comparison ignores the basic principles of immigration law that the state may control access to Canada by foreign nationals and may distinguish between them, permanent residents and citizens. It has long been recognized that the state may preclude admission, particularly for those who are reasonably believed on the information available to the Ministers to a present danger to national security. Release from detention of a person certified as one who presents a threat to national security is simply not comparable to release on bail of one detained in regular criminal or extradition proceedings.

Almrei v. Canada (Minister of Citizenship & Immigration) (2003), 245 F.T.R. 27, 2003 CarswellNat 4425, 2003 FC 1523, 2003 CarswellNat 4152 — The applicant made an application for an order pursuant to s. 84(2) that he should be released from detention (s. 84(2) does not contain any provision with respect to the procedure to be followed in the detention review). The proceedings commenced by the issuance of the security certificate continue so long as the subject of the certificate remains in detention or is released on bail pending removal. If a certificate is determined to be reasonable under subs. 80(1), it is conclusive proof that the permanent resident or foreign national is inadmissible. Conclusive proof of inadmissibility is not conclusive proof that the person will pose a danger to national security or the safety of any person. The second branch of the detention review test is not automatically met where there is, in existence, a valid security certificate.

The requirements of subs. 84(2) necessitate incorporation of s. 78 procedures. Consideration of the second branch of the test, that release will not pose a danger to national security or to the safety of any person, requires that the judge assess the basis upon which the applicant is detained.

Canada (Minister of Citizenship & Immigration) v. Mahjoub (2003), [2004] 1 F.C.R. 493, 2003 CarswellNat 3857, 2003 CarswellNat 2332, [2003] F.C.J. No. 1183, 2003 FC 928, 238 F.T.R. 12 — This is an application by Mr. Mahjoub for an order releasing him from detention. The applicant entered Canada on December 30, 1995 and immediately claimed refugee status. In October 1996, he was found to be a refugee. On June 27, 2000 under the former Act, the Solicitor General and Minister of Citizenship and Immigration caused a copy of a security certificate signed by them to be referred to the court for determination, as to whether the certificate should be quashed. On the basis of the certificate, Mr. Mahjoub was detained on June 26, 2000 and has been in custody ever since. In October 2001, the certificate was found to be reasonable and in March 2002 the adjudication division found Mr. Mahjoub to be inadmissible based on the security certificate and issued a deportation order. On June 28, 2002, the present Act came into effect and on October 28, 2002, this motion was commenced.

The wording now found in subs. 84(?) is not to be construed in a significantly different fashion than the similar provisions under the former Act.

The applicant bears the onus of showing that he meets the statutory criteria for release. The criteria require a judge to be satisfied that the applicant will not be removed within a reasonable time and that the release of the applicant will not pose a danger to the public. The standard of proof is the ordinary civil standard. The certificate is conclusive proof that the person is inadmissible on the grounds of security. Release under subs. 84(2) cannot be automatic because the persons to whom that section applies had been found to be inadmissible on the grounds of security, violating human or international rights, serious criminality or organized criminality. Finally, a person cannot be detained indefinitely without good reason.

The applicant has a right to be reasonably informed as to the basis upon which his release from detention is opposed. Such right must be viewed against the state's interest to protect information which, if disclosed, would be injurious to national security or the safety of any person. The court's duty to ensure that national security is protected is not lessened on an application for release from detention.

The reference to a period of 120 days in subs. 84(2) reflects Parliament's intent, that once a certificate has been determined to be reasonable, the person named in the certificate should be removed expeditiously by requiring as one of the criteria for release that the court consider whether removal will take place within a reasonable time. Parliament contemplated that in some circumstances removal will not have occurred within 120 days. The right to apply for release after 120 days undoubtedly acts as an impetus to officials to assure an expeditious removal, and at the same time assures that any post 120-day delay can be the subject of judicial scrutiny.

While it is the applicant's right to exhaust all avenues of legal recourse, the time required for those challenges cannot be relied upon by the applicant for the purpose of arguing that he or she will not be removed from Canada within a reasonable time. An individual is free to take those steps available to him or her at law to remain in Canada. If he or she does so however, they may not claim that, on the basis of their own actions, they will not be removed from Canada within a reasonable time.

The court, having regard to the fact that the uncertainty about when the applicant may be removed from Canada was in a large part the result of pending and contemplated Court challenges initiated by the applicant, concluded that the applicant had not met the burden on a balance of probabilities of proving that he would not be removed from Canada within a reasonable time.

For the purpose of subs. 84(2), evidence which grounds an objectively reasonable suspicion of substantial threatened harm, would establish a danger to national security. Because the onus is on the applicant for release to satisfy the court on a balance of probabilities, that his or her release will not pose a danger to national security or the safety of any person, the onus may be difficult to meet given that an objectively reasonable suspicion of substantial threatened harm may establish the danger.

76. Definitions — The following definitions apply in this Division.

"information" means security or criminal intelligence information and information that is obtained in confidence from a source in Canada, the government of a foreign state, an international organization of states or an institution of such a government or international organization. *("renseignements")*

"judge" means the Chief Justice of the Federal Court or a judge of that Court designated by the Chief Justice. *("juge")*

2002, c. 8, s. 194(d); 2008, c. 3, s. 4

Certificate

[Heading added 2008, c. 3, s. 4.]

77. (1) Referral of certificate — The Minister and the Minister of Citizenship and Immigration shall sign a certificate stating that a permanent resident or foreign national is inadmissible on grounds of security, violating human or international rights, serious criminality or organized criminality, and shall refer the certificate to the Federal Court.

(2) Filing of evidence and summary — When the certificate is referred, the Minister shall file with the Court the information and other evidence that is relevant to the ground of inadmissibility stated in the certificate and on which the certificate is based, as well as a summary of information and other evidence that enables the person named in the certificate to be reasonably informed of the case made by the Minister but that does not include anything that, in the Minister's opinion, would be injurious to national security or endanger the safety of any person if disclosed.

(3) Effect of referral — Once the certificate is referred, no proceeding under this Act respecting the person who is named in the certificate — other than proceedings relating to sections 79.1, 82 to 82.31, 112 and 115 — may be commenced or continued until the judge determines whether the certificate is reasonable.

2002, c. 8, s. 194(a)(ii); 2005, c. 10, s. 34(1)(o)(ii); 2008, c. 3, s. 4; 2015, c. 20, s. 54

Case Law

Harkat, Re (2014), 24 Imm. L.R. (4th) 1, 69 Admin. L.R. (5th) 177, 10 C.R. (7th) 225, 458 N.R. 67, 2014 SCC 37, 2014 CarswellNat 1463, 2014 CarswellNat 1464, [2014] S.C.J. No. 37 — Harkat is alleged to have come to Canada to engage in terrorism. In 2002, a security certificate was issued against him under the scheme then contained in the *IRPA*. The certificate declared Harkat inadmissible to Canada on national security grounds; however, after a successful constitutional challenge of the then existing *IRPA* security certificate scheme and subsequent amendments to the *IRPA*, a second security certificate was issued against Harkat and referred to the Federal Court for a determination as to its reasonableness. The designated judge found the security scheme under the amended *IRPA* to be constitutional, and concluded that the certificate declaring Harkat inadmissible to Canada was reasonable. On appeal, the Federal Court of Appeal upheld the constitutionality of the scheme but found that the identity of CSIS human sources is not protected by privilege. It also excluded from the evidence the summaries of intercepted conversations to which Harkat had not been privy, and remitted the matter to the designated Judge for redetermination on the basis of what remained of the record after the exclusion of the summaries.

The Supreme Court of Canada concluded that the *IRPA* scheme is constitutional and that CSIS human sources are not protected by a class privilege. The Supreme Court of Canada reinstated the designated judge's conclusion that the security certificate was reasonable.

The *IRPA* scheme remains an imperfect substitute for full disclosure in an open court, and the designated judge has an ongoing responsibility to assess the overall fairness of the process and to grant remedies under s. 24(1) of the *Charter* where appropriate. The *IRPA* scheme's requirement that the named person be "reasonably informed" of the case should be read as a recognition that the person named must receive an incompressible minimum amount of disclosure. The level of disclosure required for a named person to be reasonably informed is case-specific, depending on the allegations and evidence against him or her. Only information and evidence that raises a serious risk of injury to national security or a danger to the safety of a person can be withheld from the named person. The designated judge must be vigilant and sceptical with respect to claims of national security confidentiality and must ensure that only information or evidence that would injure national security or endanger the safety of a person is withheld from the named person. Systematic over-claiming would infringe the named person's right to a fair process or undermine the integrity of the judicial system requiring a remedy under s. 24(1) of the *Charter*. Parliament's choice to adopt a categorical prohibition against disclosure of sensitive information, as opposed to a balancing approach, does not as such constitute a breach of the right to a fair process.

CSIS human sources are not protected by a class privilege. First, police informer privilege does not attach to CSIS human sources. The differences between traditional policing and modern intelligence-gathering preclude automatically applying traditional police informer privilege to CSIS human sources. While evidence gathered by the police is traditionally used in criminal trials that provide the accused with significant evidentiary safeguards, the intelligence gathered by CSIS may be used to establish criminal conduct in proceedings that have relaxed rules of evidence and allow for the admission of hearsay evidence. Second, the Supreme Court of Canada should not create a new privilege for CSIS human sources. If Parliament deems it desirable that CSIS human sources' identities and related information be privileged, it can enact appropriate protections. The *IRPA* scheme already affords broad protection to human sources by precluding the public disclosure of information that would injure national security or endanger a person.

Jaballah, Re (2010), 88 Imm. L.R. (3d) 268, 2010 FC 224, 2010 CarswellNat 1174, 2010 CarswellNat 448 — Mahmoud Jaballah was named in a security certificate signed by the Minister of Citizenship & Immigration and the Minister of Public Safety and Emergency Preparedness. Mr. Jaballah moved for an order to restrict the Ministers from using his evidence given in previous proceedings. What was in issue was a very unique situation: where there had been three prior reasonableness hearings, and a number of associated detention review hearings, years later the question arose whether the Ministers could use Mr. Jaballah's prior testimony against him in support of their case in the court proceeding. The court held that the evidence could not be used to build the Ministers' case in chief, but could be used in cross examination should Mr. Jaballah decide to testify. This finding represented a balance between protecting Mr. Jaballah's right to a fair hearing and protecting the public's right to have all relevant evidence available in search of the truth.

Almrei, Re (2009), 86 Imm. L.R. (3d) 212, 355 F.T.R. 222 (Eng.), [2009] F.C.J. No. 1579, 2009 FC 1263, 2009 CarswellNat 4286, 2009 CarswellNat 5657 — On February 22, 2008, the Ministers signed a certificate in which they stated that Hassan Almrei was a foreign national inadmissible to Canada on security grounds. Pursuant to s. 77(1) of IRPA, the certificate was referred to the court for determination as to whether it was reasonable. The Court held the reasons for determining the certificate were not reasonable.

The duties of utmost good faith and candour imply that the party relying upon the presentation of *ex parte* evidence will conduct a thorough review of the information in its possession and make representations based on all of the information including that which is unfavourable to their case. That was not done in this instance. The 2008 security intelligence report was assembled with information that could only be construed as unfavourable to Mr. Almrei without any serious attempt to include information to the contrary, or to update their assessment.

The court held that Hassan Almrei of 2009 was not the same person as in 2001 when the certificate was initially issued. The service's assessment in a February 2008 Security Intelligence Review was prepared, in the court's view, without sufficient consideration of all the information within its possession and without considering whether the state of knowledge about the risk to national security posted by Islamic extremists had evolved since Mr. Almrei was detained in 2001. That task fell on the court with the assistance of counsel for both parties and the special advocates. The Federal Court struck down the national security certificate.

Charkaoui, Re, [2008] 2 S.C.R. 326, (sub nom. *Charkaoui v. Canada (Minister of Citizenship & Immigration))* 70 Imm. L.R. (3d) 1, [2008] S.C.J. No. 39, 175 C.R.R. (2d) 120, 294 D.L.R. (4th) 478, 58 C.R. (6th) 45, 376 N.R. 154, 2008 CarswellNat 1898, 2008 CarswellNat 1899, 2008 SCC 38 — The appellant appealed against the dismissal in Federal Court of his application for a stay of proceedings relating to the security certificate issued against him under s. 77 of the IRPA. He alleged that the government breached its duty to disclose relevant information in its possession, and its auxiliary duty to do so in a timely manner. He alleged as well that the respondent Ministers relied impermissibly on evidence obtained subsequent to the issuance of the security certificate. They did so, he alleged, upon the designated judge's review of reasonableness of the certificate and again during the judge's review of the appellant's applications for release from custody. The Court concluded that the appellant's appeal should succeed. The Canadian Security Intelligence Service ("CSIS") is bound to disclose to the Ministers responsible all information in its possession regarding the person named in a security certificate. The Ministers must convey this information to the designated judge. The judge must then disclose the information to the person named in the security certificate, except to the extent that disclosure might, in the judge's view, endanger Canada's security. These obligations of disclosure cannot be properly discharged when CSIS has destroyed what it was bound to disclose. As a matter of text and context, the court concluded that CSIS was bound to retain the information it gathers within the limits established by the legislation governing its activities. In accordance with its prior practice, it did not do so here. Nevertheless, the court was satisfied that a stay of proceedings would not be an appropriate remedy in this case. It would be premature at this stage of the proceedings for the court to determine how the destruction of the notes affects the reliability of the evidence. The designated judge will be in a position to make that determination as he will have all of the evidence before him and will be able to summon and question as witnesses those who took the interview notes. If he concludes that there is a reasonable basis for the security certificate but that the destruction of the notes had a prejudicial effect, he will then consider whether the appellant should be granted a remedy. A stay would be an inappropriate remedy here.

The only appropriate remedy is to confirm the duty to disclose the appellant's entire file to the designated judge and, after the judge has filtered it, to the appellant and his counsel. The appeal from the decision of the Federal Court of Appeal was allowed in part. The application for a stay of proceedings was dismissed.

Proposed Addition — 77.1

77.1 (1) Conditions — inadmissibility on grounds of security — If a certificate stating that a permanent resident or foreign national is inadmissible on grounds of security is referred to the Federal Court and no warrant for the person's arrest and detention is issued under section 81, the Minister of Public Safety and Emergency Preparedness shall impose the prescribed conditions on the person who is named in the certificate.

(2) Duration of conditions — The prescribed conditions imposed under subsection (1) cease to apply only when

(a) the person is detained;

(b) the certificate stating that the person is inadmissible on grounds of security is withdrawn;

(c) a final determination is made that the certificate is not reasonable;

(d) the Minister makes a declaration under subsection 42.1(1) or (2) in relation to the person; or

(e) a removal order is enforced against the person in accordance with the regulations.

2013, c. 16, s. 25 [Not in force at date of publication.]

78. Determination — The judge shall determine whether the certificate is reasonable and shall quash the certificate if he or she determines that it is not.

2005, c. 10, s. 34(2); 2008, c. 3, s. 4

79. Appeal — An appeal from the determination may be made to the Federal Court of Appeal only if the judge certifies that a serious question of general importance is involved and states the question. However, no appeal may be made from an interlocutory decision in the proceeding.

2002, c. 8, s. 194(b)(ii); 2008, c. 3, s. 4

79.1 (1) Appeal by Minister — Despite section 79, the Minister may, without it being necessary for the judge to certify that a serious question of general importance is involved, appeal, at any stage of the proceeding, any decision made in the proceeding requiring the disclosure of information or other evidence if, in the Minister's opinion, the disclosure would be injurious to national security or endanger the safety of any person.

(2) Effects of appeal — The appeal suspends the execution of the decision, as well as the proceeding under section 78, until the appeal has been finally determined.

2015, c. 20, s. 55

80. Effect of certificate — A certificate that is determined to be reasonable is conclusive proof that the person named in it is inadmissible and is a removal order that is in force without it being necessary to hold or continue an examination or admissibility hearing.

2008, c. 3, s. 4

Detention and Release

[Heading added 2008, c. 3, s. 4.]

81. Ministers' warrant — The Minister and the Minister of Citizenship and Immigration may issue a warrant for the arrest and detention of a person who is named in a certificate if they have reasonable grounds to believe that the person is a danger to national security or to the safety of any person or is unlikely to appear at a proceeding or for removal.

2008, c. 3, s. 4

[Heading repealed 2008, c. 3, s. 4.]

82. (1) Initial review of detention — A judge shall commence a review of the reasons for the person's continued detention within 48 hours after the detention begins.

(2) Further reviews of detention — before determining reasonableness — Until it is determined whether a certificate is reasonable, a judge shall commence another review of the reasons for the person's continued detention at least once in the six-month period following the conclusion of each preceding review.

(3) Further reviews of detention — after determining reasonableness — A person who continues to be detained after a certificate is determined to be reasonable may apply to the Federal Court for another review of the reasons for their continued detention if a period of six months has expired since the conclusion of the preceding review.

(4) Reviews of conditions — A person who is released from detention under conditions may apply to the Federal Court for another review of the reasons for continuing the conditions if a period of six months has expired since the conclusion of the preceding review.

(5) Order — On review, the judge

    (a) shall order the person's detention to be continued if the judge is satisfied that the person's release under conditions would be injurious to national security or endanger the safety of any person or that they would be unlikely to appear at a proceeding or for removal if they were released under conditions; or

    (b) in any other case, shall order or confirm the person's release from detention and set any conditions that the judge considers appropriate.

Proposed Addition — 82(6)–(9)

(6) Conditions — inadmissibility on grounds of security — If the judge orders the release, under paragraph (5)(b), of a person who is named in a certificate stating that they are inadmissible on grounds of security, the judge shall also impose the prescribed conditions on the person.

(7) No review of conditions — The prescribed conditions imposed under subsection (6) are not subject to review under subsection (4).

(8) Variation of conditions — If a person is subject to the prescribed conditions imposed under subsection (6), any variation of conditions under subsection 82.1(1) or paragraph 82.2(3)(c) is not to result in the person being subject to conditions that do not include those prescribed conditions.

(9) Duration of conditions — The prescribed conditions imposed under subsection (6) cease to apply only when one of the events described in paragraphs 77.1(2)(a) to (e) occurs.

2013, c. 16, s. 26 [Not in force at date of publication.]

2005, c. 10, s. 34(1)(o)(iii); 2008, c. 3, s. 4

Case Law

Chaudhary v. Canada (Minister of Public Safety & Emergency Preparedness) (2015), 38 Imm. L.R. (4th) 210, 127 O.R. (3d) 401, 92 Admin. L.R. (5th) 147, 390 D.L.R. (4th) 598, 343 C.R.R. (2d) 146, 340 O.A.C. 211, 2015 ONCA 700, 2015 CarswellOnt 15828, [2015] O.J. No. 5438 — The applications judge concluded that the court should decline to exercise its *habeas corpus* jurisdiction, in light of the fact that IRPA put into place a comprehensive statutory review mechanism as broad and advantageous as *habeas corpus*. The Ontario Court of Appeal disagreed and allowed the appeals.

The prerogative writ of *habeas corpus* is "a cornerstone of liberty" and "a means of judicial control over the arbitrary behaviour of the executive government." It is "one of the most important safeguards of the liberty of the subject": M. Groves, "*habeas corpus*, Justiciability and Foreign Affairs" (2013) 11:3 N.Z. J. Pub. & Int'l L. 587, at p. 588. It is also "the most significant means of protecting individual liberty": R.S. Sharpe, J. Farbey & S. Atrill, *The Law of Habeas Corpus*, 3rd ed. (New York: Oxford University Press, 2011), at p. 1. Most significantly in Canada, it is guaranteed by s. 10(c) of the Charter which reads as follows: "Everyone has the right on arrest or detention . . . to have the validity of the detention determined by way of *habeas corpus* and to be released if the detention is not lawful."

The question a *habeas corpus* application would answer is whether the detentions, because of their length and their uncertain duration, have become illegal and in violation of the appellants' ss. 7 and 9 Charter rights. As such, the immigration status of the applicants will not be affected. They will still be subject to removal. All that will be decided is whether there continues to be a constitutionally valid basis for their detentions pending those immigration decisions and dispositions. This court has previously held that, although immigration matters will generally be best dealt with under the comprehensive scheme established under the immigration legislation, "there will be situations in which the Federal Court is not an effective and appropriate forum in which to seek the relief claimed. In those rare cases, the Superior Court can properly exercise its jurisdiction":

Francis (Litigation Guardian of) v. Canada (Minister of Citizenship and Immigration) (1999), 49 O.R. (3rd) 136 (C.A.); leave to appeal granted (2000), 138 O.A.C. 199 (note) (S.C.C.), at para. 12. The exception set out in *Peiroo v. Minister of Employment and Immigration* (1989), 69 O.R. (2d) 253 (C.A.); leave to appeal refused (1989), 37 O.A.C. 160 (note) (S.C.C.), is not a blanket exclusion of *habeas corpus* in all matters related to immigration law. Therefore, because the issue raised by the appellants is not a core immigration issue as was *Peiroo* and seeks only the determination of the legality of the appellants' continued detentions, these are cases that warrant a "careful evaluation" as prescribed in *May v. Ferndale Institution*, [2005] 3 S.C.R. 809. There are three critical differences between the IRPA process and *habeas corpus* that, taken together, make *habeas corpus* broader and more advantageous to the appellants when the issue is whether continued detentions have become illegal due to their length and the uncertainty of their continued duration. Those three differences are:

(i) the question the court is to answer;

(ii) the onus; and

(iii) the review process.

In addition, the Supreme Court in *May v. Ferndale Institution* identified the weaknesses in the statutory process for the review of prisoner transfer decisions, went on to assess the differences between the statutory scheme and *habeas corpus* purposively.

This involved consideration of five factors that the court found mitigated in favour of concurrent jurisdiction and provided additional support for allowing federal prisoners access to *habeas corpus*. The following five factors were also considered in this case:

(i) the choice of remedies and forum;

(ii) the expertise of provincial superior courts;

(iii) the timeliness of the remedy;

(iv) local access to the remedy; and

(v) the nature of the remedy and the burden of proof.

In conclusion, the applicants, who have been in immigration detentions for lengthy periods and whose detentions are to continue for uncertain duration, should not be deprived of their Charter right to *habeas corpus*. They have the right to choose whether to have their detention-related issues heard in the Federal Court through judicial review of the ID decisions, or in the Superior Court through *habeas corpus* applications. The appeals were allowed.

Almrei, Re (2009), 78 Imm. L.R. (3d) 167, 337 F.T.R. 160 (Eng.), 2009 CarswellNat 17, 2009 FC 3 — The applicant had been detained since October 2001 for his removal from the country as a risk to Canada's national security. The court concluded that his continued detention could no longer be justified and that he should be released under strict conditions pending a determination of the reasonableness of the security certificate under which he was presently detained, and if the certificate should be found to be reasonable, until a determination whether he can be removed from Canada to his country of nationality or some other country.

The length of detention in the applicant's case exceeded seven years. It is difficult to find any comparable cases in the common law world where a person detained on security grounds has been held for so long. While this factor does not outweigh all other considerations, it must count heavily in favour of his release. The government's case against the applicant had remained substantially unchanged for seven years. The Minister conceded that there was no certain date in relation to the applicant's removal. This factor will weigh in favour of release "if there will be a lengthy detention before deportation or if the future detention cannot be ascertained." The applicant's principle difficulty thus far had been the fact that he had no family network in Canada and had thus far been unable to come up with a proposal for supervising sureties similar to those that were relied upon in the release decisions respecting the other security certificate detainees.

The court did not agree with the view expressed by the Ministers that it was in some way an inappropriate delegation of supervisory responsibility to government. The court held that it is a responsibility which stems from the legislative scheme in the same way that the burden of supervision of an offender on probation or parole is borne by the state. It is the Ministers who seek the restriction of the applicant's liberty and are prepared to accept the responsibility of detaining him. They must equally accept the responsibility of supervising his release on conditions. The applicant was released from detention subject to conditions imposed.

82.1 (1) Variation of orders — A judge may vary an order made under subsection 82(5) on application of the Minister or of the person who is subject to the order if the judge is satisfied that the variation is desirable because of a material change in the circumstances that led to the order.

(2) Calculation of period for next review — For the purpose of calculating the six-month period referred to in subsection 82(2), (3) or (4), the conclusion of the preceding review is deemed to have taken place on the day on which the decision under subsection (1) is made.

2008, c. 3, s. 4

Case Law

Jaballah, Re (2011), 419 N.R. 394, 2011 FCA 175, 2011 CarswellNat 1832, 2011 CarswellNat 3385 — This was an appeal from an order of the Federal Court dismissing the appellant's application to review the conditions of his release under subs. 82(4) of IRPA and, in the alternative, to "vary" the terms and conditions of his release under subs. 82.1(1). The appellant argued that the absence of a deeming provision similar to subs. 82.1(2) in relation to the other release or detention reviews under s. 82 suggests that Parliament intended the date of "the conclusion of the preceding review" to be computed otherwise than by reference to the date of the last review order. There is no basis for such an inference. The deeming provision in subs. 82.1(2) has a limited application because although a variation on the basis of a material change in circumstances may be sought at any time, i.e. without regard to the six-month limitation applicable to reviews, it was thought logical, given the close connection between the review and variation proceedings, to compute the six-month period for the next review by reference to the date of this order. This was achieved by deeming the preceding review under subs. 82(2), (3) or (4) to have concluded on the day on which the variation decision is made, rather than the earlier date when the decision on the preceding review was in fact made. The "conclusion of the preceding review" means the date on which the review decision is rendered, that the six-month period set out in subs. 82(4) runs from that date, and therefore in this case, the appellant's application was accordingly premature. The questions certified were answered in the negative and the appeal dismissed.

82.2 (1) Arrest and detention — breach of conditions — A peace officer may arrest and detain a person released under section 82 or 82.1 if the officer has reasonable grounds to believe that the person has contravened or is about to contravene any condition applicable to their release.

(2) Appearance before judge — The peace officer shall bring the person before a judge within 48 hours after the detention begins.

(3) Order — If the judge finds that the person has contravened or was about to contravene any condition applicable to their release, the judge shall

(a) order the person's detention to be continued if the judge is satisfied that the person's release under conditions would be injurious to national security or endanger the safety of any person or that they would be unlikely to appear at a proceeding or for removal if they were released under conditions;

(b) confirm the release order; or

(c) vary the conditions applicable to their release.

(4) Calculation of period for next review — For the purpose of calculating the six-month period referred to in subsection 82(2), (3) or (4), the conclusion of the preceding review is deemed to have taken place on the day on which the decision under subsection (3) is made.

2008, c. 3, s. 4

82.3 Appeal — An appeal from a decision made under any of sections 82 to 82.2 may be made to the Federal Court of Appeal only if the judge certifies that a serious question of general importance is involved and states the question. However, no appeal may be made from an interlocutory decision in the proceeding.

2008, c. 3, s. 4

82.31 (1) Appeal by Minister — Despite section 82.3, the Minister may, without it being necessary for the judge to certify that a serious question of general importance is involved, appeal, at any stage of the proceeding, any decision made in the proceeding requiring the disclosure of information or other evidence if, in the Minister's opinion, the disclosure would be injurious to national security or endanger the safety of any person.

(2) Effects of appeal — The appeal suspends the execution of the decision until the appeal has been finally determined.

2015, c. 20, s. 56

82.4 Minister's order to release — The Minister may, at any time, order that a person who is detained under any of sections 82 to 82.2 be released from detention to permit their departure from Canada.

2008, c. 3, s. 4

Protection of Information

[Heading added 2008, c. 3, s. 4.]

83. (1) Protection of Information — The following provisions apply to proceedings under any of sections 78 and 82 to 82.2:

(a) the judge shall proceed as informally and expeditiously as the circumstances and considerations of fairness and natural justice permit;

(b) the judge shall appoint a person from the list referred to in subsection 85(1) to act as a special advocate in the proceeding after hearing representations from the permanent resident or foreign national and the Minister and after giving particular consideration and weight to the preferences of the permanent resident or foreign national;

(c) at any time during a proceeding, the judge may, on the judge's own motion — and shall, on each request of the Minister — hear information or other evidence in the absence of the public and of the permanent resident or foreign national and their counsel if, in the judge's opinion, its disclosure could be injurious to national security or endanger the safety of any person;

(c.1) on the request of the Minister, the judge may exempt the Minister from the obligation to provide the special advocate with a copy of information under paragraph 85.4(1)(b) if the judge is satisfied that the information does not enable the permanent resident or foreign national to be reasonably informed of the case made by the Minister;

(c.2) for the purpose of deciding whether to grant an exemption under paragraph (c.1), the judge may ask the special advocate to make submissions and may communicate with the special advocate to the extent required to enable the special advocate to make the submissions, if the judge is of the opinion that considerations of fairness and natural justice require it;

(d) the judge shall ensure the confidentiality of information and other evidence provided by the Minister if, in the judge's opinion, its disclosure would be injurious to national security or endanger the safety of any person;

(e) throughout the proceeding, the judge shall ensure that the permanent resident or foreign national is provided with a summary of information and other evidence that enables them to be reasonably informed of the case made by the Minister in the proceeding but that does not include anything that, in the judge's opinion, would be injurious to national security or endanger the safety of any person if disclosed;

(f) the judge shall ensure the confidentiality of all information or other evidence that is withdrawn by the Minister;

(g) the judge shall provide the permanent resident or foreign national and the Minister with an opportunity to be heard;

(h) the judge may receive into evidence anything that, in the judge's opinion, is reliable and appropriate, even if it is inadmissible in a court of law, and may base a decision on that evidence;

(i) the judge may base a decision on information or other evidence even if a summary of that information or other evidence is not provided to the permanent resident or foreign national;

(j) the judge shall not base a decision on information or other evidence provided by the Minister, and shall return it to the Minister, if the judge determines that it is not relevant or if the Minister withdraws it; and

(k) the judge shall not base a decision on information that the Minister is exempted from providing to the special advocate, shall ensure the confidentiality of that information and shall return it to the Minister.

(1.1) **Clarification** — For the purposes of paragraph (1)(h), reliable and appropriate evidence does not include information that is believed on reasonable grounds to have been obtained as a result of the use of torture within the meaning of section 269.1 of the *Criminal Code*, or cruel, inhuman or degrading treatment or punishment within the meaning of the Convention Against Torture.

(1.2) **Appointment of special advocate** — If the permanent resident or foreign national requests that a particular person be appointed under paragraph (1)(b), the judge shall appoint that person unless the judge is satisfied that

(a) the appointment would result in the proceeding being unreasonably delayed;

(b) the appointment would place the person in a conflict of interest; or

(c) the person has knowledge of information or other evidence whose disclosure would be injurious to national security or endanger the safety of any person and, in the circumstances, there is a risk of inadvertent disclosure of that information or other evidence.

(2) **For greater certainty** — For greater certainty, the judge's power to appoint a person to act as a special advocate in a proceeding includes the power to terminate the appointment and to appoint another person.

2008, c. 3, s. 4; 2015, c. 20, s. 57

Case Law

Section 83(1)

Harkat, Re (2014), 24 Imm. L.R. (4th) 1, 69 Admin. L.R. (5th) 177, 10 C.R. (7th) 225, 458 N.R. 67, 2014 SCC 37, 2014 CarswellNat 1463, 2014 CarswellNat 1464, [2014] S.C.J. No. 37 — Harkat is alleged to have come to Canada to engage in terrorism. In 2002, a security certificate was issued against him under the scheme then contained in the *IRPA*. The certificate declared Harkat inadmissible to Canada on national security grounds; however, after a successful constitutional challenge of the then existing *IRPA* security certificate scheme and subsequent amendments to the *IRPA*, a second security certificate was issued against Harkat and referred to the Federal Court for a determination as to its reasonableness. The designated judge found the security scheme under the amended *IRPA* to be constitutional, and concluded that the certificate declaring Harkat inadmissible to Canada was reasonable. On appeal, the Federal Court of Appeal upheld the constitutionality of the scheme but found that the identity of CSIS human sources is not protected by privilege. It also excluded from the evidence the summaries of intercepted conversations to which Harkat had not been privy, and remitted the matter to the designated Judge for redetermination on the basis of what remained of the record after the exclusion of the summaries.

The Supreme Court of Canada concluded that the *IRPA* scheme is constitutional and that CSIS human sources are not protected by a class privilege. The Supreme Court of Canada reinstated the designated judge's conclusion that the security certificate was reasonable.

The *IRPA* scheme remains an imperfect substitute for full disclosure in an open court, and the designated judge has an ongoing responsibility to assess the overall fairness of the process and to grant remedies under s. 24(1) of the *Charter* where appropriate. The *IRPA* scheme's requirement that the named person be "reasonably informed" of the case should be read as a recognition that the person named must receive an incompressible minimum amount of disclosure. The level of disclosure required for a named person to be reasonably informed is case-specific, depending on the allegations and evidence against him or her. Only information and evidence that raises a serious risk of injury to national security or a danger to the safety of a person can be withheld from the named person. The designated judge must be vigilant and sceptical with respect to claims of national security confidentiality and must ensure that only information or evidence that would injure national security or endanger the safety of a person is withheld from the named person. Systematic over-claiming would infringe the named person's right to a fair process or undermine the integrity of the judicial system requiring a remedy under s. 24(1) of the *Charter*. Parliament's choice to adapt a categorical prohibition against disclosure of sensitive information, as opposed to a balancing approach, does not as such constitute a breach of the right to a fair process.

CSIS human sources are not protected by a class privilege. First, police informer privilege does not attach to CSIS human sources. The differences between traditional policing and modern intelligence-gathering preclude automatically applying traditional police informer privilege to CSIS human sources. While evidence gathered by the police is traditionally used in criminal trials that provide the accused with significant evidentiary safeguards, the intelligence gathered by CSIS may be used to establish criminal conduct in proceedings that have relaxed rules of evidence and allow for the admission of hearsay evidence. Second, the Supreme Court of Canada should not create a new privilege for CSIS human sources. If Parliament deems it desirable that CSIS human sources' identities and related information be privileged, it can enact appropriate protections. The *IRPA* scheme already affords broad protection to human sources by precluding the public disclosure of information that would injure national security or endanger a person.

Harkat, Re (2009), 312 D.L.R. (4th) 464, 198 C.R.R. (2d) 275, 350 F.T.R. 143 (Eng.), 2009 CarswellNat 3192, 2009 FC 1050, 2009 CarswellNat 5823, [2009] F.C.J. No. 1242 — CSIS failed to include relevant information in the source matrix. Three CSIS witnesses were given the opportunity to explain their failure to provide important information to the court. The court recognized the importance of human source information to Canada's national security and the need to protect the identity of sources. The importance of human sources to intelligence gathering is not in question. However, when human source information is used to support serious allegations against an individual, the Court and the special advocates must be able to effectively test the credibility and reliability of that information. To conform to the law, CSIS and the Ministers must give the court all the information necessary to test the credibility of the source and not just the information that a witness, trained as an intelligence officer, considers operationally necessary. CSIS must also ensure that nothing prevents its legal counsel from fulfilling his role as legal advisor to CSIS or his ability to act as an officer of the court. A lawyer has an obligation to represent his client to the utmost subject to an overriding duty to the court and to the administration of justice. Without access to all the information available, counsel is unable to effectively advise his or her client and is unable to ensure that the administration of justice is being served. It is also clear that despite his best efforts, counsel for CSIS had been overwhelmed by the magnitude of this file. Adequate administrative and legal resources must be dedicated to these complex and time-consuming files.

The evolution of the security certificate proceedings post-*Charkaoui 1* (2007), 59 Imm. L.R. (3d) 1 and *Charkaoui 2* (2008), 70 Imm. L.R. (3d) 1, require the Ministers to adapt to the requirements of the law as propounded by the Supreme Court of Canada and as set out by Parliament. Counsel representing the Ministers must thoroughly understand the evolving jurisprudence and law and be able to adequately prepare CSIS employees who have been asked to appear as witnesses before the court. The Ministers' decision in relation to what evidence must be adduced should not be left in the hands of a legally inexperienced witness. A process must be put in place to ensure that decisions are made after a proper consultation with all stakeholders and upon receipt of legal advice. Such a process must be followed by the institution and its employees.

The court found that Mr. Harkat's rights as guaranteed by the *Charter* had not been violated and consequently s. 24(1) was not engaged. However, the Court found the failure of CSIS, and of its witnesses, to act in accordance with the obligations of utmost good faith recognized in *Charkaoui* has undermined the integrity of the court's process. By failing to make full and frank disclosure, CSIS and the Ministers do not protect the confidentiality of their human sources; they put it at risk. The judge, not the Ministers, is charged with determining the reasonableness of a security certificate pursuant to s. 78 of IRPA. With the coming into force of Bill C-3, Special Advocates are appointed by the court to protect Mr. Harkat's interest by, among other things, testing the reliability of the information that is heard in closed proceedings. The Ministers and CSIS intelligence officers may have their own views as to the reliability of the human source information but they may not impose that view by limiting the information provided to the court and the Special Advocates. Filtering evidence even with the best of intentions is unacceptable.

The explanations provided by the three witnesses did not convince the court that all the relevant evidence was before it. Accordingly, the court determined it was necessary to order the production of the files of other human sources relied on by the Ministers in this proceeding. Such an order will ensure that there is no further concern in relation to the Special Advocate's ability to fully test the evidence; it is necessary to repair the damage done to the administration of justice and to reestablish the necessary climate of trust and confidence which must be present in such an exceptional legal proceeding.

Harkat, Re (2009), 80 Imm. L.R. (3d) 89, 2009 FC 167, 2009 CarswellNat 436, [2009] F.C.J. No. 228 — Special advocates do not have the jurisdiction to act in public on behalf of a named person, nor are they permitted to communicate with him while acting as special advocate. They are not counsel of record in the proceeding. They do not, therefore, have standing to seek a confidentiality order which would prevent public access to court records; only counsel for the applicant may seek such an order. The objection made by the special advocates that the three summaries of conversation be kept confidential was granted on an interim basis. The three summaries of conversations were disclosed to the applicant and his counsel. The applicant and his counsel were given 10 days to serve and file a motion asking the court to continue treating the three summaries of conversations confidentially. In the absence of any such motion, the summaries would become part of the public amended security intelligence report.

Canada (Minister of Citizenship & Immigration) v. Jaballah, 2009 CarswellNat 840, 2009 FC 279 — This decision explains why the court allowed an employee of the Canadian Security Intelligence Service to testify in public under the name "David" without disclosing his proper legal name.

The open court principle requires a witness to be identified by their proper legal name. However, in s. 83 of the IRPA, Parliament has evidenced its intent that the open court principle be infringed to the extent necessary to protect Canada's national security and the safety of persons. Such infringement is only warranted, however, where the designated judge forms the opinion that the disclosure of information that the Ministers seek to protect would be injurious to national security or endanger the safety of any person. In order to ascertain the need to protect information, the designated judge may hold a hearing in the absence of the person concerned and the public to hear pertinent evidence and submissions. It is the Ministers who bear the burden of establishing that disclosure not only could, but would, be injurious to national security, or endanger the safety of a person. Once satisfied that the disclosure would be injurious to national security, or endanger the safety of any person, the designated judge must, pursuant to para. 83(1)(d) of the Act, ensure the confidentiality of the information. The designated judge is given no discretion in this regard. This renders irrelevant the balancing of interests test.

Of particular importance to this case was the fact that the applicant was unable to properly name the officer in an Ontario court lawsuit even though the officer gave evidence that he had identified himself to the applicant on two occasions. On the basis of this evidence, which supported the conclusion that the applicant did not know the officer's identity, the court concluded that the officer's identity retained the necessary quality of confidentiality such that it was appropriate to protect it. For these reasons, an order issued permitting the officer to testify publicly in court identifying himself only as "David."

Almrei, Re, [2010] 2 F.C.R. 165, 342 F.T.R. 27 (Eng.), 2009 CarswellNat 690, 2009 FC 240 — By order dated January 2, 2009, the Chief Justice ordered that the court adjudicate upon two common issues of law that have arisen in four proceedings. The two common issues were identified in the order as follows:

> (a) What is the role of the designated judge with respect to the additional information disclosed by the Ministers pursuant to the decision of the Supreme Court of Canada in *Charkaoui v. Canada (Citizenship & Immigration) (Charkaoui 2)*, [2008] 2 S.C.R. 326, 70 Imm. L.R. (3d) 1, [2008] S.C.J. No. 39, 294 D.L.R. (4th) 478, 58 C.R. (6th) 45, 376 N.R. 154, 175 C.R.R. (2d) 120, 2008 CarswellNat 1898, 2008 SCC 38? More specifically, does para. 62 of that decision require the judge to "verify" all information disclosed by the Ministers if the special advocates and counsel for the Ministers all agree that a portion of that information is irrelevant to the issues before the court?

> (b) Should the information disclosed to the named persons and their counsel be placed on the court's public files in these proceedings? If so, when?

The Federal Court concluded that:

> (a) Where the Ministers and the special advocate agree that the material disclosed by the Ministers pursuant to *Charkaoui 2* is irrelevant to the issues before the court, the court may rely upon that agreement. In such a case, the court need not verify information that the Ministers and the special advocates agree to be irrelevant.

(b) No information filed with the court in confidence pursuant to *Charkaoui 2* can be disclosed to the person named in a security certificate without the prior approval of the court.

(c) Information or evidence disclosed to the named persons pursuant to *Charkaoui 2* should be disclosed directly to counsel for each person named in a security certificate. The *Charkaoui 2* disclosure should not be placed on the court's public file. Such information or evidence would only become public if it is relied upon by a party and placed into evidence.

(d) Summaries of evidence or information made pursuant to para. 83(1)(e) of the Act must be placed on the court's public file because they relate to information relied upon by the Ministers and to what transpired in the *in camera* proceedings.

Section 83(1.1)

Mahjoub, Re (2010), 90 Imm. L.R. (3d) 76, 2010 FC 787, 2010 CarswellNat 2473, 373 F.T.R. 36 (Eng.) — The applicant brought the motion with respect to the admissibility of the information relied on by the Ministers, which was obtained from foreign agencies. He sought to exclude from the record information that was relied on by the Ministers and is believed, on reasonable grounds, to have been obtained as a result of the use of torture or cruel, inhumane or degrading treatment or punishment, pursuant to subs. 83(1.1) of IRPA. The Ministers bear the burden of establishing that information they rely upon is reliable and appropriate. They must establish that this information is admissible. Where torture or CIDT is alleged by the named person, it is for the named person to raise the issue that information relied upon by the Ministers is obtained as a result of the use of torture or CIDT. To meet this initial burden, the named person need only show a plausible connection between the use of torture or CIDT and the information proffered by the Ministers. Depending on the cogency of the evidence of the named person, the Ministers may adduce responding evidence. The Court will then, after hearing submissions, decide on all of the evidence before it whether the proposed evidence is believable on reasonable grounds to have been obtained as a result of use of torture or CIDT. On the record before the Court, notwithstanding the policies in practice implemented by the Service, the approach adopted by the Service in [text omitted] [*filtering*] information collected in compliance with its mandate is insufficient to ensure that all the information obtained from countries with a poor human rights record and relied upon by the Ministers in this proceeding meets the admissibility criteria of para. 83(1)(h) and subs. 83(1.1) of IRPA. Paragraph 83(1)(h) and subs. 83(1.1) exclude from the security certificate proceedings both primary and derivative evidence believed on reasonable grounds to have been obtained as a result of the use of torture or CIDT.

The court ordered the Ministers to review the information relied upon in the Security Intelligence Report for the purpose of excluding therefrom any information that is inadmissible pursuant to para. 83(1)(h) and subs. 83(1.1) of IRPA.

84. Protection of information on appeal — Section 83 — other than the obligation to provide a summary — and sections 85.1 to 85.5 apply in respect of an appeal under section 79, 79.1, 82.3 or 82.31 and in respect of any further appeal, with any necessary modifications.

2008, c. 3, s. 4; 2015, c. 20, s. 58

Special Advocate

[Heading added 2008, c. 3, s. 4.]

85. (1) List of persons who may act as special advocates — The Minister of Justice shall establish a list of persons who may act as special advocates and shall publish the list in a manner that the Minister of Justice considers appropriate to facilitate public access to it.

(2) Statutory Instruments Act — The *Statutory Instruments Act* does not apply to the list.

(3) Administrative support and resources — The Minister of Justice shall ensure that special advocates are provided with adequate administrative support and resources.

2008, c. 3, s. 4

Case Law

Section 85(3)

Harkat, Re, 2009 CarswellNat 626, 2009 FC 173 — The special advocates sought the ability to communicate with an administrative support person to assist them with the organization of the documents which were to be disclosed pursuant to a previous order in this proceeding.

The court concluded that where a person is not representing the interest of a named person, has the requisite security clearance, agrees to become permanently bound to secrecy and is subject to the same restrictions on communication as other participants in the proceeding, the disclosure of the confidential information to her by the court for administrative support purposes will not injure national security or endanger the safety of an individual.

Case Law

Former Section 86

Sogi v. Canada (Minister of Citizenship & Immigration) (2004), 36 Imm. L.R. (3d) 1, 2004 CarswellNat 2880, 2004 CarswellNat 1599, 322 N.R. 2, 2004 FCA 212, 121 C.R.R. (2d) 137, [2005] 1 F.C.R. 171, [2004] F.C.J. No. 947; leave to appeal refused 2004 CarswellNat 4104, 2004 CarswellNat 4105, 121 C.R.R. (2d) 188 (note), [2004] S.C.C.A. No. 354 — As long as the availability of judicial review provides the appellant with an opportunity to have a Federal Court judge decide the propriety of keeping information confidential, the IRPA procedure must be found to be in accordance with the principles of fundamental justice.

Subsection 86(2) provides that the procedures set out in s. 78 apply to the determination of an application for non-disclosure before an Immigration Division member. If the member decides that the information or evidence is not relevant, or that it is relevant but should be included in the summary provided to the individual, para. 78(f) requires the information to be returned to the Minister. Section 78(g) allows the member to consider relevant but potentially injurious material without disclosing it. That subsection makes no mention of subsequently returning the considered material to the Minister. Any information considered by the member under para. 78(g) forms part of the Immigration Division's record, albeit a confidential portion.

Under Rule 14 of the *Federal Court Immigration and Refugee Protection Rules*, where a judge considers the documents in the possession or control of a tribunal are required for a proper disposition of the application for leave, the judge may order the Immigration Division to produce the documents. Once leave is granted, Rule 17 requires the Board to prepare a record including all documents in possession or control of the tribunal and submit it to the Court. When the confidential information is produced to the court, the Minister may make an application under subs. 87(1) for continued non-disclosure.

If information is to be returned to CSIS, an undertaking must be given that the precise information that was before the Immigration Division member will be produced for judicial review purposes. The confidential information must be retained intact, in a format that allows for precise identification of what information was considered by the Immigration Division member. The information that has been considered by the member and returned to CSIS must be considered "information under the control of the tribunal for the purposes of its production to the Federal Court on judicial review." If information is returned to CSIS, the onus is on the Minister to satisfy the judge hearing the judicial review that the precise record that was before the member has been provided to the court. In the event that the evidence was not transcribed, an affidavit attesting to the evidence given before the member would be required.

The standard of review, for a decision on whether information supplied by the Minister *in camera* should have been considered by the member without completely disclosing it, is correctness. Considering the correctness of the Immigration Division member's decision, the judge will make his or her own assessment of whether disclosure of the confidential information would be injurious to national security or the safety of any person.

If the judicial review is allowed, the information will not immediately be disclosed, rather, in remitting the matter to the Immigration Division, the judge may direct that some or all of the information be included in the summary to be provided to the affected individual. In such a case, it will be up to the Minister to decide whether that information should be disclosed to the individual in order to allow it to be considered by the Immigration Division member or withdrawn from consideration in order to maintain the confidentiality of the information.

The precise record that was before the Immigration Division member will be before the judge conducting the judicial review and the member's decision not to disclose will be reviewed on a correctness standard. For these reasons, the IRPA procedure is in accordance with the principles of fundamental justice.

85.1 (1) Special advocate's role — A special advocate's role is to protect the interests of the permanent resident or foreign national in a proceeding under any of sections 78 and 82 to 82.2 when information or other evidence is heard in the absence of the public and of the permanent resident or foreign national and their counsel.

(2) Responsibilities — A special advocate may challenge

> (a) the Minister's claim that the disclosure of information or other evidence would be injurious to national security or endanger the safety of any person; and

(b) the relevance, reliability and sufficiency of information or other evidence that is provided by the Minister and is not disclosed to the permanent resident or foreign national and their counsel, and the weight to be given to it.

(3) **For greater certainty** — For greater certainty, the special advocate is not a party to the proceeding and the relationship between the special advocate and the permanent resident or foreign national is not that of solicitor and client.

(4) **Protection of communications with special advocate** — However, a communication between the permanent resident or foreign national or their counsel and the special advocate that would be subject to solicitor-client privilege if the relationship were one of solicitor and client is deemed to be subject to solicitor-client privilege. For greater certainty, in respect of that communication, the special advocate is not a compellable witness in any proceeding.

2008, c. 3, s. 4

Case Law

Harkat, Re (2009), 80 Imm. L.R. (3d) 252, 345 F.T.R. 143 (Eng.), 2009 FC 553, 2009 CarswellNat 1681 — A request was made by the special advocates to access the human source file in question. Access to the file would inevitably result in the special advocates learning the identity of the source in question.

The court found that as a result of the review of the Minister's letter, the special advocates have a "need to know" the contents of the human source file even if this results in a revelation of the source's identity. The rule of law requires no less. Once the court has evidence that leads it to question the completeness of the information being provided to it by the Ministers, in apparent violation of their obligation of utmost good faith, it must allow the special advocates access to all information which they have a need to know. To do otherwise would bring the administration of justice into disrepute.

Almrei, Re, [2010] 2 F.C.R. 165, 342 F.T.R. 27 (Eng.), 2009 CarswellNat 690, 2009 FC 240 — By order dated January 2, 2009, the Chief Justice ordered that the court adjudicate upon two common issues of law that have arisen in four proceedings.

The Federal Court concluded that:

(a) Where the Ministers and the special advocate agree that the material disclosed by the Ministers pursuant to *Charkaoui 2* is irrelevant to the issues before the court, the court may rely upon that agreement. In such a case, the court need not verify information that the Ministers and the special advocates agree to be irrelevant.

(b) No information filed with the court in confidence pursuant to *Charkaoui 2* can be disclosed to the person named in a security certificate without the prior approval of the court.

(c) Information or evidence disclosed to the named persons pursuant to *Charkaoui 2* should be disclosed directly to counsel for each person named in a security certificate. The *Charkaoui 2* disclosure should not be placed on the court's public file. Such information or evidence would only become public if it is relied upon by a party and placed into evidence.

(d) Summaries of evidence or information made pursuant to para. 83(1)(e) of the Act must be placed on the court's public file because they relate to information relied upon by the Ministers and to what transpired in the *in camera* proceedings.

85.2 Powers — A special advocate may

(a) make oral and written submissions with respect to the information and other evidence that is provided by the Minister and is not disclosed to the permanent resident or foreign national and their counsel;

(b) participate in, and cross-examine witnesses who testify during, any part of the proceeding that is held in the absence of the public and of the permanent resident or foreign national and their counsel; and

(c) exercise, with the judge's authorization, any other powers that are necessary to protect the interests of the permanent resident or foreign national.

2008, c. 3, s. 4

Case Law

Almrei, Re, 2009 CarswellNat 1491, 2009 CarswellNat 2098, 2009 FC 314 — This decision concerns the exclusion of the special advocates from a closed hearing in which the court heard evidence from a witness presented by the Ministers with respect to one of the conditions of the applicant's release from detention. A redacted version of the transcript of the evidence heard on that occasion was provided to the special advocates and the court invited submissions from them and counsel for the Ministers as to whether the procedure adopted was correct. The court concluded that a complete transcript of the evidence from the hearing must be provided to the special advocates and an opportunity provided to them to cross-examine the witness and make further submissions. The transcript of evidence was to remain confidential pending any further determination by the court, but this decision was entered on the public record of proceedings.

In general, information which could cause injury to national security should only be assessed by persons who have a genuine need to know the information in order to carry out their responsibilities. The statute does not contain an explicit "need to know" test that would restrict the special advocates' participation in the closed hearing in which the Minister presents information or other evidence to the court which may affect the named person's interests. Nor does the law implicitly recognize such a test that would override the express terms of the statute. Special advocates are not empowered to have access to all information within the possession of the government, particularly privileged information. The special advocates have not requested that the government provide access to privileged information which is not before the Court, but are asking that they be allowed to perform the role which Parliament has assigned to them to question evidence that the Ministers have chosen to present in Court. The court may need to review information provided by the Ministers in the absence of the special advocates to determine whether it pertains to the proceedings or is privileged for reasons other than national security claims. The summary and the redacted transcript of the testimony given to the special advocates did not serve as an adequate substitute for the right to "participate in and cross-examine witnesses who testify during any part of the proceeding that is held in the absence of the public" as set out in subs. 85.2(b) of IRPA.

85.3 Immunity — A special advocate is not personally liable for anything they do or omit to do in good faith under this Division.

2008, c. 3, s. 4

85.4 (1) Obligation to provide information — Subject to paragraph 83(1)(c.1), the Minister shall, within a period set by the judge,

(a) provide the special advocate with a copy of the information and other evidence that is relevant to the case made by the Minister in a proceeding under any of sections 78 and 82 to 82.2, on which the certificate or warrant is based and that has been filed with the Federal Court, but that is not disclosed to the permanent resident or foreign national and their counsel; and

(b) provide the special advocate with a copy of any other information that is in the Minister's possession and that is relevant to the case made by the Minister in a proceeding under any of sections 78 and 82 to 82.2, but on which the certificate or warrant is not based and that has not been filed with the Federal Court.

(2) Restrictions on communications — special advocate — After that information or other evidence is received by the special advocate, the special advocate may, during the remainder of the proceeding, communicate with another person about the proceeding only with the judge's authorization and subject to any conditions that the judge considers appropriate.

(3) Restrictions on communications — other persons — If the special advocate is authorized to communicate with a person, the judge may prohibit that person from communicating with anyone else about the proceeding during the remainder of the proceeding or may impose conditions with respect to such a communication during that period.

2008, c. 3, s. 4; 2015, c. 20, s. 59

Case Law

Almrei, Re, [2010] 2 F.C.R. 165, 342 F.T.R. 27 (Eng.), 2009 CarswellNat 690, 2009 FC 240 — By order dated January 2, 2009, the Chief Justice ordered that the court adjudicate upon two common issues of law that have arisen in four proceedings. The two common issues were identified in the order as follows:

(a) What is the role of the designated judge with respect to the additional information disclosed by the Ministers pursuant to the decision of the Supreme Court of Canada in *Charkaoui v. Canada (Citizenship & Immigration) (Charkaoui 2)*, [2008] 2 S.C.R. 326, 70 Imm. L.R. (3d) 1, [2008] S.C.J. No. 39, 294 D.L.R. (4th) 478, 58 C.R. (6th) 45, 376 N.R. 154, 175 C.R.R. (2d) 120, 2008 CarswellNat 1898, 2008 SCC 38? More specifically, does para. 62 of that decision require the judge to "verify" all information disclosed by the Ministers if the special advocates and counsel for the Ministers all agree that a portion of that information is irrelevant to the issues before the court?

(b) Should the information disclosed to the named persons and their counsel be placed on the court's public files in these proceedings? If so, when?

The Federal Court concluded that:

(a) Where the Ministers and the special advocate agree that the material disclosed by the Ministers pursuant to *Charkaoui 2* is irrelevant to the issues before the court, the court may rely upon that agreement. In such a case, the court need not verify information that the Ministers and the special advocates agree to be irrelevant.

(b) No information filed with the court in confidence pursuant to *Charkaoui 2* can be disclosed to the person named in a security certificate without the prior approval of the court.

(c) Information or evidence disclosed to the named persons pursuant to *Charkaoui 2* should be disclosed directly to counsel for each person named in a security certificate. The *Charkaoui 2* disclosure should not be placed on the court's public file. Such information or evidence would only become public if it is relied upon by a party and placed into evidence.

(d) Summaries of evidence or information made pursuant to para. 83(1)(e) of the Act must be placed on the court's public file because they relate to information relied upon by the Ministers and to what transpired in the *in camera* proceedings.

Harkat, Re, 2009 CarswellNat 540, 2009 CarswellNat 99 (F.C.) — The special advocates in this proceeding sought judicial authorization to communicate with special advocates appointed in other certificate proceedings "concerning the Orders that should be issued in IRPA proceedings where special advocates are appointed." The special advocates submitted that one of the goals of the amendments made to the IRPA by Parliament in Bill C-3 was to put the special advocates in the same position as counsel for the Ministers, that is, provide for an equity of arms in the closed portion of security certificate proceedings. It was therefore asserted that special advocates should be authorized to discuss common issues since it is believed that ministerial counsel have that ability. The Ministers opposed the request on the grounds that the authorization sought is overly vague and seeks to displace the designated judge's role to authorize specific communication requests by special advocates appointed in a proceeding. The order sought, according to the Ministers, goes against the intent of the legislation which is to prevent the inadvertent disclosure of confidential information by constant judicial supervision.

The court held that the request was not so vague that it was impossible to determine what can be discussed. A person with legal training, who is qualified to be a special advocate, has the knowledge necessary to determine the meaning of "common issues and questions of jurisdiction, procedure, and substantive law." He or she is also capable of distinguishing legal from factual issues although whenever there is a doubt, the guidance of the court should be sought. The court granted permission for the special advocates to communicate with other special advocates (who have obtained the same judicial authorization from their respective designated judge) appointed in other security certificate proceedings to discuss common issues related to questions of jurisdiction, procedure, and substantive law and orders rendered or orders to be sought. They are not authorized to refer directly or indirectly to any information or evidence which has been provided to them or to which they have been privy in their capacity as special advocates. These communications were only authorized at meetings organized by the support resources group for special advocates.

85.5 Disclosure and communication prohibited — With the exception of communications authorized by a judge, no person shall

　　(a) disclose information or other evidence that is disclosed to them under section 85.4 and that is treated as confidential by the judge presiding at the proceeding; or

(b) communicate with another person about the content of any part of a proceeding under any of sections 78 and 82 to 82.2 that is heard in the absence of the public and of the permanent resident or foreign national and their counsel.

2008, c. 3, s. 4

85.6 (1) Rules — The Chief Justice of the Federal Court of Appeal and the Chief Justice of the Federal Court may each establish a committee to make rules governing the practice and procedure in relation to the participation of special advocates in proceedings before the court over which they preside. The rules are binding despite any rule of practice that would otherwise apply.

(2) Composition of committees — Any committee established shall be composed of the Chief Justice of the Federal Court of Appeal or the Chief Justice of the Federal Court, as the case may be, the Attorney General of Canada or one or more representatives of the Attorney General of Canada, and one or more members of the bar of any province who have experience in a field of law relevant to those types of proceedings. The Chief Justices may also designate additional members of their respective committees.

(3) Chief Justices shall preside — The Chief Justice of the Federal Court of Appeal and the Chief Justice of the Federal Court — or a member designated by them — shall preside over their respective committees.

2008, c. 3, s. 4

Other Proceedings

[Heading amended 2008, c. 3, s. 4.]

86. Application for non-disclosure — The Minister may, during an admissibility hearing, a detention review or an appeal before the Immigration Appeal Division, apply for the non-disclosure of information or other evidence. Sections 83 and 85.1 to 85.5 apply to the proceeding with any necessary modifications, including that a reference to "judge" be read as a reference to the applicable Division of the Board.

2008, c. 3, s. 4

[Heading repealed 2008, c. 3, s. 4.]

86.1 (1) Judicial review — The Minister may, at any stage of the proceeding, apply for judicial review of any decision made in a proceeding referred to in section 86 requiring the disclosure of information or other evidence if, in the Minister's opinion, the disclosure would be injurious to national security or endanger the safety of any person. The application may be made without an application for leave.

(2) Effects of judicial review — The making of the application suspends the execution of the decision and, except in the case of a detention review, the proceeding referred to in section 86, until the application has been finally determined.

2015, c. 20, s. 60

87. Application for non-disclosure — judicial review and appeal — The Minister may, during a judicial review, apply for the non-disclosure of information or other evidence. Section 83 — other than the obligations to appoint a special advocate and to provide a summary — applies in respect of the proceeding and in respect of any appeal of a decision made in the proceeding, with any necessary modifications.

2008, c. 3, s. 4; 2015, c. 20, s. 60

Case Law

Sellathurai v. Canada (Minister of Public Safety & Emergency Preparedness) (2010), 375 F.T.R. 181 (Eng.), 93 Imm. L.R. (3d) 219, 2010 FC 1082, 2010 CarswellNat 4172, 2010 CarswellNat 5654 — The Minister sought the return of material inadvertently forwarded to counsel for the applicant. The Minister maintained that three unredacted confidential documents (the "disputed documents") attract national security privilege, that certain portions of the disputed documents should not have been disclosed, and that the inadvertent disclosure of the disputed documents did not waive the claimed privilege. A Federal Court judge granted the motion and concluded the court had jurisdiction to apply s. 87 of IRPA to the disputed documents. On appeal the Federal Court of Appeal held that the court's jurisdiction to consider the Minister's motion for the return of the material was grounded in s. 44 of the *Federal Courts Act*, R.S.C. 1985, c. F-7, and the Federal Court's plenary jurisdiction over disclosure in immigration matters, and not s. 87 of IRPA. Section 87 applies only to protect information that is producible in a pending application for judicial review. The linkage to a future, perhaps related, judicial review is insufficient to make s. 87 applicable to documents or information not otherwise producible in the pending application for judicial review.

The judge concluded on the evidence before her that the claim to national security privilege over portions of the three documents was not waived by their inadvertent disclosure. That conclusion was not challenged on appeal.

The appeal was allowed to the limited extent of remitting the matter back to the Federal Court for the purpose of considering whether in the circumstances an *amicus curiae* should be appointed to assist the court and what, if any, remedy is required by application of the principles of procedural fairness as a result of the inadvertent disclosure to the applicant of three documents that contained privileged information. In all other respects the appeal was dismissed.

87.01 (1) Appeal by Minister — The Minister may, without it being necessary for the judge to certify that a serious question of general importance is involved, appeal, at any stage of the proceeding, to the Federal Court of Appeal any decision made in a judicial review requiring the disclosure of information or other evidence if, in the Minister's opinion, the disclosure would be injurious to national security or endanger the safety of any person.

(2) Effects of appeal — The appeal suspends the execution of the decision, as well as the judicial review, until the appeal has been finally determined.

2015, c. 20, s. 60

87.1 Special advocate — **If the judge during the judicial review, or a court on appeal from the judge's decision, is of the opinion that considerations of fairness and natural justice require that a special advocate be appointed to protect the interests of the permanent resident or foreign national, the judge or court shall appoint a special advocate from the list referred to in subsection 85(1). Sections 85.1 to 85.5 apply to the proceeding with any necessary modifications.**

2008, c. 3, s. 4

Case Law

Farkhondehfall v. Canada (Minister of Citizenship & Immigration) (2009), 2 Admin. L.R. (5th) 240, 2009 FC 1064, 2009 CarswellNat 3344 — The Minister of Citizenship & Immigration brought motions for the non-disclosure of portions of a certified tribunal record in accordance with s. 87 of IRPA. The Minister asserted that the disclosure of the redacted information would be injurious to national security or to the safety of any person. In response to the Minister's s. 87 motions, the applicant brought motions of his own seeking the appointment of a special advocate to protect his interest in the s. 87 proceedings in each application. The court concluded that considerations of fairness and natural justice do not require the appointment of a special advocate to protect the applicant's interest in either application and dismissed the applicant's motion seeking a special advocate.

While the amendments made to IRPA in the wake of *Charkaoui* (2007), 59 Imm. L.R. (3d) 1 (S.C.C.), made the appointment of special advocates mandatory in security certificate proceedings, the appointment of special advocates in other types of cases under the Act is left to the discretion of the presiding designated judge. That is, s. 87.1 of IRPA gives the court the discretion to appoint a special advocate if it "is of the opinion that considerations of fairness and natural justice require" such an appointment in order to protect the interest of an applicant. A number of factors should be weighed by the court in accessing whether considerations of fairness and natural justice require the appointment of a special advocate to protect the interests of the individual. No one factor will necessarily be determinative; rather, the task for the court should be to balance all of the competing considerations in order to arrive at a just result. One set of related factors to be considered involves the importance of the decision in issue to the individual, the nature of the interests affected, and the degree of procedural fairness to which the individual is entitled in the case at hand. Other relevant considerations are the amount of information that has been disclosed and the extent to which the affected individual has been made aware of the case that they have to meet.

Regulations

[Heading added 2008, c. 3, s. 4.]

87.2 (1) Regulations — **The regulations may provide for any matter relating to the application of this Division and may include provisions respecting conditions and qualifications that persons must meet to be included in the list referred to in subsection 85(1) and additional qualifications that are assets that may be taken into account for that purpose.**

Proposed Amendment — 87.2(1)

(1) Regulations — The regulations may provide for any matter relating to the application of this Division and may include provisions respecting

(a) the conditions that must be imposed under subsection 77.1(1) or 82(6); and

(b) the conditions and qualifications that persons must meet to be included in the list referred to in subsection 85(1) and the additional qualifications that are assets that may be taken into account for that purpose.

2013, c. 16, s. 27 [Not in force at date of publication.]

(2) Requirements — The regulations

(a) shall require that, to be included in the list, persons be members in good standing of the bar of a province, not be employed in the federal public administration, and not otherwise be associated with the federal public administration in such a way as to impair their ability to protect the interests of the permanent resident or foreign national; and

(b) may include provisions respecting those requirements.

2008, c. 3, s. 4

DIVISION 10 — GENERAL PROVISIONS

Instructions on Processing Applications and Requests
[Heading added 2008, c. 28, s. 118.]

87.3 (1) Application — This section applies to applications for visas or other documents made under subsections 11(1) and (1.01), other than those made by persons referred to in subsection 99(2), to sponsorship applications made under subsection 13(1), to applications for permanent resident status under subsection 21(1) or temporary resident status under subsection 22(1) made by foreign nationals in Canada, to applications for work or study permits and to requests under subsection 25(1) made by foreign nationals outside Canada.

(2) Attainment of immigration goals — The processing of applications and requests is to be conducted in a manner that, in the opinion of the Minister, will best support the attainment of the immigration goals established by the Government of Canada.

(3) Instructions — For the purposes of subsection (2), the Minister may give instructions with respect to the processing of applications and requests, including instructions

(a) establishing categories of applications or requests to which the instructions apply;

(a.1) establishing conditions, by category or otherwise, that must be met before or during the processing of an application or request;

(b) establishing an order, by category or otherwise, for the processing of applications or requests;

(c) setting the number of applications or requests, by category or otherwise, to be processed in any year; and

(d) providing for the disposition of applications and requests, including those made subsequent to the first application or request.

(3.1) Application — An instruction may, if it so provides, apply in respect of pending applications or requests that are made before the day on which the instruction takes effect.

(3.2) Clarification — For greater certainty, an instruction given under paragraph (3)(c) may provide that the number of applications or requests, by category or otherwise, to be processed in any year be set at zero.

(4) Compliance with instructions — Officers and persons authorized to exercise the powers of the Minister under section 25 shall comply with any instructions before processing an application or request or when processing one. If an application or request is not processed, it may be retained, returned or otherwise disposed of in accordance with the instructions of the Minister.

(5) Clarification — The fact that an application or request is retained, returned or otherwise disposed of does not constitute a decision not to issue the visa or other document, or grant the status or exemption, in relation to which the application or request is made.

(6) Publication — Instructions shall be published in the *Canada Gazette*.

(7) Clarification — Nothing in this section in any way limits the power of the Minister to otherwise determine the most efficient manner in which to administer this Act.

[Editor's Note: According to section 120 of 2008, c. 28, section 87.3 applies only to applications and requests made on or after February 27, 2008.]

2008, c. 28, s. 118; 2012, c. 17, s. 29; 2012, c. 19, ss. 706(1), (3), (5), 710(2); 2012, c. 31, ss. 311, 314

Case Law

Jia v. Canada (Minister of Citizenship and Immigration) (2014), 26 Imm. L.R. (4th) 1, 457 F.T.R. 73, 82 Admin. L.R. (5th) 1, 2014 FC 596, 2014 CarswellNat 2228, 2014 CarswellNat 2451; affirmed 2015 FCA 146, 2015 CarswellNat 2294 — The applicant made an application for permanent residence as a member of the investor class, a class of economic immigrants provided for in s. 90 of the Regulations. His application was not being processed due to a large number of similar applications from other would-be investor class immigrants and also, possibly, as a result of certain changes to the way in which Citizenship and Immigration Canada processed applications under the federal Immigrant Investor Program ("IIP"). These changes resulted in applications like his being slowed down in the processing queue because the Minister adopted amended processing criteria, which provided for the concurrent processing of older applications — like the applicant's — at the same time as newer applications filed under amended and more demanding criteria. The applicant argued that if the Minister had not changed the processing priorities or had not set the quota for applications at artificially low levels, his application would have been granted by now and he would have been landed as a member of the investor class. He sought an order of *mandamus* to direct the respondent to process his IIP application.

The IRPA and the Regulations did not cast any obligation on the Minister to set any particular quota or target for the number of IIP applications that may be accepted in a year or to adhere to any particular processing priority. Likewise, there was no requirement to tie the IIP quota to the numbers that might be set under the Quebec Investor Program, an entirely separate immigration program. Nor can any such duties be inferred from the general purpose clauses set out in s. 3 of IRPA. Would-be immigrants have no right to force the Minister to set any particular quota for any economic class. The extent of the duty owed by the Minister in this case was to process the applicants' IIP applications within a reasonable period of time. There was no unreasonable delay in the processing and the applicants' IIP applications. The application for judicial review was dismissed.

Jiang v. Canada (Minister of Citizenship & Immigration), 2014 CarswellNat 420, 2014 FC 95 — This is an application for judicial review of the respondent's failure to process and render a decision with respect to the applicant's application for permanent residence in the investor category. The applicant sought an order of *mandamus* which was dismissed. The court certified the following question:

> Are individuals who will be subject to a lengthy waiting period, prior to the assessment of their immigration applications under the Investor Class, due to the effect of annual targets and Ministerial Instructions made under s. 87.3 of the *IRPA*, entitled to an order of *mandamus* to compel immediate processing?

Fang v. Canada (Minister of Citizenship & Immigration) (2014), 65 Admin. L.R. (5th) 259, 2014 CarswellNat 180, 2014 CarswellNat 621 — The applicant sought an order of *mandamus* requiring the Minister to process and render a final decision on her application for permanent residence as an investor. The applicant was of the view that the Minister had failed to honour his "processing pledge" and commence the processing within the timelines that were provided to the applicant upon filing. The applicant argued that the underlying reasons for the processing delays were the new selection criteria, the quotas and the processing priorities that were set out by the Ministerial Instructions and the Operational Bulletin.

The court concluded that the immigrant investor program scheme was legally set out and implemented in full contemplation of the law, and the powers adopted by Parliament pursuant to the new s. 87.3 of the Act. It is important to take a broad view when determining if the processing of an application took longer than the nature of the process required, more specifically when there are more applications than Canada can accept. The application for judicial review was dismissed.

The following question was certified:

> Are individuals who will be subject to a lengthy waiting period, prior to the assessment of their immigration applications under the Investor class, due to the effect of annual targets and Ministerial Instructions made under s. 87.3 of the *IRPA*, entitled to an order of mandamus to compel immediate processing?

Ansari v. Canada (Minister of Citizenship & Immigration), 2013 CarswellNat 2870, 2013 CarswellNat 3879, 2013 FC 849 — The officer found that the applicant did not have sufficient evidence that he had performed the actions described in the lead statement for the occupation and that he had performed all of the essential duties and a substantial number of the main duties. The refusal letter stated that the duties described in the employment letter submitted were "closely paraphrased from occupational descriptions of the NOC, diminishing the overall credibility of the employment letter." There is a need to determine whether the concern is about credibility or sufficiency before determining if a duty of procedural fairness is owed. If a concern about copying or paraphrasing from the NOC is characterised as related to credibility, without assessing whether it is in fact a credibility concern, the applicants who copy the NOC duties may come to expect an opportunity to provide further information or respond to the officer's concerns. This could lead to delays in processing FSW applications and is inconsistent with the instructions provided to applicants to provide all the relevant documents with their applications and to visa officers to assess the application as presented. The officer was entitled to give the evidence less weight, and as a result, the applicant did not meet the burden of providing sufficient information. There was no breach of procedural fairness.

Jordano v. Canada (Minister of Citizenship & Immigration), 2013 CarswellNat 4162, 2013 CarswellNat 4718, 2013 FC 1143 — The applicant wished to sponsor her mother to come to Canada as a member of the family class pursuant to s. 117(1) of the *IRPR*. Under normal circumstances, she would have been able to sponsor her mother pursuant to para. 117(1)(c) of the Regulations. However, a Ministerial Instruction was issued which imposed a temporary freeze on the acceptance for processing of new family class applications for a sponsor's parents or grandparents. The applicant chose to proceed under para. 117(1)(h) which is intended to provide for sponsorship by persons who do not have family members, such as persons who are orphans or do not have the more common relations described in other paragraphs of s. 117(1), i.e. spouses, dependent children, parents and grandparents. Interpreting the effect of an administrative implementation measure in a fashion that would aggravate the problem it was intended to resolve would constitute a perverse interpretation of both para. 117(1)(h) of the Regulations and s. 87.3 of the *IRPA*. The application for judicial review was dismissed.

Jin v. Canada (Minister of Citizenship & Immigration) (2009), 86 Imm. L.R. (3d) 13, 357 F.T.R. 309 (Eng.), 2009 FC 1234, 2009 CarswellNat 4162 — This was an application for judicial review concerning the interpretation of ministerial instructions issued in 2008 pursuant to s. 87.3 of IRPA introduced into the Act by s. 118 of the *Budget Implementation Act, 2008*. The applicant sought to have the court interpret the words "[a]pplications submitted [. . .] by foreign nationals residing legally in Canada for at least one year as [. . .] International Students" set out in the instructions as including foreign nationals who, *at any time in the past*, resided legally in Canada for at least one year as International Students. This interpretation would allow an International Student who resided in Canada for at least one year at any time in the past to benefit from priority processing for federal skilled workers permanent residence applications.

The terms of the instructions are clear on the residency requirements. The words "applications submitted by foreign nationals residing legally in Canada for at least one year as Temporary Foreign Workers or International Students" suffer no ambiguity. The choice of verb tense makes it abundantly clear that the Temporary Foreign Worker or the International Student must have been residing legally in Canada for at least one year immediately prior to his or her application. The French wording is also unambiguous and conveys the same meaning. Where the ministerial instructions wish to convey that a past period of time can be considered, they state so clearly, such as in the footnote concerning applications from skilled workers with evidence of experience which clearly provides for recognition of past experience in the following terms: "[a]t least one year of continuous full-time or equivalent paid work experience in the last ten years." The court also commented that the unfortunate use of form letters in responding to applications where multiple fact situations are involved can easily lead to ambiguity and misunderstanding. In this case the whole litigation could have easily been avoided had a proper and cogent response been provided to the applicant setting out in unambiguous terms the basis for which her application could not be processed as an International Student. The form letter stated that the applicant did not indicate in her application that she was legally residing in Canada for at least one year as an International Student. The true reason for not processing the application is thus stated, but in such a convoluted and ambiguous manner as to render the decision almost impossible to understand without further inquiry. Although the decision was legally correct, the communication of the reasons for which it was made were deficient. Nevertheless, returning the matter to the decision maker on the basis of the original application would not provide the applicant with the result she sought. The application for judicial review was dismissed.

Federal Skilled Workers

[Heading added 2012, c. 19, s. 707.]

87.4 (1) Application made before February 27, 2008 — An application by a foreign national for a permanent resident visa as a member of the prescribed class of federal skilled workers that was made before February 27, 2008 is terminated if, before March 29, 2012, it has not been established by an officer, in accordance with the regulations, whether the applicant meets the selection criteria and other requirements applicable to that class.

(2) Application — Subsection (1) does not apply to an application in respect of which a superior court has made a final determination unless the determination is made on or after March 29, 2012.

(3) Effect — The fact that an application is terminated under subsection (1) does not constitute a decision not to issue a permanent resident visa.

(4) Fees returned — Any fees paid to the Minister in respect of the application referred to in subsection (1) — including for the acquisition of permanent resident status — must be returned, without interest, to the person who paid them. The amounts payable may be paid out of the Consolidated Revenue Fund.

(5) No recourse or indemnity — No person has a right of recourse or indemnity against Her Majesty in connection with an application that is terminated under subsection (1).

2012, c. 19, s. 707

Case Law

Liu v. Canada (Minister of Citizenship & Immigration) (2014), 22 Imm. L.R. (4th) 212, 2014 FC 42, 2014 CarswellNat 113, 2014 CarswellNat 33 — This was a judicial review by way of *mandamus* concerning an application for a visa under the federal skilled worker class. The visa application was deemed terminated by retrospective legislation, set out in s. 87.4. The Minister issued Operational Bulletin 400 instructing that as of March 29, 2012, processing should not commence or continue for a federal skilled worker visa application received before February 27, 2008, for which a selection decision had not been made before March 29, 2012. Operational Bulletin 400 was rescinded. The Minister subsequently issued Operational Bulletin 413 on April 27, 2013, that instructed to continue processing all federal skilled worker applications until Bill C-38 came into force, which it did on June 29, 2013. On June 21, 2012, an officer determined that the applicant had met the selection criteria for his occupation and he was instructed to complete the medical examinations and pay the requisite fees. His application was returned to him in October 2012 on the grounds that the application was terminated by operation of law. The court concluded that the purpose and intent of the legislation was to expunge as of March 29, 2012, existing rights in pre-February 27, 2008, visa applications unless an applicant had fully complied on that date with the federal skilled worker visa requirements. The applicant did not nor had he complied when s. 87.4 came into effect on June 29, 2012. Therefore the application for judicial review was dismissed.

Tabingo v. Canada (Minister of Citizenship and Immigration) (2014), 27 Imm. L.R. (4th) 175, 86 Admin. L.R. (5th) 194, 377 D.L.R. (4th) 151, 318 C.R.R. (2d) 267, 462 N.R. 124, 2014 FCA 191, 2014 CarswellNat 3180, 2014 CarswellNat 6290; leave to appeal to S.C.C. refused 2015 CarswellNat 1278, 2015 CarswellNat 1279 (S.C.C.) — The applicants applied for federal skilled worker permanent resident visas before February 27, 2008. They sought an order of *mandamus* directing the respondent to process their applications and have filed Notices of Constitutional Question alleging that s. 87.4 violates the rule of law and the *Canadian Charter of Rights and Freedoms*. Eight applicants were identified to represent approximately 1400 other individuals, all of whom had commenced applications under s. 18.1 of the *Federal Courts Act*.

The court accepted that the applicants have experienced stress and hardship, and that the circumstances of some of the applicants are compelling. However, immigration is not of such an intimate, profound and fundamental nature as to be comparable with a woman's right of reproductive choice, or the freedom of parents to care for their children. The ability to immigrate, particularly as a member of an economic class, is not among the fundamental choices relating to personal autonomy which would engage s. 7. While it may have life-altering consequences, the possibility of immigrating to Canada as a successful federal skilled worker applicant does not engage life or liberty interests. The loss of the expectation or hope is understandably distressing. Given the passage of time, the effect on the points awarded on the basis of age and the shift in occupational priorities reflected in successive ministerial instructions, the opportunity of re-applying has evaporated. Nevertheless, the interests protected by s. 7 are not engaged in these circumstances. Section 87.4 merely terminated the opportunity. Section 87.4 is valid legislation, compliant with the rule of law, the Bill of Rights and the Charter. The applications have been terminated by operation of law and the court cannot order *mandamus*.

The Federal Court of Appeal dismissed all the appeals and concluded as follows:

(a) Subsection 87.4(1) terminated the applications automatically on June 29, 2012. After that date, the Minister had no legal obligation to continue to process the applications. The appellants were not entitled to *mandamus*.

(b) The *Canadian Bill of Rights* does not mandate notice and an opportunity to make submissions prior to termination of an application under subs. 87.4(1) of the IRPA.

(c) Section 87.4 of the IRPA is not unconstitutional or contrary to the rule of law or ss. 7 and 15 of the *Charter*.

Federal Investor and Entrepreneur Classes
[Heading added 2014, c. 20, s. 303.]

87.5 (1) Pending applications — An application by a foreign national for a permanent resident visa as a member of the prescribed class of investors or of entrepreneurs is terminated if, before February 11, 2014, it has not been established by an officer, in accordance with the regulations, whether the applicant meets the selection criteria and other requirements applicable to the class in question.

(2) Application — Subsection (1) does not apply to

(a) an application in respect of which a superior court has made a final determination unless the determination is made on or after February 11, 2014; or

(b) an application made by an investor or entrepreneur who is selected as such by a province whose government has entered into an agreement referred to in subsection 9(1).

(3) Effect — The fact that an application is terminated under subsection (1) does not constitute a decision not to issue a permanent resident visa.

(4) Fees returned — Any fees paid to the Minister in respect of the application referred to in subsection (1) — including for the acquisition of permanent resident status — must be returned, without interest, to the person who paid them. The amounts payable may be paid out of the Consolidated Revenue Fund.

(5) Investment returned — If an application for a permanent resident visa as a member of the prescribed class of investors is terminated under subsection (1), an amount equal to the investment made by the applicant in respect of their application must be returned, without interest, to the applicant. The amount may be paid out of the Consolidated Revenue Fund.

(6) Provincial allocation — If the provincial allocation of an investment made in respect of an application for a permanent resident visa as a member of the prescribed class of investors that is terminated under subsection (1) has been transferred to an approved fund, as defined in subsection 88(1) of the *Immigration and Refugee Protection Regulations*, the province whose government controls the approved fund must return an amount equal to that provincial allocation to the Minister without delay. The return of the amount extinguishes the debt obligation in respect of that provincial allocation.

(7) No recourse or indemnity — No right of recourse or indemnity lies against Her Majesty in right of Canada in connection with an application that is terminated under subsection (1), including in respect of any contract or other arrangement relating to any aspect of the application.

2014, c. 20, s. 303

Case Law

Kearney v. Canada (Minister of Citizenship and Immigration), 2015 FCA 144, 2015 CarswellNat 2295 — The appeals are moot. The applications that were before the Federal Court judges in these appeals were for orders of *mandamus* to compel the Minister of

Citizenship and Immigration to process applications for permanent residence under the federal Immigrant Investor Program in the IRPA that had not been processed as fast as the applicants desired. The decision under appeal was rendered four days after s. 87.5 of the IRPA came into force. Its effect was to terminate all of the applications of the appellants in these appeals. As a result the issue of whether the Minister could be forced to process these applications was no longer a live controversy.

Loans

88. (1) Loans — **The Minister of Finance may, from time to time, advance to the Minister out of the Consolidated Revenue Fund, up to the maximum amount that is prescribed, sums that the Minister may require in order to make loans for the purposes of this Act.**

(2) Regulations — **The regulations may provide for any matter relating to the application of this section, and may include provisions respecting classes of persons to whom, and the purposes for which, the loans may be made.**

Fees

89. (1) Regulations — **The regulations may govern fees for services provided in the administration of this Act, and cases in which fees may be waived by the Minister or otherwise, individually or by class.**

(1.1) User Fees Act — **The** *User Fees Act* **does not apply to a fee for the provision of services in relation to a request for an assessment provided by the Department of Employment and Social Development with respect to an application for a work permit.**

(1.2) User Fees Act — **The** *User Fees Act* **does not apply to a fee for the provision of services in relation to the processing of an application for a temporary resident visa, work permit, study permit or extension of an authorization to remain in Canada as a temporary resident.**

(2) User Fees Act — **The** *User Fees Act* **does not apply to a fee for the provision of services in relation to an application referred to in subsection 11(1.01).**

(3) User Fees Act — **The** *User Fees Act* **does not apply to a fee for the provision of services in relation to the collection, use and disclosure of biometric information and for the provision of related services.**
2012, c. 17, s. 30 [Amended 2012, c. 31, s. 313(4).]; 2012, c. 31, s. 312; 2013, c. 33, s. 162; 2013, c. 40, s. 237(1)(i); 2014, c. 39, s. 310

Case Law

Toussaint v. Canada (Minister of Citizenship & Immigration), 2011 FCA 146, 2011 CarswellNat 1943, 2011 CarswellNat 1446; application/notice of appeal to S.C.C. filed 2011 CarswellNat 2875 (S.C.C.) — On a proper interpretation of subs. 25(1) of IRPA, the Minister is obligated to consider a request for an exemption from the requirement in para. 10(1)(d) of the Regulations to pay a fee for processing an application under subs. 25(1).

The Governor in Council's failure to enact regulations permitting the waiver of fees for foreign nationals living in poverty who wish to make an in-Canada application for permanent residence status pursuant to subs. 25(1) of IRPA does not infringe an applicant's s. 7 or 15 of the *Charter of Rights* nor does it infringe the rule of law or the common law constitutional right of access to the courts.

Proposed Addition — 89.01

89.01 Fees for rights and privileges — assessments — The regulations may

(a) govern fees to be paid for rights and privileges in relation to an assessment provided by the Department of Employment and Social Development with respect to an application for a work permit; and

(b) govern cases in which the fees referred to in paragraph (a) are waived.

2014, c. 39, s. 311 [Not in force at date of publication.]

89.1 (1) Fees for rights and privileges — The regulations may

(a) govern fees to be paid for rights and privileges conferred by means of a work permit; and

(b) waive the fees referred to in paragraph (a) for certain work permits or certain classes of work permits.

(2) User Fees Act — The *User Fees Act* does not apply to fees referred to in paragraph (1)(a).

2013, c. 33, s. 163

89.2 Fees — compliance regime — (1) The regulations may

(a) govern fees to be paid in respect of the compliance regime that applies to employers in relation to their employment of foreign nationals whose authorizations to work in Canada do not require an assessment provided by the Department of Employment and Social Development;

Proposed Amendment — 89.2(1)(a)

(a) govern fees to be paid in respect of the compliance regime that applies to employers in relation to their employment of foreign nationals whose authorizations to work in Canada do not require an assessment provided by the Department of Employment and Social Development; and

2015, c. 36, s. 173 [Not in force at date of publication.]

(b) govern cases in which the fees referred to in paragraph (a) are waived;

(c) require employers to pay the fees referred to in paragraph (a) by means of an electronic system; and

Proposed Repeal — 89.2(1)(c)

(c) [Repealed 2015, c. 36, s. 173. Not in force at date of publication.]

(d) include provisions respecting that system, respecting the circumstances in which those fees may be paid by other means and respecting those other means.

Proposed Repeal — 89.2(1)(d)

(d) [Repealed 2015, c. 36, s. 173. Not in force at date of publication.]

(2) User Fees Act — The *User Fees Act* does not apply to fees referred to in paragraph (1)(a).

2014, c. 39, s. 312

Social Insurance Numbers

[Heading amended 2012, c. 19, s. 311.]

90. Minister directs special numbers to be issued — The Minister may direct the Canada Employment Insurance Commission to assign to persons, other than Canadian citizens or permanent residents, Social Insurance Numbers identifying those persons as persons who may be required under this Act to obtain authorization to work in Canada.

2012, c. 19, s. 311

Representation or Advice

[Heading amended 2011, c. 8, s. 1.]

91. (1) Representation or advice for consideration — Subject to this section, no person shall knowingly, directly or indirectly, represent or advise a person for consideration — or offer to do so — in connection with the submission of an expression of interest under subsection 10.1(3) or a proceeding or application under this Act.

(2) Persons who may represent or advise — A person does not contravene subsection (1) if they are

    (a) a lawyer who is a member in good standing of a law society of a province or a notary who is a member in good standing of the Chambre des notaires du Québec;

    (b) any other member in good standing of a law society of a province or the Chambre des notaires du Québec, including a paralegal; or

    (c) a member in good standing of a body designated under subsection (5).

(3) Students-at-law — A student-at-law does not contravene subsection (1) by offering or providing representation or advice to a person if the student-at-law is acting under the supervision of a person mentioned in paragraph (2)(a) who is representing or advising the person — or offering to do so — in connection with the submission of an expression of interest under subsection 10.1(3) or a proceeding or application under this Act.

IRP Act

(4) Agreement or arrangement with Her Majesty — An entity, including a person acting on its behalf, that offers or provides services to assist persons in connection with the submission of an expression of interest under subsection 10.1(3) or an application under this Act, including for a permanent or temporary resident visa, travel documents or a work or study permit, does not contravene subsection (1) if it is acting in accordance with an agreement or arrangement between that entity and Her Majesty in right of Canada that authorizes it to provide those services.

(5) Designation by Minister — The Minister may, by regulation, designate a body whose members in good standing may represent or advise a person for consideration — or offer to do so — in connection with the submission of an expression of interest under subsection 10.1(3) or a proceeding or application under this Act.

(5.1) Revocation of designation — For greater certainty, subsection (5) authorizes the Minister to revoke, by regulation, a designation made under that subsection.

(6) Regulations — required information — The Governor in Council may make regulations requiring the designated body to provide the Minister with any information set out in the regulations, including information relating to its governance and information to assist the Minister to evaluate whether the designated body governs its members in a manner that is in the public interest so that they provide professional and ethical representation and advice.

(7) Regulations — transitional measures — The Minister may, by regulation, provide for measures respecting any transitional issues raised by the exercise of his or her power under subsection (5), including measures

(a) making any person or member of a class of persons a member for a specified period of a body that is designated under that subsection; and

(b) providing that members or classes of members of a body that has ceased to be a designated body under that subsection continue for a specified period to be authorized to represent or advise a person for consideration — or offer to do so — in connection with the submission of an expression of interest under subsection 10.1(3) or a proceeding or application under this Act without contravening subsection (1).

(7.1) An Act respecting immigration to Québec — For greater certainty, *An Act respecting immigration to Québec*, R.S.Q., c. I-0.2, applies to, among other persons, every person who, in Quebec, represents or advises a person for consideration — or offers to do so — in connection with a proceeding or application under this Act and

(a) is authorized to do so under regulations made under paragraph (7)(b); or

(b) is a member of a body designated under subsection (5).

(8) Persons made members of a body — For greater certainty, nothing in measures referred to in paragraph (7)(a) exempts a person made a member of a body under the measures from the body's disciplinary rules concerning suspension or revocation of membership for providing — or offering to provide — representation or advice that is not professional or is not ethical.

(9) Penalties — Every person who contravenes subsection (1) commits an offence and is liable

(a) on conviction on indictment, to a fine of not more than $100,000 or to imprisonment for a term of not more than two years, or to both; or

(b) on summary conviction, to a fine of not more than $20,000 or to imprisonment for a term of not more than six months, or to both.

(10) Meaning of "proceeding" — For greater certainty, in this section, "proceeding" does not include a proceeding before a superior court.

2011, c. 8, s. 1; 2013, c. 40, s. 292

Case Law

Kavihuha v. Canada (Minister of Citizenship and Immigration), 2015 FC 328, 2015 CarswellNat 3439, 2015 CarswellNat 828 — The applicants challenged the decision of the Refugee Board, concluding that they are not Convention refugees or persons in need of protection. They argued that they were denied procedural fairness and natural justice because their counsel was incompetent. Refugee claimants have a statutory right to be represented by counsel during Board proceedings. There is a reason competent counsel meets with and prepares witnesses for their testimony. This is especially the case where, as here, the process is new and in a foreign country. Where, as here, the relevant events occurred years before the hearing, it is only common sense that memory will not be as sharp on dates of those events if the witness has not had an opportunity to review those facts with counsel. Here, on the evidence of the applicants, there was no such opportunity. It is no answer for counsel to assert that she was waiting to be "properly retained." In this case, counsel had acted for these applicants in making their claim and if she was not prepared to do a competent job representing them because of a lack of financial retainer, then she ought to have removed herself as counsel of record. The court did not accept the respondent's submission that the result would have been the same in regards to the credibility finding had the solicitor done a competent job of representing the applicants. Nor did the court agree that the result was, at least in part, dependent on the lack of the documents that counsel ought to have obtained herself or advised her clients to obtain. It is impossible to reach a conclusion that the result would have been the same, without seeing what those documents would have been. The application for judicial review was allowed.

Canadian Society of Immigration Consultants v. Canada (Minister of Citizenship & Immigration) (2012), 8 Imm. L.R. (4th) 233, 434 N.R. 14, 41 Admin. L.R. (5th) 298, 2012 FCA 194, 2012 CarswellNat 2165, 2012 CarswellNat 3063; leave to appeal to the S.C.C. refused 2012 CarswellNat 5001, 2012 CarswellNat 5002 (S.C.C.) — This appeal by the Canadian Society of Immigration Consultants was from a decision of the Federal Court where an application for judicial review had been dismissed. The Federal Court judge certified the following question:

> Are the *Regulations Amending the Immigration and Refugee Protection Regulations* (SOR/2011-129), the *Order Fixing June 30, 2011 as the Day on which Chapter 8 of the Statutes of Canada, 2011, Comes into Force* (SI/2011-57) and/or the *Regulations Designating a Body for the Purposes of paragraph 91(2)(c) of the Immigration and Refugee Act* (SOR/2011-142) *ultra vires*, illegal and/or invalid in law?

The Federal Court of Appeal was not persuaded that the Regulations were invalid. The appeal was dismissed.

Kim v. Canada (Minister of Citizenship & Immigration), 2012 CarswellNat 1749, 2012 FC 687 — This was an application for judicial review of an immigration officer's decision denying the application for an exemption under H&C grounds, to apply for permanent residence from within Canada. The sole issue to be determined was whether the consultant's conduct amounted to incompetence. The consultant overlooked, in his preparation of the file, the financial aspect of the applicants' situation. In this particular context, where the officer specifically refers to the lack of evidence, and where the submissions by the consultant are limited, the court concluded that the failure to submit evidence caused a prejudice to the applicants amounting to a miscarriage of justice. The application for judicial review was allowed.

Thamotharampillai v. Canada (Minister of Citizenship & Immigration), 2011 FC 438, 2011 CarswellNat 1107, 2011 CarswellNat 1938 — As a general rule, a party is bound by the actions of his or her agent. However, there are times when a lawyer or an authorized representative has failed to mail a completed humanitarian and compassionate application, or has failed to inform the Board of the applicant's change of address. This is a different category altogether, and the category which is applicable in this instance. In this case, the consultant did absolutely nothing. The applicant was denied natural justice because he was represented by an incompetent immigration consultant. Had the consultant been competent and done his duty, the decision may well have been different. The immigration consultant failed to make any submissions with respect to the PRRA application.

Onuschak v. Canadian Society of Immigration Consultants (2009), 86 Imm. L.R. (3d) 78, 357 F.T.R. 22 (Eng.), 3 Admin. L.R. (5th) 214, 2009 FC 1135, 2009 CarswellNat 5491, 2009 CarswellNat 4214 — The applicant was a member of the Canadian Society of Immigration Consultants and a would-be director. She applied to the court for various declarations pertaining to her eligibility to run for office and as to the validity of the nomination and election procedures currently in place and other relief. The issue was whether the society is a federal board, commission or other tribunal within the meaning of the *Federal Courts Act* and, if so, whether the activities in question had a public aspect or a connotation to them or whether they were merely incidental to the society's status as a corporation incorporated under the *Canada Corporations Act*.

The Minister delegated to the society the power to set the rules to license third parties on standards set by the Minister and has prohibited immigration consultants from charging fees or having a right of standing in administrative proceedings unless they are members of the society. Thus licensing, standards and membership all form part of a single whole. A society is a federal board, commission or other tribunal, and was acting as such with respect to all aspects of the application for judicial review. Whether the Federal Court has any jurisdiction over the society other than by way of judicial review was a question to be left to another day.

Domantay v. Canada (Minister of Citizenship & Immigration) (2008), 73 Imm. L.R. (3d) 241, 2008 CarswellNat 3997, 2008 CarswellNat 1968, 2008 FC 755 — The sole issue raised by this application was whether by allowing the applicant's former representative, allegedly someone who was not a "member in good standing of a bar of a province, Chamber des notaires du Québec or the Canadian Society of Immigration Consultants," as required by the *Immigration and Refugee Protection Regulations*, to represent the applicant, the Board committed a breach of procedural fairness or natural justice. The court concluded that there is an onus on the applicant to choose his representative. It is not the obligation of the Board to police the applicant's right to counsel, while the applicant bears the onus of establishing the circumstances surrounding his allegation that any duty owed to him was not met, and that as a result he suffered a breach of natural justice. The applicant retained the office of a Max Chaudhary to act on his behalf in his appeal before the Board and someone was sent by Chaudhary's office to act on his behalf at his hearing. That person was neither a member of the Law Society nor a member of the Canadian Society of Immigration Consultants. The court concluded that the applicant accepted the representative delegated to him by Chaudhary's firm and that the Board fulfilled any verification duties that were incumbent upon it and that applicant had not established that the Board failed to meet its verification obligations pursuant to the Regulations, or that it committed a breach of procedural fairness or natural justice. Therefore the application was dismissed.

Shapovalov v. Canada (Minister of Citizenship & Immigration), 2007 CarswellNat 7011 (F.C.) — The applicant sought judicial review of an immigration officer's decision to refuse the applicant's request to have counsel present at his inadmissibility interview. The respondent relied primarily on the fact that the questions posed to the applicant were not of a legal or complex nature and did not warrant the presence of counsel at the interview. The court held that other factors identified by the applicant outweighed this consideration. Specifically, this interview was not occurring at the early stages of the process, since the applicant had previously been interviewed and a finding had been made that he met the selection criteria; the interview was to determine whether he was inadmissible and was a last crucial step in the process. Further, the rejection of an application on the ground of inadmissibility identified in this case may well hinder any future chance of success and therefore was of importance to the applicant. Thirdly, permitting counsel to attend in these circumstances to observe would not unduly encumber the efficient administration of the process. Finally, given the nature of the inquiry at which the questions were directed coupled with the fact that the application had already been the subject of a judicial review proceeding weighed in favour of concluding that the duty of fairness in these circumstances encompasses the right to have counsel present at the interview. The application for judicial review was allowed.

Law Society of Upper Canada v. Canada (Minister of Citizenship & Immigration) (2006), 55 Imm. L.R. (3d) 238, 2006 CarswellNat 2717, 2006 FC 1042 — The applicant Law Society of Upper Canada sought a declaration that the *Regulations Amending the Immigration and Refugee Protection Regulations* are *ultra vires*. The Regulations at issue provided that, subject to certain "grandfathering," only the certain persons may, for a fee, represent, advise or consult with a person who is the subject of an IRPA proceeding, before the Minister, an officer or the Board.

The Regulations were not discriminatory. The federal government has the power to choose persons who can represent others for the IRPA purposes including representations before the Board, and such persons need not be lawyers. Not to select a group of persons such as lawyers' employees, is not, in itself, discriminatory.

The following question has been certified: Are the *Regulations Amending the Immigration & Refugee Protection Regulations* (SOR/2004-59), which were enacted pursuant to s. 91 of the *Immigration and Refugee Protection Act, ultra vires*?

Chinese Business Chamber of Canada v. R. (2005), 45 Imm. L.R. (3d) 40, 2005 CarswellNat 250, 2005 FC 142 — On April 13, 2004, regulations came into effect that governed who may represent, advise or consult with persons subject to immigration proceedings or those making immigration applications. Since that date, only lawyers, members of the Chambre des Notaries du Québec or members of the Canadian Society of Immigration Consultants may act for a fee in immigration matters.

Notwithstanding that the *Immigration Act* conferred the statutory power to regulate who could appear before the Immigration and Refugee Board or the Governor-in-Council, there was some question as to whether the federal government could in fact legislate in this area, or whether this would be an encroachment on provincial jurisdiction. In 2001, the Supreme Court of Canada decided that while the provinces do indeed have the power to regulate professions, including the legal profession, it is Parliament that has jurisdiction over the areas of immigration and naturalization. Flowing from this is the authority to provide for the powers of immigration tribunals. One of these powers is the power to regulate who may appear. In June 2002, the *Immigration and Refugee Protection Act* came into effect. With the jurisdiction question resolved, the regulations determining who could act in immigration matters were passed.

There has been a long recognized need to regulate immigration consultants. Unqualified and unscrupulous consultants have been known to take advantage of vulnerable prospective immigrants and refugees. On October 8, 2003, CSIC was incorporated. The mandate of CSIC was to regulate immigration consultants in the public interest and, in so doing, to establish a code of conduct, a complaints and disciplinary process and a compensation fund. In January 2004, CSIC published an announcement advising that non-lawyer immigration consultants could file an "intent to register" in order to be recognized as a registered consultant at the time the regulations came into force. CSIC's by-laws, which contain the details of the regulatory scheme governing immigration consultants, were published on March 29, 2004. On April 1, 2004, the immigration consultant regulations were approved by the Governor-in-Council and came into force on April 13, 2004.

In accordance with its by-laws, CSIC has developed membership requirements, a code of conduct and a complaints and discipline process. CSIC has established errors and omissions insurance requirements and competency testing. Of the estimated 6,000–7,000 immigration consultants, approximately 1,400 have become "transitional" members.

This application for a stay of the enforcement of the regulations was refused because the applicants could not demonstrate irreparable harm.

Hak v. Canada (Minister of Citizenship & Immigration) (2005), 54 Imm. L.R. (3d) 98, 2005 CarswellNat 3669, 2005 CarswellNat 5007, 2005 FC 1488 — The law is clear that an individual must bear the consequences of hiring poor counsel. There may be circumstances where the negligent or incompetent actions of an individual's representative may result in the person being denied a fair hearing. In this case, the applicant claimed that the failure of her immigration consultant to notify her of the date for her interview resulted in her being denied procedural fairness in the process. The applicant failed to persuade the court that she had been denied procedural fairness in the process.

Toor v. Canada (Minister of Citizenship & Immigration), 2005 CarswellNat 3256, 2005 FC 1386 — The applicants, having been unsuccessful Convention refugees, made an application for humanitarian and compassionate consideration pursuant to s. 25 of the IRPA. They also made an application for consideration as Post-determination Refugee Claimants. Their lawyer wrote to the processing centre in Vegreville, Alberta, in anticipation that the file would be transferred to Vancouver and might be determined concurrently with the PRRA application, advising that he would make complete representations in support of their request once the applicants received their notice to make representations and file evidence in support of the PRRA. The H&C request was turned down. No additional information was supplied by the applicants' lawyer because Vegieville ignored the fact that the lawyer's address was listed as the place to communicate with the applicants, and wrote directly to the applicants instead. The decision maker's notes to file indicate that she did not appear to have focused on what was before her and consequently the decision was held to be patently unreasonable.

Khan v. Canada (Minister of Citizenship & Immigration) (2005), 47 Imm. L.R. (3d) 278, 2005 CarswellNat 1716, 2005 CarswellNat 5405, 2005 FC 833 — There is no doubt that the onus of notifying immigration of change of addresses rests with the refugee claimant. However, where the negligence of counsel is egregious and there has been no contributing negligence or fault on the part of the applicant, the Immigration Refugee Board's decision to refuse to reopen the applicant's claim after it had been declared abandoned when the applicant failed to appear for a hearing and failed to appear at an abandonment show cause hearing can be set aside. In this case, the applicants put their trust in a consultant who led them to believe that he would take care of all correspondence with the Board, that they need not contact the Board directly and that he would advise them of any scheduled proceedings. Consequently, the court was prepared to accept that their fault was not of such a degree that the applicants should be held accountable for their counsel's failures.

Shirvan v. Canada (Minister of Citizenship & Immigration), 2005 FC 1509, 2005 CarswellNat 3744, 2005 CarswellNat 5233, [2005] F.C.J. No. 1864 — Before examining allegations of incompetence, the court must first determine whether the applicants have met their preliminary burden of giving notice of the allegations to their former counsel. In this case, new counsel for the applicants wrote to the Canadian Society of Immigration Consultants to complain of their former counsel's treatment and to request that he immediately be prohibited from practising as an immigration consultant. The letter provided sufficient corroborating evidence and provided sufficient notice of the allegation to the applicants' former counsel.

Although the Immigration Appeal Division transcript demonstrated that the former counsel was unfamiliar with the hearing procedure, the applicants were still able to present their case. The only major ground the applicants claimed their former counsel should have raised was the best interest of the child consideration. Since the child was aged 19 or older at the time of the initial determination and at the time of the Immigration Appeal Division hearing, the Immigration Appeal Division did not err in its decision not to consider the best interest of the applicant's daughter. Accordingly, the applicants failed to demonstrate the result of their hearing would have been different but for their former counsel's alleged incompetence.

Material Incorporated in Regulations

92. (1) Incorporated material — A regulation may incorporate by reference the following material:

  (a) material produced by a person or body other than the Governor in Council;

(b) material referred to in paragraph (a) that has been subsequently adapted or edited in order to facilitate its incorporation for the purposes of the regulation;

(c) material that has been developed jointly with another government or government agency for the purpose of harmonizing the regulation with other laws; and

(d) material that is technical or explanatory in nature, such as specifications, classifications, illustrations or graphs, as well as examples that may assist in the application of the regulation.

(1.1) Incorporated material — instructions — An instruction given by the Minister or the Minister of Employment and Social Development under this Act may incorporate by reference any material, regardless of its source.

(2) Amended from time to time — Material may be incorporated by reference on a specified date or as amended from time to time.

(3) Incorporated material is not a regulation — For greater certainty, material that is incorporated by reference in a regulation made under this Act is not a regulation for the purposes of the *Statutory Instruments Act*.

2012, c. 19, s. 708; 2013, c. 33, s. 164; 2013, c. 40, s. 238(1)(h)(ii)

93. Statutory Instruments Act — Instructions given by the Minister or the Minister of Employment and Social Development under this Act and guidelines issued by the Chairperson under paragraph 159(1)(h) are not statutory instruments for the purposes of the *Statutory Instruments Act*.

2013, c. 33, s. 165; 2013, c. 40, s. 238(1)(h)(iii)

Report to Parliament

94. (1) Annual report to Parliament — The Minister must, on or before November 1 of each year or, if a House of Parliament is not then sitting, within the next 30 days on which that House is sitting after that date, table in each House of Parliament a report on the operation of this Act in the preceding calendar year.

(2) Contents of report — The report shall include a description of

(a) the instructions given under section 87.3 and other activities and initiatives taken concerning the selection of foreign nationals, including measures taken in cooperation with the provinces;

(b) in respect of Canada, the number of foreign nationals who became permanent residents, and the number projected to become permanent residents in the following year;

(b.1) in respect of Canada, the linguistic profile of foreign nationals who became permanent residents;

(c) in respect of each province that has entered into a federal-provincial agreement described in subsection 9(1), the number, for each class listed in the agreement, of persons that became permanent residents and that the province projects will become permanent residents there in the following year;

(d) the number of temporary resident permits issued under section 24, categorized according to grounds of inadmissibility, if any;

(e) the number of persons granted permanent resident status under each of subsections 25(1), 25.1(1) and 25.2(1);

(e.1) any instructions given under subsection 30(1.2), (1.41) or (1.43) during the year in question and the date of their publication; and

(f) a gender-based analysis of the impact of this Act.

2008, c. 28, s. 119; 2010, c. 8, s. 9; 2012, c. 1, s. 207; 2013, c. 33, s. 166

PART 2 — REFUGEE PROTECTION

DIVISION 1 — REFUGEE PROTECTION, CONVENTION REFUGEES AND PERSONS IN NEED OF PROTECTION

95. (1) Conferral of refugee protection — Refugee protection is conferred on a person when

(a) the person has been determined to be a Convention refugee or a person in similar circumstances under a visa application and becomes a permanent resident under the visa or a temporary resident under a temporary resident permit for protection reasons;

(b) the Board determines the person to be a Convention refugee or a person in need of protection; or

(c) except in the case of a person described in subsection 112(3), the Minister allows an application for protection.

Proposed Amendment — 95(1)(c)

(c) the Board allows their application for protection.

2012, c. 17, s. 31(1) [Not in force at date of publication.]

(2) Protected person — A protected person is a person on whom refugee protection is conferred under subsection (1), and whose claim or application has not subsequently been deemed to be rejected under subsection 108(3), 109(3) or 114(4).

Proposed Amendment — 95(2)

(2) Protected person — A protected person is a person on whom refugee protection is conferred under subsection (1) and whose claim or application has not subsequently been deemed to be rejected under subsection 108(3) or 109(3).

2012, c. 17, s. 31(2) [Not in force at date of publication.]

[Editor's Note: SOR/2002-227, s. 338 provides that refugee protection under the Immigration and Refugee Protection Act, S.C. 2001, c. 27 (the "new Act") is conferred on a person who

(a) has been determined in Canada before June 28, 2002 to be a Convention refugee and

(i) no determination was made to vacate that determination, or

347

(ii) no determination was made that the person ceased to be a Convention refugee;

(b) as an applicant or an accompanying dependant was granted landing before June 28, 2002 after being issued a visa under

(i) s. 7 of the Immigration Regulations, 1978, *SOR/78-172 (the "former Regulations"), or*

(ii) s. 4 of the Humanitarian Designated Classes Regulations, *SOR/97-183; or*

(c) was determined to be a member of the post-determination refugee claimants in Canada class before June 28, 2002 and was granted landing under s. 11.4 of the former Regulations or who becomes a permanent resident under s. 21(2) of the new Act.

SOR/2002-227, s. 339 further provides that a determination made in Canada before June 28, 2002 that a person is not a Convention refugee is deemed to be a claim for refugee protection rejected by the Immigration and Refugee Board.]

Case Law

Section 95(1)

Canada (Minister of Citizenship and Immigration) v. Esfand (2015), [2016] 2 F.C.R. 282, 2015 FC 1190, 2015 CarswellNat 6443, 2015 CarswellNat 5161 — The respondent is a citizen of Iran who became a permanent resident of Canada upon her arrival in the country on June 13, 2006. She was a dependant of her husband, who was determined to be a Convention refugee by a visa officer overseas. Under a policy of family unity, the respondent, her husband, and their son became members of the Convention Refugees Abroad class. The overseas visa officer's notes show the officer analyzed and considered whether the respondent's husband was a Convention refugee. The officer concluded that the respondent's husband had a well-founded fear of persecution based on political opinion. There was no similar finding for the respondent. It seems that, upon finding that the respondent's husband was a Convention refugee, it was considered unnecessary to assess other family members' risks in Iran. Under the policy of family unity, the other family members were accepted without assessment. The respondent has since returned to Iran on two occasions (the second time after having renewed her Iranian passport). This prompted the Minister to seek the cessation of the respondent's Convention refugee status on the basis of para. 108(1)(a) of IRPA for voluntarily re-availing herself of the protection of Iran. However, s. 108 of IRPA applies only to Convention refugees and persons in need of protection: subs. 95(1) of IRPA. The current dispute arose as a result of the respondent's assertion that she does not in fact have this status. The court concluded that the RPD's decision was reasonable noting the following important points:

1. it makes no sense for the respondent to face negative consequences for visiting Iran, where she never claimed to be at risk;

2. the applicable statutory and regulatory provisions do not support the Minister's position; and

3. the Minister's position would work against the clearly stated policy of family unity.

The application was dismissed and the RPD's decision that the respondent was not a Convention refugee as contemplated in s. 95(1)(a) of IRPA was maintained.

The following serious question of general importance was certified:

> Where a person has become a permanent resident under a visa application in the overseas Refugee and Humanitarian Resettlement Program by virtue of a member of the person's family listed in the visa application having been determined to be a Convention refugee (though the person was not themselves assessed as a Convention refugee), is that person a Convention refugee as contemplated in para. 95(1)(a) of IRPA who is subject to cessation of refugee status pursuant to subs. 108(2) of IRPA?

Seyoboka v. Canada (Minister of Citizenship & Immigration), 2009 CarswellNat 237, 2009 FC 104 — This was an application for judicial review of a decision of the Immigration and Refugee Board dismissing the applicant's motion to reopen his claim for refugee protection pursuant to s. 72(1) of the IRPA. The applicant contends that the Minister had a duty to disclose exculpatory evidence in vacation proceedings and the Minister breached her duty to disclose the exculpatory evidence.

The Refugee Protection Division of the Board is an administrative tribunal with specialized knowledge, not bound by legal or technical rules of evidence. As a result, the disclosure to standards delineated in *Stinchcombe*, [1991] 3 S.C.R. 326, do not necessarily apply automatically in the context of a refugee hearing and may require some adaptation. On the other hand, the level of disclosure owed to an applicant cannot be decided by a simple invocation of the distinction between criminal and administrative proceedings, and the consequences of an adverse finding on the applicant must be taken into consideration. The application for judicial review was dismissed. The following four questions were certified:

> 1. Within the context of the judicial review hearing where the Minister intervenes to seek the exclusion of the claimant, is the Minister under a duty to disclose all relevant evidence in his possession including exculpatory evidence subject only to any claims to privilege which would be assessed by the tribunal?

> 2. Is that duty contingent on any request from the claimant or does the duty exist independently of any request from the claimant?

> 3. Can the right to disclosure be waived? If so, must the waiver be explicit, or can it be inferred from the conduct of the claimant?

> 4. If there is a duty to disclose, does that duty include a duty to disclose evidence in the possession of other government agencies when Minister's counsel is aware that that government agency has a file on the person which might contain relevant evidence?

Quintanilla v. Canada (Minister of Citizenship & Immigration) (2006), 55 Imm. L.R. (3d) 112, 2006 CarswellNat 1595, 2006 FC 726 — The applicants were citizens of El Salvador. They lost their permanent residence status and currently face removal from Canada. The applicants contested the validity of the direction to report for removal issued against them on the grounds that they are protected from *refoulement*.

The applicants were granted permanent residence status in December 1995 under the political prisoners and oppressed persons designated class Regulations (PPOP). The applicants sought re-settlement in Canada on the basis of a well-founded fear of persecution on a Convention ground. Four months after their arrival in Canada as permanent residents in December 1995, the applicants returned to El Salvador. They stayed for more than six years in El Salvador until their second return to Canada in June 2002. In July 2002, the applicants were issued removal orders for failing to comply with their residency obligations. The applicants' appeals of these removal orders were denied by the IAD in July 2003. As a result, the applicants lost their permanent residence status and their removal orders came into force.

The court concluded that the applicants did not have a vested right not to be returned to El Salvador. The concept of "protected person" was created by IRPA. The determinative factor is that the applicants entered Canada in 1995 as permanent residents under the PPOP designated class. The applicants were subject to the same rights and obligations as any other permanent resident. In 1996, the applicants voluntarily returned to El Salvador and remained there for six years. The only right the applicants acquired under the PPOP Regulations was permanent resident status and that status was lost in light of the applicants' failure to comply with their residency requirements. Upon their second entry to Canada, the applicants were found to be inadmissible. The argument made by the applicants that the members of the PPOP designated class are permanently protected from *refoulement*, unless steps are taken by the Minister to cease or vacate their status under s. 108(3) or 109(3) of the IRPA, was dismissed by the Federal Court.

A question was certified: Under the *Immigration and Refugee Protection Act* and Regulations, is "refugee protection" conferred on a person who was landed in Canada as a member of the political prisoners and oppressed persons designated class but who has never been determined to be a Convention refugee or a person in need of protection?

Ha v. Canada (Minister of Citizenship & Immigration), 34 Imm. L.R. (3d) 157, 2004 CarswellNat 247, [2004] F.C.J. No. 174, 11 Admin. L.R. (4th) 306, 2004 FCA 49, 236 D.L.R. (4th) 485, 316 N.R. 299, 2004 CarswellNat 5581, [2004] 3 F.C.R. 195, 247 F.T.R. 314 (note) — This was an appeal from a decision of a motions judge dismissing the appellants' application for judicial review of the decision of a visa officer at the Canadian High Commission in Singapore denying the appellants' application for permanent residents as Convention refugees seeking resettlement.

The duty of fairness owed to the appellants, in the particular circumstances of this case, entitled them to have counsel attend and observe their interviews. The respondent's refusal to allow counsel to be present, accordingly, breached the appellants' right to procedural fairness.

The policy contained in the operations memorandum stating that counsel should not attend interviews is invalid because it fettered the visa officer's discretion and duty to consider the particular facts of each case when deciding whether counsel should be permitted to attend interviews.

96. Convention refugee — A Convention refugee is a person who, by reason of a well-founded fear of persecution for reasons of race, religion, nationality, membership in a particular social group or political opinion,

> **(a) is outside each of their countries of nationality and is unable or, by reason of that fear, unwilling to avail themself of the protection of each of those countries; or**

> **(b) not having a country of nationality, is outside the country of their former habitual residence and is unable or, by reason of that fear, unwilling to return to that country.**

Case Law

Tretsetsang v. Canada (Minister of Citizenship and Immigration) (2016), 40 Imm. L.R. (4th) 189, 398 D.L.R. (4th) 685, 483 N.R. 383, 2016 FCA 175, 2016 CarswellNat 2158 — Under international law, refugee protection is surrogate protection. It is available only when a person's country of nationality is unable or unwilling to protect against risks identified by the 1951 Convention relating to the Status of Refugees. In consequence, refugee claimants with multiple nationalities must prove that none of their countries of nationality will protect them. Consistent with this principle, foreign nationals seeking refugee protection in Canada must establish that they either have no country of nationality or that their country of nationality will not offer them protection against the threats identified in ss. 96 or 97 of IRPA.

The RAD concluded that the appellant had Indian citizenship and had failed to establish that his Indian citizenship rights would not provide him with protection. The Federal Court of Appeal held that these conclusions were reasonable. The Indian statute clearly established the appellant's Indian citizenship and the only decisions of the Indian courts that were referred to by the parties supported that view. Since the appellant did not take any steps to determine whether India would recognize him as a citizen without requiring him to litigate this matter, it followed that he had failed to establish that there was any impediment, much less any significant impediment, to his ability to access the state protected rights inherent in his Indian citizenship.

The appeal was dismissed. The Court held that any impediment that a refugee claimant may face in accessing state protection in a country in which the claimant is a citizen is not sufficient to exclude that country from the scope of the expressions "countries of nationality" and "country of nationality" in s. 96 of IRPA.

Balog v. Canada (Minister of Citizenship & Immigration), 2014 CarswellNat 1657, 2014 CarswellNat 2285, 2014 FC 449 — The Refugee Protection Division ("RPD") issued a decision to refuse the applicants' refugee claim. In doing so, however, the RPD failed to address a *sur place* claim arising from a tragic event in Canada and the response to it by extremists in Hungary. That failure in the particular circumstances of this matter required that the decision be overturned. A *sur place* claim normally arises where an individual expresses his views or engages in activities that jeopardize the possibility of safe return to their state. The key issue is usually whether the activities abroad are likely to have come to the attention of the authorities in the claimant's country of origin where the state is the agent of persecution. The court has recognized *sur place* claims where the agent of persecution is not the state but a third party. The court has also held that credible evidence of an applicant's activities in Canada that are likely to substantiate harm upon return must be expressly considered by the Board even if the motivation behind the activities is not genuine.

In this case, there was no suggestion that the applicants were responsible for the publicity and resulting threats that the death of their child in Canada engendered in Hungary. They were not seeking attention in an effort to provoke an adverse reaction in their country of origin. Rather, the situation evolved from the decision of a Canadian press outlet to publish a story of their tragic loss of their child and efforts to obtain protection from this country. Credible evidence submitted to the Board was to the effect that this family alone, out of all the Hungarian Roma who have sought protection in Canada, had been publicly identified and vilified by extremist elements in that country. This presented a personal risk to the applicants distinct from the type of generalized discrimination and street violence that they had previously experienced. The question of whether the protection of the state would be adequate in those circumstances had to be squarely addressed by the Board. The application for judicial review was allowed.

Horvath v. Canada (Minister of Citizenship & Immigration), 2013 FC 788, 2013 CarswellNat 2587, 2013 CarswellNat 3182, [2013] F.C.J. No. 852 — This was an application for judicial review of a decision of the Refugee Protection Division denying the applicants refugee protection. A state protection cannot be determined in the vacuum. The willingness and ability of states to protect their citizens may be linked to the nature of the persecution in question. When undertaking a contextual approach to determine whether a refugee claimant has rebutted the presumption of state protection, a number of factors need to be taken into consideration including: (1) the nature of the human rights violation; (2) the profile of the alleged human right abuser; (3) the efforts that the victim took to seek protection from authorities; (4) the response of the authorities to requests for their assistance; and (5) the available documentary evidence. In the present case, the credibility findings that the court is not in a position to review are of great importance and they are related to all of the above-mentioned factors, except for the last one. Therefore, the court is not in a position to assess the reasonability of the state protection analysis as it is closely linked to the credibility findings made by the RPD. Since the state protection determination is intertwined with the credibility findings related to the applicants' fear of persecution and efforts to seek protection, the court is not in a position to draw a conclusion as to the reasonability of the state protection analysis. The decision was returned to a different RPD panel.

Galyas v. Canada (Minister of Citizenship & Immigration) (2013), 50 Admin. L.R. (5th) 180, 2013 FC 250, 2013 CarswellNat 1927, 2013 CarswellNat 490 — The applicant sought judicial review of a decision of the Refugee Protection Division ("RPD") which refused the applicant's application to be deemed a Convention refugee or a person in need of protection under ss. 96 and 97 of the Act. The court considered whether there was a breach of natural justice due to the incompetence of the applicant's former counsel. The threshold for establishing breach of procedural fairness on the basis of incompetent counsel is very high. Incompetence will only constitute a breach of natural justice under extraordinary circumstances. It is generally recognized that if an applicant wishes to establish a breach of fairness on this ground, he or she must: (a) provide corroboration by giving notice to former counsel and providing them with an opportunity to respond; (b) establish that former counsel's act or omission constituted incompetence without the benefit and wisdom of hindsight; and (c) establish that the outcome would have been different but for the incompetence.

Former counsel disputed the evidence put forward by the applicant but the Court found that there could be no dispute in the inadequacies that appear on the face of the applicant's PIF narrative which clearly support his allegation that he was left to prepare this important document by himself, without guidance on what it should contain and what the RPD would be looking for in such a narrative. Competent counsel would have known that the applicant's narrative does not comply with the expectations of the RPD and that it would be extremely detrimental to the applicant at the hearing. Anyone with experience before the RPD knows that it consistently and relentlessly draws negative credibility findings from a failure to include important incidents in the PIF and that, where an applicant is assisted by a lawyer, it will not accept a lack of knowledge as to what should be included in the PIF as a reasonable explanation. In that regard, the applicant's PIF is a negative credibility finding waiting to happen.

The evidence before the court was undisputed that the applicant was left to write his PIF on his own and that, after doing so, he was not advised that what he had written did not conform with the requirements set out in question 31 as to what should be in a PIF narrative. At least as regards the PIF, incompetent representation caused the RPD to find the applicant was not credible with regard to his fear of persecution in Hungary and that the result could very well have been different had the applicant been guided to prepare a PIF that met the expectations of the RPD. The application for judicial review was allowed.

Canada (Minister of Citizenship & Immigration) v. B472, 2013 FC 151, 2013 CarswellNat 345, 2013 CarswellNat 868, [2013] F.C.J. No. 192 — B472, a young Tamil, from Sri Lanka was found to be a refugee. The Minister sought judicial review on the basis that it was unreasonable to find that the Tamil passengers on board the M.V. "Sun Sea" were a "particular social group" for the purposes of s. 96 of IRPA and that the wrong standard of proof was used in the Board's findings of fact. The Minister argued it should have used the "balance of probabilities" standard rather than the "serious possibility" standard.

In accordance with s. 96 of the IRPA, a Convention refugee is one who has a well-founded fear of persecution "for reasons of race, religion, nationality, membership in a particular social group or political opinion. . ." Section 96 is to be contrasted with s. 97 which gives protection to persons who are not Convention refugees, but if returned to their country would be personally subjected to a danger of torture or to a risk to life or to a risk of cruel and unusual treatment or punishment. The standard of proof differs. Under s. 96, the burden is on the claimant to establish a reasonable chance of persecution, which is something less than the balance of probabilities. However, under s. 97, the applicant must make out a case on the balance of probabilities.

The case turned on the legal definition of "membership in a particular social group" within the meaning of s. 96 of IRPA. Although non-exhaustive, there are three categories of groups: (a) groups defined by an innate or unchangeable characteristic; (b) groups whose members voluntarily associate for reasons so fundamental to their human dignity that they should not be forced to forsake the association; and (c) groups associated by a former voluntary status, unalterable due to its historical permanence. The historical fact of having come together voluntarily in a particular way for the purpose of travelling to Canada to seek refugee status was not a sufficient basis upon which to become a member of a "particular social group" within the meaning of s. 96. Otherwise, every group of people including a small family who came together for that purpose would have a nexus to s. 96 and the words "race, religion, nationality — or political opinion" would be superfluous.

The court concluded that it may well be that Mr. B472 faces a serious risk of persecution were he to be returned to Sri Lanka, but not because of his membership in a particular social group, the Tamil passengers on the ship. The Board erred in its interpretation of s. 96. The application for judicial review was allowed.

The following question was certified:

> Is review by this Court of the meaning of "membership in a particular social group" in s. 96 of the *Immigration and Refugee Protection Act* as determined by a member of the Refugee Protection Division of the Immigration and Refugee Board on the correctness or reasonableness standard?

Cruz v. Canada (Minister of Citizenship & Immigration), 2012 CarswellNat 1698, 2012 FC 664 — This was an application for judicial review of the decision of the IRB that concluded that the applicants were neither Convention refugees nor persons in need of protection under ss. 96 and 97 of IRPA. Domestic violence is frequent in Mexico. The Board should have conducted a separate analysis of the children's situation. As the court reviewed the evidence adduced with respect to the children, it was obvious that each child's fear was distinct and relied on different facts and circumstances that should have been assessed. The Board failed to take into consideration these claims in their own right. It is not sufficient to merely rely on a review of existing measures with respect to changes of address or the existence of organizations to help families caught with problems of domestic violence. The evidence adduced with respect to the situation of each individual child should have triggered separate analysis of risk and the ability of the Mexican state to protect these children and whether they could reasonably access such protection taking into consideration each child's individual circumstance. The country conditions should have been contextualized in respect of each child's respective situation. The application for judicial review was allowed.

Ahanin v. Canada (Minister of Citizenship & Immigration), 2012 FC 180, 2012 CarswellNat 1849, 2012 CarswellNat 381 — The applicant sought judicial review of a decision to refuse his claim for protection as a Convention refugee. The applicant claimed that the RPD made an unreasonable plausibility finding in concluding that it would be improbable that he would return to Iran just to be with his adult son. The applicant says that the bond between parent and child is no less strong than a political opinion, and is such that to find that parents will not face danger to be reunited with their children is an unreasonable basis to reject credibility. In this case, the implausibility finding was a significant part of the overall credibility determination and accordingly the RPD should have explored the issue further and provided more justification than it did for its conclusions on point. Its assessment has to be objective and reasonable but a decision to face danger in order to protect an isolated child is plausible depending upon the personality and beliefs of the person involved. The applicant specifically asked the RPD not to look at this issue from the perspective of Canadian society, but "to look at things through Iranian. A 20 year old might be considered an adult in Canada, but in Iran even older age, children rely on their parents."

There was no indication that the RPD addressed this cultural issue in a reasonable way. The conduct of an applicant cannot be reasonably assessed by applying Canadian norms and cultural assumptions to foreign cultures. The application was allowed.

Rezmuves v. Canada (Minister of Citizenship & Immigration), 2012 CarswellNat 864, 2012 FC 334 — The applicants were found not to be Convention refugees and sought judicial review of the decision. The Board failed to review or acknowledge the recent evidence which the applicants described in their memorandum as follows: "there has been a severe upswing of extremism directed against Roma and further that there is extensive evidence of the government's shortcomings in actually preventing violence against Roma (for example the European Roma Rights Centre report and a recent Amnesty International report, both lengthy and detailed on this very point)." The failure to address the real issue and examine current evidence on that point must lead to the conclusion that the decision on state protection was unreasonable.

Fontenelle v. Canada (Minister of Citizenship & Immigration) (2011), 5 Imm. L.R. (4th) 14, 2011 FC 1155, 2011 CarswellNat 4093, 2011 CarswellNat 5023 — The Gender Guidelines exist to assist the Board in dispelling myths and understanding the behaviour of a claimant fleeing domestic violence. By failing to properly consider and apply the guidelines to the applicant's claim, the Board erred. The Board found that the applicant would have told her high school teachers about the abuse. The guidelines are supposed to make the board member sensitive enough to know that abused women often do not disclose the abuse, as recognized by the Supreme Court of Canada. This basic lack of sensitivity shows that the member did not understand or apply the guidelines. The application for judicial review was granted.

Mosqueda Costa v. Canada (Minister of Citizenship & Immigration), 2011 FC 1388, 2011 CarswellNat 5078, 2011 CarswellNat 5801 — The applicant made a refugee claim in May 2009 and represented herself at the hearing before the Board. An issue arose as to whether the applicant should have been given the opportunity at, or after, the hearing to file further evidence as to the denunciations she made to the Mexican authorities with respect to the persons she alleged were troubling her. The transcript of the hearing made it clear that the applicant had offered to provide further evidence as to these denunciations, but the members said she could not do so.

The dismissal by the member of what amounted to the self-represented applicant's attempt to do so, without advising the applicant or considering Rule 37, was an error in law and failure to provide due process. It was clear from the member's reasons that the denunciations were material to the decision being made. Refusal or neglect or oversight in not permitting the applicant an opportunity to provide such documentation was a reviewable error. The application was allowed.

Nyota v. Canada (Minister of Citizenship & Immigration) (2011), 391 F.T.R. 108, 2 Imm. L.R. (4th) 83, 2011 FC 675, 2011 CarswellNat 2273 — Recent jurisprudence from the Federal Court indicates that in some instances, extortion may amount to persecution. For example, in *Sinnasamy v. Canada (Minister of Citizenship & Immigration)* (2008), 68 Imm. L.R. (3d) 246, de Montigny J. held at para. 25:

> As demands for bribes by the police are a form of extortion, they may also, in relevant circumstances, amount to "persecution" for the purposes of the Convention: see *Kularatnam v. Canada (Minister of Citizenship & Immigration)*, 2004 FC 1122, at paras. 10–13.

Accordingly, the Board is required to assess whether the risk of extortion amounts to persecution under s. 96 or risk under s. 97. The application for judicial review was allowed.

Josile v. Canada (Minister of Citizenship & Immigration) (2011), 95 Imm. L.R. (3d) 62, 2011 FC 39, 2011 CarswellNat 116 — The applicant was a female Haitian national born in 1980. She left Haiti in 2005 and had her refugee claim rejected by the United States the same year. In 2007, she made her Canadian refugee claim based on political opinion and membership in a particular group (Haitian women) or other social group (family). The Board rejected the applicant's argument based on membership in a social group (family). The Board accepted that Haitian women do constitute a particular social group, but they do not face persecution because of their membership therein. The applicant contested the correctness of the Board's legal approach and reasonableness of its analysis of the evidence regarding the political nature of gang violence in Haiti and the gender-targeted nature of rape in Haiti.

Women, at large, should be recognized as a particular social group, provided that the evidence proves that they are subject to severe violations of their fundamental human rights because of their gender. The Board's conclusion was untenable. The decision was set aside and referred back for a new hearing.

IRP Act

Zheng v. Canada (Minister of Citizenship & Immigration), 2011 FC 181, 2011 Car-swellNat 1321, 2011 CarswellNat 640 — The applicant sought judicial review of a decision to refuse her claim for refugee protection after determining that she was neither a Convention refugee nor a person in need of protection. It was unreasonable for the Board to base its determination on the premise that the applicant could leave her infant son in Canada, and since the Board's treatment of the applicant's risk as speculative was also unreasonable, and since the Board's failure to deal with country conditions also constituted a reviewable error, the application for judicial review was allowed.

John v. Canada (Minister of Citizenship & Immigration), 2011 FC 387, 2011 Car-swellNat 978, 2011 CarswellNat 1799 — The present application challenges the decision of the Refugee Protection Division in which the applicant's claim for protection was rejected, in large measure, on the basis of a negative credibility finding. The decision was set aside. When dealing with gender-related claims it is critical that RPD pays special attention to *Guideline 4: Women Refugee Claimants Fearing Gender-Related Persecution: Guidelines Issued by the Chairperson* in reaching a determination. It is a reviewable error to first determine that a claimant is not credible and then to use that lack of credibility as a basis for rejecting or giving little weight to evidence that is submitted to corroborate the claimant's testimony. In the present case, the psychological report is tendered, not to prove the truth of the applicant's statements to the psychologist, but to prove her current state of mind. The applicant's impaired state of mind can be found to support the truth of her evidence of the abuse she suffered. And second, the applicant's state of mind was an important factor to be taken into consideration by the RPD when evaluating her evidence: to do so constitutes a practical application of *Guideline 4.*

R. v. Laboucan, [2010] S.C.J. No. 12, 73 C.R. (6th) 235, (sub nom. *R. v. Briscoe)* 400 N.R. 200, 22 Alta. L.R. (5th) 62, 253 C.C.C. (3d) 129, [2010] 6 W.W.R. 13, 316 D.L.R. (4th) 590, (sub nom. *R. v. Briscoe)* 477 A.R. 70, 483 W.A.C. 70, 2010 SCC 12, 2010 CarswellAlta 591, 2010 CarswellAlta 590 — The fact that a witness has an interest in the outcome of the proceedings is common sense and a relevant factor, among others, to take into account when assessing the credibility of the witness's testimony. A trier of fact, however, should not place undue weight on the status of a person in the proceeding as a factor going to credibility. For example, it would be improper to base a finding of credibility regarding a parent's or a spouse's testimony solely on the basis of a witness's relationship to the complainant or to the accused. Regard should be given to all relevant factors in assessing credibility.

Smith v. Canada (Minister of Citizenship & Immigration) (2009), 86 Imm. L.R. (3d) 114, 358 F.T.R. 189 (Eng.), 2009 FC 1194, 2009 CarswellNat 3800, 2009 CarswellNat 3801 — The applicant, an American citizen, claimed refugee protection pursuant to ss. 96 and 97(1) of IRPA as a homosexual member of the U.S. Army, from which she had deserted. She alleged a fear of persecution on the part of a colleague and superiors because of her sexual orientation. She also claimed that she would be personally facing a risk to her life or cruel and unusual treatment or punishment if she were returned to the United States. Her claim was rejected by the Refugee Board on the ground that she failed to seek state protection that would have been adequate.

Contrary to the situation in *Hinzman, Re* (2006), 55 Imm. L.R. (3d) 54 (F.C.), where the appellants had not made an adequate attempt to avail themselves of the protections afforded by the Uniform Code of Military Justice (UCMJ), the applicant in this case provided evidence that she did approach her superiors to try to obtain a discharge. According to the evidence, she went so far as to ask her superior for permission to speak to a higher authority, but was denied. She also testified that one supervisor scoffed at her and said they would figure out the paper work when she returned from her tour of duty in Afghanistan. The case law of this Court requires more than one attempt to obtain state protection. It is often said that an applicant must usually follow up with his complaint, and seek assistance from higher authorities if unsuccessful at the first stage. Yet, one must take into account the particular environment that an applicant finds himself in. It is clear that in the Army there is an atmosphere of unconditional obedience to the hierarchy. The Board member did not seem to be sensitive to this special context.

The duty of the Board member was to determine whether she would suffer persecution as a result of the relevant substantive law or of the process whereby the law would be applied to her. It was not enough for the Board member to state that he is "not in a position to defend or criticize." It is part of the assessment of a refugee claim to determine whether a claimant has a well-founded fear of persecution for reasons, *inter alia*, of her membership in a particular social group, if he/she is returned to his/her home country. The applicant provided evidence to the Board that the punishment she would be exposed to under the court-martial process relates to a breach of a law that is in conflict with a fundamental human right and therefore adversely differentiates on a Convention ground in its application. This evidence could not simply be ignored by the Board member and had to be properly discussed and analyzed before he could conclude that the UCMJ was a law of general application and applied in a non-discriminatory fashion. It was therefore the duty of the Board member to assess the fairness of the court-martial process in light of the particular set of facts and of the evidence that was before him. The application for judicial review was allowed.

Alexander v. Canada (Minister of Citizenship & Immigration (2009), 88 Imm. L.R. (3d) 75, 357 F.T.R. 222 (Eng.), 2009 FC 1305, 2009 CarswellNat 5510, 2009 CarswellNat 4566, [2009] F.C.J. No. 1682 — The Refugee Protection Panel accepted that the applicant had been beaten up by her boyfriend, that she had taken refuge with her aunt on one of the Grenadian Islands, that her boyfriend had threatened to burn down her mother's house if she did not return to Kingstown and that he continued to make terrifying threats by telephone. The only issue was that of state protection. The panel found that St. Vincent and the Grenadines was a democracy and that the applicant did not "take all reasonable steps in the circumstances of this case to pursue the available state protection," and that she "did not provide any persuasive evidence of similarly-situated individuals let down by the state protection arrangements." The conclusion was that she had failed to rebut the presumption of state protection with clear and convincing evidence.

Taken at its face value, the decision appears to be reasonable. This Court is supposed to show deference to the RPD panels that allegedly have greater expertise in country conditions than the court itself. However, there comes a time when it becomes obvious that deference should be earned, particularly when the panel apparently pays no attention to the cases coming out of this Court which specifically deal with St. Vincent and the Grenadines. The analysis of country conditions was clearly a *pro forma* one, or a "cookie cutter analysis." This Court does not sit in a *de novo* appeal and so cannot do its own country analysis. It was "absolutely astonishing" that the IRB publishes information on country conditions but failed to mention that the Consul General has admitted that the state cannot guarantee the effectiveness of a restraining order. That would be relevant information in any assessment as would an analysis of the types of threats the applicant received. The application for judicial review was granted.

Perez v. Canada (Minister of Citizenship & Immigration) (2009), 85 Imm. L.R. (3d) 118, 2009 FC 1065, 2009 CarswellNat 5598, 2009 CarswellNat 3345 — Refugee law does not require altruism from those who seek protection from persecution nor does it exclude those who publicize their fears. In this case, the board member repeatedly criticized the applicant's recourse to the media to call attention to her victimization. The member's comments that the applicant "failed frequently to address corruption before it affected her," used "duplicity and threats" to press her case and lacked "altruistic intent," reflect judgments about the applicant's integrity that are legally irrelevant and taint the entire decision. The application for judicial review was allowed.

Key v. Canada (Minister of Citizenship & Immigration) (2008), 73 Imm. L.R. (3d) 278, 331 F.T.R. 137, 85 Admin. L.R. (4th) 157, 2008 CarswellNat 3031, 2008 FC 838, 2008 CarswellNat 2152, [2008] F.C.J. No. 1003 — It is clear that officially condoned military misconduct falling well short of a war crime may support a claim to refugee protection. Indeed, authorities indicate that military action which *systematically* degrades, abuses or humiliates either combatants or noncombatants is capable of supporting a refugee claim where that is the proven reason for refusing to serve. The Board erred in this case by imposing a too restrictive legal standard upon the applicant. The Board's assertion that his past combat participation would not be sufficient to support his claim to asylum unless it constituted excludible conduct cannot be correct. This would give rise to an unacceptable "Catch-22" situation where the factual threshold for obtaining protection would necessarily exclude a claimant from that protection. That, however, does not end the matter because the court has made it very clear in *Hinzman* (C.A.), *infra*, that soldiers facing punishment in the United States for desertion must, as a rule, pursue the available options for state protection at home before seeking protection in Canada. In light of this decision, there is no question that the Board erred by adopting the "state of persecutor" principle as a basis for finding that state protection was not available to the applicant. There is not much doubt that he would likely face some form of punishment for desertion if he returned to the United States and, indeed, the Board found that he would, in all probability, be court martialled and sentenced to a year of imprisonment. While the *Hinzman* decision has certainly set the bar very high for deserters from the United States military seeking refuge in Canada, the Court of Appeal acknowledged in that case that one's failure to fully pursue state protection opportunities will not always be fatal to a refugee claim. Clear and convincing evidence about similarly situated individuals who unsuccessfully sought to be excused from combat duty or who were persecuted and imprisoned for a refusal to serve, may be sufficient to rebut the presumption of state protection in the United States. Since the applicant would have been deployed back to Iraq within two weeks of his arrival in the United States, the opportunity to pursue a release or re-assignment may not have been realistic. Because the outcome of this case could not be considered to be a foregone conclusion, the applicant was given the opportunity to address fully the issue of state protection in a rehearing before the Board. The application for judicial review was allowed and the matter remitted to a differently constituted panel of the Board for reconsideration on the merits.

Guney v. Canada (Minister of Citizenship & Immigration), 2008 CarswellNat 5579, 2008 CarswellNat 3687, 2008 FC 1134 — The applicant tried to bolster his claim for refugee status more than a year later, by inventing an additional basis for protection. The Board found that this new lie rendered the applicant's evidence, as a whole, not to be credible and thus did no real analysis of the rest of his story. The fact that a witness has been caught in one lie, in itself, is insufficient to discredit all of his evidence where, as here, the evidence is otherwise plausible and consistent. This approach was unreasonable and the decision was set aside.

Munderere v. Canada (Minister of Citizenship & Immigration) (2008), 69 Imm. L.R. (3d) 129, 291 D.L.R. (4th) 68, 2008 CarswellNat 600, 2008 CarswellNat 601, 2008 FCA 84 — Considering s. 53 of the United Nations Handbook on Procedures and Criteria for Determining Refugee Status, and in particular the last sentence of that paragraph, "This will necessarily depend on all the circumstances, including the particular geographical, historical and ethnological context," it is not an error in law to limit the analysis of the cumulative grounds to the events that occurred within one country of nationality or habitual residence, when the claimant alleges persecution on the basis of the same Convention ground in the two (or more) countries, and where the claimant's subject fear is related to events that occurred in more than one country, except where the events which occur in a country other than that in respect of which a claimant seeks refugee status are relevant to the determination of whether the country where a claimant seeks refugee status can protect him or her from persecution.

Carrillo v. Canada (Minister of Citizenship & Immigration) (2008), 9 Imm. L.R. (3d) 309, 2008 FCA 94, 2008 CarswellNat 1953, 2008 CarswellNat 605, [2008] F.C.J. No. 399 — A refugee who claims that the state protection is inadequate or non-existent bears the evidentiary burden of adducing evidence to that effect and the legal burden of persuading the trier of fact that his or her claim in this respect is founded. The standard of proof applicable is the balance of probabilities and there is no requirement of a higher degree of probability than what that standard usually requires. As for the quality of the evidence required to rebut the presumption of state protection, the presumption is rebutted by clear and convincing evidence that the state protection is inadequate or non-existent. The appeal was allowed, the decision of the Federal Court set aside and the decision of the Board restored.

Sanchez v. Canada (Minister of Citizenship & Immigration) (2007), 360 N.R. 344, 2007 CarswellNat 572, 2007 FCA 99 — The appellants, a husband and wife, were Colombian nationalists. One appellant was employed full-time by the Colombian Ministry of Agriculture as an engineer, with a specialty in environmental clean-up. In addition, he ran a side-line business with his brother that reported violations of signage by-laws to the city authorities. He and his brother received a percentage of the fine that was levied against the guilty person or business. The appellant was threatened by the Fuerzas Armadas Revolucionarias de Colombia ("FARC") due to his part-time business. The appellant sought refugee status. The Board found no indication that the lives or well being of the appellants would have been at risk had the appellant simply chosen to comply with the warning and cease his side business. The Board was of the view that it was not unreasonable to expect him to cease his side business and that his inability to continue this endeavour was not a denial of his core human rights or of his general ability to earn a living. The applications judge found the Board's decision to be reasonable and legally correct with respect to this part-time business.

Although it was not possible in the context of this case to attempt to develop an exhaustive list of the factors that should be taken into account in assessing whether a person is in need of protection, persons claiming to be in need of protection solely because of the nature of the occupation or business in which they are engaged in their own country generally will not be found to be in need of protection unless they can establish that there is no alternative occupation or business reasonably open to them in their own country that it would eliminate the risk of harm.

Hinzman, Re (2006), 55 Imm. L.R. (3d) 54, *(sub nom. Hinzman v. Canada (Minister of Citizenship & Immigration))* [2007] 1 F.C.R. 561, *(sub nom. Hinzman v. Canada (Minister of Citizenship & Immigration))* 290 F.T.R. 8 (Eng.), 266 D.L.R. (4th) 582, 2006 FC 420, 2006 CarswellNat 1779, [2006] F.C.J. No. 521; affirmed 2007 FCA 171, 2007 CarswellNat 950, [2007] F.C.J. No. 584 — The applicant is an American soldier who deserted the United States Army after his unit was deployed to fight in Iraq. He says he deserted because of his strong moral objections to the war in Iraq, and his belief that the American-led military action in that country is illegal. The applicant made a refugee claim which was rejected. He then sought judicial review of the Board's decision, asserting that the Board erred in refusing to allow him to lead evidence with respect to the alleged illegality of the American military action in Iraq. He also argued that in ignoring evidence with respect to the alleged condoning of ongoing human rights violations perpetrated by the American military in Iraq, and with respect to the systemic nature of those violations, the Board further erred. Finally, he argued that the Board imposed too heavy a burden on him to demonstrate that he would have been involved in unlawful acts had he gone to Iraq and that the Board erred in failing to properly consider the fact that an objection to a particular war is not recognized as a legitimate basis on which to grant conscientious objector status in the United States.

The application for judicial review was dismissed. The court concluded that there was no internationally recognized right to object to a particular war, other than in the circumstances specifically identified in para. 171 of the United Nations High Commission for Refugees Handbook on Procedures and Criteria for Determining Refugee Status. The court stated that the reality is that states, including Canada, can and do punish their citizens for acting in accordance with their sincerely held moral, political and religious views when those individuals break laws of general application.

Note: The Federal Court of Appeal refused to answer the certified question, since the appellants failed to satisfy the fundamental requirement that claimants seek protection from their home state before going abroad to obtain protection through the refugee system. It was impossible for a Canadian Court or tribunal to assess the availability of protections in the United States.

Rey Nunez v. Canada (Minister of Citizenship & Immigration) (2005), 51 Imm. L.R. (3d) 291, 2005 CarswellNat 4127, 2005 FC 1661 — The Board's conclusion that the applicants had not rebutted the presumption of state protection available to them in Bolivia was unreasonable in light of the evidence before it. With regard to the standard of review applicable to a state protection determination, it is clear that the findings of fact can only be set aside if made in a perverse and capricious manner, or without regard to the material before the tribunal. Once the findings of fact are made, they must be assessed to determine if they constitute "clear and convincing confirmation of a state's inability to protect." That is a question of mixed fact and law for which less deference should be shown to the tribunal's decision. The appropriate standard of review for a finding of state protection is reasonableness *simpliciter*. Therefore, the decision of the Board will be set aside only if there is no line of analysis within the given reasons that could reasonably lead the tribunal from the evidence before it to the conclusion at which it arrived. If any of the reasons that are sufficient to support the conclusion are tenable in the sense that they can stand up to a somewhat probing examination, then the decision will not be unreasonable and a reviewing court must not interfere.

In the case at hand, the principal applicant and his family had made at least four attempts at seeking protection from state authorities and there was no analysis in the Board's reasons as to why these efforts were not enough to demonstrate a lack of state protection.

Manzi Williams v. Canada (Minister of Citizenship & Immigration), 2005 CarswellNat 950, 2005 CarswellNat 1805, 253 D.L.R. (4th) 449, 2005 FCA 126 — Refugee protection will be denied where it is shown that an applicant is entitled to acquire, by mere formalities, the citizenship of a particular country with respect to which he has no well founded fear of persecution.

If it is within the control of the applicant to acquire the citizenship of a country with respect to which he has no well founded fear of persecution, the claim for refugee status will be denied. The control test also reflects the notion, which is transparent in the definition of a refugee, namely that the unwillingness of an applicant to take steps required from him to gain state protection is fatal to his refugee claim unless that unwillingness results from the very fear of persecution itself.

Whether the citizenship of another country was obtained at birth, by naturalization, or by state succession is of no consequence provided it is within the control of the applicant to obtain it.

The condition of not having a country of nationality must be one that is beyond the power of the applicant to control.

Fernandopulle v. Canada (Minister of Citizenship & Immigration), 2005 CarswellNat 610, 253 D.L.R. (4th) 425, 2005 FCA 91, 331 N.R. 385 — Evidence of past persecution may support a finding of fact that a claimant has a well-founded fear of persecution. Whether such a finding is made in a particular case will depend on all of the evidence including evidence of current country conditions. There is, however, no rebuttable legal presumption to this effect.

De Barros v. Canada (Minister of Citizenship & Immigration), 2005 CarswellNat 535, 2005 FC 283 — A basic principle of refugee law is to grant status to those requiring surrogate protection and not to those who have a ready and automatic right to another country's nationality and protection. A person who is able to obtain citizenship in another country by complying with mere formalities is not entitled to avail themselves of protection in Canada.

Chaves v. Canada (Minister of Citizenship & Immigration) (2005), 45 Imm. L.R. (3d) 58, 2005 CarswellNat 333, 2005 FC 193, [2005] F.C.J. No. 232 — This was an application to review a negative decision respecting the applicant's application for protection. The onus lies on the applicant to rebut the presumption of state protection. The claimant's subjective fear of persecution is not at issue. The issue is whether the fear is objectively justifiable and that requires an examination into the existence or non-existence of state protection. The mere refusal by the police or authorities to aid a claimant will not suffice to displace the presumption of state protection. The burden of proof on the individual increases in proportion to the democratic nature of the particular state's institutions. An individual will not be required to exhaust all avenues before the presumption of state protection is rebutted. Where agents of the state are themselves the source of the persecution in question, and where the applicant's credibility is not undermined, the applicant can successfully rebut the presumption without exhausting every conceivable recourse in the country. The very fact that agents of the state are the alleged perpetrators of persecution undercuts the apparent democratic nature of the state's institutions, and correspondingly, the burden of proof

Ozdemir v. Canada (Minister of Citizenship & Immigration) (2004), 256 F.T.R. 154, 38 Imm. L.R. (3d) 237, 2004 CarswellNat 2232, 2004 FC 1008, [2004] F.C.J. No. 1242 — Pursuant to s. 97(1) of the IRPA, the Board is required to evaluate whether a claimant is in need of protection owing to the danger of torture or risk of cruel and unusual punishment. The separate analysis of a claimant's refugee claim under s. 96 and the enumerated risks under s. 97(1) is required. Further, a negative credibility determination in respect of a refugee claim under s. 96 is not necessarily dispositive of the considerations under s. 97(1).

Kadoura c. Canada (Ministre de la Citoyenneté & de l'Immigration), 2003 FC 1057, 2003 CarswellNat 4831, 2003 CarswellNat 2789, [2003] F.C.J. No. 1328 — The terms "refugee" and "person in need of protection" apply in particular to persons who do not have a country of nationality and who find themselves outside the country of their former "habitual residence." If a claimant resided in more than one country, it is not necessary to prove that he or she was persecuted in each of those countries. The claimant must show that he or she was persecuted in at least one of these countries and that he or she is unable or unwilling to return to the countries where he had his habitual residence.

The definition of "country of habitual residence" should not be so unduly restrictive as to pre-empt providing shelter to a stateless person who has demonstrated a well-founded fear of persecution on any of the grounds listed in the Convention. The claimant does not have to be legally able to return to a country of a habitual residence. The denial of the right to return, in fact, may in itself constitute an act of persecution by the State.

Ranjha v. Canada (Minister of Citizenship & Immigration) (2003), 29 Imm. L.R. (3d) 59, 2003 CarswellNat 4495, 2003 CarswellNat 1686, 234 F.T.R. 132, 2003 FCT 637 — The applicant sought to overturn a negative determination of his refugee claim. The tribunal determined, in part, that the applicant had not suffered past persecution. The tribunal analyzed separately the incidents of persecution but found that they were not repetitive, persistent and systematic and therefore, did not cumulatively amount to persecution.

Security measures to unmask terrorists can never justify torture of and physical violence to innocent civilians. While the tribunal made an error in its analysis, the panel had found the applicant to be a credible witness. It had to determine whether the quality of the incidents constituted a fundamental violation of human dignity. Reading the tribunal's decision as a whole, the Court concluded that the tribunal took the view that the absence of past persecution necessarily impacted on its view as to whether the applicant would be persecuted should he return and accordingly set aside the decision of the panel.

Kovacs v. Kovacs, [2002] O.J. No. 3074, 59 O.R. (3d) 671, 2002 CarswellOnt 1429, 21 Imm. L.R. (3d) 205, 212 D.L.R. (4th) 711, [2002] O.T.C. 287 (S.C.J.) — The respondent arrived at Pearson Airport from Hungary with her 3-year-old son and immediately claimed refugee status for herself and on behalf of her child. Eventually, the applicant learned of the respondent's whereabouts and launched this application for an order for the immediate return of the child to Hungary.

An order for the immediate return of the child can be made despite the fact there is a refugee claim pending.

Editor's Note

The following case summaries were collected under the provisions of the former Act relating to the definition of Convention refugee. The previous jurisprudence interpreting refugee concepts may still be relevant.

Bin v. Canada (Minister of Citizenship & Immigration) (2001), 213 F.T.R. 47, 2001 FCT 1246, 2001 CarswellNat 2600 — The applicant was aged 17 at the time the refugee claim was made. The applicant was transported to Canada by human smugglers or "snakeheads." The applicant also claimed that he was a refugee *sur place* on the basis that the Chinese government will view his illegal exit and the refugee claim as expressing a political opinion.

There are few guidelines and little jurisprudence on the proper evaluation of *sur place* claims. A person can become a refugee *sur place* for reasons other than a change in circumstances in her or his country of origin. The person can become such a refugee as a result of his own actions such as associating with refugees already recognized or expressing his political views in his country of residence. Regard should be had in particular to whether such actions may have come to the notice of the authorities of the person's country of origin and how they are likely to be viewed by those authorities.

There was no evidence before the panel, documentary or otherwise, that substantiated the *sur place* allegation. The panel limited its analysis to documentary evidence of punishment for illegal exit in China. The court did not agree that the panel should have determined how the Chinese government might view making a claim for refugee status, even in the absence of specific documentary evidence. If there is a distinction to be made respecting the treatment given to returnees who have claimed refugee status in Canada and other returnees, and if that amounts to discrimination based on imputed political opinion, it should have been a matter of evidence before the panel. In the absence of such evidence it was reasonable for the panel to draw no conclusion based upon evidence of publicity. It was not open to the panel to engage in speculation whether it is to the applicant's benefit or detriment.

Reul v. Canada (Minister of Citizenship & Immigration) (2000), 9 Imm. L.R. (3d) 79, 2000 CarswellNat 2318 (Fed. T.D.) — The applicants sought to review a negative determination of their claim for refugee status. The applicants are Jehovah's Witnesses. The principal applicant's mother was also a Jehovah's Witness. During her final illness, she and the principal applicant received advice that she required a blood transfusion. The principal applicant's mother declined to accept the transfusion. The principal applicant supported her in this decision. The principal applicant's mother died. The principal applicant's siblings accused him of causing their mother's death. They sent threatening letters and made threatening phone calls to the principal applicant.

The principal applicant and his family members feared persecution by reason of the principal applicant's choice to live his conviction, flowing from his religious beliefs, a conviction shared by his mother based on her religious beliefs, that it was inappropriate to receive a blood transfusion. The principal applicant thus established a subjectively and objectively well-founded fear of persecution in Mexico on the ground of religious belief. Religion encompasses both the beliefs that one may choose to hold and behaviour which stems from those beliefs.

Ranganathan v. Canada (Minister of Citizenship & Immigration) (2000), 11 Imm. L.R. (3d) 142, [2001] 2 F.C. 164, 266 N.R. 380, 193 F.T.R. 320 (note), 2000 CarswellNat 3134, 2000 CarswellNat 3459 (C.A) — The sole issue before the panel of the Immigration and Refugee Board was whether there was an internal flight alternative in Colombo that was reasonably available to the respondent. In order for an IFA to be unreasonable, it requires nothing less than the existence of conditions which would jeopardize the life and safety of a claimant in travelling or temporarily relocating to a safe area. In addition, it requires actual and concrete evidence of such conditions. The absence of relatives in a safe place, whether taken alone or in conjunction with other factors, can only amount to such a condition if it meets that threshold, that is to say, if it establishes that, as a result, a claimant's life or safety would be jeopardized. This is in sharp contrast with undue hardship resulting from loss of employment, loss of status, reduction in quality of life, loss of aspirations, loss of loved ones and frustration of one's wishes and expectations.

Zhuravlvev v. Canada (Minister of Citizenship & Immigration), [2000] 4 F.C. 3, 187 F.T.R. 110, 2000 CarswellNat 706, 2000 CarswellNat 3264, [2000] F.C.J. No. 507 — The applicant sought to overturn a negative decision of a panel of the CRDD. The question of state protection must be considered two times: the first time, in relation to the question of a well-founded fear of persecution; and the second time, in relation to the claimant's unwillingness or inability to avail him- or herself of state protection. Given that a lack of state protection is inherent in the finding of a well-founded fear of persecution, it is unlikely that the question of willingness or inability to avail oneself of state protection will require serious inquiry.

Refugees are generally not political scientists who can establish systemic lack of state protection. The object of the refugee system is to deal with state failure to protect its citizens. The Convention refugee system was designed to deal with the failure of national governments to protect their citizens from persecution.

When the agent of persecution is not the state, the lack of state protection has to be assessed as a matter of state capacity to provide protection rather than from the perspective of whether the local apparatus provided protection in a given circumstance. Local failures to provide effective policing do not amount to a lack of state protection. Where the evidence, including the documentary evidence, situates the individual claimant's experience as part of a broader pattern of state inability or refusal to extend protection, then the absence of state protection is made out. The question of a refusal to provide protection should be addressed on the same basis as the inability to provide protection. A local refusal to provide protection is not a state refusal in the absence of evidence of a broader state policy not to extend state protection to a target group.

There is an additional element in the question of refusal which is that the refusal by the state to extend protection may not be overt. The state organs may justify their failure to act by reference to various factors which, in their view, would make any state action ineffective. It is for the CRDD to assess the bona fides of those assertions in light of all the evidence.

The issue of internal flight alternative must be considered in relation to the state's inability or refusal to provide protection. A reasonable response to a local failure to provide protection is the internal migration to an area where state protection is available. Where internal movement is restricted, a failure to remedy local conditions may amount to state failure to provide protection. If state policy restricts a claimant's access to the whole of the state's territory, then the state's failure to provide local protection can be seen as a state failure to provide protection and not a mere local failure.

In this case, the CRDD's analysis of state protection was perfunctory with the result that the decision of the panel was set aside.

Klinko v. Canada (Minister of Citizenship & Immigration), [2000] 3 F.C. 327, 184 D.L.R. (4th) 14, 251 N.R. 388, 179 F.T.R. 253 (note), 2000 CarswellNat 283, 2000 CarswellNat 3251, [2000] F.C.J. No. 228 (C.A.) — This was an appeal against the decision of a motions judge dismissing an application for judicial review of a decision denying the appellant's refugee status. The central issue was whether the opinion expressed by the appellants in this case was a political opinion or not. The standard of review of such decisions is that of correctness. In the present case, while the motions judge did not explicitly discuss the standard, the court was satisfied that he applied the standard of correctness in reviewing the Convention Refugee Division's interpretation of the law with respect to the notion of political opinion. An opinion can be political for the purposes of subs. 2(1) of the Act whether or not that opinion accorded with the official government position. The words "political opinion" were broad enough to cover all instances where the political opinion expressed or imputed attracted persecution, including those where the government officially agreed with that opinion. The court declined to follow *Femenia v. Canada (Minister of Citizenship & Immigration)*, 1995 CarswellNat 2579 (T.D.).

Montchak v. Canada (Minister of Citizenship & Immigration), 1999 CarswellNat 1323 (Fed. T.D.) — The applicant was a citizen of Ukraine, claimed refugee status and stated that he was a successful businessman and for that reason organized criminals stole his property, extorted money from him and attempted to kill him. He further alleged that he received no adequate protection from the Ukrainian police.

There is ample authority for the proposition that those who had made money in business do not comprise a particular social group and therefore if they attract the attention of criminals by virtue of their wealth they cannot be said to fear persecution on a Convention ground.

Serrano v. Canada (Minister of Citizenship & Immigration) (1999), 166 F.T.R. 227, 1999 CarswellNat 636, [1999] F.C.J. No. 57 — This was an application to review a decision of a panel of the CRDD. The applicants were citizens of Mexico who claim to be at risk of being killed or seriously injured if returned there. The applicant operated a small trucking business in Acapulco. In 1996, he hired a new driver who introduced him to people who wished to hire his truck for the purpose of transporting drugs. The applicant refused to deal with them and a few days later his truck was found abandoned and damaged. Subsequently, the applicant and his family received threatening phone calls and a threatening letter. A friend of the applicant's who had agreed to work for drug traffickers was killed after he changed his mind.

The applicants' claims initially were based on a fear of persecution by reason of membership in a particular social group or political opinion. The CRDD concluded that as a matter of law the applicants were not members of a particular social group. In this case, the social group was described as "law abiding Mexican citizens." The court agreed with the CRDD that "law abiding citizens of Mexico" were not a particular social group within the meaning of the Convention.

The court found that to hold that everyone who fears persecution solely because of a family connection may be entitled to the protection of the Convention, would be to stretch the category of "particular social group" far beyond its proper limits. The court did not accept that family connection was an attribute requiring Convention protection in the absence of an underlying Convention ground for the claimed protection. Accordingly, the application for judicial review was dismissed.

Ali v. Canada (Minister of Citizenship & Immigration) (1999), 235 N.R. 316, 160 F.T.R. 292 (note), 1999 CarswellNat 128 (C.A.) — The appeal in this matter was dismissed. The Court of Appeal noted that the test for persecution in a civil war context was set out in *Salibian v. Canada (Minister of Employment & Immigration)*, [1990] 3 F.C. 250, 11 Imm. L.R. (2d) 165 (C.A.) and *Rizkallah v. Canada (Minister of Citizenship & Immigra-*

tion) (1992), 156 N.R. 1 (Fed. C.A.). The court also approved page 6 of the Refugee Board Guidelines issued on March 7, 1996, pursuant to s. 65(3) of the *Immigration Act*, dealing with refugee claims of civilian non-combatants in a civil war situation.

Canada (Minister of Citizenship & Immigration) v. Bob Smith (1998), 47 Imm. L.R. (2d) 305, [1999] 1 F.C. 310, 154 F.T.R. 92; additional reasons at 1998 CarswellNat 2423 (Fed. T.D.) — The respondent, Bob Smith, aged 14, is a citizen of the United States and the United Kingdom. He was a victim of ongoing sexual abuse. The principal aggressor was his natural father. The Minister sought judicial review of the determination by the CRDD that the respondent, his mother and his step-father were Convention refugees. The quantum of clear and convincing evidence required to rebut the presumption of a state's ability to protect depends on its democratic processes. In a democracy such as the United States with a free and independent judicial system, it would be necessary to impeach substantially the relevant jury selection process for the independence and fair-mindedness of the judiciary.

In this case, the evidence was simply insufficient to rebut the presumption of state protection. The tribunal's finding of no state protection in the United Kingdom and the United States was made in a perverse manner and without regard to the evidence. Accordingly, the decision of the tribunal was set aside.

Ramanathan v. Canada (Minister of Citizenship & Immigration) (1998), 44 Imm. L.R. (2d) 294, 152 F.T.R. 305 — This was an application to review a decision of the CRDD. The Board acknowledged that the applicant would probably not be able to attend to his daily living activities without the aid of his son, daughter-in-law and grandchildren. Notwithstanding this fact, the Board found a viable IFA in Columbo. There was no issue with respect to the fact that Colombo was a place where the applicant could live without fear of persecution. The panel refused to consider humanitarian and compassionate considerations in applying the second branch of the IFA test. A test of whether the IFA is unreasonable or unduly harsh in all the circumstances is bound to involve the consideration of some factors, at least, which will undoubtedly be the same sort of considerations that are taken into account in humanitarian and compassionate relief.

Thabet v. Canada (Minister of Citizenship & Immigration) (1998), 48 Imm. L.R. (2d) 195, [1998] 4 F.C. 21, 151 F.T.R. 160 (note), 227 N.R. 42, 160 D.L.R. (4th) 666 (C.A.) — The appellant was born in Kuwait and is a stateless Palestinian. He lived in Kuwait on a residency permit sponsored by his father. In 1983, the appellant left Kuwait to study in the United States where he obtained an engineering degree. In 1986, his residency status in Kuwait came to an end, and he returned to Kuwait to make an independent application to renew his residency permit, which was denied. The appellant then returned to the United States on a visitor's visa, where he lived for 11 years. After the outbreak of the Gulf War the appellant sought asylum in the United States. His application was rejected and he was ordered deported. He filed an appeal, but abandoned it and came to Canada where he applied for refugee status. Before a panel of the IRB, the appellant based his claim on the ground that Kuwait was his country of formal habitual residence and that he feared persecution if returned there. He also claimed to fear persecution in the United States, because while living in Louisiana he experienced harassment threats and violence at the hands of the Ku Klux Klan.

A panel of the IRB found that both Kuwait and the U.S. were countries of formal habitual residence and that the appellant had to demonstrate a well-founded fear of persecution against both in order to be granted refugee status. According to the Board, the appellant had not made out his fear of persecution in either country, and denied his claim.

The Trial Division judge found that the Board had erred in not asking itself whether the denial of a right to return to Kuwait was in itself an act of persecution. The Trial Division judge went on to find that a stateless person who has habitually resided in more than one country before making a refugee claim must establish his or her claim by reference to the last country of formal habitual residence. Accordingly, notwithstanding the error made by the panel in this matter the application for judicial review was dismissed.

On appeal, it was held that a stateless person must show on a balance of probabilities that he or she would suffer persecution in any country of formal habitual residence. In addition, the court observed that so long as a claimant does not face persecution in a country of formal habitual residence that will take him or her back, he or she could not be determined to be a refugee.

Shahpari v. Canada (Minister of Citizenship & Immigration) (1998), 44 Imm. L.R. (2d) 139, 146 F.T.R. 102 — The applicants sought to review the question of whether section E of Article I of the *Geneva Convention* applied to them. The applicants were citizens of Iran. In 1984 they moved to France and after seven years of temporary residence were issued a "Carte de Résident" which was valid for 10 years. After residing in France until 1994, the applicants came to Canada and within one month made a refugee application.

The burden of proving that section E applies rests with the party asserting it, in this case the respondent. It did not assist the applicant in this case that she allowed her visa to expire. The evidence allowed the panel to conclude that the visa could be renewed. Applicants should remember that actions they themselves take, which are intended to result in their not being able to return to a country which has already granted them refugee status, may well evidence an absence of the subjective fear of persecution in their original country. Further, if applicants are entitled to renounce the protection they receive from one country and claim protection from another, it gives them a right to emigrate to another country without complying with the usual requirements, solely by reason of their unilateral renunciation of the protection that they have been afforded by the country they are leaving.

Pour-Shariati v. Canada (Minister of Employment & Immigration) (1997), 39 Imm. L.R. (2d) 103, 215 N.R. 174 (Fed. C.A.) — Indirect persecution does not constitute persecution within the meaning of Convention refugee. The concept of indirect persecution goes directly against the decision of the Court of Appeal in *Rizkallah v. Canada (Minister of Employment & Immigration)* (1992), 156 N.R. 1 (Fed. C.A.), where it was held that there had to be a personal nexus between the claimant and the alleged persecution on one of the Convention grounds. The Convention ground of "membership in a particular social group" is a ground which allows for family concerns in an appropriate case. In addition s. 46.04(1) and 46.04(3) allow for the landing of dependants of refugees.

Martinez v. Canada (Minister of Citizenship & Immigration) (1996), 114 F.T.R. 113, 1996 CarswellNat 1033 — The applicant sought to review a negative decision of the CRDD. The applicant is a citizen of El Salvador, by reason of his mother's nationality, and of Belize, by reason of his birth. The applicant's mother alleged before the CRDD a well-founded fear of persecution in El Salvador based on her membership in a particular social group.

The applicant's mother and two of her three children were found to be Convention refugees as against El Salvador, but the applicant as a citizen of Belize was found not to have a well-founded fear of persecution in that country.

It is unnecessary to extend the plain meaning of the words Convention refugee to include the principle of family unity. The principle of family unity is enshrined in the *Immigration Act* by s. 46.04(1) and (3). None of the exceptions or limitations provided for in the two subsections in any way limit the applicant's mother's right to apply for landing in Canada for herself and the applicant, or the obligation of an immigration officer to grant landing in the event of such an application is made. Accordingly the application for judicial review was dismissed.

Wassiq v. Canada (Minister of Citizenship & Immigration) (1996), 33 Imm. L.R. (2d) 238, 112 F.T.R. 143 — The applicants applied to review a negative decision of the IRB. The applicants were citizens of Afghanistan. In 1981, they successfully applied as Convention refugees in Germany. In 1991, they left Germany and came to Canada and sought refugee status here.

A panel of the IRB had decided that the applicants had a well-founded fear of persecution in respect of Afghanistan, but that Canada had assumed responsibility for them and that Germany was obliged to allow them to return. Therefore, the Board found that the convention did not apply to the applicants by virtue of section E of Article 1.

Refugee claims were never meant to allow a claimant to seek out better protection than that from which he or she already benefitted. If by reason of their absence from Germany and sojourn in Canada, the applicants were in effect entitled to renounce the protection they received from Germany and claim protection from Canada, such a result would be anomalous. In substance, it would give a person who had Convention refugee status in one country the right to emigrate to another country without complying with the usual requirements.

Whether Canada or Germany should be responsible for the applicants should ideally be determined as between the governments of Canada and Germany. A decision of a panel of IRB, that Germany should have responsibility for the applicants which is in effect the decision in this case, is not binding on Germany. The real issue is whether Germany recognizes that the applicants may return.

On the evidence before it, the panel could not have arrived at such a conclusion and therefore could not have found that section E of Article 1 was applicable to the applicants. Accordingly, the application for judicial review was allowed and the matter remitted back to a differently constituted panel.

Badran v. Canada (Minister of Citizenship & Immigration) (1996), 111 F.T.R. 211 — The applicant sought judicial review of a negative decision of the IRB. The applicant in the instant case was a member of a particular social group: his family. He was also a member of a group which can be labelled "The Children of Police Officers Who Are Anti-terrorist Supporters." The evidence before the tribunal established that the authorities were effectively unable to protect the children of police officers and the documentary evidence supported that statement.

It is very difficult for a state to effectively protect its citizens against terrorism. In most cases, the inability to protect against random terrorist attacks will not constitute an inability of the state to protect. There is a limited exception to this however, where past, personal incidents qualify an individual as a member of the particular social group which the state is unable to protect. In the present case, there was a specifically and directly targeted applicant who was a member of a small targeted group and this distinguished the applicant's case from most cases which involved random instances of terrorism.

The negative decision of the IRB was set aside and the matter sent back to the same panel on the same record for a redetermination in the manner not inconsistent with the court's reasons.

Kanagaratnam v. Canada (Minister of Employment & Immigration) (1996), 36 Imm. L.R. (2d) 180, 194 N.R. 46 (Fed. C.A.) — The Refugee Board determined that the appellant, a native of Sri Lanka, had an internal flight alternative (IFA) within her country, and did not think it necessary to decide that the appellant otherwise had a well-founded fear of persecution. A motion was brought for judicial review and the trial judge dismissed the motion but certified a question for appeal, namely, whether a determination of whether a claimant has a well-founded fear of persecution in the area from which he or she originates, is a prerequisite to the consideration of an IFA.

In assessing whether a viable IFA exists, the Board, of course, must have regard to all the appropriate circumstances. Since an IFA existed, therefore, the claimant, by definition, could not have a well-founded fear of persecution in her country of nationality. Thus, while the Board may certainly do so if it chooses, there was no need, as a matter of law, for the Board to decide whether there was persecution in the area of origin as a prerequisite to the consideration of an IFA.

Chan v. Canada (Minister of Employment & Immigration), [1995] 3 S.C.R. 593, 187 N.R. 321, 128 D.L.R. (4th) 213 — The appellant held a managerial position at a manufacturing company, and owned a restaurant business. He fled to Hong Kong in 1990 and proceeded to Canada where he sought Convention refugee status based on his fear of persecution because of his political opinion and membership in a particular social group. The panel found that the appellant did not have good grounds for fearing persecution based on his membership in a particular social group, relying on the fact that there was no evidence adduced to suggest that the appellant was persecuted beyond the period of the Cultural Revolution. A panel of the CRDD also found that the appellant did not have good grounds for fearing persecution by reason of his political opinion manifested through his pro-democracy activities.

The appellant, who was a male, also claimed to fear sterilization due to the fact that he had fathered more children than the government of China's family planning policy permitted. Sterilization was found by the panel not, in itself, to be a form of persecution. Further, due to the fact that the appellant testified that he did not wish to have any more children, and due to a lack of evidence to suggest that the appellant would be physically abused during the sterilization process, the CRDD panel found that the appellant's fear of persecution was not well founded. The appellant appealed only on the issue of forced sterilization. The appeal was dismissed with one justice dissenting.

The appellant was required to demonstrate a well-founded fear of sterilization. The majority accepted the fact that the United Nations Handbook on Procedures and Criteria for Determining Refugee Status (Geneva 1979) although not binding on the court was highly persuasive authority in Canada. The appellant was not required to prove that persecution would be more likely than not in order to meet the objective portion of the refugee test. That test is more appropriately described as requiring the appellant to demonstrate a serious possibility of persecution.

The appellant testified with the assistance of an interpreter. The task of an interpreter in a judicial or quasi-judicial hearing is an extremely difficult one. Simultaneous translation can lead to minor infelicities of style. The Board and the court, when reviewing the written record, are well equipped to look past grammatical errors and to grasp the general import of a claimant's testimony, particularly when that testimony is considered as a whole. This is a fundamental part of the sympathetic approach to the evidence. It is the responsibility of the presiding member of the Board to ensure that the interpretation provided to the Board and reflected in the written record is as accurate as possible. The appellant's testimony, even with respect to his own fear of forced sterilization, was equivocal and inconsistent.

The evidence of the appellant with respect to his subjective fear of forced sterilization was equivocal, however, in the absence of an explicit finding by the Board on this point, it would not be appropriate for the Supreme Court of Canada to determine that the appellant did not have a subjective fear. Even if the appellant is given the benefit of the doubt on the question of his subjective fear it is the responsibility of the appellant to lay an evidentiary foundation upon which the Board can conclude not only that the fear existed in the mind of the appellant, but also that it was objectively well founded.

The objective component of the refugee test requires an examination of the objective situation and the relevant factors include the conditions in the appellant's country of origin, and the laws in that country, together with the manner in which they are applied. The appellant did not meet the burden of proof on the objective aspect of the test. The appellant failed to adduce any evidence that his fear of forced sterilization was objectively well founded. The appellant failed to adduce any evidence that forced sterilization was actually carried out and not merely threatened by the local authorities in his area. Evidence with respect to the enforcement procedures utilized in the particular region where the appellant lives, at the relevant time, should be presented to the Board. Where such evidence is not available in documentary form, the appellant may still be able to establish that the fear was objectively well founded by providing testimony with respect to similarly situated individuals. This liberal approach to establishing the facts represents a relaxation of the usual rules of evidence and is intended to grant the appellant the benefit of the doubt in cases where strict documentary evidence may be lacking.

The appellant failed to provide either documentary evidence or anecdotal evidence to substantiate his claim that the pressure from the Chinese authorities to submit to sterilization would extend beyond psychological and financial pressure to actual physical coercion. The benefit of the doubt should only be given to a refugee claimant when all available evidence has been obtained and checked and a panel is satisfied as to the claimant's general credibility. The refugee claimant's statements must be coherent and plausible, and must not run counter to generally known facts.

With respect to sterilization the available evidence shows that the Chinese authorities attempt to persuade couples with more than one child to submit to sterilization by psychological, social and financial pressure, including heavy fines. The primary agent of enforcement is the woman's work unit, but such measures can include other family members, specifically, in the case of government control licenses such as driver's licenses. The generally known facts suggest that some, but not all local authorities exceed these measures and resort to physical compulsion primarily against women.

In light of the fact that not all persons who have breached the one-child policy in China face a reasonable chance of forced sterilization, the appellant was required to establish a well-founded fear of forced sterilization before he could attempt to rely on that type of persecutory treatment. On the basis of the oral testimony, and the documentary evidence presented, forced sterilization remained no more than a mere possibility. In the absence of that evidence it was open to the Board to conclude that it could not determine that the appellant had a well-founded fear of persecution in the form of a forced sterilization. Accordingly, in the opinion of the majority, the appeal was dismissed.

Al-Maisri v. Canada (Minister of Employment & Immigration) (1995), 183 N.R. 234 (Fed. C.A.) — The appellant, a citizen of Yemen, claimed a well-founded fear of persecution by reason of political opinion. Yemen had supported Iraq during the invasion of Kuwait and the appellant, when he was called up to serve in the Yemenese army, deserted rather than go to Iraq by way of Jordan, to fight in the Iraqi Army.

The Refugee Division rejected the claim on the ground that the appellant would face prosecution in Yemen for deserting his country's military rather than persecution for political opinion.

Iraq's invasion of Kuwait was condemned by the United Nations and the annexation of Kuwait by Iraq was declared by the U.N. to be null and void.

The court was persuaded that Iraq's actions were contrary to the basic rules of human conduct and following the guidance afforded by para. 171 of the UNHCR Handbook, concluded that any punishment for desertion visited upon the appellant if he returned to Yemen would amount to persecution of which the appellant had a well founded fear.

The appeal was allowed and the applicant was declared to be a Convention refugee.

Isa v. Canada (Secretary of State) (1995), 91 F.T.R. 71 — The applicant comes from Somalia. The applicant fled Mogadishu and went to live in the Gedo region of Somalia. Subsequent to that the applicant and his family fled to Kenya and then eventually came to Canada. The applicant's claim was dismissed on the basis that the applicant demonstrated merely a general fear arising out of civil war and anarchy, and not persecution for a Convention reason.

A situation of civil war does not preclude an individual being found a Convention refugee. The individual must demonstrate that his or her fear arose because reprehensible acts were likely to be committed against members of a group to which he or she belonged, or against all citizens as a result of one of the reasons identified in the Convention definition of a refugee. A case will fail if it falls short of establishing that the applicants were collectively targeted differently from the general victims of a civil war. Many, if not most, civil war situations are racially or ethnically based. If racially motivated attacks in civil war circumstances alone could constitute grounds for Convention refugee status, then all individuals on either side of the conflict would qualify for refugee status.

Ramirez v. Canada (Solicitor General) (1994), 88 F.T.R. 208 — This was an application to review a negative decision of the CRDD. The panel declined to describe the harm suffered by the applicant in her native Nicaragua as persecution. The court noted that discrimination will only amount to persecution where it is serious or systematic enough to be characterized as persecution and, secondly, that the dividing line between discrimination and persecution is difficult to establish with the result that the court will not intervene unless the conclusion reached by the panel "appears to be capricious or unreasonable."

In this case the conclusion reached by the panel was neither and the application for judicial review was dismissed.

Fosu v. Canada (Minister of Employment & Immigration) (1994), 27 Imm. L.R. (2d) 95, 90 F.T.R. 182 — The applicant is a Jehovah's Witness and claimed religious persecution based on the enforcement of legislation in Ghana restricting the public activities of the applicant's religion. The claim was unsuccessful because a panel determined that the legislation prohibited religious services but did not prevent individual members from worshipping God.

The right to freedom of religion also includes the right to demonstrate one's religion or belief in public or in private by teaching, practise, worship and the performance of rites. The persecution of the practise of religion can take various forms such as prohibiting worshipping in public, or giving or receiving religious instruction or the implementation of serious discriminatory practises against persons on account of their religion. The prohibition against Jehovah's Witnesses to practice their religion could amount to persecution and the panel was obliged to consider this matter which it failed to do. Accordingly, the decision of the panel was set aside and the matter remitted for determination.

Gil v. Canada (Minister of Employment & Immigration) (1994), 25 Imm. L.R. (2d) 209, 174 N.R. 292, 119 D.L.R. (4th) 497, [1995] 1 F.C. 508 (C.A.) — This case raised the question of what is meant by the phrase a "serious non-political crime" in section F of Article 1 of the Convention.

The appellant is an Iranian citizen, the son of a wealthy family which had been an active supporter of the Shah's regime. The family experienced considerable difficulties after the coming into power of the government that overthrew the Shah. The appellant joined an underground student group and, in due course, became associated with a larger militant group of anti-government activists. In the years 1980 and 1981 the appellant personally took part in five or six incidents of bombing and arson. Those attacks were directed against wealthy supporters of the regime. These incidents led to the injury and death of innocent bystanders. The appellant was arrested and interrogated by the authorities but never confessed to his activities and he was ultimately released by the authorities, without being charged, and eventually fled to Canada.

A panel of the CRDD found that the appellant had a well-founded fear of persecution but that he was excluded by the provision in section 1F(b) of the Convention.

A panel of the CRDD concluded that the appellant's crimes were non-political. Accordingly, the appeal raised the question of what was meant by political crime. The characterization of crimes as political is found in both extradition and refugee law. The court noted that there was a need for even greater caution characterizing the crime as political for the purposes of applying section 1F(b) than for the purpose of denying extradition. The court developed an incidence test as a means of resolving whether a crime is political. The appellant met the first branch of the test because Iran, in the years in question, was a turbulent society in which a number of armed groups were in conflict with the regime and the appellant's testimony that he was a member of one such group was accepted as credible. The appellant's claim failed the second branch of the test. There was no objective rational connection between injuring the commercial interests of certain wealthy supporters of the government and any realistic goal of forcing the regime itself to fall or change. Further, the means used by the appellant excluded his crimes from any claim to be political in nature. The attacks were not carried out against armed adversaries and were bound to injure innocent bystanders. The use of deadly force against unarmed civilian commercial targets in circumstances where serious injury or death to innocent bystanders was inevitable rendered the violence used wholly disproportionate to any legitimate political objective.

Khatib v. Canada (Minister of Citizenship & Immigration) (1994), 83 F.T.R. 310 — The court noted that in *Ward v. Canada (Minister of Employment & Immigration)*, [1993] 2 S.C.R. 689, the applicant was a citizen of a state which admitted that it could not provide protection, The discussion and conclusions reached in *Ward*, in the opinion of the Court, applied only to citizens of a state, and not to stateless people. A stateless person is not expected to avail himself or herself of state protection when there is no duty on the state to provide such protection.

Bediako v. Canada (Minister of Employment & Immigration), 1994 CarswellNat 1590 (Fed. T.D.) — The applicant had a well-founded subjective and objective fear of persecution when he left Ghana. The Board concluded that the objective fear of the applicant had been removed by changes in the country conditions between December 31, 1991, when the applicant left that country, and December 30, 1992, when the Board heard evidence of the applicant's claim.

The Board, in deciding whether there has been a change in country conditions, is required to give a sufficient analysis of the conflicting documentary evidence before it. There was, in this case, a very extensive analysis of the change in country conditions and, accordingly, that aspect of the Board's decision cannot be criticized.

Country changes have to be meaningful, effective and durable. In this case there was documentary evidence that showed that democracy was not working perfectly in Ghana, however, the Board addressed in detail the changes in country conditions and found them to be fundamental and durable enough to eliminate the objective basis for the applicant's fear. Accordingly, the application was dismissed.

Hassan v. Canada (Minister of Employment & Immigration) (1994), 174 N.R. 74 (Fed. C.A.) — The appellant claimed refugee status for herself and for her four children. She was a member of the Issaq clan. She and her husband operated a small grocery store in Northern Somalia. She and her husband suffered at the hands of police in the months leading up to the outbreak of hostilities in 1988. After that time their grocery store was destroyed and her husband fled the country never to be seen again. The appellant herself fled to Canada and claimed refugee status in 1989.

The decision of the Board was set aside. The issue was not whether the difficulties the appellant had experienced in the past constituted persecution, nor was it whether the appellant had been singled out for harassment while in Somalia. The issue was whether the appellant could reasonably fear persecution in the future simply by being a member of the Issaq clan.

It is clear that the status of refugee is attached to an individual and is granted on the basis that this individual needs protection from personal harm and persecution that he or she may suffer in his or her country over and above what would come from a state of general oppression affecting all the inhabitants of the country. This principle relates to the objective fear, not to its well-foundedness or reasonability. It has nothing to do with the question of whether one may have a reasonable fear of being personally a victim of persecution for the sole reason that he or she belongs to a specific targeted group whose members are indiscriminately subject to persecution. It is this question which was at the heart of the appellant's claim. The Board missed the point and as a result its decision did not dispose of the real issue.

Papu v. Canada (Minister of Employment & Immigration), 1994 CarswellNat 1587 (Fed. T.D.) — It is well established that the determination of whether an individual's treatment is sufficiently serious to constitute persecution is to be left to the members of the Board.

Most states have measures which provide for the derogation of civil rights temporarily in a time of emergency. This derogation of civil rights does not necessarily amount to "persecution."

Chun v. Canada (Minister of Employment & Immigration), 1994 CarswellNat 1605 (Fed. T.D.) — The court construed the Federal Court of Appeal decision in *Cheung v. Canada (Minister of Employment & Immigration)* (1993), 19 Imm. L.R. (2d) 81 (Fed. C.A.), as standing for the proposition that women in China who have more than one child and are faced with forced sterilization form a particular social group so as to come within the meaning of the definition Convention refugee. The court also determined that the Court of Appeal found in *Cheung* that even if forced sterilization was accepted as a law of general application, that fact would not necessarily prevent a claim to Convention refugee status.

The court allowed this application for judicial review because the panel that reached a negative decision in this case did not have the benefit of the decision of the Court of Appeal in *Cheung*.

Equizabal v. Canada (Minister of Employment & Immigration), [1994] 3 F.C. 514, 24 Imm. L.R. (2d) 277, 170 N.R. 329 (C.A.) — The appellant was denied refugee status on the basis that he was included in Article 1F of the Convention and therefore excluded from the definition of refugee. The specific finding of the CRDD was that the appellant had committed crimes against humanity by torturing civilians. The appellant sought and obtained leave to apply for judicial review, which application was dismissed. The Trial Division judge certified a serious question of general importance.

The appellant was a citizen of Guatemala who was forcibly recruited by the Guatemalan military. He described in his evidence before the CRDD four military missions which involved the torture of civilians. A crime against humanity is not only a domestic offence, but is rather an offence with the additional component of barbarous cruelty. On the uncontradicted evidence of the appellant, it is obvious that he was guilty of barbarous cruelty in the four incidents he described in his evidence.

The defence of obedience to the orders of a superior based on compulsion was also considered. The first matter to be assessed was whether the orders in issue were manifestly unlawful. A manifestly unlawful order must be one that offends the conscience of every reasonable right-thinking person. It must be an order which is obviously and flagrantly wrong. The court had no difficulty in concluding that the orders here in issue were manifestly unlawful. The appellant and two other soldiers were ordered on one occasion to beat four persons and torture them over a period of three hours. Torturing the truth out of someone is manifestly unlawful, by any standard.

On the question of compulsion, the issue was whether the appellant faced an imminent, real and inevitable threat to his life. Stern punishment or demotion would not be sufficient. The appellant's evidence summarized two reasons why, notwithstanding his understanding that the penalty for desertion was only 12 months in jail, he would be killed: first, he knew of three other deserters who were apprehended and never heard from again; second, he believed he would be killed by his lieutenant because of his knowledge of relatives of persons whom the lieutenant had tortured personally. The first reason was dismissed as it was pure speculation without any credible evidence to support it. The second reason was not supported by the record. The record established that before the third mission, the appellant advised his lieutenant that he would no longer participate in such torture. As a result he was never forced to torture anyone again. He was thereafter, on two occasions, assigned to act as a guard while others did the torturing. There was, therefore, no evidence that the appellant was facing an imminent, real and inevitable threat to his life.

Accordingly, the appeal was dismissed and the decision that the appellant had committed a crime against humanity, as that expression appears in Article 1F of the Convention relating to the status of refugees, was upheld.

Gonzalez v. Canada (Minister of Employment & Immigration), [1994] 3 F.C. 646, 24 Imm. L.R. (2d) 229, 170 N.R. 302, 115 D.L.R. (4th) 403 (C.A.) — This was an appeal from a decision of the Refugee Division, which found the appellant excluded from the definition of Convention refugee by reason of section F(a) of Article 1 of The United Nations Convention Relating to the Status of Refugees because the Board found there was serious reason to believe that the appellant had committed a crime against humanity. The Board proceeded directly to that finding and made no finding on the merits of the refugee claim. The appellant had admitted to killing civilians on two occasions when his military unit in Nicaragua encountered armed counter-revolutionaries. The court noted that as a practical matter it would have been better had the Refugee Division dealt with the merits of the claim as well as the applicability of the exclusion. The court noted that if the claim was well founded but for the application of the exclusion and if it were found on appeal that the exclusion had been wrongly applied to the appellant, then the Court could have made the necessary declaration without requiring the Refugee Division to deal with the matter again. The court found that, on the particular facts and circumstances of this case, the appellant was a soldier engaged in an action against an armed enemy and that his actual participation in the killing of innocent civilians fell short of a crime against humanity. The court indicated that it did not wish to be understood as saying that the killing of civilians by a soldier while engaged in an action against an armed enemy could never amount to a war crime or a crime against humanity; each case will depend on its own individual facts and circumstances.

Roble v. Canada (Minister of Employment & Immigration) (1994), 169 N.R. 125 (Fed. C.A.) — The appellant was born in Somalia and claimed a fear of persecution if he were returned at the hands of the National Security Service, which had been the security service used by former President Mohammed Siad Barre. The Board found as a fact that the National Security Service was no longer a factor in Somalia because the Barre government had been toppled.

The appellant submitted that when the political situation in a country is unstable and uncertain and an interim government is not yet in control, it is inappropriate for the appellant to be required to seek the protection of his state. There are situations in which the political and military circumstances in a country at a given time are such that it is impossible to speak of a government with control of the territory and able to provide effective protection. The non-existence of a government is not an obstacle to an application for refugee status. However, this statement of the law only applies to cases where a claimant has demonstrated a prospective risk of persecution based on one of the grounds enumerated in the definition. The finding that the agent of persecution — the NSS — was no longer a factor meant that the inability of the state to protect the appellant was not in itself sufficient basis for his claim.

Fathi-Rad v. Canada (Secretary of State) (1994), 77 F.T.R. 41 — The applicant sought review of a decision determining that she was not a Convention refugee. The applicant was a 51-year-old woman whose family supported the pre-revolutionary government and the People's Democratic Front in Iran. The applicant was arrested, detained and questioned approximately once every two months between 1985 and 1988 for her failure to conform to the Islamic dress code. In overruling the Board's decision, the court concluded that the Islamic dress code in Iran was not a law of general application. The dress code applied only to women. It dictated the manner in which women must dress to comply with the religious beliefs of the governing regime and prescribed punishments for violation of that law. A law which specifically targets the manner in which women dress may not properly be characterized, as it was in this case, as a law of general application which applies to all citizens.

For this and other reasons the decision of the Board was set aside and the matter returned to a differently constituted panel for rehearing and redetermination.

Rodriguez-Hernandez v. Canada (Secretary of State) (1994), 76 F.T.R. 107 — The applicant, a citizen of Cuba, claimed persecution on the basis of religion and political opinion. The applicant left Cuba for Canada while he was in possession of a valid travel permit, which allowed him to be absent for 30 days. In determining whether the applicant faced persecution for overstaying his exit visa, the Board considered that Cuban exit laws are of general application. This finding alone did not end the matter, however, for the law must still be examined to determine whether it is persecutory. One indication that a general law is persecutory is a penalty which is disproportionate to the offence. The Board did not err in concluding that the potential punishment for violation of the Cuban exit laws by the applicant did not amount to persecution. The onus was on the applicant to bring evidence before the Board of the punishment to be faced upon return and to demonstrate that the punishment is disproportionate to the offence. This onus had not been met, and the application for judicial review was dismissed.

Thirunavukkarasu v. Canada (Minister of Employment & Immigration) (1993), [1994] 1 F.C. 589, 22 Imm. L.R. (2d) 241, 109 D.L.R. (4th) 682, 163 N.R. 232 (C.A.) — The appellant was a citizen of Sri Lanka and a Tamil. The appellant's claim that he faced serious risk to his life in the north of Sri Lanka was accepted but his claim for refugee status was refused on the basis that there was an internal flight alternative (IFA) available to him.

The court had occasion to review the law on the question of IFAs in this judgment.

The notion of an IFA is not a legal defence and it is not a legal doctrine. It is a convenient, short-hand way of describing a fact situation in which a person may be in danger of persecution in one part of a country, but not in another. The idea of an IFA is inherent in the definition of a Convention refugee; it is not something separate. The definition requires that claimants have a well-founded fear of persecution which renders them unwilling or unable to return to their home country. If claimants are able to seek refuge within their own country, there is no basis for finding that they are unable or unwilling to avail themselves of the protection of that country.

The burden of proof with respect to an IFA is on the claimant. The claimant must show, on a balance of probabilities, a serious possibility of persecution throughout the country, including the area which is alleged to afford an IFA.

There is an obligation on the Minister or the Board to warn a claimant that the IFA issue will be raised. If the possibility of an IFA is raised, the claimant must demonstrate that there is a serious possibility of persecution in the area alleged to constitute an IFA. A refugee claimant enjoys the benefit of the privilege of natural justice in hearings before the Refugee Division. A basic and well-established component of the right to be heard includes notice of the case to be met. The purpose of this notice is to allow a person to prepare an adequate response. The right to notice of the case against the claimant is acutely important where the claimant may be called upon to provide evidence to show that no valid IFA exists in response to an allegation by the Minister. Therefore, neither the Minister nor the Refugee Division may spring the allegation of an IFA upon a complainant without notice that an IFA will be in issue at the hearing.

A claimant must seek and resort to an IFA if it is not unreasonable to do so in the circumstances of the individual claimant. This aspect of the test is a flexible one, that takes into account the particular situation of the claimant and the particular country involved. It is an objective test and the onus of proof rests on the claimant on this issue, just as it does with all other aspects of a refugee claim. Consequently, if there is a safe haven for claimants in their own country, where they would be free of persecution, they are expected to avail themselves of it unless they can show that it is objectively unreasonable for them to do so. It is not a question of whether the IFA is more or less appealing to the claimant than a new country. The question is whether, given the persecution in the claimant's part of the country, it is objectively reasonable to expect him or her to seek safety in a different part of that country before seeking a haven in Canada or elsewhere. Stated another way, the question to be answered is, would it be unduly harsh to expect the claimant, who is being persecuted in one part of his country, to move to another less hostile part of the country before seeking refugee status abroad?

An IFA cannot be speculative or theoretical. The alternative place of safety must be realistically accessible to the claimant. Any barriers getting there should be reasonably surmountable. The claimant cannot be required to encounter great physical danger or undergo undue hardship in travelling there or staying there. For example, claimants should not be required to cross battle lines where fighting is going on at great risk to their lives in order to reach a place of safety. Similarly, claimants should not be compelled to hide out in isolated regions of their country, like a cave in the mountains, or in a desert or in a jungle, if those are the only areas of internal safety. Neither is it enough for refugee claimants to say that they do not like the weather in a safe area, or that they have no friends or relatives there, or that they may not be able to find suitable work there. If it is objectively reasonable in these latter situations to live in those places, without fear of persecution, then an IFA exists and the claimant is not a refugee.

It is not a matter of a claimant's convenience or the attractiveness of the IFA, but whether one should be expected to make do in that location, before travelling half-way around the world to seek a safe haven in another country.

The finding of an IFA, in this case, by the IRB was not sustained. The Country Profile of Sri Lanka and the Amnesty International Reports on the country did not show "quite clearly" that Tamils were safe in the southwest of the country. The reports, at the time this case was argued, spoke of several violent incidents in which Tamils were persecuted by the Sri Lankan government in the southwest in retaliation for the activities of the LTTE and other Tamil groups. Accordingly, there was no IFA for this appellant and the appeal was allowed.

Petrescu v. Canada (Solicitor General) (sub nom. Petrescu c. Canada (Solliciteur général)) (1993), 73 F.T.R. 1. — The applicant was a Romanian claiming refugee status on account of his political opinion and membership in a particular social group. The court elaborated on what was meant by a reasonable possibility of persecution and referred to

Ponniah v. Canada (Minister of Employment & Immigration) (1991), 13 Imm. L.R. (2d) 241, 132 N.R. 32 (Fed. C.A.):

> "Good grounds" or "reasonable chance" is defined in *Adjei* as occupying the field between upper and lower limits; it is less than a 50 per cent chance (*i.e.* a probability), but more than a minimal or mere possibility. There is no intermediate ground: what falls between the two limits is "good grounds."

> If the claimant, as the Board said, "... may face slightly more than a mere possibility ..." of persecution, he had crossed the lower limit and had made his case of "good grounds" or a "reasonable chance" for fearing persecution.

In this case, it was said that the claimant, when he argued that he feared a repetition of what he had suffered if he returned home and that he was in danger of losing his liberty or being the victim of a staged accident, did not persuade the panel. The Refugee Division imposed too high a standard of proof. Accordingly, the decision of the Refugee Division was quashed.

Kahlon v. King (1993), 66 F.T.R. 219 — The CRDD determined that the applicant was not a Convention refugee because a viable internal flight alternative (IFA) existed. The CRDD erred in failing to take into account the situations of individuals who were similarly situated to the applicant. It was not sufficient to take into account Sikhs in general living in India outside the Punjab or all Sikh men living in India outside the Punjab. The question before the tribunal was whether there was a serious possibility of the applicant being persecuted elsewhere in India. Accordingly, the decision of the CRDD was set aside and the matter referred back for rehearing before a differently constituted panel.

Chan v. Canada (Minister of Employment & Immigration), [1993] 3 F.C. 675, 20 Imm. L.R. (2d) 181, 156 N.R. 279 (C.A.); affirmed [1995] 3 S.C.R. 593, 128 D.L.R. (4th) 213, 187 N.R. 321 — This was an appeal with leave from a decision of the Convention Refugee Determination Division of the Immigration and Refugee Board deciding that the appellant was not a Convention refugee.

The appellant was a citizen of the People's Republic of China (PRC). During the Cultural Revolution the appellant's family was persecuted due to his father's background as a landowner. During the students' pro-democracy demonstrations in 1989 the appellant expressed his support of the movement by giving food and drink to the students from his restaurant in Guangzhou Province. After the students' movement was crushed by the authorities and the appellant voluntarily reported his pro-democracy activities to the Public Security Bureau (PSB); officers visited his restaurant at least 13 times, interrogating him, his staff and his customers. In November 1989, the appellant's wife gave birth to a second child. When the PSB learned of this birth, they accused the appellant of violating the birth control policy of the PRC. Officers visited his home on a number of occasions after the birth of his child. The appellant was advised that either he or his wife would have to undergo sterilization. The appellant agreed to be sterilized but fled the PRC before the operation took place. The appellant claimed that after his departure his family continued to be harassed for violating the one-child policy.

There were three decisions given by the court, namely: the majority (Heald J.A. and Desjardins J.A.) dismissed the appeal; the minority (Mahoney J.A.) would have allowed the appeal.

Heald J.A. was not convinced on the evidence that the appellant had a well-founded fear of persecution and this determination would normally have been sufficient to dispose of the appeal. However, His Lordship went on to discuss the meaning of the phrase "particular social group" and "political opinion" in his judgment. The particular social group was defined to be parents in China with more than one child, who disagree with forced sterilization. This group was found by Heald J.A. not to be encompassed by any of the categories identified by the Supreme Court of Canada in the *Ward* decision (*Ward v. Canada (Minister of Employment & Immigration)* (1993), 20 Imm. L.R. (2d) 85, [1993] 2 S.C.R. 689). This group was found to be defined solely by the fact that its members face a particular form of persecutory treatment. Membership in the group was dictated by the finding of persecution. This logic reversed the statutory definition and voided enumerated grounds of content. The appellant's fear stemmed from what he did and not from what he was.

Disagreement with the one-child policy is a political statement. There was no evidence that persons who simply voiced their opposition to this policy or to forced sterilization were not tolerated. On the question of whether the appellant who had breached the policy and failed to submit to the resulting demand for sterilization faced a well-founded fear of persecution, Heald J.A. answered in the negative. The persecutory treatment emanated not from a refusal to submit to sterilization, but from a breach of the policy. There was no indication that a breach of the one-child policy and a reluctance to undergo sterilization would be perceived by the central government or the local authorities as anything more than a breach of a law and a reluctance to undergo the ensuing penalty. The one-child policy is well within the jurisdiction of the Chinese government and there was a plethora of documentary evidence which articulated the rationale for this policy in China. Sanctions, in general, imposed for a breach of the policy must be accepted. A finding of persecution would have to be based uniquely on an abhorrence of the penalty. In other words the persecution alone motivates the determination of refugee status. Heald J.A. found that the definition of Convention refugee did not permit such a conclusion.

Desjardins J.A. agreed in the result and noted that, with respect to the phrase "particular social group," what links the members of the group together must be so fundamental that it cannot be changed and if it were to be changed, would destroy the person as a person. The unchangeable characteristic of a particular social group must be distinguished from the basic human right which the group might decide to defend. The innate characteristic must be so strong a factor that it makes a group of individuals what they are and it must exist independently of what they are fighting for. The appellant was one of a number of persons who, individually, had resisted the one-child policy and, like the others of his category, faced the general sanction, namely forced sterilization. This was not a group that was affiliated in a fundamental way so as to qualify as a particular social group. The group of which the appellant claimed to be a member was cognizable by the decision of the local Chinese authorities to use forced sterilization as a means of enforcing government policy. Thus, what linked the group together was an external factor and this was insufficient to meet the definition of the term particular social group.

With respect to the ground of "political opinion," Desjardins J.A. accepted that any opinion on any matter related to state affairs expressed or imputed to a claimant may constitute the basis for a claim under political opinion. Her Lordship, however, was unable to infer that the local authorities would impute to the appellant a political opinion in this case on account of his resistance to a general government policy. The evidence showed that there was continuing popular resistance to family planning in China and that birth rates soared the moment the pressure was eased. Her Lordship noted that the treatment, in the case at bar, related to forced sterilization. The court assumed that this was carried out through normal procedures currently in use by those who voluntarily opt for this procedure elsewhere, including Canada. What was objected to was the absence of consent. Her Lordship concluded that, unless amended, the *Convention Relating to the Status of Refugees* would not cover violations of human rights imposed by local authorities in the pursuit of what the record showed is a legitimate state objective, namely population control.

Mahoney J.A. dissented and found this case undistinguishable from *Cheung v. Canada (Minister of Employment & Immigration)* (1993), 19 Imm. L.R. (2d) 81, [1993] 2 F.C. 314 (Fed. C.A.). He further found that none of the reasons which would justify a Court departing from its previous decisions were present in this case and therefore *Cheung* had to be followed. Thus, the appellant could not be said not to belong to a particular social group. Further, he was in profound disagreement with the notion that the legitimacy of population control excluded persecution in pursuit of it from the Convention refugee definition.

Zolfagharkhani v. Canada (Minister of Employment & Immigration) (1993), 20 Imm. L.R. (2d) 1, [1993] 3 F.C. 540, 155 N.R. 311 (C.A.) — This was an appeal of a decision denying Convention refugee status to the appellant.

The appellant was an Iranian citizen who had served 27 months in the Iranian military during the Iran Iraq war. Subsequent to his discharge, the Revolutionary Guards requested him to report for a further six months of military service as a paramedic. The appellant reported for a one-month training course and during the last week of training discovered the apparent intention of his government to engage in chemical warfare against the Kurds. His conscience being troubled by this, he deserted and fled the country.

No issue was raised as to conscientious objection in relation to war in general. Since the appellant had no objection to serving in an active capacity in the Iranian military in the Iran/Iraq war, the issue as to conscientious objection relates solely to participation in chemical warfare.

The probable use of chemical weapons, which the Board accepted as a fact, was clearly judged by the international community to be contrary to basic rules of human conduct. Consequently, the ordinary Iranian conscription law of general application, as applied to a conflict in which Iran intended to use chemical weapons, amounted to persecution for political opinion.

The court set forth the following general propositions relating to the status of an ordinary law of general application in determining the question of persecution:

1. The statutory definition of Convention refugee makes the intent or any principal effect of an ordinary law of general application, rather than the motivation of the claimant, relevant to the existence of persecution.

2. The neutrality of an ordinary law of general application, *vis-à-vis* the five grounds for refugee status, must be judged objectively by Canadian tribunals and courts when required.

3. In such consideration, an ordinary law of general application, even in non-democratic societies, should be given a presumption of validity and neutrality, and the onus should be on a claimant, as is generally the case in refugee cases, to show that the laws are either inherently or for some other reason persecutory.

4. It will not be enough for the claimant to show that a particular regime is generally oppressive, but rather that the law in question is persecutory in relation to a Convention ground.

The appeal was allowed and the matter returned to a differently constituted panel for reconsideration not inconsistent with the reasons of the court.

Bouianova v. Canada (Minister of Employment & Immigration) (1993), 67 F.T.R. 74 — The applicant was born in Komi, near Moscow in the former USSR. The applicant's place of birth is located in what is now Russia. Before coming to Canada the applicant had lived in Latvia for 14 years. The applicant claimed a well-founded fear of persecution in Latvia based on discrimination against ethnic Russians in that country. Latvia had been her country of habitual residence. The panel found that the applicant was a citizen of the Russian Federation and that there was no evidence that she had a well-founded fear of persecution in Russia. In order to become a Russian citizen, all that the applicant had to do was make an application to the Russian Embassy requesting Russian citizenship and have her USSR passport so stamped. The applicant did not do this and her counsel in this proceeding sought to claim that she was therefore stateless.

Statelessness was not an option for the applicant. The condition of not having a country of nationality must be one that is beyond the power of the applicant to control. Otherwise, a person could claim statelessness merely by renouncing his or her former citizenship.

Ward v. Canada (Minister of Employment & Immigration) (1993), 20 Imm. L.R. (2d) 85, [1993] 2 S.C.R. 689, *(sub nom. Canada (Attorney General) v. Ward)* 103 D.L.R. (4th) 1, 153 N.R. 321, [1993] S.C.J. No. 74, [1997] I.N.L.R. 42, 1993 CarswellNat 1382, 1993 CarswellNat 90 — The appellant was born in Northern Ireland in 1955. He joined the Irish National Liberation Army (INLA) in 1983 as a volunteer. The INLA is a paramilitary organization, more violent than the Irish Republican Army (IRA), with a military-like hierarchy and strict discipline. The appellant's first task as a member of the INLA was to assist in guarding two of the organization's hostages. After he commenced his duties the INLA ordered the hostages executed. The appellant underwent what he described as "a predicament of moral conscience" and released the hostages without revealing himself to the INLA. Sometime later the police let slip to an INLA member that one of their own had assisted the hostages in their escape. The appellant was court-martialled and sentenced to death, but managed to escape. He was charged in the hostage incident and while in police custody the INLA kidnapped his wife and children to prevent him from becoming an informant.

The appellant was sentenced to three years in prison. He did not become an informant and never publicly admitted having released the hostages. Toward the end of his prison sentence he obtained a Republic of Ireland passport and on his release entered Canada as a visitor in December, 1985. He claimed refugee status in 1986. Under the procedures that were in effect at that time the Minister determined that the appellant was not a Convention refugee. The appellant applied for redetermination of his claim to the Immigration Appeal Board, as it was then known. The Board allowed the redetermination and found him to be a Convention refugee.

The Attorney General brought an application in the Federal Court to set aside the Board's decision, which decision was successful. The result of the Federal Court decision was that the appellant's case was referred back to the Immigration Appeal Board for reconsideration.

The Board again found the appellant to be a Convention refugee. The Minister appealed the Board's decision to the Federal Court of Appeal, which set aside the Board's decision. The appellant then appealed that decision to the Supreme Court of Canada.

International refugee law was formulated to serve as a back-up to the protection one expects from the state of which an individual is a national. It was meant to come into play only in situations when that protection is unavailable, and then only in certain situations. The international community intended that persecuted individuals be required to approach their home state for protection before the responsibility of other states became engaged.

The onus of proof in a refugee proceeding is on the claimant and it is for the claimant to show a well-founded fear of persecution in all countries of which the claimant is a national. In this case the appellant was a national not only of the Republic of Ireland, but also of Great Britain and there was therefore a burden upon him to prove that he was a refugee from both countries before Canada's obligation could be engaged.

State complicity in persecution is not a prerequisite to a valid refugee claim. The claimant must establish a "well-founded fear." The claimant must be outside his or her country of nationality because of that fear and unable to avail him- or herself of its protection. Alternatively, the claimant must be both outside his or her country of nationality and unwilling to avail himself or herself of its protection by reason of that well-founded fear. If a state is able to protect a claimant, then his or her fear is not, objectively speaking, well founded. Persecution under the Convention includes situations where the state is not an accomplice to the persecution, but is simply unable to protect its citizens.

Being unable to avail oneself of state protection implies circumstances that are beyond the will of the person concerned. There may, for example, be a state of war, civil war or other grave disturbance which prevents the country of nationality from extending protection. Protection by the country of nationality may also have been denied to the claimant. Such denial may confirm or strengthen the claimant's fear of persecution and may indeed be an element of the persecution. The term "unwilling" in the definition refers to refugees who refuse to accept the protection of the country of nationality. Where a person is willing to avail himself or herself of the protection of his or her home country, such willingness would be incompatible with a claim that he or she is outside that country owing to a well-founded fear of persecution. Whenever the protection of the country of nationality is available and there is no ground based on well-founded fear for refusing it, the person concerned is not in need of international protection and is not a refugee. Ineffective state protection is encompassed within the concept of "unable" and "unwilling." In cases of "inability," protection is denied to the claimant, whereas when the claimant is "unwilling," he or she opts not to approach the state by reason of his or her fear on one of the enumerated bases. In either case, the state's involvement in the persecution is not a necessary consideration.

Where the existence of a fear is established and where the state's inability to protect is established, it is not assuming too much to say that the fear is well founded. The burden of showing a state's inability to protect rests on the claimant and can only be discharged by the adducing of clear and convincing confirmation of this inability to protect. In this particular case the proof was unnecessary as representatives of the state authorities conceded their inability to protect the appellant. Nations should be presumed to be capable of protecting their citizens. Security of nationals is the essence of sovereignty. Absent a situation where the state apparatus has completely broken down, such as that recognized in Lebanon in the *Zalzali* case, [1991] 3 F.C. 605, it should be assumed that the state is capable of protecting its nationals.

The appellant justified his claim to refugee status on the basis of a well-founded fear of persecution at the hands of the INLA by reason of his membership in a particular social group, *i.e.*, the INLA. A good working rule to determine the meaning of "particular social group" is set out in the test proposed in *Canada (Minister of Employment & Immigration) v. Mayers* (1992), 97 D.L.R. (4th) 729; *Acosta, Re* 2986, 919850 WL 56042 (B.I.A.); and *Cheung v. Canada (Minister of Employment & Immigration)*, (1993), 19 Imm. L.R. (2d) 81 (Fed. T.D.). Those cases identify three possible categories:

1. groups defined by an innate or unchangeable characteristic;

2. groups whose members voluntarily associate for reasons so fundamental to their human dignity that they should not be forced to forsake the association; and

3. groups associated by a former voluntary status, unalterable due to its historical permanence.

The INLA did not meet these three tests and was therefore not a particular social group.

However, it is for the examiner to decide whether the Convention definition is met; usually there will be more than one ground for the well-founded fear of persecution. In this case the court considered whether the appellant had a well-founded fear of persecution for reasons of his political opinion. He believed that the killing of innocent people to achieve political change was unacceptable and thus his persecution by the INLA stemmed from that belief, which was held by the Supreme Court of Canada to be a political opinion. Any opinion on any matter in which the machinery of state, government and policy may be engaged is a political opinion. The political opinion need not have been expressed outright by the claimant and need not conform to the claimant's true beliefs. Not just any dissent to any organization will unlock the gates to Canadian asylum; the disagreement has to be rooted in political conviction.

The appeal was allowed. The decision of the Court of Appeal was set aside. The case was remitted back to the Immigration and Refugee Board so that it could determine whether the appellant was also a refugee from Great Britain, his second country of nationality.

Ling v. Canada (Minister of Employment & Immigration) (1993), 64 F.T.R. 182 — The expression "a reasonable chance of persecution" has been held by the Appeal Division of the Federal Court to be an apt equivalent for a "well-founded fear of persecution."

The court approved the following comments of MacGuigan J.A. in *Adjei v. Canada (Minister of Employment & Immigration)*, [1989] 2 F.C. 680, 7 Imm. L.R. (2d) 169, 57 D.L.R. (4th) 153, 132 N.R. 24 (C.A.):

> The fear of persecution in the definition has a two-fold aspect. On the one hand, the applicant must experience a subjective fear. A man with great fortitude may not have a subjective fear of persecution until adverse circumstances are worse for him than for his less courageous fellow countryman; nevertheless such a fear must be present in the mind of the applicant for the definition of Convention refugee to be met. The appropriate test as to whether or not a subjective fear exists is that appropriate for determining the existence of other matters of fact in a case of this kind, namely balance of probabilities.

> The second aspect is the objective element. The subjective fear of the applicant ... must have an objective basis.

The decision of the Board was unexceptionable, and not to be disturbed. Accordingly, the application to quash the decision of the Convention Refugee Determination Division was dismissed.

Ghazizadeh v. Canada (Minister of Employment & Immigration) (1993), 154 N.R. 236 (Fed. C.A.) — The whole concept of a refugee *"sur place"* requires an assessment of the situation in the applicant's country of origin after she or he has left it. The fact that the departure may have been perfectly legal is nothing to the point.

Cheung v. Canada (Minister of Employment & Immigration) (1993), 19 Imm. L.R. (2d) 81, 153 N.R. 145 (Fed. C.A.) — In 1984 Ting Ting Cheung gave birth to a baby boy in the People's Republic of China. She had another child in 1987 and came to the attention of the Family Planning Bureau in her native province. Shortly after the pro-democracy demonstrations in Beijing she came to Canada and claimed to be a refugee.

The first question was whether women in China who have more than one child and are faced with forced sterilization constitute a social group within the meaning of the definition of "Convention refugee." The court indicated that the following criteria provide a useful basis for consideration in constructing a test for being a particular social group:

> (1) a natural or non-natural group of persons with (2) similar shared background, habits, social status, political outlook, education, values, aspirations, history, economic activity or interests, often interests contrary to those of the prevailing government, and (3) sharing basic, innate, unalterable characteristics, consciousness, and solidarity or (4) sharing a temporary but voluntary status, with the purpose of their association being so fundamental to their human dignity that they should not be required to alter it.

The court concluded that women in China who have one child and are faced with forced sterilization satisfy enough of the above criteria to be considered a particular social group. This did not mean that all women in China who have more than one child may automatically claim Convention refugee status. It is only those women who also have a well-founded fear of persecution as a result of membership in that social group who can claim such status.

The next question was whether forced or strongly coerced sterilization in the context of China's one-child policy constituted persecution. The Immigration and Refugee Board had concluded that forced sterilization in that context was not persecution. The court disagreed.

The court noted that forced sterilization of women was a violation of Articles 3 and 5 of the United Nations Universal Declaration of Human Rights. This declaration was adopted and proclaimed December 10, 1948 by the General Assembly of the United Nations.

Karen Lee Cheung was the second child, whose birth was contrary to the one-child policy. The court found that the minor could also claim the benefit of Convention refugee status on the principle of family unity. Finally, there being no problems as to the credibility of the adult claimant, nor any factual questions that needed to be resolved by the Board, the court exercised its discretion under subs. 52(c)(i) of the *Federal Court Act* and declared both appellants to be Convention refugees.

Canada (Minister of Employment & Immigration) v. Villafranca (1992), 18 Imm. L.R. (2d) 130, 99 D.L.R. (4th) 334, 150 N.R. 232 (Fed. C.A.) — The respondent was a Philippine national who served in his home country as a policeman. He fled because he had been marked for death by a communist terrorist guerilla group and he feared for his life. The Refugee Division found him credible and held that he did have a well-founded fear of persecution by reason of his political opinion.

The Refugee Division failed to address the question of whether the respondent was unable or unwilling to avail himself of the protection of the Philippines. Where the claimant is himself an agent of the state, it makes no sense to speak of him as being unwilling to seek the state's protection. The claim can only succeed if he shows that he is unable to do so. The burden of showing that one is not able to avail oneself of the protection of one's own state is not easily satisfied. The test is an objective one and involves the claimant showing either that he is physically prevented from seeking his government's aid or that the government itself is in some way prevented from giving it. No government that makes any claim to democratic values can guarantee the protection of all of its citizens at all times. Thus, it is not enough for a claimant to show that his government has not always been effective at protecting persons in his particular situation. Where the state is so weak and its control over all or part of its territories so tenuous as to make it a government in name only, a refugee may justly claim to be unable to avail himself of its protection. Situations of civil war, invasion or the total collapse of internal order will normally be required. The Refugee Division having failed to address this question, its decision was quashed and the matter referred back to a differently constituted panel of the Board for a new hearing.

Orelien v. Canada (Minister of Employment & Immigration) (1991), [1992] 1 F.C. 592, 15 Imm. L.R. (2d) 1, 135 N.R. 50 (C.A.) — Canada's obligations in the area of refugees stem from the 4th Geneva Convention of August 12, 1949, and protocol due to the Geneva Convention of August 12, 1949, both approved by Acts of Parliament (*Geneva Conventions Act*, R.S.C. 1985, c. G-3, s. 2, as am. S.C. 1990, c. 14, s. 1), as well as a customary norm of temporary refuge. To return a person to Haiti in the circumstances that presently exist and have existed at relevant times in this case would have violated Canada's obligations under the Convention, the protocol and the customary norm of international law prohibiting the forceable repatriation of foreign nationals who have fled generalized violence and other threats to their lives and security arising out of internal armed conflict within their state of nationality. The Convention, the protocol and the customary norm of international law have the force of domestic law in Canada and can be enforced in the courts of Canada at the suit of a private individual. The intention to execute a deportation order, which if executed would breach those laws, does not colour the process under the *Immigration Act* by which a person from such a country may be ordered deported. This is not to denigrate the importance of the Convention, the protocol and the customary norms of international law. It would be a grave and justiciable matter if Canada were to execute deportation orders in circumstances which breached obligations under international law and put the life, liberty or security of persons in peril.

Canada (Minister of Employment & Immigration) v. Obstoj, [1992] 2 F.C. 739, 93 D.L.R. (4th) 144, 142 N.R. 81 (C.A.) — The Minister applied to set aside a credible basis determination. The first-level tribunal found that given the present day change of circumstances in Poland there was no realistic possibility of the respondent suffering persecution if she would return. They found, however, that the respondent fell under the provisions of s. 2(3) of the *Immigration Act* and that there were compelling reasons for her refusing to avail herself of the protection of Poland and that therefore her claim had a credible basis. The three judges of the Court of Appeal that heard the matter gave three different judgments. Hugessen J. ruled that since the Refugee Division, when conducting the hearing into the claim for refugee status, was able to hear evidence and consider questions raised by s. 2(3), the credible basis tribunal, when deciding whether or not there is credible or trustworthy evidence on which the division could decide in a claimant's favour, is likcwise able to consider such evidence. Subs. 2(2) and (3) were found to deal not only with the loss of a refugee status which had already been acquired, but also to have been incorporated into the definition of a Convention refugee by virtue of para. (b) of the definition.

Section 2(3) extends to anyone who has been recognized as a refugee at any time, even long after the date of the Convention. It should also be read as requiring Canadian authorities to give recognition to refugee status on humanitarian grounds to a special and limited category of persons, in particular, those persons who have suffered such appalling persecution that the experience alone is a compelling reason not to return them even though they may no longer have reason to fear further persecution.

Desjardins J.A. was of the view that para. (b) contained in the definition of a Convention refugee was an integral part of that definition and that a claimant must meet the requirements of both paragraphs (a) and (b) at the time that status is claimed and continuously thereafter. There is a constant relationship between the cases mentioned in para. (b) and the requirement of a well-founded fear mentioned in para. (a). Subsection (2) referred to in para. (b) contains five categories. Paragraphs (a), (b), (c) and (d) presuppose the case of an individual who does something contrary to the idea of a Convention refugee. Such an individual could then never claim that his or her fear was well founded. Such a person ceases to be a refugee first because of the requirements in para. (b) of the definition, and second because the fear of such a person is not well founded. Paragraph 2(2)(e) does not deal with an act committed by a claimant which conflicts with the idea of a well-founded fear, but rather with changes that occurred in the country of origin so that the reasons for the fear have ceased. Such a claimant does not meet para. (b) of the definition and further his fear is no longer well founded as required by para. (a) of the definition. Subsection 2(3) creates justification which excludes the application of para. 2(2)(e). While the fear of a person described in s. 2(3) is not well founded, Parliament intended to recognize that such persons could claim refugee status despite this fact. Such a claim could only initially be made at a first-level tribunal, and accordingly a first-level tribunal can consider whether there is credible evidence of the justification set out in s. 2(3).

Pratte J.A. dissented and would have allowed the application and ruled that a foreigner who no longer has a reason to fear persecution in his country may not be determined to be a Convention refugee for the sole reason that the persecution he suffered in the past justifies his refusal to avail himself of the protection of that country.

[Editor's note: Although decided under a different statutory framework the principles discussed may still be of interest.]

Zalzali v. Canada (Minister of Employment & Immigration) (1991), 14 Imm. L.R. (2d) 81, 126 N.R. 126, [1991] 3 F.C. 605 (C.A.) — The appellant, a Lebanese national, claimed he was persecuted on account of his nationality, political opinion and membership in a particular social group. In most cases of claims for refugee status, the state, while it may not itself be the agent of persecution, makes itself an accomplice by tolerance or inertia. It is then possible to speak in terms of persecution attributable to the state and to conclude that the refugee claimant had good reason to be unwilling to claim protection which the state was, in all likelihood, not going to give him. There can be persecution within the meaning of the convention and the *Immigration Act* where there is no form of guilt, complicity or participation by the state. The definition of a refugee refers to "the fear of persecution without saying that this persecution must be by the government." The natural meaning of the words "is unable" assumes an objective inability on the part of the complainant and the fact that "is unable" is not qualified by "reason of that fear" confirms that the inability in question is governed by objective criteria which can be verified independently of the fear experienced. Seeing a connection of any kind between "is unable" and "complicity by the government" would be a misreading of the definition. Persecution by someone other than the government is possible when the government is unable to offer protection. There are several reasons beyond the person's control why he or she might be unable to claim the protection of the state. One of those reasons is the non-existence of a government to which that person may resort. In this case, the decision of the Refugee Division was set aside and the matter was remitted back for a rehearing in accordance with the reasoning of the court.

[Editor's note: The cases which discuss the phrase "is unwilling" are Rajudeen (1984), 55 N.R. 129; Surujpal (1985), 60 N.R. 73; and Satiacum (1985), 99 N.R. 171.]

Hilo v. Canada (Minister of Employment & Immigration) (1991), 15 Imm. L.R. (2d) 199, 130 N.R. 236 (Fed. C.A.) — The Refugee Division was under a duty to give its reasons for casting doubt upon the appellant's credibility in clear and unmistakeable terms. The Board's credibility assessment was defective because it was couched in vague and general terms. The claimant had only attended informal meetings of a political group inside Syria. The Refugee Division viewed this group as loosely knit with apparently charitable aims, no official title or status and noted further that the claimant was only 14 years of age at the time of his attendance. The court found that characterizing the group in this way was irrelevant. The Syrian authorities had sought to persecute the appellant because of his perceived political opinion. The proper test for evaluating political activities is not whether the division or members considered that the appellant had engaged in political activities but whether the ruling government of the country from which he claimed to be a refugee so considered his conduct.

Hoang v. Canada (Minister of Employment & Immigration) (1990), 13 Imm. L.R. (2d) 35, 120 N.R. 193 (Fed. C.A.) — The appellant was ordered deported because he was a permanent resident who had been convicted of an offence for which a term of imprisonment of more than six months had been imposed; he had also been convicted of an offence for which the maximum term was five years or greater. The appellant had come to Canada as a stateless person from Vietnam and had been determined by the Minister in 1986 to be a Convention refugee. The court noted that the Immigration Appeal Board (which had decided this matter) correctly determined that its jurisdiction is only over whether a person should be removed from Canada and not as to the country of removal. Until the issue of deportation is settled the Minister cannot make a decision as to the country of removal. Thus, a statement by the Minister's representative as to the Minister's disposition to deport the appellant to Vietnam was not taken as a formal expression of the Minister's decision since the Minister was not, at the date of that statement, empowered to make the decision.

The court determined that in dealing with the "double jeopardy" provisions of s. 11(h) of the *Charter*, deportation was not to be seen as a punishment of the person deported but a protection of those who remained. Further, deportation for serious offences affects neither s. 7 nor s. 12 of the *Charter of Rights and Freedoms* since it is not to be conceptualized as either a deprivation of liberty or a punishment. Finally, the court noted that with respect to Canada's international obligations the United Nations convention relating to the status of refugees contained an exception to the prohibition against *refoulement* where the deportee had been convicted in the country where he was making the refugee claim of a particularly serious crime. The court noted that the phrase "particularly serious crime" and "danger to the community" were not defined in the convention and therefore presumed that Parliament responsibly fulfilled its obligation when it enacted the *Immigration Act.*

Accordingly, the appellant's appeal was dismissed.

Adjei v. Canada (Minister of Employment & Immigration), [1989] 2 F.C. 680, 7 Imm. L.R. (2d) 169, 57 D.L.R. (4th) 153, 132 N.R. 24 (C.A.) — This application focuses on the proper interpretation of the definition of Convention refugee. An accurate way of describing the requisite test is in terms of "reasonable chance": is there a reasonable chance that persecution would take place were the applicant returned to his country of origin. There need not be more than a 50 per cent chance that persecution will occur (that is, a probability). On the other hand, there must be more than a minimal possibility of persecution. This application was allowed because the Board, in describing the test set out in the definition, stated that it was whether there was a reasonable chance or "substantial grounds" for thinking that the persecution may take place. The use of the term "substantial grounds" introduced an element of ambiguity into the Board's formulation of the correct test under the refugee definition. Accordingly, the Board's decision was set aside and the matter remitted back to the Board for reconsideration.

Surujpal v. Canada (Minister of Employment & Immigration) (1985), 60 N.R. 73 (Fed. C.A.) — The applicant brought an application to quash a decision of the Immigration Appeal Board finding that the applicant was not a Convention refugee. The decision of the Immigration Appeal Board was quashed because the evidence disclosed that the police were complicit in the broader sense in the persecution and harassment of the applicant. It is not required that state participation in persecution be direct; it is sufficient that it is indirect provided that there is proof of state complicity.

Rajudeen v. Canada (Minister of Employment & Immigration) (1984), 55 N.R. 129 (Fed. C.A.) — The definition of Convention refugee does not include a definition of persecution. "Persecute" was defined by reference to a dictionary as "to harass or afflict with repeated acts of cruelty or annoyance; to afflict persistently; to afflict or punish because of particular opinions or adherence to a particular creed or mode of worship." "Persecution" was defined as "a particular course or period of systematic infliction of punishment directed against those holding a particular (religious belief); persistent injury or annoyance from any source."

There is a subjective and objective component necessary to satisfy the definition of Convention refugee. The subjective component relates to the existence of the fear of persecution in the mind of the refugee. The objective component requires that the refugee's fear be evaluated objectively to determine if there is a valid basis for that fear.

In determining whether refugee status has been extended to cover a particular case, reference should be made to the expression of underlying policy in s. 3(g) of the Act. To satisfy the definition, the persecution complained of must have been committed or been condoned by the state itself and consist either of conduct directed by the state toward the individual or in the state knowingly tolerating the behaviour of private citizens or refusing or being unable to protect the individual from such behaviour.

Naredo v. Canada (Minister of Employment & Immigration) (1981), 130 D.L.R. (3d) 752, 40 N.R. 436 (Fed. C.A.) — The Federal Court held that the Immigration Appeal Board erred in imposing upon the applicant and his wife the requirement that they be subject to persecution. The statutory definition requires only that they establish a well-founded fear of persecution.

97. (1) Person in need of protection — A person in need of protection is a person in Canada whose removal to their country or countries of nationality or, if they do not have a country of nationality, their country of former habitual residence, would subject them personally

(a) to a danger, believed on substantial grounds to exist, of torture within the meaning of Article 1 of the Convention Against Torture; or

(b) to a risk to their life or to a risk of cruel and unusual treatment or punishment if

(i) the person is unable or, because of that risk, unwilling to avail themself of the protection of that country,

(ii) the risk would be faced by the person in every part of that country and is not faced generally by other individuals in or from that country,

(iii) the risk is not inherent or incidental to lawful sanctions, unless imposed in disregard of accepted international standards, and

(iv) the risk is not caused by the inability of that country to provide adequate health or medical care.

(2) Person in need of protection — A person in Canada who is a member of a class of persons prescribed by the regulations as being in need of protection is also a person in need of protection.

Case Law

Roberts v. Canada (Minister of Citizenship & Immigration), 2013 FC 298, 2013 CarswellNat 679, 2013 CarswellNat 1344, [2013] F.C.J. No. 325 — The applicant brought an application for judicial review of the Immigration and Refugee Board's dismissal of his claim for protection under ss. 96 and 97 of IRPA. The applicant took issue with the panel's finding that he was not a person in need of protection under subpara. 97(1)(b)(ii) because although he was personally targeted by a criminal gang, his alleged risk was a generalized one in his country of origin.

There is divided authority within the jurisprudence of the Federal Court over the issue of the appropriate interpretation to be given to the notion of "generalized risk" as contemplated in para. 97(1)(b) of IRPA and what is required to establish that a refugee claimant's risk is not a generalized one. In the decision under review, the panel suggested that there was no requirement of a personalized risk under subpara. 97(1)(b)(ii), which in turn lead the panel to completely disregard the applicant's personal circumstances and evidence of alleged risk. There was no analysis of the applicant's testimony and corroborating documents tendered in support of the allegation that he was particularly and personally at risk if he was to return to Saint Vincent. The panel's conclusion was based on its unsupported and unexplained finding that the threats of future harm made to the applicant did not place him at any greater risk than the rest of the population.

The starting point for the required analysis under s. 97 of IRPA is to first appropriately determine the nature of the risk faced by the claimant. This requires an assessment of whether the claimant faces an ongoing or future risk, what the risk is, whether such risk is one of cruel and unusual treatment or punishment and the basis for the risk. The next required step in the analysis under s. 97, after the risk has been appropriately characterized, is the comparison of the correctly described risk faced by the claimant to that faced by a significant group in the country to determine whether the risks are of the same nature and degree. If the risk is not the same, then the claimant will be entitled to protection under s. 97 of IRPA.

The panel erred in conducting both steps of the required analysis. First, it made an unreasonable characterization of the nature of the risk faced by the applicant, stating on one hand that the applicant was "a victim in a criminal vendetta situation" in Saint Vincent and yet determining his risk as being a generalized risk due to a generalized crime activity. The panel's failure to conduct an individualized assessment in light of the applicant's evidence in its entirety constituted a reviewable error. The application for judicial review was allowed.

Also see *Fontenelle v. Canada (Minister of Citizenship & Immigration)* (2011), 5 Imm. L.R. (4th) 14, 2011 FC 1155, 2011 CarswellNat 4093, 2011 CarswellNat 5023, at s. 96 of IRPA.

See the *Mosqueda Costa, Ahanin, Nyota, Cruz, Josile,* and *Zheng* summaries under s. 96 of IRPA. And see *John v. Canada (Minister of Citizenship & Immigration)*, 2011 FC 387, 2011 CarswellNat 978, 2011 CarswellNat 1799.

— The present application challenges the decision of the Refugee Protection Division in which the applicant's claim for protection was rejected, in large measure, on the basis of a negative credibility finding. The decision was set aside. When dealing with gender-related claims it is critical that RPD pays special attention to *Guideline 4: Women Refugee Claimants Fearing Gender-Related Persecution: Guidelines Issued by the Chairperson* in reaching a determination. It is a reviewable error to first determine that a claimant is not credible and then to use that lack of credibility as a basis for rejecting or giving little weight to evidence that is submitted to corroborate the claimant's testimony. In the present case, the psychological report is tendered, not to prove the truth of the applicant's statements to the psychologist, but to prove her current state of mind. The applicant's impaired state of mind can be found to support the truth of her evidence of the abuse she suffered. And second, the applicant's state of mind was an important factor to be taken into consideration by the RPD when evaluating her evidence: to do so constitutes a practical application of *Guideline 4*.

Paz Guifarro v. Canada (Minister of Citizenship & Immigration), 2011 FC 182, 2011 CarswellNat 356, 2011 CarswellNat 1350 — Given the conjunctive nature of the two elements contemplated by para. 97(1)(b)(ii), a person applying for protection under s. 97 must demonstrate not only a likelihood of a personalized risk contemplated by that section, but also that such risk "is not faced generally by other individuals in, or from, that country." Accordingly, it is not an error for the RPD to reject an application for protection under s. 97 where it finds that a personalized risk that would be faced by the applicant as a risk that is shared by a sub-group of the population that is sufficiently large that the risk can reasonably be characterized as being widespread or prevalent in that country. This is so even where that sub-group may be specifically targeted. It is particularly so when the risk arises from criminal conduct or activity.

Given the frequency with which claims such as those that were advanced in the case at bar continue to be made under s. 97, it is necessary to underscore that it is now settled law that claims based on past and likely future targeting of the claimant will not meet the requirement of para. 97(1)(b)(ii) of IRPA where: (i) such targeting in the claimant's home country occurred or is likely to occur because of the claimant's membership in a sub-group of persons returning from abroad or perceived to have wealth for other reasons;

and (ii) that sub-group is sufficiently large that the risk can reasonably be characterized as being widespread or prevalent in that country. A sub-group of such persons numbering in the thousands would be sufficiently large as to render the risk they face widespread or prevalent in their home country, and therefore "general" within the meaning of para. 97(1)(b)(ii), even though that sub-group may only constitute a small percentage of the general population in that country. The application for judicial review was dismissed.

See *R. v. Laboucan*, [2010] 6 W.W.R. 13, 73 C.R. (6th) 235, (sub nom. *R. v. Briscoe*) 400 N.R. 200, 22 Alta. L.R. (5th) 62, 253 C.C.C. (3d) 129, 316 D.L.R. (4th) 590, (sub nom. *R. v. Briscoe*) 477 A.R. 70, 483 W.A.C. 70, 2010 SCC 12, 2010 CarswellAlta 591, 2010 CarswellAlta 590 at s. 96 of IRPA. Also see *Smith v. Canada (Minister of Citizenship & Immigration)* (2009), 86 Imm. L.R. (3d) 114, 358 F.T.R. 189 (Eng.), 2009 FC 1194, 2009 CarswellNat 3800, 2009 CarswellNat 3801 and *Alexander v. Canada (Minister of Citizenship & Immigration* (2009), 88 Imm. L.R. (3d) 75, 357 F.T.R. 222 (Eng.), 2009 FC 1305, 2009 CarswellNat 5510, 2009 CarswellNat 4566, [2009] F.C.J. No. 1682

Also see *Perez v. Canada (Minister of Citizenship & Immigration)* (2009), 85 Imm. L.R. (3d) 118, 2009 FC 1065, 2009 CarswellNat 5598, 2009 CarswellNat 3345 at s. 96.

Odetoyinbo v. Canada (Minister of Citizenship & Immigration), 2009 CarswellNat 1328, 2009 FC 501 — The applicant, a citizen of Nigeria, challenged the legality of a decision of the Refugee Protection Division of the Immigration and Refugee Board wherein the Board held he was not a Convention refugee or a person in need of protection. The applicant's claim is based on his alleged bisexuality. Since homosexuality is illegal in Nigeria, the applicant feared persecution because of his sexual orientation.

The Board's failure to make an explicit determination as to the applicant's bisexuality constituted a reviewable error and justified a redetermination of the applicant's claim. It is well settled that an adverse credibility finding, though it may be conclusive of a refugee claim under s. 96 of the IRPA, is not necessarily conclusive of a claim under s. 97(1). The reason is that the evidence necessary to establish a claim under s. 97 differs from that required under s. 96. When considering s. 97, the Board must decide whether the claimant's removal would subject him personally to the dangers and risks stipulated in para. 97(1)(a) and (b) of the Act. Further, there are objective and subjective components to s. 96, which is not the case for para. 97(1)(a): a person relying on this paragraph must show on a balance of probabilities that he or she is more likely than not to be persecuted.

In the case at bar, the Board did not explicitly state in its reasons that it did not believe that the applicant was bisexual. Accordingly, it could not ignore compelling objective evidence on record demonstrating the abuses which gay men are subjected to in Nigeria. Therefore, even if the Board rejected the applicant's account of what happened to him in Nigeria, it still had a duty to consider whether the applicant's sexual orientation would put him personally at risk in his country. The application was allowed and returned to the Board for redetermination by a different member.

See *Guney v. Canada (Minister of Citizenship & Immigration)*, 2008 CarswellNat 5579, 2008 CarswellNat 3687, 2008 FC 1134 at s. 96 of IRPA.

Prophète v. Canada (Minister of Citizenship & Immigration) (2009), 78 Imm. L.R. (3d) 163, 387 N.R. 149, 2009 FCA 31, 2009 CarswellNat 282, 2009 CarswellNat 1393, [2009] F.C.J. No. 143 — The Refugee Protection Division of the Immigration and Refugee Board determined that the applicant was not a Convention refugee. The appellant, a citizen of Haiti, claimed to have been the target of gang violence on multiple occasions. The appellant submitted that kidnapping was rampant in Haiti, but businessmen are especially at risk because the goal of kidnapping for ransom is to obtain money. The appellant argued, given the fact that in Haiti most of the population is poor, those with money or those perceived to have money are at a greater risk than the general population. He claimed s. 97 of the Act was to be interpreted as indicating that there can be a subgroup within a generalized group that faces an even more acute risk than the larger group. The lower Court concluded that the appellant did not face a personalized risk that is not faced generally by other individuals in or from Haiti. The risk of all forms of criminality is general and felt by all Haitians. While a specific number of individuals may be targeted more frequently because of their wealth, all Haitians are at risk of becoming the victims of violence. The application for judicial review was dismissed by the Federal Court and the following question was certified:

> Where the population of a country faces a generalized risk of crime, does the limitation of s. 97(1)(b)(ii) of the IRPA apply to a subgroup of individuals who face a significantly heightened risk of such crime.

The Federal Court of Appeal concluded that unlike s. 96, s. 97 of the Act is meant to afford protection to an individual whose claim "is not predicated on the individual demonstrating that he or she is [at risk] . . . for any enumerated grounds of s. 96." The examination of a claim under subs. 97(1) necessitates an individualized inquiry, which is to be conducted on the basis of the evidence adduced by a claimant "in the context of a *present or prospective* risk" for him. As drafted, the Court of Appeal found the certified question was too broad. Taking into consideration the broader federal scheme of which s. 97 is a part, answering the certifying question in a factual vacuum would, depending on the circumstances of each case, result in unduly narrowing or widening the scope of subparagraph 97(1)(b)(ii) of the Act. The Federal Court of Appeal declined to answer the certified question and dismissed the appeal.

See *Carrillo v. Canada (Minister of Citizenship & Immigration)* (2008), 69 Imm. L.R. (3d) 309, 2008 FCA 94, 2008 CarswellNat 1953, 2008 CarswellNat 605, [2008] F.C.J. No. 399 and *Sanchez v. Canada (Minister of Citizenship & Immigration)* (2007), 360 N.R. 344, 2007 CarswellNat 572, 2007 FCA 99 at s. 96 of IRPA.

Covarrubias v. Canada (Minister of Citizenship & Immigration) (2006), 56 Imm. L.R. (3d) 178, 354 N.R. 367, 148 C.R.R. (2d) 45, [2007] 3 F.C.R. 169, 2006 CarswellNat 3653, [2006] F.C.J. No. 1682, 2006 FCA 365 — The male appellant had a serious health condition and required life-sustaining medical treatment which he is unable to afford in his native Mexico, and which he says his country will not freely provide. The Federal Court of Appeal declined to consider the certified question of whether the exclusion of a risk to life caused by the inability of a country to provide adequate medical care to a person suffering a life-threatening illness under s. 97 of the IRPA infringed the *Canadian Charter of Rights and Freedoms* in a manner that does not accord with the principles of fundamental justice, and which cannot be justified under s. 1 of the *Charter*. Since the appellant had failed to provide sufficient evidence of a risk to his life on account of inadequate medical care should he be deported to Mexico? The allegations of specific *Charter* violation were without evidentiary foundation. Hence, there was no factual basis for entering into a *Charter* analysis in this case.

The provision in issue (s. 97) is meant to be broadly interpreted so that only in rare cases would the onus on the applicant be met. The applicant must establish on the balance of probabilities, not only that there is a personalized risk to his or her life, but that this was not caused by the inability of his or her country to provided adequate health care. Proof of a negative is required, that is, that the country is not able to furnish medical care that is adequate for this applicant. This is no easy task and the language and the history of the provision show that it was not meant to be. The words "inability to provide adequate medical services" must include situations where a foreign government decides to allocate its limited funds in a way that obliges some of its less prosperous citizens to defray part or all of their medical expenses. The exclusion in subparagraph 97(1)(b)(iv) should not be interpreted so broadly as to exclude any claim in respect of health care. The wording of the provision clearly leaves open the possibility for protection where an applicant can show that he faces a personalized risk to life on account of his country's unjustified unwillingness to provide him with adequate medical care, where the financial ability is present.

The phrase "not caused by the inability of that country to provide adequate health care or medical care" in subparagraph 97(1)(b)(iv) of the IRPA excludes from protection persons whose claims are based on evidence that their native country is unable to provide adequate medical care because it chooses in good faith, for legitimate, political and financial priority reasons, not to provide such care to its nationals. If it can be proved that there is an illegitimate reason for denying the care, such as persecutorial reasons, that may suffice to avoid the operation of the exclusion.

Kandiah v. Canada (Minister of Citizenship & Immigration), 2005 FC 1815, 2005 CarswellNat 390, [2005] F.C.J. No. 27 — There may well be instances where a refugee claimant, whose identity is not disputed, is found to not have a valid basis for his subjective fear of persecution, but the country conditions are such that the claimant's particular circumstances, make him or her a person in need of protection. A negative subjective fear determination is not necessarily determinative of a claim under s. 97. A claim under s. 97 requires that the Board determine whether a claimant's removal would subject him personally to the dangers and risks stipulated in paragraphs 97(1)(a) and (b).

Li v. Canada (Minister of Citizenship & Immigration) (2005), 249 D.L.R. (4th) 306, 41 Imm. L.R. (3d) 157, 2005 CarswellNat 30, 2005 CarswellNat 1128, 2005 FCA 1, 329 N.R. 346, [2005] F.C.J. No. 1; leave to appeal refused 2005 CarswellNat 1112, 2005 CarswellNat 1113, [2005] S.C.C.A. No. 119 — Section 97 requires that a person establish, on a balance of probabilities, that he or she will face the danger or risks described in paragraphs 97(1)(a) and (b). The test for the degree of danger of torture in para. 97(1)(a) is a balance of probabilities or "more likely than not." Proof on a balance of probabilities is the standard of proof that the panel will apply in assessing the evidence adduced before it for the purposes of making its factual findings. The test for determining the danger of torture is whether, on the facts found by the panel, the panel is satisfied that it is more likely than not the individual would be personally subjected to a danger of torture.

Xie v. Canada (Minister of Citizenship & Immigration) (2004), 37 Imm. L.R. (3d) 163, 2004 CarswellNat 2036, 2004 CarswellNat 3972, 325 N.R. 255, [2005] 1 F.C.R. 304, 243 D.L.R. (4th) 385, 2004 FCA 250, [2004] F.C.J. No. 1142; leave to appeal refused 2005 CarswellNat 748, 2005 CarswellNat 749 (S.C.C.) — The appellant, a citizen of the People's Republic of China, was a senior official in the Guangzhou Commission for Foreign Economic Relations and Trade. She fled China and arrived in Canada in 2001 and made a claim for refugee protection. In the course of processing her claim, two facts emerged. Firstly, the appellant and her daughter had to their names bank accounts containing $2.7 million. Second, at the request of the Chinese authorities, there was an international warrant for the arrest of the appellant and a charge of embezzlement. On the basis of the appellant's unexplained wealth, the Board applied the exclusion in Article 1(F)(b) of the

IRP Act

Convention. The Board also decided that, in light of the offence with which the appellant was charged, she faced a risk of torture at the hands of the Chinese authorities if she were to return to China.

The Board was entitled to presume that the warrant for the appellant's arrest was issued in the belief that she was guilty of misconduct. The presumption of innocence does not apply so as to prevent the Board from taking the Chinese State's belief in the appellant's guilt into account in deciding if there are serious reasons to consider that she committed the crime with which she is charged. There are three ways in which refugee protection can be obtained. Refugee protection is extended to persons falling within the definition of Convention refugee which has not been changed by the new Act. Refugee protection is also extended to those persons who are found to be in the need of protection, a class defined by the risk of harm as opposed to the motivation of those inflicting harm. The grounds upon which such an application can be made are found in s. 97 and include those who are in "danger, believed on substantial grounds to exist, of torture within the meaning of Article 1 of the Convention Against Torture." Finally, a person can be extended refugee protection by means of an application for protection pursuant to s. 112 of the Act. Persons facing deportation may apply to the Minister for protection on the basis that they face a risk of harm if they return to their country of origin. If the application for protection is granted, such persons acquire refugee protection pursuant to para. 95(1)(c) of the Act. Subsection 112(3) of the Act lists those persons who are ineligible for refugee protection, including persons who are described in Article 1, Section F of the Convention. The exclusion from refugee protection is not an exclusion from protection altogether. Section 113 stipulates that persons described in 112(3) are to have their applications for protection decided on the basis of the factors set out in s. 97, with additional consideration given to the issue of whether such persons are a danger to the public in Canada or to the security of Canada. For all except those described in subs. 112(3), a successful application for protection results in the grant of refugee protection in the status of protected person. For persons described in subs. 112(3) the result is a stay of the deportation order in force against them. One consequence of the distinction is that protected persons have access to the status of permanent residence and are subject to the principle of non-refoulement.

Thus, the structure of the Act has two streams, claims for refugee protection and claims for protection in the context of pre-removal risk assessments. The person who is excluded from refugee protection is eligible to apply for protection at the PRRA stage. The basis on which the claim for protection may be advanced is the same, but the Minister can have regard to whether the granting of protection would affect the safety of the public or the security of Canada. If protection is granted, the result is a stay of the deportation order. The claimant does not have the same access to permanent resident status as does a successful claimant for refugee protection.

Once a panel of the Refugee Protection Division found that the appellant was excluded pursuant to Section F of Article 1, it had done everything that it was required to do. The appellant was, thereby, excluded from refugee protection, a matter within the Board's confidence, and was limited to applying for protection, a matter within the Minister's jurisdiction. Accordingly, the Board's conclusions as to the appellant's risk of torture were gratuitous and were an infringement upon the Minister's responsibilities.

Singh (H.) v. Canada (Solicitor General), [2004] 3 F.C.R. 323, (sub nom. *Singh v. Canada (Minister of Citizenship & Immigration)*) 39 Imm. L.R. (3d) 261, 248 F.T.R. 114, (sub nom. *Singh v. Canada (Minister of Citizenship & Immigration) (No. 2))* 117

C.R.R. (2d) 239, 2004 CarswellNat 2091, 2004 CarswellNat 549, 2004 FC 288 — A risk to life under s. 97 does not include having to assess whether there is appropriate health and medical care available in the country in question.

Pre-removal risk assessment officers do not have the jurisdiction to consider constitutional questions.

See also *Kadoura c. Canada (Ministre de la Citoyenneté & de l'Immigration)*, 2003 FC 1057, 2003 CarswellNat 4831, 2003 CarswellNat 2789, [2003] F.C.J. No. 1328, at s. 96 of IRPA.

Li v. Canada (Minister of Citizenship & Immigration) (2003), 39 Imm. L.R. (3d) 216, [2004] 3 F.C.R. 501, 2003 CarswellNat 4150, 2003 CarswellNat 4739, [2003] F.C.J. No. 1934, 2003 FC 1514, 243 F.T.R. 261; affirmed (2005), 41 Imm. L.R. (3d) 157, 2005 CarswellNat 30, [2005] F.C.J. No. 1, 2005 CarswellNat 1128, 2005 FCA 1, 329 N.R. 346, 249 D.L.R. (4th) 306; leave to appeal refused 2005 CarswellNat 1112, 2005 CarswellNat 1113, [2005] S.C.C.A. No. 119 — The applicant was seeking to quash a negative decision with respect to his refugee claim.

Pursuant to subs. 97(1), there must be persuasive evidence (that is a balance of probabilities) establishing the facts on which a claimant relies to say that he or she faces a substantial danger of being tortured on his or her return. Second, the danger or risk must be such that it is more likely than not that he or she would be tortured or subjected to other cruel or other degrading treatments. This does not mean that the Refugee Protection Division will not continue to give the benefit of the doubt to the claimant, in fact, it must do so.

Bouaouni v. Canada (Minister of Citizenship & Immigration), 2003 FC 1211, 2003 CarswellNat 3266, 2003 CarswellNat 3267, [2003] F.C.J. No. 1540 — This is an application to review a negative decision of a panel of the Refugee Protection Division.

A claim under s. 97 must be evaluated with respect to all the relevant considerations and with a view to the country's human rights record. While the Board must assess the applicant's claim objectively, the analysis must still be individualized. There may well be instances where a refugee claimant, whose identity is not disputed, is found to be not credible with respect to his subjective fear of persecution but the country conditions are such that the claimant's particular circumstances make him a person in need of protection. A negative credibility determination which may be determinative of a refugee claim under s. 96 is not necessarily determinative of a claim under s. 97(1).

A claim under s. 97 requires that the Board determine whether the applicant's removal would subject him or her personally to the dangers and risks stipulated in paragraphs 97(1)(a) and (b) of the Act.

98. Exclusion — Refugee Convention — A person referred to in section E or F of Article 1 of the Refugee Convention is not a Convention refugee or a person in need of protection.

[Editor's note: Also see case summaries under the Schedule — Sections E and F of Article 1 of the United Nations Convention Relating to the Status of Refugees.]

Case Law

Hernandez Febles v. Canada (Minister of Citizenship & Immigration), [2014] 3 S.C.R. 431, (sub nom. *Febles v. Canada (Citizenship and Immigration)*) 376 D.L.R. (4th) 387,

30 Imm. L.R. (4th) 1, (sub nom. *Febles v. Canada (Minister of Citizenship and Immigration))* 464 N.R. 7, 2014 SCC 68, 2014 CarswellNat 4175, 2014 CarswellNat 4176 — The appellant, a national of Cuba, was convicted in the United States in 1984 and in 1993 of assault with a deadly weapon. He came to Canada in 2008 after completing his prison sentences and claimed refugee status. The Refugee Protection Division held that Article 1F(b) of the *Refugee Convention* excluded him from the definition of a refugee. This was because his convictions in the US provided reasons for considering that he had committed "a serious non-political crime" outside of Canada.

Exclusion clauses should not be enlarged in a manner inconsistent with the Refugee Convention's broad humanitarian aims, but neither should overly narrow interpretations be adopted which ignore the contracting states' need to control who enters their territory. Ultimately, the purpose of an exclusion clause is to exclude, and broad purposes do not invite interpretations of exclusion clauses unsupported by the text. Article 1F(b) is not directed solely at fugitives and neither is it directed solely at some subset of serious criminals who are undeserving at the time of the refugee application. In excluding all claimants who have committed serious non-political crimes, Article 1F(b) expresses the contracting states' agreement that such persons by definition would be undeserving of refugee protection by reason of their serious criminality.

The Board was correct to conclude that he was ineligible for refugee protection in Canada pursuant to s. 98 of the IRPA. If his removal to Cuba would place him at risk of death, torture or cruel and unusual treatment or punishment his recourse is to apply for a stay of removal.

The appeal was dismissed.

Ezokola c. Canada (Ministre de la Citoyenneté & de l'Immigration), [2013] 2 S.C.R. 678, 361 D.L.R. (4th) 1, 18 Imm. L.R. (4th) 175, (sub nom. *Ezokola v. Canada (Minister of Citizenship and Immigration))* 447 N.R. 254, 2013 SCC 40, 2013 CarswellNat 2463, 2013 CarswellNat 2464 — The applicant began his career with the Government of the Democratic Republic of Congo ("DRC") in 1999 and resigned in January 2008 and fled to Canada. He claimed he could no longer work for the government of President Kabila, which he considered corrupt, antidemocratic and violent. He claimed that his resignation would be viewed as an act of treason by the DRC government, and that the DRC's intelligence service had harassed, intimidated, and threatened him. He sought refugee protection for himself and his family in Canada.

The Refugee Protection Division excluded the applicant from the definition of "refugee" under article 1F(a) of the *Convention Relating to the Status of Refugees* finding that he was complicit in crimes against humanity committed by the government of the DRC. The Federal Court allowed his application for judicial review, but certified a question concerning the nature of complicity under article 1F(a). The Federal Court of Appeal held that a senior official in a government could demonstrate personal and knowing participation and be complicit in the crimes of the government by remaining in his or her position without protest and continuing to defend the interests of his or her government while being aware of the crimes committed by the government. The Supreme Court of Canada allowed the appeal and remitted the matter to a new panel of the RPD for redetermination in accordance with its reasons.

Exclusions based on the criminal activities of the group and not on the individual's contribution to that criminal activity must be firmly foreclosed in Canadian law. Whether an individual's conduct meets the *actus reus* and *mens rea* for complicity will depend on the facts of each case, including (i) the size and nature of the organization; (ii) the part of the organization with which the claimant was most directly concerned; (iii) the claimant's duties and activities within the organization; (iv) the claimant's position or rank in the organization; (v) the length of time the claimant was in the organization, particularly after acquiring knowledge of the group's crime or criminal purpose; and (vi) the method by which the claimant was recruited and the claimant's opportunity to leave the organization. These factors are not necessarily exhaustive, nor will each of them be significant in every case. Their assessment will necessarily be highly contextual, the focus must always remain on the individual's contribution to the crime or criminal purpose, and any viable defences should be taken into account.

Liu v. Canada (Minister of Citizenship & Immigration) (2009), 83 Imm. L.R. (3d) 228, 353 F.T.R. 132 (Eng.), 2009 FC 877, 2009 CarswellNat 2750, 2009 CarswellNat 4523, [2009] F.C.J. No. 1110 — This was an application for judicial review of a decision of a Minister's delegate refusing the applicant's pre-removal risk assessment decision. The PRRA officer concluded that the applicant was a person described under Article 1F(b) of the Convention based on an analysis of the criminal charges against him. The charges include: criminal fraud in China; immigration fraud in the United States of America; criminal fraud in the US; and immigration fraud in Canada. However, the PRRA officer concluded that "if the applicant is returned to China he will more likely than not be at risk of cruel or unusual treatment or punishment due to his being denied his right to a fair trial guaranteed under the *Universal Declaration of Human Rights and the International Covenant on Civil Political Rights*." The Minister's delegate disagreed with the assessment and concluded that there were no humanitarian and compassionate grounds to consider in this matter.

The applicant says that the decision is wrong because there is no basis in the Act or the Regulations that allows a PRRA officer to consider a claim for refugee protection and reject it on the basis of section F of Article 1 of the Convention. The applicant imposed upon the PRRA officer a full consideration of his ss. 96 and 97 rights without the benefit of a determination by the RPD. The Act appears to contemplate this alternative approach, but it was the applicant's choice to use the PRRA system and was not something that was forced upon him. He was not made to relinquish rights and safeguards he would otherwise have had. He then argued that since the PRRA officer made a positive risk assessment under s. 97, the effect of that decision was to confer refugee protection on him by virtue of subs. 114(1) of the Act. The court concluded it was not Parliament's intent to provide a means for a claimant to bypass the RPD and to have his or her ss. 96 and 97 rights considered *de novo* by the PRRA officer, without any reference to serious criminality and 1F(b) of the Convention. Neither the PRRA officer nor the delegate acted without jurisdiction or committed an error of law in their determination of the applicant's claim insofar as it related to serious criminality outside of Canada in the Article 1F(b) exclusion issue. The application for judicial review was dismissed. The following questions were certified:

> Do pre-removal risk assessment officers have the jurisdiction to exclude persons from refugee protection under s. 98 of IRPA and find them described in s. 112(3)(c) of IRPA?

> Does s. 112(3)(c) of the IRPA only apply to rejections by the Refugee Protection Division on the basis of section F of Article 1 of the *Refugee Convention* or does it apply to rejections by pre-removal risk assessment officers on the basis of section F of Article 1 of the *Refugee Convention*?

Murillo v Canada (Minister of Citizenship & Immigration) (2008), 333 F.T.R. 149 (Eng.), 2008 FC 966, 2008 CarswellNat 3002, 2008 CarswellNat 3705 — There is no obligation or requirement on the Refugee Protection Division of the Immigration and Refugee Board to conduct a "balancing" exercise to determine whether a claimant is excludable under Article 1F(b) of the *United Nations Convention Relating to the Status of Refugees.* It is reasonable for the RPD to use as a measurement of a "serious" crime, the view which Canadian law takes of that offence. Any offence for which a maximum sentence of 10 years could be imposed under Canadian law is a "serious" crime. There is also no requirement that the RPD consider a claimant's "good character" under Article 1F(b) of the Refugee Convention. The only consideration that may be salient to the RPD's determination is whether the claimant already served a sentence outside of Canada for the crime in question. The application for judicial review to set aside the RPD's decision was dismissed.

Jayasekara v. Canada (Minister of Citizenship & Immigration) (2008), 76 Imm. L.R. (3d) 159, 305 D.L.R. (4th) 630, 384 N.R. 293, 2008 CarswellNat 5525, 2008 CarswellNat 4718, 2008 FCA 404 — The Board excluded the appellant from refugee protection under s. 98 of the IRPA and Article 1F(b) of the Convention because there were serious reasons for considering that he had committed a serious non-political crime outside of Canada and that he had not completed his sentence, as he fled the United States during his probation. Moreover, it found that, even if the appellant were not excludable under Article 1F(b) of the Convention, he did not meet the criteria for either Convention refugee status or as a person requiring protection. These findings based on credibility were not contested. The appellant sought judicial review before the Federal Court only of his exclusion under s. 98 of the IRPA and Article 1F(b) of the Convention.

The Federal Court of Appeal confirmed that the Federal Court judge did not commit an error when he concluded that it was reasonable for the Board to conclude on these facts that the appellant's conviction in the United States gave it a serious reason to believe that he had committed a serious non-political crime outside the country. Serving a sentence for a serious crime prior to coming to Canada does not allow one to avoid the application of Article 1F(b) of the Convention relating to the Status of Refugees.

Parshottam v. Canada (Minister of Citizenship & Immigration) (2008), 75 Imm. L.R. (3d) 165, 303 D.L.R. (4th) 672, 382 N.R. 186, 2008 CarswellNat 4154, 2008 CarswellNat 5358, 2008 FCA 355 — This was an appeal of a decision to dismiss an application for judicial review of a rejection of the appellant's application for protection by a pre-removal risk assessment officer. The question certified by Justice Mosley was found not to be dispositive of the appeal and the court declined to answer the question. The court did add that they did not share Justice Mosley's view that it was "settled law" that whether a claimant for protection in Canada is a permanent resident of a third country for the purpose of Article 1E and s. 98 of the IRPA is invariably determined as of the time of the claimant's arrival in Canada and that subsequent events are irrelevant. It was common ground that if the appellant was a permanent resident of the United States at the relevant time, he was excluded by Article 1E from claiming refugee status in Canada. Counsel for the appellant argued that the PRRA officer had erred in law by applying the wrong standard of proof. That is, the officer required the appellant to prove as a matter of certainty that he had lost his permanent residence status in the United States. The court found that although the PRRA officer did not articulate the standard of proof that she was applying, it was to be assumed in the absence of indications to the contrary that she applied the correct one, namely, a balance of probabilities. The officer's reasons, including her observation that whether the appellant was still a permanent resident would ultimately be determined by an immigration judge in the United States, did not establish that she had applied some standard other than a balance of probabilities. The appeal was dismissed. However, Justice Sharlow would have answered the certified question even though the issue may not have been dispositive of the appeal. He would have answered the certified question as follows:

> If the claimant presents new evidence (as contemplated by paragraph 113(a) of IRPA that Article 1E does not apply as of the date of the pre-removal risk assessment, the PRRA officer may determine on the basis of the new evidence that Article 1E currently applies, in which case the claim for protection is barred. Alternatively, the PRRA officer may determine on the basis of the new evidence that Article 1E does not currently apply although it did apply at the time of the claimant's admission to Canada (or at the date of the RPD decision). If such a change of status has occurred, the PRRA officer should consider why the change of status occurred and what steps, if any, the claimant took or might have taken to cause or fail to prevent the change of status. If the acts or omissions of the claimant indicate asylum shopping, Article 1E may be held to apply despite the change in status.

Al Husin v. Canada (Minister of Citizenship & Immigration) (2006), 59 Imm. L.R. (3d) 142, 2006 CarswellNat 4250, 2006 FC 1451 — The applicant's refugee claim was denied on the basis of the exclusion in Article 1F(b) of the *United Nations Convention Relating to the Status of Refugees*. The Board found that it had serious grounds to believe that the applicant had committed a serious non-political crime and that he had not completed his sentence for that crime before entering Canada. The Board's decision was overturned.

The applicant was a citizen of Jordan and while studying in the United States was convicted of an offence and upon being released on probation was arrested by federal Immigration and Naturalization Services and deported to Jordan. A bench warrant for his arrest was issued for involuntarily violating his probation by leaving the country. The Board erred in concluding that the American offence was the equivalent of a Canadian offence of aiding and abetting. It is clear that the applicant's probation imposed under state law was rendered impossible by action of U.S. federal authorities to deport him. The Board's conclusion that the applicant had not served his sentence was correct.

The following questions were certified:

> 1. Does serving a sentence for a serious crime prior to coming to Canada allow one to avoid the application of Article 1F of the Convention?

> 2. If the answer to Question 1 is affirmative, when and in what circumstances is a sentence deemed served, specifically does a deportation have the effect of deeming a sentence served?

Also see *Xie v. Canada (Minister of Citizenship & Immigration)* (2004), 37 Imm. L.R. (3d) 163, 2004 CarswellNat 2036, 2004 CarswellNat 3972, 325 N.R. 255, [2005] 1 F.C.R. 304, 243 D.L.R. (4th) 385, 2004 FCA 250, [2004] F.C.J. No. 1142; leave to appeal refused 2005 CarswellNat 748, 2005 CarswellNat 749 (S.C.C.) at s. 97 of IRPA.

Chowdhury v. Canada (Minister of Citizenship & Immigration) (2003), 28 Imm. L.R. (3d) 299, 235 F.T.R. 271, 2003 CarswellNat 1797, 2003 CarswellNat 2640, 2003 FCT 744 — This is an application to review a negative decision of the Refugee Protection Division. The applicant was found not be a refugee or a "person in need of protection" because he was referred to in Article 1F(c) of the refugee Convention and was excluded from claiming asylum by s. 98 of IRPA. The question of the applicant's exclusion refugee process was first raised by the presiding member during the course of the applicant's hearing. No objection was raised by the applicant's counsel, however, in oral submissions counsel objected to the fact that the Minister's representative had not committed to invoking or not invoking the exclusion clause.

The decision of the panel was set aside. There had been no notice provided to the claimant prior to the hearing that the exclusion issue was to be raised. The presiding member raised the issue and the Minister's counsel replied that the exclusion "could be raised." This was a tentative answer and did not meet the requirements of procedural fairness. Notice in advance of the hearing or an adjournment of the hearing, once the issue was raised, would have given the applicant and his counsel time to prepare submissions. In the circumstances, the presiding member only allowed for written submissions to be filed after the hearing. This was insufficient to ensure procedural fairness at the hearing. Accordingly, the decision of the panel was set aside.

98.1 (1) Requirement to report — A designated foreign national on whom refugee protection is conferred under paragraph 95(1)(b) or (c) must report to an officer in accordance with the regulations.

(2) Obligation when reporting — A designated foreign national who is required to report to an officer must answer truthfully all questions put to him or her and must provide any information and documents that the officer requests.

2012, c. 17, s. 32

98.2 Regulations — The regulations may provide for any matter relating to the application of section 98.1 and may include provisions respecting the requirement to report to an officer.

2012, c. 17, s. 32

DIVISION 2 — CONVENTION REFUGEES AND PERSONS IN NEED OF PROTECTION

Claim for Refugee Protection

99. (1) Claim — A claim for refugee protection may be made in or outside Canada.

(2) Claim outside Canada — A claim for refugee protection made by a person outside Canada must be made by making an application for a visa as a Convention refugee or a person in similar circumstances, and is governed by Part 1.

(3) Claim inside Canada — A claim for refugee protection made by a person inside Canada must be made to an officer, may not be made by a person who is subject to a removal order, and is governed by this Part.

(3.1) Claim made inside Canada — not at port of entry — A person who makes a claim for refugee protection inside Canada other than at a port of entry must provide the officer, within the time limits provided for in the regulations, with the documents and information — including in respect of the basis for the claim — required by the rules of the Board, in accord-ance with those rules.

(4) Permanent resident — An application to become a permanent resident made by a protected person is governed by Part 1.

2012, c. 17, s. 33

Examination of Eligibility to Refer Claim

100. (1) Referral to Refugee Protection Division — An officer shall, within three working days after receipt of a claim referred to in subsection 99(3), determine whether the claim is eligible to be referred to the Refugee Protection Division and, if it is eligible, shall refer the claim in accordance with the rules of the Board.

[Editor's Note: SOR/2002-227, s. 342 provides that a claim made in Canada to be a Convention refugee in respect of which a determination of eligibility was not made before June 28, 2002 is deemed to be a claim for refugee protection made in Canada that is received on June 28, 2002.

SOR/2002-227, s. 343 provides that, subject to s. 191 of the Immigration and Refugee Protection Act, *S.C. 2001, c. 27 (the "new Act"), a claim of a person who was determined eligible before June 28, 2002 to have a claim to be a Convention refugee determined by the Convention Refugee Determination Division, and in respect of which no determination was made by the Convention Refugee Determination Division, is a claim that:*

(a) is referred under the new Act to the Refugee Protection Division unless an officer gives notice under s. 104(1) of the new Act; and

(b) is subject to the provisions of the new Act.]

(1.1) Burden of proof — The burden of proving that a claim is eligible to be referred to the Refugee Protection Division rests on the claimant, who must answer truthfully all questions put to them.

(2) Decision — The officer shall suspend consideration of the eligibility of the person's claim if

(a) a report has been referred for a determination, at an admissibility hearing, of whether the person is inadmissible on grounds of security, violating human or international rights, serious criminality or organized criminality, or

(b) the officer considers it necessary to wait for a decision of a court with respect to a claimant who is charged with an offence under an Act of Parliament that is punishable by a maximum term of imprisonment of at least 10 years.

(3) Consideration of claim — The Refugee Protection Division may not consider a claim until it is referred by the officer. If the claim is not referred within the three-day period referred to in subsection (1), it is deemed to be referred, unless there is a suspension or it is determined to be ineligible.

(4) Documents and information to be provided — A person who makes a claim for refugee protection inside Canada at a port of entry and whose claim is referred to the Refugee Protection Division must provide the Division, within the time limits provided for in the regulations, with the documents and information — including in respect of the basis for the claim — required by the rules of the Board, in accordance with those rules.

(4.1) Date of hearing — The referring officer must, in accordance with the regulations, the rules of the Board and any directions of the Chairperson of the Board, fix the date on which the claimant is to attend a hearing before the Refugee Protection Division.

(5) Quarantine Act — If a traveller is detained or isolated under the *Quarantine Act*, the period referred to in subsections (1) and (3) does not begin to run until the day on which the detention or isolation ends.

2005, c. 20, s. 81; 2010, c. 8, s. 11 [Amended 2012, c. 17, s. 56.]

101. (1) Ineligibility — A claim is ineligible to be referred to the Refugee Protection Division if

(a) refugee protection has been conferred on the claimant under this Act;

(b) a claim for refugee protection by the claimant has been rejected by the Board;

(c) a prior claim by the claimant was determined to be ineligible to be referred to the Refugee Protection Division, or to have been withdrawn or abandoned;

(d) the claimant has been recognized as a Convention refugee by a country other than Canada and can be sent or returned to that country;

(e) the claimant came directly or indirectly to Canada from a country designated by the regulations, other than a country of their nationality or their former habitual residence; or

(f) the claimant has been determined to be inadmissible on grounds of security, violating human or international rights, serious criminality or organized criminality, except for persons who are inadmissible solely on the grounds of paragraph 35(1)(c).

[Editor's Note: SOR/2002-227, s. 340 provides that a determination made before June 28, 2002 that a person is not eligible to have his or her Convention refugee claim determined by the Convention Refugee Determination Division is deemed to be a determination that the claim is ineligible to be referred to the Refugee Protection Division.

SOR/2002-227, s. 341 further provides that a claim to be a Convention refugee that was withdrawn or declared to be abandoned before June 28, 2002 is deemed to be a claim determined to be withdrawn or abandoned under the Immigration and Refugee Protection Act, *S.C. 2001, c. 27.]*

(2) Serious criminality — A claim is not ineligible by reason of serious criminality under paragraph (1)(f) unless

(a) in the case of inadmissibility by reason of a conviction in Canada, the conviction is for an offence under an Act of Parliament punishable by a maximum term of imprisonment of at least 10 years; or

(b) in the case of inadmissibility by reason of a conviction outside Canada, the conviction is for an offence that, if committed in Canada, would constitute an offence under an Act of Parliament punishable by a maximum term of imprisonment of at least 10 years.

[Editor's Note: SOR/2002-227, s. 326(1) provides that a claim to be a Convention Refugee by a person described in subparagraph 19(1)(c.1)(i) of the Immigration

Act, *R.S.C. 1985, c. I-2 (the "former Act") in respect of whom the Minister was of the opinion under subparagraph 46.01(1)(e)(i) of the former Act that the person constitutes a danger to the public in Canada is deemed, if no determination was made by a senior immigration officer under s. 45 of the former Act, to be a claim for refugee protection made by a person described in paragraph 101(2)(b) of the* new Immigration and Refugee Protection Act, *S.C. 2001, c. 27 who is inadmissible and in respect of whom the Minister is of the opinion that the person is a danger to the public.]*

2012, c. 17, s. 34

Case Law

Section 101(1)

Hernandez Febles v. Canada (Minister of Citizenship & Immigration), [2014] 3 S.C.R. 431, (sub nom. *Febles v. Canada (Citizenship and Immigration)*) 376 D.L.R. (4th) 387, 30 Imm. L.R. (4th) 1, (sub nom. *Febles v. Canada (Minister of Citizenship and Immigration)*) 464 N.R. 7, 2014 SCC 68, 2014 CarswellNat 4175, 2014 CarswellNat 4176 — The appellant, a national of Cuba, was convicted in the United States in 1984 and in 1993 of assault with a deadly weapon. He came to Canada in 2008 after completing his prison sentences and claimed refugee status. The Refugee Protection Division held that Article 1F(b) of the *Refugee Convention* excluded him from the definition of a refugee. This was because his convictions in the US provided reasons for considering that he had committed "a serious non-political crime" outside of Canada.

Exclusion clauses should not be enlarged in a manner inconsistent with the Refugee Convention's broad humanitarian aims, but neither should overly narrow interpretations be adopted which ignore the contracting states' need to control who enters their territory. Ultimately, the purpose of an exclusion clause is to exclude, and broad purposes do not invite interpretations of exclusion clauses unsupported by the text. Article 1F (b) is not directed solely at fugitives and neither is it directed solely at some subset of serious criminals who are undeserving at the time of the refugee application. In excluding all claimants who have committed serious non-political crimes, Article 1F(b) expresses the contracting states' agreement that such persons by definition would be undeserving of refugee protection by reason of their serious criminality.

The Board was correct to conclude that he was ineligible for refugee protection in Canada pursuant to s. 98 of the IRPA. If his removal to Cuba would place him at risk of death, torture or cruel and unusual treatment or punishment his recourse is to apply for a stay of removal.

The appeal was dismissed.

Tsering v. Canada (Minister of Citizenship & Immigration), 2008 CarswellNat 3295, 2008 CarswellNat 2054, 2008 FC 799 — In 2007, the applicant tried to come to Canada from the United States where she had been living and working. She was stopped at the border and found to be ineligible to make a refugee claim in Canada. Normally, a person entering Canada from the United States is ineligible because Canada recognizes the United States as a "safe third country" in which to make a refugee claim. However, stateless persons who are former habitual residents of the United States are exempted from the safe third country rule. Similarly, persons who are family members of permanent residents of Canada are exempted. The immigration officer found the applicant to be stateless and neither a former habitual resident of the United States nor a family member of a

IRP Act

permanent resident of Canada. The officer's findings did not constitute adequate reasons for deciding that the applicant was not a former habitual resident of the United States. The officer's notes mention only a few of the many factors that might have been relevant to an assessment of whether the applicant had formed any significant attachment to the United States, but which do not, in themselves, suggest that she had not been a habitual resident there. The fact is that she lived and worked in the United States for seven years. The proper test is whether the claimant has established a significant period of actual residence in the country in question. The application for judicial review was allowed.

Wangden v. Canada (Minister of Citizenship & Immigration) (2008), 76 Imm. L.R. (3d) 52, 336 F.T.R. 242 (Eng.), 2008 CarswellNat 4077, 2008 CarswellNat 5516, 2008 FC 1230; affirmed (2009), 86 Imm. L.R. (3d) 165, 398 N.R. 265, 2009 FCA 344, 2009 CarswellNat 3878, 2009 CarswellNat 4975 — The Minister's delegate determined that the applicant was ineligible to be referred to the Refugee Protection Division pursuant to para. 101(1)(d) as he had been "recognized as a Convention refugee by the U.S.A. and to which [he] could be sent and returned." The delegate signed an exclusion order against the applicant. Pursuant to para. 49(2)(b) of the IRPA, the order did not come into force for seven days and the applicant was not required to return to the U.S. immediately. His removal to the United States was stayed until the final disposition of this application by the order of the Chief Justice issued on April 8, 2008.

In the case at bar, the delegate's ineligibility decision is consistent with the primary objective of the IRPA, which is about saving lives and offering protection to the displaced and persecuted, since the applicant can be returned to the United States where he will not be at risk of persecution. Based on the objectives of the IRPA and on the wording of para. 101(1)(d), the court concluded that Parliament did not intend for this provision to include consideration of whether a person could *remain* indefinitely in the country in which he or she has been recognized as a Convention refugee and to which he or she can be returned. Of importance is whether the individuals are protected from risk, not whether they have the full panoply of rights provided for under the 1951 Convention. It would be incompatible with the expeditious and relatively straightforward administrative process of screening certain claims out of the RPD's jurisdiction to require front line immigration officers to conduct a more expansive review of claimants' status in another country to determine whether the particular features of that jurisdiction's domestic law satisfies the definition of "refugee" under the Convention. This is not their role; the Refugee Protection Division level is tasked with this assessment. In this case, the decision makers acted reasonably and within the scope of their authority. The application was dismissed. The following question was certified:

> Is the legal remedy or status of "withholding of removal" in the United States of America equivalent to being "recognized as a Convention refugee," pursuant to s. 101(1)(d) of the IRPA?

The Federal Court of Appeal agreed with the decision of Justice Mosley and dismissed the appeal. The Federal Court of Appeal answered the certified question positively. The legal remedy or status of "withholding of removal" in the United States of America is equivalent to being "recognized as a Convention refugee," pursuant to s. 101(1)(d) of IRPA.

Bouttavong v. Canada (Minister of Citizenship & Immigration) (2005), 344 N.R. 134, 2005 CarswellNat 3527, 2005 CarswellNat 5559, 2005 FCA 341 — Former public danger opinions are irrelevant to the determination of danger to the public under subs.

113(d)(i). This does not mean that the underlying criminal convictions may not be taken into account, only that the danger opinions are irrelevant.

Section 101(2)

Feimi v. Canada (Minister of Citizenship & Immigration) (2012), 353 D.L.R. (4th) 536, 442 N.R. 374, 2012 FCA 325, 2012 CarswellNat 5724, 2012 CarswellNat 5013, [2012] F.C.J. No. 1610 — The appellant, a national of Albania, appealed a Federal Court decision to dismiss a decision of the Refugee Protection Division from denying his application for refugee status. The RPD rejected his claim for refugee protection on the ground that he was excluded from the definition of a refugee by Article 1F(b) of the United Nations Convention relating to the Status of Refugees. The RPD held that there were serious reasons for considering that the appellant had committed a "serious non-political crime" within the meaning of Article 1F(b) as a result of his conviction in Greece in 1997 for a crime of murder in a fit of anger.

The appellant's argument that the Minister of Public Safety and Emergency Preparedness improperly exercised his discretion to intervene at the exclusion hearing was largely based on the fact that the Minister of Citizenship and Immigration had declined to give an opinion that the appellant was a danger to the public in Canada and that his claim was therefore not ineligible to be referred to the RPD. The appellant argued that the fact that the Minister of Citizenship and Immigration did not consider him a danger in effect estops the Minister of Public Safety and Emergency Preparedness from intervening before the RPD to argue for exclusion on essentially the same materials as those on which the Minister of Citizenship and Immigration denied a request for a danger opinion.

Since the Federal Court of Appeal held in *Hernandez Febles v. Canada (Minister of Citizenship & Immigration)* (2012), 357 D.L.R. (4th) 343, that current dangerousness is not an issue at an exclusion hearing, there is no possible basis for concluding that the Minister of Citizenship and Immigration's refusal of a danger opinion at the eligibility stage made it unreasonable for the Minister of Public Safety and Emergency Preparedness to intervene at the appellant's exclusion hearing to argue that his crime was serious and Article 1F(b) applied. The issues at the eligibility and exclusion stages of processing a refugee claim are not the same. Thus, no question of estoppel can arise, even when the same criminal conduct underlies both the danger opinion at the eligibility stage and intervention at the exclusion hearing.

The broad scope of the decision of the Minister of Public Safety and Emergency Preparedness to intervene before the RPD imposes a heavy burden on the applicant to establish that it was exercised unreasonably. The appellant did not come close to discharging it. The appeal was dismissed.

102. (1) Regulations — **The regulations may govern matters relating to the application of sections 100 and 101, may, for the purposes of this Act, define the terms used in those sections and, for the purpose of sharing responsibility with governments of foreign states for the consideration of refugee claims, may include provisions**

> **(a) designating countries that comply with Article 33 of the Refugee Convention and Article 3 of the Convention Against Torture;**

> **(b) making a list of those countries and amending it as necessary; and**

(c) respecting the circumstances and criteria for the application of paragraph 101(1)(e).

(2) **Factors** — The following factors are to be considered in designating a country under paragraph (1)(a):

(a) whether the country is a party to the Refugee Convention and to the Convention Against Torture;

(b) its policies and practices with respect to claims under the Refugee Convention and with respect to obligations under the Convention Against Torture;

(c) its human rights record; and

(d) whether it is party to an agreement with the Government of Canada for the purpose of sharing responsibility with respect to claims for refugee protection.

(3) **Review** — The Governor in Council must ensure the continuing review of factors set out in subsection (2) with respect to each designated country.

Case Law

Canadian Council for Refugees v. R. (2008), 74 Admin. L.R. (4th) 79, 2008 CarswellNat 1995, 2008 CarswellNat 2197, 2008 FCA 229; leave to appeal to S.C.C. refused 2008 CarswellNat 5170, 2008 CarswellNat 5171 (S.C.C.) — This was an appeal from a decision of the applications judge granting an application for judicial review by the respondents the Canadian Council for Refugees, the Canadian Council of Churches, Amnesty International and John Doe, declaring invalid sections of 159.1 to 159.7 of the Immigration and Refugee Protection Regulations, and the Agreement between the Government of Canada and the Government of the United States of America for Co-operation in the Examination of Refugee Status Claims from Nationals of Third Countries (the "Safe Third Country Agreement"). The Regulations at issue implement into domestic law a Safe Third Country Agreement between Canada and the United States whereby if a refugee enters Canada from the U.S. at a land border port-of-entry, Canada will, subject to specified exceptions, send the refugee back to the U.S. The same applies for refugees crossing by land from Canada to the U.S. The appeal was allowed and the decision of the applications judge set aside. The appropriate standard of review in respect of the decision of the Governor In Council ("GIC") to designate the United States as a "Safe Third Country" pursuant to s. 102 of the Immigration and Refugee Protection Act is correctness. The Federal Court of Appeal took issue with the applications judge's suggestion that unless "compliance" is made a condition precedent to the designation of a country, the GIC would have discretion to designate a country that does not comply. Subsection 101(2) does not refer to "actual" compliance or compliance "in absolute terms" nor does it otherwise specify the type and extent of compliance contemplated. However, Parliament has specified the four factors to be considered in determining whether a country can be designated. These factors are general in nature and are indicative of Parliament's intent that the matter of compliance be assessed on the basis of an appreciation by the GIC of the country's policies, practices and human rights record. Once it is accepted, as it must be in this case, that the GIC has given due consideration to these four factors, and formed the opinion that the candidate country is compliant with the relevant articles of the Conventions, there is nothing left to be reviewed judicially. The Federal Court of Appeal concluded there was no factual basis on which to assess the alleged Charter breaches. The respondents' main contention was directed at a border officer's lack of discretion to forego returning a claimant to the U.S. for reasons other than the enumerated exceptions set out in s. 159.5 of the Regulations. This challenge, however, should be assessed in a proper factual context — that is, when advanced by a refugee who has been denied asylum in Canada pursuant to the Regulations and faces a real risk of *refoulement* in being sent back to the U.S. pursuant to the Safe Third Country Agreement. In this case the refugee never came to Canada, and instead claimed that he would have sought asylum in Canada but for the Regulations.

Suspension or Termination of Consideration of Claim

103. (1) Suspension — **Proceedings of the Refugee Protection Division in respect of a claim for refugee protection are suspended on notice by an officer that**

> **(a) the matter has been referred to the Immigration Division to determine whether the claimant is inadmissible on grounds of security, violating human or international rights, serious criminality or organized criminality; or**

> **(b) an officer considers it necessary to wait for a decision of a court with respect to a claimant who is charged with an offence under an Act of Parliament that may be punished by a maximum term of imprisonment of at least 10 years.**

(2) Continuation — **On notice by an officer that the suspended claim was determined to be eligible, proceedings of the Refugee Protection Division must continue.**

2012, c. 17, s. 35

Case Law

Also see cases under s. 104.

Tjiueza v. Canada (Minister of Safety & Emergency Preparedness) (2009), 86 Imm. L.R. (3d) 176, 357 F.T.R. 179 (Eng.), 2009 FC 1247, 2009 CarswellNat 4168, 2009 CarswellNat 5296 — This was an application for judicial review of a notice given by an enforcement officer of the Pacific Region Enforcement Centre of the Canadian Border Services Agency under s. 104(1)(b) of the Act. The officer found the applicant's claim for refugee protection ineligible to be referred to the Refugee Protection Division because the Immigration Division had determined the applicant to be inadmissible on grounds of security. The issue raised by the applicant is reviewable on a correctness standard. Determining whether or not the officer had the discretion to issue the notice requires statutory interpretation and is therefore a question of law. If he had discretion, whether he failed to exercise it was either an issue of law or of procedural fairness, both of which are reviewable against the standard of correctness. Finally, where it is found that he had discretion and exercised it, whether he exercised that discretion properly is reviewable on a standard of reasonableness.

While s. 104 of IRPA does generally give an officer discretion as to whether or not to re-determine the eligibility of the claim, that discretion does not exist in the case of a claim that has been suspended under s. 103. In the case of a claim that has been suspended, any discretion that may exist regarding re-determining the eligibility of a claim would have been exercised in making the decision under s. 103 to suspend the RPD proceeding. Once a claim is suspended, IRPA only provides for two possible results: either the proceedings are continued because an officer notifies the RPD that the claim is eligible, or the proceedings are terminated because an officer notifies the RPD that the claim is not eligible. The Manual confirms that the officer generally has discretion under s. 104. However, it states that the officer would only exercise his discretion because situations may arise where the RPD ought to make a decision on the claim (for example, in cases involving exclusion clauses). Since a claim that has been suspended under s. 103 will remain suspended indefinitely, the RPD will never make a decision on this sort of claim. Thus it seems that the discretion in s. 104 was never meant to apply to this situation. This is consistent with the provisions of IRPA and the objective of this Act that require refugee protection claims to be dealt with efficiently and expeditiously. Furthermore, this interpretation is supported by the fact that an indefinite suspension would not give any practical benefit to the applicant. Having come to the conclusion that the officer had no discretion, and was required to determine the eligibility of the applicant's claim according to the ID finding and to notify the RPD of his determination, there is no need to address the other questions raised by the applicant. He may still have his risk assessed by making a PRRA application. The application for judicial review was dismissed. The following question was certified:

> After an RPD hearing has been suspended under s. 103 of the *Immigration and Refugee Protection Act* pending the outcome of an ID hearing and re-determination of a claim's eligibility, if the ID determines that the claimant is inadmissible for security reasons, does the officer have discretion under the *Immigration and Refugee Protection Act* to not re-determine the claim's eligibility and to not notify the RPD of the officer's decision on eligibility, and thereby suspend the RPD hearing indefinitely?

104. (1) Notice of ineligible claim — An officer may, with respect to a claim that is before the Refugee Protection Division or, in the case of paragraph (d), that is before or has been determined by the Refugee Protection Division or the Refugee Appeal Division, give notice that an officer has determined that

(a) the claim is ineligible under paragraphs 101(1)(a) to (e);

(b) the claim is ineligible under paragraph 101(1)(f);

(c) the claim was referred as a result of directly or indirectly misrepresenting or withholding material facts relating to a relevant matter and that the claim was not otherwise eligible to be referred to that Division; or

(d) the claim is not the first claim that was received by an officer in respect of the claimant.

(2) Termination and nullification — A notice given under the following provisions has the following effects:

(a) if given under any of paragraphs (1)(a) to (c), it terminates pending proceedings in the Refugee Protection Division respecting the claim; and

(b) if given under paragraph (1)(d), it terminates proceedings in and nullifies any decision of the Refugee Protection Division or the Refugee Appeal Division respecting a claim other than the first claim.

Case Law

Also see cases under s. 103.

Haqi v. Canada (Minister of Public Safety and Emergency Preparedness) (2015), 39 Imm. L.R. (4th) 122, 479 N.R. 368, 2015 FCA 256, 2015 CarswellNat 6209 — The applicant sought refugee protection, but before his claim could be heard, his case was referred to the Immigration Division for a determination as to his admissibility. The Immigration Division found him inadmissible for being a member of an organization for which there were reasonable grounds to believe had engaged in the subversion by force of the Iranian government. After this decision, a Canadian Border Services Agency officer gave notice under s. 104 of IRPA, which had the effect of ending his refugee claim. The applicant argued that the CBSA officer had the discretion not to terminate his refugee claim, and that he erred in failing to exercise that discretion.

The court concluded s. 104 does not confer discretion on CBSA officers to decline to give notice terminating a refugee claim once an officer has concluded that the claim is ineligible for consideration by the Refugee Protection Division on security ground. The applicants sought appeal to the Federal Court which was dismissed. The Federal Court of Appeal concluded that after a Refugee Protection Division proceeding has been suspended under para. 103(1)(a) of IRPA pending the outcome of an Immigration Division hearing into a refugee claimant's admissibility, if the Immigration Division determines that the claimant is inadmissible for security reasons under s. 34(1)(f) of IRPA, a CBSA officer does not have any discretion under subs. 104(1)(b) of IRPA to not determine the claimant's eligibility and to not notify the Refugee Protection Division of the officer's decision on eligibility. The fact that it is a human actor, the officer, who takes notice of facts and communicates the legal consequence imposed by the Act to the affected party and to the Refugee Protection Division does not make that person a decision maker with discretion.

Extradition Procedure

105. (1) Suspension if proceeding under *Extradition Act* — **The Refugee Protection Division and Refugee Appeal Division shall not commence, or shall suspend, consideration of any matter concerning a person against whom an authority to proceed has been issued under section 15 of the *Extradition Act* with respect to an offence under Canadian law that is punishable under an Act of Parliament by a maximum term of imprisonment of at least 10 years, until a final decision under the *Extradition Act* with respect to the discharge or surrender of the person has been made.**

(2) Continuation if discharge under *Extradition Act* — If the person is finally discharged under the *Extradition Act*, the proceedings of the applicable Division may be commenced or continued as though there had not been any proceedings under that Act.

(3) Rejection if surrender under *Extradition Act* — If the person is ordered surrendered by the Minister of Justice under the *Extradition Act* and the offence for which the person was committed by the judge under section 29 of that Act is punishable under an Act of Parliament by a maximum term of imprisonment of at least 10

Decision on Claim for Refugee Protection

Editor's Note

[Procedural decisions regarding refugee hearings under the former Act are collected and tabbed separately for your information. Decisions concerning the sufficiency of reasons in a refugee case are collected under Refugee Protection Division Rule 61.]

107. (1) Decision — **The Refugee Protection Division shall accept a claim for refugee protection if it determines that the claimant is a Convention refugee or person in need of protection, and shall otherwise reject the claim.**

[Editor's Note: SOR/2002-227, s. 343 provides that, subject to s. 191 of the Immigration and Refugee Protection Act, *S.C. 2001, c. 27 (the "new Act"), a claim of a person who was determined eligible before June 28, 2002 to have a claim to be a Convention refugee determined by the Convention Refugee Determination Division, and in respect of which no determination was made by that Division, is a claim that:*

(a) is referred under the new Act to the Refugee Protection Division unless an officer gives notice under s. 104(1) of the new Act; and

(b) is subject to the provisions of the new Act.]

(2) No credible basis — **If the Refugee Protection Division is of the opinion, in rejecting a claim, that there was no credible or trustworthy evidence on which it could have made a favourable decision, it shall state in its reasons for the decision that there is no credible basis for the claim.**

Case Law

Section 107(1)

Avci v. Canada (Minister of Citizenship & Immigration), 35 Imm. L.R. (3d) 19, 2003 CarswellNat 3039, 244 F.T.R. 320 (note), 2003 FCA 359, 313 N.R. 307, [2003] F.C.J. No. 1424 — If the Board reserves its decision at the end of the Refugee determination hearing, it renders its decision and becomes *functus officio* when it signs written reasons for the decision and transmits them to the registrar.

Yu v. Canada (Minister of Citizenship & Immigration), 2003 CarswellNat 1694, 2003 CarswellNat 2639, [2003] F.C.J. No. 932, 2003 FCT 720 (T.D.) — The applicant sought to review a negative decision of his refugee claim. The appropriate standard of review is one of patent unreasonableness, which means that findings of credibility and of fact must be supported by the evidence and must not be made capriciously. These findings must not be based on erroneous findings of fact or made without regard to the evidence. When the Board finds a claimant not credible based on implausibility findings which are open to it on the evidence, the court should not interfere unless an overriding error has been made.

The panel did not commit a reviewable error when it failed to confront the applicant with the inconsistencies in his testimony regarding his arrival in Canada. The Board was not obligated by the duty of fairness to put all of its concerns regarding credibility before the applicant.

Contradictions or discrepancies in the evidence of a refugee claimant are a well-accepted basis for a finding of a lack of credibility. The application in this case was dismissed.

107.1 Manifestly unfounded — If the Refugee Protection Division rejects a claim for refugee protection, it must state in its reasons for the decision that the claim is manifestly unfounded if it is of the opinion that the claim is clearly fraudulent.

2010, c. 8, s. 11.1 [Amended 2012, c. 17, s. 57.]

Cessation of Refugee Protection

108. (1) Rejection — A claim for refugee protection shall be rejected, and a person is not a Convention refugee or a person in need of protection, in any of the following circumstances:

(a) the person has voluntarily reavailed themself of the protection of their country of nationality;

(b) the person has voluntarily reacquired their nationality;

(c) the person has acquired a new nationality and enjoys the protection of the country of that new nationality;

(d) the person has voluntarily become re-established in the country that the person left or remained outside of and in respect of which the person claimed refugee protection in Canada; or

(e) the reasons for which the person sought refugee protection have ceased to exist.

[Editor's Note: SOR/2002-227, s. 339 provides that a determination made in Canada before June 28, 2002 that a person is not a Convention refugee is deemed to be a claim for refugee protection rejected by the Immigration and Refugee Board.]

(2) Cessation of refugee protection — On application by the Minister, the Refugee Protection Division may determine that refugee protection referred to in subsection 95(1) has ceased for any of the reasons described in subsection (1).

(3) Effect of decision — If the application is allowed, the claim of the person is deemed to be rejected.

[Editor's Note: SOR/2002-227, s. 344 provides that a determination made in Canada before June 28, 2002 that a person has ceased to be a Convention refugee is deemed to be a determination by the Immigration and Refugee Board that refugee protection has ceased.]

(4) Exception — Paragraph (1)(e) does not apply to a person who establishes that there are compelling reasons arising out of previous persecution, torture, treatment or punishment for refusing to avail themselves of the protection of the country which they left, or outside of which they remained, due to such previous persecution, torture, treatment or punishment.

Case Law

Section 108(1)

Abadi v. Canada (Minister of Citizenship and Immigration), 2016 FC 29, 2016 CarswellNat 1916, 2016 CarswellNat 68; additional reasons 2016 FC 196, 2016 CarswellNat

367, 2016 CarswellNat 2168 — The applicant, a citizen of Iran, applied for judicial review of a decision of the RPD. He arrived in Canada in 1996 at the age of 12. He, his mother and his two siblings were granted refugee status in September of 1999. The precise basis upon which he received refugee status in Canada was unclear. However, the parties agreed that he was granted refugee status on the basis of his mother's well-founded fear of gender-based persecution in Iran. In 2006, he applied for and was issued an Iranian passport. He used the passport to travel to Iran to attend his sister's wedding. He renewed his Iranian passport in 2011 in anticipation of a vacation to Mexico. He used it to return to Iran in 2014, to visit his aging father. Upon return to Canada, he was questioned by an agent with the CBSA who recommended to the Minister that his refugee status be "cessated" pursuant to s. 108(1)(e) of the IRPA due to a change in country conditions in Iran. The RPD granted the application of the Minister. The Federal Court upheld the decision of the RPD.

Siddiqui v. Canada (Minister of Citizenship and Immigration) (2016), 40 Imm. L.R. (4th) 1, 2016 FCA 134, 2016 CarswellNat 1681, 2016 CarswellNat 16 — This was a judicial review of a decision of the Refugee Protection Division which allowed the Minister of Public Safety and Emergency Preparedness's application pursuant to para. 108(1)(a) of IRPA. The refugee protection claim of the applicant was deemed to be rejected. The RPD stated that s. 108 of IRPA places the burden of proof on the Minister to demonstrate that an individual who had been determined a Convention refugee under IRPA has ceased to be a Convention refugee. The applicant must then answer to the allegations of the Minister, once a *prima facie* case has been established. Here, the Minister met his burden. Thus, pursuant to para. 108(1)(a), the applicant voluntarily reavailed himself of the protection of Afghanistan. The applicant did not rebut the allegations against him on a balance of probabilities. The RPD conducted the proper analysis for a determination of cessation of refugee status by applying the three requirements: (a) voluntariness: the refugee must act voluntarily; (b) intention: the refugee must intend by his action to reavail himself of the protection of the country of his nationality; and (c) reavailment: the refugee must actually obtain such a protection. The applicant first voluntarily obtained an Afghan passport. He could have used a travel document from Canada for his travels, but instead voluntarily decided to obtain an Afghan passport because it was faster, and subsequently used his passport to travel to Afghanistan. He had the intention to reavail himself of the protection of Afghanistan by using his Afghan passport for travel to China and to Afghanistan, along with travelling to Afghanistan for business purposes and enrolling one of his sons in school during his last trip to Afghanistan demonstrating his intention to reavail. The court's intervention was not warranted. The application for judicial review was dismissed.

An appeal of this decision was considered by the Federal Court of Appeal and subsequently dismissed. The Federal Court of Appeal answered the certified question in the affirmative. In a cessation application pursuant to para. 108(1)(a) of IRPA, the same or substantially the same considerations, precedents and analysis apply to persons found to be Convention refugees as to persons found to be in need of protection as members of the country of asylum class.

Canada (Minister of Public Safety and Emergency Preparedness) v. Zaric (2015), 37 Imm. L.R. (4th) 135, [2016] 1 F.C.R. 407, 2015 FC 837, 2015 CarswellNat 2874, 2015 CarswellNat 4021 — The Board concluded that the Minister's application to vacate was moot and declined to exercise its discretion to hear the application. The Board held that s. 108(2) of IRPA provides one manner of terminating an individual's status as a Convention refugee, but it does not preclude the automatic operation of s. 108(1)(c) when a Convention refugee acquires a new nationality. The Board noted that s. 108(1) of the Act is worded differently from s. 109(1), and the latter provision clearly operates only upon the application of the Minister. The Board reasoned that if Parliament had intended s. 108(1) to apply only upon the application of the Minister, it would have stated this explicitly in the same manner as it did in s. 109(1). The Board concluded that a person who has been granted refugee status in Canada ceases to be a refugee when he or she becomes a Canadian citizen. The Board therefore concluded that the respondent ceased to be a Convention refugee when he became a Canadian citizen in 2001, and the refugee status which the Minister sought to vacate no longer existed. The Board found that there was no longer a live controversy between the parties and the Minister's Application to Vacate was moot. The Minister sought judicial review of the Board's decision. The Federal Court concluded that the Board was wrong to interpret s. 108(1) of the IRPA, which deals only with the rejection of a claim before it has been determined, as causing the respondent's refugee status to disappear the moment he became a Canadian citizen. The application for judicial review was allowed and the court certified the following question:

> Does refugee protection conferred pursuant to a s. 95(1) of the *Immigration and Refugee Protection Act* automatically cease by operation of s. 108(1)(c) when a Convention refugee becomes a Canadian citizen, thereby preventing the Minister of Public Safety and Emergency Preparedness from applying to the Immigration and Refugee Board pursuant to s. 109(1) to vacate the Board's previous decision to confer refugee protection?

Balouch v. Canada (Minister of Public Safety and Emergency Preparedness), 2015 FC 765, 2015 CarswellNat 2263, 2015 CarswellNat 3851 — The applicant sought judicial review of a decision of the Board to grant the Minister's application to cease her status as a refugee, pursuant to s. 108(2) of IRPA. The Board determined that the Minister had established grounds for cessation of the applicant's refugee status on the ground she had reavailed herself of the protection of her country of nationality. She had applied for an Iranian passport to visit her grandmother and to undergo foot surgery during her visit in 2010. She then returned in 2013 to visit an uncle who was being treated for colon cancer and during this visit had surgery on her nose and dental work on her teeth.

Three requirements must be shown: that the refugee has acted voluntarily; that the refugee has shown an intention to reavail; and that the refugee has actually obtained protection of his or her country or nationality. The applicant argued that the Board failed to consider whether a forward-looking current risk of persecution is a relevant consideration under s. 108.

The court concluded the Board considered all the evidence and reasonably concluded the applicant had met the three factors for reavailment and that she had failed to give a compelling explanation for her return to her country of nationality. A refugee claimant's voluntary reavailment indicates that the individual is no longer either unable or unwilling to avail him- or herself of the protection of their country of nationality. The issue of risk will be assessed if the applicant seeks a pre-removal risk assessment pursuant to s. 112.

The application was dismissed, the following question was certified:

> When deciding whether to allow an application by the Minister for cessation of refugee status pursuant to s. 108(1)(a) of the *Immigration and Refugee Protection Act* based on past actions, can the Board allow the Minister's application

without addressing whether the person is at risk of persecution upon return to their country of nationality at the time of the cessation hearing?

Canada (Minister of Public Safety and Emergency Preparedness) v. Dashi, 2015 FC 51, 2015 CarswellNat 3435, 2015 CarswellNat 83 — The Minister of Public Safety and Emergency Preparedness applied for a judicial review of the decision by the Refugee Protection Division to reject an application made by the Minister to cease the refugee protection of the respondent pursuant to para. 108(1)(a) of IRPA. The Board found that the respondent had not reavailed himself of the protection of his country of nationality, Pakistan, when he applied for and obtained a Pakistani passport.

There is no logical reason to irrefutably presume that as soon as a refugee states that he intends to travel abroad with a national passport, he is deemed to have had the intention of reavailing himself of the protection of his country of nationality. Each situation must turn on its own circumstances and it falls on the Board to assess these circumstances. The Board was not required to proceed to the third prong of the analysis in paragraph 119 of the UNHCR Handbook given its conclusion on intention. The requirements of paragraph 119 are cumulative and conjunctive. The cumulative nature of these requirements appears from the wording of paragraph 119. If one of the criteria is not met, the refugee status cannot be deemed ceased. Since the Board concluded that the respondent did not have the intention to reavail himself of the protection of the Pakistani authorities when he renewed his Pakistani passport, it was not necessary for it to pursue its analysis any further. The application of the Minister was dismissed.

The following questions were certified:

1. Does applying for and obtaining a passport from one's country of nationality with the intention to use it to travel outside Canada, but not in one's country of nationality, constitute, in all circumstances, irrefutable proof that the refugee had the intention of reavailing himself of the protection of his country of nationality?

2. Does applying for and obtaining a passport from one's country of nationality with the intention to use it to travel outside Canada, but not in one's country of nationality constitute, in all circumstances, a circumstance that can never serve to rebut the presumption created at paragraph 121 of the UNHCR Handbook?

Editor's note: The following case summaries were collected under the provisions of the former Act relating to the cessation of Convention refugee status. The previous jurisprudence interpreting refugee concepts may still be relevant.

Chandrakumar v. Canada (Minister of Employment & Immigration), 1997 CarswellNat 792 (Fed. T.D.) — The applicant sought to review a negative decision of the CRDD. A panel of the CRDD found that the applicant's renewal of his Sri Lanka passport indicated that he had re-availed himself of the protection of Sri Lanka. A person who applies for a passport must have the intention to re-avail himself or herself of the protection of the state. Such an intention cannot simply be assumed. The panel of the CRDD in this case did not engage in an analysis of the intention of the principal applicant in renewing his passport. The panel seems to have assumed that the simple action of renewing the passport without more was sufficient to establish re-availment of the protection of Sri Lanka. Such an inference is unreasonable. Accordingly, the decision of the CRDD was set aside.

Yusuf v. Canada (Minister of Employment & Immigration) (1995), 179 N.R. 11 (Fed. C.A.) — A change in the political situation in the claimant's country of origin is only relevant if it may help in determining whether or not there is, at the date of the hearing, a reasonable and objectively foreseeable possibility that the claimant will be persecuted in the event of a return there. The use of words such as meaningful, effective or durable are only helpful if one keeps clearly in mind that the only question, and therefore the only test, is that derived from the definition of Convention refugee. The issue of so-called change in circumstances is simply one of fact. It is not a question of law.

See annotation for *Canada (Minister of Employment & Immigration) v. Obstoj*, [1992] 2 F.C. 739, 93 D.L.R. (4th) 144, 142 N.R. 81 (C.A.), under s. 96 of the Act.

Section 108(2)

See the summary of *Canada (Minister of Citizenship and Immigration) v. Esfand* (2015), [2016] 2 F.C.R. 282, 2015 FC 1190, 2015 CarswellNat 6443, 2015 CarswellNat 5161, at s. 95(1) of the Act.

Canada (Minister of Citizenship and Immigration) v. Bermudez (2016), 40 Imm. L.R. (4th) 11, 483 N.R. 115, 2016 FCA 131, 2016 CarswellNat 1428, [2016] F.C.J. No. 468 — At issue in this appeal was whether a CBSA hearings officer had the discretion to consider circumstances or factors that are not explicitly listed in s. 108 of the IRPA, more precisely, humanitarian and compassionate factors and the best interests of the child, when assessing whether an application for cessation of refugee protection should be submitted to the Refugee Protection Division for a determination that refugee protection has ceased for any of the reasons described in subs. 108(1) of the IRPA, particularly in instances involving a refugee who acquired permanent resident status in Canada. A Federal Court judge held that a hearings officer has the discretion to consider H&C factors when assessing whether a cessation application should be filed with the RPD. The judge granted the application for judicial review and set aside the decision made by the hearings officer. The Minister appealed. The appeal was allowed. A CBSA hearings officer, or the hearings officer, as the Minister's delegate, does not have the discretion to consider H&C factors and the best interests of the child when deciding whether to make his cessation application pursuant to subs. 108(2) in respect of a permanent resident.

See annotation for *Canada (Minister of Employment & Immigration) v. Obstoj*, [1992] 2 F.C. 739, 93 D.L.R. (4th) 144, 142 N.R. 81 (C.A.), under s. 96, *supra*.

Section 108(4)

Brovina v. Canada (Minister of Citizenship & Immigration) (2004), 254 F.T.R. 244, 2004 CarswellNat 2841, 2004 CarswellNat 1243, 2004 FC 635, [2004] F.C.J. No. 771 — For a panel to embark on a compelling reasons analysis, it must first find that there was a valid refugee or protected person claim and that the reasons for the claim have ceased to exist. It is only then that the Board should consider whether the nature of the claimant's experiences in the former country were so appalling that he or she should not be expected to return and put himself or herself under the protection of that state.

Editor's note: The following case summaries were collected under the provisions of the former Act relating to the cessation of Convention refugee status. The previous jurisprudence interpreting refugee concepts may still be relevant.

Elemah v. Canada (Minister of Citizenship & Immigration), 2001 CarswellNat 1530, 2001 FCT 779 (T.D.) The applicant sought to review a negative decision of a panel of the CRDD. The decision of the panel was set aside. The panel determined that the applicant had not suffered appalling persecution which would bring him within the ambit of subs. 2(3). Subsection 2(3) does not establish a test which necessitates that persecution reach a level to qualify it as atrocious and appalling. Rather, the subsection requires that the Board must thoroughly canvass all the documentary and oral evidence, including the nature of the incidents of torture and the medical reports provided by the parties, in order to determine, as stated in the legislation, if there are "compelling reasons" not to return the claimant.

Kulla v. Canada (Minister of Citizenship & Immigration), 2000 CarswellNat 1912, [2000] F.C.J. No. 1347 (T.D.) — The applicant's claim for refugee status was rejected by a panel of the CRDD. The panel also concluded that subs. 2(3) of the Immigration Act was not of any assistance to the applicant. The panel found that the claimant's past experience, at the hands of the authorities in Albania, was "cruel and harsh" but not "atrocious" and "appalling" and, therefore, not caught by s. 2(3). The issue is not whether a claimant's past experience can be characterized as "atrocious" and "appalling," adjectives used in other jurisprudence, but rather, if the person has established that there are compelling reasons arising out of any previous persecution for the applicant refusing to avail himself or herself of the protection of the country that he or she has left.

Yamba v. Canada (Minister of Citizenship & Immigration) (2000), 254 N.R. 388, 181 F.T.R. 132 (note), 2000 CarswellNat 543, [2000] F.C.J. No. 457 (C.A.) — The motions judge was correct in holding that the Refugee Division is under an obligation to consider the applicability of subs. 2(3) once it is satisfied that refugee status cannot be claimed because of a change in country conditions under para. 2(2)(e). The evidentiary burden is upon the claimant to establish that there are compelling reasons for not returning to the country in which the past persecution arose.

Jiminez v. Canada (Minister of Citizenship & Immigration) (1999), 162 F.T.R. 177 — In order to bring himself within the provisions of s. 2(3) of the *Immigration Act*, the applicant is not required to show that he is suffering continual psychological after-effects from the persecution which he suffered in his country of nationality. The Board accepted as a fact that the applicant had been beaten, burned, raped, shot and left for dead. However, it did not comment on whether the nature of the applicant's persecution was sufficiently appalling and atrocious to warrant the application of s. 2(3), rather it focused exclusively on whether the applicant was currently suffering from "the continued effect of past persecution." In so deciding, the Board erred in law, and the matter was remitted back for redetermination.

Shahid v. Canada (Minister of Citizenship & Immigration) (1995), 89 F.T.R. 106 — The applicant claimed that by virtue of s. 2(3) of the *Immigration Act* he should not be returned to Pakistan. The Board, in refusing to apply s. 2(3) determined that it required an ongoing fear of persecution. For this reason the decision was set aside. The Board, once it embarked upon the assessment of the applicant's claim under s. 2(3) had the duty to consider the level of atrocity of the acts inflicted upon the applicant, the repercussions upon his physical and mental state, and determine whether this experience alone constituted a compelling reason not to return him to his country of origin. The panel failed to do this and accordingly its decision was quashed and the matter returned for a new hearing before a differently constituted tribunal.

Hassan v. Canada (Minister of Employment & Immigration) (1994), 77 F.T.R. 309 — The respondent conceded that the Board had erred in this case. However, counsel for the applicants was of the view that the panel had erred in its interpretation of s. 2(3) of the *Immigration Act* and that if it had not been for this error the applicants would have been found to be Convention refugees.

Before the court will refer a matter back for redetermination in accordance with a direction that the applicants be found to be Convention refugees, the following circumstances must apply:

1. the evidence must be so clearly conclusive that the only possible conclusion is that the claimant is a Convention refugee;

2. the sole issue to be decided must be a pure question of law which will be dispositive of the case;

3. the legal issue must be based on uncontroverted evidence and accepted facts; and

4. there must be no factual issues which involve conflicting evidence which are central to the claim.

To require that before s. 2(3) could apply, there would have to be a Convention refugee determination in respect of an applicant, would make the application of s. 2(3) dependent on timing alone. Section 2(3) does not require an on-going fear of persecution. It only applies to a tiny minority of present day claimants who can demonstrate that they have suffered such appalling persecution that their experience alone is a compelling reason not to return them to the country in which they suffered the persecution. Section 2(3) only applies to extraordinary cases in which the persecution is relatively so exceptional that, even in the wake of changed circumstances, it would be wrong to return refugee claimants. The court did not direct that on a rehearing of the matter the Board find the applicants to be Convention refugees. The Board with its experience and expertise was best able to assess whether, having regard to the special and limited application of s. 2(3), the applicants fell within its ambit.

Arguello-Garcia v. Canada (Minister of Employment & Immigration) (1993), 21 Imm. L.R. (2d) 285, 64 F.T.R. 307, 70 F.T.R. 1 — The Refugee Division found the applicant not to be a Convention refugee. The Board erred in law when it found that the facts did not amount to previous persecution. The court noted that it had accepted a broad range of harassment and ill-treatment as constituting persecution and, furthermore, that neither deprivation of physical liberty nor physical mistreatment were essential elements of persecution.

The Board, notwithstanding its findings that there was no persecution, found that there had been a change of circumstance in El Salvador. The second issue before the court was whether the applicant fell within the special or limited category of persons to which s. 2(3) of the *Immigration Act* applies. Section 2(3) is based on a general humanitarian principle which permits a person who has suffered serious past persecution to retain or obtain Convention refugee status despite fundamental changes in his or her country of origin.

The court referred to the Concise Oxford Dictionary of Current English, Clarendon Press, Oxford, 1990 definition of atrocious and appalling. Atrocious was defined as very bad or unpleasant or alternatively extremely savage or wicked. An atrocity was defined as an extremely wicked or cruel act, especially one involving physical violence or injury. Appalling was defined as shocking, unpleasant or bad.

In this case, the torture and sexual assault experienced by the applicant qualified as atrocious and appalling acts as defined above. The right not to be subject to torture and cruel, inhuman and degrading treatment is a fundamental right which enjoys the highest international protection.

Further, there was ample evidence before the Board to show that the applicant continued to suffer severe psychological hardship as a result of the very serious persecution which he and his family members suffered in El Salvador. A psychiatric report entered in evidence stated that the applicant was suffering from post-traumatic stress disorder, related to his personal and family history of violent persecution, torture and massacre. The finding by the Board that the applicant did not fit within the criteria set out in s. 2(3) was on a misconstruction of the applicable test and constituted an error in law.

The application was granted and the matter returned to a differently constituted panel of the IRB to reconsider the evidence in accordance with the reasons of the court.

Applications to Vacate

109. (1) Vacation of refugee protection — The Refugee Protection Division may, on application by the Minister, vacate a decision to allow a claim for refugee protection, if it finds that the decision was obtained as a result of directly or indirectly misrepresenting or witholding material facts relating to a relevant matter.

[Editor's Note: SOR/2002-227, s. 345 provides that a decision made in Canada before June 28, 2002 to approve an application to reconsider and vacate a determination that a person is a Convention refugee is deemed to be a determination by the Immigration and Refugee Board to vacate a decision to allow a claim for refugee protection.]

(2) Rejection of application — The Refugee Protection Division may reject the application if it is satisfied that other sufficient evidence was considered at the time of the first determination to justify refugee protection.

[Editor's Note: SOR/2002-227, s. 339 provides that a determination made in Canada before June 28, 2002 that a person is not a Convention refugee is deemed to be a claim for refugee protection rejected by the Immigration and Refugee Board.]

(3) Allowance of application — If the application is allowed, the claim of the person is deemed to be rejected and the decision that led to the conferral of refugee protection is nullified.

Case Law

Bortey v. Canada (Minister of Citizenship & Immigration), 2006 CarswellNat 327, 2006 CarswellNat 2422, 2006 FC 190 — The Board found that the applicant obtained refugee status on the basis of misrepresentations and the withholding of material facts. The Board also concluded that once these misrepresentations were set aside, there was no other sufficient evidence considered at the time of the first determination on which a decision in favour of the applicant could have been based. The Board was required, under subs. 109(2) of the IRPA, to decipher whether any of the evidence cited in support of the original positive determination is left "untainted" by the fact of the newly discovered material misrepresentations.

Iliev v. Canada (Minister of Citizenship & Immigration), 2005 CarswellNat 2010, 2005 FC 395 — The applicant, a citizen of Bulgaria, made a claim to be a Convention refugee and was found to be a Convention refugee. However, the Minister of Citizenship and Immigration obtained leave to vacate the determination of the Convention Refugee Determination Division pursuant to s. 109 of the IRPA on the basis that the applicant had obtained refugee status on fraudulent means, misrepresentation, suppression and concealment of material facts, specifically with respect to the entry of two criminal convictions in Bulgaria. The Minister relied on certificates of conviction that had been issued by the Bulgarian court. The Board accepted the Minister's argument and concluded that pursuant to Article 1F(b) of the *Refugee Convention*, the applicant was a person who was excluded from consideration as a Convention refugee as a result of having committed a serious non-political offence. The Board's conclusion was set aside by the Federal Court as it was made in the absence of any evidence about the equivalency between the Bulgarian criminal law and the Canadian criminal law. A factual finding made without evidence is a ground for judicial intervention, pursuant to s. 18.1(4) of the Federal Courts Act, R.S.C. 1985, c. F-7, as amended.

Calixto v. Canada (Minister of Citizenship & Immigration) (2005), 49 Imm. L.R. (3d) 36, 2005 CarswellNat 2165, 2005 CarswellNat 4919, 2005 FC 1037 — The applicant arrived in Canada and was granted refugee status, and then applied for landed immigrant status. At a CSIS interview, the applicant was confronted with information that he had lied about his past activities, including a criminal record in the United States that arose during the time he claimed he was being persecuted in Mexico. The applicant admitted this misrepresentation and as a result of the admission, the applicant's refugee status was vacated pursuant to s. 109(1) of the IRPA. A report was prepared pursuant to s. 44(1) setting out that the applicant was inadmissible pursuant to s. 40(1)(c). An immigration officer found the report well founded and consequently made a deportation order against the applicant pursuant to s. 44(2). The applicant argued that s. 40(1)(c) would render him inadmissible only if he made a misrepresentation in the course of the vacation proceeding before the Refugee Protection Division. The court held that whether the applicant made any misrepresentations during the vacation hearing was not a relevant consideration. Instead, the use of the term "misrepresentation" in s. 40(1)(c) should be read as denoting statements of fact which operate to make a person inadmissible, that is, if either of the events mentioned in this section are proved to have occurred, a person is considered, or "deemed," inadmissible for "misrepresentation."

Designated Countries of Origin

[Heading added 2010, c. 8, s. 12.]

109.1 (1) Designation of countries of origin — The Minister may, by order, designate a country, for the purposes of subsection 110(2) and section 111.1.

(1.1) [Repealed 2012, c. 17, s. 58.]

(1.2) [Repealed 2012, c. 17, s. 58.]

(2) Limitation — The Minister may only make a designation

(a) in the case where the number of claims for refugee protection made in Canada by nationals of the country in question in respect of which the Refugee Protection Division has made a final determination is equal to or greater than the number provided for by order of the Minister,

(i) if the rate, expressed as a percentage, that is obtained by dividing the total number of claims made by nationals of the country in question that, in a final determination by the Division during the period provided for in the order, are rejected or determined to be withdrawn or abandoned by the total number of claims made by nationals of the country in question in respect of which the Division has, during the same period, made a final determination is equal to or greater than the percentage provided for in the order, or

(ii) if the rate, expressed as a percentage, that is obtained by dividing the total number of claims made by nationals of the country in question that, in a final determination by the Division, during the period provided for in the order, are determined to be withdrawn or abandoned by the total number of claims made by nationals of the country in question in respect of which the Division has, during the same period, made a final determination is equal to or greater than the percentage provided for in the order; or

(b) in the case where the number of claims for refugee protection made in Canada by nationals of the country in question in respect of which the Refugee Protection Division has made a final determination is less than the number provided for by order of the Minister, if the Minister is of the opinion that in the country in question

(i) there is an independent judicial system,

(ii) basic democratic rights and freedoms are recognized and mechanisms for redress are available if those rights or freedoms are infringed, and

(iii) civil society organizations exist.

(3) Order of Minister — The Minister may, by order, provide for the number, period or percentages referred to in subsection (2).

(4) Statutory Instruments Act — An order made under subsection (1) or (3) is not a statutory instrument for the purposes of the *Statutory Instruments Act*. However, it must be published in the *Canada Gazette*.

2010, c. 8, s. 12 [Amended 2012, c. 17, s. 58.]

Appeal to Refugee Appeal Division

110. (1) Appeal — Subject to subsections (1.1) and (2), a person or the Minister may appeal, in accordance with the rules of the Board, on a question of law, of fact or of mixed law and fact, to the Refugee Appeal Division against a decision of the Refugee Protection Division to allow or reject the person's claim for refugee protection.

(1.1) Notice of appeal — The Minister may satisfy any requirement respecting the manner in which an appeal is filed and perfected by submitting a notice of appeal and any supporting documents.

(2) Restriction on appeals — No appeal may be made in respect of any of the following:

(a) a decision of the Refugee Protection Division allowing or rejecting the claim for refugee protection of a designated foreign national;

(b) a determination that a refugee protection claim has been withdrawn or abandoned;

(c) a decision of the Refugee Protection Division rejecting a claim for refugee protection that states that the claim has no credible basis or is manifestly unfounded;

(d) subject to the regulations, a decision of the Refugee Protection Division in respect of a claim for refugee protection if

(i) the foreign national who makes the claim came directly or indirectly to Canada from a country that is, on the day on which their claim is made, designated by regulations made under subsection 102(1) and that is a party to an agreement referred to in paragraph 102(2)(d), and

(ii) the claim — by virtue of regulations made under paragraph 102(1)(c) — is not ineligible under paragraph 101(1)(e) to be referred to the Refugee Protection Division;

(d.1) a decision of the Refugee Protection Division allowing or rejecting a claim for refugee protection made by a foreign national who is a national of a country that was, on the day on which the decision was made, a country designated under subsection 109.1(1);

(e) a decision of the Refugee Protection Division allowing or rejecting an application by the Minister for a determination that refugee protection has ceased;

(f) a decision of the Refugee Protection Division allowing or rejecting an application by the Minister to vacate a decision to allow a claim for refugee protection.

(2.1) Making of appeal — The appeal must be filed and perfected within the time limits set out in the regulations.

(3) Procedure — Subject to subsections (3.1), (4) and (6), the Refugee Appeal Division must proceed without a hearing, on the basis of the record of the proceedings of the Refugee Protection Division, and may accept documentary evidence and written submissions from the Minister and the person who is the subject of the appeal and, in the case of a matter that is conducted before a panel of three members, written submissions from a representative or agent of the United Nations High Commissioner for Refugees and any other person described in the rules of the Board.

(3.1) Time limits — Unless a hearing is held under subsection (6), the Refugee Appeal Division must make a decision within the time limits set out in the regulations.

(4) Evidence that may be presented — On appeal, the person who is the subject of the appeal may present only evidence that arose after the rejection of their claim or that was not reasonably available, or that the person could not reasonably have been expected in the circumstances to have presented, at the time of the rejection.

(5) Exception — Subsection (4) does not apply in respect of evidence that is presented in response to evidence presented by the Minister.

(6) Hearing — The Refugee Appeal Division may hold a hearing if, in its opinion, there is documentary evidence referred to in subsection (3)

    (a) that raises a serious issue with respect to the credibility of the person who is the subject of the appeal;

    (b) that is central to the decision with respect to the refugee protection claim; and

    (c) that, if accepted, would justify allowing or rejecting the refugee protection claim.

[Editor's Note: S.C. 2001, c. 27, s. 191 provides that every application, proceeding or matter before the Convention Refugee Determination Division under the Immigration Act, *R.S.C. 1985, c. I-2 (the "former Act") that is pending or in progress immediately before June 28, 2002, in respect of which substantive evidence has been adduced but no decision has been made, shall be continued under the former Act by the Refugee Protection Division of the Immigration and Refugee Board.*

S.C. 2001, c. 27, s. 194 [not in force at date of publication] provides that in cases referred to in S.C. 2001, c. 27, s. 191, a decision by the Refugee Protection Division following a hearing that has been commenced by the Convention Refugee Determination Division is not subject to an appeal under s. 110 of the Immigration and Refugee Protection Act, *S.C. 2001, c. 27 (the "new Act").*

S.C. 2001, c. 27, s. 195 [not in force at date of publication] further provides that a decision made by the Convention Refugee Determination Division before June 28, 2002 is not subject to an appeal under s. 110 of the new Act.

S.C. 2001, c. 27, s. 198 provides that the Refugee Protection Division has jurisdiction to consider decisions of the Convention Refugee Determination Division that are set aside by the Federal Court or the Supreme Court of Canada, and shall dispose of those matters in accordance with the provisions of the new Act.

S.C. 2001, c. 27, s. 199 still further provides that sections 112 to 114 of the new Act apply to a redetermination of a decision set aside by the Federal Court with respect to an application for landing as a member of the post-determination refugee claimants in Canada class within the meaning of the Immigration Regulations, 1978, *SOR/78-172.]*

2010, c. 8, s. 13; 2012, c. 17, ss. 36, 84(2)

Case Law

Section 110(2)

Z. (Y.) v. Canada (Minister of Citizenship and Immigration) (2015), 35 Imm. L.R. (4th) 217, [2016] 1 F.C.R. 575, 93 Admin. L.R. (5th) 187, 387 D.L.R. (4th) 676, 339 C.R.R. (2d) 24, 2015 FC 892, 2015 CarswellNat 3181, 2015 CarswellNat 4106, [2015] F.C.J. No. 880 — As part of the reforms enacted by the *Protecting Canada's Immigration System Act*, S.C. 2012, c 17, Parliament added para. 110(2)(d.1) to IRPA. This new paragraph became effective on December 10, 2012, the same date as when the Refugee Appeal Division ("RAD") of the Immigration and Refugee Board ("IRB") became operational under s. 110 of IRPA. Paragraph 110(2)(d.1) denies access to the RAD for all refugee claimants from any country designated by the Minster of Citizenship and Immigration pursuant to s. 109.1 of IRPA. The applicants challenged the constitutionality of para. 110(2)(d.1) and the mechanism for selecting which countries to designate.

IRP Act

Paragraph 110(2)(d.1) of the IRPA does not violate s. 7 of the Charter, therefore the court did not consider whether that section could be saved vis-à-vis s. 1 of the Charter and did not address whether the review process for designation was prescribed by law. However, the court did consider whether an appeal to the RAD for a designated country of origin ("DCO") claimant is a reasonable limit prescribed by the law that can be demonstrably justified in a free and democratic society. The court agreed with the respondents that the denial of an appeal to the RAD by DCO refugee claimants in para. 110(2)(d.1) of the IRPA is "prescribed by law" and, therefore, s. 1 of the Charter is engaged. The court recognized that Canada has a pressing and substantial objective in effecting the reforms. Prior to such reforms, it took approximately 20 months before a refugee claim could be heard and failed claimants took an average of 4.5 years to deport. The objective of para. 110(2)(d.1) specifically is to reduce the layers of recourse and ensure that failed claimants from DCOs can be removed faster; a shorter expected stay could act as a disincentive for those claimants who might otherwise come to Canada and make a fraudulent refugee claim. Even if it may have been reasonable to suppose that denying an appeal to the RAD might further such objectives, it cannot be said that para. 110(2)(d.1) is minimally impairing. Just because every refugee claimant still gets a full hearing before the RPD, and even though there may be provisions in the IRPA, the Regulations and the RPD Rules to seek adjournments, or to extend filing deadlines if the expedited timelines cannot be obeyed, or to reopen an application, these factors cannot justify the fact that some claimants can and others cannot make an appeal to the RAD.

Inasmuch as one of the goals of the reforms was to deter abusive or unfounded claims, this can be achieved by the RPD either declaring a claim manifestly unfounded under s. 107.1 of the IRPA or finding that there is no credible basis for the claim under subs. 107(2). In both cases, an appeal to the RAD is precluded by virtue of para. 110(2)(c). Claimants who abandon or withdraw their claims are also denied an appeal to the RAD. The respondents lead no evidence to suggest RPD members cannot competently detect non-credible or fraudulent claims. It was not necessary for Parliament to differentiate between DCO and non-DCO claimants to preclude appeals to the RAD since the stated goal of deterring abusive or unfounded claims could be achieved by the combined effect of s. 107.1, subs. 107(2) and paras. 110(2)(b) and (c) of the IRPA.

An appeal to the RAD is a significant benefit for claimants, and denying an appeal to some claimants based on their country of origin is a serious impairment of their right to equality. Furthermore, unlike non-DCO claimants who cannot be removed from Canada until after the Federal Court has dismissed any applications for judicial review of their RAD appeals, DCO claimants do not benefit from an automatic stay of removal while seeking judicial review of a negative RPD decision. They must seek a stay from the court to request an administrative deferral of removal or, in certain circumstances, request a PRRA. These avenues do not mitigate any risk of refoulement from the lack of an RAD appeal.

Denying an appeal to all claimants from DCOs is not proportional to the government's objectives; it is an inequality that is disproportionate and overbroad and cannot be saved by s. 1 of the Charter. Accordingly, para. 110(2)(d.1) of the IRPA is inconsistent with subs. 15(1) of the Charter and has no force and effect. The applications for judicial review were granted in part.

The following questions were certified:

    1. Does para. 110(2)(d.1) of the IRPA comply with subs. 15(1) of the Charter?

2. If not, is para. 110(2)(d.1) of the IRPA a reasonable limit on Charter rights that is prescribed by law and can be demonstrably justified under s. 1 of the Charter?

Section 110(4)

Canada (Minister of Citizenship and Immigration) v. Singh (2016), 40 Imm. L.R. (4th) 32, 397 D.L.R. (4th) 353, (sub nom. *Singh (Parminder) v. Canada (Minister of Citizenship and Immigration))* 482 N.R. 149, 2016 FCA 96, 2016 CarswellNat 867, 2016 CarswellNat 868, [2016] F.C.J. No. 315 — This was an appeal from Federal Court, which allowed the respondent's application for judicial review of a decision of the Refugee Appeal Division regarding his claim for refugee protection. The appeal raised for the first time the issue as to how to interpret subs. 110(4) of the Act, which governs admissible evidence before the RAD. This provision was enacted as part of the *Balanced Refugee Reform Act*, the objective of which was to amend and implement unproclaimed provisions in the IRPA providing for the creation of the RAD.

The appeal was allowed, the Federal Court judgment was set aside and the RAD decision was confirmed. Accordingly, the respondent is not a Convention refugee or a person in need of protection within the meaning of ss. 96 and 97 of the IRPA.

The RAD's interpretation of subs. 110(4) of the Act must be reviewed in light of the reasonableness standard, in accordance with the presumption that an administrative agency's interpretation of its home statute should be shown deference by the reviewing court.

To determine the admissibility of evidence under subs. 110(4) of the IRPA, the RAD must always ensure compliance with the explicit requirements set out in this provision. It was also reasonable for the RAD to be guided, subject to the necessary adaptations, by the considerations made by this Court in *Raza v. Canada (Minister of Citizenship and Immigration)*, 2007 FCA 385. However, the requirement concerning the materiality of the new evidence must be assessed in the context of subs. 110(6), for the sole purpose of determining whether the RAD may hold a hearing.

Akuffo v. Canada (Minister of Citizenship and Immigration) (2014), 31 Imm. L.R. (4th) 301, 86 Admin. L.R. (5th) 112, 2014 FC 1063, 2014 CarswellNat 4487, 2014 CarswellNat 5273, [2014] F.C.J. No. 1116 — The applicant was a citizen of Ghana and alleged that he had a well-founded fear of persecution based on his homosexuality and, as homosexuality is illegal in Ghana, that he is a person in need of protection. The Refugee Protection Division found him not to be credible. Specifically, the RPD was of the opinion that someone who was a homosexual and who was seeking refugee status based on that issue would not have omitted to mention until the very end of the hearing that he was now seeing a man in Canada. The applicant appealed to the Refugee Appeal Division which confirmed the RPD's decision. The RAD held that the RPD, as a first instance tribunal, is owed deference, and so its credibility findings must be assessed on a reasonableness standard. The rationale is that the appeal did not qualify for a hearing and only the RPD held a hearing directly questioning the applicant and reviewed the evidence before reaching its conclusion. The RAD added that it was not intended to act as a *de novo* appeal board, but rather to review the RPD decision for reasonableness. The RAD also found that it was within the range of possible, acceptable outcomes with respect to the credibility determination. The court concluded that deference was only owed by the RAD to the RPD's credibility findings. Accordingly, it was reasonable for the RAD to defer to the RPD's credibility findings and that the overall reassessment of the evidence was reasonable. The application for judicial review was dismissed.

The following questions were certified:

> What standard of review should be applied by this Court when reviewing the Refugee Appeal Division's interpretation of sections 110, 111, 162 and 171 of the *Immigration and Refugee Protection Act*, and more specifically when reviewing its determination of the level of deference owed to the Refugee Protection Division's credibility findings?

— and —

> Within the Refugee Appeal Division's statutory framework where the appeal proceeds on the basis of the Refugee Protection Division record of the proceedings, what is the level of deference owed by the Refugee Appeal Division to the Refugee Protection Division findings of fact and of mixed fact and law, more specifically to its credibility findings?

Section 110(6)

Zhou v. Canada (Minister of Citizenship and Immigration) (2015), 37 Imm. L.R. (4th) 275, 2015 FC 911, 2015 CarswellNat 3277, 2015 CarswellNat 5691 — The legislation clearly states that the Refugee Appeal Division "may" hold a hearing where the statutory criteria are met. An oral hearing will generally be required when the statutory criteria has been satisfied. The RAD retains the discretion on this question but that discretion must be exercised reasonably in the circumstances. In particular, the mere fact that a party has not requested a hearing will generally not be sufficient reason to justify a refusal to convene one when the circumstances appear to require it. While the RAD rules allow an appellant to request a hearing, IRPA does not actually impose a burden either to request, or to satisfy the RAD that the circumstances merit, an oral hearing. The onus rests with the RAD to consider and apply the statutory criteria reasonably. In this case, the RAD should have convened an oral hearing before dismissing the appellant's appeal on credibility grounds. The court overturned the decision of the RAD and made an order directing another panel of the RAD to reconsider the appeal.

111. (1) Decision — **After considering the appeal, the Refugee Appeal Division shall make one of the following decisions:**

(a) confirm the determination of the Refugee Protection Division;

(b) set aside the determination and substitute a determination that, in its opinion, should have been made; or

(c) refer the matter to the Refugee Protection Division for re-determination, giving the directions to the Refugee Protection Division that it considers appropriate.

(1.1) [Repealed 2012, c. 17, s. 37.]

(2) Referrals — **The Refugee Appeal Division may make the referral described in paragraph (1)(c) only if it is of the opinion that**

(a) the decision of the Refugee Protection Division is wrong in law, in fact or in mixed law and fact; and

(b) it cannot make a decision under paragraph 111(1)(a) or (b) without hearing evidence that was presented to the Refugee Protection Division.

2010, c. 8, s. 14; 2012, c. 17, s. 37

Case Law

Canada (Minister of Citizenship and Immigration) v. Huruglica (2016), 39 Imm. L.R. (4th) 185, 481 N.R. 207, 3 Admin. L.R. (6th) 283, 396 D.L.R. (4th) 527, 2016 CarswellNat 843, [2016] F.C.J. No. 313 — The appellant Minister of Citizenship and Immigration appealed from the decision of Justice Michael L. Phelan of the Federal Court allowing the three respondents' application for judicial review. In their application, the respondents had contested the validity of the decision of the Refugee Appeal Division which dismissed their appeal from the Refugee Protection Division. The judge certified the following question:

> What is the scope of the Refugee Appeal Division's review when considering an appeal of a decision of the Refugee Protection Division?

The Federal Court of Appeal concluded after a statutory analysis that with respect to findings of fact (and mixed fact and law) such as the one involved here, which raised no issue of credibility of oral evidence, the RAD is to review RPD decisions applying the correctness standard. Thus, after carefully considering the RPD decision, the RAD carries out its own analysis of the record to determine whether, as submitted by the appellant, the RPD erred. Having done this, the RAD is to provide a final determination, either by confirming the RPD decision or setting it aside and substituting its own determination of the merits of the refugee claim. It is only when the RAD is of the opinion that it cannot provide such a final determination without hearing the oral evidence presented to the RPD that the matter can be referred back to the RPD for redetermination. No other interpretation of the relevant statutory provisions is reasonable. Thus, the RAD erred by applying the reasonableness standard to the RPD's analysis of the objective evidence regarding state protection and to its conclusion in that respect. The appeal was dismissed.

It was certainly expected in 2001 that the workload of the RAD would be important and the IRB's intent was to equip the new division with a corresponding level of staff and resources. The then-chairman of the IRB appeared to have no issue with respect to the capacity of the RAD to substantively review RPD decisions on the merits and remedy errors made by the RPD. There is no indication that this exercise was viewed as a useless duplication of the work of the RPD, for this is exactly what justified reducing the number of members on the RPD panel involved in reviewing each refugee claim. It would certainly be more efficient to have only one instead of two decision makers routinely involved in preparing and holding a hearing.

Nnah v. Canada (Minister of Citizenship and Immigration, 2015 FC 77, 2015 CarswellNat 1929, 2015 CarswellNat 1930 — The applicants sought to set aside a decision of the Refugee Appeal Division dismissing their appeal and confirming a decision of the Refugee Protection Division that they were not persons in need of protection.

The RAD reviewed the decision of the RPD on the standard of reasonableness and most judges of the Federal Court have held that to be the incorrect basis on which to conduct an appeal of an RPD decision. The application was allowed on this basis. However, a second issue was raised, and the court commented on the issue of a lack of transcript before the RAD and the availability of only the audio recording of the RPD. The applicant challenged that there was a breach of procedural fairness because of the lack of a proper audio file or written transcript. The applicant alleged the audio tape was not audible. The RAD held there was no breach. The Refugee Appeal Division rules are silent on who is to provide the transcript and there is no case law on this exact point. If there is a request for a transcript in the redetermination, the RAD will have to decide, based on the facts offered, whether the burden of doing so lies with it, or lies with the appellants.

The application was allowed, the decision of the RAD quashed and the appeal remitted back to be determined by a differently constituted panel. The following question was certified:

> What is the scope of the Refugee Appeal Division's review when considering an appeal of a decision of the Refugee Protection Division?

Regulations

[Heading added 2010, c. 8, s. 14.1.]

111.1 (1) Regulations — The regulations may provide for any matter relating to the application of this Division, and may include provisions respecting

(a) time limits for the provision of documents and information under subsection 99(3.1) or 100(4);

(b) time limits for the hearing referred to in subsection 100(4.1);

(c) exceptions to the application of paragraph 110(2)(d);

(d) time limits for the filing and perfecting of an appeal under subsection 110(2.1); and

(e) time limits for the making of a decision by the Refugee Appeal Division, the extension of those time limits and the circumstances in which they do not apply.

(2) Clarification — regulations made under paragraph (1)(b) — With respect to claimants who are nationals of a country that is, on the day on which their claim is made, a country designated under subsection 109.1(1), regulations made under paragraph (1)(b) may provide for time limits that are different from the time limits for other claimants.

(3) [Repealed 2012, c. 17, s. 59.]

(4) [Repealed 2012, c. 17, s. 59.]

2010, c. 8, s. 14.1 [Amended 2012, c. 17, s. 59.]

DIVISION 3 — PRE-REMOVAL RISK ASSESSMENT

Protection

112. (1) Application for protection — A person in Canada, other than a person referred to in subsection 115(1), may, in accordance with the regulations, apply to the Minister for protection if they are subject to a removal order that is in force or are named in a certificate described in subsection 77(1).

Proposed Amendment — 112(1)

(1) Application for protection — Subject to subsection (1.1), a person in Canada, other than a person referred to in subsection 115(1), may, in accordance with the regulations and the rules of the Board, apply to the Refugee Protection Division for protection if they are subject to a removal order that is in force.

2010, c. 8, s. 15(1) [Not in force at date of publication.]

Proposed Addition — 112(1.1)–(1.7)

(1.1) Application to Minister — In the case of a person described in subsection (3), the application for protection must be made to the Minister in accordance with the regulations.

(1.2) Suspension of application — Despite subsection 105(1), proceedings of the Refugee Protection Division in respect of an application are suspended on notice by an officer that

(a) a report has been referred to the Immigration Division for a determination of whether the applicant is inadmissible on grounds of security, violating human or international rights, serious criminality — as referred to in paragraph (3)(b) — or organized criminality; or

(b) the applicant is the subject of an authority to proceed issued under section 15 of the *Extradition Act*.

(1.3) Transfer — inadmissibility — On notice by an officer that the Immigration Division has made a determination that the applicant is inadmissible on the grounds referred to in paragraph (1.2)(a), consideration of the application is transferred to the Minister.

(1.4) Continuation — On notice by an officer that the Immigration Division has made a determination that the applicant is not inadmissible on the grounds referred to in paragraph (1.2)(a), consideration of the application is continued by the Refugee Protection Division.

(1.5) Termination after surrender under *Extradition Act* — If the applicant is ordered surrendered by the Minister of Justice under the *Extradition Act*, consideration of the application is terminated.

(1.6) Continuation — If the applicant is finally discharged under the *Extradition Act*, consideration of the application is continued by the Refugee Protection Division.

(1.7) Transfer: Refugee Convention — If the Refugee Protection Division makes a determination that the applicant is referred to in section F of Article 1 of the Refugee Convention, consideration of the application is transferred to the Minister.

2010, c. 8, s. 15(1) [Not in force at date of publication. Amended 2012, c. 17, s. 60(1).]

(2) Exception — Despite subsection (1), a person may not apply for protection if

Proposed Amendment — 112(2) opening words

(2) Exception — Despite subsections (1) and (1.1), a person may not apply for protection if

2010, c. 8, s. 15(2) [Not in force at date of publication.]

(a) they are the subject of an authority to proceed issued under section 15 of the *Extradition Act*;

(b) they have made a claim to refugee protection that has been determined under paragraph 101(1)(e) to be ineligible;

(b.1) subject to subsection (2.1), less than 12 months, or, in the case of a person who is a national of a country that is designated under subsection 109.1(1), less than 36 months, have passed since their claim for refugee protection was last rejected — unless it was deemed to be rejected under subsection 109(3) or was rejected on the basis of section E or F of Article 1 of the Refugee Convention — or determined to be withdrawn or abandoned by the Refugee Protection Division or the Refugee Appeal Division;

(c) subject to subsection (2.1), less than 12 months, or, in the case of a person who is a national of a country that is designated under subsection 109.1(1), less than 36 months, have passed since their last application for protection was rejected or determined to be withdrawn or abandoned by the Refugee Protection Division or the Minister.

(d) [Repealed 2012, c. 17, s. 38(1.1).]

(2.1) **Exemption** — The Minister may exempt from the application of paragraph (2)(b.1) or (c)

(a) the nationals — or, in the case of persons who do not have a country of nationality, the former habitual residents — of a country;

(b) the nationals or former habitual residents of a country who, before they left the country, lived in a given part of that country; and

(c) a class of nationals or former habitual residents of a country.

(2.2) **Application** — However, an exemption made under subsection (2.1) does not apply to persons in respect of whom, after the day on which the exemption comes into force, a decision is made respecting their claim for refugee protection by the Refugee Protection Division or, if an appeal is made, by the Refugee Appeal Division.

(2.3) **Regulations** — The regulations may govern any matter relating to the application of subsection (2.1) or (2.2) and may include provisions establishing the criteria to be considered when an exemption is made.

(3) **Restriction** — Refugee protection may not be conferred on an applicant who

(a) is determined to be inadmissible on grounds of security, violating human or international rights or organized criminality;

(b) is determined to be inadmissible on grounds of serious criminality with respect to a conviction in Canada of an offence under an Act of Parliament punishable by a maximum term of imprisonment of at least 10 years or with respect to a conviction outside Canada for an offence that, if committed in Canada, would constitute an offence under an Act of Parliament punishable by a maximum term of imprisonment of at least 10 years;

(c) made a claim to refugee protection that was rejected on the basis of section F of Article 1 of the Refugee Convention; or

Proposed Amendment — 112(3)(c)

(c) made a claim to refugee protection that was rejected on the basis of section F of Article 1 of the Refugee Convention;

2010, c. 8, s. 15(5) [Not in force at date of publication.]

Proposed Addition — 112(3)(c.1)

(c.1) made an application for protection and the consideration of that application was transferred to the Minister under subsection (1.7); or

2010, c. 8, s. 15(5) [Not in force at date of publication.]

(d) is named in a certificate referred to in subsection 77(1).

[Editor's Note: S.C. 2001, c. 27, s. 199 provides that sections 112 to 114 of the Immigration and Refugee Protection Act, *S.C. 2001, c. 27 (the "new Act") apply to a redetermination of a decision set aside by the Federal Court with respect to an application for landing as a member of the post-determination refugee claimants in Canada class within the meaning of the* Immigration Regulations, 1978, SOR/78-172.

SOR/2002-227, s. 346(1) provides that an application for landing as a member of the post-determination refugee claimants in Canada class in respect of which no determination of whether the applicant is a member of that class was made before June 28, 2002 is an application for protection under sections 112 to 114 of the new Act and those sections apply to the application.

SOR/2002-227, s. 346(2) provides that before a decision is made on the application, the applicant shall be notified that he or she may make additional submissions in support of his or her application.

SOR/2002-227, s. 346(3) provides that a decision on the application shall not be made until 30 days after notification is given to the applicant.

SOR/2002-227, s. 346(4) provides that notification is given

(a) when it is given by hand to the applicant; or

(b) if it is sent by mail, seven days after the day on which it was sent to the applicant at the last address provided by him or her to the Department.]

2010, c. 8, s. 15(3), (4) [Amended 2012, c. 17, s. 60(2), (3).]; 2012, c. 17, ss. 38, 84(3); 2015, c. 3, s. 114

Case Law

Section 112(1)

Arango v. Canada (Minister of Citizenship and Immigration) (2015), 29 Imm. L.R. (4th) 215, 468 N.R. 197, *(sub nom. Gil Arango v. Canada (Minister of Citizenship and Immigration))* 2015 FCA 10, 2015 CarswellNat 51 — This was an appeal of a dismissal of an application for judicial review challenging a decision by a senior immigration officer rejecting the appellant's pre-removal risk assessment application. According to the affidavit of the officer, her initial decision rejecting the application was rendered on February 20, 2013. The appellant deposed that this decision was served on him on February 22, 2013. On February 28, 2013, supplemental reasons were provided dealing with the February 20th document package sent by the appellant to the officer. According to the officer's affidavit, she was unaware of the February 20th document package until her return to the office on February 28. The appellant argued that the process filed by the officer was unfair, that she was *functus officio* after serving her initial decision in that she effectively usurped the jurisdiction of the Federal Court when she rendered supplemental reasons in the face of the application for judicial review which was filed on February 27, 2013.

The Federal Court found that the officer realized that her initial decision did not address all the submitted evidence. She considered the new evidence and found it was not persuasive. Her analysis of the new evidence was reasonable and could not be faulted. This was a valid exercise of the discretion to reconsider and not an illegitimate attempt to justify a poorly crafted decision. The application for judicial review was dismissed by the Federal Court. The Federal Court of Appeal dismissed the appeal and confirmed that a PRRA officer may revisit or reconsider a final decision for the appropriate circumstances because the doctrine of *functus officio* does not strictly apply in non-adjudicative administrative proceedings.

Zazai v. Canada (Minister of Citizenship & Immigration), 2012 FC 162, 2012 CarswellNat 428, 2012 CarswellNat 1046 — The applicant sought judicial review of an officer's decision that there were insufficient H&C grounds to warrant an exception allowing the applicant's permanent residence application to be made from within Canada. In assessing PRRA applications, officers must consider new, credible, relevant and material evidence of facts that might have affected the outcome of the applicant's refugee claim hearing if this evidence had been presented and thereby assess the risk against the country of removal. Conversely, when assessing H&C applications, officers must "have regard to public policy considerations and humanitarian grounds, including family-related interests." Compared to PRRA assessments, H&C assessments are a lower threshold and are not limited to specific parameters of persecution.

Due to these differences between the two processes, the officer's reliance in this case on a future PRRA assessment, and a "restricted" one at that, did not show how the best interests of the children would be considered prior to removal. Further, although the officer clearly stated that the best interests of the children were the most compelling H&C considerations in this case, her limited discussion on these interests did not meet the standard of examining them in great detail. The existence of a TRP that can be cancelled at any time did not remove the requirement to consider these interests thoroughly and carefully.

Although it was up to the officer to determine what weight to grant the best interests of the children, she did not conduct an adequate analysis of these interests before proceeding with the balancing exercise. The officer's reliance on a future restricted PRRA did not guarantee that these interests would be addressed prior to a future removal that remained a possibility due to the impermanent nature of TRPs. The application for judicial review was allowed.

Divakaran v. Canada (Minister of Citizenship & Immigration), 2011 CarswellNat 2079, 2011 FC 633 — The applicant sought judicial review of two decisions by a pre-removal risk assessment officer wherein the officer refused the applicant's application under subs. 25(1) of the Act to have his application for permanent residence processed from within Canada on H&C grounds, and the officer determined that the applicant would not be subject to risk of persecution, torture, risk to life or risk of cruel and unusual treatment or punishment, if he returned to Sri Lanka.

The Federal Court of Appeal and the Federal Court have both held that a series of discriminatory events that individually do not give rise to persecution may amount to persecution when considered cumulatively. The officer failed to consider cumulative persecution. For example, in the H&C decision, the officer accepted that the applicant may have to register with police and be questioned by state security agencies if he wishes to reside in Colombo, or, if he resides in Jaffna, the applicant might be required to proceed through security checkpoints and register with the police. These findings of facts were absent from the PRRA decision. As both decisions were made on the same day by the same officer, these findings should have formed part of the PRRA decision and the officer should have assessed whether the applicant would face more than a mere possibility of persecution on the basis of these discriminatory actions. The application for judicial review for both the PRRA and H&C applications was allowed. If the PRRA is faulty, then the same would follow for the H&C.

Krohmalnik v. Canada (Minister of Citizenship & Immigration), 2009 CarswellNat 1635, 2009 FC 589 — The applicant sought judicial review of a negative decision made in relation to her application for a pre-removal risk assessment. It is clearly the role of the PRRA officer to weigh the available information relating to the issues of risk and the availability of state protection. However, where, as here, there is important evidence that runs directly contrary to the officer's finding on a central issue, there is an obligation on the officer to analyze that evidence, and to explain why he or she prefers other evidence on the point in question. The failure of the officer to do so means that the decision lacks the justification, transparency and intelligibility required of a reasonable decision. The application for judicial review was allowed.

Perez v. Canada (Minister of Citizenship & Immigration) (2009), 82 Imm. L.R. (3d) 167, 393 N.R. 332, 2009 FCA 171, 2009 CarswellNat 1522, 2009 CarswellNat 5164, [2009] F.C.J. No. 691 — This is an appeal from a decision of Justice Martineau dated May 26, 2008 wherein he dismissed the appellants' application for judicial review of a pre-removal risk assessment officer's decision on the ground that the matter was moot because the appellant was no longer in Canada. The Court further held that it would not exercise its discretion to hear the judicial review. After having sought, without success, to stay the removal order issued subsequent to the negative decision of the PRRA officer, the appellant returned to Mexico. Subsequently, leave to seek judicial review of the decision of the PRRA officer was granted. Justice Martineau dismissed the application on the grounds of mootness, applying the decision in *Borowski v. Canada (Attorney General)*, [1989] 1 S.C.R 342. The Federal Court of Appeal agreed with Justice Martineau that the judicial review was moot.

Parliament intended that the PRRA should be determined before the PRRA applicant was removed from Canada, to avoid putting her or him at risk in her or his country of origin. To this extent, if a PRRA applicant is removed from Canada before a determination is made on the risks to which the person would be subject to in her or his country of origin, the intended objective of the PRRA system cannot be met. This explains why s. 112 of the Act specifies that a person applying for protection is a "person in Canada."

By the same logic, a review of a negative decision of a PRRA officer after the subject person has been removed from Canada, is without object. The appeal was dismissed.

Oshurova c. Canada (Ministre de la Citoyenneté & de l'Immigration), 2006 CarswellNat 5301, 2006 FCA 301 — The Federal Court of Appeal was asked to answer whether there was an appearance of bias, *in this case*, because the same officer decided the application for a visa exemption on humanitarian and compassionate grounds as well as the pre-removal risk assessment.

There is no apprehension of institutional bias of all officers who have been or are involved with these two types of applications. The appeal was dismissed.

Varga v. Canada (Minister of Citizenship & Immigration) (2006), 57 Imm. L.R. (3d) 159, 357 N.R. 333, 277 D.L.R. (4th) 762, 2006 CarswellNat 4183, 2006 FCA 394, [2006] F.C.J. No. 1828 — A PRRA officer has no obligation to consider, in the context of the PRRA, the interests of a Canadian-born child when assessing the risks involved in removing at least one of the parents of that child.

Ragupathy v. Canada (Minister of Public Safety & Emergency Preparedness) (2006), 58 Imm. L.R. (3d) 101, 2006 CarswellNat 3734, 2006 FC 1370 — The applicant was a Convention refugee and became a permanent resident of Canada. He then became inadmissible on grounds of serious criminality within the meaning of s. 36 of the IRPA. The Minister's delegate issued an opinion concluding that the applicant was a danger to the public in Canada (the danger opinion). The applicant was subject to removal from Canada under para. 115(2)(a) of the Act. The enforcement officer had discretion to defer the applicant's removal. The enforcement officer stated in her affidavit that the reason for not deferring removal was because there was no specific reason to do so. The enforcement officer also stated that she relied on the risk assessment provided by the Minister's delegate in the danger opinion. Both statements indicated that the enforcement officer was not alert and alive to the possibility that the alleged change in country conditions gave rise to an enhanced risk of torture or persecution upon the applicant's return to Sri Lanka. By relying on the existing risk assessment pre-dating the events identified by the applicant in his request for deferral, the enforcement officer failed to acknowledge the basis for the applicant's concern. The applicant was entitled to an updated risk assessment before removal. Recognizing an applicant's right under s. 7 of the *Charter* to a risk assessment before removal requires that the risk assessment occur proximate in time to the removal and is not incompatible with the need for finality in the system. Whatever the period of delay between the issuance of a danger opinion and the scheduled removal, the onus is on the applicant to demonstrate that there has been a material change in circumstances warranting a re-assessment of his risk upon removal. If an enforcement officer declines to exercise the discretion to defer the removal of a deportee pending re-assessment, a judicial stay of the removal order will only be granted where the deportee can satisfy the well-established tri-partite test. The requirements of a serious issue, irreparable harm and the balance of convenience are appropriate safeguards to ensure that vexatious attempts to forestall removal are dealt with accordingly.

The applicant was entitled to an updated risk assessment in light of the considerable passage of time since the issuance of the danger opinion. The application for judicial review was allowed in part. The enforcement officer was correct in determining that the applicant was not eligible for a PRRA under subs. 112(1) of the Act. However, the enforcement officer erred in declining to suspend the applicant's removal pending a re-assessment of the risk faced by him on removal in light of the significant change of circumstances alleged by the applicant.

Qazi v. Canada (Minister of Citizenship & Immigration), 2005 FC 1667, 2005 CarswellNat 4129, 2005 CarswellNat 5566, [2005] F.C.J. No. 2069 — The question of when a PRRA becomes unreasonably stale is not solely dependent on the length of time that has passed, but also depends on the applicant establishing that he has been prejudiced by the delay. In this case, nearly two years had elapsed from the time the applicant replied to the negative risk assessment. While the delay was unfortunate, nevertheless there was no evidence that the applicant had been prejudiced by it. The court concluded that he had not been denied procedural fairness or natural justice.

Say v. Canada (Solicitor General), 2005 CarswellNat 1510, 2005 FC 739 — This application raised the issue of institutional bias or lack of independence on the part of PRRA assessment officers during the period from December 12, 2003 to October 8, 2004 when such officers were situated, in an organizational sense, within the Canada Border Services Agency. The pre-removal risk assessment program was first created on the coming into force of the *Immigration and Refugee Protection Act* on the 28th of June, 2002.

The policy basis for assessing risk prior to removal is found in Canada's domestic and international commitments to the principle of non-refoulement. This principle holds that persons should not be removed from Canada to a country where they would be at risk of persecution, torture, risk to life or risk of cruel and unusual treatment or punishment. Such commitments require that risk be reviewed prior to removal.

While a first-time application for a pre-removal risk assessment is being reviewed and assessed, a statutory stay of removal is in effect by virtue of s. 232 of the IRPA Regulations.

The Canada Border Services Agency was created within the Canadian Public Service on the 12th of December, 2003. On that same day, control and supervision of pre-removal risk assessments was transferred to the agency. On the 8th of October 2004, control and supervision of pre-removal risk assessments was transferred back to the Department of Citizenship and Immigration. The fact that the government, within 10 months of transferring the PRRA program from the Department of Citizenship and Immigration to the CBSA, determined to transfer it back because it concluded the function was more in the nature of a protection function than an enforcement and removal function, does not lead to a presumption that while the program was with CBSA, it was subject to institutional bias. Accordingly, the application for judicial review was dismissed.

Thamotharampillai v. Canada (Solicitor General), 2005 CarswellNat 1503, 2005 FC 756 — A judicial review application directed against a negative PRRA decision is moot where the applicant for judicial review has been removed from Canada following a finding by a judge that the applicant is not entitled to a stay of removal by reason that he or she has failed to meet the "irreparable harm" element of the test for a stay.

Ratnasingham v. Canada (Minister of Citizenship & Immigration), 2005 CarswellNat 1504, 2005 FC 740 — This was an application to review a decision of a pre-removal risk assessment officer. The analysis of the officer of the impact of changed country conditions is extensive and detailed. The failure, however, to in any way relate that analysis to the risk of forced recruitment of the children by the Tamil Tigers amounts to a reviewable error. The court was satisfied that the deference owed to a PRRA officer was minimal. The decision of the officer was set aside.

Hausleitner v. Canada (Minister of Citizenship & Immigration), 2005 CarswellNat 1202, 2005 FC 641 — The risk assessment to be carried out at the PRRA stage is not to be a reconsideration of the Board's decision, but instead, is limited to an evaluation of new evidence that either arose after the applicant's refugee hearing or was not previously reasonably available to the applicant. An extensive risk assessment should be carried out where a PRRA applicant has not already had their claim to be at risk assessed by the Refugee Protection Division.

Rasiah v. Canada (Minister of Citizenship & Immigration), 2005 CarswellNat 1073, 2005 FC 583 — The purpose of a PRRA application is to assess whether the applicant is in need of protection in Canada because removal to her country of nationality would subject her personally to a danger of torture, a risk to her life or a risk of cruel and unusual treatment or punishment. The PRRA officer should focus the assessment on risk, and not whether the applicant has the personal financial resources to care for herself, if she is removed from Canada.

Sherzady v. Canada (Minister of Citizenship & Immigration), 2005 CarswellNat 971, 2005 FC 516 — A pre-removal risk assessment officer has the delegated authority to decide a properly constituted H&C application. However, when a person applies for a PRRA and appends a request for H&C consideration, without making the H&C application through the appropriate channels, it does not follow that the PRRA officer must consider H&C factors.

Vasquez v. Canada (Minister of Citizenship & Immigration), 2005 CarswellNat 89, 2005 FC 91, [2005] F.C.J. No. 96 — This was an application for a judicial review of the decision of the PRRA officer. The officer had no duty to disclose the analysis of the risk of return and to give the applicant an opportunity to make comments before reaching a final decision because the same officer is making both the PRRA risk assessment and the H&C decision.

Canada (Minister of Citizenship & Immigration) v. Jaballah (2004), 38 Imm. L.R. (3d) 157, 2004 CarswellNat 3451, 2004 CarswellNat 2123, (sub nom. *Jaballah, Re)* 325 N.R. 90, 242 D.L.R. (4th) 490, 2004 FCA 257 — This was an appeal by the Minister from a decision of the designated judge that the delay by the MCI in deciding the protection application constituted an abuse of process. A protection application involves two risk assessments. One relates to the risk faced by the individual if removed from Canada, and the other assesses the risk the individual poses to the security of Canada. Based on these two assessments and any submissions made by the individual, the Minister decides the protection application.

The decision of the designated judge, made in the course of security certificate proceedings under ss. 78 and 80, is not a judicial review and therefore para. 74(d) of IRPA is not applicable.

A decision by a designated judge made under s. 80 is subject to the privative clause in subs. 80(3). The finding that the MCI's delay in deciding the application for protection constituted an abuse of process is not protected from review.

Pursuant to s. 112, a person named in a security certificate may make an application for protection to the MCI. The application must be made before the certificate is determined to be reasonable. If the individual in question makes an application for protection, the designated judge is required to suspend the security certificate proceedings.

In remedying abuses of their process, courts are to be flexible and provide a remedy that is suitable to the circumstances. The decision of how best to remedy an abuse is a discretionary one. An appellate court may only overturn such a decision if it reaches the clear conclusion that there has been a wrongful exercise of discretion.

Zamora v. Canada (Minister of Citizenship & Immigration) (2004), 41 Imm. L.R. (3d) 276, 2004 CarswellNat 5619, 2004 CarswellNat 3709, 260 F.T.R. 155 (Eng.), 2004 FC 1414 — The unilateral use of internet information by a PRRA officer is unfair unless the applicant has been given an opportunity to examine the material and make submissions respecting it.

Nosa v. Canada (Solicitor General) (2004), 41 Imm. L.R. (3d) 32, 2004 CarswellNat 5095, 2004 CarswellNat 3180, 2004 FC 1248 — On December 12, 2003, the Governor General-in-Council transferred various duties from the Minister of Citizenship and Immigration to the Canada Border Services Agency. A pre-removal risk assessment was one of these functions. The Canada Border Services Agency is presided over by the Solicitor General with the result that the style of cause in this matter was amended removing the Minister of Citizenship and Immigration and adding the Solicitor General of Canada.

This was an application to review a negative decision made by a pre-removal risk assessment officer. The applicant included in her submissions her husband's personal information form and the favourable determination that his refugee application had received from Canadian immigration. The applicant had taken the position with the PRRA officer that she faced persecution from this same group of people, namely the State Security Service. The officer's failure to consider and explain her analysis of this separate risk made her finding that the applicant had an IFA patently unreasonably. Accordingly, the officer's decision was set aside.

Harkat v. Canada (Minister of Citizenship & Immigration), 2004 CarswellNat 2870, 2004 CarswellNat 1957, *(*sub nom. *Harkat, Re)* 325 N.R. 298, 2004 FCA 244 — After a security certificate was issued against the appellant, he brought a motion requesting that the hearing into the reasonableness of the certificate be suspended pursuant to subs. 79(1) in order that he might make an application for protection under s. 112(1). The designated judge declined to suspend the proceedings into the reasonableness of the security certificate on the grounds that the appellant was not entitled to apply for protection under subs. 112(1) because he had already been determined to be a Convention refugee and therefore was already a protected person under subs. 95(2) of the Act. In the Court of Appeal's opinion the designated judge's decision in this regard was correct.

The appeal with respect to the second order, having to do with the production of a CSIS employee as a witness, was not pursued although the issue of whether there had been an abuse of process was left to the Court of Appeal for its decision. The Court of Appeal decided that there had been no abuse of process to this point in the proceedings against the appellant.

Singh (H.) v. Canada (Solicitor General), [2004] 3 F.C.R. 323, *(*sub nom. *Singh v. Canada (Minister of Citizenship & Immigration))* 39 Imm. L.R. (3d) 261, 248 F.T.R. 114, *(*sub nom. *Singh v. Canada (Minister of Citizenship & Immigration) (No. 2))* 117 C.R.R. (2d) 239, 2004 CarswellNat 2091, 2004 CarswellNat 549, 2004 FC 288 — A risk to life under s. 97 does not include having to assess whether there is appropriate health and medical care available in the country in question.

Pre-removal risk assessment officers do not have the jurisdiction to consider constitutional questions.

Sidhu v. Canada (Minister of Citizenship & Immigration), 2004 FC 39, 2004 CarswellNat 4182, 2004 CarswellNat 118, [2004] F.C.J. No. 30 — The standard of review to be applied to a pre-removal risk assessment officer's determination is one of reasonableness *simpliciter.*

Kaybaki v. Canada (Solicitor General), 2004 FC 32, 2004 CarswellNat 149, 2004 CarswellNat 5940, [2004] F.C.J. No. 27 — This was an application to review the decision of a pre-removal risk assessment officer. The decision of a PRRA officer is to be accorded deference since it involves findings of fact; however, the decision must be supported by the evidence. The presumption that the decision maker has considered all the evidence is a rebuttable one, and where the evidence in question is of significant probative value, the court can make a negative inference from the decision maker's failure to mention it.

Zolotareva v. Canada (Minister of Citizenship & Immigration) (2003), 241 F.T.R. 289, 2003 CarswellNat 3360, [2003] F.C.J. No. 1596, 2003 FC 1274, 2003 CarswellNat 5082 — The applicant sought to review a decision of a pre-removal risk assessment officer which found insufficient humanitarian and compassionate grounds to permit the applicant to remain. The officer has jurisdiction to make a determination under subs. 25(1). The officer had no duty to disclose the analysis of the risk of return and to give the applicant an opportunity to make comments before reaching a final decision. There is no obligation on the PRRA officer to do so where there is no third party involved in the decision making.

Section 112(2)

Atawnah v. Canada (Minister of Public Safety and Emergency Preparedness) (2016), 39 Imm. L.R. (4th) 173, 397 D.L.R. (4th) 177, 483 N.R. 219, 2016 FCA 144, 2016 CarswellNat 1459; notice of appeal filed (August 8, 2016), Doc. 37122 (S.C.C.) — The applicant and three of her children are citizens of Israel who sought refugee protection in Canada. Their refugee claims were never decided on their merits because the Refugee Protection Division declared their claims to be abandoned. As a result of this declaration, the appellants were unable to obtain a pre-removal risk assessment; para. 112(2)(b.1) of IRPA precludes access to the PRRA process by individuals from designated countries of origin who have abandoned their refugee claim until 36 months pass from the date the refugee claim is declared to be abandoned. The appellants moved in the Federal Court for declaratory relief, arguing that both their removal from Canada without a full risk assessment being conducted by a competent decision maker in accordance with the principles of fundamental justice and para. 112(2)(b.1) of the Act violated rights guaranteed to them under s. 7 of the Charter. The Federal Court dismissed the application and the appellant sought to appeal the decision. The appeal was dismissed and the Federal Court of Appeal concluded that the prohibition contained in s. 112(2)(b.1) of IRPA against bringing a PRRA application until 36 months had passed since the claim for refugee protection was abandoned, did not violate s. 7 of the Charter.

Section 112(3)

Liu v. Canada (Minister of Citizenship & Immigration) (2009), 83 Imm. L.R. (3d) 228, 353 F.T.R. 132 (Eng.), 2009 FC 877, 2009 CarswellNat 2750, 2009 CarswellNat 4523, [2009] F.C.J. No. 1110 — This was an application for judicial review of a decision of a Minister's delegate refusing the applicant's pre-removal risk assessment decision. The PRRA officer concluded that the applicant was a person described under Article 1F(b) of the Convention based on an analysis of the criminal charges against him. The charges include: criminal fraud in China; immigration fraud in the United States of America; criminal fraud in the US; and immigration fraud in Canada. However, the PRRA officer concluded that "if the applicant is returned to China he will more likely than not be at risk of cruel or unusual treatment or punishment due to his being denied his right to a fair trial guaranteed under the *Universal Declaration of Human Rights and the International Covenant on Civil Political Rights*." The Minister's delegate disagreed with the assessment and concluded that there were no humanitarian and compassionate grounds to consider in this matter.

The applicant says that the decision is wrong because there is no basis in the Act or the Regulations that allows a PRRA officer to consider a claim for refugee protection and reject it on the basis of section F of Article 1 of the Convention. The applicant imposed upon the PRRA officer a full consideration of his ss. 96 and 97 rights without the benefit of a determination by the RPD. The Act appears to contemplate this alternative approach, but it was the applicant's choice to use the PRRA system and was not something that was forced upon him. He was not made to relinquish rights and safeguards he would otherwise have had. He then argued that since the PRRA officer made a positive risk assessment under s. 97, the effect of that decision was to confer refugee protection on him by virtue of subs. 114(1) of the Act. The court concluded it was not Parliament's intent to provide a means for a claimant to bypass the RPD and to have his or her ss. 96 and 97 rights considered *de novo* by the PRRA officer, without any reference to serious criminality and 1F(b) of the Convention. Neither the PRRA officer nor the delegate acted without jurisdiction or committed an error of law in their determination of the applicant's claim insofar as it related to serious criminality outside of Canada in the Article 1F(b) exclusion issue. The application for judicial review was dismissed. The following questions were certified:

> Do pre-removal risk assessment officers have the jurisdiction to exclude persons from refugee protection under s. 98 of IRPA and find them described in s. 112(3)(c) of IRPA?

> Does s. 112(3)(c) of the IRPA only apply to rejections by the Refugee Protection Division on the basis of section F of Article 1 of the *Refugee Convention* or does it apply to rejections by pre-removal risk assessment officers on the basis of section F of Article 1 of the *Refugee Convention*?

Sogi v. Canada (Minister of Citizenship & Immigration) (2004), 254 F.T.R. 129, 2004 CarswellNat 1908, 2004 FC 853 — The Minister's delegate denied an application made by the applicant for protection under s. 112 of IRPA. The applicant claimed refugee status; however, he became the subject of a report under subs. 44(1) of IRPA. This report led to an admissibility hearing where a decision was made that the applicant was inadmissible because he was a member of a Sikh terrorist organization.

Since the applicant was found to be inadmissible, two assessments were prepared pursuant to subs. 172(2). The first was a pre-removal risk assessment. The PRRA was conducted under paragraphs 112(3)(a) and 113(d)(ii) of IRPA. These paragraphs provide that applicants who were inadmissible on security grounds will have their PRRA applications considered based only on the factors in s. 97 of IRPA. The PRRA concluded that the applicant would be at risk of torture if deported to India. There was a second assessment which determined that the applicant represented a present and future danger to the security of Canada. The Minister's delegate balanced these two assessments, decided to deport the applicant to India, despite the likelihood that the applicant would be tortured.

Canadian jurisprudence does not suggest that Canada may never deport a person to face treatment elsewhere that would be unconstitutional if imposed by Canada directly, on Canadian soil.

The Minister's delegate erred in determining that the applicant should be deported. The decision did not address any alternatives to deportation to torture. A decision to deport to torture must consider, in the balancing exercise, any alternatives proposed to reduce the threat.

In the circumstances of this case, it was patently unreasonable to decide to deport the applicant without considering the applicant's proposal to observe curfews, reporting requirements and wear a tracking device.

Xie v. Canada (Minister of Citizenship & Immigration) (2004), 37 Imm. L.R. (3d) 163, 2004 CarswellNat 2036, 2004 CarswellNat 3972, 325 N.R. 255, [2005] 1 F.C.R. 304, 243 D.L.R. (4th) 385, 2004 FCA 250, [2004] F.C.J. No. 1142; leave to appeal refused 2005 CarswellNat 748, 2005 CarswellNat 749 (S.C.C.) — The appellant is a citizen of the People's Republic of China where she was a senior official in the Guangzhou Commission for Foreign Economic Relations and Trade. She fled China and arrived in Canada in 2001 and made a claim for refugee protection. In the course of processing her claim, two facts emerged. The first was that the appellant and her daughter had to their names bank accounts containing $2.7 million dollars. Second was, at the request of the Chinese authorities, an international warrant for the arrest of the appellant and a charge of embezzlement. On the basis of the appellant's unexplained wealth, the Board applied the exclusion in Article 1(F)(b) of the Convention. The Board also decided that, in light of the offence with which the appellant was charged, she faced a risk of torture at the hands of the Chinese authorities if she were to return to China.

The Board was entitled to presume that the warrant for the appellant's arrest was issued in the belief that she was guilty of misconduct. The presumption of innocence does not apply so as to prevent the Board from taking the Chinese State's belief in the appellant's guilt into account in deciding if there are serious reasons to consider that she committed the crime with which she is charged. There are three ways in which refugee protection can be obtained. Refugee protection is extended to persons falling within the definition of Convention refugee which has not been changed by the new Act. Refugee protection is also extended to those persons who are found to be in the need of protection, a class defined by the risk of harm as opposed to the motivation of those inflicting harm. The grounds upon which such an application can be made are found in s. 97 and include those who are in "danger, believed on substantial grounds to exist, of torture within the meaning of Article 1 of the Convention Against Torture." Finally, a person can be extended refugee protection by means of an application for protection pursuant to s. 112 of the Act. Persons facing deportation may apply to the Minister for protection on the basis that they face a risk of harm if they return to their country of origin. If the application for protection is granted, such persons acquire refugee protection pursuant to para. 95(1)(c) of the Act. Subsection 112(3) of the Act lists those persons who are ineligible for refugee protection including persons who are described in Article 1, Section F of the Convention. The exclusion from refugee protection is not an exclusion from protection altogether. Section 113 stipulates that persons described in 112(3) are to have their applications for protection decided on the basis of the factors set out in s. 97 with additional consideration given to the issue of whether such persons are a danger to the public in Canada or to the security of Canada. For all except those described in subs. 112(3), a successful application for protection results in the grant of refugee protection in the status of protected person. For persons described in subs. 112(3) the result is a stay of the deportation order in force against them. One consequence of the distinction is that protected persons have access to the status of permanent residence and are subject to the principle of non-refoulement.

Thus, the structure of the Act has two streams, claims for refugee protection and claims for protection in the context of pre-removal risk assessments. The person who is excluded from refugee protection is eligible to apply for protection at the PRRA stage. The basis on which the claim for protection may be advanced is the same, but the Minister can have regard to whether the granting of protection would affect the safety of the public or the security of Canada. If protection is granted, the result is a stay of the deportation order.

The claimant does not have the same access to permanent resident status as does a successful claimant for refugee protection.

Once a panel of the Refugee Protection Division found that the appellant was excluded pursuant to Section F of Article 1, it had done everything that it was required to do. The appellant was thereby excluded from refugee protection, a matter within the Board's confidence, and was limited to applying for protection, a matter within the Minister's jurisdiction. Accordingly, the Board's conclusions as to the appellant's risk of torture were gratuitous and were an infringement upon the Minister's responsibilities.

113. Consideration of application — Consideration of an application for protection shall be as follows:

(a) an applicant whose claim to refugee protection has been rejected may present only new evidence that arose after the rejection or was not reasonably available, or that the applicant could not reasonably have been expected in the circumstances to have presented, at the time of the rejection;

Proposed Amendment — 113(a)

(a) an applicant whose claim for refugee protection or whose most recent application for protection, as the case may be, has been rejected may present only evidence that arose after the rejection or was not reasonably available, or that the applicant could not reasonably have been expected in the circumstances to have presented, at the time of the rejection;

2010, c. 8, s. 16 [Not in force at date of publication.]

(b) a hearing may be held if the Minister, on the basis of prescribed factors, is of the opinion that a hearing is required;

Proposed Amendment — 113(b)

(b) in the case of an applicant described in subsection 112(3), a hearing may be held if the Minister, on the basis of prescribed factors, is of the opinion that a hearing is required;

2010, c. 8, s. 16 [Not in force at date of publication.]

Proposed Addition — 113(b.1)–(b.3)

(b.1) subject to paragraphs (a) and (b.3), in the case of an applicant not described in subsection 112(3), the Refugee Protection Division must proceed without a hearing and may accept documentary evidence and written submissions from the Minister and the applicant;

(b.2) in the case of an applicant not described in subsection 112(3), paragraph (a) does not apply in respect of evidence that is presented in response to evidence presented by the Minister;

(b.3) in the case of an applicant not described in subsection 112(3), the Refugee Protection Division may hold a hearing if, in its opinion, there is documentary evidence referred to in paragraph (b.1)

(i) that raises a serious issue with respect to the credibility of the applicant,

(ii) that is central to the decision with respect to the application, and

441

(iii) that, if accepted, would justify allowing the application;

2010, c. 8, s. 16 [Not in force at date of publication.]

(c) in the case of an applicant not described in subsection 112(3), consideration shall be on the basis of sections 96 to 98;

(d) in the case of an applicant described in subsection 112(3) — other than one described in subparagraph (e)(i) or (ii) — consideration shall be on the basis of the factors set out in section 97 and

(i) in the case of an applicant for protection who is inadmissible on grounds of serious criminality, whether they are a danger to the public in Canada, or

(ii) in the case of any other applicant, whether the application should be refused because of the nature and severity of acts committed by the applicant or because of the danger that the applicant constitutes to the security of Canada; and

(e) in the case of the following applicants, consideration shall be on the basis of sections 96 to 98 and subparagraph (d)(i) or (ii), as the case may be:

(i) an applicant who is determined to be inadmissible on grounds of serious criminality with respect to a conviction in Canada punishable by a maximum term of imprisonment of at least 10 years for which a term of imprisonment of less than two years — or no term of imprisonment — was imposed, and

(ii) an applicant who is determined to be inadmissible on grounds of serious criminality with respect to a conviction of an offence outside Canada that, if committed in Canada, would constitute an offence under an Act of Parliament punishable by a maximum term of imprisonment of at least 10 years, unless they are found to be a person referred to in section F of Article 1 of the Refugee Convention.

[Editor's Note: S.C. 2001, c. 27, s. 199 provides that sections 112 to 114 of the Immigration and Refugee Protection Act, *S.C. 2001, c. 27 (the "new Act") apply to a redetermination of a decision set aside by the Federal Court with respect to an application for landing as a member of the post-determination refugee claimants in Canada class within the meaning of the* Immigration Regulations, 1978, *SOR/78-172.*

SOR/2002-227, s. 346(1) provides that an application for landing as a member of the post-determination refugee claimants in Canada class in respect of which no determination of whether the applicant is a member of that class was made before June 28, 2002 is an application for protection under sections 112 to 114 of the new Act and those sections apply to the application.

SOR/2002-227, s. 346(2) provides that before a decision is made on the application, the applicant shall be notified that he or she may make additional submissions in support of his or her application.

SOR/2002-227, s. 346(3) provides that a decision on the application shall not be made until 30 days after notification is given to the applicant.

SOR/2002-227, s. 346(4) provides that notification is given

(a) when it is given by hand to the applicant; or

(b) if it is sent by mail, seven days after the day on which it was sent to the applicant at the last address provided by him or her to the Department.]

2012, c. 17, s. 39

Case Law

Aboud v. Canada (Minister of Citizenship and Immigration), 2014 FC 1019, 2014 CarswellNat 4156, 2014 CarswellNat 5198 — The PRRA officer determined the applicant would not be subject to risk of persecution, torture, risk to life or risk of cruel and unusual treatment or punishment if returned to Somalia, on the basis that the applicant had not proven his country of nationality or his identity. In making this decision, the PRRA officer concluded that much of the material submitted by the applicant was not new evidence and therefore not admissible before him.

When assessing whether evidence satisfies the newness requirement, the date on which it was created is not determinative; rather, what is important is the event or circumstance sought to be proved by the documentary evidence. The onus to produce acceptable documentation establishing a claimant's identity is on the claimant him- or herself. Whether owing to a lack of diligent effort or to strategic choices, the applicant failed to produce evidence capable of establishing his identity before the RPD. This is critical as well as basic. Having counsel now that is better able or willing to track down persons to make statutory declarations, affidavits, linguistics reports, etc. is not a compelling argument that this evidence should have been admissible before the PRRA officer. The court concluded that the decision to reject evidence that was not available or reasonably available at the time of the RPD hearing but was available or reasonably available at the time of the applicant's first PRRA application was reasonable. A prior PRRA meets the statutory language of subs. 113(a) of IRPA: it is a "claim to refugee protection [that] has been rejected." Accordingly, subs. 113(a) can be used to limit the admissibility of evidence submitted to a subsequent PRRA application.

In addition to determining that the applicant had not adduced new admissible evidence, the PRRA officer also conducted alternative analyses regarding the probative value of the information. The court concluded that the PRRA officer's decision fell within the range of possible acceptable outcomes that were defensible on the facts and law. The burden was on the applicant to establish, on a balance of probabilities, that the PRRA officer's decision was not reasonable. The application for judicial review was dismissed.

Chen v. Canada (Minister of Citizenship & Immigration), 2009 CarswellNat 973, 2009 FC 379 — The applicant sought judicial review of a decision of a pre-removal risk assessment officer. The basis of the officer's decision appears to be that nothing submitted with the PRRA application changed what the Refugee Protection Division decided. However, the PRRA officer did proceed further because she recognized an obligation to go beyond the applicant's evidence and review country condition documents. The officer was correct to conclude that, notwithstanding the continuing identity problems, she was still obliged to assess risk against the country of removal. The failure to establish identity means that there is no need to proceed further with an analysis of persecution. This does not mean that the PRRA officer need not go further in assessing risk if identity is a continuing problem. In this case the officer proceeded beyond the identity issue. That being the case, the officer's analysis of the country conditions documents was inadequate. There was reliable documentation before the officer of the torture mistreatment of Falun Gong supporters in China that was not referred to and that directly contradicted the of-years, the order of surrender is deemed to be a rejection of a claim for refugee protection based on paragraph (b) of Section F of Article 1 of the Refugee Convention.

(4) **Final decision** — The deemed rejection referred to in subsection (3) may not be appealed, and is not subject to judicial review except to the extent that a judicial review of the order of surrender is provided for under the *Extradition Act*.

(5) **Limit if no previous claim** — If the person has not made a claim for refugee protection before the order of surrender referred to in subsection (3), the person may not do so before the surrender.

Claimant Without Identification

106. **Credibility** — The Refugee Protection Division must take into account, with respect to the credibility of a claimant, whether the claimant possesses acceptable documentation establishing identity, and if not, whether they have provided a reasonable explanation for the lack of documentation or have taken reasonable steps to obtain the documentation.

Case Law

Flores v. Canada (Minister of Citizenship & Immigration), 2005 CarswellNat 2332, 2005 FC 1138 — The applicant claimed refugee protection in Canada, but a panel of the Immigration and Refugee Board dismissed his claim because it felt he had not provided acceptable evidence of identity. On the day of his hearing, the applicant provided two documents he hoped would constitute good evidence of his identity and nationality. The first was a photocopy of one page of a Salvadoran passport. The second was a faxed copy of a birth certificate. The Board found that the applicant had failed to prove his identity and, therefore, that it was unnecessary to consider the merits of the claim. The Board stated that it "rejected" the applicant's identity documents for the following reasons: the photocopy of the passport did not resemble the applicant; the documents were mere photocopies; the originals were not available, and the applicant could not provide a reasonable explanation why he could not get them; the applicant had nearly a year between making his refugee claim and the date of his hearing to obtain acceptable identity documents; the documents were filed very late, on the date of the hearing; and the applicant claimed to have spent a period of time in the United States but, without a complete passport, it was impossible to verify the duration of his stay there. Since the Board did not reject the documents solely because they were photocopies, its decision was not out of keeping with the requirements of the IRPA or the Rules.

Rasheed v. Canada (Minister of Citizenship & Immigration) (2004), 251 F.T.R. 258, 35 Imm. L.R. (3d) 299, 2004 CarswellNat 1086, 2004 FC 587, 2004 CarswellNat 4478, [2004] F.C.J. No. 715 — The determination made by a panel with respect to the identity of the applicant should be examined on the reasonableness *simpliciter* standard.

Gasparyan v. Canada (Minister of Citizenship & Immigration), 2003 FC 863, 2003 CarswellNat 2140, 2003 CarswellNat 5121, [2003] F.C.J. No. 1103 — The appropriate standard for reviewing the Refugee Division's assessment of identity documents is patent unreasonableness. The panel had firsthand access to the identity documents and the testimony of the applicants and also possesses a high level of expertise in this area.

ficer's conclusions. This means that important evidence was overlooked and the reasons do not provide an adequate assessment of that evidence. For these reasons, the decision was unreasonable. The application for judicial review was allowed and the matter returned for reconsideration.

Raza v. Canada (Minister of Citizenship & Immigration), 289 D.L.R. (4th) 675, 68 Admin. L.R. (4th) 225, 370 N.R. 344, [2007] F.C.J. No. 1632, 2007 CarswellNat 4905, 2007 FCA 385 — This was an appeal from a judgment ((2006), 304 F.T.R. 46) dismissing the appellants' application for judicial review of the decision of a pre-removal risk assessment officer, who rejected their application for protection under subs. 112(1) of the IRPA. The principal issue in this appeal is the interpretation of para. 113(a) of the IRPA.

Paragraph 113(a) deals with the circumstances in which a failed refugee claimant who makes a PRRA application may present evidence to the PRRA officer that was not before the refugee protection division ("RPD") of the Immigration and Refugee Board. A PRRA application is not an appeal or reconsideration of the decision of the RPD to reject a claim for refugee protection; nevertheless, it may require consideration of some or all of the same factual or legal issues as a claim for refugee protection. In such cases, there is an obvious risk of wasteful and potentially abusive relitigation. The IRPA mitigates that risk by limiting the evidence that may be presented to the PRRA officer. The limitation is found in para. 113(a).

Paragraph 113(a) is based on the premise that a negative refugee determination by the RPD must be respected by the PRRA officer, unless there is new evidence of facts that might have affected the outcome of the RPD hearing if the evidence had been presented to the RPD. Paragraph 113(a) asks a number of questions, some expressly and some by necessary implication, about the proposed new evidence. Those questions are summarized as follows:

1. *Credibility*: Is the evidence credible, considering its source and the circumstances in which it came into existence? If not, the evidence need not be considered.

2. *Relevance*: Is the evidence relevant to the PRRA application, in the sense that it is capable of proving or disproving a fact that is relevant to the claim for protection? If not, the evidence need not be considered.

3. *Newness*: Is the evidence new in the sense that it is capable of:

   (a) proving the current state of affairs in the country of removal or an event that occurred, or a circumstance that arose after the hearing in the RPD, or

   (b) proving a fact that was unknown to the refugee claimant at the time of the RPD hearing, or

   (c) contradicting a finding of fact by the RPD (including a credibility finding)?

   If not, the evidence need not be considered.

4. *Materiality*: Is the evidence material, in the sense that the refugee claim probably would have succeeded if the evidence had been made available to the RPD? If not, the evidence need not be considered.

5. *Express statutory conditions*:

   (a) If the evidence is capable of proving only an event that occurred or circumstances that arose prior to the RPD hearing, then has the applicant established either that the evidence was not reasonably available to him or her for presentation at the RPD hearing, or that he or she could not reasonably have been expected, in the circumstances, to have presented the evidence at the RPD hearing? If not, the evidence need not be considered.

(b) If the evidence is capable of proving an event that occurred or circumstances that arose after the RPD hearing, then the evidence must be considered (unless it is rejected because it is not credible, not relevant, not new or not material).

The first four questions, relating to credibility, relevance, newness and materiality, are necessarily implied from the purpose of para. 113(a) within the statutory scheme of the IRPA relating to refugee claims and pre removal risk assessments. The remaining questions are asked expressly by para. 113(a).

The questions listed above need not be asked in any particular order. It is not necessary that the PRRA officer ask each question. What is important is that the PRRA officer must consider all evidence that is presented, unless it is excluded on one of the grounds stated above.

In this case, the appellant and his family submitted a number of documents in support of their PRRA application. All of the documents were created after the rejection of their claim for refugee protection. The PRRA officer concluded that the information in the documents was essentially a repetition of the same information that was before the RPD. This conclusion was reasonable. The documents were not capable of establishing that state protection in Pakistan, which had been found by the RPD to be adequate, was no longer adequate as of the date of the PRRA application. Therefore, the proposed new evidence fails at the fourth question listed above.

The appeal was dismissed.

Elezi v. Canada (Minister of Citizenship & Immigration), 2007 CarswellNat 577, 2007 FC 240 — The applicant applied for refugee status after escaping Albania. His claim was dismissed. He applied for pre-removal risk assessment. A PRRA officer rejected his application. The applicant sought judicial review of the PRRA officer's decision. The proper standard of review for a PRRA decision, when considered globally and as a whole, is reasonableness. When assessing the issue of new evidence under subs. 113(a) of IRPA, two separate questions must be addressed. The first one is whether the officer erred in interpreting the section itself. This is a question of law, which must be reviewed against a standard of correctness. If he made no mistake interpreting the provision, the court must still determine whether he erred in his application of the section to the particular facts of the case. This is a question of mixed fact and law, to be reviewed on a standard of reasonableness. The applicant submitted to the PRRA officer various documents that predated the Board's decision. All of this evidence was obviously extremely probative, and to a large extent, refutes all of the Board's conclusions against the applicant. Had he submitted this evidence at his Board hearing, the Board may have written a very different decision. These documents did not raise any "new" risks, *per se*. The risks outlined were the same as those the applicant claimed during his hearing before the Board. It was not reasonable for the PRRA officer to exclude all these documents on that basis.

The nature of the information, its significance for the case, the credibility of its source, are all factors that can and should be taken into consideration in determining whether it can be considered "new evidence," when it appears to have been created after the Board's decision. The letters created after the Board's decision qualified as "new evidence." As for the evidence that predated the Board's decision, the PRRA officer erred in excluding it. The error related to the second and third branches of subs. 113(a). Not only were all these documents extremely helpful in assessing the applicant's claim but he could not reasonably have been expected, in the circumstances, to have presented them to the Board. The Board's hearing took place only three months after he arrived in Canada, and it does not require a stretch of the imagination to consider that this is not much time to gather that kind of evidence. The application for judicial review was granted. The court certified four questions:

1. Is "new evidence" for the purposes of s. 113(a) of the IRPA limited to evidence that postdates and is "substantially different" from the evidence that was before the RPD?

2. Does the standard for the reception of "new evidence" under s. 113(a) of the IRPA require the PRRA officer to accept any evidence created after the RPD determination, even where that evidence was reasonably available to the applicant or he/she could reasonably have been expected to present it at the refugee hearing?

3. In determining whether evidence has arisen after the Board rejects a refugee claim and is therefore "new," must the PRRA officer look only for new facts or new risks, or can he or she take into consideration other factors like the nature of the information, its significance for the case, and the credibility of its source?

4. In light of paragraphs 3(3)(d) and (f) of the IRPA, is the PRRA officer precluded from considering personalized evidence that goes to the heart of an applicant's claim and establishes that he would be at risk if returned, when that evidence could conceivably have been presented to the Board?

Sing v. Canada (Minister of Citizenship & Immigration), [2006] F.C.J. No. 851, 2006 CarswellNat 1420, 2006 FC 672 — The applicants were accused by the Chinese government of masterminding a massive smuggling and bribery operation. It wants the couple returned home to face prosecution for their alleged crimes. The applicants have consistently maintained that China has fabricated all the allegations against them. The applicants and their three children claimed refugee status. The Board found the parents were excluded from Convention refugee status under Article 1F(b) of the *United Nations Convention Relating to the Status of Refugees.* The Board also found the parents not to be Convention refugees because there was no nexus between their claims and any Convention refugee grounds. The Board described the couple as criminals fleeing from justice, not persecution. In their PRRA application, the applicants made submissions alleging bias, charter violations and breaches of procedural fairness. Their submissions on risk included a number of challenges to the Chinese legal system. They maintained the same theory raised at their Board hearing. They argued that they could not get a fair trial in China, and that they faced torture and the death penalty despite a diplomatic note from China assuring the contrary. After a probing review of their submissions, the PRRA officer rejected all of their claims.

The applicants' PRRA decision, although well reasoned and quite comprehensive in its assessment of the facts and of the submissions made by both counsel, was deficient in its assessment of the risk of torture. The application for judicial review was granted. The following questions were certified:

1. Where the Minister takes a public position on pre-removal risk to an applicant before a pre-removal risk assessment application is decided, is there a reasonable apprehension that the Minister's decision on pre-removal risk assessment application will be biased?

2. What is the appropriate standard of review for the interpretation of a diplomatic note providing assurances against the death penalty or the infliction of torture or other cruel or unusual treatment?

3. Is it appropriate to rely on assurances against torture in assessing an applicant's risk under s. 97 of the IRPA, when there are credible reports that torture prevails in the country where the applicant is to be removed? If so, under what circumstances?

4. If there is a risk of torture in an individual case, what are the requirements that an assurance against torture should fulfil to make that risk less likely than not? Should the assurance provide for monitoring to allow for verification of compliance for that assurance to be found reliable? In the absence of a monitoring mechanism, is the notoriety of the person to be removed a relevant, and a sufficient, consideration for the PRRA officer in determining whether it is more likely than not that the assuring state will adhere to the diplomatic assurance?

Jaballah v. Canada (Minister of Citizenship & Immigration), [2006] F.C.J. No. 747, 353 N.R. 6, (sub nom. *Jaballah, Re)* 2006 CarswellNat 1362, 2006 CarswellNat 2227, 2006 FCA 179 — A principle of international law acknowledged by a treaty to which Canada is a signatory, such as the prohibition against deportation to death or torture, may be relevant in interpretation of Canadian law, but it is not determinative of that interpretation unless it is specifically incorporated by legislation. The prohibition in this case is not expressly incorporated in the IRPA or other legislation.

Chudal v. Canada (Minister of Citizenship & Immigration), 2005 CarswellNat 2227, 2005 CarswellNat 4713, 2005 FC 1073 — A PRRA officer has an obligation to receive all evidence which may affect the decision until the time that such decision is made. It is reasonable to consider that such decision is not made until it has been written and signed and notice of the decision, even if not its contents, has been delivered to the applicant.

Bouttavong v. Canada (Minister of Citizenship & Immigration) (2005), 344 N.R. 134, 2005 CarswellNat 3527, 2005 CarswellNat 5559, 2005 FCA 341 — Former public danger opinions are irrelevant to the determination of danger to the public under subs. 113(d)(i). This does not mean that the underlying criminal convictions may not be taken into account, only that the danger opinions are irrelevant.

Jaballah, Re (2005), 44 Imm. L.R. (3d) 181, 2005 CarswellNat 754, 2005 FC 399 — This decision was the court's reasons for finding that the decision on behalf of the Minister on the application of protection by the applicant was not lawfully made. There was no question that the applicant faced a substantial risk of death or torture if he were returned to Egypt.

The Minister's delegate erred in law by undue reliance on certain matters, *i.e.* (1) an earlier decision by the court that the Minister's opinion was reasonable, a decision quashed by the Court of Appeal and (2) by failing to describe the danger to Canada's security that the applicant represented. Further, the delegate failed to consider as a factor the effect of the applicant's continued restraint, in one form or another, while he remains in Canada. Finally, the delegate failed to consider adequately the best interests of the applicant's children.

Mojzisik v. Canada (Minister of Citizenship & Immigration), [2004] F.C.J. No. 33, 40 Imm. L.R. (3d) 204, 245 F.T.R. 183, 2004 CarswellNat 68, 2004 CarswellNat 872, 2004 FC 48 — The applicant was denied refugee status under the former *Immigration Act*. He submitted a Post-Determination Refugee Claim In-Canada application which was converted to a pre removal risk assessment application on the coming into effect of the *Immi-*

gration and Refugee Protection Act. This application was dismissed and the applicant now sought to judicially review that refusal.

The PRRA is an innovation in the new Act which is designed to ensure that the vast majority of individuals facing removal from Canada are given a full but expedited chance to establish that they face a risk of torture or gross mistreatment on their return to a home country.

This case was caught in the transition from the former Act to the *Immigration and Refugee Protection Act.*

The definition of "new evidence" in the kit which accompanied the PRRA application form was woefully inadequate. The letter informing the applicant of the conversion of his application should have informed him that the PRRA officer now had additional authority to determine whether the applicant was in need of protection and that any evidence in that respect would qualify as new evidence and should be presented.

Proposed Addition — 113.1

113.1 Regulations — **The regulations may include provisions respecting the time limits for the making of a decision by the Refugee Protection Division with respect to an application for protection, the extension of those time limits and the circumstances in which they do not apply.**

2012, c. 17, s. 40 [Not in force at date of publication.]

114. (1) Effect of decision — A decision to allow the application for protection has

    (a) in the case of an applicant not described in subsection 112(3), the effect of conferring refugee protection; and

    (b) in the case of an applicant described in subsection 112(3), the effect of staying the removal order with respect to a country or place in respect of which the applicant was determined to be in need of protection.

(2) Cancellation of stay — **If the Minister is of the opinion that the circumstances surrounding a stay of the enforcement of a removal order have changed, the Minister may re-examine, in accordance with paragraph 113(d) and the regulations, the grounds on which the application was allowed and may cancel the stay.**

(3) Vacation of determination — **If the Minister is of the opinion that a decision to allow an application for protection was obtained as a result of directly or indirectly misrepresenting or witholding material facts on a relevant matter, the Minister may vacate the decision.**

(4) Effect of vacation — **If a decision is vacated under subsection (3), it is nullified and the application for protection is deemed to have been rejected.**

[Editor's Note: SOR/2002-227, s. 339 provides that a determination made in Canada before June 28, 2002 that a person is not a Convention refugee is deemed to be a claim for refugee protection rejected by the Immigration and Refugee Board.]

[Editor's Note: S.C. 2001, c. 27, s. 199 provides that sections 112 to 114 of the Immigration and Refugee Protection Act, *S.C. 2001, c. 27 (the "new Act") apply to a redetermination of a decision set aside by the Federal Court with respect to an application for*

landing as a member of the post-determination refugee claimants in Canada class within the meaning of the Immigration Regulations, 1978, *SOR/78-172.*

SOR/2002-227, s. 346(1) provides that an application for landing as a member of the post-determination refugee claimants in Canada class in respect of which no determination of whether the applicant is a member of that class was made before June 28, 2002 is an application for protection under sections 112 to 114 of the new Act and those sections apply to the application.

SOR/2002-227, s. 346(2) provides that before a decision is made on the application, the applicant shall be notified that he or she may make additional submissions in support of his or her application.

SOR/2002-227, s. 346(3) provides that a decision on the application shall not be made until 30 days after notification is given to the applicant.

SOR/2002-227, s. 346(4) provides that notification is given

(a) when it is given by hand to the applicant; or

(b) if it is sent by mail, seven days after the day on which it was sent to the applicant at the last address provided by him or her to the Department.]

Proposed Addition — 114.1

114.1 (1) Limitation — Subsections 114(3) and (4) apply in respect of a decision to allow an application for protection only if the application was made to the Minister under subsection 112(1.1) or transferred to the Minister under subsection 112(1.3) or (1.7).

(2) Application of section 109 — Section 109 applies to a decision made by the Refugee Protection Division to allow an application for protection as if it were a decision to allow a claim for refugee protection.

2010, c. 8, s. 16.1 [Not in force at date of publication.]

Principle of Non-refoulement

115. (1) Protection — A protected person or a person who is recognized as a Convention refugee by another country to which the person may be returned shall not be removed from Canada to a country where they would be at risk of persecution for reasons of race, religion, nationality, membership in a particular social group or political opinion or at risk of torture or cruel and unusual treatment or punishment.

(2) Exceptions — Subsection (1) does not apply in the case of a person

(a) who is inadmissible on grounds of serious criminality and who constitutes, in the opinion of the Minister, a danger to the public in Canada; or

(b) who is inadmissible on grounds of security, violating human or international rights or organized criminality if, in the opinion of the Minister, the person should not be allowed to remain in Canada on the basis of the nature and severity of acts committed or of danger to the security of Canada.

[Editor's Note: SOR/2002-227, s. 326(3) provides that a person whose removal on June 28, 2002 was allowed by the application of paragraphs 53(1)(a) to (d) of the former

Immigration Act, *R.S.C. 1985, c. I-2 is a person referred to in s. 115(2) of the new* Immigration and Refugee Protection Act, *S.C. 2001, c. 27.]*

(3) **Removal of refugee** — **A person, after a determination under paragraph 101(1)(e) that the person's claim is ineligible, is to be sent to the country from which the person came to Canada, but may be sent to another country if that country is designated under subsection 102(1) or if the country from which the person came to Canada has rejected their claim for refugee protection.**

Case Law

Section 115(2)

Canada (Minister of Public Safety & Emergency Preparedness) v. Samuels (2009), 85 Imm. L.R. (3d) 226, 2009 FC 1152, 2009 CarswellNat 5632, 2009 CarswellNat 3739 — This is an application by the Minister for judicial review of an order of a member of the Immigration Division to release the respondent from detention. The respondent was born in Panama but lived for 39 years in Jamaica. He is a citizen of both countries and came to Canada in 1991 and became a permanent resident. By September 1992, he was diagnosed as having schizophrenia. In total, the respondent has 27 or 30 criminal convictions, as well as over 10 provincial convictions. Following his last criminal conviction on March 14, 2005, he was immediately placed in immigration hold. He was released from immigration hold on October 12, 2006, under the Toronto Bail Program, for which he was supervised by Steven Sharp. Contrary to the terms of his release, the respondent repeatedly left his residence unescorted. Mr. Sharp was of the opinion that public safety would be a concern if the respondent remained in the community. The respondent was re-arrested and returned to immigration hold, remaining in detention ever since. A risk assessment officer reached a positive decision in June 2009 and the Minister then sought a danger opinion against the respondent, which would lead to his removal from Canada. Following the success of the PRRA application, the respondent sought to be released from detention. The member of the Immigration Division determined that while a danger opinion was being sought, it was likely to take a considerable time — and might yet turn out to be negative, so that it "wouldn't be fair" to keep the respondent in detention. Although the member noted that the respondent had "a pretty impressive criminal file," the member concluded that "if there's no removal in sight, the Immigration Division is not responsible to protect Canadian society anymore."

The court held that the Immigration Division had jurisdiction to order the respondent's continued detention if it was satisfied that he was a danger to the public. The court also found that the Immigration Division member failed to exercise its statutory duty, and quashed the decision to release the respondent. A removal order that is stayed is not void. Although it cannot be executed pending a ruling on a protected person's application for permanent residence, or the passing of the deadline to file such an application, it still exists and is valid and, in the opinion of the court, the person against whom it was issued is still "subject to it." Accordingly, the Immigration Division had jurisdiction to order the continued detention of the respondent, if it was satisfied that he was a danger to the public.

Villanueva Cruz v. Canada (Minister of Citizenship & Immigration) (2008), 78 Imm. L.R. (3d) 68, 2008 CarswellNat 5281, 2008 CarswellNat 4628, 2008 FC 1341 — The applicant was found to be a Convention refugee in 1999. He was subsequently convicted of trafficking in a controlled substance and sentenced to serve three years and 10 months.

A delegate of the Minister of Citizenship and Immigration determined that the applicant constituted a danger to the public in Canada pursuant to s. 115(2)(a) of the IRPA. The applicant sought judicial review of that decision.

The test to be used by the Minister in forming a danger opinion was summarized by Justice Strayer in *Williams v. Canada (Minister of Citizenship & Immigration)*, [1997] 2 F.C. 646 (C.A.) at para. 29:

> In the context the meaning of "public danger' is not a mystery: it must refer to the possibility that a person who has committed a serious crime in the past may seriously be thought to be a potential re-offender. It need not be proven — indeed it cannot be proven — that the person will reoffend. What I believe the subs. adequately focusses the Minister's mind on is consideration of *whether, given what she knows about the individual and what that individual has had to say in his own behalf, she can form an opinion in good faith that he is a possible re-offender whose presence in Canada creates an unacceptable risk to the public.*

Justice Beaudry offered further comments on this standard as it related to individuals convicted of narcotics-related offences in *Do v. Canada (Minister of Citizenship & Immigration)*, [2003] 2 F.C. 493 at paragraphs 42-43:

> This Court has consistently held, including in cases dealing with narcotics-related offences, that the mere fact of conviction on one or more criminal offences does not itself support a determination that a person is, may be, or is likely to pose a danger to the public, although some offences by their nature may be of a type that invite such conclusion: *Salilar v. Canada (Minister of Citizenship & Immigration)* [1995] 3 F.C. 150 at page 159 (T.D.); *Thai v. Canada (Minister [page 510] of Citizenship & Immigration)* (1998), 42 Imm. L.R. (2d) 28 at para. 16 (F.C.T.D.); *Tewelde v. Canada (Minister of Citizenship & Immigration)* (2000), 89 F.T.R. 206 (F.C.T.D.).

> Rather, in forming an opinion as to whether an individual constitutes a danger to the public, natural justice and procedural fairness require the Minister to take into account all of the relevant and particular circumstances of each case, and the circumstances of each case must, over and above the conviction, indicate a danger to the public: *Fairhurst v. Canada (Minister of Citizenship & Immigration)* (1996), 124 F.T.R. 142 at para. 10 (F.C.T.D.); *Thompson v. Canada (Minister of Citizenship & Immigration)* (1996), 41 Admin. L.R. (2d) 10 at para. 19 (F.C.T.D.).

The court concluded that the Minister's delegate misconstrued the evidence and did not have regard to the evidence before her. The application for judicial review was allowed.

Hasan v. Canada (Minister of Citizenship & Immigration) (2008), 75 Imm. L.R. (3d) 64, 180 C.R.R. 286, 2008 CarswellNat 3445, 2008 FC 1069 — The applicant was reported as an inadmissible permanent resident because of serious criminality pursuant to s. 44 of the IRPA. The Canadian Border Services Agency informed the applicant of their intention to seek the opinion, pursuant to s. 115(2)(a), from the Minister of Citizenship and Immigration that he was a danger to the public and, thus, could be returned to Iraq. There is no requirement in s. 115(2) that the Minister must assess the risk to the person who has been found to be a danger. That obligation arises from the operation of s. 7 of the Charter, as decided by the Supreme Court of Canada in *Suresh*, [2002] 1 S.C.R. 3. Thus, there is no parallel between the cessation provisions of s. 108, which explicitly require the Minister to demonstrate that the reasons for which the person sought refugee protection have ceased to exist, and s. 115, where the only obligation arises as a result of the Charter. The jurisprudence is clear that, once the applicant is found to be a danger to the public, he must establish that he would be at risk.

Therefore, the delegate did not erroneously place the onus on the applicant to prove that he faced the risk of torture or risk to life if returned to Iraq. The delegate properly engaged in an assessment of the current risks facing the applicant should he be removed to Iraq. The applicant was told that he could make written representations or arguments deemed necessary and relevant, including those related to whether his life or freedoms were threatened by removal from Canada. This was adequate notice to the applicant.

The applicant also argued that the delegate failed to have regard to the fact that the Minister had imposed a stay on removals to Iraq pursuant to s. 230 of the Regulations. Not only had the applicant not initially raised this argument in his submissions to the CBSA, but more importantly, the s. 230(1) moratorium does not apply to the applicant since s. 230(3) explicitly states that the stay under s. 230(1) does not apply to a person who is inadmissible on grounds of serious criminality or criminality. In this case, the applicant had been found to be inadmissible on grounds of serious criminality and he could not rely on the stay provisions of s. 230. The application for judicial review was dismissed.

Nagalingam v. Canada (Minister of Citizenship & Immigration) (2008), 292 D.L.R. (4th) 463, 70 Imm. L.R. (3d) 54, 2008 CarswellNat 1221, 2008 FCA 153 — In the preparation of an opinion under para. 115(2)(b) of the IRPA, where the Minister finds that a refugee who is inadmissible on grounds of organized criminality does not face a risk of persecution, torture, cruel and unusual punishment or treatment upon return to his country of origin, such a finding does not render the Minister's consideration of the "nature and severity of acts committed" under para. 115(2)(b) unnecessary.

The exception of para. 115(2)(b) regarding organized criminality will apply to a Convention refugee or a protected person if, in the opinion of the Minister, that person should not be allowed to remain in Canada on the basis of the nature and substantial gravity of acts committed (in the context of organized criminality) personally or through complicity, as defined by Canadian domestic laws, but established on a standard of reasonable grounds. In this case, the Delegate had to reasonably link the appellant to the acts of the organization in which he was a member, taking into consideration, if applicable, his role and responsibilities within the criminal organization. In doing so, the Delegate had to caution himself that it is only in exceptional cases that a Convention refugee or a protected person will lose the benefit of subs. 115(1). Only acts which are of substantial gravity will meet this high threshold. The appeal was allowed and the matter remitted back to the Delegate for re-determination.

Balathavarajan v. Canada (Minister of Citizenship & Immigration), [2006] F.C.J. No. 1550, 56 Imm. L.R. (3d) 1, 354 N.R. 320, 2006 CarswellNat 3297, 2006 FCA 340 — The court considered whether the IAD must consider hardship to a permanent resident who had been issued a deportation order, and who had been declared a Convention refugee, where the deportation order did not specify the country of removal, and where it is uncertain what that country might be. The Minister had not specified the country of deportation, and at the time of the IAD appeal had not taken the necessary steps under subs. 115(2) of the IRPA to remove the appellant. It was, at the time of the IAD appeal, not only unlikely but legally improper to remove the appellant to Sri Lanka. For the IAD to consider potential hardship the appellant might face if deported to Sri Lanka would have been a hypothetical and a speculative exercise. Therefore it did not need to do this. Accordingly, the certified question was answered in the negative by the Court of Appeal.

Section 173 of the IRPA permits the IAD to receive and base a decision on evidence adduced in immigration proceedings that it considers to be credible and trustworthy in the circumstances. It is up to the IAD, not the court, to decide the weight to be given to the evidence. Therefore the appellant also failed to demonstrate that the judge had committed a palpable and overriding error in upholding the IAD's decision. The appeal was dismissed.

Ragupathy v. Canada (Minister of Public Safety & Emergency Preparedness) (2006), 58 Imm. L.R. (3d) 101, 2006 CarswellNat 3734, 2006 FC 1370 — The applicant was a Convention refugee and became a permanent resident of Canada. He then became inadmissible on grounds of serious criminality within the meaning of s. 36 of the IRPA. The Minister's delegate issued an opinion concluding that the applicant was a danger to the public in Canada (the danger opinion). The applicant was subject to removal from Canada under para. 115(2)(a) of the Act. The enforcement officer had discretion to defer the applicant's removal. The enforcement officer stated in her affidavit that the reason for not deferring removal was because there was no specific reason to do so. The enforcement officer also stated that she relied on the risk assessment provided by the Minister's delegate in the danger opinion. Both statements indicated that the enforcement officer was not alert and alive to the possibility that the alleged change in country conditions gave rise to an enhanced risk of torture or persecution upon the applicant's return to Sri Lanka. By relying on the existing risk assessment pre-dating the events identified by the applicant in his request for deferral, the enforcement officer failed to acknowledge the basis for the applicant's concern. The applicant was entitled to an updated risk assessment before removal. Recognizing an applicant's right under s. 7 of the *Charter* to a risk assessment before removal requires that the risk assessment occur proximate in time to the removal and is not incompatible with the need for finality in the system. Whatever the period of delay between the issuance of a danger opinion and the scheduled removal, the onus is on the applicant to demonstrate that there has been a material change in circumstances warranting a re-assessment of his risk upon removal. If an enforcement officer declines to exercise the discretion to defer the removal of a deportee pending re-assessment, a judicial stay of the removal order will only be granted where the deportee can satisfy the well-established tri-partite test. The requirements of a serious issue, irreparable harm and the balance of convenience are appropriate safeguards to ensure that vexatious attempts to forestall removal are dealt with accordingly.

The applicant was entitled to an updated risk assessment in light of the considerable passage of time since the issuance of the danger opinion. The application for judicial review was allowed in part. The enforcement officer was correct in determining that the applicant was not eligible for a PRRA under subs. 112(1) of the Act. However, the enforcement officer erred in declining to suspend the applicant's removal pending a re-assessment of the risk faced by him on removal in light of the significant change of circumstances alleged by the applicant.

Ragupathy v. Canada (Minister of Citizenship & Immigration), 2006 CarswellNat 1100, 2006 FCA 151 — The applicant was recognized as a refugee and was granted permanent residence status. He was subsequently convicted of criminal offences. Following a report by immigration officials requesting a "danger opinion," the delegate of the Minister of Citizenship and Immigration formed the opinion that the applicant's continued presence in Canada presented a high level of danger to the public and that this outweighed the small chance he would be persecuted or tortured if he was returned to Sri Lanka.

Since a finding that a protected person is a danger to the public by virtue of his criminality is a prerequisite of removal, this is a logical starting point in a delegate's analysis. Without a positive opinion on this issue, the delegate's inquiry must end, because the person cannot be deported. Proceeding in this manner also avoids the possibility that the delegate will assess whether a protected person is a "danger to the public" by having regard to the risk of persecution.

Neither the text of the IRPA nor the jurisprudence dictates, as a matter of law, in what order the Minister's delegates' reasons must deal with the various elements of the "danger opinion." This is more a matter of elegance than substance and does not rise to the level of a legal requirement, especially given the degree of discretion entrusted to delegates in the formation of their opinion. The preferred ordering is not required either for a protected person to understand the bases of a delegate's opinion, or for a court to determine whether the delegate had committed reviewable error in performing the legal tasks entrusted to her. While analytical clarity will generally be enhanced if the delegate considers the criminal aspects of the "danger opinion" before opining on the gravity of the risk of persecution, if necessary, and balancing one against the other, there is no legal requirement to follow this format.

Akuech v. Canada (Minister of Citizenship & Immigration), 2005 CarswellNat 624, 2005 FC 337 — The delegate's opinion was quashed. Nowhere in her reasons did the Minister's delegate conclude that the applicant was a danger to the public in Canada. Rather, she decided "on balance" that the applicant's ongoing presence in Canada was a greater danger to the public than the risk he might face upon his return to Sudan. It is incumbent on the Minister's delegate to develop a clear, distinct and separate rationale and decision respecting whether the applicant was a danger to the public in Canada. She is required to make this determination separate from, and prior to, any analysis of the risks which may result from the applicant's return to Sudan. A discrete finding under s. 115(2) that the applicant is a danger to the public in Canada must be made before the non-refoulement rights the applicant has under s. 115(1) can be said not to apply to him.

Almrei v. Canada (Minister of Citizenship & Immigration) (2005), 262 F.T.R. 7, 2005 CarswellNat 653, 2005 FC 355 — The applicant applied for judicial review of the PRAA decision determining that the applicant was not at risk if returned to Syria.

In making her decision, the Minister's delegate considered both secret evidence and evidence which was publicly disclosed. The secret evidence consisted of the narrative portion of the report (SIR) which led to the issuance of the security certificate. The delegate did not have before her the secret appendices which contained the information that supported the SIR.

Section 115(2) requires that the applicant establish that there are substantial grounds upon which to believe that, if removed to Syria, he would be at risk of persecution on a Convention ground or at risk of torture, death, or cruel or unusual treatment or punishment. If the risk is not established, there is no need to pursue the analysis since the applicant is not entitled to the protection afforded by subs. 115(1). The risk that must be assessed goes beyond mere theory or suspicion. The risk, however, can be something less than highly probable. The risk of torture must be personal and present.

The delegate could not rely on the SIR, the ensuing security certificate, and the motion judge's decision that the certificate was reasonable as proof that the applicant posed a danger to Canada.

A reviewing in court must be able to know and assess the evidentiary basis upon which findings are made in order to determine if they are properly based on the evidence. In making her decision, the delegate could not substitute the beliefs of the security service or the opinions of the designated judge for her own. The decision maker must independently consider and assess all of the evidence upon which she relies relating to the danger posed to Canada's security. The delegate must be in a position to weigh the factors which go to the reliability, cogency and value of that information.

The decision of the delegate was set aside.

Mahjoub v. Canada (Minister of Citizenship & Immigration) (2005), 45 Imm. L.R. (3d) 135, 2005 CarswellNat 339, 2005 CarswellNat 1058, 2005 FC 156 — In the spring of 2000, the Solicitor General of Canada and the Minister of Citizenship and Immigration signed a security certificate, evincing their opinion that the applicant was a member of an inadmissible class of persons. The security certificate was found to be reasonable. Finally, by a decision dated July 22, 2004, a delegate of the Minister decided that the applicant should be removed to Egypt. The applicant sought to review that decision.

Section 115(1) generally prohibits the government from returning a protected person to a country where he or she would be at risk of persecution or torture or cruel or unusual treatment or punishment. Subsection 115(2) sets out certain exceptions to that general principle. One such exception is in the case of a person who poses a danger to the security of Canada.

Both the decision whether the applicant constitutes a danger to the security of Canada and the decision whether the applicant faces a substantial risk of torture if deported to Egypt ought not to be set aside unless patently unreasonable. Whether there is a real possibility of an adverse effect on Canada if the individual remained in Canada must be weighed against the possible injustice to the individual if deported. Anyone exercising discretion under s. 115(2) must have evidence that allows the conclusion that the person concerned poses a danger to the security of Canada. The decision maker cannot rely simply upon the fact that the person is described in subs. 34(1) of the Act. The decision maker must carefully analyse all of the relevant evidence. The delegate must consider all of the evidence before him or her relating to the danger posed to Canada's security, and weigh the factors which go to the reliability of that information.

Conflicting evidence relating to danger must be weighed and reasons given for rejecting evidence of significance. The effect of the passage of time, and the effect of the person's apprehension and detention, should be considered so that not just the person's past actions but their future behaviour may be assessed. The fact of apprehension and disclosure may neutralize the future ability of the person concerned to conduct clandestine activities. After considering these factors, the nature of the danger posed by the person concerned should be articulated. By articulating the nature of the danger posed, the decision maker may, at the final stage of the analysis, properly balance the competing interests.

Thuraisingam v. Canada (Minister of Citizenship & Immigration), [2004] F.C.J. No. 746, 40 Imm. L.R. (3d) 145, 251 F.T.R. 282, 2004 CarswellNat 2725, 2004 CarswellNat 1179, 2004 FC 607 — There are two elements that must be established in order to support the issuance of a danger opinion under s. 115. The individual must be inadmissible on the basis of serious criminality and in the opinion of the Minister must constitute a danger to the public in Canada. The phrase "danger to the public" is not a mystery. It must refer to the possibility that the person who has committed a serious crime in the past may seriously be thought to be a potential re-offender. The subsection adequately focuses the Minister's mind on the question of whether, given what the Minister knows about the individual and what the individual had to say in his or her own behalf, the Minister can form an opinion in good faith that the individual is a possible re-offender whose presence in Canada creates an unacceptable risk.

The fact that an individual has been convicted of a serious offence is not, in and of itself, a sufficient foundation for the opinion.

The fact that someone has been charged with an offence proves nothing. It is simply an allegation. The evidence underlying the charge may indeed be sufficient to provide the foundation for a good faith opinion that the individual poses a present or future danger to others in Canada.

Section 115 creates an exception to the principle of non-refoulement, that is, a person who has been found to be a Convention refugee should not be returned to the country where they would be at risk of persecution. Determining whether the return of such a person offends s. 7 of the Charter, a balancing exercise must be carried out weighing the protection of Canada's security interest against the refugee's interest in not being deported or tortured. A similar exercise must be carried out when the danger opinion is based on serious criminality.

The assessment of risk is largely outside the expertise of reviewing courts and does not possess a significant legal dimension. As such, significant deference must be accorded to the risk assessment.

116. Regulations — The regulations may provide for any matter relating to the application of this Division, and may include provisions respecting procedures to be followed with respect to applications for protection and decisions made under section 115, including the establishment of factors to determine whether a hearing is required.

PART 3 — ENFORCEMENT

Human Smuggling and Trafficking

117. (1) Organizing entry into Canada — No person shall organize, induce, aid or abet the coming into Canada of one or more persons knowing that, or being reckless as to whether, their coming into Canada is or would be in contravention of this Act.

(2) Penalties — fewer than 10 persons — A person who contravenes subsection (1) with respect to fewer than 10 persons is guilty of an offence and liable

    (a) on conviction on indictment

        (i) for a first offence, to a fine of not more than $500,000 or to a term of imprisonment of not more than 10 years, or to both, or

        (ii) for a subsequent offence, to a fine of not more than $1,000,000 or to a term of imprisonment of not more than 14 years, or to both; and

(b) on summary conviction, to a fine of not more than $100,000 or to a term of imprisonment of not more than two years, or to both.

(3) Penalty — 10 persons or more — A person who contravenes subsection (1) with respect to a group of 10 persons or more is guilty of an offence and liable on conviction by way of indictment to a fine of not more than $1,000,000 or to life imprisonment, or to both.

(3.1) Minimum penalty — fewer than 50 persons — A person who is convicted on indictment of an offence under subsection (2) or (3) with respect to fewer than 50 persons is also liable to a minimum punishment of imprisonment for a term of

(a) three years, if either

(i) the person, in committing the offence, endangered the life or safety of, or caused bodily harm or death to, any of the persons with respect to whom the offence was committed, or

(ii) the commission of the offence was for profit, or was for the benefit of, at the direction of or in association with a criminal organization or terrorist group; or

(b) five years, if both

(i) the person, in committing the offence, endangered the life or safety of, or caused bodily harm or death to, any of the persons with respect to whom the offence was committed, and

(ii) the commission of the offence was for profit, or was for the benefit of, at the direction of or in association with a criminal organization or terrorist group.

(3.2) Minimum penalty — 50 persons or more — A person who is convicted of an offence under subsection (3) with respect to a group of 50 persons or more is also liable to a minimum punishment of imprisonment for a term of

(a) five years, if either

(i) the person, in committing the offence, endangered the life or safety of, or caused bodily harm or death to, any of the persons with respect to whom the offence was committed, or

(ii) the commission of the offence was for profit, or was for the benefit of, at the direction of or in association with a criminal organization or terrorist group; or

(b) 10 years, if both

(i) the person, in committing the offence, endangered the life or safety of, or caused bodily harm or death to, any of the persons with respect to whom the offence was committed, and

(ii) the commission of the offence was for profit, or was for the benefit of, at the direction of or in association with a criminal organization or terrorist group.

(4) No proceedings without consent — **No proceedings for an offence under this section may be instituted except by or with the consent of the Attorney General of Canada.**

2012, c. 17, s. 41(1), (4)

Case Law

Section 117(1)

R. v. Appulonappa, [2015] 3 S.C.R. 754, 332 C.C.C. (3d) 1, 24 C.R. (7th) 385, 390 D.L.R. (4th) 425, 35 Imm. L.R. (4th) 171, 379 B.C.A.C. 3, 345 C.R.R. (2d) 74, 478 N.R. 3, 654 W.A.C. 3, 2015 SCC 59, 2015 CarswellBC 3427, 2015 CarswellBC 3428, [2015] S.C.J. No. 59 — The accused argued that s. 117 attempted to criminalize any person who committed any of the acts referred to in this section; it casts too wide a net. Inadvertently, it captures the acts of certain categories of persons (humanitarian workers and close family members) and conduct, which the Crown agrees are not intended to be prosecuted under the section and which the government has no intention of prosecuting under the section. The lower court concluded the section was vague and/or overbroad and inconsistent with principles of fundamental justice and accordingly s. 117 was unnecessarily broad in that it captures a broader range of conduct and persons than is necessary to achieve the government's objective and therefore infringed s. 7 of the *Charter*. The British Columbia Court of Appeal overturned that decision.

The Supreme Court of Canada allowed the appeals and remitted the charges for trial. Section 117 was found to be unconstitutional insofar as it permits prosecution for humanitarian aid to undocumented entrants, mutual assistance among asylum seekers or assistance to family members. Participating in the unauthorized entry of other people into Canada may result in prosecution and imprisonment and/or substantial fines upon conviction under s. 117 of IRPA. The migrants contended that s. 117 violated s. 7 of the Charter because the provision catches two categories of people outside its purpose — people who assist close family members to come to Canada and humanitarians who assist those fleeing persecution to come to Canada, in each case without required documents. The purpose of s. 117 is to criminalize the smuggling of people into Canada in the context of organized crime, and does not extend to permitting prosecution for simply assisting family or providing humanitarian or mutual aid to undocumented entrants to Canada. A broad punitive goal that would prosecute persons with no connection to and no furtherance of organized crime is not consistent with Parliament's purpose as evinced by the text of s. 117 read together with Canada's international commitments, s. 117's role within the IRPA, the IRPA's objectives, the history of s. 117, and the parliamentary debates.

The scope of s. 117 is overbroad and interferes with conduct that bears no connection to its objective. The fact that the Attorney General could not permit the prosecution of such people does not cure the overbreadth problem created by s. 117(1). Ministerial discretion, whether conscientiously exercised or not, does not negate the fact that s. 117(1) criminalizes conduct beyond Parliament's objective, and that people whom Parliament did not intend to prosecute are therefore at risk of prosecution, conviction and imprisonment. Section 117 cannot be justified under s. 1 of the Charter. While the objective of s. 117 is clearly pressing and substantial and some applications of s. 117 are rationally connected to the legislative objective, the provision fails the minimum impairment branch of the s. 1 analysis. It follows that s. 117 is of no force or effect to the extent of its inconstancy with the Charter.

R. v. Alli, 2015 ONSC 1716, 2015 CarswellOnt 4729, [2015] O.J. No. 1629 — The Crown's theory was that the accused was knowingly complicit in an organization formed to smuggle humans across the US-Canada border, crossing the river at Cornwall for transport to Toronto. *Mens rea* may be established through the use of the wilful blindness doctrine. It is not sufficient to establish that the accused ought to have known. The evidence must establish suspicion combined with a conscious decision to refrain from inquiry. An accused cannot deliberately remain ignorant and thereby escape criminal responsibility. The Crown proved from the accused's own words that he knew that by driving these passengers to Toronto he was aiding in an offence under IRPA. If such knowledge lacked certainty and particulars at the time, he did, in fact, harbour real suspicion and chose to close his eyes to inquiry and the implications. The accused was found guilty as charged and convictions were entered.

Gomravi v. Canada (Attorney General), 2015 FC 431, 2015 CarswellNat 1263, 2015 CarswellNat 3805 — The applicant sought judicial review of a decision to revoke his passport and deny him access to a passport after concluding he had used his Canadian passport while acting as an escort to assist an unidentified individual who was unlawfully using another passport in order to board a flight to Canada. Paragraph 10(2)(b) of the Canadian Passport Order was not ambiguous, in that the term "committed" indicates that the commission of the act is sufficient, and that a conviction is not a precondition to its application. CIC had the jurisdiction to revoke Mr. Gomravi's passport and deny him passport services on the basis that he acted in contravention of s. 117, in conjunction with s. 135 of IRPA, in "committing" an act that would constitute an indictable offence if committed in Canada. The application for judicial review was denied.

R. v. Abdulle (2014), 32 Imm. L.R. (4th) 53, 124 O.R. (3d) 111, 2014 ONSC 7455, 2014 CarswellOnt 18232, [2014] O.J. No. 6177 — The applicant brought an application for an order declaring s. 117 of IRPA overbroad, and as such unconstitutional and specifically he argued that s. 117 was overbroad in scope for the offence of human smuggling and captured within its application individuals who assist refugees to enter Canada for humanitarian purposes. The applicant was charged between May 4, 2006, and January 31, 2011, of organizing or attempt to organize the coming to Canada of 10 or more potential refugees who were not in possession of a visa, passport or other documents contrary to s. 117. Some of the refugees were known to him as family members, friends, or family or friends of persons he knew. Many of the refugees were not personally known to the applicant. He claimed that based on his personal experience and knowledge, the lives of the refugees wanting to come to Canada were in danger so long as they remained in Somalia. He was also charged with misrepresentation, submitting false information and bribery under the IRPA, as well as frauds on the government, forgery, use of fraudulent documents and possession of identity documents contrary to the *Criminal Code*.

The applicant argued that there were two clearly enunciated sentiments surrounding s. 117. First, Parliament had indicated that the demographic targeted are those who seek to take advantage of refugees, smuggling them into Canada for malicious purposes. Second, there had been a continuous desire to exclude from the application of penalties workers who for humanitarian purposes assist refugees. The applicant asked the court to recognize these sentiments, and to find that s. 117 was not intended to apply to an individual who facilitates the flight of refugees into Canada, and as such the provision is overly and impermissibly broad in its scope.

The court concluded that the immigration objectives of s. 3(1) cannot be overlooked and that these were much broader and specifically included the protection of the health and safety of Canadians and the maintenance of the security of a Canadian society. Motive cannot be confused with intent; however, motive may be a sentencing factor as set out in s. 121(b) and (c). Importantly, the offence of s. 117 can be made out without either motive being present. Part 2 of the IRPA deals extensively with refugee protection and sets out a comprehensive scheme for Canada to meet its international obligations. The court accepted the government's argument that the primary objective of s. 117 is border security and control. Parliament intended to create an offence that is broad in scope that would not contain any "loopholes" that would undermine border security and control. The objective of s. 117 is aligned with its scope, and is therefore constitutional. The application was dismissed.

Also see *B010 v. Canada (Minister of Citizenship and Immigration)*, [2015] 3 S.C.R. 704, 92 Admin. L.R. (5th) 1, 390 D.L.R. (4th) 385, 36 Imm. L.R. (4th) 64, 478 N.R. 57, 2015 CarswellNat 6186, 2015 SCC 58, 2015 CarswellNat 6186, 2015 CarswellNat 6187, [2015] S.C.J. No. 58, at s. 37(1) of IRPA.

R. v. Toor, 2009 CarswellOnt 8881 (S.C.J.) — The accused was a licensed taxi driver in 2002. On seven occasions he drove people from Toronto to the Windsor area and left them there. Arrangements had been made by others to smuggle the passengers into the United States. The accused was charged with conspiring to illegally smuggle the immigrants into the United States and was found guilty under s. 117 of IRPA. When relying on s. 117 the Crown has to establish that the accused knew or was willfully blind as to whether the migrants had the required documents to enter the United States. The American legislation makes it an offence to bring someone into the United States at a location other than a regular border crossing location or someone who the accused knows or in reckless disregard of the fact that an alien has not received prior official authorization to come to, enter or reside in the United States. The Canadian legislation makes it an offence to enter Canada without reporting immediately to Canadian authorities. Accordingly, the accused was presumed by law to have known that he agreed to participate in a human smuggling offence in which people were taken to the United States at a port of entry after a lawful inspection and authorization by an immigration officer or at a location other than a port of entry. In those circumstances, he would know or at the very least be willfully blind to the fact that the migrants did not have prior authorization to enter the United States. That prior authorization could be given in advance of the attendance at the port of entry. Knowing that they were to be secreted into the United States he knew or was at least willfully blind that they did not have prior official authorization.

R. v. Alzehrani (2008), 75 Imm. L.R. (3d) 304, 237 C.C.C. (3d) 471, 2008 CarswellOnt 6556 (S.C.J.) — This was a trial alleging a conspiracy between one or both of the accused, together with others, to smuggle people across the border between Canada and the United States. The defence moved for a directed verdict and the trial judge found on 23 of the 30 counts there was no evidence on one or more of the essential elements of the offence and that those counts could not be left to the jury. The remaining seven counts went to the jury and the jury convicted on all of them.

An issue arose during the course of the trial as to whether the Crown was required to prove that the persons being brought into Canada did not have the required documents to enter, and if so, the means by which that could be proven. Initially, the issue was cast by the defence simply as an admissibility of evidence issue on the final telephone intercept relied upon by the Crown in respect of Count 11 on the indictment. However, it became apparent in the course of argument that the defence position related to all counts on the indictment. The defence argument was that the failure of the Crown to tender any direct evidence as to the lack of documentation and knowledge of the accused was fatal to the Crown's case, that no reasonable inferences of guilt could be drawn from the limited circumstantial evidence on these points, and that there was, therefore, no case to go to the jury on any of the counts before the court.

In the majority of the charges before the court, the Crown presented no direct evidence as to whether the persons being smuggled had the required documents for legal entry, and also no evidence of the knowledge or belief of the accused. All of the counts on the indictment involved some surreptitious manner of crossing the border so as to avoid the scrutiny of border crossing authorities. However, even though in some of these cases the persons crossing illegally were apprehended, there was no evidence as to their status in the country they were entering and whether they had any documentation that would permit their entry. In respect of those counts, the position of the Crown was that both the lack of documentation and the knowledge of the accused could be determined by drawing inferences from the manner in which the persons involved were taken across the border.

The statute is very explicit about requiring proof that the person being brought into the country does not have appropriate documentation. Parliament could have made it an offence to assist any person to cross the border surreptitiously. If that was the language of the statute, there would be no problem with these 23 counts. However, the statute is not worded that way, and ought not to be interpreted as if it was. The plain meaning of the statute is clear. It is only the assisting of persons who do not have passports or similar documents that is the subject matter of this offence. Something beyond surreptitious entry is required in order to establish a lack of documentation.

There was also no evidence of the accused's state of knowledge with respect to the 23 counts. Wilful blindness is not a route for imputing knowledge unless the true facts to which the accused has shut his eyes are known. Therefore, unless there was some evidence that the people being transported did not have documents, the doctrine of wilful blindness had no application. Why s. 117 of the IRPA was limited to the smuggling of persons across the border who are without the required documents, as opposed to simply smuggling people across the border for whatever reason, is not apparent. However, if the manner in which the legislation is drafted makes it difficult to prosecute wrongdoers (which it does), and the wrongdoing is serious (which it is), the remedy lies in legislative reform, not by judicial interpretation that violates the plain meaning of the existing statutory language.

Section 117(2)

R. v. Alli, 2015 ONSC 3961, 2015 CarswellOnt 9446, [2015] O.J. No. 3281 — The accused was convicted under s. 117(2) of IRPA for his part in smuggling six Nigerians from the US to Canada. Although it was a close call, a conditional sentence was imposed. The accused was not involved in planning. This was a first offense. There was evidence of family and community support and he was the family breadwinner. He spent seven days in prison and was subject to interim release for three years without offending. The conviction and disposition will result in another three years of direct institutional intrusion and a lifetime of indirect intrusion in his life. Any rational person faced with assessing the cost and benefit of such activity should be deterred. The court stated it strongly denounced human smuggling, takes it very seriously and imposes meaningful consequences in the measure of proportionality. A sentence of 15 months imprisonment was to be served conditionally in the community, subject to mandatory terms. The first 10 months include full house arrest, save for demands of employment, medical treatment and three hours weekly for household necessaries, all to be approved by his supervisor in writing beforehand. For the remaining five months a curfew is imposed, followed by two years of probation, to include statutory terms, report as directed subject to supervision, attend and participate in assessment, rehabilitation and counseling as recommended by the probation officer. The accused was to perform 100 hours of community service as part of the probationary rehabilitation process.

R. v. Ng (2008), 241 C.C.C. (3d) 340, 263 B.C.A.C. 300, 2008 CarswellBC 2823, 2008 BCCA 535 — The appellant kept a common bawdy house for almost two years and employed more than two prostitutes. He was convicted of procuring two of them to have illicit sexual intercourse, one of them over a lengthy period of time. He ran a prostitution business from which he profited. Deterrence is a significant factor in sentencing for these offences. Because of the moral turpitude involved, denunciation is an equally significant factor. The sentences imposed for the prostitution offences do not adequately speak to these factors and are unfit. The global sentence was inadequate. The Crown's leave to appeal to increase the global sentence by one year to 27 months was allowed. The court did not disturb the sentences for the immigration offences. The appellant had been convicted under s. 117(1) of the IRPA for inducing, aiding or abetting the coming into Canada of a person who was not in possession of a valid visa, passport or other document required by the IRPA and of inducing, aiding or abetting or attempting to counsel, induce, aid or abet a person, to directly or indirectly misrepresent or withhold material facts relating to a relevant matter that induces or could induce an error in the administration of the IRPA under s. 126 of the IRPA.

The immigration sentencing cases relied upon by the Crown involved more serious circumstances and, in some cases at least, offenders with existing criminal records. The appellant, who had no prior record, assisted one person to illegally enter Canada, apparently without compromising her physical safety. It seems that there are no reported sentencing decisions in immigration cases that involve comparable facts. If the two immigration offences were the only offences for which the appellant had been convicted, it would have been the court's opinion that the concurrent nine-month sentences were at the low end of the scale but not unfit. The sentences for the immigration offences were not varied on appeal.

R. v. Wasiluk, 2005 CarswellOnt 4728, 2005 ONCJ 407 — The increase in the maximum penalty to life imprisonment for organizing entry into Canada of a group of 10 persons or more is reflective of the seriousness with which Parliament views these types of activities and the need to increase the sentences for these types of offences. Accordingly, a statutorily increased penalty is a legislative signal that the sentencing paradigm has shifted towards a regime of tougher sentences than that which previously existed.

The accused transported three migrants across the river to the United States. Their role was limited to transporting the migrants across the river in their boat and they were not involved in the arrangements which resulted in the migrants coming to Canada. A sentence of 14 months' house arrest was imposed with the exception of attending work.

Section 117(3)

R. v. Hallal, 2008 ONCA 210, 2008 CarswellOnt 1644 — The defendant pleaded guilty to Count 22, which concerned the conspiracy in relation to the newly enacted Immigration and Refugee Protection Act. Approximately 200 persons were smuggled from Canada to the United States and charged between $2,500 and $3,000 U.S. The evidence showed that in less than four months following that the defendant was involved in the movement of 30 migrants and those 30 migrants were part of 10 different operations. The evidence showed that the defendant was actively involved and he was assertive with other members of the conspiracy about business being directed to him and not to others. As far as this defendant was concerned, his actions were planned and deliberate. It was done for profit.

Unless a conditional sentence is an obvious outcome on sentencing there is an evidentiary burden on the defendant to show that he is not a risk in the community for re-offending. It is true that the court has greater concern with respect to this factor when one is dealing with violent offences, but being involved in a non-violent offence alone is not a ticket to a conditional sentence. Looking at the bigger picture, this is a serious offence. It has international implications. In mitigation there was a plea of guilty. The plea was significant. A term of custody of 18 months is appropriate. In light of the defendant's financial circumstances and length of time in jail, the victim fine surcharge was waived. The Ontario Federal Court of Appeal affirmed the lower Court's decision with respect to the sentencing.

118. (1) Offence — trafficking in persons — No person shall knowingly organize the coming into Canada of one or more persons by means of abduction, fraud, deception or use or threat of force or coercion.

(2) Definition of "organize" — For the purpose of subsection (1), "organize", with respect to persons, includes their recruitment or transportation and, after their entry into Canada, the receipt or harbouring of those persons.

Case Law

R. v. Orr (2013), 20 Imm. L.R. (4th) 456, 2013 BCSC 1883, 2013 CarswellBC 4173, [2013] B.C.J. No. 2257 — The accused was convicted of one count under each of ss. 118(1), 124(1)(c) and 127(a) of IRPA. This was the first conviction in Canada under s. 118 of IRPA. Sentences have been imposed for human trafficking under s. 279.01 of the *Criminal Code* which involves an essential ingredient of exploitation which is not present under s. 118 of IRPA. Offences under s. 118 of IRPA will fall across a broad continuum of conduct. Aggravating factors can include whether bodily harm or death occurred, whether the life or safety of a person was endangered, whether the commission of the offence involved criminal organization, whether the commission of the offence was for profit or whether the victim was subject to humiliating and degrading treatment. The lack of significant aggravating factors puts this offence at the low end of the continuum. Individuals cannot be allowed to disregard the immigration laws of this country with impunity. The main sentencing objectives in the circumstance of this case must be those of denunciation and general deterrence. A conditional sentence would not be consistent with these objectives.

The accused was sentenced to 18 months in jail with respect to s. 118 and six months with respect to ss. 124 and 127. Since all three offences arose from the same general circumstances, the court must take into account the concept of totality and proportionality; therefore, the sentence on counts 2 and 3 dealing with ss. 124 and 127 were to be served concurrently with the 18-month sentence under s. 118.

R. v. Ng, 2006 CarswellBC 723, 2006 BCPC 111 — The defendant was charged with committing offences under s. 118 of the IRPA and challenged the constitutionality of the section. Specifically, he submitted that inclusion of the terms fraud and deception as means of committing the offence renders the section vague or overly broad or both.

The use of the terms fraud and deception as legislative means of achieving the object of the IRPA are not grossly disproportionate to the section's objective. Accordingly, s. 118(1) of the IRPA is neither vague nor overly broad, and as such, this section does not violate s. 7 of the *Charter of Rights and Freedoms*.

119. Disembarking persons at sea — A person shall not disembark a person or group of persons at sea for the purpose of inducing, aiding or abetting them to come into Canada in contravention of this Act.

120. Penalties — A person who contravenes section 118 or 119 is guilty of an offence and liable on conviction by way of indictment to a fine of not more than $1,000,000 or to life imprisonment, or to both.

121. (1) Aggravating factors — The court, in determining the penalty to be imposed under section 120, shall take into account whether

    (a) bodily harm or death occurred, or the life or safety of any person was endangered, as a result of the commission of the offence;

    (b) the commission of the offence was for the benefit of, at the direction of or in association with a criminal organization;

    (c) the commission of the offence was for profit, whether or not any profit was realized; and

    (d) a person was subjected to humiliating or degrading treatment, including with respect to work or health conditions or sexual exploitation as a result of the commission of the offence.

(2) [Repealed 2012, c. 17, s. 42(3).]

2012, c. 17, s. 42(1), (3)

121.1 (1) Definition of "criminal organization" — For the purposes of subparagraphs 117(3.1)(a)(ii) and (b)(ii) and (3.2)(a)(ii) and (b)(ii) and paragraph 121(b), "criminal organization" means a criminal organization as defined in subsection 467.1(1) of the *Criminal Code*.

(2) Definition of "terrorist group" — For the purposes of subparagraphs 117(3.1)(a)(ii) and (b)(ii) and (3.2)(a)(ii) and (b)(ii), "terrorist group" means a terrorist group as defined in subsection 83.01(1) of the *Criminal Code*.

2012, c. 17, s. 43

Offences Related to Documents

122. (1) Documents — No person shall, in order to contravene this Act,

    (a) possess a passport, visa or other document, of Canadian or foreign origin, that purports to establish or that could be used to establish a person's identity;

(b) use such a document, including for the purpose of entering or remaining in Canada; or

(c) import, export or deal in such a document.

(2) Proof of offence — Proof of the matters referred to in subsection (1) in relation to a forged document or a document that is blank, incomplete, altered or not genuine is, in the absence of evidence to the contrary, proof that the person intends to contravene this Act.

Case Law

R. v. Mahamoud (2015), 37 Imm. L.R. (4th) 79, 2015 CarswellOnt 12265 (C.J.) — The defendant was charged under the *Immigration and Refugee Protection Act* with possession of a fraudulent passport and aiding and abetting his adolescent niece, originally from Somalia, to enter the country by making a refugee claim. The court found that the charge was not proven beyond a reasonable doubt. The defence conceded that the defendant possessed the passport that could be used to establish a person's identity. However, the Crown was required to prove more than mere possession, but also that it was for the purpose of contravening the Act. The agreed statement of facts and the evidence showed that the defendant possessed the passport to aid his niece in leaving Dubai and coming through Amsterdam to get to Toronto; however, it was never used thereafter. The presumption in subs. 122(2) of IRPA assists the Crown in proving the charge. This presumption provides that possession of a forged document, or a document that is blank, incomplete, altered or not genuine is, in the absence of evidence to the contrary, proof that the person intends to contravene the Act. However, the subject passport, according to the agreed statement of facts was deemed "genuine." It was not forged, blank, or incomplete. As for being "altered," this word implies that it was issued by the embassy and then something was done to it subsequently to change it. There was insufficient evidence, however, to support this. Since no passport was ever used by the niece to try to enter Canada, the only evidence was that she came to make a refugee claim, which is not contrary to the Act. Therefore, the defendant's possession of the passport was merely part of the history of the events but did not constitute an offence. Although it may be attractive to convict, it would be dangerous to do so in all of the circumstances on a principled basis. The charges were dismissed.

R v. Oladapo, 2013 ONCJ 156, 2013 CarswellOnt 3527, [2013] O.J. No. 1403 — The accused entered a guilty plea to possessing a genuine Nigerian passport that could be used to establish identity, contrary to s. 122(1)(a) of IRPA, and misrepresenting or withholding material facts relating to the true identity of his passenger that could induce an error in the administration of the Act, contrary to s. 127(a). The court held that this was an appropriate case for a conditional sentence.

Neither of the aggravating factors set out in s. 123(2) of IRPA were in play. There was no evidence put before the court that the accused was associated with any criminal organization or that he committed these offences for profit.

A sentence of imprisonment would certainly make it clear that as a society we are not prepared to tolerate such behaviour, and would hopefully serve as a deterrent to such offences being committed in the future, either by the accused or by other like-minded individuals. However, the court was aware of a number of cases where a non-custodial sentence was imposed with respect to similar or even more serious offences. In each of these cases, the sentencing judge was satisfied that the principles of denunciation and deterrence could both be met by either a large fine or by the imposition of a conditional sentence of imprisonment.

123. (1) Penalty — Every person who contravenes

(a) paragraph 122(1)(a) is guilty of an offence and liable on conviction on indictment to a term of imprisonment of up to five years; and

(b) paragraph 122(1)(b) or (c) is guilty of an offence and liable on conviction on indictment to a term of imprisonment of up to 14 years.

(2) Aggravating factors — The court, in determining the penalty to be imposed, shall take into account whether

(a) the commission of the offence was for the benefit of, at the direction of or in association with a criminal organization as defined in subsection 121.1(1); and

(b) the commission of the offence was for profit, whether or not any profit was realized.

2012, c. 17, s. 44(2)

Case Law

R. v. Daskalov, 2011 BCCA 169, 2011 CarswellBC 793, [2011] B.C.J. No. 623 — The respondent was convicted under s. 122(1)(a) of IRPA and pled guilty in Provincial Court. The respondent was sentenced to a conditional discharge and six months' probation. The Crown appealed the sentence arguing that the trial judge gave improper consideration to the immigration consequences of the sentence, and allowed that factor to override the purpose and principles of sentencing. The Crown further argued that a conditional discharge falls outside the range of sentences for an offence of this nature, which typically include a period of imprisonment and that the discharge was granted in order to avoid recording a conviction for the offence against the respondent and thus avoid the effect of s. 36(2)(a) of IRPA.

The B.C. Court of Appeal concluded that the sentencing judge erred in principle by taking into account an irrelevant fact, that being the effect of s. 36(2)(a) of IRPA on the respondent's future inadmissibility into Canada, which resulted in his granting the respondent a conditional discharge with a period of six months' probation. Given the absence of an exceptional or unique circumstance, the sentence was unfit, the appeal was allowed and the sentence was varied to a period of imprisonment of one day resulting in an effective sentence of four months.

R. v. Agbor, 2010 BCCA 278, 2010 CarswellBC 1494 — The appellant pled guilty to one count of using a false document to enter or remain in Canada, contrary to s. 122(1)(b) of IRPA. He then sought to have the conviction quashed. The charge in which the conviction was entered related to the appellant's entry into Canada on January 27, 2008, using a fake French passport. The fake passport was detected at the time of attempted entry, and the appellant was found to be inadmissible to Canada. A removal order was issued against him. The appellant subsequently attempted to make a refugee claim, but was ineligible to do so because s. 99(3) of the Act does not allow a person who is subject to a removal order to make such a claim. He was allowed, however, under s. 112 of the Act to make an application to the Minister for protection, and he did so on September 28, 2008. Section 113 of the Act provides that a successful application for protection confers refugee protection on the applicant. The appellant was ultimately successful in his application for protection. He now has refugee protection in Canada. Section 133 of the Act prevents refugee claimants from being charged with certain immigration offences unless and until their claims have been rejected. An application for protection under s. 112 constitutes a claim for refugee protection and for the purposes of s. 133. Accordingly, the accused should not have been charged with the offence under s. 122 pending determination of his claim for protection. As the claim for protection has now succeeded, the appellant cannot be charged with the offence. The guilty plea was struck and the conviction quashed.

R. v. Zelaya (2009), 77 Imm. L.R. (3d) 163, 2009 CarswellAlta 37, 2009 ABPC 7 — Although the *Immigration and Refugee Protection Act* was enacted in 2001, there have been few prosecutions taken in Alberta. The penalty provisions are a guide as to how seriously Parliament (and thus, the Canadian people) consider the current offences. The accused was sentenced with respect to four guilty pleas entered including: possession of a false passport — s. 123(1)(a); using a false passport to wrongfully enter Canada — s. 123(1)(b); lying about his identity and nationality to gain entry to Canada — s. 128(a); and, return to Canada without the correct authorization — s. 124(1)(a).

In this case, a conditional sentence order would not address the fundamental principle of proportionality found in s. 718.1 of the Code, or the principles of denunciation, punishment and deterrence. The sentence must account for relevant aggravating and mitigating circumstances and be tailored to fit the individual accused before the court. The accused received four months in jail for having a false passport; 7½ months for using a false passport to enter Canada; six months for lying about his identity and nationality to enter Canada; and three months for merely returning to Canada without authorization. All of these terms of imprisonment were concurrent one to another for a global sentence of one year in jail; however, accounting for pre-sentence custody credit of 140 days (70 actual days), the sentence of 7½ months was made consecutive to any other sentence imposed by any Court, should there be any.

R. v. Lin (2006), 62 Imm. L.R. (3d) 196, 2006 CarswellNfld 371 (T.D.); affirmed (2007), 62 Imm. L.R. (3d) 199, 263 Nfld. & P.E.I.R. 273, 798 A.P.R. 273, 2007 CarswellNfld 155, 2007 NLCA 13, [2007] N.J. No. 74 — The accused was a Chinese national who used a forged Korean passport. When individuals use false passports to enter Canada they undermine the *Immigration and Refugee Protection Act*. Authorities have the right to run background on all persons wishing to enter Canada in order to ensure compliance with Canadian laws and regulations. Authorities also have the duty to screen persons entering our country for the purposes of national security and public safety. There needs to be a message sent that using a false passport for the purpose of illegally entering Canada will result in a deterrent sentence of imprisonment. A sentence that was considered a mere slap on the wrist would only be encouragement for like-minded individuals to illegally enter our country. Deterrence has to be the guiding principle in sentencing such individuals. A sentence of one year was appropriate.

General Offences

124. (1) Contravention of Act — Every person commits an offence who

(a) contravenes a provision of this Act for which a penalty is not specifically provided or fails to comply with a condition or obligation imposed under this Act;

(b) escapes or attempts to escape from lawful custody or detention under this Act; or

(c) employs a foreign national in a capacity in which the foreign national is not authorized under this Act to be employed.

(2) Deemed knowledge — For the purposes of paragraph (1)(c), a person who fails to exercise due diligence to determine whether employment is authorized under this Act is deemed to know that it is not authorized.

(3) Due diligence defence — A person referred to in subsection 148(1) shall not be found guilty of an offence under paragraph (1)(a) if it is established that they exercised all due diligence to prevent the commission of the offence.

Case Law

R. v. Orr (2013), 20 Imm. L.R. (4th) 456, 2013 BCSC 1883, 2013 CarswellBC 4173, [2013] B.C.J. No. 2257 — The accused was convicted of one count under each of ss. 118(1), 124(1)(c) and 127(a) of IRPA. This was the first conviction in Canada under s. 118 of IRPA. Sentences have been imposed for human trafficking under s. 279.01 of the *Criminal Code* which involves an essential ingredient of exploitation which is not present under s. 118 of IRPA. Offences under s. 118 of IRPA will fall across a broad continuum of conduct. Aggravating factors can include whether bodily harm or death occurred, whether the life or safety of a person was endangered, whether the commission of the offence involved criminal organization, whether the commission of the offence was for profit or whether the victim was subject to humiliating and degrading treatment. The lack of significant aggravating factors puts this offence at the low end of the continuum. Individuals cannot be allowed to disregard the immigration laws of this country with impunity. The main sentencing objectives in the circumstance of this case must be those of denunciation and general deterrence. A conditional sentence would not be consistent with these objectives.

The accused was sentenced to 18 months in jail with respect to s. 118 and six months with respect to ss. 124 and 127. Since all three offences arose from the same general circumstances, the court must take into account the concept of totality and proportionality; therefore, the sentence on counts 2 and 3 dealing with ss. 124 and 127 were to be served concurrently with the 18-month sentence under s. 118.

R. v. Choi (2013), 21 Imm. L.R. (4th) 1, 301 C.C.C. (3d) 390, 5 C.R. (7th) 85, [2013] 12 W.W.R. 711, 294 Man. R. (2d) 261, 2013 MBCA 75, 2013 CarswellMan 442, [2013] M.J. No. 282 — The accused entered a guilty plea to one count under s. 124(1)(c) of IRPA with respect to multiple incidents involving six refugees. The accused was the director and president of the corporation whose interests included two restaurants in Winnipeg. Six individuals named in the information had worked for the accused at his restaurant without being properly authorized.

The accused was sentenced to an 18-month conditional discharge and placed on a period of supervised probation with a number of terms including 50 hours of community service work at the time and place as directed by probation services and a charitable donation of $6,000 to the International Centre and $6,000 to Welcome Place within the first nine months of the order.

The Crown appealed the sentence. The Court of Appeal concluded that the imposition of a condition in a probation order which forms part of a conditional discharge sentence requiring that an accused make a donation of $6,000 to each of two named charities is not a sentencing option available under the *Criminal Code*. It was not apparent in the circumstances of this case, nor did the sentencing judge give any explanation or appear to give any consideration as to how such a condition could or would protect society or facilitate the accused's successful reintegration into the community. Furthermore, conditions of a probation order cannot be punitive. A condition requiring payment of $12,000 is clearly punitive.

The granting of a conditional discharge in the circumstances of this case was an unfit sentence. The sentencing judge did not place sufficient emphasis on denunciation of the accused and his conduct in the circumstances or the need for general deterrence by sending a clear message to other employers of the consequences of a wilful violation of the IRPA in illegally employing foreign workers. In this case the breach of IRPA was not the result of carelessness, mistake or lack or due diligence, but was willful conduct in knowingly violating the rules. Not only had he done this in the past but financial records showed he distinguished between the wage he paid workers without a work permit compared with that which he paid foreign nationals, including the same workers doing the same work after they obtained their work permit.

The conditional discharge and probation order were set aside and a conviction was imposed with a fine of $15,000.

R. v. Beltran (2010), 89 Imm. L.R. (3d) 1, 2010 ABPC 113, 2010 CarswellAlta 602 — The accused entered a guilty plea to an offence of returning to Canada without the prescribed authorization, contrary to IRPA. The Crown sought a sentence of five months' incarceration. The accused sought a conditional discharge. A discharge was not a fit disposition in this case. The offence is a problematic one in that it is difficult to detect and quantify the cost to taxpayers. The accused entered Canada unauthorized for his own personal gain and to avoid the proper and lawful mechanisms in place for application. The offence was planned, deliberate and ongoing. There were no facts presented to show that the accused intended at any time to address his unlawful act or remove himself from the country to properly apply for admission. He is currently willing to leave Canada but it appears only because he was prosecuted.

Any hardship on the accused's family was inflicted by his act. There are no exceptional circumstances in this case that would compel the court to put the accused in a position he would have been in but for his third illegal entry. The accused was sentenced to four months and 13 days in custody. Without credit for pre-sentence custody, the jail term imposed would have been five months. The time spent in custody prior to this sentencing hearing was nine days. The amount of time credited was 18 days.

See the *R. v. Zelaya* summary under s. 123 of IRPA.

125. Penalties — **A person who commits an offence under subsection 124(1) is liable**

    (a) on conviction on indictment, to a fine of not more than $50,000 or to imprisonment for a term of not more than two years, or to both; or

    (b) on summary conviction, to a fine of not more than $10,000 or to imprisonment for a term of not more than six months, or to both.

126. Counselling misrepresentation — Every person who knowingly counsels, induces, aids or abets or attempts to counsel, induce, aid or abet any person to directly or indirectly misrepresent or withhold material facts relating to a relevant matter that induces or could induce an error in the administration of this Act is guilty of an offence.

Case Law

See the summary of *R. v. Mahamoud* (2015), 37 Imm. L.R. (4th) 79, 2015 CarswellOnt 12265 (C.J.), at s. 122, *supra.*

R. v. Al-Awaid (2015), 364 N.S.R. (2d) 350, 1146 A.P.R. 350, 2015 NSPC 52, 2015 CarswellNS 733, [2015] N.S.J. No. 369 — The accused pleaded guilty to eight offences under IRPA and 10 offences under the *Citizenship Act*. He had worked as an immigration consultant. Prospective citizenship applicants and permanent residents used his services to deal with the residency requirements associated with their applications for citizenship or to maintain their permanent resident status. Mr. Al-Awaid's serious health issues were taken into consideration. He was sentenced to a conditional sentence of two years less a day on each charge under IRPA to run concurrently. A $400 fine for each charge under the *Citizenship Act* totalling $4,000 was also imposed. He was required to perform 240 hours of community service. The incarceration was house arrest with significant conditions imposed.

R. v. Ren, 2015 ONSC 3397, 2015 CarswellOnt 7830, [2015] O.J. No. 2722 — The accused pleaded guilty to five counts and formally admitted the allegations in relation to the remaining 16 counts of counselling misrepresentation, contrary to s. 126 of the *Immigration and Refugee Protection Act*. Given the importance of public confidence and the integrity of Canada's immigration processes, the paramount objectives of sentencing must be denunciation and deterrence. Accordingly, a sentence of imprisonment of two years less one day was required. Ordering the sentence to be served in the community could dilute its denunciatory and deterrent impact. However, with the imposition of punitive conditions the accused's liberty can be restricted in a fashion that will make it clear both to her and to the community that she is truly serving a significant sentence of imprisonment. Accordingly, her term of imprisonment will be served in accordance with the terms of a conditional sentence order. For a substantial portion of her sentence, the accused should be under complete house arrest, with only those exceptions that are necessary to ensure her health and that of her parents and to enable the supervisor to administer the order. Apart from that, she should be subject to the same kind of restrictions on her liberty that she would be if serving the sentence in a custodial facility.

R. v. Lwamba, 2012 ONCJ 263, 2012 CarswellOnt 5371, [2012] O.J. No. 1964 — The defendants pleaded guilty to attempting to aid or abet a foreign national to misrepresent a material fact that could induce an error in the administration of IRPA by providing her with a Canadian passport which was fraudulently used to attempt to enter Canada, contrary to s. 126 of IRPA, thereby committing an offence contrary to s. 128. The court accepted the fact that this case fell into the less serious category of this type of offender. Their crimes were not motivated by financial gain. Instead, each defendant was attempting to assist an apparently harmless woman jump the queue to get into Canada in a misguided effort to affect a humanitarian purpose. Each was fined $5,000.

R. v. Dhalla, 2007 CarswellOnt 2095 (S.C.J.) — The respondent was sentenced on one count of counseling, aiding or abetting contrary to s. 126 of the IRPA to a fine of $5,000.

The appellant appealed the sentence. At the sentencing hearing, the Crown counsel had asked for six months incarceration due to the seriousness of child smuggling, the abandonment of the child, and the financial benefit to the respondent. Defence counsel took no position during the sentencing hearing.

While it was open to the trial judge to impose a custodial sentence, the sentence imposed was within the appropriate range for this type of offence, taking into account both the nature and gravity of the offence as well as the particular circumstances and antecedents of the respondent. The appeal was dismissed.

127. Misrepresentation — No person shall knowingly

    (a) directly or indirectly misrepresent or withhold material facts relating to a relevant matter that induces or could induce an error in the administration of this Act;

    (b) communicate, directly or indirectly, by any means, false or misleading information or declarations with intent to induce or deter immigration to Canada; or

    (c) refuse to be sworn or to affirm or declare, as the case may be, or to answer a question put to the person at an examination or at a proceeding held under this Act.

Case Law

R. v. Orr (2013), 20 Imm. L.R. (4th) 456, 2013 BCSC 1883, 2013 CarswellBC 4173, [2013] B.C.J. No. 2257 — The accused was convicted of one count under each of ss. 118(1), 124(1)(c) and 127(a) of IRPA. This was the first conviction in Canada under s. 118 of IRPA. Sentences have been imposed for human trafficking under s. 279.01 of the *Criminal Code* which involves an essential ingredient of exploitation which is not present under s. 118 of IRPA. Offences under s. 118 of IRPA will fall across a broad continuum of conduct. Aggravating factors can include whether bodily harm or death occurred, whether the life or safety of a person was endangered, whether the commission of the offence involved criminal organization, whether the commission of the offence was for profit or whether the victim was subject to humiliating and degrading treatment. The lack of significant aggravating factors puts this offence at the low end of the continuum. Individuals cannot be allowed to disregard the immigration laws of this country with impunity. The main sentencing objectives in the circumstance of this case must be those of denunciation and general deterrence. A conditional sentence would not be consistent with these objectives.

The accused was sentenced to 18 months in jail with respect to s. 118 and six months with respect to ss. 124 and 127. Since all three offences arose from the same general circumstances, the court must take into account the concept of totality and proportionality; therefore, the sentence on counts 2 and 3 dealing with ss. 124 and 127 were to be served concurrently with the 18-month sentence under s. 118.

Kandhai v. Canada (Minister of Citizenship & Immigration) (2009), 81 Imm. L.R. (3d) 144, 2009 FC 656, 2009 CarswellNat 1919, 2009 CarswellNat 5681 — The applicant sought judicial review of a decision refusing his application for humanitarian and compassionate exemption. The court determined it was appropriate to consider the application, notwithstanding the applicant's history of repeatedly lying to Canadian immigration authorities. The reasons given for refusing the H&C application were also insufficient. The officer's "reasons" essentially consisted of a review of facts coupled with a statement of conclusion, without any analysis to back it up. Consequently the application for judicial review was allowed. The decision under review was the applicant's third H&C application. He admitted that he was not truthful on his most recent H&C application, as he indicated on the form that he was divorced when in fact he was living in a common-law relationship with his ex-wife. The applicant argued that while the misrepresentation as to his marital situation was undoubtedly an error in judgment, it was not made with the intent of securing an advantage in relation to his H&C application, and thus had no negative effect on the integrity of the Canadian immigration process. In fact, the presence of a common-law partner in Canada may have strengthened his H&C application. In two prior H&C applications, the applicant indicated that he had never been charged with, or convicted of, a criminal offence in another country, when that was not, in fact, the case. These misrepresentations were made in order to gain an advantage in relation to those applications, and thus had the potential to undermine the integrity of the immigration process. In this case, since the misrepresentations did not appear to be made to gain an advantage, and the applicant appeared to have come forward voluntarily with his admission of misrepresentation, the court concluded that for the purposes of this "clean hands" analysis it was a very strong case.

The court relied on the Federal Court of Appeal decision in *Thanabalasingham v. Canada (Minister of Citizenship & Immigration)* (2006), 51 Imm. L.R. (3d) 1, where the court held that the task for the reviewing court is to strike a balance between "maintaining the integrity of, and preventing the abuse of, judicial and administrative processes," and "the public interest in ensuring the lawful conduct of government in the protection of fundamental human rights."

Koo v. 5220459 Manitoba Inc. (2010), 89 Imm. L.R. (3d) 140, 2010 MBQB 132, 2010 CarswellMan 248 — The issue on this *de novo* hearing under the Court of Queen's Bench Small Claims Practices Act was whether the Labour Market Opinion (LMO) obtained by the defendant and furnished to the plaintiff for submission by him in support of his application for a work permit gives the plaintiff the right to recover from the defendant in contract or tort for failure to pay him the wage referred to in the document. The LMO refers to a salary of $14.50 per hour. The defendant paid less than that to the plaintiff and it was agreed that if the plaintiff succeeded in his claim he was entitled to judgment for $9,057.06.

There is no provision in the statute or regulation expressly spelling out the consequences if incorrect information is given in the application for an LMO or if the employer chooses to pay the foreign national a salary less than indicated in the application.

It would be difficult to find that the LMO in itself or the providing of the LMO creates a contract, express or implied, between the plaintiff and defendant. The LMO is an expression of opinion by Service Canada of the matter set out therein. None of the essentials of a contract is present: offer, acceptance, privity, consideration and intention to create legal relations. The fundamental policy being to protect Canadian citizens or persons who are landed immigrants, it would be impossible for a member of that class to sustain an action against the defendant if the defendant had paid the plaintiff a salary greater than $14.50 per hour. It would be impossible for Service Canada to sustain an action against either party for breach of the terms of the document. There is no basis in contract for allowing the plaintiff to recover on the facts of this case. Nor is there a duty of care sufficient to support a tort action.

Is an employer free to disregard the salary set out in the LMO? Perhaps, perhaps not. If there is a false statement in the LMO, it may make it impossible for the employer to justify a finding of genuineness in a second or later application for an LMO. If there is a misrepresentation made knowingly, an employer may be subject to prosecution. Whatever the answer to the question, the plaintiff could have discussed the proposed salary with the defendant before receiving the LMO. He could have sought clarification from the defendant or refused to come to Canada. As it happens, the court found the parties did have a discussion, and the plaintiff agreed to accept a lesser salary. He was not entitled to recover from the defendant the difference between the salary stated in the LMO and the salary paid. The claim was dismissed.

R. v. Pandher (2009), 83 Imm. L.R. (3d) 322, 2009 CarswellOnt 5198 (C.J.) — The accused entered a plea to two counts of making a material misrepresentation by including falsified documents in applications for sponsorship under s. 127(a) of the IRPA and the Crown proceeded by indictment. The accused did so as a consultant to clients who retained him to file the applications on their behalf. The court concluded that it is people like the accused who give immigration consultants such a bad name and why they are held in such low regard and with such great suspicion. Accordingly, any sentence, because of the significant criminal acts, should reflect not only the court's extreme denunciation of his actions, which again strike at the heart of the security of this country, but also take advantage of desperate people who are trying to get their families into the country, and expose them to prosecution, all for the almighty dollar. Normally any sentence for these offences should be considerable jail sentences. The accused had suffered a heart attack and had some significant health issues in 2007 and accordingly the court acceded to the joint submission and conditional sentence. The accused was sentenced to 18 months conditional; for the first six months he was subject to house arrest, save and except traveling to and from his place of employment in a schedule to be provided to his supervisor at least once a week and to any medical appointments and medical emergencies for himself or his immediate family. For the remaining 12 months he was to observe a curfew except for medical emergencies or medical appointments. During the entire conditional sentence he will not be involved directly or indirectly with any sponsorship matters whatsoever. He was also prohibited from working in any form as a consultant on immigration matters.

R. v. Zhong (2008), 72 Imm. L.R. (3d) 287, [2008] B.C.J. No. 723, 2008 CarswellBC 815, 2008 BCSC 514 — The appellant appealed his conviction for making false statements on his immigration application to renew his student visa. He was charged and convicted of one count under s. 128 of the IRPA for misrepresenting facts relating to a relevant matter that could induce an error in the administration of the Act, by providing false transcripts and acceptance documents in support of his study permit renewal application, contrary to s. 127(a) of the Act.

The appellant testified that he was not aware that something illegal would happen with his application, that it was not his signature on the application document, that he never lived, at and was unaware of, the Surrey address given on the application, and that he did not see the fraudulent documents until his arrest in July 2007. He acknowledged that all of his previous study permit applications had been prepared with the assistance of the staff at the college that he was attending and they did not charge a large fee. Any fee charged was considerably less than the $8,000 he had paid the consultant who prepared this application. Intent was the only issue before the trial judge. The trial judge concluded that it was incredible that the appellant did not know that his payment of $8,000 was to obtain fraudulent papers. He questioned why a $2,000 deposit would be paid for something that had cost "next to nothing" on other occasions. He concluded that it was "probable" that the $8,000 was for obtaining false documents, that this is what $8,000 would get you, that anybody who did not realize that was "beyond willfully blind," and that the appellant was desperate.

On appeal, the court found a reasonable inference on the whole of the evidence that a payment of $8,000 must have been for more than completion of an application. The fact that the appellant had paid a minimum amount on several occasions previously was evidence of a reasonable amount to be paid for an application. The Appeal Court did not accept that the trial judge had to consider that the immigration consultant's self description as an immigration consultant automatically put his fees into a different service category than the school-based consultant. Accordingly, the reasons of the trial judge, taken as a whole, did not reflect a reversible error.

R. v. Hupang, 2007 CarswellBC 3491 (Prov. Ct.); varied (2008), 76 Imm. L.R. (3d) 1, 261 B.C.A.C. 298, 440 W.A.C. 298, 2008 CarswellBC 2498, 2008 BCCA 4 — The accused pled guilty to a charge under s. 127(a) of the IRPA that he knowingly misrepresented material facts relevant to the administration of the Act. In this case the accused, through searching the Internet, found an individual who was prepared to provide false university or college transcripts and false acceptance letters for a fee. The accused paid $3,000 to receive the false documentation.

It is incumbent on the court to impose a sentence that is fit in all the circumstances, including the circumstances of the accused. The accused had no criminal history in Canada, and the court accepted that he probably had no criminal history where he came from. By all accounts, he was seeking to improve his life. However, the court had to consider the issue of general deterrence and that issue, with respect to this case, is the issue of people lying to either get into or stay in this country. Once somebody does that they become a security risk, not only to Canada but to the US. It is unquestionable that security is a major concern in these times. The court has to send a message, not only to the accused, but to anybody who may be willing to search the Internet to get false documentation to stay in the country.

Although a discharge might well have been in the accused's best interests, it would be contrary to the public interest. The public interest in this case was paramount. The court stated: "the public interest includes the issue of national security and international security. Canada must be seen as a nation that will not tolerate illegal immigrants. It must be seen as a nation that will protect the integrity of our national security and the security of our neighbour to the south. If we do not do that, all of our borders will be closed, the walls will be built, and we will be in a very isolated and dangerous situation."

The accused was sentenced to two months in jail as well as a $2,500 fine. The Court of Appeal varied the sentence by setting aside the custodial sentence and imposing a sentence of 17 days imprisonment, representing time already served. The fine was not altered.

R. v. Tongo, 2002 CarswellBC 2657, 2002 BCPC 463 — The accused pleaded guilty under s. 127(a) of the IRPA. IRPA was a strong response by Parliament to a growing problem of illegal migration. Part 3 recognizes the role of organized crime and persons who would profit from such activity and establishes severe penalties which are considered to be aggravated by profit, by involvement of organized crime and by the inhuman treatment of the migrants, including humiliation, degradation, death or bodily harm. The

Act establishes a number of general offences to discourage persons from engaging in enabling activities such as employing illegal migrants and withholding relevant information. The accused were charged, and plead guilty to, the general enabling offence of withholding material facts relating to a relevant matter. The material fact, in this case, was the presence onboard the ship of the three Chinese migrants who were being transported to Canada for illegal entry. The accused were sentenced to two months incarceration, in addition to the equivalent of six weeks already spent, for their involvement in this activity.

128. Penalties — **A person who contravenes a provision of section 126 or 127 is guilty of an offence and liable**

    (a) on conviction on indictment, to a fine of not more than $100,000 or to imprisonment for a term of not more than five years, or to both; or

    (b) on summary conviction, to a fine of not more than $50,000 or to imprisonment for a term of not more than two years, or to both.

Case Law

See the *R. v. Zelaya* summary (2009), 77 Imm. L.R. (3d) 163, 2009 CarswellAlta 37, 2009 ABPC 7, under s. 123 of the Act.

R. v. Pandher (2009), 83 Imm. L.R. (3d) 322, 2009 CarswellOnt 5198 (C.J.) — The accused entered a plea to two counts of making a material misrepresentation by including falsified documents in applications for sponsorship under s. 127(a) of the IRPA and the Crown proceeded by indictment. The accused did so as a consultant to clients who retained him to file the applications on their behalf. The court concluded that it is people like the accused who give immigration consultants such a bad name and why they are held in such low regard and with such great suspicion. Accordingly, any sentence, because of the significant criminal acts, should reflect not only the court's extreme denunciation of his actions, which again strike at the heart of the security of this country, but also take advantage of desperate people who are trying to get their families into the country, and expose them to prosecution, all for the almighty dollar. Normally any sentence for these offences should be considerable jail sentences. The accused had suffered a heart attack and had some significant health issues in 2007 and accordingly the court acceded to the joint submission and conditional sentence. The accused was sentenced to 18 months conditional; for the first six months he was subject to house arrest, save and except traveling to and from his place of employment in a schedule to be provided to his supervisor at least once a week and to any medical appointments and medical emergencies for himself or his immediate family. For the remaining 12 months he was to observe a curfew except for medical emergencies or medical appointments. During the entire conditional sentence he will not be involved directly or indirectly with any sponsorship matters whatsoever. He was also prohibited from working in any form as a consultant on immigration matters.

R v. Ng (2008), 241 C.C.C. (3d) 340, 263 B.C.A.C. 300, 2008 CarswellBC 2823, 2008 BCCA 535 — The appellant kept a common bawdy house for almost two years and employed more than two prostitutes. He was convicted of procuring two of them to have illicit sexual intercourse, one of them over a lengthy period of time. He ran a prostitution business from which he profited. Deterrence is a significant factor in sentencing for these offences. Because of the moral turpitude involved, denunciation is an equally significant factor. The sentences imposed for the prostitution offences do not adequately speak to these factors and are unfit. The global sentence was inadequate. The Crown's leave to appeal to increase the global sentence by one year to 27 months was allowed. The court did not disturb the sentences for the immigration offences. The appellant had been convicted under s. 117(1) of the IRPA for inducing, aiding or abetting the coming into Canada of a person who was not in possession of a valid visa, passport or other document required by the IRPA and of inducing, aiding or abetting or attempting to counsel, induce, aid or abet a person, to directly or indirectly misrepresent or withhold material facts relating to a relevant matter that induces or could induce an error in the administration of the IRPA under s. 126 of the IRPA.

The immigration sentencing cases relied upon by the Crown involved more serious circumstances and, in some cases at least, offenders with existing criminal records. The appellant, who had no prior record, assisted one person to illegally enter Canada, apparently without compromising her physical safety. It seems that there are no reported sentencing decisions in immigration cases that involve comparable facts. If the two immigration offences were the only offences for which the appellant had been convicted, it would have been the court's opinion that the concurrent nine-month sentences were at the low end of the scale but not unfit. The sentences for the immigration offences were not varied on appeal.

R. v. Dhalla, 2007 CarswellOnt 2095 (S.C.J.) — The respondent was sentenced on one count of counseling, aiding or abetting contrary to s. 126 of the IRPA to a fine of $5,000. The appellant appealed the sentence. At the sentencing hearing, the Crown counsel had asked for six months incarceration due to the seriousness of child smuggling, the abandonment of the child, and the financial benefit to the respondent. Defence counsel took no position during the sentencing hearing.

While it was open to the trial judge to impose a custodial sentence, the sentence imposed was within the appropriate range for this type of offence, taking into account both the nature and gravity of the offence as well as the particular circumstances and antecedents of the respondent. The appeal was dismissed.

129. (1) **Offences relating to officers** — Every person is guilty of an offence who

(a) being an officer or an employee of the Government of Canada, knowingly makes or issues any false document or statement, or accepts or agrees to accept a bribe or other benefit, in respect of any matter under this Act or knowingly fails to perform their duties under this Act;

(b) gives or offers to give a bribe or consideration to, or makes an agreement or arrangement with, an officer to induce the officer not to perform their duties under this Act;

(c) falsely personates an officer or by any act or omission leads any person to believe that the person is an officer; or

(d) obstructs or impedes an officer in the performance of the officer's duties under this Act.

(2) Punishment — Every person who is guilty of an offence under subsection (1) is liable

    (a) on conviction on indictment, to a fine of not more than $50,000 or to imprisonment for a term of not more than five years, or to both; or

    (b) on summary conviction, to a fine of not more than $10,000 or to imprisonment for a term of not more than six months, or to both.

[Heading repealed 2011, c. 8, s. 2.]

130. [Repealed 2001, c. 32, s. 81(3)(a).]

131. Counselling offence — Every person who knowingly induces, aids or abets or attempts to induce, aid or abet any person to contravene section 117, 118, 119, 122, 124 or 129, or who counsels a person to do so, commits an offence and is liable to the same penalty as that person.

2001, c. 32, s. 81(3)(b)

132. [Repealed 2001, c. 32, s. 81(3)(c).]

Prosecution of Offences

133. Deferral — A person who has claimed refugee protection, and who came to Canada directly or indirectly from the country in respect of which the claim is made, may not be charged with an offence under section 122, paragraph 124(1)(a) or section 127 of this Act or under section 57, paragraph 340(c) or section 354, 366, 368, 374 or 403 of the *Criminal Code*, in relation to the coming into Canada of the person, pending disposition of their claim for refugee protection or if refugee protection is conferred.

Case Law

R. v. Agbor, 2010 BCCA 278, 2010 CarswellBC 1494 — The appellant pled guilty to one count of using a false document to enter or remain in Canada, contrary to s. 122(1)(b) of IRPA. He then sought to have the conviction quashed. The charge in which the conviction was entered related to the appellant's entry into Canada on January 27, 2008, using a fake French passport. The fake passport was detected at the time of attempted entry, and the appellant was found to be inadmissible to Canada. A removal order was issued against him. The appellant subsequently attempted to make a refugee claim, but was ineligible to do so because s. 99(3) of the Act does not allow a person who is subject to a removal order to make such a claim. He was allowed, however, under s. 112 of the Act to make an application to the Minister for protection, and he did so on September 28, 2008. Section 113 of the Act provides that a successful application for protection confers refugee protection on the applicant. The appellant was ultimately successful in his application for protection. He now has refugee protection in Canada. Section 133 of the Act prevents refugee claimants from being charged with certain immigration offences unless and until their claims have been rejected. An application for protection under s. 112 constitutes a claim for refugee protection and for the purposes of s. 133. Accordingly, the accused should not have been charged with the offence under s. 122 pending determination of his claim for protection. As the claim for protection has now succeeded, the appellant cannot be charged with the offence. The guilty plea was struck and the conviction quashed.

133.1 (1) Limitation period for summary conviction offences — A proceeding by way of summary conviction for an offence under section 117, 126 or 127, or section 131 as it relates to section 117, may be instituted at any time within, but not later than, 10 years after the day on which the subject-matter of the proceeding arose, and a proceeding by way of summary conviction for any other offence under this Act may be instituted at any time within, but not later than, five years after the day on which the subject-matter of the proceeding arose.

(2) Application — Subsection (1) does not apply if the subject-matter of the proceeding arose before the day on which this section comes into force.

2011, c. 8, s. 3; 2012, c. 17, s. 46

134. Defence — incorporation by reference — No person may be found guilty of an offence or subjected to a penalty for the contravention of a provision of a regulation that incorporates material by reference, unless it is proved that, at the time of the alleged contravention,

   (a) the material was reasonably accessible to the person;

   (b) reasonable steps had been taken to ensure that the material was accessible to persons likely to be affected by the regulation; or

   (c) the material had been published in the *Canada Gazette*.

135. Offences outside Canada — An act or omission that would by reason of this Act be punishable as an offence if committed in Canada is, if committed outside Canada, an offence under this Act and may be tried and punished in Canada.

136. (1) Venue — A proceeding in respect of an offence under this Act may be instituted, tried and determined at the place in Canada where the offence was committed or at the place in Canada where the person charged with the offence is or has an office or place of business at the time of the institution of those proceedings.

(2) Where commission outside Canada — A proceeding in respect of an offence under this Act that is committed outside Canada may be instituted, tried and determined at any place in Canada.

Forfeiture

137. (1) Forfeiture — A court that convicts a person of an offence under this Act may, in addition to any other punishment imposed, order that any offence-related property seized in relation to the offence be forfeited to Her Majesty in right of Canada.

(2) Regulations — The regulations may define the expression "offence-related property" for the purposes of this section, may provide for any matter relating to the application of this section, and may include provisions respecting the return to their lawful owner, disposition, or disposition of the proceeds of disposition, of offence-related property that has been seized.

Officers Authorized to Enforce Act

138. (1) Powers of peace officer — An officer, if so authorized, has the authority and powers of a peace officer — including those set out in sections 487 to 492.2 of the *Criminal Code* — to enforce this Act, including any of its provisions with respect to the arrest, detention or removal from Canada of any person.

(2) Temporary assistants — An officer may, in cases of emergency, employ a person to assist the officer in carrying out duties under this Act. That person has the authority and powers of the officer for a period of no more than 48 hours, unless approved by the Minister.

139. (1) Search — An officer may search any person seeking to come into Canada and may search their luggage and personal effects and the means of transportation that conveyed the person to Canada if the officer believes on reasonable grounds that the person

    (a) has not revealed their identity or has hidden on or about their person documents that are relevant to their admissibility; or

    (b) has committed, or possesses documents that may be used in the commission of, an offence referred to in section 117, 118 or 122.

(2) Search by person of same sex — A search of a person under this section must be performed by a person of the same sex as the person being searched. If an officer of the same sex is not available, any suitable person of the same sex may be authorized by an officer to perform the search.

140. (1) Seizure — An officer may seize and hold any means of transportation, document or other thing if the officer believes on reasonable grounds that it was fraudulently or improperly obtained or used or that the seizure is necessary to prevent its fraudulent or improper use or to carry out the purposes of this Act.

[Editor's Note: SOR/2002-227, s. 332 provides that a thing seized under the former Immigration Act, *R.S.C. 1985, c. I-2 continues to be seized on June 28, 2002, and the seizure is governed by the provisions of the new* Immigration and Refugee Protection Act, *S.C. 2001, c. 27.]*

(2) Interpretation — Despite subsection 42(2) of the *Canada Post Corporation Act*, a thing or document that is detained under the *Customs Act* and seized by an officer is not in the course of post for the purposes of the *Canada Post Corporation Act*.

(3) Regulations — The regulations may provide for any matter relating to the application of this section and may include provisions respecting the deposit of security as a guarantee to replace things that have been seized or that might otherwise be seized, and the return to their lawful owner, and the disposition, of things that have been seized.

[Editor's Note: SOR/2002-227, s. 331 provides that a performance bond posted or security deposited under the former Immigration Act, R.S.C. 1985, c. I-2 that remains posted or deposited immediately before June 28, 2002 continues as a deposit or a guarantee under the new Immigration and Refugee Protection Act, S.C. 2001, c. 27 and is governed by its provisions.]

141. Oaths and evidence — Every officer has the authority to administer oaths and to take and receive evidence under oath on any matter arising out of this Act.

Peace Officers

142. Duties of peace officers to execute orders — Every peace officer and every person in immediate charge or control of an immigrant station shall, when so directed by an officer, execute any warrant or written order issued under this Act for the arrest, detention or removal from Canada of any permanent resident or foreign national.

143. Authority to execute warrants and orders — A warrant issued or an order to detain made under this Act is, notwithstanding any other law, sufficient authority to the person to whom it is addressed or who may receive and execute it to arrest and detain the person with respect to whom the warrant or order was issued or made.

Ticketable Offences

144. (1) Prosecution of designated offences — In addition to other procedures set out in this Act or in the *Criminal Code* for commencing a proceeding, proceedings in respect of any offence that is prescribed by regulation may be commenced in accordance with this section.

(2) Procedure — An officer may commence a proceeding by

(a) completing a ticket that consists of a summons portion and an information portion;

(b) delivering the summons portion of the ticket to the accused or mailing it to the accused at the accused's latest known address, and

(c) filing the information portion of the ticket with a court of competent jurisdiction before or as soon as practicable after the summons portion has been delivered or mailed.

(3) Content of ticket — The summons and information portions of a ticket must

(a) set out a description of the offence and the time and place of its alleged commission;

(b) include a statement, signed by the officer, that there are reasonable grounds to believe that the accused committed the offence;

(c) set out the amount of the prescribed fine for the offence and the manner in which and period within which it must be paid;

(d) include a statement that, if the accused pays the fine within the period set out in the ticket, a conviction will be entered and recorded against the accused; and

(e) include a statement that if the accused wishes to plead not guilty or for any other reason fails to pay the fine within the period set out in the ticket, the accused must appear in the court and at the time set out in the ticket.

(4) Consequences of payment — Payment of the fine by the accused within the period set out in the ticket constitutes a plea of guilty to the offence described in the ticket and, following the payment,

(a) a conviction shall be entered against the accused and no further action shall be taken against the accused in respect of that offence; and

(b) any thing seized from the accused under this Act relating to the offence described in the ticket, or any proceeds realized from its disposition, are forfeited to Her Majesty in right of Canada and may be disposed of as the Minister directs.

(5) Regulations — The regulations may provide for any matter relating to the application of this section, and may include provisions prescribing

(a) the offences referred to in subsection (1) and the manner in which those offences may be described in tickets; and

(b) the amount of the fine, not exceeding $10,000, for a prescribed offence.

Debt Due to Her Majesty

145. (1) Debts due — The following amounts are debts due to Her Majesty in right of Canada payable on demand:

(a) a debt incurred by Her Majesty for which any person is liable under this Act;

(b) an amount that a person has agreed to pay as a deposit or guarantee of performance of an obligation under this Act;

(b.1) the amount of a penalty imposed under any regulation made under paragraph 32(d.4);

(c) the costs incurred in removing a prescribed foreign national from Canada;

(d) an amount that is ordered to be paid under section 147 on account of an unpaid liability; and

(e) an amount referred to in paragraph 148(1)(g).

[Editor's Note: SOR/2002-227, s. 331 provides that a performance bond posted or security deposited under the former Immigration Act, *R.S.C. 1985, c. I-2 that remains posted or deposited immediately before June 28, 2002 continues as a deposit or a guarantee under the new* Immigration and Refugee Protection Act, *S.C. 2001, c. 27 and is governed by its provisions.]*

(2) Debts due — sponsors — Subject to any federal-provincial agreement, an amount that a sponsor is required to pay under the terms of an undertaking is payable on demand to Her Majesty in right of Canada and Her Majesty in right of the

province concerned and may be recovered by Her Majesty in either or both of those rights.

(3) Recovery of debt — **A debt may be recovered at any time.**

[Editor's Note: SOR/2002-227, s. 333 provides that any debt under s. 118(3) of the former Immigration Act, *R.S.C. 1985, c. I-2 continues as a debt on June 28, 2002 and is governed by the provisions of the new* Immigration and Refugee Protection Act, *S.C. 2001, c. 27.]*

2014, c. 20, s. 304

Case Law

Mavi v. Canada (Attorney General) (2011), 97 Imm. L.R. (3d) 173, [2011] 2 S.C.R. 504, 19 Admin. L.R. (5th) 1, 2011 SCC 30, 2011 CarswellOnt 4429, 2011 CarswellOnt 4430 — The present proceedings were initiated by eight sponsors whose relatives received social assistance and are therefore deemed to have defaulted on their undertakings. The sponsors deny liability under the undertakings and sought various declarations. The result of which, if granted, would be to avoid payment either temporarily or permanently.

Parliament's legislation manifests an unambiguous intent to require the full sponsorship debt to be paid if and when the sponsor is in a position to do so, even incrementally over many years pursuant to an agreement under the Regulations. In dealing with defaulting sponsors, the government must however act fairly having regard to their financial means to pay and the existence of circumstances that would militate against enforcement of immediate payment. In the exercise of this discretion, which Parliament has made clear is narrow in scope, the Crown is bound by a duty of procedural fairness. Nevertheless the content of the duty of fairness in these circumstances is less ample than was contemplated in the decision of the Court of Appeal and, contrary to its opinion, the requirements of procedural fairness were met in the cases of the eight respondent sponsors. The Supreme Court of Canada held the undertakings were valid but that they were also structured, controlled and supplemented by federal legislation. The debts created thereby are not only contractual but statutory, and as such their enforcement is not exclusively governed by the private law of contract. The Crown does have a limited discretion to delay enforcement action having regard to the sponsors' circumstances and to enter into agreements respecting terms of payment, but this discretion does not extend to the forgiveness of the statutory debt. Debt collection without any discretion would not advance the purposes of IRPA. Excessively harsh treatment of defaulting sponsors may risk discouraging others from bringing their relatives to Canada which would undermine the policy of promoting family reunification.

Collection of Debts Due to Her Majesty

146. (1) Certificates — **An amount or part of an amount payable under this Act that has not been paid may be certified by the Minister**

    (a) without delay, if the Minister is of the opinion that the person liable for that amount is attempting to avoid payment; and

    (b) in any other case, on the expiration of 30 days after the default.

(1.1) Minister of Employment and Social Development — When a penalty is imposed as a result of the Minister of Employment and Social Development exercising a power conferred on him or her by regulation made under paragraph 32(d.4), that Minister is responsible for the recovery of the debt referred to in paragraph 145(1)(b.1).

(2) Judgments — The certificate is to be filed and registered in the Federal Court and, when registered, has the same force and effect, and all proceedings may be taken, as if the certificate were a judgment obtained in the Court for a debt of the amount specified in the certificate plus interest to the day of payment.

(3) Costs — The costs of registering the certificate are recoverable in the same manner as if they had been included in the certificate.

[Editor's Note: SOR/2002-227, s. 333 provides that any debt under s. 118(3) of the former Immigration Act, *R.S.C. 1985, c. I-2 continues as a debt on June 28, 2002 and is governed by the provisions of the new* Immigration and Refugee Protection Act, *S.C. 2001, c. 27.]*

2014, c. 20, s. 305

147. (1) Garnishment — If the Minister is of the opinion that a person is or is about to become liable to make a payment to a person liable to make a payment under this Act, the Minister may, by written notice, order the first person to pay to the Receiver General, on account of the second person's liability, all or part of the money otherwise payable to the second person.

(2) Applicability to future payments — If the Minister, under subsection (1), orders an employer to pay to the Receiver General money otherwise payable to an employee as remuneration,

> (a) the order is applicable to all future payments of remuneration until the liability is satisfied; and

> (b) the employer shall pay to the Receiver General out of each payment of remuneration the amount that the Minister stipulates in the notice.

(3) Discharge of liability — The receipt of the Minister is a good and sufficient discharge of the original liability to the extent of the payment.

(4) Regulations — The regulations may provide for any matter relating to the application of this section.

Transportation Companies

148. (1) Obligation of operators of vehicles and facilities — A person who owns or operates a vehicle or a transportation facility, and an agent for such a person, must, in accordance with the regulations,

> (a) not carry to Canada a person who is prescribed or does not hold a prescribed document, or who an officer directs not be carried;

> (b) hold the prescribed documentation of a person whom it carries to Canada until an examination begins, present the person for examination and hold the person until the examination is completed;

(c) **arrange for a medical examination and medical treatment and observation of a person it carries to Canada;**

(d) **provide prescribed information, including documentation and reports;**

(e) **provide facilities for the holding and examination of persons being carried to Canada;**

(f) **carry from Canada a person whom it has carried to or caused to enter Canada and who is prescribed or whom an officer directs to be carried;**

(g) **pay for all prescribed costs and fees relating to paragraphs (a), (b), (c) and (f); and**

(h) **provide security for compliance with its obligations under paragraphs (a) to (g).**

(2) **Seizure of security for compliance** — **If a person who owns or operates a vehicle or a transportation facility, or an agent of such a person, fails to comply with an obligation under this Act, all or part of any security provided by the person and any vehicle or other prescribed good owned or operated by the person may be detained, seized or forfeited to Her Majesty in right of Canada.**

[Editor's Note: SOR/2002-227, s. 332 provides that a thing seized under the former Immigration Act, *R.S.C. 1985, c. I-2 continues to be seized on June 28, 2002, and the seizure is governed by the provisions of the new* Immigration and Refugee Protection Act, *S.C. 2001, c. 27.]*

Case Law

KLM Royal Dutch Airlines v. Canada (Soliciteur général), 2004 CarswellNat 5196, 2004 CarswellNat 536, 2004 FC 308, (sub nom. *KLM Royal Dutch Airlines v. Canada (Attorney General))* 258 F.T.R. 261 (Eng.) — This was an application to review a decision by Citizenship and Immigration Canada that the applicant owes $114,000 to the respondent for removal costs of one Mohamed Moussa Mouhoumed. Mr. Mouhoumed came to Canada on January 19, 1999 from France. He arrived with a false passport. A deportation order was issued the same day but stayed because Mr. Mouhoumed claimed refugee status. The respondent advised the applicant that it had an obligation to transport Mr. Mouhoumed to Djibouti. The applicant agreed to transport Mr. Mouhoumed but could not because of Mr. Mouhoumed's resistance and violent behaviour. The applicant refused to pay the cost of chartering a private plane and finally the respondent removed Mr. Mouhoumed of its own initiative and asked the applicant to reimburse the costs which request was refused. The respondent advised the applicant that unless the amount was paid the amount of the security provided by the applicant could be forfeited under subs. 148(2) of IRPA.

The applicable standard of review is that of reasonableness *simpliciter.*

On the facts of this case, the decision by the respondent that the applicant had not been prompt in fulfilling its obligation to remove Mr. Mouhoumed was reasonable. The application for judicial review was dismissed.

149. Use of information — The following provisions govern information provided under paragraph 148(1)(d):

(a) the information may be used only for the purposes of this Act or the *Department of Citizenship and Immigration Act* or to identify a person for whom a warrant of arrest has been issued in Canada; and

(b) notice regarding use of the information must be given to the person to whom it relates.

2004, c. 15, s. 71

150. Regulations — The regulations may provide for any matter relating to the purposes of sections 148 and 149, may define, for the purposes of this Act, terms used in those sections and may include provisions respecting

(a) the requirements and procedures applicable to a person who owns or operates a vehicle or a transportation facility;

(b) the costs and fees for which a person who owns or operates a vehicle or a transportation facility is liable;

(c) the procedures to be followed when a vehicle or other security is detained, seized, forfeited to Her Majesty in right of Canada or returned; and

(d) the procedures by which a person may make claim that their interest in a vehicle or other good is not affected by it being detained, seized or forfeited to Her Majesty in right of Canada.

Sharing of Information
[Heading added 2004, c. 15, s. 72.]

150.1 (1) Regulations — The regulations may provide for any matter relating to

(a) the collection, retention, use, disclosure and disposal of information, including a Social Insurance Number, for the purposes of this Act or for the purposes of program legislation as defined in section 2 of the *Canada Border Services Agency Act*;

Proposed Addition — 150.1(1)(a.1)

(a.1) the collection, retention and use of a Social Insurance Number by the Minister of Employment and Social Development in respect of an assessment provided by the Department of Employment and Social Development or in respect of the compliance regime that applies to an employer, in relation to the employment of a foreign national or a permanent resident;

2014, c. 39, s. 313(2) [Not in force at date of publication.]

(b) the disclosure of information for the purposes of national security, the defence of Canada or the conduct of international affairs, including the implementation of an agreement or arrangement entered into under section 5 or 5.1 of the *Department of Citizenship and Immigration Act* or section 13 of the *Canada Border Services Agency Act*;

(c) the disclosure of information relating to the professional or ethical conduct of a person referred to in any of paragraphs 91(2)(a) to (c) in connection with a proceeding — other than a proceeding before a superior court — or application under this Act to a body that is responsible for governing or investigating that conduct or to a person who is responsible for investigating that conduct, for the purposes of ensuring that persons referred to in those paragraphs offer and provide professional and ethical representation and advice to persons in connection with such proceedings and applications;

(d) the retention, use, disclosure and disposal by the Royal Canadian Mounted Police of biometric information and any related personal information that is provided to it under this Act for the enforcement of any law of Canada or a province; and

Proposed Amendment — 150.1(1)(d)

(d) the retention, use, disclosure and disposal by the Royal Canadian Mounted Police of biometric information and any related personal information that is collected under this Act and provided to it for the enforcement of any law of Canada or a province; and

2015, c. 36, s. 174 [Not in force at date of publication.]

(e) the disclosure of information for the purposes of cooperation between the Government of Canada and the government of a province.

(2) **Conditions** — Regulations made under subsection (1) may include conditions under which the collection, retention, use, disposal and disclosure may be made.
2004, c. 15, s. 72; 2005, c. 38, s. 119; 2011, c. 8, s. 4; 2012, c. 17, s. 47; 2014, c. 39, s. 313(1), (3)

PART 4 — IMMIGRATION AND REFUGEE BOARD

Composition of Board

151. Immigration and Refugee Board — The Immigration and Refugee Board consists of the Refugee Protection Division, the Refugee Appeal Division, the Immigration Division and the Immigration Appeal Division.

152. Composition — The Board is composed of a Chairperson and other members as are required to ensure the proper functioning of the Board.

152.1 Oath or affirmation of office — The Chairperson and other members of the Board must swear the oath or give the solemn affirmation of office set out in the rules of the Board.

2010, c. 8, s. 17

153. (1) Chairperson and other members — The Chairperson and members of the Refugee Appeal Division and Immigration Appeal Division

(a) are appointed to the Board by the Governor in Council, to hold office during good behaviour for a term not exceeding seven years, subject to removal by the Governor in Council at any time for cause, to serve in a regional or district office of the Board;

(b) [Repealed 2010, c. 8, s. 18(2).]

(c) are eligible for reappointment in the same or another capacity;

(d) shall receive the remuneration that may be fixed by the Governor in Council;

(e) are entitled to be paid reasonable travel and living expenses incurred while absent in the course of their duties, in the case of a full-time member, from their ordinary place of work or, in the case of a part-time member, while absent from their ordinary place of residence;

(f) are deemed to be employed in the public service for the purposes of the *Public Service Superannuation Act* and in the federal public administration for the purposes of the *Government Employees Compensation Act* and any regulations made under section 9 of the *Aeronautics Act*;

(g) may not accept or hold any office or employment or carry on any activity inconsistent with their duties and functions under this Act; and

(h) if appointed as full-time members, must devote the whole of their time to the performance of their duties under this Act.

(1.1) [Repealed 2012, c. 17, s. 84(4).]

(2) **Deputy Chairperson and Assistant Deputy** — One Deputy Chairperson for each Division referred to in subsection (1) and not more than 10 Assistant Deputy Chairpersons are to be designated by the Governor in Council from among the full-time members of those Divisions.

(3) **Full-time and part-time appointments** — The Chairperson and the Deputy Chairpersons and Assistant Deputy Chairpersons of the Divisions referred to in subsection (1) are appointed on a full-time basis and the other members are appointed on a full-time or part-time basis.

(4) **Qualification** — The Deputy Chairperson of the Immigration Appeal Division and a majority of the Assistant Deputy Chairpersons of that Division and at least 10 per cent of the members of the Divisions referred to in subsection (1) must be members of at least five years standing at the bar of a province or notaries of at least five years standing at the Chambre des notaires du Québec.

2003, c. 22, s. 173; 2010, c. 8, s. 18; 2012, c. 17, ss. 48, 84(4)

Case Law

Mroshaj v. Canada (Minister of Citizenship & Immigration), 2004 CarswellNat 5302, 2004 CarswellNat 3635, 262 F.T.R. 118, 2004 FC 1395 — The applicant sought to review a negative determination of his claim for protection. The member who dismissed the claim was on extended medical leave at the time she decided the case.

Section 153(1)(h) does not deprive a full-time member who, is on extended medical leave, from deciding cases that she heard before her leave began.

154. Disposition after member ceases to hold office — A former member of the Board, within eight weeks after ceasing to be a member, may make or take part in a decision on a matter that they heard as a member, if the Chairperson so requests. For that purpose, the former member is deemed to be a member.

155. Disposition if member unable to take part — If a member of a three-member panel is unable to take part in the disposition of a matter that the member has heard, the remaining members may make the disposition and, for that purpose, are deemed to constitute the applicable Division.

156. Immunity and no summons — The following rules apply to the Chairperson and the members in respect of the exercise or purported exercise of their functions under this Act:

    (a) no criminal or civil proceedings lie against them for anything done or omitted to be done in good faith; and

    (b) they are not competent or compellable to appear as a witness in any civil proceedings.

Case Law

Bourbonnais c. Canada (Procureur général) (2006), 267 D.L.R. (4th) 120, *(sub nom. Bourbonnais v. Canada (Attorney General))* 348 N.R. 28, 2006 CarswellNat 318, 2006 CarswellNat 1030, 2006 FCA 62 — Close to 100 charges were laid against a member of the IRB for fraud against the government, breach of trust, and obstruction of justice. More particularly, the charges were with respect to having solicited and accepted money for the purpose of issuing favourable decisions to certain persons in cases that were being heard by the Board member.

The Board member claimed the right to be indemnified for his legal costs and fees incurred in defending himself on the charges against him. His claim was premised on the principle of judicial independence and its essential components: security of tenure, financial security and institutional independence. The Board member in this case was charged with soliciting and accepting money in exchange for favourable decisions. Consequently, the sole purpose of the trial he would have to undergo was to determine his guilt on those charges. Those proceedings do not challenge the notion of security of tenure, an essential component of judicial independence. The Board member was not entitled to obtain from the IRB the payment of legal costs and fees he would have to incur in defending himself against the charges laid against him. The Board member did not act in good faith, and accordingly, was not entitled to immunity.

Head Office and Staff

157. (1) Head office — The head office of the Board shall be in the National Capital Region as described in the Schedule to the *National Capital Act*.

(2) Residence — Chairperson — The Chairperson must live in the National Capital Region or within reasonable commuting distance of it.

158. Personnel — The Executive Director and other personnel necessary for the proper conduct of the business of the Board shall be appointed in accordance with the *Public Service Employment Act*, and the personnel are deemed to be employed in the public service for the purposes of the *Public Service Superannuation Act*.

[Editor's Note: S.C. 2001, c. 27, s. 188(4) provides that the person who, on June 28, 2002, held the office of Executive Director of the Immigration and Refugee Board is deemed to have been appointed to that office under section 158 of the new Immigration and Refugee Protection Act, *S.C. 2001, c. 27, without prejudice to any salary and benefits he or she may receive by virtue of having held that office before June 28, 2002.]*

2003, c. 22, s. 225(z.3)

Duties of Chairperson

159. (1) Chairperson — The Chairperson is, by virtue of holding that office, a member of each Division of the Board and is the chief executive officer of the Board. In that capacity, the Chairperson

(a) has supervision over and direction of the work and staff of the Board;

(b) may at any time assign a member appointed under paragraph 153(1)(a) to the Refugee Appeal Division or the Immigration Appeal Division;

(c) may at any time, despite paragraph 153(1)(a), assign a member of the Refugee Appeal Division or the Immigration Appeal Division to work in another regional or district office to satisfy operational requirements, but an assignment may not exceed 120 days without the approval of the Governor in Council;

(d) may designate, from among the full-time members appointed under paragraph 153(1)(a), coordinating members for the Refugee Appeal Division or the Immigration Appeal Division;

(e) assigns administrative functions to the members of the Board;

(f) apportions work among the members of the Board and fixes the place, date and time of proceedings;

(g) takes any action that may be necessary to ensure that the members of the Board carry out their duties efficiently and without undue delay;

(h) may issue guidelines in writing to members of the Board and identify decisions of the Board as jurisprudential guides, after consulting with the Deputy Chairpersons, to assist members in carrying out their duties; and

(i) may appoint and, subject to the approval of the Treasury Board, fix the remuneration of experts or persons having special knowledge to assist the Divisions in any matter.

(2) Delegation — The Chairperson may delegate any of his or her powers under this Act to a member of the Board, except that

(a) powers referred to in subsection 161(1) may not be delegated;

(b) powers referred to in paragraphs (1)(a) and (i) may be delegated to the Executive Director of the Board;

(c) powers in relation to the Immigration Appeal Division and the Refugee Appeal Division may only be delegated to the Deputy Chairperson, the Assistant Deputy Chairpersons, or other members, including coordinating members, of either of those Divisions; and

(d) powers in relation to the Immigration Division or the Refugee Protection Division may only be delegated to the Deputy Chairperson, the Assistant Deputy Chairpersons or other members, including coordinating members, of that Division.

2010, c. 8, s. 19

Case Law

Section 159(1)

Benitez v. Canada (Minister of Citizenship & Immigration), 2007 CarswellNat 1393, 2007 FCA 199 — The Federal Court consolidated a number of applications for judicial review impugning the validity of Guideline 7. Guideline 7 was issued by the Chairperson of the Board in 2003, pursuant to the power conferred by para. 159(1)(h) of the *Immigration and Refugee Protection Act,* S.C. 2001, c. 27, to issue guidelines to assist members of the Board in carrying out their duties ("the Guideline 7 issue"). Guideline 7 provides that the standard order of questioning at a refugee protection hearing by the Refugee Protection Division of the Board will be that the claimant is questioned first by the Refugee Protection officer and/or by the Refugee Protection Division member conducting the hearing. However, in exceptional cases members may permit claimants to be questioned first by their own counsel.

Guideline 7 does not breach the duty of fairness by either denying the claimants an effective opportunity to make representations or so distorting the role of the member of the Refugee Protection Division hearing the claim as to give rise to a reasonable apprehension of bias. Nor is it an unlawful fetter on members' discretion, and it was not legally required to have been issued under the Chairperson's statutory power to issue rules of procedure, subject to cabinet approval.

Thamotharem v. Canada (Minister of Citizenship & Immigration), 2006 CarswellNat 1588, 2006 FCA 218 — This appeal concerns the validity of Guideline 7 (preparation and conduct of a hearing in the Refugee Protection Division) issued in 2003 by the Chairperson of the Board pursuant to the statutory power to "issue guidelines. . .to assist members in carrying out their duties": *Immigration and Refugee Protection Act*, S.C. 2001, c. 27, para. 159(1)(h). The key paragraphs of Guideline 7 provide as follows:

> "In a claim for refugee protection, the standard practice will be for the Refugee Protection Officer to start questioning the claimant," although the member of the Refugee Protection Division ("RPD") hearing the claim "may vary the order of questioning in exceptional circumstances."

Guideline 7 is not, on its face, invalid on the ground of procedural unfairness, although, as the Minister and the Board conceded, fairness may require that, in certain circumstances particular claimants should be questioned first by their own counsel. Guideline 7 is not incompatible with the impartiality required of a member when conducting a hearing which is inquisitorial in form. Guideline 7 is not an unlawful fetter on the exercise of members' discretion on the conduct of refugee protection hearings. The Guideline expressly directs members to consider the facts of the particular case before them to determine whether there are exceptional circumstances warranting a deviation from the standard order of questioning. The evidence did not establish that members disregarded this aspect of Guideline 7 and slavishly adhered to the standard order of questioning, regardless of the facts of the case before them. Nor does it follow that the fact that Guideline 7 could have been issued as a statutory rule of procedure that it is invalid because it was not approved by the Governor in Council. The Minister's appeal was allowed, the appellant's cross-appeal was dismissed, the order of the Federal Court set aside, and the application for judicial review dismissed.

Karanja v. Canada (Minister of Citizenship & Immigration), 2006 CarswellNat 1265, 2006 CarswellNat 2533, 2006 FC 574 — Pursuant to the Gender Guidelines (*Women Refugee Claimants Fearing Gender-Related Persecution*, 9 March 1993, by the chairperson of the Immigration and Refugee Board pursuant to para. 159(1)(h) of the Immigration Act), the Board should be particularly sensitive to a female applicant's difficulty in testifying. However, the gender guidelines, in and of themselves, are not intended to serve as a cure for all deficiencies in the applicant's claim or evidence. The applicant bears the onus of proving her claim. The Guidelines cannot be treated as corroborating any evidence of gender-based persecution so that the giving of the evidence becomes proof of its truth.

Instead, the Guidelines are an aid for the panel in the assessment of the evidence of women who allege that they have been victims of gender-based persecution. The Guidelines do not create new grounds for finding a person to be a victim of persecution. A board's failure to specifically mention the Gender Guidelines does not mean that they were not considered and is not material or fatal to the Board's decision.

The Gender Guidelines specifically state that the female refugee claimant must demonstrate that the harm feared is sufficiently serious to amount to persecution. In this case, there were numerous negative credability findings by the Board and such findings are open to the Board to make. Accordingly, the applicant failed to demonstrate that the Board's decision was patently unreasonable so as to warrant the intervention of the court.

160. Absence, incapacity or vacancy — In the event of the absence or incapacity of the Chairperson, or if the office of Chairperson is vacant, the Minister may authorize one of the Deputy Chairpersons or any other member of the Board to act as Chairperson.

Functioning of Board

161. (1) Rules — Subject to the approval of the Governor in Council, and in consultation with the Deputy Chairpersons, the Chairperson may make rules respecting

    (a) the referral of a claim for refugee protection to the Refugee Protection Division;

    (a.1) the factors to be taken into account in fixing or changing the date of the hearing referred to in subsection 100(4.1);

    (a.2) the activities, practice and procedure of each of the Divisions of the Board, including the periods for appeal, other than in respect of appeals of decisions of the Refugee Protection Division, the priority to be given to proceedings, the notice that is required and the period in which notice must be given;

    (b) the conduct of persons in proceedings before the Board, as well as the consequences of, and sanctions for, the breach of those rules;

(c) the information that may be required and the manner in which, and the time within which, it must be provided with respect to a proceeding before the Board; and

(d) any other matter considered by the Chairperson to require rules.

(1.1) Distinctions — The rules made under paragraph (1)(c) may distinguish among claimants for refugee protection who make their claims inside Canada on the basis of whether their claims are made at a port of entry or elsewhere or on the basis of whether they are nationals of a country that is, on the day on which their claim is made, a country designated under subsection 109.1(1).

(2) Tabling in Parliament — The Minister shall cause a copy of any rule made under subsection (1) to be laid before each House of Parliament on any of the first 15 days on which that House is sitting after the approval of the rule by the Governor in Council.

2010, c. 8, s. 20 [Amended 2012, c. 17, s. 61.]; 2012, c. 17, ss. 49, 84(5)

Provisions that Apply to All Divisions

162. (1) Sole and exclusive jurisdiction — Each Division of the Board has, in respect of proceedings brought before it under this Act, sole and exclusive jurisdiction to hear and determine all questions of law and fact, including questions of jurisdiction.

(2) Procedure — Each Division shall deal with all proceedings before it as informally and quickly as the circumstances and the considerations of fairness and natural justice permit.

Case Law

Kamtasingh v. Canada (Minister of Citizenship & Immigration) (2010), 87 Imm. L.R. (3d) 118, 2010 FC 45, 2010 CarswellNat 801, 2010 CarswellNat 101 — This was an application for judicial review challenging a decision of the Immigration Appeal Division which determined the applicant's marriage was not genuine. The applicant states that the IAD member denied him procedural fairness by preventing him from calling all of his proposed witnesses.

The IAD has the right to limit repetitive testimony, but not by effectively excluding witnesses who could offer evidence going to the central issues of the case. The place to control excessive or repetitive evidence on issues of controversy which are central or determinative is generally not at the entrance to the witness box, but once the witness is testifying — and even then the member must grant some latitude to ensure that all important matters are covered. The IAD can, of course, limit the scope of evidence by stipulating certain points that are not in dispute. In a case like this one where the credibility of the applicant is clearly an issue and where the genuineness of a marriage is in doubt, the evidence of immediate family and close acquaintances is highly relevant and should be heard without reservation. Indeed, it was difficult to see how this matter could be fairly determined after only two hours of evidence, particularly when the applicant was self-represented and was initially intending to lead evidence from several witnesses. This was a situation where the duty to allow the applicant to fully present his case was sacrificed for the desire for administrative efficiency. That is not a permissible trade-off. The application for judicial review was allowed.

Canada (Minister of Citizenship & Immigration) v. Peirovdinnabi (2010), 87 Imm. L.R. (3d) 162, 2010 FC 64, 2010 CarswellNat 108, 2010 CarswellNat 726 — The issue considered was whether, in 2010, the respondent made a misrepresentation by answering "yes" to the question "are you living with your spouse," posed in a form entitled "Supplemental Information Spouse in Canada." This issue arose in the course of the respondent's sponsorship of his second wife to Canada in 2005. In the course of that application he was questioned about his living circumstances with his first wife three years before and he answered that he thought that the question posed at the time required an answer as to whether he and his first wife were living "together." To this question the respondent said that, while they were living together, he and his first wife maintained separate residences and lived in both after their marriage. The problem that arose was that the applicant interpreted the question answered by the respondent to mean "are you living together with your wife in the same residence." This conflict in interpretation set a course of decision making in motion which has resulted in the present application for judicial review of an IAD decision that found that the respondent did not make a misrepresentation.

The central argument advanced by the applicant in the present review of the IAD decision is that, as a matter of law, the IAD was required to determine the genuineness of the respondent's first marriage. The position that the applicant takes is that since the hearing before the IAD was *de novo*, all issues with respect to the respondent's first marriage were required to be determined. The court rejected this argument and found that the IAD took the appeal as it came: there was only one question to be addressed and that was whether the respondent made a misrepresentation. The question of whether the marriage was genuine was not determined in the first and second level decisions, and it was not in play in the IAD decision. The IAD's decision was upheld and the application for judicial review dismissed. The following question was certified:

> Does the IAD have an obligation in law to determine the genuineness of a marriage on a *de novo* appeal brought with respect to an issue of misrepresentation when the issue of the genuineness of the marriage concerned was not specifically raised for determination in the appeal?

Ferri v. Canada (Minister of Citizenship & Immigration) (2005), 51 Imm. L.R. (3d) 177, [2005] F.C.J. No. 1941, [2006] 3 F.C.R. 53, 2005 CarswellNat 3878, 2005 CarswellNat 5009, 2005 FC 1580 — Subsection 68(4) of the IRPA limits the jurisdiction of the IAD to determining whether the factual requirements of this subsection are met. The IAD can only consider whether it has previously stayed a removal order; whether the individual in question is a permanent resident or a foreign national who was found inadmissible on grounds of serious criminality or criminality; and whether the individual has been convicted of another offence coming within subs. 36(1) of the IRPA. Once the IAD determines that the factual requirements of this subsection have been met, it then loses jurisdiction over the individual, by operation of law. The IAD does not have jurisdiction to consider the constitutionality of subs. 68(4).

Alwan v. Canada (Minister of Citizenship & Immigration), 2004 CarswellNat 5221, 2004 CarswellNat 1689, 2004 FC 807 — The applicant's refugee claim was rejected under Article 1(F)(a) of the Refugee Convention. At the end of the hearing, the Refugee Protection Division panel asked counsel for the applicant, the refugee protection officer and the Minister's counsel for written submissions concerning the exclusion under Article 1(F)

Counsel for the Minister indicated that he would not be providing written submissions as he was of the view that the evidence before the Board in this respect was not compelling and that the test had not been made out. He left it to the RPD to draw its own conclusions. The Refugee Protection officer and counsel for the applicant provided written submissions. The Refugee Protection Division found that the test had been met and excluded the applicant.

The Refugee Protection Division was not required to defer to the opinion of the Minister's counsel. Subsection 162(1) vests the Refugee Protection Division with sole and exclusive jurisdiction to hear and determine all questions of law and fact including questions of jurisdiction.

163. Composition of panels — **Matters before a Division shall be conducted before a single member unless, except for matters before the Immigration Division, the Chairperson is of the opinion that a panel of three members should be constituted.**

164. Presence of parties — **Where a hearing is held by a Division, it may, in the Division's discretion, be conducted in the presence of, or by a means of live telecommunication with, the person who is the subject of the proceedings.**

Case Law

Sundaram v. Canada (Minister of Citizenship & Immigration), 2006 CarswellNat 499, 2006 CarswellNat 2426, 2006 FC 291 — When the IRB receives requests for a change of venue because a person cannot attend at a scheduled hearing location, it has an obligation to consider all relevant matters including its own discretionary powers relevant to the request. In this case, the applicant had moved from Toronto to Vancouver. As there was no indication in the conclusionary reasons that the Refugee Protection Division ever turned its mind to the issue of alternative means and locations of hearing, the decision not to reopen the dismissal of the applicant's refugee claim was quashed.

165. Powers of a commissioner — **The Refugee Protection Division, the Refugee Appeal Division and the Immigration Division and each member of those Divisions have the powers and authority of a commissioner appointed under Part I of the *Inquiries Act* and may do any other thing they consider necessary to provide a full and proper hearing.**

2010, c. 8, s. 22

Case Law

Canada (Minister of Public Safety & Emergency Preparedness) v. Kahlon (2005), 35 Admin. L.R. (4th) 213, 2005 CarswellNat 2255, 2005 CarswellNat 5610, 2005 FC 1000 — The proper procedure when there is a requirement to produce documents, whether by subpoena or otherwise, and there is a genuine dispute as to their relevance or as to whether they are privileged, is to have the documents produced, so that the tribunal charged with determining their relevance will have them available for examination. If any of the documents then turned out to be irrelevant, the privacy interest of the owner would be protected as the documents would not then be provided to the party making the demand. In this case, the Refugee Protection Division improperly exercised its powers to compel evidence and did not follow its own procedural rules.

166. Proceedings — all Divisions — Proceedings before a Division are to be conducted as follows:

(a) subject to the other provisions of this section, proceedings must be held in public;

(b) on application or on its own initiative, the Division may conduct a proceeding in the absence of the public, or take any other measure that it considers necessary to ensure the confidentiality of the proceedings, if, after having considered all available alternate measures, the Division is satisfied that there is

(i) a serious possibility that the life, liberty or security of a person will be endangered if the proceeding is held in public,

(ii) a real and substantial risk to the fairness of the proceeding such that the need to prevent disclosure outweighs the societal interest that the proceeding be conducted in public, or

(iii) a real and substantial risk that matters involving public security will be disclosed;

(c) subject to paragraph (d), proceedings before the Refugee Protection Division and the Refugee Appeal Division must be held in the absence of the public;

(c.1) subject to paragraph (d), proceedings before the Immigration Division must be held in the absence of the public if they concern a person who is the subject of a proceeding before the Refugee Protection Division or the Refugee Appeal Division that is pending or who has made an application for protection to the Minister that is pending;

(d) on application or on its own initiative, the Division may conduct a proceeding in public, or take any other measure that it considers necessary to ensure the appropriate access to the proceedings if, after having considered all available alternate measures and the factors set out in paragraph (b), the Division is satisfied that it is appropriate to do so;

(e) despite paragraphs (b) to (c.1), a representative or agent of the United Nations High Commissioner for Refugees is entitled to observe proceedings concerning a protected person or a person who has made a claim for refugee protection or an application for protection; and

(f) despite paragraph (e), the representative or agent may not observe any part of the proceedings that deals with information or other evidence in respect of which an application has been made under section 86, and not rejected, or with information or other evidence protected under that section.

2008, c. 3, s. 5; 2012, c. 17, s. 50(1), (3)

167. (1) Right to counsel — A person who is the subject of proceedings before any Division of the Board and the Minister may, at their own expense, be represented by legal or other counsel.

(2) Representation — **If a person who is the subject of proceedings is under 18 years of age or unable, in the opinion of the applicable Division, to appreciate the nature of the proceedings, the Division shall designate a person to represent the person.**

2010, c. 8, s. 23 [Amended 2012, c. 17, s. 63.]

Case Law

Section 167(1)

Charles v. Canada (Minister of Citizenship & Immigration) (2011), 99 Imm. L.R. (3d) 310, 37 Admin. L.R. (5th) 8, 2011 FC 852, 2011 CarswellNat 2765, 2011 CarswellNat 3654 — While the Federal Court has recognized that right to counsel is not absolute (*Sandy v. Canada (Minister of Citizenship & Immigration)* (2011), 41 Imm. L.R. (3d) 123, at para. 50), at the hearing, the applicant testified that he was in the process of obtaining a Legal Aid certificate that would take approximately two weeks and that would result in allowing him the representation he clearly sought. The Board erred in not taking into account the timing of the hearing *vis-à-vis* his release from detention, together with the fact that this was the first time the applicant had requested the adjournment. The respondent was correct to note that the Board's decision with respect to granting post-ponements or adjournments is discretionary in nature and there is no presumption of enti-tlement. At the same time, however, as articulated in *Baker v. Canada (Minister of Citizenship & Immigration)*, [1999] 2 S.C.R. 817: "The values underlying the duty of procedural fairness relate to the principle that the individual or individuals affected should have the opportunity to present their case fully and fairly [. . .]." The application was granted and the matter returned to a differently constituted panel for the applicant to have the hearing with representation that he was denied.

Thamotharampillai v. Canada (Minister of Citizenship & Immigration), 2011 FC 438, 2011 CarswellNat 1107, 2011 CarswellNat 1938 — As a general rule, a party is bound by the actions of his or her agent. However, there are times when a lawyer or an authorized representative has failed to mail a completed humanitarian and compassionate applica-tion, or has failed to inform the Board of the applicant's change of address. This is a different category altogether, and the category which is applicable in this instance. In this case, the consultant did absolutely nothing. The applicant was denied natural justice be-cause he was represented by an incompetent immigration consultant. Had the consultant been competent and done his duty, the decision may well have been different. The immi-gration consultant failed to make any submissions with respect to the PRRA application.

Cha v. Canada (Minister of Citizenship & Immigration), [2006] F.C.J. No. 491, 53 Imm. L.R. (3d) 1, 267 D.L.R. (4th) 324, 349 N.R. 233, 2006 CarswellNat 751, 2006 FCA 126 — The intent of Parliament is clear. The Minister's delegate is only empowered under subs. 44(2) of the Act to make the removal orders in prescribed cases which are clear and non-controversial and where the facts simply dictate the remedy. The Minister's delegate could not look at the gravity of the offence, and the particular circumstances of the applicant and his conviction, in determining not to issue the removal order. It is sim-ply not open to the Minister's delegate to indirectly or collaterally go beyond the actual conviction. To do so would ignore Parliament's clearly expressed intent that the breaking of the condition of non-criminality be determinative. Although the manual indicates that the personal circumstances of the offender will be considered at the front-end of the pro-cess before any decision is taken to remove an individual from Canada, these views and statements have been expressed in respect to permanent residents convicted of serious offences in Canada. No such assurances were given by specific reference to foreign nationals. A foreign national may wish to invoke humanitarian and compassionate considerations and is at liberty to make a request to the Minister pursuant to s. 25 of the Act or to stay a removal order pursuant to s. 233 of the Regulations, or avail himself of the pre-removal risk assessment proceeding pursuant to s. 112 of the Act.

Absent a Charter right to be notified of a right to counsel on arrest or detention, there is no authority for the proposition that a person is entitled, as of right, to be notified before a hearing that he or she has either a statutory right or a duty-of-fairness right to counsel. Once a person is sufficiently informed of the object and possible effects of a forthcoming hearing — absent sufficient notice, the decision rendered will in all likelihood be set aside — the decision maker is under no duty to go further.

It may be sound practice, in certain cases, to give notice in advance that counsel may be retained, but there is no duty to do so unless the statute requires it. The responsibility lies with the person to seek leave from the decision maker to be accompanied by counsel or to come to the hearing accompanied by counsel.

In the recent IRPA, the right to be informed of one's right to counsel in admissibility matters has disappeared and the right to counsel has been preserved only with respect to hearings before the Immigration Division. There is no provision concerning the right to counsel and proceedings before the immigration officer or the Minister's delegate under subs. 44(1) and (2) of the IRPA. In this case, the respondent did not seek leave to have counsel present during the interview or to attend accompanied by counsel.

If leave is denied or if counsel is not allowed to be present, that could become an issue in a judicial review of the decision ultimately rendered.

Mallette v. Canada (Minister of Citizenship & Immigration) (2005), 51 Imm. L.R. (3d) 267, 2005 CarswellNat 3224, 2005 FC 1400 — The applicant was ordered deported because she had been convicted of possession of narcotics for purposes of trafficking. She was granted a stay of execution of the deportation order for five years on 10 expressed conditions. The Minister's representative requested an early review of the stay of execution alleging breaches of the conditions imposed. The breaches included further criminal offences, the use of illegal drugs, sale of drugs including problems with keeping the peace and being of good behaviour. The Board did not cancel the stay but modified the initial conditions imposed on the applicant. The Board advised the applicant that an oral interim reconsideration of the case would take place the next year and that a final reconsideration would take place four years later or at such date as it determined. The applicant received a notice of the hearing date, however, arrived at the hearing without a lawyer and testified on her own behalf. The Board cancelled the order staying the applicant's removal and directed that she be removed from Canada as soon as reasonably possible.

The right to counsel is not absolute. Immigration case law indicates that a decision is invalid should the absence of counsel deprive the applicant of his or her right to a fair hearing. In *Mervilus v. Canada (Minister of Citizenship & Immigration)*, [2004] F.C.J. No. 1460, the law from the Federal Court and the Federal Court of Appeal was reviewed and summarized as follows at page 25:

> The following principles can therefore be drawn from the case law: although the right to counsel is not absolute in an administrative proceeding, refusing an individual the possibility to retain counsel by not allowing a postponement is reviewable if the following factors are in play: the case is complex, the consequences of

the decision are serious, the individual does not have the resources — whether in terms of intellect or legal knowledge — to properly represent his interests.

The court found all of the above factors present in this case and that it was clear the applicant was not capable of representing herself.

The applicant was formerly notified twice of the Board's intention to review her compliance with the conditions; it was evident that she understood the purpose of the hearing to be a yearly review of her progress and recovery, similar to her monthly stay interviews. It was for this reason she claimed that she did not bring in a lawyer. The Board's failure to provide an adjournment in order that the applicant might retain counsel deprived her of the right to a fair hearing.

Hak v. Canada (Minister of Citizenship & Immigration) (2005), 54 Imm. L.R. (3d) 98, 2005 CarswellNat 3669, 2005 CarswellNat 5007, 2005 FC 1488 — The law is clear that an individual must bear the consequences of hiring poor counsel. There may be circumstances where the negligent or incompetent actions of an individual's representative may result in the person being denied a fair hearing. In this case the applicant claimed that the failure of her immigration consultant to notify her of the date for her interview resulted in her being denied procedural fairness in the process. The applicant failed to persuade the court that she had been denied procedural fairness in the process.

Toor v. Canada (Minister of Citizenship & Immigration), 2005 CarswellNat 3256, 2005 FC 1386 — The applicants, having been unsuccessful Convention refugees, made an application for humanitarian and compassionate consideration pursuant to s. 25 of the IRPA. They also made an application for consideration as Post-determination Refugee Claimants. Their lawyer wrote to the processing centre in Vegreville, Alberta, in anticipation that the file would be transferred to Vancouver and might be determined concurrently with the PRRA application, advising that he would make complete representations in support of their request once the applicants received their notice to make representations and file evidence in support of the PRRA. The H&C request was turned down. No additional information was supplied by the applicants' lawyer because Vegreville ignored the fact that the lawyer's address was listed as the place to communicate with the applicants, and wrote directly to the applicants instead. The decision maker's notes to file indicate that she did not appear to have focused on what was before her and consequently the decision was held to be patently unreasonable.

Shirvan v. Canada (Minister of Citizenship & Immigration), 2005 FC 1509, 2005 CarswellNat 3744, 2005 CarswellNat 5233, [2005] F.C.J. No. 1864 — Before examining allegations of incompetence, the court must first determine whether the applicants have met their preliminary burden of giving notice of the allegations to their former counsel. In this case, new counsel for the applicants wrote to the Canadian Society of Immigration Consultants to complain of their former counsel's treatment and to request that he immediately be prohibited from practising as an immigration consultant. The letter provided sufficient corroborating evidence and provided sufficient notice of the allegation to the applicants' former counsel.

Although the Immigration Appeal Division transcript demonstrated that the former counsel was unfamiliar with the hearing procedure, the applicants were still able to present their case. The only major ground the applicants claimed their former counsel should have raised was the best interest of the child consideration. Since the child was aged 19 or older at the time of the initial determination and at the time of the Immigration Appeal Division hearing, the Immigration Appeal Division did not err in its decision not to consider the best interest of the applicant's daughter. Accordingly, the applicants failed to demonstrate the result of their hearing would have been different but for their former counsel's alleged incompetence.

Mervilus v. Canada (Ministre de la Citoyenneté & de l'Immigration), 2004 CarswellNat 5673, 2004 CarswellNat 3104, 262 F.T.R. 186, 2004 FC 1206 — The applicant was ordered to leave Canada in 1996. The execution of that order was stayed by order of the Appeal Division in March 1997. The stay was for a five year period with a review six months later and every year thereafter. On September 16, 2003 the Immigration Appeal Division set aside the stay of the deportation order and dismissed the appeal of this order.

The applicant appeared before the Appeal Division for the annual review of the stay. For the first time since the proceedings began he did not have counsel. At the outset of the proceedings he requested a postponement. The applicant explained that he had been in Haiti and that he had only arrived back in Canada a few days before the review of his appeal. The member presiding over the hearing decided to proceed.

Although the right to counsel is not absolute in an administrative proceeding, refusing an individual the possibility to retain counsel by not allowing a postponement is reviewable if the following factors are in play: the case is complex, the consequences of the decision are serious, the individual does not have resources whether in terms of intellect or legal knowledge to properly represent his interests. The decision of the Board member was quashed and the matter referred for re-determination by a differently constituted panel.

Robles v. Canada (Minister of Citizenship & Immigration) (2003), 2 Admin. L.R. (4th) 315, 2003 CarswellNat 815, 2003 CarswellNat 1819, 2003 FCT 374, [2003] F.C.J. No. 520 (T.D.) — This was an application to review a negative decision of a panel of the CRDD. The applicants argued that they were denied natural justice due to the incompetence of their former counsel who was himself an immigration consultant and not a lawyer. *Law Society (British Columbia) v. Mangat* (2001), 16 Imm. L.R. (3d) 1, [2001] 3 S.C.R. 113, 2001 CarswellBC 2168, 2001 CarswellBC 2169, [2001] S.C.J. No. 66, 2001 SCC 67, 205 D.L.R. (4th) 577, 157 B.C.A.C. 161, 256 W.A.C. 161, 96 B.C.L.R. (3d) 1, 276 N.R. 339, [2002] 2 W.W.R. 201, established that the participation of non-lawyer consultants as a matter within federal, not provincial, jurisdiction. A precise factual foundation must exist in order for the court to find that prejudice resulted to a person as a result of the incompetence of counsel. Incompetence is determined by a reasonableness standard. The analysis proceeds upon a strong presumption that counsel's conduct fell within the wide range of reasonable professional assistance. The onus is on the applicant to establish the acts or omissions of counsel that are alleged not to have been the result of reasonable professional judgment. The wisdom of hindsight has no place in this assessment.

Miscarriages of justice may take many forms. In some instances, counsel's performance may have resulted in procedural unfairness. In others, the reliability of the trial's result may have been compromised.

In the present case, the principal applicant filed an affidavit in which he addressed the alleged incompetent performance of his immigration consultant. The applicant also filed the affidavit of a person with expertise in the immigration area who attested to the fact that the immigration consultant was incompetent.

In this case the evidence was held not to have been sufficient and the application was dismissed.

Dehghani v. Canada (Minister of Employment & Immigration), [1993] 1 S.C.R. 1053, 18 Imm. L.R. (2d) 245, 10 Admin. L.R. (2d) 1, 20 C.R. (4th) 34, 101 D.L.R. (4th) 654, 150 N.R. 241, 14 C.R.R. (2d) 1, 1993 CarswellNat 57, 1993 CarswellNat 1380, EYB 1993-67290, [1993] S.C.J. No. 38 — The appellant, a citizen of Iran, arrived in Canada without valid travel or identity documents and claimed Convention refugee status. He was interviewed at the secondary examination and extensive written notes were made by an immigration officer, which notes were later entered in evidence at the credible-basis hearing. At the conclusion of that hearing the first level tribunal decided that there was no credible basis to the appellant's claim.

When the appellant was taken to a secondary examination at Canadian Immigration at Pearson International Airport, he was not detained in the sense contemplated by s. 10(b) of the Charter. Further, the principles of s. 10(b) do not require that the appellant be provided with counsel at the pre-inquiry or pre-hearing stage of the refugee claim determination process. The secondary examination of the appellant at the port-of-entry is not analogous to a hearing. The purpose of the port-of entry interview was to aid in the processing of the appellant's application for entry and to determine the appropriate procedures which should be invoked in order to deal with the appellant's application for Convention refugee status. The principles of fundamental justice do not include a right to counsel in these circumstances of routine information gathering.

[*Editor's note: Although* Dehghani *was decided under the former Act, it may still be relevant.*]

Section 167(2)

Hillary v. Canada (Minister of Citizenship & Immigration) (2011), 96 Imm. L.R. (3d) 197, 331 D.L.R. (4th) 338, 414 N.R. 292, 2011 FCA 51, 2011 CarswellNat 285; affirming (2010), 370 F.T.R. 199 (Eng.), 320 D.L.R. (4th) 118, 2010 FC 638, 2010 CarswellNat 3091, 2010 CarswellNat 1740; leave to appeal to S.C.C. refused 2011 CarswellNat 1898, 2011 CarswellNat 1899 (S.C.C.) — The appellant, a citizen of Jamaica in his early 40s, came to Canada as a permanent resident in 1982 when he was only 13 years old. He was deported on the basis of a string of criminal convictions starting in 1987. He was diagnosed as suffering from schizophrenia, is HIV positive and had been addicted to crack cocaine. The appellant claimed that the IAD's dismissal of his appeal against deportation should be reopened because the IAD denied him a fair hearing when it failed to inquire whether he appreciated the nature of the proceeding, in order to determine whether he required the assistance of the designated representative.

The right to representation in an administrative proceeding normally means the right of a party to appoint someone, often legal counsel, to conduct the case before the tribunal on their behalf. However, subs. 167(2) of IRPA recognizes that, if their interests are to be adequately protected in a proceeding before the Board, minors, and those unable to appreciate the nature of the proceedings, also require the assistance of a designated representative who is sensitive to the particular needs of the individual concerned and alert to their best interests. It is always within the discretion of the IAD to raise the issue itself and inquire into the appellant's capacity. However, if the IAD makes no so such inquiry, the court should intervene only if satisfied on the basis of an examination of the entire context that the Board's inaction was unreasonable and fairness required the IAD to be proactive. Given the adversarial nature of the IAD's procedure, it will only be in the most unusual circumstances that a panel is obligated to make inquiries in a case where the appellant is represented by counsel who has not raised the issue of the client's ability to understand the nature of the proceedings. Such is not the case here. The appeal was dismissed.

Duale v. Canada (Minister of Citizenship & Immigration), [2004] F.C.J. No. 178, 40 Imm. L.R. (3d) 165, 2004 CarswellNat 198, 2004 CarswellNat 2401, 2004 FC 150 — The obligation to designate a representative for a claimant who is a minor, or who is otherwise unable to appreciate the nature of the proceedings, arises at the earliest point in time at which the Refugee Protection Division becomes aware of facts which reveal the need for the designated representative. The need for the designation of a representative applies to the entirety of the proceedings in respect of a refugee claim and not just to the actual hearing of the claim.

The duties of the designated representative are:

a) to retain counsel;

b) to instruct counsel or to assist the child in instructing counsel;

c) to make other decisions with respect to the proceedings or to help the child make those decisions;

d) to inform the child about the various stages and proceedings of the claim;

e) to assist in obtaining evidence in support of the claim;

f) to provide evidence and be a witness in the claim;

g) to act in the best interest of the child.

168. (1) Abandonment of proceeding — A Division may determine that a proceeding before it has been abandoned if the Division is of the opinion that the applicant is in default in the proceedings, including by failing to appear for a hearing, to provide information required by the Division or to communicate with the Division on being requested to do so.

(2) Abuse of process — A Division may refuse to allow an applicant to withdraw from a proceeding if it is of the opinion that the withdrawal would be an abuse of process under its rules.

Case Law

Section 168(1)

Revich c. Canada (Ministre de la Citoyenneté & de l'Immigration) (2004), 44 Imm. L.R. (3d) 129, 2004 CarswellNat 5036, 2004 CarswellNat 2631, 2004 FC 1064 — The *Refugee Protection Division Rules* clearly provide how the Division must proceed in order to declare a claim abandoned. The Division must give the claimant the opportunity to explain why the claim should not be declared abandoned, must take into account the claimant's explanations and must take into account any other relevant factor, in particular the claimant's intention to pursue the matter. The standard of review to apply to abandonment claim decisions is that of reasonableness *simpliciter*. The case law provides that the question the Division must ask itself is whether the applicant truly intended to abandon the claim.

The claimant did not behave like a person indifferent to the outcome of her claim. She informed her counsel of her absence, consulted a physician who confirmed the seriousness of her state of health. She came to the abandonment proceeding with the necessary documentary evidence. The chairperson dismissed the applicant's explanation but did not explain why. The chairperson drew an invalid inference from the evidence in declaring that the claim had been abandoned.

Aslam v. Canada (Minister of Citizenship & Immigration), [2004] F.C.J. No. 620, 35 Imm. L.R. (3d) 100, 2004 CarswellNat 920, 2004 FC 514, 250 F.T.R. 307 — This is an application to judicially review a decision that a refugee claim had been abandoned. The member declared that the applicant had abandoned his claim because the applicant would not proceed to a hearing without his counsel. Approximately 3 weeks before the hearing of the applicant's application, his immigration consultant informed him that he would be unable to assist him. The applicant made other arrangements but the new counsel could not proceed on the day set for the hearing. A day before the hearing the applicant was informed that his counsel's request for a postponement was denied. The applicant's consultant was unable to proceed and the applicant refused to proceed without counsel with the result that the applicant's claim was declared abandoned.

The decision of the member was set aside.

Rules of procedure are to be interpreted and to be applied to bring about the most expeditious and least expensive determination of proceedings on their merits. Fundamental rights can never be sacrificed at the altar of administrative efficiency and the right to a full and fair hearing cannot be compromised.

Gapchenko v. Canada (Minister of Citizenship & Immigration), 2004 CarswellNat 767, 2004 FC 427 — In order for the Board to find that a claim has been abandoned, the claimant must be in default either because he/she failed to appear for a hearing, failed to provide information, or failed to communicate with the Board. In addition, the Board must give the claimant an opportunity to be heard at the hearing, unless the circumstances provided for in subs. 58(1) of the Rules exist.

There is an onus on the applicant to act diligently in pursuing his/her refugee claim.

The decided cases of the court on a review of abandonment claim decisions indicate the test or question to be asked is whether the refugee claimant's conduct amounts to an expression of intention by that person that he or she did not wish, or had shown no interest, to pursue the refugee claim with diligence.

It is the duty of the applicants at the last minute, before changing counsel, to verify that a new one is available.

169. Decisions and reasons — **In the case of a decision of a Division, other than an interlocutory decision:**

> **(a) the decision takes effect in accordance with the rules;**
>
> **(b) reasons for the decision must be given;**
>
> **(c) the decision may be rendered orally or in writing, except a decision of the Refugee Appeal Division, which must be rendered in writing;**
>
> **(d) if the Refugee Protection Division rejects a claim, written reasons must be provided to the claimant and the Minister;**
>
> **(e) if the person who is the subject of proceedings before the Board or the Minister requests reasons for a decision within 10 days of notification of the decision, or in circumstances set out in the rules of the Board, the Division must provide written reasons; and**

(f) the period in which to apply for judicial review with respect to a decision of the Board is calculated from the giving of notice of the decision or from the sending of written reasons, whichever is later.

Proposed Amendment — 169

169. (1) Decisions and reasons — In the case of a decision of a Division, other than an interlocutory decision:

(a) the decision takes effect in accordance with the rules;

(b) reasons for the decision must be given;

(c) the decision may be rendered orally or in writing, except for a decision of the Refugee Protection Division in respect of an application for protection under subsection 112(1), which must be rendered in writing;

(d) if the Refugee Protection Division rejects a claim, written reasons must be provided to the claimant and the Minister;

(e) if the person who is the subject of proceedings before the Board or the Minister requests reasons for a decision within 10 days of notification of the decision, or in circumstances set out in the rules of the Board, the Division must provide written reasons;

(e.1) notice of a decision of the Refugee Protection Division in respect of an application for protection, as well as written reasons for the decision, must, in accordance with the regulations, be provided to the Minister, who must then provide the notice and reasons to the applicant in accordance with the regulations; and

(f) the period in which to apply for judicial review with respect to a decision of the Board is calculated from the giving of notice of the decision or from the sending of written reasons, whichever is later.

(2) Regulations — The regulations may govern the time within which and the manner in which notice of a decision of the Refugee Protection Division in respect of an application for protection, as well as written reasons for the decision, must be provided.

2010, c. 8, s. 25 [Not in force at date of publication.]

Case Law

Section 169(b)

Bajraktarevic v. Canada (Minister of Citizenship & Immigration) (2006), 52 Imm. L.R. (3d) 5, 2006 CarswellNat 258, 2006 CarswellNat 1134, 2006 FC 123 — The applicant argued that the officer committed a reviewable error in failing to provide any analysis or assessment of the basis put forward by the applicant, in support of her application for permanent residence on humanitarian and compassionate grounds, and consequently provided inadequate and insufficient reasons. The officer's refusal letter and the notes in the applicant's Computer Assisted Immigration Processing System cannot be deemed to constitute sufficient and adequate reasons. The applicant was entitled to know why her application was rejected. Reasons must be accompanied by a sufficient analysis.

Agalliu v. Canada (Minister of Citizenship & Immigration) (2005), 49 Imm. L.R. (3d) 1, 34 Admin. L.R. (4th) 214, 2005 CarswellNat 2112, 2005 FC 1035 — The Board's reasons disclosed a number of superficial errors, in footnotes and in references to the documentary evidence. However, the Board's other errors and its failure to explain its conclusions adequately disclosed more fundamental problems. Taken together, these errors led to the conclusion that the Board's decision was out of keeping with the evidence before it. Sometimes, little errors in a written decision represent no more than a lack of final polishing. Other times, they are symptomatic of inadequate care on the part of the decision maker.

Torres v. Canada (Minister of Citizenship & Immigration), [2005] F.C.J. No. 812, 45 Imm. L.R. (3d) 313, 2005 CarswellNat 1206, 2005 FC 660 — The applicant expressed her fear of the lack of police support and the difficulty of her taking advantage and having recourse to the existing legislative and procedural framework of state protection in Nicaragua. The Board never engaged with the applicant's concern that the police and other support groups could not provide effective protection. The applicant's evidence was clear and convincing that the state could not protect her against her father in the past and would not be able to do so in the future. The Board should have turned its mind to this issue and addressed it directly in its reasons.

Yontem v. Canada (Minister of Citizenship & Immigration), 2005 CarswellNat 197, 26 Admin. L.R. (4th) 115, 2005 FC 41 — It is well established that a Board may draw a negative inference from inconsistencies between statements made at the port of entry and the content of subsequent testimony. The Board acted appropriately by notifying the applicant that the port of entry notes were an issue and providing him with a reasonable opportunity to explain the inconsistency before it drew an adverse inference. The Board also provided cogent reasons for rejecting the applicant's explanation. There was nothing in the applicant's port of entry notes to suggest that the Board translation was faulty. Many of the details recorded in the notes appear to be accurate since they were repeated and relied on by the applicant during the hearing. It was reasonably open to the Board to reject the applicant's explanation regarding the inconsistencies arising from the port of entry notes.

If the applicant had wanted to challenge the accuracy of the notes, he could have subpoenaed both the immigration officer and the interpreter to testify at the hearing.

Cobo v. Canada (Minister of Citizenship & Immigration), 2005 CarswellNat 93, 2005 CarswellNat 1553, 2005 FC 69 — This was an application to review a negative decision on an application for protection. The Board's bare statement that the Board "was not satisfied with the explanation" (of the applicant) does not provide satisfactory reasons for not accepting the applicant's evidence.

Ahmed v. Canada (Minister of Citizenship & Immigration), 2004 CarswellNat 5683, 2004 CarswellNat 2586, 2004 FC 1076 — It is an error for a Board not to deal with the applicants' reasonable explanations for the tribunal's concerns in its reasons. While it is open to the Board to disbelieve explanations which appear reasonable on their face, the Board has an obligation to address them in its reasons and explain why it did not find the explanations convincing.

Coitinho v. Canada (Minister of Citizenship & Immigration), [2004] F.C.J. No. 1269, 2004 CarswellNat 3892, 2004 FC 1037, 2004 CarswellNat 2577 — In the absence of stating that the applicant's evidence was not credible, the Board concluded that it would give more weight to the documentary evidence because it came from knowledgeable sources, none of whom had any interest in the outcome of the particular hearing. This statement was tantamount to stating that documentary evidence should always be preferred to that of a refugee claimant. Further, the decision did not inform the reader why the applicant's evidence was considered suspect. The decision of the Board was overturned.

Shahid v. Canada (Minister of Citizenship & Immigration), 2004 CarswellNat 5919, 2004 CarswellNat 4311, 2004 FC 1607 — This was an application to review a decision of a Board member dismissing the applicant's motion to reopen his refugee claim. The decision not to reopen a refugee claim is a final decision. Reasons are required by s. 169(b).

Sawyer v. Canada (Minister of Citizenship & Immigration), [2004] F.C.J. No. 1140, 37 Imm. L.R. (3d) 114, 2004 CarswellNat 4460, 2004 CarswellNat 2104, 2004 FC 935 — The applicant sought to judicially review the rejection of his claim to refugee protection. The Minister's operating manual instructs officers, to whom a claim for refugee status is made, to ask the standard questions on the refugee claim and record the answers of the claimant. The officers are instructed not to ask the claimant to elaborate on the basis of the claim unless the information relates to admissibility and eligibility. In the face of this instruction, it was patently unreasonable for the panel to reject, summarily, the applicant's evidence that he was told by an immigration officer not to give his full story and that it is was for that reason that everything the applicant claimed he told the officer was not found in the officer's notes.

Muliri v. Canada (Ministre de la Citoyenneté & de l'Immigration), [2004] F.C.J. No. 1376, 42 Imm. L.R. (3d) 139, 2004 CarswellNat 5052, 2004 CarswellNat 2813, 2004 FC 1139 — Judicial deference does not amount to a blind acceptance of the findings of fact drawn by a panel, without any critical analysis by the court. The judicial review process exists to ensure that administrative tribunals do not venture into the absurd, thinking that they can make findings of fact which simply do not stand up.

The applicant, a citizen of the Democratic Republic of Congo, obtained a visa to come to Canada from South Africa. The visa application contains facts which contradicted the applicant's testimony before the panel. The applicant told the panel that he lied to Canadian authorities at the Canadian Embassy in South Africa in order to obtain a Canadian visa. The panel did not believe the applicant because it was of the view that the information he submitted to the Canadian authorities would have been easy for them to verify. There was nothing in the record to indicate that the information had been verified and accordingly the panel's finding of credibility was unreasonable and its decision set aside.

Hussain v. Canada (Ministre de la Citoyenneté & de l'Immigration), 2004 CarswellNat 3996, 2004 CarswellNat 766, 2004 FC 430 — This is an application to judicially review a negative decision respecting the applicants' request for protection.

An initial hearing took place on July 29, 2002. During this hearing, the panel asked the refugee protection officer for information about the applicants' passage through the United States. A second hearing took place on August 7, 2002. On August 9, 2002, the officer received a report from the American authorities which indicated that they had no indication that the applicants had crossed the American border. The officer informed the panel of this and it was evident that additional evidence would be required. On September 27, 2002, the applicants' counsel gave birth to a child. On October 16, two months after the report was received, the panel asked the officer to contact counsel to ask her to respond within six days. Counsel was informed of this letter at home by her secretary and submitted a written reply informing that it was not necessary to reconvene because her client had informed her that it had been a smuggler who had made the arrangements. Three months later the panel rendered its decision.

The panel was aware that counsel was on maternity leave for several months due to the fact that she had appeared before the panel in the final months of her pregnancy and had discussed it with the panel informally. Further, the panel had been informed by the officer of the receipt of the report in August, while counsel was still available. Despite this, it was only two months later that, at the panel's request, the officer wrote to counsel giving her only six days to respond, knowing that she was on maternity leave. There was no urgency in this matter. The panel did not render its decision until three months later. The short time given to reply was totally unjustified given that counsel was at home with a newborn and not in a position to make an enlightened decision about how to deal with the file and present the applicants' position fully and fairly. The decision of the panel was set aside.

Nagulesan v. Canada (Minister of Citizenship & Immigration), [2004] F.C.J. No. 1690, 44 Imm. L.R. (3d) 99, 2004 CarswellNat 5903, 2004 CarswellNat 3637, 2004 FC 1382 — The applicant sought to review a negative decision respecting his claim under ss. 96 and 97. A few days after his hearing, the applicant delivered to the RPD a letter addressed to the member presiding at his hearing indicating that he wished to file additional evidence to corroborate his testimony. The proposed evidence was attached to the letter. The letter and the documents attached thereto were not in the certified copy of Tribunal Record and RPD did not refer to the evidence at all in its decision.

The applicant's letter satisfied the requirement of Rule 37. This meant that the RPD had to deal with the applicant's request. It could simply mention that having reviewed the letter, it decided not to consider the evidence because of factors listed in Rule 37(3), or it could accept the new evidence and deal with it in its decision. The failure to deal with the matter at all was a breach of procedural fairness and the decision was set aside.

Begollari v. Canada (Minister of Citizenship & Immigration), [2004] F.C.J. No. 1613, 2004 CarswellNat 5098, 2004 CarswellNat 3437, 2004 FC 1340 — The reviewing Court could not determine whether the Board had applied a balance of probabilities test to the objective component of a well founded fear of persecution, or the reasonable chance or serious possibility of a fear of persecution test. The balance of probabilities test was an erroneous test and since the court could not determine whether it was used or not, the decision was set aside.

Mann v. Canada (Minister of Citizenship & Immigration) (2004), 43 Imm. L.R. (3d) 230, 2004 CarswellNat 5099, 2004 CarswellNat 3438, (sub nom. *Canada (Minister of Citizenship & Immigration) v. Mann)* 258 F.T.R. 139 (Eng.), 2004 FC 1338 — This is an application to review a decision of the Immigration Appeal Division wherein the Appeal Division allowed an appeal from a visa officer's refusal to grant the respondent's wife an immigrant visa.

In dealing with the adequacy of reasons, the court relied upon the Federal Court of Appeal decision in *VIA Rail Canada Inc. v. Canada (National Transportation Agency)* (2000), [2001] 2 F.C. 25, 2000 CarswellNat 2531, 2000 CarswellNat 3453, 261 N.R. 184, 193 D.L.R. (4th) 357, 26 Admin. L.R. (3d) 1, [2000] F.C.J. No. 1685 (C.A.). Reasons foster better decision making. By ensuring that issues and reasoning are well articulated and therefore more carefully thought out, the process of writing reasons for a decision by itself may be a guarantee of a better decision. Reasons provide the parties with the assurance that their representations have been considered.

Reasons allow the parties to effectuate any right of appeal or judicial review that they might have. They provide a basis for an assessment of possible grounds of appeal or review. They allow the appellate or reviewing body to determine whether the decision maker erred and thereby render him or her accountable. This is particularly important when the decision is subject to a deferential standard of review.

In a case of a regulated industry, the regulator's reasons provide guidance to others who are subject to the regulator's jurisdiction.

The duty to give reasons is only fulfilled if the reasons provided are adequate. What constitutes adequate reasons is a matter to be determined in the light of the circumstances of each case. As a general rule, adequate reasons are those that serve the functions for which the duty to provide them was imposed.

The obligation to provide adequate reasons is not satisfied by merely reciting the submissions and evidence of the parties and stating a conclusion. The decision maker must set out its findings of fact and the principal evidence upon which those findings were based. The reasons must address the major points at issue. The reasoning process followed by the decision maker must be set out and must reflect consideration of the main relevant factors.

In this case, s. 4 of the *Hindu Marriage Act* was an important factor in the case. The interpretation of this section is a matter on which the IAD's reasons are silent, and due to this silence, the reasons are inadequate.

Machedon v. Canada (Minister of Citizenship & Immigration), [2004] F.C.J. No. 1331, 2004 CarswellNat 3551, 2004 CarswellNat 2665, 256 F.T.R. 211, 2004 FC 1104 — The Board found that the fact that the applicants, who were citizens of Romania, had abandoned refugee claims in Ireland lacked a subjective fear of persecution. The applicants explained their abandonment of their Irish refugee claims by stating that their initial intention was to come to Canada and that they were told Romanian refugee claimants were not successful in obtaining protection from Irish authorities.

The standard of review on this issue is patent unreasonableness. An applicant's failure to seek refugee status in transit countries is relevant to a determination of their subjective fear of persecution. In this case the Board did not analyze the explanation offered by the applicants for the abandonment of their Irish claims, nor did it state that it disbelieved their explanation for abandoning the Irish claims. The Board simply stated that there was no persuasive, trustworthy and reliable evidence to show that Ireland would not fulfil its obligations. The Board did not make a negative finding of credibility and therefore drew a negative inference with regard to the evidence before it. The decision of the Board was set aside.

Eminidis v. Canada (Ministre de la Citoyenneté & de l'Immigration), 2004 CarswellNat 2769, 2004 CarswellNat 1403, 2004 FC 700 — The fact that the panel preferred the documentary evidence even though the applicants had been considered credible was not an error. It was within the panel's jurisdiction to do so and open to the panel to decide what weight to give the evidence before it.

Refugee Protection Division

169.1 (1) Composition — The Refugee Protection Division consists of the Deputy Chairperson, Assistant Deputy Chairpersons and other members, including coordinating members, necessary to carry out its functions.

(2) Public Service Employment Act — The members of the Refugee Protection Division are appointed in accordance with the *Public Service Employment Act*.

2010, c. 8, s. 26

170. Proceedings — The Refugee Protection Division, in any proceeding before it,

Proposed Amendment — 170 opening words

170. Proceedings — Except in respect of an application for protection made under subsection 112(1), the Refugee Protection Division, in any proceeding before it,

2010, c. 8, s. 27(1) [Not in force at date of publication.]

(a) may inquire into any matter that it considers relevant to establishing whether a claim is well-founded;

(b) must hold a hearing;

(c) must notify the person who is the subject of the proceeding and the Minister of the hearing;

(d) must provide the Minister, on request, with the documents and information referred to in subsection 100(4);

(d.1) may question the witnesses, including the person who is the subject of the proceeding;

(e) must give the person and the Minister a reasonable opportunity to present evidence, question witnesses and make representations;

(f) may, despite paragraph (b), allow a claim for refugee protection without a hearing, if the Minister has not notified the Division, within the period set out in the rules of the Board, of the Minister's intention to intervene;

(g) is not bound by any legal or technical rules of evidence;

(h) may receive and base a decision on evidence that is adduced in the proceedings and considered credible or trustworthy in the circumstances; and

(i) may take notice of any facts that may be judicially noticed, any other generally recognized facts and any information or opinion that is within its specialized knowledge.

2010, c. 8, s. 27(2)

Case Law

Section 170(b)

Reyes v. Canada (Minister of Citizenship & Immigration), 2005 CarswellNat 806, 2005 FC 418 — It is open to the Board to ask for corroborating evidence if such evidence is material and could reasonably be expected to be available. If an applicant is unwilling or unable to comply with such a request, he or she bears the onus of explaining the non-compliance.

Balson v. Canada (Minister of Citizenship & Immigration), 2005 CarswellNat 311, 2005 FC 197 — The applicant sought to review a negative decision respecting her application for protection. On August 24, 2002 the applicant received a notice which informed her that if her counsel was unable to proceed on the hearing date, she should find another counsel who is able to proceed and warned her that she may have to proceed without counsel if no counsel attended with her on the date of her hearing. In September 2002, the applicant identified her counsel. In July 2003 the applicant and her counsel were asked to attend in August 2003 to set a hearing date. In August 2003 the applicant attended, set a hearing date and received a form entitled "A Notice to Appear" which advised her that her claim would be heard in November 2003. In September 2003 the applicant and her counsel were asked to confirm their readiness to proceed in November. The day before the hearing, the applicant's counsel faxed a letter to the Board requesting an adjournment. On the date set for the hearing the request for an adjournment was denied and the applicant's refugee claim proceeded.

It was made very clear to the applicant that her case would proceed on the date set, with or without counsel. It was open to the Board to exercise its discretion to refuse the request for an adjournment and accordingly the application for judicial review was dismissed.

Herrera v. Canada (Minister of Citizenship & Immigration) (2005), 2005 CarswellNat 2128, 2005 CarswellNat 140, 2004 FC 1724 — The applicant sought to overturn a negative decision respecting his application for protection. At the hearing, the applicant was not allowed to lead his evidence, but instead the refugee protection officer was instructed to question first, and then the RPD followed with its own questions. The applicant's lawyer consented to the procedure but the consent was not binding. There was no way that the lawyer would have known the nature and intensity of the questioning to come. As the procedure was highly unusual it was incumbent on the RPD to state a reason why the procedure was adopted. The decision of the RPD was set aside.

Guermache v. Canada (Ministre de la Citoyenneté & de l'Immigration), [2004] F.C.J. No. 1058, 43 Imm. L.R. (3d) 195, 2004 CarswellNat 3999, 2004 CarswellNat 1853, (sub nom. *Guermache v. Canada (Minister of Citizenship & Immigration)*) 257 F.T.R. 272 (Eng.), 21 Admin. L.R. (4th) 37, 2004 FC 870 — The applicant sought to review the negative decision of his protection application. The applicant successfully maintained that the member's conduct at the hearing was such that it raised a reasonable apprehension of bias. Members have a difficult but essential role to play. Because of their workload, the stress is enormous. Nevertheless, even if they may have heard the same "story" hundreds of times, individuals are different, each application for protection deserves the same degree of care. Canada offers protection to those who have well-founded fears of persecution for a Convention reason, as well as those in danger of torture or risk of cruel and unusual treatment or punishment. At the same time, the objectives of the Act grant, as a fundamental expression of Canada's humanitarian ideals, fair consideration to those seeking protection. The scale of the members' tasks must not cause them to lose sight of the fact that the rules of natural justice must be observed and that their conduct during hearings and applications for protection must be irreproachable. There is neither place for intimidation, contempt, and offensive innuendo, nor for harshness or inappropriate language. The neutral attitude expected from members during hearings suggests that they adhere to their own responsibilities as much as possible, and let the claimant's counsellor, the refugee claim officer and, if applicable, the Minister's representative, play their respective roles.

The court found that the chairperson had crossed the line from the role of an impartial adjudicator by his constant interference which prevented the applicant from presenting his case. Accordingly, the decision was set aside.

Upul v. Canada (Minister of Citizenship & Immigration) (2004), 41 Imm. L.R. (3d) 284, 2004 CarswellNat 4747, 2004 CarswellNat 3741, (sub nom. *Kankanagme v. Canada (Minister of Citizenship & Immigration))* 259 F.T.R. 268 (Eng.), 2004 FC 1451 — Where the full extent of the member's animus towards the applicant was not entirely evident until the decision was rendered, the failure of counsel to object to the conduct of the Board member is not fatal to the applicant's right to argue that there exists a reasonable apprehension of bias.

Geza v. Canada (Minister of Citizenship & Immigration) (2004), 44 Imm. L.R. (3d) 57, 2004 CarswellNat 5179, 2004 CarswellNat 2970, 20 Admin. L.R. (4th) 79, 257 F.T.R. 114 (Eng.), 2004 FC 1039, 2004 FC 1163, 244 D.L.R. (4th) 218, [2004] F.C.J. No. 1401 — In 1998, the Immigration and Refugee Board decided to produce a precedent, coined a "lead case," out of concern for growing numbers of Roma refugee claimants from Hungary. The stated purpose of the exercise was to establish a base line of legal and factual issues to promote consistency in subsequent claim decisions. The Applicants agreed to participate in the test case on the advice of counsel, however, after their claims were rejected, they challenged the jurisdiction of the Board to conduct such an exercise.

No reasonable apprehension of bias was created on the part of the Board when the lead case idea was conceived and conducted.

A lead case conducted to promote consistency in decision-making is a matter of procedure that was clearly within the jurisdiction of the Board on the basis of the common-law and by necessary implication by virtue of the *Immigration Act*. No reasonable apprehension of bias is created by the Board acting in this manner.

The evidence does not prove that there was a decline in acceptance rates for Hungarian Roma directly as result of the lead case.

Caceres v. Canada (Minister of Citizenship & Immigration), 2004 CarswellNat 2539, 2004 CarswellNat 1821, 2004 FC 843 — The applicant sought to review a negative decision of a panel of the Refugee Protection Division. The panel concluded that there was no credible or trustworthy evidence on which the applicant could establish his claim. The applicant forwarded written submissions to the Board by fax after the hearing had been concluded but before the Board had rendered its decision. The fax transmission sheet shows that seven pages of material were sent to the Board in a sensible timeframe and to the Board's correct fax number. The court, therefore, presumed that the submission was received at the Board's fax machine. The faxed material correctly described the case and the hearing date. There is no evidence that this submission reached the relevant panel members. They did not mention it in their decision and it does not appear in the tribunal records.

The court concluded that on a balance of probabilities that through error at the Board's offices, the panel did not receive the submission. To disregard written submissions on the sole basis of the delay of their delivery would be absurd. Such a breach of natural justice is, in itself, sufficient to warrant intervention by the court.

Section 170(e)

Chohan v. Canada (Minister of Citizenship & Immigration), 2006 CarswellNat 819, 2006 CarswellNat 2501, 2006 FC 390 — The Board has an obligation to deal with a request for an adjournment in a principled way. To have denied the applicant the benefit of a short adjournment was manifestly unfair and contravened the requirement of s. 170 of the IRPA that the applicant be given a reasonable opportunity to present evidence.

The Board's reasons for denying the adjournment request also failed to address the factors required by s. 48 of the *Refugee Protection Division Rules*. Had these factors been considered and applied, the adjournment would also certainly have been granted.

Canada (Ministre de la Citoyenneté & de l'Immigration) c. Deffo, 2005 CarswellNat 3924, 2005 CarswellNat 5117, 2005 FC 1589 — The Refugee Protection Division of the Immigration and Refugee Board has a duty to formally notify the counsel representing the Minister pursuant to s. 170(e) of the IRPA and s. 22 of the Rules. There is no discretionary authority for the Board to dispense of this duty. In failing to notify the counsel of record for the Minister after he had filed a notice of intervention in accordance with subs. 25(1) of the Rules, the Board erred in law.

Bokhari v. Canada (Minister of Citizenship & Immigration), 2005 CarswellNat 1092, 2005 FC 574 — The applicants sought to review a negative decision concerning their application for refugee status. At the hearing, after counsel had finished questioning the applicant, the Board member made a statement to counsel which suggested that credibility, objective and subjective fear, had been established and that state protection and the IFA were the issues that the Board member was concerned about.

The claim was dismissed, however, on the basis that there was insufficient credible and trustworthy evidence to establish the principal claimant's allegation that he was a high profile Shia leader in Peshawar.

Such misleading of counsel, thereby effectively depriving an applicant from making submissions on crucial points, amounts to a denial of natural justice.

Section 170(h)

Kovacs v. Canada (Minister of Citizenship & Immigration) (2005), [2006] 2 F.C.R. 455, 2005 CarswellNat 3524, 2005 CarswellNat 4487, 2005 FC 1473 — The principle applicant, a citizen of Hungary, arrived in Canada and claimed protection in Canada for herself and two minor children: a daughter, who subsequently returned to Hungary, and a son. The refugee claim was refused. Subsequent to the applicant's arrival in Canada, and prior to the refugee determination hearing, the applicant's husband brought an application in the Ontario Superior Court of Justice, pursuant to the Hague Convention on the Civil Aspects of International Child Abduction (October 25, 1980) for the removal of his son, in accordance with a Hungarian custody order. The Ontario Superior Court judge made several findings with respect to the credibility of both parties and findings that the applicant's husband was a wanted fugitive with a history of criminal behaviour.

Upon judicial review of the decision to refuse the applicant's refugee claim, the court considered the extent to which the Refugee Protection Board was bound by or could rely on the decision of the Ontario Superior Court. The Ontario Superior Court's decision was not binding on the Refugee Protection Board. Nevertheless, it was relevant and important evidence and the Board was entitled to and, in fact, should have taken into account the findings of the Ontario Superior Court where they were directly relevant to the facts before the Refugee Protection Board. The Refugee Protection Board must carry out its own analysis and reach its own conclusions on the matters before it and cannot be bound by the actions of the Ontario Superior Court, particularly where the issues and questions are different.

Application Under s. 83.28 of the Criminal Code, Re, [2004] S.C.J. No. 40, 2004 CarswellBC 1378, 2004 CarswellBC 1379, [2004] 2 S.C.R. 248, 33 B.C.L.R. (4th) 195, 121 C.R.R. (2d) 1, [2005] 2 W.W.R. 605, 21 C.R. (6th) 82, 322 N.R. 205, (sub nom. *R. v. Bagri*) 184 C.C.C. (3d) 449, (sub nom. *R. v. Bagri*) 240 D.L.R. (4th) 81, 199 B.C.A.C. 45, 2004 SCC 42 — The appeal raised, for the first time in the Supreme Court, fundamental questions about the Constitutional validity of provisions of the *Anti-Terrorism Act*. The Act was a legislative component of Canada's response to the tragedy of September 11, 2001. The appellant was ordered to attend a judicial investigative hearing. This case dealt with the Constitutional validity of the "judicial investigative hearing" provision.

There were essentially two acts of alleged terrorism. Firstly, an explosion killed two baggage handlers, and injured four others at Narita Airport, as baggage was being transferred onto Air India Flight 301. A second explosion occurred just one hour later, causing Air India Flight 182 to crash off the west coast of Ireland, killing all passengers and crew.

The first accused, Inderjit Singh Reyat, was arrested in England and extradited to Canada where he was convicted in connection with the explosion at Narita Airport. Mr. Reyat pleaded guilty to manslaughter in connection with the explosion of Air India Flight 182. Two other accused were jointly charged with offences in relation to both explosions and while their trial was ongoing, the Crown brought an application to examine the appellant in this matter pursuant to s. 83.28.

The challenge for democracies in the battle against terrorism is not whether to respond, but rather how to do so. Canadians value the importance of human life and liberty and the protection of society through respect for the rule of law. A democracy cannot exist without the rule of law. Terrorism challenges the context in which the rule of law must operate, but does not call for the abdication of the law. At the same time, the Constitution must not become a suicide pact. The challenge for a democratic state's answer to terrorism calls for a balancing of what is required for an effective response to terrorism in a way that appropriately recognizes the fundamental values of the rule of law. In a democracy, not every response is available to meet the challenge of terrorism.

The international scope of terrorism raised concerns about the potential uses of information gathered pursuant to s. 83.28. Section 83.28 specifically provides use and derivative use immunity in the context of criminal proceedings. The legislation did not speak to the safeguards in relation to other types of hearings. Deportation and extradition hearings must accord with the principles of fundamental justice. In order to meet the requirements of s. 7 of the Charter, use and derivative use immunity respecting information gathered under s. 83.28 must be extended to extradition and deportation hearings. Therefore, the hearing judge must make and, if necessary, vary the terms of an order to properly provide use and derivative use immunity in extradition and deportation proceedings.

Section 170(i)

Sadeghi-Pari v. Canada (Minister of Citizenship & Immigration) (2004), 37 Imm. L.R. (3d) 150, 2004 CarswellNat 1672, 2004 CarswellNat 483, 2004 FC 282 — The applicant sought to review a negative decision of a panel of the Refugee Protection Division. The Board may rely on its general expertise on country conditions in evaluating the plausibility of an applicant's testimony. Documentary evidence on the standardized country file that is not specifically relied on by the Board does not necessarily need to be reproduced on the tribunal record. The Board's power, in this regard, is not open ended. In this case, the Board relied on several specific observations about life in Tehran without referring to any sociological, human rights or other country evidence in support of its conclusions. Accordingly, the decision of the Board was set aside.

Proposed Addition — 170.1

170.1 Application for protection — In respect of an application for protection under subsection 112(1), the Refugee Protection Division

(a) may inquire into any matter that it considers relevant to establishing whether an application is well-founded;

(b) must provide the Minister, on request, with the documentary evidence and written submissions of the applicant that are referred to in paragraph 113(b.1);

(c) must give notice of any hearing to the Minister and the applicant;

(d) subject to paragraph 113(a), must — if a hearing is held — give the applicant and the Minister the opportunity to present evidence, question witnesses and make submissions;

(e) may question the witnesses, including the applicant;

(f) is not bound by any legal or technical rules of evidence;

(g) may receive and base a decision on evidence that is adduced in the proceedings and considered credible or trustworthy in the circumstances; and

(h) may take notice of any facts that may be judicially noticed and of any other generally recognized facts and any information or opinion that is within its specialized knowledge.

2010, c. 8, s. 27.1 [Not in force at date of publication.]

170.2 No reopening of claim or application — The Refugee Protection Division does not have jurisdiction to reopen on any ground — including a failure to observe a principle of natural justice — a claim for refugee protection, an application for protection or an application for cessation or vacation, in respect of which the Refugee Appeal Division or the Federal Court, as the case may be, has made a final determination.

2012, c. 17, s. 51

Case Law

O. (N.) v. Canada (Minister of Citizenship and Immigration), [2016] 2 F.C.R. 378, 2015 FC 1186, 2015 CarswellNat 5463, 2015 CarswellNat 9250 — The applicant sought judicial review of a decision of the RPD refusing to reconsider an application to reopen a refugee claim. The RPD did not commit a reviewable error. The language of s. 170.2 of the Act is clear. The fact is that a "final decision" had been made upon the applicant's claim for protection when the Federal Court dismissed the application for leave and judicial review, without certifying a question pursuant to para. 74(d) of the Act. The absence of a certified question means that no appeal was available to the applicant. This application for judicial review was therefore dismissed.

IRP Act

The following questions were certified:

(1) Does s. 170.2 of the *Immigration and Refugee Protection Act*, where it states, "The Refugee Protection Division does not have jurisdiction to reopen on any ground — including a failure to observe a principle of natural justice — a claim for refugee protection . . . in respect of which the Refugee Appeal Division or the Federal Court . . . has made a final determination," withdraw jurisdiction from the Refugee Protection Division to *decide* questions of law and, by implication, constitutionality, arising under that provision?

(2) In spite of the availability of other possible applications under the *Immigration and Refugee Protection Act*, does s. 170.2 of the *Immigration and Refugee Protection Act* unjustifiably breach a claimant's rights under s. 7 of the *Charter of Rights and Freedoms* such that the provision must be found unconstitutional and declared to be of no force and effect?

Refugee Appeal Division

171. Proceedings — **In the case of a proceeding of the Refugee Appeal Division,**

(a) the Division must give notice of any hearing to the Minister and to the person who is the subject of the appeal;

(a.1) subject to subsection 110(4), if a hearing is held, the Division must give the person who is the subject of the appeal and the Minister the opportunity to present evidence, question witnesses and make submissions;

(a.2) the Division is not bound by any legal or technical rules of evidence;

(a.3) the Division may receive and base a decision on evidence that is adduced in the proceedings and considered credible or trustworthy in the circumstances;

(a.4) the Minister may, at any time before the Division makes a decision, after giving notice to the Division and to the person who is the subject of the appeal, intervene in the appeal;

(a.5) the Minister may, at any time before the Division makes a decision, submit documentary evidence and make written submissions in support of the Minister's appeal or intervention in the appeal;

(b) the Division may take notice of any facts that may be judicially noticed and of any other generally recognized facts and any information or opinion that is within its specialized knowledge; and

(c) a decision of a panel of three members of the Refugee Appeal Division has, for the Refugee Protection Division and for a panel of one member of the Refugee Appeal Division, the same precedential value as a decision of an appeal court has for a trial court.

2010, c. 8, s. 28(1); 2012, c. 17, s. 52

Case Law

K. (R.) v. Canada (Minister of Citizenship and Immigration) (2015), 38 Imm. L.R. (4th) 260, 2015 FC 1304, 2015 CarswellNat 7833, 2015 CarswellNat 8532 — Once the RAD advised that it would accept new evidence on behalf of the applicants and proceed with a hearing, it should have dealt with all the evidence on a *de novo* basis. The RAD committed a reviewable error by failing to conduct a full *de novo* hearing. It is no answer to refer to subs. 171(a.2) of the Act and say that the RAD is a master of its own process. The process chosen must give effect to the appeal right conferred by the Act. The application for judicial review was allowed.

The following question was certified:

> Is there any deference owed by the Refugee Appeal Division ("RAD") to the Refugee Protection Division's ("RPD") credibility findings where the RAD holds a hearing under s. 110(6) of IRPA?

171.1 No reopening of appeal — **The Refugee Appeal Division does not have jurisdiction to reopen on any ground — including a failure to observe a principle of natural justice — an appeal in respect of which the Federal Court has made a final determination.**

2012, c. 17, s. 53

Immigration Division

172. (1) Composition — **The Immigration Division consists of the Deputy Chairperson, Assistant Deputy Chairpersons and other members necessary to carry out its functions.**

(2) Public Service Employment Act — **The members of the Immigration Division are appointed in accordance with the *Public Service Employment Act*.**

2010, c. 8, s. 29

173. Proceedings — **The Immigration Division, in any proceeding before it,**

(a) **must, where practicable, hold a hearing;**

(b) **must give notice of the proceeding to the Minister and to the person who is the subject of the proceeding and hear the matter without delay;**

(c) **is not bound by any legal or technical rules of evidence; and**

(d) **may receive and base a decision on evidence adduced in the proceedings that it considers credible or trustworthy in the circumstances.**

Case Law

Balathavarajan v. Canada (Minister of Citizenship & Immigration), [2006] F.C.J. No. 1550, 56 Imm. L.R. (3d) 1, 354 N.R. 320, 2006 CarswellNat 3297, 2006 FCA 340 — The court considered whether the IAD must consider hardship to a permanent resident who had been issued a deportation order, and who had been declared a Convention refugee, where the deportation order did not specify the country of removal, and where it is uncertain what that country might be. The Minister had not specified the country of deportation, and at the time of the IAD appeal had not taken the necessary steps under subs. 115(2) of the IRPA to remove the appellant. It was, at the time of the IAD appeal, not only unlikely but legally improper to remove the appellant to Sri Lanka. For the IAD to consider potential hardship the appellant might face if deported to Sri Lanka would have been a hypothetical and a speculative exercise. Therefore it did not need to do this. Accordingly, the certified question was answered in the negative by the Court of Appeal.

Section 173 of the IRPA permits the IAD to receive and base a decision on evidence adduced in immigration proceedings that it considers to be credible and trustworthy in the circumstances. It is up to the IAD, not the court, to decide the weight to be given to the evidence. Therefore the appellant also failed to demonstrate that the judge had committed a palpable and overriding error in upholding the IAD's decision. The appeal was dismissed.

Application Under s. 83.28 of the Criminal Code, Re, [2004] S.C.J. No. 40, 2004 CarswellBC 1378, 2004 CarswellBC 1379, [2004] 2 S.C.R. 248, 33 B.C.L.R. (4th) 195, 121 C.R.R. (2d) 1, [2005] 2 W.W.R. 605, 21 C.R. (6th) 82, 322 N.R. 205, (sub nom. *R. v. Bagri)* 184 C.C.C. (3d) 449, (sub nom. *R. v. Bagri)* 240 D.L.R. (4th) 81, 199 B.C.A.C. 45, 2004 SCC 42 — The appeal raised, for the first time in the Supreme Court, fundamental questions about the Constitutional validity of provisions of the *Anti-Terrorism Act*. The Act was a legislative component of Canada's response to the tragedy of September 11, 2001. The appellant was ordered to attend a judicial investigative hearing. This case dealt with the Constitutional validity of the "judicial investigative hearing" provision.

There were essentially two acts of alleged terrorism. Firstly, an explosion killed two baggage handlers, and injured four others at Narita Airport, as baggage was being transferred onto Air India Flight 301. A second explosion occurred just one hour later, causing Air India Flight 182 to crash off the west coast of Ireland, killing all passengers and crew.

The first accused, Inderjit Singh Reyat, was arrested in England and extradited to Canada where he was convicted in connection with the explosion at Narita Airport. Mr. Reyat pleaded guilty to manslaughter in connection with the explosion of Air India Flight 182. Two other accused were jointly charged with offences in relation to both explosions and while their trial was ongoing, the Crown brought an application to examine the appellant in this matter pursuant to s. 83.28.

The challenge for democracies in the battle against terrorism is not whether to respond, but rather, how to do so. Canadians value the importance of human life and liberty and the protection of society through respect for the rule of law. A democracy cannot exist without the rule of law. Terrorism challenges the context in which the rule of law must operate, but does not call for the abdication of the law. At the same time, the Constitution must not become a suicide pact. The challenge for a democratic state's answer to terrorism calls for a balancing of what is required for an effective response to terrorism in a way that appropriately recognizes the fundamental values of the rule of law. In a democracy, not every response is available to meet the challenge of terrorism.

The international scope of terrorism raised concerns about the potential uses of information gathered pursuant to s. 83.28. Section 83.28 specifically provides use and derivative use immunity in the context of criminal proceedings. The legislation did not speak to the safeguards in relation to other types of hearings. Deportation and extradition hearings must accord with the principles of fundamental justice. In order to meet the requirements of s. 7 of the Charter, use and derivative use immunity respecting information gathered under s. 83.28 must be extended to extradition and deportation hearings. Therefore, the hearing judge must make and, if necessary, vary the terms of an order to properly provide use and derivative use immunity in extradition and deportation proceedings.

Immigration Appeal Division

174. (1) Court of record — The Immigration Appeal Division is a court of record and shall have an official seal, which shall be judicially noticed.

(2) Powers — The Immigration Appeal Division has all the powers, rights and privileges vested in a superior court of record with respect to any matter necessary for the exercise of its jurisdiction, including the swearing and examination of witnesses, the production and inspection of documents and the enforcement of its orders.

Case Law

Canada (Minister of Citizenship & Immigration) v. Peirovdinnabi (2010), 87 Imm. L.R. (3d) 162, 2010 FC 64, 2010 CarswellNat 108, 2010 CarswellNat 726 — The issue considered was whether, in 2010, the respondent made a misrepresentation by answering "yes" to the question "are you living with your spouse," posed in a form entitled "Supplemental Information Spouse in Canada." This issue arose in the course of the respondent's sponsorship of his second wife to Canada in 2005. In the course of that application he was questioned about his living circumstances with his first wife three years before and he answered that he thought that the question posed at the time required an answer as to whether he and his first wife were living "together." To this question the respondent said that, while they were living together, he and his first wife maintained separate residences and lived in both after their marriage. The problem that arose was that the applicant interpreted the question answered by the respondent to mean "are you living together with your wife in the same residence." This conflict in interpretation set a course of decision making in motion which has resulted in the present application for judicial review of an IAD decision that found that the respondent did not make a misrepresentation.

The central argument advanced by the applicant in the present review of the IAD decision is that, as a matter of law, the IAD was required to determine the genuineness of the respondent's first marriage. The position that the applicant takes is that since the hearing before the IAD was *de novo*, all issues with respect to the respondent's first marriage were required to be determined. The court rejected this argument and found that the IAD took the appeal as it came: there was only one question to be addressed and that was whether the respondent made a misrepresentation. The question of whether the marriage was genuine was not determined in the first and second level decisions, and it was not in play in the IAD decision. The IAD's decision was upheld and the application for judicial review dismissed. The following question was certified:

> Does the IAD have an obligation in law to determine the genuineness of a marriage on a *de novo* appeal brought with respect to an issue of misrepresentation when the issue of the genuineness of the marriage concerned was not specifically raised for determination in the appeal?

175. (1) Proceedings — The Immigration Appeal Division, in any proceeding before it,

(a) must, in the case of an appeal under subsection 63(4), hold a hearing;

(b) is not bound by any legal or technical rules of evidence; and

(c) may receive and base a decision on evidence adduced in the proceedings that it considers credible or trustworthy in the circumstances.

(2) Presence of permanent resident — **In the case of an appeal by a permanent resident under subsection 63(4), the Immigration Appeal Division may, after considering submissions from the Minister and the permanent resident and if satisfied that the presence of the permanent resident at the hearing is necessary, order the permanent resident to physically appear at the hearing, in which case an officer shall issue a travel document for that purpose.**

Case Law

Kamtasingh v. Canada (Minister of Citizenship & Immigration) (2010), 87 Imm. L.R. (3d) 118, 2010 FC 45, 2010 CarswellNat 801, 2010 CarswellNat 101 — This was an application for judicial review challenging a decision of the Immigration Appeal Division which determined the applicant's marriage was not genuine. The applicant states that the IAD member denied him procedural fairness by preventing him from calling all of his proposed witnesses.

The IAD has the right to limit repetitive testimony, but not by effectively excluding witnesses who could offer evidence going to the central issues of the case. The place to control excessive or repetitive evidence on issues of controversy which are central or determinative is generally not at the entrance to the witness box, but once the witness is testifying — and even then the member must grant some latitude to ensure that all important matters are covered. The IAD can, of course, limit the scope of evidence by stipulating certain points that are not in dispute. In a case like this one where the credibility of the applicant is clearly an issue and where the genuineness of a marriage is in doubt, the evidence of immediate family and close acquaintances is highly relevant and should be heard without reservation. Indeed, it was difficult to see how this matter could be fairly determined after only two hours of evidence, particularly when the applicant was self-represented and was initially intending to lead evidence from several witnesses. This was a situation where the duty to allow the applicant to fully present his case was sacrificed for the desire for administrative efficiency. That is not a permissible trade-off. The application for judicial review was allowed.

Ayele v. Canada (Minister of Citizenship & Immigration) (2007), 60 Imm. L.R. (3d) 197, 2007 CarswellNat 253, 2007 FC 126 — The duty of fairness requires that a party to a proceeding should have the opportunity to present his or her case fully and fairly. This generally includes the right to call witnesses in order to establish the evidentiary basis of a claim or defence. The applicant applied to sponsor his wife. A visa officer rejected the wife's application for permanent residence on the ground that the marriage was not genuine and was entered into for immigration purposes. The applicant appealed to the Immigration Appeal Division (IAD). After hearing the applicant's testimony, the IAD was anxious to conclude the hearing and to dismiss the appeal. In the words of the presiding member, "[i]t will be a waste of the tribunal's time to continue to indulge the appellant in this waste of taxpayer's money." The IAD refused to hear a witness that the applicant wished to call. The Minister claimed that the IAD refused to allow the witness to testify because the applicant was in breach of Rule 37 of the *Immigration Appeal Division Rules* which required the applicant to have provided, in writing, witness information.

The Minister's reliance upon Rule 37 in order to justify the refusal of the IAD to hear the witness was misplaced. At the outset of the hearing, after hearing submissions with respect to the applicant's late disclosure of information, including late disclosure of witness information, the presiding member ruled "I will allow you to deal with the witness, but obviously the identity and credibility of the witness will be an issue." Any hurdle posed by Rule 37 was overcome when the IAD ruled it would exercise its discretion to allow the witness to testify. When the IAD later ruled it would not allow the witness to testify, it did not refer to Rule 37. Instead, the presiding member stated, "Even if the witness corroborates the testimony, in assessing the testimony it's not credible. So, there's no point in calling the witness and even if it is characterized as a breach of natural justice, there is no prejudice suffered when the evidence is of no use and calling the witness is futile."

It is not within the purview of a tribunal bound by the requirement of procedural fairness to dispense with those requirements because, in its view, the result of the hearing will be the same. Rather, it is for a court reviewing a decision of the tribunal that has erred to determine whether, as a matter of administrative law, the consequences of a failure to comply with the requirements of procedural fairness are such that the discretionary remedy available to the reviewing court should be withheld.

The withholding of relief in the face of a breach of procedural fairness is exceptional. One can never rule on the credibility of evidence that has not yet been heard. The presiding member violated the principle when he stated that even if the witness corroborated the applicant's testimony, that subsequent testimony would not be credible.

The essence of adjudication is the ability to keep an open mind until all evidence has been heard. The reliability of evidence is to be determined in light of all the evidence in a particular case. The application for judicial review was allowed.

Canada (Ministre de la Citoyenneté & de l'Immigration) c. Nkunzimana (2005), 54 Admin. L.R. (4th) 122, 2005 CarswellNat 177, 2005 CarswellNat 4820, 2005 FC 29 — The applicant, a Canadian citizen, successfully appealed a visa officer's decision to refuse an application to sponsor five orphaned children of whom he claimed to be the uncle. The mothers of the children were the applicant's two deceased sisters. The key evidence the applicant relied on was a letter from the Burundian Ambassador to Canada, attesting that, following a verification of the adopting father's attestation of family composition and the birth certificates of the children to be adopted, the applicant was the uncle of the children he wanted to sponsor. On judicial review the Minister argued the Appeal Division erred in law by stating it was bound by the legal and technical rules of evidence of the Civil Code of Quebec and Code of Civil Procedure when determining that the contents of the letter from the Ambassador of Burundi was true. This approach incorporated a form of evidentiary rigidity that was not intended by Parliament and in this case had the effect of reversing the burden of proof and placing it on the Minister's shoulders. Section 175(1)(c) of the current Act "has the purpose and effect of freeing the Board's hearings from all technical rules of evidence and particularly the 'best evidence' and 'hearsay' rules."

Although the Federal Court agreed that the Appeal Division panel erred, it decided that the panel's decision should not be set aside, since on a balance of probabilities, the Federal Court concluded the children were members of the family class.

Application Under s. 83.28 of the Criminal Code, Re, [2004] S.C.J. No. 40, 2004 CarswellBC 1378, 2004 CarswellBC 1379, [2004] 2 S.C.R. 248, 33 B.C.L.R. (4th) 195, 121 C.R.R. (2d) 1, [2005] 2 W.W.R. 605, 21 C.R. (6th) 82, 322 N.R. 205, (sub nom. *R. v. Bagri*) 184 C.C.C. (3d) 449, (sub nom. *R. v. Bagri*) 240 D.L.R. (4th) 81, 199 B.C.A.C.

45, 2004 SCC 42 — The appeal raised, for the first time in the Supreme Court, fundamental questions about the Constitutional validity of provisions of the *Anti-Terrorism Act*. The Act was a legislative component of Canada's response to the tragedy of September 11, 2001. The appellant was ordered to attend a judicial investigative hearing. This case dealt with the Constitutional validity of the "judicial investigative hearing" provision.

There were essentially two acts of alleged terrorism. Firstly, an explosion killed two baggage handlers, and injured four others at Narita Airport, as baggage was being transferred onto Air India Flight 301. A second explosion occurred just one hour later, causing Air India Flight 182 to crash off the west coast of Ireland, killing all passengers and crew.

The first accused, Inderjit Singh Reyat, was arrested in England and extradited to Canada where he was convicted in connection with the explosion at Narita Airport. Mr. Reyat pleaded guilty to manslaughter in connection with the explosion of Air India Flight 182. Two other accused were jointly charged with offences in relation to both explosions and while their trial was ongoing, the Crown brought an application to examine the appellant in this matter pursuant to s. 83.28.

The challenge for democracies in the battle against terrorism is not whether to respond, but rather, how to do so. Canadians value the importance of human life and liberty and the protection of society through respect for the rule of law. A democracy cannot exist without the rule of law. Terrorism challenges the context in which the rule of law must operate, but does not call for the abdication of the law. At the same time, the Constitution must not become a suicide pact. The challenge for a democratic state's answer to terrorism calls for a balancing of what is required for an effective response to terrorism in a way that appropriately recognizes the fundamental values of the rule of law. In a democracy, not every response is available to meet the challenge of terrorism.

The international scope of terrorism raised concerns about the potential uses of information gathered pursuant to s. 83.28. Section 83.28 specifically provides use and derivative use immunity in the context of criminal proceedings. The legislation did not speak to the safeguards in relation to other types of hearings. Deportation and extradition hearings must accord with the principles of fundamental justice. In order to meet the requirements of s. 7 of the Charter, use and derivative use immunity respecting information gathered under s. 83.28 must be extended to extradition and deportation hearings. Therefore, the hearing judge must make and, if necessary, vary the terms of an order to properly provide use and derivative use immunity in extradition and deportation proceedings.

Remedial and Disciplinary Measures

176. (1) Request — **The Chairperson may request the Minister to decide whether any member of the Immigration Appeal Division or the Refugee Appeal Division should be subject to remedial or disciplinary measures for a reason set out in subsection (2).**

(2) Reasons — **The request is to be based on the reason that the member has become incapacitated from the proper execution of that office by reason of infirmity, has been guilty of misconduct, has failed in the proper execution of that office or has been placed, by conduct or otherwise, in a position that is incompatible with due execution of that office.**

2010, c. 8, s. 30

177. Measures — On receipt of the request, the Minister may take one or more of the following measures:

(a) obtain, in an informal and expeditious manner, any information that the Minister considers necessary;

(b) refer the matter for mediation, if the Minister is satisfied that the issues in relation to the request may be appropriately resolved by mediation;

(c) request of the Governor in Council that an inquiry be held under section 178; or

(d) advise the Chairperson that the Minister considers that it is not necessary to take further measures under this section or sections 178 to 185.

178. Appointment of inquirer — On receipt of a request referred to in paragraph 177(c), the Governor in Council may, on the recommendation of the Minister of Justice, appoint a judge of a superior court to conduct an inquiry.

179. Powers — The judge has all the powers, rights and privileges that are vested in a superior court, including the power

(a) to issue a summons requiring any person to appear at the time and place mentioned in the summons to testify about all matters within that person's knowledge relative to the inquiry and to produce any document or thing relative to the inquiry that the person has or controls; and

(b) to administer oaths and examine any person on oath.

180. Staff — The judge may engage the services of counsel and other persons having technical or specialized knowledge to assist the judge in conducting the inquiry, establish the terms and conditions of their engagement and, with the approval of the Treasury Board, fix and pay their remuneration and expenses.

181. (1) Exceptions to public hearing — An inquiry must be held in public. However, the judge may, on application, take any appropriate measures and make any order that the judge considers necessary to ensure the confidentiality of the inquiry if, after having considered all available alternate measures, the judge is satisfied that there is

(a) a real and substantial risk that matters involving public security will be disclosed;

(b) a real and substantial risk to the fairness of the inquiry such that the need to prevent disclosure outweighs the societal interest that the inquiry be conducted in public; or

(c) a serious possibility that the life, liberty or security of a person will be endangered.

(2) Confidentiality of application — If the judge considers it appropriate, the judge may take any measures and make any order that the judge considers necessary to ensure the confidentiality of a hearing held in respect of an application under subsection (1).

182. (1) Rules of evidence — In conducting an inquiry, the judge is not bound by any legal or technical rules of evidence and may receive, and base a decision on, evidence presented in the proceedings that the judge considers credible or trustworthy in the circumstances of the case.

(2) Intervenors — An interested party may, with leave of the judge, intervene in an inquiry on any terms and conditions that the judge considers appropriate.

Case Law

Jalota v. Canada (Minister of Citizenship & Immigration) (2013), 21 Imm. L.R. (4th) 114, 2013 FC 1176, 2013 CarswellNat 4607, 2013 CarswellNat 4239 — An application to restore the applicant's temporary resident status as a student was refused and he sought judicial review of that decision. The application was denied because the officer was not satisfied that the applicant was a genuine temporary resident and student, that the applicant had sufficient funds, that he would leave Canada at the end of the authorized study, and that the co-op component of his studies met some specified criteria.

The government's own checklist did not ask for any financial information *per se* as part of the restoration application, although it is listed as a requirement for study permit applications. The court held that if the government wished to have financial or other documents, it should have asked for them either in the checklist or by additional request. Any confusion in the checklist lies at the feet of the government and it is a further breach of procedural fairness to have a misleading document supplied to the public. This breach was particularly so where the applicant had confirmed his financial situation and informed the government that he was prepared to provide evidence if asked. It is incumbent on the respondent to state the reasons for loss of status in sufficient terms that an applicant can address those reasons in any further relief he may claim. The government's reliance on financial issues is a new-found basis, not the basis for the original loss of status which concerned whether he was a genuine student, and not that he had lacked sufficient funds. The applicant addressed the issue of his genuineness as a student in his restoration application. It was a further breach of procedural fairness to rely on a ground not cited in the original decision without giving the applicant notice that this ground of financial sustainability was now an issue. The government also put forward no basis for concluding that the applicant would not leave Canada. It is not sufficient to just run through the various grounds for denial of the application, as if checking off a list, without giving reasons for the conclusion. The application for judicial review was granted.

183. Right to be heard — The member who is the subject of the inquiry shall be given reasonable notice of the subject-matter of the inquiry and of the time and place of any hearing and shall be given an opportunity, in person or by counsel, to be heard at the hearing, to cross-examine witnesses and to present evidence.

184. (1) Report to Minister — After an inquiry has been completed, the judge must submit a report containing the judge's findings and recommendations, if any, to the Minister.

(2) Recommendations — The judge may, for any of the reasons set out in subsection 176(2), recommend in the report that the member be suspended without pay or removed from office or that any other disciplinary measure or any remedial measure be taken.

185. Transmission of report to Governor in Council — If the Minister receives a report of an inquiry in which the judge makes a recommendation, the Minister shall send the report to the Governor in Council who may, if the Governor in Council considers it appropriate, suspend the member without pay, remove the member from office or impose any other disciplinary measure or any remedial measure.

186. Rights not affected — Nothing in sections 176 to 185 affects any right or power of the Governor in Council in relation to the removal of a member from office for cause.

Proposed Addition — 186.1–186.4

PART 4.1 — ELECTRONIC ADMINISTRATION

[Heading added 2015, c. 36, s. 175. Not in force at date of publication.]

186.1 (1) Powers — The Minister may administer this Act using electronic means, including as it relates to its enforcement.

(2) Exception — This Part does not apply to the Minister of Employment and Social Development in respect of any activity the administration of which is the responsibility of that Minister under this Act.

(3) Officer — For greater certainty, any person or class of persons who are designated as officers by the Minister to carry out any purpose of this Act may, in the exercise of their powers or the performance of their duties and functions, use the electronic means that are made available or specified by the Minister.

(4) Delegation — For greater certainty, a person who has been authorized by the Minister to do anything that may be done by the Minister under this Act, may do so using the electronic means that are made available or specified by the Minister.

(5) Decision, determination or examination by automated system — For greater certainty, an electronic system, including an automated system, may be used by the Minister to make a decision or determination under this Act, or by an officer to make a decision or determination or to proceed with an examination under this Act, if the system is made available to the officer by the Minister.

2015, c. 36, s. 175 [Not in force at date of publication.]

186.2 Conditions for electronic version — A requirement under this Act to provide a signature, or to make an application, request, claim, decision or determination, or to submit or issue any document, or to give notice or provide information, or to submit a document in its original form, is satisfied by its electronic version, if

(a) the electronic version is provided by the electronic means, including an electronic system, that are made available or specified by the Minister; and

(b) any other requirements that may be prescribed have been met.

2015, c. 36, s. 175 [Not in force at date of publication.]

186.3 (1) Regulations — The regulations may provide for any matter respecting the application of section 186.1 and paragraph 186.2(b), and may include provisions respecting

(a) the technology or format to be used, or the standards, specifications or processes to be followed, including for the making or verifying of an electronic signature and the manner in which it is to be used; and

(b) the date and time when, and the place where, an electronic version of an application, request, claim, notice, decision, determination, document or any information is deemed to be sent or received.

(2) Requirement to use electronic means — The regulations may require a foreign national or another individual who, or entity that, makes an application, request or claim, submits any document or provides information under this Act to do so using electronic means, including an electronic system. The regulations may also include provisions respecting those means, including that system, respecting the circumstances in which that application, request or claim may be made, the document may be submitted or the information may be provided by other means and respecting those other means.

(3) Minister's power — The regulations may prescribe the circumstances in which the Minister may require a foreign national or another individual who, or an entity that, makes an application, request or claim, submits any document or provides information under this Act to do so using any means that are specified by the Minister.

(4) Electronic payments — The regulations may

(a) require that payments that are required to be made or evidence of payment that is required to be provided under this Act must be made or provided by means of an electronic system;

(b) include provisions respecting such a system, respecting the circumstances in which those payments may be made or evidence of payments may be provided by other means, and respecting those other means; and

(c) include provisions respecting the date and time when, and the place where, an electronic payment or evidence of payment is deemed to be sent or received.

(5) Incorporation by reference — The regulations may incorporate by reference the standards or specifications of any government, person or organization, either as they exist on a specified date or as amended from time to time.

2015, c. 36, s. 175 [Not in force at date of publication.]

186.4 Clarification — If any provision of this Act or the regulations authorizes an officer or another individual to require a foreign national or another individual or an entity to submit a visa or other document or to provide information, the officer or individual is not precluded by this Part from requiring the foreign national, other individual or entity to submit the visa or other document or to provide the information, as the case may be, in accordance with that provision.

2015, c. 36, s. 175 [Not in force at date of publication.]

PART 5 — TRANSITIONAL PROVISIONS, CONSEQUENTIAL AND RELATED AMENDMENTS, COORDINATING AMENDMENTS, REPEALS AND COMING INTO FORCE

Transitional Provisions

187. Definition of "former Act" — For the purposes of sections 188 to 201, "former Act" means the *Immigration Act*, chapter 1-2 of the Revised Statutes of Canada, 1985, and, where applicable, the regulations and rules made under it.

188. (1) Continuation — The Immigration and Refugee Board continued by section 57 of the former Act is hereby continued.

(2) Chairpersons, Deputy Chairpersons, Assistant Deputy Chairpersons — The Chairperson, Deputy Chairpersons and Assistant Deputy Chairpersons appointed under the former Act continue in the same capacity with the Board until the expiry or revocation of their respective appointments.

(3) Continuation — members — A member appointed under the former Act to the Convention Refugee Determination Division or the Immigration Appeal Division continues in office as a member of the Board until the expiry or revocation of their appointment.

(4) Executive Director — The person who, on the coming into force of this section, held the office of Executive Director of the Board is deemed to have been appointed to that office under section 158, without prejudice to any salary and benefits he or she may receive by virtue of having held that office before that coming into force.

189. Powers — Sections 94.6, 102.001 to 102.003 and 107.1 of the former Act are, despite paragraph 274(a), deemed not to be repealed and the Minister may exercise any of the powers described in those sections with respect to any business or fund that was approved by the Minister before the coming into force of paragraph 274(a).

190. Application of this Act — Every application, proceeding or matter under the former Act that is pending or in progress immediately before the coming into force of this section shall be governed by this Act on that coming into force.

Case Law

Lopez v. Canada (Minister of Citizenship & Immigration), 2003 CarswellNat 4893 (Imm. & Ref. Bd. (App. Div.)) — The appellant made an application to re-open his removal order appeal. This application is governed by s. 190 of the Act. Section 192 applies only in proceedings where a Notice of Appeal has been filed with the Appeal Division. Filing a Notice of Appeal involves a standard practice related to the filing of a recognized form in an appeal from a refused sponsorship or the issuance of a removal order. Once filed, a Notice of Appeal serves to create or initiate an appeal where before there was none. A re-opening application seeks to re-open an already existing appeal and as such is governed by s. 190 of IRPA.

Mafuala v. Canada (Minister of Citizenship & Immigration), 2003 CarswellNat 3291, 2003 CarswellNat 4685, 2003 FC 1221 — The applicant came to Canada from Congo in 1966. He made a refugee claim which was dismissed, subsequently left Canada for the United States and returned in 1999 when he made another refugee claim which was also dismissed. He then went back to the United States and returned to Canada in 2001 and once again applied for refugee status. The former *Immigration Act* permitted repeat claims so long as the applicant spent more than 90 days outside of Canada between each one. The applicant was informed that his third claim could not be heard because he was no longer eligible under the new *Immigration and Refugee Protection Act*. This decision was upheld. The *Immigration and Refugee Protection Regulations* state the general rule that applicants for refugee protection who are eligible to make claims under the former Act are entitled to have their claims determined under the new Act, unless, an immigration officer notifies them that they are no longer eligible. The Act specifically provides that the person is no longer eligible if his or her claim has already been rejected even if it was dealt with under the former legislation.

Section 90 of the IRPA Regulations does not permit the applicant's claim to go forward despite the fact that he was told in October 2001 that he was eligible to have his third claim heard.

Dragan v. Canada (Minister of Citizenship & Immigration) (2003), 27 Imm. L.R. (3d) 157, 227 F.T.R. 272, 224 D.L.R. (4th) 738, [2003] 4 F.C. 189, 2003 CarswellNat 467, 2003 CarswellNat 1525, 2003 FCT 211, [2003] F.C.J. No. 260; additional reasons at (2003), 27 Imm. L.R. (3d) 185, 2003 CarswellNat 588, 2003 CarswellNat 1580, 2003 FCT 281, 228 F.T.R. 52, [2003] F.C.J. No. 404; affirmed (2003), 27 Imm. L.R. (3d) 194, 2003 CarswellNat 1419, 2003 FCA 233, 224 D.L.R. (4th) 764, [2003] F.C.J. No. 813 — This consolidated application involved 124 applicants who applied for permanent residence in Canada before June 28, 2002, the day that the IRPA came into force. The applicants sought a writ of *mandamus* requiring the respondent to assess them in accordance with the former Act and the former Regulations. Sections 190 and 201 of the IRPA indicate that Parliament intended the new Act to apply retrospectively and to authorize regulations with retrospective effect. Parliament can expressly enact retroactive or retrospective legislation. The clear expression of Parliamentary intent in this regard overrides the presumption against retroactivity or retrospectively in s. 43 of the *Interpretation Act*. Section 361 of the IRPA Regulations is validly authorized respective legislation and operates according to its terms, which means that applications filed after January 1, 2002, are to be assessed under the new Regulations and applications filed before January 1, 2002 are to be assessed under the old Regulations up until March 31, 2003.

The following conditions need to be satisfied for the court to issue a writ of *mandamus*:

1. There must be a public legal duty to act.

2. The duty must be owed to the applicant.

3. There must be a clear right to the performance of that duty, in particular,

   (a) the applicant must have satisfied all conditions precedent giving rise to the duty and;

b) there was a prior demand for the performance of the duty, a reasonable time to comply with the demand and a subsequent refusal which can either be expressed or implied, e.g. unreasonable delay.

4. No other adequate remedy is available to the applicant.

5. The order sought will be of some practical value or effect.

6. The court finds no equitable bar to the relief sought.

7. On a balance of convenience an order should issue.

The court found all of these conditions satisfied and granted a writ of *mandamus* with respect to 102 of the applicants requiring the respondent on or before March 31, 2003 to assess the 102 applicants and award units of assessment in accordance with the former Regulations. Applications for judicial review with respect to applicants who filed after January 1, 2002 will be assessed under the selection criteria in the IRPA. The applicants who applied in this category had notice of the new selection criteria at the time of their application.

Karmali v. Canada (Minister of Citizenship & Immigration) (2003), 30 Imm. L.R. (3d) 90, 2003 CarswellNat 800, 2003 CarswellNat 2109, 2003 FCT 358, 230 F.T.R. 140 — Section 190 of IRPA and s. 350 of the Regulations do not apply retroactively. They do not state that IRPA should govern as though it was enforced in 1997, rather they state that applications still pending, and specifically applications sent back for re-determination after IRPA came into force, are to be dealt with under IRPA.

The applicant does not have a vested right to have his application re-determined under the law as it existed at the date of the application. Section 190 of IRPA and s. 350 of the Regulations deal with, in clear terms, the manner in which a matter sent back for re-determination is to be re-considered.

The language of s. 190 is not permissive. When s. 190 of IRPA and s. 350 of the Regulations are read together they clearly provide a complete framework for dealing with applications that are referred back by the court for re-determination.

Section 350 of the Regulations is not *ultra vires* the framework of s. 190. Section 201 of the IRPA allows for Regulations regarding the transition between the former Act and IRPA.

Finally s. 190 of IRPA does not offend subs. 2(e) of the *Canadian Bill of Rights* as it does not deprive a person of the right to a fair hearing.

191. Convention Refugee Determination Division — Every application, proceeding or matter before the Convention Refugee Determination Division under the former Act that is pending or in progress immediately before the coming into force of this section, in respect of which substantive evidence has been adduced but no decision has been made, shall be continued under the former Act by the Refugee Protection Division of the Board.

Case Law

Molnar v. Canada (Minister of Citizenship & Immigration), 2004 CarswellNat 5334, 2004 CarswellNat 1840, 254 F.T.R. 221, 2004 FC 834 — The filing of a PIF does not constitute "substantive evidence adduced in the proceeding" for the purposes of s. 191, because evidence is only "adduced" when it is identified on the record and entered as an exhibit at the hearing.

Borcsok v. Canada (Minister of Citizenship & Immigration), 2004 CarswellNat 1516, 2004 CarswellNat 799, 2004 FC 445, [2004] F.C.J. No. 552 — The filing of a Personal Information Form does not constitute substantive evidence for the purpose of s. 191.

192. Immigration Appeal Division — **If a notice of appeal has been filed with the Immigration Appeal Division immediately before the coming into force of this section, the appeal shall be continued under the former Act by the Immigration Appeal Division of the Board.**

Case Law

Lopez v. Canada (Minister of Citizenship & Immigration), 2003 CarswellNat 4893 (Imm. & Ref. Bd. (App. Div.)) — The appellant made an application to re-open his removal order appeal. This application is governed by s. 190 of the Act. Section 192 applies only in proceedings where a Notice of Appeal has been filed with the Appeal Division. Filing a Notice of Appeal involves a standard practice related to the filing of a recognized form in an appeal from a refused sponsorship or the issuance of a removal order. Once filed, a Notice of Appeal serves to create or initiate an appeal where before there was none. A re-opening application seeks to re-open an already existing appeal and as such is governed by s. 190 of IRPA.

193. Continuation by Immigration Division — **Every application, proceeding or matter before the Adjudication Division under the former Act that is pending or in progress immediately before the coming into force of this section, in respect of which substantive evidence has been adduced but no decision has been made, shall be continued under this Act by the Immigration Division of the Board.**

194. Refugee Protection Division — **In cases referred to in section 191, a decision by the Refugee Protection Division following a hearing that has been commenced by the Convention Refugee Determination Division is not subject to an appeal under section 110.**

195. Convention Refugee Determination Division — **A decision made by the Convention Refugee Determination Division before the coming into force of this section is not subject to an appeal under section 110.**

196. Appeals — **Despite section 192, an appeal made to the Immigration Appeal Division before the coming into force of this section shall be discontinued if the appellant has not been granted a stay under the former Act and the appeal could not have been made because of section 64 of this Act.**

Case Law

Medovarski v. Canada (Minister of Citizenship & Immigration), [2005] 2 S.C.R. 539, 50 Imm. L.R. (3d) 1, 135 C.R.R. (2d) 1, 258 D.L.R. (4th) 193, [2005] S.C.J. No. 31, 339 N.R. 1, EYB 2005-95306, 2005 CarswellNat 2943, 2005 CarswellNat 2944, 2005 SCC

51 — The appellant was a permanent resident and had been ordered deported for serious criminality. Her removal order was automatically stayed when she appealed the deportation order to the Immigration Appeal Division. The appeal was discontinued as a result of s. 196 of the IRPA (a transitional provision), which took away the right to appeal an order for removal unless a party had, under the former Act, been "granted a stay." The trial judge set aside the decision to discontinue. However, the Federal Court of Appeal allowed the Minister of Citizenship and Immigration's appeal, holding that the purpose of the IRPA transitional provision was to deny the right of appeal in the case of an automatic stay. Section 196 of the IRPA, properly interpreted, applies only to actively granted stays. The objectives of the IRPA, as expressed in s. 3, indicate an intent to prioritize security. In keeping with these objectives, the IRPA creates a new scheme whereby a person sentenced to more than six months in prison is inadmissible pursuant to s. 36; if they have been sentenced to a prison term of more than two years, they are denied a right to appeal their removal order under s. 64 of the IRPA. The purpose in enacting the IRPA, and in particular s. 64, was to efficiently remove from the country persons who have engaged in serious criminality. Since s. 196 refers explicitly to s. 64, the transitional provision should be interpreted in light of these legislative objectives.

The deportation of a non-citizen cannot in itself implicate the liberty and security interests protected by s. 7 of the Canadian Charter of Rights and Freedoms. Even if the liberty and security of the person were engaged, any unfairness resulting from s. 196 would be inadequate to constitute a breach of principles of fundamental justice.

Kang v. Canada (Minister of Citizenship & Immigration), 2005 CarswellNat 531, 2005 FC 297, [2005] F.C.J. No. 367 — Section 196 applies to sponsorship appeals. The jurisdictional question for the IAD is not whether the foreign national is in fact inadmissible but rather whether the individual in question has been found to be inadmissible on one of the enumerated bases. Once that question is answered in the affirmative, the statute is clear. The IAD is without jurisdiction to deal further with the matter.

Canada (Minister of Citizenship & Immigration) v. Bhalrhu, [2004] F.C.J. No. 1498, 40 Imm. L.R. (3d) 238, 2004 CarswellNat 3184, 2004 FC 1236 — The Minister sought to review a decision of the IRB not to discontinue the respondent's appeal.

Section 196 applies to sponsorship appeals. The legislator excluded from the application of s. 196, appellants who were granted a stay under the former Act out of deference to the IAD and therefore only appeals where the IAD has in fact been involved and granted a stay are excluded by s. 196.

Williams v. Canada (Minister of Citizenship & Immigration), [2004] F.C.J. No. 814, 36 Imm. L.R. (3d) 235, 2004 CarswellNat 2979, 2004 CarswellNat 1310, 2004 FC 662, 254 F.T.R. 224 — Section 196 is designed to put the appellants, including sponsors, under the provisions of the new legislation.

Canada (Minister of Citizenship & Immigration) v. Sohal, [2004] F.C.J. No. 813, 36 Imm. L.R. (3d) 91, 2004 CarswellNat 1309, 2004 FC 660, 2004 CarswellNat 4467, 252 F.T.R. 267 — Section 196 does not apply to sponsorship appeals.

Medovarski v. Canada (Minister of Citizenship & Immigration), [2004] F.C.J. No. 366, 35 Imm. L.R. (3d) 161, 2004 CarswellNat 2709, 2004 CarswellNat 543, 318 N.R. 252, 238 D.L.R. (4th) 328, 2004 FCA 85, (sub nom. *Medovarski c. Canada (Minister of Citizenship & Immigration)*) [2004] 4 F.C.R. 48, 119 C.R.R. (2d) 187 (note), 248 F.T.R. 319 (note), 116 C.R.R. (2d) 268; leave to appeal allowed 2004 CarswellNat 4019, 2004 CarswellNat 4020 (S.C.C.); leave to appeal allowed 2004 CarswellNat 4021, 2004 Car-

swellNat 4022, 119 C.R.R. (2d) 187 (S.C.C.); affirmed 2005 CarswellNat 1533, 2005
CarswellNat 1534 (S.C.C.); affirmed 2005 CarswellNat 1535, 2005 CarswellNat 1536
(S.C.C.) — With respect to the statutory transitional scheme, the general rule is that
IRPA applies to every application, proceeding or matter under the former Act that is
pending or in progress immediately before the coming into force of s. 190. Section 192
creates an exception to s. 190 by enacting the opposite general rule for appeals to the
IAD. If the Notice of Appeal has been filed immediately before the coming into force of
s. 190 then the appeal shall be continued under the former Act.

Section 196 carves a specific exception out of s. 192 by providing that appeals to the IAD
filed before the coming into force of s. 192 shall be discontinued if the appellant has not
been granted a stay under the former Act and the appeal could not have been made because of s. 64. Section 196 discontinues appeals only when a stay has not been granted on
the disposition of an appeal under the former Act para. 73(1)(c). Section 196 does not
include an automatic statutory stay.

Esteban v. Canada (Minister of Citizenship & Immigration), [2003] F.C.J. No. 1181, 31
Imm. L.R. (3d) 47, 2003 CarswellNat 4360, 2003 CarswellNat 2279, 2003 FC 930; reversed (2004), 35 Imm. L.R. (3d) 161, 2004 CarswellNat 2709, 2004 CarswellNat 543,
[2004] F.C.J. No. 366, 318 N.R. 252, 238 D.L.R. (4th) 328, 2004 FCA 85, (sub nom.
Medovarski c. Canada (Minister of Citizenship & Immigration)) [2004] 4 F.C.R. 48, 119
C.R.R. (2d) 187 (note), 248 F.T.R. 319 (note), 116 C.R.R. (2d) 268; affirmed 2005 CarswellNat 1533, 2005 CarswellNat 1534 (S.C.C.); affirmed (2005), 2005 CarswellNat
1535, 2005 CarswellNat 1536 (S.C.C.) — The applicant, since 1990, had been convicted
of a number of criminal offences. In consequence of his last conviction he was reported
under the former *Immigration Act* and ordered deported. The applicant had a right of
appeal from the issuance of the deportation order because he was a permanent resident of
Canada and filed a Notice of Appeal at the end of the hearing. On June 28, 2002 the
IRPA was proclaimed and the Appeal Division advised the applicant that his appeal was
discontinued. The applicant in this action is reviewing the decision of the IAD to treat his
appeal as discontinued.

Section 192 is the general transitional provision applicable to appeals pending before the
IAD when the IRPA came into force. This section generally continues, under the former
Act, appeals before the IAD. Section 196 limits this provision. Section 196 only has any
meaning if it contemplates a statutory stay. Sections 196 and 197 should be read together
because they both limit the general provision in s. 192, continuing appeals under the
former Act. Section 196 applies to appeals launched but not heard or disposed of, while s.
197 applies to appeals heard but still extant because a stay was issued by the IAD.

The interpretation that s. 196 contemplates a statutory stay, avoids the result that there
would never be a granted stay in respect of an appeal pending with the IAD but not heard.
Under this interpretation there are some cases where s. 196 of the Act would operate to
remove an appeal pending to the IAD.

Accordingly, the decision of the registrar concluding that the applicant's appeal was discontinued was set aside.

Jones v. Canada (Minister of Citizenship & Immigration), 2003 CarswellNat 1655, 2003
FCT 661 (T.D.); reversed [2004] F.C.J. No. 366, 35 Imm. L.R. (3d) 161, 2004 CarswellNat 543, 2004 CarswellNat 2709, 318 N.R. 252, 238 D.L.R. (4th) 328, 2004 FCA
85, (sub nom. *Medovarski c. Canada (Minister of Citizenship & Immigration))* [2004] 4
F.C.R. 48, 119 C.R.R. (2d) 187 (note), 248 F.T.R. 319 (note), 116 C.R.R. (2d) 268; leave

to appeal allowed 2004 CarswellNat 4019, 2004 CarswellNat 4020 (S.C.C.); leave to appeal allowed 2004 CarswellNat 4021, 2004 CarswellNat 4022, 119 C.R.R. (2d) 187 (S.C.C.); affirmed 2005 CarswellNat 1533, 2005 CarswellNat 1534 (S.C.C.); affirmed 2005 CarswellNat 1535, 2005 CarswellNat 1536 (S.C.C.) — The word "stay" in s. 196 contemplates a stay that came into effect as a result of the operation of para. 49(1)(b) of the former Act.

Medovarski v. Canada (Minister of Citizenship & Immigration), [2003] 4 F.C. 227, 28 Imm. L.R. (3d) 50, [2003] F.C.J. No. 811, 234 F.T.R. 101, 2003 CarswellNat 1486, 2003 FCT 634; reversed (2004), 35 Imm. L.R. (3d) 161, 2004 CarswellNat 2709, 2004 CarswellNat 543, [2004] F.C.J. No. 366, 318 N.R. 252, 238 D.L.R. (4th) 328, 2004 FCA 85, (sub nom. *Medovarski c. Canada (Minister of Citizenship & Immigration))* [2004] 4 F.C.R. 48, 119 C.R.R. (2d) 187 (note), 248 F.T.R. 319 (note), 116 C.R.R. (2d) 268; leave to appeal allowed 2004 CarswellNat 4019, 2004 CarswellNat 4020 (S.C.C.); leave to appeal allowed 2004 CarswellNat 4021, 2004 CarswellNat 4022, 119 C.R.R. (2d) 187 (S.C.C.); affirmed 2005 CarswellNat 1533, 2005 CarswellNat 1534 (S.C.C.); affirmed 2005 CarswellNat 1535, 2005 CarswellNat 1536 (S.C.C.) — This is an application to review a decision of the IAD which had discontinued the applicant's appeal for lack of jurisdiction. The applicant, a permanent resident of Canada, had appealed her deportation order to the IAD. She received a notice to appear dated April 24, 2002 stating that her appeal would be heard on September 26, 2002. On June 28, 2002 the *Immigration and Refugee Protection Act* and its accompanying regulations came into force. On August 12, 2002 the IAD advised the applicant that her appeal would be discontinued pursuant to ss. 196 and 64 of the IRPA.

Parliament acknowledges that a change from one legislative framework to another will affect parties who have commenced some actions under the appeal legislation. This group of affected parties is usually easily defined. While those caught in the transition are subject to the new statute as a whole, they form a unique group to whom the general objectives of both the new law and the old law will apply. Thus, almost every statute that is intended to replace an existing statute contains transitional provisions. The objective of Parliament is to treat those caught by the transition as fairly as possible. Where a right previously held is being affected, the transitional provisions should be interpreted in a manner that respects not only the overall intent of the IRPA, but also the more limited intent of treating those individuals fairly. Where the right to an appeal is being removed, the context requires an interpretation that minimizes the negative impact on the applicant.

The word "stay" in s. 196 of the IRPA contemplates a stay that came into effect as a result of the operation of para. 49(1)(b) of the former Act. As a result, the IAD was held to have erred in concluding that s. 196 had the effect of extinguishing the applicant's appeal rights under s. 192.

197. Stays — **Despite section 192, if an appellant who has been granted a stay under the former Act breaches a condition of the stay, the appellant shall be subject to the provisions of section 64 and subsection 68(4) of this Act.**

Case Law

Canada (Minister of Citizenship & Immigration) v. Hyde, [2006] F.C.J. No. 1747, 57 Imm. L.R. (3d) 165, 359 N.R. 165, 2006 CarswellNat 4146, 2006 FCA 379 — The effect of s. 197 of IRPA is to terminate the IAD's jurisdiction with respect to a person who falls within the sections ambit. Section 197 precludes the IAD from staying a removal order in the exercise of its jurisdiction under s. 68 of IRPA. A permanent resident whose removal the IAD stayed before IRPA came into effect, and who breaches a condition of the stay, cannot continue an appeal to the IAD if either the basis of the deportation order was a criminal conviction with a sentence of two years or more, or if the offence committed after the IAD had stayed the removal was punishable by a maximum of 10 years or a sentence of more than six months was imposed.

The appellant had been ordered deported on the basis of a s. 64 offence (that is, one for which he received a sentence of two years or more). Therefore, his appeal was automatically terminated by IRPA when he breached the conditions imposed on his stay. It is irrelevant that the breaches did not involve the commission of offences referred to in subs. 68(4). The appeal was allowed.

Singh v. Canada (Minister of Citizenship & Immigration), [2006] 3 F.C.R. 70, 344 N.R. 244, 51 Imm. L.R. (3d) 49, 2005 CarswellNat 4113, 2005 CarswellNat 5141, 2005 FCA 417 — The appellant was a permanent resident of Canada. After being convicted of robbery he was found inadmissible on the grounds of serious criminality and ordered deported. He appealed his deportation and was granted a stay of removal that contained, among others, the condition "keep the peace and be of good behaviour." Subsequently, the appellant committed another serious offence and was convicted of that crime. It is the offence itself that constitutes the breach of the condition to keep the peace and to be of good behaviour. In this regard, a breach may be established without a conviction where there is other clear evidence of the offensive behaviour.

Between the time of the assault and the conviction, on June 28, 2002, the *Immigration Act*, R.S.C. 1985, c. I-2, was replaced by the IRPA. A provision of the IRPA addressed individuals such as the appellant, who were found inadmissible on grounds of serious criminality, had obtained a stay of their removal order, and were then convicted of another serious offence. Specifically, the IRPA mandates the cancellation of the stay and the termination of the appeal.

The appellant argued that the transitional provision of the IRPA, s. 197(1) should not apply to a breach of condition that occurred before s. 197 was enacted. The Federal Court concluded that Parliament clearly intended that the provision of the IRPA that cancels the stay and terminates the appeal apply to individuals such as the appellant, regardless of whether the condition of the stay was breached before or after the IRPA came into force.

Leite v. Canada (Minister of Citizenship & Immigration), 2005 CarswellNat 2006, 2005 CarswellNat 5148, 2005 FC 984 — In this case, the applicant was subject to a stay order. The IAD had issued a stay of a deportation and had attached specific terms and conditions to the stay, including detailed reporting requirements and an oral review of the case. The actual stay order did not refer to a four-year term. The applicant was convicted of trafficking a controlled substance and the conviction triggered the application of s. 197 of the IRPA which required the stay to be cancelled by operation of law pursuant to subs. 68(4) of the IRPA. The applicant argued that the stay had expired at the time the conviction occurred and that the applicant should have a hearing where he could lead new evidence and the Board could determine what to do with his case on the merits. The court concluded the stay ordered by the Board was in effect and the applicant was convicted of an offence during that time and, consequently, s. 68(4) applied.

Ferri v. Canada (Minister of Citizenship & Immigration) (2005), 51 Imm. L.R. (3d) 177, [2005] F.C.J. No. 1941, [2006] 3 F.C.R. 53, 2005 CarswellNat 3878, 2005 CarswellNat

5009, 2005 FC 1580 — Subsection 68(4) of the IRPA limits the jurisdiction of the IAD to determining whether the factual requirements of this subsection are met. The IAD can only consider whether it has previously stayed a removal over order; whether the individual in question is a permanent resident or a foreign national who was found inadmissible on grounds of serious criminality or criminality; and whether the individual has been convicted of another offence coming within subs. 36(1) of the IRPA. Once the IAD determines that the factual requirements of this subsection have been met, it then loses jurisdiction over the individual, by operation of law. The IAD does not have jurisdiction to consider the constitutionality of subs. 68(4).

198. Refugee Protection Division — The Refugee Protection Division has jurisdiction to consider decisions of the Convention Refugee Determination Division that are set aside by the Federal Court, the Federal Court of Appeal or the Supreme Court of Canada, and shall dispose of those matters in accordance with the provisions of this Act.

2002, c. 8, s. 194(e)

199. Redetermination — Sections 112 to 114 apply to a redetermination of a decision set aside by the Federal Court with respect to an application for landing as a member of the post-determination refugee claimants in Canada class within the meaning of the *Immigration Regulations, 1978*.

200. Exclusion — Subsection 31(1) does not apply with respect to persons who were permanent residents, within the meaning of the former Act, on the coming into force of this section.

201. Regulations — The regulations may provide for measures regarding the transition between the former Act and this Act, including measures regarding classes of persons who will be subject in whole or in part to this Act or the former Act and measures regarding financial and enforcement matters.

Proposed Addition — 201.1

201.1 Subsection 15(1) of Balanced Refugee Reform Act — The regulations may provide for measures regarding the transition — in respect of an application for protection — between this Act, as it read immediately before the day on which subsection 15(1) of the *Balanced Refugee Reform Act* comes into force, and this Act, as it read on the day on which that subsection comes into force.

2012, c. 17, s. 54 [Not in force at date of publication.]

· · · · ·

Repeals

274. Repeals — The following Acts are repealed:

(a) the *Immigration Act*, chapter I-2 of the Revised Statutes of Canada, 1985;

[*Editor's Note: S.C. 2001, c. 27, s. 189 provides that sections 94.6, 102.001, 102.002, 102.003 and 107.1 of the* Immigration Act, *R.S.C. 1985, c. I-2 (the "for-*

mer Act") are, despite paragraph 274(a) of the Immigration and Refugee Protection
Act, *S.C. 2001, c. 27 (the "new Act"), deemed not to be repealed and the Minister
may exercise any of the powers described in sections 94.6, 102.001, 102.002,
102.003 and 107.1 with respect to any business or fund that was approved by the
Minister before the repeal of the former Act on June 28, 2002.*

*However, S.C. 2001, c. 27, s. 190 provides that every application, proceeding or
matter under the former Act that is pending or in progress immediately before June
28, 2002 shall be governed by the new Act.]*

**(b) An Act to amend the Immigration Act and other Acts in consequence thereof,
chapter 49 of the Statutes of Canada, 1992;**

**(c) An Act to amend the Immigration Act and the Citizenship Act and to make a
consequential amendment to the Customs Act, chapter 15 of the Statutes of Canada, 1995; and**

**(d) An Act to amend the Citizenship Act and the Immigration Act, chapter 22 of
the Statutes of Canada, 1997.**

Coming Into Force

275. Order in council — **Sections 73, 110, 111, 171, 194 and 195 come into force
on a day to be fixed by order of the Governor in Council.**

2010, c. 8, s. 31; 2012, c. 17, s. 55

SCHEDULE — SECTIONS E AND F OF ARTICLE 1 OF THE UNITED NATIONS CONVENTION RELATING TO THE STATUS OF REFUGEES

(Subsection 2(1))

E. This Convention shall not apply to a person who is recognized by the competent authorities of the country in which he has taken residence as having the rights and obligations which are attached to the possession of the nationality of that country.

F. The provisions of this Convention shall not apply to any person with respect to whom
there are serious reasons for considering that:

(a) he has committed a crime against peace, a war crime, or a crime against humanity, as defined in the international instruments drawn up to make provision in respect of such crimes;

(b) he has committed a serious non-political crime outside the country of refuge
prior to his admission to that country as a refugee;

(c) he has been guilty of acts contrary to the purposes and principles of the United
Nations.

Article 1 of the Convention Against Torture and Other Cruel, Inhuman and Degrading Treatment or Punishment

1. For the purposes of this Convention, torture means any act by which severe pain or
suffering, whether physical or mental, is intentionally inflicted on a person for such pur-

poses as obtaining from him or a third person information or a confession, punishing him for an act he or a third person has committed or is suspected of having committed, or intimidating or coercing him or a third person, or for any reason based on discrimination of any kind, when such pain or suffering is inflicted by or at the instigation of or with the consent or acquiescence of a public official or other person acting in an official capacity. It does not include pain or suffering arising only from, inherent in or incidental to lawful sanctions.

2. This article is without prejudice to any international instrument or national legislation which does or may contain provisions of wider application.

Case Law

Section E

Majebi v. Canada (Minister of Citizenship and Immigration), 2016 FC 14, 2016 CarswellNat 18, 2016 CarswellNat 292, [2016] F.C.J. No. 12 — The applicant and his three children brought an application for judicial review of the RAD. The RAD confirmed the decision of the RPD that the applicant and his children were excluded from refugee protection pursuant to s. 98 of IRPA and Article 1E of the United Nations Convention Relating to the Status of Refugees, because they were found to have residency status substantially similar to that of Italian nationals at the time their claims were heard by the RPD, and they therefore did not need refugee protection in Canada. The RAD reasonably rejected new evidence that was offered by the applicant in support of the appeal. It was open to the RAD to assess their residency status as of the date of the hearing before the RPD, rather than the date of the RPD's decision. The application for judicial review was dismissed.

The following question was certified:

> In determining whether an individual is excluded from refugee protection under Article 1E of the United Nations Convention Relating to the Status of Refugees, is the assessment of whether the individual has the rights and obligations which are attached to the possession of the nationality of the country in which the person has taken residence to be made at the time of the hearing before the Refugee Protection Division, at the time of the RPD's decision, or at the time of any appeal before the Refugee Appeal Division?

Zeng v. Canada (Minister of Citizenship & Immigration) (2010), 402 N.R. 154, 2010 FCA 118, 2010 CarswellNat 1295, 2010 CarswellNat 2439 — This appeal concerns Section E of Article 1 (Article 1E) of the *United Nations Convention Relating to the Status of Refugees* and more particularly, the issue of asylum shopping. Article 1E is an exclusion clause. It precludes the conferral of refugee protection if an individual has surrogate protection in a country where the individual enjoys substantially the same rights and obligations as nationals of that country. Asylum shopping refers to circumstances where an individual seeks protection in one country, from alleged persecution, torture, or cruel or unusual punishment in another country (the home country), while entitled to stay in a "safe" country (the third country). The appellant Minister of Citizenship and Immigration appealed the judgment of Justice Gibson of the Federal Court on an application for judicial review of a decision of the Refugee Protection Division of the Immigration and Refugee Board. The RPD determined that the respondents, Zeng and Feng, were excluded from refugee protection pursuant to Article 1E. In allowing the application for judicial review, Justice Gibson identified a discrepancy in the jurisprudence regarding the appropriate date for assessing the applicability of Article 1E exclusion (date of application or date of hearing). He concluded that a more fluid approach was required and proposed a three-step test to be followed in Article 1E exclusion determinations. The applicants were citizens of the PRC. The daughter was born in China and has always lived there. Their son was born in Chile. Mr. Zeng obtained permanent residence status in Chile and his wife obtained temporary residence status. Upon their return to China, they faced persecution for breaching the one-child policy. On their return trip to Chile, they remained in Toronto where they made refugee claims.

The Federal Court of Appeal allowed the appeal and set aside the decision of the application judge and dismissed the application for judicial review. The Federal Court of Appeal set out a test to be applied to Article 1E determinations as follows:

> Considering all relevant factors to the date of the hearing, does the claimant have status, substantially similar to that of its nationals, in the third country? If the answer is yes, the claimant is excluded. If the answer is no, the next question is whether the claimant previously had such status and lost it, or had access to such status and failed to acquire it? If the answer is no, the claimant is not excluded under Article 1E. If the answer is yes, the RPD must consider and balance various factors. These include, but are not limited to, the reason for the loss of status (voluntary or involuntary), whether the claimant could return to the third country, the risk the claimant would face in the country, Canada's international obligations, and any other relevant factors.

It will be for the RPD to weigh the factors and arrive at a determination as to whether the exclusion will apply in the particular circumstances.

See also *Parshottam v. Canada (Minister of Citizenship & Immigration)* (2008), 75 Imm. L.R. (3d) 165, 303 D.L.R. (4th) 672, 382 N.R. 186, 2008 CarswellNat 4154, 2008 CarswellNat 5358, 2008 FCA 355 at s. 98 of IRPA.

Shahpari v. Canada (Minister of Citizenship & Immigration) (1998), 44 Imm. L.R. (2d) 139, 146 F.T.R. 102 — The applicants sought to review the question of whether Section E of Article I of the *Convention* applied to them. The applicants were citizens of Iran. In 1984 they moved to France and after seven years of temporary residence in France were issued a "Carte de Resident" which was valid for 10 years. After residing in France until 1994, the applicants came to Canada and within one month made a refugee application.

The burden of proving that Section E applies rests with the party asserting it, in this case the respondent. It did not assist the applicant in this case that she allowed her visa to expire. The evidence allowed the panel to conclude that the visa could be renewed. Applicants should remember that actions they themselves take, which are intended to result in their not being able to return to a country which has already granted them refugee status, may well evidence an absence of the subjective fear of persecution in their original country. Further, if applicants are entitled to renounce the protection they receive from one country and claim protection from another, it gives them a right to emigrate to another country without complying with the usual requirements, solely by reason of their unilateral renunciation of the protection that they have been afforded by the country they are leaving.

Hamdan v. Canada (Minister of Citizenship & Immigration) (1997), 38 Imm. L.R. (2d) 20 (Fed. T.D.) — This was an application to review a negative decision of the CRDD. The applicant, a citizen of Iraq, claimed refugee status in February 1995. Before coming to Canada the applicant had resided in the Philippines since May 1986. From 1986 until

1992 he had legal status in the Philippines as a student. After the expiry of his student visa, he stayed in the Philippines illegally for approximately one year. He tried to come to Canada with false travel documents, but was turned back in Hong Kong. He returned to the Philippines and subsequently filed a refugee claim with the United Nations High Commissioner for Refugees. His claim was accepted. The fact that the applicant has a well-founded fear of persecution in Iraq was confirmed by the Board and was not at issue in this application. The Board determined that the applicant was not a convention refugee on the basis of the exclusion in Article 1(E) of the Convention.

Article 1(E) is incorporated into Canadian law under s. 2 of the Immigration Act under the definition of Convention refugee. The primary source for understanding the meaning and application of Article 1(E) must be the text of the article itself. It is clear that the article is intended to operate where a person has been recognized "as having the rights and obligations which are attached to the possession of the nationality" of the country in which he has taken residence. With respect to the criteria in *Shamlou v. Canada* (1995), 103 F.T.R. 241, the court observed that the relevant criteria would change depending on the rights which normally accrue to citizens in the country which is being scrutinized. The court did not comment on whether all the criteria set out in the *Shamlou* case must be satisfied for exclusion under Article 1(E). In this case, the court found it to be critical that the applicant had neither the right to work nor the right to receive social services in the Philippines.

Accordingly, the court concluded that the Board had applied the wrong test in determining that the applicant had the rights and obligations attaching to nationality of the Philippines. The decision of the Board was set aside and the matter remitted back for rehearing by a freshly constituted panel.

Also see *Wassiq v. Canada (Minister of Citizenship & Immigration)* (1996), 33 Imm. L.R. (2d) 238, 112 F.T.R. 143 at s. 96 of IRPA.

Kanesharan v. Canada (Minister of Citizenship & Immigration) (1996), 35 Imm. L.R. (2d) 185, 120 F.T.R. 67 — The applicant, a Sri Lankan Tamil, fled Sri Lanka and went to the United Kingdom in 1990. In 1991, the applicant unsuccessfully applied for Convention refugee status in the U.K. The applicant was however given permission to remain in the U.K. until September 1993. This right to remain included the right to make trips from and to the United Kingdom during that period. This right was extended to May 1997. The applicant eventually made his way to Canada where he made a claim which was the subject of this application.

A panel of the IRB decided that Article 1(E) of the 1951 U.N. Convention applied to the applicant. Thus, the issue before the Federal Court was whether, with respect to the United Kingdom, the applicant had the rights and obligations which are normally attached to persons possessing U.K. nationality.

The court noted that in the United Kingdom, the home office reserved the right to remove persons similarly situated to the applicant to their country of nationality should the prevailing circumstances change significantly in a positive manner. Further, the court noted it was only in 1997, when the applicant's extended right to remain in the U.K. had concluded that the applicant would be considered by the home office to be eligible for indefinite leave to remain in that country.

Accordingly, the court found that Article 1(E) of the U.N. Convention did not apply to the applicant, quashed the decision of the IRB and remitted the matter back for reconsideration.

Kroon v. Canada (Minister of Employment & Immigration) (1995), 89 F.T.R. 236 — The applicant, his wife and children sought to set aside a negative decision of the CRDD. The panel concluded that although the claimants may subjectively fear persecution in Estonia, what they suffered or might suffer is discrimination at most. Their claims that they face a reasonable chance of persecution were held to be not well founded. The purpose of Article 1E of the U.N. Convention is to support regular immigration laws of countries in the international community. If a person faces threat of persecution in his own country but is living in another country, with or without refugee status, and there faces no threat of persecution, but rather enjoys the same basic rights as nationals of the second country, then the function of Article 1E is to exclude such a person as a potential refugee claimant in Canada. The panel did not err by considering the basic rights which the applicant was apparently entitled to under the Constitution and laws of Estonia, and comparing those with the rights acknowledged for Estonian nationals. The tribunal's assessments of the rights to which the male applicant would be entitled were he to return and register in Estonia as a foreign national cannot be said to be in error. In light of the special role and expertise of the CRDD the court should defer to the tribunal's assessment on issues of this sort which fall within its particular specialized capacities, unless the tribunal's finding is found to be patently unreasonable.

Section F

See *Kanagendren* (2015), 382 D.L.R. (4th) 562, 2015 FCA 86, 2015 CarswellNat 815, [2015] F.C.J. No. 382, at s. 34 of IRPA.

Gama Sanchez v. Canada (Minister of Citizenship and Immigration) (2014), 28 Imm. L.R. (4th) 228, (sub nom. *Sanchez v. Canada (Minister of Citizenship and Immigration)*) 464 N.R. 333, 2014 FCA 157, 2014 CarswellNat 2177; leave to appeal to S.C.C. refused 2014 CarswellNat 4636, 2014 CarswellNat 4637 (S.C.C.) — The Refugee Protection Division found the applicant had committed a serious non-political crime outside Canada and was excluded from refugee protection pursuant to article 1F(b) of the United Nations *Convention Relating to the Status of Refugees* and s. 98 of the *Immigration and Refugee Protection Act*. The central issue before the Federal Court was when the seriousness of the crime under article 1F(b) of the Convention should be assessed. Should it be assessed at the time of the commission of the crime or at the time of the Refugee Protection Division's determination? The Federal Court concluded that the relevant time for assessment is the time of determination. The Federal Court of Appeal upheld this decision. In assessing the penalty for the equivalent crime under Canadian law, the Refugee Protection Division cannot close its eyes to the law that is on the books at the time of its determination. The appeal was dismissed.

See also *Hernandez Febles v. Canada (Minister of Citizenship & Immigration)*, [2014] 3 S.C.R. 431, (sub nom. *Febles v. Canada (Citizenship and Immigration)*) 376 D.L.R. (4th) 387, 30 Imm. L.R. (4th) 1, (sub nom. *Febles v. Canada (Minister of Citizenship and Immigration)*) 464 N.R. 7, 2014 SCC 68, 2014 CarswellNat 4175, 2014 CarswellNat 4176 at s. 98 of IRPA.

Feimi v. Canada (Minister of Citizenship & Immigration) (2012), 353 D.L.R. (4th) 536, 442 N.R. 374, 2012 FCA 325, 2012 CarswellNat 5724, 2012 CarswellNat 5013, [2012] F.C.J. No. 1610 — The appellant, a national of Albania, appealed a Federal Court decision to dismiss a decision of the Refugee Protection Division from denying his application for refugee status. The RPD rejected his claim for refugee protection on the ground that he was excluded from the definition of a refugee by Article 1F(b) of the United

Nations Convention relating to the Status of Refugees. The RPD held that there were serious reasons for considering that the appellant had committed a "serious non-political crime" within the meaning of Article 1F(b) as a result of his conviction in Greece in 1997 for a crime of murder in a fit of anger.

The appellant's argument that the Minister of Public Safety and Emergency Preparedness improperly exercised his discretion to intervene at the exclusion hearing was largely based on the fact that the Minister of Citizenship and Immigration had declined to give an opinion that the appellant was a danger to the public in Canada and that his claim was therefore not ineligible to be referred to the RPD. The appellant argued that the fact that the Minister of Citizenship and Immigration did not consider him a danger in effect estops the Minister of Public Safety and Emergency Preparedness from intervening before the RPD to argue for exclusion on essentially the same materials as those on which the Minister of Citizenship and Immigration denied a request for a danger opinion.

Since the Federal Court of Appeal held in *Hernandez Febles v. Canada (Minister of Citizenship & Immigration)* (2012), 357 D.L.R. (4th) 343, that current dangerousness is not an issue at an exclusion hearing, there is no possible basis for concluding that the Minister of Citizenship and Immigration's refusal of a danger opinion at the eligibility stage made it unreasonable for the Minister of Public Safety and Emergency Preparedness to intervene at the appellant's exclusion hearing to argue that his crime was serious and Article 1F(b) applied. The issues at the eligibility and exclusion stages of processing a refugee claim are not the same. Thus, no question of estoppel can arise, even when the same criminal conduct underlies both the danger opinion at the eligibility stage and intervention at the exclusion hearing.

The broad scope of the decision of the Minister of Public Safety and Emergency Preparedness to intervene before the RPD imposes a heavy burden on the applicant to establish that it was exercised unreasonably. The appellant did not come close to discharging it. The appeal was dismissed.

Also see *Ezokola c. Canada (Ministre de la Citoyenneté & de l'Immigration)*, [2013] 2 S.C.R. 678, 361 D.L.R. (4th) 1, 18 Imm. L.R. (4th) 175, (sub nom. *Ezokola v. Canada (Minister of Citizenship and Immigration))* 447 N.R. 254, 2013 SCC 40, 2013 CarswellNat 2463, 2013 CarswellNat 2464, at s. 98 of IRPA.

The Refugee Protection Division excluded the applicant from the definition of "refugee" under article 1F(a) of the *Convention Relating to the Status of Refugees* finding that he was complicit in crimes against humanity committed by the government of the DRC. The Federal Court allowed his application for judicial review, but certified a question concerning the nature of complicity under article 1F(a). The Federal Court of Appeal held that a senior official in a government could demonstrate personal and knowing participation and be complicit in the crimes of the government by remaining in his or her position without protest and continuing to defend the interests of his or her government while being aware of the crimes committed by the government. The Supreme Court of Canada allowed the appeal and remitted the matter to a new panel of the RPD for redetermination in accordance with its reasons.

Exclusions based on the criminal activities of the group and not on the individual's contribution to that criminal activity must be firmly foreclosed in Canadian law. Whether an individual's conduct meets the *actus reus* and *mens rea* for complicity will depend on the facts of each case, including (i) the size and nature of the organization; (ii) the part of the organization with which the claimant was most directly concerned; (iii) the claimant's duties and activities within the organization; (iv) the claimant's position or rank in the organization; (v) the length of time the claimant was in the organization, particularly after acquiring knowledge of the group's crime or criminal purpose; and (vi) the method by which the claimant was recruited and the claimant's opportunity to leave the organization. These factors are not necessarily exhaustive, nor will each of them be significant in every case. Their assessment will necessarily be highly contextual, the focus must always remain on the individual's contribution to the crime or criminal purpose, and any viable defences should be taken into account.

Rudakubana v. Canada (Minister of Citizenship & Immigration), 2010 FC 940, 2010 CarswellNat 3449, 2010 CarswellNat 4186 — The Immigration and Refugee Board found the applicant to be complicit in crimes against humanity committed by organizations he had been a member of and his status within those organizations and knowledge of their persecuting activities.

While the findings of foreign authorities are not, except in the most unusual circumstances, binding on the Board, it is appropriate to give recognition to decisions by those other authorities where there is sufficient similarity in practices, policies and values to those in Canada. In this instance, the Swedish decision, along with the evidence before the Board, provided a reasonable basis for the Board's conclusions. The application for judicial review was dismissed.

See also *Jayasekara v. Canada (Minister of Citizenship & Immigration)* (2008), 76 Imm. L.R. (3d) 159, 305 D.L.R. (4th) 630, 384 N.R. 293, 2008 CarswellNat 5525, 2008 CarswellNat 4718, 2008 FCA 404, at s. 98 of IRPA.

Zazai v. Canada (Minister of Citizenship & Immigration) (2005), 50 Imm. L.R. (3d) 107, 259 D.L.R. (4th) 281, 339 N.R. 201, 2005 CarswellNat 2933, 2005 CarswellNat 4771, 2005 FCA 303, [2005] F.C.J. No. 1567 — The appellant came to Canada as a stowaway and made a refugee claim. The Refugee Board determined that he was excluded from the definition of Convention refugee under subs. 2(1) of the *Immigration Act*, R.S.C. 1985, because of Section F(a) of Article 1 of the United Nations Convention relating to the status of refugees. The Board found that there were serious reasons for considering that he had committed crimes against humanity. His application for leave with respect to the Refugee Board's decision was denied. He subsequently submitted an application for landing as a post-determination refugee claimant in Canada. A report under s. 27(2) of the former Act was prepared and a s. 27(3) direction for inquiry was issued. The inquiry was held before an adjudicator who concluded that the appellant was a person described in para. 27(2)(a) coupled with para. 19(1)(j) of the former Act. As a result, the adjudicator determined that he was subject to a deportation order. The appellant successfully sought leave to apply for judicial review of the adjudicator's decision. The Federal Court Trial Division allowed the application and the Minister appealed. The appeal to the Federal Court of Appeal was allowed and the order of the applications judge was set aside and remitted back to the Federal Court for re-determination.

The Federal Court of Appeal concluded that the definition of "crime against humanity" found at subs. 6(3) of the *Crimes Against Humanity and War Crimes Act* includes complicity.

As a matter of fact, as found by the adjudicator and agreed by the reviewing judge, there was sufficient cogent evidence that the appellant was, knowingly and voluntarily, a participating and active member for five years in a secret service organization within the Ministry of State Security known as KHAD that tortured and eliminated people who were against the government. The evidence revealed that the appellant entered as a lieutenant and rose to the level of captain. Not only did he share and espouse the views of the brutal organization, he attended training sessions and provided the names of those who did not cooperate.

According to the evidence, the appellant was willingly and to his benefit a member of an organization that only existed for a limited brutal purpose. Under both Canadian and international jurisprudence, the behaviour of the appellant amounted to complicity in the commission of crimes against humanity. Consequently, the Federal Court judge properly confirmed the decision of the adjudicator that the appellant was inadmissible pursuant to para. 19(1)(j) of the former Act or para. 35(1)(a) of the new Act.

The Supreme Court's decision in *Mugesera vs. Canada (Minister of Citizenship & Immigration)*, [2005] S.C.J. No. 39, was distinguished on the basis that the Supreme Court in that case was not confronted with an issue of complicity in the commission of a crime by someone else. In that case, Mr. Mugesera was the actual perpetrator. Complicity is not a crime at common law and under Canadian criminal law, it was, and still is, a mode of commission of a crime. It refers to the act or omission of a person who helps, or is done for the purpose of helping, the furtherance of a crime. An accomplice is then charged with, and tried for, the crime that was actually committed and that he assisted or furthered. In other words, whether one looks at it from the perspective of our domestic law or of international law, complicity contemplates a contribution to the commission of a crime. Complicity must not be confused with the inchoate crimes of conspiracy, attempt and incitement to commit a crime. Unlike complicity, they are not modes or means of committing a crime.

Lai v. Canada (Minister of Citizenship & Immigration), 2005 CarswellNat 886, 332 N.R. 344, 2005 FCA 125 — This was an appeal from a decision of an applications judge who dismissed the appellants' application for judicial review of their failed refugee claims. While various purposes of Article 1F have been identified, the primary purpose of the Article is to ensure that perpetrators of serious, non-political crimes are not entitled to international protection. The exclusion hearing under Article 1F is not in the nature of a criminal trial. In both the extradition and criminal law context, signed foreign statements taken in accordance with foreign procedural law are not inadmissible on the ground that the foreign procedural requirements are different than Canadian procedural requirements if the admission would not make the trial unfair. Enforcement processes on foreign soil are governed by the laws and codes of the foreign jurisdiction. In order for the Board to admit interrogation statements produced abroad by foreign government agencies, the Minister need only provide general evidence as to the credible or trustworthy nature of the statements offered. The Board may take into consideration specific evidence presented by the Minister or by the applicant as to the voluntariness or involuntariness of a particular statement. The legal rules normally associated with the criminal process, when dealing with the voluntariness of a statement, simply do not apply in a refugee context. Subsection 20(3) of the *Refugee Protection Division Rules* requires the Minister to state in the notice the facts and law on which he relies if he believes that Section E or F of Article 1 applies to a claim.

One of the purposes of Article 1F(b) is to protect the integrity of the refugee determination system of the receiving state by screening out serious ordinary criminals because of their criminal activities in a foreign state.

Whether a crime is political for the purposes of Article 1F(b) is determined by the motivation of the offender at the time the crime was committed.

Once excluded under Article 1F(b), claimants are not entitled to have their inclusionary claims determined. Because in this appeal the children's actions were not subject to Article 1F(b) their derivatives claims must be determined. Accordingly, it was proper for the Board to conduct an inclusionary analysis with respect to all five of the appellants in order to determine if the children's derivative claims could be successful.

Bitaraf v. Canada (Minister of Citizenship & Immigration), 2004 CarswellNat 2909, 2004 CarswellNat 1941, 254 F.T.R. 277, 2004 FC 898 — This application for judicial review raised issues concerning the interpretation of the exclusion found in Article 1(F)(c) of the United Nations Convention Relating to the Status of Refugees.

The purpose of Article 1(F)(c) can be characterized in the following terms: to exclude those individuals responsible for serious, sustained or systemic violations of fundamental human rights which amount to persecution in a non-war setting. Two categories of acts qualify as being contrary to the purposes and principles of the United Nations: (i) those acts which have been expressly determined by the United Nations or the International Court of Justice to be contrary to the purposes and principles of the United Nations; and (ii) certain types of serious, sustained and systemic violations of human rights constituting persecution.

In order to make a finding under Article 1(F)(c) given its potential breadth, the panel ought to have had regard for such matters as the United Nations Security Council Resolution 1377, both as regards to the MEK and, more importantly, the specific conduct of the applicant.

Mere membership in an organization is insufficient to incur exclusion except where the organization is one of limited brutal purpose and absence of membership is likewise insufficient where there is personal and knowing participation. It is essential that the panel focus on the specific acts of the person, their nature, quality and the circumstances thereof and their relationship of those acts to the offending acts or practices of the subject organization.

In order for the applicant to be an accomplice, the Board has to address whether he had a shared common purpose with MEK and whether there was personal and knowing participation in the organization.

Xie v. Canada (Minister of Citizenship & Immigration) (2003), [2004] 2 F.C.R. 372, 34 Imm. L.R. (3d) 220, 2003 CarswellNat 4640, 2003 CarswellNat 2942, 239 F.T.R. 59, 2003 FC 1023; affirmed (2004), 37 Imm. L.R. (3d) 163, 2004 CarswellNat 2036, 2004 FCA 250, [2004] F.C.J. No. 1142, 2004 CarswellNat 3972, 325 N.R. 255, [2005] 1 F.C.R. 304, 243 D.L.R. (4th) 385; leave to appeal refused 2005 CarswellNat 748, 2005 CarswellNat 749 (S.C.C.) — This is an application to review a negative decision of a panel of the Refugee Protection Division. The applicant was excluded under Article 1F(b) of the 1951 Convention. The standard of review for decisions under Article 1F(b) was described as follows: 1) the standard of patent unreasonableness will be applied to the panel's finding of fact and its credibility finding; 2) the determination that there were serious reasons for considering the applicant to have committed fraud or embezzlement will be reviewed according to a standard of reasonableness *simpliciter*; and 3) the standard of review of correctness will be applied to the determination that a purely economic offence can constitute a serious non-political crime, because interpreting Articles of the Convention is a determination of law. The court determined that a serious crime should he determined by having reference to the applicable maximum sentence that could have been imposed had the crime had been committed in Canada. An examination of all the relevant surrounding circumstances can still be conducted. The fact that the offence is punishable in this case by a maximum sentence of 10 years is not the end of the analysis. Surrounding circumstances can be looked at to determine whether Article 1F(b) is applicable.

On the facts of this case, the finding of the panel that a serious non-political crime had been committed was upheld.

Zrig c. Canada (Ministre de la Citoyenneté & de l'Immigration) (2003), 32 Imm. L.R. (3d) 1, (sub nom. *Zrig v. Canada (Minister of Citizenship & Immigration))* 229 D.L.R. (4th) 235, 307 N.R. 201, 239 F.T.R. 319 (note), [2003] 3 F.C. 761, 2003 FCA 178, 2003 CarswellNat 924, 2003 CarswellNat 1978, [2003] F.C.J. No. 565 — The appellant sought to review the dismissal of his application for judicial review of a decision of the Immigration and Refugee Board. A panel of the Refugee Division had concluded that the applicant was not a refugee on the grounds that he should be excluded because of the provisions of Articles 1(F)(b)(c). The question on appeal was whether the rules laid down by the court in *Sivakumar v. Canada (Minister of Employment & Immigration)*, [1994] 1 F.C. 433, 163 N.R. 197, 1993 CarswellNat 242, [1993] F.C.J. No. 1145 (C.A.), on complicity by association for the purposes of implementing Article 1F(a) of the Convention were applicable in connection with an exclusion under Article 1F(b). The majority of the court concluded that the rules laid down in Sivakumar on complicity by association were applicable for the purpose of an exclusion under Article 1F(b). Decary J.A. concurred in the result but found that the rules complicity by association developed with respect to Article 1F(a) of the Convention did not apply, as such, to Article 1F(b).

Harb v. Canada (Ministre de la Citoyenneté & de l'Immigration) (2003), 27 Imm. L.R. (3d) 1, 238 F.T.R. 194 (note), 302 N.R. 178, 2003 CarswellNat 1279, 2003 CarswellNat 180, 2003 FCA 39, [2003] F.C.J. No. 108 — Article 1 F(a) of the United Nations Convention relating to the status of refugees should be interpreted so as to include international instruments concluded since it was adopted.

Zrig c. Canada (Ministre de la Citoyenneté & de l'Immigration), 2001 CarswellNat 2228, 2001 CarswellNat 2782, 2001 FCT 1043 — A majority of the judges in the House of Lords in *T. v. Secretary of State for the Home Department*, [1996] 2 All E.R. 865, defined a political crime for purposes of para. 1F(b) as follows: a crime is a political crime for the purposes of Article 1F(b) if and only if (1) it is committed for a political purpose, that is to say with the object of overthrowing or subverting or changing the government of the State or inducing it to change its policy; and (2) there is a sufficiently close and direct link between the crime and the alleged political purpose. The court will bear in mind the means used to achieve the political end and will have particular regard to whether the crime was aimed at a military or government target on the one hand, or a civilian target on the other, and in either event, whether it was likely to involve the indiscriminate killing or injuring of members of the public.

The word "serious" means that these are crimes that warrant an especially severe punishment thus making clear the commitment of signatories of the Convention to withhold protection from those who have committed truly abhorrent wrongs.

Bermudez v. Canada (Minister of Citizenship & Immigration) (2000), 6 Imm. L.R. (3d) 135, 24 Admin. L.R. (3d) 65, 191 F.T.R. 72, 2000 CarswellNat 1174; additional reasons at (2001), 17 Imm. L.R. (3d) 273, 2001 CarswellNat 1335, 35 Admin. L.R. (3d) 145, 206

F.T.R. 188 — The applicant sought to review an unsuccessful decision of a panel of the CRDD. In that decision, the panel found that the female applicant and her minor children did not have a well-founded fear of persecution. The panel also found that the male applicant did have a fear of persecution but was excluded from status as a convention refugee by Article 1(F)(A) as a person who had committed war crimes in Nicaragua.

The panel did not give the applicants notice that an exclusion based on the commission of war crimes would be considered. There are two possible grounds for exclusion under clause 1(F)(A), namely, crimes against humanity and war crimes. These two types of crimes are sufficiently different to require different evidence in argument and different submissions in response. Accordingly, the panel was required to · give the applicants proper notice of the ground on which the exclusion would be considered.

War crimes have come to be understood internationally in the context of international conflict. The foundation documents for the concept of the international war crime are the London Agreement of August 8, 1945 and the Charter of the International Military Tribunal, Article 6. An inhumane action that would be a war crime, during war time, may well be a crime against humanity in the absence of international war. In this case, the activities of the applicant have to do with the mistreatment of prisoners in the course of a civil war. The ill treatment of civilians as a war crime is limited to crimes against the population of, or in the territory of, a country other than that of the perpetrator in the course of an international war. The CRDD made an erroneous determination of the law in relation to war crimes. The applicant may have committed a crime against humanity. The Trial Division however does not accord the CRDD deference on a matter of law. The standard is correctness and the panel erred. The decision of the panel was overturned.

Chan v. Canada (Minister of Citizenship & Immigration), [2000] 4 F.C. 390, 190 D.L.R. (4th) 128, 260 N.R. 376, 10 Imm. L.R. (3d) 167, 2000 CarswellNat 1512, 2000 CarswellNat 3277 (C.A.) — Article 1F(b) cannot be invoked in cases where a refugee claimant has been convicted of a crime and served his/her sentence outside Canada prior to his or her arrival in this country.

Wajid v. Canada (Minister of Citizenship & Immigration) (2000), 185 F.T.R. 308, 2000 CarswellNat 978 — The applicant sought to overturn a negative decision of a panel of the Convention Refugee Determination Division (CRDD). The applicant was the general secretary of the TNSM in his village in Pakistan. The TNSM described itself as a peaceful movement seeking the imposition of traditional Islamic law upon certain administrative units of the northwest frontier in Pakistan. When it became clear to the TNSM that the central government was not able to satisfy its demands more militant activity resulted in the course of which hostages were taken, the local airport seized and closed and people killed. The applicant was excluded from being considered a Convention refugee because there were "serious reasons to consider that he had committed a crime against peace, a war crime or a crime against humanity. . . ." It was incumbent upon the panel to identify the crime in question and to show what made it an international crime instead of merely a domestic crime. The onus of establishing that a person is excluded lies on the person asserting the exclusion. It is not for the applicant to show that the acts did not constitute international crimes.

Sumaida v. Canada (Minister of Citizenship & Immigration) (2000), 3 Imm. L.R. (3d) 169, 183 D.L.R. (4th) 713, 252 N.R. 380, [2000] 3 F.C. 66, 179 F.T.R. 148, 2000 CarswellNat 23, 2000 CarswellNat 1751 (C.A.) — The respondent was a citizen of Iraq and Tunisia. He claimed to be a Convention refugee by reason of a well-founded fear of peroocution in Iraq and Tunisia on the ground of his political opinion. The applicant's claim was rejected because a panel of the Convention Refugee Determination Division (CRDD) found serious reasons for believing that the respondent had committed crimes against humanity. The panel's finding that civilians were targeted victims of the respondent's crimes against humanity referred to two classes of civilians, students in the United Kingdom and their families in Iraq. Such a finding was sufficient to meet the definition "crime against humanity."

When an informant such as the respondent has knowingly directed those at the most violent point in the chain of command to their victims, it hardly lies in his mouth to say, "you can't prove anyone I informed on was actually killed or tortured." Evidence that any harm befell the alleged victims or that any crime was committed specifically against them was not required.

Brzezinski v. Canada (Minister of Citizenship & Immigration), [1998] 4 F.C. 525, 45 Imm. L.R. (2d) 262, 148 F.T.R. 296 — The applicants claimed Convention refugee status and they were determined by the tribunal to be excluded from the definition by reason of the fact that they had committed serious non-political crimes outside the country of refuge.

The evidence was that the applicants, who described themselves as gypsies, supported themselves by stealing, both prior to seeking refuge in Canada and subsequently. Their stealing was by way of shoplifting.

The extent of theft and shoplifting in Canada may be a serious social problem. The acts of stealing acknowledged by the applicants are crimes. They are serious matters. They are not, however, serious crimes within the meaning of Article 1(F)(b), which is part of the laws of Canada through its incorporation in the *Immigration Act*. On the evidence in this case it appears that the applicants were charged with summary conviction offences in Canada. Their sentences ranged between fines and one 14-day period of detention. The sanction against the applicants' repeated conduct, should they succeed in establishing their well-founded fear of persecution in Poland, must be found in Canada's criminal and immigration laws. The response, however, cannot be Article 1(F)(b).

Bamlaku v. Canada (Minister of Citizenship & Immigration) (1998), 142 F.T.R. 140 — The applicant sought to review a negative decision of the CRDD, which was based on the applicant being excluded from protection pursuant to Section F(a) of Article 1 of the Convention. The applicant joined the Marine Transportation Authority in Ethiopia where he was assigned to security duties at a strategic facility comprised of a port and oil refinery. The applicant informed on some or all of the individuals he investigated to security forces of the government notwithstanding his opposition to the government. He also secretly joined the Ethiopian People's Revolutionary Party. The applicant then informed against persons who were enemies of the Ethiopian People's Revolutionary Party and turned them over to the security forces of the Ethiopian government. The result was that these persons were arrested, detained and probably tortured. The applicant expressed no remorse at this result. He acknowledged that his motivation was mixed — partly they were enemies of the Ethiopian People's Revolutionary Party, and partly he feared they represented threats of terrorist activity against the oil refinery in respect of which he was employed. The applicant testified that any such terrorist activity would have resulted in significant civilian casualties.

The CRDD made no reviewable error. The applicant in informing on the persons in question was not motivated by humanitarian considerations alone. The applicant was also motivated by the fact that such persons were enemies of the Ethiopian People's Revolutionary Party. The tribunal had reasons for considering that the applicant was a person within the scope of Section F and accordingly its decision was not reviewable.

Pushpanathan v. Canada (Minister of Employment & Immigration) (1998), 43 Imm. L.R. (2d) 117, (sub nom. *Pushpanathan v. Canada (Minister of Citizenship & Immigration))* [1998] 1 S.C.R. 982, 226 N.R. 201, (sub nom. *Pushpanathan v. Canada (Minister of Citizenship & Immigration))* 160 D.L.R. (4th) 193, 11 Admin. L.R. (3d) 1 (S.C.C.); additional reasons (sub nom. *Pushpanathan v. Canada (Minister of Citizenship & Immigration))* [1998] 1 S.C.R. 1222, 11 Admin. L.R. (3d) 130 (S.C.C.) — This appeal raised two questions: first, the standard of judicial review over decisions of the IRB and second, the meaning of the exclusion from refugee status set out in Article 1F(c) of the *United Nations Convention Relating to the Status of Refugees.* The appellant left Sri Lanka in 1983 and spent time in India and France before arriving in Canada via Italy in March 1985. He claimed Convention refugee status. The claim was never adjudicated because the appellant was granted permanent resident status in May 1987 under an administrative program. In December 1987, the appellant was arrested and charged with conspiracy to traffic in heroin. The appellant was convicted and sentenced to eight years in prison.

In September 1991, the appellant, then on parole, renewed his claim to Convention refugee status. In June 1992, a conditional deportation order was issued against the appellant. Deportation was conditional upon a determination that the claimant was not a Convention refugee and accordingly the appellant's claim was referred to the CRDD. The Board decided that the appellant was not a Convention refugee. The Federal Court Trial Division and the Federal Court of Appeal refused to reverse that decision on an application for judicial review.

A correctness standard applies to the determinations of law by the IRB.

Conspiracy to traffic in a narcotic is not a violation of Article 1F(c) of the *United Nations Convention Relating to the Status of Refugees.*

Even though international trafficking in drugs is an extremely serious problem that the United Nations has taken extraordinary measures to eradicate, in the absence of clear indications that the international community recognizes drug trafficking as a sufficiently serious and sustained violation of fundamental human rights as to amount to persecution, either through a specific designation, as an act contrary to the purposes and principles of the United Nations, or through international instruments which otherwise indicate that trafficking is a serious violation of fundamental human rights, individuals should not be deprived of the essential protections contained in the Convention for having committed those acts.

Ledezma v. Canada (Minister of Citizenship & Immigration), 1997 CarswellNat 2277, [1997] F.C.J. No. 1664 (T.D.) — The applicants sought to review a negative decision with respect to their claim for refugee status.

The Board rejected the refugee claim because of a lack of credible and trustworthy evidence from the principal applicant with respect to his persecution for his political beliefs. In addition, the Board concluded that the applicant was excluded under Article 1(F)(a) of the UN convention for being an accomplice to crimes against humanity.

The court elected to review the exclusion order to ensure that it was error free, even though the decision about the exclusion would not be dispositive of the judicial review application. Exclusion by Canada under Article 1(F)(a) of the Convention is a serious matter which could affect the applicant for the rest of his life and accordingly, even though the Board's decision would stand on the basis of its credibility findings, the court agreed to undertake a review of the exclusion order.

Suliman v. Canada (Minister of Citizenship & Immigration) (1997), 133 F.T.R. 178 — The applicants sought to review a negative decision of a panel of the CRDD. The Board found that the male applicant was excluded under Article 1(F)(a) of the Convention on the basis that he committed crimes against humanity. The decision of the panel was set aside. The Board did not expressly consider whether the crimes committed by the police constituted crimes against humanity. Crimes against humanity must generally be committed in a wide spread systematic fashion. This requirement does not mean that a crime against humanity cannot be committed against one person, but in order to elevate a domestic crime such as murder or assault to the realm of international law an additional element will have to be found. This element is that the person who has been victimized is a member of a group which has been targeted systematically and in a widespread manner for one of the crimes of murder, extermination, enslavement, deportation or other inhuman acts. The Board should have considered whether the victims of police abuse in this case were ". . . members of a group which have been targeted systematically and in a widespread manner for one of the crimes mentioned . . ."

Bazargan v. Canada (Ministre de l'Emploi & de l'Immigration) (1996), 205 N.R. 282, 119 F.T.R. 240 (note) (C.A.) — The respondent joined the Iranian national police in 1960 and pursued his career there until 1980. Between 1960 and 1977, he climbed the ranks of the military hierarchy and became a colonel. From 1974 to 1977, he worked in Tehran as the officer in charge of liaison between the police forces and SAVAK. SAVAK, from which the respondent had received some of his training, was an internal security agency under the Shah's personal authority. During that period, the respondent was in charge of the network for exchanging classified information between the police forces and SAVAK. The respondent was appointed to that position because of his knowledge of intelligence, espionage and counterespionage. In 1977, the respondent became a chief of the police forces in a province in southwestern Iran and held that position until the fall of the monarchist regime in 1979.

A panel of the IRB had determined that the respondent was a refugee within the meaning of subs. 2(1) but that he was excluded from Convention protection due to Article 1(F). This decision was overturned by the motions judge on a judicial review application. A court of appeal allowed the appeal and reinstated the decision of the panel of the IRB.

The court has expressly refused to make formal membership in an organization a condition for the exclusion to apply. Membership in an organization that committed atrocities helps to determine whether the condition of personal and knowing participation has been met. It is important not to turn what is actually a factual presumption into a legal condition.

The Minister does not have to prove the respondent's guilt. The minister has to show that there is serious reason for considering that the respondent is guilty, the burden of proof resting on a minister is "less than a balance of probabilities."

In this appeal the inferences and the conclusions of the panel were based on the evidence and were reasonable. The IRB is a specialized tribunal and it has complete jurisdiction to draw the inferences that can reasonably be drawn.

Pushpanathan v. Canada (Minister of Citizenship & Immigration) (1995), 191 N.R. 247 (Fed. C.A.) — The appellant left Sri Lanka in May 1983 and spent nearly two years in India. He then proceeded to Canada by way of France and Italy arriving here on March

21, 1985 where upon he made a claim for Convention refugee status. In December, 1987 the appellant was among 8 individuals arrested on charges of conspiracy to traffic in heroin. He received an 8 year sentence and was released on parole. A panel of the IRB determined that the appellant was excluded from entitlement to claim the status of a Convention refugee due to para. F(c) of Article 1 of the International Convention on the Status of Refugees.

The Court of Appeal upheld the decision of the Trial Division and concluded that para. F(c) of Article 1 can apply to acts committed by a refugee claimant after his arrival in Canada. It was also held that the paragraph can apply to persons otherwise within its terms, even with respect to acts not committed in the name of, or on behalf of a state. Article 1 of the Convention is dedicated to defining which individuals may have the right, in international law, to be recognized as refugees. The exceptions, found in para. F, deny refugee status to certain individuals who might otherwise be within the global definition. Finally, the court concluded that trafficking in narcotics was an act contrary to the purposes and principles of the United Nations. The court pointed out that the United Nations adopted a Convention against the illicit traffic in narcotics in 1988 and that this Convention was ratified by Canada in 1988. This Convention called upon Canada and other signatory states to establish criminal offenses domestically to prevent, among other things, trafficking in narcotics. In Canada, such a measure was the *Narcotic Control Act*, which is the law under which the appellant was convicted. Accordingly, trafficking in narcotics is contrary to the purposes and principles of the United Nations and the appellant was properly excluded from the refugee process. Accordingly, the appeal was dismissed.

Atef v. Canada (Minister of Citizenship & Immigration), [1995] 3 F.C. 86, 96 F.T.R. 217, 32 Imm. L.R. (2d) 106 — This was an application to review a negative decision of a panel of the CRDD which had concluded that the applicant was a person to whom Section F(c) of Article 1 of the *United Nations Convention Relating to the Status of Refugees* applied.

The applicant, a citizen of Iran, was convicted in Canada of possession of heroin for the purpose of trafficking.

It was not necessary for the panel to determine whether the applicant was a Convention refugee within the meaning of the definition. There is no requirement for the Board to determine this question when applying Article 1F(c) of the Convention. The panel could have conducted an inclusion analysis, but there was no error in not so doing.

The applicant raised arguments suggesting that his rights under ss. 7 and 12 of the Charter had been infringed. The panel correctly determined that these arguments were premature. The panel was dealing with the question of whether the applicant was entitled to claim refugee status and not with the execution of the deportation order. The exclusion of an individual from claiming such status does not, by itself, imply or lead to any positive act which may affect the life, liberty or security of the person. This type of reasoning also lead to a conclusion that the applicant's arguments with respect to s. 12 of the Charter were also premature.

Finally, the applicant contended that the definition of Convention refugee, which incorporated Article 1F(c) of the Convention, violated the applicant's right to fundamental justice under s. 7 of the Charter on account of vagueness. It was argued that Article 1F(c) provided no substantive notice to society in the sense that society was given no notice of what actions are contrary to the principles and purposes of the United Nations. Further, it was argued that Article 1F(c) did not provide meaningful boundaries of conduct or delineate areas of risk because the general public is unaware of the initiatives taken by the United Nations to curb drug trafficking.

The doctrine of vagueness is founded on the principles of fair notice to citizens and the limitation of enforcement discretion. Fair notice comprises two aspects:

1. A formal aspect, namely, an acquaintance with the actual text of the statute; and,

2. A substantive aspect, namely, an understanding that certain conduct is the subject of legal restrictions.

The limitation of enforcement discretion relates to the fact that a law must not be so imprecise that the power to decide becomes fused with the power to prosecute. The various factors to be considered in determining whether a law is vague are:

A. The need for flexibility and the interpretative role of the courts;

B. The impossibility of achieving absolute certainty, a standard of intelligibility being more appropriate; and,

C. The possibility that many varying judicial interpretations of a given disposition may exist and perhaps co-exist.

Applying those factors, the court concluded that Article 1F(c) was not unconstitutionally vague.

Arica v. Canada (Minister of Employment & Immigration) (1995), 182 N.R. 392 (Fed. C.A.) — The appellant was denied refugee status because there were serious reasons for considering that he had been involved in acts constituting crimes against humanity.

Under s. 69.1(5) there is no obligation on the Minister to give notice to claimants of the former's intention to participate in the hearing. The purpose of the notice, which is directed solely at the Board, is to empower the Minister to question a claimant and other witnesses and to make representations, otherwise the Minister's participation is limited to the presentation of evidence.

Further, the Board was not required to balance the nature of the crimes committed by the appellant against the fate that awaits him should he be returned to Peru. This was the finding of the court in *Gonzalez v. Canada (Minister of Employment & Immigration)* (1994), 24 Imm. L.R. (2d) 229. Section 7 of the Charter, which was not argued in the *Gonzalez* case, does not alter the extant law. A decision in which it was found that the appellant was not entitled to claim refugee status does not, by itself, imply or lead to any positive act which may affect the life, liberty or security of the person.

Kabirian v. Canada (Solicitor General) (1995), 93 F.T.R. 222 — The panel of the CRDD concluded that there was a reasonable possibility that the applicant would be persecuted if he were to return to Iran. Despite this conclusion, the tribunal found that the applicant was excluded from the definition of Convention refugee under Section F(c) of Article 1 of the Convention.

The applicant deserted the Iranian Army and took refuge in Canada in 1985. In October, 1986 he was convicted of trafficking 26 grams of heroin and sentenced to 3 years in prison. In view of the unresolved ambiguity concerning the intention of the signatories to the Convention with respect to the scope of Section F(c), the subsequent conventions and protocols of the United Nations concerning the struggle against drug trafficking should be considered when interpreting the words ". . .contrary to the purposes and principles of the United Nations."

Section F(c) of Article 1 of the Convention is applicable to someone convicted of heroin trafficking in Canada, even in the absence of proof of an international aspect to his crime. The activities of the United Nations in the struggle against illegal drug trafficking are conducted both internationally and nationally. Further, a trafficker constitutes an indispensable link in the chain of distribution of drugs.

The panel did not err in concluding that Section F(c) of Article 1 of the Convention applied to the applicant.

Srour v. Canada (Solicitor General) (1995), 91 F.T.R. 24 — The applicant, a citizen of Lebanon, was denied refugee status on the basis that he was a person covered by Section F(a) of Article 1 of the U.N. Convention. The court reviewed the principles that govern this exclusion and reaffirmed that it was unnecessary to analyze the validity of the applicant's fear of persecution if the exclusion applied.

After reviewing the principles the court applied them in this case and concluded that the applicant was rightly excluded from the definition.

Malouf v. Canada (Minister of Citizenship & Immigration) (1994), 26 Imm. L.R. (2d) 20, 86 F.T.R. 124, [1995] 1 F.C. 537 — The applicant sought to overturn an unfavourable decision of the CRDD. The applicant, who was a citizen of Lebanon, left there in 1977 and obtained permanent resident status in the United States. The applicant pleaded guilty to possession of cocaine for the purpose of trafficking and fled to Canada before his sentencing.

The panel excluded the applicant from the refugee process by applying the exclusion in Section F(b) of Article 1 of the Convention. That section excluded the applicant from the protection of the Geneva Convention on the basis that he had committed a serious, non-political crime outside of Canada and prior to his admission to Canada. Once the panel concluded that the exclusion clause might apply to the applicant, it should have, through the refugee hearing officer, given notice to the Minister and provided an opportunity for the Minister to make representations. Then, whether or not the Minister intervened, it would have been open to the panel to conclude that the exclusion clause applied to the applicant.

For purposes of Section F(b) the country of refuge was Canada, notwithstanding the fact that there was more than one country of refuge. There were reasons for considering that the applicant had committed a serious non-political crime outside of Canada, prior to his admission to Canada as a refugee claimant, that is, in the United States.

The CRDD erred in failing to consider the applicant's Convention refugee claim as against Lebanon and in failing to balance the risk to the applicant that would flow from his return to Lebanon by reason of the exclusion clause against the seriousness of the non-political crime here at issue. Once that balancing was conducted, the panel would have been in a position to determine whether the serious non-political crimes were of such a nature as to warrant the application of the exclusion clause, and the imposition on the applicant of the risk that would flow from his return to Lebanon. No balancing would be required had the panel concluded that the applicant was not, in fact, a refugee from Lebanon.

Gil v. Canada (Minister of Employment & Immigration) (1994), 25 Imm. L.R. (2d) 209, 174 N.R. 292, 119 D.L.R. (4th) 497, [1995] 1 F.C. 508 (C.A.) — This case raises the question of what is meant by the phrase a "serious non-political crime" in Section F of Article 1 of the Convention.

The appellant is an Iranian citizen, the son of a wealthy family which had been an active supporter of the Shah's regime. The family experienced considerable difficulties after the coming into power of the government that overthrew the Shah. The appellant joined an underground student group and, in due course, became associated with a larger militant group of anti-government activists. In the years 1980 and 1981 the appellant personally took part in five or six incidents of bombing and arson. Those attacks were directed against wealthy supporters of the regime. These incidents lead to the injury and death of innocent bystanders. The appellant was arrested and interrogated by the authorities but never confessed to his activities and he was ultimately released by the authorities, without being charged, and eventually fled to Canada.

A panel of the CRDD found that the appellant had a well-founded fear of persecution but that he was excluded by the provision in Section 1F(b) of the Convention.

A panel of the CRDD concluded that the appellant's crimes were non-political. Accordingly, the appeal raised the question of what was meant by political crime. The characterization of crimes as political is found in both extradition and refugee law. The court noted that there was a need for even greater caution characterizing the crime as political for the purposes of applying Section 1F(b) than for the purpose of denying extradition. The court developed an incidence test as a means of resolving whether a crime is political. The appellant met the first branch of the test because Iran, in the years in question, was a turbulent society in which a number of armed groups were in conflict with the regime and the appellant's testimony that he was a member of one such group was accepted as credible. The appellant's claim failed the second branch of the test. There was no objective rational connection between injuring the commercial interests of certain wealthy supporters and any realistic goal of forcing the regime itself to fall or change. Further, the means used by the appellant excluded his crimes from any claim to be political in nature. The attacks were not carried out against armed adversaries and were bound to injure innocent bystanders. The use of deadly force against unarmed civilian commercial targets in circumstances where serious injury or death to innocent bystanders was inevitable rendered the violence used wholly disproportionate to any legitimate political objective.

Thamotharampillai v. Canada (Minister of Employment & Immigration), [1994] 3 F.C. 99, 77 F.T.R. 114 — This was an application for judicial review of a negative decision of the CRDD. The applicant was found, by the relevant minister of the Government of Canada in February of 1985, to be a Convention refugee. On the 30th day of August, 1990 he was convicted of conspiracy to traffic in a narcotic and sentenced to three years. The CRDD found the applicant to have a well-founded fear of persecution. It found the applicant not to have an internal flight alternative. Despite these findings, it found the applicant not to be a Convention refugee as he was a person to whom the Convention did not apply because, in the terms of Article 1F(c) of the Convention, he was a person with respect to whom there were serious reasons for considering that he had been guilty of acts contrary to the purposes and principles of the United Nations. The crime committed by the applicant was one with international implications. Heroin was not a locally-produced narcotic. The crime in question was a crime against which the United Nations has initiated, coordinated and undertaken a range of international initiatives. It was a crime within Canada that potentially had fearful social, cultural and humanitarian, to say nothing of its economic, repercussions. Accordingly, the CRDD was correct in concluding that Article 1F(c) of the Convention excluded the applicant from Convention refugee status.

Gonzalez v. Canada (Minister of Employment & Immigration), [1994] 3 F.C. 646, 24 Imm. L.R. (2d) 229, 170 N.R. 302, 115 D.L.R. (4th) 403 (C.A.) — This was an appeal from a decision of the Refugee Division, which found the appellant excluded from the definition of Convention refugee by reason of Section F(a) of Article 1 of the *United Nations Convention Relating to the Status of Refugees* because the Board found that there was serious reason to believe that the appellant had committed a crime against humanity. The Board proceeded directly to that finding and made no finding on the merits of the refugee claim. The appellant had admitted to killing civilians on two occasions when his military unit in Nicaragua encountered armed counter-revolutionaries. The court noted that as a practical matter it would have been better had the Refugee Division dealt with the merits of the claim as well as the applicability of the exclusion. The court noted that if the claim was well founded but for the application of the exclusion and if it were found on appeal that the exclusion had been wrongly applied to the appellant, then the Court could have made the necessary declaration without requiring the Refugee Division to deal with the matter again. The court found that, on the particular facts and circumstances of this case, the appellant was a soldier engaged in an action against an armed enemy and that his actual participation in the killing of innocent civilians fell short of a crime against humanity. The court indicated that it did not wish to be understood as saying that the killing of civilians by a soldier while engaged in an action against an armed enemy could never amount to a war crime or a crime against humanity, rather, each case will depend on its own individual facts and circumstances.

Equizabal v. Canada (Minister of Employment & Immigration), [1994] 3 F.C. 514, 24 Imm. L.R. (2d) 277, 170 N.R. 329 (C.A.) — The appellant was denied refugee status on the basis that he was included in Article 1(F) of the Convention and therefore excluded from the definition of refugee. The specific finding of the CRDD was that the appellant had committed crimes against humanity by torturing civilians. The appellant sought and obtained leave to apply for judicial review, which application was dismissed. The Trial Division judge certified a serious question of general importance.

The appellant was a citizen of Guatemala who was forcibly recruited by the Guatemalan military. He described in his evidence before the CRDD four military missions which involved the torture of civilians. A crime against humanity is not only a domestic offence, but is rather an offence with the additional component of barbarous cruelty. On the uncontradicted evidence of the appellant, it is obvious that he was guilty of barbarous cruelty in the four incidents he described in his evidence.

The defence of obedience to the orders of a superior based on compulsion was also considered. The first matter to be assessed was whether the orders in issue were manifestly unlawful. A manifestly unlawful order must be one that offends the conscience of every reasonable right-thinking person. It must be an order which is obviously and flagrantly wrong. The court had no difficulty in concluding that the orders here in issue were manifestly unlawful. The appellant and two other soldiers were ordered on one occasion to beat four persons and torture them over a period of three hours. Torturing the truth out of someone is manifestly unlawful, by any standard.

On the question of compulsion, the issue was whether the appellant faced an imminent, real and inevitable threat to his life. Stern punishment or demotion would not be sufficient. The appellant's evidence summarized two reasons why, notwithstanding his understanding that the penalty for desertion was only twelve months in jail, he would be killed: first, he knew of three other deserters who were apprehended and never heard from again; second, he believed he would be killed by his lieutenant because of his knowledge of relatives of persons whom the lieutenant had tortured personally. The first reason was dismissed as it was pure speculation without any credible evidence to support it. The second reason was not supported by the record. The record established that before the third mission, the appellant advised his lieutenant that he would no longer participate in such torture. As a result he was never forced to torture anyone again. He was thereafter, on two occasions, assigned to act as a guard while others did the torturing. There was, therefore, no evidence that the appellant was facing an imminent, real and inevitable threat to his life.

Accordingly, the appeal was dismissed and the decision that the appellant had committed a crime against humanity, as that expression appears in Article 1F of the *Convention Relating to the Status of Refugees*, was upheld.

Cardenas v. Canada (Minister of Employment & Immigration) (1994), 74 F.T.R. 214 — The applicant was unsuccessful in his claim for refugee status because he was found to have been an accomplice to crimes against humanity. The applicant was from Chile and had an association with the political faction, the Manuel Rodriguez Patriotic Front. In quashing the Board's decision, the court noted that the Board had made little effort to link the applicant to specific criminal activities. Rather, it chose to refer only in general terms to shootings and bombings. The Board should have endeavoured to carefully detail the criminal acts which it considered the applicant to have committed.

The Board's decision was quashed on this and other grounds.

Nehru, Re (1993), 21 Imm. L.R. (2d) 53 (Imm. & Ref. Bd. (Ref. Div.)) — The issue before the Refugee Division was whether the claimant was described in Schedule F as referred to in the definition of a Convention refugee. The Minister's representative referred to the fact that the claimant had been convicted of trafficking in a narcotic and sentenced to four months' imprisonment and that trafficking in narcotics was contrary to the purposes and principles of the United Nations.

The panel was of the opinion that countering world drug trafficking was a purpose of the United Nations. The panel was prepared to find that persons who committed acts that are contrary to this initiative do not deserve international protection by countries who are signatories to the 1951 Convention and the 1967 Protocol.

In this case, however, the panel viewed the claimant's involvement in the illicit drug trafficking as marginal. It noted that the length of sentence (four months) did not persuade it of the seriousness of the offence committed by the claimant. Further, the court that convicted the claimant recommended that monies possessed by the police at the time of his arrest be returned to him. Thus, the panel concluded that the claimant should not be excluded from protection and that he was not a person described in Schedule F of the definition.

CAN. REG. 2002-227 — IMMIGRATION AND REFUGEE PROTECTION REGULATIONS

made under the *Immigration and Refugee Protection Act* and the *Financial Administration Act*

SOR/2002-227, as am. S.C. 2002, c. 8, s. 182(3)(a); SOR/2002-326; SOR/2002-332; SOR/2003-97; SOR/2003-197; SOR/2003-260; SOR/2003-383; SOR/2004-34; SOR/2004-59; SOR/2004-111; SOR/2004-167, ss. 1(1), (2) (Fr.), 2–4, 5(1), (2) (Fr.), 6–9, 10–14 (Fr.), 15–19, 20(1), (2), (3) (Fr.), 21, 22(1) (Fr.), (2), 23, 24 (Fr.), 25, 26(1)–(4), (5) (Fr.), (6), (7), 27, 28(1) (Fr.), (2), 29, 30(1)–(3), (4) (Fr.), (5)–(7), 31–43, 44(1) (Fr.), (2), 45, 46 (Fr.), 47–49, 50(1), (2), (3) (Fr.), 51 (Fr.), 52 (Fr.), 53–63, 64(1) (Fr.), (2)–(4), 65–73, 74(1), (2), (3) (Fr.), 75–79, 80 (Fr.); SOR/2004-217; SOR/2005-61; SOR/2005-63; SOR/2006-89; SOR/2006-116; SOR/2006-228; SOR/2007-238; SOR/2008-54; SOR/2008-188; SOR/2008-193; SOR/2008-202, ss. 1–8, 9 (Fr.), 10 (Fr.), 11; SOR/2008-253; SOR/2008-254; SOR/2008-308; SOR/2008-309; SOR/2009-105; SOR/2009-163, ss. 1, 2–13 (Fr.), 14–17, 18 (Fr.); SOR/2009-164; SOR/2009-207; SOR/2009-208; SOR/2009-210; SOR/2009-290, ss. 1, 2, 3–5 (Fr.), 6; SOR/2010-54; SOR/2010-78; SOR/2010-121, ss. 1, 2, 3 (Fr.); SOR/2010-172; SOR/2010-195, ss. 1–6 (Fr.), 7, 8 (Fr.), 9, 10 (Fr.), 11(1)–(3), (4) (Fr.), (5), (6), 12, 13, 14(1), (2) (Fr.), 15 (Fr.); SOR/2010-208; SOR/2010-218; SOR/2010-252; SOR/2010-253; SOR/2010-265; SOR/2011-54; SOR/2011-124, ss. 1, 2(1) (Fr.), (2); SOR/2011-125; SOR/2011-126, ss. 1–3, 4 (Fr.), 5–7; SOR/2011-129; SOR/2011-222; SOR/2011-262; SOR/2012-20; SOR/2012-77; SOR/2012-154; SOR/2012-171; SOR/2012-225; SOR/2012-227; SOR/2012-244; SOR/2012-252; SOR/2012-272; SOR/2012-274; SOR/2013-73; SOR/2013-149; SOR/2013-150; SOR/2013-201; SOR/2013-210; SOR/2013-245, ss. 1–4, 5(1)–(5), (6) (Fr.), 6(1), (2) (Fr.), (3)–(5), (6) (Fr.), (7)–(10), (11) (Fr.), (12)–(14), 7; SOR/2013-246; 2013, c. 40, ss. 237(3)(a), 238(3)(a); SOR/2014-6; SOR/2014-14; SOR/2014-19; SOR/2014-83; SOR/2014-84; SOR/2014-133; SOR/2014-139, ss. 1 (Fr.), 2, 3 (Fr.), 4, 5 (Fr.), 6 (Fr.); SOR/2014-140, ss. 1 (Fr.), 2 (Fr.), 3, 4 (Fr.), 5, 6 (Fr.), 7 (Fr.), 8–10, 11 (Fr.), 12, 13 (Fr.), 14, 15(1) (Fr.), (2), (3) (Fr.), 16, 17 (Fr.), 18 (Fr.); SOR/2014-169; SOR/2014-170; SOR/2014-185; SOR/2014-237; SOR/2014-256; SOR/2014-267; SOR/2014-269; SOR/2015-25; SOR/2015-46; SOR/2015-77; SOR/2015-95; SOR/2015-138; SOR/2015-139; SOR/2015-144; SOR/2015-147; SOR/2016-37, ss. 1–3, 4 (Fr.), 5–11, 12(1) (Fr.), (2), (3), 13–19 [ss. 18, 19 not in force at date of publication.]; SOR/2016-136, ss. 1, 2, 3 (Fr.), 4–7, 8 (Fr.), 9 (Fr.), 10, 11–13 (Fr.), 14.

[Editor's Note: The Immigration Act, *R.S.C. 1985, c. I-2 has been repealed by 2001, c. 27, s. 274(a) and replaced by the* Immigration and Refugee Protection Act, *2001, c. 27, effective June 28, 2002.*

Despite the repeal of the Immigration Act, *R.S.C. 1985, c. I-2, the "former Act," there are substantial transitional provisions that may apply to the particular proceeding or transaction. Reference should be made to the transitional provisions which speak to the continuing application of the former Act in certain situations in 2001, c. 27, ss. 187–201, either by express reference therein or as prescribed by the new* Immigration and Refugee Protection Regulations, *SOR/2002-227.*

The Immigration Regulations, 1978, *SOR/78-172, the* Refugee Claimants Designated Class Regulations, *SOR/90-40, the* Immigration Act Fees Regulations, *SOR/97-22, and the* Humanitarian Designated Classes Regulations, *SOR/97-183, the "former Regulations," have been repealed by ss. 364(a), (b), (c), (d), respectively, of the* Immigration and Refugee Protection Regulations, *SOR/2002-227, effective June 28, 2002. Despite the repeal of the former Regulations, there are substantial transitional provisions that may apply to the particular proceeding or transaction. Reference should be made to the transitional provisions which speak to the continuing application of the former Act in certain situations and as previously prescribed by the former Regulations in SOR/2002-227, ss. 316–363.]*

PART 1 — INTERPRETATION AND APPLICATION

DIVISION 1 — INTERPRETATION

1. (1) Definitions — The definitions in this subsection apply in the Act and in these Regulations.

"common-law partner" means, in relation to a person, an individual who is cohabiting with the person in a conjugal relationship, having so cohabited for a period of at least one year. *("conjoint de fait")*

"excessive demand" means

(a) a demand on health services or social services for which the anticipated costs would likely exceed average Canadian per capita health services and social services costs over a period of five consecutive years immediately following the most recent medical examination required under paragraph 16(2)(b) of the Act, unless there is evidence that significant costs are likely to be incurred beyond that period, in which case the period is no more than 10 consecutive years; or

(b) a demand on health services or social services that would add to existing waiting lists and would increase the rate of mortality and morbidity in Canada as a result of an inability to provide timely services to Canadian citizens or permanent residents.

("fardeau excessif")

"health services" means any health services for which the majority of the funds are contributed by governments, including the services of family physicians, medical specialists, nurses, chiropractors and physiotherapists, laboratory services and the supply of pharmaceutical or hospital care. *("services de santé")* "social services" means any social services, such as home care, specialized residence and residential services, special education services, social and vocational rehabilitation services, personal support services and the provision of devices related to those services,

(a) that are intended to assist a person in functioning physically, emotionally, socially, psychologically or vocationally; and

(b) for which the majority of the funding, including funding that provides direct or indirect financial support to an assisted person, is contributed by governments, either directly or through publicly-funded agencies.

("services sociaux")

"student" [Repealed SOR/2014-14, s. 1.]

"studies" [Repealed SOR/2014-14, s. 1.]

"study permit" [Repealed SOR/2014-14, s. 1.]

(2) **Interpretation — common-law partner** — For the purposes of the Act and these Regulations, an individual who has been in a conjugal relationship with a person for at least one year but is unable to cohabit with the person, due to persecution or any form of penal control, shall be considered a common-law partner of the person.

(3) **Definition of "family member"** — For the purposes of the Act, other than section 12 and paragraph 38(2)(d), and for the purposes of these Regulations, other than paragraph 7.1(3)(a) and sections 159.1 and 159.5, "family member" in respect of a person means

(a) the spouse or common-law partner of the person;

(b) a dependent child of the person or of the person's spouse or common-law partner; and

(c) a dependent child of a dependent child referred to in paragraph (b).
SOR/2004-217, s. 1; SOR/2009-163, s. 1; SOR/2012-154, s. 1; SOR/2014-14, s. 1; SOR/2015-77, s. 1

Case Law

Section 1(1)

Common-Law Partner

Gebreselassie v. Canada (Minister of Citizenship and Immigration), 2015 FC 609, 2015 CarswellNat 1444, 2015 CarswellNat 2940 — The applicant challenged a decision of the Minister's delegate in which the officer refused the applicants' application for permanent residence as members of the family class. The principal applicant applied as the common-law partner of her sponsor. The application was rejected because the officer did not accept that the principal applicant had resided with her sponsor for the required one year and, therefore, was not the common-law partner of her sponsor. It was clear that the officer approached the evidence with a suspicious mind. There was no clear reasoning provided for not accepting the applicant's evidence at face value. Most importantly, there was no reason provided for rejecting the applicant's answer to the question of why her family would accept her and her partner to live together in the family home. Rather than accept the applicant's evidence, the officer depended upon an unverified understanding of the "cultural context." This finding constitutes an implausibility finding which is unsupported by any evidence on the record at the time the decision was made. It was incumbent on the officer to explain the source of the understanding so that its accuracy could be considered against the evidence supplied by the applicant. If the officer's understanding arose from experience, the details of that experience were required to be stated in the decision. The application for judicial review was allowed.

Xuan v. Canada (Minister of Citizenship & Immigration), 2013 FC 92, 2013 CarswellNat 193, 2013 CarswellNat 372 — The applicant sought judicial review of a decision of an immigration officer denying an application for permanent residence under the "spouse in Canada" class. It is a requirement of this class that not only must an applicant be a spouse or common-law partner but they must cohabitate with the sponsor. The couple claimed to live in Markham, both prior to and subsequent to being married. More importantly, it was where they claimed to live together at the time of the home visit by CBSA officers. They had also bought a property in Stouffville in 2010. The CBSA officers visited the Markham house and the applicant let them in. They then questioned the applicant about her husband's clothes and personal hygiene/grooming supplies. Concluding that the answers were unsatisfactory and that she might be a flight risk, the applicant was arrested and held in detention for 11 days. The applicant was later interviewed by a different CBSA officer. There was no evidence that this was a "warrantless search," the applicant never objecting to the CBSA entering the premises. She showed them the location of clothes and of personal items. She never claimed to insist or ask for an interpreter and she responded to their questions. There was no breach of natural justice in respect to the home visit. It was legal, entry was consensual, responses were apparently voluntary and questions appeared to be understood. In terms of the test for "cohabitation," the term is not defined in the Regulations. There is no one controlled test or factor. Documents showing joint interest are consistent with marriage but not necessarily of cohabitation. The officer placed greater weight in what was observed or said at the home visit and in the home visit and solo interview of the applicant than in the answers given at the joint interview two months later. The choice to assign greater weight to the less prepared, extemporaneous evidence lies within the discretion of the officer. It is a reasonable choice given the nature of the inquiry which is to determine how a person lives not merely how they say they live. The officer's decision that cohabitation had not been established was reasonable.

Walia v. Canada (Minister of Citizenship & Immigration), 2008 CarswellNat 1079, 2008 CarswellNat 2640, 2008 FC 486 — The applicants sought judicial review of a decision that they were inadmissible to Canada for directly or indirectly misrepresenting or withholding material facts contrary to para. 40(1)(a) of the IRPA. The principal applicant had indicated that she was divorced and did not cohabitate with one Mr. Ashok Raikhywalia. An officer from the High Commission visited the applicant's village and house and discovered that she was still in cohabitation with Mr. Ashok Raikhywalia. The applicant was given an opportunity to address the officer's concerns about the misrepresentation.

The officer's finding as to the making of a material misrepresentation within the scope of para. 40(2)(a) of the Act was grounded in the finding that Mrs. Raikhywalia continued to cohabitate with her former husband. The question of "cohabitation" means more than simple shared residence, if that is indeed the situation here. The word "cohabitate" has been interpreted as meaning a "marriage-like" relationship characterized by the features of financial interdependence, a sexual relationship, a common principal residence, mutual obligations to share the responsibility of running the home and the "expectation each day that there be continued mutual dependency." The evidence in the record fell short of establishing these facts. The decision of the visa officer did not meet the standard of reasonableness. The application for judicial review was allowed.

Cai v. Canada (Minister of Citizenship & Immigration), 2007 CarswellNat 2274, 2007 CarswellNat 5843, 2007 FC 816 — The applicant's application for permanent resident status under the Spouse or Common-Law Partner in Canada Class was refused on the basis that the applicant did not comply with Regulation 125(1)(d). At the time of the sponsor's application for permanent residence, she did not list the applicant as a non-accompanying family member and the applicant was not examined. The court considered whether the immigration officer erred in determining that the applicant was his sponsor's common-law partner when the sponsor applied to be a permanent resident of Canada. In her application to sponsor an undertaking, the applicant's sponsor stated that her relationship with the applicant began on June 1, 2002. The applicant argued that, despite the fact that the relationship with the sponsor traces back to 2002, his relationship with his sponsor did not meet the requirements of common-law relationship as of that date. When the applicant and his sponsor began living together they were young students, and as such, they may not have made a "mutual commitment to a shared life" when they decided to live together. There was accordingly no basis on which the immigration officer could reasonably conclude that the applicant was a common-law partner of his sponsor when she submitted her application for permanent residence in January, 2005 and did not identify the applicant as a non-accompanying family member. The meaning of "common-law partner" means that the conjugal relationship is one of some permanence where the couple has made a serious commitment to one another. The applicant's application for judicial review was allowed.

1.1 (1) Definition of "agent" — section 148 of the Act — For the purposes of section 148 of the Act, "agent" includes any person — whether or not an independent contractor — who provides services as a representative of a vehicle owner, operator or charterer.

(2) Definition of "agent" — paragraph 148(1)(d) of the Act — For the purposes of paragraph 148(1)(d) of the Act, "agent" includes, in addition to a person referred to in subsection (1), a charterer and an owner or operator of a reservation system.

SOR/2016-37, s. 1

2. Interpretation — The definitions in this section apply in these Regulations.

"Act" means the *Immigration and Refugee Protection Act*. *("Loi")*

"administration fee" means a portion of the average cost incurred by Her Majesty in right of Canada in respect of foreign nationals referred to in subsection 279(1), and includes the costs relating to

(a) examinations;

(b) detention;

(c) investigations and admissibility hearings in respect of inadmissible foreign nationals;

(d) fingerprinting, photographing and the verification of documents with other governments and national or international police agencies;

(e) translation and interpretation; and

(f) proceedings before the Immigration Division.

("frais administratifs")

"agent" [Repealed SOR/2016-37, s. 2(1).]

"authorized representative" [Repealed SOR/2011-129, s. 1.]

[Editor's note: See Can. Reg. 2011-142, Regulations Designating a Body for the Purposes of Paragraph 91(2)(c) of the Immigration and Refugee Protection Act. Also see case summaries under section 91 of the IRPA regarding Representation or Advice.]

"Canadian citizen" means a citizen referred to in subsection 3(1) of the *Citizenship Act. ("citoyen canadien")*

"Canadian Language Benchmarks" means, for the English language, the *Canadian Language Benchmarks: English as a Second Language for Adults* developed by the Centre for Canadian Language Benchmarks, as amended from time to time. *("Canadian Language Benchmarks")*

"commercial transporter" means a transporter who operates a commercial vehicle. *("transporteur commercial")*

"commercial vehicle" means a vehicle that is used for commercial purposes. *("véhicule commercial")*

"conjugal partner" means, in relation to a sponsor, a foreign national residing outside Canada who is in a conjugal relationship with the sponsor and has been in that relationship for a period of at least one year. *("partenaire conjugal")*

"Department" means the Department of Citizenship and Immigration. *("ministère")*

"dependent child", in respect of a parent, means a child who

    (a) has one of the following relationships with the parent, namely,

        (i) is the biological child of the parent, if the child has not been adopted by a person other than the spouse or common-law partner of the parent, or

        (ii) is the adopted child of the parent; and

    (b) is in one of the following situations of dependency, namely,

        (i) is less than 19 years of age and is not a spouse or common-law partner, or

        (ii) is 19 years of age or older and has depended substantially on the financial support of the parent since before the age of 19 and is unable to be financially self-supporting due to a physical or mental condition.

("enfant à charge")

"guardianship" [Repealed SOR/2005-61, s. 1.]

"Hague Convention on Adoption" means the Convention on the Protection of Children and Cooperation in respect of Inter-Country Adoption that was concluded on May 29, 1993 and came into force on May 1, 1995. *("Convention sur l'adoption")*

"Indian" means any person registered as an Indian under the *Indian Act*. *("Indien")*

"in-flight security officer" means a person who is on board a commercial passenger aircraft and whose duty it is to protect the passengers and the members of the crew as well as the aircraft itself. *("agent de sécurité aérien")*

"in-transit passenger" means a person who arrives by aircraft at a Canadian airport from another country for the sole purpose of reboarding their flight or boarding a connecting flight departing from that airport to a country other than Canada. *("passager en transit")*

"in-transit preclearance passenger" means an in-transit passenger who is subject to a preclearance procedure in accordance with the *Preclearance Act*. *("passager en transit bénéficiant d'un précontrôle")*

"live-in caregiver" means a person who resides in and provides child care, senior home support care or care of the disabled without supervision in the private household in Canada where the person being cared for resides. *("aide familial")*

"marriage", in respect of a marriage that took place outside Canada, means a marriage that is valid both under the laws of the jurisdiction where it took place and under Canadian law. *("mariage")*

"minimum necessary income" means the amount identified, in the most recent edition of the publication concerning low income cut-offs that is published annually by Statistics Canada under the *Statistics Act*, for urban areas of residence of 500,000 persons or more as the minimum amount of before-tax annual income necessary to support a group of persons equal in number to the total number of the following persons:

    (a) a sponsor and their family members,

    (b) the sponsored foreign national, and their family members, whether they are accompanying the foreign national or not, and

    (c) every other person, and their family members,

        (i) in respect of whom the sponsor has given or co-signed an undertaking that is still in effect, and

        (ii) in respect of whom the sponsor's spouse or common-law partner has given or co-signed an undertaking that is still in effect, if the sponsor's spouse or common-law partner has co-signed with the sponsor the undertaking in respect of the foreign national referred to in paragraph (b).

("revenu vital minimum")

"Minister" means the Minister referred to in section 4 of the Act. *("ministre")*

"National Occupational Classification" means the *National Occupational Classification* developed by the Department of Employment and Social Development and Statistics Canada, as amended from time to time. *("Classification nationale des professions")*

"Niveaux de compétence linguistique canadiens" means, for the French language, the *Niveaux de compétence linguistique canadiens : français langue seconde pour adultes* developed by the Centre for Canadian Language Benchmarks, as amended from time to time. *("Niveaux de compétence linguistique canadiens")*

"officer" means a person designated as an officer by the Minister under subsection 6(1) of the Act. *("agent")*

"port of entry" means

 (a) a place set out in Schedule 1; and

 (b) a place designated by the Minister under section 26 as a port of entry, on the dates and during the hours of operation designated for that place by the Minister.

("point d'entrée")

"relative" means a person who is related to another person by blood or adoption. *("membre de la parenté")*

"social assistance" means any benefit in the form of money, goods or services provided to or on behalf of a person by a province under a program of social assistance, including a program of social assistance designated by a province to provide for basic requirements including food, shelter, clothing, fuel, utilities, household supplies, personal requirements and health care not provided by public health care, including dental care and eye care. *("assistance sociale")*

"sterile transit area" means an area in an airport where in-transit passengers, in-transit preclearance passengers or goods that are in transit or precontrolled are physically separated from other passengers and goods. *("espace de transit isolé")*

"study permit" means a written authorization to engage in academic, professional, vocational or other education or training in Canada that is issued by an officer to a foreign national. *("permis d'études")*

"time of departure" means

 (a) in the case of a commercial vehicle that carries persons or goods by air, the time of take-off from the last point of embarkation of persons before the vehicle arrives in Canada; and

 (b) in the case of a commercial vehicle that carries persons or goods by water or land, the time of departure from the last point of embarkation of persons before the vehicle arrives in Canada.

("moment du départ")

"transporter" means

 (a) a person who owns, operates, charters or manages a vehicle or fleet of vehicles;

 (b) a person who owns or operates an international tunnel or bridge;

 (c) a designated airport authority as defined in subsection 2(1) of the *Airport Transfer (Miscellaneous Matters) Act*; or

 (d) an agent for a person or authority referred to in paragraphs (a) to (c).

("transporteur")

"vehicle" means a means of transportation that may be used for transportation by water, land or air. *("véhicule")*

"vessel" means a vessel within the meaning of section 2 of the *Canada Shipping Act*. *("bâtiment")*

"work" means an activity for which wages are paid or commission is earned, or that is in direct competition with the activities of Canadian citizens or permanent residents in the Canadian labour market. *("travail")*

"work permit" means a written authorization to work in Canada issued by an officer to a foreign national. *("permis de travail")*

[Editor's Note: SOR/2002-227, s. 352 provides that a person is not required to include in an application a non-accompanying common-law partner or a non-accompanying child who is not a dependant son or a dependant daughter within the meaning of s. 2(1) of the Immigration Regulations, 1978, *SOR/78-172 (the "former Regulations") and is a dependant child as defined in s. 2 of the* Immigration and Refugee Protection Regulations, *SOR/2002-227 if the application was made under the* Immigration Act, R.S.C. 1985, c. I-2 *(the "former Act") before June 28, 2002.*

SOR/2002-227, s. 356 provides that if a person referred to in paragraph (f) of the definition "member of the family class" in s. 2(1) of the former Regulations made an application under the former Regulations for a permanent resident visa before June 28, 2002, the application is governed by the former Act.]

SOR/2004-59, s. 1; SOR/2004-167, s. 1(1); SOR/2005-61, s. 1; SOR/2010-253, s. 1; SOR/2010-172, s. 5(a); SOR/2011-129, s. 1; SOR/2012-274, s. 1; 2013, c. 40, s. 237(3)(a); SOR/2014-14, s. 2; SOR/2014-133, s. 1; SOR/2016-37, s. 2; SOR/2016-136, s. 1

Case Law

Section 2

Conjugal Partner

Leroux v. Canada (Minister of Citizenship & Immigration) (2007), 64 Imm. L.R. (3d) 123, 2007 FC 403, 2007 CarswellNat 2813, 2007 CarswellNat 984 — The applicant in this proceeding alleged that the applicant for permanent residence, a 26-year-old Moroccan citizen, was his conjugal partner. An immigration officer concluded that the applicant for permanent residence was excluded from the family class under s. 4 of the Regulations. The applicant appealed to the IAD. In dismissing the appeal, the IAD concluded that "the Appellant had failed to establish on the preponderance of the evidence, that his relationship with the Applicant is a conjugal relationship within the meaning of s. 2 of the *Regulations*" and reaffirmed the immigration officer's opinion that the relationship was not genuine.

The Federal Court has not rendered any decision about the criteria to be used in an immigration context to determine whether there is a conjugal relationship; however, several IAD decisions have recognized the criteria in *M. v. H.*, [1999] 2 S.C.R. 3, which specifies seven non-exhaustive factors used to identify a conjugal relationship, namely, shared shelter, sexual and personal behaviour, services, social activities, economic support, children, and the societal perception of the couple. The IAD decisions recognize that the criteria in *M. v. H.* were established for couples living in Canada and must be modified for couples living in different countries. The Federal Court agreed with this approach stating that it was important to keep in mind the restrictions which apply because the partners live in different countries, some of which have different moral standards and customs which may have an impact on the degree of tolerance for conjugal relationships, especially where same-sex partners are concerned. Nevertheless, the alleged conjugal relationship must have a sufficient number of features of a marriage to show that it is more than just a means of entering Canada as a member of the family class. A conjugal relationship is more than a precursor, or plan, to share a conjugal relationship in future.

The application for judicial review was allowed. The IAD erred in law in its interpretation of s. 2 of the Regulations by restricting its analysis to the one-year period preceding the filing of the application for permanent residence. It was also impossible on reading the reasons to conclude that the IAD applied the criteria in a flexible manner on the basis of all the relevant facts in order to determine whether or not the relationship was genuine.

Canada (Ministre de la Citoyenneté & de l'Immigration) c. Savard (2006), 292 F.T.R. 10 (Eng.), 2006 FC 109, 2006 CarswellNat 4609, [2006] F.C.J. No. 126 — The respondent, a Canadian citizen, met Mr. Samadi, a citizen of Morocco, through the internet. The respondent filed a sponsorship application to sponsor Mr. Samadi in the family reunification class as a "conjugal partner." The visa officer rejected the sponsorship application. The visa officer found Mr. Samadi did not belong in the family class as he was not maintaining a conjugal relationship with the applicant within the meaning of ss. 2 and 121 of the *Immigration and Refugee Protection Regulations*. She appealed the visa officer's decision before the Immigration Appeal Division (IAD). The IAD found that the respondent had discharged her burden of proof and that there was a conjugal relationship between her and Mr. Samadi. The IAD also found the record indicated that the couple were in love and intended to live together once he was in Canada.

The Minister argued that the IAD erred in law and in fact in finding the couple had discharged their onus of establishing that they are conjugal partners within the meaning of the IRPA and ss. 2 and 121 of the IRPR. Section 2 of the IRPR requires that the individuals be in a conjugal relationship for a period of at least one year at the time of filing of the sponsorship application. A conjugal partner need not cohabitate for at least one year. The IAD may in fact consider all of the evidence that is adduced before it. However, in this case, the IAD made no distinction between the evidence pertaining to the relevant period and the subsequent evidence. The Minister argued that the IAD considered the subsequent evidence in order to determine that the two were indeed conjugal partners, and that the IAD did not correctly interpret the language in s. 2 of the IRPR, which requires that the individuals have been in a conjugal relationship for a period of at least one year at the time of filing of this sponsorship application. The problem in this case was that it is impossible to determine from the IAD's reasons how the decision maker arrived at the finding that the respondent and Mr. Samadi were conjugal partners within the meaning of s. 2 of the IRPR. Absent a precise distinction between the evidence relating to the sponsorship period and the evidence subsequent to the application, the court must assume that the subsequent evidence was considered. The application for judicial review was allowed.

Gibbs v. Canada (Minister of Citizenship & Immigration, 2004 CarswellNat 6212, [2004] I.A.D.D. No. 1221 (Imm. & Ref. Bd. (App. Div.)) — The appellant applied to sponsor the applicant to Canada as a permanent resident under the family class category. The application was refused because the visa officer concluded that the appellant and applicant had not established a conjugal relationship.

The definition of "conjugal partner" sets out three basic requirements. Firstly, the foreign national must reside outside Canada; second, the relationship must be conjugal in nature; and third, the conjugal relationship has subsisted for a one-year period.

The Board stated that in looking at other relevant factors it is significant that the parties, although living within reasonable proximity of each other in the United Kingdom and apparently able to reside together, consciously chose not to do so for economics and other reasons of convenience. The couple did not have any routine joint habits with respect to meals, housekeeping, shopping, household maintenance or other domestic duties. With respect to their financial interdependence there was none. Each was responsible for his/her own financial affairs and adequately managed their respective separate income and debt issues. The couple did not own property together and, in the relevant period, did not have any particular plans in place for the future acquisition of joint property.

The balance of evidence did not support the conclusion that the relationship between the appellant and applicant was of a conjugal nature for one year or more, as required by the legislation. While the relationship may have had some conjugal characteristics, when all was taken together, the relationship as between the appellant and applicant during the applicant's period of residence overseas was at best a precursor, or plan, to have a conjugal relationship in the future.

Dependent Child

Cheshenchuk v. Canada (Minister of Citizenship & Immigration) (2014), 22 Imm. L.R. (4th) 57, 2014 FC 33, 2014 CarswellNat 22, 2014 CarswellNat 967 — This application under s. 18.1 of the *Federal Courts Act* was for judicial review of a decision of a delegate of the Minister of Citizenship & Immigration refusing to grant citizenship to the applicant's adopted children under subsec. 5.1(1) of the *Citizenship Act*. The applicant was a citizen of both Canada and Ukraine and adopted two young children in Ukraine through a domestic private adoption approved by a Ukrainian court on August 11, 2011. She then applied to have her adopted children recognized as Canadian citizens under subsec. 5.1(1). The application was refused by a citizenship officer at the Canadian Embassy in Kiev on the basis that the adoptions were not completed in accordance with Ukrainian law.

The applicant argued that she was a citizen of both Canada and Ukraine, and had residence in both countries, and thus was eligible to proceed with a domestic adoption. International adoptions involve adoption agencies in both Canada and Ukraine, which make significant profits from such adoptions, as well as staff of the Canadian Embassy in Kiev. This results in a lengthy and costly process. A private domestic adoption, available only to Ukrainian citizens, does not involve the adoption agencies or the Embassy. The applicant followed, and argued that she was entitled by law to follow, the second route.

The officer decided that the adoption was not legally valid or was obtained through misrepresentation. Canadian courts have consistently ruled that an adoption documented by a final order of a foreign court should be presumed to be valid, and such an order is the best evidence that the adoption was carried out in accordance with the laws of the country in question. The officer's reviewing notes suggested that she was legitimately concerned that the applicant, in obtaining the Ukrainian court order, had not disclosed her residence in Canada, her Canadian citizenship, or that she was married to a non-Ukrainian who lived in Canada. The applicant claimed that she was legally separated from her husband when she was in Ukraine, although she provided nothing to support this. It was clear that at the material time, she was married. The court found that the officer had good reason to conclude that a serious irregularity had allowed the applicant to obtain the Ukrainian adoption order. The evidence before the officer revealed that the adoption order could not have been obtained if the applicant had revealed that she was a Canadian citizen who had been living in Canada for a number of years.

The Ukrainian court was not provided with fundamental information relevant to its jurisdiction to grant the order, and the Ukrainian government was deprived of its right to assess and approve an adoption of children younger than age 5 in a situation where the applicant, a Canadian citizen, intended to take the children out of the country. These were serious matters. The explanations offered by the applicant for what she did were unconvincing and did not, in any event, explain why she told the Ukrainian court that she was divorced. Accordingly, the high threshold required to set aside a foreign judgment for "fraud or irregularity" was satisfied. There were sufficient grounds for the officer to disregard the Ukrainian court order, and the officer came to the correct conclusion. The application was dismissed.

Dhillon v. Canada (Minister of Citizenship & Immigration), 2012 FC 192, 2012 CarswellNat 394, 2012 CarswellNat 1112 — The application to sponsor the applicant as a permanent resident on the basis of his being a family member was dismissed since the visa officer was not satisfied that an adult older than age 22 was unable to be financially self-supporting. The officer accepted that he had a physical disability as a result of polio, but was not satisfied that his physical or mental condition rendered him unable to be financially self-supporting.

The officer did not deal with the uncontradicted country conditions that people with disabilities were among the most excluded in Indian society and that the majority of Indians in the applicant's situation, some 62 per cent, cannot find employment. Thus, on the balance of probabilities, he was unable to support himself because of the attitude of the society in which he lives. One must not only be willing to work, someone must be willing to hire. Furthermore, the officer refused to give any weight to the affidavits because they were generated for the purpose of supporting the submission. This did not mean that they were untrue. Evidence cannot be rejected simply by reason of association to the applicant. His ability to support himself financially cannot be considered in the abstract. The question is whether he is able to financially support himself where he lives, and not whether his physical condition would prevent him from becoming self-sufficient in Canada, where the federal and provincial human rights commissions would give short shrift to those who would not hire him because of his disability. The application for judicial review was granted.

Sha v. Canada (Minister of Citizenship & Immigration), 2010 FC 434, 2010 CarswellNat 1109, 2010 CarswellNat 2281 — The applicant sought judicial review of a decision to reject the inclusion of Quan Sha as a dependent child on his father's permanent residence application. The basis for the rejection was the officer's determination that the vocational school Quan Sha was attending did not meet the requirements of the *Immigration and Refugee Protection Regulations*. The officer was clearly concerned with whether Quan Sha's school met the requirements described under the "dependent child" definition in the Regulations. The Regulations require that the post-secondary institution to be "accredited by the relevant government authority." The officer's request for a China Academic Degrees and Graduate Education Development Center (CADGEDC) report was in relation to this accreditation.

In this case, the applicants were given an opportunity to respond to the officer's concerns. Consequently, the reasons were adequate and the officer satisfied the duty of fairness. What was problematic, in the court's view, was the officer's reliance on the lack of a CADGEDC report. Neither the Regulations nor the respondent's guidelines stipulate how an officer is to determine whether a post-secondary institution "is accredited by the relevant authority." In this case, the applicants provided an answer as to why the report would not be forthcoming, and tendered evidence that Quan's school was "accredited by the relevant government authority." The officer failed to explain why this evidence, a copy of the school's licence from the Ministry of Education, was rejected. The application for judicial review was allowed.

Yao v. Canada (Minister of Citizenship & Immigration), 2009 CarswellNat 271, 2009 FC 114 — The applicants sought judicial review of the decision of a visa officer to exclude the son from his father's application for permanent residence on the basis that he did not meet the definition of "dependent child" in s. 2 of the Regulations. The father applied for permanent residence under the economic class including himself, his wife and his son shortly after May 2, 2007. In December 2003, the son turned 22. At that time, he was enrolled and studying at the Language College of the Immigration Services Society of British Columbia ("ISS"). He completed these programs in April 2004 and in the fall of 2004 he started the Arts and Science Program at Langara College, where he studied until August 2007, obtaining a total of 67 credits in the process.

The visa officer informed the applicants that the son was not eligible for inclusion in the application as a "dependent child" because the ISS was not a post-secondary institution and the courses in which he was enrolled from December 24, 2003, to April 15, 2004, did not constitute "a course of academic, professional or vocation training" within the meaning of s. 2 of the Regulations, and from April 16, 2004, to at least August 31, 2004, he was not enrolled and studying in any educational institution. As well, in the fall semester of 2006, the son concluded only one four credit course at Langara College and therefore was not pursuing a course on a full-time basis as defined in subs. 78(1) of the Regulations or by Langara College.

The requirement of dependency contained at s. 2 of the Regulations under the definition of "dependent child" is a public recognition of the value which our society and Parliament places on higher education. These requirements are susceptible to being applied to a number of different countries and educational systems. It is thus understandable that the definition of "dependent child" at s. 2 refers to concepts that include some flexibility in order to achieve its goals. In that sense, although an officer applies objective criteria, he or she has some discretion in their application. Although there is no obligation on a visa officer to provide a running account to the applicants of concerns with any specific answers or impressions they have given, a visa officer should provide an opportunity to applicants to comment when he or she comes to a conclusion based on their own specific standards or tests for interpreting the documentary evidence before them with a view of applying the Regulations. In the present instance, this entails that, for example, before reaching any conclusion based on s. 78 of the Regulations which is expressly said to apply only to the part of the Regulations dealing with the "federal skilled workers class," the officer should have given an opportunity to the applicants to comment in respect of her concerns that their son was not studying full time. The same reasoning would apply to the particular interpretation given by the officer to Langara College policy, as this institution offers its programs on a flexible three-semester basis as opposed to a traditional two-semester basis. If there were any doubts as to whether or not "Learn English Now" and "TOEFL Preparation" courses qualified as "courses of academic, professional or vocational training," the answer may well lie in whether these courses were part of a study plan or were prerequisites to the ability of a foreign student to enroll in a college or university in Canada. The application of the Regulations in such respects raises important policy issues which should be clarified for it appears to be dealt with differently depending on the officer. The officer should have raised her concerns with respect to these courses. The court also found that the decision did not disclose adequate reasons, specifically as to why the officer concluded that ISS was not a post-secondary institution and whether or not the "Learn English Now" and "TOEFL Preparation" courses fell within the meaning of the expression used in clause (b)(ii)(B) of the definition of "dependent child" at s. 2 of the Regulations. The application for judicial review was granted.

Gill v. Canada (Minister of Citizenship & Immigration), 2008 CarswellNat 793, 2008 CarswellNat 2416, 2008 FC 365 — The applicant indicated to the visa officer that she had taken leave from school on certain occasions — the period of her grandmother's illness — to assist in preparing for her sister's wedding. These leaves or absences from studies, however, did not, in and of themselves, constitute a sufficient period of time for her to abandon her studies. Her school transcripts and certificates attested she continued with her studies, uninterrupted; neither of the educational institutions specified considered that she had either withdrawn or abandoned her studies for any given year. No intention existed, on the part of the applicant, to withdraw or abandon her studies. Following an interview by a visa officer at the High Commission of Canada, in New Delhi, India, the applicant was deleted from the application as she was found not to have been in continuous studies nor was she found to be actively pursuing post-secondary education prior to the age of 22. The fact that the applicant had failed one year of her studies was not due to her absence or withdrawal from her studies, but was the result of poor marks and, more particularly, to "difficult personal circumstance." The visa officer was unreasonable in determining that the applicant was not "continuously enrolled in and attending a post-secondary institution" and that she was not a "dependent child" within the meaning of s. 2 of the Regulations. The application for judicial review was allowed.

Dehar v. Canada (Minister of Citizenship & Immigration), 2007 CarswellNat 1401, 2007 FC 558 — The applicant sought judicial review of the decision of a visa officer that she no longer met the definition of a "dependent child" in s. 2 of the Immigration Refugee Protection Regulations. The officer correctly determined that the applicant did not meet the criteria in s. 2(b)(ii) of the definition of "dependent child" because she was married after the age of 22. This would be sufficient to dismiss the application for judicial review. Nevertheless, the court commented on the second ground raised by the applicants for the purpose of assessing whether questions should be certified. The applicant submitted that the reasons of the visa officer do not adequately explain why attending a distant education wing of a post-secondary institution offends the definition of "dependent child."

The evidence *prima facie* suggests that the applicant was continuously enrolled and attending a post-secondary institution. The officer's notes and the decision letter made no reference to any of those documents nor did they provide an explanation for the officer's conclusion that attending a distant education program does not amount to "attending a post secondary institution" within the meaning of the definition of "dependent child." The officer's decision that the applicant was not attending full-time classes was therefore unreasonable. However, since the applicant had to meet all the requirements set out in the definition of a "dependent child," the application for judicial review was dismissed.

Dhillon v. Canada (Minister of Citizenship & Immigration), 2006 CarswellNat 3928, 2006 FC 1430 — The applicant sought to include his two children — each of whom is older than 22 years of age — as accompanying family members in his visa application. To do so, it must be established that each were "continuously enrolled in and attending" and "actively pursuing" their education in a post-secondary institution.

The parties agreed that a decision issued prior to IRPA by the Federal Court of Appeal in *Sandhu v. Canada (Minister of Citizenship & Immigration)* (2002), 23 Imm. L.R. (3d) 8, 287 N.R. 97, 211 D.L.R. (4th) 567, [2002] 3 F.C. 280, 2002 FCA 79, 2002 CarswellNat 454, [2002] F.C.J. No. 299, is instructive in the application of the definition of "dependent child" to the fact situation in this case. The visa officer must make "sufficient enquiries" to assure that the student understood the courses and made a *bona fide* attempt to assimilate the material. On the other hand, the student need not have "a mastery of the subject."

Shah v. Canada (Minister of Citizenship & Immigration) (2006), 56 Imm. L.R. (3d) 43, 2006 CarswellNat 2957, 2006 FC 1131 — This was an application for judicial review of a decision by a visa officer that the applicant was not a dependent child according to the *Immigration and Refugee Protection Regulations*; she was deleted from the permanent residence application of her parents, her brother and herself — sponsored by her sister — and her sister's husband, both citizens of Canada. The application for permanent residence was filed in November 2002. The applicant turned 22 years of age on July 27, 2001, prior to the sponsorship being filed. The applicant alleged that she was in full-time attendance at an educational institution in India and was completely dependent upon her parents for support at all times since her 22nd birthday. The only issue arising on this application was whether the post-secondary institution that the applicant had been enrolled in and attending since before the age of 22 was "accredited" by the relevant government authority. The shorter Oxford English Dictionary defines "accredited" to mean "furnished with credentials; authoritatively sanctioned." It does not equate to "recognized" in some informal sense. The onus is on the applicant to establish that she fills the criteria that entitled her to a visa to enter Canada. On a standard of review of reasonableness *simpliciter*, and taking into account the totality of evidence before the decision maker, the decision maker made no reviewable error in determining that the school was not a post-secondary institution accredited by the relevant government authority in India. The fact that graduates of the school may be "recognized" by certain government institutions in India as possessing certain academic or technical qualifications for employment simply does not equate to "accreditation by a relevant government authority."

Hamid v. Canada (Minister of Citizenship & Immigration), 2006 CarswellNat 1592, 2006 FCA 217 — The applicant applied for permanent residence and included his accompanying family members in his application. His oldest two sons qualified as dependent children because they were financially dependent on him and full-time students. However, when the officer assessed the application 2½ years after it had been received, both sons had graduated and were no longer enrolled in full-time studies. The question to be decided in this appeal was whether the visa officer was correct to remove them from the applicant's application on the ground that they did not meet the eligibility requirement of being students when the visa application was both made and assessed.

The Federal Court of Appeal found a child of a federal skilled worker who has applied for a visa, who was 22 years of age or over, and who was considered dependent on the skilled worker on the date of the application by virtue of his or her financial dependence and full time study, but who does not meet the requirements of "a dependent child" within the meaning of para. 2(b)(ii) of the *Immigration and Refugee Protection Regulations*, when the visa application is determined, cannot be included as part of his or her parent's application for permanent residence in Canada. The appeal by the Minister was allowed and the order of the Federal Court was set aside and the application for judicial review was dismissed.

Gilani v. Canada (Minister of Citizenship & Immigration) (2005), 51 Imm. L.R. (3d) 190, 2005 CarswellNat 3692, 2005 CarswellNat 4513, 2005 FC 1522 — The relevant portions of the definition "dependent child" simply do not require that an applicant demonstrate that a "physical or mental" condition causing an applicant child to be unable to be financially self-supporting has existed at all times since the applicant became 22 years of age and that the condition was diagnosed before the applicant reached that age. A question was certified which read as follows: "must the condition of the inability of the child to be financially self-supporting due to a physical or mental condition be established only at the time the claim to dependency is being asserted or must it be established that such condition existed and was diagnosed prior to the child attaining the age of 22 years?"

Lee v. Canada (Minister of Citizenship & Immigration) (2004), 38 Imm. L.R. (3d) 220, 2004 CarswellNat 2213, 2004 CarswellNat 4989, [2005] 2 F.C.R. 3, 256 F.T.R. 172, 2004 FC 1012, [2004] F.C.J. No. 1232 — The definition of dependent child in the regulations expresses the intent to codify the test articulated by the Court of Appeal in *Sandhu*. Sub-part (A) of the definition carries forward the requirement of full-time enrolment and attendance in an educational program. Sub-part (B) articulates the requirement for a mental presence in the educational program in the form of a genuine, *bona fide* effort on the part of a student.

Marriage

Manuvelpillai v. Canada (Minister of Citizenship & Immigration) (2010), 88 Imm. L.R. (3d) 156, 2010 FC 286, 2010 CarswellNat 2340, 2010 CarswellNat 558 — The applicant was a citizen of Sri Lanka who intended to marry a man who was a lawful landed immigrant resident in Canada. This man traveled to Sri Lanka where he and the applicant engaged in a ceremony in a church including exchange of rings. The evidence is equivocal as to whether the ceremony was "registered as a marriage in Sri Lanka." The Board seems to have found that it was. In any event the applicant and this man came to Canada, in particular Ontario, where, within 90 days a marriage ceremony took place and the marriage was "registered in Ontario." Later there was a falling out between the two spouses and they divorced. An appropriate order of divorce was granted by the appropriate Ontario court. The applicant remarried a man who is a citizen of Sri Lanka. She sought to sponsor him so that he may obtain a permanent resident visa and enter Canada as a member of the family class as her husband. This application was refused and came before the Immigration Refugee Board. The Board concluded that the applicant's first marriage had taken place in Sri Lanka and since it was not "dissolved" in Sri Lanka she could not sponsor a second husband. The Board did not state any basis for its determination as to why a dissolution of the first marriage had to be obtained in Sri Lanka. It did not state why it would not consider the Ontario divorce adequate to terminate the marriage.

The *Divorce Act* does not restrict the appropriate Canadian court from granting a divorce only in respect of marriages performed in Canada. Once a divorce has been granted it is effective throughout Canada, including, for the purposes of the *Immigration and Refugee Protection Act*. The Board, therefore, was in error in not finding that the applicant's first marriage had been terminated by the divorce.

The following question was certified:

> Whether a person legally married outside Canada who has come to Canada and subsequently receives a divorce from an appropriate court of the Canadian province in which they reside, must also secure a divorce from the country in which they were married before they can sponsor the new spouse who is resident outside Canada to enter Canada as an applicant for permanent residence in Canada.

Relative

Chen v. Canada (Minister of Citizenship & Immigration) (2003), 232 F.T.R. 118, 2003 FCT 447, 2003 CarswellNat 2908, 2003 CarswellNat 1052 — The applicant sought to review a negative decision on a Humanitarian and Compassionate application. In 1959 the applicant and his wife put their daughter in the care of her aunt and uncle when she was only a baby. In 1961, the aunt and uncle moved from Tianjin to Hong Kong. In order to bring the little girl with them to Hong Kong the aunt and uncle needed to show authorities there a document indicating that the child had been adopted. Therefore, the applicant and his wife signed an agreement to that effect. In 1975, the aunt and uncle immigrated to Canada and brought their adopted daughter with them. The daughter was landed as a dependent daughter and not as an adopted daughter. In 1993, the applicant and his wife were reunited with their daughter. Since their reunification the applicant has been living with his daughter who was providing him with all the necessary care. The officer found that the daughter was not an eligible sponsor as she was not satisfied that a parent/child relationship existed between the applicant and daughter. Under subs. 3(c) of the *Immigration Act*, the immigration objective established is "to facilitate the reunion in Canada of Canadian citizens and permanent residents with their close relatives from abroad." In the new *Immigration and Refugee Protection Act 2001*, at subs. 3(1)(d), the related objective is "to see that families are reunited in Canada." In IRPA, s. 2, the word "relatives" means a person who is related by blood or adoption. There is room for interpretation of the law with respect to the immigration objectives and the new definition of "relative" so as not to preclude a person from sponsoring a biological parent, if he or she already has an adoptive parent. There is enough evidence to show that there is a sufficient parent/child relationship to conclude that the immigration officer made a capricious finding of fact, which fettered her discretion.

Work

Juneja v. Canada (Minister of Citizenship & Immigration), 2007 CarswellNat 636, 2007 FC 301 — While in Canada on a valid study permit, the applicant was observed to be working at a local car dealership in Edmonton. He was arrested for working without authorization contrary to s. 30(1) of the Act. An admissibility hearing was then convoked under s. 44(2) of the Act. The applicant was declared inadmissible and was issued an exclusion order requiring him to leave Canada. The Board was satisfied that his activity did constitute "work" under the Act and Regulations. The applicant was performing work-like tasks for the dealership but was not being paid. The employer was banking or keeping track of his hours, presumably for the purposes of paying wages if and when the applicant received an authorization to work from the department. The agreed wage was $8.00 per hour. The employer's agreement to bank the applicant's hours and to pay a wage of $8.00 per hour — albeit conditionally — was either an activity for which wages are paid or was, otherwise, in direct competition with the employment activities of Canadians or permanent residents. The Board's finding was upheld and the application for judicial review was dismissed.

3. (1) Interpretation — member of a crew — For the purposes of these Regulations,

(a) "member of a crew" means a person who is employed on a means of transportation to perform duties during a voyage or trip, or while in port, related to the operation of the means of transportation or the provision of services to passengers or to other members of the crew, but does not include

(i) any person whose fare is waived in exchange for work to be performed during the voyage or trip,

(ii) any person who performs maintenance or repairs under a service contract with a transporter during the voyage or trip or while the means of transportation is in Canada,

(iii) any other person who is on board the means of transportation for a purpose other than to perform duties that relate to the operation of the means of transportation or to provide services to passengers or members of the crew, or

(iv) any in-flight security officer; and

(b) a person ceases to be a member of a crew if

(i) they have deserted;

(ii) an officer believes on reasonable grounds that they have deserted;

(iii) they have been hospitalized and have failed to return to the means of transportation or leave Canada after leaving the hospital, or

(iv) they have been discharged or are otherwise unable or unwilling to perform their duties as a member of a crew and failed to leave Canada after the discharge or after they first became unable or unwilling to perform those duties.

(2) Interpretation — adoption — For the purposes of these Regulations, "adoption", for greater certainty, means an adoption that creates a legal parent-child relationship and severs the pre-existing legal parent-child relationship.

SOR/2004-167, s. 2; SOR/2010-253, s. 2

Case Law

Section 3(2)

Cheshenchuk v. Canada (Minister of Citizenship & Immigration) (2014), 22 Imm. L.R. (4th) 57, 2014 FC 33, 2014 CarswellNat 22, 2014 CarswellNat 967 — This application under s. 18.1 of the *Federal Courts Act* was for judicial review of a decision of a delegate of the Minister of Citizenship & Immigration refusing to grant citizenship to the applicant's adopted children under subsec. 5.1(1) of the *Citizenship Act*. The applicant was a citizen of both Canada and Ukraine and adopted two young children in Ukraine through a domestic private adoption approved by a Ukrainian court on August 11, 2011. She then applied to have her adopted children recognized as Canadian citizens under subsec. 5.1(1). The application was refused by a citizenship officer at the Canadian Embassy in Kiev on the basis that the adoptions were not completed in accordance with Ukrainian law.

The applicant argued that she was a citizen of both Canada and Ukraine, and had residence in both countries, and thus was eligible to proceed with a domestic adoption. International adoptions involve adoption agencies in both Canada and Ukraine, which make significant profits from such adoptions, as well as staff of the Canadian Embassy in Kiev. This results in a lengthy and costly process. A private domestic adoption, available only to Ukrainian citizens, does not involve the adoption agencies or the Embassy. The applicant followed, and argued that she was entitled by law to follow, the second route.

The officer decided that the adoption was not legally valid or was obtained through misrepresentation. Canadian courts have consistently ruled that an adoption documented by a final order of a foreign court should be presumed to be valid, and such an order is the best evidence that the adoption was carried out in accordance with the laws of the country in question. The officer's reviewing notes suggested that she was legitimately concerned that the applicant, in obtaining the Ukrainian court order, had not disclosed her residence in Canada, her Canadian citizenship, or that she was married to a non-Ukrainian who lived in Canada. The applicant claimed that she was legally separated from her husband when she was in Ukraine, although she provided nothing to support this. It was clear that at the material time, she was married. The court found that the officer had good reason to conclude that a serious irregularity had allowed the applicant to obtain the Ukrainian adoption order. The evidence before the officer revealed that the adoption order could not have been obtained if the applicant had revealed that she was a Canadian citizen who had been living in Canada for a number of years.

The Ukrainian court was not provided with fundamental information relevant to its jurisdiction to grant the order, and the Ukrainian government was deprived of its right to assess and approve an adoption of children younger than age 5 in a situation where the applicant, a Canadian citizen, intended to take the children out of the country. These were serious matters. The explanations offered by the applicant for what she did were unconvincing and did not, in any event, explain why she told the Ukrainian court that she was divorced. Accordingly, the high threshold required to set aside a foreign judgment for "fraud or irregularity" was satisfied. There were sufficient grounds for the officer to disregard the Ukrainian court order, and the officer came to the correct conclusion. The application was dismissed.

Garcia Rubio v. Canada (Minister of Citizenship & Immigration) (2011), 385 F.T.R. 284, 2011 FC 272, 2011 CarswellNat 1361, 2011 CarswellNat 630 — The applicant was a minor when his Canadian uncle applied to adopt him. However, he had become an adult by the time the Canadian adoption order was made. In a decision dated January 26, 2010, his subsequent application for citizenship was denied. An application for judicial review pursuant to s. 18.1 was allowed. There had been a failure of natural justice in that the reasons were wholly inadequate. They omitted two important facts. First, that the affidavit evidence showed that the applicant's uncle had paid for his schooling in Mexico since kindergarten and, second, that the uncle initially tried to adopt the applicant under Mexican law when he was aged 14. At that time, his parents had just been divorced. As well, the reasons do not explain the relevance of the conclusion that "the ties with your biological parents have not been severed." This is important because the legislation speaks of "legal ties" and they were clearly severed when the applicant's parents consented to the adoption. Finally, the six facts listed in the final paragraph of the reasons appear to be irrelevant. At a minimum, the decision should have included an explanation of their significance.

Jardine v. Canada (Minister of Citizenship & Immigration), 2011 FC 565, 2011 CarswellNat 1981, 2011 CarswellNat 2986 — Although decided under the *Citizenship Act*, this case may also be relevant for purposes of the *Immigration and Refugee Protection Act* and Regulations.

The applicants immigrated to Canada in 2003 and applied for citizenship for their adopted child, Melissa, in 2009 under the new "direct route" provided by s. 5.1 of the *Citizenship Act*. An immigration officer at the High Commission in Port of Spain, Trinidad and Tobago refused the application on the grounds that a genuine parent-child relationship had not been established, that it was in the best interest of the child to remain in Guyana, and that the officer could not be satisfied that it was not an adoption of convenience entered into for the sole purpose of acquiring status in Canada.

There was sufficient evidence on the record to suggest that this adoption was genuine, was in the best interest of the adoptive child and was not entered into for the purpose of acquiring status or benefit. However, deference may still have been owed to the officer and the decision found to fall within the range of acceptable outcomes defensible in respect of the facts and law had it been clear that the officer properly considered the totality of the evidence. The officer's failure to articulate her rationale for attributing no weight to certain key pieces of evidence, especially significant evidence that is contrary to her alternate determination, requires a finding that the decision was made in error. The application for judicial review was allowed.

DIVISION 2 — FAMILY RELATIONSHIPS

4. (1) Bad faith — **For the purposes of these Regulations, a foreign national shall not be considered a spouse, a common-law partner or a conjugal partner of a person if the marriage, common-law partnership or conjugal partnership**

    (a) was entered into primarily for the purpose of acquiring any status or privilege under the Act; or

    (b) is not genuine.

(2) Adopted children   **A foreign national shall not be considered an adopted child of a person if the adoption**

    (a) was entered into primarily for the purpose of acquiring any status or privilege under the Act; or

(b) did not create a genuine parent-child relationship.

(3) Sponsorship of adopted children — Subsection (2) does not apply to adoptions referred to in paragraph 117(1)(g) and subsections 117(2) and (4).

SOR/2004-167, s. 3; SOR/2010-208, s. 1

Case Law

Canada (Minister of Citizenship and Immigration) v. Young (Litigation Guardian of Patrice Young) (2016), 40 Imm. L.R. (4th) 173, 398 D.L.R. (4th) 709, 2016 FCA 183, 2016 CarswellNat 2261 — Patrice Young, a Canadian citizen, adopted her cousin's daughter, Abreyah. As part of the adoption process, Ms Young submitted character references and medical information. In addition, she was the subject of a detailed home study conducted by an Alberta child welfare agency which found that Ms Young's home was appropriate for reception of an adopted child. A visa officer refused Ms Young's application for Canadian citizenship on behalf of her adopted daughter because, in the visa officer's opinion, the adoption did not meet any of the statutory requirements set out in 5.1(1) of the *Citizenship Act*. Federal Court allowed the application for judicial review and returned the matter for reconsideration by a different visa officer. However, the Minister appealed the Federal Court decision.

The mere fact of enabling a child to benefit from Canada's "generous" health and education systems is not an indication of an adoption of convenience. Something more is required. Awareness of the material advantages which will accrue to a child as a result of an adoption does not necessarily lead to the conclusion that the adoption is entered into *primarily* to provide the child with those material advantages. This is particularly true in the case of adoption of young children who will require care and nurturing for an extended period of time. A genuine commitment on the part of the adoptive parents to provide that care and nurturing militates against the conclusion that the adoption was entered into *primarily* for the purpose of gaining an advantage or a privilege with respect to citizenship or immigration.

The Act applies to all adoptions of minor children, without regard to their ages. It is difficult to know how one could find a genuine parent-child relationship in the case of the adoption of an infant when parent and child meet each other for the first time when the parents attend in the foreign country to take the child into their care. Clearly, there is no pre-existing relationship between those parents and that child. Any genuine parent-child relationship will develop over time as the parties live with each other. As a result, it is unlikely that Parliament meant to impose the obligation that there be a pre-existing relationship between parent and child as a condition of granting Canadian citizenship.

Paragraph 5.1(1)(b) does not require the adoptive parent to pass an emotional litmus test. It is designed to deal with the situation where the adoptive parents would essentially operate as a boarding house for their adopted child with the natural parents continuing to meet the child's material needs. This type of situation is more likely where the child is older and more able to function independently. This condition is best understood in the negative: is there reason to believe that the adoption will not, in the future, result in a genuine parent-child relationship?

A visa officer must be alive to indications that there is no intention to establish a genuine parent-child relationship, as opposed to passing judgment on the quality of the current quality of the relationship. The visa officer's conclusion was unreasonable on this point. The appeal was dismissed.

Huung v. Canada (Minister of Citizenship and Immigration), 2015 FC 905, 2015 Car-swellNat 3193, 2015 CarswellNat 5058 — The applicant sought judicial review of a decision of an officer to refuse the spousal sponsorship application on the basis that the applicant and her sponsor did not "share a level of financial and emotional interdependence expected of a genuinely married couple." The content of the duty of procedural fairness is ensuring that administrative decisions are made using a fair and open procedure, appropriate to the decision being made and its statutory, institutional, and social context, with an opportunity for those affected by the decision to put forward their views and evidence fully and have them considered by the decision maker. It makes sense to interview spouses separately where concerns arise about the genuineness of the marriage. However, that does not mean that applicants must also be denied knowledge of what their spouse said and not be afforded some opportunity to argue that the officer had misunderstood their statements. Once the spouses had been interviewed separately, there is no longer any danger of collusion. If an applicant or his or her spouse should try to retract any of their statements when confronted with inconsistencies, this could simply affect their credibility. A duty to confront the spouses with any inconsistencies would not be unduly onerous. In this case, had the applicant been confronted with the supposed inconsistencies, she might have been able to convince the officer that they were just misunderstandings. The application for judicial review was allowed.

Sandhu v. Canada (Minister of Citizenship and Immigration), 2014 FC 834, 2014 CarswellNat 3712, 2014 CarswellNat 4595 — The IAD dismissed the spousal-sponsorship appeal of the applicant on the basis that the matter was *res judicata* or, in the alternative, the marriage was entered into for the primary purpose of acquiring status under the Act. *Res judicata* attracts a different standard of review. The pre-conditions of *res judicata* existed on the facts of this case. The only issue was the second step — whether special circumstances existed to justify an exception. This is a discretionary decision. The reasonableness standard of review applied. A finding that a marriage is genuine weighs significantly in favour of a marriage that was not entered into for the purpose of gaining status in Canada. However, the finding that a marriage is genuine is not determinative of primary purpose. Evidence of commitment subsequent to the marriage can be used to prove the primary purpose of the marriage. This might include evidence of a continuing relationship or the birth of a child. Additionally, new evidence may be relevant to the analysis of genuineness of the marriage or primary purpose, even if similar evidence was adduced in the first IAD hearing. The nature of new evidence must be carefully analyzed by the decision maker. On the facts of some cases, the birth of a child may be sufficient to warrant the non-application of *res judicata*. However, where the facts on which the previous decision was decided very strongly support the finding that the primary purpose of a marriage is to acquire a status under the Act, it is less likely that this will be sufficient. In order to be decisive new evidence, the evidence must genuinely affect the analysis or evaluation of the intention. Evidence which simply bolsters or attempts to create the intention after the fact will be insufficient. In this case, the respondent admitted that the new evidence established the genuineness of the marriage. In this case, the IAD expressly adopted the reasoning of the first decision in the analysis of whether *res judicata* should apply. However, what was required was consideration of whether the evidence that was not available at the time of the previous IAD could genuinely alter the analysis of the primary purpose of the marriage. In this case, there was clear evidence that might alter the outcome if properly considered in its totality: in particular, evidence of the continuing relationship, two to three trips to India of several months in duration, and the birth of a child. The application for judicial review was allowed.

Singh v. Canada (Minister of Citizenship and Immigration), 2014 FC 1077, 2014 Car-swellNat 4532, 2014 CarswellNat 5205 — The IAD determined that the applicant's marriage met the definition of the exclusion in subs. 4(1) of the Regulations. The Federal Court dismissed the application for judicial review.

The Regulations are *intra vires*. The Regulations and Parliament's intent was to create a disjunctive relationship between the genuineness and the primary purpose aspects of subs. 4(1) of the Regulations. Furthermore, subs. 4(1) of the Regulations operates to support the IRPA's objective of family reunification rather than to frustrate it. This was found to be the case with other analogous exceptions to this general objective. For example, the Federal Court of Appeal found that excluding a family member as a member of the family class under para. 117(9)(d) of the Regulations is not inconsistent with or *ultra vires* to the IRPA's family reunification objective.

The court concluded the IAD did not act unreasonably regarding both the primary purpose and the genuineness test. The applicant only succeeded on the issue of genuineness even though the court found that the IAD acted unreasonably in respect of its assessment of the evidence and, in addition, applied the wrong legal test. The application for judicial review was dismissed.

The court certified the following question:

> Is the disjunctive element of subsection 4(1) of the *Immigration and Refugee Protection Regulations ultra vires* the enabling statute because subsection 4(1) would prohibit the sponsorship of a spouse when the marriage was found to be entered into primarily for the purpose of gaining status, notwithstanding a finding that the marriage always was or subsequently became genuine, and would therefore frustrate the aims and objectives of the Act, in particular section 3(1)(d), "to see that families are reunited in Canada"?

Cheshenchuk v. Canada (Minister of Citizenship & Immigration) (2014), 22 Imm. L.R. (4th) 57, 2014 FC 33, 2014 CarswellNat 22, 2014 CarswellNat 967 — This application under s. 18.1 of the *Federal Courts Act* was for judicial review of a decision of a delegate of the Minister of Citizenship & Immigration refusing to grant citizenship to the applicant's adopted children under subsec. 5.1(1) of the *Citizenship Act*. The applicant was a citizen of both Canada and Ukraine and adopted two young children in Ukraine through a domestic private adoption approved by a Ukrainian court on August 11, 2011. She then applied to have her adopted children recognized as Canadian citizens under subsec. 5.1(1). The application was refused by a citizenship officer at the Canadian Embassy in Kiev on the basis that the adoptions were not completed in accordance with Ukrainian law.

The applicant argued that she was a citizen of both Canada and Ukraine, and had residence in both countries, and thus was eligible to proceed with a domestic adoption. International adoptions involve adoption agencies in both Canada and Ukraine, which make significant profits from such adoptions, as well as staff of the Canadian Embassy in Kiev. This results in a lengthy and costly process. A private domestic adoption, available only to Ukrainian citizens, does not involve the adoption agencies or the Embassy. The applicant followed, and argued that she was entitled by law to follow, the second route.

The officer decided that the adoption was not legally valid or was obtained through misrepresentation. Canadian courts have consistently ruled that an adoption documented by a final order of a foreign court should be presumed to be valid, and such an order is the best evidence that the adoption was carried out in accordance with the laws of the country in question. The officer's reviewing notes suggested that she was legitimately concerned that the applicant, in obtaining the Ukrainian court order, had not disclosed her residence in Canada, her Canadian citizenship, or that she was married to a non-Ukrainian who lived in Canada. The applicant claimed that she was legally separated from her husband when she was in Ukraine, although she provided nothing to support this. It was clear that at the material time, she was married. The court found that the officer had good reason to conclude that a serious irregularity had allowed the applicant to obtain the Ukrainian adoption order. The evidence before the officer revealed that the adoption order could not have been obtained if the applicant had revealed that she was a Canadian citizen who had been living in Canada for a number of years.

The Ukrainian court was not provided with fundamental information relevant to its jurisdiction to grant the order, and the Ukrainian government was deprived of its right to assess and approve an adoption of children younger than age 5 in a situation where the applicant, a Canadian citizen, intended to take the children out of the country. These were serious matters. The explanations offered by the applicant for what she did were unconvincing and did not, in any event, explain why she told the Ukrainian court that she was divorced. Accordingly, the high threshold required to set aside a foreign judgment for "fraud or irregularity" was satisfied. There were sufficient grounds for the officer to disregard the Ukrainian court order, and the officer came to the correct conclusion. The application was dismissed.

Gonzalez v. Canada (Minister of Citizenship & Immigration), 2014 FC 201, 2014 CarswellNat 439, 2014 CarswellNat 1011 — Judicial review was granted on the basis of a breach of natural justice. The decision maker did not approach the hearing with an open mind. One is entitled to be heard before an impartial decision maker. Remarks during the hearing show a bias, rather than the required neutrality. In any event the decision was unreasonable. The only conclusion the court could draw from reading the transcript was that the tribunal member had a fixed idea of how romances should develop, and that one should keep a specific diary of events, rather than treat an ongoing developing relationship as a continuum.

To say that the burden of proof was upon the applicant is not the same as saying there was a presumption that the marriage was entered into for immigration purposes. The tribunal appears to have presumed bad faith and that the marriage was entered into as an abuse of the immigration laws and set out to prove it. The tribunal member concluded that the minor inconsistencies led to bad faith. This was not a reasonable inference, but simply outright speculation which had no value.

Canada (Minister of Citizenship & Immigration) v. Xie, 2013 FC 666, 2013 CarswellNat 2026, 2013 CarswellNat 225 — The officer refused to issue a permanent resident visa to the respondent's spouse. The spouse admitted to relying on two pages of preparatory material, referred to by the officer as "cheat sheets." The officer refused the application for permanent residence on two grounds: pursuant to subsec. 4(1) of the Regulations, that the marriage was not genuine and was entered into primarily for the purpose of the spouse gaining entry into Canada; and, pursuant to para. 40(1)(a) of the Act, that the applicant was inadmissible for misrepresentation due to the reliance on the so-called "cheat sheets." The Board allowed the appeal and concluded that the couple did indeed have a genuine marriage. The Minister sought judicial review of the Board's decision. The Board found that the "cheat sheets" were used only as a memory aid and not for any improper purpose. One sheet of notes had been prepared by the spouse's Canadian lawyer and the other by his niece based on information on the internet. The Board accepted that

IRP Regulations

such preparation was reasonable and that the contents were true. The Minister did not cross-examine the niece on her affidavit regarding the spouse's poor memory. As this was the only evidence before the Board regarding the spouse's nervousness and poor memory, the Board was entitled to consider the evidence and give it the appropriate weight. The Board considered all the evidence, including the inconsistencies, and determined that, as a whole, the positive features of the marriage outweighed the minor inconsistencies and/or were explained to the satisfaction of the Board. It is not the role of the court to re-weigh the evidence considered by the Board. The application for judicial review was dismissed.

Kaur v. Canada (Minister of Citizenship & Immigration), 2012 CarswellNat 659, 2012 FC 273 — The applicant first applied for a permanent resident visa under the skilled worker class but subsequently withdrew her application. She then married and reapplied for permanent residence on January 4, 2010, including her husband as an accompanying spouse. A visa officer assigned the applicant a score of 69 points but determined that an interview was required due to concerns that the applicant's husband was seven years older than her, which was not common in local culture; that the spouse held a master's degree but had been unemployed since he graduated in April 2007; that the applicant and spouse had been married only one month before she applied for permanent residence; that her new passport issued February 2010 did not indicate she was married; and the applicant's PCC from India issued in May 2010 did not indicate she was married. The visa officer concluded that the applicant had misrepresented her marital status in order to bring her husband to Canada and to pass selection with enough points gained from the spouse's education. After review the manager determined on a balance of probabilities it was more probable that the applicant had misrepresented the facts and deemed the applicant inadmissible for misrepresentation under s. 40 of IRPA.

The court concluded that the manager's decision was taken under s. 40 and that no determination was made under s. 4 of IRPA. As a result, the manager was not guided by the proper legal considerations and committed a reviewable error. The officer and manager made their findings based strictly on concerns about the *bona fides* of the marriage. Such a determination should have been made under s. 4 of IRPA. It would then have been open to them to also conclude there was a misrepresentation based on s. 40. Without first determining under s. 4 that the marriage was entered into in bad faith, however, the officer and manager could not simply conclude misrepresentation had occurred based on an unconfirmed doubt as to the *bona fides* of the marriage. The application for judicial review was allowed.

Brar v. Canada (Minister of Citizenship & Immigration), 2011 FC 929, 2011 CarswellNat 2961, 2011 CarswellNat 3784 — The applicant's application to sponsor her adopted daughter in 2005 was refused. The officer found that the adoption was not genuine and was entered into for the purpose of gaining permanent resident status in Canada for the adoptive daughter. The applicant's appeal to the IAD was dismissed. The IAD accepted that the applicant and her husband had originally wanted to adopt a child because they were having trouble conceiving a child of their own. But after the adoption, and after they had children of their own, it appeared more likely they were trying to help provide a better life and opportunities for a relative. The IAD considered the following factors: the motivation for the adoption; the extent to which the adoptive parents have maintained care and control over the child since the adoption; the nature and extent of contact between the adoptive parents and the child; the extent of the party's knowledge of one another; and the plans and arrangements for the child's future. The IAD's reasons as a whole and its conclusion were not unreasonable. The application for judicial review was dismissed.

Garcia Rubio v. Canada (Minister of Citizenship & Immigration) (2011), 385 F.T.R. 284, 2011 FC 272, 2011 CarswellNat 1361, 2011 CarswellNat 630 — The applicant was a minor when his Canadian uncle applied to adopt him. However, he had become an adult by the time the Canadian adoption order was made. In a decision dated January 26, 2010, his subsequent application for citizenship was denied. An application for judicial review pursuant to s. 18.1 was allowed. There had been a failure of natural justice in that the reasons were wholly inadequate. They omitted two important facts. First, that the affidavit evidence showed that the applicant's uncle had paid for his schooling in Mexico since kindergarten and, second, that the uncle initially tried to adopt the applicant under Mexican law when he was aged 14. At that time, his parents had just been divorced. As well, the reasons do not explain the relevance of the conclusion that "the ties with your biological parents have not been severed." This is important because the legislation speaks of "legal ties" and they were clearly severed when the applicant's parents consented to the adoption. Finally, the six facts listed in the final paragraph of the reasons appear to be irrelevant. At a minimum, the decision should have included an explanation of their significance.

Jardine v. Canada (Minister of Citizenship & Immigration), 2011 FC 565, 2011 CarswellNat 1981, 2011 CarswellNat 2986 — Although decided under the *Citizenship Act*, this case may also be relevant for purposes of the *Immigration and Refugee Protection Act* and Regulations.

The applicants immigrated to Canada in 2003 and applied for citizenship for their adopted child, Melissa, in 2009 under the new "direct route" provided by s. 5.1 of the *Citizenship Act*. An immigration officer at the High Commission in Port of Spain, Trinidad and Tobago refused the application on the grounds that a genuine parent-child relationship had not been established, that it was in the best interest of the child to remain in Guyana, and that the officer could not be satisfied that it was not an adoption of convenience entered into for the sole purpose of acquiring status in Canada.

There was sufficient evidence on the record to suggest that this adoption was genuine, was in the best interest of the adoptive child and was not entered into for the purpose of acquiring status or benefit. However, deference may still have been owed to the officer and the decision found to fall within the range of acceptable outcomes defensible in respect of the facts and law had it been clear that the officer properly considered the totality of the evidence. The officer's failure to articulate her rationale for attributing no weight to certain key pieces of evidence, especially significant evidence that is contrary to her alternate determination, requires a finding that the decision was made in error. The application for judicial review was allowed.

Gill vs. Canada (Minister of Citizenship & Immigration) (2010), 362 F.T.R. 281(Eng.), 2010 FC 122, 2010 CarswellNat 446 — The applicant sought judicial review of the Immigration Appeal Division's decision finding her marriage not to be genuine under s. 4 of the Regulations. When the Board is required to examine the genuineness of a marriage under s. 63(1) of IRPA, it must proceed with great care because the consequences of a mistake will be catastrophic to the family. This is particularly obvious where the family includes a child born of the relationship. The Board's task is not an easy one because the genuineness of personal relationships can be difficult to assess from the outside. Behaviour that may look suspicious at first glance may be open to simple explanation or interpretation. An example of this from this case involves the officer's concern that the wedding photos looked staged and the parties appeared uncomfortable. The simple answer, of course, is that almost all wedding photos are staged and, in the context of an arranged marriage, some personal awkwardness might well be expected. The subsequent birth of a child would ordinarily be sufficient to dispel any lingering concern of this sort. Similarly, the Board's concern that the applicant rushed into a second marriage may perhaps be explained by the fact that her divorce may have substantially reduced her prospects for remarriage.

When assessing the genuineness of an arranged marriage, the Board must be careful not to apply expectations that are more in keeping with a western marriage. By its very nature, an arranged marriage, when viewed through a North American cultural lens, will appear non-genuine. When a relationship involves parties exposed to two cultures, Indian norms and traditions concerning marriage and divorce must also be applied with some caution.

The cumulative deficiencies in the Board's analysis were sufficiently grave enough to return the matter for reconsideration on the merits.

Lin v. Canada (Minister of Citizenship & Immigration), 2010 FC 659, 2010 CarswellNat 2758, 2010 CarswellNat 1862 — The applicant's application for permanent resident status under the spouse or common-law partner in Canada class was refused. The applicant first arrived in Canada under a study permit in 2000. The permit was extended and he subsequently obtained a work permit valid until December 31, 2005. At some point during this time, he and two friends purchased a home furnishings supply business. He was refused an extension of his work permit but remained in the country awaiting the results of his application for permanent residence as a foreign skilled worker which was refused on October 19, 2006. At the end of June 2006, the applicant met Evelyn Wong while at a party. They began to date and moved in together in October 2006 and were married on June 5, 2007. The applicant applied for permanent resident status under the spouse or common-law partner in Canada class. The application was refused. The officer did not believe the applicant cohabitated with his sponsor, and he did not believe that the marriage was genuine and was not entered into primarily for the purpose of acquiring status under the Act.

The timing of a marriage can be a relevant factor in assessing the genuineness of the marriage. The factor can weigh in favour of an applicant or, as in this case, can lead the officer to draw a negative inference. Furthermore, the consideration of this factor is not contrary to the policy set out in the Spousal Policy (IP 8 — Spouse or Common-law Partner in Canada Class). That policy requires the applicant to prove that there is a *bona fide* relationship as one of the required criteria for the exemption and timing of the marriage can clearly be used to assess the *bona fides* of the relationship. The applicant and Ms. Wong submitted bank statements, bills and other correspondence showing that they shared an address, copies of their driver's licenses showing the same address as well as leases and a joint bank account statement. The officer did not explain why she found the T4 slips outweighed the other evidence contrary in reaching her determination. There were photos of the applicant and Ms. Wong at different points in time and statements on their relationship. The notes taken during the interview showed both provided roughly the same answers to the questions asked about their relationship. Although these pieces of evidence are not determinant in assessing the genuineness of the marriage, the court found that these pieces of evidence were relevant but were not noted by the officer and were not weighed against the others. In this case, there was relevant evidence that ran contrary to the officer's conclusion on a central issue and the officer should have explained why she did not accept it or preferred other evidence. The application for judicial review was allowed.

Elahi v. Canada (Minister of Citizenship & Immigration), 2011 FC 858, 2011 CarswellNat 2727 — The applicant applied to sponsor her spouse as a member of the family class. The visa officer was not satisfied that the marriage was genuine. The applicant appealed to the IAD. The IAD concluded that the applicant's marriage to her spouse was not *bona fide* and was entered into primarily for the purpose of her husband gaining permanent resident status under IRPA. The applicant sought judicial review of that decision. The Federal Court concluded that it does not follow that just because this applicant's spouse was looking to establish himself in Canada, that the couple's marriage was not genuine. The IAD erred in using the spouse's immigration history as a basis for finding a lack of *bona fides* of the marriage. In doing so, it failed to properly appreciate the distinction between what may traditionally constitute a "genuine marriage" in Canada and what may constitute a genuine marriage in other cultures.

Despite the fact that the IAD clearly considered the majority of the evidence before it, the applicant correctly pointed to pertinent evidence that was not mentioned in the decision under review. This evidence supports the applicant's position and could be considered to be contradictory evidence. As such, the court concluded that it was overlooked or ignored. Accordingly, the application for judicial review was allowed and remitted to a differently constituted panel of the IAD.

In oral argument, counsel for the applicant requested that if the matter were returned to the IAD that the court's reasons for judgment and judgment included direction that the IAD apply the conjunctive test as it was before the September 30, 2010, amendments of the Regulations. Fairness, the applicant argued, demanded that the law be applied as it was when the original decision was made. The respondent noted that if returned, the hearing before the IAD would be *de novo* and argued that the new, disjunctive test would apply as required under the current Regulations. There are no transitional provisions in the Regulations. The court agreed with the applicant after considering s. 43 of the *Interpretation Act*, R.S.C. 1985, c. I-21, which indicates that the repealing of a provision in whole or in part should not have an effect on any rights or privileges once they have begun to accrue. The court also relied on case law which stands for the principle that a person cannot be prejudiced by giving retroactive effect to new and additional requirements in a regulation. The court concluded that would be the effect of sending this matter back for reconsideration if the new disjunctive test were applied. When sending a matter back for redetermination, the Federal Court should not, except in the [clearest] of circumstances, direct the tribunal to reach a specific decision. Although acknowledging the limits of the court's ability to exercise its discretion in the applicant's favour, it was within the ambit of the court's powers to direct the IAD to apply the law as it read when the applicant initiated her appeal and it was first determined by the IAD. Not to do so would render the remedy which the applicant has obtained on this application in nullity and deny her natural justice.

Abbasi v. Canada (Minister of Citizenship & Immigration) (2010), 88 Imm. L.R. (3d) 174, 2010 FC 288, 2010 CarswellNat 1675, 2010 CarswellNat 560 — The applicant challenged a refusal of a visa officer to grant him a permanent resident visa as a member of the family class. The applicant was a Pakistan national being sponsored for landing in Canada by his wife. The refusal of the sponsorship application was based on the finding that the marriage was not genuine. Two grounds were advanced for setting aside the visa officer's decision: the finding that the marriage is not genuine is unreasonable; and that the process applied to reaching the decision offends the *Official Languages Act*, R.S.C. 1985, c. 31 (4th Supp.), because the visa officer's interview of the applicant was conducted in Urdu.

The circumstances of the marriage were unusual which, not surprisingly, raised suspicion. But the unusual circumstances should give cause for very careful consideration. A marriage is a union between two individuals, and where suspicion exists as to the genuineness of the union because an expected standard of conduct is not met, to fairly and properly deal with the suspicion, the evidence of each individual must be carefully considered. There is no evidence on the record that the visa officer provided the applicant's spouse with an opportunity to give her evidence with respect to the quality of the marriage before the decision under review was made. In a case such as this, the visa officer was required to interview both the applicant and his spouse by the best means available whether by teleconference, video conference, or personal interview. The decision under review was unreasonable.

In this case there was no breach of the *Official Languages Act*. The interview was conducted in Urdu at the applicant's request. This choice was confirmed by the visa officer at the opening of the interview. No interpreter was required as the visa officer was fluent in this language. The applicant argued that as a matter of law the visa officer was required to conduct the interview in either English or French through an interpreter who could interpret the visa officer's questions to the applicant in Urdu and his answers back in English or French to the visa officer.

Section 20(1) of the *Charter* provides a right to any member of the public in Canada to communicate with and receive available services from federal institutions in English and French. This right imposes an obligation and practical requirement on federal institutions to comply with the right. This rights based concept does not inhibit federal institutions to offer services in languages other than English or French if the members of the public involved do not wish to exercise their right under s. 20(1) of the *Charter*, and, indeed wish to conduct business in any other language to which the institution's officials are capable of reliably communicating without an interpreter. This point was made by Justice Pinard in *Toma v. Canada (Minister of Citizenships & Immigration)* (2006), 295 F.T.R. 158 (Eng.) (F.C.) at paragraph 33 where a visa officer conducted an interview in Arabic without an interpreter:

> If the officer speaks the applicant's language — as was the case here — it would be strange indeed for the officer to use an interpreter. There would be no need to do so. The preferable options, as the Manual suggests [Overseas Processing Manual (OP) 5], is to conduct the interview in the applicant's language.

The application for judicial review was allowed on the first ground.

Chen v. Canada (Minister of Public Safety & Emergency Preparedness), 2010 FC 584, 2010 CarswellNat 2957, 2010 CarswellNat 1506 — The applicant, a Chinese citizen, married Ms. Zou, a Canadian resident. She then sponsored him for permanent residence. When he arrived in Canada about a year later, he found her pregnant with another man's child. After a month or two, the marriage fell apart. After their divorce, he married an old flame in China and as a Canadian permanent resident endeavoured to sponsor her. At this stage, the immigration authorities became suspicious. Not only was the sponsorship of his second wife disallowed, he was also declared inadmissible for misrepresentation by directly withholding information and representing that his first marriage was genuine. The applicant appealed that decision to the Immigration Appeal Division of the Immigration and Refugee Board. His appeal was dismissed. This was the judicial review of that decision.

The basis for holding that the marriage was not genuine was that it only lasted for a short time, and that he did not immediately return to China when the marriage broke up but returned a short time later to pursue a former flame. These facts cannot establish an evidentiary basis that the marriage was not genuine in the first place. He could not know at the time of the marriage that his wife would become pregnant with another man's child a year later. As to not immediately returning to China when the marriage broke down, he said that as a cuckold he would be the laughing stock of his village. There was no evidence to contradict that statement. When he returned thereafter, it was in a different context altogether. As to not sharing the rumours regarding his wife's affair at the time of the interview, he withheld no material fact. The only fact was that he had heard rumours. Even if they were true, it did not mean that the marriage was necessarily at an end. The *Divorce Act* specifically contemplates a possible reconciliation and the divorce papers jointly signed by the parties, which are to be found in the tribunal record, contain their joint statement that reconciliation was not possible. The duty of candour did not oblige the applicant to share his worries with an immigration officer. There was no misrepresentation and no fact was withheld. The application for judicial review was granted.

Tamber v. Canada (Minister of Citizenship & Immigration), 2008 CarswellNat 2867, 2008 CarswellNat 3913, 2008 FC 951 — Both the visa officer and the Board concluded that the marriage between the applicant and a Mr. Singh was not genuine. The applicant sought judicial review of the Board's decision. She had given birth to a baby boy on March 11, 2005, and DNA testing confirmed Mr. Singh as the alleged father with a 99.98 per cent probability of paternity. The Board rejected the DNA evidence even though the supporting test documentation was on its face reliable and the respondent acknowledged that the analysis had been carried out by a reputable Canadian laboratory. That, however, was not the primary problem with the Board's approach to this highly determinative evidence. If the Board had reservations about the reliability of this testing or about the continuity of the blood samples, it had a clear duty to advise the applicant's counsel of its concerns. This was a proceeding that spanned two hearings separated by almost three months and there was no justification for ambushing the applicant by essentially ignoring the issue during the testimonial phase. It was open to the Minister to supervise the DNA testing and to control the continuity of the evidence obtained; it was not appropriate for the Minister to sit silently until all the evidence was in and then criticize the process as deficient. For the same reason it was unfair for the Board to reject this evidence as unreliable. It is a well-accepted principle of natural justice that the Board's concerns about the reliability of important documentary evidence must be put to the claimant either for an explanation or to allow for additional corroboration. The application was allowed.

Chen v. Canada (Minister of Citizenship & Immigration) (2008), 75 Imm. L.R. (3d) 282, 2008 FC 1227, 2008 CarswellNat 4076 — The applicant applied for permanent residence as a member of the skilled worker category. Included as family members were his wife and her son by a previous marriage. The visa officer refused the application because the officer was not satisfied the applicant answered truthfully about his marriage to Ms. Zhao. The applicant was inadmissible pursuant to s. 40(1) of the IRPA because he misrepresented material facts relating to his marriage. Accordingly, the officer was concerned whether the marriage was entered into in order for the applicant to serve as a "courier" husband and stepfather and thereby assist Ms. Zhao and her son to gain admission to Canada as family members. The officer did not advise the applicant or Ms. Zhao that the purpose for the scheduled interview was to ascertain whether their marriage was genuine.

The question of whether the officer had jurisdiction to look at the question of the *bona fides* of a marriage in a skilled worker application involves a matter of statutory interpretation. This question goes to the fundamental issue of whether s. 4 of the *Immigration and Refugee Protection Regulations*, confers jurisdiction upon an officer processing an application in the skilled worker class. The applicant had never been married before his marriage to Ms. Zhao 2½ months before applying for permanent residence and the circumstances of the marriage were inconsistent with local and Chinese customs that an unmarried young man should marry a woman 11 years his senior with a dependent child.

The court concluded that s. 4 was not limited to family class sponsorships. Section 4 applied to family members of an applicant in the skilled worker class. However, the court concluded that the officer denied the applicant's procedural fairness when, having not given advance notice of the purpose of the examination, she did not afford the applicants the opportunity to supply further documentation and submissions. Had the applicants been notified in advance about this issue, the potential for being denied a permanent resident visa, and the consequence of being ruled inadmissible, they could have had the opportunity to obtain additional documents and make focused submissions to the officer. The application for judicial review of both the decision of the visa officer and the immigration program manager was granted and the matter referred back for reconsideration.

Leroux v. Canada (Minister of Citizenship & Immigration) (2007), 64 Imm. L.R. (3d) 123, 2007 CarswellNat 2813, 2007 CarswellNat 984, 2007 FC 403 — The applicant in this proceeding alleged that the applicant for permanent residence, a 26-year-old Moroccan citizen, was his conjugal partner. An immigration officer concluded that the applicant for permanent residence was excluded from the family class under s. 4 of the Regulations. The applicant appealed to the IAD. In dismissing the appeal, the IAD concluded that "the Appellant had failed to establish on the preponderance of the evidence, that his relationship with the applicant is a conjugal relationship within the meaning of section 2 of the *Regulations*" and reaffirmed the immigration officer's opinion that the relationship was not genuine.

The Federal Court has not rendered any decision about the criteria to be used in an immigration context to determine whether there is a conjugal relationship; however, several IAD decisions have recognized the criteria in *M. v. H.*, [1999] 2 S.C.R. 3, which specifies seven non-exhaustive factors used to identify a conjugal relationship, namely, shared shelter, sexual and personal behaviour, services, social activities, economic support, children, and the societal perception of the couple. The IAD decisions recognize that the criteria in *M. v. H.* were established for couples living in Canada and must be modified for couples living in different countries. The Federal Court agreed with this approach stating that it was important to keep in mind the restrictions which apply because the partners live in different countries, some of which have different moral standards and customs which may have an impact on the degree of tolerance for conjugal relationships, especially where same-sex partners are concerned. Nevertheless, the alleged conjugal relationship must have a sufficient number of features of a marriage to show that it is more than just a means of entering Canada as a member of the family class. A conjugal relationship is more than a precursor, or plan, to share a conjugal relationship in future.

The application for judicial review was allowed. The IAD erred in law in its interpretation of s. 2 of the Regulations by restricting its analysis to the one-year period preceding the filing of the application for permanent residence. It was also impossible on reading the reasons to conclude that the IAD applied the criteria in a flexible manner on the basis of all the relevant facts in order to determine whether or not the relationship was genuine.

Canada (Minister of Citizenship & Immigration) v. Nahal, 2007 CarswellNat 178, 2007 FC 92 — The IAD found that the adoption was genuine because it was legally solemnized, without considering other factors to determine the *bona fides* of the adoption. This interpretation ". . . to interpret 'genuine' as 'legal' would render s. 4 of the *Regulations* redundant." The IAD erroneously addressed the questions of whether the adoption was valid or legal in the local country and did not analyze whether there was a genuine parent-child relationship created. Relevant factors to be considered under the s. 4 analysis such as the circumstances of the adoption, the whereabouts of the child's natural parents and their personal and living circumstances, financial and emotional support provided by the adoptive parents, the reasons for the adoption, and the social and legal practices in the local country, were not considered. The IAD's decision was set aside and the matter sent back for re-determination.

Owusu v. Canada (Minister of Citizenship & Immigration), 2006 CarswellNat 3100, 2006 FC 1195 — The applicant's application for permanent residence based on a spousal sponsorship was denied on the basis that the marriage was not genuine. The Immigration and Appeal Division came to the same conclusion. The applicant sought judicial review of the Immigration and Appeal Division's decision.

"Sometimes it can be difficult to realize that many of our attitudes derive from our own culture and may not be universally shared. If these attitudes, or bias if you will, are not recognized, it is impossible to cast them aside and try to walk a mile in someone else's shoes. That is what happened in this case.

. . . . .

"Reweighing evidence is improper within the limits of the scales of justice. Those limits are set by the functional and pragmatic approach to judicial review. The range or swing of deference is narrow if the scale has been set to correctness, broader if based on reasonableness, and broader yet if based on patent unreasonableness. In this case, the simplest probing, or weighing if you will, shows that the decision cannot stand up to scrutiny.

"The panel's focus was on this being a marriage of convenience. No fault was given to the inconvenience to [the applicant] if the marriage was not genuine. The analysis was woefully inadequate. The panel engaged in conjecture, which cannot serve as an evidentiary basis for finding that the marriage was not genuine or entered into '*primarily*' for the purpose of acquiring status in Canada."

The application for judicial review was granted.

Apaza v. Canada (Minister of Citizenship & Immigration), 2006 CarswellNat 606, 2006 CarswellNat 1415, 2006 FC 313 — The applicant's inland application for permanent residence based on humanitarian and compassionate grounds was rejected. The decision letter also stated that the case had been assessed under the spouse or common-law partner in Canada class and was rejected on that ground as well. In the opinion of the immigration officer, there was little evidence to show there was a genuine marriage and that the marriage had not been entered into primarily for the purpose of acquiring permanent residence status in Canada. The refusal letter provided no detailed reasons. The immigration officer's lengthy notes were produced only in the course of the application for judicial review. The court concluded that the officer ignored relevant evidence that, if believed, would have significant probative value. Specifically, the immigration officer ignored evidence about the ages of the applicants, the period of cohabitation before marriage, and supporting documents, including doctors' notes, employer reference letters and the filing of joint income tax returns, in reaching her conclusion about the genuineness of the marriage. Instead, the officer focused on irrelevant matters, for example the contents of bedside tables and the timing of the wife's divorce from her previous husband, and details of the mode of transportation used for their first date, in assessing the genuineness of the marriage. The application for judicial review was allowed and referred to a different officer for redetermination.

Gavino v. Canada (Minister of Citizenship & Immigration), [2006] F.C.J. No. 385, 2006 CarswellNat 561, 2006 FC 308 — Section 4 of the Regulations requires the focus of the inquiry to be the "marriage," its genuineness and its primary purpose. In deciding these issues, the evidence of both spouses is relevant.

Mohammed c. Canada (Ministre de la Citoyenneté & de l'Immigration), [2005] F.C.J. No. 1786, 2005 CarswellNat 3499, 2005 CarswellNat 4868, 2005 FC 1442 — In November of 1998, a visa officer rejected an application to sponsor the applicant as a spouse on the basis that the marriage was not *bona fide*. The Appeal Division, on a balance of probability, also concluded that the marriage was not *bona fide* and dismissed the appeal. In July 2001, a second spousal sponsorship application was filed and in February 2003 a visa officer rejected that application again on the grounds that the marriage was not *bona fide*. On appeal to the Appeal Division, the Minister's representative filed a motion to dismiss the second appeal on the ground that there was *res judicata*. The doctrine of *res judicata* applies when three conditions are satisfied: the parties in the previous proceeding are the same as those in the second proceeding; the previous decision was final; and the issue is the same. The Appeal Division properly concluded that the issue to be decided was the same, after having compared the meaning of subs. 4(3) of the *Immigration Regulations*, 1978 and s. 4 of the *Immigration Refugee Protection Regulations*. Both subs. 4(3) of the old Regulations and subs. (4) of the new Regulations are intended to exclude spouses whose spousal status is not based on the creation of a *bona fide* marriage.

4.1 New relationship — For the purposes of these Regulations, a foreign national shall not be considered a spouse, a common-law partner or a conjugal partner of a person if the foreign national has begun a new conjugal relationship with that person after a previous marriage, common-law partnership or conjugal partnership with that person was dissolved primarily so that the foreign national, another foreign national or the sponsor could acquire any status or privilege under the Act.

SOR/2004-167, s. 4

5. Excluded relationships — For the purposes of these Regulations, a foreign national shall not be considered

    (a) the spouse or common-law partner of a person if the foreign national is under the age of 18 years;

    (b) the spouse of a person if

        (i) the foreign national or the person was, at the time of their marriage, the spouse of another person, or

(n) the person has lived separate and apart from the foreign national for at least one year and is the common-law partner of another person; or

(c) the spouse of a person if at the time the marriage ceremony was conducted either one or both of the spouses were not physically present unless the person was not physically present at the ceremony as a result of their service as a member of the Canadian Forces and the marriage is valid both under the laws of the jurisdiction where it took place and under Canadian law.

SOR/2015-139, s. 1

PART 2 — GENERAL REQUIREMENTS

DIVISION 1 — DOCUMENTS REQUIRED BEFORE ENTRY

6. Permanent resident — A foreign national may not enter Canada to remain on a permanent basis without first obtaining a permanent resident visa.

7. (1) Temporary resident — A foreign national may not enter Canada to remain on a temporary basis without first obtaining a temporary resident visa.

(2) Exception — Subsection (1) does not apply to a foreign national who

(a) is exempted under Division 5 of Part 9 from the requirement to have a temporary resident visa;

(b) holds a temporary resident permit issued under subsection 24(1) of the Act; or

(c) is authorized under the Act or these Regulations to re-enter Canada to remain in Canada.

(3) When certificat d'acceptation du Québec required — In addition to any visa required under this section, a foreign national who is seeking to enter and remain in Canada on a temporary basis to receive medical treatment in the Province of Quebec must hold a *certificat d'acceptation du Québec* if the laws of that Province require the foreign national to hold that document.

7.1 (1) Electronic travel authorization — A foreign national referred to in paragraph 7(2)(a) who is exempt from the requirement to obtain a temporary resident visa and who, on or after March 15, 2016, is seeking to enter Canada by air to remain on a temporary basis is, nevertheless, required to obtain an electronic travel authorization before entering Canada, unless they are exempted by subsection (3) from the requirement to obtain one.

(2) Holder of temporary resident visa — Subsection (1) does not apply to a foreign national who holds a temporary resident visa.

(3) Exempt persons — The following persons are exempt from the requirement to obtain an electronic travel authorization:

(a) Her Majesty in right of Canada and any member of the Royal Family;

(b) a national of the United States;

(c) a foreign national referred to in paragraph 190(2)(a);

(d) a foreign national seeking to enter and remain in Canada solely

(i) as a member of a crew of a means of transportation that may be used for transportation by air or to become a member of such a crew, or

(ii) to transit through Canada after working, or to work, as a member of a crew of a means of transportation that may be used for transportation by air, if they possess a ticket for departure from Canada within 24 hours after their arrival in Canada;

(e) a citizen of France who is a resident of St. Pierre and Miquelon who seeks to enter Canada directly from St. Pierre and Miquelon; and

(f) a foreign national referred to in any of paragraphs 190(3)(b), (b.1), (c), (d), (f), (g) or (h).

SOR/2015-77, s. 2

8. (1) Work permit — A foreign national may not enter Canada to work without first obtaining a work permit.

(2) Exception — Subsection (1) does not apply to a foreign national who is authorized under section 186 to work in Canada without a work permit.

Case Law

Gupta v. Canada (Minister of Public Safety and Emergency Preparedness), 2015 FC 1086, 2015 CarswellNat 4449, 2015 CarswellNat 8173 — This is a judicial review of a decision by a Minister's delegate of the Canada Border Services Agency ("CBSA") issuing an exclusion order against the applicant pursuant to s. 41(a) of IRPA for failing to comply with para. 20(1)(b). This provision requires that a foreign national seeking entry into Canada establish that she/he hold the visa or other document required by the Regulations. In this case, the Minister's delegate determined that the applicant was entering to work without first obtaining a work permit, contrary to subs. 8(1) of the Regulations.

The applicant received a two-year work permit to work as a server for a Preeceville, Saskatchewan restaurant, the employer (the "Employer"). In January 2015, Mr. Gupta travelled to British Columbia to visit his girlfriend and while there, underwent training in bread baking at a Surrey, B.C. restaurant. He also worked in other roles at the Surrey restaurant. He and his girlfriend travelled to the United States. In March 2015 upon re-entry, he was interviewed by the CBSA. As part of the interview, he provided a signed declaration to CBSA stating that his employer had asked him to work at the Surrey, B.C. restaurant to learn how to make bread and that the applicant would receive pay from the employer as if he were still working in Saskatchewan and that the applicant would return to Saskatchewan on April 3, 2015. A s. 44 report was issued following the interview by the CBSA. A one-year exclusion order was issued.

Regardless of whether the exclusion order was based on past violation of the work permit, or concern about possible future violations, one key issue in the present application is whether a person can be found to have entered Canada without first obtaining a work permit (in contravention of s. of the Regulations) where they have a work permit, but intended to work in violation of its conditions. It appears that there is no jurisprudence directly on point. The Minister's delegate's decision reads in a requirement that is not included in s. 8: that the work to be done under the work permit be in compliance with the conditions thereof.

Certainly, violations of the terms of a work permit are of concern, and there are measures that can be taken against the holder of a work permit who ignores its conditions. However, there is no indication that s. 8 was intended to address such a situation. A reading of s. 8 in its grammatical and ordinary sense harmoniously with the scheme and object of IRPA and the intention of Parliament does not permit this.

The applicant also argued that an exclusion order is not the appropriate sanction in these circumstances. He asserted that concerns about alleged violations of the work permit should instead be referred to the Immigration Division for consideration and, if necessary, sanction. The court agreed. The possibility of issues surrounding the contravention of the conditions of this work permit demonstrate that this type of situation should be referred to the Immigration Division and was not intended to be dealt with by means of an exclusion order. The application for judicial review was granted and the Minister's decision was found to be unreasonable in both respects and the exclusion order was quashed.

9. (1) Study permit — A foreign national may not enter Canada to study without first obtaining a study permit.

(2) Exception — Subsection (1) does not apply to a foreign national who is authorized under section 188 or 189 to study in Canada without a study permit.

DIVISION 2 — APPLICATIONS

10. (1) Form and content of application — Subject to paragraphs 28(b) to (d) and 139(1)(b), an application under these Regulations shall

(a) be made in writing using the form provided by the Department, if any;

(b) be signed by the applicant;

(c) include all information and documents required by these Regulations, as well as any other evidence required by the Act;

(d) be accompanied by evidence of payment of the applicable fee, if any, set out in these Regulations; and

(e) if there is an accompanying spouse or common-law partner, identify who is the principal applicant and who is the accompanying spouse or common-law partner.

(2) Required information — The application shall, unless otherwise provided by these Regulations,

(a) contain the name, birth date, address, nationality and immigration status of the applicant and of all family members of the applicant, whether accompanying or not, and a statement whether the applicant or any of the family members is the spouse, common-law partner or conjugal partner of another person;

(b) indicate whether they are applying for a visa, permit or authorization;

(c) indicate the class prescribed by these Regulations for which the application is made;

589

(c.1) if the applicant is represented in connection with the application, include the name, postal address and telephone number, and fax number and electronic mail address, if any, of any person or entity — or a person acting on its behalf — representing the applicant;

(c.2) if the applicant is represented, for consideration in connection with the application, by a person referred to in any of paragraphs 91(2)(a) to (c) of the Act, include the name of the body of which the person is a member and their membership identification number;

(c.3) if the applicant has been advised, for consideration in connection with the application, by a person referred to in any of paragraphs 91(2)(a) to (c) of the Act, include the information referred to in paragraphs (c.1) and (c.2) with respect to that person;

(c.4) if the applicant has been advised, for consideration in connection with the application, by an entity — or a person acting on its behalf — referred to in subsection 91(4) of the Act, include the information referred to in paragraph (c.1) with respect to that entity or person; and

(d) include a declaration that the information provided is complete and accurate.

(3) Application of family members — The application is considered to be an application made for the principal applicant and their accompanying family members.

(4) Sponsorship application — An application made by a foreign national as a member of the family class must be preceded or accompanied by a sponsorship application referred to in paragraph 130(1)(c).

(5) Multiple applications — No sponsorship application may be filed by a sponsor in respect of a person if the sponsor has filed another sponsorship application in respect of that same person and a final decision has not been made in respect of that other application.

(6) Invalid sponsorship application — A sponsorship application that is not made in accordance with subsection (1) is considered not to be an application filed in the prescribed manner for the purposes of subsection 63(1) of the Act.

SOR/2004-59, s. 2; SOR/2004-167, s. 5(1); SOR/2011-129, s. 2; SOR/2012-225, s. 1

Case Law

Su v. Canada (Minister of Citizenship and Immigration) (2016), 39 Imm. L.R. (4th) 1, 2016 FC 51, 2016 CarswellNat 293, 2016 CarswellNat 64 — The applicant's application for permanent residence was returned to her as it was incomplete and did not meet the requirements of s. 10 of the Regulations. The sole issue was whether the officer's interpretation of s. 10 of the Regulations was reasonable. Section 10 employs mandatory language regarding the content of applications, making them preconditions to a valid application. Section 12 of the Regulations instructs that an application is to be returned when the mandatory requirements in ss. 10 and 11 are not met. The applicant had failed to include two forms to be completed and signed by her dependent child who was over the age of 18 at the time the application was submitted.

Sections 10 and 12 make no reference to an application remaining alive and pending after it and all documentation pertaining to it have been returned. Nor do they provide any authority for visa officers to maintain incomplete applications or to treat them as continuations of the prior applications following resubmission. IRPA's stated objectives of "consistent standards and prompt processing" to attain the government's immigration goals under s. 3(1)(f) of the Act also supports the officer's interpretation. Where an application is unperfected, there is no duty to process the application. If the application is not processed and is returned, it cannot be considered to still exist and, even if it did, it would not serve to "lock in" and thereby hold a place in line for the applicant. Therefore, the application is not immune from the impact of regulatory changes that come into force before the application is perfected. The application for judicial review was dismissed.

The following question was certified:

> If an application for permanent residence is incomplete as it fails to meet the requirements prescribed by s. 10 of the *Immigration and Refugee Protection Regulations* ("IRPA Regulations") and the application and all supporting documents are returned to the applicant pursuant to s. 12 of the IRPA Regulations, does the application still "exist" such that it preserves or "locks in" the applicant's position in time so that a subsequently submitted complete application must be assessed according to the regulatory scheme that was in effect when the first, incomplete application was submitted?

Doron v. Canada (Minister of Citizenship and Immigration), 2016 FC 429, 2016 CarswellNat 1172, 2016 CarswellNat 2722 — The applicant applied for permanent residence through the express entry program administered by Citizenship and Immigration Canada. CIC advised the applicant that he had been accepted in the express entry pool of candidates and subsequently that he had been invited to apply and must submit a complete application within 60 days. The applicant wrote to CIC stating he was facing technical difficulty in submitting his online application and supporting documents on March 4, 2015. His letter also stated that he had uploaded a police clearance from the Philippines issued November 21, 2014, and referred to difficulties obtaining police clearances from Saudi Arabia and the United Arab Emirates. The police clearance certificate from the Philippines was issued by the National Police Commission not the National Bureau of Investigations as required by CIC. On April 8, 2015, the applicant received a letter from CIC confirming that his application had been received and was being checked to determine whether it met the requirements of a complete application under s. 10 of the Regulations, and would be rejected as incomplete if it did not meet the requirements of this section. On May 14, 2015, CIC sent another letter requesting certain information and documents including passports, birth certificates, and medical information related to members of the applicant's family. On July 2, 2015, an officer issued the decision rejecting the application.

The applicant's evidence was that he submitted a police certificate from the National Police Commission and that he did not understand that he was required to submit one specifically from the National Bureau of Investigations ("NBI"). It appears that CIC's practice was to advise an applicant of the requirement of the NBI's certificate with a checklist but in this case the practice was not followed. Consequently, the court was not prepared to rely on a series of website screenshots, attached to written submissions but not proven through an affidavit, to reach the conclusion that CIC had advised the applicant of the requirement that the police certificate be obtained from the NBI. Accordingly,

CIC did not give the applicant the initial notice of the requirement he was obliged to meet necessary to discharge the obligation of procedural fairness. The decision was set aside.

Campana v. Canada (Minister of Citizenship & Immigration) (2014), 22 Imm. L.R. (4th) 219, 2014 FC 49, 2014 CarswellNat 295, 2014 CarswellNat 58 — The applicants were a husband who sought to sponsor his spouse. The applicants argued that they made their application before the Regulations were amended. Specifically s. 130(3) of the Regulations precluded a sponsor who became a permanent resident after being sponsored as a spouse or partner from sponsoring a spouse or partner, unless the sponsor became a permanent resident not less than five years immediately preceding the day on which the application was filed. Their application was returned with instructions to "resubmit." The court could not find anything in s. 10 to confirm that a lack of compliance resulted in an application not being in existence. Rather, the section provides in clear terms what an application under the Regulations must contain. That an incomplete application may not be processed is one thing. Suggesting that it does not even exist is quite another. The regulatory impact analysis statement speaks of the requirements of applications for them to be "considered" or "processed." It does go as far as to state that "(F)ailure to provide the necessary documentation in its required form may result in a refusal of the application." That is a far cry from concluding that an application that fails on any of the requirements of s. 10 is deemed to have never existed. In order to be able to conclude that an application does not exist, language much clearer than that found in s. 10 is needed. The application for judicial review was allowed. The matter was returned for rehearing and redetermination by a different officer on the basis that the application was made on February 29, 2012, and the five-year requirement for the applicant's sponsor did not apply in the circumstances.

Toussaint v. Canada (Minister of Citizenship & Immigration), 2011 FCA 146, 2011 CarswellNat 1943, 2011 CarswellNat 1446; application/notice of appeal to S.C.C. filed 2011 CarswellNat 2875 (S.C.C.) — On a proper interpretation of subs. 25(1) of IRPA, the Minister is obligated to consider a request for an exemption from the requirement in para. 10(1)(d) of the Regulations to pay a fee for processing an application under subs. 25(1). The Governor in Council's failure to enact regulations permitting the waiver of fees for foreign nationals living in poverty who wish to make an in-Canada application for permanent residence status pursuant to subs. 25(1) of IRPA does not infringe an applicant's ss. 7 or 15 of the *Charter of Rights* nor does it infringe the rule of law or the common law constitutional right of access to the courts.

Wang v. Canada (Minister of Citizenship & Immigration), 2008 CarswellNat 3897, 2008 CarswellNat 2051, 2008 FC 798 — The officer concluded that the applicant had insufficient points to qualify for immigration to Canada. She noted that no points were awarded for the male applicant's brother living in Canada. She determined that the evidence provided by the applicants in support of this allegation was insufficient to establish that the brother resided in Canada at the time of the decision, based on the fact that the majority of the documentation provided related to the brother's wife and not him. The brother's notice of assessment was the only document which specifically related to him. It indicated he earned a total of $2,000 in 2006. The officer noted that her records indicated that the brother had prolonged absences from Canada in the past. The Notice of Assessment was therefore insufficient evidence to convince her that he was a resident of Canada at the time the decision was made. The officer's decision was based on the insufficiency of evidence establishing the brother's residence in Canada. The burden of adducing sufficient evidence to support the application falls to the applicant. The application for judicial review was dismissed.

11. (1) Place of application for permanent resident visa — An application for a permanent resident visa — other than an application for a permanent resident visa made under Part 8 — must be made to the immigration office that serves

(a) the country where the applicant is residing, if the applicant has been lawfully admitted to that country for a period of at least one year; or

(b) the applicant's country of nationality or, if the applicant is stateless, their country of habitual residence other than a country in which they are residing without having been lawfully admitted.

(2) Place of application for temporary resident visa, work permit or study permit — An application for a temporary resident visa — or an application for a work permit or study permit that under these Regulations must be made outside of Canada — must be made to an immigration office that serves as an immigration office for processing the type of application made and that serves, for the purpose of the application,

(a) the country in which the applicant is present and has been lawfully admitted; or

(b) the applicant's country of nationality or, if the applicant is stateless, their country of habitualresidence other than a country in which they are residing without having been lawfully admitted.

(3) Applications to remain in Canada as permanent residents — An application to remain in Canada as a permanent resident as a member of one of the classes referred to in section 65 or subsection 72(2), and an application to remain in Canada under subsection 21(2) of the Act, must be made to the Department's Case Processing Centre in Canada that serves the applicant's place of habitual residence.

(4) Applications for permanent resident cards — An applicant for a permanent resident card must send the application to the Department's Case Processing Centre in Canada that serves the applicant's place of habitual residence.

(5) Sponsorship applications — A person who applies to sponsor a foreign national, other than a foreign national who is making an application for a permanent resident visa under Division 1 of Part 8, must send the application to the Department's Case Processing Centre in Canada that serves the applicant's place of habitual residence.

[Editor's Note: SOR/2002-227, s. 358(1) provides that a fee paid for processing an application in respect of which no decision has been made before June 28, 2002 or an application that has been refused but the refusal has not been communicated to the applicant before June 28, 2002 shall be applied to the cost of completing the processing of the application under the new Immigration and Refugee Protection Act, 2001, c. 27.

SOR/2002-227, s. 358(2) provides, however, that SOR/2002-227, s. 358(1) does not apply in respect of an application for a returning resident permit.]

SOR/2004-167, s. 6; SOR/2012-154, s. 2; SOR/2012-225, s. 2

Case Law

Ramos-Frances v. Canada (Minister of Citizenship & Immigration), 2007 FC 142, 2007 CarswellNat 278, [2007] F.C.J. No. 192 — The applicant, a citizen of Spain, applied for permanent residence as a skilled worker. At the time of his application, he was working in Canada as authorized by a work permit. Therefore, his application for permanent residence was filed at the Canadian Consulate in Buffalo. The applicant received a letter advising that he was required to attend a personal interview at the Canadian Consulate in Detroit, Michigan. He responded advising that he no longer had legal status in the United States so would be unable to attend an interview in Detroit. He stated that he was now living in Chile and requested his file be transferred to the Canadian Embassy in Santiago, Chile, to attend an interview there. This request was refused.

The applicant claimed he was denied procedural fairness because his request for the transfer of his file was unfairly and unreasonably refused. The requirements of s. 11 of the Regulations applied to this application. Chile is not the applicant's country of nationality and he provided no information in his request for file transfer with respect to how long he had been in Chile, or what his legal status in Chile was.

The applicant did not attend the scheduled interview and his application was based on the information contained within his file. The application was rejected. Given that there is no absolute entitlement to an interview, and the fact that the onus is on the applicant for permanent residence to ensure that his or her file is complete, the officer did not breach the duty of fairness, either by failing to advise about her concerns under subs. 11(1) of the Regulations or by failing to transfer the file. The application was dismissed.

Ponomarenko v. Canada (Minister of Citizenship & Immigration) (2003), 26 Imm. L.R. (3d) 315, 2003 CarswellNat 562, 2003 CarswellNat 1906, 2003 FCT 259 (Fed. T.D.) — The applicant, originally from Russia, applied for permanent residence at the Canadian Consulate General in Buffalo, USA. The file was transferred to New York for an interview and a visa officer there decided to transfer the file to Moscow. The applicant failed to attend his interview in Moscow with the result that the application for permanent residence was dismissed. The applicant's attempt to quash that decision failed. Visa applicants have no statutory right to have their applications processed at any particular visa post. While efforts should be made to accommodate applicants, in the end the place of the interview must remain at the discretion of the visa officer.

12. Return of application — **Subject to section 140.4, if the requirements of sections 10 and 11 are not met, the application and all documents submitted in support of it shall be returned to the applicant.**

SOR/2012-225, s. 3

Case Law

Stanabady v. Canada (Minister of Citizenship and Immigration) (2015), [2016] 3 F.C.R. 3, 2015 FC 1380, 2015 CarswellNat 7163, 2015 CarswellNat 7768 — The applicants were in Canada as temporary residents. An exclusion order was issued against them on the grounds that they had remained in Canada after their permits had expired. The applicants' position is that the exclusion order was invalid because they had applied for an extension of their permits before they had expired, so they had maintained Canadian status under the Regulations until their applications were refused on the merits. The applicants applied for an extension of time on June 16, 2014. The application forms and documents were returned to them because they had failed to make sufficient payment and provide necessary photos in passport form for each family member. By the time the applicants received notice of the deficient application, their temporary resident permits had already expired. On August 25, 2014, their application forms were sent back in and were again sent back indicating deficiencies in information and photographs missing. On July 4, 2015, the Minister's delegate signed an exclusion order pursuant to s. 44(2) of IRPA on the ground that they had violated s. 29(2) of the Act by failing to leave Canada at the expiry of their temporary resident permits.

Section 183 of the Regulations must be read together with ss. 10 and 12 of the Regulations. The fact that Citizenship and Immigration Canada had sent the applicants a form letter, after their temporary resident permits had expired, which stated that if they wished to reapply they had to send back a copy of the letter together with an application form complete in all respects, did not result in their status being locked in until a negative decision was made on the merits. In this case, it was impossible to render a decision extending the temporary resident permits before they expired. Had the applications been complete in every way, the officer may or may not have granted the extension after the permits expired, as permitted under s. 183(5) of the Regulations. There are two decisions of the Federal Court that came to different conclusions. Justice Roy was of the view that an incomplete application was still an application in *Campana v. Canada (Citizenship and Immigration)* (2014), 22 Imm. L.R. (4th) 219 (F.C.). While Justice Rennie concluded that an incomplete application was not an application at all in *Ma v. Canada (Citizenship and Immigration)* (2015), 475 F.T.R. 148. Accordingly, although the application for judicial review in this case was dismissed, the court certified the following question:

> When a temporary resident has applied for an extension of the period authorized for his or her stay, but the application is returned to the applicant, due to the incompleteness, in accordance with s. 12 of the *Immigration and Refugee Protection Regulations*, does the applicant benefit from implied status until he or she actually submits a complete application and that application is either refused or allowed?

See also *Su v. Canada (Minister of Citizenship and Immigration)*, [2016] 3 F.C.R. 275, 39 Imm. L.R. (4th) 1, 2016 FC 51, 2016 CarswellNat 293, 2016 CarswellNat 64, at s. 10 of the IRPR.

Mashtouli v. Canada (Minister of Citizenship & Immigration), 2006 CarswellNat 205, 2006 FC 94 — The Regulations set out a 180-day deadline for successful refugee claimants to file an application for permanent residence. The Regulations, however, do not stipulate that incomplete applications submitted on time should be rejected. On the contrary, s. 12 of the Regulations simply says that incomplete applications should be returned to the applicants. Had the Governor in Council intended that incomplete applications be rejected entirely, it would have said so. In contrast, a sponsorship application that is deficient is considered not to be an application filed in the prescribed manner: see s. 10(6) of the *Immigration and Refugee Protection Regulations*.

12.01 (1) Invitation to apply for permanent residence — application by electronic system — Subject to subsection 12.02(1), an application for permanent residence that is made in response to an invitation issued by the Minister under Division 0.1 of the Act must be made by means of an electronic system that is made available by the Department for that purpose.

(2) Effect of electronic application — For greater certainty,

(a) an application referred to in subsection (1) that is made by means of the electronic system meets the requirements of paragraph 10(1)(a); and

(b) the applicant's electronic signature in that application meets the requirement of paragraph 10(1)(b).

(3) Electronic application — requirements — When an application referred to in subsection (1) is made by means of the electronic system

(a) the information, documents and evidence referred to in paragraph 10(1)(c) must be submitted by means of that electronic system at the time the application is made; and

(b) the applicant must, at the time the application is made,

(i) pay electronically the applicable fee, if any, referred to in section 295, or

(ii) submit electronically the evidence of payment referred to in paragraph 10(1)(d).

SOR/2014-256, s. 1

12.02 (1) Invitation to apply for permanent residence — application by other means — If an applicant is unable to make the application referred to in subsection 12.01(1) by means of the electronic system because of a physical or mental disability, it may be made by another means made available by the Department for that purpose that would enable the applicant to make the application, including a paper application form.

(2) Evidence of payment of fee — An application that is made under subsection (1) must be accompanied by the evidence of payment referred to in paragraph 10(1)(d).

SOR/2014-256, s. 1

12.03 Non-application — Subsections 11(1) and (3) do not apply in respect of an application referred to in subsection 12.01(1) that is made by means of an electronic system under that subsection or made by another means under subsection 12.02(1).

SOR/2014-256, s. 1

12.04 (1) Electronic travel authorization — application by electronic system — Despite section 10 and subject to subsection (2), an application for an electronic travel authorization under subsection 11(1.01) of the Act must be made by means of an electronic system that is made available by the Department for that purpose.

(2) Electronic travel authorization — application by other means — If the applicant is unable to make the application by means of the electronic system because of a physical or mental disability, it may be made by another means, made available for that purpose, that would enable the applicant to make the application, including a paper application form.

(3) **Payment of fee** — The fee referred to in subsection 294.1(1) must be paid at the time the application is made and, unless the application is made under subsection (2), it must be paid by electronic means.

(4) **Required information** — The application must contain the following information:

  (a) the applicant's name;

  (b) the applicant's date and place of birth;

  (c) the applicant's gender;

  (d) the applicant's address;

  (e) the applicant's nationality;

  (f) the number of the applicant's passport or other travel document, together with its date of issue and its expiry date and the country or the authority that issued it;

  (g) if the applicant is an applicant referred to in any of paragraphs 10(2)(c.1) to (c.4), the information required under that paragraph;

  (h) if the applicant is making the application by means of the electronic system referred to in subsection (1), the applicant's email address; and

  (i) a declaration that the information provided in the application is complete and accurate.

(5) **Combined application** — An application for a work permit or study permit that is made by a foreign national who is required under subsection 7.1(1) to obtain an electronic travel authorization is considered to constitute an application for an electronic travel authorization.

SOR/2015-77, s. 3

12.05 Period of validity — An electronic travel authorization is valid for a period of five years from the day on which it is issued to the applicant or until the earliest of the following days, if they occur before the end of that period:

  (a) the day on which the applicant's passport or other travel document expires,

  (b) the day on which the electronic travel authorization is cancelled, or

  (c) the day on which a new electronic travel authorization is issued to the applicant.

SOR/2015-77, s. 3

12.06 Cancellation — An officer may cancel an electronic travel authorization that was issued to a foreign national if

  (a) the officer determines that the foreign national is inadmissible; or

  (b) the foreign national is the subject of a declaration made under subsection 22.1(1) of the Act.

SOR/2015-77, s. 3

DIVISION 2.1 — COLLECTION OF BIOMETRIC INFORMATION
[Heading added SOR/2013-73, s. 1.]

12.1 (1) Prescribed foreign nationals — For the purposes of section 11.1 of the Act and subject to subsection (2), a foreign national referred to in any of the following paragraphs who makes an application for a temporary resident visa under section 179, an application for a study permit under section 213, 214 or 215 or an application for a work permit under section 197, 198 or 199 must, as of the applicable date set out in that paragraph, follow the procedure set out in subsection (3) for the collection of the biometric information set out in subsection (4):

(a) September 4, 2013, in the case of a foreign national who is a citizen of Colombia, Haiti or Jamaica;

(b) October 23, 2013, in the case of a foreign national who is a citizen of Albania, Algeria, Democratic Republic of Congo, Eritrea, Libya, Nigeria, Saudi Arabia, Somalia, South Sudan, Sudan or Tunisia;

(c) December 11, 2013, in the case of a foreign national who is a citizen of Afghanistan, Bangladesh, Burma, Cambodia, Egypt, Iran, Iraq, Jordan, Laos, Lebanon, Pakistan, Sri Lanka, Syria, Vietnam or Yemen;

(d) December 11, 2013, in the case of a foreign national who holds a passport or travel document issued by the Palestinian Authority.

(2) Exemption — A foreign national referred to in subsection (1) is exempt from the requirement to follow the procedure set out in subsection (3) if the foreign national is

(a) under the age of 14;

(b) over the age of 79;

(c) a person who is seeking to enter Canada in the course of official duties as a properly accredited diplomat, consular officer, representative or official of a country other than Canada, of the United Nations or any of its agencies or of any intergovernmental organization of which Canada is a member, or is a family member of one of them;

(d) a holder of a valid United States entry visa who is destined to or returning from that country, is seeking to enter Canada for a period of less than 48 hours and is

(i) travelling by transporter's vehicle to a destination other than Canada, or

(ii) transiting through or stopping over in Canada for refuelling or for the continuation of their journey in another transporter's vehicle; or

(e) a foreign national who makes an application for a study permit or a work permit and is

(i) a person in Canada who has made a refugee claim that has not yet been determined by the Refugee Protection Division,

(ii) a person in Canada on whom refugee protection has been conferred, or

(iii) a person who is a member of the Convention refugees abroad class or a member of a humanitarian-protected persons abroad class.

(3) Prescribed procedure — A foreign national referred to in subsection (1) must present themselves in person at one of the following points of service to have the biometric information set out in subsection (4) collected from them:

(a) a location where services for the collection of biometric information are provided by an entity under an agreement or arrangement with the Minister for that purpose; or

(b) an immigration office if authorized or directed by an officer to do so for

(i) reasons relating to the national interest,

(ii) reasons relating to operational requirements, or

(iii) any other reason that may be necessary in the circumstances.

(4) Prescribed biometric information — The biometric information that is to be collected from a foreign national referred to in subsection (1) consists of the following:

(a) their photograph; and

(b) their fingerprints.

SOR/2013-73, s. 1

DIVISION 3 — DOCUMENTS AND CERTIFIED COPIES

13. (1) Production of documents — Subject to subsection (2), a requirement of the Act or these Regulations to produce a document is met

(a) by producing the original document;

(b) by producing a certified copy of the original document; or

(c) in the case of an application, if there is an application form on the Department's website, by completing and producing the form printed from the website or by completing and submitting the form on-line, if the website indicates that the form can be submitted on-line.

(2) Exception — Unless these Regulations provide otherwise, a passport, a permanent resident visa, a permanent resident card, a temporary resident visa, a temporary resident permit, a work permit or a study permit may be produced only by producing the original document.

DIVISION 4 — DISCLOSURE OF INFORMATION

[Heading repealed SOR/2011-129, s. 3. Added SOR/2012-77, s. 1.]

13.1 Authorized disclosure — If a member of the Board or an officer determines that the conduct of a person referred to in any of paragraphs 91(2)(a) to (c) of the Act in connection with a proceeding — other than a proceeding before a superior court — or application under the Act is likely to constitute a breach of the person's professional or ethical obligations, the Department, the Canada Border Services Agency or the Board, as the case may be, may disclose the following

IRP Regulations

information to a body that is responsible for governing or investigating that conduct or to a person who is responsible for investigating that conduct:

(a) any information referred to in paragraphs 10(2)(c.1) to (c.3); and

(b) any information relating to that conduct, but — in the case of any information that could identify any other person — only to the extent necessary for the complete disclosure of that conduct.

SOR/2011-129, s. 3; SOR/2012-77, s. 1

[Editor's note: See Can. Reg. 2011-142, Regulations Designating a Body for the Purposes of Paragraph 91(2)(c) of the Immigration and Refugee Protection Act. Also see case summaries under section 91 of the IRPA regarding Representation or Advice.]

DIVISION 4.1 — USE AND DISCLOSURE OF BIOMETRIC INFORMATION AND RELATED PERSONAL INFORMATION

[Heading added SOR/2013-73, s. 2.]

13.11 (1) Disclosure of information — Any biometric information and related personal information set out in subsection (2) that is provided to the Royal Canadian Mounted Police under the Act may be used or disclosed by it to a law enforcement agency in Canada for the following purposes, if there is a potential match between fingerprints collected under the Act and fingerprints collected by it or submitted to it by a law enforcement agency in Canada:

(a) to establish or verify the identity of a person in order to prevent, investigate or prosecute an offence under any law of Canada or a province; and

(b) to establish or verify the identity of a person whose identity cannot reasonably be otherwise established or verified because of a physical or mental condition or because of their death.

(2) Information that may be used or disclosed — The following information in respect of a foreign national or a permanent resident may be used or disclosed by the Royal Canadian Mounted Police under subsection (1):

(a) their fingerprints and the date on which they were taken;

(b) their surname and first name;

(c) their other names and aliases, if any;

(d) their date of birth;

(e) their gender; and

(f) any file number associated with the biometric information or related personal information.

SOR/2013-73, s. 2; SOR/2014-83, s. 1

DIVISION 5 — DESIGNATED BODY — INFORMATION REQUIREMENTS

[Heading added SOR/2012-77, s. 1.]

13.2 (1) General requirement — A body that is designated under subsection 91(5) of the Act must provide to the Minister, within 90 days after the end of each of its fiscal years, the following information and documents:

(a) its most recent annual report;

(b) its most recent financial statement and the auditor's report on that financial statement;

(c) its instrument of incorporation, with an indication of any changes that have been made to that document since the last time it provided that document to the Minister in accordance with this section;

(d) its by-laws, with an indication of any changes that have been made to those by-laws since the last time it provided them to the Minister in accordance with this section;

(e) the minutes of each of the general meetings of its members that has been held during its last completed fiscal year;

(f) the terms of reference of its board of directors, if any, with an indication of any changes that have been made to those terms of reference since the last time it provided them to the Minister in accordance with this section;

(g) the conflict of interest code for its directors, if any, with an indication of any changes that have been made to that code since the last time it provided the code to the Minister in accordance with this section;

(h) the name, professional qualifications and term of office of each of its directors, with any change in the board of director's composition that has occurred since the last time it provided the names of its directors to the Minister in accordance with this section;

(i) the minutes of each meeting of its board of directors that has been held during its last completed fiscal year;

(j) the name, terms of reference and composition of each of its executive committees, if any, as well as the name and professional qualifications of each of their members;

(k) the minutes of each meeting of its executive committees, if any, that has been held during its last completed fiscal year;

(l) any sums disbursed to its directors and officers as remuneration and any cash benefits or financial advantages granted to them, during its last completed fiscal year;

(m) the name and membership number of each of its members;

(n) the rules that govern the conduct of its members, with an indication of any changes that have been made to those rules since the last time it provided them to the Minister in accordance with this section;

(o) information, made anonymous, concerning the number and type of any complaints that it received during its last completed fiscal year in relation to the conduct of any of its members, including the distribution of those complaints by type, country of origin and, in the case of Canada, province of origin, the measures that it took to deal with those complaints and any decision that it rendered and sanction that it imposed as a consequence of those complaints;

(p) information in aggregate form, made anonymous, concerning any investigation by it, during its last completed fiscal year, into the conduct of any of its members if that conduct likely constitutes a breach of their professional or ethical obligations;

(q) the amount of any fees charged by it to its members, including its membership fees, with any change in those fees that has occurred since the last time it provided that information to the Minister in accordance with this section;

(r) the nature and amount of its entertainment, hospitality, meal, transport, accommodation, training and incidental expenses, if any, that were incurred by any person during its last completed fiscal year, as well as the name of the person;

(s) any training requirements that it imposes on its members; and

(t) information concerning any training made available by it to its members during its last completed fiscal year, including

    (i) the professional qualifications required of trainers,

    (ii) the identification of the mandatory courses from among those on offer,

    (iii) any evaluation methods and applicable completion standards, and

    (iv) the name and professional qualifications of each trainer.

(2) **Special requirement** — If the ability of the designated body to govern its members in a manner that is in the public interest so that they provide professional and ethical representation and advice appears to be compromised, the body must provide to the Minister — within 10 business days after the day on which the body receives from the Minister a notice indicating the existence of such a situation and setting out any information or documents from among those referred to in paragraphs (1)(c) to (t) that are necessary to assist the Minister to evaluate whether the body governs its members in a manner that is in the public interest so that they provide professional and ethical representation and advice — the documents or information set out in the notice.

(3) **Redacted information** — The information and documents set out in subsections (1) and (2) may be provided in redacted form to exclude from them information that is subject to litigation privilege or solicitor-client privilege or, in civil law, to immunity from disclosure or professional secrecy of advocates and notaries.

(4) **Electronic means** — Despite subsection 13(1), any information or document set out in subsection (1) or (2) may be provided to the Minister by electronic means.

SOR/2012-77, s. 1

PART 3 — INADMISSIBILITY

14. Application of par. 34(1)(c) of the Act — For the purpose of determining whether a foreign national or permanent resident is inadmissible under paragraph 34(1)(c) of the Act, if either the following determination or decision has been rendered, the findings of fact set out in that determination or decision shall be considered as conclusive findings of fact:

(a) a determination by the Board, based on findings that the foreign national or permanent resident has engaged in terrorism, that the foreign national or permanent resident is a person referred to in section F of Article 1 of the Refugee Convention; or

(b) a decision by a Canadian court under the *Criminal Code* concerning the foreign national or permanent resident and the commission of a terrorism offence.

15. Application of par. 35(1)(a) of the Act — For the purpose of determining whether a foreign national or permanent resident is inadmissible under paragraph 35(1)(a) of the Act, if any of the following decisions or the following determination has been rendered, the findings of fact set out in that decision or determination shall be considered as conclusive findings of fact:

(a) a decision concerning the foreign national or permanent resident that is made by any international criminal tribunal that is established by resolution of the Security Council of the United Nations, or the International Criminal Court as defined in the *Crimes Against Humanity and War Crimes Act*;

(b) a determination by the Board, based on findings that the foreign national or permanent resident has committed a war crime or a crime against humanity, that the foreign national or permanent resident is a person referred to in section F of Article 1 of the Refugee Convention; or

(c) a decision by a Canadian court under the *Criminal Code* or the *Crimes Against Humanity and War Crimes Act* concerning the foreign national or permanent resident and a war crime or crime against humanity committed outside Canada.

16. Application of paragraph 35(1)(b) of the Act — For the purposes of paragraph 35(1)(b) of the Act, a prescribed senior official is a person who, by virtue of the position they hold or held, is or was able to exert significant influence on the exercise of government power or is or was able to benefit from their position, and includes

(a) heads of state or government;

(b) members of the cabinet or governing council;

(c) senior advisors to persons described in paragraph (a) or (b);

(d) senior members of the public service;

(e) senior members of the military and of the intelligence and internal security services;

(f) ambassadors and senior diplomatic officials; and

(g) members of the judiciary.

SOR/2016-136, s. 2

Case Law

Segasayo v. Canada (Minister of Citizenship & Immigration) (2010), 89 Imm. L.R. (3d) 7, 2010 FC 173, 2010 CarswellNat 323, 2010 CarswellNat 324 — The applicant was Rwanda's ambassador to Canada from 1991 to 1995. After the new government in Rwanda recalled him, he and his family applied for and were given refugee status by the Immigration and Refugee Board in 1996. He submitted that as a member of the Hutu intelligentsia and as ambassador to Canada appointed by the former government he feared persecution and reprisal by the new Tutsi government. He is now subject to a deportation order because he was found inadmissible to Canada for violating human or international rights. He sought judicial review of that decision. The Board determined that the applicant was a person described in s. 35(1)(a) of IRPA. The Member was of the view that the deeming provision in s. 16 of the Regulations created an irrebuttable presumption that an ambassador in the service of a government on the Minister's list was inadmissible on the grounds of violating human or international rights. In other words, once it was shown that the applicant was the ambassador of the government designated by the Minister (facts that the applicant had never disputed), then he was inadmissible and had no defence based on lack of complicity in crimes against humanity or human rights violations. The member also dismissed the argument that the provisions in question were unconstitutional as violating s. 7 of the *Canadian Charter of Rights and Freedoms*. The court upheld the Board's decision that the applicant was inadmissible, dismissed his *Charter* argument and dismissed the application for judicial review.

The following question was certified:

> Are ss. 35(1) of the *Immigration and Refugee Protection Act* and 16 of the *Immigration and Refugee Protection Regulations* in accordance with the principles stated by the Supreme Court in *Singh v. Canada (Minister of Citizenship & Immigration)*, [1985] 1 S.C.R. 177 and *Charkaoui v. Canada (Citizenship & Immigration)* (2007), 59 Imm. L.R. (3d) 1, and with s. 7 of the *Canadian Charter of Rights and Freedoms* when a person targeted by those provisions had already obtained the refugee or protected person status and does not have the right to defend him/herself against the allegations made against him/her under those provisions?

Sungu c. Canada (Ministre de la Citoyenneté & de l'Immigration) (2002), 26 Imm. L.R. (3d) 242, [2003] 3 F.C. 192, 2002 CarswellNat 3326, 2002 CarswellNat 4178, 2002 FCT 1207, 230 F.T.R. 67 (T.D.) — The male applicant was an elected deputy or member of Parliament for the city of Kinshasa in the Congo from 1982 to 1987. From 1987 to 1990 he remained an active but unpaid cadre within the MPR as an honorary deputy and member of a political judicial committee. The applicant participated in foreign missions to Brussels, France and Portugal as well as participating, while he was a deputy, in a sub-commission on national defence and security. The panel determined that the applicant had not demonstrated a well-founded fear of persecution, that his testimony lacked credibility and that he was excluded from refugee protection pursuant to para. 1(F)(a) of the Convention because of his complicity with the Mobutu regime and crimes against humanity that were committed by that regime. The position of deputy or member of Parliament is not listed in s. 16 of the Regulations. Deputies are not persons who, by virtue of the position they hold or held, are or were necessarily persons able to exert significant influence on the exercise of governmental power. This does not exclude a situation in which such influence could be established in light of the evidence, where appropriate. There is no evidence to show that the applicant, as a deputy, participated in the promotion or preparation of laws supporting the criminal objectives of the Mobutu regime.

17. Prescribed period — For the purposes of paragraph 36(3)(c) of the Act, the prescribed period is five years

(a) after the completion of an imposed sentence, in the case of matters referred to in paragraphs 36(1)(b) and (2)(b) of the Act, if the person has not been convicted of a subsequent offence other than an offence designated as a contravention under the *Contraventions Act* or an offence under the *Young Offenders Act*; and

(b) after committing an offence, in the case of matters referred to in paragraphs 36(1)(c) and (2)(c) of the Act, if the person has not been convicted of a subsequent offence other than an offence designated as a contravention under the *Contraventions Act* or an offence under the *Young Offenders Act*.

18. (1) Rehabilitation — For the purposes of paragraph 36(3)(c) of the Act, the class of persons deemed to have been rehabilitated is a prescribed class.

(2) Members of the class — The following persons are members of the class of persons deemed to have been rehabilitated:

(a) persons who have been convicted outside Canada of no more than one offence that, if committed in Canada, would constitute an indictable offence under an Act of Parliament, if all of the following conditions apply, namely,

(i) the offence is punishable in Canada by a maximum term of imprisonment of less than 10 years,

(ii) at least 10 years have elapsed since the day after the completion of the imposed sentence,

(iii) the person has not been convicted in Canada of an indictable offence under an Act of Parliament,

(iv) the person has not been convicted in Canada of any summary conviction offence within the last 10 years under an Act of Parliament or of more than one summary conviction offence before the last 10 years, other than an offence designated as a contravention under the *Contraventions Act* or an offence under the *Youth Criminal Justice Act*,

(v) the person has not within the last 10 years been convicted outside Canada of an offence that, if committed in Canada, would constitute an offence under an Act of Parliament, other than an offence designated as a contravention under the *Contraventions Act* or an offence under the *Youth Criminal Justice Act*,

(vi) the person has not before the last 10 years been convicted outside Canada of more than one offence that, if committed in Canada, would constitute a summary conviction offence under an Act of Parliament, and

(vii) the person has not committed an act described in paragraph 36(2)(c) of the Act;

(b) persons convicted outside Canada of two or more offences that, if committed in Canada, would constitute summary conviction offences under any Act of Parliament, if all of the following conditions apply, namely,

(i) at least five years have elapsed since the day after the completion of the imposed sentences,

(ii) the person has not been convicted in Canada of an indictable offence under an Act of Parliament,

(iii) the person has not within the last five years been convicted in Canada of an offence under an Act of Parliament, other than an offence designated as a contravention under the *Contraventions Act* or an offence under the *Youth Criminal Justice Act*,

(iv) the person has not within the last five years been convicted outside Canada of an offence that, if committed in Canada, would constitute an offence under an Act of Parliament, other than an offence designated as a contravention under the *Contraventions Act* or an offence under the *Youth Criminal Justice Act*,

(v) the person has not before the last five years been convicted in Canada of more than one summary conviction offence under an Act of Parliament, other than an offence designated as a contravention under the *Contraventions Act* or an offence under the *Youth Criminal Justice Act*,

(vi) the person has not been convicted of an offence referred to in paragraph 36(2)(b) of the Act that, if committed in Canada, would constitute an indictable offence, and

(vii) the person has not committed an act described in paragraph 36(2)(c) of the Act; and

(c) persons who have committed no more than one act outside Canada that is an offence in the place where it was committed and that, if committed in Canada, would constitute an indictable offence under an Act of Parliament, if all of the following conditions apply, namely,

(i) the offence is punishable in Canada by a maximum term of imprisonment of less than 10 years,

(ii) at least 10 years have elapsed since the day after the commission of the offence,

(iii) the person has not been convicted in Canada of an indictable offence under an Act of Parliament,

(iv) the person has not been convicted in Canada of any summary conviction offence within the last 10 years under an Act of Parliament or of more than one summary conviction offence before the last 10 years, other than an offence designated as a contravention under the *Contraventions Act* or an offence under the *Youth Criminal Justice Act*,

(v) the person has not within the last 10 years been convicted outside of Canada of an offence that, if committed in Canada, would constitute an offence under an Act of Parliament, other than an offence designated as a contravention under the *Contraventions Act* or an offence under the *Youth Criminal Justice Act,*

(vi) the person has not before the last 10 years been convicted outside Canada of more than one offence that, if committed in Canada, would constitute a summary conviction offence under an Act of Parliament, and

(vii) the person has not been convicted outside of Canada of an offence that, if committed in Canada, would constitute an indictable offence under an Act of Parliament.

SOR/2004-167, s. 7

Case Law

Sun v. Canada (Minister of Citizenship & Immigration), 2011 FC 708, 2011 CarswellNat 3443, 2011 CarswellNat 2305 — The applicant's application for permanent residence as a skilled worker was refused on the basis of criminal inadmissibility pursuant to para. 36(1)(b) of IRPA. The applicant had been convicted of a criminal offence pursuant to article 268 of the *Korean Criminal Act*, namely, "death and injury by occupational gross negligence." The applicant had been driving with a blood-alcohol level of 0.12 percent when he crossed the centre line and collided with a truck, seriously injuring its passengers. As a result of the conviction, he paid a fine. The applicant had a clean criminal record otherwise. The applicant argued that he was deemed to be rehabilitated. It was agreed that more than 10 years had lapsed since his conviction and the payment of the fine when the officer reviewed his application and that he met all the conditions set out in para. 18(2)(a) of the Regulations except for subpara. 18(2)(a)(i), namely that the offence is punishable in Canada by a maximum term of imprisonment of *less than 10 years*, which is at the centre of the dispute. The only issue in this application is whether the term "not exceeding 10 years" in the *Criminal Code* falls within the maximum term of "less than 10 years" in s. 18 of the Regulations. The following was held to apply:

d) Serious criminality is defined at subs. 36(1) as including offences committed outside of Canada that could have been punishable by a maximum term of at least 10 years, meaning 10 years or more.

e) Subs. 249(3) of the *Criminal Code* provides for a term not exceeding 10 years, meaning 10 years or less.

f) Pursuant to paragraph 36(3)(c) of IRPA and s. 18 of the Regulations, the benefit of deemed rehabilitation only applies to offences punishable by a maximum of less than 10 years, meaning up to nine years, 364 days.

18.1 (1) Prescribed class — The class of foreign nationals who are inadmissible solely on the basis of having been convicted in Canada of two or more offences that may only be prosecuted summarily, under any Act of Parliament, is a prescribed class for the application of paragraph 36(2)(a) of the Act.

(2) Exemption — A member of the class prescribed in subsection (1) is exempt from the application of paragraph 36(2)(a) of the Act if it has been at least five years since the day after the completion of the imposed sentences.

SOR/2004-167, s. 8

607

19. Transborder crime — For the purposes of paragraph 36(2)(d) of the Act, indictable offences under the following Acts of Parliament are prescribed:

    (a) the *Criminal Code*;

    (b) the *Immigration and Refugee Protection Act*;

    (c) the *Firearms Act*;

    (d) the *Customs Act*; and

    (e) the *Controlled Drugs and Substances Act*.

20. Assessment of inadmissibility on health grounds — An officer shall determine that a foreign national is inadmissible on health grounds if an assessment of their health condition has been made by an officer who is responsible for the application of sections 29 to 34 and the officer concluded that the foreign national's health condition is likely to be a danger to public health or public safety or might reasonably be expected to cause excessive demand.

21. Financial reasons — Protected persons within the meaning of subsection 95(2) of the Act are exempted from the application of section 39 of the Act.

22. Misrepresentation — Persons who have claimed refugee protection, if disposition of the claim is pending, and protected persons within the meaning of subsection 95(2) of the Act are exempted from the application of paragraph 40(1)(a) of the Act.

23. Prescribed circumstances — family members — For the purposes of paragraph 42(1)(a) of the Act, the prescribed circumstances in which the foreign national is inadmissible on grounds of an inadmissible non-accompanying family member are that

    (a) the foreign national is a temporary resident or has made an application for temporary resident status, an application for a permanent resident visa or an application to remain in Canada as a temporary or permanent resident; and

    (b) the non-accompanying family member is

        (i) the spouse of the foreign national, except where the relationship between the spouse and foreign national has broken down in law or in fact,

        (ii) the common-law partner of the foreign national,

        (iii) a dependent child of the foreign national and either the foreign national or an accompanying family member of the foreign national has custody of that child or is empowered to act on behalf of that child by virtue of a court order or written agreement or by operation of law, or

        (iv) a dependent child of a dependent child of the foreign national and the foreign national, a dependent child of the foreign national or any other accompanying family member of the foreign national has custody of that child or is empowered to act on behalf of that child by virtue of a court order or written agreement or by operation of law.

SOR/2014-269, ss. 1, 6(a)

Case Law

Anderson v. Canada (Minister of Citizenship and Immigration), 2015 FC 495, 2015 CarswellNat 1230, 2015 CarswellNat 3158 — The applicant sought judicial review of an officer's decision to refuse his request to waive the medical examination of his dependent son as part of the applicant's application for permanent residence in Canada as a member of the spouse or a common-law partner in Canada class. This decision ultimately lead to the refusal of the applicant's permanent resident application. The officer's decision was a reasonable one. The law is clear that family members must be admissible in order for the applicant to obtain permanent residence. Section 23 of the IRPA creates an exception when children are in the sole custody of a separated or former spouse. However, in order to benefit from the s. 23 exception, the applicant must provide proof of custody arrangements for non-accompanying children. In this case, the applicant had asserted, from the beginning, that he did not have custody of his children. However, the applicant did not make sufficient efforts to demonstrate that such an examination would be infeasible. For instance, the applicant did not engage the justice system in Jamaica to obtain court approval, nor did he make any effort to go to Jamaica and facilitate the examination in person. The application for judicial review was dismissed.

Nguyen v. Canada (Minister of Citizenship and Immigration), 2014 FC 1191, 2014 CarswellNat 7288, 2014 CarswellNat 5647 — The applicant sought judicial review of an officer's decision to refuse the applicant's request to waive the medical examination of her dependent son with respect to her application for permanent residence in Canada as a member of the spouse or common-law partner in Canada class. She advised Citizenship and Immigration Canada that her son was living with his father and not interested in coming to Canada. She provided a translated copy of her divorce judgment and a letter from a lawyer. CIC advised the applicant that she had provided conflicting information with respect to the custody of her son. On the one hand, she had stated that he was in the custody of his father, and on the other, she had provided documents indicating that he was looked after by his grandparents. Her counsel wrote to advise that the son was with the biological father who had refused to allow the medical examination and asked that the medical examination be waived as there may be a need for the son to come to Canada in the future.

The intention and requirements of the Act are to compel all family members to undergo a medical examination, and the focus is on whether, in this fact scenario, the principal applicant had exhausted all reasonable avenues to have her dependent child examined. The applicant did not provide sufficient proof that she could not make her son available for examination. She did not provide evidence that the divorce judgment had ever been amended; evidence from her ex-husband that he refused to allow the son to undergo the medical examination (or any sworn statements speaking to these issues); evidence that she could not have visited Vietnam and taken her son to a medical examination; evidence that she legally required the consent of her ex-husband for her parents to take her son for the examination, or an explanation for why her parents did not take her son for the examination. The officer's decision was completely reasonable. The application for judicial review was dismissed.

Zhang v. Canada (Minister of Citizenship & Immigration) (2012), 13 Imm. L.R. (4th) 95, 2012 FC 1093, 2012 CarswellNat 3526, 2012 CarswellNat 4190, [2012] F.C.J. No. 1179; affirmed (2013), 446 N.R. 382, 2013 FCA 168, 2013 CarswellNat 2197, [2013] F.C.J. No. 764 — Despite the fact that the applicant's son, who was diagnosed with "moderate mental retardation," was a non-accompanying family member, the applicant and the other

IRP Regulations

accompanying family members were deemed to be inadmissible in conformity with para. 38(1)(c) and s. 42 of IRPA on the grounds that the son suffers from a health condition that might reasonably be expected to cause excessive demand on health or social services. There was no clear undertaking by the applicant that he would not sponsor the son, while it was even questionable whether an applicant seeking the issuance of a visa to gain permanent resident status, can legally renounce to the right to sponsor a non-accompanying family member. It was up to the applicant to discharge the onus by providing a credible plan for mitigating the excessive demand on social services in Canada. The fact that the son would apparently be taken care of in China by an aunt did not really respond to the visa officer's concern that nothing prevented the applicant, in the future, from sponsoring his son once he himself gained permanent resident status. Accordingly, it was reasonable to require the applicant to submit an individualized plan addressing the problem of excessive demand on social services in Canada, considering that the son could be sponsored in the future without regard to his inadmissibility. The application for judicial review was dismissed and the following question was certified:

> In the aftermath of *Hilewitz v. Canada (Minister of Citizenship & Immigration*, 2005 SCC 57, when an applicant is required to submit an individualized plan to ensure that his family member's admission will not cause an excessive demand on social services, is it acceptable for this applicant to state that the inadmissible family member will not be accompanying him to Canada, considering that he could be sponsored in the future without regard to his inadmissibility pursuant to paragraph 38(2) of the *Immigration and Refugee Protection Act*?

The Federal Court of Appeal dismissed the applicant's appeal because the certified question did not meet the test for certification and could not be determinative of the appeal. The Court of Appeal affirmed that pursuant to subpara. 23(b)(iii) of the regulations, in circumstances where a child is in the legal custody of someone other than an applicant or an accompanying family member of an applicant, a visa officer might conclude that the child's inadmissibility does not render the applicant inadmissible.

24. Exception to excessive demand — **For the purposes of subsection 38(2) of the Act, a foreign national who has been determined to be a member of the family class is exempted from the application of paragraph 38(1)(c) of the Act if they are**

    (a) in respect of the sponsor, their conjugal partner, their dependent child or a person referred to in paragraph 117(1)(g); or

    (b) in respect of the spouse, common-law partner or conjugal partner of the sponsor, their dependent child.

SOR/2005-61, s. 2

PART 4 — PROCEDURES

DIVISION 1 — VISA ISSUANCE

25. When unenforced removal order — **A visa shall not be issued to a foreign national who is subject to an unenforced removal order.**

25.1 (1) General rule — one-step process — For the purposes of determining whether a child is a dependent child, the lock-in date for the age of a child of a person who is a member of any of the classes set out in these Regulations, other than in those cases referred to in subsections (2) to (9), and who makes an application under Division 5, 6 or 7 of Part 5 is the date on which the application is made.

(2) **Certificat de sélection — distressful situation** — For the purposes of determining whether a child is a dependent child, the lock-in date for the age of a child of a person who is referred to in section 71, to whom a *Certificat de sélection du Québec* has been issued declaring that that person is in a particularly distressful situation and who makes an application under Division 6 of Part 5 is the date on which the application for selection was made to Quebec.

(3) **Quebec economic candidate** — For the purposes of determining whether a child is a dependent child, the lock-in date for the age of a child of a person who is referred to in section 86, 96, 99 or 101, to whom a *Certificat de sélection du Québec* has been issued and who makes an application under Division 6 of Part 5 is the date on which the application for selection was made to Quebec.

(4) **Provincial nominee** — For the purposes of determining whether a child is a dependent child, the lock-in date for the age of a child of a person who is a member of the provincial nominee class, who is nominated by the province and who makes an application under Division 6 of Part 5 is the date on which the application for nomination was made to the province.

(5) **Live-in caregiver** — For the purposes of determining whether a child is a dependent child, the lock-in date for the age of a child of a person who is a member of the live-in caregiver class and who makes an application under Division 6 of Part 5 is the date on which the initial application for a work permit as a live-in caregiver was made.

(6) **Sponsorship — refugee** — For the purposes of determining whether a child is a dependent child, the lock-in date for the age of a child of a person who is referred to in paragraph 139(1)(h), who makes an application under Division 6 of Part 5 and in respect of whom an undertaking application is made by a sponsor who meets the requirements of sponsorship set out in section 158 is the date on which the undertaking application was made to Quebec.

(7) **Refugee** — For the purposes of determining whether a child is a dependent child, the lock-in date for the age of a child of a person who submits an application for a permanent resident visa under Division 1 of Part 8 along with one of the referrals set out in section 140.3 is the date on which the referral was made.

(8) **Family member who does not accompany applicant** — For the purposes of determining whether a child who submits an application under paragraph 141(1)(b) is the dependent child of a person who has submitted an application under paragraph 139(1)(b), the lock-in date for the age of that child is the date on which that person submitted the application.

(9) **Refugee protection** — For the purposes of determining whether a child is a dependent child, the lock-in date for the age of a child of a person who has submitted a claim for refugee protection inside Canada under subsection 99(3) of the Act,

who has acquired protected person status and who has made an application for permanent residence is the date on which the claim for refugee protection was made.

SOR/2014-133, s. 2

DIVISION 1.1 — ISSUANCE OF ELECTRONIC TRAVEL AUTHORIZATION

[Heading added SOR/2015-77, s. 4.]

25.2 Electronic travel authorization not to be issued — An electronic travel authorization shall not be issued to a foreign national who is subject to an unenforced removal order.

SOR/2015-77, s. 4

DIVISION 2 — AUTHORIZATION TO ENTER CANADA

26. Designation of ports of entry — The Minister may, on the basis of the following factors, designate a place as a port of entry as well as the port of entry's dates and hours of operation:

(a) the frequency or anticipated frequency of persons arriving from abroad in the area under consideration;

(b) the need for the Department's services in that area;

(c) the operational requirements of commercial transporters; and

(d) administrative arrangements with other departments or agencies of the Government of Canada.

27. (1) Obligation on entry — Unless these Regulations provide otherwise, for the purpose of the examination required by subsection 18(1) of the Act, a person must appear without delay before an officer at a port of entry.

(2) Seeking entry at a place other than a port of entry — Unless these Regulations provide otherwise, a person who seeks to enter Canada at a place other than a port of entry must appear without delay for examination at the port of entry that is nearest to that place.

(3) Refused entry elsewhere — For the purposes of section 18 of the Act, every person who has been returned to Canada as a result of the refusal of another country to allow that person entry is a person seeking to enter Canada.

DIVISION 3 — CONDUCT OF EXAMINATION

General

28. Examination — For the purposes of subsection 15(1) of the Act, a person makes an application in accordance with the Act by

(a) submitting an application in writing;

(b) seeking to enter Canada;

(c) seeking to transit through Canada as provided in section 35; or

(d) making a claim for refugee protection

29. Medical examination — For the purposes of paragraph 16(2)(b) of the Act, a medical examination includes any or all of the following:

(a) physical examination;

(b) mental examination;

(c) review of past medical history;

(d) laboratory test;

(e) diagnostic test; and

(f) medical assessment of records respecting the applicant.

30. (1) Exemptions from medical examination requirement — For the purposes of paragraph 16(2)(b) of the Act, the following foreign nationals are exempt from the requirement to submit to a medical examination:

(a) foreign nationals other than

(i) subject to paragraph (g), foreign nationals who are applying for a permanent resident visa or applying to remain in Canada as a permanent resident, as well as their family members, whether accompanying or not,

(ii) foreign nationals who are seeking to work in Canada in an occupation in which the protection of public health is essential,

(iii) foreign nationals who

(A) are seeking to enter Canada or applying for renewal of their work or study permit or authorization to remain in Canada as a temporary resident for a period in excess of six consecutive months, including an actual or proposed period of absence from Canada of less than 14 days, and

(B) have resided or stayed for a period of six consecutive months, at any time during the one-year period immediately preceding the date that they sought entry or made their application, in an area that the Minister determines, after consultation with the Minister of Health, has a higher incidence of serious communicable disease than Canada,

(iv) foreign nationals who an officer, or the Immigration Division, has reasonable grounds to believe are inadmissible under subsection 38(1) of the Act,

(v) foreign nationals who claim refugee protection in Canada, and

(vi) foreign nationals who are seeking to enter or remain in Canada and who may apply to the Minister for protection under subsection 112(1) of the Act, other than foreign nationals who have not left Canada since their claim for refugee protection or application for protection was rejected;

(b) a person described in paragraph 186(b) who is entering or is in Canada to carry out official duties, unless they seek to engage or continue in secondary employment in Canada;

(c) a family member of a person described in paragraph 186(b), unless that family member seeks to engage or continue in employment in Canada;

(d) a member of the armed forces of a country that is a designated state as defined in the *Visiting Forces Act*, who is entering or is in Canada to carry out official duties, other than a person who has been designated as a civilian component of those armed forces, unless that member seeks to engage or continue in secondary employment in Canada;

(e) a family member of a protected person, if the family member is not included in the protected person's application to remain in Canada as a permanent resident;

(f) a non-accompanying family member of a foreign national who has applied for refugee protection outside Canada; and

(g) a foreign national who has applied for permanent resident status and is a member of the live-in caregiver class.

(2) **Subsequent examination** — Every foreign national who has undergone a medical examination as required under paragraph 16(2)(b) of the Act must submit to a new medical examination before entering Canada if, after being authorized to enter and remain in Canada, they have resided or stayed for a total period in excess of six months in an area that the Minister determines, after consultation with the Minister of Health, has a higher incidence of serious communicable disease than Canada.

(2.1) [Repealed SOR/2012-154, s. 3.]

(3) **Medical certificate** — Every foreign national who must submit to a medical examination, as required under paragraph 16(2)(b) of the Act, and who seeks to enter Canada must hold a medical certificate — based on the most recent medical examination to which they were required to submit under that paragraph and which took place within the previous 12 months — that indicates that their health condition is not likely to be a danger to public health or public safety and, unless subsection 38(2) of the Act applies, is not reasonably expected to cause excessive demand.

(4) [Repealed SOR/2012-154, s. 3.]

SOR/2004-167, s. 9; SOR/2010-78, s. 1; SOR/2012-154, s. 3

Case Law

Rarama v. Canada (Minister of Citizenship & Immigration) (2014), 22 Imm. L.R. (4th) 228, 2014 FC 60, 2014 CarswellNat 54, 2014 CarswellNat 359 — The applicant listed her daughter as a non-accompanying overseas dependant. Immigration advised the applicant that her daughter must be medically examined to ensure that she was not inadmissible. The applicant explained that due to a refusal to cooperate by her former husband, the applicant was unable to have her young daughter comply with this requirement. Immigration advised that without documentary evidence that the applicant's daughter was in the sole custody of another person, the medical examination was required and that failure to comply may result in a refusal of the application. The applicant asked Immigration to remove the daughter from her application so that it could continue to be processed. Immigration refused. Her application for permanent residence was subsequently refused. The applicant had provided a statutory declaration in advance of the refusal. Although the officer was not compelled to accept the statutory declaration as *de facto* evidence that the applicant's daughter was in the sole custody of her ex-husband, the officer was required to provide a reasonable basis upon which to refuse to accept that evidence. The court found the officer's refusal, without explanation, to accept the statutory declaration was unreasonable. Of significance was the fact that the applicant had unambiguously waived her right to sponsor her daughter at a later date. Furthermore, there was evidence before the officer that the applicant had started a new relationship with a new common-law spouse and had given birth to a child with her new spouse. The officer also had the applicant's Certificate of Divorce from an Ontario superior court as further evidence that the relationship with her former husband was concluded. The application was allowed and the decision set aside and the matter remitted for redetermination.

31. Public health — Before concluding whether a foreign national's health condition is likely to be a danger to public health, an officer who is assessing the foreign national's health condition shall consider

(a) any report made by a health practitioner or medical laboratory with respect to the foreign national;

(b) the communicability of any disease that the foreign national is affected by or carries; and

(c) the impact that the disease could have on other persons living in Canada.

32. Conditions — In addition to the conditions that are imposed on a foreign national who makes an application as a member of a class, an officer may impose, vary or cancel the following conditions in respect of any foreign national who is required to submit to a medical examination under paragraph 16(2)(b) of the Act:

(a) to report at the specified times and places for medical examination, surveillance or treatment; and

(b) to provide proof, at the specified times and places, of compliance with the conditions imposed.

SOR/2012-154, s. 4

33. Public safety — Before concluding whether a foreign national's health condition is likely to be a danger to public safety, an officer who is assessing the foreign national's health condition shall consider

(a) any reports made by a health practitioner or medical laboratory with respect to the foreign national; and

(b) the risk of a sudden incapacity or of unpredictable or violent behaviour of the foreign national that would create a danger to the health or safety of persons living in Canada.

34. Excessive demand — Before concluding whether a foreign national's health condition might reasonably be expected to cause excessive demand, an officer who is assessing the foreign national's health condition shall consider

(a) any reports made by a health practitioner or medical laboratory with respect to the foreign national; and

(b) any condition identified by the medical examination.

Case Law

Hossain v. Canada (Minister of Citizenship & Immigration), 2006 CarswellNat 993, 2006 FC 475 — The applicant's application for permanent residence under the skilled worker category was refused on the basis that he was found to have a medical condition that "would or might reasonably be expected to place excessive demands on health or social services in Canada, and thus would render him inadmissible to Canada under s. 38(1) of the IRPA." The applicant had had a kidney transplant performed in 2000 because of renal failure. His renal function was currently normal and he took medication on a daily basis. These medications were expensive and would have been paid by the provincial health care.

The applicant had personally borne all of the medical costs since his transplant and was ready to undertake not to claim medical costs from Canadian health care services relating to his current medical condition. He also was prepared to undertake to subscribe to all necessary private insurance coverage and he provided evidence of more than C$200,000 of savings that would enable him to meet the costs of his medicines from his own financial sources. There was no indication that the medical officer or the visa officer considered the applicant's offer to assume the cost of the medication relating to his current medical condition or his personal financial situation.

The decision was set aside and referred back to ensure that the next decision maker considered the financial situation of the applicant.

Hilewitz v. Canada (Minister of Citizenship & Immigration), [2005] 2 S.C.R. 706, 50 Imm. L.R. (3d) 40, 33 Admin. L.R. (4th) 1, 340 N.R. 102, 259 D.L.R. (4th) 244, [2005] S.C.J. No. 58, 2005 CarswellNat 3234, 2005 CarswellNat 3235, 2005 SCC 57 — The appellant and another both applied for permanent residence, respectively, under the "investor" and "self-employed" classes set out in the *Immigration Act*. These categories require that applicants have substantial financial resources to qualify. Both qualified, but were denied admission because the intellectual disability of a dependent child "would cause or might reasonably be expected to cause excessive demands on . . . social services" in Canada, which made them inadmissible pursuant to s. 19(1)(a)(ii) of the former *Immigration Act*.

The visa officers' decisions were set aside by the Supreme Court of Canada. The Supreme Court of Canada concluded that the personal circumstances of the families of disabled dependants are relevant factors in an assessment of their anticipated impact on social services. Since the "investor" and "self-employed" categories under which the appellants were qualified for admission to Canada were, to a large extent, concerned with an individual's assets, it would be incongruous to interpret the legislation in such a way that the very assets that qualify these individuals for admission to Canada can simultaneously be ignored in determining the admissibility of their disabled children.

The applicants' ability and willingness to attenuate the burden on the public purse that would otherwise be created by their intellectually disabled children was a relevant factor in determining whether those children could reasonably be expected to cause excessive demands on Canada's social services. The fears were articulated in the rejections of the applications, such as possible bankruptcy, mobility, school closure or parental death, represent contingencies that could be raised in relation to any applicant. Using such contingencies to negate a family's genuine ability and willingness to absorb some of the burdens created by a child's disabilities anchors an applicant's admissibility to conjecture, not reality. The visa officers erred by confirming the medical officers' refusal to account for the potential impact of the families' willingness to assist. Moreover, the visa officers' failure to read the families' responses to the fairness letters sent to them meant that their decisions were not based on all the relevant available information.

[Note: Although decided under former legislation (the Immigration Act, *R.S.C. 1985, c. I-2) this decision may still be useful.]*

35. (1) Transit — **Subject to subsection (2), the following persons are not seeking to enter Canada but are making an application under subsection 15(1) of the Act to transit through Canada:**

> **(a) in airports where there are United States' in-transit preclearance facilities, in-transit preclearance passengers; and**

> **(b) in any airport, passengers who are arriving from any country and who are transiting to a country other than Canada and remain in a sterile transit area.**

(2) Obligatory examination — Any person seeking to leave a sterile transit area must appear immediately for examination.

36. Actions not constituting a complete examination — An inspection carried out aboard a means of transportation bringing persons to Canada or the questioning of persons embarking on or disembarking from a means of transportation, or the examination of any record or document respecting such persons before they appear for examination at a port of entry, is part of an examination but does not constitute a complete examination.

37. End of examination — The examination of a person who seeks to enter Canada, or who makes an application to transit through Canada, ends only when

> **(a) a determination is made that the person has a right to enter Canada, or is authorized to enter Canada as a temporary resident or permanent resident, the person is authorized to leave the port of entry at which the examination takes place and the person leaves the port of entry;**

> **(b) if the person is an in-transit passenger, the person departs from Canada;**

> **(c) the person is authorized to withdraw their application to enter Canada and an officer verifies their departure from Canada; or**

> **(d) a decision in respect of the person is made under subsection 44(2) of the Act and the person leaves the port of entry.**

Alternative Means of Examination

38. Means — For the purposes of subsection 18(1) of the Act, the following persons may — unless otherwise directed by an officer — be examined by the means indicated as alternative to appearing for an examination by an officer at a port of entry:

(a) persons who have previously been examined and hold an authorization issued under section 11.1 of the *Customs Act*, in which case examination is effected by the presentation of the authorization by those persons at a port of entry;

(b) persons who are seeking to enter Canada at a port of entry where facilities are in place for automatic screening of persons seeking to enter Canada, in which case examination is performed by automatic screening;

(c) persons who leave Canada and proceed directly to a marine installation or structure to which the *Oceans Act* applies, and who return directly to Canada from the installation or structure without entering the territorial waters of a foreign state, in which case examination is conducted by an officer by telephone or other means of telecommunication;

(d) members of a crew of a ship that transports oil or liquid natural gas and that docks at a marine installation or structure to which the *Oceans Act* applies, for the purpose of loading oil or liquid natural gas, in which case examination is conducted by an officer by telephone or other means of telecommunication;

(e) members of a crew of a ship registered in a foreign country, other than members of a crew referred to in paragraph (d), in which case examination is conducted by an officer by telephone or other means of telecommunication;

(f) members of a crew of a ship registered in Canada, in which case examination is conducted by an officer by telephone or other means of telecommunication;

(g) citizens or permanent residents of Canada or the United States who are seeking to enter Canada at remote locations where no officer is assigned or where there are no means by which the persons may report for examination, in which case examination is conducted by an officer by telephone or other means of telecommunication; and

(h) citizens or permanent residents of Canada or the United States who seek to enter Canada at places, other than a port of entry, where no officer is assigned, in which case examination is conducted by an officer by telephone or other means of telecommunication.

Permitted Entry

39. Entry permitted — An officer shall allow the following persons to enter Canada following an examination:

(a) persons who have been returned to Canada as a result of a refusal of another country to allow them entry after they were removed from or otherwise left Canada after a removal order was made against them;

(b) persons returning to Canada under a transfer order made under the *Mutual Legal Assistance in Criminal Matters Act* and who, immediately before being transferred to a foreign state under the transfer order, were subject to an unenforced removal order; and

(c) persons who are in possession of refugee travel papers issued to them by the Minister that are valid for return to Canada.

SOR/2015-46, s. 1(a)

Conduct of Examination Measures

40. (1) Direction to leave — Except in the case of protected persons within the meaning of subsection 95(2) of the Act and refugee protection claimants, an officer who is unable to examine a person who is seeking to enter Canada at a port of entry shall, in writing, direct the person to leave Canada.

(2) Service — A copy of the direction shall be served on the person as well as on the owner or person in control of the means of transportation, if any, that brought the person to Canada.

(3) Ceasing to have effect — The direction ceases to have effect when the person appears again at a port of entry and an officer proceeds to examine the person.

41. Direct back — Unless an authorization has been given under section 23 of the Act, an officer who examines a foreign national who is seeking to enter Canada from the United States shall direct them to return temporarily to the United States if

(a) no officer is able to complete an examination;

(b) the Minister is not available to consider, under subsection 44(2) of the Act, a report prepared with respect to the person; or

(c) an admissibility hearing cannot be held by the Immigration Division.

42. (1) Withdrawing application — Subject to subsection (2), an officer who examines a foreign national who is seeking to enter Canada and who has indicated that they want to withdraw their application to enter Canada shall allow the foreign national to withdraw their application and leave Canada.

(2) Exception — report — If a report is being prepared or has been prepared under subsection 44(1) of the Act in respect of a foreign national who indicates that they want to withdraw their application to enter Canada, the officer shall not allow the foreign national to withdraw their application or leave Canada unless the Minister does not make a removal order or refer the report to the Immigration Division for an admissibility hearing.

(3) Obligation to confirm departure — A foreign national who is allowed to withdraw their application to enter Canada must appear without delay before an officer at a port of entry to confirm their departure from Canada.

Application of Section 23 of the Act

43. (1) Conditions — An officer must impose the following conditions on every person authorized to enter Canada under section 23 of the Act:

(a) to report in person at the time and place specified for the completion of the examination or the admissibility hearing;

(b) to not engage in any work in Canada;

(c) to not attend any educational institution in Canada; and

(d) to report in person to an officer at a port of entry if the person withdraws their application to enter Canada.

(2) Effect of authorization to enter — A foreign national who is authorized to enter Canada under section 23 of the Act does not, by reason only of that authorization, become a temporary resident or a permanent resident.

Obligation to Appear at an Admissibility Hearing

44. (1) Class — The class of persons who are the subject of a report referred for an admissibility hearing under subsection 44(2) of the Act is prescribed as a class of persons.

(2) Members — The members of the class of persons who are the subject of a report referred for an admissibility hearing under subsection 44(2) of the Act are the persons who are the subject of such a report.

(3) Obligation — Every member of the class prescribed under subsection (1) must appear at their admissibility hearing before the Immigration Division if they are given notice of the hearing by the Division.

Deposits or Guarantees

45. (1) Deposit or guarantee required on entry — An officer can require, in respect of a person or group of persons seeking to enter Canada, the payment of a deposit or the posting of a guarantee, or both, to the Minister for compliance with any conditions imposed.

(2) Amount — The amount of the deposit or guarantee is fixed by an officer on the basis of

(a) the financial resources of the person or group;

(b) the obligations that result from the conditions imposed;

(c) the costs that would likely be incurred to locate and arrest the person or group, to detain them, to hold an admissibility hearing and to remove them from Canada; and

(d) in the case of a guarantee, the costs that would likely be incurred to enforce it.

46. Application   Sections 47 to 49 apply to deposits and guarantees required under subsection 44(3), section 56 and subsection 58(3) of the Act and section 45 of these Regulations.

47. (1) General requirements — A person who pays a deposit or posts a guarantee

(a) must not have signed or co-signed another guarantee that is in default; and

(b) must have the capacity to contract in the province where the deposit is paid or the guarantee is posted.

(2) Requirements if guarantee posted — A person who posts a guarantee must

(a) be a Canadian citizen or a permanent resident, physically present and residing in Canada;

(b) be able to ensure that the person or group of persons in respect of whom the guarantee is required will comply with the conditions imposed; and

(c) present to an officer evidence of their ability to fulfil the obligation arising from the guarantee.

(3) Money illegally obtained — If an officer has reasonable grounds to believe that a sum of money offered by a person as a deposit was not legally obtained, or that a sum of money that a person may be obliged to pay under a guarantee would not be legally obtained, the officer shall not allow that person to pay a deposit or post a guarantee.

48. (1) Conditions if guarantee posted — In addition to any other conditions that are imposed, the following conditions are imposed on a person or group of persons in respect of whom a guarantee is required:

(a) to provide the Department with the address of the person posting the guarantee and to advise the Department before any change in that address; and

(b) to present themself or themselves at the time and place that an officer or the Immigration Division requires them to appear to comply with any obligation imposed on them under the Act.

(2) Conditions if deposit paid — In addition to any other conditions that are imposed, the following conditions are imposed on a person or group of persons in respect of whom a deposit is required:

(a) to provide the Department with their address and to advise the Department before any change in that address; and

(b) to present themself or themselves at the time and place that an officer or the Immigration Division requires them to appear to comply with any obligation imposed on them under the Act.

IRP Regulations

49. (1) Acknowledgment of consequences of failure to comply with conditions — A person who pays a deposit or posts a guarantee must acknowledge in writing

(a) that they have been informed of the conditions imposed; and

(b) that they have been informed that non-compliance with any conditions imposed will result in the forfeiture of the deposit or enforcement of the guarantee.

(2) Receipt — An officer shall issue a receipt for the deposit or a copy of the guarantee, and a copy of the conditions imposed.

(3) Return of deposit — The Department shall return the deposit paid on being informed by an officer that the person or group of persons in respect of whom the deposit was required has complied with the conditions imposed.

(4) Breach of condition — A sum of money deposited is forfeited, or a guarantee posted becomes enforceable, on the failure of the person or any member of the group of persons in respect of whom the deposit or guarantee was required to comply with a condition imposed.

Case Law

Section 49(4)

Ferzly v. Canada (Minister of Citizenship & Immigration) (2007), 65 Imm. L.R. (3d) 293, 2007 CarswellNat 3440, 2007 CarswellNat 4426, 2007 FC 1064 — The applicant paid a cash deposit of $10,000 to secure the release of Mr. Bassolé from immigration detention. One of the conditions of release imposed by the Canadian Border Services Agency enforcement officer, was for Mr. Bassolé to report to the Pierre Elliott Trudeau Airport in Montreal, on June 28, 2006, to board a flight, bound for Burkina Faso. This condition was imposed on him as a result of the airline ticket which Mr. Bassolé had purchased and presented in order to secure his release from detention. Instead, Mr. Bassolé unilaterally chose to attempt to leave Canada, on June 28, 2006, via Ottawa, on a flight for Boston, United States, thereby breaching a term of his release. As a result of this breach, the director of the investigations and removal section of the CBSA declared the $10,000 deposit forfeited. The applicant sought judicial review of that decision. The standard of review for whether the director's decision to forfeit the security deposit was properly made is reasonableness. This decision is a question of mixed law and fact that attracts considerable deference by the court. The decision was made in good faith. There was no evidence of malice. The director considered several factors which are referenced in his decision. Under the circumstances, the decision was logical and reasonably sound as it was based on all of the evidence on the record before the Director. The decision was exercised in good faith, in accordance with the principles of natural justice; none of the considerations were irrelevant nor extraneous to the statutory purpose. Therefore, the court did not intervene.

Kang v. Canada (Minister of Public Safety & Emergency Preparedness), 2006 CarswellNat 1441, 2006 FC 652 — The applicant paid a cash deposit of $5,000 to secure her elderly mother's release from immigration detention. One of the release conditions was that the mother reside at her daughter's address "at all times." The mother was absent one day when Canada Border Services Agency officers visited to enquire about other family members. Several months later, after the mother had returned to Korea, the operations manager of the Greater Toronto Enforcement Centre declared the $5,000 deposit forfeited. The applicant sought judicial review of that decision. The decision to forfeit a cash bond should withstand scrutiny on the reasonableness standard.

The applicant contended that the notes contained the interviewing officer's conclusions rather than statements fairly attributable to her or her mother. A close reading of the notes suggests that what may appear to be admissions against interest by the applicant and her mother are no more than a repetition of the conclusion reached by the immigration officer based on what the applicant's son may have mistakenly told the officer during the visit to the applicant's house. The case, therefore, was complicated by the involvement of other members of the family subject to arrest and removal and the language barrier. There was no fault on the part of the immigration officers, but the possibility of confusion and error should have been considered by the operations manager when there was contradictory affidavit evidence before her. The manager's factual finding that the release condition had been breached was patently unreasonable in light of that evidence. Furthermore, no rational explanation was provided as to why the evidence did not provide a justification for not forfeiting the deposit. Accordingly the decision was found to be unreasonable and was overturned.

The current Act is silent on the question of ministerial discretion for the forfeiture of security deposits or performance bonds but provides, in s. 61, for the making of regulations for the application of Division 6 with respect to detention and release. It was clear from the evidence that the operations manager did not consider whether a lesser amount, including no amount, would be sufficient to satisfy the purpose of imposing the cash deposit, particularly where, as here, the subject of the release condition had returned to her country of origin. Further, it was impossible to ascertain from the brief reasons endorsed on the applicant's submissions or from the terse letter communicating the decision what factors the manager took into consideration in deciding that the bond should be forfeited. The court had no way to determine whether the manager relied upon considerations that were irrelevant or extraneous to the legislative purpose for which she exercised discretion. Accordingly, the manager's error in this regard amounted to another ground for concluding that the application must be granted and remitted for reconsideration by another officer.

Khalife v. Canada (Minister of Citizenship & Immigration), [2006] F.C.J. No. 293, 52 Imm. L.R. (3d) 267, 2006 CarswellNat 456, 2006 CarswellNat 1135, 2006 FC 221 — The statute and the Regulations say little about the decisions to impose and to forfeit a cash deposit. The authority to require a cash deposit is found in the IRPA at subs. 58(3). The manager's decision to forfeit the deposit appears to have been made in accordance with the principles in the Immigration Canada Enforcement Manual. The manager exercised his statutory discretion in good faith, in accordance with the principles of natural justice and did not rely upon considerations irrelevant or extraneous to the statutory purpose. Instead, the manager verified that the applicant was fully aware of the conditions of his release and determined that the applicant had in fact breached these terms. The manager received and considered the applicant's representations and then followed the direction provided by s. 49(4) of the Regulations and the Manual and determined on the merits that it was appropriate to forfeit only part of the applicant's deposit.

Tsang v. Canada (Minister of Public Safety & Emergency Preparedness), [2006] F.C.J. No. 576, 2006 CarswellNat 941, 2006 CarswellNat 2380, 2006 FC 474 — A regional director of the Canadian Border Services Agency decided that a performance bond granted by the applicant in the amount of $80,000 was forfeited. The bond had been provided for the release of the applicant's husband. He had violated a term of the release order and as a result was arrested. In consequence of this violation, the performance bond was forfeited. The decision to forfeit the $80,000 bond was set aside since the officer failed to appreciate that he had the discretion to make a decision that resulted in less than $80,000 being forfeited.

Documents Required

50. (1) Documents — permanent residents — In addition to the permanent resident visa required of a foreign national who is a member of a class referred to in subsection 70(2), a foreign national seeking to become a permanent resident must hold

(a) a passport, other than a diplomatic, official or similar passport, that was issued by the country of which the foreign national is a citizen or national;

(b) a travel document that was issued by the country of which the foreign national is a citizen or national;

(c) an identity or travel document that was issued by a country to non-national residents, refugees or stateless persons who are unable to obtain a passport or other travel document from their country of citizenship or nationality or who have no country of citizenship or nationality;

(d) a travel document that was issued by the International Committee of the Red Cross in Geneva, Switzerland, to enable and facilitate emigration;

(e) a passport or travel document that was issued by the Palestinian Authority;

(f) an exit visa that was issued by the Government of the Union of Soviet Socialist Republics to its citizens who were compelled to relinquish their Soviet nationality in order to emigrate from that country;

(g) a passport issued by the United Kingdom to a British National (Overseas), as a person born, naturalized or registered in Hong Kong;

(h) a passport issued by the Hong Kong Special Administrative Region of the People's Republic of China; or

(i) a passport issued by the United Kingdom to a British Subject.

(2) Exception — protected persons — Subsection (1) does not apply to a person who is a protected person within the meaning of subsection 95(2) of the Act and holds a permanent resident visa when it is not possible for the person to obtain a passport or an identity or travel document referred to in subsection (1).

(3) [Repealed SOR/2010-54, s. 1.]

SOR/2008-253, s. 1; SOR/2010-54, s. 1; SOR/2011-125, s. 1

Case Law

Andryanov v. Canada (Minister of Citizenship & Immigration) (2007), 60 Imm. L.R. (3d) 202, 2007 CarswellNat 429, 2007 FC 186 — The applicant and his wife attended a marriage interview at an inland immigration office. The officer who conducted the interview was satisfied the marriage was genuine. A considerable amount of correspondence then ensued between the applicant and the respondent's officials with respect to para. 50(1)(a) or (b) of the *Immigration and Refugee Protection Regulations*, namely that he provide a passport or a travel document issued by his country of origin. The result was a "Catch 22" situation. The respondent's officials refused to accept that the applicant was who he said he was without the passport, and the Russian Embassy refused to give him one without a request from the respondent's officials. The respondent's officials refused to make such a request as the onus to provide the passport rested on the applicant. As a result, the applicant's application was denied.

At no point in either the refusal letter or the FOSS notes was it explained how the officer reached his conclusion that the applicant had not provided a passport, a travel document or other suitable identification, or reasonable explanation. Though this conclusion was ultimately open to the officer, in light of the fact that the applicant provided his Seaman's Passport, internal identity card, his birth certificate, and his valid Russian driver's licence, in addition to multiple explanations, something further was required on the part of the officer to meet the adequacy test for his reasons. The officer had a duty to explain why the evidence and explanations were insufficient. At no time did CIC indicate that they had a concern regarding the validity of the Seaman's Passport. It had been issued by the country of which the applicant was a citizen, and it was subsisting at the time it was submitted.

It was also not clear why the applicant's internal identity card was not accepted as sufficient identification. Although CIC had concerns regarding whether or not the document was subsisting, in light of the fact it did not have an expiry date, the applicant clearly explained that the document was issued for life. Absent a conclusion on the part of CIC that either the document was fraudulent or that they did not believe the explanation of the applicant, it was not open to them to conclude that the document was not subsisting. No analysis was provided for CIC's conclusion that the document was not subsisting. Moreover, neither para. 50(1)(a) nor (b) include the words "valid and subsisting" as had been the case in subs. 46.4(8) of the former *Immigration Act*.

The decision to refuse the application on the ground that the applicant had been unable to provide a passport or suitable identifications to satisfy CIC officials as to his identity was unreasonable. The decision was set aside and was remitted for reconsideration.

50.1 (1) Designation of unreliable travel documents — The Minister may designate, individually or by class, passports or travel or identity documents that do not constitute reliable proof of identity or nationality.

(2) Factors — The Minister shall consider the following factors in determining whether to designate any passport or travel or identity document, or class of passport or travel or identity document, as not being reliable proof of identity or nationality:

(a) the adequacy of security features incorporated into the passport or document for the purpose of deterring its misuse or unauthorized alteration, reproduction or issuance; and

(b) information respecting the security or integrity of the process leading to the issuance of the passport or document.

(3) Effect of designation — A passport or travel or identity document that has been designated under subsection (1) is not a passport or travel or identity document for the purpose of subsection 50(1) or 52(1).

(4) Public notice — The Minister shall make available to the public a list of all passports or travel or identity documents designated under subsection (1).

SOR/2010-54, s. 2

51. Examination — permanent residents — A foreign national who holds a permanent resident visa and is seeking to become a permanent resident must, at the time of their examination,

  (a) inform the officer if

  (i) the foreign national has become a spouse or common-law partner or has ceased to be a spouse, common-law partner or conjugal partner after the visa was issued, or

  (ii) material facts relevant to the issuance of the visa have changed since the visa was issued or were not divulged when it was issued; and

  (b) establish that they and their family members, whether accompanying or not, meet the requirements of the Act and these Regulations.

[Editor's Note: SOR/2002-227, s. 354 provides that if a person makes an application before June 28, 2002, his or her non-accompanying dependent children, referred to in s. 352 of the Immigration and Refugee Protection Regulations, *SOR/2002-227 (the "new Regulations"), and his or her non-accompanying common-law partner shall not, for the purposes of that application, be considered inadmissible non-accompanying family members referred to in paragraph 42(a) of the new* Immigration and Refugee Protection Act, *S.C. 2001, c. 27, and are not subject to the requirements of paragraph 30(1)(a) or 51(b) of the new Regulations.]*

SOR/2008-253, s. 2

Case Law

Ivanov v. Canada (Minister of Citizenship & Immigration) (2006), 56 Imm. L.R. (3d) 56, 2006 CarswellNat 2335 (Imm. & Ref. Bd. (App. Div.)) — The appellant made an application for permanent residence as an independent in May 2001. At the time he disclosed that he had never been married and had no dependants. The application was successful and he was issued a permanent resident visa in June 2003. The appellant married his girlfriend on October 3, 2003. The appellant arrived in Canada on October 7, 2003. He disclosed his recent marriage to Canadian immigration officials upon his arrival in Toronto. At the time of his examination at Pearson Airport, he could not establish that his wife met the requirements of IRPA and the Regulations. His counsel wrote to the Canadian Embassy in Vienna in November 2003 advising that the immigration official at the port of entry had no objection regarding the release of the landed documents to the appellant subject to the appellant's wife meeting the medical and security requirements. The Embassy replied that there was no legal basis on which they were required to assess the wife against the admissibility criteria of IRPA. The appellant was issued an exclusion order on the basis that he was unable to establish at the time of his examination that his wife met the requirement of the Act and the Regulations. The appellant appealed the exclusion order.

The Appeal Board concluded that the exclusion order was valid in law. The appeal, however, was allowed under s. 67(1)(c) and the matter referred back to an immigration officer at the port of entry for reconsideration. The Board found that the appellant made an honest mistake in not informing the visa officer of his marriage prior to appearing for landing, but had disclosed the marriage immediately upon landing. As a result of the appellant's error, the Board concluded that he had suffered financial hardship upon his arrival in Canada, exhausting his savings because he could not legally work here. The Board found that the appellant had established humanitarian and compassionate considerations to warrant the granting of special relief in light of all the circumstances of the case. The Board directed that the department take all steps required to facilitate the examination of the appellant's wife and to provide the appellant with the necessary immigration documents to allow the appellant to attend before an immigration officer at a port of entry for reconsideration.

52. (1) Documents — temporary residents — In addition to the other requirements of these Regulations, a foreign national seeking to become a temporary resident must hold one of the following documents that is valid for the period authorized for their stay:

(a) a passport that was issued by the country of which the foreign national is a citizen or national, that does not prohibit travel to Canada and that the foreign national may use to enter the country of issue;

(b) a travel document that was issued by the country of which the foreign national is a citizen or national, that does not prohibit travel to Canada and that the foreign national may use to enter the country of issue;

(c) an identity or travel document that was issued by a country, that does not prohibit travel to Canada, that the foreign national may use to enter the country of issue and that is of the type issued by that country to non-national residents, refugees or stateless persons who are unable to obtain a passport or other travel document from their country of citizenship or nationality or who have no country of citizenship or nationality;

(d) a laissez-passer that was issued by the United Nations;

(e) a passport or travel document that was issued by the Palestinian Authority;

(f) a document that was issued by the Organization of American States and is entitled "Official Travel Document";

(g) a passport issued by the United Kingdom to a British Overseas Citizen;

(h) a passport issued by the United Kingdom to a British National (Overseas), as a person born, naturalized or registered in Hong Kong;

(i) a passport issued by the Hong Kong Special Administrative Region of the People's Republic of China; or

(j) a passport issued by the United Kingdom to a British Subject.

(1.1) [Repealed SOR/2003-260, s. 1(1).]

(2) Exceptions — Subsection (1) does not apply to

(a) citizens of the United States;

(b) persons seeking to enter Canada from the United States or St. Pierre and Miquelon who have been lawfully admitted to the United States for permanent residence;

(c) residents of Greenland seeking to enter Canada from Greenland;

(d) persons seeking to enter Canada from St. Pierre and Miquelon who are citizens of France and residents of St. Pierre and Miquelon;

(e) members of the armed forces of a country that is a designated state for the purposes of the *Visiting Forces Act* who are seeking entry in order to carry out official duties, other than persons who have been designated as a civilian component of those armed forces;

(f) persons who are seeking to enter Canada as, or in order to become, members of a crew of a means of air transportation and who hold an airline flight crew licence or crew member certificate issued in accordance with International Civil Aviation Organization specifications; or

(g) persons seeking to enter Canada as members of a crew who hold a seafarer's identity document issued under International Labour Organization conventions and are members of the crew of the vessel that carries them to Canada.

(3) [Repealed SOR/2010-54, s. 3.]

SOR/2003-197, s. 1; SOR/2003-260, s. 1; SOR/2010-54, s. 3; SOR/2011-125, s. 2

PART 5 — PERMANENT RESIDENTS

DIVISION 1 — PERMANENT RESIDENT CARDS

53. (1) Document indicating status — For the purposes of subsection 31(1) of the Act, the document indicating the status of a permanent resident is a permanent resident card that is

(a) provided by the Department to a person who has become a permanent resident under the Act; or

(b) issued by the Department, on application, to a permanent resident who has become a permanent resident under the Act or a permanent resident who obtained that status under the *Immigration Act*, chapter I-2 of the Revised Statutes of Canada, 1985, as it read immediately before the coming into force of section 31 of the Act.

(2) Property of Her Majesty — A permanent resident card remains the property of Her Majesty in right of Canada at all times and must be returned to the Department on the Department's request.

SOR/2004-167, s. 15

Case Law

Section 53(2)

Salewski v. Canada (Minister of Citizenship & Immigration) (2008), 74 Imm. L.R. (3d) 57, 83 Admin. L.R. (4th) 167, 2008 CarswellNat 2565, 2008 CarswellNat 5094, 2008 FC 899 — This was an application for judicial review of Citizenship and Immigration Canada's ("CIC") decision to recall and cancel the permanent resident card issued to the applicant. The applicant, a citizen of Germany, became a permanent resident of Canada in 1958. She left Canada in 1968 following the breakup of her marriage. There was no indication that the applicant returned to Canada at any time from 1968 to 2007. The applicant entered Canada in February 2007. It is not clear whether she entered Canada as a visitor or a permanent resident. However, on June 19, 2007, she sought to extend her visitor's status. She also made an application for a permanent resident card on June 4, 2007. During that application process she informed CIC that she had resided in Canada for 10 years (from 1958 to 1968); she had three Canadian born children; she returned to Germany in June 1968 for personal reasons and had remained there until February 5, 2007. She currently intends to remain in Canada to be with her children, who are residents and citizens of Canada, and she requested the card be issued on H&C grounds. The card was issued on August 16, 2007. In September 2007, CIC discovered that no residency determination had been made with respect to the applicant and according to CIC the residency card had been issued in error. The applicant was asked to return her card and she refused, and requested CIC's reasons for recalling the card.

Neither the Act nor the Regulations provide that a holder of a permanent resident card is to be provided an opportunity to make submissions before his or her card is recalled. Instead, Regulation 53(2) explicitly states that the card "remains the property of Her Majesty . . . at all times and must be retuned to the Department on the Department's request." There is a general common law principle, a duty of procedural fairness, lying on every public authority making an administrative decision which is not of a legislative nature and which affects the rights, privileges or interests of an individual. Where a permanent resident card has been issued in error, the canceling or rendering the card void is not beyond the jurisdiction of an officer or, more generally, the issuing department. It was not Parliament's intent to confer the authority upon CIC to recall a permanent resident card but to limit its power to cancel or render null a permanent resident card, especially where the card has been issued in error and the person to whom it was issued has refused to return it. The officer did not act beyond his jurisdiction by recalling, canceling and rendering void the applicant's permanent resident card in this case. The applicant has no entitlement to the card and she is simply refusing to return it. The application for judicial review was dismissed.

54. (1) Period of validity — Subject to subsection (2), a permanent resident card is valid for five years from the date of issue.

(2) Exception — A permanent resident card is valid for one year from the date of issue if, at the time of issue, the permanent resident

    (a) is subject to the process set out in paragraph 46(1)(b) of the Act;

    (b) is the subject of a report prepared under subsection 44(1) of the Act;

(c) is subject to a removal order made by the Minister under subsection 44(2) of the Act and the period for filing an appeal from the decision has not expired or, if an appeal is filed, there has been no final determination of the appeal; or

(d) is the subject of a report referred to the Immigration Division under subsection 44(2) of the Act and the period for filing an appeal from the decision of the Immigration Division has not expired or, if an appeal is filed, there has been no final determination of the appeal.

Case Law

Kuang v. Canada (Minister of Citizenship & Immigration), 2013 FC 663, 2013 CarswellNat 2164, 2013 CarswellNat 2511 — The applicant sought a mandamus order compelling Citizenship & Immigration Canada to release his permanent resident card. The applicant was employed by a Canadian business in China. He and his wife and son applied for travel documents and this application was refused as a visa officer found that the applicant's employment with the Canadian business was not genuine and he and his family had not satisfied their residency obligations under s. 28 of the Act for the five-year period under consideration. The family appealed the decision to the Immigration Appeal Division. The IAD determined that the applicant had satisfied s. 28 residency requirements. As such, the family maintained their permanent resident status. The family's applications for renewal of their PR cards were approved and CIC notified them that they were to pick up their cards in Vancouver. In Vancouver they were questioned by CBSA at the airport. The interview raised questions about the applicant's compliance with his residency obligation. The applicant and his wife were not given their PR cards at the CIC office in Vancouver. Instead, they were required to complete additional residency questionnaires and submit additional supporting documents regarding the applicant's overseas employment by the Canadian business. CIC is in the process of deciding whether to issue the applicant a five-year or one-year PR card along with a subsec. 44(1) report. The court concluded that a *mandamus* order would be premature in this case. The request for a *mandamus* order was denied. The following question was certified:

> In light of subsec.s 54(2) and 59(1) of the Immigration and Refugee Protection Regulations, SOR/2002-227, where an applicant is not the subject of a report prepared under subsec. 44(1) of the *Immigration and Refugee Protection Act*, SC 2001, c27 at the time he or she is sent a letter to pick up his or her permanent resident ("PR") card at a schedule time (the "pick up date"), but before the pick up date new concerns arise leading to an investigation under subsec. 44(1), is there a legal duty to issue a five-year PR card to the applicant on the pick up date even if the investigation under subsec. 44(1) is incomplete?

An appeal was discontinued by the appellant on August 28, 2014.

55. Delivery — **A permanent resident card shall only be provided or issued in Canada.**

56. (1) [Repealed SOR/2008-188, s. 1(1).]

(7) Application for a card — An application for a permanent resident card must be made in Canada and include

(a) an application form that contains the following information, namely,

(i) the applicant's name and date and place of birth,

(ii) the applicant's gender, height and eye colour,

(iii) the date on which and the place where the applicant became a permanent resident,

(iv) the applicant's mailing address,

(v) the addresses of all of the applicant's places of residence during the previous five years,

(vi) the names and addresses of the applicant's employers and educational institutions attended, during the previous five years,

(vii) the periods during the previous five years that the applicant was absent from Canada,

(viii) [Repealed SOR/2008-188, s. 1(2).]

(ix) whether a report under subsection 44(1) of the Act has been made in respect of the applicant or whether a decision was made outside of Canada that they have failed to comply with the residency obligation under section 28 of the Act, and

(x) whether the applicant has lost their permanent resident status or has been issued a removal order;

(b) [Repealed SOR/2008-188, s. 1(3).]

(c) a copy of

(i) any document described in paragraphs 50(1)(a) to (h) — or, if the applicant does not hold one of those documents, any document described in paragraphs 178(1)(a) and (b) — that is currently held by the applicant or was held by the applicant at the time they became a permanent resident,

(ii) a certificate of identity issued in Canada to the applicant by the Minister, or

(iii) refugee travel papers issued in Canada to the applicant by the Minister;

(d) a copy of

(i) the form IMM1000, entitled "Record of Landing", held by the applicant,

(ii) a provincial driver's license held by the applicant,

(iii) a photo-identity card held by the applicant and issued by a province,

(iv) a student card held by the applicant and issued by a provincially accredited college or university, or

(v) the most recent notice of assessment within the meaning of the *Income Tax Act* received in relation to the applicant's income tax return; and

(e) two identical photographs that

(i) were taken not more than 12 months before the application was made,

(ii) [Repealed SOR/2008-188, s. 1(4).]

(iii) are in black and white or colour on paper,

(iv) show a full front view of the applicant's head and shoulders and have a white background,

(v) have a view of the applicant's head that is at least 25 mm (one inch) and at most 35 mm (1.375 inches) in length,

(vi) show the applicant's face unobscured by sunglasses or any other object, and

(vii) have a dimension of 35 mm (1.375 inches) by 45 mm (1.75 inches).

(3) [Repealed SOR/2008-188, s. 1(5).]

SOR/2004-167, s. 16; SOR/2008-188, s. 1; SOR/2015-46, s. 1(b)

57. (1) Applicants — Subject to subsection (3), every person who applies for a permanent resident card must make and sign the application on their own behalf.

(2) Minor applicants 14 years of age or more — The application of a child who is 14 years of age or more but less than 18 years of age must be signed by the applicant and one of their parents unless

(a) a Canadian court has made another person responsible for the child, in which case that person must co-sign the application; or

(b) the parents are deceased, in which case the person legally responsible for the child must co-sign the application.

(3) Minor applicants less than 14 years of age — The application of a child who is less than 14 years of age must be signed by one of their parents unless

(a) a Canadian court has made another person responsible for the child, in which case that person must sign the application; or

(b) the parents are deceased, in which case the person legally responsible for the child must sign the application.

58. (1) Providing address within 180 days — In order to allow the Department to provide a permanent resident card, a permanent resident referred to in paragraph 53(1)(a) must provide to the Department, within 180 days after the day on which they become a permanent resident, their address in Canada and, on the request of an officer,

(a) a photograph of the permanent resident that satisfies the requirements of subparagraphs 56(2)(e)(i) and (iii) to (vii); and

(b) the signature of the permanent resident or, if the permanent resident is a child less than 14 years of age, the signature of one of their parents unless

(i) a Canadian court has made another person responsible for the child, in which case the signature of that person must be provided, or

(ii) the parents are deceased, in which case the signature of the person legally responsible for the child must be provided.

(2) Issuance after 180 days — If the permanent resident does not comply with subsection (1), they must make an application for a permanent resident card in accordance with section 56.

(3) Attendance required — A permanent resident who applies for a permanent resident card under section 56 must, in order to be provided with the card, attend at the time and place specified in a notice mailed by the Department. If the permanent resident fails to attend within 180 days after the Department first mails a notice, the card shall be destroyed and the applicant must make a new application in order to be issued a permanent resident card.

(4) Document verification — When attending in accordance with subsection (3), a permanent resident must produce the original documents copies of which were included in their application as required by paragraphs 56(2)(c) and (d).

SOR/2004-167, s. 17; SOR/2014-139, s. 2

59. (1) Issuance of new permanent resident card — An officer shall, on application, issue a new permanent resident card if

    (a) the applicant has not lost permanent resident status under subsection 46(1) of the Act;

    (b) the applicant has not been convicted under section 123 or 126 of the Act for an offence related to the misuse of a permanent resident card, unless a pardon has been granted and has not ceased to have effect or been revoked under the *Criminal Records Act*;

    (c) the applicant complies with the requirements of sections 56 and 57 and subsection 58(4); and

    (d) the applicant returns their last permanent resident card, unless the card has been lost, stolen or destroyed, in which case the applicant must produce all relevant evidence in accordance with subsection 16(1) of the Act.

(2) Issuance of new permanent resident card — effect — A previously issued permanent resident card is revoked on the issuance of a new permanent resident card.

SOR/2004-167, s. 18

Case Law

Kuang v. Canada (Minister of Citizenship & Immigration), 2013 FC 663, 2013 CarswellNat 2164, 2013 CarswellNat 2511 — The applicant sought a mandamus order compelling Citizenship & Immigration Canada ("CIC") to release his permanent resident card. The applicant was employed by a Canadian business in China. He and his wife and son applied for travel documents and this application was refused as a visa officer found that the applicant's employment with the Canadian business was not genuine and he and his family had not satisfied their residency obligations under s. 28 of the Act for the five-year period under consideration. The family appealed the decision to the Immigration Appeal Division. The IAD determined that the applicant had satisfied s. 28 residency requirements. As such, the family maintained their permanent resident status. The family's applications for renewal of their PR cards were approved and CIC notified them that they were to pick up their cards in Vancouver. In Vancouver they were questioned by

CBSA at the airport. The interview raised questions about the applicant's compliance with his residency obligation. The applicant and his wife were not given their PR cards at the CIC office in Vancouver. Instead, they were required to complete additional residency questionnaires and submit additional supporting documents regarding the applicant's overseas employment by the Canadian business. CIC is in the process of deciding whether to issue the applicant a five-year or one-year PR card along with a subsec. 44(1) report. The court concluded that a *mandamus* order would be premature in this case. The request for a *mandamus* order was denied. The following question was certified:

> In light of subsec.s 54(2) and 59(1) of the Immigration and Refugee Protection Regulations, SOR/2002-227, where an applicant is not the subject of a report prepared under subsec. 44(1) of the *Immigration and Refugee Protection Act*, SC 2001, c27 at the time he or she is sent a letter to pick up his or her permanent resident ("PR") card at a schedule time (the "pick up date"), but before the pick up date new concerns arise leading to an investigation under subsec. 44(1), is there a legal duty to issue a five-year PR card to the applicant on the pick up date even if the investigation under subsec. 44(1) is incomplete?

An appeal was discontinued by the appellant on August 28, 2014.

Khan v. Canada (Minister of Citizenship & Immigration) (2012), 15 Imm. L.R. (4th) 101, 2012 FC 1471, 2012 CarswellNat 4944, 2012 CarswellNat 5401 — The applicant was a permanent resident of Canada who had been issued a permanent resident card as proof of his status. PR cards are time limited and this application arises out of the applicant's failed attempt to renew his expired card. The PR card does not create or maintain one's status as a permanent resident: it merely serves as proof of that status. The applicant's application to obtain a replacement card was processed by CIC at its Case Processing Centre — Sydney (CPCS). He received a letter informing him that he could pick up his new PR card at CIC GTA Central. The letter also advised that all permanent residents of Canada are subject to a residency assessment at the time of distribution of their new PR card, and that an immigration officer would review his documents and may require additional information to determine his eligibility. The applicant went to CIC GTA Central on June 28, 2011, to pick up his new card where the CIC officer examined his former and current passport and asked why he had taken so long to pick up his new card. He told her that he had been in Pakistan for the birth of his daughter. He was then asked to list his absences in the five years preceding the appointment at CIC GTA and was advised that it appeared he did not meet the residency requirement and that she could not issue him the card. He protested saying that he thought the five-year period was from the date of his application, not the date when he picked up the card. The officer sent his file for investigation.

The court considered whether the CIC GTA Central representative acted lawfully in refusing to provide the applicant with his validly issued permanent resident card because the respondent was *functus officio* after granting the card. The court further considered whether the CIC GTA Central representative otherwise acted unlawfully since nothing in the Act mandated the review of the residency requirement when providing the card.

The court concluded that the Act requires that every permanent resident meet the residency obligation in every rolling five-year period. Therefore, although not required, it was open to the officer at CIC GTA Central to question whether the applicant met the residency obligation as at that date or as at any other earlier date. What was not open to her was to refuse to issue him the PR card once he had met the conditions set out in subsec.59(1) of the Regulations There was a refusal to acknowledge that the applicant was entitled to be issued his new card notwithstanding questions as to whether he had completed the residency obligation. Those questions could and should have been addressed later and, if it was determined that he had failed to meet the residency obligation, appropriate steps taken which would provide the applicant with appeal rights to the IAD from any adverse decision. The applicant was entitled to be placed back in the position he ought to have been on June 28, 2011, provided he produced the relevant original documents.

Although an application for a PR card must be made in Canada, there is no requirement in the Act that it must be issued to an applicant in Canada.

The court allowed the application for judicial review and directed the respondent to issue a new card to the applicant. The issuance of the card and the residency obligation are two distinct matters. The respondent is entitled to pursue an investigation as to whether the applicant has met the residency obligation if it continues to have any concerns in that regard. The court did not therefore order that the applicant was free from responding to inquiries made by the respondent in this respect.

The applicant was ordered to advise the respondent in writing within 30 days of the date of the order as to whether he is in Pakistan or Canada and to provide his current address.

The following question was certified:

> Who has the jurisdiction to make the final determination on the merits of an application for a permanent resident card application — CPCS who may authorize the production of the PR Card or the CIC local office whose mandate is to issue the PR Card pursuant to s. 59 of the Regulations?

60. Revocation — A permanent resident card is revoked if

(a) the permanent resident becomes a Canadian citizen or otherwise loses permanent resident status;

(b) the permanent resident card is lost, stolen or destroyed; or

(c) the permanent resident is deceased.

DIVISION 1.1 — COLLECTION AND DISCLOSURE OF INFORMATION
[Heading added SOR/2015-138, s. 1.]

60.1 (1) Collection of social insurance number — The Minister may collect the social insurance number of a permanent resident card applicant or a travel document applicant to verify that the applicant has complied with the obligation set out in section 28 of the Act.

(2) Disclosure of social insurance number — The Minister may disclose the social insurance number of the applicant to the Canada Revenue Agency for the purpose set out in subsection (1) if the Minister has entered into an arrangement with the Agency for the disclosure of that information.

SOR/2015-138, s. 1

DIVISION 2 — RESIDENCY OBLIGATION

61. (1) Canadian business — Subject to subsection (2), for the purposes of subparagraphs 28(2)(a)(iii) and (iv) of the Act and of this section, a Canadian business is

(a) a corporation that is incorporated under the laws of Canada or of a province and that has an ongoing operation in Canada;

(b) an enterprise, other than a corporation described in paragraph (a), that has an ongoing operation in Canada and

(i) that is capable of generating revenue and is carried on in anticipation of profit, and

(ii) in which a majority of voting or ownership interests is held by Canadian citizens, permanent residents, or Canadian businesses as defined in this subsection; or

(c) an organization or enterprise created under the laws of Canada or a province.

(2) Exclusion — For greater certainty, a Canadian business does not include a business that serves primarily to allow a permanent resident to comply with their residency obligation while residing outside Canada.

(3) Employment outside Canada — For the purposes of subparagraphs 28(2)(a)(iii) and (iv) of the Act, the expression "employed on a full-time basis by a Canadian business or in the public service of Canada or of a province" means, in relation to a permanent resident, that the permanent resident is an employee of, or under contract to provide services to, a Canadian business or the public service of Canada or of a province, and is assigned on a full-time basis as a term of the employment or contract to

(a) a position outside Canada;

(b) an affiliated enterprise outside Canada; or

(c) a client of the Canadian business or the public service outside Canada.

(4) Accompanying outside Canada — For the purposes of subparagraphs 28(2)(a)(ii) and (iv) of the Act and this section, a permanent resident is accompanying outside Canada a Canadian citizen or another permanent resident — who is their spouse or common-law partner or, in the case of a child, their parent — on each day that the permanent resident is ordinarily residing with the Canadian citizen or the other permanent resident.

(5) Compliance — For the purposes of subparagraph 28(2)(a)(iv) of the Act, a permanent resident complies with the residency obligation as long as the permanent resident they are accompanying complies with their residency obligation.

(6) Child — For the purposes of subparagraphs 28(2)(a)(ii) and (iv) of the Act, a "child" means a child who is not a spouse or common-law partner and is less than 19 years of age.

SOR/2009-290, s. 1; SOR/2014-133, s. 3

Case Law

Osba v Canada (Minister of Citizenship and Immigration), 2015 FC 1294, 2015 CarswellNat 5907, 2015 CarswellNat 10087 — The IAD accepted that SUBCOE was a Canadian company. However, since the applicant's employment contract with SUBCOE referred only to part-time employment for 16 hours a week, they concluded he did not work full-time for a Canadian business. Further, while the applicant may have worked full time for GOS, it was not a Canadian business. Therefore, the IAD concluded that the applicant did not meet the residency requirement in IRPA. The IAD then went on to consider humanitarian and compassionate factors. It found that the applicant's ties to Canada, the best interests of his children, and the hardship the removal order would have imposed on him favoured a positive decision on his behalf. On the other hand, the IAD found the negative factors outweighed the positive ones — the degree of the applicant's non-compliance with the residency requirement, his lack of establishment in Canada, and the absence of convincing reasons to remain outside Canada. The IAD dismissed the applicant's appeal.

The Federal Court found the IAD's analysis of the legality of the removal order was deficient because it did not take into account the exception set out in the IRPA, and did not address the evidence that was relevant to the issue. The evidence before the IAD clearly showed that the applicant worked full time, on assignment, for a client of SUBCOE, GOS, from June 2006 to October 2009. According to IRPA, working full time on assignment for a Canadian business or a client of that business qualifies as time spent working for the Canadian business itself. This possibility was not considered by the officer who issued the removal order, or by the IAD. Council for the Minister before the Board argued that working for a non-Canadian client of a Canadian business does not count as employment for a Canadian business. The court concluded that if the applicant had been credited for the time spent working for GOS, he would have met his residency requirement. The Board's decision was unreasonable and was set aside.

Wei v. Canada (Minister of Citizenship & Immigration) (2012), 12 Imm. L.R. (4th) 256, 2012 FC 1084, 2012 CarswellNat 3506, 2012 CarswellNat 5054, [2012] F.C.J. No. 1173 — This was an application for judicial review of a decision of the Immigration Appeal Division under subsec. 63(4) of the Act. The Appeal Division held that a visa officer's determination that the applicant had failed to comply with the residency obligations was valid in law and there were insufficient H&C grounds to warrant special relief. The applicant became a permanent resident in May 1999 and was employed by a sea product company and a chicken farm in Vancouver. In 2004, he was hired by a B.C. pharmaceutical company to represent that company in China to find a business partner for it there. The applicant's salary was paid every three months and employment and Canadian taxes were deducted. The applicant applied for a travel document in 2009 which was refused by the Canadian Embassy for failure to meet the residency obligations. The Board found that the applicant was hired for a local position in China and therefore there was no assignment within the meaning of the Regulation, s. 61(3). Accordingly, the time that he was employed in China did not count toward the fulfilment of his residence obligation. The Board found the visa officer's decision reasonable but noted it retained the discretion to allow the applicant's appeal on H&C grounds taking into account the best interest of a child directly affected by the decision. The Board noted that the applicant was not hired to work in Canada and there was no position for him in Canada should the position in China cease. The Board therefore concluded that the applicant was hired for a local job in China and thus there was no assignment as per the Regulations. The applicant argued that the Board erred in finding that his employment was full time; as his position was subject to annual renewal, it was temporary rather than full time. Further, there were several connecting factors between the applicant and his Canadian employer including his work duties, his payment of taxes and other employment deductions in accordance with Canadian law and the fact that the Canadian company controlled his assignment from its head office in Canada. The court found that the Board came to a reasonable decision in finding that there was no assignment ultimately due to the lack of a job available for the applicant to return to in Canada. There were also insufficient H&C grounds and the application for judicial review was dismissed.

Bi v. Canada (Minister of Citizenship & Immigration), 2012 CarswellNat 870, 2012 FC 293 — The IAD rejected the applicant's appeal of a determination that he had failed to comply with the residency obligation of s. 28 of IRPA. The applicant was a Chinese citizen who became a permanent resident on September 3, 2005, along with his parents and sister. He returned to China approximately one month later. Upon his return to China, the applicant remained unemployed from October 2005 to February 21, 2007, when he entered into an agreement with a Canadian business to work as an assistant general manager in China until January 20, 2010. In an application for a travel document dated April 3, 2010, the applicant indicated that he had spent 130 days in Canada over the previous $4\frac{1}{2}$ years. The visa officer refused his application for a travel document based on a lack of supporting evidence and, moreover, determined he had also failed to satisfy his residency obligation. The Federal Court in *Canada (Minister of Citizenship & Immigration) v. Jiang*, 2011 FC 349, was clearly opposed to an employee accumulating days toward meeting their residency requirement simply by being hired on a full-time basis outside of Canada by a Canadian business. Instead, it was the court's view that the permanent resident must be assigned temporarily, maintain a connection with his or her employer, and to continue working for his or her employer in Canada following the assignment. *Jiang* does not mandate that the permanent resident first worked in Canada. The emphasis is instead on the temporary nature of the assignment that requires the employee to maintain a connection with the Canadian business and then remain employed for that business in Canada.

In this case, even if a translation error occurred during the hearing which caused a misunderstanding as to the applicant's continued connection with his employer, there was no doubt that the applicant was not assigned to temporarily work abroad. Instead, his work abroad began from the moment he was hired and continued to the expiry of his contract nearly three years later. Furthermore, there was simply no evidence that his employer had agreed to keep the applicant on in Canada after this period. The applicant only indicated at the hearing that he now wanted to talk to the employer to tell him or her that he wanted to work in Canada and inquire as to whether another employee could be sent abroad in his place. As a result, the IAD's conclusion that the applicant did not meet the burden of establishing that he had satisfied the requirements under subs. 61(3) of the IRPR was reasonable. The application for judicial review was dismissed.

Durve v. Canada (Minister of Citizenship & Immigration) (2011), 99 Imm. L.R. (3d) 334, 2011 FC 995, 2011 CarswellNat 3202 — A visa officer refused to renew the applicant's permanent resident status because he had failed to comply with the residency obligations. The IAD upheld the decision and the applicant sought judicial review of the IAD's decision.

The determination of whether a Canadian corporation has an "ongoing operation" is essentially a question of fact to be determined by the nature and the degree of the activity of the companies in each individual case and no particular *indicia* is determinative. In this case, all the consulting fees were paid to the Canadian corporation; there was no evidence of any salary being paid by any other company to the applicant; and the incorporation of the Canadian company did not coincide with the applicant's entry in Canada.

It is important to examine the nature of the applicant's activities while outside of Canada in relation to the business of his or her Canadian company. It is also clear that the application of subs. 61(1) and (2) of the Regulations involves two distinct concepts. A company that does not have an ongoing operation is not necessarily a company incorporated primarily for the purpose of allowing an applicant to meet its residency obligations.

The court found that the presumption that the decision maker had considered all the evidence had been rebutted and that the decision did not meet the requirements of justification and transparency applicable under the standard of reasonableness. Although the decision was set aside, it did not imply accepting that the applicant's company fell within the parameters of subs. 61(1) of the Regulations. Instead, the court simply found that the matter had not been properly assessed on all the facts and the evidence before the decision maker, and that the decision maker had not sufficiently explained its reasonings to enable the court to properly assess the validity of its conclusion. In that respect, the court indicated it would be helpful if the IAD could be more precise as to the *indicia* it will look at when considering the application of the above-mentioned provisions to businesses started by new permanent residents on a very small scale and which involved developing clientele abroad. For example, if a one-man operation is not acceptable, it should be clearly spelled out. The application for judicial review was granted.

Canada (Minister of Citizenship & Immigration) v. Jiang, 2011 FC 349, 2011 CarswellNat 1527 — This was an application for judicial review by the Minister of Citizenship and Immigration of a decision by the Immigration Appeal Division (the "panel"). The panel allowed the appellant's appeal and determined that she had met the residency obligation imposed on permanent residents under s. 28 of IRPA. The panel found that the appellant, through her employment with Investissement Québec in China, was "assigned full-time as a term of one's employment to a position outside of Canada" within the meaning of subs. 61(3) of the *Immigration and Refugee Protection Regulations*. The panel determined that being hired locally outside Canada, i.e. in China, met the requirements of the Act and the Regulations. The Minister sought judicial review of the panel's decision.

In this case, it is difficult to argue that the appellant met the "assignment" criterion set out in the Regulations. The word "assignment" in the context of permanent resident status interpreted in light of the Act and Regulations necessarily implies a connecting factor to the employer located in Canada. The word "assigned" in s. 61 of the Regulations means that an individual who is assigned to a position outside Canada on a temporary basis and who maintains a connection to a Canadian business or to the public service of Canada or of a province, may therefore return to Canada. The memorandum's definitions of advisors and local recruited professional employees (attachés) are convincing in this regard. The appellant was hired as a local employee, where the concept of assignment is absent from the definition. The ENF 23 also refers to "assignment" and to "duration of the assignment." The clarification added by Parliament to subs. 61(3) of the Regulations creates an equilibrium between the obligation imposed on the permanent resident to accumulate the required number of days under the Act while recognizing there may be opportunities for permanent residents to work abroad. Consequently, the court was of the opinion that, in light of the evidence in the record, the panel's finding that permanent residents holding full-time positions outside Canada with an eligible Canadian company can accumulate days that would enable them to comply with the residency obligations set out in s. 25 of the Act, is unreasonable.

In *obiter*, the court sympathized with the appellant's situation and noted she was a highly qualified person and her contribution was without a doubt an asset to Canadian society in general and to Quebec society in particular. However, it was not within the purview of the court to grant special relief under the current Act in order to proceed with an assessment of the genuine connections between the appellant and Canada and the fact that she enriches and strengthens the social and cultural fabric of Canadian society in addition to being a benefit to the Canadian economy, which in and of itself reflects the purpose of the Act (s. 3(2)). The appellant's particular circumstances lend themselves to an application for humanitarian and compassionate relief. The application for judicial review was allowed.

62. (1) Calculation — residency obligation — Subject to subsection (2), the calculation of days under paragraph 28(2)(a) of the Act in respect of a permanent resident does not include any day after

    (a) a report is prepared under subsection 44(1) of the Act on the ground that the permanent resident has failed to comply with the residency obligation; or

    (b) a decision is made outside of Canada that the permanent resident has failed to comply with the residency obligation.

(2) Exception — If the permanent resident is subsequently determined to have complied with the residency obligation, subsection (1) does not apply.

DIVISION 3 — PERMIT HOLDERS

63. Period of permit's validity — A temporary resident permit is valid until any one of the following events occurs:

    (a) the permit is cancelled under subsection 24(1) of the Act;

    (b) the permit holder leaves Canada without obtaining prior authorization to re-enter Canada;

    (c) the period of validity specified on the permit expires; or

    (d) a period of three years elapses from its date of validity.

DIVISION 4 — PERMIT HOLDER CLASS
[Heading amended SOR/2004-167, s. 19.]

64. Permit holder class — The permit holder class is prescribed as a class of foreign nationals who may become permanent residents on the basis of the requirements of this Division.

SOR/2004-167, s. 19

65. Member of class — A foreign national is a permit holder and a member of the permit holder class if

(a) they have been issued a temporary resident permit under subsection 24(1) of the Act;

(b) they have continuously resided in Canada as a permit holder for a period of

(i) at least three years, if they

(A) are inadmissible on health grounds under subsection 38(1) of the Act,

(B) are inadmissible under paragraph 42(1)(a) of the Act on grounds of an accompanying family member who is inadmissible under subsection 38(1) of the Act, or

(C) are inadmissible under paragraph 42(1)(b) of the Act on grounds of being an accompanying family member of a foreign national who is inadmissible

(I) under subsection 38(1) of the Act, or

(II) under paragraph 42(1)(a) of the Act on grounds of an accompanying family member who is inadmissible under subsection 38(1) of the Act,

(ii) at least five years, if they are inadmissible on any other grounds under the Act, except sections 34 and 35 and subsections 36(1) and 37(1) of the Act;

(c) they have not become inadmissible on any ground since the permit was issued; and

(d) in the case of a foreign national who intends to reside in the Province of Quebec and is not a member of the family class or a person whom the Board has determined to be a Convention refugee, the competent authority of that Province is of the opinion that the foreign national meets the selection criteria of the Province.

SOR/2004-167, s. 20(1), (2); SOR/2014-269, ss. 6(b), (c), 7(a)

65.1 (1) Becoming a permanent resident — A foreign national in Canada who is a permit holder and a member of the permit holder class becomes a permanent resident if, following an examination, it is established that

(a) they have applied to remain in Canada as a permanent resident as a member of that class;

(b) they are in Canada to establish permanent residence;

(c) they meet the selection criteria and other requirements applicable to that class;

(d) they hold

(i) subject to subsection (4), a document described in any of paragraphs 50(1)(a) to (h), and

(ii) a medical certificate — based on the most recent medical examination to which they were required to submit under paragraph 16(2)(b) of the Act and which took place within the previous 12 months — that indicates

641

that their health condition is not likely to be a danger to public health or public safety and is not reasonably expected to cause excessive demand; and

(e) they and their family members, whether accompanying or not, are not inadmissible on any ground other than the grounds on which an officer, at the time the permit was issued, formed the opinion that the foreign national was inadmissible.

(2) **Criteria in the Province of Quebec** — For the purposes of paragraph (1)(c), the selection criterion applicable to a foreign national who intends to reside in the Province of Quebec as a permanent resident and who is not a person whom the Board has determined to be a Convention refugee is met by evidence that the competent authority of that Province is of the opinion that the foreign national meets the selection criteria of the Province.

(3) **Foreign nationals without a passport or other travel document** — The following foreign nationals who are not holders of a document described in any of paragraphs 50(1)(a) to (h) may submit with their application a document described in paragraph 178(1)(a) or (b):

(a) a protected person within the meaning of subsection 95(2) of the Act;

(b) a person who was determined to be a Convention refugee seeking resettlement under the *Immigration Regulations, 1978*, as enacted by Order in Council P.C. 1978-486 dated February 23, 1978 and registered as SOR/78-172, if under the Act or section 69.2 of the former Act, within the meaning of section 187 of the Act,

(i) no determination has been made to vacate that determination, or

(ii) no determination has been made that the person ceased to be a Convention refugee; and

(c) a member of the country of asylum class or the source country class under the *Humanitarian Designated Classes Regulations*, as enacted by Order in Council P.C. 1997-477 dated April 8, 1997 and registered as SOR/97-183.

(4) **Alternative documents** — A document submitted under subsection (3) shall be accepted in lieu of a document described in any of paragraphs 50(1)(a) to (h) if it satisfies the requirements of paragraphs 178(2)(a) or (b).

SOR/2004-167, s. 21; SOR/2012-154, s. 5

DIVISION 5 — HUMANITARIAN AND COMPASSIONATE CONSIDERATIONS

66. Request — A request made by a foreign national under subsection 25(1) of the Act must be made as an application in writing accompanied by an application to remain in Canada as a permanent resident or, in the case of a foreign national outside Canada, an application for a permanent resident visa.

67. Applicant outside Canada — If an exemption from paragraphs 70(1)(a), (c) and (d) is granted under subsection 25(1), 25.1(1) or 25.2(1) of the Act with respect to a foreign national outside Canada who has made the applications referred to in section 66, a permanent resident visa shall be issued to the foreign national if, following an examination, it is established that the foreign national meets the requirement set out in paragraph 70(1)(b) and

(a) in the case of a foreign national who intends to reside in the Province of Quebec and is not a member of the family class, the competent authority of that Province is of the opinion that the foreign national meets the selection criteria of the Province;

(b) the foreign national is not otherwise inadmissible; and

(c) the family members of the foreign national, whether accompanying or not, are not inadmissible.

SOR/2010-252, s. 3(a)

68. Applicant in Canada — If an exemption from paragraphs 72(1)(a), (c) and (d) is granted under subsection 25(1), 25.1(1) or 25.2(1) of the Act with respect to a foreign national in Canada who has made the applications referred to in section 66, the foreign national becomes a permanent resident if, following an examination, it is established that the foreign national meets the requirements set out in paragraphs 72(1)(b) and (e) and

(a) in the case of a foreign national who intends to reside in the Province of Quebec and is not a member of the family class or a person whom the Board has determined to be a Convention refugee, the competent authority of that Province is of the opinion that the foreign national meets the selection criteria of the Province;

(b) the foreign national is not otherwise inadmissible; and

(c) the family members of the foreign national, whether accompanying or not, are not inadmissible

SOR/2004-167, s. 22(2); SOR/2010-252, s. 3(b)

69. (1) Accompanying family member outside Canada — A foreign national who is an accompanying family member of a foreign national to whom a permanent resident visa is issued under section 67 shall be issued a permanent resident visa if, following an examination, it is established that

(a) the accompanying family member is not inadmissible; and

(b) in the case of an accompanying family member who intends to reside in the Province of Quebec and is not a member of the family class or a person whom the Board has determined to be a Convention refugee, the competent authority of that Province is of the opinion that the family member meets the selection criteria of the Province.

(2) Accompanying family member in Canada — A foreign national who is an accompanying family member of a foreign national who becomes a permanent resident under section 68 shall become a permanent resident if the accompanying family member is in Canada and, following an examination, it is established that

(a) the accompanying family member is not inadmissible; and

(b) in the case of an accompanying family member who intends to reside in the Province of Quebec and is not a member of the family class or a person whom the Board has determined to be a Convention refugee, the competent authority of that Province is of the opinion that the family member meets the selection criteria of the Province.

SOR/2004-167, s. 23

69.1 Requirements — family member — Subject to subsection 25.1(1), to be considered a family member of the applicant, a person shall be a family member of an applicant both at the time the application under section 66 is made and at the time of the determination of the application.

SOR/2014-133, s. 4

DIVISION 6 — PERMANENT RESIDENT VISA

70. (1) Issuance — An officer shall issue a permanent resident visa to a foreign national if, following an examination, it is established that

(a) the foreign national has applied in accordance with these Regulations for a permanent resident visa as a member of a class referred to in subsection (2);

[Editor's Note: SOR/2002-227, s. 356 provides that if a person referred to in paragraph (f) of the definition "member of the family class" in s. 2(1) of the Immigration Regulations, 1978, *SOR/78-172 (the "former Regulations") made an application under the former Regulations for a permanent resident visa before June 28, 2002, the application is governed by the former* Immigration Act, R.S.C. 1985, c. I-2.]

(b) the foreign national is coming to Canada to establish permanent residence;

(c) the foreign national is a member of that class;

(d) the foreign national meets the selection criteria and other requirements applicable to that class; and

(e) the foreign national and their family members, whether accompanying or not, are not inadmissible.

[Editor's Note: SOR/2002-227, s. 353 provides that if a person has made an application under the former Immigration Act, R.S.C. 1985, c. I-2 before June 28, 2002, *the following provisions of the* Immigration and Refugee Protection Regulations, SOR/2002-227 (the "new Regulations") *do not apply to the person in respect of any of his or her non-accompanying dependent children, referred to in s. 352 of the new Regulations, or his or her non-accompanying common-law partner:*

(a) paragraph 70(1)(e);

(b) subparagraph 72(1)(e)(i); and

(c) paragraph 108(1)(a).]

(2) Classes — The classes are

(a) the family class;

(b) the economic class, consisting of the federal skilled worker class, the transitional federal skilled worker class, the Quebec skilled worker class, the provin-

cial nominee class, the Canadian experience class, federal skilled trades class, the investor class, the entrepreneur class, the self-employed persons class, the transitional federal investor class, the transitional federal entrepreneur class and the transitional federal self-employed persons class; and

(c) the Convention refugees abroad class and the country of asylum class.

(3) Criteria in the Province of Quebec — For the purposes of paragraph (1)(d), the selection criterion for a foreign national who intends to reside in the Province of Quebec as a permanent resident and is not a member of the family class is met by evidence that the competent authority of that Province is of the opinion that the foreign national complies with the provincial selection criteria.

(4) Accompanying family members — A foreign national who is an accompanying family member of a foreign national who is issued a permanent resident visa shall be issued a permanent resident visa if, following an examination, it is established that

(a) the accompanying family member is not inadmissible; and

(b) in the case of a family member who intends to reside in the Province of Quebec and is not a member of the family class, the competent authority of that Province is of the opinion that the family member complies with the provincial selection criteria.

(5) Family member — If a permanent resident visa is not issued to a child as an accompanying family member of a foreign national or the foreign national's spouse or common-law partner, a permanent resident visa shall not be issued to a child of that child as an accompanying family member of the foreign national.

SOR/2003-383, s. 1; SOR/2008-254, s. 1; SOR/2011-222, s. 1; SOR/2012-274, s. 2

71. Issuance — particular Quebec selection cases — An officer shall issue a permanent resident visa to a foreign national outside Canada who intends to reside in the Province of Quebec as a permanent resident and does not satisfy the requirements of paragraphs 70(1)(a), (c) and (d) if, following an examination, it is established that

(a) the foreign national has applied for a permanent resident visa in accordance with these Regulations, other than paragraph 10(2)(c);

(b) the foreign national may not be issued a permanent resident visa under subsection 176(2) and is not a member of any class of persons prescribed by these Regulations who may become permanent residents or be issued permanent resident visas;

(c) the foreign national is named in a *Certificat de sélection du Québec* issued by that Province indicating that the foreign national, under the regulations made under *An Act respecting immigration to Québec*, R.S.Q., c. I-0.2, as amended from time to time, is a foreign national in a particularly distressful situation; and

(d) the foreign national and their family members, whether accompanying or not, are not inadmissible.

DIVISION 7 — BECOMING A PERMANENT RESIDENT
[Heading added SOR/2008-253, s. 3.]

71.1 (1) Foreign nationals outside Canada — A foreign national who is a member of a class referred to in subsection 70(2) and is outside Canada must, to become a permanent resident, present their permanent resident visa to an officer at a port of entry.

(2) Foreign nationals in Canada as temporary residents — A foreign national who is a member of a class referred to in paragraph 70(2)(a) or (b) and who is a temporary resident in Canada must, to become a permanent resident, present their permanent resident visa to an officer at a port of entry or at an office of the Department in Canada.

SOR/2008-253, s. 3

[Heading repealed SOR/2008-253, s. 4.]

72. (1) Obtaining status — A foreign national in Canada becomes a permanent resident if, following an examination, it is established that

(a) they have applied to remain in Canada as a permanent resident as a member of a class referred to in subsection (2);

(b) they are in Canada to establish permanent residence;

(c) they are a member of that class;

(d) they meet the selection criteria and other requirements applicable to that class;

(e) except in the case of a foreign national who has submitted a document accepted under subsection 178(2) or of a member of the protected temporary residents class,

(i) they and their family members, whether accompanying or not, are not inadmissible,

[Editor's Note: SOR/2002-227, s. 353 provides that if a person has made an application under the former Immigration Act, *R.S.C. 1985, c. I-2 before June 28, 2002, the following provisions of the* Immigration and Refugee Protection Regulations, *SOR/2002-227 (the "new Regulations") do not apply to the person in respect of any of his or her non-accompanying dependent children, referred to in s. 352 of the new Regulations, or his or her non-accompanying common-law partner:*

(a) paragraph 70(1)(e);

(b) subparagraph 72(1)(e)(i); and

(c) paragraph 108(1)(a).]

(ii) they hold a document described in any of paragraphs 50(1)(a) to (h), and

(iii) they hold a medical certificate — based on the most recent medical examination to which they were required to submit under paragraph 16(2)(b) of the Act and which took place within the previous 12 months — that indicates that their health condition is not likely to be a danger to public health or public safety and, unless subsection 38(2) of the Act applies, is not reasonably expected to cause excessive demand; and

(f) in the case of a member of the protected temporary residents class, they are not inadmissible.

(2) **Classes** — The classes are

(a) the live-in caregiver class;

(b) the spouse or common-law partner in Canada class; and

(c) the protected temporary residents class.

(3) **Criteria in the Province of Quebec** — For the purposes of paragraph (1)(d), the selection criterion applicable to a foreign national who intends to reside in the Province of Quebec as a permanent resident, and who is not a member of the family class or a person whom the Board has determined to be a Convention refugee, is met by evidence that the competent authority of that Province is of the opinion that the foreign national meets the selection criteria of the Province.

(4) **Accompanying family members** — A foreign national who is an accompanying family member of a foreign national who becomes a permanent resident under this section shall be issued a permanent resident visa or become a permanent resident, as the case may be, if following an examination it is established that

(a) the accompanying family member is not inadmissible;

(b) in the case of a family member who intends to reside in the Province of Quebec and is not a member of the family class or a person whom the Board has determined to be a Convention refugee, the competent authority of that Province is of the opinion that the family member meets the selection criteria of the Province.

SOR/2004-167, s. 26(1)–(4), (6), (7); SOR/2008-253, s. 5; SOR/2012-154, s. 6

DIVISION 8 — CONDITION APPLICABLE TO CERTAIN PERMANENT RESIDENTS

[Heading added SOR/2012-227, s. 1.]

72.1 (1) Condition — Subject to subsections (5) and (6), a permanent resident described in subsection (2) is subject to the condition that they must cohabit in a conjugal relationship with their sponsor for a continuous period of two years after the day on which they became a permanent resident.

(2) **Permanent resident subject to condition** — For the purpose of subsection (1) and subject to subsection (3), the permanent resident is a person who was a foreign national who

(a) became a permanent resident after making an application for permanent residence as a member of the family class, or an application as a member of the spouse or common-law partner in Canada class to remain in Canada as a permanent resident, as applicable;

(b) at the time the sponsor filed a sponsorship application with respect to the person under paragraph 130(1)(c) had been the spouse, common-law partner or conjugal partner of the sponsor, as applicable, for a period of two years or less; and

(c) had no child in respect of whom both they and the sponsor were the parents at the time the sponsor filed a sponsorship application with respect to the person under paragraph 130(1)(c).

(3) **Exclusion** — An application referred to in paragraph (2)(a) does not include one that was received before the day on which this section comes into force.

(4) **Evidence of compliance** — A permanent resident referred to in subsection (1) must provide evidence of their compliance with the condition set out in that subsection to an officer if

(a) the officer requests such evidence because they have reason to believe that the permanent resident is not complying or has not complied with the condition; or

(b) the officer requests such evidence as part of a random assessment of the overall level of compliance with that condition by the permanent residents who are or were subject to it.

(5) **Exception — sponsor's death** — The condition set out in subsection (1) ceases to apply in respect of a permanent resident referred to in that subsection if the sponsor dies during the two-year period referred to in that subsection, the permanent resident provides evidence to that effect to an officer and the officer determines, based on evidence provided by the permanent resident or on any other relevant evidence, that the permanent resident had continued to cohabit in a conjugal relationship with the sponsor until the sponsor's death.

(6) **Exception — abuse or neglect** — The condition set out in subsection (1) also ceases to apply in respect of a permanent resident referred to in that subsection if an officer determines, based on evidence provided by the permanent resident or on any other relevant evidence, that

(a) the permanent resident

(i) is not able to meet that condition throughout the two-year period referred to in that subsection because the permanent resident or a child of the permanent resident or the sponsor, or a person who is related to the permanent resident or the sponsor and who is habitually residing in their household, is subjected by the sponsor to any abuse or neglect referred to in subsection (7) during that period, and

(ii) continued to cohabit in a conjugal relationship with the sponsor during that period until the cohabitation ceased as a result of the abuse or neglect; or

(b) the permanent resident

(i) is not able to meet that condition throughout the two-year period referred to in subsection (1) because the sponsor has failed to protect the permanent resident or a child of the permanent resident or the sponsor, or a person who is related to the permanent resident or the sponsor and who is habitually residing in their household, from any abuse or neglect referred to in subsection (7) during that period by another person who is

648

related to the sponsor, whether that person is residing in the household or not, and

(ii) continued to cohabit in a conjugal relationship with the sponsor during that period until the cohabitation ceased as a result of the abuse or neglect.

(7) **Abuse and neglect** — For the purpose of subsection (6),

(a) abuse consists of any of the following:

(i) physical abuse, including assault and forcible confinement,

(ii) sexual abuse, including sexual contact without consent,

(iii) psychological abuse, including threats and intimidation, and

(iv) financial abuse, including fraud and extortion; and

(b) neglect consists of the failure to provide the necessaries of life, such as food, clothing, medical care or shelter, and any other omission that results in a risk of serious harm.

(8) **Related person** — For the purposes of subsections (6) and (7), a person is related to the permanent resident or the sponsor if they are related to them by birth, adoption, marriage, common-law partnership or conjugal partnership.

SOR/2012-227, s. 1

72.2 (1) Condition — accompanying family members — Subject to subsection (2), a permanent resident who became a permanent resident as an accompanying family member of a permanent resident referred to in subsection 72.1(1) is subject to the condition that the permanent resident in respect of whom they were an accompanying family member meets the condition set out in subsection 72.1(1).

(2) **Exception — accompanying family members** — Subsection (1) does not apply in respect of a permanent resident who became a permanent resident as an accompanying family member of a permanent resident referred to in subsection 72.1(1) if the permanent resident in respect of whom they were an accompanying family member is one to whom an exception referred to in subsection 72.1(5) or (6) applies.

SOR/2012-227, s. 1

72.3 (1) Condition — sponsored person and their accompanying family members — Subject to subsection (2), a permanent resident who became a permanent resident after being sponsored, either during or after the period referred to in subsection 72.1(1), by a sponsor who is a permanent resident referred to in that subsection, is subject to the condition that the sponsoring permanent resident meets the condition set out in subsection 72.1(1).

(2) **Exception — sponsored person and their accompanying family members** — Subsection (1) does not apply in respect of a permanent resident who became a permanent resident after being sponsored by a permanent resident referred to in subsection 72.1(1), if the sponsoring permanent resident is one in respect of whom an exception referred to in subsection 72.1(5) or (6) applies.

SOR/2012-227, s. 1

72.4 Clarification — For greater certainty, for the purposes of subsection 27(2) of the Act, a determination as to whether the permanent resident has failed to comply with the condition set out in subsection 72.1(1) may be made during or after the two-year period referred to in subsection 72.1(1).

SOR/2012-227, s. 1

DIVISION 9 — APPLICATION TO RENOUNCE PERMANENT RESIDENT STATUS

[Heading added SOR/2014-269, s. 2.]

72.5 Separate application — Despite subsection 10(3), a separate application must be made for each family member that would like to renounce their permanent resident status.

SOR/2014-269, s. 2

72.6 Application — conditions — An officer may approve a person's application to renounce their permanent resident status if

(a) the person has provided evidence of their citizenship, nationality or permanent legal resident status in another country; and

(b) in the case of an application in respect of a person who is less than 18 years of age, the application is signed by every person who has custody of that person or who is empowered to act on their behalf by virtue of a court order or written agreement or by operation of law, unless otherwise ordered by a court.

SOR/2014-269, s. 2

72.7 Sponsorship application suspended — If a permanent resident makes an application to renounce their permanent resident status, any sponsorship application made by them is suspended until a decision is made on the application to renounce permanent residence.

SOR/2014-269, s. 2

PART 6 — ECONOMIC CLASSES

DIVISION 0.1 — GENERAL

[Heading added SOR/2014-133, s. 5.]

72.8 Requirements — family member — Subject to subsections 25.1(3) to (5) and for the purposes of this Part, to be considered a family member of an applicant, a person must be a family member of the applicant both at the time the application under Division 6 of Part 5 is made and at the time of the determination of the application.

SOR/2014-133, s. 5

DIVISION 1 — SKILLED WORKERS

Interpretation

73. Definitions — (1) The following definitions apply in this Division.

"Canadian educational credential" means any diploma, certificate or credential, issued on the completion of a Canadian program of study or training at an educational or training institution that is recognized by the provincial authorities responsible for registering, accrediting, supervising and regulating such institutions. *("diplôme canadien")*

"educational credential" [Repealed SOR/2012-274, s. 3(2).]

"equivalency assessment" means a determination, issued by an organization or institution designated under subsection 75(4), that a foreign diploma, certificate or credential is equivalent to a Canadian educational credential and an assessment, by the organization or institution, of the authenticity of the foreign diploma, certificate or credential. *("attestation d'équivalence")*

"former Regulations" has the same meaning as in subsection 316(1). *("ancien règlement")*

"full-time work" means at least 30 hours of work over a period of one week. *("travail à temps plein")*

"language skill area" means speaking, oral comprehension, reading or writing. *("habileté langagière")*

"restricted occupation" means an occupation designated as a restricted occupation by the Minister, taking into account labour market activity on both an area and a national basis, following consultation with the Department of Employment and Social Development, provincial governments and any other relevant organizations or institutions. *("profession d'accès limité")*

(2) **Definition "work"** — Despite the definition "work" in section 2, for the purposes of this Division, "work" means an activity for which wages are paid or commission is earned.
SOR/2003-383, s. 2; SOR/2008-254, s. 2; SOR/2010-172, s. 5(b); SOR/2012-274, s. 3;
2013, c. 40, s. 237(3)(a)

General
[Heading repealed SOR/2008-253, s. 6. Added SOR/2012-274, s. 4.]

74. (1) Criteria — For the purposes of paragraphs 75(2)(d), 79(3)(a), 87.1(2)(d) and (e) and 87.2(3)(a), the Minister shall fix, by class prescribed by these Regulations or by occupation, and make available to the public, minimum language proficiency thresholds on the basis of

(a) the number of applications in all classes under this Part that are being processed;

(b) the number of immigrants who are projected to become permanent residents according to the report to Parliament referred to in section 94 of the Act; and

(c) the potential, taking into account the applicants' linguistic profiles and economic and other relevant factors, for the establishment in Canada of applicants under the federal skilled worker class, the Canadian experience class and the federal skilled trades class.

(2) **Minimum language proficiency thresholds** — The minimum language proficiency thresholds fixed by the Minister shall be established in reference to the benchmarks described in the *Canadian Language Benchmarks* and the *Niveaux de compétence linguistique canadiens.*

(3) **Designation for evaluating language proficiency** — The Minister may designate, for any period specified by the Minister, any organization or institution to be responsible for evaluating language proficiency if the organization or institution has expertise in evaluating language proficiency and if the organization or institution has provided a correlation of its evaluation results to the benchmarks set out in the *Canadian Language Benchmarks* and the *Niveaux de compétence linguistique canadiens.*

(4) **Public notice** — The Minister shall make available to the public a list of the designated organizations or institutions.

(5) **Definition "service agreement"** — For the purpose of subsection (6), "service agreement" means an agreement concluded between the Government of Canada and an organization or institution for the purpose of having the organization or institution supply the service of evaluating the language proficiency of foreign nationals.

(6) **Revocation of designation** — The Minister may revoke a designation if

(a) the organization or institution no longer meets the criteria set out in subsection (3);

(b) the organization or institution submitted false, misleading or inaccurate information or has contravened any provision of federal or provincial legislation relevant to the service provided by the organization or institution; or

(c) either the Government of Canada or the organization or institution has terminated the service agreement.

(7) **Conclusive evidence** — The results of an evaluation by a designated organization or institution are conclusive evidence of the language proficiency of an applicant under the federal skilled worker class, the Canadian experience class or the federal skilled trades class, as the case may be.

SOR/2008-253, s. 6; SOR/2012-274, s. 4

Federal Skilled Workers

Federal Skilled Worker Class

75. (1) Class — For the purposes of subsection 12(2) of the Act, the federal skilled worker class is hereby prescribed as a class of persons who are skilled workers and who may become permanent residents on the basis of their ability to become economically established in Canada and who intend to reside in a province other than the Province of Quebec.

(2) Skilled workers — A foreign national is a skilled worker if

(a) within the 10 years before the date on which their application for a permanent resident visa is made, they have accumulated, over a continuous period, at least one year of full-time work experience, or the equivalent in part-time work, in the occupation identified by the foreign national in their application as their primary occupation, other than a restricted occupation, that is listed in Skill Type 0 Management Occupations or Skill Level A or B of the *National Occupational Classification* matrix;

(b) during that period of employment they performed the actions described in the lead statement for the occupation as set out in the occupational descriptions of the *National Occupational Classification*;

(c) during that period of employment they performed a substantial number of the main duties of the occupation as set out in the occupational descriptions of the *National Occupational Classification*, including all of the essential duties;

(d) they have submitted the results of an evaluation — by an organization or institution designated under subsection 74(3) and which must be less than two years old on the date on which their application is made — of their proficiency in either English or French indicating that they have met or exceeded the applicable language proficiency threshold fixed by the Minister under subsection 74(1) for each of the four language skill areas; and

(e) they have submitted one of the following:

(i) their Canadian educational credential, or

(ii) their foreign diploma, certificate or credential and the equivalency assessment, which assessment must be less than five years old on the date on which their application is made.

(2.1) If professional body designated — If a professional body has been designated under subsection (4) in respect of the occupation identified by the foreign national in their application as their primary occupation, the foreign diploma, certificate or credential submitted by the foreign national must be relevant to that occupation and the equivalency assessment — which must be less than five years old on the date on which their application is made and must be issued by the designated professional body — must establish that the foreign diploma, certificate or credential is equivalent to the Canadian educational credential required to practise that occupation in at least one of the provinces in which the equivalency assessments issued by this professional body are recognized.

653

(3) Minimal requirements — If the foreign national fails to meet the requirements of subsection (2), the application for a permanent resident visa shall be refused and no further assessment is required.

(4) Designation for equivalency assessment — For the purposes of paragraph (2)(e) and subsection (2.1), the Minister may designate, for a period specified by the Minister, any organization or institution to be responsible for issuing equivalency assessments

   (a) if the organization or institution has the recognized expertise to assess the authenticity of foreign diplomas, certificates and credentials and their equivalency to Canadian educational credentials; and

   (b) if, in the case of a professional body, their equivalency assessments are recognized by at least two provincial professional bodies that regulate an occupation listed in the *National Occupational Classification* matrix at Skill Level A or B for which licensing by a provincial regulatory body is required.

(5) Public notice — The Minister shall make available to the public a list of the designated organizations or institutions.

(6) Definition "service agreement" — For the purpose of subsection (7), "service agreement" means an agreement concluded between the Government of Canada and an organization or institution for the purpose of having the organization or institution supply the service of assessing the authenticity of foreign diplomas, certificates and credentials and their equivalency to Canadian educational credentials.

(7) Revocation of designation — The Minister may revoke a designation if

   (a) the organization or institution no longer meets the criteria set out in subsection (4);

   (b) the organization or institution submitted false, misleading or inaccurate information or has contravened any provision of federal or provincial legislation relevant to the service provided by the organization or institution; or

   (c) either the Government of Canada or the organization or institution has terminated the service agreement.

(8) Conclusive evidence — For the purposes of paragraph (2)(e), subsection (2.1) and section 78, an equivalency assessment is conclusive evidence that the foreign diplomas, certificates or credentials are equivalent to Canadian educational credentials.

[Editor's Note: SOR/2002-227, s. 361(1) provides that if, before June 28, 2002, a foreign national referred to in SOR/2002-227, s. 361(2) has been assessed by a visa officer and awarded the number of units of assessment required by the Immigration Regulations, 1978, SOR/78-172 *(the "former Regulations"), that assessment is, for the purpose of the* Immigration and Refugee Protection Regulations, SOR/2002-227 *(the "new Regulations"), an award of points equal or superior to the minimum number of points required of*

   (a) a skilled worker, in the case of a foreign national described in paragraph (2)(a) of the new Regulations;

(b) an investor in the case of a foreign national described in paragraph (2)(b) of the new Regulations;

(c) an entrepreneur, in the case of a foreign national described in paragraph (2)(c) of the new Regulations; or

(d) a self-employed person, in the case of a foreign national described in paragraph (2)(a) of the new Regulations.

SOR/2002-227, s. 361(2) provides that SOR/2002-227, s. 361(1) applies in respect of a foreign national who submitted an application under the former Regulations, as one of the following, for an immigrant visa that is pending immediately before June 28, 2002:

(a) a person described in subparagraph 9(1)(b)(i) or paragraph 10(1)(b) of the former Regulations;

(b) an investor; or

(c) an entrepreneur.

SOR/2002-227, s. 361(5) provides that if a foreign national referred to in paragraph 2(a) of the new Regulations made an application before January 1, 2002 for an immigrant visa and has not, before April 1, 2003, been awarded the number of units of assessment required by the former Regulations, he or she must obtain a minimum of 70 points based on the factors set out in paragraph 76(1)(a) of the new Regulations to become a permanent resident as a member of the federal skilled worker class.]

SOR/2004-167, s. 27; SOR/2012-274, s. 5

Case Law

Dhaliwal v. Canada (Minister of Citizenship and Immigration), 2016 FC 131, 2016 CarswellNat 232, 2016 CarswellNat 2163 — The applicant sought judicial review of a decision of a visa officer to deny the application for permanent residence as a member of the federal skilled worker class, finding that, contrary to s. 75(1) of the Regulations, she lacked the intention to reside outside of Quebec. The applicant maintained that she intended at all times to permanently reside in Brampton, Ontario, and was only in Quebec on a study permit to complete her PhD at McGill University. The officer found that the applicant had not taken the "necessary steps" to reside in a province other than Quebec. However, there is no requirement for any necessary steps to be taken to prove intention. If there was a requirement to demonstrate compliance with subs. 75(1) of the Regulations by producing more than a simple statement of intent to permanently reside outside of Quebec as provided in Question 6 of the Generic IMM0008 form, that requirement would need to be stated somewhere explicitly, in order to provide notice to the applicant. The officer erred in imposing such a requirement.

The assessment of intention, since it is a highly subjective notion, may take into account all indicia, including past conduct, present circumstances, and future plans, as best as can be ascertained from the available evidence and context. In this case, the applicant clearly expressed her intention to permanently reside in Brampton, Ontario, as well as her intention to finish her PhD in Quebec, which required continued temporary residence in Quebec. These intentions are not contradictory; rather, they are complementary to one another. She also provided statutory declarations from herself, her parents, and her sister setting out the reasons why she intended to move to Ontario, all in cogent terms, which further buttressed here stated intention to live outside of Quebec. There were also ample objective indicia to support the applicant's sworn statements of intent, including the residence of her close family members in Brampton, their Canadian status, and the careers and languages of both the applicant and her spouse, the fact that she did not speak French and the fact that there are a few English-only university departments in Quebec made Ontario an objectively more attractive location with respect to job opportunities. There was nothing in the record which would suggest the applicant intended to reside in Quebec beyond the terms of her studies at McGill University. The application for judicial review was allowed.

Millik v. Canada (Minister of Citizenship and Immigration), 2015 FC 82, 2015 CarswellNat 82, 2015 CarswellNat 1983 — The applicant sought judicial review of a decision of a visa officer to refuse her application for permanent residence under the federal skilled worker class. The officer concluded that the applicant had not proven that she performed the duties of any of the occupations for which assessment had been requested. The Regulations require in para. 75(2)(c) that only a "substantial" number of the main duties be performed with respect to the NOC being assessed. It was unclear whether the officer turned or directed his or her mind to the question of whether subs. 75(2) had been met. The officer's decision did not provide sufficient grounds to understand the officer's reasoning and, thus, was neither intelligible nor transparent. The officer simply stated in the GCMS notes that he or she found the description of the duties in the letter from the applicant's employer "very vague" because they referred merely to "participating in" certain activities. The application for judicial review was allowed.

Katebi v. Canada (Minister of Citizenship and Immigration), 2014 FC 813, 2014 CarswellNat 3161, 2014 CarswellNat 3804 — The applicant sought judicial review of the visa officer's decision denying him permanent residence under the federal skilled workers category. The officer found that the applicant had failed to provide sufficient evidence regarding the work duties he was performing in his country of origin. Specifically, the officer noted that the reference letter the applicant's employer had provided in support of his skilled worker application did not contain any description of his job duties and that the applicant's own job duties' description had been taken *verbatim* from the NOC and did not appear, as a result, "credible."

The applicant bore the onus of putting together an application that was complete, relevant, convincing and unambiguous and the officer had no duty, according to the jurisprudence of this court, to provide him with an opportunity to address the officer's concern regarding the content of the employer's letter. With respect to the officer's concern regarding the paraphrasing of the NOC's descriptions in the applicant's skilled worker application materials, the officer's decision when read as a whole raises an issue of sufficiency of evidence, not one of credibility. Although the officer did indicate in his decision that the paraphrasing of the NOC by the applicant diminished the credibility of the job description he provided in his application materials, his key findings were clearly about the insufficiency of the applicant's evidence. All the references to the duties and experiences of the applicant paraphrased the NOC; none came from another source, including the employer's letter. In such circumstances, these references could be regarded as self-serving and the officer was therefore entitled to give them less weight and question whether they accurately described the applicants' work experience. In such circumstances, visa officers are justified in being doubtful as to whether a visa applicant meets the skilled worker visa requirements. Although these doubts may sometimes be expressed as credibility concerns, as they were in this case, they often are an indication that a visa officer was not able to make that determination based on the material before him. The court concluded the officer's decision was clear and unequivocal. The application for judicial review was dismissed.

Dinani v. Canada (Minister of Citizenship & Immigration) (2014), 23 Imm. L.R. (4th) 78, 2014 FC 141, 2014 CarswellNat 263 — This was an application for judicial review challenging a decision by a visa officer to deny an application for permanent residence as a skilled worker. The applicant applied for a skilled worker visa in the post-secondary teaching and research assistants employment category. It was incumbent upon the applicant to establish that he performed the actions of a research and teaching assistant as described in the lead statement for that occupation found in the applicable NOC. The applicant had provided letters of reference from three members of the engineering faculty setting out the nature of his employment duties. Visa officers have an obligation to bring at least a modicum of common sense and rationality to the exercise of comparing actual job descriptions to NOC employment criteria. It seemed obvious to the Federal Court that the assistance to the other members of the faculty was being provided when a PhD student is teaching, setting and supervising examinations, marking and conducting supervised research. In the absence of that assistance, the work would necessarily need to be carried out by others in the department. The decision was not reasonable and the reasons given were insufficient. The application for judicial review was allowed.

Bazaid v. Canada (Minister of Citizenship & Immigration), 2013 FC 17, 2013 CarswellNat 69, 2013 CarswellNat 993 — The applicant seeks judicial review of the refusal of an immigration officer to process his application for permanent residence under the federal skilled worker class. The applicant challenged the immigration officer's decision that he did not present sufficient evidence to establish that he met the occupational requirements for NOC 3111 — Specialist Physicians.

The lead statement and list of main duties in the NOC document describes the set of tasks generally performed by most specialist physicians. It would be unreasonable to find that a person who held the job titles of Psychiatrist, Psychiatrist (Child and Adolescent), Assistant Professor and Consultant at the Department of Psychiatry, Consultant Child and Adolescent Psychiatrist and who is a Fellow of the College would not have diagnosed and treated psychiatric disorders, ordered diagnostic procedures, prescribed medication and treatment, and acted as a consultant to other physicians. By setting out a generic list of tasks typical to most specialists, the NOC document does not command the level of detail that the respondent in this case advocated. The court was not persuaded by the respondent's arguments that the applicant's certificates from Saudi Aramco only established that he worked for an oil company and that the letter describing him as an assistant professor suggested he only worked in an academic capacity. The certificates stated that the applicant worked as a psychiatrist for Saudi Aramco. The applicant may have been an oil company employee but he was an oil company employee whose position was within the NOC 3111 class. A person who holds the job title of Psychiatrist will obviously perform the functions of a psychiatrist, practice as a psychiatrist and provide in-patient care. The application for judicial review was granted.

Porto Turizo v. Canada (Minister of Citizenship & Immigration), 2013 FC 721, 2013 CarswellNat 2834, 2013 CarswellNat 2217 — This was the judicial review of a decision by an officer to refuse the applicant's permanent residence application under the federal skilled worker program. The applicant was a professional engineer from Columbia and applied under the occupation of Construction Managers, NOC code 0711, an occupation on the ministerial instructions published November 28, 2008. The applicant met the academic qualifications; however, the officer was not satisfied that he had performed the duties associated with the lead statement, and his employment letter did not stipulate clearly that he performed some or most of the duties under NOC 0711.

The officer is supposed to be a specialist in these matters and, therefore, courts, as generalists, owe deference. The decision may only be set aside if found to be unreasonable and this decision was unreasonable. The court's comparative reading of NOC 0711 and the duties the applicant carried out indicates that he has satisfied the lead statement and carried out most of the main duties. The officer gave no reason for his decision. The court reviewed the record and found that all the material leads away from the decision reached. Reasons would have to be given as to why the employment letter was insufficient. Judicial review was granted and the application referred to another officer for redetermination.

Hussain v. Canada (Minister of Citizenship & Immigration), 2013 FC 636, 2013 CarswellNat 2613, 2013 CarswellNat 1756 — The applicant sought judicial review of a visa officer's decision that the applicant did not meet the requirements for issuance of the permanent resident visa under the federal skilled worker class. The officer's notes indicated that the applicant did not provide satisfactory evidence that he had work experience in any of the listed occupations set out in the ministerial instructions published November 28, 2008. The notes explained that the application was refused because "the main duties that [the applicant] listed do not indicate that [he] performed the actions described in the lead statement of the occupation, or that [he] performed all of the essential duties and a substantial number of the main duties, as set out in the occupational descriptions of the NOC."

The court is not an expert in the technological terms connected with the various NOC codes and cannot be required to assess the sufficiency of the applicant's application where the visa officer has provided no relevant comments or reasons in that regard. The applicant in this case was correct that the fact that the duties may "bear more resemblance" to another category is irrelevant where an officer has failed to assess the relevance of the duties in relation to the particular category in question and has provided no analysis comparing the requirements of the two codes mentioned. The question is not whether the applicant's duties bear more of a resemblance to another category than to the one sought, but whether the applicant has satisfied the requirements of the category in question. The similarity with another NOC category was the sole explanation offered by the visa officer in support of his conclusion that the information submitted was insufficient to show that the applicant satisfied the requirements of the NOC in question. The application for judicial review was allowed.

Komolafe v. Canada (Minister of Citizenship & Immigration), 2013 FC 431, 2013 CarswellNat 1390, 2013 CarswellNat 1105 — The applicant sought judicial review of a decision to refuse his application for permanent residence under the federal skilled worker class as a driller and blaster, NOC 7372. Subsec. 75(2) of the Regulations describes a skilled worker as a foreign national who has performed the tasks described in the lead statement for the occupation as set out in the NOC descriptions and performed a substantial number of the main duties of the occupation, including all "essential" duties. The officer determined that the applicant did not provide evidence that he satisfied this requirement and was not eligible for further processing pursuant to subsec. 75(3) of the Regulations. The decision was a form letter merely stating that the officer was not satisfied that the applicant had performed the actions in the lead statement for the occupation or a substantial number of the main duties. The agent subsequently swore an affidavit for the judicial review stating that the applicant's evidence only demonstrated experience in two of the listed main duties. Although decision makers may supplement their reasons by way of an affidavit to provide an explanation for their notes made contemporaneous to the decision, in this case, the officer had no contemporaneous notes which describe her reasoning process. The affidavit, therefore, was inadmissible.

It is not for the court to determine whether the applicant had in fact performed the actions described in the lead statement and a substantial number of the main duties. The visa officer must do this with some line of reasoning which provides a basis for review. In this case, the decision provided no insight into the officer's reasoning process. The application for judicial review was granted.

Benoit v. Canada (Minister of Citizenship & Immigration), 2013 FC 185, 2013 CarswellNat 422, 2013 CarswellNat 649 — The officer's decision rejecting the application for permanent residence in Canada under the Canadian experience class for not meeting the work experience described in NOC 6211 is unreasonable because the test set out in the Immigration and Refugee Protection Regulations was not applied. The officer was required to determine if the applicant "performed a substantial number of main duties." However, the officer's decision did not make it clear that the officer had at any point turned his or her mind to the real question, which was whether — on the whole — the duties were a substantial match. The respondent conceded that the applicant did perform "some" of the duties listed in NOC 6211. The Regulations clearly require that only a "substantial" number of the duties be performed. That is the test. The officer in this case singled out only parts of two of the eight main duties from NOC 6211 and on that basis concluded that the applicant's experience did not qualify. The court was satisfied that the applicant's responsibilities were far from being such a total mismatch that her application for permanent residence had no chance of success. At a glance, the duties were substantially a match. Accordingly, the application for judicial review was allowed and the application sent back for decision by a different officer to decide whether the applicant "performed a substantial number of the main duties" listed in NOC 6211.

Agama v. Canada (Minister of Citizenship & Immigration), 2013 FC 135, 2013 CarswellNat 195, 2013 CarswellNat 644 — The applicant was denied a permanent resident visa under the skilled worker class because her application fell outside the annual "cap" imposed by policy on this class. The applicant filed her application on November 14, 2011. On December 1, 2011, the website reported that the cap stood at 458. On January 13, 2012, the applicant was informed that her application was rejected because the cap of 500 applications for NOC 0631 had been reached. The applicant alleged that there had been a breach of the principles of fairness in failing to announce when the cap was reached, by leading the applicant to believe that the cap had not been reached, by creating a legitimate expectation that the cap was not reached and in failing to effectively implement the ministerial instructions.

The respondent indicates that there is a normal lag time before the cap numbers can be posted and that the website says that the figures provided are a guide only.

In applying the fairness principle, it is relevant in this case to look at the impact of the applicant's position vis-à-vis others. All those persons who filed after September 19, 2011, when the cap was reached, but before the applicant, would have just as legitimate a complaint as the applicant. Since they were prior in filing time, their applications would have priority over the applicant. Even if there was some basis for the applicant's position, it would not be equitable to grant relief without addressing the situation of these other applicants. The application for *mandamus* was dismissed.

Gulati v. Canada (Minister of Citizenship & Immigration) (2010), 89 Imm. L.R. (3d) 238, 2010 FC 451, 2010 CarswellNat 4178, 2010 CarswellNat 1743 — The visa officer refused the applicant's application for permanent residence as a member of the federal skilled worker class. The officer found that the applicant had not performed the lead statement or a substantial number of the main duties of NOC 6212 Food Services Supervisor. The applicant's Canadian employer had received an arranged employment opinion from Human Resources and Skills Development Canada ("HRSDC"). Ordinarily the job offer, and AEO that confirms it, relate to future employment and would be irrelevant to the applicant's past work experience. However, in this case the AEO confirmed a job offer for the same job that the applicant had performed in the past three years. Therefore the duties listed in the job offer were relevant in assessing the applicant's past work experience. Even if the AEO had not been relevant to the applicant's past work experience, it was certainly relevant in interpreting NOC 6212. HRSDC, a body with considerable expertise in occupational classifications, determined that the applicant's offer for a future restaurant job fell within NOC 6212. Accordingly, the officer's interpretation of the lead statement was unreasonable. The officer had interpreted it to exclude fine dining restaurants. The next question was whether the decision was unreasonable with respect to the applicant's failure to perform a substantial number of the main duties of NOC 6212. It was impossible to assess the officer's conclusion, without knowing which duties the officer thought had not been performed and why. The decision was unreasonable as it was made without regard to relevant evidence, relied on an unreasonable interpretation of the lead statement of NOC 6212 and did not meet the standards of transparency and intelligibility. Accordingly, the application for judicial review was granted.

Dash v. Canada (Minister of Citizenship & Immigration), 2010 FC 1255, 2010 CarswellNat 5567, 2010 CarswellNat 4776 — The applicant's application for permanent residence under the skilled worker category was refused. The officer determined that the applicant did not have the equivalent of one year of full-time experience within the 10 preceding her application date. When the applicant's application was initially filed in January 2007 her work experience consisted of a one-month stint as a geological technician between April and May 2000, and a position at the Bank of Nova Scotia as a teller between July 2000 and December 2001 that was mostly part time. However, after submitting her application, the applicant began working as a full-time administrative officer and still held that job when she updated her application in May 2009. The applicant argued that the visa officer ignored this employment experience. This argument counters the clear language of para. 75(2)(a) which requires that applicants have at least one year of continuous full-time employment experience within the 10 years preceding the date of the application. OP 6 instructs officers to take into account any years of work experience that occur between application and assessment, and for which the applicant has submitted the necessary documentation when assessing the experience of applicants.

If the applicant fails to meet the requirements of subs. 75(2), "the application for a permanent resident visa shall be refused and no further assessment is required." Only if the applicant had met the minimum requirements set out in para. 75(2)(a) would the officer proceed to Chapter 10 of OP 6 where he or she would find the instruction to consider post-application work experience as per s. 77 of IRPA. The application for judicial review was dismissed.

Sandhu v. Canada (Minister of Citizenship & Immigration) (2010), 90 Imm. L.R. (3d) 301, 371 F.T.R. 239, 2010 FC 759, 2010 CarswellNat 3100, 2010 CarswellNat 2412 — A visa officer refused the applicant's application for permanent residence as a skilled worker on the basis that she did not meet the requirements of s. 75(2) of the Regulations because a Banking Clerk (NOC 1434) does not meet the requirement for assessment as it is not listed in Skilled Type O, or Skill Level A or B of the National Occupational Classification matrix, and her documentation does not satisfactorily demonstrate that she has performed the main duties of a Secretary (NOC 1241) and/or a Loan Officer (NOC 1232). Consequently, the officer concluded that she was not performing the duties of an occupation in the Skill Level B, as opposed to an occupation in the Skill Level C such as a General Office Clerk.

The visa officer did not identify a basis for her assumption that a small business enterprise does not require a dedicated secretary. A review of the documentation suggests otherwise in this case. The applicant is highly educated, receives a regular salary and it is the employer who confirms travel and training responsibilities. Where the application is adequate, but the officer nevertheless entertains a doubt on the evidence, there remains a duty to clarify the information with the applicant. When a visa officer has a doubt which has no foundation in the facts and the applicant puts her best foot forward by submitting a complete application, the officer should seek clarification to either substantiate or eliminate the doubt. Without seeking clarification, the officer was in no position to do either. The application for judicial review was granted.

Shangguan v. Canada (Minister of Citizenship & Immigration), 2007 CarswellNat 181, 2007 FC 75 — The applicant sought judicial review of a decision of a visa officer refusing his application for permanent residence in the skilled worker category on the basis that she did not meet the requirements under para. 75(2) of the Regulations. The onus is on the applicant to fully satisfy the visa officer of the existence of all the positive elements in her application. The visa officer dismissed the idea that the applicant had a managerial position, in part because she found that the applicant was not privy to financial reports or profit/loss statements and that she was not tasked with the responsibility of conducting daily banking transactions or general accounting. The NOC states that persons who fit within the occupation "Restaurant and Food Service Managers" perform some or all of the duties listed under this occupation. None of the listed duties referred to financial reports or responsibility for banking transaction or general accounting. The list does include monitoring revenue; however, since an applicant need only have performed some of the duties listed, monitoring revenues is not a mandatory requirement. The officer interpreted the NOC duties relevant to the occupation in an unreasonable manner by importing extraneous criteria into the occupation's duties. The officer's error of law was sufficient to warrant setting the decision aside for reconsideration by a different officer.

Mercado v. Canada (Minister of Citizenship & Immigration) (2006), 60 Imm. L.R. (3d) 88, 2006 CarswellNat 4484, 2006 FC 1527 — The applicant argued the immigration officer incorrectly assessed his experience under s. 75 of the Regulations. He argued that he presented evidence of employment with a landscaping company. He contended that the evidence established that he met the requirements for Landscape Contractor as set out in NOC 8255. He argued that the immigration officer incorrectly rejected such evidence as it was evidence of contracting for services and not evidence of employment. Under cross-examination, the immigration officer admitted that she applied s. 75 as if it only applied to employment situations. This was a questionable interpretation as s. 75(2) applies to "continuous full-time employment experience" which could be broad enough to cover contracting. However, this was immaterial, since the applicant had to first establish that he qualified as a skilled worker. The application for judicial review was dismissed.

76. (1) Selection criteria — For the purpose of determining whether a skilled worker, as a member of the federal skilled worker class, will be able to become economically established in Canada, they must be assessed on the basis of the following criteria:

    (a) the skilled worker must be awarded not less than the minimum number of required points referred to in subsection (2) on the basis of the following factors, namely,

        (i) education, in accordance with section 78,

        (ii) proficiency in the official languages of Canada, in accordance with section 79,

        (iii) experience, in accordance with section 80,

        (iv) age, in accordance with section 81,

        (v) arranged employment, in accordance with section 82, and

        (vi) adaptability, in accordance with section 83; and

    (b) the skilled worker must

        (i) have in the form of transferable and available funds, unencumbered by debts or other obligations, an amount equal to one half of the minimum necessary income applicable in respect of the group of persons consisting of the skilled worker and their family members, or

        (ii) be awarded points under paragraph 82(2)(a), (b) or (d) for arranged employment, as defined in subsection 82(1), in Canada.

(2) Number of points — The Minister shall fix and make available to the public the minimum number of points required of a skilled worker, on the basis of

    (a) the number of applications by skilled workers as members of the federal skilled worker class currently being processed;

    (b) the number of skilled workers projected to become permanent residents according to the report to Parliament referred to in section 94 of the Act; and

    (c) the potential, taking into account economic and other relevant factors, for the establishment of skilled workers in Canada.

(3) Circumstances for officer's substituted evaluation — Whether or not the skilled worker has been awarded the minimum number of required points referred to in subsection (2), an officer may substitute for the criteria set out in paragraph (1)(a) their evaluation of the likelihood of the ability of the skilled worker to become economically established in Canada if the number of points awarded is not a sufficient indicator of whether the skilled worker may become economically established in Canada.

(4) Concurrence — An evaluation made under subsection (3) requires the concurrence of a second officer.

SOR/2004-167, s. 28(2); SOR/2012-274, s. 6

Caoc Law

Section 76(1)

Hussain v. Canada (Minister of Citizenship & Immigration) (2009), 80 Imm. L.R. (3d) 124, 2009 CarswellNat 546, 2009 CarswellNat 1117, 2009 FC 209 — The applicant sought judicial review of a visa officer's decision to refuse an application for permanent residence under the skilled worker class. The applicant was awarded 68 points out of a minimum of 67. Nonetheless, the officer undertook a negative substituted evaluation pursuant to subs. 76(3).

The officer failed to take into account the applicant's settlement funds. This is an essential element when an assessment is conducted pursuant to subs. 76(1) of the Regulations. Although an officer is presumed to have considered all the evidence, the failure in this case to refer to these funds raises the suspicion that she did not do so. This is a reviewable error.

Insofar as the exercise of discretion pursuant to subs. 76(4) is concerned, there was another error. The second officer apparently took into account the marital status of the applicant who, in accordance with Pakistan law, has two wives. His application for permanent residence showed that he intended to be accompanied by one wife if granted status in Canada. The second officer referred to his "peculiar/polygamist family situation." The court found that this was an irrelevant consideration in relation to the application before her. The application for judicial review was allowed.

Wang v. Canada (Minister of Citizenship & Immigration), 2008 CarswellNat 3897, 2008 CarswellNat 2051, 2008 FC 798 — The officer concluded that the applicant had insufficient points to qualify for immigration to Canada. She noted that no points were awarded for the male applicant's brother living in Canada. She determined that the evidence provided by the applicants in support of this allegation was insufficient to establish that the brother resided in Canada at the time of the decision, based on the fact that the majority of the documentation provided related to the brother's wife and not him. The brother's notice of assessment was the only document which specifically related to him. It indicated he earned a total of $2,000 in 2006. The officer noted that her records indicated that the brother had prolonged absences from Canada in the past. The Notice of Assessment was therefore insufficient evidence to convince her that he was a resident of Canada at the time the decision was made. The officer's decision was based on the insufficiency of evidence establishing the brother's residence in Canada. The burden of adducing sufficient evidence to support the application falls to the applicant. The application for judicial review was dismissed.

Zheng v. Canada (Minister of Citizenship & Immigration), 2008 CarswellNat 1864, 2008 CarswellNat 880, 2008 FC 430 — A visa officer rejected an application for landing by a skilled worker from China. The visa officer's entry in the CAIPS system identifies a stark conflict in the evidence the applicant tendered in obvious error: the standard application form was completed to say that the applicant attended Kunming University at the same time she completed high school there, which, of course, is impossible. Because of the conflict, and the fact that the applicant failed to file a diploma to prove her attendance at the university, the application was rejected. It was remarkably unfair for the visa officer not to have asked for clarification of the obvious error which drove the rejection of the applicant's application. The visa officer's decision was set aside.

Gay v. Canada (Minister of Citizenship & Immigration) (2007), 69 Imm. L.R. (3d) 245, 320 F.T.R. 132, 2007 FC 1280, 2007 CarswellNat 5403, 2007 CarswellNat 4277 — The applicant, an accountant by profession, applied for permanent residence under the skilled worker category. He forwarded proof of his financial situation to the Canadian Embassy, claiming US$19,592.10 as his available financial resources. A letter from the Embassy was sent to the applicant requesting that he provide evidence of availability of his financial resources in the amount of C$10,168, for the purpose of establishment in Canada for his file to be finalized. The applicant forwarded to the Canadian Embassy a certified copy of a property deed, showing his title to the land, a statement of his net assets and new bank statements. The financial evidence provided at this time had a total value of approximately C$22,000. The application was refused pursuant to para. 76(1)(b) of the Regulations. The visa officer did not consider the applicant's land assets in the calculation of his settlement funds, as the applicant did not establish that this property amounted to funds that were available, transferable and unencumbered by debts or other obligations, as required by subs. 76(1) of the Regulations. The officer did not provide the applicant with the opportunity to provide more complete information in order to address her concerns that the assets from the land were transferable and unencumbered by debts and other obligations. Her failure to mention important pieces of evidence resulted in her having made an erroneous finding of fact "without regard to the evidence" before her (i.e. the certified copy of a property deed showing the applicant's title to the land, a statement of the applicant's net assets and new bank statements). The application for judicial review was granted.

Hernandez v. Canada (Minister of Citizenship & Immigration) (2004), 43 Imm. L.R. (3d) 63, 2004 CarswellNat 5382, 2004 CarswellNat 3658, 2004 FC 1398 — The applicant applied for admission as a member of the skilled worker class. The operations manual purports to assist a visa officer in assessing an application of this type. The manual requires a visa officer to give an applicant the opportunity to supply missing documentation concerning settlement funds. The officer failed to comply with this guideline and the officer's decision was set aside.

Section 76(3)

Gharialia v. Canada (Minister of Citizenship & Immigration), 2013 CarswellNat 2278, 2013 FC 745, 2013 CarswellNat 3113 — In the present case, the officer's substituted evaluation of the applicant's ability to become economically established was both linked to the criteria and broader than the criteria set out in subsec. 76(1). The officer considered the applicant's educational qualifications, experience as an Ayurvedic doctor, the lack of regulation of Ayurvedic doctors in Canada, prospects of employment in Canada, dependants and the settlement funds. Although there was no requirement for an applicant to work in the NOC field of which they may be eligible to come to Canada, these were the skills that the applicant would likely rely on to make a living. The officer was, therefore, justified in his belief that because the applicant would not be able to practise in Canada, the points did not adequately reflect the applicant's ability to become economically established. The officer had a valid reason to turn to a substituted evaluation and he reasonably exercised his discretion to do so. The application for judicial review was dismissed.

Sharma v. Canada (Minister of Citizenship & Immigration), 2011 FC 337, 2011 CarswellNat 785, 2011 CarswellNat 1969 — An officer refused the applicant's application for permanent residence under the federal skilled worker class. Although the applicant had obtained 70 points in the assessment of his application for a permanent residence visa as a skilled worker thus meeting the passing mark set at 67 points, the points awarded did not reflect his ability to become economically established in Canada. The officer made a negative substituted evaluation under s. 76(3) of the Regulations. The applicant was a lawyer and a financial consultant. He had immigrated to New Zealand in October 2005 but since that time had been engaged in completing the necessary studies to allow himself to be licensed as a lawyer and as an accountant in New Zealand and had only worked in temporary jobs. The officer was concerned that he had not secured from the respective corporative bodies the authorization to work in these occupations.

The court allowed the judicial review on the basis that the applicant had not been afforded the opportunity to address the officer's concern with respect to his settlement plans in Canada. A review of the officer's CAIPS notes did not indicate that the officer discussed his concerns with the applicant in the course of the interview.

Philbean v. Canada (Minister of Citizenship & Immigration), 2011 FC 487, 2011 CarswellNat 1343, 2011 CarswellNat 2608 — The officer was not satisfied that the applicant would be able to become economically established in Canada as per subs. 12(2) of IRPA and s. 76 of the Regulations. The applicant was a citizen of the UK and had worked as a registered nurse for almost 30 years. In March 2007, the applicant moved with her partner to Canada. Her partner was issued a work permit to work as a long haul truck driver. The applicant was issued a temporary visitor permit which prohibited her from employment in Canada. At the expiry of their respective permits, the couple returned to the UK. The applicant submitted an application for permanent residence in Canada under the federal skilled worker class based on her qualifications and work experience as a registered nurse. Although the applicant had been assessed as having over the minimum number of required points, her application was nonetheless rejected pursuant to subs. 76(3) of the Regulations because the officer was not satisfied that the applicant would be able to become economically established in Canada.

The officer was concerned not only about the applicant's ability to find employment in Canada, but also her *willingness* in that regard. These concerns were not based solely on the applicant's age. Instead, the officer considered the applicant's age in combination with a number of other circumstances, including: the applicant had already effectively retired in the UK, that despite having lived in Canada for two years she had not taken concrete steps towards certification or towards securing future employment in Canada, and that the applicant's husband had been offered work in Canada but that an LMO for his line of unskilled work had not been issued for a second stay.

The role of the court is not to substitute its own view for that of the immigration officer. The officer's decision to substitute a negative determination under subs. 76(3) of the Regulations did not lack justification, transparency or intelligibility or fall outside the range of possible acceptable outcomes defensible in respect of the facts in the law. The application for judicial review was dismissed.

Debnath v. Canada (Minister of Citizenship & Immigration), 2010 FC 904, 2010 CarswellNat 3727, 2010 CarswellNat 3308 — This is one of the rare cases where a visa officer exercised discretion to evaluate the likelihood of an applicant to become economically established in Canada, despite the number of points earned in the usual evaluation process. In this case, the applicant secured 68 points wherein 67 points were the minimum required. At the interview, the visa officer advised the applicant of his concerns about the potential for recognition of his medical qualifications in Canada and therefore whether he was likely to become economically established. Subsequently, the applicant submitted various documents related to his medical qualifications, courses and workshops attended and newspaper articles and letters to editors which he had written. In summary, the applicant was of the view that he could become qualified in Canada within six to 12 months of arrival. The applicant also argued that the visa officer failed to consider the applicant's settlement funds in assessing his ability to become economically established in Canada. The court held that the visa officer was aware of those funds and the matter of settlement funds was irrelevant to the visa officer's decision. The court concluded that the visa officer's decision to deny the visa was reasonable. The case turned on the sufficiency of the evidence, and the applicant had failed to put forward sufficient evidence to convince the visa officer that he was likely to become economically established. The application for judicial review was dismissed.

Kisson v. Canada (Minister of Citizenship and Immigration) (2010), 88 Imm. L.R. (3d) 66, 2010 FC 99, 2010 CarswellNat 803, 2010 CarswellNat 161 — This was an application for judicial review of a visa officer's decision rejecting the applicant's application for permanent residence under the federal skilled worker category. The applicant requested substitute evaluation and exemption from the requirements of IRPA pursuant to humanitarian and compassionate considerations. The visa officer did not demonstrate that he looked beyond the selection criteria listed at subs. 76(1) of the Regulations (*i.e.* education, language, experience, age, arranged employment, adaptability). There was no evidence that the visa officer's substituted evaluation broadly assessed the likelihood of the ability of the applicant to become economically established in Canada according to his set of circumstances. The clear intent of subs. 76(3) is to allow the visa officer to substitute their evaluation taking into account a number of factors, and not just the factors listed in s. 76(1). In this case, the applicant had an existing employment offer and previous establishment in Canada which were indicative of the possibility that the applicant will once again be able to establish himself successfully in Canada. It was unreasonable that these factors do not appear to have been considered by the officer when he assessed the humanitarian and compassionate considerations under s. 25 of IRPA. The application for judicial review was allowed.

Also see *Hussain v. Canada (Minister of Citizenship & Immigration)* (2009), 80 Imm. L.R. (3d) 124, 2009 CarswellNat 546, 2009 CarswellNat 1117, 2009 FC 209, at s. 76(1) of IRPR.

Lackhee v. Canada (Minister of Citizenship & Immigration), [2008] F.C.J. No. 1615, 76 Imm. L.R. (3d) 283, 337 F.T.R. 299 (Eng.), 2008 CarswellNat 5316, 2008 CarswellNat 4270, 2008 FC 1270 — The designated immigration officer who rendered the impugned decision rejected the application for permanent residence because he "obtained insufficient points to qualify for immigration to Canada, the minimum requirement being 67 points." The applicant did not contest the points awarded to him by the officer. Nor did the applicant argue that the officer did not turn her mind to his request for substituted evaluation. Instead, the applicant argued that the officer exercised her discretion in a capricious manner without due regard to the evidence in determining that the units of assessment assigned were an accurate indication of his prospects of becoming established in Canada.

Written reasons explaining why the request for substituted evaluation was denied are not required. The court was sympathetic to the applicant's position: he was a skilled tradesman with expertise in a field that is in high demand in Canada, and his profile was compelling. It was unclear why his relative lack of formal education and modest score on his language assessment have any bearing on the question of his ability to become economically settled in Canada. However, it is not the role of the court to substitute its own view for that of the decision maker, whom the legislation has imbued with broad discretion over this matter.

Although the immigration officer referred in her notes to the $25,000 initially noted in the applicant's application, the updated information indicating the availability of dramatically more assets for establishment is nowhere mentioned in either her notes or in her refusal letter. It is not enough that she was aware of this information: she had a duty to reflect this awareness in her notes and/or reasons in the interests of "justification, transparency and intelligibility." The jurisprudence of the Federal Court leaves no doubt that settlement income is among the considerations pertinent to assessing "the likelihood of the ability of the skilled worker to become economically established in Canada." The officer's failure to make any reference to the considerable assets available to the applicant in either her decision or her notes constituted a reviewable error warranting court intervention. The application was set aside.

Esguerra v. Canada (Minister of Citizenship & Immigration), 2008 CarswellNat 864, 2008 FC 413 — Discretion under subs. 76(3) of the IRPR is clearly exceptional and applies only in cases where the points awarded are not a sufficient indicator of whether the skilled worker will become economically established. The fact that the applicant or even the court would have weighed the factors differently is not a sufficient ground for judicial review.

Fernandes v. Canada (Minister of Citizenship & Immigration) (2008), 71 Imm. L.R. (3d) 134, 2008 FC 243, 2008 CarswellNat 465 — When it is said that an officer need give no reasons for refusing to exercise a discretion, what is meant is that an officer need give no reasons for exercising the discretion negatively. But it must be clear that the visa officer did consider whether the discretion should be exercised in favour of the applicant. There was nothing to indicate that the visa officer considered exercising the discretion under subs. 76(3). Therefore, she erred in law and the decision was set aside.

Choi v. Canada (Minister of Citizenship & Immigration), 2008 CarswellNat 1372, 2008 FC 577 — The applicant applied for permanent residence under the economic class, skilled worker category, as a secondary school teacher. The applicant received an offer of employment as a music teacher at Cambridge International College of Canada in Toronto.

Under subs. 76(3) of the Regulations, a visa officer may substitute the points assessment with his or her own evaluation of an applicant's likelihood of becoming economically established in Canada. Such a power is discretionary under the Regulations and may be performed "if the number of points awarded is not a sufficient indicator of whether the skilled worker may become economically established in Canada." The applicant argued that the visa officer did not give any weight to the principal's letter, which assured the visa officer that the applicant would be able to fulfill the requirements of the job, and that her English ability would soon rise to the requirements of the job. In the court's view, it was unreasonable for the visa officer not to give this letter some weight as a sufficient indicator of the applicant's ability to perform this job to the satisfaction of the principal of the school. The applicant also argued that she had settlement funds totalling approximately C$699,000 and that it was impossible for a reasonable person to conclude that a person arriving in Canada with these funds and an offer of employment would not be able to become "economically established in Canada." The court concluded that consideration under subs. 76(3) should not be limited to the assessment of points, but rather, should be open to all factors identified in subs. 76(1), including the settlement funds possessed by the applicant. In this case, there was no evidence that the visa officer considered those funds in refusing to exercise his discretion to substitute his evaluation. The visa officer's decision was set aside and the matter remitted to another visa officer for redetermination.

Eslamieh v. Canada (Minister of Citizenship & Immigration), 2008 CarswellNat 1701, 2008 CarswellNat 2799, 2008 FC 722 — The applicant's application for permanent residence status as a skilled worker was rejected. She scored 66 out of a possible 100 points. The applicant contended that the visa officer should have considered her discretion to grant the applicant permanent residence status despite her failure to reach the threshold set by the Minister pursuant to subs. 76(3) of the IRPA Regulations.

Given that the decision of the visa officer is highly discretionary, it is to be reviewed on a standard of reasonableness with great deference shown by the court. Visa officers have the authority to consider an alternative evaluation under subs. 76(3) by their own motion. That said, it is clear from the jurisprudence that they are under no obligation to exercise that discretion unless specifically requested to do so. The applicant concedes that she did not make such a request, and therefore, the court could not find that the visa officer was unreasonable in her decision.

The applicant also raised a question of natural justice inferentially in her reply brief and at the hearing. She asserted that the officer should have considered her application in the context of her self-representation and extremely narrow failure to reach the point target. From that perspective, the officer had an obligation in the name of fairness to consider her discretion under subs. 76(3). While the court was sympathetic to this contention, it is trite law that the applicant is restricted, also for reasons of natural justice and procedural fairness, to arguing issues raised in her application for leave. She sought leave solely on the ground that the officer had erred in law. The court could not now substitute a ground which was not contained therein. The application was dismissed.

Tathgur v. Canada (Minister of Citizenship & Immigration), [2007] F.C.J. No. 1662, 321 F.T.R. 102, 2007 FC 1293, 68 Imm. L.R. (3d) 258, 2007 CarswellNat 4354, 2007 CarswellNat 4954 — The failure by the visa officer to consider exercising the statutory discretion when requested to do so is a failure to carry out a statutory responsibility the visa officer was obligated to do. Under IRPA Regulations, a visa officer may substitute the evaluation criteria if the number of points awarded is not a sufficient indicator of whether the applicant will become economically established in Canada. The respondent argued that the applicant, in requesting the exercise of discretion, did not specify the reason for believing he would become successfully established in Canada despite not meeting the assessment requirements. The court concluded that the applicant did offer "good reason" for the consideration of positive discretion, and that in any event it is clear that the Regulations impose no such requirement. The request for judicial review was granted.

Nayyar v. Canada (Minister of Citizenship & Immigration), 2007 CarswellNat 559, 2007 FC 199 — The applicant sought judicial review of a decision to refuse his application for permanent residence as a skilled worker. The applicant alleged a breach of procedural fairness in that the officer failed to consider the exercise of positive discretion or substituted evaluation when specifically requested to do so in the applicant's application for permanent residence. It was not in dispute before the court that: there is nothing on the face of the officer's decision or of the CAIPS notes supporting that decision that the officer considered the exercise of positive discretion or substituted evaluation notwithstanding the fact that the applicant was within one (1) unit of assessment from a successful score under the *Immigration and Refugee Protection Act* and related *Regulations* assessment; there was absolutely no evidence before the court that the applicant reiterated his request for an exercise of positive discretion or substituted evaluation during his interview with the officer before the decision under review was arrived at; and notwithstanding the fact a request for reconsideration of the decision under review was made, that request made no reference to the question of exercise of positive discretion or substituted evaluation.

In the application for a permanent resident visa filed on behalf of the applicant under the former Act, the applicant's immigration consultant sets out at some length the applicant's personal background and an assessment of the units of assessment the consultant thinks are justified for the applicant, and provides a rationale for the units of assessment that he urges in respect of the education and training factor, the work experience factor, the knowledge of English and other languages factor and the personal suitability factor. The court was satisfied that the consultant's presentation constitutes "some good reasons" why a units of assessment determination made by the officer, that he did not reach the threshold justifying the issuance of a permanent resident visa, would not reflect the chances of successful establishment in Canada by the applicant and would therefore justify the exercise of positive discretion or positive substituted evaluation. The application for judicial review was allowed and was referred back for consideration of the exercise of positive discretion by a different officer.

Also see *Mercado v. Canada (Minister of Citizenship & Immigration)* (2006), 60 Imm. L.R. (3d) 88, 2006 CarswellNat 4484, 2006 FC 1527, at s. 75 of IRPR.

Poblado v. Canada (Minister of Citizenship & Immigration), 2005 CarswellNat 2399, 2005 CarswellNat 4425, 2005 FC 1167 — A visa officer merely has to inform the applicant that they have considered the request for substitution of evaluation, where the applicant asked that favourable discretion be exercised.

77. Conformity — applicable times — For the purposes of Part 5, the requirements and criteria set out in sections 75 and 76 must be met on the date on which an application for a permanent resident visa is made and on the date on which it is issued.

SOR/2012-274, s. 7

Selection Grid

78. (1) Education (25 points) — Points shall be awarded, to a maximum of 25, for a skilled worker's Canadian educational credential or equivalency assessment submitted in support of an application, as follows:

    (a) 5 points for a secondary school credential;

    (b) 15 points for a one-year post-secondary program credential;

    (c) 19 points for a two-year post-secondary program credential;

    (d) 21 points for a post-secondary program credential of three years or longer;

(e) 22 points for two or more post-secondary program credentials, one of which must be a credential issued on completion of a post-secondary program of three years or longer;

(f) 23 points for a university-level credential at the master's level or at the level of an entry-to-practice professional degree for an occupation listed in the *National Occupational Classification* matrix at Skill Level A for which licensing by a provincial regulatory body is required; and

(g) 25 points for a university-level credential at the doctoral level.

(2) More than one educational credential — For the purposes of subsection (1), points

(a) except as set out in paragraph (1)(e), shall not be awarded cumulatively on the basis of more than one educational credential; and

(b) shall be awarded on the basis of the Canadian educational credentials or equivalency assessments submitted in support of an application for a permanent resident visa that result in the highest number of points.

(3) [Repealed SOR/2012-274, s. 7.]

(4) [Repealed SOR/2012-274, s. 7.]

SOR/2012-274, s. 7

Case Law

Ijaz v. Canada (Minister of Citizenship and Immigration) (2015), 32 Imm. L.R. (4th) 286, 2015 FC 67, 2015 CarswellNat 3404, 2015 CarswellNat 113 — The applicant sought judicial review of the decision to refuse her application for permanent residence as a federal skilled worker. The officer only awarded the applicant five of a potential 25 points for education. The World Education Services ("WES") organization assessed the applicant's higher secondary certificate credential as equivalent to a Canadian secondary school diploma. It assessed her foreign two-year Bachelor of Science credential as equivalent to two years of Canadian undergraduate study and her Intermediate and Professional Examination Results credential as equivalent to two years of Canadian professional study. It was open to the officer to interpret the WES educational assessment and the IRP Regulations as he did, being that the WES equivalency findings of two years of undergraduate study and two years of professional study were not the equivalent of a Canadian educational credential. The WES educational assessment did not state that the applicant's credentials were equivalent to Canadian educational credentials, and the officer relied on this as conclusive evidence as required by s. 75(8) of the IRP Regulations. While the officer had discretion in interpreting ambiguous language in the WES assessment, he had no discretion on the points to be awarded once the meaning of the report had been ascertained. The officer's decision was reasonable. The application for judicial review was dismissed.

The following question was certified:

When assessing a federal skilled worker class application for permanent residency and the points to be awarded for education under s. 78 of the *Immigration and Refugee Protection Regulations* (IRP Regulations), do the IRP Regulations require an equivalency assessment, as required by s. 75(2) and defined by s. 73(1), of a foreign diploma, certificate or credential to be evaluated and explicitly stated as being equivalent to a diploma, certificate or credential issued on the completion of a Canadian program of study or training, as defined in s. 73(1) as a "Canadian educational credential?

Or, is a determination and statement of the equivalent value of the foreign diploma, certificate or credential, expressed as a number of years of study in Canada, sufficient to award points pursuant to s. 78(1)?

Khan v. Canada (Minister of Citizenship & Immigration) (2011), 3 Imm. L.R. (4th) 1, 344 D.L.R. (4th) 739, 426 N.R. 12, 2011 FCA 339, 2011 CarswellNat 5153 — The appellant sought judicial review of the decision to refuse his application for permanent residence under the skilled worker class. He had been awarded 22 points for his education and this was a subject of the initial application for judicial review. He held a Bachelor of Commerce degree which was awarded in 1985; a Master's degree in accounting that was awarded in 1987; a Diploma in Computer Application Programming that was awarded in 1998; and a Masters in Business Administration that was awarded in 2007. He had pursued 19 years of full-time studies. The visa officer concluded that he obtained 22 points for education based on his highest level of credential of a Master's degree with the equivalent of 16 years of full-time education leading up to the completion of his highest degree (his two Master's degrees separately) in a recognized post-secondary institution. The officer held that he could not accumulate more years of education having two credentials at the same level. Progression towards obtaining his highest credential therefore was not considered by the visa officer for additional years of education.

In assessing the points for education under s. 78 of the *Immigration and Refugee Protection Regulations*, a visa officer does not award points for years of full-time or full-time equivalent studies that did not contribute to the educational credential being assessed. That is, visa officers must give credit only for those years of study which the national authorities identify as the norm for the achievement of the educational credential in issue. The appeal was dismissed.

Shahid v. Canada (Minister of Citizenship & Immigration) (2011), 96 Imm. L.R. (3d) 186, [2011] F.C.J. No. 160, 2011 FCA 40, 2011 CarswellNat 237 — The application for permanent residence as a skilled worker was refused on the basis that the respondent scored only 63 points. The officer gave the respondent no credit for his spouse's education. The evidence showed that the spouse had completed a two-year university degree and wrote exams in her first and second years. The officer, however, concluded that she was an external candidate at the university and, therefore, did not meet the requirement that she demonstrate completion of 14 years of full-time or full-time equivalent studies.

On a correct construction of the definition of "full-time equivalent," the respondent's spouse failed to meet the two requirements of subpara. 78(2)(d)(ii) in that she did not obtain an educational credential as defined or achieve 14 years of full-time or full-time equivalent studies. It follows that the immigration officer came to the proper conclusion and the applications judge erred in intervening. The definition of "full-time equivalent" applies when there is a discrepancy between the time in which a particular "educational credential" as defined is obtained by an individual and the time required to obtain the same credential on a full-time basis by reason of having followed part-time or accelerated studies at an educational or training institution recognized by the authorities. It follows that the definition requires a consideration of both the nature and quantity of instruction received by the individual.

Bano v. Canada (Minister of Citizenship & Immigration), 2011 FC 401, 2011 CarswellNat 1065, 2011 CarswellNat 2259 — An officer denied the applicant's application for permanent residence as a skilled worker. The officer awarded the applicant 15 points for her education because she completed one year of post-secondary education at Aga Khan University. The officer did not award the applicant any points for her Bachelor's degree from the University of Karachi because the documents indicated that the applicant was an external candidate. The officer noted that candidates may have prepared for their examination through self-study or with a private tutor who is not regulated by the government of Pakistan. A private/external candidate is not enrolled as a student at the institution granting the degree or recognized college. The court followed the decision in *Shahid v. Canada (Minister of Citizenship & Immigration)*, 2010 FC 130, CarswellNat 847, 2010 CarswellNat 278, where Justice O'Reilley stated "even if she studied elsewhere, or on her own, whether part-time or on an accelerated basis, it seems to me she could meet the definition of 'full-time equivalent' if she proved that the degree she obtained would ordinarily take 14 years of full-time study to obtain." In the present case, the applicant presented the same evidence as Ms. Shahid: her Bachelor degree and her record of examinations. The application for judicial review was allowed.

Rabiee v. Canada (Minister of Citizenship & Immigration), 2011 FC 824, 2011 CarswellNat 2813 (T.D.) — The applicant challenged a refusal for a permanent resident visa pursuant to the federal skilled worker program. The applicant argued that the officer made three reviewable errors: first, that the officer's assessment of the applicant under the "general practitioner" (NOC 3112) category, as opposed to the "specialist" category (NOC 3111). Second, the applicant argued that the officer erred in the assessment of the applicant's language ability in that she should have received an additional 2 points. Third, the applicant argued that the officer awarded the applicant 22 points for education, assuming that all of her credentials were at the university Bachelor's level. The applicant maintained that she should have received 25 points because of the specialty she completed in dermatology. The officer justified the decision for believing that the applicant's specialist degree was not a credential at the Master's or doctoral level. Given that there was no clear evidence showing that the specialization qualified as graduate studies, the decision was left to the officer's discretion and the court was not satisfied that the conclusion was unreasonable. The application for judicial review was dismissed.

Healey v. Canada (Minister of Citizenship & Immigration) (2009), 80 Imm. L.R. (3d) 138, 2009 CarswellNat 891, 2009 FC 355 — This was an application for judicial review of a decision of a visa officer refusing the applicant's application for permanent residence under the federal skilled worker category. There was an error made on the applicant's application in that two years of college were not accurately indicated in the educational history boxes on the application form. The applicant accidentally wrote "0" instead of "2" in the box labeled "University/College." The officer concluded that the applicant had only completed 13 years of education, and 15 points was appropriate. Counsel for the applicant attempted to clarify the mistake but received no response.

It was not possible to tell from the record why the officer felt the applicant only had 13 years of education, and the fact that the officer had recently provided a detailed affidavit justifying his calculations is a clear confirmation that the letter and CAIPS notes do not explain that issue. The officer's affidavit was given no weight by the court as it went well beyond an elaboration of the reasons and instead provided an after-the-fact rationale for the central issue in this application concerning the way that the points were calculated.

In all the circumstances of this case, the reasons were inadequate. This was a decision of importance for the applicant's future. He could not surmise from the decision why the Thurrock and BTEC certificates had been awarded 0 points. The officer's position was simply that he had no obligation to explain to the applicant why he had taken a position on the facts that the two certificates in question would not be credited. This prevented any understanding or questioning of the officer's position on the facts. It was a denial of the applicant's right to comprehend why he had been refused and an attempt to thwart any action he might take to question the officer's decision. It left him to choose between incomprehension and legal action. In fairness to the applicant, he should have the matter reviewed by someone else who will explain to him what his certificates represent and how they merit, or do not merit, points under the Regulations. A simple explanation by the officer could have prevented what became a significant waste of time and resources on both sides. The application for judicial review was allowed.

Hameed v. Canada (Minister of Citizenship & Immigration) (2009), 80 Imm. L.R. (3d) 109, 2009 FC 527, 2009 CarswellNat 1416 — The applicant's application for permanent residence as a skilled worker was turned down. The officer's assessment was based on the applicant's completion of secondary education. The applicant was given no points for his Bachelor's degree because, according to the officer, he had failed to provide conclusive proof that he had attended classes on a full-time or full-time equivalent basis on the way to achieving that degree.

The officer's conclusion was unreasonable. The Regulations do not require proof of attendance. Even if the officer was concerned that the applicant had not proved how many hours of classes he was supposed to have attended each week, his evidence showed that "the period that would have been required to complete" his degree was 14 years, according to the Higher Education Commission. In other words, even if the applicant had failed to show that his studies met the definition of "full-time," he had proved that he had obtained a degree based on a full-time equivalent of 14 years of study. Accordingly, he met the dual requirements of the Regulations. The officer's decision to the contrary is not in keeping with the law and the relevant facts and, therefore, is unreasonable. The application for judicial review was allowed.

79. (1) Official languages — A skilled worker must identify in their application for a permanent resident visa which language — English or French — is to be considered their first official language in Canada. They must have their proficiency in that language evaluated by an organization or institution designated under subsection 74(3).

(2) Proficiency in second language — If the skilled worker wishes to claim points for proficiency in their second official language they must, with the application for a permanent resident visa, submit the results of an evaluation — which must be less than two years old on the date on which their application is made — of their proficiency by an organization or institution designated under subsection 74(3).

(3) Proficiency in English and French (28 points) — Points for proficiency in the official languages of Canada shall be awarded up to a maximum of 24 points for the skilled worker's first official language and a maximum of 4 points for the applicant's second official language based on benchmarks set out in *Canadian Language Benchmarks* and the *Niveaux de compétence linguistique canadiens*, as follows:

(a) for the four language skill areas in the skilled worker's first official language,

(i) 4 points per language skill area if the skilled worker's proficiency meets the threshold fixed by the Minister under subsection 74(1) for that language skill area,

(ii) 5 points per language skill area if the skilled worker's proficiency exceeds the threshold fixed by the Minister under subsection 74(1) for that language skill area by one benchmark level, and

(iii) 6 points per language skill area if the skilled worker's proficiency exceeds the threshold fixed by the Minister under subsection 74(1) for that language skill area by at least two benchmark levels; and

(b) for the four language skill areas in the skilled worker's second official language, 4 points if the skilled worker's proficiency in that language meets or exceeds benchmark level 5 in each of the four language skill areas.

SOR/2004-167, s. 29; SOR/2008-253, s. 7; SOR/2011-54, s. 1; SOR/2012-274, ss. 7, 8

Case Law

Section 79(1)

Tan v. Canada (Minister of Citizenship & Immigration) (2012), 12 Imm. L.R. (4th) 13, 2012 FC 1079, 2012 CarswellNat 3543, 2012 CarswellNat 4298 — The applicant argued that the officer erred by assessing the applicant's language proficiency on a higher standard than specified in the AEO. The AEO merely specified that the applicant needed to have basic English oral proficiency to complete the employment. No English writing or reading skills were specified. Nevertheless, the officer found that the applicant's proposed employer would not be able to ensure that an English-speaking person was always present while the applicant was working. Therefore, the officer concluded that in addition to the basic English oral proficiency, the applicant will require sufficient English proficiency to be able to read English safety equipment instructions in the kitchen and to communicate with Canadian authorities in case of accidents or emergencies. The officer found that these requirements were important in assessing whether the applicant could perform and carry out the proposed employment and therefore become economically established in Canada. The officer incorporated a requirement not specified in the AEO. The officer erred by incorporating requirements that exceeded those specifically listed in the AEO and by denying the applicant's permanent residence application on this basis. The application for judicial review was allowed.

Grewal v. Canada (Minister of Citizenship & Immigration), 2011 FC 167, 2011 CarswellNat 301, 2011 CarswellNat 1268 — The applicant sought judicial review of a decision to refuse her permanent residence application under the skilled worker class. The applicant had arranged employment in Canada as a retail trade manager, but the immigration officer was of the opinion that she would not be able to perform the required duties as she did not have sufficient language skills. Basically, the immigration officer assessed the applicant's IELTS scores to conclude on both language proficiency and arrange employment. While it was true that the applicant's IELTS test results were not sufficient for her to be awarded more points, there was evidence before the officer that the applicant was to undertake a second examination to better her results. Her poor results were allegedly caused by health reasons.

The applicant's statements and educational background could reasonably infer some knowledge of English. When this is considered with the claims of poor health when taking the IELTS test, it seems as though the immigration officer's decision to adjudicate the matter without a fairness letter or an interview is unreasonable, especially as the officer knew that a second IELTS test was to follow. Surely, procedural fairness called for further enquiry by the officer in such a case, through a letter or an interview.

It is clear that assessing the breadth of procedural fairness in a case must be adapted to the context in which it arises. In this case, where a manual provided clear guidance that more information should be sought, where one finding on language proficiency derailed the whole claim for permanent residence and where there was evidence that another test was to be taken, it seems that procedural fairness should have extended to an interview or a fairness letter. Immigration policy must be meaningfully addressed. The application for judicial review was granted and the matter sent for redetermination.

Islam v. Canada (Minister of Citizenship & Immigration), 2006 CarswellNat 1073, 2006 FC 424 — The Regulations do not grant the visa officer the authority to administer their own "writing test" in lieu of the prescribed test.

80. (1) Experience (15 points) — Points shall be awarded, up to a maximum of 15 points, to a skilled worker for full-time work experience, or the equivalent in part-time work, within the 10 years before the date on which their application is made, as follows:

    (a) 9 points for one year of work experience;

    (b) 11 points for two to three years of work experience;

    (c) 13 points for four to five years of work experience; and

    (d) 15 points for six or more years of work experience.

(2) Listed occupation — For the purposes of subsection (1), points are awarded for work experience in occupations, other than a restricted occupation, that are listed in Skill Type 0 Management Occupations or Skill Level A or B of the *National Occupational Classification* matrix.

(3) Occupational experience — For the purposes of subsection (1), a skilled worker is considered to have experience in an occupation, regardless of whether they meet the employment requirements of the occupation as set out in the occupational descriptions of the *National Occupational Classification*, if they performed

    (a) the actions described in the lead statement for the occupation as set out in the occupational descriptions of the *National Occupational Classification*; and

    (b) at least a substantial number of the main duties of the occupation as set out in the occupational descriptions of the *National Occupational Classification*, including all the essential duties.

(4) Work in excess — A period of work experience that exceeds full-time work in one occupation, or simultaneous periods of work experience in more than one full-time occupation, shall be evaluated as a single period of full-time work experience in a single occupation.

(5) Classification code — A skilled worker must specify in their application for a permanent resident visa the four-digit code of the *National Occupational Classification* that corresponds to each of the occupations engaged in by the applicant and that constitutes the skilled worker's work experience.

(6) Officer's duty — An officer is not required to consider occupations that have not been specified in the application.

(7) [Repealed SOR/2012-274, s. 9(2).]

SOR/2010-195, s. 7; SOR/2012-274, s. 9

Case Law

Ansari v. Canada (Minister of Citizenship & Immigration), 2013 CarswellNat 2870, 2013 CarswellNat 3879, 2013 FC 849 — The officer found that the applicant did not have sufficient evidence that he had performed the actions described in the lead statement for the occupation and that he had performed all of the essential duties and a substantial number of the main duties. The refusal letter stated that the duties described in the employment letter submitted were "closely paraphrased from occupational descriptions of the NOC, diminishing the overall credibility of the employment letter." There is a need to determine whether the concern is about credibility or sufficiency before determining if a duty of procedural fairness is owed. If a concern about copying or paraphrasing from the NOC is characterised as related to credibility, without assessing whether it is in fact a credibility concern, the applicants who copy the NOC duties may come to expect an opportunity to provide further information or respond to the officer's concerns. This could lead to delays in processing FSW applications and is inconsistent with the instructions provided to applicants to provide all the relevant documents with their applications and to visa officers to assess the application as presented. The officer was entitled to give the evidence less weight, and as a result, the applicant did not meet the burden of providing sufficient information. There was no breach of procedural fairness.

Bazaid v. Canada (Minister of Citizenship & Immigration), 2013 FC 17, 2013 CarswellNat 69, 2013 CarswellNat 993 — The applicant seeks judicial review of the refusal of an immigration officer to process his application for permanent residence under the federal skilled worker class. The applicant challenged the immigration officer's decision that he did not present sufficient evidence to establish that he met the occupational requirements for NOC 3111 — Specialist Physicians.

The lead statement and list of main duties in the NOC document describes the set of tasks generally performed by most specialist physicians. It would be unreasonable to find that a person who held the job titles of Psychiatrist, Psychiatrist (Child and Adolescent), Assistant Professor and Consultant at the Department of Psychiatry, Consultant Child and Adolescent Psychiatrist and who is a Fellow of the College would not have diagnosed and treated psychiatric disorders, ordered diagnostic procedures, prescribed medication and treatment, and acted as a consultant to other physicians. By setting out a generic list of tasks typical to most specialists, the NOC document does not command the level of detail that the respondent in this case advocated. The court was not persuaded by the respondent's arguments that the applicant's certificates from Saudi Aramco only established that he worked for an oil company and that the letter describing him as an assistant professor suggested he only worked in an academic capacity. The certificates stated that the applicant worked as a psychiatrist for Saudi Aramco. The applicant may have been an oil company employee but he was an oil company employee whose position was within the NOC 3111 class. A person who holds the job title of Psychiatrist will obviously perform the functions of a psychiatrist, practice as a psychiatrist and provide in-patient care. The application for judicial review was granted.

Hosseini v. Canada (Minister of Citizenship & Immigration), 2013 CarswellNat 2323, 2013 CarswellNat 3800, 2013 FC 766, [2013] F.C.J. No. 814 — In this application for a judicial review of a decision to refuse an application for permanent residence as a member of the federal skilled worker class, the officer found that the applicant had not provided satisfactory evidence of work experience in the listed occupation. The jurisprudence of the court is that there is no requirement that he should have performed all the main duties described in NOC 0711. The applicant only had to show that he had performed a substantial number of the main duties set out in the NOC, including any essential duties. When the duties were compared with the lead statement and the duties set out in NOC 0711, it was clear that there was some overlap, but whether it can be said that the applicant had performed "a substantial number of the main duties" set out in the NOC is very much a discretionary judgment call. Parliament has said that visa officers are to make that discretionary call and, as the jurisprudence makes clear, the court cannot countermand a decision unless it falls outside of the range posited in para. 47 of *New Brunswick (Board of Management) v. Dunsmuir*, [2008] 1 S.C.R. 190 (*sub nom. Dunsmuir v. New Brunswick*). The application was dismissed.

Esmaili v. Canada (Minister of Citizenship & Immigration) (2013), 21 Imm. L.R. (4th) 756, 8 Admin. L.R. (5th) 27, 2013 FC 1161, 2013 CarswellNat 4192, 2013 CarswellNat 4740 — The decision appears clearly unreasonable on its face. The applicant had a Bachelor's and Master's degree in his field, as well as a glowing recommendation from a professor at the graduate studies level. He had risen through the ranks at his company over the course of 4½ years, performing various functions in the general area of information systems management, and had documentation showing 1½ years' experience as a full-time information systems manager directing employees and running the IT operations of the organization. In the absence of any explanation from the officer, it was neither transparent nor intelligible why this was not thought to be sufficient, and the decision does not represent a possible, acceptable outcome. The application for a judicial review was allowed setting aside the decision to refuse the applicant's application for permanent residence as a member of the federal skilled worker class.

Nauman v. Canada (Minister of Citizenship & Immigration) (2013), 20 Imm. L.R. (4th) 1, 63 Admin. L.R. (5th) 237, 2013 FC 964, 2013 CarswellNat 3393, 2013 CarswellNat 3949 — This was an application for judicial review of a decision refusing the applicant's application for permanent residence in the federal skilled worker category. The officer noted that he had concerns about the authenticity of the documentation from the applicant's employer. However, he did not send a fairness letter informing the applicant of this concern. In his refusal letter, he stated that the list of duties carried out did not demonstrate that the applicant had performed all of the essential duties and a substantial number of the main duties of the NOC.

While the application on its face may not have been sufficient to demonstrate that the applicant had performed all of the necessary tasks required, the visa officer's discretion to question whether the applicant's documents accurately describe an applicant's experience raises a duty of fairness upon his attribution of adverse inferences to the applicant regarding her creditability. The failure to question the applicant on the authenticity of her documents could have affected the decision. The application for judicial review was allowed.

Madadi v. Canada (Minister of Citizenship & Immigration), 2013 CarswellNat 2283, 2013 CarswellNat 2790, 2013 FC 716, [2013] F.C.J. No. 798 — The applicant held a Master's degree in civil engineering, and stated in his application for permanent residence under NOC 0711 "Construction Manager" that he had been working as a construction manager since September 2003. He was found not eligible for processing in the category. The letter from his current employer confirmed his title, salary, period of employment, projects worked on, and the duties he performed in this position. The officer rejected the letter stating that the duties described were either copied word for word or closely paraphrased from occupational descriptions of the NOC, diminishing the overall credibility of the employment letter.

Where an applicant provides evidence sufficient to establish that they meet the requirements of the Act or Regulations, as the case may be, and the officer doubts the "credibility, accuracy or genuine nature of the information provided" and wishes to deny the application based on those concerns, the duty of fairness is invoked. The officer erred in failing to put his or her concerns to the applicant. The decision was set aside.

Kaur v. Canada (Minister of Citizenship & Immigration), 2010 FC 442, 2010 CarswellNat 2241, 2010 CarswellNat 1305 — The application for permanent residence was refused. The visa officer found the supporting documents with respect to work experience insufficient. The applicant claimed that she provided a "detailed letter" stating that she performed the duties of a cook for 3 ½ years in India. The applicant complained that the visa officer's concern that the letter was insufficient could easily have been addressed had he notified the applicant. The question of whether an applicant has the relevant experience as required by the Regulations and is thus qualified for the trade or profession in which he or she claims to be a skilled worker is "based directly on the requirements of the legislation and regulations." Therefore, it is up to the applicant to submit sufficient evidence on this question, and the visa officer was not under a duty to apprise her of his concerns. It did not help that the applicant's own description of her duties appeared to be copied from the National Occupational Classification. It was open to the visa officer on the basis of the scant evidence before him to find the applicant had not established that she had sufficient work experience in her stated occupation, and to reject her application on that basis. The application for judicial review was dismissed.

Rodrigues v. Canada (Minister of Citizenship & Immigration), 2009 CarswellNat 864, 2009 CarswellNat 240, 2009 FC 111 — This was a judicial review of the decision of a visa officer to reject the applicant's application for permanent residence as a member of the skilled worker class. The only issue argued in this matter was with respect to the officer's evaluation of the applicant's experience under job category NOC 1221 Administrative Officers. The visa officer's function in this matter is to make a largely factual determination, which is informed by particular experience in this area. The officer concluded that the applicant worked "in customer service and logistics (not as a supervisor)." The officer found that the applicant's real functions were the coordination of cargo and some financial management. The best that could be said in respect of the applicant's qualifications under NOC 1221 is that he performed some element of oversight in an indirect manner. The function of oversight was only one element in the NOC 1221 main duties requirements. In the Federal Court of Appeal's decision in *Noman v. Canada (Minister of Citizenship & Immigration)* (2002), 24 Imm. L.R. (3d) 131, while the court outlined that an applicant was not required to perform all the main duties in an NOC job category, they did require that an applicant perform a few, meaning more than one.

The real function of the visa officer is to determine what is the pith and substance of the work performed by an applicant. Tangential performance of one or more functions under one or more job categories does not convert the job or the functions from one NOC category to another. On the evidence, it was open to the officer to reach the conclusion that the applicant did not have sufficient experience to match the requirements of NOC 1221 for the skilled worker application. The application for judicial review was dismissed.

McHugh v. Canada (Minister of Citizenship & Immigration), 2006 CarswellNat 3095, 2006 FC 1181 — In assessing an application for permanent residence in the skilled worker class, visa officers are required to give the NOC categories a liberal interpretation, and the requirements of the job in question have to be assessed with flexibility. Job requirements also have to be assessed in the operational context in which the individual has actually worked. In this case, although the visa officer found that the evidence did not demonstrate that the applicant had performed all of the essential duties of an administrative officer, NOC 1221 does not identify any essential duties for the position. It should also be noted that NOC 1221 required that applicants have performed *some or all* of the duties in question. This allows a visa officer to give greater weight to certain duties contained in the job description over others, but does not require that applicants must perform all of the duties listed in the NOC. The applicant's documented financial management skills demonstrate that she would satisfy several of the criteria for the administrative officer category, in particular, as they relate to the administration of the internal financial management of the bank, the preparation of reports, and the duties in budgetary administration. While visa officers have considerable discretion in determining whether an applicant satisfies the requirements of a given occupation, and in interpreting the provisions of a NOC, in this case the officer's conclusion that there was "no comparison" between the list of the applicant's duties provided by her employer and the duties of administrative officers was patently unreasonable. The officer's decision was set aside.

Kniazeva v. Canada (Minister of Citizenship & Immigration) (2006), 52 Imm. L.R. (3d) 298, 2006 CarswellNat 472, 2006 FC 268 — The applicant filed an application for permanent residence under the skilled worker class. New legislation was enacted following the applicant's application having been filed. Under subs. 361(4) of the *Immigration and Refugee Protection Regulations*, the applicant could have become a permanent resident as a member of the federal skilled worker class by qualifying under either the former Act's regulation or under the new legislation. Once the visa officer decided to assess the applicant under both the old and new Act, he had to inform the applicant of the new requirements with respect to language proficiency. The visa officer's failure to conduct a thorough review of her application under the new Act and failure to provide the applicant with an opportunity to provide him with the language assessment amounted to a clear breach of duty of fairness owed to the applicant.

The visa officer contacted the applicant's former employer with a view to verifying her employment. The employer confirmed the applicant had "practical training at the plant while she was a student and had worked intervals during the period between June 1997 and July 1998. Accordingly, the visa officer had a duty to inform the applicant that he only considered this work experience as part-time and therefore the experience was being disqualified as relevant work experience.

The visa officer breached the duty of procedural fairness and the application for judicial review was allowed.

81. Age (12 points) — Points shall be awarded, up to a maximum of 12, for a skilled worker's age on the date on which their application is made, as follows:

(a) 12 points for a skilled worker 18 years of age or older but less than 36 years of age;

(b) 11 points for a skilled worker 36 years of age;

(c) 10 points for a skilled worker 37 years of age;

(d) 9 points for a skilled worker 38 years of age;

(e) 8 points for a skilled worker 39 years of age;

(f) 7 points for a skilled worker 40 years of age;

(g) 6 points for a skilled worker 41 years of age;

(h) 5 points for a skilled worker 42 years of age;

(i) 4 points for a skilled worker 43 years of age;

(j) 3 points for a skilled worker 44 years of age;

(k) 2 points for a skilled worker 45 years of age;

(l) 1 point for a skilled worker 46 years of age; and

(m) 0 points for a skilled worker under 18 years of age or 47 years of age or older.

SOR/2012-274, s. 10

82. (1) Definition of "arranged employment" — In this section, "arranged employment" means an offer of employment for full-time work in Canada that is non-seasonal and indeterminate, in an occupation listed in Skill Type 0 Management Occupations or Skill Level A or B of the *National Occupational Classification* matrix, that is made by an employer other than an embassy, high commission or consulate in Canada or an employer who is referred to in any of subparagraphs 200(3)(h)(i) to (iii).

(2) Arranged employment (10 points) — Ten points shall be awarded to a skilled worker for arranged employment if they are able to perform and are likely to accept and carry out the employment and

(a) the skilled worker is in Canada and holds a work permit that is valid on the date on which their application for a permanent resident visa is made and, on the date on which it is issued, holds a valid work permit or is authorized to work in Canada under section 186, and

(i) the work permit was issued based on a positive determination by an officer under subsection 203(1) with respect to the skilled worker's employment in an occupation listed in Skill Type 0 Management Occupations or Skill Level A or B of the *National Occupational Classification* matrix,

(ii) the skilled worker is working for an employer specified on the work permit, and

(iii) the employer has made an offer of arranged employment to the skilled worker subject to the permanent resident visa being issued to the skilled worker;

(b) the skilled worker is in Canada and

(i) holds a work permit referred to in paragraph 204(a) or (c) that is valid on the date on which their application for a permanent resident visa is made and, on the date on which it is issued, holds a valid work permit or is authorized to work in Canada under section 186, and

(ii) the circumstances referred to in subparagraphs (a)(ii) and (iii) apply;

(c) the skilled worker does not hold a valid work permit and is not authorized to work in Canada under section 186 on the date on which their application for a permanent resident visa is made and

(i) an employer has made an offer of arranged employment to the skilled worker, and

(ii) an officer has approved the offer of employment based on an assessment — provided to the officer by the Department of Employment and Social Development, on the same basis as an assessment provided for the issuance of a work permit, at the request of the employer or an officer — that the requirements set out in subsection 203(1) with respect to the offer have been met; or

(d) the skilled worker holds a valid work permit or is authorized to work in Canada under section 186 on the date on which their application for a permanent resident visa is made and on the date on which it is issued, and

(i) the circumstances referred to in subparagraphs (a)(ii) and (iii) and paragraph (b) do not apply, and

(ii) the circumstances referred to in subparagraphs (c)(i) and (ii) apply.

SOR/2004-167, s. 30(1)–(3), (5)–(7); SOR/2010-172, s. 5(c); SOR/2012-274, s. 11; 2013, c. 40, s. 237(3)(a); SOR/2013-245, s. 1; SOR/2015-144, s. 1; SOR/2015-147, s. 1(a)

Case Law

Chughtai v. Canada (Minister of Citizenship and Immigration) (2016), 40 Imm. L.R. (4th) 157, 2016 FC 416, 2016 CarswellNat 1384, 2016 CarswellNat 3240 — The applicant sought judicial review of an officer's decision to refuse his application for permanent residence as a skilled worker due to a finding that he was inadmissible to Canada on the basis of misrepresentation, pursuant to para. 40(1)(a) of IRPA. In particular, the officer reviewing the applicant's file found that the applicant had submitted an AEO for a position that was not genuine, and that this submission was relevant to whether or not he met the selection criteria as a skilled worker under the ministerial instructions. This misrepresentation was material to the disposition of the application, and could have led to an error in the administration of IRPA.

The determination of misrepresentation under para. 40(1)(a) is factual in nature and calls for a differential standard of review. The court should not intervene if the decision falls within a range of possible acceptable outcomes which are defensible in respect of the facts and law.

A visa officer has the discretion to refuse an application for permanent residence as a skilled worker, even in cases where HRSDC has issued an AEO. Pursuant to s. 203(1)(a) of the Regulations, an officer must determine on the basis of an assessment provided by the Department of Employment and Social Development if the job offer is genuine. The visa officer must be satisfied that the criteria specified in s. 82 of the Regulations are met. Furthermore, HRSDC's opinion is not determinative of whether a visa should be issued. The immigration officer is the ultimate decision maker. While the officer was permitted to determine the genuineness of the job offer, taking into account the assessment provided by HRSDC, the respondent missed the crux of the issue by a mischaracterization of the impugned decision. It is true that in this case, the officer's finding that the AEO was not genuine led the officer to award the applicant zero points for that category, presumably resulting in the applicant's failure to reach the necessary 67-point threshold. The officer's primary reason for rejecting the application was the finding that the applicant was inadmissible for misrepresentation.

The officer alleged that the employer changed the education requirements of the AEO; however, the court held that rather than altering any of the employment requirements the employer simply stated in his first letter that he was aware of the applicant's educational credentials at the time the AEO was made, that he was familiar with the educational institution from which the applicant received his degree, and that he was satisfied that these credentials were sufficient, particularly in conjunction with the applicant's overall training, background and work experience. This did not rise to the level of clear and convincing evidence of a misrepresentation. Nor did the court conclude that the record suggested that the applicant or the employer misrepresented their familial relationship. While misrepresentation can occur by omission, there does not appear to be any indication that the applicant or the employer believed they were withholding material information with respect to their relationship. The information was volunteered during the interview and was not solicited prior to that time. Although, a relationship between applicant and the employer may be a factor that the officer can take into account in assessing the *bona fide* character of the contract, there is nothing in the Act or the Regulations to prevent family ties between future employer and employee. Overall, it appears that the only evidence the officer used to support the misrepresentation finding was the determination that the employer may not have had an actual business need for the position of office manager. The reasons did not support the officer's finding of misrepresentation on the basis of clear and convincing evidence. The determination of inadmissibility did not fall within the range of possible, acceptable outcomes which are defensible in respect of the facts and law. The application for judicial review was allowed.

Tan v. Canada (Minister of Citizenship & Immigration) (2012), 12 Imm. L.R. (4th) 13, 2012 FC 1079, 2012 CarswellNat 3543, 2012 CarswellNat 4298 — The applicant argued that the officer erred by assessing the applicant's language proficiency on a higher standard than specified in the AEO. The AEO merely specified that the applicant needed to have basic English oral proficiency to complete the employment. No English writing or reading skills were specified. Nevertheless, the officer found that the applicant's proposed employer would not be able to ensure that an English-speaking person was always present while the applicant was working. Therefore, the officer concluded that in addition to the basic English oral proficiency, the applicant will require sufficient English proficiency to be able to read English safety equipment instructions in the kitchen and to communicate with Canadian authorities in case of accidents or emergencies. The officer found that these requirements were important in assessing whether the applicant could perform and carry out the proposed employment and therefore become economically established in Canada. The officer incorporated a requirement not specified in the AEO. The officer erred by incorporating requirements that exceeded those specifically listed in the AEO and by denying the applicant's permanent residence application on this basis. The application for judicial review was allowed.

Osorio v. Canada (Minister of Citizenship & Immigration) (2012), 8 Imm. L.R. (4th) 250, 2012 FC 882, 2012 CarswellNat 3168, 2012 CarswellNat 2548 — The applicant applied for permanent residence in Canada after receiving a job offer as an office administrator from Christopher's Fine Drycleaning in Okotoks, Alberta. However, an immigration officer concluded that the offer was not genuine and denied the application. The officer's principal concern was that it did not make sense for the applicant to leave the Philippines to take a lower paying job in Canada; that the applicant had limited knowledge of the job she would be performing or her destination; and she had not spoken to her prospective employer for 10 months. The court concluded that the officer did not adequately consider the evidence before her. The applicant had provided evidence of her intentions to seek a balanced life in a small community and work in a 9-5 job with weekends free; she would have administrative duties similar to the responsibilities she had in the Philippines; she had researched employment opportunities in the United States and Australia but regarded these countries less appealing; she had researched the location of Okotoks; and her employer had supplied an updated job offer days before her interview. In the face of this evidence, it was difficult to understand why the officer harboured ongoing concerns about the applicant's reasons for being interested in the job, her knowledge of the business, her familiarity with the intended destination, and the lack of recent contact with the employer. The officer failed to explain why the evidence before her was insufficient to allay concerns that the applicant had other reasons for taking a job beneath her qualifications and current salary. The officer's decision was unreasonable because it was not justified, intelligible, or transparent.

Garcia Porfirio v. Canada (Minister of Citizenship & Immigration) (2011), 99 Imm. L.R. (3d) 320, 2011 FC 794, 2011 CarswellNat 2704 — The applicant sought judicial review of his application for permanent residence as a skilled worker. The officer was not satisfied that the applicant had a genuine arranged employment offer as required by the ministerial instructions. HRSDC and CIC have different goals and benchmarks to meet, and it is equally clear that they each have a different realm of expertise. In this regard, CIC has chosen to use the specialized knowledge of HRSDC to help to streamline the processing of skilled workers. However, the immigration or visa officer is still the final check and balance in the system. Although an officer might be directed to take the HRSDC arranged employment opinion (AEO) at face value, they are instructed and required to consider whether the applicant is able and likely to carry out the offer of employment by s. 82 of the Regulations. Even if an immigration officer is precluded from considering the genuineness of the job offer she is certainly not precluded from assessing the genuineness of the applicant's intentions as needed to ensure that the requirements of IRPA are fulfilled.

Generally it would be unusual for the officer to question the window-washing needs of southern Ontario and dismiss out of hand the positive AEO obtained by the window cleaners. However that is not what occurred, and the officer did not act beyond her jurisdiction in rendering her decision. The officer was entitled to refuse the application since she found the applicant to be untruthful.

Subsection 16(1) of IRPA states that a person who makes an application must answer truthfully all questions put to them for the purpose of the examination and must produce a visa and all relevant evidence and documents that the officer reasonably requires. Though the officer might be precluded from evaluating the genuineness of the offer in Canada, she is not barred from assessing the legitimacy of the applicant's overall application. In this case, that is what she attempted to do. The applicant effectively shot himself in the foot when he lied in the interview. Clearly, there was a reasonable basis for the officer's decision. The application for judicial review was dismissed.

Zhong v. Canada (Minister of Citizenship & Immigration) (2011), 100 Imm. L.R. (3d) 41, 2011 CarswellNat 3181, 2011 FC 980 — The applicant filed for permanent residence under the skilled worker program. The application included a positive Arranged Employment Opinion from Service Canada, confirming the offer of permanent employment from the owner of a firm in Oakville, Ontario. The consulate rejected the application based on the applicant's failure to meet the 67-point minimum required for success. The officer awarded no points to the applicant for his arranged employment, having found that the offer of employment was not genuine and that the applicant was not likely to accept and carry out his employment in Canada.

The decision is clear that the officer refused to consider as valid the applicant's offer of employment because of the adverse inference that she drew from the following three factors: the nature and size of the company does not justify the employer's hiring of the applicant; the employer is the firm's only company executive; and the employer operates his business through his cell phone and residential telephone.

The plurals used in the job description create a very different impression from the facts gathered by the officer concerning the actual business. It looks as though a considerable amount of exaggeration has taken place; the established facts about the business lead to a reasonable conclusion that the business does not require the applicant to perform all the duties set out in the list of job duties provided to the officer. The reasons are not extensive but they are adequate because they allow the applicant to see how and why the decision was made and they also allow the court to assess their validity. The application for judicial review was dismissed.

Kumar v. Canada (Minister of Citizenship & Immigration) (2011), 3 Imm. L.R. (4th) 93, 2011 FC 770, 2011 CarswellNat 2409, 2011 CarswellNat 3463, [2001] F.C.J. No. 970 — The applicant's application for permanent residence as a skilled worker was refused on the basis that the applicant would not be able to perform, and would be unlikely to accept and carry out his pre-arranged employment in Canada, based on the International English Language Testing System (IELTS) test score. The applicant received 0 points for arranged employment. The only explanation as to why the applicant would not be able to carry out the function of the arranged employment was his IELTS score, yet ironically, the applicant received 4 points for English proficiency. There was no indication in either the CAIPS notes or the decision letter as to how the applicant's language ability may have precluded him from carrying out the arranged employment and indeed, no acknowledgment that the employer required not only English skills but also Hindi and Punjabi language skills, both of which the applicant possessed. It was unfair for the officer to reject the application without a further and more detailed assessment.

Kiselus v. Canada (Minister of Citizenship & Immigration), 2010 FC 879, 2010 CarswellNat 3853, 2010 CarswellNat 3217 — The applicant came to Canada in 2009 under the terms of a Working Holiday Program between Canada and Latvia. She began working as a sales associate at Shoppers Drug Mart, but was promoted to the position of retail supervisor after just a few months. Shoppers offered her indeterminate employment if she became a permanent resident of Canada. She applied for permanent residence but an immigration officer determined that she was not eligible to make an application. The applicant maintained that the officer unreasonably dismissed her application and, in doing so, misconstrued the applicable *Immigration and Refugee Protection Regulations*. The applicant argued that the officer's conclusion was unreasonable because the Canada-Latvia Working Holiday Program was an "international agreement" under s. 204(a) of the Regulations. She acknowledged that the ministerial guidelines suggested that the program fell under another provision of the Regulations — s. 205(b), which applies to reciprocal employment programs which, unlike agreements under s. 204(a), are not exempt from the requirement of the labour market analysis. She maintained that the Regulations should prevail over the guidelines. The court concluded that in light of the regulatory scheme and the applicable guidelines, the officer's finding that the applicant was ineligible to apply for permanent residence was not unreasonable. The application for judicial review was dismissed.

Gill v. Canada (Minister of Citizenship & Immigration), 2010 FC 466, 2010 CarswellNat 1153, 2010 CarswellNat 3278 — The application for permanent residence was refused on the basis that the applicant did not meet the required 67 points. Had he demonstrated that his spouse's brother was a permanent resident of Canada, living in Canada, he would have been assessed 5 further points. Had he "arranged employment" he would have received 10 additional points.

It was procedurally unfair for the visa officer to render her decision without bringing to the applicant's attention concerns that the applicant's brother-in-law may or may not be a permanent resident living in Canada. This was not a case where there had been a bald statement of a relative living in Canada, without any evidence whatsoever. There was evidence. If the officer wanted more, she should have asked for it.

Having reached the conclusion with respect to the points for a relative in Canada, the court did not need to consider the arranged employment issue as it was moot. Nevertheless, *in obiter*, the court held that, read in conjunction with s. 82(2) of the Regulations, which requires the officer to assess whether a skilled worker is able to perform and is likely to accept and carry out the employment, a visa officer must determine whether the applicant is up to the job. In this case, the officer not only found that the applicant was not up to the job, but was also of the view that the job offer was not genuine. That a visa officer in India is entitled to override the Department of Human Resources and Development's opinion based on an investigation in Canada of whether the offer is genuine is best left for another day.

Singh v. Canada (Minister of Citizenship & Immigration), [2008] F.C.J. No. 65, 2008 CarswellNat 92, 2008 FC 58 — The applicant argued that the visa officer erred in finding that he did not have a work permit allowing him to work in Canada and refusing to award him any points for "arranged employment" or "adaptability." The applicant was a Sikh priest and an Indian citizen who came to Canada on a visitor's visa. His visa explicitly prohibited him from being employed while he was in Canada, but did allow him to perform religious duties in the country. The applicant contended that religious workers do not require a work permit to be allowed to work in Canada, and the fact that he did not have such a permit should not have precluded the consideration of his job offer.

The applicant's argument ignored the explicit condition contained in his visitor's visa that he was "prohibited from engaging in employment in Canada." In the face of this language, the visa cannot reasonably be interpreted as amounting to "a written authorization to work in Canada." There was no evidence that the applicant had complied with the application process required under Divisions 2 and 3 of the Regulations containing extensive provisions governing the granting of work permits. Finally, the applicant's offer of employment was never validated by Human Resources and Skills Development Canada. Consequently, there was no error in the visa officer's assessment.

Nathoo v. Canada (Minister of Citizenship & Immigration), 2007 CarswellNat 2277, 2007 CarswellNat 4924, 2007 FC 818 — The applicant was an assistant manager at a hotel in Tanzania. She was offered a similar job at the Holiday Inn Express in Calgary, Alberta. A visa officer refused her application as a skilled worker on the basis that she was not persuaded that the applicant could perform the job she had been offered. The officer noted that the applicant had no direct contact with her putative employer, knew little about the Holiday Inn Express, and knew nothing about the hotel industry in Canada. As a result, the officer gave the applicant no credit for arranged employment.

The officer took into account extraneous factors. There was nothing in the NOC, or in the description of the job the applicant was being offered, that required her to know in advance all of the various items cited by the officer. The court noted that the applicant had indirect contact with the hotel through her brother, a staffing consultant, and her mother who resided in Calgary and was acquainted with the president of the hotel. This degree of contact was not so inadequate as to deny the applicant credit for the position that she was offered. The application for judicial review was allowed.

Singh v. Canada (Minister of Citizenship & Immigration), 2007 CarswellNat 142, 2007 FC 69 — The applicant first arrived in Canada on a visitor's visa, allowing him to temporarily perform religious duties. He subsequently applied for permanent residence as a skilled worker. The applicant fell short of the required 67 points.

The applicant was correct in noting that he was exempt from the requirement to obtain a work permit before coming to Canada to work as a Sikh priest as per subs. 186(l) of the Regulations. However, no further accommodations are made in the Regulations that would grant special privileges for workers that meet the requirements of s. 186 when applying for a permanent resident visa. Given the various scenarios considered under s. 82 of the Regulations to be awarded points for arranged employment, had such an exemption been contemplated by the Canadian Government, it could easily have been included in the Regulations. The applicant argued that no such accommodations were made because the occupations listed under s. 186 have already been determined to have a "neutral and positive affect on the labour market in Canada," as required to issue a work permit under s. 203 of the Regulations, and thus, an exemption is implied from a joint reading of ss. 186, 203, and 82 of the Regulations. The court dismissed this argument. The court found it was clear on the face of the record that the applicant possessed neither a work permit nor an offer of employment validated by HRSDC, and that the decision of the visa officer not to grant the applicant any points for adaptability or arranged employment, and ultimately to refuse the application for permanent residence, was reasonable pursuant to the existing Regulations. Nevertheless, since it appeared at the time that the applicant submitted his application for permanent residence, that there was confusion at Citizenship and Immigration Canada concerning the proper awarding of points for arranged employment for priests, whose job offers were not validated by HRSDC as evidenced by the visa officer's affidavit and the email from a third party submitted by the applicant, this was sufficient to raise serious concerns that all individuals applying for permanent residence in Canada under circumstances similar to that of the applicant may not be treated alike, a situation contrary to the rules of procedural fairness. On this basis alone, the judicial review was granted.

The court strongly encouraged the Minister of Citizenship and Immigration to clarify the guidelines concerning the allocation of points in permanent resident applications, for both arranged employment and adaptability, for individuals who are permitted to work in Canada without a work permit under s. 186, and who later seek to become permanent residents under the skilled worker class.

Mercado v. Canada (Minister of Citizenship & Immigration) (2006), 60 Imm. L.R. (3d) 88, 2006 CarswellNat 4484, 2006 FC 1527 — The applicant also argued that his arranged employment should have been assessed under s. 82(2)(c) instead of s. 82(2)(a). He made his application from Canada on March 18, 2005, and went back to Mexico for his interview on October 25, 2005. While by his own admission he had worked illegally in Canada for many years and never paid any taxes, at the time of the assessment, he was in Mexico. Given that the applicant was making the application while working illegally in Canada, none of the provisions of s. 82(2) were available to him. The immigration officer rightly disqualified him under s. 82(2)(a). She could have done so equally under s. 82(2)(c).

Bellido v. Canada (Minister of Citizenship & Immigration), 2005 CarswellNat 889, 2005 FC 452 — HRDC validation is not sufficient evidence of arranged employment. Such validation does not remove the obligation of the visa officer to assess whether the applicant is able to perform the job described in the validation.

83. (1) Adaptability (10 points) — A maximum of 10 points for adaptability shall be awarded to a skilled worker on the basis of any combination of the following elements:

(a) for the skilled worker's accompanying spouse or common-law partner, other than a permanent resident residing in Canada or a Canadian citizen, the language proficiency in either official language of at least benchmark level 4 for each of the four language skill areas, as set out in the *Canadian Language Benchmarks* and the *Niveaux de compétence linguistique canadiens*, as demonstrated by the results of an evaluation by an organization or institution designated under subsection 74(3), 5 points;

(b) for a period of full-time study in Canada by the skilled worker of at least two academic years in a program of at least two years in duration whether or not they obtained an educational credential for completing the program and during which period they remained in good academic standing as defined by the institution, 5 points;

(b.1) for a period of full-time study in Canada by the skilled worker's accompanying spouse or common-law partner, other than a permanent resident residing in Canada or a Canadian citizen, of at least two academic years in a program of at least two years in duration whether or not the accompanying spouse or common-law partner obtained an educational credential for completing the program, and during which period the accompanying spouse or common-law partner remained in good academic standing as defined by the institution, 5 points;

(c) for any previous period of full-time work under a work permit or authorized under section 186 of at least one year in Canada by the skilled worker in an occupation that is listed in Skill Type 0 Management Occupations or Skill Level A or B of the *National Occupational Classification* matrix, 10 points;

(c.1) for any previous period of full-time work under a work permit or authorized under section 186 of at least one year in Canada by the skilled worker's accompanying spouse or common-law partner, other than a permanent resident residing in Canada or a Canadian citizen, 5 points;

(d) for being related to, or for having an accompanying spouse or accompanying common-law partner who is related to, a person living in Canada who is described in subsection (5), 5 points; and

(e) for being awarded points for arranged employment in Canada under subsection 82(2), 5 points.

(2) **Full-time study** — For the purposes of paragraphs (1)(b) and (b.1), full-time study means at least 15 hours of instruction per week during the academic year, authorized under a study permit or under section 188, at a secondary or post-secondary institution in Canada that is recognized by the provincial authorities responsible for registering, accrediting, supervising and regulating such institutions, including any period of training in the workplace that forms part of the course of instruction.

(3) [Repealed SOR/2012-274, s. 12(2).]

(4) [Repealed SOR/2012-274, s. 12(2).]

(5) **Family relationships in Canada** — For the purposes of paragraph (1)(d), a skilled worker shall be awarded 5 points if

(a) the skilled worker or the skilled worker's accompanying spouse or accompanying common-law partner is related by blood, marriage, common-law partnership or adoption to a person who is 18 years or older, a Canadian citizen or permanent resident living in Canada and who is

(i) their father or mother,

(ii) the father or mother of their father or mother,

(iii) their child,

(iv) a child of their child,

(v) a child of their father or mother,

(vi) a child of the father or mother of their father or mother, other than their father or mother, or

(vii) a child of the child of their father or mother;

(b) [Repealed SOR/2012-274, s. 12(4).]

SOR/2012-274, s. 12; SOR/2014-140, s. 3

Case Law

Section 83(2)

See the summary for *McLachlan v. Canada (Minister of Citizenship & Immigration)* (2009), 85 Imm. L.R. (3d) 90, 354 F.T.R. 176 (Eng.), 2009 FC 975, 2009 CarswellNat 5869, 2009 CarswellNat 2936 annotated at s. 78(2) of the Regulations.

Section 83(5)

Hadwani v. Canada (Minister of Citizenship & Immigration) (2011), 394 F.T.R. 156, 2 Imm. L.R. (4th) 53, 2011 FC 888, 2011 CarswellNat 2806, [2011] F.C.J. No. 1117 — The applicant sought to come to Canada as a permanent resident and was assessed 63 points, and did not meet the required 67 points. The essential issue turned on the award of 0 points in a category termed as "adaptability." The officer was not satisfied that the applicant had filed a government issued birth certificate in support of the otherwise satisfactory proof that the applicant had a nephew residing in Canada. The applicant had filed a document provided by a Pakistan hospital providing particulars of the birth of the nephew there. The officer apparently required a government-issued birth certificate but didn't tell the applicant or his representatives.

The checklist does not state that a government-issued birth certificate must be submitted in the case of a relative in Canada. It says documents "such as" a birth certificate must be submitted. The officer was clearly wrong in dismissing out of hand the hospital record as to the nephew's birth.

Gill v. Canada (Minister of Citizenship & Immigration), 2010 FC 466, 2010 CarswellNat 1153, 2010 CarswellNat 3278 — The application for permanent residence was refused on the basis that the applicant did not meet the required 67 points. Had he demonstrated that his spouse's brother was a permanent resident of Canada, living in Canada, he would have been assessed 5 further points. Had he "arranged employment" he would have received 10 additional points.

It was procedurally unfair for the visa officer to render her decision without bringing to the applicant's attention concerns that the applicant's brother-in-law may or may not be a permanent resident living in Canada. This was not a case where there had been a bald statement of a relative living in Canada, without any evidence whatsoever. There was evidence. If the officer wanted more, she should have asked for it.

Wang v. Canada (Minister of Citizenship & Immigration), 2008 CarswellNat 3897, 2008 CarswellNat 2051, 2008 FC 798 — The officer concluded that the applicant had insufficient points to qualify for immigration to Canada. She noted that no points were awarded for the male applicant's brother living in Canada. She determined that the evidence provided by the applicants in support of this allegation was insufficient to establish that the brother resided in Canada at the time of the decision, based on the fact that the majority of the documentation provided related to the brother's wife and not him. The brother's notice of assessment was the only document which specifically related to him. It indicated he earned a total of $2,000 in 2006. The officer noted that her records indicated that the brother had prolonged absences from Canada in the past. The Notice of Assessment was therefore insufficient evidence to convince her that he was a resident of Canada at the time the decision was made. The officer's decision was based on the insufficiency of evidence establishing the brother's residence in Canada. The burden of adducing sufficient evidence to support the application falls to the applicant. The application for judicial review was dismissed.

Requirements

84. [Repealed SOR/2008 202, s. 1.]

85. Permanent resident status — A foreign national who is an accompanying family member of a person who makes an application as a member of the federal skilled worker class shall become a permanent resident if, following an examination, it is established that

(a) the person who made the application has become a permanent resident; and

(b) the foreign national is not inadmissible.

SOR/2008-202, s. 1

Transitional Federal Skilled Workers
[Heading added SOR/2003-383, s. 3.]

Transitional Federal Skilled Worker Class
[Heading added SOR/2003-383, s. 3.]

85.1 (1) Class — For the purposes of subsection 12(2) of the Act, the transitional federal skilled worker class is hereby prescribed as a class of persons who are transitional skilled workers and who may become permanent residents on the basis of their ability to become economically established in Canada and who intend to reside in a province other than the Province of Quebec.

(2) Transitional skilled workers — A foreign national is a transitional skilled worker if they made an application before January 1, 2002 under the former Regulations for an immigrant visa as a person described in subparagraph 9(1)(b)(i) or paragraph 10(1)(b) of those Regulations, other than a self-employed person within the meaning of subsection 2(1) of those Regulations, that was

(a) refused after March 31, 2003 and before June 20, 2003; or

(b) withdrawn by the foreign national on or after January 1, 2002 and before December 1, 2003.

SOR/2003-383, s. 3

85.2 (1) Application before January 1, 2005 — Subject to subsection (2), an application for a permanent resident visa as a member of the transitional federal skilled worker class must be made in accordance with sections 10 and 11 and must be received by the applicable immigration office referred to in subsection 11(1) not later than December 31, 2004.

(2) Alternate place of application — An application referred to in subsection (1) may be made to the immigration office at the location where the application referred to in subsection 85.1(2) was made, instead of to the immigration office referred to in subsection 11(1).

SOR/2003-383, s. 3

85.3 Criteria — For the purpose of determining whether a transitional skilled worker, as a member of the transitional federal skilled worker class, will be able to become economically established in Canada, they must

(a) be awarded the number of units of assessment required by the former Regulations for a person described in subparagraph 9(1)(b)(i) or paragraph 10(1)(b) of those Regulations, other than a self-employed person within the meaning of subsection 2(1) of those Regulations; or

(b) meet the requirements of subsection 75(2) and paragraph 76(1)(b) of these Regulations and obtain a minimum of 67 points based on the factors set out in paragraph 76(1)(a) of these Regulations.

SOR/2003-383, s. 3

Requirements

[Heading added SOR/2003-383, s. 3.]

85.4 [Repealed SOR/2008-253, s. 8.]

85.5 [Repealed SOR/2008-202, s. 2.]

85.6 Permanent resident status — A foreign national who is a family member of a person who makes an application for a permanent resident visa as a member of the transitional federal skilled worker class shall become a permanent resident if, following an examination, it is established that the family member is not inadmissible.

SOR/2003-383, s. 3

Quebec Skilled Worker Class

86. (1) Class — For the purposes of subsection 12(2) of the Act, the Quebec skilled worker class is hereby prescribed as a class of persons who may become permanent residents on the basis of their ability to become economically established in Canada.

(2) Member of the class — A foreign national is a member of the Quebec skilled worker class if they

(a) intend to reside in the Province of Quebec; and

(b) are named in a *Certificat de sélection du Québec* issued to them by that Province.

(3) [Repealed SOR/2008-253, s. 9.]

(4) [Repealed SOR/2008-253, s. 9.]

(5) Requirements for accompanying family members — A foreign national who is an accompanying family member of a person who makes an application as a member of the Quebec skilled worker class shall become a permanent resident if, following an examination, it is established that

(a) the person who made the application has become a permanent resident; and

(b) the foreign national is not inadmissible.

SOR/2008-202, s. 3; SOR/2008-253, s. 9

Provincial Nominee Class

87. (1) Class — For the purposes of subsection 12(2) of the Act, the provincial nominee class is hereby prescribed as a class of persons who may become permanent residents on the basis of their ability to become economically established in Canada.

(2) Member of the class — A foreign national is a member of the provincial nominee class if

(a) subject to subsection (5), they are named in a nomination certificate issued by the government of a province under a provincial nomination agreement between that province and the Minister; and

(b) they intend to reside in the province that has nominated them.

(3) Substitution of evaluation — If the fact that the foreign national is named in a certificate referred to in paragraph (2)(a) is not a sufficient indicator of whether they may become economically established in Canada and an officer has consulted the government that issued the certificate, the officer may substitute for the criteria set out in subsection (2) their evaluation of the likelihood of the ability of the foreign national to become economically established in Canada.

(4) Concurrence — An evaluation made under subsection (3) requires the concurrence of a second officer.

(5) Exclusion — Subject to subsection (6), a foreign national who is named in a certificate referred to in paragraph (2)(a) shall not be considered a member of the provincial nominee class if

(a) the nomination was based on the provision of capital by the foreign national; or

(b) the foreign national intends to participate in, or has participated in, an immigration-linked investment scheme.

(6) Exception — Subsection (5) does not apply if

(a) the capital is provided by the foreign national to a business in the province that nominated them, other than a business operated primarily for the purpose of deriving investment income such as interest, dividends or capital gains;

(b) the foreign national controls or will control

(i) a percentage of equity in the business equal to or greater than $33\frac{1}{3}\%$, or

(ii) an equity investment in the business of at least $1,000,000;

(c) the foreign national provides or will provide active and ongoing management of the business from within the province that nominated them; and

(d) the terms of the investment in the business do not include a redemption option.

(7) [Repealed SOR/2008 253, s. 10.]

(8) [Repealed SOR/2008-253, s. 10.]

(9) **Definitions** — The following definitions apply in this section.

"immigration-linked investment scheme" means a strategy or plan

(a) where one of the objectives of the strategy or plan is to facilitate immigration to Canada and one of the objectives of the promoters of the strategy or plan is to raise capital; or

(b) where the agreement or arrangement in respect of the strategy or plan was entered into primarily for the purpose of acquiring a status or privilege under the Act.

("projet de placement lié à l'immigration")

"percentage of equity" has the same meaning as in subsection 88(1). *("pourcentage des capitaux propres")*

(10) **Non-application** — Subsections (5), (6) and (9) do not apply in respect of a foreign national who is issued a nomination certificate referred to in paragraph (2)(a) before September 2, 2008.

(11) **Transitional** — Subsections (5) and (6) as they read immediately before September 2, 2008 apply in respect of a foreign national referred to in subsection (10).

(12) **Requirements for accompanying family members** — A foreign national who is an accompanying family member of a person who makes an application as a member of the provincial nominee class shall become a permanent resident if, following an examination, it is established that

(a) the person who made the application has become a permanent resident; and

(b) the foreign national is not inadmissible.

SOR/2008-202, ss. 4, 5; SOR/2008-253, s. 10; SOR/2009-164, s. 1

Case Law

Abeywardane v. Canada (Minister of Citizenship and Immigration), 2016 CarswellNat 366, 2016 FC 209, 2016 CarswellNat 366 — The applicant sought judicial review of a decision of a visa officer's negative substituted evaluation concurring with another officer's previous assessment and refusal of the applicant's application for permanent residence as a member of the federal skilled worker class. The officer was not satisfied that the applicant and his wife would be able to economically establish in Canada. The officer was of the opinion that the applicant was very unprepared for immigration despite having almost one year to prepare before the interview. The officer had concerns about the inability to adequately explain job duties and had concerns over the credibility of employment letters.

The officer had a duty to advise the applicant of her concerns and her failure to clearly communicate concerns regarding the applicant's ability to economically establish in Canada amounted to a breach of procedural fairness. The applicant had met and surpassed the requirements of the FSW class, and in such a case, the Federal Court of Appeal has deter-

IRP Regulations

mined that it is important that officers raise their concerns with the individual in a way that enables him or her to respond (*Sadeghi v. Canada (Minister of Citizenship and Immigration)*, [2000] 4 F.C. 337 (C.A.). The application for judicial review was allowed.

Yasmin v. Canada (Minister of Citizenship and Immigration), 2015 FC 1346, 2015 CarswellNat 6430, 2015 CarswellNat 9629 — The principal applicant was named in a certificate issued by the province of Saskatchewan for a permanent resident visa application as a member of the Provincial Nominee Class as someone who may become a permanent resident on the basis of their ability to become economically established in Canada pursuant to s. 87 of the Regulations. The principal applicant had an offer of permanent full-time employment from an employer who verified that she had the skills required to perform the job, being that of a cashier working in a gas station. After exchanges with the Saskatchewan Immigration Nominee Program ("SINP") and a fairness letter being sent to the applicants, the officer acting pursuant to s. 87(3) substituted his criteria for those of the SINP. It concluded that in order for the applicants to become economically established, it is expected that they will be able to obtain employment in Canada and already have the abilities, education and work experience which will enable them to procure employment. The officer concluded that the applicant did not have the English language skills to be able to perform the duties required for the position of a cashier.

The officer did not apply a test based on reasonably acquiring the abilities in a reasonable time *after* arriving in Canada. Instead, the officer required that the applicants demonstrate that "they will be able to obtain employment in Canada and already have the abilities, education and work experience which will enable them to procure employment." The court found the officer applied an appropriate definition of "the ability to become economically established." The court distinguished Justice Russell's decision in *Rezaeiazar v. Canada (Minister of Citizenship and Immigration)*, 2013 FC 761 at para. 77 that the applicant only need to show that she can become economically established in Canada within a reasonable amount of time upon her arrival, on the basis that in that case the applicant had already surpassed the points requirement and therefore her abilities, education and work experience were not an issue.

The court went on to further state that it was understandable that the Regulations would require that persons arriving in Canada to occupy positions already possess the necessary abilities, education and work experience to discharge their duties. Otherwise the granting of permanent residency would be based upon a contingent outcome in the future. The application for judicial review was dismissed.

Shaukat v. Canada (Minister of Citizenship and Immigration), 2015 FC 1120, 2015 CarswellNat 4713, 2015 CarswellNat 8975 — The applicant sought to set aside the decision of a visa officer rejecting the applicant's application for permanent residency under the provincial nominee class pursuant to s. 87 of the Regulations. The officer was not satisfied that the applicant had the language skills to become economically established in Canada. The court concluded that a federal officer is not bound by the decision of a provincial program officer and is entitled to form his or her own opinion as to the likelihood of an immigrant to become economically established in Canada. Both the provincial agreement and the Regulations provide for this so long as the visa officer consults the provincial government that issued the certificate and a second visa officer concurs with the evaluation under subs. 87(3). In this case, both requirements were met. The application for judicial review was dismissed.

Zahid v. Canada (Minister of Citizenship and Immigration), 2015 FC 1263, 2015 CarswellNat 5666, 2015 CarswellNat 9127 — The applicant's application for a permanent resident visa was denied after she had been nominated under the Saskatchewan Immigrant Nominee Program in its family stream. Her intention was to immigrate to Saskatchewan with her husband and three children. The visa officer was not satisfied that she could economically establish herself as required by the Regulations. More particularly, he was of the view that she could not succeed in her intended profession of school teacher as her knowledge of the English language was insufficient. Furthermore, she provided no evidence that she had the skill sets to successfully perform other employment. The province of Saskatchewan had accepted that she might never make it as a teacher because of her language skills, but they were certainly adequate enough to allow her to perform other jobs. She was highly educated and there was a labour shortage in Saskatchewan at that time. The applicant's reply to a fairness letter indicated that she hoped to become a teacher but accepted that she might only be able to be employed as a teacher's assistance or indeed in other areas, such as the food and beverage industry. She also emphasized that her husband had a job offer in hand, through his brother. Her husband could not himself apply under the program as he was beyond the cut-off age of 49. Unfortunately, neither the Act nor the Regulations nor the various relevant operation manuals explain what it means to be "economically established." There is no reference to the cost of living generally, to the cost of housing, and income thresholds. These matters are apparently left to the expertise of the visa officer. It is clear that the visa officer must take into account such matters as age, education, qualifications, past employment experience, the province's views and the applicant's own initiative. Although the prime focus is obviously on the applicant, other matters should be taken into account such as an accompanying spouse and dependent children.

There was no factual basis to suggest that the applicant would be unable to carry out tasks, or to act as a retail sales person or a teacher's assistant, supervising students at lunch and at recess, for example. The court also found that the visa officer's decision was unreasonable because the officer gave short shrift to her husband's employment opportunities. Although department policy documents such as operation manuals are not law, they nevertheless may be of great assistance to the court in determining the reasonableness of a decision. In this case, the Overseas Processing Manual OP 7b section 7.7 refers to consideration of the applicant's ability to become economically established with the assistance of other family members. Accordingly, the Federal Court concluded that husbands and wives are required to mutually support each other. The application for judicial review was allowed.

Sardar v. Canada (Minister of Citizenship and Immigration), 2015 FC 1373, 2015 CarswellNat 7165, 2015 CarswellNat 10511 — The applicant challenged the decision of the visa officer to refuse his application for permanent residence. The officer refused to grant permanent residence on an exercise of s. 87(3) of the Regulations. It is clear from the reasons that the officer formed a suspicion that the job offers were not *bona fide*, and, as a result, excluded cogent evidence in support of the likelihood of the applicant's ability to become economically established in Canada. The court found that, in fairness, once the suspicion arose, the officer owed a duty of fairness to the applicant to make further concerted inquiries of the persons making the job offers, to either confirm the suspicion or negate the suspicion. Since the officer made no effort to do so, the decision under review was rendered in breach of a duty of fairness owed to the applicant. The application for judicial review was allowed and the matter referred back for redetermination.

Sran v. Canada (Minister of Citizenship & Immigration) (2012), 11 Imm. L.R. (4th) 74, 2012 FC 791, 2012 CarswellNat 2107, 2012 CarswellNat 3061 — The applicant sought judicial review of an immigration officer's decision to refuse his application for permanent resident status in the provincial nominees' class. The applicant had been nominated under the Alberta Immigrant Nominee Program in the Family Stream and approved by the Alberta program office. The immigration officer did not believe that the applicant had the ability of becoming economically established in Canada. His wife's education and experience was considered to be relevant, but insufficient to overcome the deficiencies in the application. He had not demonstrated fluency in English, did not speak French and required an interpreter for the interview. He admitted that his divinity credential was of little use in Canada. The officer also found that the applicant did not provide evidence of National Occupational Classification duties. Accordingly, the officer found that the applicant would not qualify as a skilled worker.

The officer erred in relying primarily on the skilled worker classification tool to evaluate the likelihood that the applicant would become economically established in Canada. In comparing the applicant's skills to the NOC criteria, the officer lost sight of the factors that had persuaded the Alberta government that the family could be settled including the wife's education and the parents' willingness to support the family. The application for judicial review was allowed.

Kikeshian v. Canada (Minister of Citizenship & Immigration) (2011), 98 Imm. L.R. (3d) 327, 391 F.T.R. 52, 2011 FC 658, 2011 CarswellNat 3252, 2011 CarswellNat 2103, [2011] F.C.J. No. 832 — This was an application for judicial review of a decision to refuse the applicant's application for permanent residence as a member of the Entrepreneur Class under the province of Saskatchewan's program. The visa officer was not satisfied the applicant intended to reside in the province that nominated him. Although it is clear that under this program the ultimate authority to determine whether the statutory admissibility criteria has been met rests with the visa officer, the importance of provincial participation is that exercise is recognized throughout. The department's Operation Manual OP7(b) recognizes that a provincial nomination creates a presumption that the applicant will be able to become economically established. Article 7.8 instructs that an officer must consult with provincial authorities if reasons exist to believe that a visa applicant does not intend to live in the nominating province or that he is unlikely to be able to become economically established in Canada. That same provision states that the visa officer must obtain a concurring decision from another officer before rejecting the application on established grounds. The cautionary nature of this process is further reflected in Article 7.6 which states: "Officers should request additional documentation or clarification from the applicant or the nominating province if they are not satisfied that all criteria will be met by the applicant." The failure of the visa officer to comply with his statutory obligation to consult with provincial authorities before rejecting the visa application was fatal to the decision; the application for judicial review was allowed.

Wai v. Canada (Minister of Citizenship & Immigration) (2009), 348 F.T.R. 85 (Eng.), 2009 FC 780, 2009 CarswellNat 2481, [2009] F.C.J. No. 1015 — This was an application for judicial review of a decision of a visa officer, refusing the applicant's application for permanent residence in Canada under the provincial nominee class. The officer requested additional information from the applicant, including: evidence of his current legal status in Canada; employment letter(s) and pay stubs; evidence of current funds; and a written personal statement explaining how he was supporting himself. The applicant indicated to the officer that he had been living with his mother and grandmother since his arrival and had been supported by his mother for the entire time. The officer concluded that the applicant named in the certificate issued by Manitoba was not likely to become economically established in Canada. The officer points out that the fact that a foreign national is named in the certificate is not a sufficient indicator of whether they may become economically established in Canada. An officer who has consulted with the provincial government that issued the certificate may substitute, for the criteria set out in subs. (2), their own evaluation of the likelihood of the ability of the foreign national to become economically established in Canada. The officer in this case was not satisfied that, just because the applicant was named in the certificate issued by Manitoba, he was likely to become economically established in Canada.

Under the relevant legislation, as well as the agreement between Manitoba and Canada, it is clear that the province will, in the normal course, be afforded deference once it has issued a nomination certificate, and it is also clear under s. 87(2)(b) of the Regulations that an applicant must intend to reside in Manitoba. However, s. 87(3) makes it clear that an officer can substitute their own evaluation on the likelihood of economic establishment. As Canada has the ultimate responsibility for immigration matters, the intent of this provision appears clear. Accordingly, the real issue was whether the decision was reasonable. The court found justification, transparency and intelligibility throughout the decision-making process and the decision falls within the required range.

Subsection 87(4) of the Regulations stipulates that a substitute evaluation under subs. 87(3) "requires the concurrence of a second officer." In this context "concurrence" can only mean "agreement." Concurrence requires that the second officer must read the evaluation and indicate that he or she agrees with it. The second officer adopted the reasons and conclusions of the first officer. Nothing further was required to satisfy subs. 87(4) of the Regulations or to provide adequate reasons. The application for judicial review was dismissed.

Canadian Experience Class

[Heading added SOR/2008-254, s. 3.]

87.1 (1) Class — **For the purposes of subsection 12(2) of the Act, the Canadian experience class is prescribed as a class of persons who may become permanent residents on the basis of their ability to become economically established in Canada, their experience in Canada, and their intention to reside in a province other than the Province of Quebec.**

(2) Member of the class — **A foreign national is a member of the Canadian experience class if**

(a) they have acquired in Canada, within the three years before the date on which their application for permanent residence is made, at least one year of full-time work experience, or the equivalent in part-time work experience, in one or more occupations that are listed in Skill Type 0 Management Occupations or Skill Level A or B of the *National Occupational Classification* matrix, exclusive of restricted occupations; and

(b) during that period of employment they performed the actions described in the lead statement for the occupation as set out in the occupational descriptions of the *National Occupational Classification*;

697

IRP Regulations

(c) during that period of employment they performed a substantial number of the main duties of the occupation as set out in the occupational descriptions of the *National Occupational Classification*, including all of the essential duties;

(d) they have had their proficiency in the English or French language evaluated by an organization or institution designated under subsection 74(3) and have met the applicable threshold fixed by the Minister under subsection 74(1) for each of the four language skill areas; and

(e) in the case where they have acquired the work experience referred to in paragraph (a) in more than one occupation, they meet the threshold for proficiency in the English or French language, fixed by the Minister under subsection 74(1), for the occupation in which they have acquired the greater amount of work experience in the three years referred to in paragraph (a).

(3) **Application** — For the purposes of subsection (2),

(a) any period of employment during which the foreign national was engaged in full-time study shall not be included in calculating a period of work experience;

(b) any period of self-employment or unauthorized work shall not be included in calculating a period of work experience; and

(c) the foreign national must have had temporary resident status during their period of work experience and any period of full-time study or training.

(d) [Repealed SOR/2012-274, s. 13(4).]

(e) [Repealed SOR/2012-274, s. 13(4).]

(f) [Repealed SOR/2012-274, s. 13(4).]

(g) [Repealed SOR/2012-274, s. 13(4).]

(4) [Repealed SOR/2012-274, s. 13(5).]

(5) [Repealed SOR/2012-274, s. 13(5).]

SOR/2008-254, s. 3; SOR/2011-54, s. 2; SOR/2012-274, s. 13

Case Law

Song v. Canada (Minister of Citizenship and Immigration), 2015 FC 141, 2015 CarswellNat 160, 2015 CarswellNat 1987 — The applicant sought judicial review of the decision of a visa officer to refuse his application for permanent residence as a member of the Canadian Experience class. The officer said that the applicant's letter of employment detailing his responsibilities as a front store manager did not satisfy him or her that the applicant had performed the functions listed under NOC 0621. As a result, the officer concluded that the applicant had failed to demonstrate that he had "acquired twelve months of full-time skilled work experience in Canada at a National Occupational Classification skill of type O or level A or B in the last twenty-four months prior to the submission of [his] application and after having obtained [his] Canadian educational credential."

The decision was unreasonable. It is clear that the duties listed in the employer's letter do not use the same words that appear in NOC 0621. But this will inevitably be the case because applications have been refused when an employer simply reiterates the wording of an NOC. So employers are obligated to describe in their own words exactly what applicants do. This requires officers to examine applications carefully and not to reject them because the same words are not used. The decision was quashed and the application for judicial review granted.

Gao v. Canada (Minister of Citizenship and Immigration), 2014 FC 821, 2014 CarswellNat 3158, 2014 CarswellNat 3239 — The applicant had applied under the Canadian Experience Class under NOC 6211 as a Retail Sales Supervisor and had been offered a position at Safeway Ltd. The visa officer concluded that the applicant did not provide evidence that he performed a substantial number of the main duties of a retail sales supervisor under NOC 6211, nor evidence that he performed the essential duties of the position. As such, the officer was not satisfied that the applicant met the statutory requirements to be granted permanent residence under the Canadian Experience Class and refused the application.

NOC 6211 does not list any essential duties. Therefore, it was unclear against what standard the officer assessed the application. The respondent urged the court to overlook the error in the decision letter; however, the court concluded there was a substantive difference in resorting to the record to complete, or, to supplement an otherwise deficient decision, and resorting to the record to override or negate patent error on the face of the decision in respect of a critical element. Furthermore, the decision letter focused on the fact that the employer's letter described the applicant as "helping," "assisting" and "aiding." From that, the officer concluded that the applicant did not perform three of the duties. Without greater context, evidence or information before the officer, it was unreasonable for the officer to conclude that performing a function in concert with, or parallel to others, such as is common in a team-based work environment, means that the person did not perform the function or duty. The officer unreasonably excluded evidence of three of the eight duties, and, on the face of the decision erroneously considered some of them to be essential. The application for judicial review was granted.

Madadi v. Canada (Minister of Citizenship & Immigration), 2013 CarswellNat 2283, 2013 CarswellNat 2790, 2013 FC 716, [2013] F.C.J. No. 798 — The applicant held a Master's degree in civil engineering, and stated in his application for permanent residence under NOC 0711 "Construction Manager" that he had been working as a construction manager since September 2003. He was found not eligible for processing in the category. The letter from his current employer confirmed his title, salary, period of employment, projects worked on, and the duties he performed in this position. The officer rejected the letter stating that the duties described were either copied word for word or closely paraphrased from occupational descriptions of the NOC, diminishing the overall credibility of the employment letter.

Where an applicant provides evidence sufficient to establish that they meet the requirements of the Act or Regulations, as the case may be, and the officer doubts the "credibility, accuracy or genuine nature of the information provided" and wishes to deny the application based on those concerns, the duty of fairness is invoked. The officer erred in failing to put his or her concerns to the applicant. The decision was set aside.

Qin v. Canada (Minister of Citizenship & Immigration) (2013), 21 Imm. L.R. (4th) 98, 451 N.R. 336, 2013 CarswellNat 4332, [2013] F.C.J. No. 1264 — The principal issue raised in this case concerns the evidence that a visa officer may consider in determining if a CEC applicant meets the Canadian work experience requirement. In particular, when deciding whether an applicant was employed to perform duties of the requisite level of skill, may the officer take into account the fact that the applicant's wages are below those prevailing for the occupation in which the applicant was assessed? This is an appeal from a decision of the Federal Court in which the application for judicial review was allowed and the officer's rejection of the application for permanent residence was set aside. The visa officer based his decision in part on the disparity between the applicant's wages and the relatively higher minimum wage rates prevailing locally for legal secretaries and translators/interpreters, the occupational categories in which her application was assessed. In addition, the description of the job provided by her employer did not match the duties of the Legal Secretaries as described in the NOC. Although the parties agreed that the applicant's CEC application must be determined by another visa officer because of the breach of procedural fairness, it was clear from the judge's reasons that her order implicitly permitted the officer redetermining the applicant's visa application to take comparator wage data into account. Hence, the questions of general importance certified by the judge required answering.

The Federal Court of Appeal concluded that wages are simply one of the many considerations that may be relevant to determining whether a CEC applicant satisfies the prescribed work experience requirement. The visa officer did not treat the low salary as a disqualification in itself, because he found that the description of her duties in the letter of reference was not consistent with the NOC code. The Federal Court of Appeal also held that if there was satisfactory evidence from an employer that a CEC applicant had the required Canadian work experience, an applicant may be granted a visa even though her wages are below the prevailing wage rates. When other evidence is available, an officer may be satisfied that an applicant meets the work experience requirement without having to consider comparator wage information at all. Much depends on the particular facts of an application. Therefore, it is permissible for a visa officer to consider comparator salary data when assessing the nature of the work experience of an applicant who wishes to qualify as a member of the Canadian experience class. Correctness is the applicable standard in this case for reviewing the visa officer's interpretation of s. 87.1 of the Regulations and reasonableness is the standard of review of a visa officer's findings of fact and application of s. 87.1 to the facts of a CEC application. The appeal was dismissed.

Benoit v. Canada (Minister of Citizenship & Immigration), 2013 FC 185, 2013 CarswellNat 422, 2013 CarswellNat 649 — The officer's decision rejecting the application for permanent residence in Canada under the Canadian experience class for not meeting the work experience described in NOC 6211 is unreasonable because the test set out in the Immigration and Refugee Protection Regulations was not applied. The officer was required to determine if the applicant "performed a substantial number of main duties." However, the officer's decision did not make it clear that the officer had at any point turned his or her mind to the real question, which was whether — on the whole — the duties were a substantial match. The respondent conceded that the applicant did perform "some" of the duties listed in NOC 6211. The Regulations clearly require that only a "substantial" number of the duties be performed. That is the test. The officer in this case singled out only parts of two of the eight main duties from NOC 6211 and on that basis concluded that the applicant's experience did not qualify. The court was satisfied that the applicant's responsibilities were far from being such a total mismatch that her application for permanent residence had no chance of success. At a glance, the duties were substantially a match. Accordingly, the application for judicial review was allowed and the application sent back for decision by a different officer to decide whether the applicant "performed a substantial number of the main duties" listed in NOC 6211.

Federal Skilled Trades Class

[Heading added SOR/2012-274, s. 14.]

87.2 (1) **Definition "skilled trade occupation"** — In this section, "skilled trade occupation" means an occupation, unless the occupation has been designated a restricted occupation by the Minister, in the following categories listed in Skill Level B of the *National Occupational Classification* matrix:

(a) Major Group 72, industrial, electrical and construction trades;

(b) Major Group 73, maintenance and equipment operation trades;

(c) Major Group 82, supervisors and technical occupations in natural resources, agriculture and related production;

(d) Major Group 92, processing, manufacturing and utilities supervisors and central control operators;

(e) Minor Group 632, chefs and cooks; and

(f) Minor Group 633, butchers and bakers.

(2) **Class** — For the purposes of subsection 12(2) of the Act, the federal skilled trades class is prescribed as a class of persons who are skilled trades workers and who may become permanent residents on the basis of their ability to become economically established in Canada in a skilled trade occupation and their intention to reside in a province other than the Province of Quebec.

(3) **Member of class** — A foreign national is a member of the federal skilled trades class if

(a) following an evaluation by an organization or institution designated under subsection 74(3), they meet the threshold fixed by the Minister under subsection 74(1) for proficiency in either English or French for each of the four language skill areas;

(b) they have, during the five years before the date on which their permanent resident visa application is made, acquired at least two years of full-time work experience, or the equivalent in part-time work, in the skilled trade occupation specified in the application after becoming qualified to independently practice the occupation, and during that period of employment has performed

(i) the actions described in the lead statement for the occupation as set out in the occupational descriptions of the *National Occupational Classification*, and

(ii) a substantial number of the main duties listed in the description of the occupation set out in the *National Occupational Classification*, including all of the essential duties;

(c) they have met the relevant employment requirements of the skilled trade occupation specified in the application as set out in the *National Occupational Classification*, except for the requirement to obtain a certificate of qualification issued by a competent provincial authority; and

(d) they meet at least one of the following requirements:

(i) they hold a certificate of qualification issued by a competent provincial authority in the skilled trade occupation specified in the application,

(ii) they are in Canada and hold a work permit that is valid on the date on which their application is made and, on the date on which the visa is issued, hold a valid work permit or are authorized to work in Canada under section 186, and

(A) the work permit was issued based on a positive determination by an officer under subsection 203(1) with respect to their employment in a skilled trade occupation,

(B) they are working for any employer specified on the work permit, and

(C) they have an offer of employment — for continuous full-time work for a total of at least one year in the skilled trade occupation that is specified in the application and is in the same minor group set out in the *National Occupational Classification* as the occupation specified on their work permit — that is made by up to two employers who are specified on the work permit, none of whom is an embassy, high commission or consulate in Canada or an employer who is referred to in any of subparagraphs 200(3)(h)(i) to (iii), subject to the visa being issued to the foreign national,

(iii) they are in Canada and hold a work permit referred to in paragraph 204(a) or (c) — that is valid on the date on which their application is received — and, on the date on which the visa is issued, hold a valid work permit or are authorized to work in Canada under section 186, and the circumstances referred to in clauses (ii)(B) and (C) apply,

(iv) they do not hold a valid work permit or are not authorized to work in Canada under section 186 on the date on which their application is made and

(A) up to two employers, none of whom is an embassy, high commission or consulate in Canada or an employer who is referred to in any of subparagraphs 200(3)(h)(i) to (iii), have made an offer of employment to the foreign national in the skilled trade occupation specified in the application for continuous full-time work for a total of at least one year, subject to the visa being issued to them, and

(B) an officer has approved the offer for full-time work — based on an assessment provided to the officer by the Department of Employment and Social Development, on the same basis as an assessment provided for the issuance of a work permit, at the request of up to two employers or an officer — that the requirements set out in subsection 203(1) with respect to the offer have been met, and

(v) they either hold a valid work permit or are authorized to work in Canada under section 186 on the date on which their application for a permanent resident visa is made and on the date on which it is issued, and

(A) the circumstances referred to in clauses (ii)(B) and (C) and subparagraph (iii) do not apply, and

702

(B) the circumstances referred to in clauses (iv)(A) and (B) apply.

(4) **Substitution of officer's evaluation** — If the requirements referred to in subsection (3), whether or not they are met, are not sufficient indicators of whether the foreign national will become economically established in Canada, an officer may substitute their evaluation for the requirements. This decision requires the concurrence of another officer.

(5) **Requirement for funds** — With the exception of the foreign nationals referred to in subparagraphs (3)(d)(ii), (iii) and (v), the foreign national must have, in the form of transferable and available funds, unencumbered by debts or other obligations, an amount equal to one half of the minimum necessary income applicable in respect of the group of persons consisting of the skilled trades worker and their family members.
SOR/2012-274, s. 14; 2013, c. 40, s. 237(3)(a); SOR/2013-245, s. 2; SOR/2015-144, s. 2; SOR/2015-147, s. 1(b)

DIVISION 2 — BUSINESS IMMIGRANTS

Interpretation

88. (1) **Definitions** — The definitions in this subsection apply in this Division.

"agent" means, in respect of a fund, the Minister acting as an agent on behalf of a fund that has been approved by a province. *("mandataire")*

"allocation period" means, in respect of the provincial allocation of an investor, the period of five years beginning on the first day of the second month after the month in which the agent receives the investment. *("période de placement")*

"approved fund" means a fund that is approved by the Minister under section 91. *("fonds agréé")*

"business experience", in respect of

(a) an investor, other than an investor selected by a province, means a minimum of two years of experience consisting of

(i) two one-year periods of experience in the management of a qualifying business and the control of a percentage of equity of the qualifying business during the period beginning five years before the date of application for a permanent resident visa and ending on the day a determination is made in respect of the application,

(ii) two one-year periods of experience in the management of at least five full-time job equivalents per year in a business during the period beginning five years before the date of application for a permanent resident visa and ending on the day a determination is made in respect of the application, or

(iii) a combination of a one-year period of experience described in subparagraph (i) and a one-year period of experience described in subparagraph (ii);

703

(b) an entrepreneur, other than an entrepreneur selected by a province, means a minimum of two years of experience consisting of two one-year periods of experience in the management of a qualifying business and the control of a percentage of equity of the qualifying business during the period beginning five years before the date of application for a permanent resident visa and ending on the day a determination is made in respect of the application; and

(c) an investor selected by a province or an entrepreneur selected by a province, has themeaning provided by the laws of the province and is calculated in accordance with the laws of the province.

("expérience dans l'exploitation d'une entreprise")

"debt obligation" has the same meaning as in subsection 2(1) of the *Canada Business Corporations Act*. *("titre de créance")*

"entrepreneur" means a foreign national who

(a) has business experience;

(b) has a legally obtained minimum net worth; and

(c) provides a written statement to an officer that they intend and will be able to meet

(i) in the case of an entrepreneur selected by a province,

(A) if there are provincial conditions that the entrepreneur is required by subsection 98(2) to meet, those conditions, as well as the conditions set out in subsections 98(3) to (5), and

(B) if there are no provincial conditions that the entrepreneur is required to meet, the condition set out in paragraph 98(5)(a), and

(ii) in the case of any other entrepreneur, the conditions set out in subsections 98(1) and (3) to (5).

("entrepreneur")

"entrepreneur selected by a province" means an entrepreneur who

(a) intends to reside in a province the government of which has, under subsection 8(1) of the Act, entered into an agreement referred to in subsection 9(1) of the Act with the Minister whereby the province has sole responsibility for the selection of entrepreneurs; and

(b) is named in a selection certificate issued to them by that province.

("entrepreneur sélectionné par une province")

"former Regulations" has the same meaning as in subsection 316(1). *("ancien règlement")*

"full-time job equivalent" means 1,950 hours of paid employment. *("équivalent d'emploi à temps plein")*

"fund" means a corporation that is controlled by the government of a province and is authorized to create or continue employment in Canada in order to foster the development of a strong and viable economy. *("fonds")*

"investment" means, in respect of an investor, a sum of $800,000 that

(a) in the case of an investor other than an investor selected by a province, is paid by the investor to the agent for allocation to all approved funds in existence as of the date the allocation period begins and that is not refundable during the period beginning on the day a permanent resident visa is issued to the investor and ending at the end of the allocation period; and

(b) in the case of an investor selected by a province, is invested by the investor in accordance with an investment proposal within the meaning of the laws of the province and is not refundable for a period of at least five years, as calculated in accordance with the laws of the province.

("placement")

"investor" means a foreign national who

(a) has business experience;

(b) has a legally obtained net worth of at least $1,600,000; and

(c) indicates in writing to an officer that they intend to make or have made an investment.

("investisseur")

"investor selected by a province" means an investor who

(a) intends to reside in a province the government of which has, under subsection 8(1) of the Act, entered into an agreement referred to in subsection 9(1) of the Act with the Minister whereby the province has sole responsibility for the selection of investors; and

(b) is named in a selection certificate issued to them by that province.

("investisseur sélectionné par une province")

"language skill area" means speaking, oral comprehension, reading or writing. *("habileté langagière")*

"minimum net worth" means

(a) in respect of an entrepreneur, other than an entrepreneur selected by a province, $300,000; and

(b) in respect of an entrepreneur selected by a province, the minimum net worth required by the laws of the province.

("avoir net minimal")

"net assets", in respect of a qualifying business or a qualifying Canadian business, means the assets of the business, minus the liabilities of the business, plus shareholder loans made to the business by the foreign national who is making or has made an application for a permanent resident visa and their spouse or common-law partner. *("actif net")*

"net income", in respect of a qualifying business or a qualifying Canadian business, means the after tax profit or loss of the business plus remuneration by the business to the foreign national who is making or has made an application for a permanent resident visa and their spouse or common-law partner. *("revenu net")*

"net worth", in respect of

> (a) an investor, other than an investor selected by a province, means the fair market value of all of the assets of the investor and their spouse or common-law partner minus the fair market value of all of their liabilities;

> (b) an entrepreneur, other than an entrepreneur selected by a province, means the fair market value of all of the assets of the entrepreneur and their spouse or common-law partner minus the fair market value of all of their liabilities; and

> (c) an investor selected by a province or an entrepreneur selected by a province, has the meaning provided by the laws of the province and is calculated in accordance with the laws of the province.

("avoir net")

"percentage of equity" means

> (a) in respect of a sole proprietorship, 100 per cent of the equity of the sole proprietorship controlled by a foreign national or their spouse or common-law partner;

> (b) in respect of a corporation, the percentage of the issued and outstanding voting shares of the capital stock of the corporation controlled by a foreign national or their spouse or common-law partner; and

> (c) in respect of a partnership or joint venture, the percentage of the profit or loss of the partnership or joint venture to which a foreign national or their spouse or common-law partner is entitled.

("pourcentage des capitaux propres")

"provincial allocation" means the portion of an investor's investment in an approved fund calculated in accordance with subsection (2). *("quote-part provinciale")*

"qualifying business" means a business — other than a business operated primarily for the purpose of deriving investment income such as interest, dividends or capital gains — for which, during the year under consideration, there is documentary evidence of any two of the following:

> (a) the percentage of equity multiplied by the number of full-time job equivalents is equal to or greater than two full-time job equivalents per year;

> (b) the percentage of equity multiplied by the total annual sales is equal to or greater than $500,000;

> (c) the percentage of equity multiplied by the net income in the year is equal to or greater than $50,000; and

> (d) the percentage of equity multiplied by the net assets at the end of the year is equal to or greater than $125,000.

("entreprise admissible")

"qualifying Canadian business" means a business operated in Canada by an entrepreneur — other than a business operated primarily for the purpose of deriving investment income, such as interest, dividends or capital gains — for which there is in any year within the period of three years after the day the entrepreneur becomes a permanent resident documentary evidence of any two of the following:

(a) the percentage of equity multiplied by the number of full-time job equivalents is equal to or greater than two full-time job equivalents per year;

(b) the percentage of equity multiplied by the total annual sales is equal to or greater than $250,000;

(c) the percentage of equity multiplied by the net income in the year is equal to or greater than $25,000; and

(d) the percentage of equity multiplied by the net assets at the end of the year is equal to or greater than $125,000.

("entreprise canadienne admissible")

"relevant experience", in respect of

(a) a self-employed person, other than a self-employed person selected by a province, means a minimum of two years of experience, during the period beginning five years before the date of application for a permanent resident visa and ending on the day a determination is made in respect of the application, consisting of

(i) in respect of cultural activities,

(A) two one-year periods of experience in self-employment in cultural activities,

(B) two one-year periods of experience in participation at a world class level in cultural activities, or

(C) a combination of a one-year period of experience described in clause (A) and a one-year period of experience described in clause (B),

(ii) in respect of athletics,

(A) two one-year periods of experience in self-employment in athletics,

(B) two one-year periods of experience in participation at a world class level in athletics, or

(C) a combination of a one-year period of experience described in clause (A) and a one-year period of experience described in clause (B), and

(iii) in respect of the purchase and management of a farm, two one-year periods of experience in the management of a farm; and

(b) a self-employed person selected by a province, has the meaning provided by the laws of the province.

("expérience utile")

"self-employed person" means a foreign national who has relevant experience and has the intention and ability to be self-employed in Canada and to make a significant contribution to specified economic activities in Canada. *("travailleur autonome")*

707

"self-employed person selected by a province" means a self-employed person

(a) who intends to reside in a province the government of which has, under subsection 8(1) of the Act, entered into an agreement referred to in subsection 9(1) of the Act with the Minister whereby the province has sole responsibility for the selection of self-employed persons; and

(b) is named in a selection certificate issued to them by that province.

("travailleur autonome sélectionné par une province")

"specified economic activities", in respect of

(a) a self-employed person, other than a self-employed person selected by a province, means cultural activities, athletics or the purchase and management of a farm; and

(b) a self-employed person selected by a province, has the meaning provided by the laws of the province.

("activités économiques déterminées")

(2) Provincial allocation — For the purposes of the definition "provincial allocation" in subsection (1), the provincial allocation shall be calculated as of the first day of the allocation period in accordance with the formula

$$A + B$$

where

A   equals $400,000 divided by the number of approved funds that are not suspended; and

B   equals $400,000 multiplied by the gross domestic product at market prices of the province that has approved the non-suspended fund, divided by the total of the gross domestic products at market prices of all of the provinces that have approved a non-suspended fund.

(3) Gross domestic product — For the purposes of subsection (2), the gross domestic product is the one for the calendar year before the calendar year that immediately precedesthe date of provincial allocation, as set out in the table entitled "Provincial accounts GDP at market prices by province (millions of dollars)" in the *Canadian Economic Observer Historical Statistical Supplement*, published by Statistics Canada.

SOR/2003-383, s. 4; SOR/2004-167, s. 31; SOR/2010-218, s. 1; SOR/2011-124, s. 1; SOR/2012-274, s. 15

Case Law

Section 88(1)

Business Experience

Rahim v. Canada (Minister of Citizenship & Immigration) (2008), 69 Imm. L.R. (3d) 120, 375 N.R. 210, 2008 CarswellNat 610, 2008 CarswellNat 1456, 2008 FCA 87 — The issue in this appeal related to the appropriate test to be applied with respect to the determination of whether the appellant had control of certain shares of a corporation, a condition of the definition of business experience that he was obligated to meet to succeed in his application for a permanent resident visa as a member of the entrepreneur class. The visa officer stated that the documentary evidence showed that the appellant had set up a trust whereby he had turned over his rights, titles and 60 per cent interest in the issued shares of the corporation to a Mr. Ali and accordingly, the visa officer considered that the appellant had relinquished his equity in the corporation. The visa officer concluded that the appellant did not meet the business experience requirement of the definition of an entrepreneur in subs. 88(1) of the Regulations and, therefore, rejected his application. The Federal Court upheld the visa officer's decision, holding that the test was whether the appellant had legal or *de jure* control over the shares in question.

The Federal Court of Appeal concluded that the *de jure* control test with respect to the determination of who, if anyone, controls a corporation for income tax purposes does not provide authority for the proposition that a *de jure* control test is applicable with respect to the determination of whether a person controls shares for the purposes of the definition of business experience in subs. 88(1) of the Regulations. Income tax legislation and immigration legislation are based upon significantly different considerations. Instead, the Federal Court of Appeal concluded that the effective control test in *Cloutier v. Canada (Minister of National Revenue)*, [1986] F.C.J. No. 788, [1987] 2 F.C. 222 was consistent with the language of the definitions of business experience and percentage of equity that are found in subs. 88(1) of the Regulations, as well as the purpose of the provisions of the Regulations that deal with immigration by entrepreneurs.

In the present circumstances, the appellant had always been in a position to have the shares of the corporation transferred to him by revoking the trust. His power to do so was unfettered and could be freely exercised. Accordingly, he had and always had effective control over the shares of the corporation that were held in trust for him by Mr. Ali and, therefore, demonstrated that he met the requirement of control of a percentage of equity of the qualifying business in subs. 88(1) of the Regulations. The appeal was allowed.

Entrepreneur

See the *Rahim* summary, (2008), 69 Imm. L.R. (3d) 120, 375 N.R. 210, 2008 CarswellNat 610, 2008 CarswellNat 1456, 2008 FCA 87, under Business Experience.

Li v. Canada (Minister of Citizenship & Immigration), 2006 CarswellNat 1300, 2006 CarswellNat 2280, 2006 FC 599 — The applicant applied for permanent resident status under the Canada-Quebec Investor Program. His application was denied on the basis that he failed to adequately account for the origins of his net worth. The applicant argued that the officer's decision was patently unreasonable as the decision was based on irrelevant considerations. He also argued that the information the officer requested imposed too heavy a burden on the applicant as the documents were from many years prior to the interview, and were not relevant to the current assets that had been primarily accumulated in recent years. The court held that given the money in question was the seed money that allowed the applicant to establish his own business, it was very relevant to the application and the officer was merely doing her duty under s. 16 of IRPA when enquiring into the source of the funds.

Bharaj v. Canada (Minister of Citizenship & Immigration), 2005 FC 1462, 2005 CarswellNat 3571, 2005 CarswellNat 5028, [2005] F.C.J. No. 1821 — The applicant submitted an application for a permanent resident visa as a member of the "entrepreneur class." The visa officer determined that the applicant did not meet the definition of "entrepreneur" as set out in s. 88(1) of the Regulations. In determining that the applicant did not satisfy the visa officer that Bharaj & Co. is a "qualified business," he only cited one reason, that being that the applicant indicated that the total sales of the business were 35,686,302 rupees and the auditor's report showed the actual total annual sales as 3,568,302 rupees. The single explanation or reason cited by the visa officer did not even stipulate which part of the "qualifying business" test the applicant did not meet and, accordingly, the Federal Court concluded that it could not be certain that a visa officer had considered all the relevant facts.

Zhang c. Canada (Ministre de la Citoyenneté & de l'Immigration) (2005), 281 F.T.R. 35, 2005 CarswellNat 2969, 2005 CarswellNat 5557, 2005 FC 1313 — The applicant applied for judicial review of a decision by the immigration program manager at the Canadian Embassy in Beijing with respect to the applicant's application for permanent residence. The application was refused based on a violation of para. 40(1)(a) of the Act, specifically a misrepresentation as to the source of the applicant's funds. The court concluded that where the applicant does not establish the source of her money, which is required by the Act, the visa officer is justified in denying the visa application. Therefore, misrepresenting the source of the funds is a material fact. The application for judicial review was dismissed.

Investor

Molev v. Canada (Minister of Citizenship & Immigration) (2011), 6 Imm. L.R. (4th) 1, 2011 FC 1362, 2011 CarswellNat 4921, 2011 CarswellNat 5661 — The applicant's application for permanent residence under the Federal Investor program was refused on the basis of the applicant's perceived failure to prove a single fact in a highly complex evidentiary scenario. The key issue for determination was whether the visa officer was required to give the applicant a reasonable opportunity to establish that the evidence submitted proved the fact found to be so important. Under the Overseas Processing Manual OP9, an applicant must be given an opportunity to rebut the content of any negative provincial assessment that may influence the final decision. When the veracity of the documentation is in doubt, the officer should first request further documentation. In this case, the applicant's counsel requested an opportunity for the applicant to meet the visa officer's concern upon receipt of the officer's decision. However, this request was denied. The failure to resolve the doubt by following the guidelines constituted a breach in the duty of fairness owed to the applicant. The application for judicial review was allowed.

See summaries for *Li*, 2006 CarswellNat 1300, 2006 CarswellNat 2280, 2006 FC 599, and *Zhang* (2005), 281 F.T.R. 35, 2005 CarswellNat 2969, 2005 CarswellNat 5557, 2005 FC 1313, [2005] F.C.J. No. 1594, under Entrepreneur.

Ahmed v. Canada (Minister of Citizenship & Immigration), 2006 CarswellNat 3202, 2006 FC 1203 — This was an application for judicial review of a decision of a visa officer rejecting the applicant's application for permanent residence under the Investor category. The visa officer expressed concerns about how the applicant had accumulated his wealth and asked if the applicant could provide further documentation to satisfy her of the sources of his funds. The visa officer states in her decision that the applicant replied that he did not have any further documentation and at no time did he advise that he would be sending, within 30 days of the interview, the necessary proof from his accountant showing that he was exempt from filing and paying personal income tax.

The visa officer was under no obligation to apprise the applicant of concerns unless these concerns dealt with extrinsic evidence. Although there was no obligation to do so, the visa officer did express her misgivings and invited the applicant to provide further documentation to persuade her that his wealth was not gleaned from illegitimate sources. Unfortunately, the applicant said he had no further information. The information the applicant subsequently provided was simply too late and arrived after the decision was made. There was no request from the applicant to reopen the case. The application for judicial review was dismissed as the applicant had failed to discharge himself of the onus to respect the terms of his application for permanent residence under the Investor program. Specifically, the applicant failed to clearly establish that his net worth was not gained by illegitimate means.

Net Worth

See summaries for *Li*, 2006 CarswellNat 1300, 2006 CarswellNat 2280, 2006 FC 599, and *Zhang* (2005), 281 F.T.R. 35, 2005 CarswellNat 2969, 2005 CarswellNat 5557, 2005 FC 1313, [2005] F.C.J. No. 1594, under Entrepreneur.

Qualifying Business

Thomas v. Canada (Minister of Citizenship & Immigration), 2006 CarswellNat 607, 2006 CarswellNat 1875, 2006 FC 334 — A visa officer refused the application of the applicant and his dependants for permanent residence in Canada under the entrepreneur class. The officer concluded that the applicants had not established that any of the applicants' businesses met the definition of a "qualifying business" as required by s. 88(1) of the Regulations. The visa officer did not consider the aggregate of the applicants' businesses' results under the Regulations but instead, looked at each corporate entity on its own in determining whether the applicants' business met the definition of a "qualifying business."

Since the issue of whether s. 88(1) of the Regulations authorizes the aggregation of the results of the two corporations was a question of law to which the court has greater experience than a visa officer, the appropriate standard of review was correctness.

A business is not defined in the Act or Regulations but is generally an activity carried out for the purpose of profit. The legal vehicle by which businesses are conducted is a different issue. In dealing with the term "qualifying business," the Regulation not only does not define a "business" but does not stipulate how it is structured. The definition simply excludes a business whose purpose is deriving investment income. The purpose of the definition is to ensure that the business in which the entrepreneur has management experience is an "active" business. The Regulation does not address and is not intended to address the structure or legal vehicle used to conduct the business, whether by a "business name," partnership, joint venture, trust, or corporation.

In this case, the proper question to ask was what were the results of the active businesses managed by the applicant? The visa officer put undue emphasis on the legal structure of the businesses, and ignored the results of the active business in all its components. The result was to ignore the reality of the scope of the businesses managed by the entrepreneur. Such an approach could lead to the unreasonable result that an entrepreneur who has structured his/her business through many corporations — for legitimate reasons such as liability, tax planning and so forth — is penalized for using the very business acumen that the Act and Regulations seeks to attract to Canada (see s. 3(1)(c) of the IRPA which identifies one of the objectives of the IRPA to "support the development of a strong and prosperous Canadian economy, in which the benefits of immigration are shared by all regions of Canada.")

It is more consistent with the purposes of the legislative provisions to focus the consideration of the entrepreneur on the overall results of the business activities managed by him/her. This leads to a result in keeping with the very aim of the statutory provision and the Regulations. The term "qualifying business" is not restricted to each legal entity conducting the non-investment income activity. It is more consistent with the purposes of the Act and the Regulations to include the financial results of the entrepreneur's non-investment income activities.

Bharaj v. Canada (Minister of Citizenship & Immigration), 2005 FC 1462, 2005 CarswellNat 3571, 2005 CarswellNat 5028, [2005] F.C.J. No. 1821 — The applicant submitted an application for a permanent resident visa as a member of the "entrepreneur class." The visa officer determined that the applicant did not meet the definition of "entrepreneur" as set out in s. 88(1) of the Regulations. In determining that the applicant did not satisfy the visa officer that Bharaj & Co. is a "qualified business," he only cited one reason, that being that the applicant indicated that the total sales of the business were 35,686,302 rupees and the auditor's report showed the actual total annual sales as 3,568,302 rupees. The single explanation or reason cited by the visa officer did not even stipulate which part of the "qualifying business" test the applicant did not meet and accordingly the Federal Court concluded that it could not be certain that a visa officer had considered all the relevant facts.

Self-employed person

Ding v. Canada (Minister of Citizenship & Immigration), 2010 FC 764, 2010 CarswellNat 2425, 2010 CarswellNat 2927 — The Canadian Embassy in Beijing refused the applicant's application for permanent resident status as a member of the self-employed person class. The applicant argued that the visa officer erred by failing to provide reasons as to why traditional Chinese medicine is not a cultural activity under the Regulations. Section 11.4 of the OP 8 Entrepreneurs and Self-Employed Manual stipulates that it is intended that the self-employed class enrich Canadian culture. It is clear that cultural activities are meant to be those as ordinarily understood to be part of the arts. There is no basis on which to conclude that experience in a Chinese therapeutic massage clinic and training centre falls within the meaning of cultural activities under the Regulations. The application for judicial review was dismissed.

Rolfe v. Canada (Minister of Citizenship & Immigration), 2005 CarswellNat 3686, 2005 CarswellNat 4784, 2005 FC 1514 — The obligation to provide adequate reasons is not satisfied by merely stating a conclusion. In this case, the officer concluded the applicant did not meet the definition of a "self-employed person" because she was not satisfied that his experience as an explorer, leader of northern expeditions, and husky trainer was recognized as a form of cultural activity, sports, or farming under the intent of s. 88 of the Regulations. Since the applicant was presented with a conclusion without meaningful explanation, the court concluded the officer had failed to fulfill the duty of procedural fairness owed to the applicant and set aside the decision of the immigration officer.

89. Artificial transactions — **For the purposes of this Division, an investor, an entrepreneur and a self-employed person are not considered to have met the applicable requirements of this Division if the fulfillment of those requirements is based**

on one or more transactions the purpose of which is to circumvent, directly or indirectly, the requirements of this Division.

Investors

Investors Class

90. (1) Members of the class — For the purposes of subsection 12(2) of the Act, the investor class is hereby prescribed as a class of persons who may become permanent residents on the basis of their ability to become economically established in Canada and who are investors within the meaning of subsection 88(1).

(2) Minimal requirements — If a foreign national who makes an application as a member of the investor class is not an investor within the meaning of subsection 88(1), the application shall be refused and no further assessment is required.

[Editor's Note: SOR/2002-227, s. 361(1) provides that if, before June 28, 2002, a foreign national referred to in SOR/2002-227, s. 361(2), has been assessed by a visa officer and awarded the number of units of assessment required by the Immigration Regulations, 1978, SOR/78-172 *(the "former Regulations"), that assessment is, for the purpose of the* Immigration and Refugee Protection Regulations, SOR/2002-227 *(the "new Regulations"), an award of points equal or superior to the minimum number of points required of*

> *(a) a skilled worker, in the case of a foreign national described in paragraph (2)(a) of the new Regulations;*
>
> *(b) an investor, in the case of a foreign national described in paragraph (2)(b) of the new Regulations;*
>
> *(c) an entrepreneur, in the case of a foreign national described in paragraph (2)(c) of the new Regulations; or*
>
> *(d) a self-employed person, in the case of a foreign national described in paragraph (2)(a) of the new Regulations.*

SOR/2002-227, s. 361(2) provides that SOR/2002-227, s. 361(1) applies in respect of a foreign national who submitted an application under the former Regulations, as one of the following, for an immigrant visa that is pending immediately before June 28, 2002:

> *(a) a person described in subparagraph 9(1)(b)(i) or paragraph 10(1)(b) of the former Regulations;*
>
> *(b) an investor; or*
>
> *(c) an entrepreneur.]*

Fund

91. Approval by the Minister — The Minister shall approve a fund if

(a) the fund has been approved by a province;

(b) the province provides documentation to the Minister stating that, if the fund fails to transfer the provincial allocation to the agent in accordance with paragraph 92(g), the province will be liable to transfer to the agent an amount equal to the provincial allocation in order to repay the investor in accordance with paragraph 92(i);

(c) the fund will be the only non-suspended approved fund in the province; and

(d) the fund has entered into an agreement with the Minister designating the Minister as agent for the purpose of

(i) receiving the provincial allocation and keeping it until the beginning of the allocation period, unless the provincial allocation is repaid under paragraph 92(b),

(ii) transferring the provincial allocation to the approved fund at the beginning of the allocation period in accordance with paragraph 92(d), unless the approval of the fund is suspended under subsection 93(1),

(iii) preparing and delivering to the investor a debt obligation and notifying the investor of the date of receipt of the provincial allocation at the beginning of the allocation period in accordance with paragraph 92(e),

(iv) receiving the provincial allocation transferred by the approved fund at the end of the allocation period in accordance with paragraph 92(g),

(v) if the approved fund fails to transfer the provincial allocation under paragraph 92(g), receiving the provincial allocation from the province in accordance with paragraph 92(h), and

(vi) repaying the provincial allocation to the investor in accordance with paragraph 92(i).

SOR/2010-195, s. 9

92. Terms and conditions — An approved fund is subject to the following terms and conditions:

(a) it must receive the provincial allocation through the agent;

(b) it must repay the provincial allocation through the agent to the investor within 90 days after the date of receipt by the agent of the request for repayment by the investor, if the request for repayment is received before a permanent resident visa is issued to the investor;

(c) it must repay the provincial allocation to the agent within 30 days after the agent informs the fund that the investor has chosen to withdraw their investment before the issuance of a permanent resident visa;

(d) if the approval of the fund has not been suspended, it must receive the provincial allocation through the agent on the first day of the allocation period;

(e) when it receives the provincial allocation it must

(i) on the first day of the allocation period, issue to the investor, through the agent, a debt obligation that is in an amount equal to the provincial allocation, is due and payable 30 days after the expiry of the allocation period, can be pledged as security and cannot be transferred before the expiry of the allocation period without the written consent of the approved fund provided by the agent, and

(ii) notify the investor through the agent of the date of receipt of the provincial allocation;

(f) during the allocation period, it must use the provincial allocation for the purpose of creating or continuing employment in Canada to foster the development of a strong and viable economy;

(g) at the end of the allocation period, it must transfer the provincial allocation to the agent for repayment in accordance with paragraph (i);

(h) if the approved fund fails to transfer the provincial allocation to the agent under paragraph (g), the province must transfer an amount equal to the provincial allocation to the agent for repayment in accordance with paragraph (i); and

(i) 30 days after the expiry of the allocation period, the agent must repay the provincial allocation to the investor thereby extinguishing the debt obligation in respect of that provincial allocation.

SOR/2004-167, s. 32

93. (1) Suspension — The Minister shall suspend the approval of a fund if

(a) the province that approved the fund withdraws its approval;

(b) the fund no longer qualifies as a fund within the meaning of subsection 88(1);

(c) the documentation provided by the province to the Minister in accordance with paragraph 91(b) is no longer valid and no valid documentation has been provided by the province to replace it;

(d) the agreement between the fund and the Minister referred to in paragraph 91(d) is no longer valid; or

(e) the fund is not in compliance with the terms and conditions set out in section 92.

(2) Lifting of suspension — The Minister shall lift the suspension if the circumstances that gave rise to the suspension cease to exist.

94. Revocation — The Minister shall revoke the approval of a fund if

(a) the approved fund has repaid the provincial allocation to all of its investors; and

(b) the approval of the fund has been suspended.

95. Reports — Every approved fund must submit to the Minister, until all investors in that fund have been repaid in accordance with paragraph 92(i), the following periodic reports for the purpose of demonstrating compliance with paragraph 92(f):

(a) a quarterly report on the use of provincial allocations, including

(i) the names of the recipients of the portion of the provincial allocations invested,

(ii) a description of and the terms of the security received for that investment,

(iii) the date on which the portion of the provincial allocations is invested,

715

(iv) the date on which the portion of the provincial allocations invested is recovered by the approved fund,

(v) a brief description of the use of the portion of the provincial allocations invested,

(vi) the number of full-time job equivalents created by the portion of the provincial allocations invested, and

(vii) the code for each recipient of the investment as set out in the *Canadian Standard Industrial Classification for Companies and Enterprises, 1980*; and

(b) audited annual financial statements for the approved fund, submitted within 180 days after the end of each financial year.

Investor Selected by a Province

96. Exception — A foreign national who is an investor selected by a province shall not be assessed in accordance with section 102.

SOR/2004-167, s. 33

Entrepreneurs

Entrepreneur Class

97. (1) Members of the class — For the purposes of subsection 12(2) of the Act, the entrepreneur class is hereby prescribed as a class of persons who may become permanent residents on the basis of their ability to become economically established in Canada and who are entrepreneurs within the meaning of subsection 88(1).

(2) Minimal requirements — If a foreign national who makes an application as a member of the entrepreneur class is not an entrepreneur within the meaning of subsection 88(1), the application shall be refused and no further assessment is required.

[Editor's Note: SOR/2002-227, s. 361(1) provides that if, before June 28, 2002, a foreign national referred to in SOR/2002-227, s. 361(2), has been assessed by a visa officer and awarded the number of units of assessment required by the Immigration Regulations, 1978, SOR/78-172 *(the "former Regulations"), that assessment is, for the purpose of the* Immigration and Refugee Protection Regulations, SOR/2002-227 *(the "new Regulations"), an award of points equal or superior to the minimum number of points required of*

(a) a skilled worker, in the case of a foreign national described in paragraph (2)(a) of the new Regulations;

(b) an investor, in the case of a foreign national described in paragraph (2)(b) of the new Regulations;

(c) an entrepreneur, in the case of a foreign national described in paragraph (2)(c) of the new Regulations; or

(d) a self-employed person, in the case of a foreign national described in paragraph (2)(a) of the new Regulations.

SOR/2002-227, s. 361(2) provides that SOR/2012-227, s. 361(1) applies in respect of a foreign national who submitted an application under the former Regulations, as one of the following, for an immigrant visa that is pending immediately before June 28, 2002:

(a) a person described in subparagraph 9(1)(b)(i) or paragraph 10(1)(b) of the former Regulations;

(b) an investor; or

(c) an entrepreneur.]

Case Law

Section 97(2)

See the *Bharaj* summary, 2005 CarswellNat 3571, 2005 CarswellNat 5028, 2005 FC 1462, [2005] F.C.J. No. 1821, in s. 96 of the Regulations under Qualifying Business.

Conditions

98. (1) Permanent residence — Subject to subsection (2), an entrepreneur who becomes a permanent resident must meet the following conditions:

(a) the entrepreneur must control a percentage of the equity of a qualifying Canadian business equal to or greater than 33 1/3 per cent;

(b) the entrepreneur must provide active and on-going management of the qualifying Canadian business; and

(c) the entrepreneur must create at least one incremental full-time job equivalent in the qualifying Canadian business for Canadian citizens or permanent residents, other than the entrepreneur and their family members.

(2) Conditions — par. 9(1)(d) of the Act — If at the time an entrepreneur selected by a province provides the written statement referred to in paragraph (c) of the definition "entrepreneur" in subsection 88(1) the province has established the conditions required to be met by such an entrepreneur, that statement must refer to those conditions instead of the conditions set out in subsection (1) and the entrepreneur must meet those conditions instead of the conditions set out in subsection (1).

(3) Applicable time — The entrepreneur must meet the conditions for a period of at least one year within the period of three years after the day on which the entrepreneur becomes a permanent resident.

(4) Evidence of compliance — An entrepreneur who becomes a permanent resident must provide to an officer evidence of compliance with the conditions within the period of three years after the day on which the entrepreneur becomes a permanent resident.

(5) Report and evidence of efforts to comply — An entrepreneur must provide to an officer

(a) not later than six months after the day on which the entrepreneur becomes a permanent resident, their residential address and telephone number; and

(b) during the period beginning 18 months after and ending 24 months after the day on which the entrepreneur becomes a permanent resident, evidence of their efforts to comply with the conditions.

(6) Family members — The family members of an entrepreneur are subject to the condition that the entrepreneur meets the conditions set out or referred to in this section.

(7) Non-application — If, at the time that a province issues a selection certificate to an entrepreneur, there are no provincial conditions that must be met by the entrepreneur,

(a) the entrepreneur is not required to meet the conditions set out in paragraphs (1)(a) to (c); and

(b) subsections (2) to (4), paragraph (5)(b) and subsection (6) do not apply in respect of the entrepreneur.

SOR/2004-167, s. 34; SOR/2011-124, s. 2(2)

Case Law

Section 98(1)

Gjoka v. Canada (Minister of Citizenship & Immigration) (2009), 84 Imm. L.R. (3d) 198, 352 F.T.R. 303, 2009 FC 943, 2009 CarswellNat 3058, 2009 CarswellNat 5358 (Eng.) — The applicant was selected on September 16, 2002, for permanent residence under the entrepreneur category and was issued a permanent resident visa on February 4, 2003, and landed on March 12, 2003. On May 28, 2004, in response to a letter from Canadian Immigration and Citizenship, the applicant submitted a monitoring report and an application to cancel his terms and conditions of landing. No other monitoring reports were submitted. A report alleging that the applicant had failed to comply with the terms and conditions of his landing was issued on March 18, 2008. An inadmissibility hearing was held before the ID on May 7, 2008. The respondent submitted that the applicant had not met the conditions imposed on him under the *Immigration Regulations* (the former Regulations), specifically paras. 23.1(1)(a) to (d). The applicant made his application for permanent residency under the former Act but the selection decision and his permanent resident visa were issued after the coming into force of the current Act. Furthermore, the Confirmation of Permanent Residence form signed by the applicant upon landing specified that the conditions to be met were those of the former Regulations and s. 23.1 of those Regulations was attached to the form. At the admissibility hearing, the ID member found that the conditions imposed on the applicant were of s. 98 of the current Regulations and as such, this subs. 44(1) report alleging a failure to meet the conditions under the former Regulations was unfounded. Following an appeal by the Minister, the IAD set aside the ID's decision and referred the matter back for reconsideration. The IAD accepted the conclusion that the applicant was subject to the conditions set out in s. 98 of the current Regulations and referred the matter back to the ID to determine whether or not the applicant had met the conditions imposed under the Act.

Because of the transitional provisions and s. 318 of the current Regulations, the court found that the entrepreneur class selected applicants under the former *Immigration Act* are required to comply with post-admission to Canada terms and conditions as set out in paras. 23(a) to (d) of the former *Immigration Regulations*. The interpretation of the transitional provisions of the IAD is too restrictive. It implies that s. 98 of the current Regulations can be applied retroactively to entrepreneurial applicants who filed their application prior to January 1, 2002, and were assessed and issued visas as entrepreneurs under the former *Immigration Act* and Regulations. Nothing in the Act, the current Regulations or the transitional provisions support such a proposition. The application for judicial review was allowed.

Chang v. Canada (Minister of Citizenship & Immigration), 2006 CarswellNat 2194, 2006 CarswellNat 329, [2006] F.C.J. No. 217, 2006 FC 157 — The legislatively established conditions of the entrepreneur category, if flaunted knowingly, without serious consequence, would make a mockery of the purpose for which they were established. The act of creating or participating in a front operation or a sham investment, if left unchecked, strikes a blow at the very integrity of the immigration system. In this case, the applicants were found to be in non-compliance with subs. 27(2) and s. 28. The applicants' children were also found to be in non-compliance with subs. 27(2) as they were dependants of an entrepreneur and bound by the same terms and conditions of landing as provided in s. 23.1 of the previous Regulations. Both the applicants as well as their children sought special relief on appeal in light of the circumstances of their case, specifically, that there were sufficient humanitarian and compassionate considerations that warranted the setting aside of departure orders. The IAD was of the view that the parents did not merit discretionary relief as they took part in a sham arrangement to try to fulfill the conditions of the entrepreneur category. Even though the IAD felt that the children would be excellent candidates for permanent residence, it refused to grant discretionary relief to the children because once the children became permanent residents they would be entitled to sponsor their parents which would render the removal of the parents moot.

The granting of special relief is a weighing process. Even though there were some positive elements in favour of discretionary relief being allowed to the three children, these elements did not outweigh the importance given to the integrity of maintaining the conditions in the entrepreneur category. It was open to the IAD to find that special relief should not be granted to the children because this would benefit the parents who had not respected the conditions under which they entered Canada.

Elias c. Canada (Ministre de la Citoyenneté & de l'Immigration), 2005 CarswellNat 5708, 2005 FC 1329 — The applicant sought judicial review of the IAD's decision dismissing their appeal from a removal order. The principal applicant was born in Lebanon and emigrated to Brazil, where he lived for 20 years and became a citizen of that country. The applicant was granted landing in Canada as an entrepreneur and accepted the conditions provided under s. 23.1 of the *Immigration Regulations*. The Immigration Division decided that the applicants were persons contemplated by s. 41 of the IRPA since the principal applicant had not respected the conditions imposed for entrepreneurs when he was granted landing. The IAD dismissed the applicant's appeal concluding that an order to stay the removal order would have the effect of not only calling into question the integrity of the program conceived to attract entrepreneurs, but also the integrity of the Canadian immigration system as a whole. The principal applicant argued that he had provided plausible explanations and reasons why he was unable to respect the conditions within the two-year time period. In this case, the court concluded that the IAD weighed the best interests of the children directly affected as well as the other factors alleged by the applicants in support of their appeal but, considering the other circumstances of the matter, determined that special relief was not justified. The applicants' eldest son was born in Brazil while the younger son was born in Canada. The applicants did not submit any evidence regarding the effects that the removal to Brazil could have on the eldest child, or the effects of a possible migration on the younger child. The applicants' argument regarding the children amounted to saying that the presence of children in Canada automatically implies humanitarian considerations justifying special measures. The court concluded that Parliament has not decided that the presence of children in Canada constitutes in itself an impediment to any *refoulement* of a parent illegally residing in Canada. The application for judicial review was dismissed.

Entrepreneur Selected by a Province

99. Exception — **A foreign national who is an entrepreneur selected by a province shall not be assessed in accordance with section 102.**

SOR/2004-167, s. 35

Self-employed Persons

Self-employed Persons Class

100. (1) Members of the class — **For the purposes of subsection 12(2) of the Act, the self-employed persons class is hereby prescribed as a class of persons who may become permanent residents on the basis of their ability to become economically established in Canada and who are self-employed persons within the meaning of subsection 88(1).**

(2) Minimal requirements — **If a foreign national who applies as a member of the self-employed persons class is not a self-employed person within the meaning of subsection 88(1), the application shall be refused and no further assessment is required.**

[Editor's Note: SOR/2002-227, s. 361(1) provides that if, before June 28, 2002, a foreign national referred to in SOR/2002-227, s. 361(2), has been assessed by a visa officer and awarded the number of units of assessment required by the Immigration Regulations, 1978, *SOR/78-172 (the "former Regulations"), that assessment is, for the purpose of the* Immigration and Refugee Protection Regulations, *SOR/2002-227 (the "new Regulations"), an award of points equal or superior to the minimum number of points required of*

> *(a) a skilled worker, in the case of a foreign national described in paragraph (2)(a) of the new Regulations;*

> *(b) an investor, in the case of a foreign national described in paragraph (2)(b) of the new Regulations;*

> *(c) an entrepreneur, in the case of a foreign national described in paragraph (2)(c) of the new Regulations; or*

> *(d) a self-employed person, in the case of a foreign national described in paragraph (2)(a) of the new Regulations.*

SOR/2002-227, s. 361(2) provides that SOR/2002-227, s. 361(1) applies in respect of a foreign national who submitted an application under the former Regulations, as one of the following, for an immigrant visa that is pending immediately before June 28, 2002:

> *(a) a person described in subparagraph 9(1)(b)(i) or paragraph 10(1)(b) of the former Regulations;*
>
> *(b) an investor; or*
>
> *(c) an entrepreneur.]*

Case Law

Section 100(2)

Rolfe v. Canada (Minister of Citizenship & Immigration), 2005 CarswellNat 3686, 2005 CarswellNat 4784, 2005 FC 1514 — The obligation to provide adequate reasons is not satisfied by merely stating a conclusion. In this case, the officer concluded the applicant did not meet the definition of a "self-employed person" because she was not satisfied that his experience as an explorer, leader of northern expeditions, and husky trainer was recognized as a form of cultural activity, sports, or farming under the intent of s. 88 of the Regulations. Since the applicant was presented with a conclusion without meaningful explanation, the court concluded the officer had failed to fulfill the duty of procedural fairness owed to the applicant and set aside the decision of the immigration officer.

Self-employed Person Selected by a Province

101. Exception — **A foreign national who is a self-employed person selected by a province shall not be assessed in accordance with section 102.**

SOR/2004-167, s. 36

Selection Criteria

General

102. (1) Criteria — **For the purpose of determining whether a foreign national, as a member of the investor class, the entrepreneur class or the self-employed persons class, and the foreign national's family members will be able to become economically established in Canada, an officer shall assess that foreign national on the basis of the following factors:**

(a) age, in accordance with section 102.1;

(b) education, in accordance with section 102.2;

(c) proficiency in the official languages of Canada, in accordance with section 102.3;

(d) experience, in accordance with section 103; and

(e) adaptability, in accordance with section 104 in the case of a member of the investor class or the entrepreneur class, and in accordance with section 105 in the case of a member of the self-employed persons class.

(2) Units of assessment — A foreign national who is assessed on the basis of the factors set out in paragraphs (1)(a) to (e) shall be awarded the applicable number of assessment points for each factor set out in the provision referred to in each of those paragraphs, subject to the maximum number set out in that provision for that factor.

SOR/2004-167, s. 37; SOR/2012-274, s. 16

102.1 Age (10 points) — Points shall be awarded, up to a maximum of 10, for a foreign national's age on the date on which their application is made, as follows:

(a) 10 points for a foreign national 21 years of age or older but less than 50 years of age;

(b) 8 points for a foreign national 20 or 50 years of age;

(c) 6 points for a foreign national 19 or 51 years of age;

(d) 4 points for a foreign national 18 or 52 years of age;

(e) 2 points for a foreign national 17 or 53 years of age; and

(f) 0 points, for a foreign national under 17 years of age or 54 years of age or older.

SOR/2012-274, s. 17

102.2 (1) Definitions — The following definitions apply in this section.

"full-time" means, in relation to a program of study leading to an educational credential, at least 15 hours of instruction per week during the academic year, including any period of training in the workplace that forms part of the course of instruction. *("temps plein")*

"full-time equivalent" means, in respect of part-time or accelerated studies, the number of years that would have been required to complete the equivalent of those studies on a full-time basis. *("équivalent temps plein")*

(2) Education (25 points) — Points shall be awarded, to a maximum of 25, for a foreign national's education as follows:

(a) 5 points for a secondary school educational credential;

(b) 12 points for a one-year post-secondary educational credential, other than a university educational credential, and a total of at least 12 years of completed full-time or full-time equivalent studies;

(c) 15 points for

(i) a one-year post-secondary educational credential, other than a university educational credential, and a total of at least 13 years of completed full-time or full-time equivalent studies, or

(ii) a one-year university educational credential at the bachelor's level and a total of at least 13 years of completed full-time or full-time equivalent studies;

(d) 20 points for

(i) a two-year post-secondary educational credential, other than a university educational credential, and a total of at least 14 years of completed full-time or full-time equivalent studies, or

(ii) a two-year university educational credential at the bachelor's level and a total of at least 14 years of completed full-time or full-time equivalent studies;

(e) 22 points for

(i) a three-year post-secondary educational credential, other than a university educational credential, and a total of at least 15 years of completed full-time or full-time equivalent studies, or

(ii) two or more university educational credentials at the bachelor's level and a total of at least 15 years of completed full-time or full-time equivalent studies; and

(f) 25 points for a university educational credential at the master's or doctoral level and a total of at least 17 years of completed full-time or full-time equivalent studies.

(3) **More than one educational credential** — For the purposes of subsection (2), points

(a) shall not be awarded cumulatively on the basis of more than one educational credential; and

(b) shall be awarded

(i) for the purposes of paragraphs (2)(a) to (d), subparagraph (2)(e)(i) and paragraph (2)(f), on the basis of the educational credential that results in the highest number of points, and

(ii) for the purposes of subparagraph (2)(e)(ii), on the basis of the combined educational credentials referred to in that paragraph.

(4) **Special circumstances** — For the purposes of subsection (2), if a foreign national has an educational credential referred to in any of paragraphs (2)(b) to (f), but not the total number of years of full-time or full-time equivalent studies required, the foreign national shall be awarded the same number of points as the number of years of completed full-time or full-time equivalent studies set out in the paragraph.

SOR/2012-274, s. 17

102.3 (1) **Official languages** — A foreign national must specify in their application for a permanent resident visa which language — English or French — is to be considered their first official language in Canada. They must have their proficiency in that language evaluated by an organization or institution designated under subsection (4).

(2) **Proficiency in second language** — If the foreign national wishes to claim points for proficiency in their second official language they must, with the application for a permanent resident visa, submit the results of an evaluation — which

must be less than two years old on the date on which their application is made — of their proficiency by an organization or institution designated under subsection (4).

(3) Proficiency in English and French (24 points) — Points for proficiency in the official languages of Canada shall be awarded up to a maximum of 24 points based on the benchmarks referred to in the *Canadian Language Benchmarks* and the *Niveaux de compétence linguistique canadiens*, as follows:

(a) for high proficiency

(i) in the first official language, 4 points for each language skill area if the foreign national's proficiency corresponds to a benchmark of 8 or higher, and

(ii) in the second official language, 2 points for each language skill area if the foreign national's proficiency corresponds to a benchmark of 8 or higher;

(b) for moderate proficiency

(i) in the first official language, 2 points for each language skill area if the foreign national's proficiency corresponds to a benchmark of 6 or 7, and

(ii) in the second official language, 2 points for each language skill area if the foreign national's proficiency corresponds to a benchmark of 6 or 7;

(c) for basic proficiency in either official language, 1 point for each language skill area, up to a maximum of 2 points, if the foreign national's proficiency corresponds to a benchmark of 4 or 5; and

(d) for no proficiency in either official language, 0 points if the foreign national's proficiency corresponds to a benchmark of 3 or lower.

(4) Designation for evaluating language proficiency — The Minister may designate, for any period specified by the Minister, any organization or institution to be responsible for evaluating language proficiency if the organization or institution has expertise in evaluating language proficiency and if the organization or institution has provided a correlation of its evaluation results to the benchmarks set out in the *Canadian Language Benchmarks* and the *Niveaux de compétence linguistique canadiens*.

(5) Public notice — The Minister shall make available to the public a list of the designated organizations or institutions.

(6) Definition "service agreement" — For the purposes of subsection (7), "service agreement" means an agreement concluded between the Government of Canada and an organization or institution for the purpose of having the organization or institution supply the service of evaluating the language proficiency of foreign nationals.

(7) Revocation of designation — The Minister may revoke a designation if

(a) the organization or institution no longer meets the criteria set out in subsection (4);

(b) the organization or institution submitted false, misleading or inaccurate information or has contravened any provision of federal or provincial legislation relevant to the service provided by the organization or institution; or

(c) either the government of Canada or the organization or institution has terminated the service agreement.

(8) Conclusive evidence — The results of an evaluation of a foreign national's language proficiency by a designated organization or institution and the correlation of those results with the benchmarks under subsection (4) are conclusive evidence of the foreign national's proficiency in the official languages of Canada for the purposes of subsection (1).

SOR/2012-274, s. 17

Experience

103. **(1) Investor** — A member of the investor class shall be awarded assessment points up to a maximum of 35 points for business experience during the period beginning five years before the date of their application for a permanent resident visa and ending on the day a determination is made in respect of the application as follows:

(a) for two one-year periods of experience described in subparagraph (a)(i) or (ii) of the definition "business experience" in subsection 88(1) or for a combination of two one-year periods of such experience, 20 points;

(b) for three one-year periods of experience described in subparagraph (a)(i) or (ii) of the definition "business experience" in subsection 88(1) or for any combination of three one-year periods of such experience, 25 points;

(c) for four one-year periods of experience described in subparagraph (a)(i) or (ii) of the definition "business experience" in subsection 88(1) or for any combination of four one-year periods of such experience, 30 points; and

(d) for five one-year periods of experience described in subparagraph (a)(i) or (ii) of the definition "business experience" in subsection 88(1) or for any combination of five one-year periods of such experience, 35 points.

(2) Entrepreneur — A member of the entrepreneur class shall be awarded assessment points up to a maximum of 35 points for business experience during the period beginning five years before the date of their application for a permanent resident visa and ending on the day a determination is made in respect of the application as follows:

(a) for two one-year periods of experience described in paragraph (b) of the definition "business experience" in subsection 88(1), 20 points;

(b) for three one-year periods of experience described in paragraph (b) of the definition "business experience" in subsection 88(1), 25 points;

(c) for four one-year periods of experience described in paragraph (b) of the definition "business experience" in subsection 88(1), 30 points; and

(d) for five one-year periods of experience described in paragraph (b) of the definition "business experience" in subsection 88(1), 35 points.

(3) "Self-employed person" — A member of the self-employed persons class shall be awarded assessment points up to a maximum of 35 points for relevant experience during the period beginning five years before the date of their application for a permanent resident visa and ending on the day a determination is made in respect of the application as follows:

(a) 20 points for

(i) two one-year periods of experience described in clause (a)(i)(A) or (B) of the definition "relevant experience" in subsection 88(1) or a combination of two one-year periods of such experience,

(ii) two one-year periods of experience described in clause (a)(ii)(A) or (B) of the definition "relevant experience" in subsection 88(1) or a combination of two one-year periods of such experience, or

(iii) two one-year periods of experience described in subparagraph (a)(iii) of the definition "relevant experience" in subsection 88(1);

(b) 25 points for

(i) three one-year periods of experience described in clause (a)(i)(A) or (B) of the definition "relevant experience" in subsection 88(1) or any combination of three one-year periods of such experience,

(ii) three one-year periods of experience described in clause (a)(ii)(A) or (B) of the definition "relevant experience" in subsection 88(1) or any combination of three one-year periods of such experience, or

(iii) three one-year periods of experience described in subparagraph (a)(iii) of the definition "relevant experience" in subsection 88(1);

(c) 30 points for

(i) four one-year periods of experience described in clause (a)(i)(A) or (B) of the definition "relevant experience" in subsection 88(1) or any combination of four one-year periods of such experience,

(ii) four one-year periods of experience described in clause (a)(ii)(A) or (B) of the definition "relevant experience" in subsection 88(1) or any combination of four one-year periods of such experience, or

(iii) four one-year periods of experience described in subparagraph (a)(iii) of the definition "relevant experience" in subsection 88(1); and

(d) 35 points for

(i) five one-year periods of experience described in clause (a)(i)(A) or (B) of the definition "relevant experience" in subsection 88(1) or any combination of five one-year periods of such experience,

(ii) five one-year periods of experience described in clause (a)(ii)(A) or (B) of the definition "relevant experience" in subsection 88(1) or any combination of five one-year periods of such experience, or

(iii) five one-year periods of experience described in subparagraph (a)(iii) of the definition "relevant experience" in subsection 88(1).

SOR/2004-167, s. 38

Adaptability

104. Investor and entrepreneur — A member of the investor class or the entrepreneur class shall be awarded assessment points up to a maximum of six points for adaptability on the basis of the following elements:

(a) for a business exploration trip to Canada in the period beginning five years before the date of their application for a permanent resident visa and ending on the day on which a determination is made in respect of the application, 6 points; and

(b) for participation in joint federal-provincial business immigration initiatives, 6 points.

105. (1) Self-employed person — A member of the self-employed persons class shall be awarded assessment points up to a maximum of 6 points for adaptability on the basis of any combination of the following elements:

(a) for the educational credentials of the member's accompanying spouse or common-law partner, 3, 4 or 5 points determined in accordance with subsection (2);

(b) for any previous period of study in Canada by the member or their spouse or common-law partner, 5 points;

(c) for any previous period of work in Canada by the member or their spouse or common-law partner, 5 points; and

(d) for being related to, or for having an accompanying spouse or accompanying common-law partner who is related to, a person living in Canada who is described in subsection (5), 5 points.

(2) Educational credentials of spouse or common-law partner — For the purposes of paragraph (1)(a), an officer shall evaluate the educational credentials of the accompanying spouse or accompanying common-law partner of the member of the self-employed persons class as if the spouse or common-law partner were the member, and shall award points to the member as follows:

(a) for a spouse or common-law partner who would be awarded 25 points, 5 points;

(b) for a spouse or common-law partner who would be awarded 20 or 22 points, 4 points; and

(c) for a spouse or common-law partner who would be awarded 12 or 15 points, 3 points.

(3) Previous study in Canada — For the purposes of paragraph (1)(b), a member of the self-employed persons class shall be awarded 5 points if the member or their accompanying spouse or accompanying common-law partner, on or after their 17th birthday, completed a program of full-time study of at least two years' duration at a post-secondary institution in Canada under a study permit, whether or not they obtained an educational credential for completing that program.

(4) Previous work in Canada — For the purpose of paragraph (1)(c), a member of the self-employed persons class shall be awarded 5 points if the member or their accompanying spouse or accompanying common-law partner engaged in at least one year of full-time work in Canada under a work permit.

(5) Family relationships in Canada — For the purposes of paragraph (1)(d), a member of the self-employed persons class shall be awarded 5 points if

(a) the member or their accompanying spouse or accompanying common-law partner is related by blood, marriage, common-law partnership or adoption to a person who is a Canadian citizen or permanent resident living in Canada and who is

(i) their father or mother,

(ii) the father or mother of their father or mother,

(iii) their child,

(iv) a child of their child,

(v) a child of their father or mother,

(vi) a child of the father or mother of their father or mother, other than their father or mother, or

(vii) a child of the child of their father or mother; or

(b) the member has a spouse or common-law partner who is not accompanying them and is a Canadian citizen or permanent resident living in Canada.

SOR/2004-167, s. 39; SOR/2014-140, s. 5

Requirements

106. [Repealed SOR/2008-202, s. 6.]

107. Permanent resident status — A foreign national who is an accompanying family member of a person who makes an application as a member of the investor class, the entrepreneur class or the self-employed persons class shall become a permanent resident if, following an examination, it is established that

(a) the person who made the application has become a permanent resident; and

(b) the foreign national is not inadmissible.

SOR/2008-202, s. 6

Selection

108. (1) Application for visa — Subject to subsection (5), if a foreign national makes an application as a member of the investor class, the entrepreneur class or the self-employed persons class for a permanent resident visa, an officer shall issue the visa to the foreign national and their accompanying family members if

(a) the foreign national and their family members, whether accompanying or not, are not inadmissible and meet the requirements of the Act and these Regulations;

[Editor's Note: SOR/2002-227, s. 344 provides that if a person has made an application under the former Immigration Act, R.S.C. 1985, c. I-2 before June 28, 2002, the following provisions of the Immigration and Refugee Protection Regulations, *SOR/2002-227 (the "new Regulations") do not apply to the person in respect of any of his or her non-accompanying dependent children, referred to in s. 352 of the new Regulations, or his or her non-accompanying common-law partner:*

(a) paragraph 70(1)(e);

(b) subparagraph 72(1)(e)(i); and

(c) paragraph 108(1)(a).]

(b) where the foreign national and their accompanying family members intend to reside in a place in Canada other than a province the government of which has, under subsection 8(1) of the Act, entered into an agreement referred to in subsection 9(1) of the Act with the Minister whereby the province has sole responsibility for selection, the foreign national is awarded the minimum number of points referred to in subsection (2), (3) or (4), as the case may be, and, if they are a member of the investor class, they have made an investment; and

(c) where the foreign national and their accompanying family members intend to reside in a province the government of which has, under subsection 8(1) of the Act, entered into an agreement referred to in subsection 9(1) of the Act with the Minister whereby the province has sole responsibility for selection, the foreign national is named in a selection certificate issued by that province and, if the foreign national is a member of the investor class, they have made an investment.

(2) Minimum points — investors — The Minister shall fix and make available to the public the minimum number of points required of an investor, on the basis of

(a) the number of applications made by members of the investor class currently being processed;

(b) the number of investors projected to become permanent residents according to the report to Parliament referred to in section 94 of the Act; and

(c) the potential, taking into account economic and other relevant factors, for the establishment of investors in Canada.

(3) Minimum points — entrepreneurs — The Minister shall fix and make available to the public the minimum number of points required of an entrepreneur, on the basis of

(a) the number of applications by members of the entrepreneur class currently being processed;

(b) the number of entrepreneurs projected to become permanent residents according to the report to Parliament referred to in section 94 of the Act; and

(c) the potential, taking into account economic and other relevant factors, for the establishment of entrepreneurs in Canada.

(4) Minimum points — self-employed persons — The Minister shall fix and make available to the public the minimum number of points required of a self-employed person, on the basis of

(a) the number of applications by members of the self-employed persons class currently being processed;

(b) the number of self-employed persons projected to become permanent residents according to the report to Parliament referred to in section 94 of the Act; and

(c) the potential, taking into account economic and other relevant factors, for the establishment of self-employed persons in Canada.

(5) Federal-provincial agreement — A permanent resident visa shall not be issued to an investor selected by a province, or to that investor's accompanying family members, if the Minister is engaged in consultations with the province in respect of the interpretation or implementation of the agreement, referred to in subsection 9(1) of the Act and entered into under subsection 8(1) of the Act, between the province and the Minister in respect of the selection of investors and the consultations have not been successfully completed.

SOR/2004-167, s. 40

109. (1) Substitution of evaluation — Whether or not a foreign national has been awarded the minimum number of required points referred to in subsection 108(1), an officer may substitute for the factors set out in subsection 102(1) their evaluation of the likelihood of the foreign national's ability to become economically established in Canada if the number of points awarded is not a sufficient indicator of whether the foreign national may become economically established in Canada.

(2) Concurrence — An evaluation made under subsection (1) requires the concurrence of a second officer.

Transitional Federal Investors, Entrepreneurs and Self-employed Persons

[Heading added SOR/2003-383, s. 5.]

Transitional Federal Business Classes

[Heading added SOR/2003-383, s. 5.]

109.1 (1) Classes — For the purposes of subsection 12(2) of the Act, the transitional federal investor class, the transitional federal entrepreneur class and the transitional federal self-employed persons class are hereby prescribed as classes of persons who are transitional investors, transitional entrepreneurs or transitional self-employed persons, respectively, and who may become permanent residents on the basis of their ability to become economically established in Canada and who intend to reside in a province other than the Province of Quebec.

(2) Transitional federal business immigrants — A foreign national is a transitional investor, a transitional entrepreneur or a transitional self-employed person if they made an application before January 1, 2002 under the former Regulations for an immigrant visa as an investor, an entrepreneur or a self-employed person, respectively, within the meaning of subsection 2(1) of those Regulations that was

(a) refused after March 31, 2003 and before June 20, 2003; or

(b) withdrawn by the foreign national on or after January 1, 2002 and before December 1, 2003.

SOR/2003-383, s. 5

109.2 (1) Application before January 1, 2005 — Subject to subsection (2), an application for a permanent resident visa as a member of the transitional federal investor class, the transitional federal entrepreneur class or the transitional federal self-employed persons class must be made in accordance with sections 10 and 11 and must be received by the applicable immigration office referred to in subsection 11(1) not later than December 31, 2004.

(2) **Alternate place of application** — An application referred to in subsection (1) may be made to the immigration office at the location where the application referred to in subsection 109.1(2) was made, instead of to the immigration office referred to in subsection 11(1).

SOR/2003-383, s. 5

109.3 Criteria — For the purpose of determining whether

(a) a transitional investor, as a member of the transitional federal investor class, will be able to become economically established in Canada, they must be

(i) an investor within the meaning of subsection 2(1) of the former Regulations and be awarded the number of units of assessment required by those Regulations for an investor, or

(ii) an investor within the meaning of subsection 88(1) and obtain a minimum of 35 points based on the factors set out in subsection 102(1) to become a permanent resident as a member of the investor class;

(b) a transitional entrepreneur, as a member of the transitional federal entrepreneur class, will be able to become economically established in Canada, they must be

(i) an entrepreneur within the meaning of subsection 2(1) of the former Regulations and be awarded the number of units of assessment required by those Regulations for an entrepreneur, or

(ii) an entrepreneur within the meaning of subsection 88(1) and obtain a minimum of 35 points based on the factors set out in subsection 102(1) to become a permanent resident as a member of the entrepreneur class; and

(c) a transitional self-employed person, as a member of the transitional federal self-employed persons class, will be able to become economically established in Canada, they must be

(i) a self-employed person within the meaning of subsection 2(1) of the former Regulations and be awarded the number of units of assessment required by those Regulations for a self-employed person, or

(ii) **a self-employed person within the meaning of subsection 88(1) and obtain a minimum of 35 points based on the factors set out in subsection 102(1) to become a permanent resident as a member of the self-employed persons class.**

SOR/2003-383, s. 5

Requirements

[Heading added SOR/2003-383, s. 5.]

109.4 [Repealed SOR/2008-202, s. 7.]

109.5 Permanent resident status — A foreign national who is a family member of a person who makes an application for a permanent resident visa as a member of the transitional federal investor class, the transitional federal entrepreneur class or the transitional federal self-employed persons class shall become a permanent resident if, following an examination, it is established that the family member is not inadmissible.

SOR/2003-383, s. 5

DIVISION 3 — LIVE-IN CAREGIVERS

110. Live-in caregiver class — The live-in caregiver class is prescribed as a class of foreign nationals who may become permanent residents on the basis of the requirements of this Division.

111. Processing — A foreign national who seeks to enter Canada as a live-in caregiver must make

(a) **an application for a work permit in accordance with Part 11; and**

(b) **an application for**

(i) **a temporary resident visa, if such a visa is required under Part 9, or**

(ii) **an electronic travel authorization in accordance with section 12.04, if such an authorization is required under section 7.1.**

SOR/2015-77, s. 5

112. Work permits — requirements — A work permit shall not be issued to a foreign national who seeks to enter Canada as a live-in caregiver unless they

(a) **applied for a work permit as a live-in caregiver before entering Canada;**

(b) **have successfully completed a course of study that is equivalent to the successful completion of secondary school in Canada;**

(c) **have the following training or experience, in a field or occupation related to the employment for which the work permit is sought, namely,**

(i) **successful completion of six months of full-time training in a classroom setting, or**

(ii) **completion of one year of full-time paid employment, including at least six months of continuous employment with one employer, in such a** field or occupation within the three years immediately before the day on which they submit an application for a work permit;

(d) have the ability to speak, read and listen to English or French at a level sufficient to communicate effectively in an unsupervised setting; and

(e) have an employment contract with their future employer.

Case Law

de Ocampo v. Canada (Minister of Citizenship & Immigration) (2014), 25 Imm. L.R. (4th) 329, 2014 FC 447, 2014 CarswellNat 1460, 2014 CarswellNat 1698 — The applicant sought judicial review of a decision of a visa officer that found she did not meet the requirements for a work permit as a live-in caregiver under the Live-In Caregiver Program.

The CIC Manual, s. 5.7, sets out the employment contract requirements. Employers must establish that they have sufficient income to provide the wages and benefits for the live-in caregiver based upon provincial wage rates. The position must be full time and the employer must be residing in Canada. The employer has to provide suitable accommodation for the live-in caregiver and should include privacy such as a private room with a lock. The live-in caregiver must reside at the employer's residence to qualify for the program. Of course, these requirements are meant to ensure that the job offer is *bona fides*, and this is an implicit prerequisite. Once all the requirements are met, however, the court failed to see how an application could be dismissed on the ground that the employment offer was not genuine, especially when the employer and the applicant had been given to understand that the only concerns were in relation to the property ownership and the configuration of that property. The officer acted unfairly and breached the applicant's right to procedural fairness. The application for judicial review was granted and the decision set aside to be redetermined by another visa officer.

Mehmi v. Canada (Minister of Citizenship & Immigration) (2011), 3 Imm. L.R. (4th) 231, 2011 FC 1246, 2011 CarswellNat 4495, 2011 CarswellNat 5334 — There is no statutory or case-law authority which says that procedural fairness requires, in every case, a standardized language test. In some instances, it would be pointless. OP-14 directs in these situations that "if an officer has reason to doubt an applicant's language ability, then the officer should interview the applicant." This appears to recognize that a face-to-face interview is an acceptable procedure in these circumstances. It may not suffice in all circumstances. A standardized test may be the only fair way of assessing the ability of some applicants. Much will depend upon the circumstances of each case and whether the interview has provided a particular applicant with a fair opportunity to demonstrate their proficiency and the officer's ability to make an assessment from what transpires at the interview. There was no evidence of procedural unfairness on the facts of this case. The application was dismissed.

De Luna v. Canada (Minister of Citizenship & Immigration) (2010), 90 Imm. L.R. (3d) 67, 2010 FC 726, 2010 CarswellNat 2763, 2010 CarswellNat 2090 — The applicant's application for a visa to come to Canada as a live-in care worker was refused. She had previously worked as a social welfare officer for six years in the Philippines where she says she used English regularly. She pursued training at FIL-CAN Training School for six months in 2007 and 2008 geared towards live-in care. She also spent a month and a half studying at Nursing Resource Center Inc. The applicant contends these experiences demonstrate her proficiency in English and have equipped her with the necessary knowledge and skills to be a live-in caregiver in Canada. The applicant contended that the visa officer did not follow operational procedures set out by the Minister with respect to assessing documents, knowledge and language skills. The applicant argued that she was deprived of an opportunity to address her poor performance in the "S.P.E.A.K." language test. The applicant argued that the visa officer would have arrived at a different conclusion with respect to her language and knowledge had she considered her credentials and experience. The court held that since the applicant had participated in the S.P.E.A.K. test, no breach of procedural fairness had arisen and the application for judicial review was dismissed.

Nazir v. Canada (Citizenship & Immigration) (2010), 89 Imm. L.R. (3d) 131, 369 F.T.R. 77 (Eng.), [2010] F.C.J. No. 655, 2010 FC 553, 2010 CarswellNat 2246, 2010 CarswellNat 1421 — A visa officer determined that the applicant did not meet the requirements for a work permit as a live-in caregiver pursuant to s. 112 of the Regulations. The visa officer was not satisfied that the applicant's intentions were *bona fide* and temporary in nature, and that she was a genuine temporary worker in Canada. While noting that there is no legislative restriction preventing family members from offering relatives jobs as live-in caregiver, the visa officer was not convinced that the job offer was not made primarily for the purposes of facilitating the applicant's admission in Canada.

There is nothing in the Act or Regulations to prevent family ties between future employer and employee. Furthermore, the caregiver program specifically provides that these individuals can apply for permanent residence afterward. A candidate with no intention of applying for permanent residence would be ineligible for the program (see 5.2 of the Manual). The Manual also points out that with these individuals, it is difficult to apply the normal requirement that temporary residents will leave Canada by the end of the authorized period (at section 8.4). The officer's determination was therefore clearly erroneous; he quite simply disregarded the type of program involved in this case. The application for judicial review was allowed.

Bondoc v. Canada (Minister of Citizenship & Immigration), [2008] F.C.J. No. 1063, 2008 CarswellNat 4247, 2008 CarswellNat 2327, 2008 FC 842 — The application for a work permit in Canada as a "live-in caregiver" was refused on the basis that the employment offer was not genuine, the applicant was unable to demonstrate that she had sufficient knowledge and skills to adequately provide care without supervision and that the job offer was made primarily for the purpose of facilitating the applicant's admission to Canada and that the applicant's intentions in coming to Canada were not for a temporary purpose. The HRSDC deals exclusively with the employer in Canada and is therefore not responsible for assessing the *bona fides* of the employment contract. The visa officer has the responsibility to assess the intent of both parties to the contract. As to the duties envisaged by the employment contract, the visa officer committed no unreasonable error in concluding that the applicant's duties were more in line with domestic duties, rather than providing unsupervised care to the children. With regards to the officer's consideration of the applicant's familial relationship with her future employer, the court noted that this is not the only pertinent factor considered in the officer's assessment of the *bona fides* of the employment offer. This consideration should not be isolated from the other factors that were considered in support of this finding. Nothing in the Act or its Regulations prevents employment offers between family members. On the other hand, nothing prevented the officer from considering the family relationship with the other factors that were considered to be able to convince herself that the applicant's offer of employment was not genuine. It is within the power of a visa officer to assess the genuineness of an employer's offer, and there is no requirement for her to give deference to the HRSDC officer's assessment of the validity of the employment offer.

The court agreed with the applicant that the finding that she was not a genuine visitor was not supported by the evidence and the visa officer had no basis to make it. While there is a provision entitling applicants for the LIC Program to have a dual intent in entering Canada, the visa officer must still be satisfied that ultimately the applicant would depart Canada and not remain here illegally if their application for permanent residence was denied. The visa officer in this case appeared to ignore the applicant's close ties to the Philippines, including the fact that her husband and young child resided there. It was also an error for the visa officer to ignore in her decision the dual intent nature of the LIC Program. The visa officer does not have to be satisfied that the applicant has a temporary purpose in coming to Canada, but instead, that the applicant will not remain illegally in Canada if her application for permanent residence under the LIC class is rejected.

While the visa officer did err in her finding that the applicant did not seek to come to Canada for a temporary purpose, this error had no serious consequence on the impugned decision, since the court found that the first two issues were determinative of the visa officer's decision that the applicant did not meet the LIC Program's requirements, and that this finding was reasonable. The application for judicial review was dismissed.

Duroseau v. Canada (Minister of Citizenship & Immigration), 2008 CarswellNat 130, 2008 CarswellNat 957, 2008 FC 72 — The officer refused to issue a work permit for two reasons:

> (1) She referred to the prohibition against issuing a work permit under subpara. 200(3)(e)(i) to persons having engaged in unauthorized work in Canada in the past six months. The officer believed that the applicant had engaged in such work since her arrival in Canada by helping the employer with her children.

> (2) The officer determined that the applicant did not meet the requirements of s. 112 of the Regulations because the employment contract was not genuine and constituted an offer of convenience aimed at facilitating the applicant's acquisition of status in Canada.

The definition of "work" set forth in the Regulations does not require compensation to have been received in order for an activity to be considered work. The activity merely has to be "in direct competition with the activities of Canadian citizens or permanent residents in the Canadian labour market." Child care meets the definition of work. The friendship between the applicant and the employer was just one fact among many justifying the officer's doubts as to the *bona fide* character of the contract. The fact that the applicant lived in the employer's home prior to submitting her application, the length of time before she submitted it, and the fact that the applicant was engaged in child-care activity all provided sufficient support for the officer's decision.

Salman v. Canada (Minister of Citizenship & Immigration), [2007] F.C.J. No. 1142, 63 Imm. L.R. (3d) 285, 2007 FC 877, 2007 CarswellNat 3464, 2007 CarswellNat 2749 — A visa officer determined that the applicant was not a member of the live-in caregiver class and denied his application for a work permit. He sought judicial review. The visa officer was not satisfied that the applicant had completed the equivalent of a secondary school education, as required by s. 112 of the Regulations. Following this rejection, the applicant's future employer in Canada obtained an evaluation by the Comparative Education Service of the University of Toronto, confirming that the programme of study in which the applicant was enrolled was the academic equivalent of the Ontario Secondary School

Diploma. This letter was faxed to the Embassy, and the applicant was granted a second interview with a different visa officer. Even though the officer refers to the evaluation in his CAIPS notes, he made no analysis or comments as to why he rejected that evidence. With the evidence before him, the visa officer had a duty to investigate this point more thoroughly. The error was sufficient to justify the intervention of the court. The application for judicial review was allowed.

Singh v. Canada (Minister of Citizenship & Immigration), 2006 CarswellNat 2573, 2006 CarswellNat 1474, 2006 FC 684 — The applicant challenged a decision of the visa officer who refused his application for a work permit as a live-in caregiver. The applicant was offered a position at the home of his sister and brother-in-law. The position involved looking after the needs of two young children. The applicant's request for a work permit was refused on the basis that he did not have the requisite training or work experience in the field of child care. The applicant's employment experience had been in the field of health care. He had successfully passed his examination in nursing and had been employed as a ward nurse at a well known geriatric hospital in Vienna. Although the applicant had a wealth of experience as a geriatric caregiver, he presented no evidence of experience in the area of child care. Due to the absence of child-care experience his application for a work permit was refused. The visa officer's decision was based on an interpretation that s. 112 of the Regulations required the applicant to have specific employment experience in the field of child care. The court held that the language of s. 112 was sufficiently ambiguous that it could support either of the interpretations advanced by the parties. The CIC operational guidelines applicable to s. 112 offered some limited assistance in understanding how the department applies the eligibility criteria for issuing a live-in caregiver work permit. Although the provisions of the guidelines lack clarity, the tenor of these provisions suggest that it is not the labels that are attached to the training or experience factors that are instructive, but rather the relevant skills that one acquires against which work permit eligibility is to be measured.

The adoption of a purposive approach to the interpretation of s. 112 leads to the same result. Clearly what is intended by these provisions is that caregivers have the capacity to adequately perform the tasks expected of them. There is no question that a well qualified nurse would have considerable knowledge and experience in the field of caregiving. The fact that beneficiaries of that prior work experience may not have been children does not mean that such an applicant has no transferable skills which could be applied in a child-care setting. The record in this case suggests that the applicant did enjoy a number of skills which could have been readily applied to the care of children, including those of nutrition, hygiene, first aid, supervision, home care and social skills.

What is required in the application of s. 112 to any given fact situation is to assess the applicant's employment experience with a view of identifying the transferable skills that are available to the fulfillment of the proposed Canadian employment. It could very well be that in a single household there will be children needing typical care, along with elderly or disabled individuals whose needs may be different or unique. A too-rigid approach to the interpretation of work experience or training requirements of s. 112 could deprive a family of the support that this provision was intended to accommodate.

The visa officer should have considered the caregiving skills acquired by the applicant during his more than 10 years of hospital nursing employment to determine if they would be adequate to meet the employment demands for the position he had been offered. It is not sufficient in assessing prior experience to focus only on the characteristics or the age of the intended beneficiaries of care. It is difficult to believe that more than 10 years of experience as a hospital nurse would not result in the acquisition of many skills and aptitudes which would be readily applicable to the provision of child care in a home setting.

The matter was remitted to a different visa officer for reconsideration of the application.

Ouafae c. Canada (Ministre de la Citoyenneté & de l'Immigration), [2005] F.C.J. No. 592, 2005 CarswellNat 899, 2005 CarswellNat 5098, 2005 FC 459 — The applicant's application for a work permit as a live-in caregiver was refused on the basis that she did not meet the requirements of s. 112 of the Regulations. Section 112 requires that the applicant show they have training or experience in a field or occupation related to the employment for which the work permit is sought. The applicant stated in the interview that she had worked as a teacher for two years. On that basis, the officer concluded that the applicant had failed to show she had any recent experience as a housekeeper. The officer was, therefore, not satisfied that she really was a domestic worker. The officer also concluded that since the applicant's brother was her future employer in Canada, the application was being made to facilitate her entry to Canada and she would not return to Morocco.

According to the department's manual, training and experience must be in a field or occupation related to the employment sought, and it specifies that caregivers may have training or experience in early childhood education, which was precisely the applicant's case. The visa officer's decision to disregard that experience was therefore unreasonable and inconsistent with the provisions of the manual. Both the training and the experience may be acquired in a field or occupation related to the employment.

The officer's conclusion with respect to the applicant's brother being the intended employer and the conclusion that she would not return to Morocco were purely speculative and without evidence. Furthermore, there was nothing in the Act or Regulations to prevent family ties between future employer and employee. The caregiver program specifically provides that these individuals can apply for permanent residence afterwards. A candidate with no intention of applying for permanent residence would be ineligible for the program. The manual also points out that it is difficult with these individuals to apply the normal requirement that temporary residents will leave Canada by the end of the authorized period. The officer's determination was, therefore, clearly erroneous because he disregarded the type of program the applicant was applying under.

113. (1) Permanent residence — **A foreign national becomes a member of the live-in caregiver class if**

(a) they have submitted an application to remain in Canada as a permanent resident;

(b) they are a temporary resident;

(c) they hold a work permit as a live-in caregiver;

(d) they entered Canada as a live-in caregiver and for at least two of the four years immediately following their entry or, alternatively, for at least 3,900 hours during a period of not less than 22 months in those four years,

(i) resided in a private household in Canada, and

(ii) provided child care, senior home support care or care of a disabled person in that household without supervision;

(e) they are not, and none of their family members are, the subject of an enforceable removal order or an admissibility hearing under the Act or an appeal or application for judicial review arising from such a hearing;

(f) they did not enter Canada as a live-in caregiver as a result of a misrepresentation concerning their education, training or experience; and

(g) where they intend to reside in the Province of Quebec, the competent authority of that Province is of the opinion that they meet the selection criteria of the Province.

(2) Calculation — For the purposes of paragraph (1)(d),

(a) the periods of two years and 3,900 hours may be in respect of more than one employer or household, but may not be in respect of more than one employer or household at a time; and

(b) the 3,900 hours are not to include more than 390 hours of overtime.

SOR/2010-78, s. 2

Case Law

Jacob v. Canada (Minister of Citizenship & Immigration) (2012), 14 Imm. L.R. (4th) 324, 2012 FC 1382, 2012 CarswellNat 4680, 2012 CarswellNat 5040 — The applicant sought judicial review of a decision to refuse his application for permanent residence in Canada on humanitarian and compassionate grounds. The applicant came to Canada as a student and following the school's closure looked into options for employment as a caregiver to an elderly, bed-ridden man whose wife had advertised for the job after obtaining a labour market opinion. The applicant had two years' experience as a live-in caregiver in India. He applied for a work permit from within Canada on the basis of being in Canada on a study permit and on the basis of the positive LMO. The work permit was not issued under the live-in caregiver program ("LCP"). The applicant eventually made an in-Canada application for permanent resident status under the LCP. He was advised initially that he met the requirements to apply under the live-in caretaker class, and subsequently was told in order to be considered under that class he must have been assessed under the LCP from abroad. Since his work permits were not issued under the LCP, he was never in the LCP. The applicant responded and provided an explanation as to how he had become a caregiver in Canada and his oversight in not being under the LCP and referred to the initial positive letter he had received from CIC. He asked for forgiveness and requested the continuing of the processing of the application. The application was refused. He sought judicial review arguing that he had requested that his application be assessed in the live-in caregiver class and requested he be exempted from the requirement that he enters as a live-in caregiver, and in particular from para. 113(d).

The officer did not consider that the purpose of the regulatory scheme underlying an LCP was to encourage people to come into Canada to fill a void that exists in the Canadian labour market, and in consideration for their commitment to work in the domestic field participants are virtually guaranteed permanent residence. The officer's failure led him to ignore a relevant consideration. The officer also erred in processing the application as if it was a simple exemption request from having to apply for permanent residency to Canada from abroad; in fact, the applicant was applying for permanent residency in Canada because that is what he was entitled to as a live-in caregiver, which he was, but had entered in Canada legally as a student. Finally the officer ignored the letter of evidence of the applicant's interdependency with the Thomas family and ignored Mrs. Thomas's letter as well as the doctor's letter. The application for judicial review was granted.

114. Family members — requirement — The requirement with respect to a family member of a live-in caregiver applying to remain in Canada as a permanent resident is that the family member was included in the live-in caregiver's application to remain in Canada as a permanent resident at the time the application was made.

SOR/2008-202, s. 8

114.1 Family members — permanent residence — A foreign national who is a family member of a live-in caregiver who makes an application to remain in Canada as a permanent resident shall become a permanent resident if, following an examination, it is established that

(a) the live-in caregiver has become a permanent resident; and

(b) the foreign national is not inadmissible.

SOR/2008-202, s. 8

115. Conformity — applicable times — The applicable requirements set out in sections 112 to 114.1 must be met when an application for a work permit or temporary resident visa is made, when the permit or visa is issued and when the foreign national becomes a permanent resident.

SOR/2008-202, s. 8

Case Law

Pacis v. Canada (Minister of Citizenship & Immigration), 2005 CarswellNat 1973, 2005 CarswellNat 4901, 2005 FC 931 — The live-in caregiver program requires an applicant to work a minimum of 24 months out of a 36-month period. The evidence submitted indicated that the applicant was only able to work approximately 16 months, well short of the required amount. After reviewing her work background, the officer confronted the applicant with her inability to keep steady employment and the fact she had been unemployed for more than half of her time in Canada. The officer was not satisfied with the applicant's answers and denied a fifth work permit. The court dismissed this application for judicial review, stating that if the applicant was allowed to continually apply for temporary work permits this would allow her to be permitted to stay in Canada as a live-in caregiver perpetually, without ever meeting the requirements set out for that program.

PART 7 — FAMILY CLASSES

DIVISION 1 — FAMILY CLASS

116. Family class — For the purposes of subsection 12(1) of the Act, the family class is hereby prescribed as a class of persons who may become permanent residents on the basis of the requirements of this Division.

117. (1) Member — A foreign national is a member of the family class if, with respect to a sponsor, the foreign national is

(a) the sponsor's spouse, common-law partner or conjugal partner;

(b) a dependent child of the sponsor;

[Editor's Note: SOR/2002-227, s. 357 provides that the fee set out in column III of item 19 of the schedule to the Immigration Act Fees Regulations, *SOR/97-22 is remitted and shall be repaid by the Minister to the person who paid it if the fee is paid in respect of a person before he or she becomes a permanent resident under the new* Immigration and Refugee Protection Act, *S.C. 2001, c. 27 and the person, at the time he or she made an application for landing under the* Immigration Regulations, 1978, SOR/78-172 *(the "former Regulations"), was:*

(a) a member of the family class and 19 years of age or older and, on June 28, 2002, is a foreign national referred to in paragraph 117(1)(b) or (e) of the new Immigration and Refugee Protection Regulations, *SOR/2002-227; or*

(b) an accompanying dependant of an immigrant, within the meaning of s. 2(1) of the former Regulations, 19 years of age or older and not a spouse of the principal applicant.]

(c) the sponsor's mother or father;

(d) the mother or father of the sponsor's mother or father;

(e) [Repealed SOR/2005-61, s. 3(1).]

[Editor's Note: SOR/2002-227, s. 357 provides that the fee set out in column III of item 19 of the schedule to the Immigration Act Fees Regulations, *SOR/97-22 is remitted and shall be repaid by the Minister to the person who paid it if the fee is paid in respect of a person before he or she becomes a permanent resident under the new* Immigration and Refugee Protection Act, *S.C. 2001, c. 27 and the person, at the time he or she made an application for landing under the* Immigration Regulations, 1978, SOR/78-172 *(the "former Regulations"), was:*

(a) a member of the family class and 19 years of age or older and, on June 28, 2002, is a foreign national referred to in paragraph 117(1)(b) or (e) of the new Immigration and Refugee Protection Regulations, *SOR/2002-227; or*

(b) an accompanying dependant of an immigrant, within the meaning of s. 2(1) of the former Regulations, 19 years of age or older and not a spouse of the principal applicant.]

(f) a person whose parents are deceased, who is under 18 years of age, who is not a spouse or common-law partner and who is

(i) a child of the sponsor's mother or father,

(ii) a child of a child of the sponsor's mother or father, or

(iii) a child of the sponsor's child;

(g) a person under 18 years of age whom the sponsor intends to adopt in Canada if

(i) the adoption is not being entered into primarily for the purpose of acquiring any status or privilege under the Act,

(ii) where the adoption is an international adoption and the country in which the person resides and their province of intended destination are parties to the Hague Convention on Adoption, the competent authority of the country and of the province have approved the adoption in writing as conforming to that Convention, and

(iii) where the adoption is an international adoption and either the country in which the person resides or the person's province of intended destination is not a party to the Hague Convention on Adoption

(A) the person has been placed for adoption in the country in which they reside or is otherwise legally available in that country for adoption and there is no evidence that the intended adoption is for the purpose of child trafficking or undue gain within the meaning of the Hague Convention on Adoption, and

(B) the competent authority of the person's province of intended destination has stated in writing that it does not object to the adoption; or

(h) a relative of the sponsor, regardless of age, if the sponsor does not have a spouse, a common-law partner, a conjugal partner, a child, a mother or father, a relative who is a child of that mother or father, a relative who is a child of a child of that mother or father, a mother or father of that mother or father or a relative who is a child of the mother or father of that mother or father

(i) who is a Canadian citizen, Indian or permanent resident, or

(ii) whose application to enter and remain in Canada as a permanent resident the sponsor may otherwise sponsor.

(2) **Adoption — under 18** — A foreign national who is the adopted child of a sponsor and whose adoption took place when the child was under the age of 18 shall not be considered a member of the family class by virtue of the adoption unless

(a) the adoption was in the best interests of the child within the meaning of the Hague Convention on Adoption; and

(b) the adoption was not entered into primarily for the purpose of acquiring any status or privilege under the Act.

(3) **Best interests of the child** — The adoption referred to in subsection (2) is considered to be in the best interests of a child if it took place under the following circumstances:

(a) a competent authority has conducted or approved a home study of the adoptive parents;

(b) before the adoption, the child's parents gave their free and informed consent to the child's adoption;

(c) the adoption created a genuine parent-child relationship;

(d) the adoption was in accordance with the laws of the place where the adoption took place;

(e) the adoption was in accordance with the laws of the sponsor's place of residence and, if the sponsor resided in Canada at the time the adoption took place, the competent authority of the child's province of intended destination has stated in writing that it does not object to the adoption;

(f) if the adoption is an international adoption and the country in which the adoption took place and the child's province of intended destination are parties to the Hague Convention on Adoption, the competent authority of the country and of the province have stated in writing that they approve the adoption as conforming to that Convention; and

(g) if the adoption is an international adoption and either the country in which the adoption took place or the child's province of intended destination is not a party to the Hague Convention on Adoption, there is no evidence that the adoption is for the purpose of child trafficking or undue gain within the meaning of that Convention.

(4) **Adoption — over 18** — A foreign national who is the adopted child of a sponsor and whose adoption took place when the child was 18 years of age or older shall not be considered a member of the family class by virtue of that adoption unless it took place under the following circumstances:

(a) the adoption was in accordance with the laws of the place where the adoption took place and, if the sponsor resided in Canada at the time of the adoption, the adoption was in accordance with the laws of the province where the sponsor then resided, if any, that applied in respect of the adoption of a child 18 years of age or older;

(b) a genuine parent-child relationship existed at the time of the adoption and existed before the child reached the age of 18; and

(c) the adoption was not entered into primarily for the purpose of acquiring any status or privilege under the Act.

(5) [Repealed SOR/2005-61, s. 3(2).]

(6) [Repealed SOR/2005-61, s. 3(2).]

(7) **Provincial statement** — If a statement referred to in clause (1)(g)(iii)(B) or paragraph (3)(e) or (f) has been provided to an officer by the competent authority of the foreign national's province of intended destination, that statement is, except in the case of an adoption that was entered into primarily for the purpose of acquiring any status or privilege under the Act, conclusive evidence that the foreign national meets the following applicable requirements:

(a) [Repealed SOR/2005-61, s. 3(4).]

(b) in the case of a person referred to in paragraph (1)(g), the requirements set out in clause (1)(g)(iii)(A); and

(c) in the case of a person referred to in paragraph (1)(b) who is an adopted child described in subsection (2), the requirements set out in paragraphs (3)(a) to (e) and (g).

(8) **New evidence** — If, after the statement is provided to the officer, the officer receives evidence that the foreign national does not meet the applicable requirements set out in paragraph (7)(b) or (c) for becoming a member of the family class, the processing of their application shall be suspended until the officer provides that evidence to the competent authority of the province and that authority confirms or revises its statement.

(9) **Excluded relationships** — A foreign national shall not be considered a member of the family class by virtue of their relationship to a sponsor if

(a) the foreign national is the sponsor's spouse, common-law partner or conjugal partner and is under 18 years of age;

(b) the foreign national is the sponsor's spouse, common-law partner or conjugal partner, the sponsor has an existing sponsorship undertaking in respect of a spouse, common-law partner or conjugal partner and the period referred to in subsection 132(1) in respect of that undertaking has not ended;

(c) the foreign national is the sponsor's spouse and

(i) the sponsor or the foreign national was, at the time of their marriage, the spouse of another person, or

(ii) the sponsor has lived separate and apart from the foreign national for at least one year and

(A) the sponsor is the common-law partner of another person or the sponsor has a conjugal partner, or

(B) the foreign national is the common-law partner of another person or the conjugal partner of another sponsor; or

(c.1) the foreign national is the sponsor's spouse and if at the time the marriage ceremony was conducted either one or both of the spouses were not physically present unless the foreign national was marrying a person who was not physically present at the ceremony as a result of their service as a member of the Canadian Forces and the marriage is valid both under the laws of the jurisdiction where it took place and under Canadian law;

(d) subject to subsection (10), the sponsor previously made an application for permanent residence and became a permanent resident and, at the time of that application, the foreign national was a non-accompanying family member of the sponsor and was not examined.

[Editor's Note: SOR/2002-227, s. 355 provides that if a person who made an application under the former Immigration Act, R.S.C. 1985, c. I-2 *before June 28, 2002 sponsors a non-accompanying dependent child referred to in s. 352 of the* Immigration and Refugee Protection Regulations, SOR/2002-227 *(the "new Regulations"), who makes an application as a member of the family class or the spouse or common-law partner in Canada class, or sponsors a non-accompanying common-law partner who makes such an application, paragraph 117(9)(d) of the new Regulations does not apply in respect of that dependent child or common-law partner.]*

(10) **Exception** — Subject to subsection (11), paragraph (9)(d) does not apply in respect of a foreign national referred to in that paragraph who was not examined because an officer determined that they were not required by the Act or the former Act, as applicable, to be examined.

IRP Regulations

(11) Application of par. (9)(d) — Paragraph (9)(d) applies in respect of a foreign national referred to in subsection (10) if an officer determines that, at the time of the application referred to in that paragraph,

(a) the sponsor was informed that the foreign national could be examined and the sponsor was able to make the foreign national available for examination but did not do so or the foreign national did not appear for examination; or

(b) the foreign national was the sponsor's spouse, was living separate and apart from the sponsor and was not examined.

(12) Definition of "former Act" — In subsection (10), "former Act" has the same meaning as in section 187 of the Act.

SOR/2004-59, s. 4; SOR/2004-167, s. 41; SOR/2005-61, s. 3; SOR/2010-195, s. 11(1)–(3), (5), (6); SOR/2010-208, s. 2; SOR/2015-139, s. 2

Case Law

Section 117(1)

Jordano v. Canada (Minister of Citizenship & Immigration), 2013 CarswellNat 4162, 2013 CarswellNat 4718, 2013 FC 1143 — The applicant wished to sponsor her mother to come to Canada as a member of the family class pursuant to s. 117(1) of *IRPR*. Under normal circumstances, she would have been able to sponsor her mother pursuant to para. 117(1)(c) of the Regulations. However, a Ministerial Instruction was issued which imposed a temporary freeze on the acceptance for processing of new family class applications for a sponsor's parents or grandparents. The applicant chose to proceed under para. 117(1)(h) which is intended to provide for sponsorship by persons who do not have family members, such as persons who are orphans or do not have the more common relations described in other paragraphs of s. 117(1), i.e. spouses, dependent children, parents and grandparents. Interpreting the effect of an administrative implementation measure in a fashion that would aggravate the problem it was intended to resolve would constitute a perverse interpretation of both para. 117(1)(h) of the Regulations and s. 87.3 of the *IRPA*. The application for judicial review was dismissed.

Canada (Minister of Citizenship & Immigration) v. Vong (2005), [2006] 1 F.C.R. 404, 47 Imm. L.R. (3d) 213, 2005 CarswellNat 1701, 2005 CarswellNat 3724, 2005 FC 855 — The respondent applied to sponsor his stepmother (the widow of the respondent's father). The visa officer refused the sponsorship application on the grounds that the stepmother was not a member of the family class as described in the *Immigration and Refugee Protection Regulations*. Upon appeal, the IAD determined that the absence of the definition of the word "mother" in the Regulations indicated Parliament's intention that the term be accorded a broad and liberal interpretation, in order to accommodate the changing dynamics of the modern family. It concluded that a stepmother could, in appropriate circumstances, fall within the definition of "mother." According to its reasons, the IAD considered that the presence of mutual benefits and dependencies could constitute such "appropriate circumstances."

The Minister sought judicial review of the IAD's decision on the basis that the issue to be determined was a question of statutory interpretation and the word "mother" was not defined and appeared only in the English version of the Regulations. The Federal Court held that the stepmother did not fall within the definition of "parents." The absence of an

English definition of "mother" or "parents" does not indicate that Parliament intended that step-parents be included in the family class.

The following questions were certified:

- Are step-parents included in the family class and, in particular, does the word "mother" in paragraph 117(1)(c) of the *Immigration and Refugee Protection Regulations* include a stepmother?

- Does the word "parent" in French include a "step-parent"?

Section 117(3)

Jhajj v. Canada (Minister of Citizenship and Immigration), [2013] 4 F.C.R. 507, 409 F.T.R. 277, 2012 FC 512, 2012 CarswellNat 2451, 2012 CarswellNat 1328 — The applicant and his wife adopted their 13-year-old niece in India. Shortly after, they applied to sponsor her for landing in Canada as their adopted daughter. The visa office sent a fax to Alberta's Children's Services requesting a home study. The applicant's legal adviser wrote the visa post advising that a home study could not be completed because the daughter was now over the age of 18 — the age of majority in Alberta. In the absence of a home study, the Program Manager for International Adoptions at Alberta Children's Services wrote to the visa office by way of a "Letter of No Involvement". The visa officer rejected the sponsorship application of the basis that s. 117(3) required a competent authority to conduct and approve a home study of the adoptive parents. The fact that the sponsors did not go through the appropriate steps to effect the adoption of their relative at the time of the adoption (and in the five years after the adoption) undermined the bona fides of the case, in addition to ensuring that the application did not meet the requirements of s. 117(3).

The visa officer is expected to pay considerable deference to the provincial adoption authority with respect to some matters concerning the adoption of foreign children into Canadian families. This is not surprising because provincial child welfare authorities have the necessary expertise to assess when an adoption is in the best interests of a child. In the usual case of the adoption of a foreign dependant, a home study would be completed and the provincial adoption authority would pass judgment on the appropriateness of the placement. Presumably the rationale for the statement in subsec. 117(7) that where the provincial adoption authority does not object to the proposed adoption of a foreign child, this is "conclusive evidence" that the best interests of the child requirements have been met. The interpretative problem that arises from this subsection is that not all of the "best interests" considerations that are said to be conclusively resolved by a provincial Letter of No Objection are amenable to provincial determination. In this case, the applicant did not put forward evidence from Alberta Children's Services as to what it intended by its letter or to verify that it no longer considered a home study to be necessary. The applicant failed to satisfy the Board that the Alberta Children's Services letter was sufficient to displace the requirement for a home study. The application for judicial review was dismissed.

Section 117(7)

See the *Jhajj* summary, [2013] 4 F.C.R. 507, 409 F.T.R. 277, 2012 FC 512, 2012 CarswellNat 2451, 2012 CarswellNat 1328, at s. 117(3), above.

Section 117(9)

Weng (Litigation guardian of) v. Canada (Minister of Citizenship and Immigration) (2014), 29 Imm. L.R. (4th) 152, 2014 CarswellNat 3016, 2014 CarswellNat 3673

The applicant sought judicial review of a decision of a visa officer that determined pursuant to s. 25(1) of IRPA that there were insufficient H&C grounds to grant permanent residence or an exemption from a family class exclusion arising from s. 117(9)(d) of the Regulations. The applicant was a 12-year-old minor child and a citizen of China.

The visa officer failed to address the best interest of the applicant's siblings. The visa officer must consider the scenario of the family being reunited in Canada when considering the best interests of the child. Further, where more than one child is directly affected, the officer must consider their separate interests and needs. Here, the applicant's siblings are both Canadian children and were directly affected by their sister's presence in China. As Canadian citizens being forced to move back to China with their parents, their situation was very different from that of their sister. The visa officer should have used the applicant's potential life in Canada as a point of comparison in considering her best interests. Instead, the visa officer considered only the status quo of the applicant's life in China, and whether there was any impediment to her remaining there. When an applicant has been excluded pursuant to s. 117(9)(d) of the Regulations, it is an error for an officer to give undue weight to the misrepresentation. The visa officer's fixation on the reason for the non-disclosure prevented him from genuinely assessing the H&C considerations that the applicant had raised. The application for judicial review was allowed.

Kobita v. Canada (Minister of Citizenship & Immigration) (2012), 15 Imm. L.R. (4th) 205, 2012 FC 1479, 2012 CarswellNat 4952, 2012 CarswellNat 5403 — The applicant and her two sons were denied a permanent residence visa following the sponsorship by her husband. The immigration officer concluded that the applicant and her children were not members of the family class pursuant to para. 117(9)(d) of the Regulations because her husband had failed to declare them as dependants upon his arrival in Canada in 2005 and in his application for permanent residence, which was made in 1999. The officer also found there was insufficient evidence of H&C grounds under s. 25(1) of the Act to overcome the exclusion.

The court considered the decision of *Williams v. Canada (Minister of Citizenship & Immigration)*, 2012 FC 166, at para 64, that there is no "hardship threshold" that must be met, but rather that the best interests of the child is truly the starting point of the analysis. The court also considered the three-step approach set out in the *Williams* decision, which held that the decision maker, when assessing the best interest of the child, must first establish what is in the child's best interest, second the degree to which the child's interest are compromised by one potential decision over another, and then finally, in light of the foregoing assessment determine the weight that this factor should play in the ultimate balancing of positive and negative factors assessed in the application. The court also pointed out that the *Williams* decision did not have the mandatory effect that a decision of the Supreme Court of Canada or Federal Court of Appeal would have.

In the present case, the officer concluded that the best interests of the children would be to continue to reside with their mother in Bangladesh as they did not appear to be suffering undue hardship as a result of their exclusion. The court found that the officer's assessment of the best interests of the child was unreasonable. The officer took the status quo as her starting point and determined the status quo was sufficient without considering other options, including life in Canada with both parents. The officer focused on the fact that the children were not suffering "undue hardship" due to their exclusion. There was no need to find that the children were suffering undue hardship before considering if their best interests could be met by moving them to Canada. The application for judicial review was allowed.

Nguyen v. Canada (Minister of Citizenship & Immigration), 2012 FC 331, 2012 CarswellNat 866 — The applicant tried to sponsor his daughter to become a permanent resident of Canada. A visa officer dismissed the application on the basis he had not disclosed his daughter's existence when he previously sponsored his three sons. In fact, he was unaware of his daughter's existence at that point. The applicant asked the officer to consider H&C grounds supporting his application, but the officer appeared not to have considered them. The applicant appealed the officer's decision to the IAD. The IAD confirmed that the applicant's daughter could not be sponsored because she had not been identified in his earlier application. It also stated it had no jurisdiction to consider H&C factors in the circumstances and only the Minister of Citizenship and Immigration could do so. The applicant argued that the IAD erred by failing to appreciate that he was not asking the IAD to consider the H&C factors; rather, he had argued that the officer had committed an error of law by failing to consider the H&C factors. The IAD has jurisdiction to overturn an officer's decision if it is based on an error of law. The IAD misapprehended the grounds of the applicant's appeal. The question was whether the officer had erred in law, a matter over which the IAD clearly had jurisdiction. The application for judicial review was allowed and the IAD was ordered to reconsider the appeal. The sole issue is whether the IAD erred in law by failing to consider the basis of the applicant's appeal.

Lau v. Canada (Minister of Citizenship & Immigration) (2009), 84 Imm. L.R. (3d) 261, 356 F.T.R. 206 (Eng.), 2009 FC 1089, 2009 CarswellNat 3343 — This was an application for judicial review of a decision of the Immigration Appeal Division of the Immigration and Refugee Board dismissing the appeal of a decision of a visa officer refusing to approve the permanent resident visa application made to sponsor the applicant's spouse. The IAD dismissed the appeal on the basis that the divorce in question between the applicant and Huang was not undertaken in compliance with Canadian law and was not deemed to be a valid divorce according to the laws of Canada. The Board made no determination whatsoever as to whether the divorce at issue was legally valid in the place where it was granted. Accordingly, the application for judicial review was allowed, the decision under review set aside and the applicant's appeal to the IAD referred back to the Board for rehearing and redetermination.

Sultana v. Canada (Minister of Citizenship & Immigration), 2009 CarswellNat 1418, 2009 FC 533 — The applicants contended that the immigration officer failed to adequately assess the best interests of the children affected by the decision to deny them family reunification with the sponsor, and that it did not mention, refer to or analyze the level of dependency between the child and the sponsor and how the humanitarian and compassionate decision would affect them.

The court agreed with the applicants that the decision fell far short of the duty to consider the best interests of the children and to be "alive, alert and sensitive" to those interests. The immigration officer failed to have regard to the children's specific gender, age and education related needs; that two of the children are boys and require a father figure; that the mother only had a Grade 8 education and no paid labour force experience; that Pakistan is a male-dominated society where single female households are looked down upon and how all of this would impact the children. Moreover, there was no evidence to support the immigration officer's bald assertion and presumption that the mother and her children could turn to her parents/siblings and in-laws for emotional and other support, when the evidence indicated otherwise, as they lived a few hours away. There was no consideration of the consequences of growing up without their father and it was not explained why the policy consideration underlying s. 117(9)(d) of the Regulations should outweigh the hardships faced by these children when there is no indication that they would have been inadmissible if listed and have already suffered seven years away from their father.

While an immigration official should not be left to speculate as to how a child will be impacted by his or her decision, it would be preposterous to require from an applicant a detailed and minute demonstration of the negative consequences of such a decision when they can reasonably be deducted from the facts brought to his or her attention. The application for judicial review was allowed.

Ferrer v. Canada (Minister of Citizenship & Immigration), 2009 CarswellNat 899, 2009 CarswellNat 2095, 2009 FC 356 — The applicant sought judicial review of a decision of the IAD which dismissed his plea for humanitarian and compassionate relief pursuant to s. 67(1)(c) of the IRPA. An exclusion order had been issued against the applicant based on a finding of inadmissibility for a misrepresentation made in September 1998 with respect to his permanent resident application. In his permanent resident application, the applicant testified that he was single with no children. It was not disputed that at the time he was the father of two dependent children living with their mother in the Philippines. The applicant married his spouse who was the mother of his two children on a trip back to the Philippines after he was granted permanent residence status in Canada. The applicant's spouse is not excluded from the family class pursuant to s. 117(9)(d) of the Regulations. Accordingly, the applicant's two children would be eligible to be included on the applicant's spouse's application for permanent residence as her dependent children, provided the applicant's appeal before the IAD was allowed as he would be in a position to sponsor his wife and both of his children as members of the family class.

The IAD considered only two possibilities with respect to the best interests of the children. The first possibility was that the children could remain in the Philippines and that their father would continue to have a geographically distant relationship with them while at the same time supporting them financially at a higher level than possible if he were returned to the Philippines. The second alternative was that the applicant could be returned to the Philippines where he would be able to better meet their emotional needs by having close contact with them, though he would not be able to provide the higher level of financial support in the event that he was removed from Canada. It was argued that the analysis was erroneous and that it did not take into consideration the most probable outcome should the applicant's appeal be allowed. The tribunal's failure to consider the likely chain of events should the appeal be allowed led to its conclusion that the best interests of the children were a neutral factor; in fact the best interests of the applicant's children were a positive factor which weighed in favour of allowing the appeal. In other words, the tribunal failed to appreciate that the applicant's children could have the best of both worlds by being reunited with him in Canada. Had the tribunal not committed this error, it would certainly have considered the best interests of the applicant's children to be a factor in favour of allowing his appeal and not a neutral factor — thereby negating its value. It appears that the IAD's reasoning was dominated by a consideration of the "integrity of the Canadian immigration system." This might be an important factor to consider, but only after the best interest of the children are properly addressed; only in this way can a fair and balanced approach be taken to this important statutory requirement. The application for judicial review was allowed and the matter sent back for redetermination.

Odicho v. Canada (Minister of Citizenship & Immigration) (2008), 75 Imm. L.R. (3d) 45, 2008 CarswellNat 4011, 2008 CarswellNat 3442, 2008 FC 1039 — The applicants sought judicial review of a visa officer's decision to refuse to issue a permanent resident visa to the wife. The applicants argued that the visa officer erred by failing to consider H&C grounds, pursuant to subs. 25 of the IRPA. They submit that they specifically requested that the wife's application for permanent residence in Canada be considered on the basis of s. 25. The husband had been landed in Canada in January 2005 and his initial application to sponsor his wife in May 2005 was refused on the basis that he had not disclosed his marriage when he was landed. The application on behalf of a dependent child was refused for the same reason but was subsequently reversed. The visa officer, however, maintained the rejection of the application on behalf of the wife on the basis of para. 117(9)(d) of the Regulations.

There was no dispute that the husband failed to declare his wife as a non-accompanying dependant when he landed in Canada in January 2005. There is no evidence to challenge the *bona fides* of the marriage of the applicants. There is no evidence to challenge the status of the infant as their child. The failure of the husband to declare the change in marital status when he landed in Canada gave rise to the exclusion of his wife pursuant to the terms of para. 117(9)(d). The court held that the visa officer apparently ignored the material that was submitted concerning the "circumstances" of the husband's failure to declare the change in his marital status at the time he landed in Canada. The applicants carry the burden of establishing the evidence to justify an exercise of discretion, but the discharge of this burden does not require superfluity. The visa officer's decision does not demonstrate an understanding of the purpose of subs. 25(1) of the Act, which is to overcome the consequences of being in breach of statutory requirements. The initial decision which excluded the child, as well as the wife, illustrates an excess of zeal on the part of the original decision maker, if not a misunderstanding of s. 117 of the Regulations. The application for judicial review was allowed. The matter was remitted for reconsideration by a different member of the Canadian Embassy.

David v. Canada (Minister of Citizenship & Immigration), 2007 CarswellNat 1385, 2007 FC 546 — The applicant's H&C application was denied. The exclusion mentioned at para. 117(9)(d) is a very harsh one, but does not prevent a sponsor from invoking H&C grounds considerations. Indeed, the very reason why the Court of Appeal in *De Guzman* (2005), 51 Imm. L.R. (3d) 17, found that this provision is compliant with the international instruments to which Canada is a signatory is that s. 25 of the Act enables the Act to be administered in a compliant manner.

The First Secretary, Immigration, at the Canadian Embassy did not make any findings of fact with respect to the evidence tendered by the applicants, such as the relationship between the sponsor and his wife and son, the fact that the sponsor had been supporting the family financially, the frequency of their contact, as well as the letters tendered by various members of the family and others in support of their application. The officer's notes do not provide a clear rationale of why any of the public policy considerations mentioned by the First Secretary (such as the past misrepresentations) should prevail here over the objective at para. 3(1)(d) of the Act "to see that families are reunited in Canada."

Woldeselassie v. Canada (Minister of Citizenship & Immigration) (2006), 60 Imm. L.R. (3d) 119, 2006 CarswellNat 4497, 2006 FC 1540 — The applicant had not disclosed his illegitimate daughter's existence both at the time of the processing of his application, and at the time of his landing in Canada.

The issue before the IAD was whether the applicant was precluded from sponsoring his daughter after having failed to disclose her existence at the time of his application for permanent residence in Canada. The applicant argued that one can only declare or disclose information that is known. He claimed that he did not know the existence of the child at the time that he applied for permanent residence or at the time that he landed in Canada. The IAD did not make any credibility findings or question the veracity of the applicant's testimony with respect to his explanation as to why he did not know about the pregnancy and subsequent birth of his daughter until after he arrived in Canada. It was not reasonable for the IAD to simply state its sense of incredulity at the applicant's story without providing reasons to support this reaction. The application for judicial review was granted and the matter sent back for re-determination.

dela Fuente v. Canada (Minister of Citizenship & Immigration), 2006 FCA 186, 2006 CarswellNat 1334, 2006 CarswellNat 2749, [2006] F.C.J. No. 774 — The court considered the meaning of "time of that application" referred to in para. 117(9)(d) of the Regulations. The Federal Court adopted the interpretation proposed in *Dave v. Canada (M.C.I.)* (2005), 272 F.T.R. 168, 2005 FC 510, [2005] F.C.J. No. 686, 2005 CarswellNat 4680, which held that the application process for permanent residence encompasses not only the application for a visa, but also the application for admission at the port of entry. Accordingly, the argument that the phrase "at the time of that application" comprises only the point in time when the application form was completed and submitted must fail. This interpretation was preferred as it was consistent with the objective of family unification under IRPA.

The legislative scheme requires that a prospective immigrant's family members be identified so that the family unit may be assessed as a whole as well as the eligibility of each member. Reading the phrase "at the time of that application" as referring to the life of the application allows foreign nationals to define their family unit and make appropriate changes right up to the moment when they seek to enter Canada, which in turn, facilitates the admission of disclosed family members who may seek to come to Canada in the future. This is how family unification is achieved under IRPA.

Since the respondent was married during the life of the application from the time it was initiated by the filing of the authorized form to the time when permanent resident status was granted at the port of entry and since she failed to disclose this relationship, her husband was excluded from the family class by virtue of para. 117(9)(d) of Regulations.

de Guzman v. Canada (Minister of Citizenship & Immigration), [2005] F.C.J. No. 2119, 262 D.L.R. (4th) 13, 51 Imm. L.R. (3d) 17, 137 C.R.R. (2d) 20, 345 N.R. 73, 2005 CarswellNat 4381, 2005 FCA 436; leave to appeal to S.C.C. refused [2006] S.C.C.A. No. 70, 2006 CarswellNat 1695, 356 N.R. 399 — In 1993, the appellant came to live in Canada. When she was landed in Canada, she told the immigration officials that she was single and had no dependants, other than her daughter who was accompanying her. This was not true: she also had two sons whom she left in the Philippines with their father. Eight years later, after establishing herself in Canada and becoming a citizen, the appellant applied to sponsor her sons as members of the family class. They were refused visas under para. 117(9)(d) of the Regulations on the ground that they were not members of the family class because they had not been examined for immigration purposes when the appellant applied to come to Canada.

The appellant's misrepresentation was highly material to the success of her application for a visa in the family class as an unmarried daughter. Her daughter's birth certificate stated that the appellant was unmarried, unlike her sons' birth certificates.

The Immigration Appeal Division was correct in law to dismiss the appellant's appeal pursuant to para. 74(d) of the IRPA. Specifically, the Board concluded that since the sons were not members of the family class, the Board, under s. 65 of the IRPA, had no discretionary jurisdiction to consider humanitarian and compassionate circumstances.

The Federal Court of Appeal concluded that para. 117(9)(d) of the Regulations was not invalid or inoperative. It was not unconstitutional nor did it deprive the applicant of her right to liberty and/or her right to security of person, in a manner not in accordance with the principles of fundamental justice contrary to s. 7 of the *Charter*.

118. Medical condition — **A foreign national who is an adopted dependent child or is a person referred to in paragraph 117(1)(f) or (g) shall not be issued a permanent resident visa as a member of the family class unless the sponsor has provided a statement in writing confirming that they have obtained information about the medical condition of the child or of the foreign national.**

SOR/2005-61, s. 4; SOR/2010-195, s. 12

119. Withdrawal of sponsorship application — **A decision shall not be made on an application for a permanent resident visa by a member of the family class if the sponsor withdraws their sponsorship application in respect of that member.**

120. Approved sponsorship application — **For the purposes of Part 5,**

(a) a permanent resident visa shall not be issued to a foreign national who makes an application as a member of the family class or to their accompanying family members unless a sponsorship undertaking in respect of the foreign national and those family members is in effect; and

(b) a foreign national who makes an application as a member of the family class and their accompanying family members shall not become permanent residents unless a sponsorship undertaking in respect of the foreign national and those family members is in effect and the sponsor who gave that undertaking still meets the requirements of section 133 and, if applicable, section 137.

121. Requirements — **Subject to subsection 25.1(1), a person who is a member of the family class or a family member of a member of the family class who makes an application under Division 6 of Part 5 must be a family member of the applicant or of the sponsor both at the time the application is made and at the time of the determination of the application.**

SOR/2004-167, s. 42; SOR/2014-133, s. 6

122. Requirements for accompanying family members — **A foreign national who is an accompanying family member of a person who makes an applica-**

tion as a member of the family class shall become a permanent resident if, following an examination, it is established that

(a) the person who made the application has become a permanent resident; and

(b) the family member is not inadmissible.

DIVISION 2 — SPOUSE OR COMMON-LAW PARTNER IN CANADA CLASS

123. Class — For the purposes of subsection 12(1) of the Act, the spouse or common-law partner in Canada class is hereby prescribed as a class of persons who may become permanent residents on the basis of the requirements of this Division.

124. Member — A foreign national is a member of the spouse or common-law partner in Canada class if they

(a) are the spouse or common-law partner of a sponsor and cohabit with that sponsor in Canada;

(b) have temporary resident status in Canada; and

(c) are the subject of a sponsorship application.

Case Law

Xuan v. Canada (Minister of Citizenship & Immigration), 2013 FC 92, 2013 CarswellNat 193, 2013 CarswellNat 372 — The applicant sought judicial review of a decision of an immigration officer denying an application for permanent residence under the "spouse in Canada" class. It is a requirement of this class that not only must an applicant be a spouse or common-law partner but they must cohabitate with the sponsor. The couple claimed to live in Markham, both prior to and subsequent to being married. More importantly, it was where they claimed to live together at the time of the home visit by CBSA officers. They had also bought a property in Stouffville in 2010. The CBSA officers visited the Markham house and the applicant let them in. They then questioned the applicant about her husband's clothes and personal hygiene/grooming supplies. Concluding that the answers were unsatisfactory and that she might be a flight risk, the applicant was arrested and held in detention for 11 days. The applicant was later interviewed by a different CBSA officer. There was no evidence that this was a "warrantless search," the applicant never objecting to the CBSA entering the premises. She showed them the location of clothes and of personal items. She never claimed to insist or ask for an interpreter and she responded to their questions. There was no breach of natural justice in respect to the home visit. It was legal, entry was consensual, responses were apparently voluntary and questions appeared to be understood. In terms of the test for "cohabitation," the term is not defined in the Regulations. There is no one controlled test or factor. Documents showing joint interest are consistent with marriage but not necessarily of cohabitation. The officer placed greater weight in what was observed or said at the home visit and in the home visit and solo interview of the applicant than in the answers given at the joint interview two months later. The choice to assign greater weight to the less prepared, extemporaneous evidence lies within the discretion of the officer. It is a reasonable choice given the nature of the inquiry which is to determine how a person lives not merely how they say they live. The officer's decision that cohabitation had not been established was reasonable.

Ally v. Canada (Minister of Citizenship & Immigration), 2008 CarswellNat 1869, 2008 CarswellNat 853, 2008 FC 445 — The applicant's application for permanent residence as a member of the Spouse or Common-law Partner in Canada Class was denied. Immigration received information that he had been charged by police with assault and threats; conditions of his bail release stated that he must stay away from his wife and reside with his uncle when in Canada. The onus was upon the applicant to establish that s. 124 of the Regulations was satisfied and that any separation was only temporary and short.

125. (1) Excluded relationships — A foreign national shall not be considered a member of the spouse or common-law partner in Canada class by virtue of their relationship to the sponsor if

(a) the foreign national is the sponsor's spouse or common-law partner and is under 18 years of age;

(b) the foreign national is the sponsor's spouse or common-law partner, the sponsor has an existing sponsorship undertaking in respect of a spouse or common-law partner and the period referred to in subsection 132(1) in respect of that undertaking has not ended;

(c) the foreign national is the sponsor's spouse and

(i) the sponsor or the spouse was, at the time of their marriage, the spouse of another person, or

(ii) the sponsor has lived separate and apart from the foreign national for at least one year and

(A) the sponsor is the common-law partner of another person or the sponsor has a conjugal partner, or

(B) the foreign national is the common-law partner of another person or the conjugal partner of another sponsor;

(c.1) the foreign national is the sponsor's spouse and if at the time the marriage ceremony was conducted either one or both of the spouses were not physically present unless the foreign national was married to a person who was not physically present at the ceremony as a result of their service as a member of the Canadian Forces and the marriage is valid both under the laws of the jurisdiction where it took place and under Canadian law; or

(d) subject to subsection (2), the sponsor previously made an application for permanent residence and became a permanent resident and, at the time of that application, the foreign national was a non-accompanying family member of the sponsor and was not examined.

(2) Exception — Subject to subsection (3), paragraph (1)(d) does not apply in respect of a foreign national referred to in that paragraph who was not examined because an officer determined that they were not required by the Act or the former Act, as applicable, to be examined.

(3) Application of par. (1)(d) — Paragraph (1)(d) applies in respect of a foreign national referred to in subsection (2) if an officer determines that, at the time of the application referred to in that paragraph,

   (a) the sponsor was informed that the foreign national could be examined and the sponsor was able to make the foreign national available for examination but did not do so or the foreign national did not appear for examination; or

   (b) the foreign national was the sponsor's spouse, was living separate and apart from the sponsor and was not examined.

(4) Definition of "former Act" — In subsection (2), "former Act" has the same meaning as in section 187 of the Act.

SOR/2004-167, s. 43; SOR/2010-195, s. 13; SOR/2015-139, s. 3

Case Law

Section 125(1)

Cai v. Canada (Minister of Citizenship & Immigration), 2007 CarswellNat 2274, 2007 CarswellNat 5843, 2007 FC 816 — The applicant's application for permanent resident status under the Spouse or Common-Law Partner in Canada Class was refused on the basis that the applicant did not comply with s. 125(1)(d) of the Regulation. At the time of the sponsor's application for permanent residence, she did not list the applicant as a non-accompanying family member and the applicant was not examined. The court considered whether the immigration officer erred in determining that the applicant was his sponsor's common-law partner when the sponsor applied to be a permanent resident of Canada. In her application to sponsor an undertaking, the applicant's sponsor stated that her relationship with the applicant began on June 1, 2002. The applicant argued that, despite the fact that the relationship with the sponsor traces back to 2002, his relationship with his sponsor did not meet the requirements of common-law relationship as of that date. When the applicant and her sponsor began living together they were young students, and as such, they may not have made a "mutual commitment to a shared life" when they decided to live together. There was, accordingly, no basis on which the immigration officer could reasonably conclude that the applicant was a common-law partner of his sponsor when she submitted her application for permanent residence in January, 2005 and did not identify the applicant as a non-accompanying family member. The meaning of "common-law partner" means that the conjugal relationship is one of some permanence where the couple has made a serious commitment to one another. The applicant's application for judicial review was allowed.

126. Withdrawal of sponsorship application — A decision shall not be made on an application for permanent residence by a foreign national as a member of the spouse or common-law partner in Canada class if the sponsor withdraws their sponsorship application in respect of that foreign national.

127. Approved sponsorship application — For the purposes of Part 5, a foreign national who makes an application as a member of the spouse or common-law partner in Canada class and their accompanying family members shall not become a permanent resident unless a sponsorship undertaking in respect of the foreign national and those family members is in effect and the sponsor who gave that under-taking still meets the requirements of section 133 and, if applicable, section 137.

128. Requirements — family member — The requirements with respect to a person who is a family member of a member of the spouse or common-law partner in Canada class who makes an application under Division 6 of Part 5 are the following:

(a) subject to subsection 25.1(1), the person is a family member of the applicant both at the time the application is made and at the time of the determination of the application; and

(b) at the time it is made, the application includes a request for the family member to remain in Canada as a permanent resident.

SOR/2014-133, s. 7

129. Requirements for accompanying family members — A foreign na-tional who is an accompanying family member of a person who makes an applica-tion as a member of the spouse or common-law partner in Canada class shall be-come a permanent resident if, following an examination, it is established that

(a) the person who made the application has become a permanent resident; and

(b) the family member is not inadmissible.

DIVISION 3 — SPONSORS

130. (1) Sponsor — Subject to subsections (2) and (3), a sponsor, for the purpose of sponsoring a foreign national who makes an application for a permanent resident visa as a member of the family class or an application to remain in Canada as a member of the spouse or common-law partner in Canada class under subsection 13(1) of the Act, must be a Canadian citizen or permanent resident who

(a) is at least 18 years of age;

(b) resides in Canada; and

(c) has filed a sponsorship application in respect of a member of the family class or the spouse or common-law partner in Canada class in accordance with section 10.

(2) Sponsor not residing in Canada — A sponsor who is a Canadian citizen and does not reside in Canada may sponsor a foreign national who makes an appli-cation referred to in subsection (1) and is the sponsor's spouse, common-law part-ner, conjugal partner or dependent child who has no dependent children, if the sponsor will reside in Canada when the foreign national becomes a permanent resident.

(3) Five-year requirement — A sponsor who became a permanent resident or a Canadian citizen after being sponsored as a spouse, common-law partner or conju-gal partner under subsection 13(1) of the Act may not sponsor a foreign national referred to in subsection (1) as a spouse, common-law partner or conjugal partner, unless the sponsor has been a permanent resident, or a Canadian citizen, or a com-

bination of the two, for a period of at least five years immediately preceding the day on which a sponsorship application referred to in paragraph (1)(c) is filed by the sponsor in respect of the foreign national.

SOR/2012-20, s. 1; SOR/2015-139, s. 4

Case Law

Lau v. Canada (Minister of Citizenship & Immigration) (2009), 84 Imm. L.R. (3d) 261, 356 F.T.R. 206 (Eng.), 2009 FC 1089, 2009 CarswellNat 3343 — This was an application for judicial review of a decision of the Immigration Appeal Division of the Immigration and Refugee Board dismissing the appeal of a decision of a visa officer refusing to approve the permanent resident visa application made to sponsor the applicant's spouse. The IAD dismissed the appeal on the basis that the divorce in question between the applicant and Huang was not undertaken in compliance with Canadian law and was not deemed to be a valid divorce according to the laws of Canada. The Board made no determination whatsoever as to whether the divorce at issue was legally valid in the place where it was granted. Accordingly, the application for judicial review was allowed, the decision under review set aside and the applicant's appeal to the IAD referred back to the Board for rehearing and redetermination.

131. Sponsorship undertaking — The sponsor's undertaking shall be given

(a) to the Minister; or

(b) if the sponsor resides in a province that has entered into an agreement referred to in subsection 8(1) of the Act that enables the province to determine and apply financial criteria with respect to sponsorship undertakings and to administer sponsorship undertakings, to the competent authority of the province.

SOR/2014-140, s. 8

132. (1) Undertaking — duration — Subject to subsection (2), the sponsor's undertaking obliges the sponsor to reimburse Her Majesty in right of Canada or a province for every benefit provided as social assistance to or on behalf of the sponsored foreign national and their family members during the period

(a) beginning

(i) if the foreign national enters Canada with a temporary resident permit, on the day of that entry,

(ii) if the foreign national is in Canada, on the day on which the foreign national obtains a temporary resident permit following an application to remain in Canada as a permanent resident, and

(iii) in any other case, on the day on which the foreign national becomes a permanent resident; and

(b) ending

(i) if the foreign national is the sponsor's spouse, common-law partner or conjugal partner, on the last day of the period of three years following the day on which the foreign national becomes a permanent resident,

(ii) if the foreign national is a dependent child of the sponsor or of the sponsor's spouse, common-law partner or conjugal partner or is a person referred to in paragraph 117(1)(g), and is less than 19 years of age when they become a permanent resident, on the earlier of

(A) the last day of the period of 10 years following the day on which the foreign national becomes a permanent resident, and

(B) the day on which the foreign national reaches 22 years of age,

(iii) if the foreign national is a dependent child of the sponsor or of the sponsor's spouse, common-law partner or conjugal partner and is 19 years of age or older when they become a permanent resident, on the last day of the period of three years following the day on which the foreign national becomes a permanent resident,

(iv) on the last day of the period of 20 years following the day on which the foreign national becomes a permanent resident, if the foreign national is

(A) the sponsor's mother or father,

(B) the mother or father of the sponsor's mother or father, or

(C) an accompanying family member of the foreign national described in clause (A) or (B), and

(v) if the foreign national is a person other than a person referred to in subparagraph (i), (ii), (iii) or (iv), on the last day of the period of 10 years following the day on which the foreign national becomes a permanent resident.

(2) **Undertaking to province — duration** — In the case of an undertaking to a competent authority of a province referred to in paragraph 131(b), the period referred to in subsection (1) shall end not later than

(a) if the foreign national is a sponsor's spouse, common-law partner or conjugal partner, on the last day of the period of three years following the day on which the foreign national becomes a permanent resident;

(b) if the foreign national is a dependent child of the sponsor or of the sponsor's spouse, common-law partner or conjugal partner, or is a person referred to in paragraph 117(1)(g), and is less than 19 years of age on the day on which he or she becomes a permanent resident, the later of

(i) the day on which the foreign national reaches 19 years of age, and

(ii) the last day of the period of 10 years following the day on which the foreign national becomes a permanent resident;

(c) if the foreign national is a dependent child of the sponsor or of the sponsor's spouse, common-law partner or conjugal partner and is 19 years of age or older on the day on which he or she becomes a permanent resident, on the last day of the period of 10 years following the day on which the foreign national becomes a permanent resident;

(d) on the last day of the period of 20 years following the day on which the foreign national becomes a permanent resident, if the foreign national is

(i) the sponsor's mother or father,

IRP Regulations

(ii) the mother or father of the sponsor's mother or father, or

(iii) an accompanying family member of the foreign national described in subparagraph (i) or (ii); and

(e) if the foreign national is a person other than a person referred to in paragraphs (a) to (d), on the last day of the period of 10 years following the day on which the foreign national becomes a permanent resident.

(3) **Undertaking to province — alternate duration** — Despite subsection (2), the period referred to in subsection (1) shall end not later than the day provided for by the laws of the province if that day is

(a) in the case of a foreign national referred to in paragraph (2)(a), earlier than the last day referred to in that paragraph;

(b) in the case of a foreign national referred to in paragraph (2)(b), earlier than the later of the days referred to in subparagraph (2)(b)(i) and (ii);

(c) in the case of a foreign national referred to in paragraph (2)(c), earlier than the last day referred to in that paragraph;

(d) in the case of a foreign national referred to in paragraph (2)(d), earlier than the last day referred to in that paragraph; and

(e) in the case of a foreign national referred to in paragraph (2)(e), earlier than the last day referred to in that paragraph.

(4) **Agreement** — Subject to paragraph 137(c), if the person is to be sponsored as a member of the family class or of the spouse or common-law partner in Canada class and is at least 19 years of age, or is less than 19 years of age and is the sponsor's spouse, common-law partner or conjugal partner, the sponsor, the co-signer, if any, and the person must, before the sponsorship application is approved, enter into a written agreement that includes

(a) a statement by the sponsor and the co-signer, if any, that they will provide for the basic requirements of the person and their accompanying family members during the applicable period referred to in subsection (1);

(b) a declaration by the sponsor and the co-signer, if any, that their financial obligations do not prevent them from honouring their agreement with the person and their undertaking to the Minister in respect of the person's application; and

(c) a statement by the person that they will make every reasonable effort to provide for their own basic requirements as well as those of their accompanying family members.

(5) **Co-signature — undertaking** — Subject to paragraph 137(c), the sponsor's undertaking may be co-signed by the spouse or common-law partner of the sponsor if the spouse or common-law partner meets the requirements set out in subsection 130(1), except paragraph 130(1)(c), and those set out in subsection 133(1), except paragraph 133(1)(a), and, in that case,

(a) the sponsor's income shall be calculated in accordance with paragraph 134(1)(b) or (c) or (1.1)(b), as applicable; and

(b) the co-signing spouse or common-law partner is jointly and severally or solidarily bound with the sponsor to perform the obligations in the undertaking and is jointly and severally or solidarily liable with the sponsor for any breach of those obligations.

SOR/2004-167, s. 44(2); SOR/2005-61, s. 5; SOR/2013-246, s. 1; SOR/2014-133, s. 8; SOR/2014-140, s. 9

133. (1) Requirements for sponsor — A sponsorship application shall only be approved by an officer if, on the day on which the application was filed and from that day until the day a decision is made with respect to the application, there is evidence that the sponsor

(a) is a sponsor as described in section 130;

(b) intends to fulfil the obligations in the sponsorship undertaking;

(c) is not subject to a removal order;

(d) is not detained in any penitentiary, jail, reformatory or prison;

(e) has not been convicted under the *Criminal Code* of

(i) an offence of a sexual nature, or an attempt or a threat to commit such an offence, against any person,

(i.1) an indictable offence involving the use of violence and punishable by a maximum term of imprisonment of at least 10 years, or an attempt to commit such an offence, against any person, or

(ii) an offence that results in bodily harm, as defined in section 2 of the *Criminal Code*, to any of the following persons or an attempt or a threat to commit such an offence against any of the following persons:

(A) a current or former family member of the sponsor,

(B) a relative of the sponsor, as well as a current or former family member of that relative,

(C) a relative of the family member of the sponsor, or a current or former family member of that relative,

(D) a current or former conjugal partner of the sponsor,

(E) a current or former family member of a family member or conjugal partner of the sponsor,

(F) a relative of the conjugal partner of the sponsor, or a current or former family member of that relative,

(G) a child under the current or former care and control of the sponsor, their current or former family member or conjugal partner,

(H) a child under the current or former care and control of a relative of the sponsor or a current or former family member of that relative, or

(I) someone the sponsor is dating or has dated, whether or not they have lived together, or a family member of that person.

(f) has not been convicted outside Canada of an offence that, if committed in Canada, would constitute an offence referred to in paragraph (e);

(g) subject to paragraph 137(c), is not in default of

(i) any sponsorship undertaking, or

(ii) any support payment obligations ordered by a court;

(h) is not in default in respect of the repayment of any debt referred to in subsection 145(1) of the Act payable to Her Majesty in right of Canada;

(i) subject to paragraph 137(c), is not an undischarged bankrupt under the *Bankruptcy and Insolvency Act*;

(j) if the sponsor resides

(i) in a province other than a province referred to in paragraph 131(b),

(A) has a total income that is at least equal to the minimum necessary income, if the sponsorship application was filed in respect of a foreign national other than a foreign national referred to in clause (B), or

(B) has a total income that is at least equal to the minimum necessary income, plus 30%, for each of the three consecutive taxation years immediately preceding the date of filing of the sponsorship application, if the sponsorship application was filed in respect of a foreign national who is

(I) the sponsor's mother or father,

(II) the mother or father of the sponsor's mother or father, or

(III) an accompanying family member of the foreign national described in subclause (I) or (II), and

(ii) in a province referred to in paragraph 131(b), is able, within the meaning of the laws of that province and as determined by the competent authority of that province, to fulfil the undertaking referred to in that paragraph; and

(k) is not in receipt of social assistance for a reason other than disability.

(2) Exception — conviction in Canada — Despite paragraph (1)(e), a sponsorship application may not be refused

(a) on the basis of a conviction in Canada in respect of which a pardon has been granted and has not ceased to have effect or been revoked under the *Criminal Records Act*, or in respect of which there has been a final determination of an acquittal; or

(b) if a period of five years or more has elapsed since the completion of the sentence imposed for an offence in Canada referred to in paragraph (l)(e).

(3) Exception — conviction outside Canada — Despite paragraph (1)(f), a sponsorship application may not be refused

(a) on the basis of a conviction outside Canada in respect of which there has been a final determination of an acquittal; or

(b) if a period of five years or more has elapsed since the completion of the sentence imposed for an offence outside Canada referred to in that paragraph and the sponsor has demonstrated that they have been rehabilitated.

(4) Exception to minimum necessary income — Paragraph (1)(j) does not apply If the sponsored person is

(a) the sponsor's spouse, common-law partner or conjugal partner and has no dependent children;

(b) the sponsor's spouse, common-law partner or conjugal partner and has a dependent child who has no dependent children; or

(c) a dependent child of the sponsor who has no dependent children or a person referred to in paragraph 117(1)(g).

(5) Adopted sponsor — A person who is adopted outside Canada and whose adoption is subsequently revoked by a foreign authority or by a court in Canada of competent jurisdiction may sponsor an application for a permanent resident visa that is made by a member of the family class only if the revocation of the adoption was not obtained for the purpose of sponsoring that application.

SOR/2004-167, s. 45; SOR/2005-61, s. 6; SOR/2011-262, s. 1; SOR/2013-246, s. 2; SOR/2014-140, s. 10

Case Law

Section 133(1)(e)

Canada (Minister of Citizenship & Immigration) v. Brar (2008), 76 Imm. L.R. (3d) 246, 336 F.T.R. 293 (Eng.), 2008 CarswellNat 4260, 2008 FC 1285 — The wording of subpara. 133(1)(e)(ii) of the Regulations denies the right of sponsorship to Canadian citizens and permanent residents who have committed offences involving bodily harm against only certain enumerated victims. According to the definition in s. 2 of the Regulations, "relative" means a person who is related to another person by blood or adoption. The Board accepted the submission that the respondent's sister-in-law is not a blood relative. Furthermore, the victim does not fit within the definition of "family member" as defined in subs. 1(3) of the Regulations. Section 133 of the Regulations restricts the victims of assaults causing bodily harm to the sponsored spouse or common-law partner and family members of the sponsor's spouse or common-law partner. It does not include all family members on each side of the family and is not worded so as to catch a sponsor who has committed a crime causing bodily harm against a sister-in-law. Therefore, the respondent's sister-in-law does not fit within the narrow definition of victims of offences causing bodily harm in clause 133(1)(e)(ii)(A).

In the end, the Board concluded that the word "sister-in-law" did not fit within the definition of "family member." The Board did not err in its interpretation and the application for judicial review was dismissed.

Section 133(1)(k)

Guzman v. Canada (Minister of Citizenship & Immigration) (2006), 57 Imm. L.R. (3d) 174, 146 C.R.R. (2d) 305, [2007] 3 F.C.R. 411, 2006 CarswellNat 3005, 2006 FC 1134 — This was an application for judicial review of a decision to reject the applicant's sponsorship application under para. 133(1)(k) of the *Immigration and Refugee Protection Regulations*, as the applicant, during the processing of the sponsorship application, was a recipient of social assistance for a reason other than disability. The applicant sought to quash para. 133(1)(k) of the IRPR on the basis that it violates s. 15 of the *Canadian*

Charter of Rights and Freedoms, Pt. 1 of the *Constitution Act*, 1982, being schedule B to the *Canada Act, 1982* (UK), 1982 c. 1, and it is not justifiable under s. 1 of the *Charter*. The applicant claimed that para. 133(1)(k) is discriminatory as it prevents those on social assistance from being able to sponsor a relative they would otherwise be qualified to sponsor.

The Federal Court applied the three-step framework for analyzing a claim for discrimination under subs. 15(1) of the *Charter* known as the *Law v. Canada (MEI)*, [1999] 1 S.C.R. 497 three-step framework. The court concluded that all three parts of the *Law* test failed and that para. 133(1)(k) of the IRPR does not violate s. 15 of the *Charter*.

The following question was certified: "Whether paragraph 133(1)(k) of the IRPR violates subs. 15(1) of the *Charter* in that it discriminates on the basis of the analogous ground of receipt of social assistance?"

134. (1) Income calculation rules — **Subject to subsection (3), for the purpose of clause 133(1)(j)(i)(A), the sponsor's total income shall be calculated in accordance with the following rules:**

> **(a) the sponsor's income shall be calculated on the basis of the last notice of assessment, or an equivalent document, issued by the Minister of National Revenue in respect of the most recent taxation year preceding the date of filing of the sponsorship application;**

> **(b) if the sponsor produces a document referred to in paragraph (a), the sponsor's income is the income earned as reported in that document less the amounts referred to in subparagraphs (c)(i) to (v);**

> **(c) if the sponsor does not produce a document referred to in paragraph (a), or if the sponsor's income as calculated under paragraph (b) is less than their minimum necessary income, the sponsor's Canadian income for the 12-month period preceding the date of filing of the sponsorship application is the income earned by the sponsor not including**

> > **(i) any provincial allowance received by the sponsor for a program of instruction or training,**

> > **(ii) any social assistance received by the sponsor from a province,**

> > **(iii) any financial assistance received by the sponsor from the Government of Canada under a resettlement assistance program,**

> > **(iv) any amounts paid to the sponsor under the *Employment Insurance Act*, other than special benefits,**

> > **(v) any monthly guaranteed income supplement paid to the sponsor under the *Old Age Security Act*, and**

> > **(vi) any Canada child tax benefit paid to the sponsor under the *Income Tax Act*; and**

> **(d) if there is a co-signer, the income of the co-signer, as calculated in accordance with paragraphs (a) to (c), with any modifications that the circumstances require, shall be included in the calculation of the sponsor's income.**

(1.1) Exception Subject to subsection (3), for the purpose of clause 133(1)(j)(i)(B), the sponsor's total income shall be calculated in accordance with the following rules:

(a) the sponsor's income shall be calculated on the basis of the income earned as reported in the notices of assessment, or an equivalent document, issued by the Minister of National Revenue in respect of each of the three consecutive taxation years immediately preceding the date of filing of the sponsorship application;

(b) the sponsor's income is the income earned as reported in the documents referred to in paragraph (a), not including

(i) any provincial allowance received by the sponsor for a program of instruction or training,

(ii) any social assistance received by the sponsor from a province,

(iii) any financial assistance received by the sponsor from the Government of Canada under a resettlement assistance program,

(iv) any amounts paid to the sponsor under the *Employment Insurance Act*, other than special benefits,

(v) any monthly guaranteed income supplement paid to the sponsor under the *Old Age Security Act*, and

(vi) any Canada child tax benefit paid to the sponsor under the *Income Tax Act*; and

(c) if there is a co-signer, the income of the co-signer, as calculated in accordance with paragraphs (a) and (b), with any modifications that the circumstances require, shall be included in the calculation of the sponsor's income.

(2) Updated evidence of income — An officer may request from the sponsor, after the receipt of the sponsorship application but before a decision is made on an application for permanent residence, updated evidence of income if

(a) the officer receives information indicating that the sponsor is no longer able to fulfil the obligations of the sponsorship undertaking; or

(b) more than 12 months have elapsed since the receipt of the sponsorship application.

(3) Modified income calculation rules — When an officer receives the updated evidence of income requested under subsection (2), the sponsor's total income shall be calculated in accordance with subsection (1) or (1.1), as applicable, except that

(a) in the case of paragraph (1)(a), the sponsor's income shall be calculated on the basis of the last notice of assessment, or an equivalent document, issued by the Minister of National Revenue in respect of the most recent taxation year preceding the day on which the officer receives the updated evidence;

(b) in the case of paragraph (1)(c), the sponsor's income is the sponsor's Canadian income earned during the 12-month period preceding the day on which the officer receives the updated evidence; and

(c) in the case of paragraph (1.1)(a), the sponsor's income shall be calculated on the basis of the income earned as reported in the notices of assessment, or

an equivalent document, issued by the Minister of National Revenue in respect of each of the three consecutive taxation years immediately preceding the day on which the officer receives the updated evidence.

SOR/2013-246, s. 3

Case Law

Motala v. Canada (Minister of Citizenship & Immigration), 2012 FC 123, 2012 CarswellNat 265, 2012 CarswellNat 583 — The IAD dismissed the applicant's appeal of a visa officer's decision refusing the applicant's request to sponsor 10 other family members. A Canadian who wishes to sponsor family members to come to Canada must establish that they have the financial capacity to support their family members on arrival in Canada. The applicant contended that the IAD erred by importing additional requirements into the income calculation, over and above those required by s. 134(1) of the Regulations and, in effect, going behind the Notice of Assessment and discounting the reported amounts. If the minimum necessary income was surpassed, the application would be assessed under a more favourable criteria. Hardship, as defined in the jurisprudence, need not be established when the ground of inadmissibility has been overcome.

The IAD has, as a consequence of its discretionary power to consider whether the grounds of inadmissibility have been overcome and hence whether special relief should be granted, the authority to require evidence corroborative of the income reported in the Notice of Assessment. The IAD is permitted to question the accuracy and veracity of certain financial documents submitted in support of sponsorship applications and to assign relative and proportionate evidentiary weight to them. This interpretation of the scope of the IAD jurisdiction is consistent with the objective of the Regulations as a whole, which are designed to ensure that those sponsored to come to Canada can in fact be provided for, and that the integrity of the sponsorship provisions of IRPA is not eroded through inaccurate statements of income, whether deliberate or accidental. The application for judicial review is dismissed. The following question was certified:

> Is the Appeal Division of the Immigration and Refugee Board of Canada, in hearing an appeal from a decision of a visa officer dismissing an application to sponsor family members, bound to accept as conclusive the income as reported in the applicant's Notice of Assessment, by Regulation 134 of the *Immigration and Refugee Protection Regulations*?

Dokaj v. Canada (Minister of Citizenship & Immigration) (2009), 82 Imm. L.R. (3d) 239, 2009 FC 847, 2009 CarswellNat 5484, 2009 CarswellNat 2493 — This was an application for judicial review of a decision by an immigration officer at the Case Processing Centre (CPC) in Mississauga, dated February 10, 2009, wherein the immigration officer refused the applicant's application to sponsor a member of the family class. The officer determined that the applicant did not meet the financial requirements to sponsor his family members. The officer found the applicant's co-signer ineligible to co-sign his application as she was not on the application when it was originally received. A co-signer cannot be added to the application once it has been received at the CPC. Therefore, her income could not be considered toward the financial test and the officer also did not have the authority to consider income earned outside the stated 12-month period. The officer found that the income of the applicant's common-law spouse could not be included in the sponsorship undertaking because she was not his common-law spouse when the initial sponsorship application was remitted and therefore she could not be added once the application was received by the CPC.

The immigration officer at the CPC erred in the determination of whether the applicant could sponsor members of the family class. Since the applicant's common-law spouse is to be considered in the calculation of the size of the applicant's family, her income should also be included in the sponsorship undertaking as per subs. 132(5) and para. 134(1)(c) of the Regulations. The statutory provisions do not provide for the exclusion of the spouse's income while including her as a dependent member of the applicant's family. Inclusive of his common-law spouse income, the applicant met the low income cut-off at the time the decision was made. The application for judicial review was allowed.

135. Default — For the purpose of subparagraph 133(1)(g)(i), the default of a sponsorship undertaking

    (a) begins when

        (i) a government makes a payment that the sponsor has in the undertaking promised to repay, or

        (ii) an obligation set out in the undertaking is breached; and

    (b) ends, as the case may be, when

        (i) the sponsor reimburses the government concerned, in full or in accordance with an agreement with that government, for amounts paid by it, or

        (ii) the sponsor ceases to be in breach of the obligation set out in the undertaking.

Case Law

Mavi v. Canada (Attorney General) (2011), 97 Imm. L.R. (3d) 173, [2011] 2 S.C.R. 504, 19 Admin. L.R. (5th) 1, 2011 SCC 30, 2011 CarswellOnt 4429, 2011 CarswellOnt 4430 — The present proceedings were initiated by eight sponsors whose relatives received social assistance and are therefore deemed to have defaulted on their undertakings. The sponsors deny liability under the undertakings and sought various declarations. The result of which, if granted, would be to avoid payment either temporarily or permanently.

Parliament's legislation manifests an unambiguous intent to require the full sponsorship debt to be paid if and when the sponsor is in a position to do so, even incrementally over many years pursuant to an agreement under the Regulations. In dealing with defaulting sponsors, the government must however act fairly having regard to their financial means to pay and the existence of circumstances that would militate against enforcement of immediate payment. In the exercise of this discretion, which Parliament has made clear is narrow in scope, the Crown is bound by a duty of procedural fairness. Nevertheless the content of the duty of fairness in these circumstances is less ample than was contemplated in the decision of the Court of Appeal and, contrary to its opinion, the requirements of procedural fairness were met in the cases of the eight respondent sponsors. The Supreme Court of Canada held the undertakings were valid but that they were also structured, controlled and supplemented by federal legislation. The debts created thereby are not only contractual but statutory, and as such their enforcement is not exclusively governed by the private law of contract. The Crown does have a limited discretion to delay enforcement action having regard to the sponsors' circumstances and to enter into agreements respecting terms of payment, but this discretion does not extend to the forgiveness of the statutory debt. Debt collection without any discretion would not advance the purposes of IRPA. Excessively harsh treatment of defaulting sponsors may risk discouraging others from bringing their relatives to Canada which would undermine the policy of promoting family reunification.

Manitoba v. Barkman (2007), 213 Man. R. (2d) 273, 2007 CarswellMan 86, 2007 MBQB 54 (Q.B.) — The plaintiff sued the defendant to recover the amount of income assistance payments which the plaintiff paid to immigrants sponsored by the defendant pursuant to an "undertaking of assistance," whereby the defendant undertook to provide and guaranteed their maintenance or support. The defendant maintains that the immigrants did not need to apply for social assistance; that any application for such was made at the instance of agents of the plaintiff. The defendant had sponsored his wife and four children. His wife and the children abruptly left. The defendant submitted that his wife and the children did not need to go on income assistance because he was always prepared to support them. The plaintiff's officials were quite right in concluding that the defendant's wife was genuinely in need of income assistance. The plaintiff did not follow their policy with respect to notifying the sponsor by registered mail (or at all) that legal action may be taken to recover the assistance as a result of the sponsor's breach of the undertaking. The plaintiff obtained judgment against the defendant.

136. (1) Suspension during proceedings against sponsor or co-signer — If any of the following proceedings are brought against a sponsor or co-signer, the sponsorship application shall not be processed until there has been a final determination of the proceeding:

(a) the revocation of citizenship under the *Citizenship Act*;

(b) a report prepared under subsection 44(1) of the Act; or

(c) a charge alleging the commission of an offence under an Act of Parliament punishable by a maximum term of imprisonment of at least 10 years.

(2) Suspension during appeal by sponsor or co-signer — If a sponsor or co-signer has made an appeal under subsection 63(4) of the Act, the sponsorship application shall not be processed until the period for making the appeal has expired or there has been a final determination of the appeal.

SOR/2014-140, s. 12

137. Undertaking — Province of Quebec — If the sponsor resides in the Province of Quebec, the government of which has entered into an agreement referred to in paragraph 131(b),

(a) the sponsor's undertaking, given in accordance with section 131, is the undertaking required by *An Act respecting immigration to Québec*, R.S.Q., c. I-0.2, as amended from time to time;

(b) an officer shall approve the sponsorship application only if there is evidence that the competent authority of the Province has determined that the sponsor, on the day the undertaking was given as well as on the day a decision was made with respect to the application, was able to fulfil the undertaking; and

(c) subsections 132(4) and (5) and paragraphs 133(1)(g) and (i) do not apply.

DIVISION 1.1 — COLLECTION AND DISCLOSURE OF INFORMATION
[Heading added SOR/2015-138, s. 2.]

137.1 (1) Collection of social insurance number — The Minister may collect the social insurance numbers of a sponsor and a co-signer who have submitted an application to sponsor a person set out in clause 133(1)(j)(i)(B), in order to verify that they meet the requirements set out in clause 133(1)(j)(i)(B) and in paragraph 133(1)(k).

(2) Disclosure of social insurance number — The Minister may disclose the social insurance numbers of the sponsor and the co-signer to the Canada Revenue Agency for the purposes set out in subsection (1) if the Minister has entered into an arrangement with the Agency for the disclosure of that information.

SOR/2015-138, s. 2

PART 8 — REFUGEE CLASSES

DIVISION 1 — CONVENTION REFUGEES ABROAD, HUMANITARIAN-PROTECTED PERSONS ABROAD AND PROTECTED TEMPORARY RESIDENTS
[Heading amended SOR/2011-222, s. 2.]

Interpretation

138. Definitions — The definitions in this section apply in this Division and in Division 2.

"**group**" means

(a) five or more Canadian citizens or permanent residents, each of whom is at least 18 years of age, who are acting together for the purpose of sponsoring a Convention refugee or a person in similar circumstances; or

(b) one or more Canadian citizens or permanent residents, each of whom is at least 18 years of age, and a corporation or unincorporated organization or association referred to in subsection 13(2) of the Act, acting together for the purpose of sponsoring a Convention refugee or a person in similar circumstances. (*"groupe"*)

"**referral organization**" means

(a) the United Nations High Commissioner for Refugees; or

(b) any organization with which the Minister has entered into a memorandum of understanding under section 143. (*"organisation de recommandation"*)

"**sponsor**" means

(a) a group, a corporation or an unincorporated organization or association referred to in subsection 13(2) of the Act, or any combination of them, that is

IRP Regulations

acting for the purpose of sponsoring a Convention refugee or a person in similar circumstances; or

(b) for the purposes of section 158, a sponsor within the meaning of the regulations made under *An Act respecting immigration to Québec*, R.S.Q., c. I-0.2, as amended from time to time.

("répondant")

"undertaking" means an undertaking in writing to the Minister to provide resettlement assistance, lodging and other basic necessities in Canada for a member of a class prescribed by this Division, the member's accompanying family members and any of the member's non-accompanying family members who meet the requirements of section 141, for the period determined in accordance with subsections 154(2) and (3). *("engagement")*

"urgent need of protection" means, in respect of a member of the Convention refugee abroad or the country of asylum class, that their life, liberty or physical safety is under immediate threat and, if not protected, the person is likely to be

(a) killed;

(b) subjected to violence, torture, sexual assault or arbitrary imprisonment; or

(c) returned to their country of nationality or of their former habitual residence.

("besoin urgent de protection")

"vulnerable" means, in respect of a Convention refugee or a person in similar circumstances, that the person has a greater need of protection than other applicants for protection abroad because of the person's particular circumstances that give rise to a heightened risk to their physical safety. *("vulnérable")*

SOR/2011-222, s. 3

General

139. (1) General requirements — A permanent resident visa shall be issued to a foreign national in need of refugee protection, and their accompanying family members, if following an examination it is established that

(a) the foreign national is outside Canada;

(b) the foreign national has submitted an application for a permanent resident visa under this Division in accordance with paragraphs 10(1)(a) to (c) and (2)(c.1) to (d) and sections 140.1 to 140.3;

(c) the foreign national is seeking to come to Canada to establish permanent residence;

(d) the foreign national is a person in respect of whom there is no reasonable prospect, within a reasonable period, of a durable solution in a country other than Canada, namely

(i) voluntary repatriation or resettlement in their country of nationality or habitual residence, or

(ii) resettlement or an offer of resettlement in another country;

(e) the foreign national is a member of one of the classes prescribed by this Division;

(f) one of the following is the case, namely

(i) the sponsor's sponsorship application for the foreign national and their family members included in the application for protection has been approved under these Regulations,

(ii) in the case of a member of the Convention refugee abroad class, financial assistance in the form of funds from a governmental resettlement assistance program is available in Canada for the foreign national and their family members included in the application for protection, or

(iii) the foreign national has sufficient financial resources to provide for the lodging, care and maintenance, and for the resettlement in Canada, of themself and their family members included in the application for protection;

(g) if the foreign national intends to reside in a province other than the Province of Quebec, the foreign national and their family members included in the application for protection will be able to become successfully established in Canada, taking into account the following factors:

(i) their resourcefulness and other similar qualities that assist in integration in a new society,

(ii) the presence of their relatives, including the relatives of a spouse or a common-law partner, or their sponsor in the expected community of resettlement,

(iii) their potential for employment in Canada, given their education, work experience and skills, and

(iv) their ability to learn to communicate in one of the official languages of Canada;

(h) if the foreign national intends to reside in the Province of Quebec, the competent authority of that Province is of the opinion that the foreign national and their family members included in the application for protection meet the selection criteria of the Province; and

(i) subject to subsections (3) and (4), the foreign national and their family members included in the application for protection are not inadmissible.

(2) **Exception** — Paragraph (1)(g) does not apply to a foreign national, or their family members included in the application for protection, who has been determined by an officer to be vulnerable or in urgent need of protection.

(3) **Financial inadmissibility — exemption** — A foreign national who is a member of a class prescribed by this Division, and meets the applicable requirements of this Division, is exempted from the application of section 39 of the Act.

(4) **Health grounds — exception** — A foreign national who is a member of a class prescribed by this Division, and meets the applicable requirements of this Division, is exempted from the application of paragraph 38(1)(c) of the Act.

SOR/2011-222, s. 4; SOR/2012-225, s. 4

140. Class of family members — Family members of an applicant who is determined to be a member of a class under this Division are members of the applicant's class.

140.1 Application — An application for a permanent resident visa submitted by a foreign national under this Division shall indicate that the foreign national is outside Canada and is making a claim for refugee protection and shall

(a) contain the name, address and country of birth of the applicant and of all their accompanying family members;

(b) contain the name and country of birth of all the applicant's non-accompanying family members; and

(c) indicate whether the applicant or any of their accompanying or non-accompanying family members is the spouse, common-law partner or conjugal partner of another person.

SOR/2012-225, s. 5

140.2 (1) Sponsorship of foreign national — requirement to attach applications — If the foreign national making an application for a permanent resident visa under this Division is being sponsored, the application for a permanent resident visa shall

(a) be accompanied by a sponsorship application referred to in paragraph 153(1)(b) by which the foreign national is being sponsored; or

(b) be attached to the sponsorship application sent by the sponsor in accordance with subsection 153(1.2).

(2) Place of application — The foreign national who has chosen to have their application for a permanent resident visa accompanied by the sponsorship application shall send the application for a permanent resident visa and the sponsorship application to the Department's Case Processing Centre in Canada for processing those applications.

SOR/2012-225, s. 5

140.3 (1) Referral requirement — If the foreign national making an application for a permanent resident visa under this Division is not being sponsored, a foreign national making an application for a permanent resident visa under this Division shall submit their application with one of the following referrals, if the referral has not yet been submitted to the immigration office by its issuer:

(a) a referral from a referral organization;

(b) a referral resulting from an arrangement between the Minister and the government of a foreign state or any institution of such a government relating to resettlement; or

(c) a referral resulting from an agreement relating to resettlement entered into by the Government of Canada and an international organization or the government of a foreign state.

(2) Exception — A foreign national may submit the application without a referral if they reside in a geographic area as determined by the Minister in accordance with subsection (3).

(3) Minister's determination — The Minister may determine on the basis of the following factors that a geographic area is an area in which circumstances justify the submission of permanent resident visa applications without a referral:

(a) advice from referral organizations with which the Minister has entered into a memorandum of understanding under section 143 that they are unable to make the number of referrals specified in their memorandum of understanding for the area;

(b) the inability of referral organizations to refer persons in the area;

(c) the resettlement needs in the area, after consultation with referral organizations that have substantial knowledge of the area; and

(d) the relative importance of resettlement needs in the area, within the context of resettlement needs globally.

(4) Place of application — If the foreign national who is being referred under any of paragraphs (1)(a) to (c) or if the foreign national resides in a geographic area as determined by the Minister in accordance with subsection (3), the foreign national shall submit their application to the immigration office outside Canada that serves the foreign national's place of residence.

SOR/2012-225, s. 5

140.4 Return of documents — An application for a permanent resident visa made under this Division, its related sponsorship application made under Division 2 of this Part and all documents submitted in support of the applications shall be returned to the person who sent the applications as a result of the choice made under subsection 140.2(1) if

(a) in the case of an application for a permanent resident visa, the requirements set out in paragraph 139(1)(b) are not met; or

(b) in the case of a sponsorship application, the requirements set out in paragraph 153(1)(b) and subsections 153(1.2) and (2) are not met.

SOR/2012-225, s. 5

141. (1) Non-accompanying family member — A permanent resident visa shall be issued to a family member who does not accompany the applicant if, following an examination, it is established that

(a) the family member was included in the applicant's permanent resident visa application at the time that application was made, or was added to that application before the applicant's departure for Canada;

(b) the family member submits their application to an officer outside Canada within one year from the day on which refugee protection is conferred on the applicant;

(c) the family member is not inadmissible;

(d) if the applicant is the subject of a sponsorship application referred to in paragraph 139(1)(f)(i), their sponsor has been notified of the family member's application and an officer is satisfied that there are adequate financial arrangements for resettlement; and

(e) in the case of a family member who intends to reside in the Province of Quebec, the competent authority of that Province is of the opinion that the foreign national meets the selection criteria of the Province.

(2) **Non-application of paragraph 139(1)(b)** — For greater certainty, the requirements set out in paragraph 139(1)(b) do not apply to the application of a non-accompanying family member.

SOR/2012-225, s. 6; SOR/2014-140, s. 14

142. Requirements — family members — Subject to subsections 25.1(1) and (6) to (8) and for the purposes of this Division, to be considered a family member of an applicant, a person must be a family member of the applicant

(a) at the time the application referred to in paragraph 139(1)(b) is made; and

(b) at the time of the determination of the application referred to in paragraph 141(1)(b).

SOR/2012-225, s. 7; SOR/2014-133, s. 9

143. (1) Memorandum of understanding — The Minister may enter into a memorandum of understanding with an organization for the purpose of locating and identifying Convention refugees and persons in similar circumstances if the organization demonstrates

(a) a working knowledge of the provisions of the Act relating to protection criteria; and

(b) an ability abroad to locate and identify Convention refugees and persons in similar circumstances.

(2) **Content of memorandum of understanding** — The memorandum of understanding shall include provisions with respect to

(a) the geographic area to be served by the organization;

(b) the number of referrals that may be made by the organization and the manner of referral;

(c) the training of members or employees of the organization; and

(d) the grounds for suspending or cancelling the memorandum of understanding.

Convention Refugees Abroad

144. Convention refugees abroad class — The Convention refugees abroad class is prescribed as a class of persons who may be issued a permanent resident visa on the basis of the requirements of this Division.

145. Member of Convention refugees abroad class — A foreign national is a Convention refugee abroad and a member of the Convention refugees abroad class if the foreign national has been determined, outside Canada, by an officer to be a Convention refugee.

Humanitarian-protected Persons Abroad

146. (1) Person in similar circumstances to those of a Convention refugee — For the purposes of subsection 12(3) of the Act, a person in similar circumstances to those of a Convention refugee is a member of the country of asylum class.

(2) Humanitarian-protected persons abroad — The country of asylum class is prescribed as a humanitarian-protected persons abroad class of persons who may be issued permanent resident visas on the basis of the requirements of this Division.

SOR/2011-222, s. 5

147. Member of country of asylum class — A foreign national is a member of the country of asylum class if they have been determined by an officer to be in need of resettlement because

(a) they are outside all of their countries of nationality and habitual residence; and

(b) they have been, and continue to be, seriously and personally affected by civil war, armed conflict or massive violation of human rights in each of those countries.

Case Law

El Karm v. Canada (Minister of Citizenship & Immigration), 2006 CarswellNat 2410, 2006 FC 972 — The applicant was determined, by a visa officer, not to be eligible to be sponsored as a private group-sponsored refugee to Canada because he was not outside his country of habitual residence. The applicant sought judicial review of the visa officer's decision.

The applicant, born in Jordan in 1973, was a stateless Palestinian. His family moved to Egypt in the 1980s where he completed his education. All of his siblings still live in Egypt. In June 1998, the applicant left Egypt for employment in Gaza. He remained in Gaza legally until November 1998 at which point he lost his status for failure to renew his visitor's permit. He also lost his right to return to Egypt by failing to return to Egypt every six months to renew his residency permit. In March 2003, the applicant attempted to re-enter Egypt but was caught and detained for 20 days because of his illegal entry. Since his release, he has remained in Cairo.

The visa officer, in reaching his conclusion, concluded that since the applicant was inside his country of habitual residence he did not meet the requirements of s. 147(a) of the Regulations. The court found that the visa officer's conclusion was reasonable, since it was based on the fact that the applicant completed all of his education in Egypt, lived in Egypt from the 1980s until 1998, lived in Egypt again from 2003 to 2005, had siblings living in Egypt, the applicant's right to return to Egypt had lapsed but he was allowed to stay in Egypt for the last two years and the Egyptian government has a policy of not removing long-term Palestinian residents from Egypt. Against all of that factual background, it was at least reasonable for the visa officer to conclude that Egypt was a country of habitual residence for the applicant.

148. [Repealed SOR/2011-222, s. 6.]

149. [Repealed SOR/2011-222, s. 6.]

150. [Repealed SOR/2012-225, s. 8.]

151. Travel document — An officer shall issue a temporary travel document to a foreign national who has been determined to be a member of a class prescribed by this Division and who

    (a) holds a permanent resident visa or a temporary resident permit;

    (b) does not hold a valid passport or travel document issued by their country of nationality or the country of their present or former habitual residence;

    (c) does not hold a valid travel document issued by the United Nations or the International Committee of the Red Cross and is unable to obtain such a document within a reasonable time; and

    (d) would be unable to travel to Canada if the temporary travel document were not issued.

Protected Temporary Residents

[Heading added SOR/2004-167, s. 48.]

151.1 (1) Protected temporary residents class — The protected temporary residents class is prescribed as a class of persons who may become permanent residents on the basis of the requirements of this section.

(2) Member of the class — A foreign national is a protected temporary resident and a member of the protected temporary residents class if the foreign national holds a temporary resident permit and

    (a) became a temporary resident under a temporary resident permit for protection reasons after making a claim for refugee protection outside Canada under section 99 of the Act; or

    (b) was issued a Minister's permit under section 37 of the former Act after seeking admission to Canada under section 7 of the former Regulations or section 4 of the *Humanitarian Designated Classes Regulations*.

(2.1) Application — A foreign national destined for Quebec does not become a member of the protected temporary residents class described in paragraph (2)(a) if they have not received a selection certificate from the Province of Quebec.

(3) Former Act and Regulations — In subsection (2), "former Act" has the same meaning as in section 187 of the Act and "former Regulations" and "*Humanitarian Designated Classes Regulations*" have the same meaning as in subsection 316(1) of these Regulations.

SOR/2004-167, s. 48

DIVISION 2 — SPONSORSHIP

152. (1) Sponsorship agreements — The Minister may enter into a sponsorship agreement with a sponsor for the purpose of facilitating the processing of sponsorship applications.

(2) Contents of agreement — A sponsorship agreement shall include provisions relating to

(a) settlement plans;

(b) financial requirements;

(c) assistance to be provided by the Department;

(d) the standard of conduct expected of the sponsor;

(e) reporting requirements; and

(f) the grounds for suspending or cancelling the agreement.

[Editor's Note: SOR/2002-227, s. 336 provides that a sponsorship agreement with the Minister made under the former Immigration Act, *R.S.C. 1985, c. I-2 and the former* Immigration Regulations, 1978, *SOR/78-172 does not cease to have effect for the sole reason of s. 152 of the new* Immigration and Refugee Protection Regulations, *SOR/2002-227 coming into force on June 28, 2002.]*

153. (1) Sponsorship requirements — In order to sponsor a foreign national and their family members who are members of a class prescribed by Division 1, a sponsor

(a) must reside or have representatives in the expected community of settlement;

(b) must make a sponsorship application that includes a settlement plan, an undertaking and, if the sponsor has not entered into a sponsorship agreement with the Minister, a document issued by the United Nations High Commissioner for Refugees or a foreign state certifying the status of the foreign national as a refugee under the rules applicable to the United Nations High Commissioner for Refugees or the applicable laws of the foreign state, as the case may be; and

(c) must not be — or include — an individual, a corporation or an unincorporated organization or association that was a party to a sponsorship in which they defaulted on an undertaking and remain in default.

(1.1) Non-application of paragraphs 13(1)(a) and (b) — Paragraphs 13(1)(a) and (b) do not apply to the document referred to in paragraph (1)(b) issued by the United Nations High Commissioner for Refugees or a foreign state.

(1.2) Place of application — If the foreign national has chosen to have their application for a permanent resident visa attached to the sponsorship application in accordance with paragraph 140.2(1)(b), the sponsor must send the sponsorship application and the application for a permanent resident visa to the Department's Case Processing Centre in Canada for processing those applications.

(2) Undertaking — The undertaking referred to in paragraph (1)(b) shall be signed by each party to the sponsorship.

(3) Joint and several or solidary liability — All parties to the undertaking are jointly and severally or solidarily liable.

(4) End of default — A party or a sponsor who defaults on an undertaking ceases to be in default

(a) in the case of a sponsor who defaults on a financial obligation, when the sponsor has reimbursed the government concerned, in full or in accordance with an agreement with that government, for amounts paid by the government;

(b) in the case of a party, other than an organization or association, who defaults on a financial obligation, when the defaulting party has reimbursed any other party to the sponsorship, in full or in accordance with an agreement with that party, for amounts paid by that party;

(c) in the case of a sponsor who defaults on a non-financial obligation, when the sponsor satisfies an officer that they are in compliance with the obligation; and

(d) in the case of an organization or association that was a party to a sponsorship and defaulted for any reason, when a period of five years has elapsed from the date of default.

SOR/2012-225, s. 9; SOR/2014-140, s. 15(2)

154. (1) Approval of application — An officer shall approve an application referred to in paragraph 153(1)(b) if, on the basis of the documentation submitted with the application, the officer determines that

(a) the sponsor has the financial resources to fulfil the settlement plan for the duration of the undertaking, unless subsection 157(1) applies; and

(b) the sponsor has made adequate arrangements in anticipation of the arrival of the foreign national and their family members in the expected community of settlement.

(2) Duration of sponsor's undertaking — Subject to subsection (3), the duration of an undertaking is one year.

(3) Officer's determination — An officer may, on the basis of the assessment made under paragraph 139(1)(g), require that the duration of the undertaking be more than one year but not more than three years.

[Editor's Note: SOR/2002-227, s. 337(1) provides that, subject to SOR/2002-227, ss. 337(2) and 337(3), a sponsor who made an undertaking within the meaning of paragraph (b) of the definition "undertaking" in s. 2(1) of the Immigration Regulations, 1978, *SOR/78-172, or of the definition "undertaking" in s. 1(1) of the* Humanitarian Designated Classes Regulations, *SOR/97-183, and in respect of whom an immigration officer was satisfied that the requirements of ss. 7.1(2)(d) or 5(2)(d) of those Regulations, respectively, were met is deemed to be a sponsor whose application has been approved by an officer under s. 154 of the* Immigration and Refugee Protection Regulations, *SOR/2002-227 (the "new Regulations").*

SOR/2002-227, s. 337(2) provides that SOR/2002-227, s. 337(1) does not apply to a sponsor who requests that a person be added to his or her undertaking.

SOR/2002-227, s. 337(3) further provides that SOR/2002-227, s. 337(1) does not apply to a sponsor who is ineligible to be a party to a sponsorship under s. 156 of the new Regulations.]

155. Revoking approval — An officer shall revoke an approval given in respect of an application under section 154 if the officer determines that the sponsor no longer meets the requirements of paragraph 154(1)(a) or (b) or is ineligible under subsection 156(1).

156. (1) Ineligibility to be a party to a sponsorship — The following persons are ineligible to be a party to a sponsorship:

(a) a person who has been convicted in Canada of the offence of murder or an offence set out in Schedule I or II to the *Corrections and Conditional Release Act*, regardless of whether it was prosecuted by indictment, if a period of five years has not elapsed since the completion of the person's sentence;

(b) a person who has been convicted of an offence outside Canada that, if committed in Canada, would constitute an offence referred to in paragraph (a), if a period of five years has not elapsed since the completion of the person's sentence imposed under a foreign law;

(c) a person who is in default of any support payment obligations ordered by a court;

(d) a person who is subject to a removal order;

(e) a person who is subject to a revocation proceeding under the *Citizenship Act*; and

(f) a person who is detained in any penitentiary, jail, reformatory or prison.

(2) Exception if pardoned — For the purpose of paragraph (1)(a), a sponsorship application may not be refused on the basis of a conviction in respect of which a pardon has been granted and has not ceased to have effect or been revoked under the *Criminal Records Act*, or in respect of which there has been a final determination of an acquittal.

SOR/2010-195, s. 14(1)

157. (1) Joint assistance sponsorship — If an officer determines that special needs exist in respect of a member of a class prescribed by Division 1, the Department shall endeavour to identify a sponsor in order to make the financial assistance of the Government of Canada available for the purpose of sponsorship. A sponsor identified by the Department is exempt from the financial requirements of paragraph 154(1)(a).

(2) Definition of "special needs" — In this section, "special needs" means that a person has greater need of settlement assistance than other applicants for protection abroad owing to personal circumstances, including

(a) a large number of family members;

(b) **trauma resulting from violence or torture;**

(c) **medical disabilities; and**

(d) **the effects of systemic discrimination.**

158. Settlement in the Province of Quebec — If the foreign national and their family members intend to reside in the Province of Quebec, the sponsor must meet the requirements for sponsorship that are provided by regulations made under *An Act respecting immigration to Québec*, R.S.Q., c. I-0.2, as amended from time to time. In such a case, the requirements of this Division, other than section 156, do not apply.

DIVISION 3 — DETERMINATION OF ELIGIBILITY OF CLAIM

159. Working day — For the purposes of subsections 100(1) and (3) of the Act,

(a) **a working day does not include Saturdays or holidays;**

(b) **a day that is not a working day is not included in the calculation of the three-day period; and**

(c) **the three-day period begins from the day on which the claim is received.**

159.1 Definitions — The following definitions apply in this section and sections 159.2 to 159.7.

"**Agreement**" means the Agreement dated December 5, 2002 between the Government of Canada and the Government of the United States of America for Cooperation in the Examination of Refugee Status Claims from Nationals of Third Countries. *("Accord")*

"**claimant**" means a claimant referred to in paragraph 101(1)(e) of the Act. *("demandeur")*

"**designated country**" means a country designated by section 159.3. *("pays désigné")*

"**family member**", in respect of a claimant, means their spouse or common-law partner, their legal guardian, and any of the following persons, namely, their child, father, mother, brother, sister, grandfather, grandmother, grandchild, uncle, aunt, nephew or niece. *("membre de la famille")*

"**legal guardian**", in respect of a claimant who has not attained the age of 18 years, means a person who has custody of the claimant or who is empowered to act on the claimant's behalf by virtue of a court order or written agreement or by operation of law. *("tuteur légal")*

"**United States**" means the United States of America, but does not include Puerto Rico, the Virgin Islands, Guam or any other United States of America possession or territory. *("États-Unis")*

SOR/2004-217, s. 2

Case Law

Canadian Council for Refugees v. R. (2008), 74 Admin. L.R. (4th) 79, 2008 CarswellNat 1995, 2008 CarswellNat 2197, 2008 FCA 229; leave to appeal to S.C.C. refused 2008 CarswellNat 5170, 2008 CarswellNat 5171 (S.C.C.) — This was an appeal from a decision of Phelan J. (the "applications judge"), granting an application for judicial review by the Canadian Council of Refugees, the Canadian Council of Churches, Amnesty International and John Doe ("the respondents"), declaring invalid sections of 159.1 to 159.7 of the Immigration and Refugee Protection Regulations, and the Agreement between the Government of Canada and the Government of the United States of America for Co-operation in the Examination of Refugee Status Claims from Nationals of Third Countries (the "Safe Third Country Agreement"). The Regulations at issue implement into domestic law a Safe Third Country Agreement between Canada and the United States whereby if a refugee enters Canada from the U.S. at a land border port-of-entry, Canada will, subject to specified exceptions, send the refugee back to the U.S. The same applies for refugees crossing by land from Canada to the U.S. The appeal was allowed and the decision of the applications judge set aside. The appropriate standard of review in respect of the decision of the Governor In Council ("GIC") to designate the United States as a "Safe Third Country" pursuant to s. 102 of the Immigration and Refugee Protection Act is correctness. The Federal Court of Appeal took issue with the applications judge's suggestion that unless "compliance" is made a condition precedent to the designation of a country, the GIC would have discretion to designate a country that does not comply. Subsection 101(2) does not refer to "actual" compliance or compliance "in absolute terms" nor does it otherwise specify the type and extent of compliance contemplated. However, Parliament has specified the four factors to be considered in determining whether a country can be designated. These factors are general in nature and are indicative of Parliament's intent that the matter of compliance be assessed on the basis of an appreciation by the GIC of the country's policies, practices and human rights record. Once it is accepted, as it must be in this case, that the GIC has given due consideration to these four factors, and formed the opinion that the candidate country is compliant with the relevant articles of the Conventions, there is nothing left to be reviewed judicially. The Federal Court of Appeal concluded there was no factual basis on which to assess the alleged Charter breaches. The respondents' main contention was directed at a border officer's lack of discretion to forego returning a claimant to the U.S. for reasons other than the enumerated exceptions set out in s. 159.5 of the Regulations. This challenge, however, should be assessed in a proper factual context - that is, when advanced by a refugee who has been denied asylum in Canada pursuant to the Regulations and faces a real risk of refoulement in being sent back to the U.S. pursuant to the Safe Third Country Agreement. In this case the refugee never came to Canada, and instead claimed that he would have sought asylum in Canada but for the Regulations.

Odicho v. Canada (Minister of Citizenship & Immigration) (2008), 75 Imm. L.R. (3d) 45, 2008 CarswellNat 4011, 2008 CarswellNat 3442, 2008 FC 1039 — The applicants sought judicial review of a visa officer's decision to refuse to issue a permanent resident visa to the wife. The applicants argued that the visa officer erred by failing to consider H&C grounds, pursuant to subs. 25 of the IRPA. They submit that they specifically requested that the wife's application for permanent residence in Canada be considered on the basis of s. 25. The husband had been landed in Canada in January 2005 and his initial application to sponsor his wife in May 2005 was refused on the basis that he had not disclosed his marriage when he was landed. The application on behalf of a dependent child was refused for the same reason but was subsequently reversed. The visa officer, however, maintained the rejection of the application on behalf of the wife on the basis of para. 117(9)(d) of the Regulations.

There was no dispute that the husband failed to declare his wife as a non-accompanying dependant when he landed in Canada in January 2005. There is no evidence to challenge the *bona fides* of the marriage of the applicants. There is no evidence to challenge the status of the infant as their child. The failure of the husband to declare the change in marital status when he landed in Canada gave rise to the exclusion of his wife pursuant to the terms of para. 117(9)(d). The court held that the visa officer apparently ignored the material that was submitted concerning the "circumstances" of the husband's failure to declare the change in his marital status at the time he landed in Canada. The applicants carry the burden of establishing the evidence to justify an exercise of discretion, but the discharge of this burden does not require superfluity. The visa officer's decision does not demonstrate an understanding of the purpose of subs. 25(1) of the Act, which is to overcome the consequences of being in breach of statutory requirements. The initial decision which excluded the child, as well as the wife, illustrates an excess of zeal on the part of the original decision maker, if not a misunderstanding of s. 117 of the Regulations. The application for judicial review was allowed. The matter was remitted for reconsideration by a different member of the Canadian Embassy.

159.2   Non-application — former habitual residence — Paragraph 101(1)(e) of the Act does not apply to a claimant who is a stateless person who comes directly or indirectly to Canada from a designated country that is their country of former habitual residence.

SOR/2004-217, s. 2

159.3 Designation — United States — The United States is designated under paragraph 102(1)(a) of the Act as a country that complies with Article 33 of the Refugee Convention and Article 3 of the Convention Against Torture, and is a designated country for the purpose of the application of paragraph 101(1)(e) of the Act.

SOR/2004-217, s. 2

Case Law

Editor's Note: See also case summaries under s. 101(1) of the Act.

Mendez v. Canada (Ministre de la Citoyenneté & de l'Immigration), 2005 CarswellNat 369, 2005 FC 75, [2005] F.C.J. No. 152 — Following the introduction of the regulations known as "*Safe Third Country Regulations*," as of December 29, 2004, claims made by those who arrive in Canada via the United States or other safe third country, will no longer be referred to the Refugee Protection Division. Prior to the passage of these regulations, the existing jurisprudence stated that the failure to claim in a safe third country could be considered by the Board in examining subjective fear. A short stay in a safe third country *en route* is not necessarily considered a material enough sojourn to oblige the claimant to declare themselves as a refugee on their way to Canada. This was particularly true of the United States since many claimants must travel through the United States to get to Canada.

159.4 (1) Non-application — ports of entry other than land ports of entry   Paragraph 101(1)(e) of the Act does not apply to a claimant who seeks to enter Canada at

(a) a location that is not a port of entry;

(b) a port of entry that is a harbour port, including a ferry landing; or

(c) subject to subsection (2), a port of entry that is an airport.

(2) In transit exception — Paragraph 101(1)(e) of the Act applies to a claimant who has been ordered removed from the United States and who seeks to enter Canada at a port of entry that is an airport while they are in transit through Canada from the United States in the course of the enforcement of that order.

SOR/2004-217, s. 2

159.5 Non-application — claimants at land ports of entry — Paragraph 101(1)(e) of the Act does not apply if a claimant who seeks to enter Canada at a location other than one identified in paragraphs 159.4(1)(a) to (c) establishes, in accordance with subsection 100(4) of the Act, that

(a) a family member of the claimant is in Canada and is a Canadian citizen;

(b) a family member of the claimant is in Canada and is

(i) a protected person within the meaning of subsection 95(2) of the Act,

(ii) a permanent resident under the Act, or

(iii) a person in favour of whom a removal order has been stayed in accordance with section 233;

(c) a family member of the claimant who has attained the age of 18 years is in Canada and has made a claim for refugee protection that has been referred to the Board for determination, unless

(i) the claim has been withdrawn by the family member,

(ii) the claim has been abandonned by the family member,

(iii) the claim has been rejected, or

(iv) any pending proceedings or proceedings respecting the claim have been terminated under subsection 104(2) of the Act or any decision respecting the claim has been nullified under that subsection;

(d) a family member of the claimant who has attained the age of 18 years is in Canada and is the holder of a work permit or study permit other than

(i) a work permit that was issued under paragraph 206(b) or that has become invalid as a result of the application of section 209, or

(ii) a study permit that has become invalid as a result of the application of section 222;

(e) the claimant is a person who

(i) has not attained the age of 18 years and is not accompanied by their mother, father or legal guardian,

(ii) has neither a spouse nor a common-law partner, and

(iii) has neither a mother or father nor a legal guardian in Canada or the United States;

(f) the claimant is the holder of any of the following documents, excluding any document issued for the sole purpose of transit through Canada, namely,

(i) a permanent resident visa or a temporary resident visa referred to in section 6 and subsection 7(1), respectively,

(ii) a temporary resident permit issued under subsection 24(1) of the Act,

(iii) a travel document referred to in subsection 31(3) of the Act,

(iv) refugee travel papers issued by the Minister, or

(v) a temporary travel document referred to in section 151;

(g) the claimant is a person

(i) who may, under the Act or these Regulations, enter Canada without being required to hold a visa, and

(ii) who would, if the claimant were entering the United States, be required to hold a visa; or

(h) the claimant is

(i) a foreign national who is seeking to re-enter Canada in circumstances where they have been refused entry to the United States without having a refugee claim adjudicated there, or

(ii) a permanent resident who has been ordered removed from the United States and is being returned to Canada.

SOR/2004-217, s. 2; SOR/2009-290, s. 2; SOR/2015-46, s. 1(c)

Case Law

Baron v. Canada (Minister of Citizenship & Immigration), 2008 CarswellNat 466, 2008 CarswellNat 1923, 2008 FC 245 — This review concerned a decision by a CBSA officer that the applicant did not qualify for exemption under the Safe Third Country Agreement (STCA) between Canada and the United States. He had claimed exemption on the basis of having a family member in Canada. The applicant was interviewed by a CBSA officer to determine if he qualified for exemption under the STCA as a class of persons who would otherwise be returned to the United States. He relied on the fact that his sister had made a refugee claim. The CBSA officer determined that the sister's claim had been rejected by the Immigration and Refugee Board, that there was no stay of her removal and therefore the sister did not qualify as an "anchor relative" to ground the request for exemption. Section 159.5(c)(iii) does not contemplate finality of all appeal processes. The term "rejected" should be given consistent meaning and it is not one that includes "finally rejected." Once the sister's claim was rejected, she ceased to be the anchor relative.

The court certified the following two questions:

(1) Does the term "rejected" in the phrase "unless the claim has been rejected" in s. 159.5(c)(iii) of the *Immigration and Refugee Protection Regulations* include the final determination of all reviews and appeals which may flow from the initial rejection decision?

(2) What are the consequences to those persons whose claim was denied under s. 159.5(c)(iii) if the decision in *Canadian Council for Refugees v. Canada*, 2007 FC 1262, is upheld in respect of the *ultra vires* of s. 159 of the Regulations.

159.6 Non-application — claimants at land ports of entry and in transit — Paragraph 101(1)(e) of the Act does not apply if a claimant establishes, in accordance with subsection 100(4) of the Act, that the claimant

(a) is charged in the United States with, or has been convicted there of, an offence that is punishable with the death penalty in the United States; or

(b) is charged in a country other than the United States with, or has been convicted there of, an offence that is punishable with the death penalty in that country.

(c) [Repealed SOR/2009-210, s. 1.]

SOR/2004-217, s. 2; SOR/2009-210, s. 1

159.7 (1) Temporal operation — For the purposes of paragraph 101(1)(e) of the Act, the application of all or part of sections 159.1 to 159.6 and this section is discontinued, in accordance with subsections (2) to (6), if

(a) a notice of suspension of the Agreement setting out the period of suspension is publicized broadly in the various regions of Canada by the Minister via information media and on the website of the Department;

(b) a notice of renewal of the suspension of the Agreement setting out the period of renewal of suspension is published in accordance with subsection (6);

(c) a notice of suspension of a part of the Agreement is issued by the Government of Canada and the Government of the United States; or

(d) a notice of termination of the Agreement is issued by the Government of Canada or the Government of the United States.

(2) Paragraph (1)(a) — notice of suspension of Agreement — Subject to subsection (3), if a notice of suspension of the Agreement is publicized under paragraph (1)(a), sections 159.2 to 159.6 are rendered inoperative for a period of up to three months that shall be set out in the notice, which period shall begin on the day after the day on which the notice is publicized.

(3) Paragraph (1)(b) — notice of renewal of suspension of Agreement — If a notice of renewal of the suspension of the Agreement is published under paragraph (1)(b), sections 159.2 to 159.6 are rendered inoperative for the further period of up to three months set out in the notice.

(4) Paragraph (1)(c) — suspension of part of Agreement — If a notice of suspension of part of the Agreement is issued under paragraph (1)(c), those provisions of these Regulations relating to the application of the Agreement that are referred to in the notice are rendered inoperative for a period that shall be set out in the notice. All other provisions of these Regulations continue to apply.

(5) Paragraph (1)(d) — termination of Agreement — If a notice of termination of the Agreement is issued under paragraph (1)(d), sections 159.1 to 159.6 and this section cease to have effect on the day set out in the notice.

IRP Regulations

(6) Publication requirement — *Canada Gazette* — Any notice referred to in paragraph (1)(b), (c) or (d) shall be published in the *Canada Gazette*, Part I, not less than seven days before the day on which the renewal, suspension in part or termination provided for in the notice is effective.

SOR/2004-217, s. 2

DIVISION 3.1 — CLAIM FOR REFUGEE PROTECTION — TIME LIMITS
[Heading added SOR/2012-252, s. 1.]

Documents and Information
[Heading added SOR/2012-252, s. 1.]

159.8 (1) Time limit — provision of documents and information to officer — For the purpose of subsection 99(3.1) of the Act, a person who makes a claim for refugee protection inside Canada other than at a port of entry must provide an officer with the documents and information referred to in that subsection not later than the day on which the officer determines the eligibility of their claim under subsection 100(1) of the Act.

(2) Time limit — provision of documents and information to Refugee Protection Division — Subject to subsection (3), for the purpose of subsection 100(4) of the Act, a person who makes a claim for refugee protection inside Canada at a port of entry must provide the Refugee Protection Division with the documents and information referred to in subsection 100(4) not later than 15 days after the day on which the claim is referred to that Division.

(3) Extension — If the documents and information cannot be provided within the time limit set out in subsection (2), the Refugee Protection Division may, for reasons of fairness and natural justice, extend that time limit by the number of days that is necessary in the circumstances.

SOR/2012-252, s. 1

Hearing Before Refugee Protection Division
[Heading added SOR/2012-252, s. 1.]

159.9 (1) Time limits for hearing — Subject to subsections (2) and (3), for the purpose of subsection 100(4.1) of the Act, the date fixed for the hearing before the Refugee Protection Division must be not later than

(a) in the case of a claimant referred to in subsection 111.1(2) of the Act,

(i) 30 days after the day on which the claim is referred to the Refugee Protection Division, if the claim is made inside Canada other than at a port of entry, and

(ii) 45 days after the day on which the claim is referred to the Refugee Protection Division, if the claim is made inside Canada at a port of entry; and

(b) in the case of any other claimant, 60 days after the day on which the claim is referred to the Refugee Protection Division, whether the claim is made inside Canada at a port of entry or inside Canada other than at a port of entry.

(2) **Exclusion** — If the time limit set out in subparagraph (1)(a)(i) or (ii) or paragraph (1)(b) ends on a Saturday, that time limit is extended to the next working day.

(3) **Exceptions** — If the hearing cannot be held within the time limit set out in subparagraph (1)(a)(i) or (ii) or paragraph (1)(b) for any of the following reasons, the hearing must be held as soon as feasible after that time limit:

(a) for reasons of fairness and natural justice;

(b) because of a pending investigation or inquiry relating to any of sections 34 to 37 of the Act; or

(c) because of operational limitations of the Refugee Protection Division.

SOR/2012-252, s. 1

Appeal to Refugee Appeal Division

[Heading added SOR/2012-252, s. 1.]

159.91 (1) Time limit for appeal — Subject to subsection (2), for the purpose of subsection 110(2.1) of the Act,

(a) the time limit for a person or the Minister to file an appeal to the Refugee Appeal Division against a decision of the Refugee Protection Division is 15 days after the day on which the person or the Minister receives written reasons for the decision; and

(b) the time limit for a person or the Minister to perfect such an appeal is 30 days after the day on which the person or the Minister receives written reasons for the decision.

(2) **Extension** — If the appeal cannot be filed within the time limit set out in paragraph (1)(a) or perfected within the time limit set out in paragraph (1)(b), the Refugee Appeal Division may, for reasons of fairness and natural justice, extend each of those time limits by the number of days that is necessary in the circumstances.

SOR/2012-252, s. 1

159.92 (1) Time limit for decision — Subject to subsection (2), for the purpose of subsection 110(3.1) of the Act, except when a hearing is held under subsection 110(6) of the Act, the time limit for the Refugee Appeal Division to make a decision on an appeal is 90 days after the day on which the appeal is perfected.

(2) **Exception** — If it is not possible for the Refugee Appeal Division to make a decision on an appeal within the time limit set out in subsection (1), the decision must be made as soon as feasible after that time limit.

SOR/2012-252, s. 1

DIVISION 4 — PRE-REMOVAL RISK ASSESSMENT

160. (1) Application for protection — Subject to subsection (2) and for the purposes of subsection 112(1) of the Act, a person may apply for protection after they are given notification to that effect by the Department.

(2) No notification — A person described in section 165 or 166 may apply for protection in accordance with that section without being given notification to that effect by the Department.

(3) Notification — Notification shall be given

(a) in the case of a person who is subject to a removal order that is in force, before removal from Canada; and

(b) in the case of a person named in a certificate described in subsection 77(1) of the Act, when the summary of information and other evidence is filed under subsection 77(2) of the Act.

(4) When notification is given — Notification is given

(a) when the person is given the application for protection form by hand; or

(b) if the application for protection form is sent by mail, seven days after the day on which it was sent to the person at the last address provided by them to the Department.

SOR/2008-193, s. 1

Case Law

Asfaw v. Canada (Minister of Citizenship and Immigration), 2016 FC 366, 2016 CarswellNat 1150, 2016 CarswellNat 2692 — This was an application for judicial review of the applicant's pre-removal risk assessment which was submitted before the applicant had received a notification of eligibility to apply for a PRRA pursuant to subs. 160(1). In the case before the court, there was no suggestion that the applicant is to be soon removed from Canada such that the notification requirement under s. 160(3) of the Regulations came into effect. There is no imminent removal planned, nor was it likely until the applicant left the sanctuary or the Minister took steps to forcibly remove her from the church where she now resides. A PRRA *should not* be conducted immediately, because its effectiveness in safeguarding the applicant's right of *non-refoulement* depends on it being conducted just prior to removal. Accordingly, even if the services assistant erred in taking the position that the responsibility to issue a notification was with CBSA, no notification had issued nor was there reason to think it ought to be issued when requested. The decision was reasonable as this applicant had no automatic right to a PRRA nor does she have a right to require a notification be issued to permit the PRRA at this time. If the applicant wishes to have the benefit of a PRRA, then she must be close to removal and that is unlikely to happen so long as she remains in the church. Application for judicial review was dismissed.

Enabulele v. Canada (Ministry of Public Safety & Emergency Preparedness) (2009), 81 Imm. L.R. (3d) 78, 347 F.T.R. 309 (Eng.), 2009 FC 641, 2009 CarswellNat 1876, 2009 CarswellNat 5904 — The applicant, a citizen of Nigeria married to a Canadian citizen, applied for permanent residence under the Spouse or Common-law Partner in Canada Class, pursuant to the Ministerial Policy, released in February 2005, and contained in

Appendix H of the Citizenship and Immigration of Canada's Operational Manual for Inland Processing IP8. This policy is designed to allow spouses or common-law partners in Canada to apply for permanent residence from within Canada in accordance with the same criteria as members of the Spouse or Common-law Partner in Canada Class regardless of their immigration status. The applicant was advised, by reason of having been charged with two counts of sexual assault, that he was not entitled to a 60-day administrative deferral of removal under the policy. The applicant sought to challenge the policy on the basis that it violated his s. 7 and s. 11(d) *Charter* rights. The court accepted the respondent's submission that the administrative deferral under the policy sought by the applicant would have expired even if the officer had found that the applicant was eligible for it. Notwithstanding this, the court considered the *Charter* issues raised in the application.

The applicant argued that the policy compromised his security in that it did not allow him to defend his innocence of the charges laid against him. He says the policy stigmatizes those charged but not convicted of criminal charges. The court found the applicant's argument without merit and concluded his s. 7 *Charter* rights were not engaged in the circumstances. The impugned policy renders the applicant ineligible for an administrative deferral by reason of his criminal charges. It does not follow, however, that the applicant will be removed without a proper risk assessment. The PRRA process, to which the applicant is entitled, is designed to assist foreign nationals who may be required to leave Canada. It is the means by which the applicant can have his risk assessed prior to his departure. It is the very process which provides for consideration of the applicant's life, liberty and security interest in a pre-removal context. The applicant's access to that process was in no way affected by the policy. The application for judicial review was dismissed. The following question was certified:

> Does the Minister's policy on administrative deferral of removal found under IP8 offend the applicant's sections 7 and 11(d) rights of the *Canadian Charter of Rights and Freedoms*?

Revich c. Canada (Ministre de la Citoyenneté & de l'Immigration) (2005), 280 F.T.R. 201 (Eng.), (sub nom. *Revich v. Canada (Minister of Citizenship & Immigration)*) 2005 CarswellNat 5741, 2005 FC 852 — The respondent issued a departure order against the applicant. Under the old legislation, the departure order was conditional and could not become effective until one of the conditions provided in subs. 49(2) had occurred. The applicant's refugee claim was refused and the departure order came into force 15 days after the notification of the rejection of the refugee claim. The Federal Court refused an application for leave against the decision of the RPD. The refusal ended the stay of execution of the departure order. The departure order became enforceable and became a deportation order pursuant to Reg. 224(2). The applicant was then notified of her right to file a pre-removal risk assessment (PRRA) application. The notice resulted in a stay of execution of the deportation order pending the PRRA decision. The PRRA application was rejected and the stay provided for under s. 232 of the Regulations ended with the rejection of the PRRA application.

Under para. 160(3)(a) of the Regulations, the department is required to notify the persons subject to a removal order, such as the present applicant, that they are entitled to apply for a PRRA decision. However, neither the Act nor the Regulations states at what time this notice must be issued. Meanwhile, because the person's refugee claim has been rejected, the stay of execution of the removal order is no longer in force. In other words, the removal order is "enforceable" and, after a 30-day period, the order will become a deportation order unless the person voluntarily leaves the country. The Regulations also provide for the stay of execution of a removal order when a person is notified that he or she may file a PRRA application.

The applicant in this case did not attack the combined effect of these statutory provisions but instead targeted the department's decision to send the notice under s. 160 of the Regulations after the removal order became a deportation order, and thereby depriving her of the opportunity to have the stay that the PRRA application would have triggered. So the essential question was whether it was fair for the department to act in this way.

The purpose of the PRRA is to prevent a foreign national whose refugee claim has already been rejected from being required to return to his country of residence or citizenship when the situation has changed in that country and he would be exposed to a risk of persecution. If this review is to be effective and consistent with Parliament's intention when creating it, the PRRA must coincide as closely as possible with the person's departure from the country. The court concluded that if an interested party voluntarily complies with the removal order under s. 238 of the Regulations, within the requisite period, he or she may avoid the consequences of the deportation order. Requiring the department to issue a notice before the deportation order comes into force would in turn eliminate the main incentive for people to comply voluntarily with the removal order prior to the PRRA decision. The department's decision to send a notice after the departure order became a deportation order does not fail to meet the requirements of procedural fairness having regard to the objective of the PRRA process, which is to serve as a final "safeguard" before the interested party is required to leave the country. There is nothing inequitable in the applicant asking in the future for written authorization to return to Canada since she knew that this was a consequence of her choice to not leave voluntarily. The application for judicial review was dismissed.

The following question was certified: Is the PRRA officer required to send the notice under s. 160 of the *Immigration Refugee Protection Regulations* before the departure order becomes a deportation order, thereby putting the foreign national in an irregular situation? Should the answer to the preceding question be positive, should the deportation order be set aside?

160.1 Criterion — exemption from application of paragraphs 112(2)(b.1) or (c) of the Act — For the purposes of subsection 112(2.1) of the Act, the Minister must consider, when an exemption is made, any event having arisen in a country that could place all or some of its nationals or former habitual residents referred to in that subsection in a situation similar to those referred to in section 96 or 97 of the Act for which a person may be determined to be a Convention refugee or a person in need of protection.

SOR/2012-154, s. 7

161. (1) Submissions — Subject to section 166, a person applying for protection may make written submissions in support of their application and for that purpose may be assisted, at their own expense, by a barrister or solicitor or other counsel.

(2) New evidence — A person who makes written submissions must identify the evidence presented that meets the requirements of paragraph 113(a) of the Act and indicate how that evidence relates to them.

SOR/2014-139, s. 4

162. Application within 15-day period — An application received within 15 days after notification was given under section 160 shall not be decided until at least 30 days after notification was given. The removal order is stayed under section 232 until the earliest of the events referred to in paragraphs 232(c) to (f) occurs.

163. Applications after the 15-day period — A person who has remained in Canada since being given notification under section 160 may make an application after a period of 15 days has elapsed from notification being given under that section, but the application does not result in a stay of the removal order. Written submissions, if any, must accompany the application.

164. Application that must be received within 15-day period — certificate — Despite section 163, an application by a person who is named in a certificate described in subsection 77(1) of the Act must be received within 15 days after notification was given under section 160. An application received within that period shall not be decided until at least 30 days after notification was given.

165. Subsequent application — A person whose application for protection was rejected and who has remained in Canada since being given notification under section 160 may make another application. Written submissions, if any, must accompany the application. For greater certainty, the application does not result in a stay of the removal order.

166. Application at port of entry — An application for protection by a foreign national against whom a removal order is made at a port of entry as a result of a determination of inadmissibility on entry into Canada must, if the order is in force, be received as soon as the removal order is made. Written submissions, if any, must accompany the application. For greater certainty, the application does not result in a stay of the removal order.

167. Hearing — prescribed factors — For the purpose of determining whether a hearing is required under paragraph 113(b) of the Act, the factors are the following:

(a) whether there is evidence that raises a serious issue of the applicant's credibility and is related to the factors set out in sections 96 and 97 of the Act;

(b) whether the evidence is central to the decision with respect to the application for protection; and

(c) whether the evidence, if accepted, would justify allowing the application for protection.

Case Law

Tekie v. Canada (Minister of Citizenship & Immigration), 2005 CarswellNat 190, 2005 CarswellNat 819, 2005 FC 27 — Section 167 becomes operative where credibility is an issue which could result in a negative PRRA decision. The intent of the provision is to allow an applicant to face any credibility concern which may be put at issue. In this case, the officer had concerns about the applicant's credibility. Although the case was decided principally on the basis of objective fear, if the applicant's contentions had been accepted, a positive PRRA would have resulted. The fact that in the end, the PRRA decision was based on grounds other than credibility, did not lessen the right to an oral hearing.

168. Hearing procedure — A hearing is subject to the following provisions:

(a) notice shall be provided to the applicant of the time and place of the hearing and the issues of fact that will be raised at the hearing;

(b) the hearing is restricted to matters relating to the issues of fact stated in the notice, unless the officer conducting the hearing considers that other issues of fact have been raised by statements made by the applicant during the hearing;

(c) the applicant must respond to the questions posed by the officer and may be assisted for that purpose, at their own expense, by a barrister or solicitor or other counsel; and

(d) any evidence of a person other than the applicant must be in writing and the officer may question the person for the purpose of verifying the evidence provided.

169. Abandonment — An application for protection is declared abandoned

(a) in the case of an applicant who fails to appear at a hearing, if the applicant is given notice of a subsequent hearing and fails to appear at that hearing; and

(b) in the case of an applicant who voluntarily departs Canada, when the applicant's removal order is enforced under section 240 or the applicant otherwise departs Canada.

170. Withdrawal — An application for protection may be withdrawn by the applicant at any time by notifying the Minister in writing. The application is declared to be withdrawn on receipt of the notice.

171. Effect of abandonment and withdrawal — An application for protection is rejected when a decision is made not to allow the application or when the application is declared withdrawn or abandoned.

172. (1) Applicant described in s. 112(3) of the Act — Before making a decision to allow or reject the application of an applicant described in subsection 112(3) of the Act, the Minister shall consider the assessments referred to in subsection (2) and any written response of the applicant to the assessments that is received within 15 days after the applicant is given the assessments.

(2) Assessments — The following assessments shall be given to the applicant:

(a) a written assessment on the basis of the factors set out in section 97 of the Act; and

(b) a written assessment on the basis of the factors set out in subparagraph 113(d)(i) or (ii) of the Act; as the case may be.

(2.1) Certificate — Despite subsection (2), no assessments shall be given to an applicant who is named in a certificate until a judge under section 78 of the Act determines whether the certificate is reasonable.

(3) When assessments given — The assessments are given to an applicant when they are given by hand to the applicant or, if sent by mail, are deemed to be given to an applicant seven days after the day on which they are sent to the last address that the applicant provided to the Department.

(4) Applicant not described in s. 97 of the Act — Despite subsections (1) to (3), if the Minister decides on the basis of the factors set out in section 97 of the Act that the applicant is not described in that section,

> (a) no written assessment on the basis of the factors set out in subparagraph 113(d)(i) or (ii) of the Act need be made; and

> (b) the application is rejected.

SOR/2008-193, s. 2

Case Law

Muhammad v. Canada (Minister of Citizenship & Immigration) (2014), 25 Imm. L.R. (4th) 212, 2014 CarswellNat 2984, 2014 CarswellNat 1482, 2014 FC 448 — The applicant is a citizen of Pakistan and a Sunni Muslim. He arrived in Canada in August 1999 using a false Italian passport and claimed refugee protection. His claim was denied in October 2001, because he was determined to be excluded from consideration as a Convention refugee pursuant to s. 98 of *IRPA* which incorporates Article 1F(a) and (c) of the *UNHCR 1951 Convention Relating to the Status of Refugees*. His application for judicial review of that decision was denied in 2002 as a result of his membership in a terrorist organization, His application for permanent residence on humanitarian and compassionate grounds was also refused. He submitted a first PRRA application in October 2002 which was refused in March 2003. Prior to receiving these two negative decisions, he allegedly wrote to his former counsel advising that he was leaving Montreal to go back to Pakistan, but he actually relocated to Toronto. He received a notice to attend an interview but did not attend and claimed that he feared that if he presented himself he would be jailed and returned to Pakistan. A warrant for his removal was issued in July 2003 and he was arrested in July 2011. He submitted his subsequent PRRA application claiming new facts had arisen since July 2011. Specifically, his name, photograph and last known whereabouts were on a CBSA website along with details of 29 other individuals wanted by the CBSA. He submitted that he was now a person in need of protection because of the publicity surrounding his case and the possible risk to him in Pakistan including extreme physical abuse while in custody, unlawful detention and extrajudicial killing. The PRRA officer found that the applicant would be at risk. The Minister's delegate rejected the PRRA assessment on February 16, 2012. The applicant sought judicial review of that decision which was granted on the basis that the Minister's delegate had failed to adequately justify, on the basis of the evidence, why she had concluded that the applicant would likely not be at risk.

The Minister's delegate, who conducted the redetermination on May 17, 2013, also found that the applicant had not established that he would face a risk of torture, a risk of life, or risk of cruel and unusual treatment or punishment should he be returned to Pakistan. That decision is the subject of the present judicial review.

While it is true that an administrative decision maker need not refer to every piece of evidence relied on in the decision-making process, in this situation, being aware of the PRRA assessment and knowing that the prior first restricted PRRA decision of another Minister's delegate had been found to be unreasonable, it was particularly incumbent upon the Minister's delegate to clearly identify the documentation upon which she was relying to justify her finding. She did not do so. Rather she made general references to the evidence before her and made unsupportable inferences in her reasoning. The decision was set aside and the matter remitted to a third Minister's delegate for redetermination.

Mohammad v. Canada (Minister of Public Safety & Emergency Preparedness), 2013 FC 24, 2013 CarswellNat 21, 2013 CarswellNat 293 — The applicant, a 73-year-old Afghan, had his refugee application denied in 1992. As a police officer under the Communist regime, he was excluded pursuant to Article 1F(a) of the *Convention Relating to the Status of Refugees*, 1951, Can TS 1969 No 6 [Refugee Convention] (crimes against peace, war crimes, crimes against humanity). Following a judicial review of the refugee decision, a 2006 PRRA found in accordance with IRPA, s. 97, that it was more likely than not that the applicant would face a risk of cruel and unusual treatment of punishment or risk to his life if he were returned to Afghanistan. The ministerial delegate reviewed the current circumstances in Afghanistan and determined that the applicant's personal characteristics did not match the profiles listed at risk by the UNHCR. This was a judicial review of the ministerial delegate's decision to deny a PRRA concerning a former Afghan police officer during the Communist era. The ministerial delegate erred when looking at changes to circumstances that led to the previous 2006 positive PRRA. The test is whether the current circumstances (as contrasted with the 2006 circumstances) are substantial, effective, and durable. The failure to consider effectiveness or durability of an amnesty program is significant in a country where the ministerial delegate recognizes that lawlessness is rampant. The judicial review was granted.

Jaballah, Re (2002), [2003] 3 F.C. 85, 224 F.T.R. 20, 2002 CarswellNat 2697, 2002 CarswellNat 3514, [2002] F.C.J. No. 1385, 2002 FCT 1046 — The statute specifically provides, by s. 116, for Regulations relating to the application of Pt. 1, Division 3 of the Act concerning pre-removal risk assessment. Section 116 includes authority to provide by Regulation, "for any matter relating to the application of this division," including "provisions respecting procedures to be followed with respect to applications for protection." Section 172 of the Regulations, on its face, appears to be within the broad grant of regulating authority under s. 116.

173. (1) Re-examination of stay — procedure — A person in respect of whom a stay of a removal order, with respect to a country or place, is being re-examined under subsection 114(2) of the Act shall be given

    (a) a notice of re-examination;

    (b) a written assessment on the basis of the factors set out in section 97 of the Act; and

    (c) a written assessment on the basis of the factors set out in subparagraph 113(d)(i) or (ii) of the Act, as the case may be.

(2) Assessments and response — Before making a decision to cancel or maintain the stay of the removal order, the Minister shall consider the assessments and any written response of the person in respect of whom the stay is being re-examined that is received within 15 days after the assessments are given to that person.

(3) **When assessments given** — The assessments are given to an applicant when they are given by hand to the applicant or, if sent by mail, are deemed to be given to an applicant seven days after the day on which they are sent to the last address that the applicant provided to the Department.

SOR/2009-290, s. 6

174. Reasons for decision — On request, an applicant shall be given a copy of the file notes that record the justification for the decision on their application for protection.

DIVISION 4.1 — DESIGNATED FOREIGN NATIONAL — REQUIREMENT TO REPORT TO AN OFFICER

[Heading added SOR/2012-244, s. 1.]

174.1 (1) Regular reporting intervals — For the purposes of subsection 98.1(1) of the Act, a designated foreign national referred to in that subsection who has not become a permanent resident under subsection 21(2) of the Act must report to an officer as follows:

(a) in person, not more than 30 days after refugee protection is conferred on the designated foreign national under paragraph 95(1)(b) or (c) of the Act; and

(b) once a year in each year after the day on which the foreign national first reports to an officer under paragraph (a), on a date fixed by the officer.

(2) **Reporting on request** — The designated foreign national must also report to an officer if requested to do so by the officer because the officer has reason to believe that any of the circumstances referred to in paragraphs 108(1)(a) to (e) of the Act may apply in respect of the designated foreign national.

(3) **Additional reporting requirements** — In addition to meeting the requirements of subsections (1) and (2), the designated foreign national must report to an officer

(a) any change in

(i) their address, not more than 10 working days after the day on which the change occurs, and

(ii) their employment status, not more than 20 working days after the day on which the change occurs;

(b) any departure from Canada, not less than 10 working days before the day of their departure; and

(c) any return to Canada, not more than 10 working days after the day of their return.

(4) Cessation of reporting requirements — The reporting requirements in subsections (1) to (3) cease to apply to the designated foreign national on the day on which they become a permanent resident.

SOR/2012-244, s. 1

DIVISION 5 — PROTECTED PERSONS — PERMANENT RESIDENCE

175. (1) Judicial review — For the purposes of subsection 21(2) of the Act, an officer shall not be satisfied that an applicant meets the conditions of that subsection if the determination or decision is subject to judicial review or if the time limit for commencing judicial review has not elapsed.

(2) [Repealed SOR/2012-154, s. 8.]

(3) Quebec — For the purposes of subsection 21(2) of the Act, an applicant who makes an application to remain in Canada as a permanent resident — and the family members included in the application — who intend to reside in the Province of Quebec as permanent residents and who are not persons whom the Board has determined to be Convention refugees, may become permanent residents only if it is established that the competent authority of that Province is of the opinion that they meet the selection criteria of the Province.

SOR/2012-154, s. 8

Case Law

Section 175(1)

Mashtouli v. Canada (Minister of Citizenship & Immigration), 2006 CarswellNat 205, 2006 FC 94 — The Regulations set out a 180-day deadline for successful refugee claimants to file an application for permanent residence. The Regulations, however, do not stipulate that incomplete applications submitted on time should be rejected. On the contrary, s. 12 of the Regulations simply says that incomplete applications should be returned to the applicants. Had the Governor in Council intended that incomplete applications be rejected entirely, it would have said so. In contrast, a sponsorship application that is deficient is considered not to be an application filed in the prescribed manner: see s. 10(6) of the *Immigration and Refugee Protection Regulations*.

176. (1) Family members — An applicant may include in their application to remain in Canada as a permanent resident any of their family members.

(2) One-year time limit — A family member who is included in an application to remain in Canada as a permanent resident and who is outside Canada at the time the application is made shall be issued a permanent resident visa if

   (a) the family member makes an application outside Canada to an officer within one year after the day on which the applicant becomes a permanent resident; and

   (b) the family member is not inadmissible on the grounds referred to in subsection (3).

(3) Inadmicoibility — A family member who is inadmissible on any of the grounds referred to in subsection 21(2) of the Act shall not be issued a permanent resident visa and shall not become a permanent resident.

177. Prescribed classes — For the purposes of subsection 21(2) of the Act, the following are prescribed as classes of persons who cannot become permanent residents:

(a) the class of persons who have been the subject of a decision under section 108 or 109 or subsection 114(3) of the Act resulting in the rejection of a claim for refugee protection or nullification of the decision that led to conferral of refugee protection;

(b) the class of persons who are permanent residents at the time of their application to remain in Canada as a permanent resident;

(c) the class of persons who have been recognized by any country, other than Canada, as Convention refugees and who, if removed from Canada, would be allowed to return to that country;

(d) the class of nationals or citizens of a country, other than the country that the person left, or outside of which the person remains, by reason of fear of persecution; and

(e) the class of persons who have permanently resided in a country, other than the country that the person left, or outside of which the person remains, by reason of fear of persecution, and who, if removed from Canada, would be allowed to return to that country.

SOR/2014-140, s. 16

178. (1) Identity documents — An applicant who does not hold a document described in any of paragraphs 50(1)(a) to (h) may submit with their application

(a) any identity document issued outside Canada before the person's entry into Canada; or

(b) if there is a reasonable and objectively verifiable explanation related to circumstances in the applicant's country of nationality or former habitual residence for the applicant's inability to obtain any identity documents, a statutory declaration made by the applicant attesting to their identity, accompanied by

(i) a statutory declaration attesting to the applicant's identity made by a person who, before the applicant's entry into Canada, knew the applicant, a family member of the applicant or the applicant's father, mother, brother, sister, grand-father or grandmother, or

(ii) a statutory declaration attesting to the applicant's identity made by an official of an organization representing nationals of the applicant's country of nationality or former habitual residence.

(2) Alternative documents — A document submitted under subsection (1) shall be accepted in lieu of a document described in any of paragraphs 50(1)(a) to (h) if

(a) in the case of an identity document, the identity document

(i) is genuine,

   (ii) identifies the applicant, and

   (iii) constitutes credible evidence of the applicant's identity; and

  (b) in the case of a statutory declaration, the declaration

   (i) is consistent with any information previously provided by the applicant to the Department or the Board, and

   (ii) constitutes credible evidence of the applicant's identity.

               SOR/2004-167, s. 49; SOR/2011-126, s. 1

Case Law

Nadesan v. Canada (Minister of Citizenship & Immigration), 2011 FC 1325, 2011 CarswellNat 4777, 2011 CarswellNat 5381 — The officer refused to grant permanent residence to the applicant based on the submission of statutory declarations in lieu of identity documents. Section 178 of the Regulations makes it clear that statutory declarations may be submitted where there is "a reasonable and objectively verifiable explanation related to circumstances in the applicant's country of nationality or former habitual residence" that an individual is unable to obtain identity documents. This necessitates an assessment of the reasons for providing a statutory declaration. In addition, the officer is required to accept the statutory declarations as long as they are "consistent with information previously provided by the applicant" and "constitutes credible evidence of the applicant's identity." Consideration must be given to whether the statutory declarations constitute credible evidence. They cannot simply be rejected in favour of the requirement for formal identity documents. The Regulations clearly contemplate the submission of either identity documents or statutory declarations to establish identity.

Even though the officer may have had concerns regarding the applicant's credibility generally, given his previous submissions of fraudulent documents, the decision to refuse the statutory declarations without regard to their contents does not correspond to the requirements of s. 178. Although the submission of fraudulent documents should not have completely been ignored by the officer, the Regulations prescribe a particular process for considering the statutory declarations that has to be addressed. The failure to provide reasons for this outright rejection is similarly problematic. The officer's decision therefore constitutes an error of law and is in breach of procedural fairness. The application for judicial review was allowed.

PART 9 — TEMPORARY RESIDENTS

DIVISION 1 — TEMPORARY RESIDENT VISA

179. Issuance — An officer shall issue a temporary resident visa to a foreign national if, following an examination, it is established that the foreign national

  (a) has applied in accordance with these Regulations for a temporary resident visa as a member of the visitor, worker or student class;

  (b) will leave Canada by the end of the period authorized for their stay under Division 2;

  (c) holds a passport or other document that they may use to enter the country that issued it or another country;

(d) meets the requirements applicable to that class;

(e) is not inadmissible;

(f) meets the requirements of subsections 30(2) and (3), if they must submit to a medical examination under paragraph 16(2)(b) of the Act; and

(g) is not the subject of a declaration made under subsection 22.1(1) of the Act.

SOR/2012-154, s. 9; SOR/2013-210, s. 1

Case Law

Girn v. Canada (Minister of Citizenship and Immigration), 2015 FC 1222, 2015 CarswellNat 5705, 2015 CarswellNat 9128 — The applicant's application for a temporary resident visa to visit his ailing mother, who suffered from advanced dementia, was refused on the basis that the officer was not satisfied the applicant would be motivated to depart Canada given his strong family ties to Canada (his parents, sister and brother-in-law reside in Canada) and weak ties in establishment in India. The officer noted the bank certificate showing the applicant's deposits were not detailed bank statements to show those funds and the origin of those funds.

Given the detailed submission of the applicant's finances, the officer's concern for the origin of these funds was an issue of credibility. Procedural fairness was breached by not providing the applicant with an opportunity to address the concern. The officer had a duty to give him an opportunity to address the concern related to the credibility of the information. The court also concluded that the officer ignored relevant evidence in reaching the decision making the decision unreasonable. With respect to whether the applicant would leave Canada at the end of the authorized stay, the officer did not refer to the fact that the applicant owned a business in India, had a return ticket to India, and had provided a statutory declaration that he would return to India at the end of his authorized stay. Additionally, the officer failed to mention or assess the applicant's father's and brother-in-law's statutory declaration stating that they would make sure he returned to India. The failure by the officer to assess this evidence made the decision unreasonable. The application for judicial review was allowed.

Kokareva v. Canada (Minister of Citizenship and Immigration), 2015 FC 451, 2015 CarswellNat 984, 2015 CarswellNat 2080 — The applicant sought a judicial review of a visa officer's decision to refuse her application for a temporary resident visa. The officer did not express concern about the credibility of either the applicant or her niece but nevertheless was not satisfied that the applicant would leave Canada at the end of her stay. The decision was unreasonable. The officer failed to appreciate import of some of the evidence. For example, the applicant disclosed the earlier refusals on her application showing that she was honest. As well, the officer did not recognize the importance of the applicant's visits to her granddaughter in Russia which showed an established pattern of regular returns to her home country and that she had close family that live near her home. The officer also treated the applicant's failure to visit her sister in Canada as a negative factor. This was unreasonable because, at least in recent years, she had been unable to secure a visa for such a visit. The officer was dismissive of her assets, which included a home that she owned, of her resources for her visit, and there was no reference to the financial support from a Canadian niece who was prepared to provide support. The officer was also dismissive of the applicant's ties to her home country which included professional ties and ongoing work as a tutor as well as social and family ties and emotional ties to the graves of her son and husband. The application for judicial review was allowed.

Karambamuchero v. Canada (Minister of Citizenship and Immigration) (2014), 32 Imm. L.R. (4th) 97, 2014 FC 1240, 2014 CarswellNat 6042, 2014 CarswellNat 6915 — The applicant was a citizen of Zimbabwe. She sought a TRV in order to visit her daughter, son-in-law, grandchildren, and son in Canada. She had visited her children in Canada in 2002, 2004, and 2007. However, since 2007, she had been refused a TRV four times. She was a school principal of a school she founded in 1994, so she was not a mere employee but a successful business person. She had business bank accounts and owned her own home and vehicles. She had a mother and son and other family in Zimbabwe. The visa officer observed there was a "current unstable situation in Zimbabwe" but it was unclear how this impacts the applicant. On the contrary, she appeared to be prospering in the country and one would wonder why she would voluntarily leave. She had left Zimbabwe and returned a number of times. It was troubling that the visa officer did more than note that both of the applicant's two children in Canada are landed residents, but have a "history of refugee claims." The inference was that the applicant will therefore make a refugee claim when she is in Canada. Such an inference is unreasonable on the facts. The reality is that she had previously visited Canada when the refugee claims were pending, or had been granted, and then returned to Zimbabwe. To suggest that she might make a claim for status now, when she did not previously, requires some explanation from the visa officer. The visa officer's decision cannot reasonably be supported. The application for judicial review was allowed.

Agidi v. Canada (Minister of Citizenship & Immigration), 2013 FC 691, 2013 CarswellNat 2831, 2013 CarswellNat 2167 — The applicant applied for a temporary resident visa ("TRV") in order to visit a friend in Ontario. Her application was denied. The officer who refused the application swore an affidavit. The court found the paragraphs were inappropriate and the affidavit was inadmissible. The officer was impermissibly attempting to "bootstrap" his decision. It has become far too common in applications where the "reasons" are scant to offer such bootstrap affidavits.

An applicant for a TRV need not establish that they have a "compelling" reason to travel to Canada. On the contrary, an officer "shall" issue a TRV if the conditions in s. 179 are established. The only condition in s. 179 relevant in this application for judicial review is that an applicant for a TRV establishes that he or she "will leave Canada by the end of the period authorized for their stay." In the absence of any real reasons in the Certified Tribunal Record as to why the officer reached his conclusion that the applicant had not satisfied him that the applicant would not [sic] leave Canada at the end of her intended three-week stay, the decision was unreasonable and was set aside.

Bahr v. Canada (Minister of Citizenship & Immigration), 2012 CarswellNat 1345, 2012 FC 527 — This was an application for judicial review of the refusal of an application for a study permit. The visa officer was not satisfied the main purpose of the applicant's visit to Canada was actually education or that she would leave Canada at the end of her stay. The officer found that based on the economic and security situation in Iraq, the applicant would not likely leave Canada if she were admitted. What applicants should expect is that the onus is upon them to make a convincing case and that, in assessing their applications, visa officers will use their general experience and knowledge of local conditions to draw inferences and reach conclusions on the basis of the information and documents provided by the applicant without necessarily putting any concerns that may arise to the applicant. The onus is upon the applicant to ensure that the application is comprehensive and contains all that is needed to make a convincing case. There was no reviewable error. The application for judicial review was dismissed.

Lacchar v. Canada (Minister of Citizenship & Immigration) (January 9, 2012), IMM-3042-11 (F.C.) — The applicant sought a TRV to visit her son in Ontario and attend the first birthday of her grandchild. She also made an application for permanent residence as a member of the family class which was sponsored by her son who was a Canadian citizen. The application was refused on the basis that the officer expressed concern that the applicant would take similar steps as her sister in Montreal who had arrived in Canada without a valid visa and made a failed refugee claim before being accepted on H&C grounds. The officer also questioned the applicant's financial documentation and lack of travel history outside of India.

A lack of travel history as a negative factor is unreasonable. In this case, the officer's finding that the applicant had no compelling reason to travel to Canada was held to be perverse given the applicant's stated desire to see a very young grandchild she had never seen. Her reason may not be compelling from an economic perspective but it was from a grandparent's perspective. The starting point of assessing an applicant's immigration history must be judged according to his or her own behaviour, not that of a family member. An officer may consider a relative's immigration history but that consideration must take into account both similarities and differences between the two. In this case, the applicant's conduct seeking lawful entry was strikingly different from that of her sister and it was unreasonable for the visa officer to ascribe the sister's conduct to the applicant. This was especially so, since the applicant may reasonably be assumed to abide by the TRV requirements in order not to jeopardize her permanent residence application by violating the terms of the TRV. It was incongruous to question the applicant's financial documentation without giving her an opportunity to respond to questions raised and destroying the very document questioned. The application for judicial review was allowed.

Kindie v. Canada (Minister of Citizenship & Immigration) (2011), 2 Imm. L.R. (4th) 149, 2011 FC 850, 2011 CarswellNat 2663, 2011 CarswellNat 3651 — The applicant applied for a work permit. The visa officer was not satisfied that the applicant would leave Canada by the end of the period authorized due to her social and economic situation in her country of residence, Ethiopia. There must be an objective reason to question the motivation of the applicant. It is inconsistent with the purpose and objective of the statutory and regulatory scheme authorizing temporary work visas to rely on the very factor that would induce someone to come to Canada in the first place as the basis for keeping them out. The scheme itself is predicated on the assumption that people will come to Canada to seek work in order to better their economic situation. It is for this reason that decisions of the court have consistently held that economic reasons to overstay will not, in and of themselves, support a refusal. In this case, the visa officer had objective evidence that constituted a sufficient basis for concern about the *bona fides* of the application and the applicant's commitment to return to Ethiopia at the end of the visa. The applicant's mother had been issued a visitor's visa by the same High Commission in Nairobi and claimed refugee status on arrival. She is now residing in Hamilton, Ontario where the applicant proposes to work. The second consideration, in and of itself, supports the reasonableness of the officer's conclusion that it had not been established that the applicant would return to her country of origin. Officers are required to situate applications in their broader context and it would be unreasonable to require the visa officer to turn a blind eye to the surrounding circumstances, including the recent conduct of family members. The application for judicial review was dismissed.

Paramasivam v. Canada (Minister of Citizenship & Immigration) (2010), 91 Imm. L.R. (3d) 29, [2010] F.C.J. No. 988, 2010 FC 811, 2010 CarswellNat 3413, 2010 CarswellNat 2690 — A visa officer refused the applicant's application for a temporary resident visa to Canada. The officer determined the applicant had failed to prove that she would leave Canada at the end of the temporary period if she was authorized to visit. This determination was based on consideration of her ties to Sri Lanka and factors which might motivate her to stay in Canada. The applicant's demonstrated links to Sri Lanka were as follows:

(a) the applicant was employed as the principal of a medical college;

(b) the applicant is paid a salary for her job and has been granted a temporary leave by the college;

(c) the applicant owns property in Sri Lanka;

(d) the applicant has money in Sri Lanka;

(e) the applicant has three brothers and one sister in Sri Lanka who live near her;

(f) the applicant has a 94-year-old mother in Sri Lanka who lives in the same area as the applicant;

(g) the applicant has lived all her life in Sri Lanka;

(h) the applicant is a justice of the peace in Sri Lanka.

The court concluded that these facts could not reasonably be assessed as demonstrating "very few ties to Sri Lanka." In coming to such a conclusion the officer must have overlooked significant material facts that were before him. Furthermore, the officer concluded that the applicant had limited travel history having visited South Africa and India. The court found that the requirement only asked for travel within the previous six months and, in that time, the applicant had travelled to South Africa once and to India on several occasions and had returned to Sri Lanka. The visa officer did not refer to a letter from the applicant's brother which indicated that he worked for Canada Immigration before joining the Immigration and Refugee Board as a tribunal officer. The court found this to be a material fact that was overlooked. Based on the accumulation of errors, the application for judicial review was allowed.

Kuewor v. Canada (Minister of Citizenship & Immigration), 2010 FC 707, 2010 CarswellNat 2019, 2010 CarswellNat 2648 — The applicant's application for a visa to visit Canada was refused. The applicant supplied cogent evidence that he was a 27-year-old citizen of Ghana; a mature student with sound academic background; a member of a family in which his parents and three siblings reside in Ghana; a person with an employment record dating back to 2002 who was currently employed and had been granted leave by his current employer to visit Canada; and invited to visit Canada by a responsible person employed by the Roman Catholic Arch Diocese of Toronto who was willing to sponsor the visit by providing room and board and a return airline ticket to Ghana; and, importantly as a person who has the support of a Member of Parliament of the Government of Ghana in obtaining the visa requested. The application for a visa was refused citing the applicant was not well established; showed unstable employment; cannot afford the trip on his own; showed limited funds; had no previous travel; did not show strong ties in Ghana. The evidence presented in support of the visa application was disconnected from the reasons provided for rejecting the application. It was necessary for the visa officer to carefully consider the evidence presented and, in reaching a decision, provide reasons for the results which were clear and responsive to the evidence. The decision under review failed to meet this standard and the application for judicial review was allowed.

Singh v. Canada (Minister of Citizenship & Immigration) (2010), 93 Imm. L.R. (3d) 235, 2010 FC 1111, 2010 CarswellNat 5093, 2010 CarswellNat 4251 — The applicant sought judicial review of a visa officer's decision to refuse his application for a temporary resident visa ("TRV"). The applicant's travel experience was not considered as a neutral factor by the officer. While the applicant traveled in 2006-2007 to Southeast Asia, the officer gave no reasons why the absence of travel to Europe, UK or North America should be held against the applicant. The officer made no reference or analyzed an important document pertaining to the applicant's purpose of the application for the TRV, which was an exploratory visit to Montreal to become a permanent resident as an investor under the Quebec Investor Program. The officer mentioned that the applicant had close family ties in Canada (mother and brother) but ought to have considered his family (wife and daughters) and property he had in India. The court's intervention was warranted. The application for judicial review was granted.

Groohi v. Canada (Minister of Citizenship & Immigration) (2009), 83 Imm. L.R. (3d) 129, 2009 FC 837, 2009 CarswellNat 4136, 2009 CarswellNat 2502 — The applicants were sisters who applied for temporary resident visas which were refused by a visa officer. The sisters had been invited by their brother to visit along with their parents. Their brother was a medical doctor practicing in Manitoba and had status in Canada as a permanent resident. The sisters' applications were initially refused in July 2007 on the basis that in the visa officer's estimation both sisters had "weak ties" to Iran and were unable to show that they would leave Canada at the end of an authorized stay. Applications for judicial review were granted and both visa applications were remitted to a different visa officer for determination. The applications were refused again.

These applications must succeed based simply on the absence of any true analysis of the evidence by the visa officer. It is trite law that simply listing a series of factors, and stating a conclusion, is generally insufficient to meet the test of reasonableness, the reason being that it is impossible for a reviewing court to appreciate and access the train of thought or logical process engaged in by the decision maker.

A visa officer's decision as to whether an applicant has satisfied him or her that the applicant will not overstay the visit to Canada is not one requiring a detailed and lengthy analysis. However, where the officer concludes that the applicant has failed to satisfy the officer of that essential fact, the applicant is entitled to know the facts which the officer considered, the weight accorded to those facts, and the reasoning of the officer as to why the applicant failed to meet the burden. In these decisions there was a complete lack of any explanation of the reasoning process in which the officer engaged. The applications for judicial review were allowed.

Rudder v. Canada (Minister of Citizenship & Immigration) (2009), 82 Imm. L.R. (3d) 173, 346 F.T.R. 286 (Eng.), 2009 FC 689, 2009 CarswellNat 1912, 2009 CarswellNat 5866 — The applicant, a citizen of Guyana aged 53, challenged the decision of a visa officer to refuse her application for a temporary residence visa to enable her to come to Canada to visit relatives and view the gravesites of her mother and sister. The court found the officer's decision to be contrary to paragraph 18.1(4)(d) of the *Federal Courts Act*. The officer's decision was reached ignoring the evidence before him or by drawing inferences from the evidence which are unreasonable in the perspective of the purposes and objectives for Canada granting entry to this country on a temporary resident visa (TRV)

IRP Regulations

in the category of a visitor. While there is no question an application for a foreign national for a TRV triggers a discretionary decision by an officer, administrative law has settled the principles upon which discretionary decisions of officers dealing with TRV decisions must be reviewed. The officer clearly failed to consider many of the factors identified in the ministerial guideline to access the central and only criteria spelled out in IRPA for the issuance of a TRV, namely, whether on the evidence, the officer should be satisfied an applicant will return to his or her country of residence. The application for judicial review was allowed and the matter referred to a different officer with directions that a TRV for the period of one month be issued forthwith to the applicant.

Hara v. Canada (Minister of Citizenship & Immigration) (2009), 79 Imm. L.R. (3d) 27, 2009 FC 263, 2009 CarswellNat 739 — This was an application for judicial review of a decision of a visa officer refusing the applicant's application for a work permit. On June 16, 2008, the applicant submitted a third application for a work permit as a live-in-caregiver. This application was refused on June 20, 2008. The reasons for refusal were that the applicant had failed to provide a new employment contract with her employer in Canada and the officer was not satisfied that the applicant would leave Canada at the end of her authorized stay. The officer noted in the CAIPS notes that the applicant had overstayed in Canada, had failed to mention her refusals for work permits in her previous applications, and had weak connections to Japan.

The court held that the officer was mistaken in his reasoning that the applicant had not declared being refused a visa to Canada on her first application. The first application was the applicant's first refusal of a visa to Canada. The CPC-Vegreville refusal was not a visa refusal to Canada or, in the court's opinion, analogous. The applicant, however, did give an incorrect answer to a question in her second application, when she indicated that she had not been refused a visa to Canada when, in fact, the first refusal did constitute a refused visa to Canada. However, the officer's mistaken reasoning as to the extent of the applicant's misstatements is sufficient to hold the officer's finding on this point was unreasonable. The court agreed with the applicant that the officer's finding that she would not leave Canada at the end of the authorized stay was not sufficiently supported by the evidence and was unreasonable. While the applicant did not leave as required by law once she received the September 2007 CPC-Vegreville refusal, possibly for the reason she attested to, she nevertheless did leave Canada once she became aware that she had to apply for the Live-In-Caregiver Program from outside Canada. Having received no notice to leave Canada, she claims to have only later learned after reviewing the CAIPS notes that she should have left Canada after receiving the CPC-Vegreville refusal. The applicant "did not go underground." The officer also breached the duty of procedural fairness by not providing adequate reasons why he rejected the applicant's detailed explanation of her overstay in Canada. The whole history of the applicant's relationship with Canada and her repeated comings and goings were directly against the officer's conclusions on this point. There is nothing in the Act or Regulations that prevent someone from consulting with a lawyer as to the legal means to remain in Canada. The fact that the applicant had a two-year degree from a Canadian college in early childhood education is evidence that her interest in the LIC Program was not simply a utilitarian move to remain in Canada "no matter for which purpose." The decision was set aside and the application for judicial review was allowed.

Villagonzalo v. Canada (Minister of Citizenship & Immigration), 2008 CarswellNat 4937, 2008 CarswellNat 3640, 2008 FC 1127 — This was an application for judicial review of a visa officer's decision that the applicant did not meet the requirements for a work permit. The applicant applied under the Live-In-Caregiver Program. The applicant argued that the officer failed to take into account that throughout her previous stay in Canada, the applicant undertook to maintain valid TRV status and promptly left when her request for an extension was refused. The applicant explained that she originally received a six-month TRV to come to Canada to attend her brother's wedding. Due to her child being sick, she was unable to attend the wedding. She did, however, come to Canada in November 2004 to visit her family. The applicant deposed that she told this to the visa officer at the time of her interview for a work permit. It appears that her failure to attend her brother's wedding and her failure to leave Canada between either May 17, 2005, or May 22, 2005 (the date she received the refusal to extend her status in Canada), and June 1, 2005, caused the visa officer to believe that the applicant in the future would not leave Canada by the end of any period authorized for her stay. The court concluded that the visa officer's decision was not reasonable and that there should have been some consideration of the applicant's explanations. The application for judicial review was allowed.

Singh v. Canada (Minister of Citizenship & Immigration) (2008), 68 Imm. L.R. (3d) 278, 2008 CarswellNat 894, 2008 CarswellNat 12, 2008 FC 15 — This was the judicial review of one of many refusals to grant the applicant a visa based on the fact that he is believed to be a people smuggler. The applicant first applied for a temporary residence visa in August 1996, which was refused. All the subsequent visa refusals have been based on this 1996 refusal. It was unreasonable for the visa officer to continue to rely solely on the 1996 visa refusal without considering the case in its totality. The decision was quashed. The applicant was entitled to have his visa application reviewed fully and fairly — to be able to address in a real manner the allegations (stated and implied).

Khatoon v. Canada (Minister of Citizenship & Immigration) (2008), 71 Imm. L.R. (3d) 102, 2008 CarswellNat 558, 2008 CarswellNat 1024, 2008 FC 276 — The applicant was a citizen of Pakistan who applied for a visitor permit in order to attend her granddaughter's wedding. The application was received along with a letter of invitation from the applicant's grandson. The officer refused the application, checking off the boxes corresponding to two reasons on the standard refusal letter, specifically that the applicant had not satisfied the officer that she met the requirements of Regulation s. 179 and would leave Canada at the end of her temporary period if authorized to stay and the applicant had not provided sufficient documentation to support her host's income and assets. The officer's conclusion was found to be patently unreasonable. The fact that the applicant's son was in Canada out of status could not be used to impute similar conduct to the applicant. People are to be judged according to their own behaviour, not on that of their family members. The mere fact that elderly widowed women normally, in the view of the officer, live with their sons and not daughters, could not be used to attack the *bona fides* of the applicant's application. This type of gross generalization is patently unreasonable. Finally, the officer disregarded the applicant's previous trip to Saudi Arabia, stating that "a trip to Saudi Arabia is not usually considered to be major international travel in the context in which the officer assesses applications for temporary residence." The court held that a trip from Pakistan to Saudi Arabia was international travel. The application for judicial review was allowed and the visa officer's decision was quashed.

Wang v. Canada (Minister of Citizenship & Immigration), 2006 CarswellNat 3482, 2006 FC 1298 — The applicant made two unsuccessful applications to enter Canada as a student. Her second visa application was refused because the visa officer was not satisfied that she was an intending temporary resident to Canada. The applicant argued that the visa officer's finding that the applicant was not well established in China was bizarre because the record disclosed that she "is as well established in China as any 19-year-old who has just finished high school." While there is some merit to the applicant's contention that one's establishment in a country ordinarily requires consideration of many factors, it is also the case that a visa officer has a broad discretion to weigh the evidence submitted in making a decision. Here the visa officer looked for evidence of the financial situation of the applicant's parents. The visa officer considered this to be important to the assessment of the application and she failed to find it. The applicant's parents were retired and their financial situation was unknown. The onus rested on the applicant to establish an entitlement to a student visa. The visa officer was entitled to base the refusal decision solely on the absence of that evidence of family circumstance. If the evidence had been offered and if it sufficiently answered the concerns of the visa officer, the decision may well have been different.

The applicant also complained that the refusal letter was deficient because it did not contain the reasons for the visa refusal. The CAIPS notes were provided to the applicant in compliance with the *Federal Court Immigration and Refugee Protection Rules*. CAIPS notes have been accepted as a constituent part of an administrative decision. Rule 9 contemplates that the provision of detailed reasons for an immigration decision may occur after the commencement of an application for judicial review. The court concluded that the respondent met its obligation under that Rule and cannot be taken to have breached a natural justice requirement by failure to abide by some other standard.

Toor v. Canada (Minister of Citizenship & Immigration), 2006 CarswellNat 1342, 2006 FC 573 — The applicant applied for judicial review of a decision of an immigration officer at the New Delhi High Commission, wherein the officer refused the applicant's application for a temporary resident visa. The officer was not satisfied as to the *bona fides* of the application. The applicant had been invited to an interview by a provincial government, however, the officer noted that the letter from the province of Manitoba referred to funds claimed by the applicant which could not be verified on documents and accordingly, concluded there were large inconsistencies. The officer also noted the applicant had no previous travel and only previous refusals from the United States and New Zealand.

The applicant argued that it would have been proper for the visa officer to give him an opportunity to reply to his concerns.

The court concluded that the obligation to confront an applicant with adverse conclusions applies when the conclusions arise from material not known to the applicant. Where the issue arises out of material provided by the applicant, there is no obligation to provide an opportunity for explanation since the provider of the material is taken to know of the contents of the material. There was no breach of procedural fairness.

Dhillon v. Canada (Minister of Citizenship & Immigration), 2003 CarswellNat 3954, 2003 CarswellNat 4433, 2003 FC 1446 — The applicant tried three times to obtain a visa to allow him to visit his ailing mother in Vancouver for one month. His first two applications were turned down because the officers found that "he had no ties to India." The applicant went to considerable effort to address that concern in his third application. He supplied documents showing details of his prosperous farming operation including proof of title to his land and house, financial statements and savings records. He described his responsibility as sole caregiver to his elderly grandmother and his other family connections in India. The officer who turned down the applicant's third request for a visa had an obligation to consider and respond to the new evidence of the applicant's ties to India.

The officer either failed to consider the evidence or failed to explain adequately why the third application was being refused and accordingly the decision was set aside.

Holders of Temporary Resident Visas

180. Authorization — A foreign national is not authorized to enter and remain in Canada as a temporary resident unless, following an examination, it is established that the foreign national and their accompanying family members

(a) met the requirements for issuance of their temporary resident visa at the time it was issued; and

(b) continue to meet these requirements at the time of the examination on entry into Canada.

Applications for Extension of Authorization to Remain in Canada as a Temporary Resident

181. (1) Circumstances — A foreign national may apply for an extension of their authorization to remain in Canada as a temporary resident if

(a) the application is made by the end of the period authorized for their stay; and

(b) they have complied with all conditions imposed on their entry into Canada.

(2) Extension — An officer shall extend the foreign national's authorization to remain in Canada as a temporary resident if, following an examination, it is established that the foreign national continues to meet the requirements of section 179.

Case Law

Kaur v. Canada (Minister of Citizenship & Immigration), 2011 FC 219, 2011 CarswellNat 1277, 2011 CarswellNat 434 — The applicant sought judicial review of a decision of an officer of Citizenship and Immigration Canada Case Processing Centre wherein the officer refused to restore the applicant's temporary resident status, work permit and study permit. The applicant submitted her application for a work permit on September 4, 2009. The application was returned for insufficient fees. She reapplied for restoration of her temporary resident status and a further work permit and study permit on November 10, 2009. The officer found that the applicant's application was not mailed within the prescribed 90-day period and therefore determined that she was not eligible for a work permit for post-graduation employment. The officer determined that the 90-day period began from the date on the applicant's diploma, April 30, 2009. The officer found that the applicant did not meet the requirements of a study permit; the officer was not convinced that the applicant was a genuine student. The officer had concerns about the credibility of the documents received. Several letters from the officers at Fanshawe College conflicted as to the applicant's official graduation date.

An officer is not under a duty to inform the applicant about any concerns regarding the application which arise directly from the requirements of the legislation or regulations. The onus is on the applicant to satisfy the officer on all parts of her application and the officer was under no obligation to ask for additional information where the applicant's material was insufficient. However, the officer was obligated to inform the applicant of any concerns related to the veracity of documents that formed part of the application and the officer was required to make further inquiries in such a situation. By viewing the letter as not credible or fraudulent, the officer ought to have convoked an interview with the applicant to provide her an opportunity to respond to these concerns. The officer denied the applicant procedural fairness and the judicial review was allowed. The other issues were not addressed.

Lim v. Canada (Minister of Citizenship & Immigration) (2005), 45 Imm. L.R. (3d) 271, 2005 CarswellNat 1209, 2005 FC 657 — One of the objectives of the IRPA is to facilitate the entry of temporary workers. Live-in caregivers are temporary workers and are needed in Canada. IRPA and the Regulations have established a special program for caregivers. Under that program, live-in caregivers are given an incentive to come to Canada; they can qualify for permanent residency after having worked as live-in caregivers in Canada. The program works on the basis of dual interdependent authorizations; the work permit and the temporary resident status. Both the work permit and the temporary resident status are obtained when the caregiver first arrives in Canada. If the work permit is renewed, the temporary residency status is also extended. If the work permit expires, the temporary resident status expires. Without valid, unexpired temporary residency status, a caregiver cannot apply for renewal of the work permit. Conversely, a valid unexpired work permit is a precondition for extension of the temporary residency status.

To avoid hardship or exploitation, caregivers can change employers but this is dependent on furnishing, with respect to the new employer, a validated job offer and new employment contract.

Due to the fact that there may be timeline issues, the Regulations allow for an extension for two months for those caregivers who anticipate the problem and apply prior to the expiry of their work permit and a 90 day grace period for those caregivers that missed the deadline and apply after the expiry of their work permit.

The discretion of CIC officers is circumscribed by the mandatory requirements of ss. 181 and 182.

The point of the 90 day grace period is to allow live-in caregivers to rectify their status. The applicant in this case applied within the required period. Any bureaucratic delay in handling the application should not be used as justification to curtail the applicant's rights. The applicant made her application to rectify her status within the 90 day grace period established by s. 182. She still had 19 days to correct any deficiencies. In this case, the deficiency was that in the application she did not tick off one box on the form, Box C and failed to tick off Box D and provided the wrong renewal fee.

The date of receipt of the application is to be considered the lock-in date. The applicant did not know, nor could she reasonably be expected to know, that she had also to apply for restoration of status. The CIC booklet entitled, "Applying to Change Conditions or Extend Your Stay in Canada — Worker (IMM 553-E (04-2004)" is extremely hard to understand and contains confusing and questionable statements.

It is necessary to be mindful of the fact that the actions of CIC in refusing the extension have a drastic effect. The applicant has to return to the Philippines and has to reapply which will take a minimum of two years. She has to re-qualify and start from scratch. The time that she has worked in Canada does not count towards the two years working time she needs before applying for permanent status. The rejection of the application in this case serves no discernable policy goal under IRPA, nor does it prevent any abuse of

IRPA or the Regulations. It is completely out of tune with the general nature of the Live-in Caregiver Program.

Stanislavsky v. Canada (Minister of Citizenship & Immigration) (2003), 237 F.T.R. 27, 2003 CarswellNat 1961, 2003 CarswellNat 2799, 2003 FCT 835 (T.D.) — The applicants sought judicial review of the decision of an Immigration counsellor denying the applicants' request for a restoration of their temporary resident status. The applicants who are married to each other are citizens of Ukraine. They entered Canada in July 2000 as visitors. They have two sons who are Canadian citizens and who live in Canada. In 2000, the purpose of their visit was to look after the mother of one of the applicants who was ill. The mother died in August 2001 leaving property in Canada to one of the applicants. In February 2002, their request for an extension of their visitor status was refused. They applied for a restoration of their visitor status and that was also refused. In May 2002, the applicants made an application for permanent residence sponsored by one of their sons. The Immigration counsellor refused to restore their temporary status and entered a note in the CAIPS notes advising that the immediate departure of the applicants should be effected.

A person seeking a temporary resident permit must have the intention of staying in Canada for a temporary purpose and the officer must be satisfied that such a person will leave Canada on the expiry of status. The officer did not refuse the application for restoration on the basis that the applicants were not in Canada for a temporary purpose. The officer denied the application because the applicants' stay would be for a "long temporary purpose," that is, while awaiting a decision on their application for permanent residence. The extended delay was attributed to the long processing time in Vegreville, Alberta, relative to inland sponsorship applications.

The fact that the applicants had submitted an inland sponsorship application was relevant to their intention to remain in Canada for a long temporary purpose. That is for the duration of the processing of their landing applications. This was a new and different temporary purpose from their original temporary purpose when they entered Canada in July 2000. The statutory and regulatory scheme does not say that a person's initial temporary purpose must remain constant and unchanged. The only requirement is the existence of a "temporary purpose." In the present case the officer did not address his mind to this question and this was a reversible error.

Restoration of Temporary Resident Status

182. (1) Restoration — On application made by a visitor, worker or student within 90 days after losing temporary resident status as a result of failing to comply with a condition imposed under paragraph 185(a), any of subparagraphs 185(b)(i) to (iii) or paragraph 185(c), an officer shall restore that status if, following an examination, it is established that the visitor, worker or student meets the initial requirements for their stay, has not failed to comply with any other conditions imposed and is not the subject of a declaration made under subsection 22.1(1) of the Act.

(2) Exception — Despite subsection (1), an officer shall not restore the status of a student who is not in compliance with a condition set out in subsection 220.1(1).

SOR/2013-210, s. 2; SOR/2014-14, s. 3

Case Law

Adroh c. Canada (Ministre de la Citoyenneté & de l'Immigration), 2012 CarswellNat 1390, 2012 FC 393 — An immigration officer refused the applicant's post-graduation work permit application. It is accepted that the applicant had to obtain the restoration of her temporary resident status and hold a valid study permit for the post-graduation work permit application to be granted. If an applicant does not have temporary resident status in Canada, the officer has no discretion: the officer must refuse the work permit application. The language in s. 182 of the Regulations is not discretionary: if the application for restoration is brought outside of the 90-day period imposed by law, the officer must refuse the application. The application for judicial review was dismissed.

Kaur v. Canada (Minister of Citizenship & Immigration), 2011 FC 219, 2011 CarswellNat 1277, 2011 CarswellNat 434 — The applicant sought judicial review of a decision of an officer of Citizenship and Immigration Canada Case Processing Centre wherein the officer refused to restore the applicant's temporary resident status, work permit and study permit. The applicant submitted her application for a work permit on September 4, 2009. The application was returned for insufficient fees. She reapplied for restoration of her temporary resident status and a further work permit and study permit on November 10, 2009. The officer found that the applicant's application was not mailed within the prescribed 90-day period and therefore determined that she was not eligible for a work permit for post-graduation employment. The officer determined that the 90-day period began from the date on the applicant's diploma, April 30, 2009. The officer found that the applicant did not meet the requirements of a study permit; the officer was not convinced that the applicant was a genuine student. The officer had concerns about the credibility of the documents received. Several letters from the officers at Fanshawe College conflicted as to the applicant's official graduation date.

An officer is not under a duty to inform the applicant about any concerns regarding the application which arise directly from the requirements of the legislation or regulations. The onus is on the applicant to satisfy the officer on all parts of her application and the officer was under no obligation to ask for additional information where the applicant's material was insufficient. However, the officer was obligated to inform the applicant of any concerns related to the veracity of documents that formed part of the application and the officer was required to make further inquiries in such a situation. By viewing the letter as not credible or fraudulent, the officer ought to have convoked an interview with the applicant to provide her an opportunity to respond to these concerns. The officer denied the applicant procedural fairness and the judicial review was allowed. The other issues were not addressed.

Sui v. Canada (Minister of Public Safety & Emergency Preparedness) (2006), 58 Imm. L.R. (3d) 135, [2007] 3 F.C.R. 218, 2006 CarswellNat 3554, 2006 FC 1314 — The applicant was in Canada for several years as a temporary resident on a study permit. Before his study permit expired, he applied for a post-graduation work permit. He received a letter from CIC informing him that he did not meet the requirements for a work permit and that he should leave Canada immediately, failing which enforcement action would be taken against him. Within 90 days of the expiration of his study permit and within 90 days of losing his temporary resident status, he applied to have his status restored pursuant to Regulation 182. While awaiting a decision on his application for restoration, two immigration officers attended his home and questioned him. Two inadmissibility reports were issued, the first based on para. 40(1)(a) of the IRPA and the fact that "there were reasonable grounds to believe that this foreign national was inadmissible for directly or indirectly misrepresenting or withholding material facts relating to a relevant matter that induces or could induce an error in administration of this Act." The second report was based on para. 41(a) and subs. 29(2) of the IRPA and the fact that the applicant was inadmissible for failing to comply with his obligation as a temporary resident to leave Canada by the end of the period authorized for his stay. A Minister's delegate decided to issue an exclusion order based on para. 41(a) and subs. 29(2) of the IRPA. In light of s. 225 of the Regulations, this meant that the applicant could not come back to Canada without written consent of the Minister for a period of one year following his departure. The applicant left Canada. No decision with respect to the application for restoration was ever made. In this case, the Minister's delegate had the discretion and even the duty to consider the fact that the applicant had applied for restoration well before a s. 44(1) report was issued against him in respect of his failure to leave Canada at the end of his authorized stay. It was an error of law to consider that the applicant was not entitled to make such an application for restoration simply because after the filing of his application in accordance with the Regulations, a s. 44(1) report had been issued on the sole basis of subs. 29(2) of the IRPA. The decision was set aside.

The following questions were certified:

1. Is an application for restoration pursuant to s. 182 of the Regulations a relevant consideration when the Minister's delegate considers whether or not to make an exclusion order based on a failure to comply with s. 29(2) of the IRPA?

2. Does a foreign national who has applied for restoration within the delay set out in s. 182 of the Regulations, automatically lose the benefit of his or her application when an enforcement officer considers issuing a report under s. 44(1) on the basis of a failure to comply with s. 29(2) of the IRPA?

Zhang v. Canada (Minister of Citizenship & Immigration) (2006), 59 Imm. L.R. (3d) 165, 2006 CarswellNat 3831, 2006 FC 1381 — The applicant moved to British Columbia in 2002 on a temporary student permit that was valid until August 2004. He applied for and was granted an extension to August 30, 2005. Since he wanted to continue his studies, he applied for a further extension in August 2005. The officer concluded he was not a *bona fide* student and did not intend to leave Canada at the end of his stay. The applicant did not leave Canada, nor did he seek leave of the court to challenge the decision to refuse his extension application. Instead, the applicant submitted a restoration application seeking to re-acquire the temporary status he had lost. The applicant's restoration application was refused. The officer's letter essentially quoted para. 47(a) of the IRPA and s. 182 of its accompanying Regulations, and simply stated that the applicant was refused as he was not satisfied the applicant met those criteria. It was perfectly legitimate for the applicant to apply for restoration instead of judicial review of the initial decision to extend his study permit. While the immigration officer could take the extension decision into consideration, he also had to assess the applicant's new evidence in support of his claim that the initial decision was mistaken or did not reflect his true intentions. It is true that there is nothing in the IRPA requiring an immigration officer to provide reasons to an applicant. But it is well established that the duty of procedural fairness sometimes requires that explanations be given for a particular decision. In the present case, the mere recital of the relevant sections of the IRPA and the Regulations was clearly not sufficient. The applicant submitted further evidence that he was a *bona fide* student. He is certainly entitled to some explanation as to why these further documents were inadequate to show that he was a *bona fide* student. As a result of the negative restoration decision, the applicant was found to be inadmissible to Canada and the decision that he challenged before the Federal Court would have profound implications for him. The more important a decision is to the lives of those affected and the greater its impact on that person or those persons, the more stringent the procedural protections that will be mandated. Although a relatively low degree of procedural fairness is warranted in an immigration officer's decision to grant or deny an application to restore temporary resident status, a low level of procedural fairness still imposes some obligations on officers to provide reasons for negative decisions. The application for judicial review was granted.

Patel v. Canada (Minister of Citizenship & Immigration) (2006), 54 Imm. L.R. (3d) 180, 2006 CarswellNat 454, 2006 CarswellNat 2375, 2006 FC 224 — The applicant was aged 79 and a citizen of India. She had five children and 11 grandchildren living in Canada, all of whom were Canadian citizens. Her husband was deceased and she had no more family living in India. She first came to Canada to attend the wedding of her granddaughter. Subsequently, her Canadian children decided they would sponsor her to stay in Canada as she would be alone in her mother country. She obtained three extensions of her status as a temporary resident. Her request for a fourth extension was denied after consideration of dual intent and determination that she was not a *bona fide* temporary resident. An application for restoration was denied.

The standard of review applicable to a decision refusing restoration of status is that of reasonableness *simpliciter*.

A permanent residence application does not necessarily preclude a temporary purpose for being in Canada. The current statutory and regulatory scheme does not say that a person's initial temporary purpose must remain constant and unchanged. The only requirement is the existence of a temporary purpose. The application for restoration of temporary status was not refused on the basis that the applicant would not be in Canada for a temporary purpose. On the contrary, it was denied because the applicant's stay in Canada would be for a "longer" temporary purpose, that is, while awaiting a decision on the application for permanent residence. The conclusion reached by the officer contained a reviewable error. The application was granted and the matter referred back to a different officer for redetermination.

Radics v. Canada (Minister of Citizenship & Immigration) (2004), 262 F.T.R. 211, 2004 CarswellNat 4093, 2004 FC 1590 — This is an application to review a decision refusing the applicant's request for the restoration of his status. The applicant entered as a visitor and was authorized to remain until December 18, 2003. On December 22, 2003, the applicant applied for a restoration of his temporary resident status. The applicant said that he had inadvertently failed to apply for an extension within the necessary time period.

Pursuant to s. 182, an immigration officer is required to restore an applicant's temporary resident status if he meets the initial requirements for a stay and if he has not failed to comply with any conditions imposed. Section 179 sets out the initial requirements for the issuance of a temporary visa. The applicant must have applied as either a visitor, worker or student and it must be established that the applicant will leave Canada by the end of his authorized stay. In determining whether an applicant will leave Canada, an officer will usually consider the applicant's purpose for wanting to be in Canada. The fact that an applicant applied to restore his visitor's status, and did not evade authorities, suggests that he is law abiding and that he will leave by the end of the period authorized. This fact was ignored by the officer. The officer's decision was set aside.

Duong v. Canada (Minister of Citizenship & Immigration), 2003 CarswellNat 4029, 2003 CarswellNat 3066, 2003 FC 1131 — The applicant came to Canada pursuant to a Minister's permit issued under s. 37 of the former Act. The permit was valid for 6 months. The permit expired and relying on Regulation 182, the applicant applied for restoration. The applicant wants to remain in Canada because she is now married to a Canadian citizen and has submitted an H&C application.

The applicant was not a visitor, worker or student, she was a permit holder. The Minister's delegate was accordingly without jurisdiction to restore her temporary resident status.

Stanislavsky v. Canada (Minister of Citizenship & Immigration) (2003), 237 F.T.R. 27, 2003 CarswellNat 1961, 2003 CarswellNat 2799, 2003 FCT 835 (T.D.) — The applicants sought judicial review of the decision of an Immigration counsellor denying the applicants' request for a restoration of their temporary resident status. The applicants who are married to each other are citizens of Ukraine. They entered Canada in July 2000 as visitors. They have two sons who are Canadian citizens and who live in Canada. In 2000, the purpose of their visit was to look after the mother of one of the applicants who was ill. The mother died in August 2001 leaving property in Canada to one of the applicants. In February 2002, their request for an extension of their visitor status was refused. They applied for a restoration of their visitor status and that was also refused. In May 2002, the applicants made an application for permanent residence sponsored by one of their sons. The Immigration counsellor refused to restore their temporary status and entered a note in the CAIPS notes advising that the immediate departure of the applicants should be effected.

A person seeking a temporary resident permit must have the intention of staying in Canada for a temporary purpose and the officer must be satisfied that such a person will leave Canada on the expiry of status. The officer did not refuse the application for restoration on the basis that the applicants were not in Canada for a temporary purpose. The officer denied the application because the applicants' stay would be for a "long temporary purpose," that is, while awaiting a decision on their application for permanent residence. The extended delay was attributed to the long processing time in Vegreville, Alberta, relative to inland sponsorship applications.

The fact that the applicants had submitted an inland sponsorship application was relevant to their intention to remain in Canada for a long temporary purpose. That is for the duration of the processing of their landing applications. This was a new and different temporary purpose from their original temporary purpose when they entered Canada in July 2000. The statutory and regulatory scheme does not say that a person's initial temporary purpose must remain constant and unchanged. The only requirement is the existence of a "temporary purpose." In the present case the officer did not address his mind to this question and this was a reversible error.

DIVISION 1.1 — DECLARATION UNDER SUBSECTION 22.1(1) OF THE ACT

[Heading added SOR/2013-210, s. 2.]

182.1 Notice — **If the Minister makes a declaration under subsection 22.1(1) of the Act in respect of a foreign national, the foreign national is considered to have been given notice of the declaration if**

   (a) notice is sent by mail to their last known address;

(b) notice is sent to their last known email address;

(c) notice is provided to them by hand, including at a port of entry; or

(d) notice is sent or provided by other reasonable means, if it is not possible to give notice by one of the means referred to in paragraphs (a) to (c).

SOR/2013-210, s. 2

182.2 (1) Written submissions — A foreign national who is the subject of a declaration made under subsection 22.1(1) of the Act may make written submissions to the Minister as to why the declaration should be revoked or why its effective period should be shortened.

(2) Time limit — The written submissions must be made within 60 days after the day on which the notice of the declaration is sent or provided to the foreign national, as the case may be.

SOR/2013-210, s. 2

DIVISION 2 — CONDITIONS ON TEMPORARY RESIDENTS

183. (1) General conditions — Subject to section 185, the following conditions are imposed on all temporary residents:

(a) to leave Canada by the end of the period authorized for their stay;

(b) to not work, unless authorized by this Part or Part 11;

(b.1) if authorized to work by this Part or Part 11, to not enter into an employment agreement, or extend the term of an employment agreement, with an employer who, on a regular basis, offers striptease, erotic dance, escort services or erotic massages;

(b.2) if authorized to work by this Part or Part 11, to not enter into an employment agreement, or extend the term of an employment agreement, with an employer referred to in any of subparagraphs 200(3)(h)(i) to (iii); and

(c) to not study, unless authorized by the Act, this Part or Part 12.

(2) Authorized period of stay — Subject to subsections (3) to (5), the period authorized for the stay of a temporary resident is six months or any other period that is fixed by an officer on the basis of

(a) the temporary resident's means of support in Canada;

(b) the period for which the temporary resident applies to stay; and

(c) the expiry of the temporary resident's passport or other travel document.

(3) Authorized period begins — The period authorized for the stay of a temporary resident begins on

(a) if they are authorized to enter and remain in Canada on a temporary basis, the day on which they first enter Canada after they are so authorized;

(a.1) if they have become a temporary resident in accordance with subsection 46(1.1) of the Act, the day on which their application to renounce their permanent resident status is approved; and

812

(b) in any other case, the day on which they enter Canada.

(4) **Authorized period ends** — The period authorized for a temporary resident's stay ends on the earliest of

(a) the day on which the temporary resident leaves Canada without obtaining prior authorization to re-enter Canada;

(b) the day on which their permit becomes invalid, in the case of a temporary resident who has been issued either a work permit or a study permit;

(b.1) the day on which the second of their permits becomes invalid, in the case of a temporary resident who has been issued a work permit and a study permit;

(c) the day on which any temporary resident permit issued to the temporary resident is no longer valid under section 63; or

(d) the day on which the period authorized under subsection (2) ends, if paragraphs (a) to (c) do not apply.

(5) **Extension of period authorized for stay** — Subject to subsection (5.1), if a temporary resident has applied for an extension of the period authorized for their stay and a decision is not made on the application by the end of the period authorized for their stay, the period is extended until

(a) the day on which a decision is made, if the application is refused; or

(b) the end of the new period authorized for their stay, if the application is allowed.

(5.1) **Non-application** — Subsection (5) does not apply in respect of a foreign national who is the subject of a declaration made under subsection 22.1(1) of the Act.

(6) **Continuation of status and conditions** — If the period authorized for the stay of a temporary resident is extended by operation of paragraph (5)(a) or extended under paragraph (5)(b), the temporary resident retains their status, subject to any other conditions imposed, during the extended period.

SOR/2010-172, s. 1; SOR/2013-210, s. 3; SOR/2013-245, s. 3; SOR/2014-14, s. 4; SOR/2014-269, s. 3; SOR/2015-144, s. 3

Case Law

Section 183(1)

Editor's note: With respect to the issue of the intention to leave Canada by the end of the period authorized, see also case summaries under Regulation 200(1) and Regulation 216.

Po v. Canada (Minister of Citizenship and Immigration) (2014), 31 Imm. L.R. (4th) 116, 2014 FC 1012, 2014 CarswellNat 4246, 2014 CarswellNat 4377 — The applicant, a citizen of Malaysia, was studying business pursuant to a student visa. Her program included 980 hours of coursework and 980 hours of employment through a co-op arrangement for which she held a work permit. Her student visa expired during the program. She made a timely application for its restoration. The Minister denied the application, giving only the following explanation from the examining officer:

I'm not satisfied that you meet the requirements as a genuine student as per *Regulation 183(1)* and the co-op work permit as per *Regulation 205(c)*.

The officer's notes show that the application was denied because the work component exceeded 50 per cent of the program, in violation of the Minister's policy. Originally the work component was exactly 50 per cent, but the student received an exemption from five courses. By the officer's calculation, the academic component, excluding the exempted courses, totalled 802 or 826 hours, and the work component remained at 980 hours. Since work represented 54-55 per cent of the program, she found the applicant to be ineligible. The sole issue was whether the officer breached the applicant's right to procedural fairness by not offering the opportunity to address the officer's concerns.

The Minister enjoys discretion to deny visas for programs that are nothing more than ruses to facilitate employment in Canada under the pretense of study. In the case at bar, however, an exemption reducing the academic component from 50 per cent to 45 or 46 per cent of the total does not stand out as a manifest abuse of the work-study scheme. The conclusion that the exemption changed the very nature of the program requires a stronger basis in fact than the officer provided. In such a case, the officer should have sought an explanation of the exemption before drawing that conclusion. The officer's failure to give the applicant an opportunity to respond to her concerns, on the facts of this case, amounted to a breach of natural justice. The application for judicial review was allowed.

Boughus v. Canada (Minister of Citizenship & Immigration), 2010 FC 210, 2010 CarswellNat 2171, 2010 CarswellNat 404 — The applicant's application for a temporary resident visa was refused. The applicant originally came to Canada on his mother's application as a dependant and became a permanent resident in June, 1992. Despite his permanent residence status, the applicant continued his employment overseas. In September, 1996, an inquiry was held to determine if the applicant was still a permanent resident because of the amount of time he had spent outside Canada. The inquiry found that he was still a permanent resident because he maintained his intention to reside in Canada, as demonstrated by his applying for a returning resident permit. However, the applicant was found inadmissible to Canada upon his attempt to return in July, 1999. At the time, an officer wrote a report against the applicant indicating that he had not met the terms of his residency obligation. The applicant returned to Syria prior to an inquiry being held with regards to his status in Canada. The applicant's mother became sick in 2004 and he sought a temporary resident visa (TRV) to visit her in Canada. Between May, 2004 and April, 2009, the applicant applied for a TRV on five occasions and each application was refused. While making these applications, the applicant was unaware that he retained permanent resident status and, as a result, was ineligible for a TRV. In February, 2009, the applicant was made aware of the questionable status of his permanent residency. The applicant then signed a voluntary relinquishment of permanent resident status. The applicant was advised that he could reapply for a visitor's visa after signing a waiver of appeal with regard to his relinquishment of permanent resident status. The applicant's application for a TRV was refused because the officer was not satisfied that the applicant would leave Canada at the end of his stay.

Procedural fairness did not require an interview in this case.

There was nothing to suggest the officer failed to consider family reunification objectives in making the decision. It is the officer's job to weigh competing factors and reach conclusions based upon what he or she finds to be determinative of the issue in hand. The process does not involve a fettering of discretion. Although the court concluded that a decision in the applicant's favour would have been reasonable, that in itself did not make the officer's decision unreasonable. The court cannot interfere unless the decision falls outside the acceptable reasonable range enunciated in *Dunsmuir* (2008), 69 Imm. L.R. (3d) 1 (S.C.C.). Application for judicial review was dismissed.

Murai v. Canada (Minister of Citizenship & Immigration) (2006), 53 Imm. L.R. (3d) 218, 2006 CarswellNat 367, 2006 FC 186 — The applicant came to Canada without a visa as it was not required. Her application for an extension of time to remain in Canada was refused. Her subsequent application for refugee status was denied and her leave application for judicial review was refused. Her application to defer the removal order was denied. Her pre-removal risk assessment was denied and leave for judicial review was denied. Her humanitarian and compassionate leave application was denied and leave for judicial review was also denied. She left Canada. She then made an application for a work permit as a live-in caregiver. This application was denied as the visa officer was not satisfied that the applicant would leave Canada at the end of the authorized stay period per s. 183(1)(a) of the Regulations. The officer came to this conclusion on the basis of the applicant's previous immigration history.

The officer was entitled to satisfy himself that the applicant for the Live-In Caregiver Program had an intention of leaving Canada should the application for permanent residence be refused. In this case, however, the court concluded that the officer's decision was unreasonable since the record revealed that the applicant was a law-abiding citizen, who after exhausting her remedies returned to her home country and subsequently applied under the Live-In Caregiver Program. In fact, the evidence of her previous immigration encounters supported the applicant's contention that she was law abiding and would continue to comply with the rules in the future.

The visa officer should have asked himself "will this person stay illegally in Canada if not successful under the program?" Based on the applicant's past performance, any reasonable person would say "no, she would not stay in Canada illegally."

Boni c. Canada (Ministre de la Citoyenneté & de l'Immigration), [2005] F.C.J. No. 43, 2005 CarswellNat 176, 2005 CarswellNat 4646, 2005 FC 31; affirmed [2006] F.C.J. No. 275, 57 Imm. L.R. (3d) 4, 2006 CarswellNat 414, 2006 FCA 68 (C.A.) — The applicant applied for judicial review of a visa officer's decision to deny the applicant's application for a study permit. The risk that study permit applicants will not leave Canada once the period of their stay ends is a very important factor to be considered. An officer may examine the applicant's long-term objective. That objective is a relevant point which carries some weight, in view of the evidence as a whole on whether a study permit would be granted. A visa officer's conclusions will not be disturbed unless they are so unreasonable as to require the court's intervention.

Section 183(5)

De Brito v. Canada (Minister of Citizenship & Immigration) (2003), 33 Imm. L.R. (3d) 54, 242 F.T.R. 145, 2003 CarswellNat 3719, 2003 CarswellNat 4192, 2003 FC 1379 — The applicant entered Canada and obtained a temporary work authorization. His authorization was extended on two occasions and was to expire August 31, 2002. In March 2002, the applicant entered into a common-law relationship with a Canadian citizen. The applicant also attended courses in English as a second language which were less than 6 months in duration. In April 2002, the applicant ceased her employment in Canada and was accepted in a full-time 40 week ESL program at a community college. In July 2002, the applicant submitted an application for a student authorization to the Canadian Consulate in Buffalo. The applicant, in August 2002, applied for an extension of her temporary work authorization and for a change of terms and conditions through the Case Processing Centre in Vegreville. In September 2002, the applicant received a letter stating that her application for an extension of her temporary work authorization had been transferred to the respondent's offices in Mississauga. The applicant received no further correspondence from either Mississauga or Vegreville in connection with this application for a work authorization extension. In September 2002, the applicant also received a letter from Buffalo stating that she should attend an interview there on October 1, 2002. On October 1, 2002, when the applicant attempted to enter the United States she was refused entry. Upon her return to Canada the applicant advised the Canadian authorities at the port-of-entry that she had been refused entry into the United States and an immigration officer determined that her temporary authorization to remain in Canada was no longer valid because she had left Canada prior to receiving a decision on her extension request and had not obtained a re-entry visa. The applicant was found to be inadmissible and an exclusion order was issued.

The immigration officer erred in requiring the applicant to obtain a visa prior to re-entry due to the fact that the applicant falls under an exemption found in para. 190(3) of the Regulations. The applicant was seeking to enter the US solely for the purpose of attending an interview with the Canadian Consulate. She held a work permit that had been issued prior to departing Canada. The applicant had received no decision from the respondent regarding her application for an extension of her work authorization and pursuant to s. 183(5) of the Regulations retained her status until such a decision was made.

Figueroa v. Canada (Minister of Citizenship & Immigration), 2003 CarswellNat 3657, 2003 CarswellNat 4507, 2003 FC 1339 — The applicant sought to review a decision of an immigration officer refusing the applicant's request for an extension of her temporary resident status.

The applicant is a citizen of Cuba. She met her husband, Mr. Cecil Stein, a Canadian citizen, when he was vacationing there. Mr. Stein continued to visit the applicant in Cuba after his holiday and eventually proposed to her. The applicant sought a Canadian visitor visa but was refused. Mr. Stein contacted his member of Parliament and eventually a Minister's permit was obtained for the applicant in the summer of 2002. This permit allowed the applicant temporary residence in Canada until September 30, 2002. On August 21, 2002, the applicant married Mr. Stein and on August 26, 2002, more than 30 days before the expiration of her temporary resident permit, the applicant sought an extension pending a final determination of her permanent resident application. The permanent resident application was filed in September 2002, the applicant applied as a Member of the Spouse In-Canada class. Her application was supported by Mr. Stein's sponsorship application. In December 2002, the applicant's request for an extension of her temporary resident status was refused.

The covering letter from the immigration officer indicated that she was attaching copies of the decision giving written reasons for the decision. However, it is clear that the decision did not include any written reasons.

The respondent took the position that the immigration officer acted in accordance with the instructions from the Minister. The record, however, was silent as to the content of those instructions. In the absence of any evidence as to those instructions, and without reasons, a question arose as to how the immigration officer followed the instructions. In those circumstances, the lack of reasons raised an appearance of arbitrariness on the part of the officer. Accordingly the officer's decision was set aside.

184 (1) Condition imposed on members of a crew — A foreign national who enters Canada as a member of a crew must leave Canada within 72 hours after they cease to be a member of a crew.

(2) Conditions imposed on foreign nationals who enter to become members of a crew — The following conditions are imposed on a foreign national who enters Canada to become a member of a crew:

(a) [Repealed SOR/2004-167, s. 50(2).]

(b) to join the means of transportation within the period imposed as a condition of entry or, if no period is imposed, within 48 hours after they enter Canada; and

(c) to leave Canada within 72 hours after they cease to be a member of a crew.

SOR/2004-167, s. 50(1), (2)

185. Specific conditions — An officer may impose, vary or cancel the following specific conditions on a temporary resident:

(a) the period authorized for their stay;

(b) the work that they are permitted to engage in, or are prohibited from engaging in, in Canada, including

(i) the type of work,

(ii) the employer,

(iii) the location of the work,

(iv) the times and periods of the work, and

(v) in the case of a member of a crew, the period within which they must join the means of transportation;

(c) the studies that they are permitted to engage in, or are prohibited from engaging in, in Canada, including

(i) the type of studies or course,

(ii) the educational institution,

(iii) the location of the studies, and

(iv) the times and periods of the studies;

(d) the area within which they are permitted to travel or are prohibited from travelling in Canada; and

(e) the times and places at which they must report for

(i) medical examination, surveillance or treatment, or

(ii) the presentation of evidence of compliance with applicable conditions.

Case Law

Patel v. Canada (Minister of Citizenship & Immigration) (2006), 54 Imm. L.R. (3d) 180, 2006 CarswellNat 454, 2006 CarswellNat 2375, 2006 FC 224 — The applicant was aged 79 and a citizen of India. She had five children and 11 grandchildren living in Canada, all of whom were Canadian citizens. Her husband was deceased and she had no more family living in India. She first came to Canada to attend the wedding of her granddaughter.

Subsequently, her Canadian children decided they would sponsor her to stay in Canada as she would be alone in her mother country. She obtained three extensions of her status as a temporary resident. Her request for a fourth extension was denied after consideration of dual intent and determination that she was not a *bona fide* temporary resident. An application for restoration was denied.

The standard of review applicable to a decision refusing restoration of status is that of reasonableness *simpliciter*.

A permanent residence application does not necessarily preclude a temporary purpose for being in Canada. The current statutory and regulatory scheme does not say that a person's initial temporary purpose must remain constant and unchanged. The only requirement is the existence of a temporary purpose. The application for restoration of temporary status was not refused on the basis that the applicant would not be in Canada for a temporary purpose. On the contrary, it was denied because the applicant's stay in Canada would be for a "longer" temporary purpose, that is, while awaiting a decision on the application for permanent residence. The conclusion reached by the officer contained a reviewable error. The application was granted and the matter referred back to a different officer for redetermination.

DIVISION 3 — WORK WITHOUT A PERMIT

186. No permit required — A foreign national may work in Canada without a work permit

(a) as a business visitor to Canada within the meaning of section 187;

(b) as a foreign representative, if they are properly accredited by the Department of Foreign Affairs and International Trade and are in Canada to carry out official duties as a diplomatic agent, consular officer, representative or official of a country other than Canada, of the United Nations or any of its agencies or of any international organization of which Canada is a member;

(c) if the foreign national is a family member of a foreign representative in Canada who is accredited with diplomatic status by the Department of Foreign Affairs and International Trade and that Department has stated in writing that it does not object to the foreign national working in Canada;

(d) as a member of the armed forces of a country that is a designated state for the purposes of the *Visiting Forces Act*, including a person who has been designated as a civilian component of those armed forces;

(e) as an officer of a foreign government sent, under an exchange agreement between Canada and one or more countries, to take up duties with a federal or provincial agency;

(e.1) as a cross-border maritime law enforcement officer designated by the United States under the Framework Agreement on Integrated Cross-Border Maritime Law Enforcement Operations between the Government of Canada and the Government of the United States of America, signed on May 26, 2009;

(e.2) as an in-flight security officer employed by a foreign government with which Canada has concluded an arrangement in respect of commercial passenger aircraft security;

(f) if they are a full-time student, on the campus of the university or college at which they are a full-time student, for the period for which they hold a study permit to study at that university or college;

(g) as a performing artist appearing alone or in a group in an artistic performance — other than a performance that is primarily for a film production or a television or radio broadcast — or as a member of the staff of such a performing artist or group who is integral to the artistic performance, if

    (i) they are part of a foreign production or group, or are a guest artist in a Canadian production or group, performing a time-limited engagement, and

    (ii) they are not in an employment relationship with the organization or business in Canada that is contracting for their services;

(h) as a participant in sports activities or events, in Canada, either as an individual participant or as a member of a foreign-based team or Canadian amateur team;

(i) as an employee of a foreign news company for the purpose of reporting on events in Canada;

(j) as a guest speaker for the sole purpose of making a speech or delivering a paper at a dinner, graduation, convention or similar function, or as a commercial speaker or seminar leader delivering a seminar that lasts no longer than five days;

(k) as a member of the executive of a committee that is organizing a convention or meeting in Canada or as a member of the administrative support staff of such a committee;

(l) as a person who is responsible for assisting a congregation or group in the achievement of its spiritual goals and whose main duties are to preach doctrine, perform functions related to gatherings of the congregation or group or provide spiritual counselling;

(m) as a judge, referee or similar official at an international amateur sports competition, an international cultural or artistic event or competition or an animal or agricultural competition;

(n) as an examiner or evaluator of research proposals or university projects, programs or theses;

(o) as an expert who conducts surveys or analyses that are to be used as evidence before a federal or provincial regulatory body, a tribunal or a court of law or as an expert witness before such a body, tribunal or court of law;

(p) as a student in a health field, including as a medical elective or clinical clerk at a medical teaching institution in Canada, for the primary purpose of acquiring training, if they have written approval from the body that regulates that field;

(q) as a civil aviation inspector of a national aeronautical authority conducting inspections of the flight operation procedures or cabin safety of a commercial air carrier operating international flights;

(r) as an accredited representative or adviser participating in an aviation accident or incident investigation conducted under the *Canadian Transportation Accident Investigation and Safety Board Act*;

(s) as a member of a crew who is employed by a foreign company aboard a means of transportation that

    (i) is foreign-owned and not registered in Canada, and

    (ii) is engaged primarily in international transportation;

(t) as a provider of emergency services, including medical services, for the protection or preservation of life or property;

(u) until a decision is made on an application made by them under subsection 201(1), if they have remained in Canada after the expiry of their work permit and they have continued to comply with the conditions set out on the expired work permit, other than the expiry date.

(v) if they are the holder of a study permit and

    (i) they are a full-time student enrolled at a designated learning institution as defined in section 211.1,

    (ii) the program in which they are enrolled is a post-secondary academic, vocational or professional training program, or a vocational training program at the secondary level offered in Quebec, in each case, of a duration of six months or more that leads to a degree, diploma or certificate, and

    (iii) although they are permitted to engage in full-time work during a regularly scheduled break between academic sessions, they work no more than 20 hours per week during a regular academic session; or

(w) if they are or were the holder of a study permit who has completed their program of study and

    (i) they met the requirements set out in paragraph (v), and

    (ii) they applied for a work permit before the expiry of that study permit and a decision has not yet been made in respect of their application.

SOR/2010-253, s. 3; SOR/2011-126, s. 2; SOR/2014-14, s. 5; SOR/2014-170, s. 1

Case Law

Singh v. Canada (Minister of Citizenship & Immigration), [2008] F.C.J. No. 65, 2008 CarswellNat 92, 2008 FC 58 — The applicant argued that the visa officer erred in finding that he did not have a work permit allowing him to work in Canada and refusing to award him any points for "arranged employment" or "adaptability." The applicant was a Sikh priest and an Indian citizen who came to Canada on a visitor's visa. His visa explicitly prohibited him from being employed while he was in Canada, but did allow him to perform religious duties in the country. The applicant contended that religious workers do not require a work permit to be allowed to work in Canada, and the fact that he did not have such a permit should not have precluded the consideration of his job offer.

The applicant's argument ignored the explicit condition contained in his visitor's visa that he was "prohibited from engaging in employment in Canada." In the face of this language, the visa cannot reasonably be interpreted as amounting to "a written authorization to work in Canada." There was no evidence that the applicant had complied with the application process required under Divisions 2 and 3 of the Regulations containing extensive provisions governing the granting of work permits. Finally, the applicant's offer of employment was never validated by Human Resources and Skills Development Canada. Consequently, there was no error in the visa officer's assessment.

Singh v. Canada (Minister of Citizenship & Immigration), 2007 CarswellNat 142, 2007 FC 69 — The applicant first arrived in Canada on a visitor's visa, allowing him to temporarily perform religious duties. He subsequently applied for permanent residence as a skilled worker. The applicant fell short of the required 67 points.

The applicant was correct in noting that he was exempt from the requirement to obtain a work permit before coming to Canada to work as a Sikh priest as per subs. 186(l) of the Regulations. However, no further accommodations are made in the Regulations that would grant special privileges for workers that meet the requirements of s. 186 when applying for a permanent resident visa. Given the various scenarios considered under s. 82 of the Regulations to be awarded points for arranged employment, had such an exemption been contemplated by the Canadian Government, it could easily have been included in the Regulations. The applicant argued that no such accommodations were made because the occupations listed under s. 186 have already been determined to have a "neutral and positive affect on the labour market in Canada," as required to issue a work permit under s. 203 of the Regulations, and thus an exemption is implied from a joint reading of ss. 186, 203, and 82 of the Regulations. The court dismissed this argument. It found that it was clear on the face of the record that the applicant possessed neither a work permit nor an offer of employment validated by HRSDC, and that the decision of the visa officer not to grant the applicant any points for adaptability or arranged employment, and ultimately to refuse the application for permanent residence, was reasonable pursuant to the existing Regulations. Nevertheless, since it appeared at the time that the applicant submitted his application for permanent residence, that there was confusion at Citizenship and Immigration Canada concerning the proper awarding of points for arranged employment for priests, whose job offers were not validated by HRSDC as evidenced by the visa officer's affidavit and the email from a third party submitted by the applicant, this was sufficient to raise serious concerns that all individuals applying for permanent residence in Canada under circumstances similar to that of the applicant may not be treated alike, a situation contrary to the rules of procedural fairness. On this basis alone, the judicial review was granted.

The court strongly encouraged the Minister of Citizenship and Immigration to clarify the guidelines concerning the allocation of points in permanent resident applications, for both arranged employment and adaptability, for individuals who are permitted to work in Canada without a work permit under s. 186, and who later seek to become permanent residents under the skilled worker class.

Duraisami v. Canada (Minister of Citizenship & Immigration), 2005 CarswellNat 2005, 2005 CarswellNat 4421, 2005 FC 1008 — The applicant was denied an extension of his temporary resident permit on the grounds that he did not satisfy the requirements of the *Immigration and Refugee Protection Regulations*, s. 186(l), as a religious worker. The immigration officer had not been presented any information relating to his abilities to preach doctrine or any certificates indicating he was ordained or educated in any way to perform spiritual duties. The court concluded that the officer's decision was reasonable as there was no evidence presented on the ability of the applicant to preach doctrine but instead there was only reference to the applicant's religious fervour which the court concluded could not necessarily be equated to the ability to preach. Section 186(l) has to be given a meaning and application consistent with its purpose "to grant an exemption from work permits to those who have responsibility to assist a congregation or a group in achieving its spiritual goals." There are rational limitations based on the specific facts as to the scope of the provision. Not every person who assists at a place of worship (ushers, singers, teachers of children's religious studies) *per se*, falls within the scope of s. 186(l).

187. (1) Business visitors — For the purposes of paragraph 186(a), a business visitor to Canada is a foreign national who is described in subsection (2) or who seeks to engage in international business activities in Canada without directly entering the Canadian labour market.

(2) Specific cases — The following foreign nationals are business visitors:

(a) foreign nationals purchasing Canadian goods or services for a foreign business or government, or receiving training or familiarization in respect of such goods or services;

(b) foreign nationals receiving or giving training within a Canadian parent or subsidiary of the corporation that employs them outside Canada, if any production of goods or services that results from the training is incidental; and

(c) foreign nationals representing a foreign business or government for the purpose of selling goods for that business or government, if the foreign national is not engaged in making sales to the general public in Canada.

(3) Factors — For the purpose of subsection (1), a foreign national seeks to engage in international business activities in Canada without directly entering the Canadian labour market only if

(a) the primary source of remuneration for the business activities is outside Canada; and

(b) the principal place of business and actual place of accrual of profits remain predominately outside Canada.

DIVISION 4 — STUDY WITHOUT A PERMIT

188. (1) No permit required — A foreign national may study in Canada without a study permit

(a) if they are a family member or a member of the private staff of a foreign representative who is properly accredited by the Department of Foreign Affairs and International Trade and who is in Canada to carry out official duties as a diplomatic agent, consular officer, representative or official of a country other than Canada, of the United Nations or any of its agencies or of any international organization of which Canada is a member;

(b) as a member of the armed forces of a country that is a designated state for the purposes of the *Visiting Forces Act*, including a person who has been designated as a civilian component of those armed forces;

(c) if the duration of their course or program of studies is six months or less and will be completed within the period for their stay authorized upon entry into Canada; or

(d) if they are an Indian.

(2) Exception — Despite paragraph (1)(c), a foreign national may apply for a study permit before entering Canada for a course or program of studies of a duration of six months or less.

SOR/2014-14, s. 6

189. Expired study permits — A foreign national who has made an application under subsection 217(1) is authorized to study without a study permit until a decision is made on the application if they have remained in Canada since the expiry of their study permit and continue to comply with the conditions, other than the expiry date, set out on the expired study permit.

DIVISION 5 — TEMPORARY RESIDENT VISA EXEMPTIONS

190. (1) Visa exemption — nationality — A foreign national is exempt from the requirement to obtain a temporary resident visa if they

(a) are a citizen of Andorra, Antigua and Barbuda, Australia, Austria, Bahamas, Barbados, Belgium, Brunei Darussalam, Chile, Croatia, Cyprus, Czech Republic, Denmark, Estonia, Federal Republic of Germany, Finland, France, Greece, Hungary, Iceland, Ireland, Italy, Japan, Latvia, Liechtenstein, Lithuania, Luxembourg, Malta, Monaco, Netherlands, New Zealand, Norway, Papua New Guinea, Poland, Portugal, Republic of Korea, Samoa, San Marino, Singapore, Slovakia, Slovenia, Solomon Islands, Spain, Sweden or Switzerland;

(b) are

(i) a British citizen,

(ii) a British overseas citizen who is re-admissible to the United Kingdom, or

(iii) a citizen of a British overseas territory who derives that citizenship through birth, descent, naturalization or registration in one of the British overseas territories of Anguilla, Bermuda, British Virgin Islands, Cayman Islands, Falkland Islands, Gibraltar, Montserrat, Pitcairn Island, Saint Helena or Turks and Caicos Islands; or

(c) are a national of the United States or a person who has been lawfully admitted to the United States for permanent residence.

(2) Visa exemption — documents — A foreign national is exempt from the requirement to obtain a temporary resident visa if they

(a) hold a passport that contains a diplomatic acceptance, a consular acceptance or an official acceptance issued by the Chief of Protocol for the Department of Foreign Affairs and International Trade on behalf of the Government of Canada and are a properly accredited diplomat, consular officer, representative or official of a country other than Canada, of the United Nations or any of its agencies, or of any international organization of which Canada is a member;

(b) hold a passport or travel document issued by the Holy See;

(c) hold a national Israeli passport;

823

(d) hold a passport issued by the Hong Kong Special Administrative Region of the People's Republic of China;

(e) hold a passport issued by the United Kingdom to a British National (Overseas), as a person born, naturalized or registered in Hong Kong;

(e.1) hold a passport issued by the United Kingdom to a British Subject which contains the observation that the holder has the right of abode in the United Kingdom; or

(f) hold an ordinary passport issued by the Ministry of Foreign Affairs in Taiwan that includes the personal identification number of the individual.

(2.1) [Repealed SOR/2015-77, s. 6(2).]

(3) **Visa exemption — purpose of entry** — A foreign national is exempt from the requirement to obtain a temporary resident visa if they are seeking to enter and remain in Canada solely

(a) subject to an agreement between Canada and one or more foreign countries respecting the obligation to hold such a visa,

(i) as a member of a crew of a means of transportation other than a vessel or to become a member of a crew of a means of transportation other than a vessel, or

(ii) to transit through Canada after working, or to work, as a member of a crew of a means of transportation other than a vessel, if they possess a ticket for departure from Canada within 24 hours after their arrival in Canada;

(b) to transit through Canada as a passenger on a flight stopping in Canada for the sole purpose of refuelling and

(i) they are in possession of the documents required in order to enter the United States and their flight is bound for that country, or

(ii) they were lawfully admitted to the United States and their flight originated in that country;

(b.1) to transit through Canada as a passenger on a flight that, owing to an emergency or other unforeseen circumstances, makes an unscheduled stop in Canada;

(c) to transit through Canada as a passenger on a flight if the foreign national

(i) is transported by a commercial transporter and there is a memorandum of understanding referred to in subsection (4) in effect between the Minister and the commercial transporter concerning the transit of passengers through Canada without a Canadian visa,

(ii) holds a passport or travel document that was issued by the country of which the foreign national is a citizen or national and that country is listed in the memorandum of understanding, and

(iii) is in possession of any visa required to enter the country of destination;

(d) to carry out official duties as a member of the armed forces of a country that is a designated state for the purposes of the *Visiting Forces Act*, unless they have been designated under that Act as a civilian component of those armed forces;

(e) [Repealed SOR/2015-77, s. 6(5).]

(f) to re-enter Canada following a visit solely to the United States or St. Pierre and Miquelon, if they

(i) held a study permit or a work permit that was issued before they left Canada on such a visit or were authorized to enter and remain in Canada as a temporary resident, and

(ii) return to Canada by the end of the period initially authorized for their stay or any extension to it;

(g) to conduct inspections of the flight operation procedures or cabin safety of a commercial air carrier operating international flights, if they are a civil aviation inspector of a national aeronautical authority and possess valid documentation to that effect; or

(h) to participate as an accredited representative or as an adviser to an aviation accident or incident investigation conducted under the *Canadian Transportation Accident Investigation and Safety Board Act*, if they possess valid documentation to that effect.

(3.1) Visa exemption — crew member — A foreign national who is a member of a crew and who is carried to Canada by a vessel is exempt from the requirement to obtain a temporary resident visa if they are seeking

(a) to enter Canada as a member of the crew of the vessel; and

(b) to remain in Canada solely as a member of the crew of that vessel or any other vessel.

(4) Content of memorandum of understanding — A memorandum of understanding referred to in paragraph (3)(c) shall include provisions respecting

(a) the countries to which the memorandum of understanding applies;

(b) the scheduled flights to which the memorandum of understanding applies; and

(c) the commercial transporter's obligation to control the movement of in-transit passengers.

SOR/2002-326, s. 1; SOR/2002-332, s. 1; SOR/2003-197, s. 2; SOR/2003-260, s. 2; SOR/2004-111, s. 1; SOR/2004-167, s. 53; SOR/2006-228, s. 1; SOR/2007-238, s. 1; SOR/2008-54, s. 1; SOR/2008-308, s. 1; SOR/2009-105, s. 1; SOR/2009-207, s. 1; SOR/2009-208, s. 1; SOR/2010-265, s. 1; SOR/2011-125, s. 3; SOR/2011-126, s. 3; SOR/2012-171, s. 1; SOR/2013-201, s. 1; SOR/2014-267, s. 1; SOR/2015-77, s. 6

Case Law

Section 190(3)

De Brito v. Canada (Minister of Citizenship & Immigration) (2003), 33 Imm. L.R. (3d) 54, 242 F.T.R. 145, 2003 CarswellNat 3719, 2003 CarswellNat 4192, 2003 FC 1379 — The applicant entered Canada and obtained a temporary work authorization. His authorization was extended on two occasions and was to expire August 31, 2002. In March

2002, the applicant entered into a common-law relationship with a Canadian citizen. The applicant also attended courses in English as a second language which were less than six months in duration. In April 2002, the applicant ceased her employment in Canada and was accepted in a full-time 40-week ESL program at a community college. In July 2002, the applicant submitted an application for a student authorization to the Canadian Consulate in Buffalo. The applicant, in August 2002, applied for an extension of her temporary work authorization and for a change of terms and conditions through the case processing centre in Vegreville. In September 2002, the applicant received a letter stating that her application for an extension of her temporary work authorization had been transferred to the respondent's offices in Mississauga. The applicant received no further correspondence from either Mississauga or Vegreville in connection with this application for a work authorization extension. In September 2002, the applicant also received a letter from Buffalo stating that she should attend an interview there on October 1, 2002. On October 1, 2002, when the applicant attempted to enter the United States she was refused entry. Upon her return to Canada the applicant advised the Canadian authorities at the port-of-entry that she had been refused entry into the United States and an immigration officer determined that her temporary authorization to remain in Canada was no longer valid because she had left Canada prior to receiving a decision on her extension request and had not obtained a re-entry visa. The applicant was found to be inadmissible and an exclusion order was issued.

The immigration officer erred in requiring the applicant to obtain a visa prior to re-entry due to the fact that the applicant falls under an exemption found in para. 190(3) of the Regulations. The applicant was seeking to enter the U.S. solely for the purpose of attending an interview with the Canadian Consulate. She held a work permit that had been issued prior to departing Canada. The applicant had received no decision from the respondent regarding her application for an extension of her work authorization and pursuant to s. 183(5) of the Regulations retained her status until such a decision was made.

PART 10 — VISITORS

191. Class — The visitor class is prescribed as a class of persons who may become temporary residents.

192. Visitor — A foreign national is a visitor and a member of the visitor class if the foreign national has been authorized to enter and remain in Canada as a visitor.

193. Conditions — A visitor is subject to the conditions imposed under Part 9.

PART 10.1

[Heading repealed SOR/2014-185, s. 2.]

193.1 [Repealed SOR/2014-185, s. 2.]

193.2 [Repealed SOR/2014-185, s. 2.]

193.3 [Repealed SOR/2014-185, s. 2.]

193.4 [Repealed SOR/2014 185, s. 2.]

193.5 [Repealed SOR/2008-309, s. 2.]

PART 11 — WORKERS

DIVISION 1 — GENERAL RULES

194. Class — The worker class is prescribed as a class of persons who may become temporary residents.

195. Worker — A foreign national is a worker and a member of the worker class if the foreign national has been authorized to enter and remain in Canada as a worker.

196. Work permit required — A foreign national must not work in Canada unless authorized to do so by a work permit or these Regulations.

Case Law

Brar v. Canada (Minister of Citizenship & Immigration) (2006), 59 Imm. L.R. (3d) 293, 2006 CarswellNat 4324, 2006 FC 1502 — The applicants sought judicial review in respect of a decision by a member of the Immigration and Refugee Board of Canada given collectively, but pertaining to each of them, that determined that each of the applicants had contravened the terms of the work permit issued to each of them and therefore each was to be excluded from Canada. The applicants were all adult male citizens of India. They applied for and received temporary work permits. The work permit stated:

Employer: Bombay Paradise

Conditions:

- not authorized to work in any occupation other than stated;
- not authorized to work for any employer other than stated; and
- not authorized for work in any location other than stated.

When the applicants arrived in Calgary, they found that the Bombay Paradise Restaurant was under construction and far from being completed. The owner of that business was a numbered company run by a person known as Vic. He placed them in another establishment known as Bombay Sweet House & Restaurant. Apparently, the ownership was not the same as Bombay Paradise, although pay cheques issued to the applicants were from the numbered company which was the owner of the Bombay Paradise business.

It came to the Minister's attention that the applicants were working for an employer whom the Minister believed to be other than that named in the work permit. As a result, an exclusion order was issued. Following that order, an admissibility hearing was held on March 1, 2006. The issue of the hearing was whether each of the applicants was inadmissible under s. 41(a) of the IRPA, as having contravened s. 29(2) of that Act.

The court concluded that Bombay Paradise paid the applicants and the applicants worked in Calgary, and therefore, no term as set out in the work permit had been breached. A work permit should be understandable to all interested persons, not just the worker or the government, on the face of it. The Minister has the resources to ensure that the permit is complete and understandable. If it is not, the Minister cannot be seen to rely on self-created ambiguities to derive a beneficial interpretation. It is the same concept as *contra proferentum* in the interpretation of a contract. If the contract was prepared by a party, any ambiguity must be interpreted against the interests of that party.

The applicants did not breach the terms of their work permits. Their employer, the person who pays them, was Bombay Paradise. They worked in Calgary. As a result, the exclusion order was set aside and the matter was returned to be determined by a different person.

196.1 Restrictions — A foreign national must not enter into an employment agreement, or extend the term of an employment agreement, with an employer

(a) **who, on a regular basis, offers striptease, erotic dance, escort services or erotic massages; or**

(b) **referred to in any of subparagraphs 200(3)(h)(i) to (iii).**

SOR/2013-245, s. 4; SOR/2015-144, s. 4

DIVISION 2 — APPLICATION FOR WORK PERMIT

197. Application before entry — A foreign national may apply for a work permit at any time before entering Canada.

Case Law

Villagonzalo v. Canada (Minister of Citizenship & Immigration), 2008 CarswellNat 4937, 2008 CarswellNat 3640, 2008 FC 1127 — This was an application for judicial review of a visa officer's decision that the applicant did not meet the requirements for a work permit. The applicant applied under the Live-In-Caregiver Program. The applicant argued that the officer failed to take into account that throughout her previous stay in Canada, the applicant undertook to maintain valid TRV status and promptly left when her request for an extension was refused. The applicant explained that she originally received a six-month TRV to come to Canada to attend her brother's wedding. Due to her child being sick, she was unable to attend the wedding. She did, however, come to Canada in November 2004 to visit her family. The applicant deposed that she told this to the visa officer at the time of her interview for a work permit. It appears that her failure to attend her brother's wedding and her failure to leave Canada between either May 17, 2005, or May 22, 2005 (the date she received the refusal to extend her status in Canada), and June 1, 2005, caused the visa officer to believe that the applicant in the future would not leave Canada by the end of any period authorized for her stay. The court concluded that the visa officer's decision was not reasonable and that there should have been some consideration of the applicant's explanations. The application for judicial review was allowed.

da Silva v. Canada (Minister of Citizenship & Immigration) (2007), 68 Imm. L.R. (3d) 312, 2007 CarswellNat 4883, 2007 CarswellNat 5486, 2007 FC 1138 — The duty to provide reasons is lower in the context of applications for temporary residence status. A number of factors would suggest that the duty to provide reasons is minimal: the applicant has no legal right to obtain a visa, and bears the burden of establishing the merits of his claim; the refusal of a work permit on an application from outside of Canada has less impact on the applicant than would the removal of a benefit; and the officer is better placed to evaluate the cultural and economic benefits of the applicant's prospective employment than the applicant.

198. (1) Application on entry — Subject to subsection (2), a foreign national may apply for a work permit when entering Canada if the foreign national is exempt under Division 5 of Part 9 from the requirement to obtain a temporary resident visa.

(2) Exceptions — A foreign national may not apply for a work permit when entering Canada if

(a) a determination under section 203 is required, unless

(i) the Department of Employment and Social Development has provided an assessment under paragraph 203(2)(a) in respect of an offer of employment — other than seasonal agricultural employment or employment as a live-in caregiver — to the foreign national, or

(ii) the foreign national is a national or permanent resident of the United States or is a resident of Greenland or St. Pierre and Miquelon;

(b) the foreign national does not hold a medical certificate that they are required to hold under subsection 30(3); or

(c) the foreign national is a participant in an international youth exchange program, unless they are a national or permanent resident of the United States or their application for a work permit was approved before their entry into Canada.

SOR/2004-167, s. 54; SOR/2010-172, s. 5(d); 2013, c. 40, s. 237(3)(a); SOR/2015-147, s. 1(c); SOR/2016-136, s. 4

199. Application after entry — A foreign national may apply for a work permit after entering Canada if they

(a) hold a work permit;

(b) are working in Canada under the authority of section 186 and are not a business visitor within the meaning of section 187;

(c) hold a study permit;

(d) hold a temporary resident permit issued under subsection 24(1) of the Act that is valid for at least six months;

(e) are a family member of a person described in any of paragraphs (a) to (d);

(f) are in a situation described in section 206 or 207;

(g) applied for a work permit before entering Canada and the application was approved in writing but they have not been issued the permit;

(h) are applying as a trader or investor, intra-company transferee or professional, as described in Section B, C or D of Annex 1603 of the Agreement, within the meaning of subsection 2(1) of the *North American Free Trade Agreement Implementation Act*, and their country of citizenship — being a country party to that Agreement — grants to Canadian citizens who submit a similar application within that country treatment equivalent to that accorded by Canada to citizens of that country who submit an application within Canada, including treatment in respect of an authorization for multiple entries based on a single application; or

(i) hold a written statement from the Department of Foreign Affairs and International Trade stating that it has no objection to the foreign national working at a foreign mission in Canada.

SOR/2004-167, s. 55

DIVISION 3 — ISSUANCE OF WORK PERMITS

200. (1) Work permits — Subject to subsections (2) and (3) — and, in respect of a foreign national who makes an application for a work permit before entering Canada, subject to section 87.3 of the Act — an officer shall issue a work permit to a foreign national if, following an examination, it is established that

(a) the foreign national applied for it in accordance with Division 2;

(b) the foreign national will leave Canada by the end of the period authorized for their stay under Division 2 of Part 9;

(c) the foreign national

(i) is described in section 206 or 208,

(ii) intends to perform work described in section 204 or 205 but does not have an offer of employment to perform that work or is described in section 207 but does not have an offer of employment,

(ii.1) intends to perform work described in section 204 or 205 and has an offer of employment to perform that work or is described in section 207 and has an offer of employment, and an officer has determined, on the basis of any information provided on the officer's request by the employer making the offer and any other relevant information,

(A) that the offer is genuine under subsection (5), and

(B) that the employer

(I) during the six-year period before the day on which the application for the work permit is received by the Department, provided each foreign national employed by the employer with employment in the same occupation as that set out in the foreign national's offer of employment and with wages and working conditions that were substantially the same as — but not less favourable than — those set out in that offer, or

(II) is able to justify, under subsection 203(1.1), any failure to satisfy the criteria set out in subclause (I), or

(iii) has been offered employment, and an officer has made a positive determination under paragraphs 203(1)(a) to (e); and

(d) [Repealed SOR/2004-167, s. 56(2).]

(e) the requirements of subsections 30(2) and (3) are met, if they must submit to a medical examination under paragraph 16(2)(b) of the Act.

(2) Non-application of par. (1)(b) — Paragraph (1)(b) does not apply to a foreign national who satisfies the criteria set out in section 206 or paragraph 207(c) or (d).

(3) Exceptions — An officer shall not issue a work permit to a foreign national if

(a) there are reasonable grounds to believe that the foreign national is unable to perform the work sought;

(b) in the case of a foreign national who intends to work in the Province of Quebec and does not hold a *Certificat d'acceptation du Québec*, a determination under section 203 is required and the laws of that Province require that the foreign national hold a *Certificat d'acceptation du Québec*;

(c) the work that the foreign national intends to perform is likely to adversely affect the settlement of any labour dispute in progress or the employment of any person involved in the dispute;

(d) the foreign national seeks to enter Canada as a live-in caregiver and the foreign national does not meet the requirements of section 112;

(e) the foreign national has engaged in unauthorized study or work in Canada or has failed to comply with a condition of a previous permit or authorization unless

(i) a period of six months has elapsed since the cessation of the unauthorized work or study or failure to comply with a condition,

(ii) the study or work was unauthorized by reason only that the foreign national did not comply with conditions imposed under paragraph 185(a), any of subparagraphs 185(b)(i) to (iii) or paragraph 185(c),

(iii) section 206 applies to them, or

(iv) the foreign national was subsequently issued a temporary resident permit under subsection 24(1) of the Act;

(f) in the case of a foreign national referred to in subparagraphs (1)(c)(i) to (iii), the issuance of a work permit would be inconsistent with the terms of a federal-provincial agreement that apply to the employment of foreign nationals;

(f.1) in the case of a foreign national referred to in subparagraph (1)(c)(ii.1), the fee referred to in section 303.1 has not been paid or the information referred to in section 209.11 has not been provided before the foreign national makes an application for a work permit;

(g) the foreign national has worked in Canada for one or more periods totalling four years, unless

(i) a period of forty-eight months has elapsed since the day on which the foreign national accumulated four years of work in Canada,

(ii) the foreign national intends to perform work that would create or maintain significant social, cultural or economic benefits or opportunities for Canadian citizens or permanent residents, or

(iii) the foreign national intends to perform work pursuant to an international agreement between Canada and one or more countries, including an agreement concerning seasonal agricultural workers;

(g.1) the foreign national intends to work for an employer who, on a regular basis, offers striptease, erotic dance, escort services or erotic massages; or

(h) the foreign national intends to work for an employer who is

(i) subject to a determination made under subsection 203(5), if two years have not elapsed since the day on which that determination was made,

(ii) ineligible under paragraph 209.95(1)(b), or

(iii) in default of any amount payable in respect of an administrative monetary penalty, including if the employer fails to comply with a payment agreement for the payment of that amount.

(4) Cumulative work periods — students — A period of work in Canada by a foreign national shall not be included in the calculation of the four-year period referred to in paragraph (3)(g) if the work was performed during a period in which the foreign national was authorized to study on a full-time basis in Canada.

(5) Genuineness of job offer — A determination of whether an offer of employment is genuine shall be based on the following factors:

(a) whether the offer is made by an employer that is actively engaged in the business in respect of which the offer is made, unless the offer is made for employment as a live-in caregiver;

(b) whether the offer is consistent with the reasonable employment needs of the employer;

(c) whether the terms of the offer are terms that the employer is reasonably able to fulfil; and

(d) the past compliance of the employer, or any person who recruited the foreign national for the employer, with the federal or provincial laws that regulate employment, or the recruiting of employees, in the province in which it is intended that the foreign national work.
SOR/2004-167, s. 56; SOR/2010-172, s. 2; SOR/2012-154, s. 10; SOR/2013-245, s. 5(1)–(5); SOR/2015-25, s. 1; SOR/2015-144, s. 5

Case Law

Section 200(1)

Editor's note: With respect to the issue of the intention to leave Canada by the end of the period authorized, see also case summaries under Regulation 183(1) and Regulation 216.

Portillo v. Canada (Minister of Citizenship and Immigration) (2014), 30 Imm. L.R. (4th) 254, 86 Admin. L.R. (5th) 1, 2014 FC 866, 2014 CarswellNat 3476, 2014 CarswellNat 3850 — There were four applications for judicial review of decisions denying work permits to each of the applicants. All of the decisions were made by the same officer. The applicants were recruited to work for McDonald's restaurants in Canada. The visa officer concluded that the applicants were not able to demonstrate that they adequately met the job requirements and that they had satisfied the officer that they would leave Canada by the end of the period of authorized stay. Decisions of visa officers regarding the issuance of temporary work permits are discretionary in nature and are reviewable on a standard of reasonableness.

The issue was whether the officer was entitled to evaluate and consider whether the applicants had experience. The employer indicated on its advertisement and the labour market opinion application that no experience was required and on-the-job training would be provided, "although some previous experience in the fast food industry (McDonald's) would be preferred." The officer in this case was not in a position to assess their suitability and experience, or unreasonably imported suitability requirements that the employers did not consider necessary for the employment in question. There was no dispute that the applicants were offered the position as part of an organized recruitment process on behalf of McDonald's and that they were offered positions based upon their resumés, interviews and past experience. McDonald's was entirely happy with all aspects of their applications and offered the applicants jobs. It is entirely unreasonable for the officer to say, on these facts, that he is not sure the applicants meet the requirements when the employer is sure that they do. Without some explanation for the officer's decisions to override the employer on the issue of suitability, this aspect of the decision was unreasonable.

As regards, any assessment of intent not to leave Canada, there is no clear rationale for these decisions given the facts of establishment in Belize in each case. The decisions were not reasonable because they lack justification, transparency and intelligibility. The application for judicial review was granted.

Momi v. Canada (Minister of Citizenship & Immigration), 2013 FC 162, 2013 CarswellNat 275, 2013 CarswellNat 864 — The applicant sought judicial review of the decision of a visa officer to refuse a temporary work permit. The officer concluded that the foreign national would not leave Canada by the end of the period authorized for his stay. The considerations relied on by the officer were irrelevant or neutral, or even worse, draw an inference that is not reasonable given the state of the record. The fact that the applicant sought to obtain the appropriate visa from Canada because his immigration situation in Australia would become precarious militates in favour of considering the applicant as law abiding. Past, previous immigration encounters are good indicators of an applicant's likelihood of future compliance. The fact the applicant had stayed in Australia since 2009 was not sufficient to conclude that if he were awarded a temporary work permit to Canada, he would not return to India at its expiration. At best, not wishing to return to India following a stint in Australia by seeking to obtain a temporary work visa in Canada should be considered as neutral as to whether or not the applicant will leave Canada by the end of the period authorized for their stay. Similarly, having a "permanent job" in Canada does not allow for an inference that the applicant will break the law and remain in Canada past the expiry of the work permit. There was no evidence on the record that the applicant would have ties in Canada such that he would be tempted to stay for that reason alone. Conversely, his ties with India remain as his family is there. The officer's reasons appear to be speculations, without adequate consideration given to the countervailing factors. As such, they appear to be arbitrary and do not meet the standard of reasonableness. The application for judicial review was allowed.

Li v. Canada (Minister of Citizenship & Immigration), 2012 CarswellNat 1183, 2012 FC 484 — A visa officer found that the applicant did not meet the necessary language and work experience requirements, and denied the applicant's request for a work permit. The applicant submitted school records showing passing grades in English in support of the language requirement. Nevertheless, the officer found that the applicant had not provided proof that he met the English requirements "according to the LMO [Labour Market Opinion]." The LMO merely stated that the job requires written and oral English. Further, unlike the skilled worker class, there are no levels of education specified in the Regulations for worker work permits. Although the applicant's English grades were not high, there was no evidence on which to find them inadequate for the requirements specified in the LMO. In addition, there was nothing in either the statutory provisions or the CIC policies to suggest that school records would be inadequate to establish the applicant's proficiency in English. The evidence from the applicant's previous employer, his cultural heritage and his nationality rendered it difficult to find the reasonable grounds on which the officer could find that the applicant was unable to perform the work sought. Although there is generally no obligation on an officer to make further inquiries when an application is ambiguous, this is an instance where the facts favour an exception to the rule. In this case, the officer's failure to grant the applicant the opportunity to respond to his concerns results in a denial of procedural fairness to the applicant. The officer's decision was set aside and the application for judicial review was allowed.

Calaunan v. Canada (Minister of Citizenship & Immigration), 2011 FC 1494, 2011 CarswellNat 5388, 2011 CarswellNat 5978 — The applicant's application for a work permit under the pilot project for hiring foreign workers in occupations that require lower levels of formal training was refused on the basis that the officer was not satisfied that the applicant had sufficient ties to his home country to ensure incentive to leave Canada by the end of the authorized stay.

Previous immigration encounters are the best indicators of an applicant's likelihood of future compliance. In the case at hand, there was no evidence to suggest that the applicant had previous immigration encounters, which was reaffirmed by the statements in the applicant's affidavit.

The court further noted that according to the applicable legislation, the officer must be satisfied that an applicant will not remain illegally in Canada after his authorized period of stay. It was the duty of the applicant to prove that he would leave Canada by the end of his authorized period of stay and to provide relevant documentation to that effect. However, in light of the lack of evidence supporting his strong ties to the Philippines, the existence of his ties to Canada, the apparent economic advantage of relocating to Canada — which is a necessary component of the decision — the court concluded that it was not unreasonable for the officer to reject his application. The applicant's parents, his two brothers, his cousin and his two uncles lived in Canada. Also, the applicant listed no spouse, children or any other family members in the Philippines. Although the applicant mentioned a family farm in his application, no evidence was provided in this regard. Officers are entitled to rely on their common sense and rationality in their analysis of an applicant's incentive to leave Canada at the end of their stay. As these are findings of fact, the court may not re-evaluate or reconsider the objective evidence and must defer to the decision of the officer. The application for judicial review was dismissed.

Arora v. Canada (Minister of Citizenship & Immigration), 2011 FC 241, 2011 CarswellNat 1325, 2011 CarswellNat 653 — The applicant's application for a work permit was refused for failure to demonstrate that he met the requirements of an intra-company transferee such that he should be exempted from applying for an LMO and receive a work permit and temporary resident visa. The officer found discrepancies between a letter from the applicant's employer and the applicant's submitted form with respect to his annual salary. The officer was not satisfied that the applicant worked as a senior executive or held a managerial level position due to his age (23), his level of education (Grade 12), his limited experience with the company (less than three years), his modest income and the lack of evidence with respect to his prior work experience.

The court held that while these factors may play a part in an officer's assessment, they cannot be substituted for an assessment of the qualities of a manager as outlined in the FW1 Manual. In addition, several factors noted by the officer were irrelevant to the assessment. For example, the officer was concerned that the applicant could not be a senior executive at the age of 23 years. However, age is not a factor listed in the Foreign Worker 1 Manual and not allowing the exemption under subs. 205(a) of the Regulations based on the applicant's age is inappropriate. A further problem with the officer's finding was that the Foreign Worker Manual explicitly states that the applicant must show only one year of managerial experience at the company for which he was applying for a work permit. Finally, neither the FW1 Manual nor the Regulations requires a certain salary level before an applicant can be considered a senior executive or manager. As such, it was an error for the officer to draw a negative inference from the finding that the applicant made a modest salary. The application for judicial review was allowed.

Cao v. Canada (Minister of Citizenship & Immigration), 2010 ONSC 2750, 2010 CarswellOnt 3456 (Ont. S.C.J.) — The applicant challenged the legality of a decision made by a visa officer to refuse his application for a work permit. The officer was not satisfied that the applicant was a genuine visitor who would leave Canada upon the expiry of his work permit mainly because the latter had insufficient financial and personal ties to China considering that the applicant's family is small, his salary in China was modest in light of his relatively high position, he had limited advancement opportunities in China and he would not gain experience readily bankable upon his return to China.

As is the case with virtually all applicants for temporary work permits, there is a financial incentive to work in Canada. This fact cannot be held against an applicant, as to do so would result in the rejection of the vast majority of such applications. There must be objective reasons to reasonably question the motivation of an applicant. Just to cite a few examples, past immigration attempts, overstaying in other countries, or a criminal past may provide sufficient basis to doubt that an applicant will leave Canada by the end of the authorized period. In the case at bar, the officer made no serious effort to test the strength of the applicant's ties to China, especially given that he had no family elsewhere. The impugned decision was unreasonable not simply because it is stereotypical, but also because it relied on the very factor which would induce someone to come here temporarily in the first place as the main reason for keeping the person out. The application for judicial review was allowed.

Singh v. Canada (Minister of Citizenship & Immigration) (2009), 82 Imm. L.R. (3d) 205, 2009 FC 621, 2009 CarswellNat 1820, 2009 CarswellNat 5881, [2009] F.C.J. No. 798 — The applicant, a native of Punjab province in India, is the 26-year old brother-in-law of the principal owner of the Mahek Restaurant and Lounge in Surrey, British Columbia, his prospective Canadian employer. The applicant was offered a position as a food preparer for a two-year term in connection with a positive labour market opinion (LMO) issued by Service Canada valid through September 4, 2010. This was the applicant's third failed application for a work permit for employment with Mahek Restaurant. Two previous applications were refused because of a visa officer's concerns that the applicant would not be able to perform the work of cook described in the relevant LMO, and because he was "unable to adequately clarify inconsistencies raised in [the] application" and failed to satisfy the visa officer that "his stated reasons for visiting Canada were genuine." The most recent work permit application was for a position as a food preparer and not for cook, as in the two previous applications.

The visa officer seems to have made much of the fact that the applicant had made previous work permit applications in connections with job offers from the same employer, and that this employer is his brother-in-law. There are two potential problems with this: firstly, there is no obvious justification for treating work permit applications like credit card applications, where one's credibility diminishes with every application made; and second, the visa officer's suspicion concerning the "modification" of the LMO was entirely speculative. It is fully possible, and indeed likely, that the employer was in need of both cooks and food preparers. It is not as if the two occupations are unrelated. And it is hardly surprising that a Canadian business in need of workers from India would look to family members living there. There is no obvious connection between the fact that the applicant is being offered a job by a relative and whether he is likely to return to India and the officer fails to explain why she thought this was a relevant fact.

While the officer is entitled to substantial deference in reaching her opinion, when these concerns were examined, the court found the decision reached did not fall within a range of possible, acceptable outcomes which were defensible in respect of the facts and the law, as set out by the Supreme Court in *Dunsmuir v. New Brunswick* (2008), 69 Imm. L.R. (3d) 1. The court concluded that the same result may not have been reached had the officer not placed weight on the applicant's history of previous work permits and the fact that the employer was a relative. The application for judicial review was allowed.

Baylon v. Canada (Minister of Citizenship & Immigration) (2009), 84 Imm. L.R. (3d) 24, 2009 FC 938, 2009 CarswellNat 2914, 2009 CarswellNat 4471, [2009] F.C.J. No. 1147 — The applicants are young citizens of the Philippines, part of a group of approximately 40 persons who applied for a temporary resident visa in order to come and work at a fish processing plant in Richmond, B.C. The applications were refused because they did not convince the visa officers that they would leave Canada at the end of their visas' terms. They then sought judicial review of the officers' decisions.

In her affidavit, the visa officer states that leaving family behind is not a strong incentive to return to the Philippines, as "it is not uncommon in the Philippines for one or both parents to work overseas for long periods of time, sometimes totaling several years." She added that "in fact, over a million Filipinos every year reside and work abroad, most of them in low-skilled occupations. Separation from close family members due to overseas work is accepted and common place." The court found this extraneous evidence to be unsupported and undocumented, and in any event irrelevant. The court accepted that the local conditions in the applicant's home country can be part of the broader picture which the visa officer ought to consider in assessing whether an applicant will leave Canada at the end of the period authorized for any temporary stay. But the mere fact that many low-skilled workers from the Philippines work overseas does not, in and of itself, mean that they overstay their authorized work permit, let alone that they live illegally in other countries. Oversimplified generalizations cannot, and should not, form the basis of what must always be an individualized assessment based on the particular circumstances of each individual. The applications for judicial review were granted in two of the five cases and dismissed in the balance.

Thomas v. Canada (Minister of Citizenship & Immigration) (2009), 85 Imm. L.R. (3d) 133, 2009 FC 1038, 2009 CarswellNat 5014, 2009 CarswellNat 3190 — This was an application for judicial review of a decision of a visa officer who determined that the applicant had not satisfied the requirements for obtaining a temporary work permit on the grounds that the applicant had not shown that he was well established in India and that he had not shown that he would return to India at the end of his authorized period of stay given there were better work conditions and high economic incentives to remain in Canada.

The burden rests on the applicant to provide sufficient information for a visa officer to make a determination that the requirements of the program have been met. Fairness does not require that the officer provide the applicant with an interview to address questions that might arise from the materials submitted. The officer is entitled to proceed to a determination upon considering the application as it was presented. However, to arrive at a determination of insufficient establishment in India that would fall within the range of acceptable and defensible outcomes, it was necessary for the visa officer to consider and analyze the relevant evidence on that question. In this case, the visa officer's failure to consider the applicant's property, holdings and valuations leads to the inference that the visa officer made an erroneous finding of fact without regard to the evidence. It was also difficult to understand why the officer concluded that the applicant would require moderate English language skills to perform the job duties when it was not identified as a requirement in the employment contract. Moreover, the record indicated that he had taken two secondary school courses in English, yet the decision did not explain why the officer thought that this was insufficient. The reasoning process was flawed and the resulting decision fell outside the range of possible, acceptable outcomes. The process adopted by the visa officer and its outcome did not resonate with the principles of justification, transparency, and intelligibility. The application for judicial review was allowed.

Dhanoa v. Canada (Minister of Citizenship & Immigration), 2009 FC 729, 2009 CarswellNat 2159, 2009 CarswellNat 4903 — The application for a temporary resident visa work permit was refused on the grounds that the applicant had failed to satisfy the visa officer that he would leave Canada at the end of the authorized period.

The officer's notes read: "PA has no previous travel. As per info in application form his current income in India is low. Is working as a farmer in India. I note that proposed employment in Canada is unrelated to PA's work experience. Given PA's greater earning power in Canada versus India, combined with better living and working conditions in Canada, I find that PA would have a strong socio-economic incentive to stay in Canada by any means after the end of his authorized stay. I am cognizant that PA has a wife and kids in India. However, on a balance of probabilities, I am not satisfied that PA would not bear the hardship of being separated from his family in order to take advantage of better socio-economic opportunities in Canada. Not satisfied PA meets requirements of R200(1)(b)."

The lack of previous travel can only at most be a neutral factor. If one had traveled and always returned, the visa officer's concern might be lessened. If one came to Canada, claimed refugee status and was not permitted to stay here on humanitarian and compassionate grounds, an application for a temporary work permit would obviously heighten suspicions. The remark that the employment is unrelated to the applicant's work experience as a farmer did not serve as an indication that he was unable to do the job, as that box was not checked off in the decision form. It was not apparent as to how this would be indicative of his intention not to do the job and not to leave Canada at the end of his employment. The references to greater earning power in Canada and better living and working conditions are somewhat sterile as no analysis was done of his living conditions in India, whether his declared intention to purchase a farm was feasible, and what his standard of living would be in India compared to Canada after he earned some money here. Indeed, the very basis of the pilot project is these workers will only come here if they are going to be paid more than in their home country.

The thought that he would abandon his wife and children in order to take advantage of better socio-economic opportunities here is distasteful. It was "sanctimonious" to suggest that our society is more of a draw for him than India, where he would be in the bosom of his family, simply because he would have 30 pieces of silver in his pocket.

The decision was unreasonable not simply because it was stereotypical, but also because it relied on the very factor which would induce someone to come here temporarily in the first place as a main reason for keeping that person out. The application for judicial review was granted.

Calma v. Canada (Minister of Citizenship & Immigration) (2009), 83 Imm. L.R. (3d) 135, 2009 FC 742, 2009 CarswellNat 4152, 2009 CarswellNat 2484 — The applicant sought judicial review of a refusal of his application for a work permit. The officer concluded that the applicant had not satisfied him that he would leave Canada by the end of the period authorized for his stay because he "had not demonstrated ties that would satisfy the officer of the applicant's intention to return."

The assessment of an application for a work permit involves an exercise of statutory discretion and attracts a high degree of deference from the court. Apart from the procedural fairness issues raised, the applicable standard of review in this case is reasonableness.

There was no evidence before the officer to support either conclusion that the applicant had weak economic ties in the Philippines and that he was not sufficiently well established to ensure his return. The applicant was born in the Philippines, had always lived there, had a wife and four children there, and he had been employed in the same job for 10 years that he could go back to. It was difficult to see how anyone could be more established than this, or why this meant he had weak economic ties. The officer's decision could not be reconciled with the evidence presented by the applicant. The evidence was either entirely overlooked or the decision was unreasonable. The application for judicial review was allowed.

Baylon v. Canada (Minister of Citizenship & Immigration), 2009 FC 743, 2009 CarswellNat 4153, 2009 CarswellNat 2505 — The applicant applied for judicial review of a visa officer's decision refusing his application for a work permit. The officer concluded that the applicant had not satisfied him that he would leave Canada by the end of the period authorized for his stay because he "h[ad] not demonstrated ties that would satisfy [the officer] of [the applicant's] intention to return." The applicant said that he should have had an opportunity to provide an explanation for perceived or apparent deficiencies and respond to the officer's concerns. In the present case, however, the officer was not concerned with deficiencies. He assessed the application materials and exercised his discretion as required by statute. If an officer is not convinced that an applicant will leave Canada at the end of the authorized stay, there is no obligation to interview the applicant and provide an opportunity for the applicant to try and dissuade the officer from that conclusion. The onus was on the applicant to provide all the information necessary for the decision and to convince the officer that he was a visitor and not an immigrant. The application for judicial review was dismissed.

Minhas v. Canada (Minister of Citizenship & Immigration) (2009), 82 Imm. L.R. (3d) 210, 2009 FC 696, 2009 CarswellNat 2148, 2009 CarswellNat 5682, [2009] F.C.J. No. 867 — This was an application for judicial review of a decision to refuse an application for a work permit. The only reference to English language skills before the officer was the applicant's own affidavit in which he attested that his intended employer informed him that knowledge of the English language was not necessary to the job, and that the applicant could perform the job without English language skills. There was no evidence before the officer addressing the applicant's level of English language ability; thus it was not reasonable to conclude, based on his English language ability, that he could not perform the work of a construction helper.

While higher salary in Canada is alluded to with the remark "high economic incentive," no consideration was given to the difference in cost of living and living standard between Canada and India. The differences in salary between India and Canada may indicate incentive to stay only when the cost of living is also considered. The standard of living in the home country is also important to determining where the applicant may be better off. While economic incentive to stay in Canada is a reasonable consideration on the part of the officer, the majority of applicants would have some economic incentive to come work in Canada, and this incentive therefore cannot so easily correlate with overstays since it is inconsistent with the work permit scheme. The officer failed to make a serious attempt at evaluating establishment and ties given the evidence before him. The decision was unreasonable. The application for judicial review was allowed.

Rengasamy v. Canada (Minister of Citizenship & Immigration) (2009), 86 Imm. L.R. (3d) 106, 2009 FC 1229, 2009 CarswellNat 5505, 2009 CarswellNat 4073 — Persons who apply for temporary work permits in Canada are doing so because they can earn more money here than at home. In that sense, anyone who seeks or is granted a temporary work permit will have a financial incentive to stay in Canada beyond the specified term. Accordingly, a financial incentive to remain in Canada cannot, on its own, justify refusing an application. Otherwise no application could succeed. Here, the applicants submitted evidence of their significant family connections in India where each has a parent, spouse and young children. They only have one distant cousin in Canada. Two officers reviewed the applicant's materials. The Minister suggested that the applicants could have supplemented their applications by giving more information about the quality of their family relationships. The officer stated that the applicants had the burden of proving that the personal hardship of being separated from their families indefinitely would outweigh the financial benefits of remaining in Canada. In other words, they had to show that their families meant more to them than $10.43 an hour. The officer misstated the onus on the applicants and by doing so caused the officers to discount, unreasonably, the significance of the applicants' family ties in India and, therefore, the evidence supporting their undertakings to return to India when their permits expire. As a result, the officers' decision was unreasonable. The application for judicial review was allowed.

Li v. Canada (Minister of Citizenship & Immigration), [2008] F.C.J. No. 1625, 76 Imm. L.R. (3d) 265, 337 F.T.R. 100 (Eng.), 2008 CarswellNat 4261, 2008 CarswellNat 5159, 2008 FC 1284 — Service Canada issued a positive labour market opinion (LMO) and validated the offer of employment. The applicant then applied to the Canadian Consulate in Shanghai, China for a two-year work permit. Obtaining a positive LMO is one of the requirements for a work permit. The visa officer denied the application because he was not satisfied that the applicant will leave Canada upon the expiry of the work permit.

The visa officer made no serious attempt to determine the strength of the ties of the applicant to China. According to the Act, the burden of proof rests on the applicant, who has attempted to discharge the duty by providing information on his family in China, as well as employment and education information. The officer did not sufficiently take into account the fact that the applicant's family ties to China were strong, since he had no family members elsewhere than there. On this basis, the refusal of the visa was based on an erroneous finding of fact, which did not take into account the material evidence which was presented.

The applicant also had no way of knowing that the officer would rely on the applicant's higher salary in Canada, the fact that he often changed jobs in China, the fact that his employment history was difficult to obtain or that he apparently had limited family ties in PRC. In this case, an interview would have been appropriate for the applicant to explain the extent of his family ties in China. He would have been able to communicate the information which is provided in his further affidavit. The court found the visa officer's failure to give the applicant an opportunity to respond to his concerns, on the facts of this case, amounted to a breach of the rules of natural justice. The application for judicial review was allowed.

Vairea v. Canada (Minister of Citizenship & Immigration), 2006 CarswellNat 3305, 2006 FC 1238 — This is an application for judicial review of the decision of a visa officer to dismiss the applicant's application for a work permit in Canada. The applicant received an offer of employment to work in Canada as a cement finisher. A positive labour market opinion was obtained. The visa officer was not satisfied that the applicant had a genuine offer of employment or was able to perform the work sought. The visa officer reviewed the notes on file including the electronic correspondence from the HRSDC officer, who expressed his concerns regarding the applicant's prospective employer on the basis of a published newspaper article that mentioned that a group of overseas Filipino workers in Toronto had filed a complaint of recruitment fraud against a Toronto-based employment agency and its owner-operator. The visa officer was concerned that the applicant did not know much about his prospective employer. This was supported by the fact that the applicant had never spoken directly to his prospective employer and that his friend had found the ad through the internet. The visa officer's conclusions in this regard were not patently unreasonable. The visa officer's concerns with respect to the ability of the applicant to perform the work sought were not unreasonable. The visa officer was entitled to find that the applicant's answers with regard to his work experience were unsatisfactory.

Nguyen c. Canada (Ministre de la Citoyenneté & de l'Immigration), 2005 CarswellNat 2305, 2005 CarswellNat 5511, 2005 FC 1087 — The applicant applied for judicial review of a decision by a visa officer denying the applicant's application for a permit to work in Canada. The visa officer determined that the applicant had not satisfied him he would leave Canada at the end of his authorized stay and determined that he was trying to live in Canada permanently. It was the applicant's responsibility to establish that he was not inadmissible and that he meets the requirements of the IRPA. Specifically, he must establish that he will leave Canada at the end of his stay as provided under para. 200(1)(b) of the Regulations.

The visa officer took into account the assets of the applicant held in Vietnam. The officer was of the opinion that because the applicant had left his business for nine months and decided to remain in Canada, there was no strong connection that would force him to return to Vietnam. This was evidence tending to establish the absence of a significant connection with that country. Further, the applicant expressed a desire to remain in Canada with his children, which showed a strong connection with Canada. It was therefore not unreasonable for the visa officer to determine that the applicant had not persuaded him he had strong ties with his native country and that he would leave Canada at the end of his stay.

Section 200(3)

Sulce v. Canada (Minister of Citizenship and Immigration), 2015 FC 1132, 2015 CarswellNat 4736, 2015 CarswellNat 8781 — The applicant was offered employment as a stucco technician by a construction company located in Saskatchewan. He applied for a temporary work permit and included the results of an International English Language Testing System where the applicant was found to have the language skills of an "extremely limited user." An approved labour market opinion (LMO) was also submitted with the application. The officer refused the application on the grounds that the applicant's proficiency in the English language was insufficient to allow him to perform his employment duties. A positive LMO is not determinative of how visa officers are to exercise their discretion. Here the prospective job was in the field of construction and the officer's concerns were about the applicant's understanding of instructions regarding workplace safety. Her additional concern regarding the applicant not being able to communicate with first responders in case of an emergency was, given the nature of the prospective job, a relevant and logical consideration in the context of the safety of working conditions on a construction site. The officer was not bound by the LMO confirmation and was under a duty to conduct an independent assessment of the applicant's ability to perform the prospective job duties. The officer's decision was found to be both reasonable and procedurally fair. The application for judicial review was dismissed.

Singh v. Canada (Minister of Citizenship & Immigration) (2010), 95 Imm. L.R. (3d) 83, 2010 FC 1306, 2010 CarswellNat 5221, 2010 CarswellNat 5583 — The applicants' application for a temporary work permit was rejected. The officer concluded that the applicants did not meet the requirements of the job as specified in the job offer. In addition, the officer's note indicated that the applicants had insufficient knowledge of the religion and its teachings and had provided inconsistent answers. The applicants submitted two letters outlining their previous work experience and training as Ragis. Since the officer found the applicants did not meet the requirement of the job offer, these letters were relevant and pointed to a different conclusion than the one she reached. She was required to acknowledge and analyze them. The failure to do so was a reviewable error. The officer stated in her affidavit regarding the past experience letters submitted by the applicants, that the office "sees many such letters which turned out to be fictitious." As such, she noted that she required "more than the letters, for instance, newspaper cutouts, photos of them practicing or letters of reference, to properly corroborate claims of training, knowledge and experience." However, the applicants were not put on notice that the officer was concerned with the veracity of the letters and were not requested to present further documentations to corroborate the letters. This was an error in law. The application for judicial review was allowed.

Duroseau v. Canada (Minister of Citizenship & Immigration), 2008 CarswellNat 130, 2008 CarswellNat 957, 2008 FC 72 — The officer refused to issue a work permit for two reasons:

> (1) She referred to the prohibition against issuing a work permit under subpara. 200(3)(e)(i) to persons having engaged in unauthorized work in Canada in the past six months. The officer believed that the applicant had engaged in such work since her arrival in Canada by helping Ms. Darius with her children.

> (2) The officer determined that the applicant did not meet the requirements of s. 112 of the Regulations because the employment contract was not genuine and consti-

tuted an offer of convenience aimed at facilitating the applicant's acquisition of status in Canada.

The definition of "work" set forth in the Regulations does not require compensation to have been received in order for an activity to be considered work. The activity merely has to be "in direct competition with the activities of Canadian citizens or permanent residents in the Canadian labour market." Child care meets the definition of work. The friendship between the applicant and the employer was just one fact among many justifying the officer's doubts as to the *bona fide* character of the contract. The fact that the applicant lived in Ms. Darius' home prior to submitting her application, the length of time before she submitted it, and the fact that the applicant was engaged in child-care activity all provided sufficient support for the officer's decision.

Randhawa v. Canada (Minister of Citizenship & Immigration) (2006), 57 Imm. L.R. (3d) 99, 2006 CarswellNat 3481, 2006 FC 1294 — This is an application for judicial review of a decision of a visa officer that refused the applicant's application for a work permit. The applicant was an assistant cook specializing in North Indian cuisine. The visa officer questioned the applicant about food hygiene and decided he was not qualified to perform the cook's job he was offered in Toronto. HRSDC confirmed the job offer and provided a positive labour market opinion.

The court concluded that the visa officer was not an expert on food hygiene, yet the visa officer "grilled" the applicant. The court concludes that the intense questioning of the applicant by the visa officer on his ability to "maintain high standards of hygiene and sanitation" was an unreasonable basis to form the conclusion that there were reasonable grounds to believe that the applicant is unable to perform the assistant cook job offered to him in Toronto. There was nothing in the evidence to indicate that the visa officer obtained objective standards against which to assess the applicant's level of fitness. In fact, the only objective measure of fitness was the completion of the food hygiene training course that the applicant had completed at the visa officer's request. The visa officer also refused to consider the training that the applicant would receive in the course of his employment in Toronto. While it is reasonable to require that an applicant satisfy the job requirements of a particular position before obtaining a work permit, it is unreasonable not to take into account some measure of job orientation that would inevitably be provided to the applicant. The application for judicial review was allowed.

Also see *Vairea v. Canada (Minister of Citizenship & Immigration)*, 2006 CarswellNat 3305, 2006 FC 1238, at s. 200(1) of IRPR.

Chen v. Canada (Minister of Citizenship & Immigration), 2005 CarswellNat 4950, 2005 CarswellNat 3219, 2005 FC 1378 — The applicant was a Chinese national and had applied for a temporary work permit. He only spoke Chinese and had been offered a position as a warehouse manager for a Chinese luxury food company that was owned and operated by his nephew. The visa officer refused to issue a work permit on the basis that the applicant had not satisfied the officer that he would leave Canada by the end of the period authorized for the stay and he had not satisfied the officer that he had qualifications and experience for the employment for which the work permit was sought.

The visa officer's notes indicated that he was of the view that Human Resources Development Canada (HRDC) had imposed an English knowledge requirement on the position and that was included as one of the reasons for rejecting the application for the work permit. The visa officer was under a duty to examine all the relevant evidence before him in order to come to an independent assessment of whether there are reasonable grounds to believe the applicant is unable to perform the work. The officer could not be bound by a statement by HRDC that English is or is not required and he cannot delegate his decision making to a third party such as HRDC. Conversely, a statement by an applicant or employer that English is not required cannot be binding on the officer. Instead, the officer must carry out his own evaluation based on a weighing of all of the evidence before him.

In this case, the visa officer did not simply state that English was a requirement imposed by HRDC. Rather, the visa officer explains in his notes that he cannot foresee how the applicant would train his replacement, as required to do as part of his duties. Since the visa officer viewed the ability to communicate in English as relevant to his assessment as to whether the applicant would be able to perform his duties, the officer's findings were considered to be logical and were not based upon irrelevant considerations. The officer's decision was upheld even though he may have erred by stating that English was a HRDC requirement and even relied to some extent on this error, because the officer also considered the need for English independently of the HRDC validation.

201. (1) Application for renewal — A foreign national may apply for the renewal of their work permit if

    (a) the application is made before their work permit expires; and

    (b) they have complied with all conditions imposed on their entry into Canada.

(2) Renewal — An officer shall renew the foreign national's work permit if, following an examination, it is established that the foreign national continues to meet the requirements of section 200.

SOR/2010-172, s. 3

Case Law

Kaur v. Canada (Minister of Citizenship & Immigration), 2011 FC 219, 2011 CarswellNat 1277, 2011 CarswellNat 434 — The applicant sought judicial review of a decision of an officer of Citizenship and Immigration Canada Case Processing Centre wherein the officer refused to restore the applicant's temporary resident status, work permit and study permit. The applicant submitted her application for a work permit on September 4, 2009. The application was returned for insufficient fees. She reapplied for restoration of her temporary resident status and a further work permit and study permit on November 10, 2009. The officer found that the applicant's application was not mailed within the prescribed 90-day period and therefore determined that she was not eligible for a work permit for post-graduation employment. The officer determined that the 90-day period began from the date on the applicant's diploma, April 30, 2009. The officer found that the applicant did not meet the requirements of a study permit; the officer was not convinced that the applicant was a genuine student. The officer had concerns about the credibility of the documents received. Several letters from the officers at Fanshawe College conflicted as to the applicant's official graduation date.

An officer is not under a duty to inform the applicant about any concerns regarding the application which arise directly from the requirements of the legislation or regulations. The onus is on the applicant to satisfy the officer on all parts of her application and the officer was under no obligation to ask for additional information where the applicant's material was insufficient. However, the officer was obligated to inform the applicant of any concerns related to the veracity of documents that formed part of the application and the officer was required to make further inquiries in such a situation. By viewing the letter as not credible or fraudulent, the officer ought to have convoked an interview with the applicant to provide her an opportunity to respond to these concerns. The officer denied the applicant procedural fairness and the judicial review was allowed. The other issues were not addressed.

202. Temporary resident status — A foreign national who is issued a work permit under section 206 or paragraph 207(c) or (d) does not, by reason only of being issued a work permit, become a temporary resident.

203. (1) Assessment of employment offered — On application under Division 2 for a work permit made by a foreign national other than a foreign national referred to in subparagraphs 200(1)(c)(i) to (ii.1), an officer must determine, on the basis of an assessment provided by the Department of Employment and Social Development, of any information provided on the officer's request by the employer making the offer and of any other relevant information, if

(a) the job offer is genuine under subsection 200(5);

(b) the employment of the foreign national is likely to have a neutral or positive effect on the labour market in Canada;

(c) the issuance of a work permit would not be inconsistent with the terms of any federal-provincial agreement that apply to the employers of foreign nationals;

(d) in the case of a foreign national who seeks to enter Canada as a live-in caregiver,

(i) the foreign national will reside in a private household in Canada and provide child care, senior home support care or care of a disabled person in that household without supervision,

(ii) the employer will provide the foreign national with adequate furnished and private accommodations in the household, and

(iii) the employer has sufficient financial resources to pay the foreign national the wages that are offered to the foreign national; and

(e) the employer

(i) during the period beginning six years before the day on which the request for an assessment under subsection (2) is received by the Department of Employment and Social Development and ending on the day on which the application for the work permit is received by the Department, provided each foreign national employed by the employer with employment in the same occupation as that set out in the foreign national's offer of employment and with wages and working conditions that were substantially the same as — but not less favourable than — those set out in that offer, or

(ii) is able to justify, under subsection (1.1), any failure to satisfy the criteria set out in subparagraph (i).

(1.01) Effect on labour market — language — For the purposes of paragraph (1)(b), the employment of a foreign national is unlikely to have a positive or neutral effect on the labour market in Canada if the offer of employment requires the ability to communicate in a language other than English or French, unless

(a) the employer or group of employers demonstrates that the ability to communicate in the other language is a bona fide requirement for performing the duties associated with the employment;

(b) the offer of employment relates to work to be performed under an international agreement between Canada and one or more countries concerning seasonal agricultural workers; or

(c) the offer of employment relates to other work to be performed in the primary agriculture sector, within the meaning of subsection 315.2(4).

(1.1) **Justification** — A failure to satisfy the criteria set out in subparagraph (1)(e)(i) is justified if it results from

(a) a change in federal or provincial law;

(b) a change to the provisions of a collective agreement;

(c) the implementation of measures by the employer in response to a dramatic change in economic conditions that directly affected the business of the employer, provided that the measures were not directed disproportionately at foreign nationals employed by the employer;

(d) an error in interpretation made in good faith by the employer with respect to its obligations to a foreign national, if the employer subsequently provided compensation — or if it was not possible to provide compensation, made sufficient efforts to do so — to all foreign nationals who suffered a disadvantage as a result of the error;

(e) an unintentional accounting or administrative error made by the employer, if the employer subsequently provided compensation — or if it was not possible to provide compensation, made sufficient efforts to do so — to all foreign nationals who suffered a disadvantage as a result of the error;

(f) circumstances similar to those set out in paragraphs (a) to (e); or

(g) *force majeure.*

(2) **Assessment on request** — The Department of Employment and Social Development must provide the assessment referred to in subsection (1) on the request of an officer or an employer or group of employers, none of whom is an employer who

(a) on a regular basis, offers striptease, erotic dance, escort services or erotic massages; or

(b) is referred to in any of subparagraphs 200(3)(h)(i) to (iii).

(2.01) **Offer of employment** — A request may be made in respect of

(a) an offer of employment to a foreign national; and

(b) offers of employment made, or anticipated to be made, by an employer or group of employers.

(2.1) **Basis of assessment** — The assessment provided by the Department of Employment and Social Development on the matters set out in paragraphs (1)(a) to

(e) must be based on any information provided by the employer making the offer and any other relevant information, but, for the purposes of this subsection, the period referred to in subparagraph (1)(e)(i) ends on the day on which the request for the assessment is received by that Department.

(3) **Factors — effect on labour market** — An assessment provided by the Department of Employment and Social Development with respect to the matters referred to in paragraph (1)(b) shall, unless the employment of the foreign national is unlikely to have a positive or neutral effect on the labour market in Canada as a result of the application of subsection (1.01), be based on the following factors:

(a) whether the employment of the foreign national will or is likely to result in direct job creation or job retention for Canadian citizens or permanent residents;

(b) whether the employment of the foreign national will or is likely to result in the development or transfer of skills and knowledge for the benefit of Canadian citizens or permanent residents;

(c) whether the employment of the foreign national is likely to fill a labour shortage;

(d) whether the wages offered to the foreign national are consistent with the prevailing wage rate for the occupation and whether the working conditions meet generally accepted Canadian standards;

(e) whether the employer will hire or train Canadian citizens or permanent residents or has made, or has agreed to make, reasonable efforts to do so;

(f) whether the employment of the foreign national is likely to adversely affect the settlement of any labour dispute in progress or the employment of any person involved in the dispute; and

(g) whether the employer has fulfilled or has made reasonable efforts to fulfill any commitments made, in the context of any assessment that was previously provided under subsection (2), with respect to the matters referred to in paragraphs (a), (b) and (e).

(3.1) **Period of validity of assessment** — An assessment provided by the Department of Employment and Social Development shall indicate the period during which the assessment is in effect for the purposes of subsection (1).

(4) **Province of Quebec** — In the case of a foreign national who intends to work in the Province of Quebec, the assessment provided by the Department of Employment and Social Development shall be made in concert with the competent authority of that Province.

(5) **Failure to satisfy criteria** — If an officer determines that the criteria set out in subclause 200(1)(c)(ii.1)(B)(I) or subparagraph (1)(e)(i) were not satisfied and the failure to do so was not justified by the employer under subsection (1.1), the Department must notify the employer of that determination and that the information referred to in subsection 209.997(2) will be added to the list referred to in that subsection.

(6) Publication of employer's Information — If an officer makes a determination under subsection (5), the Department must add the information referred to in subsection 209.997(2) to the list referred to in that subsection.

SOR/2004-167, s. 57; SOR/2010-172, ss. 4, 5(e); SOR/2013-150, s. 1; 2013, c. 40, s. 237(3)(a); SOR/2013-245, s. 6(1), (3)–(5), (7)–(10), (12)–(14); SOR/2014-84, s. 1(a); SOR/2015-144, s. 6; SOR/2015-147, s. 1(d)

Case Law

Babic v. Canada (Minister of Employment and Social Development) (2016), 39 Imm. L.R. (4th) 75, 2016 FC 174, 2016 CarswellNat 370, 2016 CarswellNat 2214 — The applicant sought to have a negative Labour Market Impact Assessment set aside. The Service Canada officer found the applicant had not demonstrated sufficient efforts to hire Canadians in the occupation or to train Canadians in the occupation, and the hiring would have a negative impact on the Canadian labour market. The officer determined that the employer did not offer enough when he set the wage rate for a carpenter who was also a welder. The applicant says he looked at the guideline-posted median wage rate for carpenters in Toronto, which was $22 per hour, and the median wage rate for welders which was $21.53 per hour. He then offered $25 per hour and said it was "well above what was requested in the guidelines." Simply averaging the wage rates of each individual trade and then increasing that amount slightly does not necessarily take into account whether the resulting amount is an appropriate wage rate for someone with the combination of skills the applicant sought. The officer noted that there was no premium paid for the additional required skills of some welding experience. It was, on this basis, reasonably open to the officer to find as she did that "the wage offering was insufficient to attract a qualified Canadian/PR to apply." The court found the decision was not contrary to the law and was reasonable and fair. The application for judicial review was dismissed.

Charger Logistics Ltd. v. Canada (Minister of Employment and Social Development), 2016 CarswellNat 593, 2016 FC 286 — The applicant sought judicial review of a refusal of the applicant's Labour Market Impact Assessment. The LMIA was refused on the basis of the wages the applicant was offering and based on the applicant's failure to demonstrate sufficient efforts to hire Canadians in the occupation. The wage of $30.76 per hour offered by the employer was not over the prevailing wage for the occupation which the officer held it needed to be because of an additional requirement of a language skill, combined with job duties and education. There are also gaps in the advertising.

The application for judicial review was allowed. The officer in the present case did demonstrate a willingness to depart from the strict requirements of the temporary foreign workers program, by considering advertising by the applicant other than through the job bank. However, the decision did not address the evidence related to other advertisements in a manner that would allow the court to conclude the decision was transparent, intelligible and therefore reasonable. The court concluded that the officer did not fetter discretion in analyzing whether the minimum advertising requirements were met and the court declined to certify the question of whether an employer is required to advertise for a position at a wage above the prevailing wage rate for an occupation where a prospective employee's skills warrant an increase above the prevailing wage. The application for judicial review was allowed.

Paturel International Co. v. Canada (Minister of Employment and Social Development), 2016 FC 541, 2016 CarswellNat 1669 — Paturel International sought judicial review of a decision to refuse a Labour Market Impact Assessment. The LMIA was denied on the basis that the company failed to meet the requirement to pay the prevailing wage for shellfish workers in the region according to data relating to the median wage for that occupation. The prevailing wage was set too high and the officer fettered his discretion by relying solely on data relating to median wages. The company was the largest employer of shellfish workers in the relevant region. None of its employees earned a wage as high as that established by the Minister as the median for that occupation. Other workers across Canada do earn higher wages than employees in New Brunswick but the statistics show that the median wage in the province was $11.33 per hour. Job postings in the region offer between $11.49 and $12.43. Median wages in two regions adjacent to the company's location, where its competitors operate, are $11.09 and $11.20. The Minister argued that it was not unreasonable for the officer to rely on median wage rates, calculated with reference to EI data, given that other sources of information were unavailable or unreliable at the time. While the officer has broad discretion to rely on the data that he considered to be most representative of the prevailing wages in the region, the officer sole reliance on EI data amounted to a fettering of his discretion. A conclusion reached by a decision maker who has fettered his or her discretion is, *per se*, unreasonable. The application for judicial review was allowed.

Canadian Reformed Church of Cloverdale B.C. v. Canada (Minister of Employment and Social Development), 2015 FC 1075, 2015 CarswellNat 4453, 2015 CarswellNat 8222 — Employment and Social Development Canada ("ESDC") dismissed the Labour Market Impact Assessment because the church had not shown that it had made reasonable efforts to hire or train a Canadian employee. Specifically, ESDC concluded that the advertisements did not include the business address where the translator would be working. The court concluded that the officer fettered her discretion and arrived at an unreasonable decision by relying exclusively on internal guidelines, rather than on the language in the applicable regulations. The records show that the sole reason why the officer refused the church's assessment was because of the absence of a business address in the advertisements. The officer did not determine whether the church had actually made reasonable efforts to hire or train a Canadian in accordance with the regulatory standard but rather rejected the assessment for the solitary reason that the advertisements lacked a business address. The officer appears to have treated the guidelines as mandatory obligations. The application for judicial review was allowed.

Frankie's Burgers Lougheed Inc. v. Canada (Minister of Employment and Social Development Canada) (2015), 32 Imm. L.R. (4th) 221, 2015 FC 27, 2015 CarswellNat 107, 2015 CarswellNat 3757 — The applicants sought to have two virtually identical decisions of an ESDC officer to refuse positive labour market opinions ("LMOs") set aside on the basis of being unreasonable for concluding that the applicants should have made greater efforts to recruit part-time workers, failed to demonstrate a labour shortage and had not met the minimum advertising; failing to provide an opportunity to address concerns regarding the authenticity of certain advertisements; and fettering her discretion in assessing their applications, by not taking their particular circumstances into account and by relying on operational guidelines issued by ESDC in refusing the applications.

The officer had concerns that the advertisements had only mentioned full-time positions, and did not mention the business addresses of the restaurants in question. She also questioned whether sufficient efforts had been made to target underrepresented groups. The court concluded that the officer's determination that the applicants' advertisements were insufficient because they did not include the full addresses of the two employment locations was not unreasonable. The Guidelines made it very clear that the advertisements must include both the location of work and the business address of the place of employment, and that it was reasonable to expect that potential candidates for part-time positions in a restaurant may well want to know this information before applying for an advertised position. Although the officer's concerns related to the authenticity of the advertisements that contain the full business address of the Alberta location and purportedly were posted on August 2013 were not unreasonable, the court concluded that the failure of the officer to provide the applicant in that matter with an opportunity to address her concerns was not immaterial. The applicant may have been able to alleviate these concerns, in which case the officer may well have reached a different conclusion. On this basis, the officer's decision was set aside.

It is trite law that administrative guidelines are not binding and cannot be applied in a manner that unduly fetters a decision maker's discretion, unless they constitute delegated legislation, having the full force of law. So long as the Guidelines are not binding on officers, and are applied in a manner that permit departures where warranted, it is not unreasonable for officers to apply and follow them in the majority, or even the substantial majority of cases. ESDC must process a very large volume of requests for LMOs annually. In this context, it is not reasonable to expect that the ESDC should explain why departures from the Guidelines are not made, unless the particular circumstances of an applicant's case are such that it would be reasonable for such a departure to have been given serious consideration. The court concluded that the officer did not fetter her discretion by blindly following the Guidelines. Notwithstanding this finding, the court commented that the Guidelines could be much clearer regarding their flexible application. In this regard, in an explicit statement at the beginning of the Guidelines, stating that departures from them may be made in appropriate circumstances, would have been helpful. In applying the Guidelines, officers would be well advised to avoid using language that may suggest that the Guidelines are binding in all circumstances. The application for judicial review of the B.C. matter was dismissed; however, judicial review of the Alberta matter was granted due to the failure to provide the applicant with an opportunity to address concerns.

Euro Railings Ltd. v. Canada (Minister of Employment and Social Development), 2015 FC 507, 2015 CarswellNat 1108 — This was a judicial review of a decision of a program officer to refuse a positive labour market opinion ("LMO") to hire a foreign worker — a highly skilled welder for a specialized metal railing business. The record in this case was sufficiently deficient that the respondent, without leave of the court, filed both an affidavit from the officer purporting to explain the reasons for her decision and an affidavit from the officer's supervisor in part explaining the program as she saw it and the duties of an officer assessing labour markets. Both affidavits were submitted to buttress the officer's decision — to make up for the obvious deficiencies in it. The supervisor's affidavit was struck from the record as improper evidence in a judicial review. The officer's affidavit was also struck for the same reason. The applicant received numerous applications for the welding position; 90 per cent were from individuals who did not meet the requirements. "Welders" is an occupation listed on the Federal Skills Trade Program indicating a need for such skills in Canada. The LMO refusal letter was based on an absence of a demonstrable labour shortage in the occupation. The reasons in this case were not intelligible against the background of the material before the officer. The applicant was entitled to an explanation — short, sharp and crisp — for the rejection of key evidence. The judicial review was granted.

CSWU, Local 1611 v. Canada (Minister of Citizenship & Immigration), 2013 FC 512, 2013 CarswellNat 1482, 2013 CarswellNat 1575 — The applicants challenged a decision made under Canada's Temporary Foreign Worker Program ("TFWP") which is administered by Human Resources and Skills Development Canada ("HRSDC") and CIC. The applicants challenged the decision of the HRSDC officer to issue a positive labour market opinion under s. 203 of IRPR. The officer issued these positive LMOs because he decided that offers of employment by HD Mining to 201 workers from China to do the work of extracting a bulk sample from HD Mining's coal properties in British Columbia (the Murray River Project), would likely result in "a neutral or positive effect on the labour market in Canada."

The officer's assessment of whether the employment of the foreign nationals would likely result in the creation or transfer of skills and knowledge for the benefit of Canadian citizens or permanent residents was reasonable. He found this factor weighted in HD Mining's favour, if only slightly, based on their transition plan, the discussions they had had with a local training institution, and the use of English-speaking foremen, but nevertheless had some concerns about this plan and about how the use of Mandarin would affect HD Mining's ability to attract and train Canadians. This finding is intelligible and fell within the range of possible acceptable outcomes based on the material that was before the officer. Moreover, the officer's expression of his concerns in his reasons was meant to be a useful tool for the next officer to review an LMO application from HD Mining, which was to occur within roughly two years. The court would send the wrong message and it would arguably have a chilling effect on administrative reasons to hold, in effect, that an officer cannot express his or her concerns but nevertheless make a positive determination if, on balance, it was warranted.

The applicants argued that the officer's reasons offered no source or basis for the determination of the prevailing wage rates and if it was accepted that he looked at the working in Canada ("WiC") website run by the Government of Canada, he failed to follow HRSDC policy by not looking at various sources. The court concluded that the source of the officer's prevailing wage rate information was the WiC website. Although, the officer failed to state in the assessment notes his source, it did not follow that he had no source of information. LMO decisions are administrative decisions and the duty to give reasons is at the low end of the scale. Accordingly, his failure to state the source, given the evidence before the court, was not a reason to set the decision aside.

An officer is entitled to use his discretion when examining the advertising an applicant has made both in terms of timing and accuracy. The officer did so and, as he stated, was looking at whether he felt that "any different outcome would arise" if the recruitment was done differently. There was nothing on the record that establishes that he was wrong in his assessment that sufficient efforts had been made to recruit Canadians, either when he made the assessment or in hindsight. The applicants argued that the decisions the officer made were unreasonable because of the deficiencies in the advertising done by HD Mining. The court acknowledged that another officer may take the view that HD Mining had to re-advertise for those few positions where the job title was slightly misstated, or where the advertising is slightly stale-dated, but that did not make the officer's decision to the contrary unreasonable.

The applicants also submitted that the officer ought to have been suspicious of the recruitment efforts in Canada given the few Canadians hired or interviewed, despite HD Mining having received many resumes. The court held that the program officer is not a human resources specialist or a recruitment officer. Accordingly, the review of the resumo would not likely have been more meaningful to the officer than to the court. An employer must be given some latitude in its hiring even within the TFWP. The real question is whether there was anything before the officer from which he should reasonably have concluded that the applicant had failed to make reasonable efforts to hire Canadians. In approaching that question, one must keep in mind that there was a labour shortage in the mining industry, that the mine owner's application had been approved only 12 months earlier for the same project, and that the owner and HD Mining both did recruitment. The low number of interviews alone would not have reasonably raised a concern that the recruitment process was not genuine or sincere.

It is not necessary that an applicant meet every one of the six factors listed in s. 203(3), the decision maker must examine and assess each and then perform a weighing exercise to decide whether the LMO will issue. This is exactly what the officer did. As he notes in the bulk request assessment and recommendation form, even if the job creation and skill transfer factors did not weigh in favour of a positive opinion, all of the others did and the LMO would still issue.

The application for judicial review was dismissed.

204. International agreements — A work permit may be issued under section 200 to a foreign national who intends to perform work pursuant to

    (a) an international agreement between Canada and one or more countries, other than an agreement concerning seasonal agricultural workers;

    (b) an agreement entered into by one or more countries and by or on behalf of one or more provinces; or

    (c) an agreement entered into by the Minister with a province or group of provinces under subsection 8(1) of the Act.

Case Law

Garro v. Canada (Minister of Citizenship & Immigration) (2007), 67 Imm. L.R. (3d) 263, 2007 CarswellNat 1827, 2007 CarswellNat 4509, 2007 FC 670 — This was an application for judicial review of a decision of an immigration officer, refusing the application for a work permit for the applicant and visitor status for his family. The immigration officer concluded that the applicant failed to meet the conditions required to obtain investor status under the North American Free Trade Agreement. The letter of refusal that the officer sent contained no reasons explaining why the application was denied. The officer's notes revealed that he did not consider the initial sum of $20,000 to be a substantial investment for purposes of granting the applicant a permit. However, the evidence in the record showed that the applicant invested $166,000 in commercial premises for the company, $67,000 in book stocks to sell and thousands of dollars in equipment. Given that the applicant's evidence was so compelling, the court concluded that there was absolutely no reason for the officer's decision and allowed the judicial review.

205. Canadian interests — A work permit may be issued under section 200 to a foreign national who intends to perform work that

    (a) would create or maintain significant social, cultural or economic benefits or opportunities for Canadian citizens or permanent residents;

(b) would create or maintain reciprocal employment of Canadian citizens or permanent residents of Canada in other countries;

(c) is designated by the Minister as being work that can be performed by a foreign national on the basis of the following criteria, namely,

> **(i) the work is related to a research program,**

> **(i.1) the work is an essential part of a post-secondary academic, vocational or professional training program offered by a designated learning institution as defined in section 211.1,**

> **(i.2) the work is an essential part of a program at the secondary level**

>> **(A) that is a vocational training program offered by a designated learning institution in Quebec, or**

>> **(B) that is a program offered by a designated learning institution that requires students to work in order to obtain their secondary or high school diploma or certificate of graduation, or**

> **(ii) limited access to the Canadian labour market is necessary for reasons of public policy relating to the competitiveness of Canada's academic institutions or economy; or**

(d) is of a religious or charitable nature.

SOR/2014-14, s. 7

Case Law

Appidy v. Canada (Minister of Citizenship and Immigration), 2015 FC 1356, 2015 CarswellNat 7152, 2015 CarswellNat 10510 — The officer did not grant a post-graduate work permit to the applicant on the basis that five of the six classes he completed at Niagara College were online courses and the post-graduate work permit program provides that students who participate in and complete their program of study by distance learning are not eligible for the issuance of a work permit. The officer considered only the applicant's final program of study to determine his eligibility. The applicant argued that he completed two years of full-time studies in Canada and that only 25 per cent of his courses were taken online, and even then at the suggestion of his professor, and 75 per cent of his courses were taken in-class. Specifically, the applicant obtained 42 in-class credits from Fanshawe College and three in-class credits from Niagara College. Only 15 credits were obtained online. The applicant also argues that he paid the full-time student fee under the legitimate expectation that he would be granted a three-year work permit.

The officer's decision was not reasonable because of the failure to take into account the in-class credits earned by the applicant through his study at Fanshawe College. The officer relied on the portion of the relevant Citizenship and Immigration Canada manual that required the applicant to apply for a work permit within 90 days of receiving written confirmation from the educational institution indicating that they had met the requirements for completing their program of study. It was not reasonable for the officer to interpret the manual as precluding consideration of the credits from Fanshawe College, as those credits formed part of the requirements for completing the applicant's program of study at Niagara College. The application for judicial review was allowed.

Arora v. Canada (Minister of Citizenship & Immigration), 2011 FC 241, 2011 CarswellNat 1325, 2011 CarswellNat 653 — The applicant's application for a work permit was refused for failure to demonstrate that he met the requirements of an intra-company transferee such that he should be exempted from applying for an LMO and receive a work permit and temporary resident visa. The officer found discrepancies between a letter from the applicant's employer and the applicant's submitted form with respect to his annual salary. The officer was not satisfied that the applicant worked as a senior executive or held a managerial level position due to his age (23), his level of education (Grade 12), his limited experience with the company (less than three years), his modest income and the lack of evidence with respect to his prior work experience.

The court held that while these factors may play a part in an officer's assessment, they cannot be substituted for an assessment of the qualities of a manager as outlined in the FW1 Manual. In addition, several factors noted by the officer were irrelevant to the assessment. For example, the officer was concerned that the applicant could not be a senior executive at the age of 23 years. However, age is not a factor listed in the Foreign Worker 1 Manual and not allowing the exemption under subs. 205(a) of the Regulations based on the applicant's age is inappropriate. A further problem with the officer's finding was that the Foreign Worker Manual explicitly states that the applicant must show only one year of managerial experience at the company for which he was applying for a work permit. Finally, neither the FW1 Manual nor the Regulations requires a certain salary level before an applicant can be considered a senior executive or manager. As such, it was an error for the officer to draw a negative inference from the finding that the applicant made a modest salary. The application for judicial review allowed.

206. (1) No other means of support — A work permit may be issued under section 200 to a foreign national in Canada who cannot support themselves without working, if the foreign national

(a) has made a claim for refugee protection that has been referred to the Refugee Protection Division but has not been determined; or

(b) is subject to an unenforceable removal order.

(2) Exception — Despite subsection (1), a work permit must not be issued to a claimant referred to in subsection 111.1(2) of the Act unless at least 180 days have elapsed since their claim was referred to the Refugee Protection Division.

SOR/2012-252, s. 2

207. Applicants in Canada — A work permit may be issued under section 200 to a foreign national in Canada who

(a) is a member of the live-in caregiver class set out in Division 3 of Part 6 and meets the requirements of section 113;

(b) is a member of the spouse or common-law partner in Canada class set out in Division 2 of Part 7;

(c) is a protected person within the meaning of subsection 95(2) of the Act;

(d) has applied to become a permanent resident and the Minister has granted them an exemption under subsection 25(1), 25.1(1) or 25.2(1) of the Act; or

(e) is a family member of a person described in any of paragraphs (a) to (d).

SOR/2010-252, s. 3(c)

208. Humanitarian reasons — A work permit may be issued under section 200 to a foreign national in Canada who cannot support themself without working, if the foreign national

(a) holds a study permit and has become temporarily destitute through circumstances beyond their control and beyond the control of any person on whom that person is dependent for the financial support to complete their term of study; or

(b) holds a temporary resident permit issued under subsection 24(1) of the Act that is valid for at least six months.

SOR/2004-167, s. 58

209. Invalidity — A work permit becomes invalid when it expires or when a removal order that is made against the permit holder becomes enforceable.

DIVISION 4 — CONDITIONS IMPOSED ON EMPLOYERS
[Heading added SOR/2013-245, s. 7.]

209.1 Definition of "document" — For the purposes of this Division, "document" means anything on which information that is capable of being understood by a person, or read by a computer or other device, is recorded or marked.

SOR/2013-245, s. 7

209.11 (1) Foreign national referred to in subparagraph 200(1)(c)(ii.1) — An employer who has made an offer of employment to a foreign national referred to in subparagraph 200(1)(c)(ii.1) must, before the foreign national makes an application for a work permit in respect of that employment, provide the following information to the Minister by means of the electronic system that is made available by the Department for that purpose:

(a) their name, address and telephone number and their fax number and electronic mail address, if any;

(b) the business number assigned to the employer by the Minister of National Revenue, if applicable;

(c) information that demonstrates that the foreign national will be performing work described in section 204 or 205 or is a foreign national described in section 207; and

(d) a copy of the offer of employment made in the form made available by the Department.

(2) Information provided — time — The information is deemed to be received on the date and at the time recorded in the electronic system.

(3) Other means of providing information — If an employer is unable to provide the information by means of the electronic system because of a physical or mental disability, the information may be provided by another means that is made available by the Department for that purpose and that would enable the employer to provide the information, including a paper form.

SOR/2015-25, s. 2

209.2 (1) **Foreign national referred to in subparagraph 200(1)(c)(ii.1) —** An employer who has made an offer of employment to a foreign national referred to in subparagraph 200(1)(c)(ii.1) must comply with the following conditions:

> (a) during the period of employment for which the work permit is issued to the foreign national,
>
>> (i) the employer must be actively engaged in the business in respect of which the offer of employment was made, unless the offer was made for employment as a live-in caregiver,
>>
>> (ii) the employer must comply with the federal and provincial laws that regulate employment, and the recruiting of employees, in the province in which the foreign national works,
>>
>> (iii) the employer must provide the foreign national with employment in the same occupation as that set out in the foreign national's offer of employment and with wages and working conditions that are substantially the same as — but not less favourable than — those set out in that offer, and
>>
>> (iv) the employer must make reasonable efforts to provide a workplace that is free of abuse, within the meaning of paragraph 72.1(7)(a); and
>
> (b) during a period of six years beginning on the first day of the period of employment for which the work permit is issued to the foreign national, the employer must
>
>> (i) be able to demonstrate that any information they provided under subparagraph 200(1)(c)(ii.1) or section 209.11 was accurate, and
>>
>> (ii) retain any document that relates to compliance with the conditions set out in paragraph (a).

(2) **Period of employment —** For the purposes of subsection (1), the period of employment for which the work permit is issued includes any period during which the foreign national may, under paragraph 186(u), work in Canada without a permit after the expiry of their work permit.

(3) **Justification —** A failure to comply with any of the conditions set out in paragraph (1)(a) is justified if it results from any of the circumstances set out in subsection 203(1.1).

(4) **Justification —** A failure to comply with either of the conditions set out in paragraph (1)(b) is justified if the employer made all reasonable efforts to comply with the condition.

SOR/2013-245, s. 7; SOR/2015-25, s. 3

209.3 (1) Foreign national referred to in subparagraph 200(1)(c)(iii) — An employer who has made an offer of employment to a foreign national referred to in subparagraph 200(1)(c)(iii) must comply with the following conditions:

(a) during the period of employment for which the work permit is issued to the foreign national,

(i) the employer must be actively engaged in the business in respect of which the offer of employment was made, unless the offer was made for employment as a live-in caregiver,

(ii) the employer must comply with the federal and provincial laws that regulate employment, and the recruiting of employees, in the province in which the foreign national works,

(iii) the employer, in the case of an employer who employs a foreign national as a live-in caregiver, must

(A) ensure that the foreign national resides in a private household in Canada and provides child care, senior home support care or care of a disabled person in that household without supervision,

(B) provide the foreign national with adequate furnished and private accommodations in the household, and

(C) have sufficient financial resources to pay the foreign national the wages that were offered to the foreign national,

(iv) the employer must provide the foreign national with employment in the same occupation as that set out in the foreign national's offer of employment and with wages and working conditions that are substantially the same as — but not less favourable than — those set out in that offer, and

(v) the employer must make reasonable efforts to provide a workplace that is free of abuse, within the meaning of paragraph 72.1(7)(a);

(b) during the period of employment for which the work permit is issued to the foreign national or any other period that was agreed on by the employer and the Department of Employment and Social Development at the time the assessment referred to in subsection 203(2) was provided,

(i) the employer must ensure that the employment of the foreign national will result in direct job creation or job retention for Canadian citizens or permanent residents, if that was one of the factors that led to the issuance of the work permit,

(ii) the employer must ensure that the employment of the foreign national will result in the development or transfer of skills and knowledge for the benefit of Canadian citizens or permanent residents, if that was one of the factors that led to the issuance of the work permit,

(iii) the employer must hire or train Canadian citizens or permanent residents, if that was one of the factors that led to the issuance of the work permit, and

(iv) the employer must make reasonable efforts to hire or train Canadian citizens or permanent residents, if that was one of the factors that led to the issuance of the work permit; and

(c) during a period of six years beginning on the first day of the period of employment for which the work permit is issued to the foreign national, the employer must

(i) be able to demonstrate that any information they provided under subsections 203(1) and (2.1) was accurate, and

(ii) retain any document that relates to compliance with the conditions set out in paragraphs (a) and (b).

(2) **Period of employment** — For the purposes of subsection (1), the period of employment for which the work permit is issued includes any period during which the foreign national may, under paragraph 186(u), work in Canada without a permit after the expiry of their work permit.

(3) **Justification** — A failure to comply with any of the conditions set out in paragraphs (1)(a) and (b) is justified if it results from any of the circumstances set out in subsection 203(1.1).

(4) **Justification** — A failure to comply with either of the conditions set out in paragraph (1)(c) is justified if the employer made all reasonable efforts to comply with the condition.

SOR/2013-245, s. 7; 2013, c. 40, s. 237(3)(a); SOR/2014-84, s. 1(b); SOR/2015-147, s. 1(e)

209.4 (1) Conditions imposed on all employers — An employer referred to in section 209.2 or 209.3 must

(a) report at any specified time and place to answer questions and provide documents, in accordance with section 209.6;

(b) provide any documents that are required under section 209.7; and

(c) attend any inspection referred to in section 209.8 or 209.9, unless the employer was not notified of it, give all reasonable assistance to the person conducting that inspection and provide that person with any document or information that the person requires.

(2) **Justification** — A failure to comply with any of the conditions set out in subsection (1) is justified if the employer made all reasonable efforts to comply with the condition or if it results from anything done or omitted to be done by the employer in good faith.

SOR/2013-245, s. 7

209.5 Circumstances for exercise of powers — sections 209.6 to 209.9 — The powers set out in sections 209.6 to 209.9 may be exercised in the following circumstances:

(a) an officer or the Minister of Employment and Social Development has a reason to suspect that the employer is not complying or has not complied with any of the conditions set out in section 209.2 or 209.3;

(b) the employer has not complied with the conditions set out in section 209.2 or 209.3 in the past; or

(c) the employer is chosen as part of a random verification of compliance with the conditions set out in sections 209.2 and 209.3.

SOR/2013-245, s. 7; 2013, c. 40, s. 238(3)(a); SOR/2014-84, s. 2(a)

209.6 (1) Answering questions and providing documents — If any of the circumstances set out in section 209.5 exists,

(a) an officer may, for the purpose of verifying compliance with the conditions set out in section 209.2, require an employer to report at any specified time and place to answer questions and provide documents that relate to compliance with those conditions; and

(b) the Minister of Employment and Social Development may, for the purpose of verifying compliance with the conditions set out in section 209.3, require an employer to report at any specified time and place to answer questions and provide documents that relate to compliance with those conditions.

(2) Minister of Employment and Social Development — The Minister of Employment and Social Development may exercise the powers set out in paragraph (1)(a) on the request of an officer.

SOR/2013-245, s. 7; 2013, c. 40, s. 238(3)(a); SOR/2014-84, s. 2(b)

209.7 (1) Examination of documents — If any of the circumstances set out in section 209.5 exists,

(a) an officer may, for the purpose of verifying compliance with the conditions set out in section 209.2, require an employer to provide them with any document that relates to compliance with those conditions; and

(b) the Minister of Employment and Social Development may, for the purpose of verifying compliance with the conditions set out in section 209.3, require an employer to provide him or her with any document that relates to compliance with those conditions.

(2) Minister of Employment and Social Development — The Minister of Employment and Social Development may exercise the powers set out in paragraph (1)(a) on the request of an officer.

SOR/2013-245, s. 7; 2013, c. 40, s. 238(3)(a); SOR/2014-84, s. 2(c)

209.8 (1) Entry to verify compliance with section 209.2 — Subject to subsection (5), if any of the circumstances set out in section 209.5 exists, an officer may, for the purpose of verifying compliance with the conditions set out in section 209.2, enter and inspect any premises or place in which a foreign national referred to in that section performs work.

(2) Powers on entry — The officer may, for that purpose,

(a) ask the employer and any person employed by the employer any relevant questions;

(b) require from the employer, for examination, any documents found in the premises or place;

(c) use copying equipment in the premises or place, or require the employer to make copies of documents, and remove the copies for examination or, if it is not possible to make copies in the premises or place, remove the documents to make copies;

(d) take photographs and make video or audio recordings;

(e) examine anything in the premises or place;

(f) require the employer to use any computer or other electronic device in the premises or place to allow the officer to examine any relevant document contained in or available to it; and

(g) be accompanied or assisted in the premises or place by any person required by the officer.

(3) Entering private property — An officer and any person accompanying the officer may enter on and pass through private property, other than a dwelling-house, to gain entry to a premises or place referred to in subsection (1). For greater certainty, they are not liable for doing so.

(4) Person accompanying officer — A person may, at an officer's request, accompany the officer to assist them to access the premises or place referred to in subsection (1) and is not liable for doing so.

(5) Dwelling-house — In the case of a dwelling-house, an officer may enter it without the occupant's consent only under the authority of a warrant issued under subsection (6).

(6) Issuance of warrant — On *ex parte* application, a justice of the peace may issue a warrant authorizing an officer who is named in it or the Minister of Employment and Social Development, as the case may be, to enter a dwelling-house, subject to any conditions specified in the warrant, if the justice of the peace is satisfied by information on oath that

(a) there are reasonable grounds to believe that the dwelling-house is a premises or place referred to in subsection (1);

(b) entry into the dwelling-house is necessary to verify compliance with the conditions set out in section 209.2; and

(c) entry was refused by the occupant or there are reasonable grounds to believe that entry will be refused or that consent to entry cannot be obtained from the occupant.

(7) Minister of Employment and Social Development — The Minister of Employment and Social Development may exercise the powers set out in this section on the request of an officer.

SOR/2013-245, s. 7; 2013, c. 40, s. 238(3)(a); SOR/2014-84, s. 2(d)

209.9 (1) Entry to verify compliance with section 209.3 — Subject to subsection (5), if any of the circumstances set out in section 209.5 exists, the Minister of Employment and Social Development may, for the purpose of verifying compliance with the conditions set out in section 209.3, enter and inspect any premises or place in which a foreign national referred to in that section performs work and any premises or place that the employer has provided to the foreign national as accommodation.

(2) Powers on entry — The Minister of Employment and Social Development may, for that purpose,

(a) ask the employer and any person employed by the employer any relevant questions;

(b) require from the employer, for examination, any documents found in the premises or place;

(c) use copying equipment in the premises or place, or require the employer to make copies of documents, and remove the copies for examination or, if it is not possible to make copies in the premises or place, remove the documents to make copies;

(d) take photographs and make video or audio recordings;

(e) examine anything in the premises or place;

(f) require the employer to use any computer or other electronic device in the premises or place to allow that Minister to examine any relevant document contained in or available to it; and

(g) be accompanied or assisted in the premises or place by any person required by that Minister.

(3) Entering private property — The Minister of Employment and Social Development and any person accompanying him or her may enter on and pass through private property, other than a dwelling-house, to gain entry to a premises or place referred to in subsection (1). For greater certainty, they are not liable for doing so.

(4) Person accompanying Minister of Employment and Social Development — A person may, at the Minister of Employment and Social Development's request, accompany that Minister to assist him or her to access the premises or place referred to in subsection (1) and is not liable for doing so.

(5) Dwelling-house — In the case of a dwelling-house, the Minister of Employment and Social Development may enter it without the occupant's consent only under the authority of a warrant issued under subsection (6).

(6) Issuance of warrant — On *ex parte* application, a justice of the peace may issue a warrant authorizing the Minister of Employment and Social Development to enter a dwelling-house, subject to any conditions specified in the warrant, if the justice of the peace is satisfied by information on oath that

(a) there are reasonable grounds to believe that the dwelling-house is a premises or place referred to in subsection (1);

(b) entry into the dwelling-house is necessary to verify compliance with the conditions set out in section 209.3; and

(c) entry was refused by the occupant or there are reasonable grounds to believe that entry will be refused or that consent to entry cannot be obtained from the occupant.

SOR/2013-245, s. 7; 2013, c. 40, s. 238(3)(a); SOR/2014-84, ss. 2(e), 3

209.91 [Repealed SOR/2015-144, s. 7.]

DIVISION 5 — DISCLOSURE OF INFORMATION
[Heading added SOR/2013-245, s. 7.]

209.92 Disclosure of information — An officer may, for the purposes of determining whether a work permit is to be issued to a foreign national under subsection 200(1), of making a determination under paragraphs 203(1)(a) to (e), if applicable, or of verifying compliance with the conditions set out in sections 209.2 to 209.4, disclose to the Minister of Employment and Social Development and to the competent authorities of the provinces concerned information that relates to an application for a work permit or to an employer's compliance with the conditions set out in sections 209.2 to 209.4.

SOR/2013-245, s. 7; 2013, c. 40, s. 238(3)(a); SOR/2014-84, s. 2(g)

DIVISION 6 — ADMINISTRATIVE MONETARY PENALTIES AND OTHER CONSEQUENCES FOR FAILURE TO COMPLY WITH CONDITIONS IMPOSED ON EMPLOYERS
[Heading added SOR/2015-144, s. 8.]

Interpretation
[Heading added SOR/2015-144, s. 8.]

209.93 Definitions — The following definitions apply in this Division.

"large business" means any business that is not a small business. *("grande entreprise")*

"small business" means any business, including its affiliates, that has fewer than 100 employees or less than $5 million in annual gross revenues at the time a request for an assessment under subsection 203(2) is received, or if no such request is made, at the time a copy of an offer of employment for a work permit application is provided to the Minister under paragraph 209.11(1)(d). *("petite entreprise")*

SOR/2015-144, s. 8

Purpose
[Heading added SOR/2015-144, s. 8.]

209.94 Purpose of Division — The purpose of this Division is to encourage compliance with the provisions of the Act and these Regulations and not to punish.

SOR/2015-144, s. 8

Violations

[Heading added SOR/2015-144, s. 8.]

209.95 (1) Violations — **An employer referred to in subsection 209.2(1) or 209.3(1) who fails to comply with one of the conditions set out in the provisions listed in column 1 of Table 1 of Schedule 2 — if the failure to do so is not justified under subsection 209.2(3) or (4), 209.3(3) or (4) or 209.4(2) — commits a violation and**

> **(a) is liable to an administrative monetary penalty of an amount that is determined in accordance with section 209.98 or if it is determined under that section that there is no penalty, is issued a warning informing the employer that there is no administrative monetary penalty for the violation but that the violation will be considered in the calculation of the total number of points under subparagraph 209.991(1)(a)(i) for any subsequent violation; and**

> **(b) if applicable, is ineligible to employ a foreign national for whom a work permit is required for the period determined in accordance with section 209.99.**

(2) Discrepancy — **In the event of a discrepancy between the short-form description in column 2 of Table 1 of Schedule 2 and the provision to which it pertains, the provision prevails.**

SOR/2015-144, s. 8

Rules Applicable to Violations

[Heading added SOR/2015-144, s. 8.]

209.96 (1) Separate violation multiple foreign nationals — A failure to comply — that is not justified under subsection 209.2(3) or (4), 209.3(3) or (4) or 209.4(2) — with a condition that affects more than one foreign national constitutes a separate violation for each foreign national affected.

(2) Separate violation occupation, wages or working conditions — A failure to comply — that is not justified under subsection 209.2(3) or 209.3(3) — with any one of the following elements of the condition set out in item 9 of Table 1 of Schedule 2, constitutes a separate violation:

> (a) to provide the foreign national with employment in the same occupation as the occupation that is set out in the foreign national's offer of employment;

> (b) to provide the foreign national with wages that are substantially the same as — but not less favourable than — those set out in the foreign national's offer of employment; and

> (c) to provide the foreign national with working conditions that are substantially the same as — but not less favourable than — those set out in the foreign national's offer of employment.

(3) Separate violation live-in caregivers — With respect to employers who employ foreign nationals as live-in caregivers, a failure to comply — that is not justified under subsection 209.3(3) — with either one of the following elements of the condition set out in item 10 of Table 1 of Schedule 2, constitutes a separate violation:

(a) to ensure that the foreign national resides in a private household in Canada,

(b) to ensure that the foreign national provides child care, senior home support care or care of a disabled person in that household without supervision.

(4) Separate violation abuse — A failure to comply — that is not justified under subsection 209.2(3) or 209.3(3) — with the condition set out in item 17 of Table 1 of Schedule 2 with respect to any one of the elements set out in subparagraphs 72.1(7)(a)(i) to (iv), constitutes a separate violation.

SOR/2015-144, s. 8

Classification
[Heading added SOR/2015-144, s. 8.]

209.97 Provisions — A failure to comply — that is not justified under subsection 209.2(3) or (4), 209.3(3) or (4) or 209.4(2) — with a condition that is set out in one of the provisions listed in column 1 of Table 1 of Schedule 2, is classified as a violation of Type A, Type B or Type C as set out in column 3 of that Table.

SOR/2015-144, s. 8

Administrative Monetary Penalty Amount
[Heading added SOR/2015-144, s. 8.]

209.98 Administrative monetary penalty amount — The administrative monetary penalty for a violation is the amount set out in column 2, 3 or 4 of Table 2 of Schedule 2 opposite the total number of points determined under section 209.991 as set out in column 1, depending on the type of violation and whether it is committed by an individual or small business, or a large business.

SOR/2015-144, s. 8

Period of Ineligibility
[Heading added SOR/2015-144, s. 8.]

209.99 (1) Period of ineligibility — The period of ineligibility for a violation is the period set out in column 2, 3 or 4 of Table 3 of Schedule 2 opposite the total number of points determined under section 209.991 as set out in column 1 depending on the type of violation.

(2) Beginning of period — The period referred to in subsection (1) begins on the day on which the determination referred to in subsection 209.996(1) or (2) is made in respect of the employer.

SOR/2015-144, s. 8

Total Number of Points

[Heading added SOR/2015-144, s. 8.]

209.991 (1) Calculation — The total number of points in respect of each violation is determined by

(a) considering

(i) the compliance history of the employer who committed the violation set out in column 1 of Table 4 of Schedule 2, and

(ii) the severity criteria set out in column 1 of Table 5 of Schedule 2;

(b) ascribing

(i) for the criterion described in subparagraph (a)(i), the applicable number of points set out in column 2 of Table 4 of Schedule 2,

(ii) for the criteria described in subparagraph (a)(ii), the applicable number of points set out in column 2 of Table 5 of Schedule 2 having regard to the severity or the impact of the violation, as the case may be,

(c) adding the values obtained under paragraph (b); and

(d) if the employer made an acceptable voluntary disclosure in accordance with subsections (2) and (3) and the value obtained under paragraph (c)

(i) is four or more, subtracting four points from the value obtained under that paragraph, or

(ii) is less than four, replacing that value with a value of zero.

(2) Voluntary disclosure criteria of acceptability — The voluntary disclosure made by an employer with respect to the commission of a violation by the employer is acceptable if

(a) the disclosure is complete; and

(b) at the time the voluntary disclosure is made, the powers set out in sections 209.6 to 209.9 are not being exercised in respect of the employer nor is any enforcement action related to an offence arising out of the contravention of a provision of the Act being undertaken in respect of the employer.

(3) Voluntary disclosure considerations — Despite subsection (2), an officer or the Minister of Employment and Social Development may consider that the voluntary disclosure is not acceptable after considering

(a) the severity of the impact of the violation on the foreign national;

(b) in the case of an employer described in subsection 209.2(1), the severity of the impact of the violation on the Canadian economy, or in the case of an employer described in subsection 209.3(1), the severity of the impact of the violation on the Canadian labour market;

(c) whether the disclosure was made in a timely manner;

(d) the number of times an acceptable voluntary disclosure is made by the employer; and

(e) the nature of the condition with which the employer failed to comply.

SOR/2015-144, s. 8

Multiple Violations
[Heading added SOR/2015-144, s. 8.]

209.992 (1) Cumulative amounts — If a notice of preliminary finding under section 209.993 or a notice of final determination under section 209.996 that is issued to an employer lists more than one violation, the administrative monetary penalty amounts are cumulative but the total must not exceed $1 million.

(2) Applicable period of ineligibility — If a notice of preliminary finding or a notice of final determination that is issued to an employer includes more than one period of ineligibility, the longest period of ineligibility applies.

SOR/2015-144, s. 8

Notice of Preliminary Finding
[Heading added SOR/2015-144, s. 8.]

209.993 (1) Notice issuance by officer — If an officer assesses, on the basis of information obtained by any officer or the Minister of Employment and Social Development during the exercise of the powers set out in sections 209.6 to 209.8 and any other relevant information, that an employer has committed a violation because that employer failed to comply with one of the conditions set out in the provisions listed in column 1 of Table 1 of Schedule 2 and the failure to do so was not justified under subsection 209.2(3) or (4) or 209.4(2), the officer must issue a notice of preliminary finding to the employer.

(2) Notice issuance by Minister — If the Minister of Employment and Social Development assesses, on the basis of information obtained during the exercise of the powers set out in sections 209.6, 209.7 and 209.9 and any other relevant information, that an employer has committed a violation because that employer failed to comply with one of the conditions set out in the provisions listed in column 1 of Table 1 of Schedule 2 and the failure to do so was not justified under subsection 209.3(3) or (4) or 209.4(2), that Minister must issue a notice of preliminary finding to the employer.

(3) Content of notice — The notice of preliminary finding must include the following information:

(a) the name of the employer referred to in subsection (1) or (2), as the case may be;

(b) the condition with which the employer failed to comply as well as the provision listed in column 1 of Table 1 of Schedule 2, the relevant facts surrounding the violation and the reasons for the preliminary finding;

(c) if applicable, the administrative monetary penalty amount and the period of ineligibility for the violation as well as the statement that the violation will be considered in the calculation of the total number of points under subparagraph 209.991(1)(a)(i) for any subsequent violation;

(d) if applicable, the statement that a warning may be issued to the employer informing them that there is no administrative monetary penalty for the viola-

865

tion but that the violation will be considered in the calculation of the total number of points under subparagraph 209.991(1)(a)(i) for any subsequent violation; and

(e) the statement that the employer may make written submissions within the period set out in section 209.994 with respect to the information referred to in paragraphs (b) to (d).

SOR/2015-144, s. 8

209.994 (1) Submissions by employer period — An employer to whom a notice of preliminary finding under section 209.993 or a corrected notice of preliminary finding under section 209.995 is issued may, within 30 days after the day on which it is received,

(a) make written submissions with respect to the information referred to in paragraphs 209.993(3)(b) to (d); or

(b) request an extension of that period.

(2) Deemed receipt — Despite section 3 of the *Electronic Documents and Electronic Information Regulations*, a notice of preliminary finding or a corrected or cancelled notice of preliminary finding is deemed to have been received 10 days after the day on which it is sent.

(3) Submissions by employer extension of period — An officer or the Minister of Employment and Social Development may extend the period referred to in subsection (1) if there is a reasonable explanation justifying its extension.

SOR/2015-144, s. 8

209.995 Correction or cancellation of notice — An officer or the Minister of Employment and Social Development may correct any information in a notice of preliminary finding that is issued under subsection 209.993(1) or (2), or cancel one, at any time before a notice of final determination is issued under section 209.996.

SOR/2015-144, s. 8

Notice of Final Determination

[Heading added SOR/2015-144, s. 8.]

209.996 (1) Notice issuance by officer — Subject to subsection (3), if an officer determines, on the basis of information obtained by any officer or the Minister of Employment and Social Development during the exercise of the powers set out in sections 209.6 to 209.8 and any other relevant information, that an employer has committed a violation because that employer failed to comply with one of the conditions set out in the provisions listed in column 1 of Table 1 of Schedule 2 and the failure to do so was not justified under subsection 209.2(3) or (4) or 209.4(2), the officer must issue a notice of final determination to the employer.

(2) Notice issuance by Minister — Subject to subsection (3), if the Minister of Employment and Social Development determines, on the basis of information obtained during the exercise of the powers set out in sections 209.6, 209.7 and 209.9 and any other relevant information, that an employer has committed a violation because that employer failed to comply with one of the conditions set out in the provisions listed in column 1 of Table 1 of Schedule 2 and the failure to do so was not justified under subsection 209.3(3) or (4) or 209.4(2), that Minister must issue a notice of final determination to the employer.

(3) Period — An officer or the Minister of Employment and Social Development must not make a determination before the expiry of the period set out in subsection 209.994(1) or the period extended under subsection 209.994(3) as the case may be.

(4) Content of notice — The notice of final determination must include the following information:

(a) the name of the employer referred to in subsection (1) or (2), as the case may be;

(b) the condition with which the employer failed to comply as well as the provision listed in column 1 of Table 1 of Schedule 2, the relevant facts surrounding the violation and the reasons for the determination;

(c) if applicable, the administrative monetary penalty amount and the period of ineligibility for the violation as well as the statement indicating that the violation will be considered in the calculation of the total number of points under subparagraph 209.991(1)(a)(i) for any subsequent violation;

(d) if applicable, a warning informing the employer that there is no administrative monetary penalty for the violation but that the violation will be considered in the calculation of the total number of points under subparagraph 209.991(1)(a)(i) for any subsequent violation;

(e) if applicable, a statement that the administrative monetary penalty amount must be paid within 30 days after the day on which the notice of final determination is received by the employer, unless a payment agreement for the payment of amount and interest has been reached within that period; and

(f) how the administrative monetary penalty is to be paid.

(5) Maximum amount within 12 months — If the sum of the administrative monetary penalty amount described in paragraph (4)(c) and all previous administrative monetary penalty amounts provided for in notices of final determination issued to the employer in question within 12 months before the day on which the determination is made exceeds $1 million, then the amount of the penalty must be reduced by that excess.

(6) Deemed receipt — Despite section 3 of the *Electronic Documents and Electronic Information Regulations*, a notice of final determination is deemed to have been received 10 days after the day on which it is sent.

SOR/2015-144, s. 8

List of Employers
[Heading added SOR/2015-144, s. 8.]

209.997 (1) Publication of employer's information — If an officer or the Minister of Employment and Social Development makes a determination under subsection 209.996(1) or (2) in respect of an employer, the Department or that Minister, as the case may be, must add the information referred to in subsection (2) to the list referred to in that subsection, except if the officer or that Minister issues a warning to the employer in accordance with paragraph 209.996(4)(d).

(2) Content of list — A list is posted on one or more Government of Canada websites and includes the following information:

(a) the employer's name;

(b) the employer's address;

(c) the criteria set out in subclause 200(1)(c)(ii.1)(B)(I) or subparagraph 203(1)(e)(i) that were not satisfied or the conditions set out in the provisions listed in column 1 of Table 1 of Schedule 2 with which the employer failed to comply, as the case may be;

(d) the day on which the determination was made;

(e) the eligibility status of the employer;

(f) if applicable,

(i) the administrative monetary penalty amount, and

(ii) the ineligibility period of the employer.

SOR/2015-144, s. 8

PART 12 — STUDENTS

DIVISION 1 — GENERAL RULES

210. Class — The student class is prescribed as a class of persons who may become temporary residents.

211. Student — A foreign national is a student and a member of the student class if the foreign national has been authorized to enter and remain in Canada as a student.

211.1 Definition of "designated learning institution" — In this Part, "designated learning institution" means

(a) the following learning institutions:

(i) a learning institution that is administered by a federal department or agency,

(ii) if a province has entered into an agreement or arrangement with the Minister in respect of post-secondary learning institutions in Canada that host international students, a postsecondary learning institution located in the province that is designated by the province for the purposes of these Regulations on the basis that the institution meets provincial requirements in respect of the delivery of education,

(iii) if a province has entered into an agreement or arrangement with the Minister in respect of primary or secondary learning institutions in Canada that host international students, a primary or secondary learning institution located in the province that is designated by the province for the purposes of these Regulations on the basis that the institution meets provincial requirements in respect of the delivery of education, and

(iv) if a province has not entered into an agreement or arrangement with the Minister in respect of primary or secondary learning institutions in Canada that host international students, any primary or secondary level learning institution in the province; and

(b) in the case of Quebec, the following additional learning institutions:

(i) any educational institution within the meaning of section 36 of the *Education Act* of Quebec, R.S.Q. c. I-13.3,

(ii) any college established in accordance with section 2 of the *General and Vocational Colleges Act* of Quebec, R.S.Q. c. 29,

(iii) any private educational institution for which a permit is issued under section 10 of the *Act respecting private education* of Quebec, R.S.Q. c. E-9.1,

(iv) any educational institution operated under an Act of Quebec by a government department or a body that is a mandatary of the province,

(v) the Conservatoire de musique et d'art dramatique du Québec established by the *Act respecting the Conservatoire de musique et d'art dramatique du Québec* of Quebec, R.S.Q. c. C-62.1, and

(vi) any educational institution at the university level referred to in section 1 of the *Act respecting educational institutions at the university level*, R.S.Q. c. E-14.1.

SOR/2014-14, s. 8

211.2 List of provinces — The Minister shall publish a list of those provinces with which the Minister has entered into an agreement or arrangement in respect of learning institutions that host international students.

SOR/2014-14, s. 8

212. Authorization — A foreign national may not study in Canada unless authorized to do so by the Act, a study permit or these Regulations.

SOR/2014-14, s. 9

DIVISION 2 — APPLICATION FOR STUDY PERMIT

213. Application before entry — Subject to sections 214 and 215, in order to study in Canada, a foreign national shall apply for a study permit before entering Canada.

214. Application on entry — A foreign national may apply for a study permit when entering Canada if they are

(a) a national or a permanent resident of the United States;

(b) a person who has been lawfully admitted to the United States for permanent residence;

(c) a resident of Greenland; or

(d) a resident of St. Pierre and Miquelon.

(e) [Repealed SOR/2014-14, s. 10.]

SOR/2014-14, s. 10

215. (1) **Application after entry** — A foreign national may apply for a study permit after entering Canada if they

(a) hold a study permit;

(b) apply within the period beginning 90 days before the expiry of their authorization to engage in studies in Canada under subsection 30(2) of the Act, or paragraph 188(1)(a) of these Regulations, and ending 90 days after that expiry;

(c) hold a work permit;

(d) are subject to an unenforceable removal order;

(e) hold a temporary resident permit issued under subsection 24(1) of the Act that is valid for at least six months;

(f) are a temporary resident who

(i) is studying at the preschool, primary or secondary level,

(ii) is a visiting or exchange student who is studying at a designated learning institution, or

(iii) has completed a course or program of study that is a prerequisite to their enrolling at a designated learning institution; or

(g) are in a situation described in section 207.

(2) **Family members** — A family member of a foreign national may apply for a study permit after entering Canada if the foreign national resides in Canada and the foreign national

(a) holds a study permit;

(b) holds a work permit;

(c) holds a temporary resident permit issued under subsection 24(1) of the Act that is valid for at least six months;

(d) is subject to an unenforceable removal order;

(e) is a member of the armed forces of a country that is a designated state described in paragraph 186(d);

(f) is an officer of a foreign government described in paragraph 186(e);

(g) is a participant in sports activities or events, as described in paragraph 186(h);

(h) is an employee of a foreign news company as described in paragraph 186(i); or

(i) is a person who is responsible for assisting a congregation or group, as described in paragraph 186(l).

SOR/2014-14, s. 11

DIVISION 3 — ISSUANCE OF STUDY PERMITS

216. (1) Study permits — Subject to subsections (2) and (3), an officer shall issue a study permit to a foreign national if, following an examination, it is established that the foreign national

(a) applied for it in accordance with this Part;

(b) will leave Canada by the end of the period authorized for their stay under Division 2 of Part 9;

(c) meets the requirements of this Part;

(d) meets the requirements of subsections 30(2) and (3), if they must submit to a medical examination under paragraph 16(2)(b) of the Act; and

(e) has been accepted to undertake a program of study at a designated learning institution.

(2) Exception — Paragraph (1)(b) does not apply to persons described in section 206 and paragraphs 207(c) and (d).

(3) Study in Quebec — An officer shall not issue a study permit to a foreign national who intends to study in the Province of Quebec — other than under a federal assistance program for developing countries — and does not hold a *Certificat d'acceptation du Québec*, if the laws of that Province require that the foreign national hold a *Certificat d'acceptation du Québec*.

SOR/2004-167, s. 59; SOR/2012-154, s. 11; SOR/2014-14, s. 12

Case Law

Editor's note: With respect to the issue of the intention to leave Canada by the end of the period authorized, see also case summaries under Regulation 183(1) and Regulation 200(1).

See the *Bahr* summary, 2012 CarswellNat 1345, 2012 FC 527, at s. 179 of the Regulations. And see *Loveridge* (2011), 390 F.T.R. 316, 2011 FC 694, 2011 CarswellNat 2120, under s. 22(2) of IRPA.

Hakimi v. Canada (Minister of Citizenship and Immigration), 2015 FC 657, 2015 CarswellNat 1779, 2015 CarswellNat 3850 — The applicant brought an application for judicial review to challenge a decision of the Immigration Program Manager of the Canadian Embassy in Tel Aviv to deny him a Canadian study permit. The officer was not satisfied that the applicant had sufficient available financial resources to maintain himself during the proposed period of study without working in Canada. The officer questioned the source of the funds, as this was not identified in the application. The officer was concerned that the funds were not sufficient for the long term. The officer was concerned the applicant's parents, who resided in Iran, would not be able to support him financially due to economic sanctions imposed on that country. The officer was also not satisfied that the applicant would leave Canada upon the expiration of his study permit. The officer based his decision on several factors, including the applicant's travel history; the extent of his family ties in his country of residence; the purpose of his proposed travel to Canada; his employment situation; and his personal assets and financial status.

A foreign national seeking to obtain a student visa must convince the visa officer that he is not inadmissible to Canada and that he meets the eligibility requirements set out in the legislation. There is no requirement that an applicant be permitted to respond to an officer's concerns as they arise. If an officer intends to base his decision on extrinsic information of which an applicant is unaware, then an opportunity to respond should be made available to enable the applicant to disabuse the officer of any concerns arising from that evidence. However, where the issue arises out of material provided by the applicant, as in this case, there is no obligation to provide an opportunity for explanation since the provider of the material is taken to know the contents of the material. There is a duty to provide an opportunity to respond where the credibility, accuracy or genuine nature of the information submitted by the applicant is the basis of the officer's concern. However, in this case, the officer's concern was not the applicant's credibility, but rather the sufficiency of the information that he provided in support of the application. The application for judicial review was dismissed.

Obot v. Canada (Minister of Citizenship & Immigration), 2012 FC 208, 2012 CarswellNat 436 — The applicant's request for a visa to continue his education in Canada was refused on the ground that he would be unlikely to return to Nigeria on the completion of his studies. With regards to conditions in Nigeria, there was nothing in the certified tribunal record to support the officer's statement that the country was split. This issue was not brought to the attention of the applicant and thus the applicant did not have the opportunity to make submissions on the matter. In fact, the consideration of Nigeria's current situation as a factor for denying a visa did not appear in the decision communicated to the applicant but rather only appeared in the officer's notes.

While immigration officers become well versed in the conditions within the countries from which visa applications are made, this awareness does not constitute a form of "judicial notice." In this case, there was clearly a difference of opinion about the conditions in Nigeria and whether that would have a bearing on the applicant's future return to that country. The decision to deny the applicant a student visa was unreasonable. The application for judicial review was granted.

Abdulateef v. Canada (Minister of Citizenship & Immigration), 2012 CarswellNat 1015, 2012 FC 400 — The application for a study permit was refused because the officer was not satisfied that the applicant would leave Canada at the end of the period of study if she was authorized to enter. In this case, the officer was not satisfied that the applicant was a *bona fide* temporary resident because: she failed to provide a satisfactory reason for pursuing her proposed course of study; she provided no proof of funds; she had weak ties to Iraq and Egypt; and she had presented no compelling reason for travel to Canada. The court upheld the visa officer's decision despite the court agreeing with the applicant that the statement that she provided no proof of funds was erroneous. She had submitted a letter from her father indicating he would pay all the expenses relating to her study in Canada, and she provided her father's bank statement showing considerable assets. This error did not render the officer's conclusion unreasonable in light of the officer's other findings. The application for judicial review was dismissed.

Hamad v. Canada (Minister of Citizenship & Immigration), 2012 FC 336, 2012 CarswellNat 868 — The applicants' request for visas to come to Canada so Mr. Hamad could study and his young children could attend school and his wife stay at home or work while in Canada was refused because the officer was not satisfied that the applicants would return to Libya after their visit. The officer examined their travel history, their purpose for the visits, their family ties in Egypt, Libya and Canada, their employment prospects in Libya, and incentives to return.

The decision of the officer lacked justification in the decision-making process and falls outside a range of possible, acceptable outcomes defensible in respect of the facts. The officer noted the applicant's limited travel to Egypt but completely disregarded or ignored his travel to Canada in 1991 and the fact that he returned to Libya before the expiry of his Canadian visa. The officer's conclusion that the applicants' ties to Libya were weak was unreasonable and not supported by the record. He had one brother in Canada but his mother and two brothers and their families were in Libya. His wife had no immediate family in Canada but had parents, sisters and brothers and their families in Libya. The officer's finding of limited future employment in Libya resulting from the current instability was speculative and an unreasonable conclusion not supported by the record. The applicant owned businesses in Libya which he intended to leave in the control of his brothers and business partner while in Canada. The officer's statement that "the family will seek to stay in [Canada] as long as the situation in Libya remains unstable" mischaracterizes the statements made in the application. The officer unreasonably suggested that the entire purpose of the visit to Canada was to escape the instability in Libya, which was not an accurate reflection of the information in the record which more aptly described the instability in Libya as affecting the timing of the study, not its validity. Although there was little doubt that they were all looking to Canada as a safer environment for the children, this does not imply that the study was not *bona fide*, especially when, as here, there was a description of the value of the study to the applicant as outlined in the application. The application for judicial review was allowed.

Gu v. Canada (Minister of Citizenship & Immigration), 2010 FC 522, 2010 CarswellNat 2333, 2010 CarswellNat 1337 — The applicant's application for a study permit was refused. The officer found that the applicant's intentions in Canada did not appear to be of a temporary nature. The applicant first came to Canada as a visitor and subsequently obtained a study permit which was extended. She also obtained a work permit and applied for permanent residence under the live-in caregiver class but was refused in April 2009.

The CAIPS notes indicated the officer was concerned that the applicant did not establish that she had completed any studies in Canada under previously issued study permits or worked in Canada under the work permits issued to her. The court held that these past permits had been issued and renewed by Canadian immigration authorities and there was no evidence of non-compliance with the Act and the Regulations on the part of the applicant. In circumstances where past compliance issues have never been raised, if an officer has concerns about compliance with past permits, the officer should inform the applicant of the concern and provide them with an opportunity to respond.

Patel v. Canada (Minister of Citizenship & Immigration) (2009), 82 Imm. L.R. (3d) 186, 344 F.T.R. 313 (Eng.), 2009 FC 602, 2009 CarswellNat 1786, 2009 CarswellNat 4049 — The applicant, a citizen of India, applied for a study permit and restoration of his temporary resident status to pursue a fourth diploma in information technology, this time from an accredited and statutorily recognized institution. His application was refused on the basis that the officer was not satisfied of the *bona fides* of the applicant as a genuine student and doubted whether he would leave Canada at the end of his authorized stay. In his five years since coming to Canada, the applicant had been awarded three post-secondary diplomas. In April 2008 the applicant applied for a post-graduate work permit on the strength of his certificate from the Canadian Career College and arranged employment.

This permit was refused because the Canadian Career College was not a recognized degree-conferring institution. Following this refusal, the applicant applied for a new study permit in June 2008, and also a restoration of his temporary resident status which had by that time expired. It is the refusal of this application which formed the basis of the judicial review.

The officer offered a very thin explanation for the decision to refuse to extend the applicant's student visa, stating only that he was not satisfied the applicant would leave Canada following completion of his studies, and that the applicant's pursuit of an additional degree "seems redundant" in light of previously completed studies. The applicant, however, offered a very plausible explanation. In light of this explanation, it was unreasonable for the officer to conclude that the applicant's further studies were redundant. It was clear the decision was made without regard to the evidence. Furthermore, there was no explanation as to why the officer concluded the applicant would not leave Canada at the end of the authorized study period. There was no rational basis or sufficient explanation offered by the officer for why he doubted the applicant's *bona fides* as a student, and the officer failed to address the applicant's specific evidence on this point. The application for judicial review was allowed.

Onyeka v. Canada (Minister of Citizenship & Immigration) (2009), 80 Imm. L.R. (3d) 56, 2009 CarswellNat 780, 2009 CarswellNat 2094, 2009 FC 336 — This was an application for judicial review of a decision to refuse the applicant's application for a study permit. The officer found that the applicant did not have adequate funds available to him to pay for his tuition and living expenses while in Canada and to return to his country of residence. Also, the officer was not convinced that the applicant would leave Canada by the end of the period authorized for his stay. While the court accepted the respondent's position that the decision attracted a high degree of deference from the court, the exercise of discretion in this case approached the arbitrary and capricious. The refusal of a study permit was based upon two grounds. One was that the applicant did not satisfy the officer that he would leave Canada at the end of the authorized stay. The reasons given for this are as follows:

> applicant is single, has no dependant, low paid job. Considering PA's ties to Nigeria balanced against factors which might motivate to stay in Canada, I am not satisfied PA would leave the country at the end of an authorized stay.

Although the court could see some connection between being single and having no dependants and the issue of whether, under Regulation 216(1)(b), the applicant will leave Canada at the end of the authorized period, it held that these factors merely place the applicant in the position of most students applying for study permits. The applicant had no family connections in Canada: his family was in the UK or Nigeria, and he had a highly responsible job in Nigeria. The officer did give reasons — being single and having no dependants — but these reasons were hardly sufficient to amount to a reasonable exercise of discretion when the other factors are taken into account. There was simply nothing on the facts that suggests that the applicant was not a *bone fide* student or that he would stay in Canada illegally at the end of the authorized period.

The officer's approach to the other ground of refusal — "You have not satisfied me that you have adequate funds available to you to pay for your tuition and living expenses while in Canada and to return to your country of residence" — were more significant. The applicant had confirmed financial support of $12,000 per year as well as assurances that the College of Engineering at the University of Saskatchewan makes available

$3,000 per year in the form of a "teaching assistant" payment for graduate students with the applicant's qualifications. In addition, the applicant provided evidence of personal savings. The officer, for no apparent reason, simply disregarded this money. The reasons appear entirely arbitrary in light of the evidence that was before the officer. The application for judicial review was allowed.

Ogbonnaya v. Canada (Minister of Citizenship & Immigration), 2008 CarswellNat 1525, 2008 FC 317 — The applicant sought judicial review of a visa officer's decision to refuse his application for a student visa. The visa officer's decision was patently unreasonable. In concluding that the applicant did not satisfy the visa officer that he would return to Nigeria by the end of the authorized period, the visa officer's notes suggest that this was because the applicant lacked ties to Nigeria, and would therefore have no incentive to return upon the completion of his schooling. The court found such a conclusion patently unreasonable in light of the fact that the applicant's visa application listed a large and extensive family in Nigeria consisting of his mother, father, and six siblings, all of whom are older than the applicant. As well, the applicant stated that he did not have any relatives in Canada, thereby suggesting a strong incentive to return to Nigeria upon the completion of his studies. Moreover, the applicant demonstrated strong ties to the Presbyterian Church of Nigeria, which would no doubt influence his decision to return to the country. In light of these strong connections to Nigeria, it was also patently unreasonable that the visa officer would conclude that the applicant was not a *bona fide* student. This is especially the case in view of the fact that the applicant proffered a letter of acceptance from York University demonstrating that he had been accepted into the economics programme. The visa officer's decision was set aside.

Odewole v. Canada (Minister of Citizenship & Immigration), 2008 CarswellNat 1667, 2008 CarswellNat 2786, 2008 FC 697 — The applicant sought judicial review of a visa officer's decision to refuse an application for a study permit. The application was refused because the applicant failed to demonstrate that her obligations or ties to her home country are such that they would compel her to leave Canada following the completion of her studies and because the officer was not satisfied that the applicant had dual intent pursuant to s. 22(2) of the Act. The applicant's sister had applied to sponsor the applicant's mother and the applicant was included as a dependent child in her mother's application for permanent residence.

Pursuant to subs. 22(2) of the Act, a person seeking a temporary entry into Canada may also hold the intention of establishing permanent residence. The officer was therefore required to weigh the evidence in connection with the application for a study permit and assess the applicant's intention to leave Canada at the end of her studies under para. 20(1)(b) of the Act and subs. 216(1) of the Regulations. The officer was not dealing with the family application for permanent residence, and the issue of dual intent arose only in relation to that application. The application for permanent residence was an irrelevant consideration for the purposes of the applicant's application for a study permit. Although in her affidavit the officer acknowledged that she lacked jurisdiction to assess the applicant's eligibility for permanent residence under the family class sponsorship, she nevertheless took this factor into account. Thus, the officer committed a reviewable error. The decision was set aside.

Bonilla v. Canada (Minister of Citizenship & Immigration), 2007 CarswellNat 26, 2007 FC 20 — The applicant applied for a study permit. The application was refused. The visa officer found that living in Canada during her formative high school years would have a negative impact upon the applicant's ability to function in Colombia. The applicant was therefore unable to establish that she would return to her home country following the expiration of her study permit, should she be given one. The officer concluded that the applicant's separation from her family, community, language and Colombia's education system, for such a long period of time, would result in the severance of her ties to Colombia.

The visa officer relied upon a generalization when he refused the applicant's application. The generalization in question is that all applicants who apply for a study permit which cover four years of high school should be denied, since they would automatically be unlikely to return to their home country due to long-term separation from their families and cultures. Clearly, any individual who applies to study in Canada for four years of high school would be away from the aspects of their home country noted by the visa officer. However, it is not necessarily the case that all young people in these circumstances would become unable to function in their home countries following the four-year period, and as a result, would be unlikely to leave Canada. The officer subjectively formed an opinion and should have allowed the applicant an opportunity to respond to his concerns. The applicant had no way of knowing that the visa officer would act upon his view that those in their "formative years" may not study in Canada for a four-year period, since they would be unlikely to leave the country. The visa officer's failure to give the applicant an opportunity to respond to his concerns, on the facts of this case, amounted to a breach of the rules of natural justice. The application for judicial review was allowed.

Zuo v. Canada (Minister of Citizenship & Immigration), 2007 CarswellNat 182, 2007 FC 88 — The applicant's application for a study permit was refused because he had not satisfied the officer that he was a genuine visitor who would leave Canada by the end of the authorized period of stay. It is not unreasonable for a visa officer to consider the availability of similar programs offered elsewhere at a lower cost; however, this fact will not necessarily be determinative. If this factor were determinative then many, if not most, study permit applications could be denied on this ground. Moreover, people choosing educational programs may base their choices on more than the price of a program. The availability of similar programs elsewhere at a lower cost is simply one factor to be considered by a visa officer in assessing an applicant's motives for applying for a study permit.

The applicant's father clearly believed that the ability to work in English is a valuable asset. The visa officer's determination that it would be an illogical decision for the applicant's parents to spend approximately $30,000 of their $80,000 savings on their son's education is patently unreasonable. Furthermore, her conclusion on this matter is not relevant to the issue she needed to determine, namely whether there is evidence that the applicant would stay past the authorized period. Similarly, the officer's conclusion that the applicant would not leave Canada before the authorized period given the economic opportunities and the high standard of living in Canada is also patently unreasonable. The applicant's family is well off in China and has a high standard of living. The applicant has an education as well as a family with significant ties in local government. The applicant does not lack support or opportunities in China. This court has, in a number of cases, considered the status of an applicant's family in assessing whether an applicant will leave Canada before the authorized period of stay is over, such that if an applicant's family is well established and well off then the applicant is more likely to leave Canada before the end of the authorized period of stay. This is based on the assumption that there is less incentive for applicants with high standards of living in their home countries to seek to establish themselves in Canada. Here the officer determined that there was a risk the applicant may try to stay in Canada past the authorized period because he is attracted by the high standard of living in Canada without considering the standard of living that the applicant actually enjoyed in China. The application for judicial review was allowed.

Tran v. Canada (Minister of Citizenship & Immigration) (2006), 59 Imm. L.R. (3d) 217, 2006 CarswellNat 3833, 2006 FC 1377 — The applicant sought to overturn the decision of an immigration officer who denied his application for a study permit. The visa officer was not satisfied that he was either a *bona fide* student or a *bona fide* temporary resident, sufficiently well established in Vietnam, that he would leave Canada after his authorized stay in Canada. Procedural protection that arises in the context of a student visa application is "relaxed." In other words, there is no clear requirement that an applicant be permitted to respond to an officer's concerns as they arise. Immigration manuals are primary guidelines for the assistance of the visa officers in the assessment of applications for either permanent residence or temporary visas. As such, manuals cannot be relied upon by applicants to argue lack of fairness simply because the officer did not strictly adhere to the guidelines found in the manual in question. It is trite law that the onus is on the applicant to provide a visa officer with all relevant information and documentation to satisfy the visa officer that the applicant meets the statutory requirements of the IRPA and the Regulations. In this case, the visa officer conducted a fulsome and diligent assessment of the applicant's application for a study permit. The visa officer considered a variety of factors in her assessment, including the low income of the applicant's parents in Vietnam and no proof of their employment, income or any assets. The fact that the same type of education is available locally and at a fraction of the cost is a relevant factor in determining the credibility and intentions of a potential foreign student. It was not patently unreasonable for the visa officer to consider the availability of similar courses in Vietnam and South Asia at a much less cost. The applicant's very weak English and his inability to carry even a basic conversation in English, as was revealed during his telephone conversation with the case analyst and reflected in the CAIPS notes, was a relevant factor for the visa officer to consider, given that his acceptance into Algonquin College was conditional upon him meeting the English language requirement. There were no reviewable errors in the visa officer's refusal to issue a study permit. The application for judicial review was dismissed.

Boni c. Canada (Ministre de la Citoyenneté & de l'Immigration), [2005] F.C.J. No. 43, 2005 CarswellNat 176, 2005 CarswellNat 4646, 2005 FC 31; affirmed [2006] F.C.J. No. 275, 57 Imm. L.R. (3d) 4, 2006 CarswellNat 414, 2006 FCA 68 (C.A.) — The applicant applied for judicial review of a visa officer's decision to deny the applicant's application for a study permit. The risk that study permit applicants will not leave Canada once the period of their stay ends is a very important factor to be considered. An officer may examine the applicant's long-term objective. That objective is a relevant point which carries some weight, in view of the evidence as a whole on whether a study permit would be granted. A visa officer's conclusions will not be disturbed unless they are so unreasonable as to require the court's intervention.

217. (1) Application for renewal — **A foreign national may apply for the renewal of their study permit if**

    (a) the application is made before the expiry of their study permit; and

    (b) they have complied with all conditions imposed on their entry into Canada;

    (c) [Repealed SOR/2014-14, s. 13.]

(2) Renewal — **An officer shall renew the foreign national's study permit if, following an examination, it is established that the foreign national continues to meet the requirements of section 216.**

SOR/2004-167, s. 60; SOR/2014-14, s. 13

Case Law

Dang v. Canada (Minister of Citizenship & Immigration), 2007 CarswellNat 25, 2007 FC 15 — The immigration officer's decision not to grant a study permit was based on a factual finding that the applicant had not established that she would leave Canada at the end of her authorized stay. To obtain a renewal of a study permit, the Regulations require that applicants maintain good standing at their educational institution, have sufficient and available financial resources to support their studies, and establish that they will leave Canada after the expiry of their authorized stay. The evidence before the immigration officer, which included progress reports issued to the applicant by the Canadian Conversation College, indicated that the applicant maintained satisfactory standing in her classes. The immigration officer's finding of fact that the applicant was progressing slowly was patently unreasonable. Moreover, the immigration officer erroneously found that the applicant has been studying for 4 1/2 years, when in fact it was three years. The fact that the applicant had pursued an application to permanently reside in Canada with her husband does not establish that she would not leave Canada at the end of the period authorized for her study permit as required under para. 216(1)(b) of the Regulations. The visa officer failed to recognize that the IRPA expressly allows the applicant to simultaneously seek permanent resident status and temporary resident status as a student. Without an evidentiary basis on which to support the immigration officer's findings, the conclusion that the applicant would not leave Canada at the end of the period authorized for her stay was patently unreasonable. By determining that the applicant had taken an unreasonable amount of time to learn the English language, the immigration officer based her conclusion on irrelevant factors. The Regulations in this respect only require that an applicant maintain "good standing" at her educational institution, which she had done. The application for judicial review was allowed.

218. Temporary resident status — **A foreign national referred to in paragraph 215(1)(d) and their family members do not, by reason only of being issued a study permit, become temporary residents.**

DIVISION 4 — RESTRICTIONS ON STUDYING IN CANADA

219. (1) Acceptance letter — **A study permit shall not be issued to a foreign national unless they have written documentation from the designated learning institution where they intend to study that states that they have been accepted to study there.**

(2) Exception — **Subsection (1) does not apply to**

   (a) a family member of a foreign national whose application for a work permit or a study permit is approved in writing before the foreign national enters Canada.

   (b) [Repealed SOR/2014-14, s. 14(2).]

(3) [Repealed SOR/2014-14, s. 14(3).]

SOR/2004-167, s. 61; SOR/2014-14, s. 14

220. Financial resources — An officer shall not issue a study permit to a foreign national, other than one described in paragraph 215(1)(d) or (e), unless they have sufficient and available financial resources, without working in Canada, to

(a) pay the tuition fees for the course or program of studies that they intend to pursue;

(b) maintain themself and any family members who are accompanying them during their proposed period of study; and

(c) pay the costs of transporting themself and the family members referred to in paragraph (b) to and from Canada.

220.1 (1) Conditions — study permit holder — The holder of a study permit in Canada is subject to the following conditions:

(a) they shall enroll at a designated learning institution and remain enrolled at a designated learning institution until they complete their studies; and

(b) they shall actively pursue their course or program of study.

(2) Loss of designation — In the event that the learning institution at which the holder of a study permit is enrolled loses its designated status after the issuance of the permit by virtue of any of the following events, subsection (1) shall apply to that holder for the duration of their permit as if the learning institution at which they are enrolled continues to be a designated learning institution:

(a) termination of an agreement or arrangement between the province and the Minister in respect of learning institutions that host international students under which the learning institution had been designated;

(b) the coming into force of an agreement or arrangement between the province and the Minister in respect of learning institutions that host international students under which the learning institution no longer qualifies for designation; or

(c) revocation of the designation by the province.

(3) Exception — Subsection (1) does not apply to

(a) a person described in any of paragraphs 300(2)(a) to (i); or

(b) a family member of a foreign national who resides in Canada and is described in any of paragraphs 215(2)(a) to (i).

(4) Evidence of compliance with conditions — The holder of a study permit must provide evidence to an officer of their compliance with the conditions set out in subsection (1) if

(a) the officer requests the evidence because the officer has reason to believe that the permit holder is not complying or has not complied with one or more of the conditions; or

IRP Regulations

(b) the officer requests the evidence as part of a random assessment of the overall level of compliance with those conditions by permit holders who are or were subject to them.

SOR/2014-14, s. 15

221. Failure to comply with conditions — Despite Division 2, a study permit shall not be issued to a foreign national who has engaged in unauthorized work or study in Canada or who has failed to comply with a condition of a permit unless

(a) a period of six months has elapsed since the cessation of the unauthorized work or study or failure to comply with a condition;

(b) the work or study was unauthorized by reason only that the foreign national did not comply with conditions imposed under paragraph 185(a), any of subparagraphs 185(b)(i) to (iii) or paragraph 185(c); or

(c) the foreign national was subsequently issued a temporary resident permit under subsection 24(1) of the Act.

SOR/2004-167, s. 62

DIVISION 5 — VALIDITY AND EXPIRY OF STUDY PERMITS

222. (1) Invalidity — A study permit becomes invalid upon the first to occur of the following days:

(a) the day that is 90 days after the day on which the permit holder completes their studies,

(b) the day on which a removal order made against the permit holder becomes enforceable, or

(c) the day on which the permit expires.

(2) Exception — Paragraph (1)(a) does not apply to

(a) a person described in any of paragraphs 300(2)(a) to (i); or

(b) a family member of a foreign national who resides in Canada and is described in any of paragraphs 215(2)(a) to (i).

SOR/2014-14, s. 16

PART 13 — REMOVAL

DIVISION 1 — REMOVAL ORDERS

223. Types of removal order — There are three types of removal orders, namely, departure orders, exclusion orders and deportation orders.

224. (1) Departure order — For the purposes of subsection 52(1) of the Act, an enforced departure order is a circumstance in which the foreign national is exempt from the requirement to obtain an authorization in order to return to Canada.

(2) **Requirement** — A foreign national who is issued a departure order must meet the requirements set out in paragraphs 240(1)(a) to (c) within 30 days after the order becomes enforceable, failing which the departure order becomes a deportation order.

(3) **Exception — stay of removal and detention** — If the foreign national is detained within the 30-day period or the removal order against them is stayed, the 30-day period is suspended until the foreign national's release or the removal order becomes enforceable.

SOR/2011-126, s. 5

225. (1) **Exclusion order** — For the purposes of subsection 52(1) of the Act, and subject to subsections (3) and (4), an exclusion order obliges the foreign national to obtain a written authorization in order to return to Canada during the one-year period after the exclusion order was enforced.

(2) **Exception** — For the purposes of subsection 52(1) of the Act, the expiry of a one-year period following the enforcement of an exclusion order, or a five-year period if subsection (3) applies, is a circumstance in which the foreign national is exempt from the requirement to obtain an authorization in order to return to Canada.

(3) **Misrepresentation** — A foreign national who is issued an exclusion order as a result of the application of paragraph 40(2)(a) of the Act must obtain a written authorization in order to return to Canada within the five-year period after the exclusion order was enforced.

(4) **Application of par. 42(1)(b) of the Act** — For the purposes of subsection 52(1) of the Act, the making of an exclusion order against a foreign national on the basis of inadmissibility under paragraph 42(1)(b) of the Act is a circumstance in which the foreign national is exempt from the requirement to obtain an authorization in order to return to Canada.

SOR/2011-126, s. 6; SOR/2014-269, ss. 4, 7(b)

226. (1) **Deportation order** — For the purposes of subsection 52(1) of the Act, and subject to subsection (2), a deportation order obliges the foreign national to obtain a written authorization in order to return to Canada at any time after the deportation order was enforced.

(2) **Application of par. 42(1)(b) of the Act** — For the purposes of subsection 52(1) of the Act, the making of a deportation order against a foreign national on the basis of inadmissibility under paragraph 42(1)(b) of the Act is a circumstance in which the foreign national is exempt from the requirement to obtain an authorization in order to return to Canada.

(3) **Removal order — certificate** — For the purposes of subsection 52(1) of the Act, a removal order referred to in section 80 of the Act obliges the foreign national to obtain a written authorization in order to return to Canada at any time after the removal order was enforced.

SOR/2011-126, s. 7; SOR/2014-269, s. 7(c); SOR/2016-136, s. 5

IRP Regulations

227. (1) Report — family members — For the purposes of section 42 of the Act, a report prepared under subsection 44(1) of the Act against a foreign national is also a report against the foreign national's family members in Canada.

(2) Removal — family members — A removal order made by the Immigration Division against a foreign national is also a removal order against their family members in Canada to whom subsection (1) applies if

(a) an officer informed the family members of the report, that they are the subject of an admissibility hearing and of their right to make submissions and be represented, at their own expense, at the admissibility hearing; and

(b) the family members are subject to a decision of the Immigration Division that they are inadmissible under section 42 of the Act on grounds of the inadmissibility of the foreign national.

SOR/2016-136, s. 6

DIVISION 2 — SPECIFIED REMOVAL ORDER

228. (1) Subsection 44(2) of the Act — foreign nationals — For the purposes of subsection 44(2) of the Act, and subject to subsections (3) and (4), if a report in respect of a foreign national does not include any grounds of inadmissibility other than those set out in the following circumstances, the report shall not be referred to the Immigration Division and any removal order made shall be

(a) if the foreign national is inadmissible under paragraph 36(1)(a) or (2)(a) of the Act on grounds of serious criminality or criminality, a deportation order;

(b) if the foreign national is inadmissible under paragraph 40(1)(c) of the Act on grounds of misrepresentation, a deportation order;

(b.1) if the foreign national is inadmissible under subsection 40.1(1) of the Act on grounds of the cessation of refugee protection, a departure order;

(c) if the foreign national is inadmissible under section 41 of the Act on grounds of

(i) failing to appear for further examination or an admissibility hearing under Part 1 of the Act, an exclusion order,

(ii) failing to obtain the authorization of an officer required by subsection 52(1) of the Act, a deportation order,

(iii) failing to establish that they hold the visa or other document as required under section 20 of the Act, an exclusion order,

(iv) failing to leave Canada by the end of the period authorized for their stay as required by subsection 29(2) of the Act, an exclusion order,

(v) failing to comply with subsection 29(2) of the Act as a result of non-compliance with any condition set out in section 184 or subsection 220.1(1), an exclusion order, or

(vi) failing to comply with the requirement under subsection 20(1.1) of the Act to not seek to enter or remain in Canada as a temporary resident while being the subject of a declaration made under subsection 22.1(1) of the Act, an exclusion order;

(d) subject to paragraph (e), if the foreign national is inadmissible under section 42 of the Act on grounds of an inadmissible family member, the same removal order as was made in respect of the inadmissible family member; and

(e) if the foreign national is inadmissible on grounds of an inadmissible family member in accordance with paragraph 42(2)(a) of the Act, a deportation order.

(2) **Subsection 44(2) of the Act — permanent residents** — For the purposes of subsection 44(2) of the Act, if a removal order is made against a permanent resident who fails to comply with the residency obligation under section 28 of the Act, the order shall be a departure order.

(3) **Eligible claim for refugee protection** — If a claim for refugee protection is made and the claim has been determined to be eligible to be referred to the Refugee Protection Division or no determination has been made, a departure order is the applicable removal order in the circumstances set out in any of subparagraphs (1)(c)(i) and (iii) to (v).

(4) **Reports in respect of certain foreign nationals** — For the purposes of subsection (1), a report in respect of a foreign national does not include a report in respect of a foreign national who

(a) is under 18 years of age and not accompanied by a parent or an adult legally responsible for them; or

(b) is unable, in the opinion of the Minister, to appreciate the nature of the proceedings and is not accompanied by a parent or an adult legally responsible for them.

SOR/2004-167, s. 63; SOR/2013-210, s. 4; SOR/2014-14, s. 17; SOR/2014-237, s. 1; SOR/2014-269, s. 5

Case Law

Gupta v. Canada (Minister of Public Safety and Emergency Preparedness), 2015 FC 1086, 2015 CarswellNat 4449, 2015 CarswellNat 8173 — This is a judicial review of a decision by a Minister's delegate of the Canada Border Services Agency ("CBSA") issuing an exclusion order against the applicant pursuant to s. 41(a) of IRPA for failing to comply with para. 20(1)(b). This provision requires that a foreign national seeking entry into Canada establish that she/he hold the visa or other document required by the Regulations. In this case, the Minister's delegate determined that the applicant was entering to work without first obtaining a work permit, contrary to subs. 8(1) of the Regulations.

The applicant received a two-year work permit to work as a server for a Preeceville, Saskatchewan restaurant, the employer (the "Employer"). In January 2015, Mr. Gupta travelled to British Columbia to visit his girlfriend and while there, underwent training in bread baking at a Surrey, B.C. restaurant. He also worked in other roles at the Surrey restaurant. He and his girlfriend travelled to the United States. In March 2015 upon re-entry, he was interviewed by the CBSA. As part of the interview, he provided a signed declaration to CBSA stating that his employer had asked him to work at the Surrey, B.C. restaurant to learn how to make bread and that the applicant would receive pay from the employer as if he were still working in Saskatchewan and that the applicant would return

IRP Regulations

to Saskatchewan on April 3, 2015. A s. 44 report was issued following the interview by the CBSA. A one-year exclusion order was issued.

Regardless of whether the exclusion order was based on past violation of the work permit, or concern about possible future violations, one key issue in the present application is whether a person can be found to have entered Canada without first obtaining a work permit (in contravention of s. 8 of the Regulations) where they have a work permit, but intended to work in violation of its conditions. It appears that there is no jurisprudence directly on point. The Minister's delegate's decision reads in a requirement that is not included in s. 8: that the work to be done under the work permit be in compliance with the conditions thereof.

Certainly, violations of the terms of a work permit are of concern, and there are measures that can be taken against the holder of a work permit who ignores its conditions. However, there is no indication that s. 8 was intended to address such a situation. A reading of s. 8 in its grammatical and ordinary sense harmoniously with the scheme and object of IRPA and the intention of Parliament does not permit this.

The applicant also argued that an exclusion order is not the appropriate sanction in these circumstances. He asserted that concerns about alleged violations of the work permit should instead be referred to the Immigration Division for consideration and, if necessary, sanction. The court agreed. The possibility of issues surrounding the contravention of the conditions of this work permit demonstrate that this type of situation should be referred to the Immigration Division and was not intended to be dealt with by means of an exclusion order. The application for judicial review was granted and the Minister's decision was found to be unreasonable in both respects and the exclusion order was quashed.

Mudalige Don v. Canada (Minister of Citizenship & Immigration) (2014), 20 Imm. L.R. (4th) 249, 369 D.L.R. (4th) 356, 455 N.R. 132, 2014 FCA 4, 2014 CarswellNat 14; leave to appeal to S.C.C. refused 2014 CarswellNat 1959, 2014 CarswellNat 1960 (S.C.C.) — The delegate of the Minister of Citizenship and Immigration issued an exclusion order against the applicant for his failure to respect the requirement under subsec. 184(1) of the *IRPA Regulations* to leave Canada within 72 hours after ceasing to be a member of the crew. The Federal Court judge allowed the judicial review and certified a question. The Federal Court of Appeal concluded that a Minister's issuance of an exclusion order pursuant to subpara. 228(1)(c)(v) of the Regulations before the member of a crew subject to an exclusion order has any contact with the immigration authorities does not constitute a breach of procedural fairness by depriving the foreign national of the opportunity to make a refugee claim. The Federal Court of Appeal concluded that the lower court judge's reasoning disregarded both the wording of the relevant legislation and its intent. In allowing for the timely issuance of a removal order, the Legislature must be taken to have acted coherently, in full knowledge of the impact that such order has on the right to claim refugee protection (subsec. 99(3) of the Act). The result is that persons who desert a ship in Canada in order to claim refugee protection should report to the immigration authorities and make their claim promptly. The 72-hour limitation makes it clear that they cannot expect to claim this status at a time of their choice. The appeal was allowed and the decision of the Federal Court judge set aside, and the application for judicial review by the applicant was dismissed.

229. (1) Paragraph 45(d) of the Act — applicable removal order — For the purposes of paragraph 45(d) of the Act, the applicable removal order to be made by the Immigration Division against a person is

(a) a deportation order, if they are inadmissible under subsection 34(1) of the Act on security grounds;

(b) a deportation order, if they are inadmissible under subsection 35(1) of the Act on grounds of violating human or international rights;

(c) a deportation order, in the case of a permanent resident inadmissible under subsection 36(1) of the Act on grounds of serious criminality or a foreign national inadmissible under paragraph 36(1)(b) or (c) of the Act on grounds of serious criminality;

(d) a deportation order, if they are inadmissible under paragraph 36(2)(b), (c) or (d) of the Act on grounds of criminality;

(e) a deportation order, if they are inadmissible under subsection 37(1) of the Act on grounds of organized criminality;

(f) an exclusion order, if they are inadmissible under subsection 38(1) of the Act on health grounds, unless subsection (2) or (3) applies;

(g) an exclusion order, if they are inadmissible under section 39 of the Act for financial reasons, unless subsection (2) or (3) applies;

(h) an exclusion order, if they are inadmissible under paragraph 40(1)(a) or (b) of the Act for misrepresentation, unless subsection (3) applies;

(i) a deportation order, if they are inadmissible under paragraph 40(1)(d) of the Act for misrepresentation;

(j) an exclusion order, if they are inadmissible under paragraph 41(a) of the Act for failing to comply with the requirement to appear for examination, unless subsection (2) or (3) applies;

(k) a departure order, if they are inadmissible under paragraph 41(b) of the Act;

(l) an exclusion order, if they are inadmissible under paragraph 41(a) of the Act for failing to establish that they have come to Canada in order to establish permanent residence, unless subsection (3) applies;

(m) an exclusion order, if they are inadmissible under paragraph 41(a) of the Act for failing to establish that they will leave Canada by the end of the period authorized for their stay, unless subsection (2) applies; and

(n) an exclusion order, if they are inadmissible under paragraph 41(a) of the Act for any other failure to comply with the Act, unless subsection (2) or (3) applies.

(2) Eligible claim for refugee protection — If a claim for refugee protection is made and the claim has been determined to be eligible to be referred to the Refugee Protection Division or no determination has been made, a departure order is the applicable removal order in the circumstances set out in paragraph (1)(f), (g), (j), (m) or (n).

(3) Exception — The applicable removal order in the circumstances set out in paragraph (1)(f), (g), (h), (j), (l) or (n) is a deportation order if the person

(a) was previously subject to a removal order and they are inadmissible on the same grounds as in that order;

(b) has failed to comply with any condition or obligation imposed under the Act or the *Immigration Act*, chapter I-2 of the Revised Statutes of Canada, 1985, unless the failure is the basis for the removal order; or

(c) has been convicted in Canada of an offence under an Act of Parliament punishable by way of indictment or of two offences under any Act of Parliament not arising out of a single occurrence, unless the conviction or convictions are the grounds for the removal order.

(3.1) Punishable by way of indictment — For the purposes of paragraph (3)(c), an offence that may be prosecuted either summarily or by way of indictment is deemed to be an offence punishable by way of indictment, even if it has been prosecuted summarily.

(4) Section 228 circumstances — If the Immigration Division makes a removal order against a foreign national with respect to any grounds of inadmissibility that are circumstances set out in section 228, the Immigration Division shall make

(a) the removal order that would have been applicable under subsection 228(1) or (3) if the report had not been referred to the Immigration Division under subsection 44(2) of the Act; or

(b) in the case of a foreign national described in paragraph 228(4)(a) or (b), the removal order that would have been applicable under subsection 228(1) or (3) if the foreign national had not been described in that paragraph.

SOR/2004-167, s. 64(2)–(4); SOR/2016-136, s. 7

DIVISION 3 — STAY OF REMOVAL ORDERS

Editor's Note

[All of the decisions of the Federal Court setting out the requirements an applicant must meet in order to obtain a court order staying the removal of the applicant from Canada which were collected under section 48 of the former Act may still be relevant and have been reproduced under section 18.2 of the Federal Courts Act in this text.]

230. (1) Considerations — The Minister may impose a stay on removal orders with respect to a country or a place if the circumstances in that country or place pose a generalized risk to the entire civilian population as a result of

(a) an armed conflict within the country or place;

(b) an environmental disaster resulting in a substantial temporary disruption of living conditions; or

(c) any situation that is temporary and generalized.

(2) Cancellation — The Minister may cancel the stay if the circumstances referred to in subsection (1) no longer pose a generalized risk to the entire civilian population.

(3) Exceptions — The stay does not apply to a person who

(a) is inadmissible under subsection 34(1) of the Act on security grounds;

(b) is inadmissible under subsection 35(1) of the Act on grounds of violating human or international rights;

(c) is inadmissible under subsection 36(1) of the Act on grounds of serious criminality or under subsection 36(2) of the Act on grounds of criminality;

(d) is inadmissible under subsection 37(1) of the Act on grounds of organized criminality;

(e) is a person referred to in section F of Article 1 of the Refugee Convention; or

(f) informs the Minister in writing that they consent to their removal to a country or place to which a stay of removal applies.

Case Law

Section 230(1)

Adviento v. Canada (Minister of Citizenship & Immigration) (2003), 33 Imm. L.R. (3d) 13, 9 Admin. L.R. (4th) 314, 242 F.T.R. 295, 2003 CarswellNat 3955, 2003 CarswellNat 4980, 2003 FC 1430, [2003] F.C.J. No. 1837 — It is well-established law that the discretion to defer a removal is very limited. It would be contrary to the purposes and objects to the Act to expand, by judicial declaration, a removal officer's limited discretion so as to mandate "a mini H&C" review prior to removal.

An officer is entitled to take into account a range of factors, such as whether any required travel documents are missing, whether the applicant is subject to a court order requiring his or her presence in Canada, or whether there is a health related impediment to the applicant travelling and finally whether the failure to defer will otherwise expose the applicant to the risk of death, extreme sanction or inadequate treatment. These are all factors which could result in a removal being rescheduled.

Section 230(3)

Hasan v. Canada (Minister of Citizenship & Immigration) (2008), 75 Imm. L.R. (3d) 64, 180 C.R.R. 286, 2008 CarswellNat 3445, 2008 FC 1069 — The applicant was reported as an inadmissible permanent resident because of serious criminality pursuant to s. 44 of the IRPA. The CBSA informed the applicant of their intention to seek the opinion, pursuant to s. 115(2)(a) of the IRPA, from the Minister of Citizenship and Immigration that he was a danger to the public and, thus, could be returned to Iraq. There is no requirement in s. 115(2) that the Minister must assess the risk to the person who has been found to be a danger. That obligation arises from the operation of s. 7 of the *Charter*, as decided by the Supreme Court of Canada in *Suresh* (2002), 18 Imm. L.R. (3d) 1. Thus, there is no parallel between the cessation provisions of s. 108, which explicitly require the Minister to demonstrate that the reasons for which the person sought refugee protection have ceased to exist, and s. 115, where the only obligation arises as a result of the *Charter*. The jurisprudence is clear that, once the applicant is found to be a danger to the public, he must establish that he would be at risk.

Therefore, the delegate did not erroneously place the onus on the applicant to prove that he faced the risk of torture or risk to life if returned to Iraq. The delegate properly engaged in an assessment of the current risks facing the applicant should he be removed to Iraq. The applicant was told that he could make written representations or arguments deemed necessary and relevant, including those related to whether his life or freedoms were threatened by removal from Canada. This was adequate notice to the applicant.

The applicant also argued that the delegate failed to have regard to the fact that the Minister had imposed a stay on removals to Iraq pursuant to s. 230 of the Regulations. Not only had the applicant not initially raised this argument in his submissions to the CBSA, but more importantly, the s. 230(1) moratorium does not apply to the applicant since s. 230(3) explicitly states that the stay under s. 230(1) does not apply to a person who is inadmissible on grounds of serious criminality or criminality. In this case, the applicant had been found to be inadmissible on grounds of serious criminality and he could not rely on the stay provisions of s. 230. The application for judicial review was dismissed.

231. (1) Stay of removal — judicial review — Subject to subsections (2) to (4), a removal order is stayed if the subject of the order makes an application for leave for judicial review in accordance with section 72 of the Act with respect to a decision of the Refugee Appeal Division that rejects, or confirms the rejection of, a claim for refugee protection, and the stay is effective until the earliest of the following:

  (a) the application for leave is refused,

  (b) the application for leave is granted, the application for judicial review is refused and no question is certified for the Federal Court of Appeal,

  (c) if a question is certified by the Federal Court — Trial Division,

    (i) the appeal is not filed within the time limit, or

    (ii) the Federal Court of Appeal decides to dismiss the appeal, and the time limit in which an application to the Supreme Court of Canada for leave to appeal from that decision expires without an application being made,

  (d) if an application for leave to appeal is made to the Supreme Court of Canada from a decision of the Federal Court of Appeal referred to in paragraph (c), the application is refused, and

  (e) if the application referred to in paragraph (d) is granted, the appeal is not filed within the time limit or the Supreme Court of Canada dismisses the appeal.

(2) Exception — Subsection (1) does not apply if, when leave is applied for, the subject of the removal order is a designated foreign national or a national of a country that is designated under subsection 109.1(1) of the Act.

(3) Other exceptions — There is no stay of removal if

  (a) the person is subject to a removal order because they are inadmissible on grounds of serious criminality; or

(b) the subject of the removal order resides or sojourns in the United States or St. Pierre and Miquelon and is the subject of a report prepared under subsection 44(1) of the Act on their entry into Canada.

(4) Non-application — Subsection (1) does not apply if the person applies for an extension of time to file an application referred to in that subsection.

SOR/2012-272, s. 1

232. Stay of removal — pre-removal risk assessment — A removal order is stayed when a person is notified by the Department under subsection 160(3) that they may make an application under subsection 112(1) of the Act, and the stay is effective until the earliest of the following events occurs:

(a) the Department receives confirmation in writing from the person that they do not intend to make an application;

(b) the person does not make an application within the period provided under section 162;

(c) the application for protection is rejected;

(d) [Repealed SOR/2012-154, s. 12.]

(e) if a decision to allow the application for protection is made under paragraph 114(1)(a) of the Act, the decision with respect to the person's application to remain in Canada as a permanent resident is made; and

(f) in the case of a person to whom subsection 112(3) of the Act applies, the stay is cancelled under subsection 114(2) of the Act.

SOR/2012-154, s. 12

233. Stay of removal — humanitarian and compassionate or public policy considerations — A removal order made against a foreign national, and any family member of the foreign national, is stayed if the Minister is of the opinion that the stay is justified by humanitarian and compassionate considerations, under subsection 25(1) or 25.1(1) of the Act, or by public policy considerations, under subsection 25.2(1) of the Act. The stay is effective until a decision is made to grant, or not grant, permanent resident status.

SOR/2010-252, s. 1

Case Law

Level (Litigation Guardian of) v. Canada (Minister of Public Safety & Emergency Preparedness) (2008), 71 Imm. L.R. (3d) 52, 2008 CarswellNat 423, 2008 FC 227 — This is an application for judicial review of an enforcement officer's decision to deny the applicant's request for a deferral of removal pending a decision on his application for permanent residence based on an H&C application.

An enforcement officer is statutorily bound to remove an applicant as soon as reasonably practicable. However, if the officer relies on extrinsic evidence not brought forward by the applicant, the applicant must be given an opportunity to respond to that evidence. This is a minimal duty of procedural fairness. In the application at bar, the enforcement officer relied on detailed evidence about medical conditions in Jamaica that the applicant contested in an affidavit filed in support of the applicant's successful motion for a stay of removal. With respect to tight time frames, the applicant had been in Canada for 20 years, and the duty of fairness should not be sacrificed because of an artificial deadline established by the respondent for the applicant's removal. There is no harm in allowing the applicant another week or two in order to respond to extrinsic evidence upon which the enforcement officer intends to rely. If that extrinsic evidence is incorrect, the applicant will suffer great harm. The application for judicial review was allowed.

Adviento v. Canada (Minister of Citizenship & Immigration) (2003), 33 Imm. L.R. (3d) 13, 9 Admin. L.R. (4th) 314, 242 F.T.R. 295, 2003 CarswellNat 3955, 2003 CarswellNat 4980, 2003 FC 1430, [2003] F.C.J. No. 1837 — It is well-established law that the discretion to defer a removal is very limited. It would be contrary to the purposes and objects to the Act to expand, by judicial declaration, a removal officer's limited discretion so as to mandate "a mini H&C" review prior to removal.

An officer is entitled to take into account a range of factors, such as whether any required travel documents are missing, whether the applicant is subject to a court order requiring his or her presence in Canada, or whether there is a health related impediment to the applicant travelling and finally whether the failure to defer will otherwise expose the applicant to the risk of death, extreme sanction or inadequate treatment. These are all factors which could result in a removal being rescheduled.

Brown (Litigation Guardian of) v. Canada (Minister of Citizenship & Immigration) (2003), 26 Imm. L.R. (3d) 192, 2003 CarswellNat 532, 2003 CarswellNat 1526, 2003 FCT 269 (Fed. T.D.) — The applicant applied for an order declaring that it would be a violation of the principles of fundamental justice to deport him back to Jamaica.

The declaratory action is discretionary and the two factors which will influence the court in the exercise of its discretion are the utility of the remedy if granted and whether, if it is granted, it will settle the questions at issue between the parties. The first factor is directed to the reality of the dispute. A declaration will not normally be granted when the dispute is over and has become academic, or where the dispute has yet to arise and may not arise.

The court was satisfied the dispute was real and not hypothetical.

The applicant had received approval in principle of an H&C application and by virtue of s. 233 of the IRPA regulations the removal order was stayed until a decision was made to grant, or not grant, permanent resident status. Accordingly the court concluded that the declaration if granted would have no practical effect as the applicant may be deported if his humanitarian and compassionate application is unsuccessful and in any event cannot be deported until a decision is made to grant or not grant permanent resident status. Therefore no useful purpose would be accomplished by granting a declaration at this time.

234. Application of par. 50(a) of the Act — For greater certainty and for the purposes of paragraph 50(a) of the Act, a decision made in a judicial proceeding would not be directly contravened by the enforcement of a removal order if

(a) there is an agreement between the Department and the Attorney General of Canada or the attorney general of a province that criminal charges against the foreign national will be withdrawn or stayed on the removal of the person from Canada; or

(b) there is an agreement between the Department and the Attorney General of Canada or the attorney general of a province to withdraw or cancel any summons or subpoena with respect to the foreign national on the removal of the person from Canada.

SOR/2016-136, s. 10

DIVISION 4 — ENFORCEMENT OF REMOVAL ORDERS

235. Not void — For greater certainty, and subject to section 51 of the Act, a removal order does not become void by reason of any lapse of time.

236. Providing copies — A person against whom a removal order is made shall be provided with a copy of the order when it is made.

237. Modality of enforcement — A removal order is enforced by the voluntary compliance of a foreign national with the removal order or by the removal of the foreign national by the Minister.

238. (1) Voluntary compliance — A foreign national who wants to voluntarily comply with a removal order must appear before an officer who shall determine if

(a) the foreign national has sufficient means to effect their departure to a country that they will be authorized to enter; and

(b) the foreign national intends to voluntarily comply with the requirements set out in paragraphs 240(1)(a) to (c) and will be able to act on that intention.

(2) Choice of country — Following the appearance referred to in subsection (1), the foreign national must submit their choice of destination to the officer who shall approve the choice unless the foreign national is

(a) a danger to the public;

(b) a fugitive from justice in Canada or another country; or

(c) seeking to evade or frustrate the cause of justice in Canada or another country.

Case Law

Revich c. Canada (Ministre de la Citoyenneté & de l'Immigration) (2005), 280 F.T.R. 201 (Eng.), (sub nom. *Revich v. Canada (Minister of Citizenship & Immigration)*) 2005 CarswellNat 5741, 2005 FC 852 — The respondent issued a departure order against the applicant. Under the old legislation, the departure order was conditional and could not become effective until one of the conditions provided in subs. 49(2) had occurred. The applicant's refugee claim was refused and the departure order came into force 15 days after the notification of the rejection of the refugee claim. The Federal Court refused an application for leave against the decision of the RPD. The refusal ended the stay of execution of the departure order. The departure order became enforceable and became a deportation order pursuant to Reg. 224(2) of the Regulations. The applicant was then notified of her right to file a pre-removal risk assessment (PRRA) application. The notice resulted in a stay of execution of the deportation order pending the PRRA decision. The PRRA application was rejected and the stay provided for under s. 232 of the Regulations ended with the rejection of the PRRA application.

Under para. 160(3)(a) of the Regulations, the department is required to notify the persons subject to a removal order, such as the present applicant, that they are entitled to apply for a PRRA decision. However, neither the Act nor the Regulations states at what time this notice must be issued. Meanwhile, because the person's refugee claim has been rejected, the stay of execution of the removal order is no longer in force. In other words, the removal order is "enforceable" and, after a 30-day period, the order will become a deportation order unless the person voluntarily leaves the country. The Regulations also provide for the stay of execution of a removal order when a person is notified that he or she may file a PRRA application.

The applicant in this case did not attack the combined effect of these statutory provisions but instead targeted the department's decision to send the notice under s. 160 of the Regulations after the removal order became a deportation order, and thereby depriving her of the opportunity to have the stay that the PRRA application would have triggered. So the essential question was whether it was fair for the department to act in this way.

The purpose of the PRRA is to prevent a foreign national whose refugee claim has already been rejected from being required to return to his country of residence or citizenship when the situation has changed in that country and he would be exposed to a risk of persecution. If this review is to be effective and consistent with Parliament's intention when creating it, the PRRA must coincide as closely as possible with the person's departure from the country. The court concluded that if an interested party voluntarily complies with the removal order under s. 238 of the Regulations, within the requisite period, he or she may avoid the consequences of the deportation order. Requiring the department to issue a notice before the deportation order comes into force would in turn eliminate the main incentive for people to comply voluntarily with the removal order prior to the PRRA decision. The department's decision to send a notice after the departure order became a deportation order does not fail to meet the requirements of procedural fairness having regard to the objective of the PRRA process, which is to serve as a final "safeguard" before the interested party is required to leave the country. There is nothing inequitable in the applicant asking in the future for written authorization to return to Canada since she knew that this was a consequence of her choice to not leave voluntarily. The application for judicial review was dismissed.

The following question was certified: Is the PRRA officer required to send the notice under s. 160 of the *Immigration Refugee Protection Regulations* before the departure order becomes a deportation order, thereby putting the foreign national in an irregular situation? Should the answer to the preceding question be positive, should the deportation order be set aside?

239. Removal by Minister — **If a foreign national does not voluntarily comply with a removal order, a negative determination is made under subsection 238(1) or the foreign national's choice of destination is not approved under subsection 238(2), the removal order shall be enforced by the Minister.**

240. (1) When removal order is enforced — **A removal order against a foreign national, whether it is enforced by voluntary compliance or by the Minister, is enforced when the foreign national**

    (a) appears before an officer at a port of entry to verify their departure from Canada;

(b) obtains a certificate of departure from the Department;

(c) departs from Canada; and

(d) is authorized to enter, other than for purposes of transit, their country of destination.

(2) When removal order is enforced by officer outside Canada — If a foreign national against whom a removal order has not been enforced is applying outside Canada for a visa, an authorization to return to Canada or an electronic travel authorization, an officer shall enforce the order if, following an examination, the foreign national establishes that

(a) they are the person described in the order;

(b) they have been lawfully admitted to the country in which they are physically present at the time that the application is made; and

(c) they are not inadmissible on grounds of security, violating human or international rights, serious criminality or organized criminality.

SOR/2015-77, s. 7

Case Law

Umlani v. Canada (Minister of Citizenship & Immigration) (2008), 77 Imm. L.R. (3d) 179, 2008 CarswellNat 5454, 2008 CarswellNat 4806, 2008 FC 1373 — The applicant withdrew his refugee claim and advised the Immigration Refugee Board about his departure from Canada. He did not, however, confirm his departure by checking out with CIC officials at the airport when he was leaving. This meant that a departure order came into effect when he withdrew his claim, which eventually turned into a deportation order. The applicant was then called in for a meeting with CIC. He informed CIC by telephone that he had left Canada. CIC advised him to attend at a Canadian Consulate to show evidence that he had left Canada. The applicant attended the Canadian Consulate in New York and provided the requested information. The Canadian Consulate advised him that he would require authorization to return to Canada. The applicant applied for authorization to return to Canada and this application was refused.

Given the highly discretionary and fact-driven nature of ARC decisions, the court should extend considerable deference in reviewing any such decision against the reasonableness standard. The visa officer refused the applicant's ARC request because:

1. The applicant is a failed refugee claimant;

2. A departure order was issued against the applicant and his departure was never confirmed; and

3. The stated reason for wishing to enter Canada (tourism) did not outweigh the serious import of a removal order and the applicant's non-compliance with the IRPA.

The court pointed out that the officer gives no explanation as to why the six-year gap between the date of the removal order and the decision was not of any significance or relevance. Also the court points out that the applicant was not a failed refugee claimant, but that he voluntarily withdrew his refugee application for legitimate reasons.

The only reason why the applicant had to apply for an ARC is because of his inadvertence in failing to appear before an officer to obtain the relevant certificate when he left the country. There was nothing to suggest that the applicant poses any kind of risk, that

IRP Regulations

he had not dealt openly with immigration authorities at all relevant times, or that his re-entry would be undesirable in any way. In fact, the applicant had gone out of his way to correct the mistake and to keep authorities fully informed of why and when it came about. It is obvious that, from time to time, people make the same mistake as the applicant and forget to comply with the technicalities upon leaving Canada. In fact, it happens often enough that CIC has seen fit to address the issue and provide advice on how it should be dealt with in ENF 11 Verifying Departure. Direction is given regarding the circumstances in which officers outside of Canada should enforce an unenforced removal order. Officers are cautioned to keep in mind the "CBSA's overriding priority . . . to maintain control of the removal process," but officers are also advised on what they should do regarding precisely the kind of oversight that occurred in this case. Precisely why the applicant did not receive the benefit of these guidelines was unclear. The applicant's reasons for wanting to re-enter Canada were hardly compelling (tourism) but he was forced to make an ARC request because of a harmless and inadvertent mistake that, in the court's view, fell under the "oversight" provisions of CIC's own guidelines. The application was allowed.

241. (1) Country of removal — If a removal order is enforced under section 239, the foreign national shall be removed to

(a) the country from which they came to Canada;

(b) the country in which they last permanently resided before coming to Canada;

(c) a country of which they are a national or citizen; or

(d) the country of their birth.

(2) Removal to another country — If none of the countries referred to in subsection (1) is willing to authorize the foreign national to enter, the Minister shall select any country that will authorize entry within a reasonable time and shall remove the foreign national to that country.

(3) Exception — Despite section 238 and subsection (1), the Minister shall remove a person who is subject to a removal order on the grounds of inadmissibility referred to in paragraph 35(1)(a) of the Act to a country that the Minister determines will authorize the person to enter.

242. Mutual Legal Assistance in Criminal Matters Act — A person transferred under an order made under the *Mutual Legal Assistance in Criminal Matters Act* is not, for the purposes of paragraph 240(1)(d), a person who has been authorized to enter their country of destination.

243. Payment of removal costs — Unless expenses incurred by Her Majesty in right of Canada have been recovered from a transporter, a foreign national who is removed from Canada at Her Majesty's expense shall not return to Canada if the foreign national has not paid to Her Majesty the removal costs of

(a) $750 for removal to the United States or St. Pierre and Miquelon; and

(b) $1,500 for removal to any other country.

PART 14 — DETENTION AND RELEASE

244. Factors to be considered — **For the purposes of Division 6 of Part 1 of the Act, the factors set out in this Part shall be taken into consideration when assessing whether a person**

(a) **is unlikely to appear for examination, an admissibility hearing, removal from Canada, or at a proceeding that could lead to the making of a removal order by the Minister under subsection 44(2) of the Act;**

(b) **is a danger to the public; or**

(c) **is a foreign national whose identity has not been established.**

Case Law

Dehghani v. Canada (Minister of Employment & Immigration), [1993] 1 S.C.R. 1053, 18 Imm. L.R. (2d) 245, 10 Admin. L.R. (2d) 1, 20 C.R. (4th) 34, 101 D.L.R. (4th) 654, 150 N.R. 241, 14 C.R.R. (2d) 1, 1993 CarswellNat 57, 1993 CarswellNat 1380, EYB 1993-67290, [1993] S.C.J. No. 38 — The appellant, a citizen of Iran, arrived in Canada without valid travel or identity documents and claimed Convention refugee status. He was interviewed at the secondary examination and extensive written notes were made by an immigration officer, which notes were later entered in evidence at the credible-basis hearing. At the conclusion of that hearing the first level tribunal decided that there was no credible basis to the appellant's claim.

When the appellant was taken to a secondary examination at Canadian Immigration at Pearson International Airport, he was not detained in the sense contemplated by s. 10(b) of the *Charter*. Further, the principles of s. 10(b) do not require that the appellant be provided with counsel at the pre-inquiry or pre-hearing stage of the refugee claim determination process. The secondary examination of the appellant at the port-of-entry is not analogous to a hearing. The purpose of the port-of entry interview was to aid in the processing of the appellant's application for entry and to determine the appropriate procedures which should be invoked in order to deal with the appellant's application for Convention refugee status. The principles of fundamental justice do not include a right to counsel in these circumstances of routine information gathering.

[Editor's Note: Although Dehghani *was decided under the former Act it may still be relevant.]*

245. Flight risk — **For the purposes of paragraph 244(a), the factors are the following:**

(a) **being a fugitive from justice in a foreign jurisdiction in relation to an offence that, if committed in Canada, would constitute an offence under an Act of Parliament;**

(b) **voluntary compliance with any previous departure order;**

(c) **voluntary compliance with any previously required appearance at an immigration or criminal proceeding;**

(d) **previous compliance with any conditions imposed in respect of entry, release or a stay of removal;**

(e) any previous avoidance of examination or escape from custody, or any previous attempt to do so;

(f) involvement with a people smuggling or trafficking in persons operation that would likely lead the person to not appear for a measure referred to in paragraph 244(a) or to be vulnerable to being influenced or coerced by an organization involved in such an operation to not appear for such a measure; and

(g) the existence of strong ties to a community in Canada.

Case Law

See case summaries under s. 58(1) of the Act.

246. Danger to the public — For the purposes of paragraph 244(b), the factors are the following:

(a) the fact that the person constitutes, in the opinion of the Minister, a danger to the public in Canada or a danger to the security of Canada under paragraph 101(2)(b), subparagraph 113(d)(i) or (ii) or paragraph 115(2)(a) or (b) of the Act;

(b) association with a criminal organization within the meaning of subsection 121(2) of the Act;

(c) engagement in people smuggling or trafficking in persons;

(d) conviction in Canada under an Act of Parliament for

   (i) a sexual offence, or

   (ii) an offence involving violence or weapons;

(e) conviction for an offence in Canada under any of the following provisions of the *Controlled Drugs and Substances Act*, namely,

   (i) section 5 (trafficking),

   (ii) section 6 (importing and exporting), and

   (iii) section 7 (production);

(f) conviction outside Canada, or the existence of pending charges outside Canada, for an offence that, if committed in Canada, would constitute an offence under an Act of Parliament for

   (i) a sexual offence, or

   (ii) an offence involving violence or weapons; and

(g) conviction outside Canada, or the existence of pending charges outside Canada, for an offence that, if committed in Canada, would constitute an offence under any of the following provisions of the *Controlled Drugs and Substances Act*, namely,

   (i) section 5 (trafficking),

   (ii) section 6 (importing and exporting), and

   (iii) section 7 (production).

Case Law

Capra v *Canada (Attorney General)* (2008), 76 Imm. L.R. (3d) 21, 335 F.T.R. 299 (Eng.), 2008 CarswellNat 3875, 2008 CarswellNat 5267, 2008 FC 1212 — This was an application for a declaration that subs. 128(4) of the *Corrections and Conditional Release Act*, S.C. 1992, c. 20 ("CCRA") is invalid on the ground that it breaches ss. 7, 9 and 15 of the *Canadian Charter of Rights and Freedoms*, Part 1 of the *Constitution Act, 1982*. The applicant had been granted Convention refugee status and became a permanent resident on December 2, 1992. The applicant was subsequently convicted of 80 counts of fraud in connection with credit cards and automatic bank teller machines in 2001. A deportation order was issued on the grounds of serious criminality. Both the appeal of the deportation order and his application were dismissed and the applicant lost his permanent residence status. However, because of his refugee status, he could not be removed to Romania unless the Minister of Citizenship and Immigration issued an opinion that the applicant constitutes a danger to the public. The CBSA sought the opinion of the Minister that he was a danger to the public in Canada. In the meantime, the applicant served his sentence in a medium security federal correctional facility and underwent a rehabilitation program. He became eligible for an unescorted temporary absence ("UTA") and day parole on July 2008. The CBSA informed the sentence management office of the deportation order previously issued against the applicant. As a result, by operation of subs. 128(4) of the CCRA, the applicant was ineligible for release on a UTA or day parole until his full parole eligibility date. The applicant believed that he was being treated differently in relation to day parole eligibility because he was not a Canadian citizen. He claimed that he was the subject of discrimination and regardless of whether he was allowed to stay in Canada or not, he perceived that he was being denied an opportunity to work towards his own rehabilitation simply because of his identity.

The court held that s. 128(4) of the CCRA was directed at inmates subject to removal. The operation of the subsection is triggered by the issuance of a removal order. A stay of that removal order suspends the section's effect. The application of the section is rationally tied to its purpose and cannot be called arbitrary in relation to the objectives sought to be attained. Accordingly this was not arbitrary detention within the meaning of s. 9. Furthermore, the Supreme Court of Canada had made it clear that a "change in the form in which a sentence is served, whether it be favourable or unfavourable to the prisoner, is not, in itself, contrary to any principle of fundamental justice."

Parliament has decided that offenders subject to removal should serve their sentences in different ways from other offenders, including Canadian citizens. This is to ensure that their status as offenders does not enhance their access to Canadian society over that of non-offenders who face deportation; it is also intended to ensure that their removal status does not result in their serving shorter sentences than either Canadian citizens or non-citizens who are not subject to removal. Parliament has chosen to deal with these issues by suspending day parole and UTA for offenders who are subject to removal. It is possible to disagree with this approach and with whether it achieves the objectives it is intended to achieve, but that was not the issue before the court. What is relevant is that the variation in the form of the sentence that comes about as a result of subs. 128(4) of CCRA is triggered by the existence of a removal order and whether this fact makes it part of a deportation scheme.

The court was not convinced that, if the purpose of parole is to protect society, that the loss of the possibility of that protection because of the loss of eligibility for day parole under subs. 128(4) was a disadvantage to the applicant, whether or not he was removed from Canada. Furthermore if parole was a benefit to offenders, the court was not convinced that the applicant had been disadvantaged by the loss of any such benefit in a situation where the evidence showed his deportation was being actively pursued and he did not fall into one of the exceptions specifically provided for under subs. 128(6). The applicant failed to demonstrate differential treatment between citizens and non-citizens. The application was dismissed.

Canada (Minister of Citizenship & Immigration) v. Thanabalasingham, [2004] 3 F.C.R. 572, 38 Imm. L.R. (3d) 1, [2004] F.C.J. No. 15, 247 F.T.R. 159 (note), 236 D.L.R. (4th) 329, 10 Admin. L.R. (4th) 285, 315 N.R. 91, 2004 CarswellNat 22, 2004 CarswellNat 782, 2004 FCA 4 — This was an appeal on a certified question from a decision of the motions judge. The certified question asked whether detention reviews were hearings *de novo* and whether the detained person bears the burden of establishing that he or she was not a danger to the public or a flight risk. The respondent was arrested in October 2001 on an immigration warrant and detained on grounds that he was a danger to the public because he was the leader of a Tamil gang. His detention was reviewed under the former Act and, after it came into force, under ss. 57 and 58 of IRPA. At his first five reviews the continued detention of the respondent was ordered. At his sixth review the respondent was ordered released. The Minister applied for judicial review and obtained a stay of that order until the next detention review was completed. The next detention review was completed in March 2003 and the respondent was once again ordered released. The Minister once again obtained a stay of that order and sought judicial review and it was this judicial review that was the subject of the matter in this case.

Detention reviews are the kind of essentially fact-based decision to which deference is usually shown. While prior decisions are not binding on a Member, if a Member chooses to depart from prior decisions to detain, clear and compelling reasons for doing so must be set out. The best way for the Member to provide clear and compelling reasons would be to expressly explain what has given rise to the changed opinion. It would be unacceptable for a Member to give a cursory decision which does not advert to the prior reasons for detention in a meaningful way.

Sections 57 and 58 allow persons to be detained for potentially lengthy if not indefinite periods of time without having been charged let alone having been convicted of any crime. As a result, detention decisions must be made with s. 7 of the *Charter* in mind.

It is the Minister who must establish, on a balance of probabilities, that the respondent is a danger to the public if he wants the detention to continue. The onus is always on the Minister to demonstrate that there are reasons which warrant detention or continued detention. Once the Minister has made out a *prima facie* case for the continued detention, the individual must lead some evidence or risk continued detention. The Minister may establish a *prima facie* case in a variety of ways including reliance on reasons for prior detention.

247. (1) Identity not established — For the purposes of paragraph 244(c), the factors are the following:

(a) the foreign national's cooperation in providing evidence of their identity, or assisting the Department in obtaining evidence of their identity, in providing the date and place of their birth as well as the names of their mother and father or providing detailed information on the itinerary they followed in travelling to Canada or in completing an application for a travel document;

(b) in the case of a foreign national who makes a claim for refugee protection, the possibility of obtaining identity documents or information without divulging personal information to government officials of their country of nationality or, if there is no country of nationality, their country of former habitual residence;

(c) the destruction of identity or travel documents, or the use of fraudulent documents in order to mislead the Department, and the circumstances under which the foreign national acted;

(d) the provision of contradictory information by a foreign national with respect to identity during the processing of an application by the Department; and

(e) the existence of documents that contradict information provided by the foreign national with respect to their identity.

(2) Non-application to minors — Consideration of the factors set out in paragraph (1)(a) shall not have an adverse impact with respect to minor children referred to in section 249.

SOR/2004-167, s. 65; SOR/2016-136, s. 14

248. Other factors — If it is determined that there are grounds for detention, the following factors shall be considered before a decision is made on detention or release:

(a) the reason for detention;

(b) the length of time in detention;

(c) whether there are any elements that can assist in determining the length of time that detention is likely to continue and, if so, that length of time;

(d) any unexplained delays or unexplained lack of diligence caused by the Department or the person concerned; and

(e) the existence of alternatives to detention.

Case Law

See the *Canada v. B072* summary, 2012 CarswellNat 1493, 2012 FC 563, under s. 58(1) of the Act.

Walker v. Canada (Minister of Citizenship & Immigration) (2010), 89 Imm. L.R. (3d) 151, 2010 FC 392, 2010 CarswellNat 1050, 2010 CarswellNat 2161 — Section 248 of the Regulations adds the length of detention as a consideration to be taken into account even if the person detained is considered to be a flight risk, as in this case. The length of the applicant's detention has to be considered against other factors besides his refusal to cooperate with immigration officials and to reveal his true identity. These other factors would include the immigration status of the applicant, the fact that this was the 38th detention review, the passage of time since his last criminal conviction, etc. A close reading of the Member's reasons reveals that the three-year detention of the applicant was not considered against these factors. The application for judicial review to set aside the decision of the Immigration Division of the Immigration and Refugee Board to order the applicant remain in detention, was allowed.

Canada (Minister of Public Safety & Emergency Preparedness) v. Welch, 2006 Car-swellNat 2416, 2006 FC 924 — The Minister sought judicial review of the decision of a member of the Immigration Division of the Immigration and Refugee Board, allowing the conditional release from detention of the respondents. This was the fifth review of the detention of the respondents. The Minister argued that the member did not provide clear and compelling reasons as to why he should depart from the four previous decisions and release the respondents on terms and conditions. The Minister's view was that these terms and conditions were less stringent than those considered at the previous reviews.

The respondents are citizens of the United States and are wanted in the State of Colorado on a number of charges. They fled to Canada following release on bail pending their trial in the United States. Shortly after their arrival in Canada, they were arrested by the RCMP and a decision was made to detain them, and a removal order pursuant to s. 44 of the IRPA was issued against them. The respondents claimed refugee status and this claim had yet to be determined. At the first detention hearing, it was determined that they were a flight risk but the duration of the detention contemplated was very short. It was mentioned that they had two children. At a second detention hearing, the member came to the same conclusion and continued the detention. The two respondents' children were in the audience during the second hearing. It became clear that they had been with their parents when the latter were apprehended. The children were by then in the care of their grandmother in Canada, having been in the custody of the Ministry of Children and Families. It was argued that it was not in the best interest of the children to be separated from their parents. However, the presence of the children was not found to supersede the other factors listed in s. 245 of the Regulations. A proposal for release including a curfew and a $4,000 bond was rejected. At the third detention hearing, the member considered physical restriction to an area, $25,000 cash bond for each of the respondents, a prohibition to carry weapons, daily reporting and, alternatively, the release of only one of the respondents to enable the children, who were back in the United States with their grandmother, to visit and spend some time with her. At this hearing, the Minister argued for the first time that the respondents posed a danger to the public. This argument was rejected. The member concluded that even a release subject to cash bond and very stringent reporting conditions would not be effective considering that the respondents failed to appear for their trial in the United States in spite of significant bail bonds in existence there (US$25,000 and US$100,000).

At the fourth hearing, the member concluded the detention was necessary to ensure the respondents would appear for their removal. At that time, in addition to the three conditions of release discussed earlier, the respondents proposed a release be made subject to a review once a decision was made on the refugee claim. They also alluded to the possibility of electronic tracking as an alternative to detention, but had been advised by the Minister that this was not a viable alternative as no such system was currently available. Despite the fact that the respondents were likely to remain in detention for several months pending the determination of their refugee claim, the member concluded that their continued detention was necessary and found he had no authority to give any direction to the Minister with respect to the quality of the detention and the electronic monitoring. At the fifth detention hearing, the respondents called a representative of the company Trace Canada as a witness to explain how Trace Canada would equip them with electronic tracking devices that would keep a record of their movements at all times. The company could then report this information to immigration officials who would know immediately if the respondents had breached their conditions of release. Their submission was that the flight risk would be considerably reduced if such a mechanism were in use. The member took the matter under advisement. When the hearing resumed, the member specified that he was not "reopening" the detention review, but simply wished to obtain some clarification with regard to the services offered by Trace Canada. He questioned the representative about the functioning of the electronic tracking system. The member concluded that he considered electronic monitoring to be more responsive than a self-monitored curfew and no-go zone. He also stated it was more responsive than periodic physical reporting where, according to him, the respondents could be long gone by the time they failed to show up to report. It was thus a more immediate form of reporting. He also noted that, in the end, if the person's intention is to abscond, they will do so whatever the type of monitoring and explained that:

> Alternatives to detention are not meant to provide absolute certainty of appearance for removal. They need only have the effect of reducing the risk to an acceptable degree. The fact that the persons concerned have proposed electronic monitoring and have made the effort to bring a proposal for consideration is an indication of their sincerity in seeking to address the Minister's concerns of flight.

The question the court considered was not whether or not the member was justified in ordering the release on the conditions he did, but whether he had provided clear, compelling reasons for departing from the previous decisions reached at the detention reviews. Had the superiority of electronic monitoring been the sole basis of the decision, the court would have concluded that the reasons given by the member met the low threshold set out by the Court of Appeal in *Thanabalasingham*. However, the member clearly distinguishes the situation before him from those reviewed by his colleagues on the basis of the "new evidence" with respect to the respondents' children. Since the member believed the information relating to the existence of the respondents' children was new, he could not properly turn his mind to the decisions of his colleagues on this point and consider why he should depart from the course of action they took. Since the member clearly failed to consider the contrary view expressed by the previous member on this particular point, the decision was set aside.

249. Special considerations for minor children — For the application of the principle affirmed in section 60 of the Act that a minor child shall be detained only as a measure of last resort, the special considerations that apply in relation to the detention of minor children who are less than 18 years of age are

(a) the availability of alternative arrangements with local child-care agencies or child protection services for the care and protection of the minor children;

(b) the anticipated length of detention;

(c) the risk of continued control by the human smugglers or traffickers who brought the children to Canada;

(d) the type of detention facility envisaged and the conditions of detention;

(e) the availability of accommodation that allows for the segregation of the minor children from adult detainees who are not the parent of or the adult legally responsible for the detained minor children; and

(f) the availability of services in the detention facility, including education, counselling and recreation.

250. **Applications for travel documents** — If a completed application for a passport or travel document must be provided as a condition of release from detention, any completed application provided by a foreign national who makes a claim for refugee protection shall not be divulged to government officials of their country of nationality or, if there is no country of nationality, their country of previous habitual residence, as long as the removal order to which the foreign national is subject is not enforceable.

PART 15 — THE IMMIGRATION APPEAL DIVISION

251. **Conditions** — If the Immigration Appeal Division stays a removal order under paragraph 66(b) of the Act, that Division shall impose the following conditions on the person against whom the order was made:

(a) to inform the Department and the Immigration Appeal Division in writing in advance of any change in the person's address;

(b) to provide a copy of their passport or travel document to the Department or, if they do not hold a passport or travel document, to complete an application for a passport or a travel document and to provide the application to the Department;

(c) to apply for an extension of the validity period of any passport or travel document before it expires, and to provide a copy of the extended passport or document to the Department;

(d) to not commit any criminal offences;

(e) if they are charged with a criminal offence, to immediately report that fact in writing to the Department; and

(f) if they are convicted of a criminal offence, to immediately report that fact in writing to the Department and the Division.

PART 16 — SEIZURE

252. **Custody of seized thing** — A thing seized under subsection 140(1) of the Act shall be placed without delay in the custody of the Department.

253. (1) **Notice of seizure** — An officer who seizes a thing under subsection 140(1) of the Act shall make reasonable efforts to

(a) identify the lawful owner; and

(b) give the lawful owner written notice of, and reasons for, the seizure.

(2) **Disposition after seizure** — Subject to subsection (3), a thing seized shall be disposed of as follows:

(a) if it was fraudulently or improperly obtained, by returning it to its lawful owner unless section 256 applies;

(b) if it was fraudulently or improperly used, by disposing of it under section 257 unless section 254, 255 or 256 applies;

(o) if the seizure was necessary to prevent its fraudulent or improper use

    (i) by returning it to its lawful owner, if the seizure is no longer necessary for preventing its fraudulent or improper use, or

    (ii) by disposing of it under section 257, if returning it to its lawful owner would result in its fraudulent or improper use; or

(d) if the seizure was necessary to carry out the purposes of the Act, by returning it to its lawful owner without delay if the seizure is no longer necessary to carry out the purposes of the Act.

(3) **Additional factor** — A thing seized shall only be returned if its return would not be contrary to the purposes of the Act. If its return would be contrary to the purposes of the Act, it shall be disposed of under section 257.

254. (1) **Application for return** — The lawful owner of a thing seized or the person from whom it was seized may apply for its return.

(2) **Return** — A thing seized, other than a document, shall be returned to the applicant if

(a) paragraph 253(2)(b) applies to the thing and the seizure is no longer necessary to prevent its fraudulent or improper use or to carry out the purposes of the Act; and

(b) the applicant provides cash security equal to the fair market value of the thing at the time of the seizure or, if there is no significant risk of being unable to recover the debt, a combination of cash and guarantee of performance.

(3) **Disposition of security** — Any cash deposit or guarantee of performance provided under paragraph 2(b) replaces the thing seized and, if section 257 applies, any cash deposit is forfeited to Her Majesty in right of Canada and any guarantee of performance becomes a debt due under section 145 of the Act.

255. (1) **Application by lawful owner** — For the purposes of paragraph 253(2)(b), a person who claims to be the lawful owner of a seized thing may apply in writing for its return within 60 days after the seizure.

(2) **Return of thing** — The thing seized shall be returned to an applicant if the applicant demonstrates that they

(a) were the lawful owner prior to its seizure and have remained a lawful owner;

(b) did not participate in the fraudulent or improper use of the thing; and

(c) exercised all reasonable care to satisfy themselves that the person permitted to obtain possession of the thing was not likely to fraudulently or improperly use it.

(3) **Return of vehicle** — A seized vehicle that is not returned under subsection (2) shall be returned on payment of a $5,000 fee if the applicant demonstrates that they

(a) were the lawful owner prior to its seizure and have remained a lawful owner;

(b) did not profit or intend to profit from the fraudulent or improper use of the vehicle; and

(c) are unlikely to contravene the Act in the future.

(4) **Additional factor** — A thing seized shall only be returned if its return would not be contrary to the purposes of the Act.

(5) **Notice of decision** — The applicant shall be notified in writing of the decision on the application and the reasons for it. If the applicant is notified by mail, notification is deemed to have been effected on the seventh day after the day on which the notification was mailed.

256. (1) **Application by person from whom thing was seized** — If a thing was seized on the ground that it was fraudulently or improperly obtained or used, a person from whom it was seized may apply in writing within 30 days after the seizure for its return.

(2) **Return of thing** — The thing seized shall be returned to an applicant if the applicant demonstrates that it was not fraudulently or improperly obtained or used.

(3) **Notice of decision** — An applicant shall be notified in writing of the decision on the application and the reasons for it. If the applicant is notified by mail, notification is deemed to have been effected on the seventh day after the day on which the notification was mailed.

257. (1) **Sale of a seized thing** — Subject to subsections (2) and (3), if a thing seized is not returned to its lawful owner or the person from whom it was seized under section 254, 255 or 256, the thing shall be sold unless the costs of sale would exceed the monetary value of the thing, in which case the thing shall be destroyed.

(2) **Sale suspended** — A thing seized shall not be sold

(a) during the 15 days following notification of a decision not to return it under section 255 or 256; or

(b) before a final decision is made in any judicial proceeding in Canada affecting the seizure or the return of the thing seized.

(3) **Disposition of documents** — If a document is not returned to its lawful owner or the person from whom it was seized, the document shall be retained for as long as is necessary for the administration or enforcement of Canadian laws, after which it is subject to the applicable laws relating to the disposal of public archives.

258. **Limitation period for seizures** — No seizure may be made under subsection 140(1) of the Act in respect of the fraudulent or improper obtaining or use of a thing more than six years after that obtaining or use.

PART 17 — TRANSPORTATION

258.1 Prescribed persons — For the purposes of paragraph 148(1)(a) of the Act, the following persons are prescribed:

(a) any foreign national who is the subject of a declaration made under subsection 22.1(1) of the Act, unless they hold a temporary resident permit issued under section 24 of the Act; and

(b) any foreign national who is not authorized under subsection 52(1) of the Act to return to Canada.

SOR/2013-210, s. 5; SOR/2016-37, s. 3

259. Prescribed documents — For the purposes of subsection 148(1) of the Act, the following documents that a person requires under the Act to enter Canada are prescribed:

(a) a travel document referred to in subsection 31(3) of the Act;

(b) refugee travel papers issued by the Minister;

(c) a document referred to in subsection 50(1) or 52(1);

(d) a temporary travel document referred to in section 151;

(e) a visa referred to in section 6 or subsection 7(1);

(f) a permanent resident card; and

(g) an electronic travel authorization referred to in section 7.1.

SOR/2015-46, s. 1(d); SOR/2016-37, s. 14

260. (1) Holding prescribed documentation — If a commercial transporter has reasonable grounds to believe that the prescribed documents of a person whom it carries to Canada may not be available for examination at a port of entry, the commercial transporter must give the person a receipt for the documents and hold the documents until examination.

(2) Presenting documents — A commercial transporter that holds the documents of a person must, when presenting the person for examination under paragraph 148(1)(b) of the Act, present the documents and a copy of the receipt.

SOR/2016-37, s. 5

261. (1) Obligation to hold a person — For the purposes of paragraph 148(1)(b) of the Act, a transporter has complied with the obligation to hold a person until the examination is completed when

(a) an officer informs the transporter that the examination of the person is completed;

(b) the person is authorized to enter Canada under section 23 of the Act; or

(c) the person is detained under any Canadian law.

(2) Notification — A transporter must notify an officer without delay if a person whose examination has not been completed leaves or attempts to leave the transporter's vehicle for any other purpose than examination.

262. Stowaway notification — On the arrival of a vessel at its first port of call in Canada, the transporter must notify an officer at the nearest port of entry of the presence of any stowaway and, on request of the officer, must without delay provide a written report concerning the stowaway.

263. (1) Medical examination and treatment — A commercial transporter must arrange for the medical examination of a foreign national who is required to submit to one under paragraph 16(2)(b) of the Act and for any medical examination, surveillance or treatment that is imposed under section 32.

(2) Exception — Subsection (1) does not apply if

(a) the foreign national holds a temporary or permanent resident visa at the time of their examination and the foreign national's health condition is not a result of the commercial transporter's negligence; or

(b) the foreign national has been authorized to enter and remain in Canada and is not a member of the crew.

(3) Prescribed medical costs — For the purposes of paragraph 148(1)(g) of the Act, any medical costs incurred with respect to the foreign national are prescribed costs and are to be calculated on the basis of the applicable provincial health insurance system.

SOR/2012-154, s. 13; SOR/2016-37, s. 6

264. Prescribed information — A transporter must provide without delay any of the following documents that are requested by an officer within 72 hours after the presentation for examination of a person carried by the transporter to Canada:

(a) a copy of any ticket issued to the person;

(b) a document specifying the person's itinerary, including the place of embarkation and dates of travel; and

(c) a document identifying the document number and type of passport, travel document or identity document carried by the person, the country of issue and the name of the person to whom it was issued.

265. (1) Crew list — On arrival at the first port of call in Canada of a vessel registered in a foreign country, the transporter must provide an officer at the nearest port of entry with a list of all members of the crew.

(2) Amended crew list — The transporter must maintain on board a current list of all members of the crew while the vessel is in Canada.

(3) Final crew list — Before the vessel's departure from its final port of call in Canada, the transporter must provide an officer with a copy of the list referred to in subsection (1) that includes any changes made while the vessel was in Canada.

266. Assembly — On the request of an officer, a transporter must assemble without delay aboard the vessel all members of the crew.

267. Canadian registered vessels — On the arrival of a vessel registered in Canada at its first port of call in Canada, the transporter must notify an officer at the nearest port of entry of all members of the crew who are not Canadian citizens or permanent residents and, on request, provide the officer with a list of all crew members.

268. (1) Reporting obligation — A transporter must, without delay, notify an officer at the nearest port of entry of any foreign national who ceases to be a member of the crew for a reason listed in paragraph 3(1)(b). The transporter must record that information and provide it in writing on the request of the officer.

(2) Failure to join means of transportation — A transporter must, without delay, notify an officer at the nearest port of entry when a foreign national who entered Canada to become a member of the crew of the transporter's vessel fails to join the means of transportation within the period provided in paragraph 184(2)(b).

SOR/2004-167, s. 66; SOR/2016-37, s. 7

269. (1) Prescribed information — On the request of an official of the Canada Border Services Agency, a commercial transporter that carries or expects to carry persons to Canada on board its commercial vehicle must provide the Canada Border Services Agency with the following information about each person whom it expects to carry:

(a) their surname, first name and any middle names, their date of birth, their citizenship or nationality and their gender;

(b) the type and number of each passport or other travel document that identifies them and the name of the country or entity that issued it;

(c) their reservation record locator number, if any;

(d) the unique passenger reference assigned to them by the commercial transporter, if any, or, in the case of a crew member who has not been assigned one, notice of their status as a crew member;

(e) any information about the person that is in a reservation system of the commercial transporter or its agent; and

Proposed Amendment — 269(1)(e)

(e) any information about the person that is referred to in Schedule 3 and is in a reservation system of the commercial transporter or its agent;

SOR/2016-37, s. 18(1) [Not in force at date of publication.]

(f) the following information about their carriage on board the commercial vehicle:

(i) if the person is carried or is expected to be carried on board the commercial vehicle by air, the date and time of take-off from the last point of embarkation of persons before the commercial vehicle arrives in Canada or, if the person is carried or is expected to be carried on board the vehicle by water or land, the date and time of departure from the last point of embarkation of persons before the commercial vehicle arrives in Canada,

IRP Regulations

(ii) the last point of embarkation of persons before the commercial vehicle arrives in Canada,

(iii) the date and time of arrival of the commercial vehicle at the first point of disembarkation of persons in Canada,

(iv) the first point of disembarkation of persons in Canada, and

(v) in the case of a commercial vehicle that carries persons or goods by air, the flight code identifying the commercial transporter and the flight number.

(2) **Electronic means** — The information referred to in subsection (1) must be provided by electronic means in accordance with the technical requirements, specifications and procedures for electronic data interchange set out in the document entitled *CBSA Carrier Messaging Requirements* issued by the Canada Border Services Agency, as amended from time to time.

(3) **Time of transmission — paragraphs (1)(a) to (d)** — The information referred to in paragraphs (1)(a) to (d) must be provided

(a) not later than one hour before the time of departure, if the information relates to a member of the crew; and

(b) not later than the time of check-in, if the information relates to any other person who is expected to be on board the commercial vehicle.

(4) **Time of transmission — paragraph (1)(e)** — The information referred to in paragraph (1)(e) must be provided not later than at the time of departure.

Proposed Amendment — 269(4)

(4) **Time of transmission — paragraph (1)(e)** — The information referred to in paragraph (1)(e) must be provided, for each person who is expected to be on board the commercial vehicle, not later than 72 hours before the time of departure.

SOR/2016-37, s. 18(2) [Not in force at date of publication.]

(5) **Time of transmission — paragraph (1)(d)** — The information referred to in paragraph (1)(d) must also be provided, for each passenger who is on board the commercial vehicle at the time of departure, not later than 30 minutes after the time of departure.

Proposed Amendment — 269(5)

(5) **Time of transmission — paragraph (1)(d)** — The information referred to in paragraph (1)(d) must also be provided, for each passenger who is on board the commercial vehicle at the time of departure, not later than 30 minutes after the time of departure.

SOR/2016-37, s. 18(2) [Not in force at date of publication.]

(6) **Incomplete or inaccurate information** — A commercial transporter that becomes aware before or at the time of departure that information they have provided under paragraph 148(1)(d) of the Act is incomplete or inaccurate must, in the manner described in subsection (2) and without delay, provide the Canada Border Services Agency with the missing or accurate information.

Proposed Amendment — 269(6)

(6) Incomplete or inaccurate information — A commercial transporter that becomes aware before or at the time of departure that information it has provided under paragraph 148(1)(d) of the Act is incomplete or inaccurate must, in the manner described in subsection (2) and without delay, provide the Canada Border Services Agency with the missing or accurate information.

SOR/2016-37, s. 18(2) [Not in force at date of publication.]

(7) Exception — paragraph (1)(e) — Subsection (6) does not apply in respect of information referred to in paragraph (1)(e).

Proposed Amendment — 269(7)

(7) Exception — paragraph (1)(e) — Subsection (6) does not apply in respect of information referred to in paragraph (1)(e).

SOR/2016-37, s. 18(2) [Not in force at date of publication.]

(8) Time of transmission — paragraph (1)(f) — The information referred to in paragraph (1)(f) must be provided at the same time that any information referred to in subsections (3) to (7) is provided.

Proposed Amendment — 269(8)

(8) Updates — If information referred to in paragraph (1)(e) about a person in relation to a particular carriage is added to a reservation system or changed in the system less than 72 hours before the time of departure, the commercial transporter must, in the manner described in subsection (2) and at the following times, provide the Canada Border Services Agency with all the information referred to in paragraph (1)(e) about the person in relation to that carriage:

(a) if the addition or change is made more than 24 hours before the time of departure, not later than 24 hours before the time of departure;

(b) if the addition or change is made during the period beginning 24 hours before the time of departure and ending eight hours before that time, not later than eight hours before the time of departure; and

(c) if the addition or change is made less than eight hours before the time of departure, not later than the time of departure.

SOR/2016-37, s. 18(2) [Not in force at date of publication.]

(9) Maximum retention period — The Canada Border Services Agency may retain information referred to in paragraphs (1)(a) to (d) about a person for up to three years and six months after the day of departure of the commercial vehicle that carried or was to carry the person to Canada.

Proposed Amendment — 269(9)

(9) Time of transmission — paragraph (1)(f) — The information referred to in paragraph (1)(f) must be provided at the same time that any information referred to in subsections (3) to (8) is provided.

SOR/2016-37, s. 18(2) [Not in force at date of publication.]

(10) Retention period — investigation — After the period referred to in subsection (9), the Canada Border Services Agency may retain the information referred to in that subsection about a person for as long as it is required as part of an investigation, but in no case longer than six years after the day of departure of the commercial vehicle that carried or was to carry the person to Canada.

Proposed Amendment — 269(10)

(10) Retention period — The Canada Border Services Agency may retain information referred to in paragraphs (1)(a) to (d) about a person for up to three years and six months after the day of departure of the commercial vehicle that carried or was to carry the person to Canada.

SOR/2016-37, s. 18(2) [Not in force at date of publication.]

Proposed Addition — 269(11)

(11) Retention period — investigation — After the period referred to in subsection (10), the Canada Border Services Agency may retain the information referred to in that subsection about a person for as long as it is required as part of an investigation, but in no case longer than six years after the day of departure of the commercial vehicle that carried or was to carry the person to Canada.

SOR/2016-37, s. 18(2) [Not in force at date of publication.]

SOR/2016-37, s. 8

270. (1) Notice by Canada Border Services Agency — The Canada Border Services Agency may notify a commercial transporter that a person whom it expects to carry to Canada may be a person who is prescribed under section 258.1 or may be a person who does not hold the necessary documents prescribed under section 259.

(2) Obligations unchanged — For greater certainty, subsection (1) does not relieve a commercial transporter of its obligation to comply with any requirement imposed by the Act or these Regulations.

SOR/2004-167, s. 67; SOR/2016-37, s. 8

271. (1) Facilities for holding and examination — A commercial transporter, and a transporter who operates an airport or an international bridge or tunnel, must without cost to Her Majesty in right of Canada provide and maintain facilities, including areas, offices and laboratories, that are adequate for the proper holding and examination of persons being carried to Canada.

(2) Criteria — The facilities referred to in subsection (1) are adequate if they satisfy the applicable requirements of Part II of the *Canada Labour Code*, are secure and, if necessary, sterile, and include equipment and furnishings that permit officers to discharge their duties under the Act.

272. Examination on vessels — A commercial transporter carrying persons to Canada aboard its vessel must provide facilities aboard the vessel that permit an officer to conduct examinations.

273. (1) Obligation to carry from Canada — A commercial transporter that has carried a foreign national referred to in this subsection to Canada or caused such a foreign national to be carried to Canada must, without delay, carry the foreign national from Canada

(a) to any other country, in the case of a foreign national directed to leave under subsection 40(1);

(b) to the United States, in the case of a foreign national directed back to that country under section 41;

(c) to any other country, in the case of a foreign national allowed to withdraw their application under section 42; or

(d) to the country to which the foreign national is removed under section 241, in the case of a foreign national who is subject to an enforceable removal order.

(2) **Conveyance to vehicle** — The transporter must transport a foreign national who is subject to an enforceable removal order from wherever the foreign national is situated in Canada to the vehicle in which they will be carried to another country.

SOR/2016-37, s. 9

274. (1) Members of a crew — If a transporter carries, or causes to be carried, a foreign national to Canada as a member of its crew or to become a member of its crew, and the foreign national is subject to an enforceable removal order, the transporter must carry that foreign national from Canada to the applicable country as determined under Division 4 of Part 13.

(2) **Conveyance to vehicle** — The transporter must transport the foreign national referred to in subsection (1) from wherever the foreign national is situated in Canada to the vehicle in which they will be carried to another country.

275. Notification — A transporter must notify an officer without delay if a foreign national referred to in section 273 or 274 whom they are carrying from Canada leaves or attempts to leave a vehicle before they are carried from Canada.

276. (1) Notifying commercial transporter — When a foreign national who seeks to enter Canada is made subject to a removal order and a commercial transporter is or may be required under the Act to carry that foreign national from Canada, an officer must

(a) notify the commercial transporter that it is or may be required to carry the foreign national from Canada; and

(b) when the removal order is enforceable, notify the commercial transporter of its obligation to carry the foreign national from Canada and, if an escort is necessary, request the commercial transporter to provide an escort or to make arrangements for the carriage of an escort assigned by the Minister.

(2) **Arrangements and notice** — After being notified under paragraph (1)(b), the commercial transporter must, without delay,

(a) make arrangements to carry the foreign national from Canada and notify an officer of those arrangements; or

(b) notify an officer that it is unable to make such arrangements.

(3) **Time period** — The commercial transporter must carry the foreign national from Canada within 48 hours after giving the notice required by paragraph (2)(a).

(4) **Non-compliance** — If a commercial transporter does not comply with paragraph 2(a) or subsection (3) or notifies an officer that it is unable to comply with those provisions, or if an officer notifies the commercial transporter in writing that the proposed arrangements are not acceptable, an officer must cause the foreign national to be carried from Canada and the commercial transporter must pay the costs referred to in section 278.

(5) **Requirements for acceptance of arrangements** — To be acceptable, the arrangements referred to in subsection (2) must meet the following requirements:

(a) the itinerary must begin where the foreign national is situated in Canada and end in the country and city to which the foreign national is to be removed, following the most direct routing possible;

(b) the itinerary must not include a country through which transit has not been approved; and

(c) the period of time between any connections must not exceed 12 hours.

(6) **Requirements for escort** — A commercial transporter that has been notified under paragraph 1(b) must comply with any request by an officer to provide an escort or to arrange for the carriage of the escort assigned by the Minister.

SOR/2016-37, s. 10

277. Relief from obligations — Despite sections 273 and 276, a commercial transporter is relieved of its obligation to carry a foreign national from Canada, except for a member of its crew or a foreign national who entered Canada to become a member of its crew, if the foreign national at the time of their examination

(a) was authorized to enter and remain in Canada on a temporary basis;

(b) held a temporary or permanent resident visa; or

(c) was a person prescribed under section 258.1 and the commercial transporter was not, before the person was carried to Canada, notified under section 270 that the person may have been a prescribed person.

SOR/2016-37, s. 10, 15

278. Removal costs — A transporter that is required under the Act to carry a foreign national from Canada must pay the following costs of removal and, if applicable, attempted removal:

(a) expenses incurred within or outside Canada with respect to the foreign national's accommodation and transport, including penalties for changes of date or routing;

(b) accommodation and travel expenses incurred by any escorts provided to accompany the foreign national;

(c) fees paid in obtaining passports, travel documents and visas for the foreign national and any escorts;

(d) the cost of meals, incidentals and other expenses as calculated in accordance with the rates set out in the *Travel Directive* published by the Treasury Board Secretariat, as amended from time to time;

(e) any wages paid to escorts and other personnel; and

(f) the costs or expenses incurred with respect to interpreters and medical and other personnel engaged for the removal.

279. (1) Assessment of administration fee — Subject to subsection (2), an administration fee must be assessed against a commercial transporter in respect of any of the following foreign nationals it carried or caused to be carried to Canada:

(a) a foreign national who is inadmissible under section 41 of the Act for failing to meet the requirements of section 6, subsection 7(1), section 7.1 or subsection 50(1) or 52(1);

(b) a foreign national who is prescribed under section 258.1 or whom the commercial transporter has been directed under paragraph 148(1)(a) of the Act not to carry to Canada;

(c) a foreign national who is exempt, under subsection 52(2), from the requirement to hold a passport or travel document but who fails to produce sufficient evidence of their identity;

(d) a foreign national who failed to appear for an examination on entry into Canada;

(e) a foreign national who entered Canada as a member of a crew or to become a member of a crew and is inadmissible; and

(f) a foreign national who is subject to a removal order, or is allowed under section 42 to withdraw their application to enter Canada, and who fails to leave Canada immediately.

(2) Exceptions — An administration fee shall not be assessed against a commercial transporter in respect of

(a) a person referred to in section 39;

(b) a foreign national who is prescribed under section 258.1 and in respect of whom notice under section 270 was not given before the foreign national was carried to Canada but who holds the necessary documents prescribed under section 259;

(c) a foreign national who does not hold an electronic travel authorization when one is required under section 7.1 and in respect of whom the Canada Border Services Agency did not give notice under section 270 to the commercial transporter before the foreign national was carried to Canada, but who holds one of the required prescribed documents set out in paragraphs 259(a) to (f); or

(d) a foreign national, other than a foreign national referred to in paragraph 190(3)(c), who seeks to enter Canada to obtain permanent residence and is inadmissible under paragraph 41(a) of the Act for failing to obtain a permanent resident visa as required under section 6, but who is exempted under Division 1 of Part 2 from the requirement to obtain an electronic travel authorization required under section 7.1 or exempted under Division 5 of Part 9 from the requirement to obtain a temporary resident visa.

(e) [Repealed SOR/2016-37, s. 11(3).]

SOR/2004-167, s. 68; SOR/2016-37, ss. 11, 16

280. (1) Administration fee — Subject to subsection (2), the administration fee assessed under section 279 is $3,200.

(2) Memorandum of understanding — If a memorandum of understanding in accordance with subsection (3) is in effect between the commercial transporter and the Minister, the administration fee assessed is

(a) $3,200, if the commercial transporter does not demonstrate that it complies with the memorandum of understanding, if the commercial transporter carried to Canada a foreign national who is prescribed under section 258.1 or whom the commercial transporter has been directed under paragraph 148(1)(a) of the Act not to carry to Canada, or if the administration fee is assessed in respect of a member of the crew of the transporter;

(b) $2,400, if the commercial transporter demonstrates that it complies with the memorandum of understanding;

(c) $1,600, if the commercial transporter demonstrates that it complies with the memorandum of understanding and has a number of administration fee assessments that is equal to or less than the number specified in the memorandum, for the period specified in the memorandum, for reducing the administration fee by 50%;

(d) $800, if the commercial transporter demonstrates that it complies with the memorandum of understanding and has a number of administration fee assessments that is equal to or less than the number specified in the memorandum, for the period specified in the memorandum, for reducing the administration fee by 75%; and

(e) $0, if the commercial transporter demonstrates that it complies with the memorandum of understanding and has a number of administration fee assessments that is equal to or less than the number specified in the memorandum, for the period specified in the memorandum, for reducing the administration fee by 100%.

(4) Content of memorandum of understanding — A memorandum of understanding referred to in subsection (2) shall include provisions respecting

(a) document screening;

(b) the training of personnel in document screening;

(c) the use of technological aids;

(d) fraud prevention;

(e) gate checks;

(f) information exchange;

(g) performance standards and administration fee assessments;

(h) compliance monitoring of the provisions of the memorandum of understanding;

(i) holding documents under section 260;

(j) providing information referred to in subsections 269(1) and (2);

(k) stowaways; and

(l) security screening of members of a crew.

SOR/2016-37, s. 12(2), (3)

281. (1) Notice of assessment — The assessment of an administration fee shall be served personally, by registered mail, by facsimile with acknowledgement of receipt or by electronic transmission on a representative of the commercial transporter.

(2) Service effected — Service of the assessment by registered mail is deemed to have been effected on the seventh day after the day on which the assessment was mailed.

282. (1) Submissions concerning assessment — The commercial transporter may submit written submissions to the Minister within 30 days after being served with an assessment of an administration fee.

(2) Final decision and notice — If submissions are made, the Minister must consider the submissions, confirm, vary or cancel the assessment and give written notice of the final decision to the commercial transporter.

(2.1) Elements considered — In considering the submissions, the Minister must take into account whether the commercial transporter was, before the foreign national was carried to Canada, notified under section 270 that the foreign national may have been a person prescribed under section 258.1 or a person who did not hold an electronic travel authorization when one was required by section 7.1.

(3) Liability — If no submissions are made within the 30-day period, the assessment is final and the commercial transporter is liable for the assessment at the end of that period.

(4) Liability — If the Minister confirms an assessment under subsection (2), the commercial transporter is liable for the assessment on the date the notice is sent.

SOR/2016-37, ss. 13, 17

283. (1) Security — The Minister may, on the basis of the following factors, require a commercial transporter to provide security for compliance with its obligations under paragraphs 148(1)(a) to (g) of the Act:

(a) the frequency and regularity of arrival, or anticipated arrival, of the transporter's vehicles carrying persons to Canada;

(b) the number of persons carried, or anticipated to be carried, to Canada aboard the transporter's vehicles;

(c) whether the transporter has carried an inadmissible foreign national to Canada; and

(d) the anticipated risk of inadmissible foreign nationals being carried to Canada by the transporter.

(2) Amount of security — If the Minister requires security to be provided, the Minister shall determine the amount of security on the basis of the following factors:

(a) the commercial transporter's record of compliance with the Act; and

(b) the anticipated risk of inadmissible foreign nationals being carried to Canada by the transporter and the estimated removal costs.

(3) Form of security — A commercial transporter who is required to provide security must provide it in the form of a cash deposit unless

(a) the transporter has entered into a memorandum of understanding referred to in subsection 280(2) that provides for another form of security; and

(b) the transporter demonstrates that there is no significant risk of a debt not being paid if they were to provide another form of security.

(4) Return of security — If the Minister determines on the basis of the factors set out in subsection (1) that security is no longer required, the Minister shall return the security to the commercial transporter.

284. Application of s. 148(2) of the Act — For the purposes of subsection 148(2) of the Act, a prescribed good is a good that is not land, a building or a transportation facility.

285. Object detained or seized — If an object is detained or seized under subsection 148(2) of the Act, that object shall remain detained or seized until

(a) the transporter complies with its obligations under section 148 of the Act; or

(b) the transporter's obligations are discharged by another person.

286. (1) Notice of seizure — Following a seizure under subsection 148(2) of the Act, an officer shall make reasonable efforts to

(a) identify the lawful owner of the object seized; and

(b) give notice of the seizure to that person.

(2) Disposition after seizure — A thing seized under subsection 148(2) of the Act shall be disposed of by

  (a) returning the object to the transporter on receipt of

    (i) an amount equal to the value of the object at the time of seizure and any expenses incurred in the seizure and, if applicable, detention,

    (ii) the security required under the Act or any costs and fees for which the transporter is liable, as well as an amount equal to any expenses incurred in the seizure and, if applicable, detention, or

    (iii) evidence that the transporter is in compliance with its obligations under subsection 148(1) of the Act and has reimbursed Her Majesty in right of Canada for any expenses incurred in the seizure and, if applicable, detention; or

  (b) disposing of the object under section 287.

287. (1) Sale of a seized object — If a transporter does not comply with paragraph 286(2)(a) within a reasonable time, an officer shall give notice to the transporter that the object will be sold. The object shall then be sold for the benefit of Her Majesty in right of Canada and the proceeds of the sale shall be applied to the transporter's outstanding debt to Her Majesty under the Act. Any surplus shall be returned to the transporter.

(2) Costs incurred in seizure — Any expenses incurred by Her Majesty in right of Canada in selling the object, and any expenses incurred in the seizure or, if applicable, detention of the object, shall be deducted from the proceeds of the sale.

SOR/2004-167, s. 69

PART 18 — LOANS

288. Definition of "beneficiary" — In this Part, "beneficiary", in respect of a person, means

  (a) the person's spouse, common-law partner or conjugal partner;

  (b) a dependent child of the person or of the person's spouse, common-law partner or conjugal partner; and

  (c) any other person who, at the time of their application for a permanent resident visa or their application to remain in Canada as a permanent resident, is in a relationship of dependency with the person by virtue of being cared for by or receiving emotional and financial support from the person.

289. Types of loans — The Minister may make loans to the following persons for the following purposes:

  (a) to a foreign national referred to in Part 1 of the Act for the purpose of

    (i) defraying the cost to the foreign national and their beneficiaries of transportation from their point of departure outside Canada to their point of destination in Canada, and related administrative charges,

(ii) assisting the foreign national and their beneficiaries to become established in Canada, or

(iii) defraying the fee, referred to in subsection 303(1), payable for the acquisition by the foreign national and their beneficiaries of permanent resident status;

(b) to a foreign national referred to in Part 2 of the Act for the purpose of

(i) defraying the cost to the foreign national and their beneficiaries of transportation from their point of departure outside Canada to their point of destination in·Canada, and related administrative charges,

(ii) defraying the cost to the foreign national and their beneficiaries of transportation to attend any interview relating to their application, and related administrative charges,

(iii) defraying the cost to the foreign national and their beneficiaries of a medical examination under paragraph 16(2)(b) of the Act, and related costs and administrative charges, or

(iv) assisting the foreign national and their beneficiaries to become established in Canada; and

(c) to a permanent resident or a Canadian citizen for the purpose of

(i) defraying the cost to their beneficiaries of transportation from their point of departure outside Canada to their point of destination in Canada, and related administrative charges,

(ii) defraying the cost to their beneficiaries of a medical examination under paragraph 16(2)(b) of the Act, and related costs and administrative charges, if the beneficiaries are protected persons within the meaning of subsection 95(2) of the Act, or

(iii) defraying the fee, referred to in subsection 303(1), payable for the acquisition by their beneficiaries of permanent resident status.

SOR/2012-154, s. 14

290. (1) Maximum amount — The maximum amount of advances that may be made under subsection 88(1) of the Act is $110,000,000.

(2) Total loans — The total amount of all loans made under this Part plus accrued interest on those loans shall not at any time exceed the maximum amount of advances prescribed by subsection (1).

291. (1) Repayment — Subject to section 292, a loan made under section 289 becomes payable

(a) in the case of a loan for the purpose of defraying transportation costs, 30 days after the day on which the person for whose benefit the loan was made enters Canada; and

(b) in the case of a loan for any other purpose, 30 days after the day on which the loan was made.

(2) Repayment terms   Subject to section 292, a loan made under section 289, together with all accrued interest, must be repaid in full, in consecutive monthly instalments, within

(a) 12 months after the day on which the loan becomes payable, if the amount of the loan is not more than $1,200;

(b) 24 months after the day on which the loan becomes payable, if the amount of the loan is more than $1,200 but not more than $2,400;

(c) 36 months after the day on which the loan becomes payable, if the amount of the loan is more than $2,400 but not more than $3,600;

(d) 48 months after the day on which the loan becomes payable, if the amount of the loan is more than $3,600 but not more than $4,800; and

(e) 72 months after the day on which the loan becomes payable, if the amount of the loan is more than $4,800.

292. (1) Deferred repayment — If repaying a loan, in accordance with the requirements of section 291, that was made to a person under section 289 would, by reason of the person's income, assets and liabilities, cause the person financial hardship, an officer may, to the extent necessary to relieve that hardship but subject to subsection (2), defer the commencement of the repayment of the loan, defer payments on the loan, vary the amount of the payments or extend the repayment period.

(2) Maximum extension — A repayment period shall not be extended beyond

(a) an additional 24 months, in the case of a loan referred to in paragraph 289(b); and

(b) an additional six months, in the case of any other loan.

293. (1) Rate of interest — A loan made under this Part bears interest at a rate equal to the rate that is established by the Minister of Finance for loans made by that Minister to Crown corporations and that is in effect

(a) on the first day of January in the year in which the loan is made, in the case of a loan made to a person in Canada who has no other outstanding loans under this Part; and

(b) on the first day of January in the year in which the person for whose benefit the loan is made enters Canada, in any other case.

(2) Interest on loans under paras. 289(a) and (c) — The interest on a loan made under paragraph 289(a) or (c) accrues beginning

(a) 30 days after the day on which the loan is made, in the case of a loan made to a person in Canada who has no other outstanding loans under this Part; and

(b) 30 days after the day on which the person for whose benefit the loan is made enters Canada, in any other case.

IRP Regulations

(3) Interest on loans under par. 289(b) — The interest on a loan made under paragraph 289(b) accrues

(a) if the amount of the loan is not more than $1,200, beginning on the first day of the thirteenth month after

(i) the day on which the loan is made, in the case of a loan made to a person in Canada who has no other outstanding loans under this Part, and

(ii) the day on which the person for whose benefit the loan is made enters Canada, in any other case;

(b) if the amount of the loan is more than $1,200 but not more than $2,400, beginning on the first day of the twenty-fifth month after

(i) the day on which the loan is made, in the case of a loan made to a person in Canada who has no other outstanding loans under this Part, and

(ii) the day on which the person for whose benefit the loan is made enters Canada, in any other case; and

(c) if the amount of the loan is more than $2,400, beginning on the first day of the thirty-seventh month after

(i) the day on which the loan is made, in the case of a loan made to a person in Canada who has no other outstanding loans under this Part, and

(ii) the day on which the person for whose benefit the loan is made enters Canada, in any other case.

(4) Existing loan — If a loan that was made to a person under section 289 has not been repaid and a subsequent loan is made under that section to that person, the subsequent loan bears interest at a rate equal to the rate of interest payable on the previous loan.

(5) The interest on a loan made under section 289 shall be calculated daily and, if a monthly installment referred to in subsection 291(2) is paid late or in part or is not paid, shall be compounded monthly.

(6) For greater certainty, the applicable rate of interest in respect of a loan made under section 289 remains the same until the loan is repaid in full.

SOR/2006-116, s. 1

PART 19 — FEES

DIVISION 1 — GENERAL

294. Interpretation — In this Part,

(a) a fee payable under this Part is payable not per application but for each person in respect of whom an application is made;

(b) subject to subsections 295(4), 301(2), 304(2) and 314(3), a fee payable under this Part for processing an application is payable at the time the application is made; and

(c) subject to subsections 295(4) and 301(3), if the requirement to pay a fee depends on a person's age or the amount of a fee is calculated in accordance with their age, the age of the person shall be determined as of the day the application in respect of which the fee is payable is made.

SOR/2009-163, s. 14; SOR/2013-73, s. 3; SOR/2014-19, s. 1

DIVISION 2 — FEES FOR APPLICATIONS FOR AUTHORIZATIONS, VISAS AND PERMITS

[Heading amended SOR/2015-77, s. 8.]

Electronic Travel Authorizations

[Heading amended SOR/2015-77, s. 8.]

294.1 (1) Fee — $7 — A fee of $7 is payable for processing an application for an electronic travel authorization.

(2) Exception — A person whose application for a work permit or a study permit is considered under subsection 12.04(5) to constitute an application for an electronic travel authorization is not required to pay the fee referred to in subsection (1).

SOR/2015-77, s. 8

295. (1) Permanent resident visa — The following fees are payable for processing an application for a permanent resident visa:

(a) if the application is made by a person as a member of the family class

(i) in respect of a principal applicant, other than a principal applicant referred to in subparagraph (ii), $475,

(ii) in respect of a principal applicant who is a foreign national referred to in any of paragraphs 117(1)(b) or (f) to (h), is less than 19 years of age and is not a spouse or common-law partner, $75,

(iii) in respect of a family member of the principal applicant who is a spouse or common-law partner, $550, and

(iv) in respect of a family member of the principal applicant who is a dependent child, $150;

(b) if the application is made by a person as a member of the investor class, the entrepreneur class, the self-employed persons class, the transitional federal investor class, the transitional federal entrepreneur class or the transitional federal self-employed persons class

(i) in respect of a principal applicant, $1,050,

(ii) in respect of a family member of the principal applicant who is a spouse or common-law partner, $550, and

(iii) in respect of a family member of the principal applicant who is a dependent child, $150; and

(c) if the application is made by a person as a member of any other class or by a person referred to in section 71

(i) in respect of a principal applicant, $550,

(ii) in respect of a family member of the principal applicant who is a spouse or common-law partner, $550, and

(iii) in respect of a family member of the principal applicant who is a dependent child, $150.

(2) **Exception — refugees** — The following persons are not required to pay the fees referred to in subsection (1):

(a) a person who makes an application as a member of the Convention refugees abroad class and the family members included in the member's application; and

(b) a person who makes an application as a member of a humanitarian-protected persons abroad class and the family members included in the member's application.

(2.1) **Exception — transitional skilled worker class** — The following persons are not required to pay the fees referred to in subsection (1):

(a) a person described in paragraph 85.1(2)(a) who makes an application as a member of the transitional federal skilled worker class for a permanent resident visa and the family members included in the member's application who were also included in the application referred to in subsection 85.1(2); and

(b) a person described in paragraph 85.1(2)(b) who makes an application as a member of the transitional federal skilled worker class for a permanent resident visa and the family members included in the member's application who were also included in the application referred to in subsection 85.1(2), if the fees for processing their withdrawn application have not been refunded.

(2.2) **Exception — transitional federal business classes** — The following persons are not required to pay the fees referred to in subsection (1):

(a) a person described in paragraph 109.1(2)(a) who makes an application as a member of the transitional federal investor class, the transitional federal entrepreneur class or the transitional federal self-employed persons class for a permanent resident visa and the family members included in the member's application who were also included in the application referred to in subsection 109.1(2); and

(b) a person described in paragraph 109.1(2)(b) who makes an application as a member of the transitional federal investor class, the transitional federal entrepreneur class or the transitional federal self-employed persons class for a permanent resident visa and the family members included in the member's application who were also included in the application referred to in subsection 109.1(2), if the fees for processing their withdrawn application have not been refunded.

(3) Payment by sponsor — A fee payable under subsection (1) in respect of a person who makes an application as a member of the family class or their family members

(a) is payable, together with the fee payable under subsection 304(1), at the time the sponsor files the sponsorship application; and

(b) shall be repaid in accordance with regulations referred to in subsection 20(2) of the *Financial Administration Act* if, before the processing of the application for a permanent resident visa has begun, the sponsorship application is withdrawn by the sponsor.

(4) Age — For the purposes of paragraph (1)(a), the age of the person in respect of whom the application is made shall be determined as of the day the sponsorship application is filed.

SOR/2003-383, s. 6; SOR/2005-61, s. 7; SOR/2009 163, s. 15; SOR/2011-222, s. 7; SOR/2014-133, s. 10

Case Law

Li v. Canada (Minister of Citizenship & Immigration) (2010), 90 Imm. L.R. (3d) 161, 376 F.T.R. 195 (Eng.), 2010 FC 803, 2010 CarswellNat 3411, 2010 CarswellNat 2694; affirmed (2011), 96 Imm. L.R. (3d) 1, 2011 FCA 110, 2011 CarswellNat 1944, 2011 CarswellNat 754 — The applicant sought judicial review of a decision to charge the applicant the fee payable pursuant to paras. 295(1)(a) and (3)(a) of the *Immigration and Refugee Protection Regulations*. Under the former *Immigration Act*, the sponsor paid a single fee for the processing of both applications. However, under the current Regulations made pursuant to IRPA, two separate fees are payable: one for processing the sponsorship application under subs. 304(1) ("sponsorship fee"), and one for processing the application for permanent residence under para. 295(1)(a) ("PR application fee"). Pursuant to para. 295(3)(a), the PR application fee is payable when the sponsorship application is submitted at the first step of the process, even though the fee relates to the second step (processing the application for permanent residence). In effect, this was a continuation of the practice under the former legislative regime. A significant difference is that under the former Act none of the fee was refunded if the sponsorship application was denied. Under IRPA, the PR application fee is fully refundable if the sponsorship application is rejected or withdrawn.

In this instance, the government made a policy choice to require payment of a fee in advance recognizing that in a small portion of cases the service will not be provided and the fee must be refunded. The court was not persuaded that this rendered the regulation *ultra vires*, particularly in light of the evidence that only a small percentage of sponsorship applications are rejected. The vast majority are granted and proceed to PR application. The fee is fully refundable in those cases where the sponsorship applicant is found to be ineligible and has elected not to proceed with the permanent resident application notwithstanding that result. This brings the regulation within s. 19(2) of the *Financial Administration Act*. Section 295(3)(a) is *intra vires* its enabling authority insofar as there is a clear nexus between the fee and the cost incurred in providing the service. The application for judicial review was dismissed; however, a question was certified: Is *Immigration and Refugee Protection Regulation* 295(3)(a), as applied to sponsored immigrant visa applications made by parents and grandparents, *ultra vires* on the ground it is inconsistent with s. 19 of the *Financial Administration Act*?

Temporary Resident Visas

296. (1) Single or multiple entry — $100 — A fee of $100 is payable for processing an application for a temporary resident visa to enter Canada one or more times.

(2) Exception — The following persons are not required to pay the fee referred to in subsection (1):

(a) a properly accredited diplomat, consular officer, representative or official of a country other than Canada, of the United Nations or any of its agencies or of any intergovernmental organization of which Canada is a member, the members of the suite of such a person and the family members of such a person;

(b) a member of the armed forces of a country that is a designated state for the purposes of the *Visiting Forces Act*, including a person who has been designated as a civilian component of that visiting force under paragraph 4(c) of that Act, and their family members;

(c) a person who is a member of the clergy, a member of a religious order or a lay person who is to assist a congregation or a group in the achievement of its spiritual goals, if the duties to be performed by the person are to consist mainly of preaching doctrine, presiding at liturgical functions or spiritual counselling, and their family members;

(d) persons, other than a group of performing artists and their staff, who apply at the same time and place for a work permit or a study permit;

(e) a person who is seeking to enter Canada

(i) for the purpose of attending a meeting hosted by the Government of Canada, an organization of the United Nations or the Organization of American States, as a participant,

(ii) for the purpose of attending a meeting as a representative of the Organization of American States or the Caribbean Development Bank, or

(iii) for the purpose of attending a meeting hosted by the Government of Canada, an organization of the United Nations or the Organization of American States, at the invitation of the Government of Canada;

(f) a person who is seeking to enter Canada as a competitor, coach, judge, team official, medical staff member or member of a national or international sports organizing body participating in the Pan-American Games, when held in Canada, or as a performer participating in a festival associated with any of those Games; and

(g) a person who is seeking to enter Canada for a period of less than 48 hours and who is

(i) travelling by transporter's vehicle to a destination other than Canada, or

(ii) transiting through or stopping over in Canada for refuelling or for the continuation of their journey in another transporter's vehicle.

(h) [Repealed SOR/2014-19, s. 2(2).]

(3) **Maximum fee** — The total amount of fees payable under subsection (1) by an applicant and their family members who apply at the same time and place shall not exceed $500.

SOR/2005-63, s. 1; SOR/2010-121, s. 1; SOR/2014-19, s. 2

297. [Repealed SOR/2014-19, s. 3.]

Temporary Resident Permits

298. (1) **Fee — $200** — A fee of $200 is payable for processing an application for a temporary resident permit.

(2) **Exception** — The following persons are not required to pay the fee referred to in subsection (1):

(a) a person referred to in subsection 295(2) or any of paragraphs 296(2)(c) and (d), 299(2)(a), (b), (d) to (f) and (h) to (k) and 300(2)(f) to (i);

(a.1) a properly accredited diplomat, consular officer, representative or official of a country other than Canada, of the United Nations or any of its agencies or of any intergovernmental organization of which Canada is a member, the members of the suite of such a person and the family members of such a person;

(a.2) a member of the armed forces of a country that is a designated state for the purposes of the *Visiting Forces Act*, including a person who has been designated as a civilian component of that visiting force under paragraph 4(c) of that Act, and their family members;

(a.3) a person whose work in Canada would create or maintain reciprocal employment for Canadian citizens or permanent residents of Canada in other countries and who is a family member of a person referred to in subparagraph 299(2)(g)(iii);

(b) a person in respect of whom an application for a permanent resident visa, an application to remain in Canada as a permanent resident, or an application under subsection 25(1) of the Act is pending, or in respect of whom a decision under subsection 25.1(1) or 25.2(1) of the Act is pending;

(c) a citizen of Costa Rica seeking to enter and remain in Canada during the period beginning on May 11, 2004 and ending on May 12, 2004, if the person does not hold a temporary resident visa but is not otherwise inadmissible;

(d) a person who is seeking to enter Canada

(i) for the purpose of attending a meeting hosted by the Government of Canada, an organization of the United Nations or the Organization of American States, as a participant,

(ii) for the purpose of attending a meeting as a representative of the Organization of American States or the Caribbean Development Bank, or

(iii) for the purpose of attending a meeting hosted by the Government of Canada, an organization of the United Nations or the Organization of American States, at the invitation of the Government of Canada; and

(e) a person who, while they are in transit to Canada, ceases to be exempt under paragraph 190(1)(a) from the requirement for a temporary resident visa, if, during the first 48 hours after they cease to be exempt from that requirement, they seek to enter and remain in Canada and are inadmissible to Canada for the sole reason that they do not have a temporary resident visa.
SOR/2003-197, s. 3; SOR/2004-111, s. 2; SOR/2004-167, s. 71; SOR/2010-121, s. 2; SOR/2010-252, s. 2

Work Permits

299. (1) Fee — $155 — A fee of $155 is payable for processing an application for a work permit.

(2) Exception — The following persons are not required to pay the fee referred to in subsection (1):

(a) a person in Canada who has made a refugee claim that has not yet been determined by the Refugee Protection Division, and their family members;

(b) a person in Canada on whom refugee protection has been conferred, and their family members;

(c) a person who is a member of the Convention refugees abroad class or a member of a humanitarian-protected persons abroad class, and their family members;

(d) a person who holds a study permit and is temporarily destitute, as described in paragraph 208(a);

(e) a person whose work in Canada is designated under subparagraph 205(c)(i);

(f) a person who works in Canada for a Canadian religious or charitable organization, without remuneration;

(g) a person whose work in Canada would create or maintain reciprocal employment for Canadian citizens or permanent residents of Canada in other countries and who is a family member of

(i) a properly accredited diplomat, consular officer, representative or official of a country other than Canada, of the United Nations or any of its agencies or of any intergovernmental organization of which Canada is a member,

(ii) a member of the armed forces of a country that is a designated state for the purposes of the *Visiting Forces Act*, including a person who has been designated as a civilian component of that visiting force under paragraph 4(c) of that Act, or

(iii) an officer of a foreign government sent, under an exchange agreement between Canada and one or more countries, to take up duties with a federal or provincial agency;

(h) a person who works in Canada under an agreement entered into with a country by Canada or by or on behalf of a province, that provides for reciprocal employment opportunities of an artistic, cultural or educational nature;

(i) a person whose work in Canada is pursuant to an international student or young workers reciprocal employment program;

(j) a person who works in Canada as an officer of the United States Immigration and Naturalization Service or of United States Customs carrying out pre-inspection duties, as an American member of the International Joint Commission or as a United States grain inspector, and their family members; and

(k) a United States Government official in possession of an official United States passport who is assigned to a temporary posting in Canada, and their family members.

(3) **Maximum fee** — The total amount of fees payable under subsection (1) by a group of three or more persons, consisting of performing artists and their staff, who apply at the same time and place for a work permit is $465.

SOR/2011-222, s. 8; SOR/2014-19, s. 4; SOR/2015-25, s. 4

Study Permits

300. (1) **Fee — $150** — A fee of $150 is payable for processing an application for a study permit.

(2) **Exception** — The following persons are not required to pay the fee referred to in subsection (1):

(a) a person in Canada who has made a refugee claim that has not yet been determined by the Refugee Protection Division, and their family members;

(b) a person in Canada on whom refugee protection has been conferred, and their family members;

(c) a person who is a member of the Convention refugees abroad class or a humanitarian-protected persons abroad class, and their family members;

(d) a properly accredited diplomat, consular officer, representative or official of a country other than Canada, of the United Nations or any of its agencies or of any intergovernmental organization of which Canada is a member, the members of the suite of such a person and the family members of such a person;

(e) a member of the armed forces of a country that is a designated state for the purposes of the *Visiting Forces Act*, including a person who has been designated as a civilian component of that visiting force under paragraph 4(c) of that Act, and their family members;

(f) a person who holds a study permit and is temporarily destitute, as described in paragraph 208(a);

(g) a person whose study in Canada is under an agreement or arrangement between Canada and another country that provides for reciprocity of student exchange programs;

(h) a person who works in Canada as an officer of the United States Immigration and Naturalization Service or of United States Customs carrying out pre-inspection duties, as an American member of the International Joint Commission or as a United States grain inspector, and their family members; and

(i) a United States Government official in possession of an official United States passport who is assigned to a temporary posting in Canada, and their family members.

SOR/2011-222, s. 9; SOR/2014-19, s. 5; SOR/2015-25, s. 5

DIVISION 3 — FEES FOR APPLICATIONS TO REMAIN IN CANADA AS A PERMANENT RESIDENT

301. (1) Fee — The following fees are payable for processing an application to remain in Canada as a permanent resident:

(a) if the application is made by a person as a member of the spouse or common-law partner in Canada class

(i) in respect of a principal applicant, $475,

(ii) in respect of a family member of the principal applicant who is a spouse or common-law partner, $550, and

(iii) in respect of a family member of the principal applicant who is a dependent child, $150; and

(b) if the application is made by a person as a member of the live-in caregiver class or as a protected person referred to in subsection 21(2) of the Act

(i) in respect of a principal applicant, $550,

(ii) in respect of a family member of the principal applicant who is a spouse or common-law partner, $550, and

(iii) in respect of a family member of the principal applicant who is a dependent child, $150.

(1.1) Exception — A person who is a member of the protected temporary residents class and the family members included in their application are not required to pay the fees referred to in subsection (1).

(2) Payment by sponsor — The fee payable under subsection (1) in respect of a person who makes an application as a member of the spouse or common-law partner in Canada class or their family members

(a) is payable, together with the fee payable under subsection 304(1), at the time the sponsor files the sponsorship application; and

(b) shall be repaid in accordance with regulations referred to in subsection 20(2) of the *Financial Administration Act* if, before the processing of the application to remain in Canada as a permanent resident has begun, the sponsorship application is withdrawn by the sponsor.

(3) Age — For the purposes of paragraph (1)(a), the age of the person in respect of whom the application is made shall be determined as of the day the sponsorship application is filed.

SOR/2004-167, s. 72; SOR/2009-163, s. 16; SOR/2012-154, s. 15; SOR/2014-133, s. 11

302. Fee — $325 — A fee of $475 is payable for processing an application by a person as a member of the permit holder class to remain in Canada as a permanent resident.

SOR/2004-167, s. 73

DIVISION 4 — RIGHT OF PERMANENT RESIDENCE

303. (1) Fee — $490 — A fee of $490 is payable by a person for the acquisition of permanent resident status.

(2) Exception — The following persons are not required to pay the fee referred to in subsection (1):

(a) a person who is a family member of a principal applicant and is a dependent child referred to in paragraph (b) or (c) of the definition "family member" in subsection 1(3);

(b) a principal applicant who is a foreign national referred to in paragraph 117(1)(b), (f) or (g);

(b.1) a principal applicant in Canada who has made an application in accordance with section 66 and is a dependent child of a permanent resident or of a Canadian citizen;

(b.2) a member of the permit holder class who is a dependent child of

(i) a member of the permit holder class who has made an application to remain in Canada as a permanent resident, or

(ii) a permanent resident or a Canadian citizen;

(c) a protected person within the meaning of subsection 95(2) of the Act who has applied to remain in Canada as a permanent resident, and their family members;

(c.1) a person who is a member of the protected temporary residents class and is described in paragraph 151.1(2)(b) and the family members included in their application;

(d) a person who is a member of the Convention refugees abroad class, and the family members included in their application; and

(e) a person who is a member of a humanitarian-protected persons abroad class, and the family members included in their application.

(3) Payment — The fee referred to in subsection (1) is payable

(a) in the case of an application by or on behalf of a person for a permanent resident visa, before the visa is issued; and

(b) in the case of an application by or on behalf of a foreign national to remain in Canada as a permanent resident, before the foreign national becomes a permanent resident.

(4) Remission — The fee referred to in subsection (1) is remitted if the person does not acquire permanent resident status, in which case the fee shall be repaid by the Minister to the person who paid it.

929

(5) Transitional — subsection (4) — For the purpose of subsection (4), if the fee was paid before the day on which this subsection comes into force, the amount to be remitted and repaid — except to the extent otherwise remitted — is $975.

(6) Transitional — remission — Despite subsections (4) and (5), in the case where the fee of $975 was paid in accordance with paragraph (3)(a), a portion of that fee in the amount of $485 is remitted and shall be repaid — except to the extent otherwise remitted — by the Minister to the person who paid the fee if

(a) the person in respect of whom the fee was paid has, on or before the day on which this subsection comes into force, not yet acquired permanent resident status and they are a person referred to in any of paragraphs 117(1)(a), (c), (d) or (h); or

(b) the person in respect of whom the fee was paid acquires permanent resident status on or after the day on which this subsection comes into force and they are not a person referred to in any of paragraphs 117(1)(a), (c), (d) or (h).

SOR/2004-167, s. 74(1), (2); SOR/2005-61, s. 8; SOR/2006-89, s. 1; SOR/2011-222, s. 10

DIVISION 4.1 — OTHER FEES IN RESPECT OF WORK PERMITS
[Heading added SOR/2015-25, s. 6.]

Compliance Regime — Employer Fee
[Heading added SOR/2015-25, s. 6.]

303.1 (1) Fee — $230 — A fee of $230 is payable by an employer who has made an offer of employment to

(a) a foreign national in respect of work described in section 204 or 205;

(b) a foreign national described in section 207; or

(c) a foreign national referred to in paragraph (a) or (b) who makes an application for renewal of a work permit.

(2) Electronic payment — The fee referred to in subsection (1) is payable by means of the electronic system that is made available by the Department for that purpose, before the foreign national to whom the offer of employment is made makes an application for a work permit or an application for renewal of the work permit.

(3) Fee paid — time — The fee is deemed to be paid on the date and at the time recorded in the electronic system.

(4) Other means of payment — If an employer is unable to pay the fee by means of the electronic system because of a physical or mental disability, the payment may be made by another means that is made available by the Department for that purpose and that would enable the employer to pay the fee.

(5) Exception — An employer is not required to pay the fee referred to in subsection (1) if the offer of employment is made to a foreign national — other than a person referred to in paragraph 299(2)(i) — who under subsection 299(2) is not required to pay a fee for processing an application for a work permit.

(6) Remission — The fee referred to in subsection (1) is remitted, and must be repaid by the Minister to the person who paid it, if

(a) the work permit is refused; or

(b) the employer withdraws the offer of employment and requests a remission before the work permit is issued.

(7) Maximum fee — The total amount of fees payable under subsection (1) by an employer who has made offers of employment to a group of three or more foreign nationals, consisting of performing artists and their staff, is $690, if those offers are made at the same time.

SOR/2015-25, s. 6

Rights and Privileges
[Heading added SOR/2015-25, s. 6.]

303.2 (1) Fee — $100 — A fee of $100 is payable by a person for the rights and privileges conferred by means of a work permit if that person is

(a) a foreign national who intends to perform work described in section 204 or 205 but does not have an offer of employment to perform that work;

(b) a foreign national described in paragraph 207(b) who does not have an offer of employment; or

(c) a family member of a foreign national referred to in paragraph (b).

(2) Exceptions — The following persons are not required to pay the fee referred to in subsection (1):

(a) a person — other than a person referred to in paragraph 299(2)(i) — who under subsection 299(2) is not required to pay a fee for processing an application for a work permit;

(b) a person referred to in paragraph 299(2)(i) who intends to perform work under an international agreement between Canada and one or more countries, if the agreement

(i) prohibits the payment of a fee other than a participation fee, and

(ii) is in force at the time that the person makes an application for a work permit or for renewal of the work permit; and

(c) a foreign national who has made an application for permanent residence as a member of the live-in caregiver class and the family members included in that application.

(3) Remission — The fee referred to in subsection (1) is remitted, and must be repaid by the Minister to the person who paid it, if

(a) the work permit is refused; or

(b) the foreign national withdraws their application and requests a remission before the work permit is issued.

SOR/2015-25, s. 6

DIVISION 5 — FEES FOR OTHER APPLICATIONS AND SERVICES

Sponsorship Application for Family Classes

304. (1) Fee — $75 — A fee of $75 is payable for processing a sponsorship application under Part 7.

(2) Payment — The fee referred to in subsection (1) is payable at the time the application is filed.

Extension of Authorization to Remain in Canada as a Temporary Resident

305. (1) Fee — $100 — A fee of $100 is payable for processing an application under subsection 181(1).

(2) Exception — The following persons are not required to pay the fee referred to in subsection (1):

(a) a person who makes an application for a work permit or a study permit at the same time as they make the application referred to in subsection (1);

(b) a person who has made a claim for refugee protection that has not yet been determined by the Refugee Protection Division;

(c) a person on whom refugee protection has been conferred;

(d) a person who is a member of the Convention refugees abroad class or a humanitarian-protected persons abroad class;

(e) a properly accredited diplomat, consular officer, representative or official of a country other than Canada, of the United Nations or any of its agencies or of any intergovernmental organization of which Canada is a member, the members of the suite of such a person and the family members of such a person;

(f) a member of the armed forces of a country that is a designated state for the purposes of the *Visiting Forces Act*, including a person who has been designated as a civilian component of that visiting force under paragraph 4(c) of that Act, and their family members;

(g) a person who is a member of the clergy, a member of a religious order or a lay person who is to assist a congregation or a group in the achievement of its spiritual goals, if the duties to be performed by the person are to consist mainly of preaching doctrine, presiding at liturgical functions or spiritual counselling, and their family members;

(h) an officer of a foreign government sent, under an exchange agreement between Canada and one or more countries, to take up duties with a federal or provincial agency; and

(i) a family member of any of the following persons, namely,

(i) a person who holds a study permit and is temporarily destitute, as described in paragraph 208(a),

(ii) a person whose work is designated under subparagraph 205(c)(i),

(iii) a person whose work in Canada is for a Canadian religious or charitable organization, without remuneration,

(iv) a person whose presence in Canada is as a participant in a program sponsored by the Canadian International Development Agency, or

(v) a person whose presence in Canada is as a recipient of a Government of Canada scholarship or fellowship.

SOR/2011-222, s. 11; SOR/2014-19, s. 6

Restoration of Temporary Resident Status

306. (1) **Fee — $200** — A fee of $200 is payable for processing an application under section 182.

(2) **Exception** — A person who holds an unexpired temporary resident permit is not required to pay the fee referred to in subsection (1).

Fees for a Request under Section 25 of the Act or an Examination of Circumstances under Section 25.2 of the Act

[Heading amended SOR/2015-95, s. 1.]

307. **Fees** — The following fees are payable for processing an application made in accordance with section 66 or for examining the circumstances under subsection 25.2(1) of the Act of a foreign national who applies for permanent resident status or for a permanent resident visa, if no fees are payable in respect of the same applicant for processing an application to remain in Canada as a permanent resident or an application for a permanent resident visa:

(a) in the case of a principal applicant, $550;

(b) in the case of a family member of the principal applicant who is a spouse or common-law partner, $550; and

(c) in the case of a family member of the principal applicant who is a dependent child, $150.

SOR/2014-133, s. 12; SOR/2015-95, s. 2

Permanent Resident Cards

308. (1) **Fee — $50** — A fee of $50 is payable for processing an application made under paragraph 53(1)(b) for a permanent resident card.

(2) Renewal or replacement fee — A fee of $50 is payable for processing an application for the renewal of a permanent resident card or for the replacement of a lost, stolen or destroyed permanent resident card.

(3) Replacement due to error — No fee is payable for the replacement of a permanent resident card containing an error that is not attributable to the permanent resident.

Determination of Rehabilitation

309. Fees — The following fees are payable for processing an application for a determination of rehabilitation under paragraph 36(3)(c) of the Act:

(a) in the case of a foreign national inadmissible on grounds of serious criminality under paragraph 36(1)(b) or (c) of the Act, $1,000; and

(b) in the case of a foreign national inadmissible on grounds of criminality under paragraph 36(2)(b) or (c) of the Act, $200.

Authorization to Return to Canada

310. Fee — $400 — A fee of $400 is payable for processing an application for authorization to return to Canada under subsection 52(1) of the Act.

Certification and Replacement of Immigration Document

311. (1) Certification — $30 — A fee of $30 is payable for processing an application for the certification of an immigration document, other than a permanent resident card, confirming the date on which a person became a permanent resident.

(2) Replacement — $30 — A fee of $30 is payable for processing an application to replace any immigration document, other than a permanent resident card, that is issued by the Department.

(3) Exception — The following persons are not required to pay the fee referred to in subsection (1):

(a) a federal, provincial or municipal government agency;

(b) a person in receipt of provincial social assistance payments; and

(c) a person in receipt of assistance under the Resettlement Assistance Program.

After-hours Examination

312. (1) Fee — $100 — The following fees are payable for an examination for the purpose of entering Canada that is made outside the applicable service hours of the port of entry where the officer who conducts the examination is based:

(a) a fee of $100 for the first four hours of examination; and

(b) a fee of $30 for each additional hour or part of an hour of examination.

(2) **Payment**   The fees are payable at the time of the examination

(a) if the transporter's vehicle carrying the person to be examined arrives unscheduled at a port of entry outside service hours, by the transporter; and

(b) in any other case, by the person who requests that the examination take place outside service hours.

Alternative Means of Examination

313. (1) **Fee — $30** — A fee of $30 is payable for processing an application to enroll in a program for an alternative means of examination that is administered solely by the Minister.

(2) **Payment** — The fee is payable in respect of each person to be examined by an alternative means referred to in subsection (1).

Immigration Statistical Data

314. (1) **Fee for statistical data** — The following fees are payable for processing an application for immigration statistical data that have not been published by the Department:

(a) $100 for the first 10 minutes or less of access to the Department's database in order to respond to such an application; and

(b) $30 for each additional minute or less of such access.

(2) **Exception** — The following persons are not required to pay the fees referred to in subsection (1):

(a) an employee of the Department; and

(b) an employee of the Data Development Division of the Department of Employment and Social Development.

(3) **Payment** — The fee referred to in subsection (1)(b) is payable at the time the service is rendered.

SOR/2009-163, s. 17; SOR/2010-172, s. 5(f); 2013, c. 40, s. 237(3)(a)

315. **Travel document** — A fee of $50 is payable for processing an application for a travel document issued under subsection 31(3) of the Act.

Services in Relation to the Collection, Use and Disclosure of Biometric Information

[Heading added SOR/2013-73, s. 4.]

315.1 (1) **Fee — $85** — A fee of $85 is payable for the provision of services in relation to the collection of biometric information under Division 2.1 of Part 1 in respect of an application for a temporary resident visa, a study permit or a work permit and to the use and disclosure of that information and for the provision of services related to those services.

935

IRP Regulations

(2) Exception — The following persons are not required to pay the fee referred to in subsection (1):

(a) a properly accredited diplomat, consular officer, representative or official of a country other than Canada, of the United Nations or any of its agencies or of any intergovernmental organization of which Canada is a member, the members of the suite of such a person and the family members of such a person;

(b) a member of the armed forces of a country that is a designated state for the purposes of the *Visiting Forces Act*, including a person who has been designated as a civilian component of that visiting force under paragraph 4(c) of that Act, and their family members;

(c) a person who is seeking to enter Canada

(i) for the purpose of attending a meeting hosted by the Government of Canada, an organization of the United Nations or the Organization of American States, as a participant,

(ii) for the purpose of attending a meeting as a representative of the Organization of American States or the Caribbean Development Bank, or

(iii) for the purpose of attending a meeting hosted by the Government of Canada, an organization of the United Nations or the Organization of American States, at the invitation of the Government of Canada;

(d) a person who is seeking to enter Canada as a competitor, coach, judge, team official, medical staff member or member of a national or international sports organizing body participating in the Pan-American Games, when held in Canada, or as a performer participating in a festival associated with any of those Games;

(e) a person who is seeking to enter Canada for a period of less than 48 hours and is

(i) travelling by transporter's vehicle to a destination other than Canada, or

(ii) transiting through or stopping over in Canada for refuelling or for the continuation of their journey in another transporter's vehicle;

(f) if the application is an application for a study permit or a work permit,

(i) the family members of a person in Canada who has made a refugee claim that has not yet been determined by the Refugee Protection Division,

(ii) the family members of a person in Canada on whom refugee protection has been conferred, and

(iii) the family members of a person who is a member of the Convention refugees abroad class or a member of a humanitarian-protected persons abroad class; and

(g) a person whose work in Canada would create or maintain reciprocal employment for Canadian citizens or permanent residents of Canada in other countries and who is a family member of an officer of a foreign government sent, under an exchange agreement between Canada and one or more countries, to take up duties with a federal or provincial agency.

(3) **Maximum fee** — The total amount of fees payable under subsection (1) is

(a) in relation to an application for a temporary resident visa, $170, if the applicant and their family members submit their application at the same time and place; and

(b) in relation to an application for a work permit, $255, if the applicants are a group of three or more persons, consisting of performing artists and their staff, who submit their applications at the same time and place.

SOR/2013-73, s. 4

Services in Relation to an Assessment from the Department of Employment and Social Development

[Heading added SOR/2013-149, s. 1. Amended 2013, c. 40, s. 237(3)(a); SOR/2015-147, s. 1(f).]

315.2 (1) **Fee — $1,000** — A fee of $1,000 is payable for the provision of services in relation to an assessment from the Department of Employment and Social Development that is requested by an employer or group of employers under subsection 203(2) for each offer of employment in respect of which the request is made.

(2) **Exceptions** — No fee is payable if the request is made in respect of an offer of employment that relates to

(a) work to be performed under an international agreement between Canada and one or more countries concerning seasonal agricultural workers; or

(b) any other work in the primary agriculture sector.

(3) **Payment** — The fee must be paid at the time the request is made.

(4) **Primary agriculture sector** — For the purposes of paragraph (2)(b), work in the primary agriculture sector means, subject to subsection (5), work that is performed within the boundaries of a farm, nursery or greenhouse and involves

(a) the operation of agricultural machinery;

(b) the boarding, care, breeding, sanitation or other handling of animals, other than fish, for the purpose of obtaining animal products for market, or activities relating to the collection, handling and assessment of those products; or

(c) the planting, care, harvesting or preparation of crops, trees, sod or other plants for market.

(5) **Exclusions** — Work in the primary agriculture sector does not include work involving

(a) the activities of agronomists or agricultural economists;

(b) landscape architecture;

(c) [Repealed SOR/2014-169, s. 1(2).]

(d) the preparation of vegetable fibres for textile use;

(e) activities related to commercial hunting and trapping; or

937

(f) veterinary activities.
SOR/2013-149, s. 1; 2013, c. 40, s. 237(3)(a); SOR/2014-169, s. 1; SOR/2015-147, s. 1(g)

PART 19.1 — INFORMATION SHARING BETWEEN COUNTRIES
[Heading added SOR/2014-6, s. 1.]

DIVISION 1 — AGREEMENT BETWEEN THE GOVERNMENT OF CANADA AND THE GOVERNMENT OF THE UNITED STATES OF AMERICA FOR THE SHARING OF VISA AND IMMIGRATION INFORMATION
[Heading added SOR/2014-6, s. 1.]

315.21 Interpretation — The definitions in this section apply in this Division.

"**Agreement**" means the *Agreement Between the Government of Canada and the Government of the United States of America for the Sharing of Visa and Immigration Information*, signed on December 13, 2012. *("Accord")*

"**national of a third country**" means a foreign national other than a national, citizen or permanent resident of the United States. *("ressortissant d'un pays tiers")*

"**parties**" means the parties to the Agreement, namely the Government of Canada and the Government of the United States. *("parties")*

"**query**" means a request that triggers an electronic search process requiring minimal human intervention. *("requête")*

SOR/2014-6, s. 1

315.22 Purpose — The purpose of this Division is to implement the Agreement, the objectives of which, as elaborated more specifically through its provisions, are to specify the terms, relationships, responsibilities and conditions for the parties to share information by means of a query to assist in the administration and enforcement of the parties' respective immigration laws.

SOR/2014-6, s. 1

315.23 (1) Authority to disclose information — The Minister may disclose information to the Government of the United States in making a query to that Government, or in response to a query made by that Government, only for the following purposes:

(a) to support an examination following an application made by a national of a third country for a permanent or temporary resident visa, a work or study permit, or to obtain protected person status or another immigration benefit under federal immigration legislation;

(b) to support an examination or determination as to whether a national of a third country is authorized to travel to, enter or remain in Canada or the Unites States, as the case may be; or

(c) to ensure the accuracy and reliability of biographic data or other immigration-related data.

(2) **Response to query — limitation** — In the case of a response to a query made by the Government of the United States, the Minister may disclose information only in respect of any of the following nationals of a third country:

(a) those who were previously determined to be inadmissible under the Act;

(b) those who did not meet the requirements under the Act;

(c) those in respect of whom a fingerprint match is established.

SOR/2014-6, s. 1

315.24 Necessary, relevant and proportionate information — Only information that is necessary, relevant and proportionate to achieving the purposes of this Division may be disclosed.

SOR/2014-6, s. 1

315.25 (1) Information categories — Only information belonging to the following information categories in respect of a national of a third country may be disclosed:

(a) biographic data to be used for the purposes of identity verification, such as name, alias, date of birth, country of birth, gender, citizenship and travel document number;

(b) biometric data consisting of a photograph, fingerprints or both to be used for the purposes of identity verification; and

(c) in the case of a response to a query made by the Government of the United States, other immigration-related data, including the immigration status of the national of a third country, a previous determination that the national of a third country failed to meet the requirements of Canada's immigration laws, a previous admissibility decision or determination and data relevant to the admissibility of the national of a third country if

(i) a match is established in respect of the biographic data referred to in paragraph (a); or

(ii) a match is established in respect of the biometric data referred to in paragraph (b).

(2) **Refugee claim — limitation on disclosure of data** — In the case of a response to a query made by the Government of the United States in respect of a national of a third country making a refugee claim in the United States, only information related to an application for a permanent or temporary resident visa, a work or study permit or another immigration benefit under federal immigration legislation may be disclosed.

(3) **Accuracy and reliability** — The disclosure must be made in a manner that ensures the accuracy and reliability of the information in question.

(4) Refusal to disclose — If the Minister determines that disclosing information in response to a query would be inconsistent with domestic law or detrimental to national sovereignty, national security, public policy, or other important national interests, the Minister may refuse to provide all or part of the available information or offer to provide all or part of the information subject to any terms and conditions that he or she may specify.

SOR/2014-6, s. 1

315.26 Destruction of information — Any information collected by the Minister that is determined not to be relevant to a query and that was not used for an administrative purpose, as defined in section 3 of the *Privacy Act*, must be destroyed as soon as feasible.

SOR/2014-6, s. 1

315.27 (1) Correction of previously disclosed information — If the Minister is made aware that previously disclosed information is inaccurate, the Minister must notify the Government of the United States and provide correcting information.

(2) Notification of correction and destruction of inaccurate information — If the Minister receives correcting information from the Government of the United States, the Minister must notify that Government once the necessary corrections have been made and, unless the information was used for an administrative purpose, as defined in section 3 of the *Privacy Act*, any inaccurate information and any information derived from that inaccurate information must be destroyed as soon as feasible.

(3) Note to file — If inaccurate information has been used for an administrative purpose, as defined in section 3 of the *Privacy Act*, a note must be placed in the file to that effect.

SOR/2014-6, s. 1

DIVISION 2 — ANNEX REGARDING THE SHARING OF INFORMATION ON ASYLUM AND REFUGEE STATUS CLAIMS TO THE STATEMENT OF MUTUAL UNDERSTANDING ON INFORMATION SHARING

[Heading added SOR/2014-6, s. 1.]

315.28 Interpretation — The definitions in this section apply in this Division.

"Asylum Annex" means the *Annex Regarding the Sharing of Information on Asylum and Refugee Status Claims to the Statement of Mutual Understanding on Information Sharing*, signed on behalf of Canada on August 22, 2003, as amended from time to time. (*"Annexe sur l'asile"*)

"participants" means the participants to the Asylum Annex, taking into account their successors, namely the Department of Citizenship and Immigration Canada, the Canada Border Services Agency and the Department of Homeland Security of the United States. (*"participants"*)

"refugee status claimant" means a person who has made a claim for refugee protection in Canada or at a port of entry. *("demandeur du statut de réfugié")*

SOR/2014-6, s. 1

315.29 Purpose — The purpose of this Division is to implement the Asylum Annex, the objectives of which, as elaborated more specifically through its provisions, are to

(a) preserve and protect the participants' refugee status determination systems;

(b) enhance the participants' abilities to assist those who qualify for protection from persecution or from torture;

(c) support efforts to share responsibility between the participants in providing protection to qualified refugee status claimants;

(d) identify and prevent abuse of the participants' refugee status determination systems and citizenship and immigration laws; and

(e) identify those who are excluded from protection or denied protection according to the Refugee Convention, as implemented in the participants' domestic legislation or whose refugee protection may be subject to termination, cancellation or revocation.

SOR/2014-6, s. 1

315.3 Authority to disclose information — The Minister may only disclose information to the Department of Homeland Security of the United States in respect of a refugee status claimant other than a refugee status claimant who is alleging persecution in the United States.

SOR/2014-6, s. 1

315.31 Necessary, relevant and proportionate information — Only information that is necessary, relevant and proportionate to achieving the purposes of this Division may be disclosed.

SOR/2014-6, s. 1

315.32 (1) Method of disclosure — The disclosure of information must be made in accordance with article 6 of the Asylum Annex.

(2) Accuracy and reliability — The disclosure must be made in a manner that ensures the accuracy and reliability of the information in question.

SOR/2014-6, s. 1

315.33 Data elements to be disclosed — Only information belonging to the following information categories may be disclosed:

(a) information relating to the identity of a refugee status claimant;

(b) information relating to the processing of a refugee status claimant's claim;

(c) information relevant to a decision to deny a refugee status claimant access to or to exclude such a claimant from the protection of the refugee status determination system or to cease, vacate or nullify a refugee status claimant's refugee protection; and

(d) information regarding the substance or history of a previous claim made by a refugee status claimant that will assist in determining a subsequent claim.

SOR/2014-6, s. 1

315.34 Destruction of information — Any information collected by the Minister that is determined not to be relevant to the purposes of this Division and that was not used for an administrative purpose, as defined in section 3 of the *Privacy Act*, must be destroyed as soon as feasible.

SOR/2014-6, s. 1

315.35 (1) Correction of previously disclosed information — If the Minister is made aware that previously disclosed information is inaccurate, the Minister must notify the Department of Homeland Security of the United States and provide correcting information.

(2) Notification of correction and destruction of inaccurate information — If the Minister receives correcting information from the Department of Homeland Security of the United States, the Minister must notify that Department once the necessary corrections have been made and, unless the information was used for an administrative purpose, as defined in section 3 of the *Privacy Act*, any inaccurate information and any information derived from that inaccurate information must be destroyed as soon as feasible.

(3) Note to file — If inaccurate information has been used for an administrative purpose, as defined in section 3 of the *Privacy Act*, a note must be placed in the file to that effect.

SOR/2014-6, s. 1

PART 20 — TRANSITIONAL PROVISIONS

DIVISION 1 — INTERPRETATION

316. (1) Definitions — The definitions in this subsection apply in this Part.

"former Regulations" means the *Immigration Regulations, 1978*, as enacted by Order in Council P.C. 1978-486 dated February 23, 1978 and registered as SOR/78-172. (*"ancien règlement"*)

"Humanitarian Designated Classes Regulations" means the *Humanitarian Designated Classes Regulations*, as enacted by Order in Council P.C. 1997-477 dated April 8, 1997 and registered as SOR/97-183. (*"Règlement sur les catégories d'immigrants précisées pour des motifs d'ordre humanitaire"*)

"Immigration Act Fees Regulations" means the *Immigration Act Fees Regulations*, as enacted by Order in Council P.C. 1996-2003 dated December 19, 1996 and registered as SOR/97-22. (*"Règlement sur les prix à payer — Loi sur l'immigration"*)

"Refugee Claimants Designated Class Regulations" means the *Refugee Claimants Designated Class Regulations*, as enacted by Order in Council P.C. 1989-2517 dated December 21, 1989 and registered as SOR/90-40. *("Règlement sur la catégorie admissible de demandeurs du statut de réfugié")*

(2) **Interpretation — former Act** — For greater certainty, in this Part "former Act" has the same meaning as in section 187 of the *Immigration and Refugee Protection Act*.

(3) **Interpretation — *Immigration and Refugee Protection Act*** — A reference in this Part to the *Immigration and Refugee Protection Act* includes the regulations and rules made under it.

DIVISION 2 — GENERAL PROVISIONS

317. (1) **Decisions and orders made under former Act** — A decision or order made under the former Act that is in effect immediately before the coming into force of this section continues in effect after that coming into force.

(2) **Documents issued under former Act** — A document, including a visa, that is issued under the former Act and is valid immediately before the coming into force of this section continues to be valid after that coming into force.

DIVISION 3 — ENFORCEMENT

318. **Terms and conditions** — Terms and conditions imposed under the former Act become conditions imposed under the *Immigration and Refugee Protection Act*.

Case Law

Gjoka v. Canada (Minister of Citizenship & Immigration) (2009), 84 Imm. L.R. (3d) 198, 352 F.T.R. 303, 2009 FC 943, 2009 CarswellNat 3058, 2009 CarswellNat 5358 (Eng.) — The applicant was selected on September 16, 2002, for permanent residence under the entrepreneur category and was issued a permanent resident visa on February 4, 2003, and landed on March 12, 2003. On May 28, 2004, in response to a letter from Canadian Immigration and Citizenship, the applicant submitted a monitoring report and an application to cancel his terms and conditions of landing. No other monitoring reports were submitted. A report pursuant to subs. 41(1) of the Act alleging that the applicant had failed to comply with the terms and conditions of his landing was issued on March 18, 2009. An inadmissibility hearing was held before the ID on May 7, 2008. The respondent submitted that the applicant had not met the conditions imposed on him under the *Immigration Regulations* (the former Regulations), specifically paras. 23.1(1)(a) to (d). The applicant made his application for permanent residency under the former Act but the selection decision and his permanent resident visa were issued after the coming into force of the current Act. Furthermore, the Confirmation of Permanent Residence form signed by the applicant upon landing specified that the conditions to be met were those of the former Regulations and s. 23.1 of those Regulations was attached to the form. At the admissibility hearing, the ID member found that the conditions imposed on the applicant were of s. 98 of the current Regulations and as such, this subs. 44(1) report alleging a failure to meet the conditions under the former Regulations was unfounded. Following an appeal by the Minister, the IAD set aside the ID's decision and referred the matter back for reconsideration. The IAD accepted the conclusion that the applicant was subject to the conditions set out in s. 98 of the current Regulations and referred the matter back to the ID to determine whether or not the applicant had met the conditions imposed under the Act.

Because of the transitional provisions and s. 318 of the current Regulations, the court found that the entrepreneur class selected applicants under the former *Immigration Act* are required to comply with post-admission to Canada terms and conditions as set out in paras. 23(a) to (d) of the former *Immigration Regulations*. The interpretation of the transitional provisions of the IAD is too restrictive. It implies that s. 98 of the current Regulations can be applied retroactively to entrepreneurial applicants who filed their application prior to January 1, 2002, and were assessed and issued visas as entrepreneur under the former *Immigration Act* and Regulations. Nothing in the Act, the current Regulations or the transitional provisions support such a proposition. The application for judicial review was allowed.

319. (1) Removal order — Subject to subsection (2), a removal order made under the former Act that was unexecuted on the coming into force of this section continues in force and is subject to the provisions of the *Immigration and Refugee Protection Act*.

(2) Stay of removal — The execution of a removal order that had been stayed on the coming into force of this section under paragraphs 49(1)(c) to (f) of the former Act continues to be stayed until the earliest of the events described in paragraphs 231(1)(a) to (e).

(3) Exception — Subsection (2) does not apply if

(a) the subject of the removal order was determined by the Convention Refugee Determination Division not to have a credible basis for their claim; or

(b) the subject of the removal order

(i) is subject to a removal order because they are inadmissible on grounds of serious criminality, or

(ii) resides or sojourns in the United States or St. Pierre and Miquelon and is the subject of a report prepared under subsection 44(1) of the *Immigration and Refugee Protection Act* on their entry into Canada.

(4) Conditional removal order — A conditional removal order made under the former Act continues in force and is subject to subsection 49(2) of the *Immigration and Refugee Protection Act*.

(5) Executed removal order — Section 52 of the *Immigration and Refugee Protection Act* applies to a person who immediately before the coming into force of this section was outside Canada after a removal order was executed against them.

320. (1) Inadmissibility — security grounds — A person is inadmissible under the *Immigration and Refugee Protection Act* on security grounds if, on the coming into force of this section, the person had been determined to be a member of an inadmissible class described in paragraph 19(1)(e), (f), (g) or (k) of the former Act.

(2) **Violating human or international rights** — A person is inadmissible under the *Immigration and Refugee Protection Act* on grounds of violating human or international rights if, on the coming into force of this section, the person had been determined to be a member of an inadmissible class described in paragraph 19(1)(j) or (l) of the former Act.

(2.1) **Paragraph 19(1)(l) of the former Act** — For greater certainty, an opinion of the Minister under paragraph 19(1)(l) of the former Act continues as an opinion of the Minister under paragraph 35(1)(b) of the *Immigration and Refugee Protection Act*.

(3) **Serious criminality** — A person is inadmissible under the *Immigration and Refugee Protection Act* on grounds of serious criminality if, on the coming into force of this section, the person had been determined to be a member of an inadmissible class described in paragraph 19(1)(c) or (c.1) of the former Act or had been determined to be inadmissible on the basis of paragraph 27(1)(a.1) of the former Act.

(4) **Criminality** — A person is inadmissible under the *Immigration and Refugee Protection Act* on grounds of criminality if, on the coming into force of this section, the person had been determined to be a member of an inadmissible class described in paragraph 19(2)(a), (a.1) or (b) of the former Act, or had been determined to be inadmissible on the basis of paragraph 27(1)(a.2) or (a.3) or (2)(d) of the former Act.

(5) **Paragraph 27(1)(d) of former Act** — A person who on the coming into force of this section had been determined to be inadmissible on the basis of paragraph 27(1)(d) of the former Act is

(a) inadmissible under the *Immigration and Refugee Protection Act* on grounds of serious criminality if the person was convicted of an offence and a term of imprisonment of more than six months has been imposed or a term of imprisonment of 10 years or more could have been imposed; or

(b) inadmissible under the *Immigration and Refugee Protection Act* on grounds of criminality if the offence was punishable by a maximum term of imprisonment of five years or more but less than 10 years.

(6) **Organized crime** — A person is inadmissible under the *Immigration and Refugee Protection Act* on grounds of organized criminality if, on the coming into force of this section, the person had been determined to be a member of an inadmissible class described in paragraph 19(1)(c.2) or subparagraph 19(1)(d)(ii) of the former Act.

(7) **Health grounds** — A person — other than an applicant described in section 7 of the former Regulations or section 4 of *Humanitarian Designated Classes Regulations* who made an application for admission under the former Act — is inadmissible under the *Immigration and Refugee Protection Act* on health grounds if, on the coming into force of this section, the person had been determined to be a member of the inadmissible class described in paragraph 19(1)(a) of the former Act.

(8) Financial reasons — A person is inadmissible under the *Immigration and Refugee Protection Act* for financial reasons if, on the coming into force of this section, the person had been determined to be a member of the inadmissible class described in paragraph 19(1)(b) of the former Act or had been determined to be inadmissible on the basis of paragraph 27(1)(f) or (2)(l) of the former Act.

(9) Misrepresentation — A person is inadmissible under the *Immigration and Refugee Protection Act* for misrepresentation if, on the coming into force of this section, the person had been determined to be inadmissible on the basis of paragraph 27(1)(e) or (2)(g) or (i) of the former Act.

(10) Failing to comply — A person is inadmissible under the *Immigration and Refugee Protection Act* for failing to comply with that Act if, on the coming into force of this section, the person had been determined to be a member of an inadmissible class described in paragraph 19(1)(h) or (i) or (2)(c) or (d) of the former Act, or had been determined to be inadmissible on the basis of paragraph 27(1)(b) or (2)(b), (e), (f), (h), (i) or (k) of the former Act.

SOR/2004-167, s. 75

321. (1) Reports — A report made under section 20 or 27 of the former Act is a report under subsection 44(1) of the *Immigration and Refugee Protection Act*.

(2) Equivalency — For the purpose of subsection (1)

(a) inadmissibility as a member of a class described in paragraph 19(1)(e), (f), (g) or (k) of the former Act is inadmissibility on security grounds under the *Immigration and Refugee Protection Act*;

(b) inadmissibility as a member of a class described in paragraph 19(1)(j) or (l) of the former Act is inadmissibility under the *Immigration and Refugee Protection Act* on grounds of violating human or international rights;

(c) inadmissibility as a member of a class described in paragraph 19(1)(c) or (c.1) of the former Act or inadmissibility on the basis of paragraph 27(1)(a.1) of the former Act is inadmissibility under the *Immigration and Refugee Protection Act* on grounds of serious criminality;

(d) inadmissibility as a member of a class described in paragraph 19(2)(a), (a.1) or (b) of the former Act or inadmissibility on the basis of paragraph 27(1)(a.2) or (a.3) or (2)(d) of the former Act is inadmissibility under the *Immigration and Refugee Protection Act* on grounds of criminality;

(e) inadmissibility on the basis of paragraph 27(1)(d) of the former Act is inadmissibility under the *Immigration and Refugee Protection Act* on grounds of

(i) serious criminality, if the person was convicted of an offence and a term of imprisonment of more than six months has been imposed or a term of imprisonment of 10 years or more could have been imposed, or

(ii) criminality if the offence was punishable by a maximum term of imprisonment of five years or more but less than 10 years;

(f) inadmissibility as a member of a class described in paragraph 19(1)(c.2) or subparagraph 19(1)(d)(ii) of the former Act is inadmissibility under the *Immigration and Refugee Protection Act* on grounds of organized criminality;

(g) inadmissibility as a member of the inadmissible class described in paragraph 19(1)(a) of the former Act — other than an applicant described in section 7 of the former Regulations or section 4 of the *Humanitarian Designated Classes Regulations* who made an application for admission under the former Act — is inadmissibility under the *Immigration and Refugee Protection Act* on health grounds if, on the coming into force of this section, the person had been determined to be a member of file inadmissible class described in paragraph 19(1)(a) of the former Act;

(h) inadmissibility as a member of a class described in paragraph 19(1)(b) of the former Act or inadmissibility on the basis of paragraph 27(1)(f) or (2)(l) of the former Act is inadmissibility under the *Immigration and Refugee Protection Act* for financial reasons;

(i) inadmissibility on the basis of paragraph 27(1)(e) or (2)(g) or (i) of the former Act is inadmissibility under the *Immigration and Refugee Protection Act* for misrepresentation; and

(j) inadmissibility as a member of a class described in paragraph 19(1)(h) or (i) or (2)(c) or (d) of the former Act or inadmissibility on the basis of paragraph 27(1)(b) or (2)(b), (e), (f), (h), (i) or (k) of the former Act is inadmissibility under the *Immigration and Refugee Protection Act* for failing to comply with the Act.

(3) **Reports forwarded to a senior immigration officer** — A report that was forwarded to a senior immigration officer under the former Act and in respect of which a decision has not been made on the coming into force of this section is a report transmitted to the Minister.

(4) **Inquiry** — The causing by a senior immigration officer of an inquiry to be held under the former Act is the referring by the Minister of a report to the Immigration Division under subsection 44(2) of the *Immigration and Refugee Protection Act* unless that subsection allows the Minister to make a removal order.

(5) **No substantive evidence** — If no substantive evidence was adduced before the Adjudication Division, the causing by a senior immigration officer of an inquiry to be held under the former Act is, if subsection 44(2) of the *Immigration and Refugee Protection Act* allows the Minister to make a removal order, a report on the basis of which the Minister may make a removal order.

322. (1) **Detention** — The first review of reasons, after the coming into force of this section, for the continued detention of a person detained under the former Act shall be made in accordance with the provisions of the former Act.

(2) **Period of detention** — If the review referred to in subsection (1) was the first review in respect of a person's detention, the period of detention at the end of which that review was made shall be considered the period referred to in subsection 57(1) of the *Immigration and Refugee Protection Act*.

(3) **Subsequent review** — If a review of reasons for continued detention follows the review referred to in subsection (1), that review shall be made under the *Immigration and Refugee Protection Act*.

323. Order issued by Deputy Minister — An order issued by a Deputy Minister under subsection 105(1) of the former Act continues in force and the review of reasons for continued detention shall be made under the *Immigration and Refugee Protection Act*.

324. Release — A release from detention under the former Act is the ordering of release from detention under the *Immigration and Refugee Protection Act* and any terms and conditions imposed under the former Act become conditions imposed under the *Immigration and Refugee Protection Act*.

325. (1) Warrants — A warrant for arrest and detention made under the former Act is a warrant for arrest and detention made under the *Immigration and Refugee Protection Act*.

(2) Detention orders — An order for the detention of a person made under the former Act is an order to detain made under the *Immigration and Refugee Protection Act*.

326. (1) Danger to the public — A claim to be a Convention refugee made by a person described in subparagraph 19(1)(c.1)(i) of the former Act in respect of whom the Minister was of the opinion under subparagraph 46.01(1)(e)(i) of the former Act that the person constitutes a danger to the public in Canada is deemed, if no determination was made by a senior immigration officer under section 45 of the former Act, to be a claim for refugee protection made by a person described in paragraph 101(2)(b) of the *Immigration and Refugee Protection Act* who is inadmissible and in respect of whom the Minister is of the opinion that the person is a danger to the public.

(2) Appeals — A person in respect of whom subsection 70(5) or paragraph 77(3.01)(b) of the former Act applied on the coming into force of this section is a person in respect of whom subsection 64(1) of the *Immigration and Refugee Protection Act* applies.

(3) Removal not prohibited — A person whose removal on the coming into force of this section was allowed by the application of paragraphs 53(1)(a) to (d) of the former Act is a person referred to in subsection 115(2) of the *Immigration and Refugee Protection Act*.

Case Law

Section 326(2)

Townsend v. Canada (Minister of Citizenship & Immigration) (2004), 41 Imm. L.R. (3d) 1, 2004 CarswellNat 5639, 2004 CarswellNat 4723, 331 N.R. 62, 2004 FCA 436 — If a person has been convicted of a crime that was punished in Canada by a term of imprisonment of less than two years, and found to be a danger to the public under subs. 70(5) of the former *Immigration Act* so that person had no right of an appeal to the IAD under the former *Immigration Act*, then s. 326(2) of the *Immigration and Refugee Protection Regulations* bar an appeal to the IAD.

327. Certificates — A certificate determined to be reasonable under paragraph 40.1(4)(d) of the former Act is deemed to be a certificate determined to be reasonable under subsection 80(1) of the *Immigration and Refugee Protection Act*.

328. (1) Permanent residents — A person who was a permanent resident immediately before the coming into force of this section is a permanent resident under the *Immigration and Refugee Protection Act*.

(2) Returning resident permit — Any period spent outside Canada within the five years preceding the coming into force of this section by a permanent resident holding a returning resident permit is considered to be a period spent in Canada for the purpose of satisfying the residency obligation under section 28 of the *Immigration and Refugee Protection Act* if that period is included in the five-year period referred to in that section.

(3) Returning resident permit — Any period spent outside Canada within the two years immediately following the coming into force of this section by a permanent resident holding a returning resident permit is considered to be a period spent in Canada for the purpose of satisfying the residency obligation under section 28 of the *Immigration and Refugee Protection Act* if that period is included in the five-year period referred to in that section.

329. (1) Visitors and permit holders — Any of the following persons who were in Canada immediately before the coming into force of this section are temporary residents under the *Immigration and Refugee Protection Act* and are subject to its provisions:

(a) a visitor under the former Act; and

(b) a person issued a permit under section 37 of the former Act.

(2) Permits — A permit issued by the Minister under section 37 of the former Act is deemed to be a temporary resident permit referred to in section 24 of the *Immigration and Refugee Protection Act*.

330. Examination — Any of the following persons who were in Canada immediately before the coming into force of this section are deemed to have been authorized under section 23 of the *Immigration and Refugee Protection Act* to enter Canada:

(a) a person in respect of whom an examination remains incomplete and whose examination was adjourned and referred to another immigration officer for completion under subsection 12(3) of the former Act;

(b) a person in respect of whom an examination remains incomplete and whose examination was deferred under paragraph 13(1)(a) of the former Act;

(c) a person in respect of whom an examination remains incomplete and who was authorized to come into Canada for further examination under paragraph 14(2)(b) of the former Act;

(d) a person in respect of whom an examination remains incomplete and who was authorized to come into Canada for further examination under paragraph 23(1)(b) of the former Act; and

IRP Regulations

(e) a person who has made a claim to be a Convention refugee in respect of which a determination of eligibility was not made before the coming into force of this section.

331. Performance bonds and security deposits — A performance bond posted or security deposited under the former Act that remains posted or deposited immediately before the coming into force of this section continues as a deposit or a guarantee under the *Immigration and Refugee Protection Act* and is governed by its provisions.

332. Seizures — A thing seized under the former Act continues to be seized on the coming into force of this section, and the seizure is governed by the provisions of the *Immigration and Refugee Protection Act*.

333. Debts — Any debt under subsection 118(3) of the former Act continues as a debt on the coming into force of this section and is governed by the provisions of the *Immigration and Refugee Protection Act*.

DIVISION 4 — REFUGEE AND HUMANITARIAN RESETTLEMENT PROGRAM

334. Applications for protection abroad — With the exception of subsection 140.3(1) of these Regulations, the *Immigration and Refugee Protection Act* applies to an applicant described in section 7 of the former Regulations or section 4 of the *Humanitarian Designated Classes Regulations*, who made an application for admission under the former Act if the application is pending on the day on which this section comes into force and no visa has been issued to the applicant.

SOR/2012-225, s. 10

335. Family member — An applicant described in section 7 of the former Regulations or section 4 of the *Humanitarian Designated Classes Regulations* who made an application for admission under the former Act that has not been refused may add to their application at any time prior to their departure for Canada a person included in the definition "family member" in subsection 1(3).

336. Sponsorship agreements — A sponsorship agreement with the Minister made under the former Act and former Regulations does not cease to have effect for the sole reason of section 152 coming into force.

337. (1) Sponsors — Subject to subsections (2) and (3), a sponsor who made an undertaking within the meaning of paragraph (b) of the definition "undertaking" in subsection 2(1) of the former Regulations, or of the definition "undertaking" in subsection 1(1) of the *Humanitarian Designated Classes Regulations*, and in respect of whom an immigration officer was satisfied that the requirements of paragraph 7.1(2)(d) or 5(2)(d) of those Regulations, respectively, were met is deemed to be a sponsor whose application has been approved by an officer under section 154.

(2) Additional persons sponsored — Subsection (1) does not apply to a sponsor who requests that a person be added to their undertaking.

(3) Ineligibility to sponsor — Subsection (1) does not apply to a sponsor who is ineligible to be a party to a sponsorship under section 156.

DIVISION 5 — REFUGEE PROTECTION

338. Refugee protection — Refugee protection is conferred under the *Immigration and Refugee Protection Act* on a person who

(a) has been determined in Canada before the coming into force of this section to be a Convention refugee and

(i) no determination was made to vacate that determination, or

(ii) no determination was made that the person ceased to be a Convention refugee;

(b) as an applicant or an accompanying dependant was granted landing before the coming into force of this section after being issued a visa under

(i) section 7 of the former Regulations, or

(ii) section 4 of the *Humanitarian Designated Classes Regulations*; or

(c) was determined to be a member of the post-determination refugee claimants in Canada class before the coming into force of this section and was granted landing under section 11.4 of the former Regulations or who becomes a permanent resident under subsection 21(2) of the *Immigration and Refugee Protection Act.*

339. Rejection of a claim for refugee protection — A determination made in Canada before the coming into force of this section that a person is not a Convention refugee is deemed to be a claim for refugee protection rejected by the Board.

340. Ineligibility — A determination made before the coming into force of this section that a person is not eligible to have their Convention refugee claim determined by the Convention Refugee Determination Division is deemed to be a determination that the claim is ineligible to be referred to the Refugee Protection Division.

341. Withdrawal and abandonment — A claim to be a Convention refugee that was withdrawn or declared to be abandoned before the coming into force of this section is deemed to be a claim determined to be withdrawn or abandoned under the *Immigration and Refugee Protection Act.*

342. Eligibility — A claim made in Canada to be a Convention refugee in respect of which a determination of eligibility was not made before the coming into force of this section is deemed to be a claim for refugee protection made in Canada that is received on the day on which this section comes into force.

343. Redetermination of eligibility — Subject to section 191 of the *Immigration and Refugee Protection Act*, a claim of a person who was determined eligible before the coming into force of this section to have a claim to be a Convention refugee determined by the Convention Refugee Determination Division, and in respect of which no determination was made by that Division, is a claim that

   (a) is referred under the *Immigration and Refugee Protection Act* to the Refugee Protection Division unless an officer gives notice under subsection 104(1) of that Act; and

   (b) is subject to the provisions of that Act.

344. Cessation of refugee protection — A determination made in Canada before the coming into force of this section that a person has ceased to be a Convention refugee is deemed to be a determination by the Board that refugee protection has ceased.

345. Vacation — A decision made in Canada before the coming into force of this section to approve an application to reconsider and vacate a determination that a person is a Convention refugee is deemed to be a determination by the Board to vacate a decision to allow a claim for refugee protection.

346. (1) Post-determination refugee claimants in Canada class — An application for landing as a member of the post-determination refugee claimants in Canada class in respect of which no determination of whether the applicant is a member of that class was made before the coming into force of this section is an application for protection under sections 112 to 114 of the *Immigration and Refugee Protection Act* and those sections apply to the application.

(2) Notification re additional submissions — Before a decision is made on the application, the applicant shall be notified that they may make additional submissions in support of their application.

(3) Decision — A decision on the application shall not be made until 30 days after notification is given to the applicant.

(4) Giving notification — Notification is given

   (a) when it is given by hand to the applicant; or

   (b) if it is sent by mail, seven days after the day on which it was sent to the applicant at the last address provided by them to the Department.

(5) Stay of removal — For greater certainty, the execution of a removal order made under the former Act against an applicant referred to in subsection (1) is stayed, and the stay is effective until the earliest of the applicable events described in section 232 occurs.

SOR/2004-167, s. 76

347. (1) Application for landing — Convention refugees — If landing was not granted before the coming into force of this section, an application for landing submitted under section 46.04 of the former Act is an application to remain in Canada as a permanent resident under subsection 21(2) of the *Immigration and Refugee Protection Act*.

(2) Application for landing — undocumented Convention refugee in Canada class — If landing was not granted before June 28, 2002, an application for landing as a member of the undocumented Convention refugee in Canada class is an application to remain in Canada as a permanent resident under subsection 21(2) of the *Immigration and Refugee Protection Act*.

(3) Application for landing — post-determination refugee claimants in Canada class — If landing was not granted before the coming into force of this section, an application for landing submitted by a person pursuant to a determination that the person is a member of the post-determination refugee claimants in Canada class is an application to remain in Canada as a permanent resident under subsection 21(2) of the *Immigration and Refugee Protection Act*.

SOR/2012-154, s. 16

DIVISION 6 — COURT PROCEEDINGS

348. (1) Judicial review — On the coming into force of this section, any application for leave to commence an application for judicial review and any application for judicial review or appeal from an application that was brought under the former Act that is pending before the Federal Court or the Supreme Court of Canada is deemed to have been commenced under Division 8 of Part 1 of the *Immigration and Refugee Protection Act* and is governed by the provisions of that Division and section 87.

(2) Application for non-disclosure — On the coming into force of this section, any application under subsection 82.1(10) of the former Act that is pending before the Federal Court is deemed to be an application under section 87 of the *Immigration and Refugee Protection Act*.

(3) Where no leave required — Despite subsection (1), an application for judicial review that was not subject to the requirement of an application for leave under the former Act and was pending on the coming into force of this section does not require such an application under the *Immigration and Refugee Protection Act*.

(4) Judicial review after coming into force — Any judicial review proceeding brought in respect of any decision or order made or any matter arising under the former Act after the coming into force of this section is governed by Division 8 of Part 1 and section 87 of the *Immigration and Refugee Protection Act*.

(5) Time for filing — A person in respect of whom the 30-day period provided by section 18.1 of the *Federal Courts Act* for making an application for judicial review from a decision or matter referred to in subsection 82.1(2) of the former Act has not elapsed on the coming into force of this section and who has not made such an application has 60 days from the coming into force of this section to file an application for leave under section 72 of the *Immigration and Refugee Protection Act*.

(6) Validity or lawfulness of a decision or act — The validity or lawfulness of a decision or act made under the former Act that is the subject of a judicial review procedure or appeal referred to in subsection (1) is determined in accordance with the provisions of the former Act.

2002, c. 8, s. 182(3)(a)

Case Law

Section 348(1)

Dragosin v. Canada (Minister of Citizenship & Immigration) (2003), 26 Imm. L.R. (3d) 119, 2003 CarswellNat 175, 2003 CarswellNat 988, 2003 FCT 81, 227 F.T.R. 16, 106 C.R.R. (2d) 92 (T.D.) — This was a judicial review of an exclusion order against the applicant who, as a stowaway, arrived in Halifax in November 2001. Upon his arrival ashore in Halifax, the applicant was turned over to the Immigration Department and eventually ordered detained under s. 103.1(a) of the *Immigration Act*. The applicant was interviewed after his detention. He had not, at the time of the second interview, had any contact with counsel. Pursuant to s. 348(1) of IRPA Regulations and s. 190 of IRPA, this proceeding is governed by IRPA, but s. 348(6) of IRPA Regulations provides that the lawfulness or validity of a decision made or done under the *Immigration Act* is to be determined under the provisions of the *Immigration Act*.

The applicant's right to counsel arose at the moment he was ordered detained. The immigration officers who arranged his detention had the responsibility to provide advice about, and to facilitate access to, counsel. It was an error in law not to do so. The exclusion order was set aside because of this failure and an order was issued directing reconsideration of the applicant's circumstances by a different immigration officer.

349. Other court proceedings — On the coming into force of this section, an appeal made under section 102.17 of the former Act or an application for an order made under section 102.2 of the former Act that is pending remains governed by the provisions of the former Act.

350. (1) Decisions referred back — Subject to subsections (2) and (3), if a decision or an act of the Minister or an immigration officer under the former Act is referred back by the Federal Court or Supreme Court of Canada for determination and the determination is not made before this section comes into force, the determination shall be made in accordance with the *Immigration and Refugee Protection Act*.

(2) Decisions or acts not provided for by *Immigration and Refugee Protection Act* — If the decision or act referred to in subsection (1) was made under paragraph 46.01(1)(e), subsection 70(5) or paragraph 77(3.01)(b) of the former Act and the *Immigration and Refugee Protection Act* makes no provision for the decision or act, no determination shall be made.

(3) Skilled workers and self-employed persons — If a decision or an act of the Minister or an immigration officer under the former Act in respect of a person described in subparagraph 9(1)(b)(i) or paragraph 10(1)(b) of the former Regulations is referred back by the Federal Court or Supreme Court of Canada for determination and the determination is not made before December 1, 2003, the determination shall be made in accordance with subsections 361(4) and (5.2) of these Regulations.

(4) Investors, entrepreneurs and provincial nominees — If a decision or an act of the Minister or an Immigration officer under the former Act in respect of a person described in subparagraph 9(1)(b)(ii) or (iii) of the former Regulations is referred back by the Federal Court or Supreme Court of Canada for determination and the determination is not made before December 1, 2003, the determination shall be made in accordance with subsections 361(5), (5.1) and (6) of these Regulations.

(5) Immigration Appeal Division decisions — If a decision of the Immigration Appeal Division made under the former Act is referred back by the Federal Court or Supreme Court of Canada for determination and the determination is not made before the date of the coming into force of this section, the Immigration Appeal Division shall dispose of the matter in accordance with the former Act.

(6) Adjudication Division decisions — If a decision of the Adjudication Division made under the former Act is referred back by the Federal Court or Supreme Court of Canada for determination and the determination is not made before the date of the coming into force of this section, the immigration Division shall dispose of the matter in accordance with the *Immigration and Refugee Protection Act*.

SOR/2003-383, s. 7

Case Law

Section 350(1)

Karmali v. Canada (Minister of Citizenship & Immigration) (2003), 30 Imm. L.R. (3d) 90, 2003 CarswellNat 800, 2003 CarswellNat 2109, 2003 FCT 358, 230 F.T.R. 140 (T.D.) — Section 190 of IRPA and s. 350 of the Regulations do not apply retroactively. They do not state that IRPA should govern as though it was enforced in 1997, rather they state that applications still pending, and specifically applications sent back for re-determination after IRPA came into force, are to be dealt with under IRPA.

The applicant does not have a vested right to have his application re-determined under the law as it existed at the date of the application. Section 190 of IRPA and s. 350 of the Regulations deal with, in clear terms, the manner in which a matter sent back for re-determination is to be re-considered.

The language of s. 190 is not permissive. When s. 190 of IRPA and s. 350 of the Regulations are read together they clearly provide a complete framework for dealing with applications that are referred back by the court for re-determination.

Section 350 of the Regulations is not *ultra vires* the framework of s. 190. Section 201 of the IRPA allows for Regulations regarding the transition between the former Act and IRPA.

Finally s. 190 of IRPA does not offend subs. 2(e) of the *Canadian Bill of Rights* as it does not deprive a person of the right to a fair hearing.

Section 350(3)

Chen v. Canada (Minister of Citizenship & Immigration) (2003), 27 Imm. L.R. (3rd) 18, 2003 CarswellNat 804, 2003 CarswellNat 2106, 2003 FCT 368 (T.D.) — Section 201 of IRPA provides authority for subs. 350(3) of the Regulations and therefore subs. 350(3) of the Regulations is not *ultra vires*.

Section 350(5)

Denton-James v. Canada (Minister of Citizenship & Immigration), 2004 CarswellNat 2902, 2004 CarswellNat 1942, 254 F.T.R. 290, 2004 FC 911 — Section 350(5) of the IRP Regulations applies to a decision of the IAD that is remitted for re-determination by the Federal Court after June 28, 2002.

DIVISION 7 — UNDERTAKINGS

351. (1) Application of the Act to existing undertakings — Subject to sub-section (2), an undertaking referred to in section 118 of the former Act that was given before the day on which this section comes into force is governed by the *Immigration and Refugee Protection Act*.

(2) Recovery of social assistance payments — Payments that are made to or for the benefit of a person as social assistance or as financial assistance in the form of funds from a government resettlement assistance program referred to in subparagraph 139(1)(f)(ii) as a result of the breach of an undertaking, within the meaning of subparagraph (a)(ii) or paragraph (b) of the definition "undertaking" in subsection 2(1) of the former Regulations or of the definition "undertaking" in sub-section 1(1) of the *Humanitarian Designated Classes Regulations*, that was given before the day on which this section comes into force, may be recovered from the person or organization that gave the undertaking as a debt due to Her Majesty in right of Canada or in right of a province.

(3) Duration — For greater certainty, the duration of an undertaking referred to in section 118 of the former Act that was given to the Minister before the day on which this section comes into force is not affected by these Regulations.

(4) Duration and terms — For greater certainty, if an immigrant visa was issued to a person described in section 7 of the former Regulations or section 4 of the *Humanitarian Designated Classes Regulations* before the day on which this section comes into force, the duration and terms of an undertaking, referred to in section 118 of the former Act, relating to that person are not affected by these Regulations.

DIVISION 8 — NON-ACCOMPANYING FAMILY MEMBERS

352. Not required to be included — A person is not required to include in an application a non-accompanying common-law partner or a non-accompanying child who is not a dependent son or a dependent daughter within the meaning of subsection 2(1) of the former Regulations and is a dependent child as defined in section 2 of these Regulations if the application was made under the former Act before the day on which this section comes into force.

Case Law

Natt v. Canada (Minister of Citizenship & Immigration) (2004), 36 Imm. L.R. (3d) 292, 254 F.T.R. 122, 2004 CarswellNat 1693, 2004 FC 810, [2004] F.C.J. No. 997 — This was an application to review a decision of the Immigration Appeal Division. The applicant married a Canadian citizen who then sponsored her application for permanent residence. The applicant did not disclose that she had two children and on this basis was granted permanent residence. In May 2001, the applicant sponsored applications for permanent residence for her two children. A visa officer refused these applications and the applicant appealed to the Appeal Division who dismissed her appeal.

The central issue was whether Regulation 117(9)(d) applied to the two children as members of the family class. The purpose of this provision is to ensure that foreign nationals seeking permanent residence do not omit non-accompanying dependent members from their application, thereby avoiding their examination for admissibility at that time, and then, once having obtained their own permanent residence status, seek to sponsor their dependants and benefit from the preferential processing as well as admission treatments given to members of the family class. The sole exception is with respect to the children of sponsors whose applications for permanent residence were made before June 28, 2002, where those children meet the definition of "dependent child" under the Act but do not meet the definition of "dependent child" under the former Act. This exception is articulated in ss. 352 and 355 of the Regulations and reflects the fact that the Act changed the definition of dependent child to include unmarried children as old as age 21, whereas the former Act's definition included only unmarried children up to age 18. The purpose of the exception is to enable family members to sponsor dependants who would have been considered too old to be eligible before the Act came into force.

353. Requirements not applicable — If a person has made an application under the former Act before the day on which this section comes into force, the following provisions do not apply to the person in respect of any of their non-accompanying dependent children, referred to in section 352, or their non-accompanying common-law partner:

    (a) paragraph 70(1)(e);

    (b) subparagraph 72(1)(e)(i); and

    (c) paragraph 108(1)(a).

354. Requirements not applicable — If a person makes an application under the former Act before June 28, 2002, their non-accompanying dependent children, referred to in section 352, and their non-accompanying common-law partner shall not, for the purposes of that application, be considered inadmissible non-accompanying family members, referred to in paragraph 42(1)(a) of the *Immigration and Refugee Protection Act*, and are not subject to the requirements of paragraph 16(2)(b) of the *Immigration and Refugee Protection Act* or 51(b) of these Regulations.

SOR/2012-154, s. 17; SOR/2014-269, s. 6(d)

355. Family members not excluded from family class — If a person who made an application under the former Act before June 28, 2002 sponsors a non-accompanying dependent child, referred to in section 352, who makes an application as a member of the family class or the spouse or common-law partner in Canada class, or sponsors a non-accompanying common-law partner who makes such an application, paragraph 117(9)(d) does not apply in respect of that dependent child or common-law partner.

SOR/2004-167, s. 77

IRP Regulations

Case Law

Collier v. Canada (Minister of Citizenship & Immigration), [2004] F.C.J. No. 1445, 43 Imm. L.R. (3d) 53, 2004 CarswellNat 5094, 2004 CarswellNat 2993, 260 F.T.R. 266 (Eng.), 2004 FC 1209 — A child who is between 19 and 21, although a dependent under the new Regulations, did not need to be included as a non-accompanying dependent child in the sponsor's application for landing under the former regulations. Section 355 is intended to save an application if it was filed under the former regulatory scheme and in accordance with the former definition of dependant child within that scheme.

Natt v. Canada (Minister of Citizenship & Immigration), [2004] F.C.J. No. 997, 36 Imm. L.R. (3d) 292, 254 F.T.R. 122, 2004 CarswellNat 1693, 2004 FC 810 — This was an application to review a decision of the Immigration Appeal Division. The applicant married a Canadian citizen who then sponsored her application for permanent residence. The applicant did not disclose that she had two children and on this basis was granted permanent residence. In May 2001, the applicant sponsored applications for permanent residence for her two children. A visa officer refused these applications and the applicant appealed to the Appeal Division who dismissed her appeal.

The central issue was whether Regulation 117(9)(d) applied to the two children as members of the family class. The purpose of this provision is to ensure that foreign nationals seeking permanent residence do not omit non-accompanying dependent members from their application thereby avoiding their examination for admissibility at that time, and then, once having obtained their own permanent residence status, seek to sponsor their dependants and benefit from the preferential processing as well as admission treatments given to members of the family class. The sole exception is with respect to the children of sponsors whose applications for permanent residence were made before June 28, 2002, where those children meet the definition of "dependent child" under the Act but do not meet the definition of "dependent child" under the former Act. This exception is articulated in ss. 352 and 355 of the Regulations and reflects the fact that the Act changed the definition of dependent child to include unmarried children as old as age 21, whereas the former Act's definition included only unmarried children up to age 18. The purpose of the exception is to enable family members to sponsor dependants who would have been considered too old to be eligible before the Act came into force.

DIVISION 9 — FIANCÉS

356. Pending applications — **If a person referred to in paragraph (f) of the definition "member of the family class" in subsection 2(1) of the former Regulations made an application under those Regulations for a permanent resident visa, or their sponsor submitted a sponsorship application under those Regulations, before June 28, 2002, the person's application or the sponsorship application, as the case may be, is governed by the former Act.**

SOR/2004-167, s. 78

DIVISION 10 — FEES

357. Remission — right of landing fee — The fee set out in column III of item 19 of the schedule to the *Immigration Act Fees Regulations* is remitted and shall be repaid by the Minister to the person who paid it if the fee is paid in respect of a person before they become a permanent resident under the *Immigration and Refugee Protection Act* and the person, at the time they made an application for landing under the former Regulations, was

(a) a member of the family class and 19 years of age or older and, on the day on which this section comes into force, is a foreign national referred to in paragraph 117(1)(b) or (e) of these Regulations; or

(b) an accompanying dependant of an immigrant, within the meaning of subsection 2(1) of the former Regulations, 19 years of age or older and not a spouse of the principal applicant.

358. (1) Fees to be reapplied — A fee paid for processing an application in respect of which no decision has been made before the day on which this section comes into force or an application that has been refused but the refusal has not been communicated to the applicant before that day shall be applied to the cost of completing the processing of the application under the *Immigration and Refugee Protection Act*.

(2) **Exception** — Subsection (1) does not apply in respect of an application for a returning resident permit.

359. Remission — returning resident permit fee — The fee for a returning resident permit set out in column III of item 3 of the schedule to the *Immigration Act Fees Regulations* is remitted if, before the day on which this section comes into force, no decision has been made on the application for the permit or the application has been refused and the refusal has not been communicated to the applicant. If the fee is remitted, it shall be repaid by the Minister to the person who paid it.

360. Remission — fee for review of family business employment offer — The fee set out in column III of item 16 of the schedule to the *Immigration Act Fees Regulations* for the review of an offer of employment made to an applicant in respect of a family business is remitted if, before the day on which this section comes into force, no determination has been made on the family business application or the application has been refused and the refusal has not been communicated to the applicant. If the fee is remitted, it shall be repaid by the Minister to the person who paid it.

DIVISION 11 — ECONOMIC CLASSES

361. (1) Equivalent assessment — If, before the day on which this section comes into force, a foreign national referred to in subsection (2) has been assessed by a visa officer and awarded the number of units of assessment required by the former Regulations, that assessment is, for the purpose of these Regulations, an award of points equal or superior to the minimum number of points required of

(a) a skilled worker, in the case of a foreign national described in paragraph (2)(a);

(b) an investor, in the case of a foreign national described in paragraph (2)(b);

959

(c) an entrepreneur, in the case of a foreign national described in paragraph (2)(c); or

(d) a self-employed person, in the case of a foreign national described in paragraph (2)(a).

(2) **Applicant for immigrant visa** — Subsection (1) applies in respect of a foreign national who submitted an application under the former Regulations, as one of the following, for an immigrant visa that is pending immediately before the day on which this section comes into force:

(a) a person described in subparagraph 9(1)(b)(i) or paragraph 10(1)(b) of the former Regulations;

(b) an investor; or

(c) an entrepreneur.

(3) **Application before January 1, 2002** — During the period beginning on the day on which this section comes into force and ending on March 31, 2003, units of assessment shall be awarded to a foreign national, in accordance with the former Regulations, if the foreign national is an immigrant who,

(a) is referred to in subsection 8(1) of those Regulations, other than a provincial nominee; and

(b) before January 1, 2002, made an application for an immigrant visa under those Regulations that is still pending on the day on which this section comes into force and has not, before that day, been awarded units of assessment under those Regulations.

(4) **Pending applications — skilled workers** — Beginning on December 1, 2003, a foreign national who is an immigrant who made an application under the former Regulations before January 1, 2002 for an immigrant visa as a person described in subparagraph 9(1)(b)(i) or paragraph 10(1)(b) of those Regulations, other than a self-employed person within the meaning of subsection 2(1) of those Regulations, and whose application is still pending on December 1, 2003 and who has not, before that day, been awarded units of assessment under those Regulations must, in order to become a permanent resident as a member of the federal skilled worker class,

(a) be awarded at least the minimum number of units of assessment required by those Regulations for a person described in subparagraph 9(1)(b)(i) or paragraph 10(1)(b) of those Regulations, other than a self-employed person within the meaning of subsection 2(1) of those Regulations; or

(b) meet the requirements of subsection 75(2) and paragraph 76(1)(b) of these Regulations and obtain a minimum of 67 points based on the factors set out in paragraph 76(1)(a) of these Regulations.

(5) **Pending applications — investors** — Beginning on December 1, 2003, a foreign national who is an immigrant who made an application under the former Regulations before January 1, 2002 for an immigrant visa as an investor and whose application is still pending on December 1, 2003 and who has not, before that day,

been awarded units of assessment under those Regulations must, in order to become a permanent resident as a member of the investor class,

(a) be determined to be an investor within the meaning of subsection 2(1) of those Regulations and be awarded at least the minimum number of units of assessment required by those Regulations for an investor; or

(b) be an investor within the meaning of subsection 88(1) of these Regulations and obtain a minimum of 35 points based on the factors set out in subsection 102(1) of these Regulations.

(5.1) Pending applications — entrepreneurs — Beginning on December 1, 2003, a foreign national who is an immigrant who made an application under the former Regulations before January 1, 2002 for an immigrant visa as an entrepreneur and whose application is still pending on December 1, 2003 and who has not, before that day, been awarded units of assessment under those Regulations must, in order to become a permanent resident as a member of the entrepreneur class,

(a) be determined to be an entrepreneur within the meaning of subsection 2(1) of those Regulations and be awarded at least the minimum number of units of assessment required by those Regulations for an entrepreneur; or

(b) be an entrepreneur within the meaning of subsection 88(1) of these Regulations and obtain a minimum of 35 points based on the factors set out in subsection 102(1) of these Regulations.

(5.2) Pending applications — self-employed persons — Beginning on December 1, 2003, a foreign national who is an immigrant who made an application under the former Regulations before January 1, 2002 for an immigrant visa as a self-employed person and whose application is still pending on December 1, 2003 and who has not, before that day, been awarded units of assessment under those Regulations must, in order to become a permanent resident as a member of the self-employed persons class,

(a) be determined to be a self-employed person within the meaning of subsection 2(1) of those Regulations and be awarded at least the minimum number of units of assessment required by those Regulations for a self-employed person; or

(b) be a self-employed person within the meaning of subsection 88(1) of these Regulations and obtain a minimum of 35 points based on the factors set out in subsection 102(1) of these Regulations.

(6) Provincial nominees — If, before the day on which this section comes into force, a foreign national who was a provincial nominee submitted an application for a permanent resident visa under the former Regulations that is pending immediately before that day, the foreign national shall be assessed, and units of assessment shall be awarded to them, in accordance with those Regulations.

SOR/2003-383, s. 8

Case Law

Kniazeva v. Canada (Minister of Citizenship & Immigration) (2006), 52 Imm. L.R. (3d) 298, 2006 CarswellNat 472, 2006 FC 268 — The applicant filed an application for permanent residence under the skilled worker class. New legislation was enacted following the applicant's application having been filed. Under subs. 361(4) of the *Immigration and Refugee Protection Regulations*, the applicant could have become a permanent resident as a member of the federal skilled worker class by qualifying under either the former Act's regulation or under the new legislation. Once the visa officer decided to access the applicant under both the old and new Act, he had to inform the applicant of the new requirements with respect to language proficiency. The visa officer's failure to conduct a thorough review of her application under the new Act and failure to provide the applicant with an opportunity to provide him with the language assessment amounted to a clear breach of duty of fairness owed to the applicant.

The visa officer contacted the applicant's former employer with a view to verifying her employment. The employer confirmed the applicant had "practical training at the plant while she was a student and had worked intervals during the period between June 1997 and July 1998. Accordingly, the visa officer had a duty to inform the applicant that he only considered this work experience as part-time and therefore the experience was being disqualified as relevant work experience.

The visa officer breached the duty of procedural fairness and the application for judicial review was allowed.

Kazi v. Canada (Minister of Citizenship & Immigration) (2003), 34 Imm. L.R. (3d) 38, [2004] 1 F.C.R. 161, 238 F.T.R. 99, 2003 FC 948, [2003] F.C.J. No. 1212, 2003 CarswellNat 4427, 2003 CarswellNat 2413 — This is an application to review a decision of a visa officer refusing the applicant's application for permanent residence in the skilled worker class category.

A foreign national must, before entering Canada, apply for a visa or for any other document required by the Regulations. The visas or other documents shall be issued if, following an examination, the officer is satisfied that the foreign national is not inadmissible and meets the requirements of the Act and Regulations. A foreign national may be selected as a member of the economic class on the basis of his or her ability to become economically established in Canada.

Subsection 75(1) of the new Regulations creates the "Federal Skilled Worker Class," one of the economic classes for the purposes of subs. 12(2) of the Act. It is defined as a class of persons who are skilled workers and who may become permanent residents on the basis of their ability to become economically established in Canada and who intend to reside in a province other than Quebec. The requirements that a foreign national must meet in order to be considered a skilled worker are listed in subs. 75(2) of the new Regulations. If the foreign worker fails to meet these requirements, the application for permanent residence shall be refused and no further assessment is required. The ability of the foreign national to become economically established must be assessed on the basis of the criteria enumerated at subs. 76(1) of the Regulations. The minimum number of points is to be fixed by the Minister in a manner provided in subs. 76(2). The visa officer has a discretion to substitute his or her evaluation if the number of points awarded is not an accurate indicator of whether the skilled worker may become economically established in Canada. Such an evaluation requires the concurrence of a second officer.

No one has a vested right in the continuation of the laws that stood in the past. The survival provisions of the *Interpretation Act* provide for the continued application of repealed legislation to past situations. However, subs. 43(c) of the *Interpretation Act* is no more than a presumption. This presumption is refutable if the contrary intention is set out in the statute being considered. Section 361 of the Regulations specifically addresses the case where an application has been made before January 1, 2002. Accordingly, it is reasonable to conclude that in so doing it was clearly intended that any application made after January 1, 2002 would be assessed in accordance with the new Act and Regulations.

The new Regulations have a retrospective application in the sense that they change the future legal effect of a past situation. Once the visa officer determined that the applicant's application did not fall within the ambit of the transitional provisions, he should have promptly informed the applicant that he would now be assessed under the changed criteria and given the applicant the opportunity to provide additional information and to complete his application within a reasonable period of time. The lack of proper notice constitutes a breach of rules of fairness.

The decision of the visa officer was set aside and the matter was returned to a different visa officer with directions that the applicant be allowed to complete his application and submit additional information. The court also directed that three months was a reasonable time to allow for the additional information to be provided.

Dragan v. Canada (Minister of Citizenship & Immigration) (2003), 27 Imm. L.R. (3d) 157, 227 F.T.R. 272, 224 D.L.R. (4th) 738, [2003] 4 F.C. 189, 2003 CarswellNat 467, 2003 CarswellNat 1525, 2003 FCT 211, 2003 CFPI 211, [2003] F.C.J. No. 260; additional reasons at (2003), 27 Imm. L.R. (3d) 185, 2003 CarswellNat 588, 2003 CarswellNat 1580, 2003 FCT 281, 2003 CFPI 281, 228 F.T.R. 52, [2003] F.C.J. No. 404; affirmed (2003), 27 Imm. L.R. (3d) 194, 2003 CarswellNat 1419, 2003 FCA 233, 224 D.L.R. (4th) 764, [2003] F.C.J. No. 813 — This consolidated application involved 124 applicants who applied for permanent residence in Canada before June 28, 2002, the day that the IRPA came into force. The applicants sought a writ of *mandamus* requiring the respondent to assess them in accordance with the former Act and the former Regulations. Sections 190 and 201 of the IRPA indicate that Parliament intended the new Act to apply retrospectively and to authorize regulations with retrospective effect. Parliament can expressly enact retroactive or retrospective legislation. The clear expression of Parliamentary intent in this regard overrides the presumption against retroactivity or retrospectively in s. 43 of the *Interpretation Act*. Section 361 of the IRPA Regulations is validly authorized respective legislation and operates according to its terms, which means that applications filed after January 1, 2002, are to be assessed under the new Regulations and applications filed before January 1, 2002 are to be assessed under the old Regulations up until March 31, 2003.

The following conditions need to be satisfied for the court to issue a writ of *mandamus*:

1. There must be a public legal duty to act.

2. The duty must be owed to the applicant.

3. There must be a clear right to the performance of that duty, in particular,

    (a) the applicant must have satisfied all conditions precedent giving rise to the duty and;

    b) there was a prior demand for the performance of the duty, a reasonable time to comply with the demand and a subsequent refusal which can either be expressed or implied, e.g. unreasonable delay.

4. No other adequate remedy is available to the applicant.

5. The order sought will be of some practical value or effect.

6. The court finds no equitable bar to the relief sought.

7. On a balance of convenience an order should issue.

The court found all of these conditions satisfied and granted a writ of *mandamus* with respect to 102 of the applicants requiring the respondent on or before March 31, 2003 to assess the 102 applicants and award units of assessment in accordance with the former Regulations. Applications for judicial review with respect to applicants who filed after January 1, 2002, will be assessed under the selection criteria in the IRPA. The applicants who applied in this category had notice of the new selection criteria at the time of their application.

362. Investors — If, before April 1, 1999, a foreign national made an application for an immigrant visa as an investor and signed any document referred to in clause 1(v)(iii)(A) of Schedule X to the former Regulations, as that Schedule read immediately before that date, or, in the case of an investor in a province, either applied for a selection certificate under section 3.1 of *An Act respecting immigration to Québec*, R.S.Q., c. I-0.2, as amended from time to time, or applied for an immigrant visa as an investor, and signed an investment agreement in accordance with the law of that province, the relevant provisions of the former Regulations respecting an applicant for an immigrant visa as an investor, an approved business, an investor in a province, a fund manager, an eligible business, an approved fund, a fund, an escrow agent, a privately administered venture capital fund or a government-administered venture capital fund continue to apply as they read immediately before April 1, 1999 to all persons governed by their application before that date.

363. Entrepreneurs — For greater certainty, section 98 does not apply in respect of an entrepreneur within the meaning of subsection 2(1) of the former Regulations who was issued an immigrant visa under subparagraph 9(1)(b)(ii) or (c)(i) of those Regulations.

PART 21 — REPEALS AND COMING INTO FORCE

Repeals

364. Regulations repealed — The following Regulations are repealed:

(a) the *Immigration Regulations, 1978*[1];

(b) the *Refugee Claimants Designated Class Regulations*[2];

(c) the *Immigration Act Fees Regulations*[3]; and

(d) the *Humanitarian Designated Classes Regulations*[4].

---

[1] SOR/78-172

[2] SOR/90-40

[3] SOR/97-22

[4] SOR/97-183

Coming Into Force

365. (1) Coming into force — These Regulations, except paragraph 117(1)(e), subsection 117(5) and paragraphs 259(a) and (f) come into force on June 28, 2002.

(2) [Repealed SOR/2005-61, s. 9.]

(3) Exception — Paragraphs 259(a) and (f) come into force on December 31, 2003.
SOR/2003-97, s. 1; SOR/2004-34, s. 1; SOR/2005-61, s. 9

SCHEDULE 1 — PORTS OF ENTRY
(Section 2)

Division 1 — Ontario
1. Ambassador Bridge, Windsor
2. Detroit and Canada Tunnel, Windsor
3. Fort Frances International Bridge, Fort Frances
4. Hamilton International Airport, Hamilton
5. Lansdowne (Thousand Islands Bridge), Lansdowne
6. Lester B. Pearson International Airport, Mississauga
7. Lewiston-Queenston Bridge, Queenston
8. Peace Bridge, Fort Erie
9. Pigeon River Border Crossing at Highway 61, Pigeon River
10. Rainbow Bridge, Niagara Falls
11. Rainy River International Bridge, Rainy River
12. Sarnia Blue Water Bridge, Point Edward
13. Sault Ste. Marie International Bridge, Sault Ste. Marie
14. Seaway International Bridge, Cornwall
15. Seaway Skyway International Bridge, Prescott
16. Whirlpool Bridge, Niagara Falls

Division 2 — Quebec
1. Abercorn, Abercorn
2. Armstrong, Saint-Théophile
3. Beebe, Stanstead
4. Chartierville, Chartierville
5. Clarenceville, Clarenceville
6. Dundee, Sainte-Agnès-de-Dundee
7. East Hereford, East Hereford
8. Frelighsburg, Frelighsburg
9. Glen Sutton, Sutton

10. Hemmingford, Hemmingford

11. Herdman, Athelstan

12. Hereford Road, Saint-Herménégilde

13. Highwater, Highwater

14. Lacolle Highway 15, Saint-Bernard-de-Lacolle

15. Lacolle Highway 221, Notre-Dame Du Mont-Carmel

16. Lacolle Highway 223, Notre-Dame Du Mont-Carmel

17. Montreal International Airport, Dorval

18. Montreal International Airport, Mirabel

19. Noyan, Noyan

20. Rock Island Highway 55, Stanstead

21. Rock Island Highway 143, Stanstead

22. Saint-Armand, Saint-Armand de Philipsburg

23. Stanhope, Stanhope

24. Trout River, Athelstan

25. Woburn, Woburn

Division 3 — New Brunswick

1. Andover, Carlingford

2. Campobello, Welshpool

3. Centreville, Royalton

4. Clair, Clair

5. Edmundston, Edmundston

6. Gillespie Portage, Gillespie Settlement

7. Milltown, St. Stephen

8. St. Croix, St. Croix

9. Saint Leonard, Saint Leonard

10. Woodstock Road, Belleville

11. Grand Falls, Grand Falls

Division 4 — Manitoba

1. Boissevain, Boissevain

2. Emerson West Lynne, Emerson

3. Sprague, Sprague

4. Winnipeg International Airport, Winnipeg

Division 5 — British Columbia

1. Boundary Bay, Delta

2. Douglas, Surrey

3. Huntingdon, Huntingdon

4. Kingsgate, Kingsgate

5. Osoyoos, Osoyoos

6. Pacific Highway, Surrey

7. Patterson, Rossland

8. Roosville, Grasmere

9. Stewart, Stewart

10. Vancouver International Airport, Richmond

11. Victoria International Airport, Sidney

Division 6 — Saskatchewan

1. North Portal, North Portal

2. Regway, Regway

Division 7 — Alberta

1. Calgary International Airport, Calgary

2. Coutts, Coutts

3. Edmonton International Airport, Edmonton

Division 8 — Yukon

1. Beaver Creek, Beaver Creek

SOR/2004-167, s. 79

SCHEDULE 2 — VIOLATIONS [Heading added SOR/2015-144, s. 9 (Sched.).]

(Section 209.95, subsections 209.96(2), (3) and (4), sections 209.97 and 209.98, subsections 209.99(1) and 209.991(1), section 209.993, subsections 209.996(1), (2) and (4) and paragraph 209.997(2)(c))

Table 1 — Employer Conditions

	Column 1	Column 2	Column 3
Item	Provision	Short-form Description	Classification
1.	209.2(1)(b)(i)	Be able to demonstrate that any information provided in respect of a work permit application was accurate during a period of six years, beginning on the first day of the foreign national's employment	Type A
2.	209.2(1)(b)(ii) and 209.3(1)(c)(ii)	Retain any document that relates to compliance with cited conditions during a period of six years, beginning on the first day of the foreign national's employment	Type A

	Column 1	Column 2	Column 3
Item	Provision	Short-form Description	Classification
3.	209.3(1)(a)(iii)(C)	For employers of a live-in caregiver: have sufficient financial resources to pay wages that were offered	Type A
4.	209.3(1)(c)(i)	Be able to demonstrate that any information provided for the assessment was accurate during a period of six years, beginning on the first day of the foreign national's employment	Type A
5.	209.4(1)(a)	Report at any time and place specified to answer questions and provide documents	Type A
6.	209.4(1)(b)	Provide required documents	Type A
7.	209.4(1)(c)	Attend any inspection, unless the employer was not notified, give all reasonable assistance to the person conducting the inspection and provide that person with any required document or information	Type A
8.	209.2(1)(a)(ii) and 209.3(1)(a)(ii)	Comply with the federal and provincial laws that regulate employment and the recruiting of employees in the province in which the foreign national works	Type B
9.	209.2(1)(a)(iii) and 209.3(1)(a)(iv)	Provide the foreign national with employment in the same occupation and substantially the same, but not less favourable, wages and working conditions as outlined in the foreign national's offer of employment	Type B
10.	209.3(1)(a)(iii)(A)	For employers of a live-in caregiver: ensure that foreign national resides in a private household in Canada and provides child care, senior home support care or care of a disabled person in that household without supervision	Type B
11.	209.3(1)(b)(i)	Ensure that the employment of the foreign national will result in direct job creation or retention for Canadian citizens or permanent residents, if that was a factor that led to the issuance of the work permit	Type B

	Column 1	Column 2	Column 3
Item	Provision	Short-form Description	Classification
12.	209.3(1)(b)(ii)	Ensure that the employment of the foreign national will result in the development or transfer of skills and knowledge for the benefit of Canadian citizens or permanent residents, if that was a factor that led to the issuance of the work permit	Type B
13.	209.3(1)(b)(iii)	Hire or train Canadian citizens or permanent residents, if that was a factor that led to the issuance of the work permit	Type B
14.	209.3(1)(b)(iv)	Make reasonable efforts to hire or train Canadian citizens or permanent residents, if that was a factor that led to the issuance of the work permit	Type B
15.	209.2(1)(a)(i) and 209.3(1)(a)(I)	Be actively engaged in the business in which the offer of employment was made, unless the offer was made for employment as a live-in caregiver	Type C
16.	209.3(1)(a)(iii)(B)	For employers of a live-in caregiver: provide the foreign national with adequate furnished private accommodation in the household	Type C
17.	209.2(1)(a)(iv) and 209.3(1)(a)(v)	Make reasonable efforts to provide a workplace that is free of abuse within the meaning of paragraph 72.1(7)(a) of these Regulations	Type C

Table 2 — Administrative Monetary Penalty Amounts

	Column 1	Column 2		Column 3		Column 4	
		Type A Violation		Type B Violation		Type C Violation	
Item	Total Number of Points	Individual or Small Business ($)	Large Business ($)	Individual or Small Business ($)	Large Business ($)	Individual or Small Business ($)	Large Business ($)
1.	0 or 1	none	none	none	none	none	none
2.	2	500	750	750	1,000	1,000	2,000
3.	3	750	1,000	1,250	2,000	5,000	10,000
4.	4	1,000	2,000	3,000	7,000	10,000	20,000

	Column 1	Column 2		Column 3		Column 4	
		Type A Violation		Type B Violation		Type C Violation	
Item	Total Number of Points	Individual or Small Business ($)	Large Business ($)	Individual or Small Business ($)	Large Business ($)	Individual or Small Business ($)	Large Business ($)
5.	5	4,000	6,000	7,000	12,000	15,000	30,000
6.	6	8,000	10,000	12,000	20,000	20,000	40,000
7.	7	12,000	20,000	20,000	30,000	35,000	50,000
8.	8	20,000	30,000	35,000	45,000	45,000	60,000
9.	9 or 10	30,000	45,000	50,000	60,000	60,000	70,000
10.	11 or 12	40,000	60,000	60,000	70,000	70,000	80,000
11.	13 or 14	50,000	70,000	70,000	80,000	80,000	90,000
12.	15 or more	100,000	100,000	100,000	100,000	100,000	100,000

Table 3 — Period of Ineligibility

	Column 1	Column 2	Column 3	Column 4
Item	Total Number of Points	Type A Violation	Type B Violation	Type C Violation
1.	0 to 5	none	none	none
2.	6	none	none	1 year
3.	7	none	1 year	2 years
4.	8	1 year	2 years	5 years
5.	9 or 10	2 years	5 years	10 years
6.	11 or 12	5 years	10 years	10 years
7.	13 or 14	10 years	10 years	10 years
8.	15 or more	permanent	permanent	permanent

Table 4 — Compliance History

	Column 1	Column 2
Item	Criterion	Points
1.	For Type A and Type B violations — first violation	1
2.	For Type A violations — second or subsequent violation	2
3.	For Type B violations — second violation	2
4.	For Type C violations — first violation	2
5.	For Type B violations — third or subsequent violation	3

Column 1		Column 2
Item	Criterion	Points
6	For Type C violations — second violation	3
7.	For Type C violations — third or subsequent violation	4

Table 5 — Severity of the Violation

Column 1		Column 2
Item	Criterion	Points
1.	The employer derived competitive or economic benefit from the violation	0 to 6
2.	The violation involved abuse of a foreign national (physical, psychological, sexual or financial)	0 to 10
3.	The violation negatively affected the Canadian labour market or the Canadian economy	0 to 6
4.	The employer did not make reasonable efforts to minimize or remediate the effects of the violation	0 to 3
5.	The employer did not make reasonable efforts to prevent recurrence of the violation	0 to 3

SOR/2011-222, s. 12; SOR/2015-144, s. 9 (Sched.)

Proposed Addition — Sched. 3

SCHEDULE 3 — INFORMATION ABOUT PERSONS IN A RESERVATION SYSTEM [Heading added SOR/2016-37, s. 19 (Sched.). Not in force at date of publication.]

(Paragraph 269(1)(e))

1 Their surname, first name and any middle names

2 Their reservation record locator number

3 The date of their reservation and date their ticket was issued

4 Their itinerary, including the dates of departure and arrival for each segment of carriage

5 Information about their participation in a loyalty program and the benefits earned under the program, such as free tickets or upgrades

6 The number of the other passengers included in the reservation record and their surname, first name and any middle names

7 Contact information for each person mentioned in the reservation record, including the person who made the reservation

8 Billing and payment information, including credit card number and billing address

9 Information about the travel agent or agency, including the name and contact information

10 Code share information

11 Information about whether the reservation record has been divided into several records or is linked to another record

12 Their travel status, including travel confirmation and check-in status

13 Ticketing information, including the ticket number, automated ticket fare quote and whether a one-way ticket was purchased

14 Their baggage information, including the number and weight of their bags

15 Their seating information, including seat number

16 General remarks about the person in the reservation record, including other supplementary information, special service information and special service request information

17 The information referred to in paragraphs 269(1)(a) and (b) of these Regulations

18 The history of any changes to the information referred toin items 1 to 17 of this Schedule

SOR/2016-37, s. 19 (Sched.) [Not in force at date of publication.]

CAN. REG. 2011-142 — REGULATIONS DESIGNATING A BODY FOR THE PURPOSES OF PARAGRAPH 91(2)(C) OF THE IMMIGRATION AND REFUGEE PROTECTION ACT

made under the *Immigration and Refugee Protection Act*

SOR/2011-142

INTERPRETATION

1. The following definitions apply in these Regulations.

"**Act**" means the *Immigration and Refugee Protection Act*. *("Loi")*

"**ICCRC**" means the Immigration Consultants of Canada Regulatory Council, incorporated under Part II of the *Canada Corporations Act* on February 18, 2011. *("CRCIC")*

DESIGNATION

2. For the purposes of paragraph 91(2)(c) of the Act, the ICCRC is designated as a body whose members in good standing may represent or advise a person for consideration — or offer to do so — in connection with a proceeding or application under the Act.

Case Law

Canadian Society of Immigration Consultants v. Canada (Minister of Citizenship & Immigration) (2012), 8 Imm. L.R. (4th) 233, 434 N.R. 14, 41 Admin. L.R. (5th) 298, 2012 FCA 194, 2012 CarswellNat 2165, 2012 CarswellNat 3063; leave to appeal to the S.C.C. refused 2012 CarswellNat 5001, 2012 CarswellNat 5002 (S.C.C.) — This appeal by the Canadian Society of Immigration Consultants was from a decision of the Federal Court where an application for judicial review had been dismissed. The Federal Court Judge certified the following question:

> Are the *Regulations Amending the Immigration and Refugee Protection Regulations* (SOR/2011-129), the *Order Fixing June 30, 2011 as the Day on which Chapter 8 of the Statutes of Canada, 2011, Comes into Force* (SI/2011-57) and/or the *Regulations Designating a Body for the Purposes of paragraph 91(2)(c) of the Immigration and Refugee Act* (SOR/2011-142) *ultra vires*, illegal and/or invalid in law?

The Federal Court of Appeal was not persuaded that the Regulations were invalid. The appeal was dismissed.

TRANSITIONAL MEASURES

3. (1) Any person who, on the date on which these Regulations come into force, is a member in good standing of the Canadian Society of Immigration Consultants, incorporated under Part II of the *Canada Corporations Act* on October 8, 2003, is a member of the ICCRC, for the purposes of the Act, for a period lasting until the earlier of

(a) 120 days following the date on which these Regulations come into force; and

(b) the date on which that person discontinues their status as a member of the ICCRC.

(2) For the period during which they are a member of the ICCRC in accordance with subsection (1), the persons referred to in that subsection are not required to pay membership fees to that body.

COMING INTO FORCE

4. These Regulations come into force on the day on which section 1 of *An Act to amend the Immigration and Refugee Protection Act*, chapter 8 of the Statutes of Canada, 2011, comes into force, but if they are registered after that day, they come into force on the day on which they are registered.

CAN. REG. 2012-256 — REFUGEE PROTECTION DIVISION RULES

made under the *Immigration and Refugee Protection Act*

SOR/2012-256

INTERPRETATION

1. Definitions — The following definitions apply in these Rules.

"Act" means the *Immigration and Refugee Protection Act*. *("Loi")*

"Basis of Claim Form" means the form in which a claimant gives the information referred to in Schedule 1. *("Formulaire de fondement de la demande d'asile")*

"contact information" means, with respect to a person,

(a) the person's name, postal address and telephone number, and their fax number and email address, if any; and

(b) in the case of counsel for a claimant or protected person, if the counsel is a person referred to in any of paragraphs 91(2)(a) to (c) of the Act, in addition to the information referred to in paragraph (a), the name of the body of which the counsel is a member and the membership identification number issued to the counsel.

("coordonnées")

"Division" means the Refugee Protection Division. *("Section")*

"officer" means a person designated as an officer by the Minister under subsection 6(1) of the Act. *("agent")*

"party" means,

(a) in the case of a claim for refugee protection, the claimant and, if the Minister intervenes in the claim, the Minister; and

(b) in the case of an application to vacate or to cease refugee protection, the protected person and the Minister.

("partie")

"proceeding" includes a conference, an application or a hearing. *("procédure")*

"registry office" means a business office of the Division. *("greffe")*

"Regulations" means the *Immigration and Refugee Protection Regulations*. *("Règlement")* "vulnerable person" means a person who has been identified as vulnerable under the *Guideline on Procedures with Respect to Vulnerable Persons Appearing Before the IRB* issued under paragraph 159(1)(h) of the Act. *("personne vulnérable")*

"working day" does not include Saturdays, Sundays or other days on which the Board offices are closed. *("jour ouvrable")*

COMMUNICATING WITH THE DIVISION

2. Communicating with Division — All communication with the Division must be directed to the registry office specified by the Division.

INFORMATION AND DOCUMENTS TO BE PROVIDED

Claims for Refugee Protection

3. (1) Fixing date, time and location of hearing — As soon as a claim for refugee protection is referred to the Division, or as soon as possible before it is deemed to be referred under subsection 100(3) of the Act, an officer must fix a date, time and location for the claimant to attend a hearing on the claim, within the time limits set out in the Regulations, from the dates, times and locations provided by the Division.

(2) Date fixed by officer — Subject to paragraph 3(b), the officer must select the date closest to the last day of the applicable time limit set out in the Regulations, unless the claimant agrees to an earlier date.

(3) Factors — In fixing the date, time and location for the hearing, the officer must consider

    (a) the claimant's preference of location; and

    (b) counsel's availability, if the claimant has retained counsel at the time of referral and the officer has been informed that counsel will be available to attend a hearing on one of the dates provided by the Division.

(4) Providing information to claimant in writing — The officer must

    (a) notify the claimant in writing by way of a notice to appear

        (i) of the date, time and location of the hearing of the claim; and

        (ii) of the date, time and location of any special hearing on the abandonment of the claim under subrules 65(2) and (3);

    (b) unless the claimant has provided a completed Basis of Claim Form to the officer in accordance with subsection 99(3.1) of the Act, provide to the claimant the Basis of Claim Form; and

    (c) provide to the claimant information in writing

        (i) explaining how and when to provide a Basis of Claim Form and other documents to the Division and to the Minister,

(ii) informing the claimant of the importance of obtaining relevant documentary evidence without delay,

(iii) explaining how the hearing will proceed,

(iv) informing the claimant of the obligation to notify the Division and the Minister of the claimant's contact information and any changes to that information,

(v) informing the claimant that they may, at their own expense, be represented by legal or other counsel, and

(vi) informing the claimant that the claim may be declared abandoned without further notice if the claimant fails to provide the completed Basis of Claim Form or fails to appear at the hearing.

(5) Providing information in writing and documents to Division — After providing to the claimant the information set out in subrule (4), the officer must without delay provide to the Division

(a) a written statement indicating how and when the information set out in subrule (4) was provided to the claimant;

(b) the completed Basis of Claim Form for a claimant referred to in subsection 99(3.1) of the Act;

(c) a copy of each notice to appear provided to the claimant in accordance with paragraph (4)(a);

(d) the information set out in Schedule 2;

(e) a copy of any identity and travel documents of the claimant that have been seized by the officer;

(f) a copy of the notice of seizure of any seized documents referred to in paragraph (e); and

(g) a copy of any other relevant documents that are in the possession of the officer.

(6) Providing copies to claimant — The officer must provide to the claimant a copy of any documents or information that the officer has provided to the Division under paragraphs (5)(d) to (g).

4. (1) Claimant's contact information — The claimant must provide their contact information in writing to the Division and to the Minister.

(2) Time limit — The claimant's contact information must be received by the Division and the Minister no later than 10 days after the day on which the claimant receives the information provided by the officer under subrule 3(4).

(3) Change to contact information — If the claimant's contact information changes, the claimant must without delay provide the changes in writing to the Division and to the Minister.

(4) Information concerning claimant's counsel — A claimant who is represented by counsel must without delay, on retaining counsel, provide the counsel's contact information in writing to the Division and to the Minister and notify them of

977

any limitations on the counsel's retainer. If that information changes, the claimant must without delay provide the changes in writing to the Division and to the Minister.

5. Declaration — counsel not representing or advising for consideration — If a claimant retains counsel who is not a person referred to in any of paragraphs 91(2)(a) to (c) of the Act, both the claimant and their counsel must without delay provide the information and declarations set out in Schedule 3 to the Division in writing.

Basis of Claim Form

6. (1) Claimant's declarations — The claimant must complete a Basis of Claim Form and sign and date the declaration set out in the form stating that

(a) the information given by the claimant is complete, true and correct; and

(b) the claimant understands that the declaration is of the same force and effect as if made under oath.

(2) Form completed without interpreter — If the claimant completes the Basis of Claim Form without an interpreter's assistance, the claimant must sign and date the declaration set out in the form stating that they can read the language of the form and understand what information is requested.

(3) Interpreter's declaration — If the claimant completes the Basis of Claim Form with an interpreter's assistance, the interpreter must sign and date the declaration in the form stating that

(a) they are proficient in the language and dialect, if any, used, and were able to communicate effectively with the claimant;

(b) the completed Basis of Claim Form and all attached documents were interpreted to the claimant; and

(c) the claimant indicated that the claimant understood what was interpreted.

7. (1) Providing Basis of Claim Form — inland claim — A claimant referred to in subsection 99(3.1) of the Act must provide the original and a copy of the completed Basis of Claim Form to the officer referred to in rule 3.

(2) Providing Basis of Claim Form — port of entry claim — A claimant other than a claimant referred to in subsection 99(3.1) of the Act must provide the original and a copy of the completed Basis of Claim Form to the Division.

(3) Documents to be attached — The claimant must attach to the original and to the copy of the completed Basis of Claim Form a copy of their identity and travel documents, genuine or not, and a copy of any other relevant documents in their possession. The claimant does not have to attach a copy of a document that has been seized by an officer or provided to the Division by an officer.

(4) Documents obtained after providing Basis of Claim Form — If the claimant obtains an identity or travel document after the Division has received the completed Basis of Claim Form, they must provide two copies of the document to the Division without delay.

(5) Providing Basis of Claim Form — port of entry claim — The Basis of Claim Form provided under subrule (2) must be

(a) received by the Division within the time limit set out in the Regulations, and

(b) provided in any of the following ways:

(i) by hand,

(ii) by courier,

(iii) by fax if the document is no more than 20 pages long, unless the Division consents to receiving more than 20 pages, or

(iv) by email or other electronic means if the Division allows.

(6) Original Basis of Claim Form — A claimant who provides the Basis of Claim Form by fax must provide the original to the Division at the beginning of the hearing.

8. (1) Application for extension of time — A claimant who makes an application for an extension of time to provide the completed Basis of Claim Form must make the application in accordance with rule 50, but the claimant is not required to give evidence in an affidavit or statutory declaration.

(2) Time limit — The application must be received by the Division no later than three working days before the expiry of the time limit set out in the Regulations.

(3) Application for medical reasons — If a claimant makes the application for medical reasons, other than those related to their counsel, they must provide, together with the application, a legible, recently dated medical certificate signed by a qualified medical practitioner whose name and address are printed or stamped on the certificate. A claimant who has provided a copy of the certificate to the Division must provide the original document to the Division without delay.

(4) Content of certificate — The medical certificate must set out the particulars of the medical condition, without specifying the diagnosis, that prevent the claimant from providing the completed Basis of Claim Form in the time limit referred to in paragraph 7(5)(a).

(5) Failure to provide medical certificate — If a claimant fails to provide a medical certificate in accordance with subrules (3) and (4), the claimant must include in their application

(a) particulars of any efforts they made to obtain the required medical certificate, supported by corroborating evidence;

(b) particulars of the medical reasons for the application, supported by corroborating evidence; and

(c) an explanation of how the medical condition prevents them from providing the completed Basis of Claim Form in the time limit referred to in paragraph 7(5)(a).

(6) Providing Basis of Claim Form after extension granted — If an extension of time is granted, the claimant must provide the original and a copy of the completed Basis of Claim Form to the Division in accordance with subrules 7(2) and (3), no later than on the date indicated by the Division and by a means set out in paragraph 7(5)(b).

9. (1) Changes or additions to Basis of Claim Form — To make changes or add any information to the Basis of Claim Form, the claimant must

(a) provide to the Division the original and a copy of each page of the form to which changes or additions have been made;

(b) sign and date each new page and underline the changes or additions made; and

(c) sign and date a declaration stating that

(i) the information given by the claimant in the Basis of Claim Form, together with the changes and additions, is complete, true and correct, and

(ii) the claimant understands that the declaration is of the same force and effect as if made under oath.

(2) Time limit — The documents referred to in subrule (1) must be provided to the Division without delay and must be received by it no later than 10 days before the date fixed for the hearing.

Conduct of a Hearing

10. (1) Standard order of questioning — In a hearing of a claim for refugee protection, if the Minister is not a party, any witness, including the claimant, will be questioned first by the Division and then by the claimant's counsel.

(2) Order of questioning — Minister's intervention on exclusion issue — In a hearing of a claim for refugee protection, if the Minister is a party and has intervened on an issue of exclusion under subrule 29(3), any witness, including the claimant, will be questioned first by the Minister's counsel, then by the Division and then by the claimant's counsel.

(3) Order of questioning — Minister's intervention not on exclusion issue — In a hearing of a claim for refugee protection, if the Minister is a party but has not intervened on an issue of exclusion under subrule 29(3), any witness, including the claimant, will be questioned first by the Division, then by the Minister's counsel and then by the claimant's counsel.

(4) Order of questioning — application to vacate or cease refugee protection — In a hearing into an application to vacate or to cease refugee protection, any witness, including the protected person, is to be questioned first by the Minister's counsel, then by the Division and then by the protected person's counsel.

(5) Variation of order of questioning — The Division must not vary the order of questioning unless there are exceptional circumstances, including that the variation is required to accommodate a vulnerable person.

(6) **Limiting questioning of witnesses** — The Division may limit the questioning of witnesses, including a claimant or a protected person, taking into account the nature and complexity of the issues and the relevance of the questions.

(7) **Oral representations** — Representations must be made orally at the end of a hearing unless the Division orders otherwise.

(8) **Oral decision and reasons** — A Division member must render an oral decision and reasons for the decision at the hearing unless it is not practicable to do so.

Documents Establishing Identity and Other Elements of the Claim

11. **Documents** — The claimant must provide acceptable documents establishing their identity and other elements of the claim. A claimant who does not provide acceptable documents must explain why they did not provide the documents and what steps they took to obtain them.

Application to Vacate or to Cease Refugee Protection

12. **Contact information** — If an application to vacate or to cease refugee protection is made, the protected person must without delay notify the Division and the Minister in writing of

(a) any change in their contact information; and

(b) their counsel's contact information and any limitations on the counsel's retainer, if represented by counsel, and any changes to that information.

13. **Declaration — counsel not representing or advising for consideration** — If a protected person retains counsel who is not a person referred to in any of paragraphs 91(2)(a) to (c) of the Act, both the protected person and their counsel must without delay provide the information and declarations set out in Schedule 3 to the Division in writing.

COUNSEL OF RECORD

14. (1) **Becoming counsel of record** — Subject to subrule (2), as soon as counsel for a claimant or protected person agrees to a date for a proceeding, or as soon as a person becomes counsel after a date for a proceeding has been fixed, the counsel becomes counsel of record for the claimant or protected person.

(2) **Limitation on counsel's retainer** — If a claimant or protected person has notified the Division of a limitation on their counsel's retainer, counsel is counsel of record only to the extent of the services to be provided within the limited retainer. Counsel ceases to be counsel of record as soon as those services are completed.

Case Law

Dvorianova v. Canada (Minister of Citizenship & Immigration), 2004 CarswellNat 2390, 2004 CarswellNat 789, 2004 FC 413 — The applicant is a Russian who claims to face political persecution in her home country. She sought to judicially review a decision that her refugee claim was abandoned. Her original refugee hearing was scheduled for November 27, 2002. On the day before the hearing, her immigration consultant advised her that he would seek a postponement. He further advised her not to attend the hearing and that he would do whatever it took to secure the postponement. The panel granted the postponement but scheduled a hearing on April 8, 2003, to give the applicant an opportunity to show cause why her claim should not be abandoned.

The fact that the applicant used an immigration consultant rather than a lawyer is irrelevant. She had a right to do so, but she also must accept the consequences of doing so. An applicant remains bound by the consultant's conduct as would be the case if she had retained counsel. The incompetence of counsel may be a breach of natural justice. It is not necessary that the incompetence be apparent to the decision maker. The claimant must establish the acts or omissions of counsel that are alleged are not the result of professional judgement. The claimant must also establish that there was a miscarriage of justice. Evidence of incompetence must be clear and convincing. In this particular case the application for judicial review was dismissed.

15. (1) Request to be removed as counsel of record — To be removed as counsel of record, counsel for a claimant or protected person must first provide to the person represented and to the Minister, if the Minister is a party, a copy of a written request to be removed and then provide the written request to the Division, no later than three working days before the date fixed for the next proceeding.

(2) Oral request — If it is not possible for counsel to make the request in accordance with subrule (1), counsel must appear on the date fixed for the proceeding and make the request to be removed orally before the time fixed for the proceeding.

(3) Division's permission required — Counsel remains counsel of record unless the request to be removed is granted.

16. (1) Removing counsel of record — To remove counsel as counsel of record, a claimant or protected person must first provide to counsel and to the Minister, if the Minister is a party, a copy of a written notice that counsel is no longer counsel for the claimant or protected person, as the case may be, and then provide the written notice to the Division.

(2) Ceasing to be counsel of record — Counsel ceases to be counsel of record as soon as the Division receives the notice.

LANGUAGE OF PROCEEDINGS

17. (1) Choice of language — claim for refugee protection — A claimant must choose English or French as the language of the proceedings at the time of the referral of their claim for refugee protection to the Division.

(2) **Changing language** — A claimant may change the language of the proceedings that they chose under subrule (1) by notifying the Division and the Minister in writing. The notice must be received by the Division and the Minister no later than 10 days before the date fixed for the next proceeding.

18. (1) **Choice of language — application to vacate or cease refugee protection** — The language that is chosen under rule 17 is to be the language of the proceedings in any application made by the Minister to vacate or to cease refugee protection with respect to that claim.

(2) **Changing language** — A protected person may change the language of the proceedings by notifying the Division and the Minister in writing. The notice must be received by the Division and the Minister no later than 10 days before the date fixed for the next proceeding.

INTERPRETERS

19. (1) **Need for interpreter — claimant** — If a claimant needs an interpreter for the proceedings, the claimant must notify an officer at the time of the referral of the claim to the Division and specify the language and dialect, if any, to be interpreted.

(2) **Changing language of interpretation** — A claimant may change the language and dialect, if any, that they specified under subrule (1), or if they had not indicated that an interpreter was needed, they may indicate that they need an interpreter, by notifying the Division in writing and indicating the language and dialect, if any, to be interpreted. The notice must be received by the Division no later than 10 days before the date fixed for the next proceeding.

(3) **Need for interpreter — protected person** — If a protected person needs an interpreter for the proceedings, the protected person must notify the Division in writing and specify the language and dialect, if any, to be interpreted. The notice must be received by the Division no later than 10 days before the date fixed for the next proceeding.

(4) **Need for interpreter — witness** — If any party's witness needs an interpreter for the proceedings, the party must notify the Division in writing and specify the language and dialect, if any, to be interpreted. The notice must be received by the Division no later than 10 days before the date fixed for the next proceeding.

(5) **Interpreter's oath** — The interpreter must take an oath or make a solemn affirmation to interpret accurately.

Case Law

Vakulenko v. Canada (Minister of Citizenship and Immigration), 2014 FC 667, 2014 CarswellNat 3274, 2014 CarswellNat 2506 — The sole issue for disposition was whether the duty of fairness owed to the applicant had been breached by the RPD in the treatment given to the concerns about the interpretation made available to the applicant at the hearing. The central issue was the credibility of the applicant. She was a woman aged 73 at the time of the application for judicial review. She came to Canada from her country of nationality, Russia, on a temporary resident visa. It was not completely clear what her purpose was in coming to Canada: one purpose was to attend a wedding; the other was an attempt to get away from an abusive partner and to live with her relatives in Canada. She eventually made an application based on ss. 96 and 97 of IRPA. It is from the refusal of the RPD to grant that application that judicial review is sought. The matter of the quality of interpretation was raised at the hearing by the applicant's granddaughter. A discussion ensued between counsel for the applicant and the RPD panel. The upshot of the discussion was that a "spot audit" would be done for the purpose of ascertaining the quality of the interpretation. Once it received the results of the spot audit, the RPD also chose to satisfy itself that the interpretation was adequate in the circumstances and proceeded to decide against the applicant without seeking observations or comments from her or her counsel. In other words, the RPD never shared with the applicant the results of the spot audit before making its decision on the merits, including findings on the credibility of the applicant. The issue is whether or not it was incumbent on the RPD to allow the applicant to comment on the results of the audit before a decision was to be made on the adequacy of the audit.

Persons affected by those decisions have the right to participate. Once the quality of the interpretation is considered sufficiently doubtful that an audit is ordered, the fairness of the process commands that it include the opportunity to comment on the results. If the duty to act fairly has been deficient, one never reaches the merits of the case which is reviewable on a reasonableness standard. As a result, the application for judicial review was granted.

Lamme v. Canada (Minister of Citizenship & Immigration), 2005 CarswellNat 3063, 2005 CarswellNat 4881, 2005 FC 1336 — The general standard to be met with respect to the quality of interpretation is that it must be continuous, precise, impartial and contemporaneous. In addition, for the interpretation to be considered as meeting the standard, it must be established that the applicant understood the interpretation and adequately expressed himself or herself through the interpreter.

DESIGNATED REPRESENTATIVES

20. (1) Duty of counsel or officer to notify — If counsel for a party or if an officer believes that the Division should designate a representative for the claimant or protected person because the claimant or protected person is under 18 years of age or is unable to appreciate the nature of the proceedings, counsel or the officer must without delay notify the Division in writing.

(2) Exception — Subrule (1) does not apply in the case of a claimant under 18 years of age whose claim is joined with the claim of their parent or legal guardian if the parent or legal guardian is 18 years of age or older.

(3) Content of notice — The notice must include the following information:

(a) whether counsel or the officer is aware of a person in Canada who meets the requirements to be designated as a representative and, if so, the person's contact information;

(b) a copy of any available supporting documents; and

(c) the reasons why counsel or the officer believes that a representative should be designated.

(4) Requirements for being designated — To be designated as a representative, a person must

    (a) be 18 years of age or older;

    (b) understand the nature of the proceedings;

    (c) be willing and able to act in the best interests of the claimant or protected person; and

    (d) not have interests that conflict with those of the claimant or protected person.

(5) Factors — When determining whether a claimant or protected person is unable to appreciate the nature of the proceedings, the Division must consider any relevant factors, including

    (a) whether the person can understand the reason for the proceeding and can instruct counsel;

    (b) the person's statements and behaviour at the proceeding;

    (c) expert evidence, if any, on the person's intellectual or physical faculties, age or mental condition; and

    (d) whether the person has had a representative designated for a proceeding in another division of the Board.

(6) Designation applies to all proceedings — The designation of a representative for a person who is under 18 years of age or who is unable to appreciate the nature of the proceedings applies to all subsequent proceedings in the Division with respect to that person unless the Division orders otherwise.

(7) End of designation — person reaches 18 years of age — The designation of a representative for a person who is under 18 years of age ends when the person reaches 18 years of age unless that representative has also been designated because the person is unable to appreciate the nature of the proceedings.

(8) Termination of designation — The Division may terminate a designation if the Division is of the opinion that the representative is no longer required or suitable and may designate a new representative if required.

(9) Designation criteria — Before designating a person as a representative, the Division must

    (a) assess the person's ability to fulfil the responsibilities of a designated representative; and

    (b) ensure that the person has been informed of the responsibilities of a designated representative.

(10) Responsibilities of representative — The responsibilities of a designated representative include

    (a) deciding whether to retain counsel and, if counsel is retained, instructing counsel or assisting the represented person in instructing counsel;

(b) making decisions regarding the claim or application or assisting the represented person in making those decisions;

(c) informing the represented person about the various stages and procedures in the processing of their case;

(d) assisting in gathering evidence to support the represented person's case and in providing evidence and, if necessary, being a witness at the hearing;

(e) protecting the interests of the represented person and putting forward the best possible case to the Division;

(f) informing and consulting the represented person to the extent possible when making decisions about the case; and

(g) filing and perfecting an appeal to the Refugee Appeal Division, if required.

DISCLOSURE OF PERSONAL INFORMATION

21. (1) Disclosure of information from another claim — Subject to subrule (5), the Division may disclose to a claimant personal and other information that it wants to use from any other claim if the claims involve similar questions of fact or if the information is otherwise relevant to the determination of their claim.

(2) Notice to another claimant — If the personal or other information of another claimant has not been made public, the Division must make reasonable efforts to notify the other claimant in writing that

(a) it intends to disclose the information to a claimant; and

(b) the other claimant may object to that disclosure.

(3) Request for disclosure — In order to decide whether to object to the disclosure, the other claimant may make a written request to the Division for personal and other information relating to the claimant. Subject to subrule (5), the Division may disclose only information that is necessary to permit the other claimant to make an informed decision.

(4) Notice to claimant — If the personal or other information of the claimant has not been made public, the Division must make reasonable efforts to notify the claimant in writing that

(a) it intends to disclose the information to the other claimant; and

(b) the claimant may object to that disclosure.

(5) Information not to be disclosed — The Division must not disclose personal or other information unless it is satisfied that

(a) there is not a serious possibility that disclosing the information will endanger the life, liberty or security of any person; or

(b) disclosing the information is not likely to cause an injustice.

(6) Information from joined claims — Personal or other information from a joined claim is not subject to this rule. If claims were once joined but were later separated, only personal or other information that was provided before the separation is not subject to this rule.

Case Law

Seyoboka v. Canada (Minister of Citizenship & Immigration), 2009 CarswellNat 237, 2009 FC 104 — This was an application for judicial review of a decision of the Immigration Refugee Board dismissing the applicant's motion to reopen his claim for refugee protection pursuant to s. 72(1) of the IRPA. The applicant contends that the Minister had a duty to disclose exculpatory evidence in vacation proceedings and the Minister breached her duty to disclose the exculpatory evidence.

The Refugee Protection Division of the Immigration and Refugee Protection Board is an administrative tribunal with specialized knowledge, not bound by legal or technical rules of evidence. As a result, the disclosure to standards delineated in *Stinchcombe*, [1991] 3 S.C.R. 326, do not necessarily apply automatically in the context of a refugee hearing and may require some adaptation. On the other hand, the level of disclosure owed to an applicant cannot be decided by a simple invocation of the distinction between criminal and administrative proceedings, and the consequences of an adverse finding on the applicant must be taken into consideration. The application for judicial review was dismissed. The following four questions were certified:

1. Within the context of the judicial review hearing where the Minister intervenes to seek the exclusion of the claimant, is the Minister under a duty to disclose all relevant evidence in his possession including exculpatory evidence subject only to any claims to privilege which would be assessed by the tribunal?

2. Is that duty contingent on any request from the claimant or does the duty exist independently of any request from the claimant?

3. Can the right to disclosure be waived? If so, must the waiver be explicit, or can it be inferred from the conduct of the claimant?

4. If there is a duty to disclose, does that duty include a duty to disclose evidence in the possession of other government agencies when Minister's counsel is aware that that government agency has a file on the person which might contain relevant evidence?

SPECIALIZED KNOWLEDGE

22. Notice to parties — **Before using any information or opinion that is within its specialized knowledge, the Division must notify the claimant or protected person and, if the Minister is present at the hearing, the Minister, and give them an opportunity to**

(a) make representations on the reliability and use of the information or opinion; and

(b) provide evidence in support of their representations.

Case Law

Bitala v. Canada (Minister of Citizenship & Immigration), 2005 CarswellNat 896, 2005 FC 470 — The RPD did not clearly and unequivocally give notice to the applicants of its intention to rely on its specialized knowledge and provide an opportunity to respond. The specialized knowledge, however, was essentially not in dispute. If the RPD had given, to the applicant, the specific notification required by Rule 18 the applicant's response would

Rules

not have impacted the final decision. Accordingly, the application for judicial review was dismissed.

ALLOWING A CLAIM WITHOUT A HEARING

23. Claim allowed without hearing — For the purpose of paragraph 170(f) of the Act, the period during which the Minister must notify the Division of the Minister's intention to intervene is no later than 10 days after the day on which the Minister receives the Basis of Claim Form.

CONFERENCES

24. (1) Requirement to participate at conference — The Division may require the parties to participate at a conference to fix a date for a proceeding or to discuss issues, relevant facts and any other matter to make the proceedings fairer and more efficient.

(2) Information or documents — The Division may require the parties to give any information or provide any document, at or before the conference.

(3) Written record — The Division must make a written record of any decisions and agreements made at the conference.

NOTICE TO APPEAR

25. (1) Notice to appear — The Division must notify the claimant or protected person and the Minister in writing of the date, time and location of the proceeding.

(2) Notice to appear for hearing — In the case of a hearing on a refugee claim, the notice may be provided by an officer under paragraph 3(4)(a).

(3) Date fixed for hearing — The date fixed for a hearing of a claim or an application to vacate or to cease refugee protection must not be earlier than 20 days after the day on which the parties receive the notice referred to in subrule (1) or (2) unless

    (a) the hearing has been adjourned or postponed from an earlier date; or

    (b) the parties consent to an earlier date.

Case Law

Canada (Ministre de la Citoyenneté & de l'Immigration) c. Deffo, 2005 CarswellNat 3924, 2005 CarswellNat 5117, 2005 FC 1589 — The Refugee Protection Division of the Immigration and Refugee Board has a duty to formally notify the counsel representing the Minister pursuant to s. 170(e) of the IRPA and s. 22 of the Rules. There is no discretionary authority for the Board to dispense of this duty. In failing to notify the counsel of record for the Minister after he had filed a notice of intervention in accordance with subs. 25(1) of the Rules, the Board erred in law.

EXCLUSION, INTEGRITY ISSUES, INADMISSIBILITY AND INELIGIBILITY

26. (1) Notice to Minister of possible exclusion before hearing — If the Division believes, before a hearing begins, that there is a possibility that section E or F of Article 1 of the Refugee Convention applies to the claim, the Division must without delay notify the Minister in writing and provide any relevant information to the Minister.

(2) Notice to Minister of possible exclusion during hearing — If the Division believes, after a hearing begins, that there is a possibility that section E or F of Article 1 of the Refugee Convention applies to the claim and the Division is of the opinion that the Minister's participation may help in the full and proper hearing of the claim, the Division must adjourn the hearing and without delay notify the Minister in writing and provide any relevant information to the Minister.

(3) Disclosure to claimant — The Division must provide to the claimant a copy of any notice or information that the Division provides to the Minister.

(4) Resumption of hearing — The Division must fix a date for the resumption of the hearing that is as soon as practicable,

(a) if the Minister responds to the notice referred to in subrule (2), after receipt of the response from the Minister; or

(b) if the Minister does not respond to that notice, no earlier than 14 days after receipt of the notice by the Minister.

27. (1) Notice to Minister of possible integrity issues before hearing — If the Division believes, before a hearing begins, that there is a possibility that issues relating to the integrity of the Canadian refugee protection system may arise from the claim and the Division is of the opinion that the Minister's participation may help in the full and proper hearing of the claim, the Division must without delay notify the Minister in writing and provide any relevant information to the Minister.

(2) Notice to Minister of possible integrity issues during hearing — If the Division believes, after a hearing begins, that there is a possibility that issues relating to the integrity of the Canadian refugee protection system may arise from the claim and the Division is of the opinion that the Minister's participation may help in the full and proper hearing of the claim, the Division must adjourn the hearing and without delay notify the Minister in writing and provide any relevant information to the Minister.

(3) Integrity issues — For the purpose of this rule, claims in which the possibility that issues relating to the integrity of the Canadian refugee protection system may arise include those in which there is

(a) information that the claim may have been made under a false identity in whole or in part;

(b) a substantial change to the basis of the claim from that indicated in the Basis of Claim Form first provided to the Division;

Rules

(c) information that, in support of the claim, the claimant submitted documents that may be fraudulent; or

(d) other information that the claimant may be directly or indirectly misrepresenting or withholding material facts relating to a relevant matter.

(4) **Disclosure to claimant** — The Division must provide to the claimant a copy of any notice or information that the Division provides to the Minister.

(5) **Resumption of hearing** — The Division must fix a date for the resumption of the hearing that is as soon as practicable,

(a) if the Minister responds to the notice referred to in subrule (2), after receipt of the response from the Minister; or

(b) if the Minister does not respond to that notice, no earlier than 14 days after receipt of the notice by the Minister.

28. (1) **Notice of possible inadmissibility or ineligibility** — The Division must without delay notify the Minister in writing and provide the Minister with any relevant information if the Division believes that

(a) a claimant may be inadmissible on grounds of security, violating human or international rights, serious criminality or organized criminality;

(b) there is an outstanding charge against the claimant for an offence under an Act of Parliament that is punishable by a maximum term of imprisonment of at least 10 years; or

(c) the claimant's claim may be ineligible to be referred under section 101 or paragraph 104(1)(c) or (d) of the Act.

(2) **Disclosure to claimant** — The Division must provide to the claimant a copy of any notice or information that the Division provides to the Minister.

(3) **Continuation of proceeding** — If, within 20 days after receipt of the notice referred to in subrule (1), the Minister does not notify the Division that the proceedings are suspended under paragraph 103(1)(a) or (b) of the Act or that the pending proceedings respecting the claim are terminated under section 104 of the Act, the Division may continue with the proceedings.

INTERVENTION BY THE MINISTER

29. (1) **Notice of intention to intervene** — To intervene in a claim, the Minister must provide

(a) to the claimant, a copy of a notice of the Minister's intention to intervene; and

(b) to the Division, the original of the notice, together with a written statement indicating how and when a copy was provided to the claimant.

(2) **Contents of notice** — In the notice, the Minister must state

(a) the purpose for which the Minister will intervene;

(b) whether the Minister will intervene in writing only, in person, or both; and

(o) the Minister's counsel's contact information.

(3) Intervention — exclusion clauses — If the Minister believes that section E or F of Article 1 of the Refugee Convention may apply to the claim, the Minister must also state in the notice the facts and law on which the Minister relies.

(4) Time limit — Documents provided under this rule must be received by their recipients no later than 10 days before the date fixed for a hearing.

CLAIMANT OR PROTECTED PERSON IN CUSTODY

30. Custody — The Division may order a person who holds a claimant or protected person in custody to bring the claimant or protected person to a proceeding at a location specified by the Division.

DOCUMENTS

Form and Language of Documents

31. (1) Documents prepared by party — A document prepared for use by a party in a proceeding must be typewritten, in a type not smaller than 12 point, on one or both sides of 216 mm by 279 mm (8 1/2 inches x 11 inches) paper.

(2) Photocopies — Any photocopy provided by a party must be a clear copy of the document photocopied and be on one or both sides of 216 mm by 279 mm (8 1/2 inches x 11 inches) paper.

(3) List of documents — If more than one document is provided, the party must provide a list identifying each of the documents.

(4) Consecutively numbered pages — A party must consecutively number each page of all the documents provided as if they were one document.

32. (1) Language of documents — claimant or protected person — All documents used by a claimant or protected person in a proceeding must be in English or French or, if in another language, be provided together with an English or French translation and a declaration signed by the translator.

(2) Language of Minister's documents — All documents used by the Minister in a proceeding must be in the language of the proceeding or be provided together with a translation in the language of the proceeding and a declaration signed by the translator.

(3) Translator's declaration — A translator's declaration must include translator's name, the language and dialect, if any, translated and a statement that the translation is accurate.

Disclosure and Use of Documents

33. (1) Disclosure of documents by Division — Subject to subrule (2), if the Division wants to use a document in a hearing, the Division must provide a copy of the document to each party.

(2) Disclosure of country documentation by Division — The Division may disclose country documentation by providing to the parties a list of those documents or providing information as to where a list of those documents can be found on the Board's website.

34. (1) Disclosure of documents by party — If a party wants to use a document in a hearing, the party must provide a copy of the document to the other party, if any, and to the Division.

(2) Proof that document was provided — The copy of the document provided to the Division must be accompanied by a written statement indicating how and when a copy of that document was provided to the other party, if any.

(3) Time limit — Documents provided under this rule must be received by their recipients no later than

(a) 10 days before the date fixed for the hearing; or

(b) five days before the date fixed for the hearing if the document is provided to respond to another document provided by a party or the Division.

Case Law

Flores v. Canada (Minister of Citizenship & Immigration), 2005 CarswellNat 2332, 2005 FC 1138 — The applicant claimed refugee protection in Canada, but a panel of the Immigration and Refugee Board dismissed his claim because it felt he had not provided acceptable evidence of identity. On the day of his hearing, the applicant provided two documents he hoped would constitute good evidence of his identity and nationality. The first was a photocopy of one page of a Salvadoran passport. The second was a faxed copy of a birth certificate. The Board found that the applicant had failed to prove his identity and, therefore, that it was unnecessary to consider the merits of the claim. The Board stated that it "rejected" the applicant's identity documents for the following reasons: the photocopy of the passport did not resemble the applicant; the documents were mere photocopies; the originals were not available, and the applicant could not provide a reasonable explanation why he could not get them; the applicant had nearly a year between making his refugee claim and the date of his hearing to obtain acceptable identity documents; the documents were filed very late, on the date of the hearing; and the applicant claimed to have spent a period of time in the United States but, without a complete passport, it was impossible to verify the duration of his stay there. Since the Board did not reject the documents solely because they were photocopies, its decision was not out of keeping with the requirements of the IRPA or the Rules.

Hasan v. Canada (Minister of Citizenship & Immigration), 2004 CarswellNat 5000, 2004 CarswellNat 3864, 2004 FC 1537 — The applicant sought to review a negative determination of his application for refugee status and for protection. The Board in rejecting the application, refused to admit as evidence more than 550 pages of documents. The Board paid particular attention to Rule 29 which sets out the 20-day and five-day deadlines.

The decision of the Board was set aside. The Board failed to pay attention to Rule 30, which gives it the discretion to admit documents filed outside the prescribed time. The exercise of the Board's discretion resulted in a denial of natural justice and a breach of principles of fairness. There would have been no offsetting prejudice to the respondent had the evidence been admitted.

35. Documents relevant and not duplicate — Each document provided by a party for use at a proceeding must

(a) be relevant to the particular proceeding; and

(b) not duplicate other documents provided by a party or by the Division.

36. Use of undisclosed documents — A party who does not provide a document in accordance with rule 34 must not use the document at the hearing unless allowed to do so by the Division. In deciding whether to allow its use, the Division must consider any relevant factors, including

(a) the document's relevance and probative value;

(b) any new evidence the document brings to the hearing; and

(c) whether the party, with reasonable effort, could have provided the document as required by rule 34.

Case Law

Flores v. Canada (Minister of Citizenship & Immigration), 2005 CarswellNat 2332, 2005 FC 1138 — The applicant claimed refugee protection in Canada, but a panel of the Immigration and Refugee Board dismissed his claim because it felt he had not provided acceptable evidence of identity. On the day of his hearing, the applicant provided two documents he hoped would constitute good evidence of his identity and nationality. The first was a photocopy of one page of a Salvadoran passport. The second was a faxed copy of a birth certificate. The Board found that the applicant had failed to prove his identity and, therefore, that it was unnecessary to consider the merits of the claim. The Board stated that it "rejected" the applicant's identity documents for the following reasons: the photocopy of the passport did not resemble the applicant; the documents were mere photocopies; the originals were not available, and the applicant could not provide a reasonable explanation why he could not get them; the applicant had nearly a year between making his refugee claim and the date of his hearing to obtain acceptable identity documents; the documents were filed very late, on the date of the hearing; and the applicant claimed to have spent a period of time in the United States but, without a complete passport, it was impossible to verify the duration of his stay there. Since the Board did not reject the documents solely because they were photocopies, its decision was not out of keeping with the requirements of the IRPA or the Rules.

Behaz v. Canada (Minister of Citizenship & Immigration), 2005 CarswellNat 1583, 2005 FC 791 — At the applicant's refugee hearing, his counsel attempted to have the Board admit a package of approximately 87 pages of documentary evidence that had not previously been disclosed by the applicant. The Board initially refused to accept any documents, but ultimately agreed to accept only the identity documents. The decision was set aside. The member, in refusing to admit the applicant's documents did not consider the factors outlined in Rule 30. The only reasons given by the Board for not allowing the late filing was the size of the package of documents and the lateness of the request. It was a denial of natural justice for the presiding member not to take the listed factors in Rule 30 into consideration.

Providing a Document

37. General provision — **Rules 38 to 41 apply to any document, including a notice or request in writing.**

38. (1) Providing documents to Division — **A document to be provided to the Division must be provided to the registry office specified by the Division.**

(2) Providing documents to Minister — **A document to be provided to the Minister must be provided to the Minister's counsel.**

(3) Providing documents to person other than Minister — **A document to be provided to a person other than the Minister must be provided to the person's counsel if the person has counsel of record. If the person does not have counsel of record, the document must be provided to the person.**

Case Law

Section 38(3)

Sharma v. Canada (Minister of Citizenship & Immigration), 2006 CarswellNat 206, 2006 FC 95 — The Board has a duty to give a refugee claimant an opportunity, at a hearing, to show why his or her claim should not be abandoned. Before declaring a claim abandoned, the Board must consider the explanation the claimant provides at the hearing, the claimant's readiness to proceed with his or her claim, as well as other relevant information. Obviously, these obligations would be meaningless if there were no duty to inform the claimant when and where a hearing was to take place. The Board must give a claimant notice in writing of an abandonment hearing. There is no obligation on the Board to send out a new notice when the applicant changes counsel.

39. How to provide document — **Unless these Rules provide otherwise, a document may be provided in any of the following ways:**

    (a) by hand;

    (b) by regular mail or registered mail;

    (c) by courier;

    (d) by fax if the recipient has a fax number and the document is no more than 20 pages long, unless the recipient consents to receiving more than 20 pages; and

    (e) by email or other electronic means if the Division allows.

40. (1) Application if unable to provide document — **If a party is unable to provide a document in a way required by rule 39, the party may make an applica-**

tion to the Division to be allowed to provide the document in another way or to be excused from providing the document.

(2) Form of application — The application must be made in accordance with rule 50.

(3) Allowing application — The Division must not allow the application unless the party has made reasonable efforts to provide the document to the person to whom the document must be provided.

41. (1) When document received by Division — A document provided to the Division is considered to be received by the Division on the day on which the document is date-stamped by the Division.

(2) When document received by recipient other than Division — A document provided by regular mail other than to the Division is considered to be received seven days after the day on which it was mailed. If the seventh day is not a working day, the document is considered to be received on the next working day.

(3) Extension of time limit — next working day — When the time limit for providing a document ends on a day that is not a working day, the time limit is extended to the next working day.

Original Documents

42. (1) Original documents — A party who has provided a copy of a document to the Division must provide the original document to the Division

    (a) without delay, on the written request of the Division; or

    (b) if the Division does not make a request, no later than at the beginning of the proceeding at which the document will be used.

(2) Documents referred to in paragraph 3(5)(e) or (g) — On the written request of the Division, the Minister must without delay provide to the Division the original of any document referred to in paragraph 3(5)(e) or (g) that is in the possession of an officer.

Additional Documents

43. (1) Documents after hearing — A party who wants to provide a document as evidence after a hearing but before a decision takes effect must make an application to the Division.

(2) Application — The party must attach a copy of the document to the application that must be made in accordance with rule 50, but the party is not required to give evidence in an affidavit or statutory declaration.

(3) Factors — In deciding the application, the Division must consider any relevant factors, including

    (a) the document's relevance and probative value;

(b) any new evidence the document brings to the proceedings; and

(c) whether the party, with reasonable effort, could have provided the document as required by rule 34.

Case Law

Cox v. Canada (Minister of Citizenship & Immigration) (2012), 12 Imm. L.R. (4th) 232, 2012 FC 1220, 2012 CarswellNat 4047, 2012 CarswellNat 4622 — The applicants sought judicial review of a decision of the Refugee Protection Division of the Immigration and Refugee Board in which the Board determined that the applicants were neither Convention refugees nor persons in need of protection in accordance with ss. 96 and 97 of IRPA. The applicants submitted an application for the admission of additional evidence following the hearing. The Board determined that it was inadmissible because it had not been adequately explained why the documents submitted post-hearing were not able to be requested, obtained and put before the Board within the timelines set out in the *Refugee Protection Division Rules* or even at the hearing. The documents' relevance and probative value were important facts that the Board should have considered in its treatment of the application to admit the post-hearing evidence. The Board was required to consider the relevance, probative value and newness of the documents, i.e. the factors enumerated in Refugee Protection Division Rule 37(3)(a) and (b). While the list of factors to be considered in Rule 37(3) is not exhaustive, the use of the word "including" rather than the words "such as" before the list of factors indicates the intent that each of the factors included in the sub-rule be considered. A failure to do so gives rise to a breach of procedural fairness. The application for judicial review was allowed.

[Editor's Note: This case was decided under the previous RPD Rules but is still relevant here.]

Mosqueda Costa v. Canada (Minister of Citizenship & Immigration), 2011 FC 1388, 2011 CarswellNat 5078, 2011 CarswellNat 5801 — The applicant made a refugee claim in May 2009 and represented herself at the hearing before the Board. An issue arose as to whether the applicant should have been given the opportunity at, or after, the hearing to file further evidence as to the denunciations she made to the Mexican authorities with respect to the persons she alleged were troubling her. The transcript of the hearing made it clear that the applicant had offered to provide further evidence as to these denunciations, but the members said she could not do so.

The dismissal by the member of what amounted to the self-represented applicant's attempt to do so, without advising the applicant or considering Rule 37, was an error in law and failure to provide due process. It was clear from the member's reasons that the denunciations were material to the decision being made. Refusal or neglect or oversight in not permitting the applicant an opportunity to provide such documentation was a reviewable error. The application was allowed.

Nagulesan v. Canada (Minister of Citizenship & Immigration) (2004), 44 Imm. L.R. (3d) 99, 2004 FC 1382, 2004 CarswellNat 5903, 2004 CarswellNat 3637, [2004] F.C.J. No. 1690 — The applicant sought to review a negative decision respecting his claim under ss. 96 and 97. A few days after his hearing, the applicant delivered to the RPD a letter addressed to the member presiding at his hearing indicating that he wished to file additional evidence to corroborate his testimony. The proposed evidence was attached to the letter. The letter and the documents attached thereto were not in the certified copy of the tribunal record and the RPD did not refer to the evidence at all in its decision.

The applicant's letter satisfied the requirement of Rule 37. This meant that the RPD had to deal with the applicant's request. It could simply mention that having reviewed the letter, it decided not to consider the evidence because of factors listed in Rule 37(3), or it could accept the new evidence and deal with it in its decision. The failure to deal with the matter at all was a breach of procedural fairness and the decision was set aside.

WITNESSES

44. (1) Providing witness information — If a party wants to call a witness, the party must provide the following witness information in writing to the other party, if any, and to the Division:

(a) the witness's contact information;

(b) a brief statement of the purpose and substance of the witness's testimony or, in the case of an expert witness, the expert witness's brief signed summary of the testimony to be given;

(c) the time needed for the witness's testimony;

(d) the party's relationship to the witness;

(e) in the case of an expert witness, a description of the expert witness's qualifications; and

(f) whether the party wants the witness to testify by means of live telecommunication.

(2) Proof witness information provided — The witness information provided to the Division must be accompanied by a written statement indicating how and when it was provided to the other party, if any.

(3) Time limit — Documents provided under this rule must be received by their recipients no later than 10 days before the date fixed for the hearing.

(4) Failure to provide witness information — If a party does not provide the witness information, the witness must not testify at the hearing unless the Division allows them to testify.

(5) Factors — In deciding whether to allow a witness to testify, the Division must consider any relevant factors, including

(a) the relevance and probative value of the proposed testimony; and

(b) the reason why the witness information was not provided.

Case Law

R. v. Laboucan, [2010] 1 S.C.R. 397, 73 C.R. (6th) 235, (sub nom. *R. v. Briscoe)* 400 N.R. 200, 22 Alta. L.R. (5th) 62, 253 C.C.C. (3d) 129, [2010] 6 W.W.R. 13, 316 D.L.R. (4th) 590, [2010] S.C.J. No. 12, (sub nom. *R. v. Briscoe)* 477 A.R. 70, 483 W.A.C. 70, 2010 SCC 12, 2010 CarswellAlta 591, 2010 CarswellAlta 590 — The fact that a witness has an interest in the outcome of the proceedings is common sense and a relevant factor, among others, to take into account when assessing the credibility of the witness's testimony. A trier of fact, however, should not place undue weight on the status of a person in the proceeding as a factor going to credibility. For example, it would be improper to base a finding of credibility regarding a parent's or a spouse's testimony solely on the basis of a witness's relationship to the complainant or to the accused. Regard should be given to all relevant factors in assessing credibility.

45. (1) Requesting summons — A party who wants the Division to order a person to testify at a hearing must make a request to the Division for a summons, either orally at a proceeding or in writing.

(2) Factors — In deciding whether to issue a summons, the Division must consider any relevant factors, including

  (a) the necessity of the testimony to a full and proper hearing;

  (b) the person's ability to give that testimony; and

  (c) whether the person has agreed to be summoned as a witness.

(3) Using summons — If a party wants to use a summons, the party must

  (a) provide the summons to the person by hand;

  (b) provide a copy of the summons to the Division, together with a written statement indicating the name of the person who provided the summons and the date, time and place that it was provided by hand; and

  (c) pay or offer to pay the person the applicable witness fees and travel expenses set out in Tariff A of the *Federal Courts Rules*.

Case Law

Canada (Minister of Public Safety & Emergency Preparedness) v. Kahlon (2005), 35 Admin. L.R. (4th) 213, 2005 CarswellNat 2255, 2005 CarswellNat 5610, 2005 FC 1000 — The proper procedure when there is a requirement to produce documents, whether by subpoena or otherwise, and there is a genuine dispute as to their relevance or as to whether they are privileged, is to have the documents produced, so that the tribunal charged with determining their relevance will have them available for examination. If any of the documents then turned out to be irrelevant, the privacy interest of the owner would be protected as the documents would not then be provided to the party making the demand. In this case, the Refugee Protection Division improperly exercised its powers to compel evidence and did not follow its own procedural rules.

46. (1) Cancelling summons — If a person who is summoned to appear as a witness wants the summons cancelled, the person must make an application in writing to the Division.

(2) Application — The person must make the application in accordance with rule 50, but is not required to give evidence in an affidavit or statutory declaration.

47. (1) Arrest warrant — If a person does not obey a summons to appear as a witness, the party who requested the summons may make a request to the Division orally at the hearing, or in writing, to issue a warrant for the person's arrest.

(2) Written request — A party who makes a written request for a warrant must provide supporting evidence by affidavit or statutory declaration.

(3) **Requirements for issue of arrest warrant** — The Division must not issue a warrant unless

(a) the person was provided the summons by hand or the person is avoiding being provided the summons;

(b) the person was paid or offered the applicable witness fees and travel expenses set out in Tariff A of the *Federal Courts Rules*;

(c) the person did not appear at the hearing as required by the summons; and

(d) the person's testimony is still needed for a full and proper hearing.

(4) **Content of warrant** — A warrant issued by the Division for the arrest of a person must include directions concerning detention or release.

48. Excluded witness — If the Division excludes a witness from a hearing room, no person may communicate to the witness any evidence given while the witness was excluded unless allowed to do so by the Division or until the witness has finished testifying.

APPLICATIONS

General

49. General provision — Unless these Rules provide otherwise,

(a) a party who wants the Division to make a decision on any matter in a proceeding, including the procedure to be followed, must make an application to the Division in accordance with rule 50;

(b) a party who wants to respond to the application must respond in accordance with rule 51; and

(c) a party who wants to reply to a response must reply in accordance with rule 52.

How to Make an Application

50. (1) Written application and time limit — Unless these Rules provide otherwise, an application must be made in writing, without delay, and must be received by the Division no later than 10 days before the date fixed for the next proceeding.

(2) **Oral application** — The Division must not allow a party to make an application orally at a proceeding unless the party, with reasonable effort, could not have made a written application before the proceeding.

(3) **Content of application** — Unless these Rules provide otherwise, in a written application, the party must

(a) state the decision the party wants the Division to make;

(b) give reasons why the Division should make that decision; and

Rules

(c) if there is another party and the views of that party are known, state whether the other party agrees to the application.

(4) Affidavit or statutory declaration — Unless these Rules provide otherwise, any evidence that the party wants the Division to consider with a written application must be given in an affidavit or statutory declaration that accompanies the application.

(5) Providing application to other party and Division — A party who makes a written application must provide

(a) to the other party, if any, a copy of the application and a copy of any affidavit or statutory declaration; and

(b) to the Division, the original application and the original of any affidavit or statutory declaration, together with a written statement indicating how and when the party provided a copy to the other party, if any.

How to Respond to a Written Application

51. (1) Responding to written application — A response to a written application must be in writing and

(a) state the decision the party wants the Division to make; and

(b) give reasons why the Division should make that decision.

(2) Evidence in written response — Any evidence that the party wants the Division to consider with the written response must be given in an affidavit or statutory declaration that accompanies the response. Unless the Division requires it, an affidavit or statutory declaration is not required if the party who made the application was not required to give evidence in an affidavit or statutory declaration, together with the application.

(3) Providing response — A party who responds to a written application must provide

(a) to the other party, a copy of the response and a copy of any affidavit or statutory declaration; and

(b) to the Division, the original response and the original of any affidavit or statutory declaration, together with a written statement indicating how and when the party provided a copy to the other party.

(4) Time limit — Documents provided under subrule (3) must be received by their recipients no later than five days after the date on which the party receives the copy of the application.

How to Reply to a Written Response

52. (1) Replying to written response — A reply to a written response must be in writing.

(2) Evidence in reply — Any evidence that the party wants the Division to consider with the written reply must be given in an affidavit or statutory declaration that accompanies the reply. Unless the Division requires it, an affidavit or statutory declaration is not required if the party was not required to give evidence in an affidavit or statutory declaration, together with the application.

(3) Providing reply — A party who replies to a written response must provide

(a) to the other party, a copy of the reply and a copy of any affidavit or statutory declaration; and

(b) to the Division, the original reply and the original of any affidavit or statutory declaration, together with a written statement indicating how and when the party provided a copy to the other party.

(4) Time limit — Documents provided under subrule (3) must be received by their recipients no later than three days after the date on which the party receives the copy of the response.

CHANGING THE LOCATION OF A PROCEEDING

53. (1) Application to change location — A party may make an application to the Division to change the location of a proceeding.

(2) Form and content of application — The party must make the application in accordance with rule 50, but is not required to give evidence in an affidavit or statutory declaration.

(3) Time limit — Documents provided under this rule must be received by their recipients no later than 20 days before the date fixed for the proceeding.

(4) Factors — In deciding the application, the Division must consider any relevant factors, including

(a) whether the party is residing in the location where the party wants the proceeding to be held;

(b) whether a change of location would allow the proceeding to be full and proper;

(c) whether a change of location would likely delay the proceeding;

(d) how a change of location would affect the Division's operation;

(e) how a change of location would affect the parties;

(f) whether a change of location is necessary to accommodate a vulnerable person; and

(g) whether a hearing may be conducted by a means of live telecommunication with the claimant or protected person.

(5) Duty to appear — Unless a party receives a decision from the Division allowing the application, the party must appear for the proceeding at the location fixed and be ready to start or continue the proceeding.

Case Law

Sundaram v. Canada (Minister of Citizenship & Immigration), 2006 CarswellNat 499, 2006 CarswellNat 2426, 2006 FC 291 — When the IRB receives requests for a change of venue because a person cannot attend at a scheduled hearing location, it has an obligation to consider all relevant matters including its own discretionary powers relevant to the request. In this case, the applicant had moved from Toronto to Vancouver. As there was no indication in the conclusionary reasons that the Refugee Protection Division ever turned its mind to the issue of alternative means and locations of hearing, the decision not to reopen the dismissal of the applicant's refugee claim was quashed.

CHANGING THE DATE OR TIME OF A PROCEEDING

54. (1) Application in writing — Subject to subrule (5), an application to change the date or time of a proceeding must be made in accordance with rule 50, but the party is not required to give evidence in an affidavit or statutory declaration.

(2) Time limit and content of application — The application must

(a) be made without delay;

(b) be received by the Division no later than three working days before the date fixed for the proceeding, unless the application is made for medical reasons or other emergencies; and

(c) include at least three dates and times, which are no later than 10 working days after the date originally fixed for the proceeding, on which the party is available to start or continue the proceeding.

(3) Oral application — If it is not possible for the party to make the application in accordance with paragraph (2)(b), the party must appear on the date fixed for the proceeding and make the application orally before the time fixed for the proceeding.

(4) Factors — Subject to subrule (5), the Division must not allow the application unless there are exceptional circumstances, such as

(a) the change is required to accommodate a vulnerable person; or

(b) an emergency or other development outside the party's control and the party has acted diligently.

(5) Counsel retained or availability of counsel provided after hearing date fixed — If, at the time the officer fixed the hearing date under subrule 3(1), a claimant did not have counsel or was unable to provide the dates when their counsel would be available to attend a hearing, the claimant may make an application to change the date or time of the hearing. Subject to operational limitations, the Division must allow the application if

(a) the claimant retains counsel no later than five working days after the day on which the hearing date was fixed by the officer;

(b) the counsel retained is not available on the date fixed for the hearing;

(c) the application is made in writing;

(d) the application is made without delay and no later than five working days after the day on which the hearing date was fixed by the officer; and

(e) the claimant provides at least three dates and times when counsel is available, which are within the time limits set out in the Regulations for the hearing of the claim.

(6) **Application for medical reasons** — If a claimant or protected person makes the application for medical reasons, other than those related to their counsel, they must provide, together with the application, a legible, recently dated medical certificate signed by a qualified medical practitioner whose name and address are printed or stamped on the certificate. A claimant or protected person who has provided a copy of the certificate to the Division must provide the original document to the Division without delay.

(7) **Content of certificate** — The medical certificate must set out

(a) the particulars of the medical condition, without specifying the diagnosis, that prevent the claimant or protected person from participating in the proceeding on the date fixed for the proceeding; and

(b) the date on which the claimant or protected person is expected to be able to participate in the proceeding.

(8) **Failure to provide medical certificate** — If a claimant or protected person fails to provide a medical certificate in accordance with subrules (6) and (7), they must include in their application

(a) particulars of any efforts they made to obtain the required medical certificate, supported by corroborating evidence;

(b) particulars of the medical reasons for the application, supported by corroborating evidence; and

(c) an explanation of how the medical condition prevents them from participating in the proceeding on the date fixed for the proceeding.

(9) **Subsequent application** — If the party made a previous application that was denied, the Division must consider the reasons for the denial and must not allow the subsequent application unless there are exceptional circumstances supported by new evidence.

(10) **Duty to appear** — Unless a party receives a decision from the Division allowing the application, the party must appear for the proceeding at the date and time fixed and be ready to start or continue the proceeding.

(11) **New date** — If an application for a change to the date or time of a proceeding is allowed, the new date fixed by the Division must be no later than 10 working days after the date originally fixed for the proceeding or as soon as possible after that date.

Case Law

Guylas v. Canada (Minister of Citizenship and Immigration) (2015), 33 Imm. L.R. (4th) 142, 2015 FC 202, 2015 CarswellNat 353, 2015 CarswellNat 2151 — The court concluded there was a breach of procedural fairness by the refusal to postpone the hearing to allow the applicants to be represented by counsel. The member's position was that when a new lawyer is retained with a pending hearing date determined, "he has to be ready to go at the hearing." Recent amendments to the legislation had changed the scheduling process such that dates were given for hearings at the initial meetings with refugee claimants. The applicants' circumstances of scheduling fell within the transition period for the amendments, where notice of the hearing was provided a month before the hearing date. Where dates are set long in advance of their occurrence, the need for a restrictive policy on adjournments can be understood. However, in the transition period, in the context of a one-off situation where the date was fixed in the month before the hearing, a fair and reasonable approach must consider the circumstances of the applicants. The member erred in relying upon the policy reflected in the amended Rules. The right to counsel is important and can be a determinative factor in the outcome of these decisions, particularly where there is some sense that the applicants are vulnerable. While it was commendable from an efficiency standpoint that the member was prepared to deal with both matters, the aura of urgency that pervaded the hearing undermined the process. A reading of the transcript suggests some sense of impatience and concern on the part of the member about being able to complete the hearing. The manner in which the request for an adjournment was decided smacks of unreasonableness by its peremptory nature, giving the appearance of lack of transparency.

Laidlow v. Canada (Minister of Citizenship & Immigration) (2012), 12 Imm. L.R. (4th) 33, 440 N.R. 105, 2012 FCA 256, 2012 CarswellNat 3843, 2012 CarswellNat 5564 — The appellant was diagnosed with a benign tumor affecting his brain and pituitary gland. While in the hospital he commenced the paperwork for a claim for refugee protection in Canada. The basis of the claim was that he faced a risk to his life were he to return to St. Vincent, in that he would be unable to access adequate medical treatment there. A year later, he applied for permanent residence based on humanitarian and compassionate grounds on the basis that he would be unable to afford life sustaining medication were he to return to St. Vincent. A request for an adjournment of his refugee claim pending the outcome of his humanitarian and compassionate application was refused. The Refugee Protection Division then rejected the his refugee claim and he sought judicial review of the decision to deny the adjournment.

Section 7 of the *Charter* does not impose a positive obligation on the RPD to adjourn its hearing until the determination of the humanitarian and compassionate application. The appellant's right to request an adjournment so he could exhaust his non-constitutional remedies does not create a corresponding obligation on the RPD to structure its hearing so that the appellant's constitutional arguments were heard last. The appeal was dismissed.

Chohan v. Canada (Minister of Citizenship & Immigration), 2006 CarswellNat 819, 2006 CarswellNat 2501, 2006 FC 390 — The Board has an obligation to deal with a request for an adjournment in a principled way. To have denied the applicant the benefit of a short adjournment was manifestly unfair and contravened the requirement of s. 170 of the IRPA that the applicant be given a reasonable opportunity to present evidence.

The Board's reasons for denying the adjournment request also failed to address the factors required by s. 48 of the *Refugee Protection Division Rules*. Had these factors been considered and applied, the adjournment would also certainly have been granted.

Herman v. Canada (Minister of Citizenship & Immigration), 2005 CarswellNat 1183, 2005 FC 603 — A member of the Immigration and Refugee Protection Board refused a short postponement of the commencement of the applicant's hearing, despite knowing the applicant's counsel had requested the short postponement and that the applicant wanted and expected her counsel to be present. At the time the postponement was refused, counsel was in transit to the Board hearing. The member's decision to refuse to postpone the start time of the hearing was quashed. The member failed to consider the factors set out in Rule 48(4) before ruling on the adjournment. The member did not consider that the applicant wanted counsel present, that counsel had been retained for a long period of time, that counsel was on her way to attend and that the delay was only for about half an hour. The member did not consider the prejudice to the applicant of being denied the right to counsel. Whatever may be said about counsel's actions or the reasonableness of the explanation for the short postponement, the critical matter is that the applicant who was wholly innocent in the matter suffered the consequences of the denied postponement. The Board must, as a minimum, have regard to the consequences of a refusal to postpone and to the relevant factors set out in Rule 48(4).

Sandy v. Canada (Minister of Citizenship & Immigration) (2004), 41 Imm. L.R. (3d) 123, 260 F.T.R. 1 (Eng.), 2004 CarswellNat 5110, 2004 CarswellNat 3724, 2004 FC 1468 — The applicant sought to review a negative determination of her refugee claim. The applicant's legal costs were being paid for by Legal Aid. She was sent a notice to appear for September 3, 2003, when her hearing date would be set. Her counsel could not appear on that date, and the panel set a peremptory hearing dated of October 2nd. Counsel could not appear on October 2nd and requested an adjournment for September 24th which request was denied.

The applicant attended the October 2nd hearing alone and when asked whether she was ready to proceed she replied "not to the fullest". The hearing was finished in one hour, and the applicant was found not to be a convention refugee.

The Board's decision was set aside. The Court could not determine from the transcript whether the Board had given consideration to the factors listed in Rule 48(4) of the *Refugee Protection Division Rules*.

JOINING OR SEPARATING CLAIMS OR APPLICATIONS

55. (1) Claims automatically joined — The Division must join the claim of a claimant to a claim made by the claimant's spouse or common-law partner, child, parent, legal guardian, brother, sister, grandchild or grandparent, unless it is not practicable to do so.

(2) Applications joined if claims joined — Applications to vacate or to cease refugee protection are joined if the claims of the protected persons were joined.

56. (1) Application to join — A party may make an application to the Division to join claims or applications to vacate or to cease refugee protection.

(2) Application to separate — A party may make an application to the Division to separate claims or applications to vacate or to cease refugee protection that are joined.

(3) Form of application and providing application — A party who makes an application to join or separate claims or applications to vacate or to cease refugee protection must do so in accordance with rule 50, but the party is not required to give evidence in an affidavit or statutory declaration. The party must also

(a) provide a copy of the application to any person who will be affected by the Division's decision on the application; and

(b) provide to the Division a written statement indicating how and when the copy of the application was provided to any affected person, together with proof that the party provided the copy to that person.

(4) Time limit — Documents provided under this rule must be received by their recipients no later than 20 days before the date fixed for the hearing.

(5) Factors — In deciding the application to join or separate, the Division must consider any relevant factors, including whether

(a) the claims or applications to vacate or to cease refugee protection involve similar questions of fact or law;

(b) allowing the application to join or separate would promote the efficient administration of the Division's work; and

(c) allowing the application to join or separate would likely cause an injustice.

PROCEEDINGS CONDUCTED IN PUBLIC

57. (1) Minister considered party — For the purpose of this rule, the Minister is considered to be a party whether or not the Minister takes part in the proceedings.

(2) Application — A person who makes an application to the Division to have a proceeding conducted in public must do so in writing and in accordance with this rule rather than rule 50.

(3) Oral application — The Division must not allow a person to make an application orally at a proceeding unless the person, with reasonable effort, could not have made a written application before the proceeding.

(4) Content of application — In the application, the person must

(a) state the decision they want the Division to make;

(b) give reasons why the Division should make that decision;

(c) state whether they want the Division to consider the application in public or in the absence of the public;

(d) give reasons why the Division should consider the application in public or in the absence of the public;

(e) if they want the Division to hear the application orally, give reasons why the Division should do so; and

(f) include any evidence that they want the Division to consider in deciding the application.

(5) Providing application — The person must provide the original application together with two copies to the Division. The Division must provide a copy of the application to the parties.

(6) Response to application — A party may respond to a written application. The response must

(a) state the decision they want the Division to make;

(b) give reasons why the Division should make that decision;

(c) state whether they want the Division to consider the application in public or in the absence of the public;

(d) give reasons why the Division should consider the application in public or in the absence of the public;

(e) if they want the Division to hear the application orally, give reasons why the Division should do so; and

(f) include any evidence that they want the Division to consider in deciding the application.

(7) Providing response — The party must provide a copy of the response to the other party and provide the original response and a copy to the Division, together with a written statement indicating how and when the party provided the copy to the other party.

(8) Providing response to applicant — The Division must provide to the applicant either a copy of the response or a summary of the response referred to in paragraph (12)(a).

(9) Reply to response — An applicant or a party may reply in writing to a written response or a summary of a response.

(10) Providing reply — An applicant or a party who replies to a written response or a summary of a response must provide the original reply and two copies to the Division. The Division must provide a copy of the reply to the parties.

(11) Time limit — An application made under this rule must be received by the Division without delay. The Division must specify the time limit within which a response or reply, if any, is to be provided.

(12) Confidentiality — The Division may take any measures it considers necessary to ensure the confidentiality of the proceeding in respect of the application, including

(a) providing a summary of the response to the applicant instead of a copy; and

(b) if the Division holds a hearing in respect of the application,

(i) excluding the applicant or the applicant and their counsel from the hearing while the party responding to the application provides evidence and makes representations, or

(ii) allowing the presence of the applicant's counsel at the hearing while the party responding to the application provides evidence and makes representations, upon receipt of a written undertaking by counsel not to disclose any evidence or information adduced until a decision is made to hold the hearing in public.

(13) Summary of response — If the Division provides a summary of the response under paragraph (12)(a), or excludes the applicant and their counsel from a hearing in respect of the application under subparagraph (12)(b)(i), the Division must provide a summary of the representations and evidence, if any, that is sufficient to enable the applicant to reply, while ensuring the confidentiality of the proceeding having regard to the factors set out in paragraph 166(b) of the Act.

(14) Notification of decision on application — The Division must notify the applicant and the parties of its decision on the application and provide reasons for the decision.

OBSERVERS

58. (1) Observers — An application under rule 57 is not necessary if an observer is a member of the staff of the Board or a representative or agent of the United Nations High Commissioner for Refugees or if the claimant or protected person consents to or requests the presence of an observer other than a representative of the press or other media of communication at the proceeding.

(2) Observers — factor — The Division must allow the attendance of an observer unless, in the opinion of the Division, the observer's attendance is likely to impede the proceeding.

(3) Observers — confidentiality of proceeding — The Division may take any measures that it considers necessary to ensure the confidentiality of the proceeding despite the presence of an observer.

WITHDRAWAL

59. (1) Abuse of process — For the purpose of subsection 168(2) of the Act, withdrawal of a claim or of an application to vacate or to cease refugee protection is an abuse of process if withdrawal would likely have a negative effect on the Division's integrity. If no substantive evidence has been accepted in the hearing, withdrawal is not an abuse of process.

(2) Withdrawal if no substantive evidence accepted — If no substantive evidence has been accepted in the hearing, a party may withdraw the party's claim or the application to vacate or to cease refugee protection by notifying the Division orally at a proceeding or in writing.

(3) Withdrawal if substantive evidence accepted — If substantive evidence has been accepted in the hearing, a party who wants to withdraw the party's claim or the application to vacate or to cease refugee protection must make an application to the Division in accordance with rule 50.

REINSTATING A WITHDRAWN CLAIM OR APPLICATION

60. (1) **Application to reinstate withdrawn claim** — A person may make an application to the Division to reinstate a claim that was made by the person and was withdrawn.

(2) **Form and content of application** — The person must make the application in accordance with rule 50, include in the application their contact information and, if represented by counsel, their counsel's contact information and any limitations on counsel's retainer, and provide a copy of the application to the Minister.

(3) **Factors** — The Division must not allow the application unless it is established that there was a failure to observe a principle of natural justice or it is otherwise in the interests of justice to allow the application.

(4) **Factors** — In deciding the application, the Division must consider any relevant factors, including whether the application was made in a timely manner and the justification for any delay.

(5) **Subsequent application** — If the person made a previous application to reinstate that was denied, the Division must consider the reasons for the denial and must not allow the subsequent application unless there are exceptional circumstances supported by new evidence.

61. (1) **Application to reinstate withdrawn application to vacate or to cease refugee protection** — The Minister may make an application to the Division to reinstate an application to vacate or to cease refugee protection that was withdrawn.

(2) **Form of application** — The Minister must make the application in accordance with rule 50.

(3) **Factors** — The Division must not allow the application unless it is established that there was a failure to observe a principle of natural justice or it is otherwise in the interests of justice to allow the application.

(4) **Factors** — In deciding the application, the Division must consider any relevant factors, including whether the application was made in a timely manner and the justification for any delay.

(5) **Subsequent application** — If the Minister made a previous application to reinstate that was denied, the Division must consider the reasons for the denial and must not allow the subsequent application unless there are exceptional circumstances supported by new evidence.

REOPENING A CLAIM OR APPLICATION

62. (1) **Application to reopen claim** — At any time before the Refugee Appeal Division or the Federal Court has made a final determination in respect of a claim for refugee protection that has been decided or declared abandoned, the claimant or the Minister may make an application to the Division to reopen the claim.

(2) Form of application — The application must be made in accordance with rule 50 and, for the purpose of paragraph 50(5)(a), the Minister is considered to be a party whether or not the Minister took part in the proceedings.

(3) Contact information — If a claimant makes the application, they must include in the application their contact information and, if represented by counsel, their counsel's contact information and any limitations on counsel's retainer.

(4) Allegations against counsel — If it is alleged in the application that the claimant's counsel in the proceedings that are the subject of the application provided inadequate representation,

(a) the claimant must first provide a copy of the application to the counsel and then provide the original application to the Division, and

(b) the application provided to the Division must be accompanied by a written statement indicating how and when the copy of the application was provided to the counsel.

(5) Copy of notice of appeal or pending application — The application must be accompanied by a copy of any notice of pending appeal or any pending application for leave to apply for judicial review or any pending application for judicial review.

(6) Factor — The Division must not allow the application unless it is established that there was a failure to observe a principle of natural justice.

(7) Factors — In deciding the application, the Division must consider any relevant factors, including

(a) whether the application was made in a timely manner and the justification for any delay; and

(b) the reasons why

(i) a party who had the right of appeal to the Refugee Appeal Division did not appeal, or

(ii) a party did not make an application for leave to apply for judicial review or an application for judicial review.

(8) Subsequent application — If the party made a previous application to reopen that was denied, the Division must consider the reasons for the denial and must not allow the subsequent application unless there are exceptional circumstances supported by new evidence.

(9) Other remedies — If there is a pending appeal to the Refugee Appeal Division or a pending application for leave to apply for judicial review or a pending application for judicial review on the same or similar grounds, the Division must, as soon as is practicable, allow the application to reopen if it is necessary for the timely and efficient processing of a claim, or dismiss the application.

Case Law

Emani v. Canada (Minister of Citizenship & Immigration), 2009 CarswellNat 1527, 2009 FC 520 — The applicant sought judicial review of the decision by an officer of the Immigration Refugee Board refusing the applicant's request to have his refugee claim reopened. The jurisprudence appears to be clear that the central consideration in regard to abandonment proceedings is whether the applicant's conduct amounts to an expression of his intention to diligently prosecute his claim. When presented with the application to have the claim reopened, the Board was furnished for the first time with information explaining the applicant's failure to appear, and demonstrating that it was due solely to administrative errors on the part of his counsel. In rejecting the application to reopen his claim, the Board failed to consider evidence before it of the appellant's conduct demonstrating his intention to earnestly pursue his claim. The Board erred in seeing only part of the picture and neglecting this central consideration.

Matondo v. Canada (Minister of Citizenship & Immigration) (2005), 44 Imm. L.R. (3d) 225, 2005 FC 416, 2005 CarswellNat 761, [2005] F.C.J. No. 509 — The applicant arrived at Pearson Airport in December 2003 and claimed refugee status. Two days later he was given his personal information form which was due January 20. The accompanying notice said that if the form was not filed in time the applicant would have to show cause why the claim should not be declared abandoned. The applicant provided a Toronto address and acknowledged to Citizenship and Immigration Canada that he would inform it of any change of address. The applicant retained counsel and on January 14, the day after counsel was retained, a letter was faxed to Citizenship and Immigration advising that the applicant was now in Montreal and asking for the address to which the personal information form should be mailed. No PIF form was filed by the deadline of January 20, 2004. On January 26, 2004, counsel's office wrote again to immigration asking for certain information as no reply had been received to the earlier fax communication. On February 2, the Board issued an abandonment decision. Counsel faxed again on March 15 and finally on April 5 went to the Montreal office where they were informed that the refugee claim had been declared abandoned. An application was then made under s. 55 to reopen the claim. The member who declared the claim abandoned made no mention of the futile communications the lawyer's office had with Citizenship and Immigration Canada or the applicant's visit to the immigration offices in Montreal. The member took the approach that counsel should have known better. The word abandon means "to give up absolutely". The applicant had done no such thing. Refugee Protection Division Rule 55 makes reference to the principles of natural justice. The fundamental principle is the right to be heard by an impartial decision maker. The right to be heard is at the heart of our sense of justice and fairness. The Court found this decision of the Refugee Protection Division to be aberrant and abhorrent and set it aside.

Ahmad v. Canada (Minister of Citizenship & Immigration), 2005 CarswellNat 532, 2005 FC 279 — The applicant sought to review a decision of the Refugee Protection Division refusing to reopen his refugee claim. A denial of natural justice is the correct consideration to be employed by the Board in an application to reopen. It is not the Board's function at a hearing for an application to reopen to consider issues that should have been raised in a judicial review application of the abandonment hearing.

Krishnamoorthy v. Canada (Minister of Citizenship & Immigration) (2005), 45 Imm. L.R. (3d) 126, 2005 CarswellNat 392, 2005 FC 237 — The applicant sought to review a refusal of his request to reopen his claim for refugee status which had been declared abandoned. Applications to reopen can be allowed only where a breach of natural justice can be demonstrated. Thus, on such an application, the function of the RPD is to review the file to ensure that the abandonment decision was made in a manner that did not breach the principles of natural justice.

Shahid v. Canada (Minister of Citizenship & Immigration), 2004 CarswellNat 5919, 2004 CarswellNat 4311, 2004 FC 1607 (F.C.) — This was an application to review a decision of a Board Member dismissing the applicant's motion to reopen his refugee claim. The decision not to reopen a refugee claim is a final decision. Reasons are required by s. 169(b).

Javed v. Canada (Minister of Citizenship & Immigration) (2004), 41 Imm. L.R. (3d) 118, 2004 CarswellNat 3722, 2004 FC 1458 — This was an application to review a decision refusing the applicants' motion to reopen their refugee claim. Reasons are required for refusing an application to reopen a refugee claim. The reasons in this case were not meaningful or sufficient. The Court was unable to determine why the Board made the decision to refuse to reopen.

Osagie v. Canada (Minister of Citizenship & Immigration) (2004), 262 F.T.R. 112, 2004 CarswellNat 3521, 2004 CarswellNat 5055, 2004 FC 1368 — The applicant sought to review a decision refusing to reopen her refugee claim. The applicant completed and signed her PIF form within the time period required by the IRB. The form was then given to an employee of her lawyer who was to file the form with the Board. The employee, through inadvertence, failed to do so. Because it had not received the form within the stipulated 28-day period, a notice to appear for abandonment was sent by the Board, both to the applicant and her counsel by ordinary mail. Because her counsel had inadvertently given the Board his office address, as the applicant's personal address, both notices were sent to the applicant's lawyer. The applicant's counsel then failed to appear at her abandonment hearing with a result that her claim was declared abandoned. Counsel then applied to reopen the claim and put before the Board all of the mistakes that had been made by counsel in the matter.

The effect of the various errors committed by the applicant's counsel and his employees denied the applicant natural justice and according to the mandatory language of Rule 55 the request to re-open should have been granted.

Ali v. Canada (Minister of Citizenship & Immigration) (2004), 44 Imm. L.R. (3d) 4, 2004 FC 1153, 2004 CarswellNat 5685, 2004 CarswellNat 2742, 258 F.T.R. 226 (Eng.), [2004] F.C.J. No. 1394 — The correct interpretation of Rule 55 is that applications to re-open may only be allowed where a breach of natural justice has been established.

63. (1) Application to reopen application to vacate or to cease refugee protection — At any time before the Federal Court has made a final determination in respect of an application to vacate or to cease refugee protection that has been decided or declared abandoned, the Minister or the protected person may make an application to the Division to reopen the application.

(2) Form of application — The application must be made in accordance with rule 50.

(3) Contact information — If a protected person makes the application, they must include in the application their contact information and, if represented by counsel, their counsel's contact information and any limitations on counsel's retainer, and they must provide a copy of the application to the Minister.

(4) **Allegations against counsel** — If it is alleged in the application that the protected person's counsel in the proceedings that are the subject of the application to reopen provided inadequate representation,

>   (a) the protected person must first provide a copy of the application to the counsel and then provide the original application to the Division, and

>   (b) the application provided to the Division must be accompanied by a written statement indicating how and when the copy of the application was provided to the counsel.

(5) **Copy of pending application** — The application must be accompanied by a copy of any pending application for leave to apply for judicial review or any pending application for judicial review in respect of the application to vacate or to cease refugee protection.

(6) **Factor** — The Division must not allow the application unless it is established that there was a failure to observe a principle of natural justice.

(7) **Factors** — In deciding the application, the Division must consider any relevant factors, including

>   (a) whether the application was made in a timely manner and the justification for any delay; and

>   (b) if a party did not make an application for leave to apply for judicial review or an application for judicial review, the reasons why an application was not made.

(8) **Subsequent application** — If the party made a previous application to reopen that was denied, the Division must consider the reasons for the denial and must not allow the subsequent application unless there are exceptional circumstances supported by new evidence.

(9) **Other remedies** — If there is a pending application for leave to apply for judicial review or a pending application for judicial review on the same or similar grounds, the Division must, as soon as is practicable, allow the application to reopen if it is necessary for the timely and efficient processing of a claim, or dismiss the application.

Case Law

Logeswaren v. Canada (Minister of Citizenship & Immigration) (2004), 256 F.T.R. 78, 2004 FC 886, 2004 CarswellNat 1906, 2004 CarswellNat 2983, [2004] F.C.J. No. 1086 — The applicants were granted refugee status on May 6, 1993. They applied for permanent residency, which application remains pending. The applicants' respective husband and father was also found to be a refugee and has since become a Canadian citizen. The Minister filed an application to vacate the applicants' refugee status in 1999. That application was dismissed for insufficiency of evidence. Early in 2001, the Minister applied for leave to file a second application to vacate under s. 55 of the *Refugee Protection Division Rules*. The applicants brought a motion to dismiss the application to vacate on the basis of *res judicata*. That motion was dismissed and that decision is the subject of this judicial review application.

The Minister had no right to bring a second application to vary under Rule 55. The appropriate remedy was to be found in Rule 56, which gives the Minister the specific right to apply to reopen the first application to vary, even though it has been decided.

APPLICATIONS TO VACATE OR TO CEASE REFUGEE PROTECTION

64. (1) Form of application — An application to vacate or to cease refugee protection made by the Minister must be in writing and made in accordance with this rule.

(2) Content of application — In the application, the Minister must include

(a) the contact information of the protected person and of their counsel, if any;

(b) the identification number given by the Department of Citizenship and Immigration to the protected person;

(c) the date and file number of any Division decision with respect to the protected person;

(d) in the case of a person whose application for protection was allowed abroad, the person's file number, a copy of the decision and the location of the office;

(e) the decision that the Minister wants the Division to make; and

(f) the reasons why the Division should make that decision.

(3) Providing application to protected person and Division — The Minister must provide

(a) a copy of the application to the protected person; and

(b) the original of the application to the registry office that provided the notice of decision in the claim or to a registry office specified by the Division, together with a written statement indicating how and when a copy was provided to the protected person.

ABANDONMENT

65. (1) Opportunity to explain — In determining whether a claim has been abandoned under subsection 168(1) of the Act, the Division must give the claimant an opportunity to explain why the claim should not be declared abandoned,

(a) immediately, if the claimant is present at the proceeding and the Division considers that it is fair to do so; or

(b) in any other case, by way of a special hearing.

(2) Special hearing — Basis of Claim Form — The special hearing on the abandonment of the claim for the failure to provide a completed Basis of Claim Form in accordance with paragraph 7(5)(a) must be held no later than five working days after the day on which the completed Basis of Claim Form was due. At the special hearing, the claimant must provide their completed Basis of Claim Form, unless the form has already been provided to the Division.

(3) **Special hearing — failure to appear** — The special hearing on the abandonment of the claim for the failure to appear for the hearing of the claim must be held no later than five working days after the day originally fixed for the hearing of the claim.

(4) **Factors to consider** — The Division must consider, in deciding if the claim should be declared abandoned, the explanation given by the claimant and any other relevant factors, including the fact that the claimant is ready to start or continue the proceedings.

(5) **Medical reasons** — If the claimant's explanation includes medical reasons, other than those related to their counsel, they must provide, together with the explanation, the original of a legible, recently dated medical certificate signed by a qualified medical practitioner whose name and address are printed or stamped on the certificate.

(6) **Content of certificate** — The medical certificate must set out

(a) the particulars of the medical condition, without specifying the diagnosis, that prevented the claimant from providing the completed Basis of Claim Form on the due date, appearing for the hearing of the claim, or otherwise pursuing their claim, as the case may be; and

(b) the date on which the claimant is expected to be able to pursue their claim.

(7) **Failure to provide medical certificate** — If a claimant fails to provide a medical certificate in accordance with subrules (5) and (6), the claimant must include in their explanation

(a) particulars of any efforts they made to obtain the required medical certificate, supported by corroborating evidence;

(b) particulars of the medical reasons included in the explanation, supported by corroborating evidence; and

(c) an explanation of how the medical condition prevented them from providing the completed Basis of Claim Form on the due date, appearing for the hearing of the claim or otherwise pursuing their claim, as the case may be.

(8) **Start or continue proceedings** — If the Division decides not to declare the claim abandoned, other than under subrule (2), it must start or continue the proceedings on the day the decision is made or as soon as possible after that day.

Case Law

Sharma v. Canada (Minister of Citizenship & Immigration), 2006 CarswellNat 206, 2006 FC 95 — The Board has a duty to give a refugee claimant an opportunity, at a hearing, to show why his or her claim should not be abandoned. Before declaring a claim abandoned, the Board must consider the explanation the claimant provides at the hearing, the claimant's readiness to proceed with his or her claim, as well as other relevant information. Obviously, these obligations would be meaningless if there were no duty to inform the claimant when and where a hearing was to take place. The Board must give a claimant notice in writing of an abandonment hearing. There is no obligation on the Board to send out a new notice when the applicant changes counsel.

Abrazaldo v. Canada (Minister of Citizenship & Immigration), 2005 CarswellNat 2928, 2005 CarswellNat 4995, 2005 FC 1295 — The applicable standard of review to be applied to a decision of the Refugee Protection Division declaring a refugee claim to be abandoned is reasonableness *simpliciter*. This means that the Court is not to decide whether it agrees with the decision of the Refugee Protection Division. The Court must not interfere unless the applicant shows that the decision was unreasonable.

Tajadodi v. Canada (Minister of Citizenship & Immigration) (2005), 49 Imm. L.R. (3d) 129, 2005 CarswellNat 2436, 2005 CarswellNat 5087, 2005 FC 1096 — The test of "exceptional circumstances" applies for considering a request for an extension of time to file a personal information form, and those "exceptional circumstances," if they exist, are among the relevant factors to be considered, but not the decisive test to be applied in declaring a claim abandoned.

Khan v. Canada (Minister of Citizenship & Immigration) (2005), 47 Imm. L.R. (3d) 278, 2005 CarswellNat 1716, 2005 CarswellNat 5405, 2005 FC 833 — There is no doubt that the onus of notifying immigration of change of addresses rests with the refugee claimant. However, where the negligence of counsel is egregious and there has been no contributing negligence or fault on the part of the applicant, the Immigration Refugee Board's decision to refuse to reopen the applicant's claim after it had been declared abandoned when the applicant failed to appear for a hearing and failed to appear at an abandonment show cause hearing can be set aside. In this case, the applicants put their trust in a consultant who led them to believe that he would take care of all correspondence with the Board, that they need not contact the Board directly and that he would advise them of any scheduled proceedings. Consequently, the Court was prepared to accept that their fault was not of such a degree that the applicants should be held accountable for their counsel's failures.

Andreoli v. Canada (Ministre de la Citoyenneté & de l'Immigration), 2004 CarswellNat 5550, 2004 CarswellNat 2680, 2004 FC 1111 — The applicant came to Canada with her family in July 2002. In August 2002 the applicant and her family moved and following the advice of their counsel and the interpreter, they gave their change of address to the interpreter who was working for their counsel. The interpreter had promised that she would inform the IRB of the change of address. The panel of the IRB declared the applicant's claim abandoned when the IRB was unable to reach the applicant because the interpreter had failed to notify them of the change of address. The applicant sought to review that decision.

The evidence established that the interpreter forgot to advise the panel and that it was this error alone that led to the dismissal of the applicant's claim. The applicants do not speak French or English and were therefore particularly vulnerable and dependent on the interpreter. Finding that the applicants were the authors of their own misfortune amounts to punishing them for the carelessness of a third party which is not only unfair but also disregards s. 3(2) of the Act. The decision of the Board declaring the claim abandoned was set aside.

Revich c. Canada (Ministre de la Citoyenneté & de l'Immigration) (2004), 44 Imm. L.R. (3d) 129, 2004 CarswellNat 5036, 2004 CarswellNat 2631, 2004 FC 1064 — The *Refugee Protection Division Rules* clearly provide how the Division must proceed in order to declare a claim abandoned. The Division must give the claimant the opportunity to explain why the claim should not be declared abandoned, must take into account the claimant's explanations and must take into account any other relevant factor, in particular the claimant's intention to pursue the matter. The standard of review to apply to abandonment claim decisions is that of reasonableness *simpliciter*. The case law provides that the question the Division must ask itself is whether the applicant truly intended to abandon the claim.

The claimant did not behave like a person indifferent to the outcome of her claim. She informed her counsel of her absence, consulted a physician who confirmed the seriousness of her state of health. She came to the abandonment proceeding with the necessary documentary evidence. The chairperson dismissed the applicant's explanation but did not explain why. The chairperson drew an invalid inference from the evidence in declaring that the claim had been abandoned.

Anjum v. Canada (Minister of Citizenship & Immigration) (2004), 39 Imm. L.R. (3d) 157, 250 F.T.R. 311, 2004 CarswellNat 2394, 2004 CarswellNat 917, 2004 FC 496 — The decision of a member of the Refugee Division declaring a claim to be abandoned was set aside. The member did not ask the right question. This was an abandonment case where the inquiry must be directed at the true intention and actions of the claimant, in order to conclude that the claim is abandoned. The question is whether the applicants were ready to proceed with their claim.

NOTICE OF CONSTITUTIONAL QUESTION

66. (1) Notice of constitutional question — A party who wants to challenge the constitutional validity, applicability or operability of a legislative provision must complete a notice of constitutional question.

(2) Form and content of notice — The party must complete the notice as set out in Form 69 of the *Federal Courts Rules* or any other form that includes

    (a) the party's name;

    (b) the Division file number;

    (c) the date, time and location of the hearing;

    (d) the specific legislative provision that is being challenged;

    (e) the material facts relied on to support the constitutional challenge; and

    (f) a summary of the legal argument to be made in support of the constitutional challenge.

(3) Providing notice — The party must provide

    (a) a copy of the notice to the Attorney General of Canada and to the attorney general of each province of Canada, in accordance with section 57 of the *Federal Courts Act*;

    (b) a copy of the notice to the Minister;

    (c) a copy of the notice to the other party, if any; and

    (d) the original notice to the Division, together with a written statement indicating how and when the copies of the notice were provided under paragraphs (a) to (c), and proof that they were provided.

(4) Time limit — Documents provided under this rule must be received by their recipients no later than 10 days before the day on which the constitutional argument is made.

DECISIONS

67. (1) Notice of decision and reasons — When the Division makes a decision, other than an interlocutory decision, it must provide in writing a notice of decision to the claimant or the protected person, as the case may be, and to the Minister.

(2) Written reasons — The Division must provide written reasons for the decision together with the notice of decision

(a) if written reasons must be provided under paragraph 169(1)(d) of the Act;

(b) if the Minister was not present when the Division rendered an oral decision and reasons allowing a claim for refugee protection; or

(c) when the Division makes a decision on an application to vacate or to cease refugee protection.

(3) Request for written reasons — A request under paragraph 169(1)(e) of the Act for written reasons for a decision must be made in writing.

Case Law

Gutierrez v. Canada (Minister of Citizenship & Immigration) (2005), 47 Imm. L.R. (3d) 238, 2005 CarswellNat 1706, 2005 CarswellNat 5356, 2005 FC 841 — This was an application for judicial review of the Refugee Protection Division's decision not to reopen the abandonment decision in respect of the applicant's Convention refugee claim. An abandonment decision has dramatic, potentially even fatal, implications for persons. The fact that the Refugee Protection Division did not have an address for the applicant so that it could comply with its obligation to give him notice of its abandonment decision did not relieve the RPD of its obligation under Rule 61(1) to give notice of its decision. The right to be heard is at the heart of our sense of justice and fairness. The RPD failed to observe a principle of natural justice arising out of the failure to give the applicant timely notice of the abandonment decision. The application was allowed and the decision of the RPD was set aside.

Agalliu v. Canada (Minister of Citizenship & Immigration) (2005), 49 Imm. L.R. (3d) 1, 34 Admin. L.R. (4th) 214, 2005 CarswellNat 2112, 2005 FC 1035 — The Board's reasons disclosed a number of superficial errors, in footnotes and in references to the documentary evidence. However, the Board's other errors and its failure to explain its conclusions adequately disclosed more fundamental problems. Taken together, these errors led to the conclusion that the Board's decision was not in keeping with the evidence before it. Sometimes, little errors in a written decision represent no more than a lack of final polishing. Other times, they are symptomatic of inadequate care on the part of the decision maker.

Karakeeva v. Canada (Minister of Citizenship & Immigration) (2004), 35 Imm. L.R. (3d) 219, 2004 CarswellNat 2142, 2004 CarswellNat 705, 2004 FC 416 — A tribunal may make adverse findings of credibility based on the implausibility of an applicant's story, provided the inferences drawn can be reasonably said to exist. However, plausibility findings should be made only in the clearest cases, i.e. if the facts as presented are outside the realm of what could reasonably be expected or where the documentary evidence demonstrates that the events could not have happened in the manner asserted by the claimant. A tribunal must be careful when rendering a decision based on a lack of plausibility because refugee claimants come from diverse cultures. Actions which appear implausible by Canadian standards might be plausible when considered from within the claimant's milieu.

Vlad v. Canada (Minister of Citizenship & Immigration) (2004), 38 Imm. L.R. (3d) 44, 2004 CarswellNat 2874, 2004 CarswellNat 404, 12 Admin. L.R. (4th) 150, 2004 FC 260 — This was an application to review a negative decision of a panel of the Refugee Protection Division.

Questions of procedural fairness are reviewed against a standard of correctness.

The job of a member of the Refugee Protection Division is a difficult one. The Board deals with a very significant volume of cases. Members are required to listen to tales of human misery on a daily basis, sometimes of unimaginable proportions. Their task is complicated by the fact that many claimants speak neither English nor French and must testify with the assistance of an interpreter. Many claimants suffer from psychological trauma which makes it more difficult for them to get their story across. Further, claimants come from a range of different ethnic backgrounds, each with their own cultural norms and attributes.

Sometimes, it may be necessary for Board members to take a somewhat active role in refugee hearings. Board interventions that amount to an energetic exercise in attempting to clear up inconsistencies will not necessarily result in an unfair hearing. If, at the conclusion of the examination, a Board member has concerns about a claimant's testimony the member is entitled to question the applicant in order to clarify the situation.

In this case what happened went beyond what was appropriate. Questions or comments from the Board appear on 111 pages of the 118 pages of the applicant's testimony. The majority of the interventions go beyond benign questions and come closer to what would normally be characterized as cross-examination. Questions were not reserved to the end of the applicant's examination, rather the Board's questions were interspersed throughout the examination in chief and cross-examination. Board members interrupted both the applicant, the applicant's counsel and the refugee protection officer in order to pursue their own line of questions. The Board's intervention did not clarify the situation with respect to the applicant's testimony but just added to the confusion.

The decision of the Board was set aside.

Mihajlovics v. Canada (Minister of Citizenship & Immigration), 2004 CarswellNat 1289, 2004 CarswellNat 348, 2004 FC 215 — This was an application to review a negative decision of a panel of the Refugee Protection Division.

It is well established that on findings of fact the panel is to be accorded a standard of review of patent unreasonableness. On the issue of bias or reasonable apprehension of bias, little deference is paid to the panel and the standard of review is correctness. On the issue of persecution and discrimination, which is a question of mixed law and fact, the standard of review is reasonableness *simpliciter*.

Murji v. Canada (Minister of Citizenship & Immigration) (2004), 36 Imm. L.R. (3d) 314, 2004 FC 148, 2004 CarswellNat 297, [2004] F.C.J. No. 211 — The Board stipulated that the only issues on which it wanted to hear submissions were credibility and delay, then proceeded to decide on the ground of state protection. This amounted to a gross denial of natural justice. The applicant was denied the opportunity to know and answer the case against him by the deliberate decision of the Board member presiding over the hearing.

Kilic v. Canada (Minister of Citizenship & Immigration) (2004), 245 F.T.R. 52, 2004 CarswellNat 1374, 2004 CarswellNat 428, 2004 FC 84, [2004] F.C.J. No. 84 — The applicant sought to review a negative decision of the Refugee Protection Division. The decision was set aside because the panel's reasons did not demonstrate an analysis of s. 97. Despite the Board's negative credibility finding a separate analysis having regard to the wording of s. 97 may have produced a finding that the applicant was a person in need of protection. Accordingly the applicant's application was sent back for redetermination on this ground.

Castillo v. Canada (Minister of Citizenship & Immigration), 2004 CarswellNat 73, 2004 CarswellNat 873, 2004 FC 56 — The Refugee Protection Division failed to explain why it discounted the applicants' evidence and referred solely to the evidence submitted by the Refugee Protection Officer. This created the impression that the RPD had ignored evidence that went to the crux of the matter. The application for judicial review was allowed.

Nozem v. Canada (Minister of Citizenship & Immigration) (2003), 244 F.T.R. 135, 10 Admin. L.R. (4th) 158, 2003 CarswellNat 4620, 2003 FC 1449, 2003 CarswellNat 4119 — The principle of *functus officio* has no application where the final decision in respect of the matter was issued in error.

The principle of *functus officio* is based on policy grounds which favour finality of proceedings.

Justice may require the re-opening of administrative proceedings in order to provide relief which would otherwise be available on appeal.

If the error which renders the decision a nullity is one that taints the whole proceeding then the tribunal must start afresh.

Ben Ghribi v. Canada (Minister of Citizenship & Immigration), 2003 FC 1191, 2003 CarswellNat 3452, 2003 CarswellNat 3144, [2003] F.C.J. No. 1502 — This was an application to review a negative decision of the Refugee Panel. A tribunal is not required to address arguments concerning refugee "sur place" where the applicant has been judged not to have presented any credible evidence substantiating his claim.

Ibrahimov v. Canada (Minister of Citizenship & Immigration) (2003), 32 Imm. L.R. (3d) 135, 2003 CarswellNat 3166, 2003 CarswellNat 3871, 2003 FC 1185 — The applicant sought to review a negative decision of a panel of the Refugee Protection Division. The alleged delay in the applicant's departure from Azerbaijan was a critical reason for the Board's rejection of his claim. Delay not only affected the Board's assessment of the subjective element but also was a significant factor underlying its assessment of the applicant's credibility.

When a claim is based on a number of discriminatory or harassing incidents which culminate in an event which forces a person to leave his country, then the issue of delay cannot be used as a significant factor to doubt that person's subjective fear of persecution.

Shah v. Canada (Minister of Citizenship & Immigration) (2003), 240 F.T.R. 15, 2003 FC 1121, 2003 CarswellNat 4768, 2003 CarswellNat 2983, [2003] F.C.J. No. 1418 — The applicant sought to review a negative decision of a panel of the Refugee Protection Division.

The Board's reasons are insufficient; the Board failed to deal with the documentary evidence which corroborated the applicant's claim that he was a person in need of protection. The reasons given amount to no more than an unsupported conclusion with respect to that claim.

Editor's note: The following case summaries were collected under the provisions of the former Act relating to procedural decisions interpreting the former s. 69.1(11). They may still be relevant.

Badal v. Canada (Minister of Citizenship & Immigration) (2003), 26 Imm. L.R. (3d) 132, 231 F.T.R. 26, 2003 CarswellNat 645, 2003 CarswellNat 1471, 2003 FCT 311, 2003 CFPI 27, [2003] F.C.J. No. 440 (T.D.) — The applicant claimed refugee status based on the fear of persecution in Iran because of his religion. His first claim before a panel of the IRB was denied. That decision was quashed. The evidence before the panel at the second hearing included some documents previously thought to have been lost, a transcript of the first hearing and the decisions and reasons of the first panel. The applicant did not testify at the second hearing due to post-traumatic stress disorder and related memory problems. The Board adjourned and gave counsel an opportunity to file a medical assessment of the applicant. Counsel filed the assessment and stated that he would not be calling the applicant. The Board never resumed hearing. It rendered the decision now under review.

Transcripts of previous hearings are generally admissible before the Board. A transcript should be considered trustworthy in the sense that it represents an accurate record of the oral testimony. It may be considered by the Board for the purpose of fact finding, including, where justified, making conclusions about credibility. When a panel considers a transcript from a previous hearing and relies on it to make credibility findings, its reasons should make the basis for those findings clearer. A panel can rely on the fact finding of another panel. It can for example adopt another panel's conclusions in respect of the conditions in the applicant's country of origin or the feasibility of seeking refuge within its borders. A panel may also admit in evidence and read the written reasons of a previous panel dealing with the same applicant. The question will arise, however, when this happens, concerning whether a reasonable observer would think that the Board had carried out a thorough independent and impartial analysis of all the evidence. It must be clear that the Board considered the matter afresh. A Board must not simply attach to its decisions the reasons of another panel.

Adjibi v. Canada (Minister of Citizenship & Immigration) (2002), 219 F.T.R. 54, 2002 CarswellNat 2756, 2002 CarswellNat 1011, 2002 FCT 525, [2002] F.C.J. No. 680 — Persecution, by definition, requires maltreatment which rises to the level of serious harm. Meaningful reasons require that a claimant and a reviewing court receive a sufficiently intelligible explanation as to why persecutory treatment does not constitute persecution. This requires a thorough consideration of the level of atrocity of the Acts inflicted upon the applicant, the effect upon the applicant's physical and mental state and whether the experiences constituted a compelling reason not to return the applicant to his/her country of origin.

Mukwaya v. Canada (Minister of Citizenship & Immigration) (2001), 15 Imm. L.R. (3d) 258, 209 F.T.R. 28, 2001 CarswellNat 1251, 2001 FCT 650 — The applicant's claim for refugee status was refused on the basis of his involvement with the ADF in Uganda and his complicity in war crimes and crimes against humanity. The following principles should direct a tribunal where the Minister seeks the claimant's exclusion on the basis of the claimant's role as an accomplice to an entity guilty of war crimes or crimes against humanity.

1. The Minister always has the legal burden of establishing that the refugee claimant is complicit in the commission of international crimes.

2. Complicity requires the claimant's personal and knowing participation in the commission of international crimes.

3. As a general rule mere membership in an organization involved in international crimes does not establish personal and knowing participation.

4. An exception to this general rule may arise when the tribunal is "free from doubt" that the Minister has established that the organization is "principally directed to a limited, brutal purpose".

5. Where the exception applies, mere membership in such an organization may place on the refugee claimant the evidentiary burden of showing that he had no personal and knowing participation in the commission of the organization's international crimes.

6. Mere membership in an organization principally directed to a limited, brutal purpose may allow the tribunal to infer the claimant's personal and knowing participation in the international crimes in the absence of any reliable evidence proffered by that person to explain otherwise their role in the organization.

The decision of the panel was set aside. The tribunal made no specific finding that the ADF was an organization principally directed to a limited, brutal purpose. In the absence of such a finding, the tribunal could not infer that the applicant had personal and knowing participation in the international crimes attributed to the ADF, let alone suggest that the claimant had to rebut a presumption of complicity. No properly instructed panel on this evidence could conclude that the ADF was principally directed to a limited, brutal purpose while the applicant was still in Uganda, nor that the applicant could have known that the ADF had such a purpose. The finding of the panel was set aside.

Hidri v. Canada (Minister of Citizenship & Immigration), 2001 CarswellNat 1977, 2001 FCT 949, [2001] F.C.J. No. 1362 — The applicants sought to review a decision of a panel of the CRDD denying their claim to refugee status. The applicants argued that the Board required them to meet a standard of proof well beyond that of the civil balance of probabilities, when it maintained that it was not "convinced" of the applicants' allegations. It cannot be assumed that using the word "convince" automatically connotes a higher burden of proof without a careful examination of the contextual basis of the decision. The Court held that on reading the reasons of the panel and reviewing the materials it was satisfied that the civil standard of proof was applied and that the applicants merely failed to meet that threshold.

Thanni c. Canada (Ministre de la Citoyenneté & l'Immigration) (2001), 203 F.T.R. 117, 2001 CarswellNat 2236, 2001 CarswellNat 771, 2001 FCT 353 — This was an application to review a negative decision of a panel of the CRDD. The decision was rendered orally and confirmed at a later date with written reasons. There were some additions in the written reasons which were not part of the oral decision. Some conformity is required between written and oral reasons. The test to be applied is whether the differences between the written and oral reasons are substantial. Decisions in which it has been held that the difference was substantial, related to cases in which the panel's conclusion was no longer the same in the written decision, or where some findings appeared in the oral reasons and not in the written reasons. In the present case, the panel's conclusion was the same in both the written and oral reasons. Some written reasons were added in support of the panel's conclusion. Furthermore, the panel did not reserve the right when it gave its oral reasons to make some alterations or additions to those reasons when they appeared in written form.

There was a substantial difference between the oral and written reasons in this case because a number of written reasons were added to the panel's conclusions. If a panel chooses to render its decision at the conclusion of a hearing, it must be concluded that the panel has completed its thinking about the case and that it is prepared to present its decision and the reasons for it. If the panel continues to deliberate afterward on the question and adds reasons to its decision, then one can easily be led to believe that its thinking had not ended when it gave its decision.

A panel may make some corrections in its written decision for the purposes of syntax and comprehension. To accept that a panel could perfect its decision in written reasons because it had forgotten to address one or two questions that it thought were important to the review of the case when it gave its oral reasons would constitute a miscarriage of justice.

Accordingly, the application for judicial review was allowed.

Bodokia v. Canada (Minister of Citizenship & Immigration), 2001 FCT 227, 2001 CarswellNat 552 — The applicant sought to review a negative decision of a panel of the CRDD. It was reasonable for the panel to conclude that the silence of recent reports monitoring and reporting human rights abuses in Georgia was an indication that there were no current serious problems for Abkhazians in Georgia.

Chen v. Canada (Minister of Citizenship & Immigration) (2001), 14 Imm. L.R. (3d) 82, 2001 FCT 500, 2001 CarswellNat 1019 — The applicant sought to review a negative decision of a panel of the CRDD. The applicant claimed to be adherent of the Tian Dao religion.

Judicial deference to findings of credibility cannot serve to excuse the failure of a panel to clearly express itself on primary findings of fact. It was reasonable to expect that a panel would clearly express itself on primary issues arising from a claim for refugee status. Here, the Board could not conclude that the applicant had a well-founded fear of persecution on religious grounds, unless it found she was a member of the religion in question. The Board failed to address this "primary issue" in its reasons and therefore the decision was set aside.

Koroz v. Canada (Minister of Citizenship & Immigration) (2000), 9 Imm. L.R. (3d) 12, 261 N.R. 71, 186 F.T.R. 295 (note), 2000 CarswellNat 2347, [2000] F.C.J. No. 1593 — The appellant was denied refugee status on the basis of the existence of an internal flight alternative in Moldova.

A panel of the Board may adopt the same reasoning as another panel faced with the same documentary evidence as a basis for finding the existence of an internal flight alternative in the same country. This does not mean that a panel can blindly adopt factual findings of other panels. Where the question is one of fact-finding concerning general country conditions at approximately the same time, however, a panel may rely on the reasoning of an earlier panel on the same documentary evidence. Where the analysis of one panel on the same evidence on such a question commends itself to a later panel, there is no legal bar to the second panel relying upon it. The technique of appending part of the reasons of the first panel to the reasons of the second one is a shortcut practice that should not be used.

Hartley v. Canada (Minister of Citizenship & Immigration) (2000), 189 F.T.R. 296, 2000 CarswellNat 912 — A person's political beliefs do not have to conform to the beliefs ascribed to him or her by the persecutor. Additionally, they do not have to be explicitly stated, but the perception may be based upon the actions of the claimant. It is not incumbent upon the claimant to identify the precise reasons for the persecution, it is for the examiner to decide whether the convention definition is met. Lack of a precedent is no reason to decline to consider whether the claim of an applicant for refugee status falls within the definition.

Natural justice and procedural fairness require the panel to consider the arguments put forward by the claimant. The claimant argued that he was the subject of persecution because of a perception that he was a member of a particular social group. The panel did not address whether perceived membership could give rise to Convention protection, an issue critical to the applicant's claim.

Accordingly, the application for judicial review was allowed.

Berete v. Canada (Minister of Citizenship & Immigration), 1999 CarswellNat 986, [1999] F.C.J. No. 359 (T.D.) — When documentary evidence is presented that could influence the way in which the panel handles a refugee claim, the panel must indicate its impact on the applicant's claim. The panel must comment on documentary evidence when it directly contradicts the decision made.

Numbi v. Canada (Minister of Citizenship & Immigration) (1999), 163 F.T.R. 319, 1999 CarswellNat 262, 1999 CarswellNat 4599 (T.D.) — The failure of the Board to address the specific and relevant documentary evidence which appeared to corroborate important aspects of the applicant's claim in its analysis constituted a reviewable error.

Miral v. Canada (Minister of Citizenship & Immigration) (1999), 161 F.T.R. 213, 1999 CarswellNat 314, 1999 CarswellNat 4613 — The applicant challenged a negative decision of the CRDD. The applicant who was from Sri Lanka was found not to be a credible witness by the panel.

Considerable deference is given on judicial review to credibility findings made by the CRDD. It is perfectly acceptable for a tribunal to find an applicant lacking in credibility according to implausibilities in the applicant's testimony. Where the tribunal finds a lack of credibility based on inferences, there must be a basis in the evidence to support the inferences. Such inferences must be reasonably open to this tribunal based on the evidence of the applicant. Where the tribunal's inferences are based on what seem to be "common sense or rational perceptions about how a government regime in another country might be expected to act", there is an obligation to provide an opportunity for the applicant to address those inferences on which the tribunal relies. In the case at bar, the tribunal found that the applicant's evidence was perfunctory and lacked the kind of detail that could be expected of someone as articulate and well educated as the claimant.

The Court found that the panel had engaged in speculation as to regular or normal police procedures in Sri Lanka and had no evidence before it on which to base such conclusions. The applicant offered a plausible explanation for the police's repeated acceptance of bribes. The panel, in making its finding regarding probable police procedure, made no references to any documentary evidence to support such a finding. While there may have been a basis in the evidence for such a finding, the panel neglected to point to it. In addition, the panel referred to a lack of corroborating evidence regarding the applicant's detention as significant in the negative determination of her claim. A failure to offer documentation cannot be linked to an applicant's credibility in the absence of evidence to contradict the applicant's testimony. It is not open to the CRDD to require documentary evidence to support an applicant's uncontradicted testimony regarding her arrest and detention.

The decision of the tribunal was set aside.

Gill v. Canada (Minister of Citizenship & Immigration), [1998] F.C.J. No. 1139, 1998 CarswellNat 1561 (T.D.) — The applicant sought to review a negative decision of the IRB. The panel found that the applicant was persecuted by the Punjabi police in the past. The sole issue framed by the panel was whether the applicant had an internal flight alternative. The panel's analysis, however, did not proceed. The actual analysis dealt with whether conditions had changed sufficiently in India and in particular in the Punjab such that the applicant was no longer at risk of persecution. In making its assessment of the profiles of people currently at risk, the panel relied on documentary evidence. A panel is entitled to accept, reject and weigh documentary evidence. If a panel states that it is relying on specific documentary evidence however, it cannot arbitrarily disregard integral portions of that evidence.

68. (1) When decision of single member takes effect — A decision made by a single Division member allowing or rejecting a claim for refugee protection, on an application to vacate or to cease refugee protection, on the abandonment of a claim or of an application to vacate or to cease refugee protection, or allowing an application to withdraw a claim or to withdraw an application to vacate or to cease refugee protection takes effect

(a) if given orally at a hearing, when the member states the decision and gives the reasons; and

(b) if made in writing, when the member signs and dates the reasons for the decision.

(2) When decision of three member panel takes effect — A decision made by a panel of three Division members allowing or rejecting a claim for refugee protection, on an application to vacate or to cease refugee protection, on the abandonment of a claim or of an application to vacate or to cease refugee protection, or allowing an application to withdraw a claim or to withdraw an application to vacate or to cease refugee protection takes effect

(a) if given orally at a hearing, when all the members state their decision and give their reasons; and

(b) if made in writing, when all the members sign and date their reasons for the decision.

GENERAL PROVISIONS

69. No applicable rule — In the absence of a provision in these Rules dealing with a matter raised during the proceedings, the Division may do whatever is necessary to deal with the matter.

Case Law

Benitez v. Canada (Minister of Citizenship & Immigration), 2007 CarswellNat 1393, 2007 FCA 199 — The Federal Court consolidated a number of applications for judicial review impugning the validity of Guideline 7. Guideline 7 was issued by the Chairperson of the Board in 2003, pursuant to the power conferred by paragraph 159(1)(h) of the Immigration and Refugee Protection Act, S.C. 2001, c. 27, to issue guidelines to assist members of the Board in carrying out their duties ("the Guideline 7 issue"). Guideline 7 provides that the standard order of questioning at a refugee protection hearing by the Refugee Protection Division of the Board will be that the claimant is questioned first by the Refugee Protection officer and/or by the Refugee Protection Division member conducting the hearing. However, in exceptional cases members may permit claimants to be questioned first by their own counsel.

Guideline 7 does not breach the duty of fairness by either denying the claimants an effective opportunity to make representations or so distorting the role of the member of the Refugee Protection Division hearing the claim as to give rise to a reasonable apprehension of bias. Nor is it an unlawful fetter on member's discretion, and it was not legally required to have been issued under the chairperson's statutory power to issue rules of procedure, subject to cabinet approval.

Thamotharem v. Canada (Minister of Citizenship & Immigration), 2006 CarswellNat 1588, 2006 FCA 218 — This appeal concerns the validity of Guideline 7 (preparation and conduct of a hearing in the Refugee Protection Division) issued in 2003 by the chairperson of the Board pursuant to the statutory power to "issue guidelines. . .to assist members in carrying out their duties": Immigration and Refugee Protection Act, S.C. 2001, c. 27, para. 159(1)(h). The key paragraphs of Guideline 7 provide as follows:

> "In a claim for refugee protection, the standard practice will be for the Refugee Protection Officer to start questioning the claimant," although the member of the Refugee Protection Division hearing the claim "may vary the order of questioning in exceptional circumstances."

Guideline 7 is not, on its face, invalid on the ground of procedural unfairness, although, as the Minister and the Board conceded, fairness may require that, in certain circumstances particular claimants should be questioned first by their own counsel. Guideline 7 is not incompatible with the impartiality required of a member when conducting a hearing which is inquisitorial in form. Guideline 7 is not an unlawful fetter on the exercise of members' discretion on the conduct of refugee protection hearings. The Guideline expressly directs members to consider the facts of the particular case before them to determine whether there are exceptional circumstances warranting a deviation from the standard order of questioning. The evidence did not establish that members disregarded this aspect of Guideline 7 and slavishly adhered to the standard order of questioning, regardless of the facts of the case before them. Nor does it follow that the fact that Guideline 7 could have been issued as a statutory rule of procedure that it is invalid because it was not approved by the Governor in Council. The Minister's appeal was allowed, the appellant's cross-appeal was dismissed, the order of the Federal Court set aside, and the application for judicial review dismissed.

70. Powers of Division — The Division may, after giving the parties notice and an opportunity to object,

(a) act on its own initiative, without a party having to make an application or request to the Division;

(b) change a requirement of a rule;

(c) excuse a person from a requirement of a rule; and

(d) extend a time limit, before or after the time limit has expired, or shorten it if the time limit has not expired.

71. Failure to follow rule — Unless proceedings are declared invalid by the Division, a failure to follow any requirement of these Rules does not make the proceedings invalid.

REPEALS

72. Repeal — The *Convention Refugee Determination Division Rules*[5] are repealed.

73. Repeal — The *Refugee Protection Division Rules*[6] are repealed.

COMING INTO FORCE

74. S.C. 2010, c. 8 — These Rules come into force on the day on which section 26 of the *Balanced Refugee Reform Act* comes into force, but if they are registered after that day, they come into force on the day on which they are registered.

SCHEDULE 1 — CLAIMANT'S INFORMATION AND BASIS OF CLAIM
(Rule 1)

Item	Information
1.	Claimant's name.
2.	Claimant's date of birth.
3.	Claimant's gender.
4.	Claimant's nationality, ethnic or racial group, or tribe.
5.	Languages and dialects, if any, that the claimant speaks.
6.	Claimant's religion and denomination or sect.

---

[5] SOR/93-45

[6] SOR/2002-228

Item	Information
7.	Whether the claimant believes that they would experience harm, mistreatment or threats if they returned to their country today. If yes, description of what the claimant expects would happen, including who would harm, mistreat or threaten them and what the claimant believes would be the reasons for it.
8.	Whether the claimant or the claimant's family have ever experienced harm, mistreatment or threats in the past. If yes, a description of the harm, mistreatment or threats, including when it occurred, who caused it, what the claimant believes are the reasons for it and whether similarly situated persons have experienced such harm, mistreatment or threats.
9.	Whether the claimant sought protection or help from any authority or organization in their country. If not, an explanation of why not. If yes, the authority or organization from which the claimant sought protection or help and a description of what the claimant did and what happened as a result.
10.	When the claimant left their country and the reasons for leaving at that time.
11.	Whether the claimant moved to another part of their country to seek safety. If not, an explanation of why not. If the claimant moved to another part of their country, the reasons for leaving it and an explanation why the claimant could not live there or in another part of their country today.
12.	Whether the claimant moved to another country to seek safety. If yes, details including the name of the country, when the claimant moved there, length of stay and whether the claimant claimed refugee protection there. If the claimant did not claim refugee protection there, an explanation of why not.
13.	Whether minors are claiming refugee protection with the claimant. If yes, whether the claimant is the minor's parent and the other parent is in Canada, or whether the claimant is not the minor's parent, or whether the claimant is the minor's parent but the other parent is not in Canada. If the claimant is not the minor's parent or if the claimant is the minor's parent but the other parent is not in Canada, details of any legal documents or written consent allowing the claimant to take care of the minor or travel with the minor. If the claimant does not have such documents, an explanation of why not.
14.	If a child six years old or younger is claiming refugee protection with the claimant, an explanation of why the claimant believes the child would be at risk of being harmed, mistreated or threatened if returned to their country.
15.	Other details the claimant considers important for the refugee protection claim.
16.	Country or countries in which the claimant believes they are at risk of serious harm.

Item	Information
17.	The country or countries in which the claimant is or has been a citizen, including how and when citizenship was acquired and present status.
18.	Name, date of birth, citizenship and place and country of residence of relatives, living or dead, specifically the claimant's spouse, common-law partner, children, parents, brothers and sisters.
19.	If the claimant or the claimant's spouse, common-law partner, child, parent, brother or sister has claimed refugee protection or asylum in Canada or in any other country — including at a Canadian office abroad or from the United Nations High Commissioner for Refugees — the details of the claim including the name of the person who made the claim, and the date, location, result of the claim and IRB file number or CIC client ID number, if any.
20.	Whether the claimant applied for a visa to enter Canada. If yes, for what type of visa, the date of the application, at which Canadian office the application was made and whether or not it was accepted. If the visa was issued, the date of issue and the duration of the visa. If the application was refused, the date and reasons of refusal.
21.	Claimant's contact information.
22.	Whether the claimant has counsel and if so, details concerning counsel — including what counsel has been retained to do and counsel's contact information.
23.	Claimant's choice of official language for communications with and proceedings before the Board.
24.	Whether the claimant needs an interpreter during any proceeding, and the language and dialect, if any, to be interpreted.

SCHEDULE 2 — INFORMATION TO BE PROVIDED ABOUT THE CLAIMANT BY AN OFFICER

(Paragraph 3(5)(d))

Item	Information
1.	Name, gender and date of birth.
2.	Department of Citizenship and Immigration client identification number.
3.	If the claimant is detained, the name and address of the place of detention.
4.	Claimant's contact information in Canada, if any.
5.	Contact information of any counsel for the claimant.
6.	Official language chosen by the claimant as the language of proceedings before the Board.
7.	Date the claim was referred or deemed to be referred to the Division.

Rules

Item	Information
8.	Section of the Act under which the claim is being referred.
9.	Officer's decision about the claim's eligibility under section 100 of the Act, if a decision has been made.
10.	The country or countries in which the claimant fears persecution, torture, a risk to their life or a risk of cruel and unusual treatment or punishment.
11.	Whether the claimant may need a designated representative and the contact information for any proposed designated representative.
12.	Whether the claimant needs an interpreter, including a sign language interpreter, during any proceeding, and the language and dialect, if any, to be interpreted.
13.	If a claim of the claimant's spouse, common-law partner or any relative has been referred to the Division, the name and Department of Citizenship and Immigration client identification numbers of each of those persons.
14.	When and how the officer notified the claimant of the referral of the claim to the Division.
15.	Whether the claim was made at a port of entry or inside Canada other than at a port of entry.
16.	Any other information gathered by the officer about the claimant that is relevant to the claim.

SCHEDULE 3 — INFORMATION AND DECLARATIONS — COUNSEL NOT REPRESENTING OR ADVISING FOR CONSIDERATION
(Rules 5 and 13)

Item	Information
1.	IRB Division and file number with respect to the claimant or protected person.
2.	Name of counsel who is representing or advising the claimant or protected person and who is not receiving consideration for those services.
3.	Name of counsel's firm or organization, if applicable, and counsel's postal address, telephone number, fax number and email address, if any.
4.	If applicable, a declaration, signed by the interpreter, that includes the interpreter's name, the language and dialect, if any, interpreted and a statement that the interpretation is accurate.
5.	Declaration signed by the claimant or protected person that the counsel who is representing or advising them is not receiving consideration and the information provided in the form is complete, true and correct.

Item	Information
6.	Declaration signed by counsel that they are not receiving consideration for representing or advising the claimant or protected person and that the information provided in the form is complete, true and correct.

CAN. REG. 2012-257 — REFUGEE APPEAL DIVISION RULES

made under the *Immigration and Refugee Protection Act*

INTERPRETATION

1. Definitions — The following definitions apply in these Rules.

"Act" means the *Immigration and Refugee Protection Act*. *("Loi")*

"appellant" means a person who is the subject of an appeal, or the Minister, who makes an appeal to the Division from a decision of the Refugee Protection Division. *("appelant")*

"contact information" means, with respect to a person,

> (a) the person's name, postal address and telephone number, and their fax number and email address, if any; and

> (b) in the case of counsel for a person who is the subject of an appeal, if the counsel is a person referred to in any of paragraphs 91(2)(a) to (c) of the Act, in addition to the information referred to in paragraph (a), the name of the body of which the counsel is a member and the membership identification number issued to the counsel.

("coordonnées")

"Division" means the Refugee Appeal Division. *("Section")*

"interested person" means a person whose application to participate in an appeal under rule 46 has been granted. *("personne intéressée")*

"party" means,

> (a) in the case of an appeal by a person who is the subject of an appeal, the person and, if the Minister intervenes in the appeal, the Minister; and

> (b) in the case of an appeal by the Minister, the person who is the subject of the appeal and the Minister.

("partie")

"proceeding" includes a conference, an application, or an appeal that is decided with or without a hearing. *("procédure")*

"registry office" means a business office of the Division. *("greffe")*

"Regulations" means the *Immigration and Refugee Protection Regulations*. *("Règlement")* "respondent" means a person who is the subject of an appeal in the case of an appeal by the Minister. *("intimé")*

"UNHCR" means the United Nations High Commissioner for Refugees and includes its representative or agent. *("HCR")*

"vulnerable person" means a person who has been identified as vulnerable under the *Guideline on Procedures with Respect to Vulnerable Persons Appearing Before the IRB* issued under paragraph 159(1)(h) of the Act. *("personne vulnérable")*

"working day" does not include Saturdays, Sundays or other days on which the Board offices are closed. *("jour ouvrable")*

PART 1 — RULES APPLICABLE TO APPEALS MADE BY A PERSON WHO IS THE SUBJECT OF AN APPEAL

Filing and Perfecting an Appeal

2. (1) Filing appeal — To file an appeal, the person who is the subject of the appeal must provide to the Division three copies of a written notice of appeal.

(2) Copy provided to Minister — The Division must provide a copy of the notice of appeal to the Minister without delay.

(3) Content of notice of appeal — In the notice of appeal, the appellant must indicate

(a) their name and telephone number, and an address where documents can be provided to them;

(b) if represented by counsel, counsel's contact information and any limitations on counsel's retainer;

(c) the identification number given by the Department of Citizenship and Immigration to them;

(d) the Refugee Protection Division file number, the date of the notice of decision relating to the decision being appealed and the date that they received the written reasons for the decision;

(e) the language — English or French — chosen by them as the language of the appeal; and

(f) the representative's contact information if the Refugee Protection Division has designated a representative for them in the proceedings relating to the decision being appealed, and any proposed change in representative.

(4) Time limit — The notice of appeal provided under this rule must be received by the Division within the time limit for filing an appeal set out in the Regulations.

3. (1) Perfecting appeal — To perfect an appeal, the person who is the subject of the appeal must provide to the Division two copies of the appellant's record.

(2) Copy provided to Minister — The Division must provide a copy of the appellant's record to the Minister without delay.

(3) Content of appellant's record — The appellant's record must contain the following documents, on consecutively numbered pages, in the following order:

(a) the notice of decision and written reasons for the Refugee Protection Division's decision that the appellant is appealing;

(b) all or part of the transcript of the Refugee Protection Division hearing if the appellant wants to rely on the transcript in the appeal, together with a declaration, signed by the transcriber, that includes the transcriber's name and a statement that the transcript is accurate;

(c) any documents that the Refugee Protection Division refused to accept as evidence, during or after the hearing, if the appellant wants to rely on the documents in the appeal;

(d) a written statement indicating

(i) whether the appellant is relying on any evidence referred to in subsection 110(4) of the Act,

(ii) whether the appellant is requesting that a hearing be held under subsection 110(6) of the Act, and if they are requesting a hearing, whether they are making an application under rule 66 to change the location of the hearing, and

(iii) the language and dialect, if any, to be interpreted, if the Division decides that a hearing is necessary and the appellant needs an interpreter;

(e) any documentary evidence that the appellant wants to rely on in the appeal;

(f) any law, case law or other legal authority that the appellant wants to rely on in the appeal; and

(g) a memorandum that includes full and detailed submissions regarding

(i) the errors that are the grounds of the appeal,

(ii) where the errors are located in the written reasons for the Refugee Protection Division's decision that the appellant is appealing or in the transcript or in any audio or other electronic recording of the Refugee Protection Division hearing,

(iii) how any documentary evidence referred to in paragraph (e) meets the requirements of subsection 110(4) of the Act and how that evidence relates to the appellant,

(iv) the decision the appellant wants the Division to make, and

(v) why the Division should hold a hearing under subsection 110(6) of the Act if the appellant is requesting that a hearing be held.

(4) Length of memorandum — The memorandum referred to in paragraph (3)(g) must not be more than 30 pages long if typewritten on one side or 15 pages if typewritten on both sides.

(5) **Time limit** — The appellant's record provided under this rule must be received by the Division within the time limit for perfecting an appeal set out in the Regulations.

Intervention by the Minister

4. (1) **Notice of intervention** — To intervene in an appeal at any time before the Division makes a decision, the Minister must provide, first to the appellant and then to the Division, a written notice of intervention, together with any documentary evidence that the Minister wants to rely on in the appeal.

(2) **Content of notice of intervention** — In the notice of intervention, the Minister must indicate

(a) counsel's contact information;

(b) the identification number given by the Department of Citizenship and Immigration to the appellant;

(c) the appellant's name, the Refugee Protection Division file number, the date of the notice of decision relating to the decision being appealed and the date that the Minister received the written reasons for the decision;

(d) whether the Minister is relying on any documentary evidence referred to in subsection 110(3) of the Act and the relevance of that evidence; and

(e) whether the Minister is requesting that a hearing be held under subsection 110(6) of the Act, and if the Minister is requesting a hearing, why the Division should hold a hearing and whether the Minister is making an application under rule 66 to change the location of the hearing.

(3) **Minister's intervention record** — In addition to the documents referred to in subrule (1), the Minister may provide, first to the appellant and then to the Division, the Minister's intervention record containing the following documents, on consecutively numbered pages, in the following order:

(a) all or part of the transcript of the Refugee Protection Division hearing if the Minister wants to rely on the transcript in the appeal and the transcript was not provided with the appellant's record, together with a declaration, signed by the transcriber, that includes the transcriber's name and a statement that the transcript is accurate;

(b) any law, case law or other legal authority that the Minister wants to rely on in the appeal; and

(c) a memorandum that includes full and detailed submissions regarding

(i) the grounds on which the Minister is contesting the appeal, and

(ii) the decision the Minister wants the Division to make.

(4) **Length of memorandum** — The memorandum referred to in paragraph (3)(c) must not be more than 30 pages long if typewritten on one side or 15 pages if typewritten on both sides.

(5) Proof documents were provided — The documents provided to the Division under this rule must be accompanied by proof that they were provided to the appellant.

Reply

5. (1) Reply to Minister's intervention — To reply to a Minister's intervention, the appellant must provide, first to the Minister and then to the Division, a reply record.

(2) Content of reply record — The reply record must contain the following documents, on consecutively numbered pages, in the following order:

(a) all or part of the transcript of the Refugee Protection Division hearing if the appellant wants to rely on the transcript to support the reply and the transcript was not provided with the appellant's record or by the Minister, together with a declaration, signed by the transcriber, that includes the transcriber's name and a statement that the transcript is accurate;

(b) any documentary evidence that the appellant wants to rely on to support the reply and that was not provided with the appellant's record or by the Minister;

(c) any law, case law or other legal authority that the appellant wants to rely on to support the reply and that was not provided with the appellant's record or by the Minister; and

(d) a memorandum that includes full and detailed submissions regarding

(i) only the grounds raised by the Minister,

(ii) how any documentary evidence referred to in paragraph (b) meets the requirements of subsection 110(4) or (5) of the Act and how that evidence relates to the appellant, and

(iii) why the Division should hold a hearing under subsection 110(6) of the Act if the appellant is requesting that a hearing be held and they did not include such a request in the appellant's record, and if the appellant is requesting a hearing, whether they are making an application under rule 66 to change the location of the hearing.

(3) Length of memorandum — The memorandum referred to in paragraph (2)(d) must not be more than 30 pages long if typewritten on one side or 15 pages if typewritten on both sides.

(4) Proof document was provided — The reply record provided to the Division must be accompanied by proof that it was provided to the Minister.

(5) Time limit — Documents provided under this rule must be received by the Division no later than 15 days after the day on which the appellant receives the Minister's notice of intervention, the Minister's intervention record, or any additional documents provided by the Minister, as the case may be.

Case Law

Zhou v. Canada (Minister of Citizenship and Immigration) (2015), 37 Imm. L.R. (4th) 275, 2015 FC 911, 2015 CarswellNat 3277, 2015 CarswellNat 5691 — The legislation clearly states that the Refugee Appeal Division "may" hold a hearing where the statutory criteria are met. An oral hearing will generally be required when the statutory criteria has been satisfied. The RAD retains the discretion on this question but that discretion must be exercised reasonably in the circumstances. In particular, the mere fact that a party has not requested a hearing will generally not be sufficient reason to justify a refusal to convene one when the circumstances appear to require it. While the RAD rules allow an appellant to request a hearing, IRPA does not actually impose a burden either to request, or to satisfy the RAD that the circumstances merit, an oral hearing. The onus rests with the RAD to consider and apply the statutory criteria reasonably. In this case, the RAD should have convened an oral hearing before dismissing the appellant's appeal on credibility grounds. The court overturned the decision of the RAD and made an order directing another panel of the RAD to reconsider the appeal.

Extension of Time

6. (1) Application for extension of time to file or perfect — A person who is the subject of an appeal who makes an application to the Division for an extension of the time to file or to perfect an appeal under the Regulations must do so in accordance with rule 37, except that the person must provide to the Division the original and a copy of the application.

(2) Copy provided to Minister — The Division must provide a copy of an application under subrule (1) to the Minister without delay.

(3) Content of application — The person who is the subject of the appeal must include in an application under subrule (1)

(a) their name and telephone number, and an address where documents can be provided to them;

(b) if represented by counsel, counsel's contact information and any limitations on counsel's retainer;

(c) the identification number given by the Department of Citizenship and Immigration to them; and

(d) the Refugee Protection Division file number, the date of the notice of decision relating to the decision being appealed and the date that they received the written reasons for the decision.

(4) Accompanying documents — filing — An application for an extension of the time to file an appeal under subrule (1) must be accompanied by three copies of a written notice of appeal.

(5) Accompanying documents — perfecting — An application for an extension of the time to perfect an appeal under subrule (1) must be accompanied by two copies of the appellant's record.

(6) Application for extension of time to reply — A person who is the subject of an appeal may make an application to the Division for an extension of the time to reply to a Minister's intervention in accordance with rule 37.

(7) Factors — reply — In deciding an application under subrule (6), the Division must consider any relevant factors, including

(a) whether the application was made in a timely manner and the justification for any delay;

(b) whether there is an arguable case;

(c) prejudice to the Minister, if the application was granted; and

(d) the nature and complexity of the appeal.

(8) Notification of decision on application — The Division must without delay notify, in writing, both the person who is the subject of the appeal and the Minister of its decision with respect to an application under subrule (1) or (6).

Disposition of an Appeal

7. Decision without further notice — Unless a hearing is held under subsection 110(6) of the Act, the Division may, without further notice to the appellant and to the Minister, decide an appeal on the basis of the materials provided

(a) if a period of 15 days has passed since the day on which the Minister received the appellant's record, or the time limit for perfecting the appeal set out in the Regulations has expired; or

(b) if the reply record has been provided, or the time limit for providing it has expired.

PART 2 — RULES APPLICABLE TO APPEALS MADE BY THE MINISTER

Filing and Perfecting an Appeal

8. (1) Filing appeal — To file an appeal in accordance with subsection 110(1.1) of the Act, the Minister must provide, first to the person who is the subject of the appeal, a written notice of appeal, and then to the Division, two copies of the written notice of appeal.

(2) Content of notice of appeal — In the notice of appeal, the Minister must indicate

(a) counsel's contact information;

(b) the name of the person who is the subject of the appeal and the identification number given by the Department of Citizenship and Immigration to them; and

(c) the Refugee Protection Division file number, the date of the notice of decision relating to the decision being appealed and the date that the Minister received the written reasons for the decision.

(3) **Proof document was provided** — The notice of appeal provided to the Division must be accompanied by proof that it was provided to the person who is the subject of the appeal.

(4) **Time limit** — The notice of appeal provided under this rule must be received by the Division within the time limit for filing an appeal set out in the Regulations.

9. (1) Perfecting appeal — To perfect an appeal in accordance with subsection 110(1.1) of the Act, the Minister must provide, first to the person who is the subject of the appeal and then to the Division, any supporting documents that the Minister wants to rely on in the appeal.

(2) **Content of appellant's record** — In addition to the documents referred to in subrule (1), the Minister may provide, first to the person who is the subject of the appeal and then to the Division, the appellant's record containing the following documents, on consecutively numbered pages, in the following order:

(a) the notice of decision and written reasons for the Refugee Protection Division's decision that the Minister is appealing;

(b) all or part of the transcript of the Refugee Protection Division hearing if the Minister wants to rely on the transcript in the appeal, together with a declaration, signed by the transcriber, that includes the transcriber's name and a statement that the transcript is accurate;

(c) any documents that the Refugee Protection Division refused to accept as evidence, during or after the hearing, if the Minister wants to rely on the documents in the appeal;

(d) a written statement indicating

(i) whether the Minister is relying on any documentary evidence referred to in subsection 110(3) of the Act and the relevance of that evidence, and

(ii) whether the Minister is requesting that a hearing be held under subsection 110(6) of the Act, and if the Minister is requesting a hearing, why the Division should hold a hearing and whether the Minister is making an application under rule 66 to change the location of the hearing;

(e) any law, case law or other legal authority that the Minister wants to rely on in the appeal; and

(f) a memorandum that includes full and detailed submissions regarding

(i) the errors that are the grounds of the appeal,

(ii) where the errors are located in the written reasons for the Refugee Protection Division's decision that the Minister is appealing or in the transcript or in any audio or other electronic recording of the Refugee Protection Division hearing, and

(iii) the decision the Minister wants the Division to make.

(3) **Length of memorandum** — The memorandum referred to in paragraph (2)(f) must not be more than 30 pages long if typewritten on one side or 15 pages if typewritten on both sides.

(4) **Proof documents were provided** — Any supporting documents and the appellant's record, if any, provided to the Division must be accompanied by proof that they were provided to the person who is the subject of the appeal.

(5) **Time limit** — Documents provided under this rule must be received by the Division within the time limit for perfecting an appeal set out in the Regulations.

Response to an Appeal

10. (1) **Response to appeal** — To respond to an appeal, the person who is the subject of the appeal must provide, first to the Minister and then to the Division, a written notice of intent to respond, together with the respondent's record.

(2) **Content of notice of intent to respond** — In the notice of intent to respond, the respondent must indicate

(a) their name and telephone number, and an address where documents can be provided to them;

(b) if represented by counsel, counsel's contact information and any limitations on counsel's retainer;

(c) the identification number given by the Department of Citizenship and Immigration to them;

(d) the Refugee Protection Division file number and the date of the notice of decision relating to the decision being appealed;

(e) the language — English or French — chosen by them as the language of the appeal; and

(f) the representative's contact information if the Refugee Protection Division has designated a representative for them in the proceedings relating to the decision being appealed, and any proposed change in representative.

(3) **Content of respondent's record** — The respondent's record must contain the following documents, on consecutively numbered pages, in the following order:

(a) all or part of the transcript of the Refugee Protection Division hearing if the respondent wants to rely on the transcript in the appeal and the transcript was not provided with the appellant's record, together with a declaration, signed by the transcriber, that includes the transcriber's name and a statement that the transcript is accurate;

(b) a written statement indicating

(i) whether the respondent is requesting that a hearing be held under subsection 110(6) of the Act, and if they are requesting a hearing, whether they are making an application under rule 66 to change the location of the hearing, and

(ii) the language and dialect, if any, to be interpreted, if the Division decides that a hearing is necessary and the respondent needs an interpreter;

(c) any documentary evidence that the respondent wants to rely on in the appeal;

(d) any law, case law or other legal authority that the respondent wants to rely on in the appeal; and

(e) a memorandum that includes full and detailed submissions regarding

(i) the grounds on which the respondent is contesting the appeal,

(ii) the decision the respondent wants the Division to make, and

(iii) why the Division should hold a hearing under subsection 110(6) of the Act if the respondent is requesting that a hearing be held.

(4) **Length of memorandum** — The memorandum referred to in paragraph (3)(e) must not be more than 30 pages long if typewritten on one side or 15 pages if typewritten on both sides.

(5) **Proof documents were provided** — The notice of intent to respond and the respondent's record provided to the Division must be accompanied by proof that they were provided to the Minister.

(6) **Time limit** — Documents provided under this rule must be received by the Division no later than 15 days after

(a) the day on which the respondent receives any supporting documents; or

(b) if the Division allows an application for an extension of time to perfect the appeal under rule 12, the day on which the respondent is notified of the decision to allow the extension of time.

Reply

11. (1) **Minister's reply** — To reply to a response by the respondent, the Minister must provide, first to the respondent and then to the Division, any documentary evidence that the Minister wants to rely on to support the reply and that was not provided at the time that the appeal was perfected or with the respondent's record.

(2) **Reply record** — In addition to the documents referred to in subrule (1), the Minister may provide, first to the respondent and then to the Division, a reply record containing the following documents, on consecutively numbered pages, in the following order:

(a) all or part of the transcript of the Refugee Protection Division hearing if the Minister wants to rely on the transcript to support the reply and the transcript was not provided with the appellant's record, if any, or the respondent's record, together with a declaration, signed by the transcriber, that includes the transcriber's name and a statement that the transcript is accurate;

(b) any law, case law or other legal authority that the Minister wants to rely on to support the reply and that was not provided with the appellant's record, if any, or the respondent's record; and

(c) a memorandum that includes full and detailed submissions regarding

(i) only the grounds raised by the respondent, and

(ii) why the Division should hold a hearing under subsection 110(6) of the Act if the Minister is requesting that a hearing be held and the Minister did not include such a request in the appellant's record, if any, and if the Minister is requesting a hearing, whether the Minister is making an application under rule 66 to change the location of the hearing.

(3) Length of memorandum — The memorandum referred to in paragraph (2)(c) must not be more than 30 pages long if typewritten on one side or 15 pages if typewritten on both sides.

(4) Proof documents were provided — Any documentary evidence and the reply record, if any, provided to the Division under this rule must be accompanied by proof that they were provided to the respondent.

Extension of Time

12. (1) Application for extension of time — Minister — If the Minister makes an application to the Division for an extension of the time to file or to perfect an appeal under the Regulations, the Minister must do so in accordance with rule 37.

(2) Accompanying documents — filing — An application for an extension of the time to file an appeal under subrule (1) must be accompanied by two copies of a written notice of appeal.

(3) Accompanying documents — perfecting — An application for an extension of the time to perfect an appeal under subrule (1) must be accompanied by any supporting documents, and an appellant's record, if any.

(4) Application for extension of time — person — A person who is the subject of an appeal may make an application to the Division for an extension of the time to respond to an appeal in accordance with rule 37.

(5) Content of application for extension of time to respond to appeal — The person who is the subject of the appeal must include in an application under subrule (4)

(a) their name and telephone number, and an address where documents can be provided to them;

(b) if represented by counsel, counsel's contact information and any limitations on counsel's retainer;

(c) the identification number given by the Department of Citizenship and Immigration to them; and

(d) the Refugee Protection Division file number, the date of the notice of decision relating to the decision being appealed and the date that they received the written reasons for the decision.

(6) **Factors — respond** — In deciding an application under subrule (4), the Division must consider any relevant factors, including

(a) whether the application was made in a timely manner and the justification for any delay;

(b) whether there is an arguable case;

(c) prejudice to the Minister, if the application was granted; and

(d) the nature and complexity of the appeal.

(7) **Notification of decision on application** — The Division must without delay notify, in writing, both the person who is the subject of the appeal and the Minister of its decision with respect to an application under subrule (1) or (4).

Disposition of an Appeal

13. **Decision without further notice** — Unless a hearing is held under subsection 110(6) of the Act, the Division may, without further notice to the parties, decide an appeal on the basis of the materials provided

(a) if a period of 15 days has passed since the day on which the Minister received the respondent's record, or the time limit for providing it set out in subrule 10(6) has expired; or

(b) if the Minister's reply has been provided.

PART 3 — RULES APPLICABLE TO ALL APPEALS

Communicating with the Division

14. **Communicating with Division** — All communication with the Division must be directed to the registry office specified by the Division.

15. **Change to contact information** — If the contact information of a person who is the subject of an appeal changes, the person must without delay provide the changes in writing to the Division and to the Minister.

Counsel

16. (1) **Retaining counsel after providing notice** — If a person who is the subject of an appeal retains counsel after providing a notice of appeal or a notice of intent to respond, as the case may be, the person must without delay provide the counsel's contact information in writing to the Division and to the Minister.

(2) **Change to counsel's contact information — person** — If the contact information of counsel for a person who is the subject of an appeal changes, the person must without delay provide the changes in writing to the Division and to the Minister.

(3) Change to counsel's contact information — Minister — If the contact information of counsel for the Minister changes, the Minister must without delay provide the changes in writing to the Division and to the person who is the subject of the appeal.

17. Declaration — counsel not representing or advising for consideration — If a person who is the subject of an appeal retains counsel who is not a person referred to in any of paragraphs 91(2)(a) to (c) of the Act, both the person who is the subject of the appeal and their counsel must without delay provide the information and declarations set out in the schedule to the Division in writing.

18. (1) Becoming counsel of record — Subject to subrule (2), as soon as counsel for a person who is the subject of an appeal provides on behalf of the person a notice of appeal or a notice of intent to respond, as the case may be, or as soon as a person becomes counsel after the person provided a notice, the counsel becomes counsel of record for the person.

(2) Limitation on counsel's retainer — If a person who is the subject of an appeal has notified the Division of a limitation on their counsel's retainer, counsel is counsel of record only to the extent of the services to be provided within the limited retainer. Counsel ceases to be counsel of record as soon as those services are completed.

19. (1) Request to be removed as counsel of record — To be removed as counsel of record, counsel for a person who is the subject of an appeal must first provide to the person and to the Minister a copy of a written request to be removed and then provide the written request to the Division.

(2) Proof request was provided — The request provided to the Division must be accompanied by proof that copies were provided to the person represented and to the Minister.

(3) Request — if date for proceeding fixed — If a date for a proceeding has been fixed and three working days or less remain before that date, counsel must make the request orally at the proceeding.

(4) Division's permission required — Counsel remains counsel of record unless the request to be removed is granted.

20. (1) Removing counsel of record — To remove counsel as counsel of record, a person who is the subject of an appeal must first provide to counsel and to the Minister a copy of a written notice that counsel is no longer counsel for the person and then provide the written notice to the Division.

(2) Proof notice was provided — The notice provided to the Division must be accompanied by proof that copies were provided to counsel and to the Minister.

(3) Ceasing to be counsel of record — Counsel ceases to be counsel of record when the Division receives the notice.

Refugee Protection Division Record

21. (1) Providing notice of appeal — The Division must without delay provide a copy of the notice of appeal to the Refugee Protection Division after the appeal is perfected under rule 3 or 9, as the case may be.

(2) Preparing and providing record — The Refugee Protection Division must prepare a record and provide it to the Division no later than 10 days after the day on which the Refugee Protection Division receives the notice of appeal.

(3) Content of record — The Refugee Protection Division record must contain

(a) the notice of decision and written reasons for the decision that is being appealed;

(b) the Basis of Claim Form as defined in the *Refugee Protection Division Rules* and any changes or additions to it;

(c) all documentary evidence that the Refugee Protection Division accepted as evidence, during or after the hearing;

(d) any written representations made during or after the hearing but before the decision being appealed was made; and

(e) any audio or other electronic recording of the hearing.

(4) Providing record to absent Minister — If the Minister did not take part in the proceedings relating to the decision being appealed, the Division must provide a copy of the Refugee Protection Division record to the Minister as soon as the Division receives it.

Language of the Appeal

22. (1) Choice of language — A person who is the subject of an appeal must choose English or French as the language of the appeal. The person must indicate that choice in the notice of appeal if they are the appellant or in the notice of intent to respond if they are the respondent.

(2) Language — Minister's appeals — If the appellant is the Minister, the language of the appeal is the language chosen by the person who is the subject of the appeal in the proceedings relating to the decision being appealed.

(3) Changing language — A person who is the subject of an appeal may change the language of the appeal that they chose under subrule (1) by notifying the Division and the Minister in writing without delay and, if a date for a proceeding has been fixed, the notice must be received by their recipients no later than 20 days before that date.

Designated Representatives

23. (1) Continuation of designation — If the Refugee Protection Division designated a representative for the person who is the subject of the appeal in the proceedings relating to the decision being appealed, the representative is deemed to have been designated by the Division, unless the Division orders otherwise.

(2) Duty of counsel to notify — If the Refugee Protection Division did not designate a representative for the person who is the subject of the appeal and counsel for a party believes that the Division should designate a representative for the person because the person is under 18 years of age or is unable to appreciate the nature of the proceedings, counsel must without delay notify the Division in writing.

(3) Exception — Subrule (2) does not apply in the case of a person under 18 years of age whose appeal is joined with the appeal of their parent or legal guardian if the parent or legal guardian is 18 years of age or older.

(4) Content of notice — The notice must include the following information:

(a) whether counsel is aware of a person in Canada who meets the requirements to be designated as a representative and, if so, the person's contact information;

(b) a copy of any available supporting documents; and

(c) the reasons why counsel believes that a representative should be designated.

(5) Requirements for being designated — To be designated as a representative, a person must

(a) be 18 years of age or older;

(b) understand the nature of the proceedings;

(c) be willing and able to act in the best interests of the person who is the subject of the appeal; and

(d) not have interests that conflict with those of the person who is the subject of the appeal.

(6) Factors — When determining whether a person who is the subject of an appeal is unable to appreciate the nature of the proceedings, the Division must consider any relevant factors, including

(a) whether the person can understand the reason for the proceeding and can instruct counsel;

(b) the person's statements and behaviour at the proceeding;

(c) expert evidence, if any, on the person's intellectual or physical faculties, age or mental condition; and

(d) whether the person has had a representative designated for a proceeding in a division other than the Refugee Protection Division.

(7) Designation applies to all proceedings — The designation of a representative for a person who is under 18 years of age or who is unable to appreciate the nature of the proceedings applies to all subsequent proceedings in the Division with respect to that person unless the Division orders otherwise.

(8) End of designation — person reaches 18 years of age — The designation of a representative for a person who is under 18 years of age ends when the person reaches 18 years of age unless that representative has also been designated because the person is unable to appreciate the nature of the proceedings.

(9) **Termination of designation** — The Division may terminate a designation if the Division is of the opinion that the representative is no longer required or suitable and may designate a new representative if required.

(10) **Designation criteria** — Before designating a person as a representative, the Division must

(a) assess the person's ability to fulfil the responsibilities of a designated representative; and

(b) ensure that the person has been informed of the responsibilities of a designated representative.

(11) **Responsibilities of representative** — The responsibilities of a designated representative include

(a) deciding whether to retain counsel and, if counsel is retained, instructing counsel or assisting the represented person in instructing counsel;

(b) making decisions regarding the appeal or assisting the represented person in making those decisions;

(c) informing the represented person about the various stages and procedures in the processing of their case;

(d) assisting in gathering evidence to support the represented person's case and in providing evidence and, if necessary, being a witness at the hearing;

(e) protecting the interests of the represented person and putting forward the best possible case to the Division; and

(f) informing and consulting the represented person to the extent possible when making decisions about the case.

Specialized Knowledge

24. (1) **Notice to parties** — Before using any information or opinion that is within its specialized knowledge, the Division must notify the parties and give them an opportunity to,

(a) if a date for a hearing has not been fixed, make written representations on the reliability and use of the information or opinion and provide written evidence in support of their representations; and

(b) if a date for a hearing has been fixed, make oral or written representations on the reliability and use of the information or opinion and provide evidence in support of their representations.

(2) **Providing written representations and evidence** — A party must provide its written representations and evidence first to any other party and then to the Division.

(3) Proof written representations and evidence were provided — The written representations and evidence provided to the Division must be accompanied by proof that they were provided to any other party.

Notice of Constitutional Question

25. (1) Notice of constitutional question — A party who wants to challenge the constitutional validity, applicability or operability of a legislative provision must complete a notice of constitutional question.

(2) Form and content of notice — The party must complete the notice as set out in Form 69 of the *Federal Courts Rules* or any other form that includes

(a) the party's name;

(b) the Division file number;

(c) the specific legislative provision that is being challenged;

(d) the material facts relied on to support the constitutional challenge; and

(e) a summary of the legal argument to be made in support of the constitutional challenge.

(3) Providing notice — The party must provide

(a) a copy of the notice to the Attorney General of Canada and to the attorney general of each province of Canada, in accordance with section 57 of the *Federal Courts Act*;

(b) a copy of the notice to the Minister even if the Minister has not yet intervened in the appeal;

(c) a copy of the notice to the UNHCR, if the UNHCR has provided notice of its intention to provide written submissions, and to any interested person; and

(d) the original notice to the Division, together with proof that copies were provided under paragraphs (a) to (c).

(4) Time limit — Documents provided under this rule must be received by their recipients at the same time as the Division receives the appellant's record, respondent's record or the reply record, as the case may be.

(5) Deciding of constitutional question — The Division must not make a decision on the constitutional question until at least 10 days after the day on which it receives the notice of constitutional question.

Conferences

26. (1) Requirement to participate at conference — The Division may require the parties to participate at a conference to discuss issues, relevant facts and any other matter in order to make the appeal fairer and more efficient.

(2) Information or documents — The Division may require the parties to give any information or provide any document, at or before the conference.

(3) **Written record** — The Division must make a written record of any decisions and agreements made at the conference.

Documents

Form and Language of Documents

27. (1) **Documents prepared by party** — A document prepared for use by a party in a proceeding must be typewritten, in a type not smaller than 12 point, on one or both sides of 216 mm by 279 mm (8 1/2 inches x 11 inches) paper.

(2) **Photocopies** — Any photocopy provided by a party must be a clear copy of the document photocopied and be on one or both sides of 216 mm by 279 mm (8 1/2 inches x 11 inches) paper.

(3) **List of documents** — If more than one document is provided, the party must provide a list identifying each of the documents.

(4) **Consecutively numbered pages** — A party must consecutively number each page of all the documents provided as if they were one document.

28. (1) **Language of documents — person** — All documents used by a person who is the subject of an appeal in an appeal must be in English or French or, if in another language, be provided together with an English or French translation and a declaration signed by the translator.

(2) **Language of Minister's documents** — All documents used by the Minister in an appeal must be in the language of the appeal or be provided together with a translation in the language of the appeal and a declaration signed by the translator.

(3) **Translator's declaration** — A translator's declaration must include the translator's name, the language and dialect, if any, translated and a statement that the translation is accurate.

Documents or Written Submissions not Previously Provided

29. (1) **Documents or written submissions not previously provided — person** — A person who is the subject of an appeal who does not provide a document or written submissions with the appellant's record, respondent's record or reply record must not use the document or provide the written submissions in the appeal unless allowed to do so by the Division.

(2) **Application** — If a person who is the subject of an appeal wants to use a document or provide written submissions that were not previously provided, the person must make an application to the Division in accordance with rule 37.

(3) **Documents — new evidence** — The person who is the subject of the appeal must include in an application to use a document that was not previously provided an explanation of how the document meets the requirements of subsection

110(4) of the Act and how that evidence relates to the person, unless the document is being presented in response to evidence presented by the Minister.

(4) **Factors** — In deciding whether to allow an application, the Division must consider any relevant factors, including

(a) the document's relevance and probative value;

(b) any new evidence the document brings to the appeal; and

(c) whether the person who is the subject of the appeal, with reasonable effort, could have provided the document or written submissions with the appellant's record, respondent's record or reply record.

(5) **Documents or written submissions not previously provided — Minister** — If, at any time before the Division makes a decision, the Minister, in accordance with paragraph 171(a.5) of the Act, submits documentary evidence or written submissions in support of the Minister's appeal or intervention that were not previously provided, the Minister must provide the documentary evidence or written submissions first to the person who is the subject of the appeal and then to the Division.

(6) **Proof documents or written submissions provided** — The additional documents or written submissions provided to the Division under subrule (5) must be accompanied by proof that they were provided to the person who is the subject of the appeal.

(7) **Reply to Minister's documents or written submissions** — The person who is the subject of the appeal may reply to the additional documents or written submissions in accordance with rule 5 with any modifications that the circumstances require.

Providing a Document

30. **General provision** — Rules 31 to 35 apply to any document, including a notice or request in writing.

31. (1) **Providing documents to Division** — A document to be provided to the Division must be provided to the Division's registry office that is located in the same region as the Refugee Protection Division's registry office through which the notice of decision under appeal was provided.

(2) **Providing documents to Refugee Protection Division** — A document to be provided to the Refugee Protection Division must be provided to the Refugee Protection Division's registry office through which the notice of decision under appeal was provided.

(3) **Providing documents to Minister** — A document to be provided to the Minister must be provided to the Minister's counsel.

(4) **Providing documents to person other than Minister** — A document to be provided to a person other than the Minister must be provided to the person's

counsel if the person has counsel of record. If the person does not have counsel of record, the document must be provided to the person.

32. How to provide document — A document may be provided in any of the following ways:

(a) by hand;

(b) by regular mail or registered mail;

(c) by courier;

(d) by fax if the recipient has a fax number and the document is no more than 20 pages long, unless the recipient consents to receiving more than 20 pages; and

(e) by email or other electronic means if the Division allows.

33. (1) Application if unable to provide document — If a party is unable to provide a document in a way required by rule 32, the party may make an application to the Division to be allowed to provide the document in another way or to be excused from providing the document.

(2) Form of application — The application must be made in accordance with rule 37.

(3) Allowing application — The Division must not allow the application unless the party has made reasonable efforts to provide the document to the person to whom the document must be provided.

34. (1) Proof document was provided — Proof that a document was provided must be established by

(a) an acknowledgment of receipt signed by the recipient or a statement of service, if the document was provided by hand;

(b) a confirmation of receipt if the document was provided by registered mail, courier, fax or email or other electronic means; or

(c) a statement of service if the document was provided by regular mail.

(2) Statement of service — For the purpose of paragraph (1)(a) or (c), a statement of service consists of a written statement, signed by the person who provided the document, that includes the person's name and a statement of how and when the document was provided.

(3) Statement — unable to provide proof — If a party is unable to provide proof that a document was provided in a way required by paragraph (1)(a) to (c), the party must provide a written statement, signed by the party, that includes an explanation of why they are unable to provide proof.

35. (1) When document received by division — A document provided to the Division or to the Refugee Protection Division is considered to be received on the day on which the document is date-stamped by that division.

Rules

(2) When document received by recipient other than division — A document provided by regular mail other than to the Division or to the Refugee Protection Division is considered to be received seven days after the day on which it was mailed. If the seventh day is not a working day, the document is considered to be received on the next working day.

(3) Extension of time limit — next working day — When the time limit for providing a document ends on a day that is not a working day, the time limit is extended to the next working day.

Applications

General

36. General provision — Unless these Rules provide otherwise,

(a) a party who wants the Division to make a decision on any matter in a proceeding, including the procedure to be followed, must make an application to the Division in accordance with rule 37;

(b) a party who wants to respond to the application must respond in accordance with rule 38; and

(c) a party who wants to reply to a response must reply in accordance with rule 39.

How to Make an Application

37. (1) Form of application and time limit — Unless these Rules provide otherwise, an application must be made in writing and without delay.

(2) Oral application — If a date for a hearing has been fixed, the Division must not allow a party to make an application orally at the hearing unless the party, with reasonable effort, could not have made a written application before that date.

(3) Content of application — Unless these Rules provide otherwise, in a written application, the party must

(a) state the decision the party wants the Division to make;

(b) give reasons why the Division should make that decision; and

(c) if there is another party and the views of that party are known, state whether the other party agrees to the application.

(4) Affidavit or statutory declaration — Unless these Rules provide otherwise, any evidence that the party wants the Division to consider with a written application must be given in an affidavit or statutory declaration that accompanies the application.

(5) Providing application to other party and Division — A party who makes a written application must provide

(a) to any other party, a copy of the application and a copy of any affidavit or statutory declaration; and

(b) to the Division, the original application and the original of any affidavit or statutory declaration, together with proof that a copy was provided to any other party.

How to Respond to a Written Application

38. (1) Responding to written application — A response to a written application must be in writing and

(a) state the decision the party wants the Division to make; and

(b) give reasons why the Division should make that decision.

(2) Evidence in written response — Any evidence that the party wants the Division to consider with the written response must be given in an affidavit or statutory declaration that accompanies the response. Unless the Division requires it, an affidavit or statutory declaration is not required if the party who made the application was not required to give evidence in an affidavit or statutory declaration, together with the application.

(3) Providing response — A party who responds to a written application must provide

(a) to the other party, a copy of the response and a copy of any affidavit or statutory declaration; and

(b) to the Division, the original response and the original of any affidavit or statutory declaration, together with proof that a copy was provided to the other party.

(4) Time limit — Documents provided under subrule (3) must be received by their recipients no later than seven days after the day on which the party receives the copy of the application.

How to Reply to a Written Response

39. (1) Replying to written response — A reply to a written response must be in writing.

(2) Evidence in reply — Any evidence that the party wants the Division to consider with the written reply must be given in an affidavit or statutory declaration that accompanies the reply. Unless the Division requires it, an affidavit or statutory declaration is not required if the party was not required to give evidence in an affidavit or statutory declaration, together with the application.

(3) Providing reply — A party who replies to a written response must provide

(a) to the other party, a copy of the reply and a copy of any affidavit or statutory declaration; and

1053

(b) to the Division, the original reply and the original of any affidavit or statutory declaration, together with proof that a copy was provided to the other party.

(4) Time limit — Documents provided under subrule (3) must be received by their recipients no later than five days after the day on which the party receives the copy of the response.

Joining or Separating Appeals

40. Appeals automatically joined — The Division must join any appeals of decisions on claims that were joined at the time that the Refugee Protection Division decided the claims.

41. (1) Application to join — A party may make an application to the Division to join appeals.

(2) Application to separate — A party may make an application to the Division to separate appeals that are joined.

(3) Form of application and providing application — A party who makes an application to join or separate appeals must do so in accordance with rule 37, but the party is not required to give evidence in an affidavit or statutory declaration. The party must also

(a) provide a copy of the application to any person who will be affected by the Division's decision on the application; and

(b) provide to the Division proof that the party provided the copy of the application to any affected person.

(4) Time limit — Documents provided under this rule must be received by their recipients,

(a) if the person who is the subject of the appeal is the applicant, at the same time as the Division receives the person's notice of appeal, notice of intent to respond or reply record; or

(b) if the Minister is the applicant, at the same time as the Division receives the Minister's notice of appeal, notice of intervention or reply.

(5) Factors — In deciding the application, the Division must consider any relevant factors, including whether

(a) the appeals involve similar questions of fact or law;

(b) allowing the application would promote the efficient administration of the Division's work; and

(c) allowing the application would likely cause an injustice.

Proceedings Conducted in Public

42. (1) Minister considered party — For the purpose of this rule, the Minister is considered to be a party even if the Minister has not yet intervened in the appeal.

(2) Application — A person who makes an application to the Division to have a proceeding conducted in public must do so in writing and in accordance with this rule rather than rule 37.

(3) Oral application — If a date for a hearing has been fixed, the Division must not allow a person to make an application orally at the hearing unless the person, with reasonable effort, could not have made a written application before that date.

(4) Content of application — In the application, the person must

    (a) state the decision they want the Division to make;

    (b) give reasons why the Division should make that decision;

    (c) state whether they want the Division to consider the application in public or in the absence of the public;

    (d) give reasons why the Division should consider the application in public or in the absence of the public; and

    (e) include any evidence that they want the Division to consider in deciding the application.

(5) Providing application — The person must provide the original application and two copies to the Division. The Division must provide a copy of the application to the parties.

(6) Response to application — A party may respond to a written application. The response must

    (a) state the decision they want the Division to make;

    (b) give reasons why the Division should make that decision;

    (c) state whether they want the Division to consider the application in public or in the absence of the public;

    (d) give reasons why the Division should consider the application in public or in the absence of the public; and

    (e) include any evidence that they want the Division to consider in deciding the application.

(7) Minister's notice — If the Minister responds to a written application, the response must be accompanied by a notice of intervention in accordance with subrule 4(2), if one was not previously provided.

(8) Providing response — The party must provide a copy of the response to the other party and provide the original response and a copy to the Division, together with proof that the copy was provided to the other party.

(9) Providing response to applicant — The Division must provide to the applicant either a copy of the response or a summary of the response referred to in paragraph (13)(a).

(10) Reply to response — An applicant or a party may reply in writing to a written response or a summary of a response.

(11) Providing reply — An applicant or a party who replies to a written response or a summary of a response must provide the original reply and two copies to the Division. The Division must provide a copy of the reply to the parties.

(12) Time limit — An application made under this rule must be received by the Division without delay. The Division must specify the time limit within which a response or reply, if any, is to be provided.

(13) Confidentiality — The Division may take any measures it considers necessary to ensure the confidentiality of the proceeding in respect of the application, including

(a) providing a summary of the response to the applicant instead of a copy; and

(b) if the Division holds a hearing in respect of the appeal and the application,

(i) excluding the applicant or the applicant and their counsel from the hearing while the party responding to the application provides evidence and makes representations, or

(ii) allowing the presence of the applicant's counsel at the hearing while the party responding to the application provides evidence and makes representations, on receipt of a written undertaking by counsel not to disclose any evidence or information adduced until a decision is made to hold the hearing in public.

(14) Summary of response — If the Division provides a summary of the response under paragraph (13)(a), or excludes the applicant and their counsel from a hearing in respect of the application under subparagraph (13)(b)(i), the Division must provide a summary of the representations and evidence, if any, that is sufficient to enable the applicant to reply, while ensuring the confidentiality of the proceeding having regard to the factors set out in paragraph 166(b) of the Act.

(15) Notification of decision on application — The Division must notify the applicant and the parties of its decision on the application and provide reasons for the decision.

Assignment of Three-Member Panel

43. (1) Notice of order — If the Chairperson of the Board orders a proceeding to be conducted by three Division members, the Division must without delay notify the parties — including the Minister even if the Minister has not yet intervened in the appeal — and the UNHCR in writing of the order.

(2) **Providing documents to UNHCR** — The Division must provide the UNHCR with a copy of the following documents at the same time that it provides notice of the order:

(a) the Refugee Protection Division record; and

(b) the notice of appeal, appellant's record, notice of intent to respond, respondent's record, reply record, Minister's notice of intervention, Minister's intervention record, if any, Minister's reply, and Minister's reply record, if any.

(3) **UNHCR's notice to Division** — If the UNHCR receives notice of an order, the UNHCR may provide notice to the Division in accordance with subrule 45(1) of its intention to provide written submissions.

(4) **Time limit** — The Division may, without further notice to the parties and to the UNHCR, decide the appeal on the basis of the materials provided if a period of 15 days has passed since the day on which the Minister and the UNHCR receive notice of the order.

UNHCR and Interested Persons

44. Rules applicable to UNHCR and interested persons — These Rules, with the exception of rules 25 (notice of constitutional question) and 47 to 49 (withdrawal, reinstatement, reopening), apply to the UNHCR and interested persons with any modifications that the circumstances require.

45. (1) Notice to Division — The UNHCR must notify the Division in writing of its intention to provide written submissions in an appeal conducted by a three-member panel, and include its contact information and that of its counsel, if any.

(2) **Notice to person and Minister** — The Division must without delay provide a copy of the UNHCR's notice to the person who is the subject of the appeal and to the Minister.

(3) **Providing written submissions to Division** — The UNHCR's written submissions must be received by the Division no later than 10 days after the day on which the UNHCR provided the notice.

(4) **Limitation — written submissions** — The UNHCR's written submissions must not raise new issues.

(5) **Length of written submissions** — The UNHCR's written submissions must not be more than 30 pages long if typewritten on one side or 15 pages if typewritten on both sides.

(6) **Providing written submissions** — The Division must without delay provide a copy of the UNHCR's written submissions to the person who is the subject of the appeal and to the Minister.

(7) **Response** — The person who is the subject of the appeal or the Minister may respond to the UNHCR's submissions in writing.

(8) **Limitation — response** — A response must not raise new issues.

Rules

(9) Length of response — A response must not be more than 30 pages long if typewritten on one side or 15 pages if typewritten on both sides.

(10) Providing response — The response must first be provided to the person who is the subject of the appeal or to the Minister, as the case may be, and then to the Division.

(11) Proof response provided — The response provided to the Division must be accompanied by proof that it was provided to the person who is the subject of the appeal or to the Minister, as the case may be.

(12) Time limit — Documents provided under subrules (10) and (11) must be received by their recipients no later than seven days after the day on which the person who is the subject of the appeal or the Minister, as the case may be, receives the UNHCR's submissions.

46. (1) Application by person to participate — Any person, other than the UNHCR, may make an application to the Division to be allowed to participate in an appeal conducted by a three-member panel. The person must make the application without delay and in accordance with this rule.

(2) Form and content of application — The application must be in writing and include

    (a) the applicant's name;

    (b) an explanation of why the applicant wants to participate;

    (c) the submissions the applicant wants to put forward and an explanation of how they are relevant to the appeal;

    (d) an explanation of the differences between the applicant's submissions and those of the person who is the subject of the appeal and the Minister;

    (e) an explanation of how the applicant's submissions may help the Division decide the appeal; and

    (f) the contact information of the applicant and their counsel, if any.

(3) Providing application — The Division must provide a copy of the application to the person who is the subject of the appeal and to the Minister.

(4) Response — The person who is the subject of the appeal or the Minister may respond to the application in writing.

(5) Limitation — response — A response must not raise new issues.

(6) Length of response — A response must not be more than 30 pages long if typewritten on one side or 15 pages if typewritten on both sides.

(7) Time limit — A response must be received by the Division no later than 10 days after the day on which the person who is the subject of the appeal or the Minister, as the case may be, receives the application.

(8) Nullification of decision on application — The Division must without delay notify the applicant, the person who is the subject of the appeal and the Minister in writing of its decision on the application.

(9) Providing documents — If the Division allows the application, it must without delay provide the interested person with a copy of the following documents as soon as they are available:

(a) the Refugee Protection Division record;

(b) the notice of appeal, appellant's record, notice of intent to respond, respondent's record, reply record, Minister's notice of intervention, Minister's intervention record, if any, Minister's reply, and Minister's reply record, if any; and

(c) the written submissions of any other interested person and the UNHCR.

(10) Limitation — written submissions — The interested person's written submissions must not raise new issues.

(11) Length of written submissions — The interested person's written submissions must not be more than 30 pages long if typewritten on one side or 15 pages if typewritten on both sides.

(12) Providing written submissions — The interested person's written submissions must first be provided to the person who is the subject of the appeal and to the Minister and then to the Division.

(13) Proof written submissions provided — The written submissions provided to the Division must be accompanied by proof that they were provided to the person who is the subject of the appeal and to the Minister.

(14) Response — The person who is the subject of the appeal or the Minister may respond to the written submissions in writing.

(15) Limitation — response — A response must not raise new issues.

(16) Length of response — A response must not be more than 30 pages long if typewritten on one side or 15 pages if typewritten on both sides.

(17) Providing response — The response must first be provided to the interested person, then to the person who is the subject of the appeal or to the Minister, as the case may be, and then to the Division.

(18) Proof response provided — The response provided to the Division must be accompanied by proof that it was provided to the interested person, and to the person who is the subject of the appeal or to the Minister, as the case may be.

(19) Time limit — Documents provided under subrules (17) and (18) must be received by their recipients no later than seven days after the day on which the person who is the subject of the appeal or the Minister, as the case may be, receives the interested person's written submissions.

Rules

Withdrawal

47. (1) Abuse of process — For the purpose of subsection 168(2) of the Act, withdrawal of an appeal is an abuse of process if withdrawal would likely have a negative effect on the Division's integrity. If the requirements set out in rule 7 or 13, as the case may be, for deciding an appeal on the basis of the materials provided have not been met, withdrawal is not an abuse of process.

(2) Withdrawal on notice — If the requirements set out in rule 7 or 13, as the case may be, for deciding an appeal have not been met, an appellant may withdraw an appeal by notifying the Division in writing.

(3) Application to withdraw — If the requirements set out in rule 7 or 13, as the case may be, for deciding an appeal have been met, an appellant who wants to withdraw an appeal must make an application to the Division in accordance with rule 37.

Reinstating a Withdrawn Appeal

48. (1) Application to reinstate withdrawn appeal — An appellant may apply to the Division to reinstate an appeal that was made by the appellant and was withdrawn.

(2) Form and content of application — The appellant must make the application in accordance with rule 37. If a person who is the subject of an appeal makes the application, they must provide to the Division the original and a copy of the application and include in the application their contact information and, if represented by counsel, their counsel's contact information and any limitations on counsel's retainer.

(3) Documents provided to Minister — The Division must provide to the Minister, without delay, a copy of an application made by a person who is the subject of an appeal.

(4) Factors — The Division must not allow the application unless it is established that there was a failure to observe a principle of natural justice or it is otherwise in the interests of justice to allow the application.

(5) Factors — In deciding the application, the Division must consider any relevant factors, including whether the application was made in a timely manner and the justification for any delay.

(6) Subsequent application — If the appellant made a previous application to reinstate an appeal that was denied, the Division must consider the reasons for the denial and must not allow the subsequent application unless there are exceptional circumstances supported by new evidence.

Reopening an Appeal

19. **(1) Application to reopen appeal** — At any time before the Federal Court has made a final determination in respect of an appeal that has been decided or declared abandoned, the appellant may make an application to the Division to reopen the appeal.

(2) Form and content of application — The application must be made in accordance with rule 37. If a person who is the subject of an appeal makes the application, they must provide to the Division the original and a copy of the application and include in the application their contact information and, if represented by counsel, their counsel's contact information and any limitations on counsel's retainer.

(3) Documents provided to Minister — The Division must provide to the Minister, without delay, a copy of an application made by a person who is the subject of an appeal.

(4) Allegations against counsel — If it is alleged in the application that the person who is the subject of the appeal's counsel in the proceedings that are the subject of the application provided inadequate representation,

(a) the person must first provide a copy of the application to the counsel and then provide the original and a copy of the application to the Division, and

(b) the application provided to the Division must be accompanied by proof that a copy was provided to the counsel.

(5) Copy of pending application — The application must be accompanied by a copy of any pending application for leave to apply for judicial review or any pending application for judicial review.

(6) Factor — The Division must not allow the application unless it is established that there was a failure to observe a principle of natural justice.

(7) Factors — In deciding the application, the Division must consider any relevant factors, including

(a) whether the application was made in a timely manner and the justification for any delay; and

(b) if the appellant did not make an application for leave to apply for judicial review or an application for judicial review, the reasons why an application was not made.

(8) Subsequent application — If the appellant made a previous application to reopen an appeal that was denied, the Division must consider the reasons for the denial and must not allow the subsequent application unless there are exceptional circumstances supported by new evidence.

(9) Other remedies — If there is a pending application for leave to apply for judicial review or a pending application for judicial review on the same or similar grounds, the Division must, as soon as is practicable, allow the application to reopen if it is necessary for the timely and efficient processing of appeals, or dismiss the application.

Rules

Decisions

50. (1) Notice of decision — When the Division makes a decision, other than an interlocutory decision, it must provide in writing a notice of decision to the person who is the subject of the appeal, to the Minister and to the Refugee Protection Division. The Division must also provide in writing a notice of decision to the UNHCR and to any interested person, if they provided written submissions in the appeal.

(2) Written reasons — The Division must provide written reasons for the decision, together with the notice of decision, if a hearing

(a) was not held under subsection 110(6) of the Act; or

(b) was held under subsection 110(6) of the Act and the decision and reasons were not given orally at the hearing.

(3) Request for written reasons — A request under paragraph 169(1)(e) of the Act for written reasons for a decision must be made in writing.

51. (1) When decision of single member takes effect — A decision, other than an interlocutory decision, made by a single Division member takes effect

(a) if made in writing, when the member signs and dates the reasons for the decision; and

(b) if given orally at a hearing, when the member states the decision and gives the reasons.

(2) When decision of three-member panel takes effect — A decision, other than an interlocutory decision, made by a panel of three Division members takes effect

(a) if made in writing, when all the members sign and date their reasons for the decision; and

(b) if given orally at a hearing, when all the members state their decision and give their reasons.

General Provisions

52. No applicable rule — In the absence of a provision in these Rules dealing with a matter raised during the proceedings, the Division may do whatever is necessary to deal with the matter.

53. Powers of Division — The Division may, after giving the parties notice and an opportunity to object,

(a) act on its own initiative, without a party having to make an application or request to the Division;

(b) change a requirement of a rule;

(c) excuse a person from a requirement of a rule; and

(d) extend a time limit, before or after the time limit has expired, or shorten it if the time limit has not expired.

54. Failure to follow rules — Unless proceedings are declared invalid by the Division, a failure to follow any requirement of these Rules does not make the proceedings invalid.

PART 4 — RULES APPLICABLE TO AN APPEAL FOR WHICH A HEARING IS HELD

Fixing a Date for a Hearing

55. Conference to fix date for hearing — The Division may require the parties to participate in a scheduling conference or otherwise give information to help the Division fix a date for a hearing.

Notice to Appear

56. (1) Notice to appear — When, in accordance with paragraph 171(a) of the Act, the Division gives notice to the person who is the subject of the appeal and to the Minister of any hearing, it must notify them in writing of the date, time and location fixed for the hearing and the issues that will be raised at the hearing.

(2) Date fixed for hearing — The date fixed for the hearing of an appeal must not be earlier than 10 days after the day on which the person who is the subject of the appeal and the Minister receive the notice referred to in subrule (1), unless they consent to an earlier date.

Conduct of a Hearing

57. (1) Restriction of hearing — A hearing is restricted to matters relating to the issues provided with the notice to appear unless the Division considers that other issues have been raised by statements made by the person who is the subject of the appeal or by a witness during the hearing.

(2) Standard order of questioning — Unless the Division orders otherwise, any witness, including the person who is the subject of the appeal, will be questioned first by the appellant, then by any other party, then by the appellant in reply, and then by the Division.

(3) Limiting questioning of witnesses — The Division may limit the questioning of witnesses, including the person who is the subject of the appeal, taking into account the nature and complexity of the issues and the relevance of the questions.

(4) Oral representations — Representations must be made orally at the end of a hearing unless the Division orders otherwise.

Rules

1063

(5) Limits on representations — After all the evidence has been heard, the Division must

(a) set time limits for representations, taking into account the complexity of the issues and the amount of relevant evidence heard; and

(b) indicate what issues need to be addressed in the representations.

Person Who Is the Subject of an Appeal in Custody

58. Custody — The Division may order a person who holds a person who is the subject of an appeal in custody to bring the person to a proceeding at a location specified by the Division.

Interpreters

59. (1) Need for interpreter — person — If a person who is the subject of an appeal needs an interpreter, the person must indicate the language and dialect, if any, to be interpreted in the appellant's record if they are the appellant or in the respondent's record if they are the respondent.

(2) Changing language of interpretation — A person who is the subject of an appeal may change the language and dialect, if any, that they specified under subrule (1), or if they had not indicated that an interpreter was needed, they may indicate that they need an interpreter, by notifying the Division in writing and indicating the language and dialect, if any, to be interpreted. The notice must be received by the Division no later than 20 days before the date fixed for the hearing.

(3) Need for interpreter — witness — If any party's witness needs an interpreter for a hearing, the party must notify the Division in writing and specify the language and dialect, if any, to be interpreted. The notice must be received by the Division no later than 20 days before the date fixed for the hearing.

(4) Interpreter's oath — The interpreter must take an oath or make a solemn affirmation to interpret accurately.

Observers

60. (1) Observers — An application under rule 42 is not necessary if an observer is the UNHCR or a member of the staff of the Board or if the person who is the subject of the appeal consents to or requests the presence of an observer other than a representative of the press or other media of communication at the proceeding.

(2) Observers — factor — The Division must allow the attendance of an observer unless, in the opinion of the Division, the observer's attendance is likely to impede the proceeding.

(3) Observers — confidentiality of proceeding — The Division may take any measures it considers necessary to ensure the confidentiality of the proceeding despite the presence of an observer.

Witnesses

61. (1) Providing witness information — If a party wants to call a witness, the party must provide the following witness information in writing to any other party and to the Division:

(a) the witness's contact information;

(b) a brief statement of the purpose and substance of the witness's testimony or, in the case of an expert witness, the expert witness's brief signed summary of the testimony to be given;

(c) the time needed for the witness's testimony;

(d) the party's relationship to the witness;

(e) in the case of an expert witness, a description of the expert witness's qualifications; and

(f) whether the party wants the witness to testify by means of live telecommunication.

(2) Proof witness information provided — The witness information provided to the Division must be accompanied by proof that it was provided to any other party.

(3) Time limit — Documents provided under this rule must be received by their recipients no later than 20 days before the date fixed for the hearing.

(4) Failure to provide witness information — If a party does not provide the witness information, the witness must not testify at the hearing unless the Division allows them to testify.

(5) Factors — In deciding whether to allow a witness to testify, the Division must consider any relevant factors, including

(a) the relevance and probative value of the proposed testimony; and

(b) the reason why the witness information was not provided.

62. (1) Requesting summons — A party who wants the Division to order a person to testify at a hearing must make a request to the Division for a summons, either orally at a proceeding or in writing.

(2) Factors — In deciding whether to issue a summons, the Division must consider any relevant factors, including

(a) the necessity of the testimony to a full and proper hearing;

(b) the person's ability to give that testimony; and

(c) whether the person has agreed to be summoned as a witness.

(3) Using summons — If a party wants to use a summons, they must

(a) provide the summons to the person by hand;

(b) provide a copy of the summons to the Division, together with proof that it was provided to the person by hand; and

(c) pay or offer to pay the person the applicable witness fees and travel expenses set out in Tariff A of the *Federal Courts Rules*.

63. (1) Cancelling summons — If a person who is summoned to appear as a witness wants the summons cancelled, the person must make an application in writing to the Division.

(2) Application — The person must make the application in accordance with rule 37, but is not required to give evidence in an affidavit or statutory declaration.

64. (1) Arrest warrant — If a person does not obey a summons to appear as a witness, the party who requested the summons may make a request to the Division orally at the hearing, or in writing, to issue a warrant for the person's arrest.

(2) Written request — A party who makes a written request for a warrant must provide supporting evidence by affidavit or statutory declaration.

(3) Requirements for issue of arrest warrant — The Division must not issue a warrant unless

(a) the person was provided the summons by hand or the person is avoiding being provided the summons;

(b) the person was paid or offered the applicable witness fees and travel expenses set out in Tariff A of the *Federal Courts Rules*;

(c) the person did not appear at the hearing as required by the summons; and

(d) the person's testimony is still needed for a full and proper hearing.

(4) Content of warrant — A warrant issued by the Division for the arrest of a person must include directions concerning detention or release.

65. Excluded witness — If the Division excludes a witness from a hearing room, no person may communicate to the witness any evidence given while the witness was excluded unless allowed to do so by the Division or until the witness has finished testifying.

Changing the Location of a Hearing

66. (1) Application to change location — A party may make an application to the Division to change the location of a hearing.

(2) Form and content of application — The party must make the application in accordance with rule 37, but is not required to give evidence in an affidavit or statutory declaration.

(3) Time limit — Documents provided under this rule must be received by their recipients no later than 20 days before the date fixed for the hearing.

(4) Factors — In deciding the application, the Division must consider any relevant factors, including

(a) whether the party is residing in the location where the party wants the hearing to be held;

(b) whether a change of location would allow the hearing to be full and proper;

(c) whether a change of location would likely delay the hearing;

(d) how a change of location would affect the Division's operation;

(e) how a change of location would affect the parties;

(f) whether a change of location is necessary in order to accommodate a vulnerable person; and

(g) whether a hearing may be conducted by means of live telecommunication with the person who is the subject of the appeal.

(5) Duty to appear — Unless a party receives a decision from the Division allowing the application, the party must appear for the hearing at the location fixed and be ready to start or continue the hearing.

Changing the Date or Time of a Hearing

67. (1) Application to change date or time — A party may make an application to the Division to change the date or time fixed for a hearing.

(2) Form and content of application — The party must

(a) make the application in accordance with rule 37, but is not required to give evidence in an affidavit or statutory declaration; and

(b) give at least six dates and times, within the period specified by the Division, on which the party is available to start or continue the hearing.

(3) Notice of period specified by Division — The Division must provide notice of the period referred to in paragraph (2)(b) in a manner that will allow public access to it.

(4) Hearing two working days or less away — If the party wants to make an application two working days or less before the date fixed for the hearing, the party must make the application orally on the date fixed for the hearing.

(5) Factors — In deciding the application, the Division must consider any relevant factors, including

(a) in the case of a date and time that was fixed after the Division consulted or tried to consult the party, any exceptional circumstances for allowing the application;

(b) when the party made the application;

(c) the time the party has had to prepare for the hearing;

(d) the efforts made by the party to be ready to start or continue the hearing;

Rules

(e) in the case of a party who requests more time to obtain information in support of their arguments, the Division's ability to proceed in the absence of that information without causing an injustice;

(f) whether the party has counsel;

(g) the knowledge and experience of any counsel who represents the party;

(h) any previous delays and the reasons for them;

(i) whether the date and time fixed were peremptory;

(j) whether the change is required to accommodate a vulnerable person;

(k) whether allowing the application would unreasonably delay the hearing or likely cause an injustice; and

(l) the nature and complexity of the matter to be heard.

(6) **Subsequent application** — If the party made a previous application that was denied, the Division must consider the reasons for the denial and must not allow the subsequent application unless there are exceptional circumstances supported by new evidence.

(7) **Application for medical reasons** — If a person who is the subject of an appeal makes the application for medical reasons, other than those related to their counsel, they must provide, together with the application, a legible, recently dated medical certificate signed by a qualified medical practitioner whose name and address are printed or stamped on the certificate. A person who has provided a copy of the certificate to the Division must provide the original document to the Division without delay.

(8) **Content of certificate** — The medical certificate must set out

(a) the particulars of the medical condition, without specifying the diagnosis, that prevent the person from participating in the hearing on the date fixed for the hearing; and

(b) the date on which the person is expected to be able to participate in the hearing.

(9) **Failure to provide medical certificate** — If a person who is the subject of an appeal fails to provide a medical certificate in accordance with subrules (7) and (8), the person must include in their application

(a) particulars of any efforts they made to obtain the required medical certificate, supported by corroborating evidence;

(b) particulars of the medical reasons for the application, supported by corroborating evidence; and

(c) an explanation of how the medical condition prevents them from participating in the hearing on the date fixed for the hearing.

(10) **Duty to appear** — Unless a party receives a decision from the Division allowing the application, the party must appear for the hearing at the date and time fixed and be ready to start or continue the hearing.

Abandonment

68. (1) Abandonment after hearing scheduled — In determining whether an appeal has been abandoned under subsection 168(1) of the Act after a date for a hearing has been fixed, the Division must give the appellant an opportunity to explain why the appeal should not be declared abandoned,

(a) immediately, if the appellant is present at the hearing and the Division considers that it is fair to do so; or

(b) in any other case, by way of a special hearing, after notifying the appellant in writing.

(2) Factors to consider — The Division must consider, in deciding if the appeal should be declared abandoned, the explanation given by the appellant and any other relevant factors, including the fact that the appellant is ready to start or continue the proceedings.

(3) Medical reasons — If the appellant is the person who is the subject of the appeal and the explanation includes medical reasons, other than those related to their counsel, they must provide, together with the explanation, the original of a legible, recently dated medical certificate signed by a qualified medical practitioner whose name and address are printed or stamped on the certificate.

(4) Content of certificate — The medical certificate must set out

(a) the particulars of the medical condition, without specifying the diagnosis, that prevented the person from pursuing their appeal; and

(b) the date on which the person is expected to be able to pursue their appeal.

(5) Failure to provide medical certificate — If a person who is the subject of an appeal fails to provide a medical certificate in accordance with subrules (3) and (4), the person must include in their explanation

(a) particulars of any efforts they made to obtain the required medical certificate, supported by corroborating evidence;

(b) particulars of the medical reasons included in the explanation, supported by corroborating evidence; and

(c) an explanation of how the medical condition prevented them from pursuing their appeal.

(6) Start or continue proceedings — If the Division decides not to declare the appeal abandoned, it must start or continue the proceedings without delay.

Coming Into Force

69. S.C. 2001, c. 27 — These Rules come into force on the day on which section 110 of the *Immigration and Refugee Protection Act* comes into force, but if they are registered after that day, they come into force on the day on which they are registered.

SCHEDULE INFORMATION AND DECLARATIONS — COUNSEL NOT REPRESENTING OR ADVISING FOR CONSIDERATION

(Rule 17)

Item	Information
1.	IRB Division and file number with respect to the person who is the subject of the appeal.
2.	Name of counsel who is representing or advising the person who is the subject of the appeal and who is not receiving consideration for those services.
3.	Name of counsel's firm or organization, if applicable, and counsel's postal address, telephone number and fax number and email address, if any.
4.	If applicable, a declaration, signed by the interpreter, that includes the interpreter's name, the language and dialect, if any, interpreted and a statement that the interpretation is accurate.
5.	Declaration signed by the person who is the subject of the appeal that the counsel who is representing or advising them is not receiving consideration and that the information provided in the form is complete, true and correct.
6.	Declaration signed by counsel that they are not receiving consideration for representing or advising the person who is the subject of the appeal and that the information provided in the form is complete, true and correct.

CAN. REG. 2002-229 — IMMIGRATION DIVISION RULES

made under the *Immigration and Refugee Protection Act*

SOR/2002-229, as am. S.C. 2002, c. 8, s. 182(3)(a).

DEFINITIONS

1. Definitions — The following definitions apply in these Rules.

"Act" means the *Immigration and Refugee Protection Act. ("Loi")*

"admissibility hearing" means a hearing held under subsection 44(2) of the Act. *("enquête")*

"contact information" means a person's name, postal address and telephone number and the person's fax number and electronic mail address, if any. *("coordonnées")*

"detention review" means a forty-eight hour review, a seven-day review and a thirty-day review. *("contrôle des motifs de détention")*

"Division" means the Immigration Division. *("Section")*

"forty-eight hour review" means the review of the reasons for continued detention under subsection 57(1) of the Act. *("contrôle des quarante-huit heures")*

"party" means a permanent resident or foreign national, as the case may be, and the Minister. *("partie")*

"proceeding" means an admissibility hearing, a detention review, a conference or an application. *("procédure")*

"registry office" means a business office of the Division. *("greffe")*

"seven-day review" means the review of the reasons for continued detention required to be held during the seven days following a forty-eight hour review, under subsection 57(2) of the Act. *("contrôle des sept jours")*

"thirty-day review" means the review of the reasons for continued detention required to be held during the thirty days following each previous review, under subsection 57(2) of the Act. *("contrôle des trente jours")*

COMMUNICATING WITH THE DIVISION

2. Communicating with the Division — All communication with the Division must be directed to the registry office specified by the Division.

PART 1 — RULES APPLICABLE TO ADMISSIBILITY HEARINGS

Information

3. Information provided by the Minister — When the Minister requests the Division to hold an admissibility hearing, the Minister must provide to the Division and the permanent resident or foreign national, as the case may be, any relevant information or document that the Minister may have, including

(a) the name and other contact information in Canada of the permanent resident or foreign national;

(b) the person's date of birth, sex and citizenship;

(c) whether the person is single, married, separated or divorced or is a common-law partner;

(d) the inadmissibility report and the Minister's referral;

(e) whether the person has made a claim for refugee protection;

(f) the name and address of the place of detention, if the person is detained;

(g) the language — English or French — chosen by the person for communicating with the Division;

(h) if an interpreter is required, the language or dialect to be interpreted;

(i) if the person has counsel, the counsel's contact information;

(j) the client identification number given to the person by the Department of Citizenship and Immigration;

(k) the names, sex, date of birth, citizenship, and other contact information of any family member whose case has been referred to the Division, and the client identification number given to them by the Department of Citizenship and Immigration;

(l) the date on which the Minister makes the request;

(m) the name and title of the Minister's counsel;

(n) whether the Minister has made an application for non-disclosure of information;

(o) whether the Minister believes that the person is less than 18 years of age or is unable to appreciate the nature of the proceedings; and

(p) the evidence to be presented by the Minister.

4. Change to contact information — If the contact information changes, the permanent resident or foreign national, unless detained, must without delay provide the changes in writing to the Division and the Minister.

Withdrawing a Request by the Minister for an Admissibility Hearing

5. (1) Abuse of process — Withdrawal of a request for an admissibility hearing is an abuse of process if withdrawal would likely have a negative effect on the integrity of the Division. If no substantive evidence has been accepted in the proceedings, withdrawal of a request is not an abuse of process.

(2) Withdrawal if no evidence has been accepted — If no substantive evidence has been accepted in the proceedings, the Minister may withdraw a request by notifying the Division orally at a proceeding or in writing. If the Minister notifies in writing, the Minister must provide a copy of the notice to the other party.

(3) Withdrawal if evidence has been accepted — If substantive evidence has been accepted in the proceedings, the Minister must make a written application to the Division in order to withdraw a request.

Case Law

Sheremetov v. Canada (Minister of Citizenship & Immigration) (2004), 40 Imm. L.R. (3d) 9, 2004 CarswellNat 5184, 2004 CarswellNat 3920, 331 N.R. 163, 2004 FCA 373 — The respondent was a landed immigrant. In March 2002, an officer reported to the Deputy Minister that, in his opinion, the respondent had committed an act that constituted a criminal offence both in Canada and Ukraine. The respondent was given notice to attend a hearing scheduled for September 20, 2002. The hearing resumed on November 6, 2002, when both parties requested an adjournment. The hearing then resumed on February 5, 2003 when the Minister withdrew his request for the admissibility hearing. The Immigration Division accepted the withdrawal. The judicial review judge set aside that decision and found that the division should have taken into account the fact that the documents at the heart of the Ukraine charges had not been produced.

Under Rules 5 and 6 the Minister only had to notify the Immigration Division and the respondent of withdrawal of his request for an admissibility hearing because no evidence at all had been accepted in the proceeding. The adjudicator had no jurisdiction to exercise discretion or proceed with the matter. It is only when the Minister applies to reinstate a request for an inadmissibility hearing under Rule 6 that jurisdiction is conferred on the Immigration Division to determine if it is in the interest of justice to allow the application for reinstatement.

Reinstating a Request by the Minister for an Admissibility Hearing

6. (1) Application for reinstatement of withdrawn request — The Minister may make a written application to the Division to reinstate a request for an admissibility hearing that was withdrawn.

(2) Factors — The Division must allow the application if it is established that there was a failure to observe a principle of natural justice or if it is otherwise in the interests of justice to allow the application.

Case Law

Sheremetov v. Canada (Minister of Citizenship & Immigration) (2004), 40 Imm. L.R. (3d) 9, 2004 CarswellNat 5184, 2004 CarswellNat 3920, 331 N.R. 163, 2004 FCA 373 — The respondent was a landed immigrant. In March 2002, an officer reported to the Deputy Minister that, in his opinion, the respondent had committed an act that constituted a criminal offence both in Canada and Ukraine. The respondent was given notice to attend a hearing scheduled for September 20, 2002. The hearing resumed on November 6, 2002, when both parties requested an adjournment. The hearing then resumed on February 5, 2003 when the Minister withdrew his request for the admissibility hearing. The Immigration Division accepted the withdrawal. The judicial review judge set aside that decision and found that the division should have taken into account the fact that the documents at the heart of the Ukraine charges had not been produced.

Under Rules 5 and 6 the Minister only had to notify the Immigration Division and the respondent of withdrawal of his request for an admissibility hearing because no evidence at all had been accepted in the proceeding. The adjudicator had no jurisdiction to exercise discretion or proceed with the matter. It is only when the Minister applies to reinstate a request for an inadmissibility hearing under Rule 6 that jurisdiction is conferred on the Immigration Division to determine if it is in the interest of justice to allow the application for reinstatement.

Decision

7. (1) Favourable decision — **If the decision at the conclusion of an admissibility hearing is in favour of the permanent resident or foreign national, the member making the decision must date and sign a notice of decision and provide a copy to the parties.**

(2) Unfavourable decision — **If the decision is not in favour of the permanent resident or foreign national, the member must date and sign an order indicating the applicable provisions of the Act and provide a copy to the parties. The member must also notify the permanent resident or foreign national of**

> **(a) their right to appeal to the Immigration Appeal Division; or**

> **(b) if they do not have the right to appeal, their right to file an application for judicial review in the Federal Court.**

(3) When decision takes effect — **A decision made orally at a hearing takes effect when a Division member states the decision. A decision made in writing takes effect when the member signs and dates it.**

(4) Request for written reasons — **A request made by a party for written reasons for a decision may be made orally at the end of an admissibility hearing or in writing. A request in writing must be received by the Division no later than 10 days after the decision takes effect.**

PART 2 — RULES APPLICABLE TO DETENTION REVIEWS

Information

8. (1) Information provided by the Minister — If a foreign national or a permanent resident is subject to a detention review, the Minister must provide the Division and the person detained with the following information:

(a) the person's name, sex, date of birth and citizenship;

(b) whether the person is single, married, separated or divorced or is a common-law partner;

(c) whether the person has made a claim for refugee protection;

(d) the language — English or French — chosen by the person for communicating with the Division;

(e) if an interpreter is required, the language or dialect to be interpreted;

(f) if the person has counsel, the counsel's contact information;

(g) the date and time that the person was first placed in detention;

(h) the name and address of the place where the person is being detained;

(i) whether the Minister is seeking a detention review after the first forty-eight hour detention or after a seven-day or thirty-day review;

(j) the identification number given to the person by the Department of Citizenship and Immigration;

(k) the provision of the Act under which the review of the reasons for continued detention is required;

(l) whether an application for non-disclosure of information has been made; and

(m) whether the Minister believes that the person is less than 18 years of age or is unable to appreciate the nature of the proceedings.

(2) Time limit — The information must be received by the Division and the person detained

(a) in the case of a forty-eight hour review, as soon as possible; and

(b) in the case of a seven-day or thirty-day review, at least three days before the date fixed for the review.

9. (1) Application for early review — A party may make a written application to the Division requesting a detention review before the expiry of the seven-day or thirty-day period, as the case may be.

(2) Factor — The Division may allow the application if the party sets out new facts that justify an early review of the detention.

10. Removal before detention review — The Minister must notify the Division as soon as a permanent resident or foreign national is removed from Canada prior to a scheduled detention review.

Decisions

11. (1) Notice to the parties — At the conclusion of a detention review, the member must notify the parties of the member's decision.

(2) Order — The member must date and sign an order for detention or release indicating the applicable provisions of the Act and provide a copy to the parties.

(3) When decision takes effect — A decision made orally at a hearing takes effect when a Division member states the decision. A decision made in writing takes effect when the member signs and dates it.

(4) Request for written reasons — A request made by a party for written reasons for a decision may be made orally at the end of a detention review or in writing. A request in writing must be received by the Division no later than 10 days after the decision takes effect.

PART 3 — RULES THAT APPLY TO BOTH ADMISSIBILITY HEARINGS AND DETENTION REVIEWS

Information Relating to Counsel

12. Counsel's contact information — A permanent resident or foreign national who is represented by counsel must, on obtaining counsel, provide the counsel's contact information in writing to the Division and the Minister. If that information changes, the permanent resident or foreign national must without delay provide the changes in writing to the Division and the Minister.

Counsel of Record

13. Becoming counsel of record — As soon as counsel for a permanent resident or foreign national agrees to a date for a proceeding, or becomes counsel after a date has been fixed, the counsel becomes counsel of record.

14. Withdrawal as counsel of record — To withdraw as counsel of record, counsel must notify the Division and the Minister in writing as soon as possible. Counsel is no longer counsel of record as soon as the Division receives the notice.

15. Removal of counsel of record — To remove counsel as counsel of record, the permanent resident or foreign national must notify the Division and the Minister in writing as soon as possible. Counsel is no longer counsel of record when the Division receives the notice.

Language of Proceedings

16. (1) Changing the language of proceedings — A permanent resident or foreign national may make an application to the Division to change the language of the proceedings to English or French

(a) orally or in writing in the case of a forty-eight hour or seven-day review or an admissibility hearing held at the same time; and

(b) in writing in all other cases.

(2) Time limit — A written application must be received by the Division

(a) as soon as possible, in the case of a forty-eight hour or seven-day review or an admissibility hearing held at the same time; and

(b) in all other cases, at least five days before the hearing.

17. (1) Requesting an interpreter — If a party or a party's witness needs an interpreter for a proceeding, the party must notify the Division in writing and specify the language or dialect of the interpreter. The notice must be received by the Division

(a) as soon as possible, in the case of a forty-eight hour or seven-day review or an admissibility hearing held at the same time; and

(b) in all other cases, at least five days before the hearing.

(2) Interpreter's oath — The interpreter must take an oath or make a solemn affirmation to interpret accurately.

Case Law

Lamme v. Canada (Minister of Citizenship & Immigration), 2005 CarswellNat 3063, 2005 CarswellNat 4881, 2005 FC 1336 — The general standard to be met with respect to the quality of interpretation is that it must be continuous, precise, impartial and contemporaneous. In addition, for the interpretation to be considered as meeting the standard, it must be established that the applicant understood the interpretation and adequately expressed him- or herself through the interpreter.

Designated Representatives

18. Duty of counsel to notify the Division — If counsel for a party believes that the Division should designate a representative for the permanent resident or foreign national in the proceedings because they are under 18 years of age or unable to appreciate the nature of the proceedings, counsel must without delay notify the Division and the other party in writing. If counsel is aware of a person in Canada who meets the requirements to be designated as a representative, counsel must provide the person's contact information in the notice.

19. Requirements for being designated — To be designated as a representative, a person must

(a) be 18 years of age or older;

(b) understand the nature of the proceedings;

(c) be willing and able to act in the best interests of the permanent resident or foreign national; and

(d) not have interests that conflict with those of the permanent resident or foreign national.

Conference

20. (1) Requirement to participate at a conference — The Division may require the parties to participate at a conference to discuss issues, relevant facts and any other matter that would make the proceedings more fair and efficient.

(2) Information or documents — The Division may require the parties to give any information or document at or before the conference.

(3) Decisions noted — The Division must make a written record of any decisions and agreements made at the conference or state them orally at the hearing.

Fixing a Date

21. Fixing a date — The Division must fix the date for a hearing and any other proceeding relating to the hearing. The Division may require the parties to participate in the preparation of a schedule of proceedings by appearing at a scheduling conference or otherwise providing information.

Notice to Appear

22. Notice to appear — The Division must notify the parties, orally or in writing, of the date, time and location of a hearing.

Permanent Resident or Foreign National in Custody

23. Order — The Division may order the person who holds a permanent resident or foreign national in custody to bring the permanent resident or foreign national to a hearing at a location specified by the Division.

Documents

Form and Language of Documents

24. (1) Documents prepared by party — A document prepared for use by a party in a proceeding must be typewritten on one side of 21.5 cm by 28 cm (8½" x 11") paper and the pages must be numbered.

(2) Photocopies — Any photocopy provided by a party must be a clear copy of the document photocopied and be on one side of 21.5 cm by 28 cm (8½" x 11") paper and the pages must be numbered.

(3) **Numbered documents** — A party must number consecutively each document provided by the party.

(4) **List of documents** — If more than one document is provided, the party must provide a list of the documents and their numbers.

25. (1) **Language of documents** — All documents used at a proceeding must be in English or French or, if in another language, be provided with an English or French translation and a translator's declaration.

(2) **Language of Minister's documents** — If the Minister provides a document that is not in the language of the proceedings, the Minister must provide a translation and a translator's declaration.

(3) **Translator's declaration** — A translator's declaration must include the translator's name, the language translated and a statement signed by the translator that the translation is accurate.

Disclosure of Documents

26. **Disclosure of documents by a party** — If a party wants to use a document at a hearing, the party must provide a copy to the other party and the Division. The copies must be received

(a) as soon as possible, in the case of a forty-eight hour or seven-day review or an admissibility hearing held at the same time; and

(b) in all other cases, at least five days before the hearing.

How to Provide A Document

27. **General provision** — Rules 28 to 31 apply to any document, including a notice or a written request or application.

28. (1) **Providing documents to the Division** — A document provided to the Division must be provided to a Division member at a proceeding or to the registry office specified by the Division.

(2) **Providing documents to the Minister** — A document provided to the Minister must be provided to the Minister's counsel.

(3) **Providing documents to a permanent resident or foreign national** — A document provided to a permanent resident or foreign national must be provided to them or, if they have counsel, to their counsel.

29. **How to provide a document** — A document can be provided in the following ways:

(a) by hand;

(b) by regular mail or registered mail;

(c) by courier or priority post;

(d) by fax if the recipient has a fax number and the document has no more than 20 pages, unless the recipient consents to receiving more than 20 pages; and

(e) by electronic mail if the Division allows.

30. If document cannot be provided under rule 29 — If a party after making reasonable efforts is unable to provide a document in a way required by rule 29, the party may make an application to the Division to be allowed to provide the document in another way or to be excused from providing the document.

31. (1) When a document is considered received by the Division — A document provided to the Division is considered received by the Division on the day the document is date stamped by the Division.

(2) When a document provided by regular mail is considered received by a party — A document provided by regular mail to a party is considered to be received seven days after the day it was mailed. If the seventh day is a Saturday, Sunday or other statutory holiday, the document is considered to be received on the next working day.

Witnesses

32. (1) Providing witness information — If a party wants to call a witness, the party must provide in writing to the other party and the Division the following witness information:

(a) the purpose and substance of the witness's testimony or, in the case of an expert witness, a summary of the testimony to be given signed by the expert witness;

(b) the time needed for the witness's testimony;

(c) the party's relationship to the witness;

(d) in the case of an expert witness, a description of their qualifications;

(e) whether the party wants the witness to testify by videoconference or telephone; and

(f) the number of witnesses that the party intends to call.

(2) Time limit — The witness information must be received by the Division and the other party

(a) as soon as possible in the case of a forty-eight hour or seven-day review or an admissibility hearing held at the same time; and

(b) in all other cases, at least five days before the hearing.

Case Law

R. v. Laboucan, [2010] 1 S.C.R. 397, 73 C.R. (6th) 235, [2010] S.C.J. No. 12, (sub nom. *R. v. Briscoe)* 400 N.R. 200, 22 Alta. L.R. (5th) 62, 253 C.C.C. (3d) 129, [2010] 6

W.W.R. 13, 316 D.L.R. (4th) 590, (sub nom *R. v. Briscoe*) 477 A.R. 70, 483 W.A.C. 70, 2010 SCC 13, 2010 CarswellAlta 591, 2010 CarswellAlta 590 — The fact that a witness has an interest in the outcome of the proceedings is common sense and a relevant factor, among others, to take into account when assessing the credibility of the witness's testimony. A trier of fact, however, should not place undue weight on the status of a person in the proceeding as a factor going to credibility. For example, it would be improper to base a finding of credibility regarding a parent's or a spouse's testimony solely on the basis of a witness's relationship to the complainant or to the accused. Regard should be given to all relevant factors in assessing credibility.

33. (1) Application for a summons — A party who wants the Division to order a person to testify at a hearing must make an application to the Division for a summons, either orally at a proceeding or in writing.

(2) Factors — In deciding whether to issue a summons, the Division must consider any relevant factors, including

   (a) the necessity of the testimony to a full and proper hearing; and

   (b) the ability of the person to give that testimony.

(3) Using the summons — If a party wants to use a summons, the party must

   (a) provide the summons to the summoned person by hand;

   (b) provide a copy of the summons to the Division with a written statement of how and when the summons was provided; and

   (c) pay or offer to pay the summoned person the applicable witness fees and travel expenses set out in Tariff A of the *Federal Courts Rules*.

34. Cancelling a summons — A person summoned to appear may make a written application to the Division to cancel the summons.

35. (1) Arrest warrant — If a person does not obey a summons to appear, the party who requested the summons may make a written application to the Division to issue a warrant for the arrest of the person.

(2) Supporting evidence — The party must provide supporting evidence for the written application by affidavit or statutory declaration.

(3) Requirements for issue of arrest warrant — The Division may issue a warrant if

   (a) the person was provided the summons by hand or the person is avoiding being provided the summons;

   (b) the person was paid or offered the applicable witness fees and travel expenses set out in Tariff A of the *Federal Courts Rules*;

   (c) the person did not appear at the hearing as required by the summons; and

   (d) the person's testimony is still needed for a full and proper hearing.

(4) Content of a warrant — A warrant issued by the Division for the arrest of a person must include directions concerning detention and release.

36. Excluded witness — Unless allowed by the Division, no person shall communicate to a witness excluded from a hearing room any testimony given while the witness was excluded until that witness has finished testifying.

Applications

37. General provision — Unless these Rules provide otherwise, a party

(a) who wants the Division to make a decision on any matter in a proceeding, including the procedure to be followed, must make an application to the Division under rule 38;

(b) who wants to respond to the application must respond under rule 39; and

(c) who wants to reply to a response must reply under rule 40.

How to Make an Application

38. (1) Application to the Division — Unless these Rules provide otherwise, an application must follow this rule.

(2) Time limit and form of application — The application must be made orally or in writing, and as soon as possible or within the time limit provided in the Act or these Rules.

(3) Procedure in oral application — For an application made orally, the Division determines the applicable procedure.

(4) Content of written application — A party who makes a written application must

(a) state the decision that the party wants the Division to make;

(b) give reasons why the Division should make that decision;

(c) include any evidence that the party wants the Division to consider in deciding the application; and

(d) in the case of an application that is not specified in these Rules, include supporting evidence in the form of a statutory declaration or affidavit.

(5) Providing the application — A party who makes a written application must provide

(a) to the other party, a copy of the application; and

(b) to the Division, the original application, together with a written statement of how and when the party provided the copy to the other party.

How to Respond to a Written Application

39. (1) Responding to a written application — A response to a written application must be in writing. In a response the party must

(a) state the decision the party wants the Division to make;

(b) give reasons why the Division should make that decision;

(c) include any evidence that the party wants the Division to consider when it decides the application; and

(d) include supporting evidence in the form of a statutory declaration or affidavit, if the response is to an application that is not provided for by these Rules.

(2) **Providing the response** — A party who responds to a written application must provide

(a) to the other party, a copy of the response; and

(b) to the Division, the original response, together with a written statement of how and when the party provided the copy to the other party.

(3) **Time limit** — Documents provided under this rule must be received by their recipients

(a) as soon as possible, in the case of a forty-eight hour or seven-day review or an admissibility hearing held at the same time; and

(b) in all other cases, no later than five days after the party received a copy of the application.

How to Reply to a Written Response

40. (1) **Replying to a written response** — A reply to a written response must be in writing.

(2) **Providing the reply** — A party who replies must provide

(a) to the other party, a copy of the reply; and

(b) to the Division, the original reply, together with a written statement of how and when the party provided the copy to the other party.

(3) **Time limit** — Documents provided under this rule must be received by their recipients

(a) as soon as possible, in the case of a forty-eight hour or seven-day review or an admissibility hearing held at the same time; and

(b) in all other cases, no later than three days after the party received a copy of the response.

Non-disclosure of Information

41. (1) **Application to prohibit disclosure** — An application made by the Minister for non-disclosure of information must be made in writing as soon as possible.

(2) **Exclusion from hearing room** — If an application is made during a hearing, the Division must exclude the permanent resident or foreign national, and their counsel, from the hearing room.

(3) **Providing summary to the Minister** — The summary that the Division proposes to provide to the permanent resident or foreign national under paragraph

78(h) of the Act may be provided to the Minister by any means that ensures its confidentiality.

Changing the Location of a Hearing

42. (1) Application to change the location of a hearing — A party may make an application to the Division to change the location of a hearing.

(2) Factors — In deciding the application, the Division must consider any relevant factors, including

(a) whether a change of location would allow the hearing to be full and proper;

(b) whether a change of location would likely delay or slow the hearing;

(c) how a change of location would affect the operation of the Division;

(d) how a change of location would affect the parties; and

(e) whether a change of location would endanger public safety.

(3) Duty to appear at the hearing — Unless a party receives a decision from the Division allowing the application, the party must appear for the hearing at the location fixed and be ready to start or continue the hearing.

Changing the Date or Time of a Hearing

43. (1) Application to change the date or time of a hearing — A party may make an application to the Division to change the date or time of a hearing.

(2) Factors — In deciding the application, the Division must consider any relevant factors, including

(a) in the case of a date and time that was fixed after the Division consulted or tried to consult the party, the existence of exceptional circumstances for allowing the application;

(b) when the party made the application;

(c) the time the party has had to prepare for the hearing;

(d) the efforts made by the party to be ready to start or continue the hearing;

(e) the nature and complexity of the matter to be heard;

(f) whether the party has counsel;

(g) any previous delays and the reasons for them;

(h) whether the time and date fixed for the hearing was peremptory; and

(i) whether allowing the application would unreasonably delay the proceedings or likely cause an injustice.

(3) Duty to appear at the hearing — Unless a party receives a decision from the Division allowing the application, the party must appear for the hearing at the date and time fixed and be ready to start or continue the hearing.

Case Law

For v. Canada (Minister of Citizenship & Immigration) (2009), 397 N.R. 222, 2009 FCA 346, 2009 CarswellNat 3936, 2009 CarswellNat 4896 — The appellant brought a motion for an order staying the resumption of his inadmissibility hearing before the Immigration Division. The appellant was a citizen of the United States and a permanent resident of Canada who had been convicted of importing cocaine into Canada and was sentenced to seven years and 10 months of imprisonment. A s. 44 report was prepared stating that the enforcement officer was of the opinion that the appellant was inadmissible pursuant to s. 36(a) [*sic*] of the Act on the ground of serious criminality for conviction and imprisonment in Canada. An admissibility hearing was commenced but subsequently adjourned to allow the appellant to seek legal representation. The appellant was then released from incarceration by reason of the National Parole Board's decision to grant him day parole. He was delivered to the custody of a CBSA officer by reason of a warrant issued by the CBSA for his arrest, in accordance with s. 55(1) and s. 59 of the Act. The admissibility hearing resumed and the appellant was represented by his wife who immediately sought an adjournment of the hearing to April 14, 2010, the date being the appellant's full parole eligibility date. The obvious purpose of his wife's request was to prevent her husband's re-incarceration should he be found inadmissible and thus subject to a removal order. Specifically, the appellant sought to avoid application of s. 128(5) of the *Corrections and Conditional Release Act* which provides that if a removal order is made against a person who has received day parole prior to that person's full parole eligibility, the day parole becomes inoperative on the day the removal order is made, and as a result the offender will be re-incarcerated until his full parole eligibility.

In the present matter, a determination of the stay application will likely determine the appeal in that the relief sought by the appellant in this motion is the relief which he is seeking to obtain in his appeal. The Court concluded that the appellant was unable to demonstrate a serious issue. It was not possible to argue that the Immigration Division can adjourn the appellant's admissibility hearing on the ground that a finding of inadmissibility on its part, which would lead to the issuance of a removal order, would cause injustice to the appellant. There is no statutory basis to support the Immigration Division's decision to adjourn the inadmissibility hearing. The motion for the stay was dismissed.

Joining or Separating Hearings

44. (1) Application to join hearings — A party may make an application to the Division to join hearings.

(2) Application to separate hearings — A party may make an application to the Division to separate hearings that are joined.

(3) Factors — Before deciding an application, the Division must consider any information provided by the applicant and any other relevant information, including

(a) whether the hearings involve similar questions of law or fact;

(b) whether allowing the application would promote the efficient administration of the work of the Division; and

(c) whether allowing the application would likely cause an injustice.

Proceedings Conducted in Private

45. (1) Application for proceeding conducted in private — A person who makes an application to the Division to have a proceeding conducted in private must apply in writing and follow this rule.

(2) Content of application — In the application, the person must state the decision that the person wants the Division to make, and may request that the hearing of the application be conducted in private.

(3) Providing the application — The person must provide a copy of the application to the parties and the original application to the Division.

(4) Time limit — A document provided under this rule must be received by its recipient

(a) as soon as possible, in the case of a forty-eight hour or seven-day review or an admissibility hearing held at the same time; and

(b) in all other cases, at least five days before the hearing.

(5) Hearing of the application — At the hearing, the person must give reasons why the Division should conduct the proceeding in private and present any evidence that the person wants the Division to consider in deciding the application.

Proceeding Conducted in Public

46. (1) Application for proceeding conducted in public — A person who makes an application to the Division to have a proceeding conducted in public must apply in writing and follow this rule.

(2) Content of application — In the application, the person must

(a) state the decision that the person wants the Division to make;

(b) give reasons why the Division should make that decision; and

(c) include any evidence that the person wants the Division to consider in deciding the application.

(3) Providing the application — The person must provide the original application and two copies to the Division. The Division must provide a copy of the application to the parties.

(4) Time limit — A document provided under this rule must be received by the Division

(a) as soon as possible, in the case of a forty-eight hour or seven-day review or an admissibility hearing held at the same time; and

(b) in all other cases, at least five days before the hearing.

Notice of Constitutional Question

47. (1) Notice of constitutional question — A party who wants to challenge the constitutional validity, applicability or operability of a legislative provision must complete a notice of constitutional question.

(2) Form and content of notice — The party must provide notice using either Form 69, "Notice of Constitutional Question", set out in the *Federal Courts Rules*, or any other form that includes

(a) the name of the party;

(b) the Division file number;

(c) the date, time and place of the hearing;

(d) the specific legislative provision that is being challenged;

(e) the relevant facts relied on to support the constitutional challenge; and

(f) a summary of the legal argument to be made in support of the constitutional challenge.

(3) Providing the notice — The party must provide

(a) a copy of the notice of constitutional question to the Attorney General of Canada and to the attorney general of every province and territory of Canada, in accordance with section 57 of the *Federal Courts Act*;

(b) a copy of the notice to the other party; and

(c) the original notice to the Division, together with a written statement of how and when a copy of the notice was provided under paragraphs (a) and (b).

(4) Time limit — Documents provided under this rule must be received by their recipients no later than 10 days before the day the constitutional argument will be made.

2002, c. 8, s. 182(3)(a)

Oral Representations

48. Oral representations — Representations made by a party must be made orally at the end of a hearing unless the Division orders otherwise.

General Provisions

49. No applicable rule — In the absence of a provision in these Rules dealing with a matter raised during the proceedings, the Division may do whatever is necessary to deal with the matter.

50. Powers of the Division — The Division may

(a) act on its own, without a party having to make an application or request to the Division;

(b) change a requirement of a rule;

(c) excuse a person from a requirement of a rule; and

(d) extend or shorten a time limit, before or after the time limit has passed.

51. Failing to follow a rule — Unless proceedings are declared invalid by the Division, a failure to follow any requirement of these Rules does not make the proceedings invalid.

Coming Into Force

52. Coming into force — These Rules come into force on the day on which section 161 of the Act comes into force.

CAN. REG. 2002-230 — IMMIGRATION APPEAL DIVISION RULES

made under the *Immigration and Refugee Protection Act*

SOR/2002-230, as am. S.C. 2002, c. 8, s. 182(3)(a).

[Editor's Note: S.C. 2001, c. 27, s. 192 provides that if a notice of appeal has been filed with the Immigration Appeal Division immediately before June 28, 2002, the appeal shall be continued under the Immigration Act, R.S.C. 1985, c. I-2 (the "former Act") by the Immigration Appeal Division of the Immigration and Refugee Board.

However, S.C. 2001, c. 27, s. 193 provides that every application, proceeding or matter before the Adjudication Division under the former Act that is pending or in progress immediately before June 28, 2002, in respect of which substantive evidence has been adduced but no decision has been made, shall be continued under the Immigration and Refugee Protection Act, S.C. 2001, c. 27 (the "new Act"), by the Immigration Division of the Immigration and Refugee Board.

S.C. 2001, c. 27, s. 196 further provides that despite S.C. 2001, c. 27, s. 192, an appeal made to the Immigration Appeal Division before June 28, 2002 shall be discontinued if the appellant has not been granted a stay under the former Act and the appeal could not have been made because of s. 64 of the new Act.

S.C. 2001, c. 27, s. 197 still further provides that despite S.C. 2001, c. 27, s. 192, if an appellant who has been granted a stay under the former Act breaches a condition of the stay, the appellant shall be subject to the provisions of s. 64 and s. 68(4) of the new Act.]

DEFINITIONS

1. Definitions — The following definitions apply in these Rules.

"Act" means the *Immigration and Refugee Protection Act*. *("Loi")*

"appellant" means the person who makes an appeal to the Division. *("appelant")*

"contact information" means a person's name, postal address and telephone number, and the person's fax number and electronic mail address, if any. *("coordonnées")*

"Division" means the Immigration Appeal Division. *("Section")*

"officer" means a person designated as an officer by the Minister under subsection 6(1) of the Act. *("agent")*

"party" means the appellant or the respondent. *("partie")*

"proceeding" includes a hearing, a conference, an application or an alternative dispute resolution process. *("procédure")*

"registry office" means a business office of the Division. *("greffe")*

"respondent" means the Minister or, if the Minister is appealing a decision of the Immigration Division, the person who was the subject of the Immigration Division proceeding. *("intimé")*

COMMUNICATING WITH THE DIVISION

2. Communicating with the Division — All communication with the Division must be directed to the registry office specified by the Division.

APPEAL BY A SPONSOR

3. (1) Notice of appeal — A person who has filed an application to sponsor a foreign national as a member of the family class and who wants to appeal a decision not to issue a permanent resident visa to the foreign national must provide to the Division a notice of appeal and the officer's written reasons for the refusal.

(2) Time limit — The notice of appeal and the written reasons for refusal must be received by the Division no later than 30 days after the appellant received the written reasons for the refusal.

(3) Documents provided to the Minister — The Division must provide the notice of appeal and the written reasons for the refusal to the Minister without delay.

4. (1) Appeal record — The Minister must prepare an appeal record that contains

    (a) a table of contents;

    (b) the application for a permanent resident visa that was refused;

    (c) the application for sponsorship and the sponsor's undertaking;

    (d) any document that the Minister has that is relevant to the applications, to the reasons for the refusal or to any issue in the appeal; and

    (e) the written reasons for the refusal.

(2) Providing the appeal record — The Minister must provide the appeal record to the appellant and the Division.

(3) Proof that record was provided — The Minister must provide to the Division, together with the appeal record, a written statement of how and when the appeal record was provided to the appellant.

(4) Time limit — Documents provided under this rule must be received by their recipients no later than 120 days after the Minister received the notice of appeal.

(5) Late appeal record — If the Division does not receive the appeal record within the time limit set out in subrule (4), the Division may

(a) ask the Minister to explain, orally or in writing, why the appeal record was not provided on time and to give reasons why the appeal record should be accepted late; or

(b) schedule and start the hearing without the appeal record or with only part of the appeal record.

APPEAL FROM A REMOVAL ORDER MADE AT AN ADMISSIBILITY HEARING

5. (1) Notice of appeal — If a foreign national who holds a permanent resident visa, a permanent resident, or a protected person wants to appeal a removal order made at an admissibility hearing, they must provide a notice of appeal

(a) by hand to the Immigration Division member who made the removal order; or

(b) to the Immigration Appeal Division, together with the removal order.

(2) Time limit — Immigration Division member — An appellant who provides a notice of appeal to an Immigration Division member must provide the notice at the end of the admissibility hearing. The Immigration Division must provide the notice to the Immigration Appeal Division without delay.

(3) Time limit — Immigration Appeal Division — If an appellant provides a notice of appeal to the Immigration Appeal Division, the notice of appeal and the removal order must be received by the Division no later than 30 days after the appellant received the removal order. The Immigration Appeal Division must provide the notice to the Immigration Division without delay.

(4) Documents provided to the Minister — The Immigration Appeal Division must provide the notice of appeal and the removal order to the Minister without delay.

[Editor's Note: S.C. 2001, c. 27, s. 190 provides that every application, proceeding or matter under the Immigration Act, R.S.C. 1985, c. I-2 (the "former Act") that is pending or in progress immediately before June 28, 2002 shall be governed by the Immigration and Refugee Protection Act, S.C. 2001, c. 27 (the "new Act"), effective June 28, 2002.

S.C. 2001, c. 27, s. 192 provides that if a notice of appeal has been filed with the Immigration Appeal Division immediately before June 28, 2002, the appeal shall be continued under the former Act by the Immigration Appeal Division of the Immigration and Refugee Board.

S.C. 2001, c. 27, s. 196 further provides that despite S.C. 2001, c. 27, s. 192, an appeal made to the Immigration Appeal Division before June 28, 2002 shall be discontinued if the appellant has not been granted a stay under the former Act and the appeal could not have been made because of s. 64 of the new Act.

S.C. 2001, c. 27, s. 197 still further provides that despite S.C. 2001, c. 27, s. 192, if an appellant who has been granted a stay under the former Act breaches a condition of the stay, the appellant shall be subject to the provisions of s. 64 and s. 68(4) of the new Act.]

6. (1) Appeal record — The Immigration Division must prepare an appeal record that contains

    (a) a table of contents;

    (b) the removal order;

    (c) a transcript of the admissibility hearing;

    (d) any document accepted as evidence at the admissibility hearing; and

    (e) any written reasons for the Immigration Division's decision to make the removal order.

(2) Providing the appeal record — The Immigration Division must provide the appeal record to the appellant, the Minister and the Immigration Appeal Division.

(3) Time limit — The appeal record must be received by its recipients no later than 45 days after the Immigration Division received the notice of appeal.

APPEAL FROM A REMOVAL ORDER MADE AT AN EXAMINATION

7. (1) Notice of appeal — If a foreign national who holds a permanent resident visa, a permanent resident, or a protected person wants to appeal a removal order made at an examination, they must provide a notice of appeal to the Division together with the removal order.

(2) Time limit — The notice of appeal and the removal order must be received by the Division no later than 30 days after the appellant received the removal order.

(3) Documents provided to the Minister — The Division must provide the notice of appeal and the removal order to the Minister without delay.

[Editor's Note: S.C. 2001, c. 27, s. 190 provides that every application, proceeding or matter under the Immigration Act, R.S.C. 1985, c. I-2 (the "former Act") that is pending or in progress immediately before June 28, 2002 shall be governed by the Immigration and Refugee Protection Act, S.C. 2001, c. 27 (the "new Act"), effective June 28, 2002.

S.C. 2001, c. 27, s. 192 provides that if a notice of appeal has been filed with the Immigration Appeal Division immediately before June 28, 2002, the appeal shall be continued under the former Act by the Immigration Appeal Division of the Immigration and Refugee Board.

S.C. 2001, c. 27, s. 196 further provides that despite S.C. 2001, c. 27, s. 192, an appeal made to the Immigration Appeal Division before June 28, 2002 shall be discontinued if the appellant has not been granted a stay under the former Act and the appeal could not have been made because of s. 64 of the new Act.

S.C. 2001, c. 27, s. 197 still further provides that despite S.C. 2001, c. 27, s. 192, if an appellant who has been granted a stay under the former Act breaches a condition of the stay, the appellant shall be subject to the provisions of s. 64 and s. 68(4) of the new Act.]

Case Law

Canada (Minister of Citizenship & Immigration) v. Rumpler (2008), 76 Imm. L.R. (3d) 237, 336 F.T.R. 285 (Eng.), 2008 CarswellNat 4258, 2008 CarswellNat 5085, 2008 FC 1264, 2008 CarswellNat 4258 — This was an application for judicial review of the decision of the IAD wherein the IAD concluded it had jurisdiction to hear an appeal of the respondent's removal order. Returning to Canada from Israel, an immigration officer determined that the respondent did not satisfy the residency requirements of s. 28 of the Act and undertook measures to have him removed. The period to appeal the removal order expired and the respondent voluntarily left Canada for the United States. The respondent then requested of the IAD an extension of the period, to allow him to lodge an appeal of the removal order. The IAD decided that, according to subs. 63(3) of the Act, it did not have the competence to extend the period of appeal after its expiration, because the respondent had lost his status as permanent resident by failing to appeal. Justice Blanchard of the Federal Court granted the respondent's application for judicial review, and held that the IAD did have competence under the said provision to grant the extension. Accordingly, an extension was granted by a different member of the IAD and at a new hearing before the IAD, the Minister asked the tribunal to reject the appeal of the removal order on the ground of mootness, because the respondent had voluntarily left the country and thus executed the order. The Minister's motion was rejected and the Minister brought an application for judicial review of the IAD's decision.

The IAD erred in law in finding that it had continuing jurisdiction in spite of the fact that the respondent had left Canada and had executed the removal order before he filed a notice of appeal. It is trite law that the IAD does not have jurisdiction to reopen an appeal where the motion to reopen has been filed after an appellant is removed from Canada. Since the IAD did not have the jurisdiction to cancel the removal order once it had already been executed, it necessarily had no jurisdiction to grant a request (filed after such an execution) for an extension of time to lodge an appeal of the removal order. Consequently, the application for judicial review was allowed.

8. (1) Appeal record — The Minister must prepare an appeal record that contains

    (a) a table of contents;

    (b) the removal order;

    (c) any document that the Minister has that is relevant to the removal order or to any issue in the appeal; and

    (d) any written reasons for the Minister's decision to make the removal order.

(2) Providing the appeal record — The Minister must provide the appeal record to the appellant and the Division.

(3) Proof that record was provided — The Minister must provide to the Division, together with the appeal record, a written statement of how and when the appeal record was provided to the appellant.

(4) Time limit — Documents provided under this rule must be received by their recipients no later than 45 days after the Minister received the notice of appeal.

(5) Late appeal record — If the Division does not receive the appeal record within the time limit set out in subrule (4), the Division may

(a) ask the Minister to explain, orally or in writing, why the appeal record was not provided on time and to give reasons why the appeal record should be accepted late; or

(b) schedule and start the hearing without the appeal record or with only part of the appeal record.

APPEAL FROM A DECISION MADE OUTSIDE CANADA ON THE RESIDENCY OBLIGATION

9. (1) Notice of appeal — If a permanent resident wants to appeal a decision made outside Canada on the residency obligation, the permanent resident must provide to the Division a notice of appeal and the officer's written decision. The documents must be provided to the Division registry office for the region in Canada where the appellant last resided.

(2) Return to Canada — If the appellant wants to return to Canada for the hearing of the appeal, the appellant must state this in the notice of appeal.

(3) Time limit — The notice of appeal and the written decision must be received by the Division no later than 60 days after the appellant received the written decision.

(4) Documents provided to the Minister — The Division must provide the notice of appeal and the written decision to the Minister without delay.

[Editor's Note: S.C. 2001, c. 27, s. 190 provides that every application, proceeding or matter under the Immigration Act, *R.S.C. 1985, c. I-2 (the "former Act") that is pending or in progress immediately before June 28, 2002 shall be governed by the* Immigration and Refugee Protection Act, *S.C. 2001, c. 27 (the "new Act"), effective June 28, 2002.*

S.C. 2001, c. 27, s. 192 provides that if a notice of appeal has been filed with the Immigration Appeal Division immediately before June 28, 2002, the appeal shall be continued under the former Act by the Immigration Appeal Division of the Immigration and Refugee Board.

S.C. 2001, c. 27, s. 196 further provides that despite S.C. 2001, c. 27, s. 192, an appeal made to the Immigration Appeal Division before June 28, 2002 shall be discontinued if the appellant has not been granted a stay under the former Act and the appeal could not have been made because of s. 64 of the new Act.

S.C. 2001, c. 27, s. 197 still further provides that despite S.C. 2001, c. 27, s. 192, if an appellant who has been granted a stay under the former Act breaches a condition of the stay, the appellant shall be subject to the provisions of s. 64 and s. 68(4) of the new Act.]

10. (1) Appeal record — The Minister must prepare an appeal record that contains

(a) a table of contents;

(b) any document that the Minister has that is relevant to the decision on the residency obligation or any issue in the appeal; and

(o) the officer's written decision and written reasons.

(2) **Providing the appeal record** — The Minister must provide the appeal record to the appellant and the Division.

(3) **Proof that record was provided** — The Minister must provide to the Division, together with the appeal record, a written statement of how and when the appeal record was provided to the appellant.

(4) **Time limit** — Documents provided under this rule must be received by their recipients no later than 120 days after the Minister received the notice of appeal.

(5) **Late appeal record** — If the Division does not receive the appeal record within the time limit set out in subrule (4), the Division may

(a) ask the Minister to explain, orally or in writing, why the appeal record was not provided on time and to give reasons why the appeal record should be accepted late; or

(b) schedule and start the hearing without the appeal record or with only part of the appeal record.

APPEAL BY THE MINISTER FROM A DECISION OF THE IMMIGRATION DIVISION IN AN ADMISSIBILITY HEARING

11. (1) **Notice of Appeal** — If the Minister wants to appeal a decision of the Immigration Division in an admissibility hearing, the Minister must provide a notice of appeal to the respondent, the Immigration Division and the Immigration Appeal Division.

(2) **Proof that document was provided** — The Minister must provide to the Immigration Appeal Division, together with the notice of appeal, a written statement of how and when the notice of appeal was provided to the respondent and the Immigration Division.

(3) **Time limit** — Documents provided under this rule must be received by their recipients no later than 30 days after the Immigration Division decision was made.

[Editor's Note: S.C. 2001, c. 27, s. 190 provides that every application, proceeding or matter under the Immigration Act, *R.S.C. 1985, c. I-2 (the "former Act") that is pending or in progress immediately before June 28, 2002 shall be governed by the* Immigration and Refugee Protection Act, *S.C. 2001, c. 27 (the "new Act"), effective June 28, 2002.*

S.C. 2001, c. 27, s. 192 provides that if a notice of appeal has been filed with the Immigration Appeal Division immediately before June 28, 2002, the appeal shall be continued under the former Act by the Immigration Appeal Division of the Immigration and Refugee Board.

S.C. 2001, c. 27, s. 196 further provides that despite S.C. 2001, c. 27, s. 192, an appeal made to the Immigration Appeal Division before June 28, 2002 shall be discontinued if the appellant has not been granted a stay under the former Act and the appeal could not have been made because of s. 64 of the new Act.

Rules

S.C. 2001, c. 27, s. 197 still further provides that despite S.C. 2001, c. 27, s. 192, if an appellant who has been granted a stay under the former Act breaches a condition of the stay, the appellant shall be subject to the provisions of s. 64 and s. 68(4) of the new Act.]

12. (1) Appeal record — The Immigration Division must prepare an appeal record that contains

(a) a table of contents;

(b) the Immigration Division decision;

(c) a transcript of the admissibility hearing;

(d) any document accepted as evidence at the admissibility hearing; and

(e) any written reasons for the Immigration Division decision.

(2) Providing the appeal record — The Immigration Division must provide the appeal record to the respondent, the Minister and the Immigration Appeal Division.

(3) Time limit — The appeal record must be received by its recipients no later than 45 days after the Immigration Division received the notice of appeal.

CONTACT INFORMATION

13. (1) Contact information for the subject of the appeal — A person who is the subject of an appeal must provide their contact information in writing to the Division and the Minister.

(2) Time limit — The contact information must be received by the Division and the Minister

(a) with the notice of appeal, if the person is the appellant; and

(b) no later than 20 days after the person received a notice of appeal, if the Minister is the appellant.

(3) Counsel's contact information — A person who is represented by counsel must, on obtaining counsel, provide without delay the counsel's contact information in writing to the Division and the Minister.

(4) Change to contact information — If the contact information of the person or their counsel changes, the person must without delay provide the changes in writing to the Division and the Minister.

Case Law

Dubrezil c. Canada (Ministre de la Sécurité publique & de la Protection civile), 2006 CarswellNat 918, 2006 FC 441 — The applicant applied for judicial review of the Immigration and Appeal Division's decision to refuse to reopen an appeal on the ground that the applicant had not established he was a victim of a breach of a principle of natural justice. The applicant never sent his change in contact information to the IAD. It was his obligation to do so and he could not attempt to impose that obligation on the IAD. To impose such an obligation would imply that each time a person is absent, lacks diligence or acts in such a way that clearly suggests the appeal has been abandoned, the IAD would be bound to investigate to find those persons, remind them of their obligations and summon them to a new hearing before deciding that the proceedings are abandoned. The IAD is not bound to act as the applicant's legal counsel or to remind the applicant of the seriousness of the proceedings in which he is involved, or to ensure that he properly understands that he has to show up at his scheduling conference or that he is bound to advise the IAD of his change of address.

COUNSEL OF RECORD

14. Becoming counsel of record — As soon as counsel for a person who is the subject of an appeal agrees to a date for a proceeding, or becomes counsel after a date for a proceeding has been fixed, the counsel becomes counsel of record for the person.

15. (1) Request to be removed as counsel of record — To be removed as counsel of record, counsel must make a request in writing to the Division and provide a copy of the request to the person represented and the Minister.

(2) Request received two days or less before proceeding — If counsel's request is received by the recipients two working days or less before the date of a proceeding, counsel must appear at the proceeding and make the request orally.

16. (1) Removing counsel of record — To remove counsel as counsel of record, the person who is the subject of the appeal must provide written notice to the Division, to counsel and to the Minister that counsel is no longer the person's counsel.

(2) Ceasing to be counsel of record — Counsel is no longer counsel of record when the Division receives the notice.

LANGUAGE OF THE APPEAL

17. (1) Choice of language — A person who is the subject of an appeal must choose English or French as the language of the appeal. If the person is appealing, the person must indicate their choice in the notice of appeal. If the Minister is appealing, the person must notify the Division and the Minister of their choice in writing. The notice must be received by the Division and by the Minister no later than 20 days after the person received the notice of appeal.

(2) Changing the choice of language — A person who is the subject of an appeal may change the choice of language by notifying the Division and the Minister in writing. The notice must be received by the Division and the Minister no later than 20 days before the next proceeding.

18. (1) Need for an interpreter — If a party or a party's witness needs an interpreter for a proceeding, the party must notify the Division in writing and specify the language or dialect of the interpreter. The notice must be received by the Division no later than 20 days before the proceeding.

(2) Interpreter's oath — The interpreter must take an oath or make a solemn affirmation to interpret accurately.

Case Law

Lamme v. Canada (Minister of Citizenship & Immigration), 2005 CarswellNat 3063, 2005 CarswellNat 4881, 2005 FC 1336 — The general standard to be met with respect to the quality of interpretation is that it must be continuous, precise, impartial and contemporaneous. In addition, for the interpretation to be considered as meeting the standard, it must be established that the applicant understood the interpretation and adequately expressed himself or herself through the interpreter.

DESIGNATED REPRESENTATIVE

19. (1) Duty of counsel to notify — If counsel for either party believes that the Division should designate a representative for the person who is the subject of the appeal because they are under 18 years of age or unable to appreciate the nature of the proceedings, counsel must without delay notify the Division in writing. If counsel is aware of a person in Canada who meets the requirements to be designated as a representative, counsel must provide the person's contact information in the notice.

(2) Requirements for being designated — To be designated as a representative, a person must

(a) be 18 years of age or older;

(b) understand the nature of the proceedings;

(c) be willing and able to act in the best interests of the person to be represented; and

(d) not have interests that conflict with those of the person to be represented.

Case Law

Hillary v. Canada (Minister of Citizenship & Immigration) (2011), 96 Imm. L.R. (3d) 197, 331 D.L.R. (4th) 338, 414 N.R. 292, 2011 FCA 51, 2011 CarswellNat 285; affirming (2010), 370 F.T.R. 199 (Eng.), 320 D.L.R. (4th) 118, 2010 FC 638, 2010 CarswellNat 3091, 2010 CarswellNat 1740; leave to appeal to S.C.C. refused 2011 CarswellNat 1898, 2011 CarswellNat 1899 (S.C.C.) — The appellant, a citizen of Jamaica in his early 40s, came to Canada as a permanent resident in 1982 when he was only 13 years old. He was deported on the basis of a string of criminal convictions starting in 1987. He was diagnosed as suffering from schizophrenia, is HIV positive and had been addicted to crack cocaine. The appellant claimed that the IAD's dismissal of his appeal against deportation should be reopened because the IAD denied him a fair hearing when it failed to inquire whether he appreciated the nature of the proceeding, in order to determine whether he required the assistance of the designated representative.

The right to representation in an administrative proceeding normally means the right of a party to appoint someone, often legal counsel, to conduct the case before the tribunal on their behalf. However, subs. 167(2) of IRPA recognizes that, if their interests are to be adequately protected in a proceeding before the Board, minors, and those unable to appreciate the nature of the proceedings, also require the assistance of a designated representative who is sensitive to the particular needs of the individual concerned and alert to their best interests. It is always within the discretion of the IAD to raise the issue itself and inquire into the appellant's capacity. However, if the IAD makes no so such inquiry, the Court should intervene only if satisfied on the basis of an examination of the entire context that the Board's inaction was unreasonable and fairness required the IAD to be proactive. Given the adversarial nature of the IAD's procedure, it will only be in the most unusual circumstances that a panel is obligated to make inquiries in a case where the appellant is represented by counsel who has not raised the issue of the client's ability to understand the nature of the proceedings. Such is not the case here. The appeal was dismissed.

PROCEEDINGS IN AN APPEAL

Alternative Dispute Resolution Process

20. (1) Participation in the alternative dispute resolution process — The Division may require the parties to participate in an alternative dispute resolution process in order to encourage the parties to resolve an appeal without a hearing.

(2) Dispute resolution officer — The Division must assign a member of the Division or any other person to act as a dispute resolution officer for an appeal that uses the alternative dispute resolution process. A member who acts as a dispute resolution officer for an appeal must not hear that appeal.

(3) Obligations of parties and counsel — The parties and their counsel must

(a) participate in the alternative dispute resolution process in good faith;

(b) follow the directions given by the Division with respect to the process, including the manner of participation;

(c) disclose to each other and the Division any document to be relied on in the process, and any document that the Division requires to be prepared or disclosed; and

(d) be prepared as a party, or have authority as counsel, to resolve the appeal.

(4) Confidentiality — Any information, statement or document that any person gives in an alternative dispute resolution process is confidential. It must not be disclosed later in the appeal or made public unless

(a) it was obtained in a way that was not part of the alternative dispute resolution process;

(b) it relates to an offence under the Act, or a breach of these Rules; or

(c) the person who gave the information, statement or document agrees to its disclosure.

(5) Agreement — An agreement to resolve an appeal that is reached through the alternative dispute resolution process must be in writing, signed by the parties or their counsel and approved by the Division. An agreement to resolve an appeal is not confidential under subrule (4).

CONFERENCE

21. (1) Requirement to participate at a conference — The Division may require the parties to participate at a conference to discuss issues, relevant facts and any other matter that would make the appeal more fair and efficient.

(2) Information or documents — The Division may require the parties to give any information, or provide any document, at or before the conference.

(3) Written record — The Division must make a written record of any decision or agreement made at the conference.

FIXING A DATE FOR A PROCEEDING

22. Fixing a date — The Division may require the parties to participate in a scheduling conference or otherwise give information to help the Division fix a date for a proceeding.

NOTICE TO APPEAR

23. Notice to appear — The Division must notify the parties of the date, time and location of a proceeding.

SUBJECT OF AN APPEAL IN CUSTODY

24. Custody — The Division may order a person who holds a person who is the subject of an appeal in custody to bring the person in custody to a proceeding at the location specified by the Division.

PROCEEDING IN WRITING

25. (1) Proceeding in writing — Instead of holding a hearing, the Division may require the parties to proceed in writing if this would not be unfair to any party and there is no need for the oral testimony of a witness.

(2) Exception — Subsection (1) does not apply to an appeal against a decision made outside Canada on the residency obligation.

STAY OF REMOVAL ORDER

26. (1) Application to reconsider an appeal — If the Division has stayed a removal order, a party who makes an application to the Division to reconsider the appeal must

(a) follow rule 43, but the party is not required to give evidence in an affidavit or statutory declaration; and

(b) provide with their application a written statement of whether the subject of the appeal has complied with the conditions of the stay.

(2) Response — The other party must respond to the application and provide with their response a written statement of whether the subject of the appeal has complied with the conditions of the stay.

(3) Reconsideration on Division's own initiative — If the Division reconsiders an appeal on its own initiative, the Division must notify the parties. The parties must provide to the Division and each other, within the time period specified by the Division, a written statement of whether the subject of the appeal has complied with the conditions of the stay.

27. (1) Notice requirement — cancellation of stay — If a stay of removal is cancelled under subsection 68(4) of the Act, the Minister must provide the Division and the subject of the appeal with written notice of the cancellation.

(2) Content of notice — In the notice, the Minister must state

(a) the name of the person convicted;

(b) the date and place of conviction;

(c) the offence and relevant provision of an Act of Parliament; and

(d) if the offence is not punishable by a maximum term of imprisonment of at least 10 years, the term of imprisonment that was imposed.

(3) Proof that document was provided — The Minister must provide to the Division, together with the written notice, a written statement of how and when the notice was provided to the subject of the appeal.

DOCUMENTS

Form and Language of Documents

28. (1) Documents prepared by party — A document prepared for use by a party in a proceeding must be typewritten on one side of 21.5 cm by 28 cm (8½" × 11") paper and the pages must be numbered.

(2) Photocopies — Any photocopy provided by a party must be a clear copy of the document photocopied and be on one side of 21.5 cm by 28 cm (8½" × 11") paper and the pages must be numbered.

(3) Numbered documents — A party must number consecutively each document provided by the party.

(4) List of documents — If more than one document is provided, the party must provide a list of the documents and their numbers.

29. (1) Language of documents — subject of the appeal — All documents used at a proceeding by a person who is the subject of an appeal must be in English or French or, if in another language, be provided with an English or French translation and a translator's declaration.

(2) Language of documents — Minister — All documents used by the Minister at a proceeding must be in the language of the appeal, or be provided with a translation and the translator's declaration.

(3) Translator's declaration — A translator's declaration must include the translator's name, the language translated and a statement signed by the translator that the translation is accurate.

Disclosure of Documents

30. (1) Disclosure of documents by a party — If a party wants to use a document at a hearing, the party must provide a copy to the other party and the Division.

(2) Proof that document was provided — Together with the copy provided to the Division, the party must provide a written statement of how and when a copy was provided to the other party.

(3) Time limit — general — Subject to subrule (4), documents provided under this rule must be received by the Division and the other party

   (a) no later than 20 days before the hearing; or

   (b) if the document is provided to respond to another document provided by the other party, no later than 10 days before the hearing.

(4) Time limit — medical documents — A medical document provided in an appeal based on inadmissibility on health grounds must be received by the Division and the other party no later than 60 days before the hearing or, if the document is provided to respond to another medical document, no later than 30 days before the hearing.

31. Use of undisclosed documents — A party who does not provide a document as required by rule 30 may not use the document at the hearing unless allowed by the Division.

Providing a Document

32. General provision — Rules 33 to 36 apply to any document, including a notice or request in writing.

33. (1) Providing documents to the Division — A document provided to the Division must be provided to the registry office specified by the Division.

(2) Providing documents to the Minister — A document provided to the Minister must be provided to the Minister's counsel.

(3) Providing documents to the subject of an appeal — A document provided to a person who is the subject of an appeal must be provided to the person or, if the person has counsel, to their counsel.

34. How to provide a document — A document can be provided in any of the following ways:

    (a) by hand;

    (b) by regular mail or registered mail;

    (c) by courier or priority post;

    (d) by fax if the recipient has a fax number and the document has no more than 20 pages, unless the recipient consents to receiving more than 20 pages; and

    (e) by electronic mail if the Division allows.

35. (1) If document cannot be provided under rule 34 — If a party is unable to provide a document in a way required by rule 34, the party may make an application to the Division to be allowed to provide the document in another way or to be excused from providing the document.

(2) Form of application — The application must be made under rule 43.

(3) Factor — The Division may allow the application if the party has made reasonable efforts to provide the document to the other party.

36. (1) When a document is considered received by the Division — A document provided to the Division is considered to be received by the Division on the day the document is date stamped by the Division.

(2) When a document sent by regular mail is considered received by a party — A document sent to a party by regular mail is considered to be received seven days after the day it was mailed. A document sent to a party by regular mail to or from a place outside Canada is considered to be received 20 days after the day it was mailed. If the seventh day or the twentieth day, as the case may be, is a Saturday, Sunday or statutory holiday, the document is considered to be received on the next working day.

Rules

WITNESSES

37. (1) Providing witness information — If a party wants to call a witness, the party must provide in writing to the other party and the Division the following witness information:

(a) the witness's contact information;

(b) the time needed for the witness's testimony;

(c) the party's relationship to the witness;

(d) whether the party wants the witness to testify by videoconference or telephone; and

(e) in the case of an expert witness, a report signed by the expert witness giving their qualifications and summarizing their evidence.

(2) Proof that document was provided — The witness information must be provided to the Division together with a written statement of how and when it was provided to the other party.

(3) Time limit — Documents provided under this rule must be received by their recipients no later than 20 days before the hearing.

(4) Failure to provide witness information — If a party does not provide the witness information as required under this rule, the witness may not testify at the hearing unless the Division allows the witness to testify.

Case Law

R. v. Laboucan, [2010] 1 S.C.R. 397, 73 C.R. (6th) 235, (sub nom. *R. v. Briscoe*) 400 N.R. 200, 22 Alta. L.R. (5th) 62, 253 C.C.C. (3d) 129, [2010] 6 W.W.R. 13, 316 D.L.R. (4th) 590, (sub nom. *R. v. Briscoe*) 477 A.R. 70, 483 W.A.C. 70, 2010 SCC 12, 2010 CarswellAlta 591, 2010 CarswellAlta 590, [2010] S.C.J. No. 12 — The fact that a witness has an interest in the outcome of the proceedings is common sense and a relevant factor, among others, to take into account when assessing the credibility of the witness's testimony. A trier of fact, however, should not place undue weight on the status of a person in the proceeding as a factor going to credibility. For example, it would be improper to base a finding of credibility regarding a parent's or a spouse's testimony solely on the basis of a witness's relationship to the complainant or to the accused. Regard should be given to all relevant factors in assessing credibility.

Kamtasingh v. Canada (Minister of Citizenship & Immigration) (2010), 87 Imm. L.R. (3d) 118, 2010 FC 45, 2010 CarswellNat 801, 2010 CarswellNat 101 — This was an application for judicial review challenging a decision of the Immigration Appeal Division which determined the applicant's marriage was not genuine. The applicant states that the IAD member denied him procedural fairness by preventing him from calling all of his proposed witnesses.

The IAD has the right to limit repetitive testimony, but not by effectively excluding witnesses who could offer evidence going to the central issues of the case. The place to control excessive or repetitive evidence on issues of controversy which are central or determinative is generally not at the entrance to the witness box, but once the witness is testifying — and even then the member must grant some latitude to ensure that all important matters are covered. The IAD can, of course, limit the scope of evidence by stipulating certain points that are not in dispute. In a case like this one where the credibility of the applicant is clearly an issue and where the genuineness of a marriage is in doubt, the evidence of immediate family and close acquaintances is highly relevant and should be heard without reservation. Indeed, it was difficult to see how this matter could be fairly determined after only two hours of evidence, particularly when the applicant was self-represented and was initially intending to lead evidence from several witnesses. This was a situation where the duty to allow the applicant to fully present his case was sacrificed for the desire for administrative efficiency. That is not a permissible trade-off. The application for judicial review was allowed.

Ayele v. Canada (Minister of Citizenship & Immigration) (2007), 60 Imm. L.R. (3d) 197, 2007 CarswellNat 253, 2007 FC 126 — The duty of fairness requires that a party to a proceeding should have the opportunity to present his or her case fully and fairly. This generally includes the right to call witnesses in order to establish the evidentiary basis of a claim or defense. The applicant applied to sponsor his wife. A visa officer rejected the wife's application for permanent residence on the ground that the marriage was not genuine and was entered into for immigration purposes. The applicant appealed to the Immigration Appeal Division (IAD). After hearing the applicant's testimony, the IAD was anxious to conclude the hearing and to dismiss the appeal. In the words of the presiding member, "[i]t will be a waste of the tribunal's time to continue to indulge the appellant in this waste of taxpayer's money." The IAD refused to hear a witness that the applicant wished to call. The Minister claimed that the IAD refused to allow the witness to testify because the applicant was in breach of Rule 37 of the *Immigration Appeal Division Rules* which required the applicant to have provided, in writing, witness information.

The Minister's reliance upon Rule 37 in order to justify the refusal of the IAD to hear the witness was misplaced. At the outset of the hearing, after hearing submissions with respect to the applicant's late disclosure of information, including late disclosure of witness information, the presiding member ruled "I will allow you to deal with the witness, but obviously the identity and credibility of the witness will be an issue." Any hurdle posed by Rule 37 was overcome when the IAD ruled it would exercise its discretion to allow the witness to testify. When the IAD later ruled it would not allow the witness to testify, it did not refer to Rule 37. Instead, the presiding member stated, "Even if the witness corroborates the testimony, in assessing the testimony it's not credible. So, there's no point in calling the witness and even if it is characterized as a breach of natural justice, there is no prejudice suffered when the evidence is of no use and calling the witness is futile."

It is not within the purview of a tribunal bound by the requirement of procedural fairness to dispense with those requirements because, in its view, the result of the hearing will be the same. Rather, it is for a court reviewing a decision of the tribunal that has erred to determine whether, as a matter of administrative law, the consequences of a failure to comply with the requirements of procedural fairness are such that the discretionary remedy available to the reviewing court should be withheld.

The withholding of relief in the face of a breach of procedural fairness is exceptional One can never rule on the credibility of evidence that has not yet been heard. The presiding member violated the principle when he stated that even if the witness corroborated the applicant's testimony that subsequent testimony would not be credible.

The essence of adjudication is the ability to keep an open mind until all evidence has been heard. The reliability of evidence is to be determined in light of all the evidence in a particular case. The application for judicial review was allowed.

38. (1) Requesting a summons — A party who wants the Division to order a person to testify at a hearing must make a request to the Division for a summons, either orally at a proceeding or in writing.

(2) Factors — In deciding whether to issue a summons, the Division must consider any relevant factors, including

    (a) the necessity of the testimony to a full and proper hearing;

    (b) the ability of the person to give that testimony; and

    (c) whether the person has agreed to be summoned as a witness.

(3) Using the summons — If a party wants to use a summons, the party must

    (a) provide the summons to the summoned person by hand;

    (b) provide a copy of the summons to the Division with a written statement of how and when the summons was provided; and

    (c) pay or offer to pay the summoned person the applicable witness fees and travel expenses set out in Tariff A of the *Federal Courts Rules*.

39. (1) Cancelling a summons — If a person summoned to appear as a witness at a proceeding wants the summons cancelled, the person must make an application in writing to the Division.

(2) Application — The person must follow rule 43, but is not required to provide an affidavit or statutory declaration with the application.

40. (1) Arrest warrant — If a person does not obey a summons to appear, the party who requested the summons may make a request to the Division orally at a hearing, or in writing, to issue a warrant for the arrest of the person.

(2) Written request — A party who makes a written request for a warrant must provide supporting evidence by affidavit or statutory declaration.

(3) Requirements for issue of arrest warrant — The Division may issue an arrest warrant if

    (a) the person summoned was provided the summons by hand or the person is avoiding being provided the summons;

    (b) the person was paid or offered the applicable witness fees and travel expenses set out in Tariff A of the *Federal Courts Rules*;

    (c) the person did not appear at the hearing as required by the summons; and

    (d) the person's testimony is still needed for a full and proper hearing.

(4) Content of a warrant — A warrant issued by the Division for the arrest of a person must include directions concerning detention and release.

41. Excluded witness — Unless allowed by the Division, a person must not communicate to a witness excluded from a hearing room any testimony given while the witness was excluded until that witness has finished testifying.

APPLICATIONS

42. General provision — Unless these Rules provide otherwise

(a) a party who wants the Division to make a decision on any matter in an appeal, including the procedure to be followed, must make an application to the Division under rule 43;

(b) a party who wants to respond to the application must respond under rule 44; and

(c) a party who wants to reply to a response must reply under rule 45.

Case Law

Malfeo v. Canada (Minister of Citizenship & Immigration), 2010 CarswellNat 372, 2010 CarswellNat 2169, 2010 FC 193 — The main question raised by this judicial review application was whether a member of the Immigration Appeal Division breached the principles of natural justice and/or the requirements of the law when she dismissed the applicant's request to stay his deportation to Italy. This application had been made pursuant to s. 67(1)(c) of IRPA, which enables the tribunal to grant relief if sufficient humanitarian and compassionate considerations are demonstrated in light of the circumstances.

The use of joint submissions is a concept well known in criminal law where the Crown and the defense make joint submissions, for example, in sentencing. It is not unknown in administrative law cases and has been applied by this court in the context of immigration law (see *Nguyen v. Canada (Minister of Citizenship & Immigration)* (2000), 10 Imm. L.R. (3d) 252, 196 F.T.R. 236), a case which bears similarity with the case at hand since it involved an application by Mr. Nguyen to the then-Appeal Division for the exercise of its humanitarian and compassionate jurisdiction under a provision of the now repealed *Immigration Act* similar to para. 67(1)(c) of IRPA. That case involved the failure of the tribunal to explain why the joint submissions of counsel proposing a five-year stay was not endorsed. The purpose of staying the deportation is, in that case as it is in this one, to give the applicant an opportunity to demonstrate, on the ground so to speak, becoming a decent law-abiding resident of the country.

Having received the joint submission albeit unexpectedly, the tribunal breached procedural fairness by rejecting it outright without asking for further input. The applicant in these circumstances was not given a fair hearing. The tribunal provided no analysis and did not even refer to the proposed terms and conditions. It was also clear that the tribunal did not give serious consideration to the joint submissions. Again, it provided no analysis of its terms and dismissed the joint submission in a perfunctory manner. The reasons put forward for rejecting the joint submission also lacked analysis. The application for judicial review was granted.

How to Make an Application

43. (1) Form of application and time limit — An application must be made in writing and without delay unless

(a) these Rules provide otherwise; or

(b) the Division allows it to be made orally at a proceeding after considering any relevant factors, including whether the party with reasonable effort could have made the application in writing before the proceeding.

(2) Content of application — Unless these Rules provide otherwise, in a written application the party must

(a) state what decision the party wants the Division to make;

(b) give reasons why the Division should make that decision; and

(c) if there is another party and the views of that party are known, state whether the other party agrees to the application.

(3) Affidavit or statutory declaration — Unless these Rules provide otherwise, any evidence that the party wants the Division to consider with an application in writing must be given in a statutory declaration or affidavit that is provided together with the application.

(4) Providing the application — A party who makes an written application must provide

(a) to the other party, a copy of the application and any affidavit or statutory declaration; and

(b) to the Division, the original application and any affidavit or statutory declaration, together with a written statement of how and when the party provided the copy to any other party.

How to Respond to a Written Application

44. (1) Responding to a written application — A response to a written application must be in writing. In a response the party must

(a) state what decision the party wants the Division to make; and

(b) give reasons why the Division should make that decision.

(2) Evidence in a written response — Any evidence that the party wants the Division to consider with the written response must be given in an affidavit or statutory declaration that accompanies the response. Unless the Division requires it, an affidavit or statutory declaration is not required if the party who made the application was not required to provide an affidavit or statutory declaration.

(3) Providing the response — A party who responds to a written application must provide

(a) to the other party, a copy of the response and any affidavit or statutory declaration; and

(b) to the Division, the original response and any affidavit or statutory declaration, together with a written statement of how and when the party provided the copy to the other party.

(4) Time limit — Documents provided under this rule must be received by the recipients no later than seven days after the party received the copy of the application.

How to Reply to a Written Response

45. (1) Replying to a written response — A reply to a written response must be in writing.

(2) Evidence in the reply — Any evidence that the party wants the Division to consider with the written reply must be given in an affidavit or statutory declaration together with the reply. Unless the Division requires it, an affidavit or statutory declaration is not required if the party was not required to provide a statutory declaration or affidavit with the application.

(3) Providing the reply — A party who replies to a written response must provide

(a) to the other party, a copy of the reply and any affidavit or statutory declaration; and

(b) to the Division, the original reply and any affidavit or statutory declaration, together with a written statement of how and when the party provided the copy to the other party.

(4) Time limit — Documents provided under this rule must be received by their recipients no later than five days after the party received the copy of the response.

RETURN TO CANADA TO APPEAR AT A HEARING

46. (1) Application for an order to appear — A permanent resident who appeals a decision made outside Canada on the residency obligation may make an application to the Division for an order that they physically appear at the hearing.

(2) Form of application — The application must be made under rule 43.

(3) Time limit — Documents provided under this rule must be received by their recipients no later than 60 days after the Division received the notice of appeal.

CHANGING THE LOCATION OF THE PROCEEDING

47. (1) Application to change the location of a proceeding — A party may make an application to the Division to change the location of a proceeding.

(2) Form of application — The party must follow rule 43, but is not required to give evidence in an affidavit or statutory declaration.

(3) Time limit — Documents provided under this rule must be received by their recipients no later than 30 days before the proceeding.

(4) Factors — In deciding the application, the Division must consider any relevant factors, including

(a) whether the party is residing in the location where the party wants the proceeding to be held;

(b) whether a change of location would allow the proceeding to be full and proper;

(c) whether a change of location would likely delay or slow the proceeding;

(d) how a change of location would affect the operation of the Division; and

(e) how a change of location would affect the parties.

(5) Duty to appear at the proceeding — Unless a party receives a decision from the Division allowing the application, the party must appear for the proceeding at the location fixed and be ready to start or continue the proceeding.

CHANGING THE DATE OR TIME OF A PROCEEDING

48. (1) Application to change the date or time of a proceeding — A party may make an application to the Division to change the date or time of a proceeding.

(2) Form and content of application — The party must

(a) follow rule 43, but is not required to give evidence in an affidavit or statutory declaration; and

(b) give at least six dates, within the period specified by the Division, on which the party is available to start or continue the proceeding.

(3) Application received two days or less before proceeding — If the party's application is received by the recipients two working days or less before the date of a proceeding, the party must appear at the proceeding and make the request orally.

(4) Factors — In deciding the application, the Division must consider any relevant factors, including

(a) in the case of a date and time that was fixed after the Division consulted or tried to consult the party, any exceptional circumstances for allowing the application;

(b) when the party made the application;

(c) the time the party has had to prepare for the proceeding;

(d) the efforts made by the party to be ready to start or continue the proceeding;

(e) in the case of a party who wants more time to obtain information in support of the party's arguments, the ability of the Division to proceed in the absence of that information without causing an injustice;

(f) the knowledge and experience of any counsel who represents the party;

(g) any previous delays and the reasons for them;

(h) whether the time and date fixed for the proceeding were peremptory;

(i) whether allowing the application would unreasonably delay the proceedings; and

(j) the nature and complexity of the matter to be heard.

(5) Duty to appear at the proceeding — Unless a party receives a decision from the Division allowing the application, the party must appear for the proceeding at the date and time fixed and be ready to start or continue the proceeding.

Case Law

Laidlow v. Canada (Minister of Citizenship & Immigration) (2012), 12 Imm. L.R. (4th) 33, 440 N.R. 105, 2012 FCA 256, 2012 CarswellNat 3843, 2012 CarswellNat 5564 — The appellant was diagnosed with a benign tumor affecting his brain and pituitary gland. While in the hospital he commenced the paperwork for a claim for refugee protection in Canada. The basis of the claim was that he faced a risk to his life were he to return to St. Vincent, in that he would be unable to access adequate medical treatment there. A year later, he applied for permanent residence based on humanitarian and compassionate grounds on the basis that he would be unable to afford life sustaining medication were he to return to St. Vincent. A request for an adjournment of his refugee claim pending the outcome of his humanitarian and compassionate application was refused. The Refugee Protection Division then rejected the his refugee claim and he sought judicial review of the decision to deny the adjournment.

Section 7 of the *Charter* does not impose a positive obligation on the RPD to adjourn its hearing until the determination of the humanitarian and compassionate application. The appellant's right to request an adjournment so he could exhaust his non-constitutional remedies does not create a corresponding obligation on the RPD to structure its hearing so that the appellant's constitutional arguments were heard last. The appeal was dismissed.

Quindiagan v. Canada (Minister of Citizenship & Immigration), 2005 CarswellNat 1499, 2005 FC 769 — Before the Appeal Division, counsel on behalf of the applicant requested a postponement on the basis that he wished to raise a constitutional question but had failed to complete and serve a notice of constitutional question within the time limit required by s. 52 of the *Immigration Appeal Division Rules*. The Appeal Division denied the request. Counsel for a party to a case is that party's agent. He or she acts on behalf of the party and assumes a number of obligations including those of conduct of the proceedings and receipt and issue of documents required by the proceedings. The only instance where a Court could disrupt an administrative tribunal's decision due to errors committed by counsel would be in a case where extraordinary incompetence on the part of counsel was shown to have resulted in a breach of natural justice.

PROCEEDING TO BE HELD IN PRIVATE

49. (1) Form of application — A person who wants to have a proceeding held in private, or who wants the Division to take any other measure to ensure the confidentiality of the proceedings, must make an application to the Division under rule 43.

(2) Time limit — Documents provided under this rule must be received by their recipients no later than 20 days before the proceeding.

(3) Response by non-party — Any person may make a written request to the Division to be allowed to respond to an application by another person or a party to have a proceeding held in private. If the Division allows the request, the person must respond under rule 44.

(4) Temporary confidentiality — The Division may do anything to ensure the confidentiality of the information in the application.

WITHDRAWING AN APPEAL

50. (1) Abuse of process — Withdrawal of an appeal is an abuse of process if it would likely have a negative effect on the integrity of the Division. If no substantive evidence has been accepted in the appeal, withdrawal is not an abuse of process.

(2) Withdrawal if no substantive evidence has been accepted — If no substantive evidence has been accepted in the appeal, a party may withdraw their appeal by notifying the Division orally at a proceeding or in writing.

(3) Withdrawal if subtantive evidence has been accepted — If substantive evidence has been accepted in the appeal, a party who wants to withdraw their appeal must make an application under rule 43.

REINSTATING AN APPEAL AFTER WITHDRAWAL

51. (1) Application to reinstate a withdrawn appeal — A person may apply to the Division to reinstate an appeal that was made by that person and withdrawn.

(2) Form and content of application — The person must follow rule 43 and include their contact information in the application.

(3) Factors — The Division must allow the application if it is established that there was a failure to observe a principle of natural justice or if it is otherwise in the interests of justice to allow the application.

NOTICE OF CONSTITUTIONAL QUESTION

52. (1) Notice of constitutional question — A party who wants to challenge the constitutional validity, applicability or operability of a legislative provision must complete a notice of constitutional question.

(2) **Form and content of notice** — The party must provide notice using either Form 69, "Notice of Constitutional Question", set out in the *Federal Courts Rules*, or any other form that includes

(a) the name of the party;

(b) the Division file number;

(c) the date, time and place of the hearing;

(d) the specific legislative provision that is being challenged;

(e) the relevant facts relied on to support the constitutional challenge; and

(f) a summary of the legal argument to be made in support of the constitutional challenge.

(3) **Providing the notice** — The party must provide

(a) a copy of the notice of constitutional question to the Attorney General of Canada and to the attorney general of every province and territory of Canada, according to section 57 of the *Federal Courts Act*;

(b) a copy of the notice to the other party; and

(c) the original notice to the Division, together with a written statement of how and when a copy of the notice was provided under paragraphs (a) and (b).

(4) **Time limit** — Documents provided under this rule must be received by their recipients no later than 10 days before the day the constitutional argument will be made.

2002, c. 8, s. 182(3)(a)

DECISIONS

53. Notice of decision — When the Division makes a decision, other than an interlocutory decision, it must provide a notice of decision to the parties.

54. (1) Written reasons for decision on appeal by a sponsor or that stays a removal order — The Division must provide to the parties, together with the notice of decision, written reasons for a decision on an appeal by a sponsor or for a decision that stays a removal order.

(2) **Written reasons provided on request** — A request made by a party for written reasons for a decision, other than a decision referred to in subrule (1) or an interlocutory decision, must be in writing. The request must be received by the Division no later than 10 days after the party received the notice of decision.

Case Law

Sandhu v. Canada (Minister of Citizenship & Immigration) (2005), 48 Imm. L.R. (3d) 104, 34 Admin. L.R. (4th) 307, 2005 CarswellNat 2101, 2005 CarswellNat 5263, 2005 FC 1046 — The Immigration Appeal Division dismissed the applicant's appeal of a visa officer's decision to refuse the applicant's application to sponsor his son as a member of the family class. The IAD concluded that the applicant had not shown that the visa officer's refusal was wrong in law. Accordingly, the IAD concluded that the person who was sponsored by the applicant was not a member of the family class and therefore under s. 65 of the IRPA, the IAD had no discretionary jurisdiction to consider humanitarian and compassionate considerations. The application for judicial review was allowed as the IAD provided no explanation or analysis whatsoever to conclude that the visa officer's refusal of the applicant's sponsorship application was wrong in law. Accordingly, the reasons provided by the IAD were entirely insufficient to allow the applicant and his family members to understand why they had been denied the opportunity to unite their family in Canada. The reasons were equally insufficient to allow the Federal Court to determine whether or not the tribunal was justified in deciding as it did.

Singh v. Canada (Minister of Citizenship & Immigration), 2005 FC 1673, 2005 CarswellNat 4126, 2005 CarswellNat 4892, [2005] F.C.J. No. 2071 — An appeal heard under s. 63(1) of the IRPA results in a hearing *de novo*. In such a hearing, the IAD does not need to comment on every piece of new evidence that is proffered, but it must deal with evidence that directly contradicts, or at least addresses, the concerns of the original decision maker.

Agalliu v. Canada (Minister of Citizenship & Immigration) (2005), 49 Imm. L.R. (3d) 1, 34 Admin. L.R. (4th) 214, 2005 CarswellNat 2112, 2005 FC 1035 — The Board's reasons disclosed a number of superficial errors, in footnotes and in references to the documentary evidence. However, the Board's other errors and its failure to explain its conclusions adequately disclosed more fundamental problems. Taken together, these errors led to the conclusion that the Board's decision was not in keeping with the evidence before it. Sometimes, little errors in a written decision represent no more than a lack of final polishing. Other times, they are symptomatic of inadequate care on the part of the decision maker.

Mann v. Canada (Minister of Citizenship & Immigration) (2004), 43 Imm. L.R. (3d) 230, 2004 CarswellNat 5099, 2004 CarswellNat 3438, 258 F.T.R. 139 (Eng.), 2004 FC 1338 — This was an application to review a decision of the Immigration Appeal Division wherein the Appeal Division allowed an appeal from a visa officer's refusal to grant the respondent's wife an immigrant visa.

In dealing with the adequacy of reasons, the court relied upon the Federal Court of Appeal decision in *VIA Rail Canada Inc. v. Canada (National Transportation Agency* (2000), [2001] 2 F.C. 25. Reasons foster better decision making. By ensuring that issues and reasoning are well articulated and therefore more carefully thought out, the process of writing reasons for a decision by itself may be a guarantee of a better decision. Reasons provide the parties with the assurance that their representations have been considered.

Reasons allow the parties to effectuate any right of appeal or judicial review that they might have. They provide a basis for an assessment of possible grounds of appeal or review. They allow the appellate or reviewing body to determine whether the decision maker erred and thereby render him or her accountable. This is particularly important when the decision is subject to a deferential standard of review.

In a case of a regulated industry, the regulator's reasons provide guidance to others who are subject to the regulator's jurisdiction.

The duty to give reasons is only fulfilled if the reasons provided are adequate. What constitutes adequate reasons is a matter to be determined in the light of the circumstances of each case. As a general rule, adequate reasons are those that serve the functions for which the duty to provide them was imposed.

The obligation to provide adequate reasons is not satisfied by merely reciting the submissions and evidence of the parties and stating a conclusion. The decision maker must set out its findings of fact and the principal evidence upon which those findings were based. The reasons must address the major points in issue. The reasoning process followed by the decision maker must be set out and must reflect consideration of the main relevant factors.

In this case, s. 4 of the *Hindu Marriage Act* was an important factor in the case. The interpretation of this section is a matter on which the IAD's reasons are silent, and due to this silence, the reasons are inadequate.

55. When decision of single member takes effect — A decision of the Division made orally by one Division member at a proceeding takes effect when the member states the decision. A decision made in writing takes effect when the member signs and dates the decision.

56. When decision of three-member panel takes effect — A decision of the Division made orally by a panel of three members takes effect when all the members state their decision. A decision made in writing takes effect when all members of the panel sign and date the decision.

GENERAL PROVISIONS

57. No applicable rule — In the absence of a provision in these Rules dealing with a matter raised during an appeal, the Division may do whatever is necessary to deal with the matter.

58. Powers of the Division — The Division may

(a) act on its own initiative, without a party having to make an application or request to the Division;

(b) change a requirement of a rule;

(c) excuse a person from a requirement of a rule; and

(d) extend or shorten a time limit, before or after the time limit has passed.

Case Law

Canada (Minister of Citizenship & Immigration) v. Rumpler (2008), 76 Imm. L.R. (3d) 237, 336 F.T.R. 285 (Eng.), 2008 CarswellNat 4258, 2008 CarswellNat 5085, 2008 FC 1264, 2008 CarswellNat 4258 — This was an application for judicial review of the decision of the IAD wherein the IAD concluded it had jurisdiction to hear an appeal of the respondent's removal order. Returning to Canada from Israel, an immigration officer determined that the respondent did not satisfy the residency requirements of s. 28 of the Act and undertook measures to have him removed. The period to appeal the removal order expired and the respondent voluntarily left Canada for the United States. The respondent then requested of the IAD an extension of the period, to allow him to lodge an appeal of the removal order. The IAD decided that, according to subs. 63(3) of the Act, it did not have the competence to extend the period of appeal after its expiration, because the respondent had lost his status as permanent resident by failing to appeal. Justice Blanchard of the Federal Court granted the respondent's application for judicial review, and held that the IAD did have competence under the said provision to grant the extension. Accordingly, an extension was granted by a different member of the IAD and at a new hearing before the IAD, the Minister asked the tribunal to reject the appeal of the removal order on the ground of mootness, because the respondent had voluntarily left the country and thus executed the order. The Minister's motion was rejected and the Minister brought an application for judicial review of the IAD's decision.

The IAD erred in law in finding that it had continuing jurisdiction in spite of the fact that the respondent had left Canada and had executed the removal order before he filed a notice of appeal. It is trite law that the IAD does not have jurisdiction to reopen an appeal where the motion to reopen has been filed after an appellant is removed from Canada. Since the IAD did not have the jurisdiction to cancel the removal order once it had already been executed, it necessarily had no jurisdiction to grant a request (filed after such an execution) for an extension of time to lodge an appeal of the removal order. Consequently, the application for judicial review was allowed.

Rumpler v. Canada (Minister of Citizenship & Immigration) (2006), 60 Imm. L.R. (3d) 71, 2006 CarswellNat 4492, 2006 FC 1485 — The applicant sought judicial review of a decision of the Appeal Division wherein the Appeal Division decided it did not have jurisdiction to extend time to hear an appeal from a removal order issued at an examination pursuant to s. 63(3) of the IRPA. The Board found that it did not have jurisdiction to extend the time to file an appeal under s. 63(3) once the prescribed delay had expired because the applicant was no longer a permanent resident of Canada. The Board reasoned that since no appeal had been filed in the 30-day period pursuant to paragraph 49(1)(b) of the IRPA, the removal order came into force the day the appeal period expired, and the applicant contemporaneously lost his permanent resident status, pursuant to paragraph 46(1)(c) of the IRPA. Moreover, pursuant to ss. 237 and 240 of the *Immigration and Refugee Protection Regulations* the order had been enforced by the voluntary departure of the applicant to the United States. The court found that the Appeal Division does have jurisdiction to hear the request to extend time and then decide in the exercise of its discretion if the request is justified. If the extension is granted then the effect of such determination by the Appeal Board would be to allow the appeal to be made in time and the removal order would be vitiated. As a consequence, the applicant would retain his permanent resident status and the Appeal Division would have jurisdiction to hear the appeal. This interpretation is in keeping with the statutory scheme and intention of Parliament to provide a right of appeal, a significant guarantee against arbitrary decisions when important rights are in play. Parliament could not have intended to deprive a person of his or her right to appeal from a deportation order because of a failure to respect the delay to appeal no matter the circumstances, absent express language to that effect.

The IAD Rules passed under authority of the IRPA expressly provide that the Appeal Division can extend time when time has passed. There may well be instances where an applicant is able to adequately explain the delay. Applicants have a right to appeal provided for in law. The Appeal Division's decision was set aside and remitted for re-determination in accordance with the reasons of the court.

The court certified the following question:

> Would it be lawful for the Immigration Appeal Division to entertain an application for an extension of time pursuant to subs. 58(d) of the *Immigration Appeal*

Division Rules made by an individual who has no right of appeal through the combined effect of paragraphs 48(1)(b) and 46(1)(c), ss. 2 and 63 of the IRPA?

59. Failing to follow a rule — Unless proceedings are declared invalid by the Division, a failure to follow any requirement of these Rules does not make the proceedings invalid.

COMING INTO FORCE

60. Coming into force — These Rules come into force on the day on which section 161 of the Act comes into force.

Rules

1117

CAN. REG. 2012-255 — OATH OR SOLEMN AFFIRMATION OF OFFICE RULES (IMMIGRATION AND REFUGEE BOARD)

made under the *Immigration and Refugee Protection Act*
SOR/2012-255

OATH OR SOLEMN AFFIRMATION OF OFFICE

1. Text of the oath or affirmation — The oath or solemn affirmation of office to be taken by the Chairperson and other members of the Immigration and Refugee Board under section 152.1 of the *Immigration and Refugee Protection Act* is to be in the following form:

I, ..., do swear (*or* solemnly affirm) that

    (a) I will, during the term of my appointment, and any re-appointments, faithfully, impartially and to the best of my knowledge and ability, properly carry out the duties of a (full-time *or* part-time) (*title*) of the Immigration and Refugee Board;

    (b) I will comply with the *Code of Conduct for Members of the Immigration and Refugee Board of Canada*, as amended or replaced from time to time; and

    (c) I will not disclose or make known, unless authorized, any matter that comes to my knowledge because I am holding that office.

(*In the case of an oath, add*: So help me (*Name of Deity*).)

REPEAL

2. Repeal — The *Oath or Solemn Affirmation of Office Rules (Immigration and Refugee Board)*[7] are repealed.

COMING INTO FORCE

3. S.C. 2010, c. 8 — These Rules come into force on the day on which section 17 of the *Balanced Refugee Reform Act* comes into force, but if they are registered after that day, they come into force on the day on which they are registered.

---

[7] SOR/2002-231

FEDERAL COURTS ACT

An Act respecting the Federal Court of Appeal and the Federal Court

R.S.C. 1985, c. F-7, as am. R.S.C. 1985, c. 41 (1st Supp.), s. 11; R.S.C. 1985, c. 30 (2nd Supp.), s. 61; R.S.C. 1985, c. 16 (3rd Supp.), s. 7; R.S.C. 1985, c. 51 (4th Supp.), ss. 10–12; S.C. 1990, c. 8, ss. 1–14(2), (3) (Fr.), (4), 15–19 [s. 7(2) amended 1990, c. 8, s. 78(1).]; 1990, c. 37, s. 34; 1992, c. 1, s. 68; 1992, c. 26, s. 17; 1992, c. 33, s. 69; 1992, c. 49, ss. 127, 128; 1993, c. 27, s. 214; 1993, c. 34, ss. 68 (Fr.), 69 (Fr.), 70; 1996, c. 10, s. 229; 1996, c. 22, s. 1; 1996, c. 23, s. 187(c); 1996, c. 31, ss. 82–84; 1998, c. 26, s. 73; 1999, c. 31, s. 92; 2001, c. 6, s. 115; 2001, c. 41, ss. 95, 144(2); 2002, c. 8, ss. 13–58; 2003, c. 22, ss. 167, 225(w) [s. 167 amended 2003, c. 22, s. 262; s. 225(w) amended 2003, c. 22, s. 263.]; 2004, c. 7, s. 7 [Amended 2004, c. 7, s. 38.]; 2005, c. 46, s. 56.1 [Added 2006, c. 9, s. 222.]; 2006, c. 9, ss. 5, 6, 38; 2006, c. 11, ss. 20–24; 2008, c. 22, s. 46; 2009, c. 21, s. 18; 2010, c. 8, s. 41; 2012, c. 19, ss. 110, 272, 572; 2012, c. 24, s. 86 [Not in force at date of publication. Amended 2014, c. 20, s. 236.]; 2013, c. 40, ss. 236(1)(d), 439; 2014, c. 22, s. 41; 2014, c. 39, s. 328; 2015, c. 36, s. 124.

[Note: The short title of this Act was changed from "Federal Court Act" to "Federal Courts Act" by S.C. 2002, c. 8, s. 14. The long title of this Act was changed from "An Act respecting the Federal Court of Canada" to "An Act respecting the Federal Court of Appeal and the Federal Court" by S.C. 2002, c. 8, s. 13.]

· · · · ·

BARRISTERS, ADVOCATES, ATTORNEYS AND SOLICITORS

11. (1) Barrister or advocate — Every person who is a barrister or an advocate in a province may practise as a barrister or an advocate in the Federal Court of Appeal or the Federal Court.

(2) Attorney or solicitor — Every person who is an attorney or a solicitor in a superior court of a province may practise as an attorney or a solicitor in the Federal Court of Appeal or the Federal Court.

(3) Officers of court — Every person who may practise as a barrister, an advocate, an attorney or a solicitor in the Federal Court of Appeal or the Federal Court is an officer of that Court.

2002, c. 8, s. 19

Case Law

Obando v. Canada (Minister of Citizenship & Immigration), 2003 CarswellNat 1554, 2003 CarswellNat 2613, 2003 FCT 668, 2003 CFPI 668 — The court dismissed this application for a stay of execution of a removal order. At the commencement of the hearing, the applicant, who was representing himself, sought approval of the court to be represented by a consultant who was not a lawyer. The Minister objected based on the court's own rules permitting representation by persons themselves or by solicitors retained on their behalf. The court examined the applicant and determined 1), that he was not proficient in English and would not have been able to represent himself; 2), that he had no submissions to make on his own behalf but wished submissions to be made by his consultant; and 3) that he was prepared to adopt submissions made on his behalf by his consultant as his own after those submissions were made. The court authorized the consultant to make submissions and at the conclusion asked the applicant to affirm that the submissions were adopted by him as his own. The court, at the conclusion of the submissions, dismissed the request for a stay.

Salinas v. Canada (Minister of Citizenship & Immigration), 2000 CarswellNat 1414, 2000 CarswellNat 3202, [2000] F.C.J. No. 1004 (T.D.) — The respondent Minister appealed an order of a prothonotary who dismissed the Minister's motion asking that the application for leave and judicial review be dismissed on the ground that no one acting on behalf of the applicants was qualified to represent them.

The court should not approve of third parties who are not lawyers doing things which are within the exclusive jurisdiction of members of the bar.

It is the court's role and duty to guarantee compliance with the Act and the Rules and to ensure that those who appear before it, or draft proceedings for the purpose of asserting rights, are officers of the court. Facts put in evidence in each of the respondent Minister's motions constituted evidence which pointed inexorably to the conclusion that in each case the application for leave and judicial review by the applicants had been prepared and drafted by an agent who could not act as a representative in this court. If an applicant decides to be represented, Rule 119 is clear: he or she must be represented by a solicitor.

Accordingly, the respondent Minister's appeal was allowed and the application for judicial review dismissed.

Parmar c. Canada (Ministre de la Citoyenneté & de l'Immigration) (2000), 12 Imm. L.R. (3d) 178, 2000 CarswellNat 1432, 2000 CarswellNat 3429 (Fed. T.D.) — The defendant Minister appealed an order dismissing its motion asking the court to dismiss an application for leave and judicial review. The motion had been brought on the ground that the person acting on the plaintiff's behalf was not qualified to represent him.

It is the court's function and duty to ensure that its Act and its Rules are observed and that those who appear before it or prepare pleadings to be used in asserting rights are officers of the court. The facts in this matter lead inexorably to the conclusion that the plaintiff's application for leave and judicial review had been prepared and drafted by an agent. It is true that a plaintiff may act in person, but if he or she decides to be represented then the rule is clear that he or she must be represented by a barrister or advocate.

The court concluded that the plaintiff had been represented by a person who was not authorized to do so and accordingly allowed the Minister's appeal and dismissed the plaintiff's application for leave and for judicial review.

· · · · ·

JURISDICTION OF FEDERAL COURT

[Heading amended 2002, c. 8, s. 24.]

. . . . .

18. (1) Extraordinary remedies, federal tribunals — Subject to section 28, the Federal Court has exclusive original jurisdiction

(a) to issue an injunction, writ of *certiorari*, writ of prohibition, writ of *mandamus* or writ of *quo warranto*, or grant declaratory relief, against any federal board, commission or other tribunal; and

(b) to hear and determine any application or other proceeding for relief in the nature of relief contemplated by paragraph (a), including any proceeding brought against the Attorney General of Canada, to obtain relief against a federal board, commission or other tribunal.

(2) Extraordinary remedies, members of Canadian Forces — The Federal Court has exclusive original jurisdiction to hear and determine every application for a writ of *habeas corpus ad subjiciendum*, writ of *certiorari*, writ of prohibition or writ of *mandamus* in relation to any member of the Canadian Forces serving outside Canada.

(3) Remedies to be obtained on application — The remedies provided for in subsections (1) and (2) may be obtained only on an application for judicial review made under section 18.1.

1990, c. 8, s. 4; 2002, c. 8, s. 26

Case Law

Section 18(1)

John Doe v. Canada (Minister of Citizenship & Immigration) (2006), 54 Imm. L.R. (3d) 212, 2006 CarswellNat 1105, 2006 CarswellNat 1543, 2006 FC 535 — The applicant came to Canada in 1984 and was granted refugee status in 1986. He then applied for permanent residence. After many interviews, security checks, etc., no decision was taken on his application. In 1998, the immigration officers raised security concerns. The applicant made an application for ministerial relief under what would now be subs. 34(2) of the IRPA, which would have the effect of relieving him of possible inadmissibility that might otherwise be a bar to grant permanent residence. In nearly eight years no decision had been taken on the application for ministerial relief. The applicant brought an application for *mandamus* to require the Minister to make a decision with respect to the applicant's permanent residence in Canada.

On the eve of the hearing, the Minister made an offer to settle. The Minister was prepared not to oppose the *mandamus* application but was to agree to an order that would set out time limits for progressive steps leading to an ultimate decision. The applicant found the proposal unacceptable as it contemplated steps totaling some 240 days and did not set out any limit as to how long the Minister of Public Security and Emergency Preparedness might take to decide the application for ministerial relief, which was first made in 1998. The court directed that a decision on permanent residence be made by a specific date.

Other Relevant Legislation

The court also awarded costs, finding special reasons — specifically that the Minister failed to take a decision which was requested almost 20 years previous, while the applicant had endured interview after interview, acquired a good deal of legal advice and was forced to bring the Minister to court. Even when faced with this matter being set down for hearing the Minister waited until the afternoon of the day before the hearing to offer a settlement.

Seyoboka c. Canada (Ministre de la Citoyenneté & de l'Immigration), 2005 CarswellNat 5690, 2005 FC 1290 — This was an application for judicial review in order to obtain a writ of *mandamus*, ordering the respondent to determine and make a definitive decision on the applicant's application for permanent residence which had been dated August 12, 1996. The applicant was a citizen of Rwanda and had arrived in Canada on January 17, 1996, and claimed refugee status. The IRB recognized the applicant as a Convention refugee on October 25, 1996. On August 12, 1996, the applicant filed an application for permanent residence. To date, the respondent has still not processed that application. On several occasions, the applicant tried to find out the status of his application. The respondent always replied that the security check was ongoing.

Even though at first glance nine years is a long time for someone who is waiting to be given permanent residence status, *mandamus* applications must be assessed in accordance with the particular facts of the case; the case law is used only to outline the parameters. In this case, the applicant made some significant additions to his file over the last nine years. Considering the facts presented by the applicant since his initial permanent residence application, the respondent was justified in completing its security check. When it is a matter of security, the court must not issue an order of *mandamus* having the effect of an aborted or abbreviated investigation. Further, the Minister of Public Safety applied to the IRB to annul the applicant's refugee status. That application, though late, is certainly not frivolous. If it is granted, any right to permanent residence would be annulled. In the interim, therefore, until the application by the Minister of Public Safety is decided, issuing a writ of *mandamus* would serve no purpose.

Uppal v. Canada (Minister of Citizenship & Immigration), 2005 CarswellNat 2437, 2005 CarswellNat 4845, 2005 FC 1133 — Costs are generally not awarded in applications for leave and for judicial review brought in a context of the *Immigration and Refugee Protection Act*. This is because Rule 22 of the *Federal Court Immigration and Refugee Protection Rules* provides that no costs shall be awarded in proceedings under the Rules "unless the court, for special reasons, so orders." The finding that an order of *mandamus* is warranted is not, by itself, sufficient to justify the award of costs.

Although none of the steps required to process the applicant's application were concluded expediently, and an embarrassing gaffe occurred, the pace was not so slow or lax as to give rise to special circumstances and an award of costs.

Marshall v. R., 2002 CarswellNat 2901, 2002 CarswellNat 3965, 2002 FCT 1099 — The applicant applied for an order restraining an adjudicator from continuing a hearing against the applicant until the action commenced by the applicant was heard and determined. The court concluded that it did not have jurisdiction to issue the order requested because no application for judicial review had been filed with the court. Section 18(1) of the *Federal Court Act* grants the Federal Court the jurisdiction to grant certain remedies but subs. 18(3) requires that the application for judicial review be commenced. In the present motion, the motion for an interim injunction is made incidental to an action, not an application for judicial review. The court has jurisdiction to grant a stay pursuant to s.

18.2 of the *Federal Court Act*, but only if a judicial review application has been filed. Subs. 50(1) of the *Federal Court Act* gives the court jurisdiction to grant a stay but only provides for stays in proceedings being conducted before the Federal Court. Accordingly the motion for an injunction was dismissed.

Atlantic Prudence Fund Corp. v. Canada (Minister of Citizenship & Immigration), 2000 CarswellNat 531 (Fed. T.D.) — The applicant sought to amend notices of application so as to seek declaratory relief in lieu of *mandamus* and to add to the grounds of their application for judicial review allegations of bad faith.

A notice of application may be amended at any time. The governing principle is that in the absence of prejudice to the opposing party, amendments should be allowed if they will assist in determining the real issue between the parties. Applicants must adduce some evidence to convince the court that it would be fair in the circumstances to allow them to add a further ground to their applications for judicial review. The court found that there was some evidence to convince the court that it was fair to allow the amendments. This evidence included the dissemination of rumours by representatives of the Minister around the time of the decisions which are the subject of the proceedings to the effect that one of the persons associated with the applicants had attempted to bribe an official of the respondent, and that two of the persons associated with the applicants were connected with Chinese organized crime. Further, there was evidence of an e-mail sent by an official of the Ministry which suggested a course of action which ". . . would be far more effective, in our opinion, and would be more likely to hurt the group where it really hurts."

The court found an absence of any evidence of prejudice and accordingly allowed the amendments.

Popal v. Canada (Minister of Citizenship & Immigration), [2000] 3 F.C. 532, 184 F.T.R. 161, 2000 CarswellNat 459, [2000] F.C.J. No. 352, 2000 CarswellNat 3417 — The applicant alleged that he was a citizen of Afghanistan, and was determined by a panel of the Convention Refugee Determination Division (CRDD) to be a refugee from that country. Since November 15, 1994, the date of the CRDD decision, the applicant's wife and children have been residing in Pakistan under, what the applicant attested to were, "deplorable conditions." In December 1994, the applicant submitted an application for permanent residence as a Convention refugee. More than five years have passed and the applicant remains in suspended animation in Canada. His children continue to grow older and one of his children is now of an age where he can no longer be sponsored. The applicant provided a valid passport, Afghan driver's licence, an Ontario driver's licence and Ontario Health Insurance Card as identity documents. The respondent rejected these identity documents and provided no explanation to the applicant for this decision.

The decision to reject these documents was critical to the future of the principal applicant and his family members. Accordingly, the court found that the respondent erred in a reviewable manner in not providing reasons for the rejection of the various documents.

The decision to reject these documents was set aside. The respondent was urged to make a redetermination about the satisfactory nature of the applicant's identity documents as expeditiously as possible.

Gosal v. Canada (Minister of Citizenship & Immigration), 2000 CarswellNat 433 (Fed. T.D.) — During the course of processing the applicant's application for permanent residence, the visa officer requested that the applicant undergo DNA testing to establish family relationships. The applicant sought to quash this decision. The decision to require DNA testing was interlocutory in nature and did not in any sense dispose of the proceedings. The court's jurisdiction under s. 18 is not restricted to final substantive decisions. The court can, in special circumstances, review an interlocutory decision.

The court decided not to intervene. If ultimately the applicant was refused, she could apply for judicial review and raise any argument she might have, including the DNA testing. Accordingly, the application for review was dismissed.

Van Nguyen v. R. (1997), (sub nom. *Van Nguyen v. Canada*) 134 F.T.R. 241 — The defendant moved pursuant to Rule 324 to strike out the plaintiff's action, which was for damages for wrongful detention by immigration authorities, on the basis of want for a reasonable cause of action.

The plaintiff, a permanent resident, came from Hong Kong as a stateless person in 1991. He married a Canadian permanent resident with whom he had three children. He subsequently acquired a criminal record and was ordered deported. In January 1996, he was declared a danger to the public in Canada. On completing his jail sentence the plaintiff remained in immigration custody pending his removal. However, the Vietnamese government would not provide travel documents and the plaintiff was released. The plaintiff obeyed the terms of his release, but was nevertheless arrested by immigration authorities and was in custody at the time this motion was heard. The present statement of claim set out briefly and in the clearest language that the claim was one for damages for arbitrary and unlawful arrest and detention. The absence of some new wrongdoing at the time of the plaintiff's re-arrest made it impossible for the court to say that the plaintiff's action was futile, devoid of merit, and could not possibly succeed.

Due to the fact that the plaintiff was not seeking any form of declaratory relief, the defendant could not gain any comfort from s. 18(1) of the *Federal Court Act*.

Chesters v. Canada (Minister of Citizenship & Immigration) (1997), 38 Imm. L.R. (2d) 269, 45 C.R.R. (2d) 233, 134 F.T.R. 151 — A party may, in an action, seek a declaration that legislation of Parliament is contrary to the *Charter of Rights*. The type of declaration mentioned in s. 18 of the *Federal Court Act*, is one which impugns the decision of a board, commission or other tribunal. Such a declaration can only be sought in judicial review proceedings.

Section 18(3)

Marshall v. R., 2002 CarswellNat 2901, 2002 CarswellNat 3965, 2002 FCT 1099 — The applicant applied for an order restraining an adjudicator from continuing a hearing against the applicant until the action commenced by the applicant was heard and determined. The court concluded that it did not have jurisdiction to issue the order requested because no application for judicial review had been filed with the court. Section 18(1) of the *Federal Court Act* grants the Federal Court the jurisdiction to grant certain remedies but subs. 18(3) requires that the application for judicial review be commenced. In the present motion, the motion for an interim injunction is made incidental to an action, not an application for judicial review. The court has jurisdiction to grant a stay pursuant to s. 18.2 of the *Federal Court Act*, but only if a judicial review application has been filed. Subsection 50(1) of the *Federal Court Act* gives the court jurisdiction to grant a stay but only provides for stays in proceedings being conducted before the Federal Court. Accordingly the motion for an injunction was dismissed.

Moktari v. Canada (Minister of Citizenship & Immigration) (1999), 70 C.R.R. (2d) 133, 249 N.R. 385, [2000] 2 F.C. 341, 12 Imm. L.R. (3d) 12, 1999 CarswellNat 2522, [1999] F.C.J. No. 1864, 1999 CarswellNat 3045 (C.A.) — The Federal Court possesses jurisdiction to hear constitutional challenges to legislation in judicial review proceedings. This is true whether or not the decision maker possesses the jurisdiction to make constitutional rulings. The court possesses jurisdiction to grant declaratory relief in judicial review proceedings brought pursuant to s. 18 of the *Federal Court Act*. The cases in which statements of claim have been struck for disclosing no reasonable cause of action where the relief being sought in the action was by declaration and a parallel judicial review application had been brought seeking the same result are to be followed.

To permit parallel proceedings arising from a single decision would diminish the capacity of the Federal Court to dispense justice in an expedient and efficient manner.

Sivaraj v. Canada (Minister of Citizenship & Immigration), 1996 CarswellNat 1040, [1996] F.C.J. No. 700 (C.A.) — The Court of Appeal upheld the motion judge's ruling, striking the appellant's statement of claim as disclosing no reasonable cause of action. The motions judge had done so on the basis that the declaratory and injunctive relief sought must be pursued by way of judicial review, as opposed to an action, pursuant to subs. 18(1) and (3) of the *Federal Court Act*. The Court of Appeal was in agreement with the reasons of the motions judge.

Zelzle v. Canada (Minister of Citizenship & Immigration), [1996] 3 F.C. 20, 34 Imm. L.R. (2d) 24, 110 F.T.R. 161 — This was an application to review an interlocutory decision of a panel of the CRDD, wherein it was determined that a previous CRDD panel had failed to render a decision, leaving the CRDD open to hear the applicant's refugee claim *de novo*.

The applicant made a claim for refugee status on November 26, 1992. The applicant appeared for a hearing on the 15th of November 1993. At the commencement of the hearing, a positive Notice of Decision was found in the CRDD file. This Notice of Decision was dated May 10, 1993. The decision had apparently been made pursuant to the expedited hearing process. The November 15, 1993 panel adjourned the matter pending an inquiry to the registrar. On May 4, 1994, the applicant received a letter stating that the May 10 decision had been signed and left in the file as a result of an administrative error and, as such, that the case would proceed *de novo*. At the *de novo* hearing on January 9, 1995, the applicant made a motion that the panel did not have jurisdiction. On May 29, 1995, this motion was dismissed.

Once the tribunal has rendered a final decision, that tribunal's jurisdiction ceases and the tribunal becomes *functus officio*. In the case of the administrative tribunals, however, justice may require the reopening of administrative proceedings in order to provide relief which would otherwise be available on appeal. This exception was established to allow an administrative tribunal to re-open proceedings where, if the hearing of an application had not been held according to the rules of natural justice, the administrative tribunal may treat its decision as a nullity and reconsider the matter. This exception has usually been invoked by unsuccessful refugee claimants where, for example, the CRDD failed to consider evidence of changed country conditions. While the principal of *functus officio* favours the finality of proceedings, its application is flexible in the case of administrative tribunals.

In the instant case, the CRDD discharged the function committed to it by its enabling legislation by issuing the May 10, 1993, decision, which decision was valid on its face.

The decision on May 29, 1995, resulted in the panel exceeding its jurisdiction in looking beyond the decision and determining that it was an "administrative error." The panel had no jurisdiction to question a decision validly made in conformity with the Act. Once such a decision was made, the November 15 and May 29 panels were *functus officio*, since the decision in respect of the applicant's refugee status had been made. If the Minister had concerns regarding the legitimacy of the May 10, 1993, decision, the proper method by which to address those concerns would have been by way of an application for judicial review.

18.1 (1) Application for judicial review — An application for judicial review may be made by the Attorney General of Canada or by anyone directly affected by the matter in respect of which relief is sought.

(2) Time limitation — An application for judicial review in respect of a decision or an order of a federal board, commission or other tribunal shall be made within 30 days after the time the decision or order was first communicated by the federal board, commission or other tribunal to the office of the Deputy Attorney General of Canada or to the party directly affected by it, or within any further time that a judge of the Federal Court may fix or allow before or after the expiration of those 30 days.

(3) Powers of Federal Court — On an application for judicial review, the Federal Court may

(a) order a federal board, commission or other tribunal to do any act or thing it has unlawfully failed or refused to do or has unreasonably delayed in doing; or

(b) declare invalid or unlawful, or quash, set aside or set aside and refer back for determination in accordance with such directions as it considers to be appropriate, prohibit or restrain, a decision, order, act or proceeding of a federal board, commission or other tribunal.

(4) Grounds of review — The Federal Court may grant relief under subsection (3) if it is satisfied that the federal board, commission or other tribunal

(a) acted without jurisdiction, acted beyond its jurisdiction or refused to exercise its jurisdiction;

(b) failed to observe a principle of natural justice, procedural fairness or other procedure that it was required by law to observe;

(c) erred in law in making a decision or an order, whether or not the error appears on the face of the record;

(d) based its decision or order on an erroneous finding of fact that it made in a perverse or capricious manner or without regard for the material before it;

(e) acted, or failed to act, by reason of fraud or perjured evidence; or

(f) acted in any other way that was contrary to law.

(5) Defect in form or technical irregularity — If the sole ground for relief established on an application for judicial review is a defect in form or a technical irregularity, the Federal Court may

(a) refuse the relief if it finds that no substantial wrong or miscarriage of justice has occurred; and

(b) in the case of a defect in form or a technical irregularity in a decision or an order, make an order validating the decision or order, to have effect from any time and on any terms that it considers appropriate.

1990, c. 8, s. 5; 2002, c. 8, s. 27

Case Law

Section 18.1(1)

New Brunswick (Board of Management) v. Dunsmuir, [2008] 1 S.C.R. 190, 372 N.R. 1, 69 Admin. L.R. (4th) 1, 2008 C.L.L.C. 220-020, D.T.E. 2008T-223, 329 N.B.R. (2d) 1, 170 L.A.C. (4th) 1, 291 D.L.R. (4th) 577, 64 C.C.E.L. (3d) 1, 2008 CarswellNB 124, 2008 CarswellNB 125, 2008 SCC 9, (sub nom. *Dunsmuir v. New Brunswick)* [2008] S.C.J. No. 9 — The operation of three standards of review has not been without practical and theoretical difficulties, neither has it been free of criticism. One major problem lies in distinguishing between the patent unreasonableness standard and the reasonableness simpliciter standard. The difficulty in distinguishing between those standards contributes to the problem of choosing the right standard of review. An even greater problem lies in the application of the patent unreasonableness standard, which at times seems to require parties to accept an unreasonable decision.

Even if one could conceive of a situation in which a clearly or highly irrational decision were distinguishable from a merely irrational decision, it would be unpalatable to require parties to accept an irrational decision simply because, on a deferential standard, the irrationality of the decision is not clear enough. It is also inconsistent with the rule of law to retain an irrational decision. A simpler test is needed.

In judicial review, reasonableness is concerned mostly with the existence of justification, transparency and intelligibility within the decision-making process. But it is also concerned with whether the decision falls within a range of possible, acceptable outcomes which are defensible in respect of the facts and law. The move towards a single reasonableness standard does not pave the way for a more intrusive review by courts and does not represent a return to pre-*Southam* formalism. In this respect, the concept of deference, so central to judicial review in administrative law, has perhaps been insufficiently explored in the case law.

Deference is both an attitude of the court and a requirement of the law of judicial review. It does not mean that courts are subservient to the determinations of decision makers, or that courts must show blind reverence to their interpretations, or that they may be content to pay lip service to the concept of reasonableness review while in fact imposing their own view. Rather, deference imports respect for the decision-making process of adjudicative bodies with regard to both the facts and the law. The notion of deference "is rooted in part in a respect for governmental decisions to create administrative bodies with delegated powers." There are now only two standards, reasonableness and correctness. The process of judicial review involves two steps. First, courts ascertain whether the jurisprudence has already determined in a satisfactory manner the degree of deference to be accorded with regard to a particular category of question. Secondly, where the first inquiry proves unfruitful, courts must proceed to an analysis of the factors making it possible to identify the proper standard of review.

The existing approach to determining the appropriate standard of review has in the past commonly been referred to as "pragmatic and functional." In the future, it should simply be referred to as the "standard of review analysis." The analysis must be contextual. It is dependent on the application of a number of relevant factors, including: (1) the presence or absence of a privative clause; (2) the purpose of the tribunal as determined by interpretation of enabling legislation; (3) the nature of the question at issue; and (4) the expertise of the tribunal.

The existence of a privative or preclusive clause gives rise to a strong indication of review pursuant to the reasonableness standard. Where the question is one of fact, discretion or policy, as well as questions where the legal issues cannot be easily separated from the factual issues, a standard of reasonableness is appropriate. Where an administrative tribunal has developed particular expertise, a reasonableness test is applied. A question of law that is of "central importance to the legal system. . .and outside the. . .specialized area of expertise" of the administrative decision maker will always attract a correctness standard, while a question of law that does not rise to this level may be compatible with a reasonableness standard.

Thanabalasingham v. Canada (Minister of Citizenship & Immigration) (2006), 51 Imm. L.R. (3d) 1, , 263 D.L.R. (4th) 51, 345 N.R. 388, 2006 FCA 14, 2006 CarswellNat 25, 2006 CarswellNat 1416, [2006] F.C.J. No. 20 — This was an appeal by the Minister of Citizenship & Immigration from a decision of a Federal Court judge who granted an application for judicial review by the applicant to set aside the danger opinion given by the Minister's delegate. The judge granted the application on the ground that the delegate's assessment of risk was based solely on the evidence of country conditions in Sri Lanka and had no regard to the risk resulting from the applicant's personal circumstances, and that her reasons did not adequately explain why she accepted the material submitted by the Minister and rejected that favourable to the applicant. The judge certified the following question for appeal:

> When an applicant comes to the court without clean hands on an application for judicial review, should the court in determining whether to consider the merits of the application, consider the consequences that might befall the applicant if the application is not considered on its merits?

The Minister's principal concern was the judge's decision to hear and grant the application for judicial review in the face of an admission by the applicant during the IAD proceedings that he had knowingly made false representations in earlier proceedings to review his detention following his arrest in 2001.

The jurisprudence cited by the Minister does not support the proposition that, "where it appears that an applicant has not come to the court with clean hands, the court must initially determine whether in fact the party has unclean hands, and if that is proven, the court *must* refuse to hear or grant the application on its merits." Rather, the case law suggests that, if satisfied that an applicant has lied, or is otherwise guilty of misconduct, a reviewing court may dismiss the application without proceeding to determine the merits or, even though having found reviewable error, decline to grant relief.

In exercising its discretion, the court should attempt to strike a balance between, on the one hand, maintaining the integrity of, and preventing the abuse of, judicial and administrative processes, and, on the other, the public interest in ensuring the lawful conduct of government and the protection of fundamental human rights. The factors to be taken into account in this exercise include: the seriousness of the applicant's misconduct and the extent to which it undermines the proceeding in question; the need to deter others from similar conduct; the nature of the alleged administrative unlawfulness and the apparent strength of the case; the importance of the individual rights affected; and the likely impact upon the applicant if the administrative action impugned is allowed to stand.

These factors are not intended to be exhaustive, nor are they necessarily relevant in every case. While this discretion must be exercised on a judicial basis, an appellate court should not lightly interfere with a judge's exercise of the broad discretion afforded by public law proceedings and remedies.

In this case, the judge erred in the exercise of his discretion by failing to take into account the remedy provided to Mr. Thanabalasingham by his right to appeal to the IAD against his removal and the relevance of that appeal to an assessment of the consequences if the Minister's opinion stood. The appeal was allowed. The opinion of the Minister's delegate was restored. The consideration of the consequences of not determining the merits of an application for judicial review is within a judge's overall discretion with respect to the hearing of an application and the grant of relief.

Cross v. Canada (Minister of Citizenship & Immigration) (1996), 33 Imm. L.R. (2d) 251, 111 F.T.R. 304 — This was an application to review a decision of an immigration officer who arrested the applicant at the Vancouver pre-trial detention centre and removed him to the U.S. on the same date. The applicant, an American citizen, pleaded guilty to simple assault in the state of Vermont. Upon his release from the detention centre in that state, the applicant came to Canada. At this time, there was a warrant outstanding for the applicant in the state of Vermont. As well, the applicant was a prime suspect in a rape/murder investigation occurring in that state.

The issue of mootness is to be decided in two stages. The first stage requires consideration of whether a live controversy remains. The second stage applies if no live controversy remains. The court must then consider whether to exercise its discretion to hear the appeal, notwithstanding that it is moot. With respect to the second stage, there are three criteria for the exercise of the discretion to hear a matter. One, the existence of an adversarial context; two, the concern for judicial economy; and three, the need for the court to demonstrate a measure of awareness of its proper law-making function.

At the date of the hearing of this motion, the applicant was no longer under arrest by Canadian authorities. He had been freed and then immediately turned over to the U.S. authorities sometime earlier. The applicant's removal from Canada in no way altered his legal standing within Canada. There was therefore no live controversy in this matter. Further, there was no reason to believe that this was a case of a recurring nature. Accordingly, the court declined to hear the matter.

Sivaraj v. Canada (Minister of Citizenship & Immigration) (1996), 107 F.T.R. 64; affirmed 1996 CarswellNat 1040, [1996] F.C.J. No. 700 (C.A.) — The respondent was attempting to remove the applicant to Sri Lanka. The applicant applied for a stay of the execution of the removal order and the respondent took the position that the statement of claim, which the applicant had used to commence these proceedings, did not disclose a reasonable cause of action.

The applicants came to Canada from Sri Lanka. They unsuccessfully claimed refugee status with the result that removal orders were issued. The applicants then filed a statement of claim in order to obtain declaratory relief that the removal orders violated ss. 7 and 12 of the *Canadian Charter of Rights and Freedoms*, and that they contravened the *Geneva Conventions Act*.

The Minister's decision in determining the country of removal was, in fact, a decision made by a federal board, commission, or other tribunal within the meaning of s. 18, and is therefore subject to review under s. 18.1.

The applicants should not have proceeded by way of action to obtain declaratory relief under the *Charter*. The proper procedure was by way of application for judicial review. The court has often, under the rules of judicial review, examined the constitutionality under the *Charter* of decisions made by federal boards.

The court did, however, stay the execution of the removal orders, and to avoid a vacuum being created whereby the applicants would have no proceedings before the court, the court exercised its jurisdiction under rules 2 and 303 of the *Federal Court Rules* and presumed the proceedings to have been commenced as applications for judicial review.

Rodrigues v. Canada (Secretary of State) (1994), 82 F.T.R. 111 — Pedro Rodrigues came from Brazil to Canada and made a refugee claim in 1987. He was subsequently ordered excluded. His application for judicial review was dismissed. In July 1992, he married a Canadian citizen. John Rodrigues was born a little over a year later. In the spring of 1994, Immigration Canada advised that there were insufficient humanitarian and compassionate factors to intervene in a decision that Pedro Rodrigues must leave the country.

Pedro Rodrigues brought the present proceedings under s. 18.1 of the *Federal Court Act*. The infant son, John Rodrigues, was held to be a person directly affected under s. 18.1 of the *Federal Court Act* and, therefore, an order was issued that he be joined as a party and that the style of cause be amended to reflect the addition of Assis John Rodrigues, a minor through his litigation guardian, Assis Pedro Rodrigues.

Singh (R.) v. Canada (Secretary of State) (1994), 27 Imm. L.R. (2d) 176, (sub nom. *Singh c. Canada (Secrétaire d'Etat)*) 82 F.T.R. 68 — The applicant claimed refugee status in a false name. He later approached the Immigration Commission and properly identified himself and sought to have the commission amend his name on the documents that had already been placed in his file. The commission refused.

The decision refusing to amend documents in the applicant's file did not constitute a decision within the meaning of s. 18.1 of the *Federal Court Act* and, therefore, the court had no jurisdiction to consider an application for judicial review of that decision.

Chen v. Canada (Minister of Employment & Immigration) (1994), 76 F.T.R. 235 — The applicant sought to overturn a negative decision of the CRDD. The tribunal accepted the applicant's testimony as trustworthy. In the course of giving its reasons, the tribunal mis-identified the principal issue. The respondent urged that, despite this error, the conclusions of the tribunal were reasonable on the basis of the evidence before it and the decision as a whole was supportable.

The tribunal did err by not assessing the very basis claimed by the applicant as the grounds of his fear of persecution. While the evidence before the tribunal may be said to support the conclusion it reached, such an assessment is not for the court on an application for judicial review. Aside from procedural issues, the court, on a judicial review application, must be concerned with the decision rendered by the tribunal and the reasons expressed for its conclusion.

Section 10.1(2)

Canada (Attorney General) v. Hennelly (1999), 244 N.R. 399, 167 F.T.R. 158 (note), 1999 CarswellNat 967, [1999] F.C.J. No. 846 (C.A.) — The proper test for granting an extension of time is whether the applicant has demonstrated:

1. a continuing intention to pursue his or her application;
2. that the application has some merit;
3. that no prejudice to the respondent arises from the delay; and
4. that a reasonable explanation for delay exists.

Any determination of whether or not the applicant's explanation justifies the granting of the necessary extension of time will turn on the facts of each particular case.

Brar v. Canada (Minister of Citizenship & Immigration) (1997), 140 F.T.R. 163 — The applicant applied for permanent residence. The application was made in a self-employed category and his application was refused in January 1996. Counsel wrote to the visa officer in March 1996 asking for a review. Counsel wrote again in June, enclosing an affidavit from the applicant's cousin. In July 1996, the visa officer faxed a letter to counsel referring counsel to the refusal letter in January 1996. The July letter was a courtesy letter and did not constitute a decision as that phrase is employed in s. 18.1 of the *Federal Court Act.*

The *Immigration Act* makes no provision for reconsideration of decisions by a visa officer. There is, however, a clear provision for judicial review of alleged errors. On the concept of *functus officio* and its application to administrative tribunals, the court adopted the remarks of Sopinka J. in *Chandler v. The Association of Architects*, [1989] 2 S.C.R. 848 at p. 861. The application for judicial review was dismissed.

Chan v. Canada (Minister of Citizenship & Immigration), 1996 CarswellNat 1876, [1996] F.C.J. No. 1393 (T.D.) — The applicant sought to review a decision of a visa officer refusing the applicant's application for permanent residence. This application for judicial review raises an issue of timeliness. The decision was made on October 23, 1995. The applicant's counsel, instead of proceeding to commence a judicial review application, elected to seek reconsideration. There was no evidence of reconsideration by the respondent. The applicant filed its application for judicial review on February 19, 1996, without seeking an extension of time until three weeks after the respondent had served its motion to dismiss.

The applicant's attempt to provoke a reconsideration from the respondent could not result in extending the date of the refusal and, accordingly, the application for judicial review was dismissed as being untimely.

Soimu v. Canada (Secretary of State) (1994), 83 F.T.R. 285 — In a letter dated February 8, 1994, a visa officer refused the applicant's application for permanent residence. On February 14, 1994, counsel for the applicant wrote to the visa officer requesting that she review her decision. On April 20, 1994, the visa officer replied. The April 20 letter, on the facts of this particular case, constitutes a decision by the visa officer and the applicant had, therefore, 30 days pursuant to s. 18.1 of the *Federal Court Act*, to seek judicial review. The originating notice was filed on May 19, 1994, within 30 days. Accordingly, the respondent's motion to strike the applicant's originating notice of motion was dismissed.

The court pointed out that the procedural difficulty occasioned in these proceedings might have been avoided if the applicant had sought judicial review of the February 8, 1994, decision in a timely manner. This would not have precluded the applicant from seeking a review by the visa officer. Had the April 20 letter not resulted from a true review, but merely been a "courtesy response", the applicant might well have been out of time to seek judicial review of the February 8, 1994, decision.

Section 18.1(3)

Lin v. Canada (Minister of Citizenship & Immigration), 2001 CarswellNat 2957, 2001 FCT 1368 — This was an appeal from the decision of the Appeal Division to dismiss an appeal from the issuance of a departure order against the applicants. The applicants were admitted from Taiwan as entrepreneurs and were granted conditional visas. They did not comply with the conditions in their visas and the department commenced an inquiry at which an adjudicator found that the conditions had not been obeyed. The Appeal Division of the IRB dismissed their appeal. An appeal by a person holding a visa to the Appeal Division of the IRB is a hearing *de novo*. The Federal Court in this proceeding was reviewing the Appeal Board's decision. The court was not reviewing the administrative actions of the visa officer who interviewed the applicants for the purpose of determining whether they had complied with the terms and conditions of their visa. The court will only review errors which were allegedly committed by the Board. It will not review an alleged breach of procedural fairness by the immigration officer who interviewed the applicants.

Du v. Canada (Minister of Citizenship & Immigration) (2001), 15 Imm. L.R. (3d) 64, 2001 FCT 485, 2001 CarswellNat 945 — The applicant sought to review the rejection of his application for permanent residence. The applicant objected to the units that were awarded for personal suitability. The visa officer had concerns stemming from the applicant's work for the same employer and lack of experience in a competitive labour market. This flowed from her own perception of the applicant's employment record. The officer's concerns were not shared with the applicant and accordingly, the applicant was denied procedural fairness.

The respondent argued that, despite this error, it was inconceivable that the applicant would have obtained the additional units for personal suitability that were required.

Reviewing courts have been warned not to withhold relief for a breach of the duty of fairness on the basis put forward by the respondent because it is dangerous to speculate on what might have happened if a person had been allowed to present relevant evidence and because of the importance of the values which underlie the duty of fairness.

Mohamed v. Canada (Minister of Citizenship & Immigration) (2000), 10 Imm. L.R. (3d) 90, 195 F.T.R. 137, 2000 CarswellNat 2551 — This was an application for *mandamus* and the question was whether the delay in processing the applicant's application was so unreasonable as to justify the granting of relief.

Each application for *mandamus* turns upon its own facts. Prior jurisprudence is not particularly helpful except for the purpose of outlining the parameters within which the court has issued an order in the nature of *mandamus*, where it has found an unusual delay which has not been reasonably explained.

The conditions that have to be met for granting an order are:

1. The delay in question has been longer than the nature of the process required, *prima facie*;

2. The applicant and his counsel are not responsible for the delay; and

3. The authority responsible for the delay has not provided satisfactory justification.

Gwala v. Canada (Minister of Citizenship & Immigration), [1999] 3 F.C. 404, 3 Imm. L.R. (3d) 26, 68 C.R.R. (2d) 48, 242 N.R.173, 1999 CarswellNat 908, 1999 F.C.J. No. 792 (C.A.) — Senior immigration officers do not have the implied jurisdiction to decide questions of law. The Trial Division of the Federal Court has jurisdiction in judicial review proceedings to decide constitutional questions which a senior immigration officer could not entertain.

Vuong v. Canada (Minister of Citizenship & Immigration) (1998), 47 Imm. L.R. (2d) 129, 153 F.T.R. 207 — This was an application to review and set aside a decision of the Appeal Division wherein the applicant's appeal was dismissed for lack of jurisdiction. The applicant applied to sponsor his adopted daughter. In support of his application he obtained from the People's Committee of the Socialist Republic of Vietnam in the district where he formally resided and where the adoption took place, a document confirming that Xuan was his adopted daughter. The application for landing was refused on the grounds that there was no proof that Xuan was the legally adopted daughter of the applicant. Prior to the hearing before the Appeal Division, the applicant obtained further confirmation from the People's Court of the Socialist Republic of Vietnam that Xuan was his adopted daughter. Prior to the hearing of the appeal, the Minister had also made inquiries through the Canadian Embassy. The government of Vietnam replied that according to the present law of adoption, all adoptions were required to be approved by the People's Committee and recorded in the household register. Since the adoption of the applicant's daughter was not recorded in the household register, the Vietnamese government advised that it could not confirm that the child had been adopted. The Appeal Division determined that the daughter was not a member of the family class and dismissed the appeal for want of jurisdiction.

At the hearing, the Appeal Division had considered documentary evidence and it heard from four witnesses, one of whom was a former lawyer practicing in Vietnam between 1969 and 1975 in the area of public adoption. This witness made it quite clear that customary adoption was a usual and frequent practice among the Vietnamese people and that there was apparently a lax approach to making changes in the household registers. The panel of the Appeal Division found that the applicant's own attempts to have the register changed were genuine, but were thwarted by the nature of the administrative and bureaucratic processes.

The court allowed the appeal and noted that it was the law applicable at the time of the adoption that was relevant for the purpose of determining whether there had been a valid adoption. The court noted the uncontradicted evidence of the Vietnamese lawyer and then referred the matter back to a differently constituted panel of the Appeal Division with directions to find that Xuan was the adopted daughter and a member of the family class pursuant to s. 2 of the *Immigration Regulations*.

Alleti c. Canada (Ministre de la Citoyenneté & de l'Immigration) (1998), 147 F.T.R. 310 — The scope of the powers conferred on the court under para. 18.1(3)(b) of the *Federal Court Act* do not permit the court to issue a visa to the applicant. The court can set aside a visa officer's decision and refer the matter back for re-determination in accordance with certain directions. The court cannot issue specific and conclusive directions with respect to the decision a visa officer must make, unless the conclusion is simple, obvious and inescapable. The directions that the court is authorized to make will vary with the circumstances of each case. If facts remain to be established, it is the officer who must determine them. If the court finds an error in law, all the visa officer can do is to act accordingly when re-determining the matter.

Marquez v. Canada (Minister of Citizenship & Immigration) (1996), 32 Imm. L.R. (2d) 286 (Fed. T.D.) — The judge in this case reconsidered two of his own previous decisions and came to the conclusion that pursuant to s. 18.1(3) of the *Federal Court Act*, the court has jurisdiction, when allowing an application for judicial review, to provide directions for the decision maker who has to reconsider the matter, which directions may even be specific in relation to the ultimate outcome of the matter.

On the facts of this case, the court declined to refer the matter for reconsideration with directions that the tribunal determine the applicant to be a Convention refugee. The record was not so clearly conclusive that the only possible conclusion on reconsideration was that the applicant was a Convention refugee, nor was the sole issue one of law which left the ultimate outcome uncontroverted.

Turanskaya v. Canada (Minister of Citizenship & Immigration) (1995), 111 F.T.R. 314; affirmed (1997), 145 D.L.R. (4th) 259, 125 F.T.R. 240 (note), 210 N.R. 235 (C.A.) — The applicant was found by a panel of the CRDD to be a stateless person.

The respondent conceded that the Board had erred in law in requiring the applicant to demonstrate a well-founded fear of persecution in respect of both countries of former habitual residence.

The applicant had asked the court to refer the matter back to the Board, with a direction that it declare the applicant to be a Convention refugee.

There will sometimes be situations in which by giving specific directions, the court will be able to accomplish indirectly what it is not authorized to do directly. It will be able to compel the Board to reach a specific conclusion, thereby, in effect, substituting its decision for that made by the Board. Specific directions of this type are within the jurisdiction of the court.

The discretion to give directions should be exercised in the context of the Board's decision. The court should not go behind that decision on matters unrelated to the error brought forward on judicial review.

But for the error which caused the Board to require the applicant to demonstrate a well-founded fear in respect of both countries of former habitual residence, the Board would have declared the applicant to be a Convention refugee.

Accordingly, the court issued an order directing the Board to declare the applicant to be a Convention refugee.

Memarpour v. Canada (Minister of Citizenship & Immigration) (1995), 104 F.T.R. 55 — At the opening of the hearing of the applicant's refugee claim, the presiding Board member made a statement which indicated that certain evidence about events in Iran was accepted for purposes of the hearing. The Board then, in rendering its decision, made an adverse credibility finding in respect of those events. This was held to be a failure of natural justice. There is no general duty to confront a witness with issues of credibility. Such a requirement exists if credibility becomes an issue for the Board when it has previously been deleted by the Board as a relevant issue.

Having decided that there was a denial of a fair hearing, the court then must ask itself whether it is nonsensical and contrary to notions of finality and the effective use of public funds and the Board's resources to require a re-hearing. The court relied upon *Mobil Oil Canada Ltd. v. Canada-Newfoundland Offshore Petroleum Board*, [1994] 1 S.C.R. 202 at p. 205. In this case, the court concluded that even if the applicant were to be believed about the events in Iran which were the subject matter of the application, a panel of the IRB would certainly conclude that the applicant did not have a subjective fear of persecution. In those circumstances, the application was dismissed.

Efremov v. Canada (Minister of Citizenship & Immigration) (1995), 90 F.T.R. 259 — The applicant sought to quash a negative decision of a panel of the CRDD. In order to quash a decision it must be shown that the Board made an error which was material to the decision. The cumulative effect of a number of errors can also constitute a material error. A microscopic examination of the reasons for the decision is not appropriate. The word "patently" adds nothing to the applicable test. For a decision to be unreasonable it must be plain and obvious that it is so.

Argueta v. Canada (Minister of Employment & Immigration), 1994 CarswellNat 1582 (Fed. T.D.) — The applicant sought judicial review contending that the trier of fact had made three errors of law which warranted the setting aside of the decision. The respondent conceded that the law had been misstated or misapplied in two respects, but suggested that applying the law correctly would support the conclusion of the tribunal and, implicitly, that the same result would follow any reconsideration of the matter. In an application for judicial review, aside from procedural issues, the jurisdiction of the court is concerned with the decision as it has been rendered, not with a decision that might have been but was not given. The court may review the evidence before the tribunal only in relation to the decision rendered. It is not for the court to assess what its decision might be on the evidence before the tribunal nor to speculate on the result if the matter is referred back for reconsideration, the outcome of which will be dependent upon the evidence and argument then before the reconsidering tribunal.

Ali v. Canada (Minister of Employment & Immigration) (1994), 24 Imm. L.R. (2d) 289, 76 F.T.R. 182, [1994] 3 F.C. 73, 27 Admin. L.R. (2d) 110 — Section 18.1(3) of the *Federal Court Act* provides jurisdiction for the court to issue directions of such specificity that they require the CRDD to declare an applicant to be a Convention refugee.

The court should only exercise this jurisdiction after asking itself questions of this type:

1. Is the evidence on the record so clearly conclusive that the only possible conclusion is that the claimant is a Convention refugee?

2. Is the sole issue to be decided a pure question of law which will be dispositive of the case?

3. Is the legal issue based on uncontroverted evidence and accepted facts?

4. Is there a factual issue that involves conflicting evidence which is central to the claim?

Popov v. Canada (Minister of Employment & Immigration) (1994), 75 F.T.R. 90 — The applicant emigrated to Israel from Russia under the Law of Return. He was entitled to do so because one of his grandparents was Jewish. He suffered discrimination in Israel because he was a new immigrant from Russia and because, while he was Jewish as a matter of racial ancestry, he was a member of the Russian Orthodox Christian church. The applicant applied for refugee status in Canada. The CRDD did not accept his claim, but that decision was rendered before the Supreme Court decision in *Ward v. Canada (Minister of Employment & Immigration)*, (sub nom. *Canada (Attorney General) v. Ward*) [1993] 2 S.C.R. 689 and the Federal Court decision in *Zolfagharkhani v. Canada (Minister of Employment & Immigration)*, [1993] 3 F.C. 540 (C.A.).

The application was dismissed from the bench due to the fact that notwithstanding the errors complained of, no properly instructed Board could have found the applicant to be a Convention refugee. The authority of the court on a judicial review application is not the same as on an appeal. Even though one might find errors in a Board's decision, that does not, on a judicial review application, result in a decision to send the matter back for rehearing when the court is convinced that no real purpose will be served by so doing. One does not quash and send it back just for the sake of having a new hearing. When it is clear from the evidence on the record and from the decision that no different result could be reached, the appropriate course of action is to refuse an order requiring that such be done.

The court noted that the intertwined nature of "appeals" and "judicial review" was found in a recent paper by Madame Justice Desjardins: *Review of Administrative Action in the Federal Court of Canada: The New Style in a Pluralistic Setting*, Law Society of Upper Canada Special Lectures, 1992, at 404.

Xie v. Canada (Minister of Employment & Immigration) (1994), 75 F.T.R. 125 — The court's jurisdiction on applications for judicial review is found in s. 18.1(3) of the *Federal Court Act*. There is nothing in the subs. that indicates that the court has the jurisdiction to substitute its opinion for that of the tribunal whose decision is under judicial review and make the decision that the tribunal should have made. As such words do not appear in the Act, the court does not have jurisdiction to substitute its decision for that of the tribunal in a judicial review application.

The court does have jurisdiction to refer a matter back for redetermination in accordance with such directions as it considers appropriate. The court should only issue directions to a tribunal in the nature of a directed verdict where the case is straightforward and the decision of the court on the judicial review would be dispositive of the matter before the tribunal.

Section 18.1(4)

Kennedy v. Canada (Minister of Citizenship and Immigration), 2016 FC 628, 2016 CarswellNat 3665, 2016 CarswellNat 2299 — The applicant challenged a decision of an officer refusing to continue processing the applicant's permanent resident application under the spouse or common-law partner in Canada class. The applicant was sent, by email, instructions to submit a medical examination within 30 days. The request went unanswered as the email was redirected to the applicant's email spam folder. CIC sent the applicant a letter by email, which was not redirected to the applicant's spam folder, indicating that CIC would no longer continue to process the application for not having submitted the immigration medical examination. The case law surrounding issues of email miscommunication has developed into two lines of cases. Whether the two-prong test or the fault analysis approach is applied, the result is the same, i.e. the duty of procedural fairness is satisfied. If the two-prong test approach is applied, the first step is to determine whether the communication was sent to the applicant's email, which it was. The second step is to determine whether the email failed to deliver or bounced back, which it did not because the applicant received it. If the fault-based approach is applied, there must be evidence that the document was sent (and there is) and the rebuttable presumption that the applicant received the email is confirmed by the fact that the applicant admits to having received the email communication. In both cases, there is no breach of procedural fairness.

The responsibility of managing the applicant's spam filtering system obviously rests with applicant, particularly as email programs indicate that there are items in the spam folder. The evidence in this case was insufficient, or at least inconsistent, to demonstrate what actually happened to the email. There was no screen shot showing the email was in the spam folder or how the spam folder operated to filter out communications. There was also no explanation as to why the decision letter was not filtered out, while the email to the same address a few months earlier had been.

Procedural fairness concerning the transmission of emails entails that CIC should be "required to exhaust all reasonable mechanisms available on email programs to ensure receipt of their important transmissions." As unfortunate as it is for the applicant, in the last steps of his lengthy permanent resident application, to have his application refused as a result of email miscommunication, the facts remain that while CIC did not have a "send receipt" type of mechanism in place, this in of itself does not offset the fact that the communication was properly delivered by CIC and received by the applicant. That is the purpose of the receipt option. It does not cover what amounts to fault on the part of the applicant in failing to read his emails. The application was dismissed.

Yonten v. Canada (Minister of Citizenship and Immigration), 2016 FC 588, 2016 CarswellNat 1906, 2016 CarswellNat 2860 — The applicant sought judicial review of a decision that the applicant was inadmissible pursuant to para. 38(1)(a) of IRPA. The duty of procedural fairness requires that the visa officer provide an applicant with an opportunity to comment upon the medical officer's negative opinion. In failing to do so, the visa officer commits a reviewable error. In this case, the visa officer relied upon the medical officer's opinion which considered irrelevant factors and did not consider the totality of the medical evidence. The medical officer noted the possibility that the Meena Devi Jindal Medical Institute & Research Centre was engaged in money laundering, when concluding that the applicant suffered from tuberculosis. The fact that "not infrequently" clinics like the Meena Devi Jindal Medical Institute & Research Centre are created to "process black money" is irrelevant to the assessment of the admissibility of the applicant. The application for judicial review was allowed.

Naderika v. Canada (Minister of Citizenship and Immigration) (2015), 36 Imm. L.R. (4th) 248, 2015 FC 788, 2015 CarswellNat 2839, 2015 CarswellNat 4475 — The applicant sought judicial review of a decision to refuse his application for permanent residence. The applicant argued the officer breached his duty of procedural fairness by failing to give him an opportunity to address this officer's concerns regarding the lack of proof of his relative's residency before making a final decision. Procedural fairness requires that an applicant be provided with a meaningful opportunity to present the various types of evidence relevant to his or her case and to have it fully considered. However, in the context of a visa application, the duty of fairness does not require a visa officer to inform an applicant of concerns arising directly from the requirements of the legislation or Regulations and to give the applicant an opportunity to disabuse him or her of those concerns. In this case, the officer's concerns arose directly from the Regulations. Therefore, the officer did not have an obligation to inform the applicant that he had not received these documents. In this case, it could be reasonably inferred from the response from the applicant's consultant that the consultant intended to attach the updated documentation relating to the residency in Canada of the applicant's relative. The consultant's ability to produce these documents within a day or so of the refusal decision suggested that she had them on file. The interests of justice demanded that the court review the determination on the reconsideration request as part of the judicial review of the initial decision to refuse the application for permanent residence. No useful purpose would be served by requiring the applicant to file a separate application for judicial review and to bifurcate the proceedings, and it would be contrary to the interests of justice to do so.

While there is no obligation on an immigration officer to reconsider an application for permanent residence, the case law is clear that, on the basis of fairness and common sense, a visa officer should reconsider a file if, within days of a negative decision of an application that has been outstanding for a number of years, new evidence that confirms a material fact is presented. The updated evidence on the applicant's relative, even if it was considered as new evidence that was not before the officer at the time the initial decision was made, conclusively answered the concern that had led to the refusal. The documentation provided appears to be sufficient to allow the applicant to reach the required number of points, and neither efficiency nor practicality would be served by requiring the applicant to restart the process at that point, more than four years after he submitted the initial application. The officer's decision to refuse the request for reconsideration was unreasonable in the circumstances. The officer viewed his discretion too narrowly by refusing the request on the sole basis that the applicant's application had been considered on its substantive merits based on the information in the file at the time of the refusal decision. The application for judicial review was allowed.

Huang v. Canada (Minister of Citizenship and Immigration), 2015 FC 905, 2015 CarswellNat 3193, 2015 CarswellNat 5058 — The applicant sought judicial review of a decision of an officer to refuse the spousal sponsorship application on the basis that the applicant and her sponsor did not "share a level of financial and emotional interdependence expected of a genuinely married couple." The content of the duty of procedural fairness is ensuring that administrative decisions are made using a fair and open procedure, appropriate to the decision being made and its statutory, institutional, and social context, with an opportunity for those affected by the decision to put forward their views and evidence fully and have them considered by the decision maker. It makes sense to interview spouses separately where concerns arise about the genuineness of the marriage. However, that does not mean that applicants must also be denied knowledge of what their spouse said and not be afforded some opportunity to argue that the officer had misunderstood their statements. Once the spouses had been interviewed separately, there is no longer any danger of collusion. If an applicant or his or her spouse should try to retract any of their statements when confronted with inconsistencies, this could simply affect their credibility. A duty to confront the spouses with any inconsistencies would not be unduly onerous. In this case, had the applicant been confronted with the supposed inconsistencies, she might have been able to convince the officer that they were just misunderstandings. The application for judicial review was allowed.

Tisson v. Canada (Minister of Citizenship and Immigration) (2015), 38 Imm. L.R. (4th) 124, 2015 FC 944, 2015 CarswellNat 3380, 2015 CarswellNat 5062 — The applicant sought judicial review of the decision to refuse her request to apply for permanent residence from within Canada on humanitarian and compassionate grounds. Disclosure of information may be necessary to provide the affected party with a reasonable opportunity for meaningful participation in the decision-making process. When a decision maker unilaterally consults information found on the internet, and this could not have been reasonably anticipated, then fairness may require that the person affected by the decision be given an opportunity to challenge its relevance or validity. In this case, the record disclosed to the applicant and submitted to the court did not include the on-line photographs that were viewed by the officer. It was also unclear what inferences the officer drew from viewing them. Specifically, the officer had looked up the descriptions of the applicant's daughter's medical condition on Wikipedia and followed a few of the related links. These links showed a number of photos of children with varying degrees of the medical condition. Their appearances range from mildly abnormal to severely disfigured. Because the applicant's daughter was described by her doctor as "currently ... [appearing] to be mildly affected," the implication was that the on-line photographs contributed to the officer's conclusion that she may not "experience significant problems in St. Lucia" or require "surgical care" in the future.

The court concluded that the officer's reliance on the results of the internet search that were not disclosed to the applicant denied her the opportunity to address the information, and thereby breached her right to procedural fairness. The application for judicial review was allowed.

Karimi v. Canada (Minister of Citizenship and Immigration), 2015 FC 1163, 2015 CarswellNat 5106, 2015 CarswellNat 8979 — The applicant brought an application for judicial review of the decision of an immigration officer to refuse his request to re-open his application for permanent residence. His application had been refused due to the failure to provide information requested in an email message that was sent to his immigration consultant. The applicant says he never received the disputed email message. The Minister met the burden of establishing that the disputed email message was sent. However, the applicant successfully rebutted the presumption that the disputed message was received. Accordingly, the applicant was not given a sufficient opportunity to meet the requirements of his application for permanent residence and the Minister's refusal to re-open his file was unreasonable. The application for judicial review was allowed. In this case, CIC's own records were not consistent. The disputed email message did not appear in the outgoing correspondence screen of the GCMS notes, although three other messages with the same date were duly recorded. Only the CIC file notes confirmed that the fourth message had been sent. The Minister did not provide an explanation for this apparent inconsistency. The applicant had responded promptly to the three other requests that were sent to him and since there was nothing from the fourth email message to distinguish it from the others, nor any incentive for the applicant to wilfully disregard it, he successfully rebutted the presumption that it had been received. The application for judicial review was allowed.

Asoyan v. Canada (Minister of Citizenship and Immigration) (2015), 33 Imm. L.R. (4th) 122, 2015 FC 206, 2015 CarswellNat 352 — The applicant's application for permanent residence was refused on the basis that she had failed to provide the required document requested in an email on February 14, 2013, within the 30-day deadline. The applicant contacted the Embassy upon receiving the refusal and advised that she had never received notification or email from the Embassy of the requested documents. She pointed out that there had been a previous failure to receive CIC communications in relation to the acknowledgement of receipt and that she would logically not have contacted the Embassy on March 4, 2013, requesting an update on the status of her application had she received the February 14, 2013, email requesting the documents. The visa office refused to reopen the application.

Other Relevant Legislation

Since the applicant had inquired with the CIC Sydney on March 4, 2013, that she had not received an acknowledgement of receipt for her application and this fell within the 30-day time period fixed by the respondent requesting updated information, it is clear that the respondent had an indication that the February 14 email requesting documents had not been received. Accordingly, the risk of non-delivery shifted to the respondent. It thereby breached its duty of procedural fairness in refusing the application without making inquiries to ensure that the applicant had received its email requesting additional information.

The protocol of the respondent for communicating with applicants does not contain any requirement to include an acknowledgement of receipt of emails, although a simple and quick procedure is available for this purpose. The very high self-interest of the applicant who seeks permanent residency in Canada as soon as possible is such that if no acknowledgement is received within the time period allotted, the Minister is put on notice that its message likely did not arrive in the first place. At the minimum, therefore, a second attempt to send the email to the given address can be made. All other things considered, this should normally satisfy any requirement of the respondent to demonstrate reasonable attempts to communicate with the applicant. The application for judicial review was allowed.

Gebreselassie v. Canada (Minister of Citizenship and Immigration), 2015 FC 609, 2015 CarswellNat 1444, 2015 CarswellNat 2940 — The applicant challenged a decision of the Minister's delegate in which the officer refused the applicants' application for permanent residence as members of the family class. The principal applicant applied as the common-law partner of her sponsor. The application was rejected because the officer did not accept that the principal applicant had resided with her sponsor for the required one year and, therefore, was not the common-law partner of her sponsor. It was clear that the officer approached the evidence with a suspicious mind. There was no clear reasoning provided for not accepting the applicant's evidence at face value. Most importantly, there was no reason provided for rejecting the applicant's answer to the question of why her family would accept her and her partner to live together in the family home. Rather than accept the applicant's evidence, the officer depended upon an unverified understanding of the "cultural context." This finding constitutes an implausibility finding which is unsupported by any evidence on the record at the time the decision was made. It was incumbent on the officer to explain the source of the understanding so that its accuracy could be considered against the evidence supplied by the applicant. If the officer's understanding arose from experience, the details of that experience were required to be stated in the decision. The application for judicial review was allowed.

Ni v. Canada (Minister of Citizenship and Immigration) (2014), 29 Imm. L.R. (4th) 55, 2014 FC 725, 2014 CarswellNat 2932, 2014 CarswellNat 3364 — The applicant filed an online application for a post-graduation work permit ("PGWP"). The applicant encountered numerous difficulties and problems in paying the fee for her PGWP application but eventually payment was made and made within the time. The applicant called the CIC's call centre several times and initially was told there was a technical difficulty with the website. She subsequently called again and was told to pay the fees at a financial institution and simply send the fee receipt to CIC. Notwithstanding this, CIC rejected her application for a PGWP taking the position that while it recognizes several modalities of online and mail-in filings, CIC does not recognize an online filing followed by mailing an original fee receipt to CIC. There was no evidence that CIC's call centre at any time pointed out to the applicant that mailing in a fee receipt without a paper copy of the online application was not allowed and would be rejected. Once again, the applicant called the call centre to seek instructions regarding an application to restore her temporary resident status. CIC refused the application for restoration of temporary resident status, a work permit and a study permit, because the applicant had failed to apply within 90 days of issuance of notification that she had met the requirements for her course of study program, i.e. because she was late filing her request for a PGWP. The officer concluded the applicant was not restorable. Because the applicant was deemed no longer temporary resident status in Canada, the officer also refused her application for a PGWP.

The evidence before the court is that CIC encourages people to use its online services. It makes the point that lawyers and consultants are not necessary. CIC also encourages applicants to use the services of a call centre for whose actions CIC is responsible. There was no doubt that the applicant's online filing was made well within the 90 days after she received confirmation of her diploma, as required. It was also agreed that the applicant paid the required fee associated with the PGWP. It was further agreed that the applicant paid the required fee within the 90 days allowed after obtaining confirmation of her diploma. The court concluded that the applicant's PGWP application was tantamount to and therefore a legal filing and ought to have been accepted by CIC in the circumstances of the case — circumstances which were known and reported to CIC even though not alluded to in any fashion in its decision. CIC knew that the applicant had completed an online application. It never told her that she had to mail a paper copy of the application that she had already filed online, with the mailed-in fee receipt. Nor would that be a reasonable expectation given CIC already had the online application in its possession, filed previously and within the time. The failure of justice in this case arises solely from the applicant following CIC's instructions. Therefore, as between these two parties, responsibility must fall on the party who directed the erroneous course of conduct, which is in this case, the CIC through its call centre. The applicant cannot be required to suffer the loss of her PGWP, loss of temporary student resident status and her immediate removal from Canada, simply because she followed CIC's instructions even though those turned out to be incorrect. An application for judicial review was allowed.

Vakulenko v. Canada (Minister of Citizenship and Immigration), 2014 FC 667, 2014 CarswellNat 3274, 2014 CarswellNat 2506 — The sole issue for disposition was whether the duty of fairness owed to the applicant had been breached by the RPD in the treatment given to the concerns about the interpretation made available to the applicant at the hearing. The central issue was the credibility of the applicant. She was a woman aged 73 at the time of the application for judicial review. She came to Canada from her country of nationality, Russia, on a temporary resident visa. It was not completely clear what her purpose was in coming to Canada: one purpose was to attend a wedding; the other was an attempt to get away from an abusive partner and to live with her relatives in Canada. She eventually made an application based on ss. 96 and 97 of IRPA. It is from the refusal of the RPD to grant that application that judicial review is sought. The matter of the quality of interpretation was raised at the hearing by the applicant's granddaughter. A discussion ensued between counsel for the applicant and the RPD panel. The upshot of the discussion was that a "spot audit" would be done for the purpose of ascertaining the quality of the interpretation. Once it received the results of the spot audit, the RPD also chose to satisfy itself that the interpretation was adequate in the circumstances and proceeded to decide against the applicant without seeking observations or comments from her or her counsel. In other words, the RPD never shared with the applicant the results of the spot audit before making its decision on the merits, including findings on the credibility of the applicant. The issue is whether or not it was incumbent on the RPD to allow the applicant to comment on the results of the audit before a decision was to be made on the adequacy of the audit.

Persons affected by those decisions have the right to participate. Once the quality of the interpretation is considered sufficiently doubtful that an audit is ordered, the fairness of the process commands that it include the opportunity to comment on the results. If the duty to act fairly has been deficient, one never reaches the merits of the case which is reviewable on a reasonableness standard. As a result, the application for judicial review was granted.

Kaur v. Canada (Minister of Citizenship & Immigration), 2013 FC 1023, 2013 CarswellNat 3634, 2013 CarswellNat 3916 — The applicant sought judicial review of the finding of inadmissibility by reason of misrepresentation. The officer concluded that documents concerning the applicant's son were fraudulent. As a result, he concluded that the applicant was inadmissible. Procedural fairness was not afforded. Hence, the matter was readmitted to a different officer for redetermination. The record showed that there were other documents which supported the contention that the applicant's son was a student in university. The officer proceeded to send the letter advising the applicant of the finding of inadmissibility despite two requests for an extension of time. Efficient decision-making cannot alleviate the need to allow for representations to be made.

Jalota v. Canada (Minister of Citizenship & Immigration) (2013), 21 Imm. L.R. (4th) 114, 2013 FC 1176, 2013 CarswellNat 4607, 2013 CarswellNat 4239 — An application to restore the applicant's temporary resident status as a student was refused and he sought judicial review of that decision. The application was denied because the officer was not satisfied that the applicant was a genuine temporary resident and student, that the applicant had sufficient funds, that he would leave Canada at the end of the authorized study, and that the co-op component of his studies met some specified criteria.

The government's own checklist did not ask for any financial information *per se* as part of the restoration application, although it is listed as a requirement for study permit applications. The court held that if the government wished to have financial or other documents, it should have asked for them either in the checklist or by additional request. Any confusion in the checklist lies at the feet of the government and it is a further breach of procedural fairness to have a misleading document supplied to the public. This breach was particularly so where the applicant had confirmed his financial situation and informed the government that he was prepared to provide evidence if asked. It is incumbent on the respondent to state the reasons for loss of status in sufficient terms that an applicant can address those reasons in any further relief he may claim. The government's reliance on financial issues is a new-found basis, not the basis for the original loss of status which concerned whether he was a genuine student, and not that he had lacked sufficient funds. The applicant addressed the issue of his genuineness as a student in his restoration application. It was a further breach of procedural fairness to rely on a ground not cited in the original decision without giving the applicant notice that this ground of financial sustainability was now an issue. The government also put forward no basis for concluding that the applicant would not leave Canada. It is not sufficient to just run through the various grounds for denial of the application, as if checking off a list, without giving reasons for the conclusion. The application for judicial review was granted.

Nauman v. Canada (Minister of Citizenship & Immigration) (2013), 20 Imm. L.R. (4th) 1, 63 Admin. L.R. (5th) 237, 2013 FC 964, 2013 CarswellNat 3393, 2013 CarswellNat

3949 — This was an application for judicial review of a decision refusing the applicant's application for permanent residence in the Federal Skilled Worker category. The officer noted that he had concerns about the authenticity of the documentation from the applicant's employer. However, he did not send a fairness letter informing the applicant of this concern. In his refusal letter, he stated that the list of duties carried out did not demonstrate that the applicant had performed all of the essential duties and a substantial number of the main duties of the NOC.

While the application on its face may not have been sufficient to demonstrate that the applicant had performed all of the necessary tasks required, the visa officer's discretion to question whether the applicant's documents accurately describe an applicant's experience raises a duty of fairness upon his attribution of adverse inferences to the applicant regarding her creditability. The failure to question the applicant on the authenticity of her documents could have affected the decision. The application for judicial review was allowed.

Madadi v. Canada (Minister of Citizenship & Immigration), 2013 CarswellNat 2283, 2013 CarswellNat 2790, 2013 FC 716, [2013] F.C.J. No. 798 — The applicant held a Master's degree in civil engineering, and stated in his application for permanent residence under NOC 0711 "Construction Manager" that he had been working as a construction manager since September 2003. He was found not eligible for processing in the category. The letter from his current employer confirmed his title, salary, period of employment, projects worked on, and the duties he performed in this position. The officer rejected the letter stating that the duties described were either copied word for word or closely paraphrased from occupational descriptions of the NOC, diminishing the overall credibility of the employment letter.

Where an applicant provides evidence sufficient to establish that they meet the requirements of the Act or Regulations, as the case may be, and the officer doubts the "credibility, accuracy or genuine nature of the information provided" and wishes to deny the application based on those concerns, the duty of fairness is invoked. The officer erred in failing to put his or her concerns to the applicant. The decision was set aside.

Ansari v. Canada (Minister of Citizenship & Immigration), 2013 CarswellNat 2870, 2013 CarswellNat 3879, 2013 FC 849 — The officer found that the applicant did not have sufficient evidence that he had performed the actions described in the lead statement for the occupation and that he had performed all of the essential duties and a substantial number of the main duties. The refusal letter stated that the duties described in the employment letter submitted were "closely paraphrased from occupational descriptions of the NOC, diminishing the overall credibility of the employment letter." There is a need to determine whether the concern is about credibility or sufficiency before determining if a duty of procedural fairness is owed. If a concern about copying or paraphrasing from the NOC is characterised as related to credibility, without assessing whether it is in fact a credibility concern, the applicants who copy the NOC duties may come to expect an opportunity to provide further information or respond to the officer's concerns. This could lead to delays in processing FSW applications and is inconsistent with the instructions provided to applicants to provide all the relevant documents with their applications and to visa officers to assess the application as presented. The officer was entitled to give the evidence less weight, and as a result, the applicant did not meet the burden of providing sufficient information. There was no breach of procedural fairness.

Xuan v. Canada (Minister of Citizenship & Immigration), 2013 FC 92, 2013 CarswellNat 193, 2013 CarswellNat 372 — The applicant sought judicial review of a decision of an immigration officer denying an application for permanent residence under the "spouse in Canada" class. It is a requirement of this class that not only must an applicant be a spouse or common-law partner but they must cohabitate with the sponsor. The couple claimed to live in Markham, both prior to and subsequent to being married. More importantly, it was where they claimed to live together at the time of the home visit by CBSA officers. They had also bought a property in Stouffville in 2010. The CBSA officers visited the Markham house and the applicant let them in. They then questioned the applicant about her husband's clothes and personal hygiene/grooming supplies. Concluding that the answers were unsatisfactory and that she might be a flight risk, the applicant was arrested and held in detention for 11 days. The applicant was later interviewed by a different CBSA officer. There was no evidence that this was a "warrantless search," the applicant never objecting to the CBSA entering the premises. She showed them the location of clothes and of personal items. She never claimed to insist or ask for an interpreter and she responded to their questions. There was no breach of natural justice in respect to the home visit. It was legal, entry was consensual, responses were apparently voluntary and questions appeared to be understood. In terms of the test for "cohabitation," the term is not defined in the Regulations. There is no one controlled test or factor. Documents showing joint interest are consistent with marriage but not necessarily of cohabitation. The officer placed greater weight in what was observed or said at the home visit and in the home visit and solo interview of the applicant than in the answers given at the joint interview two months later. The choice to assign greater weight to the less prepared, extemporaneous evidence lies within the discretion of the officer. It is a reasonable choice given the nature of the inquiry which is to determine how a person lives not merely how they say they live. The officer's decision that cohabitation had not been established was reasonable.

Galyas v. Canada (Minister of Citizenship & Immigration) (2013), 50 Admin. L.R. (5th) 180, 2013 FC 250, 2013 CarswellNat 1927, 2013 CarswellNat 490 — The applicant sought judicial review of a decision of the Refugee Protection Division which refused the applicant's application to be deemed a Convention refugee or a person in need of protection under ss. 96 and 97 of the Act. The court considered whether there was a breach of natural justice due to the incompetence of the applicant's former counsel. The threshold for establishing breach of procedural fairness on the basis of incompetent counsel is very high. Incompetence will only constitute a breach of natural justice under extraordinary circumstances. It is generally recognized that if an applicant wishes to establish a breach of fairness on this ground, he or she must: (a) provide corroboration by giving notice to former counsel and providing them with an opportunity to respond; (b) establish that former counsel's act or omission constituted incompetence without the benefit and wisdom of hindsight; and (c) establish that the outcome would have been different but for the incompetence.

Former counsel disputed the evidence put forward by the applicant but the court found that there could be no dispute in the inadequacies that appear on the face of the applicant's PIF narrative which clearly support his allegation that he was left to prepare this important document by himself, without guidance on what it should contain and what the RPD would be looking for in such a narrative. Competent counsel would have known that the applicant's narrative does not comply with the expectations of the RPD and that it would be extremely detrimental to the applicant at the hearing. Anyone with experience before the RPD knows that it consistently and relentlessly draws negative credibility findings from a failure to include important incidents in the PIF and that, where an applicant is assisted by a lawyer, it will not accept a lack of knowledge as to what should be included in the PIF as a reasonable explanation. In that regard, the applicant's PIF is a negative credibility finding waiting to happen.

The evidence before the court was undisputed that the applicant was left to write his PIF on his own and that, after doing so, he was not advised that what he had written did not conform with the requirements set out in question 31 as to what should be in a PIF narrative. At least as regards the PIF, incompetent representation caused the RPD to find the applicant was not credible with regard to his fear of persecution in Hungary and that the result could very well have been different had the applicant been guided to prepare a PIF that met the expectations of the RPD. The application for judicial review was allowed.

Komolafe v. Canada (Minister of Citizenship & Immigration), 2013 FC 431, 2013 CarswellNat 1390, 2013 CarswellNat 1105 — The applicant sought judicial review of a decision to refuse his application for permanent residence under the federal skilled worker class as a driller and blaster, NOC 7372. Subsec. 75(2) of the Regulations describes a skilled worker as a foreign national who has performed the tasks described in the lead statement for the occupation as set out in the NOC descriptions and performed a substantial number of the main duties of the occupation, including all "essential" duties. The officer determined that the applicant did not provide evidence that he satisfied this requirement and was not eligible for further processing pursuant to subsec. 75(3) of the Regulations. The decision was a form letter merely stating that the officer was not satisfied that the applicant had performed the actions in the lead statement for the occupation or a substantial number of the main duties. The agent subsequently swore an affidavit for the judicial review stating that the applicant's evidence only demonstrated experience in two of the listed main duties. Although decision makers may supplement their reasons by way of an affidavit to provide an explanation for their notes made contemporaneous to the decision, in this case, the officer had no contemporaneous notes which describe her reasoning process. The affidavit, therefore, was inadmissible.

It is not for the court to determine whether the applicant had in fact performed the actions described in the lead statement and a substantial number of the main duties. The visa officer must do this with some line of reasoning which provides a basis for review. In this case, the decision provided no insight into the officer's reasoning process. The application for judicial review was granted.

Agama v. Canada (Minister of Citizenship & Immigration), 2013 FC 135, 2013 CarswellNat 195, 2013 CarswellNat 644 — The applicant was denied a permanent resident visa under the skilled worker class because her application fell outside the annual "cap" imposed by policy on this class. The applicant filed her application on November 14, 2011. On December 1, 2011, the website reported that the cap stood at 458. On January 13, 2012, the applicant was informed that her application was rejected because the cap of 500 applications for NOC 0631 had been reached. The applicant alleged that there had been a breach of the principles of fairness in failing to announce when the cap was reached, by leading the applicant to believe that the cap had not been reached, by creating a legitimate expectation that the cap was not reached and in failing to effectively implement the ministerial instructions.

The respondent indicates that there is a normal lag time before the cap numbers can be posted and that the website says that the figures provided are a guide only.

In applying the fairness principle, it is relevant in this case to look at the impact of the applicant's position vis-à-vis others. All those persons who filed after September 19, 2011, when the cap was reached, but before the applicant, would have just as legitimate a complaint as the applicant. Since they were prior in filing time, their applications would have priority over the applicant. Even if there was some basis for the applicant's position, it would not be equitable to grant relief without addressing the situation of these other applicants. The application for *mandamus* was dismissed.

Charles v. Canada (Minister of Citizenship & Immigration) (2011), 99 Imm. L.R. (3d) 310, 37 Admin. L.R. (5th) 8, 2011 FC 852, 2011 CarswellNat 2765, 2011 CarswellNat 3654 — While the Federal Court has recognized that right to counsel is not absolute (*Sandy v. Canada (Minister of Citizenship & Immigration)* (2011), 41 Imm. L.R. (3d) 123, at para. 50), at the hearing, the applicant testified that he was in the process of obtaining a Legal Aid certificate that would take approximately two weeks and that would result in allowing him the representation he clearly sought. The Board erred in not taking into account the timing of the hearing vis-à-vis his release from detention, together with the fact that this was the first time the applicant had requested the adjournment. The respondent was correct to note that the Board's decision with respect to granting post-ponements or adjournments is discretionary in nature and there is no presumption of enti-tlement. At the same time, however, as articulated in *Baker v. Canada (Minister of Citizenship & Immigration)*, [1999] 2 S.C.R. 817: "The values underlying the duty of procedural fairness relate to the principle that the individual or individuals affected should have the opportunity to present their case fully and fairly [. . .]." The application was granted and the matter returned to a differently constituted panel for the applicant to have the hearing with representation that he was denied.

Zhong v. Canada (Minister of Citizenship & Immigration) (2011), 100 Imm. L.R. (3d) 41, 2011 CarswellNat 3181, 2011 FC 980 — The applicant filed for permanent residence under the skilled worker program. The application included a positive arranged employ-ment opinion from Service Canada, confirming the offer of permanent employment from the owner of a firm in Oakville, Ontario. The consulate rejected the application based on the applicant's failure to meet the 67-point minimum required for success. The officer awarded no points to the applicant for his arranged employment, having found that the offer of employment was not genuine and that the applicant was not likely to accept and carry out his employment in Canada.

The decision is clear that the officer refused to consider as valid the applicant's offer of employment because of the adverse inference that she drew from the following three factors: the nature and size of the company does not justify the employer's hiring of the applicant; the employer is the firm's only company executive; and the employer operates his business through his cell phone and residential telephone.

The plurals used in the job description create a very different impression from the facts gathered by the officer concerning the actual business. It looks as though a considerable amount of exaggeration has taken place; the established facts about the business lead to a reasonable conclusion that the business does not require the applicant to perform all the duties set out in the list of job duties provided to the officer. The reasons are not exten-sive but they are adequate because they allow the applicant to see how and why the deci-sion was made and they also allow the court to assess their validity. The application for judicial review was dismissed.

Hadwani v. Canada (Minister of Citizenship & Immigration) (2011), 394 F.T.R. 156, 2 Imm. L.R. (4th) 53, 2011 FC 888, 2011 CarswellNat 2806, [2011] F.C.J. No. 1117 — The applicant sought to come to Canada as a permanent resident and was assessed 63 points, and did not meet the required 67 points. The essential issue turned on the award of

0 points in a category termed as "adaptability." The officer was not satisfied that the applicant had filed a government issued birth certificate in support of the otherwise satisfactory proof that the applicant had a nephew residing in Canada. The applicant had filed a document provided by a Pakistan hospital providing particulars of the birth of the nephew there. The officer apparently required a government-issued birth certificate but didn't tell the applicant or his representatives.

The checklist does not state that a government-issued birth certificate must be submitted in the case of a relative in Canada. It says documents "such as" a birth certificate must be submitted. The officer was clearly wrong in dismissing out of hand the hospital record as to the nephew's birth.

Molev v. Canada (Minister of Citizenship & Immigration) (2011), 6 Imm. L.R. (4th) 1, 2011 FC 1362, 2011 CarswellNat 4921, 2011 CarswellNat 5661 — The applicant's application for permanent residence under the federal investor program was refused on the basis of the applicant's perceived failure to prove a single fact in a highly complex evidentiary scenario. The key issue for determination was whether the visa officer was required to give the applicant a reasonable opportunity to establish that the evidence submitted proved the fact found to be so important. Under the Overseas Processing Manual OP9, an applicant must be given an opportunity to rebut the content of any negative provincial assessment that may influence the final decision. When the veracity of the documentation is in doubt, the officer should first request further documentation. In this case, the applicant's counsel requested an opportunity for the applicant to meet the visa officer's concern upon receipt of the officer's decision. However, this request was denied. The failure to resolve the doubt by following the guidelines constituted a breach in the duty of fairness owed to the applicant. The application for judicial review was allowed.

Garcia Rubio v. Canada (Minister of Citizenship & Immigration) (2011), 385 F.T.R. 284, 2011 FC 272, 2011 CarswellNat 1361, 2011 CarswellNat 630 — The applicant was a minor when his Canadian uncle applied to adopt him. However, he had become an adult by the time the Canadian adoption order was made. In a decision dated January 26, 2010, his subsequent application for citizenship was denied. An application for judicial review pursuant to s. 18.1 was allowed. There had been a failure of natural justice in that the reasons were wholly inadequate. They omitted two important facts. First, that the affidavit evidence showed that the applicant's uncle had paid for his schooling in Mexico since kindergarten and, second, that the uncle initially tried to adopt the applicant under Mexican law when he was aged 14. At that time, his parents had just been divorced. As well, the reasons do not explain the relevance of the conclusion that "the ties with your biological parents have not been severed." This is important because the legislation speaks of "legal ties" and they were clearly severed when the applicant's parents consented to the adoption. Finally, the six facts listed in the final paragraph of the reasons appear to be irrelevant. At a minimum, the decision should have included an explanation of their significance.

Elahi v. Canada (Minister of Citizenship & Immigration), 2011 FC 858, 2011 CarswellNat 2727 — The applicant applied to sponsor her spouse as a member of the family class. The visa officer was not satisfied that the marriage was genuine. The applicant appealed to the IAD. The IAD concluded that the applicant's marriage to her spouse was not *bona fide* and was entered into primarily for the purpose of her husband gaining permanent resident status under IRPA. The applicant sought judicial review of that decision. The Federal Court concluded that it does not follow that just because this applicant's spouse was looking to establish himself in Canada, that the couple's marriage was not genuine. The IAD erred in using the spouse's immigration history as a basis for finding a lack of *bona fides* of the marriage. In doing so, it failed to properly appreciate the distinction between what may traditionally constitute a "genuine marriage" in Canada and what may constitute a genuine marriage in other cultures.

Despite the fact that the IAD clearly considered the majority of the evidence before it, the applicant correctly pointed to pertinent evidence that was not mentioned in the decision under review. This evidence supports the applicant's position and could be considered to be contradictory evidence. As such, the court concluded that it was overlooked or ignored. Accordingly, the application for judicial review was allowed and remitted to a differently constituted panel of the IAD.

In oral argument, counsel for the applicant requested that if the matter were returned to the IAD that the court's reasons for judgment and judgment included direction that the IAD apply the conjunctive test as it was before the September 30, 2010, amendments of the Regulations. Fairness, the applicant argued, demanded that the law be applied as it was when the original decision was made. The respondent noted that if returned, the hearing before the IAD would be *de novo* and argued that the new, disjunctive test would apply as required under the current Regulations. There are no transitional provisions in the Regulations. The court agreed with the applicant after considering s. 43 of the *Interpretation Act*, R.S.C. 1985, c. I-21, which indicates that the repealing of a provision in whole or in part should not have an effect on any rights or privileges once they have begun to accrue. The court also relied on case law which stands for the principle that a person cannot be prejudiced by giving retroactive effect to new and additional requirements in a regulation. The court concluded that would be the effect of sending this matter back for reconsideration if the new disjunctive test were applied. When sending a matter back for redetermination, the Federal Court should not, except in the [clearest] of circumstances, direct the tribunal to reach a specific decision. Although acknowledging the limits of the court's ability to exercise its discretion in the applicant's favour, it was within the ambit of the court's powers to direct the IAD to apply the law as it read when the applicant initiated her appeal and it was first determined by the IAD. Not to do so would render the remedy which the applicant has obtained on this application in nullity and deny her natural justice.

Grewal v. Canada (Minister of Citizenship & Immigration), 2011 FC 167, 2011 CarswellNat 301, 2011 CarswellNat 1268 — The applicant sought judicial review of a decision to refuse her permanent residence application under the skilled worker class. The applicant had arranged employment in Canada as a retail trade manager, but the immigration officer was of the opinion that she would not be able to perform the required duties as she did not have sufficient language skills. Basically, the immigration officer assessed the applicant's IETLS scores to conclude on both language proficiency and arrange employment. While it was true that the applicant's IETLS test results were not sufficient for her to be awarded more points, there was evidence before the officer that the applicant was to undertake a second examination to better her results. Her poor results were allegedly caused by health reasons.

The applicant's statements and educational background could reasonably infer some knowledge of English. When this is considered with the claims of poor health when taking the IETLS test, it seems as though the immigration officer's decision to adjudicate the matter without a fairness letter or an interview is unreasonable, especially as the officer knew that a second IETLS test was to follow. Surely, procedural fairness called for further enquiry by the officer in such a case, through a letter or an interview.

It is clear that assessing the breadth of procedural fairness in a case must be adapted to the context in which it arises. In this case, where a manual provided clear guidance that more information should be sought, where one finding on language proficiency derailed the whole claim for permanent residence and where there was evidence that another test was to be taken, it seems that procedural fairness should have extended to an interview or a fairness letter. Immigration policy must be meaningfully addressed. The application for judicial review was granted and the matter sent for redetermination.

Noor v. Canada (Minister of Citizenship & Immigration), 2011 FC 308, 2011 CarswellNat 1699, 2011 CarswellNat 673 — The applicant's application for permanent residence was refused for insufficient points. The applicant noted that if he had been able to prove that his sister resided in Canada he would have received five points in the adaptability category. This would have brought his total to 69 points and he would have been eligible to receive permanent residence. On an unspecified date in April 2009, following the applicant having filed his application for permanent residence, a new visa office-specific instructions package was posted on the internet. This included the new requirements for proving that a close relative was residing in Canada. The applicant had not been aware of the changes of the documentation requirements and pointed this out in his request for reconsideration.

It was clear to the visa officer that the applicant was using the older kit, which had recently been changed, yet he was afforded no opportunity to rectify this simple error. Furthermore, the respondent was incorrect in stating that the applicant was specifically advised to use the new kit. The letter sent to the applicant simply directed him to the CIC website for "Visa office — specific forms and a list of supporting documents required by the visa office." There was no specific indication at all that these requirements had changed. Even a low duty of fairness, in the specific circumstances of this case, required the visa officer to consider the new documents. The application for judicial review was allowed.

Patel v. Canada (Minister of Citizenship & Immigration), 2011 FC 571, 2011 CarswellNat 1657, 2011 CarswellNat 3016 — The case law specifies that a visa officer is not under a duty to inform an applicant about any concerns regarding the application which arise directly from the requirements of the legislation or regulations. However, a visa officer is obligated to inform an applicant of any concerns related to the veracity of the documents and will be required to make further inquiries. The onus is always on the principal applicant to satisfy the visa officer of all parts of his application. The officer is under no obligation to ask for additional information where the principal applicant's material is insufficient.

In this case, if the visa officer was concerned only that the employment letter was insufficient proof that the principal applicant met the requirements of Regulation 75, then the visa officer would not have been required to conduct an interview. However, in this case the officer states that her concern is that the duties in the employment letter have been copied directly from the NOC description and that the duties in the experience letter are identical to the letter of employment. The officer's reasons were inadequate to explain why this was problematic. The court concluded that the implication from these concerns is that the officer considered the experience letter to be fraudulent. Consequently, by viewing the letter as fraudulent, the officer ought to have convoked an interview of the principal applicant based on the jurisprudence. As such, the officer denied the principal applicant procedural fairness and the judicial review must be allowed.

Yazdani v. Canada (Minister of Citizenship & Immigration) (2010), 92 Imm. L.R. (3d) 97, 324 D.L.R. (4th) 552, 14 Admin. L.R. (5th) 74, 374 F.T.R. 149 (Eng.), 2010 FC 885, 2010 CarswellNat 3204, 2010 CarswellNat 3631 — The court considered who bears the risk when email notices are sent by a reviewing visa officer but are not received by the applicant's agent who has exercised due diligence. In the case at hand, there had been no prior successful email transmission between the Warsaw visa office and the consultant's office. Nor did the [CIC] Protocol or Email Communications contemplate and provide safeguard measures for email transmission failures (such as alternate follow-up by mailing the letter). Finally, the visa application system does not provide for reconsideration in such circumstances. The respondent chose to send an important and crucial notice to the applicant via email without safeguards in place. The respondent therefore bears the risk of an email transmission failure when it sent the crucial request to the applicant. The application for judicial review was allowed.

Alavi v. Canada (Minister of Citizenship & Immigration) (2010), 92 Imm. L.R. (3d) 170, 2010 FC 969, 2010 CarswellNat 3633 — The court quashed the refusal of the applicant's application which was based on a failure to supply information requested in a communication which the applicant's representative, in affidavit evidence, said was never received and because the respondent Minister did not put proper evidence before the court that the communication was sent. The so called "risk" involved in a failure of communication is to be borne by the Minister if it cannot be proved that the communication in question was sent by the Minister's officials. However, once the Minister proves that the communication was sent, the applicant bears the risk involved in a failure to receive the communication.

Baybazarov v. Canada (Minister of Citizenship & Immigration), 2010 FC 665, 2010 CarswellNat 2427, 2010 CarswellNat 2428 — The applicant applied in the investor category after a positive selection as a Prince Edward Island Provincial Nominee. The visa officer determined the applicant inadmissible under s. 37(1)(b) of IRPA on grounds of engaging, in the context of transnational crime, in activity such as money laundering. The officer relied on a document classified as "secret," from the Canadian Border Services Agency's Organized Crime Section, and a report from the Financial Transactions and Reports Analysis Centre of Canada citing suspicious financial activity relating to the applicant, his business partner in Canada and their corporation.

The CBSA report is an instrument of advocacy. The CBSA report discloses a number of serious allegations in considerable detail. The allegations appear to tie the applicant or his publishing company to known organized crime figures. Because of the officer's admitted reliance on the CBSA report, and the officer's suspicions of the applicant's employment income, the CBSA report ought to have been disclosed in the fairness letter. Without this disclosure, the applicant had no way of meaningfully responding to concerns that his source of income was illegitimate. The officer breached procedural fairness. The application for judicial review was allowed.

Sandhu v. Canada (Minister of Citizenship & Immigration) (2010), 90 Imm. L.R. (3d) 301, 371 F.T.R. 239, 2010 FC 759, 2010 CarswellNat 3100, 2010 CarswellNat 2412 — A visa officer refused the applicant's application for permanent residence as a skilled worker on the basis that she did not meet the requirements of s. 75(2) of the Regulations because a Banking Clerk (NOC 1434) does not meet the requirement for assessment as it is not listed in Skilled Type O, or Skill Level A or B of the National Occupational Classification matrix, and her documentation does not satisfactorily demonstrate that she has performed the main duties of a Secretary (NOC 1241) and/or a Loan Officer (NOC 1232). Consequently, the officer concluded that she was not performing the duties of an occupation in the Skill Level B, as opposed to an occupation in the Skill Level C such as a General Office Clerk.

The visa officer did not identify a basis for her assumption that a small business enterprise does not require a dedicated secretary. A review of the documentation suggests otherwise in this case. The applicant is highly educated, receives a regular salary and it is the employer who confirms travel and training responsibilities. Where the application is adequate, but the officer nevertheless entertains a doubt on the evidence, there remains a duty to clarify the information with the applicant. When a visa officer has a doubt which has no foundation in the facts and the applicant puts her best foot forward by submitting a complete application, the officer should seek clarification to either substantiate or eliminate the doubt. Without seeking clarification, the officer was in no position to do either. The application for judicial review was granted.

Nazir v. Canada (Citizenship & Immigration) (2010), 89 Imm. L.R. (3d) 131, 369 F.T.R. 77 (Eng.), 2010 FC 553, 2010 CarswellNat 2246, 2010 CarswellNat 1421, [2010] F.C.J. No. 655 — A visa officer found that the applicant did not meet the requirements for a work permit as a live-in caregiver pursuant to s. 112 of IRPA. The applicant argued that the visa officer failed to provide her with an opportunity to address concerns relating to the job being offered. The applicant explained that the sole concern expressed by the visa officer during the interview had to do with her future employer's financial capability to hire her. According to the applicant, the visa officer never expressed any concern regarding the genuineness of the offer nor of the applicant's intention to take up the job offer.

The only appropriately introduced evidence in regard to what happened during the interview was the affidavit of the applicant, since there was no affidavit by the visa officer attesting to the truth of the content of the CAIPS notes. In such cases, the jurisprudence is clearly to the effect that CAIPS notes entered by an officer following an interview can be part of the record but do not prove what happened during the interview. Since the applicant filed an affidavit, upon which she was cross-examined, explaining what happened during the interview, it is her version that must prevail.

Abbasi v. Canada (Minister of Citizenship & Immigration) (2010), 88 Imm. L.R. (3d) 174, 2010 FC 288, 2010 CarswellNat 1675, 2010 CarswellNat 560 — The applicant challenged a refusal of a visa officer to grant him a permanent resident visa as a member of the family class. The applicant was a Pakistan national being sponsored for landing in Canada by his wife. The refusal of the sponsorship application was based on the finding that the marriage was not genuine. Two grounds were advanced for setting aside the visa officer's decision: the finding that the marriage is not genuine is unreasonable; and that the process applied to reaching the decision offends the *Official Languages Act*, R.S.C. 1985, c. 31 (4th Supp.), because the visa officer's interview of the applicant was conducted in Urdu.

The circumstances of the marriage were unusual which, not surprisingly, raised suspicion. But the unusual circumstances should give cause for very careful consideration. A marriage is a union between two individuals, and where suspicion exists as to the genuineness of the union because an expected standard of conduct is not met, to fairly and properly deal with the suspicion, the evidence of each individual must be carefully considered. There is no evidence on the record that the visa officer provided the applicant's spouse with an opportunity to give her evidence with respect to the quality of the marriage before the decision under review was made. In a case such as this, the visa officer was required to interview both the applicant and his spouse by the best means available whether by teleconference, video conference, or personal interview. The decision under review was unreasonable.

In this case there was no breach of the *Official Languages Act*. The interview was conducted in Urdu at the applicant's request. This choice was confirmed by the visa officer at the opening of the interview. No interpreter was required as the visa officer was fluent in this language. The applicant argued that as a matter of law the visa officer was required to conduct the interview in either English or French through an interpreter who could interpret the visa officer's questions to the applicant in Urdu and his answers back in English or French to the visa officer.

Section 20(1) of the *Charter* provides a right to any member of the public in Canada to communicate with and receive available services from federal institutions in English and French. This right imposes an obligation and practical requirement on federal institutions to comply with the right. This rights based concept does not inhibit federal institutions to offer services in languages other than English or French if the members of the public involved do not wish to exercise their right under s. 20(1) of the *Charter*, and, indeed wish to conduct business in any other language to which the institution's officials are capable of reliably communicating without an interpreter. This point was made by Justice Pinard in *Toma v. Canada (Minister of Citizenships & Immigration)* (2006), 295 F.T.R. 158 (Eng.) (F.C.) at paragraph 33 where a visa officer conducted an interview in Arabic without an interpreter:

> If the officer speaks the applicant's language — as was the case here — it would be strange indeed for the officer to use an interpreter. There would be no need to do so. The preferable options, as the Manual suggests [Overseas Processing Manual (OP) 5], is to conduct the interview in the applicant's language.

The application for judicial review was allowed on the first ground.

Zhong v. Canada (Minister of Citizenship & Immigration) (2009), 350 F.T.R. 43 (Eng.), 2009 FC 632, 2009 CarswellNat 1867 — This application exposes a fundamental fault in the refugee claim process applied at the time the applicant made his initial statements claiming refugee protection. The initial interview was conducted through a Cantonese interpreter. The applicant gave his statements in Cantonese which were in turn given in English by the interpreter and written in English by the interviewing officer. No independent means, such as a recording, was used to verify what was said by either the applicant or the interpreter, or whether the interviewing officer's writing accurately recorded what the Cantonese interpreter said. This "Record of Examination" is the centre of a fundamental controversy in the present application. Following the preparation of the Personal Information Form (PIF) by the applicant with the help of legal counsel, the Record of Examination was made available to the applicant and his counsel. The applicant immediately asserted to his counsel that the Record of Examination did not correctly record what he said in the interview, and, as a result, counsel for the applicant made this known to the Refugee Protection Division well in advance of the hearing. Nevertheless, the RPD Member who conducted the hearing chose to use the Record of Examination as accurate and relied on the statements made in it to find contradictions between it and the PIF and oral evidence produced at the hearing. This process resulted in a negative credibility finding made against the applicant. This process constituted a breach of due process.

In the absence of a verifiable record of what was said by the applicant at his interview, it is a breach of due process for the RPD to have accepted the Record of Examination as accurate in the face of the applicant's sworn statement that it was not accurate. The Record of Examination is the result of a fundamentally flawed record keeping process and should not be used with respect to the applicant's claim for refugee protection. The application for judicial review was allowed. Counsel for the respondents requested a question for certification, however, the applicant objected and the court agreed that the finding of breach of due process in the present case was based on the facts.

Kamtasingh v. Canada (Minister of Citizenship & Immigration) (2010), 87 Imm. L.R. (3d) 118, 2010 FC 45, 2010 CarswellNat 801, 2010 CarswellNat 101 — This was an application for judicial review challenging a decision of the Immigration Appeal Division which determined the applicant's marriage was not genuine. The applicant states that the IAD member denied him procedural fairness by preventing him from calling all of his proposed witnesses.

The IAD has the right to limit repetitive testimony, but not by effectively excluding witnesses who could offer evidence going to the central issues of the case. The place to control excessive or repetitive evidence on issues of controversy which are central or determinative is generally not at the entrance to the witness box, but once the witness is testifying — and even then the member must grant some latitude to ensure that all important matters are covered. The IAD can, of course, limit the scope of evidence by stipulating certain points that are not in dispute. In a case like this one where the credibility of the applicant is clearly an issue and where the genuineness of a marriage is in doubt, the evidence of immediate family and close acquaintances is highly relevant and should be heard without reservation. Indeed, it was difficult to see how this matter could be fairly determined after only two hours of evidence, particularly when the applicant was self-represented and was initially intending to lead evidence from several witnesses. This was a situation where the duty to allow the applicant to fully present his case was sacrificed for the desire for administrative efficiency. That is not a permissible trade-off. The application for judicial review was allowed.

Khan v. Canada (Minister of Citizenship & Immigration) (2009), 88 Imm. L.R. (3d) 61, 2009 FC 1312, 2009 CarswellNat 5532, 2009 CarswellNat 4569 — The applicant applied for a permanent resident visa as a federal skilled worker. He only listed English, and professed no proficiency in French. The application needed to be accompanied by test results by an accredited language institution or by other evidence in writing of the applicant's proficiency in his selected language. The High Commission requested further documentation and strongly advised the applicant to provide the International English Language Testing System (IELTS) test results. The applicant was unable to secure a seat for the exam until February 2009. He requested a 60-day extension, through his consultant, to supply the IELTS test results. The CAIPS notes reflect the request but do not state if the consultant gave a reason for the request. The refusal to grant an extension of time was unreasonable. Administrative efficiency is important, and necessary. The underlying consideration on an application to extend time is that justice be done. Consideration should be given to the reason for the requested delay and whether there is an arguable case on the merits. Certainly the applicant had a continuing intention to pursue his application, his application had some merit, there was no prejudice to the Minister arising from the delay and a reasonable explanation existed. Thus the decision arises from procedural unfairness, upon which no deference is owed. However, in any event, the decision on the merits not to award any points for English language ability was also unreasonable. The applicant obtained both an undergraduate degree and a Masters of Administration in England, and had worked in Dubai for a number of years in English. The Regulation does not require an IELTS report and so the visa officer failed to discharge his duty by not accessing the material which was on hand. Not only did the applicant study in the UK, he was awarded 25 out of 25 points for education. It was "ludicrous" to suggest that someone who has obtained both an undergraduate and a Master's degree in England from an English language university has no ability in the English language. The application for judicial review was allowed.

Zhang v. Canada (Minister of Citizenship & Immigration) (2010), 89 Imm. L.R. (3d) 75, 2010 FC 75, 2010 CarswellNat 118 — The question for determination was whether the applicant had created a reasonable expectation that important written communication would only be conducted by regular mail. Although the language of the visa application form and the use of representative form could be more clear with respect to the potential use of e-mail communication, when those documents are considered together, no reasonable expectation could arise that the Embassy would not use e-mail to communicate with the applicant's lawyer; even if such an expectation could arise it was surely displaced when the lawyer received an e-mail from the Embassy and did nothing about it at the time. The application for judicial review was dismissed.

Kaur v. Canada (Minister of Citizenship & Immigration), 2009 CarswellNat 4918, 2009 FC 935, 2009 CarswellNat 3870, [2009] F.C.J. No. 1530 — This application for judicial review challenges a decision to refuse the applicant's request for a skilled worker visa. The applicant failed to provide additional evidence to support the application as requested by the Canadian High Commission because of an apparent failed communication between them.

The assumption that the High Commission would continue to communicate by regular mail was, as the facts attest, a dangerous one. It was not reasonable to expect the High Commission to figure out from the absence of an e-mail address on the last communication that his e-mail was no longer functioning. This was a risk which the applicant and her Canadian representative could have avoided by the simple step of advising the High Commission that the previously identified e-mail address was no longer valid, just as the representative had done for his postal address. E-mail is, after all, a standard method of business communication. It is fast, efficient and reliable and it is not unreasonable or unfair for the High Commission to have relied upon it. In these circumstances the failed e-mail delivery was solely caused by the representative's unwarranted assumption and by the failure to provide complete and accurate contact information to the High Commission.

In summary, when a communication is correctly sent by a visa officer to an address (e-mail or otherwise) that has been provided by an applicant which has not been revoked or revised and where there has been no indication received that the communication may have failed, the risk of non-delivery rests with the applicant and not with the respondent.

Sebahtu v. Canada (Minister of Citizenship & Immigration), 2010 FC 200, 2010 CarswellNat 1136, 2010 CarswellNat 408 — This was a judicial review of a decision denying the applicant a permanent resident's visa on the grounds that she was a security risk pursuant to s. 34(1)(f) of IRPA. The applicant was already a UN Convention refugee living in Sudan having fled Ethiopia with her family. Her husband was a member of the

Ethiopian Democratic Union (EDU), a group which had fought against the Derg regime in the 1970s. The applicant had a UN form filled out — she being illiterate — which indicated that she had fled Ethiopia in 1977 and her husband in 1978. The form also indicated that she had been a member of the EDU, had participated in meetings and made financial contributions. The applicant contended that she was never a member of the EDU but had merely supported her husband. The visa officer held that the applicant was not forthcoming about her EDU membership and therefore denied her application.

It is within the purview of a visa officer to make a credibility finding but the reasons for that decision must disclose, even in a summary way, the basis for the adverse findings. This is an issue which goes to the fairness of the process and the reasonableness of the result. The second difficulty in this case was the fairness of the process particularly as regards to the translation of her narrative. On the balance of probabilities, there was confusion in the translation — not the fault of either party. Nevertheless it resulted in an unfair process and an unfairness which had serious consequences. The application for judicial review was allowed.

Healey v. Canada (Minister of Citizenship & Immigration) (2009), 80 Imm. L.R. (3d) 138, 2009 CarswellNat 891, 2009 FC 355 — This was an application for judicial review of a decision of a visa officer refusing the applicant's application for permanent residence under the federal skilled worker category. There was an error made on the applicant's application in that two years of college were not accurately indicated in the educational history boxes on the application form. The applicant accidentally wrote "0" instead of "2" in the box labeled "University/College." The officer concluded that the applicant had only completed 13 years of education, and 15 points was appropriate. Counsel for the applicant attempted to clarify the mistake but received no response.

It was not possible to tell from the record why the officer felt the applicant only had 13 years of education, and the fact that the officer had recently provided a detailed affidavit justifying his calculations is a clear confirmation that the letter and CAIPS notes do not explain that issue. The officer's affidavit was given no weight by the court as it went well beyond an elaboration of the reasons and instead provided an after-the-fact rationale for the central issue in this application concerning the way that the points were calculated.

In all the circumstances of this case, the reasons were inadequate. This was a decision of importance for the applicant's future. He could not surmise from the decision why the Thurrock and BTEC certificates had been awarded 0 points. The officer's position was simply that he had no obligation to explain to the applicant why he had taken a position on the facts that the two certificates in question would not be credited. This prevented any understanding or questioning of the officer's position on the facts. It was a denial of the applicant's right to comprehend why he had been refused and an attempt to thwart any action he might take to question the officer's decision. It left him to choose between incomprehension and legal action. In fairness to the applicant, he should have the matter reviewed by someone else who will explain to him what his certificates represent and how they merit, or do not merit, points under the Regulations. A simple explanation by the officer could have prevented what became a significant waste of time and resources on both sides. The application for judicial review was allowed.

Tantash v. Canada (Minister of Citizenship & Immigration), 2008 CarswellNat 1366, 2008 FC 565 — The applicant sought judicial review of a decision to refuse his application for permanent residence in Canada under the economic skilled workers class, on the ground that he had not submitted the requested documents and was therefore inadmissible. Although the applicant made a request for an extension of time to submit an FBI clearance, at no time did the applicant attempt to provide the officer with reasons for the lengthy wait in providing the FBI clearance, nor did he provide her with any timeframe in which he anticipated receiving the documents.

The refusal resulted from the applicant's failure to provide the officer with the evidence and documents that were reasonably required. Reasonable timeframes must be respected in order to allow that applications be processed in an expeditious manner. Therefore, the officer's decision to refuse the application and refuse any further extension of time was free of any breach of procedural fairness or natural justice.

Level (Litigation Guardian of) v. Canada (Minister of Public Safety & Emergency Preparedness) (2008), 71 Imm. L.R. (3d) 52, 2008 CarswellNat 423, 2008 FC 227 — This was an application for judicial review of an enforcement officer's decision to deny the applicant's request for a deferral of removal pending a decision on his application for permanent residence based on an H&C application.

An enforcement officer is statutorily bound to remove an applicant as soon as reasonably practical. However, if the officer relies on extrinsic evidence not brought forward by the applicant, the applicant must be given an opportunity to respond to that evidence. This is a minimal duty of procedural fairness. In the application at bar, the enforcement officer relied on detailed evidence about medical conditions in Jamaica that the applicant contested in an affidavit filed in support of the applicant's successful motion for a stay of removal. With respect to tight timeframes, the applicant has been in Canada for 20 years, and the duty of fairness should not be sacrificed because of an artificial deadline established by the respondent for the applicant's removal. There is no harm in allowing the applicant another week or two in order to respond to extrinsic evidence upon which the enforcement officer intends to rely. If that extrinsic evidence is incorrect, the applicant will suffer great harm. The application for judicial review was allowed.

Thandal v. Canada (Minister of Citizenship & Immigration), 2008 CarswellNat 1085, 2008 CarswellNat 1958, 2008 FC 489 — The applicant sought judicial review of a decision to refuse her application for permanent residence as a skilled worker and her H&C application from outside Canada. With the Supreme Court of Canada's decision in *New Brunswick (Board of Management) v. Dunsmuir*, 2008 SCC 9, it is settled that procedural fairness is to be reviewed on a correctness standard while the H&C decision is to be reviewed on a reasonableness standard. The reasonableness standard admits a range of reasonable outcomes. The court was aware that an H&C decision is discretionary, an exception to the normal rules. The officer, by virtue of familiarity and having interviewed the applicant, was in an excellent position to assess the merits of the applicant's story.

It is well established that an applicant has the burden of establishing her case. Generally, an applicant is to do that once, rather than on the basis of some sort of rolling story of reply, sur-reply and so forth. The applicant had an interview at which all the relevant issues were canvassed. There is nothing unfair in the officer deciding the case on the evidence as provided by the applicant at that time. The judicial review was dismissed.

Zheng v. Canada (Minister of Citizenship & Immigration), 2008 CarswellNat 1864, 2008 CarswellNat 880, 2008 FC 430 — A visa officer rejected an application for landing by a skilled worker from China. The visa officer's entry in the CAIPS system identifies a stark conflict in the evidence the applicant tendered in obvious error: the standard application form was completed to say that the applicant attended Kunming University at the same time she completed high school there, which, of course, is impossible. Because of the conflict, and the fact that the applicant failed to file a diploma to prove her attendance at the university, the applicant's application was rejected. It was remarkably unfair for the visa officer not to have asked for clarification of the obvious error which drove the rejection of the applicant's application. The visa officer's decision was set aside.

Chadha v. Canada (Minister of Citizenship & Immigration), 2008 CarswellNat 294, 2008 CarswellNat 1119, 2008 FC 170 — A visa officer is not obligated to take the initiative to transfer a file where there is no request. Had the applicant made a clear and reasoned request for the interview to be held in the applicant's home country, for example, this might well have been done. In *obiter*, the court indicated that the visa officer did propose one option — the withdrawal of the application and the submission of a new application — and therefore the possibility of simply arranging an interview at a different office could have been suggested.

da Silva v. Canada (Minister of Citizenship & Immigration) (2007), 68 Imm. L.R. (3d) 312, 2007 CarswellNat 4883, 2007 CarswellNat 5486, 2007 FC 1138 — The duty to provide reasons is lower in the context of applications for temporary residence status. A number of factors would suggest that the duty to provide reasons is minimal: the applicant has no legal right to obtain a visa, and bears the burden of establishing the merits of his claim; the refusal of a work permit on an application from outside of Canada has less impact on the applicant than would the removal of a benefit; and the officer is better placed to evaluate the cultural and economic benefits of the applicant's prospective employment than the applicant.

Shapovalov v. Canada (Minister of Citizenship & Immigration), 2007 CarswellNat 7011 (F.C.) — The applicant sought judicial review of an immigration officer's decision to refuse the applicant's request to have counsel present at his inadmissibility interview. The respondent relied primarily on the fact that the questions posed to the applicant were not of a legal or complex nature and did not warrant the presence of counsel at the interview. The court held that other factors identified by the applicant outweighed this consideration. Specifically, this interview was not occurring at the early stages of the process, since the applicant had previously been interviewed and a finding had been made that he met the selection criteria; the interview was to determine whether he was inadmissible and was a last crucial step in the process. Further, the rejection of an application on the ground of inadmissibility identified in this case may well hinder any future chance of success and therefore was of importance to the applicant. Thirdly, permitting counsel to attend in these circumstances to observe would not unduly encumber the efficient administration of the process. Finally, given the nature of the inquiry at which the questions were directed coupled with the fact that the application had already been the subject of a judicial review proceeding weighed in favour of concluding that the duty of fairness in these circumstances encompasses the right to have counsel present at the interview. The application for judicial review was allowed.

Mekonen v. Canada (Minister of Citizenship & Immigration) (2007), 66 Imm. L.R. (3d) 222, 2007 CarswellNat 3655, 2007 FC 1133 — The applicant brought an application for judicial review of a decision of a visa officer that, as a member of the Eritrean Liberation Front, he was captured by para. 34(1)(f) of the IRPA, and therefore was inadmissible to Canada. The court found that the officer should have provided the applicant with a CBSA memorandum and an open source document, to allow him to make submissions that were responsive to that material. The court adopted the Federal Court of Appeal decision in *B. (S.) v. Canada (Minister of Citizenship & Immigration)*, 2001 CarswellNat 2008, that the question is not whether the report is or contains extrinsic evidence of facts unknown to the person affected by the decision, but whether the disclosure of the report is required to provide the person with a reasonable opportunity to participate in a meaningful manner in the decision-making process. In this case, meaningful participation included the right to highlight weaknesses in the material before the officer. Because the officer breached the duty of procedural fairness, the application for judicial review was allowed.

Garro v. Canada (Minister of Citizenship & Immigration) (2007), 67 Imm. L.R. (3d) 263, 2007 CarswellNat 1827, 2007 CarswellNat 4509, 2007 FC 670 — This was an application for judicial review of a decision of an immigration officer, refusing the application for a work permit for the applicant and visitor status for his family. The immigration officer concluded that the applicant failed to meet the conditions required to obtain investor status under NAFTA. The letter of refusal that the officer sent contained no reasons explaining why the application was denied. The officer's notes revealed that he did not consider the initial sum of $20,000 to be a substantial investment for purposes of granting the applicant a permit. However, the evidence in the record showed that the applicant invested $166,000 in commercial premises for the company, $67,000 in book stocks to sell and thousands of dollars in equipment. Given that the applicant's evidence was so compelling, the court concluded that there was absolutely no reason for the officer's decision and allowed the judicial review.

Somasundram v. Canada (Minister of Citizenship & Immigration) (2006), 56 Imm. L.R. (3d) 105, 2006 CarswellNat 2180, 2006 FC 925 — The applicant, a single Tamil female citizen of Sri Lanka, fled Colombo where she was seized and detained by the police who abused her and demanded information as to the warring factions in her local area. Upon her release by the police she fled to Canada claiming refugee protection. Once in Canada, she took up residence with relatives in the Toronto area, has been steadily employed as a cashier in a local business and settled into the community without incident. Her refugee claim was rejected in July of 2001 and in November 2001 she made a claim for exemption from visa requirements on humanitarian and compassionate grounds. This application was dismissed in October 2005 and she sought judicial review of that decision.

The application for judicial review was allowed on the basis that the reasons for the decision did not stand up to a reasonably probative examination as required. The court found that the last of the quotations from the reasons were nothing more than a recital of the general categories of materials reviewed following which was a recital of the criteria set out by the guidelines and of the decision made. The reasons failed to address any consideration given to the major points at issue. No issues were stated, no points of evidence were discussed, and no explanation of the thought process engaged by the officers was given.

Sandhu v. Canada (Minister of Citizenship & Immigration) (2006), 55 Imm. L.R. (3d) 203, 2006 CarswellNat 2360, 2006 FC 941 — The principal applicant, a citizen of India, was sponsored for permanent residence by her daughter in Canada. The applicant included in her permanent residence application her dependant children. Following an interview, the immigration officer expressed concerns about the application because two of the children did not have birth certificates and, in addition, supporting letters issued by the particular public school had, in the past, been found to be fraudulent. Following the interview, the applicant wrote to the Canadian High Commission responding to the concerns regarding the school certificates. She attached documentary evidence corroborating that the school documents provided were genuine. These documents were received by the Canadian High Commission on May 10, 2005. The immigration officer allegedly reviewed all the information in the file, including the post-interview information, and in

June 2005 sent the file to the Canadian High Commission Visa Section with her recommendation that the application for permanent residence be refused on the grounds that the applicant had misrepresented or withheld material facts. The application was refused for those reasons. There was no mention of the post-interview documents in the refusal letter.

The applicant sought leave for judicial review of the decision. The respondent took the position that the applicant had misaddressed the correspondence and post-interview documents and therefore had not proven that the Canadian High Commission ever received those post-interview documents. Leave was granted and during the subsequent judicial review proceedings, including the necessary cross-examination of the respondent's representatives, the respondent admitted that it had had the documents from the very time that the applicant had claimed. The respondent, having been "caught out", turned its argument around and through evidence and submission claimed that the documents were considered and given no weight. The immigration officer currently claimed that she had read the documents and gave them no weight — the visa officer could not recall the evidence but said that it would have had made no difference to his decision.

The failure to cite this material in the decision letter counters any weight that might be given to the officer's evidence that the material was considered. For this reason alone, the judicial review was granted. The applicant also asked for costs because of the respondent's conduct of this matter. The court concluded that the respondent's conduct was misleading to the applicant and was simply unacceptable. Therefore, "special reasons" under Rule 22 of the *Federal Courts Immigration and Refugee Protection Rules* were shown to justify an award of costs. The applicant was awarded solicitor-client costs of the whole of the matter.

Velasquez v. Canada (Minister of Citizenship & Immigration), 2006 CarswellNat 2616, 2006 FC 1024 — A decision to deny the applicant a visa to enter Canada as a permanent resident was set aside, since the officer did not give notice of concerns respecting the nature and scope of the applicant's activities nor was the applicant given a reasonable opportunity to respond. Specifically, the visa officer concluded that the applicant was involved or complicit in crimes against humanity following disclosure by the applicant during a telephone interview that he was with Mobile Brigade #2 in a particular location in Colombia in October 1992. The applicant was never confronted with the opinion formed, and was never asked questions as to what he was doing or what others known to him were doing at the relevant time or place. The visa officer concluded he was inadmissible under subs. 35(1)(a) of the IRPA.

Dhoot v. Canada (Minister of Citizenship & Immigration) (2006), 57 Imm. L.R. (3d) 153, 2006 FC 1295, 2006 CarswellNat 3480, [2006] F.C.J. No. 1625 — This is an application for judicial review of a visa officer's decision of the applicant's application for a permanent resident visa which was denied on the basis that the applicant failed to attend an interview scheduled on October 26, 2005. The applicant states that he was never informed of the interview. The visa officer insisted that the notice of the interview was provided to the applicant by letter dated August 19, 2005.

The visa officer, for whatever reason, did not send the notice by mail as would be expected given the significantly prejudicial impact non delivery would have on the applicant's interest in obtaining a permanent resident visa. It is reasonable to expect that there will be mistakes by the respondent when dealing with thousands of immigration files. When the evidence shows that there has been such a mistake the court expects that the respondent cure the mistake, *i.e.*, invite the applicant to attend another interview. It was

Other Relevant Legislation

wrong for the respondent, in a case such as this, to oppose the applicant's court case. The application for judicial review was allowed and the applicant was awarded legal costs.

Zhen v. Canada (Minister of Citizenship & Immigration), 2006 CarswellNat 758, 2006 CarswellNat 1854, 2006 FC 408 — The applicant was given only three weeks to comply with the visa officer's request for additional financial records. The visa officer's request for 20 years of financial records supported, in part, by third party verifications, went beyond what is normally required by the department. Since the visa officer requested the documentary history and then failed to afford a reasonable opportunity to the applicant to comply with the request, the handling of the application did not conform to the obligation to allow the applicant to present his case fully and fairly.

Kniazeva v. Canada (Minister of Citizenship & Immigration) (2006), 52 Imm. L.R. (3d) 298, 2006 CarswellNat 472, 2006 FC 268 — The applicant filed an application for permanent residence under the skilled worker class. New legislation was enacted following the applicant's application having been filed. Under subs. 361(4) of the *Immigration and Refugee Protection Regulations*, the applicant could have become a permanent resident as a member of the federal skilled worker class by qualifying under either the former Act's regulation or under the new legislation. Once the visa officer decided to access the applicant under both the old and new Act, he had to inform the applicant of the new requirements with respect to language proficiency. The visa officer's failure to conduct a thorough review of her application under the new Act and failure to provide the applicant with an opportunity to provide him with the language assessment amounted to a clear breach of duty of fairness owed to the applicant.

The visa officer contacted the applicant's former employer with a view to verifying her employment. The employer confirmed the applicant had "practical training" at the plant while she was a student and had worked intervals during the period between June 1997 and July 1998. Accordingly, the visa officer had a duty to inform the applicant that he only considered this work experience as part-time and therefore the experience was being disqualified as relevant work experience.

The visa officer breached the duty of procedural fairness and the application for judicial review was allowed.

Keymanesh v. Canada (Minister of Citizenship & Immigration), 2006 CarswellNat 1392, 2006 FC 641 — The applicant challenged a decision made by the officer denying his application for permanent resident status because of a failure to obtain a pardon from a conviction for impaired driving in 1998. In the absence of a pardon, the applicant was ineligible for landing and, in the result, subject to removal. The court considered whether the department owed a duty to give notice to the applicant that it was intending to determine his application for permanent residence in the absence of proof of a pardon, and if so, did it fulfil that duty. The department advised the applicant that he had been approved in principle for a visa exemption but that landing would be subject to meeting other immigration requirements including health and security assessments. When the department learned of the applicant's criminal conviction, it notified him of the need for a pardon. They also advised him that he would not be eligible to apply for a pardon for three years. This extension of time afforded by the department was generous because the applicant could have been removed immediately on the basis of his criminal conviction. The department, quite rightly, was not prepared to hold the applicant's case for landing in abeyance indefinitely. The department wrote the applicant giving him a notice to respond to its request for the pardon which was returned "undeliverable." Not hearing from the applicant, they sent him a "final notice" which was also returned as "undeliverable." The department refused the application for permanent residence. The applicant claimed not to have received the three notification letters and deposed that he had advised the department of his change of address. The applicant had a clear indication that the department required proof of a pardon before his application for landing would be finalized. However, when the department began to contemplate the possibility of revoking his interim status, it did have a duty to inform him of that risk. Indeed, the department's lengthy acquiescence may well have created some expectation in the mind of the applicant that time was not of the essence and that he would be informed of any change in the department's position.

It is difficult to contemplate any decision by the department which would have greater significance to the applicant than the one taken here. The finalization of his application for permanent residence without the required pardon had only one possible outcome: deportation. The obligation to give effective notice of a potentially adverse administrative decision is different than a situation involving the obligation to produce evidence or to meet a burden of proof. From the department's record, it was not clear that the officer who decided to refuse the application for landing was even aware that its notification correspondence had been returned as undelivered. Although the department need not exhaust every tracing possibility, some effort to that end is essential in cases like this, at least to the extent recognized by the department's own guidelines.

IP5-Immigration Application in Canada Made on Humanitarian and Compassionate Grounds, s. 17.3, suggests that where contact has been lost, some effort should be made to locate the subject. Those guidelines indicate that where an applicant does not respond to requests for information or fails to provide an updated address, a decision can be taken "based on information on file as long as previous correspondence has informed the applicant of how and when to apply and included the consequences of failing to respond." Those guidelines go on to indicate that officers should indicate in their computer notes any attempts to verify the applicant's current address such as looking in the local telephone directory, calling the most recent telephone number provided on the application form or calling other persons listed as contacts or representatives. The recommendations imply that where the department is aware that its notification letters have not been received there is some responsibility to make some enquiries with respect to whereabouts.

The department did not meet the duty of fairness owed to the applicant with respect to giving effective notice. The failure was entirely inadvertent but does require that the decision to refuse the applicant's application for permanent residence be set aside.

Shaker v. Canada (Minister of Citizenship & Immigration), 2006 FC 185, 2006 CarswellNat 271, 2006 CarswellNat 2244, [2006] F.C.J. No. 201 — The applicant submitted an application for permanent residence as a skilled worker in December 1999. An interview date was set for July 2004 and the applicant was instructed to submit additional information regarding his financial situation, employment history and identity. However, before the applicant received the notice, his counsel sent a letter to the embassy requesting that his file be transferred to the Canadian High Commission in Singapore. The Canadian Embassy in Manila sent the file to the Canadian High Commission in Singapore, returned the documents the applicant's counsel had submitted and instructed him to send them directly to the High Commission in Singapore. The applicant was then informed by the High Commission of the coming into effect of the IRPA and that his application would be processed under the new requirements. The applicant was asked to provide proof of his current level of official language proficiency. In August 2004, the applicant sent the High Commission in Singapore the documents that had been sent back by the embassy in Manila, as well as proof of his English language proficiency in the form of school transcripts, a letter from a company stating that he had taken an English course, and six pages of manuscript narrative regarding his use of English in the workplace and at home.

In September 2004, the officer stated in her assessment under the old and new Acts and Regulations that under the old Act she was not satisfied the applicant had performed the essential duties of his intended occupation in Canada, and she consequently would not award him any units of assessment under the "occupational factor" or "experience" headings. In addition to the overall pass mark of 70 units, at least one unit under these headings was necessary for an application to be granted. The officer also stated that in the context of her assessment under the new Act, there was insufficient evidence to determine the applicant's work experience or his proficiency in the English language. She instructed the applicant to submit employment references, work contracts, or any other information/documentation which demonstrates experience in the occupation described by the National Occupational Classification No. 0611, and either IELTS test results or more written evidence that can permit measurement of proficiency in the English language. In addition, the visa officer asked the applicant to pay the cost recovery fee for his wife and child and to submit proof of financial capacity to resettle in Canada. In fact, the High Commission had already sent the applicant a receipt for payment of the processing fees regarding his spouse and child on August 28, 2004.

Since the applicant had sent documents regarding all four of these subjects in August of 2004, he inferred that the officer did not have them when she assessed his application. The Minister argued that the officer did not violate procedural fairness, in that her letter of September 2, 2004, gave the applicant a chance to respond to her concerns regarding his professional qualifications and his proficiency in English. The court disagreed and held that the fact that the officer requested items that the applicant had already submitted reasonably led him to believe that she did not have any of the evidence he had submitted in the same package. In light of the ambiguity caused by her letter and the applicant's effort to notify her that he had already sent the items she requested, the duty of procedural fairness required the officer to inform the applicant that the evidence he submitted regarding his employment history and proficiency in English was still insufficient, and that she explain the confusion. The officer's decision was found to be unreasonable as she failed to offer any explanation as to why the applicant was awarded no points under the "experience" and "arranged employment" headings. Furthermore, the visa officer's decision to award zero points for English was found to be patently unreasonable. While the presence of mistakes in the applicant's manuscript evidencing his English skills and the relatively poor grades he obtained while studying English may not have warranted the attribution of full marks for English skills, he clearly demonstrated the ability to communicate in English at some level.

Karanja v. Canada (Minister of Citizenship & Immigration), 2006 CarswellNat 1265, 2006 CarswellNat 2533, 2006 FC 574 — Pursuant to the gender guidelines (Women Refugee Claimants Fearing Gender-Related Persecution, 9 March 1993, by the chairperson of the Immigration and Refugee Board pursuant to para. 159(1)(h) of the *Immigration Act*), the Board should be particularly sensitive to a female applicant's difficulty in testifying. However, the gender guidelines, in and of themselves, are not intended to serve as a cure for all deficiencies in the applicant's claim or evidence. The applicant bears the onus of proving her claim. The guidelines cannot be treated as corroborating any evidence of gender-based persecution so that the giving of the evidence becomes proof of its truth. Instead, the guidelines are an aid for the panel in the assessment of the evidence of women who allege that they have been victims of gender-based persecution. The guidelines do not create new grounds for finding a person to be a victim of persecution. A Board's failure to specifically mention the gender guidelines does not mean that they were not considered and is not material or fatal to the Board's decision.

The gender guidelines specifically state that the female refugee claimant must demonstrate that the harm feared is sufficiently serious to amount to persecution. In this case, there were numerous negative credibility findings by the Board and such findings are open to the Board to make. Accordingly, the applicant failed to demonstrate that the Board's decision was patently unreasonable so as to warrant the intervention of the court.

Bortey v. Canada (Minister of Citizenship & Immigration), 2006 CarswellNat 327, 2006 CarswellNat 2422, 2006 FC 190 — The Board found that the applicant obtained refugee status on the basis of misrepresentations and the withholding of material facts. The Board also concluded that once these misrepresentations were set aside, there was no other sufficient evidence considered at the time of the first determination on which a decision in favour of the applicant could have been based. The Board was required, under subs. 109(2) of the IRPA, to decipher whether any of the evidence cited in support of the original positive determination is left "untainted" by the fact of the newly discovered material misrepresentations.

Apaza v. Canada (Minister of Citizenship & Immigration), 2006 CarswellNat 606, 2006 CarswellNat 1415, 2006 FC 313 — The applicant's inland application for permanent residence based on humanitarian and compassionate grounds was rejected. The decision letter also stated that the case had been assessed under the spouse or common-law partner in Canada class and was rejected on that ground as well. In the opinion of the immigration officer, there was little evidence to show there was a genuine marriage and that the marriage had not been entered into primarily for the purpose of acquiring permanent residence status in Canada. The refusal letter provided no detailed reasons. The immigration officer's lengthy notes were produced only in the course of the application for judicial review. The court concluded that the officer ignored relevant evidence that, if believed, would have significant probative value. Specifically, the immigration officer ignored evidence about the ages of the applicants, the period of cohabitation before marriage, and supporting documents, including doctors' notes, employer reference letters and the filing of joint income tax returns, in reaching her conclusion about the genuineness of the marriage. Instead, the officer focused on irrelevant matters, for example the contents of bedside tables and the timing of the wife's divorce from her previous husband, and details of the mode of transportation used for their first date, in assessing the genuineness of the marriage. The application for judicial review was allowed and referred to a different officer for redetermination.

Boni c. Canada (Ministre de la Citoyenneté & de l'Immigration) (2005), 57 Imm. L.R. (3d) 4, 2005 CarswellNat 176, 2005 CarswellNat 4646, 2005 FC 31, [2005] F.C.J. No. 43; affirmed 2006 FCA 68, 2006 CarswellNat 414, [2006] F.C.J. No. 275 — The applicant applied for judicial review of a visa officer's decision to deny the applicant's application for a study permit. The risk that study permit applicants will not leave Canada once the period of their stay ends is a very important factor to be considered. An officer may examine the applicant's long-term objective. That objective is a relevant point which carries some weight, in view of the evidence as a whole on whether a study permit would be granted. A visa officer's conclusions will not be disturbed unless they are so unreasonable as to require the court's intervention.

Iliev v. Canada (Minister of Citizenship & Immigration), 2005 CarswellNat 2010, 2005 FC 395 — The applicant, a citizen of Bulgaria, made a claim to be a Convention refugee and was found to be a Convention refugee. However, the Minister of Citizenship and Immigration obtained leave to vacate the determination of the Convention Refugee Determination Division pursuant to s. 109 of the IRPA on the basis that the applicant had obtained refugee status on fraudulent means, misrepresentation, suppression and concealment of material facts, specifically with respect to the entry of two criminal convictions in Bulgaria. The Minister relied on certificates of conviction that had been issued by the Bulgarian court. The Board accepted the Minister's argument and concluded that pursuant to Article 1F(b) of the *Refugee Convention*, the applicant was a person who was excluded from consideration as a Convention refugee as a result of having committed a serious non-political offence. The Board's conclusion was set aside by the Federal Court as it was made in the absence of any evidence about the equivalency between the Bulgarian criminal law and the Canadian criminal law. A factual finding made without evidence is a ground for judicial intervention, pursuant to s. 18.1(4) of the *Federal Courts Act*.

Qazi v. Canada (Minister of Citizenship & Immigration), 2005 FC 1667, 2005 CarswellNat 4129, 2005 CarswellNat 5566, [2005] F.C.J. No. 2069 — The question of when a PRRA becomes unreasonably stale is not solely dependent on the length of time that has passed, but also depends on the applicant establishing that he has been prejudiced by the delay. In this case, nearly two years had elapsed from the time the applicant replied to the negative risk assessment. While the delay was unfortunate, nevertheless there was no evidence that the applicant had been prejudiced by it. The court concluded that he had not been denied procedural fairness or natural justice.

Huiqiao v. Canada (Minister of Citizenship & Immigration) (2000), 10 Imm. L.R. (3d) 132, 2000 CarswellNat 2509 (Fed. T.D.) — Although not made in the context of an immigration matter, the Federal Court of Appeal stated in *Stelco Inc. v. British Steel Canada Inc.*, [2000] 3 F.C. 282, 20 Admin. L.R. (3d) 159, 252 N.R. 364, 2000 CarswellNat 230, [2000] F.C.J. No. 286, 2000 CarswellNat 3248 (C.A.), at p. 284:

> When a tribunal bases a discretionary decision on findings of fact, a reviewing court must examine those findings to ensure that they are rationally based on the material before the tribunal . . . in order to establish that the tribunal committed a reviewable error the applicant and the interveners had to demonstrate on the balance of probabilities that the tribunal's finding was not rationally supported by any material before it.

Sinnathamby v. Canada (Minister of Citizenship & Immigration), 2001 FCT 473, 2001 CarswellNat 1012 — In cases seeking to review a decision of a panel of the CRDD, the standard of review is twofold. Questions of law are governed by the standard of correctness. Factual findings are regulated by the patently unreasonable standard.

Singh (S.) v. Canada (Minister of Citizenship & Immigration) (1999), 2 Imm. L.R. (3d) 191, 173 F.T.R. 280, 1999 CarswellNat 1579, [1999] F.C.J. No. 1283 — The standard of review for a panel of the Convention Refugee Determination Division is patent unreasonableness. Citing *Canada (Director of Investigation & Research) v. Southam* [1997] 1 S.C.R 748, the court concluded that the difference between unreasonable and patently unreasonable lies in the immediacy or obviousness of the defect. If the defect is apparent on the face of the tribunal's reasons then the tribunal's decision is patently unreasonable. If it takes some significant searching or testing to find the defect then the decision is unreasonable, but not patently unreasonable.

Gengeswaran v. Canada (Minister of Citizenship & Immigration) (1999), 169 F.T.R. 148 — Although there is no obligation on the Board to discuss every piece of evidence, it is required to address those pieces which contradict the Board's finding on key issues. The absence of any analysis of documentary evidence which directly contradicts the Board's finding, permits the court to infer, from the silence, that the tribunal made an erroneous finding of fact without regard to evidence.

Cepeda-Gutierrez v. Canada (Minister of Citizenship & Immigration) (1998), 157 F.T.R. 35 — This was an application to set aside a decision of a panel of the CRDD. The applicant relied on s. 18.1(4)(d) of the *Federal Court Act*. The applicant was a citizen of Mexico who arrived in Canada and claimed refugee status. The Refugee Division found that while he was a taxi driver in Mexico City he had been the subject of beatings and threats of violence by the federal police. The panel found that the claimant's evidence was credible and held that the claimant had a well-founded fear of persecution in Mexico City; however, they rejected his claim on the basis that he had an internal flight alternative.

Section 18.1(4)(d) of the Act does not authorize the court to substitute its view of the facts for that of the Board which has the benefit of not only seeing and hearing the witnesses, but also of the expertise of its members in assessing evidence relating to facts that are within their area of specialized expertise. The efficient allocation of decision-making resources between administrative agencies and the courts strongly indicates that the role to be played in fact-finding by the court on an application for judicial review should be nearly residual. Thus, in order to attract judicial intervention, the applicant must satisfy the court not only that the Board made a palpably erroneous finding of material fact, but also that the finding was made without regard to the evidence. The court may infer that the administrative agency made the erroneous finding of fact without regard to the evidence from the agency's failure to mention in its reasons some evidence before it that was relevant to the finding and pointed to a different conclusion from that reached by the agency. Just as a court will only defer to an agency's interpretation of its constituent statute if it provides reasons for its conclusion, so a court will be reluctant to defer to an agency's factual determinations in the absence of express findings and an analysis of the evidence that shows how the agency reached its results. Reasons given by an administrative agency are not to be read hypercritically, nor are agencies to be required to refer to every piece of evidence that they received that is contrary to their finding and to explain how they dealt with it. A statement by the agency in its reasons for decision that in making its findings it considered all of the evidence before it will often suffice to assure a reviewing court that the agency directed itself to the totality of the evidence. The more important the evidence that is not mentioned specifically, the more willing a court will be to infer from the silence that the agency made an erroneous finding of fact without regard to the evidence. When the agency refers in some detail to evidence supporting its finding, but is silent on evidence pointing to the opposite conclusion, it will be easier to infer that the agency overlooked the contradictory evidence when making its finding of fact. The court was not persuaded that the Board erred when it found that the applicant faced no serious possibility of persecution outside Mexico City and therefore it was unnecessary to consider whether the Board's finding was made without regard to the evidence.

The applicant called a psychologist as a witness to explain why it was not reasonable to require the applicant to return to Mexico. In making its decision the panel did not refer to the psychologist's evidence. This evidence was so important to the applicant's case that it can be inferred from the refugee division's failure to mention it that the finding made by the panel was made without regard to this evidence. This inference was made easier by the fact that the Board's reasons dealt with other items of evidence indicating that return would not be unduly harsh. The inclusion of the "boilerplate" assertion that the Board considered all the evidence was not sufficient to prevent this inference from being drawn. Accordingly, the decision of the panel was set aside and the matter remitted to a differently constituted panel.

Khakh v. Canada (Minister of Citizenship & Immigration) (1996), 116 F.T.R. 310 — The applicant was determined not to be a Convention refugee on the basis that he had fabricated incidents of persecution in order to try to obtain refugee status.

The court commented on judicial decisions about s. 18.l(4)(d) and found authority for the proposition that three conditions precedent must be met to justify judicial intervention: (1) the finding of fact must be truly erroneous; (2) the finding must be made capriciously or without regard to the evidence; and (3) the decision must be based on the erroneous finding. Further, the subs. permits review where there was no evidence to support the finding, or where, on an assessment of the evidence as a whole, the finding was unreasonable.

Further, the court adopted Webster's Third New International Dictionary definition of "capricious", which defined the word as "marked or guided by caprice: given to changes of interest or attitude according to whims or passing fancies: not guided by steady judgment, intent, or purpose."

Osaloun v. Canada (Minister of Citizenship & Immigration), 1996 CarswellNat 1059 (Fed. T.D.) — The issue in this case was whether a panel of the IRB committed an error of natural justice, and if so, whether the breach should be disregarded.

The denial of a right to a fair hearing will render a decision with respect to a refugee claim invalid, unless it can be demonstrated that the claim would in any case be hopeless.

Singh (A.) v. Canada (Minister of Citizenship & Immigration) (1995), 30 Imm. L.R. (2d) 211, 98 F.T.R. 58 — This was an application to review a decision of the Appeal Division of the IRB upholding a deportation order issued against the applicant.

The applicant, his parents and his three sisters were sponsored to come to Canada as members of the family class. The applicant completed the statutory declaration in which he declared that he had never been married and that he had no children. The applicant received an immigrant visa in July 1990 and returned for a visit to Guyana in 1992. In fact, the applicant had fathered a son in Guyana in 1990, and on his return there in 1992, he married the son's mother and then sponsored his wife and son for entrance to Canada. An adjudicator determined that the applicant had been granted landing by misrepresentation of a material fact (ie. — non-disclosure of the birth of his son).

At the outset of the proceedings before the Appeal Division, counsel for the applicant advised the Tribunal that the appeal was being taken pursuant to para. 70(3)(b) of the *Immigration Act* on the ground that having regard to the existence of compassionate or humanitarian considerations, the applicant should not be removed from Canada.

The Appeal Division dismissed the appeal and this application for judicial review related to that dismissal. In the proceedings before the Trial Division, the applicant submitted that Immigration Regulations 6(1)(a), 9(l)(a), and 10(1)(a) are *ultra vires* the *Immigration Act*.

The Trial Division is not entitled to pronounce itself on a question not faced by the administrative authority whose decision it is reviewing. This principle applies when the *vires* of regulations passed pursuant to the enabling statute is in issue. Accordingly, due to the fact that counsel before the Appeal Division did not challenge the validity of the regulations in question, that issue could not be raised before the Trial Division and the application for judicial review was dismissed.

Rehman v. Canada (Secretary of State) (1995), 92 F.T.R. 297 — The court was satisfied that there had been a breach of the duty to act fairly. The court then noted that there was an added requirement before a new hearing could be ordered. Specifically, the court was required to address its mind to the question of whether the nature of the applicant's claim to refugee status is such that the claim might be described as hopeless or one where the outcome was inevitable, in which case it would be inappropriate to set aside the decision. The court could not conclude on the facts of this matter that a differently constituted panel of the CRDD would inevitably conclude that these claims must fail. The court therefore directed that there be a new hearing before a differently constituted panel of the CRDD.

Nguy v. Canada (Minister of Employment & Immigration) (1994), 80 F.T.R. 53 — The applicant was determined not to be a Convention refugee. The applicant challenged a finding of fact by the Board that he was not stateless as he had alleged, but was a citizen of Vietnam. The application was dismissed.

In order for an alleged error of fact to be reviewable, the finding must be truly erroneous or the finding must be made capriciously or without regard to the evidence, and the decision must be based on that erroneous finding. The decision that the applicant was eligible for Vietnamese citizenship was not erroneous or capricious and was not central to the negative determination of the applicant's refugee claim.

Alfred v. Canada (Minister of Employment & Immigration) (1994), 76 F.T.R. 231 — In this application to review a negative decision of the CRDD, the applicant argued that the tribunal erred in misconstruing "persecution" and that the tribunal erred in law by ignoring or misconstruing the evidence before it. The respondent made reference to portions of the transcript of the hearing and to the documentary evidence before the tribunal, which it argued would warrant the conclusion that the findings of the tribunal were reasonable. The court must review the decision as rendered by the tribunal and not the evidence to which the decision itself makes no reference but which would have warranted the conclusions reached by the tribunal if the tribunal had expressed reasons relying upon such evidence. The simple statement that the tribunal had reached its decision "after careful consideration of all the evidence adduced at the hearing" was not sufficient when the decision made little or no reference to the principal basis of the applicant's claim. The application was allowed in this case and the matter sent back for rehearing before a differently constituted panel of the CRDD.

Gholam-Nejad v. Canada (Minister of Employment & Immigration) (1994), 25 Imm. L.R. (2d) 51, 77 F.T.R. 44 — This application to review a negative decision of the CRDD was based on the denial to the applicant of her right to counsel because of the alleged manifest incompetence of her representative at the Refugee Board hearing. Section 18.1(4) of the *Federal Court Act* provides for relief where the CRDD acted or failed to act, or failed to observe a principle of natural justice, procedural fairness or other procedure that it was required by law to observe, or erred in law, or based its decision or order on an erroneous finding of fact made in a perverse or capricious manner. Nothing on the face of that subs.

would authorize the intervention of the court where the issue is the failure on the part of the applicant's representative, rather than on the part of the CRDD itself. This is particularly true where the failure of the representative was not at all apparent to the CRDD and, therefore, the representative's failure could not be identified as a failure of the CRDD to ensure natural justice and fairness. Accordingly, this ground of attack could not succeed and the application was dismissed.

Pal v. Canada (Minister of Employment & Immigration) (1993), 70 F.T.R. 289 — The applicant sought review of a decision denying him Convention refugee status.

The applicant was not granted a recess, when he requested one, in order to review documents which were introduced into evidence and which he had not seen previously. The documents were introduced to contradict evidence which he had given. They were written in English. The applicant was testifying through an interpreter. The court found that in refusing to allow the applicant and his counsel an opportunity to review the evidence, the applicant was denied the opportunity to answer the case against him and a breach of natural justice occurred.

The court pointed out that relief under s. 18.1(4) of the *Federal Court Act* is discretionary and thus, if no prejudice is caused by an erroneous procedure or decision, an order quashing that decision will not normally be given. If no real purpose will be served by requiring another hearing, one will not be ordered.

The court was unable to conclude that the breach of natural justice that occurred in the context of this case was minor and could not appreciably affect the final decision. The breach was not cured by subsequent actions and accordingly, the decision of the tribunal was quashed.

Singh (G.) v. Canada (Minister of Employment & Immigration) (1993), 69 F.T.R. 142 — The applicants sought to set aside a decision that they were not Convention refugees. This case discusses how findings on the evidence can be successfully challenged in the Trial Division.

The court commented that s. 18.1(4)(d) of the *Federal Court Act* set out disjunctive conditions under which a decision will be set aside. For purposes of paragraph (c) of that section, the court noted that findings of fact which are unsupported by adequate evidence are errors in law — the so-called "no evidence rule." Section 18.1(4)(d) allows the court to set aside a decision which is made "without regard for the material before it." This grants a broader right of review than the traditional "no evidence" test. It compels the setting aside of tribunal decisions where they are unreasonable. The phrase "perverse or capricious manner or without regard for the material before it" is accurately discussed in J.A. Kavanagh, *A Guide to Judicial Review* (1978) at 57–58.

The findings of fact can be divided into two classifications: findings of primary facts and inferences of fact which are drawn from the primary facts. Courts are reluctant to interfere with findings of primary facts made by tribunals. In areas where a tribunal has a particular expertise in drawing inferences, courts are inclined to treat those inferences with deference. If, however, the inference is of a type which is based on common experience, then the court is in equally as good a position as the tribunal to draw the inference and in that case deference is not shown.

In this particular case, the inferences of fact drawn by the Board did not stand up upon a review of the evidence and the decision refusing refugee status was set aside.

18.2 Interim orders — On an application for judicial review, the Federal Court may make any interim orders that it considers appropriate pending the final disposition of the application.

1990, c. 8, s. 5; 2002, c. 8, s. 28

Case Law

Canada (Minister of Citizenship & Immigration) v. B456, 2011 FC 439, 2011 CarswellNat 1316 — B456 is one of 490 some Sri Lankan Tamils who came to Canada in August 2010 on board the undocumented ship The Sun Sea. He, like the others, filed a claim for refugee status. He carried no identification papers. He was detained and has been subject to 30-day detention reviews. There is public interest in dealing effectively with large scale people-smuggling operations. This applies equally to the balance of convenience. It is far better to preserve the *status quo ante*.

Rivero Ramirez v. Canada (Minister of Public Safety & Emergency Preparedness), 2010 FC 706, 2010 CarswellNat 2020, 2010 CarswellNat 2649 — The applicant sought judicial review of a decision of an enforcement officer to refuse to defer the applicant's removal from Canada. The applicant sought what amounts to a permanent deferral of his removal pending the disposition of his permanent residence application under the spouse or common-law partner in Canada class. The personal safety of the applicant was not an issue. Consequently, the principal issue in this application is whether the pending in-Canada spousal sponsorship application is a sufficient reason to defer the removal. The mere existence of an H&C application does not constitute a bar to the execution of a valid removal order. The same can be said of an in-Canada spousal application since the Act does not provide that such an application results in a deferral of a removal order. Though the Minister has developed a public policy providing for a temporary administrative deferral of removal in certain circumstances for those who have submitted an in-Canada spousal application, the applicant does not meet the eligibility criteria of this public policy. The enforcement officer has no authority to modify this policy or to develop a new policy in order to accommodate the applicant. The enforcement officer has limited discretion concerning the timing of a removal, but his or her authority does not and should not extend to delaying a removal pending the outcome of an in-Canada spousal application where the Act itself or public policy does not provide for such a deferral and where the decision on the pending application is not imminent. Moreover, with respect to the presence of Canadian-born children, an enforcement officer is not required to undertake a substantive review of the children's best interest before executing a removal order.

Adolph v. Canada (Minister of Public Safety & Emergency Preparedness) (2009), 357 F.T.R. 216 (Eng.), 2009 FC 1271, 2009 CarswellNat 4277 — This "sad and disturbing" case involved a minor child who remains alone in Canada after having been sent to Toronto by his mother and aunt on a one-way ticket from St. Lucia, purportedly to offer him an opportunity for a better life. To compound this unacceptable situation, two government agencies are working at cross purposes from each other in this case, each claiming to be taking into account the true best interest of the child. A motion to stay the removal procedure was brought pursuant to s. 18.2 of the *Federal Courts Act*. The applicant argued that the enforcement officer ignored compelling factors demonstrating that the best interests of the applicant were such that his removal should be deferred and that the officer failed to take into account Canada's obligations under the *Convention on the Rights of the Child* to provide protection and assistance to the applicant and act in his best interest. The Minister argued that contrary to the allegations of the Children's Aid Society of

Toronto the best interests of the applicant do not include an entitlement to remain in Canada to obtain a better life than he would otherwise have in St. Lucia. The Minister also adds that non-citizen parents from foreign countries should not be encouraged to send and abandon their children in Canada in the hopes of better opportunities for them.

The interpretation and application of the *Convention on the Rights of the Child* in circumstances where a child without immigration status is abandoned, and how the Convention is to be taken into account for immigration purposes in such circumstances pursuant to paragraph 3(3)(f) of IRPA raised a serious issue including who should determine the best interest of an abandoned child in such circumstances, the Children's Aid Society or the immigration authorities? Since the Social Services Agency of St. Lucia had not been contacted in order to secure an onsite report on the applicant's family situation and on potential alternative placement solutions in St. Lucia should the return to the family not be deemed feasible, the applicant was deemed to be facing irreparable harm. In light of the fact that a minor child is involved, the court preferred to act cautiously. Although the court strongly supported the Minister's contention that citizens from foreign countries should not be encouraged to send and abandon their children in Canada and although the Minister must carry out a removal order as soon as reasonably practical pursuant to subs. 48(2) of IRPA, the particular circumstances of this case required a finding that the balance of convenience lies at this time with the applicant. The stay was granted.

Baron v. Canada (Minister of Public Safety & Emergency Preparedness), [2009] F.C.J. No. 314, 387 N.R. 278, 79 Imm. L.R. (3d) 157, 2009 CarswellNat 596, 2009 FCA 81 — The court considered whether an application for judicial review of an enforcement officer's decision not to defer an applicant's scheduled removal from Canada becomes moot where the court has stayed the removal and the applicant has remained in Canada.

The jurisprudence is conclusive that the enforcement officer's discretion is limited. However, ultimately an enforcement officer is intended to do nothing more than enforce a removal order. While enforcement officers are granted the discretion to fix new removal dates, they are not intended to defer removal to an indeterminate date. On the facts before the court, the date of the decision on the H&C application was unknown and unlikely to be imminent, and thus, the enforcement officer was being asked to delay removal indeterminately. An indeterminate deferral was simply not within the enforcement officer's powers.

Over the years, the duties of enforcement officers have not changed, and yet, the basis upon which applicants rely to obtain deferrals have dramatically increased. The scope of the enforcement officer's discretion cannot be changed by virtue of the request made. An enforcement officer's role is not to assess the best interest of the children or the probability of success of any application. The enforcement officer's role should remain limited and deferral should be contemplated in very limited circumstances. The legislation has not provided a new step to claimants who desire yet another assessment of their circumstances. Claimants already have the refugee application process, the pre-removal risk assessment process and the H&C application in addition to judicial reviews of these processes and the stay before removal. In this case, it appears that the claimants want to open yet another avenue of review by asking the enforcement officer to reassess information that has already been examined by administrative tribunals and that was a subject of judicial review. For the enforcement officer to comply with this request for reassessment would be akin to the enforcement officer making a quasi-judicial order without the benefit of hearing from opposing counsel. It is time to stop this abusive cycle.

The appeal was dismissed. The removal date having passed, the determination of the reasonableness of the enforcement officer's refusal to defer the removal date in January 2007 was without consequence; the matter was rendered moot.

Palka v. Canada (Minister of Public Safety & Emergency Preparedness), 2008 CarswellNat 1309, 2008 FCA 165 — The appellants appealed from a decision of the Federal Court dismissing their application for judicial review of a refusal by an enforcement officer to defer their removal from Canada until their application for permanent residence on humanitarian and compassionate grounds had been decided. The lower court judge held that the application for judicial review was moot, and did not consider its merits. She based her finding of mootness on the fact that another judge of the Federal Court had stayed the appellants' removal scheduled for June 13, 2007, pending the disposition of their application for judicial review of the officer's refusal to defer their removal. The lower court judge rejected the position taken by both the appellants and the respondent, the Minister of Public Safety and Emergency Preparedness, that the passing of the scheduled removal date did not render the application for judicial review moot because an application for permanent residence on H&C grounds was outstanding. The lower court judge certified a question for appeal on the mootness issue. The appellants then brought a motion for a stay of removal to their country of nationality, pending the disposition of the appeal.

They argued that, if they were denied a stay, their appeal on the mootness decision will be nugatory. They claimed that this would constitute irreparable harm. The court did not agree. Even if their appeal was moot, the court may decide to hear it in its discretion, on the ground that the question certified may arise repeatedly and be evasive of review. Even if a refusal of a stay does not render the appeal nugatory, this does not necessarily constitute irreparable harm. It all depends on the facts of the individual case.

Despite numerous attempts, through administrative and legal channels, the appellants have been denied status in Canada. There has to be some finality. To grant yet another deferral of their removal was contrary to the public interest as expressed in the Act. Motion to defer removal was dismissed.

See also *Islami v. Canada (Minster of Citizenship & Immigration)*, 2008 FC 364, 2008 CarswellNat 702, 2008 CarswellNat 2952.

Maruthalingam v. Canada (Minister of Public Safety & Emergency Preparedness) (2007), 63 Imm. L.R. (3d) 242, 2007 FC 823, 2007 CarswellNat 3088, 2007 CarswellNat 2278, [2007] F.C.J. No. 1079 — The applicants were ordered to report for deportation and an enforcement officer refused the applicants' request that the removal from Canada be deferred. The applicants filed a notice of application for leave and judicial review of the enforcement officer's decision and brought a motion for a stay of their removal until the court had disposed of the application for judicial review. The motion for the stay was granted. The applicants were not removed. By the time this judicial review application was heard by the court, the serious issues identified in the stay motion were, in practical terms, academic. This application for judicial review was dismissed. The applicants raised the issue of whether the court should still rule that the issue was moot where it was asked to stay the removal until the outcome of another process. The court refused to opine as to whether the court could grant a remedy to the applicants on a free-standing basis. The applicants had not sought an order to stay the removal until the final determination of their outstanding application on humanitarian and compassionate grounds. Instead, their sole request was that the matter be referred to another enforcement officer for reconsideration.

See also *Vu v. Canada (Minister of Citizenship & Immigration)*, 2007 CarswellNat 3591 (F.C.).

Higgins v. Canada (Minister of Public Safety & Emergency Preparedness) (2007), 64 Imm. L.R. (3d) 98, 2007 CarswellNat 832, 2007 CarswellNat 1841, [2007] F.C.J. No. 516, 2007 FC 377 — By order dated June 29, 2006, the court stayed the removal of the applicant from Canada pending final determination of the current application for judicial review. The granting of the stay gave the applicant his remedy before the merits of the application for judicial review were addressed.

If the respondent remains determined to remove the applicant before his humanitarian and compassionate grounds application is determined, it would be open to the applicant to request a new deferral of removal, based on all of the current circumstances and evidence. If that request is denied, a further application for leave and for judicial review would be open to him together with a further motion before the court seeking a stay of removal pending the final determination of that new application for leave and for judicial review.

The application for judicial review was moot. The court refused to exercise discretion to hear the matter.

Kovacs v. Canada (Minister of Public Safety & Emergency Preparedness) (2007), 68 Imm. L.R. (3d) 218, 2007 FC 1247, 2007 CarswellNat 4247, 2007 CarswellNat 5009, [2007] F.C.J. No. 1625 — There will no doubt be cases where the court can provide an important precedent; in such a situation the court may decide to exercise its discretion. This is not such a case. The issue in this judicial review is simply whether the Enforcement Officer had regard to the evidence before him. A ruling on this issue would not have any practical side effects on the rights of the parties.

The judicial review was dismissed.

Higgins v. Canada (Minister of Public Safety & Emergency Preparedness) (2006), 55 Imm. L.R. (3d) 30, 2006 CarswellNat 1899, 2006 FC 831 — The applicant entered Canada in June 2004 on a seasonal farm worker visa. Within a few days he left his employment and went into hiding. An arrest warrant and an exclusion order were issued in February of 2005. In June of 2005, he presented himself to immigration authorities with the intention of making a refugee claim. Such an application could not be entertained because of the outstanding exclusion order. He was arrested and released on a $3,000 bail posted by his eventual spouse. The applicant married and his wife, a Canadian citizen, made an in-land spousal sponsorship application. The Canadian spouse has a nine-year-old son from a previous relationship who has no contact with the biological father and instead calls the applicant his father. There was unchallenged affidavit evidence that the child had recently been diagnosed with behavioural and social disabilities. The applicant, prohibited from working, was the primary caregiver to the child. The applicant's spouse was the only breadwinner in the family and is currently pregnant. The court was satisfied that the harm to the family and particularly the harm to the child would be irreparable in the long run. The applicant is of invaluable assistance and the primary caregiver to the child. Without his presence, the mother would have to give up her employment and any possible employment insurance benefits she could enjoy come the birth of her child in December of 2006. This stay was granted.

Clark v. Canada (Minister of Public Safety & Emergency Preparedness) (2006), 59 Imm. L.R. (3d) 299, 2006 CarswellNat 4518, 2006 FC 1512 — The applicant brought a motion for an order staying a deportation order against him. The applicant has lived in Canada for all of his 59 years, and was the son of Canadian-born parents. The applicant did not register the fact of his birth within two years of its occurrence as required under s. 5(1)(b) of the former *Citizenship Act*. The applicant was currently incarcerated; he was convicted of several offences. The Minister's delegate wrote a report under s. 44(1) of the IRPA stating that the applicant was a foreign national or permanent resident for whom there were reasonable grounds to believe was inadmissible. The Minister's delegate issued a deportation order stating the applicant was inadmissible on grounds of serious criminality. The applicant claimed that he is a citizen of Canada and that the issuance of the deportation order triggered a serious consequence, specifically, the automatic ineligibility for day parole for which the applicant would otherwise be eligible. The applicant raised a serious issue as to whether he was a Canadian citizen. There was a minimal prejudice to the respondents in staying the deportation order since the applicant had lived in Canada for 59 years. Therefore the balance of convenience favoured the applicant and the deportation order was stayed.

Medawatte v. Canada (Minister of Public Safety & Emergency Preparedness) (2005), 52 Imm. L.R. (3d) 109, 2005 FC 1374, 2005 CarswellNat 4486, 2005 CarswellNat 3218, [2005] F.C.J. No. 1672 — The applicants were ill-served by their former lawyer. They were ordered to leave Canada. However, had their lawyer filed an application permitting them to remain in Canada based on humanitarian and compassionate grounds, that decision would have been rendered prior to the deportation orders being enforced. When the applicants attended at the immigration office to receive the PRRA decision, they mentioned their pending humanitarian and compassionate application, to which the immigration officer indicated she knew nothing about it. She told the applicants they would not be removed until the H&C application was decided. Shortly thereafter, the applicants were told to report for their removal and discovered there was no pending H&C application as it had never been filed. The removals officer, after having reviewed a great deal of information, concluded that the deportation order was enforceable. The applicants brought an application for a stay of that decision to enforce the removal order. The removal order was stayed on the basis that there was evidence of irreparable harm in that if the H&C application were granted, the effect of children being removed from school in Canada and going to Sri Lanka to be educated in another language, only to come back to Canada in a matter of months or a year could prove devastating.

Williams v. Canada (Minister of Citizenship & Immigration), 2004 CarswellNat 1405, 2004 FC 683, 2004 CarswellNat 3274 — In order to grant the stay of a removal order, the onus is on an applicant to establish each of the elements of the tripartite test. An elevated standard applies to a stay motion arising out of a refusal to defer an applicant's removal, because the stay, if granted, effectively grants the relief sought in the underlying judicial review application. Accordingly, rather than simply applying the serious issue test, it is necessary to closely examine the merits of the underlying application.

Almrei v. Canada (Minister of Citizenship & Immigration), 2003 FC 1394, 2003 CarswellNat 4244, 2003 CarswellNat 3787, [2003] F.C.J. No. 1790 — The applicant sought an order granting a stay of the removal order in force against him which provided for the applicant's removal to Syria, his country of nationality. The issue of irreputable harm can be answered in one of two ways. The first involves an assessment of the risk of personal harm if a person is deported to a particular country which is one of the key questions at issue in the underlying application to his stay application. The second involves assessing the effect of a denial of a stay application on a person's right to have the merits of his or her case determined and to reap the benefits associated with a positive ruling.

Antablioghli v. Canada (Minister of Citizenship & Immigration), 2003 CarswellNat 3325, 2003 FC 1245, 2003 CarswellNat 5192, [2003] F.C.J. No. 1576 — This was a motion to stay the execution of a removal order. The applicant was a medical doctor from Syria. He was also a Fullbright Scholar, and had obtained two postgraduate degrees in the United States. The applicant had been living in Canada since 1998 and was married to a Canadian. The applicant's Canadian wife was expecting her first child and was financially dependent on the applicant. The applicant was employed as a supervisor of community support workers with the Canadian Red Cross.

The applicant made an application for permanent residence at the Canadian Consulate General in Buffalo. The respondent knew at the time that the applicant was living in Canada. When this matter came on before the court, the applicant's application for permanent residence as a skilled worker had been outstanding for 21 months. The relevant factor in this case was obviously pertinent and compelling and it only made common sense for the removal officer to check with his own department before removing the applicant from Canada.

A stay of execution of the removal order was granted.

Marshall v. R., 2002 CarswellNat 2901, 2002 CarswellNat 3965, 2002 FCT 1099 (T.D.) — The applicant applied for an order restraining an adjudicator from continuing a hearing against the applicant until the action commenced by the applicant was heard and determined. The court concluded that it did not have jurisdiction to issue the order requested because no application for judicial review had been filed with the court. Section 18(1) of the *Federal Court Act* grants the Federal Court the jurisdiction to grant certain remedies, but subs. 18(3) requires that the application for judicial review be commenced. In the present motion, the motion for an interim injunction is made incidental to an action, not an application for judicial review. The court has jurisdiction to grant a stay pursuant to s. 18.2 of the *Federal Court Act*, but only if a judicial review application has been filed. Subsection 50(1) of the Act gives the court jurisdiction to grant a stay, but only provides for stays in proceedings being conducted before the Federal Court. Accordingly, the motion for an injunction was dismissed.

Cruz v. Canada (Minister of Citizenship & Immigration), 2001 FCT 491, 2001 CarswellNat 1016 — This was a motion for an interim order for the issuance of an employment authorization. The applicant based her motion on the fact that she had no other recourse available that would enable her to legally earn a living while waiting for the final disposition of her case. In the judicial review proceeding within which the interim order was sought, the applicant was seeking to quash a decision of a visa officer refusing her an employment authorization pursuant to the live-in caregiver program.

It is not within the purview of the court, pursuant to s. 18.2 of the *Federal Court Act*, to issue the order sought by the applicant.

Ibrahim v. Canada (Minister of Citizenship & Immigration), 2000 CarswellNat 3070 (Fed. T.D.) — The respondent moved to strike out an affidavit filed by someone other than the applicant as well as the exhibits and arguments based upon that affidavit.

The aspects that the respondent is seeking to have corrected by this motion are not aspects that, even in the event that the respondent is correct, may be seen as so incorrect or unacceptable that there should be an intervention in the process of an application for judicial review. Any motion to strike out that is made in the course of an application for judicial review must be an exception, so that one of the primary objectives of such an application, which is to hear the applications on the merits as quickly as possible, may be met.

Muncan v. Canada (Minister of Citizenship & Immigration) (1998), 141 F.T.R. 241 — The applicant applied for a stay of a pending removal order. The applicant was convicted of a number of criminal offences and was ordered deported. The applicant appealed to the Appeal Division of the IRB against the deportation order. The Minister declared the applicant to be a danger to the public and the applicant sought to set aside the danger opinion and to stay the execution of the deportation order pending review of the opinion.

There is no jurisdictional limit to the discretion that the court is empowered to apply under s. 18.2. The whole question of whether the discretion should be exercised relates to the merits of each individual case. Regarding an application for a stay of a removal order, the issue is whether it is fair and just to grant it. In considering the entire context in deciding whether to exercise the discretion provided under s. 18.2, the court found that it was far too technical a perspective to require the deportation order to be challenged on judicial review or to limit the application of the appropriate injunctive test to the circumstances of the deportation order itself.

Solis v. Canada (Minister of Citizenship & Immigration), [1997] 2 F.C. 693, 127 F.T.R. 218 — The applicant sought to stay the execution of a removal order. The applicant came to Canada as a refugee. In 1990, he and his family were granted landed immigrant status. Since 1992, the applicant has been convicted of a number of criminal offences. On the basis of some of the convictions an inquiry was held and a conditional deportation order issued against the applicant. The applicant filed an appeal to the Appeal Division which was still outstanding at the time of this application. While the appeal was pending, the Minister determined that the applicant constituted a danger to the public in Canada. The applicant sought leave to review this opinion, and that application was pending when this application for a stay was heard. The Appeal Division, notwithstanding the issuance of the Minister's opinion, had not decided that it had no jurisdiction to entertain the applicant's appeal with the result that the appeal before the Appeal Division was still outstanding at the time this application was heard.

The application for a stay pursuant to s. 18.2 of the *Federal Court Act* was dismissed on the basis that there already existed a statutory stay pursuant to paragraph 49(1)(b). In reaching this decision the court declined to follow the decision of the Court of Appeal in *Tsang v. Canada (Minister of Citizenship & Immigration)* (1997), 37 Imm. L.R. (2d) 1 (Fed. C.A.) on the basis that the application of s. 49(1)(b) was not before the Court of Appeal in that case.

Forde v. Canada (Minister of Citizenship & Immigration) (1997), 210 N.R. 194 (Fed. C.A.) — The Minister appealed against a decision of the Trial Division in which a judge ordered that "a stay currently exists in this case and the respondent's application [for reconsideration] is dismissed with costs in the cause."

In December 1994, a deportation order was made against the respondent. He appealed to the Appeal Division of the IRB, but before the appeal was heard, a delegate of the Minister decided that the respondent was a danger to the public in Canada. In February 1996, the respondent applied for leave to judicially review that opinion but at no time did he file an application for leave to review the deportation order.

In March 1996, the Trial Division issued a stay of the deportation order "until such time as the application for judicial review is finally disposed of." This order was clearly ancillary to the leave application then pending and was authorized by s. 18.2 of the *Federal Court Act*. In August 1996, the Trial Division dismissed the application for leave, thus terminating any judicial review proceeding. The original stay, granted in March 1996, thus came to an end, however, the Trial Division in September 1996, granted a "continuation" of the already terminated stay, and when the Minister applied for reconsideration of this order and a declaration that the stay no longer existed, the learned judge of the Trial Division made the order which is now the subject of this appeal.

The Trial Division has a carefully defined judicial review jurisdiction in respect of "any decision or order made or any matter arising under the *[Immigration] Act*." The decision of the Minister pursuant to subs. 70(5) is such a decision. During the course of disposing of an application for leave to seek judicial review of such a decision, the court is authorized by s. 18.2 to make ancillary orders, such as a stay. Once the leave application was disposed of there was no longer a leave or review proceeding to which a stay could be ancillary under s. 18.2. Section 50(1)(b) of the *Federal Court Act* was never intended to give a general mandate to the Trial Division to stop deportations which are no longer under attack in the court.

This appeal was properly brought without a question having been certified as the putative stay was no longer related to any application for leave, proceeding under subs. 82.1(1), and thus an appeal was not barred by s. 82.2.

Huseyinov v. Canada (Minister of Employment & Immigration) (1994), 174 N.R. 233 (Fed. C.A.) — The appellants requested an adjournment in order that counsel may have time to consider the implications of proposed new regulations concerning failed refugee claimants.

The adjournment was refused. No such regulations had been adopted. A press release cannot create accrued rights in the appellants. It is the duty of the court to apply the law as it is, not as it might be, and to hear appeals at the time for which they are set down.

Yamani v. Canada (Solicitor General) (1994), 27 Imm. L.R. (2d) 116, 80 F.T.R. 307 — The applicant applied for injunctive relief, pursuant to s. 18.2 of the *Federal Court Act*. The injunction was granted and the court had to consider, among other issues, whether the balance of convenience favoured the granting of the stay. The public interest in the maintenance of processes must be considered even where the stay is considered an exemption from the general public requirement in question and not one involving a suspension of that requirement generally.

The court referred to *RJR-MacDonald Inc. v. Canada (Attorney General)* (1994), 164 N.R. 1 (S.C.C.) at pages 38-39. It noted that in the case of a public authority the onus of demonstrating irreparable harm is less than that of a private applicant. The test will nearly always be satisfied upon proof that the authority is charged with the duty of promoting or protecting the public interest and upon some indication that the impugned legislation, regulation or activity was undertaken pursuant to that responsibility. Once these requirements have been met the court should, in most cases, assume that irreparable harm to the public interest would result from restraint of that action.

In this case deciding that the balance of convenience favoured granting a stay, the court noted that important as the public interest is in maintaining the statutory processes, the case had not been pursued by the Crown as a matter of great urgency. Further, the grant of the stay preserved the status quo as far as the applicant was concerned and did not interfere significantly with the exercise of their lawful responsibilities by the authorities. This case, if a stay was granted, would not result in a "cascade of stays and exemptions."

The court granted a stay but only to the extent of ordering that no removal or deportation order be issued against the applicant pending the final determination of the various applications for judicial review now scheduled to be heard by the court. This interfered as little as possible with the inquiry process as established under the *Immigration Act*.

Section 48 — former *Immigration Act* (The *Immigration Act*, R.S.C. 1985, c. I-2)

[Editor's Note: What appears below are the cases which were collected under section 48 of the former Act and which deal with the requirements that an applicant must meet in order to obtain a court-ordered stay.]

48. Time of Execution — Subject to sections 49 and 50, a removal order shall be executed as soon as reasonably practicable.

John v. Canada (Minister of Citizenship & Immigration) (2003), 231 F.T.R. 248, 2003 FCT 420, 2003 CarswellNat 942, [2003] F.C.J. No. 583 — The applicants sought to review the decision of a removals officer to defer the removal of the applicant from Canada. A removals officer is entitled to rely on what the applicant's counsel determines to be the overriding factor warranting deferral. Counsel must be very selective about what he or she chooses to point out to a removals officer. The *Immigration Act* does not give a removals officer the discretion to consider the various H&C factors in determining whether or not to defer removal. There is no requirement that the removals officer consider the impact of the removal on the Canadian citizen child.

In this case, the overriding factor warranting deferral was the availability of medical treatment for the child. The officer confirmed that a pediatrician in St. Vincent would be able to treat the child with the exact medication referred to by the professionals from Sick Children's Hospital.

Accordingly, the application was dismissed.

Ahani v. R. (2002), 19 Imm. L.R. (3d) 231, (sub nom. *Ahani v. Canada (Attorney General)*) 58 O.R. (3d) 107, 2002 CarswellOnt 364, (sub nom. *Ahani v. Canada (Attorney General)*) 208 D.L.R. (4th) 66, (sub nom. *Ahani v. Canada (Attorney General)*) 156 O.A.C. 37, (sub nom. *Ahani v. Canada (Minister of Citizenship & Immigration)*) 91 C.R.R. (2d) 145, [2002] O.J. No. 431 (C.A.); leave to appeal refused 2002 CarswellOnt 1651, 2002 CarswellOnt 1652, (sub nom. *R. v. Ahani*) 92 C.R.R. (2d) 188 (note), 293 N.R. 331 (note), (sub nom. *Ahani v. Canada (Attorney General)*) 169 O.A.C. 197 (note) (S.C.C.) — The appellant challenged a decision of the Minister of Citizenship and Immigration to the effect that he was a terrorist and a danger to the security of Canada. The appellant challenged this order alleging that he would face torture in Iran. His appeal was dismissed by the Supreme Court of Canada on January 11, 2002. He then filed a communication with the United Nations Human Rights Committee for relief under the optional protocol to the international covenant on civil and political rights which Canada has ratified but not incorporated into its domestic law. The appellant/applicant applied to the Superior Court for an injunction restraining his deportation pending the committee's consideration of his communication. This application was dismissed and the applicant appealed to the Court of Appeal which stayed his deportation pending the hearing of his appeal.

The applicant's mere removal from Canada does not establish a deprivation of life, liberty or security of the person. Convention refugees and other non-citizens do not have an unqualified constitutional right to remain in Canada. To trigger the principles of fundamental justice the applicant must show a potential risk of serious harm if he is deported. The Supreme Court of Canada has found that the applicant only faces a minimal risk of harm and thus it is not open to the court in this proceeding to come to a different conclusion.

The content of the principles of fundamental justice can only be determined by balancing individual and state interests. The applicant's interest is reflected in the opportunity to seek the committee's views on whether Canada's treatment of him breached the covenant which Canada signed. Canada's interest is reflected in the fact that Canada has never incorporated the covenant or the protocol into Canadian law by implementing legislation. Further, in signing the protocol, Canada did not agree to be bound by the final views of the committee. It was decided as a matter of policy by all of the party states to the covenant, that they each be free, on a case by case basis, to accept or reject the committee's final views.

Section 7 of the *Charter* cannot be used to enforce Canada's international commitments in a domestic court. International treaties and conventions not incorporated into Canadian law have no domestic legal consequences.

This case demonstrates the difference between the proper role of the executive and the proper role of the judiciary. Judges are not competent to assess whether Canada is acting in bad faith by rejecting the committee's interim measures request and instead deporting the applicant immediately. Canada has many international obligations to balance, not the least of which is to ensure that it does not become a safe haven for terrorists.

Dias v. Canada (Minister of Citizenship & Immigration), 2001 CarswellNat 1327, 2001 FCT 677 — The applicant sought to stay his removal from Canada to Jamaica. The applicant was the subject of two danger opinions issued by the Minister.

By virtue of s. 70(5) of the *Immigration Act*, the applicant loses the benefit of an appeal of his deportation order where the Minister is of the opinion the applicant constitutes a danger to the public in Canada. Should the applicant be successful on the underlying judicial review and have the danger opinion quashed, then his right to appeal the removal order would be restored, but this would be of very little assistance to the applicant if the removal order was already executed. The execution of the removal order before the hearing of the underlying judicial review of the issuance of the danger opinion will effectively render the judicial review nugatory. The loss of the benefit of the judicial review proceedings amounts to irreparable harm for the purposes of the tripartite test for a stay.

Romans v. Canada (Minister of Citizenship & Immigration), 2001 CarswellNat 1622, 2001 FCA 244, 273 N.R. 329 — This was an application for a stay of a deportation order pending the disposition of the applicant's appeal from an order of the Trial Division dismissing his application for judicial review. The Trial Division judge had certified a question for appeal. The court found irreparable harm because there was a substantial likelihood that the appellant would suffer irreparable harm if removed to Jamaica. The court found that the appellant was a mentally incompetent person who was unable to support himself and who had lived in Canada nearly all of his life. If such a person were deported, pending the disposition of his appeal, he would be effectively denied the benefit of a decision that he had a constitutional right to under s. 7 of the *Charter*.

With respect to the balance of convenience test, the court noted that the appellant will remain in detention pending the disposition of his appeal and that to stay his removal posed no threat to the safety of anyone in Canada. It was true that the Canadian public would bear the cost of this detention. In the court's view this was a price worth paying. The appellant was a vulnerable person who, in truth, although not a citizen of Canada, was more the product and responsibility of Canadian than of Jamaican society.

Cheema v. Canada (Minister of Citizenship & Immigration), 2001 CarswellNat 1417, 2001 FCT 740 (T.D.) — The applicants applied to stay their deportation from Canada. The discretion to defer removal is a discretion vested in the Minister notwithstanding the fact that the discretion is exercised by the removal officer. The Minister, pursuant to the Act, is under a positive obligation to execute removal orders. The discretion to be exercised by a removal officer does not consist of assessing risk, but rather of assessing whether there are special circumstances that would justify deferring removal.

The removal officer properly exercised her discretion in deferring removal to allow the children to complete their school year, and at the same time refusing to defer removal pending the disposition of an outstanding H & C application.

There was, accordingly, no serious issue to be tried and the motion for a stay was refused.

Williams v. Canada (Minister of Citizenship & Immigration), 2001 CarswellNat 1713, 2001 FCT 851 — The applicant applied for a stay of the decision of a removals officer refusing to defer the removal of the applicant pending his submission of an H&C application. With respect to the first part of the three-part test to be met in order to obtain a stay, the court concluded that it is necessary only to demonstrate that an applicant's case is neither frivolous nor vexatious. The court relied upon *Turbo Resources Ltd. v. Petro-Canada Inc.*, [1989] 2 F.C. 451, 91 N.R. 341, 22 C.I.P.R. 172, 24 C.P.R. (3d) 1, 39 F.T.R. 240 (note), 1989 CarswellNat 579, 1989 CarswellNat 626, [1989] F.C.J. No. 14 (C.A.)

Odumosu v. Canada (Minister of Citizenship & Immigration), 2001 CarswellNat 2477, 2001 FCT 1174 — This was an application to stay a removal order. The applicant achieved a negative H&C decision. She had failed to update her H&C application and had failed to disclose that her second child had developed asthma. Thus, the officer who rejected the application was not aware of this fact and therefore had not taken it into consideration.

Injunctions are matters of discretion. The traditional test for an injunction did not address the interests of this ill child. The court was not comfortable removing this 16-month-old baby to Nigeria without proper evidence about the severity of the child's condition and the facilities for his care in Nigeria. Accordingly, the execution of the removal order was stayed and the applicant was given a deadline by which she was to submit a fresh H&C application. The stay order further provided that the removal order was not to be executed until the disposition of this second H & C application.

Hussein v. Canada (Minister of Citizenship & Immigration), 2001 CarswellNat 2417, 2001 FCT 1172 — The applicant sought to stay a removal order. This application was brought two days after a similar motion by the applicant was heard and dismissed by another judge of the Federal Court. The court applied the principle of *res judicata*. The court observed that even if it were to consider the matter on its merits out of judicial comity, it would not reach a different conclusion than that reached on the earlier application unless it were convinced that the judge was clearly wrong on the basis of the evidence before him. Accordingly, the application was dismissed.

Other Relevant Legislation

Essiaw v. Canada (Minister of Citizenship & Immigration), 2001 CarswellNat 2312, 2001 FCT 1108, 2001 CarswellNat 3670 — The court dismissed a motion for a stay of execution of a departure order. There is an important distinction between a departure order and a deportation order. If a person subject to a departure order leaves voluntarily he or she will be provided, upon request, with a certificate confirming her departure. The effect of the certificate is that the departure is recognized as voluntary and has no implications for the applicant's right to return to Canada in the future. If the person does not leave Canada or leaves but does not obtain the certificate, the departure order is deemed to become a deportation order. As a result, the person may then be forcibly removed if she has remained in Canada. If she is removed or leaves voluntarily but does not obtain a certificate, the result is the same. The person cannot re-enter Canada without a permit from the Minister.

The issuance of a departure order represents the exercise of a discretion in favour of the applicant based upon a belief that the applicant will leave the country within the period provided by the Act and Regulations. If applicants choose not to take the benefit of that favourable discretion, then they are treated as they would have been if it had been determined that they were not likely to leave Canada. One cannot get the benefit of a departure order by agreeing to leave Canada and then seek to retain the benefit of that order when one refuses to leave by attempting to stay the order.

At the time of the bringing of the motion, the departure order had not yet changed into a deportation order. The application for a stay was therefore refused on the basis that it was premature.

Benitez v. Canada (Minister of Citizenship & Immigration), [2001] F.C.J. No. 1802, 214 F.T.R. 282, 2001 FCT 1307, 2001 CarswellNat 3468, 2001 CarswellNat 2773 — The applicant sought to review the decision of a removals officer refusing to defer the applicant's removal from Canada. The applicant's refugee claim was refused, his PDRCC was refused and then the applicant appeared for the purpose of making removal arrangements. The applicant's counsel asked the removals officer to defer removal pending the determination of the applicant's H&C application. The submissions of the applicant amounted to calling for a full H&C application to be heard by a removals officer. This is not what s. 48 of the current *Immigration Act* provides. The proper place for the full consideration of all of an applicant's H&C factors is before the H&C officer. The removals officer is entitled to rely on what the applicant's counsel determines to be the overriding factor warranting deferral. As such, counsel must be very selective about what he or she chooses to point out to a removals officer.

The doctrine of legitimate expectation does not override the very limited statutory discretion that the statute makes available to a removals officer. Possible suicidal tendencies should be given consideration by the officer and that was done in the present case. The officer took into account the three psychological reports provided by the applicant in making his decision. The application was dismissed.

Adel c. Canada (Ministre de la Citoyenneté & de l'Immigration) (2001), [2002] 2 F.C. 73, 2001 CarswellNat 2022, 2001 CarswellNat 3085, 2001 FCT 1017 — This was an application for a stay which failed. It often happens that counsel who represent immigrants are themselves consulted at the last minute by clients who live in hope that the removal date will never arrive. Moreover, the Federal Court frequently sees cases in which there is very little time between the applicant's summons and the date of removal. What this means is that often the choice of the hearing date for such applications is outside the control of applicants' counsel. But there are other cases in which counsel know in advance that they will have to make an application for a stay. In those cases, the court has a hard time understanding why the application for a stay is tendered at the last moment. This does not do justice to either the respondent or the court, both of whom must comply with the applicants' deadlines. The respondent is often unable to file its evidence. The court, for its part, must determine complex questions on the basis of an incomplete record and without the benefit of any period of reflection.

When an application to stay an exclusion order is presented at the last minute, certain facts must be taken into consideration. The first is that the court may very well refuse to hear the application. If the court is persuaded that it should hear the case, that does not mean that everything will happen in the usual way. The applicant still has the burden of satisfying the court that he or she is entitled to the order being sought. That burden is eased if the applicant is credible. Generally speaking, a judge hearing an application to stay is not, considering the state of the record, in a position to determine issues of credibility. But when the judge agrees to hear an application to stay on the ground that there was no assessment of the risk of return, and that the risk of return is based solely on the applicant's allegations, the judge must be satisfied that there is reason for concern about the fate of the applicant. The fact that there are others who would perhaps be in a better position to assess the applicant's situation, does not mean that the judge hearing the application for a stay must accept everything that he or she is told without exercising his or her critical faculties.

The court is in a position to decide questions of credibility, even in the context of an application to stay a removal order. The court must exercise prudence and maintain a certain reserve in regard to these questions of credibility because the opportunities for a careful analysis of the evidence are frequently lacking. But when the evidence before the court gives rise to some serious questions of credibility, the court should not ignore the possibility of bad faith. The court concluded that the applicant's evidence in this case was not trustworthy and dismissed the application for a stay.

Nabut v. Canada (Minister of Citizenship & Immigration), 2001 CarswellNat 3002, 2001 FCT 1392 — The denial of bail to an accused, upon his return to the United States, is not irreparable harm. Neither is it irreparable harm to be subjected to questioning in the United States in the course of an investigation into the terrorist attacks of September 11, 2001.

Chambers v. Canada (Minister of Citizenship & Immigration), 2001 FCT 84, 2001 CarswellNat 212 — This was an application to stay a removal order and in the course of giving reasons the court agreed that the discretion that a removal officer may exercise is very limited, and in any case, is restricted to when a removal order will be executed. In deciding when it is "reasonably practicable" for a removal order to be executed, a removal officer may consider various factors such as illness, other impediments to travelling, and pending H&C applications that were brought on a timely basis but have yet to be resolved due to backlogs in the system.

Obasohan v. Canada (Minister of Citizenship & Immigration) (2001), 13 Imm. L.R. (3d) 82, 2001 FCT 92, 2001 CarswellNat 325 — This was an application to stay the execution of a removal order arguing irreparable harm to the infant child of the applicant. The infant child was a Canadian citizen, born in Canada in July of 1999. While a court is normally concerned with irreparable harm to the applicant, the interests of the infant child are inseparably linked with those of the applicant. The court considered that pending a

Other Relevant Legislation

full consideration of the serious issue, or a full consideration of the child's interests, that the applicant and her daughter were *de facto* inseparable. Accordingly, the issue of irreparable harm was made out and an order was issued staying the removal of the applicant.

Wang v. Canada (Minister of Citizenship & Immigration) (2001), 13 Imm. L.R. (3d) 289, [2001] 3 F.C. 682, 204 F.T.R. 5, 2001 FCT 148, [2001] F.C.J. No. 295, 2001 CarswellNat 406, 2001 CarswellNat 2626 — Where a motion for a stay is made from a removal officer's refusal to defer removal, the judge hearing the motion ought not simply to apply the "serious issue" test, but should go further and closely examine the merits of the underlying application. Except in the case of a person overstaying a Ministerial permit, all removal orders are made by officials acting pursuant to a specific authority conferred upon them under the *Immigration Act*. Removal orders are not administrative arrangements made by the Minister, which the Minister is at liberty to change. They are orders which have the force of law which the Minister is called upon to execute. Aside from questions of travel arrangements and fitness to travel, the execution of the order can only be effected by some other process occurring within the framework of the Act since the Minister has no authority to refuse to execute the order. Accordingly, a request for deferral can only be made in the context of some collateral process which might impinge upon the enforceability of the removal order. The appropriate inquiry is whether the process in question could result in a situation in which the execution of the removal order was no longer mandatory.

Section 46.07(4) provides that where a person who has been found to be a Convention refugee is subject to a removal order, an immigration officer or an adjudicator shall inquire whether the person has a right to remain in Canada, and if so, shall quash the removal order and allow the person to remain. Section 53 provides that no Convention refugee or a person who has been found to be a Convention refugee in another country shall be removed to a country where they face a risk to life or freedom, unless they fall within certain enumerated classes of persons. This section contemplates the existence of a removal order which cannot be executed.

Legally, the mere presence of an outstanding H&C claim is not grounds for a stay of execution and by extension a deferral of a removal order. Further, declining the discretion to defer too broadly risks creating the equivalent of a statutory stay where Parliament declined to do so.

Frankowski v. Canada (Minister of Citizenship & Immigration), 2000 CarswellNat 1360 (Fed. T.D.) — The issue on this stay application was whether irreparable harm would result to the applicant if he were deported to Poland. For the purpose of a stay application, irreparable harm implies the serious likelihood of jeopardy to the applicant's life or safety. Irreparable harm must be very grave and more than the unfortunate hardship associated with the break-up or relocation of a family.

Giwa v. Canada (Minister of Citizenship & Immigration), 2000 CarswellNat 1176 (Fed. T.D.) — The applicant sought a stay of the execution of a removal order. The applicant was approximately 13 months late in seeking leave from the Refugee Division's negative decision of April 1999. The court supports the view that it is without jurisdiction on a stay application where the underlying application for leave is subject to a decision extending time before consideration. The court noted that some judges have adopted the practice on consent on stay applications deciding the extension of time question first. The court was not satisfied that an extension of time was warranted and denied the request for an extension.

Harry v. Canada (Minister of Citizenship & Immigration) (2000), 9 Imm. L.R. (3d) 159, 195 F.T.R. 221, 2000 CarswellNat 2522, [2000] F.C.J. No. 1727 — The applicants sought the stay of a removal order while their humanitarian and compassionate application was pending. If the applicants were returned to Trinidad or remained in Canada in the care of other persons, whichever course of action might be followed, irreparable harm would result to the child even in the possibly brief period that it might take to complete the humanitarian and compassionate application review. The length of that period was entirely at the discretion of the respondent. The applicants and their child have a relatively secure life in Canada. Their future in Trinidad is uncertain at best, both economically and socially. Such uncertainty represents irreparable harm for the young child, as would leaving her in Canada without the care and attention of either of her parents. The other aspects of the test were also found to be made out in this case and, accordingly, a stay was granted.

Ilyas v. Canada (Minister of Citizenship & Immigration), 2000 CarswellNat 2998 (Fed. T.D.) — The applicant was served with a direction to report for removal on November 3, 2000. His removal was scheduled for November 10, 2000 and the applicant failed to appear. The applicant was arrested on November 23, 2000 and received a direction to report informing him that his removal was scheduled for December 3, 2000. At that point, the applicant filed an application for a stay.

The applicant chose not to file a motion to stay during the time between November 3, 2000 and November 10, 2000 but rather decided to disobey a valid deportation order.

The court refused to hear this application for a stay on the basis that to do so would just reward someone who chose to disobey a valid deportation order.

Abazi v. Canada (Minister of Citizenship & Immigration), 2000 CarswellNat 529 (Fed. T.D.) — The court found irreparable harm in the fact that the applicants were operating their own business which supported them and enabled them to accumulate savings. If deported, the applicants would lose their business and their savings would be consumed for various purposes associated with their removal. The court reasoned that if the applicants were ultimately successful in their H&C application, they would be entitled to apply for landing from within Canada but would have lost their business and their savings.

Fabian v. R. (2000), (sub nom. *Fabian v. Canada (Minister of Citizenship & Immigration)*) 255 N.R. 367, (sub nom. *Fabian v. Canada (Minister of Citizenship & Immigration)*) 179 F.T.R. 153 (note), 2000 CarswellNat 93 (C.A.) — The balance of convenience favoured the appellant. The motions judge erred when she concluded that the fact that the appellant had committed crimes in Canada as opposed to abroad weighed against him and in favour of the public interest. The motions judge failed to consider whether the public was in any danger from the appellant given the fact that the appellant was detained and that as long as he so remained there was no evidence that he was endangering the public. It is not sufficient to look at the concept of "public danger" or "danger to the public" when there is in fact no likelihood of contact between the public and the "dangerous" person during the time for which interlocutory relief is sought.

Aquila v. Canada (Minister of Citizenship & Immigration), 2000 CarswellNat 131 (Fed. T.D.) — The test for determining the balance of convenience was affirmed in *R.J.R. - MacDonald Inc.* as a determination of which of the parties will suffer greater harm from the granting or refusal of a stay. One important factor in this comparison is the public interest in the maintenance of both statutory programs and the efforts of those responsible for carrying them out. If the stay is refused, the applications for landing or for leave to seek judicial review of the deportation order will not be prejudiced in any legal sense. Without any other evidence concerning the disruption which will be visited on the applicants if no stay is granted, the court found that the respondent would suffer greater inconvenience if the stay was granted and accordingly the application to stay the order was dismissed.

Anderson v. Canada (Minister of Citizenship & Immigration), 2000 CarswellNat 520 (Fed. T.D.) — The applicant commenced two proceedings. In one, he requested that his H&C application be determined, and in the other, he sought to review a negative decision of a panel of the Convention Refugee Determination Division. The applicant brought a notice of motion for a stay in each of the proceedings. The two applications were heard together. Section 49(1)(c)(i) provides a statutory stay of a deportation order when a person has been determined not to be a Convention refugee and has filed an application for leave to commence a judicial review. The statutory stay does not apply to an application compelling a decision on an H&C application. The motions were dismissed because of the statutory stay provided in s. 49(1)(c)(i).

Melo v. Canada (Minister of Citizenship & Immigration) (2000), 188 F.T.R. 39, 2000 CarswellNat 526, [2000] F.C.J. No. 403 — The applicant faced deportation to his native Portugal as a result of his criminality. The applicant, however, was also the father of two teenage daughters who resided with their mother in British Columbia and with whom the applicant visits monthly and to whom he speaks on the telephone frequently. He was also the father of a three-year-old by his relationship with another woman.

The issue of irreparable harm does not turn upon the possibility of serious physical harm to the applicant. If deported, the applicant will be returned to a western European country. Damage to economic and other interests of the applicant can satisfy the requirement of irreparable harm. The applicant will lose a position that is apparently much better than any he has previously been able to obtain. Further, deportation will affect the applicant's ongoing psychiatric treatment which may well result in a loss of the therapeutic gains which the applicant has achieved over a long period of time. Finally, there was evidence that the applicant's children would be devastated by his departure. If the phrase "irreparable harm" is to retain any meaning at all, it must refer to some prejudice beyond that which is inherent in the notion of deportation itself. To be deported is to lose your job, to be separated from familiar faces and places, and it is accompanied by enforced separation and heartbreak. There was nothing in the applicant's circumstances which took it out of the usual consequences of deportation. This was not the case of deporting an elderly woman who cared for and in turn was cared for by an elderly husband, nor was it the case of deporting someone who was the sole caregiver for a blind and sick grandparent.

In this case, the serious issue revolved around the extent to which the children's interests were considered in the proceedings before the Appeal Division. If the applicant is deported, the children's interests will be affected prior to a ruling being made on the extent to which their interests must be considered. This will effectively render the judicial review nugatory. If there is to be any reality to the judicial review application, the *status quo* must be maintained and accordingly, the loss of the benefit of the application for judicial review constitutes irreparable harm.

S. (R.V.) v. Canada (Minister of Citizenship & Immigration) (2000), 7 Imm. L.R. (3d) 181, 188 F.T.R. 58, 2000 CarswellNat 524 — This was a motion pursuant to s. 18.2 of the *Federal Court Act*, for a stay of an exclusion order and a stay of the execution of a removal order until such time as an application for judicial review had been dealt with by the court.

The law surrounding irreparable harm is treated somewhat differently in the immigration law context than it is when other areas, such as intellectual property, are involved. The high burden of proof has been downgraded so that a moving party merely has to prove that there is a reasonable likelihood that irreparable harm will be suffered. What constitutes irreparable harm has also been modified. Courts have looked to whether a moving party's life or safety will be put in jeopardy, noting that any harm from deportation must be grave, that is, more than the mere unfortunate hardship which inevitably accompanies any removal from Canada. Irreparable harm is not a mere inconvenience which may be managed, nor is it a hardship which may be overcome, or damage which may be readily repaired.

With respect to psychological trauma, a moving party's suicidal tendencies can constitute irreparable harm. Whereas there is no evidence in this case showing that the moving party's psychological problems would lead to similarly irrevocable harm, then the evidence points to the severity of the harm but not to its irrevocability or irreparable nature. The court was not prepared to consider irreparable harm being constituted by removing the applicant from the supports that he had garnered in Canada in his battle against alcohol until evidence was adduced that no such help was available to the applicant in the country to which he was being removed.

Panchoo (Litigation Guardian of) v. Canada (Minister of Citizenship & Immigration) (2001), 3 Imm. L.R. (3d) 206, *(sub nom. Panchoo v. Canada (Minister of Citizenship & Immigration))* [2000] 3 F.C. 18, *(sub nom. Panchoo v. Canada (Minister of Citizenship & Immigration))* 255 N.R. 369, 2000 CarswellNat 165, 2000 CarswellNat 1753, [2000] F.C.J. No. 143 (C.A.) — The appellant's father was scheduled for deportation after his request to be processed for landing within Canada on humanitarian and compassionate grounds was denied. The Minister sought to deport the appellant's father prior to the Trial Division's consideration of the father's application for leave to commence judicial review proceedings. An application to stay the order was dismissed, and in response the appellant, through her litigation guardian, commenced an action seeking various forms of declaratory relief. The appellant sought a stay with respect to her father's deportation pending the disposition of the action. Her motion for a stay was dismissed. The appellant appealed the dismissal of the interlocutory stay request to the Court of Appeal.

There is no right of appeal from a refusal to grant a stay of a deportation order pending the disposition of an application for leave to commence judicial review proceedings. The court expressed serious doubts that ss. 82 and 83 of the *Immigration Act* operated to preclude any appeal of a Trial Division's refusal to grant a stay pending perfection and consideration of a leave application. The Minister's decision to effect deportation was taken before the application for leave to commence had been perfected. The Minister knew full well that in proceeding in this manner, the intended deportee would be forced to seek a stay in which it would be argued that there was a serious issue to be addressed in the judicial review proceedings. That argument is for all intents and purposes the very one that will be addressed by a Trial Division judge when considering whether to grant the leave application. The Minister's insistence that deportation be carried out forthwith effectively short-circuits the leave application. The court expressed its frustrations with respect to the Minister's refusal to allow persons to have their day in court. The court expressed the view that the Minister should only pursue deportation in the clearest and most compelling of cases.

Other Relevant Legislation

Because s. 82.2 has been interpreted to the effect that there is no appeal from a motions judge's decision, counsel for the deportee initiated an action in the name of the daughter seeking a declaration that the deportation would not be in the best interest of the daughter.

There was no serious issue in this case because the appellant had no standing to challenge the deportation order. A child has no independent legal right to launch an action to prevent her parent from being removed from Canada. Further, the appellant was seeking a remedy pursuant to s. 24(1) of the *Charter*. A person seeking a remedy under s. 24(1) must personally have been the victim of an infringement. Such a person cannot base her application on an infringement of the rights of third parties. Accordingly, it was with regret, that the stay application was dismissed.

Antonio (Litigation Guardian of) v. Canada (Minister of Citizenship & Immigration), 1999 CarswellOnt 4098 (S.C.J.) — The Minister moved for a stay of these proceedings on the ground that the Superior Court should decline jurisdiction in favour of the Federal Court. The motion was allowed, however, the court noted that there was currently an application for consideration on humanitarian and compassionate grounds which had not been heard. Given the fact that there were Canadian children in this case, the court stayed the operation of its order for 120 days to allow the applicant and her children to remain in Canada until the H&C application had been concluded. The court also allowed that any party could apply to abridge or extend the stay if the circumstances required it.

Lawson v. Canada (Minister of Citizenship & Immigration) (1999), 178 F.T.R. 147, 1999 CarswellNat 2254 — The applicant was ordered deported by reason of his criminal convictions and his failure to disclose his prior conviction and period of residence in Canada when applying for admission as a sponsored candidate. The applicant's appeal to the Immigration Appeal Division was dismissed without reasons given. The applicant asked for reasons and at the date of this application for a stay, those reasons had not been provided.

The court concluded that the applicant was entitled to have the reasons of the IAD in hand before arguing his application for his stay. Accordingly, the court issued a stay on an interim basis against the deportation order. This stay was for a period ending seven days after the applicant received the reasons of the IAD.

Ahani v. R., 1999 CarswellNat 968 (Fed. C.A.) — The motions judge issued a stay preventing the deportation of the respondent pending the determination of an action before the court. The Minister appealed. The appeal was dismissed. The jurisdiction of the Court of Appeal to interfere from a decision regarding whether to issue a stay is well established. It is only where the motions judge has misapplied the law, misapprehended the evidence or where circumstances have substantially changed after the motions judge made his or her order — in such a manner as to justify interfering with the order — that the Court of Appeal will exercise its jurisdiction to intervene.

Suresh v. Canada (Minister of Citizenship & Immigration), [1999] 4 F.C. 206, 176 D.L.R. (4th) 296, 249 N.R. 28, [1999] F.C.J. No. 1180, 1999 CarswellNat 1466 (C.A.) — This was an expedited motion for an order staying the removal of the appellant pending the disposition of his appeal. Sri Lankan authorities indicated that the appellant would be detained upon his arrival in Sri Lanka, but that he would not be subjected to torture or degrading treatment. Assuming that the appellant is deported and detained, and assuming that he is successful on his appeal, the appellant's constitutional challenge would be a hollow victory. The authorities in Sri Lanka would be unlikely to release him and he would be unable to avail himself of the fruits of his victory. This was found to constitute irreparable harm.

If judges of the Trial Division are prepared to certify questions of general importance as a condition precedent to the Court of Appeal hearing an unrestricted appeal on the merits, then it is not unreasonable to defer the execution of a deportation or removal order in circumstances where it may ultimately be found that persons such as the appellant have not been dealt with as required by law. While there may be instances in which a person can return to Canada following a successful appeal, this is not one of those cases.

The court, in concluding that the balance of convenience favoured the public interest, did not wish to be viewed as undermining the legitimate attempts of the Minister to deport those who actively support terrorist organizations. Allowing the appellant to remain in Canada until such time as his appeal had been heard would not adversely affect Canada's reputation in the international community with respect to fighting terrorism.

Francis (Litigation Guardian of) v. Canada (Minister of Citizenship & Immigration) (1999), (sub nom. *Francis v. Canada (Minister of Citizenship & Immigration)*) 125 O.A.C. 248, 179 D.L.R. (4th) 421, 49 O.R. (3d) 136, 1999 CarswellOnt 3229, [1999] O.J. No. 3853 (C.A.); leave to appeal to S.C.C. allowed (2000), 138 O.A.C. 199 (note), 257 N.R. 200 (note), 2000 CarswellOnt 1961, 2000 CarswellOnt 1962, [1999] S.C.C.A. No. 558 — This was an appeal from an order of McNeely J. who had quashed a deportation order against the respondent and directed that no further order should be made against the respondent until proceedings in which her Canadian-born children had notice, and in which their best interests were considered.

The appeal was allowed. The *lis* of the application before McNeely J. was properly characterized as an immigration matter. This court has expressed the view that, generally, immigration matters are best dealt with under the comprehensive scheme established under that Act. A provincial superior court will not always yield jurisdiction to the Federal Court. There will be situations in which the Federal Court is not an effective and appropriate forum in which to seek the relief claimed. In those rare cases the superior court can properly exercise its jurisdiction. Since the decision of *Baker v. Canada*, [1999] 2 S.C.R. 817, 243 N.R. 22, 1 Imm. L.R. (3d) 1, 14 Admin. L.R. (3d) 173, 174 D.L.R. (4th) 193, 1999 CarswellNat 1124, 1999 CarswellNat 1125, [1999] S.C.J. No. 39, it is clear that the interests of the Canadian-born children can be considered under an application made under s. 114(2). Accordingly, the order of McNeely J. was set aside.

The order of the Court of Appeal, however, was stayed for 120 days to ensure that the respondents' s. 114(2) application was dealt with while they were still in Canada.

Charles v. Canada (Minister of Citizenship & Immigration) (1999), 171 F.T.R. 304 — The court did not agree that irreparable harm for the purposes of a stay application implied a serious likelihood of jeopardy to an applicant's life or safety. The court found that the execution of the deportation order on the facts of this case more than 2 months after the applicant made his application for landing on humanitarian and compassionate grounds would result in irreparable harm.

The respondent has an obligation in law to execute an outstanding deportation order as soon as reasonably practicable. This is a flexible test. The fact that the respondent has a backlog of applications for landing from within Canada on humanitarian and compassionate grounds that has precluded her from dealing with the applicant's application, a backlog which will apparently continue to preclude her from dealing with it for a number of months, should not work against the applicant. Accordingly, in this case a stay was granted.

Mahadeo v. Canada (Minister of Citizenship & Immigration) (1999), 166 F.T.R. 315, 1999 CarswellNat 347, [1999] F.C.J. No. 294 — The applicants sought to stay a removal order made against them. On the question of irreparable harm, the applicants who were 17 and 18 years of age respectively, argued that the disruption of their education due to the execution of the removal order before the end of the school year would constitute irreparable harm. Personal difficulties of this nature, although inconvenient, do not constitute irreparable harm, as serious as they may be to the applicant.

Torres-Samuels (Guardian ad litem of) v. Canada (Minister of Citizenship & Immigration) (1998), 47 Imm. L.R. (2d) 9, 57 B.C.L.R. (3d) 357, [1999] 6 W.W.R. 207, (sub nom. *Torres-Samuels v. Canada (Minister of Citizenship & Immigration))* 113 B.C.A.C. 214, (sub nom. *Torres-Samuels v. Canada (Minister of Citizenship & Immigration))* 184 W.A.C. 214, 166 D.L.R. (4th) 611 (C.A.) — This petition was brought on behalf of the children of Jose Lino Torres Hurtado who were aged seven and two at the time the petition was launched. They were seeking to enjoin or prohibit the deportation of their father, under a valid order of deportation, on the ground that it would not be in their best interests to be deprived of his attention and care. The petition invoked the *parens patriae* jurisdiction of the Supreme Court of British Columbia. The petitioners appealed from the dismissal of their petition by Paris J.

One of the underlying principles by which the discretion must be exercised is that it is not to be used to override a statutory provision, although it may be used to fill a gap in a legislative scheme.

There is no indication in the *Immigration Act* or elsewhere of a legislative intent to leave with the provincial superior courts, a power to review the validity of a deportation order under the *parens patriae* jurisdiction. Accordingly, the appeal was dismissed.

Darboe v. Canada (Minister of Citizenship & Immigration) (1996), 37 Imm. L.R. (2d) 72, 123 F.T.R. 1 — The applicant had been ordered deported and was also facing outstanding criminal charges in the Ontario Court (General Division). A representative from the Ministry of the Attorney General of Ontario indicated that immediately upon the applicant's removal from Canada, a criminal charge outstanding against the applicant would be withdrawn. In addition, it was also indicated that bail could be varied to provide for the accused's release provided that immigration would continue to detain the accused under the *Immigration Act*. Pursuant to the outstanding criminal charge, the accused was required to report for court subsequent to the date on which the immigration officials proposed to remove him from Canada.

Section 50(1)(a) of the *Immigration Act* operated to stay the removal order so long as the criminal charge remained outstanding. The court directed, however, that the respondent could immediately execute the removal order upon the withdrawal of the Ontario court charges.

Kandasamy v. Canada (Minister of Citizenship & Immigration) (1996), 36 Imm. L.R. (2d) 237, 119 F.T.R. 262 — The applicant is aged 16, male, and a citizen of Sri Lanka. In 1983, he moved with his mother to the Federal Republic of Germany to join his father who fled Sri Lanka in 1981. In June 1995, the applicant left Germany and arrived in Canada by himself. Upon arriving at Fort Erie the applicant was questioned by an immigration officer who concluded that the applicant was a Convention refugee in Germany. Subsequently, the applicant claimed refugee status in Canada. In August 1995, the applicant was determined to be ineligible to have his claim considered on a basis that he was a Convention refugee in Germany. The applicant was ordered removed from Canada. Subsequently, the applicant learned that he had not been accepted as a Convention refugee in Germany and the applicant sought to have his eligibility reconsidered in 1996. The request to reconsider was refused and the applicant applied for judicial review of that determination and a stay of the execution of the removal order.

The court found irreparable harm. The applicant was 16; it was the respondent's intention to remove the applicant to the United States. The evidence before the court indicated that throughout his entire life and since his arrival in Canada the applicant had continued to live under the care and supervision of adults: his parents in Germany and an uncle in this country. There was no evidence that the applicant was experienced in looking after himself or an individual who had demonstrated himself to be capable of surviving on his own. Should the applicant be removed to the United States, there was no evidence before the court to suggest that arrangements existed there, so that the applicant could receive the support and care to which he was accustomed. Thus, removal to the United States in those circumstances would create irreparable harm pending determination of the application for judicial review.

Rizzo v. Canada (Minister of Citizenship & Immigration), [1996] F.C.J. No. 1111, 1996 CarswellNat 1252 (T.D.) — The issue on this stay application was the question of irreparable harm. The applicant had over 20 criminal convictions and was addicted to drugs. His irreparable harm submission was based on his need for continuing medical attention in Canada. The need for such medical attention and support has been caused by the applicant's criminal activities and his drug addiction. Criminal activities and drug addiction cannot be the foundation upon which a claim of irreparable harm can be based for purposes of staying the execution of a deportation order.

Calabrese v. Canada (Minister of Citizenship & Immigration) (1996), 115 F.T.R. 213 — The applicant sought to quash a decision of the respondent that the applicant constituted a danger to the public in Canada.

The applicant was born in Italy in 1961, came to Canada with his family at the age of three and became a permanent resident, but never acquired Canadian citizenship. The applicant's family members live in Canada, the applicant does not speak Italian, the applicant has lived in a common law relationship for the past 14 years and has an 11-year-old son who is a Canadian citizen. The applicant's companion is expecting their second child. The applicant had a long criminal record that included a number of convictions for serious offences. The applicant acknowledged a substance abuse problem.

The basis for the claim of irreparable harm was that the applicant, if deported, would be separated from the professional and community base support, upon which he was relying to remain drug free and as a consequence crime free. In addition, it was submitted that there was a lack of equivalent support in the country to which the applicant would be deported and that because of the applicant's inability to speak Italian, the applicant would be faced with significant difficulties in attempting to establish himself again in that country.

The loss of family, professional and community support are capable of constituting irreparable harm. The court found the elements in this case parallel to those in *Toth v. Canada (M.E.I.)* (1988), 6 Imm L.R. (2d) 123 (Fed. C.A.). The court disagreed with the decision of Simpson J. in *Calderon v. Canada (Minister of Citizenship & Immigration)* (1995), 92

F.T.R. 107, which decision concluded that irreparable harm implied the serious likelihood of jeopardy to the applicant's life or safety.

Shayesteh v. Canada (Minister of Citizenship & Immigration) (1996), 34 Imm. L.R. (2d) 101, 112 F.T.R. 161 — This was an application to stay the execution of a deportation order pending determination of an application for leave and for judicial review of a decision made pursuant to subs. 70(5) of the *Immigration Act*. In dealing with the balance of convenience test, the court noted that there was inconvenience to the respondent if the stay was granted and acknowledged that there was a public interest in having the respondent's duties under the *Immigration Act* fulfilled in a timely manner. The court found the balance to lie in the applicant's favour, noting that the deportation order was issued in November 1984 and the process which lead to the issuing of the Minister's opinion was not implemented until September 1995, and the opinion not communicated to the applicant until March 28, 1996. On those facts the balance of convenience was held to lie in favour of granting the stay.

Singh (R.) v. Canada (Minister of Citizenship & Immigration) (1995), 31 Imm. L.R. (2d) 281, 104 F.T.R. 35 — This was a successful application to stay a removal order. There were three applicants. The first applicant was a citizen of Sri Lanka, the second applicant was his five-year-old son, and the third applicant was the wife of the first applicant who was a citizen of India. All three made refugee claims. The refugee claim of the father and son was denied and their judicial review application was dismissed. They were thus eligible for removal from Canada. For reasons undisclosed by the evidence, the wife's claim had not been concluded at the time of the judicial review application. The court found irreparable harm in the fact that, if the Minister was allowed to execute the removal order, the child would be separated from his mother. This would occur not as a result of any actions taken by the child, but rather because the processes controlled by the respondent Minister had not dealt with all of the applications at the same time. Removal of an infant child in such circumstances should be avoided. It is a primary goal of the *Immigration Act* to foster family relationships and family unity. The fact that these persons had been treated differently under the administration of the Act raised a serious dilemma for the family. That dilemma results from the department's choice to process the mother's claim at a different time than the other two applicants.

The balance of convenience favours the applicants. This order for a stay is temporary pending disposition of the application for leave and judicial review now filed in this court which simply postpones, but does not permanently preclude, the Minister undertaking removal proceedings.

Sannes v. Canada (Minister of Citizenship & Immigration), 1995 CarswellNat 1429 (Fed. T.D.) — The applicant/plaintiff commenced an action against the respondent/defendant, then applied for a stay of the execution of a deportation order. The plaintiff had maintained in an immigration inquiry that he was a Canadian citizen but had been unable to provide proper proof of that fact. Accordingly, his deportation order was issued and the adjudicator's decision was appealed to the Appeal Division which appeal was dismissed.

The applicant/plaintiff then filed a statement of claim in the Federal Court wherein he claimed status as a Canadian citizen by virtue of the provisions of s. 3(1)(e) of the *Citizenship Act*. The applicant/plaintiff maintained that his situation was similar to the case of *Benner v. Canada (Secretary of State)* (1993), 155 N.R. 321 (Fed. C.A.), which case was before the Supreme Court of Canada at the time of the commencement of the action.

In the evaluation of irreparable harm, there are three basic elements that must be considered: a) the kind of harm, b) the level of risk, and c) whether the harm is irreparable and not compensable in damages.

Personal inconvenience, even if serious, is not equivalent to irreparable harm. Irreparable harm implies the serious likelihood of jeopardy to the applicant's life and safety if he/she were to be returned to his/her country of origin.

The court found no irreparable harm. There was no doubt that the applicant would be deprived of an extensive support network of friends in groups which he established in Canada in order to help him deal with his rehabilitation from alcoholic, drug and sexual abuse. This did not constitute irreparable harm. Similarly, being returned to Norway and thrust into a foreign environment also did not constitute irreparable harm. If the applicant requires further treatment for his alcohol and sexual problems, it is admitted that Norway is capable of providing such services.

Merely because the issue raised in the proceedings was a *Charter* issue did not mean that it was necessary for the court to assume that the harm in question was irreparable. The court distinguished *RJR-MacDonald Inc. v. Canada (Attorney General)*, [1994] 1 S.C.R. 311 on the basis that it dealt with an issue whereby the applicants would incur major expense in altering their packaging. Even though this may be quantifiable, it was determined that because of the *Charter* argument, there were special reasons to conclude there that the harm would be irreparable. Accordingly, the court found no relation between the facts in *RJR-McDonald* and the case at bar. The application for a stay was denied.

Kronenfeld v. Canada (Secretary of State) (1995), 29 Imm. L.R. (2d) 231 (Fed. T.D.) — The court declined to grant a stay in this case due to the delay occasioned by counsel for the applicant. The application for a stay was scheduled to be heard on April 10, 1995 at 9:30 in the morning. At approximately 10 a.m. on April 10, 1995 the court received a 37-page affidavit from the applicant which had been prepared on April 9, 1995.

The court noted that in urgent matters it will hear an application for a stay on weekends if counsel requests. There was no adequate explanation for counsel's delay in bringing this application and his failure to perfect it in a timely fashion. The lengthy affidavit was sworn the day before the hearing but was only provided to the court at the very last moment. The court concluded that this application for a stay was, in fact, an abuse of its processes and refused to hear the application.

Langner v. Canada (Minister of Employment & Immigration) (1995), 29 C.R.R. (2d) 184, (sub nom. *Langner v. Ministre de l'Emploi & de l'Immigration*) 184 N.R. 230, 97 F.T.R. 118 (note) (C.A.) — The appellants arrived in Canada with valid visitors visas in 1988. They did not travel to the United States but rather remained in Canada eventually claiming refugee status. While they were waiting for their refugee applications to be disposed of, the parents had two children, both of whom had, by virtue of their birth on Canadian soil, Canadian citizenship and Polish citizenship.

The appellant parents' refugee claims had been rejected. They requested a waiver under s. 114(2) of the requirement that they leave Canada in order to make an application for permanent residence. This request was refused and requests for a review of that decision were also refused. Deportation orders were issued against the parents in October 1992.

The parents proceeded by way of an action for a declaratory judgment seeking a declaration that by virtue of the fact that they had 2 children who were Canadian citizens the Canadian government was prevented from executing the deportation orders made against them.

The Canadian *Charter of Rights and Freedoms* has no application in this case. The appellant parents' decision to take their children to Poland with them, or to leave them with family members in Canada, is a decision which is their own to make. The Canadian government has nothing to do with this decision. There is no government action which could bring the *Charter* into play. The appellant children's rights and freedoms, which attach to their Canadian citizenship are not an issue. Regardless of the decision made by their parents, the children will retain their Canadian citizenship and will be subject to no constraints in the exercise of the rights and liberties associated with their citizenship other than the constraints the parents impose in the exercise of their parental authority.

Rambharose (Litigation Guardian of) v. R. (1994), 28 Imm. L.R. (2d) 109 (Fed. T.D.) — This was a motion for an order to stay the execution of a removal order issued against the plaintiff's litigation guardian (mother). The plaintiff was a Canadian born child whose parents came to Canada from Trinidad in 1988. The plaintiff's mother was the subject of a s. 20 report for not having obtained an immigrant visa prior to appearing at a port-of-entry as required by s. 9 of the Act. A subsequent humanitarian and compassionate grounds review was rejected. The mother then applied for Convention refugee status but was found not to have a credible basis for her claim and an exclusion order was issued against her. A second humanitarian and compassionate review was rejected. The plaintiff's father is still awaiting a decision on his humanitarian and compassionate review.

This action was commenced to prevent the Minister from removing the plaintiff's parents. The plaintiff, through a litigation guardian, argued that his rights under the Canadian *Charter of Rights and Freedoms* would be violated if his mother was removed from Canada and he was forced to either depart from Canada or be separated from his mother.

The court found that the plaintiff would suffer irreparable harm as a result of being separated from his mother at such a tender age. Given the serious prejudice which the plaintiff would likely suffer if the removal order was executed, the balance of convenience favoured granting a stay.

Bajwa v. Canada (Secretary of State), 1994 CarswellNat 1595 (Fed. T.D.) — The applicant applied for a stay of a deportation order, which was refused. The granting of a stay is a discretionary matter. In that regard, the conduct of the applicant is a relevant consideration. The applicant's conduct in its total context is relevant. It is not merely a question of whether there has been an excessive delay.

The applicant voluntarily undertook expanded family responsibilities knowing there was an outstanding deportation order issued against him. He had not even met his wife prior to the issuance of that order. He was married in February 1993, but did not seek an H&C review until November 1993 and, at the time he sought a stay of a deportation order, his wife was pregnant. It was not appropriate for the court to exercise its discretion to grant a stay because the applicant was now trying to rely on a situation in which he purposely placed himself.

De Medeiros v. Canada (Minister of Employment & Immigration), 1994 CarswellNat 1598, [1994] F.C.J. No. 11 (T.D.) — The court granted the stay of the execution of a deportation order until such time as it had rendered its decision in respect of an application for leave and for judicial review of a decision of the Appeal Division. On the issue of irreparable harm, the court found that the Appeal Division had an ongoing and continuing equitable jurisdiction with respect to the applicant, which jurisdiction would cease to exist upon the applicant's departure from Canada. This cessation of the Appeal Division's equitable jurisdiction was held to constitute irreparable harm.

Grar v. Canada (Minister of Employment & Immigration) (1993), 20 Imm. L.R. (2d) 301, 64 F.T.R. 6 — The fact that the applicant's removal from Canada before May 28, 1993 would mean that the applicant was not able to complete a three-year program of studies and receive a diploma, constituted irreparable harm. Deportation would mean that those studies would never be completed; if they were to be completed, it would only be after several years.

There would be no irreparable harm caused to the applicant if he were removed from Canada after the date that the studies were expected to be concluded (May 28) and for that reason the stay of execution of the deportation order was not to extend beyond May 28, when the applicant's studies were expected to be completed.

Bal v. Canada (Minister of Employment & Immigration), [1993] 2 F.C. 199, 63 F.T.R. 226 — The applicant sought a stay of a removal order pending an application for leave to seek judicial review of a decision refusing special treatment on humanitarian and compassionate grounds. Sukhjinder Bal brought his two nephews to Canada because their natural father had received demands for money from members of the All Sikh Student Federation coupled with threats against the children's lives. Upon their entry into Canada the children's citizenship was not disclosed and the immigration officer wrongly assumed them to be their uncle's children. When the true citizenship of the two young children was discovered by Immigration, a conditional deportation order was obtained. The claim for refugee status on the children's behalf was dismissed. The uncle then petitioned for an order of adoption in the Supreme Court of British Columbia. When this was completed the uncle sponsored an application for permanent residence on behalf of the children and requested that the applications be processed from within Canada. This latter request was denied and it was that decision which the applicant sought to question.

Mr. Justice Noel had previously held that the court did not have jurisdiction to issue a stay in the circumstances of this case. Other judges of the court had expressed the opposite view. His Lordship was of the view that if he had jurisdiction to grant a stay he would have done so on the facts of this case. The court determined that it was imperative that there be consistency in the manner in which fundamental issues of jurisdiction are dealt with by the court. There was an open question as to the jurisdiction to grant relief. Accordingly, the court determined that the uncertainty about the court's jurisdiction should be resolved in favour of the party seeking the relief. To do otherwise would deprive a party of a remedy on the assumption that those members of the court who have assumed the jurisdiction to grant the remedy were wrong. The court was of the view that the contrary assumption should be made unless and until the Court of Appeal decides otherwise. Accordingly, a stay in the execution of the removal orders was granted.

Harper v. Canada (Minister of Employment & Immigration) (1993), 19 Imm. L.R. (2d) 233, 62 F.T.R. 96 — This was an application to stay a deportation order. The applicant claimed refugee status, which claim was found to have no credible basis. The applicant had applied for leave to review a decision finding sufficient humanitarian and compassionate grounds in the applicant's case to warrant a positive recommendation under s. 114(2). In support of the application for a stay, the applicant's counsel filed an affidavit from his personal assistant. In the affidavit the personal assistant reiterated facts about the case that had been told to her by counsel for the applicant. There was no direct evidence from the applicant and no explanation as to why such direct evidence could not be provided. A stay application is in the nature of an interlocutory motion and an affidavit based on belief is acceptable. However, it will have little weight when it consists of hearsay upon hearsay. The courts can only make decisions on the basis of evidence. The affidavit of an employee in which the employee purports to truly believe certain facts of which she has no personal knowledge, in circumstances where she has not even spoken to the person who would have such personal knowledge, is evidence of little probative value.

Information comes to the court by way of evidence and counsel should ensure that they present evidence that the court may rely upon with confidence. This is of heightened importance when motions are brought on short notice and the respondent has no practical opportunity to cross-examine on the affidavit or to present an affidavit in response.

One of the attachments to the legal assistant's affidavits was a nine-page letter from counsel to the manager of the central removals unit in Mississauga, Ontario. She also referred to this letter during argument to establish some of the facts relating to the applicant. This raises the difficulty of counsel who was appearing before the court relying on a letter that counsel has written to establish the truth about facts relating to the client. Evidence and submissions of counsel are not one and the same. Merely because counsel has written a letter containing information about the client and attached it to an affidavit, does not make it evidence of the truth of what is contained in it. The application for a stay was refused.

Petit v. Canada (Minister of Employment & Immigration) (1993), 19 Imm. L.R. (2d) 133 (Fed. T.D.) — The applicant arrived in Canada with her two children and claimed refugee status. She married her present husband while she was in Canada. A number of requests were made by the applicant after the date of her marriage for a determination of whether there were sufficient humanitarian and compassionate grounds to allow her to apply for landing from within Canada, on the ground that she was married to a Canadian citizen. On February 5, 1993 the applicant and her husband were asked to attend a marriage interview. On February 9, 1993 the applicant was notified that she would be required to leave Canada by February 26, 1993 and that there were insufficient humanitarian and compassionate grounds to justify allowing her to apply for landing from within Canada. It is in respect of that decision that leave to commence an application for judicial review was being sought. In those circumstances, s. 18.2 of the *Federal Court Act* gave the court jurisdiction to grant a stay.

On the question of whether the applicant would suffer irreparable harm, the court noted that generally when a person is being returned to a country where there is no threat of physical danger or persecution, it would be hard to argue that irreparable harm exists. However, the court noted that the applicant and her children found themselves in an 11th-hour situation created by the respondent. The applicant had written to the respondent on two or perhaps three occasions requesting a marriage interview. Had the interview been conducted in a timely manner, the applicant would have had an opportunity to test the validity of any decision made before being required to leave Canada. On the facts, the applicant had been called in for a marriage interview on the eve of deportation. She was told by the interviewer that "everything looked good." That decision was reversed by a supervisor with no explanation. The court found that the execution of the removal order in those circumstances, before the applicant had an opportunity to obtain leave to challenge the decision, was unfair.

The court does not look favourably upon applicants who appear at the last minute, before a removal order is to be executed, with a new spouse or with new requests for humanitarian and compassionate reviews. The position in which they put themselves in those circumstances is largely of their own making. In this case, the position in which the applicant and her children found themselves was largely of the respondent's making and thus, it was appropriate to grant a stay of the removal order.

Membreno-Garcia v. Canada (Minister of Employment & Immigration) (1992), 7 Admin. L.R. (2d) 38, 17 Imm. L.R. (2d) 291, 55 F.T.R. 104, [1992] 3 F.C. 306 (C.A.) — The applicant had applied for refugee status but a first-level tribunal found that there was no credible basis to the applicant's claim. The applicant applied for leave to commence an application for judicial review, which leave was granted. The applicant then sought a stay of the deportation order pending the outcome of the appeal.

In the present case, the deportation order flowed from and was underpinned by the decision finding no credible basis to the applicant's claim. If that decision was invalid then the deportation order was invalid. In such circumstances, a challenge has in fact been made to the validity of the deportation order.

In *Lodge v. Canada (Minister of Employment & Immigration)*, [1979] 1 F.C. 775 (C.A.), the court stated the principle to be applied in deciding whether a permanent injunction should be granted to restrain a Minister of the Crown from performing his statutory duty. In *Toth v. Canada (Minister of Employment & Immigration)* (1988), 6 Imm. L.R. (2d) 123 (Fed. C.A.), the court held that it had jurisdiction to grant a stay in cases such as this one. Since that time the Trial Division's jurisdiction has been made clear by the addition of s. 18.2 of the *Federal Court Act*.

The only requirement under s. 18.2 is that the judge consider the interim order "appropriate." It may be that in the absence of at least an indirect attack on the deportation order the court would not consider a stay appropriate.

In determining when a stay order is "appropriate" the court referred to the criteria set out in *Toth*. Given that leave had been granted, the applicant clearly had an arguable case. On the basis of the applicant's affidavit evidence it would be hard to reach any other conclusion than that the applicant would suffer irreparable harm if he was returned to El Salvador. Insofar as the balance of convenience is concerned, the test set out in *Metropolitan Stores (MTS) Ltd. v. Manitoba Food & Commercial Workers, Local 832*, [1987] 1 S.C.R. 110, is not relevant. In that case, the validity of one section of the statute was under attack and thus an interlocutory injunction order in favour of one litigant would by implication lead to similar orders respecting all individuals covered by the allegedly unconstitutional section in question. The section itself would in fact be rendered inoperative pending the determination of its validity. In the present case, the legislative provisions of the statute were not challenged. One decision by an adjudicative body operating under the statute with respect to one specific individual was being challenged. Rendering an injunction or a stay order in such a case will not suspend the operation of any part of the legislation. Thus, the public interest considerations expressed in *Metropolitan Stores Ltd.* are not in issue.

When considering the balance of convenience in these types of cases, the extent to which the granting of the stay might become a practice which thwarts the efficient operation of the immigration legislation is a valid consideration. The present procedures were put in place because a practice had grown up in which cases totally devoid of merit were initiated in court for the sole purpose of buying the applicants further time in Canada. There is a public interest in having a system which operates in an efficient, expeditious and fair manner and which, to the greatest extent possible, does not lend itself to abusive practices. This is the public interest which must be weighed against the potential harm to the applicant if a stay is not granted.

The situation in this case is quite different from that which exists, for example, when applicants seek humanitarian and compassionate reviews on the eve of the execution of a deportation order and then argue that a stay should be granted because of the uncompleted nature of that review. Such a case is the type of situation in which there is a potential for creating a practice which undermines the orderly operation of the legislation.

Another significant factor in considering the balance of convenience test is the degree of delay which is incurred, if any, in prosecuting the applicant's appeal. Similarly, when the applicant knows of the decision which underlies the challenge to the deportation order and does not seek leave to commence a s. 18 proceeding until the very last moment, there is reason to assume that the seeking of leave and the subsequent request for the staying of the deportation order are primarily time-buying manoeuvres.

In the present case, the balance of convenience was said to lie with the applicant and the stay was granted.

Editor's Note: Although the refugee procedures have changed, the principle stated herein may still be useful.

Cegarra v. Canada (Minister of Employment & Immigration) (1992), 56 F.T.R. 241 — Judges who decide immigration leave applications inevitably need the whole file, including the tribunal's records, so that the judge can determine whether the tribunal apparently went as badly off the rails as the applicant alleges. If the file raises an arguable case for judicial review, leave will be granted.

The applicant applied on July 30, 1992 for an 11th-hour stay. The court convoked a telephone hearing so that the respondent could be heard on July 30, before the applicant would have been removed from Canada. The removal order was made on June 9, 1992. The applicant's motion for leave was filed on June 16, 1992. The applicant was notified on July 14, 1992 that he was to be removed from Canada on Sunday, August 2, 1992. The court observed that it could have been determined on July 14, 1992, or shortly thereafter, that the tribunal's record would not become available before the August 2nd removal date.

The execution of a removal order will inevitably be stayed if the file is not complete, and, in the absence of the tribunal's record, it is not complete and the court cannot properly determine the leave application. When the removal is scheduled for a time before that at which the court and the respondent are prepared to address an already launched application for leave to commence proceedings, then, pursuant to s. 18.1 of the *Federal Court Act*, the execution order will almost always be stayed.

Eleventh-hour emergency applications for a stay will result in a dilatory solicitor being personally ordered to pay the costs of the application. Whenever a client comes to consult a solicitor at the last moment, the client's affidavit should make clear reference to that fact, lest the emergency be seen to be an unnecessary ploy or negligence on the solicitor's part. A solicitor who has acted for an applicant at the tribunal hearing can hardly ever assert tardy consultation by the client.

The court noted in this case that counsel requesting the stay had only been retained at the last minute and was not responsible for the last-minute application.

Duggal v. Canada (Minister of Employment & Immigration) (1992), 18 Imm. L.R. (2d) 20 (Fed. C.A.) — The Court of Appeal has no power to stay the execution of a removal order where it is deprived of jurisdiction by s. 82.2(1) of the *Immigration Act* to entertain an appeal from a decision of the Trial Division. The power to stay can only be implied from the court's power to hear an appeal. If such jurisdiction is denied, then the power to stay is absent. Not even the allegation that its *Charter* right is being violated can give the Court of Appeal a statutory jurisdiction to hear an appeal where Parliament has seen fit to withhold it.

Nananso v. Canada (Minister of Employment & Immigration) (1992), 56 F.T.R. 234 — The applicant sought an interim order for prohibition pursuant to s. 18 of the *Federal Court Act*, to prohibit his removal from Canada. The failure of the applicant to perfect his application for a stay in a timely manner did not deprive the court of jurisdiction. There was no legitimate reason for the application being brought a mere two hours before the applicant's removal from Canada. The court disapproved of the practice of bringing applications to stay deportation orders on an emergency basis and agreed with the proposition that the bringing of an application for a stay of a deportation order at the very last minute may constitute a sufficient basis for rejecting the application. No adequate explanation for the failure to perfect this application was forthcoming in the affidavit material and, therefore, the application was dismissed.

Berhan v. Canada (Minister of Employment & Immigration) (1992), 56 F.T.R. 183 — The applicant sought a stay of a deportation order pending a decision by the Immigration and Refugee Board on an application to re-open the claim to refugee status. Leave to review the decision denying refugee status had been sought and denied.

No decision on the application to re-open had been given prior to the date of this application, which was immediately before the date of the applicant's deportation.

No stay was granted because the court did not have the authority to do so. Stays can be granted when the validity of a deportation order is itself being challenged. It is also arguable that stays can be given when there is a proceeding before the court to which s. 18.2 of the *Federal Court Act* applies. Neither situation pertained in this case and, accordingly, the court did not have the authority to grant a stay.

Osei v. Canada (Minister of Employment & Immigration) (1988), 8 Imm. L.R. (2d) 69, 25 F.T.R. 270 — In this case, the court reviewed a variety of judicial pronouncements dealing with the court's jurisdiction to stay an executive order in general or a deportation order in particular:

1. The court noted that the Minister cannot be enjoined from executing a deportation order when the validity of the order has not been challenged;

2. The Federal Court of Appeal cannot, in the absence of statutory authorization to do so, stay the execution of an order that it has not pronounced, which it has no power to vary, and the validity of which is not challenged;

3. The Immigration Appeal Board has no jurisdiction to reconsider its decision confirming the deportation of a person and the only grounds for so doing would be evidence of new facts; and

4. The court distinguished the *Toth* case because the issue arose in that case, not out of a refugee status determination, but with respect to a removal order made against a permanent resident of Canada where a statutory right of appeal was provided. Further, the court noted that, in the *Toth* case, the order itself was being challenged.

Espinelli v. Canada (Minister of Employment & Immigration) (1988), 6 Imm. L.R. (2d) 21 (Fed. T.D.) — The applicant had been ordered deported. She then complained to the Human Rights Commission that the deportation proceedings violated the prohibition under the *Canadian Human Rights Act* against discrimination on the basis of marital status. The applicant sought a stay of the deportation order so that she could remain in Canada until her complaint was adjudicated upon. Her application was dismissed. While the *Canadian Human Rights Act* is a fundamental law, it does not clothe the Federal Court Trial Division with the power to stay a deportation order confirmed by the Immigration Appeal Board and maintained by the Federal Court of Appeal. Where the validity of the deportation is not itself an issue, the Trial Division has no jurisdiction under the *Charter* to paralyze an otherwise valid executory order.

Wood v. Canada (Minister of Employment & Immigration) (1986), 2 F.T.R. 58 — The Minister can only defer the execution of a deportation order if the person who is to be deported is subject to a judicial order containing specific provisions that would be violated if the deportation order were to be executed. Accordingly, where the applicant was subject to a probation order, which contained no conditions compelling the presence of the applicant in Canada or his attendance in court at a specified time and place, there was no obligation on the part of the Minister to defer his responsibility to execute the valid deportation order.

18.3 (1) Reference by federal tribunal — **A federal board, commission or other tribunal may at any stage of its proceedings refer any question or issue of law, of jurisdiction or of practice and procedure to the Federal Court for hearing and determination.**

(2) Reference by Attorney General of Canada — **The Attorney General of Canada may, at any stage of the proceedings of a federal board, commission or other tribunal, other than a service tribunal within the meaning of the *National Defence Act*, refer any question or issue of the constitutional validity, applicability or operability of an Act of Parliament or of regulations made under an Act of Parliament to the Federal Court for hearing and determination.**

1990, c. 8, s. 5; 2002, c. 8, s. 28

18.4 (1) Hearings in a summary way — **Subject to subsection (2), an application or reference to the Federal Court under any of sections 18.1 to 18.3 shall be heard and determined without delay and in a summary way.**

(2) Exception — **The Federal Court may, if it considers it appropriate, direct that an application for judicial review be treated and proceeded with as an action.**

1990, c. 8, s. 5; 2002, c. 8, s. 28

Case Law

Chen v. Canada (Minister of Citizenship & Immigration) (2005), 43 Imm. L.R. (3d) 48, 2005 CarswellNat 2045, 2005 CarswellNat 320, 2005 FCA 56, 330 N.R. 387, 4 B.L.R. (4th) 189 — This was a motion on behalf of the respondents to quash an appeal by the Minister against a decision directing that an application for judicial review made by the respondents be treated and proceeded with as an action. The litigation from which this motion arose involved claims for injunctive and monetary relief by the respondents, non-Canadian citizens currently outside Canada, who at one time lived here. Their claims allege that the Minister breached their statutory and constitutional rights by unlawfully failing to process their applications for permanent resident cards.

The motion succeeded. The provisions in Division 8 of IRPA effectively preclude an appeal from a decision in an application for a judicial review respecting an immigration matter without a question being certified. The court noted that once an application for a judicial review has been converted into an action, the proceeding continues subject to the rules governing actions.

Tihomirovs v. Canada (Minister of Citizenship & Immigration), 2005 CarswellNat 906, 2005 FC 479 — The applicant sought an order directing that his application for judicial review be treated as an action. It is the applicant's intention to have the action certified as a class action brought on behalf of all skilled worker, self-employed, entrepreneur and investor applicants who submitted their applications between January 1, 2002, and June 28, 2002. Subsection 18.4(2) of the *Federal Courts Act* places no limits on the factors that can properly be considered on a conversion motion. The desirability of facilitating access to justice and avoiding unnecessary cost and delay is certainly one of them.

Because it has always been the avowed intent of the applicants to seek class action certification, and because the facts that lie behind these motions make it entirely reasonable and appropriate that they should do so, it would be tantamount to a denial of the rights of the applicants and those they seek to represent to deprive them of the opportunity to seek class action certification by denying them conversion at this stage.

Chen v. Canada (Minister of Citizenship & Immigration) (2004), 43 Imm. L.R. (3d) 31, 2004 CarswellNat 5730, 2004 CarswellNat 4062, 21 Admin. L.R. (4th) 55, 259 F.T.R. 161 (Eng.), 4 B.L.R. (4th) 172, 2004 FC 1573; affirmed (2005), 43 Imm. L.R. (3d) 48, 2005 CarswellNat 2045, 2005 CarswellNat 320, 2005 FCA 56, 330 N.R. 387, 4 B.L.R. (4th) 189 — The principal relief sought in this motion was that the judicial review applications be treated and proceeded with as actions and then these actions be joined with other actions and consolidated into one proceeding. The discretion to direct that judicial review applications be treated and proceeded with as actions is governed by s. 18.4 of the *Federal Courts Act*.

On November 21, 2002, a class action scheme was incorporated into the *Federal Court Rules*, 1998 as Rule 299.1 to Rule 299.42. Significantly, however, this scheme applies only to actions and not to applications. Hence the need for Rule 299.11 that allows for a judicial review application in the Federal Court to come under the class action regime provided it is to be treated and proceeded with as an action under subs. 18.4(2).

The rationale for Rule 299.11 appears to be that the Rules Committee concluded that because judicial review applications in the Court of Appeal, pursuant to s. 28 of the *Federal Courts Act*, should not be heard as class proceedings, a rule was needed to permit applications at the trial division level to benefit from the class action scheme.

Because it has always been the avowed intent of the applicants to seek a class action certification, and because the facts that lie behind these motions make it entirely reasonable and appropriate that they should do so is tantamount to a denial of the rights of the applicants, and those they seek to represent, to deprive them of the opportunity to seek class action certification by denying them conversion under subs. 18.4(2).

This is a fundamental access to justice issue and as such is a legitimate consideration when the court is asked to exercise its discretion under subs. 18.4(2).

Gonzalez v. Canada (Minister of Citizenship & Immigration), 2001 FCT 25, 2001 CarswellNat 218 — The applicant sought to convert his application for judicial review into an action. The key test is whether affidavit evidence will be inadequate in all of the circumstances to deal with the issues at hand. The court found that while *viva voce* evidence would be better than affidavit evidence in the context of this case, it could not be said that affidavit evidence was not adequate so as to allow a proper determination of the relevant issues. Accordingly, the motion was denied.

Singh (D.) v. R. (2001), 12 Imm. L.R. (3d) 154, 2001 FCT 32, 2001 CarswellNat 257 (T.D.) — The plaintiff sought damages and other relief in an action against the defendant. The defendant brought a motion to strike out the statement of claim without leave to amend. The statement of claim arises out of a decision of a visa officer in Buffalo to deny the plaintiff's application for permanent residence.

The proper course of action for a plaintiff is to pursue an application for judicial review pursuant to ss. 18 and 18.1 of the *Federal Court Act*, and then, if successful, to bring an action for damages. Accordingly, the action was struck out.

Kozak v. Canada (Minister of Citizenship & Immigration) (2001), 12 Imm. L.R. (3d) 123, 266 N.R. 158, 194 F.T.R. 160 (note), 2001 CarswellNat 31 (C.A.) — The appellants were unsuccessful refugee claimants. They commenced applications for leave and judicial review and then moved to have their applications converted to actions pursuant to s. 18.4(2) of the *Federal Court Act*. These motions were denied. Counsel for the appellants then asked the motions judge to certify a question. Counsel for the Crown successfully argued that the motions judge was without jurisdiction to certify a question because the decision was made in the context of the *Federal Court Act* and not s. 83(1) of the *Immigration Act*. Accordingly, the appellant filed a Notice of Appeal unsupported by a certified question. Counsel for the Crown on the appeal then took the position that the court was without jurisdiction to entertain the appeals because there was no certified question as required by s. 83(1) of the *Immigration Act*.

The Court of Appeal agreed that the decision in question, namely whether an application for judicial review in an immigration matter should be converted to an action, was a decision made under the *Immigration Act*, and accordingly, before an appeal could be filed, a question for appeal had to be certified by the motions judge.

The Court of Appeal awarded costs to the appellant because counsel for the Crown had been inconsistent in this matter, arguing before the motions judge that she had no jurisdiction to certify a question and before the Court of Appeal that subs. 83(1) of the *Immigration Act* applied and that a certified question was required before the decision could be appealed.

Shao v. Canada (Minister of Citizenship & Immigration) (1999), 1 Imm. L.R. (3d) 116, 1999 CarswellNat 378 (Fed. T.D.) — The applicant requested an expedited hearing of a permanent residency application. The delay by immigration officials in Hong Kong and the anticipated delay in hearing the matter in the Federal Court had resulted in difficulties and anxieties, both on behalf of the applicant and the applicant's niece and family who now live in Canada.

Where there is a serious issue focusing on irreparable harm and the other side will not be prejudiced, the court will usually make a judge available, provided a timetable convenient to counsel and the court can be agreed upon. The applicant in this case had at best shown a serious inconvenience. Absent irreparable harm or some other exceptional circumstances, a hearing ought not to be expedited because there is still a backlog of immigration matters to be heard by the court. To expedite an individual hearing will mean either a cancellation of an already scheduled hearing or the deferment of a matter which is also waiting for a hearing date.

Oduro v. Canada (Minister of Employment & Immigration) (1993), 73 F.T.R. 191 — The applicant sought permission to proceed by way of an action so that the entire document entitled Consistency Project — Final Report on Meetings, dated May 19, 1992, be put before the court so that Board members could be questioned on their perception of the document. Judicial review is intended to proceed in a summary manner. Proceeding by way of action pursuant to s. 18.4(2) is exceptional and not to be resorted to except in the clearest circumstances. The court referred to a decision of Pinard J. in *Edwards v. Canada (Minister of Agriculture)* (1992), 53 F.T.R. 265 at 267, which allowed an application for an injunction and a declaration to be converted into an action in circumstances where counsel submitted there would be many different issues of fact and law, and that in addition there would be a need for extensive cross-examination on the many affidavits filed by both parties. Further, it was argued that the court should have the benefit of assessing the demeanour and credibility of witnesses under cross-examination, particularly experts. In this case, the applicant referred to censored evidence. The missing portion of the documents in question was delcted pursuant to the provisions of the *Access to Information Act*. The applicant sought to have the matter treated as an action on the basis of speculation there was further evidence which had been censored which could support the allegation of bias. Such speculation did not constitute a basis upon which the court could exercise its discretion under s. 18.4(2).

18.5 Exception to sections 18 and 18.1 — Despite sections 18 and 18.1, if an Act of Parliament expressly provides for an appeal to the Federal Court, the Federal Court of Appeal, the Supreme Court of Canada, the Court Martial Appeal Court, the Tax Court of Canada, the Governor in Council or the Treasury Board from a decision or order of a federal board, commission or other tribunal made by or in the course of proceedings before that board, commission or tribunal, that decision or order is not, to the extent that it may be so appealed, subject to review or to be restrained, prohibited, removed, set aside or otherwise dealt with, except in accordance with that Act.

1990, c. 8, s. 5; 2002, c. 8, s. 28

JURISDICTION OF FEDERAL COURT OF APPEAL

27. (1) Appeals from Federal Court — An appeal lies to the Federal Court of Appeal from any of the following decisions of the Federal Court:

(a) a final judgment;

(b) a judgment on a question of law determined before trial;

(c) an interlocutory judgment; or

(d) a determination on a reference made by a federal board, commission or other tribunal or the Attorney General of Canada.

(1.1) Appeals from Tax Court of Canada, except from informal procedure — An appeal lies to the Federal Court of Appeal from

(a) a final judgment of the Tax Court of Canada, other than one in respect of which section 18, 18.29, 18.3 or 18.3001 of the *Tax Court of Canada Act* applies;

(b) a judgment of the Tax Court of Canada, other than one in respect of which section 18, 18.29, 18.3 or 18.3001 of the *Tax Court of Canada Act* applies, on a question of law determined before trial; or

(c) an interlocutory judgment or order of the Tax Court of Canada, other than one in respect of which section 18, 18.29, 18.3 or 18.3001 of the *Tax Court of Canada Act* applies.

(1.2) Appeals from informal procedure in Tax Court of Canada — An appeal lies to the Federal Court of Appeal from a final judgment of the Tax Court of Canada in respect of which section 18, 18.29, 18.3 or 18.3001 of the *Tax Court of Canada Act* applies.

(1.3) Grounds for appeal — The only grounds for an appeal under subsection (1.2) are that the Tax Court of Canada

(a) acted without jurisdiction, acted beyond its jurisdiction or refused to exercise its jurisdiction;

(b) failed to observe a principle of natural justice, procedural fairness or other procedure that it was required by law to observe;

(c) erred in law in making a decision or an order, whether or not the error appears on the face of the record;

(d) based its decision or order on an erroneous finding of fact that it made in a perverse or capricious manner or without regard for the material before it;

(e) acted, or failed to act, by reason of fraud or perjured evidence; or

(f) acted in any other way that was contrary to law.

(1.4) Hearing in summary way — An appeal under subsection (1.2) shall be heard and determined without delay and in a summary way.

(2) Notice of appeal — An appeal under this section shall be brought by filing a notice of appeal in the Registry of the Federal Court of Appeal

(a) in the case of an interlocutory judgment, within 10 days after the pronouncement of the judgment or within any further time that a judge of the Federal Court of Appeal may fix or allow before or after the end of those 10 days; and

(b) in any other case, within 30 days, not including any days in July and August, after the pronouncement of the judgment or determination appealed from or within any further time that a judge of the Federal Court of Appeal may fix or allow before or after the end of those 30 days.

(3) Service — All parties directly affected by an appeal under this section shall be served without delay with a true copy of the notice of appeal, and evidence of the service shall be filed in the Registry of the Federal Court of Appeal.

(4) Final judgment — For the purposes of this section, a final judgment includes a judgment that determines a substantive right except as to any question to be determined by a referee pursuant to the judgment.

R.S.C. 1985, c. 51 (4th Supp.), s. 11; 1990, c. 8, s. 7 [s. 7(2) amended 1990, c. 8, s. 78(1).]; 1993, c. 27, s. 214; 2002, c. 8, s. 34

Case Law

Felipa v. Canada (Minister of Citizenship & Immigration) (2011), 2 Imm. L.R. (4th) 177, 340 D.L.R. (4th) 227, 422 N.R. 288, 32 Admin. L.R. (5th) 1, 2011 FCA 272, 2011 CarswellNat 3921, 2011 CarswellNat 6334, [2012] 1 F.C.R. 3 — The Chief Justice does not have the authority under subs. 10(1.1) of the *Federal Courts Act* to request that a retired judge of a superior court act as a deputy judge of the Federal Court after attaining the age of 75.

Charkaoui, Re (2003), 38 Imm. L.R. (3d) 56, [2004] 3 F.C.R. 32, 253 F.T.R. 22, 2003 CarswellNat 3887, 2003 CarswellNat 4312, 2003 FC 1419 — The applicant was questioning the validity of several provisions of IRPA which establish a procedure for determining whether a permanent resident is a danger to national security or the safety of any person.

One of IRPA's objectives is to maintain the security of Canadian society. One method that Parliament has given the Ministers to accomplish this objective is to sign a certificate that renders the person concerned inadmissible to Canada. The signing of this certificate is a ministerial power that cannot be delegated. The certificate must be signed by the Minister of Citizenship and Immigration and by the Solicitor General, after which it is filed with the Federal Court.

Another method created by Parliament to maintain the security of Canadian society is the signing of an arrest warrant by the Ministers. The signing of this warrant is a non-delegated ministerial power. In order to sign such a warrant both Ministers must have reasonable grounds to believe that the person concerned is a danger to national security or the safety of any person or is unlikely to appear at a proceeding for removal.

Subs. 3(3) and para. 78(c) of the IRPA confer on the designated judge the power to decide constitutional questions. IRPA gives the designated judge jurisdiction over the person concerned and the subject-matter as well as the power to order a remedy.

The judgement of a designated judge deciding constitutional questions can be appealed under s. 27 of the *Federal Courts Act*.

Given the distinction that the *Charter* draws between citizens and non-citizens, Parliament is entitled to enact a policy establishing rules that a permanent resident must follow in order to be able to enter and remain in Canada. Sections 33 *et seq.* of the IRPA provide that a permanent resident can be declared inadmissible if there are reasonable grounds to believe that the permanent resident is a danger to the security of Canada; that he has participated directly in war crimes or crimes against humanity; was a senior official in the government that committed war crimes or crimes against humanity; he has been convicted of an offence punishable by a term of imprisonment of at least 10 years, or for which a term of imprisonment of more than 6 months was imposed; he has been the member of an organization that has engaged in or is engaging in organized crime; or he made misrepresentations on his application for immigration or was sponsored by a person who made misrepresentations about him.

National security is essential for the preservation of our democratic society. We live in an era when threats to our democracy frequently come from unconventional acts that cannot be detected by unsophisticated investigations or traditional means. The methods used to obtain protected information must not be revealed. At the same time, a permanent resident must be reasonably informed of the reasons for which the Ministers have determined that he is a danger to national security. This is essential to ensure that the person concerned has the opportunity to defend himself.

The procedures established by ss. 76 to 85 of the IRPA take the existence of opposing interests into consideration and strike an acceptable balance between those interests. The fact that a designated judge is involved in striking this balance adds credibility to the procedure and ensures objectivity in achieving the result.

The designated judge must analyze the evidence as a whole and determine whether it provides reasonable grounds to believe there are reasons justifying the inadmissibility or arrest warrant and continued detention of the person concerned. There must be a serious possibility that the facts exist based on reliable, credible evidence.

The system of preventative detention established by Parliament in the IRPA in regard to persons concerned who in the opinion of the Ministers represent a danger to national security or to the safety of any person are consistent with the *Charter*.

Sections 77, 80, 81,82,83 and 85 of the IRPA do not contravene the rights guaranteed by s. 15 of the *Charter* or the rights guaranteed by paragraph 1(b) of the Canadian Bill of Rights.

The expressions "danger to the national security of Canada" and "members" referred to in subs. 83(3) and paragraph 34(1)(d) of the IRPA are not vague or overbroad. Subs. 80(3) and s. 84 of the IRPA do not contravene s. 96 of the *British North America Act*.

· · · · ·

PROCEDURE

· · · · ·

48. (1) How proceeding against Crown instituted — A proceeding against the Crown shall be instituted by filing in the Registry of the Federal Court the original and two copies of a document that may be in the form set out in the schedule and by payment of the sum of $2 as a filing fee.

(2) Procedure for filing originating document — The original and two copies of the originating document may be filed as required by subsection (1) by being forwarded, together with a remittance for the filing fee, by registered mail addressed to "The Registry, The Federal Court, Ottawa, Canada".

(3) [Repealed 2002, c. 8, s. 45.]

(4) [Repealed 2002, c. 8, s. 45.]

(5) [Repealed 2002, c. 8, s. 45.]

2002, c. 8, s. 45

Case Law

Torres-Samuels (Guardian ad litem of) v. Canada (Minister of Citizenship & Immigration) (1998), 42 Imm. L.R. (2d) 290 (B.C. S.C.); affirmed (1998), 47 Imm. L.R. (2d) 9, 57 B.C.L.R. (3d) 357, [1999] 6 W.W.R. 207, 166 D.L.R. (4th) 611, (sub nom. *Torres-Samuels v. Canada (Minister of Citizenship & Immigration)*) 113 B.C.A.C. 214, (sub nom. *Torres-Samuels v. Canada (Minister of Citizenship & Immigration)*) 184 W.A.C.

214 (C.A.) — This was a petition brought by two Canadian children of Jose Torres, who was the subject of a deportation order under the *Immigration Act*.

The *parens patriae* jurisdiction of the court is founded on the obvious necessity that the law should place, somewhere, the care of persons who are not able to care for themselves. The interests of the children are engaged only incidentally in the legal process that is unfolding with respect to their father. The court questioned the extent to which it could, using its *parens patriae* jurisdiction alone, frustrate an otherwise lawful and constitutional process, the focus of which is the legal status or rights of third parties.

The court found that the petitioners wanted it, pursuant to its *parens patriae* jurisdiction, to substitute a system of immigration with respect to foreign persons who have children born in Canada whereby it will be the superior courts of the provinces that will decide which of such persons shall be permitted to remain in the country. The court found that its *parens patriae* jurisdiction did not extend that far.

The *parens patriae* jurisdiction of the court should not be resorted to in a manner that flies in the face of a legislative scheme unless there is a gap in the scheme. Section 114(2) of the *Immigration Act* permits the Minister to exempt a person from deportation, owing to the existence of compassionate or humanitarian consideration; thus there is provision under the *Immigration Act* for the best interests of the children of prospective deportees to be considered. There is no gap justifying the court's intervention on behalf of the children. The petitioners also asked for a remedy pursuant to s. 24(1) of the *Charter*. The court declined to exercise its jurisdiction in favour of the Federal Court.

· · · · ·

50. (1) Stay of proceedings authorized — **The Federal Court of Appeal or the Federal Court may, in its discretion, stay proceedings in any cause or matter**

> **(a) on the ground that the claim is being proceeded with in another court or jurisdiction; or**

> **(b) where for any other reason it is in the interest of justice that the proceedings be stayed.**

(2) Stay of proceedings required — **The Federal Court of Appeal or the Federal Court shall, on application of the Attorney General of Canada, stay proceedings in any cause or matter in respect of a claim against the Crown if it appears that the claimant has an action or proceeding in respect of the same claim pending in another court against a person who, at the time when the cause of action alleged in the action or proceeding arose, was, in respect of that matter, acting so as to engage the liability of the Crown.**

(3) Lifting of stay — **A court that orders a stay under this section may subsequently, in its discretion, lift the stay.**

2002, c. 8, s. 46

Case Law

Charkaoui c. Canada (Ministre de la Citoyenneté & de l'Immigration) (2004), 42 Imm. L.R. (3d) 159, 2004 CarswellNat 3342, 2004 CarswellNat 3884, (sub nom. *Charkaoui, Re*) 328 N.R. 39, 2004 FCA 319 — A security certificate had been issued against the moving party. The hearing on the reasonableness of the certificate was to be held in November and December. The appellant asked the court to issue an order temporarily staying the hearings until the appeal currently before the Federal Court was heard and decided.

Subs. 50(1)(b) of the *Federal Courts Act*, gives the court the discretion to stay proceedings in any cause or matter. Rule 398, which establishes the procedure to follow for stays, does not strip the Federal Court of Appeal of its power to stay a proceeding if it is in the interests of justice. If an appeal before the Court of Appeal were to be rendered unnecessary, futile or illusory, as the result of an ongoing proceeding before a Federal tribunal or the Federal Court, there is no doubt that the Court of Appeal can order a stay of that proceeding to ensure that its appellate jurisdiction and process are not impeded.

Forde v. Canada (Minister of Citizenship & Immigration) (1997), 210 N.R. 194 (Fed. C.A.) — The Minister appealed against a decision of the Trial Division in which a judge ordered that "a stay currently exists in this case and the respondent's application [for reconsideration] is dismissed with costs in the cause."

In December 1994, a deportation order was made against the respondent. He appealed to the Appeal Division of the IRB, but before the appeal was heard a delegate of the Minister decided that the respondent was a danger to the public in Canada. In February 1996, the respondent applied for leave to judicially review that opinion but at no time did he file an application for leave to review the deportation order.

In March 1996, the Trial Division issued a stay of the deportation order "until such time as the application for judicial review is finally disposed of." This order was clearly ancillary to the leave application then pending and was authorized by s. 18.2 of the *Federal Court Act*. In August 1996, the Trial Division dismissed the application for leave, thus terminating any judicial review proceeding. The original stay, granted in March 1996, thus came to an end; however, the Trial Division in September 1996 granted a "continuation" of the already terminated stay, and when the Minister applied for reconsideration of this order and a declaration that the stay no longer existed, the learned judge of the Trial Division made the order which is now a subject of this appeal.

The Trial Division has a carefully defined judicial review jurisdiction in respect of "any decision or order made or any matter arising under the *[Immigration] Act*." The decision of the Minister pursuant to subs. 70(5) is such a decision. During the course of disposing of an application for leave to seek judicial review of such a decision, the court is authorized by s. 18.2 to make ancillary orders, such as a stay. Once the leave application was disposed of there was no longer a leave or review proceeding to which a stay could be ancillary under s. 18.2. Section 50(1)(b) of the *Federal Court Act* was never intended to give a general mandate to the Trial Division to stop deportations which are no longer under attack in the court.

This appeal was properly brought without a question having been certified as the putative stay was no longer related to any application for leave, proceeding under subs. 82.1(1), and thus an appeal was not barred by s. 82.2.

. . . . .

JUDGMENTS OF FEDERAL COURT OF APPEAL
[Heading amended 2002, c. 8, s. 49.]

52. Powers of Federal Court of Appeal — The Federal Court of Appeal may

(a) quash proceedings in cases brought before it in which it has no jurisdiction or whenever those proceedings are not taken in good faith;

(b) in the case of an appeal from the Federal Court,

    (i) dismiss the appeal or give the judgment and award the process or other proceedings that the Federal Court should have given or awarded,

    (ii) in its discretion, order a new trial if the ends of justice seem to require it, or

    (iii) make a declaration as to the conclusions that the Federal Court should have reached on the issues decided by it and refer the matter back for a continuance of the trial on the issues that remain to be determined in the light of that declaration; and

(c) in the case of an appeal other than an appeal from the Federal Court,

    (i) dismiss the appeal or give the decision that should have been given, or

    (ii) in its discretion, refer the matter back for determination in accordance with such directions as it considers to be appropriate.

(d) [Repealed 1990, c. 8, s. 17.]

1990, c. 8, s. 17; 2002, c. 8, s. 50

Case Law

Punniamoorthy v. Canada (Minister of Employment & Immigration) (1994), 166 N.R. 49 (Fed. C.A.) — The appellant, a citizen of Sri Lanka, was a Tamil who claimed refugee status on the grounds that he had a well-founded fear of persecution by the LTTE. The appellant testified that the EPRLF started forcibly recruiting young men into the Tamil Army. As a result of his standing in the community and long association with the commander of the EPRLF army camp, the appellant was repeatedly asked by parents to obtain their conscripted sons' releases. As a result of his frequent visits to the EPRLF camp, the appellant believed that members of the LTTE thought that he had become a spy or informer. When the LTTE seized control of Jaffna, the appellant was arrested and released after two days in custody. He subsequently fled the country.

The Board offered no reasons for disregarding the appellant's testimony on two of the three grounds upon which it based its decision. Applying the reasoning in *Hilo v. Canada (Minister of Employment & Immigration)* (1991), 15 Imm. L.R. (2d) 199, 130 N.R. 236 (Fed. C.A.), the decision of the Board was quashed. This portion of the appeal went on consent. The parties disagreed on whether the court should exercise its discretion under s. 52(c)(i) of the *Federal Court Act* and declare the appellant a Convention refugee. This decision reviews all of the relevant cases in the last three years on this question.

In order for the court to exercise its jurisdiction under s. 52(c)(i), the evidence on the record must be "so clearly conclusive" that the "only possible conclusion" is that the claimant is a Convention refugee. If the sole issue to be decided involves a pure question of law, which is ultimately decided in favour of the claimant, the court has no difficulty in declaring a claimant to be a Convention refugee. If the issue revolves around uncontroverted evidence and accepted facts upon which a legal conclusion must be drawn, the court may be compelled to declare a claimant a Convention refugee.

The court will not invoke s. 52(c)(i) when the factual matter involves conflicting evidence which is central to the refugee determination or the claimant's credibility. It is not necessary, however, for the Board to make positive findings of credibility before the court will exercise its jurisdiction under s. 52(c)(i). The court may exercise its discretion and declare a claimant to be a Convention refugee where the inconsistencies in the testimony, although not insignificant, were not central to the claim.

The weight of authority is that it is highly improbable that a claimant will be declared a Convention refugee by the court if the Board has made an overall negative assessment with respect to credibility. The same holds true when the Board disbelieves aspects of the claimant's case which are central or critical to the making of a refugee determination. In this case, the fact that the court is dealing with matters of credibility critical to the refugee claim is sufficient for it to be cautious in exercising its discretion under s. 52(c)(i). Simply because a tribunal falls into error by failing to give adequate reasons for rejecting testimony does not of itself establish the truth of what was said.

The appeal was allowed on consent, the decision of the Board set aside and the matter remitted for rehearing.

Vakeesan v. Canada (Minister of Employment & Immigration), 1993 CarswellNat 1712 (Fed. C.A.) — The court commented that it would not exercise its jurisdiction under paragraph 52(c) of the *Federal Court Act*. The evidence before the Board was not so clearly conclusive of the issue that the Board ought to declare the appellant a Convention refugee, nor was it clear that such a declaration was the only possible conclusion that the Board could reach. The court referred to two of its own cases in determining when it would exercise its jurisdiction under paragraph 52(c). Those cases were *Nadarajah v. Canada (Minister of Employment & Immigration)*, [1992] 2 F.C. 394, 17 Imm. L.R. (2d) 1, 142 N.R. 161 (C.A.) and *Mahathmasseelan v. Canada (Minister of Employment & Immigration)* (1991), 15 Imm. L.R. (2d) 29, 137 N.R. 1 (Fed. C.A.)

. . . . .

GENERAL

57. (1) Constitutional questions — **If the constitutional validity, applicability or operability of an Act of Parliament or of the legislature of a province, or of regulations made under such an Act, is in question before the Federal Court of Appeal or the Federal Court or a federal board, commission or other tribunal, other than a service tribunal within the meaning of the *National Defence Act*, the Act or regulation shall not be judged to be invalid, inapplicable or inoperable unless notice has been served on the Attorney General of Canada and the attorney general of each province in accordance with subsection (2).**

(2) Time of notice — **The notice must be served at least 10 days before the day on which the constitutional question is to be argued, unless the Federal Court of Appeal or the Federal Court or the federal board, commission or other tribunal, as the case may be, orders otherwise.**

(3) Notice of appeal or application for judicial review — The Attorney General of Canada and the attorney general of each province are entitled to notice of any appeal or application for judicial review made in respect of the constitutional question.

(4) Right to be heard — The Attorney General of Canada and the attorney general of each province are entitled to adduce evidence and make submissions to the Federal Court of Appeal or the Federal Court or the federal board, commission or other tribunal, as the case may be, in respect of the constitutional question.

(5) Appeal — If the Attorney General of Canada or the attorney general of a province makes submissions, that attorney general is deemed to be a party to the proceedings for the purpose of any appeal in respect of the constitutional question.

1990, c. 8, s. 19; 2002, c. 8, s. 54

Case Law

Gervasoni v. Canada (Minister of Citizenship & Immigration) (1995), 101 F.T.R. 150 — This case involves a constitutional challenge to subparagraph 46.0l(l)(e)(i). Notice to the Attorney General was given prior to leave having been granted but no returnable date was set forth in the notice. A notice contemplated under s. 57 of the *Federal Courtnn Act* must contain a returnable day, date, time and location. In immigration judicial reviews such particulars are not known until leave has been granted. The proper practice, therefore, is to give notice after leave has been granted with the notice containing the appropriate information.

· · · · ·

Other Relevant Legislation

CAN. REG. 98-106 — FEDERAL COURTS RULES

made under the *Federal Courts Act*

Rules for regulating the practice and procedure in the Federal Court of Appeal and the Federal Court

SOR/98-106, as am. S.C. 2002, c. 8, ss. 182(3)(a), 183(2)(a); SOR/2002-417, ss. 1–20, 21 (Fr.), 22–24, 25 (Fr.), 26–30; SOR/2004-283, ss. 1–20, 21 (Fr.), 22–41; SOR/2005-340; SOR/2006-219, ss. 1–10, 11 (Fr.), 12–17; SOR/2007-130; SOR/2007-214; SOR/2007-301, ss. 1(1), (2) (Fr.), 2(1) (Fr.), (2), (3), (4) (Fr.), 3–11, 12 (Fr.); SOR/2009-331; SOR/2010-176, ss. 1, 2, 3 (Fr.), 4–13 [Corrected Can. Gaz. 15/09/10 Vol. 144:19.]; SOR/2010-177 [Corrected Can. Gaz. 15/09/10 Vol. 144:19.]; 2012, c. 26, s. 27(b); SOR/2013-18; SOR/2015-21, ss. 1–4, 5(1) (Fr.), (2), 6–33.

[Note: The short title of these Rules was changed from "Federal Court Rules, 1998" to "Federal Courts Rules" by SOR/2004-283, s. 2. The long title of these Rules was added by SOR/2004-283, s. 1.]

. . . . .

PART 2 — ADMINISTRATION OF THE COURT

. . . . .

Court Records

. . . . .

22. (1) Caveat register — The Administrator shall keep in the Registry a caveat register, in which all caveats, withdrawals of caveats and orders affecting caveats shall be entered.

(2) Entry of caveat — On the filing of a caveat under subsection 493(1), (2) or (3), the Administrator shall enter the caveat in the caveat register.

. . . . .

Summoning of Witnesses or Other Persons

41. (1) Subpoena for witness — Subject to subsection (4), on receipt of a written request, the Administrator shall issue, in Form 41, a subpoena for the attendance of a witness or the production of a document or other material in a proceeding.

(2) Issuance in blank — A subpoena may be issued in blank and completed by a solicitor or party.

(3) Multiple names — Any number of names may be included in one subpoena.

(4) Where leave required — No subpoena shall be issued without leave of the Court

(a) for the production of an original record or of an original document, if the record or document may be proven by a copy in accordance with an Act of Parliament or of the legislature of a province;

(b) to compel the appearance of a witness who resides more than 800 km from the place where the witness will be required to attend under the subpoena; or

(c) to compel the attendance of a witness at a hearing other than a trial or a reference under rule 153.

(5) *Ex parte* motion — Leave may be granted under subsection (4) on an *ex parte* motion.

Case Law

Zündel, Re (2004), 259 F.T.R. 249 (Eng.), 2004 CarswellNat 1904, 2004 CarswellNat 2792, 2004 FC 798 — The applicant wanted to issue subpoenas to compel certain persons to attend the hearing being held pursuant to s. 80 of the Act on the reasonableness of a security certificate issued against him.

There are two main considerations which apply to a motion to quash a subpoena:

1. Is there a privilege or other legal rule which applies such that the witness should not be compelled to testify?

2. Is the evidence from the witnesses subpoenaed relevant and significant in regard to the issues the court must decide?

With respect to two of the witnesses, the applicant sought to compel them to provide evidence of the extent to which they had lobbied ministers of the Crown to deport the applicant. Lobbying ministers is a legitimate exercise in an open and democratic society. The organizations, which two of the witnesses represented, have been rather vocal about the applicant's removal from Canada and so the testimony of the two individuals would add little to the public record. The two witnesses would not be able to testify as to their true influence on the decision of the two Ministers to issue a certificate in this case since only the decision makers know how the decision was made.

Questioning the background knowledge or intent of the ministers at the time of their decision, in this case, would merely be a fishing expedition. The court held that the evidence of two of the witnesses was not relevant to the determination and quashed the subpoena. A third subpoena was issued in respect of the author of a book. The book purported to expose a number of dealings within CSIS. In deciding whether a journalist should be compelled to testify, the following factors should be considered: the relevance and materiality of the evidence to the issues at trial; the necessity of the evidence to the accused's case and his ability to make full answer in defence; the probative value of the evidence; whether the evidence was available through other means; whether the media's ability to gather and report news would be impaired by the journalist being called to give evidence and the degree of such impairment; and finally, whether the necessity of the evidence outweighs the impairment, if any, and whether the impairment of the media's function can be minimized by confining the evidence adduced to only that which is necessary.

Other Relevant Legislation

The subpoena issued to the journalist was also quashed.

· · · · ·

PART 3 — RULES APPLICABLE TO ALL PROCEEDINGS

General

· · · · ·

Appeals of Prothonotaries' Orders

51. (1) Appeal — **An order of a prothonotary may be appealed by a motion to a judge of the Federal Court.**

(2) Service of appeal — **Notice of the motion shall be served and filed within 10 days after the day on which the order under appeal was made and at least four days before the day fixed for the hearing of the motion.**

SOR/2004-283, s. 33(e); SOR/2007-130, s. 3

Case Law

Zhou v. Canada (Minister of Citizenship & Immigration) (2003), 31 Imm. L.R. (3d) 136, 2003 CarswellNat 4487, 2003 CarswellNat 2736, 242 F.T.R. 161, 2003 FC 1060 — This was a motion to appeal a decision of the prothonotary dismissing the applicant's motion to introduce additional evidence.

Discretionary orders of prothonotaries are not to be disturbed on appeal unless they are clearly wrong, in the sense that the exercise of discretion by the prothonotary was based upon a wrong principle or upon a misapprehension of the law or they raise questions vital to the final issue in the case. In such circumstances the judge ought to exercise his or her own discretion *de novo*.

· · · · ·

Orders and Directions

· · · · ·

54. Motion for directions — **A person may at any time bring a motion for directions concerning the procedure to be followed under these Rules.**

Case Law

Patel v. Canada (Minister of Citizenship & Immigration), 1999 CarswellNat 1536 (Fed. T.D.) — The applicant made a motion for directions pursuant to Rule 54 with respect to a case summary sworn by the respondent's officer and the inclusion of that summary in the tribunal record.

It would be inappropriate to include the case summary as part of the tribunal record because it was prepared after the impugned decision. The summary, however, will assist the reviewing judge and so it was ordered, on this motion, that the respondent serve and file the original or a copy of the case summary including all exhibits identified within 10 days of the date of these directions.

. . . . .

Court Documents

. . . . .

Filing of Documents

. . . . .

72. (1) Irregular documents — Where a document is submitted for filing, the Administrator shall

(a) accept the document for filing; or

(b) where the Administrator is of the opinion that the document is not in the form required by these Rules or that other conditions precedent to its filing have not been fulfilled, refer the document without delay to a judge or prothonotary.

(2) Acceptance, rejection or conditional filing — On receipt of a document referred under paragraph (1)(b), the judge or prothonotary may direct the Administrator to

(a) accept or reject the document; or

(b) accept the document subject to conditions as to the making of any corrections or the fulfilling of any conditions precedent.

(3) [Repealed SOR/2015-21, s. 12.]

SOR/2015-21, s. 12

Case Law

Alavinejad v. Canada (Minister of Citizenship & Immigration), 2005 CarswellNat 1042, 2005 F.C. 553 — This was a motion for an extension of time. The legal assistant to the applicant's lawyer miscalculated the time for filing by one day. On the day that the record was due to be served and filed, counsel realized the error. He and a student left their office at 4:15 and reached the registry at 4:45, a quarter of an hour after closing time. The registry let them in, however, the registrar refused to accept the document. Such behaviour was not in keeping either with the position of the Federal Court as a service organization or with Federal Courts Rule 72.

It is common procedure where a registrar can be made available and the circumstances are special or warrant such, to hold the Registry open or indeed to open the Registry in an emergency or perhaps as an accommodation, in order to avoid the embarrassment of counsel and extra unnecessary work. The registrar being opened, it is unseemly to deny services. If the Registry felt concern about whether or not to file the tendered material, the Registry is required, by Rule 72, which is mandatory, either to accept a document for filing or to refer it to a judge or prothonotary without delay. In this instance an order was made accepting the application record for filing.

Chung v. Canada (Minister of Citizenship & Immigration), 2003 CarswellNat 4233, 2003 CarswellNat 3055, 2003 FC 1150 — A letter from counsel for the applicants was referred to the court for directions pursuant to Rule 72. The applicants wanted to file a memorandum of argument exceeding 30 pages in length.

A general rule limiting the length of written submissions is clearly justified otherwise the court would be unable to control its own process and the parties would be free to submit prolix and redundant submissions.

Accordingly, as a general rule, a memorandum of argument cannot exceed 30 pages in length unless a party has first obtained leave by motion in writing.

72.1 Time of filing — Unless the Court directs otherwise, a document that is accepted for filing is deemed to have been filed at the time the document was submitted for filing.

SOR/2015-21, s. 13

72.2 Paper copies — fax or electronic transmission — A person who files a document by fax or electronic transmission shall, if required by the Court, provide the Registry with the same number of paper copies of the document as would have been required had the document been filed in paper copy.

SOR/2015-21, s. 13

72.3 Retention and provision of paper copy — A person who, by electronic transmission, files a document that is originally in paper copy and that bears a signature shall retain the paper copy of the document for the duration of any appeal and for 30 days after the expiry of all appeal periods and, if required by the Court, provide that paper copy to the Registry.

SOR/2015-21, s. 13

. . . . .

Affidavit Evidence and Examinations

Affidavits

. . . . .

84. (1) When cross-examination may be made — A party seeking to cross-examine the deponent of an affidavit filed in a motion or application shall not do so until the party has served on all other parties every affidavit on which the party intends to rely in the motion or application, except with the consent of all other parties or with leave of the Court.

(2) Filing of affidavit after cross-examination — A party who has cross-examined the deponent of an affidavit filed in a motion or application may not subsequently file an affidavit in that motion or application, except with the consent of all other parties or with leave of the Court.

Case Law

Zhu v. Canada (Minister of Citizenship & Immigration), 2000 CarswellNat 2518 (Fed. T.D.) — The applicant sought leave to file additional affidavits and to add material which ought to have been part of the tribunal record from the Canadian Embassy in Manila. The applicant applied for permanent residence as an investor. When it came time to cross-examine the visa officer, which was done by telephone, about half of the documents which ought to have formed part of the tribunal record were missing. Additional affidavits may be filed if such will serve the interests of justice and assist the court in making a final determination. The applicant was required also to satisfy Rule 84(2) which requires leave to file additional material following cross-examination. The test requires a consideration of the following three items:

1. Was the information in the affidavit available before the cross-examination?

2. Are the facts to be established in the supplemental material relevant?

3. Might the supplementary material cause serious prejudice to other parties?

The court allowed the filing of extra material in this case.

. . . . .

Joinder, Intervention and Parties

Joinder

. . . . .

104. (1) Order for joinder or relief against joinder — At any time, the Court may

    (a) order that a person who is not a proper or necessary party shall cease to be a party; or

    (b) order that a person who ought to have been joined as a party or whose presence before the Court is necessary to ensure that all matters in dispute in the proceeding may be effectually and completely determined be added as a party, but no person shall be added as a plaintiff or applicant without his or her consent, signified in writing or in such other manner as the Court may order.

(2) Directions — An order made under subsection (1) shall contain directions as to amendment of the originating document and any other pleadings.

Case Law

Pelishko v. Canada (Minister of Citizenship & Immigration) (2004), 227 F.T.R. 21, [2003] 3 F.C. 517, 2003 CarswellNat 1149, 2003 FCT 88, 2003 CFPI 88, 2003 CarswellNat 188 — The applicant brought a motion for an order joining Mr. H. Watson as a party to the proceeding. The Minister is a proper party to the proceedings in which an applicant challenges a decision made in the name of the Minister by one of his agents. Immigration officers authorized to perform the functions for which discretion is given to them under the Immigration Act do so in the name of the Minister. It is the usual practice in actions against the Minister, to have the decision maker file an affidavit on behalf of the Minister and to be available for cross-examination by the applicant. Watson can participate as an affiant on behalf of the Minister should the applicant seek judicial review. This is not a case in which Watson must be added as a party in order to have the issues "effectually and completely" settled. It is not appropriate to add Watson as a party in order to render him personally bound by the determination of the court. The relief sought is against the Minister and it is only the Minister who is bound by such an order. The Minister carries out what such orders require him to do, such as having applications redetermined through his representatives. Watson is only one such representative.

105. Consolidation of proceedings — The Court may order, in respect of two or more proceedings,

    (a) that they be consolidated, heard together or heard one immediately after the other;

    (b) that one proceeding be stayed until another proceeding is determined; or

    (c) that one of the proceedings be asserted as a counterclaim or cross-appeal in another proceeding.

Case Law

Kathirkamu v. Canada (Minister of Citizenship & Immigration), 2003 CarswellNat 651, 2003 FCT 308 (T.D.) — The applicant sought to consolidate separate Federal Court proceedings pursuant to Rule 105. The policy behind consolidation is the avoidance of a multiplicity of proceedings and a promotion of expeditious and inexpensive determination of proceedings. Among the factors that a court should look at to determine if there is sufficient commonality of legal and factual issues to warrant consolidation are common parties, common legal and factual issues, similar causes of action, parallel evidence, and the likelihood that the outcome of one case will resolve the other.

. . . . .

Representation of Parties

General

119. Individuals — Subject to rule 121, an individual may act in person or be represented by a solicitor in a proceeding.

Case Law

Salinas v. Canada (Minister of Citizenship & Immigration), [2000] F.C.J. No. 1004, 2000 CarswellNat 3202, 2000 CarswellNat 1414 (T.D.) — The respondent Minister appealed an order of a prothonotary who dismissed the Minister's motion asking that the application for leave and judicial review be dismissed on the ground that no one acting on behalf of the applicants was qualified to represent them.

The court should not approve of third parties who are not lawyers doing things which are within the exclusive jurisdiction of members of the bar.

It is the court's role and duty to guarantee compliance with the *Act* and the Rules and to ensure that those who appear before it, or draft proceedings for the purpose of asserting rights, are officers of the court. Facts put in evidence in each of the respondent Minister's motions constituted evidence which pointed inexorably to the conclusion that in each case the application for leave and judicial review by the applicants had been prepared and drafted by an agent who could not act as a representative in this court. If an applicant decides to be represented, Rule 119 is clear, he or she must be represented by a solicitor.

Accordingly, the respondent Minister's appeal was allowed and the application for judicial review dismissed.

Parmar c. Canada (Ministre de la Citoyenneté & de l'Immigration) (2000), 12 Imm. L.R. (3d) 178, 2000 CarswellNat 1432, 2000 CarswellNat 3429 (Fed. T.D.) — The defendant Minister appealed an order dismissing its motion asking the court to dismiss an application for leave and judicial review. The motion had been brought on the ground that the person acting on the plaintiff's behalf was not qualified to represent him.

It is the court's function and duty to ensure that its Act and its Rules are observed and that those who appear before it or prepare pleadings to be used in asserting rights are officers of the court. The facts in this matter lead inexorably to the conclusion that the plaintiff's application for leave and judicial review had been prepared and drafted by an agent. It is true that a plaintiff may act in person, but if he or she decides to be represented then the rule is clear, he or she must be represented by a barrister or advocate.

The court concluded that the plaintiff had been represented by a person who was not authorized to do so, and accordingly, allowed the Minister's appeal and dismissed the plaintiff's application for leave and for judicial review.

. . . . .

Filing of Confidential Material

151. (1) Motion for order of confidentiality — On motion, the Court may order that material to be filed shall be treated as confidential.

(2) Demonstrated need for confidentiality — Before making an order under subsection (1), the Court must be satisfied that the material should be treated as confidential, notwithstanding the public interest in open and accessible court proceedings.

Case Law

Harkat, Re, [2009] F.C.J. No. 228, 80 Imm. L.R. (3d) 89, 2009 CarswellNat 436, 2009 FC 167 — Special advocates do not have the jurisdiction to act in public on behalf of a named person, nor are they permitted to communicate with him while acting as special advocate. They are not counsel of record in the proceeding. They do not, therefore, have standing to seek a confidentiality order which would prevent public access to court records; only counsel for the applicant may seek such an order. The objection made by the special advocates that the three summaries of conversation be kept confidential was granted on an interim basis. The three summaries of conversations were disclosed to the applicant and his counsel. The applicant and his counsel were given 10 days to serve and file a motion asking the court to continue treating the three summaries of conversations confidentially. In the absence of any such motion, the three summaries of conversations would become part of the public amended security intelligence report.

Other Relevant Legislation

C. (A.) v. Canada (Minister of Citizenship & Immigration) (2003), 33 Imm. L.R. (3d) 45, 2003 CarswellNat 3976, 2003 CarswellNat 4558, 2003 FC 1452, 243 F.T.R. 211, 2003 CFPI 1452 — As an ancillary matter to their judicial review application, the applicants brought a motion for an order sealing the record in this case. The grounds for the motion were that the applicants, as well as the witnesses who testified at the refugee hearing, face a risk of harm if returned to their country of origin, as do their relatives in that country. The harm alleged is in the form of reprisals for their having testified on behalf of the applicants at the refugee hearing. Witnesses who testify before the Refugee Division, after receiving assurances that their evidence will be treated in confidence, should not be exposed to serious and substantial risk of harm if the matter proceeds to the judicial review stage.

The Supreme Court of Canada in *Sierra Club of Canada v. Canada (Minister of Finance)*, [2002] 2 S.C.R. 522, 2002 CarswellNat 823, [2002] S.C.J. No. 42, 2002 SCC 41, (sub nom. *Atomic Energy of Canada Ltd. v. Sierra Club of Canada*) 211 D.L.R. (4th) 193, (sub nom. *Atomic Energy of Canada Ltd. v. Sierra Club of Canada*) 18 C.P.R. (4th) 1, 44 C.E.L.R. (N.S.) 161, 287 N.R. 203, 20 C.P.C. (5th) 1, 40 Admin. L.R. (3d) 1, (sub nom. *Atomic Energy of Canada Ltd. v. Sierra Club of Canada*) 93 C.R.R. (2d) 219, 223 F.T.R. 137 (note), 2002 CarswellNat 822, set out a two-part test for a confidentiality order: a) a confidentiality order should only be granted when the order is necessary to prevent a serious risk to an important interest including a commercial interest, in the context of litigation because reasonable alternative measures will not prevent the risk; and b) the salutary effects of the confidentiality order, including the effects on the right of civil litigants to a fair trial, outweigh its deleterious effects, including the effects on the open right to free expression, which in this context includes the public interest in open and accessible court proceedings.

The court was satisfied that the applicants and their witnesses genuinely felt at risk, but was not satisfied that the applicants had met the onus that would justify a departure from the principle of an open and accessible court.

The court ordered that the record of the proceeding as is maintained on the court's website should be amended to show the style of cause as set out in the order that the court was issuing. Secondly, by deleting from the text the names of the applicants and replacing those names with the initials and finally, by deleting the names of the applicant's witnesses and other identifying features from the text of any order or reasons and replacing them with such alternatives as the court considered appropriate in the circumstances.

152. (1) Marking of confidential material — Where the material is required by law to be treated confidentially or where the Court orders that material be treated confidentially, a party who files the material shall separate and clearly mark it as confidential, identifying the legislative provision or the Court order under which it is required to be treated as confidential.

(2) Access to confidential material — Unless otherwise ordered by the Court,

    (a) only a solicitor of record, or a solicitor assisting in the proceeding, who is not a party is entitled to have access to confidential material;

(b) confidential material shall be given to a solicitor of record for a party only if the solicitor gives a written undertaking to the Court that he or she will

(i) not disclose its content except to solicitors assisting in the proceeding or to the Court in the course of argument,

(ii) not permit it to be reproduced in whole or in part, and

(iii) destroy the material and any notes on its content and file a certificate of their destruction or deliver the material and notes as ordered by the Court, when the material and notes are no longer required for the proceeding or the solicitor ceases to be solicitor of record;

(c) only one copy of any confidential material shall be given to the solicitor of record for each party; and

(d) no confidential material or any information derived therefrom shall be disclosed to the public.

(3) **Order to continue** — An order made under subsection (1) continues in effect until the Court orders otherwise, including for the duration of any appeal of the proceeding and after final judgment.

Case Law

Harkat, Re, [2009] F.C.J. No. 228, 80 Imm. L.R. (3d) 89, 2009 CarswellNat 436, 2009 FC 167 — Special advocates do not have the jurisdiction to act in public on behalf of a named person, nor are they permitted to communicate with him while acting as special advocate. They are not counsel of record in the proceeding. They do not, therefore, have standing to seek a confidentiality order which would prevent public access to court records; only counsel for the applicant may seek such an order. The objection made by the special advocates that the three summaries of conversation be kept confidential was granted on an interim basis. The three summaries of conversations were disclosed to the applicant and his counsel. The applicant and his counsel were given 10 days to serve and file a motion asking the court to continue treating the three summaries of conversations confidentially. In the absence of any such motion, the three summaries of conversations would become part of the public amended security intelligence report.

· · · · ·

Summary Disposition

· · · · ·

167. Dismissal for delay — The Court may, at any time, on the motion of a party who is not in default of any requirement of these Rules, dismiss a proceeding or impose other sanctions on the ground that there has been undue delay by a plaintiff, applicant or appellant in prosecuting the proceeding.

Case Law

Bensalah v. Canada (Ministre de la Citoyenneté & de l'Immigration) (2000), 184 F.T.R. 311 (note), 2000 CarswellNat 476, 2000 CarswellNat 1956 (C.A.) — The appellant was benefiting from a statutory stay of execution of a removal order pending disposition of his appeal. Under the Federal Courts Rules the appellant was required to file his memorandum on or before November 25, 1999, but had not done so. The respondent filed a motion to dismiss the appeal alleging as the reason, undue delay. The motion was allowed. The fact that in filing a Notice of Appeal the appellant may benefit from an automatic stay of the removal order, imposes a corresponding duty to prosecute the appeal with diligence and at the very least to comply with the deadlines specified in the rules.

. . . . .

PART 4 — ACTIONS

. . . . .

Summary Judgment and Summary Trial
[Heading amended SOR/2009-331, s. 3.]

Motion and Service
[Heading added SOR/2009-331, s. 3.]

213. (1) Motion by a party — A party may bring a motion for summary judgment or summary trial on all or some of the issues raised in the pleadings at any time after the defendant has filed a defence but before the time and place for trial have been fixed.

(2) Further motion — If a party brings a motion for summary judgment or summary trial, the party may not bring a further motion for either summary judgment or summary trial except with leave of the Court.

(3) Obligations of moving party — A motion for summary judgment or summary trial in an action may be brought by serving and filing a notice of motion and motion record at least 20 days before the day set out in the notice for the hearing of the motion.

(4) Obligations of responding party — A party served with a motion for summary judgment or summary trial shall serve and file a respondent's motion record not later than 10 days before the day set out in the notice of motion for the hearing of the motion.

SOR/2009-331, s. 3

Case Law

Samimifar v. Canada (Minister of Citizenship & Immigration), [2006] F.C.J. No. 1626, 58 Imm. L.R. (3d) 24, 2006 CarswellNat 5309, 2006 FC 1301 — The applicant was granted approval-in-principle to accept and process an application for permanent residence from within Canada. He submitted his application in 1994 and until January 2003, his application appears to have been subject to inattention, inaction and delay for reasons which he alleges amount to negligence and breach of his s. 7 *Charter* rights. In January 2003, he was informed that his PR application was refused on the basis of inadmissibility to Canada under s. 34(1)(f) of the IRPA because there were reasonable grounds to believe he was a member of a terrorist organization.

In addition to pursuing his administrative efforts to become a permanent resident, the applicant commenced an action against the Minister of Citizenship and Immigration by filing a Statement of Claim. The respondent brought a motion seeking summary judgment to dismiss all or part of the claim. The court concluded that the policy considerations did not preclude the imposition of the duty of care where an immigration officer completely ignores a file. At trial, it may be possible for the defendant to be able to provide a satisfactory explanation as to why this matter languished for at least seven years. However, given the unusual nature of the claim involving allegations against a particular immigration officer in the context of the harm allegedly suffered by the applicant, the action should not be summarily dismissed on broad policy grounds.

· · · · ·

Striking Out Pleadings

221. (1) Motion to strike — On motion, the Court may, at any time, order that a pleading, or anything contained therein, be struck out, with or without leave to amend, on the ground that it

(a) discloses no reasonable cause of action or defence, as the case may be,

(b) is immaterial or redundant,

(c) is scandalous, frivolous or vexatious,

(d) may prejudice or delay the fair trial of the action,

(e) constitutes a departure from a previous pleading, or

(f) is otherwise an abuse of the process of the Court,

and may order the action be dismissed or judgment entered accordingly.

(2) Evidence — No evidence shall be heard on a motion for an order under paragraph (1)(a).

· · · · ·

PART 5 — APPLICATIONS

· · · · ·

General

· · · · ·

302. Limited to single order — Unless the Court orders otherwise, an application for judicial review shall be limited to a single order in respect of which relief is sought.

Case Law

Lee v. Canada (Minister of Citizenship & Immigration) (1999), 177 F.T.R. 210, 1999 CarswellNat 2174 — The notice of application referred to two decisions and accordingly the applicant was found not to have complied with Rule 302 of the Federal Courts Rules, which limits an application for judicial review to one order. The court then dismissed the

Other Relevant Legislation

request to review one of the two decisions and amended the application for judicial review so that it only referred to the decision that was going to be reviewed by the court.

. . . . .

312. Additional steps — With leave of the Court, a party may

(a) file affidavits additional to those provided for in rules 306 and 307;

(b) conduct cross-examinations on affidavits additional to those provided for in rule 308; or

(c) file a supplementary record.

Case Law

Zhu v. Canada (Minister of Citizenship & Immigration), 2000 CarswellNat 2518 (Fed. T.D.) — The applicant sought leave to file additional affidavits and to add material which ought to have been part of the tribunal record from the Canadian Embassy in Manila. The applicant applied for permanent residence as an investor. When it came time to cross-examine the visa officer, which was done by telephone, about half of the documents which ought to have formed part of the tribunal record were missing. Additional affidavits may be filed if such will serve the interests of justice and assist the court in making a final determination. The applicant was required also to satisfy Rule 84(2) which requires leave to file additional material following cross-examination. The test requires a consideration of the following three items:

1. Was the information in the affidavit available before the cross-examination?

2. Are the facts to be established in the supplemental material relevant?

3. Might the supplementary material cause serious prejudice to other parties?

The court allowed the filing of extra material in this case.

. . . . .

PART 7 — MOTIONS

. . . . .

369. (1) Motions in writing — A party may, in a notice of motion, request that the motion be decided on the basis of written representations.

(2) Request for oral hearing — A respondent to a motion brought in accordance with subsection (1) shall serve and file a respondent's record within 10 days after being served under rule 364 and, if the respondent objects to disposition of the motion in writing, indicate in its written representations or memorandum of fact and law the reasons why the motion should not be disposed of in writing.

(3) Reply — A moving party may serve and file written representations in reply within four days after being served with a respondent's record under subsection (2).

(4) Disposition of motion — On the filing of a reply under subsection (3) or on the expiration of the period allowed for a reply, the Court may dispose of a motion in writing or fix a time and place for an oral hearing of the motion.

Case Law

Canada (Attorney General) v. Hennelly (1999), 244 N.R. 399, 167 F.T.R. 158 (note), [1999] F.C.J. No. 846, 1999 CarswellNat 967 (C.A.) — The proper test for granting an extension of time is whether the applicant has demonstrated:

1. a continuing intention to pursue his or her application;
2. that the application has some merit;
3. that no prejudice to the respondent arises from the delay; and
4. that a reasonable explanation for delay exists.

Any determination of whether or not the applicant's explanation justifies the granting of the necessary extension of time will turn on the facts of each particular case.

Padda v. Canada (Minister of Citizenship & Immigration), 2006 CarswellNat 2516, 2006 FC 995 — The applicants brought a motion for an extension of time within which to perfect their record in support of their application for leave and for judicial review. Rather than bringing their motion in writing pursuant to Rule 369 of the *Federal Courts Rules*, as is the norm in immigration leave applications, the applicants elected to proceed orally, making their motion returnable at the general sittings. Such practice should be discouraged. To allow an applicant to obtain an oral hearing for an interlocutory motion in a leave application that is intended to be conducted entirely in writing appears antithetical to the statutory and regulatory objectives of efficiency and expediency. It could easily be abused by an unscrupulous applicant who could obtain an extended stay of removal pending determination of the application for leave by making his or her motion for extension of time returnable in the distant future. The registry should, as a rule, seek directions from the court with respect to any motion in an immigration leave application that is not brought in writing pursuant to Rule 369 of the *Federal Courts Rules*.

Desouky v. Canada (Minister of Citizenship & Immigration) (1999), 176 F.T.R. 302, 1999 CarswellNat 2083 — This was a motion made pursuant to Rule 369 to allow the applicant to file an application record. The applicant filed, in June 1999, an application for leave to review the decision of an officer refusing an application for consideration on humanitarian and compassionate grounds (H&C). The application for leave was filed out of time, and the applicant requested an extension of time pursuant to subsection 82.1(15). The applicant failed to perfect the application for leave by serving and filing an application record. Therefore, on September 1, 1999, the court dismissed the application for leave due to the failure of the applicant to file a record.

The only reason given for not having filed the record was that the applicant's lawyer was "new in the practice of law and particularly in the area of immigration law." The inexperience of the applicant's lawyer is not a reason to set aside a final judgement of the court. To set aside or vary a final judgement the court requires evidence pursuant to Rule 399(2). Accordingly, the application was dismissed.

Askar v. Canada (Minister of Citizenship & Immigration) (1999), 179 F.T.R. 1, 1999 CarswellNat 2230, [1999] F.C.J. No. 1670 — The test on a motion to strike an application for judicial review seeking a declaration and mandamus, is whether the application is so clearly improper as to be bereft of any possibility of success.

· · · · ·

PART 9 — CASE MANAGEMENT AND DISPUTE RESOLUTION SERVICES

Case Management

· · · · ·

Specially Managed Proceedings

· · · · ·

384. Order for special management — The Court may at any time order that a proceeding continue as a specially managed proceeding.

SOR/2007-214, s. 3

Case Law

Huang v. Canada (Minister of Citizenship & Immigration) (2003), 34 Imm. L.R. (3d) 33, 2003 CarswellNat 412, 2003 CarswellNat 1415, 2003 FCT 196, 2003 CFPI 196 (T.D.) — The applicant sought to have his action managed as a special managed proceeding. The applicant wanted to expedite judicial review of an interlocutory ruling from the Immigration Appeal Division to adjourn a hearing. The purpose of the adjournment was to permit the tribunal to consider whether the Minister's case may be split so that after all the evidence is in, the Minister's case might be bolstered.

In order to constitute a substantial reason for special management, special circumstances must exist to warrant judicial review intervention at the interlocutory stage. The category of special circumstances is open ended. In the present instance the special circumstance is an allegation of bias on the basis that bias goes to the very function of the tribunal which is to render impartial decisions. The transcript of the adjournment decision leads one to the view that it is most likely that rather than exhibiting bias the tribunal became confused on a number of issues, some of which the Minister's representatives could have sorted out. Accordingly, the motion for special management was dismissed.

· · · · ·

PART 10 — ORDERS

· · · · ·

397. (1) Motion to reconsider — Within 10 days after the making of an order, or within such other time as the Court may allow, a party may serve and file a notice of motion to request that the Court, as constituted at the time the order was made, reconsider its terms on the ground that

    (a) the order does not accord with any reasons given for it; or

    (b) a matter that should have been dealt with has been overlooked or accidentally omitted.

(2) Mistakes — Clerical mistakes, errors or omissions in an order may at any time be corrected by the Court.

Case Law

Ismail v. Canada (Minister of Citizenship & Immigration) (2006), 58 Imm. L.R. (3d) 179, 358 N.R. 160, 2006 CarswellNat 4247, 2006 FCA 396 — The statutory prohibition on appeals in immigration matters unless a question is certified pursuant to paragraph 74(d) of the IRPA would be meaningless if it could be circumvented simply by filing a motion under Rule 397 or 399 (*Federal Courts Rules*).

Lee v. Canada (Minister of Citizenship & Immigration), 2003 CarswellNat 2350, 2003 FC 867 (F.C.) — The applicant sought reconsideration of an Order. Rule 397(1)(b) is a technical rule, designed to address situations where a matter that should have been addressed was overlooked or accidentally omitted. The applicant, in this case, was arguing that a point raised in argument was not addressed in the Reasons for Order and, therefore, the matter should be reconsidered. This is not a proper basis for invoking Rule 397(1)(b).

Samarraie v. Canada (Minister of Citizenship & Immigration), 2003 CarswellNat 1947, 2003 FCT 755 (T.D.) — Rule 397 is not intended to be used as a method of appeal. The issue is "whether there was some matter the court overlooked in reaching its decision and if so determine if the overlooked matter changes its decision." In the present case there were two errors of fact in the order. First, the order stated that the applicant applied under the independent and assisted relative categories where, in fact, the applicant applied only as an independent. Secondly, the order has the wrong date of the applicant's immigration interview. Neither of these errors resulted in the order not being in accord with the reasons given or that a matter that should have been dealt with had been overlooked or accidentally omitted. There is no inconsistency between the reasons and the order. Accordingly, the application for reconsideration was dismissed.

Grant v. Canada (Minister of Citizenship & Immigration), 2001 CarswellNat 2770, 2001 FCT 1343 (T.D.) — The applicant applied for an extension of time to bring a motion for the reconsideration by the court of one of its orders. Due to the fact that the judge who made the original order was leaving the court after long and distinguished service, the duty judge elected to deal with the application. The extension of time for the filing of the application and the application record was granted, however, the application itself was dismissed. Jurisprudence existing at the date of the order in question, whether then known or later discovered, does not qualify as a new matter within Rule 397.

Dan v. Canada (Minister of Citizenship & Immigration) (2000), 6 Imm. L.R. (3d) 84, 189 F.T.R. 301, [2000] F.C.J. No. 638, 2000 CarswellNat 892 — The oversight or accidental omission contemplated by Rule 397 must be in the terms of the order, and not in the parties' submissions to the court prior to the issuance of the order. Rule 397 protects the finality of a court order while allowing for its reconsideration where a matter that should have been dealt with in the order was overlooked or accidentally omitted.

Haque v. Canada (Minister of Citizenship & Immigration) (2000), 188 F.T.R. 154, 2000 CarswellNat 1516, [2000] F.C.J. No. 1141 — This was an application for reconsideration. The application of Rule 397 to a failure by a judge to deal with an argument made before him or her has been considered by two different judges with different results. In *Klockner Namasco Corp. v. Federal Hudson*, [1991] F.C.J. No. 1073, the court held that the failure to consider an argument came within the meaning of the rule. In *Balasingum v. M.E.I.* (1994), 77 F.T.R. 79, 28 Imm. L.R. (2d) 107, 1994 CarswellNat 256, the court considered that failure to consider an argument did not come within the meaning of the rule. To permit what are intended to be final orders to be opened up because an argument has not been dealt with, undermines the finality of the decision. The court should not have imposed upon it the obligation of dealing with every argument made without regard for its significance or its merit.

Sizov v. Canada (Minister of Citizenship & Immigration) (2000), 189 F.T.R. 317, 2000 CarswellNat 1911 — This application was for reconsideration of a decision dismissing the applicant's application for leave due to the failure of the applicant to file a Record.

On March 17, 2000, the applicant commenced an application for leave and judicial review. In that application the applicant sought an extension of time. The Application Record was due on April 17, 2000. On May 1, 2000, the applicant obtained, with the consent of the respondent, an order extending the time for service and proof of service of the Application Record to May 6, 2000. The applicant failed to file his Record within that time. Consequently, on June 14, 2000, the court dismissed his application. The instant motion for reconsideration was not filed within the 10 days stipulated under Rule 397. The order in question does accord with the failure of the applicant to file his Record and no matter that should have been dealt with was overlooked by the judge. Rule 397 provides for an extension of time "within such other time as the court may allow". The applicant deposed in his affidavit for reconsideration that he had retained a lawyer to proceed with his application and has been unable to contact the lawyer to find out why nothing was done with respect to the filing of his Application Record. The applicant further deposed that he had retained a new solicitor in July 2000. The court considered that it had jurisdiction on this motion for reconsideration to reconsider its earlier decision and grant an extension of time for the applicant to file his Record.

McFarlane v. Canada (Minister of Citizenship & Immigration), 2000 CarswellNat 1907 (Fed. T.D.) — This was a motion for an order extending the time to reconsider a judgement of the court dismissing an application for leave due to the failure of the applicant to file an application record.

Rule 397 allows the court to reconsider an order if it does not accord with the reasons given, or a matter that should have been dealt with has been overlooked or accidentally omitted. There was no suggestion by the applicant that the court's decision was in any way inconsistent with the material before it at the time it rendered its decision. Therefore, nothing was overlooked and Rule 397 does not apply.

Velupillai v. Canada (Minister of Citizenship & Immigration) (2000), 188 F.T.R. 314, 2000 CarswellNat 1898 — When the court signed its decision on June 15, 2000, it was not aware of a decision rendered by the Federal Court of Appeal three days before. Given the number of decisions rendered by the Trial Division and by the Appeal Division, it takes a few days to become aware of these decisions. The Federal Court of Appeal decision in question could have had an impact on the court's decision and accordingly, the court reconsidered its earlier decision refusing leave and granted leave. The Court of Appeal decision constituted a matter that arose subsequent to the making of the order.

Chaudhary v. Canada (Minister of Citizenship & Immigration), 1999 CarswellNat 2312 (Fed. T.D.) — The applicant was a failed refugee claimant. He filed an application for judicial review of that decision. The record was not filed in time and an extension of time was granted. Once again, the applicant failed to file a record and the court dismissed the application for lack of an application record. Counsel then filed a notice of motion asking the court to reconsider its order.

This was not an appropriate case for reconsideration. Nothing was overlooked or accidentally omitted when the court ordered the dismissal of the application. The material in support of the motion for reconsideration reveals that the cause of the dismissal of the application was the failure of counsel for the applicant to pursue the matter with anything approaching reasonable diligence. Accordingly, the motion for reconsideration was dismissed.

Sivakumar v. Canada (Minister of Citizenship & Immigration) (1998), 150 F.T.R. 299 — The defendants sought an extension of time with which to serve and file a Notice of Appeal to the Federal Court of Appeal from a disclosure order made by a judge of the Trial Division. The Notice of Appeal was not filed within 10 days of the decision, rather the defendants brought a motion for reconsideration within the 10-day period. This motion was dismissed. The defendants argued that in filing a reconsideration application they evidenced a continuing intention to appeal and that they brought the extension application within a reasonable period of time after the dismissal of the reconsideration application. Rule 337(5) (now Rule 397), provides that the court can reconsider a judgement on the grounds that it did not accord with the reasons or that some matter was overlooked or accidentally omitted. The grounds for reconsideration are narrow. Generally they involve inadvertent mistakes or omissions that should be rectified by the judge who rendered the original judgement. Very often the mistake or omission is obvious. Except in these narrow and often obvious circumstances a dissatisfied litigant's recourse is an appeal. Reconsideration applications and appeals are not interchangeable forms of relief. Reconsideration deals with inadvertent mistakes or omissions. An appeal involves acceptance of the lower court judgement as is, but disagreement with its conclusion. Litigants must decide which recourse to seek.

Where there is doubt, it is likely that reconsideration is not the appropriate course. In any event, a Notice of Appeal should be filed in a timely manner. The application for an extension of time was dismissed.

398. (1) Stay of order — On the motion of a person against whom an order has been made,

> **(a) where the order has not been appealed, the court that made the order may order that it be stayed; or**
>
> **(b) where a notice of appeal of the order has been issued, a judge of the court that is to hear the appeal may order that it be stayed.**

(2) Conditions — As a condition to granting a stay under subsection (1), a judge may require that the appellant

> **(a) provide security for costs; and**
>
> **(b) do anything required to ensure that the order will be complied with when the stay is lifted.**

(3) Setting aside of stay — A judge of the court that is to hear an appeal of an order that has been stayed pending appeal may set aside the stay if the judge is satisfied that the party who sought the stay is not expeditiously proceeding with the appeal or that for any other reason the order should no longer be stayed.

SOR/2004-283, s. 40

Case Law

Charkaoui c. Canada (Ministre de la Citoyenneté & de l'Immigration) (2004), 42 Imm. L.R. (3d) 159, 2004 CarswellNat 3342, 2004 CarswellNat 3884, (sub nom. *Charkaoui,*

Other Relevant Legislation

Re) 328 N.R. 39, 2004 FCA 319 — A security certificate had been issued against the moving party. The hearing on the reasonableness of the certificate was to be held in November and December. The appellant asked the court to issue an order temporarily staying the hearings until the appeal currently before the Federal court was heard and decided.

Subsection 50(1)(b) of the *Federal Courts Act*, gives the court the discretion to stay proceedings in any cause or matter. Rule 398, which establishes the procedure to follow for stays, does not strip the Federal Court of Appeal of its power to stay a proceeding if it is in the interests of justice. If an appeal before the Court of Appeal were to be rendered unnecessary, futile or illusory, as the result of an ongoing proceeding before a Federal tribunal or the Federal Court, there is no doubt that the Court of Appeal can order a stay of that proceeding to ensure that its appellate jurisdiction and process are not impeded.

399. (1) Setting aside or variance — On motion, the Court may set aside or vary an order that was made

    (a) *ex parte*; or

    (b) in the absence of a party who failed to appear by accident or mistake or by reason of insufficient notice of the proceeding,

if the party against whom the order is made discloses a *prima facie* case why the order should not have been made.

(2) Setting aside or variance — On motion, the Court may set aside or vary an order

    (a) by reason of a matter that arose or was discovered subsequent to the making of the order; or

    (b) where the order was obtained by fraud.

(3) Effect of order — Unless the Court orders otherwise, the setting aside or variance of an order under subsection (1) or (2) does not affect the validity or character of anything done or not done before the order was set aside or varied.

Case Law

Ismail v. Canada (Minister of Citizenship & Immigration) (2006), 58 Imm. L.R. (3d) 179, 358 N.R. 160, 2006 CarswellNat 4247, 2006 FCA 396 — The statutory prohibition on appeals in immigration matters unless a question is certified pursuant to paragraph 74(d) of the IRPA would be meaningless if it could be circumvented simply by filing a motion under Rule 397 or 399 (*Federal Courts Rules*).

Velupillai v. Canada (Minister of Citizenship & Immigration) (2000), 188 F.T.R. 314, 2000 CarswellNat 1898 — When the court signed its decision on June 15, 2000, it was not aware of a decision rendered by the Federal Court of Appeal three days before. Given the number of decisions rendered by the Trial Division and by the Appeal Division, it takes a few days to become aware of these decisions. The Federal Court of Appeal decision in question could have had an impact on the court's decision and accordingly, the court reconsidered its earlier decision refusing leave and granted leave. The Court of Appeal decision constituted a matter that arose subsequent to the making of the order.

PART 11 — COSTS

Awarding of Costs Between Parties

. . . . .

404. (1) Liability of solicitor for costs — Where costs in a proceeding are incurred improperly or without reasonable cause or are wasted by undue delay or other misconduct or default, the Court may make an order against any solicitor whom it considers to be responsible, whether personally or through a servant or agent,

> (a) directing the solicitor personally pay the costs of a party to the proceeding; or
>
> (b) disallowing the costs between the solicitor and the solicitor's client.

(2) Show cause by solicitor — No order under subsection (1) shall be made against a solicitor unless the solicitor has been given an opportunity to be heard.

(3) Notice to client — The Court may order that notice of an order against a solicitor made under subsection (1) be given to the solicitor's client in a manner specified by the Court.

Case Law

Hafeez v. Canada (Minister of Citizenship & Immigration) (1998), 45 Imm. L.R. (2d) 195 (Fed. T.D.) — When this matter came on for hearing, counsel for the applicant advised the court that there was no evidence upon which the application was based. Both the court and representative of the respondent wasted their time preparing for a hearing when in fact there was no basis for the application proceeding. Furthermore, counsel for the applicant did not appear on the matter but retained another counsel to appear one day before the hearing was scheduled to proceed. Accordingly, the court ordered costs of $1,000 in favour of the Crown payable personally by the applicant's counsel of record.

Channa v. Canada (Minister of Citizenship & Immigration) (1996), 124 F.T.R. 290 — The applicant sought to review a decision of a visa officer refusing his application for permanent residence. The applicant scored 59 points, was at the pre-interview stage, and was not granted an interview.

In the absence of a specific statutory provision, reasons are not required when an interview is denied. Further, where the statute only requires reasons when positive discretion is exercised under section 11(3) of the regulations, the court is not prepared to conclude that reasons are also required when that discretion is not exercised.

Counsel for the applicant acknowledged that, before the hearing, he received more than one telephone call from the respondent's counsel pointing out that arguments in the memorandum of argument were without merit. The applicant abandoned those arguments when the judicial review application was heard, but substituted for them new arguments which came as a total surprise to the respondent's counsel. Counsel is not entitled to proceed without notice and, whether he was asked or not, counsel ought to have advised the respondent's counsel that he was abandoning the applicant's memorandum of argument and planning to present new arguments. There were no special reasons under Rule

16 which would justify a costs award against the applicant. It was the solicitor's conduct which brought the case forward without notice. Accordingly, the court ordered that counsel for the applicant personally pay to the respondent $100 in court costs.

. . . . .

CAN. REG. 93-22 — FEDERAL COURTS CITIZENSHIP, IMMIGRATION AND REFUGEE PROTECTION RULES

made under the *Immigration Act*

SOR/93-22, as am. SOR/98-235, ss. 1–6, 7 (Fr.), 8 (Fr.); S.C. 2002, c. 8, ss.
182(3)(a), 183(2)(a); SOR/2002-232; SOR/2005-339; SOR/2007-301, s. 13;
SOR/2015-20.

[Note: The long title of these Rules was changed from "Federal Courts Immigration and Refugee Protection Rules" to "Federal Courts Citizenship, Immigration and Refugee Protection Rules" by SOR/2015-20, s. 1. It had previously been changed from "Federal Courts Immigration and Refugee Protection Rules" by SOR/2005-339, s. 1 and had previously been changed from "Rules of the Federal Court of Canada Respecting the Practice and Procedure for Applications for Leave, Applications for Judicial Review and Appeals Under the Immigration Act" by SOR/2002-232, s. 1. The short title of these Rules was repealed by SOR/2002-232, s. 2.]

[Editor's Note: The amending rules came into force on April 25, 1998. Rule 4 applies to all proceedings including further steps taken in proceedings already commenced. See SOR/98-235, ss. 9 and 11.]

[Editor's Note: S.C. 2001, c. 27, s. 198 provides that the Refugee Protection Division has jurisdiction to consider decisions of the Convention Refugee Determination Division that are set aside by the Federal Court or the Supreme Court of Canada, and shall dispose of those matters in accordance with the provisions of the Immigration and Refugee Protection Act, *S.C. 2001, c. 27 (the "new Act").*

S.C. 2001, c. 27, s. 199 further provides that sections 112 to 114 of the new Act apply to a redetermination of a decision set aside by the Federal Court with respect to an application for landing as a member of the post-determination refugee claimants in Canada class within the meaning of the Immigration Regulations, 1978, SOR/78-172.]

[Heading repealed SOR/2002-232, s. 2.]

1. [Repealed SOR/2002-232, s. 2.]

INTERPRETATION

2. The following definitions apply in these Rules.

"Act" [Repealed SOR/2015-20, s. 2(1).]

"appeal" means an appeal referred to in paragraph 22.2(d) of the *Citizenship Act* **or paragraph 74(d) of the** *Immigration and Refugee Protection Act.* **(*"appel"*)**

"application for judicial review" means an application referred to in section 22.2 of the *Citizenship Act* or section 74 of the *Immigration and Refugee and Protection Act*. *("demande de contrôle judiciare")*

"application for leave" means an application referred to in section 22.1 of the *Citizenship Act* or section 72 of the *Immigration and Refugee and Protection Act*. *("demande d'autorisation")*

"Court" means, as the circumstances require,

(a) the Federal Court of Appeal, including, in respect of a motion, a single judge of that court; or

(b) the Federal Court, including a prothonotary acting within his or her jurisdiction.

("Cour")

"Registry" means a registry within the meaning of the *Federal Courts Act*. *("greffe")*

"tribunal" means a person or body who has disposed of a matter, referred to in subsection 22.1(1) of the *Citizenship Act* or subsection 72(1) of the *Immigration and Refugee and Protection Act*, that is the subject of an application for leave or an application for judicial review. *("tribunal administratif")*

"written reasons" includes a transcript of reasons given orally. *("motifs écrits")*
SOR/98-235, s. 1; SOR/2002-232, s. 3; SOR/2005-339, s. 2; SOR/2015-20, s. 2

APPLICATION

3. These Rules apply to the following applications and appeals under the *Citizenship Act* and the *Immigration and Refugee Protection Act*:

(a) applications for leave;

(b) applications for judicial review; and

(c) appeals to the Federal Court of Appeal from judgments of the Federal Court.
SOR/98-235, s. 2; SOR/2015-20, s. 3

4. (1) Except to the extent that they are inconsistent with the *Citizenship Act* or the *Immigration and Refugee Protection Act*, as the case may be, or these Rules, Parts 1 to 3, 5.1, 6, 7, 10 and 11 and rules 302 and 383 to 385 of the *Federal Courts Rules* apply to applications for leave, applications for judicial review and appeals.

(2) Rule 133 of the *Federal Courts Rules* does not apply to the service of an application for leave or an application for judicial review.
SOR/98-235, s. 2; SOR/2002-232, s. 4; SOR/2005-339, s. 3; SOR/2007-301, s. 13; SOR/2015-20, s. 4

Case Law

Zheng v. Canada (Minister of Citizenship & Immigration), 1998 CarswellNat 1909 (Fed. T.D.) — Appearing on your own affidavit, in addition to being in breach of a principle of the common law, is now contrary to Rule 82 which prohibits a solicitor from both deposing to an affidavit and presenting arguments based on that affidavit.

Yazdanian v. Canada (Minister of Citizenship & Immigration) (1998), 150 F.T.R. 297 — The respondent sought to strike out the affidavit of Soheil Javid and paragraphs of a supplementary affidavit of Shirin Drudian. An affidavit may be struck out where it is abusive or clearly irrelevant, or where a party has obtained leave to admit evidence which turns out to be obviously inadmissible, or where the court is convinced that the matter of admissibility should be resolved at an early date so that a hearing may proceed in an orderly manner.

The respondent's motion was dismissed. While some of the material in the affidavit may border on conjecture and speculation, there was much more to the affidavit than that. At the stage when this motion was brought, before cross-examination, it was inappropriate to strike out the whole of one affidavit and substantially all of the second affidavit. These were matters that should be determined by the trial judge.

Sivakumar v. Canada (Minister of Citizenship & Immigration) (1998), 150 F.T.R. 299 — The defendants sought an extension of time with which to serve and file a Notice of Appeal to the Federal Court of Appeal from a disclosure order made by a judge of the Trial Division. The Notice of Appeal was not filed within 10 days of the decision; rather, the defendants brought a motion for reconsideration within the 10-day period. This motion was dismissed. The defendants argued that in filing a reconsideration application they evidenced a continuing intention to appeal, and that they brought the extension application within a reasonable period of time after the dismissal of the reconsideration application. Rule 337(5) (now Rule 397), provides that the court can reconsider a judgement on the grounds that it did not accord with the reasons or that some matter was overlooked or accidentally omitted. The grounds for reconsideration are narrow. Generally they involve inadvertent mistakes or omissions that should be rectified by the judge who rendered the original judgement. Very often the mistake or omission is obvious. Except in these narrow and often obvious circumstances a dissatisfied litigant's recourse is an appeal. Reconsideration applications and appeals are not interchangeable forms of relief. Reconsideration deals with inadvertent mistakes or omissions. An appeal involves acceptance of the lower court judgement as is, but disagreement with its conclusion. Litigants must decide which recourse to seek.

Where there is doubt, it is likely that reconsideration is not the appropriate course. In any event, a Notice of Appeal should be filed in a timely manner. The application for an extension of time was dismissed.

International Chartering Services Ltd. v. Canada (Minister of Citizenship & Immigration) (1998), 45 Imm. L.R. (2d) 305, 148 F.T.R. 151 — A motion to strike out an application for leave and for judicial review can only be successful in those exceptional cases where the application is so clearly improper as to be bereft of any possibility of success.

Vilus c. Canada (Ministre de la Citoyenneté & de l'Immigration) (1998), 50 Imm. L.R. (2d) 319 (Fed. T.D.) — This was a motion by the applicant for leave to amend his application for leave to commence an application for judicial review. On March 26, 1997, the applicant applied for permanent residence as the spouse of a Canadian citizen. On February 19, 1998, the applicant was advised that his application for a ministerial exemption could not be granted and that a report had been issued against him pursuant to s. 27. After this report was issued a departure order was made on March 5, 1998. On March 18, 1998, the applicant submitted a claim for Convention refugee status. On March 27, 1998, the applicant was notified pursuant to s. 44(1) of the Act that he was not eligible to have his claim determined because a departure order had been previously made against him. On April 3, 1998, the applicant commenced his application for judicial review of the March 27th decision. Through the instant motion, the applicant sought to have the March 5th decision also set aside by means of this application.

The motion was dismissed. It would be incongruous to allow the applicant to challenge the March 5th decision when he had not previously sought such a remedy. The affidavit filed in support of the motion was silent as to why the March 5th decision had not yet been challenged in a separate application for judicial review.

FORM OF APPLICATION FOR LEAVE

[Heading amended SOR/2002-232, s. 15(a).]

5. (1) An application for leave shall be in accordance with Form IR-1 as set out in the schedule and shall set out

(a) the full names of the parties;

(b) the date and the details of the matter — the decision, determination or order made, measure taken or question raised — in respect of which relief is sought and the date on which the applicant was notified of or otherwise became aware of the matter;

(c) the name of the tribunal and, if the tribunal was composed of more than one person, the name of each person who was on the tribunal;

(d) the tribunal's file number, if any;

(e) the precise relief to be sought on the application for judicial review;

(f) the grounds on which the relief is sought, including a reference to any statutory provision or Rule to be relied on;

(g) the proposed place and language of the hearing of the application for judicial review;

(h) whether or not the applicant has received the written reasons of the tribunal; and

(i) the signature, name, address and telephone number of the individual solicitor filing the application for leave, or where the applicant acts in person, his or her signature, name, address for service in Canada, and telephone number.

(2) Unless he or she is the applicant, the respondent to an application for leave is

(a) in the case of a matter under the *Citizenship Act*, the Minister of Citizenship and Immigration; and

(b) in the case of a matter under the *Immigration and Refugee Protection Act*, each Minister who is responsible for the administration of that Act in respect of the matter for which leave is sought.

SOR/2002-232, ss. 5, 15(b), (c); SOR/2005-339, s. 4; SOR/2015-20, s. 5

EXTENSION OF TIME TO FILE AND SERVE APPLICATION FOR LEAVE

[Heading amended SOR/2002-232, s. 6.]

6. (1) A request to extend the time for filing and serving an application for leave shall be made in the application for leave.

(2) A request for an extension of time shall be determined at the same time, and on the same materials, as the application for leave.

SOR/2002-232, s. 6; SOR/2015-20, s. 6

Case Law

Bains v. Canada (Minister of Employment & Immigration) (1999), 47 Admin. L.R. 317, 109 N.R. 239 (Fed. C.A.) — The only question to be considered in disposing of an application for leave under s. 82.1(1) or 82.3(1) is whether or not a fairly arguable case is disclosed for the relief proposed to be sought if leave is granted. Further, the need for material not immediately available has to be established by the applicant and the mere stated intention to rely on such material does not, without an application and an order to that end, operate to extend the time provided by the *Federal Court Immigration Rules* for the applicant to file an affidavit and/or representations in support of the leave application. The requirement for leave is, in reality, the other side of the coin of the traditional jurisdiction to summarily terminate proceedings that disclose no reasonably arguable case. The requirement for leave does not deny refugee claimants access to the court. The right to apply for leave is, itself, a right of access to the court and the requirement that leave be obtained before an appeal or application for judicial review may proceed does not impair the right guaranteed to refugee claimants under either s. 7 or 15 of the *Charter*.

Baig v. Canada (Minister of Citizenship & Immigration) (1997), 136 F.T.R. 78, 41 Imm. L.R. (2d) 237 — In July 1997, the applicant filed an originating Notice of Motion seeking to set aside a decision of a visa officer which denied his application for permanent residence in Canada. In support of that motion, the applicant, with the assistance of counsel, filed an affidavit in which he swore that he received the refusal in June 1997, notwithstanding that the refusal letter was dated in March 1997. At a conference call in September 1997, the applicant and his counsel disclosed to the court that the visa officer's letter had been received by the applicant's counsel in April 1997. The contents had only been communicated to the applicant in June 1997, due to the fact that the applicant was travelling and unavailable to his counsel. Subsequent to the conference call in September 1997, the applicant filed a request for an extension of time and filed a further affidavit which disclosed that the applicant's counsel had been unable to contact him and for that reason had not brought the refusal letter to his attention.

The application for an extension of time was refused. If applicants and their counsel wish the court to exercise its discretion in their favour, it is imperative that full and frank disclosure be made. The court indicated to counsel for the applicant that if this type of behaviour were to recur, the court would consider ordering costs against counsel personally.

Abdi-Egeh v. Canada (Minister of Citizenship & Immigration) (1995), 29 Imm. L.R. (2d) 254, 99 F.T.R. 279 — The applicant applied for an order extending the time to perfect her application for leave and for an order requiring the respondent to produce all documents in its possession and control. The applicant, in fact, had made a request under the *Privacy Act* and was waiting for the Minister's response to that request at the time the application for an extension was made. The applicant had received from the respondent, pursuant to Rule 9, an indication that no reasons had been given for the decision under review.

The court denied the request for production. According to s. 82.1(8), applications for leave to commence applications for judicial review are to be determined without delay and in a summary way. It would be contrary to the objective of subs. 82.1(8) to allow the *Privacy Act* procedure to be invoked to frustrate the regime for dealing with applications for leave. For similar reasons, the "gap rule" in the general rules and orders of this court cannot be resorted to achieve the applicant's objective.

The letter containing the immigration officer's decision contained the following: ". . . we regret to inform you that you do not meet the eligibility criteria for this program due to the following reason(s): You hindered or delayed your removal from Canada." This sentence identified the "reason" why the applicant failed to qualify under DROC. Despite the view of the applicant and of the respondent, the applicant here did receive "reasons" for the impugned decision. That is not to say that the "reasons" given constitute an explanation of the reasoning of the Immigration officer. Such an explanation is not necessary to constitute "reasons."

The court granted the extension because both the applicant and the respondent were under the mistaken impression that reasons had not been given.

Mendoza v. Canada (Secretary of State) (1994), 24 Imm. L.R. (2d) 317, 82 F.T.R. 92 — The applicant sought and obtained an extension of time to file and serve her record on the grounds that Legal Service Society of British Columbia approval had just been obtained, and that the court reporters could not prepare a transcript of the proceedings before the CRDD in time to permit the applicant to meet the deadline for filing and serving a record.

In granting the extension, the court considered first whether the request for an extension had been made in a timely fashion; secondly, the fact that the reason for the extension did not relate exclusively to counsel's work load, but rather at least one factor beyond the control of counsel, namely the preparation of the transcript of the CRDD hearing; and finally, the court considered whether the leave application had any merit.

Chin v. Canada (Minister of Employment & Immigration) (1993), 22 Imm. L.R. (2d) 136, 69 F.T.R. 77 — On September 1, 1993, the applicant sought an extension of time for filing the application record. On July 28, 1993, he had filed an application for leave. The application record, according to the rules, was required to be filed before August 27, 1993. The application for an extension of time was filed on August 20, 1993. The reason given for seeking an extension was because counsel was going out of town from August 21 to August 27 and was unable to complete the application record. The application for an extension of time was refused. The time limits set out in the rules are meant to be complied with. If they are too short, then requests should be made to have the rules amended. Extensions are not granted because it is the first time that counsel has asked for one, or because the work load which counsel has assumed is too great. In order for an application to be successful, some reason for the delay, which is beyond the control of counsel or the applicant, must be given, for example, illness or some other unexpected or unanticipated event. There was no such unanticipated delay in the present case. Courts are often reluctant to disadvantage individuals because their counsel missed deadlines. In matters of this nature, however, counsel is acting in the shoes of his or her client. Client and counsel are one for such purposes. It is too easy a justification for non-compliance with the rules for counsel to say the delay was not in any way caused by the client, and that if an extension is not granted the client will be prejudiced.

The comments of the court occurred when counsel, after having been apprised of the court's refusal to extend the time, filed a motion for reconsideration. Such a motion is filed pursuant to Rule 337(5). The court declined the motion for reconsideration. There was no oversight on the part of the court respecting the evidence. Accordingly, the motion for reconsideration was dismissed.

Espinoza v. Canada (Minister of Employment & Immigration) (1992), 142 N.R. 158 (Fed. C.A.) — An order for an extension of the time to comply with Rule 9 does not finally dispose of any matter and issue. Such an order is always open to reconsideration whether made peremptorily or not. The policy of the *Immigration Act* and *Federal Court Immigration Rules* is transparently clear and is one of deciding leave applications expeditiously. The dilatory initiation of Legal Aid applications, delays in providing opinion letters, which counsel know will be required, and the ever slower processing of such applications by Legal Aid cannot be permitted to defeat the policy of the Act and rules. Failure to make a Legal Aid application promptly can be good reason to deny an extension.

Kazi v. Kalusny (1991), 13 Imm. L.R. (2d) 258 (Fed. T.D.) — Counsel sought an extension of the time limits provided by s. 9 of the Rules. One of the bases for the request was that counsel had occupied himself with a long-standing client who was in a more difficult situation than the applicant. The extension was refused. Counsel had an obligation to delegate the file to someone else or to make sure, in some other manner, that the deadlines which apply to these clients were met. With respect to the main motion for leave to commence a proceeding, it was dismissed. There was no material on the file to support the application for leave.

FILING AND SERVICE OF APPLICATION FOR LEAVE
[Heading amended SOR/2002-232, s. 15(d).]

7. (1) Service of an application for leave is effected by serving a certified copy of the application on each respondent.

(2) Proof of service of an application on the other parties shall be filed within 10 days after the application is served.

SOR/98-235, s. 3; SOR/2002-232, s. 7; SOR/2015-20, s. 7

NOTICE OF APPEARANCE

8. (1) A respondent who is served with an application for leave shall serve a notice of appearance in accordance with Form IR-2 as set out in the schedule on the applicant and the tribunal, and file it, together with proof of service, within 10 days after service of the application.

(2) A respondent who has failed to file a notice of appearance in accordance with subrule (1) shall not be entitled to any further notice or service of any further document in the proceeding.

SOR/2002-232, s. 15(e)

OBTAINING TRIBUNAL'S DECISION AND REASONS

9. (1) Where an application for leave sets out that the applicant has not received the written reasons of the tribunal, the Registry shall forthwith send the tribunal a written request in Form IR-3 as set out in the schedule.

(2) Upon receipt of a request under subrule (1) a tribunal shall, without delay,

(a) send a copy of the decision or order, and written reasons therefor, duly certified by an appropriate officer to be correct, to each of the parties, and two copies to the Registry; or

(b) if no reasons were given for the decision or order in respect of which the application is made, or reasons were given but not recorded, send an appropriate written notice to all the parties and the Registry.

(3) A tribunal shall be deemed to have received a request under subrule (1) on the tenth day after it was sent by mail by the Registry.

(4) The applicant shall be deemed to have received the written reasons, or the notice referred to in paragraph 9(2)(b), as the case may be, on the tenth day after it was sent by mail by the tribunal.

SOR/2002-232, s. 15(f)

Case Law

Wang v. Canada (Minister of Citizenship & Immigration), 2006 CarswellNat 3482, 2006 FC 1298 — The applicant made two unsuccessful applications to enter Canada as a student. Her second visa application was refused because the visa officer was not satisfied that she was an intending temporary resident to Canada. The applicant argued that the visa officer's finding that the applicant was not well established in China was bizarre because the record disclosed that she "is as well established in China as any 19-year-old who has just finished high school." While there is some merit to the applicant's contention that one's establishment in a country ordinarily requires consideration of many factors, it is also the case that a visa officer has a broad discretion to weigh the evidence submitted in making a decision. Here the visa officer looked for evidence of the financial situation of the applicant's parents. The visa officer considered this to be important to the assessment of the application and she failed to find it. The applicant's parents were retired and their financial situation was unknown. The onus rested on the applicant to establish an entitlement to a student visa. The visa officer was entitled to base the refusal decision solely on the absence of that evidence of family circumstance. If the evidence had been offered and if it sufficiently answered the concerns of the visa officer, the decision may well have been different.

The applicant also complained that the refusal letter was deficient because it did not contain the reasons for the visa refusal. The CAIPS notes were provided to the applicant in compliance with the *Federal Court Immigration and Refugee Protection Rules*. CAIPS notes have been accepted as a constituent part of an administrative decision. Rule 9 contemplates that the provision of detailed reasons for an immigration decision may occur after the commencement of an application for judicial review. The court concluded that the respondent met its obligation under that Rule and cannot be taken to have breached a natural justice requirement by failure to abide by some other standard.

Paul v. Canada (Minister of Employment & Immigration) (1994), 28 Imm. L.R. (2d) 37, 81 F.T.R. 14, 1994 CarswellNat 247 — This was a motion on behalf of the applicant for an order compelling the Appeal Division to provide written reasons for its denial of the applicant's appeal of a deportation order. Section 69.4(5) requires reasons to be given, where they are requested, within 10 days of the disposition of the appeal. The applicant did not request written reasons within that period of time, but nevertheless argued that Rule 9 of the *Federal Court Rules* must take precedence over the *Immigration Act*. The application was dismissed.

The true purpose of Rule 9 is to ensure that all parties are provided with reasons when they are available, and notified when they are not available. Neither the *Immigration Act* nor the Rules compel the Board to produce written reasons, unless requested to do so by one of the parties within 10 days following the communication of the decision. Absent an attack on the vires of s. 69.4(5), the Board's refusal to provide written reasons, where none were requested, must be upheld.

PERFECTING APPLICATION FOR LEAVE

10. (1) The applicant shall perfect an application for leave by complying with sub-rule (2)

    (a) where the application sets out that the applicant has received the tribunal's written reasons, within 30 days after filing the application; or

    (b) where the application sets out that the applicant has not received the tribunal's written reasons, within 30 days after receiving either the written reasons, or the notice under paragraph 9(2)(b), as the case may be.

(2) The applicant shall serve on every respondent who has filed and served a notice of appearance, a record containing the following, on consecutively numbered pages, and in the following order

    (a) the application for leave,

    (b) the decision or order, if any, in respect of which the application is made,

    (c) the written reasons given by the tribunal, or the notice under paragraph 9(2)(b), as the case may be,

    (d) one or more supporting affidavits verifying the facts relied on by the applicant in support of the application, and

    (e) a memorandum of argument which shall set out concise written submissions of the facts and law relied upon by the applicant for the relief proposed should leave be granted,

and file it, together with proof of service.

Case Law

Section 10(1)

Mishak c. Canada (Ministre de la Citoyenneté & de l'Immigration) (1999), 173 F.T.R. 144, 1999 CarswellNat 1582, 1999 CarswellNat 2157 — The applicant attempted, at the last minute, to add to her *factum* and argue an issue that had not been set out in the applicant's material. Permission to raise this argument was refused. The court relied on

Other Relevant Legislation

Lanlehin v. Canada (Minister of Employment & Immigration), 1993 CarswellNat 2301 (Fed. C.A.).

Bhui v. Canada (Minister of Citizenship & Immigration), 1996 CarswellNat 567 (Fed. T.D.) — The court had before it a motion by the applicant for an extension of the time limits set out in Rule 10(1) for serving and filing the applicant's record.

In January 1996, the applicant filed his record within the time required by the rules. The record did not include a memorandum of argument. Counsel provided the court with an affidavit indicating that he did not feel it was necessary to include a memorandum of argument in the record, and therefore did not do so.

The respondent took the position that the applicant's record was not complete and not perfected within the time period provided by the rules.

The filing and service of the applicant's record are official in the court file. There cannot, therefore, be in this case an extension of time to perform acts that have already been done.

If the motion were granted allowing the inclusion of the memorandum of argument in the applicant's record, there would be no additional delays in dealing with the application and no evidence to suggest that the respondent would otherwise be prejudiced. There was nothing in the evidence to support the suggestion that counsel for the applicant was seeking to file the applicant's record in successive steps in order to avoid the time limits set out in Rule 10.

Accordingly, the memorandum of argument was permitted to be filed with the court as part of the applicant's record.

Moreno v. Canada (Minister of Citizenship & Immigration) (1996), 33 Imm. L.R. (2d) 84, (sub nom. *Moreno c. Canada (Ministre de la Citoyenneté & de l'Immigration)*) 110 F.T.R. 57 — This was a motion pursuant to Rule 21(2) of the *Federal Court Immigration Rules* for an extension of the time limit under Rule 10(1) for serving and filing the applicant's record.

The court expects the time limit set out in the rules to be complied with and an automatic extension is not available merely because it is requested. An applicant must show that there was some justification for the delay throughout the whole period of the delay and that the applicant has an arguable case. The applicant must demonstrate some reason for the delay which was beyond its control or the control of its counsel, for example, illness, or some other unexpected or unanticipated event. This motion failed because there was a lack of an explanation for the extension and, furthermore, there were no arguments advanced to show that the applicants had an arguable case.

Amevenu v. Canada (Solicitor General) (1994), 27 Imm. L.R. (2d) 157, 88 F.T.R. 142 — The applicant failed to file a record within 30 days after the filing of the leave application. The respondent submitted that the application for judicial review should therefore be dismissed. This argument was not considered. The court granted leave despite the fact that the application record was not filed on time. The respondent, at the time the leave application was pending, did not raise the argument that the record was filed outside of the time limit. To raise the issue of the time limit over two months after leave was granted, and only a week before the judicial review application was to be argued, was unfair and the court declined to consider the respondent's argument.

Section 10(2)

Balouch v. Canada (Minister of Citizenship & Immigration) (2004), 18 Admin. L.R. (4th) 174, 2004 CarswellNat 5389, 2004 CarswellNat 4087, 2004 FC 1599 — The applicant sought to review the negative decision respecting his application for protection. Leave was granted. At the opening of the hearing, counsel for the respondent argued that the applicant had sworn a false affidavit and placed it before the court as the underpinning to the application for leave. An applicant's affidavit is critical to the just determination of the leave stage of an application. In the preparation and swearing of an affidavit, great care is required of the applicant and, where appropriate, his or her counsel, to ensure that the respondent's counsel and the court are not misled. The court found that both respondent's counsel and the court had been misled through the swearing by the applicant of a false affidavit, and therefore dismissed the application for judicial review without considering the merits of the application.

Chan v. Canada (Minister of Citizenship & Immigration), 2001 CarswellNat 2857, 2001 FCT 1339 — The applicant sought to file additional evidence in the judicial review proceedings to point out official records, relied upon by the visa officer in reaching a decision that the applicant was not a dependant, were wrong. Where it is alleged that the evidence before the visa officer which may have been the determining factor was false, whether or not that evidence was in fact false, is a decision that cannot be made on an interluctory motion. Accordingly, the court allowed the evidence to be filed so that the judge hearing the application can determine its relevance.

Parveen v. Canada (Minister of Citizenship & Immigration) (1999), 1 Imm. L.R. (3d) 305, 168 F.T.R. 103, 1999 CarswellNat 772, [1999] F.C.J. No. 660 — This was an application to review and set aside a visa officer's decision denying the applicant a permanent visa. The record that was provided to the court by the respondent was incomplete. It had been "stripped". Counsel for the respondent advised the court that this occurred because of a "thin file" policy and the difficulty of retaining the full files for all the individuals applying for immigration to Canada in the various embassies abroad.

The period of time within which a person can file an appeal from a visa officer's decision is limited. The court could not accept that the administrative burden of retaining the full file for that period of time was unduly onerous. The respondent controls the record that is put before the court, thus any disputes that arise as a result of deficiency in the record should, in general, be interpreted against the respondent. An incomplete record alone could be grounds, in some circumstances, for setting aside a decision.

Finally, the court refused to adopt the approach suggested by counsel for the respondent to the effect that visa officers have no interest in these applications. The court observed that once a visa officer's decision is challenged, he or she has an interest in justifying his or her decision. This was an entirely natural reaction and at that point the visa officer was not, in the court's view, a disinterested person.

Chen v. Canada (Minister of Citizenship & Immigration) (1999), 49 Imm. L.R. (2d) 161, 17 Admin. L.R. (3d) 11, 240 N.R. 376, 174 D.L.R. (4th) 165, 1999 CarswellNat 577 (Fed. C.A.) — This was an appeal from a judgement of the Trial Division dismissing an application to review a determination of a panel of the CRDD that the appellant was not a Convention refugee. The motions judge did not err in refusing to make the audio-tape of the proceedings part of the record, or listen to it, in coming to his decision on the matter before him. Neither the *Immigration Act* nor the relevant Rules require audio tapes to be made part of the record. The witness whose credibility was questioned by the refugee

Other Relevant Legislation

division was seen and heard by that body as the trier of fact. They enjoyed unique advantages in coming to their findings and especially so in making findings upon an assessment of the witnesses' credibility. This principle applies even where a court has asked us to review a decision in the light of an audio-taped record. The advantage of having seen the witness is lost to the reviewing court. A tape recording of a proceeding may be accepted to establish some fundamental unfairness in the conduct of a hearing amounting to a denial of natural justice.

The motions judge was under no obligation to make the audio-tape part of the record or to listen to it, so as to allow himself to make an independent assessment of the appellant's credibility.

Ou v. Canada (Minister of Citizenship & Immigration) (1999), 48 Imm. L.R. (2d) 131, 1999 CarswellNat 281 (Fed. T.D.) — In December 1996, the applicant arrived in Canada from China. He made a claim to refugee status. In July of 1997, he notified the Board of his address and telephone number in Toronto. On that same date, he was informed that his claim would be referred to the Board for determination and that he would be required to appear in September 1997. On September 18, 1997, the Board sent a notice to appear for conference to the applicant at his address. On September 25, 1997, the applicant personally delivered to the Board's registry a letter indicating that he wished to delay his hearing date in order to retain counsel. On October 7, 1997, a Board employee attempted to telephone the applicant to advise him that it was not sufficient for him to deliver a letter requesting a delay and that he was required to attend in person. The employee was told that there was "no such person at that telephone number". On October 30, 1997, the Board sent the applicant a notice to appear for abandonment of a Convention refugee claim. The applicant immediately retained counsel. On December 1, 1997, the applicant attended the abandonment hearing. The Board decided that the applicant had abandoned his claim. It is with respect to that decision that the applicant sought judicial review.

The applicant filed a supplementary affidavit from his landlord's daughter, who indicated that she had received a telephone call from Canadian immigration offices and at the time did not know the applicant's name and, as well, that her parent's had a number of tenants in the house at that time.

On an application for judicial review, an applicant, in an attempt to justify his absence from the Board hearing, may tender fresh evidence. The court noted that a finding of abandonment precludes a consideration of a Convention refugee claim on its merits. The court set aside the Board's decision that the applicant's claim had been abandoned and ordered a new hearing on that question.

Bains v. Canada (Minister of Employment & Immigration) (1999), 47 Admin. L.R. 317, 109 N.R. 239 (Fed. C.A.) — The only question to be considered in disposing of an application for leave under s. 82.1(1) or s. 82.3(1) is whether or not a fairly arguable case is disclosed for the relief proposed to be sought if leave is granted. Further, the need for material not immediately available has to be established by the applicant and the mere stated intention to rely on such material does not, without an application and an order to that end, operate to extend the time provided by the *Federal Court Immigration Rules* for the applicant to file an affidavit and/or representations in support of the leave application. The requirement for leave is, in reality, the other side of the coin of the traditional jurisdiction to summarily terminate proceedings that disclose no reasonably arguable case. The requirement for leave does not deny refugee claimants access to the court. The right to apply for leave is, itself, a right of access to the court and the requirement that leave be obtained before an appeal or application for judicial review may proceed does not impair the right guaranteed by refugee claimants under either ss. 7 or 15 of the *Charter*.

Yau v. Canada (Minister of Citizenship & Immigration), 1998 CarswellNat 1634 (Fed. T.D.) — The applicant was seeking to review a decision of a visa officer and brought two motions. The first, requested permission to file an additional affidavit, and the second, for an extension of time within which to file the record including the additional affidavit. When the applicant commenced his application for judicial review, he was of the opinion that he had been turned down as a self-employed person for two reasons mentioned by the visa officer in his letter of rejection. These reasons were that the applicant had no experience as a self-employed person and that the landing of the applicant would result in no significant economic benefit to Canada. However, in his affidavit filed in opposition to the applicant, the visa officer suggested additional reasons, namely that the applicant had not supplied him with up-to-date financial data, that the applicant's financial assets were insufficient for his purposes, that the applicant had not conducted any research into the Canadian market, and that the applicant had no business plan.

Assuming that the visa officer refused the applicant, relying on facts that were not drawn to the applicant's attention, and with respect to which the applicant at the interview was given no opportunity to comment, it was appropriate that the applicant be given an opportunity to supplement the information supplied at the original interview. The proposed affidavit was offered for the purpose of showing that evidence of such a nature was available had the visa officer indicated a need to produce it. The affidavit also explained why a business plan and a proof of net worth were not placed before the visa officer, namely, because they had been stolen some two days earlier in San Francisco.

The proposed affidavit was admitted, not for the purpose of showing that the decision of the visa officer was wrong, but for the purpose of supporting an attack on the process.

Kuchin v. Canada (Minister of Citizenship & Immigration), 1995 CarswellNat 1420 (Fed. T.D.) — The applicant sought an extension of time to file a reply. There is no provision for any reply evidence, only reply argument. If reply evidence were to be permitted, it would result in the respondent having to give its final argument before all the evidence was filed.

Awogbade v. Canada (Minister of Citizenship & Immigration) (1995), 29 Imm. L.R. (2d) 281, 94 F.T.R. 184 — The applicant applied for leave to take judicial review proceedings against a decision of the CRDD. One month after filing the originating motion, the applicant's solicitors sought to extend the time for filing her application record. Additional time was refused by the court and the applicant brought an application for reconsideration of that order.

In a solicitor/client relationship, there is a strong fiduciary obligation on the solicitor's part to act in a professional, timely manner in order to advance the client's interests. The Ontario Legal Aid plan merely authorizes the payment of fees for the lawyer's services. A professional ethical lawyer will not leave his or her client in the lurch merely because fees are not secured. It may be that allowing a client's case to turn to ashes while awaiting spurious authorization from Legal Aid is contempt of court.

There are several valid reasons for which a judge could extend the time to file an applicant's record, but waiting for a legal aid certificate is not one of them.

The absence of an application record is a substantive defect as well as a procedural one, and an order disallowing additional time for the filing of an application is a final one.

Other Relevant Legislation

It is a species of professional misconduct for a lawyer to prefer the securing of his or her own fees over the client's interests.

The court noted that the reasons of the CRDD had not been filed with the original request for an extension of time, and considered that this failure on the part of the applicant's solicitors provided it with a reason to relieve the applicant of the prejudice created by the conduct of her solicitors, and accordingly, reconsidered its order and granted to the applicant a short extension to file her application record.

Abdullahi v. Canada (Minister of Employment & Immigration) (1995), 91 F.T.R. 309 — The applicant sought to review a negative decision of the CRDD. Certain evidence referred to by counsel for the applicant was filed under cover of counsel's own affidavit. This documentary evidence post-dated the date of the hearing. The court was not satisfied of the relevance of the material on the issue of the well-foundedness of the claim in question. The issue before the court was the relevance of the material in the context of a judicial review application. The documentary evidence covered by counsel's affidavit post-dating the date of the hearing was clearly not before the CRDD and not relevant to the judicial review application and the court would not take it into account.

Lieu v. Canada (Minister of Employment & Immigration), 1994 CarswellNat 2224, [1994] F.C.J. No. 857 (T.D.) — This application for an extension of time for the filing of a record in support of an application for leave and for judicial review was denied. The applicant's record was due on March 9. The applicant's lawyer required a Legal Aid certificate and as the next monthly meeting of the area committee was on March 15, he filed his opinion with the area committee on March 12. The affidavit of the applicant's lawyer did not disclose whether or not the opinion was received in time for inclusion on the area committee's March 15 agenda. This seemed unlikely as March 12 was a Saturday. No justification for the last-minute filing of the opinion was offered. It could have been prepared as early as mid-February.

The material further disclosed that as of May 23 the area committee had not decided whether to issue a Legal Aid certificate and the court was asked to grant an open-ended indefinite extension of time. In addition, the material filed did not sufficiently address the merits of the application so as to demonstrate a good case on the merits. Finally, the court noted that bald allegations of *Charter* violations without more would not suffice when the onus was on the applicant to show a good case to justify an extension.

Accordingly, the application for an extension of time was dismissed.

Koulibaly v. Canada (Solicitor General) (1993), 93 F.T.R. 241 — The court granted an order permitting the applicant to serve and file the applicant's record outside the time allowed under s. 10(2) of the *Immigration Rules* of the Federal Court. In support of the motion, the applicant filed the affidavit of his counsel stating that he had been unable to contact the applicant within the time required. It would have been preferable to file the affidavit of the applicant himself, on this question, stating in the affidavit that the applicant had not been available.

RESPONDENT'S AFFIDAVITS AND MEMORANDUM OF ARGUMENT

11. A respondent who opposes an application for leave

    (a) may serve on the other parties one or more affidavits, and

(b) shall serve on the other parties a memorandum of argument which shall set out concise written submissions of the facts and law relied upon by the respondent,

and file them, together with proof of service, within 30 days after service of the documents referred to in subrule 10(2).

SOR/2002-232, s. 15(g)

Case Law

Li v. Canada (Minister of Citizenship & Immigration), 1999 CarswellNat 1746, [1999] F.C.J. No. 1398 (T.D.) — The applicant commenced an application for judicial review on October 2, 1998, and filed his application record on November 2, 1998. On November 23, 1998, the respondent wrote to the court stating that the respondent would not be filing any submissions with respect to the application for leave but reserving the right to do so if leave was granted. On May 27, 1999, the court granted the applicant leave to commence the judicial review proceeding. The applicant filed no further affidavit material and no further memorandum of argument. The respondent filed no affidavits but did file a memorandum of argument suggesting that the applicant's affidavit, sworn in the previous October, should be declared inadmissible. The court refused to entertain the respondent's argument that the applicant's affidavit be declared inadmissible. It was too late for the respondent to take that position. The affidavit was part of the record when the respondent chose not to make submissions on the leave application the previous November. It was part of the record that formed the basis for the court's order granting leave to proceed. It was now too late to suggest that the affidavit was inadmissible.

AFFIDAVITS

12. (1) Affidavits filed in connection with an application for leave shall be confined to such evidence as the deponent could give if testifying as a witness before the Court.

(2) Unless a judge for special reasons so orders, no cross-examination of a deponent on an affidavit filed in connection with an application is permitted before leave to commence an application for judicial review is granted.

SOR/2002-232, s. 15(h)

Case Law

Section 12(1)

Ling v. Canada (Minister of Citizenship & Immigration), 2003 CarswellNat 3261, 2003 CarswellNat 4323, 2003 FC 1198 — This was an application to set aside a decision of a visa officer. Preliminary objection was taken to the nature of the affidavit provided by the applicant in support of the application. The applicant did not file her own affidavit. She submitted instead an affidavit of an immigration consultant based in Canada.

The failure to file a proper affidavit does not lead to the automatic dismissal of an application. An affidavit must be based on matters of personal knowledge. Portions of the affidavit in question consisted of arguments and conclusions rather than facts and some matters were not within the personal knowledge of the immigration consultant.

Other Relevant Legislation

There was in the affidavit sufficient evidence to establish the application and its rejection by the visa officer. Where there is no evidence based on personal knowledge to support the application, any error asserted by the applicant must appear on the face of the record. The court proceeded with the application and dismissed it on the merits.

Zheng v. Canada (Minister of Citizenship & Immigration), 2002 CarswellNat 3199, 2002 CarswellNat 4430, 2002 FCT 1152, 2002 CFPI 1152 — This was an application to review the refusal of the applicant's application for permanent residence as a self-employed chef. A person who files an application for judicial review does not himself or herself have to file an affidavit. An affidavit filed in support of the application shall be confined to facts within the personal knowledge of the deponent. The general rule against hearsay does not displace the long-standing common-law exceptions to the hearsay rule, nor the reliability and necessity exception of more recent vintage. To admit hearsay, evidence or argument relative to necessity and reliability is required. Where hearsay evidence does not pass the necessity and reliability test, the error said to vitiate the decision must appear on the face of the record. An application will not be dismissed for want of a proper affidavit where the affidavit is sufficient to establish the fact of the application and its rejection.

Murugappah v. Canada (Minister of Citizenship & Immigration) (2000), 7 Imm. L.R. (3d) 134, 184 F.T.R. 267, 2000 CarswellNat 1367, [2000] F.C.J. No. 1075 — The applicant sought to stay the execution on a deportation order. Before dealing with the substance of the application, the court addressed a procedural issue and affirmed that counsel should not appear on a matter in which he or she has deposed an affidavit or in which a partner or associate of counsel has deposed an affidavit.

Tajgardoon v. Canada (Minister of Citizenship & Immigration) (2000), 8 Imm. L.R. (3d) 310, [2001] 1 F.C. 591, 193 F.T.R. 230, 2000 CarswellNat 2087, 2000 CarswellNat 3408, [2000] F.C.J. No. 1450 — The applicant applied to immigrate to Canada as an independent applicant and was refused because it was determined that he lacked the personal characteristics which would permit him to establish himself economically in Canada. The applicant was a graduate civil engineer, a former Iranian Ambassador to the Netherlands from 1984 to 1987, the chief of protocol in the Iranian Ministry of Foreign Affairs from 1987 to 1990, the former managing director of Iran's largest car manufacturer from 1991 to 1994, and since 1994 the deputy managing director for the Iranian Offshore Engineering and Construction Company. The applicant was interviewed by a visa officer in Syria. The interview was conducted entirely in English with no interpreter. The visa officer had no difficulty understanding the applicant, who was able to answer all questions put to him. The applicant was asked to read a paragraph in English and summarize it and was awarded six points out of a possible nine for English language proficiency.

The visa officer assessed the applicant's personal suitability and questioned why he had not learned the local languages during his foreign postings. The applicant replied that he was able to function in English. The visa officer recorded that this reflected negatively upon the applicant's adaptability. The visa officer determined that the applicant had made no efforts to contact prospective employers and indicated that this showed a lack of initiative. The applicant was awarded five out of 10 points for personal suitability. Overall the applicant received 69 points. The visa officer indicated that if the applicant had scored 70 points or more he would have exercised negative discretion.

The visa officer's notes were part of the record filed on the judicial review application but there was no affidavit from the visa officer. In these circumstances, the officer's notes are not evidence but are capable of being received as reasons for the officer's decision. Using the traditional language of the law of evidence, the applicant can be said to rely upon the admissions against interest found in the notes, while the respondent seeks to use the notes as self-serving statements made in an out-of-court document whose author is not available for cross-examination. The conclusion flowing from a traditional analysis of the law is that the notes would be admissible at the instance of the applicant and not admissible in the hands of the respondent. The court then referred to the requirements of necessity and reliability, which if demonstrated, would make the notes admissible as exceptions to the hearsay rule. The court noted that it is likely easier for the respondent to get an affidavit from its officer then it is for the applicant who is also abroad to find someone to prepare and commission his affidavit. Thus, the requirement of necessity would not normally be satisfied. The requirement of some circumstantial guarantee of trustworthiness was more problematic. The facts necessary to show a circumstantial guarantee of trustworthiness must be found in the document itself. This amounts to relying upon a document of unknown reliability to prove that the same document is reliable. Accordingly, the notes, absent an affidavit from a visa officer, are not admissible as a principled exception to the hearsay rule.

The applicant's failure to learn local languages was not indicative of adaptability because the applicant was able to learn English and function in that language. In considering adaptability, a visa officer is not free to consider only one factor in isolation and to ignore the balance of an applicant's employment history. The court noted the irony of a man who had been an ambassador of a major Middle Eastern nation to a European capital, managing director of a significant industrial concern and deputy manager of a large construction and engineering firm, should be reproached for lack of adaptability. The applicant's linguistic failings, such as they are, seem trivial compared to the breadth of the applicant's experience in a number of diverse environments. Finally, the court noted that age, a factor also taken into account by the officer, was not relevant to adaptability, motivation, initiative, ingenuity or other similar qualities. The labour market realities which confront older workers are already accounted for in the reduced points awarded to immigrants over the age of 44.

The decision of the visa officer was set aside.

Samolenko v. Canada (Minister of Citizenship & Immigration), 1997 CarswellNat 1220 (Fed. T.D.) — The applicant sought to review a negative decision by a visa officer with respect to her application for permanent residence under the independent category. The applicant listed her occupation as a computer graphics specialist. In addition, the applicant alleged that she sent a supplementary application to the visa officer prior to the refusal that was the subject matter of this proceeding. That supplementary application was said to have contained an additional occupational category, namely that of an arts supervisor. The respondent disputed receipt of the supplementary application. The applicant was not assessed as an arts supervisor.

A visa officer has a duty to assess an application with reference to each occupation represented by the applicant as one for which he or she is qualified and prepared to pursue in Canada. Further, there is the clear responsibility on the part of a visa officer to assess alternative occupations inherent in the applicant's work experience.

There was no evidence to establish that the supplementary application was in fact before the visa officer. The copy of the supplementary application submitted by the applicant as part of its application for judicial review did not contain any evidence to suggest receipt of it by the respondent. The respondent specifically denied that any supplementary application was received by the embassy. The only evidence submitted by the applicant was an affidavit of a solicitor who practised in association with counsel for the applicant. This solicitor's affidavit deposed that the source of his information and belief was the applicant's solicitor, who could not reasonably be expected to have personal knowledge of the matter.

Accordingly, the applicant had failed to prove that the supplementary application was before the visa officer and the application for judicial review was therefore dismissed.

Prajapati v. Canada (Minister of Citizenship & Immigration) (1995), 31 Imm. L.R. (2d) 182, 103 F.T.R. 37 — This was an application to review a decision of a visa officer rejecting the applicant's application for permanent residence.

The sole affidavit filed in support of the application was that of the solicitor of record. The affidavit attested to the filing of the applicant's application. It further attested to the submissions of the undertaking of assistance and annexed that document and attested to the acknowledgement of receipt of the undertaking of assistance, also annexed. The affidavit attested to the fact that the applicant was invited to a personal interview and a copy of the invitation letter was annexed. It also deposed to the fact that the applicant attended the interview and thereafter informed his solicitor that the visa officer was "fully satisfied with the applicant's answers and congratulated him". The applicant's letter to his solicitor in this regard setting out the applicants report of the interview was also annexed. Finally, the affidavit deposed to the rejection of the applicant's application and an annexed copy of the rejection letter. The paragraph referring to the applicant's report of the interview was numbered 6 in the affidavit.

Hearsay evidence is now admissible on a principle basis, the governing principles being the reliability of the evidence and its necessity. Paragraph 6 was clearly hearsay. Its reliability was brought into question by the divergencies between it and the affidavit of the visa officer filed by the respondent. Accordingly, paragraph 6 was struck out.

Due to the fact that the challenge to the affidavit in support of the applicant's application was, in fact, a challenge to the application itself, because if the affidavit was struck out the application would be without a supporting factual basis, it was appropriate for the respondent to argue this issue at the hearing of the motion itself.

Patel v. Canada (Minister of Citizenship & Immigration) (1995), 31 Imm. L.R. (2d) 24, 103 F.T.R. 21 — This was an application to set aside a decision of a visa officer refusing an application for permanent residence. The application for judicial review was supported by the affidavit of the applicant's solicitor of record. The solicitor's affidavit provided no basis for reviewing the visa officer's decision. The affidavit presented only sworn statements about the application process and a confirmation of a negative reply. There was no information about the conduct of the interview, nor any grounds for disputing the visa officer's assessment. It is wholly inappropriate for solicitors to submit their own affidavits in support of an application for judicial review. The court considered the application on its merits but accorded the solicitor's affidavit very little weight.

Section 12(2)

Kanes v. Canada (Minister of Employment & Immigration) (1993), 22 Imm. L.R. (2d) 223, 72 F.T.R. 226 — The applicant brought an interlocutory motion in the course of prosecuting an application for leave seeking permission to cross-examine one Lalita Jeethan on an affidavit she filed on the leave application.

The applicant alleged that there were inaccuracies in the affidavit. The inaccuracies in this case could not be clarified further by cross-examination. The answer, if any, must be found in the documentary evidence attached to the affidavit, namely the applicant's application for permanent residence wherein he answered "No" to the question "Have you . . . ever been convicted of or currently charged with any crime or offence. . ." Further, the deponent, Jeethan, claimed no personal involvement in the handling of the file, therefore, the court could not appreciate how it would be further enlightened by her cross-examination. On the question of when documents were received by the Commission, this issue would be resolved better, the court felt, by examining the document.

Finally, the court noted that a judge dealing with an application for leave is not required to make factual findings, but simply to determine whether a serious issue has been raised. The application for leave process is designed to provide a relatively simple and speedy process for the court to determine whether there is a serious question that should be dealt with by a normal judicial review process. Judges are not expected to make findings of fact or resolve conflicts in the evidence at that stage.

The court declined to order costs against the applicant in this case because this was a matter of first impression. It did indicate, however, that it would consider ordering costs where future interlocutory motions were brought on such an insubstantial basis.

REPLY MEMORANDUM

13. Where a respondent serves a memorandum of argument, an applicant may serve a memorandum of argument in reply thereto, and shall file it, together with proof of service, within 10 days after the day of service of the respondent's memorandum of argument.

Case Law

Beci v. Canada (Minister of Citizenship & Immigration) (1997), 130 F.T.R. 267 — The applicant sought leave to file an affidavit in reply to prove certain allegations contained in the applicant's reply.

There is no provision in the *Federal Court Immigration Rules* for evidence in reply. Where it comes to the applicant's attention after the record has been filed, that certain material was before the tribunal at the hearing which is not mentioned in the record, leave can be given for affidavit evidence to be filed in reply or alternatively, the time may be extended within which to file an amended record.

In this case, new evidence had come to the attention of the applicant's counsel, which might have altered the decision of the tribunal had it been considered. The fact that such information had been uncovered since the tribunal's decision is irrelevant to a judicial review of that decision. Accordingly, the motion for leave was dismissed.

DISPOSITION OF APPLICATION FOR LEAVE

14. (1) Where

    (a) any party has failed to serve and file any document required by these Rules within the time fixed, or

(b) the applicant's reply memorandum has been filed, or the time for filing it has expired,

a judge may, without further notice to the parties, determine the application for leave on the basis of the materials then filed.

(2) Where the judge considers that documents in the possession or control of the tribunal are required for the proper disposition of the application for leave, the judge may, by order, specify the documents to be produced and filed and give such other directions as the judge considers necessary to dispose of the application for leave.

(3) The Registry shall send to the tribunal a copy of an order made under subrule (2) forthwith after it is made.

(4) Upon receipt of an order under subrule (2), the tribunal shall, without delay, send a copy of the materials specified in the order, duly certified by an appropriate officer to be correct, to each of the parties, and two copies to the Registry.

(5) The tribunal shall be deemed to have received a copy of the order on the tenth day after it was sent by mail by the Registry.

Case Law

Karakulak v. Canada (Minister of Employment & Immigration) (1995), 98 F.T.R. 81 — This was an application for an extension of time to file a reply and it arose because the notes of the immigration officer who made the impugned decision were not available and there were no written reasons for the decision. The notes had been refused pursuant to the provisions of the *Privacy Act*. The court would not order the missing pages produced, nor would it agree to extend the time to file a reply for an unlimited period. The applicant industriously pursued the pages, and if this had not been the case, the applicant would have been required to proceed without them. Immigration Rule 14 enables a judge to order the production of documents refused by a tribunal claiming *quasi*-judicial privilege, but it does not permit a judge to order the production of documents protected by the *Privacy Act*.

Nguyen v. Canada (Minister of Employment & Immigration) (1993), 66 F.T.R. 75, [1994] 1 F.C. 96, 107 D.L.R. (4th) 186 — The applicant filed an application for leave to challenge a decision of the CRDD denying the applicant refugee status. The applicant obtained a letter from the official reporter of the Board disclosing that no official transcript of the proceedings had been prepared and questioning the accuracy of the Board's quotations of the evidence. The letter from the official reporter was included in the applicant's record. The respondent Minister took the position that there was no evidence that the portions of the testimony quoted were inaccurate. The applicant filed a reply memorandum to which was attached, under cover of an affidavit of the official reporter, a transcript of the proceedings. The respondent Minister objected to the filing of the transcript in reply.

Rule 13 of the *Federal Court Immigration Rules* states that an applicant may file a memorandum of argument in reply, but it does not specifically state that no other material may be filed. Rule 4(1) provides that Part I, and other parts of the *Federal Court Rules*, apply to immigration applications, except to the extent that they are inconsistent with the Federal Court Immigration Rules. Federal Court Rules 5 and 6 are sufficient authority for the granting of leave to the applicant to file a copy of the official transcript under cover of the affidavit of the official reporter. In addition, Federal Court Immigration Rule 14(2) provides authority to direct the filing of the transcript.

15. (1) An order granting an application for leave

(a) shall specify the language and the day and place fixed for the hearing of the application for judicial review;

(b) shall specify the time limit within which the tribunal is to send copies of its record required under Rule 17;

(c) shall specify the time limits within which further materials, if any, including affidavits, transcripts of cross-examinations, and memoranda of argument are to be served and filed;

(d) shall specify the time limits within which cross-examinations, if any, on affidavits are to be completed; and

(e) may specify any other matter that the judge considers necessary or expedient for the hearing of the application for judicial review.

(2) The Registry shall send to the tribunal a copy of an order granting leave forthwith after it is made.

(3) The tribunal shall be deemed to have received a copy of the order on the tenth day after it was sent by mail by the Registry.

SOR/2002-232, s. 8; SOR/2015-20, s. 8

Case Law

Mishak c. Canada (Ministre de la Citoyenneté & de l'Immigration) (1999), 173 F.T.R. 144, 1999 CarswellNat 1582, 1999 CarswellNat 2157 — The applicant attempted, at the last minute, to add to her *factum* and argue an issue that had not been set out in the applicant's material. Permission to raise this argument was refused. The court relied on *Lanlehin v. Canada (Minister of Employment & Immigration)*, 1993 CarswellNat 2301 (Fed. C.A.).

16. Where leave is granted, all documents filed in connection with the application for leave shall be retained by the Registry for consideration by the judge hearing the application for judicial review.

Case Law

Law Society of Upper Canada v. Canada (Minister of Citizenship & Immigration) (2006), 55 Imm. L.R. (3d) 238, 2006 CarswellNat 2717, 2006 FC 1042 — The basic approach of the *Federal Courts Immigration and Refugee Protection Rules* is to adopt a seamless procedural route to obtain judicial review, consisting of one application for both the leave request and the judicial review itself. With respect to any documents filed in connection with the application for leave, Rule 16 specifically provides that they will form part of the record for consideration by the judge hearing the application for judicial review. The purpose of Rule 16 is to ensure that all the documents filed in connection with the leave application, including affidavits, form part of the judicial review record. The affidavit filed in connection with the leave application forms part of the record for the application for judicial review and the opposing party has a *prima facie* right to cross-examine the deponent of any such affidavit.

An order permitting the withdrawal of an affidavit is in the discretion of the court. The key determining factor when a request for withdrawal is made is a clear existence of prejudice to the party seeking to withdraw if leave is not given. The court should not permit a withdrawal of an affidavit merely to prevent cross-examination. The court concluded that the affiant's current views appear to be diametrically opposed to the respondent's position and supportive of the applicant's position and, therefore, it would be unfair and prejudicial to the respondent should the respondent be bound by the affiant's answers and cross-examinations. In contrast, there was no harm or prejudice to the applicant should the affiant's affidavit be allowed to be withdrawn. The respondent had filed another affidavit that was in all material respects identical to the initial affidavit. The second affiant appeared to be as knowledgeable and well versed regarding the issues and was a proper substitute.

OBTAINING TRIBUNAL'S RECORD

17. Upon receipt of an order under Rule 15, a tribunal shall, without delay, prepare a record containing the following, on consecutively numbered pages and in the following order:

> **(a) the decision or order in respect of which the application for judicial review is made and the written reasons given therefor,**
>
> **(b) all papers relevant to the matter that are in the possession or control of the tribunal,**
>
> **(c) any affidavits, or other documents filed during any such hearing, and**
>
> **(d) a transcript, if any, of any oral testimony given during the hearing, giving rise to the decision or order or other matter that is the subject of the application for judicial review,**

and shall send a copy, duly certified by an appropriate officer to be correct, to each of the parties and two copies to the Registry.

SOR/2002-232, s. 14

Case Law

Machalikashvili v. Canada (Minister of Citizenship & Immigration) (2006), 55 Imm. L.R. (3d) 33, 2006 CarswellNat 1601, 2006 FC 622 — This was an application for judicial review of the decision of a visa officer who rejected the applicant's application for permanent residence as a non-accompanying family member of a refugee under the One Year Window of Opportunity program. The applicant's wife and two children were granted refugee status in October 2004. The visa officer concluded that he was not satisfied that the applicant was not inadmissible to Canada. The visa officer's decision was set aside since the court was unable to assess the legality of the decision because the certified record filed pursuant to Rule 17 of the *Federal Courts Immigration and Refugee Protection Rules* did not include any of the materials in the applicant's wife's file that was considered by the visa officer and upon which he based his final assessment of the applicant's credibility. A breach of Rule 17 will justify setting the decision aside when the evidence missing from the certified record was particularly material to the finding under review.

Liao v. Canada (Minister of Citizenship & Immigration) (2000), 6 Imm. L.R. (3d) 26, 2000 CarswellNat 1461, [2000] F.C.J. No. 1098 (T.D.) — The applicant sought to review the refusal of his application for permanent residence. The court adopted the comments of Reed J. in *Chou v. Canada* (2000), 3 Imm. L.R. (3d) 212, 190 F.T.R. 78, 2000 CarswellNat 405, [2000] F.C.J. No. 314 as follows:

> I accept then that the CAIPS notes should be admitted as part of the record, that is, as the reasons for the decision under review. However, the underlying facts on which they rely must be independently proven. In the absence of a visa officer's affidavit attesting to the truth of what he or she recorded as having been said at the interview the notes have no status as evidence of such.

Liang v. Canada (Minister of Citizenship & Immigration), 1999 CarswellNat 1592, [1999] F.C.J. No. 1301 (T.D.) — The applicant sought to overturn the rejection of his application for permanent residence in the assisted relative category. The Minister is under no obligation to file an affidavit from a visa officer. A visa officer's notes are part of the tribunal's record submitted to the court under Rule 317 of the *Federal Court Rules*. The notes form part of the application record on which the decision is reviewed.

Parveen v. Canada (Minister of Citizenship & Immigration) (1999), 1 Imm. L.R. (3d) 305, 168 F.T.R. 103, 1999 CarswellNat 772, [1999] F.C.J. No. 660 — This was an application to review and set aside a visa officer's decision denying the applicant a permanent visa. The record that was provided to the court by the respondent was incomplete. It had been "stripped". Counsel for the respondent advised the court that this occurred because of a "thin file" policy and the difficulty of retaining the full files for all the individuals applying for immigration to Canada in the various embassies abroad.

The period of time within which a person can file an appeal from a visa officer's decision is limited. The court could not accept that the administrative burden of retaining the full file for that period of time was unduly onerous. The respondent controls the record that is put before the court, thus any disputes that arise as a result of deficiency in the record should, in general, be interpreted against the respondent. An incomplete record alone could be grounds, in some circumstances, for setting aside a decision.

Finally, the court refused to adopt the approach suggested by counsel for the respondent to the effect that visa officers have no interest in these applications. The court observed that once a visa officer's decision is challenged he or she has an interest in justifying his or her decision. This was an entirely natural reaction and at that point the visa officer was not, in the court's view, a disinterested person.

Bertold v. Canada (Minister of Citizenship & Immigration) (1997), 126 F.T.R. 216 — On December 3, 1996, the court granted leave for the applicant to institute judicial review. The acting director general, case management branch, failed or neglected to comply with Federal Court Immigration Rule 17 in accordance with the court's order that certified copies of the tribunal record be sent before or on December 30, 1996.

Section 82.1(7) requires that a judicial review hearing must be set down for hearing no later than 90 days after leave for judicial review was granted. There is nothing in the *Immigration Act* or the *Federal Court Immigration Rules* which allows this time limit to be extended. Due to the fact that neither the *Immigration Act* nor the *Federal Court Immigration Rules* contemplate such an extension, reference may be had to the *Federal Court Rules*. However, Rule 3(1)(c) applies only to extensions of time prescribed by the Rules and to any order. It is clear that the court cannot extend the period of time prescribed by statute.

It would be unjust to leave the applicant without recourse and, of course, both parties need to have the opportunity to file further affidavits and to cross-examine in regard to the tribunal's record. It would be unjust to let the tribunal (the acting director general, case management branch) abort the applicant's right to institute judicial review through the tribunal's own failure, neglect or refusal to obey Immigration Rule 17.

The tribunal was found to have perpetrated an injustice upon the applicant by frustrating the court's powers, and was required to show cause why it ought not to be punished for contempt of court. The court ordered that either party may prosecute the contempt application under Rule 355(3).

The court observed that in the event the judicial review application was commenced on the date previously fixed, it would be open to the judge seized of the matter to adjourn the application to a later date for completion.

Sajjan v. Canada (Minister of Citizenship & Immigration) (1997), 125 F.T.R. 198; reversed (1997), 39 Imm. L.R. (2d) 56, (sub nom. *Canada (Minister of Citizenship & Immigration) v. Sajjan)* 216 N.R. 150 (Fed. C.A.) — The applicant sought judicial review of a decision of the Immigration Appeal Division of the IRB, to the effect that the applicant's adopted son was not a member of the family class and that therefore the panel was without jurisdiction to hear an appeal, under subs. 77(3), of a decision of a visa officer under subs. 77(1).

Leave of a judge of the Federal Court is not required to commence this type of application for judicial review. The Appeal Division is not under an obligation to prepare a record, including a transcript, of the oral hearing before the panel and to provide a copy of that record to the applicant. Such an obligation arises under s. 17 of the *Federal Court Immigration Rules*. The obligation under s. 17 arises "upon receipt of an order under rule 15. . ..". An order under Rule 15 is an order granting an application for leave. No application for leave is required in these circumstances and, accordingly, in the absence of such an application, no obligation is placed on the Board by Rule 17. In the result, the Board was correct in concluding that it had no obligation in law to provide to the applicant a record of the proceedings before the panel. This creates an anomalous situation under which neither an applicant nor the court has a right to require of the Board a record of its proceedings. The court observed that an amendment to the *Immigration Act* or the *Federal Court Immigration Rules* may be required.

Vergara v. Canada (Minister of Employment & Immigration) (1994), 25 Imm. L.R. (2d) 197, (sub nom. *Ortiz Vergara c. Canada (Ministre de l'Emploi & l'Immigration))* 84 F.T.R. 34 — The applicant obtained leave to file an application for judicial review from a decision of a panel of the CRDD. The applicant wanted to enter in evidence on the leave application "the Peru File". This file was entered as an exhibit at the refugee hearing.

The interests of justice do not, however, require that all documents entered at the refugee hearing be reproduced in their entirety for purposes of the judicial review application. A party wishing to use documents on the judicial review application which were part of the standardized country file, should draw the court's attention to the exhibits which it intends to use by attaching them to its submission. It should send a copy to the court and to the other party before the hearing, thus informing them of the documents to which it intends to refer at the hearing. The opposing party, in turn, can append to its own submission documents taken from the standardized country file which it intends to use.

Lemiecha v. Canada (Minister of Employment & Immigration) (1993), 72 F.T.R. 49 —
This was an application to review a decision that there were no humanitarian or compassionate grounds to permit the applicants to remain in Canada. The applicants were a married couple and their two children. They arrived in Canada during the summer and au-
tumn of 1989. They claimed Convention refugee status and these claims were denied in
August, 1990. In April, 1991, through a solicitor, they applied for a review on humanitarian and compassionate grounds. A medical update on their nine-year-old son was completed in September, 1991, but not forwarded to the Immigration Centre. Without either
of the medical reports having been brought to their attention, through no fault of the
respondent, the humanitarian and compassionate review resulted in a negative decision.
A further review was conducted on the eve of what was to be the applicants' departure
for Poland. One of the medical reports that had been prepared with respect to the son was
forwarded to the officer conducting that review. The officer, after seeking advice from a
Canada Immigration physician, refused humanitarian and compassionate relief, and it
was that decision that was the subject of this application.

The application failed. The applicants were aware of their nine-year-old son's medical
condition and its relevance to a humanitarian and compassionate review. The applicants
had many months to supply information regarding medical expertise, services and facilities available in Poland and environmental conditions in that country and their relationship to the son's asthmatic condition. The applicants did not submit this information.

Judicial review of a decision of a federal board, commission or other tribunal should
proceed on the basis of the evidence that was before the decision maker. Accordingly, the
evidence of the medical experts which was tendered on the judicial review application
but not submitted to the officer whose decision was under attack, was not admissible.
There was essentially no evidence before the officer whose decision was under attack
regarding any link between conditions in Poland, environmental or otherwise, and the
son's medical difficulties. Accordingly, the application for judicial review was dismissed.

DISPOSITION OF APPLICATION FOR JUDICIAL REVIEW

**18. (1) Before a judge renders judgment in respect of an application for judicial
review, the judge shall provide the parties with an opportunity to request that he or
she certify that a serious question of general importance, referred to in paragraph
22.2(d) of the *Citizenship Act* or paragraph 74(d) of the *Immigration and Refugee
Protection Act*, as the case may be, is involved.**

**(2) A party who requests that the judge certify that a serious question of general
importance is involved shall specify the precise question.**

(3) [Repealed SOR/2002-232, s. 9(2).]

SOR/2002-232, s. 9; SOR/2015-20, s. 9

APPEALS

19. [Repealed SOR/98-235, s. 4.]

20. (1) An appeal to the Federal Court of Appeal shall be commenced by filing a notice of appeal in Form IR-4 as set out in the schedule within

(a) 30 days after the pronouncement of the judgment under appeal; or

(b) such further time as may be ordered by a judge of the Federal Court.

(2) A notice of appeal shall be served on all parties and proof of service filed within 15 days after the notice of appeal is filed.

SOR/98-235, s. 4; SOR/2002-232, s. 10; 2002, c. 8, s. 183(2)(a); SOR/2005-339, s. 5

Case Law

Dasent v. Canada (Minister of Citizenship & Immigration) (1995), 28 Imm. L.R. (2d) 28, 92 F.T.R. 103 — The respondent moved to extend the time for filing a notice of appeal. The order that was being appealed was signed by the judge on December 8, 1994, but not entered in the registry until December 13, 1994. The order in question was pronounced upon the date on which the judge signed it, namely December 8, 1994.

The notice of appeal must be filed within 15 days after the pronouncement of the judgment which includes the order. The time in this case expired on December 23, 1994. The respondent attempted to file the notice of appeal on December 28, 1994.

In arriving at the decision to extend the time the court considered, firstly, special circumstances. In this case the court found that the respondent's counsel was probably misled by the date stamp on the judgment. The court then considered whether there was prejudice to the applicant in extending the time, whether the respondent had an intention to appeal within the 15 days, whether the delay in requesting an extension was undue, and finally whether the interests of justice mandated the granting of an extension.

TIME LIMITS

21. (1) [Repealed SOR/98-235, s. 5.]

(2) No time limit prescribed by these Rules may be varied except by order of a judge or prothonotary.

SOR/98-235, s. 5

Case Law

Section 21(2)

Muhammed v. Canada (Minister of Citizenship & Immigration) (2003), 30 Imm. L.R. (3d) 145, 237 F.T.R. 8, 2003 CarswellNat 2602, 2003 CarswellNat 2235, 2003 FC 828 — The applicants sought a nominal extension of time in which to serve and file a record.

The test for a time extension is:

1) a continuing intention to pursue the application;

2) there must be some merit in the application;

3) no prejudice to the respondent arises from the delay; and

4) that a reasonable explanation for the delay exists.

Canada (Minister of Citizenship & Immigration) v. Simakov, 2001 FCT 469, 2001 CarswellNat 952 — This was a motion by the respondent for an order allowing an extension of time for serving and filing an appearance pursuant to Rule 305, an extension of time for serving and filing the respondent's affidavits pursuant to Rule 307, and an extension of time for serving and filing the respondent's application record pursuant to Rule 310.

The criteria to be met by a party seeking an extension of time are as follows:

1. a continuing intention to pursue his or her application;

2. that the application has some merit;

3. that no prejudice to the respondent arises from the delay; and

4. that a reasonable explanation for the delay exists.

In addition, the following factors must also be considered: firstly, in the circumstances presented, to do justice between the parties an extension should be granted; and secondly, whether or not the explanation justifies the necessary extension must depend on the facts of the particular case and it would be wrong to attempt to lay down rules which would fetter a discretionary power which Parliament has not fettered.

Nguyen v. Canada (Minister of Citizenship & Immigration), 1999 CarswellNat 1687 (Fed. T.D.) — This was a motion to appeal an order refusing an extension of time. A voluntary change of counsel will not normally justify an extension of time to enable new counsel to submit additional material on an application for leave after the first counsel has filed and served a complete application record in a timely fashion.

Kurian v. Canada (Minister of Citizenship & Immigration), 1999 CarswellNat 1735 (Fed. T.D.) — The applicant sought an order extending the time for filing an application for judicial review. The applicant commenced an application for judicial review on March 9, 1999. The Minister filed a motion in response for an order dismissing the application on the basis that it was filed late. The first application was dismissed in July 1999, and no reasons for the order were given. The court concluded that, in dismissing the application, the judge implicitly rejected the argument that an extension of time was warranted, and that the application before the court was subject to the doctrine of *res judicata* and, therefore, it must be dismissed.

Counsel for the applicant could and should have filed a motion for an extension of time in response to the Minister's motion for summary dismissal of the first application so that both motions could be dealt with at the same time. It was not open for counsel to attempt that step after the Minister's motion for summary dismissal had succeeded.

Abaev v. Canada (Minister of Citizenship & Immigration) (1999), 49 Imm. L.R. (2d) 29, 163 F.T.R. 149, 1999 CarswellNat 438 — The applicant brought a motion for an extension of time to file affidavits and extensions of time for the completion of other steps in this proceeding. This was an application to review a visa officer's decision. Pursuant to Federal Court Rule 318, the tribunal (a visa officer in the Immigration Section of the Canadian Consulate General in New York) was required to "transmit" the material in its possession within 20 days of the request for such being made. Transmit means more than merely depositing in the post without regard to the amount of time it might take to reach the applicant or his counsel. The Rules intend that the applicant have access to the relevant tribunal material before his or her affidavits are required to be filed in order to review that material to see if it is relevant for the purpose of preparing the affidavits. The Rules allow for a 10-day difference between the transmitting of the material and the filing of the affidavits. The action taken in this case did not constitute the transmitting of the material to the applicant within the required time. In addition to allowing the application, the court awarded costs on the motion.

Other Relevant Legislation

Bains v. Canada (Minister of Employment & Immigration) (1999), 47 Admin. L.R. 317, 109 N.R. 239 (Fed. C.A.) — The only question to be considered in disposing of an application for leave under s. 82.1(1) or s. 82.3(1) is whether or not a fairly arguable case is disclosed for the relief proposed to be sought if leave is granted. Further, the need for material not immediately available has to be established by the applicant and the mere stated intention to rely on such material does not, without an application and an order to that end, operate to extend the time provided by the *Federal Court Immigration Rules* for the applicant to file an affidavit and/or representations in support of the leave application. The requirement for leave is, in reality, the other side of the coin of the traditional jurisdiction to summarily terminate proceedings that disclose no reasonably arguable case. The requirement for leave does not deny refugee claimants access to the court. The right to apply for leave is, itself, a right of access to the court and the requirement that leave be obtained before an appeal or application for judicial review may proceed does not impair the right guaranteed by refugee claimants under either ss. 7 or 15 of the *Charter*.

Shaker v. Canada (Minister of Citizenship & Immigration), 1998 CarswellNat 1817 (Fed. T.D.) — The applicant filed a motion for an extension of time within which to file her application record. The applicant filed, in support, an affidavit evidencing the delay and exhibiting only the cover page of the application record. There was no evidence of an arguable case and so the motion was refused with leave to reapply. The applicant reapplied and this time supported the application by the very record for which leave to file was sought. This material was filed to show an arguable case. In the ordinary course the court would have returned the record to the applicant. It may well be that all of the evidence of an arguable case is to be found in certain documents and affidavits in the application record. Those documents and affidavits, however, have an independent existence and duplicates could have been exhibited to affidavits with the appropriate explanations in the motion record. Notwithstanding the court's reservations about the materials, the court allowed an extension of time to file the application record.

Mikhail v. Canada (Minister of Citizenship & Immigration) (1998), 46 Imm. L.R. (2d) 93, 150 F.T.R. 318 — This motion sought an extension of time within which to file a reply. The motion is supported by an affidavit exhibiting the reply sought to be filed. The filing of a reply as an exhibit to an affidavit when the reply cannot be filed without leave is improper.

Canada (Minister of Citizenship & Immigration) v. Singh (S.M.) (1997), 140 F.T.R. 102, 41 Imm. L.R. (2d) 284 — The respondent sought to have the applicant Minister's application for leave struck out, on the grounds that the applicant failed to file an application record within the time allowed. The applicant sought an extension of time within which to file his record.

The applicant failed to satisfy either branch of the test for a time extension set out in *Beilin v. Canada (Minister of Employment & Immigration)* (1994), 88 F.T.R. 132 at 134. The court can grant an extension notwithstanding this fact for the purpose of doing justice between the parties.

If there had been some indication in the material that the applicant had an arguable case, then the court would have considered whether, to do justice between the parties, a time extension ought to be allowed. The absence of such evidence required that the application for an extension be dismissed and the respondent's motion seeking a dismissal of the application for judicial review was allowed.

Avalos v. Canada (Minister of Citizenship & Immigration) (1997), *(sub nom. Avalos c. Canada (Ministre de la Citoyenneté & de l'Immigration))* 136 F.T.R. 125 — The applicants sought an extension of time for filing their records. An application for an extension of time in order to be successful must be accompanied by material which shows some justification for the delay throughout the whole period of the delay, and secondly that the applicant has an arguable case. With respect to the explanation as to why it was not possible to comply with the whole of the time limit set out in subs. 10(1) of the Rules, the court noted that the reason must be beyond the control of counsel or the applicant, for example, illness or some other unexpected or unanticipated event.

The court was not satisfied that this case involved an unexpected event. The court noted that less than 5 months before, counsel for the applicants approached the court in two other cases seeking extensions of time allowed by Rule 10 and citing difficulty in filing the records on time. The court noted that neither the applicant nor counsel gave any details by affidavit which would suggest that the case was arguable on the merits and accordingly the motion for an extension of time was dismissed.

The court noted that it would have considered awarding costs against the solicitor personally had there been a request to that effect.

Iakolev v. Canada (Minister of Citizenship & Immigration), 1996 CarswellNat 3124, 1996 CarswellNat 630, [1996] F.C.J. No. 640 (T.D.) — This was an application for an extension of time to perfect an application for judicial review.

The ultimate responsibility to compute time limits under the rules rests with the party and its counsel, regardless of any conversation between a counsel's secretary and a registry officer of the court. Most of the supporting affidavits in this matter referred to what was understood by the applicant's counsel from a conversation with the registry of the court. Such evidence was of no assistance in a motion for an extension of time.

When a deadline is missed, what is required is an explanation of the efforts spent throughout the entire period prescribed by the time limit.

On the basis of the affidavit material, the application for an extension was dismissed.

Bhui v. Canada (Minister of Citizenship & Immigration), 1996 CarswellNat 567 (Fed. T.D.) — The court had before it a motion by the applicant for an extension of the time limits set out in Rule 10(1) for serving and filing the applicant's record.

In January, 1996, the applicant filed his record within the time required by the Rules. The record did not include a memorandum of argument. Counsel provided the court with an affidavit indicating that he did not feel it was necessary to include a memorandum of argument in the record, and therefore did not do so.

The respondent took the position that the applicant's record was not complete and not perfected within the time period provided by the Rules.

The filing and service of the applicant's record are official in the court file. There cannot, therefore, be in this case an extension of time to perform acts that have already been done.

If the motion were granted allowing the inclusion of the memorandum of argument in the applicant's record, there would be no additional delays in dealing with the application and no evidence to suggest that the respondent would otherwise be prejudiced. There was nothing in the evidence to support the suggestion that counsel for the applicant was seeking to file the applicant's record in successive steps in order to avoid the time limits set out in Rule 10.

Other Relevant Legislation

Accordingly, the memorandum of argument was permitted to be filed with the court as part of the applicant's record.

Moreno v. Canada (Minister of Citizenship & Immigration) (1996), 33 Imm. L.R. (2d) 84, *(sub nom. Moreno c. Canada (Ministre de la Citoyenneté & de l'Immigration))* 110 F.T.R. 57 — This was a motion pursuant to Rule 21(2) of the *Federal Court Immigration Rules* for an extension of the time limit under Rule 10(1) for serving and filing the applicant's record.

The court expects the time limit set out in the rules to be complied with and an automatic extension is not available merely because it is requested. An applicant must show that there was some justification for the delay throughout the whole period of the delay and that the applicant has an arguable case. The applicant must demonstrate some reason for the delay which was beyond its control or the control of its counsel, for example, illness, or some other unexpected or unanticipated event. This motion failed because there was a lack of an explanation for the extension and, furthermore, there were no arguments advanced to show that the applicants had an arguable case.

Milon v. Canada (Minister of Citizenship & Immigration) (1995), 100 F.T.R. 1 — The applicant sought an extension of time within which to serve and file his record. An applicant seeking an extension of time must demonstrate (1) a continuing intention to pursue his appeal, (2) that there is some merit in his application, (3) that no prejudice to the respondents arises as a result of the delay, and (4) that a reasonable explanation for the delay exists.

On an application for judicial review, the issue before the court is whether sufficient information existed in front of the decision maker to justify the decision that was made. It would be an error of law to take into account any evidence arising subsequent to the making of the decision under review.

The material in this application did not at all deal with the merits of the case, and so the application for an extension was refused.

Karakulak v. Canada (Minister of Employment & Immigration) (1995), 98 F.T.R. 81 — This was an application for an extension of time to file a reply and it arose because the notes of the immigration officer who made the impugned decision were not available and there were no written reasons for the decision. The notes had been refused pursuant to the provisions of the *Privacy Act*. The court would not order the missing pages produced, nor would it agree to extend the time to file a reply for an unlimited period. The applicant industriously pursued the pages, and if this had not been the case the applicant would have been required to proceed without them. Immigration Rule 14 enables a judge to order the production of documents refused by a tribunal claiming quasi-judicial privilege, but it does not permit a judge to order the production of documents protected by the *Privacy Act*.

Awogbade v. Canada (Minister of Citizenship & Immigration) (1995), 29 Imm. L.R. (2d) 281, 94 F.T.R. 184 — The applicant applied for leave to take judicial review proceedings against a decision of the CRDD. One month after filing the originating motion the applicant's solicitors sought to extend the time for filing her application record. Additional time was refused by the court and the applicant brought an application for reconsideration of that order.

In a solicitor-client relationship, there is a strong fiduciary obligation on the solicitor's part to act in a professional, timely manner in order to advance the client's interests. The Ontario Legal Aid plan merely authorizes the payment of fees for the lawyer's services.

A professional, ethical lawyer will not leave his or her client in the lurch merely because fees are not secured. It may be that the allowing of a client's case to turn to ashes, while awaiting spurious authorization from Legal Aid, is contempt of court.

There are several valid reasons for which a judge could extend the time to file an applicant's record, but waiting for a Legal Aid certificate is not one of them.

The absence of an application record is a substantive defect as well as a procedural one, and an order dismissing additional time for the filing of an application is a final one.

It is a species of professional misconduct for a lawyer to prefer the securing of his or her own fees over the client's interests.

The court noted that the reasons of the CRDD had not been filed with the original request for an extension of time and considered that this failure on the part of the applicant's solicitors provided it with a reason to relieve the applicant of the prejudice created by the conduct of her solicitors, and accordingly, reconsidered its order and granted to the applicant a short extension to file her application record.

Valyenegro v. Canada (Secretary of State) (1994), 88 F.T.R. 196 — This was a motion for an extension of time to file the applicant's records. An application for an extension is an interlocutory application, even if in certain circumstances a resulting order refusing an extension might be final in nature.

The burden of justifying an extension of time is on the applicant. It is not incumbent on the respondent to show there is prejudice, but rather the onus is on the applicant to show that there is prejudice to the applicant and that there is no prejudice to the respondent.

It may be assumed that an applicant would be prejudiced if he or she is denied the right to put forward their case. If, however, the applicant does not have a case, he or she cannot be prejudiced if an extension of time is denied. Here the applicant tendered no evidence of an arguable case. There was, therefore, no evidence of any prejudice to the applicant if the request was refused. Accordingly, the application for an extension of time was dismissed.

Subuncuo v. Canada (Minister of Employment & Immigration), 1992 CarswellNat 818 (Fed. T.D.) — The respondent Minister sought an order extending the time within which the respondent would be allowed to file and serve written submissions in response to the applicant's application for leave pursuant to s. 82.1. The adjudicator in this case had delayed in forwarding a copy of the transcript of the hearing and this delay was determined not to be justifiable. In requesting an extension of time in such a situation, the respondent is essentially using its own conduct as a ground for delay — something an applicant would not be allowed to do. There are no good reasons why tapes could not be used to avoid the delay which arises as a result of waiting for the preparation of a transcript. In this case, however, the applicant had requested a transcript and not a copy of the tape and, accordingly, an extension of time was granted. The result would have been different had the applicant requested a copy of the tape rather than a transcript.

Espinoza v. Canada (Minister of Employment & Immigration) (1992), 142 N.R. 158 (Fed. C.A.) — An order for an extension of the time to comply with Rule 9 does not finally dispose of any matter in issue. Such an order is always open to reconsideration whether made peremptorily or not. The policy of the *Immigration Act* and *Federal Court Immigration Rules* is transparently clear and is one of deciding leave applications expeditiously. The dilatory initiation of Legal Aid applications, delays in providing opinion letters, which counsel know will be required, and the ever slower processing of such applications by Legal Aid cannot be permitted to defeat the policy of the Act and Rules. Failure to make a Legal Aid application promptly can be good reason to deny an extension.

Metodieva v. Canada (Department of Employment & Immigration) (1991), *(*sub nom. *Metodieva v. Ministre de l'emploi et de l'immigration)* 132 N.R. 38 (Fed. C.A.) — The Convention Refugee Determination Division dismissed the applicant's claim for refugee status. An initial application for leave to appeal was dismissed in December 1990. In May 1991, the applicant made a subsequent application for leave to appeal and for an extension of the 15-day deadline imposed by s. 82.3(4) of the *Immigration Act*. This application was a request to the court to disregard the final order made by the court previously refusing leave to appeal. Once an order has been signed by a judge, it is a final order. Apart from clerical mistakes or errors arising from accidental slips or omissions, a party who is not satisfied with such an order may only challenge the order in a manner prescribed by the *Federal Courts Act* or by the Rules of the court and, in immigration matters, by the *Immigration Act* and the *Federal Court Immigration Rules*. Further, in immigration matters, no appeal lies to the Supreme Court of Canada from a judgment of a Federal Court of Appeal judge on an application for leave to commence proceedings or an application for leave to appeal.

The proceedings defined by the Rules of Court are also available to a dissatisfied party. These proceedings are an application to rehear a motion dismissed in the absence of a party, an application to rescind an order made *ex parte* or, in the absence of a party, an application to reconsider the terms of the pronouncement on the grounds (a) that the pronouncement does not accord with the reasons that were given, or (b) that some matter that should have been dealt with has been overlooked or accidentally omitted, an application for a rehearing under Rule 1103(3), or an application setting aside a judgment for a new matter or fraud (Rule 1733). Apart from these cases, the court does not have jurisdiction to reconsider a final order. In the case at bar, the original order dismissing the application for leave to appeal was based on the fact that the application was unsupported by affidavit or other material. The fact that an application was dismissed for a procedural defect does not in any way change the fact that the order made is final and not subject to reconsideration except in the allowable cases referred to above. The absence of an affidavit is a substantive defect as well as a procedural one. Rule 9(1) of the *Federal Court Immigration Rules* makes the filing of an affidavit an integral part of an application, and an application for leave not supported by an affidavit is not complete and cannot be allowed by the court. The fact that the applicant is a foreigner in Canada does not confer any privilege to be ignorant of Canadian law or any special status in respect of errors which may be made by one's counsel. Accordingly, the application for leave to appeal was dismissed.

Costs

22. No costs shall be awarded to or payable by any party in respect of an application for leave, an application for judicial review or an appeal under these Rules unless the Court, for special reasons, so orders.

SOR/2002-232, s. 11

Case Law

Paul v. Canada (Minister of Citizenship & Immigration) (2010), 92 Imm. L.R. (3d) 271, 2010 FC 1075, 2010 CarswellNat 4112, 2010 CarswellNat 4813 — The applicant was a citizen of Bangladesh. He submitted an application for permanent residence in Canada as a skilled worker to the High Commission of Canada in Singapore in July 2006. He claimed five points for having a relative in Canada because his sister was a Canadian citizen residing in Canada. The applicant received a letter from the High Commission requesting additional supporting documents; specifically, the letter requested proof of his relationship to his relative in Canada. The applicant complied and the application was refused. The officer had concluded that the applicant had not demonstrated that he had a qualifying relative residing in Canada. Specifically, the applicant had not provided a marriage certificate which would demonstrate the relationship between the applicant's sister who had a different last name than the applicant. The CAIPS notes indicated that the officer had intended for a marriage certificate of the sister and proof of her living in Canada to have been requested; however, the letter only requested proof of the relationship. The immigration officer made a clear error and in doing so committed an egregious breach of procedural fairness. The respondent's decision to oppose the applicant's application for leave and judicial review caused the applicant to incur significant legal expense. The conduct of the respondent throughout was unfair, improper and resulted in undue prolongation of the proceedings and a delay in the applicant's application being determined in a timely manner. These were sufficient special reasons to justify an award of cost.

Bageerthan v. Canada (Minister of Citizenship & Immigration) (2009), 83 Imm. L.R. (3d) 111, 2009 FC 513, 2009 CarswellNat 4030, 2009 CarswellNat 2555 — This was an application for judicial review of a visa officer's decision to reject the applicant's application for her husband to be granted permanent residence. Section 22 of the *Federal Courts Immigration and Refugee Protection Rules* requires special reasons to award costs. Special reasons include the unnecessary and unreasonable prolongation of proceedings. The file revealed an excess of delay in processing this matter due to the First Secretary in Colombo's lack of sensitivity to the situation of a Tamil who feared returning to Sri Lanka and being killed in a war. A *mandamus* was issued on May 7, 2008, ordering the respondent to process the matter within 90 days. This was not done. Seven days later the officer reviewed the file and raised concerns which he had refused to raise with the applicant or her counsel before and required an in-person interview instead of an interview by video conference or by telephone. This was a special case which justified the awarding of cost. In effect, the officer circumvented a direct court order, which requires a sanction. A sum of $3,000 was awarded. The application for judicial review was granted.

Ndererehe v. Canada (Minister of Citizenship & Immigration) (2007), 63 Imm. L.R. (3d) 291, 317 F.T.R. 23, 2007 CarswellNat 3756, 2007 CarswellNat 2754, 2007 FC 880, [2007] F.C.J. No. 1144 — The applicants' application for permanent residence in Canada as members of the Convention Refugee Abroad class or the Humanitarian-Protected Persons Abroad class was filed in January, 2005. It was denied in a letter from the visa officer dated October 5, 2006. The operative portions of the decision letter consist of no more than the officer's bald assertion of her conclusions and do not provide the applicants with any explanation as to why their application had been rejected. The requirement for reasons would have been met had an adequate explanation been set out in the officer's notes and provided to the applicants upon request. But the notes did not record any analysis or the sources of information consulted, merely a record of the interview and the decision.

It should have been apparent from a review of the file that the officer's reasons for decision would not withstand judicial review and that the matter should have been brought to a rapid conclusion. It was not necessary to wait for the production of a lengthy tribunal record. Because of the risk to their personal safety, the applicants were forced to incur additional costs in bringing a motion for an expedited leave determination and hearing. While the respondent is entitled to rely on her right to defend a proceeding as she sees fit, she should not be surprised that the court may conclude that such defence unnecessarily prolonged the proceedings and required the applicants to incur additional and needless expense. It was appropriate to attribute a portion of the applicant's costs thus far to the respondent in light of the unnecessary delay in resolving the application. A lump sum of $5,000 was ordered to be paid by the respondent.

Sandhu v. Canada (Minister of Citizenship & Immigration) (2006), 55 Imm. L.R. (3d) 203, 2006 CarswellNat 2360, 2006 FC 941 — The principal applicant, a citizen of India, was sponsored for permanent residence by her daughter in Canada. The applicant included in her permanent residence application her dependant children. Following an interview, the immigration officer expressed concerns about the application because two of the children did not have birth certificates and, in addition, supporting letters issued by the particular public school had, in the past, been found to be fraudulent. Following the interview, the applicant wrote to the Canadian High Commission responding to the concerns regarding the school certificates. She attached documentary evidence corroborating that the school documents provided were genuine. These documents were received by the Canadian High Commission on May 10, 2005. The immigration officer allegedly reviewed all the information in the file, including the post-interview information, and in June 2005 sent the file to the Canadian High Commission Visa Section with her recommendation that the application for permanent residence be refused on the grounds that the applicant had misrepresented or withheld material facts. The application was refused for those reasons. There was no mention of the post-interview documents in the refusal letter.

The applicant sought leave for judicial review of the decision. The respondent took the position that the applicant had misaddressed the correspondence and post-interview documents and therefore had not proven that the Canadian High Commission ever received those post-interview documents. Leave was granted and during the subsequent judicial review proceedings, including the necessary cross-examination of the respondent's representatives, the respondent admitted that it had had the documents from the very time that the applicant had claimed. The respondent, having been "caught out" turned its argument around and through evidence and submission claimed that the documents were considered and given no weight. The immigration officer currently claimed that she had read the documents and gave them no weight — the visa officer could not recall the evidence but said that it would have had made no difference to his decision.

The failure to cite this material in the decision letter counters any weight that might be given to the officer's evidence that the material was considered. For this reason alone, the judicial review was granted. The applicant also asked for costs because of the respondent's conduct of this matter. The court concluded that the respondent's conduct was misleading to the applicant and was simply unacceptable. Therefore "special reasons" under Rule 22 of the *Federal Courts Immigration and Refugee Protection Rules* were shown to justify an award of costs. The applicant was awarded solicitor-client costs of the whole of the matter.

Nulbandian v. Canada (Minister of Citizenship & Immigration) (2006), 56 Imm. L.R. (3d) 67, 2006 CarswellNat 2899, 2006 FC 1128 — The applicant sought judicial review of the decision that humanitarian and compassionate considerations did not justify granting the applicant permanent residence in Canada. The applicant was a citizen of Iraq in her late 60s or early 70s. She was a Christian and fled to Jordan with her daughter in 1990 due to horrific circumstances in Iraq. She did not have permanent status in Jordan. The applicant's daughter and her son subsequently fled to the Netherlands and claimed refugee status. Neither was in a position to support immigration of the applicant to the Netherlands. The applicant's three brothers and sisters all fled directly to Canada and were all citizens of Canada. They were well established in Canada and providing economic support to the applicant. They provided a detailed plan to support the applicant's settlement in Canada. The applicant also has 13 nephews and nieces who are all Canadian citizens. While the decision arrived at by the officer might well be open to her, against a standard of review of reasonableness *simpliciter*, and against the terms of para. 3(1)(d) of the Act, and the guidance provided in OP4 to persons such as the officer, the officer erred in a reviewable manner in not documenting her decision against the prescribed criteria. The judicial review was allowed and the applicant's application for permanent residence in Canada referred back for reconsideration.

Six years elapsed between the filing of the application and a decision which represented "special circumstances" justifying an award of costs.

Dhoot v. Canada (Minister of Citizenship & Immigration) (2006), 57 Imm. L.R. (3d) 153, 2006 FC 1295, 2006 CarswellNat 3480, [2006] F.C.J. No. 1625 — This is an application for judicial review of a visa officer's decision of the applicant's application for a permanent resident visa which was denied on the basis that the applicant failed to attend an interview scheduled on October 26, 2005. The applicant states that he was never informed of the interview. The visa officer insisted that the notice of the interview was provided to the applicant by letter dated August 19, 2005.

The visa officer, for whatever reason, did not send the notice by mail as would be expected given the significantly prejudicial impact non-delivery would have on the applicant's interest in obtaining a permanent resident visa. It is reasonable to expect that there will be mistakes by the respondent when dealing with thousands of immigration files. When the evidence shows that there has been such a mistake the court expects that the respondent cure the mistake, *i.e.*, invite the applicant to attend another interview. It was wrong for the respondent, in a case such as this, to oppose the applicant's court case. The application for judicial review was allowed and the applicant was awarded legal costs.

John Doe v. Canada (Minister of Citizenship & Immigration) (2006), 54 Imm. L.R. (3d) 212, 2006 CarswellNat 1105, 2006 CarswellNat 1543, 2006 FC 535 — The applicant came to Canada in 1984 and was granted refugee status in 1986. He then applied for permanent residence. There ensued many interviews, security checks, etc., without any decision being taken on his application. In 1998, the immigration officers raised security concerns. The applicant made an application for ministerial relief under what would now be subs. 34(2) of the IRPA, which would have the effect of relieving him of possible inadmissibility that might otherwise be a bar to grant permanent residence. In nearly eight years no decision had been taken on the application for ministerial relief. The applicant brought an application for *mandamus* to require the Minister to make a decision with respect to the applicant's permanent residence in Canada.

Other Relevant Legislation

On the eve of the hearing, the Minister made an offer to settle. The Minister was prepared not to oppose the *mandamus* application but was to agree to an order that would set out time limits for progressive steps leading to an ultimate decision. The applicant found the proposal unacceptable as it contemplated steps totaling some 240 days and did not set out any limit as to how long the Minister of Public Security and Emergency Preparedness might take to decide the application for ministerial relief, which was first made in 1998. The court directed that a decision on permanent residence be made by a specific date.

The court also awarded costs, finding special reasons — specifically that the Minister failed to take a decision which was requested almost 20 years previous, while the applicant had endured interview after interview, acquired a good deal of legal advice and was forced to bring the Minister to court. Even when faced with this matter being set down for hearing the Minister waited until the afternoon of the day before the hearing to offer a settlement.

Uppal v. Canada (Minister of Citizenship & Immigration), 2005 CarswellNat 2437, 2005 CarswellNat 4845, 2005 FC 1133 — Costs are generally not awarded in applications for leave and for judicial review brought in a context of the *Immigration and Refugee Protection Act*. This is because Rule 22 of the *Federal Court Immigration and Refugee Protection Rules* provides that no costs shall be awarded in proceedings under the Rules "unless the court, for special reasons, so orders." The finding that an order of *mandamus* is warranted is not, by itself, sufficient to justify the award of costs.

Although none of the steps required to process the applicant's application were concluded expediently, and an embarrassing gaffe occurred, the pace was not so slow or lax as to give rise to special circumstances and an award of costs.

Mugesera c. Canada (Ministre de la Citoyenneté & de l'Immigration), [2004] 1 S.C.R. xi, 325 N.R. 134, 40 Imm. L.R. (3d) 1, 2004 CarswellNat 2750, 2004 CarswellNat 1105, 2004 FCA 157 — The award of a lump sum in lieu of costs can serve various purposes. It is usually meant to simplify the assessment process and reduce its cost in relatively simple matters, when, for example, the parties are representing themselves or when counsel are ready, at the hearing, to submit their representations to the court, or even in particularly complex matters where a precise calculation of costs would be unnecessarily complicated. It may also, on occasion, be used to give a party costs higher than the maximum provided for by the tariff.

The court must be prudent in exercising its discretion, if only to prevent parties whose conduct is not reprehensible from being ordered to pay costs of an unforeseen quantum.

To ensure that the discretion exercised by the court is not overly dependant on the perspective of a given panel of judges, I believe that the court should be guided as much as possible by the standards established in the table to Tariff B when awarding a lump sum in lieu of assessed courts.

Jaballah v. Canada (Minister of Citizenship & Immigration) (2003), 32 Imm. L.R. (3d) 140, 240 F.T.R. 155, 2003 CarswellNat 3164, 2003 CarswellNat 4032, 2003 FC 1182 — The long delay on the part of the Immigration and Refugee Board in complying with a court order constituted "special reasons for an award of costs". While the delay could not be attributed directly to the Minister, the Minister nonetheless, on two separate motions before the court, defended the delay. It would have been open to the Minister to negotiate an agreement in the nature of the directions from the court. Accordingly, costs were awarded against the Minister on a solicitor and client basis.

Huang v. Canada (Minister of Citizenship & Immigration) (2003), 25 Imm. L.R. (3d) 116, 2003 CarswellNat 257, 2003 CarswellNat 991, 2003 FCT 126, 2003 CFPI 126 — The applicant sought judicial review of her application for permanent residence in the independent category. The visa officer improperly limited her consideration of the applicant's experience to the period 1996 to 2000 without any regard for the evidence before her addressing prior and extensive experience from the period 1988 onward.

The respondent was ordered to pay $4,500 in costs inclusive of disbursements and GST. The applicant was entitled to have her application fairly and reasonably assessed and this did not happen in this case.

Behagan v. Canada (Minister of Citizenship & Immigration) (2001), 14 Imm. L.R. (3d) 154, 202 F.T.R. 259, 2001 FCT 301, 2001 CarswellNat 675, [2001] F.C.J. No. 532 — The applicant sought an award of costs in view of the repeated failure of the Minister's representatives to have proper regard to the jurisprudence of the court dealing with medical inadmissibility and to s. 22 of the Regulations.

The court has on many occasions stated that a medical officer is not entitled to presume that a particular medical condition must necessarily result in excessive demand and that a medical opinion without an evidentiary foundation cannot be justified.

While it may well be that, in future, costs will flow from a failure to have regard to the requirements set out in the jurisprudence and in s. 22 of the Regulations, the court was not persuaded to do so in this case.

Platonov v. Canada (Minister of Citizenship & Immigration) (2000), 192 F.T.R. 260, 2000 CarswellNat 2060, [2000] F.C.J. No. 1438 — The applicant sought an order in the nature of *mandamus* requiring the completion of the applicant's application within 90 days. The applicant applied under the Immigrant Investor Program at the Buffalo Consulate office. The applicant was interviewed in Warsaw in 1997, advised in 1997 that the case had been provisionally approved, medical examinations were completed and by December of 1997 the applicant had deposited $79,000 in an investor fund as a deposit towards $350,000 which he pledged to invest if admitted to permanent residence. In March of 1998, the applicant was called in for a second interview and in July of 1998 the Embassy requested specific information from his counsel in relation to certain of the applicant's business relations. This information was provided in July of 1998. The application was held in abeyance pending background checks. Finally, in September 1999, the applicant filed this application as there was no further indication of when a decision might be made. The only advice forthcoming had been to the effect that the security checks were not completed.

Each case of this type turns on its own facts. The jurisprudence simply outlines some parameters within which the court has issued an order in the nature of *mandamus* where it has found that there has been an unusual, unexplained delay. The respondent agreed to an order and an agreement was reached as to a date by which a decision would be made.

Counsel were unable to agree on the question of costs. The applicant requested that in the event that the application was refused, the sum of $23,000 Canadian, said to be the amount of loss from an investment of $79,000 in the immigrant investor fund, be paid to the applicant.

The court declined to award this amount as costs being of the view that such an amount was more in the nature of damages.

Other Relevant Legislation

Naroditskiy v. Canada (Minister of Citizenship & Immigration), 1999 CarswellNat 2517 (Fed. T.D.) — The applicant applied for permanent residence and submitted a forged letter in support of his application. After dismissing the application for judicial review, the court found that this constituted special reasons for awarding $1,100 in costs payable to the respondent.

Wong v. Canada (Minister of Citizenship & Immigration) (1999), 3 Imm. L.R. (3d) 120, 1999 CarswellNat 2056 (Fed. T.D.) — Costs in this matter were awarded on a solicitor-and-client basis. The assessment officer reduced the item in the account that charged for the presence of two counsel at the hearing on behalf of the applicant. The officer concluded that the appearance of either one of the counsel, both of whom were very experienced in their profession, would had sufficed. The applicant's bill of costs was assessed at $5,500 for fees.

Lam v. Canada (Minister of Citizenship & Immigration) (1999), 1 Imm. L.R. (3d) 196, 169 F.T.R. 153, 1999 CarswellNat 1187 — An order had been made that the cross-examination of the respondent be video-taped. Counsel for the respondent wanted a copy of the tape but argued that the applicant should pay for the cost of producing that copy.

There is no reason to depart from the usual convention that should the examined party wish a transcript it is for the account of the examined party. Accordingly, the respondent Minister was ordered to pay the costs of making a video-tape of the cross-examination.

D'Almeida v. Canada (Minister of Citizenship & Immigration) (1999), 1 Imm. L.R. (3d) 309, 1999 CarswellNat 1114 (Fed. T.D.) — The applicant sought to review the refusal of his application for permanent residence. After the applicant commenced proceedings and filed his records the respondent agreed that the application should be allowed. The applicant then opposed the respondent's motion, he wanted his application heard on the merits so there would be a decision establishing the point of law he thought important.

The court found nothing novel in the issues of law raised by the applicant. The court found therefore that the applicant had unreasonably prolonged the proceedings and awarded costs in the amount of $1,500 against the applicant.

Said v. Canada (Minister of Citizenship & Immigration) (1999), 246 N.R. 283, 1999 CarswellNat 770, [1999] F.C.J. No. 663 (Fed. C.A.) — The applicant, who came to Canada as a Convention refugee, was found guilty in 1992, on five counts of trafficking in heroin and sentenced to five years in jail. A deportation order was issued as a result of the convictions and subsequently the appellant was found to be a danger to the public. While the appellant's appeal to the Court of Appeal was pending, he was informed that a removal order had been signed against him by the Minister and a motion for a stay was brought on an urgent basis.

The stay was granted and the court awarded costs in the amount of $1,000. The court could not understand why the removal order was brought to the appellant's attention only four days before its execution. The appellant was in custody and therefore could not flee upon service of the document. The very fact of detention made it more difficult and time consuming for his counsel to prepare the motion for stay and gather the necessary supporting material.

Akinsola v. Canada (Minister of Citizenship & Immigration) (1997), 138 F.T.R. 229 — The court determined that counsel for the applicant had acted either in bad faith or incompetently. Counsel's actions wasted the court's time and caused serious inconvenience to opposing counsel. The court awarded costs against counsel personally in the amount of $200.

Singh (I) v. Canada (Minister of Citizenship & Immigration) (1996), 35 Imm. L.R. (2d) 303, 121 F.T.R. 184 — The applicant, an Indian national, had resided in Canada continuously since 1981, pursuant to a series of student authorizations, a minister's permit and two visitor's visas. At the time of this application, the applicant was without status. Since 1981, the applicant had lived with his aunt who had adopted him in accordance with Sikh tradition and culture. After the adoption, the aunt submitted an undertaking of assistance which was approved in June 1992. The applicant then applied for permanent residence as a sponsored member of the family class. The applicant was interviewed by an officer at the Canadian Consulate in Buffalo in January 1993. Although a decision was made to refuse the application approximately 9 months after the interview, this decision was not disclosed to the applicant until April 1996 some two and a half years later.

In the period from April, 1993 to February, 1996, the applicant's counsel wrote 10 letters asking for the status of the application. Seven were written to the officer's attention. The officer personally responded to the first letter and thereafter two form letters were sent to the applicant, neither of which provided accurate information. In addition, three more letters were sent by the applicant's counsel to the senior immigration officer at the consulate describing the circumstances of the case and the extraordinary delay. The senior immigration officer did not respond to counsel's letters.

Costs were awarded for the following three reasons:

1. The delay, caused by the fact that the officer did not address the file between October 1993 and September 1995.

2. The two form letters which were sent contained inaccurate information.

3. The senior immigration officer did not respond to correspondence from the applicant's counsel.

Marques v. Canada (Minister of Citizenship & Immigration) (1996), 35 Imm. L.R. (2d) 81, (sub nom. *Marques v. Canada (Minister of Citizenship & Immigration) (No. 2))* 116 F.T.R. 243 — The respondent consented to an application to review a s. 114(2) decision of an immigration officer. The issue in this matter was a question of costs under Rule 22. The court found special reasons for an award of costs.

The applicant had first filed an application for a visa exemption invoking s. 114(2) in April 1994. This application was refused. However, the refusal was the subject of a successful application for judicial review. Following the successful judicial review application, the file was returned to Mississauga CIC, where no action was taken on the file until the fall of 1995. The immigration officer conducting this second interview had before her the previous decision and the notes of the review conducted in July 1994, which had been set aside by the court. Despite the fact that the court had ordered an entirely new review, the matter was not considered afresh. The immigration officer considered merely whether there had been a change of circumstances since the date of the first s. 114(2) decision. The officer therefore did not comply with the order of the court. Immigration officers have a duty to act in accordance with decisions from the Federal Court, as well as in a courteous and professional manner. Accordingly, the court found special reasons to award costs to the applicant.

Barbu v. Canada (Secretary of State), 1996 CarswellNat 1054 (Fed. T.D.) — This application was to review a decision of a visa officer. Specifically, the visa officer intended to use the discretion conferred by s. 11(3) of the Act to deny an application, and did so without consulting a senior immigration officer and without providing that officer with written reasons.

The only issue in this application was whether the applicant was entitled to costs pursuant to rule 1618 of the *Federal Court Rules*. Rule 1618 provides that no cost shall be payable in respect of an application for judicial review unless the court for special reason so orders. The court noted that costs have been awarded in cases where there has been an abuse of process. In very unusual cases, circumstances outside the conduct of the judicial review application could be relevant to costs. A simple fact of an error, without more, does not justify a costs award. Such a conclusion would make rule 1618 meaningless, accordingly, no costs were ordered.

Chan v. Canada (Minister of Employment & Immigration) (1994), 82 F.T.R. 244 — This was an application for costs by the respondent. Costs can be awarded only in special circumstances.

Special circumstances existed in this case. The respondent, from a very early date in the proceedings, was prepared to consent to an application for judicial review. However, the applicant, believing in the strength of the case, insisted that the matter be fully litigated to establish that certain regulations applicable to his landed immigrant status were *ultra vires*. He was unsuccessful.

The court did not think that an applicant can force a respondent, who is willing to consent, to continue proceedings thereby expending time and resources, without being accountable, at least to some extent, for the costs incurred.

Canada (Minister of Employment & Immigration) v. Ermeyev (1994), 83 F.T.R. 158 — Costs were awarded against the Minister because the court viewed that the respondents had been put through a great deal of unnecessary trouble and expense by the way that the Minister's officials had dealt with the respondents. There was, at worst, a technical error committed by the respondents at the time the events giving rise to these proceedings occurred. Once this mistake was discovered, it should not have strained the imagination of immigration officials to find a simple solution, such as the departure of the entire family temporarily to the United States from which they could return together to Canada. Instead, the entire family was put through a series of removal hearings, appeals and court applications over a four-year period. Accordingly, at the discontinuance of the Minister's application in this matter, costs were awarded to the respondents.

FEES

23. A fee of $50 shall be paid to the Registry in order to file an application for leave or a notice of appeal.

SOR/2002-232, s. 15(i)

COMING INTO FORCE

24. These Rules shall come into force on the day on which sections 73, 114, 115, 116, 117 and 118 of *An Act to amend the Immigration Act and other Acts in consequence thereof*, S.C. 1992, c. 49, come into force.

SCHEDULE

(Subrules 5(1), 6(1), 8(1), 9(1) and 20(1))

Form IR-1

Form IR-1

(Rules 5 and 6)

Court File No.

FEDERAL COURT

Between:

(Insert, as applicable, the full name of party, the Minister of Citizenship and Immigration or each Minister responsible for the administration of the Immigration and Refugee Protection Act *in respect of the matter for which leave is sought)*

Applicant(s)

and

(Insert, as applicable, the full name of party, the Minister of Citizenship and Immigration or each Minister responsible for the administration of the Immigration and Refugee Protection Act *in respect of the matter for which leave is sought)*

Respondent(s)

Application for Leave and for Judicial Review

TO THE RESPONDENT(S)

AN APPLICATION FOR LEAVE TO COMMENCE AN APPLICATION FOR JUDICIAL REVIEW has been commenced by the applicant(s) under

(Select the provision under which this application is made)

[ ]SUBSECTION 22.1(1) OF THE *CITIZENSHIP ACT*; or

[ ]SUBSECTION 72(1) OF THE *IMMIGRATION AND REFUGEE PROTECTION ACT*.

UNLESS A JUDGE OTHERWISE DIRECTS, THIS APPLICATION FOR LEAVE will be disposed of without personal appearance by the parties, in accordance with paragraph 22.1(2)(c) of the *Citizenship Act* or paragraph 72(2)(d) of the *Immigration and Refugee Protection Act*, as the case may be.

IF YOU WISH TO OPPOSE THIS APPLICATION FOR LEAVE, you or a solicitor authorized to practice in Canada and acting for you must prepare a Notice of Appearance in Form IR-2 prescribed by the *Federal Courts Citizenship, Immigration and Refugee Protection Rules*, serve it on the tribunal and the applicant's solicitor or, if the applicant does not have a solicitor, serve it on the applicant, and file it, with proof after service, in the Registry, within 10 days after the day on which this application for leave is served.

Other Relevant Legislation

Form IR-1 Can. Reg. 93-22 — Federal Courts Citizenship Rules, Schedule

IF YOU FAIL TO DO SO, the Court may nevertheless dispose of this application for leave and, if the leave is granted, of the subsequent application for judicial review without further notice to you.

Note: Copies of the relevant Rules of Court, information on the local office of the Court and other necessary information may be obtained from any local office of the Federal Court or the Registry in Ottawa, telephone: (613) 992-4238.

The applicant seeks leave of the Court to commence an application for judicial review of:

(Set out the date and details of the matter — the decision or order made, measure taken or question raised — in respect of which a judicial review is sought and the date on which the applicant was notified or otherwise became aware of the matter.)

(Set out the name, address and telephone number of the tribunal and, if the tribunal was composed of more than one person, the name of each person who was on the tribunal.)

(Set out the tribunal's file number(s), if applicable.)

(Add the following paragraph, if applicable.)

[The applicant also applies to the Court for an extension of time to file and serve the application under paragraph 22.1(2)(b) of the **Citizenship Act** *or under paragraph 72(2)(c) of the* **Immigration and Refugee Protection Act**, *as the case may be, for the following special reasons*:

(Set out the special reasons for the request for the extension of time.)]

If the application for leave is granted, the applicant seeks the following relief by way of a judicial review:

(Set out the precise relief sought should leave be granted, including any statutory provision or rule relied on.)

If the application for leave is granted, the application for judicial review is to be based on the following grounds:

(Set out the grounds to be argued, including a reference to any statutory provision or rule to be relied on.)

The applicant *(has or has not)* **received written reasons from the tribunal.**

If the application for leave is granted, the applicant proposes that the application for judicial review be heard at ...., in the *(English and/or French)* **language.**

....

(Signature of solicitor or applicant)

(Name, address and telephone of solicitor or applicant)

To: *(Name(s) and address(es) of respondent(s))*

SOR/98-235, s. 6; SOR/2002-232, s. 12; SOR/2005-339, s. 6; SOR/2015-20, s. 10

(Sched.)

Form IR-2

(Rule 8)

Registry No.

FEDERAL COURT

Between:

Applicant(s)

and

Respondent(s)

Notice of Appearance

THE RESPONDENT(S) *(name(s))* intend(s) to respond to this application for leave.

The tribunal's file number(s), as set out in the application for leave is (are)

(Date)

> *(Name, address and telephone number of respondent's solicitor, or respondent if acting in person)*

TO: *(Name and address of applicant's solicitor, or applicant if acting in person)*

AND TO: *(Name and address of tribunal)*

SOR/2002-232, s. 15(j); SOR/2005-339, s. 6; SOR/2015-20, s. 10 (Sched.)

Form IR-3

(Rule 9)

Court File No.

FEDERAL COURT

Between:

Applicant(s)

and

Respondent(s)

1273

Form IR-3 Can. Reg. 93-22 — Federal Courts Citizenship Rules, Schedule

Request to Tribunal

TO: *(Name and address of tribunal)*

RE: *(Set out the complete particulars of the matter — decision or order made, measure taken or question raised — as they appear in the application, with the tribunal's file number(s), if any.)*

DATE:

In an application filed on ...., 20.........., the applicant set out that he or she had not received written reasons for the above-captioned matter.

In accordance with rule 9 of the *Federal Courts Citizenship, Immigration and Refugee Protection Rules*, you are requested to send, without delay,

(a) a copy of the decision or order at issue and the written reasons for it, duly certified by an appropriate officer to be correct, to each of the parties and two copies to the Registry; or

(b) a written notice to each of the parties and to the Registry indicating that no reasons were given or reasons were given but not recorded, as the case may be.

(Signature of Registry Officer)
Name of Registry Officer
Telephone Number

SOR/2002-232, s. 13; SOR/2005-339, s. 6; SOR/2015-20, s. 10 (Sched.)

Form IR-4
(Rule 20)

Court File No.

FEDERAL COURT OF APPEAL

Between:

Appellant
(Applicant (or Respondent) in the Federal Court)

and

(name)

Respondent
(Applicant (or Respondent) in the Federal Court)

Notice of Appeal

THE APPELLANT *(name)* appeals from the judgment of the Honourable *(name of judge)* of the Federal Court, delivered on *(date)*.

The following serious question(s) of general importance was (were) certified:

(Set out the question(s) certified.)

The question(s) was (were) certified under:

(Select the appropriate provision.)

[ ]PARAGRAPH 22.2(d) OF THE *CITIZENSHIP ACT*; or

[ ]PARAGRAPH 74(d) OF THE *IMMIGRATION AND REFUGEE PROTECTION ACT*.

The appellant seeks the following relief on the determination of the question(s) under section 52 of the *Federal Courts Act*:

(Set out the relief sought, with reference to the specific provisions in section 52 of the Federal Courts Act *relied on.)*

The appellant requests that this appeal be heard at ....*(place)*, in the *(English and/or French)* language.

Dated at ...., this .... of ...., 20..........

> *(Name, address and telephone number of appellant's solicitor)*

TO: *(Name and address of respondent's solicitor, or respondent if acting in person)*
SOR/2002-232, s. 13; 2002, c. 8, s. 182(3)(a); SOR/2005-339, s. 6; SOR/2015-20, s. 10 (Sched.)

Other Relevant Legislation

CANADA EVIDENCE ACT

An Act respecting Witnesses and Evidence

R.S.C. 1985, c. C-5, as am. R.S.C. 1985, c. 27 (1st Supp.), s. 203; R.S.C. 1985, c. 19 (3rd Supp.), ss. 17, 18; S.C. 1992, c. 1, ss. 142 (Sched. V, item 9), 144 (Sched. VII, item 5) (Fr.); 1992, c. 47, s. 66; 1993, c. 28, s. 78 (Sched. III, item 8); 1993, c. 34, s. 15; 1994, c. 44, ss. 85–93; 1995, c. 28, s. 47; 1997, c. 18, ss. 116–118; 1998, c. 9, s. 1; 1999, c. 18, ss. 89–91; 1999, c. 28, ss. 149, 150; 2000, c. 5, ss. 52–57; 2001, c. 41, ss. 43, 44 (Sched. 2), 124, 140, 141(1), (3)–(7); 2002, c. 1, s. 166; 2002, c. 7, s. 96; 2002, c. 8, ss. 118, 119, 183(1)(b) [s. 119 repealed 2001, c. 41, s. 141(3)(a).]; 2003, c. 22, ss. 104, 105; SOR/2004-19; 2004, c. 12, ss. 18, 19; 2005, c. 32, ss. 26, 27; 2005, c. 46, s. 56 [Amended 2006, c. 9, s. 222.]; SOR/2006-80; SOR/2006-335; 2008, c. 3, s. 11; SOR/2012-220; 2013, c. 9, ss. 17, 18 (Fr.), 19, 20(1), (2), (3) (Fr.), 21–24; 2013, c. 18, ss. 45, 85; 2013, c. 40, s. 448; 2014, c. 2, s. 5; 2014, c. 25, s. 34; 2014, c. 31, s. 27; 2015, c. 3, s. 14 (Fr.); 2015, c. 13, ss. 52, 53; 2015, c. 20, s. 13; 2015, c. 23, s. 20 [Not in force at date of publication. Repealed 2015, c. 13, s. 57(2).]; 2015, c. 36, s. 43.

· · · · ·

PART I

· · · · ·

Specified Public Interest

[Heading amended 2001, c. 41, s. 43.]

37. (1) Objection to disclosure of information — Subject to sections 38 to 38.16, a Minister of the Crown in right of Canada or other official may object to the disclosure of information before a court, person or body with jurisdiction to compel the production of information by certifying orally or in writing to the court, person or body that the information should not be disclosed on the grounds of a specified public interest.

(1.1) Obligation of court, person or body — If an objection is made under subsection (1), the court, person or body shall ensure that the information is not disclosed other than in accordance with this Act.

(2) Objection made to superior court — If an objection to the disclosure of information is made before a superior court, that court may determine the objection.

(3) Objection not made to superior court — If an objection to the disclosure of information is made before a court, person or body other than a superior court, the objection may be determined, on application, by

(a) the Federal Court, in the case of a person or body vested with power to compel production by or under an Act of Parliament if the person or body is not a court established under a law of a province; or

(b) the trial division or trial court of the superior court of the province within which the court, person or body exercises its jurisdiction, in any other case.

(4) Limitation period — An application under subsection (3) shall be made within 10 days after the objection is made or within any further or lesser time that the court having jurisdiction to hear the application considers appropriate in the circumstances.

(4.1) Disclosure order — Unless the court having jurisdiction to hear the application concludes that the disclosure of the information to which the objection was made under subsection (1) would encroach upon a specified public interest, the court may authorize by order the disclosure of the information.

(5) Disclosure order — If the court having jurisdiction to hear the application concludes that the disclosure of the information to which the objection was made under subsection (1) would encroach upon a specified public interest, but that the public interest in disclosure outweighs in importance the specified public interest, the court may, by order, after considering both the public interest in disclosure and the form of and conditions to disclosure that are most likely to limit any encroachment upon the specified public interest resulting from disclosure, authorize the disclosure, subject to any conditions that the court considers appropriate, of all of the information, a part or summary of the information, or a written admission of facts relating to the information.

(6) Prohibition order — If the court does not authorize disclosure under subsection (4.1) or (5), the court shall, by order, prohibit disclosure of the information.

(6.1) Evidence — The court may receive into evidence anything that, in the opinion of the court, is reliable and appropriate, even if it would not otherwise be admissible under Canadian law, and may base its decision on that evidence.

(7) When determination takes effect — An order of the court that authorizes disclosure does not take effect until the time provided or granted to appeal the order has expired or, if the order is appealed, the time provided or granted to appeal a judgment of an appeal court that confirms the order has expired and no further appeal from a judgment that confirms the order is available.

(8) Introduction into evidence — A person who wishes to introduce into evidence material the disclosure of which is authorized under subsection (5), but who may not be able to do so by reason of the rules of admissibility that apply before the court, person or body with jurisdiction to compel the production of information, may request from the court having jurisdiction under subsection (2) or (3) an order permitting the introduction into evidence of the material in a form or subject to any conditions fixed by that court, as long as that form and those conditions, comply with the order made under subsection (5).

(9) Relevant factors — For the purpose of subsection (8), the court having jurisdiction under subsection (2) or (3) shall consider all the factors that would be relevant for a determination of admissibility before the court, person or body.

2001, c. 41, ss. 43, 140; 2002, c. 8, s. 183(1)(b); 2013, c. 9, s. 17

Case Law

Moumdjian v. Canada (Security Intelligence Review Committee) (1997), 221 N.R. 188, 141 F.T.R. 80 (note), 6 Admin. L.R. (3d) 239 (C.A.) — This was an appeal from an order of a judge of the Trial Division, sitting as a judge designated by the Chief Justice pursuant to s. 38(1) of the *Canada Evidence Act*. The issue was whether the designated judge erred in sustaining an objection to the disclosure of information that had been placed before the Security Intelligence Review Committee (SIRC) during the course of an investigation by SIRC pursuant to s. 39 of the *Immigration Act*.

In the course of its investigation and in the absence of the appellant and his counsel, SIRC received evidence in the form of oral testimony and documents. The disclosure of this evidence was objected to in the certificate filed pursuant to s. 37(1) of the *Canada Evidence Act*. The disclosure of correspondence between SIRC and CSIS containing information supplied to SIRC and miscellaneous documents containing other information supplied to SIRC by CSIS was also objected to. All of this evidence was listed in a schedule attached to the s. 37(1) certificate. The appellant was provided with a summary of the evidence that was submitted to SIRC in his absence and also with a summary of the argument that was presented to SIRC.

The court referred to *Henrie v. Canada*, [1989] 2 F.C. 229 (T.D.) for a description of the competing interests at stake and the proper balancing of these interests where an application for judicial review of a SIRC decision is brought. This decision described the balancing that must occur between the principles of openness in the judicial process and the public interest in not disclosing evidence in certain types of cases.

In order to succeed on the appeal, the appellant must satisfy the court that the Trial Division judge erred in law in refusing to order disclosure. The function of the Court of Appeal in this instance is limited to reviewing the decision of the designated judge so as to be satisfied that it does not disclose an error of the sort enumerated in subs. 18.1(4) of the *Federal Court Act*. If the decision does not reveal such an error, the matter ends and the Court is not entitled to examine any of the information which the judge found ought not to be disclosed.

· · · · ·

International Relations and National Defence and National Security

[Heading added 2001, c. 41, s. 43.]

38. Definitions — The following definitions apply in this section and in sections 38.01 to 38.15.

"judge" means the Chief Justice of the Federal Court or a judge of that Court designated by the Chief Justice to conduct hearings under section 38.04. *("juge")*

Other Relevant Legislation

"participant" means a person who, in connection with a proceeding, is required to disclose, or expects to disclose or cause the disclosure of, information. *("participant")*

"potentially injurious information" means information of a type that, if it were disclosed to the public, could injure international relations or national defence or national security. *("renseignements potentiellement préjudiciables")*

"proceeding" means a proceeding before a court, person or body with jurisdiction to compel the production of information. *("instance")*

"prosecutor" means an agent of the Attorney General of Canada or of the Attorney General of a province, the Director of Military Prosecutions under the *National Defence Act* or an individual who acts as a prosecutor in a proceeding. *("poursuivant")*

"sensitive information" means information relating to international relations or national defence or national security that is in the possession of the Government of Canada, whether originating from inside or outside Canada, and is of a type that the Government of Canada is taking measures to safeguard. *("renseignements sensibles")*

2001, c. 41, ss. 43, 141(4)

. . . . .

PRIVACY ACT

An Act to extend the present laws of Canada that protect the privacy of individuals and that provide individuals with a right of access to personal information about themselves

R.S.C. 1985, c. P-21, as am. R.S.C. 1985, c. 22 (1st Supp.), s. 11; R.S.C. 1985, c. 27 (1st Supp.), s. 187; R.S.C. 1985, c. 44 (1st Supp.), s. 5; R.S.C. 1985, c. 46 (1st Supp.), s. 9; SOR/85-612; R.S.C. 1985, c. 8 (2nd Supp.), s. 27; R.S.C. 1985, c. 19 (2nd Supp.), s. 52; R.S.C. 1985, c. 20 (2nd Supp.), s. 13; R.S.C. 1985, c. 1 (3rd Supp.), s. 12; R.S.C. 1985, c. 3 (3rd Supp.), s. 2; R.S.C. 1985, c. 18 (3rd Supp.), s. 39; R.S.C. 1985, c. 20 (3rd Supp.), s. 39; R.S.C. 1985, c. 24 (3rd Supp.), s. 53; R.S.C. 1985, c. 28 (3rd Supp.), s. 308; R.S.C. 1985, c. 1 (4th Supp.), s. 48; R.S.C. 1985, c. 7 (4th Supp.), s. 7; R.S.C. 1985, c. 10 (4th Supp.), s. 22; R.S.C. 1985, c. 11 (4th Supp.), s. 15; R.S.C. 1985, c. 21 (4th Supp.), s. 5; R.S.C. 1985, c. 28 (4th Supp.), s. 36; R.S.C. 1985, c. 31 (4th Supp.), s. 101; R.S.C. 1985, c. 41 (4th Supp.), s. 53; R.S.C. 1985, c. 47 (4th Supp.), s. 52; SOR/86-136; SOR/88-110; S.C. 1989, c. 3, s. 47; 1989, c. 27, s. 22; 1990, c. 1, s. 31; 1990, c. 3, s. 32; 1990, c. 13, s. 25; SOR/90-326; SOR/90-345; 1991, c. 3, s. 12; 1991, c. 6, s. 24; 1991, c. 16, s. 23; 1991, c. 38, ss. 29, 38; SOR/91-592; 1992, c. 1, ss. 114, 143, 144 (Fr.), 145 (Fr.), 155; 1992, c. 21, ss. 34–37; 1992, c. 33, s. 70; 1992, c. 37, s. 78; SOR/92-97; SOR/92-99; 1993, c. 1, ss. 10, 20, 32, 42; 1993, c. 3, ss. 17, 18; 1993, c. 28, s. 78; 1993, c. 31, s. 26; 1993, c. 34, ss. 104, 148; 1994, c. 26, ss. 56–58; 1994, c. 31, s. 20; 1994, c. 35, s. 39; 1994, c. 38, ss. 21, 22; 1994, c. 41, ss. 29, 30; 1994, c. 43, s. 91; 1995, c. 1, ss. 54–56; 1995, c. 5, ss. 20, 21; 1995, c. 11, ss. 31, 32; 1995, c. 12, s. 11; 1995, c. 18, ss. 89, 90; 1995, c. 28, ss. 54, 55; 1995, c. 29, ss. 15, 31, 35, 75, 84; 1995, c. 45, s. 24; 1996, c. 8, ss. 27, 28; 1996, c. 9, s. 28; 1996, c. 10, ss. 253, 254; 1996, c. 11, ss. 77–80; 1996, c. 16, ss. 46–48; SOR/96-357; SOR/96-539; 1997, c. 6, s. 84; 1997, c. 9, ss. 112, 113; 1997, c. 20, s. 55; 1998, c. 9, ss. 44, 45; 1998, c. 10, ss. 190–194; 1998, c. 25, s. 167; 1998, c. 26, ss. 77, 78; 1998, c. 31, s. 57; 1998, c. 35, s. 123; SOR/98-119; SOR/98-150; SOR/98-321 [Amended SOR/99-402.] [Repealed SOR/2001-144, s. 2.]; SOR/98-567; 1999, c. 17, ss. 174, 175; 1999, c. 31, ss. 177, 178; SOR/99-402; 2000, c. 6, ss. 45, 46; 2000, c. 7, s. 26; 2000, c. 17, s. 90; SOR/2000-176; 2000, c. 28, s. 50; 2000, c. 34, s. 94(j) (Fr.); SOR/2001-144, s. 1; 2001, c. 9, s. 590; 2001, c. 22, ss. 18, 19; SOR/2001-201; SOR/2001-330; 2001, c. 27, s. 269; 2001, c. 33, ss. 25, 26; 2001, c. 34, ss. 16(f), 78; 2001, c. 41, s. 104; SOR/2002-44; SOR/2002-72; 2002, c. 7, ss. 227, 228 [s. 227 not in force at date of publication.]; 2002, c. 8, ss. 159, 160, 182(1)(z.8), 183(1)(s); 2002, c. 10, s. 191; SOR/2002-175; 2002, c. 17, ss. 14(f), 25; SOR/2002-292; SOR/2002-344; SOR/2003-149; 2003, c. 7, s. 129; 2003, c. 22, ss. 189, 225(z.17), 248, 255, 256; 2003, c. 23, s. 81 [Not in force at date of publication. Repealed 2008, c. 22, s. 52.]; SOR/2003-422;

SOR/2003-427; SOR/2003-434; SOR/2003-439; SOR/2004-23; 2004, c. 2, s. 75; 2004, c. 7, s. 35; 2004, c. 11, ss. 37–41; 2004, c. 17, ss. 18, 19; SOR/2004-206; 2005, c. 1, ss. 106, 109; 2005, c. 9, s. 152; 2005, c. 10, ss. 30, 31; 2005, c. 27, s. 21 [Amended 2005, c. 27, s. 25(1).].]; 2005, c. 30, s. 90; 2005, c. 34, ss. 72–74; 2005, c. 35, s. 63; SOR/2005-252; 2005, c. 38, s. 138(p); 2005, c. 46, ss. 58, 58.1 [Amended 2006, c. 9, s. 224.]; SOR/2006-25; SOR/2006-29; SOR/2006-33; SOR/2006-71; SOR/2006-100; 2006, c. 4, s. 212; SOR/2006-218; 2006, c. 9, ss. 97, 98, 118, 140, 181–184, 185 (Fr.), 186–193; 2006, c. 10, ss. 33, 34; SOR/2007-216; 2008, c. 9, ss. 10, 11; SOR/2008-131; SOR/2008-136; 2008, c. 22, s. 50; 2008, c. 28, s. 99; 2008, c. 32, s. 30; 2009, c. 18, s. 23; SOR/2009-175; SOR/2009-244; SOR/2009-249; 2010, c. 7, ss. 9, 10; 2010, c. 12, s. 1677; SOR/2011-163; SOR/2011-259; 2011, c. 25, s. 63; 2012, c. 1, s. 160(j); 2012, c. 19, ss. 276, 387, 472, 502, 576, 590, 679, 749; 2012, c. 31, ss. 262, 294; 2013, c. 14, ss. 4, 19; 2013, c. 18, ss. 55, 56; 2013, c. 24, ss. 124, 125; 2013, c. 25, s. 23 [Not in force at date of publication. Amended 2014, c. 1, s. 20(6).]; 2013, c. 33, ss. 185–187; 2013, c. 38, s. 18; 2013, c. 40, ss. 227, 228, 285, 459, 460 [s. 460 repealed 2014, c. 20, s. 479.]; 2014, c. 1, s. 19; 2014, c. 2, ss. 26, 239 [s. 239 not in force at date of publication.]; SOR/2014-67; 2014, c. 11, s. 24; 2014, c. 13, ss. 103, 104; 2014, c. 20, ss. 421–427; 2014, c. 39, ss. 165, 166; 2015, c. 3, s. 147.

. . . . .

ACCESS TO PERSONAL INFORMATION

Right of Access

12. (1) **Right of access** — Subject to this Act, every individual who is a Canadian citizen or a permanent resident within the meaning of subsection 2(1) of the *Immigration and Refugee Protection Act* has a right to and shall, on request, be given access to

(a) any personal information about the individual contained in a personal information bank; and

(b) any other personal information about the individual under the control of a government institution with respect to which the individual is able to provide sufficiently specific information on the location of the information as to render it reasonably retrievable by the government institution.

(2) **Other rights relating to personal information** — Every individual who is given access under paragraph (1)(a) to personal information that has been used, is being used or is available for use for an administrative purpose is entitled to

(a) request correction of the personal information where the individual believes there is an error or omission therein;

(b) require that a notation be attached to the information reflecting any correction requested but not made; and

(c) require that any person or body to whom that information has been disclosed for use for an administrative purpose within two years prior to the time a correction is requested or a notation is required under this subsection in respect of that information

    (i) be notified of the correction or notation, and

    (ii) where the disclosure is to a government institution, the institution make the correction or notation on any copy of the information under its control.

(3) Extension of right of access by order — The Governor in Council may, by order, extend the right to be given access to personal information under subsection (1) to include individuals not referred to in that subsection and may set such conditions as the Governor in Council deems appropriate.

2001, c. 27, s. 269

Case Law

Tunian v. Canada (Chairman of the Immigration & Refugee Board) (2004), 254 F.T.R. 155, *(sub nom. Tunian v. Immigration & Refugee Board (Can.))* 2004 CarswellNat 1809, 2004 FC 849 — The applicants were refused refugee status on June 25, 2002. The applicants sought to review the decision of the respondent not to disclose draft reasons prepared by the member of the Refugee Protection Division who made the decision determining that the applicants were not refugees. After the hearing of the refugee claim, the Board member dictated his notes using the same equipment that also was used to record the proceeding. The dictation was transcribed but the Board did not retain a copy of the transcription as it was of the opinion that it belonged to the member and accordingly was not part of the official record. Therefore, the request made by the applicants to obtain these notes was denied.

The notes were not under the control of the Board and therefore not subject to production pursuant to s. 12(1) of the *Privacy Act*.

· · · · ·

APPENDIX I

GUIDELINES ISSUED BY THE CHAIRPERSON

Guideline 1 — Civilian Non-Combatants Fearing Persecution in Civil War Situations

Guidelines Issued by the Chairperson Pursuant to Section 65(3) of the *Immigration Act*

The Issue

Claims made by civilian non-combatants fearing return to situations of civil war come before the Refugee Division on a regular basis. These Guidelines address the particular difficulties raised in such claims. In claims involving situations of civil war, as in all other refugee claims, the claimants must satisfy all of the elements of the statutory definition of Convention refugee.[1] A major difficulty encountered in analyzing these claims is determining whether or not a linkage exists between the persecution feared and one or more of the Convention grounds.

The Refugee Division, in interpreting the definition of Convention refugee, has determined in many cases that civilian non-combatants fearing return to situations of civil war are included within the definition of Convention refugee. On the other hand, in a limited number of decisions, the Refugee Division has come to an opposite conclusion. It should be observed that paragraph 164 of the UNHCR *Handbook*,[2] which while persuasive is not

---

[1] In a claim before the Refugee Division, it is not unusual to address various issues which form part of the assessment of the claim for Convention refugee status. These issues can include: change of circumstances in the home country; internal flight; and the application of Articles 1E or 1F of the Convention (the "exclusion clauses"). Such issues should be dealt with following the appropriate legal principles. Section 2(1) of the *Immigration Act* (the "*Act*") provides that a person who comes within the exclusion clauses is not within the definition of Convention refugee. Similarly, the definition does not include a person who has ceased to be a Convention refugee by virtue of section 2(2) of the *Act*. While these Guidelines do not deal with the application of the exclusion clauses, and for that reason there is no reference to them in the framework of analysis, it must be noted that there may be circumstances where a claimant, even though she was a civilian non-combatant, will come within the exclusion clauses, and as such will be excluded from the definition of Convention refugee.

[2] In paragraph 164 of the *Handbook on Procedures and Criteria for Determining Refugee Status*, Office of the United Nations High Commissioner for Refugees, Geneva, January,

1285

binding on the Refugee Division, notes that persons who are compelled to leave their country of origin as a result of international or armed national conflicts are not normally considered Convention refugees. The Federal Court has provided some assistance in dealing with cases that arise within the context of civil war. However, there is still a degree of uncertainty in analyzing these claims; hence the need for these Guidelines.

A general proposition which underlies the analysis of issues in civil war claims is the following:

General Proposition

There is nothing in the definition of Convention refugee which excludes its application to claimants fearing return to situations of civil war.[3] *Conversely, those fearing return to situations of civil war ought not to be deemed Convention refugees by that fact alone.*

- In these Guidelines, the feminine includes the masculine.

These Guidelines specifically seek to address the following issues in relation to claims made by civilian non-combatants fearing return to situations of civil war:

1988 (the "UNHCR *Handbook*"), which while persuasive is not binding on the Refugee Division, it is noted that:

> Persons compelled to leave their country of origin as a result of international or national armed conflicts are not normally considered refugees under the 1951 Convention or 1967 Protocol. They do, however, have the protection provided for in other international instruments, e.g. the Geneva Conventions of 1949 on the Protection of War Victims and the 1977 Protocol additional to the Geneva Conventions of 1949 relating to the protection of Victims of International Armed Conflicts.

In considering the intention of the drafters of the Convention, James C. Hathaway in *The Law of Refugee Status* (Toronto: Butterworths, 1991) notes at p. 185, the statement of Mr. Robinson of Israel (U.N. Doc. A/CONF.2/SR.22, at 6, July 16, 1951) as follows:

> The text ... obviously did not refer to refugees from natural disasters, for it was difficult to imagine that fires, flood, earthquakes or volcanic eruptions, for instance, *differentiated between their victims* on the grounds of race, religion, or political opinion. Nor did the text cover all man-made events. There was no provision, for example, for refugees fleeing from hostilities unless they were otherwise covered by Article 1 of the Convention. [emphasis added by Professor Hathaway]

[3] The underlying issue is discussed in *Refugees in Civil War Situations*, UNHCR Branch Office, Ottawa, November, 1990 where the following is set out:

> It should be noted at the outset that individuals are considered refugees when they flee or remain outside a country for reasons pertinent to refugee status. Whether these reasons arise in a civil war situation, in international armed conflict or in peace time, is irrelevant. *There is nothing in the definition itself which excludes its application to persons caught up in a civil war.* [emphasis added]

First Issue

Does the harm feared constitute "persecution" within the definition of Convention refugee?

Second Issue

What principles should decision-makers apply when determining whether the claimant's fear of persecution is based on one or more of the grounds set out in the definition of Convention refugee?

Third Issue

What factors should be considered in determining whether the claimant's fear of persecution is well-founded?

Fourth Issue

What are the key evidentiary elements that decision-makers should look to when considering a claim arising out of a situation of civil war?

The Analysis

I. — Assessing the Harm Feared

It is necessary to assess the particular circumstances which have given rise to the claimant's fear of persecution. *Does the harm feared constitute "persecution" within the definition of Convention refugee?*

A person taking no active part in the hostilities associated with a civil war should be treated by the combatants humanely without adverse distinction.[4] Her human rights must be respected. If the combatants treat the person in a manner that is contrary to these principles, such treatment can, depending on the claimant's particular circumstances, constitute persecutory treatment. *When one is determining whether the case is one of "persecution", the question to be addressed is whether there are violations of human*

___

[4] See common article 3(1) of each of the four *Geneva Conventions of 1949* discussed *infra*. These Guidelines relate to civilians with no direct participation in the hostilities. Where a claimant provided indirect support to combatants such as supplying food, money or shelter, these actions should not have taken the claimant outside of the category of non-combatant. Any sanction imposed, or threatened to be imposed, against the claimant would have to be considered in relation to the activity engaged in by the claimant; disproportionate punishment could be found to be persecutory as that could be found not to be a legitimate imposition of a sanction. Generally, a threat to life, liberty or security of the person is persecutory regardless of the context. (However, to be within the definition, there must be a link to a Convention ground.) On the other hand, in *Antonio, Pacato Joao v. M.E.I.* (September 27, 1994), IMM-1072-93, Nadon (F.C.T.D.), the Court, in an Angolan claim, was not prepared to conclude that the death penalty when imposed for treason and sabotage constituted persecution.

rights of sufficient degree and importance to constitute persecution.[5] The fact that the treatment feared by the claimant arises from the hostility felt, or the violence engaged in, by combatants directly involved in the civil war does not exclude the possibility that it could constitute persecution.

International instruments are not binding on the Refugee Division unless they are incorporated into Canadian law.[6] However, even if a particular instrument has not been so incorporated, the principles enunciated in the instrument may assist in the application of the definition of Convention refugee. Also, the standards set out in an instrument may assist the Refugee Division in determining permissible conduct even if the instrument is not binding upon the parties to the conflict. By defining permissible conduct, the instruments may assist the Refugee Division in assessing whether or not the treatment constitutes persecution as that term is understood in Canadian case law.

Accordingly, in determining what are the fundamental human rights that must be considered in assessing persecution within the context of civil war, reference should be made to international human rights instruments which provide a framework of international standards for recognizing the protection needs of individuals. Such international human rights instruments include, but are not limited to:

i. *Universal Declaration of Human Rights*

ii. *International Covenant on Civil and Political Rights*

iii. *International Covenant on Economic, Social and Cultural Rights*

iv. *Convention Against Torture and Other Cruel, Inhuman or Degrading Treatment or Punishment*

In addition, international instruments exist that relate to the protection of civilians in time of war. These instruments should be considered as they may assist the Refugee Division in determining what constitutes permissible conduct by

---

[5] As noted in paragraph 51 of the UNHCR *Handbook*: "There is no universally accepted definition of "persecution", and various attempts to formulate such a definition have met with little success." The concept of persecution has been described on a number of occasions in Canadian case law. One such description is "the systemic and persistent infliction of threats and injury" [*Rajudeen v. M.E.I.* (1984), 55 N.R. 129 at pp. 133-4 (C.A.)]; another description requires an element of repetition and relentlessness which an isolated incident can satisfy only in very exceptional circumstances [*Valentin v. M.E.I.*, [1991] 3 F.C. 390 (C.A.)]. The Supreme Court of Canada has stated that persecution, although undefined in the Convention, has been ascribed the meaning of "sustained or systemic violation of basic human rights demonstrative of a failure of state protection." [*Canada (Attorney General) v. Ward*, [1993] 2 S.C.R. 689 at p. 734]. It should be noted that in *Murugiah, Rahjendran v. M.E.I.* (May 5, 1993), no. 92-A-6788, Noël (F.C.T.D.) and *Rajah, Jeyadevan v. M.E.I.* (September 27, 1993), no. 92-A-7341, Joyal (F.C.T.D.) the Federal Court Trial Division certified the following questions for consideration by the Federal Court of Appeal: whether persecution requires systematic and persistent acts, and whether one or two violations of basic and inalienable rights such as forced labour or beatings while in police detention is enough to constitute persecution.

[6] For more on this issue, see Anne F. Bayefsky, *International Human Rights Law -Use in Canadian Charter of Rights and Freedoms Litigation* (Markham: Butterworths, 1992).

combatants toward non-combatants, and they may therefore assist the Refugee Division in determining whether the conduct constitutes persecution. These instruments include, but are not limited to:

i. Geneva Convention Relative to the Protection of Civilian Persons in Time of War of August 12, 1949 (the "1949 Convention")

ii. Protocol II to the 1949 Convention ("Protocol II")

Article 3 of the *1949 Convention* prohibits in relation to non-combatants certain acts including:

- violence to life and person, in particular murder of all kinds, mutilation, cruel treatment and torture;
- taking of hostages;
- outrages upon personal dignity, in particular humiliating and degrading treatment.

Article 4 of *Protocol II* prohibits in relation to non-combatants certain acts including:

- violence to the life, health and physical or mental well-being of persons, in particular murder as well as cruel treatment such as torture, mutilation or any form of corporal punishment;
- collective punishments;
- taking of hostages;
- acts of terrorism;
- outrages on the personal dignity, in particular humiliating and degrading treatment, rape, enforced prostitution and any form of indecent assault.

Article 13 of *Protocol II* provides that the "civilian population and individual civilians shall enjoy general protection against the dangers arising from military operations." To give effect to this protection, certain rules, including the following are to be observed:

- the civilian population, as well as individual civilians, shall not be the object of attack;
- acts or threats of violence the primary purpose of which is to spread terror among the civil population are prohibited.

Excerpts from the above two instruments accompany these Guidelines.[7]

Other Relevant Legislation

---

[7] Common article 3 of each of the four *Geneva Conventions of 1949* sets out the minimum conduct of each party to an armed conflict of a non-international character in all circumstances of the conflict. Where a claimant has adduced credible or trustworthy evidence that there is a reasonable chance that she would face a violation of any of the provisions in this article, a panel would need to assess whether the action constituted persecutory treatment. Violations of non-derogable rights found in common article 3 likely would lead to a finding of persecution. See also Report of the Representative of the Secretary-General, Mr. Francis Deng, submitted pursuant to Commission on Human Rights resolution 1993/95, "Legal Analysis based on the needs of Internally Displaced

II. — Determining Whether Persecution is Based on a Convention Ground

General principles — Federal Court of Appeal

The determination of whether there is a link between the persecution experienced or feared by the claimant, or her group, and the grounds for persecution found in the definition, has generally proved to be the most difficult aspect of applying the definition in claims arising from civil war.[8] In considering this issue, it is useful to commence the

---

Persons" prepared on behalf of the American Society of International Law and the International Human Rights Law Group, Washington D.C., U.S.A. by Janelle M. Diller, Robert K. Goldman and Cecile E.M. Meijer (Working Draft in Progress), January 30, 1995, U.N. Doc. E/CN.4/1995/CRP.1 at pp. 47–54.

For a discussion on *Protocol II* see Charles Lysaght, "The Scope of Protocol II and its Relation to common article 3 of the *Geneva Conventions of 1949* and other Human Rights Instruments", *The American University Law Review*, Vol. 33, 1983, p. 9 and Sylvie Junod, "Additional Protocol II: History and Scope", *The American University Law Review*, Vol. 33, 1983, p. 29.

In considering the impact of international instruments on the position of children in a civil war situation reference should be made to article 4(3) of *Protocol II* and article 38 of the *Convention on the Rights of the Child*. For more on the issue, see Ilene Cohn, "The Convention on the Rights of the Child: What it means for Children in War", *International Journal of Refugee Law*, Vol. 3, no. 1, 1991, p. 100.

Where the claim involves a fear of gender-related persecution, reference should be made to the additional international instruments described in the Chairperson's *Guidelines on Women Refugee Claimants Fearing Gender-related Persecution*, Immigration and Refugee Board, Ottawa, Canada, March 9, 1993 (*the "Gender Guidelines"*). It may be necessary to use these Guidelines as well as the Gender Guidelines to analyze a claim of a woman fearing persecution within the context of a civil war.

[8] or a discussion of the approaches taken in the United States of America to the assessment of refugee claims involving civil war, see Peter Butcher, "Assessing Fear of Persecution in a War Zone", *Georgetown Immigration Law Journal*, Vol. 5, no. 1, 1991, p. 435. See also Michael G. Heyman, "Redefining Refugee: A Proposal for Relief for Victims of Civil Strife", *San Diego Law Review*, Vol. 24, 1987, p. 449; T. Alexander Aleinikoff, "The Meaning of "Persecution" in U.S. Asylum Law", *Refugee Policy — Canada and the United States* (Toronto: York Lanes Press Ltd., 1991), p. 292; Walter Kalin, "Refugees and Civil Wars: Only a Matter of Interpretation", *International Journal Of Refugee Law*, Vol. 3, no. 3, 1991, p. 435; and Mark R. Von Sternberg, "Political Asylum and the Law of Internal Armed Conflict: Refugee Status, Human Rights and Humanitarian Law Concerns", *International Journal Of Refugee Law*, Vol. 5., no. 2, 1993, p. 153.

analysis by reference to the two leading decisions of the Federal Court of Appeal. The first of these is *Salibian v. M.E.I.*,[9] which at p. 258 sets out four general principles:

> It can be said in light of earlier decisions by this Court on claims to Convention refugee status that
>
>> (1) the applicant does not have to show that he had himself been persecuted in the past or would himself be persecuted in the future;
>>
>> (2) the applicant can show that the fear he had resulted not from reprehensible acts committed or likely to be committed directly against him but from reprehensible acts committed or likely to be committed against members of a group to which he belonged;
>>
>> (3) *a situation of civil war in a given country is not an obstacle to a claim provided the fear felt is not that felt indiscriminately by all citizens as a consequence of the civil war, but that felt by the applicant himself, by a group with which he is associated, or, even, by all citizens on account of a risk of persecution based on one of the reasons stated in the definition*; and
>>
>> (4) the fear felt is that of a reasonable possibility that the applicant will be persecuted if he returns to his country of origin ... [emphasis added]

The Court goes on to adopt the following statement by Professor Hathaway:[10]

> In sum, while modern refugee law is concerned to recognize the protection needs of particular claimants, the best evidence that an individual faces a serious chance of persecution is usually the treatment afforded similarly situated persons in the country of origin. *In the context of claims derived from situations of generalized oppression, therefore, the issue is not whether the claimant is more at risk than anyone else in her country, but rather whether the broadly based harassment or abuse is sufficiently serious to substantiate a claim to refugee status. If persons like the applicant may face serious harm for which the state is accountable, and if that risk is grounded in their civil or political status, then she is properly considered to be a Convention refugee.* [emphasis added]

The second case is the very brief decision in *Rizkallah v. M.E.I.*,[11] where the Court of Appeal held that:

> To succeed, *refugee claimants must establish a link between themselves and persecution for a Convention reason*. In other words, they must be *targeted* for persecution in some way, either personally or collectively.

---

[9] *Salibian v. M.E.I.*, [1990] 3 F.C. 250 (C.A.).

[10] *Salibian* at p. 259.

[11] In *Rizkallah v. M.E.I.* (1992), 156 N.R. 1 (F.C.A.), the Court determined that the appellants were merely victims of the civil war and found that there was no linkage between the harm feared and their religious status as Lebanese Christians. Lorne Waldman in *Immigration Law and Practice* (Toronto: Butterworths, 1992), Issue 5-12/93, at p. 8.45 contrasts the result in *Rizkallah* to that of *Salibian* and *Ovakimoglu v. M.E.I.* (1983), 52 N.R. 67 (F.C.A.) in illustrating the difficulty in differentiating between a harm common to all persons living in a state of civil war and one that is linked to a Convention ground.

... the evidence, as presented to us, falls short of establishing that Christians in the claimant's Lebanese village were collectively targeted in some way different from the general victims of the tragic and many-sided civil war. [emphasis added]

The third general principle set out in *Salibian* was commented upon by the Court of Appeal in *Hersi, Nur Dirie v. M.E.I.*,[12] when the Court, on consent, held that the Refugee Division erred "in holding that refugee claimants must be able to show they are at some greater differential risk than other members of their group", a conclusion which the Court found to be at odds with its decision in *Salibian*.

Approaches to Analysis of Civil War Claims

The case law emanating from the Trial Division of the Federal Court seems to suggest that the Trial Division has taken two different approaches to civil war claims. The differences pertain to the question whether there is a nexus between the harm feared and one of the Convention grounds, and to the application of *Salibian* and *Rizkallah*.

Non-comparative Approach

The non-comparative approach to the assessment of a claim is the approach advocated in these Guidelines. This approach is more in accord with the third principle set out in *Salibian*, the decisions of the Court of Appeal in *Rizkallah* and *Hersi, Nur Dirie*, as well as the wording of the Convention refugee definition.[13] With this approach, instead of an emphasis on comparing the level of risk of persecution between the claimant and other individuals (including individuals in the claimant's own group) or other groups, the Court examines the claimant's particular situation, and that of her group, in a manner similar to any other claim for Convention refugee status.

The issue is not a comparison between the claimant's risk and the risk faced by other individuals or groups at risk for a Convention reason, but whether the claimant's risk is a risk of sufficiently serious harm and is linked to a Convention reason as opposed to the general, indiscriminate consequences of civil war.[14] A claimant should not be labelled as a "general victim" of civil war without full analysis of her personal circumstances and

---

[12] *Hersi, Nur Dirie v. M.E.I.* (November 4, 1993), no. A-1231-91, MacGuigan, Linden, McDonald (F.C.A.).

[13] Section 3(g) of the *Act* recognizes that Canadian immigration policy and the rules and regulations made under the *Act* should be designed and administered in a manner that fulfils Canada's international legal obligations with respect to refugees and the upholding of its humanitarian tradition with respect to the displaced and the persecuted. The definition of Convention refugee in the *Act* should be interpreted in a manner consistent with these objectives.

[14] The Federal Court in *Hersi, Ubdi (Ubdi) Hashi v. M.E.I.* (May 5, 1993), no. 92-A-6574, Joyal (F.C.T.D.) agreed with the Minister's argument that:

... The evidence of the applicants themselves speaks of general and indiscriminate shelling of cities and villages. Members of various clans become the victims, whether such clans could otherwise be regarded as friends or foes of the assailants.

that of any group to which she may belong. Using a non-comparative approach results in a focusing of attention on whether the claimant's fear of persecution is by reason of a Convention ground.

Comparative Approach

The other approach to assessment of the claim is comparative. This approach considers whether the claimant, or her group, is at a "differential risk" when compared to other individuals or groups in the country of origin.[15] This approach

---

A similar result was reached in *Siad v. M.E.I.* (1993), 21 Imm. L.R. (2d) 6 (F.C.T.D.) where the Court upheld the Refugee Division decision as,

> It is clear that the Refugee Division concluded that the fear felt was that felt indiscriminately by all citizens [of Somalia] as a result of the civil war and random violence, and was not related to membership in a social group. (p. 11)

In *Khalib v. M.E.I.* (1994), 24 Imm. L.R. (2d) 149 (F.C.T.D.), the Court upheld a decision of the Refugee Division in which it concluded that the claimants' fear in relation to the danger from land mines was one faced indiscriminately by all people in the area notwithstanding that members of the Issaq clan may be concentrated there and form the majority in the area. It appears that the Refugee Division was not persuaded that "the mines were intended to harm only or even mainly the Issaqs living in the area of Hargeisa, and that the mines placed by a former government and not yet removed constitute grounds for fear, recognized by the Convention, of persecution by a government that is no longer in authority." (at p. 152)

In a brief decision, the Federal Court of Appeal in *Shereen, Agha Agha v. M. E.I.* (March 21, 1994), no. A-913-90, Mahoney, MacGuigan, Linden (F.C.A.) held that a perceived political opinion is not to be ascribed to all individuals who find themselves victimized by government forces in a civil war even if they live in an area of insurgency. This case illustrates the need to provide supporting evidence as to targeting. The need to address the issue of targeting can be seen in Ahmed, Faisa *Talarer v. M.E.I.* (November 2, 1993), no. A-1017-92, Noël (F.C.T.D.) and *Abdi, Jama Osman v. M.E.I.* (November 18, 1993), no. A-1089-92, Simpson (F.C.T.D.) where, in both cases, decisions of the Refugee Division were found to be in error due to the failure to deal with documentary evidence which supported the claimant's position that the fear felt by the claimant was not the general fear felt by all in Somalia.

[15] In a similar fashion, the Refugee Division has applied the concept of "differential risk" and "comparative differential risk" in the analysis of civil war claims. Due to the concerns outlined in these Guidelines, neither mode of analysis is recommended. For a review of the relevant Canadian case law and an in-depth discussion of the issue see CRDD T93-11627, T93-11628, James, Band, March 29, 1994.

For reasons that follow the comparative approach see: CRDD T92-05687, Davis, Thomas, February 9, 1993 (The panel found that the claimant's ethnic group, the Hazara, was not targeted differentially than any other ethnic group in Afghanistan. On judicial review, the application was allowed on consent and the negative decision set aside — IMM-836-93, Reed J., March 23, 1994. A positive determination was made on the rehearing of the claim.); CRDD T93-09000, T93-09143, Davis, Grice, January 14, 1994 (Positive determinations were made as the panel found that members of the claimant's

appears to involve a consideration of the predicament faced by the claimant, or her group, as compared with the circumstances of other persons in her country of origin who face harm from the same or other agents of persecution. In other words, is the claimant's, or her group's, predicament worse or different than the predicaments of others in her country of origin?[16]

---

religious group suffer more frequently from more atrocious human rights violations differentially from any other group.); and CRDD T93-09464, T93-09465, Davis, Wolman, January 6, 1994 (The claimants, ethnic Croatians, were found not to be Convention refugees as they failed to establish that they faced a differential risk when compared to other ethnic groups in the country. A leave application for judicial review was not filed.).

In Abdi, *Jama Osman v. M.E.I.* (November 18, 1993), no. A-1089-92, Simpson (F.C.T.D.), the Court stated at p. 3 that: "As a general matter, when large numbers of civilians are being killed without regards to their beliefs or affiliations, it is difficult to demonstrate a fear of persecution based on a personal belief or membership in a particular group. However, this case was unusual because there was some documentary evidence which corroborated the claimant's fear of persecution at the hands of the Abgal subclan." This statement illustrates the need for submission of evidence which shows the targeting of the claimant and/or her group. In addition, it recognizes that even in situations where large numbers of persons suffer harm for reasons not linked to a Convention ground, targeting for a Convention ground can take place.

[16] Requiring a demonstration of greater hardship might mean any one of several things. To succeed, the claimant might have to establish: (i) that the claimant's, or her group's, level of risk is greater than the risk level of persons in other groups [rejected in *Janjicek, Davorin v. M.C.I.* (March 24, 1995), no. IMM-2242-94, Richard (F.C.T.D.), but accepted in other decisions of the Trial Division]; or (ii) that the claimant's level of risk is greater than the risk level of other persons in the claimant's own group (rejected by the Court of Appeal in *Hersi, Nur Dirie*); or (iii) that the claimant is at risk of suffering harm greater than that which threatens others.

With respect to the third alternative, the question which must be addressed by the Refugee Division is whether the treatment feared crosses the threshold of what constitutes persecution, not whether the claimant is at risk of harm greater than that to which some other group, or some other person in the claimant's own group, might be subjected. The threshold should not be raised because the claim arises out of a situation of civil war; generally, it cannot be said that something which would constitute persecution in peacetime does not meet the standard in war time. Moreover, the linkage to a Convention ground should not be negated by the mere fact that the persecution arises within the context of civil war.

In *Janjicek*, the Federal Court Trial Division, on consent, ordered a claim remitted for a new hearing on the basis that "a Convention refugee claimant need not establish that her or his ethnic group is at greater risk than members of other ethnic groups, in accordance with the decision of the Federal Court of Appeal in *Salibian v. M.E.I.*". However, in *Barisic, Rajko v. M.C.I.* (January 26, 1995), no. IMM-7275-93, Noël (F.C.T.D.), the Court held that it could not conclude that the Refugee Division acted unreasonably by holding that, like all Croatians, the claimant was a victim of a civil war. The Refugee Division concluded that the claimant was situated similarly to all citizens of Croatia and

The clearest adoption of the comparative approach has been in *Isa v. S. S.C.*[17]

Conclusion

These Guidelines advocate the use of the non-comparative approach, as this approach promotes the case law in *Salibian, Rizkallah* and *Hersi, Nur Dirie*. The Guidelines do not recommend the use of any form of "differential risk" analysis. It can lead to the use of a comparative approach, where the requirement that the

---

had not demonstrated the existence of a serious risk of persecution based on one of the reasons set out in the Convention. The claimant had been forced out of his village when it was occupied by the Serb army, and had adduced evidence of "ethnic cleansing". The Court noted that the Croats, in the spirit of revenge, were engaging in acts just as reprehensible.

[17] In *Isa v. S.S.C.* (1995), 28 Imm. L.R. (2d) 68 (F.C.T.D.), the Trial Division upheld a decision of the Refugee Division (CRDD T93-01998, Mojgani, Cole, March 8, 1994) in which the panel at p. 4 concluded that:

Given the totality of the documentary evidence before us, it appears that all clans and sub-clans are both perpetrators and victims of the ongoing violence. We do not find that the claimant's clan has been differentially targeted for persecution from any other clan nor that he had been targeted any differently from any other Somali.

The claimant was found not to be a Convention refugee notwithstanding that documentary evidence described attacks on the claimant's clan. The Court did not take issue with the Refugee Division's finding that the claimant's fear was similar to that of all Somali citizens in general and arose out of the ongoing civil strife in Somalia. In particular, at p. 72 the Court stated that:

Many, if not most, civil war situations are racially or ethnically based. If racially motivated attacks in civil war circumstances constitute a ground for Convention refugee status, then, all individuals on either side of the conflict will qualify. The passages quoted by the board from [paragraph 164 of] the United Nations Handbook (supra) indicates that this is not the purpose of the 1951 Convention.

See also *Ali, Farhan Omar v. M.C.I.* (June 26, 1995), no. A-1652-92, McKeown (F.C.T.D.) where without referring to any particular passage in Isa, that decision was cited approvingly. In *Ali*, the Court upheld the decision of the Refugee Division which found the claimants not to be Convention refugees as they had not shown that they were "differentially at risk of being persecuted despite the civil war situation" (at p. 3). *Isa* was applied in CRDD T94-06601, T94-06602, T94-06603, T94-06604, T94-06605, T94-06606, Davis, Bubrin, August 2, 1995 where the panel in considering whether an IFA existed for the claimants held at p. 10 that Shi'ite Hazaras did not face "more or different difficulties in Afghanistan." (Application for leave for judicial review filed as IMM-2456-95 with leave granted.) For a similar analysis with respect to Pashtuns in Afghanistan see CRDD T95-02614, Davis, Hope, November 24, 1995. See also, CRDD T95-02034, Davis, Bubrin, October 13, 1995 where the Refugee Division applying a similar analysis determined that members of the Majerteen clan of the Darod tribe do not face a differential risk in Somali from other Somali citizens. (Application for leave for judicial review filed as IMM-3170-95.)

Other Relevant Legislation

claimant, or her group, be exposed to hardship which is greater than the hardship of others in the country of origin, may be difficult to reconcile with certain passages in *Salibian, Rizkallah* and *Hersi, Nur Dirie*. In addition, the comparative approach may be difficult to reconcile with the Convention refugee definition.

Application of the Non-Comparative Approach: Relevant Principles

To succeed, refugee claimants must establish a link between themselves and persecution on a Convention ground. In other words, they must be targeted for persecution in some way, either personally or collectively.[18] Inasmuch as persecutory measures are often directed at groups rather than individuals, the claimant need not be personally identified ("singled out") or targeted for persecution in order to be determined a Convention refugee.[19]

---

[18] In *Ali, Hassan Isse v. M.E.I.* (June 9, 1994), no. IMM-39-93, MacKay (F.C.T.D.), the Court notes, after referring to *Salibian* and *Rizkallah, that Rizkallah* "is not authority for concluding that the civil war situation in Somalia faces all Somalis indiscriminately" (p. 7) as held by the Refugee Division. In addition, the Refugee Division had concluded "that the situation in Somalia is basically one of civil war, and that the claimant is not targeted, individually or collectively, in some way different from the general victims of civil war." The panel had not provided an explanation related to the evidence for this determination. The Court held that the panel's decision erred in not assessing the claimant's claim to a fear of persecution because of his membership in his clan, and in not referring to the particulars of the claimant's own situation. It is suggested that the Court in this case focused on the fear as it related to a Convention ground as opposed to the "differential risk" analysis found in *Abdulle, Sadia Mohamed v. M.E.I.* (September 16, 1993), no. A-1440-92, Nadon (F.C.T.D.) and *Mohamud, Nasra Ali v. M.E.I.* (January 21, 1994), no. A-614-92, Nadon (F.C.T.D.).

In T94-05955, Rucker, Cram, March 7, 1995 (signed October 11, 1995), the Refugee Division found the claimant, a Darod/Marjerteen from Mogadishu, Somalia, to be a Convention refugee based on the clan-based fighting due to its adverse impact on him personally, and on his clan.

[19] See Suzanne J. Egan, *Civil War Refugees and the Issue of "Singling Out" in a State of Civil Unrest* (Toronto: The Centre for Refugee Studies, 1991). See also David Matas, "Innocent Victims of Civil War as Refugees", Vol. 22, Fall 1993, *Manitoba Law Journal*, p. 1.

In *Osman, Ashu Farah v. M.C.I.* (January 25, 1995), no. IMM-1295-94, Cullen (F.C.T.D.), the Court upheld the Refugee Division's finding that the claimant, a Somali women whose deceased husband was of another clan, did not have a well-founded fear of persecution by reason of her clan membership. However, the decision was overturned due to the panel's failure to consider the particular situation faced by the claimant related to her marriage which put her "at a heightened risk." In coming to its decision, the Court stated at p. 5 that the "Board cannot hide behind the civil war situation and automatically find that claimants from Somalia are not refugees." In *Hotaki, Khalilullah v. M.E.I.* (November 22, 1994), no. IMM-6659-93, Gibson (F.C.T.D.), the Court found that the Refugee Division erred in failing to recognise that the "applicant was personally or differen-

Where the persecution which has occurred, or the possibility of persecution in the future, is directed at the claimant's group as a whole rather than each individual member of the group, it is the fact of membership in the group which provides the foundation for the fear. Where the targeting is due to the possession of a certain characteristic related to a Convention ground, then all those who possess the characteristic may be at risk of harm by reason of their possession of that characteristic.[20] In such a case, the linkage to a Convention ground is not negated by the fact that the persecutor does not "discriminate" between one possessor of the characteristic and another possessor of the same characteristic. What is important is that the group is targeted, or there is a reasonable possibility of targeting of the claimant or the group in the future. Moreover, the number of persons in the group is irrelevant.

Targeting should be considered from the perspective of the agent of persecution, i.e. the intention of the agent of persecution must be examined. The Supreme Court of Canada has clarified that the examination of the circumstances of a case, including the intention of the agent of persecution, should be approached from the perspective of the agent of persecution, since it is this perspective that is "determinative in inciting the persecution."[21]

> Where the intention of the agent of persecution to target a claimant, or her group, is clear from the evidence, it will be a straightforward matter to determine whether there is a link to one of the Convention grounds. Where the intention is not clear on the particular facts of the case, the link to a Convention ground may be inferred from the effect that the actions of the agent of persecution have on the claimant or her group.

A civilian non-combatant should not be fixed with a share of "collective guilt" because combatant members of the claimant's group are inflicting harm on members of other

---

tially targeted and was not simply suffering from the fear felt indiscriminately by all citizens [of Afghanistan] as a consequence of the civil war" (at p. 4).

[20] While the membership of a claimant, who is a non-combatant, in a group which is a combatant in the civil war often forms the basis for her claim of a well-founded fear of persecution, it is clear that it is not determinative of the issue as the claimant must prove that the harm feared is linked to a Convention ground. In *Abdulle, Sadia Mohamed v. M.E.I.* (September 16, 1993), no. A-1440-92, Nadon (F.C.T.D.), the Court rejected the applicant's submission that membership in one of two groups involved in a two-sided conflict is determinative of the issue. The Court, applying a "differential risk" analysis, a mode of analysis not recommended in these Guidelines, required proof of targeting of the applicant or her group, an approach in accord with the Guidelines. See also *Farah, Ali Said v. M.C.I.* (January 13, 1995), no. IMM-1141-94, Dubé (F.C.T.D.). The Court, in concluding that the Refugee Division was not unreasonable in holding that the claimant had not established that he would be targeted for persecution in some way different from the general victims of civil war in Somalia, noted that "the mere fact that the applicant is a member of a tribe or clan in Somalia does not necessarily imply that he has an objectively well-founded fear of persecution" (at pp. 1-2).

[21] *Ward* at p. 747.

groups.[22] Such actions should not disqualify a claimant from refugee status if she otherwise fulfils the definition. As noted in *Isa*, there should be a recognition that civil wars are often waged for reasons found in the Convention grounds. *In applying Salibian and Rizkallah, the Guidelines recommend that a decision-maker should exercise caution before determining that a linkage to a Convention ground does not exist in such a case.* The fact that all persons on either side of the conflict may come within the definition, should not disqualify a claimant where that claimant has a well-founded fear of persecution based on a Convention ground.

In considering whether a linkage to a Convention ground exists, it is useful for decision-makers to reflect on the following comments made by Dr. Joachim Henkel, Judge, German Federal Administrative Court with respect to the "general consequences" of civil war.[23]

> The general rule that the Geneva Refugee Convention does not provide protection against the general consequences of civil war is correct, but is often applied too broadly. Certainly, the danger of being caught up in the fighting and thus losing ones life more or less by accident is a general consequence of civil war. Furthermore, the danger of loosing [sic] a limb by treading on a land mine is a general consequence of civil war. Lack of food and water, lack of electricity and heating, lack of medical treatment and many other sufferings are general consequences of civil war. But, in my view, it amounts to persecution if one of the waring [sic] parties as part of its strategy subjects the femal[e] members of the enemy community to wide-spread rape; if the waring [sic] parties resort to the practice of "ethnic-cleansing"; if the waring [sic] parties detain all male members of the enemy community in concentration camps in which they are abused and ill-treated; if one of the waring [sic] parties after having captured a city takes to killing even civilian members of the enemy community. Even though such atrocities may be common in today's civil wars they clearly are directed against persons as individuals; they are not just the unavoidable more or less anonymous consequences of a war. Thus, if one of the waring [sic] parties singles out a person or a group of persons for reasons of race, political opinion or one of the other elements enumerated in the refugee definition and subjects it to serious human rights violations this clearly constitutes persecution...

---

[22] However, see *Barisic, Rajko v. M.C.I.* (January 26, 1995), no. IMM-7275-93, Noël (F.C.T.D.), where the Court in dismissing the application for judicial review noted that the Croats, in the spirit of revenge, were engaging in acts just as reprehensible as those committed by the Serb army.

[23] Dr. Joachim Henkel, Judge, German Federal Administrative Court. Excerpt from his contribution to the International Judicial Conference on Asylum Law and Procedures, London, England, November 1995, "Who is a refugee? (Refugees from civil war and other internal armed conflicts)", in section titled "Persecution versus "general consequences" of civil war" at pp. 3-4.

Categories of Claims Encountered

In considering the issue of whether the persecution feared is based on a Convention ground, it is beneficial to highlight the types of claims seen in the civil war context. Claims arising within civil war situations may be divided into three broad categories:

1. *Fear of persecution in a generalized civil war:*

    a. *Individualized harm that is distinguishable from the general dangers of civil war.*

    b. *Group-based harm that is distinguishable from the general dangers of civil war.*

    c. *Harm that is not distinguishable from the general dangers of civil war.*

2. *Fear of persecution arising from a civil war specifically directed against a group with which the claimant is affiliated.*

3. *Fear of persecution from circumstances unrelated to the civil war.*

These categories have been identified as they delineate factual situations within which we find the majority of civil war claims. When such claims are considered within these categories, the linkage between the harm feared and the Convention grounds is more readily discernible. The examples set out below are not meant to be exhaustive of the situations that might come within a particular category.

1. *Fear of persecution in a generalized civil war.*

    A) *Individualized harm that is distinguishable from the general dangers of civil war:*

    > Certain individuals, although not taking any part in the hostilities, may nevertheless face a reasonable chance of persecution[24] because of their civil or political status, or due to a status which is imputed to them by combatants in the civil war. For example:
    >
    > > 1. persons facing persecution for refusing to join either side in the armed struggle out of a desire to remain neutral, a conscious political choice or other valid reasons of conscience;[25]

---

[24] *Adjei v. M.E.I.*, [1989] 2 F.C. 680 (C.A.). In *Chan, Kwong Hung v. M.E.I.* (October 19, 1995), no. 23813, Major, Sopinka, Cory, Iacobucci (majority); La Forest, L'Heureux-Dubé, Gonthier (dissenting) (S.C.C.), Justice Major after citing *Adjei* phrased the test as follows: "The applicable test has been expressed as a "reasonable possibility" or, more appropriately in my view, as a "serious possibility"." (p. 13). Both of these terms, as well as "reasonable chance", are found in *Adjei.*

[25] The claimant in such a situation might fear persecution at the hands of members of her own group for attempting to maintain neutrality in the conflict. Alternatively, her fear could emanate from groups in conflict with her group, as the claimant could be perceived to be a supporter of her own group.

As noted at p. 750 of the decision of the Supreme Court of Canada in *Canada (Attorney General) v. Ward*, [1993] 2 S.C.R. 689: "Not just any dissent to any organization will unlock the gates to Canadian asylum; the disagreement has to be rooted in a political conviction." At p. 749 the Court contrasted its decision in *Ward* with a recent United

2. human rights activists, journalists or other citizens threatened with measures of persecution for investigating and/or criticizing military, paramilitary or guerilla activities and atrocities;

3. persons fearing persecution for certain views attributed or imputed to them, such as "sabotaging the war efforts" or "collaborating with the enemy".[26]

B) Group-based harm that is distinguishable from the general dangers of civil war:

Although the civil war has an adverse impact on the entire population, a particular racial, national, religious, social or political group may face a reasonable chance of persecution because of the group's identifying characteristic(s). For example:

1. members of an ethnic group might face persecution as a result of, for example, selective denial of state protection related to their ethnicity;

2. women and children may, because of their social or political role or because of their association with certain individuals (including family members) be targets of deliberate violence and abuse;[27]

3. members of a clan might be perceived as associated with another clan that had ruled the country prior to the civil war and might by reason of that perceived association, face persecution.[28]

States Supreme Court disposition in *I.N.S. v. Elias-Zacarias*, 112 S.Ct. 812 (1992), where the majority was not convinced that the claimant's motive for refusing to join an anti-government guerilla force, nor that perceived by the guerilas to be his motive, was politically based.

[26] In *Antonio, Pacato Joao v. M.E.I.* (September 27, 1994), IMM-1072-93, Nadon (F.C.T.D.), the Court, in an Angolan claim, was not prepared to conclude that the death penalty, when imposed for treason and sabotage, constituted persecution. While providing indirect support to dissident forces may be subject to prosecution by the government, such prosecution must not be carried out in a persecutory manner.

[27] Where the claim involves a fear of gender-related persecution, consideration of the Chairperson's *Guidelines on Women Refugee Claimants Fearing Gender-related Persecution*, Immigration and Refugee Board, Ottawa, Canada, March 9, 1993 (the "*Gender Guidelines*") might be required. Thus, it may be necessary to use these Guidelines as well as the *Gender Guidelines* to analyze a claim of a woman fearing persecution within the context of a civil war. For a case involving a civil war situation where the panel failed to consider the *Gender Guidelines*, see *Hazarat, Ghulam v. S.S.C.* (November 25, 1994), no. IMM-5496-93, MacKay (F.C.T.D.). However, in *Narvaez, Cecilia v. M.C.I.* (February 9, 1995), no. IMM-3660-94, McKeown (F.C.T.D.), the Court had the following to say in a domestic violence case with respect to the *Gender Guidelines*: "While the guidelines are not law, they are authorized by subsection 65(3) of the Act, and intended to be followed unless circumstances are such that a different analysis is appropriate" (p. 6). With respect to the position of children see, *supra*, note 7.

[28] See *Shirwa, Mohamed Mahmoud v. M.E.I.* (December 16, 1993), no. A-1290-92, Denault (F.C.T.D.). Also, members of the clan that had ruled the country prior to the civil war might face persecution by reason of their clan membership.

C) Harm that is not distinguishable from the general dangers of civil war.

As noted above, certain individuals and groups may face a reasonable chance of persecution on a Convention ground, notwithstanding the civil war's adverse impact on the entire population. On the other hand, there will be circumstances where the persecution feared may not be linked to a Convention ground. Reference is then made to the unavoidable, more or less anonymous consequences of a civil war. For example:

1. civilians who are the unintentional victims of cross-fire between rival militias. The lack of an intention on the part of either of the rival militias leaves the civilians as "mere victims" of the civil war as there is no linkage between the harm feared and a Convention ground;[29]

2. civilians who are the unintentional victims of arbitrary, general or indiscriminate shelling and bombing or laying of land mines where the fear of such treatment is not linked to a Convention ground;[30]

3. civilians who are subject to random violence, such as looting, where the violence is not related to a Convention ground.[31]

2. Fear of persecution arising from a civil war specifically directed against a group with which the claimant is affiliated.

The violence is directed at a group that differs from the rest of the population by virtue of specific racial, national, social or political features. For example:

1. members of an ethnic group against which a genocidal campaign is being waged;

---

[29] It is recognized that in a civil war there will be civilian casualties incidental to the fighting; while regrettable, such deaths or injuries are distinct from those resulting from an attack directed at civilian non-combatants or where the combatants show wanton disregard for the safety of civilians. Evidence of such disregard might lead the Refugee Division to find that there is a link between the persecution feared and a Convention ground. For cases illustrating this issue, see, *supra*, note 14.

[30] See *Khalib v. M.E.I.* (1994), 24 Imm. L.R. (2d) 149 (F.C.T.D.), supra, note 14. This example can be contrasted with a situation where one participant in a civil war bombs and shells an area of a town primarily inhabited by civilian non-combatants who are members of another participant in the civil war. Civilians who are not near military targets should not face direct attack by combatants. Where civilians are present in or near military targets, they may be found to have assumed the risk of death or injury incidental to attacks against such military targets.

[31] This can be contrasted with the intentional infliction of harm described by Dr. Joachim Henkel. In *Abdi, Ascia Hassan v. M.C.I.* (October 27, 1994), no. A-1016-92, Noël (F.C.T.D.), the Court in dismissing the application, concluded that its review of the evidence did not justify its interference with the Refugee Division's finding that "members of the Darod or Hawiye tribes, including the Applicants, were subject to the same risk of random violence as the general population of Somalia" (at p. 7).

2. members of a religious faith expelled from their homes and suffering other forms of persecutory treatment as part of an "ethnic cleansing" agenda.[32]

3. Fear of persecution from circumstances unrelated to the civil war.

Although the claimant comes from a country in civil war, the danger faced by the claimant is not associated, directly or indirectly, with that war. However, the claimant may still be a Convention refugee if the fear of persecution is related to one of the five grounds. In this situation the claim should be determined without reference to the civil war framework. For example:

1. union leaders threatened with measures of persecution for promoting unionism;

2. members of a minority group treated in a persecutory manner, where such treatment or lack of protection is not related to the civil war.

III. — Determining whether there is a Well-Founded Fear of Persecution

It is clear from the case law that a claimant must establish that her fear is well founded, and that the state's inability to protect must be considered at this stage of the analysis of the claim. In addition, the Supreme Court of Canada in *Ward* confirmed that a claimant is to seek out international protection only when national or state protection is unavailable.[33] The claimant must seek the protection of the country of origin before seeking international protection, unless it is objectively unreasonable to do so.[34]

The question, which must be addressed by the Refugee Division, is whether the claimant faces a reasonable chance of persecution by reason of a Convention ground: Is there a subjective fear for which there is an objective basis? As previously stated in these Guidelines, it is not required that the claimant's chance of facing persecution, individually or as a member of a group, be greater than the chance of persecution faced by others in situations of civil war; nor is it required that the persecution feared by the claimant be more severe than that feared by others.

State Protection

A state's ability to protect the claimant is a crucial element in determining whether the fear of persecution is well founded, and as such, is not an independent element of the definition of Convention refugee. The Supreme Court of Canada in *Ward* held that there were two presumptions at play in refugee determination. With respect to the first presumption, the Court concluded that it can be presumed that persecution will be likely and the fear well-founded if the fear of persecution is credible and there is an absence of state protection. As a second presumption the Court held that except in situations where the state is in a condition of complete breakdown, states must be presumed capable of pro-

---

[32] In CRDD T92-03148, Miller, Shatzky, September 9, 1992, the Refugee Division determined a Bosnian Moslem to be a Convention refugee as the panel concluded that "Muslims are not merely the victims caught in the crossfire of war, but are a targeted group selected for elimination because of their religion" (p. 5).

[33] *Ward* at p. 709.

[34] *Ward* at p. 724.

tecting their citizens. The Court found that this presumption can be rebutted by "clear and convincing" evidence of the state's inability to protect.[35]

The presumption that a state must be presumed capable of protecting its citizens can be rebutted where there is a complete breakdown of state apparatus, such as that recognized in *Zalzali v. M.E.I.*[36] in relation to the civil war, then raging, in Lebanon. However, even where there is a breakdown of state apparatus,[37] there may be several established authorities in a country able to provide protection in the part of the country controlled by them.[38] Thus, the Refugee Division must consider whether there is an established authority from which protection may be sought and adequate protection is available.[39]

---

[35] See *Ward* at pp. 722–6.

[36] *Zalzali v. M.E.I.*, [1991] 3 F.C. 605 (C.A.). As noted at p. 614 of the decision, the non-existence of a government cannot be an obstacle to claiming refugee status. It would be an absurd result that the greater the chaos in a given country, the less acts of persecution could be capable of founding a claim for refugee status. However, for the principle in *Zalzali* to apply, the claimant must demonstrate a prospective risk of persecution. Thus, in *Roble, Abdi Burale v. M.E.I.* (April 25, 1994), no. A-1101-91, Heald, Stone, McDonald (F.C.A.), where the agent of persecution (the NSS in Somalia) was no longer a factor, the Court held at p. 9 that "... the inability of the state to protect the [claimant] is not, in itself, a sufficient basis for his claim."

[37] In *Mendivil v. S.S.C.* (1994), 23 Imm. L.R. (2d) 225 (F.C.A.) at p. 232, Desjardins J.A. in analyzing the situation in Peru (on the basis of the evidence filed in the particular case) stated: "Isolated cases of persons having been victimized may not reverse the presumption [of protection]. A state of profound unrest with ineffective protection for the claimant may, however, have reversed it." In *Oblitas, Jorge v. M.C.I.* (February 2, 1995), no. IMM-2489-94, Muldoon (F.C.T.D.), at p. 9, the Court goes so far as to say that while the situation in Peru due to the terrorist activities of the Shining Path is not quite one of state breakdown (as in *Zalzali*), it comes very close.

[38] *Zalzali*, at p. 615 where the Court goes on to state:

The "country", the "national government", the "legitimate government", the "nominal government" will probably vary depending on the circumstances and the evidence and it would be presumptuous to attempt to give a general definition. I will simply note here that I do not rule out the possibility that there may be several established authorities in the same country which are each able to provide protection in the part of the territory controlled by them, protection which may be adequate though not necessarily perfect.

See also *Sami, Sami Qowdan v. M.E.I.* (June 1, 1994), no. A-629-92, Simpson (F.C.T.D.) and *Saidi, Ahmed Abrar v. M.E.I.* (September 14, 1993), no. A-749-92, Wetston (F.C.T.D.) where, in each case, the Court upheld the Refugee Division's findings that protection was available in northern Somalia

[39] The Supreme Court of Canada in *Ward* did not discuss the standard of protection that a country needs to offer its nationals. In determining what constitutes adequate protection, the Refugee Division may consider as a factor, whether the established authority is able to provide the claimant with protection from the acts prohibited by common article 3 of

Internal Flight Alternative

Even when a claimant otherwise meets all the elements of the Convention refugee definition in her home area of her country of origin,[40] the claimant may have an internal flight alternative (IFA) elsewhere in that country: *If there is an IFA, the claimant is not a Convention refugee.* The question of whether a IFA exists is an integral part of the Convention definition.[41] If it is necessary to consider the availability of an IFA, reference may be made to the *Commentary* on IFA.[42]

The key concepts concerning IFA come from two cases: *Rasaratnam and Thirunavukkarasu.*[43] From these cases it is clear that the test to be applied in determining whether there is a IFA is two-pronged. Both prongs must be satisfied for there to be a finding that the claimant has an IFA. The Court of Appeal in *Rasaratnam* at pp. 709–11 adopts the two-pronged test:

> 1. The Board must be satisfied on a balance of probabilities that there is no serious possibility of the claimant being persecuted in the part of the country to which it finds a IFA exists.
>
> 2. Moreover, conditions in the part of the country considered to be a IFA must be such that it would be not unreasonable, in all the circumstances, including those particular to the claimant, for him to seek refuge there.[44]

In determining whether there is a reasonable chance of persecution in the potential IFA, the factors considered are similar to those evaluated when the panel makes this finding with respect to the claimant's home area of the country. However, some considerations

---

the *1949 Convention.* For a discussion of the appropriate standard see *M.E.I. v. Villafranca* (1992), 18 Imm. L.R. (2d) 130 (F.C.A.); *Velarde-Alvarez v. S.S.C.* (1995), 27 Imm. L.R. (2d) 88 (F.C.T.D.); *Bobrik, Iouri v. M.C.I.* (September 16, 1994), no. IMM-5519-93, Tremblay-Lamer (F.C.T.D.); *Smirnov v. S.S.C.,* [1995] 1 F.C. 780 (T.D.).

[40] In *Kanagaratnam, Parameswary v. M.E.I.* (January 17, 1996), no. A-356-94, Strayer, Linden, McDonald (F.C.A.), the Court of Appeal in answering "no" to the certified question "Is the determination of whether a claimant has a well founded fear of persecution in the area from which he or she originates a prerequisite to the consideration of an internal flight alternative?", held at p. 2 that "while the Board may certainly do so if it chooses, there was no *need* as a matter of law for the Board to decide whether there was persecution in the area of origin *as a prerequisite* to the consideration of an IFA" (emphasis added by the Court).

[41] *Rasaratnam v. M.E.I.,* [1992] 1 F.C. 706 at p. 710 (C.A.).

[42] *Internal Flight: When is it an Alternative?,* IRB Legal Services, April 1994. The Commentary provides a detailed review of the issue and includes a suggested framework of analysis.

[43] *Thirunavukkarasu v. M.E.I.,* [1994] 1 F.C. 589 (C.A.).

[44] For an elaboration of this statement, reference should be made to *Thirunavukkarasu* at pp. 596–9.

are different in order to account for the fact that the claimant is being expected to seek out alternative refuge in the country of origin.[45]

In dealing with the second prong of the IFA test, "reasonableness in all the circumstances", the Court of Appeal has stated that the circumstances must be relevant to the IFA question: "They cannot be catalogued in the abstract. They will vary from case to case."[46]

> The Trial Division has provided some guidance in assessing the reasonableness of an IFA. In the civil war context, the Court has indicated that relevant factors include the state of infrastructure and economy in the IFA region (i.e. destroyed or not), and the stability or instability of the government that is in place there.[47] In addition, it may be necessary to consider the hardship in travelling to the IFA region.
>
> *A claimant should not be required to suffer great physical danger or undue hardship in travelling to the IFA region or in staying there.*[48] *However, if there is an IFA, the claimant is not a Convention refugee.*

IV. — Evidentiary Matters

When assessing a fear of persecution by a person fearing return to a situation of civil war the evidence must show that what the claimant fears is persecution on a Convention ground and that the fear is well-founded. The burden is on the claimant to provide the Refugee Division with credible or trustworthy evidence to show that all elements of the definition have been met; this includes establishing that there is individual or group targeting on a Convention ground.

Evidence can be provided through the claimant's own testimony. In addition, this can be done by the use of witnesses (including experts) to provide evidence on country condi-

---

[45] In particular, in determining whether there is an objective basis for fearing persecution in the IFA region, the Refugee Division must consider the personal circumstances of the claimant, and not just general evidence concerning other persons who live there.

[46] *M.E.I. v. Sharbdeen* (1994), 23 Imm. L.R. (2d) 300 at p. 301-2 (F.C.A.).

[47] *Farrah, Sahra Said v. M.E.I.* (October 5, 1993), no. A-694-92 at p. 3, Reed (F.C.T.D.). See also *Megag, Sahra Abdilahi v. M.E.I.* (December 10, 1993), no. A-822-92, Rothstein (F.C.T.D.) at p. 3 where the Court holds that instability alone is not the test of reasonableness. In *Irene, Steve Albert v. M.C.I.* (October 6, 1994), no. IMM-6275-93, Rothstein (F.C.T.D.), the Court in considering an IFA in an area controlled by one of the groups to the conflict, did not disagree with the applicant's submission that the group was not internationally recognized, had lost territory, was not an established force in the country (Liberia) and the applicant could not reasonably claim protection from that group. In those circumstances, the Court rejected the Refugee Division's finding that an IFA existed.

[48] The Trial Division has specifically addressed the issue of at what point in time IFA is to be considered. In *Dubravac v. M.C.I.* (1995), 29 Imm. L.R. (2d) 55 (F.C.T.D.) where the claimants' home town had been surrounded by opposing Serbian forces, the Court commented that the claimants "would not be required to go from their home town to the safe zone of Croatia, but ... from wherever they were relanded upon being sent back" (p. 56).

tions relating to targeting; such evidence can be introduced by way of affidavit in lieu of oral testimony.[49] The Refugee Division may take notice of any facts that may be judicially noticed and, subject to giving proper notice, of any other generally recognized facts and any information or opinion that is within its specialized knowledge.[50]

One way for the claimant to establish her case can be through evidence that other similarly situated persons face a reasonable chance of persecution, whether or not that chance is applicable to a specific group only or to large segments of the population similarly situated to the claimant.[51]

> Refugee Claim Officers under the direction of the panel and Counsel should submit documentary evidence to provide evidence of country conditions relating to targeting. *There should be recognition by the Refugee Division of the difficulty that is often encountered in acquiring information on country conditions when a country is embroiled in a civil war.* Notwithstanding that a claimant has the burden of establishing her claim, Refugee Division panels should consider the statements in the UNHCR *Handbook* at paragraph 196 on the shared burden of information gathering.
>
> > ... Thus, while the burden of proof in principle rests on the applicant, the duty to ascertain and evaluate all the relevant facts is shared between the applicant and the examiner. Indeed, in some cases, it may be for the examiner to use all the means at his disposal to produce the necessary evidence in support of the application.[52]

In addition, there should be recognition that, given the rapidly changing country conditions generally associated with civil wars, there may be problems with the timeliness of evidence and problems encountered in obtaining current information with respect to those changes. Accordingly, Refugee Claim Officers under the direction of the panel and Counsel should seek out and submit to the hearing the most current information relating to country conditions.

---

[49] The *Act* provides in section 68(3) that all proceedings before the Refugee Division shall be dealt with as informally and expeditiously as the circumstances and the considerations of fairness permit.

[50] In accordance with the requirements of natural justice, section 68(5) of the *Act* provides that before the Refugee Division takes notice of any facts, information or opinion, other than facts that may be judicially noticed, in any proceedings, notice of its intention must be given and a reasonable opportunity to make representations with respect thereto must be afforded to the claimant (and the Minister, if present).

[51] In dismissing the application for judicial review in *Ahmed, Mohamed Hassan v. M.E.I.* (May 20, 1994), no. A-818-92, McKeown (F.C.T.D.), the Court noted that "the onus is on the applicant to show that he is similarly situated to members of a social group who suffered persecution" (at p. 2).

[52] See also paragraphs 195 to 205. The need to ascertain and evaluate all relevant facts is reflected in some of the enhancements to the Convention refugee determination process implemented by the Refugee Division in October 1995.

Framework of Analysis

1. Assess the particular circumstances which have given rise to the claimant's fear of persecution. Does the harm feared constitute persecution?

For the treatment to amount to persecution, it must be a serious form of harm which detracts from the claimant's human rights and fundamental freedoms. The degree and importance of the rights and freedoms violated must be examined in relation to how the concept of persecution has been defined in Canadian jurisprudence. One objective standard is provided by international human rights instruments and international instruments that relate to the position of civilians in non-international armed conflicts. However, Canadian jurisprudence on the definition of persecution is not restricted to the violation of rights or interests protected in such international instruments.

2. Is the harm feared as a result of the targeting of the claimant or her group on the basis of any one, or a combination, of the grounds in the definition of Convention refugee? Alternatively, the question can be posed: Is the claimant's fear of persecution based on any one, or a combination, of the grounds enumerated in the definition of Convention refugee?

Considerations:

- *the intention of the agent of persecution must be assessed*
- *intention may be inferred from the effect that the actions of the agent of persecution have on the claimant or her group*
- *a claimant need not be individually targeted for persecution*
- *it is necessary to ascertain the characteristic which places the claimant or members of her group at risk and the linkage to a Convention ground*
- *the level of risk of persecution should not be compared to that of other individuals or groups in the country of origin*
- *as civil wars are often waged for reasons related to a Convention ground, caution should be exercised before determining that there is not a linkage to a ground*

3. Determine whether, under all the circumstances, the claimant's fear is well-founded. This includes an assessment of the evidence related to the availability of adequate state protection and whether there is an objective basis to the claim.

Considerations:

- *is there an established authority from which protection may be sought and adequate protection is available?*
- *recognition of the difficulty of acquiring information on country conditions is important*

4. If required, determine whether there is the possibility of an internal flight alternative (IFA), or whether other issues require analysis.

Considerations:

- *the state of infrastructure and economy in the IFA region (i. e. destroyed or not), and the stability or instability of the government that is in place there*
- *whether or not there would be undue hardship on the claimant, both in reaching the location of the IFA and in establishing residence there*
- *if there is an IFA, the claimant is not a Convention refugee*

Other Relevant Legislation

Relevant International Instruments

Geneva Convention Relative to the Protection of Civilian Persons in Time of War of August 12, 1949

Article 3 of each of the four *Geneva Conventions of 1949* set out in the schedule to the *Geneva Conventions Act*, R.S.C. 1985, c. G-3, provides as follows:

> 3. In the case of armed conflict not of an international character occurring in the territory of one of the High Contracting Parties, each Party to the conflict shall be bound to apply, as a minimum, the following provisions:
>
> (1) Persons taking no active part in the hostilities, including members of armed forces who have laid down their arms and those placed *hors de combat* by sickness, wounds, detention, or any other cause shall in all circumstances be treated humanely, without adverse distinction founded on race, colour, religion or faith, sex, birth or wealth, or any other similar criteria.
>
> To this end, the following acts are and shall remain prohibited at any time and in any place whatever with respect to the above-mentioned persons:
>
>> a. violence to life and person, in particular murder of all kinds, mutilation, cruel treatment and torture;
>>
>> b. taking of hostages;
>>
>> c. outrages upon personal dignity, in particular humiliating and degrading treatment;
>>
>> d. the passing of sentences and the carrying out of executions without previous judgment pronounced by a regularly constituted court, affording all the judicial guarantees which are recognized as indispensable by civilized peoples.

Protocol II to the Geneva Convention Relative to the Protection of Civilian Persons in Time of War of August 12, 1949

(Schedule vi of the Geneva Conventions Act as amended by S.C. 1990, c. 14, s. 1)

Article 4

1. All persons who do not take a direct part or who have ceased to take part in hostilities, whether or not their liberty has been restricted, are entitled to respect for their person, honour and convictions and religious practices. They shall in all circumstances be treated humanely, without any adverse distinction. It is prohibited to order that there shall be no survivors.

2. Without prejudice to the generality of the foregoing, the following acts against the persons referred to in paragraph 1 are and shall remain prohibited at any time and in any place whatsoever:

> a. violence to the life, health and physical or mental well-being of persons, in particular murder as well as cruel treatment such as torture, mutilation or any form of corporal punishment;
>
> b. collective punishments;
>
> c. taking of hostages;
>
> d. acts of terrorism;

e. outrages on the personal dignity, in particular humiliating and degrading treatment, rape, enforced prostitution and any form of indecent assault;

f. slavery and the slave trade in all their forms;

g. pillage;

h. threats to commit any of the foregoing acts.

3. Children shall be provided with the care and aid they require, and in particular:

(c) children who have not attained the age of fifteen years shall neither be recruited in the armed forces or groups nor allowed to take part in hostilities;...

Article 13 — Protection of the Civilian Population

1. The civilian population and individual civilians shall enjoy general protection against the dangers arising from military operations. To give effect to this protection, the following rules shall be observed in all circumstances.

2. The civilian population as such, as well as individual civilians, shall not be the object of attack. Acts or threats of violence the primary purpose of which is to spread terror among the civilian population are prohibited.

3. Civilians shall enjoy the protection afforded by this Part, unless and for such time as they take a direct part in hostilities.

Article 14 — Protection of objects indispensable to the survival of the civilian population

Starvation of civilians as a method of combat is prohibited. It is therefore prohibited to attack, destroy, remove or render useless, for that purpose, objects indispensable to the survival of the civilian population, such as foodstuffs, agricultural areas for the production of foodstuffs, crops, livestock, drinking water installations and supplies and irrigation works.

Guideline 2 — Detention

Guidelines Issued by the Chairperson, Pursuant to paragraph 159(1)(h) of the *Immigration and Refugee Protection Act*

Effective date: June 5, 2013

1. — Introduction

1.1 — Introduction

1.1.1 The purpose of this Guideline is to provide guidance in the treatment of persons who are detained under Division 6 of Part 1 of the *Immigration and Refugee Protection Act* (IRPA).[53] Chairperson's Guidelines are issued to assist Immigration Division members in carrying out their duties as decision-makers under the IRPA and to promote con-

---

[53] S.C. 2001, c. 27, as amended. Section 54 of the IRPA states that the "Immigration Division is the competent Division of the Board with respect to the review of reasons for detention under this Division."

sistency, coherence and fairness in the treatment of cases at the Immigration and Refugee Board of Canada (IRB).

1.1.2 Canadian law regards preventive detention as an exceptional measure.[54] This general principle emerges from statute and case law, and is enshrined in the *Canadian Charter of Rights and Freedoms*[55] (hereinafter referred to as the Charter). International law, as reflected in the *International Covenant on Civil and Political Rights and the Optional Protocol to the International Covenant on Civil and Political Rights*, respects the same principle.[56]

1.1.3 Parliament has established grounds for detention[57] that members of the Immigration Division must consider, when applicable, at a detention review when deciding whether to order the release or continued detention of a permanent resident or a foreign national. Members of the Immigration Division must order the release of a permanent resident or a foreign national unless they are satisfied, taking into account prescribed factors, that:

- they are a *danger to the public*;
- they are *unlikely to appear* for examination, an admissibility hearing, removal from Canada, or at a proceeding that could lead to the making of a removal order by the Minister under subsection 44(2) of the IRPA;
- the Minister is taking necessary steps to inquire into a reasonable suspicion that they are inadmissible on grounds of *security, violating human or international rights, serious criminality, criminality or organized criminality*;
- the Minister is of the opinion that the *identity of the foreign national* — other than a designated foreign national who was 16 years of age or older on the day of the arrival that is the subject of the designation in question — has not been, but may be, established and they have not reasonably cooperated with the Minister by providing relevant information for the purpose of establishing their identity or the Minister is making reasonable efforts to establish their identity;
- the Minister is of the opinion that the *identity* of the foreign national who is a designated foreign national[58] and who was *16 years of age or older on the day of the arrival that is the subject of the designation* in question has not been established.

1.1.4 Members of the Immigration Division have the power to order the continued detention of a person based on one or more of the above grounds. They may also order that a

---

[54] See Part XVI of the Canadian *Criminal Code*, R.S., 1985, c. C-46.

[55] Canadian Charter of Rights and Freedoms, Part 1 of the *Constitution Act, 1982*, being Schedule B to the *Canada Act, 1982*, c. 11 (U.K.).

[56] International Covenant on Civil and Political Rights, (1976) 999 UNTS 107, in force on March 23, 1976, sections 9, 10 and 11, and the Optional Protocol to the International Covenant on Civil and Political Rights, (1976) 999 UNTS 216, in force on March 23, 1976. These two instruments confer status in law on the civil and political rights set out in the Universal Declaration of Human Rights, U.N. Doc. A/810, p. 71 (1948).

[57] IRPA, s. 58(1).

[58] The Minister's authority and jurisdiction with respect to designated foreign nationals is found in s. 20.1 of the IRPA. This provision concerns human smuggling or other irregular arrival in Canada of a group of persons.

person be released from detention and may impose any conditions that they consider necessary, including the payment of a deposit or the posting of a guarantee for compliance with the conditions.[59] In deciding whether to continue detention or order release, the public interest must be balanced with the liberty interest of the individual.[60]

1.1.5 However, in the case of designated foreign nationals who were 16 years of age or older on the day of the arrival that is the subject of the designation in question, members of the Immigration Division must order their continued detention if they are satisfied that any of the applicable grounds exist,[61] and they may not consider any other factors at the 14-day detention review.[62] If the Immigration Division orders the release of the designated foreign national, it may impose any conditions it considers necessary, including the payment of a deposit or the posting of a guarantee for compliance with the conditions,[63] and it must also impose any condition that is prescribed in the *Immigration and Refugee Protection Regulations* (IRPR).[64]

1.1.6 Members must take into account the prescribed factors set out in Part 14 of the IRPR that relate to the grounds for detention and release. It is not sufficient for a member to just note these factors in their reasons for decision. Members are required to indicate in their reasons how these factors relate to their particular finding.

1.1.7 At each detention review the Immigration Division must come to a fresh conclusion on whether the detained person should continue to be detained. However, previous decisions by the Immigration Division to detain the person concerned must be considered at subsequent reviews and the subsequent decision-maker must give "clear and compelling

---

[59] IRPA, s. 58(3).

[60] In *M.C.I. v. B147* (May 29, 2012), F.C., no. IMM-2451-12, 2012 FC 655, Rennie, the Federal Court stated:

> [54] Section 7 interests, under the *Canadian Charter of Rights and Freedoms* (*Charter*), are rarely absolute. Rather, they imply a balancing of considerations. As stated by McLachlin J. in *Cunningham v. Canada*, [1993] 2 SCR 143, at pp 151-152:
>
>> The principles of fundamental justice are concerned not only with the interest of the person who claims his liberty has been limited, but with the protection of society. Fundamental justice requires that a fair balance be struck between these interests, both substantively and procedurally.
>
> . . .

[61] The applicable grounds are the grounds described in paragraphs 58(1)(a) to (c) and (e) of the IRPA.

[62] IRPA, s. 58(1.1), which refers to a review under s. 57.1(1). This provision removes the Immigration Division's jurisdiction to consider the factors enumerated in the IRPR, s. 248, at the 14-day detention review.

[63] IRPA, s. 58(3).

[64] IRPA, s. 58(4).

reasons" for departing from previous decisions.[65] Reasons should be sufficiently detailed to allow the reader to know what factors the decision-maker relied on in support of their decision to detain or release.

1.1.8 The credibility of the person concerned and of witnesses is often an issue at detention reviews. Where a member had the opportunity to observe the demeanour of a witness and assess credibility, the subsequent decision-maker must give a clear explanation of why the prior decision-maker's assessment of the evidence does not justify continued detention. The admission of relevant new evidence could be a valid basis for departing from a prior decision to order detention. In addition, a reassessment of the prior evidence based on new arguments could also be sufficient reason to depart from a prior decision to detain. The member must expressly explain in the reasons what the former decision stated and why they are departing from the previous decision.[66]

1.1.9 At a detention review, the onus is always on the Minister to demonstrate, on a balance of probabilities, that there are reasons which warrant continued detention.[67]

2. — Grounds for Detention

2.1 — Danger to the Public

2.1.1 The Immigration Division may order the continued detention of a permanent resident or a foreign national if they are a danger to the public. Neither IRPA nor the case law explicitly defines the phrase "danger to the public." This phrase relates to the objectives of the IRPA, namely, to protect public health and safety and to maintain the security of Canadian society.[68]

2.1.2 The concept of danger to the public is usually raised with respect to persons who have been involved in criminal activities.

2.1.3 Members of the Immigration Division must consider the following prescribed factors[69] in the IRPR relating to danger to the public:

- the person constitutes, in the opinion of the Minister, a danger to the public in Canada or a danger to the security of Canada;
- association with a criminal organization;

---

[65] *Canada (Minister of Citizenship and Immigration) v. Thanabalasingham*, [2004] 3 F.C.R. 572 (F.C.A.); 2004 FCA 4; *M.C.I. v. Li, Dong Zhe* (August 15, 2008), F.C., no. IMM-2682-08, 2008 FC 949, Martineau.

[66] *Thanabalasingham, supra*, footnote 13; *Li, supra*, footnote 13. The Court noted in *M.C.I. v. Sittampalam, Jothiravi* (December 17, 2004), F.C., nos. IMM-3876-04 and IMM-8256-04, 2004 FC 1756, Blais, that "[t]he rationale behind this principle is to safeguard the findings of a previous Member who was in a better position to hear original evidence and assess credibility. New evidence, new arguments or a different assessment on the same evidence which may give rise to a change in the status quo should be clearly laid out by the Member departing from the prior decision."

[67] Thanabalasingham, supra, footnote 13.

[68] IRPA, s. 3(1)(h).

[69] IRPR, s. 246.

- engagement in people smuggling or trafficking in persons;
- a conviction in Canada for a sexual offence or an offence involving violence or weapons;
- a conviction for an offence in Canada under the *Controlled Drugs and Substances Act* for trafficking, importing and exporting, and production;
- a conviction outside Canada or pending charges outside Canada for a sexual offence or an offence involving violence or weapons;
- a conviction outside Canada or pending charges outside Canada for trafficking, importing and exporting, and production of controlled substances.

2.1.4 The type of offences referred to in the IRPR also include those acts that would render a person inadmissible on grounds of security and violating human or international rights, for example, war crimes, crimes against humanity, acts of espionage, subversion and terrorism.[70]

2.1.5 The following advice and guidance is provided to members in relation to the concept of danger to the public:

- Members must assess whether the person represents a "present or future danger to the public." In calculating future danger, the probability of danger has to be determined from the circumstances of each case.[71]
- It will often be necessary for members to draw inferences from a person's criminal record in determining whether that person is likely to be a danger to the public.[72] The more serious the criminal offences and the greater number of offences committed the more they weigh in favour of a finding of danger to the public.
- Members must consider "the possibility that a person who has committed a serious crime in the past may seriously be thought to be a potential reoffender."[73] It is acceptable to use past conduct as a reliable indicator of future conduct, although other factors cannot be ignored.[74]
- Various factors should be weighed when considering whether a person is a danger to the public, such as the age of the convictions and the circumstances in which they were committed; the character of the person concerned (for example, drug or alcohol addiction or any other chronic condition), including the willingness to be reha-

---

[70] IRPR, s. 246(a). See also IRPA, ss. 34 and 35.

[71] *Thompson, James Lorenzo v. M.C.I.* (August 16, 1996), F.C.T.D., no. IMM-107-96, Gibson. Reported: *Thompson v. Canada (Minister of Citizenship and Immigration)* (1996), 37 Imm L.R. (2d) 9 (F.C.T.D); referred to in *Canada (Minister of Citizenship and Immigration) v. Thanabalasingham*, [2004] 3 F.C.R. 523 (F.C.); 2003 FC 1225.

[72] *McIntosh, Robert v. M.C.I.* (September 20, 1995), F.C.T.D., no. 2387-95, Rothstein. Reported: *McIntosh v. Canada (Minister of Citizenship and Immigration)* (1996), 30 Imm. L.R. (2d) 314 (F.C.T.D.).

[73] *Williams v. Canada (Minister of Citizenship and Immigration)*, [1997] 2 F.C. 646 (C.A.) at p. 668.

[74] *Willis, Joan Siddon v. M.C.I.* (July 24, 2001), F.C.T.D., no. IMM-336-01, 2001 FCT 822, Gibson.

Other Relevant Legislation

bilitated and the possibility of rehabilitation; the person's behaviour in society since the convictions and family and community support.[75] Recent convictions involving violence or weapons will favour a finding of danger to the public. If a person has been convicted of an offence and has served the related sentence, the conviction alone is not sufficient to support a finding that that person is likely to be a danger to the public.[76] However, a conviction in the past for an offence involving violence or weapons is a strong indicator that the person is a danger to the public. Members must assess the current circumstances and determine whether there is evidence that the person's behaviour has changed.

- While members should not automatically conclude that a person is a danger because one of the factors listed in the IRPR exists, the existence of one of the listed factors must be considered. The weight to be given to each factor in a particular case is left to the discretion of the member depending on the individual circumstances.[77]

- In order for a member to find that a person is a danger to the public there need not be evidence of a conviction outside Canada. A pending charge in a foreign jurisdiction for the specific types of offences listed in the IRPR, involving for example, violence or weapons, is a factor that must be considered and weighed with all the relevant circumstances of the case.

- The prescribed factors in the IRPR are not exhaustive. The Immigration Division may determine that a person is a danger to the public even if none of the prescribed factors exist if there is evidence that the person represents a "present or future danger." Members must consider evidence that the person has been involved in gang activity even if that person has no criminal convictions. Evidence of gang-related activity is a factor that weighs in favour of a finding of danger to the public.

- The Immigration Division is not bound to follow the determination of the National Parole Board as to whether the person is a danger to the public. The member must exercise independent discretion and cannot simply adopt the decision of the National Parole Board.[78] A finding by the National Parole Board that a person with a violent past may be paroled with supervision does not mean that the person is not a danger to the public since all the circumstances in the case must be considered.

- Similarly, the Immigration Division is not bound to follow determinations made in a court of law with respect to the granting of bail and with respect to the imposing of a sentence.[79] While such determinations may be considered at a detention re-

---

[75] Thanabalasingham, supra, footnote 13.

[76] *Salilar v. Canada (Minister of Citizenship and Immigration)*, [1995] 3 F.C. 150 (T.D.).

[77] Thanabalasingham, supra, footnote 13.

[78] *Lam, Bao Ngoc v. M.E.I.* (October 8, 1993), F.C.T.D., no. IMM-5528-93, Jerome; *M.C.I. v. Alyea, Kevin Richard* (September 23, 1999), F.C.T.D., no. IMM-1345-99, Campbell. Reported: *Alyea v. Canada (Minister of Citizenship and Immigration)* (1999), 3 Imm. L.R. (3d) 118 (F.C.T.D.); *Willis, supra*, footnote 22.

[79] *Canada (Minister of Citizenship and Immigration) v. Salinas-Mendoza*, [1995] 1 F.C. 251 (T.D.); *Camacho, Jairo Hidalgo v. M.C.I.* (May 1, 2000), F.C.T.D., no. IMM-1908-00, Dawson.

view, members must come to their own conclusions, taking into account all the facts in the case and the immigration context.

- The Minister's opinion that the person constitutes a danger to the public is a factor to take into account at a detention review but is not in itself sufficient for finding that the person is a danger to the public.[80]

- In determining whether a person is a danger to the public, members must consider whether the person has or had an "association" with a criminal organization as opposed to "membership" in the organization.[81] The concept of "criminal organization" in this context means a criminal organization as defined in the *Criminal Code* of Canada.[82]

- In some instances danger to the public may dissipate due to the length of time that a person has been in detention or because evidence supporting a detention order has turned stale.[83] In such circumstances members must still consider whether there is ongoing danger to the public as a result of the commission of past criminal offences or prior association with a criminal organization.

2.1.6 In the case of designated foreign nationals who were 16 years of age or older on the day of the arrival that is the subject of the designation in question, however, at the 14-day detention review the Immigration Division must consider only the prescribed grounds relating to the relevant ground for detention, and may not consider any other factors.[84]

2.1.7 If the Immigration Division orders the release of the designated foreign national who was 16 years of age or older on the day of the arrival that is the subject of the designation in question, it must impose any condition that is prescribed in the IRPR.[85]

---

[80] IRPR, s. 246(a). In *M.C.I. v. Singh, Harjit* (August 27, 2001), F.C.T.D., no. IMM-3937-01, 2001 FCT 954, McKeown, the Court recognized that in addition to the Minister's opinion on danger, there was additional evidence that taken together led to a finding that the person posed a danger to Canadian society. See also *Alyea, supra*, footnote 26; *M.P.S.E.P. v. Sall, Mohamed* (June 13, 2011), F.C., no. IMM-3081-11, 2011 FC 682, de Montigny.

[81] *M.C.I. v. Nagalingam, Panchalingam* (December 17, 2004), F.C., no. IMM-4340-03, 2004 FC 1757, O'Keefe.

[82] IRPA, s. 121.1(1) reads: ". . . "criminal organization" means a criminal organization as defined in subsection 467.1(1) of the *Criminal Code*." The previous definition of "criminal organization" found in s. 121(2) of the IRPA has been repealed.

[83] *Sittampalam, supra*, footnote 14. In *Sittampalam, Jothiravi v. M.P.S.E.P.* (September 19, 2006), F.C., no. IMM-7293-05, 2006 FC 1118, O'Reilly, the Court said the Immigration Division made an error in ordering continued detention because it did not consider that after five years in detention, the gang of which the person concerned had been a leader was essentially defunct.

[84] IRPA, s. 58(1.1), which refers to a review under s. 57.1(1). This provision removes the Immigration Division's jurisdiction to consider the factors enumerated in the IRPR, s. 248, at the 14-day detention review.

[85] IRPA, s. 58(4). At present there are no prescribed conditions in the IRPR.

Other Relevant Legislation

2.2 — Flight Risk

2.2.1 The Immigration Division may order the continued detention of a permanent resident or a foreign national if the person "is unlikely to appear for examination, an admissibility hearing, removal from Canada, or at a proceeding that could lead to the making of a removal order by the Minister under section 44(2)."[86]

2.2.2 Members must consider the following prescribed factors[87] in the IRPR when determining flight risk:

- being a fugitive from justice in a foreign jurisdiction in relation to an offence that, if committed in Canada, would constitute an offence under an Act of Parliament;
- voluntary compliance with any previous departure order;
- voluntary compliance with any previously required appearance at an immigration or criminal proceeding;
- previous compliance with any conditions imposed in respect of entry, release or a stay of removal;
- any previous avoidance of examination or escape from custody, or any previous attempt to do so;
- involvement with a people smuggling or trafficking in persons operation that would likely lead the person to not appear for a measure referred to in paragraph 244(a) of the IRPR or to be vulnerable to being influenced or coerced by an organization involved in such an operation to not appear for such a measure;
- the existence of strong ties to a community in Canada.

2.2.3 The prescribed factors in the IRPR are not exhaustive. In determining whether a person is a flight risk and potentially not suitable for release, the member should consider such factors as the person's access to a significant amount of wealth, previous use of false identity documents, prior use of aliases, prior attempts to hide their presence in Canada and a lack of credibility.[88]

2.2.4 As is the case when considering the issue of danger to the public, when determining flight risk members may consider the fact that the person was granted bail by a court of law, but they are not bound by a decision of a court to release and must come to their own conclusions taking into account all the facts in the case.

2.2.5 In the case of designated foreign nationals who were 16 years of age or older on the day of the arrival that is the subject of the designation in question, at the 14-day detention

---

[86] IRPA, s. 58(1)(b).

[87] IRPR, s. 245.

[88] *Li, supra*, footnote 13. In *S.G.C. v. Oraki, Ali Reza* (April 25, 2005), F.C., no. IMM-2187-05, 2005 FC 555, Blanchard, the person was considered a severe flight risk due to his record of past convictions, his use of false passports, and his total lack of credibility. The Court noted that there was a very good chance he would fail to comply with conditions of release and fail to report as required.

review the Immigration Division must consider only the prescribed grounds relating to the relevant ground for detention, and may not consider any other factors.[89]

2.2.6 If the Immigration Division orders the release of the designated foreign national who was 16 years of age or older on the day of the arrival that is the subject of the designation in question, it must impose any condition that is prescribed in the IRPR.[90]

2.3 — Minister Inquiring into Security, Violations of Human or International Rights, Criminality, Serious Criminality or Organized Criminality

2.3.1 Members of the Immigration Division may order the continued detention of a permanent resident or a foreign national if they are satisfied that the Minister is taking necessary steps to inquire into a reasonable suspicion that they are inadmissible on grounds of security, violating human or international rights, criminality, serious criminality or organized criminality.[91]

2.3.2 It is up to the Minister to satisfy the member that the Minister is taking necessary steps to investigate their suspicion relating to security, violating human or international rights, criminality, serious criminality or organized criminality.

2.3.3 The question that must be answered by the member is not whether the evidence relied upon by the Minister is true or compelling, but whether that evidence is reasonably capable of supporting the Minister's suspicion of potential inadmissibility. It is for the Minister to decide what further investigatory steps are needed. The member's supervisory jurisdiction on this issue is limited to examining whether the proposed steps have the potential to uncover relevant evidence bearing on the Minister's suspicion and to ensure that the Minister is conducting an ongoing investigation in good faith.[92]

2.3.4 There are no prescribed factors for this ground of detention in the IRPR. In the case of designated foreign nationals who were 16 years of age or older on the day of the arrival that is the subject of the designation in question, at the 14-day detention review the Immigration Division may not consider any other factors.[93]

---

[89] IRPA, s. 58(1.1), which refers to a review under s. 57.1(1). This provision removes the Immigration Division's jurisdiction to consider the factors enumerated in the IRPR, s. 248, at the 14-day detention review.

[90] IRPA, s. 58(4). At present there are no prescribed conditions in the IRPR.

[91] IRPA, s. 58(1)(c). A permanent resident or foreign national may be detained pursuant to this ground only on entry into Canada. See IRPA, s. 55(3)(b). Given the wording in s. 58(2) of the IRPA, the Immigration Division cannot order detention on this ground where the person is not already in immigration detention.

[92] *Canada (Citizenship and Immigration) v. X*, [2011] 1 F.C.R. 493, 2010 FC 112. The Court also stated: "It is not the role of the IRB to dictate how the Minister's ongoing investigation should be conducted. The Minister is entitled to a reasonable time to complete the admissibility investigation."

[93] IRPA, s. 58(1.1), which refers to a review under s. 57.1(1). This provision removes the Immigration Division's jurisdiction to consider the factors enumerated in the IRPR, s. 248, at the 14-day detention review.

2.3.5 If the Immigration Division orders the release of the designated foreign national who was 16 years of age or older on the day of the arrival that is the subject of the designation in question, it must impose any condition that is prescribed in the IRPR.[94]

2.4 — Identity of Foreign National Not Established (other than a Designated Foreign National 16 years of age or older on the day of the arrival that is the subject of the designation)

2.4.1 The Immigration Division may order the continued detention of a foreign national if there is evidence that the Minister is of the opinion that the identity of the foreign national has not been, but may be, established and the person has not reasonably cooperated with the Minister by providing relevant information for the purpose of establishing their identity, or the Minister is making reasonable efforts to establish their identity.[95] Only a foreign national other than a designated foreign national who was 16 years of age or older on the day of the arrival that is the subject of the designation in question may be detained under this ground.

2.4.2 It is not for the Immigration Division to determine whether the identity of the foreign national has been established as this is solely for the Minister to determine.[96] Once the Minister has indicated an opinion that the identity of the foreign national has not been established, the key issues left for the member to determine are whether the foreign national has reasonably cooperated with the Minister by providing relevant information for the purpose of establishing their identity, or whether the Minister is making reasonable efforts to establish the identity of the foreign national. Even if either of these latter two conditions has been met, the member must still consider the additional factors in section 248 of the IRPR.[97]

2.4.3 The obligation to establish one's identity rests first and always with the foreign national, and not the Minister. The Minister's obligation is to make reasonable efforts. Neither has the complete onus of proof, neither can sit back and do nothing. The determination of "reasonable efforts" is conditioned to some extent by the efforts of the foreign national. This is over and above the obligation to not obstruct and to cooperate. The member must make a qualitative evaluation of the efforts on the part of both parties.

---

[94] IRPA, s. 58(4). At present there are no prescribed conditions in the IRPR.

[95] IRPA, s. 58(1)(d). Given the wording in s. 58(2) of the IRPA, the Immigration Division cannot order detention on this ground where the person is not already in immigration detention.

[96] In *M.C.I. v. Singh, Ravinder* (November 23, 2004), F.C., no. IMM-1468-04, 2004 FC 1634, Blais, the Court found that the Immigration Division crossed the line as the discretion regarding the validity of documents belongs to the Minister, not the member. See also *M.C.I. v. Gill, Randheer Singh* (November 28, 2003), F.C., no. IMM-4191-02, 2003 FC 1398, Lemieux; *M.C.I, v. Mwamba, Junior* (September 8, 2003), F.C., no. IMM-4190-02, 2003 FC 1042, Blais; *M.C.I. v. Bains, Avtar Singh* (January 5, 1999), F.C.T.D., no. IMM-5215-97, Pinard.

[97] IRPR, s. 248. In *Gill, supra*, footnote 44, in considering whether identity of the foreign national had been established under s. 58(1)(d) of the IRPA, the Court noted that once it is determined there are grounds for detention, the Immigration Division must examine the factors provided for in s. 248 of the IRPR, namely alternatives to detention.

Members should focus on the reasonableness of what had been done and was intended to be done in the future, and not on what they thought should have been done.[98]

2.4.4 Members must exercise much caution when considering release of persons where there is evidence that the Minister is of the opinion that their identity has not been established. While a lack of identity is an important consideration, it does not mean that a member may not consider alternatives to detention.[99] If a member is considering release in these circumstances, the imposition of appropriate terms and conditions of release should be instituted.

2.4.5 Members of the Immigration Division must consider the following prescribed factors[100] when determining whether the foreign national has reasonably cooperated with the Minister or if the Minister is making reasonable efforts to establish identity. These prescribed factors, however, are not exhaustive:

- the foreign national's cooperation in providing evidence of their identity, or assisting the Department of Citizenship and Immigration in obtaining evidence of their identity, in providing the date and place of their birth as well as the names of their mother and father or providing detailed information on the itinerary they followed in travelling to Canada or in completing an application for a travel document;

- in the case of a foreign national who makes a claim for refugee protection, the possibility of obtaining identity documents or information without divulging personal information to government officials of their country of nationality or, if there is no country of nationality, their country of former habitual residence;

- the destruction of identity or travel documents, or the use of fraudulent documents in order to mislead the Department, and the circumstances under which the foreign national acted;

- the provision of contradictory information with respect to identity at the time of an application to the Department;

- the existence of documents that contradict information from the foreign national with respect to their identity.

2.5 — Identity of Designated Foreign National Not Established Where the Designated Foreign National Is 16 Years of Age or Older On the Day of the Arrival That is the Subject of the Designation

2.5.1 The Immigration Division must order the continued detention of a designated foreign national who was 16 years of age or older on the day of the arrival that is the subject of the designation in question if the Minister is of the opinion that their identity has not

Other Relevant Legislation

---

[98] *M.C.I. v. X* (November 5, 2010), F.C., no. IMM-5427-10, 2010 FC 1095, Phelan. In assessing the reasonableness of the Minister's efforts to establish identity, the Immigration Division should consider whether those steps are rationally connected to the purpose of the provision, i.e., whether they have the potential to uncover relevant evidence, and whether the Minister is acting in good faith.

[99] *M.C.I. v. B046* (July 14, 2011), F.C., no. IMM-5414-10, 2011 FC 877, Snider.

[100] IRPR, s. 247(1).

been established.[101] At the 14-day detention review the Immigration Division may not consider any other factors,[102] except for the prescribed factors relating to the relevant ground for detention.[103]

2.5.2 It is not for the Immigration Division to determine whether the identity of the designated foreign national who was 16 years of age or older on the day of the arrival that is the subject of the designation in question has been established as this is solely for the Minister to determine. The Immigration Division must only consider the Minister's opinion as to whether identity has been established.[104] The Immigration Division does not determine whether the designated foreign national reasonably cooperated with the Minister by providing relevant information for the purpose of establishing their identity, or whether the Minister is making reasonable efforts to establish the identity of the designated foreign national.

2.5.3 If the Immigration Division orders the release of the designated foreign national who was 16 years of age or older on the day of the arrival that is the subject of the designation in question, it must impose any condition that is prescribed in the IRPR.[105]

3. — Other Factors

3.1 — General

3.1.1 Parliament has required that the reasons for detention be reviewed at regular intervals[106] but it has not limited the total length of the detention period. In deciding whether to order continued detention or release, members of the Immigration Division will be guided by the legislation and certain general principles arising from the case law.

---

[101] IRPA, s. 58(1)(e).

[102] IRPA, s. 58(1.1), which refers to a review under s. 57.1(1). This provision removes the Immigration Division's jurisdiction to consider the factors enumerated in the IRPR, s. 248, at the 14-day review.

[103] It appears that the prescribed factors for "identity not established" in IRPR, s. 247, apply only to cases under IRPA, s. 58(1)(d), as they relate to such things as foreign national's cooperation in providing evidence of their identity. For cases described IRPA, s. 58(1)(e), the only issue is whether the Minister is of the opinion that the identity of the foreign national has not been established.

[104] IRPA, s. 58(1)(e).

[105] IRPA, s. 58(4). At present there are no prescribed conditions in the IRPR.

[106] IRPA, s. 57. However, as described earlier, in the case of a designated foreign national, IRPA, ss. 57.1 and 58(1)(e) and (1.1), provide different time limits for holding detention reviews and different considerations for ordering release from detention.

3.1.2 If a member determines that there are grounds for detention, the following prescribed factors[107] — also known as the *Sahin*[108] factors — must be considered before a decision is made to continue detention or order release:

- the reason for detention;
- the length of time in detention;
- whether there are any elements that can assist in determining the length of time that detention is likely to continue and, if so, that length of time;
- any unexplained delays or unexplained lack of diligence caused by the Department or the person concerned;
- the existence of alternatives to detention.

3.1.3 The weight to be placed on each of these factors will depend on the circumstances of the case.[109] These factors are not exhaustive of all the considerations that the member must consider.

3.1.4 The detention of a person under the IRPA is not for the purpose of punishment, but rather a concern that the person is a danger to the public, will not appear for examination, an admissibility hearing or removal, or concerns over security, criminality and identity.[110] However, detention, even for valid reasons, cannot be indefinite. Detention generally under the IRPA is not indefinite because it must be reviewed on a regular basis.[111]

---

[107] IRPR, s. 248.

[108] *Sahin v. Canada (Minister of Citizenship and Immigration)*, [1995] 1 F.C. 214 (T.D.); appeal dismissed in *Sahin, Bektas v. M.C.I.* (June 8, 1995), F.C.A., no. A-575-94, Stone, MacGuigan, Robertson. The Court provided a list of factors which it said was not exhaustive of all the considerations that a decision-maker must consider when deciding to order continued detention or release in the immigration context. These factors have been codified in s. 248 of the IRPR. As noted in *B046, supra*, footnote 47, the purpose of s. 248 is to address the Charter issues that can arise from an indefinite detention.

[109] *Sahin, supra*, footnote 56. The Court noted that "Parliament has dealt with the right of society to be protected from those who pose a danger to society and the right of Canada to control who enters and remains in this country. Against these interests must be weighted the liberty interest of the individual."

[110] IRPA, s. 58.

[111] IRPA, s. 57. In the decision of *Charkaoui v. Canada (Citizenship and Immigration)*, [2007] 1 S.C.R. 350, 2007 SCC 9, the Supreme Court of Canada considered the scheme of review for a person detained pursuant to a security certificate. Detention under a certificate is justified on the basis of a continuing threat to national security or to the safety of any person. The Court concluded that "extended periods of detention under the certificate provisions of the *IRPA* do not violate sections 7 and 12 of the Charter if accompanied by a process that provides regular opportunities for review of detention, taking into account all relevant factors." The five factors identified are almost identical in wording to the *Sahin* factors and also correspond to the prescribed factors in s. 248 of the IRPR. However, in, *B147, supra*, footnote 8, the Court held that in the absence of any reasonable certainty as to when the Pre-Removal Risk Assessment (PRRA) process might conclude,

3.2 — Reason for Detention

3.2.1 There is a stronger case for continuing a long detention when an individual is considered a danger to the public as opposed to the concern that the person would not appear for removal.[112] However, a person may be detained when the issue is one of flight risk only.[113]

3.3 — Length of Time in Detention

3.3.1 Lengthy detention does not mean indefinite detention.[114] The case law does not specify a time period as to what constitutes "indefinite detention." When determining whether to order continued detention, even in cases where detention has been lengthy, members must consider all applicable factors and all the circumstances of the case, including the length of the person's detention.[115]

3.3.2 Lengthy detention, even for a period greater than two years, is one factor to consider, and will not by itself support a finding of release if there are other reasons to support continued detention.[116] For example, if the person has been involved in criminal activity that involves violence and weapons or other offences referred to in the IRPR, and the member determines that the imposition of strict conditions of release will not sufficiently negate the danger to the public, this will likely support an order for continued detention, even in circumstances where the person has already been in detention for a lengthy period.

3.4 — Elements to Assist in Determining Length of Detention

3.4.1 If detention under the IRPA has been lengthy and there are still certain steps that must be taken in the immigration context, if valid reasons still remain to order continued detention, such as flight risk or danger to the public, an order for continued detention does not constitute indefinite detention.[117]

---

the existence of 30-day detention reviews did not save the detention from being characterized as indefinite in that case.

[112] *Sahin, supra*, footnote 56.

[113] *Li, supra*, footnote 13.

[114] *M.C.I. v. Liu, Xiaoquan* (November 20, 2008), F.C., no. IMM-3745-08, 2008 FC 1297, Lutfy.

[115] *Sahin, supra*, footnote 56. See also *Panahi-Dargahlloo, Hamid v. M.C.I.* (October 30, 2009), F.C., no. IMM-4335-08, 2009 FC 1114, Mandamin.

[116] *Kidane, Derar v. M.C.I.* (July 11, 1997), F.C.T.D., no. IMM-2044-96, Jerome. In that case the person concerned was a convicted drug trafficker and had been convicted of at least 15 offences. In *Singh*, 2001 FCT 954, *supra*, footnote 28, the Court, in granting a stay of release, said that despite the one-year period of time that the person had spent in detention, it cannot overcome the finding that he is a danger to the public.

[117] *Sahin, supra*, footnote 56. The Court noted that the right of liberty is enshrined in section 7 of the Charter and a person may not be deprived of their rights to liberty except in accordance with the principles of fundamental justice. The Court also said that deten-

3.4.2 The length of time required for a matter to be dealt with by the Federal Court or for other recourses is generally a "neutral" factor.[118] While a person has a right to exhaust every legal avenue that is available, "he may not claim that on the basis of his own actions, that he will not be removed from Canada within a reasonable time."[119] Even where the anticipated length of time in detention may be lengthy until all proceedings are concluded, this alone is not considered to be indefinite detention and is not an infringement of section 7 of the Charter; rather, it is one factor to consider.[120] If it is anticipated that further litigation in the Federal Court or further remedies available under the IRPA are expected before removal can take place, the person's detention may be continued and expedited time frames for subsequent steps can be achieved by the parties.[121]

3.4.3 The timeframe for determining the anticipated length of detention are the current proceedings that are already in existence, and not an estimate of what future proceedings may be brought by the person. The member must make a decision based on the proceedings that are underway, or pending, at the time of the detention review, and not on an estimate of the person's anticipated pursuit of all available processes under the IRPA and at the Federal Court.[122] Members are not obliged to come to a precise finding in terms of the exact time for proceedings that are underway or pending.[123]

3.5 — Unexplained Delays or Unexplained Lack of Diligence

3.5.1 Members must determine whether the parties have caused any delay or have not been as diligent as reasonably possible. If a party has delayed in filing submissions re-

---

tion decisions under the former *Immigration Act* must be made with section 7 Charter considerations in mind.

[118] *Canada (Minister of Citizenship and Immigration) v. Li*, [2010] 2 F.C.R. 433, 2009 FCA 85. The Court said at para. 38: "to the extent that detainees or the Government are diligently exercising recourses under the IRPA that are reasonable in the circumstances or resorting to reasonable Charter challenges, the ensuing delays should not count against either party."

[119] *Ahani, Mansour v. M.C.I.* (July 11, 2000), F.C.A., no. A-160-99, Linden, Rothstein, Malone. Reported: *Ahani v. Canada (Minister of Citizenship and Immigration)* (2000), 3 Imm. L.R. (3d) 159 (F.C.A.).

[120] *San Vicente, Roberto v. M.C.I.* (January 27, 1998), F.C.T.D., no. IMM-2615-97, MacKay. Reported: *San Vicente v. Canada (Minister of Citizenship and Immigration* (1998), 42 Imm.L.R. (2d) 138 (F.C.T.D.).

[121] *Liu, supra*, footnote 62. The Court said: "with the cooperation of counsel, any resulting Federal Court proceedings can and should be heard in at least as timely a fashion as this one. In many cases, the most satisfactory course of action will be to detain the individual but expedite the immigration proceedings, even where the person who is a flight risk may not pose a public danger."

[122] *Li, supra*, footnote 66. In this case the Court said that it was an error for the Immigration Division to speculate on potential proceedings that the parties could bring rather than making its estimation on actual pending proceedings.

[123] *Muhammad, Arshad v. M.P.S.E.P.* (February 27, 2013), F.C., no. IMM-844-13, 2013 FC 203, Martineau.

garding a danger opinion or did not file an appeal of the deportation order in a timely manner, if a reasonable explanation for the delay or lack of diligence is not provided, this should count against the offending party.[124] However, this is merely one factor to consider in determining whether the person's detention should be continued. Even if the delay caused by one of the parties will result in a lengthier detention, if the person is a danger to the public based on prior criminality and the imposition of strict conditions of release will not neutralize the danger, this will weigh in favour of continued detention.

3.5.2 A person's lack of cooperation is also a factor that favours continued detention, for example, a refusal to sign a travel document so that removal can be carried out.[125]

3.6 — Alternatives to Detention

3.6.1 The IRPA gives members of the Immigration Division the discretion to order the release of a permanent resident or a foreign national and to impose any conditions that it deems necessary,[126] subject to the provisions of the IRPA governing designated foreign nationals who are 16 years of age or older on the day of the arrival that is the subject of the designation in question.[127] Before ordering release, members must consider whether the imposition of certain conditions will sufficiently neutralize the danger to the public or ensure that the person will appear for examination, an admissibility hearing or removal from Canada.

3.6.2 On occasion, the parties will have come to an agreement on the conditions of release before the detention review and will submit the agreement to the member at the hearing. The member may endorse it if the member is of the opinion that based on the nature and degree of risk posed the conditions are sufficient to neutralize the risk. The member is entitled to reject the joint submission by the parties and either order continued detention or order release on other conditions that are deemed to be more appropriate.

3.6.3 When deciding whether to release, members must consider the availability, effectiveness and appropriateness of alternatives to detention,[128] such as release on an undertaking to comply with conditions imposed, or on the payment of a deposit or the posting of a guarantee for compliance with the conditions. Conditions could include periodic re-

---

[124] *Sahin, supra*, footnote 56. See also *Kidane, supra*, note 64.

[125] *M.C.I. v. Kamail, Nariman Zangeneh* (April 8, 2002), F.C.T.D., no. IMM-6474-00, 2002 FCT 381, O'Keefe. In this case the Court found that the person concerned had been the sole cause of the delay because he refused to sign the travel document that would have led to his removal. Despite the indefinite nature of the detention, the Court did not uphold the decision to release because "to hold otherwise would be to encourage deportees to be as uncooperative as possible as a means to circumvent Canada's refugee and immigration system."

[126] IRPA, s. 58(3). While a party may apply to the Immigration Division to vary the terms and conditions of release, the Division must give the other party the opportunity to make submissions as to the appropriateness of new terms of release. See *M.P.S.E.P. v. Sittampalam, Jothiravi* (August 31, 2009), F.C., no. IMM-5058-08, 2009 FC 863, Tannenbaum.

[127] IRPA, ss. 58(1.1) and (4).

[128] *Sahin, supra*, footnote 56.

porting, confinement to a particular location or geographic area, the requirement to report changes of address or telephone number, and detention in a form that could be less restrictive to the individual.

3.6.4 Members are required to consider the circumstances of a proposed bondsperson and the bondsperson's relationship to the person. It is up to the detained person to satisfy the member that the proposed bondsperson is acceptable in the circumstances.[129] In deciding on the appropriateness of a potential bondsperson, members must consider whether the proposed bondsperson is willing to supervise and able to influence the person concerned,[130] and whether they are in a position to monitor the activities of the person concerned.[131] Members must also consider the length of time that the bondsperson has known the person concerned in detention and the knowledge that the bondsperson has of the background history of the person concerned.[132] In determining the amount of the bond, members should assess what impact the loss of the amount will have on a particular bondsperson in ensuring compliance with the terms and conditions of release.[133]

3.6.5 The failure to allow for the cross-examination of a bondsperson upon request by the Minister could constitute a breach of natural justice and therefore it is advisable to allow such examination upon request.[134]

3.6.6 If detention has been or could be for a long period of time members may consider whether the risk may be neutralized by the imposition of strict terms and conditions. Some of these strict conditions may include a curfew, refraining from using a cell phone or a computer, house arrest, wearing of an electronic bracelet to track movements, al-

---

[129] *M.C.I. v. Zhang, Zu Fa* (May 23, 2001), F.C.T.D., no. IMM-2499-01, 2001 FCT 521, Pelletier. Reported: *Canada (Minister of Citizenship and Immigration) v. Zhang*, [2001] 4 F.C. 173 (T.D.).

[130] *M.P.S.E.P. v. Castillo, Saul* (October 8, 2009), F.C., no. IMM-4914-09, 2009 FC 1022, Lemieux. In *B147, supra*, footnote 8, the Court noted, at para. 57, that an increased length of detention "does not transform an unsuitable bondsperson into a suitable one. Nor does it mitigate the assessment of the [detainees's] flight risk . . .".

[131] *M.P.S.E.P. v. Berisha, Alfred* (September 20, 2012), F.C., no. IMM-8716-12, 2012 FC 1100, Zinn. In this case the Court held that the release order must set out with sufficient specificity the terms and conditions of electronic monitoring, including the oversight expected of the bondsperson.

[132] *M.S.P.P.C. v. Al Achkar, Talal* (July 14, 2010), F.C., no. IMM-4049-10, 2010 FC 744, Shore; *B147, supra*, footnote 8.

[133] *M.C.I. v. B001* (May 3, 2012), F.C., no. IMM-2367-12, 2012 FC 523, Snider.

[134] *M.C.I. v. Ke, Yi Le* (April 12, 2000), F.C.T.D., no. IMM-1425-00, Reed. Reported: *Canada (Minister of Citizenship and Immigration) v. Ke* (2000), 5 Imm.L.R. (3d) 159 (F.C.T.D.). In *Zhang, supra*, footnote 77, the Court held that the adjudicator was correct in rejecting the Minister's request for cross-examination made after the decision regarding release was announced,

lowing entry into the person's residence at all times by immigration officials and the restriction of contact with certain individuals.[135]

3.6.7 If, however, the imposition of very strict conditions will not contain or diminish the danger to the public, these circumstances do not weigh in favour of release.[136]

3.7 — Minors

3.7.1 A minor should be detained only as a measure of last resort. Members should consider a number of factors when determining whether to continue detention or release of a minor, including the best interests of the child.[137]

3.7.2 Members must consider the following prescribed factors[138] in the IRPR when determining the detention of a minor:

- the availability of alternative arrangements with local child-care agencies or child protection services for the care and protection of the minor children;
- the anticipated length of detention;
- the risk of continued control by the human smugglers or traffickers who brought the children to Canada;
- the type of detention facility envisaged and the conditions of detention;
- the availability of accommodation that allows for the segregation of the minor children from adult detainees who are not the parent of or the adult legally responsible for the detained minor children; and
- the availability of services in the detention facility, including education, counseling and recreation.

3.7.3 In addition, when considering whether to release or continue detention of a foreign national who is a minor — other than a designated foreign national who was 16 years of age or older on the day of the arrival that is the subject of the designation in question — under paragraph 58(1)(d) of the IRPA because identity may not have been established, factors that may apply with respect to an adult will not have an adverse impact with respect to minors.[139]

---

[135] *Mahjoub, Mohamed Zeki v. M.C.I.* (February 15, 2007), F.C., no. DES-1-00, 2007 FC 171, Mosley; *Harkat v. Canada (Minister of Citizenship and Immigration)*, [2007] 1 F.C.R. 321 (F.C.); 2006 FC 628.

[136] *Almrei, Hassan v. M.C.I. and M.P.S.E.P.* (October 5, 2007), F.C., no. DES-5-01, 2007 FC 1025, Lemieux.

[137] IRPA, s. 60.

[138] IRPR, s. 249.

[139] IRPR, s. 247(2). The factors listed in the s. 247(1)(a) relating to the establishment of identity that must not have an adverse impact in relation to minors are "the foreign national's cooperation in providing evidence of their identity, or assisting the Department in obtaining evidence of their identity, in providing the date and place of their birth as well as the names of their mother and father or providing detailed information on the itinerary they followed in travelling to Canada or in completing an application for a travel document."

4. — Statutory Timeframes

4.1 — Statutory Timeframes

4.1.1 The statutory scheme for the holding of detention reviews is set out in the IRPA.[140] The timing of detention reviews must reflect the statutory scheme as set out in the IRPA as closely as possible. While the Immigration Division has some discretion[141] to postpone or adjourn a detention review or reserve a decision with respect to the issue of detention, that discretion should be exercised very cautiously. There is an obligation on the Immigration Division to conduct a detention review and deliver a decision within the timeframes stated in the IRPA.

4.1.2 The member may conduct a detention review outside the timeframes set out in the IRPA only in limited circumstances to ensure a fair hearing. An example where a member may exercise discretion to vary the timeframes is where an interpreter is not available until the day after the scheduled detention review. Other examples where variance of the timeframes may be acceptable is where counsel asks for an additional day to prepare in cases involving voluminous and complicated evidence or where a bondsperson is not available until the next day. Any variation in the timeframes, however, should be strictly limited to the time needed to conduct a fair hearing.

4.1.3 In very limited circumstances it may be difficult for a member to give a decision following the receipt of voluminous evidence and extensive submissions by the parties or where the member is departing from previous decisions on detention. The member may reserve the decision for a brief period of time, as necessary, to consider the evidence and submissions.

4.1.4 If the Federal Court has ordered a stay of a previous release order and has not made any order as to whether or not the Immigration Division should continue to conduct detention reviews pending the outcome of the leave application and judicial review, the

---

[140] Section 57 of the IRPA provides that "within 48 hours after a permanent resident or a foreign national is taken into detention, or without delay afterward, the Immigration Division must review the reasons for the continued detention." The same section in the IRPA also provides that the Immigration Division must review the reasons for the continued detention at least once during the seven days following the preceding review and at least once during each 30-day period following each previous review.

However, in the case of designated foreign nationals who were 16 years of age or older on the day of arrival that is the subject of the designation in question. s. 57.1 of the IRPA provides that "the Immigration Division must review the reasons for their continued detention within 14 days after the day on which that person is taken into detention, or without delay afterward." Subsequently, "[t]he Immigration Division must review again the reasons for their continued detention on the expiry of six months following the conclusion of the previous review and may not do so before the expiry of that period."

[141] *Pierre v. Minister of Manpower and Immigration*, [1978] 2 F.C. 849 (F.C.A.). In this case the Court noted that if there is no specific rule governing the manner in which the tribunal should exercise its discretion to grant an adjournment, the decision to grant an adjournment is a discretionary matter for the tribunal. The tribunal must make its decision, however, taking into account the principles of natural justice.

Immigration Division should conduct detention reviews according to the timeframes in the IRPA, while taking into account the Order of the Federal Court.[142]

5. — Enquiries

For information, contact:

> Director, Policy and Procedures Directorate
> Operations Branch
> Minto Place — Canada Building
> 344 Slater Street, 14th floor
> Ottawa, Ontario K1A 0K1
> Fax: 613-952-9083

Available in English and French on the IRB's Web site at www.irb-cisr.gc.ca

Approval: Signed "Brian Goodman"	June 5, 2013
Chairperson	Date

Guideline 3 — Child Refugee Claimants: Procedural and Evidentiary Issues

Guidelines Issued by the Chairperson Pursuant to Section 65(3) of the *Immigration Act*

Children, persons under 18 years of age,[143] can make a claim to be a Convention refugee and have that claim determined by the Convention Refugee Determination Division (CRDD) of the Immigration and Refugee Board (IRB). *The Immigration Act does not set*

---

[142] *M.P.S.E.P. v. Hassan, Abdurahman Ibrahim* (November 23, 2012), F.C., no. IMM-11131-12, 2012 FC 1357, Russell. In this case the Court had ordered the release order stayed until the final determination of the application for leave and judicial review or until the next scheduled detention review. See also *M.C.I. v. B386* (February 17, 2011), F.C., no. IMM-472-11, 2011 FC 175, Blanchard.

[143] For the purpose of these *Guidelines*, "child" refers to any person under the age of 18 who is the subject of proceedings before the CRDD.

Section 69(4) provides special protection to refugee claimants under the age of 18 in the form of a designated representative in proceedings before the CRDD. Section 69(4) of the *Immigration Act*, as enacted by R.S.C. 1985 (4th Supp.), c. 28, s. 18, provides in part as follows:

> Where a person who is the subject of proceedings before the Refugee Division is under eighteen years of age ... the Division shall designate another person to represent that person in the proceedings.

> The age of 18 is consistent with the provisions of the *Convention on the Rights of the Child* (hereafter the CRC) which provides in Article 1 that "for the purposes of the present Convention, a child means every human being below the age of eighteen years unless, under the law applicable to the child, majority is attained earlier."

out specific procedures or criteria for dealing with the claims of children different from those applicable to adult refugee claimants, except for the designation of a person to represent the child in CRDD proceedings.[144] The procedures currently being followed by the CRDD for an adult claimant may not always be suitable for a child claimant.

The international community has recognized that refugee children have different requirements from adult refugees when they are seeking refugee status. The United Nations *Convention on the Rights of the Child* (CRC)[145] has recognized the obligation of a government to take measures to ensure that a child seeking refugee status receives appropriate protection.[146] In addition, the United Nations High Commissioner for Refugees (UNHCR) has issued guidelines on the protection and care of refugee children.[147]

There are three broad categories of children who make refugee claims at the IRB. In all three categories, there are procedural and evidentiary issues which affect the child claimant:

1. The *first category* consists of *children who arrive in Canada at the same time as their parents or some time thereafter*. In most cases, the parents also seek refugee status. In these situations, the child should be considered an "accompanied" child. If the child arrives at the same time as the parents, then his or her claim is usually heard jointly[148] with the parents but a separate refugee determination is made.

2. The *second category* consists of *children who arrive in Canada with, or are being looked after in Canada by, persons who purport to be members of the child's family*. If the CRDD is satisfied that these persons are related to the child, then the child should be considered an "accompanied" child. If the CRDD is not satisfied as to the family relationship, then the child should be considered an "unaccompanied" child.

3. The *third category* consists of *children who are alone in Canada without their parents or anyone who purports to be a family member*. For example, an older child may be living on his or her own or a child may be in the care of a friend of the child's family. These children should be considered "unaccompanied".

---

[144] *Ibid.*

[145] The CRC was adopted by the United Nations General Assembly on 20 November 1989. It was signed by Canada on 28 May 1990 and ratified on 13 December 1991, and came into force on 12 January 1992.

[146] See Article 22 of the CRC:

State Parties shall take appropriate measures to ensure that a child who is seeking refugee status or who is considered a refugee in accordance with applicable international or domestic law and procedures shall, whether unaccompanied or accompanied by his or her parents or by any other person, receive appropriate protection ...

[147] *"Refugee Children — Guidelines on Protection and Care"*, UNHCR, Geneva 1994.

[148] Rule 10(2) of the *Convention Refugee Determination Division Rules*, SOR/93-45. These Rules also provide for claims to be heard separately if a joined hearing is likely to cause an injustice.

Other Relevant Legislation

These *Guidelines* will address the specific procedural issue of the designation of a representative and the more general procedural issue of the steps to be followed in processing claims by unaccompanied children. The *Guidelines* will also address the evidentiary issues of eliciting evidence in a child's claim and assessing that evidence.

A. — Procedural Issues

I. — General Principle

In determining the procedure to be followed when considering the refugee claim of a child, the CRDD should give primary consideration to the "best interests of the child".

The "best interests of the child" principle has been recognized by the international community as a fundamental human right of a child.[149] In the context of these Guidelines, this right applies to the process to be followed by the CRDD. *The question to be asked when determining the appropriate process for the claim of a child is "what procedure is in the best interests of this child?"* With respect to the merits of the child's claim, all of the elements of the Convention refugee definition must be satisfied.[150]

The phrase "best interests of the child" is a broad term and the interpretation to be given to it will depend on the circumstances of each case. There are many factors which may affect the best interests of the child, such as the age, gender,[151] cultural background and past experiences of the child, and this multitude of factors makes a precise definition of the "best interests" principle difficult.[152]

---

[149] See Article 3(1) of the CRC:

> In all actions concerning children, whether undertaken by public or private social welfare institutions, courts of law, administrative authorities or legislative bodies, the best interests of the child shall be a primary consideration.

See also UNHCR Executive Committee Conclusion XXXVIII "Refugee Children", 1987:

> The Executive Committee ... [s]tressed that all action taken on behalf of refugee children must be guided by the principle of the best interests of the child ...

[150] In determining the child's fear of persecution, the international human rights instruments, such as the *Universal Declaration of Human Rights*, the *International Covenant on Civil and Political Rights*, the *International Covenant on Economic, Social and Cultural Rights* and the *Convention on the Rights of the Child*, should be considered in determining whether the harm which the child fears amounts to persecution.

[151] For female child refugee claimants, reference can also be made to the Chairperson's *Guidelines on Women Refugee Claimants Fearing Gender-Related Persecution*, Immigration and Refugee Board, Ottawa, Canada, March 9, 1993.

[152] Madame Justice McLachlin of the Supreme Court of Canada, in *Gordon v. Goertz* (May 2, 1996), no. 24622, Lamer, LaForest, L'Heureux-Dubé, Sopinka, Gonthier, Cory, McLachlin, Iacobucci, Major (S.C.C.), had occasion to discuss the interpretation to be given to the phrase "best interests of the child" and the difficulty with giving the phrase a concrete definition:

II. — Designated Representative

The *Immigration Act* requires[153] the designation of a representative for all child claimants. In cases where the child is accompanied by his or her parents, one of the parents is usually appointed as the designated representative of the child. This designation applies to *all* the "proceedings" of the refugee claim and not only to the hearing of the claim. The role of the designated representative is not the same as that of legal counsel.[154] In addition to the designated representative, the child has a right to be represented by legal or other counsel.[155]

There are certain *mandatory criteria* to apply when designating a representative:

- the person must be over 18 years of age;
- the person must have an appreciation of the nature of the proceedings;
- the person must not be in a conflict of interest situation with the child claimant such that the person must not act at the expense of the child's best interests;
- the person must be willing and able to fulfill the duties of a representative and to act in the "best interests of the child".

In addition, the linguistic and cultural background, age, gender and other personal characteristics of the designated representative are factors to consider.

The *duties* of the designated representative are as follows:

- to retain counsel;
- to instruct counsel or to assist the child in instructing counsel;
- to make other decisions with respect to the proceedings or to help the child make those decisions;
- to inform the child about the various stages and proceedings of the claim;
- to assist in obtaining evidence in support of the claim;
- to provide evidence and be a witness in the claim;
- to act in the best interests of the child.

The best interests of the child test has been characterized as "indeterminate" and "more useful as legal aspiration than as legal analysis"... The multitude of factors that may impinge on the child's best interest make a measure of indeterminacy inevitable. A more precise test would risk sacrificing the child's best interest to expediency and certainty.

[153] See *endnote 1*.

[154] Although legal counsel for the claimant may also be appointed as the designated representative, the roles of the two are distinct.

[155] Section 69(1) of the *Immigration Act,* as enacted by R.S.C. 1985 (4th Supp.), c. 28, s. 18, provides as follows:

In any proceedings before the Refugee Division ... the person who is the subject of the proceedings may, at that person's own expense, be represented by a barrister or solicitor or other counsel.

Other Relevant Legislation

Before designating a person as a representative for the child, the CRDD panel should inform the proposed designated representative of his or her duties and should make an assessment of the person's ability to fulfill those duties.

There may be situations where the person who was designated to be the representative ceases to be an appropriate representative of the child. For example, the person may prove unwilling or unable to make themselves available for pre-hearing conferences. In these situations, the CRDD should remove the person as designated representative[156] and designate another appropriate representative.

III. — Processing Claims of Unaccompanied Children

The fact that children claiming refugee status can be unaccompanied raises many unique concerns with respect to the processing of their claims. The UNHCR has recognized that this group of refugees, due to their age and the fact that they are unaccompanied, warrant special attention in the process of determining their claims to refugee status.[157]

The "best interests of the child" should be given primary consideration at all stages of the processing of these claims. This principle is reflected in the following procedures:

1. *Claims of unaccompanied children should be identified as soon as possible by Registry staff after referral to the CRDD.* The name of the child and any other relevant information should be referred to the provincial authorities responsible for child protection issues, if this has not already been done by Citizenship and Immigration Canada (CIC).[158] After referral, all notices of hearings and pre-hearing conferences should be forwarded to the provincial authority.

2. *The CRDD panel and Refugee Claim Officer (RCO) should be immediately assigned to the claim and, to the extent possible, the same individuals should retain responsibility for the claim until completion.* It may also be necessary in some cases to assign an interpreter to the claim as early as possible so that the child can develop a relationship of trust with the interpreter.[159] Before the panel, RCO and interpreter

---

[156] Section 69(1) of the *Immigration Act*, as enacted by R.S.C. 1985 (4th Supp.), c. 28, s. 18, provides as follows:

In any proceedings before the Refugee Division ... the person who is the subject of the proceedings may, at that person's own expense, be represented by a barrister or solicitor or other counsel.

[157] UNHCR Executive Committee Conclusion XXXVIII "Refugee Children", 1987:

The Executive Committee ... underlined the special situation of unaccompanied children and children separated from their parents, who are in the care of other families, including their needs as regards determination of their status ...

[158] An unaccompanied child claimant is by virtue of that status a child who may be at risk and the authority responsible for children at risk should be notified. Because CRDD proceedings are held in camera and disclosing information about the refugee claim of the child would involve releasing private information, the provisions of the *Privacy Act* (S.C. 1980-81-82-83, c. 111, Sch. II "1") must be complied with.

[159] An appropriate interpreter is vital to the processing of a refugee claim. It is important that the child trust the interpreter and that the interpreter be right for the child. The cul-

are assigned, consideration should be given to their experience in dealing with the claims of children.[160]

3. *The claim should be given scheduling and processing priority[161] because it is generally in the best interests of the child to have the claim processed as expeditiously as possible.* There may be circumstances, however, where in the best interests of the child the claim should be delayed. For example, if the child is having a great deal of difficulty adjusting to Canada, he or she may need more time before coming to the CRDD for a hearing.

4. *A designated representative for the child should be appointed as soon as possible following the assignment of the panel to the claim.* This designation would usually occur at the pre-hearing conference referred to below, but it may be done earlier. CRDD panels should refer to Section II above for guidelines on designating an appropriate representative. In determining whether a proposed representative is willing and able to act in the "best interests of the child", the panel should consider any relevant information received from the provincial authorities responsible for child protection as well as any relevant information from other reliable sources.

5. *A pre-hearing conference should be scheduled within 30 days of the receipt of the Personal Information Form (PIF).* The purposes of the conference would include assigning the designated representative (if this has not already been done), identifying the issues in the claim, identifying the evidence to be presented and determining what evidence the child is able to provide and the best way to elicit that evidence. Information from individuals, such as the designated representative, medical practitioners, social workers, community workers and teachers can be considered when determining what evidence the child is able to provide and the best way to obtain the evidence.

6. *In determining what evidence the child is able to provide and the best way to elicit this evidence, the panel should consider, in addition to any other relevant factors, the following: the age and mental development of the child both at the time of the hearing and at the time of the events about which they might have information; the capacity of the child to recall past events and the time that has elapsed since the events; and the capacity of the child to communicate his or her experiences.*

Other Relevant Legislation

---

tural and linguistic background, age, gender and other personal characteristics of an interpreter may be factors for consideration in selecting an appropriate interpreter for the child. See *"Working with Unaccompanied Minors in the Community: a family-based approach"*, UNHCR, 1994.

[160] In the context of interviewing children in emergency situations, the International Social Service in *"Unaccompanied Children in Emergencies"*, J. Williamson, A. Moser, 1987, indicated that persons interviewing unaccompanied children need experience in working with children and an understanding of how refugee situations affect children.

[161] The UNHCR document *"Refugee Children — Guidelines on Protection and Care"*, endnote 5 above, provides that "the refugee status determination must be made quickly... Keeping children in limbo regarding their status, hence their security and their future, can be harmful to them." (Page 100.)

B. — Evidentiary Issues

I. — Eliciting the Evidence

Whether accompanied or unaccompanied, a child claimant may be called upon to provide evidence through oral testimony about his or her claim.[162] Like an adult claimant, a child claimant also has a right to be heard in regard to his or her refugee claim.[163] An assessment should be made as to what evidence the child is able to provide and the best way to elicit that evidence from the child.

In general, children are not able to present evidence with the same degree of precision as adults with respect to context, timing, importance and details. They may be unable, for example, to provide evidence about the circumstances surrounding their past experiences or their fear of future persecution. In addition, children may manifest their fears differently from adults.

If the panel determines that a child is able to give oral evidence and that the panel needs to hear from the child, the following should be considered:

> 1. *The process which is to be followed should be explained to the child throughout the hearing to the extent possible, taking into account the age of the child.* In particular, the various participants and their roles at the hearing should be explained as well as the purpose of questioning the child and the sequence of questioning (that is, the fact that counsel normally questions first, followed by the RCO and then the panel).

---

[162] A child refugee claimant has a right to be present at his or her refugee proceedings. Section 69(2) of the *Immigration Act*, as enacted by R.S.C. 1985 (4th Supp.), c. 28, s. 18, provides that:

> (2) Subject to subsections (3) and (3.1), proceedings before the Refugee Division shall be held in the presence of the person who is the subject of the proceedings, wherever practicable ...

[163] Section 69.1(5)(a)(i) of the *Immigration Act*, as enacted by R.S.C. 1985 (4th Supp.), c. 28, s. 18, provides that:

> (5) At the hearing into a person's claim to be a Convention refugee, the Refugee Division
>
> (a) shall give
>
> > (i) the person a reasonable opportunity to present evidence, question witnesses and make representations ...

Further, Article 12 of the CRC provides that:

> 1. State Parties shall assure to the child who is capable of forming his or her own views the right to express those views freely in all matters affecting the child, the view of the child being given due weight in accordance with the age and maturity of the child.
>
> 2. For this purpose, the child shall in particular be provided the opportunity to be heard in any judicial and administrative proceeding affecting the child, either directly, or through a representative or an appropriate body, in a manner consistent with the procedural rules of national law.

2. *Before hearing testimony from a child, the panel should determine if the child understands the nature of an oath or affirmation to tell the truth and if the child is able to communicate evidence.*[164] If the child satisfies both of these criteria then he or she can take an oath or solemn affirmation. A child who does not satisfy these criteria can still provide unsworn testimony. The weight to be given to the unsworn testimony depends on the child's understanding of the obligation to be truthful and his or her ability to communicate evidence.

3. *The environment in which the child testifies should be informal.* It may be appropriate to use an interview-style room rather than a hearing room. It may also be appropriate to have an adult whom the child trusts present when the child is providing information about his or her claim. This person may or may not be the designated representative.[165]

4. *Questioning of a child should be done in a sensitive manner and should take into account the type of evidence the child may be able to provide.* Children may not know the specific circumstances that led to their flight from the country of origin and, even if they know the circumstances, they may not know the details of those circumstances.[166] The questions put to a child should be formulated in such a manner that the child will understand the question and be able to answer. Consideration should also be given to choosing the person who is best able to question the child.

5. *Even in an informal environment, some children may find it difficult to testify orally in front of decision-makers.* Where appropriate, the evidence of the child may also be obtained by using videotape evidence or an expert as a liaison between the CRDD and the child. For example, the panel may be able to indicate to a medical expert the questions which the panel would like the child to answer.

6. *The hearing should, if possible, conclude in one sitting. If this is not possible then the earliest possible resumption date should be scheduled.* Notwithstanding the desirability of concluding the hearing in one sitting, a child's possible need for breaks and adjournments should always be taken into consideration.

7. *During the course of the hearing, extensive use may be made of conferences with the hearing participants to resolve issues as they arise.* For example, the panel may hear some testimony on a particular issue from the child and then hold a conference with the hearing participants to determine what further testimony, if any, is required.

Other Relevant Legislation

---

[164] In the case of a nine-year-old citizen of Russia (CRDD V93-02093, Brisson, Neuenfeldt, May 4, 1994), the CRDD panel agreed that given the young age of the claimant, she would not be asked to swear an oath or make a solemn affirmation. When asked, the child indicated that she understood the necessity of telling the truth during her hearing and added that it was "not nice" to tell a lie. The CRDD found her evidence to be truthful.

[165] The UNHCR document *"Refugee Children — Guidelines on Protection and Care"*, endnote 5 above, states that arrangements should be made "to have a trusted adult accompany the child during the interviewing process, either a family member of the child, a friend or an appointed independent person." (Page 102.)

[166] As stated by the CRDD in T92-09383, Wolpert, Hunt, May 4, 1993, "[a] child might well not 'know' certain things: he is not privy to an adult's world."

In all cases, whether the child provides oral evidence or not, the following alternative or additional evidence may be considered:

- evidence from other family members in Canada or another country;
- evidence from other members of the child's community;
- evidence from medical personnel, teachers, social workers, community workers and others who have dealt with the child;
- documentary evidence of persons similarly situated to the child, or his or her group, and general country conditions.

II. — Assessing the Evidence

The CRDD is not bound by the technical rules of evidence and may base its determination on any evidence it considers credible or trustworthy in the circumstances of the case. When assessing the evidence presented in support of the refugee claim of a child, the panel should take note of the following:

1. If the child has given oral testimony, then the weight to be given to the testimony must be assessed. In determining the weight to be given, the panel should consider the opportunity the child had for observation, the capacity of the child to observe accurately and to express what he or she has observed, and the ability of the child to remember the facts as observed. These factors may be influenced by the age, gender[167] and cultural background of the child as well as other factors such as fear, memory difficulties, post-traumatic stress disorder and the child's perception of the process at the CRDD.[168]

2. A child claimant may not be able to express a subjective fear of persecution in the same manner as an adult claimant. Therefore, it may be necessary to put more weight on the objective rather than the subjective elements of the claim.[169] The Federal Court of Canada (Appeal Division) has said the following on this issue:

> ... I am loath to believe that a refugee status claim could be dismissed solely on the ground that as the claimant is a young child ... he or she was incapa-

---

[167] See endnote 9.

[168] With respect to the assessment of evidence of a child claimant, the CRDD panel in V92-00501, Burdett, Brisco, April, 1993, said as follows:

> I agree that a claimant who is a child may have some difficulty recounting the events which have led him or her to flee their country. Often the child claimant's parents will not have shared distressing events with the claimant, with the intention of protecting the child. As a result, the child claimant, in testifying at his or her refugee hearing, may appear to be vague and uninformed about important events which have led up to acts of persecution. Before a trier of fact concludes that a child claimant is not credible, the child's sources of knowledge, his or her maturity, and intelligence must be assessed. The severity of the persecution alleged must be considered and whether past events have traumatized the child and hindered his or her ability to recount details.

[169] The UNHCR document "*Refugee Children — Guidelines on Protection and Care*", endnote 5 above, provides that where a child is not mature enough to establish a well-

ble of experiencing fear the reasons for which clearly exist in objective terms.[170]

3. When assessing the evidence presented in the claim of a child refugee claimant, the panel may encounter gaps in the evidence. For example: a child may indicate that men in uniforms came to the house but not know what type of uniforms they were wearing or a child may not know the political views of his or her family. The child may, due to age, gender, cultural background or other circumstances, be unable to present evidence concerning every fact in support of the claim. In these situations, the panel should consider whether it is able to infer the details of the claim from the evidence presented.

Other Relevant Legislation

---

founded fear of persecution in the same way as an adult "it is necessary to examine in more detail objective factors, such as the characteristics of the group the child left with[,] the situation prevailing in the country of origin and the circumstances of family members, inside or outside the country of origin." (Page 100 - 101.) The same point is made in the UNHCR *Handbook on Procedures and Criteria for Determining Refugee Status* (Geneva, January 1979) which states in paragraph 217 that "it may be necessary to have a greater regard to certain objective factors."

[170] *Yusuf v. M.E.I.*, [1992] 1 F.C. 629, per Hugessen, J.A.

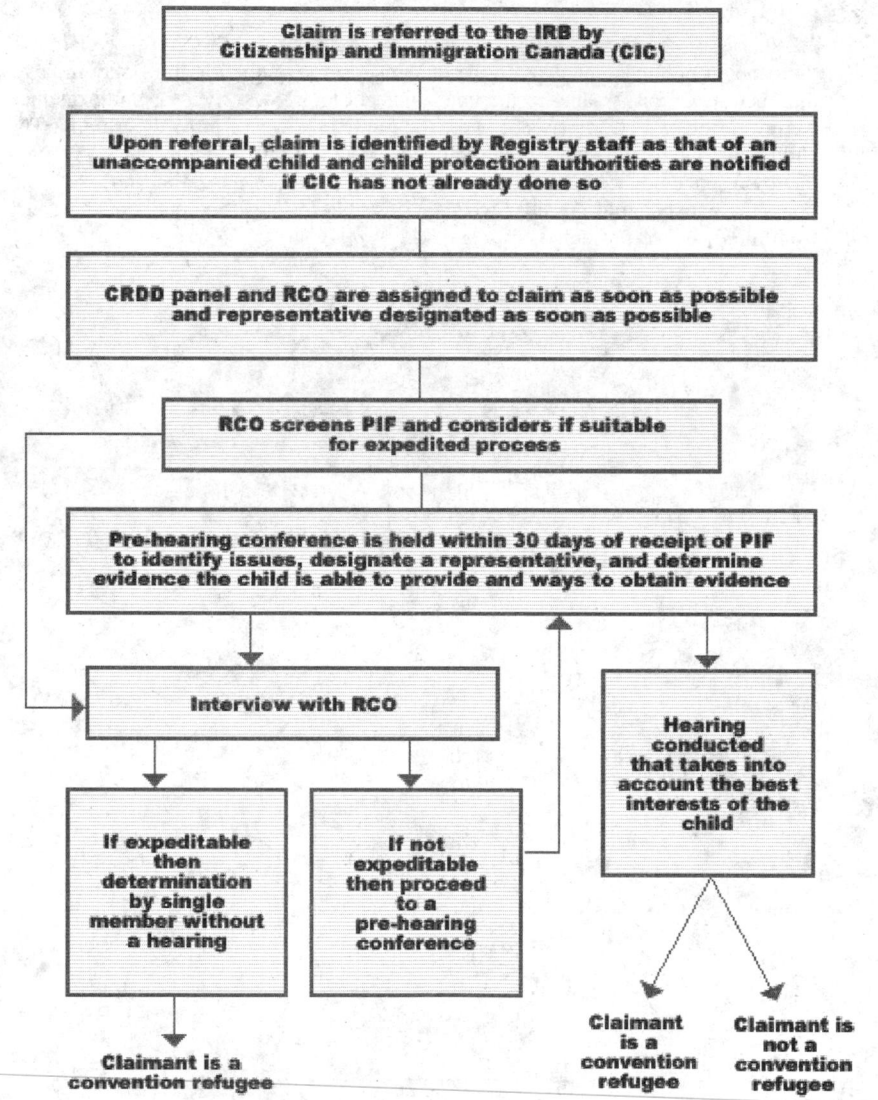

Claim is referred to the IRB by
Citizenship and Immigration Canada (CIC)

Upon referral, claim is identified by Registry staff as that of an
unaccompanied child and child protection authorities are notified
if CIC has not already done so

CRDD panel and RCO are assigned to claim as soon as possible
and representative designated as soon as possible

RCO screens PIF and considers if suitable
for expedited process

Pre-hearing conference is held within 30 days of receipt of PIF
to identify issues, designate a representative, and determine
evidence the child is able to provide and ways to obtain evidence

Interview with RCO

Hearing
conducted
that takes into
account the best
interests of the
child

If expeditable
then
determination
by single
member without
a hearing

If not
expeditable
then proceed
to a
pre-hearing
conference

Claimant is a
convention refugee

Claimant
is a
convention
refugee

Claimant is
not a
convention
refugee

1338

Guideline 4 — Women Refugee Claimants Fearing Gender-Related Persecution

Guidelines Issued by the Chairperson Pursuant to Section 65(3) of the *Immigration Act*

Update

The definition of a Convention refugee in the *Immigration Act* does not include *gender* as an independent enumerated ground for a well-founded fear of persecution warranting the recognition of Convention refugee status. As a developing area of the law, it has been more widely recognized that gender-related persecution is a *form* of persecution which can and should be assessed by the Refugee Division panel hearing the claim. Where a woman claims to have a gender-related fear of persecution, the central issue is thus the need to determine the *linkage* between gender, the feared persecution and one or more of the definition grounds.

Most gender-related refugee claims brought forward by women raise four critical issues which these Guidelines seek to address:

1. To what extent can women making a gender-related claim of fear of persecution successfully rely on any one, or a combination, of the five enumerated grounds of the Convention refugee definition?

2. Under what circumstances does sexual violence, or a threat thereof, or any other prejudicial treatment of women constitute persecution as that term is jurisprudentially understood?

3. What are the key evidentiary elements which decision-makers have to look at when considering a gender-related claim?

4. What special problems do women face when called upon to state their claim at refugee determination hearings, particularly when they have had experiences that are difficult and often humiliating to speak about?

A. — Determining the Nature and the Grounds of the Persecution

Obviously, not all claims brought forward by women are specifically gender-related. Women frequently claim fear of persecution in common with their male fellow citizens, though not necessarily of the same nature or at the same level of vulnerability, for such reasons as belonging to an ethnic or a linguistic minority, or membership in a political movement, a trade union or a religious denomination.

I. — General Proposition

Although gender is not specifically enumerated as one of the grounds for establishing Convention refugee status, the definition of Convention refugee may properly be interpreted as providing protection for women who demonstrate a well-founded fear of gender-related persecution by reason of any one, or a combination of, the enumerated grounds.

Before determining the appropriate ground(s) applicable to the claim, decision-makers must first identify the *nature* of the persecution feared by the claimant.

Other Relevant Legislation

Generally speaking, women refugee claimants may be put into four broad categories, although these categories are not mutually exclusive or exhaustive:[171]

1. *Women who fear persecution on the same Convention grounds, and in similar circumstances, as men. That is, the risk factor is not their sexual status, per se, but rather their particular identity (i.e. racial, national or social) or what they believe in, or are perceived to believe in (i.e. religion or political opinion).* In such claims, the substantive analysis does not vary as a function of the person's gender, although the nature of the harm feared and procedural issues at the hearing may vary as a function of the claimant's gender.

2. *Women who fear persecution solely for reasons pertaining to kinship, i.e. because of the status, activities or views of their spouses, parents, and siblings, or other family members.* Such cases of *"persecution of kin"* typically involve violence or other forms of harassment against women, who are not themselves accused of any antagonistic views or political convictions, in order to pressure them into revealing information about the whereabouts or the political activities of their family members. Women may also have political opinions imputed to them based on the activities of members of their family.

3. *Women who fear persecution resulting from certain circumstances of severe discrimination on grounds of gender or acts of violence either by public authorities or at the hands of private citizens from whose actions the state is unwilling or unable to adequately protect the concerned persons.* In the refugee law context, such discrimination may amount to persecution if it leads to consequences of a substantially prejudicial nature for the claimant and if it is imposed on account of any one, or a combination, of the statutory grounds for persecution. The acts of violence which a woman may fear include violence inflicted in situations of *domestic violence*[172] and situations of *civil war*.[173]

---

[171] See generally M. Meyer, "Oppression of Women and Refugee Status", in *Proceedings of the International Seminar on Refugee Women* (Amsterdam: Dutch Refugee Council, 1985) at pp. 30–33, and A.B. Johnsson, "The International Protection of Women Refugees — A Summary of Principal Problems and Issues" (1989) 1 *International Journal of Refugee Law* 221, at pp. 223-224, for a more detailed discussion of the different categories of women refugee claimants. Similar categories have been used in the Amnesty International report, *Women in the Front Line: Human Rights Violations Against Women* (New York: Amnesty International Publications, 1991) at pp. 1–3, in enumerating human rights violations against women.

[172] In this context, domestic violence is meant to include violence perpetrated against women by family members or other persons with whom the woman lives.

[173] See C. Niarchos, "Women, War and Rape: Challenges Facing the International Tribunal for the Former Yugoslavia" (1995) 17 *Human Rights Quarterly* 649. With respect to the former Yugoslavia,

> At several levels, the rapes reflect the policy of "ethnic cleansing", rape is used as a means to terrorize and displace the local population, to force the birth of children of mixed "ethnic" descent in the group, and to demoralize and destroy. The rapes are also an expression of misogyny: women are targeted not simply

4. *Women who fear persecution as the consequence of failing to conform to, or for transgressing, certain gender-discriminating religious or customary laws and practices in their country of origin.* Such laws and practices, by singling out women and placing them in a more vulnerable position than men, may create conditions for the existence of a *gender-defined social group*. The religious precepts, social traditions or cultural norms which women may be accused of violating can range from choosing their own spouses instead of accepting an arranged marriage, to such matters as the wearing of make-up, the visibility or length of hair, or the type of clothing a woman chooses to wear.

II. — Grounds Other Than Membership in a Particular Social Group

Race:

There may be cases where a woman claims a fear of persecution because of her race and her gender. For example, a woman from a minority race in her country may be persecuted not only for her race, but also for her gender.

Religion:

A woman who, in a theocracy for example, chooses not to subscribe to or follow the precepts of a state religion may be at risk of persecution for reasons of religion. In the context of the Convention refugee definition, the notion of religion may encompass, among other freedoms, the freedom to hold a belief system of one's choice or *not to hold* a particular belief system and the freedom to practise a religion of one's choice or *not to practise* a prescribed religion. In certain states, the religion assigns certain roles to women; if a woman does not fulfill her assigned role and is punished for that, she may have a well-founded fear of persecution for reasons of religion. A woman may also be perceived as expressing a political view (and have a political opinion imputed to her) because of her attitude and/or behaviour towards religion.

Nationality:

A gender-related claim of fear of persecution may be linked to reasons of nationality in situations where a national law causes a woman to lose her nationality (i.e. citizenship) because of marriage to a foreign national. What would constitute good grounds for fearing persecution is not the fact of losing her nationality as such (notwithstanding that such laws are discriminatory to the extent that they do

Other Relevant Legislation

because they are the "enemy" but also because they are women. Gender is essential to the method of assault. (at p. 658)

The author concludes that "Women's suffering in war is specifically related to gender — women are raped, forced into prostitution, forcibly impregnated." (at p. 689)

See also the Chairperson's *Guidelines on Civilian Non-Combatants Fearing Persecution in Civil War Situations*, Immigration and Refugee Board, Ottawa, Canada, March 7, 1996.

not apply to men married to foreign nationals), but the consequences she may suffer as a result.[174]

Political Opinion:

A woman who opposes institutionalized discrimination against women, or expresses views of independence from male social/cultural dominance in her society, may be found to fear persecution by reason of her *actual political opinion or a political opinion imputed to her (i.e. she is perceived by the agent of persecution to be expressing politically antagonistic views)*. Two considerations are of paramount importance when interpreting the notion of "political opinion":

1. In a society where women are "assigned" a *subordinate status* and the authority exercised by men over women results in a general oppression of women, their political protest and activism do not always manifest themselves in the same way as those of men.[175]

2. The *political nature* of oppression of women in the context of religious laws and rituals should be recognized. Where tenets of the governing religion in a given country require certain kinds of behaviour exclusively from women, contrary behaviour may be perceived by the authorities as evidence of an unacceptable political opinion that threatens the basic structure from which their political power flows.[176]

---

[174] A separate issue to be determined is whether the woman concerned has acquired her spouse's nationality, thereby enabling her to avail herself of the protection of that country.

[175] See F. Stairs & L. Pope, "No Place Like Home: Assaulted Migrant Women's Claims to Refugee Status" (1990) 6 *Journal of Law and Social Policy* 148, at p. 163, where the authors assert that, "Where an ostensibly non-political act such as choice of dress is seen to in fact be political in nature, it may provide the basis for a claim to refugee status.'"

J. Greatbatch, in "The Gender Difference: Feminist Critiques of Refugee Discourse" (1989) 1 *International Journal of Refugee Law* 518, gives examples of how the refusal by Iranian women to conform to the dress code can be viewed as opposition to the Iranian government, thereby constituting a political act. The author also discusses the development of Chilean communal kitchens and co-operative nurseries and the search for missing relatives as examples of how Chilean women demonstrated their resistance to the Pinochet regime.

See also *Shahabaldin, Modjgan v. M.E.I.* (March 2, 1987), IAB V85-6161, MacLeod, Mawani, Singh, where the former Immigration Appeal Board found the claimant to be a Convention refugee on the basis of her political opinion, because she opposed the Iranian laws governing dress.

In CRDD T90-01845, Jackson, Wright (dissenting in part), December 21, 1990, the Refugee Division was of the view that the claimant's opposition to the government's enforcement of the dress laws, "could possibly result in her being persecuted because of political opinion should she be returned to Iran." The panel noted that Iranian women are subject to "extreme discrimination".

[176] See *Namitabar v. M.E.I.*, [1994] 2 F.C. 42 (T.D.). In this case, the Court said that "I consider that in the case at bar the female applicant has demonstrated that her fear of

III. — Membership in a Particular Social Group

In considering the application of the "membership in a particular social group" ground, decision-makers should refer to the Supreme Court of Canada decision in Ward.[177] *The Ward decision indicated three possible categories of "particular social group":*

1) groups defined by an innate or unchangeable characteristic;

2) groups whose members voluntarily associate for reasons so fundamental to their human dignity that they should not be forced to forsake the association; and

3) groups associated by a former voluntary status, unalterable due to its historical permanence.

The Court gave examples of the three categories as follows:

The first category would embrace individuals fearing persecution on such bases as *gender*, linguistic background and sexual orientation, while the second would encompass, for example, human rights activists. The third branch is included more because of historical intentions, although it is also relevant to the anti-discrimination influences, in that one's past is an immutable part of the person.

Depending on the basis of the claim, women refugee claimants may belong to a group defined in any of these categories.

A further holding of the Ward decision is that a particular social group cannot be based solely on the common victimization of its members. A group is not defined *solely* by common victimization if the claimant's fear of persecution is also based on her gender, or on another innate or unchangeable characteristic of the claimant.[178]

Family as a particular social group

There is jurisprudential authority for recognizing claims grounded in familial affiliation (i.e. where kinship is the risk factor) as coming within the ambit of the "membership in a particular social group" category. See, for example, *Al-Busaidy, Talal Ali Said v. M.E.I.,*[179]

... the [Immigration and Refugee] Board has committed reviewable error in not giving due effect to the applicant's uncontradicted evidence with respect to his membership in a particular social group, namely, his own immediate family.

persecution is connected to her political opinion. In a country where the oppression of women is institutionalized any independent point of view or act opposed to the imposition of a clothing code will be seen as a manifestation of opposition to the established theocratic regime."

[177] *Canada (Attorney General) v. Ward*, [1993] 2 S.C.R. 689.

[178] The Federal Court of Canada has found "women subject to domestic abuse" to be a particular social group in two cases — *Narvaez v. M.C.I.*, [1995] 2 F.C. 55 (T.D.) and *Diluna v. M.E.I.* (1995), 29 Imm. L.R. (2d) 156 (T.D.). The issue which must then be addressed is whether the claimant's fear of persecution is well-founded.

[179] (1992), 16 Imm. L.R. (2d) 119 at 121 (F.C.A.).

The former Immigration Appeal Board also considered the family as constituting a "particular social group" in *Astudillo v. M.E.I.* (1979), 31 N.R. 121 (F.C.A.), *Barra-*

Other Relevant Legislation

Gender-defined particular social group

There is increasing international support for the application of the particular social group ground to the claims of women who allege a fear of persecution solely by reason of their gender. See *Conclusion no. 39 (XXXVI) Refugee Women and International Protection*, 1985, where the Executive Committee of the United Nations High Commissioner for Refugees (UNHCR)...

> (k) Recognized that States, in the exercise of their sovereignty, are free to adopt the interpretation that women asylum-seekers who face harsh or inhuman treatment due to their having transgressed the social mores of the society in which they live may be considered as a "particular social group" within the meaning of Article 1 A(2) of the 1951 United Nations Refugee Convention.[180]

Velasquez, Marie Mabel De La v. M.E.I. (April 29, 1981), IAB 80-6330, Hlady, Weselak, Howard, and in Zarketa, *Ignacio v. M.E.I.* (February 6, 1985), IAB M81-9776, D. Davey, Suppa, Tisshaw.

Several Refugee Division decisions have also found women to be members of a particular social group, the family. See, for example, CRDD M89-02465, Hebert, Champoux-Ohrt (dissenting), January 4, 1990, and CRDD T89-03943, Kapasi, Jew, July 25, 1990, where a political opinion was imputed to the Somali claimant because of the actions of her brothers. See also CRDD M89-00057, Wills, Gauthier, February 16, 1989, where the Iranian claimant was found to be a member of the social group, "a pro-Shah family", and CRDD M89-00971, Wolfe, Hendricks, June 13, 1989, where the Refugee Division found the Peruvian claimant to be a member of a particular social group, her family. In CRDD M89-01098, Van der Buhs, Lamarche, June 14, 1989, the Sri Lankan claimant was also found to be a refugee because she was a young Tamil in a Tamil family.

In CRDD T89-02313, T89-02314, T89-02315, Teitelbaum (dissenting), Sri-Skanda-Rajah, October 17, 1990, the Refugee Division found that the Guatemalan claimant was found to be a member of the social group, "targeted family". The Refugee Division, in CRDD C90-00299, C90-00300, Lo, Pawa, December 18, 1990, also found a Salvadoran claimant to belong to a particular social group, her husband's family.

[180] In July 1991, the UNHCR Executive Committee released *Guidelines on the Protection of Refugee Women*, EC/SCP/67 (July 22, 1991). These guidelines stress that women,

> ... fearing persecution or severe discrimination on the basis of their gender should be considered a member of a social group for the purposes of determining refugee status. Others may be seen as having made a religious or political statement in transgressing the social norms of their society.

In an *Information Note* submitted by the High Commissioner with the release of the above *Guidelines*, it was noted that "ensuring the protection of refugee women requires compliance not only with the 1951 *Convention* and its 1967 *Protocol*, but also with other relevant international instruments." (at p. 1)

During its 41st session in 1990, the UNHCR Executive Committee stated that severe discrimination experienced by women, prohibited by the *Convention on the Elimination of all Forms of Discrimination Against Women (CEDAW)*, can form the basis for the granting of refugee status. The importance of documentation regarding gender-based per-

Application of the statutory ground

In evaluating the "membership in a particular social group" ground for a fear of gender-related persecution, two considerations are necessary:

1. Most of the gender-specific claims involving fear of persecution for transgressing religious or social norms may be determined on *grounds of religion or political opinion*. Such women may be seen by the governing authorities or private citizens as having made a religious or political statement in transgressing those norms of their society, even though UNHCR *Conclusion no. 39*, above, contemplates the use of "particular social group" as an appropriate ground.

2. *For a woman to establish a well-founded fear of persecution by reason of her membership in a gender-defined particular social group*[181] *under the first category in Ward (i.e. groups defined by an innate or unchangeable characteristic)*:

- The fact that the particular social group consists of large numbers of the female population in the country concerned is *irrelevant* — race, religion, na-

---

secution and its consequences in the countries of origin of refugee women was discussed. See, in this regard, the UNHCR Executive Committee, *Note on Refugee Women and International Protection*, EC/SCP/59 (August 28, 1990) at p. 5.

The UNHCR has noted repeatedly that refugee women have special needs in the area of protection. See, for example, the discussion at the 41st session in the *Note on Refugee Women and International Protection*, cited above, at pp. 2–4. See also the United Nations General Assembly, Executive Committee of the High Commissioner's Programme, *Report on Refugee Women*, A/AC.96/727 (July 19, 1989) at p. 2.

It is interesting to observe that the European Parliament, as early as 1984, had passed a resolution similar to the 1985 UNHCR Resolution. The European Parliament called upon member states "to apply the UN treaty of 1951, as well as the 1967 Protocol regarding the status of refugees, in accordance with this interpretation." For a discussion of the resolution of the European Parliament, see the *Proceedings of the International Seminar on Refugee Women* (Amsterdam: Dutch Refugee Council, 1985) at p. 33.

In 1984, the Dutch Refugee Council issued the following policy directive:

It is the opinion of the Dutch Refugee Council that persecution for reasons of membership of a particular social group, may also be taken to include persecution because of social position on the basis of sex. This may be especially true in situations where discrimination against women in society, contrary to the rulings of international law, has been institutionalized and where women who oppose this discrimination, or distance themselves from it, are faced with drastic sanctions, either from the authorities themselves, or from their social environment, where the authorities are unwilling or unable to offer protection.

[181] Although the former Immigration Appeal Board decided few claims dealing specifically with gender-related persecution, there is one decision that merits discussion. In *Incirciyan, Zeyiye v. M.E.I.* (August 10, 1987), IAB M87-1541X, M87-1248, P. Davey, Cardinal, Angé, an Armenian claimant and her daughter who had been living in Turkey were found to be refugees on the basis of membership in a particular social group "made up of single women living in a Moslem country without the protection of a male relative (father, brother, husband, son)." Since the claimant had requested and had been refused

tionality and political opinion are also characteristics that are shared by large numbers of people.

- *Gender is an innate characteristic*[182] *and, therefore, women may form a particular social group within the Convention refugee definition.* The relevant assessment is whether the claimant, as a woman, has a well-founded fear of persecution in her country of nationality by reason of her membership in this group.

- *Particular social groups comprised of sub-groups of women may also be an appropriate finding in a case involving gender-related persecution.* These particular social groups can be identified by reference to factors, in addition to gender, which may also be innate or unchangeable characteristics. Examples of other such characteristics are age, race, marital status and economic status. Thus, for example, there may be sub-groups of women identified as old women, indigenous women, single women or poor women. In determining whether these factors are unchangeable, consideration should be given to the cultural and social context in which the woman lives, as well as to the perception of the agents of persecution and those responsible for providing state protection.

- *Because refugee status is an individual remedy, the fact that a claim is based on social group membership may not be sufficient in and of itself to give rise to refugee status.* The woman will need to show that she has a genuine fear of harm, that one of the grounds of the definition is the reason for the feared

---

the protection of the Turkish authorities on several occasions, the Board concluded that there was a lack of adequate state protection.

On several occasions, the Refugee Division has found women refugee claimants to have a well-founded fear of persecution by reason of their membership in a particular social group. In CRDD T89-06969, T89-06970, T89-06971, Nicholson, Bajwa, July 17, 1990, the Refugee Division found that the claimant and her two daughters had a well-founded fear of persecution on the basis of their membership in a particular social group, "consisting of women and girls who do not conform to Islamic fundamentalist norms." In CRDD U91-04008, Goldman, Bajwa, December 24, 1991, the Somali claimant was found to be a refugee on the basis of her membership in a particular social group, "young women without male protection." The Refugee Division, in CRDD T89-02248, Maraj, E.R. Smith, April 3, 1990, found the claimant to be a member of the particular social group composed of women who belong to a "women's organization objecting to the treatment of women in Iran."

[182] In the *Ward* decision, the Court described the first of the three possible categories of particular social group as "groups defined by an innate or unchangeable characteristic." The Court held that this category would include individuals fearing persecution on such basis as gender, linguistic background and sexual orientation. In CRDD T93-05935/36, Liebich, Larke, December 31, 1993, the Refugee Division found that a woman who was a divorced mother living under the jurisdiction of Sharia law had a well-founded fear of persecution by reason of her membership in a particular social group of "women." In CRDD T93-12198/12199/12197, Ramirez, McCaffrey, May 10, 1994 (reasons signed July 13, 1994), the panel found that "women" was a particular social group.

harm, that the harm is sufficiently serious to amount to persecution, that there is a reasonable possibility that the feared persecution would occur if she was to return to her country of origin and that she has no reasonable expectation of adequate national protection.

B. — Assessing the Feared Harm

Claims involving gender-related fear of persecution often fall quite comfortably within one of the five grounds of the Convention refugee definition. The difficulty sometimes lies in establishing whether the various forms of prejudicial treatment or sanctions imposed on women making such claims come within the scope of the concept of "persecution".

Considerations

The circumstances which give rise to women's fear of persecution are often unique to women.[183] The existing bank of jurisprudence on the meaning of persecution is based, for the most part, on the experiences of male claimants. Aside from a few cases of rape, the definition has not been widely applied to female-specific experiences, such as infanticide,

Other Relevant Legislation

---

[183] Several commentators argue that the *Convention* refugee definition,

... ignores the persecution that girls and women endure, even die under, for stepping out of the closed circle of social norms; choosing a husband in place of accepting an arranged marriage; undergoing an abortion where it is illegal; becoming politically active in the women's movement. Women are also abandoned or persecuted for being rape victims, bearing illegitimate children or marrying men of different races. See L. Bonnerjea, *Shaming the World: The Needs of Women Refugees* (London: Change, 1985) at p. 6.

See also Greatbatch, *supra*, footnote 3, at p. 218, and Stairs and Pope, *supra*, footnote 3, at pp. 163-164.

genital mutilation,[184] bride-burning, forced marriage,[185] domestic violence,[186] forced abortion or compulsory sterilization.[187]

The fact that violence, including sexual and domestic violence, against women is universal is *irrelevant* when determining whether rape, and other gender-specific crimes constitute forms of persecution. *The real issues are whether the violence — experienced or feared — is a serious violation of a fundamental human right for a Convention ground*[188]

---

[184] In CRDD T93-12198/12199/12187, Ramirez, McCaffrey, May 10, 1994 (reasons signed July 13, 1994), the Refugee Division concluded that the claimant's right to personal security would be grossly infringed if she were forced to undergo female genital mutilation. The panel found that this was a contravention of Article 3 of the *Universal Declaration of Human Rights and the United Nations Convention on the Rights of the Child*. The Federal Court of Canada in *Annan v. Canada*, [1995] 3 F.C. 25 (T.D.) in considering the case of a woman fearing female genital mutilation stated that Ghana, "according to the documentary evidence, has failed to demonstrate any intention of protecting its female citizens from the horrific torture of excision practised at various places throughout the country."

[185] In *Vidhani v. M.C.I.*, [1995] 3 F.C. 60 (T.D.), the Court held that "women who are forced into marriages against their will have had a basic human right violated."

[186] The CRDD in C93-00433, Wieler, Lazo, December 3, 1993, in dealing with the case of a woman fearing her husband and her family, found that the claimant's fear of "the violent behaviour of her husband condoned by that society, the traditional rituals which include the searing of her body with a heated instrument and the continuing domination and demands causing her to be enslaved" amounted to persecution.

[187] In L. Heise, "Crimes of Gender" (1989) 2 *Worldwatch* 12, the many forms of violence against women are discussed. The author notes that,

> Every day, thousands of women are beaten in their homes by their partners, and thousands more are raped, assaulted and sexually harassed. And, there are the less recognized forms of violence: In Nepal, female babies die from neglect because parents value sons over daughters; in Sudan, girls' genitals are mutilated to ensure virginity until marriage; and in India, young brides are murdered by their husbands when parents fail to provide enough dowry. In all these instances, women are targets of violence because of their sex. This is not random violence; the risk factor is being female.

> With respect to compulsory or forced sterilization, the Federal Court of Canada in *Cheung v. M.E.I.*, [1993] 2 F.C. 314 (C.A.) held that "The forced sterilization of women is a fundamental violation of basic human rights. It violates Articles 3 and 5 of the United Nations Universal Declaration of Human Rights... The forced sterilization of a woman is a serious and totally unacceptable violation of her security of the person. Forced sterilization subjects a woman to cruel, inhuman and degrading treatment."

[188] When considering whether sexual violence or domestic violence (both of which may involve mental and physical suffering) are forms of torture or cruel, inhuman and degrading treatment amounting to persecution, decision-makers should examine th UN *Convention Against Torture and Other Cruel, Inhuman and Degrading Treatment and Punish-*

and in what circumstances can the risk of that violence be said to result from a failure of state protection.[189]

---

ment. This Convention which, like the 1951 Refugee Convention, incorporates the principle of non-refoulement, defines "torture" as:

> ... any act by which severe pain or suffering, whether physical or mental, is intentionally inflicted on a person for such purposes as obtaining from [her] or a third person information or a confession, punishing [her] for an act [she] or a third person has committed or is suspected of having committed, or intimidating or coercing [her] or a third person, or for any reason based on discrimination of any kind, when such pain or suffering is inflicted by or at the instigation of or with the consent or acquiescence of a public official or other person acting in an official capacity. It does not include pain or suffering arising only from, inherent in or incidental to lawful sanctions. (Article 1)

> Reference should also be made to Article 16 as it relates to "... other acts of cruel, inhuman or degrading treatment or punishment which do not amount to torture as defined in Article 1 ...".

[189] In their influential study, *Sexual Violence Against Refugee Women* (The Hague, Ministry for Social Affairs, 1984) at pp. 6 & 7, C.E.J. de Neef & S.J. de Ruiter document the manner in which sexual violence "may have played a role in the flight from the country of origin in any of a variety of ways:

> 1. It may have been part of the way in which the persecution based on her political conviction was expressed; (When a woman has been imprisoned in the country of origin she may have suffered sexual violence. Both for men and women in a number of countries sexual violence is an integral part of the methods of torture.)

> 2. It may be that a woman by not conforming to the cultural traditions in the country of origin which prescribe a certain behaviour for women is fearful to be subjected to violence. (An example of this type of violence is decapitating or stoning women who have committed adultery in some Islamic cultures.)

> 3. It may be that through the threat of, or through actual sexual violence against women, conflicts between different political or religious groups are decided. (... Sexual violence against women here can be a means to hurt an entire group and to reinforce the superiority of the one group over the other.)

> 4. It may be that women who have fled because of conditions of war or of a reign of terror ... are a victim of sexual violence because they are exceptionally vulnerable when they are deprived of the men's traditional protection and have lost their status of wife."

The Dutch Refugee Council publication, *Sexual Violence: You Have Hardly Any Future Left* (Amsterdam: Dutch Refugee Council, 1987), contains a excellent discussion of the meaning and forms of sexual violence. Excerpts from this publication form part of the documentation for the workshop, "Socio-cultural Context to Refugee Claims made by Women — Case Studies: Iran, Somalia and Latin America," organized by the Toronto I CRDD Working Group on Women Refugee Claimants, Toronto, June 21, 1990. The documentation is available in the Board's regional Documentation Centres.

Other Relevant Legislation

The social, cultural, traditional and religious norms and the laws affecting women in the claimant's country of origin ought to be assessed *by reference to human rights instruments which provide a framework of international standards for recognizing the protection needs of women.* What constitutes permissible conduct by the agent of persecution towards women may be determined, therefore, by reference to international instruments such as:

> *Universal Declaration of Human Rights*
> *International Covenant on Civil and Political Rights*
> *International Covenant on Economic, Social and Cultural Rights*
> *Convention on the Elimination of All Forms of Discrimination Against Women*[190]
> *Convention on the Political Rights of Women*
> *Convention on the Nationality of Married Women*
> *Convention Against Torture and other Cruel, Inhuman or Degrading Treatment or Punishment*
> *Declaration on the Elimination of Violence Against Women*[191]

---

[190] During its 41st session in 1990, the UNHCR Executive Committee stated that severe discrimination experienced by women and prohibited by *Convention on the Elimination of All Forms of Discrimination Against Women (CEDAW)* can form the basis for the granting of refugee status. The importance of documentation regarding gender-based persecution and its consequences in the countries of origin of refugee women was discussed. See, in this regard, the UNHCR Executive Committee, *Note on Refugee Women and International Protection*, EC/SCP/59 (August 28, 1990) at p. 5.

The Refugee Division in T91-01497, T91-01498, Ramirez, Toth, August 9, 1994 (reasons signed November 1, 1994), referred to the *Convention on the Elimination of All Forms of Discrimination Against Women* in finding that the claimants, from Bulgaria, had a well-founded fear of persecution. The adult claimant had been subjected to spousal abuse throughout her marriage in the form of battering, threats of death, and rape. The panel held that despite Bulgaria's signing of the above Convention, the authorities had repeatedly ignored the violence against the adult claimant. The panel also referred to several other international human rights instruments and to the IRB's *Guidelines* on women refugee claimants, and held that the adult claimant had "an internationally protected right to protection from domestic violence and failure to give that protection is a form of gender-based discrimination."

[191] The *Declaration on the Elimination of Violence Against Women* provides in Article 2 that

> Violence against women shall be understood to encompass, but not be limited to, the following:

>> (a) Physical, sexual and psychological violence occurring in the family, including battering, sexual abuse of female children in the household, dowry-related violence, marital rape, female genital mutilation and other traditional practices harmful to women, non-spousal violence and violence related to exploitation;

>> (b) Physical, sexual and psychological violence occurring within the general community, including rape, sexual abuse, sexual harassment and intimidation at work, in educational institutions and elsewhere;

A woman's claim to Convention refugee status *cannot be based solely on the fact that she is subject to a national policy or law to which she objects.* The claimant will need to establish that:

(a) the policy or law is inherently persecutory; or

(b) the policy or law is used as a means of persecution for one of the enumerated reasons; or

(c) the policy or law, although having legitimate goals, is administered through persecutory means; or

(d) the penalty for non-compliance with the policy or law is disproportionately severe.[192]

C. — Evidentiary Matters

When an assessment of a woman's claim of gender-related fear of persecution is made, the evidence must show that what the claimant genuinely fears is persecution for a Convention reason as distinguished from random violence or random criminal activity perpetrated against her as an individual. The central factor in such an assessment is, of course, the claimant's particular circumstances in relation to both the general human rights record of her country of origin and the experiences of other similarly situated women. Evaluation of the weight and credibility of the claimant's evidence ought to include evaluation of the following considerations, among others:

1. *A gender-related claim cannot be rejected simply because the claimant comes from a country where women face generalized oppression and violence and the claimant's fear of persecution is not identifiable to her on the basis of an individualized set of facts.* This so-called "particularized evidence rule" was rejected by the Federal Court of Appeal in *Salibian v. M.E.I.*,[193] and other decisions.

2. *Decision-makers should consider evidence indicating a failure of state protection if the state or its agents in the claimant's country of origin are unwilling or unable*

(c) Physical, sexual and psychological violence perpetrated or condoned by the State, wherever it occurs.

[192] In *Fathi-Rad, Farideh v. S.S.C.*. (April 13, 1994), no. IMM-2438-93, McGillis (F.C.T.D.), the Court had to deal with the issue of whether the Islamic dress code is a policy of general application applied to all citizens of Iran. In the Court's view, "The Islamic dress code is a law applicable only to women in Iran. It dictates the manner in which Iranian women must dress to comply with the religious beliefs of the theocratic governing regime and prescribes punishments for any violation of the law. A law which specifically targets the manner in which women dress may not properly be characterized as a law of general application which applies to all citizens." In the alternative, the Court concluded that the punishment for minor infractions of the Islamic dress code was disproportionate to the objective of the law and, therefore, constituted persecution. Since the decision in *Fathi-Rad*, the Documentation, Information and Research Branch, IRB, has published a document entitled "Human Rights Brief: Women in the Islamic Republic of Iran", June 1994, which indicates that the dress code in Iran applies equally to men and women.

[193] [1990] 3 F.C. 250 at 258 (C.A.).

to provide adequate protection from gender-related persecution.[194] If the claimant can demonstrate that it was objectively unreasonable for her to seek the protection of her state, then her failure to approach the state for protection will not defeat her claim. Also, the fact that the claimant did or did not seek protection from non-government groups is irrelevant to the assessment of the availability of state protection.[195]

When considering whether it is objectively unreasonable for the claimant not to have sought the protection of the state, *the decision-maker should consider, among other relevant factors, the social, cultural, religious, and economic context in which the claimant finds herself.* If, for example, a woman has suffered gender-related persecution in the form of rape, she may be ostracized from her community for seeking protection from the state. Decision-makers should consider this type of information when determining if the claimant should reasonably have sought state protection.

In determining whether the state is willing or able to provide protection to a woman fearing gender-related persecution, *decision-makers should consider the fact that the forms of evidence which the claimant might normally provide as "clear and convincing proof" of state inability to protect, will not always be either available or useful in cases of gender-related persecution.*

For example, where a gender-related claim involves threats of or actual sexual violence at the hands of government authorities (or at the hands of non-state agents of persecution, where the state is either unwilling or unable to protect), the claimant may have difficulty in substantiating her claim with any "statistical data" on the incidence of sexual violence in her country.

In cases where the claimant cannot rely on the more standard or typical forms of evidence as "clear and convincing proof" of failure of state protection, *reference may need to be made to alternative forms of evidence to meet the "clear and convincing" test.* Such alternative forms of evidence might include the testimony of women in similar situations where there was a failure of state protection, or the testimony of the claimant herself regarding past personal incidents where state protection did not materialize.

3. *A change in country circumstances, generally viewed as a positive change, may have no impact, or even a negative impact, on a woman's fear of gender-related persecution.* In situations where a woman's fear is related to personal-status laws or where her human rights are being violated by private citizens, a change in country circumstances may not mean a positive change for the woman, as these areas are

---

[194] The Supreme Court of Canada in *Ward* held that except in situations where the state is in a condition of complete breakdown, states must be presumed capable of protecting their citizens. The Court found that this presumption can be rebutted by "clear and convincing" evidence of the state's inability to protect.

[195] It is clear that the claimant's failure to seek protection from non-government groups can have no impact on the assessment of the availability of state protection. In certain circumstances, however, the fact that the claimant did not approach existing non-government organizations in her country of origin may have an impact on her credibility or, more generally, on the well foundedness of her claim.

often the last to change. An assessment should be made of the claimant's particular fear and of whether the changes are meaningful and effective enough for her fear of gender-related persecution to no longer be well-founded.[196]

4. *In determining the reasonableness of a woman's recourse to an internal flight alternative (IFA), decision-makers should consider the ability of women, because of their gender, to travel safely to the IFA and to stay there without facing undue hardship.*[197] In determining the reasonableness of an IFA, the decision-makers should take into account factors including religious, economic, and cultural factors, and consider whether and how these factors affect women in the IFA.

John v. Canada (Minister of Citizenship & Immigration), 2011 FC 387, 2011 CF 387, 2011 CarswellNat 978, 2011 CarswellNat 1799 (F.C.) — The present application challenges the decision of the Refugee Protection Division in which the applicant's claim for protection was rejected, in large measure, on the basis of a negative credibility finding. The decision was set aside. When dealing with gender-related claims it is critical that RPD pays special attention to *Guideline 4: Women Refugee Claimants Fearing Gender-Related Persecution: Guidelines Issued by the Chairperson* in reaching a determination. It is a reviewable error to first determine that a claimant is not credible and then to use that lack of credibility as a basis for rejecting or giving little weight to evidence that is submitted to corroborate the claimant's testimony. In the present case, the psychological report is tendered, not to prove the truth of the applicant's statements to the psychologist, but to prove her current state of mind. The applicant's impaired state of mind can be found to support the truth of her evidence of the abuse she suffered. And second, the applicant's state of mind was an important factor to be taken into consideration by the RPD when evaluating her evidence: to do so constitutes a practical application of *Guideline 4.*

Section in Other Relevant Legislation, under Appendix 1, Guidelines Issued by the Chairperson, Guideline 4.

D. — Special Problems at Determination Hearings

Women refugee claimants face special problems in demonstrating that their claims are credible and trustworthy. Some of the difficulties may arise because of cross-cultural misunderstandings. For example:

1. Women from societies where the preservation of one's virginity or marital dignity is the cultural norm may be reluctant to disclose their experiences of sexual

---

[196] See *Yusuf, Sofia Mohamed v. M.E.I.* (January 9, 1995), no. A-130-92, Hugessen, Strayer, Décary (F.C.A.). See also Legal Services' Commentary on *Change of Circumstances*, IRB Legal Services, September 1994.

[197] See *Thirunavukkarasu v. M.E.I.*, [1994] 1 F.C. 589 at p. 598, where the Court ruled as follows: "The claimant cannot be required to encounter great physical danger or to undergo undue hardship in travelling there or in staying there." See also Legal Services' Commentary "*Internal Flight: When is it an Alternative?*", IRB Legal Services, April 1994.

violence in order to keep their "shame" to themselves and not dishonour their family or community.[198]

2. Women from certain cultures where men do not share the details of their political, military or even social activities with their spouses, daughters or mothers may find themselves in a difficult situation when questioned about the experiences of their male relatives.[199]

3. Women refugee claimants who have suffered sexual violence may exhibit a pattern of symptoms referred to as Rape Trauma Syndrome,[200] and may require extremely sensitive handling. Similarly, women who have been subjected to domestic violence may exhibit a pattern of symptoms referred to as Battered Woman Syndrome and may also be reluctant to testify.[201] In some cases it will be appropriate to consider whether claimants should be allowed to have the option of providing their

---

[198] The UNHCR Executive Committee notes that decision-makers should refrain from asking women refugee claimants for details of sexual abuse. They note that, "the important thing in establishing a well-founded fear of persecution is to establish that some form of it has occurred." *Guidelines on the Protection of Refugee Women, supra*, footnote 10, at p. 27.

[199] In two cases in the Federal Court of Canada, the issue of the woman's place within her society and her lack of knowledge about the activities of male family members was addressed. In *Roble v. M.E.I.* (1994), 25 Imm. L.R. (2d) 186 (F.C.T.D.), the Court stated that in Somali culture it is often the case that a wife is not privy to information concerning her husband's occupation. In *Montenegro, Suleyama v. M.C.I.* (February 29, 1996), no. IMM-3173-94, MacKay (F.C.T.D.), the Court faulted the CRDD for ignoring the claimant's explanation that her knowledge of her husband's political involvement in El Salvador was based entirely on what he had been willing to tell her, pointing out that "within their social order wives were not expected to question their husband's activities."

[200] The UNHCR Executive Committee *Guidelines on the Protection of Refugee Women, supra*, footnote 10, at p. 27, discuss the symptoms of Rape Trauma Syndrome as including "persistent fear, a loss of self-confidence and self-esteem, difficulty in concentration, an attitude of self-blame, a pervasive feeling of loss of control, and memory loss of distortion."

[201] F. Stairs & L. Pope, supra, footnote 5, at p. 202, stress that decision-makers should be,

... sensitive to the fact that women whose children are attached to their claim may also be reticent to describe the details of their persecution in front of their children. Further, if the claimant's culture dictates that she should suffer battering silently, the use of an interpreter from her community may also intimidate her.

For a discussion of the battered woman syndrome see *R. v. Lavallee*, [1990] 1 S.C.R. 852. In *Lavallee*, Madame Justice Wilson addressed the mythology about domestic violence and phrased the myth as "[e]ither she was not as badly beaten as she claims, or she would have left the man long ago. Or, if she was battered that severely, she must have stayed out of some masochistic enjoyment of it." The Court further indicated that a manifestation of the victimization of battered women is a "reluctance to disclose to others the fact or extent of the beatings". In *Lavallee*, the Court indicated that expert evidence can assist in dispelling these

testimony outside the hearing room by affidavit or by videotape, or in front of members and refugee claims officers specifically trained in dealing with violence against women. Members should be familiar with the UNHCR Executive Committee *Guidelines on the Protection of Refugee Women.*[202]

Framework of Analysis

1. *Assess the harm feared by the claimant. Does the harm feared constitute persecution?*

(a) For the treatment to likely amount to persecution, it must be a serious form of harm which detracts from the claimant's fundamental human rights.

(b) To assist decision-makers in determining what kinds of treatment are considered persecution, an objective standard is provided by international human rights instruments. The following instruments, among others, may be considered:

> *Universal Declaration of Human Rights,*
> *International Covenant on Civil and Political Rights*
> *International Covenant on Economic, Social and Cultural Right*
> *Convention on the Elimination of All Forms of Discrimination Against Women*
> *Convention on the Political Rights of Women,*
> *Convention on the Nationality of Married Women*
> *Convention Against Torture and other Cruel, Inhuman or*
> *Degrading Treatment or Punishment*
> *Declaration on the Elimination of Violence Against Women*

2. *Ascertain whether the claimant's fear of persecution is based on any of the grounds, singly or in combination, enumerated in the Convention refugee definition. Considerations*:

- It is necessary to ascertain the characteristic of the claimant which places her or members of her group at risk, and to ascertain the linkage of that characteristic to a Convention ground.

- Gender is an innate characteristic and it may form a particular social group.

- A subgroup of women may also form a particular social group. Women in these particular social groups have characteristics (possibly innate or unchangeable) additional to gender, which make them fear persecution.

- The gender-defined group cannot be defined solely by the fact that its members share common persecution.

---

myths and be used to explain why a woman would remain in a battering relationship.

[202] It should be noted that Amnesty International, in *Women in the Front Line: Human Rights Violations Against Women, supra,* footnote 1, at p. 54, recommends that:

> In procedures for the determination of refugee status governments should provide interviewers trained to recognize the specific protection needs of women refugee and asylum-seekers.

3. *Determine whether the claimant's fear of persecution is well-founded. This includes an assessment of the evidence related to the ability or willingness of the state to protect the claimant and, more generally, the objective basis of the claim. Considerations:*

- There may be little or no documentary evidence presented with respect to the inadequacy of state protection as it relates to gender-related persecution. There may be a need for greater reliance on evidence of similarly situated women and the claimant's own experiences.

- The claimant need not have approached non-state organizations for protection.

- Factors including the social, cultural, religious, and economic context in which the claimant finds herself should be considered in determining whether it was objectively unreasonable for the claimant not to have sought state protection.

- Where a woman's fear relates to personal-status laws or where her human rights are being violated by private citizens, an otherwise positive change in country conditions may have no impact, or even a negative impact, on a woman's fear of gender-related persecution.

4. *If required, determine whether there is a possibility of an internal flight alternative. Considerations:*

- Whether there would be undue hardship for the claimant, both in reaching the location of the IFA and in establishing residence there.

- Religious, economic, social and cultural factors, among others, may be relevant in determining the reasonableness of an IFA for a woman fearing gender-related persecution.

Guideline 6 — Scheduling and Changing the Date or Time of a Proceeding

Guidelines Issued by the Chairperson, Pursuant to Paragraph 159(1)(h) of the *Immigration and Refugee Protection Act*

Effective date: April 1, 2010

Amended December 15, 2012

1. — Introduction

1.1 The Immigration and Refugee Board of Canada (IRB) is a quasi-judicial, independent administrative tribunal that operates less formally and more expeditiously than a traditional court of law. Accordingly, the *Immigration and Refugee Protection Act*[203] (*IRPA*) requires that each division of the IRB deal with all proceedings before it as informally and quickly as the circumstances and the considerations of fairness and natural justice permit.[204]

1.2 The IRB originally issued Chairperson's Guideline 6 on December 1, 2003. At the time, it applied only to the Refugee Protection Division (RPD). The Guideline was ex-

---

[203] *T.S.C. 2001, c. 27.*

[204] *IRPA*, subsection 162(2).

panded to the then existing two other divisions, the Immigration Appeal Division (IAD) and the Immigration Division (ID) and was reissued in April, 2010. It is again being updated to reflect important changes to the *IRPA* set out in the *Balanced Refugee Reform Act*[205] and the *Protecting Canada's Immigration System Act.*[206] These changes include the addition of another division to the IRB, the Refugee Appeal Division (RAD), strict timelines within which the RPD must hear refugee claims, and special detention provisions for designated foreign nationals before the ID.

1.3 In this document, "counsel" refers both to counsel for the subject of a proceeding before the IRB and Minister's counsel.

2. — Purpose

2.1 The purpose of this Guideline is to explain the process the IRB follows before and during a hearing to ensure fair and efficient scheduling of its proceedings. This Guideline also sets out what the IRB expects of participants and what participants can expect from the IRB. While Chairperson's Guidelines are not mandatory, members are expected to apply them or provide a reasoned justification for not doing so.

2.2 This Guideline is to be read in conjunction with the rules of each division.[207] It is intended that it be sufficiently flexible to take into account the various circumstances that arise in the four divisions. To this end, the Guideline first sets out general principles that apply to all four divisions (section three), and then outlines particular circumstances which may give rise to special considerations in each respective division (sections four to seven).

3. — Principles Applicable to all Divisions

3.1 — General

3.1.1 The IRB has the lawful authority to control its process and to set its own procedures, as long as the principles of natural justice and fairness are followed.[208]

3.1.2 To fulfil its mandate, the IRB must schedule and conduct its proceedings so that immigration appeals, refugee appeals, admissibility hearings, detention reviews, refugee protection claims, and other proceedings are finalized as quickly as possible and, where applicable, within their legislative timeframes. The IRB must minimize the number of unnecessary postponements and adjournments and conduct cases quickly and fairly.

---

[205] *S.C. 2010, c. 8.*

[206] *S.C. 2012, c. 17.*

[207] *Refugee Protection Division Rules*, SOR/2012-0256.

[208] *Gorodiskiy, Volodimir v. Minister of Citizenship and Immigration* (July 7, 1998), F.C.T.D., no. IMM-3066-97, MacKay; *Chen, Yan v. M.C.I.* (November 7, 2011), F.C., no. IMM-1106-11, 2011 FC 1268, Rennie. See also *Siloch, Hancy v. Minister of Employment and Immigration* (January 11, 1993)(1993), F.C.A., no. A-88-92, 18 Imm L.R. (2d) 239, Stone, Desjardins, Décary (F.C.A.); *Prassad v. Minister of Employment and Immigration*, [1989] 1 S.C.R. 560 at 569.

3.2 — Procedure

3.2.1 A party who wishes to make an application to change the date or time of a proceeding must do so according to the rules of the division.[209] When the application is denied prior to the proceeding or the IRB was not able to communicate its decision to the party before the proceeding, the party and, if represented their counsel, must still appear at the IRB and be prepared to proceed; otherwise, the IRB may start abandonment proceedings.[210]

3.2.2 In cases where an application is made a second time, having previously been denied, the IRB will have careful regard for the decision and reasons for the denial of the earlier application and will only allow the new application in exceptional circumstances and where such a change is justified (for example, based on new evidence).

3.3 — Scheduling

3.3.1 The IRB schedules proceedings based on operational and legislative[211] requirements and the principles of natural justice and fairness.

3.3.2 The IRB is responsible for scheduling cases at the four divisions. The ID and RPD must schedule hearings within the time limits that are set out in the *IRPA* and its associated regulations, when applicable. At the RPD, the officer from Citizenship and Immigration Canada (CIC) or the Canada Border Services Agency (CBSA) who determines eligibility is responsible for scheduling the date for the refugee hearing at the time of referral based on criteria provided by the RPD; thereafter, scheduling is done by the RPD.

3.3.3 Except in the case of RPD hearing dates set by CIC or CBSA, as well as initial scheduling of some admissibility hearings and some detention reviews at the ID, the IRB endeavours to contact counsel for available dates in the course of assessing whether parties are ready to proceed to a hearing. When requested, counsel are required to submit their available dates for scheduling purposes to the IRB in accordance with the IRB's directions. Counsel who have submitted available dates and are no longer available on those dates must inform the IRB as soon as possible.

3.3.4 The IRB attempts to accommodate counsel's calendar based on the dates provided; however, the IRB is not bound by counsel's availability, and these attempts cannot interfere with the IRB's ability to schedule its proceedings efficiently, fairly, and within legislated timeframes. It is the division and not the parties that decides when cases will be scheduled.

---

[209] *IAD Rules* 43 and 48; *RAD Rules* 35 and 67; *ID Rules* 38 and 43; *RPD Rules* 50 and 54.

[210] *IRPA*, subsection 168(1): Abandonment of proceeding — A Division may determine that a proceeding before it has been abandoned if the Division is of the opinion that the applicant is in default in the proceedings, including by failing to appear for a hearing, to provide information required by the Division or to communicate with the Division on being requested to do so.

[211] *IRPA*, s. 57 and 57.1 (review of detention); *IRPR*, s. 159.9 (time limits for refugee hearings); and *RPD Rules* 3, 54, and 65 (fixing the date of hearings before the RPD).

3.3.5 The IRB may also require a party to participate in a scheduling conference to help the division fix a date for a proceeding.[212]

3.3.6 If counsel is retained in so many proceedings before the IRB that the IRB cannot schedule cases efficiently or within the legislated timeframes taking counsel's availability into account, the IRB may schedule proceedings on dates when counsel is not available.

3.3.7 The IRB routinely prioritizes the following types of cases, or takes other appropriate measures, to ensure fair and efficient administrative processing:

- unaccompanied minors;
- persons who are being detained under the *IRPA*;
- persons who are likely to be a danger to public health or to public safety, or would cause excessive demands on health or social services;
- persons who are serving a sentence for a criminal offence;
- persons whom the division has identified as requiring priority processing;
- persons who have had a proceeding adjourned or postponed and for which a resumption date is required; and
- cases that are remitted for redetermination by the Federal Court or the RAD.

3.4 — Vulnerable Persons

3.4.1 The IRB accommodates the special needs of persons identified as vulnerable under Chairperson's Guideline 8, *Guideline on Procedures with Respect to Vulnerable Persons Appearing before the IRB*.[213]

3.5 — Official Languages and Use of an Interpreter

3.5.1 The IRB recognizes that the parties, their counsel and witnesses have the right to participate in the official language of their choice and have the right to simultaneous interpretation of either official language if it is requested by a party.[214] Parties should inform the relevant division without delay in accordance with the division's rules if an interpreter will be required for the hearing, including the language and dialect required.

3.5.2 The IRB also recognizes that any member of the public, including counsel, has the right to communicate with the IRB in the official language of their choice. Therefore, a counsel may communicate with IRB personnel on scheduling matters in either official language,[215] even if it is not the official language chosen by the person who is the subject of the proceeding.

---

[212] *IAD Rule* 22; *RAD Rule* 24; *ID Rule* 21; and *RPD Rule* 24.

[213] *Chairperson's Guideline 8, Guideline On Procedures With Respect To Vulnerable Persons Appearing Before The IRB. December 15, 2012.*

[214] *Official Languages Act, R.S.C., 1985, c. 31 (4th Supp.). Part III — Administration of Justice, section 14 and subsections 15(1) and (2).*

[215] *Ibid.*, Part IV — Communications With and Services to the Public, section 21.

3.6 — Counsel

3.6.1 The IRB recognizes that parties have the right to be represented by counsel,[216] but this right is not absolute. The opportunity to retain counsel is not unlimited. The parties and any counsel they choose to retain must be ready and able to appear and proceed according to the scheduling requirements of the division[217] and the requirements of the legislation.

3.6.2 If counsel is retained after a date has already been set for a proceeding, the party is responsible for making sure that counsel is available and ready to proceed on the scheduled date. The IRB does not generally allow applications to change the date or time of a proceeding if a party chooses to retain counsel who is not available on a date that has already been fixed.

3.6.3 The IRB provides the parties with reasonable notice of the date and time of a proceeding in every case, which will vary according to the circumstances and the type of proceeding. The IRB therefore expects that counsel will be available and prepared to present the party's case on the date and time set by the IRB. Where, for any reason, counsel is unable to appear at a proceeding, counsel is expected to make the necessary arrangements to be replaced by another counsel who is prepared to proceed with the case on the scheduled date and time. If counsel does not appear, the IRB may decide to proceed without counsel or, if applicable, to start abandonment proceedings or to conclude that a case has been abandoned.

3.6.4 The fact that counsel wants to take time off, fulfil other professional duties or attend to personal matters that are neither urgent nor unforeseen are not sufficient reasons to allow an application to change the date or time of a proceeding.

3.7 — Medical reasons

3.7.1 If an application to change the date or time of a proceeding is made for medical reasons, other than those associated with counsel, the application should be supported by a medical certificate.[218] While there are specific requirements regarding medical certificates in the rules of some of the divisions,[219] generally all medical certificates should contain enough information to allow the member to decide the application. This information includes why the subject of the proceedings cannot participate in the proceeding on the date fixed and when it is expected that he or she will be able to do so.

3.8 — Self-represented Persons

3.8.1 The IRB will be sensitive to the situation of self-represented parties who are unfamiliar with its rules and processes.

---

[216] *IRPA*, section 167.

[217] *Pierre v. Minister of Manpower and Immigration*, [1978] 2 F.C. 849 (F.C.A.); *Aseervatham, Vimalathas v. Minister of Citizenship and Immigration* (June 1, 2000), F.C.T.D., no. IMM-1091-99, Dubé; *Kandasamy, Ratnanathan v. Minister of Citizenship and Immigration* (September 13, 2000), F.C.T.D., no. IMM-4825-99, Hansen.

[218] *Ching, Rafael Lim v. Minister of Citizenship and Immigration* (February 1, 2005), F.C., no. IMM-1825-04, 2005 FC 132, Pinard.

[219] *RAD Rules* 67(7), (8) and (9); *RPD Rules* 54(6), (7) and (8).

3.8.2 The IRB endeavours to inform self-represented parties of its process sufficiently in advance of the proceeding to help ensure that they will be ready to proceed on the scheduled date. This includes informing them of the right to be represented by counsel. The IRB expects self-represented parties to be prepared to present their case on the scheduled date.

3.9 — Time to Prepare for Proceedings

3.9.1 The IRB gives advance notice of the date and time fixed for its proceedings. The notice period will vary depending on the circumstances of the case and the type of proceeding. It is therefore expected that parties will have adequate time to prepare. An application to change the date or time of a proceeding based on the fact that parties have not had enough time to prepare must be fully substantiated. In deciding the application, the IRB considers what efforts have been made to be prepared for that proceeding.

3.10 — Other Immigration Proceedings

3.10.1 The fact that immigration or other proceedings involving the party are in progress is not generally a sufficient reason to allow an application to change the date or time of a proceeding.[220]

3.11 — Consent

3.11.1 The fact that all parties to a proceeding agree to an application to change the date or time of a proceeding does not, in itself, mean that the IRB will allow the application.[221]

3.12 — Legal Aid

3.12.1 The fact that a party is waiting for an application for legal aid to be approved is not generally a sufficient reason to allow an application to change the date or time of a proceeding.[222] However, members may consider delays in the processing of legal aid applications that were beyond the control of the party.[223]

4. — Immigration Appeal Division

4.1 The IAD allows applications to change the date or time of a proceeding only in exceptional circumstances and where such a change is justified. When considering an appli-

---

[220] *Minister of Employment and Immigration v. Lundgren, John Frederick* (September 25, 1992), F.C.T.D., no. T-682-92, Dubé; *Prassad v. Canada (Minister of Employment and Immigration)*, [1989] 1 S.C.R. 560, 7 Imm. L.R. (2d) 253 (S.C.C.); *Laidlow, Roderic v. M.C.I.* (October 10, 2012), F.C.A, no. A-77-12, 2012 FCA 256, Noël, Dawson, Stratas.

[221] *Rupolo, Pasquale v. The Queen* (October 28, 2010), F.C.A. no. A-84-10, 2010 FCA 289, Blais, Evans, Sharlow.

[222] *Flores Cabrera, Luis Enrique v. M.C.I.* (November 2, 2011), F.C., no. IMM-3751-11, 2011 FC 1251, Zinn.

[223] *Ayala Alvarez, Jose Luis v. M.C.I.* (July 29, 2010), F.C., nos. IMM-3902-09, IMM-4413-09, 2010 FC 792, O'Reilly.

cation, the member considers all relevant factors, including those set out in IAD Rule 48(4), with an important consideration being whether or not the parties were consulted by the IAD and had agreed to the date and time. Where the parties have agreed to the date and time of a proceeding, that agreement will be regarded as an explicit and positive commitment to the IAD to be present and to be prepared to proceed at that date and time.

4.2 The IAD often hears witnesses who are located in other countries, particularly in residency obligation appeals and sponsorships appeals. Parties who wish to testify from abroad or call witnesses who are situated abroad are responsible for supplying a reliable means of communication, such as valid, pre-paid calling cards and a functional land-line telephone connection, in order to facilitate their testimony. The IAD will not generally grant an application to change the date or time of a proceeding in order to make arrangements to communicate with the party or witness, if the party has not supplied such means of communication or has not acted diligently in doing so.

4.3 The fact that there are pending criminal charges or a pending appeal of a conviction on criminal charges related to the appellant is not generally a sufficient reason for the IAD to grant an application to change the date or time of a hearing.

5. — Refugee Appeal Division

5.1 The RAD holds an oral hearing only in limited circumstances.[224] While the time limits set out in the *Immigration and Refugee Protection Regulations* (*IRPR*)[225] for rendering a decision at the RAD do not apply when an oral hearing is held, the regulations signal a legislative intent for the expeditious resolution of refugee appeals.

5.2 The RAD allows applications to change the date or time of a proceeding only in exceptional circumstances and where such a change is justified. When considering an application, the member considers all relevant factors, including those set out in RAD Rule 67(5) with an important consideration being whether or not the parties were consulted by the RAD and had agreed to the date and time. Where the parties have agreed to the date and time of a proceeding, that agreement will be regarded as an explicit and positive commitment to the RAD to be present and to be prepared to proceed at that date and time.

5.3 In addition to the general requirements set out in section 3.7 of this Guideline, applications to change the date or time of a proceeding based on medical reasons, other than those related to counsel, must include the information required in *Refugee Appeal Division Rules* 67(7), (8) and (9).

6. — Immigration Division

6.1 The ID allows applications to change the date or time of a proceeding only in exceptional circumstances and where such a change is justified. When considering an application, the member considers all relevant factors, including those set out in ID Rule 43(2), with an important consideration being whether or not the parties were consulted by the ID and had agreed to the date and time. Where the parties have agreed to the date and time

---

[224] *IRPA*, s. 110(6)

[225] *SOR/2002-227, s. 159.92.*

of a proceeding, that agreement will be regarded as an explicit and positive commitment to the ID to be present and to be prepared to proceed at that date and time.

6.2 In addition, for detention reviews, compliance with mandatory statutory timeframes is a guiding principle.[226]

6.3 The ID does not generally grant applications to change the date or time of a detention review if doing so will result in the review being conducted outside the mandatory statutory timeframes. In cases where such an application is granted, the review will be rescheduled at the earliest possible date.

6.4 The ID does not grant applications to hold detention reviews outside the mandatory timeframes for the sole reason that the subject of the proceedings waives the right to have the detention reviewed within the timeframe.[227]

6.5 The ID does not grant applications to change the date or time of an admissibility hearing for the purpose of providing relief from the effect of issuing a removal order, such as avoiding the impact the issuance of a removal order may have on other legal processes.[228]

6.6 The fact that there is a pending appeal of a conviction on criminal charges related to the subject of the proceedings or a pending application for Ministerial relief from inadmissibility[229] is not generally a sufficient reason for the ID to grant an application to change the date or time of an admissibility hearing.

6.7 The fact that the subject of the proceedings is detained will be an important consideration when deciding an application to change the date and time of an admissibility hearing. In such a case, if the application is granted, the admissibility hearing will be rescheduled at the earliest possible time.

6.8 The ID expects the Minister to be prepared to proceed in an admissibility hearing from the date it is referred to the Division. The ID will not generally grant an application to change the date or time of an admissibility hearing brought by the Minister where the application is made in order to gather further evidence or prepare for the proceedings where it was reasonably foreseeable on the date of referral that such documentation or such efforts would be required.

7. — Refugee Protection Division

7.1 On December 15, 2012 substantial amendments to the *IRPA* came into force. These changes signal a clear Parliamentary shift toward an emphasis on the expeditious resolution of refugee claims. This shift was further implemented through amendments to the *IRPR*. The Regulations stipulate, for the first time, that dates for refugee hearings be

---

[226] *IRPA*, s. 57 and 57.1.

[227] *Es-Sayyid, Al-Munzir v. M.C.I.* (December 5, 2011), F.C., no. IMM-2939-11, 2011 FC 1415, Mactavish.

[228] *Fox, Timothy Roshaun v. M.C.I.* (November 26, 2009), F.C.A., no. A-393-09, 2009 FCA 346, Nadon.

[229] *Poshteh, Piran Ahmadi v. M.C.I.* (April 8, 2005), F.C.A., no. A-207-04, 2005 FCA 121, Rothstein; *Hassanzadeh, Ahmad v. M.C.I.* (June 24, 2005), F.C., no. IMM-201-05, 2005 FC 902, Mosley.

Other Relevant Legislation

fixed within specific timeframes, being 30, 45, or 60 days depending on the type of claim.[230]

7.2 In light of the amendments to *IRPA* and the Regulations, the RPD takes a strict approach to scheduling and to applications to change the date or time of a hearing. Compliance with the mandatory regulatory timeframes for conducting RPD hearings is a guiding principle.

7.3 The RPD expects parties and their counsel to be ready to proceed on the date and time scheduled for the hearing. Applications to change the date or time of the hearing will be granted only in exceptional circumstances[231] and, where the application would cause the hearing to be heard outside the statutory timeframes, only if the evidence indicates that it is necessary in order to conform with the principles of natural justice.[232]

7.4 Where an application to change the date or time of a hearing is granted, the RPD will normally reschedule the hearing within ten working days.[233] Counsel and the parties are expected to be prepared to proceed on a date fixed during that time period.

7.5 The RPD recognizes that, at the time the officer fixes the date for a refugee hearing, the claimant may not have retained counsel or may not have their counsel's available dates. Consequently, the RPD grants applications to change the date or time of a hearing that was set by the officer if the application is made in accordance with Rule 54(5) of the *Refugee Protection Division Rules*, subject only to the division's operational requirements. If the application is granted, the new date must be within the time limits set out in the Regulations for the hearing of the claim. In all other cases, the RPD will generally not grant an application to change the date or time of the proceeding based solely on the fact that the claimant chose counsel who is not available on the date the officer fixed for the hearing.

7.6 In addition to the general requirements set out in section 3.7 of this Guideline, applications to change the date or time of a proceeding based on medical reasons, other than those related to counsel, must include the information required in *Refugee Protection Division Rules* 54(6), (7) and (8).

7.7 If a party requests a change of date or time of the proceedings for the purpose of obtaining documentation, the RPD generally proceeds and will determine at the end of the hearing whether or not it is necessary to grant a delay to obtain and provide the documents.

7.8 In accordance with the *Instructions Governing the Management of Refugee Protection Claims Awaiting Front-end Security Screening*,[234] and acting on its own initiative, the RPD may administratively postpone certain proceedings when confirmation from the Canada Border Services Agency on front-end security screening of a claimant has not been received.

---

[230] *IRPR*, s. 159.9.

[231] *RPD Rule* 54(4).

[232] *IRPR*, s. 159.9(3).

[233] *RPD Rule* 54(11).

[234] *Instructions Governing the Management of Refugee Protection Claims Awaiting Front-end Security Screening*, December 15, 2012.

7.9 Despite the changes to the *IRPA* that came into force on December 15, 2012, the RPD also continues to hear transitional claims that were referred to it prior to the coming into force of those amendments. In such cases, the mandatory time limits for the hearing of refugee claims set out in the Regulations do not apply. In these transitional cases, the RPD approach to applications to change the date or time of a proceeding, and to rescheduling a hearing following an accepted application to change the date or time of a proceeding, reflects this distinct legal context within which these claims were referred to the RPD.

8. — Enquiries

For information, contact:

> Director, Policy and Procedures Directorate
> Operations Branch
> Minto Place — Canada Building
> 344 Slater Street, 14th floor
> Ottawa, Ontario K1A 0K1
> Fax: 613-952-9083

Guideline 7 — Concerning Preparation and Conduct of a Hearing in the Refugee Protection Division

Guidelines issued by the Chairperson pursuant to paragraph 159(1)(h) of the *Immigration and Refugee Protection Act*

Effective date: December 15, 2006

Amended December 15, 2012

1. — Introduction

1.1 The Refugee Protection Division (RPD) is a division of Canada's largest administrative tribunal, the Immigration and Refugee Board of Canada (IRB). Administrative tribunals operate less formally and more expeditiously than courts of law. Accordingly, the *Immigration and Refugee Protection Act* (IRPA) requires the IRB to deal with proceedings before it informally, quickly and fairly.[235] The Chairperson has issued these guidelines to explain what the RPD does before and during the hearing to make its proceedings efficient but still fair. The guidelines also set out what the RPD expects participants to do.

1.2 The guidelines apply to most cases heard by the RPD. However, in compelling or exceptional circumstances, members will use their discretion not to apply some guidelines or to apply them less strictly.

1.3 Generally speaking, the RPD will make allowances for self-represented claimants who are unfamiliar with the RPD's processes and rules. Claimants identified as particularly vulnerable will be treated with special sensitivity. The RPD may apply *Guideline 8: Guideline on Procedures with Respect to Vulnerable Persons Appearing Before the IRB*

---

[235] *Immigration and Refugee Protection Act*, subsection 162(2).

and identify as vulnerable those refugee claimants whose ability to present their case is severely impaired.

2. — The roles of members and counsel

2.1 Under the IRPA, RPD members have the same powers as commissioners who are appointed under the *Inquiries Act*.[236] They may inquire into anything they consider relevant to establishing whether a claim is well-founded.[237] This means that they define what issues must be resolved in order for them to render a decision.

2.2 A member's role is different from the role of a judge. A judge's primary role is to consider the evidence and arguments that the opposing parties choose to present; it is not to tell parties how to present their cases. Case law[238] has clearly established that the RPD has control of its own procedures. The RPD decides and gives directions as to how a hearing is to proceed. The members have to be actively involved to make the RPD's inquiry process work properly.

2.3 The role of counsel is the same whether counsel is representing a claimant or the Minister. Counsel assists the client in presenting the case in an efficient manner within the limits set by the member. Their role is essentially to protect the client's interests and right to a fair hearing.

3. — Case preparation

3.1 To make the best use of hearing time, these guidelines emphasize the importance of case preparation within the time limits set out for hearings in the *Immigration and Refugee Protection Regulations*.[239] Files will be reviewed early in the process, and the *Refugee Protection Division Rules* (*RPD Rules*) will be strictly followed.

A. — Early review of files

3.2 Prior to hearings, RPD members will review the files and provide any appropriate instructions to IRB personnel and the parties as required.

B. — Disclosure of documents

3.3 The RPD and the parties must disclose documents that they want to use at the hearing according to the *RPD Rules*.[240] Unless the member decides otherwise, a document that was not disclosed according to the *RPD Rules* cannot be used at the hearing.[241]

---

[236] *Immigration and Refugee Protection Act*, section 165.

[237] *Immigration and Refugee Protection Act*, paragraph 170(a).

[238] *Rezaei, Iraj v. M.C.I.* (December 5, 2002), F.C.T.D., No. IMM-1367-02, Beaudry, which refers to the powers of administrative tribunals according to *Prassad v. Canada (Minister of Employment and Immigration)*, [1989] 1 S.C.R. 560.

[239] *Immigration and Refugee Protection Regulations*, subsection 159.9(1).

[240] *Refugee Protection Division Rules*, rules 33 and 34.

[241] *Refugee Protection Division Rules*, rule 36.

3.4 Each document a party wants to use must be relevant and must not duplicate other documents provided by the other party, if any, or by the RPD.[242]

3.5 Members may refuse to accept documents that are not relevant to the proceeding.

3.6 The RPD will provide information on the country of reference. This means that every case will have some basic documentary evidence. The RPD may use information contained in the National Documentation Package (NDP) for the country of origin to which the refugee claim is related. In such cases, the RPD will provide a list of those documents to the parties or inform them of how to access the NDP from the IRB website.[243] Parties have the responsibility to check, prior to the hearing, for any amended version of the NDP list of documents for the country of origin in question.

C. — Information requests to IRB Research Directorate

3.7 The RPD will submit requests for country of origin and claimant-specific information to the IRB Research Directorate only where the time allows and where the RPD considers that the information is necessary to decide the case and cannot be obtained from any other source.

4. — Hearing preliminaries

4.1 The procedure for opening hearings is standardized to allow more of the hearing time to be spent on the claim itself instead of on opening formalities. Hearings proceed informally, but all the participants must show respect for the RPD and the parties.

A. — Failure to appear

4.2 The hearing will begin promptly as scheduled. Participants must be present on time and ready to proceed by the scheduled start time.

4.3 If a party or counsel does not appear by the scheduled start time, the member will note this on the record.

4.4 If a party or counsel appears within 15 minutes after the scheduled start time, the member will note the explanation for the late arrival on the record.

4.5 After 15 minutes:

- if it is a claimant who has not appeared, the member will either adjourn the hearing or the claimant will have to appear at a special hearing to explain why the claim should not be declared abandoned. This hearing must take place within the following five working days.[244]

- if it is a protected person[245] who has not appeared, the member will decide whether to proceed in the absence of that party or to adjourn the matter on a peremptory basis.

Other Relevant Legislation

---

[242] *Refugee Protection Division Rules*, rule 35.

[243] *Refugee Protection Division Rules*, subrule 33(2).

[244] *Refugee Protection Division Rules*, subrules 65(1) and (3).

[245] *Immigration and Refugee Protection Act*, subsection 95(2).

- if it is counsel who has not appeared, after giving the parties an opportunity to make submissions, the member may decide whether to proceed in counsel's absence, adjourn the proceedings or declare the claim abandoned.[246] If the member decides not to adjourn the proceedings or declare the claim abandoned, the hearing must be held the same day the decision is made or as soon as possible after that day.[247]

B. — Conference before the hearing

4.6 A brief conference with the parties will be held just before the hearing only where it would help make the proceedings fairer and more efficient.[248] When the claimant is represented, the member and counsel will participate, but the claimant will not usually be present. A represented claimant may be present if the member decides it would be useful. If the claimant was not present at the conference, before the hearing begins, the member will summarize for the claimant what was discussed and what instructions the member gave at the conference. The member will make a written record of any decisions and agreements made at the conference.[249]

C. — Interpreters

4.7 Interpreters are permanently bound by their promise to interpret accurately once they make a solemn affirmation to do so. Therefore, a member who knows that an interpreter has been sworn in before by the RPD should simply ask the interpreter to confirm that they have made the affirmation.

4.8 At the beginning of the hearing, the interpreter will confirm that they have used a standardized script to make sure that the interpreter and claimant are able to speak to and understand each other.

D. — Affirmation

4.9 Before the claimant starts testifying, the member will ask the claimant to make a solemn affirmation.

E. — Basis of Claim Form (BOC Form)

4.10 The claimant is responsible for making sure that the BOC Form was interpreted to them before the hearing. At the beginning of the hearing, the member will ask the claimant to confirm that the interpretation was done.

---

[246] *Refugee Protection Division Rules*, subrules 65(4) and (7).

[247] *Refugee Protection Division Rules*, subrule 65(7).

[248] *Refugee Protection Division Rules*, subrule 24(1). A conference should be held only where it would be more practical or efficient to consider such issues before the actual hearing or where it may be more appropriate to discuss certain sensitive issues without the presence of the claimant. For example, where there are complex legal issues to be discussed, a conference may be held to go over matters related to procedure or to evidence to be settled. A conference may also be held where the refugee claimant has been identified as vulnerable.

[249] *Refugee Protection Division Rules*, subrule 24(3).

4.11 Any changes to the BOC Form must be submitted without delay and must be received at least 10 days before the hearing according to the *RPD Rules*.[250]

F. — List of documents

4.12 The member will not create a new list of documents. The member will use a standard RPD list of documents and will update this list when a party submits documents for a proceeding.

5. — Hearing

5.1 It is an essential part of the member's inquisitorial role to be actively involved in the conduct of hearings. The member is in charge of the hearing and issues instructions as required to make the proceedings fair and efficient.

A. — Issue agenda

5.2 At the beginning of the hearing, the member will consult with counsel about the issues and will identify timelines and expectations for how the hearing will unfold.

B. — Questioning

5.3 RPD rule 10 sets out the standard order of questioning. In a claim for refugee protection where the Minister is not a party, the standard will be for the member to start the questioning, followed by counsel for the claimant.[251] Beginning the hearing in this way allows the claimant to quickly understand what evidence the member needs from the claimant in order for the claimant to prove their case.

5.4 Minister's counsel will start the questioning if the Minister is a party and has intervened on an issue of exclusion under section E or F of Article 1 of the Refugee Convention, followed by the member and then counsel for the claimant.[252]

5.5 The member will start the questioning when the Minister is a party but has not intervened on an issue of exclusion under section E or F of Article 1 of the Refugee Convention, followed by the Minister's counsel and then counsel for the claimant.[253]

5.6 The member must not vary the order of questioning unless there are exceptional circumstances[254] such as the need to accommodate a vulnerable person. Applications under *Guideline 8: Guideline on Procedures with Respect to Vulnerable Persons Appearing Before the IRB* should be made early in the process and according to the *RPD Rules*.

5.7 The member may limit the questioning of witnesses according to the nature and complexity of the issues.[255] Questioning must bring out relevant information that will help

---

[250] *Refugee Protection Division Rules*, subrule 9(2).

[251] *Refugee Protection Division Rules*, subrule 10(1).

[252] *Refugee Protection Division Rules*, subrule 10(2).

[253] *Refugee Protection Division Rules*, subrule 10(3).

[254] *Refugee Protection Division Rules*, subrule 10(5).

[255] *Refugee Protection Division Rules*, subrule 10(6).

the member make an informed decision. Questions that are answered by the claimant just repeating what is written in the BOC Form do not help the member.

C. — Representations

5.8 Parties will have an opportunity to make representations at the hearing.[256] The member will set time limits for the representations after all the evidence has been heard. The time limits will be reasonable in relation to the duration of the hearing, the number of issues and the amount of relevant evidence heard.

5.9 In general, it is expected that counsel should be ready to give oral representations after the evidence has been heard.[257] These representations must be relevant, focused and concise so that they help the member to decide the claim efficiently and make it possible for the member to give an oral decision and reasons at the end of the hearing.

D. — Oral decisions

5.10 RPD members will render oral decisions and reasons at the end of the hearing "unless it is not practicable to do so".[258]

6. — References

- *Immigration and Refugee Protection Act*, S.C. 2001, c. 27.
- *Refugee Protection Division Rules*, SOR/2012-0256.

7. — Inquiries

For more information, please contact:

> Director, Policy and Procedures Directorate
> Immigration and Refugee Board of Canada
> Minto Place — Canada Building
> 344 Slater Street, 14th Floor
> Ottawa, Ontario K1A 0K1
> Fax: 613-952-9083

Guideline 8 — Procedures With Respect to Vulnerable Persons Appearing Before the IRB

(Short title: Guideline on Vulnerable Persons)

Guideline issued by the Chairperson pursuant to paragraph 159(1)(h) of the *Immigration and Refugee Protection Act*

Effective date: December 15, 2006
Amended: December 15, 2012

---

[256] *Immigration and Refugee Protection Act*, paragraph 170(e).

[257] *Refugee Protection Division Rules*, subrule 10(7).

[258] *Refugee Protection Division Rules*, subrule 10(8).

1. — Introduction

1.1 The intention of this guideline is to provide procedural accommodation(s) for individuals who are identified as vulnerable persons by the Immigration and Refugee Board of Canada (IRB). Chairperson's guidelines are issued to assist members in carrying out their duties as decision-makers under the *Immigration and Refugee Protection Act* (IRPA)[259] and to promote consistency, coherence and fairness in the treatment of cases at the IRB.

1.2 Appearing at an IRB hearing is a process that can be difficult because of language and cultural barriers and because of the fact that the outcome of the hearing is so significant for those involved. The IRB makes decisions on immigration and refugee matters, including admissibility, detention, removal, refugee protection, permanent resident status, and family reunification — all matters that directly and profoundly affect the lives of individuals.

1.3 The IRB's four divisions, the Immigration Division (ID), the Immigration Appeal Division (IAD), the Refugee Protection Division (RPD) and the Refugee Appeal Division (RAD), are committed to providing fair proceedings to all persons appearing before them in a manner that is guided and informed by the objectives set out in section 3 of the IRPA. This guideline is intended to apply to the four divisions of the IRB.

1.4 The IRB occasionally hears cases involving persons for whom a hearing or other case process is a particularly difficult experience because their ability to present their cases is severely impaired given a physical or psychological frailty or for other reasons. The vulnerability of these persons has always required special consideration, and over the years, the IRB has adopted case-by-case procedures to deal with their cases. This guideline articulates the IRB's continuing commitment to making procedural accommodations for such persons so that they are not disadvantaged in presenting their cases.

1.5 A person's vulnerability may be due to having experienced or witnessed torture or genocide or other forms of severe mistreatment; however, it may also be due to innate or acquired personal characteristics such as a physical or mental illness, or age. What vulnerable persons appearing before the IRB have in common is their severe difficulty in going through the hearing process or other IRB processes without special consideration being given to their individual situations. Like all persons appearing before the IRB, vulnerable persons need to be treated with sensitivity and respect, but they also need to have their cases processed taking into account their specific vulnerabilities.

2. — Definition of vulnerable persons

2.1 For the purposes of this guideline, vulnerable persons are individuals whose ability to present their cases before the IRB is severely impaired. Such persons may include, but would not be limited to, the mentally ill, minors, the elderly, victims of torture, survivors of genocide and crimes against humanity, women who have suffered gender-related persecution, and individuals who have been victims of persecution based on sexual orientation and gender identity.

2.2 The definition of vulnerable persons may apply to persons presenting a case before the IRB, namely, to refugee protection claimants (in the RPD), appellants (in the IAD and in the RAD), and persons concerned (in the ID). In certain circumstances, close family

Other Relevant Legislation

---

[259] S.C. 2001, c. 27.

members of the vulnerable person who are also presenting their cases before the IRB may qualify as vulnerable persons because of the way in which they have been affected by their loved one's condition.

2.3 Persons who appear before the IRB frequently find the process difficult for various reasons, including language and cultural barriers and because they may have suffered traumatic experiences that resulted in some degree of vulnerability.[260] IRB proceedings have been designed to recognize the very nature of the IRB's mandate, which inherently involves persons who may have some vulnerabilities. In all cases, the IRB takes steps to ensure the fairness of the proceedings. This guideline addresses difficulties that go beyond those that are common to most persons appearing before the IRB. It is intended to apply to individuals who face particular difficulty and who require special consideration in the procedural handling of their cases. It applies to the more severe cases of vulnerability.

2.4 Wherever it is reasonably possible, the vulnerability must be supported by independent credible evidence[261] filed with the IRB Registry.

3. — Objectives

The objectives of this guideline are as follows:

3.1 To recognize that certain individuals face particular difficulties when they appear for their hearings or other IRB processes because their ability to present their cases is severely impaired.

3.2 To ensure that such vulnerable persons are identified and appropriate procedural accommodations are made.

3.3 To the extent possible, to prevent vulnerable persons from becoming traumatized or re-traumatized by the hearing process or another IRB process.

3.4 To ensure the ongoing sensitization of members and other hearing room participants to the impact of severe vulnerability.

4. — Procedural accommodations

4.1 Depending on the nature of a person's vulnerability, they may face particular difficulties in presenting or addressing evidence that should be taken into account in determining the procedural accommodations to be made. Such difficulties may include the following:

    a. a person's vulnerability may affect memory, behaviour and their ability to recount relevant events;

---

[260] For example, paragraph 209 of the *UNHCR Handbook on Procedures and Criteria for Determining Refugee Status under the 1951 Convention and the 1967 Protocol relating to the Status of Refugees* (Geneva, December 2011) states that "some degree of mental disturbance is frequently found in persons who have been exposed to severe persecution." Such persons regularly appear before the IRB, and the processes of the IRB have been designed to ensure that all persons are treated with sensitivity and respect. This Guideline will not necessarily apply to all such persons since it is intended to apply to those individuals whose ability to present their cases before the IRB is severely impaired.

[261] Such as a detailed report by an expert following an in-depth assessment of the person.

b. the vulnerable person may be suffering from symptoms that have an impact on the consistency and coherence of their testimony;

c. vulnerable persons who fear persons in a position of authority may associate those involved in the hearing process with the authorities they fear; and

d. a vulnerable person may be reluctant or unable to talk about their experiences.

4.2 The IRB has a broad discretion to tailor procedures to meet the particular needs of a vulnerable person, and, where appropriate and permitted by law, the IRB may accommodate a person's vulnerability by various means, including:

a. allowing the vulnerable person to provide evidence by videoconference or other means;

b. allowing a support person to participate in a hearing;

c. creating a more informal setting for a hearing;

d. varying the order of questioning;[262]

e. excluding non-parties from the hearing room;

f. providing a panel and interpreter of a particular gender;

g. explaining IRB processes to the vulnerable person; and

h. allowing any other procedural accommodations that may be reasonable in the circumstances.

5. — General principles

5.1 A person may be identified as vulnerable, and procedural accommodations made, so that the person is not disadvantaged in the presentation of their case. The identification of vulnerability will usually be made at an early stage, before the IRB has considered all the evidence in the case and before an assessment of the person's credibility has been made.

5.2 A person may be identified as vulnerable based, in part, on alleged underlying facts that are also central to the ultimate determination of their case before the IRB. An identification of vulnerability does not indicate the IRB's acceptance of the alleged underlying facts. It is made for the purpose of procedural accommodation only. Thus, the identification of a person as vulnerable does not predispose a member to make a particular determination of the case on its merits. Rather, a determination of the merits of the case will be made on the basis of an assessment of all the evidence.

5.3 Similarly, evidence initially used to identify a vulnerable person and to make procedural accommodations may not have been tested through credibility assessments or other means. If such evidence is then used to adjudicate the merits of the case, the member should ensure that the parties are given an opportunity to address this evidence as it relates to the merits of the case. This means that submissions may be made about the relevance of the evidence, and the evidence may be tested through such means as questioning by the parties and the member, and other methods. The credibility and probative value of the evidence may then be assessed by the member, even though the IRB previously ac-

Other Relevant Legislation

---

[262] See section 3.2 of IRB, *Guideline 7 — Concerning Preparation and Conduct of a Hearing in the Refugee Protection Division*. December 1, 2003. Amended December 15, 2012.

cepted the evidence, for the purpose of identifying vulnerability and making procedural accommodations.

6. — Proceedings with more than one party

6.1 Some IRB hearings are adversarial in nature, and the rules of natural justice apply equally to both parties. Identification of vulnerable persons and procedural accommodations for vulnerable persons cannot have the effect of denying any party a fair opportunity to present their case. Where the Minister[263] is a party, the Minister's views will be sought on whether a person should be identified as a vulnerable person and, if so, on the nature of any procedural accommodations to be made, except for accommodations of an administrative or minor nature.

7. — Early identification

7.1 A person can be identified as vulnerable at any stage of the proceedings. It is preferable to identify vulnerable persons at the earliest opportunity.

7.2 In the course of early review of the file, the IRB may find information disclosing that the ability of the person to present their case may be severely impaired. The IRB may initiate early contact with the person, the designated representative, counsel or any other person to gather evidence that is relevant to whether the individual should be identified as a vulnerable person and that is relevant to the types of procedural accommodations that might be made.

7.3 Counsel for a person who may be considered vulnerable is best placed to bring the vulnerability to the attention of the IRB, and is expected to do so as soon as possible. Others who are associated with the person or who have knowledge of facts indicating that the person may be vulnerable (counsel for the Minister or any other person) are encouraged to do the same. Wherever it is reasonably possible, independent credible evidence documenting the vulnerability must be filed with the IRB Registry.

7.4 Counsel for a person who wishes to be identified as a vulnerable person must make an application under the Rules of the Division.[264] The application must specify the nature of the vulnerability, the type of procedural accommodations sought and the rationale for the particular accommodations. The IRB will be sensitive to the barriers that may be created by the formal requirements related to making applications in the case of self-represented persons and other situations and will waive or modify the requirements or time limits set out in the Rules, as appropriate. The IRB may also act on its own initiative.

7.5 A member manager may identify an individual as a vulnerable person and may take appropriate measures to accommodate the person at an early stage and before a member has been assigned to conduct a proceeding. The assigned member is not bound by the IRB's early identification. The assigned member will consider this guideline and whether

---

[263] The Minister of Citizenship and Immigration and the Minister of Public Safety and Emergency Preparedness.

[264] RPD rule 50 (SOR/2012-0256), ID rule 38 (SOR/2002-229), IAD rule 43 (SOR/2002-230) and RAD rule 35 (SOR/2012-0257).

the identification and any procedural accommodations made will be maintained, amended or discontinued.

7.6 To the extent practicable, once a person has been declared a vulnerable person under this guideline, a member will be assigned at an early stage in the file and will be responsible for that file until the proceeding is concluded.

7.7 The IRB may hold conferences prior to and during hearings to assist in identifying vulnerable persons and to establish the nature of the procedural accommodations required.

8. — Expert evidence

8.1 A medical, psychiatric, psychological, or other expert report regarding the vulnerable person is an important piece of evidence that must be considered. Expert evidence can be of great assistance to the IRB in applying this guideline if it addresses the person's particular difficulty in coping with the hearing process, including the person's ability to give coherent testimony.

8.2 The IRB may suggest that an expert report be submitted but will not order or pay for it.

8.3 Generally, experts' reports should contain the following information:

a. the particular qualifications and experience of the professional that demonstrate an expertise that pertains to the person's particular condition;

b. the questions that were posed to the expert by the person who requested the expert report;

c. the factual foundation underlying the expert's opinion;

d. the methodology used by the expert in assessing the person, including whether an interview was conducted, the number and length of interviews, whether tests were administered, and, if so, what those tests were and the significance of the results;

e. whether the person is receiving treatment and, if so, the nature of the treatment and whether the treatment is controlling the condition;

f. whether the assessing expert was also treating the person at the time of producing the report; and

g. the expert's opinion about the person's condition and ability to participate in the hearing process, including any suggested procedural accommodations and why particular procedural accommodations are recommended.

8.4 Experts should not offer opinions on issues within the exclusive jurisdiction of the decision-maker, such as the merits of the person's case.

8.5 An expert's opinion is not in itself proof of the truthfulness of the information upon which it is based. The weight given to the report will depend, among other things, on the credibility of the underlying facts in support of the allegation of vulnerability.

8.6 The absence of expert evidence does not necessarily lead to a negative inference about whether the person is in fact vulnerable. The IRB will consider whether it was reasonably possible to obtain such evidence.

Other Relevant Legislation

9. — Scheduling

9.1 The IRB has a duty to determine all proceedings before it as informally and quickly as the circumstances and the considerations of fairness and natural justice permit.[265] Moreover, the uncertainty and anxiety caused by delay can be particularly detrimental to some vulnerable persons. In such cases, those persons may be given scheduling priority. Where giving scheduling priority would not facilitate the objectives of this guideline, other procedural accommodations may be provided as appropriate.

10. — Questioning the vulnerable person

10.1 The IRB ensures that all those who appear at its hearings or other proceedings are questioned with sensitivity and respect. This obligation is all the more important in the case of vulnerable persons. In probing the information provided by the person, the IRB will attempt to avoid traumatizing or re-traumatizing the vulnerable person.[266]

11. — Decisions and reasons

11.1 The uncertainty and anxiety generated by waiting for a decision and reasons for decision may be particularly stressful for vulnerable persons. Generally, decisions and reasons for decisions involving vulnerable persons will be delivered as soon as possible, and orally wherever appropriate. In individual cases, members may determine that written reasons are preferable.

12. — Designated representative

12.1 In some cases, vulnerable persons may be under 18 years of age or unable, in the opinion of the IRB, to appreciate the nature of the proceedings. In such cases, the IRB shall designate a person to represent the person, as required by subsection 167(2) of IRPA.[267]

13. — Self-represented persons

13.1 Self-represented persons are entitled to the same procedural safeguards as those who are represented, and the IRB will endeavour to ensure that the process outlined in this guideline is both accessible and understandable to these persons. The IRB will take extra care to ensure that self-represented vulnerable persons can participate as meaningfully as possible in their own hearings.

---

[265] IRPA, subsection 162(2).

[266] For a useful guide on questioning, see the *Training Manual on Victims of Torture* developed by the Learning and Professional Development directorate (LPDD) of the IRB. The principles suggested in the manual with respect to torture victims can be adopted, with necessary modifications, to the questioning of other vulnerable persons.

[267] See also RPD rule 20 (SOR/2012-0256), ID rules 18 and 19 (SOR/2002-229), IAD rule 19 (SOR/2002-230) and RAD rule 21 (SOR/2012-0257).

14. — Women fearing gender-related persecution

14.1 The RPD and the RAD will consider the IRB guideline entitled *Women Refugee Claimants Fearing Gender-Related Persecution* in all cases involving women refugee cases based on gender.[268] This guideline comprehensively sets out the relevant considerations and explicitly recognizes the special problems faced by women who fear gender-related persecution.

15. — Minors

15.1 In all cases involving minors, the RPD will continue to consider and apply the IRB guideline entitled *Child Refugee Claimants — Procedural and Evidentiary Issues*.[269]

15.2 In all cases involving minors appearing before the ID, the IAD or the RAD, these respective divisions will consider and apply the IRB guideline entitled *Child Refugee Claimants — Procedural and Evidentiary Issues*, making necessary modifications in respect of any provisions in this guideline that are not relevant to the ID, the IAD or the RAD.

16. — LGBTI individuals

16.1 Lesbian, gay, bisexual, transgender and intersex (LGBTI) individuals may have suffered negative experiences due to homophobia in their respective countries of origin, most specifically discrimination, bullying, ostracism, violence, sexual assault, and so on. The IRB has been sensitive and will continue to be sensitive and alert to the impact that these particular circumstances may have on some LGBTI individuals; it will also ensure that when identified as vulnerable, those individuals, like other persons identified as vulnerable, are not disadvantaged in presenting their cases to the IRB.

17. — References

- *Immigration and Refugee Protection Act*, S.C. 2001, c. 27.
- *Refugee Protection Division Rules*, SOR/ 2012-0256.
- *Refugee Appeal Division Rules*, SOR/2012-0257.
- *Immigration Appeal Division Rules*, SOR/2002-230.
- *Immigration Division Rules*, SOR/2002-229.
- Immigration and Refugee Board of Canada. Professional Development Branch. *Training Manual on Victims of Torture*. 2004.
- Immigration and Refugee Board of Canada. Guideline 3 — *Child Refugee Claimants: Procedural and Evidentiary Issues*. 1996.
- Immigration and Refugee Board of Canada. Guideline 4 — *Women Refugee Claimants Fearing Gender-Related Persecution*. 1996. Update.

Other Relevant Legislation

---

[268] Guideline 4 — *Women Refugee Claimants Fearing Gender-Related Persecution*. Update, November 25, 1996.

[269] Guideline 3 — *Child Refugee Claimants: Procedural and Evidentiary Issues*. September 30, 1996.

- Immigration and Refugee Board of Canada. Guideline 7 — *Concerning Preparation and Conduct of a Hearing in the Refugee Protection Division*. 2003. Amended 15 December 2012.

18. — Inquiries

For more information, please contact:

Director, Policy and Procedures Directorate
Immigration and Refugee Board of Canada
Minto Place — Canada Building
344 Slater Street, 14th Floor
Ottawa, Ontario K1A 0K1
Fax: 613-952-9083

Appendix II

An Act respecting immigration to Québec

CQLR, c. I-0.2 [S.Q. 1968, c. 68], as am. S.Q. 1978, c. 82; 1979, c. 32, ss. 9, 10; 1981, c. 9, ss. 1–8; 1981, c. 23, s. 32; U.K. 1982, c. 11, Sched. B, Pt. I, s. 33; S.Q. 1984, c. 44, s. 21; 1984, c. 47, s. 102; 1985, c. 30, s. 55; 1987, c. 75; 1988, c. 41, ss. 69–71; 1990, c. 4, s. 583; 1991, c. 3; 1992, c. 5; 1993, c. 70, ss. 1–18 [ss. 3(1), 8, 9, 11(2), (8), (9) not in force at date of publication; s. 8 repealed 1998, c. 15, s. 14.]; 1994, c. 15, ss. 12–29; 1996, c. 21, ss. 48, 49; 1997, c. 43, s. 302; 1998, c. 15, ss. 1–13; 1999, c. 40, s. 147; 1999, c. 71; 2001, c. 58 [Not in force at date of publication. Repealed 2016, c. 3, s. 115. Not in force at date of publication.]; 2004, c. 18 [ss. 2, 6, 10(5) not in force at date of publication. Repealed 2016, c. 3, s. 116. Not in force at date of publication.]; 2005, c. 24, ss. 38–40; 2013, c. 16, ss. 192–195; 2014, G.O. 1, 1242; 2015, c. 8, ss. 347–349; 2016, c. 3, s. 128 [Not in force at date of publication.].

[Note: the title of this Act was changed from "An Act respecting the Ministère de l'immigration" to "An Act respecting the Ministère des Communautés culturelles et de l'immigration" by 1981, c. 9, s. 1.]

[Note: the title of this Act was changed from "An Act respecting the Ministère des Communautés culturelles et de l'immigration" to "An Act respecting immigration to Québec" by 1994, c. 15, s. 12.]

[Note: An Act respecting immigration to Québec *repealed by 2016, c. 3, s. 128. Not in force at date of publication.]*

Division I — Definition

1. [Repealed 1994, c. 15, s. 13.]

2. "foreign national" — In this act, **"foreign national"** means a person who is neither a Canadian citizen nor a permanent resident within the meaning of the *Immigration and Refugee Protection Act* (Statutes of Canada, 2001, chapter 27) and the regulations thereunder, who settles temporarily in Québec otherwise than as the representative of a foreign government or as an international civil servant.

1968, c. 68, s. 2; 1974, c. 64, s. 1; 1978, c. 82, s. 1; 1981, c. 9, s. 3; 1994, c. 15, s. 15; 2004, c. 18, s. 1

DIVISION II — SELECTION OF FOREIGN NATIONALS

3. Selection of foreign nationals — The selection of foreign nationals wishing to settle permanently or temporarily in Québec is effected within the framework of government policy concerning immigrants and foreign nationals. The selection is intended, in particular,

(a) to contribute to the enrichment of the socio-cultural heritage of Québec, to the stimulation of its economic development and to the pursuit of its demographic objectives;

(b) to facilitate the reuniting, in Québec, of Canadian citizens and permanent residents with their close relatives from abroad;

(c) to enable Québec to assume its share of responsibilities regarding the reception of refugees and other persons in a particularly distressful situation;

(d) to favour the coming, among foreign nationals who apply therefor, of persons who will be able to become successfully established in Québec;

(e) to facilitate the conditions of the stay in Québec of foreign nationals wishing to study, work temporarily or receive medical treatment, having regard to the reasons for their coming and the capacity of Québec to receive them.

Proposed Amendment — 3(e)

(e) to facilitate the conditions of the stay in Québec of foreign nationals wishing to study or work temporarily, having regard to the reasons for their coming and the capacity of Québec to receive them.
2004, c. 18, s. 2 [Not in force at date of publication. Repealed 2016, c. 3, s. 116. Not in force at date of publication.]

1968, c. 68, s. 3; 1969, c. 9, s. 3; 1974, c. 6, s. 111; 1974, c. 64, s. 2; 1978, c. 82, s. 2; 1988, c. 41, s. 69; 1993, c. 70, s. 1; 1994, c. 15, s. 17

3.0.0.1 The Minister, having regard to government policy concerning immigrants and foreign nationals, shall formulate guidelines respecting immigration and table them in the National Assembly for examination by the appropriate committee of the Assembly. The National Assembly may, for that purpose, hear any person or organization.

2004, c. 18, s. 3

3.0.1 Annual immigration plan — The Minister, having regard to government policy concerning immigrants and foreign nationals and to its guidelines on immigration, shall establish an annual immigration plan.

Foreign nationals — The purpose of the plan is to specify planned immigration levels to promote the enrichment of the sociocultural fabric of Québec within the framework of the objectives pursued in the selection of foreign nationals.

Selection activities — The plan shall set out the maximum or estimated number of foreign nationals who may settle in Québec or of selection certificates that may be issued, and their distribution by class or within the same class; the maximum or estimated number may also be determined by source area. The plan shall take into account, among other factors, the projected overall demand for selection certificates, the projected admission and selection levels and Quéebec's capacity to welcome and integrate immigrants.

A source area may comprise a country, a group of countries, a continent or part of a continent.

Tabling — The plan shall be tabled in the National Assembly not later than 1 November or, if the Assembly is not sitting on that date, not later than the fifteenth day after resumption.

1998, c. 15, s. 1; 1999, c. 71, s. 1; 2004, c. 18, s. 4

3.1 Application for permanent residence — A foreign national wishing to settle permanently in Québec must, except for the classes and cases prescribed by regulation, file an application for a selection certificate with the Minister of Immigration and Cultural Communities in the manner determined by regulation in accordance with the procedure prescribed under paragraph f of section 3.3.

Selection certificate — The Minister shall issue a selection certificate to the foreign national who meets the conditions and criteria of selection determined by regulation.

Selection certificate — Despite the second paragraph, the Minister may, in accordance with the regulations, issue a selection certificate to a foreign national in a particularly distressful situation, in particular, in the case of Convention refugees as defined in the Act respecting immigration to Canada, or in any other case where the Minister considers that the results obtained following the application of the selection criteria do not reflect whether or not the foreign national will be able to become successfully established in Québec. Conversely, the Minister may refuse to issue such a certificate to a foreign national who meets the conditions and criteria of selection if he has reasonable grounds to believe that the foreign national does not intend to settle in Québec or is unlikely to settle successfully in Québec or that the settlement of the foreign national would be contrary to public interest.

[Editor's Note: SOR/2002-227, s. 362 provides that if, before April 1, 1999, a foreign national made an application for an immigrant visa as an investor and signed any document referred to in clause 1(v)(iii)(A) of Schedule X to the Immigration Regulations, 1978, *SOR/78-172 (the "former Regulations"), as Schedule X read immediately before April 1, 1999, or, in the case of an investor in a province, either applied for a selection certificate under s. 3.1 of* An Act respecting immigration to Québec, *chapter I-0.2, as amended from time to time, or applied for an immigrant visa as an investor, and signed an investment agreement in accordance with the law of Québec, the relevant provisions of the former Regulations respecting an applicant for an immigrant visa as an investor, an approved business, an investor in a province, a fund manager, an eligible business, an approved fund, a fund, an escrow agent, a privately administered venture capital fund or a government-administered venture capital fund continue to apply as they read immediately before April 1, 1999 to all persons governed by their application before April 1, 1999.]*

1978, c. 82, s. 3; 1992, c. 5, s. 1; 1993, c. 70, s. 2; 1994, c. 15, s. 18; 1996, c. 21, s. 48; 1998, c. 15, s. 2; 1999, c. 71, s. 2; 2005, c. 24, s. 38; 2013, c. 16, s. 192

3.1.1 Selection criteria — In the cases determined by regulation, an undertaking to assist a foreign national to settle in Québec is required.

Proposed Amendment — 3.1.1

3.1.1 Selection Criteria — Where determined by regulation, an undertaking to assist the foreign national in settling in Québec shall constitute one of the selection criteria prescribed under paragraph b of section 3.3.

1993, c. 70, s. 3(1) [Not in force at date of publication.]

Application for undertaking — The application for an undertaking shall be filed by a person or group of persons determined by regulation according to the conditions prescribed thereby. If, in the opinion of the Minister, the person or group of persons meets the conditions prescribed by regulation, the undertaking shall be subscribed to according to the terms determined by regulation. The application for an undertaking and the undertaking shall be made on the forms prescribed by the Minister.

Certificate of undertaking — The Minister shall issue a certificate of undertaking to a foreign national in whose respect an undertaking has been made and who is not required to file an application for a selection certificate.

1991, c. 3, s. 1; 1993, c. 70, s. 3; 1998, c. 15, s. 3

3.1.2 Application — A foreign national in Québec who does not hold a selection certificate may make an application to the Minister for a certificate of statutory situation. He shall file his application in accordance with the procedure prescribed under paragraph f of section 3.3.

Certificate of identity — The Minister shall issue a certificate of statutory situation to any foreign national who meets the conditions determined by regulation.

1992, c. 5, s. 2; 1993, c. 70, s. 4; 1998, c. 15, s. 4

3.1.3 Conditions — The Minister may impose conditions prescribed under paragraph f.1.2 of section 3.3 which affect the granting of permanent residence under the *Immigration and Refugee Protection Act* (Statutes of Canada, 2001, chapter 27) to a foreign national who applies for a selection certificate.

Conditions — The Minister may, in the cases determined by regulation or at the request of a permanent resident, modify, lift or cancel the conditions imposed.

1993, c. 70, s. 5; 2004, c. 18, s. 5

3.2 Temporary foreign nationals — Excepting the classes of foreign nationals excluded by regulation, every foreign national seeking temporary admission to Québec to work, study or receive medical treatment must hold a certificate of acceptance issued by the Minister. He must file an application in accordance with the procedure prescribed under paragraph f of section 3.3.

Proposed Amendment — 3.2 first para.

Excepting the classes of foreign nationals excluded by regulation, every foreign national seeking temporary admission to Québec to work or study must hold a certificate of acceptance issued by the Minister. He must file an application in accordance with the procedure prescribed under paragraph f of section 3.3.

2004, c. 18, s. 6 [Not in force at date of publication. Repealed 2016, c. 3, s. 116. Not in force at date of publication.]

Certificate of acceptance — The Minister shall issue a certificate of acceptance to the foreign national who meets the conditions determined by regulation.

Certificate of acceptance — Notwithstanding the second paragraph, the Minister may, in cases provided for by regulation, exempt a foreign national from the application of the conditions contemplated in the second paragraph and issue a certificate of acceptance to him.

1978, c. 82, s. 3; 1979, c. 32, s. 9; 1993, c. 70, s. 6; 1998, c. 15, s. 5

3.2.1 Truthfulness of declarations — Where the Minister so requires, any person must, under penalty of refusal of the application for a selection certificate, a certificate of acceptance or a certificate of statutory selection or of the application for an undertaking, demonstrate to the Minister the truthfulness of the declarations made by the person respecting the application and submit to him, in the manner and time determined by him, any document which the Minister deems to be pertinent.

In particular, the Minister may refuse any application containing any false or misleading information or document.

1991, c. 3, s. 2; 1992, c. 5, s. 3; 1993, c. 70, s. 7; 1998, c. 15, s. 6; 2004, c. 18, s. 7

3.2.2 Cancellation of certificate — The Minister may cancel a selection certificate, a certificate of acceptance, a certificate of statutory situation, an undertaking or a certificate of undertaking

    (a) where the application for a certificate or an undertaking contains any false or misleading information or document;

    (b) where the certificate was delivered or the undertaking accepted by error;

    (c) where the conditions required for the issue of the certificate or the acceptance of the undertaking cease to exist.

Minister's decision — The decision of the Minister shall take effect immediately. It must give reasons and be submitted in writing to the person concerned.

1991, c. 3, s. 2; 1992, c. 5, s. 4; 1998, c. 15, s. 7; 2004, c. 18, s. 8

3.2.2.1 The Minister may refuse to examine an application for a certificate made by a person who, in the past five years, has provided any false or misleading information or document relating to an application under this Act.

The Minister may also refuse to examine an application for an undertaking made by a person who, in the past two years, has provided such information or such a document.

2004, c. 18, s. 9

DIVISION III — INTEGRATION OF FOREIGN NATIONALS

3.2.3 Integration program — The Minister shall establish and maintain, for those persons who settle in Québec, an integration program for the purpose of favouring their introduction to Québec life.

Other Relevant Legislation

Proposed Amendment — 3.2.3

3.2.3 Integration program — The Minister shall establish and be responsible for the implementation of reception services and linguistic, social and economic integration services for immigrants.
2001, c. 58, s. 1 [Not in force at date of publication. Repealed 2016, c. 3, s. 115. Not in force at date of publication.]

1991, c. 3, s. 2

3.2.4 Linguistic integration services — The Minister, under the integration program, shall provide and take charge of the implementation of linguistic integration services consisting of services of French language instruction and introduction to Québec life.

Proposed Repeal — 3.2.4

3.2.4 [Repealed 2001, c. 58, s. 1. Not in force at date of publication. Repealed 2016, c. 3, s. 115. Not in force at date of publication.]

1991, c. 3, s. 2

3.2.5 Eligibility — Immigrants domiciled in Québec who are unable to demonstrate, according to the evaluation procedure prescribed by regulation, a knowledge of French adequate to assuring their harmonious integration with the francophone majority of Québec society and who meet the other conditions established by regulation are admissible for linguistic integration services.

Extension of services — The maintaining and extension of the services are conditional upon compliance by the student receiving them with the conditions prescribed by regulation.

Proposed Repeal — 3.2.5

3.2.5 [Repealed 2001, c. 58, s. 1. Not in force at date of publication. Repealed 2016, c. 3, s. 115. Not in force at date of publication.]

1991, c. 3, s. 2

3.2.6 Financial assistance — The Minister may allocate financial assistance to a student receiving linguistic integration services.

Proposed Amendment — 3.2.6

3.2.6 Financial assistance — The Minister may allocate financial assistance to an immigrant receiving reception or integration services.
2001, c. 58, s. 2 [Not in force at date of publication. Repealed 2016, c. 3, s. 115. Not in force at date of publication.]

1991, c. 3, s. 2; 1998, c. 15, s. 8

3.2.7 Loan — The Minister may, according to the conditions prescribed by regulation, grant a loan to an immigrant in a particularly distressful situation with a view to enabling him to discharge the cost or a part of the cost of his immigration to Québec or to assisting him to discharge the costs of becoming established in Québec.

1991, c. 3, s. 2; 1993, c. 70, s. 10; 1998, c. 15, s. 9

3.2.8 Deferment of loan repayment — The Minister may defer a loan repayment or reduce the obligations of repayment where the borrower shows that he is unable to repay his loan according to the terms and conditions prescribed by regulation.

Release from debt — Where it has been impossible to recover a debt resulting from a loan even though the appropriate recovery measures have been applied to it, the Minister may grant a release from the debt.

1991, c. 3, s. 2

DIVISION IV — REGULATIONS AND AGREEMENTS

3.3 Regulations — The Government may make regulations

(a) determining classes of foreign nationals who have filed an application for a selection certificate referred to in section 3.1;

(a.1) determining the cases where and the classes of foreign nationals for which an application for a selection certificate is not required;

(b) determining the conditions of selection applicable to each of such classes of foreign nationals, having regard, in particular, to criteria such as the vocational or professional training and experience of the foreign national, the needs of the labour market in Québec as regards his profession, the age and personal qualities, education, knowledge of languages, and financial capacity of the foreign national, the assistance he may receive from relatives or friends residing in Québec, his place of destination in Québec, and the place of establishment of his enterprise; such conditions and criteria may vary within the same class, in particular by reason of the foreign national's contribution to enriching the socio-cultural or economic heritage of Québec;

(b.1) determining the classes of foreign nationals which may be exempted from one or several of the conditions and criteria of selection prescribed under paragraph b and providing that such exemptions may vary within the same class;

(b.2) determining the classes of foreign nationals in respect of which paragraph b applies to a family member of a foreign national, as defined by regulation, and providing for cases of total or partial exemption of a family member of a foreign national from conditions or criteria of selection; such conditions and criteria may vary according to the family situation of the foreign national and also within the same class;

(b.3) determining, from among the criteria prescribed under paragraph b, those which apply to a preliminary processing for selection intended to identify the applications which will be processed, prescribing the classes of foreign nationals to which the criteria will apply and determining the cases of total or partial exemption of foreign nationals; the criteria may vary according to the class and also within the same class;

Other Relevant Legislation

(b.4) prescribing the classes of foreign nationals in respect of which a selection interview must be held, determining the cases of total or partial exemption from this obligation and providing that the obligation may vary within the same class;

(b.5) determining the conditions applicable to a person or partnership that participates in the management of an investment or deposit of a sum of money by a person who files a lawful application;

(b.6) determining the conditions applicable to an investment or deposit as well as the management and disposition of the sums invested or deposited, including their reimbursement and confiscation;

(c) determining the cases where an undertaking to assist a foreign national to settle in Québec is required and the cases where an undertaking ceases to have effect;

(c.1) determining the persons or groups of persons who may file an application for an undertaking and the conditions of the filing;

(c.2) determining the conditions which must be met by the person or group of persons who subscribe to such an undertaking and prescribing exemptions to one or several conditions by reason of the family situation or minority of the foreign national for whom the undertaking is subscribed;

(c.3) determining the terms of the undertaking and its duration, which may vary according to the age or circumstances of the foreign national or of his family;

Proposed Addition — 3.3(c.4)

(c.4) determining the cases in which an undertaking to assist a foreign national in settling in Québec constitutes one of the conditions and one of the criteria of selection referred to in paragraph b;

1993, c. 70, s. 11(2) [Not in force at date of publication.]

(d) determining the cases where and the classes of foreign nationals to whom the Minister may issue a selection certificate referred to in the third paragraph of section 3.1, and determining the procedure to be followed in a case where the Minister considers that the results obtained following the application of the selection criteria do not reflect whether or not the foreign national will be able to become successfully established in Québec;

(d.1) determining the cases where a certificate of statutory situation referred to in section 3.1.2 is to be issued and determining, according to the status of the foreign national as established under the *Immigration Act* (Revised Statutes of Canada, 1985, chapter I-2), types of certificates of statutory situation and the conditions applicable to each type;

(e) for the purposes of section 3.2, determining, while having particular regard to labour market conditions in Québec, the conditions that must be met by a foreign national seeking to stay temporarily in Québec to work, determining the conditions that must be met by a foreign national seeking to stay temporarily in Québec to study or receive medical treatment, establishing the cases where the Minister may exempt a foreign national from the application of the conditions referred to in the second paragraph of section 3.2 and issue a certificate of acceptance, and determining the classes of foreign nationals who may be excluded from the application of section 3.2;

Proposed Amendment — 3.3(e)

(e) for the purposes of section 3.2, determining, while having particular regard to labour market conditions in Québec, the conditions that must be met by a foreign national seeking to stay temporarily in Québec to work, determining the conditions that must be met by a foreign national seeking to stay temporarily in Québec to study, establishing the cases where the Minister may exempt a foreign national from the application of the conditions referred to in the second paragraph of section 3.2 and issue a certificate of acceptance, and determining the classes of foreign nationals who may be excluded from the application of section 3.2;

2004, c. 18, s. 10(5) [Not in force at date of publication. Repealed 2016, c. 3, s. 116. Not in force at date of publication.]

(f) determining the procedure that must be followed in order to obtain a selection certificate under section 3.1, a certificate of statutory situation under section 3.1.2 or a certificate of acceptance under section 3.2, or in order to subscribe an undertaking;

(f.1) determining the conditions of validity and the duration of a selection certificate, which may vary according to the class of foreign nationals or within the same class and according to whether the application is made in Québec or abroad;

(f.1.0.1) determining the conditions of validity of a certificate of acceptance, which may vary according to the class of employment or within the same class, and determining the duration of a certificate of acceptance, which may vary, in the case of a foreign national coming to Québec to study, according to whether the person is a minor or of age or according to the program of study or the duration of the studies, and in the case of a foreign national coming to Québec to work, according to the class of employment or within the same class, the duration of employment, the person's professional experience or labour market needs in the person's profession;

(f.1.0.2) determining the cases in which a selection certificate or certificate of acceptance lapses, which may vary according to the class of foreign nationals or within the same class;

(f.1.1) determining the duration of a certificate of statutory situation and the cases in which it lapses and providing that the duration and cases in which it lapses may vary by reason, in particular, of the type of certificate of statutory situation;

(f.1.2) for the purposes of section 3.1.3, providing conditions affecting the granting of permanent residence under the *Immigration and Refugee Protection Act* to a foreign national who applies for a selection certificate under section 3.1 so as to ensure, in particular, the protection of public health, the meeting of regional or sectorial needs for specialized labour, the regional or sectorial creation of enterprises or the financing of such enterprises, and the socio-economic integration of the foreign national, determining classes of foreign nationals according to which such conditions may vary and providing that such conditions may vary within the same class;

(f.1.3) determining the classes of foreign nationals which may be exempted from one or several conditions prescribed under paragraph f.1.2 and providing that such exemptions may vary within the same class;

(f.1.4) determining the duration of the conditions prescribed under section 3.1.3, determining the classes of foreign nationals according to which the duration may vary and providing that the duration may vary within the same class;

Other Relevant Legislation

(f.1.5) determining the cases in which the conditions prescribed under section 3.1.3 may be modified, lifted or cancelled;

(f.2) establishing the fees payable for processing an application for an undertaking, a certificate of statutory situation, a selection certificate or a certificate of acceptance, for issuing any such certificate or for subscribing an undertaking, and determining the cases where total or partial exemption from payment is to be granted; the fees may vary in the case of an undertaking according to the family situation of the foreign national, in the case of a certificate of statutory situation according to the authorization allowing the foreign national to be in Canada, in the case of a selection certificate according to the classes of foreign nationals or to the stages in the processing of an application or, in the case of a certificate of acceptance according to the reason for the temporary admission of the foreign national to Québec;

(f.3) establishing the fees payable for processing an application by an employer relating to a temporary or permanent job for a foreign national; the fees may vary according to whether the job is temporary or permanent or according to the class of employment;

(g) [Repealed 2013, c. 16, s. 193(2).]

(h) determining, with regard to linguistic integration services, the services offered, the teaching program, the conditions of admissibility to the services, the form and tenor of an application, the conditions of obtaining, maintaining and extending the said services, the appropriate training period and the procedure for evaluating the knowledge of French; these provisions may vary according to services and classes of immigrants or of students;

Proposed Amendment — 3.3(h)

(h) determining the conditions of eligibility for reception services and linquistic, social or economic integration services, according to services or classes of immigrants;
2001, c. 58, s. 3 [Not in force at date of publication. Repealed 2016, c. 3, s. 115. Not in force at date of publication.]

Proposed Amendment — 3.3(h)

(h) determining, with regard to linguistic integration services, the services offered, the teaching program, the conditions of admissibility to the services, the conditions of obtaining, maintaining and extending the said services, the appropriate training period and the procedure for evaluating the knowledge of French; these provisions may vary according to services and classes of immigrants or of students;
1993, c. 70, s. 11(8) [Not in force at date of publication.]

(i) [Repealed 1998, c. 15, s. 10(8).]

(j) determining, with a view to assisting the reception and settlement of immigrants in a particularly distressful situation, the classes of loans, the conditions of granting and of repayment thereof, and the applicable rate of interest;

(k) defining the expression "immigration consultant", determining classes of consultants and establishing various standards according to such classes;

(l) establishing standards of qualification for the recognition of immigration consultants and determining the conditions to be met and the information or documents to be provided to obtain recognition, the duration of the recognition, the conditions for its renewal and the fees payable for an application for recognition or for its renewal;

(m) determining the functions and powers of the Minister with respect to the recognition of immigration consultants and the supervision of their activities, and the cases in which or conditions under which recognition is to be refused, suspended, revoked or not renewed;

(n) determining conditions or obligations applicable to immigration consultants or activities they are prohibited from engaging in, in particular with respect to advertising their services;

(o) prescribing the content and amount of the professional liability insurance policy that immigration consultants are required to hold;

(p) exempting members or a class of members of a professional order from all or part of the rules applicable to immigration consultants; and

(q) determining the provisions of a regulation whose violation constitutes an offence;

(r) providing for administrative, monetary or other penalties for contraventions of this Act or the regulations.

A regulation under any of subparagraphs a to b.6, f.2 and f.3 of the first paragraph is not subject to the publication requirement set out in section 8 of the *Regulations Act* (chapter R-18.1) and, despite section 17 of that Act, comes into force on the date of its publication in the *Gazette officielle du Québec* or on any later date mentioned in the regulation.

1978, c. 82, s. 3; 1979, c. 32, s. 10; 1981, c. 23, s. 32; 1984, c. 47, s. 103; 1987, c. 75, s. 1; 1991, c. 3, s. 3; 1992, c. 5, s. 5; 1993, c. 70, s. 11; 1998, c. 15, s. 10; 2004, c. 18, s. 10(1)–(4), (6)–(9); 2013, c. 16, s. 193; 2015, c. 8, s. 347

3.4 Regulations — The Minister may, by regulation,

(a) establish the weighting of selection criteria and the passing score and, where expedient, the cutoff score determined in relation to a selection criterion, applicable to the preliminary stage of selection established under paragraph b.3 of section 3.3 and to the selection established under paragraph b of section 3.3, which weighting and which scores may vary according to the family situation of the foreign national, according to the classes of foreign nationals and within the same class of foreign nationals;

(b) determine that the regulation applies to applications that are being processed, or to applications filed after a particular date that are being processed, or to those that have not yet reached a particular stage on the date of coming into force of the regulation;

(c) if the number of selection certificate applications the Minister intends to accept is determined by a decision made under section 3.5, require a person or partnership referred to in subparagraph b.5 of the first paragraph of section 3.3 that participates in the management of an investment of a foreign national to hold a quota assigned by the Minister;

(d) set the minimum quota of the person or partnership;

Other Relevant Legislation

(e) determine the terms and conditions for assigning a quota to the person or partnership, in particular by providing a quota calculation formula and determining the value of the parameters;

(f) prescribe the administrative, monetary or other penalties applicable to a person or partnership that does not comply with the quota assigned by the Minister;

(g) determine the conditions governing the transfer of a quota.

Regulation — A regulation made under this section is not subject to the requirement to publish contained in section 8 of the *Regulations Act* (chapter R-18.1) and, notwithstanding section 17 of that Act, comes into force on the date of its publication in the *Gazette officielle du Québec*, or at any later date fixed in the regulation.

1993, c. 70, s. 12; 2015, c. 8, s. 348

3.5 Despite any other provision of this Act, the Minister may, particularly in view of the guidelines and objectives set out in the annual immigration plan and of Québec's needs and its capacity to welcome and integrate immigrants, make a decision in relation to the receipt and processing of applications for selection certificates for a specified period.

The decision may apply to all countries or a source area and to a class of foreign nationals or part of a class of foreign nationals. It may, in particular, pertain to the maximum number of applications the Minister intends to accept, the suspension of the receipt of applications, the order of priority for the processing of applications and the disposal of applications the Minister has yet to examine.

The decision stands for a maximum period of 14 months and may be modified or renewed.

The Minister shall publish the decision in the *Gazette officielle du Québec* and in any medium considered appropriate.

Decisions take effect on the date of their publication or on any later date specified. The reason for a decision must be included in the decision.

A decision may, if it so specifies, apply to applications for a selection certificate received within three months before its effective date that have yet to be examined by the Minister. In such cases, the Minister shall notify the applicant and, if applicable, return the sums received as fees.

The *Regulations Act* (chapter R-18.1) does not apply to a decision made under this section.

2004, c. 18, s. 11; 2013, c. 16, s. 194

[Editor's Note: S.Q. 2004, c. 18, s. 16 states that s. 3.5 applies only to applications for selection certificates received after May 13, 2004.]

---

4. [Repealed 1994, c. 15, s. 21.]

5. [Repealed 1988, c. 41, s. 70.]

6. Agreements — The Minister may, according to law, make any agreement with the Government of Canada or any body thereof and with any other government or body, in conformity with the interests and rights of Québec, to facilitate the carrying out of this Act.

Agreements for exchange of information — He may make any agreement, in the same manner and with the same authorities or with any department or body of the Gouvernement du Québec, for the exchange of information obtained under an Act entrusted to the administration of that Government, department or body, in order to attain the immigration objectives or to discharge the obligations incumbent upon him under this Act.

1968, c. 68, s. 7; 1991, c. 3, s. 4; 1993, c. 70, s. 13; 1994, c. 15, s. 22

DIVISION IV.1 — FEES PAYABLE

[Heading added 2013, c. 16, s. 195.]

6.1 The fees payable for the processing of an application for a selection certificate filed by a foreign national belonging to the economic class as an investor are $15,000.

The fees must be paid when the application for a selection certificate is filed.

The fees are adjusted and rounded off in accordance with section 83.3 of the *Financial Administration Act* (chapter A-6.001) and the regulation made under that Act.

The Minister publishes the results of the adjustment in the *Gazette officielle du Québec* and informs the public of the results by any means considered appropriate.

2013, c. 16, s. 195; 2014, G.O. 1, 1242; 2015, c. 8, s. 349

7.–8. [Repealed 1984, c. 44, s. 21.]

9.–12. [Repealed 1994, c. 15, s. 23.]

DIVISION V — INVESTIGATIONS

12.1 Inquiries — The Minister or any person designated by him as an investigator or inspector may make inquiries in order to ensure that this Act and the regulations are being complied with and to prevent, detect or repress contraventions to this Act.

1978, c. 82, s. 5; 1991, c. 3, s. 5; 1992, c. 5, s. 6; 1993, c. 70, s. 14

12.1.1 Powers and immunity — In conducting an investigation, the Minister and investigators are vested with the powers and immunity of commissioners appointed under the *Act respecting public inquiry commissions* (chapter C-37), except the power to order imprisonment.

1993, c. 70, s. 15

12.1.2 Information — An inspector may, for the purposes of this Act and the regulations, require any information and any document and examine and make copies of such documents.

1993, c. 70, s. 15

12.1.3 Immunity — No inspector may be prosecuted for acts performed in good faith in the carrying out of his duties.

1993, c. 70, s. 15

Other Relevant Legislation

12.1.4 Identification — On request, an inspector or investigator shall identify himself and produce the certificate signed by the Minister and attesting his capacity.

1993, c. 70, s. 15

12.2 Copy of documents — Any copy of a book, register or document produced for an investigation and certified by the Minister or an investigator as being a true copy of the original, is admissible as proof and has the same probative force as the original.

1978, c. 82, s. 5; 1991, c. 3, s. 5

DIVISION VI — PENAL PROVISIONS

12.3 Offence — Every person is guilty of an offence who communicates information he knows or should have known to be false or misleading to the Minister or to an investigator or inspector in relation to an application

(a) for a selection certificate, a certificate of acceptance, a certificate of statutory situation or an undertaking;

(b) for access to linguistic integration services;

Proposed Amendment — 12.3(b)

(b) for access to reception or integration services;
2001, c. 58, s. 4(1) [Not in force at date of publication. Repealed 2016, c. 3, s. 115. Not in force at date of publication.]

(c) for financial assistance for a student receiving linguistic integration services;

Proposed Amendment — 12.3(c)

(c) for financial assistance for a person receiving reception or integration services;
2001, c. 58, s. 4(2) [Not in force at date of publication. Repealed 2016, c. 3, s. 115. Not in force at date of publication.]

(d) for a loan for an immigrant in a particularly distressful situation.
1978, c. 82, s. 5; 1990, c. 4, s. 583; 1991, c. 3, s. 5; 1992, c. 5, s. 7; 1993, c. 70, s. 16; 1998, c. 15, s. 11

12.4 Offence — Every person who contributes to the issue of a selection certificate, a certificate of acceptance, a certificate of undertaking or a certificate of statutory situation to a foreign national or to the subscription of an undertaking in favour of a foreign national in contravention of this Act is guilty of an offence.

1991, c. 3, s. 5; 1992, c. 5, s. 8; 1998, c. 15, s. 12

12.4.1 Offence and penalty — Every person who obstructs an inspector in the carrying out of his duties is guilty of an offence.

1993, c. 70, s. 17

12.4.2 Every person who acts as an immigration consultant without being duly recognized by the Minister or while the person's recognition is suspended, non-renewed, revoked or cancelled is guilty of an offence.

2004, c. 18, s. 12

12.4.3 No person may use or evoke the expression "Immigration-Québec", "Ministère de l'Immigration et des Communautés culturelles" or "Ministère de l'Immigration du Québec" in order to hold out or lead to the belief that the person's conduct, operations or services are approved by the Minister or the Government.

No person may use or evoke the expression "Immigration-Québec", "Ministère de l'Immigration et des Communautés culturelles" or "Ministère de l'Immigration du Québec" in order the [*sic*] hold out or lead to the belief that the person's competence is recognized by the Minister or the Government, unless the person is recognized as an immigration consultant in accordance with this Act.

Every person who contravenes this section is guilty of an offence.

2004, c. 18, s. 12; 2005, c. 24, s. 39

12.4.4 Every person who contravenes a provision referred to in paragraph q of section 3.3 is guilty of an offence.

2004, c. 18, s. 12

12.5 Fine — A natural person is liable to a fine of $500 to $1 000 in the case of an offence under section 12.3, to a fine of $1 000 to $10 000 in the case of an offence under section 12.4, to a fine of $250 to $1 000 in the case of an offence under section 12.4.1 and to a fine of $1,000 to $50,000 in the case of an offence under section 12.4.2, 12.4.3 or 12.4.4.

Legal person — Where the offence is committed by a legal person, the fine shall be doubled.

Subsequent offence — In the case of a second or subsequent offence, the fine prescribed for a first offence shall be doubled.

1991, c. 3, s. 5; 1993, c. 70, s. 18; 2004, c. 18, s. 13

12.6 Parties to offence — Where a legal person is guilty of an offence described by this Act, the director, officer or representative of the legal person who prescribed or authorized the performance of the act or the omission which constitutes the offence or who consented thereto is party to the offence and liable to the penalty prescribed by law.

1991, c. 3, s. 5; 1999, c. 40, s. 147

12.7 Prescription — Prescription of penal proceedings begins to run, for an offence contemplated by section 12.3, on the date of examination of the information disclosed to the Minister or investigator and, for an offence contemplated by section 12.4, on the date of examination of the application for the selection certificate, the certificate of acceptance, the undertaking or the certificate of statutory situation.

Prescription of proceedings under section 12.4.2 or 12.4.3 begins to run on the date the Minister becomes aware of the offence.

However, no proceedings may be instituted if more than five years have elapsed from the date of the commission of the offence.

1991, c. 3, s. 5; 1992, c. 5, s. 9; 1998, c. 15, s. 13; 2004, c. 18, s. 14

13.–16. [Repealed 1994, c. 15, s. 26.]

Other Relevant Legislation

DIVISION VII — PROCEEDING BEFORE THE ADMINISTRATIVE TRIBUNAL OF QUÉBEC

17. A decision of the Minister may, within 60 days of notification of the decision, be contested before the Administrative Tribunal of Québec by

(a) any natural person whose application for an undertaking is rejected or whose undertaking is cancelled;

(b) any foreign national whose selection certificate or certificate of acceptance is cancelled;

(c) any person whose recognition as an immigration consultant is refused, suspended, revoked or cancelled.

1982, c. 21, s. 1; U.K., 1982, c. 11, Sched. B, Part I, s. 33; 1991, c. 3, s. 6; 1997, c. 43, s. 302; 2004, c. 18, s. 15

18.–39. [Repealed 1997, c. 43, s. 302.]

DIVISION VIII — FINAL PROVISION

40. The Minister of Immigration and Cultural Communities is responsible for the administration of this Act.

1994, c. 15, s. 29; 1996, c. 21, s. 49; 2005, c. 24, s. 40

APPENDIX III

QUÉBEC IMMIGRATION ACT

S.Q. 2016, c. 3 [Not in force at date of publication.]

THE PARLIAMENT OF QUÉBEC ENACTS A FOLLOWS:

Chapter I — Objects

1. The purposes of this Act are the selection of foreign nationals wishing to stay temporarily or settle permanently in Québec, family reunification of Canadian citizens and permanent residents with their close relatives who are foreign nationals, and the reception of refugees and other persons in special hardship situations.

Moreover, the goals of this Act are to promote, through a shared commitment between Québec society and immigrants, the latter's full participation, in French, in community life, in full equality and in keeping with democratic values, and to contribute, through the establishment of harmonious intercultural relations, to the cultural enrichment of Québec society.

Lastly, the aim of this Act is that immigrants contribute, in particular, to Québec's prosperity, the preservation and vitality of French — the common language knowledge of which is the key to successful participation — the vitality of the regions and Québec's international influence.

2. In this Act, a **"foreign national"** is a person who is neither a Canadian citizen nor a permanent resident within the meaning of the *Immigration and Refugee Protection Act* (Statutes of Canada, 2001, chapter 27).

Chapter II — Immigration Planning

3. To develop a multi-year immigration plan, the Minister, taking into account such elements as Québec's immigration policy, the demand for immigration, Québec's needs, including its regions' needs, and Québec's capacity to receive and integrate immigrants, submits multi-year guidelines to the Government for approval.

4. The multi-year guidelines address such matters as the composition of immigration and the projected number of persons to be admitted. They are to be tabled in the National Assembly for a general consultation to be held by the competent parliamentary committee.

5. Taking into account the multi-year plan, the Minister establishes an annual immigration plan the purpose of which is to specify projected immigration levels.

The plan indicates the projected or estimated number of foreign nationals that Québec expects to receive and the number of selection decisions concerning immigrants wishing to settle permanently in Québec that may be made. Those numbers may be broken down by class, by immigration program or by program component.

The plan is tabled in the National Assembly not later than 1 November each year or, if the Assembly is not sitting, within 15 days after resumption.

Chapter III — Temporary and Permanent Immigration

DIVISION I — IMMIGRATION CLASSES AND PROGRAMS

6. The classes of foreign nationals wishing to stay temporarily in Québec are

(1) the temporary worker class;

(2) the international student class; and

(3) the person on a temporary stay for medical treatment class.

7. The classes of foreign nationals wishing to settle permanently in Québec are

(1) the economic class;

(2) the family class; and

(3) the humanitarian class.

8. The Government may, by regulation, determine other classes in addition to those listed in sections 6 and 7.

9. For each class, the Government may, by regulation, determine immigration programs and, for each program, the selection conditions and any selection criteria applicable to foreign nationals.

10. To stay or settle in Québec, foreign nationals belonging to one of the classes listed in sections 6 and 7 must file an application with the Minister under an immigration program, unless they are covered by an exemption provided for by government regulation.

An application under a family class program must be filed by a sponsor.

11. Despite the immigration program under which a foreign national's application is filed, the Minister may decide to examine the application under a different immigration program in order to facilitate the foreign national's selection.

DIVISION II — TEMPORARY IMMIGRATION

12. A foreign national who belongs to one of the classes listed in section 6 must be selected by the Minister by obtaining the Minister's consent to the foreign national's stay. Such consent is required, unless the foreign national is covered by an exemption provided for by government regulation.

13. The Minister's consent to a foreign national's stay is given once the foreign national meets all the conditions of an immigration program under which the application is examined.

14. The Minister's consent is certified in the manner and on the conditions prescribed by government regulation.

15. An employer wishing to hire a foreign national must, in the cases and on the conditions determined by government regulation, and after filing an application, obtain from the Minister a positive assessment as to the employment offer's impact on Québec's labour market.

The conditions applicable to an employer who hires a foreign national after having obtained a positive assessment for an employment offer are determined by government regulation.

16. For the purpose of developing new temporary immigration programs, the Minister may, by regulation, implement a temporary immigration pilot program lasting up to five years.

The maximum number of foreign nationals who may be selected under a temporary immigration pilot program is 400 per year.

The Minister determines, by regulation, the conditions and required fees applicable under such a program.

DIVISION III — TRANSITION TO PERMANENT IMMIGRATION

17. A foreign national who is staying temporarily in Québec may file an application for selection under an immigration program intended to allow the foreign national to settle permanently in Québec.

The selection conditions and any selection criteria applicable to the foreign national under such a program are determined by government regulation.

Other Relevant Legislation

DIVISION IV — PERMANENT IMMIGRATION

§1. — General provisions

1. — Selection for Permanent Immigration

18. To settle permanently in Québec, a foreign national must be selected by the Minister, unless the foreign national belongs to the family class, is recognized as a refugee when already in Québec or is covered by an exemption provided for by government regulation.

19. The Minister selects a foreign national who meets all the conditions of an immigration program under which the application is examined.

20. The Minister's selection decision also applies to the family members who are included in the application filed with the Minister by the foreign national.

21. The Minister's selection decision is certified in the manner and on the conditions prescribed by government regulation.

2. — Sponsorship Undertaking

22. A person or a group of persons may, by contract, give a sponsorship undertaking to the Government to assist a foreign national and the family members accompanying the foreign national in settling permanently in Québec.

The Government determines, by regulation, which persons or groups of persons may file a sponsorship undertaking application with the Minister and the applicable conditions.

23. An undertaking is entered into according to the terms and for the time prescribed by government regulation.

24. The Government may, by regulation, determine the cases in which an undertaking may be cancelled or considered to have lapsed and the situations in which the Minister may lift the effects of a lapse.

§2. — Economic class

25. A foreign national who belongs to the economic class may be selected by the Minister under a program intended to attract persons who are able to contribute to Québec's prosperity by settling in Québec.

26. The Government may, by regulation, determine that achieving a score obtained by applying a selection grid is one of the selection conditions referred to in section 9. Such a grid is to include selection criteria such as training, work experience and knowledge of French.

27. The weighting of the selection criteria referred to in section 26, the passing score and, as applicable, the cut-off score for a selection criterion are set by ministerial regulation.

28. The Minister may, when required, in collaboration with the other ministers concerned, collate economic information, such as a list of priority areas of training or economic sectors, with a view to assessing a foreign national's ability to contribute to Québec's prosperity by settling in Québec.

That information may be published in any medium the Minister considers appropriate.

29. An employer who wishes to hire a foreign national may, in the cases and on the conditions determined by government regulation, file an application with the Minister for the validation of the employment offer.

The conditions that apply to an employer who hires a foreign national after the validation of an employment offer are determined by government regulation.

30. Subject to section 31, the conditions applicable to a person who or a partnership that participates in the management of an investment or of a deposit of a sum of money by a person who files an application in the economic class are determined by government regulation.

The Government also determines, by regulation, conditions relating to the investment, deposit, management and disposition of the sums invested or deposited, including their reimbursement and confiscation.

31. If the number of selection applications the Minister intends to receive is determined by a decision made under section 50, the Minister may, by regulation, require a person or partnership referred to in section 30 who or that participates in the management of an investment of a foreign national to hold a quota. The Minister may also, in the same manner,

(1) set the minimum quota of the person or partnership;

(2) determine the terms and conditions for assigning a quota to the person or partnership, in particular by establishing a quota calculation formula and determining the value of the parameters;

(3) prescribe the monetary administrative penalties applicable to a person who or a partnership that does not comply with the quota assigned by the Minister, set their amount and determine the applicable conditions; and

(4) determine conditions relating to the transfer of a quota.

32. For the purpose of developing new economic immigration programs, the Minister may, by regulation, implement a permanent immigration pilot program lasting up to five years.

The maximum number of foreign nationals who may be selected under a permanent immigration pilot program is 550 per year.

The Minister determines, by regulation, the conditions, selection criteria and required fees applicable under such a program.

Other Relevant Legislation

§3. — Family class

33. To settle permanently in Québec, a foreign national who belongs to the family class must be the subject of an undertaking by a natural person or a group of natural persons in accordance with sections 22 to 24.

§4. — Humanitarian class

34. A foreign national who is in a special hardship situation may be selected by the Minister in the cases and on the conditions determined by government regulation.

35. The Government determines, by regulation, the cases in which an undertaking entered into on behalf of a foreign national who is in a special hardship situation constitutes one of the elements the Minister may take into account in selecting that foreign national.

36. For the purpose of facilitating the permanent immigration of persons from countries or regions affected by a humanitarian crisis, the Government may, by regulation, if the urgency of the situation requires it, implement an immigration program with a set duration and determine its conditions.

Chapter IV — Override Power

37. Despite section 13, the Minister may consent to the stay of a foreign national who does not meet a condition of a program under which the foreign national's application is examined. The conditions the Minister may override are prescribed by government regulation.

In addition, the Minister may refuse to consent to the stay of a foreign national who meets all the conditions prescribed by regulation if the Minister has reasonable grounds to believe that the foreign national's stay in Québec would be contrary to the public interest.

38. Despite section 19 and in the cases determined by government regulation, the Minister may select for permanent immigration a foreign national who does not meet a condition or selection criterion applicable to him or her if, after examining the application, the Minister is of the opinion that the foreign national can successfully settle in Québec.

In addition, the Minister may refuse to select a foreign national who meets all the conditions determined by regulation if the Minister has reasonable grounds to believe that the foreign national has little likelihood of successfully settling in Québec or that his or her settling in Québec would be contrary to the public interest.

39. If the Minister refuses to select a foreign national for temporary or permanent immigration for a public interest reason, the Minister must indicate the nature of the reason.

40. When exercising discretion under the first paragraph of section 37 or 38, the Minister may require, in the cases prescribed by government regulation, that an undertaking be entered into on behalf of the foreign national if the Minister believes that such an undertaking is necessary for the foreign national to successfully stay or settle in Québec.

Chapter V — Application Procedure and Management

DIVISION I — CONDITIONS FOR FILING AN APPLICATION WITH THE MINISTER

41. The conditions relating to the filing of any application made under this Act are determined by ministerial regulation.

DIVISION II — EXPRESSION OF INTEREST

42. In the cases prescribed by government regulation, a foreign national may file an application for selection only if invited to do so by the Minister.

A foreign national who wishes to be invited to file such an application must submit an expression of interest in staying or settling in Québec to the Minister.

43. The Minister enters the expression of interest submitted by a foreign national who meets the submission conditions prescribed by ministerial regulation in the expressions-of-interest bank.

The conditions governing the validity of an expression of interest, including the time for which it is valid, as well as the effects of its invalidity are determined by government regulation.

44. The Minister determines the criteria or sets of criteria on the basis of which the Minister invites foreign nationals to file an application for selection in accordance with section 10 as well as their order of priority. The Minister may also rank foreign nationals, in particular by applying a score or determining whether or not the invitation criteria or sets of invitation criteria are met by each foreign national.

The Minister's decision is valid for a maximum period of 24 months and may be modified at any time during that period. The Minister publishes the decision in the *Gazette officielle du Québec* and in any medium the Minister considers appropriate. The decision takes effect on the date of its publication or on any later date specified in it.

An invitation criterion may be a score, a selection condition or criterion or any other criterion relating to a foreign national's ability to successfully stay or settle in Québec, such as training or a trade or occupation. Such an invitation criterion may notably also be a region of destination in Québec, a country or region affected by a humanitarian crisis or the existence of an international commitment.

45. The Minister invites foreign nationals to file an application for selection on the basis of the decision made under section 44.

The Minister determines the number of foreign nationals invited on the basis of an invitation criterion or a set of invitation criteria, according to the order of priority of invitation criteria or according to a ranking, taking into account, among other considerations, the Minister's processing capacity, the annual immigration plan, any decision made under sections 50 and 51, Québec's labour market needs, or labour market integration prospects.

The Minister publishes that decision in any medium the Minister considers appropriate.

46. A decision made by the Minister under section 44 or 45 is not a regulation within the meaning of the *Regulations Act* (chapter R-18.1).

47. The Minister may invite a foreign national who is subject to section 42 to file an application without the invitation criteria being applied if the Minister is of the opinion that the foreign national is able to contribute to Québec's prosperity by staying or settling in Québec.

48. The Government determines, by regulation, the cases in which the Minister invites a foreign national referred to in section 42 to file an application for selection without the invitation criteria being applied.

49. The Minister may withdraw a foreign national's expression of interest from the bank if the Minister has reasonable grounds to believe that the foreign national's staying or settling in Québec would be contrary to the public interest.

Division III — Minister's Decision Respecting Application Management

50. The Minister may make a decision on the receipt and processing of applications filed with the Minister in accordance with Chapter III. Such a decision is made taking into account such elements as the guidelines and the objectives set out in the annual immigration plan, Québec's needs and capacity to receive and integrate immigrants or the public interest.

Such a decision may pertain to the maximum number of applications the Minister intends to receive, the period for receiving applications, the terms and conditions for suspending the receipt of applications, and the order of priority for processing and disposing of applications that have yet to be examined.

The Minister's decision may, if it so specifies, apply to applications received in the three months preceding its effective date that have yet to be examined. In such cases, the Minister informs the applicant and, if applicable, returns the sums the applicant paid as fees.

51. In addition, the Minister may make a decision on the maximum number of foreign nationals that the Minister invites under section 45. The Minister may also determine the period for submitting expressions of interest or suspend the submission of expressions of interest.

52. A decision made by the Minister under section 50 or 51 may apply to an immigration class, an immigration program or a component of such a program.

A decision made by the Minister on the basis of humanitarian considerations or to ensure diversity in the origin of expressions of interest and applications for selection may also apply to a country, a region or a group of countries or regions.

A decision concerning applications filed under section 15 or 29 may, in particular, apply to a region of Québec, an economic sector, a trade or an occupation, taking into account Québec's labour market needs.

A decision stands for a maximum period of 24 months and may be modified at any time during that period. The Minister publishes the decision in the *Gazette officielle du Québec* and in any medium the Minister considers appropriate. The decision takes effect on the date of its publication or on any later date specified in it.

The reason for a decision must be included in the decision.

53. A decision made by the Minister under section 50 or 51 is not a regulation within the meaning of the *Regulations Act*.

DIVISION IV — REFUSAL TO EXAMINE, REJECTION OF AN APPLICATION AND INVALIDITY OF A DECISION

54. A person who submits an expression of interest to or files an application with the Minister must, at the Minister's request, demonstrate the truthfulness of the facts set out in his or her statements.

55. A person referred to in section 54 must also, at the time, within the time limit and in the manner specified by the Minister, provide the Minister with any information or document the Minister considers relevant.

56. The Minister may refuse to examine a person's application if

(1) the person has, in the five years preceding the examination of the application, directly or indirectly provided the Minister with false or misleading information or documents; or

(2) the person has been the subject of a decision made for a public interest reason under section 37, 38, 49 or 65.

57. The Minister may reject a person's application if

(1) the person has failed to demonstrate to the Minister, as required under section 54, the truthfulness of the facts set out in his or her statements;

(2) the person has failed to provide information or documents required by the Minister under section 55;

(3) the application contains false or misleading information or documents;

(4) the person has, in the five years preceding the examination of the application, directly or indirectly provided the Minister with false or misleading information or documents; or

(5) the person has been the subject of a decision made for a public interest reason under section 37, 38, 49 or 65.

58. A decision of the Minister is invalid if it expires, is cancelled or lapses.

The Government determines, by regulation, the time for which a decision made by the Minister is valid, the cases in which a decision lapses and the situations in which the Minister may lift the effects of any such lapse.

59. The Minister may cancel a decision in the cases prescribed by government regulation or if

(1) the application relating to the decision contained false or misleading information or documents;

(2) the decision was made in error;

(3) the conditions required for making a favourable decision cease to exist; or

(4) the public interest so requires.

The Minister's decision takes effect immediately.

Chapter VI — Participation in Québec Society

60. In collaboration with the other ministers concerned, the Minister develops reception, francization and integration programs for immigrants and programs aimed at establishing harmonious intercultural relations to promote immigrants' full participation, in French, in community life, in full equality and in keeping with democratic values, as well as their long-term settlement in the regions.

Within that framework, the Minister establishes and implements services in Québec and abroad in the areas under the Minister's responsibility and determines the eligibility requirements for those services.

61. The Minister may allocate financial assistance to an immigrant who, in accordance with the conditions determined under a program referred to in the first paragraph of section 60, has access to reception, francization or integration services.

Chapter VII — Immigration Consultant

62. A person wishing to act as an immigration consultant must, subject to the second paragraph of section 63, be recognized by the Minister.

63. The Government may, by regulation, define "immigration consultant" and determine classes of immigration consultants.

It may also exempt the members or a class of members of a professional order from all or some of the provisions applicable to immigration consultants.

64. The Minister recognizes a person as an immigration consultant or renews a person's recognition as such if the person meets all the conditions determined by regulation.

The Government also determines the cases in which the Minister must not recognize a person as an immigration consultant or renew a person's recognition as such.

65. Despite any regulation enacted under section 64, the Minister may refuse an application for recognition or for the renewal of recognition as an immigration consultant if the Minister has reasonable grounds to believe that the applicant's recognition as such would be contrary to the public interest.

66. The time for which an immigration consultant's recognition is valid is prescribed by government regulation.

67. The obligations of immigration consultants and the prohibitions applicable to them in the exercise of consulting activities are determined by government regulation.

68. The Minister may suspend or revoke an immigration consultant's recognition in the cases prescribed by government regulation or if the Minister is of the opinion that the public interest requires it.

69. The Minister keeps an up-to-date register of recognized immigration consultants, indicating those whose recognition has been suspended or revoked in the last five years.

The register is published in any medium the Minister considers appropriate.

70. Division IV of Chapter V, except sections 58 and 59, applies to applications filed with the Minister under this chapter.

Chapter VIII — Review of a Decision or Proceeding Before the Administrative Tribunal of Québec

71. A decision of the Minister may be reviewed in the cases and on the conditions the Minister determines.

72. A decision made by the Minister may be contested by the following persons before the Administrative Tribunal of Québec within 60 days after the date of its notification:

(1) a natural person whose undertaking application on behalf of a foreign national has been refused or whose undertaking on behalf of a foreign national has been cancelled;

(2) a foreign national belonging to the economic class whose application for selection for permanent immigration has been refused, unless the decision was made under the second paragraph of section 38;

(3) a foreign national in respect of whom a temporary or permanent immigration selection decision has been cancelled, unless the decision was made for a public interest reason;

(4) a person who or a partnership that has incurred a monetary administrative penalty prescribed by a regulation under paragraph 3 of section 31 or sections 101 and 102; and

Other Relevant Legislation

(5) a person whose recognition as an immigration consultant has been refused, suspended or revoked or has not been renewed, unless the decision was made for a public interest reason.

Chapter IX — Required Fees

73. The fees to be paid for the examination of an application for selection for temporary immigration filed by a foreign national are

(1) $191 for an application filed as a temporary worker; and

(2) $109 for an application filed as an international student or as a person on a temporary stay for medical treatment.

74. The fees to be paid for the examination of an application for selection for permanent immigration filed by a foreign national belonging to the economic class are

(1) $15,000 for an application filed as an investor;

(2) $1,034 for an application filed as an entrepreneur or a self-employed worker; and

(3) $765 for an application filed as a skilled worker.

75. The fees to be paid for each family member accompanying a foreign national referred to in paragraph 2 or 3 of section 74 are $164.

76. The fees to be paid for the examination of a sponsorship undertaking application regarding a foreign national who belongs to the family class are $272 for the first foreign national and $109 for every other foreign national included in the application.

77. The fees to be paid for the examination of an application for the assessment of an employment offer's impact on Québec's labour market or for the validation of an employment offer are $191.

78. The fees to be paid for the examination of an application filed by an immigration consultant are

(1) $1,600 for recognition as an immigration consultant; and

(2) $1,300 for the renewal of recognition as such.

79. The fees prescribed in this chapter are payable at the time the application is filed unless a ministerial regulation made under section 41 provides otherwise.

80. The fees are adjusted and rounded off in accordance with section 83.3 of the *Financial Administration Act* (chapter A-6.001) and the regulation made under that Act.

The Minister publishes the results of the adjustment in the *Gazette officielle du Québec* and informs the public of the results by any other means the Minister considers appropriate.

81. With the exception of the fees to be paid for the examination of applications referred to in sections 73 to 78, the Government may, by regulation, set fees for any other application or for any stage in the examination of an application.

The Government may also, in the same manner, set the fees to be paid in connection with an expression of interest or the issue or filing of any document.

82. The Government may, by regulation, determine the cases in which a foreign national is exempted from paying the required fees.

Chapter X — Delegation and Agreements

83. The Minister may, by agreement, delegate all or some of the powers conferred on the Minister by this Act to another minister or to a body of the Administration within the meaning of the *Public Administration Act* (chapter A-6.01).

84. The Minister may enter into an agreement for the administration of this Act and the regulations with another minister, an association, a partnership or a person, such as a body or a municipal authority.

Chapter XI — Inspection and Investigation

DIVISION I — INSPECTION

85. The Minister may appoint an inspector to verify compliance with this Act and the regulations.

The inspector may, in the exercise of inspection functions,

(1) enter, at any reasonable time, the establishment of a legal person, an employer or an immigration consultant;

(2) take photographs or make recordings on the premises mentioned in subparagraph 1;

(3) examine and make copies of any document containing information relating to the activities of the persons mentioned in subparagraph 1; and

(4) require that the persons present provide or communicate to the inspector, within a reasonable time, any information or document relating to the application of this Act and the regulations for examination or the making of copies.

A person having custody, possession or control of any document relating to the application of this Act and the regulations must, at the inspector's request, send the document to the inspector within a reasonable time and facilitate its examination, regardless of the medium and of the means by which it may be accessed.

86. An inspector may, by a formal demand delivered by registered mail or personal service, require any person to file by registered mail or personal service, within a reasonable time specified in the demand, information or documents relating to the application of this Act or the regulations.

The person to whom the demand is made must, within the specified time, comply with the demand, whether or not the person has already filed such information or a reply to a similar demand made under this Act.

DIVISION II — INVESTIGATION

87. The Minister may conduct an investigation or commission a person the Minister designates to conduct an investigation on any matter relating to the application of this Act and the regulations.

88. In the course of an investigation relating to an offence under this Act or a regulation, a judge of the Court of Québec may, on an *ex parte* application following an information laid in writing and under oath by an investigator, order a person, other than the person under investigation,

(1) to produce original documents, or copies of them certified by affidavit to be true copies, or to produce information; or

(2) to prepare a document based on documents or information already in existence and to produce it.

The order requires the documents or information to be produced within the time, at the place and in the form specified and to be given to the investigator named in it.

Before making such an order, the judge must be satisfied that there are reasonable grounds to believe that

(1) an offence under this Act or a regulation is being or has been committed;

(2) the documents or information will afford evidence respecting the commission of the offence; and

(3) the person who is the subject of the order has possession or control of the documents or information.

The order may contain any terms that the judge considers appropriate, including terms to protect lawyers' and notaries' professional secrecy.

Where the judge who makes the order or any other judge having jurisdiction to make such an order is satisfied, on an *ex parte* application made on the basis of an affidavit submitted by an investigator in support of the application, that the interests of justice warrant the granting of the application, the judge may vary or revoke the order or set a new time limit.

Every copy of a document produced under this section, on proof by affidavit that it is a true copy, is admissible in evidence in any proceeding and has the same probative force as the original document would have if it had been proved in the ordinary way.

DIVISION III — MISCELLANEOUS PROVISIONS

89. Legal proceedings may not be brought against inspectors and investigators for acts performed in good faith in the exercise of inspection and investigation functions.

90. Inspectors and investigators must, on request, provide identification and produce a certificate of authority signed by the Minister.

91. Any document produced for an investigation and certified by the Minister or an investigator as being a true copy of the original is admissible as proof and has the same probative force as the original.

Chapter XII — Penal Provisions

92. Anyone who

(1) acts in such a way as to falsely suggest that his, her or its conduct or activities in relation to matters to which this Act applies are authorized or approved by the Minister or the Government, notably by using the expression "Immigration-Québec", "Ministère de l'Immigration, de la Diversité et de l'Inclusion" or "Ministère de l'Immigration du Québec" or any similar expression, or

(2) makes or knowingly uses a document that falsely suggests it is made, sent or issued by the Minister or the Government, notably by using the expression "Immigration-Québec", "Ministère de l'Immigration, de la Diversité et de l'Inclusion" or "Ministère de l'Immigration du Québec" or any similar expression,

is guilty of an offence and is liable to a fine of $5,000 to $50,000 in the case of a natural person and $10,000 to $100,000 in any other case.

Immigration consultants who, by whatever means, make false, misleading or incomplete representations as to their recognition as immigration consultants or level of competence or as to the extent or effectiveness of their services are also liable to the minimum and maximum fines set out in the first paragraph.

93. Anyone who

(1) acts as an immigration consultant without being recognized as such by the Minister,

(2) directly or indirectly, by an act or omission, communicates to the Minister information or documents that he, she or it knows or should have known to be false or misleading in relation to an application filed with the Minister or an expression of interest to stay or settle in Québec, or

(3) in any way hinders an inspector or investigator in the exercise of inspection or investigation functions, or misleads the inspector or investigator by concealment or misrepresentation, or refuses to provide information or a document the inspector or investigator is entitled to obtain under this Act,

is guilty of an offence and is liable to a fine of $2,500 to $25,000 in the case of a natural person and $5,000 to $50,000 in any other case.

94. Anyone who contravenes a regulatory provision whose violation constitutes an offence is guilty of an offence and is liable to a fine of $1,000 to $50,000 in the case of a natural person and $2,000 to $100,000 in any other case.

Other Relevant Legislation

However, the Government may, by regulation, within the specified minimum and maximum limits, set the minimum and maximum amounts of a fine according to the nature of the violation and its seriousness.

95. The minimum and maximum fines prescribed by this Act or the regulations for a first offence are doubled for a second offence. Those amounts are tripled for a third or subsequent offence.

96. If an offence under this Act or the regulations is committed by a director or officer of a legal person, partnership or association without legal personality, the minimum and maximum fines are twice those prescribed for the offence.

97. Anyone who does or omits to do something in order to assist a person in committing an offence under this Act or the regulations, or advises, encourages, incites or causes a person to commit such an offence, is considered to have committed the same offence.

98. In any penal proceedings relating to an offence under this Act or the regulations, proof that the offence was committed by an agent, mandatary or employee of any party is sufficient to establish that it was committed by that party, unless the party establishes that it exercised due diligence, taking all necessary precautions to prevent the offence.

99. If a legal person or an agent, mandatary or employee of a legal person, partnership or association without legal personality commits an offence under this Act or the regulations, the directors or officers of the legal person, partnership or association without legal personality are presumed to have committed the offence unless it is established that they exercised due diligence, taking all necessary precautions to prevent the offence.

For the purposes of the first paragraph, in the case of a partnership, all partners, except special partners, are presumed to be directors of the partnership unless there is evidence to the contrary appointing one or more of them, or a third person, to manage the affairs of the partnership.

100. Penal proceedings instituted under this Act are prescribed one year from the date on which the prosecutor became aware of the commission of the offence.

However, no proceedings may be instituted if more than five years have elapsed from the date of the commission of the offence.

Chapter XIII — Regulations

101. The Government may, by regulation, prescribe administrative penalties, including monetary penalties, for contraventions of this Act or the regulations and the conditions applicable to such penalties.

102. A regulation made under section 101 may prescribe monetary administrative penalties for contraventions of

(1) a provision of a regulation made under section 9 that is a condition applicable under an economic immigration program;

(2) a provision of a regulation made under the second paragraphs of sections 15 and 29 or under section 67; and

(3) section 62.

The regulation sets the amounts of the monetary administrative penalty, taking into account the nature of the violation and its seriousness. The amounts may differ depending on whether the violation was committed by a natural person or a legal person.

103. The regulatory provisions whose violation constitutes a penal offence are determined by government regulation.

104. A regulation made under any of sections 15, 17, 18, 21, 26, 27, 29 to 31, 34, 35, 41 to 43, 48 and 81 is not subject to the publication requirement set out in section 8 of the *Regulations Act* and, despite section 17 of that Act, comes into force on the date of its publication in the *Gazette officielle du Québec* or any later date set in the regulation.

The same holds for a regulation made under any of sections 9, 10 and 101 to 103 in the case of provisions relating to a permanent immigration program.

105. A regulation made under this Act may provide for exemptions and vary for different immigration cases, classes or programs or components of an immigration program, among other things. Such a regulation may also vary for different classes of immigration consultants or different application examination stages.

106. A regulation made under this Act may apply to an application according to the date on which it was filed or to the application examination stage and may apply to an expression of interest according to the date on which it was submitted.

Chapter XIV — Amending Provisions

Individual and Family Assistance Act

107. Section 91 of the *Individual and Family Assistance Act* (chapter A-13.1.1) is amended by replacing "any dependants who accompany the foreign national, to settle in Québec must repay the amount granted under a last resort financial assistance program to the foreign national and those dependants" by "the family members accompanying the foreign national within the meaning of that Act, to settle in Québec must repay the amount granted to the foreign national and those family members under a last resort financial assistance program".

Act respecting administrative justice

108. Section 30 of the *Act respecting administrative justice* (chapter J-3) is amended by replacing "concerning an undertaking, a selection certificate or a certificate of acceptance" by "concerning a sponsorship undertaking, a temporary or permanent immigration selection decision, recognition as an immigration consultant or a monetary administrative penalty".

109. Section 6 of Schedule I to the Act is amended by replacing "17" by "72".

Act respecting the Ministère de l'Immigration et des Communautés culturelles

110. The title of the *Act respecting the Ministère de l'Immigration et des Communautés culturelles* (chapter M-16.1) is replaced by the following title:

Act respecting the Ministère de l'Immigration, de la Diversité et de l'Inclusion

111. Sections 1 to 4 of the Act are replaced by the following sections:

1. The Ministère de l'Immigration, de la Diversité et de l'Inclusion is under the direction of the Minister of Immigration, Diversity and Inclusiveness appointed under the *Executive Power Act* (chapter E-18).

The Minister is responsible for immigration, ethnocultural diversity and inclusiveness.

2. The Minister is to develop guidelines or policies on immigration and on the full participation, in French, of immigrants and ethnocultural minorities in Québec society, in full equality and in keeping with democratic values, and propose them to the Government. The Minister is notably to develop a Québec policy on those matters.

The Minister is to coordinate and monitor the implementation of those guidelines and policies in order to ensure their relevance and effectiveness.

3. The Minister is to advise the Government and government departments and bodies on any matter under the Minister's responsibility.

The Minister is to exercise the functions of office in collaboration with the other ministers concerned, in keeping with their respective missions and functions.

4. The Minister's functions in matters of immigration, ethnocultural diversity and inclusiveness are, more particularly,

(1) to plan the number of immigrants Québec wishes to receive and the composition of that immigration;

(2) to promote immigration and inform immigrants about such topics as Québec's democratic values, the integration and francization processes, Québec culture and the vitality of the regions;

(3) to select, as temporary or permanent immigrants, foreign nationals who will be able to fully participate, in French, in Québec society;

(4) to contribute, through the selection of temporary or permanent immigrants, to meeting the needs and reflecting the choices of Québec;

(5) to promote immigration's contribution to Québec's prosperity, to the preservation and vitality of French — the common language knowledge of which is the key to successful participation — to the vitality of the regions and to Québec's international influence;

(6) to ensure family reunification, participate in international solidarity efforts and respond to other humanitarian situations;

(7) to contribute, through the provision of reception, francization and integration services and through intercultural relations projects, to immigrants' full participation, in French, in community life, to their long-term settlement in the regions and to the consolidation of harmonious intercultural relations;

(8) after consultation with the other ministers concerned, to coordinate the implementation of reception, francization and integration programs for immigrants; and

(9) to foster the commitment and coordinate the actions of government departments, bodies and social actors in order to build communities that are more inclusive, thereby contributing to immigrants' long-term settlement in the regions, promote immigrants' and ethnocultural minorities' full participation, in French, in community life, in full equality and in keeping with democratic values, and contribute, through the establishment of harmonious intercultural relations, to the cultural enrichment of Québec society.

112. Sections 5 and 6 of the Act are repealed.

113. Section 7 of the Act is amended

(1) by adding ", including agreements for the sharing of information to satisfy the obligations incumbent on the Minister under the Acts for which the Minister is responsible" at the end of paragraph 2;

(2) by replacing paragraph 4 by the following paragraph:

(4) take the necessary measures, in collaboration with the other ministers and the bodies concerned, to facilitate the recognition, in Québec, of qualifications acquired abroad, such as by speeding up the recognition process;

;

(3) by replacing paragraph 5 by the following paragraphs:

(5) establish comparisons between diplomas and education obtained abroad and those obtained within Québec's education system;

(6) obtain from government departments and bodies the information necessary to develop and implement guidelines and policies and to monitor and evaluate their relevance and effectiveness.

Act to amend the Act respecting the Ministère des Communautés culturelles et de l'Immigration

114. Paragraph 1 of section 3, sections 8 and 9 and paragraphs 2, 8 and 9 of section 11 of the *Act to amend the Act respecting the Ministère des Communautés culturelles et de l'Immigration* (1993, chapter 70) are repealed.

Act to amend the Act respecting immigration to Québec

115. The *Act to amend the Act respecting immigration to Québec* (2001, chapter 58) is repealed.

Act to Amend the Act respecting immigration to Québec

116. Sections 2 and 6 and paragraph 5 of section 10 of the *Act to amend the Act respecting immigration to Québec* (2004, chapter 18) are repealed.

Regulation respecting immigration consultants

117. Section 1 of the *Regulation respecting immigration consultants* (chapter I-0.2, r. 0.2) is repealed.

118. The Regulation is amended by inserting the following section before section 5:

4.1 An immigration consultant must be recognized by the Minister in accordance with section 62 of the *Québec Immigration Act* (2016, chapter 3).

An immigration consultant who is recognized by the Minister is entered in the consultants register provided for in section 69 of the Act.

119. Section 7 of the Regulation is amended by replacing "is to deny an application for renewal" in the second paragraph by "may not grant the renewal of an immigration consultant's recognition".

120. Sections 10, 15, 24 and 25 of the Regulation are repealed.

Chapter XV — Transitional and Final Provisions

121. The multi-year guidelines and the annual plan approved by the Government under sections 3.0.0.1 and 3.0.1 of the *Act respecting immigration to Québec* (chapter I-0.2) which are in force on (*insert the date of coming into force of this Act*) are deemed to have been approved under Chapter II of this Act.

122. A selection certificate issued under section 3.1 or a certificate of acceptance issued under section 3.2 of the *Act respecting immigration to Québec* before it was replaced by this Act is valid and is deemed to be a decision made under this Act.

123. A sponsorship undertaking subscribed under section 3.1.1 of the Act respecting immigration to Québec before the replacement of that Act by this Act is valid and is deemed to have been entered into under section 23 of this Act.

124. A decision made by the Minister under section 3.5 of the *Act respecting immigration to Québec* before the replacement of that Act by this Act is deemed to have been made under the provisions of Division III of Chapter V of this Act.

125. Any civil or penal proceedings pending on (*insert the date of coming into force of this Act*) are continued, without further formality, as if the provisions under which they were brought were still in force.

126. The Government may, by a regulation made within 12 months after (*insert the date of coming into force of this Act*), enact any transitional measure applicable to applications filed with the Minister before that date.

127. The required fees prescribed in Chapter IX must, on the date of its coming into force, be adjusted in accordance with section 80 as if they had been in force since 2 December 2015.

128. This Act replaces the *Act respecting immigration to Québec*.

129. The Minister of Immigration, Diversity and Inclusiveness is responsible for the administration of this Act.

130. The provisions of this Act come into force on the date or dates to be set by the Government.

Transitional Provisions
— 2016, c. 3, ss. 121–129 [Not in force at date of publication.]:

121. The multi-year guidelines and the annual plan approved by the Government under sections 3.0.0.1 and 3.0.1 of the *Act respecting immigration to Québec* (chapter I-0.2) which are in force on (*insert the date of coming into force of this Act*) are deemed to have been approved under Chapter II of this Act.

122. A selection certificate issued under section 3.1 or a certificate of acceptance issued under section 3.2 of the *Act respecting immigration to Québec* before it was replaced by this Act is valid and is deemed to be a decision made under this Act.

123. A sponsorship undertaking subscribed under section 3.1.1 of the Act respecting immigration to Québec before the replacement of that Act by this Act is valid and is deemed to have been entered into under section 23 of this Act.

124. A decision made by the Minister under section 3.5 of the *Act respecting immigration to Québec* before the replacement of that Act by this Act is deemed to have been made under the provisions of Division III of Chapter V of this Act.

125. Any civil or penal proceedings pending on (*insert the date of coming into force of this Act*) are continued, without further formality, as if the provisions under which they were brought were still in force.

126. The Government may, by a regulation made within 12 months after (*insert the date of coming into force of this Act*), enact any transitional measure applicable to applications filed with the Minister before that date.

127. The required fees prescribed in Chapter IX must, on the date of its coming into force, be adjusted in accordance with section 80 as if they had been in force since 2 December 2015.

128. This Act replaces the *Act respecting immigration to Québec*.

129. The Minister of Immigration, Diversity and Inclusiveness is responsible for the administration of this Act.

APPENDIX IV

CHAPTER 16 OF THE NORTH AMERICAN FREE TRADE AGREEMENT (NAFTA)

Chapter Sixteen — Temporary Entry for Business Persons

Article 1601 — General Principles

Further to Article 102 (Objectives), this Chapter reflects the preferential trading relationship between the Parties, the desirability of facilitating temporary entry on a reciprocal basis and of establishing transparent criteria and procedures for temporary entry, and the need to ensure border security and to protect the domestic labor force and permanent employment in their respective territories.

Article 1602 — General Obligations

1. Each Party shall apply its measures relating to the provisions of this Chapter in accordance with Article 1601 and, in particular, shall apply expeditiously those measures so as to avoid unduly impairing or delaying trade in goods or services or conduct of investment activities under this Agreement.

2. The Parties shall endeavour to develop and adopt common criteria, definitions and interpretations for the implementation of this Chapter.

Article 1603 — Grant of Temporary Entry

1. Each Party shall grant temporary entry to business persons who are otherwise qualified for entry under applicable measures relating to public health and safety and national security, in accordance with this Chapter, including the provisions of Annex 1603.

2. A Party may refuse to issue an immigration document authorizing employment to a business person where the temporary entry of that person might affect adversely:

(a) the settlement of any labour dispute that is in progress at the place or intended place of employment; or

(b) the employment of any person who is involved in such dispute.

3. When a Party refuses pursuant to paragraph 2 to issue an immigration document authorizing employment, it shall:

(a) inform in writing the business person of the reasons for the refusal; and

(b) promptly notify in writing the Party whose business person has been refused entry of the reasons for the refusal.

4. Each Party shall limit any fees for processing applications for temporary entry of business persons to the approximate cost of services rendered.

Article 1604 — Provision of Information

1. Further to Article 1802 (Publication), each Party shall:

(a) provide to the other Parties such materials as will enable them to become acquainted with its measures relating to this Chapter; and

(b) no later than one year after the date of entry into force of this Agreement, prepare, publish and make available in its own territory, and in the territories of the other Parties, explanatory material in a consolidated document regarding the requirements for temporary entry under this Chapter in such a manner as will enable business persons of the other Parties to become acquainted with them.

2. Subject to Annex 1604.2, each Party shall collect and maintain, and make available to the other Parties in accordance with its domestic law, data respecting the granting of temporary entry under this Chapter to business persons of the other Parties who have been issued immigration documentation, including data specific to each occupation, profession or activity.

Article 1605 — Working Group

1. The Parties hereby establish a Temporary Entry Working Group, comprising representatives of each Party, including immigration officials.

2. The Working Group shall meet at least once each year to consider:

(a) the implementation and administration of this Chapter;

(b) the development of measures to further facilitate temporary entry of business persons on a reciprocal basis;

(c) the waiving of labour certification tests or procedures of similar effect for spouses of business persons who have been granted temporary entry for more than one year under Section B, C or D of Annex 1603; and

(d) proposed modifications of or additions to this Chapter.

Article 1606 — Dispute Settlement

1. A Party may not initiate proceedings under Article 2007 (Commission — Good Offices, Conciliation and Mediation) regarding a refusal to grant temporary entry under this Chapter or a particular case arising under Article 1602(1) unless:

(a) the matter involves a pattern of practice; and

(b) the business person has exhausted the available administrative remedies regarding the particular matter.

2. The remedies referred to in paragraph (1)(b) shall be deemed to be exhausted if a final determination in the matter has not been issued by the competent authority within one year of the institution of an administrative proceeding, and the failure to issue a determination is not attributable to delay caused by the business person.

Article 1607 — Relation to Other Chapters

Except for this Chapter, Chapters One (Objectives), Two (General Definitions), Twenty (Institutional Arrangements and Dispute Settlement Procedures) and Twenty-two (Final Provisions) and Articles 1801 (Contacts Points), 1802 (Publication), 1803 (Notification and Provision of Information) and 1804 (Administrative Proceedings), no provision of this Agreement shall impose any obligation on a Party regarding its immigration measures.

Article 1608 — Definitions

For purposes of this Chapter:

"business person" means a citizen of a Party who is engaged in trade in goods, the provision of services or the conduct of investment activities;

citizen means "citizen" as defined in Annex 1608 for the Parties specified in that Annex;

existing means "existing" as defined in Annex 1608 for the Parties specified in that Annex;

"temporary entry" means entry into the territory of a Party by a business person of another Party without the intent to establish permanent residence.

ANNEX 1603 — TEMPORARY ENTRY FOR BUSINESS PERSONS

Section A. — Business Visitors

1. Each Party shall grant temporary entry to a business person seeking to engage in a business activity set out in Appendix 1603.A.1, without requiring that person to obtain an employment authorization, provided that the business person otherwise complies with existing immigration measures applicable to temporary entry, on presentation of:

(a) proof of citizenship of a Party;

(b) documentation demonstrating that the business person will be so engaged and describing the purpose of entry; and

(c) evidence demonstrating that the proposed business activity is international in scope and that the business person is not seeking to enter the local labor market.

2. Each party shall provide that a business person may satisfy the requirements of paragraph 1(c) by demonstrating that:

(a) the primary source of remuneration for the proposed business activity is outside the territory of the Party granting temporary entry; and

(b) the business person's principal place of business and the actual place of accrual of profits, at least predominantly, remain outside such territory.

A Party shall normally accept an oral declaration as to the principal place of business and the actual place of accrual of profits. Where the Party requires further proof, it shall normally consider a letter from the employer attesting to these matters as sufficient proof.

3. Each Party shall grant temporary entry to a business person seeking to engage in a business activity other than those set out in Appendix 1603.A.1, without requiring that person to obtain an employment authorization, on a basis no less favourable than that provided under the existing provisions of the measures set out in Appendix 1603.A.3, provided that the business person otherwise complies with existing immigration measures applicable to temporary entry.

4. No Party may:

(a) as a condition for temporary entry under paragraph 1 or 3, require prior approval procedures, petitions, labour certification tests or other procedures of similar effect; or

(b) impose or maintain any numerical restriction relating to temporary entry under paragraph 1 or 3.

5. Notwithstanding paragraph 4, a Party may require a business person seeking temporary entry under this Section to obtain a visa or its equivalent prior to entry. Before imposing a visa requirement, the Party shall consult, on request, with a Party whose business persons would be affected with a view to avoiding the imposition of the requirement. With respect to an existing visa requirement, a Party shall consult, on request, with a Party whose business persons are subject to the requirement with a view to its removal.

Section B. — Traders and Investors

1. Each Party shall grant temporary entry and provide confirming documentation to a business person seeking to:

(a) carry on substantial trade in goods or services principally between the territory of the Party of which the business person is a citizen and the territory of the Party into which entry is sought, or

(b) establish, develop, administer or provide advice or key technical services to the operation of an investment to which the business person or the business person's enterprise has committed, or is in the process of committing, a substantial amount of capital, in a capacity that is supervisory, executive or involves essential skills,

provided that the business person otherwise complies with existing immigration measures applicable to temporary entry.

2. No Party may:

(a) as a condition for temporary entry under paragraph 1, require labor certification tests or other procedures of similar effect; or

(b) impose or maintain any numerical restriction relating to temporary entry under paragraph 1.

3. Notwithstanding paragraph 2, a Party may require a business person seeking temporary entry under this Section to obtain a visa or its equivalent prior to entry.

Section C. — Intra-Company Transferees

1. Each Party shall grant temporary entry and provide confirming documentation to a business person employed by an enterprise who seeks to render services to that enterprise or a subsidiary or affiliate thereof, in a capacity that is managerial,

executive or involves specialized knowledge, provided that the business person otherwise complies with existing immigration measures applicable to temporary entry. A Party may require the business person to have been employed continuously by the enterprise for one year within the three-year period immediately preceding the date of the application for admission.

2. No Party may:

(a) as a condition for temporary entry under paragraph 1, require labor certification tests or other procedures of similar effect; or

(b) impose or maintain any numerical restriction relating to temporary entry under paragraph 1.

3. Notwithstanding paragraph 2, a Party may require a business person seeking temporary entry under this Section to obtain a visa or its equivalent prior to entry. Before imposing a visa requirement, the Party shall consult with a Party whose business persons would be affected with a view to avoiding the imposition of the requirement. With respect to an existing visa requirement, a Party shall consult, on request, with a Party whose business persons are subject to the requirement with a view to its removal.

Section D. — Professionals

1. Each Party shall grant temporary entry and provide confirming documentation to a business person seeking to engage in a business activity at a professional level in a profession set out in Appendix 1603.D.1, if the business person otherwise complies with existing immigration measures applicable to temporary entry, on presentation of:

(a) proof of citizenship of a Party; and

(b) documentation demonstrating that the business person will be so engaged and describing the purpose of entry.

2. No Party may:

(a) as a condition for temporary entry under paragraph 1, require prior approval procedures, petitions, labor certification tests or other procedures of similar effect; or

(b) impose or maintain any numerical restriction relating to temporary entry under paragraph 1.

3. Notwithstanding paragraph 2, a Party may require a business person seeking temporary entry under this Section to obtain a visa or its equivalent prior to entry. Before imposing a visa requirement, the Party shall consult with a Party whose business persons would be affected with a view to avoiding the imposition of the requirement. With respect to an existing visa requirement, a Party shall consult, on request, with a party whose business persons are subject to the requirement with a view to its removal.

4. Notwithstanding paragraphs 1 and 2, a Party may establish an annual numerical limit, which shall be set out in Appendix 1603.D.4, regarding temporary entry of business persons of another Party seeking to engage in business activities at a professional level in a profession set out in Appendix 1603.D.1, if the Parties concerned have not agreed otherwise prior to the date of entry into force of this

Agreement for those Parties. In establishing such a limit, the Party shall consult with the other Party concerned.

5. A Party establishing a numerical limit pursuant to paragraph 4, unless the Parties concerned agree otherwise:

> (a) shall, for each year after the first year after the date of entry into force of this Agreement, consider increasing the numerical limit set out in Appendix 1603.D.4 by an amount to be established in consultation with the other Party concerned, taking into account the demand for temporary entry under this Section;

> (b) shall not apply its procedures established pursuant to paragraph 1 to the temporary entry of a business person subject to the numerical limit, but may require the business person to comply with its other procedures applicable to the temporary entry of professionals; and

> (c) may, in consultation with the other Party concerned, grant temporary entry under paragraph 1 to a business person who practices in a profession where accreditation, licensing, and certification requirements are mutually recognized by those Parties.

6. Nothing in paragraph 4 or 5 shall be construed to limit the ability of a business person to seek temporary entry under a Party's applicable immigration measures relating to the entry of professionals other than those adopted or maintained pursuant to paragraph 1.

7. Three years after a Party establishes a numerical limit pursuant to paragraph 4, it shall consult with the other Party concerned with a view to determining a date after which the limit shall cease to apply.

Appendix 1603.A.1 — Business Visitors

Research and Design

- Technical, scientific and statistical researchers conducting independent research or research for an enterprise located in the territory of another Party.

Growth, Manufacture and Production

- Harvester owner supervising a harvesting crew admitted under applicable law.
- Purchasing and production management personnel conducting commercial transactions for an enterprise located in the territory of another Party.

Marketing

- Market researchers and analysts conducting independent research or analysis or research or analysis for an enterprise located in the territory of another Party.
- Trade fair and promotional personnel attending a trade convention.

Sales

- Sales representatives and agents taking orders or negotiating contracts for goods or services for an enterprise located in the territory of another Party but not delivering goods or providing services.

- Buyers purchasing for an enterprise located in the territory of another Party.

Distribution

- Transportation operators transporting goods or passengers to the territory of a Party from the territory of another Party or loading and transporting goods or passengers from the territory of a Party, with no unloading in that territory, to the territory of another Party.
- With respect to temporary entry into the territory of the United States, Canadian customs brokers performing brokerage duties relating to the export of goods from the territory of the United States to or through the territory of Canada.
- With respect to temporary entry into the territory of Canada, United States customs brokers performing brokerage duties relating to the export of goods from the territory of Canada to or through the territory of the United States.
- Customs brokers providing consulting services regarding the facilitation of the import or export of goods.

After-Sales Service

- Installers, repair and maintenance personnel, and supervisors, possessing specialized knowledge essential to a seller's contractual obligation, performing services or training workers to perform services, pursuant to a warranty or other service contract incidental to the sale of commercial or industrial equipment or machinery, including computer software, purchased from an enterprise located outside the territory of the Party into which temporary entry is sought, during the life of the warranty or service agreement.

General Service

- Professionals engaging in a business activity at a professional level in a profession set out in Appendix 1603.D.1.
- Management and supervisory personnel engaging in a commercial transaction for an enterprise located in the territory of another Party.
- Financial services personnel (insurers, bankers or investment brokers) engaging in commercial transactions for an enterprise located in the territory of another Party.
- Public relations and advertising personnel consulting with business associates, or attending or participating in conventions.
- Tourism personnel (tour and travel agents, tour guides or tour operators) attending or participating in conventions or conducting a tour that has begun in the territory of another Party.
- Tour bus operators entering the territory of a Party:
  - (a) with a group of passengers on a bus tour that has begun in, and will return to, the territory of another Party;
  - (b) to meet a group of passengers on a bus tour that will end, and the predominant portion of which will take place, in the territory of another Party; or

(c) with a group of passengers on a bus tour to be unloaded in the territory of the Party into which temporary entry is sought, and returning with no passengers or reloading with the group for transportation to the territory of another Party.

- Translators or interpreters performing services as employees of an enterprise located in the territory of another Party.

Definitions

For purposes of this Appendix:

territory of another Party means the territory of a Party other than the territory of the Party into which temporary entry is sought;

tour bus operator means a natural person, including relief personnel accompanying or following to join, necessary for the operation of a tour bus for the duration of a trip; and

transportation operator means a natural person, other than a tour bus operator, including relief personnel accompanying or following to join, necessary for the operation of a vehicle for the duration of a trip.

Appendix 1603.A.3 — Existing Immigration Measures

1. In the case of Canada, subsection 19(1) of the *Immigration Regulations, 1978*, SOR/78-172, as amended, made under the *Immigration Act*, R.S.C. 1985, c. 1-2, as amended.

2. In the case of the United States, section 101(a)(15)(B) of the *Immigration and Nationality Act*, 1952, as amended.

3. In the case of Mexico, Chapter III of the *Ley General de Poblacion*, 1974, as amended.

Appendix 1603.D.1 — Professionals

PROFESSION[1]	MINIMUM EDUCATION REQUIREMENTS AND ALTERNATIVE CREDENTIALS
General	
Accountant	Baccalaureate or Licenciatura Degree, or C.P.A., C.A., C.G.A., C.M.A.
Architect	Baccalaureate or Licenciatura Degree; or state/provincial license[2]
Computer Systems Analyst	Baccalaureate or Licenciatura Degree; or Post-Secondary Diploma[3] or Post-Secondary Certificate,[4] and three years experience

PROFESSION[1]	MINIMUM EDUCATION REQUIREMENTS AND ALTERNATIVE CREDENTIALS
Disaster Relief Insurance Claims Adjuster (claims adjuster employed by an insurance company located in the territory of a Party, or an independent claims adjuster)	Baccalaureate or Licenciatura Degree, and successful completion of training in the appropriate areas of insurance adjustment pertaining to disaster relief claims; or three years experience in claims adjustment and successful completion of training in the appropriate areas of insurance adjustment pertaining to disaster relief claims
Economist	Baccalaureate or Licenciatura Degree
Engineer	Baccalaureate or Licenciatura Degree; or state/provincial license
Forester	Baccalaureate or Licenciatura Degree; or state/provincial license
Graphic Designer	Baccalaureate or Licenciatura Degree; or Post-Secondary Diploma or Post-Secondary Certificate, and three years experience
Hotel Manager	Baccalaureate or Licenciatura Degree in hotel/restaurant management; or Post-Secondary Diploma or Post-Secondary Certificate in hotel/restaurant management, and three years experience in hotel/restaurant management
Industrial Designer	Baccalaureate or Licenciatura Degree; or Post-Secondary Diploma or Post-Secondary Certificate, and three years experience
Interior Designer	Baccalaureate or Licenciatura Degree; or Post-Secondary Diploma or Post-Secondary Certificate, and three years experience
Land Surveyor	Baccalaureate or Licenciatura Degree; or state/provincial/federal license
Landscape Architect	Baccalaureate or Licenciatura Degree
Lawyer (including Notary in the Province of Quebec)	LL.B., J.D., LL.L., B.C.L. or Licenciatura Degree (five years); or membership in a state/provincial bar
Librarian	M.L.S. or B.L.S. (for which another Baccalaureate or Licenciatura Degree was a prerequisite)

PROFESSION[1]	MINIMUM EDUCATION REQUIREMENTS AND ALTERNATIVE CREDENTIALS
Management Consultant	Baccalaureate or Licenciatura Degree; or equivalent professional experience as established by statement or professional credential attesting to five years experience as a management consultant, or five years experience in a field of specialty related to the consulting agreement
Mathematician (including Statistician)	Baccalaureate or Licenciatura Degree
Range Manager/Range Conservationalist	Baccalaureate or Licenciatura Degree
Research Assistant (working in a post-secondary educational institution)	Baccalaureate or Licenciatura Degree
Scientific Technician/Technologist[5]	Possession of (a) theoretical knowledge of any of the following disciplines: agricultural sciences, astronomy, biology, chemistry, engineering, forestry, geology, geo-physics, meteorology or physics; and (b) the ability to solve practical problems in any of those disciplines, or the ability to apply principles of any of those disciplines to basic or applied research
Social Worker	Baccalaureate or Licenciatura Degree
Sylviculturist (including Forestry Specialist)	Baccalaureate or Licenciatura Degree
Technical Publications Writer	Baccalaureate or Licenciatura Degree; or Post-Secondary Diploma or Post-Secondary Certificate, and three years experience
Urban Planner (including Geographer)	Baccalaureate or Licenciatura Degree
Vocational Counsellor	Baccalaureate or Licenciatura Degree
Medical/Allied Professional	
Dentist	D.D.S., D.M.D., Doctor en Odontologia or Doctor en Cirugia Dental; or state/provincial license
Dietitian	Baccalaureate or Licenciatura Degree; or state/provincial license

PROFESSION[1]	MINIMUM EDUCATION REQUIREMENTS AND ALTERNATIVE CREDENTIALS
Medical Laboratory Technologist (Canada)/Medical Technologist (Mexico and the United States)[6]	Baccalaureate or Licenciatura Degree; or Post-Secondary Diploma or Post-Secondary Certificate, and three years experience
Nutritionist	Baccalaureate or Licenciatura Degree
Occupational Therapist	Baccalaureate or Licenciatura Degree; or state/provincial license
Pharmacist	Baccalaureate or Licenciatura Degree; or state/provincial license
Physician (teaching and/or research only)	M.D. or Doctor en Medicina; or state/provincial license
Physiotherapist/Physical Therapist	Baccalaureate or Licenciatura Degree; or state/provincial license
Psychologist	State/provincial license; or Licenciatura Degree
Recreational Therapist	Baccalaureate or Licenciatura Degree
Registered Nurse	State/provincial license; or Licenciatura Degree
Veterinarian	D.V.M., D.M.V., or Doctor en Veterinaria; or state/provincial license
Scientist	
Agriculturist (Agronomist)	Baccalaureate or Licenciatura Degree
Animal Breeder	Baccalaureate or Licenciatura Degree
Animal Scientist	Baccalaureate or Licenciatura Degree
Apiculturist	Baccalaureate or Licenciatura Degree
Astronomer	Baccalaureate or Licenciatura Degree
Biochemist	Baccalaureate or Licenciatura Degree
Biologist	Baccalaureate or Licenciatura Degree
Chemist	Baccalaureate or Licenciatura Degree
Dairy Scientist	Baccalaureate or Licenciatura Degree
Entomologist	Baccalaureate or Licenciatura Degree
Epidemiologist	Baccalaureate or Licenciatura Degree
Geneticist	Baccalaureate or Licenciatura Degree
Geologist	Baccalaureate or Licenciatura Degree
Geochemist	Baccalaureate or Licenciatura Degree
Geophysicist (including Oceanographer in Mexico and the United States)	Baccalaureate or Licenciatura Degree
Horticulturist	Baccalaureate or Licenciatura Degree
Meteorologist	Baccalaureate or Licenciatura Degree
Pharmacologist	Baccalaureate or Licenciatura Degree

Other Relevant Legislation

PROFESSION[1]	MINIMUM EDUCATION REQUIREMENTS AND ALTERNATIVE CREDENTIALS
Physicist (including Oceanographer in Canada)	Baccalaureate or Licenciatura Degree
Plant Breeder	Baccalaureate or Licenciatura Degree
Poultry Scientist	Baccalaureate or Licenciatura Degree
Soil Scientist	Baccalaureate or Licenciatura Degree
Zoologist	Baccalaureate or Licenciatura Degree
Teacher	
College	Baccalaureate or Licenciatura Degree
Seminary	Baccalaureate or Licenciatura Degree
University	Baccalaureate or Licenciatura Degree

Notes:

1   A business person seeking temporary entry under this Appendix may also perform training functions relating to the profession, including conducting seminars.

2   "State/provincial license" and "state/provincial/federal license" mean any document issued by a state, provincial or federal government, as the case may be, or under its authority, but not by a local government, that permits a person to engage in a regulated activity or profession.

3   "Post-Secondary Diploma" means a credential issued, on completion of two or more years of post-secondary education, by an accredited academic institution in Canada or the United States.

4   "Post-Secondary Certificate" means a certificate issued, on completion of two or more years of post-secondary education at an academic institution, by the federal government of Mexico or a state government in Mexico, an academic institution recognized by the federal government or a state government, or an academic institution created by federal or state law.

5   A business person in this category must be seeking temporary entry to work in direct support of professionals in agricultural sciences, astronomy, biology, chemistry, engineering, forestry, geology, geophysics, meterorology or physics.

6   A business person in this category must be seeking temporary entry to perform in a laboratory chemical, biological, hematological, immunologic, microscopic or bacteriological tests and analyses for diagnosis, treatment or prevention of disease.

Appendix 1603.D.4 — United States

1. Beginning on the date of entry into force of this Agreement as between the United States and Mexico, the United States shall annually approve as many as 5,500 initial petitions of business persons of Mexico seeking temporary entry under Section D of Annex 1603 to engage in a business activity at a professional level in a profession set out in Appendix 1603.D.1.

2. For purposes of paragraph 1, the United States shall not take into account:

(a) the renewal of a period of temporary entry;

(b) the entry of a spouse or children accompanying or following to join the principal business person;

(c) an admission under section 101(a)(15)(H)(i)(b) of the *Immigration and Nationality Act*, 1952, as may be amended, including the worldwide numerical limit established by section 214(g)(1)(A) of that Act; or

(d) an admission under any other provision of section 101(a)(15) of that Act relating to the entry of professionals.

3. Paragraphs 4 and 5 of Section D of Annex 1603 shall apply as between the United States and Mexico for no longer than:

(a) the period that such paragraphs or similar provisions may apply as between the United States and any other Party other than Canada or any non-Party; or

(b) 10 years after the date of entry into force of this Agreement as between such Parties,

whichever period is shorter.

ANNEX 1604.2 — PROVISION OF INFORMATION

The obligations under Article 1604(2) shall take effect with respect to Mexico one year after the date of entry into force of this Agreement.

ANNEX 1608 — COUNTRY — SPECIFIC DEFINITIONS

For purposes of this Chapter:

citizen means, with respect to Mexico, a national or a citizen according to the existing provisions of Articles 30 and 34, respectively, of the Mexican Constitution; and

existing means, as between:

(a) Canada and Mexico, and Mexico and the United States, in effect on the date of entry into force of this Agreement; and

(b) Canada and the United States, in effect on January 1, 1989.

Other Relevant Legislation

CANADA–CHILE FREE TRADE AGREEMENT (CCFTA)
CHAPTER K
DECEMBER 5, 1996

Chapter K — Temporary Entry for Business Persons

Article K-01 — General Principles

Further to Article A-02 (Objectives), this Chapter reflects the preferential trading relationship between the Parties, the desirability of facilitating temporary entry on a reciprocal basis and of establishing transparent criteria and procedures for temporary entry, and the need to ensure border security and to protect the domestic labour force and permanent employment in their respective territories.

Article K-02 — General Obligations

Each Party shall apply its measures relating to the provisions of this Chapter in accordance with Article K-01 and, in particular, shall apply expeditiously those measures so as to avoid unduly impairing or delaying trade in goods or services or conduct of investment activities under this Agreement.

Article K-03 — Grant of Temporary Entry

1. Each Party shall grant temporary entry to business persons who are otherwise qualified for entry under applicable measures relating to public health and safety and national security, in accordance with this Chapter, including the provisions of Annex K-03 and Annex K-03.1.

2. A Party may refuse to issue an immigration document authorizing employment to a business person where the temporary entry of that person might affect adversely:

(a) the settlement of any labour dispute that is in progress at the place or intended place of employment; or

(b) the employment of any person who is involved in such dispute.

3. When a Party refuses pursuant to paragraph 2 to issue an immigration document authorizing employment, it shall:

(a) inform in writing the business person of the reasons for the refusal; and

(b) promptly notify the other Party in writing of the reasons for the refusal.

4. Each Party shall limit any fees for processing applications for temporary entry of business persons to the approximate cost of services rendered.

Article K-04 — Provision of Information

1. Further to Article L-02 (Publication), each Party shall:

(a) provide to the other Party such materials as will enable it to become acquainted with its measures relating to this Chapter; and

(b) no later than one year after the date of entry into force of this Agreement, prepare, publish and make available in its own territory, and in the territory of the other Party, explanatory material in a consolidated document regarding the requirements for temporary entry under this Chapter in such a manner as will enable business persons of the other Party to become acquainted with them.

2. Each Party shall collect and maintain, and make available to the other Party in accordance with its domestic law, data respecting the granting of temporary entry under this Chapter to business persons of the other Party who have been issued immigration documentation, including data specific to each occupation, profession or activity.

Article K-05 — Working Group

The Parties hereby establish a Temporary Entry Working Group, comprising representatives of each Party, including immigration officials, to consider the implementation and administration of this Chapter and any measures of mutual interest.

Article K-06 — Dispute Settlement

1. A Party may not initiate proceedings under Article N-07 (Commission — Good Offices, Conciliation and Mediation) regarding a refusal to grant temporary entry under this Chapter or a particular case arising under Article K-02 unless:

(a) the matter involves a pattern of practice; and

(b) the business person has exhausted the available administrative remedies regarding the particular matter.

2. The remedies referred to in paragraph (1)(b) shall be deemed to be exhausted if a final determination in the matter has not been issued by the competent authority within one year of the institution of an administrative proceeding, and the failure to issue a determination is not attributable to delay caused by the business person.

Article K-07 — Relation to Other Chapters

Except for this Chapter, Chapters A (Objectives), B (General Definitions), N (Institutional Arrangements and Dispute Settlement Procedures) and P (Final Provisions) and Articles L-01 (Contacts Points), L-02 (Publication), L-03 (Notification and Provision of Information) and L-04 (Administrative Proceedings), no provision of this Agreement shall impose any obligation on a Party regarding its immigration measures.

Article K-08 — Definitions:

For purposes of this Chapter:

business person means a citizen of a Party who is engaged in trade in goods, the provision of services or the conduct of investment activities; and

temporary entry means entry into the territory of a Party by a business person of the other Party without the intent to establish permanent residence.

ANNEX K-03 — TEMPORARY ENTRY FOR BUSINESS PERSONS

Section I — Business Visitors

1. Each Party shall grant temporary entry to a business person seeking to engage in a business activity set out in Appendix K-03.I.1, without requiring that person to obtain an employment authorization, provided that the business person otherwise complies with existing immigration measures applicable to temporary entry, on presentation of:

(a) proof of citizenship of a Party;

(b) documentation demonstrating that the business person will be so engaged and describing the purpose of entry; and

(c) evidence demonstrating that the proposed business activity is international in scope and the business person is not seeking to enter the local labour market.

2. Each Party shall provide that a business person may satisfy the requirements of paragraph 1(c) by demonstrating that:

(a) the primary source of remuneration for the proposed business activity is outside the territory of the Party granting temporary entry; and

(b) the business person's principal place of business and the actual place of accrual of profits, at least, predominantly, remain outside such territory.

A Party shall normally accept an oral declaration as to the principal place of business and the actual place of accrual of profits. Where the Party requires further proof, it shall normally consider a letter from the employer attesting to these matters as sufficient proof.

3. Each Party shall grant temporary entry to a business person seeking to engage in a business activity other than those set out in Appendix K-03.I.1, without requiring that person to obtain an employment authorization, on a basis no less favourable than that provided under the existing provisions of the measures set out in Appendix K-03.I.3, provided that the business person otherwise complies with existing immigration measures applicable to temporary entry.

4. Neither Party may:

(a) as a condition for temporary entry under paragraph 1 or 3, require prior approval procedures, petitions, labour certification tests or other procedures of similar effect; or

(b) impose or maintain any numerical restriction relating to temporary entry under paragraph 1 or 3.

Other Relevant Legislation

5. Notwithstanding paragraph 4, a Party may require a business person seeking temporary entry under this Section to obtain a visa or its equivalent prior to entry. Before imposing a visa requirement, the Party shall consult with the other Party with a view to avoiding the imposition of the requirement. With respect to an existing visa requirement, a Party shall consult, on request, with the other Party with a view to its removal.

Section II — Traders and Investors

1. Each Party shall grant temporary entry and provide confirming documentation to a business person seeking to:

   (a) carry on substantial trade in goods or services principally between the territory of the Party of which the business person is a citizen and the territory of the other Party into which entry is sought, or

   (b) establish, develop, administer or provide advice or key technical services to the operation of an investment to which the business person or the business person's enterprise has committed, or is in the process of committing, a substantial amount of capital,

in a capacity that is supervisory, executive or involves essential skills, provided that the business person otherwise complies with existing immigration measures applicable to temporary entry.

2. Neither Party may:

   (a) as a condition for temporary entry under paragraph 1, require labour certification tests or other procedures of similar effect; or

   (b) impose or maintain any numerical restriction relating to temporary entry under paragraph 1.

3. Notwithstanding paragraph 2, a Party may require a business person seeking temporary entry under this Section to obtain a visa or its equivalent prior to entry.

Section III — Intra-Company Transferees

1. Each Party shall grant temporary entry and provide confirming documentation to a business person employed by an enterprise who seeks to render services to that enterprise or a subsidiary or affiliate thereof, in a capacity that is managerial, executive or involves specialized knowledge, provided that the business person otherwise complies with existing immigration measures applicable to temporary entry. A Party may require the business person to have been employed continuously by the enterprise for one year within the three-year period immediately preceding the date of the application for admission.

2. Neither Party may:

   (a) as a condition for temporary entry under paragraph 1, require labour certification tests or other procedures of similar effect; or

   (b) impose or maintain any numerical restriction relating to temporary entry under paragraph 1.

3. Notwithstanding paragraph 2, a Party may require a business person seeking temporary entry under this Section to obtain a visa or its equivalent prior to entry. Before imposing a visa requirement, the Party shall consult with the other

Party with a view to avoiding the imposition of the requirement. With respect to an existing visa requirement, a Party shall consult, on request, with the other Party with a view to its removal.

Section IV — Professionals

1. Each Party shall grant temporary entry and provide confirming documentation to a business person seeking to engage in a business activity at a professional level in a profession set out in Appendix K-03.IV.1, if the business person otherwise complies with existing immigration measures applicable to temporary entry, on presentation of:

(a) proof of citizenship of a Party; and

(b) documentation demonstrating that the business person will be so engaged and describing the purpose of entry.

2. Neither Party may:

(a) as a condition for temporary entry under paragraph 1, require prior approval procedures, petitions, labour certification tests or other procedures of similar effect; or

(b) impose or maintain any numerical restriction relating to temporary entry under paragraph 1.

3. Notwithstanding paragraph 2, a Party may require a business person seeking temporary entry under this Section to obtain a visa or its equivalent prior to entry. Before imposing a visa requirement, the Party shall consult with the other Party with a view to avoiding the imposition of the requirement. With respect to an existing visa requirement, a Party shall consult, on request, with the other Party with a view to its removal.

4. Notwithstanding paragraphs 1 and 2, a Party may establish an annual numerical limit, which shall be set out in Appendix K-03.IV.4, regarding temporary entry of business persons of the other Party seeking to engage in business activities at a professional level in a profession set out in Appendix K-03.IV.1, if the Parties have not agreed otherwise prior to the date of entry into force of this Agreement. In establishing such a limit, the Party shall consult with the other Party.

5. A Party establishing a numerical limit pursuant to paragraph 4, unless the Parties agree otherwise:

(a) shall, for each year after the first year after the date of entry into force of this Agreement, consider increasing the numerical limit set out in Appendix K-03.IV.4 by an amount to be established in consultation with the other Party, taking into account the demand for temporary entry under this Section;

(b) shall not apply its procedures established pursuant to paragraph 1 to the temporary entry of a business person subject to the numerical limit, but may require the business person to comply with its other procedures applicable to the temporary entry of professionals; and

(c) may, in consultation with the other Party, grant temporary entry under paragraph 1 to a business person who practices in a profession where accreditation, licensing, and certification requirements are mutually recognized by the Parties.

6. Nothing in paragraph 4 or 5 shall be construed to limit the ability of a business person to seek temporary entry under a Party's applicable immigration measures relating to the entry of professionals other than those adopted or maintained pursuant to paragraph 1.

7. Three years after a Party establishes a numerical limit pursuant to paragraph 4, it shall consult with the other Party with a view to determining a date after which the limit shall cease to apply.

Annex K-03.1

1. Business persons who enter Chile under any of the categories set out in Annex K-03 shall be deemed to be engaged in activities which are in the country's interest.

2. Business persons who enter Chile under any of the categories set out in Annex K-03 and are issued a temporary visa shall have that temporary visa extended for subsequent periods provided the conditions on which it is based remain in effect, without requiring that person to apply for permanent residence.

3. Business persons who enter Chile may also obtain an identity card for foreigners.

Appendix K-03.I.1 — Business Visitors

Research and Design

- Technical, scientific and statistical researchers conducting independent research or research for an enterprise located in the territory of the other Party.

Growth, Manufacture and Production

- Purchasing and production management personnel conducting commercial transactions for an enterprise located in the territory of the other Party.

Marketing

- Market researchers and analysts conducting independent research or analysis or research or analysis for an enterprise located in the territory of the other Party.
- Trade fair and promotional personnel attending a trade convention.

Sales

- Sales representatives and agents taking orders or negotiating contracts for goods or services for an enterprise located in the territory of the other Party but not delivering goods or providing services.
- Buyers purchasing for an enterprise located in the territory of the other Party.

Distribution

- Customs brokers providing consulting services regarding the facilitation of the import or export of goods.

After-sales Service

- Installers, repair and maintenance personnel, and supervisors, possessing specialized knowledge essential to a seller's contractual obligation, performing services or training workers to perform services, pursuant to a warranty or other service contract incidental to the sale of commercial or industrial equipment or machinery, including computer software, purchased from an enterprise located outside the territory of the Party into which temporary entry is sought, during the life of the warranty or service agreement.

General Service

- Professionals engaging in a business activity at a professional level in a profession set out in Appendix K-03.IV.1.

- Management and supervisory personnel engaging in a commercial transaction for an enterprise located in the territory of the other Party.

- Financial services personnel (insurers, bankers or investment brokers) engaging in commercial transactions for an enterprise located in the territory of the other Party.

- Public relations and advertising personnel consulting with business associates, or attending or participating in conventions.

- Tourism personnel (tour and travel agents, tour guides or tour operators) attending or participating in conventions or conducting a tour that has begun in the territory of the other Party.

- Translators or interpreters performing services as employees of an enterprise located in the territory of the other Party.

Definitions

For purposes of this Appendix:

territory of the other Party means the territory of the Party other than the territory of the Party into which temporary entry is sought.

Appendix K-03.I.3 — Existing Immigration Measures

1. In the case of Canada, subsection 19(1) of the *Immigration Regulations*, 1978, SOR/78-172, as amended, made under the *Immigration Act* R.S.C. 1985, c. I-2, as amended.

2. In the case of Chile, Title I, paragraph 6 of *Decree Law 1094*, Official Gazette, July 19, 1975, *Immigration Law ("Decreto Ley 1094,* Diario Oficial, julio 19, 1975, *Ley de Extranjería"),* and *Title III of Immigration Regulation ("Decreto Supremo 597 del Ministerio del Interior,* Diario Oficial noviembre 24, 1984, *Reglamento de Extranjería").*

Other Relevant Legislation

Appendix K-03.IV.1 — Professionals

PROFESSION[1]

MINIMUM EDUCATION REQUIREMENTS AND ALTERNATIVE CREDENTIALS[2]

General

Accountant	Baccalaureate or Licenciatura Degree; or C.P.A., C.A., C.G.A. or C.M.A.; or Contador auditor or Contador público (University Title)[3]
Architect	Baccalaureate or Licenciatura Degree; or state/provincial licence[4]
Computer Systems Analyst	Baccalaureate or Licenciatura Degree; or Post-Secondary Diploma[5] or Post-Secondary Certificate[6], and three years experience
Disaster Relief Insurance Claims Adjuster (claims adjuster employed by an insurance company located in the territory of a Party, or an independent claims adjuster)	Baccalaureate or Licenciatura Degree, and successful completion of training in the appropriate areas of insurance adjustment pertaining to disaster relief claims; or three years experience in claims adjustment and successful completion of training in the appropriate areas of insurance adjustment pertaining to disaster relief claims
Economist (including Commercial Engineer in Chile)	Baccalaureate or Licenciatura Degree
Engineer	Baccalaureate or Licenciatura Degree; or state/provincial licence
Forester	Baccalaureate or Licenciatura Degree; or state/provincial licence
Graphic Designer	Baccalaureate or Licenciatura Degree; or Post-Secondary Diploma or Post-Secondary Certificate, and three years experience
Hotel Manager	Baccalaureate or Licenciatura Degree in hotel/restaurant management; or Post-Secondary Diploma or Post-Secondary Certificate in hotel/restaurant management, and three years experience in hotel/restaurant management
Industrial Designer	Baccalaureate or Licenciatura Degree; or Post-Secondary Diploma or Post-Secondary Certificate, and three years experience

PROFESSION[1]	MINIMUM EDUCATION REQUIREMENTS AND ALTERNATIVE CREDENTIALS[2]
Interior Designer	Baccalaureate or Licenciatura Degree; or Post-Secondary Diploma or Post-Secondary Certificate, and three years experience
Land Surveyor	Baccalaureate or Licenciatura Degree; or state/provincial/national licence
Landscape Architect	Baccalaureate or Licenciatura Degree
Lawyer (including Notary in the Province of Quebec)	LL.B., J.D., LL.L., B.C.L. or Licenciatura Degree (five years) or Abogado, or membership in a state/provincial bar
Librarian	M.L.S. or B.L.S. or Magister en Bibliotecología (for which another Baccalaureate or Licenciatura Degree was a prerequisite)
Management Consultant	Baccalaureate or Licenciatura Degree; or equivalent professional experience as established by statement or professional credential attesting to five years experience as a management consultant, or five years experience in a field of specialty related to the consulting agreement
Mathematician (including Statistician)	Baccalaureate or Licenciatura Degree
Range Manager/Range Conservationalist	Baccalaureate or Licenciatura Degree
Research Assistant (working in a post- secondary educational institution)	Baccalaureate or Licenciatura Degree
Scientific Technician/Technologist[7]	Possession of (a) theoretical knowledge of any of the following disciplines: agricultural sciences, astronomy, biology, chemistry, engineering, forestry, geology, geophysics, meteorology or physics; and (b) the ability to solve practical problems in any of those disciplines, or the ability to apply principles of any of those disciplines to basic or applied research

PROFESSION[1]	**MINIMUM EDUCATION REQUIREMENTS AND ALTERNATIVE CREDENTIALS**[2]
Social Worker	Baccalaureate or Licenciatura Degree or Asistente Social/Trabajador social (University Title)
Sylviculturist (including Forestry Specialist)	Baccalaureate or Licenciatura Degree
Technical Publications Writer	Baccalaureate or Licenciatura Degree; or Post-Secondary Diploma or Post-Secondary Certificate, and three years experience
Urban Planner (including Geographer)	Baccalaureate or Licenciatura Degree
Vocational Counsellor	Baccalaureate or Licenciatura Degree
Medical/Allied Professional	
Dentist	D.D.S., D.M.D., Doctor en Odontologia or Doctor en Cirugia Dental or Licenciatura en Odontologia; or state/provincial licence
Dietitian	Baccalaureate or Licenciatura Degree or Dietista Nutricional (University Title); or state/provincial licence
Medical Laboratory Technologist (Canada)/Medical Technologist (Chile, Mexico and the United States of America)[8]	Baccalaureate or Licenciatura Degree; or Post-Secondary Diploma or Post-Secondary Certificate, and three years experience
Nutritionist	Baccalaureate or Licenciatura Degree or Nutricionista/Dietista Nutricional (University Title)
Occupational Therapist	Baccalaureate or Licenciatura Degree or Terapeuta Ocupacional (University Title); or state/provincial licence
Pharmacist	Baccalaureate or Licenciatura Degree; or state/provincial licence
Physician (teaching or research only)	M.D. or Doctor en Medicina or Médico Cirujano/Médico (University Title); or state/provincial licence
Physiotherapist/Physical Therapist	Baccalaureate or Licenciatura Degree or Kinesiólogo/Kinesioterapeuta (University Title); or state/provincial licence
Psychologist	State/provincial licence; or Licenciatura Degree
Recreational Therapist	Baccalaureate or Licenciatura Degree

PROFESSION[1]	MINIMUM EDUCATION REQUIREMENTS AND ALTERNATIVE CREDENTIALS[2]
Registered Nurse	State/provincial licence, or Licenciatura Degree, or Enfermera (University Title)
Veterinarian	D.V.M., D.M.V. or Doctor en Veterinaria or Médico Veterinario (University Title); or state/provincial licence
Scientist	
Agriculturist (including Agronomist)	Baccalaureate or Licenciatura Degree
Animal Breeder	Baccalaureate or Licenciatura Degree
Animal Scientist	Baccalaureate or Licenciatura Degree
Apiculturist	Baccalaureate or Licenciatura Degree
Astronomer	Baccalaureate or Licenciatura Degree
Biochemist	Baccalaureate or Licenciatura Degree
Biologist	Baccalaureate or Licenciatura Degree
Chemist	Baccalaureate or Licenciatura Degree
Dairy Scientist	Baccalaureate or Licenciatura Degree
Entomologist	Baccalaureate or Licenciatura Degree
Epidemiologist	Baccalaureate or Licenciatura Degree
Geneticist	Baccalaureate or Licenciatura Degree
Geologist	Baccalaureate or Licenciatura Degree or Geólogo (University Title)
Geochemist	Baccalaureate or Licenciatura Degree
Geophysicist (including Oceanographer in Mexico and the United States of America)	Baccalaureate or Licenciatura Degree
Horticulturist	Baccalaureate or Licenciatura Degree
Meteorologist	Baccalaureate or Licenciatura Degree
Pharmacologist	Baccalaureate or Licenciatura Degree
Physicist (including Oceanographer in Canada and Chile)	Baccalaureate or Licenciatura Degree for Physicist; Oceanógrafo (University Title) for Oceanographer
Plant Breeder	Baccalaureate or Licenciatura Degree
Poultry Scientist	Baccalaureate or Licenciatura Degree
Soil Scientist	Baccalaureate or Licenciatura Degree
Zoologist	Baccalaureate or Licenciatura Degree
Teacher	
College	Baccalaureate or Licenciatura Degree
Seminary	Baccalaureate or Licenciatura Degree
University	Baccalaureate or Licenciatura Degree

Notes:

1   A business person seeking temporary entry under this Appendix may also perform training functions relating to the profession, including conducting seminars.

2   *Accountant*:

> C.P.A.: Certified Public Accountant; C.A.: Chartered Accountant; C.G.A.: Certified General Accountant; C.M.A.: Certified Management Accountant

> *Dentist*:

> D.D.S.: Doctor of Dental Surgery; D.M.D.: Doctor of Dental Medicine

> *Lawyer*:

> LL.B.: Bachelor of Laws; J.D.: Doctor of Jurisprudence (not a doctorate); LL.L: Licence en Droit (Québec universities and University of Ottawa); BCL: Bachelor of Civil Law

> *Librarian*:

> M.L.S.: Master of Library Science; B.L.S.: Bachelor of Library Science

> *Physician*:

> M.D.: Medical Doctor

> *Veterinarian*:

> D.V.M.: Doctor of Veterinary Medicine; D.M.V.: Docteur en Médicine Vétérinaire

3   "University Title" means any document conferred by universities recognized by the Government of Chile and shall be deemed to be equivalent to the Minimum Education Requirements and Alternative Credentials for that profession. In the case of the profession of Lawyer (Abogado), the title is conferred by the Supreme Court of Chile.

4   "State/provincial licence" and "state/provincial/national licence" mean any document issued by a provincial or national government, as the case may be, or under its authority, but not by a local government, that permits a person to engage in a regulated activity or profession.

5   "Post-Secondary Diploma" means a credential issued, on completion of two or more years of post-secondary education, by an accredited academic institution in Canada or the United Sates of America.

6   "Post-Secondary Certificate" means a certificate issued, on completion of two or more years of post-secondary education at an academic institution:

> — in the case of Mexico, by the federal government or a state government, an academic institution recognized by the federal government or a state government, or an academic institution created by federal or state law; and

> — in the case of Chile, by an academic institution recognized by the Government of Chile.

7   A business person in this category must be seeking temporary entry to work in direct support of professionals in agricultural sciences, astronomy, biology, chemistry, engineering, forestry, geology, geophysics, meteorology or physics.

8   A business person in this category must be seeking temporary entry to perform in a laboratory chemical, biological, hematological, immunologic, microscopic or bacteriological tests and analyses for diagnosis, treatment or prevention of disease.

Notwithstanding Annex K-03.IV.4, for the purposes of this Agreement, neither Party shall establish an annual numerical limit regarding temporary entry of business persons of the other Party seeking to engage in business activities at a professional level set out in Appendix K-03.IV.1.

APPENDIX VI

CANADA-COSTA RICA FREE TRADE AGREEMENT
Chapter X — Temporary Entry

Article X.1 Temporary Entry

1. The Parties recognize that there is a growing importance of investment and services related to trade in goods. In accordance with their applicable laws and regulations, they shall facilitate the temporary entry of:

a. nationals who are intra-company transferees (managers, executives, specialists) and business visitors;

b. nationals who are providing after-sales services directly related to the exportation of goods by an exporter of that same Party into the territory of the other Party; or

c. spouses or common-law partners and children of nationals described in (a) above.

2. With a view to developing and deepening their relations under this Agreement, the Parties agree that within 3 years of the date of entry into force, they will review developments related to temporary entry, and consider the need for further disciplines in this area.

3. No later than 1 year after the date of entry into force of this Agreement, the Parties shall make available explanatory material regarding the requirements for temporary entry under this Article in such a manner as to enable citizens of the other Party to become acquainted with them.

4. For the purposes of this Chapter:

after-sales services include those provided by persons repairing and servicing, supervising installers, and setting up and testing commercial or industrial (including computer software) equipment, provided the services are being performed as part of an original or extended sales or lease agreement, warranty, or service contract. "Setting up" does not include hands-on installation generally performed by construction or building trades. After-sales services also includes persons providing familiarization or training sessions to potential users;

business visitors are short-term visitors who do not intend to enter the labour market of the Parties, but seek entry to engage in activities such as buying or selling of goods or services, negotiating contracts, conferring with colleagues, or attending conferences;

national means a natural person who is a citizen of a Party; and

temporary entry means the right to enter and remain for the period authorized.

Appendix VII

Canada–Peru Free Trade Agreement
Chapter 12 — Temporary Entry For Business Persons

Article 1201: General Principles

Further to Article 1202, this Chapter reflects the preferential trading relationship between the Parties, the mutual objective to facilitate temporary entry for business persons on a reciprocal basis and in accordance with Annex 1203, the need to establish transparent criteria and procedures for temporary entry and the need to ensure border security and to protect the domestic labour force and permanent employment in their respective territories.

Article 1202: General Obligations

1. Each Party shall apply its measures relating to the provisions of this Chapter in accordance with Article 1201 and, in particular, shall expeditiously apply those measures so as to avoid unduly impairing or delaying trade in goods or services or conduct of investment activities under this Agreement.

2. Nothing in this Chapter shall be construed to prevent a Party from applying measures to regulate the entry of natural persons into, or their temporary stay in, its territory, including those measures necessary to protect the integrity of, and to ensure the orderly movement of natural persons across, its borders, provided that such measures are not applied in such a manner as to unduly impair or delay trade in goods or services or conduct of investment activities under this Agreement.

Article 1203: Grant of Temporary Entry

1. Each Party shall grant temporary entry to business persons who comply with existing immigration measures applicable to temporary entry such as those relating to public health and safety and national security, in accordance with this Chapter, including the provisions of Annex 1203.

2. Subject to each Party's labour legislation, a Party may refuse to issue a work permit or authorization to a business person where the temporary entry of that person might adversely affect:

    (a) the settlement of any labour dispute that is in progress at the place or intended place of employment; or

1447

(b) the employment of any person who is involved in such dispute.

3. Each Party shall limit any fees for processing applications for temporary entry of business persons so as to not unduly impair or delay trade in goods or services or the conduct of investment activities under this Agreement.

Article 1204: Provision of Information

1. Further to Article 1901 (Transparency — Publication), and recognizing the importance to the Parties of transparency of temporary entry information, each Party shall:

(a) provide to the other Party relevant materials that will enable it to become acquainted with its measures relating to this Chapter; and

(b) no later than six months after the date of entry into force of this Agreement, make available explanatory material regarding the requirements for temporary entry under this Chapter in such a manner that will enable business persons of the other Party to become acquainted with them.

2. Each Party shall collect and maintain, and, on request, make available to the other Party in accordance with its domestic law, data respecting the granting of temporary entry under this Chapter to business persons of the other Party who have been issued immigration documentation.

Article 1205: Contact Points

1. The Parties hereby establish Contact Points:

(a) in the case of Canada, the Contact Point is:

Director

Temporary Resident Policy

Immigration Branch

Citizenship and Immigration Canada

(b) in the case of Peru, the Contact Point is:

Director

Directorate of Immigrations

General Directorate of Immigration and Naturalization

Ministry of Interior,

or the occupant of any successor position.

2. The Contact Points shall exchange information as described in Article 1204 and shall meet as required to consider matters pertaining to this Chapter, such as:

(a) the implementation and administration of the Chapter;

(b) the development and adoption of common criteria and interpretations for the implementation of the Chapter;

(c) the development of measures to further facilitate temporary entry of business persons on a reciprocal basis;

(d) proposed modifications to the Chapter; and

(e) measures that affect the temporary entry of business persons under this Chapter.

Article 1206: Dispute Settlement

1. A Party may not initiate proceedings under the general dispute settlement provisions of this Agreement regarding a refusal to grant temporary entry under this Chapter unless:

(a) the matter involves a pattern of practice; and

(b) the business person has exhausted the available administrative remedies regarding the particular matter.

2. The remedies referred to in subparagraph 1(b) shall be deemed to be exhausted if a final determination in the matter has not been issued by the competent authority within one year of the institution of an administrative proceeding, and the failure to issue a determination is not attributable to delay caused by the business person.

Article 1207: Relation to Other Chapters

1. No provision of this Agreement shall be interpreted to impose any obligation on a Party regarding its immigration measures, except as specifically identified in this Chapter and Chapters One and Nineteen to Twenty-Three (Initial Provisions and General Definitions, Transparency, Administration of the Agreement, Dispute Settlement, Exceptions and Final Provisions).

2. Nothing in this Chapter shall be construed to impose obligations or commitments with respect to other Chapters of this Agreement.

Article 1208: Transparency in Processing of Applications

1. Further to Chapter Nineteen (Transparency), each Party shall establish or maintain appropriate mechanisms to respond to inquiries from interested persons regarding applications and procedures relating to the temporary entry of business persons.

2. Each Party shall endeavour to, within a reasonable period that should not exceed 45 days after an application requesting temporary entry is considered complete under its domestic laws and regulations, inform the applicant of the decision concerning the application. At the request of the applicant, the Party shall endeavour to provide, without undue delay, information concerning the status of the application.

Article 1209: Definitions

For purposes of this Chapter:

business person means a national of a Party who is engaged in trade in goods, the supply of services or the conduct of investment activities;

contract service supplier means an employee who is a professional or technician of a foreign based company, partnership, or firm who enters the territory of the other Party temporarily in order to perform a service pursuant to a contract between his/her employer and a service consumer in the territory of the other Party, when the employer:

(a) has no commercial presence in the territory of the other Party;

(b) is a juridical person that has obtained a contract for the provision of a service in the territory of the other Party that does not consist exclusively in the supply of personnel; and

(c) provides the employee's remuneration;

executive means a business person within an organisation who primarily directs the management of the organisation, exercises wide latitude in decision-making, and receives only general supervision or direction from higher level executives, the board of directors, and/or stockholders of the business;

independent professional or technician means a professional or technician who enters the territory of the other Party temporarily in order to perform a service pursuant to a contract with a service consumer located in the territory of the other Party when:

(a) the professional or technician supplies the service as a self-employed person;

(b) the professional or technician has obtained a service contract in the territory of the Party where the service is to be supplied; and

(c) the remuneration for the contract is to be paid solely to the professional or technician in the territory of the Party where the service is to be supplied;

labour dispute means a strike between a union and employer relating to terms and conditions of employment;

management trainee on professional development means an employee with a post-secondary degree who is on a temporary work assignment intended to broaden that employee's knowledge of and experience in a company in preparation for a senior leadership position within the company;

manager means a business person within an organisation who primarily directs the organisation or a department or sub-division of the organisation, supervises and controls the work of other supervisory, professional or managerial employees, has the authority to hire and fire or take other personnel actions (such as promotion or leave authorisation), and exercises discretionary authority over day-to-day operations;

professional means a national of a Party who is engaged in a specialty occupation[270] requiring:

(a) theoretical and practical application of a body of specialized knowledge, and who is eligible to obtain the certification or license to practice, if required; and

(b) attainment of a post-secondary degree in the specialty requiring four, or more years of study as a minimum for entry into the occupation[271];

professional or technician in a subordinate relationship means a professional or technician who enters the territory of the other Party temporarily in order to perform a service under the direction of an employer in the other Party, who has the authority to regulate, direct and sanction the activities of the employee;

---

[270] With respect to Canada, a professional specialty occupation shall mean an occupation which falls within the National Occupation Classification (NOC) levels O and A.

[271] With respect to Canada, these requirements shall be those defined in the NOC. With respect to Peru, requirements for regulated professions shall be provided in accordance with Article 1204.

specialist means an employee who possesses specialized knowledge of the company's products or services and its application in international markets, or an advanced level of expertise or knowledge of the company's processes and procedures. A specialist may include, but is not limited to, professionals and technicians;

technician means a national of a Party who is engaged in a specialty occupation[272] requiring:

(a) theoretical and practical application of a body of specialized knowledge, and who is eligible to obtain the certification/license to practice, if required; and

(b) attainment of a post-secondary or technical degree requiring one, or more years of study, or the equivalent of such a degree, as a minimum for entry into the occupation;[273] and

temporary entry means entry into the territory of a Party by a business person of the other Party without the intent to establish permanent residence.

Annex 1203 — Temporary Entry for Business Persons

Section A — Business Visitors

1. Each Party shall grant temporary entry to a business person seeking to engage in a business activity set out in Appendix 1203.A.1, without requiring that person to obtain a work permit or an employment authorization, provided that the business person otherwise complies with existing immigration measures applicable to temporary entry, on presentation of:

(a) proof of nationality, citizenship or permanent residency status of a Party;

(b) documentation demonstrating that the business person will be engaged in a business activity set out in Appendix 1203.A.1 and describing the purpose of entry; and

(c) evidence demonstrating that the proposed business activity is international in scope and the business person is not seeking to enter the local labour market.

2. Each Party shall provide that a business person may satisfy the requirements of subparagraph 1(c) by demonstrating that:

(a) the primary source of remuneration for the proposed business activity is outside the territory of the Party granting temporary entry; and

(b) the business person's principal place of business and the actual place of accrual of profits, at least predominantly, remain outside the territory of the Party granting temporary entry.

A Party shall normally accept an oral declaration as to the principal place of business and the actual place of accrual of profits. Where the Party requires further proof, it shall nor-

---

[272] With respect to Canada, a technical specialty occupation shall mean an occupation which falls within the NOC level B.

[273] With respect to Canada, these requirements shall be those defined in the NOC. With respect to Peru, requirements for regulated technician occupations shall be provided in accordance with Article 1204.

Other Relevant Legislation

mally consider a letter from the employer or the representing organization attesting to these matters as sufficient proof.

3. Neither Party may:

(a) as a condition for temporary entry under paragraph 1, require prior approval procedures, labour certification tests or other procedures of similar effect; or

(b) impose or maintain any numerical restriction relating to temporary entry under paragraph 1.

4. Notwithstanding paragraph 3, a Party may require a business person seeking temporary entry under this Section to obtain a visa or an equivalent requirement prior to entry. Before imposing a visa or an equivalent requirement, the Party shall consult with the other Party whose business persons would be affected with a view to avoiding the imposition of the requirement.

Section B — Traders and Investors

1. Each Party shall grant temporary entry and provide a work permit or other authorization to a business person seeking to:

(a) carry on substantial trade in goods or services principally between the territory of the Party of which the business person is a national and the territory of the other Party into which entry is sought; or

(b) establish, develop or administer an investment to which the business person or the business person's enterprise has committed, or is in the process of committing, a substantial amount of capital,

in a capacity that is supervisory, executive or involves essential skills, provided that the business person otherwise complies with existing immigration measures applicable to temporary entry.

2. Neither Party may:

(a) as a condition for temporary entry under paragraph 1, require labour certification tests or other procedures of similar effect; or

(b) impose or maintain any numerical restriction relating to temporary entry under paragraph 1.

3. Notwithstanding paragraph 2, a Party may require a business person seeking temporary entry under this Section to obtain a visa or an equivalent requirement prior to entry. Before imposing a visa or an equivalent requirement, the Party shall consult with the other Party whose business persons would be affected with a view to avoiding the imposition of the requirement.

Section C — Intra-Company Transferees

1. Each Party shall grant temporary entry and provide a work permit or other authorization to a business person employed by an enterprise who seeks to render services to that enterprise or a subsidiary or affiliate thereof as an executive or manager, a specialist, or a management trainee on professional development, provided that the business person otherwise complies with existing immigration measures applicable to temporary entry. A Party may require the business person to have been employed continuously by the enterprise for six months within the three-year period immediately preceding the date of the application for admission.

2. Neither Party may:

(a) as a condition for temporary entry under paragraph 1, require labour certification tests or other procedures of similar effect; or

(b) impose or maintain any numerical restriction relating to temporary entry under paragraph 1.

3. Notwithstanding paragraph 2, a Party may require a business person seeking temporary entry under this Section to obtain a visa or an equivalent requirement prior to entry. Before imposing a visa or an equivalent requirement, the Party shall consult with the other Party whose business persons would be affected with a view to avoiding the imposition of the requirement.

Section D — Professionals and Technicians

1. Each Party shall grant temporary entry and provide a work permit or other authorization to a business person seeking to engage in a business activity at a professional or technical level in accordance with Appendix 1203.D.1, either as an independent professional and technician, as a professional and technician in a subordinate relationship, or as a contract service supplier, including training activities related to a particular profession, if the business person otherwise complies with existing immigration measures applicable to temporary entry, on presentation of:

(a) proof of nationality, citizenship or permanent residency status of a Party; and

(b) documentation demonstrating that the business person is seeking to enter the territory of the other Party to provide pre-arranged professional services in the field for which he/she has the appropriate qualifications.

2. Neither Party may:

(a) as a condition for temporary entry under paragraph 1, require prior approval procedures, labour certification tests or other procedures of similar effect; or

(b) impose or maintain any numerical restriction relating to temporary entry under paragraph 1.

3. Notwithstanding paragraph 2, a Party may require a business person seeking temporary entry under this Section to obtain a visa or an equivalent requirement prior to entry. Before imposing a visa or an equivalent requirement, the Party shall consult with the other Party whose business persons would be affected with a view to avoiding the imposition of the requirement.

Annex 1203.A.1 Business Visitors

Meetings and Consultations

Business persons attending meetings, seminars, or conferences; or engaged in consultations with business associates.

Research and Design

Technical, scientific and statistical researchers conducting independent research or research for an enterprise located in the territory of the other Party.

Growth, Manufacture and Production

Purchasing and production management personnel, conducting commercial transactions for an enterprise located in the territory of the other Party.

Harvester owner supervising a harvesting crew.

Marketing

Market researchers and analysts conducting independent research or analysis or research or analysis for an enterprise located in the territory of the other Party.

Trade-fair and promotional personnel attending a trade convention.

Sales

Sales representatives and agents taking orders or negotiating contracts for goods or services for an enterprise located in the territory of the other Party but not delivering goods or providing services.

Buyers purchasing for an enterprise located in the territory of the other Party.

Distribution

Transportation operators transporting goods or passengers to the territory of a Party from the territory of the other Party or loading and transporting goods or passengers from the territory of a Party, with no unloading in that territory, to the territory of the other Party.

Customs brokers providing consulting services regarding the facilitation of the import or export of goods.

After-Sales or After-Lease Service

Installers, repair and maintenance personnel, and supervisors, possessing specialized knowledge essential to a seller's contractual obligation, performing services or training workers to perform services, pursuant to a warranty or other service contract incidental to the sale or lease of commercial or industrial equipment or machinery, including computer software, purchased or leased from an enterprise located outside the territory of the Party into which temporary entry is sought, during the life of the warranty or service agreement.

General Service

Professionals and technicians engaging in a business activity at a professional or technical level as set out in Appendix 1203.D.1.

Management and supervisory personnel engaging in a commercial transaction for an enterprise located in the territory of the other Party.

Financial services personnel of an enterprise located in the territory of the other Party, engaging in the area of financial services, where the provision of such financial services does not require the authorization of the competent authority of the Party or where such financial services are listed in Annex 1105.

Public relations and advertising personnel consulting with business associates, or attending or participating in conventions.

Tourism personnel (tour and travel agents, tour guides or tour operators) attending or participating in conventions or conducting a tour that has begun in the territory of the other Party.

Cook personnel (cookers and assistants) attending or participating in gastronomic events or exhibitions, or consulting with business associates.

Translators or interpreters performing services as employees of an enterprise located in the territory of the other Party.

Information and communication technology service providers attending meetings, seminars or conferences, or engaged in consultations with business associates.

Franchise traders and developers which seek to offer their services in the territory of the other Party.

Annex 1203.D.1 Professionals

The professionals listed below, as defined in Article 1209, are not covered under this Chapter:

1. All Health, Education, and Social Services occupations and related occupations including:

    (a) Managers in Health/Education/Social & Community Services;

    (b) Physicians/Dentists/Optometrists/Chiropractors/Other Health Professions;

    (c) Pharmacists, Dietians & Nutritionists;

    (d) Therapy & Assessment Professionals;

    (e) Nurse Supervisors & Registered Nurses;

    (f) Psychologists/Social Workers;

    (g) University Professors & Assistants;

    (h) College & Other Vocational Instructors; and

    (i) Secondary/Elementary School Teachers & Counsellors.

2. All professional occupations related to cultural industries as defined in Article 2207 (Exceptions — Definitions), including:

    (a) Managers in Libraries, Archives, Museums and Art Galleries;

    (b) Managers in Publishing, Motion Pictures, Broadcasting and Performing Arts; and

    (c) Creative & Performing Artists.

3. Recreation, Sports and Fitness Program and Service Directors.

4. Managers in Telecommunication Carriers.

5. Managers in Postal and Courier Services.

6. Managers in Manufacturing.

7. Managers in Utilities.

8. Managers in Construction and Transportation.

9. Judges, Lawyers and Notaries except foreign legal consultants.

Technicians

The technicians listed below, as defined in Article 1209, are covered under this chapter:

1. Civil Engineering Technologists and Technicians;

2. Electrical and Electronics Engineering Technologists and Technicians;[274]

3. Mechanical Engineering Technologists and Technicians;

4. Industrial Engineering and Manufacturing Technologists and Technicians;

5. Construction Inspectors and Estimators;

6. Engineering Inspectors, Testers and Regulatory Officers;

7. Supervisors in the following: Machinists and Related Occupations; Printing and Related Occupations; Mining and Quarrying; Oil and Gas Drilling and Service; Mineral and Metal Processing; Petroleum, Gas and Chemical Processing and Utilities; Food, Beverage and Tobacco Processing; Plastic and Rubber Products Manufacturing; Forest Products Processing; and Textile Processing;

8. Contractors and Supervisors in the following: Electrical Trades and Telecommunications Occupations; Pipefitting Trades; Metal Forming, Shaping and Erecting Trades; Carpentry Trades; Mechanic Trades; Heavy Construction Equipment Crews; and Other Construction Trades, Installers, Repairers and Servicers;

9. Electricians;[275]

10. Plumbers;

11. Industrial Instrument Technicians and Mechanics;

12. Aircraft Instrument, Electrical and Avionics Mechanics, Technicians and Inspectors;

13. Underground Production and Development Miners;

14. Oil and Gas Well Drillers, Servicers and Testers;

15. Graphic Designers and Illustrators;

16. Interior Designers;

17. Chefs;

18. Computer and Information System Technicians; and

19. International Selling and Purchasing Agents.

Annex 1203

For Peru:

Category	Migratory Condition	Length of Stay
Business Visitor	Negocios (business)	Up to 90 days, renewable for 30 days.
Traders	Negocios (business)	Up to 90 days, renewable for 30 days.

---

[274] This includes electronic service technicians.

[275] This includes industrial electricians.

Category	Migratory Condition	Length of Stay
Investor (in the process of committing an investment)	Negocios (business)	Up to 90 days, renewable for 30 days.
Investor	Independiente-inversionista (Investor)	Up to 1 year, renewable for consecutive periods, the number of times that it is requested, to the extent that the conditions which motivated its granting are maintained.
Intra-Company Transferees	Trabajador (Worker)	Up to 1 year, renewable for consecutive periods, the number of times that it is requested, to the extent that the conditions which motivated its granting are maintained.
Professionals and Technicians (in a subordinate relationship)	Trabajador (Worker)	Up to 1 year, renewable for consecutive periods, the number of times that it is requested, to the extent that the conditions which motivated its granting are maintained.
Professionals and Technicians (Independent)	Independiente — Profesional (Independent — Professional)	Up to 1 year, renewable for consecutive periods, the number of times that it is requested, to the extent that the conditions which motivated its granting are maintained.
Professionals and Technicians (Contract service supplier)		Up to 6 months.

For Canada:

Category	Length of Stay
Business Visitors	Up to six months, extensions are possible.
Traders and Investors	Up to one year, extensions are possible.
Intra-Company Transferees	Up to three years, extensions are possible.
Professionals and Technicians	Up to one year, extensions are possible.

Other Relevant Legislation

APPENDIX VIII

CANADA–COLOMBIA FREE TRADE AGREEMENT
Chapter 12 — Temporary Entry for Business Persons

Article 1201: — General Principles

Further to Article 1202, this Chapter reflects the preferential trading relationship between the Parties, the mutual objective to facilitate temporary entry for business persons on a reciprocal basis and in accordance with Annex 1203, and the need to establish transparent criteria and procedures for temporary entry and the need to ensure border security and to protect the domestic labour force and permanent employment in their respective territories.

Article 1202: General Obligations

1. Each Party shall apply its measures relating to the provisions of this Chapter in accordance with Article 1201 and, in particular, shall expeditiously apply those measures so as to avoid unduly impairing or delaying trade in goods or services or conduct of investment activities under this Agreement.

2. Nothing in this Chapter shall be construed to prevent a Party from applying measures to regulate the entry of natural persons into, or their temporary stay in, its territory, including those measures necessary to protect the integrity of, and to ensure the orderly movement of natural persons across, its borders, provided that such measures are not applied in such a manner as to unduly impair or delay trade in goods or services or the conduct of investment activities under this Agreement.

Article 1203: — Grant of Temporary Entry

1. Each Party shall grant temporary entry to business persons who comply with its immigration measures applicable to temporary entry such as those relating to public health and safety and national security, in accordance with this Chapter, including the provisions of Annex 1203.

2. Subject to each Party's labour legislation, a Party may refuse to issue a work permit or authorization to a business person where the temporary entry of that person might affect adversely:

(a) the settlement of any labour dispute that is in progress at the place or intended place of employment; or

1459

(b) the employment of any person who is involved in such dispute.

3. Each Party shall limit any fees for processing applications for temporary entry of business persons so as to not unduly impair or delay trade in goods or services or the conduct of investment activities under this Agreement.

Article 1204: — Provision of Information

1. Further to Article 1901 (Transparency — Publication), and recognizing the importance to the Parties of transparency of temporary entry information, each Party shall:

(a) provide to the other Party relevant materials as will enable the other Party to become acquainted with its measures relating to this Chapter; and

(b) no later than six months after the date of entry into force of this Agreement, make available explanatory material regarding the requirements for temporary entry under this Chapter, in such a manner as will enable business persons of the other Party to become acquainted with those requirements.

2. Each Party shall collect and maintain, and, on request, make available to the other Party in accordance with its domestic law, data respecting the granting of temporary entry under this Chapter to business persons of the other Party who have been issued immigration documentation.

Article 1205: — Contact Points

1. The Parties hereby establish the following Contact Points:

(a) in the case of Canada:

Director
Temporary Resident Policy
Immigration Branch
Citizenship and Immigration Canada

(b) in the case of Colombia:

Coordinador
Coordinación de Visas e Immigración
Ministerio de Relaciones Exteriores

or their respective successors.

2. The Contact Points shall exchange information as described in Article 1204 and shall meet as required to consider matters pertaining to this Chapter, such as:

(a) the implementation and administration of this Chapter;

(b) the development and adoption of common criteria and interpretations for the implementation of this Chapter;

(c) the development of measures to further facilitate temporary entry of business persons on a reciprocal basis;

(d) proposed modifications to this Chapter; and

(e) measures that affect the temporary entry of business persons under this Chapter;

Article 1206: — Dispute Settlement

1. A Party may not initiate proceedings under Chapter Twenty-One (Dispute Settlement) regarding a refusal to grant temporary entry under this Chapter unless:

(a) the matter involves a pattern of practice;

(b) the business person has exhausted the available administrative remedies regarding the particular matter; and

(c) the Contact Points have been unable to resolve the issue.

2. The remedies referred to in subparagraph 1(b) shall be deemed to be exhausted if a final determination in the matter has not been issued by the competent authority within one year of the institution of an administrative proceeding, and the failure to issue a determination is not attributable to delay caused by the business person.

Article 1207: — Relation to Other Chapters

No provision of this Agreement shall be interpreted to impose any obligation on a Party regarding its immigration measures, except as specifically identified in this Chapter and Chapters One (Initial Provisions and General Definitions), Twenty-One (Dispute Settlement), Nineteen (Transparency), Twenty (Administration of the Agreement), and Twenty-Three (Final Provisions).

Article 1208: — Transparency and Processing of Applications

1. Further to Chapter Nineteen (Transparency), each Party shall establish or maintain appropriate mechanisms to respond to inquiries from interested persons regarding applications and procedures relating to the temporary entry of business persons.

2. Each Party shall endeavor to, within a reasonable period that should not exceed 30 days after an application requesting temporary entry is considered complete under its domestic laws and regulations, inform the applicant of the decision concerning the application. At the request of the applicant, the Party shall endeavor to provide, without undue delay, information concerning the status of the application

Article 1209: — Definitions

For purposes of this Chapter:

business person means a national of a Party who is engaged in trade in goods, the supply of services or the conduct of investment activities;

immigration measures applicable to temporary entry means:

(a) with respect to Canada, the *Immigration and Refugee Protection Act*, S.C. 2001, c.27, as amended and the associated *Immigration and Refugee Protection Regulations*, SOR/2002-227 as amended; and

(b) with respect to Colombia, *El Decreto 4000 de 2004*, publicado en el Diario Oficial de Colombia el 1 de diciembre de 2004, y las *Resoluciones 0255 y 0273* de enero de 2005, as amended.

immigration measure means any measure affecting the entry or sojourn of a foreign national;

labour dispute means a conflict or controversy between a union and employer relating to terms or conditions of employment;

management trainee on professional development means an employee with a post-secondary degree who is on a temporary work assignment intended to broaden that employee's knowledge of and experience in a company in preparation for a senior leadership position within the company;

professional means a national of a Party who is engaged in a specialty occupation[276] requiring:

(a) theoretical and practical application of a body of specialized knowledge and the appropriate certification/license to practice; and

(b) attainment of a post-secondary degree in the specialty requiring four or more years of study, as a minimum for entry into the occupation[277];

technician means a national of a Party who is engaged in a specialty occupation[278] requiring:

(a) theoretical and practical application of a body of specialized knowledge and the appropriate certification/license to practice; and

(b) attainment of a post-secondary or technical degree requiring two or more years of study as a minimum for entry into the occupation[279];

specialist means an employee who possesses specialized knowledge of the company's products or services and its application in international markets, or an advanced level of expertise or knowledge of the company's processes and procedures;

temporary entry means entry into the territory of a Party by a business person of the other Party without the intent to establish permanent residence.

Annex 1203 — Temporary Entry For Business Persons

Section A — Business Visitors

1. Each Party shall grant temporary entry to a business person seeking to engage in a business activity set out in Appendix 1203.A, without requiring that person to obtain a work permit or an employment authorization, provided that the business person otherwise

---

[276] In the case of Canada, a professional specialty occupation is an occupation which falls within the National Occupation Classification (NOC) levels O and A.

[277] In the case of Canada, these requirements are defined in the NOC. In the case of Colombia, the requirements are stated in the specific laws for regulated professions, which will be provided in accordance with Article 1204.

[278] In the case of Canada, a technical specialty occupation is an occupation which falls within the National Occupation Classification (NOC) level B.

[279] In the case of Canada, these requirements are defined in the NOC. In the case of Colombia, the requirements are stated in the specific laws for regulated professions, which Colombia shall provide in accordance with Article 1204.

complies with its immigration measures applicable to temporary entry, on presentation of:

(a) proof of nationality, citizenship or permanent residency status of a Party;

(b) documentation demonstrating that the business person will be engaged in a business activity set out in Appendix 1203.A and describing the purpose of entry; and

(c) evidence demonstrating that the proposed business activity is international in scope and the business person is not seeking to enter the local labour market.

2. Each Party shall provide that a business person may satisfy the requirements of paragraph 1(c) by demonstrating that:

(a) the primary source of remuneration for the proposed business activity is outside the territory of the Party granting temporary entry; and

(b) the business person's principal place of business and the actual place of accrual of profits, at least predominantly, remain outside the territory of the Party granting temporary entry.

A Party shall normally accept an oral declaration as to the principal place of business and the actual place of accrual of profits. Where the Party requires further proof, it shall normally consider a letter from the employer or the representing organization, attesting to these matters as sufficient proof.

3. Neither Party may:

(a) as a condition for temporary entry under paragraph 1, require prior approval procedures, labour certification tests or other procedures of similar effect; or

(b) impose or maintain any numerical restriction relating to temporary entry under paragraph 1.

4. Notwithstanding paragraph 3, a Party may require a business person seeking temporary entry under this Section to obtain a visa or an equivalent requirement prior to entry. Before imposing a visa or an equivalent requirement, the Party shall consult with the other Party whose business persons would be affected with a view to avoiding the imposition of the requirement.

Section B — Traders and Investors

1. Each Party shall grant temporary entry and provide a work permit or other authorization to a business person seeking to:

(a) carry on substantial trade in goods or services principally between the territory of the Party of which the business person is a national and the territory of the Party into which entry is sought, or

(b) establish, develop, administer or provide advice or key technical services to the operation of an investment to which the business person or the business person's enterprise has committed, or is in the process of committing, a substantial amount of capital,

in a capacity that is supervisory, executive or involves essential skills, provided that the business person otherwise complies with its immigration measures applicable to temporary entry.

2. Neither Party may:

(a) as a condition for temporary entry under paragraph 1, require labour certification tests or other procedures of similar effect; or

(b) impose or maintain any numerical restriction relating to temporary entry under paragraph 1.

3. Notwithstanding paragraph 2, a Party may require a business person seeking temporary entry under this Section to obtain a visa or an equivalent requirement prior to entry. Before imposing a visa or an equivalent requirement, the Party shall consult with the other Party whose business persons would be affected with a view to avoiding the imposition of the requirement.

Section C — Intra-Company Transferees

1. Each Party shall grant temporary entry and provide a work permit or other authorization to a business person employed by an enterprise who seeks to render services to that enterprise or a subsidiary or affiliate thereof as an executive or manager, a specialist, or a management trainee on professional development, provided that the business person otherwise complies with the immigration measures applicable to temporary entry. A Party may require the business person to have been employed continuously by the enterprise for six months within the three-year period immediately preceding the date of the application for admission.

2. Neither Party may:

(a) as a condition for temporary entry under paragraph 1, require labour certification tests or other procedures of similar effect; or

(b) impose or maintain any numerical restriction relating to temporary entry under paragraph 1.

3. Notwithstanding paragraph 2, a Party may require a business person seeking temporary entry under this Section to obtain a visa or an equivalent requirement prior to entry. Before imposing a visa or an equivalent requirement, the Party shall consult with the other Party whose business persons would be affected with a view to avoiding the imposition of the requirement.

Section D — Professionals and Technicians

1. Each Party shall grant temporary entry and provide a work permit or other authorization to a business person seeking to engage in an occupation at a professional or technical level in accordance with Appendix 1203.D, if the business person otherwise complies with its immigration measures applicable to temporary entry, on presentation of:

(a) proof of nationality, citizenship or permanent residency status of a Party; and

(b) documentation demonstrating that the business person is seeking to enter the other Party to provide pre-arranged professional services in the field for which the business person has the appropriate qualifications.

2. Neither Party may:

(a) as a condition for temporary entry under paragraph 1, require prior approval procedures, labour certification tests or other procedures of similar effect; or

(b) impose or maintain any numerical restriction relating to temporary entry under paragraph 1.

3. Notwithstanding paragraph 2, a Party may require a business person seeking temporary entry under this Section to obtain a visa or an equivalent requirement prior to entry. Before imposing a visa or an equivalent requirement, the Party shall consult with the other Party whose business persons would be affected with a view to avoiding the imposition of the requirement.

Section E — Spouses

1. Each Party shall grant temporary entry and provide a work permit or other authorization to a spouse of a business person qualifying for temporary entry under Section B (Traders and Investors), Section C (Intra-Company Transferees), or Section D (Professionals and Technicians), if the spouse otherwise complies with its immigration measures applicable to temporary entry.

2. Neither Party may:

(a) as a condition for temporary entry under paragraph 1, require prior approval procedures, labour certification tests or other procedures of similar effect; or

(b) impose or maintain any numerical restriction relating to temporary entry under paragraph 1.

3. Notwithstanding paragraph 2, a Party may require a spouse of a business person seeking temporary entry under this Section to obtain a visa or an equivalent requirement prior to entry. Before imposing a visa or an equivalent requirement, the Party shall consult with the other Party whose business persons would be affected with a view to avoiding the imposition of the requirement.

Appendix 1203.A — Business Visitors

Meetings and Consultations

Business persons attending meetings, seminars or conferences; or engaged in consultations with business associates.

Research and Design

Technical, scientific and statistical researchers conducting independent research or research for an enterprise located in the territory of the other Party.

Growth, Manufacture and Production

Purchasing and production management personnel, conducting commercial transactions for an enterprise located in the territory of the other Party.

Harvester owners supervising a harvesting crew.

Marketing

Market researchers and analysts conducting independent research or analysis or research or analysis for an enterprise located in the territory of the other Party.

Trade-fair and promotional personnel attending a trade convention.

Other Relevant Legislation

Sales

Sales representatives and agents taking orders or negotiating contracts for goods or services for an enterprise located in the territory of the other Party but not delivering goods or providing services.

Buyers purchasing for an enterprise located in the territory of the other Party.

Distribution

Transportation operators transporting goods or passengers to the territory of a Party from the territory of the other Party or loading and transporting goods or passengers from the territory of a Party, with no unloading in that territory, to the territory of the other Party.

Customs brokers providing consulting services regarding the facilitation of the import or export of goods.

After-Sales or After-Lease Service

Installers, repair and maintenance personnel, and supervisors, possessing specialized knowledge essential to a seller's contractual obligation, performing services or training workers to perform services, pursuant to a warranty or other service contract incidental to the sale or lease of commercial or industrial equipment or machinery, including computer software, purchased or leased from an enterprise located outside the territory of the Party into which temporary entry is sought, during the life of the warranty or service agreement.

General Service

Professionals and technicians engaging in a business activity at a professional or technician level as set out in Appendix 1203.D

Management and supervisory personnel engaging in a commercial transaction for an enterprise located in the territory of the other Party.

Financial services personnel (insurers, bankers or investment brokers) engaging in commercial transactions for an enterprise located in the territory of the other Party.

Public relations and advertising personnel consulting with business associates, or attending or participating in conventions.

Tourism personnel (tour and travel agents, tour guides or tour operators) attending or participating in conventions or conducting a tour that has begun in the territory of the other Party.

Cook personnel (cookers and assistants) attending or participating in gastronomic events or exhibitions, or consulting with business associates.

Translators or interpreters performing services as employees of an enterprise located in the territory of the other Party.

Information and communication technology service providers attending meetings, seminars, or conferences, or engaged in consultations with business associates

Franchise traders and developers who seek to offer their services in the territory of the other Party.

Appendix 1203.D — Professionals and Technicians

Professionals:

The professionals listed below are not covered under this Chapter:

1. All Health, Education, and Social Services occupations and related occupations, including:

    (a) Managers in Health/Education/Social & Community Services

    (b) Physicians/Dentists/Optometrists/Chiropractors/Other Health Professions

    (c) Pharmacists, Dieticians & Nutritionists

    (d) Therapy & Assessment Professionals

    (e) Nurse Supervisors & Registered Nurses

    (f) Psychologists/Social Workers

    (g) University Professors & Assistants

    (h) College & Other Vocational Instructors

    (i) Secondary/Elementary School Teachers & Counsellors

2. All professional occupations related to cultural industries as defined in Article 2208 (Exceptions — Definitions), including:

    (a) Managers in Libraries, Archives, Museums and Art Galleries

    (b) Managers — Publishing, Motion Pictures, Broadcasting and Performing Arts

    (c) Creative & Performing Artists

3. Recreation, Sports and Fitness Program and Service Directors

4. Managers in Telecommunication Carriers

5. Managers in Postal and Courier Services

6. Managers in Manufacturing

7. Managers in Utilities

8. Managers in Construction and Transportation

9. Judges, Lawyers and Notaries except foreign legal consultants

Technicians

The technicians listed below are covered under this chapter:

1. Civil Engineering Technologists and Technicians

2. Mechanical Engineering Technologists and Technicians

3. Industrial Engineering and Manufacturing Technologists and Technicians

4. Construction Inspectors and Estimators

5. Engineering Inspectors, Testers and Regulatory Officers

6. Supervisors in the following: Machinists and Related Occupations, Printing and Related Occupations, Mining and Quarrying, Oil and Gas Drilling and Service, Mineral and Metal Processing, Petroleum, Gas and Chemical Processing and Utilities, Food, Beverage and Tobacco Processing, Plastic and Rubber Products Manufacturing, Forest Products Processing, Textile Processing

Other Relevant Legislation

7. Contractors and Supervisors in the following: Electrical Trades and Telecommunications Occupations, Pipefitting Trades, Metal Forming, Shaping and Erecting Trades, Carpentry Trades, Mechanic Trades, Heavy Construction Equipment Crews, Other Construction Trades, Installers, Repairers and Servicers

8. Electrical and Electronics Engineering Technologists and Technicians[280]

9. Electricians[281]

10. Plumbers

11. Industrial Instrument Technicians and Mechanics

12. Aircraft Instrument, Electrical and Avionics Mechanics, Technicians and Inspectors

13. Underground Production and Development Miners

14. Oil and Gas Well Drillers, Servicers and Testers

15. Graphic Designers and Illustrators

16. Interior Designers

17. Chefs

18. Computer and Information System Technicians

19. International Purchasing and Selling Agents

---

[280] Including electronic service technicians.

[281] Including industrial electricians.

CANADA KOREA FREE TRADE AGREEMENT
Chapter Twelve: — Temporary Entry for Business Persons

Article 12.1: General Principles

This Chapter reflects the preferential trading relationship between the Parties, the desirability of facilitating temporary entry on a reciprocal basis and of establishing transparent criteria and procedures for temporary entry, and the need to ensure border security and to protect the domestic labour force and permanent employment in their respective territories.

Article 12.2: General Obligations

1. Each Party shall apply its measures relating to this Chapter in accordance with Article 12.1 and, in particular, shall apply expeditiously those measures so as to avoid unduly impairing or delaying trade in goods or services or conduct of investment activities under this Agreement.

2. This Chapter does not prevent a Party from applying measures to regulate the entry of natural persons into, or the temporary stay in, its territory, including those measures necessary to protect the integrity of, and to ensure the orderly movement of natural persons across its borders, provided that such measures are not applied in such a manner as to unduly impair or delay trade in goods or services or the conduct of activities under this Agreement. The sole fact of requiring a visa, or other document authorising entry or work for a business person, or for natural persons shall not be regarded as unduly impairing or delaying trade in goods or services or the conduct of activities under this Agreement.

Article 12.3: Grant of Temporary Entry

1. Each Party shall grant temporary entry to business persons who otherwise comply with existing immigration measures related to public health, safety and national security applicable to temporary entry, in accordance with this Chapter, including Annex 12-A.

2. A Party may refuse to issue a work permit or authorisation to a business person if the temporary entry of that person might affect adversely:

(a) the settlement of a labour dispute that is in progress at the place or intended place of employment; or

(b) the employment of a person who is involved in such dispute.

3. If a Party refuses pursuant to paragraph 2 to issue a work permit or authorisation, it shall inform in writing the business person of the reasons for the refusal.

4. Each Party shall limit fees for processing applications for temporary entry of business persons to the approximate cost of services rendered.

Article 12.4: Provision of Information

1. Recognising the importance to the Parties of transparency of information on temporary entry and further to Article 19.1 (Publication), each Party shall, after the date of entry into force of this Agreement, make available through any means, information on its measures relating to this Chapter.

2. Each Party shall collect and maintain data respecting the granting of temporary entry under this Chapter to business persons of the other Party who have been issued a work permit or authorisation. On the request of a Party, the other Party shall make such information available to the other Party in accordance with its domestic law.

Article 12.5: Contact Points

1. Each Party hereby establishes a contact point:

    (a) for Canada:

- Director
- Temporary Resident Policy
- Immigration Branch
- Citizenship and Immigration Canada; and

    (b) for Korea:

- Director
- Border Control Division
- Korea Immigration Service
- Ministry of Justice

    or their respective successors.

2. The contact points shall meet at least once each year, unless otherwise agreed, to exchange information as described in Article 12.4 and to consider matters pertaining to this Chapter, such as:

    (a) the implementation and administration of this Chapter;

    (b) the development and adoption of common criteria, definitions and interpretations for the implementation of this Chapter;

    (c) the development of measures to further facilitate temporary entry of business persons on a reciprocal basis; and

    (d) proposed modifications to this Chapter.

Article 12.6: Dispute Settlement

1. A Party shall not initiate proceedings under Chapter Twenty-One (Dispute Settlement) regarding a refusal to grant temporary entry under this Chapter unless:

(a) the matter involves a pattern of practice; and

(b) the business person has exhausted the normal administrative remedies regarding the particular matter.

2. The remedies referred to in paragraph 1(b) are deemed to be exhausted if a final determination in the matter has not been issued by the competent authority within one year of the initiation of an administrative proceeding, and the failure to issue a determination is not attributable to delay caused by the business person.

Article 12.7: Relation to Other Chapters

Except for this Chapter and Chapters One (Initial Provisions and General Definitions), Nineteen (Transparency), Twenty (Institutional Provisions and Administration) and Twenty-Three (Final Provisions), this Agreement does not impose an obligation on a Party regarding its immigration measures.

Article 12.8: Definitions

For the purposes of this Chapter:

business person means a national of a Party who is engaged in trade in goods, the provision of services or the conduct of investment activities;

contract service supplier means an employee of an enterprise who is engaged in the supply of a contracted service as an employee of an enterprise. That enterprise has a service contract from an enterprise of the other Party, who is the final consumer of the service which is supplied. The contract and duration of stay shall comply with the domestic law of the other Party;

independent professional means a self-employed professional who seeks to engage, as part of a service contract granted by an enterprise or a service consumer of the other Party, in an activity at a professional level, provided that the person possesses the necessary education, or satisfies accreditation or licensing requirements as stipulated for the profession;

management trainee on professional development means an employee who has a Bachelor or Baccalaureate degree or who has a license at a professional level concerning the intra-company activity, who is on a temporary work assignment intended to broaden an employee's knowledge of and experience in a company in preparation for a senior leadership position within the company;

pre-arranged professional service means a professional service to be provided in the territory of the other Party, the terms of which have been determined and documented prior to the entry of the professional into the territory of the other Party;

professional means a national of a Party who is engaged in a specialty occupation as stated in Appendix 12-A-2 who is not engaged in the field of education; and *temporary entry* means entry into the territory of a Party by a business person of the other Party without the intent to establish permanent residence, and does not apply to measures regarding citizenship or employment on a permanent basis.

Annex 12-A: — Temporary Entry for Business Persons

Section A — Business Visitors

1. Each Party shall grant temporary entry to a business person seeking to engage in a business activity set out in Appendix 12-A-1 without requiring that the business person obtain a work permit or authorisation, provided that the business person otherwise complies with existing immigration measures applicable to temporary entry, on presentation of:

(a) proof of citizenship or permanent resident status of the other Party;

(b) documentation demonstrating that the business person will be so engaged in a business activity set out in Appendix 12-A-1 and describing the purpose of entry; and

(c) evidence demonstrating that the proposed business activity is international in scope and that the business person is not seeking to enter the local labour market.

2. Each Party shall provide that a business person may satisfy the requirements of paragraph 1(c) by demonstrating that:

(a) the primary source of remuneration for the proposed business activity is outside the territory of the Party granting temporary entry; and

(b) the business person's principal place of business and the actual place of accrual of profits, at least predominantly, remain outside such territory.

A Party shall normally accept an oral declaration as to the principal place of business and the actual place of accrual of profits. If the Party requires further proof, it shall normally consider a letter from the employer attesting to these matters as sufficient proof.

3. A Party shall not:

(a) as a condition for temporary entry pursuant to paragraph 1 or 2, require prior approval procedures, labour certification tests or other procedures of similar effect; or

(b) impose or maintain a numerical restriction relating to temporary entry pursuant to paragraph 1 or 2.

4. Notwithstanding paragraph 3, a Party may require a business person seeking temporary entry under this Section to obtain a visa or an equivalent requirement prior to entry. Before imposing a visa or an equivalent requirement, the Party shall consult with the other Party whose business persons would be affected with a view to avoiding the imposition of the requirement.

Section B — Traders and Investors

5. Each Party shall grant temporary entry and provide a work permit or visa to a business person seeking to:

(a) carry on substantial trade in goods or services principally between the territory of the Party of which the business person is a national and the territory of the Party into which entry is sought; or

(b) establish, develop, administer or provide advice or key technical services to the operation of an investment to which the business person or the business person's enterprise has committed, or is in the process of committing, a substantial amount of capital,

in a capacity that is supervisory, executive or involves essential skills, provided that the business person otherwise complies with existing immigration measures applicable to temporary entry.

6. A Party shall not:

(a) as a condition for temporary entry pursuant to paragraph 5, require labour certification tests or other procedures of similar effect; or

(b) impose or maintain a numerical restriction relating to temporary entry pursuant to paragraph 5.

7. Notwithstanding paragraph 6, a Party may require a business person seeking temporary entry under this Section to obtain a visa or an equivalent requirement prior to entry. Before imposing a visa or an equivalent requirement, the Party shall consult with the other Party whose business persons would be affected with a view to avoiding the imposition of the requirement.

Section C — Intra-Company Transferees

8. Each Party shall grant temporary entry and provide a work permit or visa to a business person employed by an enterprise who seeks to render services to that enterprise or a subsidiary or an affiliate or a branch thereof as an executive or manager, a specialist or a management trainee on professional development, provided that the business person otherwise complies with existing immigration measures applicable to temporary entry. A Party may require the business person to have been employed continuously by the enterprise for one year within the three-year period immediately preceding the date of the application for admission.

9. A Party shall not:

(a) as a condition for temporary entry pursuant to paragraph 8, require labour certification tests or other procedures of similar effect; or

(b) impose or maintain a numerical restriction relating to temporary entry pursuant to paragraph 8.

10. Notwithstanding paragraph 9, a Party may require a business person seeking temporary entry under this Section to obtain a visa or an equivalent requirement prior to entry. Before imposing a visa or an equivalent requirement, the Party shall consult with the other Party whose business persons would be affected with a view to avoiding the imposition of the requirement.

Section D — Professionals

11. Each Party shall grant temporary entry and provide a work permit or visa to a business person who is a professional seeking to engage in a business activity at a professional level, in a profession set out in Appendix 12-A-2, if the business person otherwise complies with existing immigration measures applicable to temporary entry, on presentation of:

(a) proof of citizenship or permanent resident status of the other Party; and

Other Relevant Legislation

(b) documentation demonstrating that the business person is seeking to enter to provide pre-arranged professional services, either as a contractual service supplier, or as an independent professional, in the field for which the business person has the appropriate qualifications.

12. A Party shall not:

(a) as a condition for temporary entry pursuant to paragraph 11, require prior approval procedures, labour certification tests or other procedures of similar effect; or

(b) impose or maintain a numerical restriction relating to temporary entry pursuant to paragraph 11.

13. Notwithstanding paragraph 12, a Party may require a business person seeking temporary entry under this Section to obtain a visa or an equivalent requirement prior to entry. Before imposing a visa or an equivalent requirement, the Party shall consult with the other Party whose business persons would be affected with a view to avoiding the imposition of the requirement.

Section E — Spouses

14. Each Party shall grant temporary entry and provide a work permit or authorisation to a spouse of a business person qualifying for temporary entry under Section B, C, or D, if the spouse otherwise complies with existing immigration measures applicable to temporary entry and meets the relevant employment qualifications.

15. A Party shall not:

(a) as a condition for temporary entry pursuant to paragraph 14, require prior approval procedures, labour certification tests or other procedures of similar effect; or

(b) impose or maintain a numerical restriction relating to temporary entry pursuant to paragraph 14.

16. Notwithstanding paragraph 15, a Party may require a spouse of a business person seeking temporary entry under this Section to obtain a visa or its equivalent prior to entry. Before imposing a visa requirement on the spouse, the Party shall consult with the other Party with a view to avoiding the imposition of the requirement.

Appendix 12-A-1 — Business Visitors

Research and Design

- Technical, scientific and statistical researchers conducting independent research or research for an enterprise located in the territory of the other Party;

Growth, Manufacture and Production

- Purchasing and production management personnel conducting commercial transactions for an enterprise located in the territory of the other Party;

Marketing

- Market researchers and analysts conducting independent research or analysis or research or analysis for an enterprise located in the territory of the other Party;
- Trade-fair and promotional personnel attending a trade convention;

Sales

- Sales representatives and agents taking orders or negotiating contracts for goods or services for an enterprise located in the territory of the other Party but not delivering goods or providing services;
- Buyers purchasing for an enterprise located in the territory of the other Party;

Distribution

- Transportation operators transporting goods or passengers to the territory of a Party from the territory of the other Party or loading and transporting goods or passengers from the territory of a Party, with no unloading in that territory, to the territory of the other Party;

After-Sales or After-Lease Service

- Installers, repair and maintenance personnel, and supervisors, possessing specialised knowledge essential to a seller's contractual obligation, performing services or training workers to perform services, pursuant to a warranty or other service contract incidental to the sale or lease of commercial or industrial equipment or machinery, including computer software, purchased or leased from an enterprise located outside the territory of the Party into which temporary entry is sought, during the life of the warranty or service agreement;

General Service

- Professionals engaging in a business activity at a professional level;
- Management and supervisory personnel engaging in a commercial transaction for an enterprise located in the territory of the other Party;
- Financial services personnel (insurers, bankers or investment brokers) engaging in commercial transactions for an enterprise located in the territory of the other Party;
- Public relations and advertising personnel consulting with business associates, or attending or participating in conventions;
- Tourism personnel (tour and travel agents, tour guides or tour operators) attending or participating in a convention or conducting a tour that has begun in the territory of the other Party; and
- Translators or interpreters performing services as employees of an enterprise located in the territory of the other Party.

Appendix 12-A-2: — Listed Professionals

Independent Professionals:

Profession	Canadian Requirements	Korean Requirements
Architect*	Bachelor degree; or provincial license	Bachelor degree; or professional license
Engineer	Bachelor degree; or provincial license	Bachelor degree; or professional license
Management Consultant	Bachelor degree***	Bachelor degree***

Profession	Canadian Requirements	Korean Requirements
Veterinarian	Doctorate of Veterinary Medicine; or provincial license	Bachelor degree; or professional license

Notes:

*   Providing architectural services is subject to collaboration with architects registered under Korean law in the form of joint contracts.

***   A license may be required to perform certain activities.

Contract Service Suppliers:

Profession	Canadian Requirements	Korean Requirements
Accountant	Bachelor degree; or Chartered Professional Accountant (CPA), Chartered Accountant (CA), Certified General Accountant (CGA), or Certified Management Accountant (CMA)	Professional license**
Actuary	Bachelor degree and membership in a professional actuarial association	Professional license
Agrologist	Bachelor degree	Master degree and three years of experience; or doctorate**
Architect*	Bachelor degree; or provincial license	Bachelor degree; or provincial license
Landscape Architect	Bachelor degree	Bachelor degree
Apiculturalist	Bachelor degree	Master degree and three years of experience; or doctorate**
Auditor	Bachelor degree; or CPA, CA, CGA or CMA	Professional license
Biologist		

This category would include the following:

1. *Botanist*
2. *Biologist*
3. *Ecologist*
4. *Embryologist*

Profession	Canadian Requirements	Korean Requirements
5. Toxicologist		
6. Enzymologist		
7. Etiologist		
8. Bacteriologist		
9. Geneticist		
10. Histologist		
11. Helminthologist		
12. Human Physiologist		
13. Pathologist		
14. Immunologist		
15. Mycologist		
16. Naturalist	Bachelor degree	Master degree and three years
17. Physiologist		of experience; or doctorate**
18. Virologist		
19. Serologist		
20. Plant Pathologist		
21. Crop Scientist		
22. Anatomist		
23. Bryologist		
24. Cytochemist		
25. Ecobiologist		
26. Echthyologist		
27. Nematologist		
28. Osteologist		
29. Entomologist		
30. Epidemiologist		
31. Biochemist		
32. Plant Breeder		
33. Animal Breeder		
34. Poultry Scientist		
35. Soil Scientist		
36. Food Scientist		
37. Animal Scientist		
38. Zoologist		
39. Dairy Scientist		

Profession	Canadian Requirements	Korean Requirements
Chemist	Bachelor degree	Master degree and three years of experience; or doctorate[**]
Engineer	Bachelor degree; or provincial license	Bachelor degree; or professional license
Forester	Bachelor degree	Master degree and three years of experience; or doctorate[**]
Geoscientist		

This category would include the following:

1. Palaeontologist
2. Petrologist
3. Sedimentologist
4. Seismologist

5. Strategrapher	Bachelor degree	Master degree and three years
6. Glaciologist		of experience; or doctorate[**]

7. Hydrogeologist
8. Hydrologist
9. Mineralogist
10. Oceanographer
11. Petrophysicist
12. Quaternarist
13. Volcanologist
14. Metallurgist

Horticulturalist	Bachelor degree	Master degree and three years of experience; or doctorate[**]
Management Consultant	Bachelor degree[***]	Bachelor degree[***]
Meteorologist	Bachelor degree	Master degree and three years of experience; or doctorate[**]
Physical Scientist		

This category would include the following:

Profession	Canadian Requirements	Korean Requirements
	Post-graduate degree	Master degree and three years of experience; or doctorate[**]
1. *Physicist* 2. *Astronomer* 3. *Aerodynamicist* 4. *Cosmologist* 5. *Research Scientist* 6. *Radiation Biophysicist* 7. *Rheologist*		
Sylviculturalist	Bachelor degree	Master degree and three years of experience; or doctorate[**]
Urban and Land Use Planner	Bachelor degree[***]	Bachelor degree[***]
Veterinarian	Doctorate of Veterinary Medicine; or professional license	Bachelor degree; or professional license
Information System Analyst Database Analyst and Data Administrator	Bachelor degree in computer sciences or a related discipline and two years of experience in computer science;	Bachelor degree or Post-secondary diploma in computer science or a related discipline and seven years of experience in computer and information systems;
	Bachelor degree and five years of experience in the field of computer science and information systems; or A Canadian I.S.P. designation (Information Systems Professional of Canada) or a license or designation from a recognised foreign certification body	Bachelor degree or Post secondary diplomas and nine years of experience in computer and information systems; or Engineering Mobility Forum (EMF) license in the case of Professional engineers
	Bachelor degree in computer science or a related discipline and two years of experience in computer science;	Bachelor degree or Post secondary diploma in computer sciences or a related discipline and seven years of experience in computer and information systems;

Profession	Canadian Requirements	Korean Requirements
Computer Programmer and Interactive Media Developer	Bachelor degree and five years of experience in the field of computer science and information systems; or A Canadian I.S.P. designation (Information Systems Professional of Canada) or a license or designation from a recognised foreign certification body	Bachelor degree or Post secondary diplomas and nine years of experience in computer and information systems; or EMF license in the case of Professional engineers
Software Engineer and Designer	Bachelor degree in computer sciences or a related discipline and two years of experience in computer science; Bachelor degree and five years of experience in the field of computer science and information systems; or A Canadian I.S.P. designation (Information Systems Professional of Canada) or a license or designation from a recognised foreign certification body	Bachelor degree or Post secondary diploma in computer science or a related discipline and seven years of experience in computer and information systems; Bachelor degree or Post secondary diplomas and nine years of experience in computer and information systems; or EMF license in the case of Professional engineers

Notes:

*   Providing architectural services is subject to collaboration with architects registered under Korean law in the form of joint contracts.

**   If there is no conflict of laws in both countries, Korean educational requirements shall be deemed to be met whenever a Canadian professional has met Canadian educational requirements and the Korean client or employer has provided a letter indicating that the Canadian professional's qualifications are satisfactory and vice versa.

***   A license may be required to perform certain activities.

APPENDIX X

CONSTITUTION ACT, 1982

Canada Act 1982 (U.K.), c. 11 R.S.C. 1985, App. II, No. 44, as am. Constitution Amendment Proclamation, 1983, SI/84-102, Schedule, SI/93-54, Schedule.

. . . . . .

PART I — CANADIAN CHARTER OF RIGHTS AND FREEDOMS

Whereas Canada is founded upon principles that recognize the supremacy of God and the rule of law:

Guarantee of Rights and Freedoms

1. Rights and freedoms in Canada — The *Canadian Charter of Rights and Freedoms* guarantees the rights and freedoms set out in it subject only to such reasonable limits prescribed by law as can be demonstrably justified in a free and democratic society.

Fundamental Freedoms

2. Fundamental freedoms — Everyone has the following fundamental freedoms:

(a) freedom of conscience and religion;

(b) freedom of thought, belief, opinion and expression, including freedom of the press and other media of communication;

(c) freedom of peaceful assembly; and

(d) freedom of association.

Democratic Rights

3. Democratic rights of citizens — Every citizen of Canada has the right to vote in an election of members of the House of Commons or of a legislative assembly and to be qualified for membership therein.

4. (1) Maximum duration of legislative bodies — No House of Commons and no legislative assembly shall continue for longer than five years from the date fixed for the return of the writs at a general election of its members.

(2) Continuation in special circumstances — In time of real or apprehended war, invasion or insurrection, a House of Commons may be continued by Parliament and a legislative assembly may be continued by the legislature beyond five years if such continuation is not opposed by the votes of more than one-third of the members of the House of Commons or the legislative assembly, as the case may be.

5. Annual sitting of legislative bodies — There shall be a sitting of Parliament and of each legislature at least once every twelve months.

Mobility Rights

6. (1) Mobility of citizens — Every citizen of Canada has the right to enter, remain in and leave Canada.

(2) Rights to move and gain livelihood — Every citizen of Canada and every person who has the status of a permanent resident of Canada has the right

    (a) to move to and take up residence in any province; and

    (b) to pursue the gaining of a livelihood in any province.

(3) Limitation — The rights specified in subsection (2) are subject to

    (a) any laws or practices of general application in force in a province other than those that discriminate among persons primarily on the basis of province of present or previous residence; and

    (b) any laws providing for reasonable residency requirements as a qualification for the receipt of publicly provided social services.

(4) Affirmative action programs — Subsections (2) and (3) do not preclude any law, program or activity that has as its object the amelioration in a province of conditions of individuals in that province who are socially or economically disadvantaged if the rate of employment in that province is below the rate of employment in Canada.

Legal Rights

7. Life, liberty and security of person — Everyone has the right to life, liberty and security of the person and the right not to be deprived thereof except in accordance with the principles of fundamental justice.

8. Search or seizure — Everyone has the right to be secure against unreasonable search or seizure.

9. Detention or imprisonment — Everyone has the right not to be arbitrarily detained or imprisoned.

10. Arrest or detention — Everyone has the right on arrest or detention

(a) to be informed promptly of the reasons therefor;

(b) to retain and instruct counsel without delay and to be informed of that right; and

(c) to have the validity of the detention determined by way of *habeas corpus* and to be released if the detention is not lawful.

11. Proceedings in criminal and penal matters — Any person charged with an offence has the right

(a) to be informed without unreasonable delay of the specific offence;

(b) to be tried within a reasonable time;

(c) not to be compelled to be a witness in proceedings against that person in respect of the offence;

(d) to be presumed innocent until proven guilty according to law in a fair and public hearing by an independent and impartial tribunal;

(e) not to be denied reasonable bail without just cause;

(f) except in the case of an offence under military law tried before a military tribunal, to the benefit of trial by jury where the maximum punishment for the offence is imprisonment for five years or a more severe punishment;

(g) not to be found guilty on account of any act or omission unless, at the time of the act or omission, it constituted an offence under Canadian or international law or was criminal according to the general principles of law recognized by the community of nations;

(h) if finally acquitted of the offence, not to be tried for it again and, if finally found guilty and punished for the offence, not to be tried or punished for it again; and

(i) if found guilty of the offence and if the punishment for the offence has been varied between the time of commission and the time of sentencing, to the benefit of the lesser punishment.

12. Treatment or punishment — Everyone has the right not to be subjected to any cruel and unusual treatment or punishment.

13. Self-crimination — A witness who testifies in any proceedings has the right not to have any incriminating evidence so given used to incriminate that witness in any other proceedings, except in a prosecution for perjury or for the giving of contradictory evidence.

14. Interpreter — A party or witness in any proceedings who does not understand or speak the language in which the proceedings are conducted or who is deaf has the right to the assistance of an interpreter.

Equality Rights

15. (1) Equality before and under law and equal protection and benefit of law — Every individual is equal before and under the law and has the right to the equal protection and equal benefit of the law without discrimination and, in particular, without discrimination based on race, national or ethnic origin, colour, religion, sex, age or mental or physical disability.

(2) Affirmative action programs — Subsection (1) does not preclude any law, program or activity that has as its object the amelioration of conditions of disadvantaged individuals or groups including those that are disadvantaged because of race, national or ethnic origin, colour, religion, sex, age or mental or physical disability.

Official Languages of Canada

16. (1) Official languages of Canada — English and French are the official languages of Canada and have equality of status and equal rights and privileges as to their use in all institutions of the Parliament and government of Canada.

(2) Official languages of New Brunswick — English and French are the official languages of New Brunswick and have equality of status and equal rights and privileges as to their use in all institutions of the legislature and government of New Brunswick.

(3) Advancement of status and use — Nothing in this Charter limits the authority of Parliament or a legislature to advance the equality of status or use of English and French.

16.1 (1) English and French linguistic communities in New Brunswick — The English linguistic community and the French linguistic community in New Brunswick have equality status and equal rights and privileges, including the right to distinct educational institutions and such distinct cultural institutions as are necessary for the preservation and promotion of those communities.

(2) Role of the legislature and government of New Brunswick — The role of the legislature and government of New Brunswick to preserve and promote the status, rights and privileges referred to in subsection (1) is affirmed.

SI/93-54, Sched., s. 1

17. (1) Proceedings of Parliament — Everyone has the right to use English or French in any debates and other proceedings of Parliament.

(2) Proceedings of New Brunswick legislature — Everyone has the right to use English or French in any debates and other proceedings of the legislature of New Brunswick.

18. (1) Parliamentary statutes and records — The statutes, records and journals of Parliament shall be printed and published in English and French and both language versions are equally authoritative.

(2) New Brunswick statutes and records — The statutes, records and journals of the legislature of New Brunswick shall be printed and published in English and French and both language versions are equally authoritative.

19. (1) Proceedings in courts established by Parliament — Either English or French may be used by any person in, or in any pleading in or process issuing from, any court established by Parliament.

(2) Proceedings in New Brunswick courts — Either English or French may be used by any person in, or in any pleading in or process issuing from, any court of New Brunswick.

20. (1) Communications by public with federal institutions — Any member of the public in Canada has the right to communicate with, and to receive available services from, any head or central office of an institution of the Parliament or government of Canada in English or French, and has the same right with respect to any other office of any such institution where

(a) there is a significant demand for communications with and services from that office in such language; or

(b) due to the nature of the office, it is reasonable that communications with and services from that office be available in both English and French.

(2) Communications by public with New Brunswick institutions — Any member of the public in New Brunswick has the right to communicate with, and to receive available services from, any office of an institution of the legislature or government of New Brunswick in English or French.

21. Continuation of existing Constitutional provisions — Nothing in sections 16 to 20 abrogates or derogates from any right, privilege or obligation with respect to the English and French languages, or either of them, that exists or is continued by virtue of any other provision of the Constitution of Canada.

22. Rights and privileges preserved — Nothing in sections 16 to 20 abrogates or derogates from any legal or customary right or privilege acquired or enjoyed either before or after the coming into force of this Charter with respect to any language that is not English or French.

Minority Language Educational Rights

23. (1) Language of instruction — Citizens of Canada

(a) whose first language learned and still understood is that of the English or French linguistic minority population of the province in which they reside, or

(b) who have received their primary school instruction in Canada in English or French and reside in a province where the language in which they received that instruction is the language of the English or French linguistic minority population of the province,

have the right to have their children receive primary and secondary school instruction in that language in that province.

(2) Continuity of language instruction — Citizens of Canada of whom any child has received or is receiving primary or secondary school instruction in English or French in Canada, have the right to have all their children receive primary and secondary school instruction in the same language.

(3) Application where numbers warrant — The right of citizens of Canada under subsections (1) and (2) to have their children receive primary and secondary school instruction in the language of the English or French linguistic minority population of a province

(a) applies wherever in the province the number of children of citizens who have such a right is sufficient to warrant the provision to them out of public funds of minority language instruction; and

(b) includes, where the number of those children so warrants, the right to have them receive that instruction in minority language educational facilities provided out of public funds.

Enforcement

24. (1) Enforcement of guaranteed rights and freedoms — Anyone whose rights or freedoms, as guaranteed by this Charter, have been infringed or denied may apply to a court of competent jurisdiction to obtain such remedy as the court considers appropriate and just in the circumstances.

(2) Exclusion of evidence bringing administration of justice into disrepute — Where, in proceedings under subsection (1), a court concludes that evidence was obtained in a manner that infringed or denied any rights or freedoms guaranteed by this Charter, the evidence shall be excluded if it is established that, having regard to all the circumstances, the admission of it in the proceedings would bring the administration of justice into disrepute.

25. Aboriginal rights and freedoms not affected by Charter — The guarantee in this Charter of certain rights and freedoms shall not be construed so as to abrogate or derogate from any aboriginal treaty or other rights or freedoms that pertain to the aboriginal peoples of Canada including

(a) any rights or freedoms that have been recognized by the Royal Proclamation of October 7, 1763; and

(b) any rights or freedoms that now exist by way of land claims agreements or may be so acquired.

26. Other rights and freedoms not affected by Charter — The guarantee in this Charter of certain rights and freedoms shall not be construed as denying the existence of any other rights or freedoms that exist in Canada.

27. Multicultural heritage — This Charter shall be interpreted in a manner consistent with the preservation and enhancement of the multicultural heritage of Canadians.

28. Rights guaranteed equally to both sexes — Notwithstanding anything in this Charter, the rights and freedoms referred to in it are guaranteed equally to male and female persons.

1486

29. Rights respecting certain schools preserved — Nothing in this Charter abrogates or derogates from any rights or privileges guaranteed by or under the Constitution of Canada in respect of denominational, separate or dissentient schools.

30. Application to Territories and territorial authorities — A reference in this Charter to a province or to the legislative assembly or legislature of a province shall be deemed to include a reference to the Yukon Territory and the Northwest Territories, or to the appropriate legislative authority thereof, as the case may be.

31. Legislative powers not extended — Nothing in this Charter extends the legislative powers of any body or authority.

Application of Charter

32. (1) Application of Charter — This Charter applies

(a) to the Parliament and government of Canada in respect of all matters within the authority of Parliament including all matters relating to the Yukon Territory and Northwest Territories; and

(b) to the legislature and government of each province in respect of all matters within the authority of the legislature of each province.

(2) Exception — Notwithstanding subsection (1), section 15 shall not have effect until three years after this section comes into force.

33. (1) Exception where express declaration — Parliament or the legislature of a province may expressly declare in an Act of Parliament or of the legislature, as the case may be, that the Act or a provision thereof shall operate notwithstanding a provision included in section 2 or sections 7 to 15 of this Charter.

(2) Operation of exception — An Act or a provision of an Act in respect of which a declaration made under this section is in effect shall have such operation as it would have but for the provision of this Charter referred to in the declaration.

(3) Five year limitation — A declaration made under subsection (1) shall cease to have effect five years after it comes into force or on such earlier date as may be specified in the declaration.

(4) Re-enactment — Parliament or a legislature of a province may re-enact a declaration made under subsection (1).

(5) Five year limitation — Subsection (3) applies in respect of a re-enactment made under subsection (4).

Citation

34. Citation — This Part may be cited as the *Canadian Charter of Rights and Freedoms*.

Other Relevant Legislation

INDEX — IMMIGRATION AND REFUGEE PROTECTION ACT, REGULATIONS AND RULES

Most references in this index are as follows: Immigration Appeal Division Rules - IADR; Immigration and Refugee Protection Act - IRPA; Immigration and Refugee Protection Regulations - IRPR; Regulations - Designating a Body for the Purposes of Paragraph 91(2)(c) of the Act - IRPA Reg. 2011-142; Federal Courts Act - FCA; Immigration Division Rules - IDR; Federal Courts Rules - FCR; Federal Courts Citizenship, Immigration and Refugee Protection Rules - FCCIRP; Refugee Appeal Division Rules - RADR; and Refugee Protection Division Rules - RPDR. The "p." designations refer to a specific page of the text.

A

1489

Index

Index

Index

Index

Index

Index

Index

Index

Index

Index

Index

Index

Index

Index

Index

Index

Index

Index

Index